W9-DAZ-050

THE *Virgin* ENCYCLOPEDIA OF

JAZZ

COLIN LARKIN

Virgin

IN ASSOCIATION WITH MUZE UK LTD.

Dedicated To The Second Tier.
People like Oliver Nelson, Wynton Kelly, and Don Ellis

First published in Great Britain in 1999 by
VIRGIN BOOKS
an imprint of Virgin Publishing Ltd
Thames Wharf Studios, Rainville Road
London W6 9HT

A catalogue record for this book is available from the British Library

ISBN 1 85227 754 8

Written, edited and produced by
MUZE UK Ltd
to whom all editorial enquiries should be sent
Iron Bridge House, 3 Bridge Approach, Chalk Farm, London NW1 8BD
e-mail: nic@muze.co.uk. http://www.muze.com
Editor In Chief: Colin Larkin
Production Editor: Susan Pipe
Research Assistant: Nic Oliver
Typographic Design Consultants: Roger Kohn & Acu
Special thanks to Trev Huxley, Tony Laudico, Paul Zullo
and all the Klugettes at Muze Inc.,
and to Rob Shreeve of Virgin Publishing.
Typeset by Misterioso Studios
Printed and bound in Great Britain by Butler & Tanner Ltd, Frome and London

Introduction

The Virgin Encyclopedia Of Jazz is one of the major series of books taken from the new 8-volume *Encyclopedia Of Popular Music*. It was previously published as *The Who's Who Of Jazz*. This is now the 3rd Edition.

Other titles already available are:
The Virgin Encyclopedia Of Fifties Music
The Virgin Encyclopedia Of Sixties Music
The Virgin Encyclopedia Of Seventies Music
The Virgin Encyclopedia Of Eighties Music
The Virgin Encyclopedia Of Popular Music (Concise)
The Virgin Encyclopedia Of Indie & New Wave
The Virgin Encyclopedia Of The Blues
The Virgin Encyclopedia Of R&B And Soul
The Virgin Encyclopedia Of Reggae
The Virgin Encyclopedia Of Country Music
The Virgin Encyclopedia Of Dance
The Virgin Encyclopedia Of Heavy Rock
The Virgin Encyclopedia Of Stage & Film Musicals
The Virgin All Time Top 1000 Albums

Jazz is by far the most written about genre of popular music, with the most territorial supporters. Reading about jazz can be so inspiring that it can lead you on to music you never would have discovered. In the past year I have wallowed in two exceptional books about jazz. Gary Giddins' *Visions Of Jazz* and *Reading Jazz* by Robert Gottlieb. Both were gifts from my older brother as part of his indoctrination process. Both books have broadened and clarified my views on jazz, and armed with *The Virgin Encyclopedia Of Jazz* and Cook and Morton's indispensible *Guide To Jazz On CD*, the would-be jazz afficianado could, dare I say it, rule the world.

I steered clear of jazz for many years because of fear. It was like writing a book without having first been to University to do a degree in English Literature. How then could I begin to love jazz, or even like it, if I did not understand it? That was the insecurity and stupidity winning over my head and heart. This book is written with those misconceptions in mind. It is written for those that want a single volume about jazz, in a style that is not intimidating or elitist. Having come to jazz late in my musical life, I know how threatening this can be. I came to love jazz by entering through the door of contemporary jazz and fusion and this led me back to the jazz that I was exposed to as a child. I now know that I prefer the bebop of Mulligan, the cool romance of Bill Evans and the soul jazz of Jimmy Smith and McGriff. I respect the other areas, but they do not hit me in the stomach. Those that find other areas difficult, and own up to it, will be able to safely explore within this book. Learning, through listening to jazz, has been one of the greatest pleasures of my life over the past twenty years. Those areas that I am not experienced in, I steer clear of. I leave that to my other contributors. The playright Alan Plater had such passion for Duke Ellington, that he could not fail to fuel my interest in Ellington and Ben Webster. My friend Michael Rodwell has a similar love for Pat Metheny, and that in turn has rubbed off on me. Because of the lack of exposure that jazz receives today, we need these touchstones to influence us and open doors. The Billie Holiday entry written by the late Max Jones need never change. You cannot fail to want to be converted. I hope this book can do the same for you. And I hope that my banner waving for the likes of John Scofield and Don Ellis will at least, be considered.

Entry Style

Albums, EPs (extended play 45s), newspapers, magazines, television programmes, films and stage musicals are referred to in italics. All song titles appear in single quotes. The further reading section at the end of each entry has been expanded to give the reader a much wider choice of available books. These are not necessarily recommended titles but we have attempted to leave out any publication that has little or no merit.

We have also started to add videos at the ends of the entries. Again, this is an area that is expanding more quickly than we can easily cope with, but there are many items in the videography and further items in the filmography, which is another new section we have decided to include. Release dates in keeping with albums attempt to show the release date in the country of origin. We have also tried to include both US and UK titles where applicable.

Album Rating

Because of many requests from our readers we have now decided to rate all albums. All new releases are reviewed either by me or by our team of contributors. We also take into consideration the review ratings of the leading music journals and critics' opinions.

Our system is slightly different to most 5 Star ratings in that we rate according to the artist in question's work. Therefore, a 4 Star album from Duke Ellington may have the overall edge over a 4 Star album by Don Rendell.

Our ratings are carefully made, and consequently you will find we are very sparing with 5 Star and 1 Star albums. With Jazz, many artists play on albums on which they are not the named leader. Many albums are featured so that the ratings differ. This is not because of our own inefficiency, but simply because the musician's performance may not match that of the leader, or vice versa.

★★★★★

Outstanding in every way. A classic and therefore strongly recommended. No comprehensive record collection should be without this album.

★★★★

Excellent. A high standard album from this artist and therefore highly recommended.

★★★

Good. By the artist's usual standards and therefore recommended.

★★

Disappointing. Flawed or lacking in some way.

Poor. An album to avoid unless you are a completist.

PLAGIARISM

In maintaining the largest text database of popular music in the world we are naturally protective of its content. We license to approved licensees only. It is both flattering and irritating to see our work reproduced without credit. Time and time again over the past few years I have read an obituary, when suddenly: hang on, I wrote that line. Secondly, it has come to our notice that other companies attempting to produce their own rock or pop encyclopedias use our material as a core. Flattering this might also be, but highly illegal. We have therefore dropped a few textual 'depth charges' in addition to the original ones. Be warned, the lawyers are waiting.

ACKNOWLEDGEMENTS

Our in-house editorial team is lean and efficient. The EPM Database is now a fully grown child and needs only regular food, attention and love. Thanks to the MUZE UK team for their continuing efficiency while the cat's away: Susan Pipe, Nic Oliver and Jon Staines with the steady timing of Roger Kohn's parrot, Acu. Our outside contributors are further reduced in number, as we now write and amend all our existing text. However, we could not function without the continuing efforts and dedication of Big John Martland and Alex Ogg. By far the biggest thanks go to contributors who were with us from the early days. Graham Lock wrote a number of entries, including Anthony Braxton. Such was the quality of his work that we have barely changed the text over the years. Wherever you are Graham, thank you. Finally from his luxurious hacienda in Spain, The exceptional Bruce Crowther. He is our main house contributor. What he lacks by producing hoplessly incomplete discographies and time-wasting e-mails is more than made up by his incredible work rate and formidible thirst for jazz. It is unlikely that we are ever going to be able to get rid of him.

Other past contributors' work may appear in this volume and I acknowledge with thanks once again; Simon Adams, Mike Atherton, Alan Balfour, Michael Barnett, Chris Blackford, Keith Briggs, Paul M. Brown, Tony Burke, John Child, Linton Chiswick, Alan Clayson, Tom Collier, Paul Cross, Bill Dahl, Norman Darwen, Roy Davenport, John Eley, Lars Fahlin, John Fordham, Per Gardin, Ian Garlinge, Mike Gavin, Andy Hamilton, Mike Hughes, Arthur Jackson, Mark Jones, Max Jones, Dave Laing, Steve Lake, Paul Lewis, Graham Lock, Bernd Matheja, Chris May, Dave McAleer, York Membery, Toru Mitsui, Nick Morgan, Michael Newman, Pete Nickols, Lyndon Noon, Zbigniew Nowara, James Nye, Ken Orton, Ian Peel, Dave Penny, Alan Plater, Barry Ralph, Lionel Robinson, Johnny Rogan, Alan Rowett, Roy Sheridan, Dave Sissons, Steve Smith, Mitch Solomons, Jon Staines, Mike Stephenson, Sam Sutherland, Ray Templeton, Gerard Tierney, Christen K Thomsen, Terry Vinyard, Ben Watson, Pete Watson, Dave Wilson, Val Wilmer and Barry Witherden.

Record company press offices are often bombarded with my requests for biogs and review copies. Theirs is a thankless task, but thanks anyway to them all. Thanks for the co-operation of our colleagues at Virgin Publishing under the guidance of Rob Shreeve, in particular to elegant and diplomatic Roz Scott.

To the quite great Pete Bassett, not to forget the delicious Bassettes; Emily Williams and Emma Morris. To our owners at Muze Inc., who continue to feed the smooth running of the UK operation and are the business partners I always knew I wanted but never knew where to find. Take a dip into the formidable MUZE jazz database through their in-store kiosks, or search it out on the internet. Thanks to all my colleagues at the office on 304 Hudson Street in New York. In particular to the snazzy Ellingtonian Tony Laudico, the clean and snappy Paul Zullo, Marc 'Young Man Blues' Miller, Gary 'the mad monk' Geller, Raisa 'the dominatrix' Howe, Adam 'box of

tissues' Silver, Stephen 'Toots' Hughes and the blindingly funny Scott 'Stolen Moments' Lehr.
Not to ignore: Jim Allen, David Gil de Rubio (down by the schoolyard), Kim Osorio, Ric Hollander, Stephen Parker, Terry 'vintage' Vinyard, Deborah Freedman, Amanda 'high sweedie' Denhoff, Jannett Diaz, Tracey Brandon, Ed 'gentleman' Moore, Suzanne 'south' Park, Solomon Sabel. The unbelievably efficient Phil Fletcher, Matt 'dodgy geezer' Puccini, Bill Schmitt, Michael Doustan, Thom Pappalardo, Duncan 'scuse me pal' Ledwith, Gail 'oh my god!' Niovitch, Sandra Levanta, Paul 'funkmaster' Parreira, Marci 'marci me' Weisler, Bernadette Elliott, Myrtle Jones, Silvia Kessel and all the other Klugettes.

And to the gigantic cool dude Trev Huxley, who owns more copies of *Kind Of Blue* than anyone in the world. Finally to my musically eclectic tin lids; few children of their age know and appreciate Miles, Jimmy Smith and Louis Jordan in the way they do.

Colin Larkin, February 1999

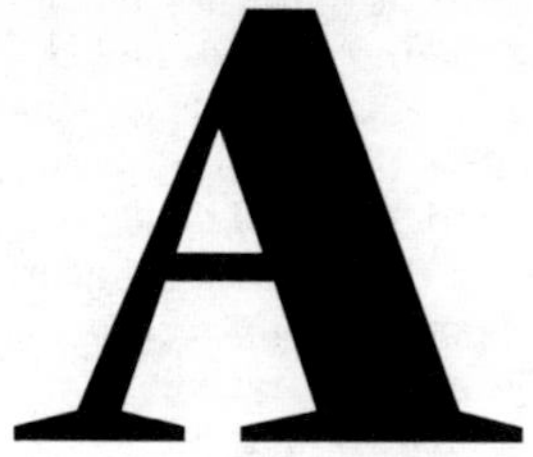

A Day In The Life - Wes Montgomery

Another performing artist whose appearances in the pop charts had the jazz purists crying 'sell out', Wes Montgomery moved to very accessible jazz music, much like the sound today produced by GRP Records. The soulful and mantric opening, with beautiful slip-note piano from Herbie Hancock, leads into the Beatles' 'A Day In The Life', of which only brief snatches are recognizable. A great deal of work went into this 1967 record, with a notable cast of accompanying musicians; the main unit in addition to Montgomery and Hancock consisted of Ron Carter (bass) and Grady Tate (drums).

- Tracks: *A Day In The Life; Watch What Happens; When A Man Loves A Woman; California Nights; Angel; Eleanor Rigby; Willow Weep For Me; Windy; Trust In Me; The Joker.*
- First released 1967
- UK peak chart position: did not chart
- USA peak chart position: 13

A Love Supreme - John Coltrane

John Coltrane's great masterpiece and one of the most profoundly moving records in all of jazz, *A Love Supreme* was recorded in 1964 by Coltrane's classic quartet (with pianist McCoy Tyner, bassist Jimmy Garrison and drummer Elvin Jones). It is a brilliantly integrated jazz suite examining four distinct stages of spiritual development, represented by four movements entitled 'Acknowledgement', 'Resolution', 'Pursuance' and 'Psalm'. The music is intense and gripping, and builds to a head on the fast and aggressive 'Pursuance' before the beautiful and soothing 'Psalm'. *A Love Supreme* is without doubt one of the most profound statements of religious conviction to have emerged in this century.

- Tracks: *Part 1 Acknowledgement; Part 2 Resolution; Part 3 Pursuance; Part 4 Psalm.*
- First released 1964
- UK peak chart position: did not chart
- USA did not chart

AACM

The Association for the Advancement of Creative Musicians was founded in 1965 in Chicago by Muhal Richard Abrams, Jodie Christian, Steve McCall and Phillip Cohran. This musically, spiritually and socially influential co-operative spawned important bands, including Air and the Art Ensemble Of Chicago, and nurtured musicians such as Anthony Braxton, Phil Wilson, Leo Smith and Chico Freeman. Abrams was the prime mover of its extra-musical ethos, encouraging members to study in other disciplines, to see themselves as part of the wider community as well as of the co-operative, and to explore sounds and textures rather than simply pursue proficiency in negotiating fast tempi and complex chord cycles. This interest in sound led to the use of a host of 'little instruments' (from swanee whistles and ocarinas to hosepipes and kitchen utensils) which became almost a trademark of Roscoe Mitchell and the Art Ensemble. The neglect of the competitive 'cutting contest' aspect of jazz was, it has been suggested, a function of the AACM's birth in Chicago rather than hectic New York City. The success of the AACM led to the formation of similar organizations in other cities, the best-known of which was probably the Black Artists Group (BAG) of St. Louis.

Aaltonen, Juhani

b. 12 December 1935, Kouvola, Finland. Although he first became widely known in Finnish jazz circles in the early 60s, saxophonist Aaltonen had begun his professional career in the previous decade. In Helsinki in the 60s, he became a sought-after studio musician while simultaneously joining the free jazz movement. He also ventured into jazz-rock. In the late 60s and early 70s he played with musicians such as Edward Vesala and, in Norway, with Arild Andersen. In addition to the alto and tenor saxophones, Aaltonen is also adept on flute. Capable of hard, driving playing, Aaltonen is also a pleasingly lyrical player, weaving fascinating filigrees of sound against the more dense ensembles of the groups with whom he works.

- ALBUMS: *Etiquette* (Love 1974)★★★.

Abate, Greg

b. 31 May 1947, Fall River, Massachusetts, USA. In the early 70s Abate attended Berklee College Of Music and followed this with on-the-road learning through two years playing lead alto saxophone with Ray Charles's touring band. However, his early influences, Charlie 'Bird' Parker, Phil Woods and Paul Desmond, were of a different order and he moved into bop, leading a quintet that featured Claudio Roditi. Nevertheless, in the early 80s he showed interesting pre-bop sensibilities in his band, Channel One, in which he teamed up with clarinettist Dick Johnson, leader of the Artie Shaw Orchestra. Throughout the 80s and 90s he has worked clubs, concerts and festivals, including, in 1998, the Toulon Jazz Festival, mostly playing in the post-bop mode. He has recorded with numerous leading jazzmen including Hilton Ruiz, Ben Riley, Kenny Barron and Frank Tiberi. Perhaps his most significant partners are Roditi and Richie Cole, and his performances with these two artists are exhilarating examples of the meeting of musical soulmates. Early in his career, Abate was noted for a forceful, frequently blistering approach but maturity revealed an intense melodic element in his style. In the late 90s Abate continued to display his instrumental and stylistic command and versatility. At this point in his career he was interestingly extending his abilities as a composer and happily exploring Latin musical concepts. In 1998 he was reported by jazz journalist Fred Bouchard to be writing books on improvisation and melodic continuity, and he is also an in-demand clinician. Abate, who also plays tenor, soprano and baritone saxophones, and flute, is at his most fluent and dynamic on his principal instrument, the alto.

● ALBUMS: *It's Christmastime* (Brownstone 1990)★★, *My Buddy* (Seaside 1990)★★★, *Broken Dreams* (Seaside 1990)★★★, *Bop City: 'Live' At Birdland* (Candid 1991)★★★, *Straight Ahead* (Candid 1992)★★★, *Dr. Jeckyll & Mr. Hyde* (Candid 1995)★★★, *Live At Chan's* (Candid 1995)★★★, *Bop Lives!* (Blue Chip 1996)★★★★, *Happy Samba* (Blue Chip 1998)★★★, with Red Rodney *Bird Lives! Tribute To Bird: Live At Town Hall* 90s recording (Muse 1998)★★★.

Abdul-Malik, Ahmed

b. Sam Gill, 30 January 1927, New York City, New York, USA, d. 2 October 1993, Long Beach, New Jersey, USA. Abdul-Malik, who adopted his Muslim name in the 50s, enjoyed successful careers in two musical areas, often combining them. As a jazz bassist, he played with enough major artists to secure a firm place in the jazz history books. He accompanied Art Blakey and Don Byas in 1948, Randy Weston for three years starting in 1954, Thelonious Monk in 1957 and 1958, Herbie Mann in 1961, Earl Hines in 1964, and Ken McIntyre in 1971, and appeared at jazz festivals in Montreux, Switzerland and New York. Abdul-Malik's other area of expertise developed after studying African and Middle-Eastern music at university. Playing the 'ud (similar to a lute), he recorded with John Coltrane in 1961, and undertook a US State Department-sponsored tour of South America the same year. Having played at the historic African Jazz Festival in Tangier in 1972, and recorded with Hamiet Bluiett in 1977, Abdul-Malik was a deserving recipient of the BMI's Pioneer in Jazz Award in 1985. From 1970 he taught at New York University and in the Department of African Studies at Brooklyn College.

● ALBUMS: *Jazz Samba* (Riverside 1958)★★★★, *East Meets West* (RCA Victor 1959)★★★, *Jazz Sahara* (Riverside 1959)★★★, *The Music Of Ahmed Abdul-Malik* (New Jazz 1961)★★★, *Ahmed Abdul-Malik/Sounds Of Africa* (New Jazz 1962)★★★, *Eastern Moods* (Prestige 1963)★★★, *Spellbound* (Status 1965)★★.

Abdullah, Ahmed

b. Leroy Bland, 10 May 1946, New York City, USA. Inspired originally by Louis Armstrong, Abdullah has played with mainstream jazzmen such as Cal Massey, R&B singers including Solomon Burke, Little Johnny Taylor and Joe Simon and with the free jazz Master Brotherhood. In the 70s he worked with the Melodic Art-tet, a co-operative that included bassist William Parker and saxophonist Charles Brackeen, and, after stints with Rashied Ali and Ed Blackwell, led his own group, Abdullah. In 1976 he joined Sun Ra's Arkestra for two years, returning for further spells in the 80s and 90s when not working with one of the three bands he leads himself. His evocative yet immediate trumpet contributed a crucial vibrancy to Billy Bang's 1985 masterpiece *The Fire From Within* and in the late 80s he recorded two albums as leader for the Swedish Silkheart label. Still shamefully under-represented on record, his free, fighting trumpet has the generous vision of the past, characteristic of post-Loft creative jazz.

● ALBUMS: *Live At Ali's Alley* (Cadence 1978)★★★, *Life's Force* (About Time 1979)★★★, *Liquid Magic* (Silkheart 1987)★★★, *Ahmed Abdullah And The Solomnic Quartet* (Silkheart 1988)★★★, *Dedication* (CIMP 1998)★★★.

Abercrombie, John

b. 16 December 1944, Portchester, New York, USA. After studying at Berklee College Of Music in Boston, Abercrombie spent four years playing guitar in Johnny 'Hammond' Smith's group. Touring with an established band offered him the kind of practical study that was ideal after Berklee's academic hothouse of the late 60s. Moving back to New York in 1969, his already unusual technical command of the instrument meant he had little difficulty finding opportunities to play with fine musicians. In the ensuing five years he played alongside Randy and Michael Brecker in the group Dreams, and toured with the Chico Hamilton Band, including an appearance at the Montreux International Jazz Festival. In demand as a sideman from countless bandleaders, from Gil Evans to Gato Barbieri, it was in Billy Cobham's fusion group Spectrum that Abercrombie's reputation quickly spread. This hard-driving, rock-influenced band was the perfect vehicle for his prodigious technique and imagination. However, by the mid-70s, Abercrombie was discovering a new and altogether different voice. Treating fusion in a similar manner to which the Modern Jazz Quartet had treated bop, he formed his highly regarded trio Timeless, playing in a softer, more delicate style. This band was replaced in 1975 by his Gateway trio, with Dave Holland and Jack DeJohnette, and then by a quartet three years later. Since 1981, Abercrombie has performed and recorded prolifically. As well as continuing to collaborate with DeJohnette, he has produced some highly regarded duet work with Ralph Towner, led a quartet featuring Michael Brecker and was involved in the all-star big band that recorded Charles Mingus's *Epitaph*. Abercrombie remains one of the most versatile and gifted guitarists of post-war jazz and appears to be enjoying a prolific period during the 90s.

● ALBUMS: *Timeless* (ECM 1974)★★★★, with Ralph Towner *Sargasso Sea* (ECM 1976)★★★★, *Pictures* (ECM 1977)★★★, *Arcade* (ECM 1979)★★★, *Abercrombie Quartet* (ECM 1980)★★★, *M* (ECM 1981)★★★, with Towner *Five Years Later* (ECM 1981)★★★★, *Solar* (Palo Alto 1982)★★★, *Night* (ECM 1984)★★★, with Peter Erskine, Marc Johnson *Current Events* (ECM 1985)★★★★, *Witchcraft* (Justin Time 1986)★★★, *Getting There* (ECM 1988)★★★, with Erskine, Johnson *John Abercrombie, Marc Johnson & Peter Erskine* (ECM 1989)★★★★, *Animato* (ECM 1990)★★★, *While We're Young* (ECM

1992)★★★★, with Erskine, Johnson, John Surman *November* (ECM 1994)★★★★, *Speak Of The Devil* (ECM 1994)★★★, with Andy LaVerne *Where We Were* (Double-Time 1996)★★★, with Adam Nussbaum, Dan Wall *Tactics* (ECM 1997)★★★.
● COMPILATIONS: *Works* (ECM 1989)★★★★.
● VIDEOS: *Jazz Guitar Improvisation* (Homespun Video 1996).

Abrahams, Brian

b. 26 June 1947, Cape Town, South Africa. Abrahams became known first for his ability as a singer. From the age of 13 he sang with local groups, but by the early 70s he was established as a drummer and percussionist, often backing vocal and dance groups. While working with a trio in Swaziland, Abrahams accompanied the American artists Sarah Vaughan and Nancy Wilson. In 1975 Abrahams moved to London where he played with a number of English bands including Ronnie Scott's, and with members of the expatriate South African community, especially Dudu Pukwana and Chris McGregor. In the early 80s, Abrahams formed his own band, District 6, named after a sector of Cape Town, which has successfully worked at fusing African folk themes with European influences. The group's patience and effort paid off, allowing a sophistication and drive rare in a unit that retains its local identity. Abrahams acknowledges the influences of Duke Ellington, Thelonious Monk, and McGregor and admires the drumming of Art Blakey, Max Roach and Jack DeJohnette. He is also a teacher and runs regular workshops, often in conjunction with District 6.
● ALBUMS: with Chris McGregor *Yes Please* (1982)★★★, with District 6 *Akuzwakale (Let It Be Heard)* (District Six 1984)★★★★, *To Be Free* (Editions EG 1987)★★★, *Imgoma Yabantwana* (District Six 1989)★★★.

Abrams, Max

b. 11 August 1907, Glasgow, Scotland, d. 12 November 1995. Abrams began playing drums with dance bands in his teens, often in the Glasgow area. In the late 20s he went to London and was soon active with a number of bands there. He toured South Africa, then returned to London where, in 1932, he joined Jack Hylton's orchestra. During the next few years he played with several leading British dance bands, including Sydney Lipton's and Carroll Gibbons's Savoy Orpheans. He was also in demand for numerous recording dates with many leaders. He recorded with his own band in 1935 and also made a series of tuition records for aspiring drummers. In the early 40s, Abrams drummed with Ambrose, Jack Payne and Stéphane Grappelli, then, in 1945, joined Sid Phillips for an engagement that lasted well into the next decade. During this period Abrams often worked with other small bands, including Humphrey Lyttelton's, and appeared regularly on radio. Abrams was a technically gifted percussionist, playing several instruments including vibraphone, xylophone and tympani. He was much sought after as a teacher and founded his own School for Drum Tuition. His admired ability drew many eager and gifted drummers to him, among them Jack Parnell.

Abrams, Muhal Richard

b. 19 September 1930, Chicago, Illinois, USA. Abrams began studying piano at Chicago Music College at the age of 17 and started working professionally a year later. In 1955 he formed Modern Jazz Two + 3 with tenor saxophonist Eddie Harris. After this group folded, he kept a low profile until 1961, when he organized the Experimental Band, a contrast to his earlier hard bop venture in its use of free jazz concepts for a fluctuating line-up. The band evolved into the AACM, emerging in 1965 with Abrams as its president. He is an accomplished pianist and composer with a deep sense of tradition, and from the mid-70s has been able to record more frequently with his own groups (including an excellent big band), but it is as the spiritual leader of the AACM that he has probably made his most lasting mark. Despite being remembered by Leroy Jenkins as a thug when he was at school, in maturity, Abrams was responsible for fostering among black musicians in Chicago (and beyond) a sense of their value and dignity as artists and for showing them the importance of the link between artists and the community.
● ALBUMS: *Levels And Degrees Of Light* (Delmark 1967)★★★, *Young At Heart/Wise In Time* (Delmark 1969)★★★, *Things To Come From Those Now Gone* (Delmark 1970)★★★, *Afrisong* (India Navigation 1975)★★★, *Sightsong* (Black Saint 1976)★★★★, *1-OQA+19* (Black Saint 1977)★★★, *Lifea Blinec* (Novus 1978)★★, *Spiral Live At Montreux* (Arista 1978)★★, with George Lewis *Spihumonesty* (Black Saint 1979)★★★, with Lewis *Mama And Daddy* (Black Saint 1980)★★★, with Amina Claudine Myers *Duet* (Black Saint 1981)★★, *Blues Forever* (Black Saint 1982)★★★, *Rejoicing With The Light* (Black Saint 1983)★★, *View From Within* (Black Saint 1984)★★, *Roots Of Blue* (RPR 1986)★★★, *Blues Forever* (Black Saint 1986)★★★★, *Colors In Thirty-Third* (Black Saint 1987)★★★, *The Hearinga Suite* (Black Saint 1989)★★★, with Roscoe Mitchell *Solos And Duets At Merkin Hall* (Black Saint 1992)★★★★, *Blu Blu Blu* (Black Saint 1992)★★★★, *Family Talk* (Black Saint 1993)★★★, *One Line, Two Views* (New World 1995)★★★★, *Think All, Focus One* (Black Saint 1996)★★★, *Song For All* (Black Saint 1997)★★★, with Barry Harris *Interpretations Of Monk, Vol. 1* 1981 recording (Koch 1997)★★★★., *The Open Air Meeting* (New World 1998★★★,

Acid Jazz Records

Fighting against the prevalent late 80s view of jazz as a soundtrack to lounge culture, Acid Jazz revived the idea that the music belonged as much to the dancefloor as to smoky cafés. The label was founded by DJ Gilles Peterson and Eddie Piller in April 1988. Piller had worked at the indie label Avator, then MCA and Stiff Records. His first label was Stiff subsidiary Countdown, then Re-elect the President, which found some degree of success with the James Taylor Quartet. This band grew out of the Prisoners, who had already spent time with Piller at Countdown. The 'acid jazz' tag was satirical, alluding to acid house in a tongue-in-cheek manner: 'We always thought about changing the name, but it stopped being a joke when our international sales started to reach a substantial level.' The first record was Galliano's 'Frederick Lies Still', followed by *Acid Jazz And Other Illicit Grooves*, packaged with rare groove and funk material. At least as significant was the huge impact made by the Brand New Heavies' debut. After a few financial setbacks, in 1989 Peterson took up an offer from Phonogram, and Piller recruited Polydor Records A&R manager Kieran Hurley. Together they took the decision to push their jazz dance sounds in a more commercial direction. As part of his agreement with Phonogram, Peterson was able to fund his own Talkin' Loud Records, which maintains a friendly rivalry with Acid Jazz to this day. Many argued that the label lost more than its fair share of high-quality acts (A Man Called Adam to Big Life Records, Galliano to Talkin' Loud, and the Sandals and Jamiroquai), but they still boasted acclaimed bands including Mother Earth, Corduroy, Night Trains and others (the James Taylor Quartet also returned to the label in 1994). The label now boasts offices in London, Milan, Sydney and Dublin, as the 'acid jazz' sound, amended to 'urban alternative' in the USA, has grown. As Piller reflects: 'To me Acid Jazz is a record label, but I can understand how it has become embodied as a style definition in social culture. It's not something we at Acid Jazz expected when we first started, but it is a term that ourselves, and the artists who are not signed to us but are often referred to as an 'Acid Jazz' act, have to accept.' Their sampler series *Totally Wired* has increased the label's profile, even though tracks are no longer selected only from the Acid Jazz roster.

● COMPILATIONS: *Totally Wired 1-7* (Acid Jazz)★★★.

ACOUSTIC ALCHEMY

Formed in the mid-80s, Acoustic Alchemy was essentially Greg Carmichael (b. 1953, London, England; nylon string guitar) and Nick Webb (b. 1954, Manchester, England, d. February 1998; steel string guitar). Their blend of instrumental music was neither jazz nor pop, but contained elements of both, together with flamenco, reggae and folk. Webb was originally influenced by John Martyn and Pentangle. He recorded one album with Simon James in the early 80s before linking up with Carmichael in 1986 (released as *Early Alchemy*). Carmichael had studied classical guitar at the London College of Music and gained experience playing with jazz groups. Their break came, when frustrated by the apathy for their music in England, they took a Virgin Atlantic Airlines in-flight gig, and literally played their way to America. They were signed to MCA as part of their Master Series, and debuted with the excellent *Red Dust And Spanish Lace*, which contained one of their finest compositions 'Mr Chow', an example of Chinese Reggae! Following *Blue Chip* they joined GRP Records, although their debut for the label, *Reference Point*, lacked the life and sparkle of their MCA work. They redressed the balance with *Back On The Case* in 1991, although subsequent albums sounded workmanlike. Webb died of pancreatic cancer in February 1998.

● ALBUMS: *Red Dust And Spanish Lace* (MCA 1987)★★★★, *Natural Elements* (MCA 1988)★★★, *Blue Chip* (MCA 1989)★★★, *Reference Point* (GRP 1990)★★, *Back On The Case* (GRP 1991)★★★, *Early Alchemy* (1992)★★, *The New Edge* (GRP 1993)★★, *Arcanum* (GRP 1996)★★, *Positive Thinking* (GRP 1998)★★★.

ADAMS, GEORGE RUFUS

b. 29 April 1940, Covington, Georgia, USA, d. 14 November 1992, New York City, New York, USA. Adams began playing piano at the age of 11, but took up the saxophone (alto first, tenor later) while still at school and was soon gigging with local R&B bands. A scholarship to Clark College, Atlanta, brought him tuition from Wayman Carver (in the 30s a mainstay of the Chick Webb band and perhaps the first man to play jazz flute, an instrument Adams also took up). Adams spent the 60s working with a wide range of musicians and in 1968, in New York, he joined Roy Haynes and subsequently worked with Gil Evans and Art Blakey. Most influential on Adams' later work was a stint with Charles Mingus in the mid-70s. At the end of the decade he was co-leader, with Don Pullen, of a quartet that also included Dannie Richmond and that stayed in existence, recording prolifically, until Richmond's death in 1988. Initially, Adams was strongly influenced by John Coltrane, but 1988's, *Nightingale*, showed him to have a deeply romantic leaning. In every aspect of his work, the often overlooked Adams always displayed a marked affinity with the blues. He also sang occasionally, in a croaky, but very effective blues voice.

● ALBUMS: *Jazz Confronto 22* (Horo 1975)★★★, *Suite For Swingers* (Horo 1976)★★★, with Don Pullen *Don't Lose Control* (Soul Note 1979)★★★★, *Paradise Space Shuttle* (Timeless 1979)★★★, *Sound Suggestions* (ECM 1979)★★★, *Hand To Hand* (Soul Note 1980)★★★, with Pullen *Lifeline* (Timeless 1981)★★★, with Pullen *Earth Beams* (Timeless 1981)★★★, with Pullen *Melodic Excursions* (Timeless 1982)★★★★, with Pullen *Live At The Village Vanguard, Volume 1* (Soul Note 1983)★★★★, with Pullen *Live At The Village Vanguard, Volume 2* (Soul Note 1983)★★★★, with Pullen *City Gates* (Timeless 1983)★★★, with Pullen *Decisions* (Timeless 1984)★★★, with Pullen *Live At Montmartre* (Timeless 1985)★★★, *More Sightings* (Enja 1985)★★★, with Pullen *Breakthrough* (Blue Note 1986)★★★, with Pullen *Song Everlasting* (Blue Note 1987)★★★, *Nightingale* (Blue Note 1988)★★★★, *America* (Blue Note 1989)★★★, *Old Feeling* (Blue Note 1991)★★★★.

ADAMS, PEPPER

b. Park Adams III, 8 October 1930, Highland Park, Michigan, USA, d. 10 September 1986, New York City, New York, USA. While Adams was still a child his family moved to Rochester, New York, where he became involved in the local jazz music scene. Inspired by Coleman Hawkins, Adams decided to become a tenor saxophone player, but quickly fell under the spell of Harry Carney, taking up the baritone in the mid-40s (somewhat self-depreciatingly, Adams later insisted that the chief reason he took up the baritone was because he was able to buy a cheap instrument). A stint with Lionel Hampton, allied to freelance work, mostly around Detroit, with Wardell Gray, Barry Harris, Frank Foster, Tommy Flanagan and others, gave Adams a broad musical base. For a time he was involved in the big bands of Stan Kenton and Maynard Ferguson, but still found time to work with Chet Baker, Donald Byrd, Benny Goodman and Thelonious Monk. His robust, big sound and forceful soloing made him an important member of the Thad Jones-Mel Lewis Jazz Orchestra for a dozen years from 1965. In the late 70s and on through the 80s he performed at festivals around the world and recorded with Kenny Wheeler, Lionel Hampton, Zoot Sims, Peter Leitch and Denny Christianson. Adams died of cancer in 1986.

● ALBUMS: *Pepper Adams 5* (Mode 1957)★★★★, *Critic's Choice* (World Pacific 1957)★★★★, *The Cool Sound Of Pepper Adams* reissued as *Pure Pepper* (Regent/Savoy 1958)★★★, with Jimmy Knepper *The Pepper-Knepper Quintet* (Metrojazz 1958)★★★, with Donald Byrd *10 To 4 At The 5 Spot* (Riverside 1958)★★★★, with Byrd *Stardust* (Bethlehem 1960)★★★, with Byrd *Out Of This World* (Warwick 1961)★★★, *The Soul Of Jazz Percussion* (Warwick 1963)★★★, *Pepper Adams Plays The Compositions Of Charles Mingus* (Workshop Jazz 1963)★★★, with Thad Jones *Mean What You Say* (Milestone 1966)★★★★, with Zoot Sims *Encounter!* (Prestige 1969)★★★★, *Ephemera* (Spotlite 1973)★★★, *Julian* (Inner City 1975)★★★, *Twelfth And Pingree* (Enja 1975)★★★, *Reflectory* (Muse 1978)★★★, *The Master* (Muse 1980)★★★★, *Urban Dreams* (Palo Alto 1981)★★★, *Conjuration: Fat Tuesday's Session* (Reservoir 1983)★★★★, *Generations* (Muse 1985)★★★, *Adams Effect* (Uptown 1985)★★★, *Live In Europe* 1977 recording (Just Jazz 1995)★★★.

ADDERLEY, CANNONBALL

b. Julian Edwin Adderley, 15 September 1928, Tampa, Florida, USA, d. 8 August 1975, Gary, Indiana, USA. Cannonball Adderley was one of the great saxophonists of his generation. His fiery, blues-soaked interpretations of Charlie Parker's alto legacy brought jazz to many people hitherto untouched by it. In the 60s he launched a new genre, 'soul-jazz', whose popularity has survived undiminished into the 90s. Cannonball was derived from 'Cannibal', a nickname earned at high school on account of his prodigious appetite. He studied brass and reed instruments there between 1944 and 1948. Until 1956 he was band director at Dillerd High School, Lauderdale, Florida, as well as leader of his own jazz quartet. While serving in the forces he became director of the 36th Army Band, an ensemble that included his younger brother Nat Adderley on trumpet. Persuaded to go to New York by legendary alto saxophonist and R&B singer Eddie 'Cleanhead' Vinson, Cannonball created a sensation at the Cafe Bohemia, playing alongside bassist Oscar Pettiford. In 1958 he signed to Riverside Records and over the next six years released a series of albums, many of them recorded live, that laid the foundations of the soul-jazz genre. As well as his brother Nat, Adderley's first group featured a superb rhythm section in Sam Jones and Louis Hayes, supplemented by pianist Bobby Timmons, who also wrote the group's first hit, 'This Here'. From 1957-59 Adderley was part of the classic Miles Davis Quintet, an astonishing group of individuals that also included John Coltrane (tenor), Bill Evans or Red Garland (piano), Paul Chambers (bass) and Philly Joe Jones (drums). As well as playing on the celebrated *Kind Of Blue*, Cannonball recorded his own album, the magnificent *Somethin' Else*, for Blue Note Records - Davis guested on the recording, a rare honour.

After leaving Davis, Cannonball re-formed his own band, with Nat still on cornet; in 1961 Yusef Lateef joined on tenor saxophone and stayed for two productive years. This band nurtured the talents of electric pianists Joe Zawinul, and then George Duke. It was Zawinul's 'Mercy, Mercy, Mercy', recorded live at the Club Delisa in Chicago, that provided Adderley with his next major hit, reaching number 11 in the US charts in February 1967. The title is indicative of the band's fondness for gospel-orientated, black consciousness themes. Their last hit was 'Country Preacher', again a Zawinul composition, which peaked in early 1970 (number 29 in the R&B charts). Straight jazz never again enjoyed such mass appeal. When asked about his inspirations, Cannonball cited the swing alto saxophonist Benny Carter and, of course, Charlie Parker - but his understanding of blues distortion also enabled him to apply the *avant garde* lessons of John Coltrane and Ornette Coleman. His alto saxophone had a special immediacy, a welcome reminder of the blues at the heart of bebop, an element that jazz rock - the bastard offspring of soul jazz - too often suppressed.

● ALBUMS: *Presenting Cannonball* (Savoy 1955)★★★, *Julian 'Cannonball' Adderley* (EmArcy 1955)★★★, *Julian 'Cannonball' Adderley And Strings* (EmArcy 1956)★★, *In The Land Of Hi-Fi* (EmArcy 1956)★★★, *Sophisticated Swing* (EmArcy 1957)★★★★, *Cannonball's Sharpshooters* (EmArcy 1958)★★★, *Jump For Joy* (EmArcy 1958)★★★, *Portrait Of Cannonball* (Riverside 1958)★★★, *Somethin' Else* (Blue Note 1958)★★★★★, *Things Are Gettin' Better* (Riverside 1958)★★★★, *Alabama Concerto* (1958)★★★, *The Cannonball Adderley Quintet In San Francisco* (Riverside 1959)★★★, *Cannonball Adderley Quintet In Chicago* (Mercury 1959)★★★, *Cannonball Takes Charge* (Riverside 1959)★★, *Cannonball Adderley Quintet At The Lighthouse* (Riverside 1960)★★★, *Them Dirty Blues* (Riverside 1960)★★★, *What Is This Thing Called Soul?* (Pablo 1960)★★★★, *The Lush Side Of Cannonball Adderley* (Mercury 1961)★★★, *African Waltz* (Riverside 1961)★★★, *Cannonball Enroute* (Mercury 1961)★★★, *Cannonball Adderley And The Poll-Winners* (Riverside 1961)★★★, *Cannonball Adderley Quintet Plus* (Riverside 1961)★★★, with Nancy Wilson *Nancy Wilson/Cannonball Adderley* (Capitol 1962)★★★, with Bill Evans *Know What I Mean* (Riverside 1962)★★★★, *The Cannonball Adderley Sextet in New York* (Riverside 1962)★★, *Cannonball's Bossa Nova* (Riverside 1963)★★, *Jazz Workshop Revisited* (Riverside 1963)★★, *Nippon Soul* (Riverside 1964)★★★, with John Coltrane *Cannonball And Coltrane* (Limelight 1964)★★★, *Domination* (Capitol 1965)★★, *Fiddler On The Roof* (Capitol 1965)★★, with Ernie Andrews *Live Session* (Capitol 1965)★★★, *Cannonball Adderley Live* (Capitol 1965)★★★, with Nat Adderley *Them Adderley's* (Limelight 1966)★★★, *Great Love Themes* (Capitol 1966)★★, *Why Am I*

Treated So Bad (Capitol 1966)★★★, with Ray Brown *Two For The Blues* (1966)★★, *Mercy Mercy Mercy Live At The Club* (Capitol 1967)★★★★, *74 Miles Away - Walk Tall* (Capitol 1967)★★, *Cannonball In Europe* (Riverside 1967)★★★, *Things Are Getting Better* (1968)★★★★, *Accent On Africa* (Capitol 1968)★★★, *Cannonball In Person* (Capitol 1969)★★★, *Planet Earth* (Riverside 1969)★★, *Country Preacher* (Capitol 1970)★★★, *Experience In E, Tensity, Dialogues* (1970)★★, *The Black Messiah* (Capitol 1970)★★★, *The Price You Got To Pay To Be Free* (Capitol 1970)★★, *Inside Straight* (Fantasy 1973)★★, *Phenix* (Fantasy 1975)★★, *Spontaneous Combustion* 1955 recording (Savoy 1976)★★★, *Cannonball In Europe* 1962 recording (1988)★★★, *In Japan* (Blue Note 1990)★★★, *Radio Nights* (Virgin 1991)★★, *Dizzy's Business* (Ace 1993)★★.

● COMPILATIONS: *Cannonball's Greatest Hits* (Riverside 1962)★★★★, *The Best Of Cannonball Adderley* (Riverside 1968)★★★★, *Cannonball Adderley Collection Volumes 1 - 7* (Landmark 1988)★★★, *Best Of Cannonball Adderley The Capitol Years* (Capitol 1991)★★★, *Quintet Plus* (Ace 1992)★★★, *Portrait Of Cannonball* (Ace 1993)★★★, *Jazz Profile* (Blue Note 1997)★★★★.

ADDERLEY, NAT

b. Nathaniel Adderley, 25 November 1931, Tampa, Florida, USA. The younger brother of Cannonball Adderley, Nathaniel was a singer until his voice broke and he took up the trumpet. In the early 50s he served in the army with his brother and played in the 36th Army Band. His professional break came in 1954, when Lionel Hampton asked him to join his riotously swinging, R&B-inflected big band; he stayed for only a year. Later he played with Woody Herman and J.J. Johnson. In 1960 he released *Work Song*, a brilliant amalgam of the soul jazz for which he is celebrated and a more 'cool'-style, chamber music instrumentation (including cello and guitar, the latter played by Wes Montgomery). Throughout the 60s and early 70s, he played in his brother's band and since the latter's death in 1975 has kept alive that special brand of warm, rootsy bop, both on his own recordings and in other contexts, such as Nathan Davis's Paris Reunion Band.

● ALBUMS: *That's Nat* (Savoy 1955)★★★, *Introducing Nat Adderley* (EmArcy 1955)★★★, *To The Ivy League From Nat* (EmArcy 1956)★★★, *Branching Out* (Riverside 1958)★★★, *Much Brass* (Riverside 1959)★★★, *That's Right!* (Riverside 1960)★★★, *Work Song* (Riverside 1960)★★★★, *Naturally!* (Jazzland 1961)★★★, *In The Bag* (Jazzland 1962)★★★★, *The Adderley Brothers In New Orleans* (1962)★★★, *Little Big Horn!* (Riverside 1964)★★★, *Autobiography* (Atlantic 1965)★★★, *Sayin' Something* (Atlantic 1966)★★★, with Cannonball *Them Adderleys* (Limelight 1966)★★★, *Live At Memory Lane* (Atlantic 1967)★★, *The Scavenger* (Milestone 1968)★★, *Comin' Out Of The Shadows* (1968)★★, *You, Baby* (A&M 1968)★★, *Natural Soul* (Milestone 1968)★★★, *Calling Out Loud* (A&M 1969)★★, *Zodiac Soul* (1970)★★, *Soul Of The Bible* (1972)★★, *Double Exposure* (1974)★★★, *Don't Look Back* (1976)★★★, *A Little New York Midtown Music* (Galaxy 1978)★★, *On The Move* (1983)★★★, *Blue Autumn* (Theresa 1983)★★, with Benny Carter, Red Norvo *Benny Carter All Stars, Featuring Nat Adderley & Red Norvo* (Sonet 1985)★★★ *That's Nat* (Savoy 1985)★★★, *Blue Autumn* (Theresa 1987)★★★, *Work Songs* (Fantasy 1987)★★★, *Talkin' About You* (Landmark 1991)★★★, *We Remember Cannon* (In & Out 1991)★★★, *The Old Country* (Enja 1992)★★★, *Working* (1993)★★★, *Mercy, Mercy, Mercy* (Evidence 1997)★★★.

● VIDEOS: *Nat Adderley Quartet* (Kay Jazz 1988).

ADDISON, BERNARD

b. 15 April 1905, Annapolis, Maryland, USA. Addison's rhythmic jazz guitar playing made him best known for his section work rather than as a soloist. In his teens he was co-leader with Claude Hopkins of a band in Washington, DC, then moved to New York, where he became a member of the house band at Small's Paradise, remaining there until 1929. Equally at home in big bands and small groups, in the early 30s Addison worked with Louis Armstrong, Fletcher Henderson, Bubber Miley, Jelly Roll Morton, Art Tatum and Fats Waller. He was also accompanist to the Mills Brothers (and later worked with the Ink Spots). Spells with Sidney Bechet, Teddy Bunn, Mezz Mezzrow and Stuff Smith led to his appearance on numerous recording dates in the 30s and 40s, including Benny Carter's 1936 London session. In the 50s he worked with musicians as diverse as Eubie Blake and Pete Brown; from the 60s onwards Bernard Addison was more concerned with teaching, although he continued to take an active interest in jazz.

AFFIF, RON

b. 30 December 1965, Pittsburgh, Pennsylvania, USA. A fluent hard bop guitarist influenced by George Benson and Joe Pass, Affif has attracted critical praise in the mid-90s with several excellent albums for the Pablo label. As a teenager Affif was taught by his uncle Ron Anthony, a guitarist with experience of playing with George Shearing and Frank Sinatra. After relocating to Los Angeles in the mid-80s, he played with Jack Sheldon, Pete Christlieb and Dave Pike and recorded as part of a quartet for the R.A. label in 1987. A move to New York brought Affif to the attention of Pass's producer Eric Miller, who signed him to Pablo. His self-titled 1992 debut set concentrated on swinging renditions of traditional material, with strong backing from bassist Essiet Essiet and drummer Colin Bailey. By 1995's *52nd Street* Affif was receiving plaudits from critics and fellow guitar players, including Benson and the late Pass. His 1997 trio set featured several strong Affif originals, and was recorded live over three days in front of invitation-only crowds at Fantasy Records' Studio A.

● ALBUMS: *Ron Affif* (Pablo 1993)★★★, *Vierd Blues* (Pablo 1994)★★★, *52nd Street* (Pablo 1996)★★★★, *Ringside* (Pablo 1997)★★★★.

AFTER HOURS

A superb 27 minute-long pilot for a US television series in 1961 that never was. The simple nightclub setting has a band led by Coleman Hawkins and Roy Eldridge with Johnny Guarnieri, Barry Galbraith, Milt Hinton and William 'Cozy' Cole. Among the songs featured are 'Lover Man' and a red-hot 'Sunday', during which

Eldridge is so carried away he overruns his solo, to the obvious delight of a momentarily upstaged Hawkins.

Ahola, Sylvester

b. 24 May 1902, Gloucester, Massachusetts, USA, d. 1995. In the early 20s, trumpeter Ahola played in Boston dance bands before moving to New York. He worked with a number of leading dance bands of the day, including Paul Specht's and Adrian Rollini's New Yorkers. While with Specht, he visited London and returned there alone in the winter of 1927/8 where he joined the Savoy Orpheans. After almost a year with the band he joined the immensely popular Ambrose band. He stayed with Bert Ambrose in London, almost without a break, until the autumn of 1931. By this time he had played on a staggeringly large number of records (perhaps as many as 3000) and earned the disapproval of UK trumpeters who saw him as a serious threat to their livelihoods. Back in New York, he continued to play in numerous studio bands and to add to his list of often uncredited appearances on record. In the early 40s Ahola retired and lived amidst accumulated memorabilia in his home-town. He continued to work, with occasional performances with a local classical orchestra. Technically, Ahola was a very assured musician, much admired by his contemporaries and many later trumpeters who recognized in his playing much that was enviable. A good jazz player, Ahola's career choices meant that his light usually gleamed, although fitfully, in the material with which he was obliged to work.

● COMPILATIONS: with various bands *Jazz In Britain: The 1920s* (Parlophone)★★★.

Air

Jazz conglomeration comprising Henry Threadgill (b. 15 February 1944, Chicago, Illinois, USA; reeds), Fred Hopkins (b. 11 October 1947, Chicago, Illinois, USA; bass), Steve McCall (b. 30 September 1933, Chicago, Illinois, USA, d. 25 May 1989; drums). Air, originally called Reflection, was formed in Chicago in 1971 when AACM colleagues Threadgill, Hopkins and McCall came together to play for a stage show about Scott Joplin. Although the trio did later record a set of Joplin and Jelly Roll Morton tunes (*Air Lore*), they are better known for the music that Threadgill wrote for them when they began to tour in 1975. He brought a new angle to jazz ensemble playing by composing 'from the bass . . . from the drums': 'It changes the whole frame of reference in terms of what accompaniment is all about, you know. It kind of kills accompaniment and puts everything on an equal footing, and that's what I'm after.' Threadgill's pieces were steeped in the AACM's structural modernisms: ambitious, democratic, unresolved; filled with space, strength (of mind, feeling, technique) and a rigorous sense of inquiry; spiced with Threadgill's particular sense of the enigmatic; and brought to life by the trio's extraordinary instrumental virtuosity. In the mid-70s Air moved to New York and in 1982, when McCall left (to be replaced by Pheeroan AkLaff, who was in turn replaced by Andrew Cyrille in 1985), they changed their name to New Air. The group's final recording, *Air Show No 1*, which featured singer Cassandra Wilson, was released in 1986. In their earlier incarnation, Air were one of the crucial new jazz groups of the 70s and - together with the Art Ensemble Of Chicago and the different groups led by Muhal Richard Abrams and Anthony Braxton - standard-bearers for the AACM's claim to have inspired the most original and exciting jazz music of the post-Coltrane era.

● ALBUMS: *Air Song* (India Navigation 1975)★★★★, *Air Raid* (1977)★★★★, *Air Time* (Nessa 1977)★★★, *Open Air Suite* (Novus 1978)★★★, *Montreux Suisse* (Novus 1978)★★★, *Air Lore* (Bluebird 1979)★★★, *Live Air* 1976/7 recording (Black Saint 1980)★★★, *Air Mail* (Black Saint 1980)★★★, *80 Degrees Below '82* (Island 1982)★★★, as New Air *Live At The Montreux International Jazz Festival* (Black Saint 1984)★★★, as New Air *Air Show No 1* (Black Saint1986)★★★.

Air Condition

(see Namyslowski, Zbigniew)

Akiyoshi, Toshiko

b. 12 December 1929, Dairen, Manchuria (of Japanese parents). Akiyoshi went to live in Japan in 1947, by which time she was already an accomplished, classically trained pianist. Turning to jazz, she soon became one of Japan's highest-paid entertainers. After recording for Norman Granz, Akiyoshi followed the advice of Oscar Peterson and moved to America, where she enrolled at Berklee College Of Music. She worked as a member of various small bop groups, including those led by Charlie Mariano (to whom she was briefly married) and Charles Mingus. Although a fleet and inventive pianist who was much influenced by Bud Powell, Akiyoshi's greatest interest lay in composing, and in particular she wished to write for big bands. In 1967 a specially assembled big band played pieces by her at a concert in New York's Town Hall. In the early 70s, now resident in Los Angeles, Akiyoshi worked with, and later married, tenor saxophonist Lew Tabackin. They formed a rehearsal band that employed many of the best available west coast session men, and was designed primarily as a showcase for Akiyoshi's talents as a composer and for Tabackin's as a forceful, freewheeling soloist. Based in New York since the mid-80s, Akiyoshi has continued to develop her big-band writing and also leads a small group, but - under-represented on records and rarely touring - she remains little-known to foreign audiences. An outstanding musician by any standards, she is one of the best living composer-arrangers of big band music in jazz and holds a very high place in the overall history of big band music. A documentary film, *Toshiko Akiyoshi: Jazz Is My Native Language* (1984), traces her life and career.

● ALBUMS: *Toshiko's Piano* 10-inch album (Norgran 1953)★★★, *Amazing Toshiko Akiyoshi* i (1954)★★★, with others *Jam Session For Musicians III: The Historic Mocambo Session '54* (1954)★★★, *The Toshiko Trio* (Storyville 1956)★★★, *Toshiko, Her Quartet* (1956)★★★, one side only *Amazing Toshiko Akiyoshi* ii (Verve 1957)★★★, *Toshiko, Her Trio Her Quartet* (Storyville 1957)★★★,

with Leon Sash *Toshiko And Leon Sash At Newport* (Verve 1958)★★★★, *The Many Sides Of Toshiko* (Verve 1958)★★★, *United Notions* (Metrojazz 1958)★★★, with Charlie Mariano *Toshiko-Mariano Quartet* (Candid 1960)★★★, *Toshiko Mariano* (Candid 1960)★★★, *Toshiko Meets Her Old Pals* (1961)★★★, with Steve Kuhn *The Country And Western Sounds Of Jazz* (Dauntless 1963)★★, *Jazz In Japan* (Vee Jay 1964)★★★, *Toshiko Akiyoshi* (1965)★★★, *Toshiko At The Top Of The Gate* (Denon 1968)★★★★, *Toshiko Akiyoshi Quartet* i (1970)★★★, *Toshiko Akiyoshi Quartet* ii (1971)★★★, *Toshiko Akiyoshi Quartet* iii (1971)★★★, *Solo Piano* (1971)★★★, with Lew Tabackin *Kogun* (RCA 1974)★★★, with Tabackin *Long Yellow Road* (RCA 1975)★★★, with Tabackin *Tales Of A Courtesan* (RCA 1975)★★★, with Tabackin *Road Time* (RCA 1976)★★★★, with Tabackin *Insights* (1976)★★★, *Dedications* (Inner City 1976)★★★, with Tabackin *March Of The Tadpoles* (1977)★★★, with Tabackin *Dedications II* (1977)★★★, with Tabackin *Toshiko Akiyoshi-Lew Tabackin Big Band Live At Newport '77* (1977)★★★★, with Tabackin *Live At Newport II* (1977)★★★, *Toshiko Akiyoshi Plays Billy Strayhorn* (1978)★★★, *Finesse* (Concord 1978)★★★, with Tabackin *Salted Ginko Nuts* (1978)★★★, *Notorious Tourist From The East* (Inner City 1978)★★★, with Tabackin *Sumi-e* (1979)★★★, with Tabackin *Farewell To Mingus* (1980)★★★, *Just Be-Bop* (1980)★★★, *Tuttie Flutie* (1980)★★★, with Tabackin *From Toshiko With Love* (1981)★★★, with Tabackin *Tanuki's Night Out* (1981)★★★, with Tabackin *European Memoirs* (1982)★★★, *Wishing Peace* (1986)★★★, *Interlude* (Concord Jazz 1987)★★★, *Remembering Bud - Cleopatra's Dream* (Evidence 1992)★★★, *Desert Lady-Fantasy* (Columbia 1994)★★★, *At Maybeck* (Concord 1997)★★★★.
● COMPILATIONS: *Collection* (Novus 1991)★★★★.
● VIDEOS: *Toshiko Akiyoshi* (Kay Jazz 1988).

AKOUSTIC BAND - CHICK COREA

Of the many albums that Chick Corea has recorded and played on, and of all the many styles that he has tackled with success, none have delighted as much as this offering. A wholly satisfying union of exemplary musicians - Corea, Dave Weckl (drums) and John Patitucci (bass). Piano, bass and drum rarely fail as the perfect jazz trio and the light but meaty covers of classics such as Mercer/Kozma/Prevert's 'Autumn Leaves', Duke Ellington's 'Sophisticated Lady' and John Coltrane's 'Bessie's Blues' are gently inspired. Corea's four compositions blend into the collection like Cinderella's slipper, with Patitucci's playing particularly inspired on 'Circles'.
● Tracks: *Bessie's Blues; My One And Only Love; So In Love; Sophisticated Lady; Autumn Leaves; Someday My Prince Will Come; Morning Sprite; T.B. C. (Terminal Baggage Caim); Circles; Spain.*
● First released 1989
● UK peak chart position: did not chart
● USA peak chart position: did not chart

ALBAM, MANNY

b. 24 June 1922, Samana, Dominican Republic. Raised in New York, Albam became interested in jazz as a child and occasionally sat in at a club in the Village, playing alto saxophone. At the age of 16 he graduated from high school and joined Muggsy Spanier's band, then worked with Bob Chester before playing baritone saxophone with Georgie Auld. Albam also played with the bands of Sam Donahue, Charlie Barnet and Charlie Spivak but, encouraged by Budd Johnson, began to make his mark as an arranger. In 1957 he wrote a jazz arrangement of Leonard Bernstein's music from *West Side Story* which met with the composer's approval. That same year he began to experiment with long works, which resulted in a succession of fine albums including *The Blues Is Everybody's Business*, *Soul Of The City* and *The Drum Suite*, with its unusual instrumentation. Rooted in late-swing era big band style, Albam's work exemplifies the best of mainstream writing. However, inspired by Dizzy Gillespie, he absorbed later concepts in jazz to become an accomplished arranger for countless small groups including those led by Stan Getz, Terry Gibbs, Gillespie and Gerry Mulligan. He also devised effective arrangements for major song stylists such as Sarah Vaughan and Carmen McRae. In the 50s Albam briefly studied classical composition under Tibor Serly and his works include 'Concerto For Trombone And Strings'. Always eager to pass on his knowledge and experience, Albam has been involved in teaching, mostly at Eastman College, since the mid-60s.
● ALBUMS: *The RCA Victor Jazz Workshop* (RCA Victor 1956)★★★, *The Drum Suite* (RCA Victor 1956)★★★, *The Blues Is Everybody's Business* (Coral 1958)★★★, *Sophisticated Lady - The Songs Of Duke Ellington* (Coral 1958)★★★, *With All My Love* (Mercury 1958)★★★, *Jazz New York* (Dot 1958)★★★, *The Jazz Greats Of Our Time Volumes 1 & 2* (Coral 1958)★★★, *West Side Story* (Coral 1958)★★★, *Steve Song* (Dot 1958)★★★, *Double Exposure* (Top Rank 1959)★★★, *Drum Feast* (United Artists 1959)★★★, *More Double Exposure* (RCA Victor 1959)★★★, with Steve Allen *And All That Jazz* (Dot 1959)★★★, *I Had The Craziest Dream* (RCA Victor 1962)★★★, *Jazz Goes To The Movies* (Impulse! 1962), *Brass On Fire* (Solid State 1966)★★★, *Soul Of The City* (Solid State 1966)★★★, *Manny Albam And His Orchestra* (1966)★★★, *The Jazz Workshop* (RCA 1983)★★★, *Sketches From The Book Of The Life* (LRC 1991)★★★.

ALBANY, JOE

b. 24 January 1924, Atlantic City, New Jersey, USA, d. 11 January 1988, New York, USA. After formal studies as a child, Albany began playing piano professionally and formed a friendship with Charlie Parker. By his mid-teens he was working extensively on the west coast, playing with Benny Carter's orchestra in 1943 and appearing with many leading jazzmen. Early in 1946 he took part in club dates with Parker and Miles Davis. Albany missed Parker's important Dial record date on 28 March 1946 when, following a quarrel with the saxophonist, he quit in the middle of the set at a club the previous night. Albany's playing was of such a high standard that, along with other white piano-playing proponents of bop, in particular Al Haig and George Wallington, he helped to establish the genre. He also worked briefly with Georgie Auld and Boyd Raeburn and recorded with Lester Young. Drug dependency severely damaged Albany's career and he did very little during the following decades, making fleeting appearances with Warne Marsh, Charles Mingus and a handful of other jazzmen. For some years he lived in Europe and his seclusion continued into the 70s; he then returned to the jazz scene, re-establishing a reputation as a formidable bop pianist and allowing latter-day audiences to understand the reason for the high regard in which, despite his erratic career, he had long been held by fellow pianists. A 1980 film documentary, *Joe Albany . . . A Jazz Life*, helped to reinforce his stature.

● ALBUMS: with Warne Marsh *The Right Combination* (Riverside 1958)★★★★, *The Legendary Jazz Pianist* (Riverside 1968)★★★★, *At Home Alone* (Spotlite 1971)★★★★, *Proto-Bopper* (Revelation 1972)★★★★, *Birdtown Birds* (Steeple Chase 1973)★★★, with Niels-Henning Ørsted Pedersen *Two's Company* (Steeple Chase 1974)★★★, *The Legendary Joe Albany* (Parlophone 1974)★★★, *This Is For My Friends* (1976)★★★, *Joe Albany Plays George Gershwin And Burton Lane* (1976)★★★, *The Albany Touch* (Trio/Sea Breeze 1977)★★★, *Bird Lives!* (Storyville 1979)★★★★, *Portrait Of An Artist* (Elektra Musician 1981)★★★★.

● FILMS: *Joe Albany . . . A Jazz Life* (1980).

Albert, Don

b. Albert Dominique, 5 August 1908, New Orleans, Louisiana, USA, d. January 1980. Albert began playing trumpet as a child, following in the footsteps of his uncle, Natty Dominique. Albert played in several bands in his hometown, including parade bands, and in other parts of the south during the 20s. At the end of the decade he formed his own band which became enormously successful in Texas and the south. Although drawing largely upon New Orleans musicians for his personnel, Albert's musical policy owed much to developments in big band music during the early 30s. Although the band played mostly in Texas, it did make occasional trips along the eastern seaboard of the USA. Active throughout most of the 30s, Albert concentrated on working in Texas and the south-east and consequently did not have an impact on the public at large. In the 40s, Albert, who had given up playing trumpet to concentrate on leading, continued to form bands. From the 50s onwards, he played occasionally in Texas. Only infrequently recorded, Albert enjoyed a high reputation among musicians for his fluent playing and skilled leadership.

● ALBUMS: *Echoes Of New Orleans* (1962)★★★.

Albright, Gerald

b. 1959, USA. A technically adroit alto saxophonist, he spent about 15 years with keyboard player Bobby Lyle. Subsequently, he played and sometimes recorded with Oscar Brashear, Anita Baker and Marlena Shaw, and he also toured with a Whitney Houston package. In 1995 he was on the Jazz Explosion tour with Rachelle Ferrell, ex-Earth, Wind And Fire drummer Michael White, and singer Will Downing. He was also on a later edition of this tour that featured Herbie Hancock. Influenced in his formative years by John Coltrane and Cannonball Adderley, with the growth of his experience he has developed a distinctive musical voice of his own, especially on alto which remains his principal instrument although he is also accomplished on tenor and soprano and additionally plays flute. His ballad playing, sumptuous and lyrical, is especially satisfying.

● ALBUMS: *Just Between Us* (MCA 1988)★★★, *Bermuda Nights* (Atlantic 1988)★★★, *Dream Come True* (Atlantic 1990)★★★, *Live At Birdland West* (Atlantic 1991)★★★, *Smooth* (Atlantic 1994)★★★, *Giving Myself To You* (Atlantic 1995)★★★, *Live To Love* (Atlantic 1997)★★★, with Will Downing *Pleasures Of The Night* (Verve 1998)★★★.

Alcorn, Alvin

b. 7 September 1912, New Orleans, Louisiana, USA. After studying trumpet as a child, Alcorn began playing professionally in the mid-20s. He played for various bands, occasionally as leader. In the early 30s he joined Don Albert, with whom he remained until 1937. From the mid-40s he worked mostly in New Orleans, then moved to the west coast to join Edward 'Kid' Ory's band in the mid-50s. Later in the decade, he played with George Lewis, Paul Barbarin and other leading New Orleans-style musicians. In the mid-60s and several times in the 70s he toured Europe and the UK. Alcorn continued to play into the 80s. A solid lead trumpeter, Alcorn's playing was ideally suited to the New Orleans tradition of collective improvisation.

Alden, Howard

b. 17 October 1958, Newport Beach, California, USA. Alden began playing guitar when he was 10 years old, using recordings by well-known jazzmen as his guide. In his early teens he played professionally in the Los Angeles area and at 16 took formal lessons from Jimmy Wyble, a former member of the Red Norvo Trio. He later met Dan Barrett, with whom he formed a friendship, and continued to find work in and around Los Angeles. In the late 70s Alden joined Norvo for a season in Atlantic City. In 1982 he relocated to New York City and was immediately in demand, working with leading jazz players such as Joe Bushkin, Ruby Braff, Joe Williams and Woody Herman. Throughout the 80s and into the 90s he continued to play in the New York area, with artists such as Warren Vaché Jnr., Kenny Davern, Benny Carter, Monty Alexander and Joe 'Flip' Phillips, and established a significant musical relationship with Dan Barrett, making records and touring the world for concert and festival appearances. Their group plays mostly in the mainstream and uses a wide range of material, in charts specially commissioned from Buck Clayton, several of which are originals. A masterly technician, Alden plays with fluency and wit. As an accompanist he is subtly supportive, while as a soloist he is assured and imaginative. One of the outstanding jazz musicians of his generation, Alden's reputation and his wide repertoire look set to make him one of the future names in jazz.

● ALBUMS: with Dan Barrett *Swing Street* (Concord Jazz 1986)★★★, with Joe 'Flip' Phillips *A Real Swinger* (1988)★★★,

Howard Alden Plays The Music Of Harry Reser (1988)★★★, with Barrett *The A-B-Q Salutes Buck Clayton* (Concord Jazz 1989)★★★, *Howard Alden Trio* (Concord Jazz 1989)★★★, with Jack Lesberg *No Amps Allowed* (Chiaroscuro 1990)★★★, *Snowy Morning Blues* (Concord Jazz 1990)★★★, with George Van Eps *13 Strings* (Concord Jazz 1991)★★★, *Misterioso* (Concord Jazz 1991)★★★, with Van Eps *Hand Crafted Swing* (Concord Jazz 1992)★★★, with Van Eps *Seven And Seven* (Concord Jazz 1993)★★★, *A Good Likeness* (Concord Jazz 1993)★★★, with Ken Peplowski *Concord Duo Series Volume 3* (Concord Jazz 1993)★★★, with Peplowski *Live At Centre Concord Encore!* (Concord Jazz 1995)★★★, with Van Eps *Keepin' Time* (Concord Jazz 1995)★★★, *Take Your Pick* (Concord Jazz 1997)★★★, with Jimmy Bruno *Full Circle* (Concord Jazz 1998)★★★.

Alemán, Oscar

b. Oscar Marcelo Alemán, 20 February 1909, Resistencia, Argentina, d. 10 October 1980. Learning guitar from his teenage years, Alemán quickly attracted attention, and before the end of the 20s he was playing in Europe, first in Spain, and then later in France, where he became even better known. In part, this was due to his leadership of the small band that accompanied the immensely popular performer Joséphine Baker. He also worked with visiting American musicians including Frank 'Big Boy' Goudie, Bill Coleman and Danny Polo. In 1941 Alemán returned to South America, settling in Buenos Aires where he remained for the rest of his life. His playing was at first replete with echoes of his native land but in Europe he fell under the spell of Django Reinhardt. Thereafter, the twin influences combined to weave a distinctively rich sound and style. His long sojourns in interwar Europe and in South America tended to keep him from a limelight he might have enjoyed had he resided in the USA.

● ALBUMS: *Oscar Alemán Y Sus Cinco Cabelleros* (Impacto 1965)★★★, *Alemán* (Redondel 1972)★★★.

● COMPILATIONS: *Swing Guitar Masterpieces* (Acoustic Disc 1998)★★★.

Alexander, Eric

b. Eric Wells Alexander, 4 August 1968, Galesburg, Illinois, USA. Born to a pair of musically inclined and encouraging parents, Alexander began taking piano lessons at eight years old and showed a great deal of promise. At 10, when instruments were distributed for the elementary school band, young Alexander chose the clarinet. He did not excel at the instrument, however, and soon found himself demoted to the bass clarinet. Upon finding a teacher at the age of 12, he switched to alto saxophone. Alexander continued in the school band programmes and state competitions, playing what classical saxophone works could be found. His interest in jazz at this age was minimal but he did gravitate towards the more contemporary saxophone artists including David Sanborn, Tom Scott and Michael Brecker. After graduating from high school, with a switch to tenor saxophone, Alexander attended Indiana University with only a partial intent to study music. It was a very influential teacher at this time, David Baker, that began to steer Alexander in the direction of becoming a serious jazz musician. His instruction and advice gave Alexander a firm musical foundation upon which he still relies heavily to this day. After a year with Baker, in 1987 Alexander made the decision to transfer to William Patterson College in New Jersey in an effort to be closer to New York City. It was here, under the guidance of teachers such as Joe Lovano, Harold Mabern and Rufus Reid, that he began to absorb the knowledge and experience that would define his musical future. While playing local bar gigs and college competitions with classmates, Alexander began an intense study of all of the saxophone masters. Sonny Stitt, Dexter Gordon, John Coltrane, George Coleman and Joe Henderson, among others, became major influences on him. After obtaining his Bachelor degree from William Patterson, Alexander made the decision to return to Chicago to try his hand at becoming a professional player in a smaller arena than New York City. Soon after arriving in Chicago, Alexander became part of organist Charles Earland's working ensemble and made his first major recording, *Unforgettable* (1991), with this group. It was this same year that Alexander competed in the Thelonious Monk Competition and placed second behind Joshua Redman. This gave him the confidence to return to New York and further pursue his career in jazz. The owner of Delmark Records had heard Alexander in Chicago and offered to record the young saxophonist. His first release as a leader, *Straight Up* (1993), included his former teacher, Harold Mabern. While playing in Philadelphia, Alexander was heard by the Criss Cross label and went on to record the aptly titled *New York Calling* (1993). It was through his association with Criss Cross producer Gary Teekens that Alexander began to work with some of the best jazz musicians in New York. He soon found himself in the company of such renowned artists as Melvin Rhyne, Cecil Payne, Kenny Barron, Irene Reid, Cedar Walton and Freddie Hubbard. Alexander continued to record for the Chicago-based Delmark label with *Up, Over And Out* (1995), *Stablemates* (1996) with saxophonist Lin Halliday, and *Mode For Mabes* (1998), with Mabern once again. At the same time, his Criss Cross releases have included *Full Range* (1995), *In Europe* (1996) and *Two Of A Kind* (1997). Between his many sessions as a sideman for other artists and his busy playing schedule, Alexander has found the time to join a group of his contemporaries in the New York-based One For All. In 1997, this group released the highly acclaimed *Too Soon To Tell* and remains an outlet for fresh ideas while still maintaining a deep sense of tradition. Alexander is a saxophonist of great lyrical ability while playing with a strength and agility beyond most of his peers. He always remains a student of his art and is constantly striving to further develop his sound and style while maintaining his grasp of the rich tradition of his instrument. He is conscious of his contemporaries and believes that acoustic jazz has a very bright future as an outlet for a world of increasing isolation by technology.

● ALBUMS: *Straight Up* (Delmark 1993)★★★, *New York Calling*

(Criss Cross 1993)★★★★, *Full Range* (Criss Cross 1995)★★★, *Up, Over And Out* (Delmark 1995)★★★, with Robert Mazurek *Badlands* (Hep 1995)★★★★, *In Europe* (Criss Cross 1996)★★★★, with Lin Halliday *Stablemates* (Delmark 1996)★★★★, with Cecil Payne *Two Of A Kind* (Criss Cross 1997)★★, *In Europe* (Criss Cross 1997)★★★, with One For All *Too Soon To Tell* (Sharp Nine 1997)★★★★, *Mode For Mabes* (Delmark 1998)★★★★, with John Hicks, George Mraz and Idris Muhammad *Solid!* (Milestone 1998)★★.

Alexander, Monty

b. 6 June 1944, Kingston, Jamaica. Resident in Miami after moving to the USA in 1961, Alexander built a reputation as a dynamic and technically brilliant pianist in the Art Tatum/Oscar Peterson seam without ever extending that virtuoso tradition. In the 60s he worked and recorded with Ray Brown and Milt Jackson before forming his own trio - the format in which he has since preferred to work. Highly popular in live performance, where the sometimes clinical accuracy of his recorded work is pleasantly animated, Alexander occasionally uses his native West Indian musical heritage to impressive effect. Indeed, on two albums of the late 80s, *Ivory And Steel* and *Jamboree*, he successfully, if improbably, incorporated jazz piano with a steel band.

● ALBUMS: *Monty Alexander* (Pacific Jazz 1965)★★★, *Alexander The Great* (1965)★★★, *Spunky* (Pacific Jazz 1965)★★★★, *Zing!* (RCA 1967)★★★, *This Is Monty Alexander* (Verve 1969)★★★, *Here Comes The Sun* (BASF 1971)★★, *We've Only Just Begun* (1971)★★★, *Perception!* (1973)★★★, *Rass* (1974)★★★, *Unlimited Love* (1974)★★★, *Live In Germany* (1974)★★, *Monty Strikes Again* (1974)★★★, *Love And Sunshine* (1974)★★, *Now's The Time* (1974)★★★, *Live! Montreux Alexander* (Pablo Jazz 1976)★★★★, *Live In Holland* (1977)★★★, *Cobilimbo* (1977)★★★, with Milt Jackson *Soul Fusion* (Original Jazz Classics 1978)★★★, *Jamento* (1978)★★★, *Monty Alexander In Tokyo* (Pablo 1979)★★★, with Jackson *The Way It Is* (1979)★★★, *Taste Of Freedom* (1979)★★★, *Facets* (Concord Jazz 1979)★★★★, *So What* (1979)★★★, *Ivory And Steel* (Concord Jazz 1980)★★★, *Solo* (L&R 1980)★★★, *Trio* (1980)★★★, *Monty Alexander And Ernest Ranglin* (1980)★★★, *Triple Treat* i (Concord 1982)★★★, *Look Up* (1982)★★★, *Duke Ellington Songbook* (Verve 1984)★★★, *Overseas Special* (Concord Jazz 1984)★★★, *Reunion In Europe* 1983 recording (Concord 1985)★★, *Ivory And Steel* (1985)★★★, *The River* (Concord Jazz 1985)★★★, *Threesome* (1985)★★★, *Full Steam Ahead* (Concord Jazz 1985)★★, *To Nat, With Love* (Master Mix 1986)★★, *Triple Treat* ii (Concord Jazz 1987)★★, *Triple Treat* iii (Concord Jazz 1987)★★, *Jamboree* (Concord Jazz 1988)★★★, *Saturday NIghts* (Timeless 1989)★★★, *Caribbean Circle* (Chesky 1992)★★★, *At Maybank* (Concord 1996)★★★★, with Ivory And Steel *To The Ends Of The Earth* (Concord Picante 1996)★★★, *Yard Movement* (Island Jamaica Jazz 1996)★★★, *Echoes Of Jilly's* (Concord Jazz 1997)★★★.

Alexander, Ray

b. 7 February 1925, Lynbrook, Long Island, USA. Born into a musical environment (his mother was a concert pianist), Alexander began playing piano as a very small child. At school, he formed a harmonica band then planned to be a trumpet player, but childhood asthma ended that ambition. After seeing Gene Krupa at New York's Paramount Theatre around 1940 Alexander decided on taking drumming lessons. He also continued to listen to jazz in New York clubs, hearing 'Big' Sid Catlett, Art Tatum, Charlie Parker, Dizzy Gillespie and many others. Occasionally Alexander sat in and accompanied musicians such as the violinists Stuff Smith and Joe Venuti. Alexander's career plans were interrupted by army service during World War II but on his return he played with many bands including Chubby Jackson and Bobby Byrne. At the end of the 40s he began playing vibraphone, studying all the time he was working as a drummer by day and vibraphone player by night. After playing drums with Claude Thornhill in the mid-50s, he joined George Shearing's Quintet, playing vibraphone, towards the end of the decade. Active mostly around New York, Alexander played with many musicians, sometimes on drums, other times on vibes, playing formal sessions and just for kicks. In this way he accompanied musicians such as Parker, Coleman Hawkins, Stan Getz and Bill Evans. In the early 60s he briefly became co-owner of a jazz restaurant in Westchester County then, also briefly, formed a band named Alexanders The Great with Mousey Alexander. He continued gigging in the New York area during the late 60s and in the 70s and in 1983 recorded his first album under his own name. In the early 90s Alexander was still mostly to be heard in and around New York although he began touring Europe, thanks in part to the success of his album which was not released in the UK until 1990. He has returned to the UK from time to time since then but is still mostly active, playing and now teaching, in New York and on Long Island.

● ALBUMS: *Cloud Patterns* (Nerus 1983)★★★, *Rain In June* (Nerus 1992)★★★.

Alexandria, Lorez

b. Delorez Alexandia Nelson, 14 August 1929, Chicago, Illinois, USA. Like so many other young black singers, Alexandria began singing in church and later performed gospel music. Her early professional career was centred in clubs and took off towards the end of the 50s with a series of well-received albums. After working with Ramsey Lewis she began to concentrate on jazz, recording extensively with Howard McGhee, Wynton Kelly and others during the early 60s. Around this time she relocated to the west coast, singing on television, recording and playing club dates. Alexandria sings with a deep, burnished tone and if her interpretations of a composer's intentions sometimes come second to her exploitation of her wide range of vocal devices, she remains one of the better, if lesser-known, jazz singers. Albums such as *A Woman Knows*, which includes what might well be the definitive version of the much-recorded song 'I Can't Get Started', and *Harlem Butterfly* are musical *tours de force*.

● ALBUMS: *This Is Lorez Alexandria With The King Fleming Quartet* (King 1957)★★★, *Lorez Sings Pres* (King 1957)★★★, *Lorez Sings Songs Everybody Knows* (King 1959)★★★, *Standards*

With A Touch Of Jazz (1959)★★★, *The Band Swings, Lorez Sings* (King 1959)★★★★, *Early In The Morning* (Argo 1960)★★★, *Deep Roots* (Argo 1960)★★★, *Sing No Sad Songs For Me* (Argo 1961)★★★, *For Swingers Only* (Argo 1963)★★★, *Alexandria The Great* (Impulse! 1964)★★★★, *More Of The Great Lorez Alexandria* (Impulse! 1965)★★★, *From Broadway To Hollywood* (1977)★★★, *How Will I Remember You* (1978)★★★, *A Woman Knows* (1978)★★★★, *The Songs Of Johnny Mercer* (1980), *Harlem Butterfly* (1984)★★★★, *Tangerine* (Trend 1984)★★★, *Singing Songs Everyone Knows* (King 1990)★★★, *May I Come In* (Muse 1991)★★★.

Ali, Rashied

b. Robert Patterson, 1 July 1935, Philadelphia, Pennsylvania, USA. When his father changed his name to Rashied Ali, Robert Patterson Junior followed suit. Ali's mother sang with the Jimmie Lunceford Orchestra and the entire family sang in their Baptist church. Saturated with music in his childhood, Ali later became a revolutionary jazz drummer who established a new kind of continuity - heated, flickering and responsive, dissolving the explicit beat into the surge required by free jazz players. John Coltrane - with whom he played between 1965 and 1967 - said, 'He allows the soloist maximum freedom, he's laying down multi-directional rhythms all the time. To me, he's definitely one of the great drummers.' Since Coltrane's death, Ali has been shamefully under-recorded, yet he continues to extend the tradition of radical black music. When the dust settles on the 80s, it may well become apparent that Phalanx, Ali (drums), Sirone (bass), George Adams (tenor saxophone) and James 'Blood' Ulmer (guitar), was one of the decade's crucial bands. Ali currently records with the Prima Materia quintet, comprising Louis Belongenis (tenor saxophone), Allan Chase (alto saxophone), Greg Murphy (piano) and Joe Gallant (bass).

● ALBUMS: with Phalanx *Original Phalanx* (DIW 1987)★★★, with Phalanx *In Touch* (DIW 1988)★★★, with Prima Materia *Peace On Earth* (Knitting Factory Works 1994)★★★★, with Prima Materia *Bells* (Knitting Factory Works 1996)★★★, with Borah Bergman, Joe McPhee, Wilber Morris *The October Revolution* (Evidence 1997)★★★.

Alix, May

b. Liza Mae Alix, 31 August 1904, Chicago, Illinois, USA. A popular if undistinguished cabaret singer in her home-town in the early 20s, Alix usually worked solo, performing in New York, Los Angeles and Paris, as well as in Chicago. Her talent for being in the right places meant she was often heard singing to the accompaniment of leading jazz orchestras, including those of Jimmie Noone, Luis Russell and Duke Ellington (with whom she appeared at the Cotton Club). For some engagements she worked in duo with Ollie Powers (Powell) and, when working the same club as the Russell band, she duetted with Louis Armstrong in a comedy routine on 'Big Butter And Egg Man'. Such connections, added to her popularity among nightclub patrons, led record producers to couple her with two leading jazzmen of the day; hence, her lacklustre singing can be heard on records by Armstrong's Hot Five (1926) and Noone's Blue Melody Boys (1929). These few records secured her lasting and largely undeserved fame. She retired in the early 40s. Although no report of Alix's death has been traced, it seems unlikely that she is still alive.

(NB: This singer should not be confused with at least three other singers, including Alberta Hunter, who sometimes used the pseudonym May Alix.)

Allan, Jack

b. Jack Clarence Allan, 28 September 1929, Sydney, Australia, d. 7 February 1995, Sunshine Coast, Queensland, Australia. Allan began playing accordion as a child before switching to piano in his teens. He worked in the Sydney cabaret and clubs and although he was heavily influenced by swing era pianists, especially Teddy Wilson, he became one of the few Australian musicians to play the early post-war modern jazz styles. His recording debut was in November 1949 on *Rex Stewart And His Sydney Six*. The visiting American jazz musician also used Allan on two subsequent sessions. In February 1950 Allan made his first recordings with his group the Katzenjammers. They performed and recorded frequently in the early 50s with variable personnel, including Ken Silver, Don Burrows, Errol Buddle, John Bamford and Edwin Duff. Allan progressed to become a reliable studio musician with the ABC and also a writer and director for musical revues. From the mid-50s he began an acting career and with his generous bulk was often cast as a villain, an amiable bar patron, or as a playing musician. His film credits include *On The Beach*, *Ned Kelly*, *They're A Weird Mob* and *Caddie* and there were also numerous television appearances. He maintained his musical prowess, but performances became spasmodic. In 1983 he recorded with percussionist John Sangster and in the following year made a tasteful, swinging solo album for the Anteater label. Moving north to the Sunshine Coast, Allan lived in semi-retirement with occasional acting and musical activity. Jack Allan was a much admired pianist, both solo and in accompaniment, but his jovial flamboyance often obscured a serious commitment to his music.

● ALBUMS: *Jack Allan's Katzenjammers* (Manhatten 1953)★★★, *Jack Allan At The Piano* (Anteater 1984)★★★.

● COMPILATIONS: two tracks only *Don Burrows - The First 50 years Volume One* (ABC 1993)★★★.

Allan, Jan

b. Jan Bertil Allan, 7 November 1934, Falun, Sweden. As a child he first studied piano but in his early teens he switched to trumpet when he became interested in jazz. He turned professional while still a teenager, playing with both jazz and dance with various groups. Allan continued to work, mostly in jazz groups and sometimes as leader, during the 50s and 60s. His music varied noticeably when he was leader, and he often sought wider audience appeal by playing in proven styles. This led him into jazz-rock fusion and a variety of Latin-influenced styles. He continued playing jazz with visiting American musicians, among them Bobby Shew, Thad Jones and Warne Marsh. A highly melodic trumpeter with a smoothly burnished sound, Allan's playing is always attractive and displays a keen intelligence at work. He has also occasionally played piano.

● ALBUMS: *Jan Allan '70* (Four Leaf Clover 1970)★★★, with Bobby Shew *Dialogic* (Four Leaf Clover 1982)★★★, with Trio Con Tromba *Fusion* (Phono Suecia 1982)★★★.

ALLEN, CARL

b. Carl Lee Allen, 25 April 1961, Milwaukee, Wisconsin, USA. Born into a large musical family, Allen began his drumming career early by banging on pots and pans at the age of three. Naturally, this activity led to drum lessons at eight with teacher Roy Sneider. Considered for playing the trumpet in the grade school band, like his older brother, a quick demonstration from Allen convinced the director that he was better suited to the drums. In high school, under the tutelage of band director Robert Siemele, who was also a drummer, Allen was educated in jazz. At 16, he played his first professional engagement with the saxophonist Sonny Stitt. In 1977, Allen began attending a series of summer jazz camps in Green Bay, Wisconsin. Eventually he won a scholarship to attend the University of Wisconsin, where he studied classical percussion for two years. This training allowed the drummer to gain a strong discipline and good practice habits that he had not developed in his younger years. When drummer Mel Lewis visited the school to conduct a clinic, he recognized Allen's talent and told the young drummer of an opening in the Count Basie band. Feeling that he was not ready to handle such an important position, Allen declined but was inspired by Lewis to transfer to William Patterson College in New Jersey in 1981 to be closer to New York City. At William Patterson, Allen was given the opportunity of studying with a number of renowned teachers, including Rufus Reid, David Samuels and Steve Bagby. Allen quickly gained notoriety, and in 1982, he joined the band of the great trumpeter Freddie Hubbard. He made his first recording in 1985, *Clarion Echoes* (Soul Note), with trumpeter Frank Gordon. From then on, Allen has performed and recorded with a multitude of great jazz artists including Jackie McLean, Dizzy Gillespie, Terence Blanchard, Benny Golson, George Coleman, Art Farmer and Branford Marsalis, to name but a few. Allen was soon given the opportunity to record as a leader and in 1988 released *Dreamboat* with his newly formed band, Manhattan Projects. As a band leader, Allen adopted the philosophy of the great Art Blakey, his most important influence, and sought out young, gifted musicians and allowed them to explore and develop a collective sound under his respectful guidance. Young prospects such as trumpeters Nicholas Payton and Roy Hargrove and pianist Cyrus Chestnut have developed into significant artists under Allen's watchful eye. Subsequent releases have included *Piccadilly Square*, *The Dark Side Of Dewey*, *The Pursuer* and *Testimonial*. In 1988, Allen co-founded his own production company, Big Apple Productions, with alto saxophonist Vincent Herring in an effort to ensure that artists should be given a chance to express their talent and not be sacrificed for reasons of marketability. So far the duo has produced in excess of 50 records for themselves and artists such as Dewey Redman, Lee Konitz, Nat Adderley and Pharoah Sanders. As a producer, Allen is very careful to make sure that the artist is as comfortable in the recording process as possible, as well as conducting the business side of the project with a careful eye for detail. Allen's high level of musicianship stems from his love of and respect for the arts, and his desire to communicate feelings of joy and celebration to his audience. His philosophy that the character of the musician must come through in the music above any technical proficiency is evident in his own playing and in that of the musicians he employs. His ultimate goal as an artist is to play in such a way as to make everyone with him feel good and play at their best. As a participant in the business of music, Allen believes that artists must strive to be in charge of their own careers and work together to break down the barriers of musical genres.

● ALBUMS: with Manhattan Projects *Dreamboat* (Alfa/Timeless 1988)★★★, with Manhattan Projects *Piccadilly Square* (Timeless 1990)★★★★, with Manhattan Projects *The Dark Side Of Dewey* (Alfa/Evidence 1992)★★★★, *Echoes Of Our Heroes* (Alfa 1993)★★★, *We Remember Cannonball* (Alfa 1994)★★★★, *The Pursuer* (Atlantic 1994)★★★★, *Testimonial* (Atlantic 1995)★★★.

ALLEN, GERI

b. 12 June 1957, Pontiac, Michigan, USA. Pianist Allen grew up in Detroit, steeped in the city's strong bebop and black pop traditions (one early gig saw her playing with Mary Wilson and the Supremes), though Eric Dolphy, Herbie Nichols and Thelonious Monk were also major influences. She studied music at Washington's Howard University and at the University of Pittsburgh (with Nathan Davis) and later with Roscoe Mitchell. Moving to New York in the early 80s she played with numerous contemporary jazz musicians, including James Newton and Lester Bowie, and recorded her debut *The Printmakers* in 1984 with a trio that featured Andrew Cyrille. She also became involved with the M-BASE and Black Rock Coalition organizations and the former's Steve Coleman and Robin Eubanks played on her *Open On All Sides In The Middle*. Later in the 80s she was a regular member of Oliver Lake's groups (*Plug It*, *Gallery*, *Impala*, *Otherside*) and toured and recorded with several leaders, including Dewey Redman (*Living On The Edge*), Frank Lowe (*Decision In Paradise*), Greg Osby (*Mindgames*) and Charlie Haden's Liberation Music Orchestra. With Haden and Paul Motian she formed an acoustic trio that has become celebrated for its intimate versions of modern mainstream jazz; and she also guested on Motian's own *Monk In Motian* and Betty Carter's *Droppin' Things*. An acutely sensitive player with a lovely touch, in the early 90s Allen signed to Blue Note Records where she recorded several strong albums. Her most acclaimed recent work, however, was *The Gathering*, her 1998 debut for the Verve label. On this album Allen was backed by Buster Williams (bass) and Lenny White (drums), with additional contributions from Vernon Reid on acoustic guitar.

● ALBUMS: *The Printmakers* (Minor Music 1984)★★★, *Homegrown* (Minor Music 1985)★★★★, *Open On All Sides In The Middle* (Minor Music 1987)★★★, with Charlie Haden, Paul Motian *Etudes* (Soul Notes 1988)★★★, with Haden, Motian *In The Year Of The Dragon* (PolyGram 1989)★★★, with Haden, Motian *Segments* (DIW 1989)★★★, *Twylight* (Verve 1989)★★★, with Haden, Motian *Live At The Village Vanguard* (DIW 1991)★★★, *The Nurturer* (Blue Note 1991)★★★, *Maroons* (Blue Note 1992)★★★, *Eyes ... In The Back Of Your Head* (Blue Note 1997)★★★, *The Gathering* (Verve 1998)★★★★, *Some Aspects Of Water* 1996 recording (Storyville 1998)★★★★.

ALLEN, HARRY

b. 12 October 1966, Washington, DC, USA. When he was aged one, Allen's parents moved to Los Angeles and it was there that he began playing music, but at that time chose the accordion and later the piano. When he was 11 years old the family moved again, this time to Rhode Island and there, at junior high school, he began playing clarinet and finally the tenor saxophone, in which instrument he decided to specialize. Encouraged by his father, Morry Allen, a schoolfriend of Paul Gonsalves who had played drums during the swing era with the Boston-based George Johnson band, he listened to jazz records. These were mainly by the likes of Louis Armstrong, Duke Ellington and Benny Goodman. Later, at Rutgers University, he was encouraged to develop his jazz playing in the formulaic John Coltrane mode but resisted, preferring instead to follow the path of the tenor players he had heard on record: Gonsalves, Ben Webster and Coleman Hawkins. By the time his formal education ended, he had already established himself as a jazz musician playing in the New York area, where he worked with leading figures such as Ruby Braff, George Masso, Bucky Pizzarelli, Kenny Barron, John Bunch and Oliver Jackson. He recorded extensively during the late 80s, often backing singers and usually on obscure and poorly promoted labels. By the early 90s, however, he was a popular figure on the international scene, playing clubs and festivals throughout Europe, Canada and the USA. An exceptionally fine interpreter of ballads, Allen belongs firmly in the late mainstream, drawing upon the great traditions of the movement but never sounding dated or lacking in originality.

● ALBUMS: *How Long Has This Been Going On?* (Progressive 1988)★★★, *I Know That You Know* (Master Mix 1991)★★★, *I'll Never Be The Same* (1992)★★★, *Someone To Light Up Your Life* (Master Mix 1992)★★★, *A Night At Birdland, Vol. 1* (Nagel-Heyer 1994)★★★★, *A Night At Birdland, Vol. 2* (Nagel-Heyer 1994)★★★, *Blue Skies* (John Marks 1994)★★★★, *Jazz Im Amerika Haus, Vol. 1* (Nagel-Heyer 1994)★★★, with Randy Sandke *The Music Of The Trumpet Kings* (Nagel-Heyer 1998)★★★, *A Little Touch Of Harry* (Master Mix 1998)★★★.

ALLEN, HENRY 'RED'

b. 7 January 1908, New Orleans, Louisiana, USA, d. 17 April 1967, New York, USA. Allen was one of the outstanding jazz trumpeters. His career found him vacillating between New Orleans traditionalism, big-band jazz, and an early kind of experimentalism that appealed to beboppers and free-form fans. His questing musical nature and deep affinity for the blues ensured his place as a major jazz player, yet, commercially and artistically (and most unfairly), he was obliged to spend much of his career in the shadow of Louis Armstrong. Allen had already worked with George Lewis, Fate Marable, Joe 'King' Oliver and Clarence Williams when, in 1928, he was hired by the Victor label as a rival attraction to Armstrong, then recording for their competitors OKeh. In 1929 Allen joined Luis Russell's New York-based band and for several years was a dominant voice in a number of important big bands of the burgeoning swing era. His musical collaborations with J.C. Higginbotham and Coleman Hawkins, during a stint with the Fletcher Henderson Orchestra, became almost legendary. A 1937 career move took him back to the Russell band, but this proved a detrimental step when the band became little more than an anonymous backing group for Armstrong. Two dominant musical personalities, both of them trumpeters, were too much for one band, so in 1940 Allen forsook big-band work to join the New Orleans Revivalist movement. However, his forward-looking nature was such that he refused to stay in a stylistic groove. Over the years, he developed an adventurous and impressive arsenal of sounds with both open horn and mute. His powerful, blues-drenched playing (and occasional singing) was shot through with burning rips and aggressive smears, to the point where he attracted the attention of notable jazz frontiersmen such as Don Ellis, who described Allen in a 1965 *Down Beat* article as 'the most *avant garde* trumpeter in New York'. Throughout the 50s and 60s Allen worked in traditional and mainstream small groups, at home and abroad, as both sideman and leader. He recorded regularly during this period and often to great effect, as on his mid-50s reunion sessions with Coleman Hawkins or the later *Feeling Good*. In an oft-quoted and somewhat inaccurate jazz trumpet lineage, Roy Eldridge is cited as the link between Armstrong and Dizzy Gillespie. In many respects Allen might be the better choice, to connect the New Orleans tradition with both bop and elements of the freer music that followed it. He died of cancer in April 1967, shortly after completing his last tour of the UK.

● ALBUMS: *Red Allen Dixielanders Featuring Big Chief Moore* (1951)★★★, *Stuyvesant Casino Nights Volume 1* (1952)★★★, with Red Norvo *Battle Of Jazz, Vol. 6* 10-inch album (Brunswick 1953)★★★, *Ridin' With Red* (X LVA 1955)★★★, *The Red Allen-Tony Parenti All Stars* (1955-57)★★★, with Kid Ory *Henry 'Red' Allen Meets Kid Ory* (Verve 1957)★★★★, with Ory *We've Got Rhythm* (Verve 1957)★★★★, *Nice* (1957)★★★, *World On A String* (RCA Bluebird 1957)★★★, *Ride, Red, Ride In Hi-Fi* (RCA Victor 1957)★★★★, *Warhorses* (1957)★★★, *Stormy Weather*

(1957-58)★★★, with Ory, Jack Teagarden *Red Allen, Jack Teagarden & Kid Ory At Newport* (Verve 1958)★★★★, *Red Allen Plays King Oliver* (Verve 1960)★★★, *Live At The London House* (1961)★★★, *Rare Red Allen Trio Performances* (1962)★★★, *Mr Allen* (Swingville 1962)★★★, *Henry Red Allen* (RCA Victor 1965)★★★, *Live 1965* (1965)★★★, with Pee Wee Russell *The College Concert Of Pee Wee Russell And Henry Red* (Impulse! 1966)★★★, *Feeling Good* (Columbia 1966)★★★.

● COMPILATIONS: *Henry Allen 1929 To 1936* (1929-36)★★★★, *The Chronological Red Allen Volumes 1 - 4* (1929-37)★★★, *Red Allen And His Friends* (1932-56)★★★, with Spike Hughes *Spike Hughes And His All-American Orchestra* (1933)★★★, with others *Red Allen And The Blues Singers Volumes 1 & 2* (1938-40)★★★★, *The Very Great Henry 'Red' Allen Volume 1* (1941-46)★★★, *Jazz Classics In Digital Stereo 1929-1936* (BBC 1990)★★★, *World On A String* (Bluebird 1991)★★★.

● FURTHER READING: *The Trumpet And Vocal Of Henry Red Allen, 1927-1942*, Jan Evensmo.

ALLEN, JACKIE

b. *c*.1960, Milwaukee, Wisconsin, USA. Growing up in a very musical family, with her father, herself and four siblings all playing brass instruments, Allen eventually went to the University of Wisconsin at Madison. She was originally torn between the relative attractions of musical drama and classical French horn, but 'as soon as I got there, the jazz department just pulled me in'. The faculty members included Richard Davis and pianist John Wildman and they helped to draw out of her a real talent for singing jazz. She began performing in clubs and other venues while still at university and after graduation she decided to return to Milwaukee. A year or so earlier, Allen had met organist Melvin Rhyne, one-time member of Wes Montgomery's group, and as he was based in Milwaukee she sought him out. They formed a musical partnership that lasted three years. The association ended in 1990, at which time Allen moved to Chicago, although continuing to hold down a regular singing engagement at Milwaukee's Wyndham Hotel and teaching vocal jazz at the city's Wisconsin Conservatory of Music. Much of her singing work was in venues that preferred the cabaret style to out-and-out jazz singing and this resulted in Allen taking a conscious decision to move her repertoire and style into this area. In particular, she sought, and continues to seek, interesting and lesser-known songs with musical and lyrical merit. Additionally, she writes some of her own material in which she echoes a bygone age of good tunes and intelligent lyrics. A relaxed, persuasive singing style, allied to a strong rhythmic feel, marks her as a talent to watch.

● ALBUMS: *Never Let Me Go* (Lake Shore Jazz 1994)★★★.

ALLEN, LEE

b. 2 July 1926, Pittsburg, Kansas, USA, d. 18 October 1994, Los Angeles, California, USA. One of the great tenor saxophonist sessionmen of the classic R&B era, Allen played with a verve and excitement equalled by few musicians. He is best known for his notable instrumental hit from 1958, 'Walkin' With Mr. Lee' (number 54 pop). Allen began his professional career in 1947 playing in the Paul Gayten band in New Orleans. By the 50s he was a key member of the famed Dave Bartholomew session band that played behind just about every R&B artist who recorded in New Orleans. Behind such artists as Fats Domino, Smiley Lewis, Amos Milburn, Lloyd Price and Little Richard, Allen played exciting solos as well as great riffs in tandem with baritone saxophonist Alvin 'Red' Tyler. Allen recorded his first solo record in 1956 for the Aladdin label, 'Rockin' At Cosimo's'. Following his 'Walkin' With Mr. Lee' hit, he charted once more in 1958 with 'Tic Toc' (number 92 pop). During much of the remainder of his career he worked in Fats Domino's touring band. During the late 60s, however, he left the music world for a time to work in an aircraft factory in Los Angeles. In the 80s, he recorded with the Los Angeles band the Blasters.

● ALBUMS: *Walking With Mr. Lee* (Ember 1958)★★★.

ALLEN, MARSHALL

b. 25 May 1924, Louisville, Kentucky, USA. At school Allen learned to play clarinet and C-melody saxophone. He studied at the National Conservatory of Music in Paris while playing jazz with pianist Art Simmons. In the early 50s he toured Europe with James Moody. On his return to the USA in 1954, Allen joined up with a bandleader whose influences - both musical and philosophical - predated bebop: Sun Ra. He was introduced by King Kolax, a trumpet player who led one of Chicago's pre-eminent R&B bands. Allen told Nat Hentoff in a 1966 *Downbeat* interview: 'I felt I wanted to play on a broader sound basis rather than on chords: I couldn't play this way until I started playing with Sun Ra.' Allen's alto saxophone became as central to Sun Ra's sound as Johnny Hodges' was to Duke Ellington's, and his tenure proved even longer. He also plays flute, oboe, cor anglais, clarinet and the *morrow*, an instrument he invented himself. As with many of Sun Ra's players, Allen's monumental contribution to modern music frequently eluded the pundits, who too often dismissed the band as Sun Ra's wacko circus. In reality, Sun Ra's monastic discipline and regular tours honed a technique that has made Marshall Allen a legend among alto saxophone players. The best-known of his rare recordings away from Sun Ra's ensemble Arkestra is a 1964 session with the Paul Bley quintet, *Barrage*.

ALLEN, PETE

b. 23 November 1953, Newbury, Berkshire, England. Although Allen has chosen to follow the well-trodden path of other British jazz traditionalists such as Freddie Randall and Kenny Ball, he has managed to maintain originality through a combination of musical flair and determination. His fluid, bluesy clarinet style is complemented by his use of alto and soprano saxophones, both of which allow him to augment the traditional Dixieland line-up to good effect. Displaying a sound business sense (on a par with that of Chris Barber), Allen has led a succession of enthusiastic young musicians, prepared to turn their backs on the new trends followed by their contemporaries. Unlike many latter-day British reed players, who have chosen to model themselves upon John Coltrane, Allen himself has followed the lineage exemplified by Edmond Hall. Largely by dint of his expressive playing and total commitment, Allen's decision to follow a traditional style has in no way limited his musical development and he continues to play an interesting and entertaining brand of jazz.

● ALBUMS: *Turkey Trot* (Black Lion 1979)★★, *Down In Honky-Tonk Town!* (Black Lion 1980)★★★, *Gonna Build A Mountain* (Platform 1982)★★★, *Jazzin' Around II* (ARB 1985)★★★, *While We Danced At The Mardi Gras* (Jazz Club 1987)★★★, *One For The Road* (PAR 1987)★★, *Wild Cat Blues* (Pete Allen 1988)★★★, *Dixie Date* (Black Lion 1988)★★★, *Martinique* (ARB 1988)★★★, *Jazz You Like It* (PAR 1991)★★★★, *Beau Sejour* (PAR 1991)★★★.

ALLEN, STEVE

b. 16 December 1921, New York City, New York, USA. A self-taught pianist, Allen was in showbusiness as a small child and when he reached his 20s, moved into radio. He gained a following as a presenter of record programmes and also turned to comedy, and as such was a natural for television. His shows regularly featured jazz, sometimes played by Allen himself, sometimes by guests. He also acted as producer for the television series *Jazz Scene USA*. His popularity was almost entirely restricted to the USA but in 1955 he became well known internationally thanks to his appearance in the title role of the film *The Benny Goodman Story*. Allen's love of jazz and the high regard in which he held musicians is evident from the calibre of the people he assembled for occasional recording dates and broadcasts: Terry Gibbs, Urbie Green, Mundell Lowe and Charlie Shavers among them.

(N.B.: This Steve Allen should not be confused with the UK broadcaster of the same name.)

● ALBUMS: *Steve Allen's All Star Jazz Concert Volume 1* (Decca 1955)★★★, *Steve Allen's All Star Jazz Concert Volume 2* (Decca 1955)★★★, *Allen Plays Allen* (Coral 1956)★★★, *Let's Dance* (Coral 1956)★★★, *Steve Sings* (Coral 1956)★★★, *Jazz For Tonight* (Coral 1956)★★★, *Tonight At Midnight* (Coral 1956)★★★, *Music For Tonight* (Coral 1956)★★★, *The Steve Allen Show* (Coral 1957)★★★, *Steve Allen At The Round Table* (Roulette 1958)★★★, with Manny Albam *And All That Jazz* (Dot 1959)★★★, *Gravy Waltz* (Dot 1963)★★★.

ALLISON, MOSE

b. Mose John Allison Jnr., 11 November 1927, Tippo, Mississippi, USA. Allison began piano lessons at the age of five, and played trumpet in high school, although he has featured the latter instrument less frequently in recent years. His music is a highly individual mix of blues and modern jazz, with influences on his cool, laconic singing and piano-playing ranging from Tampa Red and Sonny Boy 'Rice Miller' Williamson to Charlie Parker, Duke Ellington, and Thelonious Monk. He moved to New York in 1956 and worked mainly in jazz settings, playing with Stan Getz, Al Cohn, Zoot Sims and Gerry Mulligan, and recording for numerous companies. During the 60s Allison's work was much in evidence as he became a major influence on the burgeoning R&B scene. Pete Townshend, one of his greatest fans, recorded Allison's 'A Young Man's Blues' for the Who's *Live At Leeds*. Similarly, John Mayall was one of dozens who recorded his classic 'Parchman Farm', and Georgie Fame featured many Allison songs in his heyday with the Blueflames (Fame's nasal and understated vocal was similar to Allison's). In the 80s Allison saw a resurgence in his popularity after becoming a hero to the new, young audience hungry for his blend of modern jazz. In 1996 he collaborated with Fame, Van Morrison and Ben Sidran on his own tribute album, *Tell Me Something: The Songs Of Mose Allison*. Ultimately, however, his work is seen as hugely influential on other performers, and this has to a degree limited the profile afforded his own lengthy recording career.

● ALBUMS: *Back Country Suite* (Prestige 1957)★★★, *Local Color* (Prestige 1958)★★★, *Young Man Mose* (Prestige 1958)★★★, *Ramblin' With Mose* (Prestige 1958)★★★, *Creek Bank* (Prestige 1959)★★★, *Autumn Song* (Prestige 1960)★★★, *The Transfiguration Of Hiram Brown* (Columbia 1960)★★, *I Love The Life I Live* (Columbia 1960)★★★, *Take To The Hills* (Epic 1962)★★, *I Don't Worry About A Thing* (Atlantic 1962)★★★, *Swingin' Machine* (Atlantic 1962)★★★, *The World From Mose* (Atlantic 1964)★★★, *V8 Ford* (Columbia 1964)★★★, *Mose Alive!* (Atlantic 1965)★★★, *Mose Allison* (Prestige 1966)★★★, *Wild Man On The Loose* (Atlantic 1966)★★★, *Jazz Years* (Atlantic 1967)★★, *Mose Allison Plays For Lovers* (Prestige 1967)★★, *I've Been Doin' Some Thinkin'* (Atlantic 1969)★★★, *Hello There* (1969)★★, *Universe* (1969)★★, *Western Man* (Atlantic 1971)★★★★, *Mose In Your Ear* (Atlantic 1972)★★, *Your Mind Is On Vacation* (Atlantic 1976)★★★★, *That's Jazz* (1976)★★★, *Middle Class White Boy* (Elektra 1982)★★★, *Lessons In Living* (Elektra 1984)★★, *Ever Since The World Ended* (Blue Note 1987)★★, *My Backyard* (Blue Note 1990)★★★, *Sings And Plays* (Fantasy 1991)★★★, *The Earth Wants You* (1994)★★, with Georgie Fame, Van Morrison, Ben Sidran *Tell Me Something: The Songs Of Mose Allison* (Verve 1996)★★, *Gimcracks And Gewgaws* (Blue Note 1998)★★★.

● COMPILATIONS: *The Seventh Son - Mose Allison Sings* (Prestige 1963)★★★, *Down Home Piano* (Prestige 1966)★★★, *Retrospective* (Columbia 1976)★★★, *Allison Wonderland The Mose Allison Anthology* (1994)★★★, *The Best Of ...* (Sequel 1994)★★★★, *Jazz Profile* (Blue Note 1997)★★★★, *The Sage Of Tippo* (32 Jazz 1998)★★★★.

● FURTHER READING: *One Man's Blues: The Life And Music Of Mose Allison*, Patti Jones.

ALLYN, DAVID

b. Albert DiLello, 19 July 1923, Hartford, Connecticut, USA. From a musical family (his mother was a singer and his father a French horn player), Allyn became a semi-professional vocalist by the time he was 17, before joining Jack Teagarden's short-lived big band of the early 40s. After service in World War II, during which he was awarded the Purple Heart, he worked for leaders such as Van Alexander and Henry Jerome before joining the Boyd Raeburn orchestra where his musical skills were tested by the demanding work of several forward-looking arrangers, including George Handy. In the 40s, apart from his work with Raeburn, Allyn recorded with Lucky Thompson. When the Raeburn band split, Allyn moved to the west coast and became a solo act. His Dick Haymes-like vocals gained him regular club work and a recording contract with Discovery, and later, World Pacific. During the 50s he recorded some highly regarded albums with arrangements by Johnny Mandel and Bill Holman and with accompanists of the calibre of Jimmy Rowles, Frank Rosolino and Barry Harris. In the late 60s and early 70s Allyn worked infrequently in music, spending time actively involved in social work including the rehabilitation of drug users. Allyn's good pitch and diction, allied to his intense feeling for jazz and consummate musical skill, made him one of the best male singers of jazz and standard songs of his time, albeit one little known to the popular or even fringe jazz audience. In 1986, on the basis of an 'up-from-the-ashes' life story and generous recommendations from some major singers, Allyn was again receiving favourable reviews for his 'smoky instrument that he uses to glide through songs with effortless power', at clubs such as George's in Chicago. (On some recordings Allyn's name is spelled Allen.)

ALLYSON, KARRIN

b. *c.*1964, Great Bend, Kansas, USA. While still a small child, she moved to Omaha, Nebraska, where she studied classical piano. Later, living in the San Francisco Bay area, Allyson worked in the theatre, then returned to Nebraska to attend university where she majored in classical piano, graduating in 1987. It was around this time that her musical horizons broadened and she began to take an interest in jazz, playing with a college big band, and in rock, playing in an all-female group. After graduation, Allyson moved to Minneapolis and quickly found steady work playing in bars and restaurants. She then began leavening her piano-playing with singing, attracting considerable attention both in Minneapolis and in Kansas City where she appeared at the Phoenix Club. She continued to commute between the Phoenix and the Dakota, in Minneapolis, with excursions to Chicago and New York, where she appeared at Michael's Pub. In the early 90s she was signed by Concord Records, thus extending her audience worldwide, although she remains based in the Midwest. Allyson's distinctive, breathy delivery, allied as it is to a rich vocal sound, makes her a consistently interesting performer of ballads.

● ALBUMS: *Karrin Allyson* (Concord Jazz 1992)★★★, *I Didn't Know About You* (Concord Jazz 1992)★★★★, *Sweet Home Cookin'* (Concord Jazz 1993)★★★, *Azure-Té* (Concord Jazz 1994)★★, *Collage* (Concord Jazz 1996)★★★, *Daydream* (Concord Jazz 1997)★★★.

ALMEIDA, LAURINDO

b. 2 September 1917, Sao Paulo, Brazil, d. 26 July 1995, Van Nuys, California, USA. A fluent and skilled musician, famous in his native country as a classical Spanish guitar player, Almeida came to the USA in the 40s to work in film and television studios. His jazz work was first widely exposed during a spell with Stan Kenton in the late 40s. Although continuing his film and television work, Almeida also took many opportunities to play jazz, joining forces with bassist Harry Babasin, altoist Bud Shank and drummer Roy Harte in 1953. The work of this group anticipated many of the hallmarks of the bossa nova craze that came a few years later. In 1974 Almeida gained further appreciation when he was teamed with bassist Ray Brown, drummer Chuck Flores and Shank to form the LA Four. Records by this group, with Flores replaced successively by Shelly Manne and Jeff Hamilton, and later teamings with Shank in duo performances and with fellow guitarists Larry Coryell and Charlie Byrd, showcased the distinctive style that set Almeida's work apart from the mainstream of jazz guitar. During his career he won Grammy awards in 1959 for his performance on *Danzas*, and in 1960 for *The Spanish Guitars Of Laurindo Almeida* and *Conversations With The Guitar*. The following year he gained two more with *Discantos* and *Reverie For Spanish Guitars*, and in 1962 further honours with nominations for *Viva Bossa Nova!* in the Best Performance By An Orchestra For Dancing and Best Jazz Performance categories and a third nomination with *The Intimate Bach* (Best Classical performance). In 1964 the album *Guitar From Ipanema* won the Grammy for Best Instrumental Jazz Performance, and in 1972 he was nominated for the Best Soloist award with *The Art Of Laurindo Almeida*.

● ALBUMS: *Guitar Concert* 10-inch album (Capitol 1950)★★★, *A Guitar Recital Of Famous Serenades* 10-inch album (Coral 1952)★★★, *Latin Melodies* 10-inch album (Coral 1952)★★★, *Laurindo Almeida Quartet* 10-inch album (Pacific Jazz 1953)★★★, *Laurindo Almeida Quartet Volume 2* 10-inch album (Pacific Jazz 1954)★★★, with Bud Shank *The Laurindo Almeida Quartet Featuring Bud Shank* aka *Brazilliance, Volume 1* (Pacific Jazz 1955)★★★, with Chico Hamilton *Delightfully Modern* (Jazztone 1957)★★★★, *Danzas* (Capitol 1959)★★★, with Shank *Brazilliance, Volume 2* (World Pacific 1962)★★★, *Viva Bossa Nova!* (Capitol 1962)★★★, with Bud Shank *Brazilliance, Volume 3* 1953 recordings (World Pacific 1962)★★★, *Ole! Bossa Nova* (Capitol 1963)★★★, *It's A Bossa Nova World* (Capitol 1963)★★★, with Herb Ellis, Johnny Gray *Three Guitars In Bossa Nova Time* (Epic 1963)★★★, *Guitar From Ipanema* (Capitol 1964)★★★★, with MJQ *Collaboration* (Atlantic 1964)★★★, *Suenos (Dreams)* (1965)★★★, with Stan Getz *Stan Getz With Guest Artist Laurindo Almeida* (Verve 1966)★★★, with Ray Brown *Back Ground Blues And Green* (Century City 1968)★★★, *The Art Of Laurindo Almeida* (Orion 1972)★★★★, *Latin Guitar* (1974)★★★, with LA Four *The LA Four Scores!* (1975)★★★, *Virtuoso Guitar* (MCA 1976)★★★, with LA Four *Watch What Happens* (1977)★★, with LA Four *Just Friends* (1978)★★, *Laurindo Almeida Trio* (Dobre 1978)★★★, *Chamber Jazz* (Concord 1978)★★★, *Concierto De Aranjuez* (Inner City 1978)★★★★, *New Directions* (1979)★★★, *First Concerto For Guitar And Orchestra* (Concord Jazz 1979)★★★, with Charlie Byrd *Brazilian Soul* (Concord Picante 1980)★★★★, with Byrd *Latin Odyssey* (Concord Jazz 1982)★★★, with Shank *Selected Classical Works For Guitar And Flute* (1982)★★, *Artistry In*

Rhythm (Concord Jazz 1983)★★★★, *The Laurindo Almeida Trio* (1984)★★★, *Tango* (Concord Picante 1985)★★★, *New Directions Of Virtuoso Guitar* (Teldec 1987)★★, with Byrd *Music Of The Brazilian Masters* (New Note 1989)★★★, *Outra Vez (Once Again)* (Concord Jazz 1992)★★, with Shank *Baa-Too-Kee* (1993)★★★.

ALMOND, JOHNNY

b. 20 July 1946, Enfield, Middlesex, England. This accomplished saxophonist and flautist rose to prominence during the mid-60s as a member of London R&B group Tony Knight's Chessmen. In 1965 he replaced Clive Burrows in Zoot Money's Big Roll Band and two years later joined the successful Alan Price Set. This group became known as the Paul Williams Set following the original leader's departure and the same unit also formed the basis for a 1969 venture, Johnny Almond's Music Machine. Williams (vocals), Jimmy Crawford (guitar), Geoff Condon (trumpet), John Wiggins (keyboards), Roger Sutton (bass) and Alan White (drums) were featured on *Patent Pending*, a propulsive set drawing inspiration from both jazz and blues, but Almond subsequently disbanded the line-up, and a second album, *Hollywood Blues*, was completed with the aid of American musicians. A session musician on albums by Fleetwood Mac (*Mr. Wonderful*) and John Mayall (*Bluesbreakers With Eric Clapton*), the saxophonist joined the latter in 1969 in a pioneering 'drummer-less' unit captured on *The Turning Point* and *Empty Rooms*. Here Almond forged a partnership with guitarist Jon Mark, which resulted in the formation of a breakaway act, Mark-Almond in 1971. This imaginative ensemble completed a series of albums during the 70s and continued their partnership into the 80s.

● ALBUMS: *Patent Pending* (Deram 1969)★★★, *Hollywood Blues* (Deram 1970)★★★, *Enchanted* (Parlophone 1970)★★★.

● COMPILATIONS: as Mark-Almond *The Best Of Mark-Almond* (1993)★★★★.

ALPERT, HERMAN 'TRIGGER'

b. 3 September 1916, Indianapolis, Indiana, USA. After studying music at college, he played bass professionally in the late 30s and early 40s, most notably with Glenn Miller in both his civilian and armed forces bands. After the war, Alpert played with a Miller-style band led by Tex Beneke and thereafter gigged and recorded with a veritable 'who's who' of jazz and popular music, including Ella Fitzgerald, Louis Armstrong, Frank Sinatra and Woody Herman. For more than a decade, beginning in 1950, he played with studio bands at CBS Records in New York but continued to collaborate with many fine jazz artists for club and recording dates, including Artie Shaw, Coleman Hawkins, the Sauter-Finegan Orchestra, and Gene Krupa. Alpert recorded under his own name in the mid-50s, leading a band that included Zoot Sims, Tony Scott and Al Cohn (the session was later reissued under his sidemen's names). By the 70s, Alpert had retired from active playing and took up a new career in photography. A solid and thoroughly dependable bass player, Alpert was one of many unsung heroes of the middle years of jazz and popular music, content to supply a firm base for other musicians.

● ALBUMS: *Trigger Happy!* reissued as *East Coast Sounds* (Riverside 1956)★★★.

ALSTON, OVIE

b. Overton Alston, *c*.1906, Washington, DC, USA. Alston first attracted attention playing trumpet in a band in New York in the late 20s, later becoming leader of a band that had previously been led by pianist Charlie Skeets. Alston was then joined by Claude Hopkins who took over leadership in 1931. Alston stayed on, becoming an important part of this exceptional band, and remaining until 1936. He then formed his own group, with which he played a number of prestigious engagements in and around New York, including a residency at the Roseland Ballroom. The band was together for many years, although during the early days of World War II it was co-led by Noble Sissle and Eubie Blake on tours of USO camps. In 1942, once more led by Alston, the band began another residency at Roseland which lasted until after the war ended. Alston continued to lead his band into the 50s, but eventually abandoned full-time participation in music. Unusual among trumpet players of his generation, he was not a follower of the new tradition pioneered by Louis Armstrong. Alston developed a smooth legato style and played in a noticeably relaxed manner, favouring a behind-the-beat style. His muted work was interesting and his open horn playing displayed a big, burnished tone. Like the younger trumpeter Harry Edison, Alston would sometimes play repeated-note solos. Gunther Schuller suggests that he was probably an influence upon Charlie Shavers. During his time with Hopkins, Alston was a member of an exceptionally good trumpet section which also featured Sylvester Lewis and lead Albert Snaer. Records by the Hopkins band feature a number of fine solos by Alston, and trumpet trio passages with Snaer and Lewis. The latter device was a hangover from the days when Alston had been the band's leader and was for a while a welcome and popular effect, although it soon became overused. Alston was also sometimes featured as a singer when, oddly enough, he did emulate Armstrong. It is as a trumpeter, however, that his work is deserving of more attention than has been granted to date. He was co-composer with Hopkins of a number of the band's features.

● COMPILATIONS: *The Chronological Claude Hopkins 1932-1934* (Original Jazz Classics 1993)★★★★, *The Chronological Claude Hopkins 1934-1935* (Original Jazz Classics 1993)★★★★.

ALTENA, MAARTEN

b. Maarten van Regteren Altena, 22 January 1943, Amsterdam, Holland. When Altena broke his wrist falling downstairs in his Amsterdam home in 1973, he responded by also putting his bass in a plaster-cast, and the results were documented on the album *Handicaps*. On this debut solo recording it seemed safe to categorize Altena as typical of the clownish Dutch 'school' personified by Han Bennink. However, both before and after that album, Altena has been a restless explorer rather than an idiomatic musician. In the 60s he came out of the Amsterdam conservatory, then played jazz, backing artists such as Dexter Gordon, before joining Misha Mengelberg's band. In the late 70s, he threw himself wholeheartedly into the stylistic conflicts of Company, the pool of musicians headed by Derek Bailey. Within a decade, however, he had exhausted his interests in 'pure' free improvisation and formed his own Maarten Altena Ensemble, comprised of Dutch musicians from jazz, pop and classical backgrounds. In the Ensemble he took his cue from Stravinsky, aiming to make each composition a self-contained sound-world. There is enormous variety in the music, which establishes rigorous structures only to dismantle them with great energy and good humour.

● ALBUMS: *Handicaps* (1973)★★★, *Tuning The Bass* (1975)★★★, *Live Performances* (1977)★★★, *K'Ploeng* (1978), with Steve Lacy *High, Low And Order* (Claxon 1979)★★★, *Op Stap* (1980)★★★, with Peter Kowald *Two Making A Triangle* (1982)★★★, *Rondedans* (1985)★★★, *Quick Step* (1986)★★★, *Miere* (Nato 1986)★★★, *Rif* (1988)★★★, *Weerwerk* (1988)★★★, *Quotl* (1989)★★★, *Cities And Streets* (hatART 1991)★★★, *Code* (hatART 1992)★★★.

Altschul, Barry

b. 6 January 1943, New York City, New York, USA. Born into a classical music family, drummer Altschul was fascinated by the rhythms of the street. An early school report said 'He isn't doing any work, he's only playing music with Black people.' He sat in with jazz musicians in the neighbourhood - including trumpeter Charles Tolliver and tenor saxophonist Junior Cook - and learned the fundamentals of bebop touring with Johnny Griffin and Sonny Criss. His work (1970-72) with Circle, a free-improvisation quartet that featured Anthony Braxton (reeds), Chick Corea (piano) and Dave Holland (bass), established him as a pre-eminent *avant garde* player, a reputation he solidified as a member of Braxton's groundbreaking quartet of the mid-70s. His sensitivity to space and timbre means that he truly deserves the description 'percussionist'. He has also played during his career with Sam Rivers, Ray Anderson and Anthony Davis.

● ALBUMS: *You Can't Name Your Own Tune* (Muse 1977)★★★★, *Another Time/Another Place* (Muse 1978)★★★, *For Stu* (SN 1979)★★★, *Brahma* (Sackville 1980)★★★★, *Irina* (1983)★★★, *That's Nice* (1985)★★★, with Paul Bley, Gary Peacock *Virtuosi* (AI 1992)★★★.

Alvin, Danny

b. Daniel Alvin Viniello, 29 November 1902, New York, USA, d. 6 December 1958. While still in his teens Alvin played drums professionally for a number of artists in the New York area, including Sophie Tucker with whom he worked for three years. In 1922 he relocated to Chicago where he worked with numerous bands. Aside from occasional trips to Florida and back to New York, he remained based largely in Chicago through the 20s and early 30s. Between 1936 and 1947 he lived and worked again in New York. During these years he played in bands led by musicians such as Ted Fio Rito, Art Hodes, Joseph 'Wingy' Manone, Georg Brunis, Joe Marsala and Mezz Mezzrow. Back in Chicago from the late 40s onwards, Alvin played drums for artists including Doc Evans and also led his own band, which played, among other venues, at his own Alvin's Club Basin Street. Flashy and energetic, he was not ideally suited to most of the jazz styles of his time; rather, he was more in accord with the sometimes rowdy atmosphere of the 40s Dixieland revival. Nevertheless, his undoubted enthusiasm helped enliven the jazz clubs that were his milieu.

● ALBUMS: *Club Basin Street* (Stepheny 1958)★★★.

Alvis, Hayes

b. Hayes Julian Alvis, 1 May 1907, Chicago, Illinois, USA, d. 29 December 1972. As a child, Alvis played drums with the famed *Chicago Defender* Boys Band, later becoming a professional and joining Jelly Roll Morton. While with Morton he switched from drums to brass and string bass, eventually concentrating on the latter. He spent some time in Chicago, playing both types of bass with Earl Hines, for whom he also wrote arrangements. By the early 30s Alvis was in New York (and using only string bass), first with Jimmy Noone, then the Mills Blue Rhythm Band, for which he also acted as road manager. In 1935 he joined Duke Ellington for a spell of more than two years at a time when Ellington was using two bassists (the other was Billy Taylor). After leaving Ellington he briefly co-led a band with Freddie Jenkins, worked in a New York pit band, and in 1939 joined Benny Carter. During the early 40s he played with a number of bands including those led by Joe Sullivan and Louis Armstrong. While in the army during World War II, he played in a band led by Sy Oliver and after his discharge, resumed playing in New York at various venues including the Café Society. In the 50s Alvis worked with trumpeter Joe Thomas and Wilbur De Paris, where he resumed playing the brass bass (tuba). In the 60s he was active in studios and regularly backed Dionne Warwick. In the early 70s he toured Europe with Jay 'Hootie' McShann. Alvis played with firm control and his work provided a sound basis for the front-line musicians in all the bands of which he was a member. Late in his career, he worked as an official of the American Federation of Musicians. John Chilton lists among Alvis's accomplishments dentistry and interior decorating, and he also held a pilot's licence.

Ambrosetti, Franco

b. 10 December 1941, Lugano, Switzerland. Coming from a musical family, Ambrosetti started out on piano but switched to trumpet in his mid-teens. In the mid-60s he played with Gato Barbieri and was also a member of a band formed by his father, Flavio Ambrosetti, which included George Gruntz and eventually developed into Gruntz's Concert Jazz Band. Ambrosetti continued to play with Gruntz for the next decade. During the 80s he played with many different bands and also led a series of small groups that had among their sidemen musicians such as Bennie Wallace, Phil Woods and Dave Holland. Ambrosetti is a highly accomplished musician with great technical gifts. His technique is never used merely for effect but serves to underpin a freewheeling imagination. His bands have always been adventurous and forward-thinking, reflecting the leader's open mind and desire to incorporate in his work musical advances and innovations from other spheres. Like his father, Ambrosetti plays music part-time only, spending his days in the family business, which is part of the automotive industry.

● ALBUMS: *Close Encounter* (Enja 1978)★★★, *Heartbop* (Enja 1981)★★★, *Wings* (Enja 1983)★★★, *Tentets* (Enja 1985)★★★, *Movies* (Enja 1987)★★★★, *Movies, Too* (Enja 1988)★★★★, *Music For Symphony & Jazz Band* (Enja 1991)★★★, *Live At The Blue Note* (Enja 1992)★★★★, *Light Breeze* (Enja 1998)★★★.

AMERICAN GARAGE - PAT METHENY

Pat Metheny's importance in popular music is significant through his ability to transcend barriers. This is the closest he came to rock music, yet it is still a mile away. The group on this record, in addition to the ever-present keyboard player Lyle Mays, are Mark Egan (bass) and Danny Gottlieb (drums). The music is played with great ease and sounds like it was made during positive times. Metheny utilizes the acoustic 12-string that was so effective on *New Chautauqua*, in addition to his regular hollow-bodied Gibson.

● Tracks: *(Cross The) Heartland; Airstream; The Search; American Garage; Epic.*

● First released 1979

● UK peak chart position: did not chart

● USA peak chart position: 53

AMM

Formed in 1965 by jazz saxophonist Lou Gare (b. Leslie Arthur Gare, 16 June 1939, Rugby, Warwickshire, England), guitarist Keith Rowe (b. 1940) and drummer Eddie Prévost (b. 22 June 1942, Hitchin, Hertfordshire, England) with cellist and clarinettist Lawrence Sheaff (b. 1940), the UK's AMM is a vehicle for free improvisation that leaves room for the operation of chance: a mid-60s programme note suggested that the noise made by members of the audience leaving could be regarded as part of the performance. Passages of silence have also been an integral part of AMM music, and Gare, in particular, seems able to give a potent impression of phrases continuing to develop through the gaps he leaves. The structure and personnel of AMM have always fluctuated: at one period, it comprised only Gare and Prévost, when the group was perhaps at its most jazz-orientated since its inception.

The use of chance and other techniques from *avant garde* 'classical' music was imported by composer Cornelius Cardew (b. 1936, d. 1981), initially against opposition from Rowe. During the 80s other classical musicians, including pianist John Tilbury (b. 1936) and Arditti Quartet cellist Rohan de Saram (b. 1939), became members of the band.

● ALBUMS: *AMMMusic* (Impetus 1967)★★★, with MEV *Live Electronic Music Improvised* (1968)★★★, *The Crypt* (Matchless 1968)★★★, *At The Roundhouse* (1972)★★★, *To Hear And Back Again* (Matchless 1976)★★★, *It Had Been An Ordinary Enough Day In Pueblo, Colorado* (1979)★★★, *Generative Themes* (Matchless 1983)★★★, *The Inexhaustible Document* (Matchless 1987)★★★, *Combine And Laminate* 1984 recordings (Matchless 1991)★★★, *The Nameless Uncarved Block* (Matchless 1991)★★★, *Laminal* 1969-1994 recordings (Matchless 1996)★★★★, *Newfoundland* (Matchless 1996)★★★, *Live In Allentown* (Matchless 1996)★★★, *From A Strange Place* (Modern Music 1997)★★★★, *Before Driving To The Chapel We Took Coffee With Rick And Jennifer Reed* (Matchless 1997)★★★.

● COMPILATIONS: *Ammusic 1966* (ReR 1996)★★★.

AMMONS, ALBERT

b. 23 September 1907, Chicago, Illinois, USA, d. 2 December 1949, Chicago, Illinois, USA. Ammons began playing piano as a small child and worked in Chicago clubs while still a youth. In the late 20s and early 30s he played in a number of small bands but his real forte was as a soloist. After establishing himself as an important blues piano player in Chicago in the mid-30s, a period that saw him leading a small group at many of the city's top nightspots, Ammons moved to New York City. With Pete Johnson he formed a piano duo, playing in the newly popular boogie-woogie style. In New York Ammons and Johnson appeared at the Café Society and occasionally added Meade 'Lux' Lewis to their group to form a powerful boogie-woogie trio. By the mid-40s Ammons had returned to playing on his own, touring the USA before settling back in his home-town, where he died in December 1949. Although best known for his contribution to the briefly popular craze for boogie-woogie, Ammons was one of the outstanding blues piano players of all time. His influence is immense, from Erroll Garner and Ray Bryant to Jools Holland and John Cleary. His son, Gene 'Jug' Ammons, played tenor saxophone.

● ALBUMS: *Boogie Piano Stylings* 10-inch album (Mercury 1950)★★★★, *Boogie Woogie Classics* 10-inch album (Blue Note 1951)★★★★, with Pete Johnson *8 To The Bar* 10-inch album (RCA Victor 50s)★★★★.

● COMPILATIONS: with Meade Lux Lewis *The Complete Blue Note Recordings Of Albert Ammons And Meade Lux Lewis* (Mosaic 1983)★★★★, *King Of Boogie Woogie* (Blues Classics 1988)★★★★, *Albert Ammons Volumes 1 & 2* (Oldie Blues 1988)★★★★.

AMMONS, GENE 'JUG'

b. 14 April 1925, Chicago, Illinois, USA, d. 6 August 1974, Chicago, Illinois, USA. Ammons chose to make the tenor saxophone his instrument in preference to the piano played by his father, the famous boogie-woogie exponent Albert Ammons. Gene left school at the age of 18 and within two years was a member of Billy Eckstine's bebop-orientated big band. Despite working alongside leading lights of the new form such as Fats Navarro, Leo Parker and Art Blakey, Ammons proved to be very much his own man, developing a distinctive, warm sound that nevertheless fitted well into the hard-edged playing of his colleagues. After leaving Eckstine, Ammons worked mainly in small groups, sometimes as leader, but also had a short spell with Woody Herman's big band in 1949. A year later he joined forces with Sonny Stitt to co-lead a small group that played rich, soulful music overlaid with an aggressive attack - a style that moved him towards the outer edges of the bop tradition yet never quite slipped over into fully fledged soul or R&B. Ammons worked extensively in small group settings for the next dozen years but drug addiction led to prison terms that robbed his career of 10 years in total, from the late 50s through to the late 60s. Between his release from prison in 1969 and his death from cancer and pneumonia in August 1974, Ammons enjoyed considerable success thanks in part to his enthusiastic playing and the concurrent popularity of jazz-soul music throughout the 60s.

● ALBUMS: with Sonny Stitt *Battle Of The Saxes: Ammons Vs. Stitt* 10-inch album (Prestige 1951)★★★, *Tenor Sax Favorites, Volume 1* 10-inch album (Prestige 1951)★★★, *Gene Ammons Favorites Volume 2* 10-inch album (Prestige 1952)★★★, *Gene Ammons Favorites Volume 3* 10-inch album (Prestige 1953)★★★, *With Or Without* 10-inch album aka *Light Bluesy And Moody* (EmArcy 1954)★★★, *Gene Ammons Jazz Sessions* (1955)★★★, *The Gene Ammons Band* (1955)★★★, *Gene Ammons Jazz Session* 10-inch album (Prestige 1955)★★★, *Jammin' With The Gene Ammons All Stars* aka *Not Really The Blues* (Prestige 1956)★★★, *Hi-Fidelity Jam Session* aka *The Happy Blues* (Prestige 1956)★★★, *Gene Ammons All Star Session* aka *Woofin' And Tweetin'* (Prestige 1956)★★★, *Funky* (Prestige 1957)★★★, *Jammin' In Hi-Fi With Gene Ammons* aka *The Twister* (Prestige 1957)★★★★, *Gene Ammons All Stars* (1958)★★★, *The Big Sound* (Prestige 1958)★★★★, *Blue Gene* (Prestige 1958)★★★★, *Jug* (Prestige 1960)★★★★, *Nice An' Cool* (Prestige 1961)★★★★, *Gene Ammons i* (Prestige 1961)★★★, with Richard 'Groove' Holmes *Groovin' With Jug* (1961)★★★★, *Just Jug/Live! In Chicago* (Prestige 1961)★★★, *Up Tight!* (Prestige 1961)★★★★, *Groove Blues* (Prestige 1961)★★★★, *Juggin' Around* (Vee Jay 1961)★★★★, *Golden Saxophone* (Savoy 1961)★★★, with Brother Jack McDuff *Mellow Gravy - Brother Jack Meets The Boss* (Prestige 1962)★★★★, with Stitt *Boss Tenors* (Verve 1962)★★★, with Stitt *Boss Tenors* (Verve 1962)★★★, *Nothing But Soul* (1962)★★★, with Stitt, McDuff *Soul Summit* (Prestige 1962)★★★, *Twistin' The Jug* (Prestige 1962)★★★, with Stitt *Boss Tenors In Orbit* (Verve 1962)★★★, with Stitt *Dig Him!* (1962)★★★★, *Gene Ammons ii* (1962)★★★, *Blue Groove* (Prestige 1962)★★★★, with Dodo Marmarosa *Jug And Dodo* (Prestige 1962)★★★, *Gene Ammons iii* (1962)★★★, *Just Jug* (Argo 1962)★★★★, *Dig Him* (Argo 1962)★★★★, *Bad! Bossa Nova* aka *Jungle Soul* (Prestige 1962)★★★, *Swingin' The Jug* (1962)★★★, *Preachin'* (Prestige 1963)★★★, *Soul Summit Volume 2* (Prestige 1963)★★★, *The Soulful Moods Of Gene Ammons* (Moodsville 1963)★★★, *Late Hour Special* (Prestige 1964)★★★, *Velvet Soul* (Prestige 1964)★★★, *Nice And Cool* (Moodsville 1965)★★★★, *Sock!* (Prestige 1965)★★★★, *Angel Eyes* (Prestige 1965)★★★★, *Gene Ammons Live! In Chicago* (Prestige 1967)★★★, *Boss Soul!* (Prestige 1967)★★★★, *Make It Happen* (Cadet 1967)★★★★, with Stitt *Jug And Sonny* (Cadet 1967)★★★★, *The Boss Is Back!* (Prestige 1969)★★★★, *Brother Jug* (Prestige 1969)★★★★, with Stitt *We'll Be Together Again* (Prestige 1969)★★★★, *Gene Ammons iv* (1970)★★★, *Hooray For John Coltrane* (1970)★★★, with Dexter Gordon *The Chase!* (Prestige 1970)★★★, *The Black Cat* (Prestige 1970)★★★, with Stitt *You Talk That Talk* (Prestige 1971)★★★★, *My Way* (1971)★★★, with James Moody *Chicago Concert* (1971)★★★, *Free Again* (1972)★★★, *Big Bad Jug* (1972)★★★, *Gene Ammons And Friends At Montreux* (1973)★★★, *Gene Ammons In Sweden* (Enja 1973)★★★, with Stitt *Together Again For The Last Time* (1973)★★★★, *Brasswind* (1974)★★★, *Goodbye* (Prestige 1974)★★★, *Early Visions* (1985)★★★.

● COMPILATIONS: *The Best Of Gene Ammons For Beautiful People* (Prestige 1969)★★★, *Boogie Woogie And The Blues* (1987)★★.

Amram, David Werner, III

b. 17 November 1930, Philadelphia, Pennsylvania, USA. After studying classical music, Amram played horn with the National Symphony Orchestra in Washington. During his military service, he was based in Paris with the Seventh Army Symphony Orchestra. On his return to New York he studied at the Manhattan School of Music with Gunter Schuller, recorded with Charles Mingus and played in a band with Oscar Pettiford. In 1956 he began a long association with Joseph Papp and the New York Shakespeare Festival for which he wrote 25 scores over the next 10 years. He has become increasingly well known as a composer of orchestral and instrumental music including film scores and incidental music for the stage. He won a Pulitzer Prize in 1959 for the music for Archie MacLeish's *JB*. He led a group with George Barrow (tenor saxophone) that played regularly at New York's Five Spot in the mid-60s, and was composer in residence with the New York Philharmonic Orchestra (1966-67), with whom he organized concerts for children and workshops on folk music (especially Latin American) and jazz. In 1969 he went on a State Department-sponsored tour to Brazil and during the 70s visited Kenya, Cuba, the Middle East and Central America. These tours added to his 'dramatic, colourful scores', which nevertheless retain the rhythmic, improvisatory character of jazz. Amram's 1977 release, *Havana/New York*, was a particularly striking fusion of jazz and Afro-Latin rhythms.

● ALBUMS: *Jazz Studio Six* (Decca 1957)★★★, *Triple Concerto For Woodwind, Brass, Jazz Quartet And Orchestra* (1970)★★★, *Havana/New York* (Flying Fish 1977)★★★★, *No More Walls* (Flying Fish 1978)★★★, *At Home/Around The World* (Flying Fish 1980)★★, *Latin Jazz Celebration* (1982)★★★.

Amy, Curtis

b. 11 October 1929, Houston, Texas, USA. Having previously learned to play clarinet while growing up in Texas, Amy took up the tenor saxophone during his army service. Later he became a musical educator in Tennessee, following his graduation from Kentucky State College. He continued to play in nightclubs, however, and in the mid-50s he moved to the west coast, where he became extensively involved in the contemporary music scene. Amy recorded with Dizzy Gillespie, but, eager to experiment, in the early 60s he led several small groups that explored the possibilities of modal jazz. In the mid-60s he recorded with a big band led by Gerald Wilson, a swing era veteran noted for his musically adventurous ideas. Amy's later studio work found him backing many pop artists, including Carole King and the Doors.

● ALBUMS: with Paul Bryant *The Blues Message* aka *This Is The Blues* (Kimberly 1960)★★★, with Frank Butler *Groovin' Blue* (Pacific Jazz 1961)★★★, with Bryant *Meetin' Here* (Pacific Jazz 1961)★★★, with Victor Feldman *Way Down* (Pacific Jazz 1962)★★★★, *Tippin' On Through - Recorded 'Live' At The Lighthouse* (Pacific Jazz 1962)★★★, with Dupree Bolton *Katanga!* (Pacific Jazz 1963)★★★, *Sounds Of Hollywood* (Palomar 1965)★★★, *Mustang* (Verve 1966)★★★.

● VIDEOS: *Curtis Amy & Paul Horn* (Kay Jazz 1988).

Andersen, Arild

b. 27 October 1945, Oslo, Norway. Andersen's career as a jazz bassist began under the tutelage of Karel Netolicka and the influential American jazz composer and theorist George Russell, who was then resident in Sweden. From 1966-73 Andersen toured throughout Scandinavia, working with Russell's orchestra and sextet, Jan Garbarek's trio and quartet, Karin Krog, Edward Vesala and others. In West Germany he worked with Don Cherry and in France with Stan Getz. Visits to New York brought recordings with Sam Rivers, Paul Bley and Barry Altschul. In 1974 he led his own quartet, which recorded the acclaimed bop-influenced *Clouds In My Head* a year later. *Shimri* and *Green Shading Into Blue* followed a more romantic course and divided the critics. The early 80s saw the introduction of non-Norwegian musicians in Andersen-led projects, such as Americans Alphonze Mouzon and Bill Frisell, Canadian Kenny Wheeler and Briton John Taylor. From 1983 he toured and recorded with the Norwegian quintet Masqualero. *Sagn*, a series of compositions based on folk songs from the south of Norway, received its premiere at the Vossajazz festival in Norway in 1990. Andersen has received a number of awards for his bass playing, including the Buddy Award from the Norwegian Jazz Federation in 1969.

● ALBUMS: *Clouds In My Head* (1975)★★★★, *Shimri* (1976)★★★, *Green Shading Into Blue* (1978)★★★, *Lifelines* (1980)★★★, *A Molde Concert* (1981)★★★, *Sagn* (ECM 1990)★★★, with Masqualero *Masqualero* (1983)★★★, *Bande A Parte* (1985)★★★, with Ralph Towner, Nana Vasconcelos *If You Look Far Enough* (ECM 1993)★★, *Hyperborean* (ECM 1998)★★★★.

Anderson, Cat

b. William Alonzo Anderson, 12 September 1916, Greenville, South Carolina, USA, d. 29 April 1981, Norwalk, California, USA. Learning to play the trumpet while at a South Carolina orphanage, Anderson developed a fearsome technique that earned him jobs with the bands of Lucky Millinder, Lionel Hampton, Erskine Hawkins, Claude Hopkins and Sabby Lewis. In 1944, Anderson joined Duke Ellington where he remained for three years. From 1947 he alternated between leading his own bands and working for others; but he kept returning to Ellington, for whom he played more or less continuously for two long stretches, 1950-59 and 1961-71. When he finally left Ellington, Anderson settled in Los Angeles - which was where Bill Berry re-formed his Ellington-inspired big band in 1971, Anderson becoming an occasional member. Although noted for his extraordinary five-octave range, Anderson was highly accomplished in all aspects of his instrument and excelled at the colourful use of half-valve and plunger-mute techniques that made him such an integral part of Ellington's composing palette. Unlike many other high-note specialists, Anderson was able to play melodically in the top registers, not merely make noises. In the late 70s Anderson toured with Hampton's All Star band, playing festivals and making records in the USA and Europe.

● ALBUMS: *Cat Anderson Plays At 4 a.m.* (1958)★★★, *Cat On A Hot Tin Horn* (EmArcy 1958)★★★, *A Flower Is A Lovesome Thing* (1959)★★★, *A 'Chat' With Cat* (1964)★★★, *Cat Anderson/Claude Bolling & Co.* (1965)★★★, *Cat Speaks* (1977)★★★, *Cat Anderson Plays W.C. Handy (1977-1978)* (Black And Blue 1991)★★★, *Old Folks* (1979)★★★, *Cat Anderson Et Les Four Bones* (Barclay 1979)★★★.

● COMPILATIONS: *Ellingtonians In Paris 1958-1964* (DRG 1986)★★★★.

Anderson, Clifford

b. 5 October 1957, New York City, New York, USA. A bop trombonist of the J.J. Johnson school, Anderson's beguiling tones have been overshadowed by the mighty figure of his uncle, Sonny Rollins, with whom he has played since 1983. His mother's younger brother, Rollins bought the seven year old Anderson his first trombone. After graduating from New York's High School Of Music and Art and the Manhattan School Of Music, Anderson gained valuable experience working with Slide Hampton's World Of Trombones, Carlos Garnett's Cosmos Nucleus, Frank Foster's Loud Minority, McCoy Tyner's Big Band and Lester Bowie's Brass Fantasy. Fired by Rollins after only a year, Anderson was rehired and subsequently appeared on over half a dozen of the saxophonist's albums. He stepped out of Rollins's shadow in 1995 with the release of his debut as leader. *Landmarks* featured pianist Monty Alexander, bassist Bob Cranshaw, drummer Al Foster and percussionist Victor See Yuen backing Anderson on a lively and musically adventurous set.

● ALBUMS: *Landmarks* (Milestone 1995)★★★★.

Anderson, Ernestine

b. 11 November 1928, Houston, Texas, USA. Raised in Seattle, Anderson has been singing professionally since her mid-teens. She worked extensively with R&B bands in the 40s, including those led by Russell Jacquet and Johnny Otis. A year with Lionel Hampton in the early

50s and a Scandinavian tour with bop trumpeter Rolf Ericson broadened her repertoire, but she remained well rooted in the blues. In later years Anderson developed her technique and range, her rich, molten sound being especially effective on the better contemporary pop songs. Despite spending long periods overseas (including several years' residence in England from 1965), her international appeal remained limited. Indeed, the spell in Europe adversely affected her career in her homeland; even a national magazine profile that described her as the 'new Sarah Vaughan and Ella Fitzgerald' did not help. A chance appearance at the 1976 Concord Summer Jazz Festival deservedly brought her to the attention of a new and wider audience, and since then she has performed and recorded extensively for the Concord label, although she is now based chiefly on the west coast of America.

● ALBUMS: *It's Time For Ernestine* (Metronome 1956)★★★, with Rolf Ericson *Hot Cargo!* (Mercury 1956)★★★★, *Ernestine Anderson* i (Mercury 1958)★★★★, *Fascinating Ernestine* (Mercury 1959)★★★, *My Kinda Swing* (Mercury 1959)★★★, *Moanin', Moanin', Moanin'* (Mercury 1960)★★★, *Ernestine Anderson* ii (Wing 1964)★★★, *Hello Like Before* (Concord Jazz 1976)★★★★, *Live From Concord To London* (Concord 1976)★★★, *Sunshine* (Concord 1979)★★★, *Live At The Concord Jazz Festival* (Concord 1979)★★★, *Never Make Your Move Too Soon* (Concord 1981)★★★★, *Big City* (Concord 1983)★★★, *When The Sun Goes Down* (Concord 1984)★★★, *Be Mine Tonight* (Concord 1986)★★★, with Capp-Pierce Juggernaut *Live At The Alleycat* (Concord 1987)★★★, with George Shearing *A Perfect Match* (Concord 1988)★★★, *Boogie Down* (Concord 1990)★★★, *Live At The Concord Festival: The Third Set* (Concord 1990)★★★, *Late At Night* (King 1992), *Now And Then* (1993)★★★, *Blues, Dues & Love News* (Qwest 1998)★★★.

Anderson, Fred

b. 22 March 1929, Monroe, Louisiana, USA. Resident in Evanston, Illinois, just north of Chicago, since the age of 10, the self-taught Anderson was known locally as an 'outside' tenor saxophonist, his gruff, vigorous style mixing the lyricism and power of bebop with the more experimental approach of Ornette Coleman. In the mid-60s he was a founder-member of the AACM, recording on Joseph Jarman's *Song For* (which included Anderson's composition 'Little Fox Run'). A family man, he was obliged to work a day job as a carpet-fitter but remained associated with the AACM, nurturing a younger generation of talents such as Douglas Ewart and George Lewis in his regular group. In 1977 Anderson visited Europe, recording with the trio Neighbours, and in 1978 he recorded *Another Place* at the Moers Festival in Germany. Basically still a home-man, he made two further albums in Chicago and took over a Southside club, the Velvet Lounge, which he continues to run, playing frequently with long-time associates such as trumpeter Billy Brimfield and drummer Hamid Hank Drake. A strikingly original voice on tenor saxophone, Anderson is one of several AACM stalwarts who have been seriously under-recorded. In 1990 he was one of three recipients of Arts Midwest's first ever Jazz Masters Awards, and in the same year he was invited to open the AACM's 25th anniversary celebrations. He currently records with new wave *avant-garde* players the DKV trio, who comprise Ken Vandermark (reeds), Kent Kessler (bass) and Hamid Drake (drums).

● ALBUMS: *Another Place* (Moers 1978)★★★★, with Neighbours *Accents* 1977 recordings (MRC 1980)★★★, *Dark Day* 1979 recordings (Message 1982)★★★, *The Missing Link* 1979 recordings (Nessa 1984)★★★, *Vintage Duets Chicago 1-11-80* (Okkadisk)★★★, *Destiny* (Okkadisk)★★★, *Birdhouse* (Okkadisk 1996)★★★, *Fred: Chicago Chamber Music* (Southport 1997)★★★★, with DKV *Fred Anderson/DKV Trio* (Okkadisk 1997)★★★.

Anderson, Ivie

b. 10 July 1905, Gilroy, California, USA, d. 28 December 1949. Although best known for her work with Duke Ellington in the 30s, Anderson had already worked extensively both in the USA, where she sang at the Cotton Club in the mid-20s, and overseas, touring Australia with Sonny Clay towards the end of the decade. Her light-toned voice and relaxed style were well suited to the swing era and she was one of the best of her kind. Given Ellington's notoriously eccentric choice of singers for his band, the fact that he hired her at all is surprising, but once there she proved an important asset. She was with Ellington from 1931-42, making numerous records, including the first and possibly definitive version of 'It Don't Mean A Thing If It Ain't Got That Swing', and appearing on film. After leaving Ellington, Anderson retired from singing and went into the restaurant business, but she returned to the studios in 1946 for an excellent session on which she was accompanied by Charles Mingus, Willie Smith, Lucky Thompson and others.

● ALBUMS: with Lena Horne *Lena And Ivie* (Jazztone 1956)★★★.

● COMPILATIONS: *Duke Ellington Presents Ivie Anderson* (1932-40), *The Indispensable Duke Ellington Volumes 3/4/5/6* (1934-40), *Ivie Anderson And Her All Stars* (1946).

Anderson, Ray

b. 16 October 1952, Chicago, Illinois, USA. Anderson started playing trombone as soon as he was tall enough, at the age of eight. Initially inspired by his father's Dixieland record collection, he played in school alongside George Lewis, the other pre-eminent trombonist of his generation. Anderson has always involved himself with a generous spectrum of music, from harmonica player Jeff Carp's blues band as a teenager to classical orchestras. Concerts by the local black self-help organization, the AACM, were an inspiration. Lewis joined the AACM, and Anderson went to Minneapolis and then San Francisco to study music. However, Anderson has always kept in touch with the Chicago players and, like Lewis, has had a fruitful relationship with Anthony Braxton. In California he played with Charles Moffett and David Murray. In 1972 he relocated to New York, where he sat in with Charles Mingus and George Rufus Adams. In the late 70s he toured and recorded with

Braxton and Barry Altschul. In 1981 he won the *Downbeat* poll as Talent Deserving Wider Recognition and formed an entertaining funk band, Slickaphonics. His 1985 release, *Old Bottles - New Wine*, on the Enja label, had him playing standards in the formidable company of Kenny Barron, Cecil McBee and Dannie Richmond. His trio with Mark Helias and Gerry Hemingway, also known as both Oahspe and BassDrumBone, is an excellent foil for his startlingly fluid, responsive and subversive stylings. His recent collaborative work with percussionist Han Bennink and guitarist Christy Doran, and as a four trombone quartet with Craig Harris, George Lewis and Gary Valente, has produced further remarkably varied and fresh work. Anderson is a convincing representative of a generation of musicians who see no reason not to fuse the furthest outreaches of free improvisation with funk or farce as the fancy takes them. Coupled with the Louis Armstrong-style multiphonics of his singing voice, his excavation of the narrow line between emotional extension and comedy - and his staggering technique - has secured him an enthusiastic and loyal following.

● ALBUMS: *Oahspe* (1979)★★★, *Harrisburg Half Life* (Moers 1981)★★★, with Mark Helias, Gerry Hemingway *Right Down Your Alley* (Soul Note 1984)★★★, *Old Bottles - New Wine* (Enja 1985)★★★, with Helias, Hemingway *You Be* (Minor 1986)★★★, *It Just So Happens* (Enja 1986)★★★, with BassDrumBone *Wooferloo* (1987)★★★, *Blues Bred In The Bone* (Enja 1989)★★★★, *What Because* (Gramavision 1990)★★★★, *Wishbone* (Gramavision 1991)★★★, *Everyone Of Us* (Gramavision 1992)★★★, with Han Bennink, Christy Doran *Azurety* (hatART 1993)★★★★, *Don't Mow Your Lawn* (Enja 1994)★★★, with the Alligatory Band *Heads And Tails* (Enja 1996)★★★, with Craig Harris, George Lewis, Gary Valente *Slideride* (hatART 1996)★★★★, with Bennink, Doran *Cheer Up* (hatART 1996)★★★★, with BassDrumBone *Hence The Reason* (Enja 1998)★★★, *Funkorific* (Enja 1998)★★★.

ANDRADE, LENY

b. *c.*1939, Rio de Janeiro, Brazil. Andrade began as a pianist, studying formally from the age of six and won a scholarship to the Brazilian Conservatory of Music only three years later. She made her first public performance in a children's radio programme. Her first professional engagement was with Permino Gonclaves And His Orchestra. She had begun to concentrate on singing and during the 50s sang with many of her country's best musicians, including a trio led by Sergio Mendes. She appeared in musical shows, played long club residencies and made numerous records, moved to Mexico where she remained for five years, then returned to Brazil to star in the show *Gemini*. Visits to New York found her singing at the Blue Note and at Village West. Her improvisational gifts and her enthusiastic scatting endeared her to many musicians and Paquito D'Rivera composed 'Song For Leny' as a tribute to her. She has toured Spain and visited the UK with an appearance at Ronnie Scott's club in London. She has also headlined at major jazz festivals in her home-town and in São Paulo, Brazil, where her co-stars have included Ray Charles, Wynton Marsalis and David Sanborn. Andrade has a rich, strong voice and displays great dramatic flair, and she is equally comfortable with uptempo swingers and slower ballads. She also favours Latin-flavoured music, especially bossa novas and batidas. In addition to singing in English, she also sings in Spanish and, obviously, is most at home in Portuguese.

● ALBUMS: *Luz Neon* (Timeless 1990)★★, *Embraceable You* (Timeless 1992)★★★.

ANDREWS, ERNIE

b. 25 December 1927, Philadelphia, Pennsylvania, USA. Andrews was raised in Louisiana but by his mid-teens was living in Los Angeles where he attracted attention by singing at talent shows. He also sang with visiting bands, including that of Andy Kirk, and made a handful of records that were sufficiently popular to convince him that he was in the right business. Although initially leaning heavily towards ballads, sung in the currently popular fashion of Billy Eckstine, his jazz affiliation was sufficient to bring an engagement at Birdland in New York. In the 50s he recorded with Benny Carter and then spent more than five years singing with Harry James. He also recorded with Cannonball Adderley. By the 70s, and still based on the west coast, Andrews was working concerts and clubs and making occasional appearances on record, a particularly good example being a 1976 set with the Frank Capp–Nat Pierce big band. Less well known internationally than his talent deserves, Andrews continued to sing throughout the 80s and 90s making occasional well-received albums. Andrews has retained his fondness for ballads although when he does essay the blues it is with robust conviction.

● ALBUMS: *In The Dark* (GNP 1957)★★★, *Ernie Andrews* (GNP 1959)★★★★, *Travelin' Light* (GNP 1959)★★★★, *Soul Proprietor* (Dot 1965)★★★, *Hear Me Now* (Muse 1979)★★★, *From The Heart* (Discovery 1980)★★★, *The Great City* (Muse 1995)★★★, *No Regrets* 1992 recording (32 Jazz 1998)★★, *The Many Faces Of Ernie Andrews* (HighNote 1998)★★★.

ANDRIESSEN, LOUIS

b. 6 June 1939, Utrecht, Holland. Son of composer Hendrik Andriessen, Louis Andriessen writes some of the most forbidding minimalist music, and has inspired some of the most accessible. He studied under his father at Utrecht Conservatory, under Kees van Baaren at the Royal Conservatory in the Hague (where he won the composition prize in 1962) and finally with Luciano Berio in Milan and Berlin during 1964/5. Like many of the American minimalists, he revolted against the academic and elitist contemporary classical mainstream, and in 1972 he founded De Volharding, intended to allow composition for individuals rather than instruments. Since 1974 he has taught at the Royal Conservatory where, in 1976, he began a minimalist music project that developed into the band Hoketus. He later assembled another unit, Kaalslag, from musicians out of de Volharding and Hoketus. His music, which is usually rhythmic, percussive and frequently very loud, has been a major influence on a generation of Dutch minimalists and inspired the formation of the British band Icebreaker.

● ALBUMS: *Symphonies Of The Netherlands* (1974)★★★, *De Staat* (The Republic 1976)★★★, *De Tijd* (Time 1981)★★★, *Mausoleum & De Snelheid* (Velocity 1984)★★★, *De Stijl* (included on *Live* by the band Kaalslag) (1985)★★★, *Melodie & Symphony For Open Strings* (1986)★★★, *Hoketus* (included on *Balans* by the band Hoketus) (1986)★★★.

ANDRUS, CHUCK

b. Charles Edmund Andrus, 17 November 1928, Holyoke, Massachusetts, USA, d. 12 June 1997, Boca Raton, Florida, USA. Bass player Chuck Andrus came to prominence in jazz circles through his contributions to the Woody Herman Band. In this ensemble he earned the nickname 'The Arm', by virtue of his ability to play expansive bass runs at high speed. The seeds of his employment in jazz came through his experiences in World War II. Sharing a barracks with trumpeter Jerry Marshall and pianist John Williams, the three stayed together throughout their service, and for a time were stationed in Japan and Korea. In the latter country, the ever-inventive Andrus (a keen handyman) found a profitable sideline in harvesting the marijuana the locals grew to provide cloth fibre. After their discharge, the three joined Charlie Barnet's band, although Williams then left to team up with Stan Getz. Andrus then played with Terry Gibbs, Herbie Mann and Claude Thornhill until he joined Herman's band in 1961. In November 1963 the group were in the process of recording 'Satin Doll' and 'A Taste Of Honey', intended to showcase Andrus's playing, when news of President Kennedy's assassination reached them; the news added a poignancy to the recordings. Indeed, the former track is considered by many to be the definitive example of Andrus's fluid technique. During the decline of the big bands in the early 60s, Herman attempted to re-form his group, the Herd - now retitled the Swinging Herd. With the addition of musicians drawn from the Berklee College Of Music as well as Andrus, the Swinging Herd managed to turn around their fortunes, re-establishing an appetite among jazz fans for swing and big band performances, especially during their residency at New York's Metropolé Cafe. Andrus finally left the band at the peak of their popularity in 1965, thereafter working as a successful freelance bass player in and around New York. His own trio played for President Johnson at the White House - a venue to which he later returned to play at the Ambassador's Ball. During the 70s he moved back to his native Holyoke, working in a lawyer's office. Until shortly before his death, he continued to play occasional sets at the Governor's Club in Palm Beach, Florida, where he had settled in 1993.

ANTHONY, JULIE

b. Julie Moncrieff Anthony, 23 August 1951, Galga, South Australia. Anthony was born in Galga (population 15) and raised on the family farm. In her teens she began singing with a local band and in 1970 won an amateur television talent quest. Her victory and the first prize ($600 and a trip to Tasmania) led to regular appearances on the *Adelaide Tonight Show*. She moved to Sydney, making television appearances and performing on the club and cabaret circuit, and eventually embarking on international tours. An engagement at the Hong Kong Hilton in 1973 was followed by the lead role in the Australian production of *Irene*. Three years later she starred in the British version at the Adelphi Theatre. The Play and Players of London honoured her with the Best Newcomer (Actress) award for 1976. She returned to Australian television and appeared in three national specials, and in the same year she married her manager Eddie Natt. In 1977 she won the Sammy and Penquin awards for Best Television Variety Performer. Tours of America followed and Anthony worked with Bill Cosby, Roy Clarke and Merv Griffin. In 1980 she was awarded an OBE for services to the entertainment industry. Three years later she accepted the role of Maria in *The Sound Of Music*; following a season in Sydney, the show successfully toured major and regional centres. For the 1988 World Expo held in Brisbane, Anthony was invited to sing with the re-formed Seekers, joining the group as lead singer from 1988-89. In 1988 she sang the national anthem at the official opening of Australia's new Parliament House. The same year she returned to the stage in *I Do!, I Do!*. In 1990, she was awarded AM in the Order of Australia for services to the entertainment industry. In 1994, Anthony further demonstrated her versatility by teaming with jazz musician Don Burrows (b. 8 August 1928, Sydney, New South Wales; Australia; reeds, flute) for tours, including a successful appearance at the Jazz and Blues Festival at the Gold Coast International Hotel in 1995. A year later she returned to cabaret with a season at the Tilbury Hotel in Sydney. In her extensive repertoire she demonstrated great conviction, whether singing 'Amazing Grace' or material ranging from Stephen Sondheim to the Beatles, and after 25 years in the entertainment industry, Anthony continues to consolidate and develop her career. In June 1996 she accepted a cameo role as a band singer in the Bruce Beresford film *Paradise Road*, starring Glenn Close and Jean Simmons. Julie Anthony is one of the best and most durable theatre and variety performers in the post-war Australian entertainment industry. She has won the prestigious Mo Award for Entertainer Of The Year three times, and Best Female Variety Performer nine times. An admirable singer and engaging personality, she has successfully blended her career and family duties.

● ALBUMS: *Sings Just For You* (J&B 1982)★★★, *You And I* (PolyGram 1995)★★★, *Live From The Tilbury Hotel* (PolyGram 1996)★★★.

ANTHONY, RAY

b. Raymond Antonini, 20 January 1922, Bentleyville, Pennsylvania, USA. After playing in local bands in Cleveland, Anthony spent brief spells in the trumpet sections of the Al Donahue, Glenn Miller and Jimmy Dorsey orchestras. Following a four-year period in the

US Navy, where he led a services orchestra, Anthony formed his own band in 1946 and signed with Capitol Records. The band became one of the top attractions of the 50s, touring colleges and universities, producing hit singles such as 'At Last', 'Harbour Lights', the television themes from *Dragnet* and *Peter Gunn*, plus novelty dance numbers such as 'The Bunny Hop' and 'I Can't Tell A Waltz From A Tango'. From the start, the band had always had a Millerish reed sound, so when the Miller 'revival' happened they participated more successfully than most. Anthony appeared with his band in two movies, Fred Astaire's *Daddy Long Legs* and *This Could Be The Night*. He appeared on his own in the Jayne Mansfield/Tom Ewell rock 'n' roll spoof *The Girl Can't Help It*, and in an eerie piece of Hollywood casting, featured as the saxophone-playing Jimmy Dorsey in the Red Nichols biopic *The Five Pennies*. In the 60s, with a limited market for 16-piece bands, Anthony formed a sextet, with a female vocal duo, playing clubs and lounges throughout the USA. He was also active in preserving big-band music for schools and radio stations. In 1986 the Aerospace label relaunched a series of Ray Anthony titles.

● ALBUMS: *Ray Anthony's Orchestra* (Capitol 1953)★★★★, *Sweet And Lovely* (Capitol 1953)★★★★, *House Party* (Capitol 1953)★★★★, *I Remember Glenn Miller* (Capitol 1954)★★★★, *Arthur Murray Swing Foxtrots* (Capitol 1955)★★★, *Golden Horn* (Capitol 1955)★★★★, *Jam Session At The Tower* (Capitol 1956)★★★, *Dream Dancing* (Capitol 1956)★★★★, *Star Dancing* (Capitol 1957)★★★, *Young Ideas* (Capitol 1957)★★★★, *The Dream Girl* (Capitol 1958)★★★★, *Dances in Love* (Capitol 1958)★★★, *Dancing Over The Waves* (Capitol 1959)★★★, *Anthony Plays Allen* (Capitol 1959)★★★, *Sound Spectacular* (Capitol 1960)★★★, *Worried Mind* (Capitol 1962)★★★★, *More Dream Dancing* (Capitol 1983)★★★, *Plays For Dream Dancing* (Capitol 1984)★★★, *Swingin' On Campus* (Capitol 1985)★★★, *Dream Dancing Medley* (Capitol 1985)★★★, *House Party Hop* (Capitol 1985)★★★, *Dancing Alone Together* (Capitol 1986)★★★, *Sweet And Swingin' 1949-53* (Circle 1987)★★★, *Hooked On Big Bands - Live On Radio* (Aerospace 1988)★★★★, *For Dancers Only* (Capitol 1988)★★★, *Glenn Miller - Then And Now* (Aerospace 1988)★★★★, *I Get The Blues When It Rains* (Ranwood 1989)★★★, *Dancers In Love* (Memoir 1989)★★★.

● COMPILATIONS: *The Sampler* (Aerospace 1986)★★★★, *The Hits Of Ray Anthony* (Aerospace 1986)★★★★, *Show And Dance And Party* (Aerospace 1986)★★★★, *Capitol Collectors Series* (Capitol 1991)★★★★.

● FILMS: *The Girl Can't Help It* (1956).

ANTOLINI, CHARLY

b. *c.*1938, Zurich, Switzerland. Antolini decided to become a drummer after playing in a marching band at school when he was nine years old. By the time he was 15 he had become attracted to jazz and a year later joined a Dixieland band. At 18 he moved to Paris, France, and soon became a part of the city's bustling jazz scene. He played with many visiting American musicians including Albert Nicholas and Bill Coleman, and also with Sidney Bechet, then a resident in France. In Switzerland, Antolini formed his own traditional band, the Tremble Kids, and then a bop group. He also began working with radio big bands in Germany. As his reputation spread, Antolini became in much demand for bands fronted by touring jazzmen, among whom were Lew Soloff, Sal Nistico and Herb Geller. He also accompanied Earl 'Fatha' Hines, Lionel Hampton, Benny Goodman, Thad Jones and Stuff Smith. Goodman was sufficiently impressed to hire Antolini for three European and one Canadian tour. A dedicated craftsman, Antolini believes implicitly in the value of extensive practice and has drawn inspiration from many of the greatest drummers in jazz, such as Gene Krupa, Buddy Rich, Jo Jones, Art Blakey, Gus Johnson and Kenny Clarke. However, he told Ron Kirk of *Jazz Journal International* that while he has always tried to be a jazz drummer in the American way, his own playing is 'based on the Basle rudimentary technique'. Antolini made his first visit to the UK in 1991 and such is his reputation that 100 drummers attended a drum clinic at the Sonor factory. Since 1976, Antolini has led his own bands of varying sizes and repertoires but always named Jazz-Power. His musicians for these bands have come from all over the world, linked only by the highest standards of excellence. Among British musicians to have played with Jazz-Power are Danny Moss, Dick Morrissey, Brian Lemon and Brian Dee. Without doubt Antolini is a world-class instrumentalist and might well be the greatest jazzman to emerge from Switzerland.

● ALBUMS: *Bop Dance* (Jazz Publications 1981)★★★, *A Swinging Affair* (1988)★★★, *Cookin'* (Bellaphon 1991)★★★, *Jazz-Power In London* (Bellaphon 1991)★★★.

APPLEYARD, PETER

b. 26 August 1929, Cleethorpes, Lincolnshire, England. Appleyard's musical career began when he played drums in a Boys' Brigade band in his home-town. He graduated to playing drums in local dance bands before joining the popular band led by Felix Mendelssohn. During the mid-40s he played with various bands in the UK and towards the end of the decade worked in Bermuda. In 1951 he moved to Canada. By this time Appleyard had begun to play vibraphone and it was on this instrument that he made his impact on the international jazz scene. He decided to remain in Canada, playing with groups led by Calvin Jackson and others. In the late 50s he also played regularly in New York and during the following decades he toured extensively, working with Benny Goodman and in Peanuts Hucko's Pied Pipers. In Toronto, he regularly hosted a jazz show on television. He has recorded frequently, as leader and sideman, with such jazzmen as Rob McConnell, Ed Bickert, Hucko and others. A dynamic and exciting player, Appleyard's career has been musically successful and financially rewarding.

● ALBUMS: *The Peter Appleyard Quartet* (1957)★★★, *The Vibe Sound Of Peter Appleyard* (Audio Fidelity 1959)★★★★, *Per-cussive Jazz* (1960)★★★, *The Many Moods Of Peter Appleyard* (1969)★★, *On Stage With Benny Goodman And His Sextet* (1972)★★★, *The Lincolnshire Poacher* (1973)★★★, *Sophisticated Vibes* (1976)★★★, *Peter Appleyard Presents* (1977)★★★,

Barbados Heat (Concord 1990)★★, *Barbados Cool* (Concord 1991)★★★.

April In Paris - Count Basie

It is wonderful albums like this that really benefit from the age of the CD. This was crying out for reissue, and apart from the cardboard sleeve, Verve Records have treated one of Basie's greatest albums with utmost respect. The lush swing of the Count Basie band has never sounded happier and the addition of alternate takes is a joy to behold. Listeners will be reminded just how good this band was as they stroll through 'Sweety Cakes', add a sheen to Frank Foster's 'Shiny Stockings' and rip it apart with Neal Hefti's magnificent 'Dinner With Friends'. A highly recommended album just bursting with joy.

- Tracks: *April In Paris; Corner Pocket; Didn't You?; Sweetie Cakes; Magic; Shiney Stockings; What Am I Here For?; Midgets; Mambo Inn; Dinner With Friends; April In Paris; Corner Pocket; Didn't You; Magic; Magic; What Am I Here For?; Midgets.*
- First released 1961
- UK peak chart position: did not chart
- USA peak chart position: did not chart

Arbello, Fernando

b. 30 May 1907, Ponce, Puerto Rico, d. 26 July 1970. Arbello was playing the trombone before he entered his teenage years and played with bands in his homeland, mostly working in the fields of popular and classical music. In the mid-20s he went to New York where he played with many bands including the one led by Wilbur De Paris. He worked with June Clark and then with a succession of bands before settling in with Claude Hopkins for three years. After this he was with Chick Webb, Fletcher Henderson, Lucky Millinder, and others. In the early 40s he was mostly with small New York-based groups, including those led by Zutty Singleton and Marty Marsala, but then returned to big bands with spells under the leadership of Benny Carter, Henderson again, and a number of years with Jimmie Lunceford. In the 50s he briefly led his own small band and also played with Rex Stewart, and in the following decade worked with Machito. In the late 60s he returned to his homeland and led a band there for a short time before his death. Arbello was a strong and reliable section player, only rarely soloing, and was content to provide the body of the big bands of his era.

Archer, Martin

b. 9 March 1957, Sheffield, England. The leading light in the Sheffield free improvisation scene, it is surprising to note that Archer's origins are in rock. In 1972 he was in Blasé, a glam rock outfit that shared the Lou Reed/Roxy Music ethos. When punk hit in 1977 he was in Rissole, a jazz rock group inspired by the Soft Machine and Henry Cow (it broke up as a result of Archer's habit of involving non-musicians and playing saxophone solos). He was also listening to Evan Parker and Anthony Braxton, and for a few years played nothing but free improvisation. Like contemporaries Rip Rig And Panic, his next group, Bass Tone Trap, fused early 80s post-punk tribalism with free-form dazzle. In 1986 he founded the Hornweb Saxophone Quartet, which impressed critics with its innovative use of a difficult format - thanks in no small part to Archer's pithy compositions. Since then, further Hornweb releases and his own *Wild Pathway Favourites* have attracted attention to Archer's specific achievement: compositions that draw on jazz and free-form, 12-tone and monody, without a hint of self-consciousness. In the early 90s Archer was improvising with computers in a new version of Hornweb (no longer a quartet and no longer all saxophones). His own soprano saxophone playing - crystalline yet explosive - is also justly celebrated.

- ALBUMS: with Bass Tone Trap *Trapping* (1984)★★, with Hornweb *Kinesis* (1986)★★★, *Wild Pathway Favourites* (1988)★★★★, with Hornweb *Universe Works* (1989)★★★.

Archey, Jimmy

b. 12 October 1902, Norfolk, Virginia, USA, d. 16 November 1967. A highly accomplished trombone player, Archey held an important place in many of the best big bands of the 30s. Earlier, he had built an enviable reputation working in New York and recording with the bands of Edgar Hayes, Fletcher Henderson, James P. Johnson and Joe 'King' Oliver. For most of the 30s he was with Luis Russell, where he worked alongside Henry 'Red' Allen. Towards the end of the decade he played in the bands of Willie Bryant, Benny Carter, Ella Fitzgerald and Coleman Hawkins, and later deputized with Cab Calloway and Duke Ellington. In the mid-40s the decline of the big bands pointed Archey towards the New Orleans Revivalist movement, and in 1950 he became leader of Bob Wilber's band. The 50s saw Archey holding long residencies with traditional bands at clubs in Boston, New York and San Francisco (the latter alongside Earl Hines), gigs that placed few demands upon such a technically gifted player. Serious illness kept him from the scene in the early 60s, but he returned to tour the USA and Europe until his death in November 1967.

- COMPILATIONS: with Mutt Carey, Punch Miller *Jazz New Orleans* (1947)★★★★, with various artists *Jazz Dance* film soundtrack (1954)★★.

Ardley, Neil

b. 26 May 1937, Carshalton, Surrey, England. After graduating from Bristol University, Ardley studied composition and arranging under Raymond Premru and Bill Russo. In the mid- to late 60s he led the New Jazz Orchestra, and throughout the 70s continued to lead his own orchestra for recording dates, concerts and occasional tours. During this time he was able to impart his Gil Evans and Duke Ellington influences to a more contemporary audience. His groups included important musicians such as Harry Beckett, Ian Carr, Mike Gibbs, Don Rendell and Barbara Thompson. Ardley composed much of the music played by his orchestras but his sidemen were also encouraged to write. He has also written for television and is the author of numerous books on a wide range of subjects including music and several of the sciences. A much lower musical profile in recent years has resulted in his work being neglected, but, with Mike Gibbs and Mike Westbrook, he still remains an important figure in the development of 'progressive' orchestrated jazz in the 60s.

● ALBUMS: *Western Reunion* (Decca 1965)★★★, *Le Déjeuner Sur L'Herbe* (Verve 1968)★★★★, *The Greek Variations* (Columbia 1969)★★★★, *A Symphony Of Amaranths* (Regal Zonophone 1971)★★★, *Will Power* (Argo 1974)★★★, *Kaleidoscope Of Rainbows* (Gull 1975)★★★★, *The Harmony Of The Spheres* (Decca 1978)★★★★.

Argüelles, Julian

b. Julian Argüelles Clarke, 28 January 1966, Lichfield, Staffordshire, England. During his teenage years, saxophonist and composer Argüelles played with various big bands in and around Birmingham, England. He also played in the National Youth Jazz Orchestra and the European Community Big Band. In 1984 he moved to London to study at Trinity College of Music, then joined Loose Tubes, touring with this band throughout Europe. Argüelles also worked with Chris McGregor's Brotherhood Of Breath, touring Americans including Archie Shepp, and with his brother Steve Argüelles. He also formed his own small groups, usually trios and quartets, for UK tours of clubs and other venues. In the early 90s he toured with Kenny Wheeler's big band, the Mike Gibbs orchestra, John Scofield, Steve Swallow, Carla Bley, Tommy Smith, Henry Lowther, John Taylor and others. During this period he recorded with most of the aforementioned artists and also released *Phaedrus* under his own name. A gifted musician, adept on several members of the saxophone family, Argüelles plays in a distinctive style that is fully attuned to recent developments on jazz, but which also displays a thorough understanding of the music's heritage, qualities that also appear in his compositions.

● ALBUMS: *Phaedrus* (Ah-Um 1991)★★★, *Home Truths* (Babel 1996)★★★★, *Scrapes* (Babel 1996)★★, *Skull View* (Babel 1997)★★★, with Henry Lowther *Henry Lowther's Stillwaters* (Village Life 1998)★★★★.

Argüelles, Steve

b. Stephen Argüelles Clarke, 16 November 1963, Crowborough, Sussex, England. Raised in Birmingham, Argüelles began playing drums at school. He soon turned to jazz, playing in a rehearsal band with the Midland Youth Jazz Orchestra and accompanying visiting jazzmen. After leaving school he moved to London where he played with the National Youth Jazz Orchestra. He then became deeply involved in the contemporary jazz scene and was a founder-member of Loose Tubes. Continuously active, Argüelles has become one of the most accomplished and in-demand drummers in the UK. He has worked with jazzmen as diverse as George Coleman, Kenny Wheeler, Lee Konitz, Charlie Mariano, John Taylor, Hugh Masakela, Chris McGregor, Dudu Pukwana and Django Bates. With Bates he formed Human Chain and with his brother, Julian Argüelles, he formed a band known as Argüelles. This last-named group features music that happily mixes folk, country, a touch of Cajun and other exotica with hard bop. Through his broad repertoire, which includes a great many of his own compositions, Argüelles has swiftly developed into one of the most original and inventive drummers in contemporary music.

● ALBUMS: with Human Chain *Human Chain* (Loose Tubes 1986)★★★, with Human Chain *Cashin' In* (Loose Tubes 1988)★★★, with Steve Lacy *Image* 1987 recording (Ah-Um 1989)★★★★, *Steve Argüelles* (Ah-Um 1990)★★★, with Jorrit Dykstra, Mischa Kool *Dykstra, Argüelles, Kool* (1992)★★★, *Recyclers/Rhymes* (1993)★★★★, *Blue Moon In A Function Room* (Babel 1997)★★★, *Busy Listening* (Babel 1997)★★, *Circuit* (Babel 1998)★★★.

Armenra, Dolly

(see Jones, Dolly)

Armstrong, Lillian

b. Lillian Hardin, 3 February 1898, Memphis, Tennessee, USA, d. 27 August 1971, Chicago, Illinois, USA. A classically trained pianist, Hardin worked extensively in Chicago in the 20s, becoming highly popular both as a solo performer and also playing with the bands of Sugar Johnny, Freddie Keppard and Joe 'King' Oliver. It was while she was with Oliver that she met and married the band's newest recruit, Louis Armstrong. Aware of her new husband's massive talent, and being hugely ambitious for him, she persuaded Louis to start his own band, and was herself a crucial presence in his classic Hot Five and Hot Seven groups. Personality clashes later made their marriage untenable and they were divorced. Lillian Armstrong's subsequent career found her leading bands for club work and on numerous radio and recording dates. From the 50s onwards she worked mostly as a solo pianist and singer, usually in Chicago, although she sometimes played at festivals in the USA and Europe, where she also appeared in clubs. An occasional composer, one of her songs, 'Just For A Thrill', was recorded in the 50s by Ray Charles. She died in 1971 while taking part in a memorial concert for Louis, who had died a few weeks earlier.

● ALBUMS: *Satchmo And Me* (Riverside 1956)★★★, *Lil Armstrong And Her Orchestra* (Riverside 1962)★★★.

● COMPILATIONS: *Louis Armstrong Hot Five/Hot Seven* (1926-27)★★★★, *Born To Swing* (1936-37)★★★★, *Harlem On A Saturday Night* (1936-38)★★★★, *The Swing Orchestra* (1936-40)★★★★.

Armstrong, Louis

b. 4 August 1901, New Orleans, Louisiana, USA, d. 6 July 1971, New York, USA. It is impossible to overstate Louis 'Satchmo' Armstrong's importance in jazz. He was one of the most influential artists in the music's history. He was also more than just a jazz musician, he was an enormously popular entertainer (a facet upon which some critics frowned) and although other black jazz men and women would eventually be welcomed in the upper echelons of white society, Armstrong was one of the first. He certainly found his way into millions of hearts otherwise closed to his kind. Had Armstrong been born white and privileged, his achievement would have been extraordinary; that he was born black and in desperately deprived circumstances makes his success almost miraculous. Armstrong achieved this astonishing breakthrough largely by the sheer force of his personality.

Louis Armstrong was born and raised in and around the notorious Storyville district of New Orleans. His exact date of birth is unknown, although for many years he claimed it to be 4 July 1900, a date which was both patriotic and easy to remember and, as some chroniclers have suggested, might have exempted him from army service. Run-down apartment buildings, many of them converted to occasional use as brothels, honky-tonks, dance halls and even churches, were his surroundings as he grew up with his mother and younger sister (his father having abandoned the family at the time of Louis's birth). His childhood combined being free to run the streets with obligations towards his family, who needed him to earn money. His formal education was severely restricted but he was a bright child and swiftly accumulated the kind of wisdom needed for survival; long before the term existed, Louis Armstrong was 'streetwise'. From the first he learned how to hustle for money and it was a lesson he never forgot. Even late in life, when he was rich and famous, he would still regard his career as a 'hustle'. As a child, apart from regular work, among the means he had of earning money was singing at street corners in a semi-formal group. Armstrong's life underwent a dramatic change when, still in his early teens, he was sent to the Colored Waifs Home. The popularly supposed reason for this incarceration, encouraged by Armstrong's assisted autobiography, was that, in a fit of youthful exuberance he had celebrated New Year's Eve (either 1912 or 1913) by firing off a borrowed pistol in the street. Whatever the reason, the period he spent in the home changed his life. Given the opportunity to play in the home's band, first as a singer, then as a percussionist, then a bugler and finally as a cornetist, Armstrong found his métier. From the first, he displayed a remarkable affinity for music, and quickly achieved an enviable level of competence not only at playing the cornet but also in understanding harmony. Released from the home after a couple of years, it was some time before Armstrong could afford to buy an instrument of his own, but he continued to advance his playing ability, borrowing a cornet whenever he could and playing with any band that would hire him. He was, of course, some years away from earning his living through music but took playing jobs in order to supplement earnings from manual work, mainly delivering coal with a horse and cart. Through his late teens, Armstrong played in many of the countless bands that made their home in New Orleans (not all of which could be thought of as jazz groups), gradually working his way upwards until he was in demand for engagements with some of the city's best bands. The fact that Armstrong's introduction to music came through the home's band is significant in that he was inducted into a musical tradition different to that which was currently developing into the newly emergent style known as jazz. The Waif's Home band played formal brass band music that placed certain demands upon musicians, not least of which were precision and an ornate bravura style. When Armstrong put this concept of music to work with the ideals of jazz, it resulted in a much more flamboyant and personalized musical form than the ensemble playing of the new New Orleans jazz bands. Not surprisingly, this precocious young cornet player attracted the attention of the city's jazz masters, one of whom, Joe 'King' Oliver, was sufficiently impressed to become his musical coach and occasional employer. By the time that Armstrong came under Oliver's wing, around 1917, the older man was generally regarded as the best cornetist in New Orleans and few challenged his position as 'the King'.

Already displaying signs of great ambition, Armstrong knew that he needed the kind of advancement and kudos King Oliver could offer, even though Oliver's style of playing was rather simplistic and close to that of other early New Orleans cornetists, such as near-contemporaries Freddie Keppard and Buddy Petit. Much more important to Armstrong's career than musical tuition was the fact that his association with Oliver opened many doors that might otherwise have remained closed. Of special importance was the fact that through Oliver, the younger man was given the chance to take his talent out of the constrictions of one city and into the wide world beyond the bayous of Louisiana. In 1919 Oliver had been invited to take a band to Chicago (and before leaving, recommended his young protégé as his replacement with Kid Ory), and by 1922 his was the most popular ensemble in the Windy City. Back in New Orleans, Armstrong's star continued to rise even though he declined to stay with Ory when the latter was invited to take his band to Los Angeles. Armstrong, chronically shy, preferred to stay in the place that he knew; but when Oliver sent word for him to come to Chicago, he went. The reason he overcame his earlier reluctance to travel was in part his ambition and also the fact that he trusted Oliver implicitly. From the moment of Armstrong's arrival in Chicago the local musical scene was tipped onto its ear; musicians raved about the duets of the King and the young pretender and if the lay members of the audience did not know exactly what it was that they were hearing, they certainly knew that it was something special.

For two years Oliver and Armstrong made musical history and, had it not been for the piano player in the band, they might well have continued doing so for many more years. The piano player was Lillian Hardin, who took a special interest in the young cornetist and became the second major influence in his life. By 1924 Armstrong and Hardin were married and her influence had prompted him to quit Oliver's band and soon afterwards to head for New York. In New York, Armstrong joined Fletcher Henderson's orchestra, bringing to that band a quality of solo playing far exceeding anything the city had heard thus far in jazz. His musical ideas, some of which were harmonies he and Oliver had developed, were also a spur to the writing of Henderson's staff arranger, Don Redman. Armstrong stayed with Henderson for a little over a year, returning to Chicago in 1925 at his wife's behest to star as the 'World's Greatest Trumpeter' with her band. Over the next two or three years he recorded extensively, including the first of the famous Hot Five and Hot Seven sessions and as accompanist to the best of the blues singers, among them Bessie Smith, Clara Smith and Trixie Smith. He worked ceaselessly, in 1926 doubling with the orchestras of Carroll Dickerson and Erskine Tate, and becoming, briefly, a club owner with two of his closest musical companions, Earl Hines and Zutty Singleton. By the end of the decade Armstrong was in demand across the country, playing important engagements in Chicago, New York, Washington, Los Angeles (but not New Orleans, a city to which he hardly ever returned).

By the 30s, Armstrong had forsaken the cornet for the trumpet. He frequently worked with name bands yet equally often travelled alone, fronting whichever house band was available at his destination. He worked and recorded in Los Angeles with Les Hite's band (in which the drummer was Lionel Hampton), and in New York with Chick Webb. In 1932 and 1933 he made his first visits to Europe, playing to largely ecstatic audiences, although some, accustomed only to hearing him on record, found his stage mannerisms - the mugging and clowning, to say nothing of the sweating - rather difficult to accommodate. From 1935 onwards Armstrong fronted the Luis Russell orchestra, eclipsing the remarkable talents of the band's leading trumpeter, Henry 'Red' Allen. In 1938 Louis and Lillian were divorced and he married Alpha Smith. However, by 1942 he had married again, to Lucille Wilson, who survived him. In some respects, the swing era passed Louis Armstrong by, leading some observers to suggest that his career was on a downward slide from that point on. Certainly, the big band Armstrong fronted in the 30s was generally inferior to many of its competitors, but his playing was always at least as strong as that of any of the other virtuoso instrumentalist leaders of the era. His musical style, however, was a little out of step with public demand, and by the early 40s he was out of vogue. Since 1935 Armstrong's career had been in the hands of Joe Glaser, a tough-talking, hard-nosed extrovert whom people either loved or hated. Ruthless in his determination to make his clients rich and famous, Glaser promoted Armstrong intensively. When the big band showed signs of flagging, Glaser fired everyone and then hired younger, more aggressive (if not always musically appropriate) people to back his star client. When this failed to work out, Glaser took a cue from an engagement at New York's Town Hall at which Armstrong fronted a small band to great acclaim. Glaser set out to form a new band that would be made up of stars and which he planned to market under the name Louis Armstrong And His All Stars. It proved to be a perfect format for Armstrong and it remained the setting for his music for the rest of his life - even though changes in personnel gradually made a nonsense of the band's hyperbolic title.

With the All Stars, Armstrong began a relentless succession of world tours with barely a night off, occasionally playing clubs and festivals but most often filling concert halls with adoring crowds. The first All Stars included Jack Teagarden, Barney Bigard, Earl Hines and Big Sid Catlett; replacements in the early years included Trummy Young, Edmond Hall, Billy Kyle and William 'Cozy' Cole. Later substitutes, when standards slipped, included Russell Moore, Joe Darensbourg, and Barrett Deems. Regulars for many years were bassist Arvell Shaw and singer Velma Middleton. The format and content of the All Stars shows (copied to dire and detrimental effect by numerous bands in the traditional jazz boom of the 50s and 60s) were predictable, with solos being repeated night after night, often note for note. This helped to fuel the contention that Armstrong was past his best. In fact, some of the All Stars' recordings, even those made with the lesser bands, show that this was not the case. The earliest All Stars are excitingly presented on *Satchmo At Symphony Hall* and *New Orleans Nights*, while the later bands produced some classic performances on *Louis Armstrong Plays W.C. Handy* and *Satch Plays Fats*. On all these recordings Armstrong's own playing is outstanding. However, time inevitably took its toll and eventually even Armstrong's powerful lip weakened. It was then that another facet of his great talent came into its own. Apparent to any who cared to hear it since the 20s, Armstrong was a remarkable singer. By almost any standards but those of the jazz world, his voice was beyond redemption, but through jazz it became recognized for what it was: a perfect instrument for jazz singing. Armstrong's throaty voice, his lazy-sounding delivery, his perfect timing and effortlessly immaculate rhythmic presentation, brought to songs of all kinds a remarkable sense of rightness. Perfect examples of this form were the riotous '(I Want) A Butter And Egg Man' through such soulfully moving lyrics as '(What Did I Do To Be So) Black And Blue', 'Do You Know What It Means To Miss New Orleans', and countless superb renditions of the blues. He added comic absurdities to 'Baby, It's Cold Outside' and oversentimentality to 'It's A Wonderful World', which in 1968 gave him a UK number 1 hit. He added texture and warmth and a rare measure of understanding often far exceeding anything that had been put there by the songs' writers. Additionally, he was one of the first performers to sing scat (the improvisation of wordless vocal sounds in place of the formal lyrics), and certainly the first to do so with skill and intelligence and not through mere chance (although he always claimed that he began scatting when the sheet music for 'Heebie Jeebies' fell on the floor during a 1926 recording session and he had to improvise the words). It was in his late years, as a singer and entertainer rather than as a trumpet star, that Armstrong became a world figure, known by name, sight and sound to tens of millions of people of all nationalities and creeds, who also loved him in a way that the urchin kid from the wrong side of the tracks in turn-of-the-century New Orleans could never have imagined.

Armstrong's world status caused him some problems with other black Americans, many of whom believed he should have done more for his fellow blacks. He was openly criticized for the manner in which he behaved, whether on stage or off, some accusing him of being an Uncle Tom and thus pandering to stereotypical expectations of behaviour. Certainly, he was no militant, although he did explode briefly in a fit of anger when interviewed at the time of the Civil Rights protests over events in Little Rock in 1958. What his critics overlooked was that, by the time of Little Rock, Armstrong was already 60 years old, and when the Civil Rights movement hit its full stride he was past the age at which most of his contemporaries were slipping contentedly into retirement. To expect a man of this age to wholeheartedly embrace the Civil Rights movement, having been born and raised in conditions even fellow blacks of one or two generations later could scarcely comprehend, was simply asking too much. For almost 50 years he had been an entertainer - he would probably have preferred and used the term 'hustler' - and he was not about to change. Louis Armstrong toured on until almost the very end, recovering from at least one heart attack (news reports tended to be very cagey about his illnesses - doubtless Joe Glaser saw to that). He died in his sleep at his New York home on 6 July 1971. With only a handful of exceptions, most trumpet players who came after Armstrong owe some debt to his pioneering stylistic developments. By the early 40s, the date chosen by many as marking the first decline in Armstrong's importance and ability, jazz style was undergoing major changes. Brought about largely by the work of Charlie Parker and his musical collaborators, chief among whom was trumpeter Dizzy Gillespie, jazz trumpet style changed and the Armstrong style no longer had immediate currency. However, his influence was only sidetracked; it never completely disappeared, and in the post-bop era the qualities of technical proficiency and dazzling technique that he brought to jazz were once again appreciated for the remarkable achievements they were. In the early 20s Louis Armstrong had become a major influence on jazz musicians and jazz music; he altered the way musicians thought about their instruments and the way that they played them. There have been many virtuoso performers in jazz since Armstrong first came onto the scene, but nobody has matched his virtuosity or displayed a comparable level of commitment to jazz, a feeling for the blues, or such simple and highly communicable *joie de vivre*. Louis Armstrong was unique. The music world is fortunate to have received his outstanding contribution.

● ALBUMS: With such a discography it is often a problem to decide if it is a compilation or a regular album. Bearing in mind that Armstrong 'best of' and compilations have been appearing since the advent of the long-playing record, you will appreciate our problem.

New Orleans film soundtrack (1946)★★★, *Town Hall Concert Plus* (1947)★★★, *Carnegie Hall Concert With Edmond Hall's Sextet* (1947)★★★, *This Is Jazz* (1947)★★★, *A Song Is Born* film soundtrack (1947)★★★, *Satchmo At Symphony Hall* (1947)★★★, *Louis Armstrong And His All Stars At Nice* (1948)★★★, *Louis Armstrong And His All Stars Live At Ciro's, Philadelphia* (1948)★★★, *Louis Armstrong And His All Stars Live At The Empire Room, Los Angeles* (1948)★★★, *Louis Armstrong And His All Stars Live At The Clique Club Volumes 1-5* (1948-49)★★★, *Louis Armstrong At The Eddie Condon Floor Show* (1949)★★★, *Armstrong Classics* 10-inch album (Brunswick 1950)★★★, *New Orleans To New York* 10-inch album (Decca 1950)★★★, *New Orleans Days* 10-inch album (Decca 1950)★★★, *Jazz Concert* 10-inch album (Decca 1950)★★★, *Satchmo Serenades* 10-inch album (Decca 1952)★★★, *New Orleans Nights* (1950-54)★★★, *Louis Armstrong And His All Stars Live At Pasadena* i (1951)★★★, *Town Hall Concert '48* 10-inch album (Decca 1951)★★★, *The Greatest Concert* (1951)★★★, *Glory Alley* film soundtrack (1952)★★★, *Louis Armstrong Plays The Blues* 10-inch album (Riverside 1953)★★★, *Louis Armstrong And His All Stars In Yokohama* (1953)★★★, *Louis Armstrong With King Oliver's Creole Jazz Band 1923* 10-inch album (Riverside 1953)★★★, with the Mills Brothers *Louis Armstrong And The Mills Brothers* 10-inch album (Decca 1954)★★★★, *Louis Armstrong-Gordon Jenkins* 10-inch album (Decca 1954)★★★, *Latter Day Louis* 10-inch album (Decca 1954)★★★, *Satchmo At Symphony Hall* (Decca 1954)★★★★, *Louis Armstrong Plays W.C. Handy* (Columbia 1954)★★★★, *Louis Armstrong And His All Stars Live At The Crescendo Club, Los Angeles Volumes 1 And 2* (Decca 1955)★★★, *Sings The Blues* (RCA Victor 1954)★★★, *Satch Plays Fats* (Columbia 1955)★★★, *Louis Armstrong Plays W.C. Handy Volume 2* 10-inch album (Columbia 1955)★★★, *Satchmo Sings* (Decca 1955)★★★, *Ambassador Satch* (Columbia 1956)★★★, *Satchmo The Great* film soundtrack (Columbia 1956)★★, *Louis Armstrong And His All Stars Live At Pasadena* ii (Decca 1956)★★★, *Satchmo: A Musical Autobiography* 4-LP set (1956)★★★★, with Ella Fitzgerald *Ella And Louis* (Verve 1956)★★★★★, with Fitzgerald *Porgy And Bess* (Verve 1956)★★★★, with Fitzgerald *Ella And Louis Again* (Verve 1956)★★★★★, *Town Hall Concert* (RCA Victor 1957)★★★, *Louis And The Angels* (Decca 1957)★★★, *Satchmo On Stage* (Decca 1957)★★, *Louis Under The Stars* (Verve 1957)★★★, *The Five Pennies* film soundtrack (1958)★★, *Louis And The Good Book* (Decca 1958)★★★, *Satchmo In Style* (Decca 1958)★★★, *Louis Armstrong And The Dukes Of Dixieland* i (1959)★★★, *Louis Armstrong And The Dukes Of Dixieland: The Definitive Album/Sweetheart* (1959)★★★, *I've Got The World on A String* (Verve 1959)★★★, *Louis Armstrong Meets Oscar Peterson* (Verve 1959)★★★, *Snake Rag* (1959)★★★, *Louis Armstrong And The Dukes Of Dixieland* ii (1960)★★★, with Bing Crosby *Bing And Satchmo* (MGM 1960)★★★★, *A Rare Batch Of Satch* (RCA Victor 1961)★★★, *The Real Ambassador* (1961)★★★, *Louis Armstrong And Duke Ellington: The Great Reunion* (Roulette 1961)★★★, *Louis Armstrong And Duke Ellington: Together Again* (Roulette 1961)★★★★, *Satchmo Story* (1962)★★★, *I Love Jazz* (Decca 1962)★★★, *Hello, Dolly!* (Kapp 1964)★★★★, *Louis Armstrong And His All Stars Live At Juan-*

Les-Pins (1967)★★★, *What A Wonderful World* (ABC 1967)★★★★, *Disney Songs The Satchmo Way* (Disney 1968)★★, *Louis 'Country & Western' Armstrong* (1970)★, *The Great Chicago Concert 1956* (Columbia 1980)★★★.

● COMPILATIONS: *The Louis Armstrong Story Volume 1* (Columbia 1951)★★★★★, *The Louis Armstrong Story Volume 2* (Columbia 1951)★★★★★, *The Louis Armstrong Story Volume 3* (Columbia 1951)★★★★★, *The Louis Armstrong Story Volume 4* (Columbia 1951)★★★★★, *Louis Armstrong Plays King Oliver* (Audio Fidelity 1960)★★★★, *Satchmo 1930-34* (Decca 1962)★★★, *The Essential Armstrong* (Verve 1963)★★★★, *The Best Of Louis Armstrong* (Verve 1963)★★★★, *Louis Armstrong In The 30s And 40s* (RCA Victor 1964)★★★★, *King Oliver's Creole Jazz Band* recorded 1923-1924 (Milestone)★★★★, *Louis Armstrong And The Fletcher Henderson Orchestra* 1924-1926 recordings (VJM 1979)★★★★, *Louis Armstrong & Sidney Bechet* 1924-1925 recordings (Jazz Masters 1983)★★★★, *Louis In Los Angeles* 1930-1931 recordings (Swaggie 1983)★★★, *Young Louis Armstrong* 1930-1933 recordings (RCA 1983)★★★, *His Greatest Years Volumes 1-4* (1925-1928)★★★★, *Louis Armstrong And The Blues Singers* (1925-1929)★★★★, *The Louis Armstrong Legend Volumes 1-4* 1925-1929 recordings (Retrospect 1985)★★★★, *Louis Armstrong VSOP Volumes 1-8* 1925-1932 recordings (Columbia 1988)★★★, *The Hot Fives And Hot Sevens Volumes 1-4* 1925-28 recordings (Columbia 1988-1990)★★★★, *Satchmo Style* 1929-1930 recordings (DRG 1988)★★★, *Louis Armstrong And His Orchestra* 1935-1941 recordings (Swaggie 1988)★★★★, *Louis Armstrong European Tour* (1933-1934)★★★, *Louis Sings The Blues* (1933-1947)★★★, *Swing That Music* (1935-1944)★★★, *Midnight At V-Disc* (1944)★★★, *Louis Armstrong's Greatest Hits* (Curb 1990)★★★★, *The California Concerts* 1951/1955 recordings (GRP 1992)★★★, with Fletcher Henderson *Complete 1924 - 1925* (1993)★★★, *Classics 1940-42* (1993)★★★, *Gold Collection* (1993)★★★, *The Pure Genius Of* (1994)★★★, *The Ultimate Collection* (RCA 1994)★★★★★, *The Essential Recordings Of Louis Armstrong: West End Blues 1926-1933* (Indigo 1995)★★★★, *Butter And Eggman* 1929-1959 recordings (Tomato/Rhino 1995)★★★, *American Legends Volume 5* (Laserlight 1996)★★★, *Christmas Through The Years* (RCA Victor 1996)★★★, *This Is Louis* (Camden 1997)★★★, *The Complete RCA Victor Recordings* 4-CD box set (RCA Victor 1997)★★★★★, *The Complete Ella Fitzgerald & Louis Armstrong On Verve* 3-CD box set (Verve 1997)★★★★★, with King Oliver, Bessie Smith *High Society* (Tradition/Rykodisc 1997)★★★★, *Now You Has Jazz* (Rhino 1998)★★★★, *Master Of Jazz: Louis In Chicago, 1962* (Storyville 1998)★★★.

● VIDEOS: *Wonderful World* (Kay Jazz 1988), *Louis Armstrong Remembered* (1988), *Satchmo* (CMV Enterprises 1989), *Louis Armstrong* (Stylus Video 1990), *Good Years Of Jazz Volume 1* (Storyville 1990), *Louis Armstrong On Television* (Virgin 1991).

● FURTHER READING: *Satchmo: My Life In New Orleans*, Louis Armstrong. *Salute To Satchmo*, Max Jones, John Chilton and Leonard Feather. *Louis Armstrong: A Self-Portrait*, Richard Meryman. *The Louis Armstrong Story, 1900-1971*, M. Jones and J. Chilton. *Boy From New Orleans: Louis 'Satchmo' Armstrong*, Hans Westerberg. *Louis Armstrong: An American Genius*, James Lincoln Collier. *With Louis And The Duke*, B. Bigard. *Satchmo*, Gary Giddins. *Louis Armstrong: An Extravagant Life*, Laurence Bergreen.

● FILMS: *Pennies From Heaven* (1936), *Every Day's A Holiday* (1937), *Artists And Models* (1938), *Dr Rhythm* (1938), *Going Places* (1939), *The Birth Of The Blues* (1941), *Cabin In The Sky* (1943), *Hollywood Canteen* (1944), *Atlantic City* (1944), *Jam Session* (1944), *New Orleans* (1947), *A Song Is Born* (1948), *Glory Alley* (1951), *Here Comes The Groom* (1951), *The Strip* (1951), *The Glenn Miller Story* (1954), *High Society* (1956), *Satchmo The Great* (1957), *The Five Pennies* (1959), *The Beat Generation* (1959), *Jazz On A Summer's Day* (1961), *Paris Blues* (1961), *When The Boys Meet The Girls* (1962), *A Man Called Adam* (1966), *Hello Dolly* (1969).

Arodin, Sidney

b. Sidney Arnondrin, 29 March 1901, Westwego, Louisiana, USA, d. 6 February 1948. Arodin began playing clarinet in his early teens and was soon working professionally. In the early 20s he moved to New York and joined the Original New Orleans Jazz Band, then returned to the south to play in Texas and Louisiana. Arodin made records with Johnny Miller, Joesph 'Wingy' Manone and the band co-led by Lee Collins and Davey Jones, and also played with Louis Prima and other popular bands of the late 20s and 30s. In 1930 Arodin wrote the music for 'Lazy River' which, with verse and lyrics by Hoagy Carmichael, became a staple in the repertoire of Louis Armstrong. From the early 40s Arodin was plagued with poor health.

● COMPILATIONS: with Johnny Miller *New Orleans Stomp* (1928)★★★, *New Orleans Rhythm Kings Featuring Joe 'Wingy' Manone* (1934/5)★★★.

Art Blakey's Jazz Messengers With Thelonious Monk - Art Blakey

It is interesting to wonder whether, if this record was played anonymously to a major record company today, anyone there would have the foresight, understanding or courage to take it on – incredibly, this daring and advanced album was recorded in 1957. Its illustrious personnel consists of fast-fingered, prolific saxophone virtuoso Johnny Griffin, fiery trumpeter Bill Hardman, bassist Spanky DeBrest, the quirky and brilliant pianist Thelonious Monk and thunderous drummer Art Blakey, and the material features mainly Monk originals, played with as much guts, gumption and originality as ever. Monk's piano work, in particular, is full of thrilling, fascinating surprises.

● Tracks: *Evidence; In Walked Bud; Blue Monk; I Mean You; Rhythm-A-Ning; Purple Shades.*

● First released 1957

● UK peak chart position: did not chart

● USA peak chart position: did not chart

Art Ensemble Of Chicago

Founded in 1968 by trumpeter Lester Bowie, saxophonists Roscoe Mitchell and Joseph Jarman and bassist Malachi Favors, the AEC grew out of a number of projects connected with the AACM. Most directly it evolved from the Roscoe Mitchell Quartet. Mitchell has said: 'It was my band, but I couldn't afford to pay those guys what they deserved, so everybody was shouldering an equal amount of responsibility. We became a co-operative unit in order to remain committed to one another and in order to survive.' In the early days there was no regular drummer, and each member of the AEC would double on percussion. In 1969, after trying out various candidates, including William Howell and Philip Wilson, the band met Famoudou Don Moye in Paris and he became the permanent drummer, but all five continued to use an array of 'little instruments' such as whistles, bells, cooking utensils or indeed any object that could be shaken, blown, strummed or beaten rhythmically. Mitchell and Jarman between them play the full range of saxophones as well as clarinets, flutes and the oboe, and represent the two poles of the ensemble's craft: Jarman brings the bulk of the theatrical impulse, Mitchell is the musical structuralist. The music is as all-embracing as the instrumentation: basically free-form jazz. A performance will allude to New Orleans, blues, Africa, rock 'n' roll, vaudeville or anything that takes their fancy, and the ensemble is capable of playing bop as hard as any. Receiving little recognition at home, the band went to Paris in 1969 where they recorded enough material for about 14 albums within two years, including a couple that featured singer Fontella Bass. The title track of one of their French recordings, 'The Spiritual', not only charts the development of black music from early slavery to the 60s but symbolizes the progress of black people in the USA. This consciousness of social and political issues is typical of the AACM circle, and the AEC adds to it considerable theatre. Jarman once appeared on stage wearing only his saxophone sling. Bowie, whether with the ensemble or his own group, Brass Fantasy, habitually affects a doctor's white coat, while the others paint their faces and bodies and wear African styles. This dramatizing of the spirit of a culture is no less serious because of the strong element of puckish parody in their playing, which the AEC prefers to term Great Black Music rather than jazz. The Paris sessions show the ensemble defining and setting the agenda for their music: that agenda is now well settled - and has been documented on a variety of record labels, including Atlantic, ECM, DIW and the group's own AECO company - but they can still surprise and delight. Recently, however, they have taken to recording with other musicians and ensembles (including Lester Bowie's Brass Fantasy, Cecil Taylor and a South African choir) in an apparent attempt to find a fresh menu. In addition, *Eda Wobu*, a Parisian radio session from just before Don Moye joined, was released in 1991, on which Bowie is particularly impressive. Few units have stayed together for so long and it is a fine testament to their talent and longevity to find themselves back with Atlantic Records 25 years later.

● ALBUMS: *A Jackson In Your House* (BYG/Affinity 1969)★★★, *The Spiritual* (1969)★★★, *Tutankhamun* (Black Lion 1969)★★★, *People In Sorrow* (Nessa 1969)★★★, *Message To Our Folks* (Affinity 1969)★★★, *Reese And The Smooth Ones* (Freedom 1969)★★★, *Certain Blacks* (Inner City 1970)★★★★, *Go Home* (1970)★★★, *Chi Congo* (1970)★★★, *Les Stances À Sophie* (Nessa 1970)★★★, *With Fontella Bass* (1970)★★, *Live Part I* (BYG 1970)★★★, *Live Part 2* (BYG 1970)★★★, *Phase One* (Prestige 1971)★★★, *Live At Mandel Hall* (Delmark 1972)★★★★, *Bap-Tizum* (Atlantic 1973)★★★, *Fanfare For The Warriors* (Atlantic 1974)★★★★, *Kabbalaba* (AECO 1974)★★★, *Nice Guys* (ECM 1978)★★★, *Full Force* (ECM 1980)★★★, *Live In Berlin* (West Wind 1980)★★★, *Urban Bushmen* (ECM 1980)★★★★, *Among The People* (1981)★★★, *The Third Decade* (ECM 1984)★★, *Live In Japan* (DIW 1985)★★★, *Volume I Ancient In The Future* (DIW 1987)★★, *Complete Live In Japan* 1984 recording (DIW 1988)★★★, *The Alternate Express* (DIW 1989)★★★★, *Naked* 1985/1986 recordings (DIW 1989)★★★★, with Brass Fantasy *Live At The 6th Tokyo Music Joy '90* (DIW 1990)★★★, *Amabutho Male Chorus Art Ensemble Of Soweto* (DIW 1990)★★★, *Dreaming Of The Masters Suite* (DIW 1990)★★★, *Eda Wobu* 1969 recording (JMY 1991)★★★, as Art Ensemble Of Soweto *America/South Africa* 1989/1990 recordings (Columbia 1991)★★★, with Cecil Taylor *Thelonious Sphere Monk (Dreaming Of The Masters Vol. 2)* (DIW 1992)★★★★, *Coming Home Jamaica* (Atlantic 1998)★★★★.

● COMPILATIONS: *Art Ensemble: 1967/68* 5-CD set (Nessa)★★★★.

ASHBY, DOROTHY

b. 6 August 1932, Detroit, Michigan, USA, d. 1986. Born into a musical family (her father played jazz guitar) Ashby studied music at high school, where a fellow student was Donald Byrd. After graduation, she played piano and harp with several small groups, often as leader. She recorded with Richard Davis, Jimmy Cobb, Frank Wess and others in the late 50s and early 60s. During the latter period, she also had her own radio show in her home-town. Her husband, drummer John Ashby, played in her early trios and was founder of a theatre company, the Ashby Players of Detroit, for which his wife wrote scores. After relocating to the west coast she played in studio orchestras, sometimes appearing on albums featuring leading jazz musicians. One of very few harpists to play jazz convincingly, Ashby was perhaps the only such instrumentalist successfully to adapt the instrument to accommodate the language of bop.

● ALBUMS: *Dorothy Ashby - Jazz Harpist* (Regent 1957)★★★★, *Hip Harp* reissued as *The Best Of Dorothy Ashby* (Prestige 1958)★★★★, with Frank Wess *In A Minor Groove* (New Jazz 1958)★★★, *Soft Winds: The Swinging Harp Of Dorothy Ashby* (Jazzland 1961)★★★, *The Fantastic Jazz Harp Of Dorothy Ashby* (Atlantic 1965)★★★, *Soul Vibrations* (1968)★★★, *Afro-Harping* (Chess 1968)★★★★, *The Rubaiyat Of Dorothy Ashby* (1969)★★★, *Dorothy's Harp* (1969)★★★.

● COMPILATIONS: *Django - Misty* (Emarcy 1985)★★★.

ASHBY, HAROLD

b. 27 March 1925, Kansas City, Missouri, USA. After taking up the tenor saxophone as a child, Ashby played in territory bands in the Midwest. In the early 50s he settled in Chicago, playing in various bands, often in an R&B or strongly blues-based style. In the late 50s he moved to New York, working with Mercer Ellington and Duke Ellington. Ashby made records during the late 50s and early 60s, often with ex-Ellingtonians such as Lawrence Brown and Johnny Hodges, and in 1968 became a permanent member of the Ellington orchestra. After Ellington's death he played with Mercer Ellington, Benny Goodman and others, and also began playing concerts and festivals around the world, usually as a single. A striking player, moulded in the tradition of Ben Webster but with a distinctive hard-edged tone, Ashby's playing deserves the international attention it has begun to attract in the late 80s and early 90s.

● ALBUMS: *Born To Swing* (Master Jazz 1959)★★★, with Lawrence Brown *Inspired Abandon* (1965)★★★, *Duke Ellington's 70th Birthday Concert* (1969)★★★, *Scufflin'* (1978)★★★, *The Viking* (Gemini 1988)★★★, *On The Sunny Side Of The Street* (Timeless 1992)★★★, *I'm Old Fashioned* (Stash 1992)★★★, *What Am I Here For?* (Criss Cross 1993)★★★.

ASHBY, IRVING

b. 29 December 1920, Somerville, Massachusetts, USA. Ashby first came to prominence in 1947 as the guitarist in Nat 'King' Cole's popular trio. He had previously worked with Lionel Hampton, where his rock-solid rhythmic playing was often overlooked in the excitement that Hampton's band generated. After leaving Cole, Ashby gigged mainly on the west coast, then in the early 50s joined Oscar Peterson's trio. From the 60s onwards he worked mostly outside music, but continued to play occasionally when the opportunity arose.

● ALBUMS: *Memories* (1976)★★★.

ASHTON, BILL

b. 6 December 1936, Blackpool, Lancashire, England. While studying at Oxford University in the late 50s Ashton played saxophone in jazz bands, some of which he also led. By the early 60s he was teaching in London, playing occasionally at various jazz clubs. In the mid-60s, prompted by the prodigious musical talent of a student, Frank Ricotti, at an ill-equipped London school, Ashton conceived the idea of a schools orchestra. His concept was that the orchestra would allow unfledged musicians to develop their craft playing jazz and other forms of contemporary popular music. His proposals met with general indifference within the education system, and in some instances with downright hostility and sabotage. Ashton persisted, however, and his London Schools Jazz Orchestra survived, becoming the London Youth Jazz Orchestra and, eventually, the National Youth Jazz Orchestra. In 1974 NYJO became a fully professional organization and four years later Ashton was awarded the MBE for his services to youth and music, an award he sees as an honour for the organization rather than purely for him. He continues to direct the orchestra, writing arrangements, original music, and song lyrics. Tireless in his promotion of his brainchild, Ashton single-handedly produces and edits NYJO's house magazine, most of which he also writes.

ASMUSSEN, SVEND

b. 28 February 1916, Copenhagen, Denmark. Asmussen began playing violin as a small child. A superbly accomplished musician, he first played professionally in 1933. In the mid-30s he played with Kai Ewens and other Danish musicians, recording and broadcasting on the radio. He also played with visiting American stars, including Fats Waller. During World War II he continued to work in showbusiness. In the late 40s and early 50s much of his recorded output consisted of currently popular American and British songs, although there were always jazz sides interspersed among them. In the early 60s he worked with Alice Babs, Ulrik Neumann and Duke Ellington, and also with John Lewis. Despite the earlier interest of Benny Goodman, it was the Lewis recording date that drew widespread attention to his talents, and in later years he worked with many other jazz artists, including Stéphane Grappelli, Kenny Drew, Niels-Henning Ørsted Pedersen, Lionel Hampton and Bucky Pizzarelli. Throughout the 70s and 80s he continued to record and appear at international festivals, and was still active on the scene into the 90s.

● ALBUMS: *Hot Fiddle* 10-inch album (Brunswick 1953)★★★, *Svend Asmussen And His Unmelancholy Danes* 10-inch album (Angel 1955)★★★, *Rhythm Is Our Business* 10-inch album (Angel 1955)★★★, *Skol!* (Epic 1955)★★★, *Danish Imports* (1959)★★★, *Svend Asmussen* i (1961)★★★, *Svend Asmussen* ii (1961)★★★, with John Lewis *European Encounter* (Atlantic 1962)★★★★, with Duke Ellington *Jazz Violin Session* (1963)★★★★, with Stéphane Grappelli *Two Of A Kind* (Storyville 1965)★★★★, with Grappelli *Violin Summit* (1966)★★★★, *Svend Asmussen Sextet* (1966)★★★, *Svend Asmussen* iii (1968)★★★, *Amazing Strings* (1974)★★★, *Prize Winners* (Matrix 1978)★★★★, with Lionel Hampton *As Time Goes By* (1978)★★★, *String Swing* (Sonet 1983)★★★, *June Night* (Doctor Jazz 1983)★★★★, *Svend Asmussen Live At Slukafter* (1984)★★★.

● COMPILATIONS: *Musical Miracle Vol. 1, 1935-1940* (Phontastic)★★★★, *Phenomenal Fiddler* 1941-1950 recordings (Phontastic)★★★★.

AT NEWPORT - DUKE ELLINGTON

This concert marked the so-called rebirth of Duke Ellington. Of course, it was the jazz audience that had lost sight of the band, and *At Newport* saw the end of temporary obscurity. Irritated by the place on the programme and his musicians' habitual tardiness, Ellington began the second set in a do-or-die mood. They did not die. Wonderful solos by Clark Terry, Johnny Hodges and Paul Gonsalves links the two parts of 'Diminuendo In Blue' and 'Crescendo In Blue', and makes this an evening that will live forever in the annals of jazz.

● Tracks: *Newport Jazz Festival Suite - a) Festival Junction b) Blues To Be There c) Newport Up; Jeep's Blues; Diminuendo And Crescendo In Blue.*

● First released 1957

● UK peak chart position: did not chart

● USA peak chart position: 14

Atomic Basie - Count Basie

An inspired collaboration that worked so well, it is surprising that Basie and Neal Hefti did not form a long-term Sinatra/Riddle partnership. Hefti later found solace in writing musical opuses such as 'The Batman Theme'! Great for his bank balance, but little aid to his credibility. This, however, is a magnificent record that should always be played in its entirety. Basie rarely sounded so fresh and crisp. For a 1958 album, this is a staggering record. 'Splanky', in particular, spits out with an incredible force and their reading of 'Li'l Darlin' is definitive. The original engineer Bob Arnold deserves a special mention. The CD remastering is fabulous and comes with five bonus tracks.

● Tracks: *The Kid From Red Bank; Duet; After Supper; Flight Of The Foo Birds; Double-O; Teddy The Toad; Whirly-Bird; Midnite Blue; Splanky; Fantail; Li'l Darlin'; Silks And Satins; Sleepwalker's Serenade; Sleepwalker's Serenade (alternate take); The Late Late Show; The Late Late Show (vocal version).*

● First released 1958

● UK peak chart position: did not chart

● USA peak chart position: did not chart

Audience With Betty Carter, The - Betty Carter

For Betty Carter, songs are vehicles for her talent. If something does not fit her conception of how her performance should be, then she changes it. Nothing is sacred; and yet, somehow, nothing is profaned. Standards from the Great American Songbook are reworked with seemingly dismissive ease. The album title is significant: woe betide any audience that risks not being 'with' Betty Carter. In command, on display, this tough, restless tigress of jazz overshadows her contemporaries, What is more, her statement that she can see no-one coming along to challenge her superiority, looks increasingly true as the years pass by.

● Tracks: *Sounds (Movin' On); I Think I Got It Now; Caribbean Sun; The Trolley Song; Everything I Have Is Yours; I'll Buy You A Star; I Could Write A Book; Can't We Talk It Over; Either It's Love Or It Isn't; Deep Night; Spring Can Really Hang You Up The Most; Tight; Fake; So; My Favourite Things; Open The Door.*

● First released 1979

● UK peak chart position: did not chart

● USA peak chart position: did not chart

Auld, Georgie

b. John Altwerger, 19 May 1919, Toronto, Canada, d. 7 January 1990. Originally an alto saxophonist, Auld found work in the early 30s in New York, where his family had recently moved. In 1936 he switched to tenor saxophone under the influence of Coleman Hawkins and, after leading a small group, joined the big band of Bunny Berigan. In 1939, after two years with Berigan, he was hired by Artie Shaw on the recommendation of Billie Holiday. He persuaded Shaw to recruit Buddy Rich, then, after the Shaw band folded, he worked briefly for Jan Savitt, Benny Goodman and Shaw again, before forming his own modern-sounding big band in 1943. The latter included Serge Chaloff, Erroll Garner, Dizzy Gillespie and Stan Levey. After 1946 Auld worked mostly as leader of bop-orientated small groups but with occasional stints in big bands, including those of Billy Eckstine and Goodman, and he also worked with Count Basie's 1950 small band. Auld tried his hand at acting (on Broadway), and played in film and television studios, mainly in Los Angeles. Despite suffering from cancer, he toured extensively, and in the 70s proved especially popular in Japan. In 1977 he coached and ghosted for Robert De Niro in the film *New York, New York*, in which he also appeared. In the 80s Auld worked only infrequently, visiting Japan and Europe, where he appeared at the 1984 North Sea Jazz Festival.

● ALBUMS: *That's Auld* 10-inch album (Discovery 1950)★★★, *Concert In Jazz* 10-inch album (Apollo 1951)★★★, *George Auld Quintet* 10-inch album (Roost 1951)★★★, *Tenderly* 10-inch album (Coral 1952)★★★, *Manhattan* 10-inch album (Coral 1953)★★★, *Misty* (Coral 1956)★★★, *In The Land Of Hi-Fi* (EmArcy 1955)★★★, *Dancing In The Land Of Hi-Fi* (EmArcy 1956)★★★, *Georgie Auld Plays For Melancholy Babies* (ABC-Paramount 1958)★★★, *Georgie Auld With The Mellowlarks* (Top Rank 1959)★★★, *Good Enough To Keep* (Top Rank 1959)★★★, *Georgie Auld Plays The Winners* (Philips 1963)★★★, *Here's To The Losers* (Philips 1965)★★★.

● COMPILATIONS: *Jump, Georgie, Jump* (Hep Jazz 1983)★★★, *By George* (Swing House 1984)★★★, *Canyon Passage* (Musicraft 1988)★★★, *Georgie Porgie* (Musicraft 1988)★★★.

Austin, Cuba

b. *c.*1906, Charleston, West Virginia, USA, d. 60s. Starting out as a dancer, Austin turned to drums and in 1926 joined McKinney's Cotton Pickers when McKinney, himself a drummer, decided to concentrate on the full-time management of the band. In 1931 the band split into several new groups, one of which, billed as 'the Original Cotton Pickers', played under Austin's leadership. In 1934 this band folded and thereafter Austin worked outside music in Baltimore, although he continued to play part-time in local bands.

● COMPILATIONS: *McKinney's Cotton Pickers* 1928-29 recordings (Zeta 1991)★★★.

Austin, Patti

b. 10 August 1948, California, USA. Austin first sang on stage at the age of three at the famous Apollo Theatre in New York City during Dinah Washington's set. As a child performer, she appeared on television, including Sammy Davis Jnr.'s programme, and in the theatre. Her stage work included *Lost In The Stars* and *Finian's Rainbow*. At the age of nine she travelled to Europe with the bandleader/arranger Quincy Jones. As a 16-year-old, she toured with Harry Belafonte and began recording at the age of 17. Austin's first recordings were for Coral in 1965 and in 1969; 'Family Tree' (United Artists) was an R&B hit. Austin's immaculate vocals brought work on television jingles and during the 70s she was one of the busiest session singers in New York. Her session work includes credits for Paul Simon, Billy Joel,

Frankie Valli, Joe Cocker, George Benson and Roberta Flack. Her solo albums included material she had written herself, and revealed some jazz influences. Further session work during 1980 saw Austin working with Marshall Tucker, Steely Dan and the Blues Brothers. Her long-standing association with father-figure Quincy Jones continued and his composition 'The Dude' featured her lead vocal, winning a Grammy in 1982. Austin had another hit with the title track of *Every Home Should Have One* on Jones's Qwest label. Although it only just made the UK Top 100, 'Razzamatazz' (with Jones) was a UK Top 20 hit in 1981. Her duet with James Ingram, 'Baby Come To Me', became the theme music for the television soap opera *General Hospital* and was a US number 1 and a UK number 11 in 1983. Another Austin/Ingram duet, 'How Do You Keep The Music Playing?', from the film *Best Friends*, was nominated for an Oscar. She also sang themes for the films *Two Of A Kind* (1984) and *Shirley Valentine* (1988), and had an R&B hit with 'Gimme Gimme'. *The Real Me* was a collection of standards ranging from Duke Ellington's 'Mood Indigo' to 'How Long' by the UK group Ace. Her 1990 album was produced by Dave Grusin for GRP Records, while Austin was a guest vocalist on an album of George Gershwin songs released in 1992 by the Hollywood Bowl Orchestra. Already successful, Austin has yet to receive the critical acclaim her achievements merit.

● ALBUMS: *End Of A Rainbow* (CTI 1976)★★★, *Havana Candy* (CTI 1977)★★★, *Live At The Bottom Line* (CTI 1979)★★★, *Body Language* (CTI 1980)★★★, *Every Home Should Have One* (Qwest 1981)★★★★, *Patti Austin* (Qwest 1984)★★★, *Gettin' Away With Murder* (Qwest 1985)★★, *The Real Me* (Qwest 1988)★★★, *Love's Gonna Get You* (GRP 1990)★★, *Carry On* (GRP 1991)★★★, *Live* (1992)★★★.

● FILMS: *Tucker* (1988).

Austin, Sil

b. Sylvester Austin, 17 September 1929, Dunnellon, Florida, USA. A quintessential R&B tenor saxophone 'honker', Austin started his career by winning a talent contest at Harlem's Apollo theatre. He learned his craft in the big bands of Roy Eldridge and Cootie Williams. In 1956 he reached the Top 20 with 'Slow Walk' and had later hits with 'Balin' Wire', 'Birthday Party' and 'Shufflin' Home', irresistible slices of high-energy R&B. Later on, Austin recorded for Shelby Singleton's SSS label.

● ALBUMS: *Slow Walk Rock* (Mercury 1957)★★★, *Everything Is Shakin'* (Mercury 1958)★★★, *Sil Austin Plays Pretty For The People* (Mercury 1959)★★★, *Soft, Plaintive And Moody* (Mercury 1960)★★★, *Golden Saxophone Hits* (Mercury 1961)★★★, *Honey Sax* (1974)★★★.

Australian Jazz Quartet

(see Brokensha, Jack)

Autrey, Herman

b. 4 December 1904, Evergreen, Alabama, USA, d. 14 June 1980. Born into a musical family (his father and two brothers were musicians) Autrey first played alto horn before switching to trumpet. As a teenager he played in bands in and around Pittsburgh, Pennsylvania, then toured before settling in Florida. After playing in and leading bands he began working his way northwards, first to Washington, DC, then to Philadelphia and finally to New York, where he arrived in 1933. He played in the band led by Charlie 'Fess' Johnson, then became a regular associate of Fats Waller. He recorded extensively with Waller but found time to gig with many other leading bands of the day, including those led by Fletcher Henderson and Claude Hopkins. In the early and mid-40s he was active as sideman and leader, playing with Stuff Smith and Una Mae Carlisle. In the middle of the decade he returned to Philadelphia where he led a band for several years. In 1954 he sustained serious injuries in a road accident but returned to playing after a layoff lasting about a year. In the 60s he was a member of the popular Saints And Sinners touring band. By the 70s he was playing less but continued to perform as a singer. A robust and energetic trumpeter, Autrey's obvious admiration for Louis Armstrong never resulted in attempts to copy. His playing on the many records he made with Waller demonstrate his youthful ability, while his performances with Saints And Sinners and other late record dates show that in his maturity he was still a capable and dramatic performer.

● ALBUMS: *Saints And Sinners In Europe* (1968)★★★, *Finger Poppin'* (1972)★★★.

Avant garde

This term is used to describe music in the vanguard of its genre. It is associated with the development of new techniques (compositionally or instrumentally), radical aesthetic expression and non-traditional aims. The implication is that these achievements will subsequently be accepted and adopted into the mainstream, although this is by no means always the case. Perhaps the most frequent use of the term has been in connection with 20th-century classical music, initially that of Schoenberg and Webern, though it did not come into the common musical vocabulary until after World War II, when it was used in connection with composers such as Pierre Boulez and Karlheinz Stockhausen. Boulez's development of total serialism (out of possibilities already latent in Schoenberg's 12-tone system) and Stockhausen's use of electronic techniques are two of the best-known examples of recent *avant garde* music in the classical field. Aleatory composition techniques and the use of new instrumental and vocal resources are also part of this new music. A distinction sometimes made between these composers and others, such as John Cage, has been that the former are officially recognized in their role as members of the *avant garde*. The latter group, who are not, have therefore occasionally been described as experimental.

In more traditionally popular forms, *avant garde* music has also played a role. In the late 50s and early 60s jazz musicians started to develop a new language. For some of them it was no longer enough or even desirable to stay only within the chord-structures. When improvizing over a composition, chord-structures were sometimes abandoned altogether. The rhythm section also started to move away from the mainly time-keeping functions, and began to play around the beat or merely to imply it in an indirect way. This also influenced the melody players to create a new approach rhythmically. The composed part of a performed piece of music was often radically diminished and sometimes hardly present at all in favour of more improvization. The tendencies paved the way for the making of free jazz, the most *avant garde* movement in jazz at the time. Some of the most important musicians involved in this were Ornette Colman, Albert Ayler, John Coltrane, Cecil Taylor, Sun Ra and Sunny Murray. In rock there has been a similar movement. In the late 60s Frank Zappa started to create a music that contained many elements traditionally not associated with rock. Jazz, classical music modernism, extended instrumental skills, parody, protest and satire were mixed with rock into a personal style that then developed in several different directions, one of which has led into the concert world. The evolution of all cultural forms is often described as cyclical. As a general tendency, the growing popularization and commercialization of popular music, paired with a period of exhaustion of the common musical language, has led to periods of increased experimentation and *avant garde* tendencies. Be-bop was a radical innovation in jazz in the 40s and a reaction against the too commercial and worn-out (as seen by the innovators) style of swing. Jazz began to become an art music. Around 1960, as mentioned above, the same thing happened again in an even more radical way. As rock took over in popularity from jazz and started to switch from the originally more rebellious message to a more commercial and conventional appeal, the same thing happened in this field. As a rule the term *avant garde* is more of a label than a pure definition of the music.

AYERS, ROY

b. 10 September 1940, Los Angeles, California, USA. A popular jazz vibraphonist and vocalist, Ayers reached the peak of his commercial popularity during the mid-70s and early 80s. He played piano as a child and took an interest in the vibes after meeting Lionel Hampton. In high school Ayers formed his first group, the Latin Lyrics, and in the early 60s began working professionally with flautist/saxophonist Curtis Amy. Ayers' first album under his own name was *West Coast Vibes* on United Artists Records in 1964, which featured Amy. He also worked with Chico Hamilton, Hampton Hawes and Herbie Mann, with whom he first gained prominence between 1966 and 1970. He recorded three albums for Atlantic Records in the late 60s. In 1971 Ayers formed Roy Ayers Ubiquity and signed to Polydor Records, incorporating funk and R&B styles into his jazz. Using a number of prominent sidemen such as Herbie Hancock, Ron Carter, Sonny Fortune, George Benson and Billy Cobham, Ubiquity's albums helped to popularize the jazz/funk crossover style. The group charted with five albums and three R&B singles between 1974 and 1977, including the Top 20 disco-influenced R&B hit 'Running Away'. Ayers dropped the Ubiquity group name in 1978 and continued to have chart success with both his solo albums and singles through the late 80s. The 1978 single 'Heat Of The Beat' was billed as a duet with Wayne Henderson of the Crusaders. After touring Africa, Ayers recorded *Africa, Center Of The World* with Fela Kuti. He switched to Columbia Records in 1984 but released records less frequently as the 80s came to a close. During the early 90s he was under contract with Ronnie Scott's Jazz House label, but in 1995 secured a contract with RCA and the Groovetown label. The resulting album was well received.

● ALBUMS: *West Coast Vibes* (United Artists 1964)★★★, *Virgo Vibes* (Atlantic 1967)★★★, *Stoned Soul Picnic* (Atlantic 1968)★★★, *Daddy's Back* (Atlantic 1969)★★★, *Ubiquity* (Polydor 1970)★★★, *He's Coming* (Polydor 1971)★★★, *Live At Montreux* (Polydor 1972)★★★, *Red, Black And Green* (Polydor 1973)★★★, *Virgo Red* (Polydor 1974)★★★, *Change Up The Groove* (Polydor 1974)★★★, *A Tear To A Smile* (Polydor 1975)★★, *Mystic Voyage* (Polydor 1976)★★, *Everybody Loves The Sunshine* (Polydor 1976)★★, *Vibrations* (Polydor 1976)★★, *Lifeline* (Polydor 1977)★★, *Starbooty* (Polydor 1978)★★, *Let's Do It* (Polydor 1978)★★, *You Send Me* (Polydor 1978)★★, *Step Into Our Life* (Polydor 1978)★★, *Fever* (Polydor 1979)★★, *No Stranger To Love* (Polydor 1979)★★, *Love Fantasy* (Polydor 1980)★★, *Prime Time* (Polydor 1980)★★, with Fela Kuti *Africa, Center Of The World* (Polydor 1981)★★★, *Feeling Good* (Polydor 1982)★★★, *Lots Of Love* (Uno Melodic 1983)★★★, *In The Dark* (Columbia 1984)★★★, *You Might Be Surprised* (Columbia 1985)★★★, *I'm The One (For Your Love Tonight)* (Columbia 1987)★★★, *Drive* (Ichiban 1988)★★★, *Wake Up* (Ichiban 1989)★★★, *Easy Money: Live At Ronnie Scott's* (Essential 1990)★★★, *Rare* (Polydor 1990)★★★, *Rare Volume II* (Polydor 1990)★★★, *Searchin'* (Ronnie Scott's Jazz House 1993)★★★, *Hot* (Ronnie Scott's Jazz House 1993)★★★, *Naste* (Groovetown 1995)★★★.

● COMPILATIONS: *Best Of Roy Ayers* (Polydor 1979)★★★★, *Get On Up, Get On Down: Best Of Volume 2* (Polydor 1993)★★★, *A Shining Symbol: The Ultimate Collection* (Polydor 1993)★★★★, *Vibrant - The Very Best Of* (Connoisseur 1993)★★★.

● VIDEOS: *At Ronnie Scott's 1988* (Hendring Music Video 1989).

AYLER, ALBERT

b. 13 July 1936, Cleveland, Ohio, USA, d. 25 November 1970, New York, USA. In common with many of the radical figures of the 60s *avant garde*, tenor and alto saxophonist Ayler paid his dues in R&B bands. He started his musical education on alto, and played in the church attended by his family. At the age of 10 he began studying at the local academy of music, continuing to do so for some seven years. During this time he was section leader in his high-school orchestra. In his late teens he secured a job with blues legend Little Walter Jacobs. Subsequently, he formed his own R&B band, but this folded and, after giving up college due to financial difficulties, he joined the army. His national service took him to Europe, where he decided to stay following his discharge. His first few albums were taped either in Europe or for European labels, but his reputation was made with the recordings for the New York label ESP, which was established by Bernard Stollman particularly to promote Ayler's music. In 1966 Ayler signed with Impulse! Records where he continued to provoke poisonous controversy even among enthusiasts of contemporary jazz. On 25 November 1970 his body was recovered from New York City's East River. One bizarre rumour claimed that there was a bullet-hole in the back of his neck. Ayler had not been seen for some 20 days before his body was discovered, and the circumstances of his death remain unclear. The theory that he had been killed by the police has been given much currency. However, he had been very depressed about the breakdown suffered by his brother, Donald Ayler, and close friends have confirmed that he had talked about taking his own life.

Until the late 50s the tendency in the development of jazz had been one of increasing harmonic complexity and sophistication. Ornette Coleman and Ayler created styles that, although neither atonal nor entirely free, re-established the primacy of melody. Ironically, the mass of the jazz public found this music less accessible than the more technically complicated work of figures such as John Coltrane, Miles Davis, Gil Evans and Charles Mingus. Although Ayler cited Lester Young and Sidney Bechet as favourites, he seems to have owed something to Sonny Rollins, but one can also hear strong elements taken from New Orleans jazz, from gospel and work songs, and a number of techniques common in traditional African vocal music. It is, however, unwise to try to appreciate his music without paying some regard to its spiritual dimension and to the raw emotional components. In an interview with Nat Hentoff for *Downbeat* in November 1966, Ayler and his trumpeter brother Donald advised that the way to listen to their music was 'not to focus on the notes and stuff like that. Instead, try to move your imagination toward the sound . . . you really have to play your instruments to escape from notes to sound.' The Aylers were among the first to reject the term 'jazz' as redolent of Jim Crow and Uncle Tom attitudes. Standards and bop classics were still central to his repertoire, at least on record, and his articulation often sounded inadequate for the job. The cynical have suggested that this was the reason behind his predilection for dirge-like tunes, flexible, dream-like tempi and phrases that sprawl carelessly across barlines, but his proficiency, though often questioned, can scarcely be in doubt; his apprenticeship in school, church and army bands, and the recollections of those who heard him play in the 50s testify to his technical credentials. One important key to his work lies in the album of spirituals recorded for the Debut label in February 1964. Although it features some of his least inventive playing, it does provide a link between his early work with blues and mainstream modern jazz bands and the albums for ESP and Impulse! In the remarkable series of albums made in 1964, with Gary Peacock and Sunny Murray buoying him up on a tide of oblique but potent rhythm, we can hear not the strongly pulsed aspects of African music, but rather its melody-stretching and elaborate tonal and timbral play. Ayler's attitude to rhythm made even his early, inadequately realized recordings seem dangerous. At the time much attention was focused on his sound, a strident braying with an enormously exaggerated vibrato that could make his lines seem deceptively maudlin. Such tonal distortions had always been present in the playing of musicians on the borders of jazz, blues and R&B, such as Arnett Cobb and Jay McNeely, and vibrati as wide as the Mississippi delta were common with New Orleans brass band saxophonists like Emmanuel Paul and, indeed, Bechet. What alarmed people was not the sound itself, but Ayler's cavalier attitude to the beat and the way he used squeals, honks, cries and moans as an integral part of his style instead of reserving them for climactic moments. He was, however, first and foremost a melodist. He told Hentoff, 'I like to play something that people can hum . . . songs like I used to sing when I was real small. From simple melody to complicated textures to simplicity again . . .', a process that is clearly at work in all his recordings.

It was not until 1964 that Ayler was able to record with musicians who really understood what was going on. His first recordings were done in Stockholm in October 1962 with a willing but baffled bassist and drummer. With Peacock or Henry Grimes on bass, Murray on drums and Don Cherry's bright and agile pocket-trumpet it was now possible to hear Ayler's music properly realized. Gone were the rather ungainly refashionings of standards, to be replaced by Ayler compositions such as 'Mothers', 'Witches And Devils' and the ubiquitous 'Ghosts'. His broad and incantatory lines have a strange grace. In the second half of the 60s Ayler began using two bassists and, in the group that recorded the definitive *In Greenwich Village*, a violinist and cellist. With brother Donald Ayler replacing Cherry, and with one of the bassists concentrating on arco work, the music became a closely woven pattern of keening lines, developing a harder, shriller feel. These intense sides baptized his contract with Impulse! It was with this label that he made what were paradoxically his least 'way out' but most controversial albums. Even at his most abstract Ayler had been deeply rooted in spirituals and blues, but *Music Is The Healing Force Of The Universe* and *New Grass* found him involved in an uncomfortable species of pedestrian soul/funk/jazz fusion. There is some raunchy and direct sax playing, but these gems are marred by their tacky setting.

Ayler spawned fewer imitators than John Coltrane (who admitted to being influenced by Ayler) or even Coleman, but there are those - notably Matthias Schubert - who overtly base their playing on his style. Tommy Smith's first album leaned intriguingly on his example, David Murray has paid musical tribute to him, and his spirit is often heard in the work of Jan Kopinski in the otherwise harmolodics-based environment of Pinski Zoo. Ayler's ideas have been so thoroughly absorbed into the contemporary mainstream that his own work may no longer seem so startling. His effect at the time may be gauged by the fact that BBC Television, after bringing Ayler's quintet to Britain especially to record two programmes, were so alarmed by the music that the tapes were locked away and surreptitiously wiped without ever being shown.

● ALBUMS: *Something Different!* reissued as *The First Recordings* (GNP 1963)★★★★, *My Name Is Albert Ayler* reissued as *Free Jazz* (Fantasy 1963)★★★★, *Spirits* reissued as *Witches And Devils* and *Mothers And Children* (Debut 1964)★★★★, *Spiritual Unity* (ESP Disk 1965)★★★★, *Bells* (ESP Disk 1965)★★★, *Ghosts* reissued as *Vibrations* (1965)★★★, *Spirits Rejoice* (ESP Disk 1965)★★★★, *New York Eye And Ear Control* 1964 recording (ESP Disk 1966)★★★, *In Greenwich Village* (Impulse! 1967)★★★★, *Live At The Village Vanguard* (Impulse! 1967)★★★★, *Love Cry* (Impulse! 1968)★★★, *New Grass* (Impulse! 1969)★★★, *Music Is The Healing Force Of The Universe* (Impulse! 1970)★★★, *The Last Album* 1969 recording (1971)★★★, *Albert Ayler Volumes 1 &2* reissued as *Nuits De La Fondation Maeght*, *Prophecy* 1964 recordings (Shandar 1976)★★★, *The Village Concerts* recorded 1966 (ABC/Impulse! 1978)★★★, *Swing Low Sweet Spiritual* 1964 recording (80s)★★★, *Jesus* 1966 recording (1981)★★★, *Lörrach/Paris 1966* (hatART 1982)★★★, *At Slug's Saloon, Volumes 1 &2* 1966 recording (Base 1982)★★★, *The Hilversum Session* 1964 recording (Osmosis 1982)★★★★, *The Berlin Concerts - 1966* (1983)★★★★, *The First Recordings Volume 2* 1962 recordings (1990)★★★★, *Albert Ayler* 1964-1966 recordings (1991)★★★★, *Live In Greenwich Village: The Complete Impulse! Recordings* (Impulse! 1998)★★★★.

AYLER, DONALD

b. 5 October, 1942, Cleveland, Ohio, USA. The younger brother of Albert Ayler, Donald also began playing alto but, discouraged by his relative lack of facility on the saxophone, he switched to trumpet. When Albert left to work in Europe in 1964 he asked Charles Tyler, a saxophonist with whom Donald was then working, and who was a distant relation of the Aylers, to help Donald to bring his playing to a professional level. On returning home, Albert formed a band including Tyler and Donald. Donald was first heard on record on 'Holy Ghost', which appeared on an Impulse! 'sampler' called *The New Wave In Jazz*. He was also on *Bells*, the controversial single-sided pink vinyl album issued in 1965, and on the classic sides of *In Greenwich Village*. His singing tone and majestic presentation of Albert's arching themes reinforced their hymn-like grace, while his improvizations were a scurrying counterpart to the saxophone's lines. As well as his own and his brother's band he played with Paul Bley, Elvin Jones and John Coltrane. However, in 1968, when Albert disbanded the group that included Donald, the trumpeter suffered a breakdown, and his brother seems to have blamed himself. Donald returned to Cleveland, where his health improved, but it was six years before he picked up his trumpet again. He was deeply affected by Albert's death in 1970, and has only played occasionally since then. He recorded only one album under his own name.

AZIMUTH

Important and influential UK contemporary jazz group, formed in 1977 (not to be confused with the Brazilian trio formed in 1972) as a collaborative venture by its three members: pianist, composer and arranger John Taylor (b. 25 September 1942, Manchester, England), fluegelhorn player and composer Kenny Wheeler (b. 14 January 1930, Toronto, Canada) and singer and lyricist Norma Winstone (b. 23 September 1941, London, England). Although well versed in the cutting-edge styles of British jazz in the late 70s, the three musicians chose to follow a more romantic path, writing and performing richly melodic music. The group recorded for ECM Records in the late 70s and again in the mid-80s.

● ALBUMS: *Azimuth* (ECM 1977)★★★, *The Touchstone* (ECM 1978)★★★, *Depart* (ECM 1980)★★★, *Double, Double You* (1983)★★★, *Azimuth '85* (ECM 1985)★★★, *How It Was Then ... Never Again* (ECM 1997)★★★★.

AZTECA

Percussionists Pete and Coke Escovado formed this expansive unit in San Francisco, USA, upon their departure from Santana in 1972. Taking a cue from the latter group's *Abraxas*, Azteca formed a distinctly Latin American sound. A four-piece horn section emphasized the group's rhythmic style, but their strength in concert did not transfer to the recording studio. Azteca broke up in 1974, following which Pete Escovado formed a duo with his daughter Sheila. Three albums followed before he rejoined Santana. Sheila later found fame with Prince, as Sheila E.

● ALBUMS: *Azteca* (Columbia 1972)★★, *Pyramid Of Man* (Columbia 1973)★★.

AZYMUTH

Azymuth were formed in Brazil in 1971 by Jose Roberto Bertrami (keyboards), Alex Malheiros (bass) and Ivan Conte (drums - sometimes joined in his percussion duties by Aleuda). Adopting the popular jazz-funk style, they enjoyed a worldwide hit in 1980 with 'Jazz Carnival', from their *Light As A Feather* set. As such they were largely responsible for an upsurge of interest in Brazilian music, with a host of big-name American jazz acts journeying to South America to record. While commercial success for Azymuth was difficult to maintain, their subsequent releases were always of interest to the jazz-funk crowd. Both Bertrami (*Blue Wave*, 1983, and *Dreams Are Real*, 1986) and Malheiros (*Atlantic Forest*, 1985) also recorded solo outings for Milestone.

● ALBUMS: *Light As A Feather* (Black Sun 1979)★★★★, *Outubro* (Milestone 1980)★★★, *Telecommunication* (Milestone 1982)★★, *Cascades* (Milestone 1983)★★, *Flame* (Milestone 1984)★★★, *Rapid Transit* (Metronome 1984)★★★, *Spectrum* (Milestone 1986)★★, *Tightrope Walker* (Milestone 1987)★★, *Crazy Rhythm* (Milestone 1988)★★★, *Tudo Ben* (Enigma 1989)★★★, *Carioca* (Milestone 1989)★★, *Carnival* (Far Out 1996)★★★.

● COMPILATIONS: *Early Years* (Crusader 1988)★★★, *Jazz Carnival - Best Of Azymuth* (BGP 1988)★★★★.

B

Babbington, Roy

b. 8 July 1940, Kempston, Bedfordshire, England. Self-taught, Babbington began playing bass professionally in the late 50s. For several years he played in dance bands and jazz groups before moving to London. This was at the end of the 60s and he quickly became sought after for studio work. His jazz playing continued apace, and during the 70s he worked with many leading jazz musicians, including Harry Beckett, Graham Collier, Barbara Thompson, Keith Tippett and Mike Westbrook. He also worked with the jazz-rock fusion group, Soft Machine. In the 80s Babbington often played with Stan Tracey and was regularly called upon to accompany visiting American jazz artists. He has also continued to work in the studios with many broadcasting and recording bands. An accomplished technician, Babbington is also a sensitive accompanist and is comfortable backing song stylists and forward-thinking jazz players.

● ALBUMS: with Stan Tracey *Genesis* (Steam 1987)★★★.

Babs, Alice

b. Alice Nilson, 26 January 1924, Kalmar, Sweden. Well-versed in popular music and in the folk songs of her native Sweden, Babs first attracted wider attention with an appearance at the 1949 Paris Jazz Fair. Switching back and forth between jazz and popular song, she worked for a few years with fellow Scandinavians Ulrik Neumann and Svend Asmussen. In 1963 she met Duke Ellington, with whom she made concert appearances and records. The same year, her record of 'After You've Gone' reached number 43 in the UK charts. Despite such successes, her pure soprano and crystal-clear diction inclined her towards classical music, which she studied in the 60s. However, she worked again with Ellington on one of his religious concerts, which took place in Spain. Now retired in Spain, Babs regularly attends the Ellington Conferences (begun in 1983), delighting delegates with her impromptu vocal interventions, her vibrant enthusiasm and her obvious love for Ellington's music. That Ellington's feelings were reciprocal is apparent from his remark: 'Alice Babs is a composer's dream, for with her he can forget all the limitations and just write his heart out.'

● ALBUMS: *Alice And Wonderland* (1959)★★★, with Duke Ellington *Serenade To Sweden* (1963)★★★★, *Music With A Jazz Flavour* (1973)★★★, *Far Away Star* (Bluebell 1974)★★★, *Alice Babs There's Something About Me* (Bluebell 1978)★★★, *Swing It* (Pnontastic 1980)★★★.

Back Door

This jazz-rock trio from Blakey, Yorkshire, comprised Colin Hodgkinson (b. 14 October 1945, Peterborough, England; bass, vocals), Ron Aspery (saxophone, keyboards, flute, clarinet) and Tony Hicks (drums). The trio attracted much interest as a result of Hodgkinson's unique, adept full-chording bass technique. Their critically acclaimed first album, recorded in 1972, was initially released on the independent Blakey label. The praise and attention generated by the album resulted in the band signing to Warner Brothers Records, who later reissued the set. Subsequent releases, which included production work from Felix Pappalardi and Carl Palmer, failed to capture the spirit of the debut set or the fire of their live performances. By the time of the fourth album, *Activate*, in 1976, Hicks had departed (replaced by Adrian Tilbrook), and the group split the following year. Aspery went on to work with the Icelandic jazz rock group Mezzoforte, while Hodgkinson guested with various artists including Alexis Korner, Jan Hammer and Brian Auger.

● ALBUMS: *Back Door* (Blakey/Warners 1972)★★★★, *8th Street Nites* (Warners 1974)★★★, *Another Fine Mess* (Warners 1975)★★★, *Activate* (Warners 1976)★★.

Bacsik, Elek

b. 22 May 1926, Budapest, Hungary. After studying violin Bacsik took up the guitar, although he frequently returned to his first instrument in later years. Bacsik's early repertoire included gypsy music alongside classical music, but his switch to guitar coincided with a growing interest in jazz, a trend befitting a man who is believed to be distantly related to Django Reinhardt. During the 40s and 50s he was active mostly in eastern Europe but at the end of the 50s he journeyed to France, becoming resident for a time in Paris. Here he met and played with visiting American jazzmen. In the mid-60s he moved again, this time to the USA, where he worked in jazz and also became known for his dazzling violin-playing in resort hotels and casinos. He also worked with country music fiddlers, happily adapting to a rich variety of venues, audiences and accompanists. He continued his multi-faceted career throughout the 80s. Like so many other violinists who have ventured into jazz, the road has frequently been rocky; audiences and fellow musicians alike rarely take the instrument as seriously as they should. His guitar-playing is always interesting and the echoes of Tzigane add colour and excitement.

● ALBUMS: *The Electric Guitar Of The Eclectic Elek Bacsik* (Fontana 1962)★★★, with others *Bird And Dizzy: A Musical Tribute* (Flying Dutchman 1975)★★★.

Badini, Gerard

b. 16 April 1931, Paris, France. After training as a classical singer, Badini began playing clarinet in 1950. He worked in his native France and in other parts of Europe in various traditional jazz bands, including those led by Michel Attenoux and Claude Bolling. By the end of the 50s he had switched to tenor saxophone. Through the 60s and on into the 70s he worked extensively both as leader of his own small groups, which included Swing Machine, and teamed with visiting Americans, notably Helen Humes and several ex-members of Duke Ellington's band. He lived in New York for several years at the end of the 70s, but returned to France in 1982. Two years later he formed a big band, named the Super Swing Machine. Badini plays with a gutsy driving style on up-tempo pieces but is at his best playing ballads, where his warm, breathy, emotion-packed tone is reminiscent of Ben Webster.

● ALBUMS: with Helen Humes *Sneakin' Around* (Black And Blue 1974)★★★, *The Swing Machine* (1975)★★★, *French Cooking* (1980)★★★.

Bailey, Benny

b. 13 August 1925, Cleveland, Ohio, USA. Although he began playing trumpet professionally in R&B bands, including that led by Jay McShann, Bailey's work hit a peak when he began playing bop, joining Dizzy Gillespie's big band in 1947. By this time, Bailey had already greatly advanced his knowledge of music through studies with George Russell, and he brought intelligence and great finesse into all the bands with which he worked, whether as section leader or soloist. He spent five years in Lionel Hampton's All-Star Band, which included Clifford Brown, and visited Europe in 1953. Bailey liked Europe and decided to settle there, working in Sweden (with Harry Arnold's Big Band) and elsewhere before joining Quincy Jones, who also worked with Arnold. His time with Jones took Bailey back to the USA, but in 1960 he returned to Europe, where he worked on radio and in recording studios, especially in Germany. He was a founder-member of the Clarke-Boland Big Band and remained with the group until 1973. Bailey continued to be much in demand for studio work in the 70s and 80s, though he took time off for jazz festival appearances and, in 1986, a tour as a member the Paris Reunion Band. In 1988, he recorded an excellent album with Tony Coe and Horace Parlan, proving that his many years in radio and studio bands had in no way diminished his fascinating and thoughtful approach to jazz.

● ALBUMS: *Benny Bailey In Stockholm* (1959)★★★, *Big Brass* (Candid 1960)★★★★, *Bennie Bailey Plays The Music Of Quincy Jones* (Argo 1961)★★, *Benny Bailey With Strings* (1964)★★★, *Soul Eyes* (1968)★★★, *The Balkan In My Soul* (1968)★★★, *Folklore In Swing* (1970)★★, *My Greatest Love* (1975)★★★, *How Deep Can You Go?* (1976)★★★, *Islands* (Enja 1976)★★★, *Serenade To A Planet* (Ego 1976)★★★, *Grand Slam* (Storyville 1978)★★★, *East Of Isar* (1978)★★★, *For Heaven's Sake* (Hot House 1988)★★★★, *While My Lady Sleeps* (Gemini 1990)★★★.

Bailey, Buster

b. William C. Bailey, 19 July 1902, Memphis, Tennessee, USA, d. 12 April 1967, New York, USA. Bailey was one of two famous jazzmen to be taught by the Chicago-based classicist Franz Schoepp, the other being Benny Goodman. After working with bands led by W.C. Handy, Erskine Tate and Joe 'King' Oliver, Bailey joined Fletcher Henderson's orchestra in New York in 1924. He remained an important member of the band until 1937, playing alongside outstanding reed players such as Coleman Hawkins, Hilton Jefferson, Russell Procope and Ben Webster. After leaving Henderson, Bailey moved to John Kirby's musically distinguished sextet. It was in this setting, in association with perfectionists such as Procope, Charlie Shavers and Billy Kyle, that the clarinettist came into his own and the exemplary technique developed during his tuition under Schoepp was allowed to shine. The stylish playing of the Kirby band earned it great and justified popularity, both in concert and on record. Apart from minor breaks, Bailey stayed with Kirby until 1946, whereafter he played in a number of traditional or mainstream bands including those led by Wilbur De Paris and Red Allen. In 1957, he was a member of the Henderson All Star big band assembled for the Great South Bay Jazz Festival. Bailey continued working into the 60s, playing again with Red Allen and with Wild Bill Davison. In 1965, he joined Louis Armstrong's All Stars, with whom he remained until his death in April 1967.

● ALBUMS: with the Dixie All Stars *Dixiecats* (1957)★★★, *All About Memphis* (Felsted 1958)★★★.

● COMPILATIONS: *Complete Recordings 1934-40* (Rarities 1981)★★★.

Bailey, Derek

b. 29 January 1932, Sheffield, Yorkshire, England. Bailey is one of the few jazz guitarists who can accurately be described as unique and entirely original, in that there are no real precedents for his style. His father and grandfather were professional musicians and Bailey studied music and guitar formally from 1941-52. From 1952-65, he undertook all types of commercial work, including as a session man in recording studios and as a member of pit orchestras; one celebrated engagement involved accompanying Gracie Fields. In 1963, he encountered Tony Oxley and Gavin Bryars, and the interplay of ideas within this trio set off a severe evaluation of his direction which resulted in a fearsomely austere and abstract music and a long-standing commitment to total improvisation. Bailey's music is difficult to decipher, and listeners lacking a taste for stern rhetoric, subverted by unpredictable flashes of mordant humour, will get little out of it. Critics claim that his playing sounds merely random, but anyone who thinks this is the case should attempt to mimic it: his mastery of the guitar involves extreme precision, used to examine material in microscopic detail, and that material never rests on conventional melody, chords or rhythm. He strives to exclude repetition and memory. He frequently plays solo, but on the occasions when he works with other musicians (he has played with both the Spontaneous Music Ensemble and the Globe Unity Orchestra, as well as in numerous duos with musicians such as Anthony Braxton, Evan Parker and Han Bennink), it is as if he tries to avoid hearing them, playing with his head bent down over the guitar, until he suddenly produces some sharp and apposite interjection. If he has done little to attract the general jazz public, he has earned enormous respect from other musicians in the field of free jazz and improvised music. He has also contributed much to the survival of the genre, co-founding the Incus label in 1970 and running the Company festival which, surviving since 1976 against all the odds, facilitates jam sessions of both obscure toilers in the free and improvised fields and superstars such as Parker and Peter Kowald. He has recorded over 60 albums, including several with various Company line-ups, and written an influential book, *Improvisation - Its Nature And Practice In Music* (1980), which was used as the basis for the four-part television series *On The Edge*, filmed in 1990-91 and first transmitted in February 1992.

● ALBUMS: with Han Bennink *Derek Bailey/Han Bennink* (1969)★★★, with others *Instant Composers Pool* (1970)★★★, with Instant Composers Pool *Groupcomposing* (1970)★★★, *Music Improvisation Company 1968/70* (1970)★★★, with Evan Parker, Han Bennink *Topography Of The Lungs* (1970)★★★, *The Music Improvisation Company 1968-71* (1971)★★★, *Solo Guitar Volume 1* (Incus 1971)★★★★, with Dave Holland *Improvisation For Cello And Guitar* (ECM 1971)★★★, with Bennink *At Verity's Place* (1972)★★★, *Derek Bailey* (1973)★★★, *Concert In Milwaukee* (1973)★★★, *One Music Ensemble* (1973)★★★, *Lot 74 - Solo Improvisations* (1974)★★★★, *Improvisation* (1975)★★★, with Parker *The London Concert* (1975)★★★, *Domestic And Public Pieces* (1976)★★★, with Tristan Honsinger *Duo* (1976)★★★, with others *Company 1* (1976)★★★, with Anthony Braxton, Parker *Company 2* (1976)★★★, with Andrea Centazzo *Drops* (1977)★★★, with Braxton *Duo 1 & 2* 1974 recordings (1977)★★★★, with Bennink *Company 3* (1977)★★★, with Steve Lacy *Company 4* (Incus 1977)★★★, *New Sights - Old Sounds* (1978)★★★, with others *Duo And Trio Improvisations* (1978)★★★, with others *Company, Volumes 5-7* (1978)★★★, with Company *Fictions* (1978)★★★, with Tony Coe *Time* (Incus 1979)★★★, *Aida* (1980)★★★, with Company *Fables* (1980)★★★, with Christine Jeffrey *Views From Six Windows* (Metalanguage 1980)★★★, with Jamie Muir *Dart Drug* (Incus 1981)★★★, with Company *Epiphany* (1982)★★★★, with George Lewis, John Zorn *Yankees* (Celluloid 1983)★★★★, with Braxton *Royal, Volume One* 1974 recordings (1984)★★★★, *Notes* (Incus 1985)★★★, with Parker *Compatibles* (Incus 1985)★★★, with Company *Trios* 1983 recordings (1986)★★★, with Braxton *Moment Précieux* (1987)★★★, with Cyro Baptista *Cyro* 1982 recordings (Incus 1988)★★★, with Bennink *Han* 1986 recordings (Incus 1988)★★★★, with Barre Phillips *Figuring* (Incus 1988)★★★, with Company *Once* (1988)★★★, *In Whose Tradition* 1971-1987 recordings (1988)★★★, with Cecil Taylor *Pleistozaen Mit Wasser* (FMP 1989)★★★, *Lace* (Emanem 1991)★★, with Louis Moholo, Thebe Lipere *Village Life* (Incus 1992)★★★, *Solo Guitar Volume 2* (Incus 1992)★★★, *Playing* (Incus 1992)★★★, with Henry Kaiser *Wireforks* (Shanachie 1995)★★★★, as Arcana *The Last Wave* (DIW 1996)★★★, *Banter* (1996)★★, *Harras* (Avant 1996)★★, with Gregg Bendian, Pat Metheny, Paul Wertico *The Sign Of 4* 3-CD set (Knitting Factory Works 1997)★★★★, *Music And Dance* 1980 recording (Revenant 1997)★★★, *Guitar Drums And Bass* (Avant 1996)★★★★, Duo (Revenant 1996)★★, *Tohjinbo* (Paratactile 1997)★★★, *No Waiting* (Potlatch 1998)★★★, *Trio Playing* (Incus 1998)★★★★, *Takes Fakes & Dead She Dances* (Incus 1998)★★★★.

● FURTHER READING: *Improvisation - Its Nature And Practice In Music*, Derek Bailey.

BAILEY, JUDY

b. Judith Mary Bailey, 3 October 1935, Auckland, New Zealand. Raised in London, England, Bailey became infatuated with jazz at the age of 12 after hearing a Fats Waller record. Four years later she received an associate diploma in piano performance at London's Trinity College, before returning to New Zealand to play and arrange for radio groups. In 1960 Bailey moved to Sydney, Australia, and has been active there ever since. Her prolific early projects included recordings, television session work, concerts and work as musical director for various performers. On 7 May 1964 she made her first recordings as a leader, playing standards with Lyn Christie (bass) and John Sangster (drums). Bailey's inherent versatility was evident as she composed for television, musical theatre and children's radio. In 1978 she toured Asia with her quartet and when she returned became a founding teacher for the jazz studies course at New South Wales Conservatorium and lecturer and teacher for the Sydney Opera House Bennelong programme. Much of her later activities concerned jazz education, notably as director of the Sydney Youth Jazz Ensemble, but academic duties did not prohibit her performing and she was the winner of the inaugural APRA award for jazz composer and the Australian Entertainment Industry Mo Award for Female Jazz Performer. Bailey is one of Australia's leading musicians and composers. She is a talented pianist who has been influenced by players of all styles and has performed with every principal Australian jazz musician over the past two decades. As a composer her best works are already a jazz legacy. Her 1993 album, *Sundial*, featured her trio and some of Australia's best young jazz musicians including James Morrison, Sandy Evans, Graeme Lyall and Erana Clark. The material covered a typically broad spectrum, from 'I Remember Thelonious' to 'When The Saints Go Marching In'.

● ALBUMS: *The Judy Bailey Trio* (Columbia 1964)★★★, *Notwithstanding* (ABC 1980)★★★, *Judy Bailey And Friends - Sundial* (ABC 1993)★★★.

BAILEY, MILDRED

b. Mildred Rinker, 27 February 1907, Tekoa, Washington, USA, d. 12 December 1951, Poughkeepsie, New York, USA. By the early 20s Bailey was singing and playing piano in silent-picture theatres as well as working as a song demonstrator and performing in revues and on the radio. When only 18 years old, she was headlining a Hollywood nightclub, singing popular songs, blues and some of the more raunchy vaudeville numbers. She regularly worked with jazz musicians, with whom she displayed a remarkable affinity, and made her first records with guitarist Eddie Lang in 1929. That same year she was hired by Paul Whiteman, in whose band she encountered some of the best white jazz musicians of the day (her brother, Al Rinker, with Bing Crosby and Harry Barris, was a member of Whiteman's vocal trio, the Rhythm Boys). Already a well-known radio personality, she was now offered innumerable engagements and in time had her own regular show. In 1932, she had a massive hit with Hoagy Carmichael's 'Rockin' Chair' and thereafter was known as the 'Rockin' Chair Lady'. Married for a time to xylophonist Red Norvo, Bailey continued to work with jazzmen, while retaining a substantial measure of popularity with a wider audience thanks to her radio work. She sang with a fragile, sweet-toned voice that belied her exceedingly ample proportions, handling even the banalities of some 30s lyrics with uncloying tenderness. The first white female fully to deserve the term 'jazz singer', Bailey always swung effortlessly and was admired and respected (and, in her stormier moments, rather feared) by the many jazz musicians with whom she worked, among them Bunny Berigan, Buck Clayton, Benny Goodman, Coleman Hawkins, Johnny Hodges and Teddy Wilson. Never in particularly good health, she was only 44 years old and destitute when she died of heart-related problems in 1951.

● ALBUMS: *Mildred Bailey Serenade* 10-inch album (Columbia 1950)★★★, *Mildred Bailey Memorial Album* 10-inch album (Decca 1952)★★★, *Mildred Bailey Songs* 10-inch album (Allegro 1952)★★, *The Rockin' Chair Lady* 10-inch album (Decca 1953)★★★, *Mildred Bailey Sings* (Allegro 1955)★★, *Me And The Blues* (Regent 1957)★★.

● COMPILATIONS: *Mildred Bailey's Greatest Performances* 3-LP set (Columbia 1962)★★★★★, *The Uncollected Mildred Bailey - CBS Radio Show* 1944 recording (Hindsight 1979)★★, *Mildred Bailey With Paul Barron's Orchestra* 1944 recording (London/Decca 1979)★★★, *All Of Me* 1945 recording (Monmouth Evergreen 1979)★★, *Rarest Of All Rare Performances* 1944 recording (Kings Of Jazz 1982)★★, *Mildred Bailey* 1938/1939 recordings (Jazz Document 1982)★★★, *The Mildred Bailey Collection - 20 Golden Hits* (Deja Vu 1987)★★★, with Red Norvo *Red Norvo And His Big Band Featuring Mildred Bailey* 1936-1942 recordings (Sounds Of Swing)★★★★, with Norvo *Red Norvo, Featuring Mildred Bailey* 1937-1938 recordings (Portrait)★★★★.

BAILEY, PEARL

b. 29 March 1918, Newport News, Virginia, USA, d. 17 August 1990, Philadelphia, Pennsylvania, USA. Pearlie Mae, as she was known, was an uninhibited performer, who mumbled her way through some songs and filled others with outrageous asides and sly innuendoes. She entered the world of entertainment as a dancer but later sang in vaudeville, graduating to the New York nightclub circuit in the early 40s. After working with the Noble Sissle Orchestra, she became band-vocalist with Cootie Williams, with whom she recorded 'Tessa's Torch Song', previously sung by Dinah Shore in the movie *Up In Arms*. Bailey received strong critical acclaim after substituting for Sister Rosetta Tharpe in a show, and was subsequently signed to star in the 1946 Harold Arlen/Johnny Mercer Broadway musical, *St. Louis Woman*. A year later her slurred version of 'Tired' was the highlight of the movie *Variety Girl*, and she gave several other outstanding performances in films such as *Carmen Jones* (1954), *St. Louis Blues* (1958) and *Porgy And Bess* (1959). During her stay with Columbia Records (1945-50), Bailey recorded a series of duets with Frank Sinatra, trumpeter Oran 'Hot Lips' Page and comedienne Moms Mabley. She also recorded some solo tracks with outstanding arrangers/conductors, including Gil Evans and Tadd Dameron. Upon joining the Coral label in 1951, she employed Don Redman as her regular musical director, the association lasting for 10 years. In 1952, she had her biggest hit record, 'Takes Two To Tango'. In that same year she married drummer Louie Bellson and he took over from Redman as her musical director in 1961. Although few of her records sold in vast quantities, Bailey had always been a crowd-pulling live performer and, following her early stage triumph in *St. Louis Woman*, she was later cast in other shows including *The House Of Flowers*, *Bless You All*, *Arms And The Girl* and an all-black cast version of *Hello, Dolly!*. She also starred in several US television specials, playing down the double entendre that caused one of her albums, *For Adults Only*, to be 'restricted from airplay'. In 1991 Pearl Bailey was posthumously inducted into the New York Theater Hall Of Fame.

● ALBUMS: *Pearl Bailey Entertains* 10-inch album (Columbia 1950)★★★★, *Say Si Si* 10-inch album (Coral 1953)★★★, *I'm With You* 10-inch album (Coral 1953)★★★, *House Of Flowers* film soundtrack (Columbia 1954)★★★, *St. Louis Woman* film soundtrack (Capitol 1955)★★★, *The One And Only Pearl Bailey* (Mercury 1956)★★★★, *Birth Of The Blues* (Coral 1956)★★★★, *The One And Only Pearl Bailey Sings* (Mercury 1957)★★★, *Cultured Pearl* (Coral 1957)★★★, *The Intoxicating Pearl Bailey* (Mercury 1957)★★★★, *For Adults Only* (1958)★★★★, *Gems By Pearl Bailey* (Vocalion 1958)★★★★, *Pearl Bailey Sings!* (1959)★★★★, *St. Louis Blues* (1959)★★★★, *Porgy & Bess & Others* (Columbia 1959)★★★★, *More Songs For Adults* (1960)★★★, *Songs Of Bad Old Days* (1960)★★★, *Naughty But Nice* (1961)★★★, *Songs She Loves By Arlen* (1962)★★★★, *All About Good Little Girls And Bad Little Boys* (Roulette 1962)★★★, *Come On Let's Play With Pearlie Mae* (Roulette 1962)★★★, *Songs By Jimmy Van Heusen* (1964)★★★★, *Les Poupees De Paris* (RCA Victor 1964)★★★, *Hello, Dolly!* film soundtrack (RCA Victor 1964)★★★, *For Adult Listening* (60s)★★★, *C'est La Vie* (60s)★★★, *Risque World* (60s)★★★.

● COMPILATIONS: *The Definitive* (1965)★★★★, *The Best Of - The Roulette Years* (Roulette 1991)★★★★.

● FURTHER READING: *The Raw Pearl*, Pearl Bailey. *Talking To Myself*, Pearl Bailey.

● FILMS: *Variety Girl* (1947), *Isn't It Romantic* (1948), *Carmen Jones* (1954), *That Certain Feeling* (1955), *St. Louis Blues* (1957), *Porgy And Bess* (1959), *All The Fine Young Cannibals* (1960), *The Landlord* (1969).

BAKER, CHET

b. Chesney H. Baker, 23 December 1929, Yale, Oklahoma, USA, d. 13 May 1988, Amsterdam, Netherlands. One of the more lyrical of the early post-war trumpeters, Baker's fragile sound epitomized the so-called 'cool' school of west coast musicians who dominated the American jazz scene of the 50s. Baker studied music while in the army, and soon after his discharge in 1951, he was playing with Charlie Parker. He gained international prominence as a member of Gerry Mulligan's pianoless quartet, with their dynamic reading of 'My Funny Valentine' becoming a notable hit. When the quartet disbanded in 1953, Baker, after another short stint with Parker, formed his own group, which proved to be extremely popular. Baker kept this band together for the next three years, but he was not cut out for the life of a bandleader, nor was he able to withstand the pressures and temptations that fame brought him. He succumbed to drug addiction and the rest of his life was a battle against dependency. In the 80s, in control of his life, although not fully over his addiction, he was once again a regular visitor to international jazz venues and also made a few incursions into the pop world, guesting, for example, on Elvis Costello's 'Shipbuilding'. Probably his best work from this later period comes on a series of records he made for the Danish Steeplechase label with a trio that comprised Doug Raney and Niels-Henning Ørsted Pedersen. By this time his clean-cut boyish good looks had vanished beneath a mass of lines and wrinkles - fellow trumpeter Jack Sheldon, told by Baker that they were laugh-lines remarked, 'Nothing's that funny!'. In his brief prime, Baker's silvery filigrees of sound, albeit severely restricted in tonal and emotional range, brought an unmistakable touch to many fine records; however, his lack of self-esteem rarely allowed him to assert himself or to break through the stylistic bounds. The 1989 film, *Let's Get Lost*, charts the closing years of the erratic life of this largely unfulfilled musician, who died when he fell, or possibly jumped, from an Amsterdam hotel window.

● ALBUMS: *Chet Baker Quartet* 10-inch album (Pacific Jazz 1953)★★★, *Chet Baker Quartet Featuring Russ Freeman* 10-inch album (Pacific Jazz 1953)★★★, *Live At The Trade Winds 1952* (1953)★★★, *Witch Doctor* (1953)★★★, *Chet Baker Ensemble* 10-inch album (Pacific Jazz 1954)★★★★, *Chet Baker & Strings* (Columbia 1954)★★★★, *Chet Baker Sings* 10-inch album (Pacific Jazz 1954)★★★★, *Chet Baker Sextet* 10-inch album (Pacific Jazz 1954)★★★, *Chet Baker Sings And Plays With Bud Shank, Russ Freeman And Strings* (Pacific Jazz 1955)★★★★, *Jazz At Ann Arbor* (Pacific Jazz 1955)★★★, *Chet Baker In Europe* (Pacific Jazz 1956)★★★, *Exitus: Live In Europe Volume 1* (1956)★★★, *Cool Blues: Live In Europe Volume 2* (1956)★★★, *Chet Baker And Crew* (Pacific Jazz 1956)★★★, with Art Pepper *Playboys* reissued as *Picture Of Health* (Pacific Jazz 1957)★★★, *At The Forum Theater* (Fresh Sound 1957)★★★, *Grey December* (Pacific Jazz 1957)★★★, *The Route* (Pacific Jazz 1957)★★★, *Chet Baker Cools Out* (Boblicity 1957)★★★, *Chet Baker Big Band* (Pacific Jazz 1957)★★★, *It Could Happen To You - Chet Baker Sings* (Riverside 1958)★★★★, *Pretty/Groovy* (World Pacific 1958)★★★, *Chet Baker In New York* (Riverside 1959)★★★★, *Chet* (Riverside 1959)★★★★, *Chet Baker Plays The Best Of Lerner And Loewe* (Riverside 1959)★★★, *Chet Baker In Milano* (Jazzland 1959)★★★, *Chet Baker And Orchestra* (Jazzland 1960)★★★, *Chet Baker With Fifty Italian Strings* (Jazzland 1960)★★★, *Chet Baker Quintette* (Crown 1962)★★★, *Chet Is Back* (1962)★★★, *The Italian Sessions* (RCA 1962)★★★, *Baby Breeze* (Limelight 1964)★★★, *Baker's Holiday* (Limelight 1965)★★★, *Chet Baker Sings & Plays Billie Holiday* (EmArcy 1965)★★★, *Quietly There* (World Pacific 1966)★★★, *Into My Life* (World Pacific 1967)★★★, *Smokin' With The Chet Baker Quintet* 1965 recording (Prestige 1967)★★★★, *Cool Burnin' With The Chet Baker Quintet* 1965 recording (Prestige 1967)★★★★, *Boppin' With The Chet Baker Quintet* 1965 recording (Prestige 1967)★★★★, *Groovin' With The Chet Baker Quintet* 1965 recording (Prestige 1967)★★★★, *Comin' On With The Chet Baker Quintet* 1965 recording (Prestige 1967)★★★★, *Polka Dots And Moonbeams* (Jazzland 1967)★★★, *You Can't Go Home Again* (A&M 1972)★★★, *She Was Too Good To Me* (1974)★★★, *Chet Baker In Concert* (1974)★★★, *Once Upon A Summer Time* (1977)★★★, *Flic Ou Voyou* (1977)★★★, *The Incredible Chet Baker Plays And Sings* (1977)★★★, *Broken Wing* (1978)★★★, *Two A Day* (1978)★★★, *Chet Baker In Paris* (1978)★★★, *Live At Nick's* (Criss Cross 1978)★★★, *The Touch Of Your Lips* (Steeple Chase 1979)★★★, *Rendez-vous* (1979)★★★, *All Blues* (1979)★★★, *No Problem* (Steeple Chase 1979)★★★, *Daybreak* (Steeple Chase 1979)★★★, *This Is Always* (Steeple Chase 1979)★★★, with Wolfgang Lackerschmid *Chet Baker/Wolfgang Lackerschmid* (Inakustik 1979)★★★, *Live In Chateauvallon 1978* (1979)★★★, *Someday My Prince Will Come* (Philology 1979)★★★, *Deep In A Dream Of You* (1980)★★★, *Un/Deux* (1980)★★★, *In Your Own Sweet Way* (1980)★★★, *Tune Up* (1980)★★★, *Night Bird* (1980)★★★, *Salsamba* (1980)★★★, *Soft Journey* (1980)★★★, *My Funny Valentine* (1981)★★★, *Chet Baker Live: 'Round Midnight* (1981)★★★, *Peace* (Enja 1982)★★★★, *Studio Trieste* (1982)★★★, *Les Landis D'Hortense* (1983)★★★, *Chet Baker Live In Sweden* (Dragon 1983)★★★, *The Improviser* (Cadence 1983)★★★, *Chet Baker At Capolinea* (1983)★★★, *Everything Happens To Me* (Timeless 1983)★★★★, *Blues For A Reason* (Criss Cross 1984)★★★★, *Sings Again* (Timeless 1984)★★★, *The Chet Baker Trio* (1985)★★★, *Chet's Choice* (Criss Cross 1985)★★★, *My Foolish Heart* (IRD 1985)★★★, *Misty* (IRD 1985)★★★, *Time After Time* (IRD 1985)★★★, *Live From The Moonlight* (1985)★★★, *Diane* (Steeple Chase 1985)★★★, *Strollin'* (Enja 1985)★★★, *Candy* (1985)★★★, *As Time Goes By* (1986)★★★, *Night Bird* (1986)★★★, *Live At Rosenheimer* (Timeless 1988)★★★, *When Sunny Gets Blue* (Steeple Chase 1988)★★★, *Little Girl Blue* (Philology 1988)★★★, *Straight From The Heart* (Enja 1988)★★★, *Let's Get Lost* film soundtrack (RCA 1989)★★★, *Live At Fat Tuesday's* (Fresh Sounds 1991)★★★★, *Live In Brussels 1964* (1993)★★★, *Live In Buffalo* (New Note 1993)★★★, *... In Tokyo* (Evidence 1996)★★★, *Chet Baker In Bologna* 1985 recording (Dreyfus 1996)★★★, *I Remember You* (Enja 1997)★★★★.

● COMPILATIONS: *Let's Get Lost* (Pacific Jazz 1990)★★★★, *The Pacific Years* (Pacific Jazz 1994)★★★★, *The Legacy: Volume One* (Enja 1995)★★★, with Gerry Mulligan *The Complete Pacific Jazz Recordings Of The Gerry Mulligan Quartet With Chet Baker* 4-CD box set (Pacific Jazz 1996)★★★★, *Young Chet* (Blue Note 1996)★★★★, *Jazz Profile* (Blue Note 1997)★★★★, *Songs For Lovers* 1953-57 recordings (Pacific 1997)★★★, *The Art Of The Ballad* (Prestige 1998)★★★★.

● VIDEOS: *Live At Ronnie Scott's* (Hendring Music Video 1988), *Let's Get Lost* (1994).

● FILMS: *Let's Get Lost* (1989).

BAKER, DAVID NATHANIEL, JNR.

b. 21 December 1931, Indianapolis, Indiana, USA. After gaining a degree in Music Education at Indiana University, Baker played with Stan Kenton (1956) and Maynard Ferguson (1957) before leading his own band in Indianapolis (1958-9) and joining Quincy Jones's Orchestra (1961). He played with George Russell between 1959 and 1962, displaying a first-rate technique, to which he had added all the *avant garde* effects such as slides and smears. Muscular problems forced him to give up the trombone but he instead took up the cello and recorded with Charles Tyler in 1967. Baker had become increasingly involved in teaching and in 1966 joined the jazz department of Indiana University. He served as chairman of the jazz, folk and ethnic advisory panel to the NEA and on the jazz panel of the Kennedy Centre. In the late 80s he was President of the National Jazz Service Organization. He was able to return to the trombone in the 70s and again worked with George Russell. He is an interesting composer in many styles, whose jazz pieces, such as 'Honesty', have proved popular with other musicians. He has written in excess of 2,000 pieces (many of them commissioned), sometimes applying the techniques of European classical to jazz material. He was nominated for a Pulitzer Prize in 1973 for his *Concerto For Double Bass, Jazz Band, Wind And Strings*.

● ALBUMS: *Dave Baker's Twenty First Century Bebop Band* (1984)★★★, *RSVP* (1985)★★★.

BAKER, GINGER

b. Peter Baker, 19 August 1939, Lewisham, London, England. This brilliantly erratic drummer was already a vastly experienced musician when he formed the legendary Cream with Eric Clapton and Jack Bruce in 1967. He had drummed with trad-jazz bands, working with Terry Lightfoot and Acker Bilk before sitting in with Alexis Korner's Blues Incorporated and enlisting in the seminal Graham Bond Organisation. Following the unprecedented success and speedy demise of Cream, Baker joined with Steve Winwood, Rick Grech and Clapton in the 'supergroup' Blind Faith, followed by the ambitious Airforce. Baker then left Britain to live in Nigeria, where he cultivated an interest in African music and built his own recording studio (Paul McCartney's classic *Band On The Run* was recorded there). He briefly had a Nigerian band, Salt, and recorded with Fela Ransome-Kuti. Baker reputedly lost all his money on his Nigerian adventure, and returned to Britain and formed the Baker Gurvitz Army in 1973. Following the latter band's break-up he spent much of the next few years playing polo, an unlikely sport for a working-class lad from south London, but one at which he became most proficient. Baker's solo outing, *11 Sides Of Baker*, was justifiably panned in 1977. He returned with Energy in 1979 and briefly joined Atomic Rooster, Hawkwind and his own Ginger Baker's Nutters. In 1986 he played on PiL's UK Top 20 hit 'Rise'. Since then he has been unable to make any major impression and is openly bitter at the phenomenal success of Clapton. He remains, mostly through his work with Cream, one of Britain's greatest rock legends; a temperamental man who at his best showed astonishing ability on drums. His rolling, polyrhythmic playing laid the future foundation for heavy rock drumming. In 1994 he joined with Jack Bruce and Gary Moore and, as BBM, they released an accomplished and satisfying album, although friction within the group led to an early parting of the ways. Baker has since returned to his first love, jazz, and has recorded some excellent material with his trio (currently recording with Bill Frisell and Charlie Haden). Those who perceive Baker as the wild man of rock should investigate the excellent *Falling Off The Roof*.

● ALBUMS: *Stratavarious* (Polydor 1972)★★, with Fela Ransome Kuti *Fela Ransome Kuti With Ginger Baker* (Regal Zonophone 1972)★★★, *11 Sides Of Baker* (Mountain 1977)★★, *From Humble Oranges* (CDG 1983)★★, *Horses And Trees* (Celluloid 1986)★★★, *The Album* (ITM 1987)★★, *No Material* (ITM 1987)★★, *In Concert* (Onsala 1987)★★, *African Force* (ITM 1989)★★, *Middle Passage* (Axiom 1990)★★★, *Unseen Rain* (Daylight Music 1993)★★, with Bill Frisell, Charlie Haden *Going Back Home* (Atlantic 1994)★★★, with Frisell, Haden *Falling Off The Roof* (Atlantic 1996)★★★★.

● COMPILATIONS: *The Best Of Ginger Baker* (1973)★★, *The Alternative Album* (1992)★★★.

BAKER, HAROLD 'SHORTY'

b. 26 May 1914, St. Louis, Missouri, USA, d. 8 November 1966, New York, USA. An accomplished lead trumpet player and jazz soloist, Baker played in his brother's band, Winfield Baker And His St. Louis Crackerjacks, before moving on to work with riverboat bandleader Fate Marable, Eddie Johnson and Erskine Tate in the early 30s. During the late 30s, he had spells with Don Redman, Duke Ellington and Teddy Wilson's big band. In the early 40s, Baker joined Andy Kirk for about two years before leading his own combo with his wife, pianist-composer-arranger Mary Lou Williams. The 50s and early 60s were spent mostly with Duke Ellington, the Johnny Hodges combo, general freelancing, and leading his own band for a time. He featured on many records, including 'Trumpet No End', 'Beale Street Blues' and 'Jam With Sam' (all with Ellington), 'Baby Dear' and 'Harmony Blues' (with Williams) and 'Sweet As Bear Meat' (with Hodges). He was working until shortly before his death from throat cancer in 1966.

● ALBUMS: *Broadway Beat* (King 1959)★★★, *Summer Concert* (1960)★★★, with Doc Cheatham *Shorty And Doc* (Prestige 1961)★★★.

BAKER, KENNY

b. 1 March 1921, Withernsea, Yorkshire, England. After taking up the trumpet and playing in brass bands, Baker moved to London in the late 30s, to become a professional musician. During the next few years he established himself as an outstanding technician, capable of playing in any jazz or dance band. In the early 40s, he played in the bands of Lew Stone and George Chisholm before joining Ted Heath in 1944. He remained with Heath until 1949, and was featured on many recording sessions and countless concerts. In the early 50s he was regularly on the radio, leading his own band, the Baker's Dozen, on a weekly late-night show that lasted throughout the decade. In the 60s he led his own groups and recorded film soundtracks, all the time building his reputation as one of the best trumpet players in the world, even though he only rarely played outside the UK. At the end of the decade he was featured in Benny Goodman's British band. Baker's career continued throughout the 70s, with appearances as co-leader of the Best of British Jazz touring package, and with Ted Heath recreations and the bands led by Don Lusher and other former colleagues. In the early 80s, Baker turned down an invitation to take over leadership of the Harry James band after the latter's death. He could still be regularly heard playing concerts and club dates and also featured on television, usually off-camera, playing soundtracks for Alan Plater's popular UK television series *The Beiderbecke Affair* and *The Beiderbecke Tapes*. In 1989, he took part in a major recording undertaking that set out to recreate the classic recordings of Louis Armstrong using modern recording techniques. Baker took the Armstrong role, comfortably confounding the date on his birth certificate with his masterful playing. A fiery soloist with a remarkable technical capacity that he never uses simply for effect, Baker is one of the UK's greatest contributions to the international jazz scene.

● ALBUMS: *Kenny Baker's Half-Dozen* (Dormouse 1957)★★★★, *Date With The Dozen* (Dormouse 1957)★★★, *Presents The Half-Dozen* (Dormouse 1958)★★★, *Baker Plays McHugh* (1958)★★★, *The Phase 4 World Of Kenny Baker* (Decca 1977)★★★, *The Very Best Of British Jazz* (1983)★★★, *The Louis Armstrong Connection Volumes 1-7* (1989)★★★★, *Tribute To The Great Trumpeters* (1993)★★★, *The Boss Is Home* (Big Bear 1994)★★★, with Warren Vaché Jnr. *Ain't Misbehavin'* (Zephyr 1998)★★★★.

BAKER, MICKEY

b. McHouston Baker, 15 October 1925, Louisville, Kentucky, USA. After spells in reform school and a children's home, Baker moved to New York in 1941. He lived on the fringes of the criminal world but took up the guitar and quickly became a virtuoso, equally adept at jazz and blues styles. From the late 40s, Mickey 'Guitar' Baker played on hundreds of recording sessions, accompanying such artists as Ray Charles, the Coasters, Ivory Joe Hunter, Ruth Brown and Screaming Jay Hawkins. Baker occasionally recorded under his own name and in 1956 teamed up with guitarist/vocalist Sylvia Vanderpool. After an unsuccessful version of 'Walking In The Rain', the atmospheric 'Love Is Strange' (co-written by Bo Diddley) by Mickey And Sylvia was a US Top 20 hit on RCA/Groove in 1956. Later singles on Vik and RCA were only minor hits, although the duo contributed to Ike And Tina Turner's 'It's Gonna Work Out Fine' (1961), where Baker's is the male voice answering Tina's. Some of Baker's solo recordings were collected on a 1959 album for Atlantic Records. In the early 60s, he emigrated to Paris and joined the expatriate community of jazz musicians in the French capital. He toured Europe with such artists as Memphis Slim and Champion Jack Dupree, and performed at the 1973 Montreux Jazz Festival. Baker also arranged the strings for Fleetwood Mac's version of 'Need Your Love So Bad' (1968). During the 70s, he recorded several albums in Europe, including two for Stefan Grossman's guitar-instructional label, Kicking Mule.

● ALBUMS: *The Wildest Guitar* (Atlantic 1959)★★★, *But Wild* (King 1963)★★★, *The Blues In Me* (Black & Blue 1974)★★★, *Take A Look Inside* (1975)★★★, *Up On The Hill* (1975)★★★, *Blues And Jazz Guitar* (Kicking Mule 1977)★★★, *Jazz-Rock Guitar* (Kicking Mule 1978)★★★, *Rock A With A Sock* (1993)★★★.

BAKER, TOM

b. John Thomas Baker, 9 September 1952, Oakdale, California, USA. Baker first studied the piano, sang in the school choir, and at the age of 15 began to play the trumpet. His family moved to Australia in 1973. He played in the Ray Price band and then in 1975 formed the San Francisco Jazz Band, touring nationally before taking the unit to America in 1977; during this visit the group became one of the first foreign bands to be invited to the Sacramento Dixieland Jubilee. By 1980 Baker was an accomplished multi-instrumentalist, playing brass and reeds with equal authority. He again toured the USA, playing with mainstream musicians including Scott Hamilton, Dick Wellstood, Warren Vaché Jnr. and veteran artists Cab Calloway, Helen Forrest, Doc Cheatham and Ralph Sutton. During the 80s Baker toured extensively, becoming a popular performer in France and the Netherlands. He formed the Chicago Seven and the Swing Street Orchestra, both units dedicated to playing the classic swing styles of the 30s and 40s. In 1982 he formed Groove City, an outfit that allowed him to experiment more with modern styles, and they supported Oscar Peterson and Anita O'Day at a Sydney Opera House concert. Throughout the decade, Baker became a familiar figure playing in various combinations at jazz venues and festivals. In 1991 he recorded the superb *Absolutely Positively*, a collection of standards capturing the spirit and vitality of the era he admires so much. Three years later Baker successfully toured Japan. Returning to Australia, he formed a quartet with guitarist Ian Date and began a series of highly regarded albums with the independent La Brava label. Baker is a talented versatile musician in the traditional and mainstream styles and his presence on the contemporary Australian jazz scene offers a refreshing contrast to the many young musicians devoted to modernism.

● ALBUMS: *Tom Baker's San Francisco Jazz Band* (Jazz And Jazz 1976)★★★, *Absolutely Positively* (Roo Art 1991)★★★★, *The Swingcats Ball* (Dutch 1994)★★★, *Doodlin'* (La Brava 1995)★★★, *Tom Baker And Friends* (La Brava 1995)★★★★, with Dan Barrett *In Australia* (Arbors 1998)★★★.

BALDOCK, KEN

b. 5 April 1932, London, England. Baldock played the piano from the age of six and later studied piano and double bass at the Guildhall School of Music. In 1964 he played bass in the Peter King quartet at Annie's Room in London. He joined John Dankworth's Orchestra (1965-73) and also worked with Oscar Peterson at the 1972 Montreux Jazz Festival and in two television series. He had his own sextet in 1973, which featured Henry Lowther; he also played in Ronnie Scott's quartet with Louis Stewart, and then in a variety of groups with Phil Lee and John Horler, as well as accompanying musicians as diverse as Milt Jackson, Cleo Laine, Barney Kessel and Jay McShann. In the 80s, he played in Bobby Wellins' quartet and continued to work freelance. He is a reliable bass player with a solid technique who is also an able composer. In 1983, he was awarded an Arts Council grant for his composition *Kosen Rufu*. He also teaches both privately and at the Barry Summer School.

BALL, KENNY

b. 22 May 1930, Ilford, Essex, England. The most successful survivor of the early 60s 'trad boom', Ball played the harmonica and bugle in a local band before switching to the trumpet. Having previously played alongside Charlie Galbraith for a BBC radio broadcast and deputized for Britain's leading Dixieland trumpet player, Freddy Randall, Ball joined clarinettist Sid Phillips' band in 1954 and formed his own Dixieland-styled Jazzmen four years later, between which times he worked with Eric Delaney, George Chisholm, Terry Lightfoot and Al Fairweather. The Jazzmen did not record until the summer of 1959, resulting in the single 'Waterloo'/'Wabash Cannonball'. Signed to Pye Records, his first hit was in 1961 with Cole Porter's 'Samantha', originally from the Bing Crosby/Frank Sinatra movie *High Society*. This was followed by the million-selling 'Midnight In Moscow', which reached number 2 in the UK and US charts, 'March Of The Siamese Children' from *The King And I*, 'The Green Leaves Of Summer', 'Sukiyaki', and several more hits throughout the 60s. Ball featured alongside Chris Barber and Acker Bilk on a compilation album of the best of British Dixieland/trad jazz, *The Best Of Ball, Barber And Bilk*, which reached UK number 1 in 1962. The band made its film debut in 1963 in *Live It Up* with Gene Vincent, and appeared in *It's Trad Dad*. In the same year Ball was made an honorary citizen of New Orleans. For three years, from 1962-64, he received the Carl Alan Award for the Most Outstanding Traditional Jazz Band, and in 1968 the band appeared with Louis Armstrong on his last European visit. Throughout the 70s and 80s Ball extensively toured abroad while maintaining his UK popularity with regular concerts, featuring guests from the 'old days' such as Acker Bilk, Kenny Baker, Lonnie Donegan and George Chisholm. Ball claims his career peaked in 1981 when he and the Jazzmen played at the reception following the wedding of Prince Charles and Princess Diana. The early 90s Jazzmen include founder-member John Bennett (trombone), Andy Cooper (clarinet, ex-Charlie Galbraith and Alan Elsdon bands), John Benson (bass, vocals, ex-Monty Sunshine Band), John Fenner (guitar, vocals), Hugh Ledigo (piano, ex-Pasadena Roof Orchestra) and Ron Bowden (drums, ex-Ken Colyer; Lonnie Donegan and Chris Barber bands).

● ALBUMS: *Kenny Ball And His Jazzmen* (Pye 1961)★★★, *The Kenny Ball Show* (1962)★★★, with Gary Miller *Gary On The Ball* (1962)★★, *Midnight In Moscow* (Kapp 1962)★★★★, *It's Trad* (1962)★★★, *The Big Ones - Kenny Ball Style* (1963)★★★, *Jazz Band Ball* (1964)★★, *Colonel Bogey And Eleven Japanese Marches* Japan only release (1964)★, *Kenny Ball Plays For The Jet Set* US only release (1964,)★★★, *Tribute To Tokyo* (1964)★★, *The Sound Of Kenny Ball* (1968)★★★, *Kenny Ball And His Jazzmen Live In Berlin Volume 1/Volume 2* German releases (1968)★★★, *King Of The Swingers* (1969)★★, *At The Jazz Band Ball* (1970)★★★, *Fleet Street Lightning* (1970)★★, *Saturday Night With Kenny Ball And His Band* (1970)★★★, *Pixie Dust (A Tribute To Walt Disney)* (1971)★★, *My Very Good Friend ... Fats Waller* (1972)★★★, *Have A Drink On Me* (1972)★★★, *Let's All Sing A Happy Song* (1973)★★, with the Johnny Arthey Orchestra and the Eddie Lester Singers *A Friend To You* (1974)★★★, *Titillating Tango* (1976)★★★, *Saturday Night At The Mill* (Spiral 1977)★★★, *Way Down Yonder* (1977)★★★, *The Bulldog And Kangaroo* Australasian only release (1977)★★★, *In Concert* (Nevis 1978)★★, *Kenny In Concert In The USA, Volumes 1 & 2* US only releases (Jazzology 1979)★★★, *Soap* (AMI 1981)★★★, with Chris Barber, Acker Bilk *Ball, Barber And Bilk Live At The Royal Festival Hall* (Cambra 1984)★★★, *Greensleeves* (Timeless 1986)★★★, *Kenny Ball And His Jazzmen Play The Movie Greats* (MFP 1987)★★, *On Stage* (Start 1988)★★★, *Dixie* (Pickwick 1989)★★★, *Kenny Ball Plays British* (MFP 1989)★★★, *Jazz Classics* (1990)★★★, *Steppin' Out* (Castle 1992)★★★, *Strictly Jazz* (Kaz 1992)★★★, *Kenny Ball Now* (1990)★★, *Lighting Up The Town* (Intersound 1993)★★★.

● COMPILATIONS: with Chris Barber, Acker Bilk *The Best Of Ball, Barber And Bilk* (Pye Golden Guinea 1962)★★★★, *Kenny Ball's Golden Hits* (Pye Golden Guinea 1963)★★★★, *Golden Hour* (Golden Hour 1971)★★★★, *Golden Hour Presents Kenny Ball 'Hello Dolly'* (Golden Hour 1973)★★, *Cheers!* (1979)★★★, *Golden Hits* (PRT 1986)★★★★, *Kenny Ball's Cotton Club* (Conifer 1986)★★★, *The Singles Collection* (PRT 1987)★★★, *Images* (Images 1990)★★★, *Kenny Ball - The Collection* (Castle 1990)★★★★, with Barber, Bilk *The Ultimate!* (1991)★★★★, *Hello Dolly* (Spectrum 1995)★★★, *Greatest Hits* (Pulse 1997)★★★.

BALL, RONNIE

b. 22 December 1927, Birmingham, Warwickshire, England. After playing piano as a semi-pro during his teenage years, Ball emerged as a leading light of the British bop scene in the early 50s. No sooner had he made his mark than he decided to move to New York, where, from 1952 onwards, he worked and recorded with bop luminaries such as Lennie Tristano, Dizzy Gillespie, Kenny Clarke, Hank Mobley, Art Pepper and Warne Marsh. The mainstream then beckoned and by the end of the decade he had played with Buddy Rich,

Gene Krupa and Roy Eldridge. For a few years in the early 60s he was accompanist to singer Chris Connor and soon afterwards became deeply involved in studio work, providing deftly supportive accompaniment for singers and instrumentalists alike. His early bop recordings reveal a fleet, inventive soloist at ease and at one with the most distinguished company.

● ALBUMS: *All About Ronnie* (Savoy 1956)★★★.

BALLAMY, IAIN

b. 20 February 1964, Guildford, Surrey, England. Ballamy is largely self-taught, having started to learn piano before taking up reed instruments. He formed his own group, the Iains, in 1983 and in the same year worked with Graham Collier in a band that eventually became Loose Tubes. Among his closest musical associates are Django Bates (a member of the Iains and Loose Tubes) and Bill Bruford, with whose band, Earthworks, Ballamy has played since 1986. He has also worked with Gil Evans and Billy Jenkins' Voice Of God Collective. Although deriving much inspiration from John Coltrane, Ballamy has not been led into a musical *cul-de-sac*, as has happened with many of his contemporaries, and is rapidly developing into a significant leader of musical fashion. He exhibits an impressive technique, whether on alto, tenor or soprano saxophone, and a glorious, heart-on-sleeve romanticism, which he displays, for example, on one of his own compositions, 'All I Ask Of You', on his first album as leader.

● ALBUMS: *Balloon Man* (Editions EG 1988)★★★, *All Men Amen* (B&W 1995)★★★, *Acme* (B&W 1997)★★★★.

BANG, BILLY

b. Billy Walker, 20 September 1947, Mobile, Alabama, USA. Growing up in New York's South Bronx, learning violin was the last thing Bang wanted to do. 'It was the most hated instrument for me', Bang told the *LA Times*. 'It's too European and it's never been in my blood. The Temptations never played it and James Brown never sang with one.' Nonetheless, Bang learned to play, but in the early 60s abandoned the violin for percussion, becoming interested in African-Cuban rhythms. Drafted to Vietnam, he had a political awakening and returned to America to throw himself into the anti-war movement. When he began to play music again in 1971 he experimented with saxophones, but returned to the violin. Bang became known as an associate of Sam Rivers and Frank Lowe, his skidding, diabolically transgressive playing an essential component of the celebrated Loft scene. In the early 70s he formed his own group, the Survival Ensemble, and in 1977 co-founded the String Trio Of New York, which wooed audiences with seductive themes that then opened into state-of-the-art string improvisations. Associations with Sun Ra, Don Cherry, Marilyn Crispell and James 'Blood' Ulmer were also productive. Like other musicians of his generation, Bang resists categorization. *Untitled Gift*, recorded in 1982, was elegant free jazz; *Bangception* and *Outline No 12* were austere art music. In 1987, he guested on Kahil El'Zabar's *Another Kind Of Groove*, and in 1988 on Bootsy Collins' comeback, *What's Bootsy Doin'?*. His sextet album, *The Fire From Within*, launched an exotic frontline of trumpet, guitar and marimba; together with Bang's microtonal panache and his polyrhythmic vamps, it made a deliriously pretty platform for some amazing playing. *Live At Carlos 1* delivered more of the same. On other projects, such as the Jazz Doctors quartet, the presence of Cecil Taylor associate, Dennis Charles, on drums assured a precise and understated swing. In 1988 Bang toured Europe and recorded *Value No 10* with a quartet that comprised Charles, Lowe and Sirone. He also began playing in Sun Ra's Arkestra, and released a tribute album to violinist Stuff Smith, whom he considers one of the major influences on his work. Billy Bang delivers music with infectious energy and an honesty about achievement that is most moving.

● ALBUMS: *New York Collage* (Anima 1978)★★★, *Sweet Space* (Anima 1979)★★★, *Rainbow Gladiator* (Soul Note 1981)★★★★, *Untitled Gift* (1982)★★★, *Invitation* (Soul Note 1982)★★★, *Outline No 12* (Celluloid 1982)★★★, *Bangception* (hatART 1983)★★★, *Distinction Without A Difference* (hatART 1983)★★★★, with the Jazz Doctors *Intensive Care* (1984)★★★, *The Fire From Within* (Soul Note 1985)★★★★, *Live At Carlos I* (Soul Note 1987)★★★, with Kahil El'Zabar *Another Kind Of Groove* (1987)★★, *Valve No 10* 1988 recording (Soul Note 1991)★★★, *A Tribute To Stuff Smith* (Soul Note 1994)★★★★, *Bang On!* (Justin Time 1997)★★★★, *Commandment (For The Sculpture Of Alain Kirili)* (No More Records 1997)★★★, with Dennis Charles *Bangception Willisau 1982* (Hatology 1998)★★★★.

BANKS, BILLY

b. 1901, Alton, Illinois, USA, d. 19 October 1967. A mildly engaging, if somewhat eccentric, singer, Banks' chief claim to jazz fame has been the set of records he made in 1932 that featured Red Allen, Pee Wee Russell, Eddie Condon, Jess Stacy, Fats Waller, Zutty Singleton and others. These session appeared as Billy Banks And His Orchestra, The Rhythmakers or Billy Banks And The Chicago Rhythm kings. The record companies concerned claimed these were the 'hottest jazz records ever made', and for once their customary hyperbole was very nearly justified. Banks' high-pitched vocals (he was, at one time, a female impersonator) are the weakest link on these classic sides, but there is so much superb music being played all around him that his peculiarities can be happily overlooked and even enjoyed as the curiosity they really are. He also recorded under his own name and was vocalist on some tracks recorded by Eddie Edinborough. Little is known of Banks' career before 1932, although he spent four years with Noble Sissle's band from 1933, before going into a cabaret spot in 1938 at Billy Rose's Diamond Horseshoe, an engagement that continued unbroken until June 1948. From that time he worked in cabaret in New York, touring Europe in the 50s. During that decade his recordings are sparse but he did record with Freddie Randall in 1952, Cy Laurie in 1954, and with Tom Pickering in 1956. Following some gigs in the Far East, he elected to remain there and never returned to the

USA (he settled in Japan in 1959). In USA and UK terms, this largely appears to have excluded him from jazz literature (save for the the hot jazz records of the 30s). His former pianist Nick Demuth now argues, that Banks' greatest contribution to jazz was in expanding the genre in the Far East, as Buck Clayton and Teddy Weatherford had already done. He continued to work regularly in Japan up to his death in 1967.

● COMPILATIONS: *Billy Banks And The Rhythmakers* (1932 recording)★★★, 10-inch album *Pee Wee Russell/Billy Banks* (Jazz Panorama 1951)★★★.

Barbarin, Louis

b. 24 October 1902, New Orleans, Louisiana, USA, d. 12 May 1997. Barbarin was born into a musical family, taking up drums as a small child. His father, Isidore, played alto horn, his brother William played cornet and his other brothers, Lucien and Paul Barbarin, were also drummers. After playing in parade and New Orleans-style dance and jazz bands throughout the 20s, Barbarin joined Papa Celestin. This association began in the late 30s and continued until Celestin's death, and thereafter Barbarin stayed with the band when it was led by Albert French. Barbarin belonged in the tradition of unspectacular New Orleans drummers whose role was recognized as being that of timekeeper.

Barbarin, Paul

b. 5 May 1899, New Orleans, Louisiana, USA, d. 17 February 1969, New Orleans, Louisiana, USA. The best-known member of a respected New Orleans musical family, Barbarin became one of the Crescent City's best and most famous drummers. With his father, Isadore, an established brass player and a member of the Onward Brass Band, and his brothers, Louis (drums), Lucien (drums) and William (cornet) all playing jazz, Paul Barbarin could hardly have done anything but become a jazz musician. While still in his mid-teens, he was a member of Buddy Petit's band, then moved to Chicago, where he worked with the bands of Joe 'King' Oliver and Jimmy Noone. From 1928 Barbarin worked mainly in New York with the Luis Russell band, which in 1935 came under the nominal leadership of Louis Armstrong. In 1939, Barbarin returned home and, apart from occasional trips to Chicago in the 40s and 50s when he worked with Red Allen, Sidney Bechet, Art Hodes, he also led his own band. It was in New Orleans that he stayed, playing long and successful engagements and enjoying life as an elder statesman of jazz. Barbarin played with the simplistic drive of the earliest New Orleans drummers; though he lacked the polish of Baby Dodds and the flair of Zutty Singleton, he always swung any band in which he played. One of his notable compositions is 'Bourbon Street Parade'. In later years he continued the family tradition when, like his father before him, he became leader of the Onward Brass Band. It was while leading this band in a New Orleans street parade in February 1969 that he collapsed and died.

● ALBUMS: *The Streets Of The City* (1950)★★★, *New Orleans Jamboree* (Jazztone 1955)★★★, *Paul Barbarin And His New Orleans Band* (Atlantic 1956)★★★, *Barbarin's Best At Dixieland Hall* (1964)★★★.

Barber, Bill

b. John William Barber, 21 May 1920, Hornell, New York, USA. While at school Barber was persuaded to try out for the school orchestra on tuba. Very impressed with the instrument, he studied at the Manhattan and Juilliard schools of music, then was drafted during World War II. After the war he joined the Kansas City Philharmonic Orchestra and also played in several theatre pit bands. By this time, however, he was becoming deeply interested in jazz and joined Claude Thornhill's band. Later, he gigged in New York and was on hand when Miles Davis and Gil Evans were planning *Birth Of The Cool*. The band worked in New York for two weeks, playing at the Royal Roost, with Barber spending the first part of the evening in the pit band for *Magdalena*, by Villa-Lobos. Despite the latter-day popularity of the album, the Davis nonet was not especially successful and with few other jazz groups having room for a tuba, Barber continued to work in pit bands, including three years with the Broadway production of *The King And I*. During this period he performed occasional sessions with jazz musicians both live and on record, among them Charlie Ventura, the Sauter-Finegan Orchestra and Pete Rugolo. From time to time he rejoined Davis for recording dates, including *Sketches Of Spain* and *At Carnegie Hall*. He also rejoined Evans for *Out Of The Cool*. In later years, Barber began teaching on Long Island, eventually retiring. He was lured out of retirement, however, to record with Gerry Mulligan on *Rebirth Of The Cool*. Although he began playing bass in the 90s, Barber's first love remains the tuba, and the fact that this instrument is rarely used in jazz had meant that this fine musician has never been accorded his due.

Barber, Chris

b. 17 April 1930, Welwyn Garden City, Hertfordshire, England. In the 40s Barber studied trombone and bass at the Guildhall School of Music, eventually choosing the former as his principal instrument (although he occasionally played bass in later years). In the late 40s he formed his first band, which, unusually, was formed as a co-operative. Also in the band were Monty Sunshine, Ron Bowden and Lonnie Donegan. By the early 50s the band had gained a considerable following but it was nevertheless decided to invite Ken Colyer to join. The move was musically promising but proved to be unsuccessful when the personalities involved clashed repeatedly. Eventually, Colyer left and was replaced by Pat Halcox. With a remarkably consistent personnel, the Barber band was soon one of the UK's leading traditional groups and was well placed to take advantage of the surge of interest in this form of jazz in the late 50s and early 60s. The decline in popularity of 'trad', which came on the heels of the rock explosion, had a dramatic effect on many British jazz bands, but

Barber's fared much better than most. This was owing in part to his astute business sense and also his keen awareness of musical trends and a willingness to accommodate other forms without compromising his high musical standards. In the 60s Barber changed the name of the band to the Chris Barber Blues and Jazz Band. Into the traditional elements of the band's book he incorporated ragtime but also worked with such modern musicians as Joe Harriott. Among his most important activities at this time was his active promotion of R&B and the blues, which he underlined by bringing major American artists to the UK, often at his own expense. Through such philanthropy he brought to the attention of British audiences the likes of Sister Rosetta Tharpe, Brownie McGhee, Louis Jordan and Muddy Waters. Not content with performing the older blues styles, Barber also acknowledged the contemporary interest in blues evinced by rock musicians and audiences and hired such players as John Slaughter and Pete York (ex-Spencer Davis Group), who worked happily beside long-serving sidemen Halcox, Ian Wheeler, Vic Pitt and others. In the 70s, Barber focused more on mainstream music, showing a special affinity for small Duke Ellington-styled bands, and toured with visitors such as Russell Procope, Wild Bill Davis, Trummy Young and John Lewis. He also maintained his contact with his jazz roots and, simultaneously, the contemporary blues scene by touring widely with his *Take Me Back To New Orleans* show, which featured Dr. John. As a trombone player, Barber's work is enhanced by his rich sound and flowing solo style. It is, however, as bandleader and trendspotter that he has made his greatest contribution to the jazz scene, both internationally and, especially, in the UK. In the early 90s he was happily entering his fifth decade as a bandleader with no discernible flagging of interest, enthusiasm, skill or, indeed, of his audience. In 1991 he was awarded the OBE, the same year as *Panama!* was released, featuring the excellent trumpet playing of Wendell Brunious.

● ALBUMS: *Live In 1954-55* (London 1955)★★★★, *Here Is Chris Barber* (Atlantic 1958)★★★, *Ragtime* (1960)★★★, *Chris Barber At The London Palladium* (1961)★★★, *Trad Tavern* (Philips 1962)★★★★, *Getting Around* (1963)★★★, *Battersea Rain Dance* (1968)★★★, *Live In East Berlin* (Black Lion 1968)★★★, *Get Rolling!* (1971)★★★, *Sideways* (1974)★★★, *Echoes Of Ellington* (1976)★★★, *The Grand Reunion Concert* (Timeless 1976)★★★, *Take Me Back To New Orleans* (Black Lion 1980)★★★, *Creole Love Call* (Timeless 1981)★★★, *Mardi Gras At The Marquee* (Timeless 1983)★★★, with Kenny Ball, Acker Bilk *Ball, Barber And Bilk Live At The Royal Festival Hall* (Cambra 1984)★★★, *Live In 85* (Timeless 1986)★★★, *Concert For The BBC* (Timeless 1986)★★★, *In Budapest* (Storyville 1987)★★★★, *When Its Thursday Night In Egypt* (Sonet 1988)★★★, *Classics Concerts In Berlin* 1959 recording (Chris Barber Collection 1988)★★★, *Stardust* (Timeless 1988)★★★, *Mardi Gras At The Marquee* (Timeless 1989)★★★, *Get Yourself To Jackson Square* (Sonet 1990)★★★, *Echoes Of Ellington Volume I* (Timeless 1991)★★★★, *Echoes Of Ellington Volume II* (Timeless 1991)★★★, *In Concert* (Timeless 1991)★★★, with Wendell Brunious *Panama!* (Timeless 1991)★★★★, *Who's Blues* (L&R 1991)★★★, *Chris Barber And His New Orleans Friends* (Timeless 1992)★★, *With The Zenith Hot Stompers* (Timeless 1993)★★, *Chris Barber 40 Years Jubilee* (Timeless 1995)★★★★, *Elite Syncopations* 1960 recording (Lake 1994)★★, *That's It Then* (Timeless 1997)★★★.

● COMPILATIONS: with Kenny Ball, Acker Bilk *The Best Of Ball, Barber And Bilk* (Pye Golden Guinea 1962)★★★★, *30 Years, Chris Barber* (Timeless 1985)★★★★, *Can't We Get Together? (1954-84)* (Timeless 1986)★★★★, *Best Sellers* (Storyville 1987)★★★, *Everybody Knows* (Compact Collection 1987)★★★, *The Best Of Chris Barber (1959-62)* (PRT 1988)★★★★, *The Entertainer* (Polydor 1988)★★★★, *The Ultimate* (Kaz 1989)★★★★, *Essential Chris Barber* (Kaz 1990)★★★★, with Ball, Bilk *The Ultimate!* (1991)★★★★, *Petite Fleur* (Spectrum 1995)★★★★.

● VIDEOS: *Music From The Land Of Dreams Concert* (Storyville 1990), *In Concert* (Virgin Vision 1991).

BARBER, PATRICIA

b. USA. A highly gifted pianist and singer with a decidedly modern outlook to her work, Barber has attracted a good deal of attention during the 90s thanks to worldwide tours and some well-received albums. Her playing is as important as her singing, and here, too, she is forward-looking. She displays an awareness of jazz roots with funky styling while also hinting at modern classical music. In her singing she often uses her voice in wordless improvisations that evoke deep emotional responses in her listeners. Much of her work is filled with a moving melancholy that never descends into gloom and despair. Rather, there is a coolly appraising effect, as if the pianist and singer is intelligently exploring inner resources and allowing the listener to enter into her newly discovered worlds of sound.

● ALBUMS: *A Distortion Of Love* (Antilles 1991)★★★★, *Café Blue* (Premonition 1994)★★★, *Modern Cool* (Premonition 1998)★★★★.

BARBIERI, GATO

b. Leandro J. Barbieri, 28 November 1934, Rosario, Argentina. After studying clarinet while still a child, Barbieri took up alto saxophone when his family moved to Buenos Aires. He joined Lalo Schifrin's band and, despite the early influence of Charlie Parker, soon switched to tenor. He formed his own quartet, often supporting visiting American jazzmen, and his playing began to reveal the influence of John Coltrane. In 1962, Barbieri left South America for Italy, where he worked for a time with a free-form band led by Don Cherry. Although Barbieri had earlier turned his back on the music of his native land, the physical distancing he now experienced gave him more appreciation of its jazz potential. From the mid-60s onwards, his music took on a steadily more distinctive flavour as he began to incorporate the many dance rhythms of South America into a rich and ever-changing backcloth for his driving tenor-playing. Performing the commercial title track to the film *Last Tango In Paris* has since become his Albatross. Since the early 70s Barbieri has spent much time in South America, where by his example and encouragement he has helped to foster both jazz and a deeper understanding of the continent's own musical heritage. Over 15 years elapsed before Barbieri recorded again, releasing the Columbia Records session *Que Pasa?*

● ALBUMS: with Don Cherry *Gato Barbieri And Don Cherry* (Inner City 1965)★★★, *In Search Of The Mystery* (Explosive 1967)★★★, *Confluence* (Affinity 1968)★★★, *The Third World* (Flying Dutchman 1969)★★★, *Under Fire* (Flying Dutchman 1970)★★★, *Fenix* (Flying Dutchman 1971)★★★★, *Last Tango In Paris* film soundtrack (United Artists 1972)★★★★, *Chapter One: Latin America* (MCA 1973)★★★★, *Chapter Two: Hasta Siempre* (Impulse! 1974)★★★, *Chapter Three: Viva Emiliano Zapata* (Impulse! 1974)★★★★, *Bolivia* (RCA 1974)★★★, *Chapter Four: Alive In New York* (ABC/Impulse! 1975)★★★, *Caliente* (A&M 1976)★★★, *Obsession* (Affinity 1978)★★★, *Euphoria* (A&M 1979)★★, *Hamba Khale* (Affinity 1979)★★★, *Gato ... Para Los Amigos!* (Doctor Jazz 1983)★★, *Apassionado* (Polydor 1983)★★★, *The Third World Revisited* (Bluebird 1988)★★★, *Two Pictures 1965-68* (Liuto 1990)★★★, *Que Pasa?* (Columbia 1997)★★★★.

BARBOUR, DAVE

b. 28 May 1912, Long Island, New York, USA, d. 11 December 1965. In the mid-30s, having recently switched from playing banjo to the guitar, Barbour spent time with Joseph 'Wingy' Manone and Red Norvo before settling into a series of stints with leading dance-bands from the sweeter end of the swing era, including those of Glenn Miller, Hal Kemp and Raymond Scott. He also played with jazz-orientated big bands led by Charlie Barnet and Benny Goodman. Much respected as a session and studio musician, the guitarist also worked and recorded with several jazzmen of note, including Boyd Raeburn, Jack Teagarden and Teddy Wilson. In 1942, while in the Goodman band, he met and married Peggy Lee and until their divorce eight years later, he acted as his wife's musical director. In the mid-50s illness forced him to retire, although recorded with Benny Carter in the early 60s.

BAREFIELD, EDDIE

b. 12 December 1909, Scandia, Iowa, USA, d. 4 January 1991, New York, USA. After formal studies on piano, Barefield taught himself to play alto (and later tenor and soprano) saxophone. By his late teens he had begun a period of several years' work in territory bands and name bands, including those of Bennie Moten, Zack Whyte, the Cotton Pickers (under Cuba Austin) and Cab Calloway. He stayed with Calloway for three years, leaving in 1936 to settle on the west coast, where he worked with Charlie Echols and also formed a number of bands under his own leadership. Unable to stay out of the big time for long, Barefield was in New York in 1938 as a member of Fletcher Henderson's band. After leaving Henderson, he played again with Calloway, then in the early 40s he drifted in and out of big bands and small groups, working under leaders such as Don Redman, Duke Ellington, Coleman Hawkins, Benny Carter and Ella Fitzgerald, for whom he was musical director. Barefield's all-round competence as both musician and arranger ensured that he was always in demand; he was also frequently called upon by studios and established a reputation for his work in the theatre. In the 50s and 60s, he continued to work in the theatre and also played with Sy Oliver, Redman again (touring Europe with him in 1953), and with Sammy Price, Wilbur De Paris, the Dukes Of Dixieland and the Saints And Sinners band. He also appeared in a number of motion pictures including *Every Day A Holiday* (1937), *The Night They Raided Minsky's* (1968) and *L'Aventure Du Jazz* (1969). In the 70s Barefield showed no signs of slowing down, spending most of that decade in the house band for the Ringling Brothers and Barnum & Bailey Circus. He also remained active in jazz, working on into the late 80s with Dick Vance and Illinois Jacquet, among many others. Barefield's playing style carried a distinctive vibrancy and his soprano saxophone work was especially notable for its buzz-saw attack and urgency.

● ALBUMS: *L'Aventure Du Jazz* film soundtrack (1969)★★★, *The Indestructible Eddie Barefield* (Famous Door 1977)★★★.

● FILMS: *Every Day A Holiday* (1937), *The Night They Raided Minsky's* (1968), *L'Aventure Du Jazz* (1969).

BARGERON, DAVE

b. 6 September 1942, Athol, Massachusetts, USA. A vital component of several important jazz groups, Dave Bargeron's trombone has appeared on recordings by Johnny Griffin (*Dance Of Passion*), Michel Camilo (*One More Once*), Gerry Mulligan (*Re-Birth Of The Cool*) and Miles Davis/Quincy Jones *Miles & Quincy Live At Montreux*. Bargeron also recorded 11 albums over an eight-year career with Blood, Sweat And Tears, before joining the Carnegie Hall Jazz Band in the 90s. It was 1995 before he recorded his first album. He commented to the press that, 'for a long time I never felt comfortable making a record myself. It was me and this unwieldy trombone that I wanted to wrap around a post most of the time. Can you imagine having this music run around in your head, your soul, your heart, for 30 or 40 years, and not be able to play it?' It was only when he developed what he calls the Bargeron Articulating Valve Option (or BRAVO) - a special valve for his trombone's mouthpiece - that he found himself able to express himself as a true soloist on his instrument. This release came in the form of *Barge Burns ... Slide Flies*, recorded with Larry Willis (ex-Blood, Sweat And Tears) on piano, Kenwood Dennard on drums and Steve Novosel on bass. It featured a number of original compositions, some written by Bargeron and others by Willis, as well as one standard, 'There Is No Greater Love'. In February 1996 Bargeron also appeared as a soloist on Howard Johnson's *Gravity*.

● ALBUMS: *Barge Burns ... Slide Flies* (Mapleshade 1995)★★★.

BARKER, DANNY

b. 13 January 1909, New Orleans, Louisiana, USA, d. 13 March 1994, New Orleans, Louisiana, USA. One of the grand old men of jazz, Barker's career, while rooted in traditionalism, spanned a wide musical range. Before settling on the guitar as his instrument, Barker received tuition on clarinet from Barney Bigard, on drums from his uncle Paul Barbarin and then played ukelele and banjo in the Storyville district of New Orleans (often alongside blues player Cousin Joe, with whom he also recorded for Mezz Mezzrow's King Jazz label). In the early 20s he was accompanying blues singer Little Brother Montgomery and by the end of the decade was working with Lee Collins and other leading local musicians. In 1930 Barker moved to New York, where he worked clubs and recorded extensively with Red Allen, Sidney Bechet, James P. Johnson, Jelly Roll Morton (who gave him his nickname, 'Hometown', following his move from New Orleans to New York), and with his wife, singer Louis 'Blue Lu' Barker. Barker also worked with several big bands of the mid/late 30s, including those led by Lucky Millinder, Benny Carter and Cab Calloway (with whom he and Blue Lu spent nine years, while also recording for Decca). He was also to be found working on sessions by Billie Holiday, Charlie Parker and others. From the late 40s onwards he was active in the Revivalist movement, playing with Bunk Johnson, Paul Barbarin and Albert Nicholas, and enjoying one notable hit alongside his wife with 'Here's A Little Girl From Jacksonville'. In the mid-60s Barker returned to his home-town, where his great interest in and knowledge of early jazz history led to his appointment as Curator of the New Orleans Jazz Museum. He also instigated the Fairview Baptist Brass Band to maintain the marching band tradition, and engaged in a round of lectures. He wrote extensively (co-author with Jack V. Buerkle of *Bourbon Street Black* and his autobiography, *A Life In Jazz*, was published in 1986), and continued to play whenever the spirit moved him.

● ALBUMS: *Danny Barker* (1958)★★★, *Save The Bones* (Orleans 1986)★★★.

● FURTHER READING: *A Life In Jazz*, Danny Barker.

Barker, Guy

b. 26 December 1957, London, England. Barker took up the trumpet as a child and studied formally at the Royal College of Music. One of several brilliant British musicians to come up through the ranks of the National Youth Jazz Orchestra, Barker attracted media attention both then and after his departure into the wider world of the professional jazz musician. Playing with NYJO at the Cleveland Jazz Festival at Middlesbrough, England, in 1978, he was joined unexpectedly on stage by Clark Terry for a duet, a moment he took in his confident stride. At the age of 20 Barker toured the UK with his own quintet, using young American jazzmen he had met during a visit to New York. Also in the late 70s and early 80s, he played with Mike Westbrook, John Dankworth, Chris Hunter and Hubbard's Cubbard, a jazz-rock group. His major breakthrough came with a spell with Gil Evans, touring and recording, and work with Stan Tracey, Clark Tracey, with whom he toured the Far East, Europe and the UK, and Ornette Coleman. Alongside his jazz work, Barker has appeared as soloist with the London Symphony Orchestra and in groups backing Frank Sinatra, Lena Horne, Sammy Davis Jnr., Mel Tormé and Liza Minnelli. Simultaneously, he has been busy in film, television and recording studios, playing with Evans on the soundtrack of *Insignificance* (1985), and on *Absolute Beginners* (1986) and *The Living Daylights* (1987). He has also appeared on many rock albums featuring artists such as Paul McCartney, Grace Jones and Joan Armatrading. Throughout the 80s he made numerous jazz record dates with Westbrook, Evans, Stan Tracey's Hexad and big band, Clark Tracey, Peter King, Jim Mullen and the Jack Sharpe Big Band. He has continued this high level of activity into the 90s, playing on Sinatra's 1991 tour of the UK, and a tour to Hong Kong with Georgie Fame in a package paying tribute to Chet Baker. There have also been club and festival dates, a series of concerts recreating the music of Bix Beiderbecke and recording sessions with Carla Bley and with his own quintet. Barker's pure-toned melodic playing, allied to a crackling, boppish attack, makes his solo work particularly attractive and exhilarating. His wide range of musical interests, evident in his concert tours honouring trumpeters as diverse as Baker and Beiderbecke, has not resulted in his becoming a copyist. Indeed, his highly distinctive playing style is already one of the great joys of jazz in the 90s. Barker's sober onstage demeanour and dress conceal a vibrant musical personality whose future appears to have no bounds. After Barker's outstanding performance at the 1989 South Bank Jazz Festival at Grimsby, Lincolnshire, Lee Konitz remarked, 'One day that guy's gonna be a genius.' That day has seemingly already arrived, especially with the assured commerciality of *Into The Blue*.

● ALBUMS: with Clark Tracey *Suddenly Last Tuesday* (Cadillac 1986)★★★, with Tracey *Stiperstones* (Steam 1987)★★★, with Peter King *Brother Bernard* (Miles Music 1988)★★★, *Holly J* (Miles Music 1989)★★★, *Isn't It?* (Spotlite 1991)★★★, *Into The Blue* (Verve 1995)★★★★, *What Love Is* (Verve 1998)★★★★.

Barker, Louis 'Blue Lu'

b. 13 November 1913, New Orleans, Louisiana, USA, d. 7 May 1998, New Orleans, Louisiana, USA. Barker began her career as a dancer and singer in New Orleans but did not record until 1938 after her move to New York. She is almost certainly the 'Lu Blue' who recorded with Erskine Hawkins in July of that year. Under her own name she continued to record for Decca Records until 1939. She enjoyed a second period of recording activity between 1947 and 1949, with her work appearing mainly on Apollo and Capitol Records. A band singer of note, she has been cited as an influence on Billie Holiday and Eartha Kitt. Barker's blues were often slyly humorous and marked by a wonderful sense of timing, demonstrated on her most famous hit, 1938's 'Don't You Feel My Leg'. Married to New Orleans jazz guitarist Danny Barker, she usually worked in his company as well as with many of the great names in jazz.

● COMPILATIONS: *Red White And Blues* (1980)★★★, *Sorry But I Can't Take You - Woman's Railroad Blues* (1980)★★★.

Barker, Thurman

b. 8 January 1948, Chicago, Illinois, USA. Emerging from the Chicago free scene, a founder-member of the AACM, percussionist Barker first played and recorded with fellow Chicagoans Kalaparush Maurice McIntyre, Joseph Jarman, Muhal Richard Abrams and Anthony Braxton, in whose quartet he played in the late 70s. Economic survival meant periods of working in musical pit bands, but joining Cecil Taylor's Unit in 1986 brought further exposure. Taylor's dense, polyrhythmic style required the services of someone with an acute sense of structure and an incisive attack. These Barker has in abundance. At the suggestion of Billy Bang, Barker has added the marimba to his armoury, playing with exquisite grace and fire on Bang's exotic *The Fire From Within*. His drumwork on guitarist Joe Morris's *Human Rites* is equally impressive.

Barksdale, Everett

b. 28 April, 1910, Detroit, Michigan, USA, d. 29 January 1986. A multi-instrumentalist, Barksdale played in a number of bands in and around Detroit before settling on guitar. In Chicago in the early 30s, he played with Erskine Tate's popular danceband. For most of the 30s he was in Eddie South's band, then he joined Benny Carter. Most of the 40s were spent in New York, playing in small groups and also working in the studios. At the end of the decade he joined Art Tatum, with whom he played into the mid-50s. In the late 50s and most of the 60s he was again engaged in studio work, but found time for jazz gigs with Buddy Tate and others. In the 70s, Barksdale lived and occasionally worked in California. A sound rhythm player, Barksdale was an able exponent of acoustic guitar while his electric guitar playing, as shown by his work with Tate, was frequently limited.

Barlow, Dale

b. 25 December 1959, Sydney, Australia. Barlow began with piano, then studied classical flute and clarinet, switching to tenor saxophone in his teens while attending jazz courses at the New South Wales Conservatorium. His father, Bill Barlow, is a top reed player. In 1979 Dale played in the Australian Youth Orchestra at the Monterey Jazz Festival. In 1982 he went to New York, USA, ostensibly to study, but was soon playing and recording with many notable jazz musicians, including Chet Baker, Sonny Rollins, Cedar Walton, Sonny Stitt, Kenny Barron and Gil Evans, as well as pop acts, Bryan Ferry, Style Council and Mental As Anything. In addition to living in New York, Barlow toured with various groups in Europe, Indonesia and Cuba. In 1988 he was named Bicentennial Jazz Musician Of The Year. That same year he led a 10-piece band of top Australian musicians on a tour to the USA. In 1990 he recorded and toured with Art Blakey's Jazz Messengers. Barlow formed and toured with his own groups, and recorded *Wizards Of Oz* with Paul Grabowsky. From 1992-94 he was voted Jazz Instrumentalist Of The Year. Barlow, with his shaved head and hard bop tenor, became not only a musicians' favourite, but also a viable commercial property, with popular appearances on television variety and talk shows. In 1993 he toured Australia with Eddie Henderson and Mulgrew Miller and broke attendance records at Sydney's basement jazz club with vocalist Margaret Urlich. Barlow was also very much in demand as a sideman, recording with James Morrison, Tommy Emmanuel, Vince Jones and Eva Breckon. He also performed in the classical idiom, playing concerts with the Elektra String Quartet and the Western Australian Symphony Orchestra. In the mid-90s Barlow toured Europe with his quintet, playing tenor, flute and the indigenous didgeridoo. He also performed original material with the percussion ensemble Synergy. As a student of the music, Barlow has absorbed many influences but remains an individual stylist, playing with force and elegance, and his commercial success has not negated his creative artistry.

● ALBUMS: *Wizards Of Oz* (Emarcy 1988)★★★, *Hipnotation* (Spiral Scratch 1990)★★★, *Jazz Juice* (Shock 1994)★★★, *Dale Barlow* (ABC 1995)★★★.

Barnard, Bob

b. Robert Graeme Barnard, 24 November 1933, Melbourne, Victoria, Australia. Born into a musical family, Barnard began playing trumpet partly because the family band, led by his father, needed a trumpeter, but also because he had heard and was deeply impressed by a record of Muggsy Spanier. Barnard gained experience playing dance music but listened eagerly to records, notably those by his major influence, Louis Armstrong, and also to popular Australian jazz bands of the 40s, including that led by Graeme Bell. During this period and on into the 50s, Barnard had a day job, in a bank, but played extensively, touring with bands including the one led by his brother, Len Barnard. In 1957 he played in Sydney with a small group led by guitarist Ray Price. Back in Melbourne, he continued to play as a semi-pro, making occasional records, such as *The Naked Dance* with a band led by his brother. In 1957 Bell called him with a job offer in Sydney and, although the gig failed to materialize, Barnard later joined Bell's band. This led to a tour of his home country, and a visit to New Zealand and New Guinea alongside pop singer Frank Ifield. In 1963, Armstrong came to Australia, and Bell's band greeted the visitor at the airport where Barnard played briefly with his idol. In 1971 Barnard formed a band for an EMI Records date which resulted in *16 Jazz Greats*, and three years later he formed his first band. The band played in and around Sydney and in 1976 went to the USA for an appearance at the Bix Beiderbecke Festival at Davenport, Iowa, where they were a huge success. After 10 years, the band's popularity waned slightly and this, allied to the death of a key member, trombonist John Costello, motivated Barnard into cutting down to a quartet. Barnard toured extensively during the 80s and on into the 90s, playing in the USA and UK as well as in southeast Asia and various European countries. He has worked with numerous leading jazz musicians, including Ruby Braff, Peanuts Hucko, Bob Wilber, Kenny Davern, Dick Carey and Milt Hinton, recording albums with the latter pair. He and his brother, Len, also made two fine albums for Sackville Records issued under Ralph Sutton's name, *Partners In Crime* and *Easy Street*. The groups that Barnard formed for recording sessions and other dates varied from quartets to 9- and 10-piece bands and he has also recorded with strings. In the mid-90s Barnard worked on an album, partially funded by the Australian Council for the Arts, on which he celebrates the music of Australian composers. With what Barnard sees as a decline in interest in traditional jazz in his homeland, the end of the 90s saw him planning to spend more time in Europe and the USA. Barnard's playing is notable for his big, rich sound and the consummate ease of his flowing solo lines. Although his name was made, and his fame spread, through his forceful playing in the traditional jazz style this is by no means the extent of his huge talent. This would seem to lie rather in his lyrical mainstream ballad playing that emulates, without any hint of copying, the players he most admires, including Bobby Hackett, Braff, and, of course, Armstrong. Barnard has also composed a number of songs, including 'Black Stump Stomp', 'Smackarooney' and 'Rainbow Hill', an attractive ballad he included on a 1995 album recorded during a visit to New York.

● ALBUMS: *Live At The Sydney Opera House* (La Brava 1977)★★★★, *Count 'Em* (Swaggie 1980)★★★, *Cornet Chop Suey* (Opus 3 1995)★★★, *New York Notes* (Sackville 1995)★★★, *Stardust: Bob Barnard With Strings* 1979 recording (La Brava 1996)★★★, *Bob Barnard Presents Oz Originals* (La Brava 1997)★★★.

BARNARD, LEN

b. Leonard Arthur Bernard, 23 April 1929, Melbourne, Victoria, Australia. After playing drums in the family band, Barnard formed his own traditional jazz band in the late 40s. This band, one of the earliest Australian groups to make jazz records, was so popular that it remained active for more than two decades. During this same period Barnard also played with other groups, ranging through jazz to dance music and he also gigged and recorded with many musicians, including Ade Monsbourgh and Dave Dallwitz. In the early 70s, Barnard relocated to Sydney where he played with many of the country's leading musicians including Errol Buddle and John Sangster, then joined Galapagos Duck, a band led by Tom Hare. He also played on occasion with bands led by his younger brother, Bob Barnard. In the late 90s he was active with many varied artists and appeared on record with several of them, including Janet Seidel. Forceful though his playing is in the more extrovert traditional jazz setting of much of his work, Barnard's discreet and propulsive swing, and his able use of brushes, show him to be an accomplished mainstream drummer.

● ALBUMS: *The Naked Dance* (Swaggie 1961)★★★.

BARNES, ALAN

b. 23 July 1959, Altrincham, Cheshire, England. Between 1977 and 1980, Barnes studied saxophone and woodwind at the Leeds College of Music before moving to London. In the early 80s he played with the Midnite Follies Orchestra and the Pasadena Roof Orchestra, working in London and on a European tour. He stayed with the Pasadena group until 1983 when he joined the hard bop band led by Tommy Chase. The period with Chase attracted considerable attention to Barnes as a rising star of the UK jazz scene. He left Chase in 1986 to join the Jazz Renegades for a three-year stint. With this unit he travelled to Japan and also recorded. While still with the Renegades he began working with Humphrey Lyttelton and in 1989 became leader of the Pizza Express Modern Jazz Sextet. In the early 90s Barnes was still playing with Lyttelton and had also formed his own quartet, which included David Newton, and was co-leader of a quintet with John Barnes (no relation). In addition to the hectic schedule he has set, Barnes has also found time to record with Tommy Whittle, and play with the big bands formed by Bob Wilber for various engagements and with Mike Westbrook's Brass Band and Westbrook Rossini. In addition to his jazz work, Barnes plays regularly with the BBC Radio Orchestra. An outstanding musician with a distinctive and highly melodic style, Barnes is one of the most inventive and original talents to appear in the UK in recent years. His wide-ranging repertoire and arranging and composing skills make him a prospective major jazz voice of the future.

● ALBUMS: *Affiliation* (Miles Music 1987)★★★, with David Newton *Like Minds* (Fret 1993)★★★, *Thirsty Work* (Fret 1994)★★★, *A Sleepin' Bee* (Zephry 1997)★★★, *Here Comes Trouble* (Fret 1997)★★★, *Young Minds Old Hands* (Zephyr 1998)★★★★, with Tony Coe *Days Of Wines And Roses* (Zephyr 1998)★★★★.

BARNES, GEORGE

b. 17 July 1921, Chicago Heights, Illinois, USA, d. 5 September 1977, Concord, California, USA. Although first achieving a measure of national prominence by winning a Tommy Dorsey Amateur Swing Contest in 1937 when he was only 16 years old, Barnes was already a seasoned guitarist. He had previously worked extensively in the Midwest as leader of his own small group. He followed his contest success with a string of recording dates in which he accompanied leading blues singers, among them Big Bill Broonzy, Blind John Davis, Jazz Gillum and Washboard Sam. Interestingly enough, given such classical country blues associations, Barnes had been an early exponent of the electric guitar, which he had taken up in 1931. Apart from his army service, Barnes spent most of the 40s in staff jobs with NBC and ABC in Chicago and with Decca in New York. In the 60s, Barnes worked with fellow guitarists Carl Kress and Bucky Pizzarelli. Known as a decidedly prickly individual, Barnes broke up publicly with Pizzarelli before beginning an equally antagonistic - but musically profound - partnership with cornetist Ruby Braff. Barnes's blues playing was always superb, as was his melodic interpretation of the best standards. He played and recorded many fine examples of his brilliant single-line solos. His duets, especially with Braff and Joe Venuti, reveal an almost supernatural understanding of his fellow musicians. His death, in September 1977, while still very much in his prime, was a great loss to jazz guitar playing.

● ALBUMS: *Two Guitars And A Horn* (1962)★★, with Carl Kress *Something Tender* (1963)★★★★, *Guitars Anyone?* (Carney 1964)★★★★, *Swing Guitar* (Famous Door 1972)★★★, with Ruby Braff *Live At The New School* (Chiaroscuro 1974)★★★★, with Braff *The Ruby Braff/George Barnes Quartet Plays Gershwin* (Concord Jazz 1974)★★★, with Braff *The Ruby Braff/George Barnes Quartet Salutes Rodgers And Hart* (Concord 1974)★★★★, with Braff *To Fred Astaire With Love* (RCA 1975)★★★, with Joe Venuti *Gems* (Concord Jazz 1976)★★★, with Venuti *Joe Venuti-George Barnes Live At The Concord Summer Jazz Festival* (Concord Jazz 1976)★★★★.

● COMPILATIONS: *The Uncollected George Barnes* 1946 recordings (Hindsight 1979)★★★.

BARNES, JOHN

b. 15 May 1932, Manchester, Lancashire, England. Unusually, Barnes began his musical career as both a brass and reed player, but quickly abandoned the flügelhorn in favour of the clarinet. At first he played traditional jazz with the Zenith Six, Mike Daniels' Delta Jazzmen and Alan Elsdon. By the mid-60s, however, when he was with Alex Welsh, Barnes had extended his stylistic range and had also started to play alto, soprano, baritone saxophones and flute. Barnes spent a decade with Welsh, and by the time he left, in 1977, he was widely regarded as the best baritone saxophonist in Europe and one of the best in the world. Since leaving Welsh he has worked with the Midnite Follies Orchestra, Humphrey Lyttelton, as co-leader of a small group with Roy Williams and with numerous visiting American jazz musicians.

● ALBUMS: *Fancy Our Meeting* (Calligraph 1988)★★★.

BARNES, PAUL 'POLO'

b. 22 November 1902, New Orleans, Louisiana, USA. d. 13 April 1981. Born into a musical family, Barnes began playing alto saxophone while still in his teens, later adding soprano saxophone and clarinet. He played with several prominent New Orleans bands, including that led by Papa Celestin. In the late 20s he was a member of King Oliver's band, then worked with a number of bands in New York, including Chick Webb's, before joining Jelly Roll Morton. In 1931 he was again briefly with Oliver, and during the next few years he led his own band, played with various leaders, including yet another spell with Oliver, until the USA's entry into World War II. After the war Barnes spent some time with Celestin and in bands led by Alton Purnell, Paul Barbarin and others. During the 50s and 60s Barnes interspersed periods in New Orleans with long visits to California, sometimes in semi-retirement, at other times playing. He visited Europe in the early 70s but retired before the end of the decade. Polo Barnes played clarinet and soprano with flair and imaginative good taste and his recordings reveal why he was hired by such musical perfectionists as King Oliver and Jelly Roll Morton.

● ALBUMS: *The Viol, The Violet And The Vine* (1960)★★★, *Paul Barnes Quartets* (1969-74)★★★, *Portrait Of A New Orleans Clarinet Player* (1973)★★★.

BARNES, WALTER

b. 8 July 1905, Vicksburg, Mississippi, USA, d. 23 April 1940. Barnes studied clarinet and saxophone before deciding to form his own band in 1926. At first he led only a quartet but this expanded into a bigger band. Barnes and his Royal Creolians played mostly in the Chicago area but also appeared in New York. In the 30s the Royal Creolians were one of the best of the Midwest and south-west territory bands and enjoyed considerable popularity. The band grew in size during the swing era and in 1939 returned to Chicago for an engagement at the city's Savoy Ballroom. On tour in April 1940 the band reached Natchez, Mississippi, for a dance date at the Rhythm Club. The building was built of sheet steel and decorated inside with dried Spanish moss. To avoid people sneaking in without paying, all exit doors were kept locked and the windows barred. The front door was the only way in - or out. This night, a fire started and the hall's ventilation system, a fast-running fan, caused flames and smoke to spread rapidly. Reports describe how Barnes tried to calm the panic by keeping the band playing, but approximately 200 people died, including Barnes and the band, save only the bass player and drummer. The band made few records and these offer only a glimpse of the qualities that made it popular for so many years. Sadly, it is the manner of the band's passing, rather than its music, that keeps its memory alive in jazz history books.

● COMPILATIONS: *Ruff Scufflin' (1927-29)* (Retrieval 1987)★★★.

BARNET, CHARLIE

b. Charles Daly Barnet, 26 October 1913, New York City, New York, USA, d. 4 September 1991. Of all the swing era bandleaders, Barnet was the one most able to do as he pleased. Born into a rich New York family, he played piano and reed instruments while still at school and by his teens had decided that he wanted to play jazz. For a number of years he played on ocean-going liners, often as leader, and also paid his dues in numerous bands across the USA. He formed his first mainland big band in 1933 and, on and off, continued to lead a band throughout the swing era. Barnet could afford to indulge his whims and his musical preferences and did so. Although he lived riotously, marrying six times, he adopted high musical standards and refused to compromise on commercial matters. Barnet was also a leading figure in breaking racial taboos in the hiring of black musicians, and as early as 1935 he had a mixed-race band. Over the years, the roster of black artists hired by

Barnet includes such distinguished names as Frankie Newton, Peanuts Holland, Clark Terry, Charlie Shavers, Lena Horne, Dizzy Gillespie and Trummy Young. Although he never matched the huge popular success of Benny Goodman, Artie Shaw and Tommy Dorsey, Barnet had some hit records including 'Cherokee', 'Things Ain't What They Used to Be' and 'That Old Black Magic'. By the 40s Barnet's was one of the best big bands and he had several more popular records, such as 'Skyliner'. Adept on several saxophones, Barnet favoured the alto, although it was his use of the soprano that helped to give his band its distinctive sound. His arrangers, notably Billy May and Bill Holman, were particularly gifted, but while Barnet's devotion to the music of Duke Ellington ensured that he constantly strove for the highest qualities, he rarely attained the Duke's degree of perfection. By the end of the 40s, Barnet had done all that he wanted in the big band business. He folded his band and became a hotelier. In later years, he periodically formed small groups and big bands for special engagements, usually hiring top-flight musicians such as Conte Candoli, Willie Smith, Nat Pierce, Don Lamond and Al Porcino, all of whom were given free rein to play hard-swinging, big-band jazz. Barnet's autobiography is a no-stone-unturned account of his wild life.

● ALBUMS: *Charlie Barnet Plays Charlie Barnet* 10-inch album (Mercury 1952)★★★★, *Charlie Barnet Plays Charlie Barnet* 10-inch album (Clef 1953)★★★, *Dance With Charlie Barnet* 10-inch album (Clef 1953)★★★, *Charlie Barnet Dance Session, Volume 1* 10-inch album (Clef 1954)★★★, *Charlie Barnet Dance Session, Volume 2* 10-inch album (Clef 1954)★★★, *Hop On The Skyliner* (Decca 1954)★★★, *Rockin' In Rhythm* 10-inch album (RCA Victor 1954)★★★, *Redskin Romp* (RCA Victor 1955)★★★★, *Town Hall Jazz Concert* (Columbia 1955)★★★, *One Night Stand* reissued as *Dancing Party* (Clef 1955)★★★, *Dance Bash* (Verve 1956)★★★, *For Dancing Lovers* (Verve 1956)★★★, *Lonely Street* (Verve 1957)★★★, *Cherokee* (Everest 1958)★★★, *Jazz Oasis* (Capitol 1960)★★★, *Live At Basin Street East* (1966)★★★, *Charlie Barnet Big Band - 1967* (Vault 1967)★★★★.

● COMPILATIONS: *Skyliner* 1942-46 recordings (Affinity 1983)★★★, *The Indispensable Charlie Barnet Volumes 1/2* 1939-40 recordings (Jazz Tribune 1986)★★★★, *The Indispensable Charlie Barnet Volumes 3/4* 1940-41 recordings (Jazz Tribune 1986)★★★★, *Clap Hands Here Comes Charlie* (Bluebird 1988)★★★★, *Cherokee* 1939-41 recordings (Bluebird 1992)★★★, *Drop Me Off In Harlem* 1942-46 recordings (GRP 1992)★★★.

● FURTHER READING: *Those Swinging Years: The Autobiography Of Charlie Barnet*, Charlie Barnet with Stanley Dance.

● FILMS: *The Big Beat* (1957).

BARRETT, DAN

b. 14 December 1955, Pasadena, California, USA. Barrett first took up the trombone as a teenager, encouraged by a teacher named Ken Owen. He began playing professionally while still at high school, sitting in with a traditional band at a local restaurant. In 1977, by now at college, he visited Europe to take part in the Breda Jazz festival in Holland. Barrett continued to play in various parts of California, usually in a traditional jazz setting but with occasional excursions into the mainstream. A meeting with Howard Alden led to thoughts of a group of their own but the time was not yet right for either man. In 1983, he moved to New York City and was soon a member of the Widespread Depression Orchestra, often sitting in at clubs like Eddie Condon's and Jimmy Ryan's. By this time Alden was also in New York and they formed their quintet, a mainstream group with a wide swing-based repertoire, with several of the band's arrangements being supplied by Buck Clayton. The band also uses material originally written for the John Kirby band in the 30s and which was handed on from Kirby's wife, Maxine Sullivan, to Benny Carter and then, via Bill Berry, to Barrett and Alden. Barrett continued to play clubs in New York, working with Ed Polcer, Billy Butterfield, Doc Cheatham, Scott Hamilton, Warren Vaché, Benny Goodman and others. With Alden he has also played in an orchestra formed by Clayton. In the late 80s and early 90s he made several overseas tours, visiting Europe and Japan for festival and club dates, sometimes as a single, with Alden, and also with Dick Hyman, Flip Phillips, Kenny Davern, Jake Hanna and others. A highly accomplished technician, Barrett's love for and dedication to music of an earlier age in no way diminishes his status in the contemporary jazz scene; indeed, in many respects his position is enhanced by his eclecticism. A major new voice in jazz, with an engagingly melodic approach, Barrett is very much a musician for the 90s.

● ALBUMS: with Howard Alden *Swing Street* (Concord Jazz 1986)★★★★, *Strictly Instrumental* (Concord Jazz 1987)★★★, with Alden *The A-B-Q Salutes Buck Clayton* (Concord Jazz 1989)★★★, *Jubilesta!* (1993)★★★, with George Masso *Let's Be Buddies* (Arbors 1994)★★, with Rebecca Kilgore *I Saw Stars* (Arbors 1996)★★★, with Tom Baker *In Australia* (Arbors 1998)★★★.

BARRETT, SWEET EMMA

b. 25 March 1897, New Orleans, Louisiana, USA, d. 28 January 1983. After deciding upon a musical career, Barrett played piano in a number of New Orleans bands during the 20s including that led by Papa Celestin. She continued working in New Orleans bands during the 30s and 40s, with units such as those led by Sidney Desvigne and John Robichaux. In the 50s she worked with Percy Humphrey and Israel Gorman and also led her own band of New Orleans veterans, sometimes touring. In the 60s she suffered periods of ill-health but even a stroke did not stop her. Somewhat flamboyant in her younger days, she was known as the Bell Gal because of her habit of wearing bells on her garters. In her later years she developed rather grandiose ideas about her abilities. She took it as a sign of her due that during one tour her musicians clustered at one side of the stage, leaving her in isolated splendour at the other, oblivious to the fact that they were eager to stay as far away as possible from the odour of an unclean dressing on her injured foot. For all her eccentricities, however,

Barrett helped perpetuate the music of her home-town with unending enthusiasm.

● ALBUMS: *Sweet Emma* (Riverside 1960)★★★, *The Bell Gal And Her Dixieland Boys* (1961)★★★, *Sweet Emma Barrett And Her New Orleans Music* (1963)★★★, *Sweet Emma Barrett At Disneyland* (1964)★★, *Sweet Emma Barrett And Her Preservation Hall Jazz Band* (1964)★★★, *The Bell Gal And Her New Orleans Jazz Band* (1966)★★★, *Sweet Emma Barrett And Her Original Tuxedo Jass Band At Dixieland Hall* (1968)★★.

Barretto, Ray

b. 29 April 1929, Brooklyn, New York City, of Puerto Rican parentage. Barretto, raised in East Harlem and the Bronx, has been a prominent Latin bandleader for three decades. However, he started his professional career even earlier as a jazz recording session conga player. To escape the ghetto he joined the army at 17. Influenced by a record of Dizzy Gillespie with conguero Chano Pozo, Barretto started to sit in on jam sessions held at the Orlando, a GI jazz club in Munich, Germany. After military service he returned to Harlem and attended more jam sessions, studied percussion and rediscovered his Latin roots. From then on he retained a foot in both the jazz and Latin camps. Barretto jammed with Charlie Parker, Max Roach, Art Blakey and other jazz giants and recorded with Lou Donaldson, Gene Ammons, Red Garland, Eddie 'Lockjaw' Davis, Dizzy, Cannonball Adderley, Freddie Hubbard, Cal Tjader, Sonny Stitt and others. He has also sessioned with the Rolling Stones, Average White Band, Bee Gees and Bette Midler.

Barretto's first regular job was with Eddie Bonnemere's Latin Jazz Combo, followed by two years with Cuban bandleader/pianist José Curbelo. In 1957 he replaced Mongo Santamaría in Tito Puente's band, the night before the recording of *Dance Mania,* Puente's classic and best-selling album. After four years with Puente, he did a brief four-month stint with Herbie Mann. Barretto had his first leadership opportunity in 1961 when Orrin Keepnews of Riverside Records, who knew Barretto through his jazz work, asked him to form a charanga (a flute and violin band, which were highly popular at the time) for a recording date. The outcome was the album *Pachanga With Barretto,* followed by the Latin jam *Latino* (1962), on which Barretto's charanga was augmented by tenor saxophonist José 'Chombo' Silva and trumpeter Alejandro 'El Negro' Vivar (1923-79), both graduates of the historic 50s *Cuban Jam Session* albums on the Panart label. *Latino* contained the outstanding descarga (jam session) 'Cocinando Suave', described by Barretto as '. . . one of those slow burners' and cited by Chombo as one of his favourite recordings (both quoted by Latin music historian Max Salazar).

In 1962, Barretto switched to the Tico label and released the album *Charanga Moderna.* The track 'El Watusi' reached the Top 20 US pop chart in 1963 and sold a million. 'After "El Watusi", I was neither fish nor fowl - neither a good Latin nor good pop artist', he was later said. His next eight albums between 1963 and 1966 thrashed around in various directions and consistently eluded commercial success. The musical merit of some of his recorded work from this period was not appreciated until years later. His fortunes changed when he signed to Fania Records in 1967. He dropped violins for an all-brass frontline and made the R&B- and jazz-flavoured *Acid,* which won him major popularity among Latin audiences for the first time. Barretto's next nine albums on Fania between 1968 and 1975 were increasingly successful, the only body-blow being in late 1972 when his vocalist since 1966, Adalberto Santiago, and four other band members, left to found Típica 73. The title track of his 1973 *Indestructible* was aimed at his ex-accompanists; replacement lead vocalist Tito Allen sang of a blood transfusion making Barretto indestructible to any harm and Barretto is pictured as Clark Kent revealing his Superman costume on the album sleeve. His 1975 album, *Barretto,* with vocalists Rubén Blades and Tito Gómez (see Papo Lucca, Nati and Grupo Niche), was his biggest seller to date. It contained the prize-winning hit 'Guarare' and was nominated for a Grammy Award in 1976. He was also voted 'Best Conga Player of the Year' for 1975 and 1976 in *Latin NY* magazine annual poll. Meanwhile, Barretto had tired of gruelling daily night-club gigging and felt that clubs stifled creativity and gave no room for experimentation. He was also pessimistic that pure salsa could cross over to a wider audience. On New Year's Eve 1975, he played his last date with his salsa band. They continued under the name Guarare and released three albums - *Guarare* (1977), *Guarare* (1979) and *Onda Típica* (1981).

Barretto organized a fusion-orientated concert band. An agreement was struck between Fania and Atlantic Records and the first release on his new label was *Barretto Live: Tomorrow,* a two-disc recording of his successful debut concert at the Beacon Theatre, New York in May 1976. Barretto's 1977 and 1978 albums were his last on Atlantic. However, he still managed to win the *Latin NY* titles for 'Musician of the Year' and 'Best Conga Player of Year' in October 1977. However, his fusion band turned out to be a commercial flop, as he injured a hand and was unable to play for a while. In 1979 he went back to Fania and reunited with Adalberto Santiago to produce *Rican/Struction,* a return to progressive salsa. The album was a smash hit and won him the 1980 *Latin NY* titles for 'Album of the Year', 'Musician of the Year' and 'Best Conga Player'. Two albums, *Giant Force/Fuerza Gigante* (1980) and *Rhythm of Life/Ritmo de la Vida* (1982), featured the impressive voice of ex-Guarare lead singer, Ray de la Paz (see Louie Ramírez), and talented young New York-born Latino trombonist, Joe de Jesús. In 1983, Barretto teamed up with Celia Cruz and Adalberto to make the highly successful *Tremendo Trio!,* which won an ACE (The Hispanic Association of Entertainment Critics of New York) Award for 'Salsa Album of the Year'. The superb *Todo Se Vá Poder* (1984) and *Aquí Se Puede* (1987) included ex-Los Kimy singer Ray Saba (aka Del Rey Xaba) on lead vocals. Barretto and Cruz's second collaboration, *Ritmo En El Corazón,* released at the end of 1988 and issued in the UK on the Caliente label in 1989, won them a Grammy award in 1990. He joined the salsa romántica bandwagon with the weak album *Irresistible* (1989), his last on Fania. Saba, who only sang in the chorus on Barretto's 1988 and 1989 albums, launched a solo career with the album *Necesito Una Mirada Tuya* (1990) produced by former Los Kimy leader, Kimmy Solis. Since the late 80s On 30 August 1990, to mark his long-standing involvement in both jazz and Latin music, Barretto appeared with Adalberto and Puerto Rican trumpeter Juancito Torres at a tribute concert titled 'Las 2 Vidas de Ray Barretto' (The Two Lives of Ray Barretto) at the University of Puerto Rico. He switched to Concord Picante for the 1991 Latin jazz set *Handprints*. Barretto has been a member of the Fania All Stars since their inception in 1968.

● ALBUMS: *Pachanga With Barretto* (Riverside 1961)★★★★, *Latino* (Riverside 1962)★★★★, *Charanga Moderna* (Tico 1962)★★★★, *On Fire Again* (Tico 1963)★★★, *The Big Hits Latin Style* (Tico 1963)★★★, *La Moderna de Siempre* (Tico 1964)★★★, *Guajira Y Guaguanco* (Tico 1964)★★★, *Viva Watusi!* (Tico 1965)★★★, *Señor 007* (Tico 1965)★★★, *El Ray Criollo* (Tico 1966)★★★, *Latino Con Soul* (Tico 1966)★★★, *Acid* (Fania 1967)★★★, *Hard Hands* (Fania 1968)★★★, *Together* (Fania 1969)★★★, *Head Sounds* (Fania 1969)★★★, *Power* (Fania 1970)★★★, *The Message* (Fania 1971)★★★, *Que Viva La Musica* (Fania 1972)★★★, *Carnaval* reissue of first two albums (Fantasy 1973)★★★★, *The Other Road* (Fania 1973)★★★, *Indestructible* (Fania 1973)★★★, *Barretto* (Fania 1975)★★★, *Barretto Live: Tomorrow* (Atlantic 1976)★★★, *Eye Of The Beholder* (Atlantic 1977)★★★, *Can You Feel It* (Atlantic 1978)★★★, *Gracias* (Atlantic 1979)★★★, *Rican/Struction* (Fania 1979)★★★, *Giant Force/Fuerza Gigante* (Fania 1980)★★★, *La Cuna* (CTI 1981)★★★, *Rhythm Of Life/Ritmo De La Vida* (Fania 1982)★★★, with Celia Cruz, Adalberto Santiago *Tremendo Trio!* (1983)★★★★, *Todo Se Vá Poder* (Fania 1984)★★★★, *Aquí Se Puede* (Fania 1987)★★★★, with Celia Cruz *Ritmo En El Corazón* (Fania 1988)★★★★, *Irresistible* (Fania 1989)★★, *Handprints* (Concord 1991)★★, *Live In New York* (Messidor 1992)★★★, *Ancestral Messages* (Concord 1993)★★★, *My Summertime* (Owl/Blue Note 1996)★★★, with New World Spirit *Contact!* (Blue Note 1998)★★★★.

BARRITEAU, CARL

b. 7 February 1914, Trinidad, West Indies, d. 24 August 1998, Sydney, New South Wales, Australia. Raised in Venezuela, Barriteau learned music in the Trinidad Police Band, becoming proficient on clarinet and alto saxophone. He came to prominence in Britain as principal soloist and musical director for Ken 'Snakehips' Johnson, for whom he arranged 'Exactly Like You' (1938) and soloed on 'Tuxedo Junction' (1940). In 1941, he led one of two contingents at the First English Public Jam Session, where two highly influential couplings were recorded for HMV Records. Following the death of Johnson, Barriteau led the band for a broadcast and live dates, while continuing to perform as a soloist and in the reed section of notable big bands such as those led by Ambrose, Geraldo, Joe Loss, Lew Stone and Eric Winstone. Finally he formed his own band in an attempt to recreate Johnson's success but, with inadequate financial backing, was frequently forced to rely on pick-up personnel. For a while he maintained an all-white big band, and with them recorded 'Ol' Man Mose' (1944), 'A Sultan Goes To Harlem' (1945) and, with Artie Shaw's special permission, his virtuoso 'Concerto For Clarinet'. A fluent soloist on his first instrument and also a warm saxophonist in the Johnny Hodges mould, Barriteau topped the *Melody Maker* clarinet poll seven times. During the 60s he moved to Germany, and finally settled in Australia with his vocalist wife Mae Cooper in 1970.

BARRON, BILL

b. 27 March 1927, Philadelphia, Pennsylvania, USA, d. 21 September 1989. The older brother of Kenny Barron, he established his reputation in his home-town as a distinctive saxophone stylist. Strongly influenced by Dexter Gordon, he first came to national prominence in the late 50s playing and recording with Cecil Taylor. In 1962 he formed and co-led a quartet with Ted Curson, also a former Taylor sideman. To gain recognition, the group played mostly in Europe but from 1968 Barron was active in New York as director of the Muse Jazz Workshop, part of an educational programme. A distinguished teacher, he was also associated with City College of New York and in 1984 took the chair of the music department at Wesleyan University. He was also a composer of merit.

● ALBUMS: *The Tenor Stylings Of Bill Barron* (Savoy 1961)★★★, *Modern Windows* (Savoy 1962)★★★, *West Side Story Bossa Nova* (Dauntless 1963)★★, with Ted Curson *The Leopard* (Audiophile 1963)★★★, with Curson *Tears For Dolphy* (Fontana 1964)★★★, *Now Hear This* (Audio Fidelity 1964)★★★, *Hot Line* (Savoy 1964)★★★★, *Motivation* (Savoy 1972)★★★, *Jazz Caper* (Muse 1978)★★★, *Variations In Blue* (Muse 1984)★★★★, *The Next Plateau* (Muse 1987)★★★, *Nebulae* (Savoy 1988)★★★, *Higher Ground* (Joken 1996)★★★.

BARRON, KENNY

b. 9 June 1943, Philadelphia, Pennsylvania, USA. After studying piano as a child, Barron began playing professionally when still in his early teens. Performing first in R&B bands, he began to concentrate on jazz, and in the late 50s and early 60s played briefly with Philly Joe Jones and Yusef Lateef. From 1961, he was resident in New York, playing with James Moody, Lee Morgan, his older brother Bill Barron, a saxophonist, and then joined Dizzy Gillespie for an association that lasted until 1966. During his sojourn with Gillespie he toured extensively. In the late 60s he was briefly with Stanley Turrentine and then spent two years with Freddie Hubbard, following this engagement with a long stint with Lateef. By this time Barron had become established as a composer and teacher and in 1973 was appointed to a senior post at Rutgers University. During this same period he also worked with Ron Carter. In the 80s he continued teaching, writing and playing, co-leading the group Sphere, which featured Charlie Rouse, Buster Williams and Ben Riley, and recording with Frank Wess and others. He then enjoyed a long and deeply satisfying musical relationship with Stan Getz, playing on several notable albums. He has also proved to be a sensitive accompanist for singers including Judy Niemack, Sathima Bea Benjamin and Teresa Brewer. Although he has enjoyed a high profile among musicians, appearing in the rhythm sections of many bands on numerous albums, Barron's main contribution to jazz might well prove to be his teaching and composing, even though he received the Best Piano award in the *Jazz Times* poll in 1995. In 1998 he recorded with Sphere again, with Gary Bartz replacing the deceased Rouse.

● ALBUMS: *Sunset To Dawn* (Muse 1973)★★★, *Peruvian Blue* (Muse 1974)★★★, with Ted Dunbar *In Tandem* (Muse 1975)★★★, *Lucifer* (Muse 1975)★★★, with Tommy Flanagan *Together With Kenny Barron* (Denon 1978)★★★★, *Golden Lotus* (Muse 1980)★★★, *At The Piano* (Xanadu 1981)★★★, with Sphere *Four In One* (Elektra Musician 1982)★★★★, *Green Chimneys* (Criss Cross 1983)★★★★, with Sphere *Flight Path* (Elektra Musician 1983)★★★, *1+1+1* (Black Hawk 1984)★★★, *Landscape* (Limetree 1984)★★★, with Sphere *Sphere On Tour* (Red 1985)★★★, *Scratch* (Enja 1985)★★★, *What If?* (Enja 1986)★★★, with Red Mitchell *The Red Barron Duo* (Storyville 1986)★★★, with Sphere *Four For All* (Verve 1987)★★★, with Sphere *Bird Songs* (Verve 1988)★★★★, *Live At Fat Tuesday's* (Enja 1988)★★★, *Rhythm-A-Ning* (Candid 1989)★★, with Mitchell, Ben Riley *Talking* (Capri 1989)★★★ *Quickstep* (Enja 1991)★★★, *Invitation* (Criss Cross 1991)★★★, *Lemuria-Seascape* (Candid 1991)★★★, *The Only One* (1993)★★★★, *Sambao* (PolyGram 1993)★★, *Other Places* (Verve 1994)★★★★, with Roy Haynes, Charlie Haden *Wanton Spirit* (Verve 1994)★★★, with Mino Cinelu *Swamp Sally* (Verve 1996)★★★, *Things Unseen* (Verve 1997)★★★, with Haden *Night And The City* (Verve 1998)★★★★, with Sphere *Sphere* (Verve 1998)★★★.

Bartz, Gary

b. 26 September 1940, Baltimore, Maryland, USA. Bartz, whose father ran a jazz club, began playing alto saxophone at the age of 11. He played in the Alabama State Teachers College band, at his father's club, and studied at the Juilliard School, New York, and the Peabody Conservatory in Baltimore. He worked with Lee Morgan and Grachan Moncur III, but his first regular professional engagement was with the Max Roach/Abbey Lincoln band in 1964. From 1965-66 he was one of Art Blakey's Jazz Messengers, then had a second stint with Roach and periods with Charles Tolliver, Blue Mitchell and McCoy Tyner (in what Tyner once described as the happiest and most integrated band he had ever led). For 18 months beginning in August 1970 he was with Miles Davis (*Live - Evil*), in 1972 formed Nu Troop, and during the 70s moved further into the funk fusion field. In recent years he has returned to the hard bop fold, a genre that shows off his assertive and agile improvising to best advantage. Originally inspired to take up the saxophone by hearing Charlie Parker, he has helped to keep the succession alive, and his playing is in the tradition of Phil Woods and, especially, Jackie McLean, with whom he has made some fine music (*Ode To Super*). *There Goes The Neighborhood* is an exceptional album. Recorded live at New York's famous Birdland Club in November 1990, it is a vivid record from one of modern jazz's most intense and exciting living saxophonists, playing at his peak. Pianist Kenny Barron, bassist Ray Drummond and drummer Ben Riley offer firm support for Bartz's powerful, plaintive alto, as he powers his way through a well-chosen programme of standards and original tunes. Bartz, by this time, had overcome his bland jazz/pop flirtation, and was playing a strong combination of neo-bop and heavy, John Coltrane-influenced shapes. The inspired version of 'Impressions' is not to be missed. In 1998 Bartz was recruited into the ranks of the Thelonious Monk tribute band Sphere, as a replacement for the late Charlie Rouse.

● ALBUMS: *Libra* (Milestone 1967)★★★, *Another Earth* (Milestone 1968)★★★★, *Home!* (Milestone 1969)★★★, *Harlem Bush Music - Taifa* (Milestone 1970)★★★, *Harlem Bush Music - Uhuru* (1971)★★★, *Follow The Medicine Man* (Prestige 1972)★★★, *Ju-Ju Street Songs* (Prestige 1972)★★★, with Jackie McLean *Ode To Super* (Steeple Chase 1973)★★★★, *I've Known Rivers And Other Bodies* (Prestige 1974)★★★, *Singarella - A Ghetto Fairytale* (Prestige 1974)★★★, *The Shadow Do* (1975)★★★, *Music Is My Sanctuary* (Capitol 1975)★★★, *Ju-Ju Man* (Catalyst 1976)★★★, *Love Affair* (VJ 1978)★★, *Bartz* (Arista 1980)★★, *Monsoon* (Steeple Chase 1988)★★★, *Reflections Of Monk* (Steeple Chase 1989)★★, *West 42nd Street* (Candid 1990)★★★★, with Cosmo Intini *My Favourite Roots* (1990)★★★, *There Goes The Neighborhood* (Candid 1991)★★★★, *Shadows* (JSP 1992)★★★★, *Episode One: Children Of Harlem* (Jazz Challenge 1994)★★★, *Red & Orange Poems* (Atlantic 1995)★★★, with Sonny Fortune *Alto Memories* (Verve 1995)★★★, *The Blues Chronicles: Tales Of Life* (Atlantic 1996)★★★, with Sphere *Sphere* (Verve 1998)★★★.

Bascomb, Dud

b. Wilbur Odell Bascomb, 16 May 1916, Birmingham, Alabama, USA, d. 25 December 1972. Bascomb began learning trumpet while still in school and after graduation, he continued to play as a member of the 'Bama State Collegians. In 1934 the Collegians became a professional band under the leadership of Erskine Hawkins, with whom Bascomb remained until 1944. He then co-led a small group and a big band with his brother, Paul Bascomb. In the late 40s Bascomb worked with Duke Ellington and throughout the 50s and 60s continued to work, in a series of small groups, usually as leader, though one notable 1968 band was led by Buddy Tate. A sophisticated and melodic player, Bascomb's ability was for a long time overshadowed, especially through the years he spent with Hawkins, who did not allow other trumpet stars to shine in his company. Bascomb, who was co-composer of the classic 'Tuxedo Junction', died on Christmas Day 1972. His son, Dud Jnr., is a bass player.

Bascomb, Paul

b. 12 February 1910, Birmingham, Alabama, USA, d. 2 December 1986, Chicago, Illinois, USA. One of three musical brothers - Arthur (piano) and Dud Bascomb (trumpet) - Paul played tenor saxophone with the Bama State Collegians, which later became the Erskine Hawkins band. Bascomb stayed with Hawkins for several years although he occasionally had outside jobs, including deputizing in the Count Basie band in 1941. He left Hawkins in 1944 to co-lead various bands with his brother Dud. In the 50s and 60s Bascomb led his own groups in Chicago and New York. He continued playing into the 70s and 80s, including visits to European festivals.

● COMPILATIONS: *Bad Bascomb* (Delmark 1952)★★★.

Basie, Count

b. William Basie, 21 August 1904, Red Bank, New Jersey, USA, d. 26 April 1984, Hollywood, California, USA. Bandleader and pianist Basie grew up in Red Bank, just across the Hudson River from New York City. His mother gave him his first lessons at the piano, and he used every opportunity to hear the celebrated kings of New York keyboard - James P. Johnson, Willie 'The Lion' Smith and especially Fats Waller. Ragtime was all the rage, and these keyboard professors ransacked the European tradition to achieve ever more spectacular improvisations. The young Basie listened to Fats Waller playing the organ in Harlem's Lincoln Theater and received tuition from him. Pianists were in demand to accompany vaudeville acts, and Waller recommended Basie as his successor in the Katie Crippen And Her Kids troupe, and with them he toured black venues throughout America (often referred to as the 'chitlin' circuit'). Stranded in Kansas City after the Gonzel White tour collapsed, Basie found it 'wide-open'. Owing to the *laissez-faire* administration of Democrat leader Tom Pendergast, musicians could easily find work, and jazz blossomed alongside gambling and prostitution (many people trace the origins of modern jazz to these circumstances - see Kansas City Jazz). Basie played accompaniment for silent movies for a while, then in 1928 joined Walter Page's Blue Devils, starting a 20-year-long association with the bassist. When the Blue Devils broke up, Basie joined Bennie Moten, then in 1935, started his own band at the Reno Club and quickly lured Moten's best musicians into its ranks. Unfettered drinking hours, regular broadcasts on local radio and Basie's feel for swing honed the band into quite simply the most classy and propulsive unit in the history of music. Duke Ellington's band may have been more ambitious, but for sheer unstoppable *swing* Basie could not be beaten. Impresario John Hammond recognized as much when he heard them on their local broadcast. In January 1937 an augmented Basie band made its recording debut for Decca Records. By this time the classic rhythm section - Freddie Green (guitar), Walter Page (bass) and Jo Jones (drums) - had been established. The horns - which included Lester Young (tenor saxophone) and Buck Clayton (trumpet) - sounded magnificent buoyed by this team and the goadings of Basie's deceptively simple piano. Basie frequently called himself a 'non-pianist'; actually, his incisive minimalism had great power and influence - not least on Thelonious Monk, one of bebop's principal architects.
In 1938, the band recorded the classic track 'Jumpin' At The Woodside', a Basie composition featuring solos by Earle Warren (alto saxophone) and Herschel Evans (clarinet), as well as Young and Clayton. The track could be taken as a definition of swing. Basie's residency at the Famous Door club on New York's West 52nd Street from July 1938 to January 1939 was a great success, CBS broadcasting the band over its radio network (transcriptions of these broadcasts have recently been made available - although hardly hi-fi, they are fascinating documents, with Lester Young playing clarinet as well as tenor). This booking was followed by a six-month residency in Chicago. It is this kind of regular work - spontaneity balanced with regular application - that explains why the recorded sides of the period are some of the great music of the century.

In 1939 Basie left Decca for Columbia Records, with whom he stayed until 1946. Throughout the 40s the Count Basie band provided dancers with conducive rhythms and jazz fans with astonishing solos: both appreciated his characteristic contrast of brass and reeds. Outstanding tenors emerged: Don Byas, Buddy Tate, Lucky Thompson, Illinois Jacquet, Paul Gonsalves, as well as trumpeters (Al Killian and Joe Newman) and trombonists (Vic Dickenson and J.J. Johnson). On vocals Basie used Jimmy Rushing for the blues material and Helen Humes for pop and novelty numbers. Economic necessity pared down the Basie band to seven members at the start of the 50s, but otherwise Basie maintained a big band right through to his death in 1984. In 1954 he made his first tour of Europe, using arrangements by Ernie Wilkins and Neal Hefti. In June 1957 Basie broke the colour bar at New York's Waldorf-Astoria Hotel; his was the first black band to play there, and they stayed for a four-month engagement. The 1957 *The Atomic Mr. Basie* set Hefti's arrangements in glorious stereo sound and was acknowledged as a classic. Even the cover made its mark: in the 70s Blondie adapted its period nuclear-chic to frame singer Deborah Harry.

In 1960, Jimmy Rushing left the band, depriving it of a popular frontman, but the European tours continued - a groundbreaking tour of Japan in 1963 was also a great success. Count Basie was embraced by the American entertainment industry and appeared in the films *Sex And The Single Girl* and *Made In Paris*. He became a regular television guest alongside the likes of Frank Sinatra, Fred Astaire, Sammy Davis Jnr. and Tony Bennett. Arranging for Basie was a significant step in the career of Quincy Jones (later famous as Michael Jackson's producer). The onslaught of the Beatles and rock music in the 60s was giving jazz a hard time; Basie responded by giving current pop tunes the big band treatment, and Jones arranged *Hits Of The 50s And 60s*. Its resounding commercial success led to a string of similar albums arranged by Billy Byers; the brass adopted the stridency of John Barry's James Bond scores and, unlike the work of the previous decades, these records now sound dated. In 1965, Basie signed to

Sinatra's Reprise Records, and made several recordings and appearances with him.

By 1969 most of Basie's original sidemen had left the band, though Freddie Green was still with him. Eddie 'Lockjaw' Davis (tenor) was now his most distinguished soloist. The arranger Sammy Nestico provided some interesting compositions, and 1970 saw the release of *Afrique*, an intriguing and unconventional album arranged by Oliver Nelson with tunes by *avant garde* saxophonists such as Albert Ayler and Pharoah Sanders. In 1975, after recording for a slew of different labels, Basie found a home on Pablo Records (owned by Norman Granz, organizer of the Jazz At The Philharmonic showcases). This produced a late flowering, as, unlike previous producers, Granz let Basie do what he does best - swing the blues - rather than collaborate with popular singers. In 1983, the death of his wife Catherine, whom he had married 40 years earlier while he was with the Bennie Moten band, struck a heavy blow and he himself died the following year.

The later compromises should not cloud Basie's achievements: during the 30s he integrated the bounce of the blues into sophisticated ensemble playing. His piano work showed that rhythm and space were more important than technical virtuosity: his composing gave many eminent soloists their finest moments. Without the Count Basie Orchestra's sublimely aerated versions of 'Cherokee' it is unlikely that Charlie Parker could ever have created 'Koko'. Modern jazz stands indubitably in Basie's debt. For newcomers to the work of Basie the *Original American Decca Recordings* is an unbeatable starting point.

● ALBUMS: *Dance Parade* 10-inch album (Columbia 1949)★★★★, *Count Basie At The Piano* 10-inch album (Decca 1950)★★★, with Lester Young *Lester Young Quartet And Count Basie Seven* 10-inch album (Mercury 1950)★★★★, with Young *Count Basie And Lester Young* 10-inch album (Jazz Panorama 1951)★★★★, *Count Basie and the Kansas City 7* (Mercury 1952)★★★, *Count Basie And His Orchestra Collates* (Mercury 1952)★★★, *Jazz Royalty* 10-inch album (EmArcy 1954)★★★, *Count Basie And His Orchestra* (Decca 1954)★★★★, *The Old Count And The New Count - Basie* 10-inch album (Epic 1954)★★★, *Basie Jazz* (Clef 1954)★★★★, *Rock The Blues* 10-inch album (Epic 1954)★★★★, *Count Basie Sextet* (Clef 1954)★★★, *Count Basie Big Band* (Clef 1954)★★★★, *Count Basie Dance Session 1* (Clef 1954)★★★, *Count Basie* i (RCA Victor 1955)★★★★, *Lester Leaps In* (Epic 1955)★★★, *Let's Go To Prez* (Epic 1955)★★★★, *Count Basie Dance Session 2* (Clef 1955)★★★, *Basie's Back In Town* (Epic 1955)★★★, *Classics* (Columbia 1955)★★★, with Joe Williams *A Night At Count Basie's* (Vanguard 1955)★★★, with Williams *Count Basie Swings/Joe Williams Sings* (Clef 1955)★★★★, with Williams *The Greatest! Count Basie Swings/Joe Williams Sings Standards* (Verve 1956)★★★★, *Basie Bash* (Columbia 1956)★★★★, *Basie* (Clef 1956)★★★★, *Blues By Basie* 1939-1950 recordings (Columbia 1956)★★★★, with Ella Fitzgerald, Williams *One O'Clock Jump* (Columbia 1956)★★★★, *Count Basie* ii (Brunswick 1956)★★★, *The Count* (Clef 1956)★★★★, *The Swinging Count* (Clef 1956)★★★, *The Band Of Distinction* (Clef 1956)★★★, *Basie Roars Again* (Clef 1956)★★★★, *The King Of Swing* (Clef 1956)★★★, *Basie Rides Again* (Clef 1956)★★★, *Basie In Europe* (Clef 1956)★★★, *Count Basie* iii (American Record Society 1956)★★★, *April In Paris* (Verve 1957)★★★★★, *Basie's Best* (American Record Society 1957)★★★★, *Count Basie In London* (Verve 1957)★★★, *Count Basie At Newport* (Verve 1957)★★★★★, *The Atomic Mr Basie* (Roulette 1957)★★★★★, *Basie Plays Hefti* (Roulette 1958)★★★★, *Sing Along With Basie* (Roulette 1958)★★★, with Dizzy Gillespie *Dizzy Gillespie And Count Basie At Newport* (Verve 1958)★★★★, *Hall Of Fame* (Verve 1958)★★★, with Tony Bennett *Basie Swings, Bennett Sings* (Roulette 1958)★★★★, *One More Time* (Roulette 1959)★★★★, *Breakfast Dance And Barbecue* (Roulette 1959)★★★, with Billy Eckstine *Basie/Eckstine Inc.* (Roulette 1959)★★★★, *Chairman Of The Board* (Roulette 1959)★★★, with Williams *Memories Ad Lib* (Roulette 1959)★★★, with Williams *Everyday I Have The Blues* (Roulette 1959)★★★★, with Bennett *Tony Bennett In Person* (Columbia 1959)★★★, *Dance With Basie* (Roulette 1959)★★★★, *Not Now I'll Tell You When* (Roulette 1960)★★★, with Williams *Just The Blues* (Roulette 1960)★★★★, *String Along With Basie* (Roulette 1960)★★★, with Benny Carter *Kansas City Suite: The Music Of Benny Carter* (Roulette 1960)★★★★, with Sarah Vaughan *Count Basie/Sarah Vaughan* (Roulette 1960)★★★★, *The Count Basie Story* (Roulette 1961)★★★★, *The Essential Count Basie* (Verve 1961)★★★★, with Gillespie *First Time! The Count Meets The Duke* (Columbia 1961)★★★★, *Basie At Birdland* (Roulette 1961)★★★★, with Bennett *Bennett And Basie Strike Up The Band* (Roulette 1962)★★, *The Legend* (Roulette 1962)★★★, *Count Basie And The Kansas City 7* (Impulse! 1962)★★★, *The Best Of Basie Volume 2* (Roulette 1962)★★★, *Count Basie Live In Sweden* (Roulette 1962)★★★, with Fitzgerald *Ella And Basie!* (Verve 1963)★★★★, *Easin' It* (Roulette 1963)★★★, *This Time By Basie!* (Reprise 1963)★★★, *On My Way And Shouting Again* (Verve 1963)★★★★, *Lil' Ol' Groovemaker ... Basie* (Verve 1963)★★★, *More Hits Of The 50s And 60s* reissued as *Frankly Basie: Count Basie Plays The Hits Of Frank Sinatra* (Verve 1963)★★★, *Basie Land* (Verve 1964)★★★, *Our Shining Hour* (Verve 1964)★★★, *Basie Picks The Winners* (Verve 1965)★★★, with Arthur Prysock *Prysock/Basie* (Verve 1965)★★★, *Pop Goes The Basie* (Reprise 1965)★★★, *Basie's Bounce* (Affinity 1965)★★★, *Basie's Beatle Bag* (Verve 1966)★★★, *Basie's Swingin' Voices Singin'* (ABC-Paramount 1966)★★★, *Basie Meets Bond* (United 1966)★★★, *Inside Outside* (Verve 1966)★★★, *Basie's Beat* (Verve 1967)★★★★, *Live In Antibes 1968* (Esoldun 1968)★★★★, *Standing Ovation* (Dot 1968)★★★, *High Voltage* (Verve 1970)★★★, *Afrique* (Doctor Jazz 1971)★★★, *At The Chatterbox* 1937 recordings (Jazz Archives 1974)★★★, *Basie Jam, Vol. 1* (Pablo 1974)★★★, with Big Joe Turner *The Bosses* (Pablo 1974)★★★, *For The First Time* (Pablo 1974)★★★, with Oscar Peterson *Satch And Josh* (Pablo 1975)★★★, with Zoot Sims *Basie And Zoot* (Pablo 1975)★★★★, *Basie Jam At Montreux '75* (Pablo 1975)★★★, *Fun Time: Count Basie Big Band At Montreux '75* (Pablo 1975)★★★, *The Basie Big Band* (Pablo 1975)★★★, *For The Second Time* (Pablo 1975)★★★, *I Told You So* (Pablo 1976)★★★★, *Basie Jam, Vol. 2* (Pablo 1976)★★★, *Basie Jam, Vol. 3* (Pablo 1976)★★★, *Prime Time* (Pablo 1977)★★★★, *Kansas City, Vol. 5* (Pablo 1977)★★★, with Gillespie *The Gifted Ones* (Pablo 1977)★★★, *Basie Jam: Montreux '77* (Pablo 1977)★★★, *Basie Big Band: Montreux '77* (Pablo 1977)★★★, with Peterson *Satch And Josh ... Again* (Pablo

1977)★★★, with Peterson *Yessir, That's My Baby* (Pablo 1978)★★★, with Peterson *Night Rider* (Pablo 1978)★★★, with Peterson *The Timekeepers* (Pablo 1978)★★★, *Live In Japan* (Pablo 1978)★★★, with Fitzgerald *A Classy Pair* (Pablo 1979)★★★, with Fitzgerald *A Perfect Match: Basie And Ella* (Pablo 1979)★★★, *On The Road* (Pablo 1980)★★★, *Get Together* (Pablo 1980)★★★, *Kansas City, Vol. 7* (Pablo 1980)★★★, *Kansas City Shout* (Pablo 1980)★★★, *Warm Breeze* (Pablo 1981)★★★, *Farmers Market Barbecue* (Pablo 1982)★★★, *Me And You* (Pablo 1983)★★★, *88 Basie Street* (Pablo 1983)★★★, *Mostly Blues ... And Some Others* (Pablo 1983)★★★, *Fancy Pants* (Pablo 1984)★★★, with Roy Eldridge *Loose Walk* 1972 recording (Pablo 1992)★★★, the Count Basie Orchestra Directed By Grover Mitchell *Count Plays Duke* (MAMA 1998)★★★.

● COMPILATIONS: with Bennie Moten *Count Basie In Kansas City* 1929-1932 recordings (Camden 1959)★★★★, *Basie's Basement* 1929-1932 recordings (Camden 1959)★★★★, *Verve's Choice - The Best Of Count Basie* (Verve 1963)★★★★, *The World Of Count Basie* 3-LP set (Roulette 1964)★★★, *Super Chief* 1936-1942 recordings (Columbia 1972)★★★, *Good Morning Blues* 1937-1939 recordings (MCA 1977)★★★, *Basie And Friends* 1974-1981 recordings (Pablo 1982)★★★, *Birdland Era, Volumes 1 & 2* (Duke 1986)★★★★, *The Essential Count Basie, Volume 1* 1936-1939 recordings (Columbia 1987)★★★★, *The Essential Count Basie, Volume 2* 1939-1940 recordings (Columbia 1987)★★★★, *The Essential Count Basie, Volume 3* 1940-1941 recordings (Columbia 1988)★★★★, *The Swing Machine* (Giants Of Jazz 1992)★★★, *The Best Of Count Basie* (Pablo 1992)★★★, *The Complete American Decca Recordings (1937-1939)* 3-CD box set (Decca 1992)★★★★★, *The Best Of Count Basie* 1937-1939 recordings (Decca 1992)★★★★, *The Best Of Count Basie: The Roulette Years* (Roulette 1992)★★★★, *Live* 1956/1957/1959/1961 recordings, 3-CD box set (Sequel 1993)★★★★, *The Complete Atomic Basie* (Roulette 1994)★★★★★, *Count Basie And His Great Vocalists* 1939-1945 recordings (Columbia/Legacy 1995)★★★★, *The Golden Years* 1972-1983 recordings, 4-CD box set (Pablo 1996)★★★★, *One O'Clock Jump: The Very Best Of Count Basie* (Collectables 1998)★★★, *Swingsation* (GRP 1998)★★★, *The Complete Roulette Studio Count Basie* 10-CD box set (Mosaic)★★★★★, *The Complete Roulette Live Recordings Of Count Basie And His Orchestra (1958-1962)* 8-CD box set (Mosaic)★★★★, *The Last Decade* 1974/1977/1980 recordings (Artistry)★★★, *On The Upbeat* 1937-1945 recordings (Drive Archives)★★★, *Rock-A-Bye Basie, Vol. 2* 1938-1940 recordings (Vintage Jazz Classics)★★★★, *The Jubilee Alternatives* 1943-1944 recordings (Hep)★★★.

● VIDEOS: *Count Basie And Friends* (Verve Video 1990), *Swingin' The Blues* (1993).

● FURTHER READING: *Count Basie And His Orchestra: Its Music and Its Musicians*, Raymond Horricks. *Count Basie*, A. Morgan. *Count Basie: A Biodiscography*, Chris Sheridan. *Good Morning Blues: The Autobiography Of Count Basie*, Albert Murray.

● FILMS: *Jamboree* aka *Disc Jockey Jamboree* (1957), *The Big Beat* (1957).

BASS, RALPH

b. 1 May 1911, New York City, New York, USA. A pivotal figure in the history of R&B, Bass began his career during the 40s, promoting live jazz shows in Los Angeles. He subsequently worked for Black And White Records, producing 'Open The Door, Richard' for Jack McVea, but later left to found several small-scale outlets with releases by Errol Garner and Dexter Gordon. Bass also recorded (Little) Esther Phillips, the Robins and Johnny Otis for the Savoy label, and in 1951 became one of the era's first independent producers through the aegis of the Cincinnati-based King company. Armed with his own outlet, Federal, and its Armo publishing wing, he built an impressive roster of acts around Hank Ballard And The Midnighters, the Dominoes and James Brown, whom Bass signed in 1955 on hearing a demo disc at an Atlanta radio station. Although initially unimpressed by the singer's untutored delivery, King managing director Syd Nathan changed his mind when 'Please Please Please' became a bestseller. Brown remained a Federal artist until 1960 but was switched to the parent outlet when Bass departed for Chess Records. The producer brought Etta James and Pigmeat Markham to his new employers, and in turn, worked with several established acts, including Muddy Waters, Howlin' Wolf and Ramsey Lewis. Bass remained with the label until the mid-70s when its Chicago office was closed. He continued to record R&B acts, the masters from which were latterly compiled on a series of albums under the generic title *I Didn't Give A Damn If Whites Bought It*.

BASSO, GIANNI

b. 24 May 1931, Asti, Italy. Basso studied clarinet at the Conservatorio di Asti before playing with various American groups in Belgium and Germany in the late 40s. When he returned to Italy he played in dance orchestras before joining the radio orchestra of Armando Trovajoli in 1956. He co-led one of Italy's best bands with trumpeter Oscar Valdambrini (1955-60) and worked with a succession of touring American musicians including Chet Baker, Buddy Collette, Slide Hampton, Maynard Ferguson, Phil Woods and Gerry Mulligan. In the late 70s he founded the band Saxes Machine. His first influence as a tenor saxophone player was Stan Getz but he was later influenced by Sonny Rollins. His playing is characterized by the impetuosity associated with free jazz. Though he still plays club dates he now works mostly as a studio musician in Rome.

● ALBUMS: *The Best Modern Jazz In Italy* (1959)★★★★, *Lunet* (Splasc 1982)★★★, *Maestro + Maestro = Exciting Duo* (Splasc 1983)★★★, *Gianni Basso Quartet* (Pentaflowers 1992)★★★.

BATCHELOR, WAYNE

Batchelor, a skilled and stylish bass player, is one of several excellent British jazz players who have been building a reputation for years and who have come to notice in the slipstream of Courtney Pine's celebrity. In common with others of the Jazz Warriors circle he exhibits a highly serious and dedicated attitude to his music. For a while he led a fine quartet, comprising saxophonist Brian Edwards, pianist Jonathan Gee and drummer Winston Clifford. He also played as a member of the Ed

Jones Quartet and the Shelly Ambury Quartet. He has played with Steve Williamson and Williamson, in turn, has played in Batchelor's band, producing some of his finest work on a 1989 demo-disc that, sadly, is not publicly available.

Bates, Django

b. Leon Bates, 2 October 1960, Beckenham, Kent, England. A self-taught pianist, Bates formally studied the instrument, together with trumpet and violin, at London's Centre for Young Musicians in the 70s and later attended the young musicians course at Morley College. In 1978, he dropped out from the Royal College of Music (after two weeks). Bates began a series of important associations with many of the leading young musicians who graced the burgeoning British jazz scene of the 80s and several of the concurrently popular African jazz musicians. In 1983, by which time he had already experienced stints with Tim Whitehead, Steve Argüelles (with whom he formed the trio Human Chain), Bill Bruford, Harry Beckett and Dudu Pukwana's Zila, he became a founder-member of Loose Tubes. In 1986, Bates guested with the George Russell Orchestra on their UK tour, and by this time was also playing in the quartet First House, with alto saxophonist Ken Stubbs, and in Bruford's jazz rock group, Earthworks. Bates's eclectic musical tastes are evidenced by his playing and composing, neither of which can be readily pigeonholed. Whether on keyboards or on tenor horn (an unusual instrument in jazz circles and one on which Bates is particularly effective), he is a distinctive and adventurous musician and one who seems incapable of a bad or uninteresting performance. In 1990, Bates's suite *Music For The Third Policeman* (based on the novel by Flann O'Brien) was recorded by his specially formed Powder Room Collapse Orchestra, and in the summer of 1991 he assembled another big band, Delightful Precipice (named after a Loose Tubes album), for a show that also featured a circus! Earlier that year he had toured the UK in a group led by Norwegian singer Sidsel Endresen.

● ALBUMS: *First House* (1985)★★★★, with Human Chain *Human Chain* (Loose Tubes 1986)★★★, with Human Chain *Cashin' In* (Loose Tubes 1988)★★★, with First House *Cantilena* (ECM 1989)★★★, *Music For The Third Policeman* (Ah-Um 1990)★★, *Summer Fruits (And Unrest)* (PolyGram 1993)★★★, as Doran, Studer, Minton, Bates, Ali *Play The Music Of Jimi Hendrix* (Call It Anything 1994)★★, *Winter Truce (And Homes Ablaze)* (JMT 1995)★★★, *Good Evening ... Here Is The News* (Argo 1996)★★★, *Like Life* (Storyville 1998)★★★★.

Batiste, Alvin

b. 1937, New Orleans, Louisiana, USA. Batiste played jazz clarinet with Ed Blackwell in high school, which led to a long association with Ornette Coleman, with whom he jammed in Los Angeles in the mid-50s. After a spell freelancing in New Orleans, Batiste toured with the Ray Charles band in 1958. From the late 60s to the mid-80s Batiste devoted much of his time to teaching at Southern University in Baton Rouge, although he did record with Cannonball Adderley on the saxophonist's last album in 1975. In 1981 he joined John Carter, David Murray and Jimmy Hamilton in the group Clarinet Summit and in 1984 released his first album as leader, *Musique D'Afrique Nouvelle Orleans*, which comprised a suite celebrating Crescent City Culture (originally written for the New Orleans Philharmonic Orchestra) plus two pieces that revealed Batiste's deep interest in mysticism: in the sleeve-notes he also mentions that he has studied music with the Rosicrucian Order, AMORC. An eclectic player, as happy to work in classical modes as in jazz, Batiste's *Bayou Magic* is a more conventional set of post-bebop tunes but still provides an exhilarating showcase for his technique and invention on clarinet. In 1987, for a festival dedicated to Blackwell, he was reunited with various 50s associates (such as Ellis Marsalis and Blackwell himself) in the American Jazz Quintet, whose *From Bad To Badder* documented their first concert together for some 30 years.

● ALBUMS: *Musique D'Afrique Nouvelle Orleans* (India Navigation 1984)★★★, *Clarinet Summit* 1982 recording (1984)★★★, *Clarinet Summit Volume 2* 1982 recording (1985)★★★, with Clarinet Summit *Southern Belles* (1988)★★★, *Bayou Magic* (India Navigation 1991)★★★, with American Jazz Quintet *From Bad To Badder* 1987 recording (1992)★★★, *Late* (Sony 1993)★★★.

Battle, Edgar

b. 3 October 1907, Atlanta, Georgia, USA, d. 6 February 1977. Trumpet, trombone, saxophones, piano, arranger, composer. Thanks to his vast instrumental versatility, Battle played in the trumpet, trombone and reed sections of several 30s big bands, including those led by Andy Kirk, Blanche Calloway, Benny Carter and Willie Bryant. In 1937 he briefly led his own band (and in the late 40s co-led a band with Shirley Clay) before deciding to concentrate on arranging. His charts were played by the bands of Count Basie, Cab Calloway, Earl Hines, Jack Teagarden, Fats Waller and others. Battle's best-known composition is 'Topsy', which has been recorded many times and was a 50s hit for Cozy Cole.

Bauduc, Ray

b. 18 June 1909, New Orleans, Louisiana, USA, d. 8 January 1988. Bauduc's New Orleans origins instilled in him a love for two-beat drumming, which he retained even when he played with Bob Crosby's swing era big band. Before the popularity and prominence of his Crosby days, Bauduc had worked with Johnny Bayersdorffer, Eddie Lang, Joe Venuti and Freddy Rich, in whose band he was also featured as a dancer. In 1928, he joined the Ben Pollack band when Pollack decided to give up drumming and simply lead. When the Pollack band dissolved and became one of the few co-operative bands in jazz, under the nominal leadership of Bob Crosby, Bauduc was among its most important members. Unlike the majority of bands of the era, which usually played in 4/4 time, the Crosby band was spurred on by Bauduc's lively 2/4 drumming. Extensively featured with the band (and in the spin-off small groups, the Bob Cats and Four Of The Bob Cats), Bauduc's most memorable moment of glory came when an encore at the Blackhawk Ballroom found just him and bassist Bob Haggart improvising a tune, during which Haggart whistled and Bauduc drummed on the strings of the bass. The result, 'Big Noise From Winnetka', was one of the band's biggest hits. Another popular success, 'South Rampart Street Parade', was also a co-composition by Bauduc and Haggart (written on a tablecloth at the New Yorker Hotel). Bauduc's regular feature with the band, 'The Big Crash From China', provided an excellent example of his intelligent soloing and superb cymbal work. After leaving Crosby when the band broke up in 1942, Bauduc worked with Jimmy Dorsey, Jack Teagarden and others, and in the 50s became co-leader, with former Crosby colleague Nappy Lamare, of a popular west coast-based band. From 1960, Bauduc lived in Texas in semi-retirement, but visited New Orleans in 1983 where he was greeted effusively. In 1985 he showed that he had lost none of his skill in a reunion of the Crosby band at the Mid-America Jazz Festival in St Louis. Bauduc's snappy, clean, exuberant drumming gave any band in which he worked an exciting, happy sound.

● ALBUMS: with Nappy Lamare *Riverboat Dandies* (Capitol 1957)★★★, with Lamare *On A Swinging Date* (Mercury 1960)★★★.

BAUER, BILLY

b. William Henry Bauer, 14 November 1915, New York City, New York, USA. One of the few jazz guitarists of his generation to avoid the influence of Charlie Christian, Bauer's most famous associations were with Woody Herman and Lennie Tristano. During his time with Herman (the 1944-46 First Herd), Bauer also recorded extensively with small spin-off groups, including those led by Bill Harris, Chubby Jackson and Flip Phillips. One of Bauer's improvised solo features with the Herd, 'Billy Bauer's Tune', was later formalized under the title 'Pam'. When the First Herd folded, Bauer played with bands led by Tommy Dorsey, Benny Goodman and Jack Teagarden; he was also with Charlie Ventura's interesting, if short-lived, big band. This same period, the late 40s, saw him entering a somewhat different musical world as a member of Tristano's trio (later sextet). By 1949, Tristano had started to experiment with a form of jazz in which musicians improvised in unison without predetermined key signatures or orthodox structures. Bauer's precise, metallic playing fitted well into these surroundings, which proved to be of only limited appeal to fans. Bauer continued to work in jazz from the 50s onwards, recording with the band of J.J. Johnson-Kai Winding and with Tristano, Lee Konitz and others, but most of his time was spent in studio work and in operating his own music publishing company.

● ALBUMS: *Let's Have A Session* 10-inch album (Ad Lib 1953)★★★, *Plectrist* (Norgran 1956)★★★.

BAUZA, MARIO

b. 28 April 1911, Havana, Cuba, d. 11 July 1993, New York, USA. One of the outstanding, if unsung, section men of the swing era, often cited as the man who invented 'latin jazz', Bauza's trumpet playing was only one facet of his broad talent. Until 1932 Bauza had played clarinet, oboe and other reeds and woodwinds with various bands, both in Cuba, where he graduated at the Havana Municipal Conservatory of Music, and New York, where he worked for Noble Sissle's society band and Sam Wooding. It was while he was there that Bauza learned to play trumpet in just two weeks, in order to make a record date with the Cuban singer Cuarteto Machin. Bauza began to concentrate on trumpet and it was on this instrument that he joined the Missourians and later became a mainstay of the Chick Webb band. In 1938, after five years with Webb, during which he mostly played lead and also acted as musical director, he moved to the Don Redman band. He also played with Fletcher Henderson and Cab Calloway and is credited with persuading Calloway to hire Dizzy Gillespie (having previously failed to convince Webb to hire him). In 1941, Bauza joined the strongly jazz-orientated Latin American band led by his brother-in-law, Frank 'Machito' Grillo. Bauza stayed with Machito for 35 years, during which time the band enjoyed the company of many guesting jazz stars including Charlie Parker, Cannonball Adderley, Joe Newman, Doc Cheatham, Howard McGhee and Buddy Rich. Machito credited Bauza as the architect behind his sound. As musical director and principal arranger for the Machito band, Bauza was responsible for overseeing numerous shifts in taste, culminating in the 70s with the widespread popularity of salsa. After leaving Machito in 1976 Bauza continued to work, leading his own band the African-Cuban Jazz Orchestra for recording dates and appearing regularly in New York. His two albums in the 90s for the Messidor label are worthy of investigation.

● ALBUMS: *Afro-Cuban Jazz* (1986)★★★, *Tanga* (Messidor 1992)★★★★, *My Time Is Now* (Messidor 1993)★★★★.

BAY, FRANCIS

b. Frans Bayetz, 1914, Rijkevorsel, Belgium. Although he became best known for his work in the 50s with the Belgian radio dance orchestra, Bay began his career playing trombone in the 30s. He played in a variety of settings, mostly linked to dance music, in his homeland and also in the Netherlands and Germany. At the end of World War II he played with the Ramblers, a Dutch band, and also the Skymasters. He worked in western and central Europe and in Scandinavia before forming his own polished big band, which evolved into the better-known radio studio orchestra. He led this orchestra on a more or less continuous basis throughout the ensuing decades.

● ALBUMS: *Francis Bay And His Orchestra* i (Philips 1957)★★★, *All That Swing* (Philips 1958)★★★, *Charleston* (Philips 1958)★★★, *Francis Bay And His Orchestra* ii (Philips 1958)★★★, *The Bay Big Band* (Mecca/Sutton 1958)★★★, *Plays*

Ted Heath (Mecca 1958)★★★★, *Plays Glenn Miller* (Mecca 1958)★★★, *Plays Benny Goodman* (Mecca 1958)★★★★, *Francis Bay And His Orchestra* iii (Mecca 1958)★★★, *Salutes Perez Prado* (Omega *c*.1958)★★, *Plays Artie Shaw* (Mecca 1958)★★★★, *Plays Harry James* (Mecca 1958)★★★, *Plays Tommy And Jimmy Dorsey* (Golden Hour 1959)★★★, *Plays Duke Ellington* (Mecca 1959)★★★, *Plays Les Brown* (Mecca 1961)★★★, *Plays Stan Kenton* (Mecca 1961)★★★, *Plays Count Basie* (Mecca 1961)★★★, *Plays Charlie Barnet* (Mecca 1961)★★★, *Latin Beat/Hot Cha Cha Chas* (Omega 1962)★★, *Swingin' Night People* (Omega 1963)★★, *Francis Bay Swings The Cha Cha Cha/Cha Cha Beat* (Epic 1965)★★, *Francis Bay And His Orchestra* iv (Philips 1965)★★★, *Francis Bay And His Orchestra* v (Musidisc 1965)★★★, *Francis Bay And His Orchestra* vi (BASF 1968)★★★, *The Swinger's Back Again* (Baccarole 1971)★★★.

Beal, Charlie

b. 14 September 1908, Los Angeles, California, USA, d. August 1991. In the late 20s and early 30s Beal played piano with several bands, including those led by Speed Webb and Les Hite. After relocating to Chicago, Beal played with bands based there, including Erskine Tate's, and also worked with Louis Armstrong. By 1934 he was in New York, where he played a succession of long residencies at many of the city's best-known musical watering-holes. His career was interrupted by military service during World War II, after which he returned to his home-town and was thus on hand to make a brief on-screen appearance in the film *New Orleans* (1947), which also featured Armstrong (and Billie Holiday). In the late 40s Beal visited Europe, touring for some years before returning to the USA in the late 50s. He was a solid player with a penchant for the more popular end of the jazz spectrum and gained a following with this repertoire among late-night audiences at clubs and hotels. His brother, Eddie Beal (b. 1910, d. 1984) was also a pianist, having started out as a drummer; he accompanied many singers including Holiday, and also wrote and published music.

● ALBUMS: with Louis Armstrong and others *Original Motion Picture Soundtrack: New Orleans* (Giants of Jazz 1947)★★★.

Beard, Jim

b. *c*.1960, USA. Beard was raised in Philadelphia but went to New York in 1985 intent on a career as a pianist. Soon, however, he found his work as a composer in demand and thereafter pursued both aspects of his work. He toured worldwide with John McLaughlin in 1986, Wayne Shorter in 1986/87, Pat Metheny in 1992, and he has also worked with John Scofield and Randy and Michael Brecker. While it might be apt to describe his as a jazz-rock repertoire, this fails to demonstrate its astonishingly eclectic nature. He draws upon several jazz forms as well as Latin, modern pop, rock, funk, and country, and there is also an always-present atmosphere of *joie de vivre* in Beard's music. Much of his recorded work stems from his own compositions and many of his arrangements seek to underline the uninhibited enjoyment and impish pleasure he clearly has in his music. In the early and mid-90s he was associated with Didier Lockwood, Mike Stern and Chuck Loeb, playing on the latter's 1996 session *The Music Inside*. As a record producer he worked with Bob Berg (1991's *Back Roads*) and Stern (1994's *Is What It Is*), both of which were Grammy nominated. In addition to piano, Beard has also made extensive use of synthesizers in his playing and as a hobby collects old synthesizers.

● ALBUMS: *Song Of The Sun* (CTI 1991)★★★, *Lost At The Carnival* (Lipstick 1995)★★★, *Truly ...* (Escapade 1997)★★★.

Beason, Bill

b. William Beason, 1908, Louisville, Kentucky, USA. Beason began playing drums while still in high school and in the mid-20s, while attending college, he joined a band led by Horace Henderson. After Henderson's band, the Collegians, turned professional, Beason continued to play with them. During the 30s, he was resident in New York, playing with bands led by Teddy Hill, Don Redman and others. In 1939, he was hired for the unenviable task of playing in Chick Webb's band during the leader's terminal illness. Beason usually played for most of the evening, with Webb taking over the stand for the last few numbers. After Webb's death, Beason stayed on as drummer when the band continued under the nominal leadership of Ella Fitzgerald. When the outfit broke up in 1941, Beason played with Henderson again and John Kirby, then freelanced with various leaders, including Ben Webster, before rejoining Kirby. By the 50s Beason had drifted into obscurity. He was a subtly swinging drummer, at ease with small groups and discreetly propelling the big bands with which he worked, and obviously saw his own role as supportive, even anonymous.

Beau, Heinie

b. 8 March 1911, Calvary, Wisconsin, USA, d. April 1987. Although spending much of his career in film and television studios in Hollywood, Beau was an exceptionally gifted Dixieland clarinet player. In the early 40s he played with Red Nichols and his Five Pennies and with Tommy Dorsey's big band. In the 50s he broke away from his regular work long enough to write and arrange material for a Nichols comeback recording date. Although committed to his non-jazz work (which included some of the arrangements for Frank Sinatra's best recordings, often casually attributed to Billy May and Nelson Riddle), Beau's occasional jazz outings were sufficient to have earned him a quiet reputation among musicians and the few fans lucky enough to hear him perform.

● ALBUMS: *Heinie Beau And His Hollywood Jazz Quartet* (Henri 1980)★★★, *Blues For Two* (1982)★★★, *Heinie Beau And His Hollywood Sextet* (1984)★★★.

Bechet Legacy

(see Wilber, Bob)

BECHET, SIDNEY

b. 14 May 1897, New Orleans, Louisiana, USA, d. 14 May 1959, Paris, France. A major figure in early jazz, an outstanding clarinettist, and for decades the only performer of consequence on soprano saxophone, Sidney Bechet's career began in 1909. During the next few years he played clarinet in bands led by legendary musicians such as Buddy Petit, John Robichaux and Bunk Johnson. By 1917 Bechet had left New Orleans behind, both literally and musically, visiting Europe in 1919 as a member of Will Marion Cook's orchestra. While in London during this tour, Bechet purchased a straight soprano saxophone and eventually achieved mastery over this notoriously difficult instrument, thus becoming the first real jazz saxophonist. Bechet's European trip was a mixed affair: he received rave reviews, including one (much quoted) from the Swiss conductor Ernest Ansermet, and was briefly imprisoned in London after a fracas with a prostitute. Back in the USA, Bechet worked with James P. Johnson and Duke Ellington before returning to Europe for an extended visit. This time Bechet encountered problems with the law in Paris, his stay being forcibly extended by almost a year after he was involved in a shooting incident with pianist Mike McKendrick. Out of prison and back once more in the USA, Bechet settled into a long association with Noble Sissle, which lasted throughout the 30s. During this period he worked and recorded with numerous jazzmen of note, including Louis Armstrong, Tommy Ladnier and Eddie Condon. In 1938 Bechet temporarily retired from the music business and began business as a tailor in New York. However, the following year he recorded 'Summertime' for the fledgling Blue Note label and enjoyed both a popular hit and one of his greatest performances. In the 40s Bechet continued much as before but was now teaching, (he had earlier briefly schooled Johnny Hodges), and one of his pupils was Bob Wilber, who studied and worked with the master. The end of the 40s saw Bechet risking Europe again and this time there was none of the trouble that had overshadowed his previous visits. His 1949 appearance at the Salle Pleyel Jazz Festival in Paris was a massive success. Later that same year he made another trip to France and this time he stayed. Throughout the 50s Bechet was a king in his new-found homeland, experiencing a freedom and a measure of appreciation and adulation that had always escaped him in the USA. He continued to play and record extensively, visiting the USA but always considering France as home. Right until the end, his powerful playing, for example at the 1958 Brussels Exhibition, gave no indication of his approaching death from cancer, which came on 14 May 1959, his 62nd birthday. In Antibes, where he had made his home, they erected a statue and named a square after him.

A lyrical heart-on-sleeve player with a wide vibrato, Bechet was also one of the most passionate of performers, on either of his instruments. On soprano he could hold his own with anyone, even trumpeters as powerful as Louis Armstrong. Although his recorded legacy is melodically rich and immensely satisfying in its emotional intensity, only a handful of players, of whom Wilber is the outstanding example, have noticeably followed the path he signposted. Bechet's autobiography, *Treat It Gentle*, is a romantic, highly readable but not always accurate account of his life.

● ALBUMS: *Sidney Bechet's Blue Note Jazz Men* 10-inch album (Blue Note 1950)★★★, *Jazz Classics, Volume 1* 10-inch album (Blue Note 1950)★★★★, *Jazz Classics, Volume 2* 10-inch album (Blue Note 1950)★★★★, *Days Beyond Recall* 10-inch album (Blue Note 1951)★★★, *Sidney Bechet, Voume 1* 10-inch album (Jazz Panorama 1951)★★★, *Sidney Bechet, Volume 2* 10-inch album (Jazz Panorama 1951)★★★, *Sidney Bechet With The Blue Note Jazz Men, Volume 1* 10-inch album (Blue Note 1951)★★★, *Sidney Bechet's Blue Note Jazz Men Volume 2* 10-inch album (Blue Note 1951)★★★, *Deux Heures Du Matin Au Vieux Colombier* (1952)★★★, *New Orleans Style Old And New* 10-inch album (Commodore 1952)★★★, *Immortal Performances* 10-inch album (RCA Victor 1952)★★★★, *The Fabulous Sidney Bechet And His Hot Six* 10-inch album (Blue Note 1952)★★★★, *Black Stick* 10-inch album (Dial 1952)★★★, *Sidney Bechet With Wally Bishop's Orchestra* 10-inch album (Dial 1952)★★★, *Sydney Bechet Solos* 10-inch album (Atlantic 1952)★★★, *The Port Of Harlem Six* 10-inch album (Blue Note 1952)★★★, *Jazz Festival Concert, Paris 1952 Volume 1* 10-inch album (Blue Note 1953)★★★, *Jazz Festival Concert, Paris 1952 Volume 2* 10-inch album (Blue Note 1953)★★★, *Dixie By The Fabulous Sidney Bechet* 10-inch album (Blue Note 1953)★★★, *Olympia Concert* 10-inch album (Blue Note 1954)★★★, *Sidney Bechet At Storyville, Volume 1* 10-inch album (Storyville 1954)★★★, *Sidney Bechet At Storyville, Volume 2* 10-inch album (Storyville 1954)★★★, *Sidney Bechet* 10-inch album (Jolly Rogers 1954)★★★, *Sidney Bechet And New Orleans Feetwarmers* 10-inch album (X 1954)★★★★, *Sidney Bechet And His Soprano Sax* 10-inch album (Riverside 1955)★★★, *King Of The Soprano Saxophone* (Good Time Jazz 1955)★★★, *La Nuit Est Une Sorciere* 10-inch album (London 1955)★★★, with Omer Simeon *Jazz A'La Creole* (Jazztone 1955)★★★, *Sidney Bechet Duets* (Atlantic 1956)★★★, with Martial Solal *Young Ideas* (World Pacific 1957)★★★, *When A Soprano Meets A Piano* (Inner City 1957)★★★, *Refreshing Tracks* (1958)★★★, with Teddy Buckner *Parisian Encounter* (Vogue 1958)★★★, with Buck Clayton *Concert At The World's Fair, Brussels* (Columbia 1958)★★★.

● COMPILATIONS: *Sidney Bechet* i 1923-1938 recordings (Savoy 1952)★★★, *Grand Master Of The Soprano Sax And Clarinet* (Columbia 1956)★★★★, *In Memoriam* (Riverside 1961)★★★★, *Bechet* (Riverside 1961)★★★, *The Immortal Sydney Bechet* (Reprise 1963)★★★★, *Bechet Of New Orleans* (RCA Victor 1965)★★★, *The Blue Bechet* (RCA Victor 1965)★★★, *Sidney Bechet And His New Orleans Feetwarmers Volumes 1-3* 1940-41 recordings (Joker 1981)★★★★, *The Complete Sidney Bechet Volumes 1-4* 1932-41 recordings (RCA 1983)★★★★, *The Panassie Sessions* 1938-39 recordings (80s)★★★, *Jazz Classics Volumes 1 & 2* 1939-51 recordings (RCA 1983)★★★★, with Louis Armstrong *Louis Armstrong & Sidney Bechet* 1924-25 recordings (Jazz Masters 1983)★★★★, *The Sidney Bechet-Muggsy Spanier Big Four: A Jam Session* 1940 recordings (Swaggie 1983)★★★, *Sidney Bechet* ii 1945-51 recordings (Giants Of Jazz 1989)★★★★, *The Bluebird Sessions* 1932-43 recordings

(Bluebird 1989)★★★★, *In Paris; Volume 1* (Disques Vogues 1995)★★★.

● FURTHER READING: *Sidney Bechet, Ou, L'Extraordinaire Odyssee D'Un Musicien De Jazz*, Jean Roland Hippenmeyer. *Treat It Gentle*, Sidney Bechet. *Sidney Bechet, The Wizard Of Jazz*, John Chilton.

BECK, GORDON

b. 16 September 1936, London, England. Beck, unlike many of his contemporaries, did not 'pay his dues' with the show and dance bands of the era. He studied piano at school but opted for a career as a draughtsman. It was exposure in Canada to the popular playing of George Shearing and Dave Brubeck that persuaded Beck to return to music, and back in England he progressed rapidly, working with Bobby Wellins, Tony Crombie and others. In 1962, Beck joined the Tubby Hayes Quintet, with whom he recorded. In 1965 he formed a trio with Tony Oxley and Jeff Clyne, and then spent a number of years as house pianist at Ronnie Scott's club, where he played behind Joe Henderson, Lee Konitz, Helen Merrill and others. During this period Beck played with Phil Woods and when George Gruntz left Woods' band in 1969, Beck was asked to join. Tours of Europe and the USA followed, exposing the pianist to universal accolade: the critic Jean-Louis Ginibre said at the time, 'Phil called in the only other pianist in Europe who could fill the chair'. Beck developed as a composer with Woods, and his compositions have been recorded by Cleo Laine and Gary Burton. After 1972, Beck worked with his trio, his larger group, Gyroscope, with Don Sebesky and with Piano Conclave, the six-keyboard group led by Gruntz. During the 80s he has toured regularly in Europe, and most successfully in France, where he has also recorded solo projects and albums with Allan Holdsworth and Helen Merrill. Beck is one of the few English jazz musicians whose work bears comparison with his named influences, particularly Bud Powell, Bill Evans and Herbie Hancock.

● ALBUMS: with Ronnie Scott *Live At Ronnie's* (1968)★★★, trio *Experiments With Pops* (1967)★★★, *Gyroscope* (1968)★★★, *Sunbird* (1979)★★★, *The Things You See* (1980)★★, *Dreams* (JMS 1989)★★★, *For Evans Sake* (JMS 1993)★★★★, with Woods *Live At The Wigmore Hall - The Complete Concert* (JMS 1997)★★★, *Once Is Never Enough* (FMR 1997)★★.

BECK, JOE

b. 29 July 1945, Philadelphia, Pennsylvania, USA. Guitarist Joe Beck moved to New York in 1963 to take up employment in various bands. After working with musicians including Paul Winter, Charles Lloyd, Gary McFarland and Chico Hamilton, he found more permanent employment with Jeremy Steig's Satyrs in 1968. The Satyrs took him on tour with Eric Clapton and Cream throughout that year. In the meantime, Beck was developing his career as a jingles writer, contributing over 100 sequences for television and radio. However, he found a new calling in 1971, moving from the city to become a dairy farmer, but returned to the music business two years later. As well as recording and performing solo he also found new work on movie soundtracks and television documentaries, also producing and arranging for artists such as Frank Sinatra, Gloria Gaynor, Larry Coryell and Esther Phillips. In his capacity as backing musician for the latter he enjoyed several hits on Kudu Records in the late 70s. As a solo artist during the 80s he built a strong cult following for his expressive, highly musical jazz funk recordings, without ever breaking out of that musical ghetto.

● ALBUMS: *Beck & Sambora* (Columbia 1970)★★★, *Beck* (Kudu 1975)★★★★, *Nature Boy* (Verve 70s)★★★★, *Rock Encounter* (Polydor 70s)★★, *Watch The Time* (Polydor 70s)★★★ *Carioca Blues* (Polydor 1978)★★★, *Relaxin'* (DMP 1986)★★★, with Ali Ryerson *Alto* (DMP 1998)★★★.

BECKETT, HARRY

b. 30 May 1935, St Michael Parish, Barbados. Resident in the UK since 1954, trumpeter Beckett has associated with many leading post-boppers and fusionists, including Graham Collier, in whose band he worked for about 15 years, beginning in the early 60s. In 1961 Beckett worked with Charles Mingus in London, appearing in the film *All Through The Night*. Throughout the 60s and 70s, he led his own small groups, notably Joy Unlimited, and also played with John Surman, Mike Westbrook, Mike Gibbs, Stan Tracey, Dudu Pukwana and Chris MacGregor's Brotherhood Of Breath. He also touched the mainstream during engagements with Ronnie Scott and John Dankworth and made occasional forays into jazz-rock during the late 60s with the Keef Hartley Band. In the 80s he worked extensively with students and on his own compositions, touring worldwide. Beckett's playing on both trumpet and flügelhorn is characterized by a fluid lyricism shot through with dazzling and sometimes fierce bursts of free inventiveness. His 1985 *Pictures Of You* was one of the first albums on the short-lived Paladin label and in the same year he recorded *Angolan Quartet* as a member of the Johnny Dyani Quartet. In the late 80s Beckett was for a while *eminence grise* with the young Jazz Warriors and also played frequently with Courtney Pine. In the early 90s a long-time association with Elton Dean took a new twist as the pair joined up with Enrico Fazio (bass) and Fiorenzi Sardini (drums) to form the Anglo-Italian Quartet, which made its first UK tour in 1991 and released its debut album in the same year.

● ALBUMS: with Graham Collier *Deep Dark Blue Centre* (1967)★★★, *Flare Up* (1970)★★★, *Warm Smiles* (1971)★★★★, *Themes For Fega* (1972)★★★, *Joy Unlimited* (1974)★★★, *Memoirs Of Bacares* (1976)★★★, *Got It Made* (1977)★★★, *Pictures Of You* (Paladin 1985)★★★, *The Bremen Concert* (West Wind 1987)★★★, with the Anglo-Italian Quartet *Put It Right Mr. Smoothie* (Splasch 1991)★★, *All Four One* (Spotlite 1992)★★★, with Courtney Pine *Live Volume II* (West Wind 1992)★★★, *Images Of Clarity* (Evidence 1994)★★★.

BEIDERBECKE, BIX

b. Leon Bix Beiderbecke, 10 March 1903, Davenport, Iowa, USA, d. 6 August 1931, New York, USA. One of the legends of jazz, a role he would doubtless have found wryly amusing had he lived to know of it, Bix Beiderbecke entered music when he began picking out tunes on piano and cornet at the age of 15. Inspired by records of the Original Dixieland Jazz Band and by hearing bands on the Mississippi riverboats, Beiderbecke broke away from his middle-class, middle-American family background (an act for which his family appeared never to have forgiven him) and by 1923 was already achieving fame with the Wolverines. In New York and Chicago, Beiderbecke played with dance bands but spent his free time listening to the leading black musicians of the day, notably Louis Armstrong and Joe 'King' Oliver. In 1926 he worked with Frankie Trumbauer, both men moving on to the bands of Jean Goldkette and Paul Whiteman, whom they joined in 1928. Throughout his time with these two jazz-age showbands, Beiderbecke was the featured jazz soloist and was very well paid. These two facts go some way to countering the accepted wisdom that such jobs, especially that with Whiteman, destroyed his creative impulse and accelerated his decline. In fact, these same years saw Beiderbecke freelancing with numerous jazz groups, many of which included other fine jazz artists whom Goldkette and Whiteman hired. The problems that assailed Beiderbecke seem to have been largely generated by his desire to 'dignify' his work with classical overtones, his rejection by his family (his film biographer, Brigitte Berman reveals how, on a visit to his home, he found all his records that he had proudly mailed to his parents lying unopened in a cupboard) and a general weakness of character. These troubles led him to take refuge in drink and this swiftly degenerated into chronic alcoholism. This, and allied ill-health, kept Beiderbecke out of the Whiteman band for long periods, although Whiteman kept his chair empty for him and paid all his bills. By the end of 1929 he was back home in Davenport trying, vainly, to restore himself to fitness. During his last year, Beiderbecke tried out for the Casa Loma Orchestra and played with pick-up groups in New York, including sessions with Benny Goodman, Red Nichols and others.

When he died in August 1931, Beiderbecke was still only 28 years old. Set against the bold and barrier-breaking glories of Armstrong's playing, Beiderbecke's technique was limited, but within it he played with great panache. The sound of his cornet had a fragile, crystalline quality that suited his detached, introspective formalism (not surprisingly, he admired Debussy). He wrote a few pieces for piano, one of which, 'In A Mist', strongly indicated the would-be classicist within him. His recorded work, whether in small groups ('Singin' The Blues' with Trumbauer) or in big bands ('San' and 'Dardanella' with Whiteman), continually demonstrated his fertile imagination. Beiderbecke's early death and the manner of his passing helped to make him a legend, and a novel based on his life, Dorothy Baker's *Young Man With A Horn*, romanticized his life. As often happens in such cases, there was a long period when the legend substantially outweighed reality. More recently, thanks in part to extensive reissues of his recorded legacy, and accurate portrayals of his life in the Richard Sudhalter-Philip Evans biography and Berman's excellent filmed documentary, a more balanced view of Beiderbecke's work has been made possible. Although his contribution to jazz fell well short of the concurrent advances being made by Armstrong, he frequently displayed a measure of sensitivity and introspection that foreshadowed the cooler approach to jazz trumpet of a later generation.

● COMPILATIONS: *The Complete Bix Beiderbecke In Chronological Order Volumes 1-9* 1924-30 recordings (Columbia 1950)★★★★, *Bix Beiderbecke And The Wolverines* (Riverside 1954)★★★, *Bix Beiderbecke And The Chicage Cornets* 1925 recording (Milestine 1980)★★★, *Bix Beiderbecke Volumes 1-14* (Joker 1981)★★★★, *The Studio Groups* 1927 recordings (Retrospect 1985)★★★★, *Bix Beiderbecke Collection* (Deja Vu 1985)★★★, *The Bix Beiderbecke Story* (Columbia 1986)★★★★, *Bixology Volumes 1-14* 1924-30 recordings (Giants Of Jazz 1988)★★★★, *At The Jazz Band Ball* 1924-28 recordings (Living Era 1991)★★★.

● FURTHER READING: *Remembering Bix*, Ralph Berton. *Bix: Man And Legend*, Richard M. Sudhalter and Philip R. Evans. *Bix Beiderbecke*, B. James.

BEKKER, HENNIE

b. *c*.1932, Nkana, Zambia. Multi-instrumentalist and songwriter Hennie Bekker pursued a long and varied musical career before eventually realizing his potential in his mid-60s. By that time he had been based in Toronto, Canada, for over a decade. Bekker was raised in the small town of Mufulira, 10 miles south of the Congo/Zaire border. At the age of 15 he began playing piano in the Bulawayo, Zimbabwe-based Youth Marvels. His own jazz band, the Hennie Bekker Band, was formed in 1959. His apprenticeship as a session musician and arranger began in Johannesburg, South Africa, where he was forced to flee after his group's engagement at a Zairean nightclub was curtailed by the Katanga revolution. In Johannesburg he became a staff music director and producer for Gallo Records, and also worked periodically in England. He returned to South Africa to work as a highly successful composer of television and radio commercials, subsequently becoming a respected film composer. He then settled in Canada in 1987, forced there by racial tensions in Johannesburg. He worked for a time composing stock music for the John Parry library, before collaborating with Dan Gibson on combined wildlife/new age recordings. *Harmony* was the first in a series of 13 such albums recorded by the pair up to 1996. In the 90s Bekker began to release his own, new age-themed records. He quickly made up for lost time, issuing numerous records in two thematic series - the 'Kaleidoscope' cycle (*Summer Breeze, Spring Rain, Winter Reflections, Lullabies, Autumn Magic*) and the 'Tapestry' cycle (*Silk & Satin, Vivaldi, Temba*). In addition there has been a Christmas album, plus a television-marketed ambient music series of albums for Quality Music. Bekker is also part of a trio including Greg Kavanagh and DJ Chris Sheppard who record contemporary techno as BKS.

Their albums, *For Those About To Rave ... We Salute You* (1992), *Dreamcatcher* (1993) and *Astroplane* (1996), have sold a combined 100,000 copies in Canada.

Bekker continues to take great pleasure in shocking adolescent fans when they discover one of Canada's most successful techno groups is spearheaded by a man in his mid-60s. However, it is as one of the most successful and prolific new age composers on the North American continent that Bekker is best known.

● ALBUMS: with Dan Gibson *Harmony* (Holborne 1989)★★★, *Summer Breeze* (Holborne 1993)★★, *Spring Rain* (Holborne 1993)★★★, *Winter Reflections* (Holborne 1994)★★★, *Tranquillity Volume 1* (Quality Music 1994)★★★, *Awakenings* (Quality Music 1994)★★★, *Silk & Satin* (Holborne 1995)★★★★, *Vivaldi* (Holborne 1995)★★, *Temba* (Holborne 1995)★★★, *Classic Moods And Nature* (Quality Music 1995)★★★, *Christmas Spirit* (Holborne 1996)★★, *Christmas Noel* (Quality Music 1996)★★, *Transitions* (Quality Music 1996)★★★, *Classics By The Sea* (Holborne 1996)★★, *Lullabies* (Holborne 1997)★★, *Autumn Magic* (Holborne 1997)★★★, *Mirage* (Avalon 1997)★★★.

Belden, Bob

b. 31 October 1956, Charleston, South Carolina, USA. An accomplished tenor saxophonist, Belden played in college bands before joining Woody Herman for a spell. In New York in the 80s he was in demand as a sideman (on keyboard and synthesizers in addition to his main instrument) and, increasingly, for his talents as an arranger. Towards the end of the decade he led his own big band and among his regular sidemen was Tim Hagans. In the 90s he was frequently engaged as a producer, arranger and musical director for Columbia Records' Legacy series and for the Verve, GRP, Atlantic and Criss Cross labels. He was extensively involved in Blue Note Records' 'cover' series in the later years of the decade. Among these are sets with featured artists such as Cassandra Wilson, Dianne Reeves and Hagans, that displayed an off-beat liking for exploring the work of composers not usually associated with the jazz repertoire. Released under the banner 'Bob Belden Presents' are samplings of the compositions of Sting, Beatles, Carole King and classical composer Giacomo Puccini. He has also written numerous liner notes for albums.

● ALBUMS: *Treasure Island* (Sunnyside 1989)★★★, *Straight To My Heart: The Music Of Sting* (Blue Note 1991)★★★★, *When Doves Cry: The Music Of Prince* (Blue Note 1993)★★★, *Bob Belden's Shades Of Blue* (Blue Note 1996)★★★, *Tapestry* (Blue Note 1998)★★★, *La Cigale* (Sunnyside 1998)★★.

Bell, Graeme

b. 7 September 1914, Melbourne, Victoria, Australia. Early in the 40s, Bell played piano in local jazz groups with his trumpet-playing brother, Roger. In addition to playing jazz, he was one of the leading promoters of the music in Australia. He was greatly responsible for building a jazz following in the country and by the late 40s he took his band to the UK, where he delighted the local scene, thanks in part to his policy of encouraging young people to dance to his music. At the end of the 40s he formed his own recording company, Swaggie, and both then and during the 50s toured internationally. Bell also brought American jazz stars to Australia, among them Rex Stewart, with whom he broadcast (a 1949 show being captured on record). He continued his tireless promotion of jazz by performing and by various other activities throughout the 70s and into the early 80s. Direct and uncomplicated, the bands Bell led were filled with energetic and cheerful musicians, among them Ade Monsbourgh, John Sangster and Dave Dallwitz. Bell's musical policy was such that, in common with England's Chris Barber, he was never content merely to rehash material from original sources. Instead, he stamped it with his own style, writing and arranging with skill and integrity within the format of a traditional band.

● ALBUMS: *Top Of The Town* (1950)★★★, *Cakewalkin' Babies Back Home* (1951)★★★, *Inside Jazz Down Under* 10-inch album (Angel 1954)★★★, *Hernando's Hideaway* (1962)★★★, *Graeme Bell And His Australian Jazz Band* 1949-1952 recordings (Swaggie 1983)★★★★, *Czechoslovak Journey* (Swaggie 1983)★★★, *Paris 1948* (Swaggie 1983)★★.

Bell, Jimmy

b. 29 August 1910, Peoria, Illinois, USA, d. 31 December 1987, Peoria, Illinois, USA. A minor figure who made few recordings, Bell was typical of the journeyman musician who plays what he must to earn a living, while harbouring greater ambitions. Beginning violin lessons at the age of 10, he moved on to the guitar, trumpet and trombone before settling on piano. Bell spent his early musical life around St. Louis, where he led a small group in the late 30s, Jimmie 'Lightning' Bell And His Swinging Cats. Prior to that, he had worked with bands such as Earl Van Dyke's Plantation Cotton Pickers and Al Williams' St. Louis Syncopators. In the late 40s, Bell formed the six-piece Gentlemen Of Swing, including Andrew Harris on bass. Harris and guitarist Leo Blevins accompanied him on a 1948 session that produced two singles, one on Aristocrat, the other constituting the third single on the then new Chess label. Although he claimed never to have been a user, Bell was imprisoned twice for possession of heroin. A further three years was served from 1970 for aiding and abetting an abortion. In 1978, he released three singles on his own GDS label, and was imprisoned yet again, this time for possession of counterfeit food stamps. His only album was made up of songs recorded in Shreveport in 1949, along with a 1978 concert at Illinois Central College and material recorded in his own home just before his incarceration.

● ALBUMS: *Stranger In Your Town* (JSP 1979)★★★.

Bellson, Louie

b. Luigi Paulino Balassoni, 6 July 1924, Rock Falls, Illinois, USA. Drummer Bellson first gained public attention by winning a Gene Krupa talent contest in 1940 and one of his early professional jobs was with Krupa's old boss, Benny Goodman. Bellson also worked with the big bands of Tommy Dorsey, Harry James and in 1951 joined Duke Ellington, where his dynamic and aggressive style was startlingly different to that of his sometimes lackadaisical predecessor, Sonny Greer. Ellington used a number of Bellson's compositions, including 'The Hawk Talks' (written for James) and 'Skin Deep', a marathon drum feature. After leaving Ellington, Bellson recorded and toured with small groups and sporadic big bands. In the mid-50s he returned briefly to Tommy Dorsey and also recorded for Norman Granz, accompanying Louis Armstrong, Benny Carter, Ella Fitzgerald, Oscar Peterson, Art Tatum and others. In these settings he proved to be a restrained accompanist, thus confounding those who had considered him merely a thunderer. From the early 60s until her death he was musical director/accompanist to his wife, singer Pearl Bailey, but continued to record and tour with small and large bands under his own name and (in the mid-60s) made brief return visits to Ellington and James. Apart from his jazz compositions, Bellson has also written for the ballet and for jazz and symphony orchestra combinations. He is wholly ambidextrous, displays remarkable finger control, and is one of the most technically accomplished drummers jazz has known. A sought-after teacher and clinician, he is greatly admired by fellow musicians. When on tour Bellson frequently visits orphanages and the like, putting on free shows. Onstage, he is a spectacular and exciting performer. He popularized a kit with twin-bass drums, but unlike most of his imitators, he uses this set-up in a logical and gimmick-free fashion. Offstage, he is quiet, sincere and shy, and is one of the best-liked musicians of his era of jazz.

● ALBUMS: *Just Jazz All Stars* 10-inch album (Capitol 1952)★★★, *The Exciting Mr Bellson And His Big Band* 10-inch album (Norgran 1954)★★★, *Louis Bellson With Wardell Gray* 10-inch album (Norgran 1954)★★★, *Journey Into Love* (Norgran 1954)★★★, *Louis Bellson And His Drums* reissued as *Skin Deep* (Norgran 1954)★★★, with Benny Carter, Art Tatum *Tatum-Carter-Bellson* reissued as *The Three Giants* (Clef 1955)★★★, *The Driving Louis Bellson* reissued as *The Hawk Talks* (Norgran 1955)★★★, *Concerto For Drums* (Norgran 1956)★★★, *Drumorama!* (Verve 1957)★★★, *Louis Bellson At The Flamingo* (Verve 1958)★★★, *Lets Call It Swing* (Verve 1958)★★★, *Music Romance And Especially Love* (Verve 1958)★★★, with Carter, Tatum *Makin' Whoopee* (Verve 1958)★★★, *Drummers Holiday* (Verve 1959)★★★, *The Brilliant Bellson Sound* (Verve 1960)★★★, *Louis Bellson Swings Jules Styne* (Verve 1960)★★★, *Big Band Jazz AtThe Summit* (Roulette 1962)★★★, *With Bells On* (Vogue 1962)★★★, *Around The World In Percussion* (Roulette 1962)★★★, with Gene Krupa *The Mighty Two* (Roulette 1962)★★★, *Thunderbird* (Impulse! 1963)★★★, with Lalo Schifrin *Explorations* (Roulette 1964)★★★, *The Dynamic Drums Of Louie Bellson* (1968)★★★, *Louie In London* (1970)★★★, with Duke Ellington *Duke's Big 4* (Pablo 1974)★★★★, *150 MPH* (Concord Jazz 1974)★★★, *The Louie Bellson Explosion* (Pablo 1975)★★★, *Louie Bellson's 7* (Concord Jazz 1976)★★★, *Ecué - Ritmos Cubanos* (Pabo 1977)★★★, *Prime Time* (Concord Jazz 1977)★★★, *Sunshine Rock* (Pablo 1977)★★★, *Note Smoking* (1978)★★★, *Raincheck* (Concord Jazz 1978)★★★, *Intensive Care* (1978)★★★, *Louie Bellson Jam* (Pablo Jazz 1978)★★★, *Matterhorn* (Pablo 1978)★★★, *Side Track* (Concord Jazz 1979)★★★, *Dynamite!* (1979)★★★, *Originals* (Stash 1979)★★★, *Louie Bellson's Big Band Explosion Live* (PRT 1979)★★★, *London Scene* (Concord Jazz 1980)★★★, *The London Concert* (1981)★★★, *Cool Cool Blue* (Pablo 1982)★★★, *The London Gig* (Pablo 1982)★★★, *Louis Bellson Jam* (Pablo 1982)★★★, *East Side Suite* (Music Masters 1987)★★★, *Live At Jazz Showcase* (Concord Jazz 1987)★★★, *Hot* (Music Masters 1987)★★★, *Jazz Giants* (Limelight 1989)★★★, *1959 At The Flamingo Hotel* (Jazz Hour 1993)★★★, *Raincheck* (Concord Jazz 1995)★★★, *Their Time Was The Greatest!* (Concord Jazz 1996)★★★, *Air Bellson* (Concord Jazz 1997)★★★, *The Art Of The Chart* (Concord Jazz 1998)★★★★.

BELONGING - KEITH JARRETT

The spine on the CD cites Keith Jarrett as the recording artist, but many regard this as a Jan Garbarek album. Jarrett was the non-Scandinavian in a superb quartet that comprised Garbarek (saxophones), Palle Danielsson (bass) and Jon Christensen (drums). Garbarek and Jarrett constantly interplay, offering melancholy, romance, sadness and emotional, musical bliss on 'Spiral Dance' and 'Blossom', and manage to groove along with the out-of-character 'Long As You Know You're Living Yours'. One of the finest moments from ECM Records' exceptional and now sizeable catalogue; perhaps Jarrett and Garbarek need to work with each other sporadically in order to recharge each other.

● Tracks: *Spiral Dance; Blossom; Long As You Know You're Living Yours; Belonging; The Windup; Solstice.*

● First released 1974

● UK peak chart position: did not chart

● USA peak chart position: did not chart

BEMBEYA JAZZ

This group was formed in Beyla, Guinea, in 1961, under the patronage of President Sekou Toure, who was keen to foster indigenous musical expression, then under threat from the wholesale importation of western rock and soul. Bembeya Jazz have arguably made the biggest contribution to the thriving state of local, traditionally based dance music in Guinea today. In 1966, the group was appointed Guinea's national band - a position not entirely unconnected to their penchant for such lyrics as 'Ahmed Sekou Toure, you are honest, you are good, you are the person Guinea needs.' However, the honour was nonetheless wholly deserved: Bembeya presented dance music steeped in authentic Guinean folk culture, and employed a line-up that placed traditional instruments such as the kora (harp), balafon (xylophone) and tam-tam (drum) in the frontline, alongside western imports such as guitars, reeds and brass. Bembeya's first hit, 'Ballake', praised a celebrated Guinean freedom fighter from colonial times. From there, they went on to become one of Africa's greatest and most influential bands. Their reputation rested on musical excellence, their mix of roots instrumentation, hypnotic folk-informed guitar styles and dazzling horn arrangements, and partly on their own personalities. Vocalist Aboudacar Demba Camara established himself as one of the great African singers, while guitarist Sekou Diabeté, a flamboyant showman, forged an entirely original and much-imitated solo style. Camara's death in a car crash in 1973 seemed to mark the end of the band, but after a short period of reorganization, they returned to the scene with no less than three new singers, the Trio Ambiance from Tazouka, and carried on their historic role. In 1977, following an appearance at the Festac pan-African cultural Olympics in Lagos, Nigeria, Diabeté was voted 'The Hendrix of Africa'. For much of Sekou Toure's presidency, Guinea remained closed to the west. Links with Communist countries were encouraged, and in the 60s Bembeya played in Cuba, and in the early 70s in Moscow. After Toure's death in 1984, the band turned its attention to Europe, and at the end of that year played a gig at London's Africa Centre. This was followed by the release of several albums recorded in Paris, where for the first time the studio production matched the quality of the band's music. In 1985, Diabeté released the towering solo album *Diamond Fingers,* supported by musicians from the band. Bembeya continue to be one of the most popular and respected bands in West Africa, seemingly unaffected by passing trendse.

● ALBUMS: *Djanf Amagni* (Syliphone 1970)★★★, *Parade Africaine* (Syliphone 1970)★★★, *Spécial Recueil Souvenir* (Syliphone 1970)★★★, *10 Ans De Success* (Syliphone 1971)★★★★, *Bembeya Jazz* (Syliphone 1974)★★★, *Le Defi* (Syliphone 1978)★★★, *Memoire De Aboudacar Camara* (Syliphone 1982)★★★, *La Continuité* (Syliphone 1982)★★★, *Regard Sur Le Passé* (Syliphone 1982)★★★★, *Telegramme* (Sonodisc 1985)★★★, *Montagne* (Sonodisc 1985)★★★, *Bembeya Jazz National* (Sonodisc 1986)★★★★, *Yekeke* (Sonodisc 1986)★★★, *Sabu* (Sonodisc 1988)★★★, *Paris-Conakry* (Sonodisc 1989)★★★, *Wa Kele* (Sonodisc 1989)★★★.

Beneke, Tex

b. Gordon Beneke, 12 February 1914, Fort Worth, Texas, USA. Starting out on soprano saxophone, Beneke switched to tenor, working with various bands in the south-west. In 1938 he joined Glenn Miller where, in addition to featured tenor, he was also a regular vocalist. Beneke sang with engaging charm, if limited ability, on such classic hits as 'I Gotta Gal In Kalamazoo' and 'Chattanooga Choo Choo'. Strongly influenced by the driving, big-toned tradition of Texas tenors, Beneke's playing added a jazz flavour to many Miller dance hits, including 'In The Mood' and 'String Of Pearls', on which he duetted with fellow tenor Al Klink. At the outbreak of World War II, Beneke worked with Miller's singing group, the Modernaires, then joined the US Navy where he played in a navy band. After the war, following Miller's death, Beneke was invited by Miller's executors to direct the Miller orchestra. In 1950 he relinquished this role but continued to lead his own band which played Miller-style music. He continued leading bands into the late 80s, bringing enthusiasm to a somewhat overexposed corner of popular music.

● COMPILATIONS: *With No Strings* 1949-51 recordings (Hep Jazz 1981)★★★★, *Beneke On Broadway* (Bulldog 1982)★★★, *Shooting Star* 1948 recordings (Magic 1983)★★★, *Memories* 1949 recordings (First Heard 1984)★★★, *Loose Like* 1946 recordings (Hep Jazz 1988)★★★, *Tex Beneke Salutes Glenn Miller* 40s recordings (Jazz Band 1990)★★★★.

● VIDEOS: *Tex Beneke And The Glenn Miller Orchestra* (Kay Jazz 1988).

Benford, Tommy

b. 19 April 1905, Charleston, West Virginia, USA, d. 24 March 1994, Mount Vernon, New York, USA. Benford began playing drums as a child and with his tuba-playing brother, Bill, was a member of the famous Jenkins Orphanage band that toured the USA in the early years of the 20th century, visiting England in 1914 (when he was still only nine years old). By the early 20s, the brothers were in New York where they worked with the bands of Elmer Snowden (in whose ranks were Jimmie Lunceford and Bubber Miley), Jelly Roll Morton, Edgar Hayes and others. Forming their own band in 1929, the Benfords played New York's Rainbow Gardens. In 1935 Benford was in Eddie South's short-lived and unrecorded big band and the following year toured Europe with the Willie Lewis orchestra. In Europe he recorded extensively with pick-up groups featuring local and visiting musicians. Through the 40s Benford played with Jimmy Archey, Muggsy Spanier and Rex Stewart. Benford remained in demand throughout the next three decades and was still touring the USA and Europe and recording into the early 80s. Among the bands he graced with his immaculate timekeeping and sensitive accompaniment were those led by Joe Thomas, Edmond Hall, Buck Clayton, Clyde Bernhardt, Bob Wilber and Kenny Davern's Soprano Summit.

● ALBUMS: *The Stride Piano Of Dick Wellstood* (1954)★★★, *Soprano Summit* (1977)★★★.

Benjamin, Sathima Bea

b. 17 October 1936, Cape Town, South Africa. Benjamin began singing in the 50s, and towards the end of the decade met pianist Abdullah Ibrahim (formerly Dollar Brand), whom she later married. In 1962 Benjamin and Ibrahim visited Switzerland, where they met Duke Ellington, who invited them to Paris for a recording date. Ibrahim's records were released, but hers were not. Three years later, Benjamin sang with Ellington at the Newport Jazz Festival. For the next decade Benjamin worked mostly with her husband, but in 1976 their declaration of membership of the outlawed African National Congress forced the couple into exile. Living in New York since then, Benjamin has continued to work mostly on the east coast, although her regular recording sessions, on which she is often accompanied by such leading contemporary musicians as Billy Higgins and Buster Williams, helped to bring her unusual talents to the attention of a worldwide audience. Her background gives her material, some of which she writes herself, an angle unusual among artists of her generation. This and her distinctive singing style, filled with nuances of meaning that show a deep appreciation of the lyrics she sings, help to make

Benjamin's work particularly rewarding. Like so many other fine contemporary singers, Benjamin's repertoire extends far beyond the limitations implied by the term 'jazz singer', incorporating as it does popular standards and songs from musical comedies and Broadway shows.

● ALBUMS: *African Songbird* (1976)★★★, *Sathima Sings Ellington* (Ekapa 1979)★★★★, *Dedications* (1982)★★★, *Memories And Dreams* (Ekapa 1983)★★, *Wind Song* (Black Hawk 1985)★★★, *Lovelight* (Enja 1987)★★★, *Southern Touch* (Enja 1992)★★★.

BENNETT, BETTY

b. 23 October 1921, Lincoln, Nebraska, USA. Bennett studied piano and singing, with the intention of becoming an opera singer. She was attracted to jazz when her mother introduced her to the music of Ellington and Basie. She joined Georgie Auld's band, then worked with big bands led by Claude Thornhill, Alvino Rey and Charlie Ventura, where she replaced Jackie Cain and Roy Kral, and was also briefly with Stan Kenton and Woody Herman. In the 50s, she played and recorded with her then husband, André Previn, and also appeared at the Monterey Jazz Festival. In 1975 she married Mundell Lowe at a ceremony held at the Monterey festival. Later, although semi-retired for some years, she returned to singing in the USA and UK. Initially concerned with singing jazz, during her time with Ventura Bennett took an increasing interest in the lyrics of the songs she sang, eventually developing into a very good, all-round and musically intelligent song stylist.

● ALBUMS: *Betty Bennett* 10-inch album (Trend 1953)★★★, with André Previn *Nobody Else But Me* (Atlantic 1955)★★★, *Blue Sunday* (Kapp 1957)★★★, *I Love To Sing* (United Artists 1959)★★★, *The Song Is You* 1990 recording (Fresh Sounds 1992)★★★.

BENNETT, CUBAN

b. Theodore Bennett, *c.*1902, USA, d. 28 November 1965, Pittsburgh, Pennsylvania, USA. Although he never recorded, Bennett is frequently cited by other trumpeters as an outstanding talent with ideas well ahead of his time. His cousin, Benny Carter, considered him to be so harmonically advanced that in the 20s he was playing in a way others would not emulate for another two decades. Bennett worked for many bands in and around New York but was footloose and showed little interest in a steady job, preferring instead to hang out and play the way he wanted. Bennett eventually disappeared from the scene.

BENNINK, HAN

b. 17 April 1942, Zaandam, Netherlands. Bennink is an intense, energetic percussionist with a strong streak of anarchic, deadpan mockery that seems to be common among Dutch jazz musicians. He tends not to confine his playing to the kit, frequently venturing away from the stool to play on the floor, walls or anything else within reach that he considers will make the sound he wants: the personnel details on the sleeve of *Outspan No 2* lists him as using 'dr, perc, everything, anything' and those of *Schwardzwaldfahrt*, recorded in the open air, credit him with playing 'wood, trees, sand, land, water, air'. He is notoriously hard on sticks, habitually breaking several per gig, often to the peril of members of the audience. While he is primarily associated with the European free improvisation scene he has worked with a wide variety of players, including Ben Webster, Dexter Gordon, Don Byas and Johnny Griffin from the jazz mainstream, musicians such as Sonny Rollins and Lee Konitz who have at least flirted with the *avant garde*, as well as free players such as Derek Bailey, Evan Parker and Peter Brötzmann. He also played with Eric Dolphy on one of the saxophonist's final recordings (*Last Date*). In the late 80s he toured with Steve Lacy and his long-time associate Misha Mengelberg as part of the Monk Project, and for many years he has been involved with the Instant Composers Pool, which he founded in 1967 with Mengelberg and Willem Breuker. His favourite drummers include Chick Webb, Big Sid Catlett, Jo Jones and Philly Joe Jones. Bennink also learned from his father, who was in a radio orchestra and did many commercial engagements in bands accompanying dancers and singers. Han's first instrument was clarinet, and he will still sometimes break off from drumming in mid-gig to play a tune on it, or on banjo, viola or saxophone. He has appeared on many records, mostly for musician-run labels such as FMP, ICP and Incus, and in the early 90s featured with Andy Sheppard's *Soft On The Inside* big band.

● ALBUMS: with Willem Breuker *New Acoustic Swing Duo* (1967)★★★, with Misha Mengelberg, John Tchicai *Instant Composers Pool* (1968)★★★, with Derek Bailey *Derek Bailey And Han Bennink* (1969)★★★, with others *Instant Composers Pool* (1970)★★★, with Instant Composers Pool *Groupcomposing* (1970)★★★, with Bailey, Evan Parker *The Topography Of The Lungs* (1970)★★★, with Peter Brötzmann, Fred Van Hove *Balls* (1970)★★★, with Mengelberg *Instant Composers Pool* (1971)★★★, *Han Bennink Solo* (1972)★★★★, with others *Elements* (1972)★★★, with others *Couscouss De La Mauresque* (1972)★★★, with others *The End* (1972)★★★, with Bailey *At Verity's Place* (1972)★★★, with Brötzmann, Van Hove *Free Jazz Und Kinder* (1972)★★★, *Brötzmann, Van Hove, Bennick* (1973)★★★, with Brötzmann, Van Hove *Einheitsfrontlied* (1973)★★★, with Mengelberg *Eine Partie Tischtennis* (1974)★★★, with others *Outspan* i (1974)★★★, with others *Outspan* ii (1974)★★★, with Mengelberg 1973-75 recordings *Coincidents* (1975)★★★, with Mengelberg (untitled album) (1975)★★★, with Brötzmann, Van Hove *Tscüs* (1975)★★★, with Bailey *Company 3* (1977)★★★, with Brötzmann *Ein Halber Hund Kann Nicht Pinkeln* (1977)★★★, with Brötzmann *Schwarzwaldfahrt* (1977)★★★, with Mengelberg *Midwoud 77* (1977)★★★, with others *Company, Volumes 5-7* (1978)★★★, with Mengelberg, Dudu Pukwana *Yi Yole* (1978)★★★, with Mengelberg *A European Proposal* (1978)★★★, with Kees Hazevoet *Calling Down The Flevo Spirit* (1978)★★★, *Solo West Ost* (1978)★★★, with Brötzmann, Mengelberg *Three Points And A Mountain* (1979)★★★, *Mengelberg-Bennink* (1980)★★★, with Brötzmann *Atsugi Concert* (1980)★★★, *Tempo Comodo* (1982)★★★, with others *Regeneration* (1983)★★★, with

Breuker *Sendai Sjors/Sendai Sjimmie* (1984)★★★, with Bailey *Han* 1986 recording (Incus 1988)★★★, with Steve Beresford *Directly To Pyjamas* (1988)★★★, with Cecil Taylor *Spots, Circles, And Fantasy* (1989)★★★, with Ray Anderson, Christy Doran *Azurety* (hat Art 1993)★★★★, with Anderson, Doran *Cheer Up* (hat Art 1996)★★★★, with Myra Melford *Eleven Ghosts* (hatOLOGY 1998)★★★, *Serpentine* (Songlines 1998)★★★★.

● FURTHER READING: *New Dutch Swing*, Kevin Whitehead.

Benoit, David

b. 1953, Bakersfield, California, USA. Benoit gained an early appreciation of music from his parents, who played guitar and piano. He began piano lessons at the age of 14, by which time he was steeped in the influences of both Ramsey Lewis and Henry Mancini. Following his musical studies at El Camino College, he met with composer Richard Baskin and played piano on the movie soundtrack to *Nashville* in 1975. He gained valuable experience playing in clubs and bars and became Gloria Lynne's pianist. He toured with the Duke Ellington Orchestra in 1976 as Lainie Kazan's arranger and accompanist. His debut recording was with drummer Alphonse Mouzon and it was during these sessions he met with Dave Grusin, who became an important figure in his future career. He recorded a number of albums on a small label that demonstrated his fluid and skilful playing, although these recordings suffered from an overall blandness that resulted in disappointing sales. *This Side Up* in 1985 changed everything. It contained the stunning 'Beach Trails', put Benoit in the US jazz bestseller lists and led to a call from Larry Rosen, Dave Grusin's partner at GRP Records. Benoit has now become one of their leading artists, with a series of bestselling albums of easy, yet beautifully constructed, music, forging a similar path to that of Grusin and bridging the gap between jazz and pop. Each album contains a balanced mixture but it is Benoit's delicate rippling style on some of the quieter numbers that best demonstrates his dexterity. 'Kei's Song' from *Freedom At Midnight* and 'The Key To You' from *Every Step Of the Way* are fine compositions. His pure acoustic style was highlighted on *Waiting For Spring*, a concept album featuring Emily Remler and Peter Erskine. Imaginative readings of 'Cast Your Fate To the Wind', 'Secret Love' and 'My Romance' were mixed with Benoit originals. He maintained this high standard with *Inner Motion* in 1990, which opened with the Grusin-styled 'M.W.A.' and peaked with the sublime tribute to the late Remler, 'Six String Poet'. His *Letter To Evan* was another acoustic excursion, enlisting the talent of Larry Carlton. The collaboration with guitarist Russ Freeman in 1994 was a whole-hearted success and stayed in the *Billboard* jazz chart for many weeks. That same year, Benoit attempted another theme album, this time echoing his remembrances of the 60s, as good as *Shaken Not Stirred* was, it sounded just like another David Benoit album, clean, accessible and easy. Benoit is now an established artist, having refined his brand of music to perfection. His collaboration with Russ Freeman in 1994 was particularly inspiring. In his own words, 'I didn't want instant stardom like those artists whose fall is as quick as their rise'. Jazz purists may throw their arms up in horror but until another genre is invented, jazz remains the closest category for his music.

● ALBUMS: *Can You Imagine* (1980)★★, *Stages* (Bluemoon 1981)★★, *Waves Of Raves* (1982)★★, *Digits* (Bluemoon 1983)★★, *Heavier Than Yesterday* (1983)★★, *Christmastime* (1984)★★, *This Side Up* (GRP 1985)★★★★, *Freedom At Midnight* (GRP 1987)★★★, *Every Step Of The Way* (GRP 1988)★★★★, *Urban Daydreams* (GRP 1989)★★★, *Waiting For Spring* (GRP 1989)★★★★, *Inner Motion* (GRP 1990)★★★, *Shadows* (GRP 1991)★★★, *Letter To Evan* (GRP 1993)★★★, with Russ Freeman *The Benoit/Freeman Project* (GRP 1994)★★★, *Shaken Not Stirred* (GRP 1994)★★★, *Remembering Christmas* (GRP 1996)★★, *American Landscape* (GRP 1997)★★★.

● COMPILATIONS: *The Best Of David Benoit 1987-1995* (GRP 1995)★★★★.

Benson Orchestra

Edgar A. Benson, a cellist, was a contractor who ran a number of bands in the Chicago area in the 20s. Among the musicians he hired were many who wanted to play jazz but needed the regular money danceband work provided in order to live. Through the various Benson Orchestras passed men such as drummer Gene Krupa, pianist-arranger Roy Bargy, pianist Don Bestor, clarinettist Volly De Faut and saxophonist Frank Trumbauer. Both Bargy and Bestor later followed Benson's example and formed their own bands. In his hey-day, Benson was one of the few rivals to the immensely popular Paul Whiteman.

Benson, George

b. 22 March 1943, Pittsburgh, Pennsylvania, USA. This guitarist and singer successfully planted his feet in both the modern jazz and easy-listening pop camps in the mid-70s when jazz-pop as well as jazz-rock became a most lucrative proposition. Before a move to New York in 1963, he had played in various R&B outfits local to Pittsburgh, and recorded a single, 'It Should Have Been Me', in 1954. By 1965, Benson was an established jazz guitarist, having worked with Brother Jack McDuff, Herbie Hancock - and, crucially, Wes Montgomery, whose repertoire was drawn largely from pop, light classical and other non-jazz sources. When Montgomery died in 1969, critics predicted that Benson - contracted to Columbia Records in 1966 - would be his stylistic successor. Further testament to Benson's prestige was the presence of Hancock, Earl Klugh, Miles Davis, Joe Farrell and other jazz musicians on his early albums. Four of these were produced by Creed Taylor, who signed Benson to his own CTI label in 1971. Benson was impressing audiences in concert with extrapolations of songs such as 'California Dreamin'', 'Come Together' and, digging deeper into mainstream pop, 'Cry Me A River' and 'Unchained Melody'. From *Beyond The Blue Horizon*, an arrangement of Jefferson Airplane's 'White Rabbit' was a turntable hit, and chart success seemed inevitable - especially as he was now recording a majority of vocal items. After *Bad Benson* reached the US album lists and, via disco floors, the title song of *Supership* cracked European charts, he was well placed to negotiate a favourable contract with Warner Brothers Records, who immediately reaped a Grammy-winning harvest with 1976's *Breezin'* (and its memorable 'This Masquerade'). As a result, companies with rights to the prolific Benson's earlier product cashed in, with reissues such as *The Other Side Of Abbey Road*, a track-for-track interpretation of the entire Beatles album. Profit from film themes such as 'The Greatest Love Of All' (from the Muhammed Ali biopic *The Greatest*), the million-selling *Give Me The Night* and the television-advertised *The Love Songs* have allowed him to indulge artistic whims, including a nod to his jazz roots via 1987's excellent *Collaboration* with Earl Klugh, and a more commercial merger with Aretha Franklin on 'Love All The Hurt Away'. Moreover, a fondness for pop standards has also proved marketable, epitomized by revivals of 'On Broadway' - a US Top 10 single from 1978's *Weekend In LA* - and Bobby Darin's 'Beyond The Sea (La Mer)'. Like Darin, Benson also found success with Nat 'King' Cole's 'Nature Boy' (a single from *In Flight*) - and a lesser hit with Cole's 'Tenderly' in 1989, another balance of sophistication, hard-bought professionalism and intelligent response to chart climate. In 1990 he staged a full-length collaboration with the Count Basie Orchestra, accompanied by a sell-out UK tour. Benson is one of a handful of artists who have achieved major critical and commercial success in different genres - soul, jazz and pop, and this pedigree makes him one of the most respected performers of the past 30 years.

● ALBUMS: with the Brother Jack McDuff Quartet *The New Boss Guitar Of George Benson* (Prestige 1964)★★★★, *It's Uptown* (Columbia 1965)★★★★, *Most Exciting* (Columbia 1966)★★★, *Benson Burner* (Columbia 1966)★★★★, *The George Benson Cook Book* (Columbia 1967)★★★, *Giblet Gravy* (Verve 1968)★★★, *Goodies* (Verve 1969)★★★, *Shape Of Things To Come* (A&M 1969)★★, *Tell It Like It Is* (A&M 1969)★★, *The Other Side Of Abbey Road* (A&M 1970)★★★, *Beyond The Blue Horizon* (CTI 1971)★★★, *White Rabbit* (CTI 1972)★★, *Body Talk* (CTI 1973)★★★, *Bad Benson* (CTI 1974)★★, *Supership* (CTI 1975)★★★, *Breezin'* (Warners 1976)★★★★, *Good King Bad* (CTI 1976)★★★, with Joe Farrell *Benson And Farrell* (CTI 1976)★★★, *George Benson In Concert: Carnegie Hall* (CTI 1977)★★, *In Flight* (Warners 1977)★★★★, with Jack McDuff *George Benson And Jack McDuff* (Prestige 1977)★★★, *Weekend In LA* (Warners 1978)★★, *Living Inside Your Love* (Warners 1979)★★, *Give Me The Night* (Warners 1980)★★★★, *Blue Benson* (Polydor 1983)★★★, *In Your Eyes* (Warners 1983)★★★, *Stormy Weather* (Columbia 1984)★★, *20/20* (Warners 1985)★★, *The Electrifying George Benson* (Affinity 1985)★★★, *In Concert* (Premier 1985)★★, *Love Walked In* (Platinum 1985)★★, *While The City Sleeps* (Warners 1986)★★, with Earl Klugh *Collaboration* (Warners 1987)★★★★, *Love For Sale* (Masters 1988)★★★, *Twice The Love* (Warners 1988)★★, *Detroit's George Benson* (Parkwood 1988)★★★, *Tenderly* (Warners 1989)★★, with the Count Basie Orchestra *Big Boss Band* (Warners 1990)★★★, *Lil' Darlin'* (Thunderbolt 1990)★★★, *Live At The Casa Caribe Volumes 1-3* (Jazz View 1992)★★★, *Love Remembers* (Warners 1993)★★, *That's Right* (GRP 1996)★★★, *Standing Together* (GRP 1998)★★.

● COMPILATIONS: *The George Benson Collection* (Warners 1981)★★★★, *Early Years* (CTI 1982)★★★, *Best Of George Benson* (A&M 1982)★★★, *The Wonderful Years* (Proton 1984)★★★, *The Love Songs* (K-Tel 1985)★★★★, *The Silver Collection* (Verve 1985)★★★, *Compact Jazz* (Verve 1988)★★★, *Best Of* (Epic 1992)★★, *Guitar Giants* (Pickwick 1992)★★★, *The Best Of George Benson* (Warners 1995)★★★, *Essentials - The Very Best Of* (Jive 1998)★★★.

BENT, PHILLIP

b. London, England. Bent played the recorder at school then went on to study flute because he wanted a bigger sound. Sound itself, the exploration of textures, is important to him, but there is nothing academic or abstract about his music. He uses amplified flute - essential when there are electric instruments in his band - and rhythms from rock, funk and reggae. Like many of his generation of black British players he grew up on reggae, funk and soul and was attracted to jazz by hearing Louis Armstrong, Harold McNair and Miles Davis. Davis is clearly the most important influence in his work, but Bent is dedicated to developing his own voice on his own terms. He was a member of the Jazz Warriors, appearing on their live debut, *Out Of Many One People* (1987).

● ALBUMS: *Get Wise* one track only (1986)★★★, *Mellow Mayhem* one track only (1989)★★★, *The Pressure* (1993)★★★.

BERG, BOB

b. 7 April 1951, Brooklyn, New York, USA. Studying for a short time at the New York School of Performing Arts, before leaving prematurely to take a year's practical course at the Juilliard School of Music, as a young tenor saxophonist, Berg's interests were very much in the free jazz scene and the later work of John Coltrane. He involved himself in this area of jazz from 1966 onwards. In 1969 he became tired of its uncertainties and, deciding to study bop's solid harmonic schemes, joined Brother Jack McDuff's band. The next 15 years were spent in traditional hard-bop environments, where Berg could practise and expand his harmonic knowledge. Between 1973 and 1976 he worked in Horace Silver's band, and then followed this with seven years in Cedar Walton's group, touring regularly and recording. However, Berg's present musical identity was really formed after Miles Davis invited him to join his fusion band in 1984. After a series of worldwide tours, he left with a reputation as one of the more interesting Michael Brecker-influenced saxophonists in the New York studio style. His solo career has produced some undulating albums with Denon and Stretch, with *In The Shadows* so far being the most satisfying.

● ALBUMS: *New Birth* (Xanadu 1978)★★★, *Steppin': Live In Europe* 1982 recording (Red 1987)★★, *Short Stories* (Denon 1987)★★★, *Cycles* (Denon 1988)★★★, *In The Shadows* (Denon 1990)★★★★, *Back Roads* (Denon 1991)★★★, *Virtual Reality* (Denon 1993)★★★★, *Enter The Spirit* (Stretch/GRP 1993)★★★,

Riddles (Stretch 1994)★★★, *Another Standard* (Stretch 1998)★★★★.

BERG, THILO

b. Germany. A gifted drummer, at home in small group and big band settings, Berg has established a secure reputation in several areas of the jazz music business. When working with his own big band, Berg makes able use of vigorous young German musicians and the overall effect is one of the most exciting modern big bands of the 90s. For recording dates he also happily introduces into the band's ranks musicians from elsewhere, such as Gerard Presencer, Mark Nightingale, Slide Hampton and Martin Shaw. He has also used the big band as a setting for recordings with singer Barbara Morrison (1993's *Blues For Ella*). This album was released on Berg's own label, Mons Records, on which he has recorded not only his own performances but also those of artists such as Don Braden and Allan Harris.

● ALBUMS: *Carnival Of Life* (Mons 1991)★★★, *Footing* (Mons 1992)★★★, *Blues For Ella* (Mons 1993)★★★.

BERGER, KARL

b. 30 March 1935, Heidelberg, Germany. Berger studied piano, musicology and philosophy at his home-town university. In 1960, he took up vibes in order to play jazz. After gaining his PhD in 1963 he left for Paris, where he joined Don Cherry's quintet, with whom he worked for a year and a half. In 1966 he relocated to New York, finding a ready welcome in the free scene. His recording debut, *Tune In*, featured drummer Ed Blackwell, bassist Dave Holland and alto saxophonist Carlos Ward. An energetic educationalist, he established a music school in Woodstock where students were taught by *avant garde* luminaries, including George Russell, Roscoe Mitchell, John Cage and Sam Rivers, until its closure in the early 80s. Berger continues to record, often in collaboration with his wife, Ingrid, who is a singer.

● ALBUMS: *Karl Berger* (ESP 1967)★★★, *Tune In* (Milestone 1969)★★★★, *With Silence* (1972)★★★, *Changing The Time* (1977)★★★, with the Woodstock Workshop Orchestra *New Moon* (1980)★★★, *All Kinds Of Time* (Sackville 1981)★★★, *Transit* (Black Saint 1987)★★★★, *Around* (Black Saint 1991)★★★, *With Silence* (Enja 1992)★★★, *Crystal Fire* (Enja 1992)★★★★, *Conversations* (In+Out 1996)★★★★, *No Man Is An Island* (Douglas 1996)★★.

BERGH, TOTTI

b. 5 December 1935, Oslo, Norway. Before choosing the tenor saxophone he had played clarinet, having been attracted to jazz by hearing records. By the early 50s he was active in jazz groups in Norway and late in the decade played on cruise ships on the line plying between Norway and New York. In New York he was able to advance his awareness of jazz by hearing top-flight musicians at first hand. Nevertheless, by 1962, with jazz gigs few and far between, he went into industry, working as finance manager for a British company's Norwegian office. He continued to play jazz whenever possible, accompanying visiting British and American musicians. He also regularly accompanied his wife, singer Laila Dalseth, leading a regular quintet. In 1990, Bergh again became a full-time professional musician. Alone and with Dalseth, he has toured Scandinavia, the USA and the Far East, playing clubs, concerts and festivals. Among artists with whom he has worked are Al Cohn, Louis Stewart, Plas Johnson, and George Masso. A fine, sensitive interpreter of ballads, and a solid, straight-ahead swinger, Bergh's playing deserves attention. His accompaniment to his wife's singing is also exemplary. He plays with a full, breathy sound, phrasing elegantly and with understanding.

● ALBUMS: with Per Borthen *Wrap Your Troubles* (Swift 1968)★★★, with Laila Dalseth, Borthen *Swinging Departure* (Talent 1979)★★★, with Karin Krog, Borthen *Swinging Arrival* (Talent 1980)★★★★, with Dalseth, Louis Stewart *Daydreams* (Hot Club 1984)★★★, with Cohn *I Hear A Rhapsody* (Gemini 1985)★★★★, with Cohn *Tenor Gladness* (Gemini 1986)★★★, with George Masso, Major Holley *Major Blues* (Gemini 1990)★★★, with Plas Johnson *On The Trail* (Gemini 1992)★★★★, with Joe Cohn, Dalseth *Remember* (Gemini 1995)★★★, *Warm Valley* (Gemini 1996)★★★.

BERGHOFER, CHUCK

b. Charles Curtis Berghofer, 14 June 1937, Denver, Colorado, USA. Born into a musical family (his grandfather had played with John Philip Sousa), Berghofer began playing trumpet at the age of eight, by which time his family had moved to California. He played various other brass instruments before turning to the double bass in his mid-teens. An admirer of Ralph Peña, he persuaded the older man to give him lessons. Two years after taking up the bass, Berghofer joined the orchestra led by Skinnay Ennis for a Midwest tour. He then joined pianist Bobby Troup where he remained for a number of years accompanying the pianist and his wife, singer Julie London. He replaced Peña in a duo with Pete Jolly, the group later expanding to a trio with drummer Nick Martinis, and then, in 1960, became a member of Shelly Manne's house band at the drummer's newly opened club, the Manne Hole. During the early 60s, Berghofer played with numerous leading jazzmen, including Jack Sheldon, Conte Candoli, Frank Rosolino, Rahsaan Roland Kirk and Philly Joe Jones. Like many other leading musicians on the west coast, Berghofer began playing in the film, television and recording studios. Although most such musicians are doomed to a measure of anonymity, one of Berghofer's first recording gigs, backing Nancy Sinatra on a date on which she made 'These Boots Are Made For Walking', gave him a prominent role. As he told *Jazz Journal International*'s Gordon Jack, 'That little semi-tone figure on the bass seemed to make the record and as a result I started doing about three pop record dates a day all over town.' Among the pop singers with whom he recorded in the 60s were the Everly Brothers and Elvis Presley. He also worked on television with Glen Campbell, recorded with Frank Sinatra, and played on the soundtrack of Barbra Streisand's *Funny Lady*. His film work extends to a staggering 400 appearances leading to his being awarded in the mid-80s the National Academy of Recording Arts and Sciences Award as the most valuable bass player for four consecutive years. In that decade he recorded with Mel Tormé and later recorded again with Sinatra on *Duets*. Despite all his studio activities Berghofer continued to play jazz, working with many noted artists during a spell when, with pianist Frank Strazzeri and drummer Nick Ceroli, he formed the semi-regular house band at Donte's in Los Angeles. An excellent video, recorded at Donte's in 1970, features Berghofer with pianist Roger Kellaway and drummer Larry Bunker backing Zoot Sims. Among others he accompanied were Art Pepper, Bob Cooper, Gerry Mulligan and Stan Getz. Berghofer continued his eclectic gigging in the 90s, recording with Frank Capp's Juggernaut, Jolly, Buddy Greco and Keely Smith, and also visiting Europe. Berghofer has declared his influences to be Leroy Vinnegar, Paul Chambers and Ray Brown. He also admired the work of Scott La Faro and told Jack that, 'The best soloist on the instrument was Red Mitchell . . . I loved to hear him solo.' Berghofer's playing is distinguished by his huge, rich tone and the sense of relaxed power he brings his music.

BERGONZI, JERRY

b. 1947, Boston, Massachusetts, USA. Of all the legions of John Coltrane-inspired saxophonists to have emerged in the 80s in the USA, Jerry Bergonzi has been one of the most distinctive, and yet has had to wait the longest for his personal break. He played clarinet and alto saxophone from the age of eight, and took up the tenor at 12, being taught by instructors from the nearby Berklee College Of Music while still at high school. Bergonzi graduated from Lowell State University in 1972 and went to New York that year, soon beginning what was to be a 10-year association with Dave Brubeck, first in the Two Generations band, then as the featured horn in Brubeck's quartet. Bergonzi returned to Boston in 1987, and began a series of recording projects under his own name for his own label, and also for Italy's Red Records. He ran his own bands, the quartet Con Brio and the Trio Gonz, and when Mike Brecker's young pianist Joey Calderazzo got his recording debut for Blue Note Records in 1990, he called on Brecker, Branford Marsalis and Bergonzi to be the horns. Bergonzi's spirited performance convinced Blue Note to record his major-label debut.

● ALBUMS: *Con Brio* (1985)★★★, *Jerry On Red* (Red 1989)★★★, *Lineage* (1989)★★★, with Joey Calderazzo *In The Door* (1990)★★★, with Calderazzo *To Know One* (1991)★★★, *Standard Gonz* (Blue Note 1991)★★★★, *Lieage* (Red 1991)★★★, *Etc Plus One* (Red 1992)★★★, *Tilt* (Red 1992)★★★, *Signed By* (Deux 1992)★★★★, with Trio Idea *Napoli Connection* (1994)★★★, *Peek-A-Boo* (Evidence 1995)★★★★, with Hal Galper *Rebop* (Enja 1996)★★★, with Victor Lewis, Guido Manusardi, Dave Santoro *Within* (Soul Note 1997)★★★, *Just Within* (Double-Time 1998)★★★.

BERIGAN, BUNNY

b. Rowland Bernart Berigan, 2 November 1908, Hilbert, Calumet, Wisconsin, USA, d. 2 June 1942, New York, USA. One of the outstanding trumpeters of the swing era, Berigan was heavily influenced by Louis Armstrong and at his best played with much of his idol's attack and zest. In the early 30s he worked with numerous bands, including those of Paul Whiteman, Fred Rich, Tommy Dorsey and Benny Goodman (with whom he was playing when the band made its popular breakthrough at the Palomar Ballroom in Los Angeles in August 1936, the gig that launched the swing era). Berigan also worked in the studios, playing in house bands, and in 1937 formed his own big band. The band was very popular and had several hits, including a version of 'I Can't Get Started' on which the leader sings engagingly and plays one of the most celebrated jazz solos of the era. Berigan played with a full and gorgeous sound, his open horn having a burnished quality that brought added texture to his interpretation of the more melodic yet soulful tunes he loved to play. Unfortunately, he lacked discipline in his playing, which could spiral out of control, in much the same way that it was absent from his personal life. Berigan's big band folded in 1940, by which time the leader's drinking was severely damaging his health. He rejoined Dorsey for a while, then re-formed his own band in mid-1941. Early the following year he was taken ill with pneumonia but continued working - and drinking cheap liquor - until he collapsed at the end of May and died in June 1942.

● COMPILATIONS: *Bunny Berigan 1937-38* (RCA Victor 1951)★★★★, *Bunny Berigan Plays* Again (RCA Victor 1952)★★★★, *Take It Bunny* (Epic 1955)★★★, *Bunny Berigan And His Orchestra* (RCA Victor 1959)★★★, *Bunny* (RCA Victor 1966)★★★,*The Indispensable Bunny Berigan* 1937-39 recordings (RCA 1983)★★★★, *Bunny Berigan* (Charly 1986)★★★, *Portrait Of Bunny Berigan* (Living Era 1989)★★★, *1938 Broadcasts, Paradise Restaurant* (Jazz Hour 1993)★★★★.

● FURTHER READING: *Bunny Berigan: Elusive Legend Of Jazz*, Robert Dupuis.

BERKLEE COLLEGE OF MUSIC

An establishment founded in 1945 by Berk Lee Elliot in Boston, Massachusetts. The college developed into one of the world's finest educational centres for jazz. The roll call of jazz talent to benefit from tuition at Berklee is testimony to the remarkable qualities of the teaching staff, of whom a leading figure is Herb Pomeroy, a former student. Several graduates have returned there as teachers, among them Alan Dawson and Gordon Brisker. A list of students who have attended Berklee would extend to many pages and include noted figures in the world of jazz and popular music, such as Alan Broadbent, Miroslav Vitous, Roger Neumann, Pat La Barbera, Tommy Smith, Pat Metheny, John Scofield, John Abercrombie, Sadao Watanabe, Mike Gibbs, Gary Burton, Harold Galper, Steve Marcus, Joe Viola, Bill Chase and Gabor Szabo.

BERMAN, SONNY

b. Saul Berman, 21 April 1925, New Haven, Connecticut, USA, d. 16 January 1947. A child prodigy, Berman was playing trumpet in Louis Prima's band by his early teens. He followed this early induction into the big time with a rapid swing through the bands of Georgie Auld, Tommy Dorsey, Sonny Dunham, Benny Goodman and Harry James, before settling into Woody Herman's First Herd at the beginning of 1945. He remained with Herman until the band folded at the end of the following year. A musician of immense if undeveloped talent, Berman's solo playing ranged over intensely felt dramatic works, such as 'Nocturne', '125th Street Prophet' and 'Sidewalks Of Cuba' to the raw excitement of 'Apple Honey'. Influenced by the early bebop playing of Dizzy Gillespie, Berman's career ended abruptly when he suffered heart failure, apparently as a result of a drugs overdose, and died in January 1947 when still only 21 years old.

● COMPILATIONS: *Sonny Berman 1946* (Esoteric 1954)★★★.

BERNARD, WILL

Versatile guitarist Bernard shot to attention as a sideman, playing in Charlie Hunter's weird and wonderful tribute band, TJ Kirk. The Berkley native also appeared regularly with the Peter Apfelbaum Sextet and Jai Uttal's Pagan Love Orchestra, skipping adeptly between a variety of musical styles ranging from ambient dub to funk jazz. A Berkeley graduate with a degree in composition, Bernard's current projects illustrate the range of his talents. He co-leads the dub/jazz collective Pothole, and leads his own Will Bernard 4tet. The latter's debut recording for the Antilles label, featuring Bernard regulars Rob Burger (organ/accordion), John Shifflet (bass) and Scott Amendola (drums), demonstrated the guitarist's mastery of slide playing and the blues and funk idioms, and his ability to stretch the boundaries of groove-orientated music.

● ALBUMS: with Pothole *Dirty Picnic* (Intuition 1998)★★★, *Medicine Hat* (Antilles 1998)★★★★.

BERNE, TIM

b. 16 October 1954, Syracuse, New York, USA. One of the outstanding young members of New York's *avant garde* jazz scene, alto saxophonist Berne did not begin to play the instrument until he was 19 years old. After studying with both Anthony Braxton and, especially, Julius Hemphill, he set up his own record label, Empire Productions, and in 1979 travelled to the west coast to record his debut album because he found New York musicians 'too aggressive'. His second album, *7X*, also features west coast players (Vinny Golia, Alex Cline and Roberto Miranda are on both records), but subsequent releases *Spectres* and *Songs And Rituals In Real Time . . .* were recorded in New York and included appearances by Olu Dara, Ed Schuller and Paul Motian. The latter pair also formed the rhythm section on Berne's next two albums, *The Ancestors* and *Mutant Variations*, both released on the Italian Soul Note label. His final album on his own Empire Productions was *Theoretically*, a 1984 duo with upcoming guitarist Bill Frisell (and later reissued on the German Minor Music label with an extra track). With his career at a temporary standstill, Berne took a job serving behind the counter at New York's Tower Records shop, where a chance meeting turned his luck around: a childhood friend, Gary Lucas (ex-Captain Beefheart guitarist and then working as an advertising executive for Columbia Records), spotted Berne in Tower and persuaded CBS Records to sign him up. His two records for the label, *Fulton Street Maul* and *Sanctified Dreams*, won huge critical acclaim and, although the company refused to renew his contract ('The people in the higher echelon positions didn't like the music, they had a real negative attitude to it.'), Berne was now established as a major voice in contemporary jazz. He formed the co-operative trio Miniature, with Hank Roberts and Joey Baron; guested on John Zorn's Ornette Coleman tribute, *Spy Vs Spy*; and in 1991 toured Europe in a duo with pianist Marilyn Crispell. However, his own group remains his top priority: usually a five or six-piece that often includes long-time associates Baron, Roberts, Mark Dresser and Herb Robertson, Berne describes their music as 'about rhythms, textures, harmonic ideas, tonal things, non-tonal things, moods, shapes . . . (I use) little motifs and fragments . . . to set up a context for spontaneity'. The result is a fresh-sounding, small-group jazz that looks set to lead the field into the 90s.

● ALBUMS: *The Five-Year Plan* (Empire 1979)★★★, *7X* (Empire 1980)★★★★, *Spectres* (Empire 1981)★★★, *Songs And Rituals In Real Time...* (Empire 1982)★★★★, *The Ancestors* (Soul Note 1983)★★★★, *Mutant Variations* (Soul Note 1984)★★★, with Bill Frisell *Theoretically* (Minor 1984)★★★, *Fulton Street Maul* (Columbia 1986)★★★, *Sanctified Dreams* (Columbia 1987)★★★, with Hank Roberts, Joey Baron *Miniature* (1988)★★★, *Fractured Fairy Tales* (JMT 1989)★★★, *Peace Yourself* (JMT 1991)★★★, with Miniature *I Can't Put My Finger On It* (1991)★★★, with Michael Formanek, Jeff Hirshfield *Loose Cannon* (1993)★★★, *Diminutive Mysteries* (JMT 1993)★★★★, *Nice View* (JMT 1994)★★★★, *Lowlife: The Paris Concert* (JMT 1996)★★★★, *Poisoned Minds: The Paris Concert* (JMT 1996)★★★, *Memory Select: The Paris Concert* (JMT 1996)★★★, with Formanek *Ornery People* (Little Brother 1998)★★★★, *Unwound* (Screwgun 1998)★★★, *Big Satan* (Winter And Winter 1998)★★★★, *Visitation Rites* (Screwgun 1998)★★★, with Bloodcount *Discretion* (Screwgun 1998)★★★.

BERNHARDT, CLYDE

b. 11 July 1905, Gold Hill, North Carolina, USA, d. 20 May 1986, Newark, New Jersey, USA. Trombonist Bernhardt, aka Ed Barron, paid the usual dues of the jazzman by playing in myriad small territory bands in the Midwest, before moving to New York City in 1928. In 1930, he hit the big time when he was hired by Joe 'King' Oliver to play and sing with his Harlem Syncopators; later with Vernon Andrade, Edgar Hayes (with whom he made his recording debut for Decca), Horace Henderson, Oran 'Hot Lips' Page, Stuff Smith, Fats Waller, Jay McShann, Cecil Scott, Luis Russell,

Claude Hopkins and Dud Bascomb. After World War II, Bernhardt formed his own R&B jump combo. Bernhardt's strong feeling for the blues made him a natural for the R&B scene and he led his own band, the Blue Blazers, with whom he recorded in his own right for several small specialist labels between 1946 and 1953, and also backed Wynonie Harris on his debut session for King Records. On these recordings, Bernhardt proved himself to be a talented blues singer in the Jimmy Rushing/Big Joe Turner mould (he once claimed he had been shouting the blues in this style since playing with King Oliver in 1930). From the mid-50s, apart from the occasional gig, Bernhardt worked mainly outside music, but was rediscovered in 1968 when he was brought out of retirement to record for Saydisc Matchbox's Blues Series. He formed his own label in 1975 and began touring with his Harlem Blues & Jazz Band, which remained hugely popular in Europe, even after Bernhardt's death.

● ALBUMS: *Blowin' My Top* (1968)★★★, *Blues And Jazz From Harlem* (1972)★★★, *Sittin' On Top Of The World!* (1975)★★★★, *Clyde Bernhardt And The Harlem Blues And Jazz Band* (1975)★★★★, *Clyde Bernhardt And The Harlem Blues And Jazz Band At The 7th International Jazz Festival, Breda* (1977)★★★★, *Clyde Bernhardt & The Harlem Blues Jazz Band* (1978)★★★, *More Blues & Jazz From Harlem* (1979)★★★.

● FURTHER READING: *I Remember: Eighty Years Of Black Entertainment, Big Bands And Blues*, Clyde E. B. Bernhardt and Sheldon Harris.

Bernhardt, Warren

b. November 1938, Wausau, West Indies. As a child Bernhardt studied classical piano and also performed. While attending college in the USA he began playing jazz piano, thereafter touring nationally and overseas. In the early 60s he went to New York where he worked as a studio session musician, backing many pop artists, and also playing in clubs with jazzmen such as Gerry Mulligan, Clark Terry and George Benson. In the 70s he was a member of Jack DeJohnette's Directions, and also of small groups, often as co-leader, with Mike Mainieri, Peter Erskine, Eddie Gomez, and others. In the mid-80s he was reunited with several of these musicians as co-leader, with Michael Brecker, of Steps Ahead. His recording credits include appearances with artists as diverse as Art Garfunkel and Chuck Loeb. Bernhardt's playing style is uncompromisingly modern in outlook, vigorously post-bop and at times he explores modal developments. Bernhardt has also composed music, in some instances for motion pictures, and he is a noted teacher. He has produced a three-volume video, *You Can Play Jazz Piano*.

● ALBUMS: *Solo Piano* (Arista Novus 1977)★★★, *Free Smiles* (Arista Novus 1978)★★★, *Floating* (Arista Novus 1979)★★, *Trio '83* (DMP 1983)★★★, *Hands On* (DMP 1987)★★★, *Heat Of The Moment* (DMP 1989)★★★, *Ain't Life Grand* (DMP 1990)★★★★, *Reflections* (DMP 1992)★★★, *Family Album* (DMP 1993)★★★.

Bernstein, Artie

b. Arthur Bernstein, 4 February 1909, New York, USA, d. 4 January 1964. Before taking up the bass Bernstein played cello, working in dance bands. After abandoning a career in law, he became a professional musician and worked in New York with several noted jazzmen of the early 30s, including Red Nichols and Tommy and Jimmy Dorsey. Bernstein played extensively with pick-up bands on recording sessions, both on jazz and pop dates. In mid-1939 he joined Benny Goodman, playing in his big band and sextet, recording and appearing at the band's second, and much less well-known, Carnegie Hall Concert. He left Goodman early in 1941, deciding upon a career as a studio musician in Hollywood. This new career was interrupted by service during World War II when he continued to play, this time with an Army Air Force band. His film and television studio work continued through the late 40s and 50s and until shortly before his death. Bernstein was a strong and technically accomplished musician, and he provided a solid, swinging base to the bands with which he worked.

Berry, Bill

b. 14 September 1930, Benton Harbor, Michigan, USA. A largely self-taught cornetist, Berry's first job was with Don Strickland, who led a Midwest territory band. In the mid-50s Berry worked with Herb Pomeroy's Boston-based band and from there went into one of Woody Herman's lesser-known bands ('We called it the un-Herd'). After leaving Herman he joined Maynard Ferguson and in 1961 was invited to join Duke Ellington, an experience which he readily admits changed his whole life. After two years with Ellington, Berry worked extensively in New York studios, but also played and recorded with jazz artists such as Coleman Hawkins and Jimmy Rushing. He played with the Thad Jones-Mel Lewis band in New York in the mid-60s and also formed a rehearsal band that met with local success. When the television show on which he worked every week was abruptly relocated to Los Angeles, Berry took up the offer of continued employment and has been based on the west coast ever since. In 1971 he re-formed his rehearsal band, through whose ranks have passed a remarkable group of players, including Cat Anderson, Conte and Pete Candoli, Blue Mitchell, Jimmy Cleveland, Buster Cooper, Richie Kamuca, Bob Cooper, Jake Hanna, Dave Frishberg and Teddy Edwards. Although he still worked extensively in film and television studios (including ghosting for Frank Sinatra Jnr. in *A Man Called Adam* and for Bruce Willis in an episode of *Moonlighting*), Berry concentrated more and more on jazz, until by the 80s he was fully engaged in tours of Europe and Japan. He is especially popular in Japan, appearing there as a single, with fellow visitors such as Benny Carter, and as musical director of the Monterey Jazz Festival's All Stars and annual all-star university students' band. In 1989 and 1990 Berry played several UK concerts as a guest artist with the Brian Priestley Special Septet and recorded with them on a limited-edition cassette release, *Bilberry Jam*. He also performs regularly with small groups and his own big band in and around Los Angeles. Preferring cornet to trumpet, Berry plays ballads with considerable melodic grace and charm, while on up-tempo tunes his playing crackles with boppish phrases. He also favours playing tightly muted, working close to the microphone to create an exhilarating sound. In 1991 he broke new ground with an appearance in an acting role, as an American trumpeter, in Alan Plater's *Misterioso*, a film made for British television. His LA big band was host to the 1991 Ellington Conference in Los Angeles, receiving rave press notices. The same year, his big band accompanied Mel Tormé in concert at the Hollywood Bowl. Held in great respect by his peers, both for his musical abilities and for his personal warmth and enthusiasm, Berry is also a skilled arranger and composer. Among his compositions are 'Bloose' and 'Betty', the latter a delightful ballad written for his wife, a former singer. Throughout the 90s Berry continued to tour extensively, especially to Japan. He and his wife promote the annual Jazz Party that unites American and Japanese musicians in a popular festival of mainstream music.

● ALBUMS: *Jazz And Swinging Percussion* (Directional Sound 1963)★★★, *The Bill Berry Quartet* (1963)★★★★, *Hot And Happy* (Beez 1974)★★★, *Hello Rev* (Concord 1976)★★★, *A Tribute To Duke* (1977)★★★★, *Shortcake* (Concord 1978)★★★, *For Duke* (1978)★★★, with Brian Priestley *Bilberry Jam* (1990)★★★, with Jack Nimitz *Live At Capozzoli's* (Woofy 1997)★★, with Eiji Kitamura *Jazz Party* (Jazz Cook 1998)★★★.

Berry, Chu

b. Leon Berry, 13 September 1910, Wheeling, West Virginia, USA, d. 30 October 1941, Conneaut, Oklahoma, USA. In the early 30s Berry played tenor saxophone with a number of New York bands, including sessions for Spike Hughes and spells with the bands of Benny Carter and Fletcher Henderson. He was in great demand among leaders who were setting up recording and club sessions and played on memorable dates with Roy Eldridge and Lionel Hampton. In 1937, he was added to the Cab Calloway band, where his musical influence helped to build the band's reputation as a fine jazz outfit. An eloquent soloist, Berry's playing was in the mould of Coleman Hawkins, with a rich and emotional sound. However, before he was able to forge a completely distinctive style, he received severe head injuries in a car crash while touring with Calloway and died a few days later.

● ALBUMS: with Lester Young *Tops On Tenor* (Jazztone 1956)★★★.

● COMPILATIONS: *Chu Berry Memorial* 10-inch album (Commodore 1952)★★★, *Chu* (Epic 1955)★★★, *Sittin' In* (Mainstream 1965)★★★★, *The Rarest 1937-40* (Everybody's 1982)★★★, *The Indispensable* 1936-1939 recordings (RCA 1985)★★★★, *Giant Of The Tenor Sax* 1938-1941 recordings (Commodore Class 1986)★★★, *The Calloway Years (1937)* (Meritt 1988)★★★.

Berry, Emmett

b. 23 July 1915, Macon, Georgia, USA. In 1933, within a year of his first professional job, Berry was in New York and playing trumpet with leading bands of the day. In 1936 he joined Fletcher Henderson's band, replacing Roy Eldridge. He remained with Henderson for three years, moving on to the band led by Fletcher's brother, Horace. In the early 40s Berry was with Teddy Wilson's elegant sextet and also worked with Lionel Hampton, Benny Carter, John Kirby and Roy Eldridge's Little Jazz Trumpet Ensemble. Most of the second half of the decade was spent with Count Basie. In the 50s he played with Jimmy Rushing, Johnny Hodges, Cootie Williams and Sammy Price, recording extensively. In the 60s he settled in Los Angeles but was soon back on the road again with Peanuts Hucko and Wilbur De Paris. A masterly player, Berry's solos were always immaculately conceived and executed with fire and passion. Retired since 1970, he left his distinctive mark on countless records.

Bert, Eddie

b. 16 May 1922, Yonkers, New York, USA. After studying trombone with Benny Powell, Bert's first name-band job was with Sam Donahue in 1940. After Army service, he continued his apprenticeship with bands led by Red Norvo, Charlie Barnet and Woody Herman. In 1946, Bert began a period of sustained big band work, during which time he had two important spells with Stan Kenton. Throughout the 50s Bert worked mostly in small groups (sometimes as leader), including Charles Mingus's Jazz Workshop and a regular Monday night gig at Birdland. Towards the end of the 50s and throughout most of the 60s, he worked in the theatre in New York and also advanced his musical education with formal studies. Whenever possible he played jazz, working for leaders such as Mingus, Benny Goodman (with whose band he had briefly played in the late 40s) and Thelonious Monk. Although a flexible player, capable of blending into small bebop groups and mainstream bands, Bert's power and attack lend themselves best to a big band setting, as he proved when with the Thad Jones-Mel Lewis band and on the festival circuit with Lionel Hampton's all-star orchestra in 1978.

● ALBUMS: *Eddie Bert Quintet* (Discovery 1953)★★★, *Let's Dig Bert* reissued as *Like Cool* (Trans-World 1955)★★★★, *Musician Of The Year* (Savoy 1955)★★★, *Encore* (Savoy 1955)★★★, *Modern Moods* (Jazztone 1956)★★★★, *East Coast Sounds* (Jazztone 1959)★★★, *Westchester Workshop* (60s)★★, *Skeleton Of The Band* (1976)★★★, with J.R. Monterose *Live At Birdland* (1993)★★★.

Berton, Vic

b. Victor Cohen, 6 May 1896, Chicago, Illinois, USA, d. 26 December 1951. Berton began playing piano and violin while still a child, and when he was seven years old was playing drums in the pit band at the Alhambra Theatre, Milwaukee. In his early teens he studied percussion and worked with classical orchestras; later he was with a band led by John Philip Sousa during World War I. In the early 20s, Berton played with several small-time jazz groups in Chicago and also became involved in management. In 1924 he managed the Wolverines, with whom he also occasionally played. Later in the decade he played with the show bands of Roger Wolfe Kahn, Sam Lanin, Vincent Lopez and Paul Whiteman, and recorded extensively with numerous bands playing popular music and jazz, notably those of Miff Mole, Bix Beiderbecke and Red Nichols. One of the early personalities in jazz, Berton was a student of occultism and often received visitors while attired in long black robes. In 1931 he hit the headlines when he was arrested with Louis Armstrong for smoking marijuana. In the 30s and 40s Berton worked mainly in Hollywood film studios and also played with symphony orchestras in Los Angeles and New York. Berton's technical qualities were never in doubt, although his playing lacked the free-flowing swing of the best jazz drummers. In some respects this failing rested with his classical training, although he did use this to good effect in jazz, as when playing tympanis with Nichols. He is also credited with inventing a form of hi-hat cymbal in the mid-20s.

BERTRAND, JIMMY

b. James Bertrand, 24 February 1900, Biloxi, Mississippi, USA, d. August 1960. Born into a highly musical family (a cousin was New Orleans drummer Andrew Hilaire) Bertrand first played drums professionally in his late teens. At that time he was living in Chicago and for many years he was with Erskine Tate's popular band, which headlined at the Vendome Theater. He recorded with Tate and also gigged betweentimes with several other bands, including the Washboard Wizards, of which he was leader, featuring Louis Armstrong. Among the musicians with whom he played and recorded were Dave Peyton, Lee Collins and Eddie South. During the 30s and into the mid-40s Bertrand continued to gig and lead small bands in the Chicago area. Bertrand was a good drummer with a penchant for flamboyant accoutrements. His drum kit was equipped with little electric lightbulbs that flashed on and off when he took solos. It was this gimmick that attracted the attention of Lionel Hampton, whose uncle, Richard Morgan, bought him a kit with similar gimmickry. Bertrand appears also to have given lessons to Hampton, Sid Catlett and others.

● ALBUMS: *Jimmy Bertrand's Washboard Wizards* (Ace Of Hearts 1926)★★★, with Eddie South *No More Blues* (RCA 1927-33)★★★.

BEST, DENZIL DE COSTA

b. 27 April 1917, USA, d. 24 May 1965, New York, USA. A multi-instrumentalist, playing trumpet, piano and bass, Best did not begin playing drums until he was in his mid-20s. Despite this late start, he was almost instantly in demand as a session musician, playing and recording with such leading 40s jazz artists as Coleman Hawkins, Illinois Jacquet, Lee Konitz, Thelonious Monk (with whom he wrote 'Bemsha Swing') and Ben Webster. In 1949 he was a member of George Shearing's original quintet, and in the 50s worked extensively with Erroll Garner. A subtle and discreet player, especially effective on brushes, Best suffered from a progressive disease in which calcium deposits on the bones in his wrists gradually made it impossible for him to play. Best composed several bop standards including 'Move' and 'Wee'. He died in 1965 from injuries sustained from a fall on a New York subway staircase.

BEST, JOHNNY

b. John McClanian Best Jnr., 20 October 1913, Shelby, North Carolina, USA. Although he first learned to play piano, by the start of his teenage years he had switched to trumpet. Best quickly became highly proficient and was soon working with dance bands and from there joined several big bands of the swing era. He played with Les Brown, Charlie Barnet, Artie Shaw and had a long spell with Glenn Miller. During military service in World War II he was in Shaw's and Sam Donahue's US Navy bands. After the war he played with Benny Goodman and Bob Crosby, with whom he briefly worked in the early 40s. During the late 40s and into the 50s he profitably mixed work in studio bands with name band tours and revivals, including Crosby, Billy May and, some years later, Ray Conniff. This activity continued into the 80s when he worked with Crosby at Disneyland (1980), a Miller-band reunion (1984) and Crosby again (1985). Best was originally influenced by Louis Armstrong, as were so many trumpeters of his generation. He developed into a triple-threat player, combining sterling section work with disciplined and inspiring lead trumpet playing, and with original, powerful soloing. His reputation and his recorded legacy are both rather less than he so clearly deserves.

BEY, ANDY

b. *c.* 1940, Newark, New Jersey, USA. One of the most underrated vocalists currently plying their trade, Bey was belatedly championed with the release of *Ballads Blues & Bey* in 1996. Bey was brought up in Newark and attended Arts High, a college with a prestigious roll call of jazz alumni including Sarah Vaughan, Wayne Shorter, Woody Shaw and James Moody. Vaughan was a primary influence on Bey, and the great singer made several visits to Bey's sisters, Salome and Geraldine, at the family house. Later on during his career, Bey often found time to sing with Vaughan during informal sessions at club venues. A precocious talent, the eight-year old Bey was accompanied by tenor saxophonist Hank Mobley at several concerts, and in 1952, when he was 13, released his debut album. During the late 50s Bey toured with his sisters as Andy & The Bey Sisters, and the trio recorded three albums on the RCA-Victor and Riverside labels before disbanding in 1967. Bey later worked with Max Roach, Duke Pearson, Gary Bartz, Philly Joe Jones, and had a long association with Horace Silver during the 1970s, appearing on many of the pianist's self-released and obtuse metaphysical albums. Bey recorded a solitary date for Atlantic Records in the 70s, followed by several sessions as a leader in the following decades on independent labels. In 1996 Bey was deservedly placed back in the limelight when Evidence Records released *Ballads Blues & Bey*. On a powerful and emotional set of American classics, Bey's baritone effortlessly cuts to the heart of every song, bringing out delicate nuances often glossed over by lesser singers.

● ALBUMS: *Mama's Little Boy's Got The Blues* (1952)★★★, with The Bey Sisters *Now Hear* (Prestige 1964)★★★★, with The Bey Sisters *'Round About Midnight* (Prestige 1965)★★★, *Experience And Judgement* (Atlantic 1970)★★★, *As Time Goes By* (Jazzette 1991)★★★, *Ballads Blues & Bey* (Evidence 1996)★★★★, *Shades Of Bey* (Evidence 1998)★★★★.

BICKERT, ED

b. Edward Isaac Bickert, 29 November 1932, Hochfeld, Manitoba, Canada. A highly gifted guitarist, Bickert was active in Toronto in the 50s, playing with several leading musicians including Ron Collier, Paul Desmond and Rob McConnell. He attracted wider attention thanks in part to his regular accompaniment for visiting American jazz musicians, including Dave McKenna, and through his contributions to Desmond's last recordings in the mid-70s. It was not until the late 70s, however, that Bickert took full advantage of the manner in which fellow musicians accepted his gently understated skills. He toured overseas with Milt Jackson, recorded with Oscar Peterson, Scott Hamilton, Benny Carter and Rosemary Clooney, and also made records under his own name. In the 80s he visited the UK with Peter Appleyard and also appeared there with George Shearing. He continued to make records, including *Mutual Street*, an interesting duo set with McConnell. In 1990 he appeared at the Concord Summer Jazz Festival in California, playing with Marshal Royal, Ernestine Anderson and others. A highly musical player, interestingly combining introspection with a curiously unassertive authority, Bickert is clearly a major, if still widely unrecognized, talent.

● ALBUMS: *Ed Bickert* (PM 1975)★★★, with Don Thompson *The Ed Bickert-Don Thompson Duo* (Sackville 1978)★★★, *From Canada With Love* (PM 1979)★★★, *In Concert At The Garden Party* (Sackville 1981)★★, *The Ed Bickert 5 At Toronto's Bourbon Street* (Concord Jazz 1983)★★★, *Bye Bye Baby* (Concord Jazz 1983)★★★, *Border Crossing* (Concord 1983)★★★, with Thompson *Dance To The Lady* (Sackville 1983)★★★, with Rob McConnell *Mutual Street* (Innovation 1984)★★★, *I Wished On The Moon* (Concord Jazz 1985)★★★, *Third Floor Richard* (Concord Jazz 1989)★★★★, *Ed Bickert/Lorne Lofsky: This Is New* (Concord Jazz 1989)★★★★, with McConnell, Thompson *Three For The Road* (Concord Picante 1997)★★★.

BIDDELL, KERRIE

b. 8 February 1947. Biddell studied piano for many years before starting a singing career. She sang commercials before her first major job as a backing vocalist for Dusty Springfield at The Chequers in Sydney, Australia. In 1968 Biddell joined the pop group the Affair, and performed with them in England before returning to Australia to work with the exciting new Daly Wilson Big Band. She became the featured vocalist with the band, from 1970-71, singing in a vibrant, forceful style that perfectly matched the band's dynamics. Upon leaving the group she became busy with television work, studio session back-ups and voice-overs. She started a solo career in Sydney clubs and won the *Music Maker* poll as Best Female Jazz Singer. In 1974, she made her first trip to the USA and Canada. In Australia the ABC radio programme, *Kerrie Biddell And Friends*, was well received; even more so was her first solo album, which won The Australian Record Award's Best Female Vocal Album. Returning to America, she appeared on *The Merv Griffen Show* and enjoyed a residency at the MGM Grand Hotel in Las Vegas. She formed the jazz fusion band Compared To What, which recorded the first Australian digital album for EMI Records. In 1983 she joined the faculty of the Jazz Diploma Course at the Conservatorium of New South Wales and taught masterclasses and vocal workshops for seven years. Working with Julian Lee, she won the Bicentennial Music award for Best Jazz Vocalist in 1988 and the Mo Award for Best Female Jazz Performer in 1990. In 1992 Biddell wrote her, *Legends* show and was musical director for the play *Lipstick*. Another Mo Award in 1994 preceded a residency in Sydney's Tilbury Hotel. Two years later she sang in the Sydney Theatre Company production of *As You Like It* and worked on a new album. Biddell is a good choice as Australia's best contemporary female jazz singer. Her voice, style and versatility inspired a critic to suggest, 'her talents are so formidable that she is impossible to categorise. She is without doubt the most underrated talent in Australia'.

● ALBUMS: *The Exciting Daly Wilson Big Band Featuring Kerrie Biddell* (Festival 1972)★★★, *Kerrie Biddell* (EMI 1975)★★★★, *Only The Beginning* (EMI 1976)★★★, *Compared To What* (EMI 1980)★★★, *There Will Never Be Another You* (1992)★★★, *The Singer* (1996)★★★.

BIG BAND BOSSA NOVA - STAN GETZ

Stan Getz's name is synonymous with the bossa nova movement. A profoundly lyrical tenor saxophonist, full of melodic surprises and aided by a flawless, virtuoso technique, he was, along with guitarist Charlie Byrd and the Gilbertos, one of the key figures fusing bossa with jazz in the 60s. This 1962 Verve Records big band date (recorded a year before the hugely successful 'The Girl From Ipanema') features four classic compositions by Bonfa, Gilberto and Antonio Carlos Jobim, and four authentic-sounding original tunes by arranger Gary McFarland. Getz is on inspired form throughout, and there is a characteristically beautiful contribution by guitarist Jim Hall on the opening 'Manha De Carnival'.

● Tracks: *Manha De Carnival; Balanco No Samba; Melancolico; Entre Amigos; Chega De Sandade; Noite Triste; Samba De Uma Nota So; Bim Bam.*

● First released 1962

● UK peak chart position: did not chart

● USA peak chart position: 13

BIG GUNDOWN, THE - JOHN ZORN

New York-based alto saxophonist, composer and controversial avant gardist John Zorn recorded this tribute to the brilliant soundtrack composer Ennio Morricone (the man behind the music in Sergio Leone's westerns) in 1984/5, and called upon a huge and disparate roster of musicians to give the record its stunning sense of variety. There are appearances by fellow experimenters Bobby Previte (drums), Wayne Horvitz (piano), Tim Berne (alto saxophone) and Christian Marclay (turntables), as well as more mainstream stars, like Toots Thielemans (harmonica) and 'Big' John Patton (organ), but these powerful revisions of Morricone's often disturbing and trippy themes clearly comes out of Zorn's own wacky, offbeat and thoroughly original vision.

● Tracks: *The Big Gundown; Peur Sur La Ville; Poverty (Once Upon A Time In America); Milano Odea; Erotico (The Burglars); Battle Of Algiers; Giu La Testa (Duck, You Sucker!); Metamorfosi (La Classe Operaia Va In Paradiso); Tre Nel 5000; Once Upon A Time In The West.*

● First released 1986

● UK peak chart position: did not chart

● USA peak chart position: did not chart

BIGARD, BARNEY

b. Albany Leon Bigard, 3 March 1906, New Orleans, Louisiana, USA, d. 27 June 1980, Culver City, California, USA. Born into a highly musical family, Bigard began studying clarinet at the age of seven, taking lessons from the noted teacher, Lorenzo Tio Jnr. He worked in street parades but then switched to tenor saxophone in 1922 to join the band led by Albert Nicholas. During the next two years, Bigard played in several bands in New Orleans before going to Chicago to join Joe 'King' Oliver. While with Oliver he reverted to clarinet. In the mid-20s he played in Chicago and New York in the bands of Charlie Elgar and Luis Russell before joining Duke Ellington in December 1927. In common with so many Ellingtonians, he remained a member of the band for many years, but eventually left in midsummer 1942 and for the next few years he led his own small bands, worked in the film studios of Hollywood and was also briefly with Freddy Slack. In 1947 he joined Louis Armstrong's newly formed All Stars. He was with Armstrong for five years and then, after a period leading his own band, returned for a further two years in the mid-50s. After working with several bands in the late 50s he rejoined Armstrong for another stint in the early 60s and then played in various bands, including those led by Johnny St. Cyr, Muggsy Spanier, Rex Stewart and Art Hodes. In the 70s he toured with Hodes, Eddie Condon and many others, including the Legends Of Jazz.

In his later years he worked in many places, appeared on television and radio, thoroughly enjoying his role as an elder statesman of jazz. Bigard's was one of the most distinctive jazz voices, his playing characterized by a rich, flowing sound and his habitual use of the lower, chalumeau, register of the clarinet. After joining Ellington, Bigard lost his previous close affinity with the musical forms traditionally associated with his birthplace. Nevertheless, there were always echoes of his origins in his best work, which came mostly during his years with Ellington.

Among his classic recordings from this period of his career are 'Clarinet Lament' ('Barney's Concerto'), 'Mood Indigo', 'Saturday Night Function', 'Barney Goin' Easy' and 'C Jam Blues'. Some of these tunes originated in ideas and fragments Bigard created and that were fashioned by Ellington into minor masterpieces. Although this was Ellington's common practice, in later years Bigard would occasionally disconcert interviewers by ferociously declaring, 'I wrote that!' whenever almost any Ellington composition was mentioned. Although Bigard was a pleasure to hear in later years, there was a great deal of repetition in his work. Indeed, some of his solos, especially on such famous features as 'C Jam Blues', 'Rose Room' and 'Tea For Two', were repeated night after night, year upon year regardless of the company he was keeping. In fairness, it might be added that, having achieved a kind of perfection, he might well have thought there was little point in tampering with what he knew was his best.

● ALBUMS: *Barney Bigard* (Liberty 1957)★★★★, *Bucket's Got A Hole In It* (Delmark 1968)★★★, *Easy On The Ears* (1973)★★★, *Clarinet Gumbo* (RCA 1973)★★★, *Barney Bigard And The Legends Of Jazz* (1974)★★★★, *Jazz Giants In Nice* (1974)★★★, *From Rag To Swing* (1975)★★★★, *Barney Bigard And The Pelican Trio* (1976)★★★, with Claude Luter *Paris December 1960* (Vogue 1990)★★★.

● COMPILATIONS: *Barney Goin' Easy* (1937-40)★★★, *Fantasy For Clarinet And Strings* (1944)★★★.

● FILMS: *St. Louis Blues* (1957).

BILK, ACKER

b. Bernard Stanley Bilk, 28 January 1929, Pensford, Somerset, England. A self-taught clarinettist, Bilk made his first public appearance in 1947 while on National Service in Egypt. On his return to the UK, he played as a semi-professional around the Bristol area, before gaining his big break with the Ken Colyer band in 1954. Four years later, under the name 'Mr' Acker Bilk, he enjoyed his first UK Top 10 hit with 'Summer Set'. Backed by the Paramount Jazz Band, and promoted by his Bilk Marketing Board, he was at the forefront of the British traditional jazz boom of the early 60s. With their distinctive uniform of bowler hats and striped waistcoats, Bilk and company enjoyed a number of jazzy UK hits in the 60s, including 'White Cliffs Of Dover', 'Buona Sera', 'That's My Home', 'Stars And Stripes Forever', 'Frankie And Johnny', 'Gotta See Baby Tonight' and 'A Taste Of Honey'. However, it was with the Leon Young String Chorale that Bilk achieved his most remarkable hit. 'Stranger On The Shore' was a US number 1 in May 1962, and peaked at number 2 in the UK, staying for a record-breaking 55 weeks in the bestsellers. Although the beat boom all but ended the careers of many traditional jazzmen, Bilk has continued to enjoy a successful career in cabaret and concerts, and returned to the Top

10 in 1976, again with a string backing, with 'Aria'. He continues to tour regularly alongside contemporaries such as Kenny Ball and Chris Barber. The trio had a number 1 album, *The Best Of Ball, Barber And Bilk*, in 1962. Bilk remains a major figure in traditional jazz, and more than 30 years after 'Stranger On The Shore' gained an Ivor Novello Award for 'Most Performed Work'. In 1995 it featured in a UK television commercial for Volkswagen cars.

● ALBUMS: *Mr. Acker Requests* (Pye Nixa 1958)★★★, *Mr. Acker Marches On* (1958)★★★, *Mr. Acker Bilk Sings* (1959)★★, *Mr. Acker Bilk Requests (Part One)* (1959)★★★, *Mr. Acker Bilk Requests (Part Two)* (1959)★★★, *The Noble Art Of Mr. Acker Bilk* (1959)★★★, *Seven Ages Of Acker* (Columbia 1960)★★★★, *Mr. Acker Bilk's Omnibus* (Pye 1960)★★★, *Acker* (Columbia 1960)★★★, *A Golden Treasury Of Bilk* (Columbia 1961)★★★★, *Mr. Acker Bilk's Lansdowne Folio* (1961)★★★, *Stranger On The Shore* (Columbia 1961)★★★★, *Above The Stars And Other Romantic Fancies* (1962)★★★, *A Taste Of Honey* (Columbia 1963)★★★★, *Great Themes From Great European Movies* (1965)★★, *Acker In Paris* (1966)★★, *Blue Acker* (1968)★★★★, *Some Of My Favourite Things* (PRT 1973)★★★, *That's My Desire* (1974)★★★, *Serenade* (1975)★★★, *The One For Me* (PRT 1976)★★★, *Invitation* (PRT 1977)★★★, *Meanwhile* (1977)★★★, *Sheer Magic* (Warwick 1977)★★★, *Extremely Live In Studio 1* (1978)★★, *Free* (1978)★★★, *When The Lights Are Low* (1978)★★★, with Max Bygraves *Twogether* (Piccadilly 1980)★★, *Unissued Acker* (1980)★★★, *Made In Hungary* (PRT 1980)★★★, *The Moment I'm With You* (1980)★★★, *Mama Told Me So* (PRT 1980)★★★, *The Moment I'm With You* (PRT 1981)★★★, *Relaxin'* (PRT 1981)★★★, *Wereldsuccessen* (Philips 1982)★★★, *I Think The Best Thing About This Record Is The Music* (Bell 1982)★★, *Acker Bilk In Holland* (Timeless 1985)★★, *Nature Boy* (PRT 1985)★★★, *Acker's Choice* (Teldec 1985)★★★, *John, Paul And Acker* (1986)★★, *Love Songs My Way* (Topline 1987)★★, *On Stage* (Start 1988)★★★, with Ken Colyer *It Looks Like A Big Time Tonight* (Stomp Off 1988)★★★, *That's My Home* (1988)★★★, *The Love Album* (Pickwick 1989)★★★, with Chris Barber, Kenny Ball *Trad Days 1959/60* (1990)★★★★, *Imagine* (Pulse 1991)★★, *Blaze Away* (Timeless 1990)★★★★, *The Ultimate!* (1991)★★★, *Heartbeats* (Pickwick 1991)★★★, with Humphrey Lyttelton *At Sundown* (Calligraph 1992)★★★★, with Lyttelton *Three In The Morning* (Calligraph 1995)★★★★, *Chalumeau That's My Home* (Apricot 1995)★★★★, *Oscar Winners* (Carlton 1995)★★.

● COMPILATIONS: *The Best Of Ball, Barber And Bilk* (Pye 1962)★★★★, *Golden Hour Of Acker Bilk* (Knight 1974)★★★★, *Very Best Of Acker Bilk* (1978)★★★★, *Evergreen* (Warwick 1978)★★★, *The Acker Bilk Saga* (Polydor 1979)★★★, *Sheer Magic* (1979)★★★, *The Best Of Acker Bilk, Volume Two* (1979)★★★, *Mellow Music* (1980)★★★, *Spotlight On Acker Bilk* (PRT 1980)★★★, *100 Minutes Of Bilk* (PRT 1982)★★★★, *Spotlight On Acker Bilk Volume 2* (PRT 1982)★★★, *I'm In The Mood For Love* (Philips 1983)★★★, *Finest Moments* (Castle 1986)★★★, *Magic Clarinet Of Acker Bilk* (K-Tel 1986)★★★, *16 Golden Memories* (Spectrum 1988)★★★, *Best Of Acker Bilk His Clarinet And Strings* (PRT 1988)★★★, *Hits Blues And Classics* (Kaz 1988)★★★, *The Collection* (Castle 1989)★★★, *Images* (Knight 1989)★★★, *After Midnight* (Pickwick 1990)★★★, *In A Mellow Mood* (Castle 1992)★★★, *Reflections* (Spectrum 1993)★★★, *Acker Bilk Songbook* (Tring 1993)★★★, *Bridge Over Troubled Water* (Spectrum 1995)★★.

● FURTHER READING: *The Book Of Bilk*, P. Leslie and P. Gwynn-Jones.

● FILMS: *It's Trad, Dad!* (1962), *It's All Over Town* (1964).

BILLIE'S BLUES - BILLIE HOLIDAY

An album that collects her work between 1935 and 1939. Fifteen tracks recorded with Teddy Wilson And His Orchestra, including historically important tracks such as 'The Way You Look Tonight' and 'A Sunbonnet Blue'. The remastering using 3-Dimensional Sound has removed the obligatory crackles and pops, which were standard issue in the 30s. The remaining 10 tracks are those recorded with her own orchestra, which features some excellent playing from band members such as Buck Clayton, Artie Shaw, Irving Fazola and Bunny Berigan. 'I Cried for You' and 'Night And Day' are particularly impressive. Vital stuff for any student of the magnificent Lady Day.

● Tracks: *A Sunbonnet Blue; What A Little Moonlight Can Do; Billie's Blues; Eeny Meeny Miny Mo; These 'N' That 'N' Those; One, Two, Button Your Shoe; The Way You Look Tonight; With Thee I Swing; The Man I Love; A Fine Romance; It's Like Reaching For The Moon; Let's Call A Heart A Heart; I Cried For You; No Regrets; Who Loves You?; That's Life, I Guess; On The Sentimental Side; What A Night, What A Moon, What A Boy!; I Must Have That Man; Spreadin' Rhythm Around; You Go To My Head; Yankee Doodle Never Went To Town; Night And Day; Easy To Love; Yesterdays.*

● First released (1935-1939 recordings)

● UK peak chart position: did not chart

● USA peak chart position: did not chart

BIONDI, RAY

b. Remo Biondi, 5 July 1905, Cicero, Illinois, USA, d. 28 January 1981. A gifted multi-instrumentalist, in his younger days Biondi played mostly violin with several Chicago dance bands. His repertoire at that time included light classical music, influenced by his training at the American Conservatory of Music in Chicago. He added mandolin and trumpet to his accomplishments, playing with Chicago bands including one led by Joseph 'Wingy' Manone. He also played in clubs with Bud Freeman. In the mid-30s he went to New York where he played with Joe Marsala, doubling on violin and trumpet, and first began to use the guitar extensively. It was on this instrument that he played with Gene Krupa's band, with which he remained for most of the leader's big band-leading career. In Krupa's band-with-strings periods, Biondi returned to his first instrument. After a brief spell running a nightclub in the late 40s, he continued to play, again with Krupa in the early 50s, and then with various bands, mostly appearing on recording dates rather than as a regular touring member, preferring to remain close to his Chicago base. The bands with which he played in these years included those led by Ray Anthony, Woody Herman and Louis Armstrong. He was also called on by recording studio bands and backed many pop artists including Pat

Boone. In the 60s he was active again in jazz circles and also taught extensively, the latter role occupying much of his time in his later years. Biondi's guitar-playing helped to provide a strong rhythmic pulse for the Krupa band although he was always discreet and sometimes audible more to the band members than to the public. His violin-playing was also usually anonymously hidden, but he did record with a country music band led by Johnny Wicks, an occasion on which he used electrical amplification to good effect.

BIRD

In defence of any biopic about a seminal figure in the arts, it has to be said that depicting on film the creative process and the manner in which an individual can inspire a generation is nearly impossible - so it proves in this account of the life of Charlie Parker. This 1988 film also misses Parker's articulateness and his sharp and ready wit. For all these shortcomings, however, *Bird* is an honestly conceived and well-made attempt at portraying this erratic genius of jazz. Drawing heavily upon Chan Parker's account of her common-law husband's life, rather than upon reminiscences of his musical peers, the film frequently but perhaps misleadingly stresses the turbulent life of one of the half-dozen greatest figures in jazz history, while allowing his importance to jazz slip by as if it were almost incidental to his private life. Nevertheless, director Client Eastwood's admiration and affection for his subject makes up for most of the film's historical uncertainty, and is infinitely superior to the rag-tag 50s biopics of swing era favourites such as Benny Goodman, Gene Krupa and Glenn Miller. Clearly, Eastwood worked on the project for love not money, and with a solid, if uncharismatic, central performance from Forest Whitaker, *Bird* surprisingly proved to have box-office appeal that far transcended the hardcore jazz audience. The soundtrack is a brilliant display of latter-day technology, allied to astute and perceptive musical understanding. Overseen by Lennie Niehaus, Parker's solos from some of his original recordings were detached from their sometimes scrappy surroundings, and provided with newly recorded accompaniment by leading latter-day bop musicians. The end result is musical excellence, even if, predictably perhaps, the film and its re-jigged music was received in some quarters with a marked lack of enthusiasm. Among the musicians appearing on the soundtrack are Monty Alexander, Chuck Berghofer, Ray Brown, Conte Candoli, Ron Carter, Pete Christlieb, Bob Cooper, Walter Davis Jnr., Jon Faddis, John Guerin, Barry Harris, Pete Jolly, Bill Watrous and Red Rodney (portrayed in the film by Michael Zelniker and Charles McPherson, who provided all of the non-original Parker performances).

BIRDS OF FIRE - JOHN MCLAUGHLIN AND THE MAHAVISHNU ORCHESTRA

The jazz/rock band the Mahavishnu Orchestra was formed by John McLaughlin shortly after the virtuoso guitarist's brilliant contributions to Miles Davis's masterpiece *Bitches Brew*. Orchestral in power, but in fact just a five-piece, the first Mahavishnu featured keyboardist Jan Hammer, violinist Jerry Goodman, bassist Rick Laird and the advanced drumming of Billy Cobham, and established the fusion vocabulary of noisy, electric virtuosity and complex time signatures. Highlights of *Birds Of Fire* include the climactic and funky 'One Word', featuring a mesmerizing bass figure and an exciting three-way improvisation, and the subtle groove on 'Miles Beyond'.

- Tracks: *Birds Of Fire; Miles Beyond; Celestial Terrestial Commuters; Sapphire Bullets Of Pure Love; Thousand Island Park; Hope; One Word; Sanctuary; Open Country Joy; Resolution.*
- First released 1973
- UK peak chart position: 20
- USA peak chart position: 15

BIRTH OF THE BLUES

Released by Paramount in 1941, this film is remembered mainly for one song, Johnny Mercer's 'The Waiter And The Porter And The Upstairs Maid', which was performed in exuberant fashion by Bing Crosby, Jack Teagarden and Mary Martin. Harry Tugend and Walter DeLeon's screenplay was set in New Orleans at a time when the 'devil' jazz music was threatening the cosy world of opulent operettas. Throughout his life, Crosby was associated with jazz and many of its exalted exponents, including Louis Armstrong, with whom he collaborated so memorably in *High Society*. In *Birth Of The Blues*, as well as crooning, Crosby is the clarinet-playing leader of the Hot Shots, a swinging group supposedly based on the Original Dixieland Jazz Band. Brian Donlevy, an actor who later made a career out of playing the tough guy with a heart of gold, was the hot trumpeter for the Hot Shots, and Mary Martin obliged with the cool vocals. The rest of the numbers included 'Wait 'Til The Sun Shines, Nellie' (Harry Von Tilzer, Andrew Stirling), 'My Melancholy Baby' (George A. Norton, Ernie Burnett), 'Cuddle Up A Litle Closer' (Karl Hoschna, Otto Harbach), 'By The Light Of The Silvery Moon' (Gus Edwards, Edward Madden), 'The Birth Of The Blues' (De Sylva, Brown And Henderson), 'St. Louis Blues' (W.C. Handy), and several other jazzy oldies. Jack Benny's long-time comic companion, Eddie 'Rochester' Anderson, was also in the cast, and the film was directed by Victor Schertzinger.

BIRTH OF THE COOL - MILES DAVIS

Although this album is credited to Miles Davis, the importance of Gerry Mulligan's playing and, especially, his stellar compositions 'Jeru', 'Rocker' and the gorgeous 'Venus De Milo', make this 1956 album special. Although it is generally considered to be less accomplished than *Kind Of Blue*, this album is, arguably, in some ways more important. It would be churlish to say this was the birth of the cool, but the songs recorded by the legendary nonet and collected together here certainly mark the birth of something significant. Hearing all the tracks on the newly available CD version makes it more complete, and therefore, more necessary than ever. It is an indispensable album.

- Tracks: *Move*; *Jeru*; *Moon Dreams*; *Venus De Milo*; *Budo*; *Deception*; *Godchild*; *Boplicity*; *Rocker*; *Israel*; *Rouge*.
- First released 1950
- UK peak chart position: did not chart
- USA peak chart position: did not chart

Biscoe, Chris

b. 5 February 1947, East Barnet, Hertfordshire, England. Biscoe taught himself to play alto saxophone in 1963, later adding tenor, soprano and baritone saxophones and the comparatively rare alto clarinet. From 1970-73 he played with the National Youth Jazz Orchestra, then worked with various groups in London, including Redbrass. In 1979, he began a long (and continuing) association with Mike Westbrook, making outstanding contributions to many Westbrook projects, notably the brass band (*Bright As Fire*), the orchestra (*The Cortege* and *On Duke's Birthday*) and the trio (*A Little Westbrook Music* and *Love For Sale*). From 1983 he also worked with Chris McGregor's Brotherhood Of Breath (*Country Cooking*) and in 1985 he released a cassette of his own music, *Quintet And Duo*, followed the next year by a sextet album on his own Walking Wig label, which featured Italian trombonist Danilo Terenzi. In the late 80s and 90s Biscoe toured and recorded with both George Russell (*The London Concert*) and Andy Sheppard (*Soft On The Inside*), as well as playing in France with Didier Levallet's groups and in the collective band Zhivaro, which includes Levallet and Henri Texier. He continues to lead his own quartet and also plays with improvisers Full Monte (Brian Godding, Tony Marsh, Marcio Mattos). In 1991 he released a second cassette of his own music, *Modern Alarms*, and recorded in the Dedication Orchestra on the *Spirits Rejoice* project. An exciting, modern stylist, especially inventive on baritone saxophone, Biscoe has yet to receive the attention and the recording opportunities as leader that his creativity warrants.

- ALBUMS: *Quintet And Duo* (1985)★★★, *The Chris Biscoe Sextet* (Walking Wig 1986)★★, with Full Monte *Life In The Grand Hotel* (1991)★★★, *Modern Alarms* (1991)★★.

Bishop, Joe

b. 27 November 1907, Monticello, Arkansas, USA, d. 12 May 1976. As a child and young man Bishop played piano and various brass instruments including trumpet. After working with numerous bands in the south-western states during the late 20s and into the early months of 1930, Bishop joined the esteemed dance band led by Isham Jones. He remained with Jones from 1930 until the leader's retirement in 1935. When the band continued under the leadership of another member, Woody Herman, Bishop stayed on, now playing flügelhorn and, importantly, arranging. Bishop's arranging talents helped to give the Herman band its distinctive sound and, thanks to his arrangement of 'Woodchopper's Ball', a major hit. Poor health forced Bishop from the band in 1940 but a few years later he resumed work as a staff arranger. Among Bishop's compositions are 'Blue Prelude' and, in 1941, 'Blue Flame', which became the Herman band's theme tune and which thus, along with 'Woodchopper's Ball', echoed down the decades with countless performances. Bishop's health deteriorated still further in the early 50s, leading to the premature retirement of a man with considerable talent.

Bishop, Wallace

b. Wallace Henry Bishop, 17 February 1906, Chicago, Illinois, USA, d. 2 May 1986. Like so many other youngsters in Chicago's black ghettos, he played drums with the *Chicago Defender* Boys Band (Lionel Hampton and Hayes Alvis were others). Bishop subsequently studied drumming with Jimmy Bertrand before touring with several noted blues and jazz artists, including Thomas A. Dorsey, Richard M. Jones and Jelly Roll Morton. In the late 20s he worked with Les Hite, Erskine Tate and others, then in 1931 he joined Earl Hines until 1936. During the late 30s and on into the 40s, Bishop played drums with many noted jazz artists, including Coleman Hawkins, Louis Armstrong and Buck Clayton, with whom he visited Europe in late 1949. He decided to make his home in Europe, playing through the 50s and 60s with numerous touring Americans (Ben Webster, Buddy Tate, Kid Ory, Tiny Grimes) as well as with noted local musicians (Rob Pronk, Pia Beck). In the late 60s he teamed up briefly with his old boss, Hines, for a European tour. A sound and workmanlike drummer, Bishop's career decision to spend a substantial part of his working life in Europe tended to keep his name from the attention of many, although it undoubtedly provided him with steady work and more respect than might well have been the case had he remained in his homeland.

Bishop, Walter, Jnr.

b. 10 April 1927, New York City, New York, USA, d. 24 January 1998, New York, USA. Bishop began playing piano as a child, encouraged by his father, a Jamaican songwriter whose 'Swing, Brother, Swing' was recorded by, among others, Billie Holiday with Count Basie. During the 40s Bishop's musical direction was dictated by his interest in the work of Bud Powell and he played with numerous small groups, including those led by Charlie Parker, Miles Davis and Oscar Pettiford. A period of drug addiction interrupted Bishop's career in the 50s, but the following decade proved successful both musically and in terms of conquering his habit. He worked with Curtis Fuller and also led his own small groups, with which he recorded. He resumed his musical studies too, and after relocating in Los Angeles at the end of the 60s he took up teaching. In the late 70s he was back on the east coast, playing and teaching. Rarely performing outside the New York area, and with only a few recordings that fully demonstrate his skills, Bishop remained largely unknown to the wider jazz audience, despite being held in high regard by his fellow musicians. He also wrote a book on jazz theory.

● ALBUMS: *Speak Low* (Muse 1961)★★★, *Bish Bash* (Xanadu 1964)★★★★, *Walter Bishop Trio: 1965* 1962-63 recordings (Prestige 1965)★★★, *Summertime* (Fresh Sound 1964)★★★, *Walter Bishop* (Cotillion 1969)★★★, *Coral Keys* (Black Jazz 1971)★★★, *Keeper Of My Soul* (1973)★★, *Valley Land* (Muse 1974)★★★, *Old Folks* (1976)★★★, *Soliloquy* (Sea Breeze 1976)★★★★, *Soul Village* (Muse 1977)★★★, with others *I Remember Bebop* (1977)★★★, *Hot House* (Muse 1978)★★★, *Cubicle* (Muse 1978)★★★, *Just In Time* (Interplay 1988)★★★, *Milestones* (Black Lion 1989)★★★, *What's New* (DIW 1990)★★★★, *Midnight Blue* (Red 1993)★★★.

Bitches Brew - Miles Davis

A thoroughly unsaintly concoction of jazz experimentation and rock psychedelia, *Bitches Brew* took the loose, exploratory, collective improvisation and rock beat approach that Miles Davis had developed on *In A Silent Way*, and painted it a slightly harsher and more sinister hue. This is a long work, sold as a double album, with a mesmerizing feel to its collection of strange funk-rock grooves. Benny Maupin's bass clarinet adds an unnerving dimension to the group's sound, creaking threateningly from deep within, while Davis himself plays lean, but fragmented, trumpet lines. An inspired and intense work, *Bitches Brew* dramatically influenced the course of jazz history, and ushered in the fusion movement.

● Tracks: *Pharaoh's Dance; Bitches Brew; Spanish Key; John McLaughlin; Miles Runs The Voodoo Down; Sanctuary.*

● First released 1970

● UK peak chart position: 71

● USA peak position: 35

Bivona, Gus

b. 25 November 1915, New London, Connecticut, USA, d. January 1996. Born into a very musical family, he was actively encouraged to play and became adept on several instruments, including the violin, before turning to the clarinet as his principal instrument. He played with several local bands in the late 20s and early 30s before moving to New York. There, he played in a number of bands, including those led by Will Hudson and Eddie De Lange, Hudson alone, Bunny Berigan and Teddy Powell. In the early 40s he was briefly with Benny Goodman, Jan Savitt and Les Brown. Military service interrupted, but he was able to continue playing, now as leader of a US Navy band. After the war, he continued his tour of name bands with spells under the leadership of Tommy Dorsey and Bob Crosby, but then a more settled lifestyle beckoned and he moved to Hollywood where he played in the MGM studio orchestra. During these years he also worked in television and led his own big band, making records and performing with Steve Allen. Although influenced by Goodman, as were the majority of clarinet players of his generation, Bivona's forte was as a sound and reliable sideman. He continued working into the 80s.

● ALBUMS: with Glen Grey *Sounds Of The Great Casa Loma Band* (Capitol 1957)★★★, with Steve Allen *Steve Allen At The Round Table* (Roulette 1958)★★★.

Black And Tan

Directed by Dudley Murphy in 1929, who, in the same year, made *St. Louis Blues* with Bessie Smith, this early talkie short remains one of the few films to use jazz as its *raison d'être*. A slight but melodramatic storyline has showgirl Fredi Washington literally dancing her life away to ensure her musical colleagues get the big break they have been waiting for. The musicians involved are Duke Ellington And His Orchestra (their screen debut) including Barney Bigard, Harry Carney, Johnny Hodges, Joe Nanton, Artie Whetsol and Cootie Williams. Among the musical numbers are 'The Duke Steps Out', 'Black Beauty' and, of course, an eloquent version of 'Black And Tan Fantasy'.

Black Artists Group

Formed in the late 60s in St. Louis, Missouri, USA, by drummer Charles 'Bobo' Shaw and actor-poet Ajule Rutlin, BAG was directly inspired by Chicago's AACM. It was an attempt to promote black artists and encourage co-operation rather than competition. Its most famous members were Oliver Lake (alto saxophone), Joe Bowie (trombone), Baikida Carroll (trumpet) and Julius Hemphill and Marty Ehrlich (both tenor saxophone). The need to pursue individual careers destroyed the organization when five leading members left for a European tour. Unlike the AACM, there were not enough younger members to sustain its existence, but BAG is a reminder of when musicians sought to control their destiny.

Black Coffee - Peggy Lee

In 1952, Capitol Records would not allow Peggy Lee to record 'Lover' because the label already had a big hit with Les Paul's version of the song. She switched to Decca Records for the next five years and made a number of excellent recordings, including this set of standards on which she is accompanied by the cream of America's session musicians. It was originally issued as a 10-inch LP in 1953, and later extended to 12-inch with four additional tracks: 'It Ain't Necessarily So', 'Gee Baby, Ain't I Good To You', 'You're My Thrill' and 'There's A Small Hotel'. Forty years after its release, it is still regarded as one of the definitive jazz-tinged vocal albums of all time.

● Tracks: *Black Coffee; I've Got You Under My Skin; Easy Living; My Heart Belongs To Daddy; It Ain't Necessarily So; Gee Baby Ain't I Good To You; Woman Alone With The Blues; I Didn't Know What Time It Was; When The World Was Young; Love Me Or Leave Me; You're My Thrill; There's A Small Hotel.*

● First released 1961

● UK peak chart position: 20

● USA peak chart position: did not chart

Black Saint And Soul Note Records

In 1974 Italian schoolteacher Giovanni Bonandrini and four business associates established IREC, which rapidly grew into one of Italy's leading record distribution companies. In 1978 they bought the small, three-year-old, Milan-based *avant garde* jazz label Black Saint, and Bonandrini retired from teaching to become the label's full-time producer. The following year he started a sister label, Soul Note, to cater for more mainstream contemporary artists (although the distinction between the labels has become increasingly blurred). Throughout the 80s, the Black Saint/Soul Note axis established themselves as the world's leading modern jazz labels, winning the *Down Beat* annual 'best label' poll for several years in succession. In particular, the labels championed the more experimental end of American jazz. In 1984 critic Francis Davis praised Black Saint's 'landmark releases' by artists such as David Murray, Muhal Richard Abrams, Anthony Braxton and the World Saxophone Quartet, pointing out that 'No label, foreign or domestic, has been more vigilant in tracing the movements of the post-AACM Chicago diaspora and the post-Coltrane New York *avant garde*. Soul Note, he added, had helped to bring about 'the resurgence of hard bop' and also provided 'a badly needed outlet' for 'maverick talents' such as George Russell, Bill Dixon and Ran Blake. Since then Bonandrini has earned further kudos by re-igniting the recording careers of both Jimmy Giuffre (with *Dragonfly*) and Andrew Hill (with the superb *Shades*), and by releasing two outstanding Cecil Taylor projects - a double-album set of duos with Max Roach (*Historic Concerts*) and the first ever recording of Taylor's big band music (*Winged Serpent (Sliding Quadrants)*). In the late 80s, recession and the switch to CDs hit the labels financially, as did persistent distribution problems in the USA and the rise of rival companies such as JMT, Hat Hut and DIW. However, 1991 releases by the likes of Henry Threadgill, Billy Bang and Giorgio Gaslini showed that Bonandrini had not lost his taste for music's cutting edge. Whatever happens in the 90s, it is no exaggeration to say that Black Saint and Soul Note were as crucial to jazz in the 80s as Blue Note had been in the 50s and 60s: their back catalogues read like a who's who guide to the best of modern jazz.

● COMPILATIONS: *Black Saint/Soul Note: Critics' Pick Sampler (Vol. 1)* (Black Saint/Soul Note 1997)★★★★, *Black Saint/Soul Note: Critics' Pick Sampler (Vol. 2)* (Black Saint/Soul Note 1997)★★★★.

Black Saint And The Sinner Lady, The - Charles Mingus

In many ways the essential Mingus album, *The Black Saint And The Sinner Lady* is a powerful suite, embracing in one work the elements of blues, gospel, funk and Latin music that infused Mingus's sound and made it what it was. As well as featuring some of the best group arrangement outside the work of Duke Ellington, it boasts superb contributions by pianist Jaki Byard and alto saxophonist Charlie Mariano. This album is also revealing for its early use (in jazz) of studio dubbing, heard on the occasions when Mariano can be identified in the ensemble at the same time as he is soloing.

● Tracks: *Solo Dancer (Stop! Look! And Listen, Sinner Jim Whitney); Duet Solo Dancers (Heart's Beat And Shades In Physical Embraces); Group Dancers ([Soul Fusion] Freewoman); Trio And Group Dancers (Stop! Look! And Sing Songs Of Revolutions!); Single Solos And Group Dance (Saint And Sinner Join In Merriment On Battle Front); Group And Solo Dance (Of Love, Pain, And Passioned Revolt, Then Farewell, My Beloved).*

● First released 1963

● UK peak chart position: did not chart

● USA peak chart position: did not chart

Black, James

b. 1 February 1940, New Orleans, Louisiana, USA, d. 30 August 1988. Born into a musical family, Black studied music at Southern University, Baton Rouge, and also drummed in the quintessential training ground for New Orleans rhythm, a marching band. His first professional break came with an R&B outfit in 1958. He replaced Ed Blackwell in Ellis Marsalis's band when Blackwell left to join Ornette Coleman in California. In the early 60s he relocated to New York with R&B singer Joe Jones and toured with Lionel Hampton. It is Black playing drums on the Dixie Cups' 'Chapel Of Love'. He played and recorded with Cannonball Adderley, Yusef Lateef and Horace Silver. If Black had not subsequently returned to New Orleans (working with artists including Professor Longhair, the Meters, Fats Domino and Lee Dorsey), his unerring beat would have made him a big name in jazz.

Blackbyrds

The original Blackbyrds were formed in 1973 by jazz trumpeter Donald Byrd. A doctor of ethnomusicology, Byrd lectured at Washington, DC's Howard University and the group, named after *Black Byrd*, the artist's million-seller, was drawn from his students. The Blackbyrds' debut album charted in the soul, jazz and pop listings, while the follow-up, *Flying Start*, featured their 1975 US Top 10 single, 'Walking In Rhythm'. This infectious performance became the group's first major success, by which point founder-members Kevin Toney (keyboards) and Keith Killgo (vocals, drums) had been joined by Joe Hall (bass), Orville Saunders (guitar) and Jay Jones (flute, saxophone). The following year the group hit the US charts again with 'Happy Music' reaching the Top 20. Sadly, the unit's adventurousness gave way to a less spirited direction. The compulsive rhythmic pulse became increasingly predictable as the group, once so imaginative, pursued a style reliant on a safe and tested formula, the repetitiveness of which brought about their demise.

● ALBUMS: *The Blackbyrds* (Fantasy 1974)★★★, *Flying Start* (Fantasy 1974)★★★★, *Cornbread, Earl And Me* (Fantasy 1975)★★, *City Life* (Fantasy 1975)★★, *Unfinished Business* (Fantasy 1976)★★, *Action* (Fantasy 1977)★★, *Better Days* (Fantasy 1980)★★.

● COMPILATIONS: *Night Grooves - The Blackbyrds Greatest Hits* (Fantasy 1978)★★★, *The Best Of The Blackbyrds Volume 1* (Fantasy 1988)★★★★, *The Best Of The Blackbyrds Volume 2* (Fantasy 1988)★★★.

BLACKMAN, CINDY

b. 18 November 1959, Yellow Springs, Ohio, USA. One of a growing number of female drummers, Blackman is a powerful but unbombastic player, part of the tradition that includes Max Roach and one of her main influences, Tony Williams. Her mother and grandmother were classical musicians and an uncle was a vibes player. She studied classical percussion at the University of Hartford, then went on to the Berklee College Of Music, where she was taught by Alan Dawson and Lennie Nelson. In 1982 she moved to New York and played with Freddie Hubbard, Sam Rivers and Jackie McLean, whose regular drummer she became in 1987. By then she had served a tough apprenticeship as house-drummer in Ted Curson's all-night jam sessions at the Blue Note Club, and playing for several hours at a time in a band that performed on the corner of 42nd Street and 6th Avenue. Her recording debut with an all-star band displayed her skills as leader, composer and percussionist. In 1990, she joined Don Pullen's trio for some well-received festival appearances. Since then she has concentrated on her solo career.

● ALBUMS: *Arcane* (Muse 1987)★★★, *Autumn Leaves* (1989)★★★, *Code Red* (Muse 1992)★★★, *Trio + Two* (Freelance 1992)★★★★, *Telepathy* (Muse 1994)★★★, *In The Now* (HighNote 1998)★★★★.

BLACKWELL, ED

b. 10 October 1929, New Orleans, Louisiana, USA, d. 7 October 1992, Hartford, Connecticut, USA. Blackwell began playing drums in his home-town, where he took careful notice of the rudiments of jazz-playing as demonstrated by local past-masters of the trade, such as Baby Dodds and Zutty Singleton. Despite these traditional affiliations, Blackwell's first jobs were with mainstream bands and he also played R&B. Meeting Ornette Coleman changed his musical ideas and he played with Coleman on the west coast in the early 50s. However, he returned to New Orleans, and resumed playing mainstream and R&B music, including a spell with Ray Charles. At the start of the 60s he was back with Coleman, this time in New York. It was here that he also began a long-lasting association with Don Cherry. In the mid-60s he played in bands led by Cherry, Coleman and Randy Weston. He and Weston lived for a while in Morocco, where Blackwell extended his knowledge of percussion, later incorporating several additional instruments into his kit to increase his tonal palette. In the early 70s he was again with Coleman and also played with Thelonious Monk. This period also saw him cutting back on playing through a combination of poor health and a teaching engagement. Later in the 70s he resumed his association with Cherry when he joined the quartet, Old And New Dreams, to pursue further Coleman's music. The other members of the band were Charlie Haden and Dewey Redman. In 1981 he joined fellow drummers Sunny Murray, Dennis Charles and Steve McCall to form Drums Inter-Actuel, and also recorded with Anthony Braxton and others. A vigorous player with a brilliant sound and subtle beat, he had a sharp awareness of the needs of his front-line comrades. Blackwell was one of the outstanding free jazz drummers and his fast-thinking polyphonic interplay with Coleman was frequently awesome in its complexity. His work with Cherry was also remarkable for the manner in which he stayed abreast of the trumpeter's quicksilver thinking and playing.

● ALBUMS: with Don Cherry *Mu* (BYG 1970)★★★★, with Dewey Redman *Redman And Blackwell In Willisau* (Black Saint 1980)★★★, *Playtime* (1981)★★★★, with Cherry *El Corazón* (ECM 1982)★★★, *What It Is?* (Enja 1993)★★★, *What It Be Like?* (Enja 1994)★★★, *Walls-Bridges* 1992 recording (Black Saint 1997)★★★★.

BLAINE, TERRY

b. USA. Blaine grew up in a music-loving household; her mother was a concert pianist. She displayed an early interest in music and learned to play piano, clarinet and flute, graduating with a degree in music. She enjoyed singing and gradually moved in this direction. After college, she dropped her classical training and went on the road with a pop group, performing five or six gigs a nights, six nights a week. Not surprisingly, she lost her voice and used this setback to study singing. Working club dates and parties, she met pianist Mark Shane and through his enthusiasm and encouragement began to listen to the songs and singers of the 30s, including Billie Holiday and Fats Waller. Instinctively recognizing that the songs and the style suited her vocal talents, she and Shane began to develop a repertoire, and after two years, they decided to go out as a duo and to work with small bands. As a result of asthma in the late 80s and having a baby in 1993, she found her breathing changing, and once again took singing lessons. During the early 90s, Blaine began recording and her first two albums to be issued in the UK drew rave reviews in *Jazz Journal International*. Blaine's phrasing is exceptional and she sings with an easy, natural swing and a joyous sense of enthusiasm for her material. Her influences include Holiday, Waller, Louis Armstrong, Frank Sinatra, the Beatles, Patsy Cline and Mel Tormé. Blaine's musical associates, in live performances and on record, have included Shane, responsible for most of the arrangements, Ken Peplowski, Ed Polcer and Allan Vaché. Her achievements to date, bearing in mind that she is little known outside of the USA, suggest that a great career lies ahead.

● ALBUMS: *Whose Honey Are You?* (Jukebox Jazz 1994)★★★★, *In Concert With The Mark Shane Quintet* (Jukebox Jazz 1994)★★★.

BLAKE, EUBIE

b. James Hubert Blake, 7 February 1883, Baltimore, Maryland, USA, d. 12 February 1983, New York, USA. Eubie Blake grew up to the sounds of ragtime music, and before the turn of the century was playing piano in sporting houses and other similar establishments. He was a composer too, and in 1915 joined forces with Noble Sissle; they played in vaudeville as a double act and wrote together extensively. In 1921 Sissle and Blake wrote the score for a Broadway show - a remarkable accomplishment for blacks at that time. *Shuffle Along*, which starred Flournoy Miller, Aubrey Lyles, Gertrude Saunders, and Sissle himself (with Blake on the piano), included several admirable songs, including 'Bandana Days', 'Gypsy Blues', 'Love Will Find A Way', 'Everything Reminds Me Of You', 'Shuffle Along' and 'If You've Never Been Vamped By A Brown Skin (You've Never Been Vamped At All)'. There was also one enormous hit, 'I'm Just Wild About Harry', which became popular at the time for artists such as Marion Harris, Ray Miller, and Paul Whiteman, among others, and gave a boost to Harry S. Truman's election campaign in 1948. Blake contributed to other Broadway musicals and revues such as *Elsie*, *Andre Charlot's Revue Of 1924*, and Lew Leslie's *Blackbirds Of 1930*. For the latter, he and Andy Razaf wrote 'Baby Mine', 'That Lindy Hop', 'My Handy Man Ain't Handy No More', and another substantial hit, the lovely reflective ballad 'Memories Of You'. After one more Broadway musical, *Swing It* (1937), Blake reunited with Sissle for a time, and then spent much of World War II entertaining troops with the USO. In the 50s Blake demonstrated and lectured on ragtime but his day seemed to be past. Then, in 1969, at the age of 86, Blake's fortunes were revived when John Hammond recorded the old man playing piano and talking about his life. The concurrent vogue for ragtime helped his comeback and the next years were filled with honours, recordings, concerts, festivals and television appearances; in 1978, his life and music were celebrated in a Broadway show, *Eubie*, which was also televised in the USA and later staged in London. In 1983 Blake contributed to the lists of favourite quotations when, on the occasion of his 100th birthday, he said: 'If I'd known I was going to live this long, I would've taken better care of myself.' He died five days later.

● ALBUMS: *The Wizard Of Ragtime* (1959)★★★, *The Eighty-six Years Of Eubie Blake* (Columbia 1969)★★★★, *At The Piano* (1974)★★★, *Eubie Blake In Concert* (Stash 1987)★★★.

● COMPILATIONS: *Eubie Blake, Blues And Rags: His Earliest Piano Rolls* 1917-21 recordings ★★★★.

● FURTHER READING: *Reminiscing With Sissle And Blake*, Robert Kimball and William Bolcom.

BLAKE, JOHN

b. 3 July 1947, Philadelphia, Pennsylvania, USA. In 1980, John Coltrane's pianist McCoy Tyner found John Blake's soaring violin congenial and recruited him for his band, also writing liner notes for John Blake's debut in 1983. Taking Coltrane's interest in Indian music seriously, Blake studied southern Indian Carnatic music and incorporates aspects of this in his playing.

● ALBUMS: *Maiden Dance* (Gramavision 1983)★★★, *Rhythm And Blues* (Gramavision 1986)★★★, *A New Beginning* (Rhino 1988)★★★.

BLAKE, RAN

b. 20 April 1935, Springfield, Massachusetts, USA. Growing up in Springfield and later in Suffield, Connecticut, Blake began piano lessons at the age of four but was largely self-taught. A film buff from childhood, his interest in soundtracks led him to an appreciation of 20th-century European composers such as Bartok, Debussy and Prokofiev. A simultaneous love of gospel music was sparked by the records of Mahalia Jackson and, particularly, by his exposure to the choir at the local Church of God in Christ in Hartford, Connecticut. Blake studied at Bard College from 1956-60, devising his own jazz course there, and also began to work with singer Jeanne Lee - they recorded together in 1961 and toured Europe in 1963. Studies with Gunther Schuller, then a leading proponent of Third Stream Music, gave Blake the confidence to pursue his personal synthesis of African-American, European classical and various ethnic folk musics. When Schuller became President of Boston's New England Conservatory of Music in 1967, Blake went to work there too and in 1973 was made Chairperson of the Third Stream Department, where he has since remained. Although many of his recordings are solo, he has also worked with singers such as Lee, Chris Connor and Eleni Odoni, and saxophonists Anthony Braxton, Steve Lacy, Houston Person and Ricky Ford, whom Blake 'discovered' playing in Boston at the age of 16. Other notable projects include his work with the New England Conservatory Symphony Orchestra (on *Portfolio Of Doktor Mabuse*) and his appearance as featured guest artist on Franz Koglmann's 1989 *Orte Der Geometrie*. Typical Blakean characteristics, usually evident in his music in some guise, include his anti-racism and radical social perspectives, his abiding love of spirituals and his continuing fascination with film and its relationship to music (*Film Noir* and *Vertigo*). His utterly individual piano style is like a distillation of Thelonious Monk and Erik Satie: very terse, very quiet and capable of both acute dissonance and delicate romanticism - his phrases often resemble shards or beads of sound that float and trickle across great chasms of silence.*That Certain Feeling* featured the tunes of George Gershwin and was the second of a series of homages that has also included *Duke Dreams* (dedicated to Duke Ellington and Billy Strayhorn) and *Unmarked Van* (dedicated to Sarah Vaughan).

● ALBUMS: *Plays Solo Piano* (ESP 1965)★★★, *The Blue Potato* (Milestone 1969)★★★★, *Breakthru* (Improvising Artists 1976)★★★, *Wende* (1977)★★★, *Crystal Trip* (1977)★★★, *Open City* (1977)★★★, *Take One* (1977)★★★, *Take Two* (1977)★★★, *Realization Of A Dream* (1978)★★★, *Rapport* (1978)★★★, *Third Stream Recompositions* 1977 recording (1980)★★★, *Film Noir* (Novus 1980)★★★, with Jaki Byard *Improvisations* (Soul Note 1981)★★★, *Duke Dreams* (Soul Note 1982)★★★, *Portfolio Of Doktor Mabuse* 1977/79 recordings (1983)★★★, with Houston Person *Suffield Gothic* (Soul Note 1984)★★★★, *Painted Rhythms Volume I* (GM 1986)★★★★, *Vertigo* 1984 recording (1987)★★★, *Short Life Of Barbara Monk* (Soul Note 1987)★★★, *Painted Rhythms Volume II* 1985 recording (GM 1988)★★★★, with Lee *You Stepped Out Of A Cloud* (Owl 1990)★★★, *That Certain Feeling (George Gershwin Songbook)* (hatART 1991)★★★, *Epistrophy* (Soul Note 1991)★★★★, *Unmarked Van (A Tribute To*

Sarah Vaughan) (Soul Note 1997)★★★★, with Anthony Braxton *A Memory Of Vienna* 1988 recording (hatOLOGY 1998)★★★★.

BLAKENEY, ANDY

b. Andrew Blakeney, 10 June 1898, Quitman, Mississippi, USA, d. February 1992. After learning to play the piano as a child, he took up the trumpet while living in Chicago. He played professionally there with various bands, including a very short spell with King Oliver, and he also rehearsed with a band directed by Jelly Roll Morton. This band later made the famous Red Hot Pepper sides but by then Blakeney had uprooted and travelled to Los Angeles. There, he played with many bands, obscure and famous. Among the latter were those led by Les Hite, Charlie Echols and Lionel Hampton. From the mid-30s until the outbreak of World War II he played in Hawaii. Back in the USA he played in theatre bands and showbands, his forte during the majority of the preceding years. Soon after the war, however, Blakeney had drifted to the periphery of the music business. Then, in 1947, he was invited to join Edward 'Kid' Ory's band, where he replaced Mutt Carey. Although the Ory band's musical style, hard-driving Dixieland jazz, was not entirely to his liking, he persisted in this idiom, even leading his own similarly styled band in various parts of California. His location led to occasional work in motion pictures, including appearances on screen in some feature films: *Imitation Of Life* (1959), *Hotel* (1967), *The Great White Hope* (1970) and *Mame* (1974). Film-making practices being what they are, in the latter film at least, his playing was ghosted by a different trumpeter on the soundtrack - in this case by Johnny Best. Blakeney also coached young musicians and by the 70s was a respected elder statesman of jazz. In this decade he visited Europe as a member of Barry Martyn's Legends Of Jazz, gaining many admirers. He continued to play in his 80s, working with Roger Jamieson's New Orleanians. Although much of Blakeney's long career was spent in jazz bands, his prime years found him either in showbands or with bands that only rarely recorded. On the basis of his playing in the 70s and afterwards, by which time he was well past his prime, he was clearly a highly competent musician with a good sense of style, but was perhaps a shade too elaborate (and, it must be said, refined) for the direct and occasionally rowdy settings in which he was latterly heard.

BLAKEY, ART

b. Arthur Blakey, 11 October 1919, Pittsburgh, Pennsylvania, USA, d. 16 October 1990. Although renowned as a drummer, Blakey was a pianist first. His move to the drums has been variously attributed to Erroll Garner's appearance on the scene, the regular session drummer being ill and (Blakey's favourite) a gangster's indisputable directive. Blakey drummed for Mary Lou Williams on her New York debut in 1942, Fletcher Henderson's mighty swing orchestra (1943/4) and the legendary Billy Eckstine band that included Charlie Parker, Dexter Gordon, Dizzy Gillespie, Miles Davis and Thelonious Monk (1944-47). The classic bebop sessions predominantly featured Max Roach or Kenny Clarke on drums, but Blakey soon became the pre-eminent leader of the hard bop movement. In contrast to the baroque orchestrations of the West Coast Jazz 'cool' school, hard bop combined bebop's instrumental freedoms with a surging gospel backbeat. Ideally suited to the new long-playing record, tunes lengthened into rhythmic epics that featured contrasting solos. Blakey's hi-hat and snare skills became legendary, as did the musicians who passed through the ranks of the Jazz Messengers: the band became an on-the-road 'college' (pianist JoAnne Brackeen was one of his discoveries). His playing combined musicianship with risk, and his drumming encouraged daring and brilliance. He would lean with his elbow on the surface of the drum to change its intonation: such 'press rolls' became a musical trademark. That his power was not from want of subtlety was illustrated by his uncanny sympathy for Thelonious Monk's sense of rhythm: his contribution to Monk's historic 1957 group, which included both Coleman Hawkins and John Coltrane, was devastating, and the London trio recordings he made with Monk in 1971 (*Something In Blue* and *The Man I Love*) are perhaps his most impressive achievements as a player. For a period following his conversion to Islam, Blakey changed his name to Abdullah Ibn Buhaina, which led to his nickname 'Bu'.

Blakey inspired and encouraged the creativity and drive of acoustic jazz through the electric 70s; Miles Davis once remarked 'If Art Blakey's old-fashioned, I'm white'. This comment was substantiated in the 80s when hard bop became popular, a movement led by ex-Jazz Messengers Wynton Marsalis and Terence Blanchard. In England, a televised encounter in 1986 with the young turks of black British jazz, including Courtney Pine and Steve Williamson, emphasized Blakey's influence on generations of jazz fans. Until his death in 1990, Art Blakey continually found new musicians and put them through his special discipline of heat and precision. When he played, Blakey invariably had his mouth open in a grimace of pleasure and concentration: memories of his drumming still makes the jaw drop today. As a drummer Blakey will not be forgotten, but as a catalyst for hundreds of past messengers he will be forever praised.

● ALBUMS: *Blakey* (EmArcy 1954)★★★, *A Night At Birdland Volume 1* (Blue Note 1954)★★★★★, *A Night At The Birdland Volume 2* (Blue Note 1954)★★★★★, *A Night At The Birdland Volume 3* (Blue Note 1954)★★★★, *At The Cafe Bohemia Volume 1* (Blue Note 1956)★★★★★, *At The Cafe Bohemia Volume 2* (Blue Note 1956)★★★★★, *Hard Bop* (Columbia 1956)★★★, *The Jazz Messengers* (Columbia 1956)★★★, *Drum Suite* (Columbia 1957)★★★, *Cu-Bop* (Jubilee 1957)★★★, *Orgy In Rhythm Volume 1* (Blue Note 1957)★★★, *Orgy In Rhythm Volume 2* (Blue Note 1957)★★★, *A Midnight Session With The Jazz Messengers* (Elektra 1957)★★★, *Play Selections From Lerner And Loewe* (Vik 1957)★★, *The Hard Bop Academy* (Affinity 1958)★★★, *Art Blakey's Jazz Messengers With Thelonius Monk* (Atlantic 1958)★★★★, *Ritual* (Pacific Jazz 1958)★★★, *Holiday*

For Skins Volume 1 (Blue Note 1958)★★★, *Moanin'* (Blue Note 1958)★★★★, *At The Jazz Corner Of The World Volume 1* (Blue Note 1958)★★★★, *At The Jazz Corner Of The World Volume 2* (Blue Note 1958)★★★★, *Art Blakey's Big Band* (Bethlehem 1958)★★★, *Hard Drive* (Bethlehem 1958)★★★, *Holiday For Skins Volume 2* (Blue Note 1959)★★★, *A Night In Tunisia* (Blue Note 1960)★★★★, *The Big Beat* (Blue Note 1960),★★★ *Like Someone In Love* (1960)★★★, *Meet You At The Jazz Corner Of The World Volume 1* (Blue Note 1960)★★★★, *Meet You At The Jazz Corner Of The World Volume 2* (Blue Note 1960)★★★★, *Paris Concert* (Epic 1960)★★★, *Art Blakey In Paris* (Epic 1961)★★★, *The African Beat* (Blue Note 1961)★★★, *Roots & Herbs* (1961)★★★★, *Jazz Messengers !!!!!* (Impulse! 1961)★★★, *Mosaic* (Blue Note 1962)★★★★, *Buhaina's Delight* (Blue Note 1962)★★★★, *Three Blind Mice* (United Artists 1962)★★★, *Caravan* (Riverside 1962)★★★, *Ugetsu* (Riverside 1963)★★★, *The Freedom Rider* (Blue Note 1963)★★★, *Indestructible* (Blue Note 1963)★★★, *Like Someone In Love* (Blue Note 1963)★★★★, *A Jazz Message* (Impulse! 1963)★★★, *Free For All* (Blue Note 1964)★★★, *Tough!* (Cadet 1965)★★, *'S Make It* (Limelight 1965)★★, *Soul Finger* (Limelight 1965)★★, *Buttercorn Lady* (Limelight 1966)★★, *Kyoto* (Riverside 1966)★★★, *Hold On I'm Coming* (Limelight 1966)★★, *Art Blakey Live* (Mercury 1968)★★★, *Mellow Blues* (Moon 1969)★★★, with Thelonious Monk *Something In Blue* (1971)★★★, *Gypsy Folk Tales* (Roulette 1977)★★, *In This Corner* (Concord 1979)★★★, *Messages* (Vogue 1979)★★★, *Straight Ahead* (Concord 1981)★★★, *Album Of the Year* (Timeless 1981)★★★★, *In My Prime Volume 1* (Timeless 1981)★★★, *Blues Bag* (Affinity 1981)★★★, *Keystone 3* (Concord 1982)★★★, *In Sweden* (Amigo 1982)★★★, *Oh, By The Way* (Timeless 1982)★★★, *New York Scene* (Concord 1984)★★★, *Blue Night* (Timeless 1985)★★★, *Dr Jeckyl* (Paddle Wheel 1985)★★★, *Blues March* (Vogue 1985)★★★, *Farewell* (Paddle Wheel 1985)★★, *In My Prime Volume 2* (Timeless 1986)★★★, *Live At Ronnie Scott's* (Hendring 1987)★★★, *Not Yet* (Soul Note 1988)★★, *Feeling Good* (Delos 1988)★★, *Hard Champion* (Electric Bird 1988)★★★, with Freddie Hubbard *Feel The Wind* (Timeless 1988)★★★, *I Get A Kick Out Of Bu* (Soul Note 1989)★★, *Live In Berlin 1959-62* (Jazzup 1989)★★★, *One For All* (A&M 1990)★★, *Live In Europe 1959* (Creole 1992)★★★, *Live In Leverkusen* (In & Out 1996)★★.

● COMPILATIONS: *The Best Of Art Blakey* (Emarcy 1980)★★★, *Art Collection* (Concord 1986)★★★, *The Best Of Art Blakey And The Jazz Messengers* (Blue Note 1989)★★★★★, *Compact Jazz* (Verve 1992)★★★★, *The History Of Art Blakey & The Jazz Messengers* 3-CD box set (Blue Note 1992)★★★★, *Jazz Profile* (Blue Note 1997)★★★★.

● VIDEOS: *Notes From Jazz* (Kay Jazz 1988), *At Ronnie Scotts* (Hendring Video 1988), *Art Blakey & The Jazz Messengers* (Kay Jazz 1988), *Jazz At The Smithsonian Volume 2* (Parkfield Publishing 1990), *Concerts And Jam Sessions On Video* (Greenline 1991), *A Lesson With Art Blakey* (CPP Media Master 1996).

BLANCHARD, TERENCE

b. 13 March 1962, New Orleans, Louisiana, USA. One of several brilliant young musicians emerging from New Orleans in the 80s, Blanchard began playing piano at the age of five and sang with a vocal group, the Harlem Harmony Kings. He took up the trumpet at the age of eight and began lessons in his early teens while studying at the New Orleans Center for Creative Arts under Ellis Marsalis, father of Blanchard's contemporaries and fellow New Orleanians, Branford and Wynton Marsalis. A year later, Blanchard was studying composition and in 1980 went to Rutgers University. That same year he joined Lionel Hampton, with whom he played for two years before replacing Wynton Marsalis in Art Blakey's Jazz Messengers. At the same time, Donald 'Duck' Harrison, a fellow student from his days in New Orleans, replaced Branford in the Messengers. Blanchard stayed with Blakey until 1986 when he formed his own band with Harrison. In the 90s he became involved with films, writing scores for Spike Lee's *Jungle Fever* and *Malcolm X* and for the BBC Television documentary about black migration, *The Promised Land*. *The Heart Speaks* featured some outstanding vocals from the Brazilian Ivan Lins; one reviewer described the meeting as 'Rio meeting New Orleans'. A technically gifted musician, Blanchard's playing displays a marked awareness of the lyricism of some of the early bop trumpeters, such as Clifford Brown. Although much less well known than Marsalis, Blanchard's work displays a similar restraint but stronger jazz feeling. His status continues to rise, notably with his most recent work, especially *Romantic Defiance*.

● ALBUMS: with Donald Harrison *New York Second Line* (George Wein Collection 1983)★★★★, with Harrison *Discernment* (George Wein Collection 1985)★★★, with Harrison *Nascence* (Columbia 1986)★★★, with Harrison *Crystal Stair* (Columbia 1987)★★★, with Harrison *Black Pearl* (Columbia 1988)★★★★, *Terence Blanchard* (Columbia 1991)★★★, *Simply Stated* (Columbia 1992)★★★, *X* (Columbia 1994)★★★, *The Billie Holiday Songbook* (Columbia 1994)★★★, *Romantic Defiance* (Columbia 1995)★★★★, *The Heart Speaks* (Columbia 1996)★★★.

BLANTON, JIMMY

b. October 1918, Chatanooga, Tennessee, USA, d. 30 July 1942. Starting out as a violinist, Blanton studied musical theory before switching to bass while still at school. He played in several local bands and during 1936/7 worked with the Jeter-Pillars Orchestra in St. Louis and Fate Marable's Cotton Pickers. In October 1939 he was hired by Duke Ellington and celebrated this event by changing from three-string to four-string bass. For a few months he shared the spot with Billy Taylor, but from early 1940 he was on his own. A remarkably dextrous player, Blanton's technique, his range, harmonic sense and unfailing swing gave the Ellington band enormous lift. His work attracted the attention of countless other bass players whose own work subsequently bore echoes of his innovations. Off duty from the Ellington band, Blanton also played with early bop musicians at Minton's Playhouse where he was a major contributor to the changes taking place in jazz. While with Ellington, Blanton recorded extensively, not only with the band but also in duets with the leader. Blanton's death, when only 23 years old, was an exceptional loss, but his influence on jazz bass playing remains profound.

BLANTON-WEBSTER YEARS, THE - DUKE ELLINGTON

A special kind of magic surrounds the Duke Ellington band that featured Ben Webster and Jimmy Blanton; the former's tenor solos, breathily romantic or fiercely swinging, the latter changing the role of the bass in jazz. Yet these two were far from being the only stars. Not least among others were the liquid beauty of Johnny Hodges's alto and Cootie Williams' plangent trumpet. In addition, there was always the arranging-composing skills of Billy Strayhorn, another new arrival, and the maestro himself. Together, they brought to eternal life masterpieces such as 'Just A-Settin' And A-Rockin'', 'Ko-Ko', 'Jack The Bear', 'Cotton Tail' and 'Concerto For Cootie'.

● Tracks: *You, You Darlin'; Jack The Bear; Ko Ko; Morning Glory; So Far, So Good; Conga Brava; Concerto For Cootie (Do Nothin' Till You Hear From Me); Me And You; Cotton Tail; Never No Lament; Dusk; Bojangles; A Portrait Of Bert Williams; Blue Goose; Harlem Air Shaft; At A Dixie Roadside Diner; All Too Soon; Rumpus In Richmond; My Greatest Mistake; Sepia Panorama; There Shall Be No Night; In A Mellow Tone; Five O'clock Whistle; Warm Valley; The Flaming Sword; Jumpin' Punkins; Across The Track Blues; John Hardy's Wife; Blue Serge; After All; Chloe; Bakiff; Are You Sticking?; I Never Felt This Way Before; Just A-Settin' And A-Rockin'; The Giddybug Gallop; The Sidewalks Of New York; Chocolate Shake; Flamingo; I Got It Bad (And That Ain't Good); Clementine; Brown Skin Gal; The Girl In My Dreams Tries To Look Like You; Jump For Joy; Moon Over Cuba; Take The 'A' Train; Five O'clock Drag; Rocks In My Bed; Blip Blip; Chelsea Bridge; Raincheck; What Good Would It Do?; I Don't Mind; Someone; My Little Brown Book; Main Stem; Johnny Come Lately; Hayfoot Strawfoot; Sentimental Lady; A Sip Of The Lip (Can Sink A Ship); Sherman Shuffle.*

● First released 1987 (1940-1942 recordings)

● UK peak chart position: did not chart

● USA peak chart position: did not chart

BLEY, CARLA

b. Carla Borg, 11 May 1938, Oakland, California, USA. Borg began to learn piano from her father, who was a piano teacher and church organist, at an early age, but discontinued the formal lessons when she was five years old. Her main musical experience was in church choirs and as a church organist until she became interested in jazz at the age of 17. On moving to New York City she had to work as a waitress, unable to earn a living either as a pianist or composer. In 1957 she married Paul Bley and from 1959 began writing many fine compositions, still using her maiden name initially; thus, the composer credit was to 'Borg' when George Russell first recorded one of her pieces ('Dance Class') in 1960. Russell used several of her tunes, as did husband Paul. As her reputation grew, her compositions were sought by the likes of Jimmy Giuffre, Art Farmer, Gary Burton and Charlie Haden (with whom she would work on his various Liberation Music Orchestra projects). In 1964 Bill Dixon invited her to be a charter member of the Jazz Composers' Guild, and at the end of the year she and Michael Mantler, who was later to become her second husband, led the Jazz Composers' Guild Orchestra in a series of concerts at Judson Hall. Her critical standing really began to blossom after she joined the Jazz Composers' Orchestra Association, founded by Mantler in 1966 on the model of the defunct Guild. The Association and its associated Orchestra (JCO) gave writers the opportunity to write works of an epic scale for large forces, and Carla grasped the opportunity. Two of her works, *A Genuine Tong Funeral* (Dark Opera Without Words) (recorded by a band centred on the Gary Burton Quartet) and the massive *Escalator Over The Hill* (taking up six album sides) were conceived as a kind of music theatre, and were widely acclaimed; *Escalator*, in particular, remains a genre in itself. Many of her small-scale pieces have also achieved standard status, including 'Mother Of The Dead Man' (originally part of *Tong Funeral*), 'Closer', 'Ida Lupino' and 'Sing Me Softly Of The Blues'. She became a full-time musician in 1964, working with Pharoah Sanders and Charles Moffett at the beginning of that year. From December she co-led the JCO with Mantler. Her first orchestral piece, 'Roast', dates from this time, but she was also heavily committed to free jazz at this point. After the JCO appeared at the 1965 Newport Jazz Festival, Bley organized the Jazz Realities Quintet, which also included Mantler and Steve Lacy, to tour Europe. It was during another tour of Europe, this time with Peter Brötzmann and Peter Kowald in 1966, that she became disillusioned with free jazz, a change of heart that led ultimately to the production of *Funeral*. For some years she concentrated on writing, though there was a spell with Jack Bruce's band in 1974, but from 1976 she again began leading a band on a regular basis. Throughout the 80s she continued to play keyboards and to lead medium to small-sized bands but, as she pointed out herself on a visit to London in 1990, although she is not among the great pianists she is a unique writer. Her association with composer and former Gary Burton bassist Steve Swallow contributed to the flavour of her successful and accessible Sextet, which toured regularly in the late 80s. While the critics (though not the jazz public) began to grow cool towards the Sextet by the end of the decade, her tour with the Very Big Carla Bley Band at the end of 1990 confirmed that she had not lost her individual writing voice, nor her ability to deal convincingly with orchestral forces. Bley's contribution on the 'administrative' side of music deserves recognition too. She has been part of the movement to give musicians a degree of control, self-determination and independence from the industry's establishment. With Paul Bley she was a member of the Jazz Composers' Guild, a co-operative formed in autumn 1964, and subsequently helped establish the JCOA. She and Mantler also set up two record labels, Watt for their own recordings and JCOA Records to promote the work of others. Her compositions have been recorded by a number of musicians.

● ALBUMS: with Kent Carter, Steve Lacy, Mike Mantler, Aldo

Romano *Jazz Realities* (Fontana 1966)★★★, with Gary Burton *A Genuine Tong Funeral* (RCA 1967)★★★★, with Charlie Haden *Liberation Music* (1969)★★★, *Escalator Over The Hill* (ECM 1971)★★★★, *Tropic Appetites* (1974)★★★, with Michael Mantler *The Hapless Child* (1976)★★★, *Dinner Music* (Watt 1977)★★★, *Carla Bley Band European Tour 1977* (Watt 1978)★★★, *Musique Mecanique* (Watt 1979)★★★, *Social Studies* (Watt 1981)★★★, *Carla Bley Live!* (Watt 1982)★★, *Ballad Of The Fallen* (1983)★★★, *Mortelle Randonnee* (IMS 1983)★★★, *I Hate To Sing* (Watt 1984)★★★, *Heavy Heart* (Watt 1984)★★★, *Night-Glo* (ECM/Watt 1985)★★★, *Sextet* (ECM/Watt 1987)★★★, *European Tour 1977* (Watt 1987)★★★, with Swallow *Duets* (ECM 1988)★★★, *Fleur Carnivore* (Watt 1990)★★★, *The Very Little Big Carla Bley Band* (Watt 1991)★★★★, with Swallow *Go Together* (ECM 1993)★★★, *Big Band Theory* (ECM 1993)★★★, with Swallow, Andy Sheppard *Songs With Legs* (Watt 1994)★★★, *The Carla Bley Big Band Goes To Church* (Watt 1997)★★★★, *Fancy Chamber Music* (Watt 1998)★★★.

BLEY, PAUL

b. 10 November 1932, Montreal, Canada. Pianist Bley would merit a place in jazz history on the strength of his instincts as a talent scout alone. The legendary Ornette Coleman Quartet (with Don Cherry, Charlie Haden and Billy Higgins) made its earliest impact as four-fifths of Bley's quintet. He encouraged the emergence of wife Carla Bley and Annette Peacock as composers, building his repertoire in the 60s and 70s around their tunes. He had Pat Metheny and Jaco Pastorius in his band when both were callow youths, and was the first to record them. All of this, however, is of less significance than his own music, the earliest examples of which still seem entirely 'modern'. For 40 years Bley has remained on the cutting edge of creative music, from bebop to free jazz and beyond. At the age of 20, he befriended and played with Charlie Parker. On New York's 52nd Street, Jackie McLean and Donald Byrd regularly augmented Bley's trio. Charles Mingus was responsible for initiating Bley's recording career, and played bass on *Introducing Paul Bley*; Art Blakey was the drummer. Bley has always been drawn to the most creative players, and they to him. In the 60s, he put his stamp on every area of the new music. He played piano duets with Bill Evans inside George Russell's orchestra, helped to set in motion an introspective, intellectual improvisatory music in the trios of Don Ellis and Jimmy Giuffre, and recorded the classic *Footloose* - these endeavours setting the scene for, for example, ECM's development of a 'chamber jazz'. *Footloose*'s concentrated, quiet improvisation was counterbalanced by Bley's ferocious quintet on *Barrage*, featuring Sun Ra saxophonist Marshall Allen. Albert Ayler and John Gilmore also played with Bley in 1964. At the decade's end, Bley was playing Arp synthesizer and utilizing all the noise potential of electronics, and the drummers who passed through his group included Han Bennink (see *Improvisie* and *Dual Unity*) and Soft Machine's Robert Wyatt. The common denominator through all these activities is Bley's sense of form; his improvisations have the rightness and logic of composition. Bley returned to acoustic music in the 70s - his bleak, haunting *Open, To Love* setting the direction for future work - and formed his own label, IAI, donning the producer's hat to record Sun Ra, Ran Blake, Marion Brown, Sam Rivers and others. Through the 80s and 90s, Bley issued a steady stream of albums, of consistently high quality, which proved that emotional expressiveness is not the exclusive preserve of the shouters and screamers. 'Music', Bley once said, 'is the business of pain', and he can wound the heart with his carefully chosen notes.

● ALBUMS: *Introducing Paul Bley* (Debut 1954)★★★, *Paul Bley* (EmArcy 1955)★★★, *Solemn Meditation* (GNP Crescendo 1958)★★★, *Footloose* (Savoy 1963)★★★★, *Barrage* (ESP 1965)★★★★, *Closer* (ESP 1966)★★★★, *Touching* (Black Lion 1966)★★★★, *Ramblin'* (1967)★★★, *Blood* (1967)★★★★, *Paul Bley In Haarlem* (1967)★★★, *Mr Joy* (Limelight 1968)★★★, *The Fabulous Paul Bley Quintet* 1958 recording (Musidisc 1969)★★★, *Paul Bley Trio In Canada* (1969)★★★, *Paul Bley With Gary Peacock* 1963-1968 recordings (ECM 1970)★★★, *Ballads* 1967 recording (1970)★★★★, *The Paul Bley Synthesizer Show* (1971)★★★★, *Improvisie* (1971)★★★, with Annette Peacock *Dual Unity* (1972)★★★, with Peacock *Revenge - The Bigger The Love The Greater The Hate* 1969 recording (1972)★★★, *Paul Bley And Scorpio* (1973)★★★, *Open To Love* (ECM 1973)★★★, *Paul Bley/NHOP* (1974)★★★, with Bill Connors, Giuffre *Quiet Song* (Improvising Artists 1975)★★★, *Alone Again* (DIW 1975)★★★★, *Copenhagen And Haarlem* 1965-1966 recordings (1975)★★★★, *Turning Point* 1964-68 recordings (Improvising Artists)★★★, *Virtuosi* 1967 recording (1975)★★★★, *Bley/Metheny/Pastorius/Ditmas* re-released as *Jaco* 1978 (1975)★★★★, *Japan Suite* (Improvising Artists 1976)★★★, with Connors, Giuffre, Lee Konitz *IAI Festival* (Improvising Artists 1978)★★★★, *Axis* (Improvising Artists 1978)★★★, *Sonor* (1983)★★★, *Tango Palace* (Soul Note 1983)★★★★, *Tears* (Owl 1984)★★★, with Chet Baker *Diane* (1985)★★★, *Questions* (1985)★★★, *Hot* (1986)★★★, *My Standard* (1986)★★★★, *Paul Bley & Jesper Lundgaard Live* (1986)★★★, *Fragments* (ECM 1986)★★★, with Jesper Lundgaard *Live Again* (1987)★★★, with Peacock, Barry Altschul *Ballads* (ECM 1987)★★★★, *The Paul Bley Quartet* (ECM 1988)★★★, with Paul Motian *Notes* (Soul Note 1988)★★★, *Solo* (Justin Time 1988)★★★, *Solo Piano* (Steeple Chase 1988)★★★, *Floater Syndrome* 1962-63 recordings (1989)★★★, *The Nearness Of You* (Steeple Chase 1990)★★★★, with Gary Peacock *Partners* (Owl 1990)★★★, *Bebopbebopbebopbebop* (Steeple Chase 1990)★★★★, *Rejoicing* (Steeple Chase 1990)★★★★, with Giuffre, Swallow *The Diary Of A Trio: Saturday* (Owl 1990)★★★★, with Giuffre, Swallow *The Diary Of A Trio: Sunday* (Owl 1990)★★★, *12 + 6 (In A Row)* (hatART 1991)★★★★, *Blues For Red* (Red 1991)★★★★, *Live At Sweet Basil* 1988 recording (Soul Note 1991)★★★, *Memoirs* (Soul Note 1991)★★★★, *Lyrics* (Splasc 1991)★★★, *Indian Summer* 1987 recording (Steeple Chase 1991)★★★★, with Gary Burton *Right Time, Right Place* (1991)★★★, with John Ballentyne *A Musing* (1991)★★★★, with Gary Peacock, Altschul *Japan Suite* (1992)★★★, with Barry Altschul, Peacock *Virtuosi* (AI 1992)★★★, *Changing Hands* (Justin Time 1992)★★★, *Paul Plays Carla* (Steeple Chase 1992)★★★★, *Caravan Suite* (Steeple Chase 1993)★★★, with Franz Koglmann, Peacock *Annette* (hatART 1993)★★★, *In The Evenings Out There* (ECM 1993)★★★★, with Keshavan Maslak *Not To Be A Star*

(1993)★★★, with Maslak *Romance In The City* (Leo 1993)★★★, with Sonnie Greenwich *Outside In* (Justin Time 1994)★★★, with Evan Parker, Barre Phillips *Time Will Tell* (ECM 1995)★★★★, with Giuffre, Swallow *Conversations With A Goose* (Soul Note 1996)★★★★, *Synth Thesis* (Postcards 1996)★★, *Reality Check* (Steeplechase 1996)★★★★, with Kenny Wheeler *Touché* (Justin Time 1997)★★★, with Gary Peacock *Mindset* (Soul Note 1998)★★★★, with Furio Di Castri, Tony Oxley *Chaos* (Soul Note 1998)★★★.

● FURTHER READING: *Bley Play*, Henk Kluck.

BLOOM, JANE IRA

b. 1955, Newtown, Massachusetts, USA. Bloom studied music as a child and mastered the saxophone in her teens. She turned down an opportunity to tour with the Duke Ellington orchestra in favour of taking BA and MA degrees at Yale University. In 1977, she studied under George Coleman in New York and in 1979 formed her own record label, Outline. She recorded two albums, the second with Marimba and vibes player David Friedman, who introduced her to a wider public through his contact with the German label, Enja. In 1982 Bloom recorded with Charlie Haden and Ed Blackwell, establishing herself as one of the most prominent players and composers to emerge from the 70s. She recorded two more albums during the late 80s, and continues to play in a variety of settings (she has appeared solo in the Houston baseball Astrodome). *The Nearness* featured Kenny Wheeler, Fred Hersch and Julian Priester. Bloom recently declared that her aim is 'to bring more *avant garde* improvising to people who don't usually listen to it'.

● ALBUMS: *Second Wind* (Outline 1980)★★★, *Mighty Lights* (Enja 1983)★★★, *Modern Drama* (Columbia 1987)★★★★, *Shalom* (Columbia 1988)★★★★, with Fred Hersch *As One* (JMI 1992)★★★, *Art & Aviation* (Arabesque 1993)★★★, *The Nearness* (Arabesque 1996)★★★.

BLOWERS, JOHNNY

b. 21 April 1911, Spartanburg, South Carolina, USA. In his early teens, Blowers deputized on drums for his father in the pit band at a local theatre. He also worked with local groups in Florida and Georgia while still at college. In 1937 he went to New York where he played with Lou McGarity, Bobby Hackett and also spent some time with Bunny Berigan's big band. From 1940 Blowers was heavily involved in studio work but continued to play in jazz clubs and on recording dates. In 1944 he worked with Billie Holiday. Among the artists with whom Blowers played from the 40s through to the late 60s were Louis Armstrong, Georg Brunis, Eddie Condon, Johnny Mince and other exponents of Dixieland, the musical form in which he excelled. He was still playing in the mid-80s, happily working with the Harlem Blues And Jazz Band.

● ALBUMS: with Warren Vache Snr. *Jazz: It's A Wonderful Sound* (1977)★★★.

BLUE NOTE RECORDS

Founded in New York by Alfred Lion, the Blue Note record label became synonymous with the best in bebop and soul jazz. Its origins were, however, somewhat differently orientated. Born in Berlin, Germany, in 1908, Lion visited New York when he was 20 years old, mainly to hear music. Back in Germany he watched the rising tide of fascism with alarm and left the country before things became too dangerous, eventually making his way back to New York in 1938. Prompted by his admiration of boogie-woogie pianists Albert Ammons and Meade 'Lux' Lewis at John Hammond's *Spirituals To Swing* concert at Carnegie Hall, he decided to record them at his own expense. He followed this session with others featuring established jazzmen of the day, including Edmond Hall, James P. Johnson and Sidney Bechet. By the early 40s Lion had begun to record many of the most influential figures in the newly emergent strand of jazz known as bebop. Lion's dedication and ear for talent, allied as it was to the perspicacity of his A&R man, tenor saxophonist Ike Quebec, caused him to bring to his Blue Note studios many newcomers who could not find opportunities with the major record companies. In Blue Note's studios, the music was superbly recorded thanks to the skills of sound engineer Rudy Van Gelder. The list of artists recorded during this period reads like a bebop hall of fame; among them were Bud Powell, Thelonious Monk, Tadd Dameron, Wynton Kelly, Horace Silver, Fats Navarro, Howard McGhee, Clifford Brown, Lee Morgan, Freddie Hubbard, Dexter Gordon, Hank Mobley, Jackie McLean, Johnny Griffin, Kenny Barron, Clifford Jordan and Art Blakey. Thanks to such enormous talents, Blue Note's reputation grew, and over the next decade or so, many of the most important figures in contemporary jazz were persuaded to record for Lion and his partner Francis Wolff, whose photographs were often featured on the label's strikingly designed record sleeves. Following Quebec's death in 1963, Lion again appointed a musician as A&R man, this time choosing Duke Pearson. After the unexpected popular success of Lee Morgan's 'The Sidewinder' single in 1964, the label became associated with the 60s soul-jazz movement, including Big John Patten, Jimmy Smith, Grant Green, Kenny Burrell, Stanley Turrentine, Lou Donaldson and Brother Jack McDuff. During this inspired period, the record covers featured the immaculate typography of designer Reid Miles. Lion also released many notable *avant garde* records, including sessions by Ornette Coleman, Andrew Hill, Sam Rivers, Wayne Shorter, Cecil Taylor, Anthony Williams and Larry Young. Ill-health forced Lion to sell Blue Note to Liberty Records, with Wolff and Pearson continuing to control the company's musical policy. Eventually, commercial considerations affected the nature of the music with which Blue Note was associated, but an intelligent reissue programme was instigated by producer Michael Cuscuna in the mid-70s and continued into the early 90s. In the 80s Liberty became a part of the EMI group, and, in addition to the reissue programme, the label began to record many new jazz stars, including Bobby McFerrin, John Scofield and Stanley Jordan, while continuing to record such established figures as Hubbard, Woody Shaw, McCoy Tyner and Don Pullen. Alfred Lion died in 1987, his partner Wolff having died in 1971. The label is currently run by Bruce Lundval and Michael Cuscuna.

● COMPILATIONS: *Critics' Choice* (1992)★★★, *The Best Of Blue Note Volume 2* (Blue Note 1993)★★★, *A Story Of Modern Jazz* (Blue Note 1997)★★★★, *Hot Jazz On Blue Note* (Blue Note 1998)★★★, *The Blue Note Years* 14-CD box set (Blue Note 1998)★★★★★.

● FURTHER READING: *The Cover Art Of Blue Note Records*, Graham Marsh, Glyn Callingham and Felix Cromey (eds.). *The Cover Art Of Blue Note Records Volume 2*, Graham Marsh and Glyn Callingham (eds.).

BLUE TRAIN - JOHN COLTRANE

Although it would seem that Alfred Lion's Blue Note label would have been the perfect home for a Bluetrane, this is his only record for the label as a leader. Notwithstanding, this 1957 recording shows a confident John Coltrane before he became a giant in the field. The opening track is the leader; although a straightforward blues, it is a warming and familiar song. He is supported adequately by Lee 'Sidewinder' Morgan (trumpet), Kenny Drew (piano), Paul Chambers (bass), Curtis Fuller (trombone) and Philly Joe Jones (drums). Coltrane may have made more important albums, but none swung as effectively as this one.

● Tracks: *Blue Train; Moments Notice; The Locomotion; I'm Old Fashioned; Lazy Bird.*

● First released 1957

● UK peak chart position: did not chart

● USA peak chart position: did not chart

BLUEBIRD SESSIONS, THE - SIDNEY BECHET

An unashamed romantic, Sidney Bechet was a balladeer with a majestic playing style. He commanded attention on clarinet and soprano saxophone. On the former instrument he ranked with the best; on the latter there was simply no competition during his lifetime. Bechet soars gloriously over his accompanists, receiving all the attention his full-blooded, heart-on-sleeve romanticism demands. Swinging remorselessly, he demonstrates over and over again that his was a talent unique among his contemporaries. Although he had a handful of disciples, hardly anyone followed Bechet's path - a fact which makes his work even more worthy of interest today.

● Tracks: *Including - Sweetie Dear; I Want You Tonight; I've Found A New Baby; Lay Your Racket; Maple Leaf Rag; Shag; Ja Da; Really The Blues; When You And I Were Young Maggie; Weary Blues; Oh, Didn't He Ramble; High Society; I Thought I Heard Buddy Bolden Say; Winin' Boy Blues; Indian Summer; One O'clock Jump; Preachin' Blues; Sidney's Blues; Shake It And Break It; Old Man's Blues; Nobody Knows The Way I Feel This Morning; Wild Man Blues; Make Me A Pallet On The Floor; St. Louis Blues; Blues In Thirds; Blues For You, Johnny; Ain't Misbehavin'; Save It Pretty Mama; Stompy Jones; Muskat Ramble; Coal Black Shine; Egyptian Fantasy; Baby Won't You Please Come Home; Slippin' And Slidin'; The Sheik Of Araby; Blues Of Bechet; Swing Parade.*

● First Released (1932-1943 recordings)

● UK peak chart position: did not chart

● USA peak chart position: did not chart

BLUES AND THE ABSTRACT TRUTH - OLIVER NELSON

Beautifully recorded and easily the best album of Oliver Nelson's career, which, early on, had included stints with Louis Jordan and Quincy Jones, and conducting and arranging for Jimmy Smith (notably 'Walk On The Wild Side'). The personnel on this record is formidable and probably enhances the album's high standing - Eric Dolphy (alto and flute), Bill Evans (piano), Roy Haynes (drums), Freddie Hubbard (trumpet), George Barrow (baritone) and Nelson (alto, tenor and writer/arranger). It is hard to imagine that the man wholly behind this exceptional album was responsible for the *Six Million Dollar Man* television series theme.

● Tracks: *Stolen Moments; Hoe Down; Cascades; Yearnin'; Butch And Butch; Teenie's Blues.*

● First released 1961

● UK peak chart position: did not chart

● USA peak chart position: did not chart

BLUIETT, HAMIET

b. 16 September 1940, Lovejoy, Illinois, USA. Bluiett was taught music by his aunt, who directed a choir, and began to play the clarinet at the age of nine. He later studied flute and baritone saxophone at Southern Illinois University, then spent several years in the navy. In the mid-60s he moved to St. Louis, where he studied with George Hudson and became part of a collective of black musicians, later to be called BAG (Black Artists Group). In 1969 he relocated to New York, where he worked with the Sam Rivers Large Ensemble, the Thad Jones/Mel Lewis Big Band, Abdullah Ibrahim, Julius Hemphill, Charles Mingus and Don Pullen as well as soul artists Aretha Franklin and Stevie Wonder. In December 1976 he helped to form the World Saxophone Quartet for a concert in New Orleans, and this has since become the most visible showcase for his arrangements and sterling baritone saxophone. In 1981, he recorded with Lester Bowie on the trumpeter's *The Great Pretender*, adding hilarious, growling saxophone to the title track. Bluiett has also recorded an impressive series of albums as leader (featuring musicians such as Pullen, Fred Hopkins, Don Moye, John Hicks and Marvin 'Smitty' Smith), including a concert with his clarinet group, the Clarinet Family.

● ALBUMS: *Endangered Species* (India Navigation 1976)★★★★, *Bars* (1977)★★★, *Birthright* (India Navigation 1977)★★★★, *Orchestra, Duo & Septet* (1977)★★★, *Resolution* (Black Saint 1978)★★★, *S.O.S.* (India Navigation 1980)★★★, *Dangerously Suite* (Soul Note 1981)★★★, *Ebu* (Soul Note 1984)★★★, *The Clarinet Family* 1984 recording (Black Saint 1987)★★, *Nali Kola* (Soul Note 1989)★★★, *You Don't Need To Know ... If You Have To Ask* (Tutu 1991)★★★, *Sankofa/Rear Garde* (Soul Note

1993)★★★, *Young Warrior, Old Warrior* (Mapleshade 1995)★★★★, *Live At Carlos* 1986 recording (Just A Memory 1997)★★★, *Live At The Village Vanguard: Ballads & Blues* (Soul Note 1998)★★★.

Blythe, Arthur

b. 5 July 1940, Los Angeles, California, USA. From infancy Blythe lived in San Diego, returning to Los Angeles when he was 19 years old. He had taken up alto saxophone at the age of nine, playing R&B until his mid-teens when he discovered jazz. He studied with David Jackson and ex-Jimmie Lunceford altoist Kirtland (Kirk) Bradford. In the mid-60s he was part of UGMAA (The Underground Musicians and Artists Association), a west coast counterpart to Chicago's AACM founded by Horace Tapscott, on whose 1969 *The Giant Is Awakened* he made his recording debut. Blythe, aka Black Arthur, began leading his own group in 1970, often using unusual instrumentation, including tuba and cello, as well as James 'Blood' Ulmer's remarkable guitar, and during the early 70s he did some rock session work. Although he first went to New York City in 1968 he did not settle there until 1974. He was soon able to give up his job as security man at a pornography cinema when he was invited to join Chico Hamilton's group. Amongst other bands with whom he has played are those of Ray Charles, Tapscott (1963-73), Owen Marshall, Stanley Crouch (1967-73), Black Music Infinity, Leon Thomas, Julius Hemphill, Chico Hamilton, Ted Daniel, Lester Bowie (1978-80), Gil Evans (1976-80), Jack DeJohnette and all-star band the Leaders (with Bowie, Chico Freeman, Kirk Lightsey, Cecil McBee and Famoudou Don Moye). He has also guested with Craig Harris's homage to James Brown, Cold Sweat. At the end of the 70s he added a conventional saxophone and rhythm quartet, In The Tradition, to his ventures, running this alongside the guitar and cello group into the 80s. In 1990 he replaced founder-member Hemphill as the alto voice in the World Saxophone Quartet. A distinctive alto and soprano saxophonist, Blythe appears to be in the Albert Ayler tradition, though he cites Eric Dolphy, Thelonious Monk and John Coltrane as his major influences: basically a melodist, with clear gospel influences, he often uses a pronounced vibrato, though he has a generally lighter, more translucent sound than Ayler's. He has explained that his wide vibrato stems from using reeds that were too hard for him to control as a youth rather than a desire to emulate Ayler. Not a free player, Blythe nevertheless ranges far and wide in his improvisations, though an attempt at disco music with 1985's *Put Sunshine In It* (reputedly at the behest of his record label, Columbia) was neither a critical nor a commercial success. Despite living in New York for many years he still considers himself a Californian player; he once told writer Francis Davis that a musician's style was affected by his/her accent and dialect, 'because your music is a direct reflection of your speech'.

● ALBUMS: *The Grip* (India Navigation 1977)★★★, *Metamorphosis* (India Navigation 1977)★★★, *Bush Baby* (Echo 1977)★★★, *In Concert* (India Navigation 1978)★★★★, *Lenox Avenue Breakdown* (Columbia 1979)★★★★, *In The Tradition* (Columbia 1979)★★★, with In The Tradition *Illusions* (Columbia 1980)★★★★, *Blythe Spirit* (Columbia 1981)★★★, *Elaboration* (Columbia 1982)★★★, *Light Blue* (Columbia 1983)★★★, *Put Sunshine In It* (Columbia 1985)★★, *Da-Da* (Columbia 1986)★★★, with the Leaders *Mudfoot* (Black Hawk 1986)★★★, with the Leaders *Out Here Like This* (Black Saint 1987)★★★, *Basic Blythe* (Columbia 1987)★★★, with the Leaders *Unforeseen Blessings* (Black Saint 1989)★★★, with the World Saxophone Quartet *Metamorphosis* (1991)★★★, *Hipmotism* (Enja 1991)★★★★, *Retroflection* (Enja 1994)★★★, *Calling Card* (Enja 1996)★★, *Night Song* (Clarity 1997)★★★.

Blythe, Jimmy

b. *c*.1901, Louisville, Kentucky, USA, d. 21 June 1931. Growing up in Chicago, Blythe was taught to play piano and made his first records in 1924. He recorded extensively, if often anonymously, being first-call accompanist for numerous record dates by singers. He also formed and led many pick-up bands for record dates, using such names as the State Street Ramblers, the Chicago Footwarmers and the Washboard Ragamuffins. Along the way, Blythe worked with many fine jazzmen of the 20s, among them Johnny Dodds and Freddie Keppard. By the end of the 20s he was in less demand and he died in 1931.

● COMPILATIONS: *Cutting The Boogie: Piano Blues And Boogie Woogie* 1924-41 recordings (Swaggie)★★★, *Stomp Your Stuff* 1927-31 recordings (Swaggie 1983)★★★.

Bobo, Willie

b. William Correa, 28 February 1934, Spanish Harlem, New York City, USA, of Puerto Rican parentage, d. 15 September 1983, Los Angeles, California, USA. Growing up in New York's El Barrio, Bobo was exposed to substantial doses of Latin music, jazz and R&B. These genres later jostled together in his work as a bandleader. He started playing Latin percussion at the age of 14 (the timbales became his preferred instrument) and managed to get hired as Machito's bandboy. Bobo befriended Mongo Santamaría shortly after the congo player's arrival in New York. Mongo gave him percussion lessons and Bobo acted as his translator. He was dubbed 'Bobo' by jazz pianist Mary Lou Williams during an early 50s recording session. Bobo received his first major exposure as a sideman in 1955 with *The Shearing Spell* by George Shearing. After stints with Tito Puente (1954-57), Cal Tjader (1958 -61), Santamaría's charanga (1961-62), René Bloch and René Touzet, Bobo formed his own group and recorded for Tico and Roulette Records between 1963 and 1964. At that stage his attempts to 'build a bridge between Latin music and jazz' did not prove to be very popular, and gigs were few and far between. However, he was determined to fight against the stereotype that expected Latino musicians to play only typical Latin music. The smash hit success of Cal Tjader's 1965 bestseller *Soul Sauce*, on which he performed, inspired Willie to organize another Latin fusion group. The title track of his 1965 debut on Verve

Records, *Spanish Grease*, became a popular R&B hit. This and a string of other albums on the label kept him in steady work. In 1969 he returned to the west coast of America (he had been based there in the late 50s and early 60s while with Tjader and Mongo's charanga), where he continued to work regularly, including weekly appearances on Bill Cosby's national television show. In the 70s, Bobo issued albums on the Sussex, Blue Note and CBS labels. During his career, Willie sessioned with Miles Davis, Stan Getz, Cannonball Adderley, Sonny Stitt, Herbie Mann and Terry Gibbs, among others.

● ALBUMS: *Sabroso!* (1961)★★★, *Do That Thing/Guajira* (Tico 1963)★★★★, *Bobo's Beat* (Roulette 1964)★★★★, *Let's Go Bobo* (1964)★★★, *Latino* (1965)★★★★, *Soul Sauce* (1965)★★★★, as leader *Spanish Grease* (Verve 1965)★★★★, *Uno, Dos, Tres 1.2.3* (Verve 1966)★★★, *Feelin' So Good* (Verve 1967)★★★, *Juicy* (Verve 1967)★★★, *Bobo Motion* (Verve 1967)★★★, *Spanish Blues Band* (Verve 1967)★★★, *A New Dimension* (Verve 1968)★★★, *Evil Ways* (Verve 1968)★★★★, *Do What You Want To Do, Tomorrow Is Here* (1977)★★★, *Hell Of An Act To Follow* (1978)★★★, *Bobo* (1979)★★★.

Bocage, Peter

b. 31 July 1887, New Orleans, Louisiana, USA. d. 3 December 1967. A gifted multi-instrumentalist, Bocage came from a musical family. In the early years of the century he played violin in several dance bands in New Orleans. Later, he began playing cornet in bands including that led by Papa Celestin, before joining Armand J. Piron for a lengthy spell. He stayed with Piron until the end of the 20s, becoming a member of the Creole Serenaders, a band led by Louis Warneke. Resident in the north-east, by the beginning of the 40s Bocage was playing only part-time but gigged and recorded with Sidney Bechet and others. In the mid-40s he returned to New Orleans where he remained for the rest of his life, playing with Emile Barnes, the Eureka Brass Band and other local groups. Bocage's instrumental versatility (he also played guitar, xylophone, baritone horn, trombone, trumpet and banjo), allied to a inherent good taste, made him a popular figure with audiences and colleagues.

● ALBUMS: *The Barnes-Bocage Big Five* (1954)★★★, *Peter Bocage And His Creole Serenaders* (1961)★★★, *Peter Bocage And His Creole Serenaders* (1962)★★★, *Peter Bocage Quartet* (1963)★★★, *Peter Bocage At The San Jacinto Hall* (Jazzology 1964)★★★, *New Orleans - The Legends Live* (Jazzology 1986)★★★.

Body And Soul - Coleman Hawkins

This 1958 release features Coleman Hawkins' definitive interpretation of the title track. Although he did not write 'Body And Soul', he managed to engrave his own soul into it, and on the strength of this recording, should be entitled to claim it as his own. Regardless of recording techniques and location, the sparse, breathy tone produced by Hawkins is breathtaking. Without denigrating the other tracks on this record, the title track alone justifies its importance (as significant as *Kind Of Blue*) in any comprehensive record collection. Beautifully preserved from 10-inch disc and recorded in 1939, also included on this album is the 1956 recording, on which even the subtle clicks of the saxophone keys are discernible.

● Tracks: *Meet Doctor Foo; Fine Dinner; She's Funny That Way; Body And Soul; When Day Is Done; The Sheik Of Araby; My Blue Heaven; Bouncing With Bean; Say It Isn't So; Spotlight; April In Paris; How Strange; Half Step Down Please; Jumping For Jane; I Love You; There Will Never Be Another You; Little Girl Blue; Dinner For One, Please James; I Never Knew; His Very Own Blues; Thirty Nine Inches; Bean Stalks Again; I'm Shooting High; Have You Met Miss Jones?; The Day You Came Along; The Essence Of You.*

● First released 1958

● UK peak chart position: did not chart

● USA peak chart position: did not chart

Bofill, Angela

b. 1954, West Bronx, New York City, USA, Bofill began writing songs at the age of 12. She formed her first group while still at high school, the Puerto Rican Supremes, who performed in church and at local school dances. Her father, another Latin music singer, had once sung with Cuban bandleader Machito. After graduating from the Manhattan School of Music, she toured with Ricardo Morrero and recorded her first single, 'My Friend', which earned her a nomination as best Latin female vocalist from *Latin New York* magazine. Encouraged by this success, she embarked on a solo career, writing and performing the jazz suite 'Under The Moon And Over The Sky' in conjunction with the Brooklyn Academy of Music. She then became lead vocalist with the Dance Theater of Harlem Chorus, and performed alongside Stan Getz and Benny Goodman at Madison Square Garden. Following an introduction by Dave Valentin, she was signed as a soloist with Dave Grusin's GRP record label. The debut, *Angie*, included a reworking of 'Under The Moon', as well as 'Baby, I Need Your Love' and 'The Only Thing I Would Wish For'. Straying from jazz, Bofill worked in more conventional soul and R&B territory on her albums for Arista, where she teamed with producer Narada Michael Waldren before the System production team helmed her final three efforts for the label. She moved to Capitol later in the decade, where producers including Norman Connors were invited to assist. Bofill continued to tour widely between recording sessions, often with the New York Jazz Explosion, and also guested on Stanley Clarke's 'Where Do We Go' cut (from his *Hideaway* album). Although she has yet to chart a hit single outside the *Billboard* R&B lists, she has recorded increasingly impressive albums in the 90s within the jazz-soul style, and has established herself as an accomplished vocalist.

● ALBUMS: *Angie* (GRP 1978)★★★, *Angel Of The Night* (GRP 1979)★★, *Something About You* (Arista 1981)★★★, *Too Tough* (Arista 1983)★★★, *Teaser* (Arista 1983)★★, *Let Me Be The One* (Arista 1984)★★★, *Tell Me Tomorrow* (Arista 1985)★★, *Intuition* (Capitol 1988)★★★, *I Wanna Love Somebody* (Jive 1993)★★★,

Love In Slow Motion (Cachet/Shanachie 1996)★★★.
● COMPILATIONS: *Best Of Angela Bofill* (Arista 1986)★★★, *Best Of Angie (Next Time I'll Be Sweeter)* (Arista 1991)★★★.

BOLAND, FRANCY

b. François Boland, 6 November 1929, Namur, Belgium. A classically trained musician, Boland's first exposure to jazz came through concerts and records that he heard during World War II. His first contributions to the music were arrangements written for the bands of Bobby Jaspar, Henri Renaud and others. In the early 50s he spent much time in Paris, arranging and playing piano, and worked with visiting Americans such as Chet Baker and Nat Peck. In the late 50s he was writing for Kurt Edelhagen's German-based, multinational big band. In 1958 he visited New York, writing charts for Count Basie. At the same time, Boland met drummer Kenny Clarke and with the financial backing of entrepreneur Gigi Campi they formed the Clarke-Boland Big Band. This, too, was a multinational band and featured players such as Peck, Derek Humble, Benny Bailey, Jimmy Deuchar, Aake Persson, Sahib Shihab, Ronnie Scott and Johnny Griffin. Boland played piano in the band and also composed for it, but his principal contribution was his arranging, which magnificently combined the band's members into a powerful collective whole without ever subduing their potential for inventive soloing. The band was on the brink of folding in the early 70s, but stayed together thanks to the desire of the musicians to continue playing even when the financial burden was almost intolerable. Since 1976 Boland has lived and worked in Europe (mostly based in Switzerland), writing and arranging for artists such as Sarah Vaughan.
● ALBUMS: as the Clarke-Boland Big Band *The Golden Eight* (Blue Note 1961)★★★, as the Clarke-Boland Big Band *Jazz Is Universal* (Atlantic 1963)★★★, as the Clarke-Boland Big Band *The Clarke-Boland Big Band* (Atlantic 1963)★★★★, as the Clarke-Boland Big Band *Now Hear Our Meanin'* (Columbia 1965)★★★, as the Clarke-Boland Big Band *Fire, Soul, Heat & Guts* (Prestige 1968)★★★★, as the Clarke-Boland Big Band *Let's Face The Music* (Prestige 1969)★★★, as Francy Boland Orchestra *Blue Flame* (1976)★★★.

BOLDEN, BUDDY

b. Charles Joseph Bolden, 6 September 1877, New Orleans, Louisiana, USA, d. 4 November 1931. The first great jazz legend, Bolden's reputation depends largely upon the reminiscences of the next generation of cornet and trumpet players of early jazz. They recalled him as being an inspiration, a driving, rhythmic and emotional player, and the 'first jazz trumpeter'. Research by writer Don Marquis suggests that Bolden was merely an adequate musician who became immensely popular in turn-of-the-century New Orleans, thanks mainly to his powerful playing of the kind of music the crowds wanted to hear, allied to enormous personal magnetism. In the early 1900s Bolden began to drink heavily and by 1906 was showing signs of mental disorder. In 1907 he was incarcerated in the Jackson Mental Institution, where he remained until his death in 1931. Bolden never recorded, although rumours still abound that he made some cylinder recordings in the 1890s, but his stylistic influence was ostensibly apparent in the work of many early New Orleans cornetists, including Bunk Johnson. A fictional account of Bolden's life was the basis for Michael Ondaatje's brilliantly inventive 1976 novel, *Coming Through Slaughter*.
● FURTHER READING: *In Search Of Buddy Bolden, First Man Of Jazz*, Don Marquis.

BOLLING, CLAUDE

b. 10 April 1930, Cannes, France. After showing prodigious talent as a child pianist, Bolling began playing professionally while still in his early teens. Strongly influenced by ragtime and early jazz pianists and by other figures as diverse as Duke Ellington and Art Tatum, Bolling swiftly became recognized in France as a major pianist. He played at concerts, festivals and on record with many visiting jazzmen including Paul Gonsalves, Lionel Hampton and Rex Stewart. He also led his own small groups from the late 40s onwards, forming bigger bands in the 50s including the Show Biz Band, which remained in intermittent existence for the next three decades. In addition to playing jazz, Bolling has also written for films. He has composed and recorded music that mixes jazz and the classical form, although he has done so in a manner that remains closer to the mainstream than the so-called third stream. Bolling makes infrequent appearances outside his homeland but has played in the UK, leading his powerful big band from the piano.
● ALBUMS: *Claude Bolling Plays Duke Ellington* (1959)★★★★, *Cat Anderson, Claude Bolling And Co.* (1965)★★★, *Original Ragtime* (1966)★★★, *Original Boogie Woogie* (1968)★★★, *Original Piano Blues* (1969)★★★, *Original Jazz Classics* (1970)★★★, *Original Piano Greats* (1972)★★★, *Swing Session* (1973)★★★★, *Jazz Party* (1974)★★★, *Suite For Violin And Jazz Piano* (1975)★★★, *With The Help Of My Friends* (1975)★★, *Keep Swingin' Volume 4* (1975)★★★, *Suite For Flute And Jazz Piano* (1975)★★★, *Hot Sounds* (1976)★★★, *Concerto For Classic Guitar And Jazz Piano* (HMV 1975)★★★, *Suite For Chamber Orchestra And Jazz Piano Trio* (1978)★★★, *Jazz Gala 79* (1979)★★★, *Just For Fun* (1980)★★★, *Toot Suite* (1981)★★★, *Claude Bolling* (RCA 1981)★★★, *Suite For Cello And Jazz Piano Trio* (1982)★★★, *Jazz À La Française* (Columbia 1984)★★★, *Live At The Meridien* (Columbia 1985)★★★, *Nuances* (DRG 1988)★★★, *A Drum Is A Woman* (Milan Jazz 1997)★★.

BONANO, SHARKEY

b. Joseph Bonano, 9 April *c.*1902, Milneburg, Louisiana, USA, d. 27 March 1972. A powerful, hot trumpeter, Bonano played in and around his home-town as a teenager. In 1920 he went to New York to work with Eddie Edwards but was soon back home playing with various lesser-known New Orleans bands, including Norman Brownlee's, with whom he made his first recordings in 1925. During this same period he made sporadic attempts to enter the big time, auditioning for the Wolverines and working with the band led by

Jimmy Durante (before the pianist turned comic). In 1927, Bonano was briefly with Jean Goldkette and also worked with Larry Shields in Los Angeles. In the late 20s Bonano temporarily stopped striving for the national big time and settled instead for being a popular figure in New Orleans where he led his own band. He also worked in harness with Louis Prima's brother, Leon. In 1936 he tried New York again, this time with much more success, working with Ben Pollack and also leading his own band. The Revival movement helped Bonano to retain his popularity and he worked throughout the 40s and into the 50s, sometimes leading a band, often appearing as a solo act, singing and playing trumpet. Bonano's playing was variable but on a good day he was an exciting, aggressive and thoroughly entertaining player. Fortunately, some of his best work was captured on recording dates, especially those of the early 50s. Bonano played into the 60s, but ill-health gradually curtailed his activity and he died in 1972.

● ALBUMS: *Midnight On Bourbon Street* (1951)★★★, *Dixieland At The Roundtable* (1960)★★★.

● COMPILATIONS: *Sharkey Bonano And His New Orleans Boys And Sharks Of Rhythm* 1936 recordings (Holmia 1986)★★★, *Sharkey And His Kings Of Dixieland* (GHB 1986)★★★, *Sharkey Bonano 1928-1937* (Timeless 1992)★★★.

BONEY, JAMES

b. James Oppenheim, *c.*1962, Lowell, Massachusetts, USA. Raised in New Rochelle, New York, Boney played clarinet at school, then the tenor saxophone and later the alto and soprano. His early musical tastes leaned towards contemporary pop, fusion and rock, including Stevie Wonder, Earth, Wind And Fire and Grover Washington Jnr. His family moved to Los Angeles in 1975 where he began to play in garage bands and then became a session musician. In this capacity he backed many artists including the Isley Brothers and Randy Crawford. It was on a Scandinavian tour with Crawford in the mid-80s that he picked up the nickname by which he has since been known professionally. By the early 90s his eclectic taste in music and its sometimes diffusing effect upon his playing had given way to a distinctive style, mostly on tenor, which strongly favours a melodic approach. This led to popularity on radio stations with a liking for smooth jazz. Indeed, in 1995 *Seduction* spent 17 weeks as number 1 on *R&R*'s NAC chart, 16 weeks in top spot on *Gavin*'s Smooth Jazz and Vocal chart, and was on *Billboard*'s Top 10 Contemporary Jazz list for a year. Also in the mid-90s he toured as opening act with Al Jarreau and the Rippingtons, thus attracting even more attention to his playing. However, during this same period his interest in developing a parallel career as a composer was growing steadily and signposting likely future trends.

● ALBUMS: *Backbone* (Warners 1994)★★★, *Trust* 1991 recording (Warners 1995)★★, *Seduction* (Warners 1995)★★★, *Boney's Funky Christmas* (Warners 1996)★★, *Sweet Thing* (Warners 1997)★★★.

BOOTH, PAUL ERIC

b.15 April 1977, England. Booth first played tenor saxophone in public with his accordionist father in Spanish bars and restaurants. He was then 11 years old and the following year, also in Spain, he played with Diz Disley. At 13, while still at school, he was playing regularly in clubs in the north-east of England, often working with the Dick Straughan band. At the age of 15 he appeared on television and played several prestigious engagements including one with Spike Robinson. The following year, he entered the Royal Academy of Music to begin a Bachelor of Music degree course. During this same year he accompanied Harry Connick Jnr. and won the award for Most Promising Jazz Player Of The Year Under 21. The following year he won the Best Modern Jazz Player award in the Young Jazz Player Of The Year competition. One of the judges at this was Ronnie Scott, who likened Booth's playing to that of the late Tubby Hayes and who also booked him to lead a quartet at his London club. In 1995 Booth toured extensively in the UK with his own group and also played in Victor Hugo's band and with Williams Cumberbath's salsa band Tumbaito. This same year he became the first non-American to win the First Level Award and a Clifford Brown/Stan Getz fellowship at the NFAA/Arts Week. This award was presented in Miami where he was heard by Dave Grusin who invited him to play with him. From here, Booth went to Atlanta where he performed at the International Association of Jazz Educators Annual Conference. In 1996 he spent several months in Australia as an exchange student and while there played extensively and also recorded at the ABC studios. Late in 1996 and early the following year Booth was resident in several London venues, including the Café de Paris and Annabell's. He also toured the north-east of England with the Supremes. His New Year's Eve gig at the start of 1997 was in São Paulo, Brazil. Booth's technical skills are outstanding and despite his youth he is a long-standing master of his instrument, but his performing style goes far beyond the merely technical. He plays with a deep understanding of the musical roots of jazz, interpreting ballads with enormous skill and sensitivity, and improvising fluently and inventively. Still only 20 in 1997, Booth is quite clearly a major talent and one who will carry the banner of excellence in jazz into the 21st century. In 1997 he was negotiating a recording contract with a leading American jazz label.

BORBETOMAGUS

An incredibly prolific, powerful and adventurous *avant garde* jazz group, the core element of Borbetomagus comprises Don Dietrich (wind instruments), Jim Sauter (wind instruments) and Donald Miller (guitar). They formed in Hudson Valley, New York, USA, in 1978, both Dietrich and Sauter having been friends since kindergarten. They continued their musical collaborations through high school, eventually linking with Miller (ex-Slick Dick And The Volkswagens) after meeting him on an experimental radio show. Their self-titled 1980 debut album, which also featured keyboard player Brian Doherty, provided an abrasive, almost overwhelming sonic introduction, with Miller's layered feedback counterpointing the unfettered dual saxophone playing of his partners. The additional musician for *Work On What Has Been Spoiled* was English producer Hugh Davies, while *Sauter, Dietrich, Miller* was recorded at live shows between 1979 and 1981 to clearly bemused audiences. Beginning with 1983's *Industrial Strength* set, Borbetomagus embarked on a series of collaborations with obscure and well-known musicians. Many of these recordings are taken from free improvisation sessions, making them less concisely vital as the band's unaccompanied albums. There have also been several further live collections, including the double album *Zurich* (live at the Rote Fabik), *New York Performances* and *Live At Inroads*. Further collaborations with Swiss duo Voice Crack, bass player Adam Nodelman and Shaking Ray Levis were all artistically successful, though more attention was focused on their comparatively accessible 1990 album, *Barefoot In The Head*, named after a Bryan Aldiss science fiction novel, recorded with Thurston Moore of Sonic Youth. Uncompromisingly innovative, even within the free-form jazz world, Borbetomagus have produced a rich discography that combines the eloquent expressionism of the best jazz music with the attack and vigour of rock.

● ALBUMS: *Borbetomagus* (Agaric 1980)★★★, *Work On What Has Been Spoiled* (Agaric 1981)★★★, *Sauter, Dietrich, Miller* (Agaric 1982)★★, *Barbed Wire Maggots* (Agaric 1983)★★★, *Life At Inroads* (Agaric 1983)★★★, with Toshinori Kondo, Tristan Honsinger, Peter Kowald, Milo Fine *Industrial Strength* (Leo 1983)★★, *Zurich* (Agaric 1984)★★, with Kondo, Honsinger, Kowald, Fine *Borbeto Jam* (Cadence 1985)★★★, with Jim Sauter, Don Dietrich *Bells Together* (Agaric 1985)★★★, *New York Performances* (Agaric 1986)★★★, *Seven Reasons For Tears* (Purge 1988)★★★, with Voice Crack *Fish That Sparkling Bubble* (Agaric 1988)★★, *Snuff Jazz* (Agaric 1990)★★★, Sauter, Dietrich, Thurston Moore *Barefoot In The Head* (Forced Exposure 1990)★★★, with Voice Crack *Asbestos Shake* (Agaric 1992)★★★, *Buncha Hair That Long* (Agaric 1993)★★★, with Shaking Ray Levis *Coelacanth* (Agaric/Lyndhurst Society 1994)★★★.

Born To Swing

An outstanding documentary made in 1973 by John Jeremy, which draws on interviews (with Buck Clayton, John Hammond, Andy Kirk, Gene Krupa and others), still photographs (by Valerie Wilmer), archive film of the Count Basie band of the early 40s, and, most tellingly, ex-Basie sidemen in musical action. Among those still playing (in 1972) and swinging magnificently, are Eddie Durham, Jo Jones, Joe Newman, Gene Ramey, Buddy Tate, Earle Warren and Dicky Wells. Made in the UK and first screened on BBC TV, the film has a linking commentary spoken by Humphrey Lyttelton.

Bose, Sterling

b. 23 February 1906, Florence, Alabama, USA, d. June 1958. A gifted but wayward cornetist and trumpet player, Bose worked with various bands in New Orleans and St. Louis before joining Jean Goldkette in 1927. Bose subsequently worked in radio, then became a member of Ben Pollack's band in 1930. During the next decade, Bose drifted in and out of numerous big bands of the swing era, including those led by Joe Haymes (which became the Tommy Dorsey band while Bose was in its ranks), Ray Noble, Benny Goodman, Glenn Miller, Bob Crosby, Bobby Hackett, Jack Teagarden and Bud Freeman. In the 40s he worked mostly in small group settings with Georg Brunis, Art Hodes and Miff Mole, and freelanced in several major cities. Bose's playing on record shows a variety of influences, which range from occasional flashes of Bix Beiderbecke to a powerful plunger-muted solo on 'I'm Praying Humble' (with Crosby). Despite his experience and a reputation for sound musical ability, Bose's restlessness, allied to his heavy drinking, prevented his career from ever blossoming.

Bostic, Earl

b. Eugene Earl Bostic, 25 April 1913, Tulsa, Oklahoma, USA, d. 28 October 1965, Rochester, New York, USA. The romantic and smooth sound of Bostic's band, usually featuring the vibes of Gene Redd, piano of Fletcher Smith, bass of Margo Gibson, drums of Charles Walton, guitar of Alan Seltzer, and the marvellous alto saxophone of Bostic, was one of the great and distinctive sounds of both R&B and pop music, and his records became perennials on the juke-boxes during the 50s. Bostic was best known for his alto saxophone sound but he also played tenor saxophone, flute and clarinet on his records. Bostic was formally trained in music, having received a degree in music theory from Xavier University. He moved to New York City and formed a jazz combo in 1938. In the early 40s he was playing in the Lionel Hampton band. He left Hampton in 1945 to form a combo, recording tracks for Majestic, but did not make much of an impression until he signed with New York-based Gotham in 1948. He had immediate success with 'Temptation' (US R&B number 10). During the 50s he recorded prolifically for Cincinnati-based King Records, and had two big singles, 'Sleep' (US R&B number 6) and 'Flamingo' (US R&B number 1), in 1951. The smooth but perky performance on the latter became his signature tune and made him something of a Beach Music artist in the Carolinas.

● ALBUMS: *The Best of Earl Bostic* (King 1956)★★★★, *Bostic For You* (King 1956)★★★, *Alto-Tude* (King 1956)★★★, *Dancetime* (King 1957)★★★★, *Let's Dance With Earl Bostic* (King 1957)★★★★, *Invitation To Dance* (King 1957)★★★, *C'mon & Dance With Earl Bostic* (King 1958)★★★★, *Bostic Rocks-Hits From The Swing Age* (King 1958)★★★, *Bostic Showcase Of Swinging Dance Hits* (King 1958)★★★, *Alto Magic In Hi-Fi* (King 1958)★★, *Sweet Tunes Of The Fantastic 50's* (King 1959)★★★, *Workshop* (King 1959)★★★, *Sweet Tunes Of The Roaring 20's*

(King 1959)★★, *Sweet Tunes Of the Swinging 30's* (King 1959)★★★, *Sweet Tunes Of The Sentimental 40's* (King 1959)★★, *Musical Pearls* (King 1959)★★★, *Hit Tunes Of The Big Broadway Shows* (King 1960)★★, *25 Years Of Rhythm And Blues Hits* (King 1960)★★★, *By Popular Demand* (King 1962)★★★, *Earl Bostic Plays Bossa Nova* (King 1963)★★, *Jazz As I Feel It* (King 1963)★★, *The Best Of Earl Bostic* (King 1964)★★★, *New Sound* (King 1964)★★★, *The Great Hits Of 1964* (King 1964)★★★, *The Song Is Not Ended* (Philips 1967)★★★, *Harlem Nocturne* (King 1969)★★, *Sax'O Boogie* (Oldie Blues 1984)★★, *Blows A Fuse* (Charly 1985)★★★, *That's Earl, Brother* (Spotlite 1985)★★★, *Bostic Rocks* (Swingtime 1987)★★★, *Dance Time* (Sing 1988)★★★, *Bostic For You* (Sing 1988)★★★, *Dance Music From The Bostic Workshop* (Charly 1988)★★★, *Flamingo* (Charly 1995)★★★.

BOSWELL SISTERS

The Boswell Sisters were Connee Boswell (b. 3 December 1907, Kansas City, Missouri, USA, d. 11 October 1976), Martha (b. 1908, d. 1958) and Helvetia, known as Vet (b. 1909, d. 12 November 1988). Born into a white middle-class family and raised in New Orleans, the sisters broke with convention by developing a close interest in black music and forming themselves into a vocal group. Among the first white female groups to sing in this manner, their extensive musical skills, which derived from childhood lessons, ensured that what they did was free of gimmickry. Martha played piano, Helvetia played banjo, guitar and violin, while Connee was remarkably multi-instrumental. While in their early teenage years, the sisters began working on radio and, concurrently with Bing Crosby, quickly discovered the confidential style of singing made possible by intelligent use of microphones. The sisters' early exposure to jazz in their home-town ensured that they worked with a marked feeling for this kind of music, and they often recorded with noted jazzmen of their day, among them Bunny Berigan, Jimmy Dorsey and Tommy Dorsey. The sisters became enormously popular on radio and in films and through records and personal appearances across the USA and in Europe. In the mid-30s all three women married and, with only Connee wanting to continue singing, they broke up their act. In the following decade the groundwork laid by the Boswell Sisters was successfully exploited by numerous all-female singing groups, of which the Andrews Sisters came closest to the originals.

● COMPILATIONS: *Syncopating Harmonists From New Orleans* 1930-1935 recordings (Take Two)★★★, *That's How Rhythm Was Born* 1931-1934 recordings (Sony)★★★★, *The Boswell Sisters Collection, Vol. 1* 1931/1932 recordings (Collector's Classics)★★★★, *Okay America! Alternate Takes And Rarities* 1931-35 recordings (Vintage Jazz)★★★, with Connee Boswell *Sand In My Shoes* 1935-1941 recordings (MCA)★★★★, *La Selection* 1930-1936 recordings (1994)★★★★.

BOSWELL, CONNEE

b. 3 December 1907, Kansas City, Missouri, USA, d. 11 October 1976. An outstanding singer with enormous but often uncredited influence, Boswell claimed to have been inspired by singers as diverse as Bessie Smith and Enrico Caruso. According to outside sources, Connee and her sisters, Martha and Helvetia, were both influenced and encouraged by the New Orleans cornetist Emmett Hardy. In her work it is possible also to discern the effect of the stylistic advances being made by Ethel Waters and Louis Armstrong. Certainly, she was interested in the blues and when she made her first record as a pre-teenager she sang a blues written by Martha. The sisters formed a close-harmony singing group, the Boswell Sisters, but Connee's career extended far beyond this. Despite being in a wheelchair since contracting polio at the age of four, she grew up to be a determined, talented performer, carving a highly successful solo career after the sisters' act folded in 1935. A skilled musician, adept on saxophone, trombone, cello and piano, she worked extensively in radio, television and films. Essentially a two-beat singer, with a calculatedly casual sound, she considerably affected the manner in which later singers approached their work. Although few acknowledge their debt to Connee Boswell, the fact that one who did was Ella Fitzgerald suggests that her influence is widespread throughout popular music, even if her emulators do not always realize the original source of their inspiration. She worked steadily into the 60s, mostly on television. A rare opportunity to enjoy her work on CD came in 1998 with the reissue of her 1958 album celebrating the 50th anniversary of songwriter Irving Berlin's career.

● ALBUMS: *The Star Maker* 10-inch album (Decca 1951)★★★, *Connee Boswell* 10-inch album (Decca 1951)★★★, *Singing The Blues* 10-inch album (Decca 1951)★★★, *Connee* (Decca 1956)★★★, *Connee Boswell & The Original Memphis 5* (RCA Victor 1956)★★★, *Connee Boswell Sings Irving Berlin* (Design 1958)★★★★.

● COMPILATIONS: with the Boswell Sisters *Sand In My Shoes* 1935-1941 recordings (MCA)★★★★.

BOURELLY, JEAN-PAUL

b. 23 November 1960, Chicago, Illinois, USA. Raised in Chicago, Bourelly's parents were first-generation Haitians - he learned about Yoruba music from his grandmother while absorbing the electrified blues of Muddy Waters; his brother Carl went on to become house keyboardist with Def Jam (the rap and heavy metal label). When Bourelly was 10 years old he sang Rossini at the Lyric Opera House in whiteface ('to make us look like little Italian boys'). He had piano and drum lessons with Von Freeman but took up guitar in 1974 after hearing Jimi Hendrix. In 1979 he moved to New York, sharing an apartment with Steve Coleman. Chico Hamilton was the first bandleader to hire him: gigs with Muhal Richard Abrams, Roy Haynes, McCoy Tyner and Elvin Jones quickly followed. The latter particularly impressed him with his understanding of the African polyrhythms at the heart of jazz. He was also welcomed by the new generation *avant garde* - trumpeter Olu Dara and alto saxophonist Henry Threadgill - and acted in Francis Ford Coppola's *The Cotton Club*. In 1989, Miles Davis employed him to play on *Amandla*. Bourelly calls his music Blue Wave: 'a natural progression from growing up in the 60s, going through the 70s and putting up with the 80s'. Without perhaps the harmolodic detachment of James Blood Ulmer, he is a better popularizer, and his blues-drenched, stinging guitar fuses jazz outreach with gutter groove more convincingly than 70s fusion ever did. 'Hope You Find Your Way' on *Jungle Cowboy* shows why: Bourelly's voice and guitar are a genuine extension of the expressionist intensity of southern blues.

● ALBUMS: with Cassandra Wilson *Days Aweigh* (1987)★★★, *Jungle Cowboy* (1989)★★★★, with the Blue Wave Bandits *Saints & Sinners* (1993)★★★, *Blackadelic Blu* (DIW 1994)★★★.

Boutté, Lillian

b. 6 August 1949, New Orleans, Louisiana, USA. After singing in a church choir and studying music, Boutté became a professional singer in her early 20s. Initially, she sang R&B but her striking personality and wide-ranging musical knowledge brought her a key role in the show *One Mo' Time*. Her first European tour began in 1980 and she created a substantial following, particularly in France and the UK. In 1983 she collaborated with saxophonist Thomas l'Etienne, whom she married, to form the group Music Friends and, later, the Boutté-l'Etienne Jazz Ensemble. Her touring schedule was stepped up with important appearances at many festivals around the world, including Ascona where she headlined for several years from 1985, Brecon, the 1988 Ellington Convention, and other prestigious engagements. Also in the late 80s she performed with Humphrey Lyttelton. A vibrant and exceptionally talented singer, Boutté's predilection for the traditional end of the jazz song spectrum may have shielded her from the attention of fans of contemporary music. This is unfortunate, because her powerful, imaginative, blues-based style makes her one of the few singers of her generation who can evoke with ease the important place held by the blues in the art of jazz song.

● ALBUMS: *Music Is My Life* (Timeless 1984)★★★★, *A Fine Romance* (1985)★★★, *New Orleans Gospel* (Herman 1986)★★★, *Let Them Talk* (Storyville 1988)★★★, *Lillian Boutte With Humphrey Lyttelton And Band* (Calligraph 1988)★★★, *I Sing Because I'm Happy* (Timeless 1988)★★★, *Having A Good Time!* (Calligraph 1989)★★★, *Birthday Party* (Music Mecca 1989)★★★, *Lipstick Traces* (Blues Beacon 1991)★★★, *Live In Tivoli* (Music Mecca 1993)★★, *But . . . Beautiful* (Dinosaur 1996)★★★.

Bowie, Joe

b. 1958, St. Louis, Missouri, USA. Younger brother of trumpeter Lester Bowie, Joseph learned piano and congas but finally settled with trombone. At the age of 15 he played with bluesmen Albert King and Little Milton and soul saxophonist Oliver Sain. He spent two years in Paris with other members of BAG (Black Artists Group), then in the late 70s recorded with Charles 'Bobo' Shaw in the Human Arts Ensemble and the St. Louis Creative Ensemble before returning to New York to work with the Contortions, James Chance's harmolodic/punk No Wave group. The horn section became an opening act and then a band in its own right: Defunkt. This unit combined jazz chops and *nouveau*-funk cheer; they toured with the Clash and Talking Heads. After a heroin-induced hiatus, Bowie returned in 1985 with an amazing physique and an excellent album, *In America*, which featured Kim Annette Clarke's bass guitar (described by one reviewer as 'funky as the chain on Judge Dredd's motorbike'). Since then, Bowie has steered between dance music and *avant garde* jazz with a verve that makes nonsense of the usual pigeonholes.

● ALBUMS: *Joseph Bowie - Oliver Lake* (1976)★★★, with St. Louis Creative Ensemble *I Can't Figure Out* (1979)★★, *Defunkt* (1980)★★★, *Thermonuclear Sweat* (1982)★★★, *In America* (1988)★★★★, with Michael Marcus *Under The Wire* (1991)★★★.

Bowie, Lester

b. 11 October 1941, Frederick, Maryland, USA. After taking up the trumpet as a child Bowie played in several R&B bands in and around St. Louis, Missouri. He led his own R&B bands and married singer Fontella Bass, accompanying her as musical director. Despite this and earlier connections with the R&B scene, Bowie's chief musical interests lay elsewhere. Based in Chicago from the mid-60s, he was actively involved with the Association for the Advancement of Creative Musicians (AACM) and was co-founder of the Art Ensemble Of Chicago. From its inception in 1969 into the 80s, he remained closely linked with AEC, touring and recording extensively, especially in France. Always eager to experiment with fusions of seemingly differing aspects of the jazz tradition, he has constantly brought traditional blues roots into his work with such forward-thinking musicians as Archie Shepp, Roscoe Mitchell and David Murray. Bowie is also involved with the groups Brass Fantasy and From The Root To The Source, and has played with reggae groups in Jamaica and spent time in Nigeria playing in Fela Kuti's Egypt 80 band. He was also a member of the Chicago based supergroup The Leaders, alongside alto saxophonist Arthur Blythe, tenor saxophonist Chico Freeman, pianist Kirk Lightsey, drummer Famoudou Don Moye and bassist Cecil McBee. Bowie composed many numbers recorded by AEC and by other groups with which he has been associated. Among his extended works are 'Gittin' To Know Y'All', originally performed by the Baden-Baden Free Jazz Orchestra. Bowie happily works with groups of all sizes, from the smallest to a 60-piece orchestra assembled for some of his concerts. Bowie appeared on David Bowie's (no relation) *Black Tie White Noise* in 1993. A remarkably gifted trumpeter, with a full, rich tone and a comprehensive range of effects, Bowie's work frequently contains welcome elements of self-parodying humour and witty inventiveness.

● ALBUMS: with Roscoe Mitchell *Congliptious* (1968)★★★, *Gittin' To Know Y'All* (1969)★★★, *Fast Last!* (1974)★★★, *Rope A Dope* (1976)★★★, *The Fifth Power* (Black Saint 1978)★★★★, *African Children* (1978)★★★, *The Great Pretender* (ECM 1982)★★★★, *All The Magic* (ECM 1983)★★, *I Only Have Eyes*

For You (ECM 1985)★★★, with Jack DeJohnette *Zebra* (Pan 1985)★★★, *Avant Pop* (ECM 1986)★★★★, with the Leaders *Mudfoot* (Black Hawk 1986)★★★, with the Leaders *Out Here Like This* (Black Saint 1987)★★★, *Twilight Dreams* (Venture 1987)★★★★, *Serious Fun* (DIW 1989)★★★, with the Leaders *Unforseen Blessings* (Black Saint 1989)★★★, *My Way* (DIW 1990)★★★, *The Organizer* (DIW 1991)★★★, *The Fire This Time* (In And Out 1993)★★★, with Phil Wilson *Duet* (1993)★★★, with Brass Fantasy *The Fire This Time* (In & Out 1995)★★★.
● COMPILATIONS: *Works* (ECM 1989)★★★★.

BOWMAN, DAVE

b. 8 September 1914, Buffalo, New York, USA, d. 28 December 1964. Bowman began playing piano as a child, and later went on to study formally. He was in the UK in the mid-30s, playing in Jack Hylton's band in London. At the end of the 30s he was resident in New York, working in small traditional bands with such leading jazzmen as Sidney Bechet and Bud Freeman. During the early 40s he was with Jack Teagarden, Muggsy Spanier and others. He drifted into radio work, becoming adept at accompanying singers both in the jazz field, with Lee Wiley, and elsewhere, with Perry Como. In the 50s he was again with Freeman and also played as a single. He continued playing jazz into the early 60s but was rarely in the big time. A competent pianist, he was at his best as a relatively anonymous member of the rhythm section of several solid traditional bands. He died in a car accident in December 1964.

BOWN, PATTI

b. *c*.1937, Seattle, Washington, USA. Bown began playing piano at the age of two, but had to wait another four years before taking lessons. This was because four of her seven siblings were already having music lessons and there was simply not enough money to feed another hungry musical mind. As she later told Sally Placksin, even from the start she was affected by jazz and in particular the music of Duke Ellington and Billy Strayhorn. While still at school, Bown extended her studies into harmony, counterpoint and composition, but her interest in jazz was largely self-motivated. She played piano in church and for dances and had her mind set upon a career as a professional pianist. The futility of pursuing a career as a classical pianist was driven home to her when an older sister, who had studied in France, returned to give a concert in New York. Although receiving rave reviews, she was flatly informed that there was no way that a career as a concert pianist was viable for a black woman. For all the reactions her sister drew, Bown was determined to go ahead with her own career plans and took up one of the many scholarships she was offered when she completed high school. Nevertheless, she found the form of musical education stifling to her creative and improvisational impulses and eventually reverted to teaching herself as she had done when she was a small child. She had played with Dizzy Gillespie in Seattle while still a child and when she decided to try her luck in New York he was able to help her find some work. This was in the mid-50s and by the end of the decade she had begun to establish a small and localized reputation. In 1960 she was hired for the big band Quincy Jones took to Europe. She had known Jones when they were both growing up in Seattle and he clearly had no reservations about her ability. The band was formed for the Harold Arlen show, *Free And Easy*, and although the show did not run for long the band toured on its own, eventually clocking up a year on the continent of Europe. Upon her return to the USA, Bown began working in radio and television studios and in Broadway theatre pit bands. She played and recorded with many well-known artists, including Aretha Franklin, Dinah Washington, Benny Carter, Ellington, George Russell and Sarah Vaughan. She has composed several works, including jazz compositions, and music for films and television. In the late 70s and early 80s she was active with the Universal Arts and Folklore organization, of which she was co-founder, helping to promote interracial harmony and understanding. A remarkable and gifted pianist and composer with a highly idiosyncratic style, Bown's career has at times suffered from her duties to her family and from the continuing refusal in some quarters to accept women in jazz on equal terms with their male counterparts.
● ALBUMS: *Patti Bown Plays Big Piano* (Columbia 1959)★★★★.

BRACKEEN, CHARLES

b. 13 March 1940, White's Chapel (renamed Eufaula), Oklahoma, USA. As a child Brackeen studied piano and violin before taking up saxophone at the age of 10. After living briefly in Texas and New York, he moved to Los Angeles in 1956, where he met musicians such as Don Cherry, Ornette Coleman, Charlie Haden, Billy Higgins and Paul Bley, so furthering an interest in new jazz already sparked by his love for the records of John Coltrane and Sonny Rollins. In 1960 he married pianist JoAnne Brackeen (they later divorced) and in 1965 moved back to New York. After playing 'all types of music', including gigs with West Indian musicians, Brackeen recorded *Rhythm X* in 1969; with Haden, Cherry and Ed Blackwell as his associates, the record was virtually a homage to Coleman. From 1970-72, he played in the Melodic Art-tet (with Ahmed Abdullah, bassist Ronnie Boykins and drummer Roger Blank), performing regularly on New York's *avant garde* loft scene. Brackeen next worked with Blackwell again, with Ronald Shannon Jackson and with Paul Motian, playing on the latter's *Dance* (1977) and *Le Voyage* (1979). After recording with Blackwell's quartet in 1982 (the album remains unreleased), Brackeen returned to Los Angeles the following year and is still living there. In 1987 he was invited by Dennis Gonzalez to record for the Silkheart label and has so far issued three albums as leader as well as appearing on records by Abdullah (*Liquid Magic*) and Gonzalez (*Namesake, Debenge-Debenge*). A compelling tenor saxophonist, with echoes of Rollins and Albert Ayler in his playing style and the influence of Ornette Coleman discernible in his writing, Brackeen plays a disciplined post-free jazz that is shot through with a broad streak of lyricism. He is also a persuasive, if rare, performer on soprano saxophone.

● ALBUMS: *Rhythm X* (Strata East 1970)★★★, *Banner* (Silkheart 1987)★★★★, *Attainment* (Silkheart 1988)★★★, *Worshippers Come Nigh* (Silkheart 1988)★★★★.

BRACKEEN, JOANNE

b. Joanne Grogan, 26 July 1938, Ventura, California, USA. Brackeen was self-taught; academic tuition did not suit her, and she left the Los Angeles Conservatory of Music after three days. Despite this, her piano playing became much in demand among the most exacting jazz leaders on the west coast: Harold Land, Teddy Edwards and Charles Lloyd. Unimpeded by marriage (to saxophonist Charles Brackeen) and four children, she relocated to New York in 1965, playing with Woody Shaw and Dave Liebman. From 1969-71 she worked with Art Blakey's Jazz Messengers: that a woman (and a white woman at that) could hold down such a position says much about her abilities. Like all the essential pianists in jazz, Brackeen has a touch with a ballad that is utterly unique yet reverberates with the whole tradition. The high quality of her accompanists - Cecil McBee (bass), Al Foster (drums), Branford Marsalis (saxophone) - is another example of her achievements.

● ALBUMS: *Snooze* (Choice 1975)★★★, *New True Illusion* (Timeless 1976)★★★, *Tring-A-Ling* (Choice 1977)★★★★, *Invitation* (1978)★★★, *AFT* (Timeless 1979)★★★, *Ancient Dynasty* (Columbia 1980)★★★, with Ryo Kawaski *Trinkets And Things* (Timeless 1981)★★, *Special Identity* (Antilles 1982)★★★, *Havin' Fun* (Concord 1985)★★★, *Fi-fi Goes To Heaven* (Concord 1987)★★★, *Live At Maybeck Recital Hall, Volume 1* (Concord 1990)★★★, *Where Legends Dwell* (Ken 1992)★★★★, *Breath Of Brazil* (Concord 1992)★★, *Take A Chance* (Concord 1994)★★★, *Power Talk* (Turnipseed 1995)★★★★, *Turnaround* (Evidence 1995)★★★.

BRADDY, PAULINE

b. *c.*1920, Mississippi, USA. Braddy attended Piney Woods Country Life School where her musical inclinations were encouraged. She started out playing clarinet but had her heart set on the alto saxophone. When the school's founder formed an all-girl jazz orchestra she was included, but was asked to switch to drums when the intended drummer dropped out. Although she was unhappy with the move, she proved to be a natural, playing with enormous flair and swing. Braddy admired many of the popular drummers of the day, including 'Big' Sid Catlett, Gene Krupa and Jo Jones, and was by no means a second-division player. Indeed, had she been a man, her reputation would have soared. Listening to records by the band, which eventually became known as the International Sweethearts Of Rhythm, it is hard to realize that this is not one of the leading swing bands of the day, and much of the verve of the band stems from Braddy's powerful drumming. With the Sweethearts Braddy toured Europe to entertain US Army personnel during World War II, and later recorded, made movie shorts, and appeared at New York's Apollo Theatre. By the end of the 40s the Sweethearts' day had passed and the band broke up. Braddy remained outside music for some time, but in 1950 she played in a trio with former Sweetheart Carline Ray and bass player Edna Smith. In 1956 Braddy was in a band formed by former Sweethearts frontwoman Anna Mae Winburn. Much admired by many male jazz musicians, including Jones, Braddy appeared always to take a sanguine view of the fact that her name is barely known outside a few cognoscenti of women's jazz groups. The reality is that jazz lost a great deal by not giving this fine musician and superbly swinging drummer an opportunity to play and record with leading jazzmen of her era.

BRADEN, DON

b. 20 November 1963, Cincinnati, Ohio, USA. Raised in Louisville, Kentucky, Braden began playing tenor saxophone at the age of 13, making his professional debut two years later. Through Jamey Aebersold he became interested in jazz and played in the McDonald's All American High School Jazz Band. In the early 80s he attended Harvard University, studying Engineering and Applied Sciences. While at Harvard he played in the university's jazz band and also took the opportunity of studying saxophone with Boston-based teachers Bill Pierce and Jerry Bergonzi. In 1984 he went to New York and was soon attracting favourable notices. In the late 80s he toured with Wynton Marsalis, recorded with Betty Carter and also played with leaders such as Roy Haynes, Tony Williams, Freddie Hubbard and J.J. Johnson. In the 90s he continued to work in distinguished company, including Winard Harper, Tom Harrell, Mingus Big Band Workshop, Christian McBride, Benny Green, Steve Turré, Randy Brecker and organists Brother Jack McDuff and Larry Gold. He toured extensively, gaining followings in Japan and Europe, recording *Landing Zone* in the Netherlands. Braden was also increasingly sought out as an arranger and composer and towards the end of the decade worked in films and television and as a record producer. His film credits include the orchestration and playing of music composed by Benny Golson for *Ed's Next Move* (1996). He was musical supervisor and performer for television's *Cosby* in 1998, and, with Golson, co-produced *The Voice Of The Saxophone*. Highly accomplished in many areas of the music business, as a performer Braden's playing of the tenor and soprano saxophones, and sometimes flute, displays an artist at the height of his creative powers. Playing tenor with a sinewy sound and great power, he also has a rich seam of romanticism that makes his work accessible to a wide-ranging audience. There is also aural evidence that his listening has taken him back to absorb the blues-drenched playing of the Texas tenor saxophonists. His charts for the bands assembled for his recording sessions indicate a strong liking for hard bop, some of the small group dates evoking memories of Art Blakey. Braden also composes music for his various bands.

● ALBUMS: *The Time Is Now* (Criss Cross 1992)★★★, *After*

Dark (Criss Cross 1993)★★★★, *Wish List* (Criss Cross 1994)★★★, *Landing Zone* (Landmark 1994)★★★★, *Organic* (Columbia 1995)★★★, with Joris Teepe *Pay As You Earn* (Mons 1995)★★★, *The Open Road* (Double-Time 1996)★★★, *The Voice Of The Saxophone* (RCA Victor 1997)★★★★.

Bradford, Bobby

b. 19 July 1934, Cleveland, Mississippi, USA. Bradford's family moved to Dallas in 1946 and he took up the cornet in 1949. He was at high school with James Clay, Cedar Walton and David Newman and played in a dance band with Leo Wright. He also worked around Dallas with Buster Smith and John Hardee. He moved to Los Angeles in 1953 and, although he had known and played with Ornette Coleman since their teens in Dallas-Fort Worth, it was not until the move to Los Angeles that their musical collaboration really began, and Bradford did not record with Coleman until the early 70s, when he appeared on some of the tracks on *Science Fiction* and *Broken Shadows*. In California he had worked with Wardell Gray, Gerald Wilson and Eric Dolphy. In 1961, after completing his military service, he went to New York to rejoin Coleman for two years, replacing Don Cherry in Coleman's quartet. He then returned to Los Angeles and co-led the New Art Jazz Ensemble with John Carter from 1965-74. When the Ensemble split up, Carter and Bradford continued to work together in a workshop, the Little Big Horn. For a short time Bradford also led a group that comprised Stanley Crouch, Mark Dresser and then-teenagers David Murray and James Newton. In the meantime, Bradford had been to Europe in 1971, where he recorded with John Stevens' Spontaneous Music Ensemble (SME) in London and Paris. After the *Science Fiction* date he returned to Europe for an extended stay (1972-74), during which he recorded with the SME again, as he did on a further visit in 1986. In 1974, he returned to California to teach. In 1980 Bradford was featured in Peter Bull's documentary *The New Music*. In 1986 he was reunited with Stevens in the trio Detail, which also included bassist Johnny Dyani (*Way It Goes/Dance Of The Soul*). He had also resumed his partnership with Carter, playing on the clarinettist's five-album suite, *Roots And Folklore* (1982-89), and on the co-led *Comin' On* (1989). A melodic and rhythmically subtle player, Bradford has been a vital catalyst of Californian new jazz for more than 25 years.

● ALBUMS: with New Art Jazz Ensemble *Seeking* (1969)★★★, with NAJE *Flight For Four* (1970)★★★, with NAJE *Self-Determination Music* (1971)★★★, *Bobby Bradford With The Spontaneous Music Ensemble* (Nessa 1971)★★★★, with NAJE, John Carter *Secrets* (1973)★★★, with SME *Love Dreams* (1973)★★★, with Carter *Variations On Selected Themes For Jazz Quintet* (1978)★★★, with Carter *A Suite Of American Folk Pieces For Solo Clarinet* (1979)★★, with Carter *Dauwhe* (1982)★★★, with David Murray *Murray's Steps* (1982)★★★, *Lost In LA* (Soul Note 1983)★★★, with Carter *Castles Of Ghana* (1985)★★★, *One Night Stand* (Soul Note 1986)★★★★, with Carter *Fields* (1988)★★★, with Carter *Shadows On A Wall* (1989)★★★, with Carter *Comin' On* (hatART 1989)★★★.

Bradford, Perry 'Mule'

b. 14 February 1893, Montgomery, Alabama, USA, d. 20 April 1970. Although Bradford began his professional career as a performer, playing piano in tent shows, it was as a songwriter that he made his greatest impact. In 1920 he was managing blues singer Mamie Smith when she was invited by OKeh Records to record two of his vaudeville songs (Bradford had originally written the songs for Sophie Tucker, but at the last minute she was unable to make the date). The records were sufficiently successful for OKeh's boss, Fred Hager, to want more; therefore, on her subsequent session of 20 August 1920, Mamie Smith became the first singer to record the blues when she sang Bradford's 'Crazy Blues'. Bradford enjoyed considerable success in the blues boom that followed and during the 20s he also assembled some fine all-star bands to make records. Perry Bradford's Jazz Phools included Louis Armstrong, Buster Bailey, James P. Johnson and Don Redman. After the 20s, however, Bradford seemed incapable of keeping abreast of changes in musical taste and he drifted into obscurity. He published his autobiography five years before his death.

● COMPILATIONS: *Perry Bradford, Pioneer Of The Blues* (1920-27 recordings).

● FURTHER READING: *Born With The Blues*, Perry Bradford.

Bradley, Will

b. Wilbur Schwichtenberg, 12 July 1912, Newton, New Jersey, USA, d. July 1989. Bradley played trombone with various bands in New York in the late 20s and at the beginning of the next decade established the working pattern for his whole career, combining studio work with playing in name bands. In the early 30s he recorded with Red Nichols and in 1935 was in the band assembled by Glenn Miller that played under the leadership of Ray Noble. In 1939 Bradley formed a big band with drummer Ray McKinley that enjoyed great popular success, thanks in part to a string of orchestrated boogie-woogie numbers, including 'Beat Me, Daddy, Eight To The Bar'. Bradley found the format somewhat limiting and the band folded in 1942, when McKinley entered the armed forces, and thereafter, Bradley concentrated on studio work. In the 50s he played briefly with the Sauter-Finegan orchestra, and in 1959 successfully joined forces with Johnny Guarnieri to recreate the big band boogie style with a studio-assembled band. His musical interests were extensive and he composed for symphony orchestras and chamber groups. His son, Bill, became a bop drummer, working with Tony Scott, Kai Winding and with Woody Herman's 1956 big band.

Bradshaw, Tiny

b. Myron Bradshaw, 23 September 1905, Youngstown, Ohio, USA, d. 26 November 1958. While studying psychology at Wilberforce University, Ohio, Bradshaw became involved in the campus's flourishing musical subculture. He joined Horace Henderson's Collegians as the band's singer. In 1932 he went to New York where

he played drums with several bands, including the Savoy Bearcats and the Mills Blue Rhythm Band. In the same year he sang with Luis Russell and then formed his own band, which toured extensively, playing several long engagements at hotels and dancehalls. During this period, Bradshaw modelled his style on that of Cab Calloway, both men having spent time in Marion Hardy's Alabamians. He had some success on record in the 30s, notably with 'Shout, Sister, Shout' and 'The Darktown Strutters' Ball'. During World War II Bradshaw led a US Army big band.
After the war he kept a band together by adapting to the popularity of R&B, attracting the attention of several young white performers, among whom was Buddy Holly. In the mid-50s poor health forced Bradshaw to fold his band and he died in November 1958. A lively entertainer, Bradshaw never quite made the big time. Indeed, at one time he suffered the mild indignity of being billed as the 'super Cab Calloway'. Bradshaw often hired first-rate musicians and arrangers for his bands, among them Shad Collins, Russell Procope, Happy Caldwell, Charlie Shavers, Billy Kyle, Charlie Fowlkes, Bobby Plater, Shadow Wilson, Fred Radcliffe, Sonny Stitt, Gil Fuller, Big Nick Nicholas, Gigi Gryce and Red Prysock.
● COMPILATIONS: *Tiny Bradshaw 1934* (Harlequin 1987)★★★, *The Great Composer (1950-58)* (King 1988)★★★★, *Stomping Room Only* (Krazy Kat 1984)★★, *Breaking Up The House (50s)* (Charly 1985)★★★, *A Tribute To The Late Tiny Bradshaw* (Sing 1987)★★, *I'm A High Ballin' Daddy* (Juxebox Lil 1988)★★★, *Bird Nest On The Ground* (Antone's 1994)★★★.

BRAFF, RUBY

b. Reuben Braff, 16 March 1927, Boston, Massachusetts, USA. Although Braff did not make a notable impact on the jazz scene until the mid-50s, he was already an accomplished and experienced cornet player. He had worked extensively in the Boston area from the late 40s, playing with Pee Wee Russell and Edmond Hall, recording with the latter in 1949. It was, however, Braff's 1953 recordings with Vic Dickenson that drew the attention of jazz fans. Between the boppers and the Revivalist movement lay the mainstream jazzmen of which Braff was a singularly attractive example. His lyrical and expressive style, shot through with bursts of white-hot excitement, lent itself especially well to ballads, and during the rest of the 50s, he made several excellent records in distinguished company such as Buck Clayton, Mel Powell, Bud Freeman and Benny Goodman. Despite this period of remarkable creativity, Braff's career then stalled, thanks in part to his determination to play the way he wanted, rather than as the public or club owners might demand. A second factor that hindered his progress was his habitual bluntness in manner and speech; Braff said what he thought, regardless of the effect that this might have on his chances of a return engagement. His circumstances improved in the 60s, although there were no signs that he was any easier to get on with; perhaps people had simply grown accustomed to his manner. In a succession of concert and festival appearances, and in numerous recordings, Braff proved his continuing excellence both in taste and performance. His musical partnerships included one with George Barnes, which resulted in superb music and countless arguments. He also worked with Dick Hyman and Scott Hamilton. In the 80s Braff continued to work, displaying his elegant, melodic and full-toned playing all around the world, and still possessing enough of the old prickliness to frighten off all but the most determined interviewers. In the mid-90s he recorded with pianist Roger Kellaway.
● ALBUMS: with Buck Clayton, Mel Powell *Buck Meets Ruby* 10-inch album (Vanguard 1954)★★★★, *Ruby Braff Swings* reissued as *A Ruby Braff Omnibus* (Bethlehem 1954)★★★, *Holiday In Braff* 10-inch album (Bethlehem 1955)★★★★, *Ball At Bethlehem With Braff* 10-inch album (Bethlehem 1955)★★★, *Little Big Horn* (Concert Hall 1955)★★★, *The Ruby Braff Special* (Vanguard 1955)★★★, *Hustlin' And Bustlin'* 10-inch album (Storyville 1955)★★★, *Adoration Of The Melody* (Bethlehem 1955)★★★, *The Mighty Braff* (Affinity 1955)★★★, *To Fred Astaire With Love* (RCA Victor 1955)★★★, with Ellis Larkins *Inventions In Jazz - Volume 1* 10-inch album (Vanguard 1955)★★★★, with Larkins *Inventions In Jazz - Volume 2* 10-inch album (Vanguard 1955)★★★★, with Larkins *Two By Two* (Vanguard 1956)★★★, *The Magic Horn Of Ruby Braff* (RCA Victor 1956)★★★, *Ruby Braff Featuring Dave McKenna* (ABC-Paramount 1956)★★★, *Braff!* (Epic 1957)★★★, *Salute To Bunny In Hi Fi* (RCA Victor 1957)★★★, *This Is My Lucky Day* (Bluebird 1957)★★★★, with Clayton, Powell *Buckin' The Blues* (Vanguard 1957)★★★★ *Easy Now* (RCA Victor 1959)★★★, *You're Getting To Be A Habit With Me* (Stereo-Craft 1959)★★★, *Ruby Braff Goes Girl Crazy* (Warners 1959)★★★, *Blowing Around The Around* (United Artists 1959)★★★, with Marshall Brown *Ruby Braff-Marshall Brown Sextet* (United Artists 1961)★★★, *Hear Me Talkin'* (Black Lion 1967)★★★, *On Sunnie's Side Of The Street* (1968)★★★, *Ruby Braff Plays Louis Armstrong* (1969)★★★, *Swing That Music* (Affinity 1970)★★★, with Larkins *The Grand Reunion* (1972)★★★, *The Music Of Ruby Braff And His International Jazz Quartet* (1972)★★★, with George Barnes *Live At The New School* (Chiaroscuro 1974)★★★★, *The Ruby Braff/George Barnes Quartet Plays Gershwin* (Concord 1974)★★★, *The Ruby Braff/George Barnes Quartet Salutes Rodgers And Hart* (Concord 1974)★★, with Barnes *To Fred Astaire With Love* (RCA 1975)★★★, with Dick Hyman *Fats Waller's Heavenly Jive* (1976)★★★, *Them There Eyes* (1976)★★★, *Pretties* (1978)★★★, *Swinging On A Star: Braff Plays Bing Volume 1* (1978)★★★, *Ruby Braff With The Ed Bickert Trio* (1979)★★★, *Braff Plays Bing* (Pizza Express 1979)★★★, *Very Sinatra* (1981)★★★, with Hyman *A Pipe Organ Recital Plus One* (Concord 1982)★★★, with Scott Hamilton *Mr. Braff To You* (Phontastic 1983)★★★★, *Easy Now* (RCA 1983)★★★, *Best I've Heard* (Vogue 1983)★★★, with Hyman *America The Beautiful* (George Wein Collection 1984)★★★, with Hyman *Manhattan Jazz* (1985)★★★, with Hamilton *A Fine Match* (Concord Jazz 1985)★★★★, with Hamilton *A First* (Concord Jazz 1985)★★★★, with Hamilton *A Sailboat In The Moonlight* (Concord Jazz 1986)★★★★, *Bravura Eloquence* (Concord 1988)★★★, *Me, Myself And I* (Concord 1988)★★★, with Hyman *Younger Than Swingtime* (Concord 1990)★★★, *Music From My Fair Lady* (Concord 1990)★★, with Hyman *Music From South Pacific* (Concord 1991)★★★, *And His*

New England Songhounds: Volumes 1 and 2 (Concord 1991)★★★, *Cornet Chop Suey* (1991)★★★★, with Roger Kellaway *Inside & Out* (Concord Jazz 1996)★★★★, with Hyman *Ruby Braff & Dick Hyman Play Nice Tunes* (Arbors 1996)★★★, *Ruby Braff & His Buddies: Controlled Nonchalance At The Regattabar* (Arbors 1997)★★★, *Ruby Braff And His Quartet: Live At The Regattabar* (Arbors 1997)★★★, with Larkins *Calling Berlin: Vol. 2* (Arbors 1997)★★★, *As Time Goes By* (Candid 1997)★★★, *Being With You: Ruby Braff Remembers Louis Armstrong* (Arbors 1997)★★★★, *First Set* (Zephyr 1998)★★★, *Second Set* (Zephyr 1998)★★★, *You Can Depend On Me* (Arbors 1998)★★★.

BRAND X

Brand X was one of the most commercially successful of the British jazz/rock groups of the late 70s and early 80s. *Moroccan Roll* reached number 37 in the UK album chart in May 1977 while *Is There Anything About* crept in at number 93 in September 1982. The original line-up of the band was John Goodsall (guitar), Robin Lumley (keyboards), Percy Jones (bass, ex-Liverpool Scene), Phil Collins (drums) and Maurice Pert (percussion). This was the band that Collins considered second only to Weather Report. There were similarities, especially in that each group of musicians had great technical ability and a desire to play popular music, but Brand X's individuality shone through in their compositions. They produced sharp arrangements of appealing melodies, often with a gangling counterpoint provided by Jones' slurred fretless bass lines. Collins and Pert could contribute anything from the lightest colouring to a furiously propulsive rhythm and both Goodsall and Lumley were exciting soloists. All the musicians were also busy with studio work and Collins had been expanding his role with Genesis after Peter Gabriel's departure. He had also released a solo album and, as his second career as a solo artist took off, he left Brand X to be replaced by Chuck Burgi, and then by Mike Clarke. A little later, Percy Jones left and was replaced by John Gilbin.

● ALBUMS: *Unorthodox Behaviour* (Charisma 1976)★★★, *Livestock* (Charisma 1977)★★, *Moroccan Roll* (Charisma 1977)★★★, *Masques* (Charisma 1978)★★★, *Product* (Charisma 1979)★★★, *Do They Hurt* (Charisma 1980)★★★, *Is There Anything About* (Columbia 1982)★★★, *Live At The Roxy LA 1979* (Zok 1996)★★.

● COMPILATIONS: *The Plot Thins - A History Of* (1992)★★★★.

BRAND, DOLLAR

(see Ibrahim, Abdullah)

BRAUD, WELLMAN

b. Wellman Breaux, 25 January 1891, St. James Parish, Louisiana, USA, d. 27 October 1966. A gifted player of several string instruments in New Orleans during his youth, Braud settled in Chicago in 1917 and began to play string bass long before it had become universally popular. In the early 20s he worked with Charlie Elgar and Will Vodery, with whose band he toured Europe. In New York, later in the decade, Braud played with a number of bands before joining Duke Ellington in 1927. He remained with Ellington until 1935 and thereafter worked mostly with small groups and led his own trio. In the early 40s he played with several musicians enjoying the benefits of the Revival movement, notably Jelly Roll Morton, Sidney Bechet and Bunk Johnson. During this period Braud owned a pool room, the day-to-day running of which interrupted his musical career, but in the mid-50s he worked full-time in music again, touring with Kid Ory. He semi-retired to California in the 60s but still played with visiting bands, including Ellington's, and worked with singer Barbara Dane. Wellman, a strong, rhythmic musician, was a great asset to any band with which he played. Although his work with Ellington was overshadowed by his successors (in particular Jimmy Blanton), he added considerable power and swing to the band during his tenure.

BRAUN, RICK

b. *c.* 1955, Allentown, Pennsylvania, USA. A busy session musician and producer, trumpeter/flugelhornist Braun has mapped out a diverse musical career. While studying at the Eastman School of Music in Rochester Braun formed the fusion band Auracle, who released two late 70s albums recorded with Miles Davis's producer Teo Macero. In the early 80s, Braun released a pop record in Japan before moving into songwriting and soundtrack work. Braun co-wrote the Top 20 REO Speedwagon hit, 'Here With Me', and played lead trumpet on the television show *Night Caller*. He also worked as a touring and recording session musician for several mainstream pop artists including Tina Turner, War, Crowded House, Glenn Frey, Rod Stewart, Tom Petty and Natalie Cole. In 1992 he was offered a contract by the small Californian label, Mesa/Bluemoon, and promoted as a smooth jazz artist. Touring as a backup singer and soloist with Sade brought Braun to the attention of radio promoters, and his seductive blend of smooth instrumental jazz and urban-orientated R&B soon became a staple of adult contemporary stations. *Beat Street* was one of the strongest selling smooth jazz albums of 1995, and Braun has subsequently built on his success for new label Atlantic Records.

● ALBUMS: *Intimate Secrets* (Mesa 1992)★★, *Night Walker* (Bluemoon 1994)★★★, *Christmas Present: Music Of Warmth & Celebration* (Bluemoon 1994)★★, *Beat Street* (Bluemoon 1995)★★★, *Body And Soul* (Bluemoon 1996)★★★, *South Of Midnight* (Atlantic 1998)★★★★, *Full Stride* (Atlantic 1998)★★★.

BRAXTON, ANTHONY

b. 4 June 1945, Chicago, Illinois, USA. Braxton began playing clarinet in high school, studied music for one semester at Wilson Junior College, then joined the US Army, where he played clarinet and alto saxophone. In 1966 he joined Chicago's Association for the Advancement of Creative Musicians (the AACM), a newly formed musicians' co-operative whose leading members included Muhal Richard Abrams and Roscoe Mitchell. Braxton formed his own group (later called the Creative Construction Company) with Leroy Jenkins and Leo Smith and their first release, *Three*

Compositions Of New Jazz, was recorded in 1968. Their music typified the Chicagoans' new experimentalism, with its emphasis on sound, space, texture - as opposed to the John Coltrane-led energy music prevalent in New York. Braxton also followed the AACM trend towards multi-instrumentalism, becoming an accomplished master on most members of the saxophone, clarinet and flute families. However, alto sax had become his main instrument and in late 1968 he recorded his epochal double album, *For Alto*, the first ever full-length recording of solo saxophone music. In 1969 the Creative Construction Company moved to Paris, only to disband within a year. Braxton returned to the USA, lodged with Ornette Coleman and for several months earned a living as a professional chess player. In 1970 he joined Chick Corea, Dave Holland and Barry Altschul to form the group Circle, but disagreements with Corea over their involvement with the Scientology movement broke up the band and Braxton returned to Paris, where he began to play with various European improvisers, leading to later appearances with Alex Von Schlippenbach's Globe Unity Orchestra and at Derek Bailey's Company festivals. In 1974 producer Michael Cuscuna offered him a contract with Arista Records and he returned to the USA, recording and performing with a regular quartet that comprised Holland, Altschul and Kenny Wheeler (the latter replaced briefly by George Lewis). For the next six years, the Arista contract meant Braxton's music had a relatively high profile.

Already regarded as eccentric because he titled his compositions with enigmatic diagrams, Braxton quickly became a controversial figure in jazz circles as releases such as *For Trio* (1978), *For Four Orchestras* (1978) and *For Two Pianos* (1982), inspired in part by the work of Schoenberg, Stockhausen and John Cage, revealed his growing interest in contemporary composition. However, Braxton never denied his love for jazz, constantly citing Coltrane, Paul Desmond and Warne Marsh as major influences on his saxophone playing; in 1974 he had anticipated the 80s' obsession with traditional jazz repertoire by recording the two *In The Tradition* sessions (later followed by others, including outstanding tribute records to Thelonious Monk and Lennie Tristano). Also in the 70s he recorded two sets of improvised duos with the great bebop drummer Max Roach, a superb live quartet concert in Dortmund (not released until 1991) and a collection of *avant garde* big band pieces, the prize-winning *Creative Orchestra Music 1976*, which many people still regard as one of his finest releases.

In the 80s Braxton's music showed a growing concern with mysticism, theatre and collage-structures. He developed a series of 'ritual and ceremonial' works, which incorporated elements of astrology, numerology, costume and dance, and which culminated in his latest, ongoing project - a series of 12 operas, entitled *Trillium*. (The visual basis of much of this music is perhaps attributable to his chromesthetic vision; that is, like the composer Scriabin, he *sees* sounds as colours and shapes.) His quartet music, often the chief focus of his jazz-related experimentalism, has also became increasingly complex. On *Four Compositions (Quartet) 1983* he introduced the concept of 'pulse track structures' as an alternative to chord changes and modal music. A little later he began playing 'multiple logics music', in which members of the quartet (with the regular line-up of Marilyn Crispell, Mark Dresser and Gerry Hemingway) might be playing two, three or four compositions simultaneously (*Quartet (London) 1985*, *Quartet (Birmingham) 1985*, *Quartet (Willisau) 1991*). Although he started teaching at Wesleyan College, Connecticut, Braxton remained formidably prolific in the 80s. He has written nearly 400 compositions, made over 70 records as leader and appeared on at least 50 others. In 1985 he published his three-volume, philosophical *Tri-axium Writings* and in 1988 the first five volumes of his *Composition Notes*. His latest recordings include further sets of solo, duo, trio, quartet and large ensemble works, plus collaborations with the ROVA Saxophone Quartet and the London Jazz Composers Orchestra. In the mid-90s he created further controversy by recording prolifically on the piano, with stellar sidemen including Marty Ehrlich (reeds) and drummer Pheeroan AkLaff. Recent concerts showed that his music is now reaching new levels of intensity, abstraction and gracefulness while continuing to explore fresh concepts of form. Though still regarded with suspicion by some hardline traditionalists (and black nationalists), Braxton's importance as an innovator is increasingly evident in the jazz world, his influence proclaimed by newer players such as Tim Berne and John Zorn. 'The challenge of creativity', he has said, 'is to move towards the highest thought that you can think of', and in pursuit of that goal he has played at the extremes of register and tempo, and forged a unique musical synthesis of new and old, Africa and Europe, structure and freedom.

● ALBUMS: *Three Compositions Of New Jazz* (Delmark 1968)★★★★, *Anthony Braxton* (Affinity 1969)★★★, *B-X°-NO/47A* (1970)★★★, *This Time* (1970)★★★, *For Alto Saxophone* 1968 recording (Delmark 1971)★★★★, *Recital Paris '71* (1971)★★★, *Steps Out* (1971)★★★, *Donna Lee* (1972)★★★, *Saxophone Improvisations Series F* (America 1972)★★★, *Town Hall 1972* (Pausa 1972)★★★, with Gunter Hampel, Jeanne Lee *Familie* (1972)★★★, *Four Compositions (1973)* (1973)★★★, *Silence* 1969 recording (Freedom 1974)★★★, with Joseph Jarman *Together Alone* 1972 recording (Delmark 1974)★★★, *In The Tradition, Vol. One* (Steeple Chase 1974)★★★, *Solo: Live At Moers Festival* (1974)★★★, *Live At Moers Festival* (1974)★★★, with Leo Smith *Trio & Duet* (Sackville 1975)★★★★, *New York Fall 1974* (Arista 1975)★★★, with Creative Construction Company *CCC Volume One* 1970 recording (1975)★★★, *Creative Music Orchestra: RBN - 3°/K12* 1972 recording, 3-LP box set (1975)★★★, *Five Pieces 1975* (Arista 1975)★★★, with Creative Construction Company *CCC Volume Two* 1970 recording (1976)★★★, *In The Tradition, Vol. Two* 1974 recording (Steeple Chase 1976)★★★, with George Lewis *Creative Orchestra Music 1976* (Bluebird 1976)★★★★, with Lewis *Elements Of Surprise* (Moers 1976)★★★, with Muhal Richard Abrams *Duets 1976* (Arista 1976)★★★, with Bailey, Evan Parker *Company 2* (1976)★★★, *The Complete Braxton* 1971 recording (Arista

1977)★★★, with Derek Bailey *Duo 1 & 2* 1974 recording (1977)★★★★, *The Montreux/Berlin Concerts* (1977)★★★, with Richard Teitelbaum *Time Zones* (Freedom 1977)★★★, *For Trio* (1978)★★★, with Roscoe Mitchell *Duets With Anthony Braxton* (Sackville 1978)★★★★, *For Four Orchestras* 3-LP box set (Arista 1978)★★★, with Max Roach *Birth/Rebirth* (1978)★★★, *Alto Saxophone Improvisations 1979* (Arista 1979)★★★★, with Roach *One In Two - Two In One* (1980)★★★, *Seven Compositions 1978* (1980)★★★, *Performance 9/1/79* reissued as *Performance (Quartet)* (hatART 1981)★★★, *Composition 96* (hatART 1981)★★★, *For Two Pianos* (1982)★★★, with Giorgio Gaslini *Four Pieces* (1982)★★★, *Six Compositions: Quartet* (Antilles 1982)★★★★, with Teitelbaum *Open Aspects '82* (hatART 1982)★★★, with John Lindberg *Six Duets 1982* (1982)★★★, *Four Compositions (Quartet) 1983* (1983)★★★★, with Bailey *Royal, Volume One* 1974 recording (1984)★★★★, with Neighbours *With Anthony Braxton* 1980 recording (1984)★★★, *Composition 113* (Sound Aspects 1984)★★★, with Gyorgy Szabados *Szabraxtondos* (1985)★★★, *Six Compositions (Quartet) 1984* (Leo 1985)★★★★, *Seven Standards 1985 Volume One* (Magenta 1985)★★★, *Seven Standards 1985 Volume Two* (Magenta 1986)★★★, *Anthony Braxton/Robert Schumann String Quartet* 1979 recording (1986)★★★, *Five Compositions (Quartet) 1986* (Black Saint 1986)★★★, with Bailey *Moment Précieux* (1987)★★★, with Gino Robair *Duets 1987* (1987)★★★, *Six Monk's Compositions, 1987* (Black Saint 1988)★★★, with the London Jazz Composers Orchestra *Zurich Concerts* (1988)★★★★, *Composition 96* 1981 recording (1989)★★★, *Quartet (London) 1985* 3-LP box set (1989)★★★★, with ROVA Saxophone Quartet *The Aggregate* (1989)★★★★, with Lewis *Ensemble (Victoriaville) 1988* (Victo 1989)★★★★, *19 (Solo) Compositions, 1988* (1989)★★★, *Compositions 99, 101, 107 & 139* 1982-88 recordings, reissued as *Four Compositions (Solo, Duo & Trio) 1982/1988* (hatART 1989)★★★★, *Seven Compositions (Trio) 1989* (1989)★★★, with Andrew Voigt *Kol Nidre* 1988 recording (1990)★★★, with Marilyn Crispell *Duets Vancouver 1989* (1990)★★★, *Eight (+3) Tristano Compositions 1989 For Warne Marsh* (hatART 1990)★★★, *Prag 1984 (Quartet Performance)* 1984 recording (1991)★★★, with Lewis *Dortmund (Quartet) 1976* (hatART 1991)★★★★, *Solo (London) 1988* (1991)★★★, *Eugene (1989)* (1991)★★★, *Quartet (Birmingham) 1985* (1992)★★★, with Peter Niklas Wilson *Eight Duets (Hamburg) 1991* (1992)★★★, *Composition No. 165* (New Albion 1992)★★★, *Two Compositions (Ensemble) 1989-91* (1992)★★★, *Quartet (Willisau) 1991* 1991 recording, 4-CD box set (hatART 1992)★★★★, *Quartet (Coventry) 1985* (1993)★★★, *Wesleyan (12 Altosolos)* (hatART 1993)★★★, *Duo (London) 1993* (Leo 1993)★★★, *Charlie Parker Project 1993* (hatART 1995)★★★, *Composition 174* (Leo 1996)★★★, *Duet: Live At Merkin Hall* (Music & Arts 1996)★★★, *Piano Music Notated 1968-1988* (hatART 1996)★★★★, *Four Composition; Quartet 1995* (Braxton House 1996)★★★★, *Sextet: Istanbul 1995* (Braxton House 1996)★★★★, *Ensemble New York 1995* (Braxton House 1996)★★★★, *Knitting Factory (Piano/Quartet) 1994, Vol. 1* (Leo 1996)★★★, *Piano Quartet, Yoshi's 1994* 4-CD box set (Music & Arts 1996)★★★, with Mario Pavone *Seven Standards 1995 Quintet* (Knitting Factory Works 1996)★★★, *Solo Piano (Standards)* (No More 1996)★★, *Composition No. 173* (Black Saint 1996)★★★, with David Rosenboom *Two Lines* (Lovely Music 1996)★★★, *Octet New York 1995* (Braxton House 1996)★★★★, with Brett Larner *11 Compositions Duo 1995* (Leo 1997)★★★, *Santa Cruz 1993* (hatART 1997)★★★★, *Composition 192* (Leo 1997)★★★, *Tentet New York 1996* (Braxton House 1997)★★★, *Composition 102* (Braxton House 1997)★★★★, with Ran Blake *A Memory Of Vienna* 1988 recording (hatART 1998)★★★★, *Compositions No 10 and 16* (hatART 1998)★★★.

● FURTHER READING: *Tri-axium Writings, Volumes 1-3*, Anthony Braxton. *Composition Notes, Books A-E*, Anthony Braxton. *Forces In Motion: Anthony Braxton & The Meta-reality Of Creative Music*, Graham Lock. *New Musical Figurations: Anthony Braxton's Cultural Critique*, Ronald M. Radno.

BREACH, JOYCE

b. 27 February 1944, Alameda, California, USA. While studying journalism at West Virginia University, she began singing with the Joe Belcastro Trio. After graduation Breach moved to Pittsburgh, Pennsylvania, where she began her professional career as a singer. She continued to sing there for 25 years with occasional forays into recording studios, which gradually increased awareness of her exceptional talent. In February 1996 she capitalized on this growing appreciation of her work by moving to New York, appearing at clubs, hotels and other venues. She has sung with Loonis McGlohon, the highly gifted pianist-accompanist to many singers, William Roy, Richard Rodney Bennett and Ronny Whyte. Breach's highly melodic voice is particularly suited to ballads and her acute awareness of lyrics makes her one of the best latter-day interpreters of popular song. Unpretentious, subtle and distinctive, Breach's decision to work in the cabaret tradition of the wide field of jazz-influenced popular music might have kept her from international recognition but, thanks to her fine albums for Audiophile, the singer's label, the world can now hear what Pittsburgh and New York have enjoyed for decades.

● ALBUMS: *Confessions* (Audiophile 1991)★★★, with Loonis McGlohon *A Christmas Memory* (Audiophile 1992)★★, *Lovers After All* (Audiophile 1993)★★★, *Songbird* (Audiophile 1995)★★★★, *This Moment* (Audiophile 1996)★★★.

BREAU, LENNY

b. Leonard Breau, 5 August, 1941, Auburn, Maine, USA, d. 12 August 1984, Los Angeles, California, USA. Before turning to jazz, guitarist Breau played in the same field as his country music-singing parents, Hal Lone Pine And Betty Cody. Playing from the age of seven, he worked in the family's act, billed as 'Lone Pine Jr. - The Guitar Wizard', throughout the northeastern states and in Canada. He had established himself in this field in a minor way when, under the guidance of pianist Bob Erlandson, he began to turn to jazz. In 1962, in Toronto, he formed the group, Three, with singer Don Francks and bass player Ian Henstridge. Later, he worked as a solo, appearing on television in his own show for the Canadian Broadcasting Company. When he was in his late twenties, he formed a jazz trio and made two widely acclaimed albums. This was in the late 60s and during the following decade he performed with many leading jazz artists. Breau's reputation spread when it was perceived that he could comfortably hold his own when teamed with other guitarists of note, such as Chet Atkins, with whom he made *Standard Brands*, and George Benson. During the 70s, Breau widened his range as he drew into his repertoire not only the styles and techniques of all aspects of jazz but also some ethnic musical forms, including those of India and Spain. Constantly seeking new ways of expressing his seemingly boundless ideas, in the early 80s he experimented with a seven-string guitar. In 1981 he appeared briefly on film in a documentary about Tal Farlow. Also in the early 80s he had a successful group that included then newcomer Dave Young. This band was recorded at Bourbon Street, a Toronto nightclub, but the set remained unreleased for almost 15 years (the Guitarchives label was set up after Breau's death to release his private tapes). Breau also taught at the Musicians Institute in Los Angeles and was the author of a regular column in the magazine *Guitar Player*. He was found dead in a swimming pool and the subsequent Los Angeles coroner's report decided that he had been strangled, a crime that remains unsolved. Breau's great talent, allied as it was to exceptional technique and a thorough understanding of many diverse musical forms, made him one of the most interesting players of his day.

● ALBUMS: *The Guitar Sounds Of Lenny Breau* (RCA 1968)★★★★, *The Velvet Touch Of Lenny Breau* (RCA 1969)★★★★, *Five O'Clock Bells* (Adelphi 1979)★★★, *Mo' Breau* (Adelphi 1979)★★★, *Lenny Breau Trio* (Direct Disk 1979)★★★, *Quietude* (Electric Muse 1983)★★★, *Legacy* (Relaxed Rabbit 1984)★★★, *The Livingroom Tapes, Vol. 1* 1978 recordings (MHS)★★★, *The Livingroom Tapes, Vol. 2* 1978 recordings (MHS)★★★, *Live At Bourbon St., 1983* (Guitarchives 1995)★★★, *Cabin Fever* 70s recordings (Guitarchives 1997)★★★, with Tal Farlow *Chance Meeting* 1980 recording (Guitarchives 1997)★★★★, *Boy Wonder* 1956 recordings (Guitarchives 1998)★★.

BREAUX, ZACHARY

b. Zachary Charles Breaux, 1960, Port Arthur, Texas, USA, d. 20 February 1997, Miami Beach, Florida, USA. Breaux began playing guitar while still a small child and later attended North Texas State University where he majored in Musical Composition. He was spotted by Donald Byrd who advised him to go to New York and it was there that he met vibraphonist Roy Ayers and became a member of his band, an engagement that lasted for six years. During this period Ayers appeared at many noted venues including visits to Ronnie Scott's in London. He also appeared with Brother Jack McDuff and Dee Dee Bridgewater. Breaux was later heard as a solo performer and made a number of attractive albums. During his spell with Ayers, Breaux was often a rather self-effacing player, using a laid-back funky style. In his solo performances he showed a wider range of musical styles and interests, including post-bop, and was clearly well versed in the broad base of jazz music. Possessed of an enviable technique, he was always careful to subordinate this to the needs of the music, clearly preferring to offer music that was, at least on the surface, uncomplicated and rhythmically supple. While holidaying with his wife and three daughters in Miami, Breaux went to the aid of a female swimmer in distress, having saved a man from drowning in Italy in 1988. This time, the swimmer died and on reaching the shore Breaux suffered a fatal heart attack.

● ALBUMS: *Groovin'* (NYC/Ronnie Scott's Jazz House 1992)★★★, *Laid Back* (NYC 1994)★★, *Uptown Groove* (Zebra 1995)★★★.

BRECKENRIDGE, DARDANELLE

(see Dardanelle)

BRECKER BROTHERS

Randy (b. 27 November 1945, Philadelphia, Pennsylvania, USA) and Michael Brecker (b. 29 March 1949, Philadelphia, Pennsylvania, USA) are two of the most in-demand musicians around, having supplied the horn licks to untold major records over the last 25 years. Randy originally attended Indiana University to study under David Baker, and undertook a lengthy State Department tour with the university's band, directed by Jerry Coker. He relocated to New York in 1966 and joined Blood, Sweat And Tears, staying for a year before joining up with Horace Silver's quintet. Michael, another Indiana University student, turned professional at the age of 19 with Edwin Birdsong's band, before teaming up with his older brother, Billy Cobham, Chuck Rainey and Will Lee in the pop-jazz co-operative Dreams. Both became in demand for session work (notably on Cobham's three Atlantic albums of the mid-70s), but by 1974, the brothers were ready to branch out on their own. They signed with Arista early the following year, releasing their debut, 'Sneakin' Up Behind You', in a style reminiscent of the Average White Band. It received heavy club rotation, although it was 'East River' from their second album that broke onto the singles charts in 1978. The group split in 1982, with both brothers recording solo albums in addition to session work (Michael with Ashford And Simpson and Spyro Gyra, Randy with Breakwater, among others). The success of the *Collection* issues reunited the brothers in 1992.

● ALBUMS: *The Brecker Brothers* (Arista 1975)★★★★, *Back To Back* (Arista 1976)★★★, *Don't Stop The Music* (Arista 1977)★★★, *Heavy Metal Be-Bop* (Arista 1978)★★★, *Detente* (Arista 1980)★★, *Straphangin'* (Arista 1981)★★, *Return Of The Brecker Brothers* (GRP 1992)★★★, *Out Of The Loop* (GRP 1994)★★.

● COMPILATIONS: *The Brecker Bros. Collection Volume One* (RCA 1989)★★★, *The Brecker Bros. Collection Volume Two* (RCA 1992)★★.

● VIDEOS: *Return Of The Brecker Brothers: Live In Barcelona* (1993).

BRECKER, MICHAEL

b. 29 March 1949, Philadelphia, Pennsylvania, USA. Like many musicians of his generation, saxophonist Brecker was attracted in equal measure to R&B and the music of John Coltrane. In 1970 he left home for New York and joined a band led by drummer Billy Cobham. Subsequent gigs included work with the jazz rock group Dreams, Horace Silver, James Taylor and Yoko Ono. With his brother, Randy Brecker, he formed the Brecker Brothers, which became one of the pre-eminent fusion units. In the early 80s he toured and recorded with David Sancious and recorded as Steps Ahead, for many the definitive jazz rock group. Much in demand, Brecker also freelanced with a wide variety of jazz and pop artists, including Charles Mingus, John Lennon, Pat Metheny, Eric Clapton, Herbie Hancock and John Abercrombie. In 1987, at the prompting of Impulse! Records, he started recording as a leader. Brecker's smooth, strong version of Coltrane's middle-period playing has been much imitated by mainstream and session players. In 1991 he was a featured soloist on Paul Simon's Rhythm Of The Saints tour. *Tales From The Hudson* became a major success for him in 1996 and he won a Grammy in 1996 for the Best Instrumental Solo (on *Impressions*) and in 1997 for Best Jazz Performance.

● ALBUMS: *Michael Brecker* (MCA 1987)★★★, *Don't Try This At Home* (MCA 1989)★★★, *Now You See It ... Now You Don't* (GRP 1990)★★, *Impressions* (Impulse! 1995)★★★★, with McCoy Tyner *Infinity* (Impulse! 1995)★★★★, *Tales From The Hudson* (Impulse! 1996)★★★★, *Two Blocks From The Edge* (Impulse! 1998)★★★★.

Brecker, Randy

b. 27 November 1945, Philadelphia, Pennsylvania, USA. Brecker studied classical trumpet at school, at the same time playing in local R&B bands. He turned to jazz when at Indiana University and was a member of a student band that visited Europe. He quit the band and the university, remaining in Europe for a while before returning to the USA to take up a career in music. In 1967 he was with Blood, Sweat And Tears and thereafter played with various jazz groups including those led by Horace Silver, Art Blakey and Clark Terry. He also accompanied performers from the worlds of rock and pop, including Janis Joplin, Stevie Wonder and James Brown. In 1969 he became co-leader with his brother, Michael Brecker, of the band Dreams. In the early 70s he worked in the studios, playing jazz gigs with Larry Coryell, Billy Cobham, Hal Galper and others. He also formed another band with his brother, this time simply named the Brecker Brothers, which made some enormously successful albums and became one of the most popular and musically skilled and influential jazz-rock bands. In the late 70s he played with Charles Mingus and in the early 80s Brecker led his own groups and also worked with his wife, Eliane Elias, and with various jazzmen including Lew Tabackin. An exceptionally talented musician with great technical facility and flair, Brecker has become one of the major figures in jazz-rock.

● ALBUMS: *Amanda* (Sonet 1986)★★★, *In The Idiom* (Denon 1987)★★, *Live At Sweet Basil* (Sonet 1988)★★★, *Toe To Toe* (MCA 1989)★★, *Mr Max!* (Nable 1990)★★, *Score* (Blue Note 1993)★★★, *Into The Sun* (Concord Vista 1997)★★★.

Breezin' - George Benson

Benson earned his reputation as a superior jazz guitarist through his partnership with soul/jazz organist Brother Jack McDuff. Several solo albums for the CTI label ensued before a switch to Warner Brothers Records resulted in extraordinary chart success with this release. Benson's remake of the title track, originally a hit for fellow guitarist Gabor Szabo, set the tone for the entire set wherein mellifluous funk underscores the artist's sweet voice and soft-touch technique. Like Nat 'King' Cole before him, Benson left jazz to court a wider audience and with *Breezin'* he did so with considerable aplomb.

● Tracks: *This Masquerade; Six To Four; Breezin'; So This Is Love; Lady; Affirmation.*

● First released 1976

● UK peak chart position: did not chart

● USA peak chart position: 1

Breuer, Carolyn

b. 4 July 1969, Munich, Germany. Raised in a musical atmosphere, she began piano lessons at the age of seven, switching to alto saxophone at 12. She studied saxophone classically but from the age of 15 was encouraged to pay attention to jazz by her piano-and trombone-playing father, Hermann Breuer. In 1988 she began studying at a music conservatory in Hilversum, the Netherlands. She recorded with her father in the early 90s on *A Family Affair*, and also teamed up with singer Fee Claassen. As well as leading her own bands, she plays with Five Up High, Cees Slinger, and has accompanied the German singer Silvia Droste. Technically accomplished, Breuer brings a passionate intensity to her playing.

● ALBUMS: *A Family Affair* (Enja 1991)★★★, with Fee Claassen *Simply Be* (Challenge 1995)★★★★, with Klaus Weiss *A Message From Santa Klaus* (Minor Music 1995)★★★, with others *Brand New* (Arcade 1996)★★★, with Five Up High *The Deep* (A-Records 1996)★★★, *Acquaintance* (A-Records 1997)★★★.

Breuker, Willem

b. 4 November 1944, Amsterdam, Holland. At school Breuker wanted to play piano but economic circumstances in post-war Holland made that impossible. He learned to read music and play the recorder at the Labour Music school, and later took up the clarinet, still one of his main instruments, alongside various saxophones. He began improvising when, as he tells it, he was too lazy to turn the pages of his music exercises. At the start of his teens he discovered the *avant garde* classical music of Arnold Schoenberg and Edgard Varèse, and was prompted to compose. He joined a marching band and, during the 50s, worked his way through the evolution of jazz. In the early 60s he met Misha Mengelberg, who was outraging musicians and audiences with his piano-playing, and recognized a kindred spirit. In 1966 he organized a 23-piece orchestra to play his composition 'Litany', which was so controversial it made the front pages of the national newspapers. He was involved in setting up De Volharding with Louis Andriessen, and in 1967 he, Han Bennink and Mengelberg founded the Instant Composers Pool, which is still flourishing. The Dadaist, absurdist approach of those days (for radio broadcasts Mengelberg might not play a note, but would, for example, read a newspaper) is still very much a part of Breuker's act. In 1974 he left the ICP to found the BVHaast label and also initiated the Willem Breuker Kollektief, a remarkable band that mixes various schools of jazz (from New Orleans to the *avant garde*), marching band music, film and theatre scores, cabaret, Latin, and classical (light and heavy) with hilarious, deadpan clowning. Their live performances are an experience that it is difficult to compare or describe, the audience simultaneously laughing while appreciating the precision routines interspersed with virtuoso improvisation. Breuker writes most of the music but also arranges composers as varied as Prokofiev, Ennio Morricone, Kurt Weill, Reginald Foresythe and Duke Ellington or audacious parodies of, for example, Ravel's 'Bolero', which somehow incorporates fragments of songs including 'Little Drummer Boy' and 'Never On A Sunday'. The overall effect is like a hybrid of Spike Jones, the Bonzo Dog Doo-Dah Band, Gerard Hoffnung, Archie Shepp and Ellington. One of the most disconcerting aspects of the Kollektief's performances is Breuker's lampooning of the corrosive, all-stops-out free jazz that he plays for real in other bands - for example, his appearance on the still-notorious *Machine Gun* with Peter Brötzmann's octet.

● ALBUMS: with Han Bennink *New Acoustic Swing Duo* (1967)★★★, with others *Instant Composers Pool* (1970)★★★, *Renais Sense* (1972)★★★, *Bertolt Brecht/Herman Heijermans* (BVHAAST 1974)★★★, *Baal-Brecht-Breuker-Handke* (BVHAAST 1974)★★★, *Live In Berlin* (FMP 1975)★★★★, *The European Scene* (1976)★★★, with Leo Cuypers *Superstars* (1978)★★★, *Doodzonde* (1979)★★★, *In Holland* (1981)★★★, *Rhapsody In Blue* (1982)★★★, *Driebergen-Zeist* (1984)★★★, *Willem Breuker Kollektief/Willem Breuker Collective* (1984)★★★, with Bennink *Sendai Sjors/Sendai Sjimmie* (1984)★★★, *De Illusionist, Kkkomediant* (BVHAAST 1986)★★★, *Klap Op De Vuurpijl 1985* (BVHAAST 1986)★★★, *Bob's Gallery* (BVHAAST 1988)★★★★, *George Gershwin* (1988)★★★, *George Gershwin-Willem Breuker-Ennio Morricone-Alex Von Schlippenbach* (1988)★★★, *Metropolis* (BVHAAST 1989)★★★, *Parade* (BVHAAST 1990)★★★, *To Remain* (BVHAAST 1990)★★★★, *Heijermans/Brecht* 1983-89 recordings (1990)★★★, *Heibel* (1991)★★★★, *De Onderste Steen* (Entr'acte 1992)★★★, *Meets Djazzex* (BVHAAST 1992)★★★, *Summer Music A Paris* (1993)★★★, *Deze Kant Op, Dames/This Way, Ladies* (BVHAAST 1993)★★★, *Sensemaya* BVHAAST 1996)★★★★, *Psalm 122* (BVHAAST 1998)★★★.

● COMPILATIONS: with Johan van der Keuken *Music For His Films 1967/1994* (BVHAAST 1998)★★★★.

● FURTHER READING: *New Dutch Swing*, Kevin Whitehead.

BRIDGES, HENRY

b. *c.*1908, Oklahoma City, Oklahoma, USA. He played tenor saxophone in various territory bands in the Midwest in the late 20s and early 30s. Best-known of these bands was that led by Alphonso Trent, and he also often worked alongside Charlie Christian. In 1939 Bridges joined Harlan Leonard's Rockets but his career was interrupted by military service, after which he played often in and around Los Angeles and also visited Europe, but made very little impact in either location. On the evidence of his recordings with Leonard, and especially 'A La Bridges', Bridges was a gifted and technically assured player with considerable imagination. It might well be that the Leonard recordings were exceptions rather than the rule, or it could simply be a matter of personal whim that kept him from greater things; if the latter, then the jazz world seems to have lost a player of merit.

BRIDGEWATER, DEE DEE

b. Denise Garrett, 27 May 1950, Memphis, Tennessee, USA. After making her first public performances singing in the American north-west, she became featured vocalist with a university big band. In 1970 she married trumpeter Cecil Bridgewater, thereafter using her married name, even after their divorce. The couple recorded together, including the well-received *Afro-Blue*, which also featured tenor saxophonist Ron Bridgewater. In New York during the early 70s she sang regularly with the Thad Jones-Mel Lewis Jazz Orchestra. She also began a parallel career as a performer in stage musicals, including *The Wiz*, for which she won a Tony award in 1975. By the late 70s she had opted to work outside jazz, singing pop music on the west coast of America. A long sojourn in Europe found her working more in the jazz field and making further stage appearances, this time in London in the leading role in *Lady Day*. At the end of the decade she was back in the USA and a frequent visitor to jazz festivals in various parts of the world. A powerful singer, with a style well-rooted in gospel, to which she brings a fresh and contemporary feeling, Bridgewater has all the qualities needed to make a lasting mark as a jazz singer. However, her successes in other fields may well persuade her to broaden her repertoire still further, which might tend to dilute her jazz core. *Precious Things* featured an excellent duet with Ray Charles on 'Til The Next Somewhere'. Similarly sensitive was her excellent tribute to Ella Fitzgerald, *Dear Ella*.

● ALBUMS: *Brains On Fire Volumes 1 & 2* (1967)★★, *Afro-Blue* (1974)★★, with Thad Jones-Mel Lewis *Suite For Pops* (1972)★★, *Just Family* (Elektra 1978)★★★, *Bad For Me* (Elektra 1979)★★★, *Dee Dee Bridgewater* (Atlantic 1980)★★★, *Live In Paris* (Affinity 1986)★★, *Precious Things* (Prestige 1992)★★★★, *Love And Peace: A Tribute To Horace Silver* (Verve 1995)★★, *Prelude To A Kiss: The Duke Ellington Album* (Philips 1996)★★★, *Dear Ella* (Verve 1997)★★★★.

BRIGNOLA, NICK

b. 17 July 1936, Troy, New York, USA. A largely self-taught baritone saxophonist, Brignola played professionally for some years before learning to read music. Later, he studied at Berklee College Of Music where he worked and recorded with Herb Pomeroy. In 1957 he was a member of the band voted best college jazz group in *Down Beat* magazine. After briefly leading his own band in the late 50s, he played for various leaders, including Woody Herman and Ted Curson. From the mid-60s he led a jazz-rock group before reuniting with Curson. Brignola also taught, both privately and at college. In the 70s, he played with Dave Holland, Bill Watrous and Pepper Adams and also recorded with Sal Nistico and Sal Salvador. In the 80s Brignola recorded with Kenny Barron and others and he played in the Mingus Superband at the Nice Jazz Festival. In the early 90s he played with Phil Woods. A gifted player, adept also on most members of the saxophone family, Brignola has a distinctive veiled sound. An admirer of many kinds of music and different schools of jazz, Brignola brings to his work a delightful fluency that admirably suits the post-bop urgency of his modern-mainstream playing. (This artist is unrelated to the baritone saxophonist Mike Brignola who played with Herman in the 80s.)

● ALBUMS: *This Is It!* (Priam 1967)★★★, *Baritone Madness* (Bee Hive 1977)★★★★, *New York Bound* (Interplay 1979)★★★, *LA Bound* (Night Life 1979), *Burn Brigade* (1979)★★★, *Triste* (1981-84 recordings)★★★, *Signals ... In From Somewhere* (Discovery 1983)★★★, *Northern Lights* (Discovery 1984)★★★, *Raincheck* (Reservoir 1988)★★★, *On A Different Level* (Reservoir 1989)★★★, *What It Takes* (Reservoir 1990)★★★★, *It's Time* (Reservoir 1992)★★★, *Live At Sweet Basil: First Set* (Reservoir 1993)★★★, *The Flight Of The Eagle* (Reservoir 1997)★★★★, *Poinciana* (Reservoir 1998)★★★, as Three Baritone Saxophone Band *Three Baritone Saxophone Band Plays Mulligan* (Dreyfus 1998)★★★, *Spring Is Here* (Koch Jazz 1998)★★.

BRISE-GLACE

Brise-Glace is one of the many guises adopted by US experimentalist Jim O'Rourke in a prolific recording career. As a solo composer he had previously worked with the Kronos Quartet, and played with artists such as Henry Kaiser, Derek Bailey and AMM. Other collaborations have included sessions with Faust, K.K. Null and Gastr Del Sol, of whom he is a founding member. He formed Brise-Glace in order to give vent to what he described as 'rock-concrete'. In order to do so he recruited collaborative members drawn from similarly unconventional backgrounds. Thymme Jones is also a member of Chicago's Cheer Accident and Illusion Of Safety and has played with many other bands on rock's left-field fringe. Dylan Posa is a veteran of Chicago jazz-rock experimentation collective the Flying Luttenbachers. Final member Darin Gray was recruited from his (predominantly solo) work with Dazzling Killmen of St. Louis, Missouri. The idea behind Brise-Glace's debut album, 1994's *When In Vanitas ...*, was to 'explore the concept of what 'rock music' is'. A typically dense, multi-textural recording, it included guests such as Kaiser, David Grubbs (Gastr Del Sol) and German *avant garde* artist Cristoph Heemann (HNAS).

● ALBUMS: *When In Vanitas ...* (Skingraft 1994)★★★.

BRISKER, GORDON

b. 6 November 1937, Cincinnati, Ohio, USA. Educated at the Cincinnati Conservatory of Music, Brisker began playing professionally while still at high school. He played tenor saxophone in jazz and dance bands and once played piano in a Las Vegas rock 'n' roll show. He later studied at Berklee College Of Music, where he also wrote arrangements for the Herb Pomeroy band. In 1960 he joined Woody Herman's big band and by the time he left, in 1963, had attracted attention in the jazz world. Since then Brisker has written for, and played with several leaders, including Louie Bellson, Freddie Hubbard, Stanley Clarke, Jack DeJohnette, Airto, Pat Longo and Bobby Shew. Brisker's musical tastes are wide: in addition to recording with numerous jazz musicians he has worked with the Los Angeles Philharmonic and the Cincinnati and Boston Symphony Orchestras, and has written for both James Brown and Rosemary Clooney. In the mid-80s he was back at Berklee, this time teaching and once again writing charts for the Pomeroy band. He has also taught at universities in Oregon, Hawaii and California. In 1987 he recorded an album of his arrangements for his own big band. Two years later he was touring as musical director and accompanist to singer Anita O'Day. A robust, bop-orientated player, it is as a writer that Brisker seems destined to make his biggest mark on jazz in general and on big band music in particular.

● ALBUMS: *New Beginning* (Discovery 1987)★★★, with Anita O'Day *In A Mello Tone* (1989)★★★, *The Gift* (Naxos 1998)★★★★.

BROADBENT, ALAN

b. 23 April 1947, Auckland, New Zealand. After studying piano and musical theory in his homeland, in the mid-60s Broadbent moved to the USA to study at the Berklee College Of Music. After studying with Lennie Tristano he began arranging for Woody Herman, his work appearing on the 1973 album, *Giant Steps*. In the 70s, Broadbent composed music in the classical form while simultaneously playing with jazz groups including those led by John Klemmer, Bill Berry and Bud Shank. In the 80s Broadbent played with Warne Marsh, Charlie Haden and others. Having previously shown himself to be adept at accompanying singers (he recorded with Irene Kral in the early 70s), in the 90s Broadbent arranged for and accompanied Sue Raney. A fleet and inventive soloist with imaginative gifts, Broadbent is also an ideal section player, effectively accompanying soloists and lending authority to ensembles. Nevertheless, his writing, especially his jazz arranging, may well prove to be his most important contribution to music.

● ALBUMS: *Live At Maybeck Vol 14* (Concord 1992)★★★★, *Alan Broadbent/ Gary Foster Duo Series Vol 4* (Concord 1994)★★★, *Pacific Standard Time* (Concord 1996)★★★, *Personal Standards* (Concord Jazz 1997)★★★★.

BROKENSHA, JACK

b. John Joseph Brokensha, 5 January 1926, Adelaide, South Australia, Australia. During the later part of World War II, Brokensha, who was in the Royal Australian Air Force, was involved in entertainment. From this he developed an interest in jazz, playing drums and taking up other percussion instruments notably the vibraphone. After the war he formed various small bands usually for hotel and similar work and also played at concerts. Among his sidemen during this period was Errol Buddle. In the 50s he toured Australia and also visited Canada where, together with fellow countrymen Buddle, saxophonist Dick Healey and pianist Bryce Rohde, he helped form the Australian Jazz Quartet. With this group, Brokensha made several interesting but long-deleted albums for Bethlehem Records. The band was regularly expanded with the addition of a bassist, perhaps John Fawcett or Jim Gannon or Jack Lander, and a drummer, Nick Stabulas or Osie Johnson or Frank Capp. On their final date, Brokensha, who usually played vibes, switched to drums and a vibraphone player, probably Teddy Charles, was brought in. At the end of the 50s, after again touring his homeland, Brokensha took up residence in the USA where for a time he ran a music production company and also made occasional appearances on records.

● ALBUMS: with the Australian Jazz Quartet *The Australian Jazz Quartet* 10-inch album (Bethlehem 1955)★★★, with the Australian Jazz Quartet *The Australian Jazz Quartet* ii (Bethlehem 1956)★★★, with the Australian Jazz Quartet *The Australian Jazz Quartet* iii (Bethlehem 1956)★★★, with the Australian Jazz Quartet *The Australian Jazz Quartet* iv (Bethlehem 1956)★★★, with the Australian Jazz Quartet *The* Australian Jazz Quartet *At The Varsity Drag* (Bethlehem 1956)★★★, with the Australian Jazz Quartet *The Australian Jazz Quartet + One* (Bethlehem 1957)★★★, with the Australian Jazz Quartet *The Australian Jazz Quartet Plays Rogers & Hammerstein* (Bethlehem 1958)★★★, with the Australian Jazz Quartet *Free Style* (Bethlehem 1959)★★★, with the Australian Jazz Quartet *Three Penny Opera* (Bethlehem 1959)★★★, with the Australian Jazz Quartet *Jazz For Beach-Niks* (Bethlehem 1961)★★★, with the Australian Jazz Quartet *Jazz For Surf-Niks* (Bethlehem 1961)★★★, *And Then I Said* (Savoy 1962)★★★.

BROOKMEYER, BOB

b. 19 December 1929, Kansas City, Missouri, USA. Although he began his career as a pianist, it was when he took up the valve trombone in the early 50s that Brookmeyer began attracting serious attention. In 1953 he joined Gerry Mulligan, making numerous concert appearances and recordings, all of which demonstrated his considerable technical ability. His precise playing fitted well into Mulligan's rather thoughtful approach. He worked with Clark Terry in the early 60s and also played in the Thad Jones-Mel Lewis big band. A gifted arranger for both small and big bands, Brookmeyer also composes, but it is as a player that he has made his chief contribution.

● ALBUMS: *The Dual Role Of Bob Brookmeyer* (Prestige 1955)★★★, *Quintets* (Vogue 1956)★★★, with Zoot Sims *Tonight's Jazz Today* (Storyville 1956)★★★, with Sims *Whoo-eeee!* (Storyville 1956)★★★, *Traditionalism Revisited* (World Pacific 1957)★★★★, with Jim Hall, Jimmy Raney *Street Swingers* reissued as *Bob Brookmeyer And Guitars* (World Pacific/Kimberly 1957)★★, *Kansas City Revisited* (United Artists 1958)★★★, with Ivory Joe Hunter *The Ivory Hunters - Double Barrelled Piano* (United Artists 1959)★★★, *Jazz Is A Kick* (Mercury 1960)★★★, *The Blues Hot And Cold* (Verve 1961)★★★, *Gloomy Sunday And Other Bright Moments* (Verve 1961)★★★, *Stan Getz/Bobby Brookmeyer* (Verve 1961)★★★★, *Trombone Jazz Samba* (Verve 1962)★★★, *Bob Brookmeyer And Friends* (Columbia 1964)★★★★, *The Power Of Positive Swinging* (1964)★★★, with Clark Terry *Clark Terry Tonight* (Mainstream 1965)★★★, *Suitably Zoot* (1965)★★★, with Terry *Gingerbread Men* (Mainstream 1966)★★★, *Back Again* (Sonet 1978)★★, *The Bob Brookmeyer Small Band* (Gryphon 1978)★★★★, with Mel Lewis *Live At The Village Vanguard* (Rhapsody 1980)★★★★, *Through A Looking Glass* (1982)★★★, *Bobby Brookmeyer And His Orchestra* (RCA 1983)★★★, *Traditionalism Revisited* (Affinity 1984)★★★, *Oslo* (Concord 1987)★★, *Kansas City Revisited* (Fresh Sounds 1988)★★★, *Dreams* (Dragon 1989)★★★, *Bob Brookmeyer With The Stockholm Jazz Orchestra* (Dragon 1989)★★★, with the New Quartet *Paris Suite* (Challenge 1995)★★★, with Tony Coe, Danish Radio Jazz Orchestra *Captain Coe's Famous Racearound* (Storyville 1996)★★★★, *Electricity* 1991 recording (ACT 1997)★★★, *Old Friends* (Storyville 1997)★★★★.

BROOKS, TINA

b. Harold Floyd Brooks, 7 June 1932, Fayetteville, North Carolina, USA, d. 13 August 1974, New York, USA. Brooks acquired his sobriquet 'Tina' after his previous nickname 'Teeny'. He studied C Melody, alto and tenor saxophones at school before turning professional in 1950. At first he played with R&B and local New York Latin bands, recording in 1951 with Sonny Thompson, but Brooks soon tired of the restrictions of section work and looked for opportunities to play jazz. He played with Lionel Hampton in early 1955, but his break came when the trumpeter Little Benny Harris coached his playing and introduced him to other jazz musicians. Harris was instrumental in bringing the young tenor player to the attention of Blue Note label boss Alfred Lion, who immediately hired Brooks to play on the mammoth Jimmy Smith session that produced his album *The Sermon*. Brooks's playing was assured, showing that he had already assimilated the work of influences Lester Young and Sonny Rollins to create a style of his own. Between 1958-61 Brooks appeared on a series of albums with leading players Jackie McLean, Freddie Redd, Kenny Burrell and Freddie Hubbard. He also recorded four sessions as leader, but at the time only one, *True Blue* (1960), was released. After 1961, Brooks recorded no more. He continued to play in New York for a number of years but ill-health and a drug problem finally led to his early death in 1974. His shyness and inability to succeed in the highly competitive world of the professional musician prevented Brooks from fully establishing himself as a leading saxophonist.

It is only now, with all his albums issued, that Brooks can be seen as an influential and original player and composer.

● ALBUMS: *Minor Move* (Blue Note 1958)★★★, *True Blue* (Blue Note 1960)★★★★, *Back To The Tracks* (Blue Note 1960)★★★.

● COMPILATIONS: *The Complete Blue Note Recordings* 1958-61 recordings (Mosaic 1985)★★★★.

Broom, Bobby

b. 18 January 1961, New York City, New York, USA. He began playing guitar at the age of 13 but was not interested in jazz until he heard Grover Washington Jnr. and George Benson. Broom's studies broadened his interests and he also learned to play bass, but it was the lineage of jazz guitar that most attracted his attention. Moving away from the rock and fusion influences of the 70s, he concentrated upon the guitar heritage of musicians such as Wes Montgomery and Grant Green. He studied for a year at Berklee College Of Music, then returned to New York where he was offered the chance to work with jazz-funk trumpet player Tom Browne and also with Art Blakey's Jazz Messengers. He chose Browne but in the early 80s was with Sonny Rollins. He resumed studying in the mid-80s, then played with Kenny Burrell and Miles Davis. Into the 90s, Broom continued to be much sought after, his eclectic style and tastes allowing him to work in many genres and always to very good effect. In 1993 he played in London with Courtney Pine's American Band. Interviewed by *Jazz Journal International*'s Mark Gilbert in 1993, Broom was still eagerly seeking a sound that satisfied him, contemplating wood-bodied acoustic guitars, while pursuing the latest technological advances in electrical instruments and equipment. Throughout it all, his essential musicality remains paramount and makes him a worthy successor to Montgomery and Green and someone capable of advancing jazz guitar into the next century.

● ALBUMS: *Clean Sweep* (GRP 1981)★★★, *Waitin' And Waitin'* (Criss Cross 1998)★★★.

Brotherhood Of Breath

(see McGregor, Chris)

Brötzmann, Peter

b. 6 March 1941, Remscheid, Germany. Once the holder of the dubious title of loudest saxophonist in the world, Brötzmann plays several varieties of saxophone and clarinet (including the Hungarian taragato) with awesome skill, power and intensity. He started playing Dixieland at school but was more interested in art than music. While at art college he played in a semi-professional swing band. During this time music became more important to him, and he began to explore new areas of free improvised music. In 1966, he toured with Jazz Realities, including Carla Bley, Michael Mantler and Steve Lacy, and made his record debut in 1967 with Peter Kowald and Sven-Ake Johannsen. In 1969 he, Kowald, Hans Reichel and several other musicians set up the FMP label as a co-operative, and ever since he has recorded a stream of outstanding albums for the label in various contexts from solo to big bands, though few have surpassed the ferocity of his octet's 1968 recording, *Machine Gun*, now regarded as one of the early classics of European free jazz. In 1986, he formed Last Exit with Bill Laswell, Sonny Sharrock and Ronald Shannon Jackson. In 1990 he toured and recorded with B-Shops For The Poor in Britain and Nicky Skopelitis, Sharrock and Ginger Baker in the USA, but at the time of writing the albums had not been released. He has also worked with Don Cherry, Albert Mangelsdorff, the Globe Unity Orchestra and his guitarist son, Caspar, who leads the rock trio Massaker.

● ALBUMS: *For Adolphe Saxe* (FMP 1967)★★★, *Machine Gun* (FMP 1968)★★★★★, *Nipples* (1969)★★★, with Fred Van Hove, Han Bennink *Balls* (FMP 1970)★★★, with others *Elements* (1971)★★★, with others *Couscouss De La Mauresque* (1971)★★★, with others *The End* (1971)★★★, *The Berlin Concert* (1972)★★★, with Van Hove, Bennink *Free Jazz Und Kinder* (1972)★★★, *Brötzmann, Van Hove, Bennink* (1973)★★★, with Van Hove, Bennink *Einheitsfrontlied* (1973)★★★, with others *Hot Lotta* (1973)★★★, with others *Outspan 1* (FMP 1974)★★★, with others *Outspan 2* (FMP 1974)★★★, with Van Hove, Bennink *Tschüs* (1975)★★★, *Solo* (1976)★★★, with Bennick *Ein Halber Hund Kann Nicht Pinkeln* (1977)★★★, with Bennink, Misha Mengelberg *Three Points And A Mountain* (1979)★★★, with Harry Miller, Louis Moholo *The Nearer The Bone The Sweeter The Meat* (FMP 1979)★★★, with Bennink *Atsugi Concert* (1980)★★★, with Miller, Moholo *Opened, But Hardly Touched* (FMP 1980)★★★, with Willi Kellers *Edelgard-Maar-Helaas* (1980)★★★, *Alarm* (1981)★★★, *Andrew Cyrille Meets Peter Brötzmann In Berlin* (FMP 1982)★★★, with Albert Mangelsdorff, Günter Sommer *Pica Pica* (1982)★★★, *14 Love Poems - Solo* (1984)★★★, *Berlin Djungle* (FMP 1984)★★★, with Company *Trios* 1983 recording (1986)★★★, with Bill Laswell *Low Life* (Celluloid 1987)★★★, with Alfred 23 Harth *Go-No-Go* (1987)★★★, with others *No Material* (1987)★★★, with others *In A State Of Undress* (1989)★★★, *Reserve* (FMP 1989)★★★, *Wie Das Leben So Spielt* (FMP 1990)★★★, *Last Home* (Pathological 1990)★★★, *No Nothing* (FMP 1991)★★★★, *Songlines* (FMP 1992)★★, *Dare Devil* (DIW 1992)★★★★, *The Marz Combo* (FMP 1992)★★★, *Sacred Scrape* (Rastascan 1993)★★, *The Dried Rat Dog* (Okkadisk 1995)★★★★, *Evolving Blush Or Driving Original Sin* (1998)★★★, with Hamid Drake, Mahmoud Ghania *The 'WELS' Concert (Parts 1-3)* (Okkadisk 1998)★★★★.

Brown, Boyce

b. 6 April 1910, Rock Island, Illinois, USA, d. 30 January 1959. Born into a musical family Brown learned to play clarinet and alto saxophone. In his mid-teens he played professionally with various bands, and for a while was based in Chicago. In the early and mid-30s he worked in bands led by Paul Mares, Wingy Manone and others, and he also appeared on a few records. During the late 30s and on through the 40s, he played in many bands including those led by Charles LaVere, Jimmy McPartland and Wild Bill Davison and sometimes led his own small group. Eddie Condon, who always approved of eccentrics, remarked of Brown that he was, 'A slow reader, blind in one eye with about one tenth vision in the other.' In the early 50s Brown changed the direction of his life and entered a Servite monastery, emerging for a short while to play at fund-raisers. He also recorded for similar reasons using his new name, Brother Matthew.

● ALBUMS: *Brother Matthew With Eddie Condon's Jazz Band* (ABC-Paramount 1956)★★★.

BROWN, BRIAN

b. 29 December 1933, Melbourne, Victoria, Australia. After teaching himself to play various reed instruments Brown played with several bands before forming an *avant garde* group in the late 50s. Active throughout the next 30 years as player and composer, again largely self-taught, Brown was prominent in extending the boundaries of the Australian jazz scene. He has also been eager to pursue his ideas and concepts through teaching and was responsible for establishing a jazz studies course. Although he played mostly tenor saxophone in the early stages of his career, doubling on soprano, later he leaned more towards the soprano and also played flute. On all these instruments, Brown plays with considerable verve, forcefully developing complex and always interesting lines while retaining, especially on tenor, a warm and expansive lyricism.

● ALBUMS: *Winged Messenger* (AIJA 1986)★★★.

BROWN, CAMERON

b. Cameron Langdon Brown, 21 December 1945, Detroit, Michigan, USA. Although he spent some years studying piano, Brown switched to bass while still at school and later, while studying at university, attracted attention for his playing in a jazz quartet. In the mid-60s he spent some time in Europe, playing with musicians of the calibre of George Russell, Don Cherry and Donald Byrd. On his return to the USA he taught for a few years before becoming a member of the house band at a New York nightclub. In this capacity he accompanied many leading jazz musicians and also recorded with Sheila Jordan before returning to Europe, this time to tour with Archie Shepp in the mid-70s. During this period he also visited Japan with Art Blakey and three years later recorded with Beaver Harris, with whom he had first played in New York some years earlier. In 1979 he joined the newly-formed quartet co-led by George Adams and Don Pullen. He recorded with them on *Live At The Village Vanguard* (Soul Note 1983) and *Decisions* (Timeless 1984). During the 80s he was active with bands led by Dannie Richmond, Cherry and Shepp. Brown's enormous technical gifts have always served him well in the often demanding company in which he has spent much of his performing life. The solid rhythmic pulse he imparts, and his keen sense of time, have been very important in providing an anchor for the freewheeling complexities of the various bands of which he has been an invaluable part.

BROWN, CLEO

b. 8 December 1909, DeKalb, Mississippi, USA. Born into a musical household, Brown began singing in her father's church and after the family moved to Chicago in 1919, she studied music, learning to play piano. In the 20s she worked in clubs and tent shows, and was a frequent broadcaster with her own radio show. From the early 30s she worked steadily for two decades, performing in cities across the USA, usually in clubs such as New York's Three Deuces. Brown's voice was tiny and twee, and opened the way for the extremes of Rose Murphy, but her records sold well, thanks mostly to her piano playing (she was an above-average boogie-woogie pianist) and to her accompanists, who included leading jazzmen of the day. In the late 40s Brown underwent a religious experience and after an unsettled period, retired from music in 1953. She took up nursing; but when this career ended, she began performing again, this time playing religious music. In the mid-80s, thanks to the efforts of Marion McPartland, Brown was 'rediscovered' living in Colorado. She was persuaded to visit New York to appear on McPartland's radio show, following which she was the subject of an article by jazz writer Whitney Balliett in the *New Yorker*, which was later reprinted in his book *American Singers* (1988).

● ALBUMS: with Marian McPartland *Live In The Afterglow* (1987)★★★.

● COMPILATIONS: *The Legendary Cleo Brown* (President 1996)★★★.

BROWN, CLIFFORD

b. 30 October 1930, Wilmington, Delaware, USA, d. 26 June 1956, Pennsylvania, USA. As a young high school student Brown began playing trumpet and within a very short time was active in college and other youth bands. By his late teens he had attracted the favourable attention of leading jazzmen, including fellow trumpeters Dizzy Gillespie, Miles Davis and Fats Navarro. At the end of the 40s he was studying music at Maryland University and in 1952, following recovery from a serious road accident, he made his first records with Chris Powell and Tadd Dameron. In the autumn of 1953 he was a member of the big band Lionel Hampton took to Europe. Liberally filled with precocious talent, this band attracted considerable attention during its tour. Contrary to contractual stipulations, many of the young musicians moonlighted on various recordings and Brown in particular was singled out for such sessions. Back in the USA, Brown was fired along with most of the rest of the band when Hampton learned of the records they had made. Brown then joined Art Blakey and in mid-1954 teamed up with Max Roach to form the Clifford Brown-Max Roach Quintet. The quintet was quickly recognized as one of the outstanding groups in contemporary jazz and Brown as a major trumpeter and composer. In June 1956, while driving between engagements during a nationwide tour, Brown and another quintet member, pianist Richie Powell, were killed in a road accident. The early death of musicians in jazz, and of talented artists in other fields, has often led to the creation of legends. Inevitably, in many cases the legend greatly exceeds the reality, and speculation on what might have been relies more upon the imagination of the recounter than upon any hard evidence. In the case of Clifford Brown, the reality of the legend is impossible to refute. At a time when many modern jazz trumpeters sought technical expertise at the expense of tone, Brown, in common with his friend and paradigm, Navarro, had technique to spare but also developed a rich, full and frequently beautiful tone. At the same time, whether playing at scorching tempos or on languorous ballads, his range was exhaustive. He was enormously and brilliantly inventive but his search for original ideas was never executed at the expense of taste. In all his work, Brown displayed the rare combination of supreme intelligence and great emotional depths. His playing was only one aspect of his talent; he was also a fine composer, creating many works that have become modern jazz standards. Although his career was brief, Brown's influence persisted for a while in the work of Lee Morgan and throughout succeeding decades in that of Freddie Hubbard. Fortunately for jazz fans, Brown's own work persists in the form of his recordings, almost any of which can be safely recommended as outstanding examples of the very best of jazz. Indeed, all of his recordings with Roach are classics.

● ALBUMS: *New Star On The Horizon* 10-inch album (Blue Note 1953)★★★, *Clifford Brown Quartet* 10-inch album (Blue Note 1954)★★★★, with Max Roach *Clifford Brown & Max Roach* 10-inch album (EmArcy 1954)★★★★, with Roach *Brown And Roach Incorporated* (EmArcy 1954)★★★★, *Clifford Brown With Strings* (EmArcy 1955)★★★★, with Roach *A Study In Brown* (EmArcy 1955)★★★★, *The Clifford Brown Ensemble* 10-inch album (Pacific Jazz 1955)★★★★, *Clifford Brown All-Stars* (EmArcy 1956)★★★★, *Clifford Brown Memorial Album* (Blue Note 1956)★★★, with Roach *Clifford Brown & Max Roach At Basin Street* (EmArcy 1956)★★★★, with Roach, Sonny Rollins *Sonny Rollins Plus Four* reissued as *Three Giants* (Prestige 1956)★★★★, with Roach, Rollins *Pure Genius* 1956 recording (Elektra 1982)★★★★.

● COMPILATIONS: *Clifford Brown Volumes 1-4* (Jazz Reactivations 1983)★★★★, *Compact Jazz* (Emarcy 1990)★★★★, *The Complete Paris Sessions Volumes 1-3* (Vogue 1994)★★★★, *Ultimate Clifford Brown* (Verve 1998)★★★, *The Complete Blue Note-Pacific Jazz* 4-CD/5-LP box set (Mosaic)★★★★, *Brownie: The Complete EmArcy Recordings Of Clifford Brown* 10-CD box set (EmArcy)★★★★, *The Beginning And The End* 1952/1956 recordings (Columbia)★★★★.

Brown, Gerry

b. 9 November 1951, Philadelphia, Pennsylvania, USA. After training in a conservatory in the early 70s, Brown came to Europe in 1972 playing drums for John Lee. He stayed and recorded with Chris Hinze, Joachim Kuhn, Toots Thielemans and Charlie Mariano. On his return to New York in 1976 he played with Stanley Clarke before joining Chick Corea's Return To Forever. He is a deft musician, able to provide a firm rhythmic bass for any band. In 1979 he returned to Europe to play the Montreux International Jazz Festival with Didier Lockwood. He remained in France and Germany for a while, but by 1984 was back in New York recording with Arthur Blythe.

Brown, Jeri

b. St. Louis, Missouri, USA. Based in Nova Scotia, Canada, Jeri Brown is one of that country's foremost contemporary jazz singing talents. Raised in St. Louis, Brown studied classical piano, percussion and vocals at the St. Louis Institute, before studying voice with Rosa Henderson of the Metropolitan Opera. During her 20s she sang with the St. Louis Symphony Orchestra and toured Europe. However, by now her interest in jazz had grown, sparked by conversations with her uncle, trumpeter Virgil Carter, who had at one time brought Miles Davis home to practise in the family basement. After her light opera tour of Europe in 1973, Brown moved to Chicago to work with Young-Holt Unlimited for a year. Subsequent work included stints with musicians such as Joe Lovano and Ernie Krivda. She made her solo debut in 1982 with *Captain Bad* for the Atlanta-based Antelope Records. One further album for the same label followed before her first release on her own Jongleur label. An extended period as a music teacher at the Cleveland State University, Oberlin Conservatory of Music in Ohio and the University of Massachusetts in Boston served as a prelude to her move to Canada in 1989. She took a position teaching at Concordia University, but began performing immediately in Montreal clubs. Eventually she came to the attention of Justin Time Records, who released three further sets. *Fresh Start* saw her return to her own imprint, Jongleur, which she had reactivated a year previously to provide exposure to an album by the Nova Scotia Mass Choir. In keeping with her previous release, *A Timeless Place*, this collection saw Brown adopt a gruffer, more natural approach to singing by dropping her register. Her decision not to worry too much about tone refinement - a hangover from her classical training - resulted in a set with more emotive resonance than any of her previous recordings.

● ALBUMS: *Captain Bad* (Antelope 1982)★★★, *Blue And Green* (Antelope 1983)★★★, *Softly* (Jongleur 1984)★★★, with Fred Hersch *Mirage* (Justin Time 1991)★★★, *Unfolding - The Peacocks* (Justin Time 1993)★★★★, *A Timeless Place* (Justin Time 1995)★★★★, *Fresh Start* (Justin Time 1996)★★★★, *April In Paris* (Justin Time 1997)★★★.

Brown, Lawrence

b. 3 August 1907, Lawrence, Kansas, USA, d. 5 September 1988. Having previously mastered piano, violin and tuba, Brown settled with the trombone while studying medicine in California. At this time he was moonlighting with school and local bands and by 1926 he had abandoned his academic studies in favour of a career in music. After first working with Charlie Echols, he played with several popular west coast-based bands, including those of Paul Howard (where one of his fellow sidemen was Lionel Hampton), Curtis Mosby and Les Hite. In 1932 Brown joined Duke Ellington, with whom he remained for the greater part of the next two decades. After leaving Ellington in 1951, Brown worked with another ex-Ellingtonian, Johnny Hodges, until

1955. After studio work in New York, Brown rejoined Ellington in 1960 and stayed with the band for another decade. One of the most musicianly trombonists in jazz, Brown's first appearance with Ellington shocked some fans accustomed to the more aggressive playing of his predecessors and contemporaries. His melodic and gently lyrical playing seemed at first to be at odds with the music that was happening around him; his early feature number with the band, the ballad 'Trees', with its echoes of Victorian parlours, only added to the impression. Brown also kept apart from the general drinking and good-timing that the rest of the band enjoyed, thus earning the nickname the Deacon. In time both the fans and his fellow musicians began to recognize him for what he was - a remarkably gifted player with a beautiful tone and the ability to immerse himself totally in the needs of the Ellington orchestra. Indeed, Brown was so ready to commit himself to Ellington's music that, during his second spell with the band, he acquired the arsenal of effects that had been perfected in the 30s by fellow Ellington trombonist Joe 'Tricky Sam' Nanton, even though he felt that excessive use of the plunger mute risked damaging his lip and was detrimental to his own legato style. Brown retired from music in 1970 and lived in California, where he worked as a business and political consultant until his death.

● ALBUMS: *Lawrence Brown* (Clef 1956)★★★, *Inspired Abandon* (Jasmine 1965)★★★.

BROWN, LES

b. Lester Brown, 14 March 1912, Reinerton, Pennsylvania, USA. By 1932, when he entered Duke University at Durham, North Carolina, Brown had already attended Ithaca College and the New York Military Academy and had studied harmony, arranging and composing. At Duke he joined the university's dance band, the Duke Blue Devils, became its leader and built a substantial local reputation. In 1937 he moved to New York where he worked as an arranger for Jimmy Dorsey and Isham Jones. In 1938 he formed his own band for an engagement at the Hotel Edison and signed a recording contract. By 1940 the band was playing the Arcadia Ballroom and deputizing for Charlie Barnet at the Lincoln Hotel. During this spell, Brown lured Doris Day away from the Bob Crosby band to work for his. Although the draft damaged many bands, Brown managed to find replacements and his popularity gained strength even when Day left. In 1943 he persuaded the singer to rejoin and this time they had a massive hit with 'Sentimental Journey'. The band's style remained rooted in easy swinging dance music, with deceptively simple arrangements by Frank Comstock and Skippy Martin (whose chart for 'I've Got My Love To Keep Me Warm' was another hit). Nevertheless, at the end of 1946 Brown felt that he had not achieved the measure of success he wanted, and so folded the band - but he still had a contract (which he had temporarily forgotten) to play the Hollywood Palladium in March 1947. He re-formed the band and was promptly hired as resident orchestra for Bob Hope's weekly radio show. Brown remained with the show when it transferred to television, and also toured the world on the comedian's many trips to entertain US troops who were stationed overseas. Since then Les Brown and his Band Of Renown have remained popular on television and in public appearances; 1987 saw a succession of concerts celebrating his 50 years as a bandleader. In 1997 he was officially named as the longest playing group (leader) in the history of popular music and entered the *Guinness Book Of World Records*.

● ALBUMS: *Les Brown From The Cafe Rouge* i (1944)★★★, *One Night Stand With Les Brown* i (1945)★★★, *Les Brown From The Cafe Rouge* ii (1945)★★★, *One Night Stand With Les Brown* ii (1949)★★★, *Over The Rainbow* 10-inch album (Coral 1951)★★★, *That Sound Of Renown* 10-inch album (Coral 1951)★★★★, *You're My Everything* 10-inch album (Coral 1952)★★★★, *All Weather Music* (1952)★★★, *Concert At The Hollywood Palladium* (Coral 1953)★★★, *Dance To South Pacific* (1958)★★, with Vic Schoen Band *Suite For Two Bands* (1959)★★★, *Swing Song Book* (1959)★★★, *Jazz Song Book* (Coral 1959)★★★, *New Horizons* (1972)★★★, *Les Brown Today* (Harmonia Mundi 1974)★★, *The Century Masters* (1977)★★★, *Les Brown At The Aurex Festival, Tokyo* (1983)★★★.

● COMPILATIONS: *The 1943 Band* (Fanfare 1979)★★★, *Sentimental Thing* 1946-53 recordings (First Heard 1979)★★★, *Les Brown And His Orchestra, Volumes 1 & 2* 1944-46 recordings (Decca 1979)★★★★, *Les Brown And His Orchestra, Volumes 1, 2 & 3* 1944-49 recordings (Decca 1979)★★★, *The Duke Blue Devils* 30s recordings (Golden Era 1982)★★★, *The 1946 Band* (Circle 1986)★★★, *Les Brown And His Band Of Renown, Volumes 1-4* 1944-57 recordings (Columbia 1990)★★★★.

BROWN, MARION

b. 8 September 1935, Atlanta, Georgia, USA. Brown made his name as an alto saxophonist after mastering clarinet and oboe. In the 50s he studied music at Clark College, Atlanta and law at Howard University, Washington, DC - an experience that contrasted sharply with his poor southern background. He spent 18 months playing the clarinet in an army band on the Japanese island of Hokkaido. In 1962 he moved to New York and was helped by Ornette Coleman. His first musical exposure came with Archie Shepp and he played on John Coltrane's historic *Ascension*. Sun Ra also recruited him; Brown commented, 'it was all rehearsing and no jobs', but treasured the experience. He toured Europe with vibes player Gunter Hampel in the early 70s, made a series of extremely individual records with *avant gardists* such as Leo Smith, Muhal Richard Abrams and Steve McCall, and led his own groups into the 90s. He has continued to investigate African American ethnomusicology both musically and academically, and recordings have included the solo *Recollections* and two duos with pianist Mal Waldron, *Songs Of Love And Regret* and *Much More*. He has written a book of essays on his life and music, also titled *Recollections*, which was published in Germany in 1985. Brown's dry, breathy alto sound and the tenacious logic of his improvisations mark him as a great player.

● ALBUMS: *Marion Brown Quartet* (ESP 1966)★★★★, *Why Not?*

(ESP 1966)★★★, *Three For Shepp* (Impulse! 1967)★★★★, *Porto Nova* (Arista 1967)★★★★, *In Sommerhausen* (1969)★★★, *Afternoon Of A Georgia Faun* (ECM 1970)★★★, with Leo Smith *Duets* 1970 recording (Freedom 1973)★★★★, *Geechee Recollections* (Impulse! 1973)★★★★, *Sweet Earth Flying* (Impulse! 1974)★★★, *Vista* (Impulse! 1975)★★★★, *Solo Saxophone* (Sweet Earth 1977)★★★, with Gunter Hampel *Reeds 'N' Vibes* (IAI 1978)★★★, *La Placita - Live In Willisau* 1977 recording (Timeless 1979)★★★, *Gemini* (Birth 1983)★★★, *Recollections: Ballads And Blues For Saxophone* (Creative Works 1985)★★★★, *Marion Brown Quartet* (ESP 1988)★★★, *Back To Paris* 1980 recording (Freelance 1989)★★, with Mal Waldron *Songs Of Love And Regret* (Freelance 1985)★★★, with Waldron *Much More!* (Freelance 1988)★★★, *Native Land* (ITM 1991)★★★.

● FURTHER READING: *Recollections*, Marion Brown.

BROWN, MARSHALL

b. 21 December 1920, Framingham, Massachusetts, USA, d. 13 December 1983. Self-taught on several instruments, principally the trombone, Brown later formalized his musical expertise through intensive study. He formed a number of bands, one of which played at the 1957 Newport Jazz Festival and established him as a major figure on the jazz circuit. Although he often played with leading jazzmen such as Pee Wee Russell, Ruby Braff, Bobby Hackett and Lee Konitz, Brown turned much of his energy towards education. He taught music, and formed numerous youth bands in the USA and Europe. Appearing in many of these bands were musicians who subsequently became prominent figures on the international jazz scene, among them Albert Mangelsdorff, Dusko Goykovicz, George Gruntz and Jimmy Owens. Active also as a composer, Brown left a substantial body of jazz work and a number of popular songs.

● ALBUMS: *International Youth Band At Newport 1958* (1958)★★★, *Newport Youth Band At The Newport Festival* (1959)★★★, with Ruby Braff *Ruby Braff-Marshall Brown Sextet* (United Artists 1961)★★★.

BROWN, PETE

b. 9 November 1906, Baltimore, Maryland, USA, d. 20 September 1963. Although adept on trumpet, piano, violin and tenor saxophone, it was on alto that Brown made his mark on jazz. After working extensively in his home-town and in Atlantic City in the mid-20s, Brown moved to New York in 1927 and remained there, more or less continuously, for the rest of his life. Brown sometimes led his own groups and also played with a wide range of bands, including those led by John Kirby and Frankie Newton. A quirkily distinctive player, Brown's style was rooted in the blues and he was at his best playing in the hard-swinging jump bands popular along New York's 52nd Street during the 30s. When bop began to make its appearance in the early 40s, Brown was one of the few swing era musicians who made a serious attempt to come to terms with it. To some extent his clipped, aggressive yet witty sound suited certain elements of the new music, but he never wholly assimilated its implications into his style. In many respects his playing was better suited to the concurrent rhythm and blues explosion and his tough, rasping sound was aped with varying degrees of success by many saxophonists working in that field. Brown was one of several musicians whose divergences from the norm attracted the attention of Charlie Parker during his formative years, and he has also been cited by Paul Desmond as an influence. In his later years Brown was frequently in poor health, but continued to work and teach. Numbered among his pupils are Cecil Payne and Joe 'Flip' Phillips.

● ALBUMS: *Peter The Great* 10-inch album (Bethlehem 1954)★★★, *From The Heart* (Verve 1959)★★★.

● COMPILATIONS: *Jump, Blues & Swing* 1944 recordings (1980)★★★.

BROWN, PUD

b. Albert J. Brown, 22 January 1917, Wilmington, Delaware, USA, d. 27 May 1996. Born into a musical family, at the age of five he was performing with the Brown Family Band where he was billed as The World's Youngest Saxophone Player. The band toured widely, eventually folding in 1933, but he continued working in pit and territory bands across the USA. He was resident in Chicago for a while and also worked on the west coast, playing with many distinguished musicians including Jimmy Dorsey, Pete Daily, Jack Teagarden and Kid Ory. Apart from a five-year spell running a motorcycle repair shop in Shreveport, Louisiana, Brown was active in music throughout his long life. Usually playing clarinet, but equally adept on tenor saxophone, or, when the spirit moved him, on trumpet and cornet, he favoured traditional music and had a deep-seated love affair with the music of New Orleans. In the early 70s he returned to Shreveport and then to New Orleans where he became a much-loved and respected performer. In the city he played and sometimes recorded with bands such as those led by Clive Wilson and Trevor Richards, with whom he toured the Far East in the mid-80s. Towards the end of his life he led his own band at the Palm Court Café in the French Quarter of New Orleans for several years, playing his last gig there on the night before he died. A talented musician with the additional skills that allowed him to repair and rebuild musical instruments (and motor-cycles), he played clarinet with a delightfully flowing style that echoed the past masters of his adopted city.

● ALBUMS: *Lee Collins-Ralph Sutton's Jazzola Six* (Rarities 1953)★★★, *Palm Court Strut* (Jazzology 1992)★★★.

BROWN, RAY

b. 13 October 1926, Pittsburgh, Pennsylvania, USA. One of the outstanding bass players in jazz history, Brown's top-league experience began when, in 1945, at the age of 19, he joined Dizzy Gillespie. Two years later he was leading a trio accompanying Ella Fitzgerald, to whom he was married from 1948-52. In 1951 Brown joined the Oscar Peterson trio and stayed for most of the next 15 years. In 1966 he left Peterson and settled in Los

Angeles, which has remained his base ever since. Dividing his time between teaching, working in film and television studios, personal management and playing jazz clubs and festivals, Brown is in constant demand. A founder-member of the LA Four, he has also recorded with Duke Ellington. In 1989-90 he was a member of the Philip Morris Superband (led by Gene Harris). Although essentially a mainstream musician, Brown is thoroughly at home in bop, and plays with a great blues feeling. Remarkable for the accuracy of his playing and his lovely tone, Brown's work is a constant lesson to all other bass players, regardless of the field of music in which they perform.

● ALBUMS: *Bass Hit!* (Verve 1957)★★★, *This Is Ray Brown* (Verve 1958)★★★, *Jazz Cello* (Verve 1960)★★★, with Cannonball Adderley *Ray Brown With The All Star Big Band Featuring Cannoball Adderley* reissued as *Two For The Blues* (Verve 1962)★★★★, with Milt Jackson *Much In Common* (Verve 1964)★★★, with Jackson *Ray Brown-Milt Jackson* (Verve 1965)★★★★, with Laurindo Almeida *Back Ground Blues And Green* (Century City 1968)★★★, with Duke Ellington *This One's For Blanton* (Pablo 1972)★★★★, with Herb Ellis *Soft Shoe* (Concord Jazz 1974)★★★, *Brown's Bag* (Concord 1975)★★★, with Ellis *Hot Tracks* (Concord Jazz 1975)★★★, *The Most Special Joint* (1977)★★★, with Jackson *Live-Montreux '77* (Pablo 1978)★★★, with Jimmy Rowles *As Good As It Gets* (Concord Jazz 1978)★★★, with Rowles *Tasty!* (1979)★★★, *Something For Lester* (Contemporary 1979)★★★★, *Live At The Concord Festival* (Concord 1979)★★★, *Summerwind* (Bell 1980)★★★, with Almeida *Moonlight Serenade* (Bell 1981)★★★, with LA Four *Montage* (1981)★★★, *A Ray Brown Three* (Concord Jazz 1983)★★★, with LA Four *Soular Energy* (Concord Jazz 1984)★★★, with LA Four *Don't Forget The Blues* (Concord 1985)★★★, *The Red Hot Ray Brown Trio* (Concord Jazz 1986)★★★, *The Gene Harris Trio Plus One* (1986)★★★, *Gene Harris And The Philip Morris Superband* (1989)★★★, *Bam Bam Bam* (Concord Hazz1989)★★★, *Live At The Loa - Summer Wind* (Concord Jazz 1989)★★★, *Super Bass* (Capri 1990)★★★, *3 Dimensional* (Concord Jazz 1991)★★★★, *Black Orpheus* (Paddle Wheel 1992)★★★★, *Moore Makes 4* (Concord Jazz 1992)★★★★, *Bass Face* (Telarc 1993)★★★, with various artists *Some Of My Best Friends Are ... The Sax Players* (Telarc 1996)★★★, with Milt Jackson *Much In Common* (Verve 1997)★★★★, with John Clayton, Christian McBride *Super Bass* (Telarc 1997)★★★★, *Live At Scullers* (Telarc 1998)★★★, with Ulf Wakenius *Summertime* (Telarc 1998)★★★.

BROWN, ROB

b. 27 February 1962, Hampton, Virginia, USA. A striking new voice on alto saxophone, Brown began on piano as a child but switched to saxophone at the age of 13. He studied briefly at James Madison University, Berklee College Of Music and New York University, but credits the celebrated Philadelphia teacher Dennis Sandole (whose students have included John Coltrane, Art Farmer and Tommy Flanagan) as his major influence - together with recordings by Sonny Rollins, Ornette Coleman, Albert Ayler and Roscoe Mitchell. While based in Boston in the early 80s, Brown met pianist Matthew Shipp, with whom he has continued to work in New York (where both men relocated in 1985). They co-lead a trio, Right Hemisphere, and their debut recording was the duo *Sonic Explorations*. Brown also leads his own trio, with William Parker and Dennis Charles; their *Breath Rhyme* was one of the outstanding new jazz releases of 1990. Brown plays essentially a fiery free jazz, but with superb control and self-discipline.

● ALBUMS: with Matthew Shipp *Sonic Explorations* (1988)★★★, *Breath Rhyme* (Silkheart 1990)★★★★, *Youniverse* (Riti 1993)★★★, *High Wire* (Soul Note 1996)★★★, *Blink Of An Eye* (No More 1997)★★★★.

BROWN, RUTH

b. 30 January 1928, Portsmouth, Virginia, USA. Brown started her musical career singing gospel at an early age in the church choir led by her father. In 1948 she was singing with a band led by her husband Jimmy in Washington, DC, when Willis Conover (from the radio show *Voice Of America*) recommended her to Ahmet Ertegun of the newly formed Atlantic Records. Ertegun signed her, despite competition from Capitol, but on the way up to New York for an appearance at the Apollo Theatre, she was involved in a car crash. Hospitalized for nine months, her medical bills were paid by Atlantic and she rewarded them handsomely with her first big hit, 'Teardrops From My Eyes', in 1950. More hits followed with '5-10-15 Hours' (1952) and 'Mama, He Treats Your Daughter Mean' (1953). Atlantic's first real star, Brown became a major figure in 50s R&B, forming a strong link between that music and early rock 'n' roll. Her records were characterized by her rich and expressive singing voice (not unlike that of Dinah Washington) and accompaniment by breathy saxophone solos (initially by Budd Johnson, later by Willie Jackson). Between 1949 and 1955 her songs were on the charts for 129 weeks, including five number 1s. Brown's concentration upon R&B has not kept her from associations with the jazz world; very early in her career she sang briefly with the Lucky Millinder band, and has recorded with Jerome Richardson and the Thad Jones-Mel Lewis big band. She also brought a distinctively soulful treatment to varied material such as 'Yes, Sir, That's My Baby', 'Sonny Boy', 'Black Coffee' and 'I Can Dream, Can't I?'. In 1989 she won a Tony Award for her performance in the Broadway show *Black And Blue*, and was receiving enthusiastic reviews for her nightclub act in New York, at Michael's Pub and the Blue Note, into the 90s. In 1993 Brown was to be heard broadcasting on a New York radio station, and was inducted into the Rock And Roll Hall Of Fame. In 1994 she undertook a European tour, much to the delight of her small but loyal group of fans. On that tour she was recorded live at Ronnie Scott's club for an album that appeared on their own Jazzhouse label.

● ALBUMS: *Ruth Brown Sings Favorites* 10-inch album (Atlantic 1952)★★★, *Ruth Brown* (Atlantic 1957)★★★★, *Late Date With Ruth Brown* (Atlantic 1959)★★★★, *Miss Rhythm* (Atlantic 1959)★★★★, *Along Comes Ruth* (Philips 1962)★★★★, *Gospel Time* (Philips 1962)★★★, *Ruth Brown '65* (Mainstream

1965)★★★, *Black Is Brown And Brown Is Beautiful* (Rhapsody 1969)★★★, with Thad Jones, Mel Lewis *Thad Jones & Mel Lewis Featuring Miss Ruth Brown* (Solid State 1969)★★★★, *The Real Ruth Brown* (70s)★★★, *You Don't Know Me* (70s)★★, *Touch Me In The Morning* (70s)★★, *Sugar Babe* (President 1977)★★★, *Takin' Care Of Business* (1980)★★★, *The Soul Survives* (1982)★★, *Brown Sugar* (Topline 1986)★★★, *Sweet Baby Of Mine* (Route 66 1987)★★, *I'll Wait For You* (Official 1988)★★, *Blues On Broadway* (Fantasy 1989)★★★, with Linda Hopkins, Carrie Smith *Black And Blue* (1989)★★★, *Fine And Mellow* (1992)★★★, *The Songs Of My Life* (Fantasy 1993)★★★, *Live In London* (Jazzhouse 1995)★★, *R+B=Ruth Brown* (Bullseye 1997)★★★★.

● COMPILATIONS: *The Best Of Ruth Brown* (Atlantic 1963)★★★★, *Rockin' With Ruth* 1950-60 recordings (Charly 1984)★★★★, *Brown Black And Beautiful* (SDEG 1990)★★★, *Miss Rhythm, Greatest Hits And More* (Atlantic 1993)★★★★, *Blues On Broadway* (Ace 1994)★★★★, *You Don't Know Me* (Indigo 1997)★★★★.

● FURTHER READING: *Miss Rhythm*, Ruth Brown with Andrew Yule.

BROWN, SANDY

b. Alexander Brown, 25 February 1929, Izatnagar, Bareilly, India, d. 15 March 1975. Raised in Edinburgh from the age of six, Brown began playing clarinet with Al Fairweather and Stan Greig, fellow-students at the Royal High School. He made his first important impression on the UK jazz scene in the mid-50s, when the Fairweather-Brown All Stars were formed. This was the period of the trad jazz boom, and Brown's skilful yet impassioned clarinet playing was one of that era's highlights. Unlike many of his fellow trad bandleaders. Brown's interests were ever-expanding, and any bands under his leadership were home to adventurous musical souls, such as Brian Lemon and Tony Coe. Through the 50s and 60s Brown pursued musical excellence, making a string of classic albums, including *McJazz* and *The Incredible McJazz*, and working with such diverse jazz personalities as George Chisholm and Kenny Wheeler. In addition to his playing activity, he was a perceptive and witty writer (*The McJazz Manuscripts*), and was heavily involved in running an architectural practice that specialized in building acoustic recording studios. His health began to fail in the 70s, although he was able to visit the USA where he recorded with Earle Warren. His death came when he still had much to offer the jazz world.

● ALBUMS: *Fifty-Fifty Blues* (1956)★★★, *Sandy's Sidemen* (1956)★★★, *McJazz* (1957)★★★, *Doctor McJazz* (1960)★★★★, *The Incredible McJazz* (1962)★★★★, *Hair At Its Hairiest* (1968)★★★, *Barrelhouse And Blues* (1969)★★★, with the Brian Lemon Trio *In The Evening* (Hep Jazz 1971)★★★, with Earle Warren *Everybody Loves Saturday Night* (1974)★★★, *Splanky* (Spotlite 1983)★★★★, *Clarinet Opening* (CSA 1988)★★★.

● FURTHER READING: *The McJazz Manuscripts*, Sandy Brown.

BROWN, STEVE

b. 13 September 1968, Manchester, Lancashire, England. Brown began playing drums at the age of 15, studying in his hometown with David Hassel. In the early 90s he continued his studies in New York, with John Riley and Carl Allen, meanwhile developing his skills and reputation in performance. He accompanied numerous artists, including Harry Allen, and was also a member of the Jim Hunt Quartet, finalists in the 1993 European Jazz Competition at the Cologne Festival. In 1996 he relocated to London and during the next few years played with many leading jazz musicians. During his relatively short professional career he has worked with a strikingly large number of important artists, including Art Farmer, Harry 'Sweets' Edison, Teddy Edwards, Conte Candoli, Ken Peplowski, Dan Barrett, Mundell Lowe, Randy Johnston, Spike Robinson, Bill Watrous, David Newton, Alan Barnes, Stan Tracey, Guy Barker, Digby Fairweather, Stacey Kent, Harry Beckett, Iain Ballamy, Dave Cliff and Geoff Simkins. Brown is a lithely swinging drummer, playing in the late mainstream and post-bop idiom with insouciant ease. As an accompanist he displays equal parts drive and sympathetic lift. His is a rare talent, and the rapidity of his progress demonstrates the value placed upon his work by his peers.

BROWN, TOM

b. 3 June 1888, New Orleans, Louisiana, USA. d. 25 March 1958. After briefly playing violin, Brown began playing trombone. He also occasionally played bass, as did his brother, Steve Brown, who became a member of the New Orleans Rhythm Kings and the Jean Goldkette band. In the early years of the century, Brown worked in various New Orleans bands, playing for dances and parades, and also led his own band. He took a band to Chicago in 1915 and also played in New York. By the mid-20s Brown was back in New Orleans where he continued to play, often on bass, for the next several years. By the late 30s he was playing only part-time, but made occasional records with his own band and with bands led by musicians such as Johnny Wiggs. A solid, competent player, Brown's early ventures to Chicago and New York helped the spread of jazz.

● ALBUMS: *Tom Brown's Band From Dixie Land* (1954)★★★★.

BROWN, VERNON

b. 6 January 1907, Venice, Illinois, USA, d. 18 May 1979. While still a teenager, Brown was playing jazz trombone in the Midwest with Frank Trumbauer and Bix Beiderbecke. In 1928 he was with them in Jean Goldkette's orchestra, after which he played in numerous bands and studio groups in and around New York, including Mezz Mezzrow's Disciples Of Swing. In 1937 he joined Benny Goodman, and following his two-year stint there he had periods with Artie Shaw, Jan Savitt, Muggsy Spanier and the Casa Loma Orchestra before settling into studio work, mostly with NBC Broadcasting. A highly skilled craftsman, Brown was capable of powerful and entertaining solos but was at his best as a confident section player.

BROWN, WALTER

b. August 1916, Dallas, Texas, USA, d. June 1956, Lawton, Oklahoma, USA. Discovered by bandleader Jay McShann just a few days before his band's debut recording session for Decca Records in Dallas in April 1941, Brown became the band's biggest selling point, with his laid-back blues style on such successful titles as 'Hootie Blues', 'Lonely Boy Blues', and the million-selling 'Confessin' The Blues'. In 1945, owing to a drugs problem, Brown left the band to work and record as a soloist, although he often used McShann and/or old colleagues on his later recordings for King (1945/6), Signature (1947), Mercury (1947), Capitol (1949) and Peacock (1951). He is reported to have retired to Lawton, Oklahoma, during the early 50s, where he opened his own nightclub. He died in June 1956 from drug-related disorders. In spite of his personal life, Walter 'Confessin' The Blues' Brown recorded over 50 individual blues in his unique lazy drawl during his 10-year recording career and seldom produced a less than outstanding performance. He has been named as a major influence by artists as diverse as Chuck Berry and Clarence 'Big' Miller.

● ALBUMS: *Confessin' The Blues* (Affinity/Charly 1981)★★★★.

BROWNE, TOM

b. New York City, New York, USA. Browne started to learn the piano at the age of 11 and continued his studies at the Manhattan School of Music and Art. Later, he graduated in physics from Kingsborough College. It was listening to an Ornette Coleman album that sparked his interest in jazz. His first gig was with the Weldon Irvine Group in 1975, followed by stints with 'Sonny' Fortune and the Fatback Band. In 1979, he recorded his debut *Browne Sugar*, with the 14-year-old Marcus Miller playing the bass. There has been a succession of similar albums, notably 1980's *Love Approach* featuring 'Funkin' In Jamaica'.

● ALBUMS: *Browne Sugar* (GRP 1979)★★★, *Love Approach* (GRP 1980)★★★★, *Magic* (GRP 1981)★★, *Yours Truly* (GRP 1981)★★★, *Rockin Radio* (Arista 1983)★★, *Tommy Gun* (Arista 1984)★★★, *Mo' Jamaica Funk* (Hip Bop 1994)★★★, *Another Shade Of Browne* (Hip Bop 1996)★★★.

BROZMAN, BOB

b. 1954, New York City, New York, USA. Born and raised in the Hudson River Delta, blues musician, author and musicologist Bob Brozman began playing the piano at the age of four, gravitating to guitar by the age of six. Eventually he adopted the National steel guitar in 1968, and from then on developed a keen interest in and long-standing commitment to the blues. At college he undertook a degree in musicology, his thesis a comparative study of Tommy Johnson and Charley Patton that argued that they must have met at some point. Outside of the blues, he also stumbled across Hawaiian National guitar player Solomon Ho'op'i'i of the Ho'op'i'i Brothers, and began acquiring a huge collection of pre-war Hawaiian 78 rpm records. When he discovered that Ho'op'i'i had been influenced by jazz players such as Bix Beiderbecke, it convinced him of the interconnected nature of much modern music: 'For me the real interesting definition of World Music is where the First World and the Third World intersect. Third Worlders use the industrialised world's instruments to create more interesting music than anybody in the industrialised world has.' Since that time he has travelled extensively, documenting his discovery of the musics of several different continents, both academically and also in his own guitar-playing techniques. He is a virtuoso performer in his own right, his skill conditioned by what he estimates as some 11,000 45-minute bar sets played between 1973 and 1980. His love of the National steel guitar has led to his amassing a collection of over 100. Although he maintained a low profile as a performer, that situation changed dramatically in the early 90s when his *Truckload Of Blues* set for Sky Ranch Records achieved massive popularity in France. As a result he was signed to Virgin Records in that country, and released two more highly successful albums, *Slide A Go-Go* and *Blues Around The Bend*.

● ALBUMS: *Truckload Of Blues* (Sky Ranch 1992)★★★★, *Slide A Go-Go* (Sky Ranch 1993)★★★, with the Thieves Of Sleep *Blues Around The Bend* (Sky Ranch 1995)★★★.

BRUBECK, DAVE

b. David Warren Brubeck, 6 December 1920, Concord, California, USA. Initially taught piano by his mother, Brubeck showed an immediate flair for the instrument, and was performing with local professional jazz groups throughout northern California at the age of 15 while still at high school. Enrolling at the College of the Pacific in Stockton, California, as a vetinary major, he transferred to the music conservatory at the suggestion of his college advisor. His involvement in jazz continued by establishing a 12-piece band, but most of his time was spent in the study of theory and composition. After he graduated from Pacific, Brubeck decided to continue his formal classical training. His studying was interrupted by military service in World War II. Returning from Europe in 1946, he went to Mills College as a graduate student under the tutorship of Darius Milhaud, and at about this time he formed his first serious jazz group - the Jazz Workshop Ensemble, an eight-piece unit that recorded some sessions, the results of which were issued three years later on Fantasy Records as the *Dave Brubeck Octet*.

He began a more consistent professional involvement in the jazz scene in 1949, with the creation of his first trio, with Cal Tjader and Ron Crotty. It was with the addition of alto saxophonist Paul Desmond in 1951 that Brubeck's group achieved major critical acclaim, even though the trio had won the Best Small Combo award in *Downbeat*. Replacing Tjader and Crotty with Gene Wright (in 1958) and Joe Morello (in 1956) towards the end of the 50s, Brubeck led this celebrated and prolific quartet as a unit until 1967, when he disbanded the group. Brubeck toured as the Dave Brubeck Trio with Gerry Mulligan, together with Alan Dawson (drums) and Jack Six (bass) for seven years to widespread critical acclaim. He began using a new group in 1972 involving his three sons, touring as the Darius Brubeck Ensemble and the Dave Brubeck Trio, with either Mulligan or Desmond as guest soloists, until 1976. From 1977 to 1979 the New Brubeck Quartet consisted of four Brubecks, Dave, Darius, Chris and Dan. Apart from a brief classic quartet reunion in 1976, most of his now rare concert appearances have since been in this setting, with the addition at various times of Randy Jones (drums), Jack Six, Bill Smith (clarinet) and Bobby Militello (alto saxophone).

Brubeck's musical relationship with Desmond was central to his success. The group's 1959 classic 'Take Five' was composed by Desmond, and it was the saxophonist's extraordinary gift for melodic improvisation that gave the group much of its musical strength. Always seeing himself primarily as a composer rather than a pianist, Brubeck, in his own solos, tended to rely too much on his ability to work in complex time-signatures (often two at once). His work in the field of composition has produced over 300 pieces, including several jazz standards such as the magnificent 'Blue Rondo A La Turk', as well as 'In Your Own Sweet Way' and 'The Duke'. Additionally, he has composed two ballets, a musical, a mass, works for television and film, an oratorio and two cantatas. However, Brubeck will always be primarily associated with his pivotal quartet recordings with Paul Desmond, and with Desmond's 'Take Five', in particular. Throughout the 60s, when jazz was able to cross over into other territories, it was primarily Miles Davis, John Coltrane and Brubeck that were quoted, cited and applauded. His band was a central attraction at almost all the major international jazz festivals, and during the 50s and 60s, he frequently won both *Downbeat* and *Metronome* polls. As early as 1954, Brubeck appeared on the cover of *Time* magazine, and 10 years later was invited to play at the White House by Ronald Reagan (which he repeated on numerous occasions, including the 1988 Gorbachev Summit in Moscow). He later received the National Medal of the Arts from President Clinton. Brubeck remains a household name in modern jazz, and was still working on projects during the 90s. His family of talented musicians presently touring with him are Darius Brubeck (piano), Dan Brubeck (drums), Matthew Brubeck (cello) and Chris Brubeck (bass, bass trombone). His resurgence continued in 1995 with his 75th birthday and the release of *Young Lions & Old Tigers*, featuring Jon Hendricks, Gerry Mulligan, Joshua Redman, George Shearing, Joe Lovano and Michael Brecker.

By making pop charts all over the world, Dave Brubeck has brought jazz to unsuspecting ears. He has done much to popularize jazz to the masses and is both a legend and jazz icon. In later years his work will surely be added to classical music reference books, notably his mass *To Hope! A Celebration*, his cantata *La Fiesta De La Posada* and his Bach-influenced *Chromatic Fantasy Sonata*.

● ALBUMS: *Dave Brubeck Octet* (Fantasy 1949/56)★★★, *Dave Brubeck Trio* (Fantasy 1951/56)★★★, *Dave Brubeck Trio* reissued as *Distinctive Rhythm Instrumentals* (Fantasy 1951/56)★★★, *Dave Brubeck Trio* (Fantasy 1952)★★★, *Dave Brubeck Quartet* reissued as *Brubeck Desmond* (Fantasy 1952/56)★★★, *Dave Brubeck Quartet* (Fantasy 1952/56)★★★, *Jazz At Storyville* (Fantasy 1953/57)★★★, *Jazz At The Blackhawk* (Fantasy 1953/56)★★★, *Jazz At Oberlin* (Fantasy 1953/57)★★★, *Stardust* (Fantasy 1953)★★★★, *Jazz At The College Of Pacific* (Fantasy 1954/56)★★★★, *Old Sounds From San Fransisco* (Fantasy 1954)★★★, *Jazz Goes To College* (Columbia 1954)★★★★, *Jazz Goes To College, Volume 2* (Columbia 1954)★★★, *Dave Brubeck At Storyville: 1954* (Columbia 1954)★★★, *Interchanges '54* (Columbia 1954)★★★, *Paul And Dave's Jazz Interwoven* (Fantasy 1955)★★★, *Brubeck Time* (Columbia 1955)★★★, *Jazz: Red Hot And Cool* (Columbia 1955)★★★, *Brubeck Plays Brubeck* (Columbia 1956)★★★, shared with J.J. Johnson and Kai Winding *American Jazz Festival At Newport '56* (Columbia 1956)★★★, *Brubeck And Desmond At Wilshire-Ebell* (Fantasy 1957)★★★, *Jazz Impressions Of The USA* (Columbia 1957)★★★, *Jazz Goes To Junior College* (Columbia 1957)★★★, *Dave Digs Disney* (Columbia 1957)★★, *Dave Brubeck Plays And Plays And Plays . . .* (Fantasy 1958)★★★, *Re-union* (Fantasy 1958)★★★, *Dave Brubeck Quartet In Europe* (Columbia 1958)★★★, *Newport 1958* (Columbia 1958)★★★, *Jazz Impressions Of Eurasia* (Columbia 1958)★★★, *Two Nights At The Black Hawk* (Fantasy 1959)★★★, *Gone With The Wind* (Columbia 1959)★★★, *Time Out Featuring 'Take Five'* (Columbia 1959)★★★★★, *Brubeck A La Mode* (Fantasy 1960)★★★, *Southern Scene* (Columbia 1960)★★★, *The Riddle* (Columbia 1960)★★★, with the New York Philharmonic Orchestra *Bernstein Plays Brubeck Plays Bernstein* (Columbia 1960)★★★, *Brubeck And Rushing* (Columbia 1960)★★★, *Near-Myth* (Fantasy 1961)★★★, with Carmen McRae *Tonight Only!* (Columbia 1961)★★★, *Time Further Out* (Columbia 1961)★★★, *Countdown - Time In Outer Space* (Columbia 1962)★★★, *Bossa Nova USA* (Columbia 1963)★★★, *Dave Brubeck Quartet At Carnegie Hall* (Columbia 1963)★★★★, *Brandenburg Gate: Revisited* (Columbia 1963)★★★, *The Great Concerts* (Columbia 1963)★★★★, *Time Changes* (Columbia 1964)★★★★, *Jazz Impressions Of Japan* (Columbia 1964)★★★, *Jazz Impressions Of New York* (Columbia 1965)★★★★, *Take Five* (Columbia 1965)★★★, *Angel Eyes* (Columbia 1965)★★★, *My Favorite Things* (Columbia 1966)★★★, *Time In* (Columbia 1966)★★★, *Anything Goes! Dave Brubeck Quartet Plays Cole Porter* (Columbia 1966)★★★, *Bravo! Brubeck!* (Columbia 1967)★★★, *Jackpot* (Columbia 1967)★★★, *The Last Time We Saw Paris* (Columbia 1968)★★★, with Gerry Mulligan *Compadres* (Columbia 1969)★★★, *Brubeck In Amsterdam* (Columbia 1969)★★★, *Brubeck/Mulligan/Cincinnati* (MCA 1971)★★★★, *Adventures In Time* (1972)★★★, *Two Generations Of Brubeck* (Atlantic 1973)★★★, *We're All Together For The First Time* (Atlantic 1973)★★★, with Paul Desmond *Brubeck And Desmond - 1975: The Duets* (Horizon 1975)★★★, *All The Things We Are* (Atlantic 1975)★★★, *The Dave Brubeck Quartet 25th Anniversary Reunion* (A&M 1976)★★★, *Live At Montreaux* (Tomato 1978)★★★, *Paper Moon* (Concord 1982)★★★, *Concord On A Summer Night* (Concord 1982)★★, *For Iola* (Concord 1985)★★, *Reflections* (Concord 1986)★★★, *Blue Rondo* (Concord 1987)★★★, *Moscow Night* (Concord 1987)★★★, *New Wine* (Limelight 1988)★★★, *Trio Brubeck* (Limelight 1988)★★★,

Quiet As The Moon (Limelight 1991)★★★, *Once When I Was Very Young* (Limelight 1992)★★★★, *Nightshift* (Telarc 1994)★★★, *Young Lions & Old Tigers* (Telarc 1995)★★★★, *A Dave Brubeck Christmas* (Telarc 1996)★, *In Their Own Sweet Way* (Telarc 1997)★★★, *So What's New?* (Telarc 1998)★★★.

● COMPILATIONS: *Dave Brubeck's Greatest Hits* (Columbia 1966)★★★★, *Twenty-Four Classic Early Recordings* (Fantasy 1982)★★★★, *Collection: Dave Brubeck* (Deja Vu 1985)★★★, *The Essential Dave Brubeck* (Sony 1991)★★★★, *Time Signatures: A Career Retrospective* 4-CD box set (Columbia/Legacy 1993)★★★★★, *This Is Jazz No. 3* (Columbia/Legacy 1996)★★★.

● VIDEOS: *Musical Portrait* (BBC Video 1988).

● FURTHER READING: *It's About Time: The Dave Brubeck Story*, Fred M. Hall.

BRUCE, JACK

b. John Symon Asher, 14 May 1943, Glasgow, Lanarkshire, Scotland. Formerly a piano student at the Royal Scottish Academy of Music, he was awarded a RSAM scholarship for cello and composition. Bruce has utilized his brilliant bass playing to cross and bridge free jazz and heavy rock, during spells with countless musical conglomerations. As a multi-instrumentalist he also has a great fondness for the piano, cello and acoustic bass, and is highly accomplished on all these instruments. At 19 years of age he moved to London and joined the R&B scene, first with Alexis Korner's band and then as a key member of the pioneering Graham Bond Organisation. Following brief stints with John Mayall's Bluesbreakers and Manfred Mann, Bruce joined with his former colleague in the Bond band, Ginger Baker, who, together with Eric Clapton, formed Cream. The comparatively short career of this pivotal band reached musical heights that have rarely been bettered. During this time Bruce displayed and developed a strident vocal style and considerable prowess as a harmonica player. However, it was his imaginative and sometimes breathtaking bass playing that appealed. He popularized an instrument that had previously not featured prominently in rock music. Dozens of young players in the 70s and 80s cited Bruce as being the reason for them taking up the bass guitar. Upon the breakup of Cream, Bruce released an exemplary solo album, *Songs For A Tailor.* A host of top jazz/rock musicians were present on what was his most successful album. On this record he continued the songwriting partnership with Pete Brown that had already produced a number of Cream classics, 'White Room', 'Politician', 'I Feel Free', 'Sunshine Of Your Love' and 'SWLABR' ('She Was Like A Bearded Rainbow'). Brown's imaginative and surreal lyrics were the perfect foil to Bruce's furious and complex bass patterns. Evocative songs such as 'Theme For An Imaginary Western' and 'The Weird Of Hermiston' enabled Bruce's ability as a vocalist to shine, with piercing clarity. Throughout the early 70s, a series of excellent albums and constantly changing line-ups gave him a high profile. His involvement with Tony Williams' Lifetime and his own 'supergroup', West, Bruce And Laing, further enhanced his position in the jazz and rock world. A further aggregation, Jack Bruce And Friends, included jazz guitarist Larry Coryell and former Jimi Hendrix drummer Mitch Mitchell. During this busy and fruitful period Bruce found time to add vocals to Carla Bley's classic album *Escalator Over The Hill*, and Bley was also a member of the 1975 version of the Jack Bruce Band. In 1979 he toured as a member of John McLaughlin's Mahavishnu Orchestra.

The 80s started with a new Jack Bruce Band which featured former Bakerloo, Colosseum and Humble Pie guitarist Dave 'Clem' Clempson and David Sancious. They found particular favour in Germany and played there regularly. The ill-fated heavy rock trio BLT formed in 1981 with guitarist Robin Trower and drummer Bill Lordan but disintegrated after two albums; their debut, *BLT*, reached the US Top 40. During the 80s Bruce kept a low profile after having experienced severe drug problems in the mid-70s. In 1987 the perplexing album *Automatic* appeared. This obviously low-budget work had Bruce accompanied by a Fairlight machine, an odd coupling for a musician whose previous collections had consistently teamed him with highly talented drummers. Much more impressive was 1990's *A Question Of Time* which attempted to restore Bruce's now lapsed career to its former glory. Other than his long-term admirers Bruce has found it difficult to reach a wide new audience. Those that have followed his career understand his major shifts from jazz to heavy rock, but his position in today's musical climate is hard to place. His vocal work accompanied by his emotional piano playing has been his particularly strong point of late. In 1994 he formed BBM, with Gary Moore and Baker. Two parts Cream, the unit might have been more aptly called Semi-Skimmed. This was his most rock-orientated project for many years and clearly showed that Bruce was in sparkling form, fit and well. Bruce remains forever (probably because of Cream) the most renowned and respected of all rock bassists, although his Mingus-style bass lines make him a perfect choice for any jazz ensemble.

● ALBUMS: *Songs For A Tailor* (Polydor 1969)★★★★★, *Things We Like* (Polydor 1970)★★★, *Harmony Row* (Polydor 1971)★★★★, *Out Of The Storm* (Polydor 1974)★★★★, *How's Tricks* (RSO 1977)★★★, *I've Always Wanted To Do This* (Epic 1980)★★★, with Robin Trower *Truce* (Chrysalis 1982)★★, *Automatic* (President 1987)★★, *A Question Of Time* (Epic 1990)★★★★, And Friends *Live At The Bottom Line* (Traditional Line 1992)★★★, *Something Else* (1993)★★★, *Cities Of the Heart* (CMP 1994)★★★★, with Paul Jones *Alexis Korner Memorial Concert Volume 1* (Indigo 1995)★★★, *Live On The Test* (Strange Fruit 1998)★★★★.

● COMPILATIONS: *Jack Bruce At His Best* (Polydor 1972)★★★, *Greatest Hits* (Polydor 1980)★★★, *Willpower* (Polydor 1989)★★★★, *The Collection* (Castle 1992)★★★.

BRUFORD, BILL

b. 17 May 1949, Sevenoaks, Kent, England. A founder-member of Yes in 1968, Bruford left the group four years later at the height of its popularity. An accomplished drummer, he opted to join King Crimson, where his skills were put to even greater test, and remained there until leader Robert Fripp dissolved the line-up in 1974. Bruford subsequently worked with Pavlov's Dog, before forming the jazz-rock ensemble, UK. The initial line-up also featured guitarist Allan Holdsworth, who joined the drummer for his solo debut, *Feels Good To Me*. The two musicians then broke away to found Bruford, which was completed by Dave Stewart (keyboards) and Jeff Berlin (bass). However, the artist's independent career was sidelined in 1981 when Fripp invited him to join the reconstituted King Crimson. Following the second collapse of King Crimson, Bruford toured with Al Di Meola and David Torn. Bruford subsequently formed his own jazz-based group, Bill Bruford's Earthworks, which included keyboardist Django Bates and saxophonist Iain Ballamy. He became involved with the reunion of Yes in the late 80s, touring and recording under the banner of Anderson, Bruford, Wakeman And Howe until such legal matters as to the ownership of the Yes name had been resolved, becoming once more the Yes drummer in 1990, and he was part of the re-formed King Crimson for *Thrak* in 1995. One of the finest drummers in British rock, Bruford continues to progress, rather than rest on his laurels.

● ALBUMS: *Feels Good To Me* (Polydor 1978)★★, *One Of A Kind* (Polydor 1979)★★, *The Bruford Tapes* (Editions EG 1980)★★★★, *Gradually Going Tornado* (Editions EG 1980)★★★, *Earthworks* (Editions EG 1987)★★★★, *Dig* (Editions EG 1989)★★★, *All Heaven Broke Loose* (1991)★★★, *Earthworks Live* (Virgin 1994)★★, with Eddie Gomez, Ralph Towner*If Summer Had Its Ghosts* (Discipline 1997)★★.

● COMPILATIONS: *Master Strokes 1978-1985* (Editions EG 1986)★★★.

BRUNINGHAUS, RAINER

b. 21 November 1949, Bad Pyrmont, Germany. Bruninghaus studied piano and music at Cologne Conservatory (1973-6). After graduation he joined Volker Kriegel's group Spectrum before moving on to Eberhard Weber's influential band Colours (1975-80). Though it infuriated Weber when critics sometimes spoke of the band as a European counterpart to Weather Report, there were times when Bruninghaus's compositions leaned very close to the Americans' style, particularly on Colour's later albums. He made a crucial contribution to the success of the band both in composition and in his keyboard playing, which demonstrated great technical facility and a keen sensitivity. When he left Colours he worked with Manfred Schoof's quintet, then in 1981 formed his own trio with Markus Stockhausen (trumpet) and Fredy Studer (drums). Their *Continuum* won the German Record Critics' Prize in 1984. Throughout his career Bruninghaus has worked with a wide range of musicians including Kenny Wheeler, Albert Mangelsdorff, Toots Thielemans, Archie Shepp, Carla Bley and Bobby McFerrin. He composes and arranges for big bands and has continued with classical composition. When there is opportunity, he also teaches at a music college in Cologne.

● ALBUMS: with Colours: *Yellow Fields* (ECM 1975)★★★★, *Silent Feet* (ECM 1977)★★★, *Little Movements* (ECM 1980)★★★★, *Freigeweht* (1980)★★★, *Continuum* (1983)★★★★.

BRUNIS, GEORG

b. George Clarence Brunies, 6 February 1900, New Orleans, Louisiana, USA, d. 19 November 1974. The best-known member of a distinguished musical family, Brunis (who changed the spelling of his first and last names on the advice of a numerologist) had played trombone from his pre-teen years. In New Orleans he worked with Leon Roppolo and Elmer Schoebel; by 1920 he was working in Chicago with Paul Mares's Friars Society Orchestra. The band later became known as the New Orleans Rhythm Kings but Brunis moved on, joining Ted Lewis in 1924, with whom he remained for a decade. From 1934 he worked extensively in New York, recording and playing in numerous bands and playing at clubs, especially Nick's, where he was a semi-permanent fixture through the late 30s and into the 40s. From then until the end of the 60s he worked steadily, partnering Art Hodes, Wild Bill Davison, Muggsy Spanier and others, making some classic recordings. A tough, gutsy player, not above playing to the audience, Brunis was a skilful trombonist who preferred to stay within a framework that was far more limited than his technical ability warranted.

● ALBUMS: *King Of The Tailgate Trombone* 10-inch album (Commodore 1950)★★★, *Georg Brunis & The Original New Orleans Rhythm Kings* 10-inch album (Riverside 1954)★★★★, with Wild Bill Davison *Reunion In Brass* (1973)★★★.

● COMPILATIONS: with Davison *Davison-Brunis Sessions Volume 1* (Decca 1980)★★★, *Davison-Brunis Sessions Volume 2* (Decca 1980)★★★, *Friars Inn Revisited* (Delmark 1990)★★★.

BRUNSKILL, BILL

b. 1920, London, England. He began playing the guitar as a teenager, receiving instruction at the Bethnal Green Men's Institute. Soon, he was playing at dances in London's East End, the kind known locally as 'tanner hops'. During World War II he switched to trumpet, inspired by Louis Armstrong and Muggsy Spanier. After leaving the armed forces he played with Cy Laurie and began organizing jamming sessions in and around London. Having formed his own band, he played long residencies at two Surrey public houses, the Fighting Cocks in Kingston-on-Thames and the Lord Napier in Thornton Heath. He introduced many young musicians into his band over the years, among them Mike Pointon, Mike Sherborne, Les Allen, Hugh Crozier, Bill Stagg and, most notably, Sammy Rimington. In the mid-90s Brunskill was still leading his band, still blowing fiery Armstrong-inspired trumpet, and still at the Lord Napier. His dedication to jazz was recognized in 1995 by a television documentary called *Whatever Happened To Bill Brunskill*.

BRYAN, MIKE

b. Michael Neely Bryan, 1916, Byhalia, Mississippi, USA, d. 20 August 1972. A self-taught guitarist, Bryan played with various bands in the south before spending some time in Chicago where, in 1935, he played with Red Nichols. In the late 30s he had his own band in Mississippi, then joined Benny Goodman in the early 40s and also played in other swing era bands including Artie Shaw's. After military service during World War II, Bryan played with several small groups including some led by emerging bebop musicians, including Dizzy Gillespie and Charlie Parker. After a brief return visit to Goodman, he settled in Los Angeles, playing in studio bands. He was involved in the short-lived television show sponsored by the Goodyear Tyre Co., both playing and as host. In the early 70s he returned to performing as a touring musician. Content to be a relatively anonymous member of the rhythm sections of the bands with which he played, Bryan remains best known for his stint with Goodman and also for the Goodyear television shows, preserved today on video.

BRYANT, CLORA

b. *c*.1929, Denison, Texas, USA. Bryant began playing trumpet when her brother was away in the army and his instrument was available to her. She played in a school dance band and then in an all-girl orchestra at Prairie View College in Houston, Texas. Later, she attended UCLA, then left music and education behind for a short time to work in domestic service. This quickly palled and she returned to playing trumpet, and sometimes drums, in and around Los Angeles. She accompanied singer Billy Daniels, and played in the Darlings Of Rhythm, an all-female band, and various other groups. In 1947, during Dizzy Gillespie's engagement at Billy Berg's club, where he was with Charlie Parker, Bryant heard the frequent broadcasts made from the club. Entranced by Gillespie's playing, she redirected her musical career from this point onwards. However, marriage and the birth of her first child kept her from music for a couple of years, but she was soon active again, sitting in at after-hours sessions with musicians such as Lee Morgan. She appeared on television in the 50s and made an album, but the decade was difficult in Los Angeles and she drifted into regular employment with bands in Denver, Colorado, and on tour, notably a two-year gig with Billy Williams. In 1964 she formed a double act with her brother, but for most of the rest of the decade and into the 70s she freelanced, spending much time bringing up her four children. By the late 70s she was studying music and playing whenever she had the opportunity, including gigs with Bill Berry's LA Band. A lively and engaging entertainer, doing Louis Armstrong and Rose Murphy impersonations when the fancy takes her, Bryant is a thoroughly convincing bop trumpeter. Her admiration for Gillespie has not wavered since she first heard him in 1947, although there has never been any hint that in her trumpet playing she needs to fall back upon mimicry; hers is too rich a talent for that.

● ALBUMS: *The Gal With The Horn* (Mode 1957)★★★.

BRYANT, JIMMY

b. 2 June 1929, Tarrant, Birmingham, Alabama, USA. Bryant began singing at the age of five and six years later was touring Florida with the Dixie Boys Choir. He was educated at Birmingham-Southern College and the Birmingham Conservatory of Music before receiving a scholarship in composition at the New England Conservatory of Music. In 1953 he began working in New York City as an arranger, orchestrator, singer and after three years moved to California where he worked as a string bass player in various hotels and clubs, including Puccini's, which was then owned by Frank Sinatra. During this period, he also worked as a group singer, making records, movies, and appearing on television. In this capacity he performed with many leading entertainers of the period, including Sinatra, Nat 'King' Cole, Dean Martin, Fred Astaire, Bing Crosby, Dinah Shore, Doris Day and Rosemary Clooney. In 1959 he ghosted the singing voice of actor Richard Beymer, who played the role of Tony in the film version of *West Side Story*, famously singing 'Maria'. Another 'unknown' credit, also heard by millions, is Bryant's singing in the group that performed the theme for the 60s television series *Batman* - 'that's actually me singing the G above high C at the end!' During the following decades Bryant worked as an orchestrator, arranger, composer, most notably for John Williams and James Horner, and orchestrated hundreds of television shows and television movies, and in 1990 won an EMMY Achievement Award for orchestrating *Stephen King's 'It'*. He composed and orchestrated many projects for various Disney theme parks and also orchestrated and arranged for numerous production shoes in Las Vegas, as well as the Lido de Paris, in Paris. For several years he had a company, Jimmy Bryant Creative Music Service, and composed music for radio and television commercials; he wrote jingles for clients including motor companies, wine and beer makers. The most prominent of these was the theme for a Toyota advertisement written in 1973. Entitled 'Come Run With Me', it was developed into a full song and recorded by Al Martino and the Brady Bunch, among others. In the late 90s, when many of his age might have decided to drift into leisurely retirement, Bryant was hard at work on a new major project, this time for Tokyo Disneyland.

BRYANT, RAY

b. 24 December 1931, Philadelphia, Pennsylvania, USA. Coming from a musical family gave Bryant an advantage - his mother played piano and his sister sang in a gospel choir. He started on bass, but passed it to his older brother Tom, in order to play piano. The Bryant Brothers became the house band for Philadelphia's Blue Note Club, where they played with Charlie Parker and Miles Davis. It was these contacts that led to recordings with Davis, Sonny Rollins and Carmen McRae. He led a trio at New York's Village Vanguard in 1959. In 1960 he had a surprise hit with the infectious and memorable 'Little Susie', named after his daughter, and 'Cubano

Chant' and 'Slow Freight'. Initially inspired by the style of Teddy Wilson, Bryant's gospel inflections give his playing a modern, rootsy edge. For a number of years much of his work was unavailable; fortunately, in recent years, notably with the advent of the compact disc, Bryant's highly underrated work has been reissued. He continues to perform and record prolifically as both a soloist and leader of a trio. *Through The Years Volumes 1 & 2* was an excellent recording, covering Bryant's entire career, and demonstrating, if anything, that Bryant's technique is more fluid and improved with age.

● ALBUMS: with Betty Carter *Meet Betty Carter And Ray Bryant* (Epic 1955)★★★★, *Ray Bryant Trio* (Epic 1956)★★★, *Alone With The Blues* (New Jazz 1959)★★★★, *Madison Time* (Columbia 1960)★★★★, *Con Alma* (Columbia 1961)★★★★, *Ray Bryant Plays* (Signature 1960)★★★, *Little Susie* (Columbia 1962)★★★★, *Dancing The Big Twist* (Columbia 1962)★★★, *Hollywood Jazz Beat* (Columbia 1962)★★★, *Groove House* (Sue 1963)★★★★, *Live At Basin Street* (Sue 1964)★★★, *Cold Turkey* (Sue 1964)★★★, *Ray Bryant Soul* (Sue 1964)★★★★, *Gotta Travel On* (Cadet 1966)★★★, *Slow Feight* (Cadet 1967)★★★, *Lonesome Traveler* (Cadet (Cadet 1967)★★★, *Ray Bryant Touch* (Cadet 1967)★★★★, *Take A Bryant Step* (Cadet 1967)★★★, *Up Above The Rock* (Cadet 1968)★★★, *Sound Ray* (Cadet 1969)★★★, *Alone At Montreaux* (Atlantic 1973)★★★, *Hot Turkey* (Black And Blue 1975)★★★, *Montreaux 77* (Original Jazz Classics 1978)★★★, *Here's Ray Bryant* (Pablo 1982)★★★, *Ray Bryant* (1982)★★★, *Solo Flight* (Pablo 1982)★★★, *Potpourri* (Pablo 1982)★★★, *All Blues* (Pablo 1982)★★★, *Ray Bryant Trio* (JVC 1987)★★★, *Trio* (1987)★★★, *Con Alma* (Columbia 1988)★★★, *Plays Basie And Ellington* (Emarcy 1988)★★★, *Blue Moods* (Emarcy 1989)★★★, *All Mine All Yours* (Emarcy 1990)★★★, *Through The Years (Volumes 1 & 2) - The 60th Birthday Recordings* (Emarcy 1992)★★★★, *No Problem* (Emarcy 1995)★★★★, *Ray's Tribute To His Jazz Piano Friends* (JMI 1998)★★★.

● COMPILATIONS: *Best Of Ray Bryant* (Pablo 1982)★★★★.

Bryant, Willie

b. 30 August 1908, New Orleans, Louisiana, USA, d. 9 February 1964. Starting out as a singer and dancer, Bryant worked extensively in vaudeville during the 20s and early 30s. At one time he partnered Bessie Smith and sang with Buck And Bubbles. In 1934 from the remnants of the Benny Carter orchestra, he formed a big band that stayed in existence for four years, enjoying some success with engagements at the Savoy Ballroom. After it folded, he returned to work on the stage and on radio. In 1946 Bryant re-formed his band, which this time lasted only two years. Although his indifferent singing was heavily promoted, performances by Bryant's bands were always interesting because he hired outstanding jazz players. Among his sidemen were Carter, Cozy Cole, Eddie Durham, David 'Panama' Francis, Taft Jordan, Ben Webster and Teddy Wilson. Unfortunately, the group's potential was never fully realized, largely because he depended upon arrangers who were hired casually and so unable to develop a personality for the band.

Bryden, Beryl

b. 11 May 1920, Norwich, Norfolk, England, d. 14 July 1998, London, England. In the mid-40s Bryden was active in local jazz circles, organizing concerts and club dates and singing with various bands. In London in the late 40s she sang and played washboard with many of the important bands of the British trad-jazz explosion, including those of George Webb, Freddy Randall, Alex Welsh, Humphrey Lyttelton and Chris Barber. She made her recording debut in 1948 on Randall's 'Hurry Me Down', and formed her own Beryl's Backroom Boys to reproduce the music of the pre-bop era. Despite all this activity and a growing following, singing was only a part-time occupation for her, and it was not until the early 50s that she became a full-time performer. In the 50s and 60s her career was perhaps stronger in mainland Europe than the UK, and she played with visiting Americans including Sidney Bechet and Mary Lou Williams. In 1954 she played washboard on a cover version of Lead Belly's 'Rock Island Line' from Barber's *New Orleans Joy* album. Featuring skiffle singer Lonnie Donegan on vocals, the single went on to sell two million copies and reached the US Top 10. Bryden achieved her biggest hit, 'Gimme A Pigfoot And A Bottle Of Beer', in 1961 during the short-lived 'trad' boom. She waited until the early 70s before visiting the USA. In the 70s she toured extensively, sometimes as a solo artist or with her Jazzaholics Anonymous group, other times in the company of jazz musicians such as Pete Allen and Monty Sunshine. A robust performer of songs from the classic period of the blues and vaudeville, Bryden's popularity with audiences was matched by the fellow-feeling she induced in her musical companions (a quality singers often lack). Apart from performing, Bryden also developed a second-string career as a good jazz photographer. Her retirement in the 80s was not taken too seriously, either by her fellow artists or by Bryden herself. In the early 90s she was still on the road and delighting her many fans and friends, before her death from cancer in 1998.

● ALBUMS: *Way Down Yonder In New Orleans* (1975)★★★, *Basin Street Blues* (Columbia 1991)★★★, *Big Daddy* (Columbia 1991)★★★★, *Two Moods Of Beryl Bryden* (Audiophile 1994)★★★★.

Buckner, Milt

b. 10 July 1915, St. Louis, Missouri, USA, d. 27 July 1977. Orphaned as a child, Buckner was taught music by an uncle in Detroit. Playing piano and arranging for local bands, he attracted the attention of McKinney's Cotton Pickers, for whom he wrote arrangements. In November 1941 he joined Lionel Hampton's newly formed big band, acting as pianist and staff arranger, and remained there for seven years. For the next two years he led his own short-lived big band, and then rejoined Hampton. It was at this time that Buckner began to concentrate on playing organ, and he worked as a solo or in harness with Jo Jones, Sam Woodyard and Illinois Jacquet, frequently returning to Hampton for record and concert dates. From the early 30s Buckner had experimented with a technique of piano playing that became known as the 'locked hands' style and was later developed by George Shearing and Buckner himself. Buckner's playing was always strongly rhythmic and any band of which he was a member was guaranteed to swing, but his solos, especially on organ, were often little more than technical exercises.

● ALBUMS: *Milt Buckner Piano* 10-inch album (Savoy 1953)★★★★, *Rockin' With Milt* (Capitol 1955)★★★★, *Rockin' Hammond* (Capitol 1956)★★★★, *Send Me Softly* (Capitol 1958)★★★, *Mighty High* (Argo 1960)★★★, *Please, Mr. Organ Player* (Argo 1961)★★★, *Midnight Mood* (Argo 1962)★★★, *The New World Of Milt Buckner* (Bethlehem 1962)★★★★, *Milt Buckner Plays Chords* (1966)★★★, with Buddy Tate *Midnight Slows, Volume 1* (Black And Blue 1967)★★★, with Tate *Crazy Rhythm* (1968)★★★, *Locked Hands* (1968)★★★, *Them There Eyes* (Black And Blue 1968)★★★★, *More Chords* (1969)★★, *Birthday Party For H.G.B.S.* (1970)★★, *Milt Buckner And Jo Jones* (1971)★★★, with Illinois Jacquet *Genius At Work* (1971)★★★, *Rockin' Again* (1972)★★★, *Black And Blue Stomp* (1973)★★★★, *Requiem Pour Un Chat* (1973)★★★, with Arnett Cobb, Clarence 'Gatemouth' Brown *Midnight Slows, Volume 3* (1973)★★★, with Tate *Midnight Slows, Volume 5* (1974)★★, *Blues For Diane* (1974)★★★, *Green Onions* (1975)★★, *A Night At The Popcorn* (1975)★★★, *Pianistically Yours* (1975)★★★, with Cobb *Midnight Slows, Volume 6* (1976)★★★, *The Gruntin' Genius* (1976)★★★, *Green Onions* (Black And Blue 1977)★★★★, *Boogie Woogie USA* (1977)★★★, with Guy Lafitte *Midnight Slows Volume 7* (1977)★★★, with Lionel Hampton *Blues In Toulouse* (1977)★★★, with Tate *Midnight Slows, Volume 7* (1977)★★★, *Unforgettable* (MPS 1979)★★★, *Rockin' Hammond* (Capitol 1983)★★★, *Please Mr Organ Player* (1992)★★★.

● COMPILATIONS: *The Early Years, 1947-53* (Official 1985)★★★.

BUCKNER, TEDDY

b. 16 July 1909, Sherman, Texas, USA, d. 25 September 1994, Los Angeles, California, USA. A fervent disciple of Louis Armstrong from his youth, Buckner remained so all his life. Although his technique was strong enough for him to have worked in whatever style he chose, he deliberately modelled his trumpet playing upon that of his idol, even when it became unfashionable. During the 20s and early 30s Buckner worked mostly in California with bands such as those led by Sonny Clay, Curtis Mosby, Buck Clayton (with whom he visited China in 1934) and Lionel Hampton. When Hampton left California, in order to take up an offer to join Benny Goodman, Buckner took over the band. In the 40s he worked with several stylistically disparate bands, among them Benny Carter, Gerald Wilson and Johnny Otis, although he always stuck to his favoured style. In the early 50s he was with Kid Ory's band and was playing as well as ever. In the mid-60s Buckner became a popular attraction at Disneyland, California, playing old favourites and popular songs of the day.

● ALBUMS: *Teddy Buckner* (1955), with Sidney Bechet *Parisian Encounter* (Vogue 1958)★★★★, *An Evening With Teddy Buckner* (1978)★★★, *La Grand Parade De La Nouvelle Orleans* (Vogue 1988)★★★, *Teddy Buckner At The Cresendo* (Dixieland Jubilee 1988)★★, *Teddy Buckner In Concert* (Dixieland Jubilee 1988)★★, *Martinique* (Vogue 1989)★★★.

BUDD, ROY

b. 14 March 1947, Mitcham, Surrey, England, d. 7 August 1993. A self-taught pianist, Budd appeared on television and in London's theatreland when only 12 years old. In his teenage years he formed a trio that at one time included bassist Dave Holland, and was for a time house pianist at one of London's leading jazz venues, the Bull's Head at Barnes. He continued to appear on television and on stage and was soon lured to write music for films, first in the UK and, later, in Hollywood. In addition to writing film scores, Budd also composed classical music. His scores include *Soldier Blue* (1970), *Get Carter* (1971), *Fear Is The Key* (1972) and in the 90s he scored for the re-release of the silent classic, *Phantom Of The Opera*. In the 70s he married singer Caterina Valente but they were later divorced. His sudden death, from a brain haemorrhage, came while he was still at work on a symphony. Stylistically, Budd's jazz playing owed a considerable debt to Oscar Peterson, yet while he may have started out as a copyist, his maturity brought an individual stamp beautifully exemplified on seemingly unpromising material such as that displayed on a 1989 set of Christmas songs.

● ALBUMS: *Budd 'N' Bossa Nova* (60s)★★★, *Roy Budd Plays And Conducts Great Themes* (60s)★★★, *Fear Is The Key* (70s)★★★, *Have A Jazzy Christmas* (Master Mix 1989)★★★.

BUDDLE, ERROL

b. Errol Leslie Buddle, 29 April 1928, Adelaide, South Australia, Australia. Buddle became a professional musician in the mid-40s, playing tenor saxophone and other reed instruments with various bands including that led by Jack Brokensha, with whom he recorded. In the early 50s he left Australia and for a while took up residence in North America, playing mostly in Canada where, in 1954, he was reunited with Brokensha when they formed the Australian Jazz Quartet together with Bryce Rohde and Dick Healey. Buddle's plangent style is always well in evidence in his tenor playing, but he also offers intriguing colourings in his use of a wide range of alternative instruments, including the bassoon, on which he is especially adept.

● ALBUMS: *Buddle's Doubles* (M7 1977)★★.

BUDWIG, MONTY

b. 26 December 1929, Pender, Nebraska, USA, d. 9 March 1992, Los Angeles, USA. Budwig began playing bass while still at high school and turned professional soon after graduating. His first name-band engagement was a brief spell with Vido Musso in 1951, after which he served in the armed forces where he played in an air force band. On his discharge Budwig moved to California where he remained based, playing with bands led by Barney Kessel, Zoot Sims, Red Norvo and Woody Herman. He also worked frequently with Shelly Manne and made occasional tours with Benny

Goodman, but concentrated on studio work and played jazz whenever the opportunity presented itself. Either as a member of Bill Berry's LA band, or as house musician for Concord Records, Budwig made his mark on the west coast scene of the 70s and 80s. A fluid, strong and rhythmic player, his presence in any rhythm section was a guarantee of impeccable timekeeping and solid swing.

BUGGER ALL STARS

The Bugger All Stars were formed in London in 1980. It was one of the few bands keeping the faith of free improvisation at a time when this uncommercial genre was probably at its most unsaleable. Mike Hames (alto saxophone, bass clarinet) invited Hugh Metcalfe, (guitar, electronics) to form a band with him. Metcalfe suggested Jim Lebaigue (drums) and Lebaigue recommended Phil Wachsmann, (violin, electronics, miscellaneous instruments). Originally inspired by Eric Dolphy (hence his choice of instruments) and an authority on Albert Ayler, Hames is not an obvious follower of either, and the band has more in common with the abstract Improvised Music tradition of Europe (and, perhaps, with the AACM school of Chicago in its concern for exploring sounds and textures rather than melody, harmony and rhythms) than with the fiery, headlong music of the 60s New Thing. The other three remain active on the improvised music scene but Hames retired from playing in 1986 when he began a degree course.

● ALBUMS: *Bugger All Stars* (1981)★★★, *Bonzo Bites Back* (1983)★★★.

BULL, SANDY

b. 25 February 1941, New York, USA. Having learned to play guitar while in his teens, Bull gravitated to banjo, which he studied under Erik Darling, one of the instrument's leading practitioners. The young musician became immersed in folk circles while studying at Boston, and later began adapting such forms to accommodate elements drawn from different traditions, including jazz, Arabic and Indian. He returned to New York in 1961 where he worked with the Washington Square Singers and performed solo in Greenwich Village cafes. His debut, *Sandy Bull (Fantasias For Guitar And Banjo)*, featured accompaniment from Billy Higgins, drummer with *avant garde* saxophonist Ornette Coleman. Its highlight, arguably, was 'Blend', a lengthy composition based on modal scale improvisation and hinged to a revelatory pattern of drone-like figures. This inventive, freewheeling style was maintained on ensuing releases, notably *E Pluribus Unum*, which contained two pieces, 'No Deposit, No Return' and 'Electric Blend', a self-explanatory adaptation of the earlier opus. Bull's career was badly undermined by drug abuse; he re-emerged in 1972 with the typically enthralling *Demolition Derby*, wryly denying his death in attendant interviews, and in 1988 he was featured in an acting role in the film *'68*, which also starred Neil Young. Despite the brevity of Bull's musical output, the innovatory nature of his work should not be underemphasized.

● ALBUMS: *Sandy Bull (Fantasias For Guitar And Banjo)* (1963)★★★, *Inventions* (1965)★★★, *E Pluribus Unum* (1967)★★★★, *Demolition Derby* (1972)★★★★.

● COMPILATIONS: *The Essential Sandy Bull* (1978)★★★.

BULLOCK, CHICK

b. 16 September 1908, Mutte, Massachusetts, USA, d. 15 September 1981, California, USA. Bullock's English parents had wanted him to become a doctor, but he was attracted to vaudeville and became a singer. He began as a time-filler, singing to a series of pictures changing on a screen behind him. This led naturally enough to small parts in silent movies. He also provided vocals for records by Duke Ellington, Luis Russell, Cab Calloway and others, and turned down an offer from Paul Whiteman to become his vocalist. A disfiguring eye ailment forced him to concentrate on records and radio broadcasts rather than live appearances. During the 30s he worked with his Levee Loungers which was strictly a house band for ARC - and recorded prolifically. He was able to attract a stream of fine musicians including trumpeters Bunny Berigan and Bill Coleman, trombonists Jack Teagarden and Tommy Dorsey, plus Jimmy Dorsey, Joe Venuti and Eddie Lang. The musicians' strike of the 40s ended Bullock's recording activities. Unwilling to work with only vocal groups, he moved to California and took up a new career in real estate.

BUNCH, JOHN

b. 1 December 1921, Tipton, Indiana, USA. After studying piano as a child, Bunch began playing semi-professionally while barely in his teenage years. Through listening to records he learned to appreciate the work of musicians such as Fats Waller, Count Basie and Duke Ellington. As he later recalled for interviewer Martin Richards, while still a child he was taken to hear the Basie band, which then included Lester Young, Jo Jones and Jimmy Rushing. Despite this early start, Bunch remained on the fringes of the jazz scene until he was well into his 30s. Part of the problem lay in the effects of the Depression on his family and his need to try to earn a living. With America's entry into World War II, Bunch enlisted in the air force, was shot down and served out the war in a prison camp. In the post-war years Bunch's early tuition was shown to be inadequate and his poor reading ability meant that he was unable to gain a place in a music college. However, he persisted in his ambition to become a professional musician and endured several years scuffling for low pay until he began to make an impact on the Los Angeles jazz scene, where he worked with Georgie Auld. In the mid- to late 50s he became well known through his work with the bands of Woody Herman, Benny Goodman, Maynard Ferguson and Buddy Rich. In the 60s and 70s he recorded and sometimes played club and festival dates with several leading jazzmen, including Goodman, Zoot Sims and Gene Krupa and also led his own group. From the mid-60s into the early 70s he was also active outside jazz, serving for more than seven years as Tony Bennett's musical director. In the 80s he continued his round of recording sessions and live performances, usually in company with important mainstream artists, among them Joe 'Flip' Phillips and Scott Hamilton. Highly regarded by his fellow musicians, Bunch is one of an unfortunately long list of jazzmen whose work is not as well-known to audiences as his talent deserves. Festival appearances in many parts of the world in the late 80s and 90s, and some excellent records, have helped to improve his profile in the jazz market.

● ALBUMS: *John Bunch Plays Kurt Weill* (Chiaroscuro 1975)★★★★, *John's Bunch* (1975)★★★, *John's Other Bunch* (1977)★★★, *Slick Funk* (1977)★★, *It's Love In The Spring* (1977)★★★, *The Swinging Young Scott Hamilton* (1977)★★★, with Joe 'Flip' Phillips *A Sound Investment* (1987)★★★, *Jubilee* (Audiophole 1988)★★★, *The Best Thing For You* (Concord 1988)★★★★, with Bucky Pizzarelli *NY Swing* (LRC 1992)★★★, with Phil Flanigan *Struttin'* (Arbors 1997)★★★, *John Bunch Solo: Arbors Piano Series AT Mike's Place, Vol. 1* (Arbors 1998)★★★.

BUNKER, LARRY

b. 4 November 1928, Long Beach, California, USA. A gifted percussionist, Bunker's career has ably straddled the worlds of jazz and classical music, together with the commercial demands of film and television studios. On the west coast in the early 50s, he played drums with Gerry Mulligan, Stan Getz, Warne Marsh and others. From 1963, he spent almost two years as a member of the Bill Evans trio. Subtle and always listening, Bunker has worked effectively behind singers. He occasionally plays vibraphone and his classical and studio work has also made him a master of a wide range of percussion instruments.

● ALBUMS: *Live At Shelly's Manne-Hole* (Vault 1966)★★★.

BUNN, TEDDY

b. *c.*1909, Freeport, Long Island, New York, USA, d. 20 July 1978, Lancaster, California, USA. A remarkably gifted self-taught guitarist, Bunn freelanced for most of his life. Perhaps as a result of his never being long in one place, his achievements are often overlooked. He was an inventive soloist, skilfully weaving intriguing patterns from deceptively simple single lines. In this respect, he pre-dated Charlie Christian, whose arrival on the jazz scene effectively obliterated the efforts of every other guitarist. In Bunn's case this was unfortunate and his subsequent neglect is unfair. He switched from acoustic to electric guitar around 1940. Bunn was also a vocalist (he started out as a calypso singer) and this led him into an important musical collaboration with Leo Watson. Their group, the Spirits Of Rhythm, was one of the most original vocal outfits of the 30s and 40s. During this same period, Bunn played guitar with several leading blues and jazzmen, including Duke Ellington, John Kirby, Jimmy Noone, Bob Howard, Johnny Dodds, Oran 'Hot Lips' Page, Peetie Wheatstraw, Mezz Mezzrow, Sidney Bechet and Lionel Hampton. Bunn was able to move comfortably into R&B in the 50s, working with Jack McVea and Louis Jordan. By the end of the decade he had taken the extra step into rock 'n' roll. During the last decade of his life Bunn was in very poor health and worked only rarely.

● COMPILATIONS: *Teddy Bunn 1930-39* (Blues Document 1989)★★★, *The Spirits Of Rhythm* 1932-1934 recordings (JSP 1989)★★★.

BUNNETT, JANE

b. 22 October 1956, Toronto, Canada. Bunnett originally studied classical piano before tendonitis forced her to concentrate on the saxophone and the flute, and she has rapidly become one of the finest soprano players of the 90s. Bunnett is married to trumpeter Larry Cramer, who has appeared on all her recordings since her 1988 debut for Dark Light. Remarkably strong for a first recording, *In Dew Time* also featured two greats of the *avant garde*, pianist Don Pullen and tenor saxophonist Dewey Redman. Pullen was a regular on Bunnett's albums until his untimely death in 1995, and the two recorded an exciting duet set in 1989 which demonstrated not only Pullen's mastery of free jazz but Bunnett's fully-formed talent on only her second recording. Her most exciting projects to date have been her recordings with Cuban musicians, *Spirits Of Havana* and *Jane Bunnett And The Cuban Piano Masters*. The former was recorded in Havana, during September and October 1991, with several generations of Cuban players including pianists Gonzalo Rubalcaba, Hilario Duran and Frank Emilio, Yoruban singer Merceditas Valdes and Guillermo Barreto. Bunnett and Cramer's work with Cuban musicians have led to bureaucratic wrangles with US officials keen to implement the Helms-Burton Law, which imposes penalties on foreigners who do business with Cuba. It also led to cancelled concerts and an aborted recording deal with Sony Records, but Bunnett and Cramer have persisted in the face of official hostility. They regularly visit Cuba and tour America with visiting Cuban musicians, and Blue Note Records released a vibrant 1993 recording session with pianists Jose Maria Vitier and Frank Emilio.

● ALBUMS: *In Dew Time* (Dark Light 1988)★★★★, with Don Pullen *New York Duets* (Music & Arts 1989)★★★★, *Live At Sweet Basil* (Denon 1990)★★★, *Spirits Of Havana* (Denon 1992)★★★★, *Water Is Wide* (Evidence 1994)★★★★, *Rendez-Vous* (Justin Time 1995)★★★, *Jane Bunnett And The Cuban Piano Masters* 1993 recording (Blue Note 1996)★★★★.

BURBANK, ALBERT

b. 25 March 1902, New Orleans, Louisiana, USA, d. 15 August 1976. One of the great classical New Orleans clarinettists, Burbank rarely worked outside his hometown. In his youth he worked with the bands of Buddy Petit, Chris Kelly and Punch Miller, but his best period was the decade following his discharge from the armed forces in 1945. Working and recording with 'Wooden' Joe Nicholas, Paul Barbarin, Herb Morand, Kid Howard, Kid Ory and others, he gave consistent demonstrations of his powerful, sobbing vibrato. Perhaps the most distinctive feature of Burbank's playing was the rich sonority of his lower register. From the mid-50s onwards,

Burbank worked continuously in New Orleans, mostly with lesser musicians. However, he did record with Kid Thomas in the 60s, and in the 70s worked with Percy Humphrey and the Preservation Hall Jazz Band.

● ALBUMS: *Kid Howard's Olympia Band Featuring Albert Burbank The Clarinet Wizard* (1962)★★★, *Albert Burbank* (1969)★★.

Burchell, Chas

b. Charles Burchell, 30 October 1925, London, England, d. 3 June 1986. Originally a George Formby fan, Burchell began to learn the ukelele, then guitar, before hearing an Artie Shaw record which inspired him to take up the clarinet and play jazz. Switching to alto saxophone, he started his own quintet in 1943, then tried tenor sax before he was drafted into the Royal Air Force. Transferred to the army in 1944, he played in Greece with the British Divisional Band and, following his discharge in 1947, worked in London with the Toni Antone big band. In 1949 he gave up full-time musicianship and worked in a factory so that he would not have to perform music he did not like in order to make a living: 'All my playing is playing for love,' he told writer Victor Schonfield in 1978. A disciple of Lennie Tristano and a devoted admirer of Warne Marsh, Burchell continued to play part-time, leading his own quintet for more than 20 years, guesting with distinguished visitors such as Clark Terry, Emily Remler and Nathan Davis, and recording for Peter Ind's Wave label, as well as playing with Ind in the group that supported Tristano on his only UK concert, at Harrogate in 1968. A wonderfully supple, lyrical tenor saxophonist whose unpredictable twists and turns of phrase recall the style of his idol Marsh, Burchell died of a heart attack in 1986. He remains, in the words of his friend and musical associate, journalist Mike Hennessey, 'one of the great unsung heroes of British jazz'.

● ALBUMS: *Jazz At The 1969 Richmond Festival* (1969)★★★, *No Kidding* (1974)★★★, *Peter Ind Sextet* (Wave 1975)★★★.

● COMPILATIONS: *Unsung Hero* (1994)★★★.

Burke, Ray

b. Raymond Barrois, 6 June 1904, New Orleans, Louisiana, USA, d. 21 March 1986. A self-taught clarinettist, Burke played in several New Orleans bands in his teens. He recorded in 1927 but the results were not released. Throughout the 20s and 30s Burke played in bands, mostly in New Orleans. In the 40s he led his own band but also recorded with 'Wooden' Joe Nicholas. Burke continued to play in New Orleans during the 50s and 60s, content to stay in his home-town. He was still playing in the late 70s and early 80s, lending to several bands his discreet and elegant sound.

● ALBUMS: *Contemporary New Orleans Jazz* 10-inch album (Southland 1955)★★★★, with Wendell Eugen *West India Blues* (1978)★★★.

● COMPILATIONS: *Ray Burke's Speakeasy Boys* i 1937-1945 recordings (New Orleans 1989)★★★, *Ray Burke's Speakeasy Boys* ii 1937-1949 recordings (American Music 1994)★★★.

Burnap, Campbell

b. 10 September 1939, Derby, England. Burnap caught the New Orleans jazz bug in his school days, playing washboard with a group of like-minded fellow pupils. His switch to trombone happened in the late 50s, when he emigrated to New Zealand, joining the Omega Jazz Band in 1958 and recording with them in 1961. Four years later, after gigging around and recording in Australia, he returned to England, playing regularly with Terry Lightfoot. Another four years on, after visiting both Australia and New Orleans he joined Ian Armit. This time his wanderlust seems to have abated - his subsequent freelance career has included two long spells with regular bands Alan Elsdon (1970-75) and Acker Bilk (1980-87). As well as playing with virtually every well-known New Orleans/mainstream band in England, Burnap has appeared with visiting American jazz musicians including Billy Butterfield, Bud Freeman, Bob Haggart, and Kenny Davern. Burnap also broadcast regularly as a jazz presenter with London's JFM and BBC Radio 2, where he was also heard as a panellist on the quiz-show *Jazz Score*. He also writes on jazz topics - his short story *A Bit Of A Scrape* appeared in Quartet Books' 1986 collection *B-Flat, Bebop, Scat*. With a playing and singing style much indebted to that of Jack Teagarden, possessing great warmth and a strong personal touch, Burnap deserves his reputation as 'one of Britain's most stylish trombonists'.

Burns, Norman

b. 11 March 1920, London, England, d. June 1994. Burns began playing drums as a child and while still a teenager worked as a professional musician on P&O ocean-going liners. In the late 30s and early 40s he was active in dance band circles in London, playing with many leading bands including those of Lew Stone, Ambrose, Frank Weir, Ted Heath and Geraldo. He also played with George Shearing and with Tito Burns (no relation). The drummer was one of the coterie of London-based jazzmen who dedicated themselves to the new music of the 40s, bop, and was a member of an all-star bebop band formed in 1948. In the early 50s Burns formed a quintet which he modelled upon the currently popular group being led in the USA by his former leader, Shearing. The cibraphone player in this group of Burns's was Victor Feldman. Burns eventually left music and emigrated to Australia where he remained for the rest of his life. A skilled dance band drummer, Burns questing nature and his feeling for bop helped to make him one of the most important if unacclaimed figures in British drumming of the 30s and 40s.

Burns, Ralph

b. 29 June 1922, Newton, Massachusetts, USA. After studying music at the New England Conservatory in Boston, Burns worked with several late swing-era bands, including Charlie Barnet's, as both pianist and arranger. His best-known period was as a member of Woody Herman's First Herd, during which time he was not only one quarter of a superb rhythm section (the others being Billy Bauer, Chubby Jackson and Dave Tough), but also arranged some of the band's most successful numbers (in some cases formalizing classic head arrangements, like that of 'Apple Honey'). In 1945 Burns decided to concentrate on writing and arranging, and contributed some exciting charts for Herman's Four Brothers band. He also composed some longer works, among which are 'Lady McGowan's Dream' and 'Summer Sequence', both recorded by Herman. When the record company decided to reissue 'Summer Sequence', they requested that a further section be added to the original three-part suite to fill the fourth side of a pair of 78 rpm releases. Burns obliged, and although some years had elapsed since the recording of the first three parts and the Herman band's personnel and style had substantially altered, he was able to recapture the mood successfully. The new piece, entitled 'Early Autumn', became a favourite of many jazz players, including Stan Getz. Freelancing in the 50s and 60s, Burns gradually moved away from jazz and into the film studios, although even here, as in *New York, New York* (1977), he was sometimes able to make use of his extensive knowledge of the jazz world. He won Academy Awards for his work on *Cabaret* (1972) and *All That Jazz* (1979), and continued to score for a mixture of feature and television movies such as *Lenny*, *Piaf*, *Lucky Lady*, *Movie Movie*, *Make Me An Offer*, *Urban Cowboy*, *Golden Gate*, *Pennies From Heaven*, (with Marvin Hamlisch), *Annie*, *Kiss Me Goodbye*, *My Favourite Year*, *Star 80*, *Ernie Kovacs-Between The Laughter*, *A Chorus Line*; *Moving Violations*, *The Christmas Star*, *In The Mood*, *Bert Rigby*, *You're A Fool*, *Sweet Bird Of Youth*, *All Dogs Go To Heaven*, and *The Josephine Baker Story* (1991).

● ALBUMS: *Free Forms* 10-inch album (Mercury 1952)★★★★, *Ralph Burns Among The JATP's* (Norgran 1955)★★★, *Spring Sequence* 10-inch album (Period 1955)★★★, *Bijou* 10-inch album (Period 1955)★★, *Jazz Studio 5* (Decca 1956)★★★★, with Mary Lou Williams *Composers - Pianists* (Jazztone 1956)★★★, *The Masters Revisited* (Decca 1957)★★★, *The Swinging Seasons* (MGM 1958)★★★★, *New York's A Song* (Decca 1959)★★★, *Very Warm For Jazz* (Decca 1959)★★★, *Porgy And Bess* (Decca 1959)★★★, *Where There's Burns There's Fire* (Warwick 1961)★★, *Piaf* film soundtrack (1974)★★★, *Ralph Burns Conducts* 1951-1954 recordings (Raretone 1988)★★★, *Bijou* 1955 recordings (Fresh Sounds 1988)★★★.

BURNSIDE, VI

b. *c.*1920, USA. An outstanding tenor saxophonist, Burnside played in an all-female band led by Bill Baldwin before joining the International Sweethearts Of Rhythm when Jesse Stone reorganized the band in the early 40s. With the Sweethearts she toured Europe, playing to American servicemen and at the end of the 40s she stayed on when the Sweethearts disbanded to reform under the leadership of Anna Mae Winburn. During the late 40s and early 50s Burnside also led her own quintet which featured trumpet players Norma Carson and Flo Dreyer. A driving player with a breathy forceful tone, Burnside was one of the best soloists the Sweethearts had, and there was no shortage of them. Had she come along a generation or so later, there seems little doubt that she would have been acclaimed as the truly world-class saxophonist she was.

BURRAGE, RONNIE

b. James Ronaldo Burrage, 19 October 1959, St. Louis, Missouri, USA. Burrage grew up in a musical atmosphere, with his mother playing classical piano. He sang in the St. Louis Cathedral boys' choir and played drums/percussion in various funk bands. Burrage only worked a term of his scholarship at Howard University, drawn like so many other jazz musicians to New York City. In the early 80s, as part of the St Louis Metropolitan Jazz Quintet, he accompanied Arthur Blythe and visitors Jackie McLean, Andrew Hill and McCoy Tyner. Between 1983 and 1985 he drummed in the Woody Shaw quintet. In 1986, he formed Third Kind Of Blue with multi-reedsman John Purcell and bassist Anthony Cox, a suave mix of *avant garde* and more commercial, bebop-orientated elements. He has recently worked with Barbara Dennerlein and Courtney Pine. Burrage plays vibes and marimba as well as drums and his playing is informed by a feel for texture that is decidedly original.

● ALBUMS: *Third Kind Of Blue* (1986)★★★, *Shuttle* 1993 recording (Sound Hills 1996)★★★★.

BURRELL, DAVE

b. Herman Davis Burrell, 10 September 1940, Middleton, Ohio, USA. Burrell's mother was a singer, organist and choir director. Dave Burrell studied music (Berklee College Of Music for four years, Hawaii University for nine) and composed film scores (*Crucifado*), proving himself a sophisticated musical organizer in the face of criticisms that late 60s jazz freedom was merely improvised excess. He went straight from his academic studies into the maelstrom of the black *avant garde*, playing with Archie Shepp, Marion Brown and Grachan Moncur III. He played at the 1969 Pan-African Music Festival in Algiers, the historic encounter of the New Thing with ethnic Africa. Shortly afterwards he recorded *Echo* for the Parisian BYG label, a towering blast of revolutionary energy. Since then Burrell has actively involved himself with both Rastafarian and Haitian off-shoots of African music/ritual and composed a version of Puccini's *La Boheme*. In 1988 he participated in the series of classic recordings David Murray made for the Japanese DIW label, his deep grasp of gospel particularly arresting on *Spirituals*. Burrell's feel for untempered intensity interacts with his academic sophistication in a complex yet exciting dialectic: like the better-known Andrew Hill, he demonstrates how jazz can be the real confrontation between the street and the academy.

● ALBUMS: *High* (Douglas 1969)★★★, *Echo* (BYG/Affinity 1969)★★★★, *La Vie De Bohème* (1969)★★★, *After Love* (1971)★★★, *Dreams* (1973)★★★, *Only Me* (1973)★★★, *Black Spring* (1977)★★★, *Teardrops For Jimmy* (1977)★★★, *Lush Life*

(Denon 1978)★★★, *Round Midnight* (1978)★★★, *Dave Burrell Plays Ellington And Monk* (Denon 1979)★★★, *Round Midnight* (Denon 1982)★★★, with others *Lucky Four* (1989)★★★, *Daybreak* (Gazell 1990)★★★, *Jelly Roll Joys* (Gazell 1991)★★★★, with David Murray *In Concert* (Victo 1992)★★★★, *Brother To Brother* (Gazell 1993)★★★★, *High Won - High Two* (Black Lion 1996)★★★★, with Murray *Windward Passages* 1993 recording (Black Saint 1997)★★★.

Burrell, Kenny

b. Kenneth Earl Burrell, 31 July 1931, Detroit, Michigan, USA. Coming from a family that encouraged music (all his three brothers were musicians), Burrell studied classical guitar for a mere 18 months (1952-53). In 1955 he received a Bachelor of Music degree from Detroit's Wayne University. He played guitar with the Candy Johnson Sextet in 1948, with Count Belcher in 1949 and Tommy Barnett in 1950. In 1951 Dizzy Gillespie visited Detroit and they recorded together. In March 1955 he stood in for Herb Ellis in the Oscar Peterson trio and in 1957 saw work with Benny Goodman. Discovered by the prestigious Blue Note label, he formed an association with organist Jimmy Smith, and recorded with John Coltrane under the name The Cats. Like all jazz guitarists of his generation Burrell was primarily influenced by Charlie Christian, but developed his own particular playing style. His series of 60s albums for Blue Note Records and Verve Records contain his classic work. Arguably, *Midnight Blue*, featuring Stanley Turrentine (with its famous Reid Miles typography and the inspiration behind English singer-songwriter Elvis Costello's *Almost Blue* sleeve), is his best album. The track 'Midnight Blue' has also been cited as the influence for Van Morrison's 'Moondance'. The excellent *Guitar Forms*, recorded with Gil Evans in December 1964, is another important work, the ambitious suite demonstrating wide influences. Along with Grant Green, there is no finer exponent of 'smokey guitar jazz'. In the late 80s his encouragement of young black talent - especially the drummer Kenny Washington - gave his trio an edge that belied his reputation for classy easy listening. In 1994 he was once again touring with the Jimmy Smith Trio. In the late 90s he was also to be found teaching at UCLA, and became a professor of music in 1997.

● ALBUMS: *Introducing Kenny Burrell* (Blue Note 1956)★★★★, *Kenny Burrell, Volume 2* (Blue Note 1957)★★★, *Kenny Burrell* reissued as *Blue Moods* (Prestige 1957)★★★★, with Jimmy Raney *Two Guitars* (Prestige 1957)★★★★, *Blue Lights, Volume 1* (Blue Note 1958)★★★★, *Blue Lights, Volume 2* (Blue Note 1959)★★★★, *Night At The Vanguard* reissued as *Man At Work* (Argo/Cadet 1959)★★★, *On View At The Five Spot Cafe* (Blue Note 1960)★★★★, *Weaver Of Dreams* (Columbia 1961)★★, *Lotsa Bossa Nova* (Kapp 1962)★★, with John Coltrane *Kenny Burrell With John Coltrane* (New Jazz 1962)★★★★, *Bluesy Burrell* reissued as *Out Of This World* (Moodsville/Prestige 1963)★★★, *All Day Long* (Prestige 1963)★★★, with Jimmy Smith *Blue Bash* (Verve 1963)★★★★, *Midnight Blue* (Blue Note 1963)★★★★★, *Soul Call* (Prestige 1964)★★★, *Crash* (Prestige 1964)★★★, with Donald Byrd, Hank Mobley *Donald Byrd, Hank Mobley & Kenny Burrell* (Status 1965)★★★, with Tiny Grimes, Bill Jennings *Guitar Soul* (Status 1965)★★★, with Gil Evans *Guitar Forms* (Verve 1965)★★★★, *A Generation Ago Today* (Verve 1966)★★★, *The Tender Gender* (Cadet 1966)★★, *Have Yourself A Soulful Little Christmas* (Cadet 1966)★★, *For Charlie Christian And Benny Goodman* (Verve 1967)★★, *Ode To 52nd Street* (Cadet 1967)★★, *Blues - The Common Ground* (Verve 1968)★★★, *Night Song* (Verve 1968)★★★, *Asphalt Canyon Suite* (Verve 1969)★★★, *God Bless The Child* (CTI 1971)★★★, *Ellington Is Forever, Volume 1* (Fantasy 1975)★★★★, *Ellington Is Forever, Volume 2* (Fantasy 1976)★★★★, *Tin Tin Deo* (Concord Jazz 1977)★★★, *Handcrafted* (Muse 1978)★★★, *When Lights Are Low* (Concord Jazz 1979)★★★, *Live At The Village Vanguard* (Muse 1979)★★★, *Moon And Sand* (Concord Jazz 1980)★★★, *Heritage* (AudioSource 1980)★★★, *Listen To The Dawn* (Muse 1981)★★★, *Ellington À La Carte* (Muse 1983)★★★, *Bluesin' Around* 1961/1962 recordings (Columbia 1983)★★★, with Grover Washington Jr. *Togethering* (Blue Note 1984)★★, *Generations* (Blue Note 1987)★★★, *Pieces Of Blue And The Blues* (Blue Note 1987)★★★, *Groovin' High* (Muse 1987)★★★, *Recapitulation* (Charly 1989)★★, *Guiding Spirit* (Contemporary 1990)★★★, *Sunup To Sundown* (Contemporary 1992)★★★, *Lotus Blossom* (Concord Jazz 1995)★★★, *Midnight At The Village Vanguard* (Evidence 1996)★★★, with the Jazz Heritage All-Stars *Live At The Blue Note* (Concord Jazz 1997)★★★, *Love Is The Answer* (Concord Jazz 1998)★★★.

● COMPILATIONS: *The Best Of Kenny Burrell* (Prestige 1967)★★★.

Burroughs, Alvin

b. 21 November 1911, Mobile, Alabama, USA, d. 1 August 1950. He began playing drums as a child and in his early teens lived in Pittsburgh, Pennsylvania. At the age of 16 Burroughs joined a band led by another 16-year-old, Roy Eldridge, which was stranded during a tour with a show. Burroughs then played with several Midwest territory bands, including two of the best and most famous, Walter Page's Blue Devils and Alphonso Trent's. He later moved to Chicago where, during the 30s, he played with a number of bands culminating in Horace Henderson's, and, in 1938, the band led by Earl Hines at the Grand Terrace. He remained with Hines for two years, moving on to another famed territory band, Milt Larkins', then Benny Carter and for a while led his own band. After a spell with Red Allen he joined George Dixon's band in Chicago. Burroughs played with great swing and his subtle urging of the bands with which he worked, notably Hines's, played an important part in their popularity with dancers. His early death ended what might well have been a successful career in the mainstream of jazz in the following decades.

Burrows, Don

b. Donald Vernon Burrows, 8 August 1928, Sydney, New South Wales, Australia. Burrows became interested in music as a child, playing flute in a school band, and in his very early teens was sufficiently developed to work regularly in clubs playing various reed instruments, mostly clarinet. He studied at the Sydney Conservatorium of Music in the early 40s and despite his youth, but perhaps in part as a result of the loss of musicians to the armed forces, he became principal clarinettist with the Australian Broadcasting Company's Symphony Orchestra. He also played with the ABC Dance Band, helping him build a career in radio and later in television. However, he continued to play jazz whenever the opportunity was presented, recording in 1945 with George Trevare's Jazz group. In the 60s he worked for a while with George Golla, touring internationally. In the early years of the following decade he led his own band on overseas trips making acclaimed appearances at major festivals, and became a recipient of the MBE. In the 80s he turned more and more to teaching, having earlier established a jazz studies programme at the New South Wales Conservatorium of Music (of which he became the director in 1980). Burrows also continued his television work, this time presenting his own music series, *The Burrows Collection*. He continued to tour, visiting China, and time and again proved his consistency and the breadth of a range that covers post-swing and bop. Burrows's command of his instruments allows him to play with great fluency, delivering thoughtful and technically demanding solos with wit and a great sense of swing.

● ALBUMS: *Live At Montreux* (Cherry Pie 1972)★★★, *The Don Burrows Quartet At The Sydney Opera House* (Cherry Pie 1974)★★★, *Don Burrows And The Brazilian Connection* (Cherry Pie 1977)★★, *The Babinda Trilogy* (Warners 1995)★★★.

● COMPILATIONS:*The First 50 Years Vols. 1-5, 1944-1992* (ABC Jazz 1995)★★★.

Burton, Gary

b. 23 January 1943, Anderson, Indiana, USA. After teaching himself to play piano Burton studied music formally before switching to the vibraphone. In 1960 he recorded with Hank Garland, a country guitarist, but then moved into jazz with a two-year stint at Berklee College Of Music, where he began an important musical association with Mike Gibbs. In 1963 he became a member of George Shearing's group, following this with two years with Stan Getz. Later in the 60s, Burton formed his own small band, playing jazz-rock. Throughout the decade and on into the 70s, Burton led a succession of fine bands that included such musicians as Larry Coryell, Steve Swallow, Roy Haynes, Pat Metheny and Eberhard Weber. He was also teamed on record with Stéphane Grappelli, Carla Bley, Keith Jarrett, Chick Corea, Michael Brecker, Peter Erskine and others. From 1971 Burton taught at Berklee, often finding empathetic musicians among his students. In the 80s his musical associates included Tommy Smith. Although he followed many more famous vibraphonists, not least Lionel Hampton and Milt Jackson, Burton was the first player of this instrument to create a new and wholly original musical style. His extensive simultaneous use of four mallets gave him a less percussive sound, allowing him to develop more complex ideas in a manner usually available only to pianists and players of wind instruments. Burton's *Six Pack* in 1993 was a refreshing excursion featuring six guitar players: B.B. King, John Scofield, Jim Hall, Kurt Rosenwinkel Kevin Eubanks and familiar partner Ralph Towner. *Like Minds*, released through Concord Jazz in 1998, was a sublime all-star gathering that featured Burton playing with Pat Metheny, Corea and Dave Holland. His early musical experience of country and rock have all been thoroughly absorbed into a strongly jazz-orientated concept. Burton's interests and enthusiasm, allied as they are to a virtuoso technique, have made him a leading exemplar of contemporary music. However, although others have followed his example, he remains the only vibraphonist of his generation to be measured alongside the other major interpreters and innovators in jazz.

● ALBUMS: *New Vibe Man In Town* (RCA Victor 1961)★★★, *Who Is Gary Burton?* (RCA Victor 1963)★★★, shared with Sonny Rollins, Clark Terry *3 In Jazz* (RCA Victor 1963)★★★, *Something's Coming* (RCA Victor 1964)★★★, *The Groovy Sound Of Music* (RCA Victor 1965)★★★, *The Time Machine* (RCA Victor 1966)★★★, *Tennessee Firebird* (RCA Victor 1966)★★★, *Duster* (RCA Victor 1967)★★★, *Lofty Fake Anagram* (RCA Victor 1967)★★★, with Carla Bley *A Genuine Tong Funeral* (RCA Victor 1968)★★★★, *Gary Burton In Concert* (RCA Victor 1968)★★★★, *Country Roads & Other Places* (RCA Victor 1969)★★★★, with Stéphane Grappelli *Paris Encounter* (1969)★★★, *Throb* (Atlantic 1969)★★★★, with Keith Jarrett *Gary Burton And Keith Jarrett* (Atlantic 1970)★★★★, *Alone At Last* (Atlantic 1972)★★★, with Chick Corea *Crystal Silence* (ECM 1973)★★★★, *The New Quartet* (ECM 1973)★★★, with Steve Swallow *Hotel Hello* (ECM 1974)★★★, *Matchbook* (ECM 1974)★★★, *Dreams So Real* (ECM 1975)★★, with Eberhard Weber *Ring* (ECM 1974)★★★, with Weber *Passengers* (ECM 1976)★★★★, with Chick Corea *Duet* (ECM 1978)★★★★, *Easy As Pie* (ECM 1980)★★★, *Picture This* (ECM 1983)★★★, with Corea *Lyric Suite For Sextet* (ECM 1983)★★★, *Somethings Coming* (RCA 1984)★★, *Real Life Hits* (ECM 1984)★★★, with Ralph Towner *Slide Show* (ECM 1986)★★★, *Whiz Kids* (ECM 1986)★★, *Times Like These* (GRP 1988)★★, with Pat Metheny *Reunion* (ECM 1989)★★★★, *Cool Nights* (GRP 1990)★★, with Paul Bley *Right Time Right Place* (Sonet 1991)★★★, *Six Pack* (GRP 1993)★★★, with Makoto Ozone *Face To Face* (GRP 1995)★★★, *Departure* (Concord Jazz 1997)★★★★, *Astor Piazzolla Reunion* (Concord Jazz 1997)★★★, with Corea *Native Sense: The New Duets* (Concord Jazz 1998)★★★, *Duster* (Koch Jazz 1998)★★★★, *Like Minds* (Concord Jazz 1998)★★★★.

● COMPILATIONS: *Artist's Choice* 1963-1968 recordings (RCA 1987)★★★★, *Works* (ECM 1989)★★★, *Collection* (GRP 1996)★★★.

Bushell, Garvin

b. Garvin Payne Bushell, 25 September 1902, Springfield, Ohio, USA, d. 31 October 1991. Born into a very musical family, he studied piano and then clarinet and by his late teens was a professional musician. In his youth he accompanied some noted singers, including Mamie Smith and Ethel Waters and in 1925 joined Sam Wooding's orchestra. With Wooding he visited Europe and then, late in the 20s, began a sustained round of gigging and recording with numerous jazz musicians. Among the leaders with whom he played and recorded were Bessie Smith, Otto Hardwick, Fletcher

Henderson, Cab Calloway and Chick Webb. He stayed on in this band after Webb's death when it was under the nominal leadership of Ella Fitzgerald. In the early 40s he had spells with Tony Pastor, his own band and, in 1947, Bunk Johnson. In the 50s he played with Wilbur De Paris's band, and in the Fletcher Henderson reunion orchestra. His spell with De Paris continued into the 60s but he found time to record with other musicians, including, perhaps surprisingly, John Coltrane. With Coltrane, he played double bassoon on a 1961 record date (having played bassoon with the Chicago Civic Orchestra a decade earlier and with the Louisiana Sugar Babes more than two decades before that). In the mid-60s he lived for a while in Puerto Rico, then settled in Las Vegas, Nevada, where he taught music. A versatile and technically assured musician, Bushell's skill on various woodwinds made him a valuable member of any band. His principal instrument, the clarinet, was also his favourite for soloing and he displayed imaginative gifts to equal his proficiency.

● ALBUMS: with Wilbur De Paris *The Wild Jazz Age* (Atlantic 1960)★★★, *Wilbur De Paris On The Riviera* (Atlantic 1960)★★★, with John Coltrane *The Other Village Vanguard Tapes* (Impulse! 1961)★★★★.

Bushkin, Joe

b. 7 November 1916, New York City, New York, USA. While still in his early teens Bushkin played piano (and trumpet) with New York dance bands, and by the mid-30s was a regular sitter-in along 52nd Street, playing and recording with Eddie Condon, Muggsy Spanier and Billie Holiday. He joined Bunny Berigan's big band in 1935 and spent several years with Joe Marsala before taking up an offer from Tommy Dorsey in 1940. One of Bushkin's songs, 'Oh Look At Me Now', was recorded by Dorsey and the band's singer, Frank Sinatra, and became a success. After war service Bushkin worked with Benny Goodman and Louis Armstrong and accommodated changes in musical taste by easily shifting into a more commercial mode during the 60s and 70s. Although semi-retired, in the mid-70s Bushkin was tempted back into the spotlight by an invitation to accompany Bing Crosby on a tour of the USA and Europe. In the mid-80s Bushkin was still hard at work, effortlessly blending with latter-day mainstream jazzmen such as Warren Vaché Jnr.

● ALBUMS: *I Love A Piano* 10-inch album (1950)★★★, *Piano Moods* 10-inch album (1950)★★★, *After Hours* 10-inch album (1950)★★★, *Piano After Midnight* (Epic 1956)★★★, *Skylight Rhapsody* (Capitol 1956)★★★, *A Fellow Needs A Girl* (Capitol 1957)★★★, *Bushkin Spotlights Berlin* (Capitol 1958)★★★, *Night Sounds Of San Francisco* (Decca 1965)★★★, *Joe Bushkin Celebrates 100 Years Of Recorded Sound* (1977)★★★.

● COMPILATIONS: *World Is Waiting* 1942-46 recordings (Commodore 1982)★★★.

Butler, Frank

b. 18 February 1928, Kansas City, Missouri, USA, d. 24 July 1984. Learning to play drums in school, Butler played in his home-town where he took tuition from the city's finest drummer, Jo Jones. Despite such swing era roots, however, and notwithstanding a brief stint deputizing with Duke Ellington, Butler's interest lay in modern developments. From the late 50s onwards he worked with Curtis Counce, Art Pepper, Harold Land and other west coast luminaries and also played in groups led by Miles Davis and John Coltrane. His career faltered in the mid-60s but he returned a decade later, playing with great drive and flair, and was at ease in the milieu of the hard-bop resurgence.

● ALBUMS: with Red Mitchell *Rejoice* (Pacific Jazz 1961)★★★.

Butler, Henry

b. 1948, New Orleans, Louisiana, USA. A pianist, vocalist and composer, Henry Butler's work explores ethnic, gospel, blues and European classical traditions as part of a refreshingly eclectic take on contemporary jazz. Blind since birth, he has also become one of the most prominent sightless photographers in America with exhibitions in several major cities. He began to write his first melodies as a child, working on a neighbour's piano, and by the age of eight he began more disciplined musical studies at the Louisiana State School for the Blind in Baton Rouge. Later he attended Southern University where he received a Bachelor's degree as a voice major. He was a protégé of clarinettist Alvin Batiste, but also studied with Professor Longhair. A parallel apprenticeship in the live performance of New Orleans piano blues helped to pay his tuition fees. A scholarship to Michigan State University followed for his masters in vocal music, while he also received grants to study with Sir Roland Hanna, George Duke and Cannonball Adderley. Other influences included Errol Garner, Art Tatum, Chick Corea and Keith Jarrett, in addition to Bartok and Debussy. His interest in ethnomusicology also led him to explore cantorial, operatic and Slavic vocal techniques. Duly empowered with musical knowledge and technique, he returned to New Orleans in the mid-70s to share his wisdom with students at the New Orleans Center for the Creative Arts, teaching vocal technique, chorus technique and theory. However, he still maintained ambitions to become a composer and performer in his own right and in 1980 he moved to Los Angeles. His first collaborator was Oz Scott, for whose docudrama *Dreamland* he composed and arranged the score (he also took a small acting role). Regular income was achieved by becoming the talent development consultant for both Motown Records and the Stevie Wonder Organization. He also performed regularly in clubs and restaurants, with a repertoire including the works of Professor Longhair, James Booker, Fats Domino and Ray Charles. He also worked in a duo with Leo Nocentelli (ex-Meters). After collaborating with bass player Charlie Haden and drummer Billy Higgins at the Comeback Inn in Venice, he encouraged them to join him on the recording of his debut album, *Flyin' Around*. The album also featured Freddie Hubbard (trumpet), Azar Lawrence (saxophone), Steve Kujala (flute) and Jeff Clayton (oboe). The follow-up, *The Village*, was a double-length set that reunited him with Batiste and again utilized a wide mix of styles and traditions. Butler employed a series of long-standing collaborators, included a seasoned New Orleans rhythm section of Chris Severin and Herman Jackson, plus Nocentilli and keyboard player Michael Goods.

● ALBUMS: *Flyin' Around* (MCA 1984)★★★, *The Village* (MCA 1987)★★★★, *Orleans Inspiration* (Windham Hill Jazz 1994)★★★, *For All Seasons* (Atlantic 1996)★★★, *Blues After Sunset* (Black Top 1998)★★★★.

BUTTERFIELD 8

Butterfield 8 were the brainchild of former Higsons multi-instrumentalist Terry Edwards (b. Hornchurch, Essex, England) in collaboration with ex-Madness bassist Mark 'Bedders' Bedford (b. 24 August 1961, London, England). Edwards' long-time fascination with film and show scores fused with his love of blues-tinged jazz in the Butterfield 8. The group provided a welcome outlet after the restriction of the funk-influenced Higsons. Named after the 1960 film starring Laurence Harvey and Elizabeth Taylor, the Butterfield 8's debut album included versions of Herbie Hancock's 'Watermelon Man' and the Viscounts 'Harlem Nocturne'. Among Edwards' other projects and collaborations was the 70s glitter-glam parody, the Eight Track Cartridge Family. He has also performed with, and produced, Yeah Jazz, worked with the Simon Lewis Partnership and in 1991 he released two EPs celebrating the music of the Jesus And Mary Chain and the Fall.

● ALBUMS: *Blow* (Go! Discs 1988)★★★.

BUTTERFIELD, BILLY

b. 14 January 1917, Middleton, Ohio, USA, d. 18 March 1988, North Palm Beach, Florida, USA. As a child Butterfield was taught by cornetist Frank Simons, but as a teenager he began to study medicine. He continued playing music to such good effect that he was soon working regularly with the bands of Austin Wylie and Andy Anderson and eventually quit his medical studies. Although adept on several instruments he concentrated on trumpet, later adding flügelhorn, and in 1937 was hired by the Bob Crosby band. Butterfield's gorgeous, fat-toned sound was particularly suited to ballads and his recording of Bob Haggart's 'What's New?', originally entitled 'I'm Free', was a hit. In 1940 he joined Artie Shaw, then worked with Benny Goodman and Les Brown, but soon entered the more reliable area of studio work. After the war Butterfield indulged himself with every sideman's dream and formed his own big band, in collaboration with former Crosby colleague Bill Stegmeyer. Butterfield took the enterprise seriously, commissioning arrangements from Ralph Burns, Bob Haggart, Bob Peck and Neal Hefti. For all his good intentions, however, the band proved to be a financial disaster. For a while he returned to studio work but then began freelancing, working with old comrades such as Eddie Condon, recording with Louis Armstrong (playing the trumpet obbligato to Satchmo's vocal on the 1949 recording of 'Blueberry Hill') and leading small groups. In the late 60s he became a member of the World's Greatest Jazz Band alongside former Crosby sidemen Bob Haggart and Yank Lawson. In the 70s he worked with Joe 'Flip' Phillips and toured extensively, usually as a solo. Much admired by fellow musicians, and eventually attracting the kind of attention from fans he had always deserved, Butterfield enjoyed a late flowering of his career although suffering from emphysema.

● ALBUMS: *Stardusting* 10-inch album (Capitol 1950)★★★★, *Classics In Jazz* 10-inch album (Capitol 1953)★★★★, *Far Away Places* 10-inch album (1954)★★★, *Billy Butterfield And His Orchestra* (Westminster 1954)★★, *Billy Butterfield Goes To NYU* (Essex 1955)★★★, *New York Land Dixie* (RCA Victor 1956)★★★, *Billy Butterfield Quintet* (1959)★★★, *Billy Plays Bix* (Epic 1962)★★★★, with WGJB *Live At The Roosevelt Grill* (1970)★★★, with WGJB *Century Plaza* (1972)★★★, *In A Mellow Tone* (1975)★★★, *For Better Blues And Ballads* (1975)★★★, *International Session* (1975)★★★, *Billy Butterfield Plays George Gershwin* (1977)★★★★, *Watch What Happens* (Flyright 1977)★★★, *The Incomparable Butterfield Horn* (1977)★★★, *Swinging At The Elks* (1978)★★, *Rapport* (77 1979)★★★, *You Can Depend On Me* (1980)★★★.

● COMPILATIONS: *The Uncollected Billy Butterfield Orchestra* (Hindsight 1989)★★★.

BYARD, JAKI

b. John Byard, 15 June 1922, Worcester, Massachusetts, USA. A gifted multi-instrumentalist, Byard learned trumpet and piano as a child and later took up guitar, drums, trombone and tenor saxophone too. In 1949 he played piano in Earl Bostic's R&B band, and followed that with a spell as a solo pianist and then joined Herb Pomeroy's big band on tenor. After the Pomeroy stint he returned to playing piano, this time with the Maynard Ferguson band. Throughout the 60s Byard was deeply involved in what was often a very adventurous musical scene, working with Eric Dolphy, Don Ellis, Booker Ervin, Charles Mingus, Rahsaan Roland Kirk and others. In the 70s Byard worked mostly solo, but found time to experiment with his own big band, the Apollo Stompers, and to teach at Boston's New England Conservatory. Byard's wide-ranging musical interests make his work particularly interesting as he effectively incorporates ideas and styles from different periods of jazz and the classical repertoire: just one indication of his range is the series of piano duo albums he has made with players as diverse as Earl Hines, Ran Blake and Howard Riley.

● ALBUMS: *Blues For Smoke* (Candid 1961)★★★★, *Here's Jaki* (New Jazz 1961)★★★, *Hi-Fly* (New Jazz 1962)★★★, *Out Front!* (Prestige 1964)★★★★, *Live! At Lennie's On The Turnpike - Volume 1* (Prestige 1965)★★★, *Freedom Together* (Prestige 1966)★★★, *Live! At Lennie's On The Turnpike - Volume 2* (Prestige 1966)★★★, *On The Spot!* (Prestige 1967)★★★, *The Sunshine Of My Soul* (Prestige 1967)★★★, *Jaki Byard With Strings!* (Prestige 1968)★★★★, *The Jaki Byard Experience* (Prestige 1968)★★★, *Solo Piano* (Prestige 1969)★★★★, *Parisian Solos* (1971)★★★, *Live At The Jazz Inn* (1971)★★★, *Duet* (1972)★★★, *The Entertainer* (1972)★★★, *There'll Be Some*

Changes Made (Muse 1972)★★★, *Empirical* (Muse 1973)★★★★, *Flight Of The Fly* (1976)★★★, *Family Man* (Muse 1978)★★★, *To Them - To Us* (Soul Note 1981)★★★, *Phantasies* (Soul Note 1984)★★★, *Foolin' Myself* (Soul Note 1988)★★★★, *Phantasies II* (Soul Note 1988)★★★★, with Howard Riley *Live At The Royal Festival Hall* (Leo 1988)★★★, *Live At Maybeck Recital Hall, Vol. 17* (Concord Jazz 1992)★★★★, with Michael Marcus *This Happening* (Justin Time 1998)★★★, with David Eyges *Night Leaves* (Brownstone 1998)★★★.

BYAS, DON

b. 21 October 1912, Muskogee, Oklahoma, USA, d. 24 August 1972. In his teens, Byas played alto saxophone with the Midwest bands of Bennie Moten, Terrence Holder and Walter Page, but switched to tenor in the early 30s while working on the west coast. He played in Lionel Hampton's band at the Paradise Club in Los Angeles and, when Hampton joined Benny Goodman, Byas moved restlessly through the bands of Eddie Barefield, Buck Clayton, Don Redman, Benny Carter, Lucky Millinder and many others. In 1941 he succeeded Lester Young in the Count Basie band. In 1943 Byas quit Basie and began playing with small groups in clubs, mostly in New York, where his musical associates were emergent beboppers such as Dizzy Gillespie and Charlie Parker. Byas had known Parker as a young teenager and the two friends would jam together, with Byas claiming later that Parker had been his pupil (Parker always denied this and the two men almost came to blows after a row in Paris). Despite his bebop associations, however, Byas remained deeply rooted in the swinging sounds of the south-west. Given the period in which he worked, it was inevitable that he would start out by emulating the tenor saxophone style of Coleman Hawkins, but Byas always cited Art Tatum as his greatest influence, declaring: 'I haven't got any style. I just blow, like Art.' He took up residence in Paris in the late 40s, followed by long periods living in Amsterdam and in Copenhagen, and became enormously popular as a balladeer. His full, rich sound, allied to his harmonically complex playing, made him an instantly identifiable soloist. Byas was a significant player in the history of the development of the tenor saxophone and one whose contribution should not be, but (despite the exaggerated claims of his own importance) often is, overlooked.

● ALBUMS: *Tenor Saxophone Concerto* 10-inch album (Dial 1951)★★★, *Don Byas Solos* 10-inch album (Atlantic 1952)★★★, *Don Byas Sax* 10-inch album (Savoy 1952)★★★★, *In France 'Don Byas Et Ses Rhythmes'* 10-inch album (Norgran 1954)★★★, *Don Byas Favorites* 10-inch album (Seeco 1955)★★★★, with Buck Clayton, Alix Combelle, Mary Lou Williams *Messin' Round In Montmarte* (Storyville 1956)★★★, *Jazz - Free And Easy* (Regent 1957)★★★, with Bernard Peiffer *Jazz From Saint-Germain Des Pres* (Verve 1957)★★★★, with Bud Powell *A Tribute To Cannonball* (Columbia 1961)★★★★, *Don Byas With Strings* (1962)★★★, *All The Things You Are* (Jazz Hour 1963)★★★, *A Night In Tunisia* (Black Lion 1963)★★★, *Walkin'* (Black Lion 1963)★★★, *Anthropology* (Black Lion 1964)★★★★, with Ben Webster *Ben Webster Meets Don Byas In The Black Forest* (Saba 1968)★★★, *Don Byas In Japan* (1971)★★★, *Ambiences Et Slows* (Barclay 1979)★★★.

● COMPILATIONS: with various artists *Midnight At Minton's* 1941 (Onyx)★★★, with others *Savoy Jam Party* 1944-46 (Savoy 1985)★★★, *Don Byas On Blue Star* 1947-1952 recordings (ECM 1988)★★★★.

BYRD, CHARLIE

b. 16 September 1925, Chuckatuck, Virginia, USA. Byrd began playing guitar while still a small child and by the start of World War II was already highly proficient. During the war he met and played with Django Reinhardt and soon after the end of the war he became a full-time professional musician. He played in a number of popular dance bands but at the end of the 40s abandoned ambitions to play jazz and turned instead to the study of classical guitar. After studying under several leading tutors, including Andrès Segovia, he returned to the USA where he formed his own band in Washington, DC. With this group he played jazz but brought to his interpretations many of the techniques and some of the forms of the classical repertoire. In the late 50s he was with Woody Herman and in the early 60s played with Stan Getz, with whom he developed his interest in Latin American music, thus helping to generate the jazz-bossa nova craze. In 1973 he became co-founder, with Barney Kessel and Herb Ellis, of Great Guitars. During the rest of the 70s and on through the 80s he performed regularly on the international club and festival circuit, sometimes as a single, sometimes in duo and often with Great Guitars. In 1992 he recorded with the Washington Guitar Quintet for the Concord Concerto label. Byrd's jazz work is distinguished by his classical training and his interest in other musical forms. As a jazz soloist he sometimes lacks the fluid swing of such contemporaries as Kessel and Ellis, but he is a masterly technician.

● ALBUMS: *Jazz Recital/The Spanish Guitar Of Charlie Byrd* (Savoy 1957)★★★, *Blues For The Night People* (Savoy 1957)★★★★, *Midnight Guitar* (Savoy 1957)★★★, *First Flight* (1957)★★★, *Jazz At The Showboat/Byrd's Word* (Offbeat 1958)★★★, *Jazz At The Showboat Volume 2* (Offbeat 1959)★★★, *Byrd In The Wind* (1959)★★★★, *Jazz At The Showboat, Vol. 3* (Offbeat 1959)★★★, *Charlies Choice* (Offbeat 1960)★★★, *The Guitar Artistry Of Charlie Byrd* (Riverside 1960)★★★★, *Charlie Byrd At The Village Vanguard* (Riverside 1961)★★★★, *Blues Sonata* (Riverside 1961)★★★★, *Latin Impressions* (Riverside 1962)★★★★, with Stan Getz *Jazz Samba* (Verve 1962)★★★★★, *Bossa Nova Pelos Passaros* (Riverside 1962)★★★, *Byrd At The Gate* (Riverside 1963)★★★★, *Byrd's Word* (Riverside 1963)★★★, *Once More! Bossa Nova* (Riverside 1963)★★★★, *Byrd In The Wind* (Riverside 1963)★★★★, *Mr Guitar* (Riverside 1963)★★★, *The Guitar Artistry Of Charlie Byrd* (Riverside 1963)★★★★, with Herb Ellis *Herb Ellis & Charlie Byrd* (1963)★★★, *Brazilian Byrd* (Columbia 1965)★★★★, *Byrd Song* (Riverside 1965)★★★★, *Travelin' Man Recorded Live* (Columbia 1966)★★★, *Hit Trip* (Columbia 1966)★★★, *A Touch Of Gold* (Columbia 1966)★★★, *Christmas Cards For Solo Guitar* (Columbia 1966)★★★, *Solo Flight* (Riverside 1967)★★★, *Byrdland* (Columbia 1967)★★★, *Hollywood Byrd* (Columbia

1967)★★★, *More Brazilian Byrd* (Columbia 1967)★★★, *Charlie Byrd Plays Villa-Lobos* (Columbia 1968)★★★, *Delicately* (Columbia 1968)★★★, *The Great Byrd* (Columbia 1969)★★★, *Greatest Hits Of The 60s* (Columbia 1969)★★, *Bryd Man With Strings* (Riverside 1969)★★, *Crystal Silence* (1973)★★, *Byrd By The Sea* (Fantasy 1974)★★★, *Tambu* (Fantasy 1974)★★★, as Great Guitars *Great Guitars* (Concord Jazz 1974)★★★, *Top Hat* (1975)★★★, *Three Guitars* (Concord 1975)★★★, *Triste* (1976)★★★, *Blue Byrd* (Concord Jazz 1978)★★, as Great Guitars *Great Guitars: Straight Tracks* (Concord Jazz 1978)★★★, *Sugarloaf Suite* (Concord Jazz 1979)★★, with Laurindo Almeida *Brazilian Soul* (Concord Picante 1980)★★★, *Latin Byrd* (Milestone 1980)★★★★, as Great Guitars *Great Guitars At The Winery* (Concord Jazz 1980)★★★, *Brazilville* (Concord Jazz 1981)★★, with Almeida *Latin Odyssey* (Concord Jazz 1982)★★★, *Christmas Album* (Concord Jazz 1982)★, as Great Guitars *Great Guitars At Charlie's, Georgetown* (Concord Jazz 1982)★★★, *Isn't It Romantic* (Concord Jazz 1984)★★★, *Byrd & Brass* (Concord Jazz 1986)★★★, *Byrd At The Gate* (Original Jazz Classics 1987)★★★, with Scott Hamilton *It's A Wonderful World* (Concord Jazz 1988)★★, with Almeida *Music Of The Brazilian Masters* (New Note 1989)★★★, *The Bossa Nova Years* (Concord Jazz 1991)★★★★, *Charlie Byrd/The Washington Guitar Quintet* (Concord Jazz 1992)★★★★, *Jazz Recital* (Savoy 1992)★★★, *Aquarelle* (Concord 1994)★★, *Moments Like This* (Concord 1994)★★★★, *Du Hot Club De Concord* (Concord Jazz 1995)★★★, as Great Guitars *The Return Of The Great Guitars* (Concord Jazz 1996)★★★, *Au Courant* (Concord Jazz 1998)★★★.

● VIDEOS: *Contemporary Jazz Acoustic Guitar* (Hot Licks 1996).

BYRD, DONALD

b. 9 December 1932, Detroit, Michigan, USA. In the early 50s Byrd studied trumpet and composition and also played in bands during his military service. Later in the decade he was often called upon to record with leading bop musicians, including John Coltrane, Jackie McLean, Phil Woods, Sonny Rollins, Art Blake, Kenny Clarke and Gigi Gryce (with whom he co-led the Jazz Lab quintet). At the end of the 50s until 1961, he was in a partnership with Pepper Adams. Shortly after, Byrd resumed his studies, this time in Europe. In the mid-60s he began a long and parallel career as a jazz educator, teaching at some of the USA's most important seats of learning, including Rutgers and Howard universities. However, he continued to record, playing with musicians including Dexter Gordon. During the 70s, Byrd experimented with jazz-rock and achieved some commercial success with his records. Much of this work was soul- and funk-inspired and he founded the Blackbyrds with this in mind. Their series of albums represents pure funk, and the jazz hardliners were often critical of this musical heresy. He continued his teaching, however, and retained his strong links with the hard bop movement in jazz. In 1993 he recorded with Gang Starr rapper Guru on his adventurous jazz/rap fusion project *Jazzmatazz*. A leading bop trumpet stylist, Byrd's striking technique and rich and beautiful tone make him one of the most lyrical of his generation of jazzmen.

● ALBUMS: *First Flight* (Delmark 1955)★★★, *Long Green* (Savoy 1955)★★, *Byrd's Eye View* (Transition 1956)★★★, *Byrd Jazz* (Transition 1956)★★★, *Byrd Blows On Beacon Hill* (Transition 1956)★★★, *Byrd's Word* (Savoy 1956)★★★, with Art Farmer *Two Trumpets* (Prestige 1956)★★★, *The Jazz Message Of* (Savoy 1956)★★★, with Farmer, Idriss Suliman *Three Trumpets* (Prestige 1957)★★★★, with Phil Woods *The Young Bloods* (Prestige 1957)★★★★, *September Afternoon* (Discovery 1957)★★★, with Gigi Gryce *Jazz Lab* reissued as *Gigi Gryce/Donald Byrd* (Jubilee/Josie 1957)★★★★, with Gryce *Modern Jazz Perspective/Jazz Lab, Volume 2* (Columbia 1957)★★★★, with Gryce *Gigi Gryce And The Jazz Lab Quintet* (Riverside 1957)★★★★, with Hank Mobley, Lee Morgan *Hank Mobley With Donald Byrd And Lee Morgan* (Blue Note 1957)★★★, *X-tacy* (1957)★★★, *Jazz Eyes* (Savoy 1957)★★★, *Byrd In Paris, Volumes 1 & 2* (Polydor 1958)★★★★, with Pepper Adams *10 To 4 At The 5 Spot* (Riverside 1958)★★★★, *Off To The Races* (Blue Note 1959)★★★, *Byrd In Hand* (Blue Note 1959)★★★, *Byrd In Flight* (Blue Note 1960)★★★, *Fuego* (Blue Note 1960)★★★★, with Adams *Stardust* (Bethlehem 1960)★★★, with Adams *Out Of This World* (Warwick 1961)★★★, *Donald Byrd At The Half Note Volume 1* (Blue Note 1961)★★★★, *Donald Byrd At The Half Note Volume 2* (Blue Note 1961)★★★★★, *Chant* (Blue Note 1961)★★★★, *The Cat Walk* (Blue Note 1961)★★★★, *Royal Flush* (Blue Note 1962)★★★, *Groovin' For Nat* (Black Lion 1962)★★★★, *Free Form* (Blue Note 1962)★★★, with Kenny Burrell, Herbie Hancock *A New Perspective* (Blue Note 1964)★★★★, *I'm Tryin' To Get Home* (Blue Note 1965)★★★, with Kenny Burrell, Mobley *Donald Byrd, Hank Mobley & Kenny Burrell* (Status 1965)★★★, *Mustang!* (Blue Note 1966)★★★, *The Creeper* (1967)★★★★, *Blackjack* (Blue Note 1967)★★★★, *Slow Drag* (Blue Note 1968)★★★, *Fancy Free* (Blue Note 1969)★★★, *Electric Byrd* (Blue Note 1970)★★★★, *Ethiopian Knights* (Blue Note 1971)★★★, *Blackbyrd* (Blue Note 1973)★★★, *Street Lady* (Blue Note 1974)★★★, *Steppin' Into Tomorrow* (Blue Note 1975)★★★, *Places And Spaces* (Blue Note 1975)★★★, *Caricatures* (Blue Note 1977)★★★, *Thank You...For F.U.M.L. (Funking Up My Life)* (Elektra 1978)★★★, *Love Byrd* (Elektra 1981)★★★, *Words, Sounds, Colors And Shapes* (1982)★★★, *Harlem Blues* (Landmark 1987)★★★, *And 125th Street NYC* (Elektra 1988)★★★, *Getting Down To Business* (Landmark 1989)★★, *A City Called Heaven* (Landmark 1993)★★, *Kofi* (Blue Note 1994)★★★.

● COMPILATIONS: *Donald Byrd's Best* (Blue Note 1976)★★★★, *Early Byrd - The Best Of* (Blue Note 1993)★★★★.

BYRNE, BOBBY

b. 10 October 1918, Columbus, Ohio, USA. Byrne took up the trombone as a child and by the age of 16 he was sufficiently proficient to be hired for the Dorsey Brothers Orchestra. After Tommy Dorsey walked out, Byrne stayed with the band, which was now led by Jimmy Dorsey. Byrne had the unenviable task of attempting to fill the shoes of one of the greatest trombone players in the history of the instrument and it is to his credit that he acquitted himself well in what was essentially an impossible task. Byrne's talent was sufficient to gain him a following and at the end of the 30s he decided to form his own big band. As much a musical perfectionist as Tommy Dorsey, Byrne was eager to do well and he hired Don Redman as his arranger, an experienced bass player in Abe Siegel, a new young drummer, Shelly Manne, and a competent and popular singer, Dorothy Claire. A change of arranger in 1942 brought a change of style and although new man Sid Brantley was not Redman's equal, he was more attuned to Byrne's needs. Nevertheless, the band folded the following year when Byrne entered military service. In the immediate post-war years Byrne formed another big band, which included Larry Elgart and Charles Albertine, whose arrangements were later a significant factor in Elgart's success. The new band was short-lived and Byrne led a small group for a while, played in various studio sessions and in the 50s made occasional records leading his own specially assembled big band. By the 60s he had opted out of performing, turning instead to work in the recording industry.

● ALBUMS: *Bobby Byrne Plays Great Themes* (Grand Award 1958)★★★★, *The Jazzbone's Connected To The Trombone* (Grand Award 1959)★★★.

BYRNE, DONNA

b. USA. Based in Boston in the 90s, Byrne has recorded with Herb Pomeroy, Dick Johnson, Dave McKenna and Ken Peplowski. Singing in a clear, soft-toned, unmannered style, using a slight and well-controlled vibrato, she eloquently performs standards from the Great American Song Book. To this kind of material she brings a subtle sense of swing. When taking on the up-tempo jazz standards which pepper her repertoire her restraint is admirable, as is her sparing use of scat. She is at her best when backed by a swinging small group.

● ALBUMS: *Let's Face The Music And Dance* (Stash 1992)★★★★, *It Was Me* (Daring 1997)★★, *Walking On Air* (Arbors 1997)★★★.

BYRON, DON

b. 8 November 1958, New York City, New York, USA. A single-minded individualist and eclectic, clarinettist Byron has performed in classical, klezmer, salsa, classic jazz and free-music contexts, earning a reputation for an intense artistic curiosity, and helping to re-establish credibility for the clarinet as a contemporary jazz instrument. Growing up in the Bronx, he was constantly exposed to music by his parents (who played piano and bass in amateur bands) and was inevitably influenced by the thriving local Hispanic music, with its daring and exuberant improvisations over swinging rhythms. Byron would pay regular visits to the nearby Garden Of Roses, where he could hear Machito's awesome group, and would use his classical clarinet training to transcribe salsa music by Ray Barretto and Luis 'Perico' Ortiz for local bands. Continuing his studies at the New England Conservatory of Music, the proximity of Berklee College Of Music's prestigious jazz hot-house led to a greater degree of interest in the jazz tradition, and some creative exchanges with jazz students Donald 'Duck' Harrison, Jean Toussaint and Greg Osby. However, it was the Klezmer Conservatory Band and its clarinet-led Jewish folk music that really captured Byron's imagination, sowing the seeds for his highly acclaimed klezmer project *Don Byron Plays The Music Of Mickey Katz*. Katz was a Jewish bandleader, composer and paradist who embodied the 'mischief' in the music that Byron says first attracted him, and his work provided Byron with exactly the right mix of music and narrative to deal with an ever-present political content. Since leaving college, Byron's jazz credits have included tours with the David Murray Big Band, Bobby Previte, the Mercer Ellington Orchestra (in which he played Harry Carney's lines on the baritone saxophone), Bill Frisell and Ralph Peterson, and appeared in a free, *avant garde* context in the 1993 Company line-up. His debut album, *Tuskegee Experiments*, addressed an American racist outrage, in which a large number of black syphilis patients were left untreated in a 'medical experiment', and features contributions from Bill Frisell, Ralph Peterson Jnr., Reggie Workman and a powerful poem by Sadiq. He followed this up with an album by the Katz project. The traditional tunes on *Bug Music* helped it become a bestseller in the American jazz charts in 1997, but at the same time Byron collaborated with San Francisco's President's Breakfast on *Bar.B.Que Dali*, a set of grinding industrial soundscapes.

● ALBUMS: *Tuskegee Experiments* (Nonesuch 1992)★★★★, *David Murray Big Band Conducted By Butch Morris* (1992)★★★, with Ralph Peterson *Presents The Fo'tet* (Blue Note 1990)★★★, with Bobby Previte *Weather Clear Track Fast* (Enja 1992)★★★, with Peterson *Ornettology* (Blue Note 1992)★★★, *Don Byron Plays The Music Of Mickey Katz* (Elektra Nonesuch 1993)★★★★, with Bill Frisell *This Land* (Nonesuch 1993)★★★★, with Frisell *Have A Little Faith* (Nonesuch 1993)★★★, *Music For Six Musicians* (Nonesuch 1995)★★★, *Bug Music* (Nonesuch 1996)★★★★, *No-Vibe Zone: Live At The Knitting Factory* (Knitting Factory Works 1996)★★★, *Nu Blaxploitation* (Blue Note 1998)★★★★.

● COMPILATIONS: *Live At The Knitting Factory Volume 3* (Knitting Factory Works 1991)★★★.

Cables, George

b. George Andrew Cables, 14 November 1944, New York City, New York, USA. After studying piano at Mannes College, Cables' reputation as a flawless accompanist was quickly established. Playing with Art Blakey in 1969, Sonny Rollins in the same year, Joe Henderson between 1969 and 1971, and Freddie Hubbard between 1971 and 1976, he was always in demand from touring bandleaders. Through the late 70s and 80s he played and recorded with Dexter Gordon (1976 to 1978), George Benson (1981), Bebop And Beyond (1984), and was Art Pepper's last pianist (1979 to 1982). Cable's best work has been produced in the role of sideman, although his tribute to George Gershwin (*By George*) is particularly affecting.

● ALBUMS: *Circles* (Contemporary 1979)★★★, *Cables' Vision* (Original Jazz Classics 1980)★★★, with Bruce Forman *Dynamics With George Cables* (Concord Jazz 1985)★★★, *Phantom Of The City* (Contemporary 1985)★★★★, *By George* (Contemporary 1987)★★★★, *Night And Day* (DIW 1991)★★★★, *Cables Fables* Steeplechase 1992)★★★, *Beyond Forever* (Steeplechase 1992)★★★, *I Mean You* (Steeplechase 1994)★★★, *Maybeck Recital Hall Vol 35* (Concord 1995)★★★, *Quiet Fire* (Steeplechase 1995)★★, *Person To Person* (Steeplechase 1997)★★★★, *Skylark* (1998)★★, *Dark Side Light Side* (Steeplechase 1998)★★★.

Caceres, David

b. David DeLeon Caceres, 24 July 1967, San Antonio, Texas, USA. Caceres was born into a very musical family. His grandfather was violinist Emilio Caceres, and his great uncle was the distinguished baritone saxophonist Ernie Caceres. At the age of four he first played piano and then studied formally for a few years before, at the age of 11, he took up the alto saxophone. At 18 he went to the Berklee College Of Music, graduating in 1989 by which time had already begun making an impression on the music scene in the USA and abroad. In the early 80s he played with the Texas All-State Jazz Band and in 1985 performed at the North Sea and Montreux jazz festivals with the band Jazz Abroad. During the 90s he played extensively at clubs and concerts in his hometown and in Houston, Texas, and for several years has performed regularly at the San Antonio Jazz Alive Festival. He also recorded with, among others, the Latin Playerz, *Under The Influence* (Richport 1992), pianist Paul English, *Beauty* (Capstone 1994), and Stratus, *Iconoclast* (Virtual 1995) and *Live At The Ale House* (Guild 1997). He also made radio broadcasts, including one, in the company of veterans Jim Cullum and John Frigo, on which tribute was paid to the earlier generation of the Caceres family. For several years he led his own quartets which included bassist-composer Dave Nichols, the producer of Caceres's first album. Although his background has made him adept in various aspects of jazz and Latin music, Caceres is especially notable when he plays bop and post-bop alto. His ballad playing is filled with elegant phrasing and understated emotionalism. On appropriate material he improvises fluently and with burning intensity. In addition to serving the roots and branches of jazz by ably perpetuating the family name, since the late 80s Caceres has ensured the continuation of the music through his activities as a jazz educator.

● ALBUMS: *Innermost* (Mayfly 1995)★★★, *David Caceres* (Guild 1999)★★★.

Caceres, Ernie

b. 22 November 1911, Rockport, Texas, USA, d. 10 January 1971. A highly skilled musician, Caceres played guitar early in his career before turning to reed instruments. His first professional engagements took him from Texas to Detroit and New York, often playing in small groups organized and led by his brother, violinist Emilio. In 1938 Caceres joined Bobby Hackett, then played briefly with big bands led by Jack Teagarden, Bob Zurke, Glenn Miller, Tommy Dorsey, Benny Goodman, Woody Herman, Billy Butterfield and Hackett again. With these bands he mostly played clarinet and alto and baritone saxophones, but occasionally doubled on tenor. His recording career also included sessions with Sidney Bechet and Eddie Condon. For many years Caceres was one of the two most highly regarded baritone players in jazz, and although he never attained the sonority of Harry Carney, he was a forceful and flexible player. Although his roots were in big bands and Dixieland, he ventured successfully into more modern company when he played on Metronome All Stars recordings in 1949, including musicians such as Dizzy Gillespie, Miles Davis, Fats Navarro, and Charlie Parker. In the 60s Caceres returned to Texas and played with various bands, including Jim Cullum's San Antonio-based outfit. His great-nephew, David Caceres, is a fine bop alto saxophonist.

● ALBUMS: with Emilio Caceres *No More Blues* (1937)★★, *Ernie And Emilio Caceres* (Audiophile 1969)★★★★, with Bobby Hackett, Eddie Condon *Jam Session (1948)* (1986)★★★★, with Metronome All Stars *Victory Ball (1949)* (1988)★★★.

Cage, John

b. 5 September 1912, Los Angeles, California, USA, d. 12 August 1992, New York, USA. Renowned as an *avant garde* composer and experimental musician, Cage was also a poet, teacher, writer, commercial artist and lecturer. After studying with Arnold Schoenberg and Adolph Weiss in the 30s, he moved on to his own compositions, heavily influenced by the work of Edgar Varese. By his 20s he was a leading exponent of the *musique concrete* movement that combined electronics with traditional sounds and eventually led to the development of the synthesizer. His 'utilized sounds' included doors slamming, pouring water and radio static and he is credited with the invention of the prepared piano technique, wherein the piano has everyday objects lodged inside the instrument in order to produce unusual sounds when played. He studied Zen Buddhism in the Far East during the 50s and used the principles of the I Ching (Book Of Changes) to develop his own brand of experimental music. Far and away his most famous piece of music is '4 minutes 33 seconds', which consists of complete silence (barring natural environmental sounds). The performer, usually a pianist, is expected to show the audience which of the piece's four movements he is 'performing' by the use of his fingers, as if a composer. Cage encouraged performers to add their own artistic input to the composition. He remained one of the biggest influences on many of the electronic and industrial exponents of the 70s and 80s, from the Grateful Dead through to the Pet Shop Boys.

● ALBUMS: *Music Of Changes* (1951)★★★, *Imaginary Landscape No. 4* (1951)★★★, *Concerto For Prepared Piano And Orchestra* (1968)★★★★, *Cartridge Music* (1969)★★★, *HPSCHD* (Nonesuch 1970)★★★, *Child Of Tree* (1975)★★★, *Sonata And Interlude For Prepared Piano* (1976)★★★★, *Telephones And Birds* (1977)★★★★, *John Cage* (1979)★★★★, *Atlas Eclipticals For Three Flutes* (1992)★★★, *Fontana Mix & Solo For Voice 2* (1993)★★★★.

● FURTHER READING: *For The Birds*, John Cage and Daniel Charles. *John Cage*, Heinz-Klaus Metzger and Rainer Riehn.

Cagnolatti, Ernie

b. 2 April 1911, Madisonville, Louisiana, USA, d. 7 April 1983. Cagnolatti studied trumpet in his teens, and spent most of the 30s in a big band. In the 40s and 50s he played in various brass bands at parades and funerals in New Orleans. He also played in bands led by Alphonse Picou, Bill Matthews and Paul Barbarain. Cagnolatti continued to play in New Orleans, sometimes with Jim Robinson, through the 60s and 70s. A solid, if sometimes unimaginative player, Cagnolatti lent a measure of authority to ensembles of which he was a member.

Caiazza, Nick

b. 20 March 1914, New Castle, Pennsylvania, USA. In his late teens, Caiazza worked with territory bands in the Midwest before joining Joe Haymes' popular dance band in 1936. He played with a number of swing era big bands including Woody Herman's, but produced his best work of the era on his recordings with Muggsy Spanier's Ragtimers. A gifted musician, playing clarinet and tenor saxophone, Caiazza worked for many years in New York radio and television studios and also played with the New York Philharmonic Orchestra. His interest in classical music led to extensive studies and a number of compositions. He also taught at Boston's Berklee College Of Music. A fluent, driving player, Caiazza was comfortable in the most exalted company, as he displayed on the *Midnight At V-Disc* album with Louis Armstrong, Jack Teagarden and Oran 'Hot Lips' Page.

● ALBUMS: with various artists *Midnight At V-Disc* (1944)★★.

Cain, Jackie

(see Kral, Roy)

Caiola, Al

b. Alexander Emil Caiola, 7 September 1920, Jersey City, New Jersey, USA. A highly respected studio guitarist, Caiola played with many renowned musical directors such as Percy Faith, Hugo Winterhalter and Andre Kostelanetz. After serving as musical arranger and conductor for United Artists Records, Caiola released several singles on RCA during the 50s, including 'Delicado', a Brazilian song written by Walter Azevedo, which became a hit for Percy Faith, Stan Kenton, Ralph Flanagan and Dinah Shore. Caiola also released *Serenade In Blue* and *Deep In A Dream*, recorded by his Quintet. In 1961 he entered the US Top 40 charts with the movie theme *The Magnificent Seven* and *Bonanza*, the title music from the popular western television series; he had his own television show for a short time in the USA.

● ALBUMS: *Deep In A Dream* (Savoy/London 1955)★★, *Serenade In Blue* (Savoy/London 1956)★★★, *High Strung* (RCA Victor 1959)★★★, *Music For Space Squirrels* (Atco 1960)★★, with Don Arnone *Great Pickin'* (Chancellor 1960)★★★, *Salute Italia* (Roulette 1960)★★, *Percussion Espanol* (Time 1960)★★★, *Spanish Guitars* (Time 1960)★★★, *Gershwin And Guitars* (Time 1961)★★★, *Soft Guitars* (1962)★★★, *Guitar Of Plenty* (1962)★★★, *Cleopatra And All That Jazz* (United Artists 1963)★★★, *Tough Guitar* (United Artists 1964)★★, *Music To Read James Bond By* (1965)★★★, *Sounds For Spies And Private Eyes* (United Artists 1965)★★★.

Caldwell, Happy

b. Albert W. Caldwell, 25 July 1903, Chicago, Illinois, USA, d. 29 December 1978. After starting out on clarinet, Caldwell switched to tenor saxophone. He became one of the earliest jazzmen to adopt this instrument and in the 20s and 30s worked with several bands, including those led by Bernie Young, Vernon Andrade, Tiny Bradshaw, Fletcher Henderson and Elmer Snowden. He also accompanied singer Mamie Smith. He appeared on many recording dates, including some with Louis Armstrong and Jelly Roll Morton. Mostly based in New York, Caldwell played many club engagements through the 40s and into the 50s and 60s. In the 70s he joined Clyde Bernhardt's band with which he recorded and toured. A sound craftsman, he was related to and took lessons from Buster Bailey. Despite his early groundbreaking use of the tenor saxophone, Caldwell chose not to move with the musical times and this has rather unfairly led to his neglect.

California Ramblers

Between 1921 and 1937 entrepreneur and sometime singer Ed Kirkeby regularly formed a band for a series of recording dates, usually to accompany his own undistinguished singing. Kirkeby's choice of musicians was felicitous and the Ramblers used some of the best white players of the 20s and early 30s. Jimmy and Tommy Dorsey played with the band, as did Miff Mole, Adrian Rollini, Stan King and Red Nichols. Although the music of the band is clearly rooted in the jazz of the time, the arrangements they used show the band to have been forward-thinking and to have had great collective skill and dexterity. They made numerous records, switching from label to label, and usually changing their name as they did so, the most common of the alternative names being the Golden Gate Orchestra. Smaller groups from the same stable included the Goofus Five and the Varsity Eight. Despite the vocals by Kirkeby, who is best known in jazz circles for his management of Fats Waller, the band played with infectious swing and there were fine solos. The band was briefly re-formed in the 70s and 80s under the direction of Dick Sudhalter.

CALLENDER, RED

b. George Sylvester Callender, 6 March 1916, Haynesville, Virginia, USA, d. 8 March 1992, Saugus, California, USA. Callender began performing in jazz groups, playing bass, while still in his teens. By the mid-30s he had settled in California and during the next few years worked with a succession of bands, including those led by Buck Clayton, Louis Armstrong, Erroll Garner and Lester Young. From the early 40s Callender was deeply involved in bebop, adapting comfortably to the new concept. He recorded extensively with prominent beboppers such as Charlie Parker, Wardell Gray and Dexter Gordon. As well as appearing in the Nat 'King' Cole trio during this period, Callender also led his own small groups, usually a trio, one of which included Lester Young. In the 50s Callender's skilled musicianship led to his becoming a sought-after studio player; he subsequently worked on record dates with artists as diverse as Frank Sinatra and Stevie Wonder, but also continued to work with jazzmen. A particularly noteworthy set of recordings came in the mid-50s when he was signed by Norman Granz to accompany Art Tatum. In later years Callender frequently turned to playing tuba, an instrument on which he proved to possess remarkable dexterity. In addition to his playing, Callender also composed and arranged, and in 1985 published his compelling autobiography, *Unfinished Dream*.

● ALBUMS: with Nat 'King' Cole, Lester Young *King Cole-Lester Young-Red Callender Trio* reissued as *Lester Young-Nat King Cole Trio* (Aladdin/Score 1953)★★★★, *Swinging Suite* (Modern 1956)★★★, *Red Callender Speaks Low* (Crown 1957)★★★★, *The Lowest* (Metrojazz 1958)★★★★, *Basin Street Blues* (1973)★★★, with Gerry Wiggins *Night Mist Blues* (Hemisphere 1983)★★★, with Jeannie and Jimmy Cheatham *Homeward Bound* (Concord Jazz 1987)★★.

● FURTHER READING: *Unfinished Dream: The Musical World Of Red Callender*, Red Callender with Elaine Cohen.

CALLOWAY, CAB

b. Cabell Calloway, 25 December 1907, Rochester, New York, USA, d. 8 November 1994, Cokebury Village, Delaware, USA. Involved in showbusiness from an early age, vocalist Calloway was an occasional drummer and MC, working mostly in Baltimore, where he was raised, and Chicago, where he relocated in the late 20s. He worked with his sister Blanche, and then, in 1929, he became frontman for the Alabamians. Engagements with this band took him to New York; in the same year he fronted the Missourians, a band for which he had briefly worked a year earlier. The Missourians were hired for New York's Savoy Ballroom; although the band consisted of proficient musicians, there is no doubt that it was Calloway's flamboyant leadership that attracted most attention. Dressing outlandishly in an eye-catching 'Zoot Suit' - knee-length drape jacket, voluminous trousers, huge wide-brimmed hat and a floor-trailing watch chain - he was the centre of attraction. His speech was peppered with hip phraseology and his catchphrase, 'Hi-De-Hi', echoed by the fans, became a permanent part of the language. The popularity of the band and of its leader led to changes. Renamed as Cab Calloway And His Orchestra, the band moved into the Cotton Club in 1931 as replacement for Duke Ellington, allegedly at the insistence of the club's Mafia-connected owners. The radio exposure this brought helped to establish Calloway as a national figure. As a singer Calloway proved difficult for jazz fans to swallow. His eccentricities of dress extended into his vocal style, which carried echoes of the blues, crass sentimentality and cantorial religiosity. At his best, however, as on 'Geechy Joe' and 'Sunday In Savannah', which he sang in the 1943 film *Stormy Weather*, he could be highly effective. His greatest popular hits were a succession of songs, the lyrics of which were replete with veiled references to drugs that, presumably, the record company executives failed to recognize. 'Minnie The Moocher' was the first of these, recorded in March 1931 with 'Kicking The Gong Around', an expression that means smoking opium, released in October the same year. Other hits, about sexual prowess, were Fats Waller's 'Six Or Seven Times' and the Harold Arlen-Ted Koehler song 'Triggeration'. For the more perceptive jazz fans who were patient enough to sit through the razzmatazz, and what one of his sidemen referred to as 'all that hooping and hollering', Calloway's chief contribution to the music came through the extraordinary calibre of the musicians he hired. In the earlier band he had the remarkable cornetist Reuben Reeves, trombonist Ed Swayzee, Doc Cheatham and Bennie Payne. As his popularity increased, Calloway began hiring the best men he could find, paying excellent salaries and allowing plenty of solo space, even though the records were usually heavily orientated towards his singing. By the early 40s the band included outstanding players such as Chu Berry, featured on 'Ghost Of A Chance' and 'Tappin' Off', Hilton Jefferson ('Willow Weep For Me'), Milt Hinton ('Pluckin' The Bass'), Cozy Cole

('Ratamacue' and 'Crescendo In Drums') and Jonah Jones ('Jonah Joins The Cab'). Further musicians included Ben Webster, Shad Collins, Garvin Bushell, Mario Bauza, Walter 'Foots' Thomas, Tyree Glenn, J.C. Heard and Dizzy Gillespie, making the Calloway band a force with which to be reckoned and one of the outstanding big bands of the swing era. In later years Cab worked on the stage in *Porgy And Bess* and *Hello, Dolly!*, and took acting roles in films such as *The Blues Brothers* (1980). His other films over the years included *The Big Broadcast* (1932), *International House, The Singing Kid, Manhattan Merry Go Round, Sensations Of 1945, St. Louis Blues, The Cincinnati Kid* and *A Man Called Adam* (1966). Calloway enjoyed a resurgence of popularity in the 70s with a Broadway appearance in *Bubbling Brown Sugar*. In the 80s he was seen and heard on stages and television screens in the USA and UK, sometimes as star, sometimes as support but always as the centre of attention. In 1993 he appeared at London's Barbican Centre, and in the same year celebrated his honorary doctorate in fine arts at the University of Rochester in New York State by leading the 9,000 graduates and guests in a singalong to 'Minnie The Moocher'. Calloway died the following year.

● ALBUMS: *Cab Calloway* 10-inch album (Brunswick 1954)★★★★, *Cab Calloway* ii (Epic 1956)★★★, *Hi De Hi, Hi De Ho* (RCA Victor 1958)★★★★, *The Cotton Club Revue Of 1958* (Gone 1959)★★★, *Blues Make Me Happy* (Coral 1962)★★★.

● COMPILATIONS: *Club Zanzibar Broadcasts* (Unique Jazz 1981)★★★, *Kicking The Gong Around* (Living Era 1982)★★★, *The Hi-De-Ho Man* (RCA 1983)★★★★, *Cab & Co.* (RCA 1985)★★★, *Cab Calloway Collection - 20 Greatest Hits* (Deja Vu 1986)★★★★, *Missourians* (1986)★★★, *The Cab Calloway Story* (Deja Vu 1989)★★★★, *Best Of The Big Bands* (Columbia 1991)★★★, *Classics 1941-42* (1993)★★★★, *Jumpin' Jive* (Camden 1998)★★★.

● FURTHER READING: *Of Minnie The Moocher And Me*, Cab Calloway. *The New Cab Calloway's Hepster's Dictionary*, Cab Calloway.

● FILMS: *The Big Broadcast* (1932), *International House* (1933), *Stormy Weather* (1943), *Sensations Of 1945* (1945), *St. Louis Blues* (1958), *A Man Called Adam* (1966), *The Blues Brothers* (1980).

CAMARATA, TUTTI

b. Salvatore Camarata, 11 May 1913, Glen Ridge, New Jersey, USA. Although a proficient trumpet player, Camarata's chief talent lay in his imaginative arranging. After studying at New York's Juilliard School, he played in studio bands and also developed his arranging and composing ability. In the early 30s he arranged for Charlie Barnet, before joining the Jimmy Dorsey band as lead trumpeter. It was, however, as an arranger that Camarata made an indelible mark on the fortunes of the Dorsey band. He dreamed up a highly effective and musically ingenious gimmick for the band during its long run on the *Twenty Grand* radio show. Faced with the need to demonstrate all that the band could do in one three-minute spot, he created a three-in-one arrangement that began with a song smoothly sung by Bob Eberly, moved on to a jumping up-tempo section featuring Dorsey's alto, and then slowed it down to showcase Helen O'Connell's sexy wailing. The first song treated this way was 'Amapola', then came 'Yours', while the third, 'Green Eyes', was a runaway hit, as was the later 'Tangerine'. After leaving Dorsey, Camarata wrote for the Casa Loma Orchestra, Benny Goodman (for whom he wrote an arrangement of Prokoviev's 'Peter And The Wolf') and Paul Whiteman. Camarata was also the arranger of some of the string-accompanied recordings made by Billie Holiday, which included his own composition 'No More' (lyrics by Bob Russell). Camarata also wrote lyrics, his best known being 'The Breeze And I'. For a number of years he was musical director of ABC and Decca Records and was a co-founder of both London Records and Disneyland Records. Apart from his experience with big bands and in popular music, Camarata has also written a religious piece, 'Portrait Of Jesus', and worked in the classical field, transcribing operas.

CAMERO DE GUERRA, CANDIDO

(see Candido)

CAMILO, MICHEL

b. 4 April 1954, Santo Domingo, Dominican Republic. Composing his first song at the age of five, Camilo was heavily influenced by Art Tatum, Oscar Peterson and McCoy Tyner, as well as great classical composers for piano, and the Cuban composer Ernesto Lecuona. He attended the National Conservatory of the Dominican Republic for 13 years and earned a professorship in music. At 16 he became a member of the country's National Symphony Orchestra, but wishing to continue his musical education, in 1979 he moved to New York to study at Mannes and the Juilliard School of Music. A pianist of tremendous technique and agility, Camilo's mixture of his native Caribbean rhythms with traditional jazz harmony began to attract notice, and he began playing with the New York group French Toast and saxophonist Paquito D'Rivera, with whom he first recorded his most well-known composition, 'Why Not!'. A vocal version of the song was recorded by Manhattan Transfer, for which Camilo won a Grammy award in 1983. In 1985, he made his debut at Carnegie Hall as the opening act for Tania Maria. The Michel Camilo Trio was soon appearing regularly in the USA, Caribbean, Japan and Europe. Camilo's first two recordings as a leader, *Why Not!* and *Suntan*, were recorded on the Japanese label King Records/Electric Bird and later released in the USA by Projazz and Evidence Music (1992). In December 1987, Camilo was invited to conduct the National Symphony Orchestra of the Dominican Republic in a recital of classical works, including his own 'Goodwill Games Theme', for which he received an Emmy Award. He was also named the director of the Dominican Republic's Heineken Jazz Festival at this time. In November 1988, Camilo's major label debut came with *Michel Camilo*, which met with great critical and popular acclaim. In 1991/2, Camilo began to branch out into new areas of expression with performances with Katia and Marielle Labeque, the London Philharmonia Orchestra, and the Atlanta Symphony Orchestra. He also found time to compose and record the score of the award-winning European film, *Amo Tu Cama Rica*, and composed the commissioned 'Rhapsody For Two Pianos And Orchestra'. A reunion with his original trio in 1993 resulted in the recording of *Rendezvous*, a highly acclaimed album of muscular trio music, featuring long-time collaborators Dave Weckl and Anthony Jackson. Camilo's many solo piano performances at this time included a televised concert event at the White House celebrating the 40th anniversary of the Newport Jazz Festival. In 1994 Camilo composed the score for the film *Los Peores Anos De Nuestra Vida* and released *One More Once*, a recording of his best songs arranged for a big band. The following two years continued with more extensive tours with the trio, and solo concerts that included appearances at the Kennedy Center, Radio City Music Hall and Carnegie Hall. Camilo also composed and performed his third film score for the romantic comedy *Two Much*. The release of *Thru My Eyes* (1997) allowed Camilo a vehicle to interpret some of his favourite jazz standards in his own style. At this time Camilo was honoured by The Duke Ellington School of the Arts in Washington, DC, with the establishment of the Michel Camilo Piano Scholarship. Camilo continues to lead the way in the world of jazz piano and Latin/jazz composition. His blending of Caribbean dance styles with American jazz has proved to be a highly regarded formula and his astonishing technique and powers of improvisation have made him a concert favourite all over the world.

● ALBUMS: *Why Not!* (King/Electric Bird 1986)★★★★, *Suntan* (King/Electric Bird 1987)★★★, *Michel Camilo* (Columbia 1988)★★★★, *On Fire* (Columbia 1989)★★★, *On The Other Hand* (Columbia 1990)★★★, *Rendezvous* (Columbia 1993)★★★★, *One More Once* (Columbia 1994)★★★, *Thru My Eyes* (TropiJazz 1997)★★★★.

CAMPBELL, MIKE

b. Los Angeles, California, USA. Campbell's family was very musical, his father and a brother being drummers. He began playing guitar at the age of 15 but soon decided that he really wanted to be a singer. His early leanings were towards swing music, with special favourites being Benny Goodman, Duke Ellington and Count Basie. Campbell began his singing career with a vocal group, the Doodletown Pipers, performing in resort towns such as Las Vegas and Lake Tahoe. He became the group's lead singer, but after three and a half years decided to strike out on his own. He formed a band to perform in the Vegas show band tradition (and which included actress Lindsay Wagner in its ranks), but he really wanted to sing jazz. He returned to his hometown, bringing with him pianist-arranger Tom Garvin, and began building a large repertoire of songs with all manner of settings, including solo, trio and big band. He soon developed a local reputation that gradually spread through his recordings, occasional tours and his extensive work as a teacher and clinician. From 1983-92 he was Vocal Program Director at the Dick Grove School of Music, later holding a similar post at the Musicians Institute in Hollywood. He toured Europe in 1992 and again the following year, and visited Australia in 1994. He writes songs, and has also written music for films and television. His wife, Elaine Blakely Campbell, is a singer and actress. Campbell's relaxed and unassuming singing style conceals a lifetime of dedication to his craft. Although he admires singers as diverse as Nat 'King' Cole, Randy Newman, Mark Murphy and Donny Hathaway, his own style is distinctive and in no way derivative. He is especially effective with ballads and pays the lyric great heed: 'For me it's all about the words and the story. I consider myself a storyteller.' Campbell often works with jazz musicians such as Steve Hufstetter, Lanny Morgan and John Heard, and Garvin continues to be a close musical associate. Campbell's repertoire includes original material by himself, Garvin, Heard and others, together with songs by the likes of Jimmy Rowles, Dave Frishberg, Roger Kellaway and Matt Dennis; there are also the standards from the Great American Song Book composers, such as Ralph Rainger and Leo Robin, Richard Rodgers and Lorenz Hart, Alec Wilder and Johnny Mandel.

● ALBUMS: *Secret Fantasy* (Palo Alto 1984)★★★, *Blackberry Winter* (ITI)★★, *One On One* (Audiophile)★★, *Easy Chair Jazz* (Audiophile)★★★★, *Loving Friends* (Audiophile 1994)★★★, *Let's Get Away From It All* (Audiophile 1998)★★★.

CANDIDO

b. Candido Camero de Guerra, 22 April 1921, Havana, Cuba. Turning to percussion in his early teenage years, after a brief flirtation with bass and guitar, Candido became an important member of the Cuban musical hierarchy. Despite his popularity in Cuba, in 1952 he was tempted to the USA by Dizzy Gillespie, with whom he played and later recorded. During the mid-50s, he played with Billy Taylor, Stan Kenton and others, usually performing on conga and bongo drums. Eclectic in taste and style, Candido was able to blend his urgent, exhilarating Latin roots with the demands of bop and mainstream artists alike. A list of his musical associates from the late 50s through to the late 70s rings with important names such as Erroll Garner, Al Cohn, Art Blakey, Phil Woods, Sonny Rollins, Wes Montgomery, Elvin Jones and Lionel Hampton. In the 80s, Candido was still active in the USA but was heard less in jazz circles, more often playing in studio orchestras. A seminal figure in the growth of popularity of Latin rhythms in jazz in the third quarter of the century, Candido's skill, dexterity and propulsive swing has set standards achieved by only a few of his successors.

● ALBUMS: *Candido Featuring Al Cohn* (ABC-Paramount 1956)★★★★, *The Volcanic Candido* (ABC-Paramount 1957)★★★, *Candido In Indigo* (ABC-Paramount 1958)★★★★, *Latin Fire* (ABC-Paramount 1959)★★★, *Beautiful* (RCA Victor 1959)★★★, *Conga Soul* (Roulette 1962)★★★, *Candido's Comparsa* (1963)★★★, *Candido, Featuring Al Cohn* (1965)★★★★, *Thousand Finger Man* (Solid State 1970)★★, *Drum Fever* (1973)★★.

Candoli, Conte

b. Secondo Candoli, 12 July 1927, Mishawaka, Indiana, USA. At the age of 13 Candoli was already showing a prodigious talent playing the trumpet, and studying alongside his older brother, Pete Candoli, with whom he performed briefly in the Woody Herman band at the age of 16. He went back home to finish school, then rejoined Herman, but was drafted into the army. After leaving the services he joined a small group led by ex-Herman bassist Chubby Jackson, with whom he toured Scandinavia in 1947. During the next few years Candoli worked with several bands, including Charlie Ventura's, but spent most of the early 50s, very successfully, with Stan Kenton. Candoli worked with numerous small groups, sometimes as leader, and was an important contributor to the development of west coast jazz, the so-called 'cool school'. In the 60s he played with Terry Gibbs, with Herman again, worked extensively with Shelly Manne, and returned to Kenton with the LA Neophonic Orchestra. From time to time he has also worked in a small group as co-leader with his brother and through the 70s and 80s continued to perform in clubs and at festivals, making regular recordings with a wide range of musical associates, and was a member of Supersax. Candoli's playing is characterized by a fluid, reflective approach while his warm and full sound adds immeasurably to his inventive solos.

● ALBUMS: with Howard Rumsey *In The Solo Spotlight* (Fantasy 1954)★★★, *Sincerely, Conte Candoli* 10-inch album (Bethlehem 1954)★★★★, *Conte Candoli, Volume 2* 10-inch album (Bethlehem 1955)★★★, *West Coast Wailers* (Atlantic 1955)★★★★, *Mucho Calor* (Andex 1957)★★★★, *The Conte Candoli Quartet* (Mode 1957)★★★★, *Sessions, Live* (1958)★★, with Pete Candoli *The Brothers Candoli Sextet* (1959)★★★★, *Little Band, Big Jazz* (Crown 1960)★★★, *Conversation* (1973)★★★, *Echo* (1982)★★★, *Portrait Of A Count* (Fresh Sound 1998)★★★.

Candoli, Pete

b. Walter J. Candoli, 23 June 1923, Mishawaka, Indiana, USA. Despite having learnt to play the bass and French horn by the time he was 12 years old, Candoli was by his mid-teens making his name as a trumpeter, working in swing era big bands where his musicianship made him a valuable sideman. At first he worked in the more commercial end of the music scene, playing in the bands of Sonny Dunham and Will Bradley/Ray McKinley. In 1942 Candoli was briefly with Benny Goodman and then worked with Tommy Dorsey, Freddie Slack, Teddy Powell, Alvino Rey and Charlie Barnet. Candoli's precocity and startling technique (as a high-note man he was second only to Cat Anderson) first attracted the attention of jazz fans when he joined Woody Herman's First Herd. His playing on hits such as 'Caldonia', 'Apple Honey' and 'Northwest Passage' was forceful and exciting and he lived up to his 'Superman' nickname by wearing a Superman suit for his featured solos. He also worked with Boyd Raeburn's musically adventurous band, but later in the 40s returned to rather more prosaic territory with Tex Beneke, Jerry Grey and Les Brown, eventually settling on the west coast where he became a studio musician, working in films such as *The Man With The Golden Arm* (1956). The call of jazz was too strong to ignore altogether, and Candoli worked with Milt Bernhart's Brass Ensemble and joined Stan Kenton's New Concepts and LA Neophonic bands. In the early 70s he also worked as a double act with his then wife, singer Edie Adams, and has periodically worked in tandem with his brother, Conte Candoli. A bold, fiercely attacking player, Candoli's tone is warm and his solos are filled with rhythmically dramatic lines and great flair.

● ALBUMS: *Bell, Book And Candoli* (1958)★★★, with Conte Candoli *The Brothers Candoli Sextet* (1959)★★★★, *For Pete's Sake* (Kapp 1960)★★★, *Blues, When Your Lover Has Gone* (Somerset 1963)★★★.

Capp, Frank

b. 20 August 1931, Worcester, Massachusetts, USA. In his late teens, while studying music at the Berklee College Of Music in Boston, Massachusetts, Capp was invited to join Stan Kenton's Orchestra as replacement drummer for Shelly Manne. This was in early 1952; by the end of the year Capp had left to join Neal Hefti's band. As he later admitted, this was the wrong way round; the Hefti band, a commercially orientated dance band, was a better training ground than the powerhouse Kenton band. Capp then became accompanist to Peggy Lee before joining the big bands of Billy May and Harry James and small groups led by Charlie Barnet and Shorty Rogers. Through the 50s and into the 60s, Capp spent much of his working life in television and film studios but also made numerous albums with Benny Goodman, Terry Gibbs, Barney Kessel, and several with André Previn. In the mid-70s Capp formed a big band with Nat Pierce, which became known as the Capp-Pierce Juggernaut. In the 80s Capp continued to play in small and big bands, using his extensive technical proficiency and bringing enthusiasm and hard-swinging excitement to every performance. In the mid-90s, Capp continued his big band playing with Juggernaut, the concept proving sufficiently durable to survive Pierce's death.

● ALBUMS: with Rickey Woodard *Quality Time* (Concord Jazz 1996)★★★, with Sammy Nestico *'Play It Again Sam"* (Concord Jazz 1997)★★★.

Capp-Pierce Juggernaut

In 1975 American big band drummer Frank Capp temporarily took over Nat Pierce's duties as contractor for the Neal Hefti Orchestra. When the band abruptly folded, Capp was left with an engagement, for which the club owner asked him to provide an alternative band. Capp formed the group from leading west coast session men and decided to use the occasion as a tribute to Hefti's great arranging skills. A disagreement with Hefti led to Capp contacting Pierce, whose own arranging talents had graced the bandbooks of both Woody Herman and Count Basie. Using Pierce's Basie-style charts and with the pianist as his co-leader, the band was a great success; they began to make more dates and eventually were heard by writer Leonard Feather, who headlined his newspaper article: 'A Juggernaut On Basie Street'. Renaming their band accordingly, Capp and Pierce made records, the first of which sold well, and continued to work whenever and wherever they could, concentrating on Basie-style material played with enormous zest and enthusiasm, but also displaying great versatility when the occasion demanded. Unfortunately, the collective personnel make it a band far too expensive ever to tour. Among the personnel have been Bill Berry, Bobby Shew, Marshal Royal, Blue Mitchell, Herb Ellis, Chuck Berghofer and Richie Kamuca, while the singers who have worked and sometimes recorded with the band have been Ernie Andrews, Joe Williams, Ernestine Anderson and Nancy Wilson. In the mid-90s, led by Capp, Juggernaut proved sufficiently well-founded to survive Pierce's death.

● ALBUMS: with Ernie Andrews *Juggernaut* (Concord 1976)★★★★, *Juggernaut Live At Century Plaza* (Concord 1978)★★★, *The Capp-Pierce Juggernaut* (Concord 1979)★★★, *Juggernaut Strikes Again!* (Concord 1981)★★★, with Ernestine Anderson *Live At The Alley Cat* (Concord 1987)★★★★, *In A Hefti Bag* (Concord 1994)★★★★.

Carcasses, Bobby

b. 29 August 1928, Kingston, Jamaica. Born into a Cuban family (his maternal grandfather worked as a diplomat in Jamaica at the time of his birth), Carcasses moved with his family back to Cuba aged four, where he was surrounded by the various forms of local music. However, he started out as an opera singer before switching to Cuban music and working as a vocalist at the famous Tropicana nightclub. It was here that he first began to experiment with incorporating scat and bebop influences into his vocal style. By 1960 he was also known as a dancer and athlete (he was Cuba's Long Jump Champion for that year) and as a multi-instrumentalist (playing trumpet, bass, congas and drums). Later in the decade he travelled, including a year in Paris playing with resident jazz greats Bud Powell and Kenny 'Klook' Clarke. On his return to Cuba he formed his own jazz group, as well as acting in films and television. In 1980 he organized the first Jazz Plaza Festival, bringing to Cuba a host of international artists including Dizzy Gillespie, Charlie Haden and Airto Moreira. The festival became an annual event, with Carcasses and his band performing each year. He also toured extensively throughout Europe and the USA, performing alongside Tito Puente, Eddie Palmieri and many other big names of Latin jazz. *Jazz Timbero* was recorded in Havana in 1997 with an all-star Cuban big band (including members of Irakere and Los Van Van), playing a funky mix of Latin and jazz.

● ALBUMS: *Jazz Timbero* (Tumi 1998)★★★.

Carelli, Gerard

b. USA. A New York-based trombonist and singer, Carelli has attracted the respectful attention of many leading musicians. Noted New York session trombonist Wayne André considers him to be 'an excellent improviser' and singer-composer Matt Dennis admires his singing and playing in equal measure. Technically assured, Carelli's trombone playing displays great flair and he has an easy, relaxed approach to the instrument, particularly suitable for the ballads that form a substantial part of his repertoire. This repertoire is dominated by the classic songs of the 30s and 40s, although he brings to his performances touches that clearly demonstrate that he is very much a musician of today. His singing is also relaxed and he has a pleasant, warm sound suited to the late-night ambience of the supper-club circuit.

● ALBUMS: *Beautiful Dancer* (GC 1993)★★★.

Carey, Mutt

b. Thomas Carey, 1891, Hahnville, Louisiana, USA, d. 3 September 1948. Born into a musical family, 'Papa' Mutt Carey played drums and guitar throughout his early years before taking up the cornet, and later the trumpet, when in his early 20s. He worked in New Orleans with several bands, many of them marching bands, before teaming up with Kid Ory in 1914. After touring in a show with Johnny Dodds, Carey returned to New Orleans where he played alongside Chris Kelly, Wade Whalley and others, then rejoined Ory who was by this time working in California. From 1919 the two remained together until 1925 when Carey took over as leader, gradually increasing the size of the band throughout the late 20s and into the early swing era. Despite the revival of interest in New Orleans music, the early 40s found Carey no longer able to sustain a living as a full-time musician but he continued to play whenever possible. In 1944 he once more plunged into full-time playing and a renewed association with Ory, a partnership that lasted until 1947. A gifted trumpeter with unusual sensitivity and great melodic gifts, Carey's playing was characterized by a wide vibrato and he brought to the traditional trumpet playing of New Orleans music a distinction rarely equalled.

● ALBUMS: *Mutt Carey Plays The Blues* 10-inch album (Riverside 1954)★★★.

Carisi, Johnny

b. 23 February 1922, Hasbrouck Heights, New Jersey, USA, d. 3 October 1992, New York, USA. A jazz trumpeter turned composer, Carisi began arranging while in Glenn Miller's US Air Force Band at Yale between 1938 and 1943. 'I'd run and find out who wasn't going into New York for the weekend and write for whoever was left - whether it was a cello and a French horn, or a piano and a tuba. Two people and we had a band', he commented. Carisi's use of non-jazz instrumentation was celebrated for 'Israel', one of the stand-out pieces on Miles Davis's *Birth Of The Cool* sessions. Influenced by his time with Claude Thornhill, Carisi's small number of compositions are nearly all masterpieces. He arranged for Gil Evans in 1960 and for trumpeter Marvin Stamm in 1968. 'Moon Taj', released in 1960 on *Into The Hot* (on album presented by Gil Evans and featuring tracks by Carisi and Cecil Taylor), was a gem of tremulous Third Stream enchantment. Although his subsequent involvement in jazz has been minimal, Carisi continued to work in music, both as a pop arranger and a composer of highly individual classical pieces that included a saxophone quartet and a tuba concerto.

CARLISLE, UNA MAE

b. 26 December 1915, Xenia, Ohio, USA, d. 7 November 1956. Playing piano and singing professionally while still in her teens, Carlisle was heard by Fats Waller in 1932. Hired by the latter, with whom she established a close relationship, Carlisle made several records in the late 30s. Waller joined her on some of these, notably a delightful version of 'I Can't Give You Anything But Love', but she also established a name for herself in her own right. Shortly before the outbreak of World War II she became highly successful in England, Germany and France, where she worked at the Boeuf sur le Toit in Paris. She then returned to New York where she undertook several successful engagements and record dates. In 1941 she recorded with John Kirby and was nominal leader of several small bands, which featured such leading jazzmen as Russell Procope, Charlie Shavers, Ray Nance, Lester Young and Benny Carter. Also in the early 40s she became popular on radio and, before the decade was out, she had successfully transferred to television. In the early 50s she was still popular, playing with artists such as Don Redman, but her health was failing and she retired in 1954. A competent pianist with a stylistic debt to Waller, Carlisle sang in a huskily intimate manner, her warm sensual voice proving especially effective on ballads. Her use of delayed phrasing gave her jazz performances a highly effective lazy swing.

● COMPILATIONS: *Una Mae Carlisle & Savannah Churchill 1944* (Harlequin 1982)★★★★.

CARLTON, LARRY

b. 2 March 1948, Torrance, California, USA. Often cited as the guitarist's guitarist, Carlton has courted rock, jazz and acoustic 'new age' with considerable success. The former member of the Crusaders carved a career during the 70s as a sought-after session musician. His profile improved following some outstanding, fluid playing over a number of years with Steely Dan (in particular, his solo on 'Kid Charlemagne' from 1976's *The Royal Scam*). His distinctive 'creamy' Gibson 335 guitar sound was heard on countless records and his work on numerous Joni Mitchell albums arguably contributed to their success, with notable examples including *Court And Spark* and *Hejira*. His major label debut appeared in 1978. It was not until *Sleepwalk*, including its title track (formerly a hit for Santo And Johnny), that Carlton was fully accepted as a solo artist in his own right. *Alone But Never Alone* found Carlton playing acoustic guitar and the record proved a critical and commercial success. Both that album and *Discovery* broadened Carlton's following. The live *Last Nite*, however, saw a return to his jazz roots, and contained flashes of breathtaking virtuosity, in particular on his stand-out version of Miles Davis' 'So What'. With *On Solid Ground* Carlton demonstrated a stronger rock influence and produced a credible cover version of Eric Clapton's 'Layla' and Steely Dan's 'Josie'. He was awarded a Grammy in 1981 and again in 1987 for his version of 'Minute By Minute'. The following year Carlton was shot in the neck by an intruder at his studio. After an emergency operation and many months of physiotherapy he made a full recovery. Carlton joined the GRP stable in 1991 and found a home that perfectly suited his music. His duet with labelmate Lee Ritenour in 1995 was wholly satisfying, and boded well for future collaborations. Carlton remains a master musician with a catalogue of accessible and warming music.

● ALBUMS: *With A Little Help From My Friends* (Uni 1968)★★, *Singing/Playing* (Blue Thumb 1973)★★★, *Larry Carlton* (Warners 1978)★★, *Live In Japan* (Flyover 1979)★★★, *Strikes Twice* (MCA 1980)★★★, *Sleepwalk* (MCA 1981)★★★, *Eight Times Up* (Warners 1983)★★★, *Friends* (MCA 1983)★★★, *Alone But Never Alone* (MCA 1986)★★★★, *Discovery* (MCA 1986)★★★★, *Last Nite* (MCA 1986)★★★★, *On Solid Ground* (MCA 1989)★★★, *Renegade Gentleman* (GRP 1991)★★★, *Kid Gloves* (GRP 1992)★★★, with Lee Ritenour *Larry And Lee* (GRP 1995)★★★★, *The Gift* (GRP 1996)★★★.

● COMPILATIONS: *The Collection* (GRP 1990)★★★★.

CARMEL

This UK group was formed in Manchester in 1981 by Carmel McCourt (b. 24 November 1958, Scunthorpe, Lincolnshire, England; vocals) and former members of Bee Vamp, Jim Paris (b. 13 January 1957, Finchley, London, England; double bass) and Gerry Darby (b. 13 October 1959, Finchley, London, England; drums, percussion). On the release of the single 'Storm' and a mini-album in 1982 on the independent Red Flame label, Carmel drew praise for the fiery passion of all three members. Paris and Darby remarkably conjured the effect of a full ensemble backing to McCourt's powerful vocals, and were able to alternate between soulful ballads, gospel, blues and stomping jazz. The stand-out 'Tracks Of My Tears' was performed with confidence, as though the song had been a group original rather than a new arrangement of the Smokey Robinson classic. An appearance at the 1983 ICA Rock Week led to the group signing to London Records, while a sell-out date at the prestigious Ronnie Scott's jazz club confirmed Carmel's status within the British 'new jazz/pop' scene. In accentuating the 'jazz' motif, the music and 'style' press unfortunately saddled the group with an unwanted Billie Holiday image, which was eventually passed on to future 'rival', Sade. Carmel tasted success for the first time that year in the UK Top 20 singles chart, with the glorious, gospel-tinged 'Bad Day', featuring the Attractions' Steve Nieve and the swooping backing vocals of Helen Watson and Rush Winters. Carmel's '50s jazz club' image was evocatively captured on the single's cover by Serge Clerc, who supplied the artwork to the subsequent 'Willow Weep For Me', the Top 30 hit

'More More More', and the album, *The Drum Is Everything*. Despite attaining UK Top 20 status, the album failed to capture the vitality of the singles or of the earlier Red Flame issues. While the jazz fashion faded in the UK, Carmel found a much more attentive and appreciative audience in Europe, particularly France. A more satisfying release in *The Falling* saw the trio achieve their most successful studio performance up to that time, aided by several producers including Brian Eno and Hugh Johns. Subsequent albums displayed a increasing maturity that manifested itself in original compositions such as 'Easy For You', 'Nothing Good', 'Napoli' and 'I'm Over You'. The group's earlier talent for producing imaginative cover versions saw them tackling Randy Newman's 'Mama Told Me Not To Come', Charles Dawes and Carl Sigman's hit for Tommy Edwards, 'It's All In The Game', and Duke Ellington's 'Azure'. Despite the disappointing lack of mass appeal in the home market, Carmel continue to command respect from critics and fans alike and the group are able to work equally well within the confines of an intimate jazz club (selling out a season of dates at Ronnie Scott's in 1991) or in the larger auditoriums. After a long association with London Records, Carmel split from the label in 1991, signing with Warner Brothers Records/East West in 1992, but they subsequently moved to Musidisc in 1996.

● ALBUMS: *Carmel* (Red Flame 1982)★★★, *The Drum Is Everything* (London 1984)★★, *The Falling* (London 1986)★★★, *Everybody's Got A Little ... Soul* (London 1987)★★★, *Set Me Free* (London 1989)★★★, *Good News* (East West 1992)★★★, *World's Gone Crazy* (East West 1995)★★★, *Live In Paris* (Musidisc 1997)★★★★.

● COMPILATIONS: *Collected* (London 1990)★★★.

● VIDEOS: *Collected: A Collection Of Work 1983-1990* (London 1990).

CARNEY, HARRY

b. 1 April 1910, Boston, Massachusetts, USA, d. 8 October 1974, New York City, New York, USA. Carney began his professional musical career at the age of 13, playing clarinet and later the alto and baritone saxophone in Boston bands. Among his childhood friends were Johnny Hodges and Charlie Holmes, with whom he visited New York in 1927. Carney played at the Savoy Ballroom with Charlie 'Fess' Williams before joining Duke Ellington, who was about to play in the young musician's home-town. When this engagement was over Carney left for a tour with Ellington, who had taken on the role of guardian. The job with Ellington lasted until the latter's death 47 years later. Shortly after joining Ellington, Carney was persuaded to play alto saxophone but soon gravitated to the baritone, an instrument he proceeded to make his own. Carney's rich sonority became an essential element in Ellington's tonal palette and for decades listeners gloried in the full-throated lower register that, in a band brimming with individualists, had a character all its own. Nevertheless, despite his virtuosity on the baritone, Carney took up the clarinet on frequent occasions to demonstrate his mastery of reed instruments. Carney's relationship with Ellington transcended that of musician and leader; he was Ellington's confidante and for decades he drove the Duke from gig to gig. The closeness of their relationship was underlined by Carney: 'It's not only been an education being with him but also a great pleasure. At times I've been ashamed to take the money.' After Ellington's death, at the end of May 1974, Carney said, 'Without Duke I have nothing to live for.' He died a little over four months later.

● ALBUMS: *Harry Carney With Strings* (Clef 1955)★★★★, *Moods For Girl And Boy* (Verve 1956)★★★.

CARNEY, JAMES

b. 1964, USA. Los Angeles based pianist, composer and bandleader Carney, a runner up in the 1997 Thelonious Monk Institute/BMI International Jazz Composers Competition, was originally schooled in the classical and rock idioms. A fan of the Beatles, Who and Allman Brothers Band, Carney first turned to jazz when he was 21 after playing in rock groups for several years. He studied at the California Institute of the Arts alongside fellow students Charlie Haden, James Newton, John Carter and David Roitstein, graduating with a BFA in Jazz Piano Performance. The Institute also opened Carney's ears to a range of ethnic musical styles, playing an important part in the development of his own richly multi-cultural compositions. He has recorded two highly acclaimed sessions for the Jacaranda label, backed by a stellar range of young players including trumpeter Ralph Alessi and tenor saxophonists Ravi Coltrane and Chuck Manning. Through his compositions Carney makes a deliberate attempt to break with jazz tradition, exploring a range of musical styles from avant bop through country, funk and roots instead of recycling traditional jazz riffs.

● ALBUMS: *Fables From The Aqueduct* (Jacaranda 1994)★★★★, *Offset Rhapsody* (Jacaranda 1997)★★★★.

CARPENTER, THELMA

b. *c*.1920, New York City, New York, USA, d. 7 June 1997. Carpenter began singing as a very small child, and at the age of five made her radio debut. Six years later she had her own show on WNYC. She played the Apollo in 1938 on one of their justly famous amateur nights, where she won, and later appeared at the Onyx Club. She was heard by John Hammond Jnr. who recommended her to Teddy Wilson for his newly formed big band. She then sang with Coleman Hawkins' band, recording with them both but only scantily. In 1944 she played on Broadway with Bill 'Bojangles' Robinson, then sang with Count Basie for two years but recorded only one side. During the late 40s and early 50s she appeared regularly on stage, on radio, and made records, but widespread popularity and fame eluded her. In Europe in the 50s, she sang at Bricktop's in Paris and also worked in Rome, and on her return to the USA had some fairly successful records in the currently popular rocking ballad market. Largely ignored, but encouraged by budding entrepreneur Alan Eichler and others, in the 60s she stood in for Joséphine Baker at Carnegie Hall, was understudy for Pearl Bailey in the all-black version of *Hello, Dolly!* on Broadway, and played a regular role in the television series *Barefoot In The Park*. In 1970 she recorded tracks for a projected album with pianist Ellis Larkins, although it remained unreleased, and in 1975 recorded conversations and songs with Loonis McGlohon and Alec Wilder. She continued a rollercoaster career with long periods of 'resting' interspersed with work on television, in films and the theatre, among which were good roles in *The Wiz* (1978), a touring version of *Pippin*, and *The Cotton Club* (1984). In 1993 she appeared on the television special *Apollo Hall Of Fame*, and a few months before her death appeared on television's *Cosby*. Shamefully under-recorded during her lifetime, shortly after her death Carpenter's 70s recordings were eventually assembled on *A Souvenir*, decades after their making, as a tribute to an artist of great talent who deserved better respect and treatment from the public and from the music industry during her lifetime. Well-educated, she could speak several languages and, as McGlohon recalled, could express herself vividly in most of them. Her singing style, born out of admiration for her idols, Mabel Mercer and Ethel Waters, was unmistakably her own, and she invariably displayed an acute understanding of the meaning of a lyric.

● ALBUMS: *Thinking Of You Tonight* (Coral *c.*1962)★★★, *A Souvenir* 1970, 1975 recordings (Audiophile 1997)★★★.

CARPENTER, WINGIE

b. Theodore Carpenter, 15 April 1898, St. Louis, Missouri, USA, d. date unknown. While still a teenager, he lost an arm following an accident (John Chilton records that the surgeon carrying out the amputation was the uncle of trumpeter Doc Cheatham). Carpenter later began playing trumpet, working in various travelling shows in the south-western and Midwestern states. Among the territory bands with which he played were those led by Zack Whyte and Speed Webb during the 20s and in the 30s he was playing with lesser-known bands in the south and south-east. During this decade he moved to New York, playing with many different bands and also leading his own small groups. Carpenter continued to play into late middle-age. A sound and usually reliable player, his career was spent mostly in minor bands and well outside the main centres of music and recording.

CARR, IAN

b. 21 April 1933, Dumfries, Scotland. Carr taught himself trumpet from the age of 17. Between 1952 and 1956 he studied English literature at Newcastle University, and has had a career as writer, broadcaster, teacher and musician, all furthering the cause of jazz. Between 1960 and 1962 he played with the EmCee Five, the Newcastle bop quintet, before moving to London to work with tenor saxophonist Don Rendell. The Rendell-Carr group lasted until 1969, recording five albums and making international tours. Carr left to form Nucleus, which followed Miles Davis into the world of amplified jazz rock. *Elastic Rock*, their debut, was released in 1970. Tours followed, including Europe and the USA. Leonard Feather wrote, 'Many listeners and critics have agreed that Nucleus has been a seminal influence on jazz-rock groups in Europe and elsewhere'. In 1973 his book on contemporary UK jazz, *Music Outside*, was published. Carr's sometimes academic approach to music has resulted in long compositions, including *Solar Plexus* (1971) and *Labyrinth* (1974). In 1982 he became an associate professor at the Guildhall School of Music in London and was given the Calabria award for 'outstanding contribution in the field of jazz'. The same year saw the publication of his acclaimed biography of Miles Davis, which has now become one of the standard works on the artist. In 1986 he composed *Spirit Of Place* for Tony Coe and Eberhard Weber. His *Jazz: The Essential Companion* (1987, co-written with Digby Fairweather and Brian Priestley) was for some time the most in-depth jazz encyclopedia available in the UK, although some registered disquiet at Carr's apparent lack of sympathy for free improvisation, harmolodics and the black *avant garde*. In 1987 Carr also worked with the Mike Gibbs Orchestra and was the featured soloist with the Hamburg Radio Orchestra under Gibbs' direction.

Carr's recent projects include a trilogy of jazz compositions inspired by his years in Newcastle-upon-Tyne. The first piece, *Old Heartland*, inspired by the highly underrated novelist Sid Chaplin, was recorded in 1988; the second part, *Going Home*, was performed alongside Alan Plater's play of the same name; and the third, a suite entitled *North Eastern Song Lives*, was commissioned by Jazz North East to mark their 25th anniversary and first performed in Newcastle in October 1991. Since then, Carr has had a further jazz biography published, *Keith Jarrett: The Man And His Music*, and has performed with the United Jazz And Rock Ensemble. In the 90s he additionally worked with George Russell and Mike Gibbs as well as completing a new edition of his *Rough Guide To Jazz*. Carr is one of the most literate and emotional artists to come out of the 60s UK jazz scene.

● ALBUMS: with Don Rendell *Shades Of Blue* (Columbia 1964)★★★★, with Rendell *Phase III* (Columbia 1968)★★★, with Rendell *Change Is 1* (Columbia 1969)★★★, with Rendell *Dusk Fire* (Columbia 1970)★★★, with Rendell, Neil Ardley *Greek Variations* (1970)★★★, *Belladonna* (Core 1972)★★★, *Old Heartland* (MMC 1988)★★★★. See also Nucleus discography.

● FURTHER READING: *Music Outside-Contemporary Jazz In Britain*, Ian Carr. *Miles Davis*, Ian Carr. *Keith Jarrett: The Man And His Music*, Ian Carr.

CARR, MIKE

b. Michael Anthony Carr, 7 December 1937, South Shields, Co. Durham, England. The brother of trumpet-player Ian Carr, Mike taught himself the organ, piano, and vibes, and gained a reputation in the Newcastle-based EmCee Five. By the late 60s, he was running a trio that included John McLaughlin and accompanied distinguished visiting musicians. He toured with

Ronnie Scott's group between 1971 and 1975, appearing with them at Carnegie Hall in 1974. Since then his own quartet have toured Europe, and he has established Cargo - a jazz-rock group who recorded a successful album in 1985. The Mike Carr Trio continues to appear around the country, playing a hard-swinging, dynamic music rooted in bebop.

● ALBUMS: with the Emcee Five *Let's Take Five* (1961)★★★, with Tony Crombie *Hammond Under Pressure* (1968)★★★★, *Live At Ronnie Scott's* (1979)★★★, *Good Times & The Blues* (Cargogold 1993)★★★★.

CARRINGTON, TERRI LYNE

b. 1965, Medford, Massachusetts, USA. Her father and uncle, Sonny and Matt Carrington, were musicians, saxophonist and drummer respectively. Although she began playing the saxophone as a tiny child she very quickly turned to the drums. While still pre-teen, she sat in with musicians of the calibre of Dizzy Gillespie, Oscar Peterson and Clark Terry, and while at first there might have been an element of novelty in associations such as these it quickly became apparent that hers was a very real talent. Terry invited her to appear at the Wichita Jazz Festival and while there she encountered Buddy Rich, who featured her on television. When still only 11 years old she was awarded a full scholarship at the Berklee College Of Music, where she studied harmony, composition, piano and a variety of percussion instruments. Among her instructors was Alan Dawson and during this period of her life Carrington also met and played drums with numerous leading jazz musicians, including Kevin Eubanks, Branford Marsalis, Pat Metheny, Kenny Barron and Greg Osby. In 1983, with the encouragement of Jack DeJohnette, she settled in New York, playing there with jazz notables such as Stan Getz, Lester Bowie, David Sanborn and Wayne Shorter. She also accompanied a number of rising young singers, among them Cassandra Wilson and Dianne Reeves. At the end of the decade she moved to Los Angeles, playing with Herbie Hancock and Al Jarreau among others. She has appeared on many records, and also in films and on television. While still at high school Carrington had taught and conducted clinics, and her activities now extended to include not only this but also songwriting, arranging, and record production. In the latter capacity she produced and co-produced albums for many jazz and pop performers including Reeves, Sanborn and pianist, Niels Lan Doky. A technically accomplished drummer, Carrington's enormous enthusiasm for her work in so many behind-the-scenes areas of the music industry has tended to keep her from the wide attention she clearly merits as a performer.

● ALBUMS: *Real Life Story* (Verve 1989)★★★.

CARROLL, BAIKIDA

b. 15 January 1947, St Louis, Missouri, USA. Carroll studied trumpet and flügelhorn at Southern Illinois University and the Armed Forces School of Music, directing the Third Infantry Division Ensemble. He also studied music in Germany. Like many other black musicians of his generation in St. Louis, Carroll gained exposure to the world of creative music via BAG (the Black Artists Group). Although associated with the *avant garde*, Carroll has an impressive résumé, including work with blues singers Albert King and Little Milton, soul saxophonist Oliver Sain, Fontella Bass and Sam And Dave. In 1973 he left the USA to live in Europe. In 1974 he issued *Orange Fish Tears*, a deft combination of world music evocation and free jazz. Back in the USA he has worked with Oliver Lake, guitarist Michael Gregory Jackson, Muhal Richard Abrams, Jack DeJohnette, Anthony Braxton, Michele Rosewoman and David Murray, playing in the latter's octet and big band. His long association with Julius Hemphill has been particularly productive; Carroll plays on several of Hemphill's albums who returns the favour on *Shadows And Reflections*. Since 1985 he has been a regular member of Charlie Haden's Liberation Music Orchestra. Baikida's vocalized playing is supported by an unerring grasp of thematic continuity, admirably demonstrated by *The Spoken Word*, a two-record set of unaccompanied trumpet. He has also composed scores for films.

● ALBUMS: *Orange Fish Tears* (1974)★★★★, *The Spoken Word* (1978)★★★, *Shadows And Reflections* (Soul Note 1982)★★★, *Door Of The Cage* (Soul Note 1995)★★★.

CARROLL, BARBARA

b. Barbara Carole Coppersmith, 25 January 1925, Worcester, Massachusetts, USA. Carroll studied piano formally and in her early 20s became well known in New York playing bop with her own trio, which at one time included Charlie Byrd. Many leading bop musicians played with the group, finding Carroll's good ears and technical virtuosity to be ideal accompaniment. Carroll played widely throughout the 50s but then left music for some time in order to raise a family. In the mid-70s she returned to play clubs and festivals. Carroll's classical training, allied as it is to an early influential liking for Nat 'King' Cole's piano playing, have helped bring a distinctive flavour to her work. She plays with deftness and a sure sense of the harmonic complexities of bop. She occasionally also sings in an engagingly diffident manner.

● ALBUMS: *Piano Panorama* 10-inch album (Atlantic 1952)★★★, *Barbara Carroll Trio* (RCA Victor 1954)★★★, *Lullabies In Rhythm* (RCA Victor 1955)★★★, *Have You Met Miss Carroll?* (RCA 1955)★★★, *We Just Couldn't Say Goodbye* (RCA Victor 1956)★★, *It's A Wonderful World* (RCA Victor 1957)★★★, *Funny Face* (Verve 1957)★★★, *Barbara* (Verve 1957)★★★, *Flower Drum Song* (Kapp 1958)★★★, *Why Not?* (SeSeac 1959)★★★, *'Hello, Dolly' & 'What Makes Sammy Run?'* (Warners 1964)★★, *Barbara Carroll 'Live'* (Warners 1968)★★★, *Barbara Carroll* (Blue Note 1976)★★★, *From The Beginning* (United Artists 1977)★★★, *At The Piano* (Discovery 1980)★★, *Old Friends* (Audiophile 1988)★★★, *Live At The Carlyle* (DRG 1991)★★★, *This Heart Of Mine* (DRG 1993)★★★, *All In Fun* (After 9 1998)★★★.

Carroll, Joe

b. 25 November 1919, Philadelphia, Pennsylvania, USA, d. 1 February 1981. Rooted in Louis Armstrong's singing style, but shaped by that of Leo Watson and the musical thought of Lester Young, Carroll was one of the first singers in jazz to fully assimilate bebop. He worked with Dizzy Gillespie from 1949-53, writing with him one of the bop vocal anthems, 'Oo-Shoo-Be-Do-Be'. He made a number of recordings in the 50s and early 60s under his own name and in 1964 toured with Woody Herman. Carroll's hard-edged, rough-toned voice had a limited range but he compensated with his exuberant swing and inventive lines.

● ALBUMS: *Joe Carroll: Man With A Happy Sound* (1962)★★.

Carry, Scoops

b. George Dorman Carry, 23 January 1915, Little Rock, Arkansas, USA, d. 4 August 1970. Born into a musical family, Carry was first trained by his mother and then at music colleges in Chicago. He worked with various bands in Chicago, playing both clarinet and alto saxophone. Among the leaders with whom he played were Lucky Millinder, Zutty Singleton, Roy Eldridge and Art Tatum. At the start of the 40s he joined Earl Hines for a long spell during which he played lead alto and also acted as the band's straw boss. In 1947 he left the Hines band and also left full-time music, turning to law. After studying law, he passed his bar examination and established a practice in Chicago, eventually rising to prominence with the Illinois state legislature. Carry (whose name is sometimes misspelled as Carey) was a good section player and a compelling soloist with an imaginative and questing mind.

Carter, Benny

b. Bennett Lester Carter, 8 August 1907, New York City, New York, USA. Carter was born and raised in the area of New York known as San Juan Hill, a tough neighbourhood. His working-class parents encouraged their children to take up music and Carter and his two sisters received piano tuition from their mother, Sadie Bennett Carter. A cousin, Theodore 'Cuban' Bennett, was a well-known trumpeter in New York jazz clubs in the 20s, while another cousin, Darnell Howard, played clarinet with the bands of W.C. Handy, Joe 'King' Oliver and Carroll Dickerson in the 20s. Apart from his mother's tuition, Carter took early lessons on the C-melody saxophone from a succession of teachers, among them Harold Proctor and Lt. Eugene Mickell Snr. Musician neighbours of Carter, in his youth, included Bubber Miley, Freddy Johnson, Rudy Powell, Russell Procope and Bobby Stark. Carter was already familiar with the Harlem jazz scene when, in 1923, his family settled there. By the late 20s, Carter, who had by then switched to the alto saxophone, was becoming known as a reliable and dedicated young musician who had gained valuable experience in bands led by Billy Fowler, Duke Ellington and Fletcher Henderson. In 1928 he was working in the band led by Fletcher's brother, Horace Henderson. When Horace left, Carter took over as leader. Despite engagements at top dancehalls, the band proved short-lived, owing, in part, to Carter's personal manner and attitude towards music. A naturally elegant man and musically a perfectionist and utter professional, Carter refused to resort to the kind of flash and showmanship audiences expected. After the band folded, Carter worked as musical director of McKinney's Cotton Pickers, a period during which he began to develop his interest in arranging. During the early 30s Carter also played trumpet, surprising fellow musicians with the ease at which he switched from reeds to brass and back again. By this time he was also adept on clarinet, tenor saxophone, trombone and piano. He pursued his interest in writing, providing arrangements for many leading bands of the day, including those of Chick Webb, for whom he also played alto, and Benny Goodman. In 1933 he formed a new big band, which featured Chu Berry and Dicky Wells. In this same year he also played on recording dates organized by British composer-bass player Spike Hughes. In 1935 Carter joined Willie Lewis's band, with which he visited Europe. In all, Carter was away for three years, working in several countries including France, Holland and Denmark. At the urging of writer Leonard Feather, Carter was hired by Henry Hall as staff arranger for the BBC Dance Orchestra in London. In 1938, aware of the commercial successes of the swing era back in the USA, he returned home and formed a new big band. Once again, his refusal to compromise his standards meant that the band enjoyed little commercial success. He also recorded extensively on small group sessions, such as Lionel Hampton's RCA recordings, for some of which he wrote arrangements. Other bands included the Chocolate Dandies, in which he played alongside Coleman Hawkins and Roy Eldridge, and the Varsity Seven. In 1942 Carter settled in California, formed a new big band and signed with agent Carlos Gastel, who also handled Nat 'King' Cole, Sonny Dunham and Stan Kenton. Employed to write for films, Carter proved a fast learner and, although he was sometimes uncredited, because blacks had yet to achieve full status in Hollywood, he worked on numerous scores for 20th Century-Fox, Warner Brothers and MGM. In the winter of 1946/7 Carter folded his big band for the last time but continued to re-form it for special recording dates. In the early 50s he began touring with Jazz At The Philharmonic and made numerous records for Norman Granz. He also arranged and provided orchestral backing for a host of singers, notably Peggy Lee, Ella Fitzgerald and Mel Tormé. A heart attack in January 1956 barely slowed him down and he remained active in his writing and playing; the same year he married for the fourth time. The late 50s and early 60s were especially fruitful times and he composed, arranged and played on a succession of important albums, including *Aspects*, *Further Definitions* and *Additions To Further Definitions*. He also wrote a major work for Count Basie, the *Kansas City Suite*. By now he was also working in television and touring the international festival circuit.

In the early 70s Carter began a continuing association with Princeton University, where he became Visiting Lecturer in the Council of Humanities and the African-American Studies Programme. His personal contact with Morroe Berger at Princeton led to the appearance of Berger's major biography, *Benny Carter: A Life In American Music* (1982). During the 70s Carter began a regular string of visits to Japan, where he became extremely popular, and also continued to record, again for Norman Granz. In the 80s Carter toured and recorded, on many occasions scoring and composing extensively.

As a player, on any of his many instruments, Carter is skilled and always inventive and delightful to hear. It is on alto saxophone, however, that he has made his greatest contribution. A liquid player in the tradition of Johnny Hodges and Willie Smith, the two contemporary giants with whom he is usually grouped, Carter displays a striking pungency and an effortless capacity for creating solos of interest and fascination. As a composer of tunes such as 'Doozy' and 'When Lights Are Low' he has contributed greatly to the jazz catalogue. As an arranger in the 30s he was a major force in shaping big band music and has continued to demonstrate his skills in this area and in small group settings to lasting effect. His longevity and the fact that neither his playing nor writing skills have shown any signs of diminishing are truly remarkable. In 1987 he joined forces with John Lewis and the All-American Jazz Orchestra, an occasionally assembled repertory band dedicated to the performance of music especially written for big bands. For a concert and subsequent recording date, Carter composed and arranged a new major work, *Central City Sketches*. Additionally, Carter rehearsed the orchestra, conducted, played solo alto and drew from the musicians taking part admiration, enthusiasm and a sparkling performance. In the late summer of 1989 the Classical Jazz series of concerts at New York's Lincoln Center celebrated Carter's 82nd birthday with a set of his songs, sung by Ernestine Anderson and Sylvia Syms. In the same week, at the Chicago Jazz Festival, he presented a recreation of his *Further Definitions* album, using some of the original musicians. In February 1990, Carter led an all-star big band at the Lincoln Center in a concert tribute to Ella Fitzgerald. Events such as these added to the endless and imperishable catalogue of achievements of this remarkable man. In 1995 a tribute album of sorts was issued, and unusually, Carter was present on the project. It featured some beautiful vocal treatments of Carter's work, including tracks from Ruth Brown, Diana Krall, Dianne Reeves and Peggy Lee. It was probably Ben Webster who first dubbed Carter 'The King', a name that stuck because, unlike titles bestowed by outsiders, this one was offered in tribute to qualities that jazz musicians themselves esteemed.

● ALBUMS: *Jazz Off The Air* (1944)★★★, *Cosmopolite* 10-inch album (Clef 1953)★★★, *The Urbane Mr Carter* 10-inch album (Norgran 1954)★★★★, *The Formidable Benny Carter* 10-inch album (Norgran 1954)★★★★, *Benny Carter Plays Pretty* reissued as *Moonglow - Love Songs By Benny Carter* (Norgran 1955)★★★, *Benny Carter* (Norgran 1955)★★★★, *New Jazz Sounds* (Norgran 1955)★★★, with Louis Bellson, Art Tatum *Tatum-Carter-Bellson* reissued as *The Three Giants* (Clef 1955)★★★, *Alone Together* (Norgran 1956)★★★, *Sessions, Live* (1957)★★★★, with Roy Eldridge *The Urbane Jazz Of Roy Eldridge And Benny Carter* (American Recording Society 1957)★★★, with Bellson, Tatum *Makin' Whoopee* (Verve 1958)★★★★, *Jazz Giant* (Contemporary 1958)★★★, *Swingin' The Twenties* (Contemporary 1959)★★★, *'Can Can' And 'Anything Goes'* (United Artists 1959)★★★, *Aspects* (United Artists 1959)★★★★, *The Fabulous Benny Carter* (Audio Lab 1959)★★★★, *Jazz Calendar* (United Artists 1960)★★★, *Sax A La Carter* (United Artists 1960)★★★, *Further Definitions* (Impulse! 1961)★★★★, *B.B.B. & Co.* (1962)★★★, *The World Of Sight And Sounds* (1963)★★★, *Benny Carter In Paris* (20th Century Fox 1963)★★★, *Additions To Further Definitions* (Impulse! 1966)★★★★, *Benny Carter 1933* (Prestige 1969)★★★, *The King* (Pablo 1976)★★★, *Carter, Gillespie Inc.* (1976)★★★, *Wonderland* (Pablo 1976)★★★, *Benny Carter At Montreux '77* (Original Jazz Classics 1977)★★★, *Live And Well In Japan* (Original Jazz Classics 1977)★★★, *Jazz Allstar Orchestra Live In Japan '79* (1979)★★★★, *Summer Serenade* (Storyville 1980)★★★, with Teddy Wilson *Gentlemen Of Swing* (1980)★★★, *Skyline Drive* (1982)★★★, with Nat Adderley, Red Norvo*The Benny Carter All Stars Featuring Nat Adderley & Red Norvo* (Sonet 1985)★★★★, *Benny Carter Meets Oscar Peterson* (Pablo 1986)★★★, *A Gentleman And His Music* (Concord 1986)★★★, with the All-American Jazz Orchestra *Central City Sketches* (Limelight 1987)★★★, *In The Mood For Swing* (Limelight 1987)★★★, *My Kind Of Trouble* (Pablo 1988)★★★, *Cooking At Carlos 1* (Limelight 1989)★★★, *My Man Benny, My Man Phil* (Limelight 1990)★★★, *All That Jazz Live At Princeton* (Limelight 1991)★★★★, *Harlem Renaissance* (1993)★★★, *Songbook* (Music Masters 1996)★★★, with Phil Woods *Another Time, Another Place* (Evening Star 1996)★★★★.

● COMPILATIONS: *The Best Of Benny Carter* (Pablo 1982)★★★★, *Benny Carter 1928-52* (RCA 1983)★★★★, *The Benny Carter Collection - 16 Golden Greats* (Deja Vu 1987)★★★★, *When Lights Are Low* (Happy Days 1987)★★★, *3,4,5 - The Verve Small Group Sessions* (1991)★★★★, *The Complete Recordings* (Affinity/Charly 1992)★★★★, *These Foolish Things* (Tring 1993)★★★, with Dizzy Gillespie, Quincy Jones *Journey To Next* (Lightyear 1996)★★★, *New Jazz Sounds: The Urbane Sessions* 2-CD set (Verve 1996)★★★★.

● VIDEOS: *Symphony In Riffs* (Rhapsody 1995).

● FURTHER READING: *The Alto Saxophone, Trumpet And Clarinet Of Benny Carter, 1927-1946*, Jan Evensmo. *Benny Carter: A Life In American Music*, M. and E. Berger.

CARTER, BETTY

b. Lillie Mae Jones, 16 May 1930, Flint, Michigan, USA, d. 26 September 1998, New York, USA. Growing up in Detroit, Carter sang with touring jazzmen, including Charlie Parker and Dizzy Gillespie. In her late teens, she joined Lionel Hampton, using the stage name Lorene Carter. With Hampton she enjoyed a love-hate relationship; he would regularly fire her only to have his wife and business manager, Gladys Hampton, rehire her immediately. Carter's predilection for bop earned from Hampton the mildly disparaging nickname of 'Bebop Betty', by which name she became known thereafter. In the early 50s she worked on the edge of the R&B scene, sharing stages with blues artists of the calibre of Muddy Waters. Throughout the remainder of the 50s and into the 60s she worked mostly in and around New York City, establishing a reputation as a fiercely independent and dedicated jazz singer. She took time out for tours with packages headlined by Ray Charles (with whom she recorded a highly regarded album of duets), but preferred to concentrate on her own shows and club performances. She also found time for marriage and a family. Her insistence upon certain standards in her recording sessions eventually led to the formation of her own record company, Bet-Car. During the 80s, Carter continued to perform in clubs in New York and London, occasionally working with large orchestras but customarily with a regular trio of piano, bass and drums, the ideal setting for her spectacular improvisations. Taking her inspiration from instrumentalists such as Parker and Sonny Rollins rather than from other singers, Carter's technique draws little from the vocal tradition in jazz. Her kinship with the blues is never far from the surface, however complex and contemporary that surface might be. In performance, Carter mainly employed the lower register of her wide range. Always aurally witty Carter frequently displayed scant regard for the lyrics of the songs she sang, her inventiveness was ably displayed on performances such as 'Sounds', a vocalese excursion which, in one recorded form, lasts for more than 25 minutes. Despite such extraordinary performances and the breakneck tempos she employed on 'The Trolley Song' and 'My Favourite Things', she could sing ballads with uncloying tenderness. In concert, Carter dominated the stage, paced like a tigress from side to side and delivered her material with devastating attack. The authority with which she stamped her performances, especially in vocalese and the boppish side of her repertoire, helped to make unchallenged her position as the major jazz singer of the 80s and 90s.

● ALBUMS: *Meet Betty Carter And Ray Bryant* (Epic 1955)★★★★, *The Bebop Girl* (1955)★★★, *Social Call* (Sony 1956)★★★, *Out There With Betty Carter - Progressive Jazz* (Peacock 1958)★★★, *The Modern Sound Of Betty Carter* (ABC-Paramount 1960)★★★, *I Can't Help It* (Impulse! 1961)★★★, with Ray Charles *Ray Charles And Betty Carter* (ABC 1961)★★★★, *'Round Midnight* (Atco 1963)★★★, *Inside Betty Carter* (United Artists 1963)★★★, *Finally* (Roulette 1969)★★★, *Live At The Village Vanguard* (Verve 1970)★★★★, *The Betty Carter Album* (Verve 1972)★★★, *Now It's My Turn* (Roulette 1976)★★★, *What A Little Moonlight Can Do* (Impulse! 1977)★★★★, *I Didn't Know What Time It Was* (Verve 1979)★★★, *The Audience With Betty Carter* (Verve 1979)★★★★, *Whatever Happened To Love?* (Verve 1982)★★★, *Look What I Got* (Verve 1988)★★★★, *Droppin' Things* (Verve 1990)★★★, *It's Not About The Melody* (Verve 1992)★★★★, *Feed The Fire* (Verve 1993)★★★, *I'm Yours, You're Mine* (Verve 1996)★★★★.

● COMPILATIONS: *Compact Jazz* (Philips 1990)★★★.

CARTER, JAMES

b. 1969, Detroit, Michigan, USA. Saxophonist James Carter has won praise throughout the jazz world, and also from several critics writing for the popular music press, with his explosive stage show and firebrand technique. Combining an adventuristic streak, born of his love of the *avant garde*, with a respectful familiarity with the works of Coleman Hawkins and Lester Young, Carter has risen to a position of astonishing visibility in jazz circles within a relatively short space of time. The youngest of five musical siblings, Carter grew up surrounded by music, his father being a keen radio listener while his brother played occasional dates as guitarist with Funkadelic and Parliament. Early sessions included work with the Julius Hemphill ensemble (*The Fat Man And The Hard Blues*) and the Lester Bowie quintet (*Organizer*). His solo albums each attracted gradually increasing critical praise, incorporating every conceivable contemporary influence from the opera of Enrico Caruso to the gritty rap narratives of the Wu-Tang Clan. His 1996 set, *Conversin' With The Elders*, followed the direction of its title by pairing him with jazz masters such as saxophonist Buddy Tate and trumpeter Harry 'Sweets' Edison.

● ALBUMS: *J.C. On The Set* (DIW/Columbia 1993)★★★, *Jurassic Classics* (DIW/Columbia 1995)★★★, *The Real Quietstorm* (Atlantic Jazz 1995)★★★★, *Conversin' With The Elders* (Atlantic Jazz 1996)★★★, *In Carterian Fashion* (Atlantic 1998)★★★★.

● FILMS: *Kansas City* (1996).

CARTER, JOHN WALLACE

b. 24 September 1929, Fort Worth, Texas, USA, d. 31 March 1991. Like his contemporary and fellow townsman Ornette Coleman, Carter played in numerous jazz and blues groups in the south-west in the late 40s before moving to Los Angeles in the mid-50s. At that time he played with Coleman and drummer Charles Moffett, developing a highly original style on clarinet, flute, alto and tenor saxophones - free yet melodic. In 1965 he conducted a festival orchestra playing Coleman's scores. On the west coast he joined forces with trumpeter Bobby Bradford and they formed his New Art Jazz Ensemble, which recorded a series of outstanding records that built on the early explorations of the Coleman quartet. From 1974 Carter concentrated solely on clarinet, becoming one of modern jazz's most celebrated practitioners on the instrument. He was leader of Clarinet Summit (with Alvin Batiste, Jimmy Hamilton and David Murray), played in James Newton's Wind Quintet and in 1982 founded the Wind College in LA. He continued to record through the 80s with Bradford, Newton, Horace Tapscott and his own various groups; however, his crowning achievement was the five-album suite *Roots And Folklore - Episodes In The Development Of American Folk Music* (1982-90), which traced the African roots of black music and the subsequent stages of its evolution in the USA through some intense and spontaneous playing. Carter was always involved with education; he was a graduate of Lincoln University and held teaching posts at California State University.

● ALBUMS: with the New Art Jazz Ensemble *Seeking* (1969)★★★, with the NAJE *Flight For Four* (Flying Dutchman 1969)★★★, with the NAJE *Self-Determination Music* (Flying Dutchman 1971)★★★, with the NAJE *Secrets* (1973)★★★, *Echoes From Rudolph's* (1977)★★★, with Bradford *A Suite Of American Folk Pieces For Solo Clarinet* (1979)★★, *Variations On Selected Themes For Jazz Quartet* (1980)★★★★, *Night Fire* (1981)★★★, *Dauhwe* (Black Saint 1982)★★★, *Clarinet Summit* (1984)★★★★, *Clarinet Summit Volume 2* (1985)★★, with Bradford *Castles Of Ghana* (Gramavision 1986)★★★, *Dance Of The Love Ghosts* (Gramavision 1987)★★★, with Bradford *Fields* (Gramavision 1988)★★★, with Clarinet Summit *Southern Belles* (1988)★★★, with Bradford *Shadows on A Wall* (Gramavision 1989)★★★, with Bradford *Comin' On* (hatART 1989)★★★★.

CARTER, REGINA

b. Detroit, Michigan, USA. One of the most highly regarded jazz violinists of the nineties, Carter has the potential to raise the instrument's profile to that achieved by Jean-Luc Ponty two decades earlier. Proficient on the violin since early childhood, Carter studied at the New England Conservatory and Oakland University in Michigan before joining rock band Straight Ahead, and recording with them for Atlantic Records. Carter moved to New York in the mid-90s, working with the disparate talents of Max Roach, Oliver Lake and the String Trio Of New York. She achieved most acclaim, however, for her solo work on the road production of Wynton Marsalis' compelling *Blood On The Fields*. Carter's appearances on releases by Steve Turré and Mark Helias, and her own major label debut, have helped to foster a growing chorus of critical acclaim for her startling improvisational skills.

● ALBUMS: *Regina Carter* (Atlantic 1995)★★★, *Something For Grace* (Atlantic 1997)★★★.

CARTER, RON

b. 4 May 1937, Ferndale, Michigan, USA. As a child Carter played cello, hoping for a career in classical music. Adept on several instruments, including violin, clarinet and trombone, he eventually settled on bass. He also opted for a career in jazz when he became aware of the difficulties confronting any black youth with musical ambitions centred upon the concert platform. He was in his early 20s before he began to perform regularly in jazz, securing a place in Chico Hamilton's quintet. In the early 60s he worked with Eric Dolphy, Don Ellis, Cannonball Adderley, Mal Waldron and Thelonious Monk, among many leading modern jazzmen. In 1963 he joined Miles Davis, remaining in the group until 1968, where his rhythm section partners were Herbie Hancock and Tony Williams. In addition to his work with Davis, Carter was in constant demand for studio sessions, recording many hundreds of albums. He continued this double life, playing on studio dates with, among others, George Benson and Stanley Turrentine. He also played concerts with the New York Jazz Sextet/Quartet, Sonny Rollins, V.S.O.P. (a band which featured Hancock, Williams, Freddie Hubbard and Wayne Shorter), McCoy Tyner and the Milestone All Stars. Also, he occasionally led bands for record and club and concert dates. In the 80s he continued his tireless round of concerts, festivals and recording sessions, always in company with leading artists like Hubbard, Cedar Walton, Jim Hall and George Duke. He was also once again reunited with Hancock and Williams for a USA tour with Wynton Marsalis. As one of the greatest bass players jazz has ever known, Carter's impeccable technique and the powerful propulsive swing of his playing enhance any rhythm section in which he appears. As an accompanist for singers he is beyond praise, regularly working with Lena Horne, recording with Aretha Franklin and others, while his solo accompaniment to Helen Merrill's 1968 recording of 'My Funny Valentine' is an object lesson in bass playing. His soloing on compositions such as 'The Third Plane' is similarly immaculate. Nevertheless, his greatest strength lies in his section playing and within that context his period with Hancock and Williams in the Davis band stands as eloquent testimonial to a master of his craft, caught at a peak from which, a quarter of a century on, he has yet to descend.

● ALBUMS: *Where?* (New Jazz 1961)★★★★, *Out Front* (Prestige 1966)★★★, *Uptown Conversation* (Atlantic 1969)★★★★, *Blues Farm* (Columbia 1973)★★★, *All Blues* (CTI 1974)★★★, *Spanish Blue* (Columbia 1975)★★★★, *Yellow And Green* (Columbia 1976)★★★, *Pastels* (Milestone 1977)★★★★, *Piccolo* (Milestone 1977)★★★★, *Third Plane* (Milestone 1977)★★★★, *Peg Leg* (Milestone 1978)★★★★, *A Song For You* (Milestone 1978)★★★, *1 + 3* (Milestone 1978)★★★, *Parade* (Milestone 1979)★★★, *New York Slick* (Milestone 1980)★★★, *Patrao* (Milestone 1980)★★★★, *Parfait* (Milestone 1981)★★★, with Cedar Walton *Heart And Soul* (Timeless 1982)★★★, *Etudes* (Elektra 1983)★★★★, with Jim Hall *Telephone* (Concord Jazz 1984)★★★★, *All Alone* (EmArcy 1988)★★★, *Ron Carter Plays Bach* (Blue Note 1988)★★★★, *Panamanhattan* (Evidence 1990)★★★, *Friends* (Blue Note 1993)★★★, with Hall *Live At Village West* 1982 recording (Concord Jazz 1993)★★★, *Jazz, My Romance* (Blue Note 1994)★★★, with Hancock, Wallace Roney, Wayne Shorter, Tony Williams *A Tribute To Miles* (QWest/Reprise 1994)★★, *Mr. Bow-Tie* (Blue Note 1995)★★★★, with Akio Sasaiima *Akioustically Sound* (Muse 1996)★★, *Brandenburg Concerto* (Blue Note 1996)★★★★, *The Bass And I* (Blue Note 1998)★★★★, *Ron Carter Trio* (Blue Note 1998)★★★★, *So What* (Blue Note 1998)★★★.

● FURTHER READING: *Spielmethode Fur Jazz-Bass*, Ron Carter. *Building A Jazz Bass Line*, Ron Carter.

CARTWRIGHT, DEIRDRE

b. Deirdre Josephine Cartwright, 27 July 1956, London, England. Born into a musical family, Cartwright began playing piano as a child, switching to guitar at 15. She abandoned studies towards a degree in Social Sciences to become a professional musician. Among her earliest engagements was with the noted British bandleader, Ivy Benson. During the 70s she played in several groups including Jam Today and at the start of the next decade joined the all-female band, Guest Stars, with whom she toured extensively, including visits to the USA. She also recorded with this band, *The Guest Stars* (Guest Stars 1984) and *Out At Night* (Guest Stars 1985). She was featured on BBC Television's *Rockschool* and at the end of the 80s, with bassist Alison Rayner, she formed Blow The Fuse. In the 90s she toured Britain and Europe and, in addition to playing with her own band, also worked with many leading artists including Peter King, Ian Shaw, Annie Whitehead, Steve Lodder, Carol Grimes, tenor saxophonist Louise Elliot, and the Jamaican pianist Marjorie Whylie. Cartwright's repertoire draws from an intriguing mix of contemporary jazz styles and modern pop. Her playing, mostly on nylon-stringed acoustic guitar with occasional outings on Fender bass guitar, is potent and driving. Her solos are intelligently conceived and fully realized and at all times she retains a strong feeling for the more melodic aspects of the music.

● ALBUMS: *Debut* (Blow The Fuse 1994)★★★.

Carver, Wayman

b. 25 December 1905, Portsmouth, Virginia, USA, d. 6 May 1967. Carver's first professional job was as a saxophonist with J. Neal Montgomery's Collegiate Ramblers and by his early 20s he had led his own band. In 1931 he was in New York where he worked with Elmer Snowden and two years later was in Benny Carter's big band. In 1934 he joined Chick Webb, remaining in the band as saxophone section leader and arranger until after Webb's death, when Ella Fitzgerald took over the leadership. Carver was among the first jazz musicians to play flute, using it on sessions with Spike Hughes in 1933 and soloing extensively with Webb where he was featured in duets with clarinettist Chauncey Haughton as a member of the Little Chicks small group. In the late 40s Carver retired from performing, becoming a teacher of music at Clark College, Atlanta, Georgia, where his students included George Adams. Carver continued teaching until his death in 1967.

● FURTHER READING: *The Flute Of Wayman Carver*, Jan Evensmo.

Cary, Dick

b. 10 July 1916, Hartford, Connecticut, USA, d. 6 April 1994, Glendale, California, USA. A formally trained violinist, Cary played with a local symphony orchestra while still in his teens but by the early 40s was regularly playing piano in various Dixieland bands, notably those led by Joe Marsala and Wild Bill Davison. Around this time Cary also arranged music for Benny Goodman and other big bands of the day, playing briefly with the Casa Loma Orchestra, but his heart was in the more traditional areas of jazz. Throughout the 40s he worked extensively, sometimes as a soloist, occasionally with Muggsy Spanier, Eddie Condon and Davison. In 1947 he became a founder-member of Louis Armstrong's All Stars but left, ostensibly pleading boredom, to advance his musical studies. From the 50s Cary worked as a freelance, arranged and played with a wide range of artists, always exhibiting considerable skill and refusing to compromise his exacting standards. In addition to his keyboard skills he also practised trumpet, trombone and alto horn. He relocated from New York to Los Angeles in 1959, where he also arranged as well as playing with top-flight Dixieland teams. His scores, often accentuated by oboes and bassoons, included a transcription of Bix Beiderbecke's 'In A Mist' for Jimmy McPartland.

● ALBUMS: *Dixieland Goes Progressive* (Golden Crest 1957)★★★, *Hot And Cool* (1958)★★★, *Dick Cary And His Dixieland Doodlers* (1959)★★★, *The Amazing Dick Cary* (1975)★★★, *California Doings* (1980)★★, *Dick Cary And His Tuesday Night Friends* (Arbors 1995)★★★, *Dick Cary With Ted Easton's Jazzband* (Southland 1988)★★.

Casa Loma Orchestra

Canadian tycoon Sir Henry Pellatt had delusions of grandeur similar to those exhibited by William Randolph Hearst. Pellatt's equivalent to Hearst's castle at San Simeon was Casa Loma, a house he built near Toronto. In 1929 a group of musicians, originally controlled by contractor Jean Goldkette and working as the Orange Blossoms, mainly in Canada, decided to strike out on their own. Forming a co-operative band under the nominal leadership of alto saxophonist Glen Gray, the musicians decided to adopt the name of Pellatt's folly and soon showed the musical world that their venture was based upon firm foundations. In its heyday the band was regarded by black and other white musicians as one of the hottest around. The Casa Lomans featured several good musicians, including Sonny Dunham and Clarence Hutchenrider, and also a very popular singer, Kenny Sargent. Musically, the band's key-man was guitarist Gene Gifford, whose excellent arrangements provided a distinctive sound. Precision playing and a smooth, subtly dynamic swing brought the band widespread popularity during the early 30s. Although often overlooked in swing era surveys, the band continued to play prestigious residencies into the 40s, when musicians of the calibre of Herb Ellis and Bobby Hackett were in its ranks. Later, the band continued to record, although Gray died in 1963, and still attracted attention thanks to an impressive array of sidemen, including Jonah Jones and Nick Fatool.

● COMPILATIONS: with Glen Gray *Glen Gray And The Casa Loma Orchestra 1943-46* (London-American 1979)★★★★, with Gray *Solo Spotlight* (Capitol 1986)★★★, *Casa Loma Stomp (1929-30)* (Hep Jazz 1986)★★★, *White Jazz (1931-34)* (Old Bean 1988)★★★, *Glen Gray And The Casa Loma Orchestra 1939-40* (Hindsight 1988)★★★★, *Glen Gray And The Casa Loma Orchestra 1943-46* (Hindsight 1988)★★★★, *Glen Gray And The Casa Loma Orchestra* (Columbia 1990)★★★.

Casey, Al

b. 15 September 1915, Louisville, Kentucky, USA. Casey's first professional job as a guitarist was with Fats Waller, with whom he recorded extensively from 1934 until Waller's death in 1943. Also in the 30s, Casey worked with Teddy Wilson in his small groups, sometimes accompanying Billie Holiday, and big band. After switching from acoustic to electric guitar, on which instrument he proved to be an able disciple of Charlie Christian, Casey extended his range into R&B, recording with King Curtis. In demand for recording dates with artists such as Helen Humes, Casey was briefly confined to the studio, but in the 80s was back in full flow, touring extensively and delighting international audiences with his vigour and inventiveness.

● ALBUMS: *Buck Jumpin'* (Prestige 1960)★★★★, *The Al Casey Quartet* (Moodsville 1960)★★★★, *Jumpin' With Al* (Black And Blue 1973)★★★, *Six Swinging Strings* (JSP 1981)★★, *Best Of Friends* (JSP 1981)★★★, *Genius Of Jazz Guitar* (JSP 1981)★★★, *Al Casey And George Kelly With Fessor's Session Boys* (1983)★★, *Al Casey Remembers King Curtis* (1985)★★★.

Cash, Bernie

b. 18 January 1935, Scarborough, Yorkshire, England, d. 7 October 1988. Cash began performing as a trumpet player and during the traditional jazz boom of the 50s worked with Bruce Turner, among others. In the 60s he switched to bass and although adept enough to teach the flute, piccolo and most of the saxophone family, it was on bass that he established his musical reputation. Also in the 60s he began a long musical partnership with fellow bass player Peter Ind, with whom he played and recorded. In the late 70s Cash formed his Great Jazz Solos Revisited Orchestra, designed to feature his arrangements of transcribed classic solos by past masters such as Charlie Parker and Louis Armstrong. Among the musicians Cash admired was Lester Young; in 1982 he obtained his MA degree at the University of Hull with a thesis on his idol. Four years later, Cash wrote the score for the jazz opera *Prez*, with book and lyrics by Alan Plater. Apart from his jazz work Cash also played regularly with the BBC Northern Symphony Orchestra, Yorkshire Opera and the Royal Philharmonic Orchestra. It was during a European tour with the RPO that he collapsed and died on 7 October 1988.

● ALBUMS: with Peter Ind *Jazz At The 1969 Richmond Festival* (1969)★★★, with Ind *Contra Bach* (Wave 1975)★★, *Great Jazz Solos Revisited* (1978)★★★.

Cassidy, Eva

b. 2 February 1963, Oxon Hill, Maryland, USA, d. 2 November 1996. Growing up in a musical family on the outskirts of Washington, DC, Cassidy sang as a small child and later learned to play the guitar. Her father, a teacher of children with learning disabilities and a part-time musician, formed a family band with Eva, her brother, Danny, on violin, and himself on bass. She endured school, preferring her own company and, whenever possible, being involved with music and painting. In 1986 she did the art work for a projected album by a band, Method Actor, led by a friend, Dave Lourim. She was asked to sing on the album and was heard by producer Chris Biondi who, impressed by her raw talent, encouraged her and introduced her to other musicians. Cassidy appeared on several albums as a backing singer, including E-40's *I Wanna Thank You*. Meantime, Biondi was stockpiling tapes by Cassidy and in 1991, while recording Chuck Brown And The Soul Searchers, played examples for the group's leader. Brown was immediately taken with her sound, as indeed would be other artists including Roberta Flack and Shirley Horn, and in 1992 Brown and Cassidy recorded *The Other Side* (Liaison). Early the following year Brown and Cassidy began performing live, including an appearance at Washington's Blues Alley, and went on the road. Later in the year, following a medical check-up, Cassidy had outpatient surgery for a malignant skin lesion. Early in 1994 she recorded for Blue Note Records and toured with the group Pieces Of A Dream, but, unlike the sessions with Brown, she found this musically unsatisfying. In January 1996 she appeared at Blues Alley again, a session that was recorded, but when summer came she was unwell. This time the check-up revealed advanced melanoma and she was told that she had three to five months to live. In September a tribute concert was organized at which she sang, as did Brown. She died two months later. Cassidy's singing voice was a crystalline soprano, ideal for the ballads and folk songs she performed. But she also had tremendous power and when she turned to soul and gospel-flavoured material her voice resounded with emotional sincerity. Her repertoire drew from all these areas and from the more melodic aspects of contemporary pop. While she might be placed only on the edges of jazz her conviction and integrity would often ably carry her over the hazy boundary. The interpretation of Sting's 'Fields Of Gold', on *Live At Blues Alley*, is breathtaking in clarity and delivery. Most of her recorded work displays a remarkable and unspoiled talent, and almost all of it has been released posthumously.

● ALBUMS: *Live At Blues Alley* (Blix Street 1996)★★★★, *Eva By Heart* (Blix Street 1997)★★★★.

● COMPILATIONS: *Songbird* (Blix Street 1998)★★★★.

Castle, Lee

b. Aniello Castaldo, 28 February 1915, New York City, New York, USA, d. 16 November 1990. While still a teenager, Castle, then known by his real name of Castaldo, began working professionally, securing the featured trumpet solo spot in several name bands of the early swing era. He worked with artists such as Joe Haymes, Artie Shaw and Red Norvo before joining Tommy Dorsey in 1937. Despite his already extensive knowledge and skill, Castle studied music with Dorsey's father before returning to the band. As the 30s ended, he worked with Glenn Miller and Jack Teagarden, led his own unsuccessful band, rejoined Shaw and then played in the band of Will Bradley. In 1942, by now using the name Castle, he tried bandleading once again, but still to no avail. During the late 40s and early 50s he worked with various bands, including those led by Benny Goodman, Shaw and the Dorsey Brothers, and made periodic attempts to lead his own band. He was a member of Jimmy Dorsey's band when the latter died in 1957 and he took over as leader, this time finding some measure of the success that had previously eluded him. A fluent, jazz-loving trumpeter with eclectic tastes, Castle continued to lead the Jimmy Dorsey band into the mid-80s.

● ALBUMS: *Dixieland Heaven* (Davis 1951)★★★, *The Lee Castle Jazztette* (1952)★★★★, *Jimmy Dorsey's Greatest Hits, On Tour* (1960)★★★, *Goodies But Gassers* (1960)★★★, *Lee Castle Plays Bacharach/David* (1966)★★, *Big Band Beatles Bag* (1966)★.

CATHCART, DICK

b. 6 November 1924, Michigan City, Indiana, USA, d. 8 November 1993, Woodland Hills, California, USA. A fine trumpeter, his first major band appearance was with Ray McKinley. He later played in bands in the US Army during World War II, and after the war was with Bob Crosby before a spell in the Hollywood studios. Among the film soundtracks on which he can be heard are *Dragnet* (1954), *Battle Stations* (1955), *Nightmare* (1956), in which he dubbed for the on-screen Billy May, who was more than capable of blowing his own trumpet, and *The Five Pennies* (1959). Cathcart played in other name bands in the late 40s and 50s but became best known, by sound if not by name, when he played trumpet for the leading character in a 1952 US radio series entitled *Pete Kelly's Blues*. When the programme also became a feature film in 1955 and transferred to television later in the decade, Cathcart again ghosted for the star (Jack Webb in the film, William Reynolds on television), although he also appeared on-camera in the small-screen version. Cathcart made a series of successful small-group jazz albums, not surprisingly taking the sound marketing step of naming his band 'Pete Kelly's Big Seven'. Apart from playing trumpet with a bell-like tone, Cathcart also sang; it was in this capacity that he was most active in the 60s and 70s. During the 80s he returned to jazz stages, playing trumpet as well as ever.

● ALBUMS: *Pete Kelly At Home* (1956)★★★★, *Bix MCMLIX* (Warners 1959)★★★.

CATHERINE, PHILIP

b. 27 October 1942, London, England. Born of a Belgian father, Philip Catherine came to notice in 1969 as the guitarist on Scott Bradford's *Rock Slide*, thereby initiating an extremely busy period of session work. During this time Catherine contributed to the works of musicians such as Jean-Luc Ponty, Larry Coryell, Alphonse Mouzon and Zbigniew Seifert. When not doing sessions, Catherine found time to record a series of solo albums on which he also played bass and keyboards. However, in 1976 when Jan Akkerman suddenly left the Scandinavian rock band Focus, Catherine replaced him, winning considerable praise for his lyrical playing. Prior to joining Focus, Catherine had played with the Chris Hinze Combination during 1974. His solo career blossomed in the 90s, and in keeping with John Scofield, in recent years, he has developed in leaps and bounds and has hit a particularly prolific period.

● ALBUMS: *Stream* (1972)★★, *September Man* (1974)★★★, with Passport *Doldinger Jubilee 75* (1975)★★★★, *Guitars* (Atlantic 1975)★★★, with Larry Coryell *Twin House* (Elektra 1976)★★★★, with Joachim Kuhn *Spring Fever* (1977)★★, *Zbigniew Seifert* (1977)★★, with Coryell, Alphonse Mouzon *Back Together* (Warners 1977)★★★, with Coryell *Splendid* (1978)★★★, *Sleep My Love* (CMP 1979)★★★, with Seifert *We'll Remember Zbiggy* (1980)★★★, *Babel* (Elektra 1980)★★★★, *End Of August* (1982)★★, *Transparence* (Inak 1987)★★, *September Sky* (September 1989)★★★, *I Remember You* (Criss Cross 1991)★★★★, *Moods Volume 1* (Criss Cross 1992)★★★, *Spanish Nights* (Enja 1992)★★★, *Oscar* (Igloo 1992)★★★, *Moods Volume 2* (Criss Cross 1993)★★★, *'Live'* (Dreyfus 1997)★★★.

CATINGUB, MATT

b. 25 March 1961, North Hollywood, California, USA. Born into a musical family (his mother is singer Mavis Rivers), Catingub taught himself to play the piano at the age of seven and four years later was also proficient on the clarinet. At 16 he began arranging and composing and additionally took up formal music studies. The following year he switched to alto saxophone. In 1978 he was a member of the California All-Star High School big band which annually appears at the Monterey Jazz Festival. His composition 'Monterey I' was played at the festival and helped him to win a festival scholarship. That same year he visited Japan as a member of the Monterey All-Stars in company with artists such as Thad Jones, Mel Lewis and Dizzy Gillespie. In 1979 (and again in 1981), he joined Louis Bellson's big band, for which he also composed and arranged. In 1980 Catingub formed his own big band, filling it with fellow prodigies; the group played festivals and made its first record in 1983. In the early 80s he regularly accompanied his mother in concert appearances, on recordings and foreign tours. In 1982 he took the lead alto position in the big band led by Toshiko Akiyoshi and Lew Tabackin and toured with it extensively. By the mid-80s he was an established touring and recording artist and had formed the Woodshed Music School. A forceful soloist with an edgy tone, Catingub is an outstanding contemporary talent with an abiding interest in big band music which he finds challenging and a continuing inspiration. Catingub demonstrated his remarkable versatility with an album, *Hi-Tech Big Band*, on which, aided by multi-tracking techniques, he played every instrument.

● ALBUMS: *My Mommy And Me* (1983)★★★, *Your Friendly Neighborhood Big Band* (1984)★★★★, *Hi-Tech Big Band* (Sea Breeze 1985)★★★★, *Land Of The Long White Cloud* (Sea Breeze 1988)★★★, *Matt Catingub Big Band With Mavis Rivers* (Sea Breeze 1990)★★, *George Gershwin 100* (Concord Jazz 1998)★★★.

CATLETT, 'BIG' SID

b. 17 January 1910, Evansville, Indiana, USA, d. 25 March 1951. After briefly trying piano, Catlett switched to drums and received formal tuition when his family settled in Chicago. After working with Darnell Howard, Catlett moved to New York where he played with Elmer Snowden and Benny Carter, following these sessions by drumming with McKinney's Cotton Pickers, Fletcher

Henderson and Don Redman. Catlett happily switched from big bands to small groups, such as those led by Eddie Condon and Lionel Hampton, without any discernible difficulty. In 1941 he joined Benny Goodman, giving that band an overwhelming plangency it never received from any other drummer. In the late 30s and early 40s Catlett worked and played endlessly, appearing on countless recording sessions with a staggeringly wide variety of musicians. The advent of bebop appeared not to trouble him and if he never fully adapted his style he certainly gave his front-line colleagues few problems. In the early 40s Catlett was a member of the superb Teddy Wilson Sextet; when this engagement ended he led his own bands until he joined Louis Armstrong's All Stars in 1947. He remained with Armstrong until 1949 when the years of all-night jam sessions began to catch up with him. Ill or not, Catlett continued to work, but on 25 March 1951 he collapsed and died while visiting friends backstage at a Oran 'Hot Lips' Page benefit concert at the Chicago Opera House. Although a brilliant technician, Catlett chose to play in a deceptively simple style. With the fleet, smoothly swinging Wilson sextet he was discreet and self-effacing; with Goodman he rolled the band remorselessly onward, with Armstrong he gave each of his fellow musicians an individualized accompaniment that defied them not to swing. Instantly identifiable, especially through his thundercrack rimshots, Catlett always swung mightily. On stage, he was a spectacular showman, clothing his massive frame in green plaid suits, tossing his sticks high in the air during solos and generally enjoying himself.

Caton, Lauderic

b. 1920, Trinidad, West Indies. Cited by some as 'Britain's first champion of the electric guitar', Caton passed on his knowledge of that instrument, first imported into Britain shortly before World War II, to legions of students - some of whom would become world-famous. Among his most famous pupils, for one lesson at least, was Hank B. Marvin. After a brief spell in Paris and Belgium, Caton settled in England in an effort to flee the Nazis. There he became a key figure in the emergent London jazz scene, playing alongside other electric guitar pioneers such as Pete Chilver and Dave Goldberg. Initially he was hired by Cuban pianist Marino Barretto for performances at Mayfair's Embassy Hotel, before introducing his electric guitar in the confines of small Soho clubs. There, at Jig's club in St. Anne's Square, he was discovered by visiting US jazz luminaries Fats Waller and Duke Ellington. Four 78rpm records were subsequently recorded at the club, credited to bandleader and trumpeter Cyril Blake - though Caton's riveting guitar lines, quite unlike anything else available at that time, were the real attraction. For the rest of the war he broadcast regularly on radio as guitarist with clarinettist Harry Parry's band. However, more important in forging his reputation was his tenure at Soho's Caribbean Club, as leader of a trio who later became the nucleus of Ray Ellington's Quartet. In this configuration Caton recorded a number of 78s for the Regal label. As the popularity of the electric guitar grew, Caton's services as a maker of amplifiers became as sought after as his teaching skills. However, although he continued to tutor sporadically, by the 50s he had stopped playing guitar live, devoting himself to yoga and meditation. He still lives in London, surrounded by his beloved electronic gadgetry and momentos of the 'gin mill' London party scene.

Cauld Blast Orchestra

A coalition of eight talented musicians, Cauld Blast Orchestra have been at the forefront of Scotland's cultural renaissance in the 90s. They were formed when clarinettist Karen Wimhurst (who had worked in several musical spheres including a spell with experimental group Kiva while in America) was invited to piece together a group and write the music for the 1990 production of *Jock Tamson's Bairns*. Performed by Communicado Theatre, this play opened Glasgow's year as European City Of Culture in 1990. Wimhurst named the assembled group Cauld Blast Orchestra, taking their name from Robbie Burns' last song, 'Wert Thou In The Cauld Blast', with the material composed between them over a three-month period. Wimhurst recruited violinist Anne Wood, like her a former member of Communicado, and also a backing musician to Deacon Blue on tour. The other members of the group are Ron Shaw (cello), Iain Johnstone (piano, tenor horn, tuba, accordion), Mike Travis (drums; also a member of Clan Alba and EH15), Steve Kettley (saxophone, flute; also EH15), Jack Evans (guitar, bass, whistles, mandolin) and Norman Chalmers (various instruments). The last-named pair ironically worked together first as part of Jock Tamson's Bairns - the band rather than the play. With such prodigious talent and varied experience between them, the Cauld Blast Orchestra's instrumental songs were bound to outlive the theatre play they worked on: 'Though the theatre brought us together, it's not something we want to emphasise . . . It's been a couple of years since then: there's been new material written, and it's melded; it's much more communicative to the outside now.' They subsequently appeared at the 1992 WOMAD Festival, and received the *Scotland On Sunday* Jazz Award, despite the fact that they only loosely fit that category. When their other individual interests did not collide, they have also visited Scandinavia, and worked with singers such as Michael Marra and Rod Paterson. In 1992 they also appeared on television during an 'alternative Burns night' presentation, and released their debut album for Gordon Stevenson's Eclectic Records. A second album followed in 1994, though on CD the group were destined to struggle to capture their live essence.

● ALBUMS: *Savage Dance* (Eclectic 1992)★★★, *Durga's Feast* (Eclectic 1994)★★★.

Celestin, Oscar 'Papa'

b. 1 January 1884, Napoleonville, Louisiana, USA, d. 15 December 1954. When he was 20 years old Celestin relocated to New Orleans and, having previously dabbled in music on a variety of instruments, he finally chose the trumpet. Working first in marching bands, including the Indiana Brass Band, Celestin soon attracted a good deal of attention and in 1910 formed the first of several bands that he would lead. In 1917 his band, the Original Tuxedo Brass Band, featured many leading musicians of the formative years of jazz. Although he recorded in the early 20s, Celestin stayed close to his origins, mostly restricting his tours to the southern states. In the 30s he worked outside music but continued to play part-time. After a street accident in the mid-40s, he began playing more and recorded again. Celestin benefited from the resurgence of interest in early jazz during the New Orleans Revival Movement and, apart from recording, also appeared on radio and television. Although his technique was rather limited, as was his inventiveness, Celestin was a good ensemble player and the sidemen in his bands responded to his cheerful and encouraging leadership.

● COMPILATIONS: *Papa Celestin And His New Orleans Ragtime Band* (Jazzology 1986)★★★★, *Papa Celestin And His New Orleans Jazz Band* (Folklyric 1986)★★★★, *Celestin's Original Tuxedo Jazz Band (1926-28)* (VJM 1988)★★★★, with Sam Morgan *New Orleans Classics* (Azure 1992)★★★.

CEROLI, NICK

b. 22 December 1939, Warren, Ohio, USA, d. 11 August 1985. Although adept in all settings, Ceroli's early career marked him out as a big band drummer. In the early 60s he worked with Ray Anthony and Gerald Wilson before joining Stan Kenton's LA Neophonic Orchestra in 1965. For the next four years he was with Herb Alpert's Tijuana Brass but then settled in Los Angeles, where he was soon in demand as a studio musician and also in a wide range of jazz groups for club and recording dates. Among the musicians eager to hire him for small group work were Zoot Sims, Richie Kamuca, Warne Marsh, Pete Christlieb (with whom he recorded a sizzling performance at a Los Angeles club, Dino's, in 1983) and Bill Berry. But his experience and skill in big band music drew him inevitably into that area of performing, and his association with Bob Florence produced some of the finest big band jazz of the late 70s and early 80s. His playing on 'Party Hearty' on Florence's *Concerts By The Sea* album is an object lesson for all aspiring big band drummers. Ceroli's interest in all kinds of music was comprehensive; he owned a huge record collection of music by Beethoven and Duke Ellington, and he communicated his enthusiasm through his playing. A fluid, supple drummer, Ceroli gave a tremendous lift to any band he worked with. His death in 1985 came when he was still very much in his prime.

CHADBOURNE, EUGENE

b. 4 January 1954, Mount Vernon, New York, USA. Raised in Boulder, Colorado, Chadbourne took up guitar at the age of 11: 'I was the third boy in my grade school to actually get a guitar following the Beatles' appearance on the *Ed Sullivan Show*. I was the first to actually learn how to play.' The example of Jimi Hendrix led him to explore the wah-wah pedal and the fuzzbox. Dissatisfied with teenage inertia, he traded in his rock electric for a Harmony six-string acoustic and began studying bottleneck blues styles. Then came exposure to John Coltrane and Roland Kirk; puzzled at first, he became hooked to the whole gamut of the 60s black jazz revolution: Charles Mingus, Eric Dolphy, Pharoah Sanders, Ornette Coleman, as well as discovering England's free improviser, Derek Bailey. His first release, *Solo Acoustic Guitar* had a suite dedicated to 'Mr Anthony Braxton'. In 1977 he made contact with New York's black *avant garde*, playing on Frank Lowe's *Lowe & Behold* alongside Billy Bang. In the late 70s he, John Zorn and cellist Tom Cora made notorious forays into the Midwest with country-and-western-and-improvisation implosions, and his trio Shockabilly made rock covers into nightmare noise-rides, an east coast reply to the Residents. Two albums that Chadbourne made with members of Camper Van Beethoven include one side of Tim Buckley songs. Reaffirming his commitment to improvisation, he played at Derek Bailey's Company Week in August 1990. Chadbourne's scabrously noisy guitar, his considered politics and smart songwriting have made him an unexpected rock cult. As with fellow traveller Zorn, his genre-transgressions are, in fact, what it takes to harness the best elements of rock and jazz without a trace of fusion's middle-road. He would like to be remembered as the inventor of the electric rake and dogskull harmonica.

● ALBUMS: *Solo Acoustic Guitar* (1974)★★★★, *Solo Acoustic Guitar Volume 2* (1975)★★★, *Improvised Music From Acoustic Piano And Guitar* (1977)★★★, *Vermin Of the Blues* (1985)★★★★, with Camper Van Beethoven *Camper Van Chadbourne* (Fundamental 1988)★★, with Camper Van Beethoven *The Eddie Chatterbox Double Trio Love Album* (1988)★★, *I've Been Everywhere* (1988)★★★, *Country Music In The World Of Islam* (1990)★★, *Strings* (1993)★★★, with Jimmy Carl Black *Locked In A Dutch Coffeeshop* (Fundamental 1996)★★★, with Black *Pachuco Cadaver* (Fireant 1996)★★★.

CHAIX, HENRI

b. 1925, Geneva, Switzerland. Chaix played piano from an early age, becoming professional while in his late teens. He played with a number of Swiss bands, eventually becoming a leader in the early 60s. He gained a strong local reputation and during the 50s, 60s and 70s was constantly on call as accompanist for visiting American jazz musicians. Among those with whom he played during these years were Sidney Bechet, Buck Clayton, Rex Stewart and Albert Nicholas. He also played an important role at many Swiss jazz festivals and throughout western and central Europe. A powerful and dynamic player, he displays a marked penchant for the blues, and his solid accompaniment is of considerable merit. His solos demonstrate an imaginative approach to mainstream jazz. He occasionally plays trombone.

● ALBUMS: with Rex Stewart *Rex Stewart Meets Henri Chaix*

(1966)★★★, with the Tremble Kids *25 Jahre: The Tremble Kids* (Intercord 1977)★★★, *Jumpin' Pumpkins* (Sackville 1992)★★★★, *Jive At Five* (Sackville 1995)★★★.

CHALLIS, BILL

b. 8 July 1904, Wilkes-Barre, Pennsylvania, USA. A versatile musician, Challis played piano and saxophone before becoming a staff arranger for band contractor Jean Goldkette in 1926, when Goldkette's band included several enthusiastic young jazzmen, notably Bix Beiderbecke and Frankie Trumbauer. In 1927 Challis was among the group who deserted Goldkette for Paul Whiteman, with whom he remained until 1930. From then on he freelanced, writing arrangements for many big bands of the swing era, including those led by Fletcher Henderson, Jimmy and Tommy Dorsey and Artie Shaw. He also wrote for the Casa Loma Orchestra and trumpeter Bobby Hackett. For most of his career Challis's work was notably ahead of its time. Although often disregarded in assessments of the role played by arrangers in the development of big band music, his charts for Whiteman's sometimes ponderous orchestra are brilliant technical exercises which counter accusations that this band never swung. Importantly, Challis's long association with Beiderbecke and other top-flight jazzmen meant that many of their best jazz solos appear in his arrangements of tunes such as 'Lonely Melody', 'Dardanella' and 'San'.

● COMPILATIONS: *The Goldkette Project* (Circle 1986)★★★★, *Bill Challis And His Orchestra 1936* (Circle 1988)★★★, *More 1936* (Circle 1988)★★★.

CHALOFF, SERGE

b. 24 November 1923, Boston, Massachusetts, USA, d. 16 July 1957. Coming from a musical family, Chaloff studied formally on piano and clarinet but, entranced by the playing of Harry Carney, he taught himself to play baritone saxophone. In the early 40s he worked with a number of swing era big bands; however, his interest in the musical developments of the beboppers drew him to Boyd Raeburn's adventurous band, which he joined in 1945. Thereafter he played with Georgie Auld and Jimmy Dorsey, extending the appeal of his instrument through his ability to play complex material without losing either his feeling for swing or the sonority that Carney achieved on baritone. In 1947 Chaloff became a member of Woody Herman's Four Brothers band and for the next two years he was the most talked-about baritone player in jazz. Later he worked with Count Basie, but Chaloff had fallen victim to drug addiction and the remainder of his career was blighted. He taught for a while, continued to record, mostly with small groups, and proved on these recordings that his talent was undiminished and continuing to develop. Partially paralyzed, Chaloff appeared at a Four Brothers reunion date in February 1957 but on 16 July that year he died.

● ALBUMS: *Pumpernickel* (1947)★★★, *Gabardine And Serge* (1947)★★★, *The Most* (1949)★★★, *Serge Chaloff And Boots Mussulli* 10-inch album (Storyville 1954)★★★, *The Fable Of Mable* 10-inch album (Storyville 1954)★★★★, *Boston Blow-Up!* (Capitol 1955)★★★, *Blue Serge* (Capitol 1956)★★★★.

● COMPILATIONS: *The Complete Capitol Recordings Of Serge Chaloff* (Mosaic 1993)★★★★.

CHAMBERS, HENDERSON

b. 1 May 1908, Alexandria, Louisiana, USA, d. 19 October 1967. After gaining experience, playing the trombone with a number of territory bands, including those of Zack Whyte, Speed Webb and Tiny Bradshaw, Chambers settled in New York in 1939. During the next few years he worked with a number of bands, notably Louis Armstrong's. During the 40s and 50s he worked with small and big bands led by men such as Edmond Hall, Don Redman, Sy Oliver, Lucky Millinder, Count Basie and Cab Calloway. Additionally, he played for short spells, sometimes as substitute, with Duke Ellington and in the 60s with Ray Charles and Basie again. He appeared on numerous recording sessions, including some outstanding ones with Buck Clayton. A powerful player and a valued member of the brass section of any band with which he played, Chambers was less well-known as a soloist, although when given the opportunity he showed that he could shine as well as most of his contemporaries.

CHAMBERS, JOE

b. 25 June 1942, Stoneacre, Virginia, USA. Joseph Arthur Chambers studied music theory at the Philadelphia Conservatory and the American University in Washington while drumming with the JFK Quintet. In 1964 he moved to New York to play with Eric Dolphy, Freddie Hubbard and Andrew Hill, doyens of the Blue Note label, while also attending Hall Overton's composition classes. Chambers shone on vibist Bobby Hutcherson's records as both drummer and composer, contributing the title tracks to *Dialogue* and *Oblique* and a masterful, side-long suite to *Components* that pursued Hall Overton's Third Stream inclinations between Thelonious Monk and Igor Stravinsky. Since the early 70s he has also appeared with and composed for Max Roach's percussion ensemble M'Boom. In 1974 his 'The Almoravid' was played at Carnegie Hall. A ferociously accurate drummer with a feel both for swing and space, his compositional imagination informs every nuance.

● ALBUMS: *The Almoravid* (Muse 1973)★★★★, *Double Exposure* (Muse 1978)★★★, with M'Boom *Collage* (1984)★★★, *Phantom Of The City* (Candid 1991)★★★.

CHAMBERS, PAUL

b. Paul Laurence Dunbar Chambers Jnr., 22 April 1935, Pittsburgh, Pennsylvania, USA, d. 4 January 1969, New York City, New York, USA. Chambers' early death deprived jazz of one of its most influential, creative and lyrical bassists who had been present on several of the most important and enduring recordings of the 50s and early 60s. He grew up in Detroit, where he studied tuba before taking up the string bass. He worked with Paul Quinichette (1954), Bennie Green (1955), Jay and Kai (J.J. Johnson and Kai Winding) (1955), George

Wallington (1955), Les Jazz Modes (1956-58), and was with Miles Davis from 1955-63. He then joined Wynton Kelly, another Davis alumnus, until 1966. The Miles Davis Quintet of which Chambers was a member was then nicknamed 'The D & D Band' (drink and drugs), but despite his heroin habit Chambers was a fine, dependable bass player. While with Davis he popularised the use of arco (bowed) solos. His light, agile phrasing was coupled with a firm tone, which provided strong, telling accompaniment, a sturdy foundation for the explorations of soloists such as Davis and John Coltrane, who wrote the tune 'Mr P.C.' in his honour. During his short but prolific and brilliant career he also worked with, among many others, Art Pepper, Sonny Rollins, Bill Evans, Sonny Clark and Johnny Griffin.

● ALBUMS: with John Coltrane *High Step* 1955-56 recordings (Blue Note 1956)★★★, *A Jazz Delegation From The East - Chambers' Music* (Jazz: West 1956)★★★, *Whims Of Chambers* (Blue Note 1956)★★★, *The East West Controversy* (Xanadu 1957)★★★, *Paul Chambers Quintet* (Blue Note 1957)★★★★, *Bass On Top* (Blue Note 1957)★★★★, with Roy Haynes, Phineas Newborn *We Three* (New Jazz 1958)★★★★, with Cannonball Adderley *Ease It* (Affinity 1959)★★★★, *Go ...* (Vee Jay 1960)★★★, *First Bassman* (Vee Jay 1960)★★★★.

CHAMBLEE, EDDIE

b. 24 February 1920, Atlanta, Georgia, USA. Music was Chamblee's second choice, having begun to study law. In the early 40s, during his army service, he became deeply involved in music, playing the tenor saxophone, and performing in, and sometimes directing, army bands. From 1946 until he joined Lionel Hampton in 1955, Chamblee led a small band in Chicago. His tenure with Hampton lasted two years but it was long enough for him to build a reputation in Europe. Married briefly to Dinah Washington, he recorded with her, sometimes singing duets in a style similar to that which Washington adopted for her later successes with Brook Benton. Chamblee continued to lead small groups into the mid-70s, when he again visited Europe with both Milt Buckner and Hampton. In the early 80s he switched to alto saxophone for a short stint with Count Basie. Although derivative, Chamblee's playing has an urgent, earthy quality that blended well into the hard-swinging Hampton style.

● ALBUMS: with Dinah Washington *The Fats Waller Songbook* (EmArcy 1957)★★★, *Chamblee Music* (EmArcy 1958)★★★, *Doodlin'* (EmArcy 1958)★★★, *The Rockin' Tenor Sax Of Eddie Chamblee* (Prestige 1964)★★, *Twenty Years After* (1976)★★★.

CHANCE ELEMENT

Chance Element play music that is particularly hard to pigeonhole. Most of its members had a standard, classical college training, but all subsequently worked in rock and jazz contexts. All these influences are there, but the music is hardly rock, certainly not jazz, and would not be recognized as classical by most people. The UK band was formed in 1983 when Rod Arran (soprano saxophone, reed synthesizer, recorders), John Thomas (keyboards) and Brian Lenehan (guitar), all at London's Trinity School of Music, got together to try out some compositions using tapes and live instruments. The band still uses taped material, devised, realized and assembled by Arran, as an underpinning for the live performers. There is virtually no improvisation (nor any random procedures, despite the band's name) and Chance Element has been primarily a vehicle for Arran's compositions, which draw on a variety of traditions. This has not stopped the band being labelled (more than somewhat inaccurately) as jazz-funk. Chance Element also comprises former Itchy Fingers member Martin Speake (flute, alto saxophone). Their are plans for the group to realize their intention of phasing out much of the use of tapes and sequencers and bring in a bassist and drummer.

CHANGE OF THE CENTURY - ORNETTE COLEMAN

Listening to these pioneering free-jazz sessions a quarter of a century later, it is hard to understand the violently outraged responses Ornette Coleman received at the time. Gentle, spacey, melodic and certainly very beautiful, his piano-less quartet, with trumpeter Don Cherry, bassist Charlie Haden and drummer Billy Higgins, ran a quirky, blues-oriented groove with grace and wit. This is music that swings as hard as any jazz, but harmonically follows its own spontaneous laws, relying on Haden's astonishing versatility and quick thinking to establish its order.

● Tracks: *Ramblin'; Free; The Face Of The Bass; Forerunner; Bird Food; Una Muy Bonita; Change Of The Century.*

● First released 1960

● UK peak chart position: did not chart

● USA peak chart position: did not chart

CHARLES, DENNIS

b. 4 December 1933, St. Croix, Virgin Islands, d. 26 March 1998, New York City, New York, USA. Charles moved to New York in 1945 but his roots were nevertheless Caribbean: he began by playing congas in calypso and mambo bands. He taught himself on the drumkit and a year later (1955) was playing in Harlem with Cecil Taylor and recorded on the pianist's first album. Citing Art Blakey as his hero, Charles was also a close friend of polyrhythmic drummer Ed Blackwell. In 1957 he played at the Newport Jazz Festival with Taylor, Steve Lacy and Buell Neidlinger and in 1961 performed with Taylor and Archie Shepp in the Living Theatre production of *The Connection*. In 1962 he supplied calypso beats for Sonny Rollins. Unfortunately the theme of *The Connection* (heroin addiction) proved a little too close to home and Charles dropped out of the music scene for over a decade. He re-emerged as one of the Jazz Doctors, an ensemble that included Billy Bang and Frank Lowe, in the early 80s. In 1982 he recorded *Bangception*, a delightful duet album, with Bang on violin. Charles's incisive, regular time was a perfect foil to wildmen like Taylor and Bang, having the imagination and suppleness to both answer and contain them. Later recordings with Bang's quartet (*Valve No. 10*) and new alto saxophonist Rob Brown (*Breath Rhyme*) were capped by his own debut as leader on 1991's *Queen Mary*. Charles died of pneumonia in March 1998, on the day his second album as leader was released.

● ALBUMS: with Billy Bang *Bangception* (1982)★★★, with the Jazz Doctors *Intensive Care* (1983)★★, *Queen Mary* (Silkheart 1991)★★★, *Captain Of The Deep* (Eremite 1998)★★★.

CHARLES, TEDDY

b. Theodore Charles Cohen, 13 April 1928, Chicopee Falls, Massachusetts, USA. After studying percussion at the New York Juilliard School of Music, Charles worked in a number of late-swing era big bands, including those led by Benny Goodman and Artie Shaw. From the late 40s onwards he performed with numerous small groups, some of which were still dedicated to swing, but his interest lay in more progressive musical styles. Although he worked with many beboppers, Charles was attracted to the possibilities of extending the range of jazz through advanced composing techniques. Apart from experimenting with modality himself he encouraged others, such as George Russell, in similar areas. The complexities of such music made Charles appear inaccessible to many jazz fans and his reputation as a composer and arranger is valued more within the profession than with the general public. Conversely, his driving vibes playing has strong audience appeal even if he gives it rather less of his time. From the mid-50s onwards Charles became involved in record production, working with leading modern jazz artists such as Herbie Hancock and John Coltrane.

● ALBUMS: *Teddy Charles Vibe Solos* 10-inch album (Prestige 1952)★★★, *Teddy Charles' West Coasters* (Prestige 1953)★★★★, *New Directions Quartet* 10-inch album (New Jazz 1955)★★, *Collaboration: West* (Prestige 1956)★★★★, *The Teddy Charles Tentet* (Atlantic 1956)★★★★, *A Word From Bird* (Atlantic 1956)★★★, *Evolution* (Prestige 1957)★★★★, *Three For Duke* (Jubilee 1957)★★★, *Salute To Hamp: Flyin' Home* (Bethlehem 1958)★★, with Booker Little, Booker Ervin *Sounds Of Inner City* (1960)★★★, *On Campus!: Ivy League Concert* (Fresh Sound 1960)★★★,with Miles Davis, Lee Konitz *Ezz-Thetic* (New Jazz 1962)★★★, *Live At The Verona Jazz Festival 1988* (Soul Note 1988)★★.

CHARLIE PARKER ON DIAL VOLS. 1-6 - CHARLIE PARKER

Alto saxophonist Charlie Parker turned jazz on its head in the years following World War II, playing an original and highly demanding music that furthered the emphasis on improvisation, and gave jazz a greater technical complexity and psychological depth. His numerous recordings for the west coast Dial label began in 1946, and represent one of the greatest bodies of work to be found anywhere in the music. The six volumes available today represent the complete works, and feature contributions by a host of leading musicians of the time, including Dizzy Gillespie, Miles Davis, Lucky Thompson, Errol Garner, Duke Jordan, Max Roach, Teddy Wilson, Red Norvo, and J.J. Johnson. Essential.

● Tracks: *Volume 1 - Diggin' Diz; Moose The Mooche (three takes); Yardbird Suite (two takes); Ornithology (three takes); The Famous Alto Break; Night In Tunisia (two takes); Max Making Wax; Loverman; The Gypsy; Bebop. Volume 2 - This Is Always (two takes); Bird's Nest (three takes); Cool Blues (four takes). Volume 3 - Relaxin' At Camarillo; Cheers; Carvin' The Bird; Stupendous Theme Cooking (three takes). Volume 4 - Dexterity (two takes); Bongo Bop; Dewey Square (three takes); The Hymn (two takes); Bird Of Paradise (three takes); Embraceable You (two takes). Volume 5 - Bird Feathers; Klart-oveeseds-tere (two takes); Scapple From The Apple; My Old Flame; Out Of Nowhere (three takes); Don't Blame Me; Moose The Mooche; Dark Shadows; Hallelujah. Volume 6 - Drying On A Reed (three takes); Quasimodo (two takes); Charlie's Wig (three takes); Bongo Beep; Crazeology (two excerpts); How Deep Is The Ocean (two takes).*

● First released 1974

● UK peak chart position: did not chart

● USA peak chart position: did not chart

CHASE, ALLAN

b. Phoenix, Arizona, USA. Alto and soprano saxophonist Allan Chase moved to Boston in 1980 to study with pianist Jaki Byard. Interestingly, when he came to record in the 90s, it was very much piano pieces that informed his musical doctrine, leading some critics to describe his *Dark Clouds With Silver Linings* set as a 'pianoless record of piano pieces.' Among the tunes collected were pieces by artists as diverse as Lorraine Geller, Sun Ra, Bud Powell and Horace Silver. By this time Chase had established his name performing in the John Coltrane-influenced group Prima Materia, alongside Rashied Ali. He had also written an ethnomusicology thesis on Sun Ra for his master's degree. His other musical activities included playing with the Boston four-piece, Your Neighborhood Saxophone Quartet, and a stint in New York as part of Walter Thompson's big band. *Dark Clouds With Silver Linings* was his attempt to establish himself as a solo artist rather than merely to embellish his growing reputation as a collaborator. It featured long-standing associates Ron Horton (trumpet), Tony Scherr (bass) and Matt Wilson (drums), and as *Down Beat* magazine noted, displayed 'a pristine melodicism and spacious sense of time.'

● ALBUMS: *Dark Clouds With Silver Linings* (Accurate 1996)★★★.

CHASE, BILL

b. 1935, Boston, Massachusetts, USA, d. 9 August 1974, Jackson, Minnesota, USA. In the mid-50s Chase studied trumpet at Berklee College Of Music under Herb Pomeroy. Towards the end of the decade he played with Maynard Ferguson, Stan Kenton and Woody Herman. Throughout the 60s he frequently returned to the Herman band but turned increasingly to jazz-rock, later forming his own band Chase in 1971; three years later he toured with a re-formed version of the band. It was while on tour that he and other members of the band - John Emma (guitar), Walter Clark (drums) and Wally York (keyboards) - were killed in an airplane crash.

● ALBUMS: as Chase *Chase* (Epic 1971)★★★, *Ennea* (Epic 1972)★★★, *Pure Music* (Epic 1974)★★★.

CHASE, TOMMY

b. 22 March 1947, Manchester, England. Largely self-taught at the drums, Chase had to wait for a jazz revival pioneered by the next generation to bring his chosen genre - steaming soul jazz - into favour. Professional since the mid-60s he began playing pure jazz in London from the early 70s, with tenor saxophonist Art Themen and trumpeter Harry Beckett. The jazz dancers of the mid-80s responded to a band of young-bloods (including tenor saxophonist Alan Barnes, 1983-86), bringing out the lindy-hop basis of break-dancing to tunes such as 'Night In Tunisia'. Later on, his use of a Hammond organ featuring the excellent Gary Baldwin, confirmed what many people had suspected: boasting that he was the Art Blakey of British jazz, in actual fact he is its Dr Feelgood - playing unpretentious, driving music with a great feel for stage dynamics. His quartet in 1992 was arguably his finest, featuring the inspired driving string bass of Australian Les Miller, Chris Watson (guitar) and Dave Lewis (tenor saxophone, saxello). Chase is in complete control of his drumkit, changing pace in breath-taking fashion, willing his musicians on to follow his extraordinary timing.

● ALBUMS: with Ray Warleigh *One Way* (Spotlite 1983)★★★, *Hard* (Boplicity 1984)★★★, *Drive!* (Paladin 1985)★★★, *Groove Merchant* (Stiff 1987)★★★★, *Rebel Fire* (Mole 1990)★★★.

CHEATHAM, DOC

b. Adolphus Anthony Cheatham, 13 June 1905, Nashville, Tennessee, USA, d. 2 June 1997, Washington, D.C., USA. Cheatham's remarkably long career began in the early 20s when he worked in vaudeville theatre pit bands, often accompanying important blues singers of the era. In the middle of the decade he worked in Chicago where he encountered the main influence on his life, Louis Armstrong. Until this point Cheatham had dabbled with the saxophone, playing soprano with Ma Rainey, but now he concentrated on trumpet, developing a striking technique but never sacrificing his lovely tone. During the second half of the 20s and on into the early 30s, Cheatham played with many bands, including those of Wilbur De Paris, Chick Webb, Sam Wooding (who took him a tour of Europe in 1928-29), and Cab Calloway, with whom he remained for six years, during which time he again toured Europe. In 1939 Cheatham became a member of Teddy Wilson's big band and followed this with a spell in the equally elegant orchestra of Benny Carter. Through the 40s he worked in big and small bands, bringing to each job the graceful presence that was echoed in his playing. In the 50s Cheatham worked as a section player for the Latin orchestras of Machito and Perez Prado, and accompanied Billie Holiday in December 1957 for *The Sound Of Jazz* telecast. In New York in the 60s he led his own band for several years and also played frequently with Benny Goodman. Contrary to the limitations age usually imposes on brass players, his public performances and numerous recording sessions proved that he was, in fact, playing even better than before. In the 70s and on into the 80s he defied age and changing tastes in music, visiting Europe for festival and club dates and playing with his still-faultless technique and magnificent sound. Even in the 90s he was still playing, astonishing listeners and fellow musicians several generations his junior. At the end of May 1997 he played a gig with rising trumpet star Nicholas Payton, with whom he had made a record a few months earlier. Three days after his final gig he died in his sleep after suffering a stroke. He was 11 days short of his 92nd birthday.

● ALBUMS: *Doc Cheatham* (1950)★★★★, *Adolphus 'Doc' Cheatham* (Jezebel 1973)★★★, *Hey Doc!* (Black And Blue 1975)★★, with Sammy Price *Doc And Sammy* (Sackville 1976)★★, *Black Beauty* (Sackville 1979)★★★★, *John, Doc And Herb* (1979)★★★, *It's A Good Life* (Parkwood 1982)★★★, *Too Marvellous For Words* (1982)★★★, *I've Got A Crush On You* (1982)★★, *The Fabulous Doc Cheatham* (Parkwood 1983)★★★★, with George Kelly *Highlights In Jazz* (1985)★★, *Art Hodes, Carrie Smith And Doc Cheatham* (1985)★★★, *A Tribute To Billie Holiday* (1987)★★, with Price *In New Orleans* (1988)★★★, *Dear Doc* (Orange Blue 1989)★★★, *I've Got A Crush On You Volume 2* (New York 1989)★★, with Jim Galloway *At The Bern Jazz Festival* 1983-85 recordings (Sackville 1992)★★★, *The Eighty-Seven Years Of Doc Cheatham* (Columbia 1993)★★★★, *Swinging Down In New Orleans* (Jazzology 1993)★★, *You're A Sweetheart* (Sackville 1993)★★, *Doc Cheatham Live* (Natasha 1993)★★, with Nicholas Payton *Doc Cheatham & Nicholas Payton* (Verve 1997)★★★★.

● FURTHER READING: *I Guess I'll Get The Papers And Go Home: The Life Of Doc Cheatham*, Adolphus 'Doc' Cheatham.

CHEATHAM, JEANNIE

b. Jeannie Evans, *c*.1936, Akron, Ohio, USA. As a small child Cheatham began playing piano by ear and took lessons from the age of six and was soon accompanying a church choir of which her mother was a member. When she was 14 she played piano with a 16-piece rehearsal band which thus gave her her first experience in jazz. In the early 60s she began playing jazz in small bop groups. She also began singing but as a group member rather than as a soloist. Gradually, Cheatham began to develop a reputation not only as an excellent pianist but also as a leader and a reliable businesswoman. She and her band teamed up with alto saxophonist Jimmy Colvin and moved into somewhat bigger time, playing in Cleveland, Pittsburgh, Minneapolis and occasionally New York. They were managed by Moe Gale, manager of Ella Fitzgerald until the early 50s, and he found steady work for the group, known now as the Colvinaires, in the northern states and Canada. When Colvin quit, she resumed leadership until 1957 when she disbanded. That same year she married trombonist Jimmy Cheatham and continued working as a single or accompanist in and around Buffalo and Albany. Eventually moving to New York, she continued to play and sang more but also raised two children and, as she told Helen Oakley Dance for *Jazz Journal International*, she also found time to study accounting and business management. In 1977 the Cheathams relocated to the west coast and soon settled in San Diego where they continue to work and carry on a successful recording career for Concord. Cheatham is an exceptionally gifted piano player. Pete Johnson once asked her, 'Girl, you from Kansas City?', while the mild and whimsical Count Basie said on another occasion, 'Stay away from that piano or I'll break your fingers'. She sings the blues very well and all her singing is deeply imbued with the spirit of the blues.

● ALBUMS: all with Jimmy Cheatham and the Sweet Baby Blues Band: *Sweet Baby Blues* (Concord Jazz 1985)★★★, *Midnight Mama* (Concord Jazz 1986)★★★, *Homeward Bound* (Concord Jazz 1987)★★, *Back To The Neighborhood* (Concord Jazz 1988)★★★★, *Luv In The Afternoon* (Concord Jazz 1990)★★★, *Basket Full Of Blues* (Concord Jazz 1992)★★★, *Blues & The Boogie Masters* (Concord Jazz 1993)★★★, *Gud Nuz Bluz* (Concord Jazz 1996)★★★.

CHEKASIN, VLADIMIR

b. 24 February 1947, Sverdlovsk, Russia. For the past decade, Chekasin has been the most highly regarded saxophonist in the former Soviet Union, his style a blend of the late Rahsaan Roland Kirk's high-pressure hard bop (Chekasin frequently plays two or more horns at once), 60s New York free-jazz tenor and wild Peter Brötzmann-like howls, mixed with a great deal of onstage clowning and theatricality. A composer and keyboard player as well as a saxophonist, Chekasin was originally a violinist (he took it up at the age of six), then shifted to clarinet and alto saxophone, beginning to lead jazz bands around 1967. He graduated from the M.P. Mussorgsky University in Sverdlovsk as a clarinettist and moved to Vilnius in 1971, meeting two classical musicians with extra-curricular jazz enthusiasms in the pianist Vyacheslav Ganelin and the percussionist Vladimir Tarasov, with whom he worked and recorded often in the next 15 or so years. Also in 1971 Chekasin won first prize in a jazz competition in Prague and made his first record. He later taught at the Lithuanian State Conservatory in Vilnius, forming a big band with his students there in 1982, and subsequently led a variety of small groups and big bands of his own. Some of these line-ups can be heard on the eight-CD compilation *Document: New Music From Russia* and the four-CD set *Conspiracy: Soviet Jazz Festival, Zurich 1989*. With the Ganelin Trio Chekasin toured the UK in 1984 and USA in 1986. He is as likely to quote Xenakis or Lutoslawski among his influences as Ben Webster, and remains among the most energetic and inventive of contemporary jazz artists in the Republics.

● ALBUMS: *Exercises* (1983)★★★, *Nostalgia* (1984)★★★★, *Prisiminimai* (1985)★★★★, *Anti-Show* (1988)★★★.

CHERRY, DON

b. 18 November 1936, Oklahoma City, Oklahoma, USA, d. 19 October 1995. Cherry began playing trumpet while still attending high school in Los Angeles, where he was raised. He also played piano and some of his first public performances were on this instrument when he worked in R&B bands. An early musical associate was Billy Higgins and in the mid-50s the two men, by then playing bebop, joined Ornette Coleman and began to adapt their musical thought to the new concept of free jazz. Cherry and Higgins played on Coleman's 1958 quintet album, *Something Else!!!!*, an album which represents an early and important flowering of the freedom principle. Coleman's group became a quartet, the fourth member being Charlie Haden. The quartet's success was recognized by an extended engagement at New York's Five Spot Cafe which began in November 1959 and continued into the following spring when Higgins was replaced by Ed Blackwell. Later, Haden too was succeeded by Scott La Faro and then Jimmy Garrison. The group made several important albums, which established the concept of free jazz as a major 60s movement in jazz and also demonstrated the qualities of the individual musicians. During this same period, Cherry recorded with John Coltrane and with Archie Shepp, in whose group he played alongside John Tchicai and Bill Dixon. In 1964 Cherry and Tchicai joined Albert Ayler's group for a recording session which was later used as soundtrack for the film, *New York Eye And Ear Control*. Later that year Cherry visited Europe with Ayler and also recorded *Vibrations* with him. Cherry's next association was with Gato Barbieri, with whom he led a small band which toured and recorded in Europe and the USA. While in Europe, he also worked with George Russell. Towards the end of the decade, Cherry began touring Europe, Africa and Asia, absorbing ethnic musical concepts and learning to play a variety of instruments including wooden flutes from northern Europe and the doussn'gouni (a kind of guitar). He was also using a Pakistani pocket trumpet with a distorted mouthpiece, an instrument which he favoured in much of his subsequent work. He began to adapt Asian ideas and sounds into his own music, becoming one of the few jazz musicians to do so successfully. By the early 70s, Cherry, who was then living in Sweden with his wife, Moki, was the most authoritative voice in the development of a musical style which was eventually established as 'world music'. Together with his wife, he created performances which depended almost as much upon visual and other senses as upon sounds. In the mid-70s Cherry again teamed up with Haden and Blackwell and, with Dewey Redman, formed a quartet which created new concepts of Coleman's music alongside original material. This group, which took its name, Old And New Dreams, from the title of its first album, was only one of Cherry's musical ventures of the late 70s and early 80s. He also played with rock bands, guested with Abdullah Ibrahim and formed a trio, Codona, with Collin Walcott and Nana Vasconcelos. His continued association with Blackwell, himself a gatherer of musical concepts and instruments, added to Cherry's status as a major figure in world music in the late 80s and early 90s. In his trumpet playing, especially on the pocket trumpet, Cherry might not have dazzled in the manner of many of his contemporaries who remained more closely linked to bop, but he nevertheless achieved a bright, incisive sound. As a composer, both in the formal sense of that term and in the manner in which he created musical happenings, Cherry was one of the most distinctive contributors to stretching the boundaries of contemporary music.

● ALBUMS: with Steve Lacy *Evidence* (New Jazz 1962)★★★★, with Gato Barbieri *Gato Barbieri And Don Cherry* (Inner City 1965)★★★, *Complete Communion* (Blue Note 1965)★★★★, *Symphony For Improvisers* (Blue Note 1966)★★★, *Where Is Brooklyn?* (Blue Note 1966)★★★, *Live At The Montmartre Volumes 1* and *2* (Magnetic 1966)★★★, *Eternal Rhythm* (Saba 1968)★★★, with Charlie Haden *Liberation Music Orchestra* (1969)★★★, *Human Music* (1970)★★★, with Ed Blackwell *Mu* (BYG 1970)★★★★, *Orient* (Affinity 1973)★★★, *Eternal Now* (Sonet 1973)★★★, *Hear And Now* (Atlantic 1976)★★, *Brown Rice* (A&M 1976)★★★, *Live In Ankara* recorded 1969 (Sonet 1978)★★★, with Blackwell *El Corazón* (ECM 1982)★★★, *Home Boy* (Decca 1985)★★, *Art Deco* (A&M 1988)★★★, *Multikulti* (A&M 1990)★★★★, *Dona Nostra* (ECM 1994)★★★.

CHESTNUT, CYRUS

b. 17 January 1963, Baltimore, Maryland, USA. Chestnut is a gifted and deeply religious young pianist with a style equally rooted in the jazz and gospel idioms. Chestnut's grandfather was a musical churchman, and his musical legacy was passed down to his son, who in turn taught Cyrus to play piano at the age of five. When Chestnut was nine he attended the Peabody Preparatory Institute, before moving on to the Berklee College Of Music. While at Berklee he was the recipient of the Eubie Blake Fellowship, the Oscar Peterson Scholarship and the Quincy Jones Scholarship, and graduated with a degree in jazz composition and arranging. Chestnut played with several notable jazz figures, including Jon Hendricks, Terence Blanchard, Donald Harrison, Wynton Marsalis and Betty Carter before he released his solo debut in 1992, working with fellow young musicians, bassist Christian McBride and drummer Carl Allen. Chestnut signed to Atlantic Records in 1994, and has released three acclaimed albums that combine the swagger of his swinging jazz piano with the spirituality of gospel. Nowhere is this more apparent than on *Blessed Quietness*, where Chestnut covers a choice selection of hymns, carols and spirituals.

● ALBUMS: *Nut* (Alfa/Evidence 1992)★★★★, *Another Direction* (Evidence 1993)★★★★, *Revelation* (Atlantic 1994)★★★ *Dark Before The Dawn* (Atlantic 1995)★★★, *Earth Stories* (Atlantic 1996)★★★★, *Blessed Quietness: Collection Of Hymns, Spirituals, Carols* (Atlantic 1996)★★★.

CHILDERS, BUDDY

b. Marion Childers, 12 February 1926, St. Louis, Missouri, USA. Childers began playing trumpet as a small child and was soon performing in bands in Belleville, Illinois, just across the Mississippi River from his home-town. In 1942, at the age of 16, Childers was hired by Stan Kenton. Although he would later wryly suggest that this was because all the other trumpeters were being drafted into the armed forces, his new boss thought enough of him to make him lead trumpet in his powerful band. On and off, Childers played with Kenton until the mid-50s but during this same period he also worked in bands led by Woody Herman, Tommy Dorsey and others. Settling in Los Angeles, he began working in film and television studios but found time for occasional jazz gigs and recording dates. The role of the lead trumpet is such that his importance is often more apparent to fellow musicians than to audiences. For this reason, Childers is one of several unsung heroes of big band jazz.

● ALBUMS: *Sam Songs* (Liberty 1956)★★★, *Buddy Childers Quartet* (Liberty 1956)★★★, *West Coast Quintet* (Candid 1997)★★★.

CHILDS, BILLY

b. *c.*1960, Los Angeles, California, USA. While still a student at the University of Southern California, Childs played piano with Freddie Hubbard. This was in 1978 but he was discouraged by a faculty member from continuing with his playing and was redirected instead into composition. After graduating, however, he returned to playing piano in Hubbard's band for six years. Childs continued to develop his compositional skills, writing several long works that nudge healthily at the boundary lines rigidly drawn between jazz and other musical forms. He has twice been commissioned by the Akron Symphony Orchestra; one work having operatic overtones and which in performance featured singer Carmen Lundy, the other, in progress in the winter of 1996/7, using a full symphony orchestra and a large choir. He has also written two works for the Los Angeles Philharmonic Orchestra, and a percussion concerto, and he continues to extend this facet of his talent. As a pianist, Childs is highly melodic, perhaps a result of his tenure with Hubbard. His questing mind, as evidenced by his desire to write without regard for externally imposed restrictions, places him at the forefront of contemporary musicians. However, even by the late 90s he had still to break through into widespread international recognition; clearly his is a name to follow in the twenty-first century.

● ALBUMS: *Take For Example This . . .* (Hip Pocket 1988)★★★, *I've Known Rivers* (Stretch 1993)★★★, *Twilight Is Upon Us* (Windham Hill 1993)★★, *His April Touch* (Windham Hill 1994)★★, *Portrait Of A Player* (Windham Hill 1995)★★★, *The Child Within* (Shanachie 1996)★★★, as composer the St. Louis Orchestra *Concerto For Percussion And Concert Band* (Collins 1996)★★★★.

CHILTON, JOHN

b. 16 July 1932, London, England. A sound trumpeter and skilful arranger, Chilton led his own band in the mid-50s before joining the Bruce Turner Jump Band in 1958. He remained with Turner for five years, playing and writing arrangements. In the early 60s he was with Alex Welsh and Mike Daniels before forming another band of his own. At the end of the 60s he became coleader with Wally Fawkes of a band they named the Feetwarmers, taking over as leader in 1974. Almost at once, Chilton became musical director for George Melly and ever since has toured, recorded and broadcast with the singer. As far as the wider public is concerned, Chilton's place in British jazz may rest on his relationship with Melly, but for the cognoscenti it is his role as a writer and tireless researcher into jazz history that makes him a figure of considerable importance. Among his many publications are *Who's Who Of Jazz: Storyville To Swing Street*, a work that ably demonstrates the awe-inspiring meticulousness of his research; *Louis: The Louis Armstrong Story*, a biography written in collaboration with Max Jones; *Jazz*, a history written for the 'Teach Yourself' series of publications; *Billie's Blues*, a partial biography of Billie Holiday, plus historical accounts of the Jenkins Orphanage bands, McKinney's Cotton Pickers, the Bob Crosby Bobcats, and definitive biographies of Sidney Bechet and Coleman Hawkins. In the early 90s Chilton was still on the road with Melly and writing about his branch of jazz, on which he is an acknowledged expert.

CHISHOLM, GEORGE

b. 29 March 1915, Glasgow, Scotland, d. 6 December 1997, Milton Keynes, England. In his early 20s Chisholm arrived in London, where he played trombone in the popular dance bands led by Teddy Joyce and Bert Ambrose. Inspired originally by recordings of Jack Teagarden, Chisholm naturally gravitated towards the contemporary jazz scene and was thus on hand for informal sessions and even the occasional recording date with visiting American stars such as Benny Carter, Coleman Hawkins and Fats Waller. During World War II he played with the Royal Air Force's dance band, the Squadronaires, with whom he remained in the post-war years. Later he became a regular studio and session musician, playing with several of the BBC's house bands (including *The Goon Show*). In the late 50s and on through the 60s Chisholm's exuberant sense of humour led to a succession of television appearances in *The Black And White Minstrel Show*, both as musician and comic, and if his eccentric dress, black tights and George Robey-style bowler hat caused jazz fans some displeasure, the music he played was always excellent. During this period he made many records with leading British and American jazz artists including Sandy Brown and Wild Bill Davison. In the 80s, despite having had heart surgery, Chisholm played on, often working with Keith Smith's Hefty Jazz or his own band, the Gentlemen of Jazz. He continued to delight audiences with his fluid technique and his ability to blend an urgent attack with a smooth style of playing and endless touches of irreverent humour. He was awarded an OBE in 1984. In 1990 he was still on the road, touring with visiting Americans, such as Spike Robinson. Soon afterwards, however, his state of health forced him to retire from active playing but did nothing to damage his high spirits and sense of humour.

● ALBUMS: *George Chisholm And His Band* (1956)★★★★, *Stars Play Jazz* (1961)★★★★, *George Chisholm* (1967)★★★, with Sandy Brown *Hair At Its Hairiest* (1968)★★, *Along The Chisholm Trail* (1971)★★★, *In A Mellow Mood* (1973)★★★, *Trombone Showcase* (1976)★★★, *The Swingin' Mr C* (Zodiac 1986)★★★, *That's A-Plenty!* (Zodiac 1987)★★★, with John Petters *Swinging Down Memory Lane* (CMJ 1989)★★★.

CHITTISON, HERMAN

b. 15 October 1908, Flemingsburg, Kentucky, USA, d. 8 March 1967. After studying piano formally at school and college, Chittison joined Zack Whyte's Chocolate Beau Brummels in 1928. He stayed with Whyte for three years and then freelanced as an accompanying pianist to singers Adelaide Hall and Ethel Waters, and also made recordings with Clarence Williams. In 1934 he joined the Willie Lewis band, which was bound for Europe. Although he remained associated with Lewis for the next few years Chittison continued to work with other jazzmen, including Louis Armstrong, and also began a career as a solo recording artist. A band he co-led with Bill Coleman, the Harlem Rhythm Makers, worked extensively in Egypt, but with the outbreak of World War II he returned to the USA. From this point onwards, Chittison rarely left the east coast, leading his own small group, working as a solo, occasionally accompanying visiting singers, and appearing on a weekly radio show. He was a deft and often exciting soloist.

● ALBUMS: *Herman Chittison* 10-inch album (Columbia 1950)★★★★, *The Herman Chittison Trio* 10-inch album (Columbia 1951)★★★★, *Keyboard Capers* (1950)★★★★, *The Elegant Piano Styling Of Herman Chittison, Volumes 1 & 2* (1962)★★★★, *The Elegant Piano Styling Of Herman Chittison, Volume 3* (1964)★★★.

● COMPILATIONS: *At The Piano* (Holmia Classics 1986)★★★, *In Paris 1925-37* (1988)★★★, *Piano Genius* (Musicraft 1988)★★, *The Master Of Stride Piano* (Meritt 1988)★★★★, *Cocktail Piano Favourites* (Columbia 1989)★★★, *Herman Chittison 1933-41* (Classic Jazz Masters 1993)★★★.

CHOCOLATE DANDIES

Taking their name from a show written by Noble Sissle and Eubie Blake, a small group led by Don Redman recorded in the late 20s as the Chocolate Dandies. Redman also used the name for some McKinney's Cotton Pickers record dates but during the early 30s the name was picked up by other musicians, notably Benny Carter, who used it for a string of fine recordings he made with Coleman Hawkins and others. Carter revived the name in the early 40s, again with Hawkins in the band and often creating timeless miniature masterpieces of small group jazz.

● COMPILATIONS: *The Chocolate Dandies (1928-33)* (Disques Swing 1983)★★★.

CHRISTENSEN, JON

b. 20 March 1943, Oslo, Norway. Christensen won the Norwegian Jazz Amateur Competition at the age of 17 and soon became the regular drummer behind visiting American musicians. For the last two decades he has pursued two concurrent musical careers. On the international jazz festival circuit he has played with artists as varied as Dexter Gordon, Gary Burton, Sonny Rollins,

Terje Rypdal and Stan Getz. However, perhaps more importantly, he has become the central drummer in the impressionist European style characterized by the ECM Records label, drumming for Keith Jarrett's European Quartet, Eberhard Weber's Colours, and Jan Garbarek's Quartet. Voted number 1 drummer by the Polish magazine *Jazz Forum* from 1973-84, Christensen remains one of the most versatile jazz drummers around.

● ALBUMS: *Masqualero* (1983)★★★, *Bande A Part* (1985)★★, with Anders Jormin, Bobo Stenson *Reflections* (ECM 1997)★★★★.

Christian, Charlie

b. 29 July 1916, Dallas, Texas, USA, d. 2 March 1942, New York, USA. Much of Christian's early life is shadowy but he grew up in Oklahoma City where, thanks to the research of eminent writer Ralph Ellison, something of his deprived background has emerged. His father, who was blind, was an itinerant guitarist-singer and Christian's two brothers were also musically inclined. Too poor to buy an instrument of his own, Christian made a guitar out of cigar boxes and soon developed an impressive if localized reputation among musicians. In the early 30s he worked professionally with territory bands led by Anna Mae Winburn, who later led the International Sweethearts Of Rhythm, Nat Towles, Alphonso Trent, with whom he played bass, and others. As early as 1937 he was experimenting with electrical amplification and had built upon his early reputation. In 1939, at the urging of Mary Lou Williams, he was heard at the Ritz Cafe in Oklahoma City by entrepreneur and jazz enthusiast John Hammond, who tried to persuade Benny Goodman to hire him for a Los Angeles recording date. (Goodman denied this well-documented event, however). Goodman wasn't convinced about the concept of an electric guitar and Christian's appearance - he favoured vividly coloured clothes. Hammond persisted and that evening he helped Christian to haul his cumbersome amplifiers onto the stage at the Victor Hugo Restaurant in Beverly Hills, where Goodman was appearing. When Goodman returned to the stand after the interval he was dismayed and angry but was too professional to create a scene and instead counted off 'Rose Room', a tune he did not expect the newcomer to know. When it was Christian's turn to solo, he played 25 brilliant choruses that had the audience, the other musicians, and Goodman, yelling for more. This performance of 'Rose Room', unfortunately not recorded that night, lasted 45 minutes and, not surprisingly, Christian was thereafter a member of the Goodman entourage. Goodman's small groups had been steadily increasing in size and Christian was featured in the Sextet. Being with Goodman gave him maximum exposure to the public and enormous fame. However, Christian was more interested in new musical developments and became an important member of the underground movement which eventually flowered into bebop. Sadly, Christian was unable to adjust to the fame and fortune that had come his way. Apart from playing music whenever and wherever he could, he indulged in alcohol and promiscuous behaviour, rarely slept and by the middle of 1941 was seriously ill with tuberculosis. In hospital his friends decided to continue their numerous parties at his bedside. It was all too much for Christian's wasted constitution and he died on 2 March 1942. It is difficult to overstate the importance of Charlie Christian in the history of jazz and popular music. His after-hours sessions at Minton's Playhouse in New York, some of which were recorded by a fan, show him to have been an important fellow-architect of bebop with Charlie Parker and Dizzy Gillespie. A brilliantly inventive soloist, his deceptively simple, single-line solos radicalized thinking not only among fellow guitarists but also among front-line soloists. Although he was not the first guitarist to electrically amplify his instrument, he was one of a tiny number to achieve widespread attention and, thanks to his recordings with Goodman, this concept attained a level of popularity that it has never lost. Any of his records stands as an example of a genius of jazz sadly cut off before his full potential had been realized.

● ALBUMS: with Dizzy Gillespie *Dizzy Gillespie With Charlie Christian* 10-inch album (Esoteric 1953)★★★★.

● COMPILATIONS: *Jazz Immortal* 10-inch album (Esoteric 1951)★★★★, *Live Sessions, At Mintons* (Saga 1974)★★★, *1941 Historical Performances* (1988)★★★★, *Solo Flight Genius Of The Electric Guitar* (Columbia 1988)★★★★, *Charlie Christian Live 1939-41* (Music Memorial 1992)★★★, *Charlie Christian* 8-CD box set (Media 7 1994)★★★★.

● VIDEOS: *The Genius Of Charlie Christian* (View Video 1992), *Solo Flight* (View Video 1997).

● FURTHER READING: *Charlie Christian: The Story Of The Seminal Electric Guitarist*, Peter Broadbent.

Christie, Keith

b. 6 January 1931, Blackpool, Lancashire, England, d. 16 December 1980. Christie began playing trombone while in his early teens. After performing in local bands he moved to London to study and in 1949 became a member of Humphrey Lyttelton's band. In the early 50s he was co-leader with his clarinettist brother, Ian, of the Christie Brothers Stompers. He then switched musical camps, leaving the traditionalists to join Johnny Dankworth. Also in the 50s he played in the small group led by Tommy Whittle and with Ted Heath's big band. In the 60s he played in studio bands, but also played jazz with Tubby Hayes and other leading figures, effortlessly switching styles, such was his professionalism and musicianship. For all his skills and the high regard in which he was held by his peers, Christie led a troubled private life and his alcoholism led to an early death in 1980.

Christlieb, Pete

b. 16 February 1945, Los Angeles, California, USA. Formally educated in music as a violinist, Christlieb then began playing tenor saxophone in his early teenage years. In his late teens he became a professional musician working with big bands and small groups under the leadership of Si Zentner, Jerry Grey, Woody Herman and others. In 1967 he became a regular member of Louie Bellson's big band, an association which lasted for the next two decades. During this period Christlieb worked with many other leaders, among them Doc Severinsen, whose *Tonight Show* band included many of the best musicians on the west coast, Count Basie, Benny Goodman, Bill Berry, Mel Lewis and Bob Florence. He also played in small groups at clubs and for record dates, most notably a band he co-led with Warne Marsh whose *Apogee* was well received. He regularly led his own quartet, which included Mike Melvoin, Jim Hughart and Nick Ceroli. A technically proficient player, Christlieb has a zestful, attacking style which makes his playing on up-tempo numbers particularly exciting, while his ballads always have an undercurrent of urgency.

● ALBUMS: *Jazz City: A Quartet With Pete Christlieb* (1971)★★★, with Warne Marsh *Apogee* (Warners 1978)★★★★, with Marsh *Conversations With Warne, Volume 1* (Criss Cross 1978)★★★★, with Bob Florence *Concerts By The Sea* (Trend 1979)★★★★, with Florence *Westlake* (Westlake 1981)★★★, *Going My Way* (1982)★★★, *Live At Dino's '83* (Bosco 5 1983)★★, *Live* (Capri 1991)★★★, with Ernie Watts, Rickey Woodard *The Tenor Trio* (JVC 1997)★★★.

CHRISTMANN, GÜNTER

b. 1942, Srem, Poland. Trombonist and bassist Christmann, although influenced by the new jazz of John Coltrane, Ornette Coleman, and Cecil Taylor, was among the first European improvisers to reject the idea of free music as pure emotional catharsis. Though still committed to spontaneous creation he aims for the clarity and concentrated expression of such 20th-century composers as Anton Webern and Arnold Schoenberg and has worked as much on the *avant garde* 'straight music' circuit as in the jazz clubs. He has made new developments in trombone playing by doctoring his sound with electronics. His group Vario, whose line-up fluctuates constantly, aims to move between the arts, and often features the interaction of musicians and dancers. Christmann resides in Germany and has been a member of Alexander Von Schlippenbach's Globe Unity Orchestra since 1973.

● ALBUMS: with Detlef Schönenberg *We Play* (1973)★★★, with Schönenberg and Harald Bojé *Remarks* (1975)★★★★, with Schönenberg *Topic* (1976)★★, with Schönenberg *Live At Moers Festival '76* (1977)★★★, *Solomusik Für Posaune Und Kontrabass* (1977)★★★, with Tristan Honsinger *Earmeals* (1978)★★★, with Gerd Dudek, Albert Mangelsdorff, Kenny Wheeler, Paul Rutherford and Manfred Schoof *Horns* (1979)★★★★, *Off* (1980)★★★, with Maarten Altena and Paul Lovens *Weavers* (1980)★★, *Vario II* (1981)★★★, *Vario* (1986)★★★, with Torsten Müller *Carte Blanche* (1986)★★★.

CHRISTY, JUNE

b. Shirley Luster, 20 November 1925, Springfield, Illinois, USA, d. 21 June 1990. Christy first came to prominence with the bands of Boyd Raeburn and Stan Kenton, although her chirpy singing style sometimes sat oddly with the earnestly progressive experiments of her employers. Her bright, bubbling personality glowed through her performances and she was especially effective on up-tempo swingers. However, she was also adept on reflective ballads and was never afraid to have fun with a song. With Kenton she had successes in all of these areas. One of her first recordings with the band was 'Tampico', which became a million-seller; another was 'How High The Moon'. During the late 40s she was one of the band's main attractions. Kenton and his chief arranger, Pete Rugolo, responded by providing effective settings for her voice which, while of limited range, was engaging and her performances were always highly professional. In January 1947 she married Kenton's tenor saxophonist Bob Cooper, with whom she made some fine recordings backed by his small group. After leaving Kenton in 1948 Christy worked as a solo artist, making many successful recordings for Capitol Records, including three US Top 20 albums, *Something Cool* (imaginatively arranged for her by Rugolo), *The Misty Miss Christy* and *June - Fair And Warmer!*. After many years in retirement, she died in June 1990 of kidney failure.

● ALBUMS: *Something Cool* 10-inch album (Capitol 1954)★★★★, with Stan Kenton *Duets* (Capitol 1955)★★★★, *The Misty Miss Christy* (Capitol 1956)★★★★, *June - Fair And Warmer!* (Capitol 1957)★★★, *Gone For The Day* (Capitol 1957)★★★, *June's Got Rhythm* (Capitol 1958)★★★★, *The Song Is June!* (Capitol 1959)★★★★, *June Christy Recalls Those Kenton Days* (Capitol 1959)★★★, *Ballads For Night People* (Capitol 1959)★★★, with Kenton *The Road Show, Volumes 1 & 2* (Capitol 1960)★★★, with Kenton *Together Again* (Capitol 1960)★★★, *The Cool School* (Capitol 1960)★★★, *Off Beat* (Capitol 1961)★★★, *Do-Re-Mi* film soundtrack (Capitol 1961)★★, *That Time Of Year* (Capitol 1961)★★★, *Big Band Specials* (Capitol 1962)★★, *The Intimate June Christy* (Capitol 1962)★★★★, *Something Broadway, Something Latin* (Capitol 1965)★★, *Impromptu* (Interplay 1977)★★★, *Willow Weep For Me* (1979)★★★, *Interlude* (Discovery 1985)★★★.

● COMPILATIONS: *This Is June Christy!* (Capitol 1958)★★★★, *The Best Of June Christy* (Capitol 1962)★★★★, *The Capitol Years* (Capitol 1989)★★★★, *A Lovely Way To Spend An Evening* (Jasmine 1989)★★★.

CIRCLE

Circle was born in a jam session at New York's Village Gate in 1970 when Anthony Braxton sat in with the Chick Corea Trio. They comprised Braxton (alto and soprano saxophons, flute, clarinet, contrabass clarinet, percussion), Corea (piano, flute, vibes, marimba, percussion), Dave Holland (bass, cello, guitar, percussion), and Barry Altschul (drums, percussion, marimba). Corea and Holland were weary of being tied to the beat in Miles Davis's jazz rock group and were looking for alternative creative options. They had already toyed with the idea of a quartet completed by Lee Konitz, but Braxton's ideas, drawn as much from the music of Stockhausen and Xenakis as from jazz, were altogether more exciting and opened up a new world of possibilities. The group gave the saxophonist a needed shot of enthusiasm, too. Braxton was beginning to despair of finding an audience for his challenging compositions and on the brink of abandoning music for a career as a professional chess player. Circle took Europe by storm with its intellectually alert yet fiery improvising. The prize-winning *Paris Concert* is the best recorded example of the group's work. By the time of its release, however, the unit had fallen apart. Corea, in thrall to L. Ron Hubbard's ideas about 'communication', wanted to simplify the music. Holland, Altschul and Braxton, who had neither the desire nor ability to play Corea's bossa novas, put their own flirtation with Scientology behind them and continued to work together in the saxophonist's quartet until the winter of 1976.

● ALBUMS: *Paris Concert* (1972)★★★★, *Live In German Concert* (1972)★★, *Gathering* (1973)★★★.

● COMPILATIONS: *Circling In* (1975)★★, *Circulus* (1978)★★★.

CITROEN, SOESJA

b. Holland. A highly gifted singer whose style and musical interests are firmly rooted in post-bop, Citroen's work deserves much wider attention than has so far been the case. Her voice is rich and fluid and her phrasing clearly demonstrates an excellent ear for the intricate nuances of bop. Although customarily working with fellow countrymen, she has also recorded with Dusko Goykovich and John Clayton. She is a gifted lyricist and on album of music by Thelonious Monk, she contributed lyrics to several modern jazz standards, including 'Crepescule With Nellie' ('In Twilight'), 'Monk's Mood' ('Underneath This Cover') and 'Let's Cool One' ('Come With Me').

● ALBUMS: *To Build* (Coreco 1980)★★★, *Soesja Citroen Sings Thelonious Monk* (Timeless 1983)★★, *Key Largo* (Timeless 1983)★★★, *Shall We Dance* (Timeless 1985)★★★★.

CLAASSEN, FEE

b. Holland. An excellent singer with a distinctively contemporary approach to her work, she customarily uses her voice as an instrumental part of the groups with which she sings. She often works with singer Carolyn Breuer, pianist Sebastien Altekamp, bassist Stephan Van Wylick and drummer Joost Patocka.

● ALBUMS: with Carolyn Breuer *Simply Be* (Challenge 1994)★★★.

CLARE, ALAN

b. 31 May 1921, London, England, d. 29 November 1993, London, England. A self-taught pianist, Clare became a professional musician at the age of 15 and during the next few years became a familiar figure on the London jazz scene. He played with Carlo Krahmer, Sid Phillips and others in the early 40s before military service intervened. Wounded soon after D-Day, he returned to civilian life, playing in the comedy band led by Sid Milward and also began a long sporadic association with Stéphane Grappelli. From the 50s onwards, Clare was busy playing jazz in small groups, some of which he led, mostly in nightclubs but also appearing occasionally on television. An exceptionally gifted pianist with a light, subtle touch, he had a seemingly endless knowledge of tunes and chord progressions. Allied to a gift for accompaniment and the ability to play with unflagging swing, Clare was an outstanding figure of British jazz. His chosen milieu, however, and the relatively few recordings he made, often deleted with indecent haste, conspired to keep his gleaming talent from the widespread audience he so richly deserved.

● ALBUMS: *Jazz Around The Clock* (1958)★★★, *Midnight Moods* (Ditto 1988)★★★.

CLARE, KENNY

b. 8 June 1929, London, England, d. 21 December 1984. Clare played drums as a teenager and in 1949 joined the popular broadcasting danceband led by Oscar Rabin. In 1954 he moved over to the Jack Parnell band for a while before settling into the John Dankworth orchestra. He was with Dankworth until the early 60s, when he joined Ted Heath. During this period he also recorded with a band he co-led with fellow drummer Ronnie Stephenson. Later in the decade, he became a member of the Clarke-Boland Big Band. From 1972 he worked with many bands, large and small, played in studio orchestras for recording sessions, television and radio programmes, and on film soundtracks. He also toured extensively as accompanist to Tom Jones. Amongst his recording dates are sessions with Ella Fitzgerald, Joe Pass and Stéphane Grappelli. Clare was a gifted all-round percussionist, filled with enormous enthusiasm.

● ALBUMS: with Ronnie Stephenson *Drum Spectacular* (1966)★★★, with Colin Busby *Big Swing Favourites* (1984)★★★.

CLARK, BUDDY

b. 10 July 1929, Kenosha, Wisconsin, USA. After starting to learn trombone and piano Clark took up the bass at high school and studied at the Chicago Musical College (1948-49). He played with Bud Freeman and Bill Russo, before touring with the bands of Tex Beneke and Les Brown. In the early 50s he moved to Los Angeles and worked with Peggy Lee, Red Norvo, Dave Pell and Jimmy Giuffre, among others. In addition to continuing this busy studio life into the 60s he worked with Gerry Mulligan whose usually pianoless band exposes the bass player more than is usual: Brown's round, bright tone and fluid lines suited the context well. In 1972 he joined with Med Flory to found Supersax, a band dedicated to playing the music of Charlie Parker - not just the themes but arranged transcriptions of the solos too. Clark's arrangements for the saxophone section usually featured the lead alto and baritone in octaves with the other saxophones filling in the harmonies. In 1975 he returned to studio work.

● ALBUMS: *Supersax Plays Bird* (1972)★★★, *Supersax Plays Bird With Strings* (1975)★★★.

CLARK, GARNET

b. *c*.1914, Washington, DC, USA, d. 1938. While still in his teens Clark played piano professionally with several bands in his home-town. He arrived in New York in 1933 and was an overnight sensation, reputedly recording with Alex Hill and Benny Carter. In 1935 he went to Europe with Carter as a member of the Willie Lewis band. While there he recorded with Django Reinhardt, giving only a hint of the talent that had so excited New York, and served as accompanist to Adelaide Hall. Still in Europe, in 1937, he suffered a mental breakdown and was confined to an asylum for the insane where he died late the following year.

CLARK, JUNE

b. Algeria Junius Clark, 24 March 1900, Long Branch, New Jersey, USA, d. 23 February 1963. Clark learned to play several instruments as a child, eventually settling on the cornet. He became a professional musician and joined a travelling show in which James P. Johnson also played. Clark and Johnson eventually teamed up with Jimmy Harrison and the three men backed various musicians and singers, sometimes on recording dates. In the early 20s Clark was often in New York where he played with Willie 'The Lion' Smith and also led his own band, which featured Benny Carter in its ranks. He continued to play with various bands, making occasional records, but by 1937 was forced into retirement through poor health. He retained his links with the music business in general, however, and the jazz world in particular, becoming road manager and/or musical adviser and assistant to artists such as Louis Armstrong and Earl 'Fatha' Hines. John Chilton records that Clark subsequently became road manager for the boxer Sugar Ray Robinson before poor health again intervened.

CLARK, SONNY

b. Conrad Yeatis, 21 July 1931, Herminie, nr Elizabeth, Pennsylvania, USA, d. 13 January 1963, New York, USA. An underrated piano genius of the hard-bop era, Clark cast a glorious ray of sunshine over some of the Blue Note label's most memorable sessions. Art Tatum, one of his childhood heroes, and Count Basie, whose big band radio broadcasts were a popular feature of his youth, are two pianists whose influence *can* be heard in his minimal and understated style. However, his succinct and melodic approach drew as much from wind players as other pianists, his left hand providing the barest of occasional accompaniments, while he stressed instead an elegant and sophisticated single note approach. He moved to the west coast in the early 50s, and soon began working with saxophonist Vido Musso and bassist Oscar Pettiford. Throughout the mid-50s, he was an active element of the west coast scene, touring with clarinettist Buddy De Franco, saxophonist Sonny Criss and others. In 1957 he moved to New York, working first with vocalist Dinah Washington, and enjoying a new boom of attention, leading various small groups (his *Sonny's Crib* features John Coltrane) and working as a sideman with saxophonists Sonny Rollins, Clifford Jordan, and Hank Mobley and trombonist Curtis Fuller, before the combined ravages of alcohol and hard drugs took their toll. Recommended listening are *Leapin' And Lopin'* on Blue Note – an inspired 1961 date with saxophonists Ike Quebec and Charlie Rouse – the popular *Cool Struttin'* and baritone saxophone genius Serge Chaloff's classic *Blue Serge*. In 1986 the radical New York pianist Wayne Horvitz led the Sonny Clark memorial Quartet (featuring John Zorn) on *Voodoo*, a tribute album of Clark compositions.

● ALBUMS: *Dial S For Sonny* (Blue Note 1957)★★★, *Sonny's Crib* (Blue Note 1957)★★★★, *Sonny Clark Trio* (Blue Note 1958)★★★, *Cool Struttin'* (Blue Note 1958)★★★★, *Cool Struttin' Volume 2* (Blue Note 1959)★★★, *The Sonny Clark Memorial Album* (1959)★★★, *Sonny Clark* (Time 1960)★★★, *Leapin' And Lopin'* (Blue Note 1961)★★★, with George Duvivier, Max Roach *Max Roach, Sonny Clark, George Duvivier* (Time 1962)★★★★, *A Swinging Affair* (1962)★★★★, *Oakland 1955* (Uptown 1995)★★★.

● COMPILATIONS: with Grant Green *The Complete Blue Note Recordings With Sonny Clark* 4-CD box set (Mosaic 1991)★★★★, with Green *The Complete Quartets With Sonny Clark* (Blue Note 1997)★★★★.

CLARKE, KENNY 'KLOOK'

b. 9 January 1914, Pittsburgh, Pennsylvania, USA, d. 26 January 1985, Paris, France. Clarke began playing drums as a child and while in his teens played in several bands in his home-town. He later joined Roy Eldridge and also played in the Jeter-Pillars Orchestra and in those led by Edgar Hayes, Claude Hopkins and Teddy Hill. In Hill's band at the time (1939) was Dizzy Gillespie, in whom Clarke found a kindred revolutionary spirit. Both in the band and at after-hours sessions at Minton's Playhouse, Clarke began to develop new concepts of jazz drumming. His seemingly eccentric playing, 'dropping bombs' (see below), confused many musicians but was greeted with enthusiasm by the more radical newcomers. During this period, Clarke worked with leading jazzmen such as Charlie Parker, Thelonious Monk, Bud Powell and Charlie Christian. After a mid-40s hiatus for military service, Clarke was soon active in recording studios with Gillespie and other modernists, but his skills were also in demand for other, more orthodox sessions and he recorded with stalwarts of the traditional scene such as Sidney Bechet. In 1951 he was a member of Milt Jackson's quartet, a group that later evolved into the Modern Jazz Quartet. In the mid-50s he appeared on scores of albums, playing in different contexts and styles but usually favouring contemporary sounds. In 1956 Clarke relocated to Paris, France, where he worked with Powell and other visiting Americans, including Miles Davis and Dexter Gordon. From 1961 he co-led the impressive Clarke-Boland Big Band with Francy Boland. This band stayed in existence for over a decade, playing as often as was possible given its international personnel. In the 70s and early 80s he continued to live and work in Europe, in demand for concerts, recording dates, as a writer for films and as a tutor.

The founding father of bop drumming, Clarke was almost single-handedly responsible for the shift away from strict-tempoed drumming that harnessed the 4/4 beat to the bass drum. Clarke maintained the pulse on the ride cymbal, using bass and snare drums for explosive bursts of sound, as effective punctuation for the soloists. This style established the pattern and set the standards for all other bop drummers. His technique was comprehensive and he seldom allowed his enthusiasm for his work to run away with what he saw as an essentially supportive role. Despite his importance in establishing bop drumming, by the late 50s and especially during his period with the big band he co-led in Europe, Clarke had abandoned that style to concentrate upon hard-swinging drumming, which reflected his admiration for the earlier work of Jo Jones. Clarke was a major contributor to jazz and one of the few jazz innovators on his chosen instrument.

● ALBUMS: *Kenny Clarke, Vol. 1* 10-inch album (Savoy 1955)★★★★, *Kenny Clarke, Vol. 2* 10-inch album (Savoy 1955)★★★★, *Telefunken Blues* (Savoy 1955)★★★★, *Bohemia After Dark* (Savoy 1955)★★★★, with Ernie Wilkins *Plenty For Kenny* (Savoy 1955)★★★, *Klook's Clique* (Savoy 1956)★★★★, *Kenny Clarke Meets The Detroit Jazzmen* (Savoy 1956)★★★★, *Kenny Clarke Plays Andre Hodeir* (Epic 1957)★★★★, as the Clarke-Boland Big Band *The Golden Eight* (Blue Note 1961)★★★, as the Clarke-Boland Big Band *Jazz Is Universal* (Atlantic 1963)★★★, as the Clarke-Boland Big Band *The Clarke-Boland Big Band* (Atlantic 1963)★★★★, as the Clarke-Boland Big Band *Now Hear Our Meanin'* (Columbia 1965)★★★, as the Clarke-Boland Big Band *Fire, Soul, Heat & Guts* (Prestige 1968)★★★★, as the Clarke-Boland Big Band *Let's Face The Music* (Prestige 1969)★★★, *Live At Ronnie Scott's* (MPS 1969)★★★, *Rue Chaptal* (1969)★★★, *All Blues* (1969)★★★, *More Smiles* (1969)★★★, *At Her Majesty's Pleasure* (1969)★★★, *The Francy Boland-Kenny Clarke Trio* (1970)★★★, *Off Limits* (1970)★★★, *Our Kind Of Sabi* (1970)★★★, *Change Of Scenes* (1971)★★, *Jazz A Confronto* (1974)★★★, *Kenny Today* (1980)★★★, *Pieces Of Time* (Soul Note 1984)★★★, *Kenny Clarke In Paris, Vol. 1* 1957 recording (Disques Swing 1986)★★★★, *Live TNP Paris 1969* (1993)★★★, *Calipso Blues* 1964-1965 recording (Rearward 1998)★★★, with the Francy Boland Sextet *Calypso Blues* (Rearward 1998)★★★★.

● COMPILATIONS: *Paris Bebop Sessions* 1948-1950 (Prestige 1969)★★★★.

● FURTHER READING: *Klook: The Story Of Kenny Clarke*, Mike Hennessy.

CLARKE, STANLEY

b. 21 July 1951, Philadelphia, Pennsylvania, USA. Clarke started on violin, then transferred to cello, double bass and finally the bass guitar. After formal training at school and at the Philadelphia Musical Academy, his first experience was in funk outfits; he then got a taste for playing jazz working with Horace Silver for six months in 1970. He played with tenor saxophonist Joe Henderson and with Pharoah Sanders on the latter's *Black Unity*. A spell with Chick Corea and his Return For Forever band reminded Clarke of his aptitude for the electric bass, and he became a pioneer of fusion as 'cosmic' as it was commercial: *Journey To Love* (1975) had glossy production a million miles from Sanders' abrasive poly-rhythms. A partnership with George Duke, also a fugitive from acoustic jazz, provided audiences with spectacular virtuoso work-outs. Gifted with jaw-dropping technique, Clarke's rise to fame coincided with a period when demonstrating 'chops' was considered to be at the cutting edge of the music. His slapping style has produced a host of imitators, though none can quite match his speed and confidence. In 1995 he formed Rite Of Strings with guitarist Al Di Meola and violinist Jean-Luc Ponty.

● ALBUMS: with Pharoah Sanders *Black Unity* (Impulse! 1972)★★★, with Return To Forever *Return To Forever* (Polydor 1972)★★★★, *Stanley Clarke* (Nemperor 1974)★★★★, *Journey To Love* (Nemperor 1975)★★★, *School Days* (Nemperor 1976)★★, *Modern Man* (Nemperor 1978)★★, *I Wanna Play For You* (Nemperor 1979)★★, *Rocks, Pebbles And Sand* (Epic 1980)★★, You/Me Together (Epic 1980)★★, with George Duke *The Clarke/Duke Project* (Epic 1981)★★★, *Let Me Know You* (Epic 1982)★★, with Duke *The Clarke/Duke Project II* (Epic 1983)★★★, *Time Exposure* (Epic 1984)★★, *Find Out* (Epic 1985)★★, *Hideaway* (Epic 1986)★★, *Shieldstone* (Optimism 1987)★★, *If This Bass Could Only Talk* (Epic 1988)★★★, with Duke *3* (Epic 1990)★★★, *East River Drive* (1993)★★★, with Al Di Meola, Jean-Luc Ponty *The Rite Of Strings* (IRS 1995)★★★.

● COMPILATIONS: *The Collection* (Castle 1990)★★★.

CLARKE-BOLAND BIG BAND

(see Boland, Francy; Clarke, Kenny)

CLAUSEN, THOMAS

b. 5 October 1949, Copenhagen, Denmark. A pianist and composer formally trained at the Copenhagen Music Conservatory, Clausen's career took off as accompanist with visiting Americans including Dexter Gordon, Jackie McLean and Eddie 'Lockjaw' Davis, and the active encouragement of Kenny Drew who recorded him on his label Matrix. In the 70s Clausen worked with the Danish Radio Big Band. He performs his own compositions with a brilliant sense of motivic development and continuity, and like his early inspiration, Bill Evans, he can bring out new aspects of standards by subtle reharmonization (e.g. 'Blueberry Hill' on *Rain*). Clausen has accomplished his best work in a trio setting with either Niels-Henning Ørsted Pedersen or Mads Vinding on bass, but two recordings with Gary Burton show a fine consonance of minds. In the 90s Clausen worked with Brazilian musicians.

● ALBUMS: *Mirror* (1979)★★★, *Rain* (1980)★★, *The Shadow Of Bill Evans* (1983)★★★★, *She Touched Me* (1988)★★★, *Piano Music* (1989)★★★, *Café Noir* (1991)★★★, *Flowers And Trees* (1992)★★★, *Psalm* (1995)★★★.

CLAXTON, ROZELLE

b. 5 February 1913, Memphis, Tennessee, USA, d. 30 March 1995. Born into a musical family, he studied formally and at a very early age was playing piano on radio in his home-town. He studied for a while under Jimmie Lunceford, then joined a touring band which was fronted by W.C. Handy. In the early 30s Claxton played with several bands in the Midwest, including those led by Bennie Moten and Harlan Leonard. In the early 40s he was based in Chicago where he played with Eddie South and Roy Eldridge. After military service in

World War II, Claxton played with George Dixon's band in Chicago before attending college again both as a mature student and as a teacher. Over the years, he wrote arrangements for several bands, including those led by Lunceford, Count Basie, Earl Hines and Andy Kirk. In the late 50s he was briefly accompanist for Pearl Bailey and returned to her in 1978 for a five-year stint. In the 80s he retired to his home-town but from time to time could be heard performing back in Chicago. His playing was always interesting but his chosen milieu meant that he was often overlooked, although a spell in the early 60s with Franz Jackson's Original Jass All Stars brought him to wider notice. His arranging talents were also sound and he occasionally also played organ.

● ALBUMS: all with Franz Jackson *Jass, Jass, Jass* (Philips 1959)★★★★, *A Nite At The Red Arrow* (Pinnacle 1961)★★★, *Chicago: The Living Legends* (Riverside 1961)★★★.

CLAY, SHIRLEY

b. 1902, Charleston, Missouri, USA, d. 7 February 1951. In his youth he played trumpet in several territory bands, mostly in his home state, the most notable of which was that led by John 'Bearcat' Williams. After moving to Chicago, Clay played with bands led by Carroll Dickerson, Louis Armstrong and Earl Hines. In the early 30s he was often called upon for recording dates and played in several bands of the day. Among the leaders with whom he either gigged or recorded were Benny Goodman, Ben Pollack, Putney Dandridge and Claude Hopkins. In the 40s he was with Hines again, Horace Henderson and Cootie Williams. In 1944 Clay formed his own band which he led intermittently for the rest of his life, sometimes co-leading with Edgar Battle. Although some of his recordings with Hines show Clay in an unfavourable light, he was generally sound and could play interesting solos. His duets with trumpeter George Mitchell while with Hines were well conceived, although somewhat constrained by the arranger's intentions to recreate the famous Armstrong-King Oliver duets of an earlier day. A good example of Clay's abilities as a soloist can be heard on Billie Holiday's second recording date where he plays on 'Riffin' The Scotch', a track on which Goodman and Jack Teagarden also play.

● COMPILATIONS: *The Chronological Earl Hines 1928-1932* (Classics 1928-32)★★★★, *The Chronological Billie Holiday 1933-1937* (Classics 1933-37)★★★★.

CLAYTON, BUCK

b. Wilbur Dorsey Clayton, 12 November 1911, Parsons, Kansas, USA, d. 8 December 1991, New York City, New York, USA. By his late teens Clayton was already an accomplished trumpeter, having worked locally in Kansas and briefly in California. He returned to the west coast, playing in several Los Angeles-based bands including that led by Charlie Echols. He also formed his own unit, which he took to China for two years. Back in California he found that his reputation had spread and in 1936 he was invited to join Count Basie. He remained with Basie until drafted for military service in 1943, by which time his fame was guaranteed thanks to a succession of fine solos on many of the Basie band's best recordings. After the war he worked mostly with small bands and also appeared as a member of Jazz At The Philharmonic. He worked, too, with a former Basie colleague Jimmy Rushing and occasionally formed bands, big and small, under his own leadership. He toured extensively and made numerous records, including a series of very highly-regarded jam sessions in the early and mid-50s which brought together several major mainstream musicians. These sessions used Clayton's marvellously loose arrangements and became exemplars of their kind. He had begun arranging with Basie, and other bandleaders who used his charts included Benny Goodman and Harry James.
In the 50s he toured with Mezz Mezzrow, Eddie Condon and Sidney Bechet. A gifted soloist with a clean, mellow tone, his arranging skills stood him in good stead when, in the late 60s, he began to suffer from severe lip problems. Extensive surgery failed to improve matters and he eventually abandoned playing in favour of arranging. In the late 70s he led a number of bands on international tours under the auspices of the US State Department and occasionally played a little. His activities as bandleader, lecturer and arranger continued into the late 80s. A major figure in the establishment of mainstream jazz who was greatly respected by his peers.

● ALBUMS: with Ruby Braff, Mel Powell *Buck Meets Ruby* 10-inch album (Vanguard 1954)★★★★, *Hucklebuck And Robbin's Nest* (Columbia 1954)★★★★, *How High The Fi* (Columbia 1955)★★★★, *Moten Swing - Sentimental Journey* 10-inch album (Columbia 1955)★★★★, *Buck Clayton Jams Benny Goodman* (Columbia 1955)★★★★, *Jumpin' At The Woodside* (Columbia 1955)★★★★, *Jazz Spectacular* (Columbia 1956)★★★★, *All The Cats Join In* (Columbia 1956)★★★, *Meet Buck Clayton* (Jazztone 1956)★★★, with Don Byas, Alix Combelle, Mary Lou Williams *Messin' Round In Montmarte* (Storyville 1956)★★★, with Braff, Powell *Buckin' The Blues* (Vanguard 1957)★★★★, with Wild Bill Davison *Singing Trumpets* (Jazztone 1957)★★★★, with Sidney Bechet *Concert At The World's Fair, Brussels* (Columbia 1958)★★★, with Harry 'Sweets' Edison *Harry Edison Swings Buck Clayton And Vice-Versa* (Verve 1958)★★★, *Tenderly* (Inner City 1959)★★★, *Copenhagen Concert* (Steeple Chase 1959)★★★, *Songs For Swingers* (Columbia 1959)★★★, with Pee Wee Russell *A Salute To Newport* (Dot 1959)★★★★, with Russell *Memorial Album* (Prestige 1960)★★★, with Buddy Tate *Buck & Buddy* (Swingville 1961)★★★, *Olympia Concert/Live In Paris* (Vogue 1961)★★★★, *Buck Clayton All-Stars, 1961* (Storyville 1961)★★★, *Passport To Paradise* (Inner City 1961)★★★, with Tate *Buck & Buddy Blow The Blues* (Vanguard 1962)★★★, with Humphrey Lyttleton *With Humphrey Lyttelton And His Band* (Harlequin 1965)★★★, with Big Joe Turner *Buck Clayton Meets Joe Turner* (Black Lion 1965)★★★, *Baden, Switzerland 1966* (Sackville 1966)★★★★, *A Swingin' Dream* (Stash 1989)★★★, *The Buck Clayton Swing Band Live From Greenwich Village* 1990 recording (Nagel-Heyer 1997)★★.

● COMPILATIONS: *Buck Clayton Rarities, Vol. 1* 1945-1953 recordings (Swingtime 1988)★★, *Complete CBS Buck Clayton*

Jam Sessions 3-CD box set (Mosaic)★★★★, *The Essential Buck Clayton* 1953-1957 recordings (Vanguard)★★★★.

● FURTHER READING: *Buck Clayton's Jazz World*, Buck Clayton.

CLAYTON, JEFF

b. 16 February 1955, Venice, California, USA. Clayton's musical education began at a local Baptist church, where his mother was pianist and conductor of the choir. He began playing various reed instruments, including clarinet, but concentrated on alto saxophone. He later added soprano saxophone and flute, extending his studies during high school and university where his principal instrument was the oboe. He dropped out of university before graduating in order to go on tour with Stevie Wonder. Later, he mixed studio work with touring, playing with artists as diverse as Gladys Knight and Kenny Rogers, Patti Labelle and Michael Jackson. He gradually shifted towards a more jazz-orientated repertoire and although he continued to work in orchestras backing popular singers such as Frank Sinatra, Mel Tormé, Lena Horne and Sammy Davis Jnr., it was in the jazz world that he established his reputation during the 80s. He played in the Tommy Dorsey Orchestra under the direction of Murray McEachern, with Count Basie, the continuing Basie band under Thad Jones, Alphonse Mouzon, Juggernaut, Woody Herman, Lionel Hampton, Ella Fitzgerald, the Phillip Morris Superband led by Gene Harris, Monty Alexander, Ray Brown and many others. Clayton continued to work with pop stars, playing saxophone solos on an album by Madonna and on the soundtrack of the film *Dick Tracy* (1990), in which she starred. Clayton has worked extensively in partnership with his brother, John Clayton, and they both co-lead a big band with Jeff Hamilton. A hugely talented musician, Clayton's playing of the alto saxophone is especially distinguished. Although he has developed a distinctive style of his own, his playing reveals his respect and admiration for the sensitive manner in which Johnny Hodges richly interpreted ballads and the harder-edged drive and phrasing of Cannonball Adderley. In addition to his performing, which has recently included playing classical music with the Icelandic Philharmonic Orchestra, Clayton also teaches, conducts clinics, and writes. In his capacity as a writer he has composed songs for Jon Hendricks. In the early 90s Clayton continued to play numerous festivals, concerts and make records either under his own name or with major stars of jazz and popular music. Clearly a leading figure in contemporary music, his continuing career is one to watch.

● ALBUMS: with John Clayton *Jeff & John* (1978)★★★, with John Clayton *It's All In The Family* (1980)★★★, with Clayton-Hamilton Big Band *Groove Shop* (Capri 1989)★★★, *Gene Harris And The Phillip Morris Superband* (1990)★★, with Ray Brown *Evergreen* (1990)★★★, with John Clayton *The Sweet Man* (Capri 1991)★★★, as the Clayton Brothers *The Music* (1993)★★★, with Clayton-Hamilton Big Band *Heart And Soul* (Capri 1993)★★★★, as the Clayton Brothers *Expressions* (Qwest 1997)★★★.

CLAYTON, JOHN

b. 1952, Los Angeles, California, USA. Born into a musical family, Clayton took up the bass and at the age of 16 was studying with Ray Brown. Three years later he was in the orchestra for the US television series *The Mancini Generation,* but left to resume his studies. His playing career continued via stints with Monty Alexander and the Count Basie band and he also served for five years as principal bass with the Amsterdam Philharmonic Orchestra. Aside from playing, Clayton teaches bass and has appeared on a number of instructional videos with Brown and Milt Hinton. He is also an accomplished composer, drawing inspiration from Henry Mancini and especially Johnny Mandel. In 1989 he spent time in Germany, writing for the Cologne Radio Orchestra. He has appeared regularly in the Doc Severinson Orchestra on the *Tonight* television show and was a member of the Gene Harris/Philip Morris Superband for its 1989 world tour. He has recorded with Ernestine Anderson, the Cunninghams, Brown, Mancini, Rosemary Clooney and with the big band he has co-led with his brother, Jeff Clayton, and Jeff Hamilton since 1985. Many of the charts played by the Clayton-Hamilton band are written by him and he has deliberately set out to emulate Duke Ellington in seeking to create formats which effectively draw upon the abilities of individual musicians within the orchestra. An outstanding technician, Clayton is one of the most respected and sought-after jazz bassists in the 90s.

● ALBUMS: with Jeff Clayton *Jeff & John* (1978)★★★, with Jeff Clayton *It's All In The Family* (1980)★★★, with Clayton-Hamilton Big Band *Groove Shop* (Capri 1989)★★★, with Jeff Clayton *The Sweet Man* (Capri 1991)★★★, as the Clayton Brothers *The Music* (1993)★★★, with Clayton-Hamilton *Heart And Soul* (Capri 1993)★★★★, as the Clayton Brothers *Expressions* (Qwest 1997)★★★, with Ray Brown, Christian McBride *Super Bass* (Telarc 1997)★★★★.

CLESS, ROD

b. 20 May 1907, Lennox, Iowa, USA, d. 8 December 1944. After playing clarinet in local bands while still a schoolboy, Cless met Frank Teschemacher, then a member of the Wolverines, in 1925 and two years later played with him in Chicago. Influenced by Teschemacher and his brother-in-law Bud Freeman, the next few years found Cless, playing with numerous bands in the mid-western and southern states and establishing a sound reputation. In 1939 he joined Muggsy Spanier, then worked around New York and up into Canada with musicians including Art Hodes, Wild Bill Davison and Bobby Hackett. In 1944, by now drinking heavily, he worked regularly with Max Kaminsky at New York's Pied Piper Club. Walking home from the club one night he fell, was severely injured, and died four days later. In his short career Cless won the respect of musicians for his skilled, inventive playing which was captured on his recordings with Spanier.

● ALBUMS: with Muggsy Spanier *The Great Sixteen* (1939)★★★★.

CLEVELAND, JIMMY

b. 3 May 1926, Wartrace, Tennessee, USA. By the time he joined Lionel Hampton in 1950 Cleveland was already a highly-experienced trombonist, having worked with a band formed by his musical family and in the orchestra of Tennessee State University. With Hampton he played with surging power, a wonderfully rich and warm tone and great blues feeling. A brilliant technician, his playing always has great authority and his prowess makes him a much sought-after studio and session musician. After his time with Hampton he played with numerous other big bands, mostly those gathered for one-off recording dates or club and concert engagements. Among the leaders with whom he has performed are Gerry Mulligan, Quincy Jones, Dizzy Gillespie, Miles Davis, Gil Evans, Oliver Nelson, Bill Berry and Gerald Wilson.

● ALBUMS: *Introducing Jimmy Cleveland And His All Stars* (1955)★★, with Sonny Rollins *Sonny Rollins Plays/Jimmy Cleveland Plays* (Period 1956)★★★, *Gil Evans Plus Ten* (1957)★★★★, *The Great Wide World Of Quincy Jones* (1959)★★★, with Bill Berry *Hello Rev* (1976)★★★, with Urbie Green, Frank Rehak *Trombone Scene* (1988)★★.

CLEYNDERT, ANDY

b. 8 January 1963, Birmingham, West Midlands, England. Cleyndert began playing bass while still at school and, on completing his studies in 1981, immediately became a professional musician. His first engagements were at a Manchester club where he was a member of the Tony Mann Trio, which backed visiting jazzmen such as Peter King and Art Farmer. He moved to London where he played with Bobby Wellins, Don Weller and other leading figures on the British jazz scene. Naturally associating with other rising young stars, he worked with Clark Tracey and Iain Ballamy and was briefly with the National Youth Jazz Orchestra. In 1983 he recorded with Tommy Chase and the following year toured with Ted Curson. In 1985 he toured with Bobby Watson and broadcast with the Kenny Wheeler big band. In 1986 he began teaching at music summer schools. In the late 80s he was a member of the Bryan Spring Trio and was regularly called upon to accompany visiting American jazzmen, including Bud Shank, Red Rodney, Charlie Rouse and Spike Robinson. He also toured overseas with Slim Gaillard, Spirit Level, Louis Stewart and Martin Taylor. In 1990 Cleyndert was a member of the Anglo-American band led by George Coleman Jnr. Despite the intense level of work he has sustained throughout his career, Cleyndert found time to study, and in 1990 gained a degree in mathematics and psychology. One of the best of the new generation of jazz musicians to emerge on the UK scene, Cleyndert's broad musical base allied to his already wide experience assures him of an important place in the future of jazz.

CLOONEY, ROSEMARY

b. 23 May 1928, Maysville, Kentucky, USA. While very young, Rosemary and her sister Betty sang at political rallies in support of their paternal grandfather. When Rosemary was 13 the Clooney children moved to Cincinnati, Ohio, and appeared on radio station WLW. In 1945 they auditioned successfully for tenor saxophonist Tony Pastor and joined his band as featured vocalists, travelling the country doing mainly one-night shows. Rosemary made her first solo record in 1946 with 'I'm Sorry I Didn't Say I'm Sorry When I Made You Cry Last Night'. After around three years of touring, Betty quit, and Rosemary stayed on as a soloist with the band. She signed for Columbia Records in 1950 and had some success with children's songs such as 'Me And My Teddy Bear' and 'Little Johnny Chickadee', before coming under the influence of A&R manager Mitch Miller, who had a penchant for folksy, novelty dialect songs. In 1951 Clooney's warm, husky melodious voice registered well on minor hits, 'You're Just In Love', a duet with Guy Mitchell, and 'Beautiful Brown Eyes'. Later that year she topped the US chart with 'Come On-A-My House' from the off-Broadway musical *The Son*, with a catchy harpsichord accompaniment by Stan Freeman. During the next four years Clooney had a string of US hits including 'Tenderly', which became her theme tune, 'Half As Much' (number 1), 'Botcha-Me', 'Too Old To Cut The Mustard' (a duet with Marlene Dietrich), 'The Night Before Christmas Song' (with Gene Autry), 'Hey There' and 'This Ole House' (both number 1 hits), and 'Mambo Italiano'. UK hits included 'Man', with the b-side, 'Woman', sung by her husband, actor/producer/director Jose Ferrer, and the novelty, 'Where Will The Dimple Be'. Her last singles hit was 'Mangos', in 1957. Her own US television series regularly featured close harmony vocal group the Hi-Lo's, leading to their communal album *Ring Around Rosie*. Clooney's film career started in 1953 with *The Stars Are Singing* and was followed by three films the next year, *Here Come The Girls* with Bob Hope, *Red Garters* (1954) with Guy Mitchell and the Sigmund Romberg biopic, *Deep In My Heart*, in which she sang 'Mr And Mrs' with Jose Ferrer. In the same year she teamed with Bing Crosby in *White Christmas*. Highly compatible, with friendly, easy-going styles, their professional association was to last until Crosby died, and included, in 1958, the highly regarded album *Fancy Meeting You Here*, a musical travelogue with special material by Sammy Cahn and James Van Heusen, arranged and conducted by Billy May. Semi-retired in the 60s, her psychiatric problems were chronicled in her autobiography, *This For Remembrance*, later dramatized on television as *Escape From Madness*. Her more recent work has been jazz-based, and included a series of tributes to the 'great' songwriters such as Harold Arlen, Cole Porter and Duke Ellington, released on the Concorde Jazz label. In 1991 Clooney gave an 'assured performance' in concert at Carnegie Hall, and duetted with her special guest artist, Linda Ronstadt. Throughout the early 90s she has continued to play US clubs, including her much appreciated annual stint at the Rainbow & Stars in New York. She also made occasional appearances in the US medical drama *ER*.

● ALBUMS: *Hollywood's Best* (Columbia 1952/55)★★★, *Deep In My Heart* film soundtrack (MGM 1954)★★★, *Rosemary Clooney* 10-inch album (Columbia 1954)★★★, *White Christmas* 10-inch album (Columbia 1954)★★★★, *Red Garters* film soundtrack (Columbia 1954)★★★, *Tenderly* 10-inch album (Columbia 1955)★★★★, *Children's Favorites* 10-inch album (Columbia 1956)★★, *Blue Rose* (Columbia 1956)★★★, *A Date With The King* 10-inch album (Columbia 1956)★★★, *On Stage* 10-inch album (Columbia 1956)★★, *My Fair Lady* 10-inch album (Columbia 1956)★★, *Clooney Tunes* (Columbia 1957)★★★, with the Hi-Lo's *Ring A Round Rosie* (Columbia 1957)★★★★, *Swing Around Rosie* (Coral 1958)★★★, with Bing Crosby *Fancy Meeting You Here* (RCA Victor 1958)★★★★, *Rosemary Clooney In Hi-Fidelity* (Harmony 1958)★★★, *The Ferrers At Home* (1958)★★★, *Hymns From The Heart* (MGM 1959)★★, *Oh Captain!* (MGM 1959)★★, *Rosemary Clooney Swings Softly* (MGM 1960)★★★★, *A Touch Of Tabasco* (RCA Victor 1960)★★★, *Clap Hands, Here Comes Rosie* (RCA Victor 1960)★★★, *Rosie Solves The Swingin' Riddle* (RCA Victor 1961)★★★★, *Country Hits From The Heart* (RCA Victor 1963)★★, *Love* (Reprise 1963)★★★, *Thanks For Nothing* (Reprise 1964)★★★, with Crosby *That Travelin' Two Beat* (Capitol 1965)★★★, *Look My Way* (United Artists 1976)★★★, *Nice To Be Around* (United Artists 1977)★★★, *Here's To My Lady* (Concord 1979)★★★, *With Love* (Concord 1981)★★★, *Sings The Music Of Cole Porter* (Concord 1982)★★★★, *Sings Harold Arlen* (Concord 1983)★★★★, *My Buddy* (Concord 1983)★★★, *Sings The Music Of Irving Berlin* (Concord 1984)★★★★, *Rosemary Clooney Sings Ballads* (Concord 1985)★★★, *Our Favourite Things* (Dance Band Days 1986)★★★, *Mixed Emotions* (Columbia 1986)★★★, *Sings The Lyrics Of Johnny Mercer* (Concord 1987)★★★★, *Sings The Music Of Jimmy Van Heusen* (Concord 1987)★★★★, *Show Tunes* (Concord 1989)★★★, *Everything's Coming Up Rosie* (Concord 1989)★★★, *Sings Rodgers, Hart And Hammerstein* (Concord 1990)★★★, *Rosemary Clooney Sings The Lyrics Of Ira Gershwin* (Concord 1990)★★★★, *For The Duration* (Concord 1991)★★★, *Girl Singer* (Concord 1992)★★★, *Do You Miss New York?* (Concord 1994)★★★, *Still On The Road* (Concord 1994)★★★★, *Demi-Centennial* (Concord 1995)★★★, *Dedicated To Nelson* (Concord 1995)★★★★, *Mothers & Daughters* (Concord Jazz 1997)★★★, *White Christmas* (Concord 1997)★★, with the Count Basie Orchestra *At Long Last* (Concord 1998)★★★★.

● COMPILATIONS: *Rosie's Greatest Hits* (Columbia 1957)★★★★, *Rosemary Clooney Showcase Of Hits* (Columbia 1959)★★★★, *Greatest Hits* (Columbia 1983)★★★★, *The Best Of Rosemary Clooney* (Creole 1984)★★★★, *The Rosemary Clooney Songbook* (Columbia 1984)★★★★, *Come On-A My House* 7-CD box set (Bear Family 1997)★★★★, *Rosemary Clooney 70: A Seventieth Birthday Celebration* (Concord Jazz 1998)★★★.

● FURTHER READING: *This For Remembrance*, Rosemary Clooney.

CLOUDS OF JOY

A jazz group led by Andy Kirk (b. 1898, Newport, Kentucky, USA), who played saxophone and tuba. They were closely associated with the term 'Kansas City Jazz'. At various times between 1929 and 1948 (when they disbanded) such soloists as Dick Wilson, Ted Donnelly, Harold 'Shorty' Baker, Howard McGhee and Mary Lou Williams played with them. Williams was the real star with her eclectic piano virtuosity ranging from ragtime and blues to Earl Hines in approach. The biggest hit for the outfit was 'Until The Real Thing Comes Along' (1936), this featured Pha (Fay) Terrell whose style was something of an acquired taste. Although capable of playing great quality, Clouds Of Joy gained a repuation for inconsistency.

● COMPILATIONS: *Andy Kirk And The Clouds Of Joy* (1988)★★★★.

CLYNE, JEFF

b. 29 January 1937, London, England. An admirer of Scott La Faro, Eddie Gomez, Jaco Pastorius and Stanley Clarke, Clyne is a versatile performer on the electric and conventional basses and was much in demand throughout the 60s and 70s for his ability to contribute to a wide range of styles. He fitted in equally comfortably with the fusion of Turning Point or the free experimentalism of the Spontaneous Music Ensemble (SME). He is primarily self-taught, although he did spend some time studying with orchestral players and, like the majority of British players of this vintage, gained valuable experience during his National Service in the mid-50s. After spells with Tony Crombie's Rockets and Stan Tracey he joined the Jazz Couriers, co-led by tenorists Ronnie Scott and Tubby Hayes, in 1958. His association with Hayes continued for the next 10 years or so, but he also worked with a whole string of influential bands during the following two decades. He was an original member of the SME, and a partner in its sister band, Trevor Watts's Amalgam. In the mid-60s he worked with Tracey again, his warm sound contributing much to the acclaimed *Under Milk Wood*. After taking up the bass guitar he became a founder member of Ian Carr's Nucleus, from 1969-71. Turning Point was founded with Pepi Lemer in 1976. He has also worked with Gary Boyle's Isotope, John McLaughlin, Tony Oxley, Keith Tippett's Centipede, Dudley Moore, Blossom Dearie, Norma Winstone, 'Lucky' Thompson, Zoot Sims, Phil Woods, Phil Lee and Eddie 'Lockjaw' Davis and the London Jazz Composers' Orchestra.

● ALBUMS: with Tubby Hayes *Tubby's Groove* (1959)★★★★, with Stan Tracey *Under Milk Wood* (1965)★★★★, with John Stevens (including SME) *Challenge* (1965)★★★, with Stevens *Springboard* (1966)★★★, with Hayes *100% Proof* (1966)★★, with Gordon Beck *Experiments With Pops* (1967)★★★, *Gyroscope* (1968)★★★, with Michael Gibbs *Tanglewood '63* (1970)★★★★, with Nucleus *Elastic Rock* (Vertigo 1970)★★★★, with Nucleus *We'll Talk About It Later* (Vertigo 1970)★★★★, with Turning Point *Creatures Of The Night* (1977)★★, with Turning Point *Silent Promise* (1978)★★★, with Stevens *Freebop* (1982)★★★, with Phil Lee *Twice Upon A Time* (Cadillac 1987)★★★.

COBB, ARNETT

b. 10 August 1918, Houston, Texas, USA, d. 24 March 1989. Cobb began playing the tenor saxophone professionally in 1933. He spent several of his early years in the fine territory band led by Milt Larkins, a unit which numerous musicians of the older generation still hold in awe. Approached in 1941 by Lionel Hampton, who was then in the process of forming a new band after deciding to leave Benny Goodman, Cobb chose to stay with Larkins and Hampton took on Larkins's altoist, Illinois Jacquet instead, persuading him to switch to tenor and try to imitate Cobb. In 1942 Hampton proffered a second invitation and this time Cobb joined him. In 1947 he briefly fronted his own band, through to the early 50s, interrupted briefly by an illness.

In 1956 he was seriously injured in a road accident while driving his band's bus and spent the rest of his life on crutches and in considerable pain. None of this stopped him from playing and he worked extensively, often back in Texas, where he raised a daughter after the death of his wife. In later years he became a familiar and popular figure on the international festival circuit, playing in small groups, then in big bands, and occasionally working with his old boss, Hampton. A powerful, gritty player, drenched in the blues, Cobb is an outstanding member of the distinguished school of 'Texas tenors'. His sound, shifting constantly between breathy confidentiality and eruptive, emotion-packed roars, brought pleasure to many who could never imagine from his playing the grave physical discomfort which he courageously disguised for more than 30 years.

● ALBUMS: *Swingin' With Arnett Cobb* (Apollo 1952)★★★★, *Arnett Cobb And His Mob* (1952)★★★, *Blow, Arnett, Blow* (Prestige 1959)★★★★, *Smooth Sailing* (Prestige 1959)★★★★, *Party Time* (Prestige 1959)★★★★, *More Party Time* (Prestige 1960)★★, *Movin' Right Along* (Prestige 1960)★★★, *Sizzlin'* (Prestige 1960)★★★, *Ballads By Cobb* (Moodsville 1960)★★★★, *Blue And Sentimental* (Prestige 1961)★★★, *Again With Milt Buckner* (1973)★★, *Jumping At The Woodside* (1974)★★★, *Live In Paris* (1974)★★, with Milt Buckner *Again With Milt Buckner* (Black And Blue 1974)★★★, *Midnight Show Vol. 2* (Black And Blue 1974)★★★, *The Wild Man From Texas* (Black And Blue 1974)★★★, *Arnett Cobb Is Back!* (Progressive 1978)★★★★, *Live At Sandy's!* (Muse 1978)★★★, *Live At Sandy's! More* (1978)★★★, *Funky Butt* (Progressive 1980)★★★, *Live* (Timeless 1982)★★, *Keep On Pushin'* (1984)★★★, *Show Time* (Fantasy 1988)★★★, *Tenor Tribute* (Soul Note 1989)★★, *Tenor Tribute Vol 2* (Soul Note 1991)★★.

● COMPILATIONS: *The Best Of Arnett Cobb* (Prestige 1969)★★★★, *The Complete Apollo Sessions* (Vogue 1984)★★★★.

COBB, JIMMY

b. 20 January 1929, Washington DC, USA. A self-taught drummer, Cobb gained a great deal of experience working in his home town behind such visiting jazz artists as Charlie Rouse, Leo Parker and Billie Holiday. In 1951 he joined Earl Bostic and later that year married and became musical director for Dinah Washington. In the mid-50s, now located in New York, Cobb worked with many leading jazz players including Dizzy Gillespie, John Coltrane and Stan Getz and in 1958 he began a five-year period with Miles Davis. During a large part of the 60s Cobb was with Wynton Kelly after whose death he began a long association as Sarah Vaughan's regular drummer. A dynamic, aggressive player in the mould of leading hard bop drummers such as Kenny Clarke and Art Blakey, Cobb is always a welcome member of any band in which he plays and a constant encouragement to his front line.

● ALBUMS: *Only For The Pure At Heart* (Fable 1998)★★★.

COBB, JUNIUS

b. Junius C. Cobb, *c.*1896, Hot Springs, Arkansas, USA, d. *c.*1970. After playing piano as a child and with the band led by trumpeter Johnny Dunn, Cobb moved to Chicago, formed his own band and began to expand his range, playing various instruments. He played clarinet, banjo, and, a little later, alto and tenor saxophones. During the 20s he played most of these instruments in various settings including spells with King Oliver and Jimmie Noone. He was briefly in Europe but continued to make Chicago his base where for some years he performed a double act with singer Annabelle Calhoun. In the mid-40s he was mostly to be heard playing piano, often for long engagements at clubs and hotels. In the mid-50s he retired from full-time music but continued to sit in and take occasional gigs during the rest of his life. In addition to all his performing talents, Cobb also wrote a number of songs.

● ALBUMS: *Jimmy Bertrand's Washboard Wizards* (Ace Of Hearts 1926)★★★★.

COBHAM, BILLY

b. 16 May 1944, Panama. Cobham began playing drums while growing up in New York City, to where his family had moved while he was still a small child. He studied at the city's High School of Music before entering military service. In the army he played in a band and by the time of his discharge had achieved a high level of proficiency. In the late 60s he played in the New York Jazz Sextet and with Horace Silver. In 1969 he formed a jazz-rock band, Dreams, with Michael and Randy Brecker. The growing popularity of jazz-rock kept Cobham busy with recording dates, including some with Miles Davis, and he then joined John McLaughlin's Mahavishnu Orchestra, one of the most influential and highly regarded jazz-rock bands. *Birds Of Fire*'s success owes as much to Cobham's extraordinary drumming as it does to McLaughlin's stellar guitar. In 1973 Cobham capitalized upon his international fame by forming his own band and continued to lead fusion bands for the next several years. He played all around the world, at festivals and in concert, teaching and presenting drum clinics. In 1984 he and McLaughlin were reunited in a new version of the Mahavishnu Orchestra. Perhaps the best and most technically accomplished of all the jazz-rock drummers, Cobham's rhythmic dexterity, all-round ability and his dedication to musical excellence has resulted in many copyists. For all his spectacular pyrotechnics, however, Cobham's talent runs deep and his abilities as a teacher and clinician ensure that his methods are being handed on to future generations of drummers.

● ALBUMS: with Horace Silver *Serenade To A Soul Sister* (1968), with Miles Davis *A Tribute To Jack Johnson* (Columbia 1970)★★★★, *Dreams* (1970), with the Mahavishnu Orchestra *The Inner Mounting Flame* (Columbia 1972)★★★★, with the Mahavishnu Orchestra *Birds Of Fire* (Columbia 1973)★★★★, with the Mahavishnu Orchestra *Between Nothingness And Eternity* (Columbia 1973)★★★, *Spectrum* (Atlantic 1973)★★★★, *Total Eclipse* (Atlantic 1974)★★, *Crosswinds* (Atlantic 1974)★★★, *Life And Times* (Atlantic 1976)★★, *Live - On Tour In Europe* (Atlantic 1976)★★, *Inner Conflicts* (Atlantic 1978)★★★, *Simplicity Of Expression-Depth Of Thought* (Columbia 1979)★★★, *B.C.* (Columbia 1979)★★★, *Flight Time* (Inak 1981)★★★, *Stratus* (Inak 1981)★★★, *Smokin'* (Elektra 1983)★★★, *Warning* (GRP 1985)★★★, *Power Play* (GRP 1986)★★★, *Picture This* (GRP 1987)★★★, *Same Ol Love* (GRP 1987)★★, *Live On Tour In Europe* (Atlantic 1988)★★★, *By Design* (1992)★★★, *The Traveller* (WMD 1994)★★, *Focused* (Eagle 1998)★★.

● COMPILATIONS: *Best Of Billy Cobham* (Columbia 1980)★★★, *Billy's Best Hits* (GRP 1987)★★★, *Best Of Billy Cobham* (Atlantic 1988)★★★.

CODONA

This jazz group was formed in 1977 by Collin Walcott (sitar, tabla, sanza, dulcimer, timpani, voice), Don Cherry (trumpet, flutes, doussn'gouni, melodica, organ, voice) and Nana Vasconcelos (berimbau, talking drum, cuica, percussion, voice). Codona's three members came together at the instigation of ECM Records producer Manfred Eicher, Cherry and Walcott playing on the latter's *Grazing Dreams* and Vasconcelos encountering Walcott at the session for Egberto Gismonti's *Sol Do Meio Dia*. At the first trio recording the following year the players revelled in a shared enthusiasm for what Cherry called 'Universal World Folklore', this being defined by Walcott as an attempt to merge the most divergent musical forms 'without turning the whole world into milktoast'. 'Love and respect for the traditions was vital,' he said. Ten years ahead of the 'world music' boom, Codona would playfully mix ragas with Japanese music, write a piece dedicated to both Stevie Wonder and Ornette Coleman, or showcase the sitar on a standard blues. The group's potential was cut short by the death of Walcott in a tour bus crash in East Germany in 1984.

● ALBUMS: *Codona* (ECM 1978)★★★★, *Codona 2* (ECM 1981)★★★★, *Codona 3* (ECM 1983)★★★.

COE, TONY

b. 29 November 1934, Canterbury, Kent, England. A formally-trained musician proficient on clarinet, bass clarinet and tenor saxophone, Coe's early jazz experience was as a member of Humphrey Lyttelton's band (1957-62). Later he led his own group for a while, then worked with John Dankworth's Orchestra in the late 60s, as well as playing with the Kenny Clarke-Francy Boland big band (1967-73) and beginning a long association with Stan Tracey on 1969's *We Love You Madly*. During the 70s and 80s, Coe extended his horizons dramatically, moving away from the more traditional areas of jazz to explore a variety of musics, including total improvisation with Derek Bailey, classical music with Alan Hacker's Matrix ensemble and film music - he plays on the soundtracks of *The Devils*, *The Boy Friend* and the *Pink Panther* films. He also continued to lead his own modern jazz groups, with line-ups that featured Kenny Wheeler and Tony Oxley; wrote an extended piece, *Zeitgeist*, which mixed elements of jazz, rock and classical music; and toured with both the United Jazz And Rock Ensemble and the Mike Gibbs band. In the 80s, he recorded a wide range of material for the French Nato and Chabada labels, sometimes with the comedy-vocal group Melody Four (actually a trio, with Lol Coxhill and Steve Beresford). His 1988 *Canterbury Song* is a beautiful example of modern mainstream jazz, while a continuing association with Franz Koglmann has recently been taking him back into more abstract areas (*L'Heure Bleue*). A versatile and gifted player, Coe is one of the UK's most celebrated instrumentalists, an outstanding performer in all forms of jazz and classical music.

● ALBUMS: *Swingin' Til The Girls Come Home* (1962)★★★, *Zeitgeist* (1976)★★★★, *Coe-Existence* (Lee Lambert 1978)★★★, with Derek Bailey *Time* (Incus 1979)★★★, with Al Grey *Get It Together* (1979)★★, *Tournée* (Nato French 1981)★★★, *Nutty On Willisau* (hatART 1983, remixed as *Nutty*)★★★, *Le Chat Se Retourne* (Nato 1984)★★★, *Mainly Mancini* (Nato 1986)★★★★, *Canterbury Song* (Hot House 1988),★★★★ *Tony Coe* (Hep Jazz 1988)★★★★, *Les Voix D'Itxassou* (Nato 1991)★★★, *Some Other Autumn* (Hep Jazz 1993)★★★, *Blue Jersey* (AB 1996)★★★★, *Captain Coe's Famous Racearound* (Storyville 1996)★★★, *In Concert* (AB 1998)★★, with Alan Barnes *Days Of Wine And Roses* (Zephyr 1998)★★★★.

COETZEE, BASIL 'MANENBERG'

b. 2 February 1944, Cape Town, South Africa, d. 12 March 1998. Playing penny whistle on the streets of his home-town by the age of 14, Coetzee had taught himself the flute by 16 and mastered the saxophone five years later. He became a part of the vibrant local jazz scene of the time, playing alongside Abdullah Ibrahim, Hugh Masekela and Chris McGregor, among others. While many of his contemporaries went into exile in Europe and the USA in the 60s, Coetzee remained in Cape Town, playing saxophone in local nightclubs and working in a shoe factory by day. In 1974 his tough but lyrical playing was heard on Ibrahim's classic *Manenberg - Where It's Happening*, giving rise to his nickname. He subsequently toured in Europe as part of Ibrahim's band. From the 80s until his death from lung cancer in 1998, Coetzee led his own band, Sabenza (a Xhosa word meaning 'work'). The eight-piece band also included Robbie Janson, a fellow saxophonist and former member of Ibrahim's band. Coetzee and the group toured extensively throughout Southern Africa and, following the release of *Sabenza*, performed in Europe. Coetzee was one of the founders of Music Power for People Power, a Cape Town music school.

● ALBUMS: *Sabenza* (Mountain 1988)★★★.

COHEN, ALAN

b. 25 November 1934, London, England. A skilled, formally trained saxophonist, Cohen made his first impact on the UK jazz scene in the late 60s as both bandleader and arranger. His charts ranged widely, being played by the more traditional bands of Humphrey Lyttelton and Chris Barber and by several European radio orchestras. An abiding interest in the music of Duke Ellington led to the formation in 1971 of a big band for recording dates and occasional public appearances, and later in the decade he was co-founder (with Keith Nichols) of the Midnite Follies Orchestra. This orchestra existed into the early 80s but, thereafter, he continued to arrange, sometimes for his own small groups and also for other large orchestras including the mammoth big band organized by the Rolling Stones' drummer Charlie Watts in 1985. Cohen retains his dedication to Ellington's music, appearing as guest conductor at the 1988 Ellington Convention for a performance of 'Black, Brown And Beige' which he had recorded in 1972.

● ALBUMS: *Duke Ellington's Black, Brown And Beige* (1972)★★★, *Hotter Than Hades* (1978)★★★.

COHN, AL

b. 24 November 1925, New York City, New York, USA, d. 15 February 1988, Stroudsburg, Pennsylvania, USA. As a teenager Cohn gained experience playing the tenor saxophone with Joe Marsala and Georgie Auld, for whom he also arranged. A forward-thinking musician, Cohn worked extensively in big bands during the mid-late 40s, most famously as a member of Woody Herman's Four Brothers band. He continued to perform, and write for, big bands, including those of Artie Shaw and Elliot Lawrence, with whom he was associated for a substantial part of the 50s. In 1957 Cohn teamed up with Zoot Sims, a partnership that lasted into the 80s. During this period he also worked as leader of small groups and as a touring soloist, releasing several excellent sets for Xanadu and Concord during a creative renaissance that lasted until his final recordings in 1987. Cohn's writing continued throughout this time and he was responsible for scoring a number of stage musicals. A warm-toned melodic player, Cohn was stylistically in the mould of Lester Young but incorporated into his music many elements that were his own. Respected in jazz circles for his playing, he was also very popular with musicians for his ready wit. Towards the end of his life he sometimes worked with his guitarist son, Joe.

● ALBUMS: *Al Cohn Quartet* 10-inch album (Progressive 1953)★★★★, *Al Cohn Quintet* 10-inch album (Progressive 1953)★★★★, with Shorty Rogers *East Coast-West Coast Scene* (RCA Victor 1954)★★★★, *Mr. Music* (RCA Victor 1955)★★★★, *The Natural Seven* (RCA Victor 1955)★★★, with Richie Kamuca, Bill Perkins *The Brothers!* (RCA Victor 1955)★★★★, *Four Brass One Tenor* (RCA Victor 1956)★★★, *That Old Feeling* (RCA Victor 1956)★★★, *Cohn On The Saxophone* reissued as *Be Loose* (Dawn/Biograph 1956)★★★, *Cohn's Tones* reissue of Progressive material (Savoy 1956)★★★★, with Zoot Sims *From A To Z* (RCA Victor 1956)★★★★, *Al Cohn Quintet* (Coral 1957)★★★, with Sims *Al And Zoot* (Coral 1958)★★★, with Herman 'Trigger' Alpert, Tony Scott, Zoot Sims *East Coast Sounds* (Jazzland 1960)★★★, *Son Of Drum Suite* (RCA Victor 1960)★★★, with Sims *Either Way* (Abundance 1960)★★★, with Sims *You 'N Me* (Mercury 1960)★★★, *Jazz Mission To Moscow* (Colpix 1962)★★★, *Broadway* 1954 recording (Prestige 1970)★★★, *Body And Soul* (Muse 1973)★★★★, with Sims *Motoring Along* (Sonet 1974)★★★, *Play It Now* (Xanadu 1975)★★★★, *True Blue* (Xanadu 1976)★★★, *Silver Blue* (Xanadu 1976)★★★, *Al Cohn's America* (Xanadu 1976)★★★★, with Jimmy Rowles *Heavy Love* (Xanadu 1977)★★★, *No Problem* (Xanadu 1979)★★★★, *Night Flight To Dakar* (Xanadu 1980)★★★, *Nonpareil* (Concord Jazz 1981)★★★★, with Scott Hamilton, Buddy Tate *Tour De Force* (Concord Jazz 1981)★★★, *Overtones* (Concord Jazz 1982)★★★, with Sims *Zoot Case* (Sonet 1983)★★★, *Standards Of Excellence* (Concord Jazz 1984)★★★★, with Totti Bergh *I Hear A Rhapsody* (Gemini 1985)★★★, with Bergh *Tenor Gladness* (Gemini 1986)★★★, with Al Porcino *In Oblivion* (Jazz Mark 1986)★★★, with Porcino *The Final Performance* (Red Baron 1987)★★★, *Keeper Of The Flame* (Frog 1987)★★★, *Rifftide* (Timeless 1987)★★★.

COHN, ZINKY

b. Augustus Cohn, 18 August 1908, Oakland, California, USA, d. 26 April 1952. While he was still a small child, Cohn's family moved to Chicago where he attended music college, studying piano. He played piano with various bands in Chicago, other parts of Illinois and also in Michigan. Among the musicians with whom he played were Don Pasquall and Jimmie Noone. He travelled to Europe in the early 30s but was soon back in Chicago, again working with several bands including Erskine Tate's, Eddie South's and Carroll Dickerson's. In the mid-30s he led his own small band but soon afterwards moved into teaching and administrative work linked to the music business. He continued to play occasionally and in the mid-40s was briefly accompanist to Ethel Waters. During the last few years of his life he was again involved in administrative, managerial and promotional work.

COKER, HENRY

b. 24 December 1919, Dallas, Texas, USA, d. 23 November 1979. Coker's first professional engagement, in 1935, playing the trombone, was with a band led by John White and two years later, his reputation was such that he was hired by Nat Towles, one of the most esteemed territory bands. After leaving Towles he worked in the Hawaiian Islands, returning home after the bombing of Pearl Harbor. On the west coast in the mid-40s, he mixed studio work with jobs in bands led by Benny Carter and Eddie Heywood, then joined Illinois Jacquet. Starting in 1952 he enjoyed a decade as a member of Count Basie's band, contributing powerful solos. After Basie he returned to studio work, this time in New York, and then, in 1966, joined Ray Charles with whom he remained until 1971. In the 70s he was mostly engaged in film and television work in Los Angeles but played brief return engagements with both Basie and Charles.

COLE, FREDDY

b. Frederick Coles, 15 October 1931, Chicago, Illinois, USA. Following in the footsteps of his musical brothers, most notably, Nat 'King' Cole, he became a musician at a very early age, playing piano and singing professionally in Chicago clubs while still a teenager. Later, he studied at Juilliard College and at the New England Conservatory of Music, continuing to develop his technique and stagecraft at numerous clubs. In succeeding years Cole worked regularly in the USA, touring more as time passed and establishing a reputation as a good performer at the jazzier end of the pop music envelope. He had a minor hit with his second single, 'Whispering Grass', released through OKeh Records in 1953. On record he is often accompanied by noted jazz musicians, among them Steve Turré, Houston Person and, perhaps surprisingly, fellow-pianists such as Cyrus Chestnut and Larry Willis. It is largely the presence of musicians such as these that shifts consideration of Cole into a jazz context. Inevitably, Cole (who, like his brother, changed the spelling of the family name) is subjected to sibling comparisons. While he is undoubtedly a good pianist, in jazz terms he falls short of Nat Cole's astonishing abilities. As a singer, he sings with rhythmic assurance and sometimes displays a profound understanding of the lyrics of his material. Even so, like many pop singers, he is heavily dependent upon his material for impact and when he tackles quality songs he proves to be an attractive performer in the mould of the great supper club entertainers.

● ALBUMS: *I'm Not My Brother, I'm Me* (Sunnyside 1991)★★, *Live At Birdland West* (Laserlight 1992)★★★, *This Is The Life* (Muse 1993)★★★, *Always* (Fantasy 1995)★★★, *It's Crazy, But I'm In Love* (After 9 1996)★★★, *I Want A Smile For Christmas* (Fantasy 1996)★★, *Live At Vartan Jazz* (Vartan Jazz 1996)★★★, *A Circle Of Love* (Fantasy 1997)★★, *To The Ends Of The Earth* (Fantasy 1997)★★★, *Love Makes The Changes* (Fantasy 1998)★★★.

COLE, HOLLY

b. 1964, Canada. By specialising in a repertoire of show tunes, jazz and popular classics Holly Cole has established herself as a major star in her native Canada and north America. Working with a talented backing team of Aaron Davis, a respected Toronto pianist and composer, and David Piltch, a veteran of work with Chet Baker and k.d. lang, Cole's explorations of her musical sources is much more rigorous than might be imagined by a simple perusal of her catalogue. Her contralto has detected new nuances in familiar material and liberated everything from jazz to country standards from their historical context, encouraging critical comparisons to artists as diverse as Jane Siberry, Edith Piaf and Sarah Vaughan. This radical approach has inspired readings of songs such as 'On The Street Where You Live' and 'Que Sera Sera' that complement rather than compromise the originals. In 1995 Cole dedicated an entire album to a single artist for the first time, and her selection of its source - Tom Waits - surprised many. She justified the decision thus: 'In some ways I feel like he's a kindred spirit. There are so many reasons why I relate to his writing. His songs are like poems but are not at all obtuse. Also, he loves to champion the little guy and although the characters are often down-and-outers, they are never pathetic and always have integrity.' The sessions were produced by Craig Street, previously a collaborator with Cassandra Wilson, and included many 'first takes' to capture the spontaneity which has always been a component of Waits' compositions. Percussion expertise came from Dougie Bowne (Iggy Pop, Lounge Lizards) and Brazilian master drummer Cyro Baptista. *Dark Dear Heart* was a conscious attempt to break the mainstream pop market. The album was produced by Joni Mitchell's former husband, the bass player Larry Klein.

● ALBUMS: *Temptation* (Metro Blue 1995)★★, *It Happened One Night* (Metro Blue 1996)★★★, *Dark Dear Heart* (Metro Blue 1997)★★★.

COLE, NAT 'KING'

b. Nathaniel Adams Coles, 17 March 1916, Montgomery, Alabama, USA, d. 15 February 1965. Cole was born into a family that was both deeply religious and intensely musical. He learned to play piano at home when only four years old through his mother, Perlina Adams Coles, and, later, played organ at the church of which his father, Edward James Coles, was pastor. By then, the family was living in Chicago where they had moved in the early 20s. He took lessons in the classics but this was Chicago and jazz was the exciting popular music of the younger generation. At school, he led a dance band and also played piano in a group led by his bass-playing older brother, Eddie. Like Eddie, he dropped the last letter of the family name for professional purposes. It was with Eddie, who had played with Noble Sissle's band, that he made his first recordings, in 1936, by which time he had decided firmly upon a career as a professional musician. He and Eddie joined the pit band for a touring revival of *Shuffle Along*, a show in which one of the chorus line, Nadine Robinson, attracted Cole's eye and they were married. Stranded in Los Angeles when the show folded, Cole looked for club work and found it along Central Avenue, a kind of west coast equivalent of New York's 52nd Street, and most successfully at the Century Club in Santa Monica. It was a hangout for musicians and the young pianist made a splash, in particular he was heard by Bob Lewis of the Swannee Inn who hired him but also, and portentously, suggested he add a guitar and bass to form a trio. The new additions were guitarist Oscar Moore and bassist Wesley Prince. This was late in 1937 and for the next seven years the group rose in popular but still largely local acclaim despite having a weekly NBC radio show for a time in 1938. Almost from the start of the trio's existence, Cole's sparkling piano playing, his near-telepathic interplay with Moore, and the lithe ensembles, had been interspersed with songs from Cole. Sometimes currently popular novelties, sometimes ballads, although reports of the time suggest he sang more in the recording studios than at live engagements. But, as Cole later observed, 'The vocals caught on'. An understatement indeed. Then, late in 1943, the group, which had been dubbed 'The King Cole Trio' by either Lewis or Prince, was signed by the fledgling Capitol Records. Before then, Cole had recorded for Decca Records as well as various indies, notably Excelsior, but was not heavily promoted. His career at Capitol was very different; he became the company's flagship recording star and his first title on his first session, 'Straighten Up And Fly Right', became a hit. He continued to make hit records for Capitol - their famous landmark studios becoming known as 'the tower that Nat built' - but, gradually at first and then with increasing momentum, there was a shift away from his jazz-oriented work towards a superior form of popular ballad singing as he became one of the most acclaimed international superstars of his generation. In some critical writings, Cole's success as a pop singer has been declared a loss to jazz, and in particular bop piano playing. But the implication of 'selling out' in such statements is a too narrow view and largely unjustified. Without question, Cole was a major figure in the development of jazz piano. Stylistically indebted to Earl Hines in early years, he developed a fluid approach to emergent bop which miraculously blended the swing of Hines, the intricacies of Art Tatum, the elegance of Teddy Wilson, and the contemporaneous advances of Bud Powell. And yet he did it all - once he had outgrown his early idolisation of Hines - without being a copyist. His was a distinctive piano style, breathtaking in its dexterity, ingenuity and inventiveness, yet always melodic and subtle. His singing, first an adjunct to his piano playing, had many instrumental qualities. He swung, he was comfortably relaxed, managing the difficult task of singing fractionally behind the beat of his own accompaniment, and he was always melodic and tuneful - even when singing novelties. As for up-tempo songs, with Cole there was never any hint of rushing. Like a good jazz instrumentalist, even the flagwavers were delivered with controlled elegance. As for ballads, over the years he became incomparable among male vocalists. His years at Capitol, which fully document his shift from jazz star to pop superstardom, included hits such as Mel Tormé's 'The Christmas Song', 'Sweet Lorraine' (his theme, which he had also recorded pre-Capitol), 'Nature Boy', 'Baby, Won't You Say You Love Me' and 'Mona Lisa'. In areas outside music, Cole was a discreet propagandist for racial equality - so discreet that he was sometimes slighted by more outwardly radical black groups who objected to what he saw as necessary compromises. He bought a house in Los Angeles' fashionable Hancock Park, overcoming objections from entrenched white neighbours who sought to buy him off; was dignified in his response to being physically assaulted on stage in Birmingham during a concert tour with the British swing band led by Ted Heath; and he hosted a weekly television show with enormous charm despite the fact that there was a long-running and eventually fruitless struggle to secure a sponsor as no national company wanted its products associated with a black man. Before his death from lung cancer, in 1965, he was planning a production of James Baldwin's play, *Amen Corner*, showing an interest in radical black literature at odds with his image as a popular singer of often sentimental songs. In his earliest vocal recordings his pronunciation of certain words, vowel sounds and the dropping of final consonants particularly, show his southern roots. although he changed this over the years, according to some observers at the behest of his second wife, Marie Ellington, some of the original sound was still there at the end thus helping give him a delightfully melismatic way with certain words that helped enhance his vocal style. This, his innate good taste, dignity and sheer musicality contributed to his undying appeal. After his death, biographies, television documentaries and tributes, and albums galore appeared - not all showing the gentlemanly dignity with which he had conducted himself throughout his life. In the end, his greatest legacy - the only one that matters - is that he remains to this day an immensely popular artist. His jazz records remain highlights in any collection, especially for those interested in the development of jazz piano. His vocal records display a hugely talented, pleasant-voiced, intensely musical singer, blessed with almost flawless good taste who has, by some magical process, proved capable of appealing to audiences which cross class, race, nationality, and age. Such is the quality of the records of this modest man, that they have found popularity with people not born at the time of his tragically early death. Nat 'King' Cole's life and career shine like beacons from a dark period of American history and have continued ever since to illuminate popular music.

● ALBUMS: *The King Cole Trio* 10-inch album (Capitol 1950)★★★★, *The King Cole Trio Volume 2* 10-inch album (Capitol 1950)★★★★, *The King Cole Trio Volume 3* 10-inch album (Capitol 1950)★★★★, *At The Piano* 10-inch album (Capitol 1950)★★★, *The King Cole Trio Volume 4* 10-inch album (Capitol 1950)★★★, *Harvest Of Hits* 10-inch album (Capitol 1950)★★★, with Buddy Rich, Lester Young *The Lester Young Trio* 10-inch album (Mercury 1951)★★★★, *Penthouse Serenade* 10-inch album (Capitol 1952)★★★, *Unforgettable* (Capitol 1952)★★★★, with Red Callender, Young *King Cole-Lester Young-Red Callender Trio* reissued as *Lester Young-Nat King Cole Trio* (Aladdin/Score 1953)★★★★, *Nat 'King' Cole Sings For Two In Love* 10-inch album (Capitol 1953)★★★, *8 Top Pops* (Capitol 1954)★★★, *Tenth Anniversary Album* (Capitol 1955)★★★, *Vocal Classics* (Capitol 1955)★★★, *Instrumental Classics* (Capitol 1955)★★, *The Piano Style of Nat King Cole* (Capitol 1956)★★★, *In The Beginning* (Decca 1956)★★, *Ballads Of The Day* (Capitol 1956)★★★, *After Midnight* (Capitol 1957)★★★, *Love Is The Thing* (Capitol 1957)★★★★, *This Is Nat 'King' Cole* (Capitol 1957)★★★★, *Just One Of Those Things* (Capitol 1957)★★★, *St. Louis Blues* film soundtrack (Capitol 1958)★★, *Cole Espanol* (Columbia 1958)★★, *The Very Thought Of You* (Capitol

1958)★★★★, *Welcome To The Club* (Capitol 1959)★★★, *To Whom It May Concern* (Capitol 1959)★★★, *A Mis Amigos* (Capitol 1959)★★, *Tell Me All About Yourself* (Capitol 1960)★★★, *Every Time I Feel The Spirit* (Capitol 1960)★★★, *Wild Is Love* (Capitol 1960)★★★, *The Magic Of Christmas* (Capitol 1960)★★★, *The Touch Of Your Lips* (Capitol 1961)★★★★, *String Along With Nat 'King' Cole* (Capitol 1961)★★★★, *Nat 'King' Cole Sings/George Shearing Plays* (Capitol 1962)★★★★, *Ramblin' Rose* (Capitol 1962)★★★, *Sings The Blues* (Capitol 1962)★★★, *Dear Lonely Hearts* (Capitol 1962)★★★, *Where Did Everyone Go?* (Capitol 1963)★★★, *Those Lazy-Hazy-Crazy Days Of Summer* (Capitol 1963)★★★, *Sings The Blues Volume 2* (Capitol 1963)★★★, *The Christmas Song* (Capitol 1963)★★★, *I Don't Want To Be Hurt Anymore* (Capitol 1964)★★★, *My Fair Lady* (Capitol 1964)★★★, *L-O-V-E* (Capitol 1965)★★★, *Songs From 'Cat Ballou' And Other Motion Pictures* (Capitol 1965)★★★, *Looking Back* (Capitol 1965)★★★, *Nat 'King' Cole At The Sands* (Capitol 1966)★★★, *At JATP* (Verve 1966)★★★, *At JATP 2* (Verve 1966)★★★, *The Great Songs!* 1957 recording (Capitol 1966)★★★, with Dean Martin *White Christmas* (Capitol 1971)★★★, *Christmas With Nat 'King' Cole* (Stylus 1988)★★★.

● COMPILATIONS: *The Nat King Cole Story* 3-LP box set (Capitol 1961)★★★★, *The Best Of Nat King Cole* (Capitol 1968)★★★★, *20 Golden Greats* (Capitol 1978)★★★★, *Greatest Love Songs* (Capitol 1982)★★★★, *Trio Days* (Affinity 1984)★★★, *The Complete Capitol Recordings Of The Nat King Cole Trio* 18-CD box set (Mosiac 1990)★★★★, *The Unforgettable Nat 'King' Cole* (EMI 1991)★★★★, *The Nat King Cole Gold Collection* (1993)★★★★, *World War II Transcriptions* (1994)★★★.

● VIDEOS: *Nat King Cole* (Missing In Action 1988), *Unforgettable* (PMI 1988), *Nat King Cole Collection* (Castle Music Pictures 1990), *Nat King Cole 1942-1949* (Verve Video 1990), *Nat King Cole* (Virgin Vision 1992).

● FURTHER READING: *Nat King Cole: The Man And His Music*, Jim Haskins and Kathleen Benson. *Unforgettable: The Life and Mystique of Nat King Cole*, Leslie Gourse.

COLE, RICHIE

b. 29 February 1948, Trenton, New Jersey, USA. Cole took up the guitar as a small child, having heard jazz at two clubs, the Harlem and Hubby's Inn, owned by his father. Before reaching his teens he had switched to alto saxophone on which instrument he studied with Phil Woods. Later, he attended Berklee College Of Music and then, in 1969, he joined Buddy Rich. In the early 70s he played in several bands, including Lionel Hampton's, led his own small bands and worked with Eddie Jefferson. On and off, Cole was with Jefferson from 1973 until the singer's murder in 1979. Next to Woods, Jefferson was the major influence on Cole's musical life and in a 1987 interview, he indicated that he was writing a symphony dedicated to Jefferson. Throughout the 80s and into the 90s Cole has led his own band, Alto Madness, with considerable success. His open musical mind is evident from the eagerness with which he has absorbed the techniques of artists as diverse as Jefferson and country music's Boots Randolph, with whom he recorded *Yakety Madness*. A saxophonist in the tradition of Charlie Parker and his mentor, Woods, Cole's playing is filled with a burning urgency. His performances are always exciting, but only as he matures is he starting to underpin the surface with greater emotional depths.

● ALBUMS: with Buddy Rich *Keep The Customers Satisfied* (1970)★★★★, *Trenton Makes - The World Takes* (1975),★★★ *Starburst* (1976)★★★, with Eddie Jefferson *The Live-liest* (1976)★★★, *New York Afternoon* (Muse 1977)★★, *Still On The Planet* (Muse 1977)★★, *Alto Madness* (Muse 1977)★★★, *Keeper of The Flame* (1978)★★★, *Hollywood Madness* (Muse 1979)★★★, *Side By Side* (Muse 1980)★★★, *Some Things Speak For Themselves* (1981)★★, *Cool 'C'* (Muse 1981)★★★, *Richie Cole...Alive! At The Village Vanguard* (Muse 1981)★★★★, *Return To Alto Acres* (Palo Alto 1982)★★★, *Yakety Madness* (1982)★★, *Popbop* (Milestone 1987)★★★, *Pure Imagination* (Concord 1987)★★, *Signature* (Milestone 1988)★★★, *Bossa Nova International* (Milestone (1988)★★★, *Kush* (Heads Up 1995)★★★.

COLE, WILLIAM 'COZY'

b. 17 October 1909, East Orange, New Jersey, USA, d. 29 January 1981. Cole took up drumming as a child and by his early teens was studying and developing his craft. His first professional engagement was with clarinet virtuoso Wilbur Sweatman who led bands in several New York clubs and theatres. By the end of the 20s Cole had already briefly led his own band and in 1930 he recorded with Jelly Roll Morton. During the early 30s he worked successively with Blanche Calloway, Benny Carter and Willie Bryant and then, in 1936, joined the Onyx Club band co-led by Stuff Smith and Jonah Jones. In 1938 he began a four-year tenure with Cab Calloway during which he was given solo space in shows and on record. He also made many records with the small groups led by Lionel Hampton for his classic RCA sessions. Following his departure from Calloway, Cole returned to his studies, this time at Juilliard, and did theatrical work which included a featured spot in *Carmen Jones*. He led his own groups in the mid-40s and all-star 'pick-up' bands for record dates which are today usually issued under the names of one or another of his more illustrious sidemen, Coleman Hawkins and Earl Hines. In the late 40s he led various small groups and then joined Louis Armstrong's All Stars where he remained for a little over three years. During this period he was extensively featured on the soundtrack of a film, *The Strip* (1951), which starred Mickey Rooney as a drummer with Armstrong's band. In the early and mid-50s Cole was active in New York where he ran a drum school in partnership with Gene Krupa. He appeared in a number of films including *The Glenn Miller Story* (1953) in which he duetted with Krupa. In the late 50s he became a member of the all-star band co-led by Jack Teagarden and Earl 'Fatha' Hines which toured Europe and in 1958 had a surprising double-sided US hit single with 'Topsy I'/'Topsy II' - 'Turvy' reached the Top 40 later that same year. In 1961 he appeared in an excellent television pilot, *After Hours*, with Coleman Hawkins and Roy Eldridge, the soundtrack of which was later bootlegged on an obscure Dutch label. Throughout the 60s and 70s Cole worked in a variety of settings, notably in a group which reunited him with Jonah Jones, touring internationally and appearing at numerous festivals. A brilliant technician with a meticulous sense of time, Cole could sometimes sound a little stiff. He dramatically altered the sound of the Armstrong All Stars to that which his more loosely swinging predecessor, 'Big' Sid Catlett, had created but he could be relied upon to push front-line soloists along with an urgency they rarely received from other, more famous drummers. Cole died of cancer in January 1981.

● ALBUMS: *The Strip* film soundtrack (1951)★★, *Cozy Cole* (Audition 1955)★★★★, *Jazz At The Metropole Cafe* (Bethlehem 1955)★★★, *Cozy Cole And His All-Stars* (Paris 1958)★★★, *Topsy* (Love 1958)★★★★, *Earl's Backroom And Cozy's Caravan* (Felsted 1958)★★★, *Cozy Cole* (King 1959)★★★, *A Cozy Conaption Of Carmen* (Charlie Parker 1962)★★★, *Drum Beat Dancing Feet* (Coral 1962)★★★, *It's A Cozy World* (Coral 1964)★★★, *It's A Rocking Thing* (Columbia 1965)★★★, *Concereto For Cozy* (Savoy 1966)★★★★, *Lionel Hampton Presents Cozy Cole And Marty Napoleon* (1977)★★★, *1944* (Classice 1996)★★.

COLEMAN HAWKINS ENCOUNTERS BEN WEBSTER - COLEMAN HAWKINS

Although both Coleman Hawkins and Ben Webster could play with power and authority, the two men shared a love for rhapsodic and romantic music. Teaming them for a session of gorgeous ballads proved to be a wise decision. Fluid, graceful, rich in promise and fulfilment, these are solos and duets that are echoed every time two tenor saxophonists play together. Only rarely does any other pairing reach these heights and never have they been surpassed. Hawkins' barrel-chested muscular sound and Webster's breathy sensuality bring to the songs they perform profound depths of emotional understanding. This is jazz balladry at its very best.

● Tracks: *Blues For Yolande; It Never Entered My Mind; Rosita; You's Be So Nice To Come Home To; Prisoner Of Love; Tangerine; Shine On Harvest Moon.*

● First released 1959

● UK peak chart position: did not chart

● USA peak chart position: did not chart

COLEMAN, BILL

b. 4 August 1904, Centreville, Kentucky, USA, d. 24 August 1981. Despite trying various reed instruments, Coleman switched to trumpet after hearing records by Louis Armstrong and served his apprenticeship during the late 20s and early 30s in a string of amateur, semi-pro and professional bands, including those led by J.C. Higginbotham, Edgar Hayes, Lloyd and Cecil Scott, Luis Russell, Charlie 'Fess' Johnson, Lucky Millinder, Benny Carter, Teddy Hill and Fats Waller. By the mid-30s Coleman's wide experience meant that he was in great demand, but wanderlust led him to join all-round entertainer Freddy Taylor, whom Coleman had taught to play trumpet while in the Millinder band. The Taylor band spent time in Paris and then Coleman headed for Bombay, India, with Leon Abbey, returning to Paris for an engagement with Willie Lewis. In 1938 he co-led a band with Herman Chittison, which worked in Egypt until shortly after the outbreak of World War II. Back in the USA in 1940 he worked again with Benny Carter and Fats Waller and thereafter with the bands of Andy Kirk, Noble Sissle, Mary Lou Williams and John Kirby. After World War II he returned to Paris, where he resided for the rest of his life, touring other European countries and making only rare trips back to his homeland. A fluid, inventive player, Coleman was an elegant trumpeter with a full, rich sound which echoed his childhood idolization of Armstrong, but which he cloaked in his own, unmistakable style.

● ALBUMS: *Town Hall Concert* (1945)★★★, *At The Salle Pleyel* (1952)★★★, *Eartha Kitt, Doc Cheatham, Bill Coleman In Paris* (1956)★★★★, *Reunion In Paris* (1956)★★★★, *Album Of Cities* (1956)★★★, *Swingin' In Switzerland* (1957)★★, *The Great Parisian Session* (1960)★★★, *From Boogie To Funk* (1960)★★★, *Swing Low, Sweet Chariot/Bill Coleman Sings And Plays Spirituals* (1967)★★, with Ben Webster *Swingin' In London* (Black Lion 1967)★★★, *Together At Last* (1968)★★★, *Bill And The Boys* (1968)★★★, *Three Generations Jam* (1969)★★★, *Bill Coleman With The Original Jazz Band Of Raymond Fonsèque* (1971)★★★, *Bill Coleman In Milan With Lino Patruno & Friends* (1972)★★★, *Mainstream At Montreux* (1973)★★★, *Paris 1973* (1973)★★★★, *Hommage A Duke Ellington* (1974)★★★★, *Meeting The New Ragtime Band* (1976)★★★, *Cave's Blues* (1979)★★★, *Really I Do* (1980)★★★, *Au Caveau De La Huchette* (1980)★★.

● COMPILATIONS: *Bill Coleman In Paris Volume 1 (1935-8)* (1983)★★★★, *1935-37* (1984)★★★★, *Bill Coleman In Paris Volume 2 (1936-8)* (1988)★★★, *1929-40* (1993)★★★.

● FURTHER READING: *Trumpet Story*, Bill Coleman. *Bill Coleman On Record*, John Chilton.

COLEMAN, GEORGE

b. 8 March 1935, Memphis, Tennessee, USA. A self-taught musician, Coleman began playing alto saxophone and worked in the early 50s with B.B. King. While with King he switched to tenor and began to shift his musical base until, in 1958, he joined Max Roach. During the 60s Coleman worked mostly in small post-bebop bands, including those led by Slide Hampton, Wild Bill Davis, Miles Davis, becoming the first permanent replacement for John Coltrane and featuring on Davis's brilliant *My Funny Valentine* live album, and Lee Morgan. He also worked in Lionel Hampton's big band but it was as a small group player that Coleman excelled. From the early 70s he worked mostly as leader of such groups, which varied from quartet to octet in size, and which regularly included Frank Strozier and Harold Mabern. A gifted and highly-accomplished technician, Coleman's playing is often more attractive than that of many of his better-known contemporaries who have attained more popular success.

● ALBUMS: *Revival!* (1976)★★★, with Tete Montoliu *Meditation* (1977)★★★, *Big George* (Charly 1977)★★★, with Montoliu *Duo* 1977 recording (1979)★★★, *Playing Changes* (1979)★★,

Amsterdam After Dark (Timeless 1980)★★★★, *Bongo Joe* (Arhoolie 1981)★★★, *Manhatten Panorama* (Evidence 1983)★★★, *At Yoshi's* (Evidence 1987)★★★, with Junior Cook *Stablemates* (Affinity 1990)★★★, *My Horns Of Plenty* (PolyGram 1991)★★, *I Could Write A Book: The Music Of Richard Rogers* (Telarc 1998)★★★.

COLEMAN, ORNETTE

b. 19 March 1930, Fort Worth, Texas, USA. The evolution of any art form is a complex process and it is always an over-simplification to attribute a development to a single person. If there is anyone apart from Louis Armstrong for whom that claim could be made, however, Ornette Coleman would be a tenable candidate. Charlie Parker and John Coltrane were great forces for progress, but they focused and made viable certain concepts that were already in the air and which only awaited some exceptionally talented artist to give them concrete shape. They accelerated evolution, but did not change the direction of jazz in the way that Armstrong and Coleman seem to have done. Of course, certain elements of Coleman's music, including free improvisation, had been tried previously and he certainly did not reject what had gone before: his playing is well-rooted in the soil of Parker's bop tradition, and in R&B - Coleman's playing is a logical development from both, but he set the melody free and jolted jazz out of its 30-year obsession with chords. His role is somewhat analogous to that of Arnold Schoenberg in European classical music, although, unlike Schoenberg, Coleman did not forge a second set of shackles to replace the ones he burst. Those who do not recognize Coleman's contribution to music select two sticks from his early career with which to beat him. The first is that, when he acquired his first saxophone at the age of 14, he thought the low C on the alto was the A in his instruction book. Of course, he discovered his mistake after a while, but the realization of his error caused him to look at pitch and harmony in a fresh way, and this started the process which led to a style based on freely moving melody unhindered by a repetitive harmonic sub-structure, and, eventually, to the theory of harmolodics. The second was that, when in Pee Wee Crayton's band, he was playing so badly that he was paid to keep silent. Crayton remembered it slightly differently: he said that Coleman was quite capable of playing the blues convincingly, but chose not to, so Crayton told him forcefully that that's what he was paid to do. In 1946 Coleman had taken up the tenor saxophone and joined the 'Red' Connors band. He played in blues and R&B bands for some time, sat in with Stan Kenton on one occasion, and in 1949 took the tenor chair in a touring minstrel show. He recorded several of his own tunes in Natchez, Mississippi, in the same year, but these have never resurfaced. He was stranded in New Orleans, where he found it hard to get anyone to play with him, and eventually hooked up with Crayton's band, which took him to Los Angeles in 1950. He took a number of jobs unconnected with music, but continued his study of theory when he could. In the early and mid-50s he began to establish contact with musicians who were in sympathy with his ideas, such as Bobby Bradford, Ed Blackwell and Don Cherry, and in 1958 he recorded for Contemporary in Los Angeles. He met John Lewis, who arranged for the Coleman quartet - then comprising Cherry, Charlie Haden and Billy Higgins - to play a two-week engagement at New York's Five Spot Cafe; this turned into a legendary 54-month stay during which Coleman was physically assaulted by an irate bebop drummer, described as 'psychotic' by Miles Davis, and hailed as the saviour of jazz by others. Lewis also secured Coleman a recording contract with Atlantic Records, where he made a series of influential but controversial albums, most notably *Free Jazz*, a collective improvisation for double quartet. After signing him, Atlantic sponsored Coleman and Don Cherry at the Lennox School of Jazz. At this time he earned the admiration of classical composer/academics like Gunther Schuller, who involved him in a number of Third Stream works (e.g. on the John Lewis album *Jazz Abstractions*). During 1963/4 he went into retirement, learning trumpet and violin, before appearing again in 1965 with the highly influential trio with David Izenzon and Charles Moffett that he had introduced on the 1962 *Town Hall* album. It was during the currency of this trio that Coleman began to promote his 'classical' writing (*Saints And Soldiers*). Also in the mid-60s, Coleman turned his attention to writing film scores, the best-known of which is *Chappaque Suite*, which features Pharoah Sanders. He also made a guest appearance - on trumpet! - on Jackie MacLean's *Old And New Gospel*. In 1968 a second saxophonist, Dewey Redman, was added to the group, and Izenzon and Moffett were replaced by Jimmy Garrison and Elvin Jones, John Coltrane's former bassist and drummer.

By the end of the 60s, Coleman was again playing with his early associates, such as Haden, Cherry, Bradford, Higgins and Blackwell, various combinations of which can be heard on *Crisis*, *Paris Concert*, *Science Fiction* and *Broken Shadows*. In the mid-70s Coleman began using electric guitars and basses and some rock rhythms with a band that eventually evolved into Prime Time, which continues to this day. The theory of harmolodics has underpinned his music for the last 20 years in particular. Even musicians who have worked with Coleman extensively confess that they do not understand what the theory is about, but there are some threads which can be discerned: two of the most readily understood are that all instruments have their own peculiar, natural voice and should play in the appropriate range, regardless of conventional notions of key, and, secondly, that there is a sort of democracy of instruments, whereby the distinction between soloist and accompanist, leader and sidemen, front-line instruments and rhythm section, is broken down. Coleman is such a powerful improviser that in performance the soloist-accompanist division often remains, but the concept of harmolodics has been quite influential, and is evident in the music of James 'Blood' Ulmer, Ronald Shannon Jackson and the Decoding Society (Ulmer and Jackson were both members of the proto-Prime Time and Coleman guests on the former's 1978 *Tales Of Captain Black*) and Pinski Zoo. While Coleman is seen by many as the father of free jazz his music has never been as abstract, as centred on pure sound as that of the Chicago AACM circle or of many European exponents of improvised music. His playing is always intensely personal, with a 'human vocalized' sound especially notable on alto, and there is usually a strong, if fluid, rhythmic feel which has become increasingly obvious with Prime Time. There is often a sense of a tonal centre, albeit not one related to the European tempered system, and melodically, both as a writer and improviser, he evinces an acute talent for pleasing design. This he manages without the safety-net of a chord-cycle: instead of the more traditional method of creating symmetrical shapes within a pre-existing structure, his improvisations are based on linear, thematic development, spinning out open-ended, spontaneous compositions which have their own rigorous and indisputable internal logic. Since the mid-70s, with Prime Time and its immediate predecessors, this method began to give way to a more fragmented style, the edgy but elegant depth of emotion being replaced by an intensely agitated feel which sometimes seems to cloak an element of desperation. His 1987 double album, *In All Languages*, featured one disc by a re-formed version of the classic late 50s/early 60s quartet, and one by Prime Time, with most themes common to both records, and is an ideal crash-course in Coleman's evolution. As a composer he has written a number of durable themes, such as 'Beauty Is A Rare Thing', 'Focus On Sanity', 'Ramblin'', 'Sadness', 'When Will The Blues Leave', 'Tears Inside' and the ravishing 'Lonely Woman' as well as the massive and rather baffling suite *Skies Of America* written for his group and a symphony orchestra. In the 80s and early 90s he turned increasingly to his notated musics, writing a series of chamber and solo pieces that, excepting *Prime Time/Time Design* (for string quartet and percussion), remain unrecorded.

● ALBUMS: *Something Else!* (Contemporary 1958)★★★, *Tomorrow Is The Question* (Contemporary 1959)★★★, *The Shape Of Jazz To Come* (Atlantic 1959)★★★★, *Change Of The Century* (Atlantic 1960)★★★★, *This Is Our Music* (Atlantic 1961)★★★★, *Free Jazz* (Atlantic 1961)★★★★, *Ornette!* (Atlantic 1962)★★★★, *Ornette On Tenor* (Atlantic 1962)★★★★, *The Town Hall Concert 1962* (1963)★★★★, *The Music Of Ornette Coleman* (RCA 1965)★★★, *Chappaque Suite* (1965)★★★, *The Great London Concert* aka *An Evening With Ornette Coleman* (1966)★★★, *At The Golden Circle, Volumes 1 & 2* (Blue Note 1966)★★★★, *The Empty Foxhole* (Blue Note 1966)★★★, *Music Of Ornette Coleman* aka *Saints And Soldiers* (1967)★★★★, *The Unprecedented Music Of Ornette Coleman* (1967)★★★, with Jackie McLean *New And Old Gospel* (Blue Note 1967)★★★, *New York Is Now!* (Blue Note 1968)★★★, *Love Call* (Blue Note 1968)★★★, *Ornette At 12* (Impulse! 1969)★★★, *Crisis* (Impulse! 1969)★★★, *Friends And Neighbours* (1970)★★★, *The Art Of Improvisers* recorded 1959-61 (Atlantic 1970)★★★, *Twins* recorded 1959-1961 (Atlantic 1972)★★★, *Science Fiction* (1972)★★★, *Skies Of America* (1972)★★★, *To Whom Who Keeps A Record* (Atlantic 1975)★★★, *Dancing In Your Head* (1976)★★★★, *Body Meta* (1976)★★★, *Paris Concert* recorded 1971 (1977)★★★, *Coleman Classics Volume One* recorded 1958 (1977)★★★★, with Charlie Haden *Soapsuds, Soapsuds* 1977 recordings (Artists House 1979)★★★★, *Broken Shadows* recorded 1971/72 (Moon 1982)★★★, *Of Human Feelings* 1979 recording (1982)★★★, *Who's Crazy* (Affinity 1983)★★★, *Opening The Caravan Of Dreams* (1985)★★★, *Prime Time/Time Design* (1985)★★★, with Pat Metheny *Song X* (Geffen 1986)★★★, *In All Languages* (1987)★★★, *Virgin Beauty* (Columbia 1988)★★★, *Live In Milano 1968* (1989)★★★, *Jazzbuhne Berlin 88* (1990)★★★, *Naked Lunch* (1992)★★★, *Languages* (1993)★★★, *The Empty Foxhole* (Connoisseur 1994)★★★, with Prime Time *Tone Dialing* (Verve 1995)★★★, *Sound Museum: Three Women* (Harmolodic/Verve 1996)★★★, *Sound Museum: Hidden Man* (Harmolodic/Verve 1996)★★★, with Joachim Kühn *Colors Live From Leipzig* (Verve 1997)★★★★.

● COMPILATIONS: *Beauty Is A Rare Thing: The Complete Atlantic Recordings* 6-CD box set (Rhino/Atlantic 1993)★★★★.

● FURTHER READING: *Ornette Coleman*, Barry McCrae. *Four Lives In The Bebop Business*, A.B. Spellman.

COLEMAN, STEVE

b. 20 September 1956, Chicago, Illinois, USA. Growing up surrounded by dance music - funk, rock, soul and blues - in Chicago's south side gave Coleman a taste for rhythm he never lost. He learned violin in school, but abandoned it for the alto saxophone at the age of 15, playing in James Brown cover bands. At Illinois Wesleyan University he was the only black person in the music department, quite a shock for someone who says he 'did not know any white people until he was 17 or something'. Told to improvise in his jazz band, he checked out his record collection to find that his father - a 'Bird' fanatic - had slipped in a Charlie Parker album. He learned the solos, just as he had Maceo Parker's. Returning to Chicago he hooked up with Von Freeman, the legendary tenor player and pedagogue, learning the rudiments of bebop on the bandstand. He moved to New York in 1978 to join the Mel Lewis-Thad Jones Big Band, later playing in the Cecil Taylor Orchestra and Sam Rivers' Winds Of Manhattan group. Active and articulate, he and kindred spirits - including singer Cassandra Wilson - formed M-Base, a self-help organization for black musicians, seeking to integrate all forms of black music into a new ecumenical style. Refreshingly, they by-passed the John Coltrane/Michael Brecker style of the Berklee College mainstream for a quirky, electric jazz/funk with a dash of Thelonious Monk and harmolodics too. Coleman has been hailed as the successor to Charlie Parker and attacked as a self-hyped mediocrity. Critics have favoured his work with Dave Holland's group, playing relatively straight ahead bop, but Coleman claims to play the same style in his group Five Elements. Certainly Coleman and M-Base are important movers for black music in the 90s.

● ALBUMS: *Motherland Pulse* (JMT 1985)★★★, *On The Edge of Tomorrow* (JMT 1986)★★★, *World Expansion* (JMT 1987)★★★★, *Sine Die* (Pangaea 1988)★★★, with Five Elements

Rhythm People (The Resurrection Of Creative Black) (Novus 1990)★★★★, *Black Science* (Novus 1991)★★★★, *Rhythm In Mind (The Carnegie Project)* (Novus 1992)★★★, *Drop Kick* (Novus 1992)★★★, with Dave Holland *Phase = Space* 1991 recording (DIW 1993)★★★, *The Tao Of Mad Phat* (Novus 1993)★★★★, *The Live At The Hot Brass Trilogy: Curves Of Life/The Way Of The Cipher/Myths, Modes And Means* 3-CD box set (BMG France 1996)★★★★, with Five Elements *Curves Of Life* Vol 3 (BMG/RCA Victor 1996)★★★, *The Way Of The Cipher Vol 2* (RCA 1996)★★, *The Sign And The Seal (Transmissions Of The Metaphysics Of A Culture)* (BMG/RCA Victor 1997)★★★★, *Live In Paris* (RCA 1997)★★, *Genesis & The Opening Of The Way* (BMG/RCA Victor 1998)★★★★.

COLES, JOHNNY

b. 3 July 1926, Trenton, New Jersey, USA, d. 21 December 1997, Philadelphia, Pennsylvania, USA. A self-taught trumpet and flügelhorn player, Coles attended the Mastbaum Vocational School of Music in Philadelphia and played with US Army bands during WWII. Coles joined John Coltrane and Red Garland in Eddie 'Cleanhead' Vinson's band in 1948, and then went on to work with Philly Joe Jones, Earl Bostic, Bullmoose Jackson, and James Moody in the 50s. He performed and recorded with the Gil Evans Orchestra between 1958 and 1964, and was featured as the soloist on four of the six tracks on 1960's classic *Out Of The Cool* album, earning favourable comparisons with Miles Davis for his ability to exploit musical space. He then toured with the Charles Mingus Workshop, recorded with Duke Pearson and Astrud Gilberto, and joined Herbie Hancock in 1968. Coles then graced the big bands of Ray Charles (1969-84), Duke Ellington (1971-74), and Count Basie (1984-86) with his warm and lyrical style. In 1989 Coles retired to Philadelphia where he lived for the remainder of his life.

● ALBUMS: *The Warm Sound Of Johnny Coles* (Epic 1961)★★★, *Little Johnny C* (Blue Note 1964)★★★★, *Katumbo Dance* (Mainstream 1972)★★★, *New Morning* (Criss Cross 1982)★★★, with Frank Wess *Two At The Top* (Uptown 1983)★★★★.

COLLETTE, BUDDY

b. William Marcel Collette, 6 August 1921, Los Angeles, California, USA. A masterly player on any of his many instruments, Collette worked mostly in and around his home town until World War II. During his military service he directed a dance band and later played with many leading jazzmen including Eli 'Lucky' Thompson, Edgar Hayes, Benny Carter and Gerald Wilson. By the 50s Collette was working extensively in film, television and radio studios where his musical expertise gained him a great reputation. In 1955 he became a member of the Chico Hamilton Quintet where his flute-playing helped give the group its distinctive sound and win its brief moments of popular success. During the 60s Collette turned more and more to writing, especially for films, but found time to work with Thelonious Monk and Stan Kenton. In the 70s he continued the pattern much as before, interspersing writing chores with performances using such musicians as Benny Carter.

● ALBUMS: *Buddy Collette i* (1954)★★★, *The Chico Hamilton Quartet With Buddy Collette* (1955)★★★★, *Tanganyka* (Dig 1956)★★, *Man Of Many Parts* (Contemporary 1956)★★, *Nice Day With Buddy Collette* Contemporary 1956)★★, *Sessions. Live i* (1956)★★★, *Calm, Cool And Collette* (ABC 1957)★★★, *Buddy's Best* (Dooto 1957)★★★, *Everybody's Buddy* (Challenge 1957)★★★, *Sessions, Live* ii (1957)★★★, *Jazz Loves Paris* (Specialty 1958)★★★★, *Swingin' Shepherds* (Emarcy 1958), *Buddy Collette* ii (1958),★★★ *Star Studded Cast: Buddy Collette* iii (Tampa 1959)★★★, *At The Cinema* (Mercury 1959)★★, *Polynesia* (Music & Sound 1959)★, *Modern Interpretations Of Porgy And Bess* (Interlude 1959)★★★, *Buddy Collette* iv (1960)★★★, *Buddy Collette* v (1960)★★★, *Buddy Collette In Italy* (1961)★★★, *Warm Winds* (World Pacific 1964)★★, *Now And Then* (1973)★★, *Blockbuster* (1973)★★★, *Flute Talk* 1988 recording (Soul Note 1992)★★, *Jazz For Thousand Oaks* (UFO-Bass 1998)★★★.

COLLIE, MAX

b. 21 February 1931, Melbourne, Victoria, Australia. After achieving some success as a semi-pro trombonist in his homeland, Collie visited the UK in 1962 with the Melbourne New Orleans Jazz Band. He stayed behind when the band returned home and joined the London City Stompers. He spent the rest of the 60s building a reputation for the band, now renamed Max Collie's Rhythm Aces. Their success exceeded Collie's expectations thanks to their hard work, unbridled enthusiasm and the application of marketing expertise learnt at university. Tours of the USA established the Aces as one of the top post-Revival bands in the world and they won the so-called World Championship of Jazz in 1975. Collie soldiered on into the 80s playing his fiery brand of rough-hewn traditional jazz and unmoved by the commercial success achieved by other British traditionalists who had long since shifted their ground. In 1984 he co-led the *New Orleans Mardi Gras* road show alongside fellow veterans Ken Colyer and Cy Laurie.

● ALBUMS: *At The Beiderbecke Festival* (1975)★★★, *World Champions Of Jazz* (1976)★★★★, *Ten Years Together* (1976)★★★, *Gospel Train* (Black Lion 1977)★★, *Max Collie Rhythm Aces* (1977)★★★★, *Jazz Rools OK* (1978)★★★, *By Popular Demand* (Black Lion 1979)★★★★, *Live In Sweden* (Sweet Folk All 1981)★★★, *Ten Years Together* (Sweet Folk All 1981)★★★, *Live: Max Collie* (1983)★★★★, *20 Years Jubilee* (Timeless 1986),★★★ *Battle Of Trafalgar* (1987)★★★, *Sensation* (Timeless 1988)★★★, *The Thrill Of Jazz* (1989)★★★.

● COMPILATIONS *Max Collie's Rhythm Aces, Volume 1* and *2* (both 1987)★★★★, *The High Society Show* (Reality 1992)★★★.

COLLIER, GRAHAM

b. 21 February 1937, Tynemouth, Northumberland, England. Collier began his musical career playing trumpet in bands in the north of England before entering the British Army as a bandsman. He was in the army, playing dance music and jazz as well as military music, for six years and then won a scholarship to Berklee College Of Music. He worked for a while in the USA, playing bass in the Jimmy Dorsey Orchestra. From 1964 he led his own band in the UK, largely performing his own music. Amongst Collier's sidemen have been many outstanding British musicians of his generation including Harry Beckett, Mike Gibbs, John Surman and Kenny Wheeler. Varying the size and format of his bands, Collier encouraged new concepts and young musicians, establishing the orchestral base from which Loose Tubes sprang. In addition to his career as a performer, Collier has also formed his own recording company, Mosaic, teaches jazz at London's Royal Academy of Music, has composed music for films and television, and has written a number of books on jazz. In 1987 his considerable services to jazz were recognized with an OBE. His compositions are inventive, thoroughly modern and carefully structured, while allowing full and free rein to the improvisational abilities of his soloists.

● ALBUMS: *Down Another Road* (1969)★★★, *Songs For My Father* (1970)★★★★, *Mosaics* (1971)★★★★, *Darius* (1974)★★★★, *Midnight Blue* (Mosaic 1975)★★★, *New Conditions* (Mosaic 1976)★★★, *Symphony Of Scorpions* (Mosaic 1976)★★★, *Day Of The Dead* (Mosaic 1978)★★★, *Something British* (1985)★★★, *Charles River Fragments* (Boathouse 1995)★★★★.

Collins, Cal

b. Calvin Collins, 5 May 1933, Medora, Indiana, USA. Collins was born and raised in an atmosphere of bluegrass and country music. Although he had taken up the guitar, he began listening to jazz piano players, particularly Art Tatum, Fats Waller, George Shearing and Nat 'King' Cole. In the 50s he settled in Cincinnati, Ohio, playing guitar in local clubs where he sometimes accompanied visiting jazzmen including Andy Simpkins and Harold Jones. It was not until the mid-70s that he achieved wider recognition when he joined Benny Goodman, an engagement that lasted almost four years. This exposure led to a recording contract with Carl Jefferson's Concord Records where he has been teamed with Warren Vaché Jnr., Buddy Tate, Al Cohn, Marshal Royal and Scott Hamilton. Collins has also been recorded by Helen Morr of Mopro Records, who allied him with John Von Ohlen and the rest of the excellent house band's rhythm section at Cincinnati's Blue Wisp Club. During the 80s and early 90s Collins has worked regularly with all-star groups, as a solo and also as accompanist to jazz-orientated singers, notably Rosemary Clooney, playing numerous club, college and festival engagements across the USA and in other countries. Collins is also in demand as a teacher and clinician. In 1991 he was a member of the Woody Herman All Stars led by Terry Gibbs on a tour of Germany and was featured at a series of concerts in California under the generic title, 'Masters of the String Guitar'. Although he drew his early inspiration from jazz pianists Collins was also influenced by country music's Merle Travis. His jazz guitar mentors were Django Reinhardt and Charlie Christian and some of the latter's flowing single-line artistry is echoed in Collins's best work, especially when he plays the blues. His interest in pianists led to his developing an unconventional style of playing in which he uses his left thumb to create a walking bass line while playing intricate patterns with all five fingers of his right hand.

● ALBUMS: *Benny Goodman: Live At Carnegie Hall, 40th Anniversary Concert* (1978)★★★★, *Cincinnati To LA* (1978)★★★, with Warren Vaché *Cal Collins* (Concord 1979)★★, *Ohio Boss Guitar* (Famous Door 1979)★★, *Polished Brass* (1979)★★★, with Scott Hamilton, Buddy Tate *Scott's Buddy* (1980)★★★, *Cross Country* (Concord 1981)★★★, *Crack'd Rib* (1984)★★, *Ohio Style* (Concord 1990)★★★.

Collins, John

b. John Elbert Collins, 20 September 1913, Montgomery, Alabama, USA. After briefly playing clarinet, he switched to guitar and worked for a while in a band led by his mother, Georgia Gorham. From the mid-30s he was active in Chicago, then New York, with several noted jazz musicians including Art Tatum and Roy Eldridge. From 1940 he accompanied and recorded with Billie Holiday and Lester Young and also played in bands led by Benny Carter and Fletcher Henderson. After military service during World War II, Collins played in a trio led by Slam Stewart and was then with pianists Erroll Garner, Billy Taylor and Art Tatum. In the autumn of 1951 he joined yet another pianist-leader, Nat 'King' Cole, and this time settled into a spot that lasted until Cole's death in 1965. He continued playing through the late 60s and 70s with Patti Page, Bobby Troup, Carmen McRae, Snooky Young, Cat Anderson and others. By this time he was based in Los Angeles where he also taught. Collins' career was spent largely on the edges of the limelight enjoyed by others, but he was a gifted player and an outstanding accompanist. Although his role in the Cole trio was less overt than that of Oscar Moore, Cole's first guitarist, when opportunities arose, Collins was a very good soloist.

Collins, Joyce

b. 5 May 1930, Battle Mountain, Nevada, USA. Collins began playing piano professionally at the age of 15 while still attending Reno High School in Nevada. Later, while studying music and teaching at San Francisco State College, she played in groups and solo at various jazz clubs, eventually going on tour with the Frankie Carle band. In the late 50s Collins settled in Los Angeles, working there and also in Reno and Las Vegas, where she became the first women to conduct one of the resort's show bands. During this time Collins worked in film and television studios, spending 10 years in the band on the *Mary Tyler Moore Show* and also on comedian Bob Newhart's shows. In 1975 she recorded with Bill Henderson and their subsequent *Street Of Dreams* and *Tribute To Johnny Mercer* were Grammy nominees. Collins continued to work in films, coaching actors Jeff and Beau Bridges for their roles in *The Fabulous Baker Boys* (1989). Since 1975 Collins has been associated with the Dick Grove Music School where she teaches jazz piano. Collins has also written and arranged extensively, including a programme, performed live and on radio, tracing the involvement of women in jazz as composers and lyricists. Although she performs mostly in solo, duo and trio work, Collins occasionally sits in with big bands, such as that led by Bill Berry. She has also recorded with Paul Horn and under her own name. Her first album appeared in 1961, her next, *Sweet Madness*, after an inappropriately long gap. Centred mainly upon Los Angeles, Collins has worked farther afield in places such as Mexico City, Paris and, in recent years, New York and Brazil. A gifted, fluent pianist with a strong sense of time and the historical role of the piano in jazz, Collins makes a considerable impression as a performer. Her composing and arranging talents are also worthy of mention and she also sings pleasantly and with a delicate understanding of the lyricists intentions.

● ALBUMS: *Girl Here Plays Mean Piano* (1961)★★★, with Gene Estes *Westville* (1968)★★★, *The Paul Horn Concert Ensemble* (1969)★★★, with Bill Henderson *Live At The Times* (1975)★★★★, with Henderson *Street Of Dreams* (1981)★★★, with Henderson *Tribute To Johnny Mercer* (1984)★★, *Moment To Moment* (Discovery 1988)★★★, *Sweet Madness* (Audiophile 1990)★★★.

Collins, Lee

b. 17 October 1901, New Orleans, Louisiana, USA, d. 3 July 1960. As a youth, Collins gained valuable experience playing trumpet in several marching bands in his home town and also worked with George 'Pops' Foster, Oscar 'Papa' Celestin and Zutty Singleton. By the early 20s his reputation was such, that when Louis Armstrong left the King Oliver band Collins was called to Chicago as his replacement. He later toured extensively, often leading his own bands but failed to achieve widespread recognition. He worked steadily throughout the 30s and 40s but by the early 50s he was in failing health. He suffered from emphysema which inevitably limited his career but he toured Europe with a Franco-American band in 1951, which included Mezz Mezzrow and Zutty Singleton, and returned for a second tour in 1954. This time the strain was too much and he ceased playing, living on for another six years. Despite such moments of glory as when he replaced Armstrong with Oliver and also when he took Red Allen's place in the Luis Russell band in 1930, Collins however was not in their class. He was a gifted player with a rich tone and, on occasions, an exhilarating and inventive soloist.

● ALBUMS: *A Night At The Victory Club* (New Orleans 1979)★★★, *Lee Collins In The 30s* (1986)★★★.

● FURTHER READING: *Oh, Didn't He Ramble: The Life Story Of Lee Collins*, Lee Collins and Mary Collins, F.J. Gillis and J.W. Miner (Eds).

Collins, Shad

b. Lester R. Collins, 27 June 1910, Elizabeth, New Jersey, USA, d. June 1978. The early years of Collins's career were spent playing trumpet in a succession of top-flight New York-based jazz bands, including those led by Chick Webb, Benny Carter and Tiny Bradshaw. In 1936 he toured Europe with Teddy Hill, remained in Paris for a while, and then returned to the USA to join Count Basie in 1939 when the Basie band was then in full and glorious flight. Collins worked in a trumpet section which also included Buck Clayton and Harry Edison and he was thus somewhat overshadowed as a soloist. In the early 40s Collins played in small groups in New York and then returned to big band music by replacing Dizzy Gillespie in the Cab Calloway orchestra. He stayed with Calloway until 1946 and thereafter worked in various small groups. One of these, led by Sam 'The Man' Taylor, was involved in the R&B boom of the early and mid-50s. However, Collins occasionally recorded with outstanding mainstream groups, including one which featured trombonist Vic Dickenson and rising cornet star, Ruby Braff. Collins retired from active participation in music during the 60s and died in 1978.

● ALBUMS: with Vic Dickenson *Vic Dickenson Showcase* (1954)★★★.

Colours

(see Weber, Eberhard)

Colston, Mary

(see Kirk, Mary)

Coltrane, Alice

b. Alice McLeod, 27 August 1937, Detroit, Michigan, USA. Alice came from a musical family (bassist Ernie Farrow is her brother), and studied piano in Detroit, where she worked in a trio and with vibes-player Terry Pollard, before going to Europe and coming under the influence of Bud Powell's playing. She worked with Terry Gibbs on her return to the USA and it was during her stint with Gibbs (1962-63) that she first met John Coltrane. After his divorce from Naima, Alice married him in 1966 and they had three children together. At the end of 1965 she had replaced McCoy Tyner in Coltrane's band, and while she is not the pianist Tyner was, her tentative, gently probing style fitted the requirements of Trane's music at that point. After Coltrane's death in 1967 she carried on promoting his music, issuing through Impulse! Records a number of sessions which might not otherwise have seen the light of day. On some sessions she added her own harp playing and strings arranged by Ornette Coleman, an extremely controversial move. In an interview with writer Pauline Rivelli, she said 'I am really not concerned with results, my only concern is the work, the effort put forth . . . if I give you a leaf or a pearl that you trample in the dust I'm sorry. It's my gift, or offering to you. You do with it as you wish'. Playing mostly piano and organ, she subsequently led her own groups which have featured Frank Lowe, Archie Shepp, Jimmy Garrison, Clifford Jarvis and Jack DeJohnette. From the mid-70s she was less active in music, instead pursuing the spiritual and mystical interests that had already led to her adopting the name Turiya Aparana. But in 1987, to mark the 20th anniversary of her husband's death, she toured with the Coltrane Legacy band, featuring sons Oran and Ravi on saxophones, Reggie Workman on bass and Rashied Ali on drums.

● ALBUMS: *A Monastic Trio* (Impulse! 1968)★★★, *Ptah The El*

Daoud (Impulse! 1970)★★★★, *Universal Consciousness* (Impulse! 1971)★★★, *Lord Of Lords* (1972)★★★, with Joe Henderson *The Elements* (Milestone 1973)★★★, *Journey In Satchidanada* (MCA 1974)★★, with Carlos Santana *llluminations* (1974)★★★★, *Eternity* (1976)★★★, *Cosmic Music* (1977)★★, *Reflection On Creation And Space* (1977)★★.

COLTRANE, JOHN

b. John William Coltrane, 23 September 1926, Hamlet, North Carolina, USA, d. 17 July 1967, New York, USA. Coltrane grew up in the house of his maternal grandfather, Rev. William Blair (who gave him his middle name), a preacher and community spokesman. While he was taking clarinet lessons at school, his school band leader suggested his mother buy him an alto saxophone. In 1939 his grandfather and then his father died, and after finishing high school he joined his mother in Philadelphia. He spent a short period at the Ornstein School of Music and the Granoff Studios, where he won scholarships for both performance and composition, but his real education began when he started gigging. Two years' military service was spent in a navy band (1945-46), after which he toured in the King Kolax and Eddie 'Cleanhead' Vinson bands, playing goodtime, rhythmic big-band music. It was while playing in the Dizzy Gillespie Big Band (1949-51) that he switched to tenor saxophone. Coltrane's musical roots were in acoustic black music that combined swing and instrumental prowess in solos, the forerunner of R&B. He toured with Earl Bostic (1952), Johnny Hodges (1953-54) and Jimmy Smith (1955). However, it was his induction into Miles Davis's band of 1955 - rightly termed the Classic Quintet - that brought him to notice. Next to Davis's filigree sensitivity, Coltrane sounds awkward and crude, and Davis received criticism for his choice of saxophonist. The only precedent for such modernist interrogation of tenor harmony was John Gilmore's playing with Sun Ra. Critics found Coltrane's tone raw and shocking after years in which the cool school of Lester Young and Stan Getz had held sway. It was generally acknowledged, however, that his ideas were first rate. Along with Sonny Rollins, he became New York's most in-demand hard bop tenor player: 1957 saw him appearing on 21 important recordings, and enjoying a brief but fruitful association with Thelonious Monk. That same year he returned to Philadelphia, kicking his long-time heroin habit, and started to develop his own music (Coltrane's notes to the later *A Love Supreme* refer to a 'spiritual awakening'). He also found half of his 'classic' quartet: at the Red Rooster (a nightclub that he visited with trumpeter Calvin Massey, an old friend from the 40s), he discovered pianist McCoy Tyner and bassist Jimmy Garrison.

After recording numerous albums for the Prestige label, Coltrane signed to Atlantic Records and, on 15 August 1959, he recorded *Giant Steps*. Although it did not use the talents of his new friends from Philadelphia, it featured a dizzying torrent of tenor solos that harked back to the pressure-cooker creativity of bebop, while incorporating the muscular gospel attack of hard bop. Pianist Tommy Flanagan (later celebrated for his sensitive backings for singers such as Ella Fitzgerald and Tony Bennett) and drummer Art Taylor provided the best performances of their lives. Although this record is rightly hailed as a masterpiece, it encapsulated a problem: where could hard bop go from here? Coltrane knew the answer; after a second spell with Davis (1958-60), he formed his best-known quartet with Tyner, Garrison and the amazing polyrhythmic drummer Elvin Jones. Jazz has been recovering ever since.

The social situation of the 60s meant that Coltrane's innovations were simultaneously applauded as *avant garde* statements of black revolution and efficiently recorded and marketed. The Impulse! label, to which he switched from Atlantic in 1961, has a staggering catalogue that includes most of Coltrane's landmark records, plus several experimental sessions from the mid-60s that still remain unreleased (although they missed *My Favorite Things*, recorded in 1960 for Atlantic, in which Coltrane established the soprano saxophone as an important instrument). Between 1961 and his death in 1967, Coltrane made music that has become the foundation of modern jazz. For commercial reasons, Impulse! Records had a habit of delaying the release of his music; fans emerged from the live performances in shock at the pace of his evolution. A record of *Ballads* and an encounter with Duke Ellington in 1962 seemed designed to deflect criticisms of coarseness, although Coltrane later attributed their relatively temperate ambience to persistent problems with his mouthpiece. *A Love Supreme* was more hypnotic and lulling on record than in live performance, but nevertheless a classic. After that, the records became wilder and wilder. The unstinting commitment to new horizons led to ruptures within the group. Elvin Jones left after Coltrane incorporated a second drummer (Rashied Ali). McCoy Tyner was replaced by Alice McLeod (who married Coltrane in 1966). Coltrane was especially interested in new saxophone players and *Ascension* (1965) made space for Archie Shepp, Pharoah Sanders, Marion Brown and John Tchicai. Eric Dolphy, although he represented a different tradition of playing from Coltrane (a modernist projection of Charlie Parker), had also been a frequent guest player with the quartet in the early 60s, touring Europe with them in 1961. *Interstellar Space* (1967), a duet record, pitched Coltrane's tenor against Ali's drums, and provides a fascinating hint of new directions.

Coltrane's death in 1967 robbed *avant garde* jazz of its father figure. The commercial ubiquity of fusion in the 70s obscured his music and the 80s jazz revival concentrated on his hard bop period. Only Reggie Workman's Ensemble and Ali's Phalanx carried the huge ambition of Coltrane's later music into the 90s. As soloists, however, few tenor players have remained untouched by his example. It is interesting that the saxophonists Coltrane encouraged did not sound like him; since his death, his 'sound' has become a mainstream commodity, from the Berklee College Of Music style of Michael Brecker to the 'European' variant of Jan Garbarek. New stars such as Andy Sheppard have established new audiences for jazz without finding new ways of playing. Coltrane's music - like that of Jimi Hendrix - ran parallel with a tide of mass political action and consciousness. Perhaps those conditions are required for the creation of such innovative and intense music. Nevertheless, Coltrane's music reached a wide audience, and was particularly popular with the younger generation of listeners who were also big fans of rock music. *A Love Supreme* sold sufficient copies to win a gold disc, while the Byrds used the theme of Coltrane's tune 'India' as the basis of their hit single 'Eight Miles High'. Perhaps by alerting the rock audience to the presence of jazz, Coltrane can be said to have - inadvertently - prepared the way for fusion. Coltrane's work has some challenging moments and if you are not in the right mood, he can sound irritating. What is established without doubt is his importance as a true messenger of music. His jazz came from somewhere inside his body. Few jazz musicians have reached this nirvana, and still have absolute control over their instrument.

● ALBUMS: with Paul Chambers *High Step* 1955-1956 recordings (Blue Note 1956)★★★, with Elmo Hope *Informal Jazz* reissued as *Two Tenors* (Prestige 1956)★★★, with various artists *Tenor Conclave* (Prestige 1957)★★★, *Dakar* (Prestige 1957)★★★, *Coltrane* reissued as *The First Trane* (Prestige 1957)★★★, *John Coltrane With The Red Garland Trio* reissued as *Traneing In* (Prestige 1957)★★★, with various artists *Wheelin' And Dealing* (Prestige 1957)★★★, *Blue Train* (Blue Note 1957)★★★★★, with Thelonious Monk *Thelonious Monk With John Coltrane* (Jazzland 1957)★★★★, with Miles Davis *Miles And Coltrane* (Columbia 1958)★★★★, *Lush Life* (Prestige 1958)★★★, *Soultrane* (Blue Note 1958)★★★★, *John Coltrane* (Prestige 1958)★★★★, *Settin The Pace* (Prestige 1958)★★★, with Paul Quinichette *Cattin' With Coltrane And Quinichette* (Prestige 1959)★★★, *Coltrane Plays For Lovers* (Prestige 1959)★★★, *The Believer* (Prestige 1959)★★★, *Black Pearls* (Prestige 1959)★★, *The Stardust Session* (Prestige 1959)★★★, *Standard Coltrane* (Prestige 1959)★★★, *Bahia* (Prestige 1959)★★★, *Giant Steps* (Atlantic 1959)★★★★★, *Coltrane Jazz* (Atlantic 1960)★★★★, with Don Cherry *The Avant-Garde* (Atlantic 1960)★★★, with Milt Jackson *Bags And Trane* (Atlantic 1961)★★★★, *My Favorite Things* (Atlantic 1961)★★★★, *Olé Coltrane* (Atlantic 1961)★★★, *Africa/Brass: Volumes 1 & 2* (Impulse! 1961)★★★★, with Kenny Burrell *Kenny Burrell With John Coltrane* (New Jazz 1962)★★★★, *Live At The Village Vanguard* (Impulse! 1962)★★★, *Coltrane Plays The Blues* (Atlantic 1962)★★★★, *Coltrane Time* originally released as Cecil Taylor's *Hard Driving Jazz* (United Artists 1962)★★★, *Coltrane* (Impulse! 1962)★★★★, with Duke Ellington *Duke Ellington And John Coltrane* (MCA/Impulse! 1962)★★★★, *Ballads* (Impulse! 1962)★★★★, with Johnny Hartman *John Coltrane And Johnny Hartman* (Impulse! 1963)★★★★, *Coltrane Live At Birdland* (Impulse! 1963)★★★, *Impressions* (Impulse! 1963)★★★★, *Coltrane's Sound* (Atlantic 1964)★★★★, *Crescent* (Impulse! 1964)★★★, *The Last Trane* (Prestige 1965)★★★, *A Love Supreme* (Impulse! 1965)★★★★★, *The John Coltrane Quartet Plays* (Impulse! 1965)★★★, with Archie Shepp *New Thing At Newport* (Impulse! 1965)★★★, *Ascension - Edition 1* (Impulse! 1965)★★★★, *Transition* (Impulse! 1965)★★★★, *Ascension - Edition 2* (Impulse! 1966)★★★★, *Kulu Se Mama* (Impulse! 1966)★★★, *Meditations* (Impulse! 1966)★★★★, *Expression* (Impulse! 1967)★★★, *Live At The Village Vanguard Again!* (Impulse! 1967)★★★, *Om* (Impulse! 1967)★★, *Selflessness* 1963, 1965 recordings (Impulse! 1969)★★★, *Sun Ship* 1965 recording (1971)★★★, *Dear Old Stockholm* (Impulse! 1965)★★★, *Live In Seattle* 1965 recording (Impulse! 1971)★★★, *Africa Brass, Volume Two* 1961 recording (1974)★★★★, *Interstellar Space* 1967 recording (Impulse! 1974)★★★, *First Meditations - For Quartet* 1965 recording (Impulse! 1977)★★★, *The Other Village Vanguard Tapes* 1961 recording (1977)★★★, *Afro-Blue Impressions* 1962 recording (Pablo 1977)★★★, *The Paris Concert* 1962 recording (Pablo 1979)★★★, *The European Tour* 1962 recording (Pablo 1980)★★★, *Bye Bye Blackbird* 1962 recording (1981)★★★, *Live At Birdland - Featuring Eric Dolphy* 1962 recording (1982)★★★, *Stellar Regions* 1967 recording (Impulse! 1995)★★★.

● COMPILATIONS: *The Best Of John Coltrane* (Atlantic 1969)★★★★, *The Best Of John Coltrane - His Greatest Years (1961-1966)* (MCA/Impulse! 1972)★★★★, *The Best Of John Coltrane - His Greatest Years, Volume 2 (1961-1967)* (MCA/Impulse! 1972)★★★★, *The Mastery Of John Coltrane, Volumes 1-4* (1978)★★★★, *The Art Of John Coltrane (The Atlantic Years)* (Pablo 1983)★★★★, *The Gentle Side Of John Coltrane* (Impulse! 1992)★★★★, *The Major Works Of John Coltrane* (Impulse! 1992)★★★★, *The Impulse! Years* (Impulse! 1993)★★★★, *The Heavyweight Champion: The Complete Atlantic Recordings* 7-CD box set (Rhino/Atlantic 1995)★★★★★, *The Complete 1961 Village Vanguard Recordings* 4-CD box set (Impulse! 1997)★★★★, *The Classic Quartet - Complete Impulse! Studio Recordings* 8-CD box set (Impulse! 1998)★★★★★.

● CD ROM: *John Coltrane - The Ultimate Blue Train* (Blue Note 1997).

● VIDEOS: *The World According To John Coltrane* (1993).

● FURTHER READING: *Trane 'N' Me*, Andrew Nathaniel White. *About John Coltrane*, Tim Gelatt (ed.). *John Coltrane, Discography*, Brian Davis. *The Artistry Of John Coltrane*, John Coltrane. *The Style Of John Coltrane*, William Shadrack Cole. *Chasin' The Trane*, J.C. Thomas. *Coltrane*, Cuthbert Ormond Simpkins. *John Coltrane*, Brian Priestley. *John Coltrane*, Bill Cole. *Ascension: John Coltrane And His Quest*, Eric Nisenson.

COLTRANE JAZZ - JOHN COLTRANE

Coltrane Jazz features a number of takes from the 'Naima' session, with Wynton Kelly, Paul Chambers and Jimmy Cobb, as well as a track with Cedar Walton and Lex Humphries and an early outing by his newly formed quartet featuring pianist McCoy Tyner, Steve Davis and Elvin Jones. While lacking the conceptual strength of many of Coltrane's greatest works, *Coltrane Jazz* includes some memorable original tunes. Particularly, 'Harmonique', a theme involving polyphonics (more than one note played simultaneously), and a beautiful ballad, 'I'll Wait And Pray'.

● Tracks: *Little Old Lady; Village Blues; My Shining Hour; Fifth House; Harmonique; Like Sonny; I'll Wait And Pray; Some Other Blues.*

● First released 1961

● UK peak chart position: did not chart

● USA peak chart position: did not chart

COLVILLE, RANDOLPH

b. 23 May 1942, Glasgow, Scotland. Clarinettist 'Randy' Colville began his diverse musical career as a graduate from, and later as a teacher at, the Northern School of Music (now the Royal Northern College of Music) in Manchester, where he earned a high reputation on the hectic 60s jazz scene with leading local bands the Jazz Aces and the Saints Jazz Band. Moving south in the late 70s to take up a post at Kent Music School, Colville quickly found himself much in demand both in the classical and commercial fields, and on the jazz scene, working and recording regularly throughout the 70s, 80s and 90s with Keith Nichols' Ragtime Orchestra, the Midnite Follies Orchestra (with Nichols and co-leader Alan Cohen), Alan Elsdon and Humphrey Lyttelton, and with American artists such as Teddy Wilson, Billy Butterfield, Benny Waters, Yank Lawson, Ralph Sutton, and Al Casey. Colville is active too as a classical soloist, appearing often at Kenwood House and other venues on the London circuit. His meticulous arrangements are featured by many of the bands he works with, including his own Septet, the Colville Collection, whose repertoire spans mid-period jazz to bebop. Colville often combines both worlds with jazz stylings for clarinet and string quartet. In addition to his main instrument, Colville is an accomplished all-round performer on soprano, alto and tenor saxophones, and while often labelled as a Matty Matlock stylist, sees himself rather as a `versatile player at ease in jazz of all periods'.

● ALBUMS: *Gonna Call My Children Home* (1986)★★, with Alan Elsdon *Hotter Than Hades* (1987)★★★, with Keith Nichols, Benny Waters *Cotton Club Orchestra/Jazz Kings* (1990)★★★★.

COLYER, KEN

b. 18 April 1928, Great Yarmouth, Norfolk, England, d. 8 March 1988, south of France. Of all the musicians involved in the British Revivalist movement of the late 40s and early 50s, trumpeter Colyer was the only one to achieve the status of a jazz legend. He achieved this through a gritty determination to adhere to what he believed to be the true spirit of jazz. Colyer first demonstrated his obsession with the great traditions of New Orleans jazz in the early 50s. He joined the Merchant Navy in order to visit the USA, where he promptly jumped ship and headed for the Crescent City. In New Orleans he sat in with local grandmasters, including George Lewis and Emile Barnes, before the authorities caught up with him and he was deported. Before his visit to the USA, Colyer had already worked with the Crane River Jazz Band and the Christie Brothers Stompers, but his American exploits had made him a big name in the UK and he was invited to front the co-operative band formed a little earlier by Chris Barber and Monty Sunshine. Although this unit was working regularly and building a reputation, Barber and Sunshine felt that Colyer's fame would be an asset. For a while this assumption proved correct, but personality clashes developed, particularly when Colyer appeared to lose sight of the fact that the band he was leading was not his own but was a collective venture. In 1954 Barber took over the reins and Colyer formed his own band, which, with various personnel changes, he continued to lead for the next 30 years. Among the many musicians who worked under Colyer's leadership were Acker Bilk, Diz Disley, Ian Wheeler and Sammy Rimington. Conceding that his technique was limited, Colyer overcame any deficiencies in style through an unflinching determination not to be swayed by changing public tastes or commercial considerations, although he did play guitar and sing in a skiffle group in the mid-50s. In 1957 he returned to the USA and joined the George Lewis band, arranging their trips to Europe. His last significant work was as part of the touring jazz show *New Orleans Mardi Gras.* Colyer defeated cancer, and the temporary retirement this necessitated, playing on into the 80s. A year after he died, a commemorative blue plaque was placed on the wall of the 100 Club in London, and many of his former colleagues took part in a concert organized by the Ken Colyer Trust. A hugely important figure in British jazz.

● ALBUMS: *Ken Colyer In New Orleans* (Vogue 1954)★★★★, *New Orleans To London* (Decca 1954)★★★★, *In The Beginning ...* (1954)★★★★, *Back To The Delta* (Decca 1954)★★★★, *Ken Colyer's Jazzmen* (Tempo 1956)★★★, *Club Session With Colyer* (Decca 1957)★★★, *A Very Good Year* (1957)★★★, *In Gloryland* (Decca 1958)★★★, *In Hamburg* (Decca 1959)★★★, *Plays Standards* (Decca 1959)★★★, *Sensation* (Lake 1960)★★★, *This Is Jazz* (Columbia 1960)★★★, *This Is Jazz Volume 2* (Columbia 1961)★★★, *When I Leave The World Behind* (Lake 1963)★★★, *Out Of Nowhere* (1965)★★★, *Wandering* (KC 1965)★★★, *Live At The Dancing Slipper* (1969)★★★, *Ken Colyer And His Handpicked Jazzmen* (1972)★★★, *Watch That Dirty Tone Of Yours* (Joy 1974)★★★, *Spirituals, Volumes 1 & 2* (Joy 1974)★★★, *Swinging And Singing* (1975)★★★, *Painting The Clouds With Sunshine* (Black Lion 1979)★★★, *Darkness On The Delta* (Black Lion 1979)★★★, *Ken Colyer With John Petters' New Orleans Allstars* (1985)★★★, with Max Collie, Cy Laurie *New Orleans Mardi Gras* (1985)★★★, *Too Busy* (CMJ 1985)★★★, with Acker Bilk *It Looks Like A Big Time Tonight* (Stomp 1988)★★★.

● COMPILATIONS: *The Decca Years, Volume 1 (1955-59)* (Lake 1985)★★★★, *The Decca Years, Volume 2 (1955-59)* (Lake 1986)★★★★, *The Decca Years, Volume 3 (1955-59)* (Lake 1987)★★★★, *The Decca Years, Volume 4 (Skiffle Sessions 1954-57)* (Lake 1987)★★★★, *The Decca Years, Volume 5 (Lonesome Road)* (Lake 1988)★★★★, *The Decca Years, Volume 6 (In The Beginning)* (Lake 1988)★★★★, *The Guv'nor (1959-61)* (Polydor 1989)★★★★.

● FURTHER READING: *When Dreams Are In The Dust (The Path Of A Jazzman)*, Ken Colyer.

COMBELLE, ALIX

b. 15 June 1912, Paris, France, d. 27 February 1978. Although his father was a saxophonist Combelle began playing drums but later switched to clarinet and tenor saxophone. He played in various bands in the 30s, sometimes with visiting American jazzmen, including Coleman Hawkins. He worked with the Quintette Du Hot Club Du France and with Django Reinhardt. During most of the war years Combelle led a band in Paris and after the war was again on call as accompanist to touring Americans including Bill Coleman, with whom he had first played in the late 30s, Buck Clayton and Lionel Hampton. In the 60s Combelle operated his own club and worked in promotion. His son, Phillipe, continues the family's musical tradition into a third generation, playing drums. Combelle's playing style was gutsy and driving, showing the distinct influence of Hawkins. Persuaded to join in a 1953 Paris recording date by Hampton, he delivered an inspired solo. Something very similar had happened on a 1937 date with Hawkins, demonstrating that in the right company, Combelle could play as well as any of his European contemporaries.

● ALBUMS: with Don Byas, Buck Clayton, Mary Lou Williams *Messin' Round In Montmarte* (Storyville 1956)★★★.

COMMODORE RECORDS

(see Gabler, Milt)

COMPANY

Derek Bailey established the Company week/festival in 1977 and, despite all the odds, several changes of venue and the occasional annual hiccup, the unpredictability of its financial success (or otherwise) it is still going, strong and ever-surprising, in the early 90s. Bailey's idea was to bring together musicians with a shared interest in improvisation, and the label they laboured under (jazz or not: Bailey would rather avoid the name) was irrelevant. He will assemble a collection of musicians and see what happens, the musicians themselves forming and dissolving playing units as the week goes on. Potentially a recipe for disaster, the results are never less than intriguing, and frequently splendid. Music from many of the sessions has been recorded and some has been issued on Bailey's Incus label.

● ALBUMS: *Company 1* (1976)★★★, *Company 2* (1976)★★★, *Company 3* (1977)★★★, *Company 4* (Incus 1977)★★★, *Company 5* (1978)★★★, *Company 6* (Incus 1978)★★★, *Company 7* (Incus 1978)★★★, *Fictions* (1978)★★★, *Fables* (1980)★★★, *Epiphany* (1982)★★★★, *Trios* recorded 1983 (1986)★★★, *Once* (1988)★★★, *Company 91* (Incus 1992)★★★, *Company 91 Vol 2* (Incus 1992)★★★, *Company 91 Vol 3* (Incus 1992)★★,

COMPLETE BENNY GOODMAN VOLS. 1-7 BENNY GOODMAN

Although there were jazzier bands than Benny Goodman's, more musical and more creative bands, none had the popular and commercial appeal that his enjoyed for two or three glorious years in the 30s. After his breakthrough appearance at the Palomar Ballroom in Los Angeles on 21 August 1935, nothing could stop him. Labelled the 'King of Swing', Goodman offered the public what it wanted: punchy dance music, soloists like Harry James, magnetic showmen like Gene Krupa, and his own impeccable clarinet playing. The personnel was ever-changing thanks to Goodman's irascibility but the band thundered unmistakably on.

● Tracks: including - *He Ain't Got Rhythm; Never Should Have Told You; This Year's Kisses; You Can Tell She Comes From Dixie; Goodnight My Love; I Want To Be Happy; Chloe; Rosetta; Ida, Sweet As Apple Cider; Tea For Two; Runnin' Wild; Peckin'; Can't We Be Friends; Sing, Sing, Sing; Roll 'Em; When It's Sleepytime Down South; Afraid To Dream; Changes; Avalon; Handful Of Keys; The Man I Love; Smiles; Liza (All The Clouds Will Roll Away); Bob White; Sugarfoot Stomp; I Can't Give You Anything But Love Baby; Minnie The Moocher's Wedding Day; Let That Be A Lesson To You; Can't Teach My Old Heart New Tricks; I've Hitched My Wagon To A Star; Pop Corn Man.*

● First Released (recorded 1935-1939)

● UK peak chart position: did not chart

● USA peak chart position: did not chart

COMPLETE LIVE AT THE PLUGGED NICKEL 1965, THE - MILES DAVIS

With Wayne Shorter on sax, Herbie Hancock on piano, Ron Carter on bass and Tony Williams (just 20 years old) on drums, this is regarded as Miles Davis's most creative line-up. *Plugged Nickel* covers seven sets over two days and is an important historical document, not least in demonstrating how the chemistry between five strong musical personalities changes between sessions. To those unable to see him live, Davis's studio albums created a relatively mainstream impression. It was only when this material started to emerge in 1975 that his groundbreaking work in applying chromatic techniques to classic compositions became widely appreciated.

● Tracks: i) *If I Were A Bell; Stella By Starlight; Walkin'; I Fall In Love Too Easily; The Theme* ii) *My Funny Valentine; Four; When I Fall In Love* iii) *Agitation; 'Round About Midnight; Milestones; The Theme* iv) *All Of You; Oleo; I Fall In Love Too Easily; No Blues; I Thought About You; The Theme* v) *If I Were A Bell; Stella By Starlight; Walkin'; I Fall In Love Too Easily; The Theme* vi) *All Of You; Agitation; My Funny Valentine; On Green Dolphin Street; So What; The Theme* vii) *When I Fall In Love; Milestones; Autumn Leaves; I Fall In Love Too Easily; No Blues; The Theme* viii) *Stella By Starlight; All Blues; Yesterdays; The Theme.*

● First Released 1997

● UK peak chart position: did not chart

● USA peak chart position: chart

COMPLETE SAVOY SESSIONS, THE - CHARLIE PARKER

Although they do not contain the number of classic sides found within the Dial collection, the importance of Charlie Parker's Savoy recordings is more than justified by the involvement of bebop piano genius Bud Powell (perhaps the only other true bebopper playing with the level of invention and profundity of Parker himself) and the fascinating play-off between a young and troubled Miles Davis and his own hero Dizzy Gillespie. The Savoy records include the legendary 'KoKo' (a breakneck torrent of improvisation based around the tricky 'Cherokee' chord sequence), and two classic blues in F major: 'Billie's Bounce' and 'Now's The Time'.

● Tracks: *including - Billie's Bounce; Now's The Time i; Now's The Time ii; Thriving On A Riff i; Thriving On A Riff ii; Meandering;*

KoKo; Dizzy Boogie i; Dizzy Boogie ii; Flat Foot Floogie i; Flat Foot Floogie ii; Popity Pop; Slim's Jam.

● First released 1982

● UK peak chart position: did not chart

● USA peak chart position: did not chart

CONCERT BY THE SEA - ERROLL GARNER

Erroll Garner's place in the history of jazz piano is unusual. He demonstrates no obvious influences of any other pianist, he appears to have influenced no-one; and yet his is such a thoroughly engaging, happy, always enjoyable style. Here, he deftly picks his way through a sprightly selection of songs. Throughout, the Elf happily indulges his love for lengthy introductions that defy listeners to identify the coming tune, yet, when he finally arrives at the song as the composer wrote it, everything seems just right. Ageless music in an impishly droll style that defies categorization; it's just Erroll's way. Ask Dudley Moore, he'll tell you.

● Tracks: *I'll Remember April; Teach Me Tonight; Mambo Carmel; It's Alright With Me; Red Top; April In Paris; They Can't Take That Away From Me; Where Or When; Erroll's Theme.*

● First released 1958

● UK peak chart position: did not chart

● USA peak chart position: 12

CONDON, EDDIE

b. 16 November 1905, Goodland, Indiana, USA, d. 4 July 1973. After working in local bands, guitarist and banjoist Condon moved to Chicago in the early 20s. He quickly associated himself with the very finest young white musicians based there: Bix Beiderbecke, Frank Teschemacher, Jimmy McPartland, Bud Freeman, Dave Tough and other members of the Austin High School Gang. In 1928, soon after making his first record, he tried his brand of music in New York, happily starving in between recording dates with, among others, Fats Waller and Louis Armstrong. Despite some indifference amongst audiences, local musicians were impressed both with Condon and some of the friends he had brought along, including Gene Krupa and, later, Jack Teagarden. Condon stayed on in New York, building a reputation as an organizer of concerts and recording dates. A regular at several clubs, notably Nick's, he eventually opened his own which became synonymous with the best of Chicago-style jazz as played by such long-time friends and musical partners as Wild Bill Davison and Pee Wee Russell. A tough-talking, hard-drinking, wisecracking entrepreneur, Condon never lost his abiding love for the music of his youth, dismissing bebop with a joke 'They play their flatted fifths, we drink ours', just as he did to outside criticism 'Do we tell those Frogs how to jump on a grape?'. Unlike many wits, Condon was able to retain his humour in print and his three books provide fascinating and funny insights into the world in which he lived and worked. In his later years he made occasional overseas tours and continued to make record dates. Although a good rhythm player, Condon was often disinclined to perform, leaving his instrument, nicknamed 'Porkchop', in its case while he got on with the serious business of talking to customers and drinking. His reluctance to play often infiltrated record dates and on many he either laid out or contented himself with providing a discreet pulse which only the other musicians could hear. Consequently, he is not necessarily always audible on the records which bear his name.

● ALBUMS: *We Call It Music* (Decca 1950)★★★, *George Gershwin Jazz Concert* (Decca 1950)★★★★, *Jazz Concert At Eddie Condon's* (Decca 1950)★★★, *Eddie Condon* (Jazz Panorama 1951)★★★, *Jam Session Coast To Coast* (1953)★★★, *Eddie Condon's Hot Shots* (X 1954)★★★, *Jammin' At Condon's* (Columbia 1955)★★★★, *Eddie Condon And His Orchestra Featuring Pee Wee Russell* (Jolly Roger 1955)★★★, *Bixieland* (Columbia 1955)★★★, *Ringside At Condon's* (Savoy 1956)★★★, *Treasury Of Jazz* (Columbia 1956)★★★, *Dixieland Dance Party* (Dot 1958)★★★★, *The Roaring 20s* (Columbia 1958)★★★, *Eddie Condon Is Uptown Now* (MGM 1960)★★★, *Jam Session At Commodore* (Stateside 1962), *Condon A La Carte* (Staeside 1962)★★★, *Live In Tokyo* (1964)★★★, *Eddie Condon A Legend* (Mainstream 1965)★★★★, with Wild Bill Davison, Gene Krupa *Jazz At The New School* (1972)★★★★.

● COMPILATIONS: *The Spirit Of Condon* (1979)★★★, *Intoxicating Dixieland (1944-45)* (1981)★★★★, *The Eddie Condon Band (1945)* (1981)★★★★, *The Eddie Condon Floorshow, Volumes 1 and 2 (1949)* (Queendisc 1981)★★★, *His Windy City 7 Jam Sessions At Commodore (1935)* (1985)★★★★, *Chicago Style (1927-33)* (VJM 1985)★★★, *The Town Hall Broadcasts (1944-45)* (1986)★★★, *The Town Hall Concerts, Volumes 1-6 (1944-45)* (Jazzology 1988)★★★, *At The Jazz Band Ball (1944-50)* (1986)★★★★, *The Liederkranz Sessions* (1987)★★★, *Jazz On The Air - Eddie Condon Floorshow* (Delta 1988)★★★, *Dixieland Jam* (CBS 1991)★★★, *We Dig Dixieland Jazz* (Savoy 1993)★★★.

● VIDEOS: *Good Years Of Jazz Volume 4* (Storyville 1990).

● FURTHER READING: *We Called It Music*, Eddie Condon and T. Sugrue. *Eddie Condon's Treasury Of Jazz*, no editor listed. *The Eddie Condon Scrapbook Of Jazz*, Eddie Condon and Hank O'Neal.

CONFERENCE OF THE BIRDS - DAVE HOLLAND

A challenging but hugely rewarding ECM Records classic, *Conference Of The Birds* is a delicate balance of Ornette Coleman-influenced free improvisation with rhythm and more fragmented response playing. Sam Rivers and Anthony Braxton share the dynamic front line, both playing assorted reeds and flute, while drums, percussion and marimba are provided by Barry Altschul. Dave Holland has always been a fine composer, and his distinctive tunes and rich, resonant and flawlessly accurate bass playing stamp a subtle identity on this work. The title track, in particular, is a sombre and painfully beautiful masterpiece, shifting gently on a tapestry of flute, soprano saxophone and marimba.

● Tracks: *Four Winds; Q&A; Conference Of The Birds; Interceprion; Now Here (Nowhere); See-Saw.*

● First released 1972

● UK peak chart position: did not chart

● USA peak chart position: did not chart

Connor, Chris

b. 8 November 1927, Kansas City, Missouri, USA. After singing publicly while still at school, Connor worked with the bands of Claude Thornhill, where she was a member of the vocal group, the Snowflakes, and Herbie Fields in the late 40s and early 50s. Audibly influenced by Anita O'Day, Connor quickly developed her own recognizable style and built a localized reputation. Having sung in high school with a Kenton-style band it was especially appropriate when June Christy, in 1953, recommended Connor to Stan Kenton as her replacement, after this period her career was much enhanced. She continued singing for the next 30-plus years, working mostly as a soloist and usually with jazz musicians in her backing group. In the late 80s she was to be heard singing in Europe showing a few signs of deterioration in her voice while, stylistically, she was as good as ever. In 1990 she was a featured artist at London's Soho Jazz Festival.

● ALBUMS: *Chris Connor Sings Lullabys Of Birdland* 10-inch album (Bethlehem 1954)★★★★, *Chris Connor Sings Lullabys For Lovers* 10-inch album (Bethlehem 1954)★★, *This Is Chris* (Bethlehem 1955)★★, *Chris* (Bethlehem 1956)★★★, *Chris Connor* (Atlantic 1956)★★★, *He Loves Me, He Loves Me Not* (Atlantic 1956)★★★, *I Miss You So* (Atlantic 1956)★★★, with Julie London, Carmen McRae *Bethlehem Girl Friends* (Bethlehem 1956)★★★, *Chris Connor Sings The George Gershwin Almanac Of Song* (Atlantic 1957)★★★★, *A Jazz Date With Chris Connor* (Atlantic 1958)★★★★, *Chris Craft* (Atlantic 1958)★★★, *Ballads Of The Sad Cafe* (Atlantic 1959)★★★, *Chris In Person* (Atlantic 1959)★★★, *Witchcraft* (Atlantic 1959)★★★, *A Portrait Of Chris* (Atlantic 1960)★★, with Maynard Ferguson *Double Exposure* (Atlantic 1961)★★★, with Ferguson *Two's Company* (Roulette 1961)★★★, *Free Spirits* (Atlantic 1962)★★★, *Chris Connor At The Village Gate* (FM 1963)★★★★, *A Weekend In Paris* (FM 1964)★★★, *Gentle Bossa Nova* (ABC-Paramount 1965)★★★, *Chris Connor Now* (ABC-Paramount 1966)★★★, *Sketches* (1972)★★★, *Chris Moves* (1976)★★★, *Sweet And Swinging* (Progressive 1978)★★★, *Alone Together* (1978)★★★, *Chris Connor Live* (1981)★★, *I Hear Music* (Affinity 1983)★★★, *Love Being Here With You* (Stash 1983)★★★, *Classic* (Contemporary 1987)★★★, *New Again* (Contemporary 1987)★★★, *As Time Goes By* (Enja 1991)★★★★, *London Connection* (Audiophile 1993)★★★.

Connors, Bill

b. 24 September 1949, Los Angeles, California, USA. Like so many young men of his generation, Connors was attracted to rock music and the electric guitar. His interest underwent a slight shift of direction and he became a leading figure of the jazz/rock scene of the early 70s. He toured with Chick Corea's then current Return To Forever band and also played with fellow jazz/rock bass guitarist Stanley Clarke. By the late 70s, Connors, ever searching, had also moved into free jazz and during these years he worked with Lee Konitz, Gary Peacock, Jan Garbarek and others. In addition to playing electric guitar, Connors also occasionally plays the acoustic instrument, for example on his solo album, *Theme To The Guardian*. His first love, however, remained the electric guitar and stylistically he has always been most at home playing jazz/rock.

● ALBUMS: *Theme To The Guardian* (ECM 1974)★★★★, *Step It* (Core 1985)★★★, *Double Up* (Core 1985)★★★, *Assembler* (Line 1989)★★★★, *Swimming With A Hole In My Body* (ECM 1992)★★★★, *Of Mist And Melting* (ECM 1993)★★★.

Connors, Chuck

b. Charles Raymond Connors, 18 August 1930, Maysville, Kentucky, USA, d. 11 December 1994. He took up the trombone, studying extensively and taking a degree in music at Boston University in 1956. Preferring the bass trombone, he joined Dizzy Gillespie the year after graduation but then found work hard to come by. He worked in industry for a while but then, in 1961, he joined Duke Ellington where the rich sonority of his uncommon instrument was an additional colour for the composer's palette. He remained with Ellington until the leader's death in 1974 and thereafter stayed with the band under the direction of Mercer Ellington. During the 60s and 70s Connors recorded with several small groups under the leadership of various Ellingtonians. The nature of his instrument meant that Connor's work was reserved almost exclusively for the brass section but he can be heard interestingly on 'I Love To Laugh' on the 1964 *Mary Poppins* with Ellington.

Connors, Gene 'Mighty Flea'

b. 28 December 1930, Birmingham, Alabama, USA. Flea's family was musical and as a youngster he learned to play trombone and subsequently worked with many jazz legends, including Bunk Johnson, Lionel Hampton, and Count Basie. He enjoyed a very long association with Johnny Otis, and even had a minor R&B hit in 1968 with 'Ode To Billie Joe' on the Eldo label. He has recorded with a long list of jazz, blues, R&B, and soul artists, and came to Europe with Otis in 1972, when he made an album for Big Bear Records which showed that he also has a light, pleasant singing voice. Since then, he has been based in Europe and has recorded and worked in a variety of musical settings; as his calling-card states, he plays 'Rhythm And Blues-Swing-Dixie'.

● ALBUMS: *Let The Good Times Roll* (Big Bear 1972)★★★, *Sanctified* (1981)★★★.

Connors, Norman

b. 1 March 1948, Philadelphia, USA. Connors took up drums and was writing his own music from the age of five. After graduating from school he pursued music as a career, working with Billy Paul, Jack McDuff, John Coltrane and Charles Earland. He moved to New York in 1971 and was immediately hired by Pharaoh Sanders, touring the world with his band and appearing on five of his albums. In 1972 he signed as a solo artist with the Buddah subsidiary Cobblestone Records, recording his first album, *Dance Of Magic*, that same year. After recording a follow-up, *Dark Of Light*, Cobblestone

Records folded and Connors was switched to the main Buddah label. After two albums (*Live From The Sun* and *Slewfoot*) had enhanced his reputation on the UK jazz-funk scene, he began to achieve major success in his US homeland, owing to his championing the talents of artists such as Michael Henderson, Jean Carne and Phyllis Hyman. He collaborated with singer-songwriter Henderson on 'Valentine Love' from *Saturday Night Special*, a Top 100 hit in 1975 and then, a year later, broke into the US Top 30 with the title track of *You Are My Starship* (incidentally, the boat used on the cover of this album belonged to the actor John Wayne). Connors recorded five more albums for Buddah in a similar vein, showcasing the talents of Eleanor Mills, Prince Philip Mitchell, Glenn Jones, the Jones Girls and Beau Williams (and featuring Henry Fonda's aeroplane on the cover of *Romantic Journey*), although without breaking back into the pop charts. He also successfully developed a career as an outside producer, forming and guiding the Starship Orchestra and producing Aquarian Dream, Pharaoh Sanders, Al Johnson, Phyllis Hyman and Jean Carne. In 1988 he signed as a solo artist with Capitol Records, releasing one album, *Passion*, and producing Angela Bofill for the label before being chosen to spearhead Motown's jazz launch, MoJazz, recording *Remember Who You Are* in 1993.

● ALBUMS: *Dance Of Magic* (Cobblestone 1972)★★★, *Dark Of Light* (Cobblestone 1972)★★★, *Live From The Sun* (Buddah 1973)★★, with Jean Carne *Slewfoot* (Buddah 1974)★★, with Carne *Saturday Night Special* (Buddah 1975)★★, *You Are My Starship* (Buddah 1976)★★, *Romantic Journey* (Buddah 1977)★★★, with Carne *This Is Your Life* (Buddah 1978)★★, with Carne *Invitation* (Buddah 1979)★★★, *Take It To The Limit* (Arista 1980)★★★, *Mr C* (Buddah 1981)★★★, *Passion* (Capitol 1988)★★★, *Remember Who You Are* (MoJazz 1993)★★★.

● COMPILATIONS: *Best Of Norman Connors And Friends* (Buddah 1979)★★★, *Best Of ...* (Sequel 1990)★★★.

CONSPIRACY

This free-improvising group was formed in May 1989 by Adam Bohman (b. 12 August 1959, Leicester, England; prepared strings) and Nick Couldry (b. 1 July 1958, Epsom, Surrey, England; keyboards) who met at Phil Wachsmann's improvisation class at the City Literary Institute in London. They were joined by Barry Edgar Pilcher (b. 10 June 1943, Beckenham, Kent, England; saxophone) and Andy Hammond (b. 22 June 1958, Maidstone, Kent, England; electric guitars), the latter from the rock-influenced band Yo Seagull. In July 1989 Conspiracy were chosen from 50 entries to perform at the Society For The Promotion Of New Music's Improvisation Day at London's Donmar Warehouse. *The Beaufort Scale* confirmed the group's growing reputation as purveyors of intelligent abstract music with a strong emotional charge. *Wire* magazine called it, 'a magnificent debut . . . very original and unnervingly powerful'. In autumn 1990 Pilcher departed to be replaced by John Telfer (b. 11 January 1963, Gillingham, Kent; baritone and alto saxophones/flute). Throughout 1991 the group worked intensively in London, occasionally with percussionists Eddie Prévost and Mark Sanders. They also collaborated on a mixed-media project with the sculptor Chris Dorsett, performing in museums and other spaces not usually associated with music. Their influences range from contemporary classical composers like Xenakis and Berio, to the experimental rock of Fred Frith and 60s improvisers AMM. Conspiracy also founded the Polar Bear Club in London which is devoted to the promotion of improvised and experimental music.

● ALBUMS: *The Beaufort Scale* (1990)★★★.

CONTE, PAULO

b. Asti, Piemonte, Italy. After spending much of his professional life as a lawyer, jazz enthusiast Paulo Conte eventually decided to act on his impulse to become a performer in the 80s. He quickly amassed a huge audience for his gentle, acoustic jazz, which often incorporates native Latin elements such as the tango, samba and quadrille. Particular praise has been reserved for his evocative, and often exotic, lyrics. His live performances are usually interspersed with poetry readings, and have won him an international following stretching beyond linguistic boundaries. As evidence of this, he performed a sell-out concert at the Barbican Centre in London, England, in March 1995, prompting *Billboard* magazine to conclude that he had become 'an essential name-drop at UK dinner parties.'

● ALBUMS: *Novecento* (CGD 1992)★★★, *Tournee* live album (CGD 1994)★★, *Una Faccia In Prestito* (CDG/East West 1995)★★★.

CONTEMPORARY RECORDS

Formed in 1951 by Lester Koenig (b. 1918, d. 1977), this US label became synonymous with the best in west coast jazz. Previously, Koenig had formed Good Time Jazz, which specialized in traditional jazz and the bands of the post-war revival movement. The first records by the Lighthouse All Stars, originally released on Lighthouse, were reissued by Contemporary which utilized the Lighthouse trademark and logo. Koenig then invited Shelly Manne to build the new label's repertoire. Manne recorded under his own name and also organized sessions led by Shorty Rogers which produced several outstanding albums, including *Cool And Crazy*. Among the musicians involved in Contemporary's swiftly-growing catalogue were Art Pepper, Bud Shank, Curtis Counce, Lennie Niehaus, Hampton Hawes, André Previn, Sonny Rollins, Harold Land, Jack Sheldon, Marty Paich, Don Cherry and Ornette Coleman. Under Koenig, Contemporary flourished for a quarter of a century, chronicling the development of west coast jazz. In addition to his interest in all kinds of jazz, Koenig also recorded classical music. After his death, Koenig's company was run by his son until it was taken over by Fantasy Records. A massive reissue programme in the 90s and new recordings by familiar west coast names continues to make Contemporary a major force in modern jazz.

Cook, Doc

b. Charles L. Cooke, 3 September 1891, Louisville, Kentucky, USA, d. 25 December 1958. As a young man he came to Detroit where he worked as a pianist and arranger. Moving to Chicago, he studied at the Musical College, gaining a doctorate in music, and a lifelong nickname. From 1922 until the end of the decade he led dance bands for long residencies at several noted venues including Harmon's Dreamland Café. Although primarily aimed at the popular audience, his bands included from time to time several noted jazzmen of the day, including Freddie Keppard, Jimmie Noone, Don Pasquall and Andrew Hilaire. From 1930 Cook was resident in New York working mostly as a staff arranger for Radio-Keith-Orpheum (RKO) and Radio City Music Hall. He continued these activities for more than a decade, retiring in the mid-40s. Although a good pianist, Cook's long years as a bandleader and arranger form the greater part of his contribution to the music industry.

Cook, Junior

b. Herman Cook, 22 July 1934, Pensacola, Florida, USA, d. 3 February 1992, New York City, New York, USA. Raised in a musical family, Cook began playing alto saxophone, then later switched to tenor. He joined Dizzy Gillespie in the late 50s and also played with Horace Silver. He remained with Silver for about five years, after which he teamed up with Blue Mitchell for another long stint. In the early 70s he taught at Berklee College Of Music. During the early and mid-70s he played with Freddie Hubbard, then with Louis Hayes. During the late 70s and early 80s Cook recorded with several artists, including Mickey Tucker, Clifford Jordan and Eddie Jefferson and led his own small group for club and festival dates. He also formed a band with Bill Hardman, Jnr. (1979-81). A highly talented post-bop saxophonist, Cook's abilities, while well-served on record, were not fully recognized by the international jazz world.

● ALBUMS: *Junior's Cookin'* (Jazzland 1961)★★★★, *Pressure Cooker* (Affinity 1978)★★★, with Bill Hardman *Good Cookin'* (Muse 1979)★★★, *Somethin's Cookin'* (Muse 1981)★★★★, *The Place To Be* (Steeple Chase 1988)★★★, *On A Misty Night* (Steeple Chase 1989)★★★, with George Coleman *Stablemates* (Affinity 1990)★★★, *You Leave Me Breathless* (Steeple Chase 1992)★★★.

Cook, Willie

b. 11 November 1923, Tangipahoa, Louisiana, USA. After studying music in school, Cook began his professional career in the early 40s and quickly graduated to the bands of Jay McShann and Earl Hines where he stayed for five years. In 1948 he was briefly in the Jimmie Lunceford band which was struggling on after the leader's sudden death. He then worked with Dizzy Gillespie and Gerald Wilson and for a while acted as musical director to Billie Holiday. After fleetingly working outside music he joined Duke Ellington in 1951 and remained an intermittent member of the band until the early 70s. During this same period Cook, a first-class lead trumpeter, also worked with several Ellingtonians and toured solo. He left music again for a while, resuming playing in the late 70s mainly in Europe and Scandinavia. He settled and married in Sweden, recording extensively there and briefly visiting other countries including the UK in the mid-80s. Highly regarded by fellow musicians, and especially by Ellington, Cook's playing is melodic, his sound fresh and clear.

● ALBUMS: *Christl Mood* (1984)★★★.

Cooke, Micky

b. 6 August 1945, Hyde, Cheshire, England. Trombonist Cooke began his career as a semi-pro player with Manchester band the Blue Lotus Jazzmen in the early 60s, and also played with many other local outfits including the Smoky City Jazzband, Johnny Tippet's Jazzmen, and the Red River Jazzmen. In 1967 he left Manchester for Birmingham, before moving further south to join Terry Lightfoot in 1968. Following spells with bandleaders Alan Elsdon and Alex Welsh, Cooke worked as a freelance with Digby Fairweather, Lennie Hastings and Dave Shepherd, before beginning a seven-year association with Keith Smith, with whose 'Hefty Jazz' he recorded and toured extensively, visiting the US in 1985. He has a justified reputation as one of Britain's most technically-gifted trombonists, and plays in a hot, shouting style, strongly influenced by Abe Lincoln. In mid-1987 Cooke replaced Campbell Burnap in the Acker Bilk band.

Cookin' - Miles Davis

One of a series of important albums recorded for Prestige Records during the 50s that also included the excellent *Workin'* and *Steamin'*. Miles Davis's dream quintet also included John Coltrane and Red Garland (piano), Paul Chambers (bass) and the breathing brushwork of Philly Joe Jones. Of the dozens of line-ups over many years, this unit is still spoken of with sparkling eyes by those who saw them play during their two years together. One of his best recordings of 'My Funny Valentine' is on this disc, as well as a definitive 'Blues By Five'. The title was Davis's: 'after all, that's what we did, came in and cooked'.

● Tracks: *My Funny Valentine; Blues By Five; Airegin; Tune Up.*
● First released 1957
● UK peak chart position: did not chart
● USA peak chart position: did not chart

Cool Blues - Jimmy Smith

Of all the albums recorded by Jimmy Smith for Blue Note Records, this is the best example of what he could do before he started to coast, both as a purveyor of orchestrated organ music, but more importantly in his awareness that he was the world's greatest and most successful jazz organist. Both *House Party* and *The Sermon* are excellent albums, but this is more worthy because it is captured live. Recorded at a New York club it features, among others, Lou Donaldson (alto), and Art

Blakey and Donald Bailey (drums). Smith plays as though he means it, especially on 'Groovin' At Small's' and 'A Night In Tunisia'.

- Tracks: *Dark Eyes; Cool Blues; A Night In Tunisia; What's New; Small's Minor; Once In A While; Groovin' At Small's.*
- First released 1958
- UK peak chart position: did not chart
- USA peak chart position: did not chart

Cooper, Al

(see Savoy Sultans)

Cooper, Alan

b. 15 February 1931, Leeds, Yorkshire, England. Playing several instruments, notably different members of the clarinet family, Cooper has made a valuable contribution to various traditional jazz bands in the UK. In particular, he was a member of the Yorkshire Jazz Band and also played with the Temperance 7. Although settings such as these might have proved to be confining for a lesser musician, Cooper was able to display a large measure of originality in his playing. As distinguished an observer of the British jazz scene as Digby Fairweather, with whom Cooper has recorded, has likened him, with considerable justification, to Sandy Brown which is praise indeed. Not surprisingly, therefore, Cooper was chosen by Fairweather to play on a tribute to Brown.

- ALBUMS: *Songs For Sandy* (Hep 1982)★★★.

Cooper, Bob

b. 6 December 1925, Pittsburgh, Pennsylvania, USA, d. 5 August 1993, Hollywood, California, USA. After studying music at high school, Cooper showed early prowess on tenor saxophone and by the age of 20 was hired by Stan Kenton, with whom he remained for the next six years. During this period Cooper made numerous records with the band and also led a small group largely drawn from fellow sidemen. On some engagements he accompanied Kenton's singer, June Christy, whom he married in 1947. After Kenton, Cooper stayed on the west coast working in the studios and playing jazz with like-minded musicians, especially Shelly Manne and Shorty Rogers. Throughout the 60s, 70s and 80s, Cooper continued working, mainly on the coast, dividing his time between the studios and jazz groups including those led by Terry Gibbs and his old stablemate Rogers. He was also called upon by several of the big bands formed in California, including those led by Bob Florence, Frank Capp-Nat Pierce and Bill Berry. A fluent and inventive soloist, Cooper's bop and post-bop leanings were often submerged in his freewheeling, swing-orientated playing.

- ALBUMS: *Bob Cooper* (Capitol 1954)★★★, *Shifting Winds* (Capitol 1955)★★★, *The Travelling Mr Cooper* (1957)★★★, *Bob Cooper Swings TV* (World Pacific 1958)★★, *Coop!* (Contemporary 1958)★★★★, *Do Re Mi* (Capitol 1961)★★★★, *Tenor Sax Jazz Impressions* (Trend 1979)★★★, *Bob Cooper Plays The Music Of Michel Legrand* (Discovery 1980)★★, *Group Activity (1954-55)* (Affinity 1981)★★★, *Shifting Winds (1954-55)* (Affinity 1981)★★★, *In A Mellotone* (1985)★★, with Bob Florence *Trash Can City* (1986)★★★, *For All We Know* (Fresh Sound 1991)★★★, *Mosaic* (Capri 1993)★★★, *Bob Cooper/Conte Condoli Quintet* (VSOP 1995)★★★.

Cooper, Buster

b. George Cooper, 4 April 1929, St. Petersburg, Florida, USA. Coming from a musical family - his brother Steve plays bass-trombonist Cooper worked briefly in a band led by a cousin, then joined Nat Towles's famous Texas-based band. He later advanced his musical knowledge studying in New York before joining Lionel Hampton in 1953. He spent the rest of the 50s working with various bands including those led by Benny Goodman and Lucky Millinder and also co-leading a band with his brother. In 1962 he joined Duke Ellington, who would sometimes dryly introduce him as 'Trombonio-Bustoso-issimo', where he remained for seven years before returning to his home state and another joint band with his brother. In the early 70s he decided to relocate to the west coast and since then has worked with several big bands, notably those led by Frank Capp-Nat Pierce and Bill Berry. He has also toured both as a soloist and with Berry and Marshal Royal as an Ellington alumni group. A powerful player with a brilliant technique, Cooper's solos are frequently characterized by humour and extraordinary cadenzas which leave audiences and fellow musicians breathless. In a more mellow mood, when he performs ballads, he brings to his playing an attractive and delicately-romantic touch.

Cooper, Jerome

b. 14 December 1946, Chicago, Illinois, USA. Cooper came up drumming with blues bands on Chicago's south side and stormed awhile with Rahsaan Roland Kirk. In Paris, he worked with Steve Lacy and the Art Ensemble Of Chicago, then quit the freelancing life to commit his energies to the influential Revolutionary Ensemble (1970-1977), which he co-founded. Despite surfacing briefly as Cecil Taylor's drummer, Cooper has, since 1978, concentrated primarily on solo performances in which he augments his drum kit with African talking drum and balafon and also plays chirimia (a high-pitched oboe of Spanish origin) and synthesizer. He cites shamanism as an important influence on his work and collaborates periodically with the similarly-inspired English performance artist Colin Gilder, Cooper providing the live soundtrack - both improvised and composed - to Gilder's plays and happenings.

- ALBUMS: *Positions 369* (1977)★★★, *Root Assumptions* (1978)★★★, *For The People* (1979)★★★, *The Unpredictability Of Predictability* (1980)★★, *Outer And Interactions* (1988)★★★.

Cooper, Lindsay

b. March 1951, London, England. Multi-instrumentalist Cooper studied at Dartington College and the Royal Academy Of Music, becoming proficient on bassoon, sopranino and alto saxophones, oboe, flute, piano and accordion, though in recent years she concentrated almost exclusively on the first three of these instruments. After working briefly as a classical bassoonist, she turned her attention to theatre, pop and improvised musics. From 1974-78 she was a member of experimental rock group Henry Cow; in 1977 she co-founded the Feminist Improvising Group, its name indicating the primary concern of much of her subsequent work, notably in projects with other FIG and EWIG (European Women's Improvising Group) artists such as Maggie Nicols, Anna Marie Roelofs, Joëlle Léandre and Irène Schweizer. In the early 80s she was a regular performer on the European jazz scene, playing on various Mike Westbrook projects (*The Cortege, Westbrook-Rossini*) and joining the Maarten Altena Octet (*Tel*). She also kept a foot in the rock camp, recording with David Thomas's Pedestrians (*Winter Comes Home, More Places For Ever*) and as part of the group News From Babel (with Chris Cutler), Dagmar Krause and Zeena Parkins). A talented composer, her own *Rags*, *The Gold Diggers* and *Music For Other Occasions* comprised pieces she had written for various film, television and theatre projects, often in association with singer/director Sally Potter. In 1989 Cooper's song-cycle *Oh Moscow* was recorded live at Canada's Victoriaville Festival; 1991 saw the release of both the classically-oriented *An Angel On The Bridge* and a collection of contemporary dance pieces, *Schrodinger's Cat*. In 1992 her 'Concerto For Sopranino Saxophone And Strings' was premiered in London by the European Women's Orchestra, and her new 'Songs For Bassoon And Orchestra' was presented in Bologna. The same year, her chamber pieces 'The Road Is Wider Than Long' was included on Lontrano's *British Women Composers Volume 1*, and the long jazz vocal composition *Sahara Dust* (lyrics by Robyn Archer) was released, reaffirming her rare gift of versatility across so many musical genres.

● ALBUMS: *Feminist Improvising Group* (1979)★★, *Rags*, (1980)★★★, *The Gold Diggers* (1983)★★★, with Maggie Nicols, Joëlle Léandre *Live At The Bastille* 1982 recording (1984)★★, with News From Babel *Work Resumed On The Tower* (1984)★★★, with News From Babel *Letters Home* (1986)★★★, *Music For Other Occasions* (1986)★★★, *An Angel On The Bridge* (1991)★★★, *Schrodinger's Cat* (Femme 1991)★★★, with others *British Women Composers Volume 1* (1992)★★★★, *Sahara Dust* (1992)★★★, *Oh Moscow* (Victor 1993)★★★.

Copeland, Ray

b. 17 July 1926, Norfolk, Virginia, USA, d. 18 May 1984, Norfolk, Virginia, USA. Copeland was taught classical trumpet before he started to play with jazz groups in Brooklyn in the mid-40s. He then played with the bands of Mercer Ellington, Andy Kirk, Sy Oliver, Lionel Hampton, Oscar Pettiford and the Savoy Sultans. He settled in New York to play for the Roxy Theatre Orchestra (1959-61), for Bellson And Bailey (1962-64) and for Ella Fitzgerald (1965). He was a technically excellent musician who played with a firm, clear tone. In 1966 he joined Randy Weston's band (piano) and journeyed with him to the African continent (1967) and Morocco (1970). Between these trips he toured Europe with Thelonious Monk (piano). In the 70s he had his own orchestra in New York and premiered his *Classical Jazz Suite In Six Movements* at the Lincoln Centre (1970). He brought the review *A Musical Life of Charlie Parker* to Europe in 1974. During the 80s he taught at Hampshire College, Massachusetts. He later died of a heart attack in 1984.

Copland, Marc

b. 27 May 1948, Philadelphia, Pennsylvania, USA. Playing saxophone, Copland was a part of the vibrant music scene in Philadelphia before going to New York where he met John Abercrombie and also played with Chico Hamilton, Ralph Towner and others. He experimented with the electric alto saxophone but gradually became dissatisfied with the direction his music was taking and quit playing saxophone in order to study piano. He was gone for almost a decade but upon his return to the jazz world in the mid-80s his piano playing was a revelation. At first he might have displayed hints of influences such as Bill Evans, Keith Jarrett and Herbie Hancock, but before the decade was out his own vividly original style was firmly in place. During these years he played with Joe Lovano, Jane Ira Bloom, Tim Hagans, James Moody, Wallace Roney and many others, including recording sessions at which he was reunited with Abercrombie. He also built long-lasting musical relationships with bassist Gary Peacock and drummer Billy Hart. In the late 90s Copland's international fame was spreading, owing in part to several well-received albums and tours, including one late 1998 European date which brought him once again into partnership with Abercrombie. Copland's playing is harmonically rich and filled with colour that especially enhances his ballad playing. On up-tempo numbers his playing not only demonstrates quicksilver thinking, but also the technical skills needed to realize his brilliant conceptions. As an accompanist Copland is especially gifted, fashioning an undercurrent of swing that makes any band burn. In addition to playing piano, Copland is also an accomplished composer and teacher.

● ALBUMS: *All Blues At Night* (Jazz City 1990)★★★, *My Foolish Heart* (Jazz City 1991)★★★, with Stan Sulzmann *Never At All* (Future Music 1993)★★, *Songs Without End* (Jazz City 1993)★★★, *At Night* (Sunnyside 1995)★★★, *What's Goin' On?* (Jazzline 1995)★★, *Stompin' With Savoy* (Savoy Jazz 1995)★★★★, *Second Look* (Savoy Jazz 1997)★★★★, with Dieter Ilg *Two Way Street* (Jazzline 1997)★★★, *Paradiso* (Soul Note 1997)★★★, *Softly ...* (Savoy Jazz 1998)★★★★.

Corea, Chick

b. Armando Anthony Corea, 12 June 1941, Chelsea, Massachusetts, USA. After a very musical home environment, pianist Corea's first notable professional engagements were in the Latin bands of Mongo Santamaría and Willie Bobo (1962-63), playing a style of music that continues to influence him today. Joining Blue Mitchell's band in 1964, he spent two years with the trumpeter, and had a chance to record some of his own compositions on Blue Note Records. Corea's first recordings appeared in 1966 with *Tones For Joan's Bones*, and show a pianist influenced mainly by hard-bop. In 1968, he joined Miles Davis for the trumpeter's first real experiments with fusion. Playing on some of Davis's most important albums, Corea's electric piano became integral to the new sound. Leaving Davis in 1970 to explore free music within an acoustic setting, he formed Circle with Dave Holland, Barry Altschul, and later Anthony Braxton. Although Circle lasted only a year, it managed to make some important recordings before Corea, now involved in Scientology, became interested in a style with more widespread appeal. Forming the first of three bands called Return To Forever in 1971, he played a Latin-influenced fusion featuring the vocalist Flora Purim and percussionist Airto Moreiro, before he changed the band's line-up to produce a more rock-orientated sound in the mid-70s. The final Return To Forever hinted at classical music with string and brass groups, but disbanded in 1980 after only moderate success. After playing with numerous top musicians in the early 80s (including Herbie Hancock and Michael Brecker), since 1985 he has concentrated on his Akoustic and Elektric Bands and now records for GRP Records. Joined by John Patitucci (bass) and Dave Weckl (drums), he is presently involved in a music that challenges the extremes of virtuosity, mixing passages of complex arrangement with solos in the fusion style.

● ALBUMS: *Tones For Joan's Bones* reissued as *Inner Space* (Atlantic 1966)★★★, *Now He Sings, Now He Sobs* (Solid State 1969)★★★★, *Is* (Solid State 1969)★★★, *The Song Of Singing* (Blue Note 1970)★★★★, with Circle *Circulus* (Blue Note 1970)★★★, with Circle *Early Circle* (Blue Note 1971)★★★, with Circle *Paris-Concert* (ECM 1971)★★★★, with Barry Altshcul, Dave Holland *A.R.C.* (ECM 1971)★★★, *Piano Improvisations Vol. 1* (ECM 1971)★★★★, *Piano Improvisations Vol. 2* (ECM 1971)★★★★, with Gary Burton *Crystal Silence* (ECM 1973)★★★★, *Sun Dance* 1969 recording (People 1974)★★, *Chick Corea* 1968-1970 recordings (Blue Note 1975)★★★★, *Chick Corea Quartet: Live In New York City, 1974* (Oxford 1975)★★★, *My Spanish Heart* (Polydor 1976)★★★★, *Circling In* 1968-1970 recordings (Blue Note 1976)★★★★, *The Mad Hatter* (Polydor 1978)★★★, *Friends* (Polydor 1978)★★★, *Secret Agent* (Polydor 1978)★★★, with Burton *Duet* (ECM 1978)★★★★, with Herbie Hancock *An Evening With Herbie Hancock And Chick Corea* (Columbia 1979)★★★, with Hancock *Homecoming: Corea And Hancock* (Polydor 1979)★★★, *Delphi 1: Solo Piano Improvisations* (Polydor 1979)★★★, *In Concert, Zurich, October 28, 1978* (ECM 1980)★★★, *Delphi 2 & 3* (1980), *Tap Step* (Warners 1980)★★★, *Three Quartets* (Warners 1981)★★★, with Haynes *Trio Music* (ECM 1981)★★★★, *Touchstone* (Streych 1982),★★★ with Nicolas Economou *On Two Pianos* (1982)★★★, with Friedrich Gulda *The Meeting* (1982)★★★, *Again And Again (The Joburg Sessions)* (Elektra 1983)★★★, *Children's Songs* (ECM 1983)★★★★, with Burton *Lyric Suite For Sextet* (ECM 1983)★★★, *Trio Music, Live In Europe* (ECM 1984)★★★★, *Septet* (ECM 1985)★★★, with Steve Kujala *Voyage* (ECM 1985)★★★★, *Early Days* 1969 recordings (LRC 1986)★★★, *The Chick Corea Elektric Band* (GRP 1986)★★★★, with Haynes, Vitous *Trio Music: Live In Europe* (1987)★★, *Light Years* (GRP 1987)★★, *Eye Of The Beholder* (GRP 1988)★★, *Chick Corea Akoustic Band* (GRP 1989)★★★★, *Inside Out* (GRP 1990)★★★, *Beneath The Mask* (GRP 1991)★★, *Alive* (GRP 1991)★★★, with Bobby McFerrin *Play* (1992)★★★, *Inner Space* (Atlantic 1993)★★★, *Paint The World* (GRP 1993)★★★, *Expressions* (GRP 1994)★★★, with Chick Corea Quartet *Time Warp* (Stretch 1995)★★★, *Remembering Bud Powell* (Stretch 1997)★★★★, with Burton *Native Sense: The New Duets* (Concord Jazz 1998)★★★, *Origin: Live At The Blue Note* (Concord Jazz 1998)★★★★.

● COMPILATIONS: *Verve Jazz Masters* (Verve 1979)★★★, *Chick Corea Works* (ECM 1985)★★★★, *Early Days* 1969 recording (LRC 1988)★★★, *Compact Jazz: Chick Corea* 1972-1976 recordings (Verve 1991)★★★, *Music Forever & Beyond: The Selected Works Of Chick Corea 1964-1996* 5-CD box set (GRP 1996)★★★★.

● VIDEOS: *Live In Madrid* (Channel 5 1987), *Inside Out* (GRP Video 1992), *Time Warp - One World Over* (GRP Video 1995).

CORNFORD, BOB

b. Robert Leslie Cornford, 15 May 1940, Brazil, d. 18 July 1983. Encouraged in his musical interests, in particular the piano, by his family (his British parents were resident in South America at the time of his birth), Cornford studied at London's Royal College of Music. While in his twenties he developed an interest in jazz and became a member of John Dankworth's band and also arranged and orchestrated for the BBC. He was also a composer of note, writing extended works in tribute to Bill Evans, his earliest piano idol, and Ben Webster, both of which were performed by the German radio orchestra, NDR. His music has also been performed by the Danish State Radio Orchestra. He played with many important jazz artists, among them Mark Murphy, Norma Winstone, Bobby Wellins, Lee Konitz and Tony Coe, with whom he recorded *Tournée* (Nato French 1981). Cornford's great talent, sadly cut off while still very much at its height, lay not only in his discreet skills as a pianist but in his remarkable ability as a composer. His longer works, like the tributes to Evans and Webster, 'In Memoriam' and 'Coalescence' respectively, show him to have been a writer with considerable and highly original skill.

CORTEZ, DAVE 'BABY'

b. David Cortez Clowney, 13 August 1938, Detroit, Michigan, USA. Cortez played piano in church as a boy and progressed from there to Hammond organ, performing on the chittlin' circuit through the Midwest and California in the late 50s. From 1955-57 he performed with vocal group the Pearls and in 1956-57 also worked with the Valentines. In 1956 he made his first recording (under the name of Dave Clooney) for the Ember label. He recorded for RCA-Victor in September 1959 and had a hit with Clock Records ('Happy Organ') in the same year. In 1962 he hit again with 'Rinky Dink', a crude 'Louie Louie'-type instrumental that could define 60s teen rock naïvety. He recorded an album for Chess Records in 1963 called, predictably, *Rinky Dink* and then signed with Roulette Records, who issued 'Shindig', 'Tweetie Pie' and 'In Orbit'. In February 1966

The Fabulous Dave 'Baby' Cortez appeared on Metro. In 1972 All Platinum released *Soul Vibration* with Frank Prescod (bass) and Bunky Smith (drums). Producer Joe Richardson gave the bass a funk depth comparable to reggae dub experiments. The hilarious dialogue of 'Tongue Kissing', plus liner notes by the organist's mum, make the album a gem. Signed to the T-Neck label - a Buddha subsidiary - he worked with the Isley Brothers to produce *The Isley Brothers Go All The Way*.

● ALBUMS: *Dave 'Baby' Cortez And His Happy Organ* (RCA Victor 1959)★★★★, *Dave 'Baby' Cortez* (Clock 1960)★★★, *Rinky Dink* (Chess 1962)★★★, *Organ Shindig* (Roulette 1965)★★★, *Tweety Pie* (Roulette 1966)★★★, *In Orbit With Dave 'Baby' Cortez* (Roulette 1966)★★★, *The Fabulous Dave 'Baby' Cortez* (Metro 1966)★★★, *Soul Vibration* (All Platinum 1972)★★★.

● COMPILATIONS: *Happy Organs, Wild Guitars And Piano Shuffles* (Ace 1993)★★★★.

Coryell, Larry

b. 2 April 1943, Galveston, Texas, USA. Coryell grew up in the state of Washington. Coryell first worked as a guitarist in 1958 when he formed a rock 'n' roll band with keyboard player Michael Mandel. In 1965 he relocated to New York and joined Chico Hamilton's band, overlapping with the legendary guitarist Gabor Szabo, whom he eventually replaced. In 1966 he formed Free Spirits with American Indian tenor player Jim Pepper. He toured with Gary Burton (1967-68) and played on Herbie Mann's 1968 session, *Memphis Underground*. Coryell was impressed with the exploits of Jimi Hendrix and Eric Clapton with Cream, and his performance on Michael Mantler's *Jazz Composers Orchestra* project in 1968 was scarifying electric guitar at its best. Coryell's early solo albums featured strong support from Elvin Jones and Jimmy Garrison (*Lady Coryell*), and John McLaughlin and Billy Cobham (*Spaces*). *Fairyland*, recorded live at Montreux in 1971 with soul veterans Chuck Rainey (bass) and Bernard 'Pretty' Purdie (drums), a power trio format, was packed with sublime solos. *Barefoot Boy*, recorded the same year at Electric Lady Studios (built by Hendrix), was notable for its simultaneous use of non-pareil jazz drummer Roy Haynes and electric feedback and distortion. Coryell formed Eleventh House with Mandel, honing his experimental music into a dependable showcase for his virtuosity. Coryell, seeming to have sensed that a spark had gone, broke up the band and gave up electricity for a while. He began playing with other guitarists - Philip Catherine, McLaughlin, Paco De Lucia and John Scofield. He played on Charles Mingus's *Three Or Four Shades Of Blue* in 1977 and recorded arrangements of Stravinsky for Nippon Phonogram. In the mid-80s Coryell started playing electric again, with Bunny Brunel (bass) and Alphonse Mouzon (drums). In 1990 he recorded with Don Lanphere, using his considerable name to spotlight an old friend's rekindled career, and produced easy, unassuming acoustic jazz. Despite his extraordinary technique and his early promise, Coryell has never really created his own music, instead playing with undeniable finesse in a variety of contexts.

● ALBUMS: *Lady Coryell* (Vanguard 1969)★★★★, *Coryell* (Vanguard 1969)★★★, *Spaces* (Vanguard 1970)★★★★, *Fairyland* (1971)★★★, *Larry Coryell At The Village Gate* (Vanguard 1971)★★★★, *Barefoot Boy* (Flying Dutchman 1971)★★★, *Offering* (Vanguard 1972)★★★, *The Real Great Escape* (Vanguard 1973)★★★, *Introducing The Eleventh House* (Vanguard 1974)★★★, *The Restful Mind* (Vanguard 1975)★★★, *Planet End* (Vanguard 1975)★★★, *Level One* (Arista 1976)★★★, *Basics* 1968 recordings (1976)★★, *Aspects* (Arista 1976)★★★, *Lion And The Ram* (1976)★★★, with Steve Kahn *Two For The Road* (1976)★★★, with Philip Catherine *Twin House* (Elektra 1976)★★★★, *Back Together* (Warners 1977)★★★, *Splendid* (1978)★★★, *European Impressions* (1978)★★★, *Standing Ovation* (Mood 1978)★★★★, with Joe Beck, John Scofield *Tributaries* (Novus 1979)★★★, *Return* (Vanguard 1979)★★★, *Bolero* (String 1981)★★★, *A Quiet Day In Spring* (Steeple Chase 1984)★★★, *Scheherazade* (1984)★★★, with Brian Keane *Just Like Being Born* (Flying Fish 1984)★★★, *The Firebird And Petrouchka* (Philips 1984)★★★, *Coming Home* (Muse 1984)★★, with Emily Remler *Together* (Concord Jazz 1986)★★★★, *Equipoise* (Muse 1987)★★★, *Toku Du* (Muse 1988)★★★ *Just Like Being Born* (Flying Fish 1989)★★★, *Shining Hour* (Muse 1990)★★★, *Plays Ravel And Gershwin* (Soundscreen 1990)★★★, *Dragon Gate* (Shanachie 1990)★★★, *Twelve Frets To One Octave* (Shanachie 1991)★★★, *Live From Bahia* (CTI 1992)★★★, *Fallen Angel* (CTI 1994)★★, *Sketches Of Coryell* (Shanachie 1996)★★★, as Great Guitars *The Return Of The Great Guitars* (Concord Jazz 1996)★★★, *Spaces Revisited* (Shanachie 1997)★★★★, with Tom Coster and Steve Smith *Cause And Effect* (Tone Center 1998)★★★★.

Costa, Eddie

b. Edwin James Costa, 14 August 1930, Atlas, Pennsylvania, USA, d. 26 July 1962, New York City, New York, USA. After studying piano formally, Costa began playing jazz and later took up the vibraphone. While still in his teens, he played with a band led by Joe Venuti, and in the 50s worked and sometimes recorded with several artists including Tal Farlow, Kai Winding, Sal Salvador, Michel Legrand, Eric Dolphy and Woody Herman. He also led his own small group which, on record if not always live, included Phil Woods, Art Farmer and Paul Motian. He attracted considerable and always highly favourable critical attention, and was a 1957 *Down Beat* poll winner as a new star in the piano and vibraphone categories. Costa's playing displayed fleet inventiveness and at the time of his death in an automobile accident he was confidently moving beyond bop into modal forms.

● ALBUMS: *Eddie Costa Quintet* (Mode 1957)★★★, *Guys And Dolls Like Vibes* (Coral 1958)★★★, *Eddie Costa With Rolf Kühn & Dick Johnson/Mat Matthews & Don Elliott At Newport* (Verve 1958)★★★, *The House Of Blue Lights* (Dot 1959)★★★★, with Art Farmer *In Their Own Sweet Way* (Premier 1962)★★★.

Costa, Johnny

b. 17 January 1922, Arnold, Pennsylvania, USA, d. 11 October 1996. Although he lived and worked for most of his life in and around Pittsburgh, Costa's piano playing elicited glowing praise from Art Tatum, Teddy Wilson, Tommy Dorsey, Dick Hyman and numerous other jazz stars. He began playing the violin as a small child, at the age of 10 he switched to accordion, finally choosing piano. He studied formally and after leaving school played briefly in New York with a dance band. His career was interrupted by service in the army during World War II but after the war he resumed his studies this time at the Carnegie Institute of Technology. He left with degrees in music composition and music education. As he told Hugh W. Glenn, for *Jazz Journal International*, 'I completed a degree in music education just in case I was a flop as a professional musician'. He was not.

After graduating, in 1951, he promptly began a 16-year job as musical director of Pittsburgh's KDKA-TV.

During the 50s Costa also made several albums, all long out of print, but his most important work was with the television station's children's programme, *Mister Rogers' Neighborhood*. A musical programme, Costa refused to play down to his audience, 'Children understand good music', and regularly featured jazz musicians. The programme began in 1967 and was still going strong in the mid-90s. Guests have included Mary Lou Williams and Wynton Marsalis. Steeped in jazz, quality popular music and the classics, Costa's playing was powerful and dynamic. His technical ability was extraordinary. Reputedly Tatum visiting a Pittsburgh club in 1960, heard the piano and remarked, 'You've got my record on'. It wasn't, it was Costa.

In the early 90s, thanks to the efforts of friends and admirers, Costa returned to the recording studios in his own right and, after a 35-year absence, proved that he was as skilled and as inventive as ever. The new albums were received with warm praise but it took more than that to persuade Costa to move far from his family and home, or from his career in television. He died in October 1996.

● ALBUMS: *Play Piano Solos* (Coral 1952)★★★★, *Plays For The Most Beautiful Girl In The World* (Coral 1953)★★★, with others *A Gallery Of Gershwin* (Coral 1953)★★, *In My Own Quiet Way* (Dot 1954)★★★, *Introducing Johnny Costa* (Savoy 1954)★★★, *The Amazing Johnny Costa/Neighborhood* (Savoy 1955)★★★, *Classic Costa* (Chiaroscuro 1990)★★★, *Flying Fingers* (Chiaroscuro 1992)★★★, *A Portrait Of George Gershwin* (Chiaroscuro 1993)★★★★.

Costanzo, Sonny

b. 7 October 1932, New York City, New York, USA, d. 30 December 1993. Academically trained, and with on-the-road experience playing trombone with big bands such as those led by Woody Herman and Thad Jones and Mel Lewis, Costanzo became a highly-respected musician. After touring Europe with Clark Terry, Costanzo made his own forays outside the USA and established a reputation as a teacher and clinician, especially in the 80s. During this decade he recorded in Czechoslovakia and also appeared on television in the USSR. His work in the USA was centred upon his own big band and he was especially noted for his accompaniment to singers, including Tony Bennett, Johnny Mathis, Mel Tormé and Marlene VerPlanck.

● ALBUMS: with Marlene VerPlanck *A Quiet Storm* (Audiophile 1989)★★★, *Splendor In The Brass* (1992)★★★.

Cotton, Mike

b. 12 August 1939, London, England. Trumpeter Cotton had led the Mike Cotton Jazzband during the 'Trad' craze of the early 60s, but incurred the wrath of purists by increasingly adopting beat-styled material. In 1963 the group, now known as the Mike Cotton Sound, enjoyed a Top 30 entry with 'Swing That Hammer', and the following year completed their lone, highly regarded album. The group included Dave Rowberry (keyboards), later of the Animals, and future Argent and Kinks bassist Jim Rodford (b. 7 July 1941, St. Albans, Hertfordshire, England), while Johnny Crocker (trombone) Derek Tearle (bass) and Jim Garforth (drums) were among the other musicians featured in its changeable line-up. Vocalist Lucas was added in 1967 as the group switched from jazz-based R&B to soul, but by the end of the decade Cotton had jettisoned its now-anachronistic name, replacing it with Satisfaction. This new aggregation broke up on completing its sole album, following which the trumpeter retained the brass section for session work, notably with the Kinks, whom they supported both live and in the studio throughout the early 70s.

● ALBUMS: *The Mike Cotton Sound* (Columbia 1964)★★★.

Cottrell, Louis, Jnr.

b. 7 March 1911, New Orleans, Louisiana, USA. d. 21 March 1978. Born into a musical family, Cottrell studied clarinet with Lorenzo Tio. After playing with local bands he spent the 30s touring with Don Albert with whom he also played tenor saxophone. At the end of the decade he returned to New Orleans where he played with bands such as those led by Paul Barbarin and Sidney Desvigne. He continued to play through the 50s and 60s with the bands of Barbarin and others, then formed his own band which he led for the remainder of his life. A sound and professional player, Cottrell's spell with Albert displayed his ability to work effectively in surroundings other than the New Orleans style he favoured. His father was Louis Cottrell Snr. (1878-1927), an influential New Orleans drummer.

● ALBUMS: *Bourbon Street Parade* (1961)★★★, *Louis Cottrell And His New Orleans Jazz Band* (1964)★★★.

Coughlan, Frank

b. Francis James Coughlan, 10 September 1904, Emmaville, New South Wales, Australia, d. 7 April 1979. Born into a musical family, Coughlan was the third son to be taught by his father who was Band Master of the Emmaville Brass Band. Adept on trombone and trumpet, during the 20s he played with various dance bands in his homeland and also, in 1924, with the visiting Californians. Towards the end of the decade he travelled to London. While there he played in and recorded with several popular bands, including that led by Jack

Hylton. Throughout the 30s he led his own bands in Australia, playing swing-influenced dance music. After military service during World War II he returned to bandleading with considerable success. A residency at Sydney's prestigious Trocadero lasted in all for more than 30 years. A highly accomplished and thoroughly professional musician, his long-lasting career gives some measure of his popularity with audiences. His trombone playing was elegant and always pleasingly melodic.

● ALBUMS: *King Of The Trocadero* (Larrikin 1996)★★★, *The Troc* (MBS 1996)★★★.

COUNCE, CURTIS

b. 23 January 1926, Kansas City, Missouri, USA, d. 31 July 1963. After studying various instruments, bassist Counce gained early professional experience playing with Nat Towles's territory band. This was in the early 40s and he subsequently worked for three years with Edgar Hayes. By the end of the decade Counce had begun a period of intensive association with many of the leading west coast beboppers currently engaged in creating the 'cool school' of jazz. In 1953 he recorded with Teddy Charles and was on the Shorty Rogers *Cool And Crazy* album. The powerful swing engendered by Rogers' big band, made up almost entirely of Stan Kenton sidemen, was due in no small part to the rhythm section of Marty Paich, Shelly Manne and Counce. That same year, Counce recorded with small groups led by Manne. In 1954 Counce was available for a record date with an expanded version of the Max Roach-Clifford Brown quintet, the surging powerhouse playing of one breakneck-tempoed tune, 'Coronado', effectively demolishing charges of effeteness frequently levelled at the west coast school. The following year he was again with Rogers, this time for a record date as a member of the Giants, which resulted in two extremely well-received albums, *The Swinging Mr Rogers* and *Martians Come Back*. By now, Counce was an established figure and one of few black musicians to be working extensively in the studios.

In 1956 he joined Stan Kenton with whom he toured Europe. On his return he formed his own band which, musically, was in tune with the east coast-based Jazz Messengers of Horace Silver. Counce's group featured Harold Land, Jack Sheldon, Carl Perkins and Frank Butler and was musically successful. The band's records sold well although it failed to garner the critical or popular credit of the Messengers. They stayed together until 1958, making their last recording shortly before Perkins's death. Restructured and renamed as the Curtis Counce Quintet, the unit made another album later in 1958, but did not quite measure up to the remarkable earlier standards. The Curtis Counce Group was one of the most exciting of the many 50s Los Angeles-based bands and while the individual members can all be credited for their part in its success, the leader in particular must be singled out for the care with which he selected his sidemen. Counce's premature death was a great loss for the jazz world.

● ALBUMS: *The Curtis Counce Group/Landslide* (1956)★★★, *You Get More Bounce With Curtis Counce* (Original Jazz Classics 1957)★★★★, *Landslide* (Original Jazz Classics 1958)★★★★, *Carl's Blues* (1958)★★★, *Exploring The Future* (Boblicity 1958)★★★, *Sonority* (Contemporary 1959)★★★.

● COMPILATIONS: *Counceltation* (1981)★★★, *Carl's Blues* (Contemporary 1987)★★★.

COURSIL, JACQUES

b. 1939, Paris, France. Coursil's parents were immigrants from Martinique and he grew up listening to Creole songs, the beguines. After a false start trying to play the violin at the age of nine, he attended the local conservatory, ostensibly to learn clarinet - his idol was Sidney Bechet, then living in Paris - but took up a cornet when it was handed him. Arriving in New York in the early 60s he studied with Jaki Byard for two years and involved himself in the burgeoning black *avant garde*, playing with tenor saxophonist Frank Wright. In 1966 he recorded with Sunny Murray for ESP-Disk. He also played lead trumpet in the Sun Ra Arkestra. However, although he loved the music he could not swallow Sun Ra's philosophy and left to play with Rashied Ali and Marion Brown. Interested in serial procedures, Coursil wrote *Black Suite* in 1967, released by BYG Records of Paris in 1969 and features Anthony Braxton. It is a powerful and highly original piece, making one regret Coursil's subsequent neglect by the record labels. He has, though, made another contribution to modern music: it was while teaching John Zorn French that he introduced the young composer to jazz.

● ALBUMS: *Sunny Murray Quintet* (1966)★★★, *Black Suite* (1969)★★★.

COUSIN JOE

b. Pleasant Joseph (aka Brother Joshua and Smilin' Joe), 20 December 1907, Wallace, Louisiana, USA, d. 2 October 1989, New Orleans, Louisiana, USA. Joe began singing at an early age, playing the ukulele at sporting events and around the gambling joints and brothels of the Crescent City. His professional career started around 1930 with the formation of his band, the Jazz Jesters. After teaching himself to play the piano, he was associated with several local orchestras (with A.J. Piron, Harold Dejan and Joseph Robichaux) as well as leading his own Smilin' Joe's Blues Trio. In 1942 Joe decided to try his luck in New York. His recording career began in 1945 with Mezz Mezzrow's King Jazz label, and he went on to record for Philo/Aladdin, Savoy, Gotham, DeLuxe, Signature, Decca, Flip and Imperial between 1945 and 1954. In the 60s and 70s, Joe became a favourite at US and European jazz and blues concerts, making a number of appearances on British television. He resumed his recording career with albums for a variety of labels. He had left New York in 1948 to avoid the heavy drugs scene - obviously a sensible move, since he lived to the respectable age of 81, dying of the rare complaint (at least for a blues or jazz musician) of 'natural causes'.

● ALBUMS: *Bad Luck Blues* (Black & Blue 1972)★★★, *Cousin*

Joe Of New Orleans (Bluesway 1973)★★★, *Gospel-Wailing, Jazz-Playing, Rock 'N' Rolling, Soul-Shouting,Tap-Dancing Bluesman from New Orleans* (Big Bear 1974)★★★★, *Cousin Joe From New Orleans: In His Prime* (1984)★★★★, *Relaxin' In New Orleans* (Great Southern 1985)★★★.

COWELL, STANLEY

b. 5 May 1941, Toledo, Ohio, USA. Cowell began playing piano as a tiny child and later studied extensively, including taking degrees at Oberlin and the University of Michigan. During the mid- and late 60s he performed with several noted figures, including Marion Brown, Max Roach and in a band co-led by Bobby Hutcherson and Harold Land. In the 70s he began a fruitful musical and business association with Charles Tolliver, one outcome of which was Strata-East Records. The same decade also saw his involvement in the establishment of important developments in black music, including Collective Black Artists, Inc. From the mid-70s to the mid-80s he regularly performed with the Heath brothers and Larry Coryell. Cowell continued to perform and to teach on into the 90s, gradually displaying an increasing interest in writing music, and sometimes lyrics, for many good songs. Several of his songs were recorded on *Mandara Blossoms*, which introduced the young singer Karen Francis. Cowell's piano style displays the brilliance associated with early idols Art Tatum and Bud Powell, and his solos demonstrate a remarkable level of sustained inventiveness. This aspect of his playing is allied with stylish and effective accompaniment to other soloists.

● ALBUMS: *Travellin' Man (Blues For The Viet Cong)* (Freedom 1969)★★★★, *Brilliant Circles* (Freedom 1969)★★★★, *Illusion Suite* (ECM 1973), *Regeneration* (Strata-East 1975), *Waiting For The Moment* (Galaxy 1977)★★★, *New World* (Galaxy 1977)★★★, *Talkin' 'Bout Love* (Galaxy 1978)★★★, *Equipoise* (Galaxy 1978)★★★, *Bright Passion* (Steeple Chase c.1984)★★★, *Hear Me One* (Steeple Chase c.1984)★★★, *Live At Cafe Des Copains* (Unisson 1985)★★★, *Sienna* (Steeple Chase 1989)★★★★, *Back To The Beautiful* (Concord Jazz 1989)★★★, *Departure #2* (Steeple Chase 1990)★★★, *Live At Maybeck Recital Hall Series, Vol. 5* (Concord Jazz 1990)★★★, *Close To You Alone* (DIW/Columbia 1991)★★★★, *Games* (Steeple Chase 1991)★★★, *Angel Eyes* (Steeplechase 1993)★★★★, *Bright Passion* (Steeplechase 1993)★★★, *Setup* (Steeplechase 1994)★★★★, *Angel Eyes* (Steeple Chase 1982)★★★, *Setup* (Steeple Chase 1982)★★★,with Marian McPartland *Marian McPartland's Piano Jazz With Guest Stanley Cowell* 1981 recording (Concord Jazz 1995)★★★, *Mandara Blossoms* (Steeple Chase 1995)★★★, *Hear Me One* (Steeplechase 1997)★★★★.

COWENS, HERBERT

b. 24 May 1904, Dallas, Texas, USA, d. date unknown. Born into a very musical family where his four siblings included a singer, a dancer and two drummers, he started out dancing for pennies on street corners and eventually began playing drums. While still a youngster he played with various bands in Texas, interrupting his studies to do so. By the mid-20s he was a full-time musician, touring and visiting major centres including New York. He occasionally led a band of his own but mostly played for others, including Lucky Millinder, Eubie Blake, Charlie Johnson and Fats Waller. In 1938 he began a three-year spell with Stuff Smith, then played with Fletcher Henderson and Garvin Bushell before forming a wartime band with which he made USO tours around the world. After the war he again led his own small groups and also played with Louis Metcalf, Buck Clayton and others through the 50s and 60s. In the 70s he was still active.

● COMPILATIONS: with Stuff Smith *The Varsity Sessions* (Storyville 1938-40)★★★, *The Quintessential Billie Holiday Vol. 9 1940-42* (Columbia 1940-42)★★★★.

COX, IDA

b. Ida Prather, 25 February 1896, Toccoa, Georgia, USA, d. 10 November 1967. Like many early blues vocalists, Cox's origins are vague and details of the date and place of her birth vary widely. One of the classic blues singers, Cox began her career as a child, appearing on stage when barely in her teens. She made her first recordings in 1923 and for the rest of the decade recorded extensively for Paramount, often accompanied by Lovie Austin. Cox's singing style, a brooding, slightly nasal monotone, was less attractive than that of some of her contemporaries, but there was no denying the heartfelt passion with which she imbued the lyrics of her songs, many of which took death as their text. Among her greatest performances were 'Bone Orchard Blues', 'Death Letter Blues', 'Black Crepe Blues', 'Worn Down Daddy' and 'Coffin Blues' (on which she was accompanied by her husband, organist Jesse Crump). Her accompanying musicians were usually of the highest calibre; in particular, she worked with Tommy Ladnier, whose intense trumpet-playing beautifully counterpointed her threatening drone. Cox toured extensively during the 30s but was absent from the recording studios. In 1939 she was invited by John Hammond to appear at the Carnegie Hall 'Spirituals To Swing' concert, after which she made more records, this time accompanied by several top-flight jazzmen who included Oran 'Hot Lips' Page, Edmond Hall, Charlie Christian, Lionel Hampton, Red Allen and J.C. Higginbotham. In the early 40s Cox again toured with her own shows, but in 1945 she suffered a stroke and thereafter worked only sporadically. She did, however, make a welcome return to the recording studios in 1961. While these final performances inevitably showed the signs of her advancing years, she was still recognizably Ida Cox, 'The Blues Queen'.

● ALBUMS: with Tommy Ladnier *Ida Cox With Tommy Ladnier* 10-inch album (Riverside 1953)★★★, *Sings The Blues* (London 1954)★★★★, *Wild Women Don't Have The Blues* (1961)★★★, *Blues For Rampart Street* (Riverside 1961)★★★.

● COMPILATIONS: *Ida Cox Volume 1* (Fountain 1971)★★★, *Ida Cox Volume 2* (Fountain 1975)★★★, *Paramount Recordings* 6-LP box set (Garnet 1975)★★★★.

Coxhill, Lol

b. Lowen Coxhill, 19 September 1932, Portsmouth, Hampshire, England. Coxhill first attracted attention in the early 60s playing soprano saxophone with a startlingly wide variety of bands. In his early career, he was at home playing with R&B singers, rock groups, free jazz ensembles and was especially adept playing unaccompanied solos. On occasion, he would also happily sit in with traditional bands, making no attempt to adapt his forthright and contemporary style and yet improbably making the results work. In the 70s and 80s Coxhill was involved with such musicians as Chris McGregor's Brotherhood Of Breath, Bobby Wellins, Evan Parker, Derek Bailey and Tony Coe; he worked frequently with pianist Steve Miller, was co-leader of the now-defunct Johnny Rondo Trio, and is now a member of two regular groups - the Recedents (with Mike Cooper and Roger Turner) and the Melody Four (actually a trio, with Tony Coe and Steve Beresford). For a while in the early 80s, he was a guest member of the punk group, the Damned. In the 70s he also began to develop a sideline career as an actor, and has appeared in a number of plays in the theatre and on television: he was also the subject of the documentary film, *Frog Dance*. A strikingly original player, Coxhill's fiercely independent approach to his music has always been leavened by his droll sense of humour and a broad-minded eclecticism - in the early 90s he was playing early jazz with bassist Dave Green, singing with the Melody Four and continuing his total improvisations both solo and with the Recedents.

● ALBUMS: *Ear Of The Beholder* (Dandelion 1971)★★★, *Toverbal Sweet* (Mushroom 1971)★★★, with Steve Miller *Coxhill/Miller* (Caroline 1973)★★★★, *The Story So Far ... Oh Really, One Side?* (Caroline 1974)★★★★, *Lol Coxhill And The Welfare State* (Caroline 1975)★★★, *Fleas In The Custard* (Caroline 1975)★★★, *Diverse* (Ogun 1977)★★★, *Lid* (Ictus 1978)★★★, *The Joy Of Paranoia* (Ogun 1978)★★★, *Moot* (Ictus 1978)★★★, with Morgan Fisher *Slow Music* (1978)★★★, *Digwell Duets* (Random Radar 1979)★★★, *Chantenay '80* (1980)★★★, *Slow Music* (Pipe 1980)★★★, *The Dunois Solos* (Nato 1981)★★★★, *Instant Replay* (1982)★★★, with Eyeless In Gaza *Home Produce* (1982)★★★, *Cou$ Cou$* (Nato 1983)★★★, with Fred Frith *French Gigs* (AAA 1983)★★★, *Frog Dance* (1986)★★★, with Daniel Deshays *10:02* (Nato 1986)★★★, *Instant Replay* (Nato 1986)★★★, *The Inimitable* (Chabada 1986)★★★, *Café De La Place* (1986)★★★, *Before My Time* (1987)★★★, *Looking Back Forwards* (1990)★★★, *Lol Coxhill* (1990)★★★, *The Bald Soprano Companion* (Tak 1990)★★★, *Hollywood Concert* (Slam 1990)★★★, with Steve Lacy, Evan Parker 1992 recordings *Three Blokes* (FMP 1994)★★★★, *Halim* (Nato 1994)★★, *One Night In Glasgow* (Scatter 1995)★★, Boundless (Emanem 1998)★★★★.

● FURTHER READING: *The Bald Soprano*, Jeff Nuttall.

Crane, Ray

b. Raymond Crane, 31 October 1930, Skegness, Lincolnshire, England, d. 29 June 1994. Crane began playing trumpet in and around his home town, refusing to be discouraged by a music teacher who considered his teeth unsuitable for his intended profession. After working in the East Midlands for a number of years, playing in groups such as the Mercia Jazz Band, in 1963 he joined Bruce Turner's Jump Band. This brought him to the attention of a much wider audience through concerts and records, such as *Going Places* (Philips 1963). He later played in bands led by Brian Lemon, with whom he had worked while both men were still in the Midlands, and Stan Greig. Crane often accompanied visiting American jazzmen, including several fellow trumpeters, such as Red Allen, Ray Nance and Bill Coleman, all of whom expressed admiration for his playing. Crane, who sometimes played piano, also worked as a schoolteacher, and ran a youth jazz orchestra, which at various times included up-and-coming jazz musicians Martin Taylor and Guy Barker. Trombonist Pete Strange, who played alongside him in the Turner band, described his style as 'a mixture of Rex Stewart, Louis Armstrong, Roy Eldridge and Clifford Brown.' As this description suggests, Crane was a fiery, swing-era-rooted trumpet player with an ear for the more melodic aspects of the contemporary scene.

Cranshaw, Bob

b. Melbourne Robert Cranshaw, 10 December 1932, Evanston, Illinois, USA. Taking up bass in high school, Cranshaw began his professional career in Chicago. After travelling to New York in 1960 with Walter Perkins' MJT+3, he joined Sonny Rollins (a musical relationship that lasted into the 80s), and worked with Carmen McRae (1961) and Junior Mance (1962-63). Between 1962 and 1973, Cranshaw played regularly with Duke Pearson's small groups and big band, during which time he took up the electric bass and became orientated towards the recording studio, working for television as well as recording with, amongst others, Coleman Hawkins, Horace Silver, Wes Montgomery and Lee Morgan.

Crawford, Hank

b. Bennie Crawford, 21 December 1934, Memphis, Tennessee, USA. One of the most prolific jazz/blues saxophonists, Crawford came to prominence as a member of the Ray Charles band in the late 50s. After studying at the University of Tennessee, he joined Charles in 1958, playing baritone saxophone and working closely with the leader on arrangements and new material. Eventually he was given the title musical director. Crawford later switched to alto-saxophone and while still a member of the Charles band, he was signed in 1961 to a solo recording contract with Atlantic Records. His earliest recordings included fellow Charles sideman David 'Fathead' Newman on tenor saxophone and reproduced the funky feel of Charles' own work. Crawford left Ray Charles and formed his own group in 1964, the year after Hollywood arranger Marty Paich had worked with him on an album of standards such as 'Stardust' and 'Stormy Weather', but the bulk of Crawford's Atlantic output consisted of booting soul-blues material. From 1972, he recorded for Kudu, an easy-listening jazz label set up by Creed Taylor. His repertoire was now drawn from current hits (Kris Kristofferson's 'Help Me Make It Through The Night') and Ray Charles standards ('I Can't Stop Loving You') as well as original compositions. On several of the albums he was accompanied by members of the New York session mafia, notably Richard Tee (keyboards), Eric Gale and Hugh McCracken (guitars), Randy Brecker (trumpet) and Bernard Purdie (drums). After Kudu closed down, Crawford recorded for Milestone. *Soul Survivors* was made with master organist Jimmy McGriff and produced by Rudy van Gelder. It included a new version of the Charles classic 'One Mint Julep'. The same year, Dr. John played and sang in a strong Crawford band that included Purdie, Brecker and Newman. His albums during the late 80s were very much a formula, albeit a good formula - featuring the likes of McGriff, Billy Preston, George Benson and Mel Lewis.

● ALBUMS: *More Soul* (Atlantic 1961)★★★, *The Soul Clinic* (Atlantic 1961)★★★, *From The Heart* (Atlantic 1962)★★★, *Soul From The Ballad* (Atlantic 1963)★★★, *True Blue* (Atlantic 1964)★★★, *Dig These Blues* (Atlantic 1965)★★★★, *After Hours* (Atlantic 1967)★★★, *Mr Blues* (Atlantic 1967)★★★, *Double Cross* (Atlantic 1968)★★★, *Mr Blues Plays Lady Soul* (Atlantic 1969)★★★, *Help Me Make It Through The Night* (1972)★★★, *Wildflower* (CBS 1973)★★, *Don't You Worry 'Bout A Thing* (1974)★★, *I Hear A Symphony* (1975)★★, *Hank Crawford's Back* (Kudu 1976)★★, *Tico Rico* (Kudu 1977)★★★, *Cajun Sunrise* (Polydor 1979)★★, *Midnight Ramble* (Milestone 1983)★★★, *Indigo Blue* (Milestone 1983)★★★, *Roadhouse Symphony* (Milestone 1986)★★★, *Mr Chips* (Milestone 1986)★★★, *Soul Survivors* (1986)★★, *Steppin' Up* (Milestone 1988)★★, *Night Beat* (Milestone 1989)★★★, with Jimmy McGriff *Soul Brothers* (Milestone 1989)★★★, *On The Blue Side* (Milestone 1990)★★, with Johnny 'Hammond' Smith *Portrait* (Milestone 1990)★★★, *Groove Master* (Milestone 1991)★★★, *South-Central* (Milestone 1993)★★, with McGriff *Blues Groove* (Telarc 1996)★★★, *Tight* (Milestone 1996)★★★, *After Dark* (Milestone 1998)★★★★.

● COMPILATIONS: *Heart And Soul* (Rhino 1993)★★★★.

CRAWFORD, JIMMY

b. 14 January 1910, Memphis, Tennessee, USA, d. 28 January 1980. Crawford began his musical career in good company when, at Manassas County High School in the late 20s, he met Jimmie Lunceford, Moses Allen and other young musicians who played together in the Lunceford-led Chickasaw Syncopators. When Lunceford took the band on tour, Crawford went along as the drummer, contributing greatly to the band's gradual progress until, in 1933, they made their breakthrough into the big-time at New York's Lafayette Theater. In 1934 they were booked into the Savoy, a severe test for any band - and especially its drummer, as this was where Chick Webb dominated. The success of the Lunceford band was built largely upon the extraordinary talents of its arrangers, Eddie Wilcox, Eddie Durham and especially Sy Oliver, also the playing and the exacting standards set by lead alto saxophonist Willie Smith, and the urgent, exuberant drumming of Crawford was a permanent encouragement to the band, helping it gain both the admiration of other musicians and enthusiasm of the fans. Unusually among big band drummers of the swing era, Crawford favoured a two-beat style which gave the silky-smooth ensemble playing of this extremely well-rehearsed and talented band an enormous lift. After leaving Lunceford in 1943 Crawford worked mostly with small groups, including those of Ben Webster, Harry James, Edmond Hall and Benny Goodman. In the 50s he was extensively involved in the theatre, playing in the pit bands of many Broadway shows (including *Pal Joey*) and also performed with Ella Fitzgerald, Dizzy Gillespie and Count Basie. At heart, Crawford was a big band drummer and he proved his worth in the 1957 Henderson All Stars recording date, on which his playing and shouts of encouragement helped make this one of the best of big band albums.

● ALBUMS: with Henderson All Stars *Big Reunion* (1957)★★★★.

● COMPILATIONS: with Jimmie Lunceford *The Jimmie Lunceford And His Orchestra (1935-41)* (1982)★★★★, *The Complete Set* (1986)★★★.

CRAWFORD, RANDY

b. Veronica Crawford, 18 February 1952, Macon, Georgia, USA. Raised in Cincinnati, from the age of 15 Randy Crawford was a regular performer at the city's nightclubs. She later moved to New York and began singing with several jazz musicians including George Benson and Cannonball Adderley. Crawford was subsequently signed to Warner Brothers Records as a solo act, but achieved fame as the (uncredited) voice on 'Street Life', a major hit single for the Crusaders. Crawford toured extensively with the group, whose pianist, Joe Sample, provided her with 'Now We May Begin', a beautiful ballad that established the singer's independent career. Crawford enjoyed further successes with 'One Day I'll Fly Away' (UK number 2), 'You Might Need Somebody', 'Rainy Night in Georgia' (both UK Top 20 hits) and her 1981 album *Secret Combination*, considered by many to be her finest, reached number 2 in the UK. After a five-year respite, she made a return to the top flight of the chart in 1986 with 'Almaz' which reached the Top 5. Curiously, this soulful, passionate singer has found greater success in the UK than in her homeland and the album *Rich And Poor* was recorded in London.

● ALBUMS: *Miss Randy Crawford* (Warners 1977)★★★, *Raw Silk* (Warners 1979)★★★★, *Now We May Begin* (Warners 1980)★★★, *Everything Must Change* (Warners 1980)★★, *Secret Combination* (Warners 1981)★★★★, *Windsong* (Warners 1982)★★, *Nightline* (Warners 1983)★★★, *Abstract Emotions* (Warners 1986)★★★, *Rich And Poor* (Warners 1989)★★★, *Naked And True* (Bluemoon 1995)★★★★, *Every Kind Of Mood: Randy, Randi, Randee* (Atlantic 1998)★★★.

● COMPILATIONS: *Miss Randy Crawford - Greatest Hits* (K-Tel 1984)★★★, *Love Songs* (Telstar 1987)★★★, *The Very Best Of* (Dino 1992)★★★, *The Best Of* (Warners 1996)★★★★.

Crawford, Ray

b. 7 February 1924, Pittsburgh, Pennsylvania, USA. A much underrated musician throughout his career, Crawford played clarinet and saxophone with Fletcher Henderson in the early 40s before tuberculosis forced a change to guitar. He established his reputation playing with the influential first Ahmed Jamal trio in Pittsburgh and Chicago (1951-56), and later played with organist Jimmy Smith and with Gil Evans. Crawford was a principal soloist on Evans' seminal *Out Of The Cool*, and his individual approach and percussive effects on his instrument can be heard on the track 'La Nevada'. A move to Los Angeles led to the formation, in 1961, of a sextet with Johnny Coles and Cecil Payne. During the 60s and 70s he played as an accompanist with Sonny Stitt and Sonny Criss; his association with Jimmy Smith continued into the 80s.

● ALBUMS: *Smooth Groove* (Candid 1961)★★★.

Crayton, Pee Wee

b. Connie Curtis, 18 December 1914, Liberty Hill, Texas, USA, d. 25 June 1985, Los Angeles, California, USA. After learning to play ukulele and banjo as a child, Crayton took up the guitar in his mid-20s. He was inspired by Charlie Christian and T-Bone Walker, the latter of whom taught Crayton the basics of electric guitar playing. His tutelage was completed at the side of another legendary guitarist, John Collins, and he began playing with local bands before graduating to Ivory Joe Hunter's bay area band in 1946. After making his recording debut with Hunter for Pacific Records, he recorded his first efforts under his own name and these were later issued on 4 Star Records after his success with Modern Records. In 1947 Crayton formed a trio, and after an obscure release on the tiny Gru-V-Tone label, began recording for Modern between 1948 and 1951, finding success with 'Blues After Hours', 'Texas Hop', and his biggest hit 'I Love You So', soon after he switched to Aladdin and Recorded In Hollywood for one-off sessions. Imperial Records took Crayton to New Orleans in 1954-55 to record with Dave Bartholomew's band, and the following year he moved to Detroit to record for Fox and Vee Jay Records in nearby Chicago. During this period he was admired by and became the inspiration for a local young guitarist called Kenny Burrell. Moving back to Los Angeles in 1960, he recorded an unissued session for Kent Records (Modern) and subsequently recorded single sessions for the Jamie/Guyden, Smash and Edco labels, before leaving the music business in 1964 for five years, after recording the obscure *Sunset Blues Band* for Liberty's Sunset subsidiary. Rediscovered in the blues boom of the late 60s, he recommenced his recording career with an unissued session for Blue Horizon Records, a well-received album, *Things I Used To Do*, and an explosive appearance with Johnny Otis' band at the 1970 Monterey Festival. The five years or so before his death coincided with another resurgence of interest in blues and R&B, and this saw Crayton reaching an even wider audience with albums recorded for his friend Johnny Otis, solo albums and albums with Big Joe Turner on Pablo, new blues projects for the Murray Brothers, and Ace Records initiating a large-scale reissue programme.

● ALBUMS: *Pee Wee Crayton* (Crown 1959)★★★★, *After Hours* (1960)★★★, *Sunset Blues Band* (Sunset 1965)★★★, *Things I Used To Do* (Vanguard 1970)★★★, *Monterey Festival* (1970)★★★★, *Blues Guitar Genius* (1980)★★★, *Great R&B Oldies* (1982)★★★, with Big Joe Turner *Every Day I Have The Blues* (1982)★★★★, *Peace Of Mind* (1982)★★★, *Rocking Down Central Avenue* (1982)★★★, *Blues Before Dawn* (1986)★★★, *Memorial Album* (1986)★★★, *Make Room For Pee Wee* (1987)★★★, *Early Hours* (1987)★★★, *After Hours Boogie* (1988)★★★, *Blues After Dark* (1988)★★★★, *Blues After Hours* (1988)★★★.

● COMPILATIONS: *The Modern Legacy Volume 1* (Ace 1996)★★★★, *The Complete Aladdin And Imperial Recordings* (Capitol 1996)★★★★.

Creath, Charlie

b. Charles Cyril Creath, 30 December 1890, Ironton, Missouri, USA, d. 23 October 1951. He started out playing alto saxophone but later switched to trumpet and also occasionally played accordion. His two sisters, including Margie Creath Singleton, also played piano. In his mid-teens, Creath played with various touring and circus bands before becoming a leader in his own right. He ran several bands based in St. Louis and also on riverboats. In some of these ventures he was partnered by Fate Marable. He continued his activities as a band leader and contractor during the 30s, later moving to Chicago, where he worked in a munitions factory during World War II. By the late 40s, however, he had drifted out of music and suffered from poor health. Contemporary accounts suggest that Creath was a highly talented trumpet player and a good saxophonist. His main activity, however, was that of a band contractor.

Creative Orchestra Music 1976 - Anthony Braxton

One of the *avant garde*'s eccentric trail-blazers, Braxton is a virtuoso flute and reeds multi-instrumentalist, and one of a number of leading experimental musicians to have developed out of Chicago's AACM hothouse during the second half of the 60s. His innovations have included the first ever album of improvisations performed on solo saxophone, unorthodox techniques for naming compositions (including algebraic formulae or, in this case, diagrams) and a clever balance between large group composition and improvisation. *Creative Orchestra Music 1976* consists of compositions for a number of large groups, and features bassist Dave Holland, pianist Muhal Richard Abrams, saxophonist Roscoe Mitchell and trumpeters Kenny Wheeler, Jon Faddis and Leo Smith.

● Tracks: *Piece One; Piece Two; Piece Three; Piece Four; Piece Five; Piece Six.*

● First released 1977

● UK peak chart position: did not chart

● USA peak chart position: did not chart

CREESE, MALCOLM

b. 24 August 1959, Bristol, Avon, England. After singing in the St. John's College, Cambridge choir as a boy, he studied classical cello at the Guildhall School of Music and Drama in London, worked as a freelance with various classical orchestras and then in 1985, switched instruments and style. As a bass player he quickly began to make a name in London jazz circles and in 1990 joined Stan Tracey. The following year he was invited to join the group led by John Dankworth and Cleo Laine. During the 90s he continued playing with Dankworth and Laine and also appeared on numerous recording dates with pop artists, including Sting, Rod Stewart, Depeche Mode, Chris De Burgh and Shara Nelson. In these same years he also played with jazz groups and led his own trio with John Horler and Tony Coe. Creese has also played on many movie soundtracks and on television (shows and commercials). In addition to his extensive jazz and pop work, Creese has continued to work in the classical field. He is also active as a record producer and runs several labels including ABCDs and Black Box Jazz on which he has recorded singer Liz Fletcher, Matt Wates, Coe and Dankworth. Creese's sound musical background and wide experience has resulted in his becoming a much sought-after session player and he brings to all his work a deep sense of commitment and enormous technical and rhythmic skills.

● ALBUMS: *The Malcolm Creese Trio* (ABCDs 1997)★★★.

CRIMMINS, ROY

b. 2 August 1929, Perth, Scotland. A self-taught musician, trombonist Crimmins began his professional career during the early 50s traditional jazz boom. He worked with various bands, including the Galleon Jazz Band and those led by Mick Mulligan and Freddy Randall before becoming a founder member of Alex Welsh's highly popular outfit in 1954. It was more than a decade before he decided to move on. After forming his own band in 1965, Crimmins toured Germany, remaining there for the next 13 years, though he worked too in Austria, where he appeared frequently on television, and in Switzerland. In 1978 he returned to the UK and rejoined Welsh, staying with the band until the leader's death in 1982. Since then Crimmins has worked in various bands, including those of Harry Gold and Bob Wilber and the popular trombone-dominated group, Five-a-Slide. A powerful player with excellent technique, Crimmins's long association with the more traditional forms of jazz conceal the fact that his is a wide-ranging talent.

● ALBUMS: with Fatty George *Chicagoan All Stars* (1973)★★.

CRIMSON CANARY, THE

Amongst the ingredients of *film noir* was jazz-inflected music as background to shady on-screen happenings. A low-budget, generally ineffective, and decidedly borderline entry for the genre, this 1945 film went one better by setting the plot in the jazz world. When a band singer is found beaten to death with a trumpet ('how I wish' many trumpet-section members must have cried), two of the band's sidemen are suspected. The detective in charge of the investigation is a jazz fan and digs into the case with finger-snapping enthusiasm. In keeping with Hollywood's tradition of hiring the band for filming one day and the band for the recording another, who you see does not often, if ever, match who you hear. Amongst those you see are Denzil De Costa Best, Coleman Hawkins, Howard McGhee, Oscar Pettiford and Sir Charles Thompson (current winners in the *Esquire* poll). Josh White performs his hit song, 'One Meat Ball'. Oh, yes, the club owner did it.

CRISPELL, MARILYN

b. Marilyn Braune, 30 March 1947, Philadelphia, Pennsylvania, USA. Crispell began piano lessons at the age of seven, later studying classical piano at the Peabody Music School in Baltimore, where she spent her later childhood, and piano and composition at the New England Conservatory of Music in Boston. After graduating in 1969, she gave up music for marriage and medical work. Six years later she divorced and moved to Cape Cod, where a local pianist, George Kahn, introduced her to modern jazz on record. One night, listening to John Coltrane's *A Love Supreme*, 'something in the music - its feeling, its energy - caught me: I became incredibly moved. I said to myself, I have to learn to play this music. I loved it so much.' She studied jazz harmony with teacher Charlie Banacos in Boston, then attended Karl Berger's Creative Music Studio in Woodstock, later staying on to work as a teacher. At the studio, she met Anthony Braxton and toured Europe in his Creative Music Orchestra in 1978, later recording on his *Composition 98* in 1981. By the early 80s she had started to develop her own music, both solo (*Rhythms Hung In Undrawn Sky*, *Concert In Berlin*) and in a group that featured Billy Bang and drummer John Betsch (*Spirit Music, Live In Berlin*). This sudden flurry of releases was followed by a series of albums on the UK Leo Records label: *And Your Ivory Voice Sings* (a duo with drummer Doug James), *Quartet Improvisations - Paris 1986* and *Gaia*, a trio with James and Reggie Workman that *Wire* magazine later voted one of the top 50 albums of the 80s. Crispell continued to work with Braxton, becoming a regular member of his quartet in 1983, and also joined Workman's Ensemble (*Synthesis, Images*), as well as playing occasional concerts with a wide range of artists: Andrew Cyrille (one duo track on the compilation *Live At The Knitting Factory Volume Three*), Leo Smith, Anthony Davis (in his opera, *X*), Pauline Oliveros, Tim Berne Marcio Mattos and Eddie Prevost, with whom she toured in the UK as a duo in 1991. Recent recordings of her own music have included the solos *Labyrinths* and *Live In San Francisco*, duos with Braxton and Irène Schweizer, two trio sets - *The Kitchen Concert*, with her Braxton Quartet colleagues Mark Dresser and Gerry Hemingway; *Live In Zurich*, with Workman and Paul Motian - and an electrifying ensemble session, *Circles*, with Workman, Hemingway and saxophonists Peter Buettner and Oliver Lake, which had writer Ben Watson enthusing that she had 'tapped into the physical assault of late Trane'. In fact, while Coltrane remains an idol - and her versions of his 'Dear Lord' and 'After The Rain' show an astonishing power and beauty - it is Cecil Taylor, with his phenomenal force, speed and intensity, who is her primary musical influence; and she also cites Thelonious Monk, Paul Bley, Leo Smith, African pop music (for its rhythmic qualities) and Braxton (for his use of space and structure) as important models. Taylor has lauded her work as spearheading 'a new lyricism', but - although recent albums have explored more reflective modes - the essential components of her music are, as she stated in 1988, counterpoint, pointillism and, especially, energy: 'I think of energy as carrying itself forward (in the music), being directed but not decided . . . When you're really hooked into the music, you can reach another level of energy that goes beyond the mechanics of it; a feeling of going higher, to a non-mundane state.' One of the most exciting improvisers to have appeared in the last 20 years, Crispell is the first and perhaps to date the only genuine member of a post-Taylor era of jazz pianism: she has not merely accommodated elements of his style into her playing, but has used his language as the launching-pad from which she has developed her own, entirely personal and utterly distinctive music. To quote Braxton, 'she has the kind of facility that is awesome'.

● ALBUMS: *Spirit Music* (1983)★★★★, *Rhythms Hung In Undrawn Sky* (Leo 1983)★★★, *Concert In Berlin* (1983)★★, *Live In Berlin* (Black Saint 1984)★★, with Doug James *And Your Ivory Voice Sings* (Leo 1985)★★★, *Quartet Improvisations - Paris 1986* (Leo 1987)★★★, *Gaia* (Leo 1988)★★★★, *Labyrinths* (1988)★★★, *Live In San Francisco* (Music And Arts 1990)★★★★, *For Coltrane* (Leo 1990)★★★★, *Live In Zurich* (Leo 1990)★★★, with Anthony Braxton *Duets Vancouver 1989* (1990)★★★, *The Kitchen Concert* 1989 recording (Leo 1991)★★, with Irène Schweizer *Overlapping Hands: Eight Segments* (FMP 1991)★★★★, *Circles* (1991)★★★★, *Highlights From The 1992 American Tour* (1993)★★★, with Georg Graewe *Piano Duets (Tuned & Detuned Pianos)* (Leo 1993)★★★★, *Santuerio* (Leo 1993)★★★★, *Duo* (Knitting Factory 1993)★★★, *Stellar Pulsations/Three Composers* (Leo 1993)★★★★, with Eddie Prévost *Band On The Wall* (Matchless 1994)★★★★, *Destiny* (Okka 1995)★★★★, *The Woodstock Concert* (Music & Arts 1996)★★★, *Contrasts, Live At Yoshi's* (Music & Arts 1996)★★★, *Live At Mills College 1995* (Music & Arts 1995)★★★★, with Paul Motian, Gary Peacock *Nothing Ever Was, Anyway: Music Of Annette Peacock* (ECM 1997)★★★★, with Evan Parker *Natives And Aliens* (Leo 1998)★★★★.

CRISS, SONNY

b. William Criss, 23 October 1923, Memphis, Tennessee, USA, d. 19 November 1977. Criss first came to prominence in Los Angeles in the mid-late 40s, playing with Howard McGhee, Billy Eckstine, Gerald Wilson and Jazz At The Philharmonic. One of the first alto saxophonists to absorb the lessons of Charlie Parker, Criss developed into a fluent, intense bebopper whom Ornette Coleman later described as 'the fastest man alive'. In the mid-50s he worked with Buddy Rich's quintet and also led his own groups, including line-ups with Sonny Clark and Wynton Kelly. In 1961 he settled in Paris for a number of years, then returned to Los Angeles and recorded a series of mostly excellent albums for Prestige (1966-69). Perhaps most outstanding was the big band *Sonny's Dream (Birth Of The New Cool)*, which featured the compositions and arrangements of Criss's west coast colleague Horace Tapscott. Following a breakdown, Criss became involved in social work, chiefly with alcoholics but also playing and teaching in schools. In 1974 he revisited Europe and a little later began recording again, making a trio of superb small-group albums that displayed as well as ever the uniquely affecting alto tone which writer Mark Gardner called 'a piercing, passionate sound from the heart'. Two later albums that laden Criss with strings and a supposedly funky beat were less successful artistically. In November 1977, shortly before a scheduled tour of Japan, Criss died at home from gunshot wounds that were possibly the result of an accident but, it is generally believed, were more probably self-inflicted.

● ALBUMS: *Sonny Criss Collates* (Mercury 1953)★★★★, *Jazz USA* (Imperial 1955)★★★, *Go Man It's Sonny Criss And Modern Jazz* (Imperial 1956)★★★, *Plays Cole Porter* (Imperial 1956)★★, *At The Crossroads* (Peacock 1959)★★, *Criss Cross* (Imperial 1962)★★★★, *Blues Pour Flirters* (1963)★★★, *This Is Sonny Criss!* (Prestige 1966)★★★, *Portrait Of Sonny Criss* (Prestige 1967)★★★★, *Up, Up And Away* (Prestige 1968)★★, *The Beat Goes On* (Prestige 1968)★★, *Rockin' In Rhythm* (Prestige 1968)★★, *Sonny's Dream* (Prestige 1968)★★★★, *I'll Catch The Sun* (Prestige 1969)★★★, *Crisscraft* (Muse 1975)★★★, *Saturday Morning* (Xanadu 1975)★★★, *Out Of Nowhere* (Muse 1976)★★★★, *Warm And Sunny* (1976)★★, *The Joy Of Sax* (1977)★★, *Live In Italy* (Fresh Sounds 1988)★★★, *Sonny Criss In Paris* (Fresh Sounds 1988)★★★.

● COMPILATIONS: with Kenny Dorham *The Bopmasters* 1959 recording (1978)★★★.

CRITCHENSON, JOHN

b. 24 December 1934, London, England. Pianist Critchenson seemed to spring from nowhere in 1979 when he joined Ronnie Scott's Quintet. In fact he had played semi-professionally for many years while retaining his non-musical 'day job'. He had taken piano lessons early on, but he was a good player 'by ear' and was thus effectively self-taught. From 1980-83 he was with the highly successful Morrissey-Mullen band and continued with Scott: indeed he once toured with both bands simultaneously. He is still with Scott's house band and also works with Scott drummer Martin Drew's own group.

● ALBUMS: *Summer Afternoon* (1982)★★★, *New Night* (1984)★★.

CROMBIE, TONY

b. 27 August 1925, London, England. Active among the eager young British beboppers of the early 40s, Crombie, a self-taught drummer, broadened his musical knowledge by securing work on post-war transatlantic liners. The main objective of many British musicians, like Crombie, who obtained such employment, was not to play dance music for the passengers but to get to New York to hear American bebop artists in person. In the late 40s and early 50s he was still playing in London clubs and also working as an accompanist to visiting American stars, including singers Lena Horne and Carmen McRae. In the 50s he worked regularly with Ronnie Scott and Victor Feldman and was much in demand to accompany jazz solo musicians touring the UK. Anything but narrow in his musical tastes, in 1956 Crombie formed a rock 'n' roll band, the Rockets (a name he also used, confusingly, for a 1958 band which featured many of the outstanding British jazzmen of the period, including Scott and Tubby Hayes). Crombie's roots were in jazz, however, and he was a member of the resident rhythm section at Ronnie Scott's club.

In the late 50s and throughout the 60s, he turned more and more to writing: he wrote scores for films and television and also composed tunes recorded by a wide range of artists including Miles Davis, who featured 'So Near, So Far' on *Seven Steps To Heaven*. A duo he formed with organist Alan Haven had considerable popular success. In the 70s and 80s he continued to write but also played frequently at clubs and in concert, often with Scott but also with the popular jazz-loving singer/organist Georgie Fame. A highly versatile musician, Crombie also plays piano and vibraphone. His piano playing, especially on his own compositions, has a sombre beauty which reflects his love and admiration for the music of Duke Ellington.

● ALBUMS: *At The Royal Festival Hall With The Ronnie Scott Orchestra And Tony Crombie* (1956)★★★★, *Atmosphere* (1958)★★★★, *Relaunch* (1958)★★★, *Man From Interpol* (1960)★★★, *Tony Crombie (i)* (1960)★★★, *Tony Crombie (ii)* (1960)★★★, *Sweet, Wild And Blue* (1960)★★★, with Alan Haven *Through Till Two* (1966)★★★★, with Mike Carr *Hammond Under Pressure* (1968)★★★★, *Tony Crombie And Friends* (Renaissance 1989)★★★.

Crosby, Bob

b. George Robert Crosby, 25 August 1913, Spokane, Washington, USA, d. 9 March 1993, La Jolla, California, USA. For most of his early career, Crosby was inevitably overshadowed by his older brother, Bing Crosby. Nevertheless, he achieved modest success thanks to a pleasant voice and a matching personality. In the immediate pre-swing era years he sang with Anson Weeks and then joined the band co-led by brothers Jimmy and Tommy Dorsey. In 1935 the disaffected musicians who had left the Ben Pollack band decided to form a co-operative group but wanted a frontman. They approached Crosby, who accepted the job, bringing a casual, relaxed air to one of the swing era's liveliest bands. Unusually, the band favoured an energetic, two-beat Dixieland style that became extremely popular. The leading musicians in the band were trumpeters Billy Butterfield and Yank Lawson, saxophonists Eddie Miller, Irving Fazola and Matty Matlock and rhythm players Bob Zurke, Hilton 'Nappy' Lamare, Bob Haggart and Ray Bauduc. After the band folded in 1942 Crosby continued to make films and personal appearances, sometimes as leader of reconstituted Dixieland-style bands, sometimes of more contemporary-sounding bands. Generally, by the 70s and 80s, these groups bore little resemblance to the original Bob Crosby band, but the fans loved it all. Crosby died of cancer at Scripps Memorial Torrey Pines Convalescent Hospital in 1993.

● ALBUMS: *One Night Stand* (1946)★★★, *Swinging At The Sugar Bowl* 10-inch album (Coral 1950)★★★, *Dixieland Jazz 1* 10-inch album (Coral 1950)★★★, *Marches In Dixieland Style* 10-inch album (Coral 1950)★★★, *St. Louis Blues* 10-inch album (Coral 1950)★★★, *Bob Crosby And His Bobcats* (Capitol 1952/54)★★★, *The Golden Days Of Jazz* (1954)★★★★, *Five Feet Of Swing* (Decca 1954)★★★, *Bob Crosby's Bobcats* (Decca 1954)★★★, *The Bobcats' Ball* (Coral 1955)★★★, *Bobcats' Blues* (Coral 1956)★★★, *Bobcats On Parade* (Coral 1956)★★★, *Bob Crosby In Hi Fi* (Coral 1956)★★★, *The Bobcats In Hi Fi* (Coral 1958)★★★, *Petite Fleur* (Dot 1959)★★, *The Sounds Of The Swing Years* (1960)★★★, *Live At The Rainbow Grill* (1960)★★, *Mardi Gras Parade* (1960)★★★.

● COMPILATIONS: *Bob Crosby 1936 - 1956* (Coral 1957)★★★, *The Hits Of Bob Crosby's Bobcats* (Capitol 1961)★★★, *Bob Crosby's Bobcats - Their Greatest Hits* (Decca 1966)★★★★, *Bob Crosby On The Air, 1940* (Aircheck 1979)★★★, *Bob Crosby And His Orchestra, 1935-36* (Rarities 1981)★★★★, *20 Golden Pieces* (Bulldog 1981)★★★★, *Camel Caravans - The Summer Of '39* (Giants Of Jazz 1985)★★★, *Suddenly It's 1939* (Giants Of Jazz 1985)★★★★, *Accent On Swing* (Giants Of Jazz 1986)★★★, *The Big Apple, 1936-40* (Bandstand 1988)★★★, *Sugar Foot Strut (1936-42)* (Bandstand 1988)★★★★, *Bob Crosby - Jazz Classics In Digital Stereo* (BBC 1988)★★★.

● FURTHER READING: *Stomp Off, Let's Go! The Story Of Bob Crosby's Bob Cats & Big Band*, John Chilton.

Crosby, Gary

b. 26 January 1955, London, England. Born in London of Jamaican parents, and nephew of the unjustly-neglected guitarist Ernest Ranglin, Crosby was (along with a few others, like the fine tenor saxophonist Ray Carless) one of the pioneer black British jazz talents, making his reputation before the scene blossomed so dramatically in the mid-80s. He began to study trumpet at the age of 13, although he had played around on various other instruments at home. He took trumpet lessons at a community centre in Fulham for a couple of years, but subsequently switched to bass, studying with Peter Ind between the ages of 19 and 23. His first gig was with Ed Bentley alongside Carless. Later on, he was an original member of the Jazz Warriors. He has established a group of his own which is designed to give young musicians space for a year or two so they can develop themselves, strike out on their own and be replaced by other young musicians, generally from the Warriors circle. The band played regular sessions at London's Jazz Café. Like most bassists he gets far less of the limelight than the saxophonists, pianists and drummers, and certainly far less than his talent deserves. An excellent, thoroughly dependable bass player, he has worked with, amongst many others, Steve Williamson and John Stevens.

● ALBUMS: with Bukky Leo *River Nile* (1990)★★, with Steve Williamson *Waltz For Grace* (1990)★★★★, with Cleveland Watkiss *Blessing In Disguise* (1991)★★, with Williamson *Rhyme Time* (1991)★★★.

CROSBY, ISRAEL

b. 19 January 1919, Chicago, Illinois, USA, d. 11 August 1962. A musical prodigy, Crosby had mastered several instruments before taking up the bass in 1934. Within a year he was noticed by John Hammond and had made his first recordings with Gene Krupa and Jess Stacy and among the results was 'Blues For Israel' which attained classic status. On this track he demonstrated a new style of bass-playing in jazz which was to blossom more fully a little later with the emergence of the better-known Jimmy Blanton. Crosby went on to work with Fletcher Henderson and made records with several small groups including those of Teddy Wilson, Roy Eldridge and Coleman Hawkins. A master musician with a virtuoso technique, Crosby was mostly engaged in studio work throughout the 40s and 50s but also struck up an musical partnership with Ahmad Jamal, and he also played jazz with Benny Goodman and George Shearing.

CROSSFIRE

This jazz-rock group was formed in 1974 and based in Sydney, Australia. The band comprised Jim Kelly (guitar), Greg Lyon (bass), Ian Bloxsom (percussion), Michael Kenny (piano), Steve Hopes (drums) and Tony Buchanan (saxophone). Crossfire were of a high enough standard of musicianship to gather worldwide recognition, the band served a long apprenticeship in jazz venues, often as the backing band for other artists, with the various members still concentrating on session work. Early on the band showed a lot of blues influence in their playing probably due to members having played in R&B and soul bands previously. By the late 70s the band was touring widely overseas, spending time in Asia, Europe and America, having played such prestigious gigs as the Newport Jazz Festival and Ronnie Scott's in London, as well as recording modest-selling albums at home. The band have backed many jazz soloists on their visits to Australia, including Michael Franks, which resulted in the release of a live album.

● ALBUMS: *Crossfire* (1975)★★★, *Direct To Dist* (1977)★★★, *East Of Where* (1980)★★, *Hysterical Rockords* (1981)★★.

CROTHERS, CONNIE

b. 2 June 1941, Palo Alto, California, USA. Crothers moved to New York in 1962 to study piano with Lennie Tristano and has since worked chiefly with fellow-Tristanoites. In the 70s she played with Warne Marsh, recorded the solo and trio set *Perception* and, in 1979, performed at the Lennie Tristano Memorial Concert. She continued to record in the 80s, both solo and in duos with altoist Richard Tabnik and the great percussionist Max Roach. Her latest releases have been with the quartet she co-leads with Lenny Popkin (tenor saxophone), featuring Cameron Brown (bass) and Tristano's daughter, Carol (drums). In common with other Tristano disciples, Crother's repertoire comprises a handful of standards that she endlessly reshapes in improvisations based on her advanced harmonic understanding.

● ALBUMS: *Perception* (1974)★★★★, *Connie Crothers Trio* (1974)★★★, with others *Lennie Tristano Memorial Concert* (1979)★★, *Solo* (1980)★★★, with Max Roach *Swish* (1982)★★★, *Concert At Cooper Union* (1984)★★★, with Richard Tabnik *Duo Dimension* (1987)★★★, *Love Energy* (1988)★★★, *New York Night* (1990)★★★.

CROUCH, STANLEY

b. 14 December 1945, Los Angeles, California, USA. Cousin of gospel super-star Andrae Crouch, Stanley was a self-taught drummer who started playing in 1966 to accompany poet Jayne Cortez. In 1967 he formed a quartet with altoist Arthur Blythe and trumpeter Bobby Bradford. In the early 70s he taught drama at Claremont College and led the Black Music Infinity Orchestra that included James Newton (flute), David Murray (tenor saxophone) and Mark Dresser (bass). In 1975 he moved to New York, contributing to Alan Douglas's celebrated *Wildflowers* anthologies. He also started writing for *Village Voice*, his career as a critic gradually eclipsing his work on the drums. He applauded the restoration of bop values represented by Wynton Marsalis, writing controversial sleevenotes that blamed 60s free music and fusion for a decline in standards, quoting conservative culture critic Christopher Lasch to bolster his case. America's black middle-class had found its aesthetic spokesman.

CROWDER, BOB

b. Robert Henry Crowder, 1912, USA. During the early 30s he played tenor saxophone with various territory bands based mostly in Milwaukee, Wisconsin. He then moved to Chicago where he performed in big bands led by Horace Henderson, Earl Hines and others, and in small groups with Coleman Hawkins. Although continuing to play, his career decision to remain in Chicago and not tour kept him from the sight and awareness of jazz audiences. A secure and reliable player, Crowder's work as a section man is beyond reproach.

CRUMBLEY, ELMER

b. 1 August 1908, Kingfisher, Oklahoma, USA. As a child he was raised in various parts of the Midwest and eventually began playing trombone with territory bands including those led by Lloyd Hunter and George E. Lee, the latter in Kansas City. During the late 20s and early 30s he worked in a succession of bands, including Erskine Tate's, before joining Jimmie Lunceford in 1934. He remained in this band until 1947 when the band broke up after Lunceford's death. During the rest of the decade and into the early 50s, he played with bands including Lucky Millinder's and Erskine

Hawkins', then toured Europe with Sammy Price. In the 60s he was based mostly in New York and was often called upon to participate in big band revivals, playing with Cab Calloway, Earl 'Fatha' Hines and, in the early 70s, Hawkins. A good section player, Crumbley also sang rather unremarkably.

CRUSADERS

This remarkably versatile group was formed in Houston, Texas, as the Swingsters. During the 50s, Wilton Felder (b. 31 August 1940, Houston, Texas, USA; reeds), Wayne Henderson (b. 24 September 1939, Houston, Texas, USA; trombone), Joe Sample (b. 1 February 1939, Houston, Texas, USA; keyboards) and Nesbert 'Stix' Hooper (b. 15 August 1938, Houston, Texas, USA; drums), forged a reputation as an R&B group before moving to California. Known as the Jazz Crusaders, they were signed by the Pacific Jazz label for whom they recorded a series of melodious albums. In 1970 the quartet truncated their name to the Crusaders in deference to an emergent soul/funk perspective. In truth the group exaggerated facets already prevalent in their work, rather than embark on something new. A 1972 hit, 'Put It Where You Want It', established a tight, precise interplay and an undeniably rhythmic pulse. The song was later recorded by the Average White Band, the kind of approval confirming the Crusaders' newfound status. Henderson left the group in 1975, and several session musicians, including master guitarist Larry Carlton, augmented the remaining nucleus on their subsequent recordings. In 1979 the Crusaders began using featured vocalists following the success of 'Street Life'. This international hit helped launch Randy Crawford's solo career, while a further release, 'I'm So Glad I'm Standing Here Today', re-established Joe Cocker. Although Hooper left the line-up in 1983, and was replaced by Leon Ndugu Chancler, Felder and Sample continued the group's now accustomed pattern. *The Good And Bad Times*, released in 1986, celebrated the Crusaders 30th anniversary and featured several 'special guests' including jazz singer Nancy Wilson.

● ALBUMS: as the Jazz Crusaders: *Freedom Sound* (Pacific Jazz 1961)★★★, *Lookin' Ahead* (Pacific Jazz 1962)★★★★, *The Jazz Crusaders At The Lighthouse* (Pacific Jazz 1962)★★★, *Tough Talk* (Pacific Jazz 1963)★★★, *Heat Wave* (Pacific Jazz 1963)★★★, *Stretchin' Out* (Pacific Jazz 1964)★★★, *The Thing* (Pacific Jazz 1964)★★★, *Chile Con Soul* (Pacific Jazz 1965)★★, *The Jazz Crusaders At Lighthouse '66* (Pacific Jazz 1966)★★★, *Talk That Talk* (Pacific Jazz 1966)★★★, *The Festival Album* (Pacific Jazz 1967)★★, *The Jazz Crusaders At Lighthouse '68* (Pacific Jazz 1968)★★★, *Powerhouse* (Pacific Jazz 1969)★★★, *The Jazz Crusaders At Lighthouse '69* (Pacific Jazz 1969)★★★, *Uh Huh* (Pacific Jazz 1969)★★★, *Old Socks New Shoes, New Socks Old Shoes* (Chisa 1970)★★★★. As the Crusaders: *Pass The Plate* (Blue Thumb 1971)★★★, *Crusaders 1* (Blue Thumb 1972)★★★★, *Second Crusade* (Blue Thumb 1973)★★★★, *Unsung Heroes* (Blue Thumb 1973)★★★, *Scratch* (Blue Thumb 1974)★★★★, *Southern Comfort* (Blue Thumb 1974)★★★, *Chain Reaction* (Blue Thumb 1975)★★★★, *Those Southern Nights* (Blue Thumb 1976)★★★, *Free As The Wind* (Blue Thumb 1977)★★★, *Images* (Blue Thumb 1978)★★★, *Street Life* (MCA 1979)★★★★, *Rhapsody And Blues* (MCA 1980)★★★, with Joe Cocker *Standing Tall* (MCA 1981)★★, *Live Sides* (1981)★★, with B.B. King and the Royal Philharmonic Orchestra *Royal Jam* (MCA 1982)★★, *Ongaku-Kai: Live In Japan* (Crusaders 1982)★★★, *Free As The Wind* (ABC 1983)★★, *Ghetto Blaster* (MCA 1984)★★★, *The Good And Bad Times* (MCA 1986)★★★, *Life In The Modern World* (MCA 1988)★★★, *Healing The Wounds* (GRP 1991)★★★.

● COMPILATIONS: *Best Of The Crusaders* (Blue Thumb 1976)★★★★, *The Vocal Album* (MCA 1987)★★★, *The Story So Far* (1988)★★★, *Sample A Decade* (Connoisseur Collection 1989)★★★, *The Golden Years* 3-CD set (1992)★★★, *The Greatest Crusade* 2-CD set (Calibre 1995)★★★★, *Soul Shadows* (Connoisseur Collection 1995)★★★, *Way Back Home* 4-CD box set (GRP 1996)★★★★, *The Crusaders* (GRP 1998)★★★.

CUBANISMO

This all-star Cuban big band was formed in 1995 by Jesús Alemañy (b. 14 October 1962, Guanabacoa, Havana, Cuba; trumpet, ex-Sierra Maestra), initially for a recording session at Egrem studios in Havana with producer Joe Boyd. Also in the line-up were Alfredo Rodriquez, veteran percussionist Tata Gianes, trumpeters Louis Alemany and Louis Alemany Jnr. (Jesus's uncle and cousin, respectively) and various members of Irakere. *Jesús Alemañy's ¡Cubanismo!* (the word 'Cubanismo' translates as 'typical of Cuba') featured a selection of mostly instrumental tracks, based around classic Cuban dance rhythms, all performed with the raw energy and improvisational flair of the best Latin jazz. Critical response to the album was highly favourable and it featured in many world music polls for 1996, in the Best Of Latin category. The band subsequently toured and recorded a follow-up, *Malembe*. Released in 1997, it utilized the same formula of Cuban dance rhythms performed in a big-band Latin jazz style. 1998's *Reencarnación* introduces pianist Nachito Herrera, replacing Alfredo Rodriquez. A more straight-ahead Latin album, with less of a big band feel and more vocals (vocalist Rollo Martinez had also been added to the line-up). The band promoted it with an extensive tour of Europe and the USA, which included performances at the Montreux and North Sea Jazz Festivals.

● ALBUMS: *Jesús Alemañy's ¡Cubanismo!* (Hannibal 1996)★★★★, *Malembe* (Hannibal 1997)★★★, *Reencarnación* (Hannibal 1998)★★★★.

CUBER, RONNIE

b. Ronald Edward Cuber, 25 December 1941, New York City, New York, USA. Born into a highly musical family of Polish immigrants, Cuber began playing clarinet when he was aged about seven. Later, he switched to tenor saxophone but when he auditioned for the Newport Youth Band in 1959 he was asked by band director Marshall Brown to play baritone, the instrument upon which he then settled. Cuber had already gained valuable knowledge from studies at the Brooklyn Conservatory of Music and after appearing with the Brown-led youth band at the 1959 Newport Jazz Festival he became a reliable section man with Slide Hampton and Maynard Ferguson in the early to mid-60s. In 1966 he joined George Benson's quartet and began to solo more, gradually widening appreciation of his skills. He played with Lionel Hampton and Woody Herman in the late 60s and then moved through a succession of bands performing a wide variety of musical styles including Latin, with Eddie Palmieri, and rock and soul, with King Curtis and Aretha Franklin amongst others. During the 70s and into the early 80s he often led his own small outfits, and also worked in Lee Konitz's nine-piece band, with Mickey Tucker, Nick Brignola and other jazzmen. He was also regularly called upon for sessions with pop recording artists including Paul Simon, the Average White Band, Carly Simon and Steely Dan where he was partnered by Donald Fagen. In the late 80s Cuber was again leading his own small groups and also toured with the Mingus Epitaph Orchestra. In his playing, he constantly refers to all the many musical styles he has experienced over the years. Owing to his early playing of the tenor, he has brought a lightness of touch and sound to the baritone saxophone and is one of the instrument's foremost jazz practitioners.

● ALBUMS: *Cuber Libre* (Xanadu 1976)★★★, *The Eleventh Day Of Aquarius* (Xanadu 1978)★★★★, *Live At The Blue Note* (Pro Jazz 1982)★★★★, *Cubism* (Fresh Sound 1991)★★★, *The Scene Is Clean* (Milestone 1993)★★★, *Airplay* (Steeplechase 1993)★★, *In A New York Minute* (Steeple Chase 1996)★★★★, *The Scene Is Clean* (Milestone 1996)★★★, *NY Cats* (Steeplechase 1998)★★★, as Three Baritone Saxophone Band *Three Baritone Saxophone Band Plays Mulligan* (Dreyfus 1998)★★★.

CUFFEE, ED

b. Edward Emerson Cuffee, 7 June 1902, Norfolk, Virginia, USA, d. 3 January 1959. During the mid- and late 20s he played trombone with several bands, based mostly in New York, among which were Clarence Williams and McKinney's Cotton Pickers. In 1936 he joined Fletcher Henderson's orchestra where he remained for nearly three years. He then played in various bands, including Count Basie's. By the late 40s, when he recorded with Bunk Johnson, Cuffee was playing only part-time and thereafter worked mostly outside music. An interesting and sometimes inspired player, Cuffee had a penchant for the blues, and was always a dependable sideman.

CULLEY, WENDELL

b. Wendell Phillips Culley, 8 January 1906, Worcester, Massachusetts, USA. Culley began playing trumpet as a young man, working mostly in and around his hometown and in Boston. In 1930 he went to New York, played briefly with Horace Henderson and Cab Calloway, then began the first of three long spells with big bands. First came Noble Sissle's where he stayed for 11 years. In 1944 he joined Lionel Hampton for a five-year period before returning for a couple of years to Sissle. In 1951 his third long-running engagement was with Count Basie where he remained until the end of the decade when he retired from music. Almost always an anonymous sideman, Culley's solid playing was eminently well suited to the controlled dance music played by Sissle and to the disciplined fire of 50s Basie. In this sense he seemed a little out of his milieu in the often raucous Hampton band of the late 40s. The reality of that band was, of course, that beneath the frenzied soloing by the leader and some sidemen, the rest of the band concentrated upon laying down a solid foundation for the up-front shenanigans. When Culley did have an occasional solo spot, as on Hampton's 1947 version of 'Midnight Sun', or 'Two Finger Boogie' from 1945, he handled them very well. On the former, he plays a smooth passage on the second bridge, using a near-classical style with a well-controlled vibrato. On the later, he plays tightly muted and develops his solo with intelligence.

CULLUM, JIM

b. 20 September 1941, San Antonio, Texas, USA. Although little known outside his home state for many years, cornetist Cullum has played an important part in preserving interest in traditional jazz in America. He first played in a band led by his namesake father, later taking over leadership and running both the family recording company and a jazz room at San Antonio's Landing Hotel. Visiting guest musicians or resident old-timers like Ernie Caceres always fitted in well with the band's style. Cullum's records show his band to be a lively, entertaining group with good solos and a tight ensemble sound - what they lack in profundity they certainly make up in spirit. In 1991, his band was one of the musical attractions of the San Antonio Centennial Fiesta.

● ALBUMS: *'Tis The Season To Be Jamming* (1985)★★★, *Super Satch* (Stomp Off 1986)★★★, *Porgy And Bess* (CBS 1987)★★★★, *Hooray For Hoagy* (Audiophile 1990)★★★, *Music Of Jelly Roll Morton* (Stomp Off 1993)★★★.

CUNNINGHAMS

After playing alto saxophone and a variety of percussion instruments, Don Cunningham (b. 14 January 1931, St Louis, Missouri, USA), spent time in the US Army where he played in military bands. After army service, he joined the orchestra for the touring Johnny Mathis show as percussionist. After a few years he decided to form his own group, a quartet, in which he also began to feature his singing. The quartet played mostly in and around St. Louis but in the early 70s he moved to Los Angeles where he met and married a young vocalist. Alicia Cunningham (b. 5 October 1946, Los Angeles, California, USA), was classically trained as a singer and pianist and had worked in studios and as a teacher. The combination of Don's jazz-influenced energetic singing style and Alicia's fluid clear and lyrical sound proved exciting and interesting and they began to develop a solid reputation in Los Angeles. For several years the Cunninghams built their act upon a wide range of music, attempting to please all kinds of audiences without necessarily satisfying their own musical needs. In the early 80s they concentrated on singing only what they wanted to sing and soon built a substantial, if still parochial, following on the west coast. Occasional engagements in the Caribbean and the Orient helped to expand their horizons but the big international breakthrough proved elusive. Towards the end of the decade they were a big hit at the UK Hayfield Jazz Festival. Their records were played on the radio and organizers of such major festivals as Cork and Edinburgh expressed an interest in them. Their disparate singing styles provide an attractive musical mix, owing in part to Alicia's intricate and melodic harmonizing and to her arranging skills. The Cunninghams' stage presentation has enormous panache. They perform with skill, gusto and great attack.

● ALBUMS: *Something For Everyone* (1985)★★★, *Make Me (A Sweet Potato Pie)* (1987)★★★★, *I Remember Bird* (1988)★★★, *Scat Tones 'N' Bones* (1989)★★★.

Cuppini, Gil

b. Gilberto Cuppini, 6 June 1924, Milan, Italy, d. June 1996. Cuppini was in his twenties before he began playing drums but quickly reached proficiency and popularity. He played at the first Paris Jazz Fair in 1949 and began recording in the 50s. He played in and led several bands, mostly small groups, and worked with Gianni Basso and others. In 1958 he travelled to the USA with the International Youth Band directed by Marshall Brown and which also played the World's Fair at Brussels. During the 70s he was a first-call accompanist to American jazzmen visiting Italy. An accomplished technician, Cuppini played with a subtle sense of swing and blended well with fellow rhythm section players to provide support and encouragement to soloists.

● ALBUMS: *Not So Quiet Please* (Columbia 1950)★★★.

Curson, Ted

b. Theodore Curson, 3 June 1935, Philadelphia, Pennsylvania, USA. Trumpeter Curson played carnival gigs at the age of 12 and studied with tenor player Jimmy Heath. In the mid-50s he relocated to New York and worked with top pianists Mal Waldron, Red Garland and Cecil Taylor. He made his name with Charles Mingus, playing alongside Eric Dolphy and Booker Ervin in the 1959-60 band. Next he co-led a band with Philadelphian tenor saxophonist Bill Barron, recording the moving *Tears For Dolphy* in 1964; but then left for Europe in 1965. In 1973 he played in Zurich's Playhouse orchestra and in the 70s freelanced in Paris and New York, playing with pianists Andrew Hill and Kenny Barron among others. Keen to spread jazz interest he has frequently played and lectured at UCLA, the University of Vermont and at Denmark's Vallekilde Music School. In the 80s he ran a New York City jazz radio show. He brings a fervent tone to everything he plays, combining it with an assured grasp of the history of the music.

● ALBUMS: *Plenty Of Horn* (Old Town 1961)★★★, *Plays Fire Down Below* (Prestige 1963)★★★★, with Bill Barron *The Leopard* (Audiophile 1963)★★★, with Barron *Tears For Dolphy* (Black Lion 1964)★★★, *Now Hear This* (Audio Fidelity 1964)★★★★, *The New Thing And The Blue Thing* (Atlantic 1965)★★, *Jubilant Power* (1976)★★★, *The Trio* (Interplay 1979)★★★, *I Heard Mingus* (Interplay 1980)★★★, *Ted Curson And Co* (India Navigation 1984)★★★, *Canadian Concert Of Ted Curson* (Can-Am 1987)★★★, *Traveling On* (Evidence 1997)★★★★.

Cuscuna, Michael

b. 20 September 1948, Stamford, Connecticut, USA. Cuscuna developed an interest in jazz and began to learn drums at the age of 12, also exploring saxophone and flute. Realizing he would not make it as a professional player, he enrolled at the University of Pennsylvania Wharton School of Business in 1966 with the idea of creating his own record label. Business studies were not congenial and he switched to English literature. Later he began a nightly jazz radio show (WXPN), which led to part-time work for ESP-Disk, the legendary New York free music label of the 60s. He started writing about jazz (*Jazz And Pop*, *Downbeat*) and promoting in Philadelphia (Joe Henderson, Paul Bley). Producing a session for guitarist George Freeman (subsequently released on Delmark Records), Cuscuna became interested in the blues, recording Buddy Guy and Junior Wells. He pioneered underground rock radio at WMMR (Philadelphia), then WABC FM (New York), but left due to the imposition of formats and playlists in 1971. Next he recorded singer-songwriter Bonnie Raitt, started to produce for Atlantic Records (Dave Brubeck, Art Ensemble Of Chicago) then went freelance, producing for Atlantic, Motown, ABC (where he initiated a famous reissue series of 60s jazz from the Impulse! label), Muse and Arista. In 1977 he worked with Alan Douglas on the *Wildflower* series, the famous document of the black *avant garde* loft scene. Jazz editor of the trade magazine *Record World* (1971-76) he was also producer of a magnificent set of Anthony Braxton recordings for Arista (1974-82), where he helped to set up the Freedom and Novus labels as outlets for new jazz. Artists who recorded for him included Oliver Lake, Julius Hemphill, Henry Threadgill, Leo Smith, Cecil Taylor, Andrew Hill and Marion Brown. After five years of trying, he finally gained access to the vaults of Blue Note Records and began releasing unissued material (100 albums came out between 1975 and 1981). In 1983 he set up Mosaic Records to release limited-edition box-sets, mostly of bebop-related music from the 40s, 50s and 60s: music issued to date includes complete sessions by Thelonious Monk, Clifford Brown, Ike Quebec, Charles Mingus, Herbie Nichols, Tina Brooks, Nat 'King' Cole and many others, much of the material culled from the vaults of the Blue Note and Pacific Jazz labels and often including previously unreleased material. In 1984 he was involved with the reactivation of Blue Note, producing new sessions by McCoy Tyner, Tony Williams and Don Pullen among others as well as overseeing the label's latest reissue programme. In 1979 he was voted

Down Beat's 'Producer Of The Year' and has been voted number one or two ever since. Michael Cuscuna is a prime example of those enthusiasts who fight within the industry to give jazz more space on the record shelves.

CUTSHALL, CUTTY

b. Robert Dewees Cutshall, 29 December 1911, Huntington County, Pennsylvania, USA, d. 16 August 1968 After working with several bands in and around Pittsburgh, trombonist Cutshall worked with Charley Dornberger and Jan Savitt before joining Benny Goodman in 1940. Together with Lou McGarity, Cutshall helped give the Goodman band a remarkably solid sound achieved by bands with larger trombone sections. After war service, Cutshall again played with Goodman but with the sudden decrease in the number of name bands he began working more with smaller units, especially those performing at Nick's in New York. It was here that he established a long-lasting association with Eddie Condon. For two decades Cutshall played at Nick's and Condon's own club, then occasionally touring with like-minded musicians. He was involved with Yank Lawson and his old partner McGarity, in a series of bands labelled the Greats Of Jazz which would eventually metamorphose into the World's Greatest Jazz Band. Before this happened, however, Cutshall died on 16 August 1968.

● ALBUMS: with Nine Greats Of Jazz *Jazz In The Troc* (1966)★★★, with Ten Greats Of Jazz *Jazz In The Troc* (1968)★★★.

CYRILLE, ANDREW

b. 10 November 1939, Brooklyn, New York, USA. Cyrille graduated from the Juilliard School in 1958 and studied drums with Philly Joe Jones in the same year. In the early 60s he worked with the *risqué* nightclub singer Nellie Lutcher and tenor saxophonists Coleman Hawkins and Illinois Jacquet. In 1965 he started a 15-year association with Cecil Taylor, also working with musicians in the soul jazz camp such as Stanley Turrentine and Junior Mance. In 1969 he recorded *What About?* in Paris for BYG, one of the few completely successful solo drum records. In 1971 he formed Dialogue Of The Drums with Milford Graves and Rashied Ali. In the 70s he was artist-in-residence at Antioch College, Ohio. Cyrille is capable of playing time, free and everything in between, contributing rhythmic clarity to Taylor's music and supplying a flexible rhythmic base to the compositions of Muhal Richard Abrams and John Carter. In 1977 he toured Europe with Carla Bley and in the 80s he recorded several albums with his group Manao, which often featured trumpeter Ted Daniel, saxophonist David S. Ware and bassist Nick de Geronimo. He also recorded two duo albums with his Cecil Taylor Unit colleague, Jimmy Lyons and a trio album with Lyons and Jeanne Lee. In recent years, Cyrille has worked with the Reggie Workman Ensemble, played live duets with Marilyn Crispell and recorded with a wide range of artists, from Horace Tapscott and Geri Allen to Anthony Braxton and Billy Bang. In 1990 he toured the UK with a trio that featured free improviser Paul Rogers on bass and ex-Lou Reed guitarist Mark Hewins playing everything from John Coltrane to power psychedelia. Cyrille's open-minded attitude complements his consummate musicality.

● ALBUMS: *What About?* (Affinity 1969)★★★, with Milford Graves *Dialogue Of The Drums* (1974)★★★, *Metamusicians' Stomp* (Black Saint 1978)★★★★, with Jeanne Lee, Jimmy Lyons *Nuba* (Black Saint 1979)★★★★, *Junction* (IPS 1980)★★★, *Celebration* (IPS 1980)★★★, *Special People* (1981)★★★, with Lyons *Something In Return* 1981 recording (1988)★★, *The Navigator* (1984)★★, with Lyons *Burnt Offering* 1982 recording (1991)★★★, *Galaxies* (Music And Arts 1991)★★★, *My Friend Louis* (DIW 1992)★★★, *Good To Go: A Tribute To Bu* (Soul Note 1997)★★★★, with Oliver Lake, Reggie Workman *Live In Willisau* (Dizim 1998)★★★.

D'Amico, Hank

b. Henry D'Amico, 21 March 1915, Rochester, New York, USA, d. 3 December 1965. After working in bands in upstate New York, clarinettist and alto saxophonist, D'Amico worked with Paul Specht and Red Norvo during the mid-30s. Towards the end of the decade he played on radio with his own group, an octet, and also worked with the band of Richard Himber before joining Bob Crosby in 1940. The following year he formed his own big band which failed to make the grade then worked with Les Brown, Norvo again and Benny Goodman, upon whose playing D'Amico moulded his own clarinet style. In 1943 he became a staff musician at CBS Records, later moving to the ABC label. Throughout this period, until the mid-50s, D'Amico also played in a number of small jazz groups.

● ALBUMS: *Holiday With Hank* 10-inch album (Bethlehem 1954)★★★★, with Aaron Sachs *We Brought Our Axes* (Bethlehem 1957)★★★.

D'Andrea, Franco

b. 8 March 1941, Merano, Italy. D'Andrea developed his piano playing style during the 60s in the bands of Ninzio Rotondo, Gato Barbieri and Franco Ambrosetti. From 1968 he led the Modern Art Trio. In 1972 he formed the jazz rock band Rava Quartet and started to use synthesizers as well as the piano. His playing is technically adept and reflects an interest in pianists as diverse as James P. Johnson and Martial Solal. From the 60s onwards he accompanied and recorded with visiting Americans such as Dexter Gordon (tenor saxophone), Slide Hampton (trombone), Max Roach (drums), Lee Konitz (alto saxophone), Johnny Griffin (tenor saxophone) and Lucky Thompson (tenor saxophone). D'Andrea played with the Rava Quartet in 1979 before forming his own quartet in 1981. His work has won many prizes in Italy and he was twice voted Italian Jazz Musician of the Year (1982 and 1984) in the magazine Musica Jazz.

● ALBUMS: *Modern Art Trio* (1971)★★★, *Nuvolao* (1978)★★★, *From East To West* (1979)★★★, *My One And Only Love* (1983)★★★, *No Idea Of Time* (1984)★★, *Earthcake* (Label Bleu 1991)★★★, *Endrosadira* (Red 1992)★★★, *Airegin* (1993)★★★, *Flavours* (Penta Flowers 1995)★★★★, *Current Changes* (Penta Flowers 1995)★★★★, *Live In Perugia* (Penta Flowers 1996)★★, with Lee Konitz *Inside Cole Porter* (NelJazz 1998)★★★, with the New Quartet *Jobim* (Philology 1998)★★★★, *Chromatic Phrygian* 1989 recording (1998)★★★★, *3 Lines* (Philology 1998)★★, *Jobim* (Philology 1998)★★.

D*Note

The skills behind D*Note's brand of jazz, rap and rare groove belong chiefly to Matt Winn (Matt Wienevski), who is helped by scratcher Charlie Lexton and occasional keyboard player Matt Cooper (who records for Dorado in his own right as Outside). Their debut album housed the singles 'Now Is The Time', 'Bronx Bull', 'Scheme Of Things' and 'The More I See', each of which had had good reviews in their original formats. Wienevski's first film, a 10-minute short entitled *Round the Block*, was shown on the UK's Channel 4. *Criminal Justice* built on the energy level of the debut, but *Coming Down* was a marked disappointment, with only the forceful 'Waiting Hopefully' standing out.

● ALBUMS: *Babel* (Dorado 1993)★★★, *Criminal Justice* (Dorado 1995)★★★, *Coming Down* (VC 1997)★★.

Dahlander, Bert

b. Nils-Bertil Dahlander, 13 May 1928, Göteborg, Sweden. After studying various instruments, Dahlander chose the drums and first attracted wide attention with recordings accompanying Lars Gullin in the early 50s. From 1954 he was resident in the USA, playing in Chicago and, the following decade, in Aspen, Colorado. He occasionally toured Europe with American jazzmen, including Chet Baker and Terry Gibbs, and was also reunited with Gullin for European concerts. He was accompanist to some noted pianists, including Teddy Wilson, Earl Hines and Ralph Sutton. In the 70s he was often to be found back in Scandinavia. A deftly swinging drummer, Dahlander's subtle interplay with his fellow musicians is evidenced by the quality of artists who chose him for their rhythm sections.

● ALBUMS: *Skal* (Verve 1958)★★★, with Teddy Wilson *Mr Wilson And Mr Gershwin* (Columbia 1959)★★★, *Jazz With A Swedish Accent* (Everyday 1976)★★★.

Dailey, Albert

b. Albert Preston Dailey, 16 June 1938, Baltimore, Maryland, USA, d. 26 June 1984, Denver, Colorado, USA. After studying music intensively during early childhood, in his teens Dailey played piano in the pit band at a local theatre. His studies continued throughout much of the 50s and in 1960 he became accompanist to singer Damita Jo, then formed his own small band before moving to New York in 1964. Dailey began associating with leading jazzmen including Freddie Hubbard, with whom he recorded, and in 1967 he appeared with Woody Herman at the Monterey Jazz Festival. He was then hired by Art Blakey for the first of two spells with his Jazz Messengers. In the early 70s he worked with Sonny Rollins and Stan Getz, and, later in the decade, with other important figures, including Phil Woods and Elvin Jones. He continued working, mostly in and around New York, into the early 80s, recording with Getz (1983's *Poetry*) and Buddy De Franco. Although modern in his outlook and style, Dailey's playing carried a distinctive awareness of the long history of jazz piano. In addition to his playing, he also composed music and before his untimely death had completed several short and some longer pieces, all of which strongly suggested a powerful and still developing talent in this area of jazz.

● ALBUMS: *The Day After The Dawn* (Columbia 1972)★★★, *That Old Feeling* (Steeple Chase 1978)★★★, *Textures* (Muse 1981)★★★, with Stan Getz *Poetry* (Elektra 1983)★★★.

Daily, Pete

b. Thaman Pierce Daily, Portland, 5 May 1911, Indiana, USA, d. 23 August 1986. A dixieland cornetist, with his own popular combos in the USA in the 40s and 50s, Daily initially played the tuba before switching to cornet, and was still in his teens when he made his first records. During the 30s he was based mostly in Chicago, working with musicians such as Frank Melrose, Art Van Damme and Bud Freeman. He played with Mike Riley and Ozzie Nelson in the Los Angeles area in the early 40s, was in the navy during World War II, then returned to California in the late 40s. He formed his own band, Pete Daily's Chicagoans, in 1946, which became extremely popular and which he continued to lead throughout the 50s. Their records for Capitol Records included 'Johnson Rag', 'Take Me Out To The Ball Game', 'Dixieland Shuffle', 'Walkin' The Dog', and many more. In the 60s he returned to his home state and also switched to valve trombone. He played on through the 70s but early the following decade ill-health intervened. A strong, gutsy player, Daily's style was admirably suited to the commercial demands of the 50s on the west coast where Dixieland bands vied with one another for success. Daily's committed playing and considerable musicianship gave him an edge over his rivals.

● ALBUMS: with Phil Napoleon *Pete Daily/Phil Napoleon* 10-inch album (Decca 1950)★★★, *Dixieland Band* (Capitol 1950/54)★★★, *Dixie By Daily* (Capitol 1953/54)★★★.

● COMPILATIONS: *Pete Daily And His Chicagoans* (Jump 1946/48)★★★.

Dallwitz, Dave

b. 25 October 1914, Freeling, Australia. Dallwitz led a Dixieland jazz band called the Southern Jazz Group in the late 40s before turning to write and perform classical music. He returned to jazz in 1972 and has led a variety of bands including a scholarly ragtime ensemble which plays the classic rags as well as his own compositions in that style. He more often writes in a mainstream style which reflects his classical background. Among the musicians with whom he has worked is John Sangster (vibraphone).

● ALBUMS: *Melbourne Suite* (1973)★★★, *Ern Malley Suite* (1975)★★★.

Dalseth, Laila

b. 1940, Norway. An entirely self-taught singer, her first jazz influences came through listening to *Voice Of America* radio programmes as well as some Norwegian jazz programmes in the 50s. Her interest was captured by Ella Fitzgerald, Louis Armstrong and especially, Billie Holiday. In later years Dalseth also paid close attention to the work of Carmen McCrae, Sarah Vaughan, Mel Tormé and Cleo Laine. But of all of these it was Holiday who most affected Dalseth's style. Building repertoire intuitively from the Great American Song Book and from the jazz standards of the bop era, she has made some excellent records although it is yet to be heard much outside her homeland. When she has travelled, however, it has been to prestigious engagements such as the Nice Jazz Festival, the Playboy Jazz Festival in Hollywood, and jazz cruises on the *SS Norway*. She has appeared on radio and television in Norway, Germany and the UK. Her accompanists, on club dates and on record, include Howard Alden, Al Cohn, Kenny Davern, Arne Domnerus, Joe 'Flip' Phillips, Louis Stewart, Bob Wilber, and her husband, tenor saxophonist Totti Bergh.

● ALBUMS: *Metropol Jazz* (1963)★★★, *Laila Dalseth With Stokstad/Jensen* (1973)★★★, *Laila Dalseth With Wild Bill Davison* (1974)★★, *Just Friends* (1975)★★★, *Glad There Is You* (1978)★★★, *Swinging Departure* (1979)★★, *Daydreams* (Gemini 1984)★★★, *Time For Love* (Gemini 1986)★★★★, *Travelin' Light* (Gemini 1987)★★★, *Jazzmania* (1988)★★, *Nice Work* (Gemini 1990)★★★, *Some Other Time* (Gemini 1991)★★★, *The Judge And I* (Gemini 1992)★★★, *Remember* (Gemini 1995)★★★, *A Woman's Intuition* (Gemini 1995)★★★.

Daly Wilson Big Band

Australia's most commercially successful jazz orchestra was formed in 1968 by Sydney musicians, drummer Warren Daly and trombonist/arranger Ed Wilson. The band's debut was at Sydney's Stage Club in August 1969 and the personnel consisted of top jazz and session musicians including Dieter Vogt, Graeme Lyall, Bob McIvor, Col Nolan, Tony Buchanan and Kerrie Biddell. Ed Wilson, Paul McNamara and Doug Foskett provided the bulk of the arrangements. The 18-piece big band played a balanced repertoire of pop songs and originals which appealed to a mainstream youth audience. The band built up a strong following as a result of interstate touring and in September 1970 they recorded their debut *At The Cell Block*. The album was well received and followed by *Featuring Kerrie Biddell*. Financial and logistical problems led to the band giving a final concert at the Cremorne Orpheum in December 1971. Two years later corporate sponsorship enabled the outfit to be reformed and they toured and held concerts in New Zealand, Far East, Russia, and the Baltic States in 1975. Australian musical honours became frequent, including Mo awards in 1981 and 1982. *On Tour*, reached double gold status, while *Featuring Marcia Hines*, was successful in the pop market. The band became a subject of an excellent television special and continued to record and perform. Suddenly in September 1983 it was over. Sponsorship had been withdrawn and finances were as strained as the leaders' acrimonious relationship. The unit introduced jazz to a large commercial market, although some purists criticised its jazz/rock approach, but there were many future jazz greats that passed through its ranks and the Daly Wilson Big Band now enjoy a prominent place in Australian jazz history.

● ALBUMS: *Daly Wilson Big Band At The Cellblock* (Festival 1971)★★★, *The Exciting Daly Wilson Big Band Featuring Kerrie Biddell* (Festival 1972)★★, *On Tour* (Reprise 1973)★★★, *Featuring Marcia Hines* (Reprise 1975)★★★, *In Australia '77* (Hammard 1977)★★★★, *On The Road With The Daly Wilson Big Band* (Hammard 1978)★★★, *Too Good For A One Night Stand* (Hammard 1979)★★★.

● COMPILATIONS: *The Best Of...* (Hammard 1981)★★★★.

DALY, WARREN

b. Warren James Daly, 22 August 1943, Sydney, New South Wales, Australia. Daly entered the music profession in the 50s as a drummer with pop groups. During the following decade he broadened his field, playing in studio bands and also with jazz groups. By the late 60s he was concentrating on jazz, and visited the USA where he worked with musicians such as Buddy De Franco. On his return to his homeland he formed a big band with Ed Wilson. This band, which drew its fluctuating personnel from the best of Australian jazz and studio musicians, had an off and on existence during the 70s. During these years, Daly also worked in television as both player and as leader of studio orchestras. In the early 80s, Daly again showed his liking for the big band format, forming his own group along lines similar to the Daly-Wilson band. A powerful player with a strong sense of swing, throughout his continuing career Daly has made an important contribution to the Australian jazz scene.

● ALBUMS: with Ed Wilson *The Daly-Wilson Big Band On Tour* (Reprise 1973)★★★.

DAMERON, TADD

b. Tadley Ewing Peake Dameron, 21 February 1917, Cleveland, Ohio, USA, d. 8 March 1965, New York, USA. Dameron's early career found him working in several territory bands including those of Freddie Webster, Zack Whyte and Blanche Calloway, for whom he played piano and wrote arrangements. His first major impact on jazz came in 1939 when he joined Harlan Leonard's Kansas City-based band, the Rockets. One of the best of the lesser-known KC bands, the Rockets achieved considerable success in the mid-west and Dameron's charts for his own tunes 'A La Bridges' and 'Dameron Stomp' were outstanding, the first featuring Hank Bridges with both numbers giving solo space to the magnificent trombonist Fred Beckett. Dameron's arrangements subtly combined the loping swing which characterized KC bands, and the new ideas entering jazz from the bebop movement. During the early 40s, Dameron often sat in on New York after-hours sessions with Dizzy Gillespie and Charlie Parker but simultaneously worked on arrangements for some of the big swing bands, including those of Jimmie Lunceford and Count Basie, and more appropriately, the forward-thinking bands led by Georgie Auld and Billy Eckstine. In the late 40s Dameron wrote for Gillespie's big band and his composition 'Good Bait' became a bop standard. He also formed his own small (rising to 10-piece) groups which featured Fats Navarro and, later, Miles Davis. At the end of the 40s he spent some time in Europe working with Kenny Clarke and writing for the Ted Heath band. In the early 50s Dameron worked briefly with Clifford Brown but the mid-50s found him wrestling with drug addiction problems. He wrote for such diverse musicians as Artie Shaw and Carmen McRae, but his addiction led to periods of inactivity in music and eventually a spell in prison commencing in 1958. Released in 1960, he wrote for artists including Sonny Stitt and Milt Jackson and also recorded again. He died in March 1965. Throughout his troubled career, Dameron wrote with skill and finesse, displaying a marked appreciation of the more melodic aspects of bebop which he integrated into medium and big band formats with more success than most of his contemporaries or successors were able to achieve. In the early 80s, Philly Joe Jones, who had played in a 1953 Dameron band, formed a group, Dameronia, which recreated his music.

● ALBUMS: with Gil Evans *A Study in Dameronia* 10-inch album (Prestige 1953)★★★, *Clifford Brown Memorial* (1953)★★★, with John Coltrane *Mating Call* (Prestige 1956)★★★★, with Evans *Fontainebleau* (Prestige 1956)★★★★, *The Magic Touch Of Tadd Dameron* (Prestige 1962)★★★★, with Fats Navarro *Featured With The Tadd Dameron Quintet* (Jazzland 1962)★★★, *The Tadd Dameron Band* (Jazzland 1962)★★★, *Dameronia* (New Jazz 1963)★★★, *Good Bait* (Riverside 1968)★★★.

● COMPILATIONS: with Gil Evans *The Arrangers Touch* 1953/1956/1957 recordings (Prestige 1975)★★★★, *Keybop* (Jazz Live 1981)★★★.

DANDRIDGE, PUTNEY

b. 13 January 1902, Richmond, Virginia, USA, d. 15 February 1946. In the years immediately following the end of World War I Dandridge toured with tent shows. He also worked in vaudeville but settled for a while in upstate New York. In the early 30s he became accompanist to the celebrated dancer Bill 'Bojangles' Robinson. Dandridge worked on the fringes of jazz, playing piano as either a single or leader of a small group. His recordings are more jazz-orientated, featuring some excellent sidemen, including Red Allen, Roy Eldridge, Buster Bailey and Chu Berry. Although a competent pianist, Dandridge mainly sang on his record dates leaving the piano chores to artists such as Teddy Wilson and Ram Ramirez, composer of 'Lover Man'. Dandridge died in February 1946.

● COMPILATIONS: *Putney Dandridge Volumes 1-3* 1935-36 recordings (Rarities 1981)★★★.

DANIELE, PINO

b. Naples, Italy. A pioneering force in the development of a uniquely Italian jazz sound, guitarist Pino Daniele's work combines elements of trad jazz with new age and acid-jazz textures. His 1995 album, *Non Calpestare I Fiore Nel Deserto* (*Don't Tread On The Flowers In The Desert*), demonstrated the vitality of this approach, and in selling over 600,000 copies, became his nation's second biggest-selling record of the year. The album included guest appearances by singer/songwriter Irene

Grandi and the Italian rapper, Jovanotti. Manu Katche featured on drums and Jimmy Earl on bass. The tour which accompanied its release, jointly headlined by Pat Metheny, was voted the best of the year in the Premio Della Musica Italiana awards, while the single, 'Lo Per Lei', dominated the Italian pop charts during the summer months. Previously, Daniele had recorded in a more traditional jazz vein, working alongside world-renowned artists such as Chick Corea and Wayne Shorter.

● ALBUMS: *Non Calpestare I Fiore Nel Deserto* (CGC/East West 1995)★★★★.

DANIELS, EDDIE

b. 19 October 1941, New York City, New York, USA. Before choosing the clarinet as his principal instrument, Daniels played both alto and tenor saxophones. A graduate of the New York High School of the Performing Arts, Brooklyn College and the Juilliard School of Music, he worked as a teenager with Marshall Brown's Youth Band and Tony Scott. In the mid-60s, he began a six-year association with the Thad Jones-Mel Lewis big band and also played and recorded with leading jazz figures such as Freddie Hubbard, Sonny Rollins and Richard Davis. Gifted with a phenomenal technique, Daniels has been tempted into third-stream music, recording with Friedrich Gulda and has performed several works in a classical vein. His bright, clearly articulated playing has attracted a considerable following. As always with technically proficient musicians in jazz, there are some who question the depths of his jazz feeling. Clarinettist predecessors who also attracted criticism of this kind include Benny Goodman and Buddy De Franco, so if this is a flaw then Daniels is certainly in good company. In a period when the clarinet has been in the shadows of jazz, Daniels' work has been one of the few bright lights that have helped maintain the instrument's role. His work in the 80s and 90s has produced a steady flow of technically perfect albums for GRP Records, which for some are too 'digital' and crisp to fully appreciate this instrument. He moved to Shanachie Records in 1995 and issued a beautiful concept album *The Five Seasons*, a reworking of Vivaldi's masterpiece for chamber orchestra and jazz quartet.

● ALBUMS: *First Prize!* (Prestige 1967)★★★, *Muses For Richard Davis* (1969)★★★, *The Hub Of Hubbard* (1969)★★★, with Bucky Pizzarelli *A Flower For All Seasons* (1973)★★★, *Brief Encounter* (Muse 1977)★★★, *Morning Thunder* (Columbia 1978)★★, *Blackwood* (GRP 1979)★★★, *Breakthrough* (GRP 1985)★★★, *To Bird With Love* (GRP 1987)★★★★, *Memo's From Paradise* (GRP 1988)★★★★, *Blackwood* (GRP 1989)★★★, *Nepenthe (No Sorrow)* (GRP 1990)★★, *This Is Now* (GRP 1991)★★, *Benny Rides Again* (GRP 1992)★★★, *Under The Influence* (GRP 1993)★★★, with the Jazz Arts Group *Rodgers Roars, Porter Soars* (Sea Breeze 1995)★★★, *The Five Seasons* (Shanachie/Cachet 1996)★★★★, *Beautiful Love* (Shanachie 1997)★★.

DANIELS, JOE

b. 9 March 1908, Zeerust, Transvaal, South Africa, d. 2 July 1993. South African-born, bandleader/drummer Daniels moved to London when he was two years old. By the age of 10 he was a confident drummer. Four years later Daniels was working in London, playing in various bands at clubs and restaurants including that led by Harry and Burton Lester (the Cowboy Syncopaters). Among the other units in which he played were those led by Al Kaplan, Billy Mason, Fred Elizalde, and Sid Roy brother of Harry Roy. In the mid-20s Daniels formed his own group, which featured trumpeter Max Goldberg. For most of the 30s Daniels was with Harry Roy, and also made many records under his own name as leader of the hugely successful Hotshots. After World War II Daniels continued his bandleading career, playing mostly an engaging if not very profound brand of dixieland. He regularly filled the Slough Palais where he was resident for many years, in addition to playing at numerous holday camps. When the Big Band boom had subsided in the late 50s he also ran his own Wimpy Bar. During this musically barren time he recorded as Washboard Joe And The Scrubbers. His regular band was an early home for the excellent clarinettist Dave Shepherd and trumpeter Alan Wickham.

● COMPILATIONS: *Steppin' Out To Swing* 1940-45 recordings (Saville/Conifer 1984)★★★, *Swing High, Swing Low* 1935-37 recordings (Harlequin/Interstate 1988)★★★.

DANIELS, MAXINE

b. Gladys Lynch, 2 November 1930, Stepney, London, England. The sister of entertainer Kenny Lynch, and an accomplished and affectionately regarded jazz singer, Daniels won a local talent contest held at her local cinema when she was 14 years old. Later, she enjoyed a long residency with the Denny Boyce Band at the Orchid Room, Purley, and took first place on UK television's *Youth Takes A Bow* in 1953. Signed to the Delfont Agency and Oriole Records, she played smart London cabaret venues and toured the Moss Empires circuit, and appeared frequently on UK television programmes, including the *Sunday Night At The London Palladium*. In 1962 Daniels suffered a severe nervous breakdown, and it was several years before she returned to work. Her gradual rehabilitation was completed in the 80s when she made two fine albums, appeared with Humphrey Lyttelton and the Dutch Swing College Band, and sang at legendary trumpeter Nat Gonella's 80th birthday celebrations. In the early 90s she toured with George Chisholm in Swinging Down Memory Lane, and with Terry Lightfoot And His Band in *Basin Street To Broadway*. In 1995 she was appearing with artists such as Buddy Greco, Humphrey Lyttelton, Helen Shapiro, Dave Shepherd and Digby Fairweather, in the first UK Jazz And Swing Festival. Maxine Daniels was also featured on Laurie Johnson's *London Big Band Volume One*.

● ALBUMS: *A Beautiful Friendship* (Maxam 1985)★★★, *Every Night About This Time* (Calligraph 1986)★★★.

DANIELS, MIKE

b. 13 April 1939, Stanmore, Middlesex, England. One of many bands which took advantage of the UK's early 50s traditional jazz boom, Mike Daniels and his Delta Jazz Band were much more credible than all but a handful of other groups. Adhering closely to, but not directly imitating the music of Jelly Roll Morton, Joe 'King' Oliver and early Louis Armstrong, Daniels built a reputation for the high quality of his band's performances and won an enthusiastic following. As the trad scene faded, Daniels formed a big band, but eventually retired from the UK jazz scene and emigrated. In 1985 a return trip to the UK and the reformation of his old band attracted enormous attention from an army of devoted fans. Daniels' trumpet playing, while never spectacular, always offered a cogent reminder of the fire and sensitivity of his idol, King Oliver.

● ALBUMS: *Mike Daniels And His Delta Jazzmen* 1957-59 recordings (Harlequin 1986)★★★, *Together Again - Thirty Years On* (1988)★★★, *Mike Daniels* (Stomp Off 1991)★★★.

DANKWORTH, JACQUI

b. February 1963, England. The daughter of John Dankworth and Cleo Laine, she was steeped in music during her formative years. Her singing voice is light, almost ethereal at times, and is particularly well suited to the repertoire she has developed, which, while acknowledging jazz, nudges gently at the edges of world music. She has also shown the eclectic nature of her musical interests by performing the work of poet A.E. Houseman in musical settings arranged by her father and other leading musicians. Her accompanists on an album of these songs included jazz and classical players. On her debut album she worked with vibraphonist Anthony Kerr and was responsible for many of the lyrics. She has also recorded with her mother. Attuned to the musical trends of the late 90s, Dankworth's career is soundly based and will doubtless continue into the twenty-first century, adjusting to the shifting demands of the younger audience.

● ALBUMS: *First Cry* (EFZ 1994)★★★★, *Houseman Settings And Other Works* (Spotlight 1996)★★★.

DANKWORTH, JOHN

b. 20 September 1927, London, England. Dankworth started playing clarinet as a child and in the early 40s was a member of a traditional jazz band. In the mid-40s he studied at the Royal Academy of Music and extended his knowledge of jazz by taking work on transatlantic liners, so that he could hear leading jazzmen in New York. Among his influences at this time was Charlie Parker, and Dankworth began to concentrate on alto saxophone. He was an active participant in the London bebop scene of the late 40s and early 50s, often playing at the Club 11. In 1950 he formed his own band, the Johnny Dankworth Seven, which included Jimmy Deuchar and Don Rendell. Three years later he formed a big band, playing his own, sometimes innovative, arrangements. The band's singer was Cleo Laine whom Dankworth married in 1958. For his big band Dankworth drew upon the best available modern jazzmen; at one time or another, artists such as Dick Hawdon, Kenny Wheeler, Rendell, Danny Moss, Peter King, Dudley Moore and Kenny Clare were in its ranks. Dankworth's writing, especially for the big band, demonstrated his considerable arranging skills, although for many fans it is the performances by the Seven that linger longest in fond memory. In the 60s Dankworth was in demand for film work, which, together with the growing popularity of Laine, led to a shift in policy. In the early 70s Dankworth became Laine's musical director, touring extensively with her and making many records. Dankworth's musical interests extend beyond jazz and he has composed in the classical form, including a nine-movement work, 'Fair Oak Fusions', written for cellist Julian Lloyd Webber. He has also experimented with third-stream music. His deep interest in music education led in 1969 to the founding of the Wavendon Allmusic Plan, which has continued to attract performers, students and audiences from around the world to concerts, classes, courses and lectures. Although a reliable performer on alto, it is as an arranger and tireless promoter of music that Dankworth has made his greatest contributions to the international jazz scene. In 1974, in recognition of his work, he became a Companion of the British Empire.

● ALBUMS: *Five Steps To Dankworth* (Parlophone 1957)★★★★, *London To Newport* (Top Rank 1960)★★★, *Jazz Routes* (Columbia 1961)★★★, *Curtain Up* (Columbia 1963)★★★, *What The Dickens!* (Fontana 1963)★★, *Zodiac Variations* (Fontana 1965)★★★, *Shakespeare - And All That Jazz* (1965)★★★, *Fathom* film soundtrack (Stateside 1967)★★, *The $1,000,000 Collection* (Fontana 1968)★★★, *Full Circle* (1972)★★★, *Lifeline* (1973)★★★, *Movies 'N' Me* (1974)★★, *. . . And The Philharmonic* (Boulevard 1974)★★, with Cleo Laine *Lover And His Lass* (Esquire 1976)★★★, *Sepia* (1979)★★★, *Fair Oak Fusions* (1982)★★★, *Metro* (Repertoire 1983)★★★, *Gone Hitchin'* (Sepia 1983)★★★, *Octavius* (Sepia 1983)★★★, *Symphonic Fusions* (Pickwick 1985)★★★, *Innovations* (Pickwick 1987)★★★, *Live At Ronnie Scott's* (Total 1992)★★★, with Alec Dankworth *Generation Big Band* (Jazz House 1994)★★★★.

● COMPILATIONS: *Johnny Dankworth Seven And Orchestra* 1953-57 recordings ()★★★★, *Featuring Cleo Laine* 1953-58 recordings (Retrospect 1984)★★★, with others *Bop At Club 11* 1949 recordings (Esquire 1986)★★, *The John Dankworth Big Band, Vintage Years 1953-1959* (Sepia 1990)★★★★, with Humphrey Lyttelton *All That Jazz* (MFP 1990)★★★★, *The Roulette Years* (Roulette 1991)★★★★.

● FURTHER READING: *Jazz In Revolution*, John Dankworth.

DARDANELLE

b. Marcia Marie Mullen, 27 December 1917, Avalon, Mississippi, USA, d. 8 August 1997, Memphis, tennessee, USA. Playing piano and singing from childhood, Dardanelle developed her skills throughout high school and university. In the late 30s and early 40s she worked with several bands along the east coast and in Washington, DC, and Philadelphia. Eventually she decided to form her own group with Paul Edenfield and

Tal Farlow. The trio became successful and in 1945 started a year-long residency at the Copacabana club in New York. During the rest of the decade the trio played in several top New York hotels, made records and toured the USA. In addition to playing piano and singing, Dardanelle also played vibraphone. In 1949 Dardanelle married Walter Hadley and gave up her New York-based career. During the next few years she devoted her time to raising a family, but in 1956, now resident in Chicago, she became staff organist at a local radio and television station and appeared for four years on a childrens' show. In the early 60s she freelanced in Chicago, was active in church work, including conducting choirs, and began broadcasting a regular family show from home. In 1966 her husband's business effected another move, this time to New Jersey, where she formed a new trio with her son, Skip Hadley, on drums. The trio played largely for private functions and in local clubs for several years. In the mid-70s Dardanelle again began performing with leading jazz artists including Bucky Pizzarelli and George Duvivier. In 1978 she returned to the recording studios for an album with Duvivier, Pizzarelli and Grady Tate. In the late 70s Dardanelle survived a divorce and the tragic death of her son, Skip, and by the early 80s was a popular figure at jazz clubs, festivals and concerts, appearing at the Cookery, Carnegie Hall and many other prestigious venues. She continued to record, most commonly in good jazz company. She also appeared on television as performer and host of the *Music In Our Lives* show and on cruise ships, including the *QEII*. Although victim of a brutal assault, Dardanelle made many club and record dates during the next few years, including a long residency in Tokyo. From 1984 she made her home in Mississippi, but still played concerts, festivals, radio and television and made records. In many performances she was joined by her second son, Brian Hadley, on bass. For a period in the late 80s she was artist-in-residence at the University of Mississippi. At the end of the decade she began writing her autobiography, reading extracts of work in progress on radio in Mississippi and Tennessee. A distinctive song stylist with a penchant for reflective ballads which spoke of love for people and places, especially the deep south, Dardanelle made an important contribution to popular music, not only through her singing and playing but also through the enthusiastic manner in which she transmitted her love of music to audiences and students.

● ALBUMS: *Songs For New Lovers* (1978)★★★, *Colors Of My Life* (Stash 1982)★★★★, *The Two Of Us* (1983)★★★, *Dardanelle Down Home* (Audiophile 1986)★★★, *Dardanelle Echoes Singing Ladies* (Audiophile 1986)★★, *Gold Braid* (Audiophile 1986)★★★, *Woman's Intuition* (Audiophile 1988)★★★★, *That's My Style* (1989)★★★, *Swingin' In London* (Audiophile 1994)★★★.

● COMPILATIONS: *Gold Braid* 1945 recording (Audiophile 1986)★★★.

DARENSBOURG, JOE

b. 9 July 1906, Baton Rouge, Louisiana, USA, d. 24 May 1985. After trying various other instruments, Darensbourg chose the clarinet, receiving tuition from noted masters such as Alphonse Picou. His progress was such that before the end of the 20s he had played in New Orleans bands led by eminent figures such as Buddy Petit, Fate Marable, Charlie Creath and Mutt Carey. Starting in 1929, Darensbourg spent 15 profitable, but somewhat obscure, years playing mostly in the Seattle area and also in western Canada. In the mid to late 40s he played briefly with Kid Ory and Wingy Manone but it was not until the 50s that he began to make an impact on the jazz world with his recordings of his own compositions, 'Yellow Dog Blues' and 'Lou-easy-an-ia', and a period with Teddy Buckner's popular band. In the early 60s he joined Louis Armstrong's All Stars, touring extensively and playing to a wider audience than ever before. Although his was, in some respects, a dated style of playing, Darensbourg was a capable musician and brought to his work a dedication to the old traditions of New Orleans music that was never conventional. His autobiography was published in 1987.

● ALBUMS: with Teddy Buckner *Salute To Armstrong* (1956)★★★, *On A Lark In Dixieland* (1957)★★★, *Joe Darensbourg And His Dixie Flyers* (1958)★★★.

● COMPILATIONS: *Barrelhousin' With Joe* (GHB 1988)★★★, *Petite Fleur* (Dixieland Jubilee 1988)★★★, *Yellow Dog Blues* (Dixieland Jubilee 1988)★★★.

● FURTHER READING: *Telling It Like It Is*, Joe Darensbourg and Peter Vacher. *Jazz Odyssey: The Autobiography Of Joe Darensbourg*, Joe Darensbourg.

DARLING, DAVID

b. 4 March 1941, Elkhart, Indiana, USA. Darling studied the piano and cello as well as playing the double bass and alto saxophone in the school dance band of which he eventually became the leader. He studied the cello and music education at Indiana University from where he graduated in 1965. After teaching for four years he played with the Paul Winter Consort throughout the 70s and then formed the band Radiance with other Winter alumni. Getting acquainted with ethnic music with the Consort and trying to play it on the cello 'was mind-blowing'. He was able to develop his particular style as he turned to the use of a solid bodied eight-string electric cello and was able to introduce electronic effects into his playing through the use of an echoplex and other devices. Although he turned increasingly to classical composition after 1978, he played with Spiro Gyra in 1980. The following year he formed the band Gallery, and recorded with Glen Moore and Ralph Towner. He later worked in a duo with Terje Rypdal. Darling does not see his music as new age but as music 'that doesn't have the busyness of progressive jazz, that has a meditative quality'.

● ALBUMS: with Ralph Towner *Trios/Solos* (ECM 1972)★★★, with Terje Rypdal *Journal October* (ECM 1979)★★★, with

Gallery *Gallery* (1981)★★★, with Rypdal *Cycles* (ECM 1981)★★★★, with Rypdal *Eos* (ECM 1984)★★★, *Cello* (ECM 1992)★★★★, with Ketil Bjørnstad *The River* (ECM 1997)★★.

DASH, JULIAN

b. 9 April 1916, Charleston, South Carolina, USA, d. 25 February 1974. Although he had played in school bands, Dash did not at first intend to become a musician but began playing alto saxophone in local bands in Charleston and Alabama before heading for New York. In 1936, still unsure about his career, he decided to study embalming. He continued playing, however, leading his own small band, but in 1938, now playing tenor, he joined Erskine Hawkins. He stayed with the band until 1955, receiving co-composer credit for the band's biggest hit, 'Tuxedo Junction', and then drifted in and out of music, sometimes leading small groups for club dates and appearing occasionally on record. The best known of his recordings are the Buck Clayton jam sessions of 1953. He died in February 1974.

● ALBUMS: *A Portrait Of Julian Dash* (1970)★★★.

DAUNER, WOLFGANG

b. 30 December 1935, Stuttgart, Germany. Brought up by his aunt, a piano teacher, Dauner has been playing piano since the age of five. He turned professional at the age of 22, then studied piano and trumpet at Stuttgart College of Music. In 1963 he formed a trio with bassist Eberhard Weber and forceful American drummer Fred Braceful. On-stage destruction of instruments and stunts like presenting a choir in stocking masks ran a musical parallel to the neo-dada of artists like Joseph Beauys. In 1967 he recorded *Free Action* and *Sunday Walk*, both with violinist Jean-Luc Ponty: the first is free jazz, the second dense, John Coltrane-ish bop. Since 1969 Dauner has led the Stuttgart Radio jazz group, backing guests on a monthly basis. ECM Records released a trio recording called Output in 1970: Dauner's use of ringmodulator and clavinet was extravagantly creative, a combination of chaos and funk reminiscent of the Mothers Of Invention. Dauner founded the United Jazz And Rock Ensemble in 1975 and also started a record company, Mood. In 1983 he recorded a duet album with Albert Mangelsdorff and two years later wrote a concerto for him. Dauner combines superb pianistic ability with an interest in electronics and modern painting that keeps his projects fresh and lively.

● ALBUMS: *Dream Talk* (1964)★★★, with Jean-Luc Ponty *Free Action* (1967)★★, with Ponty *Sunday Walk* (1967)★★★, *Output* (1970)★★★, *Changes* (Mood 1979)★★, *Dauner-Mangelsdorff* (1982)★★★, *Dauner Solo Piano* (Mood 1983)★★★, *Two Is Company* (Mood 1983)★★★, *One Night In '88* (Mood 1989)★★★★, *Pas De Trois* (Mood 1989)★★★★.

DAVENPORT, CHARLES EDWARD 'COW COW'

b. 23 April 1894, Anniston, Alabama, USA, d. 3 December 1955, Chicago, Illinois, USA. One of the most distinctive themes utilized in boogie-woogie is the train imitation 'Cow Cow Blues' from which this consummate performer derived his nickname. Charles Davenport's father, a preacher, wanted to see his son follow him to a career in the church but it was not to be. Instead the piano laid claim to Charles at an early age and he took up the insecure life of the medicine show musician. He joined Barhoot's Travelling Carnival working the backwaters of Alabama. Here his basically rag-time piano style was subjected to the influence of Bob Davis and the lusty, rolling result was to be the basis of Davenport's success on record throughout the 20s. He moved into vaudeville with blues singer Dora Carr as 'Davenport And Co'. Davenport made his first recordings for Gennett (unissued) and Paramount in 1927. Thereafter he linked up with Vocalion both as performer and talent scout. As well as recording under his own name (and as George Hamilton, the Georgia Grinder and Bat The Hummingbird) he supported many other artists, forming a particularly successful liaison with singer Ivy Smith. During this period he tried several ventures outside music, failing as a record shop owner and opening his own café. He also fell foul of southern law and spent six months in jail. In 1938 he suffered an attack of apoplexy which left him deficient in his right hand. He continued to perform as a singer but a move to New York found him eventually washing dishes in the Onyx Club, from where he was rescued by pianist Art Hodes. He recovered sufficiently to record again as a pianist, for the Comet and Circle labels, in 1945 and 1946. Davenport worked towns as far apart as Atlanta, Cleveland and Nashville. He has composer credit for two much-played standbys of the traditional jazz scene, 'Mama Don't Allow' and '(I'll Be Glad When You're Dead) You Rascal You' and was sole composer of the 40s hit, 'Cow Cow Boogie'.

● COMPILATIONS: *Cow Cow Blues* (Oldie Blues 1978)★★★, *Alabama Strut* (Magpie 1979)★★★, *Cow Cow Davenport 1926-38* (Best Of Blues 1988)★★★, *Cow Cow Davenport 1927-29* (Document 1989)★★★, *The Accompanist 1924-29* (Blues Document 1993)★★★.

DAVERN, KENNY

b. 7 January 1935, Huntington, New York, USA. A professional musician at the age of 16, Davern worked with Jack Teagarden and Phil Napoleon in the mid-50s, moving on to play with Red Allen and Buck Clayton. In the early 60s he led his own small group and also played with the Dukes Of Dixieland. Later in the decade he worked with Ruby Braff. In the early 70s, he teamed up with Bob Wilber to form Soprano Summit. This band featured Davern and Wilber on clarinets, occasionally altos, but, as the name implies, mostly soprano saxophones. Backed by a variety of rhythm sections, Soprano Summit made a string of enormously successful concert and festival dates and numerous record albums which enjoyed good sales. In 1979 the partnership ended and Davern thereafter concentrated more on clarinet. Throughout the 80s and into the 90s, Davern led several small groups, played briefly in the World's Greatest Jazz Band, co-led the Blue Three, with

Bobby Rosengarden and Dick Wellstood, and toured and recorded extensively. Although best-remembered by many fans for his work with Wilber, all of which displayed staggering technical dexterity and magnificent musicianship, Davern is a fully-rounded artist whose latterday clarinet-playing shows him to be one of the hottest players on this instrument. Although his early work was in the traditional area of jazz, and most of his later work is in the mainstream, Davern has shown himself to be attuned to new musical developments and his enormous technical proficiency allows him to play confidently in any style. Very much his own man, and with a devastatingly accurate and pungent wit, Davern is one of the latest in a short but important line in dynamic, contemporary clarinettists whose strong feeling for the past does not deter them from experimenting with new ideas.

● ALBUMS: with Dick Wellstood *Dick Wellstood And His Famous Orchestra Featuring Kenny Davern* (1973)★★★★, with Soprano Summit *Soprano Summit* (World Jazz 1973)★★★★, with Soprano Summit *Soprano Summit II* (World Jazz 1974)★★★★, with Soprano Summit *Chalumeau Blue* (Chiaroscuro 1976)★★★, with Soprano Summit *Soprano Summit At The Big Horn Jazzfest* (Concord Jazz 1976)★★★★, with Soprano Summit *Soprano Summit In Concert* (Concord Jazz 1976)★★★★, with Soprano Summit *Soprano Summit Live At Concord* (Concord Jazz 1977)★★★★, *Unexpected* (Kharma 1978)★★★, *The Hot Three* (Jazzology 1979)★★★, with the Blue Three *The Blue Three At Hanratty's* (1981)★★★★, *Stretchin' Out* (Jazzology 1984)★★★, *Live Hot Jazz* (1984)★★★, *The Very Thought Of You* (Milton Keynes 1984)★★★, *Live And Swinging* (1985)★★★, *This Old Gang Of Ours* (1985)★★★, *Playing For Kicks* (Jazzology 1985)★★★, *I'll See You In My Dreams* (Music Masters 1988)★★★, *One Hour Tonight* (Music Masters 1988)★★★, with Soprano Summit *Summit Reunion* (Chiaroscuro 1990)★★★, *My Inspiration* (Limelight 1991)★★★, with Soprano Summit *Summit Reunion 1992* (Chiaroscuro 1992)★★★, *East Side, West Side* (Arbors 1994)★★★, with Soprano Summit *Jazz Im Amerika Haus, Vol. 5* (Nagel-Heyer 1995)★★★, with Soprano Summit *Yellow Dog Blues* (Chiaroscuro 1995)★★★★, *Kenny Davern And The Rhythm Men* (Arbors 1996)★★★, with Soprano Summit *Soprano Summit* 1976 recording (Storyville 1996)★★★, *Breezin' Along* (Arbors 1997)★★★★, with Bob Wilber *Reunion At Arbors* (Arbors 1998)★★★.

● COMPILATIONS: with Bobby Rosengarden, Dick Wellstood *Dick Wellstood And His Famous Orchestra Featuring Kenny Davern* 1973-1981 recordings (Chiaruscuro 1981)★★★★.

DAVIES, JOHN R.T.

b. John Ross Twiston Davies, 20 March 1937, Wivelsfield, Sussex, England. Before founding the Temperance Seven in 1955, this self-taught multi-instrumentalist played the slide trombone in Sandy Brown's trad jazz outfit. During his eight years in the Temperance Seven, Davies also deputized in the Crane River Band (in which his brother Julian played tuba) and other more purist groups. From 1963 he performed in various Anglo-American combos including the New Paul Whiteman Orchestra, which accompanied him on 1975's *Running Wild*. He also led the drummerless John R.T.'s Gentle Jazz and established two record labels specializing in 20s dance band reissues.

● ALBUMS: *Running Wild* (1975)★★★.

DAVIES, LITSA

b. Litsa Jane Davies, 27 June 1963, Hampshire, England. Growing up in Poole, Dorset, Davies attended Harry Harbin school where her music teacher, Dave Lewin, recognized her singing talent. At 14 she was singing with him on jazz gigs and appeared locally on television in 1977. In 1979 she gigged with pianist Mike Hatchard and the following year began a six-year stint with the National Youth Jazz Orchestra with whom she appeared on television. While with NYJO Davies sang on three albums, notably *Why Don't They Write Songs Like This Anymore?*, which featured her throughout. She also sang with her own quintet and toured with the European Jazz Orchestra. She sang on radio with the BBC Big Band, her own group, and the bands Night Owls and Bone Structure. During the early and mid-80s she was most often heard at festivals with her quintet which usually comprised Steve Melling, Rick Taylor, Steve Pearce, Mike Paxton and Dave Barlow. In 1986 Davies sang with the Burch Trio and with saxophonist Iain Ballamy. The following year she joined the cast of the West End musical Chess at the Prince Edward Theatre going on to play the lead until the show closed in 1989. She continued to sing on BBC radio. From 1990 Davies was occupied with looking after her two young children, but she was able to sing as a backing vocalist to Tom Jones at the Glastonbury Festival and to perform with various bands including the Ian Pearce Big Band, the Ross Mitchell Dance Orchestra and the Mark Graham Dance Band. In 1995 she reappeared in the jazz bigtime with a week-long engagement at Ronnie Scott's Club backed by Melling, Simon Woolf and Dave Ohm. In 1996 she was working on a planned musical entertainment for children and a programme of songs on which she was to be accompanied by a string quartet. An extremely gifted singer, with fine interpretative skills allied to intelligent phrasing, Davies is at her considerable best and is most pleasing on ballads. On uptempo songs, she sings with zesty attack and great swing.

● ALBUMS: with Ross Mitchell *Dance And Listen Music* (1994)★★★.

DAVIS, ANTHONY

b. 20 February 1951, Paterson, New Jersey, USA. Coming from an academic background (his father was the first black faculty member at Princeton University and, as chairman of African-American Studies at Yale, devised one of the first and best black studies programmes in the USA), Davis grew up in Princeton and State College in Pennsylvania. He began to take classical piano lessons at the age of seven. He studied music at Yale University and played in nearby New Haven with trombonist George Lewis and drummer Gerry Hemingway in a group called Advent. He graduated with a BA in 1975, forming a quartet which featured the master drummer Ed Blackwell in the same year. From 1974-77 he was a member of Leo Smith's New Dalta Ahkri. In 1977 he moved to New York and became involved with the burgeoning Loft scene (documented in the *Wildflowers* series), later recording with Oliver Lake (*Shine*), Anthony Braxton (*Six Compositions: Quartet*) and Leroy Jenkins (*The Legend of A. Glatson, Space Minds, New Worlds, Survival Of America*). In 1978 he formed a long-standing partnership with flautist James Newton: they co-lead the group which plays on *Hidden Voices*, work together in a trio with Abdul Wadud and Davis has recorded on Newton's *Paseo Del Mar* and *James Newton*. In 1981 Davis said 'I don't see the need to be self-consciously avant garde', proving as much with the octet Episteme, which, whilst recognising Ornette Coleman's innovations, represented a return to tonality. In 1982 he started teaching at Yale. In 1985 he wrote *X*, an opera about Malcolm X and his politics. Davis lists Messiaen and Stravinsky alongside the great jazz pianists as influences, and a 'composer's' approach characterizes his work. Sometimes criticized for his supposedly 'European' leanings, Davis's riposte was 'If somebody uses tradition as a way of limiting your choices, in a way that's as racist as saying you have to sit at the back of the bus.'

● ALBUMS: *Song For The Old World* (India Navigation 1978)★★★★, *Past Lives* (Red Rhino 1979)★★★, *Of Blues And Dreams* (Sackville 1979)★★★★, with James Newton *Hidden Voices* (India Navigation 1980)★★★, *Lady Of The Mirrors* (India Navigation 1980)★★★, *Under The Double Moon* (1980)★★★, *Episterie* (Gramavision 1981)★★★, with Newton, Abdul Wadud *I've Known Rivers* (Gramavision 1982)★★★★, *Hemispheres* (Gramavision 1983)★★★, *Middle Passage* (Gramavision 1984)★★, *Undine* (Mesa Blue Moon 1987)★★★, *The Ghost Factory* 1987/1988 recordings (Gramavision 1989)★★★, *Trio - Volume 1* (Gramavision 1990)★★★, with Newton, Wadud *Trio - Volume 2* (Gramavision 1990)★★★, *X: The Life And Times Of Malcolm X* (Gramavision 1993)★★★.

DAVIS, ART

b. Arthur D. Davis, 12 May 1934, near Harrisburg, Pennsylvania, USA. Trained at the Juilliard School of Music and an active symphonic player, bassist Davis was prominent in jazz from the late 50s, notably with Max Roach. He was occasionally involved with John Coltrane, appearing on *Africa/Brass* and an unreleased sextet version of *A Love Supreme* also involving Archie Shepp. In the late 60s Davis sued the New York Philharmonic over racial discrimination, which allegedly helped bring an end to a burgeoning career in session work and television orchestras; he was also reputed to be depressed at the state of jazz since Coltrane's passing. After studying psychology for several years - he received his doctorate in 1981 - he began playing again, with artists including Arthur Blythe and David Murray, and produced teaching materials in book and cassette form. Davis recorded a 1985 session for Soul Note, but it was over ten years before he released the wonderfully affecting *A Time Remembered*, featuring Herbie Hancock, Marvin 'Smitty' Smith and Ravi Coltrane.

● ALBUMS: *Life* (Soul Note 1985)★★★, *A Time Remembered* (Jazz Planet 1996)★★★★.

DAVIS, EDDIE 'LOCKJAW'

b. 2 March 1922, New York City, New York, USA, d. 3 November 1986, Culver City, California, USA. Davis began to make his mark on the jazz scene in his home town when he worked at Clark Monroe's Uptown House in the late 30s. Despite this establishment's close ties with the emergence of bebop a few years later, Davis's tenor saxophone playing was rooted in swing and the blues, and early in his career he displayed a marked affinity with the tough school of Texas tenors. In the early 40s he worked with a number of big bands, including those of Cootie Williams, Lucky Millinder and Andy Kirk. He also led his own small group for club and record dates. In 1952 he made the first of several appearances with the Count Basie band which extended through the 60s and into the 70s. It was with Basie that he made his greatest impact, although in between these stints he continued to lead his own small groups, notably with fellow-tenorist Johnny Griffin in the early 60s, Roy Eldridge in the mid-70s and Harry Edison in the late 70s and early 80s. Davis' playing style showed him to be at ease on both gutsy, hard-driving swingers and slow, tender ballads. The former are most evident in his partnership with Griffin and his showstoppers with Basie, such as 'Whirlybird' on *The Atomic Mr Basie*, while the latter facet of his musical character came to the fore on a fine album of ballads he made with Paul Gonsalves.

● ALBUMS: *Goodies* reissued as *Eddie Davis Trio* (Roost 1954)★★★, with Sonny Stitt *Battle Of Birdland* (Roost 1955)★★★, *Modern Jazz Expression* (King 1958)★★★, *Jazz With A Horn* (King 1958)★★★, *Jazz With A Beat* (King 1958)★★★, *Count Basie Presents Eddie Davis* (Roulette 1958)★★★, *Eddie Davis Trio* (Roulette 1958)★★★, with Shirley Scott *The Eddie 'Lockjaw' Davis Cookbook* (Prestige 1958)★★★★, *Big Beat Jazz* (King 1959)★★★, with Scott *Jaws* (Prestige 1959)★★★, *The Eddie 'Lockjaw' Davis Cookbook, Vol. 2* (Prestige 1959)★★★★, *Very Saxy* (Prestige 1959)★★★★, with Scott *Jaws In Orbit* (Prestige 1959)★★★, with Scott *Bacalao* (Prestige 1960)★★★, with Scott *Eddie 'Lockjaw' Davis With Shirley Scott* (Moodsville 1960)★★★, with Johnny Griffin *The Tenor Scene* reissued as *Live! The Breakfast Show* (Prestige 1960)★★★, with Griffin *Tough Tenors* (Jazzland 1960)★★★, *Trane Whistle* (Prestige 1961)★★★, with Scott *The Eddie 'Lockjaw' Davis Cookbook, Vol. 3* (Prestige 1961)★★★★, with Griffin *Lookin' At Monk* (Jazzland 1961)★★★, with Griffin *Griff & Lock* (Jazzland 1961)★★★, with Griffin *Blues Up & Down* (Jazzland 1961)★★★★, *Afro Jaws* reissued as *Alma Alegre* (Riverside/Jazzland 1961)★★★, with Harry 'Sweets' Edison *Jawbreakers* (Riverside 1962)★★★★, with Griffin *Tough Tenor Favorites* (Jazzland 1962)★★★★, *Goin' To The Meeting* (Prestige 1962)★★★, with Scott *Misty* (Moodsville 1963)★★★, *I Only Have Eyes For You* (Prestige 1963)★★★, *Trackin'* (Prestige 1963)★★★, with Griffin *Battle Stations* (Prestige 1963)★★★, with Griffin *The First Set - Recorded Live At Minton's* (Prestige 1964)★★★, with Griffin *Live! The Midnight Show At Minton's Playhouse* (Prestige 1964)★★★, with Scott *Smokin'* (Prestige 1964)★★★★, with Griffin *The Late*

Show Recorded Live! (Prestige 1965)★★★, *Lock The Fox* (RCA Victor 1966)★★★, *The Fox And The Hounds* (RCA Victor 1967)★★★, *Love Calls* (RCA Victor 1967)★★★, with Griffin *Tough Tenors Again 'N Again* (MPS 1970)★★★, *Leapin' On Lenox* (1974)★★★, *Chewin' The Fat* (1974)★★★, *What's New?* (1975)★★★, with Edison *Sweet And Lovely* (Black & Blue 1975)★★★, *Jaws Strikes Again* (Black & Blue 1976)★★★, *Swingin' Till The Girls Come Home* (Steeple Chase 1976)★★★★, *Straight Ahead* (Pablo 1976)★★★★, with Edison *Edison's Lights* (Pablo 1976)★★★, with Edison *Harry 'Sweets' Edison And Eddie 'Lockjaw' Davis, Vol. 1* (Storyville 1976)★★★, with Edison *Harry 'Sweets' Edison And Eddie 'Lockjaw' Davis, Vol. 2* (Storyville 1976)★★★, with Michel Attenoux *Eddie 'Lockjaw' Davis With Michel Attenoux* (Storyville 1976)★★★, *Eddie 'Lockjaw' Davis 4/Montreux '77* (Pablo 1977)★★★★, *The Heavy Hitter* (Muse 1979)★★★, *Jaw's Blues* (Enja 1981)★★★, *Land Of Dreams* (1982)★★★, *Live At The Widder, Vols. 1 & 2* (Enja 1982)★★★, *All Of Me* (Steeple Chase 1983)★★★, with Johnny Griffin *Tough Tenors Back Again* 1984 recording (Storyville 1998)★★★.

● COMPILATIONS: *Best Of Eddie 'Lockjaw' Davis* (Bethlehem 1961)★★★★, with Shirley Scott *The Best Of Eddie Davis And Shirley Scott* (Prestige 1969)★★★★, *Save Your Love For Me* 1966/1967 recordings (Bluebird 1989)★★★, *Rarest Sessions Of The '40s* 1946-1948 recordings (Pinnacle)★★★★.

DAVIS, ERNESTINE 'TINY'

b. *c.*1913, USA. Raised in Memphis, Tennessee, she began playing trumpet in her early teens while attending Booker T. Washington High School. She heard very little jazz, however, and played popular music of the day, marches and the like with the band. In Kansas City, she played in a club and at after-hours sessions and began hearing musicians such as Count Basie, Jo Jones, Mary Lou Williams and Eddie Durham. Davis based her early jazz style on that of Louis Armstrong and over the years delivered many trumpet and vocal imitations of her idol. In the mid-30s she joined an all-female band, the Harlem Playgirls, formed by Sylvester Rice, then joined the leading female orchestra of the era, the International Sweethearts Of Rhythm, where she remained for almost a decade. Davis was a featured attraction with the Sweethearts, playing hot jazz solos and occasionally singing. After the Sweethearts disbanded, David stayed with a nucleus of players who continued under the leadership of Ann Mae Winburn, then, in the early 50s, formed her own small group, the Hell Divers, which, with shifting personnel, stayed together for a number of years. Later, she formed a quartet and played several residencies in Chicago where she had settled. Davis continued to play at festivals and reunions, plus finding the time to raise three children. A gifted, driving player, Davis's long career is testimony to her ability; that this career was largely overlooked by the jazz world speaks volumes about attitudes towards women in jazz.

DAVIS, JESSE

b. New Orleans, Louisiana, USA. Davis began playing alto saxophone as a child, drawing his first influence from Grover Washington Jnr. but was encouraged by Ellis Marsalis to listen to Charlie Parker. As Davis told Alyn Shipton in an interview for *Jazz Journal International*, 'this helped me get really serious about wanting to be a jazz musician . . . '. He went to college in Chicago, studying and sitting-in, and later, in 1986, attended William Patterson College in New Jersey where he studied with Rufus Reid. Davis began recording in 1990, with Reid and Akira Tana, and two years later made his first album under his own name. A remarkably gifted soloist with an unceasing flow of ideas, Davis is well placed to become one of the major names in jazz. He is well aware of the high level of playing ability amongst present-day young musicians. He is equally alert to the way the future might develop for him, declaring to Shipton, 'the challenge for my generation is to be something with the music that's comparable to what the generations before us did'. More than most of his contemporaries, Davis has the ability and, in the late 90s at least, is being given the opportunity.

● ALBUMS: *As We Speak* (Concord Jazz 1992)★★, *Horn Of Passion* (Concord Jazz 1993)★★, *Young At Art* (Concord Jazz 1993)★★★★, *High Standards* (Concord Jazz 1994)★★★★, *From Within* (Concord Jazz 1997)★★★★, *First Insight* (Concord Jazz 1998)★★★.

DAVIS, LEM

b. Lemuel A. Davis, 22 June 1914, Tampa, Florida, USA, d. 16 January 1970. Davis began playing alto saxophone in high school and worked in semi-pro bands before coming to New York in the early 40s. He played in several small groups active in the thriving club scene of the period, switching back and forth between swing and early bop. He played in bands led by Coleman Hawkins and Rex Stewart and enjoyed a period of popular success with Eddie Heywood. While with Heywood he participated in a 1944 record date with Billie Holiday. In the mid-40s he was with John Kirby, recorded with Joe Thomas, Eddie Safranski and under his own name, leading a band which included Emmett Berry, Vic Dickenson and Dodo Marmarosa. In the 50s he worked in and around New York, appearing on one of the famous Buck Clayton jam session record dates. Davis' attempts to be a musician for all seasons at the time of the bebop revolution might well have led casual observers to dismiss him. Certainly, he seems to have failed to adapt fully to bop but his earlier playing suggests a man of great enthusiasm allied to considerable skill. He died in 1970.

DAVIS, MILES

b. 25 May 1926, Alton, Illinois, USA, d. 28 September 1991. Davis was born into a comparatively wealthy middle-class family and both his mother and sister were capable musicians. He was given a trumpet for his thirteenth birthday by his dentist father, who could not have conceived that his gift would set his son on the road to becoming one a giant in the development of jazz. Notwithstanding his outstanding talent as master of the trumpet, Davis's versatility encompassed flügelhorn and keyboards together with a considerable gift as a composer. This extraordinary list of talents earned Davis an unassailable reputation as the greatest leader/catalyst in the history of jazz. Such accolades were not used lightly, and he can justifiably be termed a 'musical genius'. Davis quickly progressed from his high school band into Eddie Randall's band in 1941, after his family had moved to St. Louis. He studied at the Juilliard School of Music in New York in 1945 before joining Charlie 'Bird' Parker, with whom he had previously played in the Billy Eckstine band. By 1948 Davis had played or recorded with many jazz giants, most notably Coleman Hawkins, Dizzy Gillespie, Benny Carter, John Lewis, Illinois Jacquet and Gerry Mulligan. That year was to be a landmark for jazz; Davis, in collaboration with Gil Evans, made a series of 78s that were eventually released in 1956 as the highly influential album *Birth Of The Cool*. Davis had now refined his innovative style of playing, which was based upon understatement rather than the hurried action of the great bebop players.

During the early 50s Davis became dependent on heroin and his career was put on hold for a lengthy period. This spell of inactivity lasted until as late as 1954. The following year his seminal quintet included, variously, Red Garland, John Coltrane, Charles Mingus, Paul Chambers, Philly Joe Jones, Bill Evans and Sonny Rollins. Among their output was the acclaimed series of collections *Cookin'*, *Relaxin'*, *Workin'* and *Steamin'*. During this time Davis was consistently voted the number 1 artist in all the major jazz polls. No longer dependent on drugs by this time, he set about collaborating with Gil Evans once again. The orchestral albums made with Evans between 1957 and 1959 have all become classics: *Miles Ahead*, *Porgy And Bess* and the sparsely beautiful *Sketches Of Spain* (influenced by composer Joaquin Rodrigo). Evans was able to blend lush and full orchestration with Davis's trumpet - allowing it the space and clarity it richly deserved. Davis went on further, assembling a sextet featuring a spectacular line-up including Coltrane, Chambers, Bill Evans, Jimmy Cobb and Cannonball Adderley. Two further landmark albums during this fertile period were the aptly titled *Milestones*, followed by *Kind Of Blue*. The latter album is cited by many critics as the finest in jazz history. More than 30 years later his albums are still available, and form an essential part of any jazz record collection, with *Kind Of Blue* at the top of the list. 'So What', the opening track, has been covered by dozens of artists, the most recent offerings from guitarist Ronnie Jordan, Larry Carlton, saxophonist Candy Dulfer and reggae star Smiley Culture, who added his own lyrics and performed it in the film *Absolute Beginners*. Ian Carr, Davis's leading biographer, perceptively stated of *Kind Of Blue* in 1982: 'The more it is listened to, the more it reveals new delights and fresh depths'.

In 1959, following the bizarre arrest and beating he received at the hands of the New York Police, Davis took out a lawsuit, which he subsequently and wisely dropped. Davis entered the 60s comfortably, still the leading innovator in jazz, and shrugged off attempts from John Coltrane to dethrone him in the jazz polls. Davis chose to keep to his sparse style, allowing his musicians air and range. In 1964 while the world experienced Beatlemania, Davis created another musical landmark when he assembled arguably his finest line-up. The combination of Herbie Hancock, Wayne Shorter, Ron Carter and Tony Williams delivered the monumental *E.S.P.* in 1965. He continued with this acoustic line-up through another three recordings, including *Miles Smiles* and ending with *Nefertiti*. By the time of *Filles De Kilimanjaro*, Davis had gradually electrified his various groups and took bold steps towards rock music, integrating multiple electric keyboards and utilizing a wah-wah pedal connected to his electrified trumpet. Additionally, his own fascination with the possibilities of electric guitar, as demonstrated by Jimi Hendrix, assumed an increasing prominence in his bands. Young American west coast rock musicians had begun to produce a form of music based upon improvisation (mostly through the use of hallucinogenics). This clearly interested Davis, who recognized the potential of blending traditional rock rhythms with jazz, although he was often contemptuous of some white rock musicians at this time. The decade closed with his band being accepted by rock fans. Davis appeared at major festivals with audiences appreciating his line-up, which now featured the brilliant electric guitarist John McLaughlin, of whom Davis stated in deference to black musicians: 'Show me a black who can play like him, and I'd have him instead'. Other outstanding musicians Davis employed included Keith Jarrett, Airto, Chick Corea, Dave Holland, Joe Zawinul, Billy Cobham and Jack DeJohnette. Two major albums from this period were *In A Silent Way* and *Bitches Brew*, which unconsciously invented jazz rock and what was later to be called fusion. These records were marketed as rock albums, and consequently appeared in the regular charts. By the early 70s Davis had alienated himself from the mainstream jazz purists by continuing to flirt with rock music. In 1975, after a succession of personal upheavals including a car crash, further drug problems, a shooting incident, more police harassment and eventual arrest, Davis, not surprisingly, retired. During this time he became seriously ill, and it was generally felt that he would never play again, but, unpredictable as ever, Davis returned healthy and fit six years later with the comeback album, *The Man With The Horn*. He assembled a new band and received favourable reviews for live performances. Among the personnel were guitarist John Scofield and saxophonist Bill Evans. On the predominantly funk-based *You're Under Arrest*, he tackled pure pop songs, and although unambitious by jazz standards, tracks such as Cyndi Lauper's 'Time After Time' and Michael Jackson's 'Human Nature' were given Davis's brilliant master touch. The aggressive disco album *Tutu* followed, featuring his trumpet played through a synthesizer. A soundtrack recording for the Dennis Hopper film *The Hot Spot* found Davis playing the blues alongside Taj Mahal, John Lee Hooker, Tim Drummond and Roy Rogers.

During his final years Davis settled into a comfortable pattern of touring the world and recording, able to dictate the pace of his life with the knowledge that ecstatic audiences were waiting for him everywhere. Following further bouts of ill health, during which times he took to painting, Davis was admitted to hospital in California and died in September 1991. The worldwide obituaries were neither sycophantic nor morose; great things had already been said about Davis for many years. Django Bates stated that his own favourite Davis recordings were those between 1926 and mid-1991. Ian Carr added, in his impressive obituary, with regard to Davis's music: 'unflagging intelligence, great courage, integrity, honesty and a sustained spirit of enquiry always in the pursuit of art - never mere experimentation for its own sake'. Miles Davis' influence on rock music is considerable; his continuing influence on jazz is inestimable.

● ALBUMS: *Bopping The Blues* 1946 recording (Black Lion)★★★, *Cool Boppin'* 1948-49 recordings (Fresh Sounds)★★★, *Young Man With A Horn* 10-inch album (Blue Note 1952)★★★, *The New Sounds Of Miles Davis* 10-inch album (Prestige 1952)★★★★, *Miles Davis Volume 2* (Blue Note 1953/55)★★★★, *Blue Period* 10-inch album (Prestige 1953)★★★, *Miles Davis Plays Al Cohn Compositions* 10-inch album (Prestige 1953)★★★, *Miles Davis Quintet* 10-inch album (Prestige 1953)★★★★, *Miles Davis Quintet Featuring Sonny Rollins* 10-inch album (Prestige 1953)★★★, *Miles Davis Volume 3* (Blue Note 1954)★★★, *Miles Davis Sextet* 10-inch album (reissued as *Walkin'*) (Prestige 1954)★★★★, *Jeru* 10-inch album (Capitol 1954)★★★★★, *Miles Davis All Stars Volume1* 10-inch album (Prestige 1955)★★★★, *Miles Davis All Stars Volume 2* 10-inch album (Prestige 1955)★★★★, *Blue Moods* (Debut 1955)★★★, *Musings Of Miles* reissued as *The Beginning* (Prestige 1955)★★★, with Sonny Rollins *Dig Miles Davis/Sonny Rollins* reissued as *Diggin'* (Prestige 1956)★★★★, *Collectors Item* (Prestige 1956)★★★, *Miles - The New Miles Davis Quintet* reissued as *The Original Quintet* (Prestige 1956)★★★, *Blue Haze* (Prestige 1956)★★★, *Birth Of The Cool* 1949-50 recordings (Capitol 1956)★★★★★, *Miles* (Original Jazz Classics 1956)★★★, *Miles Davis And Horns* reissued as *Early Miles* (Prestige 1956)★★★, *Miles Davis And Milt Jackson Quintet/Sextet* reissued as *Odyssey* (Prestige 1956)★★★, *Cookin' With The Miles Davis Quintet* (Prestige 1957)★★★★, *Relaxin' With The Miles Davis Quintet* (Prestige 1957)★★★★, *Bags Groove* (Prestige 1957)★★★★, *Round About Midnight* (Columbia 1957)★★★★, *Miles Ahead* (Columbia 1957)★★★★★, *Miles Davis And The Modern Jazz Giants* (Prestige 1958)★★★, with John Coltrane *Miles And Coltrane* (Columbia 1958)★★★★, *Milestones* (Columbia 1958)★★★★★, *Porgy And Bess* (Columbia 1958)★★★★, *'58 Miles* (Columbia 1958)★★★★, *Jazz Track* (Columbia 1958)★★★, *Workin' With The Miles Davis Quintet* (Prestige 1959)★★★★, *Kind Of Blue* (Columbia 1959)★★★★★, *Sketches Of Spain* (Columbia 1960)★★★★, *On Green Dolphin Street* 1960 recording (Jazz Door 1960)★★★, *Live In Zurich* (Jazz Unlimited 1960)★★★, *Live In Stockholm 1960* (Royal Jazz 1960)★★★, *Steamin' With The Miles Davis Quintet* (Prestige 1961)★★★★, *Miles Davis In Person (Friday And Saturday Nights At The Blackhawk, San Fransisco)* (Columbia 1961)★★★★, *Someday My Prince Will Come* (Columbia 1961)★★★★, with Teddy Charles, Lee Konitz *Ezz-Thetic* (New Jazz 1962)★★★, with Dizzy Gillespie, Fats Navarro *Trumpet Giants* (New Jazz 1962)★★★★, *Miles Davis At Carnegie Hall* (Columbia 1962)★★★★, *Seven Steps To Heaven* (Columbia 1963)★★★, *Miles Davis In Europe* (Columbia 1963)★★★, *Quiet Nights* (Columbia 1963)★★★, *Miles In Antibes* (Columbia 1964)★★★, with Thelonious Monk *Miles And Monk At Newport* (Columbia 1964)★★★, *My Funny Valentine* (Columbia 1964)★★★★, *E.S.P.* (Columbia 1965)★★★★, *Miles Davis Plays For Lovers* (Prestige 1965)★★★, *Jazz Classics* (Prestige 1965)★★★, *'Four' And More - Recorded Live In Concert* (Columbia 1966)★★★, *Miles Smiles* (Columbia 1966)★★★, *Milestones* (Columbia 1967)★★★★, *Sorcerer* (Columbia 1967)★★★, *Nefertiti* (Columbia 1967)★★★, *Miles In The Sky* (Columbia 1968)★★★, *Filles De Kilimanjaro* (Columbia 1968)★★★★, *Miles Orbits* (Columbia 1968)★★★, *In A Silent Way* (Columbia 1969)★★★★★, *Double Image* (Moon 1969)★★★, *Paraphernalia* (JMY 1969)★★★, *Bitches Brew* (Columbia 1970)★★★★★, *Miles Davis At The Fillmore* (Columbia 1970)★★★★, *A Tribute To Jack Johnson* (Columbia 1971)★★★★, *What I Say? Volumes 1 & 2* (JMY 1971)★★★, *Live-Evil* (Columbia 1971)★★★★, *On The Corner* (Columbia 1972)★★★, *In Concert* (Columbia 1972)★★★★, *Tallest Trees* (Prestige 1973)★★★, *Black Beauty* (Columbia 1974)★★★★, *Big Fun* (Columbia 1974)★★★, *Get Up With It* (Columbia 1974)★★★, *Jazz At The Plaza Volume 1* (1974)★★★, *Agharta* (Columbia 1976)★★★★, *Pangaea* (Columbia 1976)★★★, *Live At The Plugged Nickel* (Columbia 1976)★★★★, *Water Babies* (Columbia 1977)★★★, *The Man With The Horn* (Columbia 1981)★★★, *A Night In Tunisia* (Star Jazz 1981)★★★, *We Want Miles* (Columbia 1982)★★★, *Star People* (Columbia 1983)★★★, *Blue Christmas* (Columbia 1983)★★★, *Heard 'Round the World* 1964 concert recordings (Columbia 1983)★★★, with the Lighthouse All Stars *At Last* (Boplicity 1985)★★★, *Decoy* (Columbia 1984)★★★, *You're Under Arrest* (Columbia 1985)★★★★, *Tutu* (Warners 1986)★★★★, *Blue Haze* (Prestige 1988)★★★, *Music From Siesta '88* (Warners 1988)★★★, *Amandla* (Warners 1989)★★★, *Aura* (Columbia 1989)★★★★, *The Hot Spot* (1990)★★★, with Michel Legrand *Dingo* (Warners 1991)★★★, *Doo-Bop* (Warners 1992)★★★, *The Complete Concert: 1964* (Columbia 1992)★★★★, *Live In Europe 1988* (1993)★★★, with Quincy Jones *Miles And Quincy Jones Live At Montreux* 1991 recording (Reprise 1993)★★★★, *Live Around The World* (Warners 1996)★★★, *The Complete Birth Of The Cool* (Capitol 1998)★★★★★, *The Complete Bitches Brew Sessions* 4-CD box set (Columbia/Legacy 1998)★★★★★, *Miles Davis At Carnegie Hall* 1961 recording (Columbia/Legacy 1998)★★★★.

● COMPILATIONS: *Miles Davis' Greatest Hits* (Prestige 1957)★★★★, *Greatest Hits* (Columbia 1969)★★★★, *Basic Miles - The Classic Performances Of Miles Davis* 1955-58 recordings (Columbia 1973)★★★★, *Circle In The Round* 1955-70 recordings (Columbia 1979)★★★, *Directions* unreleased recordings 1960-70 (Columbia 1981)★★★, *Chronicle: The Complete Prestige Recordings* (Prestige 1987)★★★★, *The Columbia Years 1955-1985* (Columbia 1988)★★★★, *Ballads* 1961-63 recordings (Columbia 1988)★★★★, *Mellow Miles* 1961-63 recordings (Columbia 1989)★★★, *First Miles* (Savoy 1989)★★★, *The Collection* (1990)★★★★, *The Essence Of Miles Davis* (Columbia 1991)★★★★, *Gold Collection* (1993)★★★★, *The Complete Live At The Plugged Nickel 1965* 8-CD box set (Columbia 1995)★★★★★, *Highlights From The Plugged Nickel* (Columbia

1995)★★★★, *Ballads And Blues* (Blue Note 1996)★★★★, *This Is Jazz No. 8 - Miles Davis Acoustic* (Legacy 1996)★★★, with Gil Evans *Miles Davis/Gil Evans: The Complete Columbia Studio Recordings* 6-CD/11-LP box set (Columbia/Mosaic 1996)★★★★★, *Miles Davis Plays Ballads; This Is Jazz No. 22* (Legacy 1997)★★★★, *Miles Davis Live And Electric: Live Evil* (Legacy 1997)★★★★, *Miles Davis Live And Electric: Miles Davis At The Fillmore East* (Legacy 1997)★★★★, *Miles Davis Live And Electric: Black Beauty, Miles Davis Live At The Fillmore West* (Legacy 1997)★★★★, *Miles Davis Live And Electric: Dark Magus, Live At Carnegie Hall* (Legacy 1997)★★★★, *Miles Davis Live And Electric: Miles Davis In Concert, Live At The Philharmonic Hall* (Legacy 1997)★★★★, *The Complete Studio Recordings Of The Miles Davis Quintet 1965-June 1968* 7-CD/10-LP box set (Columbia/Mosaic 1998)★★★★, remix collection by Bill Laswell *Panthalassa: The Music Of Miles Davis 1969-1974* (Columbia 1998)★★★★.

● VIDEOS: *Miles Davis And Jazz Hoofer* (Kay Jazz 1988), *Miles In Paris* (Warner Music Video 1990), *Miles Davis And Quincy Jones: Live At Montreux* (1993), *Dingo* (1997).

● FURTHER READING: *Miles Davis Transcribed Solos*, Miles Davis. *Miles: The Autobiography*, Miles Davis. *Milestones: 1. Miles Davis, 1945-60*, J. Chambers. *Milestones: 2. Miles Davis Since 1960*, J. Chambers. *Miles Davis*, Barry McRae. *Miles Davis: A Critical Biography*, Ian Carr. *Miles Davis For Beginners*, Daryl Long. *The Man In The Green Shirt: Miles Davis*, Richard Williams. *Miles Davis: The Early Years*, Bill Cole. *'Round About Midnight: A Portrait Of Miles Davis*, Eric Nisenson. *The Miles Davis Companion*, Gary Carner (ed.).

● FILMS: *Dingo* (1991).

Davis, Nathan

b. 15 February 1937, Kansas City, Kansas, USA. Davis began to play trombone at the age of 17, but soon switched to reeds and is now an accomplished player on flute, bass clarinet, tenor and soprano saxophones. His first noteworthy job was with the Jay McShann band, and a little later he became one of the few males who has ever played with the usually all-female International Sweethearts Of Rhythm. While studying at Kansas University, Davis lead a group with Carmell Jones; then army service in 1960 took him to Berlin. On leaving the army in 1963 he remained in Europe and was invited to Paris by Kenny Clarke, with whom he played for most of the next six years. In 1964 Davis joined Eric Dolphy for a brief residency at the Chat Qui Peche club and also played on the revolutionary reedsman's last recordings, made for the French radio station ORTF. The next year Davis toured Europe with Art Blakey's Jazz Messengers and was asked to join the band on a permanent basis; however, he declined, feeling that the touring life was too precarious. After making a series of excellent (but long-deleted) albums for small European labels - featuring players such as Jones, Clarke, Woody Shaw, Larry Young, Mal Waldron and Hampton Hawes - Davis returned to the USA in 1969 to teach jazz at Pittsburgh University, where he has since remained. He continued to record sporadically, making two albums for the small Pittsburgh company Segue followed by three more for his own Tomorrow International label, on which he tried his hand at fusion: but, as with his European releases, these were never widely distributed. Davis has had bad luck with recordings: not only are most of his own albums unavailable, but his work with Blakey, Clarke and Dolphy remains largely unreleased. The situation began to change in the 80s: the London-based Hot House label reissued his 1967 John Coltrane homage, *Rules Of Freedom*, and later released the new *London By Night*. Davis also formed the neo-bebop Paris Reunion Band, comprising various USA musicians who had lived in Paris in the 60s, recording and touring with them in the late 80s: personnel, at different times, has included Johnny Griffin, Joe Henderson, Shaw, Nat Adderley, Dizzy Reece, Slide Hampton, Kenny Drew, Jimmy Woode and Idris Muhammad. Nevertheless, it is early albums such as *Hip Walk* (1966) and *Sixth Sense Of The 11th House* (1972) that represent Davis' finest work. In particular, his superb tenor on the former's 'While Children Sleep' and his glorious bass clarinet on the latter's 'The Shadow Of Your Smile' suggest he is one of the great balladeers of modern jazz.

● ALBUMS: *Happy Girl* (1965)★★★, *Hip Walk* (1966)★★★★, *Rules Of Freedom* (Hot House 1968)★★★, *Live At Schola Cantorum* (1969)★★★, *Makatuka* (1970)★★★, *Sixth Sense Of The 11th House* (1972)★★★★, *If* (1976)★★★, *A Tribute To Dr. Martin Luther King* (1976)★★★, *Faces Of Love* (1982)★★★, *London By Night* (DIW 1987)★★★, *Nathan Davis Sextet* 1965 recordings (1990)★★★, with Arthur Blythe, Chico Freeman, Sam Rivers *Roots* (1992)★★★, *I'm A Fool To Want You* (Tomorrow International 1996)★★★★.

Davis, Richard

b. 15 April 1930, Chicago, Illinois, USA. A superbly accomplished jazz bass player, Davis worked in and around his home town during the late 40s and early 50s while continuing his musical studies. Between 1953 and 1955 he worked with Sun Ra, Ahmad Jamal and Don Shirley and later in the decade began a long association with Sarah Vaughan. In the 60s Davis worked with a number of musicians associated with the more forward-thinking areas of jazz. Notable among these was Eric Dolphy and also Jaki Byard. Davis' eclecticism was such that he was called upon for recording dates and public appearances with musicians as diverse as Earl Hines, Ben Webster, Stan Getz, Billy Cobham and Igor Stravinsky. For a long period at the end of the 60s he was also first-call bass player for the Thad Jones-Mel Lewis Jazz Orchestra. In 1977 Davis began teaching at the University of Wisconsin. A masterly technician, Davis plays with a full sound and his accompaniment is a great benefit to soloists. His own solos are conceived with intelligence and a powerful plangency.

● ALBUMS: *Muses For Richard Davis* (1969)★★★, *Epistrophy And Now's The Time* (Muse 1972)★★★, with Jill McManus *As One* (1975)★★, with Walt Dickerson *Divine Gemini* (1977)★★★, *Fancy Free* (Galaxy 1977)★★★, *Way Out West* (Muse 1981)★★★, with Dickerson *Tenderness* (1985)★★★, *Harvest* (Muse 1988)★★★, *Persia My Dear* (DIW 1988)★★★★, *One For Frederick* (Hep 1989)★★★★, *Dealin'* (Sweet Basil 1991)★★★.

DAVIS, WALTER

b. 1 March 1912, Grenada, Mississippi, USA, d. 22 October 1963, St. Louis, Missouri, USA. Based in St. Louis for most of his life, Davis learned piano at an early age. Between 1930 and 1941 he made many records, mainly issued on the Bluebird label, establishing himself as one of the most popular blues artists of the era. At first he was accompanied by another pianist, Roosevelt Sykes, but from 1935 onwards he developed a very distinctive style based around his own straightforward, but instantly recognizable, piano playing, a melancholy vocal and thoughtful, well-developed lyrics. Many of these records featured accompanying guitarists such as Big Joe Williams and Henry Townsend, the latter in particular demonstrating considerable musical empathy with Davis. After World War II, the Victor company released a further two records by Davis, but without recapturing his former commercial success. Nevertheless, in the late 40s he made several records for the Nashville-based Bullet label, and another two for Victor in 1952, which included some of his finest and most affecting performances.

● COMPILATIONS: *The Bullet Sides* (Krazy Kat 1986)★★★★, *Let Me In Your Saddle* (Bluetime 1987)★★★, *First Recordings 1920-1932* (1993)★★★.

DAVIS, WILD BILL

b. William Strethan Davis, 24 November 1918, Glasgow, Missouri, USA, d. 17 August 1995. Davis' early career found him playing piano, guitar, or simply writing arrangements for the bands of Milt Larkins, Earl Hines and Louis Jordan. At the end of the 40s he began concentrating on playing the Hammond organ. His organled trio was very successful and he also worked with Duke Ellington, Lionel Hampton and Count Basie. He was due to record his arrangement of Vernon Duke's 'April In Paris' with Basie but arrived late at the studio so Basie proceeded without him and as a result had one of his best-selling hits. Davis worked extensively in Europe, recording with a succession of visiting Americans including Buddy Tate and Al Grey. In the late 70s and early 80s he once again worked with Hampton but was mostly engaged in leading his own small groups and appearing solo at concerts and festivals around the world. He died in 1995 while he was recovering from a road accident.

● ALBUMS: *Here's Wild Bill Davis* 10-inch album (Epic 1954)★★★, *On The Loose* (Epic 1955)★★★, *Wild Bill Davis At Birdland* (Epic 1955)★★★★, *Evening Concerto* (Epic 1956)★★★, *Wild Bill Davis On Broadway* (Imperial 1956)★★★, *Wild Bill Davis In Hollywood* (Imperial 1956)★★★, *Flying High* (Everest 1959)★★★, *Dance The Madison* (Everest 1960)★★★, *Dis Heah* (Everest 1961)★★★, *The Music From 'Milk And Honey'* (Everest 1961)★★★, with Johnny Hodges *Johnny Hodges And Wild Bill Davis* (Verve 1961)★★★, *One More Time* (Coral 1962)★★★, *Lover* (Coral 1962)★★★, with Hodges *Mess Of Blues* (Verve 1964)★★★, with Hodges *Blue Rabbit* (Verve 1964)★★★, with Hodges *Blue Pyramid* (Verve 1965)★★★★, with Hodges *Wings And Things* (Verve 1965)★★★, *Con Soul & Sax* (1965)★★★, *Live At Count Basie's* (1966)★★★, *Wild Bill Davis In Atlantic City* (1966)★★★, *Impulsions* (Black & Blue 1972)★★★, with Illinois Jacquet *Illinois Jacquet With Wild Bill Davis* (Black & Blue/Classic Jazz 1973)★★★★, *All Right, Okay, You Win* (1976)★★★, with Lionel Hampton *Live In Emmen, Holland* (1978)★★, *Swing System 'D'* (1978)★★★.

DAVISON, WILD BILL

b. 5 January 1906, Defiance, Ohio, USA, d. 14 November 1989. As a youth Davison played with local bands, making occasional trips to Cincinnati and even New York in the mid-20s. While playing with the Seattle Harmony Kings, Davison made his first visit to Chicago, the city where he was to remain stylistically linked for the rest of his long life. This first visit to Chicago lasted five years; then, after a spell of bandleading with Frank Teschemacher, he worked in Milwaukee for several years, and, from 1941, played mostly in New York. For the next few years, broken only by military service during World War II, he was a regular at the city's popular Dixieland clubs, including Nick's, Ryan's and Condon's. With Eddie Condon, Davison made numerous recordings and also toured Europe. In the 60s he divided his time between jobs on the east and west coasts, recording and touring, often as a single, but sometimes in harness with some of his old musical comrades. A tough-talking, hard-drinking in his younger days, and driving cornetist, Davison's aggressive playing won him a host of admirers and was viewed by many as the epitome of Chicago style. In fact, as can be seen from his career summary, Davison's connection with Chicago was assumed rather than real. Although his rasping, forceful sound, replete with searing rips and flares, was most readily appropriate to the traditional repertoire, he had a fine way with ballads, and an album he recorded with strings late in his career showed him to have a warm-hearted, almost rhapsodic side to his personality. Remarkably, Davison retained his playing ability into old age and still practised daily when in his 80s.

● ALBUMS: *Dixieland Jazz Jamboree* 10-inch album (Commodore 1950)★★★, *Showcase* 10-inch album (Circle 1951)★★★★, with Eddie Condon *Jam Session Coast To Coast* (1953)★★★, with Helen Ward *Wild Bill Davison With Helen Ward* 10-inch album (Pax 1954)★★★, with Condon *Dixieland* (1955)★★★★, *Jazz At Storyville* (Savoy 1955)★★★, *Sweet And Hot* (Riverside 1956)★★★★, *Pretty Wild* (Columbia 1956)★★★, *Wild Bill Davison With Strings Attached* (Columbia 1956)★★★, with Buck Clayton *Singing Trumpets* (Jazztone 1957)★★★★ *Mild And Wild* (Commodore 1959)★★★, *S'Wonderful* (Davison 1962)★★★★, *Rompin' 'N' Stompin'* (Jazzology 1965)★★★, *Wild Bill Davison With Freddie Randall And His Band* (Black Lion 1965)★★★, *After Hours* (Jazzology 1966)★★★, *Surfside Jazz* (Jazzology 1966)★★★, *I'll Be A Friend With Pleasure* (Fat Cat Jazz 1968)★★★, *The Jazz Giants* (Sackville 1968)★★★, *Jazz On A Saturday Afternoon Volume 1* (Jazzology 1971)★★★, *Jazz On A Saturday Afternoon Volume 2* (Jazzology 1971)★★★, with Condon, Gene Krupa *Jazz At The New School* (1972)★★★, *In A Mellow Tone* (Jazzology 1971)★★★, *Big Horn Jazz Fest '72* (Big Horn 1972)★★★★, *Wild Bill Davison Live At The Rainbow Room* (Chiaroscuro 1973)★★★, *Tie A Yellow Ribbon 'Round The Old*

Oak Tree (Fat Cat Jazz 1973)★★★, *Just A Gig* (Jazzology 1973)★★★, *Beautifully Wild* (Audiophile 1974)★★★★, *Driftin' Down The River* (Storyville 1975)★★★, *Wild Bill In New Orleans* (Jazzology 1975)★★★, *Wild Bill Meets The Colonial Boys* (Fat Cat Jazz 1975)★★★, *Sweet And Lovely* (Storyville 1976)★★★, with Ralph Sutton *Together Again* (Storyville 1977)★★★, *Wild Bill Davison At The King Of France Tavern* (Fat Cat Jazz 1979)★★★★, *Wild Bill Davison In London* (Jazzology 1980)★★★, *Wild Bill Davison's 75th Anniversary Jazz Band* (Jazzology 1981)★★★, with Eddie Miller *Wild Bill Davison And Eddie Miller Play Hoagy Carmichael* (Real Time 1981)★★, *Solo Flight* (Jazzology 1981)★★★★, *Wild Bill Davison Live At The Memphis Jazz Festival* (Jazzology 1982)★★★, *Wild Bill Davison All-Stars* (Timeless 1986)★★★.

● COMPILATIONS: *But Beautiful* 1974-1975 recordings (Storyville 1986)★★★, *Showcase* 1947/1976 recordings (Jazzology 1992)★★★★, *Wild Bill In Denmark, Vol. 1* 1974-1977 recordings (Storyville 1996)★★★★, *Wild Bill In Denmark, Vol. 2* 1974-1975 recordings (Storyville 1996)★★★★, *The Commodore Master Takes* 1943-1946 recordings (Commodore 1997)★★★★, *But Beautiful* (Storyville 1998)★★★.

● VIDEOS: *Wild Bill Davison* (1992).

● FURTHER READING: *The Wildest One*, Hal Willard.

DAWSON, ALAN

b. George Alan Dawson, 14 July 1929, Marietta, Pennsylvania, USA, d. 23 February 1996. After studying extensively in Boston, where he also worked with the Sabby Lewis band, drummer Dawson joined Lionel Hampton. In 1953 he travelled to Europe with the band. This put Dawson in company with many outstanding young musicians, including Gigi Gryce and Clifford Brown. They made some excellent recordings although this went expressly against Hampton's orders, and when the band returned home most were dismissed. Dawson returned to Boston where he rejoined the Lewis band and later in the 50s began a career teaching at Berklee College Of Music. A regular in Boston clubs, he played with a wide range of visiting jazz artists and also recorded occasionally with artists such as Dave Brubeck, Tal Farlow, Dexter Gordon and Phil Woods. In 1965 he appeared at the Berlin Jazz Festival with Sonny Rollins and Bill Evans. Gifted as a performer, Dawson also had the rare ability to fully communicate his skills; and among his pupils were Tony Williams and Pat LaBarbera.

DE FRANCO, BUDDY

b. Boniface Ferdinand Leonardo De Franco, 17 February 1923, Camden, New Jersey, USA. A child prodigy, De Franco won an amateur contest playing the clarinet while still only 14 years old. Four years later he was in Gene Krupa's band, then joined Charlie Barnet; and in 1944 became a featured player with Tommy Dorsey, who had been sponsor of the amateur contest that launched De Franco's career. After abortive attempts to establish his own big band, De Franco worked mostly with small groups, including those of Count Basie and Art Blakey and in 1954 toured Europe with Billie Holiday. He premiered *Nelson Riddle*'s *Cross-Country Suite* at the Hollywood Bowl in 1958, later recording the suite for Dot Records. In the 60s, he continued playing in small groups, sometimes under his own leadership, and also taught. He led a clarinet, accordion, bass, drums quartet in the early 60s with Tommy Gumina. In 1966 he became leader of the Glenn Miller Orchestra, a job which lasted until 1974. Since then he has mixed teaching with playing, touring extensively, recording and developing a long-standing musical relationship with Terry Gibbs. A marvellously accomplished player, De Franco has been criticized for sacrificing emotional depth for the sake of technique. While to some extent justifiable, this censure unfairly condemns a gifted musician who has consistently set for himself, and attained, the highest standards of performance.

● ALBUMS: *King Of The Clarinet* 10-inch album (MGM 1952)★★★★, *Buddy De Franco Takes You To The Stars* 10-inch album (Gene Norman 1954)★★★, *Buddy De Franco With Strings* 10-inch album (MGM 1954)★★★★, *Buddy De Franco Quartet* 10-inch album (Norgran 1954)★★★★, *Pretty Moods By Buddy De Franco* 10-inch album (Norgran 1954)★★★, *The Progressive Mr. De Franco* reissued as *Odalisque* (Norgran 1954)★★★★, *Buddy De Franco And His Clarinet* reissued as *Autumn Leaves* (Norgran 1954)★★★, with Oscar Peterson *Buddy De Franco And Oscar Peterson Play George Gershwin* (Norgran 1955)★★★, *Buddy De Franco Quartet* reissued as *Mr. Clarinet* (Norgran 1955)★★★, *Jazz Tones* (Norgran 1956)★★★, *In A Mellow Mood* (Norgran 1956)★★★, with Art Tatum *The Art Tatum-Buddy De Franco Quartet* (American Recording Society 1956)★★★★, *The Buddy De Franco Wailers* (Norgran 1956)★★★, *Broadway Showcase* (Verve 1957)★★★, *Cross-Country Suite* (Dot 1958)★★★, *Buddy De Franco Plays Benny Goodman* (Verve 1958)★★★, *Buddy De Franco Plays Artie Shaw* (Verve 1958)★★★, *Cooking The Blues* (Verve 1958)★★★★, *Sweet And Lovely* (Verve 1958)★★★★, *Bravura* (Verve 1959)★★★, *I Hear Benny Goodman And Artie Shaw* (Verve 1960)★★★, *Generalissimo* (Verve 1960)★★★, *Wholly Cats* (Verve 1960)★★★, *Closed Session* (Verve 1960)★★★, *Live Date!* (Verve 1960)★★★, with Tommy Gumina *Presenting The Buddy De Franco - Tommy Gumina Quintet* (Mercury 1960)★★★, with Gumina *Kaleidoscope* (Mercury 1961)★★★, *University Of New Mexico Stage Band* (Advance Guard 1961)★★, *Pacific Standard Swingin' Time* (Decca 1961)★★★★, with Gumina *Polytones* (Mercury 1963)★★★, with Gumina *The Girl From Ipanema* (Mercury 1963)★★★, *Blues Bag* (Affinity 1964)★★★, *Buddy De Franco And His Orchestra At The Glen Island Casino* (1967)★★★, *Free Fall* (Choice 1974)★★★, *Boronquin* (1975)★★★, *Like Someone In Love* (Mosaic 1977)★★★★, *Waterbed* (1977)★★★, *Love Affair With A Clarinet* (1977)★★★, *Listen And Sit-In* (1978)★★★, *Buddy de Franco In Argentina* (1980)★★★, *The Liveliest* (1980)★★★, with Terry Gibbs *Jazz Party: First Time Together* (1981)★★★, with Gibbs *My Buddy* (1982)★★★, *On Tour: UK* (1983)★★★, *Buddy De Franco Presents John Denman* (1984)★★★, *Garden Of Dreams* (1984)★★★, *Groovin'* (1984)★★★, *'Hark': Buddy De Franco Meets The Oscar Peterson Quartet* (1985)★★★, with Gibbs *Chicago Fire* (Contemporary 1987)★★★★, with Al Raymond *Born To Swing!* (1988)★★★, *Like Someone In Love* (1989)★★★, *A Chip Off The Old Bop* (Concord 1992)★★★, with Dave McKenna *You Must Believe In Swing* (Concord Jazz 1997)★★★.

DE PARIS, SIDNEY

b. 30 May 1905, Crawfordsville, Indiana, USA, d. 13 September 1967, New York, USA. In the early 20s De Paris played trumpet in bands in Washington, DC, before moving to New York where he joined Andy Preer's band. In the late 20s he worked in units led by Charlie 'Fess' Johnson, by his brother, Wilbur De Paris, and then into the 30s with a succession of bands with which he briefly worked: Benny Carter, McKinney's Cotton Pickers, Don Redman, Noble Sissle, Willie Bryant and Mezz Mezzrow. At the end of the 30s, despite the all-pervading swing era, De Paris began to move towards an association with traditional jazz which was to continue for the rest of his life. In 1939 and 1940 he worked with Zutty Singleton, Jelly Roll Morton and Sidney Bechet. He later played with Art Hodes and had brief spells deputizing in the big bands of Benny Carter, Charlie Barnet and Roy Eldridge; but from 1947 he was principally in permanent collaboration with his brother. Their band offered a high standard of traditional jazz performances, always played with reverence for the past but with a sprightly sense of the present.

● ALBUMS: *Sidney De Paris And His Blue Note Stompers* 10-inch album (Blue Note 1951)★★★, *Wilbur De Paris And His Rampart Street Ramblers* (1952)★★★, *Wilbur De Paris At Symphony Hall* (1956)★★★.

DE PARIS, WILBUR

b. 11 January 1900, Crawfordsville, Indiana, USA, d. 3 January 1973, New York, USA. After working in tent shows and carnivals, trombonist De Paris appeared in New Orleans in the early 20s where he played with Louis Armstrong and other young musicians. Throughout the 20s he toured extensively, working with a wide range of small groups and big bands. He continued this pattern into the 30s where his jobs included playing in the band Teddy Hill brought to Europe and another spell with Armstrong. In 1940 he joined the old Chick Webb band which was continuing under Ella Fitzgerald's leadership. During the early and mid-40s he also played with Roy Eldridge and Duke Ellington but in 1947 formed his own band which featured his brother, Sidney De Paris, and stayed in existence for the next two decades. The De Paris brothers' band employed the music and inspiration of the New Orleans masters of an earlier generation but it was overlaid with a skilful blend of contemporary stylization and up-to-the-minute projection. Enormously popular in concert and on records, the band was one of the most successful of its kind.

● ALBUMS: *Wilbur De Paris And His Rampart Street Ramblers* 10-inch album (Atlantic 1952)★★★★, *Wilbur De Paris, Volume 2* 10-inch album (Atlantic 1953)★★★★, *New New Orleans Jazz* 10-inch album (Atlantic 1954)★★★, *Wilbur De Paris* (Heritage 1956)★★★, *Wilbur De Paris & His New Orleans Jazz* (Atlantic 1956)★★★, *Marchin' And Swingin'* (Atlantic 1956)★★★, *Wilbur De Paris At Symphony Hall* (Atlantic 1957)★★★★, *New Orleans Blues* (Atlantic 1957)★★★★, *Wilbur De Paris Plays Cole Porter* (Atlantic 1958)★★★, *That's A-Plenty* (Atlantic 1959)★★★, *The Wild Jazz Age* (Atlantic 1960)★★★, *Wilbur De Paris On The Riviera* (Atlantic 1961)★★★.

DEAN, ELTON

b. 28 October 1945, Nottingham, England. Dean is a fiery, self-taught saxophonist, who mainly features alto but sometimes uses saxello. He had lessons on piano from four years old and on violin from the age of 11. He hated these and took up clarinet and tenor saxophone, picking up the techniques himself and playing in various trad bands as a semi-professional. He went to Germany with a soul band, Lester Square and the GTs, and then joined the Irish Crickets, a showband. Regular work and wages enabled him to return to England, where he formed his own group, the Soul Pushers. In 1967 he joined Bluesology, who were at the start of their association with Long John Baldry. It was here that he first played with Marc Charig, later a front-line partner in the Keith Tippett Sextet. (For lovers of trivia, when Bluesology split up, the organist, Reg Dwight, took his stage name from colleagues Elton Dean and John Baldry to become Elton John.) Dean first met Tippett at the 1967 Barry (Wales) Summer School. He was a member of the Tippett Sextet which, in 1968, was the first beneficiary of the London Jazz Centre Society's scheme to give six-week residencies to new bands at its Monday sessions at London's 100 Club. As a result of these exciting gigs the reputation of the band and its individual members spread rapidly. From 1969-72 Dean was with Soft Machine at a time when the group's evolution from art rock to jazz-rock was becoming settled. Dean was with the edition of the Softs which was invited to play at the Proms, and it was usually his acerbic sax which would pull the band's fascinating but often diffuse improvisations into focus. After leaving Soft Machine, he led or co-led a series of bands, including Just Us, EDQ, Ninesense, and El Skid (co-led with Alan Skidmore.) More recently he has toured Europe and South America with his own bands of various line-ups, and has started his own label to issue new recordings of his group. Since 1990 he has had a powerful trio with Paul Rogers and Mark Sanders featuring Dean's long, a stringently lyrical improvisations. He has also worked with the London Jazz Composers Orchestra, Georgie Fame, Carla Bley and with Dutch rock band Supersister. *Newsense* was a live nonet recording featuring trombonists Paul Rutherford, Annie Whitehead and Roswell Rudd.

● ALBUMS: *Elton Dean* (1971)★★, *Oh For The Edge* (1976)★★★, *They All Be On This Old Road* (1976)★★★, *The Cheque Is In The Mail* (Ogun 1977)★★★, *Happy Daze* (Ogun 1977)★★★, *El Skid* (1977)★★★, *Boundaries* (1981)★★★, *Welcomet* (Impetus 1987)★★★, *The Bologna Tape* (Ogun 1988)★★★★, *Oh For The Edge* (Ogun 1988)★★★, *Duos* (ED 1989)★★★, *Trios* (ED 1989)★★★, *Unlimited Saxophone Company* (Ogun 1989)★★★★, *Elton Dean Quartet Live* (ED 1989)★★★★, *Two's And Three's* (ED 1989)★★★, with Howard Riley *All The Tradition* (Slam 1991)★★★, *The Vortex Tapes* (Slam 1992)★★★★, *If Dubois Only Knew* (Voiceprint 1996)★★★★, *Bladik* (Cuneiform 1997)★★★, *Newsense* (Slam 1998)★★★.

Dean, Roger

b. Roger Thornton Dean, 6 September 1948, Manchester, Lancashire, England. Although set on a scientific career, Dean took music lessons and began playing semi-professionally while at university. Developing into a gifted multi-instrumentalist, playing piano, bass and vibraphone, he embarked upon a career in music and in the early 70s became a member of Graham Collier's group. In the middle of the decade he formed his own group, Lysis, and was involved with the London Jazz Composers Orchestra. In addition to performing, Dean established a growing reputation as a composer, his work in both areas ranging over various aspects of contemporary music. Throughout this crowded working schedule Dean's scientific career continued apace, and in the 80s he taught at Brunel University.

● ALBUMS: *Cycles* (Mosaic 1977)★★★, *Lysis Play Dualyses* (Soma 1978)★★★, *Lysis Plus* (Mosaic 1979)★★★.

Dearie, Blossom

b. 28 April 1928, East Durham, New York, USA. A singer, pianist and songwriter, with a 'wispy, little-girlish' voice, Dearie is regarded as one of the great supperclub singers. Her father was of Scottish and Irish descent; her mother emigrated from Oslo, Norway. Dearie is said to have been given her unusual first name after a neighbour brought peach blossoms to her house on the day she was born. She began taking piano lessons when she was five, and studied classical music until she was in her teens, when she played in her high school dance band and began to listen to jazz. Early influences included Art Tatum, Count Basie, Duke Ellington and Martha Tilton, who sang with the Benny Goodman Band. Dearie graduated from high school in the mid-40s and moved to New York City to pursue a music career. She joined the Blue Flames, a vocal group within the Woody Herman Big Band, and then sang with the Blue Reys, a similar formation in the Alvino Rey Band. In 1952, while working at the Chantilly Club in Greenwich Village, Dearie met Nicole Barclay who, with her husband, owned Barclay Records. At her suggestion she went to Paris and formed a vocal group, the Blue Stars. The group consisted of four male singers/instrumentalists, and four female singers; Dearie contributed many of the arrangements. They had a hit in France and the USA with one of their first recordings, a French version of 'Lullaby Of Birdland'. While in Paris, Dearie met impresario and record producer Norman Granz, who signed her to Verve Records, for whom she eventually made six solo albums, including the highly regarded *My Gentleman Friend*. Unable to take the Blue Stars to the USA because of passport problems (they later evolved into the Swingle Singers), she returned to New York and resumed her solo career, singing to her own piano accompaniment at New York nightclubs such as the Versailles, the Blue Angel and the Village Vanguard. She also appeared on US television with Jack Paar, Merv Griffin and Johnny Carson. In 1966 she made the first of what were to become annual appearances at Ronnie Scott's Club in London, receiving excellent reviews as 'a singer's singer', whose most important asset was her power to bring a personal interpretation to a song, while showing the utmost respect for a composer's intentions'. In the 60s she also made some albums for Capitol Records, including *May I Come In?*, a set of standards arranged and conducted by Jack Marshall. In the early 70s, disillusioned by the major record companies' lack of interest in her kind of music, she started her own company, Daffodil Records in 1974. Her first album for the label, *Blossom Dearie Sings*, was followed by a two-record set entitled *My New Celebrity Is You*, which contained eight of her own compositions. The album's title song was especially written for her by Johnny Mercer, and is said to be the last piece he wrote before his death in 1976. During the 70s Dearie performed at Carnegie Hall with former Count Basie blues singer Joe Williams and jazz vocalist Anita O'Day in a show called *The Jazz Singers*. In 1981 she appeared with Dave Frishberg for three weeks at Michael's Pub in Manhattan. Frishberg, besides being a songwriter, also sang and played the piano, and Dearie frequently performed his songs, such as 'Peel Me A Grape', 'I'm Hip' and 'My Attorney Bernie'. Her own compositions include 'I Like You, You're Nice', 'I'm Shadowing You' and 'Hey John'. From 1983, she performed regularly for six months a year at the Ballroom, a nightclub in Manhattan, and in 1985 was the first recipient of the Mabel Mercer Foundation Award, which is presented annually to an outstanding supperclub performer. Appreciated mostly in New York and London, where she appeared several times in the late 80s/early 90s at the Pizza On The Park, Dearie, with her intimate style and unique voice, remains one of the few survivors of a specialized art.

● ALBUMS: *Blossom Dearie* (Verve 1957)★★★★, *Give Him The Ooh-La-La* (Verve 1958)★★★, *Once Upon A Summertime* (Verve 1958)★★★★, *Blossom Dearie Sings Comden And Green* (Verve 1959)★★★, *My Gentleman Friend* (Verve 1959)★★★★, *Broadway Song Hits* (Verve 1960)★★★, *May I Come In?* (Capitol 1966)★★★, *Blossom Dearie Sings* (Daffodil 1974)★★★, *My New Celebrity Is You* (Daffodil 1975)★★★, *Winchester In Apple Blossom Time* (Daffodil 1979)★★★, *Et Tu Bruce?* (Larrikin 1984)★★★, *Blossom Dearie Sings Rootin' Songs* (DIW 1987)★★★, *Songs Of Chelsea* (Daffodil 1987)★★★, *Needlepoint Magic* (Daffodil 1988)★★★, *Featuring Bobby Jasper* (1988)★★★.

● COMPILATIONS: *The Special Magic Of Blossom Dearie* (1975)★★★.

Dederick, Rusty

b. 7 December 1918, New York, USA. Dederick completed teacher training at Fredonia (New York) College before studying composition with Paul Geston and Stefan Wolpe. He started his professional career as a trumpeter in the band of Dick Stabile before moving on to Red Norvo, Claude Thornhill and Ray McKinley. He worked throughout the 50s and 60s as a trumpet player and arranger for NBC Television and in New York studios. In 1971 he joined the faculty of the Manhattan College of Music, in which he later became director of jazz studies. He plays and writes in a swing style.

● ALBUMS: *Rhythm And Winds* 10-inch album (Esoteric 1955)★★★, Rusty Dederick (Keynote 1955)★★★, *Salute To Bunny* (Counterpoint 1955)★★★, *Rusty Dederick And His Orchestra* (Four Corners 1964)★★★, *A Jazz Journey* (Monument 1965)★★★.

Deems, Barrett

b. 1 March 1914, Springfield, Illinois, USA, d. 15 September 1998, Chicago, Illinois, USA. Throughout the 30s Deems worked with Paul Ash and led his own small bands. Towards the end of the decade he worked extensively with Joe Venuti, an association that lasted until the mid-40s. Thereafter, Deems played in bands led by Red Norvo, Charlie Barnet and Muggsy Spanier. Billed as the 'World's Fastest Drummer', Deems had an eccentric onstage personality that was captured on film during a solo-feature in *Rhythm Inn* (1951). In 1954 he joined Louis Armstrong's All Stars, touring several countries and again appearing on film, this time in a feature, *High Society*, and the Ed Morrow television documentary *Satchmo The Great* (both 1956). In the 60s he worked with Jack Teagarden and the Dukes Of Dixieland before settling in Chicago, where he played in clubs, often backing visiting jazzmen. In 1976 he toured with Benny Goodman, and in the 80s worked with Wild Bill Davison and as a member of Keith Smith's package celebrating the music of Louis Armstrong. At this time, Deems' eccentricity was enhanced by his wild, bearded appearance and his offstage volubility. Despite the flamboyance of his appearance and self-billing, Deems played with a powerful attack and his spell with Armstrong included the album of W.C. Handy tunes, which proved to be a classic of the leader's later work.

● ALBUMS: *Deems* (Champion 1979)★★★, *Barrett Deems Big Band* (Delmark 1994)★★★, *Groovin' Hard* (Delmark 1998)★★★.

DeFaut, Volly

b. Voltaire De Faut, 14 March 1904, Little Rock, Arkansas, USA, d. 29 May 1973. After studying violin, De Faut switched to clarinet in his early teens. By this time he was living with his family in Chicago; and when aged 19 replaced Leon Roppolo, whose style he emulated, in the New Orleans Rhythm Kings. Later in the 20s he worked with Merrit Brunies, Muggsy Spanier and Jelly Roll Morton. In the pre-swing years he played with some of the best dance bands, including that led by Isham Jones and one of contractor Jean Goldkette's bands. A highly gifted musician, Benny Goodman always spoke well of him, and one who could have commanded a high salary during the swing era, De Faut nevertheless chose to have a succession of jobs in radio orchestras throughout the 30s. From the 50s onwards De Faut worked mostly outside music but made occasional appearances with small bands, some of which, like that led by Art Hodes, made records.

Defries, David

b. 24 May 1952, London, England. A multi-instrumentalist specializing in the trumpet, Defries stayed for just two terms of his course at Leeds College of Music, gaining experience in the Surrey County Youth Orchestra instead. During his twenties he played in Don Weller's Major Surgery, Julian Bahula's Jabula, and Dudu Pukwana's Zila. In the early 80s, as well as playing with Chris MacGregor's Brotherhood Of Breath, he co-led Sunwind with guitarist Mark Wood, which won the 1982 Greater London Arts Council Jazz Competition. He has more recently worked with the Breakfast Band and Loose Tubes.

Defunkt

This hard-funk act from the USA centred on trombonist Joseph Bowie who rose to prominence as a member of the Black Artists Group, an *avant garde* collective, based in St. Louis, and patterned after the Art Ensemble Of Chicago. Defunkt drew on this 'new wave' tradition but fused such radical jazz with the dancefloor punch of Parliament and Funkadelic to create an thrilling, invigorating style. Bowie, the brother of trumpeter Lester Bowie, was an inspired frontman and several propulsive albums, notably *Thermonuclear Sweat*, captured their exciting style. Defunkt undertook an enforced four-year sabbatical while its leader battled heroin addiction but emerged anew with *In America*. Bill Bickford, Ronnie Drayton (guitars), John Mulkerik (trumpet), Kim Annette Clarke (bass) and Kenny Martin (drums) joined Bowie for this compulsive set which, if shorn of melody, compensated with sheer excitement.

● ALBUMS: *Defunkt* (Hannibal 1980)★★★, *Thermonuclear Sweat* (Hannibal 1984)★★★, *In America* (Antilles/New Direction 1988)★★★, *Cum Funky* (1993)★★★.

● COMPILATIONS: *Avoid The Funk* (Hannibal 1988)★★★.

Dejan, Harold

b. 4 February 1909, New Orleans, Louisiana, USA. After studying clarinet with Lorenzo Tio Jnr., Dejan began playing professionally while still in his early teenage. He played in several New Orleans-style bands in the 20s and 30s. After military service Dejan took up the alto saxophone, playing with various bands into the 50s. In 1958 he formed his Olympia Brass Band, inspired by the brass bands he saw and heard during his childhood. A vigorous and enthusiastic performer, Dejan communicated his love of jazz through a wide-ranging repertoire. For all his love for the traditions, he did not hesitate to incorporate currently popular styles, including R&B and even bop-inflected numbers. Dejan continued to lead his band into the late 80s.

● ALBUMS: *Harold Dejan's Olympia Brass Band* (1962)★★★, *The Mighty Four* (1963)★★★, *Dejan's Olympia Brass Band In Europe* (1968)★★★, *Harold Dejan's Olympia Brass Band In London* (1968)★★★, *Harold Dejan's Olympia Brass Band In Berlin* (1968)★★★, *The Olympia Brass Band Of New Orleans* (1971)★★★.

DEJOHNETTE, JACK

b. 9 August 1942, Chicago, Illinois, USA. DeJohnette studied piano for 10 years, graduating from the American Conservatory of Music in Chicago. He also played saxophone, but was inspired by the example of Max Roach to take up drums, which he played with the high school band. He would practise for four hours on drums and four on piano, and played in all sorts of situations, from free jazz to R&B. Finally settling on drums, in 1963 he became a member of Muhal Richard Abrams' Experimental Band and was later involved with the AACM. In 1966 he played with John Coltrane during the interregnum between the departure of Elvin Jones and the final choice of Rashied Ali as his replacement. In the same year he settled in New York, playing with 'Big' John Patton, Jackie McLean, Betty Carter and Abbey Lincoln. At the end of the year he joined the Charles Lloyd Quartet, where he stayed until 1969, but during that time he also gigged with Thelonious Monk, Freddie Hubbard, Bill Evans, Keith Jarrett, Chick Corea and Stan Getz. In August 1969 he took part in sessions for Miles Davis's *Bitches Brew*, and in April 1970 he formally joined Davis. After departing in mid-1971 he set up his own band, Compost.

During the 70s he became virtually a session drummer for ECM Records, recording with Jan Garbarek, Kenny Wheeler and John Abercrombie among others. With Abercrombie and Dave Holland, he played in the occasional trio Gateway. DeJohnette also recorded with his Directions and New Directions bands, which involved Abercrombie and Lester Bowie, and in 1980 formed the acclaimed Special Edition, whose varying personnel has featured David Murray, Chico Freeman and Arthur Blythe. In 1985, reverting temporarily to his earlier talent, he released a solo piano album. During the late 80s and early 90s DeJohnette was part of Keith Jarrett's Standards Trio with Gary Peacock and toured as a duo with John Surman, both of them doubling on keyboards and electronics. (He had earlier featured on Surman's 1981 *The Amazing Adventures Of Simon Simon*.) He has also worked with Michael Brecker, Tommy Smith and with Ornette Coleman and Pat Metheny on their *Song X* collaboration. His further collaborations with Metheny in 1990 with *Parallel Realities* and with Lyle Mays and Marc Johnson in 1993 were both inspiring excursions. In some contexts, DeJohnette's approach to the rhythm can be so oblique that his grip on time can seem precarious, but this is deceptive. He is a powerfully propulsive percussionist with an exceptional sense of structure and texture, perhaps heard at its most exotic in his vivid splashes of colour with the Lloyd Quartet.

● ALBUMS: *The Jack DeJohnette Complex* (Milestone 1969)★★, *Have You Heard?* (Milestone 1970)★★★, with Compost *Take Off Your Body* (1972)★★★, with Keith Jarrett *Rutya And Daitya* (ECM 1973)★★★, *Sorcery* (Prestige 1974)★★★, *Cosmic Chicken* (Prestige 1975)★★, *Directions* (ECM 1976)★★★★, with Directions *New Rags* (ECM 1977)★★★, with New Directions *New Directions* (ECM 1978)★★★★, *Special Edition* (ECM 1980)★★★, with New Directions *New Directions In Europe* (ECM 1980)★★★, *Tin Can Alley* (ECM 1981)★★★, *Inflation Blues* (ECM 1982)★★, *Album Album* (ECM 1984)★★★★, *The Piano Album* (Landmark 1985)★★★, with Lester Bowie *Zebra* (Pan 1985)★★★, with David Murray *In Our Style* (DIW 1986)★★★, *Irresistible Force* (MCA 1987)★★★, *Audio-Visualscapes* (MCA 1989)★★, with Pat Metheny *Parallel Realities* (MCA 1990)★★★, *Earth Walk* (Blue Note 1991)★★★★, with Lyle Mays, Marc Johnson *Fictionary* (Geffen 1993)★★★★, *Music For The Fifth World* (Capitol 1993)★★★, *Pictures* (ECM 1993)★★★, with Michael Cain, Steve Gorn *Dancing With Nature Spirits* (ECM 1996)★★★, with Keith Jarrett, Gary Peacock *Tokyo '96* (ECM 1998)★★★, *Oneness* (ECM 1998)★★★★, with World Saxophone Quartet *Selim Sivad: A Tribute To Miles Davis* (Justin Time 1998)★★★.

● COMPILATIONS: *Works* (ECM 1985)★★★★.

● VIDEOS: *Musical Expression On The Drum Set* (Homespun Video 1998), *Talking Drummers: A Journey Of Music, Friendship And Spirit* (Homespun Video 1998).

DELMAR, ELAINE

b. 13 September 1939, Harpenden, Hertfordshire, England. Delmar was a popular singer in the UK, whose style was doubtless influenced by her Jamaican-born father, the jazz trumpeter, Leslie 'Jiver' Hutchinson. After studying music from the age of six, she made her first broadcast, as a pianist, seven years later on *Children's Hour*. While still at school, she sang with her father's band at US Air Force bases in Britain, and was on tour with him at the time of his fatal accident in 1959. In 1952 she appeared in a revival of Finian's Rainbow in Liverpool. For a while she was a member of the Dominoes group, before going solo and playing the club circuit and touring overseas. From the early 60s, she made several appearances on the London stage in shows such as No Strings, *Cowardy Custard*, *Bubbling Brown Sugar* (with Billy Daniels), The Wiz and *Jerome Kern Goes To Hollywood* (1985), which marked the centenary of the composer's birth. After the latter show's brief Broadway run, Delmar made her New York cabaret debut at the Ballroom in New York. In 1991, she co-starred with actor and singer, Paul Jones, in the concert tour of *Let's Do It*, another centenary celebration of the great American songwriter, Cole Porter. In the following year, Delmar teamed with Jones again for a series of concerts entitled *Hooray For Hollywood*, which featured songs from movies such as Porgy And Bess, Annie Get Your Gun and Top Hat. Amongst her albums, which contained popular standards, she has also released the highly acclaimed *Elaine Sings Wilder*, a tribute to one of America's lesser known composers, Alec Wilder. The pianist and musical director on the record was Colin Beaton, one of Delmar's mentors and early influences. The antithesis of Wilder would be Gustav Mahler, and Delmar played the part of the Princess in Ken Russell's 1974 film biography of the famous composer. In 1983, she appeared at London's National Theatre in the straight play, *Map Of The World*. A popular regular at Ronnie Scott's club, she has appeared in concert with jazz giants such as Benny Carter, Herb Ellis and Stéphane Grappelli. A polished performer whose execution is faultless, jazz remains her first love; her accompanists are always impeccable improvisers and have included Eddie Thompson, Brian Dee and Jeff Clyne.

● ALBUMS: *Elaine Sings Wilder* (1966)★★★★, *Sneaking Up On You* (1968)★★★, *La Belle Elaine* (1968)★★★, *I've Got The World On A String* (Retrospect 1976)★★★, *Elaine Delmar And Friends* (Polydor 1980)★★★, *Yours Sincerely* (1985)★★★, with Spike Robinson *In Town* (1986)★★★, *Spirit Of The Song* (1990)★★★, *S'Wonderful* (1992)★★★.

Demuth, Nick

b. 17 May 1925, Bognor Regis, Sussex, England. Jazz pianist, arranger and composer was well grounded in working with touring bands by the time he joined Billy Banks in 1954. During the second half of the 50s Demuth toured the world with Banks, being particularly well recieved in Australia and the Far East. After a Hiatus he teamed up with Banks again in 1962, this time they worked in Tokyo for three years. From his base in Hong Kong, Demuth had a variety of jobs including working for a radio station, gigging with the Victoria Jazz Band, scoring the music for two Hong Kong made English language films and wrote a track for the UK film *Ferry To Hong Kong*.

He settled in Manila in 1990 where he continues to play at least four nights a week. He co-owns a club (which oddly specialises in C&W music not Jazz) and is the Far East correspondent for *Jazz Journal International*. He is at present working on his autobiography *Nobody Claps The Piano Player*.

Deniz, Joe

b. José William Deniz, 10 September 1913, Butetown, Cardiff, Wales, d. 24 April 1994. Deniz's musical apprenticeship was served on the docks of his native Butetown district (now known as Tiger Bay), where he played impromptu calypso to deprive sailors of their small change. He was born one of three sons to a black American mother raised in Bristol, and each of the offspring would make their mark on the British jazz dance scene as a guitarist. Joe himself learned the ukulele first, before upgrading to the fuller fretboard. As his skill increased so he would join with other vagrant musicians travelling through the ethnic centres of Cardiff, playing engagements at houses in exchange for drinks. Eventually a nucleus of black musicians, Victor Parker, George Glossop and Don Johnson, in addition to Deniz, found work in Soho clubs. After a brief sojourn to his hometown he returned as drummer at an after hours London club entitled the Nest. A haunt of visiting Afro-Caribbean musicians, it saw him introduced to the likes of Fats Waller and his idol, Django Reinhardt. His next engagement came as part of Ken 'Snakehips' Johnson's black orchestra, once again on guitar, where he remained until 1941 (when Johnson was killed in a Café De Paris bombing). Deniz too was injured (spending the rest of his life in discomfort owing to shrapnel in the leg), but went on to find session work with many top-flight band leaders, as well as violinist Stephane Grappelli. His personal notoriety also rose via solos with Harry Parry's Radio Rhythm Club Sextet. Turning away from jazz, he joined his brothers in the Latin-styled Hermanos Deniz, before joining the West End run of *Ipi Tombi*, a South African musical which featured his duets with brother Frank. He retired from music in 1980, contenting himself with his memories and passion for DIY.

Dennerlein, Barbara

b. 25 September 1965, Munich, Germany. Dennerlein started to learn organ when she was 11-years-old and soon acquired a Hammond B3, the classic instrument; she was performing in Munich jazz clubs by the age of 15. She played alongside Jimmy Smith on his German tour and with altoist Sonny Fortune. Her self-produced albums *Jazz Live At The Munich Domicile* and *Bebop* both won German Record Critics awards. Her trio with Christopher Widmoser (guitar) and Andreas Witte (drums) toured, played festivals and made radio and television appearances in the mid-80s. Playing foot-pedal bass in the authentic manner, Dennerlein's combination of down-home groove and modernist freakishness was well documented on *Straight Ahead* (1988), for which drummer Ronnie Burrage supplied his fantastic swirling drum textures, and Ray Anderson bravura trombone. After enthusiastic critical reception in England, Dennerlein recorded *Hot Stuff* in 1990 with drummer Mark Mondesir and saxophonist Andy Sheppard, prominent figures in the English jazz revival of the 1980s. In 1991 she played London's Jazz Cafe and toured Europe with Widmoser and drummer Stephan Eppinger. Altoist Bobby Watson also sat in with her. She has customised her Hammond with a Midi interface so that she can unleash synthesizer sounds, but it is her understanding of classic black organ music - blues and bebop - that makes her playing so forceful.

● ALBUMS: *Jazz Live At The Munich Domicile* (80s)★★, *Orgelspiele* (Bebab 1985)★★, *Bebop* (Bebab 1986)★★★, *Straight Ahead* (Enja 1988)★★★★, with Andreas Witte *Duo* 1988 recordings (1990)★★, *Live On Tour* (Bebab 1989)★★, *Hot Stuff* (Enja 1990)★★★★, *Plays Classics* (Bebab 1991)★★★, *That's Me* (Enja 1992)★★★, *Take Off!* (Verve 1996)★★★, *Junkanoo* (Verve 1997)★★★.

Desmond, Johnny

b. Giovanni Alfredo de Simone, 14 November 1920, Detroit, Michigan, USA, d. 6 September 1985, Los Angeles, California, USA. Shortly before he took off on his fatal final flight, Glenn Miller told Desmond: 'I have great plans for you when this war is over. You're going to be a great success'. Then Miller disappeared forever - but his prophecy was fulfilled. A performer on local radio during his childhood days, Desmond's voice changed from tenor to baritone when he was 15 years old. He temporarily gave up his showbusiness career and settled for the security of a job in his father's grocery store. After attending Detroit Conservatory of Music, he began appearing at local clubs both singing and playing piano before forming the Downbeats, a vocal group who were signed by Bob Crosby in 1940 and appeared with the Crosby band as the Bob-O-Links. In common with many other Crosby vocalists they stayed only a short time with the band, and by 1941 Desmond had moved on to replace Howard Dulaney as solo singer with the Gene Krupa Orchestra. After a brief stay with Krupa he enlisted in the US Air Force soon after the outbreak of war. By 1943 he had joined Major Glenn Miller's Allied Expeditionary Forces Band and travelled to Europe, obtaining his own BBC radio show *A Soldier And A Song*. The possessor of a smooth, Frank Sinatra-influenced singing style, Desmond became a popular solo performer after the war, with a long stay on the *Breakfast Club* show. He recorded a hit record, 'C'est Ci Bon', for MGM Records, before switching to Coral and enjoyed further chart success with 'The High And The Mighty', 'Play Me No Hearts And Flowers', 'Yellow Rose Of Texas', 'Sixteen Tons' and 'A White Sport Coat'. During 1958 Desmond appeared in the Broadway show *Say Darling*, and later succeeded Sydney Chaplin as Nicky Arnstein in the stage version of Funny Girl. He continued to be popular on television and in night clubs throughout the 60s and 70s, and was working in New York a few months before his death in September 1985.

● ALBUMS: *Dream Of Paris* (1958)★★★★, *Once Upon A Time* (Columbia 1959)★★★, *Johnny Desmond Swings* (1958)★★★★, *Hymns* (1959)★★, *Blue Smoke* (1960)★★★, *So Nice!* (1961)★★★.

● COMPILATIONS: *Memorial Album* (1985)★★★★.

Desmond, Paul

b. Paul Breitenfeld, 25 November 1924, San Francisco, California, USA, d. 30 May 1977, New York, USA. Alto saxophonist Desmond is best known as a member of the Dave Brubeck quartet, in which he played from 1951-67 and to whose popular success he greatly contributed by writing the hit 'Take Five'. However, aficionados and critics alike agree that much of his best work was done away from Brubeck's often stiff improvisations and tricky time signatures, in particular on two albums with Gerry Mulligan (*Blues In Time*, *Two Of A Mind*) and five with Jim Hall (*East Of The Sun*, *Bossa Antigua*, *Glad To Be Unhappy*, *Take Ten*, *Easy Living*), which Mosaic Records later reissued in one of their splendidly packaged box sets. Influenced by Lee Konitz, but very much his own man, Desmond's pure tone and fluid, inventive solos - into which he often wove witty quotes from other songs - marked him out as one of modern jazz's most original and distinctive voices. A noted humorist too, he once declared his aim was to make his saxophone 'sound like a dry martini' and also claimed to have won prizes as 'the world's slowest alto player'. In fact, Desmond's pellucid tone and relaxed, floating style required an architect's sense of structure and the lightning reflexes of a master improviser. In the late 60s/early 70s he sometimes sounded out of place on the CTI label, amid fusion, strings, Simon And Garfunkel songs and the other accoutrements of Creed Taylor's production; but a 1971 date with the Modern Jazz Quartet, and two albums from a 1975 concert with his own quartet, catch him back at his best. In 1975 he also recorded a set of duets with Brubeck and rejoined the pianist's quartet for a reunion tour. In 1976 his doctor diagnosed lung cancer - 'I only went with swollen feet,' Desmond wryly remarked - and he died the following May. Desmond is remembered as one of the most literate, amusing and reflective of jazzmen.

● ALBUMS: *Paul Desmond* 10-inch album (Fantasy 1954)★★★, with Gerry Mulligan *Gerry Mulligan Quartet/Paul Desmond Quintet* (Fantasy 1956)★★★★, *The Paul Desmond Quartet Featuring Don Elliot* (Fantasy 1956)★★★, with Mulligan *Blues In Time* (Fantasy 1957)★★★★, with Mulligan *The Gerry Mulligan-Paul Desmond Quartet* (Verve 1958)★★★★, with Jim Hall *East Of The Sun* (Musicraft 1959)★★★★, *First Place Again!* (Warners 1960)★★★, *Desmond Blue* (RCA Victor 1961)★★★★, with Hall *Take Ten* (RCA Victor 1962)★★★, with Mulligan *Two Of A Mind* (RCA Victor 1962)★★★★★, with Hall *Bossa Antigua* (RCA Victor 1965)★★★, with Hall *Glad To Be Unhappy* (RCA Victor 1965)★★★, with Hall *Easy Living* (RCA Victor 1966)★★★, *Polka Dots And Moonbeams* (Bluebird 1966)★★★, *Summertime* (A&M 1969)★★★, *From The Hot Afternoon* (A&M 1969)★★★, *Crystal Illusions* (1969)★★★, *Bridge Over Troubled Water* (A&M 1970)★★, *Skylark* (Columbia 1974)★★★★, *Pure Desmond* (CTI 1975)★★★, *The Paul Desmond Quartet Live* (A&M 1976)★★★★, *Like Someone In Love* (Telarc 1976)★★★★, *Paul Desmond* 1975 recording (1978)★★★, with the MJQ *The Only Recorded Performance* 1971 recording (1984)★★★.

● COMPILATIONS: *Greatest Hits* (RCA 1986)★★★, *The Complete Recordings Of The Paul Desmond Quartet With Jim Hall* recorded 1959-1965, 6-LP box set (1987)★★★★, *Late Lament* recorded1961/1962 (RCA 1987)★★★, *The Complete RCA Victor Recordings* 5-CD box set (RCA Victor 1997)★★★★.

Desmond, Trudy

b. USA. Desmond displayed an interest in singing from a very early age, and while still at school sang with jazz groups. Her professional career extends to incorporate work with small groups and big bands in clubs, at festivals, and on radio and television in the USA and Canada. Surviving cancer, she has also worked on behalf of various medical charities and support groups. Her voice is poised and clear, and she sings with a subtle sense of swing. Her repertoire is wide but centres upon the great standards, and always demonstrates a vital understanding of the lyrics of the songs she chooses to perform.

● ALBUMS: *RSVP* (Unisson/Jazz Alliance 1989)★★★, *Tailor Made* (Jazz Alliance 1993)★★, *Make Me Rainbows* (Koch 1995)★★★, *My One And Only: A Gershwin Celebration* (Justin Time 1997)H★★★.

Deuchar, Jimmy

b. 26 June 1930, Dundee, Scotland, d. 9 September 1993. Like so many of the young British musicians entering jazz in the immediate post-World War II years, trumpeter Deuchar was involved in regular bebop sessions at a handful of London clubs. Arising from this came his first important professional engagement, with the John Dankworth Seven. In the early 50s he worked with a number of popular dancebands, playing jazz with artists including Ronnie Scott and Tony Crombie.

In the mid-50s he worked with Lionel Hampton, then became a member of Kurt Edelhagen's radio big band alongside musicians such as Derek Humble and Dusko Goykovich. During his association with Edelhagen, Deuchar turned more to arranging, although he found time to perform with Scott and Tubby Hayes. In the second half of the 60s, still based in Europe, Deuchar became a member of the multi-national big band co-led by Kenny Clarke and Francy Boland. In the 70s Deuchar relocated to his native Scotland, concentrating upon arranging with only occasional recording dates as a performer, showing that he had lost none of his considerable ability. His arranging continued into the 80s despite ill-health, and included a fine album by Spike Robinson, *The Gershwin Collection*, on which Deuchar showed a clear grasp of how an arranger should overcome the problems associated with blending strings into a jazz performance.

● ALBUMS: *Jimmy Deuchar Sextet* (1953)★★, *Thou Swell* (1954)★★★, *Pub Crawling* (Contemporary 1955)★★★★, *Jimmy Deuchar Quartet* (1955)★★★, *Presenting The Ronnie Scott Sextet* (1957)★★★, *Kurt Edelhagen Presents* (1957)★★, *Pal Jimmy* (1958)★★★, *The Scots Connection* (1979)★★★.

DI MEOLA, AL

b. 22 July 1954, Jersey City, New Jersey, USA. After learning the drums at a very early age, Di Meola was inspired by the Beatles to take up the guitar, at the age of nine. Private lessons continued until, at the age of 15, he was performing in a C&W context. A growing interest in jazz led Di Meola to enter Berklee College Of Music in 1971, but he soon left to join Barry Miles' fusion group, returning in 1974 to study arranging. He was invited by Chick Corea to join his popular and influential Return To Forever. During this time Di Meola made a name for himself with his furious and sometimes spellbinding playing. It was 1976 before Di Meola began working as a leader and recording for Columbia, mostly in a jazz-rock style. In 1982 and 1983 he recorded two flamenco-influenced albums with John McLaughlin and Paco de Lucia, as part of an acoustic trio. The Al Di Meola Project was born in 1985 and remains his most celebrated venture. Recording on Manhattan and touring internationally, this group mixed his delicate, classically influenced acoustic guitar with the futuristic synthesizer work of Phil Markowitz and ethnic percussion of Airto Moreiro to form a new and influential sound. In 1995 he formed Rite Of Strings, a trio with bassist Stanley Clarke and violinist Jean-Luc Ponty.

● ALBUMS: *Land Of The Midnight Sun* (Columbia 1976)★★, *Elegant Gypsy* (Columbia 1977)★★★, *Casino* (Columbia 1978)★★★, *Splendido Hotel* (Columbia 1979)★★★★, *Roller Jubilee* (Columbia 1980)★★★, *Electric Rendevous* (Columbia 1982)★★★, *Tour De Force Live* (Columbia 1982)★★★★, *Scenario* (Columbia 1983)★★★★, *Cielo e Terra* (EMI 1983)★★★★, *Soaring Through A Dream* (EMI 1985)★★★, *Tiramu Su* (EMI 1988)★★★, *Heart Of The Immigrants* (Tomato 1993)★★★, *Kiss My Axe* (Tomato 1993)★★★, *World Sinfonia* (Tomato 1993)★★★, *Orange And Blue* (Blue Moon 1994)★★★, with Stanley Clarke, Jean-Luc Ponty *The Rite Of Strings* (IRS 1995)★★★, with Paco De Lucia, John McLaughlin *Paco De Lucia, Al Di Meola, John McLaughlin* (Verve 1996)★★★, *Di Meola Plays Piazzolla* (Blue Moon 1996)★★, *The Infinite Desire* (Verve 1998)★★★.

● COMPILATIONS: *The Best Of Al Di Meola* (Manhattan 1993)★★★.

DIAL, HARRY

b. 17 February 1907, Birmingham, Alabama, USA, d. 25 January 1987. Dial began playing drums as a child in St. Louis where his family had settled in 1909. He worked extensively in the city and also on the riverboats that were based there, playing in bands led by, among others, Fate Marable. In the late 20s he played in Chicago, making records, including some under his own name. In the early 30s he was in bands led by Don Pasquall and, in 1933, by Louis Armstrong. He recorded with Armstrong, although it must be said that some of the sessions were poor examples even of the leader's work. The following years he moved to New York where he played with Fats Waller and was also with one of the house bands at the Cotton Club, and in bands at the Log Cabin and Small's Paradise. In the 40s he often led his own band, again appearing at Small's Paradise. He continued to be active, as sideman and as leader, during the 60s and 70s.

DIALOGUE - BOBBY HUTCHERSON

Vibraphone player Bobby Hutcherson is another gifted contemporary jazz musician associated with the Blue Note label scene of the 60s. His incredible versatility left him uniquely at home on both gentle, mellow grooves and more robust and demanding *avant garde* dates. *Dialogue* is from the more modern end of the spectrum, and is a six-way musical give and take, featuring a group of the best new players on the label. Freddie Hubbard takes care of trumpet, the underrated Sam Rivers is on saxophones, bass clarinet and flute, the brilliant Andrew Hill plays piano, bass is by Richard Davis and Joe Chambers is on drums.

● Tracks: *Catta; Idle While; Les Noirs Marchent; Dialogue; Ghetto Lights.*

● First released 1965

● UK peak chart position: did not chart

● USA peak chart position: did not chart

DICKENSON, VIC

b. 6 August 1906, Xenia, Ohio, USA, d. 16 November 1984. A self-taught musician, Dickenson's early experience came playing trombone in the territory bands of Speed Webb and Zack Whyte. By the 30s he was ready for the big time and worked with bands led by Luis Russell, Claude Hopkins, Benny Carter and Count Basie. Throughout the 40s he was active mostly with small groups, including those of Sidney Bechet, Frankie Newton, Eddie Heywood (for a long spell), and as leader of his own groups. This pattern continued into the 50s and 60s when he worked with Bobby Hackett, Red Allen and others. Although rooted in the more traditional jazz style, Dickenson's big band experience, allied to his instinctive melodic grace, made him an ideal musician to enter the mainstream. Indeed, his record albums of the early and mid-50s, especially dates with Ruby Braff, were important milestones in the emergence of this strand of jazz. In addition to his mastery of his instrument, Dickenson brought a refreshing sense of humour to his playing, inserting little musical asides that help to make his work readily identifiable.

● ALBUMS: *The Vic Dickenson Septet, Volume 1* 10-inch album (Vanguard 1953)★★★★, *The Vic Dickenson Septet, Volume 2* 10-inch album (Vanguard 1953)★★★★, *Vic Dickenson Septet, Volume 3* 10-inch album (Vanguard 1953)★★★★, *The Vic Dickenson Septet, Volume 4* 10-inch album (Vanguard 1954)★★★★, *Vic's Boston Story* (Storyville 1957)★★★, with Joe Thomas *Mainstream* (Atlantic 1958)★★★, *Yacht Club Swing* (1964)★★★, with Bobby Hackett *This Is My Bag* (1968)★★★, *Bobby Hackett, Vic Dickenson, Maxine Sullivan At The Fourth Manassas Jazz Festival* (Jazzology 1969)★★★, with Bobby Hackett *Bobby Hackett-Vic Dickenson Septet* (1973)★★★, *Jive At Five* (1975)★★★, *Gentleman Of The Trombone* (1975)★★★, *Vic Dickenson In Holland* (1975)★★★, *Plays Bessie Smith - Trombone Cholly* (1976)★★★, *The Vic Dickenson Quintet* (1976)★★★, *Vic Dickenson In Sessions* (1978)★★★.

● COMPILATIONS: *The Essential Vic Dickenson* (Vanguard 1998)★★★★.

● FURTHER READING: *Ding! Ding! A Bio-Discographical Scrapbook On Vic Dickenson*, Manfred Selchow.

DICKERSON, CARROLL

b. 1895, USA, d. October 1957. Although little is known of his early life, Dickerson became highly popular in Chicago in the 20s. His own violin playing was inadequate, but he had a keen ear for good jazz musicians and employed a succession of leading players in his band, among them Johnny Dunn, Tommy Ladnier, Buster Bailey and Earl Hines (who had recalled that Dickerson would get so drunk he would sometimes try to play his violin with the back of the bow or continue to conduct the band long after the tune was over). Dickerson's most important acquisition arrived in 1926 when Louis Armstrong joined the band. After a second spell in the band, in 1927/8, Armstrong became the leader and Dickerson formed a rival band. In early 1929, once again with Armstrong, Dickerson took his band to New York where they enjoyed great success in clubs and theatres. During his time with Dickerson, Armstrong made some of his classic Hot Five recordings using sidemen from the band, among them Hines and Zutty Singleton. In 1930 Dickerson's band folded and he worked briefly with Joe 'King' Oliver and the Mills Blue Rhythm Band before returning to Chicago and reforming his own band. He continued to lead bands in Chicago through the 30s and into the 40s, but never attained the prominence he had enjoyed when Armstrong was with him.

DICKERSON, WALT

b. Walter Roland Dickerson, 16 April 1928, Philadelphia, Pennsylvania, USA. Vibraharpist Dickerson first made his mark in California in the late 50s, leading a group that included Andrew Hill and Andrew Cyrille. He moved to New York in 1960 and played with *avant garde* jazz musicians such as John Coltrane and Sun Ra, the latter of whom appeared as a sideman on his *Impressions Of A Patch Of Blue* (based on Jerry Goldsmith's music for the film *A Patch Of Blue*). Dickerson was reunited with Hill on *To My Queen*, dedicated to his wife, Elizabeth, and probably the best-known of his early albums. Following a 10-year break from performing (1965-75), Dickerson returned to music, working chiefly in Europe and recording for Denmark's Steeplechase label. He played again with Sun Ra on the duo *Visions* and also recorded with Richard Davis, Pierre Dorge and - in another reunion - Cyrille, as well as recording solo. One of the few truly contemporary vibists, Dickerson's playing is noted for his speed of execution (he uses half-length mallets) and his inventive approach to sonority, employing both bitonality and polytonality to colour music that writer Chris Sheridan has described as 'labyrinthine geometry' and 'towering monoliths of sound which shimmer like glass before dissolving'.

● ALBUMS: *This Is Walt Dickerson* (New Jazz 1961)★★★, *A Sense Of Direction* (New Jazz 1961)★★★, *Relativity* (New Jazz 1962)★★★★, *To My Queen* (New Jazz 1963)★★★★, *Jazz Impressions Of 'Lawrence Of Arabia'* (Dauntless 1963)★★★★, *Walt Dickerson Plays Unity* (Audio Fidelity 1964)★★★★, *Impressions Of A Patch Of Blue* (MGM 1965)★★★, *Vibes In Motion* (Audio Fidelity 1968)★★★, *Peace* (1975)★★★, *Serendipity* (1977)★★★, with Richard Davis *Divine Gemini* (1977)★★★, *Shades Of Love* (1978)★★★, *To My Queen Revisited* (1978)★★★, with Pierre Dorge *Landscapes With Open Door* (1979)★★★, with Sun Ra *Visions* (Steeple Chase 1979)★★★, *To My Son* (1980)★★★, with Jimmi Johnsun *I Hear You John* (1981)★★★, with Andrew Cyrille, Sirone *Life Rays* (1982)★★★, with Richard Davis *Tenderness* (1985)★★★.

DILLARD, BILL

b. 20 July 1911, Philadelphia, Pennsylvania, USA, d. 1995. Initially self-taught, Dillard received some tuition in high school but by the age of 18 he was working professionally in New York City. His name band experience began with Jelly Roll Morton and he also worked with Joe 'King' Oliver. In 1933 he was with Benny Carter and appeared on important recording dates with the band. Throughout the 30s Dillard worked in a succession of different sized units including those of Lucky Millinder, Teddy Hill and Coleman Hawkins. In the early 40s he was in Louis Armstrong's band and also worked with Red Norvo. In 1943 Dillard diversified into acting and thereafter concentrated on this aspect of his career, although his acting roles sometimes called for him to play trumpet and/or sing. Among the shows in which he appeared over the next four decades were Carmen Jones on Broadway in 1943, *Anna Lucasta* (1945), *Green Pastures* (1951), *One Mo' Time* (1981). During these years Dillard made occasional appearances on recording dates, but acting had clearly taken over as the driving force in his life.

DiNovi, Gene

b. 26 May 1928, New York City, New York, USA. He began playing piano seriously at the age of 12, when his brother arranged for piano lessons from a teacher who owed money for a painting job. Soon, more important lessons took place, again on piano, but this time from guitarist Chuck Wayne, followed by professional work with the Henry Jerome band. Amongst his fellow sidemen were Al Cohn and Zoot Sims. DiNovi's influences at this stage in his career, he was still only 16, were largely boppers but then, as he entered his twenties, he worked with Joe Marsala, with whom he made his first records, and then with Lester Young. He also played with Tiny Kahn, Don Fagerquist, and Anita O'Day. In the early 50s he gigged mostly in New York and in 1956 became Lena Horne's regular accompanist. He had previously accompanied Peggy Lee and a later job with Tony Bennett established a reputation for working with singers which stood him in good stead for a spell in west coast film and television studios. In the 70s DiNovi moved to Canada where he remained for some years re-emerging on the international jazz scene in the late 80s after successful recording sessions with Ruby Braff. In the early 90s he visited Japan, the UK and also played with classical clarinettist James Campbell. Although his early influences amongst pianists included Art Tatum and Teddy Wilson, he was particularly affected by hearing Bud Powell and for a time, still in his teens, was used by proto-boppers such as Dizzy Gillespie along with Joe Albany, George Wallington and Al Haig. The heady influence of these early days and associations has indelibly marked DiNovi's playing and in the mid-90s he is one of the very few keepers of that particular flame still demonstrating his art around the world.

● ALBUMS: *Scandinavian Route* (Roulette 1960)★★★★, *Softly As I Leave You* (Pedimega 1977)★★★, with Ruby Braff *My Funny Valentine* (Pedimega 1985)★★★★, *Precious Moments* (1990)★★★, *Renaissance Of A Jazz Master* (Candid 1993)★★★, *Live At The Montréal Bistro, Toronto* (Candid 1996)★★★.

DiPasqua, Michael

b. 4 May 1953, Orlando, Florida, USA. Born into a highly musical family, DiPasqua began his professional career very early, gigging on drums with a band co-led by Zoot Sims and Al Cohn when still only in his mid-teens. During the next few years DiPasqua played with several other musicians of note, including Don Elliott and Gerry Mulligan and he also accompanied singers Jackie Cain and Roy Kral. Towards the end of the 70s, DiPasqua was for a number of years co-leader of Double Image. He then co-led Gallery and followed that with a spell in Later That Evening, a band led by Eberhard Weber, before joining Jan Garbarek. DiPasqua has consistently proved himself to be a sleekly inventive percussionist with the ability to comfortably co-exist in a range of musical styles, from the modern end of the mainstream through jazz-rock to the cutting edge of improvisational music.

● ALBUMS: *Double Image* (Enja 1977)★★★, *Gallery* (ACM 1981)★★★, *It's OK To Listen To The Grey Voice* (ECM 1984)★★★.

Dirty Dozen Brass Band

Originally formed in the mid-70s to recreate the traditional sounds of the New Orleans marching bands, but with an overlay of contemporary music such as funk and latterday R&B, the Dozen attained considerable popularity. Using a line-up of two trumpets, trombone, sousaphone, tenor and soprano (doubling baritone) saxophones, snare drum and two bass drummers, the band has worked at festivals and parades around the world and has also made club appearances and records. A lively, high-spirited group, all but one of whom hail from New Orleans, the Dozen has undoubtedly helped draw into jazz an audience which might otherwise have sought entertainment elsewhere.

● ALBUMS: *My Feet Can't Fail Me Now* (George Wein Collection 1984)★★★★, *Live: Mardi Gras In Montreux* (Rounder 1985)★★★, *Voodoo* (Columbia 1989)★★★, *New Orleans Album* (Columbia 1990)★★★, *Open Up - Whatcha Gonna Do For The Rest Of Your Life?* (Columbia 1991)★★★, *Jelly* (Columbia 1993)★★★, *Ears To The Wall* (Mammoth 1996)★★★.

Disley, Diz

b. William C. Disley, 27 May 1931, Winnipeg, Manitoba, Canada. Disley grew up in Wales and the north of England, where he learned to play banjo, switching to guitar at the age of 14 when he heard Django Reinhardt. Among his earliest jazz gigs was a period with the Yorkshire Jazz Band. In the 50s he lived in London, working as a newspaper cartoonist and playing in a variety of bands. Although many of Disley's engagements in the 50s and 60s were with traditional bands, he also played skiffle and folk music. Eager to restore the place of the acoustic guitar in the face of the pop-scene successes of its electric counterpart, he gradually developed a substantial reputation as a leading mainstream guitarist. In the early 70s he began a fruitful association with Stéphane Grappelli, persuading the organizers of the Cambridge Folk Festival to book the violinist. With the group rounded out by guitarist Denny Wright, who had worked with Grappelli in 1944, they were a huge success and Grappelli's resurgence was assured. Later, Disley added Len Skeat and continued to accompany the violinist on some of the most memorable moments of his career comeback. On and off, Disley was with Grappelli for about a decade, a period which also saw record dates with Teresa Brewer and others, and tours of Australia, Europe and the USA. Undoubtedly, Disley's acute business sense, allied to his impeccable musical taste and dedication to Reinhardt was a significant factor in the renewal of Grappelli's career. Subsequently, Disley formed his own group which worked mostly in London through the 80s. He continues to play, bringing wit and invention, allied to an urgent unflagging swing to all his sessions.

● ALBUMS: with Stéphane Grappelli *I Got Rhythm* (1973)★★★, with Grappelli *Violinspiration* (1975)★★★, *Zing Went The Strings* (Waterfront 1986)★★★.

DISTEL, SACHA

b. 28 January 1933, Paris, France. This scion of a well-heeled showbusiness family was a professional jazz guitarist at the age of 16, often sitting in with distinguished Americans visiting Parisian clubland. With the Modern Jazz Quartet sincerely loud in his praise, Distel was recognized as one of his country's foremost jazz instrumentalists by the mid-50s. He also gained publicity for his liaisons with Brigitte Bardot and beatnik icon Juliet Greco, while becoming a businessman with interests in music publishing. In 1956, his debut single 'Shoubi-doubidou' made the French hit parade. His marriage to skiing champion Francie Breaud in 1963, and the birth of their son, Laurent, did not affect the growth of a following that had extended beyond France to North America, where he starred in his own television spectacular. Nevertheless, he continued recording a French-language version (with cover girl Johanna Shimus) of Frank Sinatra and Nancy Sinatra's 'Somethin' Stupid' in 1967. His biggest moment on disc, however, was with 'Raindrops Keep Falling On My Head', an Oscar-winning number from the film *Butch Cassidy And The Sundance Kid*, which outsold the B.J. Thomas original in the UK chart, where it peaked at number 10 in January 1970, making no less than three re-entries throughout that year. An attendant album sold well in Britain and the USA, and Distel remained a top cabaret draw throughout the world. In 1993, he co-starred with the television hostess and compère, Rosemarie Ford, on the UK tour of *Golden Songs Of The Silver Screen*.

● ALBUMS: with John Lewis *Afternoon In Paris* (Atlantic 1957)★★★★, with Slide Hampton *Slide Hampton And Sacha Distel* (1968)★★, *Sacha Distel* (Warners 1970)★★★, *Love Is All* (Pye 1976)★★★, *Forever And Ever* (1978)★★★, *20 Favourite Love Songs* (1979)★★★, *From Sacha With Love* (Mercury 1979)★★, *Move Closer* (Towerbell 1985)★★, *More And More* (Warners 1987)★★★, *Dedications* (1992)★★★.

● COMPILATIONS: *Golden Hour Of Sacha Distel* (Golden Hour 1978)★★, *The Sacha Distel Collection* (Pickwick 1980)★★★, *The Very Best Of Sacha Distel* (Temple 1997)★★★.

DIXON, BILL

b. William Robert Dixon, 5 October 1925, Nantucket Island, Massachusetts, USA. Though born of the generation that brought bebop to fruition, Dixon did not rise to prominence until the early 60s, when he emerged as one of the leading pioneers of the New Music. He grew up in New York, started on trumpet at the age of 18, studied painting at Boston University and then attended the Hartnott School of Music (1946-51). In the 50s he freelanced in the New York area as a trumpeter and arranger, and struck up friendships with Cecil Taylor and, later, Archie Shepp, with whom he co-lead a quartet and helped to found the New York Contemporary Five (which also featured Don Cherry, John Tchicai and J.C. Moses: Dixon himself never actually played with the group). In 1964 he organized the October Revolution - six nights of concerts by young *avant gardists* such as Taylor, Shepp, Roswell Rudd, Paul Bley, Milford Graves and the not-so-young Sun Ra - which is generally acknowledged as the event which gave the New Thing its identity as a movement. Its success led him to form the short-lived Jazz Composers Guild, one of the first musicians' self-help organizations (its history is recounted in Val Wilmer's *As Serious As Your Life*). In 1965 Dixon met dancer/choreographer Judith Dunn, with whom he worked for many years, their first notable collaboration being at the Newport Jazz Festival in 1966. That same year Dixon played on Taylor's *Conquistidor*, his tersely lyrical style a rare counterweight to the pianist's volcanic energy, and also recorded his own *Intents And Purposes*, with tracks by a 10-piece orchestra, a quintet and two brief, overdubbed solo pieces. Dixon's insistence on total artistic control over his music and its presentation has meant that *Intents And Purposes* (on RCA Records) remains the only recording he has been able to release on a major USA label. Already known as a teacher of art history, he became involved in music education, helping to initiate New York's University of the Streets community programme and, in 1968, taking up a teaching post at Bennington College in Vermont, where he set up a Black Music department (and where he continues to work). In 1976 he was invited to perform at the Paris Autumn Festival, where he premiered his 'Autumn Sequences From A Paris Diary' over five days with regular associates Stephen Horenstein (saxophones) and bassist Alan Silva. Throughout the 70s and 80s, Dixon has been recording his music himself, a little of which has appeared on European labels such as Soul Note and Fore, while a limited-edition two-album box-set of his solo music was released by the independent USA Cadence label in 1985. A painter too, who has exhibited widely in Europe and the USA, Dixon's music could be described as painterly, though its attention to form, line, texture and colour is as much the mark of a composer (and of a superb instrumental technique). His musical evocations of times, seasons, moods etc. are more abstract than representational and record titles such as *Considerations* and *Thoughts* indicate the essentially reflective quality of his music. In his small-group recordings he has often shown a preference for darker sonorities, sometimes using two or three bassists, and the results are remarkable for their balance of intellectual freight, sensitivity to nuance and implicit structural coherence. One of America's most original, and neglected, instrumentalist/composers, Dixon published *L'Opera* in 1986, a collection of letters, writings, musical scores and drawings.

● ALBUMS: with Archie Shepp *The Archie Shepp-Bill Dixon Quartet* (Savoy 1962)★★★★, with Shepp *Archie Shepp & The New Contemporary 5/The Bill Dixon 7-Tette* (Savoy 1964)★★★, *Intents And Purposes* (RCA Victor 1967)★★★★, with Franz Koglmann *Opium/For Franz* (Pipe 1976)★★★, *Bill Dixon In Italy - Volume One* (Soul Note 1980)★★★★, *Bill Dixon In Italy - Volume Two* (Soul Note 1981)★★★, *Considerations 1* 1972-76 recordings (1981)★★★, *Considerations 2* 1972-76 recordings (1981)★★★, *November 1981* (Soul Note 1982)★★★★, *Bill Dixon 1970-73* (1983)★★★, *Collection* box set (Cadence 1985)★★★★,

Thoughts 1985 recording (Soul Note 1987)★★★, *Son Of Sisyphus* 1988 recording (Soul Note 1990)★★★, *Vade Mecum* 1993 recording (Soul Note 1995)★★★★, with the Tony Oxley Celebration Orchestra *The Enchanted Messenger: Live From The Berlin Jazz Festival* (Soul Note 1997)★★★, *Vade Mecum II* 1993 recording (Soul Note 1997)★★★★.

● FURTHER READING: *L'Opera*, Bill Dixon.

DIXON, CHARLIE

b. c.1898, Jersey City, New Jersey, USA, d. 6 December 1940. In 1922, banjo player, Dixon joined the orchestra of Sam Wooding before moving on to play with Fletcher Henderson. Although often overlooked in potted accounts of the development of big band music, Dixon was a skilled arranger and provided many musical scores for the Henderson band, which helped establish it as the forerunner of the commercial successes of the swing era. After leaving the band he continued in music mostly as an arranger. During the next few years he wrote for Henderson and, notably, Chick Webb, for whom he arranged 'That Naughty Waltz' and 'Harlem Congo'.

DIXON, ERIC

b. 28 March 1930, New York City, New York, USA, d. 19 October 1989. Through his early teens Dixon studied the tenor saxophone, then gained practical experience in a military band. After leaving the army he began working as a professional musician in New York, playing tenor in bands led by Cootie Williams and Johnny Hodges. During the late 50s he played in theatre orchestras and also toured Europe, working with various bands including one led by Quincy Jones. In 1961 he joined Count Basie, playing tenor and flute, remaining with the band for a decade. During this period he appeared often on record with the band, including *On My Way And Shoutin' Again*, and also in small group recordings with Roy Eldridge, including 1966's *The Nifty Cat Strikes West*. After a three year retirement, Dixon rejoined Basie in 1975 and was still there in 1984 when the leader died. Subsequently, he played in the posthumous Count Basie Band. A sound section player and a fluent improviser, Dixon contributed numerous striking solos during his long periods with Basie.

● ALBUMS: *Eric's Edge* (Master Jazz 1974)★★.

DIXON, FOSTINA

b. *c*.1953, Delaware, USA. Taking her early musical inspiration from the church, Dixon began playing clarinet at school, later adding the baritone saxophone. After leaving school, she studied medicine but a year later changed track and began studying at Berklee College Of Music. There she added bass clarinet and flute to her instrumental range, eventually becoming adept also on alto and soprano saxophones. As a child she had listened to pop music, much of it Motown Records, and while still at Berklee was hired to play in the band backing Marvin Gaye where she stayed for the next two years. Settling in Los Angeles, Dixon found work with several bands, backing artists such as Sammy Davis Jnr. and Nancy Wilson. She also formed a group of her own, named Collage, in which she pursued her own musical identity. She was also discovering jazz and gradually incorporating this into her work. In addition to her considerable instrumental ability, Dixon is also a composer of distinction and a vocalist. With a broad appreciation of many varied musical forms, Dixon's commitment is total, and she is also eager to extend her audience by finding a style in both playing and composing that appeals beyond the merely intellectual. She is acutely aware of the strictures placed upon her as a woman in jazz which, added to her being black has placed unwarranted pressures upon her. As she told Sally Placksin, 'you have to do it ten times as good'. Although she often works in groups with other women, including Melba Liston and Company, her band, Collage, happened to be all-male. This was not from deliberate choice but occurred because the musicians whose sounds she felt to be compatible with her aural image of how the group should play were men. A musician of great skill, imagination and integrity, Dixon's future appears unlimited.

DIZ AND GETZ - DIZZY GILLESPIE AND STAN GETZ

A meeting of two giants can often be a disaster, especially with two quite different characters musically and personally, both used to having most of the solo limelight. However, this fusion works to perfection, individual yet totally together. The recording level, even on the CD, puts Stan Getz a few watts behind. In 1953 they forgot to balance the harshness of Dizzy Gillespie's trumpet against the smoothness of Getz's tenor, a minor gripe on a fine recording. The line-up is faultless and impressive: Oscar Peterson (piano), Herb Ellis (guitar), Ray Brown (bass) and Max Roach (drums), who play on all tracks except 'One Alone', which is supported by Hank Mobley (tenor), Wade Legge (piano), Lou Hackney (bass), and Charlie Persip (drums). It all makes for a very amiable and solid set.

● Tracks: *It Don't Mean A Thing (If It Ain't Got That Swing); I Let My Heart Go Out Of My Heart; Exactly Like You; It's The Talk Of The Town; Impromptu; One Alone; Girl Of My Dreams; Siboney (Part I), Siboney (Part II).*

● First released 1955

● UK peak chart position: did not chart

● USA peak chart position: did not chart

DIZZY GILLESPIE AND HIS ORCHESTRA - DIZZY GILLESPIE

Dizzy Gillespie is usually remembered as one of a handful of musicians who led the way to a new small-group sound in the post-war period, when the swing big bands were suffering economical problems. Along with Charlie Parker, Thelonious Monk and Bud Powell, Gillespie helped revolutionize and complicate the music, with an extended harmonic vocabulary and, most strikingly, an incredible virtuoso technique. However, Gillespie's own bebop-based big band work resulted in some of the most exciting dates of his career, providing a climactic background for his own trumpet fireworks, and a good place for him to test his burgeoning interest in Latin American musics.

- Tracks: *A Night In Tunisia; Ol' Man Rebop; Ow; Oop-Pop-A-Da; Two Bass Hit; Stay On It; Algo Bueno; Overtime; Manteca; Good Bait; Cool Breeze; Cubana Be; Cubana Bop; Minor Walk; Swedish Suite; Victory Ball.*
- First released (1946-1949 recordings)
- UK peak chart position: did not chart
- USA peak chart position: did not chart

Django Reinhardt

This movie was a good examination of the work of the first European to achieve international status in jazz. Directed by Paul Paviot, this 1958 film features several musicians associated with Reinhardt, including his brother, Joseph, and Stéphane Grappelli.

Dobrogosz, Steve

b. 26 January 1956, Belfont, Pennsylvania, USA. Educated at Berklee College Of Music, Dobrogosz moved from North Carolina to Stockholm, Sweden in 1978. His lushly textured solo playing is strongly affected by a fluent, virtuoso command of post-romantic piano. Dobrogosz has a fine lyric gift which is most fully realized in his highly expressive accompaniments to singers such as Radka Toneff and Berit Andersson. He has also recorded with bassist Arild Andersen and saxophonist Joakim Milder.

- ALBUMS: *Songs* (Caprice 1980)★★★, *Pianopieces* (Proprius 1982)★★★, with Radka Toneff *Fairy Tales* (Odin 1982)★★, with Berit Andersson *Scary Bright* (Dragon 1984)★★★, *The Child's Gift* (Proprius 1986)★★★, *The Final Touch* (Dragon 1990)★★★★, *Jade* (Dragon 1990)★★★, *Skin Baloon* (Sand Castle 1993)★★★.

Dodds, Baby

b. Warren Dodds, 24 December 1898, New Orleans, Louisiana, USA, d. 14 February 1959, Chicago, Illinois, USA. Dodds began taking drum lessons in his early teens and made appearances in street parades. Among his first professional engagements were stints in the bands of Bunk Johnson, Willie Hightower, Papa Celestin and Fate Marable, with whom he stayed for three years until 1921. He then joined King Oliver, who was working in San Francisco, and travelled with the band to Chicago the following year. From 1924 he played in a succession of leading bands, mostly in Chicago, among them those of Honore Dutrey, Freddie Keppard and his older brother, Johnny Dodds. Throughout the 30s Dodds was still based in Chicago, playing with his brother, and recorded with many leading traditionalists. In the early 40s Dodds again worked with Bunk Johnson, now a rediscovered trumpet legend. He also played with Mezz Mezzrow, Art Hodes and Miff Mole. In 1950 he suffered a stroke but was soon back, playing with Natty Dominique and also performing in pick-up groups at various clubs in New York and Chicago. Persistent ill-health eventually resulted in partial paralysis and he died in 1959. Generally held to be the master of New Orleans drumming, Dodds's style was based upon immaculate timekeeping and faultless technique. Eagerly studied by young drummers in Chicago during his many years there, he was a formative influence upon Dave Tough, who urged his slightly younger colleague Gene Krupa to listen to the same source. In practice, few of his devotees ever played like him, mainly because, in performance, Dodds did much more than merely keep time. His accompaniment, especially for soloists, was usually a display of all of his many skills and was, consequently, much fussier than many front-line players liked. Although he adhered closely to the New Orleans tradition, Dodd used his drum patterns in a manner that was in advance of his time and which was not fully exploited until the advent of bebop. In 1946 he recorded a session for Circle Records, during which he explained his technique and played several demonstration solos.

- ALBUMS: *Baby Dodds Drum Method - Band* (American Music 1951)★★★, *The Baby Dodds Drum Method - Trio* (American Music 1951)★★, *The Baby Dodds Drum Method - Solo* (American Music 1951)★, *Footnotes To Jaz, Volume 1 - Baby Dodds' Drum Solos* 10-inch album (Folkways 1951)★★★.
- FURTHER READING: *The Baby Dodds Story*, Warren 'Baby' Dodds and Larry Gara.

Dodds, Johnny

b. 12 April 1892, New Orleans, Louisiana, USA, d. 8 August 1940, Chicago, Illinois, USA. Dodds did not begin playing clarinet until he was aged 17, but in taking lessons from Lorenzo Tio ensured that his late start did not hamper his career. In the years before World War I he played with Kid Ory and Fate Marable, mostly in his home town, and also worked with a minstrel show where he met Mutt Carey. In 1920 he joined King Oliver in Chicago. After leaving Oliver at the end of 1923 he worked with among others Honore Dutrey and Freddie Keppard. During this period he appeared on the classic Hot Five and Hot Seven records with Louis Armstrong. In the 30s he worked mostly in Chicago, leading bands at various clubs. A heart attack in 1939 withdrew him from music for a few months. However, he returned in early 1940 but ill-health persisted and he died in August that year. A striking performer with a fluent style, Dodds made an important contribution to jazz, and to clarinet-playing in particular. His death occurred when clarinettists were in the ascendancy. Not only were big band leaders Benny Goodman and Artie Shaw enjoying great commercial success, but also more traditionally inclined players such as Sidney Bechet, Jimmy Noone and George Lewis were benefiting from a resurgence of interest in early forms of jazz. Despite the passage of time and the wide-ranging developments in jazz, not least the decline in popularity of the clarinet as a front-line instrument, Dodds' recordings of the 20s and 30s are still highpoints in the history of jazz recording and are rarely out of print.

- ALBUMS: *The King Of New Orleans Clarinets* 10-inch album (Brunswick 1950)★★★★, *Johnny Dodds, Volume 1* 10-inch album (Riverside 1953)★★★, *Johnny Dodds, Volume 2* 10-inch album (Riverside 1953)★★★, with Jimmy Noone *Battle Of Jazz, Volume 8* (Brunswick 1953)★★★, *Johnny Dodds' Washboard Band* (X 1954)★★★, *Johnny Dodds' New Orleans Clarinet* (Riverside 1956)★★★★, with Kid Ory *Johnny Dodds And Kid Ory* (Epic 1956)★★★★, *Sixteen Rare Recordings* (RCA Victor 1965)★★, *The Stomp* (Rhapsody 1983)★★★★, *Johnny Dodds* 1928-29 recordings (Swaggie 1989)★★★★, *Blue Clarinet Stomp* 1926-29 recordings (Bluebird 1990)★★★★, *King Of The New Orleans Clarinet* 1926-1938 recordings (Black And Blue 1992)★★★★, *Johnny Dodds Volumes 1-2* (Village Jazz 1992)★★★.

● FURTHER READING: *Johnny Dodds*, G.E. Lambert.

Dodgion, Dottie

b. Dorothy Giaimo, 23 September 1929, Brea, California, USA. After working as a singer, Dodgion began playing drums when she was in her early twenties, following the example of her father, Chuck Giaimo. She played drums first with a trio, gradually learning her new trade sitting in with various bands and at after-hours sessions. When she married saxophonist Jerry Dodgion in the mid-50s, she was actively encouraged to develop her skills and was soon working in Las Vegas with musicians such as Carl Fontana. Whilst there, she jammed with her husband, who was playing with Benny Goodman, and Goodman heard her and also sat in. A short time later, in New York, she was hired by Goodman. This was in 1959 when the band included Red Norvo, Fontana, Buddy Childers, Jimmy Rushing and Zoot Sims. She became quite popular with audiences which was a sure way to be fired, Goodman having a well known antipathy towards drummers who might upstage him. She continued to work throughout the 60s and 70s, mostly in and around New York, also in Lake Tahoe, Nevada, and Washington, DC. Amongst the artists with whom she has worked are Lee Konitz, Randy and Michael Brecker, Ruby Braff, Carol Sloane, Mary Osborne, Melba Liston and Thad Jones. An instinctive timekeeper with a subtle flair for accompaniment, Dodgion is deeply conscious of the need for a drummer in jazz to support and lift soloists and ensemble. A committed professional, she has an enviable reputation amongst musicians although the general jazz public is often unaware of her subtle and much-valued skills.

● ALBUMS: with others *Now Is The Time* (Halcyon 1977)★★★.

Doggett, Bill

b. 16 February 1916, Philadelphia, Pennsylvania, USA, d. 13 November 1996, New York City, New York, USA. In 1938 pianist Doggett formed his first band, partly drawing his sidemen from the band of Jimmy Goreham, with whom he had played for the past few years. Later that year he worked with Lucky Millinder, with whom he also played in the early 40s - Millinder having taken over leadership of Doggett's band. During this period Doggett wrote many arrangements for various bands, including Lionel Hampton and Count Basie, and also worked as staff arranger and accompanist with the popular vocal group the Ink Spots. He made a number of recordings with Buddy Tate and Illinois Jacquet, then worked with Willie Bryant, Johnny Otis and Louis Jordan. In the mid-40s he began playing organ, and when he formed his own R&B band in 1951, concentrated on this instrument. He had big hits with 'Honky Tonk', which reached number 1 in the R&B charts and number 2 in the US charts in 1956, and was in the Top 10 for 14 weeks with 'Slow Walk'. He showed his versatility by arranging and conducting Ella Fitzgerald's 1963 album *Rhythm Is Our Business.* Doggett continued leading a swinging R&B-orientated band into the 80s.

● ALBUMS: *Bill Doggett - His Organ And Combo* 10-inch album (King 1955)★★★, *Bill Doggett - His Organ And Combo Volume 2* 10-inch album (King 1955)★★★, *All-Time Christmas Favorites* 10-inch album (King 1955)★, *Sentimentally Yours* 10-inch album (King 1956)★★, *Moondust* (King 1957)★★, *Hot Doggett* (King 1957)★★, with Earl Bostic *C'mon And Dance With Earl Bostic* (King 1958)★★★★, *As You Desire* (King 1958)★★★, *A Salute To Ellington* (King 1958)★★★, *Goin' Doggett* (King 1958)★★★, *The Doggett Beat For Dancing Feet* (King 1958)★★★, *Candle Glow* (King 1958)★★★, *Dame Dreaming* (King 1958)★★★, *Everybody Dance To The Honky Tonk* (King 1958)★★★, *Man With A Beat* (King 1958)★★★, *Swingin' Easy* (King 1959)★★★, *Dance Awhile With Doggett* (King 1959)★★, *Hold It* (King 1959)★★★, *High And Wide* (King 1959)★★★, *Big City Dance Party* (King 1959)★★★, *Bill Doggett On Tour* (King 1959)★★★, *Bill Doggett Christmas* (King 1959)★★, *For Reminiscent Lovers, Romantic Songs* (King 1960)★★★, *Back Again With More Bill Doggett* (King 1960)★★★, *Focus On Bill Doggett* (King 1960)★★, *Bonanza Of 24 Songs* (King 1960)★★★, *The Many Moods Of Bill Doggett* (King 1963)★★, *American Songs In The Bossa Nova Style* (King 1963)★★, *Impressions* (King 1964)★★★, *Honky Tonk Popcorn* (King 1969)★★★, *Bill Doggett* (1971)★★★, *Lionel Hampton Presents Bill Doggett* (1977)★★★★, *Midnight Shows Volume 9* (1978)★★★.

● COMPILATIONS: *The Best Of Bill Doggett* (King 1964)★★★, *Bonanza Of 24 Hit Songs* (King 1966)★★★, *14 Original Greatest Hits* (King 1988)★★★.

Doky Brothers

Brothers Niels Lan Doky (b. 3 October 1963, Copenhagen, Denmark; piano) and Christian Minh Doky (b. 7 February 1969, Copenhagen, Denmark; bass) play an intriguing mix of mainstream jazz and contemporary pop music. The Doky brothers were raised in a musical family; their physician father was a classical guitar player, and their mother was a Danish pop singer. Niels began playing the piano professionally at the age of 13, and accompanied trumpeter Thad Jones two years later, leading to a scholarship at Boston's Berklee College Of Music. Attending the college between 1981 and 1984, Niels graduated with a degree in professional music and performed with artists including Terri Lyne Carrington, Cyrus Chestnut and Branford Marsalis. Relocating to New York he recorded the first in a series of albums for Storyville Records, and began playing as co-leader with his brother. After an early flirtation with piano, Chris took up electric bass when he was 15, switching to acoustic two years later. He moved to New York in 1988, performing with musicians of the calibre of John Scofield and Randy Brecker, and releasing a debut set on the Storyville label. While performing together both brothers continued to record solo sessions, and Niels worked extensively as a producer. In 1995 they finally recorded as a duo for Blue Note Records, with guests including the Brecker brothers, Carrington, guitarist Ulf Wakenius and MOR singer Curtis Stigers. A follow-up set repeated the beguiling formula of Doky originals and interpretations of contemporary pop hits, and featured guest appearances by singers Al Jarreau, Dianne Reeves and Gino Vannelli.

● ALBUMS: *Doky Brothers* (Blue Note 1996)★★★★, *Doky Brothers 2* (Blue Note 1998)★★★.

Solo: Chris Minh Doky *Appreciation* (Storyville 1989)★★★. Niels Lan Doky *Here Or There* (Storyville 1986)★★★★, *Target* (Storyville 1987)★★★★, *The Truth* (Storyville 1987)★★★, *Daybreak* (Storyville 1989)★★★, *Close Encounter, Vol. 1* (Storyville 1989)★★★, *Close Encounter, Vol. 2* (Storyville 1989)★★★, *Dreams* (Milestone 1990)★★★★, *Friendship* (Milestone 1991)★★★, *Paris By Night* (Soul Note 1992)★★★.

Doky, Chris Minh

(see Doky Brothers)

Doky, Niels Lan

(see Doky Brothers)

Doldinger, Klaus

b. 12 May 1936, Berlin, Germany. Doldinger studied classical piano and clarinet at the Robert Scumann Institut der Musichochshule Rheinland, Dusseldorf. He played traditional jazz as an amateur in the early 50s before turning to the tenor saxophone and developing a more modern style. In the 60s he toured extensively in a quintet with Ingfried Hoffman: Europe, Africa, South America and Asia. Then he formed a jazz-rock group Passport, with which he found success in the 70s. He also began to write film scores, the best known of which are the music for *Das Boot* and *The Eternal Story*.

● ALBUMS: *Live At The Blue Note, Berlin* (1963)★★★★, *The Ambassador* (1969)★★★, with Passport *Lookin Thru* (1973)★★★, *Cross Collateral* (1974)★★★, *Infinity Machine* (1976)★★.

Dollar Brand

(see Ibrahim, Abdullah)

Dolphy, Eric

b. 20 June 1928, Los Angeles, California, USA, d. 29 June 1964, Berlin, Germany. A fluent performer on several reed instruments, Dolphy began to play clarinet while still at school. On the west coast of America in the second half of the 40s he worked with Roy Porter's band, before spending a couple of years in the US army. After his discharge, he played with several leading musicians, including Gerald Wilson, before becoming a member of the popular Chico Hamilton quintet. The stint with Hamilton brought Dolphy to the attention of a wide audience and many other young musicians. In New York in 1959 Dolphy joined Charles Mingus, all the time freelancing at clubs and on recording dates with such influential musicians as George Russell and John Coltrane. In the early 60s, Dolphy began a hugely prolific and arduous period of touring and recording throughout the USA and Europe. He played in bands led by Ornette Coleman (on the seminal *Free Jazz* sessions), John Lewis, Ron Carter, Mal Waldron, Oliver Nelson, Max Roach, Gil Evans, Andrew Hill, Booker Little, Abbey Lincoln, Mingus and Coltrane, with whose quartet he toured Europe in 1961. He also recorded a series of albums as leader, perhaps most notably the *At The Five Spot* sessions, with the brilliant young trumpeter Booker Little (later reissued as *The Great Concert Of Eric Dolphy*), and his Blue Note debut Out To Lunch! The latter, with its dislocated rhythms and unusual instrumental textures (Bobby Hutcherson's vibes sharing front line duties with Freddie Hubbard's trumpet and Dolphy's reeds), is a landmark of modern music, and was voted best post-war jazz LP in a 1984 poll of *Wire* magazine critics. Shortly after recording *Out To Lunch!* Dolphy left the USA to live in Europe because, as he told writer A.B. Spellman, 'if you try to do anything different in this country, people put you down for it'. He was working in Germany when he suffered a complete circulatory collapse caused by too much sugar in the bloodstream (he was diabetic), and died suddenly on 29 June 1964.

During his short career Dolphy established himself as a significant force, playing alto, flute and bass clarinet, an instrument before and since unusual in jazz. He was comfortable in the varied idioms of the bands in which he played, from the relatively orthodox Hamilton to the forward-thinking Coltrane and the third-stream innovations of Gunther Schuller. He was, however, very much his own man, creating strikingly original solo lines, frequently dashed off at breakneck tempos and encompassing wide intervallic leaps. Although he is rightly associated with the concept of free jazz, Dolphy brought to this area of music his own carefully reasoned attitude, and he is perhaps better thought of as someone who stretched bebop to its very limits. Thirty years after his death, the importance of Dolphy's contribution to jazz is still being explored by musicians.

● ALBUMS: *Out There* (New Jazz 1960)★★★★, *Outward Bound* (New Jazz 1960)★★★★, *Candid Dolphy* (Candid 1961)★★★, with Mal Waldron *The Quest* (New Jazz 1961)★★★★, *Eric Dolphy At The Five Spot* (New Jazz 1961)★★★★, *Stockholm Sessions* (Enja 1961)★★★, *Far Cry* (New Jazz 1962)★★★★, *Eric Dolphy Quartet* (Tempo 1962)★★★, *Music Matador* (1963)★★★, *Conversations* (FM 1963)★★★, *Naima* (West Wind 1964)★★★, *The Memorial Album* (Vee Jay 1964)★★★★, *Last Date* (EmArcy 1964)★★★, *Eric Dolphy At The Five Spot Volume 2* (Prestige 1964)★★★★, *Out To Lunch!* (Blue Note 1964)★★★★★, *Eric Dolphy In Europe Volume 1* (Prestige 1964)★★★, *Eric Dolphy In Europe Volume 2* (Prestige 1965)★★, *Eric Dolphy In Europe Volume 3* (Prestige 1965)★★, *Here And There* (Prestige 1965)★★★★, with Cannonball Adderley *Eric Dolphy And Cannonball Adderley* (Archive Of Folk And Jazz 1968)★★★, *Iron Man* (Douglas 1969)★★★.

● COMPILATIONS: *The Great Concert Of Eric Dolphy* 3-LP set

(Prestige 1965)★★★★, *Other Aspects* 1960-1962 recordings (Blue Note 1982)★★★, *The Complete Prestige Recordings* 9-CD box set (Prestige 1995)★★★★, *Vintage Dolphy* 1962/1963 recordings (GM 1996)★★★★.

● FURTHER READING: *Like A Human Voice - The Eric Dolphy Discography*, Uwe Reichardt. *Eric Dolphy: A Musical Biography & Discography*, Vladimir Simosko and Barry Tepperman. *The Importance Of Being Eric Dolphy*, Raymond Horricks.

DOMINIQUE, NATTY

b. 2 August 1896, New Orleans, Louisiana, USA, d. 30 August 1982. Born into a musical environment with Barney Bigard as a cousin, Dominique studied trumpet with Manuel Perez before heading north in 1913 to play in Chicago. In the early 20s he joined Carroll Dickerson's band. Later that decade he played with Johnny Dodds, with whom he remained substantially throughout the 30s. In the early 40s ill health forced him to leave music, but he reappeared in 1949 and began leading his own band in the 50s, employing such kindred spirits as Baby Dodds and Volly De Faut. He continued playing into the mid-60s but then faded from sight. He died in August 1982.

● ALBUMS: *Natty Dominique And His New Orleans Hot Six* (1954)★★★.

DOMNÉRUS, ARNE

b. 20 December 1924, Stockholm, Sweden. Alto saxophonist and clarinettist Domnérus is virtually a Swedish jazz institution by himself. He led bands professionally in the 40s that included exceptionally talented players like Lars Gullin, Rolf Ericson, and Putte Wickman. American musicians including Charlie Parker, had already come to know the high standard of Domnérus's playing through the Paris Jazz Fair Festival in 1949. His bands since the 60s have usually include bassist and composer Georg Riedel, pianists Bengt Hallberg or Jan Johansson and guitarist Rune Gustafsson. Although the cool manner of Lee Konitz and Paul Desmond were formative on Swedish alto players in the 50s, Domnérus's tone and phrasing are now closer to Benny Carter's.

● ALBUMS: with Lars Gullin *New Sounds From Sweden, Volume 3* 10-inch album (Prestige 1952)★★★★, *New Sounds From Sweden, Volume 4 - Arne Domnerus Clarinet Solos* 10-inch album (Prestige 1952)★★★, *Around The World In Jazz - Sweden* 10-inch album (RCA Victor 1953)★★★, *Arne Domnérus Nalenorkester 1951-55* (Odeon 1956)★★★, *Mobil* (Megafon 1965)★★★, *Dedikation. En Tribut Til Johnny Hodges* (Megafon 1971)★★, *I Let A Song Go Out* (RCA 1972)★★★, *Jazz I Kyrkan* (1976)★★★, *Jazz At The Pawnshop* (Proprius 1976)★★★, *Ja, Vi Älskar* (Zarepta 1977)★★★, *Downtown Meeting* (Phontastic 1978)★★★, *Duets For Duke* (Sonet 1978)★★★, *The Sheik: Featuring Jimmy Rowles* (Four Leaf Clover 1979)★★★★, *Jumpin At The Woodside* (Four Leaf Clover 1979)★★★★, *A.D. 1980* (Phontastic 1980)★★, *Duke's Melody* (Phontastic 1981)★★★, *Blue And Yellow* (Phontastic 1982)★★★, *Fragment* (Phontastic 1982)★★★, *When Lights Are Low* (Salut 1988)★★★, *Swedish Rhapsody* 1980-1982 recordings (Phontastic 1984)★★★★, *Blatoner Fra Troldhaugen* (1986)★★, *Dompan At The Savoy* (Phontastic 1992)★★, *Sugar Fingers* (Phontastic 1993)★★★★, *Shall We Dance* (Proprius 1994)★★★, *Portrait Of Arne Domnérus* (Phontastic 1994)★★★, *Happy Together* (Ladybird 1997)★★★★, *In Concert, Live 1996* (Caprice 1997)★★★.

DONAHUE, SAM

b. 8 March 1918, Detroit, Michigan, USA, d. 22 March 1974, Reno, Nevada, USA. Among the most respected of swing era musicians, tenor saxophonist Donahue formed his first group in the mid-30s, leaving Sonny Burke as leader when he later joined Gene Krupas band. In the early 40s he played with Harry James and Benny Goodman. He returned to leading his old group again but in 1942 was drafted into the US Navy. When Artie Shaw was discharged from military service in 1944, Donahue took over Shaw's navy band. In the next two years he built it into a first-class swinging unit, much admired by musicians and fans alike. After the war, Donahue formed a new unit, hiring many of his former service personnel, which he led during the uneasy commercial decline of big bands. He worked in other bands, including those of Stan Kenton, Billy May and Tommy Dorsey. In 1961, five years after the latter's death, Donahue became leader of the official Tommy Dorsey orchestra which toured extensively, and featured Frank Sinatra Jnr. as singer. A highly skilled musician and one capable of drawing the best from his musicians, Donahue remained one of the lesser-known names of the swing era but to the end retained a faithful following. In later years he became musical director for the Playboy Club in New York.

● ALBUMS: *For Young Moderns In Love* (Capitol 1954)★★★, *Classics In Jazz* (Capitol 1955)★★★★, one side only *Double Date* (1957)★, *Dance Date With Sam Donahue* (1958)★★★, *The New Tommy Dorsey Orchestra Under The Direction Of Sam Donahue* (1963)★★★.

● COMPILATIONS: *Hollywood Hop* 1944-8 recordings (Hep Jazz 1983)★★★.

DONALD, BARBARA

b. 9 February 1942, Minneapolis, Minnesota, USA. Donald began to learn trumpet at school, but when her family moved to California in 1955, a sexist teacher refused to let her join her new high school band. She formed her own group, and before long she had more gigs than the school band. After playing R&B in New York and touring the south in a big band, Donald came to notice in Los Angeles bebop sessions with Dexter Gordon and Stanley Cowell. From 1962-73 she played and recorded free jazz with Sonny Simmons, whom she married in 1964, supplying excellent trumpet on a series of albums, notably *Burning Spirits*. In the mid-60s she also worked with John Coltrane, Richard Davis, Prince Lasha and Roland Kirk. After a four-year break (which also saw her separate from Simmons), she returned to music in 1978, since when she has been leading her own groups, which have included Gary Peacock and Carter Jefferson in the line-up.

● ALBUMS: *Olympia Live* (Cadence 1981)★★★★, *The Past And Tomorrow's* (Cadence 1984)★★★.

DONALD, PETER

b. 15 May 1945, San Francisco, California, USA. In his late teens, Donald studied at Berklee College Of Music, Boston and received drum tuition from Alan Dawson. In the early 70s he returned to California, this time taking up residence in Los Angeles, where he became noted for his sensitive accompaniment to singers who included Carmen McRae. He achieved notable success, however, as a member of the powerful big band co-led by Toshiko Akiyoshi and Lew Tabackin. When Akiyoshi decided to return to New York, Donald remained in Los Angeles, working in films and television studios and playing with musicians including John Abercrombie and Warne Marsh. In 1985, following the death of Nick Ceroli, he took his place in Bob Florence's Limited Edition big band. An all-round percussionist equally at home in jazz, pop and rock, Donald is very much a part of the new generation of jazz artists, but partly through his early tutelage under Dawson retains strong links with earlier strands of jazz.

DONALDSON, LOU

b. 1 November 1926, Badin, North Carolina, USA. Donaldson started on clarinet but, while playing in a band in the US Navy alongside Willie Smith and Clark Terry, he switched to alto saxophone. In the early 50s he was in New York, playing with Thelonious Monk, Horace Silver, Blue Mitchell, Art Blakey and other leading jazzmen. In 1954 he and Clifford Brown joined Blakey's Jazz Messengers. During the 60s and 70s he toured extensively, usually as leader of a small band, playing concerts and festivals in the USA and Europe. He recorded prolifically for Blue Note, producing a number of excellent soul-jazz albums, including *Alligator Boogaloo*. During this period, Donaldson made some stylistic changes, experimenting with an R&B-inflected style and playing jazz-funk; by the 80s he was back in a hard bop groove, where his striking technique and inventiveness assured him of a welcome place on the international circuit.

● ALBUMS: *Lou Donaldson Quintet-Quartet* 10-inch album (Blue Note 1953)★★★, *Lou Donaldson With Clifford Brown* 10-inch album (Blue Note 1953)★★★, with Art Blakey *A Night At The Birdland* (Blue Note 1954)★★★★★, *Lou Donaldson Sextet, Volume 2* (Blue Note 1955)★★★, *Wailing With Lou* (Blue Note 1955)★★★, *Lou Donaldson Quartet Quintet Sextet* (Blue Note 1957)★★★, *Swing And Soul* (Blue Note 1957)★★★, *Lou Takes Off* (Blue Note 1958)★★★, *Blues Walk* (Blue Note 1958)★★★, *LD+3* (Blue Note 1959)★★★, *The Time Is Right* (Blue Note 1960)★★★, *Sunny Side Up* (Blue Note 1960)★★★★, *Light Foot* (Blue Note 1960)★★★, *Here 'Tis* (Blue Note 1961)★★★★, *The Natural Soul* (Blue Note 1962)★★★★, *Gravy Train* (Blue Note 1962)★★★, *Good Gracious* (Blue Note 1963)★★★, *Signifyin'* (Argo 1963)★★★, *Possum Head* (Argo 1964)★★★, *Cole Slaw* (Argo 1964)★★★, *Musty Rusty* (Cadet 1965)★★★, *Rough House Blues* (Cadet 1965)★★★, *At His Best* (1966)★★★, *Lush Life* (Blue Note 1967)★★★★, *Alligator Boogaloo* (Blue Note 1967)★★★★, *Mr. Shing-A-ling* (Blue Note 1967)★★★, *Blowin' In The Wind* (Cadet 1967)★★★, *Fried Buzzard-Lou Donaldson Live* (Cadet 1968)★★★, *Midnight Creeper* (Blue Note 1968)★★★, *Say It Loud!* (Blue Note 1969)★★★, *Hot Dog* (Blue Note 1969)★★★, *Pretty Things* (Blue Note 1970)★★★, *Everything I Play Is Funky* (Blue Note 1970)★★, *Sophisticated Lou* (1972)★★★, *Back Street* (Muse 1972)★★★, *Sassy Soul Strut* (Blue Note 1973)★★★, *Sweet Lou* (Blue Note 1974)★★★, *A Different Scene* (1976)★★★, *Sweet Poppa Lou* (Muse 1981)★★★, *Forgotten Man* (Timeless 1981)★★★, *Life In Bologna* (Timeless 1984)★★★, *Play The Right Thing* (Milestone 1990)★★★, *Birdseed* (Milestone 1992)★★★, *Caracas* (Milestone 1992)★★★.

DONEGAN, DOROTHY

b. 6 April 1922, Chicago, Illinois, USA, d. 16 June 1998, Los Angeles, California, USA. Encouraged by her mother to learn music, Donegan studied classical piano, attending Chicago's Du Sable High School and the Chicago Conservatory of Music, but thereafter turned to jazz. A meeting with Art Tatum in the early 40s led to her becoming his protege. The following year she made her first record date and became a popular figure at Chicago clubs, playing a mixture of jazz, boogie woogie and cocktail music with a strong visual appeal. She also made an appearance in the film *Sensations Of 1945*, a back stage musical featuring Cab Calloway and W.C. Fields, and was presented in concert at the Orchestra Hall. Having started her jazz career as a single, she formed a trio in 1945 and continued to work in that format. Later in her career she was inclined to work as a soloist again, after being unable to appoint suitable drummers. In subsequent interviews she indicated a clear desire to return to playing classical music, a form which she used for her daily practise. A powerful performer with dazzling technique, she played with enormous swing and had a solid following. The audience at a 1980 appearance in New York's Sheraton Centre Hotel broke previous attendance records. In 1992 she was given an American Jazz Masters Award from the National Endowment of the Arts, and enjoyed renewed popularity in the years before her death from cancer in 1998.

● ALBUMS: *Dorothy Donegan Piano* 10-inch album (MGM 1954)★★★★, *Dorothy Donegan Trio* 10-inch album (Jubilee 1954)★★★, *September Song* (Jubilee 1956)★★★, *Dorothy Donegan At The Embers* (Roulette 1959)★★★★, *Dorothy Donegan Live!* (Capitol 1959)★★★★, *Donneybrook With Dorothy* (Capitol 1960)★★★, *Swingin' Jazz In Hi-Fi* (Regina 1963)★★★, *The Many Faces Of Dorothy Donegan* (1975)★★★, *The Dorothy Donegan Trio & Quartet* (1975)★★★, *Makin' Whoopee* (Black & Blue 1979)★★★, *Sophisticated Lady* (1980)★★★, *The Explosive Dorothy Donegan* (Progressive 1980)★★★★, *Live At The Widder Bar* (Timeless 1986)★★★, *Live At The 1990 Floating Jazz Festival* (Chiaroscuro 1990)★★★.

DØRGE, PIERRE

b. 28 February 1946, Copenhagen, Denmark. Composer and guitarist Dørge, after brief stints as sideman, led his own bands from the mid-60s inspired by the *avant garde* rock of Frank Zappa. Crucial learning years followed as participant in trumpeter Hugh Steinmetz' and John Tchicai's Cadentia Nova Danica big band (1969-71), which opened Danish jazz to a broad range of styles and genres of non-Western music. Since 1980 Dørge has led the New Jungle Orchestra which plays Duke Ellington as reinterpreted through Ornette Coleman. Dørge's compositions and arrangements reinterpret the jazz tradition in a genial, yet iconoclastic manner characteristic of Charles Mingus's music. Dørge has brilliantly shown how jazz can be creatively transformed and developed by music outside the USA, from Balkan, Gambia and Bali.

● ALBUMS: *Thermænius Live* (Pick Up 1979)★★★, with John Tchicai *Ballad Round The Left Corner* (Steeple Chase 1980)★★, *Pierre Dørge And The New Jungle Orchestra* (1982)★★★★, *Brikama* (1984)★★★, *Even The Moon Is Dancing* (1985)★★, *Different Places, Different Bananas* (Olufsen 1986)★★★, *Canoe* (Olufsen 1986)★★★, *La Luna* (Olufsen 1987)★★★★, *Live In Chicago* (Olufsen 1987)★★★, *Johnny Lives* (Steeple Chase 1987)★★★★, *Karawane* (Olufsen 1992)★★★, *Absurd Bird* (Olufsen 1994)★★★, *Music From The Danish Jungle* (Dacapo 1996)★★★, *China Jungle* (Dacapo 1998)★★★.

DORHAM, KENNY

b. McKinley Howard Dorham, 30 August 1924, Fairfield, Texas, USA, d. 5 December 1972, New York, USA. After learning to play trumpet while at high school, Dorham played in several late 40s big bands, including Lionel Hampton's and, more significantly given his musical leanings, the bop-orientated outfits of Dizzy Gillespie and Billy Eckstine. In 1948 he succeeded Miles Davis as trumpeter with Charlie Parker's quintet, and in 1954 joined Horace Silver in the first edition of what became Art Blakey's long-running Jazz Messengers. He also worked with Max Roach (stepping in when Roach's co-leader, Clifford Brown, was killed), Sonny Rollins and Charles Mingus. From the mid-50s onwards Dorham mostly led his own groups, which included the excellent Jazz Prophets, modelled as the name suggests, upon the Messengers, and made many fine recordings notably both as leader and with artists Joe Henderson, Herb Geller and Jackie McLean - making several outstanding performances for the Blue Note label. Although rightly viewed as one of the outstanding bebop trumpeters, stylistically Dorham's playing reflected his awareness of the roots of jazz and the blues. Universally admired among his contemporaries, Dorham's death led unfairly to a decline in awareness of his stature as a fine modern musician.

● ALBUMS: *Kenny Dorham Quintet* 10-inch album (Debut 1954)★★★★, *Afro-Cuban Holiday* 10-inch album (Blue Note 1955)★★★★, *Kenny Dorham's Jazz Prophets Volumes 1 & 2* (ABC-Paramount 1956)★★★, *'Round About Midnight At The Café Bohemia* (Blue Note 1956)★★★★, *Jazz Contrasts* (Riverside 1957)★★★, *2 Horns, 2 Rhythm* (Riverside 1957)★★★★, *This Is The Moment! Kenny Dorham Sings And Plays* (Riverside 1958)★★★, *Blue Spring* (Riverside 1959)★★★, *Quiet Kenny* (New Jazz 1959)★★★, *The Arrival Of Kenny Dorham* (Jaro 1959)★★★, *Jazz Contemporary* (Time 1960)★★★, *Showboat* (Time 1960)★★★★, with Clark Terry *Top Trumpets* (Jazzland 1960)★★★, *The Swingers* (Jazzland 1960)★★★, *Kenny Dorham And Friends* (Jazzland 1960)★★★, *Osmosis* (Black Lion 1961)★★★, *Ease It* (Muse 1961)★★★, *Whistle Stop* (Blue Note 1961)★★★, *West 42nd Street* (Black Lion 1961)★★★, *Hot Stuff From Brazil* (West Wind 1961)★★★, *Inta Somethin' - Recorded 'Live' At The Jazz Workshop* (Pacific Jazz 1962)★★★, *Matador* (United Artists 1962)★★★, *Una Mas - One More Time* (Blue Note 1963)★★★★, *Scandia Skies* (Steeple Chase 1963)★★★, *Short Story* (1963)★★★, *Trumpet Toccata* (Blue Note 1964)★★★★, *New York 1953-56* (Landscape 1993)★★★.

● COMPILATIONS: *The Art Of The Ballad* (Prestige 1998)★★★★.

DOROUGH, BOB

b. Robert L. Dorough, 12 December 1923, Cherry Hill, Arkansas, USA. After playing piano as a youth he studied piano and composition at college in Texas before attending Columbia University in New York. During this time he also played in New York clubs and soon began singing to his own accompaniment. In the 50s he worked in New York and Paris where he was resident for a while, playing as a solo act and also in small groups accompanying visiting American artists. He was back in the USA at the end of the decade, and in the early 60s recorded with Miles Davis. During the 70s and 80s he combined playing clubs, usually as a solo, with work in television as a composer. He made a belated return to a major label for 1997's excellent *Right On My Way Home*. His songwriting activities encompass music and lyrics. Dorough's singing style displays his appreciation of the songwriter's art and he is an especially interesting interpreter of lyrics. His sound reveals his links with the jazz world through his subtle and rhythmic phrasing.

● ALBUMS: *Devil May Care* (Bethlehem 1957)★★★, *Oliver* (Music Minus One 1963)★★★, *Just About Everything* (Focus 1965)★★, *That's The Way I Feel Now* (1983)★★, *Right On My Way Home* (Blue Note 1997)★★★★.

DORSEY, JIMMY

b. 29 February 1904, Shenandoah, Pennsylvania, USA, d. 12 June 1957, New York, USA. Musically active as a small child under the tutelage of his father, who was a coal miner turned music teacher, Dorsey switched from brass to reed instruments while still in his early teens. Concentrating on clarinet and alto saxophone, he played in various bands, mostly with his brother, Tommy Dorsey. Their co-led group, Dorseys Novelty Six, later renamed Dorseys Wild Canaries, was one of the first jazz bands to broadcast on the radio. Dorsey later joined the California Ramblers. Sometimes with his brother, sometimes alone, Dorsey played in a number of leading bands, including those led by Jean Goldkette, Paul Whiteman, Red Nichols and Ted Lewis. He also recorded frequently, often in company with Nichols and his Goldkette/Whiteman colleague, Bix Beiderbecke. He continued to associate with his brother, and in 1934 they formed the Dorsey Brothers Orchestra, which became extremely popular. Unfortunately for the band, the brothers frequently disagreed, sometimes violently, and after one such argument, on the stand at the Glen Island Casino in May

1935, Tommy walked out leaving Jimmy to run the band on his own. One of the most accomplished of the white bands of the swing era, Jimmy Dorsey's band retained a strong jazz element but also catered to popular demands. Particularly successful in this respect was a series of hit records devised by arranger Tutti Camarata. In an attempt to present all aspects of the band's work in one three-minute radio spot, Camarata made an arrangement of a song which featured first the band's male singer, Bob Eberly, in ballad mood, then the leader with an up-tempo jazz solo on alto, and finally, a wailing sensual vocal chorus by the band's other singer, Helen O'Connell (b. 23 May 1920, Lima, Ohio, USA, d. 9 September 1993, San Diego, California, USA). The first song treated in this manner was 'Amapola', followed by 'Yours' and then 'Green Eyes', which was a runaway hit, as was the later 'Tangerine'. Records like these ensured Dorsey's success and, by the mid-40s, his was one of the most popular of the big bands. This ensured Dorsey's survival over the hard winter of 1946/7, a time which saw many big bands fold, but the 50s proved difficult too, and in 1953 he was reunited with his brother who promptly renamed his own still-successful band as the Dorsey Brothers Orchestra. Jimmy remained with the band until Tommy's death, by which time he too was terminally ill, dying only a few months after his brother. An outstanding technician, Jimmy Dorsey was one of the finest jazz saxophonists of his era and a major influence on many of his contemporaries and successors.

● ALBUMS: *Latin American Favorites* 10-inch album (Decca 1950)★★, *Contrasting Music, Volume 1* 10-inch album (Coral 1950)★★★★, *Contrasting Music, Volume 2* 10-inch album (Coral 1950)★★★, *Gershwin Music* 10-inch album (Coral 1950)★★★, *Dixie By Dorsey* 10-inch album (Columbia 1950)★★★, *Dorseyland Band* 10-inch album (Columbia 1950)★★★, as the Dorsey Brothers *Dixieland Jazz* 10-inch album (Decca 1951)★★★, as the Dorsey Brothers *Jazz Of The Roaring Twenties* 10-inch album (Riverside 1953)★★★★, as the Dorsey Brothers *The Dorsey Brothers With The California Ramblers* 10-inch album (Riverside 1955)★★★, as the Dorsey Brothers *A Backward Glance* (Riverside 1956)★★★, as the Dorsey Brothers *The Fabulous Dorseys In Hi-Fi Volumes 1 & 2* (Columbia 1958)★★★★.

● COMPILATIONS: *Mostly 1940* 1939-40 recordings (Circle 1984)★★★, as the Dorsey Brothers *Spotlighting The Fabulous Dorseys* 1942-45 recordings (Giants Of Jazz 1984)★★★★, *Contrasts* recorded 1945 (Decca 1987)★★★★, *The Early Years* 1936-41 recordings (Bandstand 1988)★★★, *Don't Be That Way* 1935-40 recordings (Bandstand 1988)★★★, *The Uncollected Jimmy Dorsey Volumes 1-5* 1939-50 recordings (Hindsight 1989)★★★, *The Essential V-Discs* 1943-45 (Sandy Hook)★★★★.

● FURTHER READING: *Tommy And Jimmy: The Dorsey Years*, Herb Sanford.

● FILMS: *The Fabulous Dorseys* (1947).

DORSEY, TOMMY

b. 19 November 1905, Shenandoah, Pennsylvania, USA, d. 26 November 1956, Greenwich, Connecticut, USA. Like his older brother, Jimmy Dorsey, Tommy was taught as a small child by his father, a music teacher. He first learned to play trumpet, but switched to trombone while still very young. He played in various bands, often with his brother, their co-led group known first as Dorseys Novelty Six, later renamed Dorseys Wild Canaries. With his brother, Dorsey later played in a number of leading bands, including those led by Jean Goldkette and Paul Whiteman. He also recorded frequently, often in the company of leading jazzmen of the day.

In 1934 he and Jimmy formed the Dorsey Brothers Orchestra, which became extremely popular. Despite, or perhaps because of, their close relationship, the brothers frequently argued, sometimes violently, and after one such disagreement in May 1935, Tommy walked out leaving Jimmy to take over leadership of the orchestra. Tommy then took over the excellent dance-band led by Joe Haymes. Highly ambitious, Dorsey set about turning the band, which was already a sound and well-disciplined unit, into the finest dance orchestra of the era. Over the years he employed first rate arrangers, including Axel Stordahl, Carmen Mastren, Paul Weston and, most influential of all in ensuring the band's success and musical stature, Sy Oliver. Dorsey also engaged the services of several strong jazz players, including Bunny Berigan, Buddy Rich, Johnny Mince, Yank Lawson, Pee Wee Erwin, Buddy De Franco, Gene Krupa, Charlie Shavers and Bud Freeman. Alert to the demands of audiences, Dorsey also employed some of the finest singers ever to work with the big bands. An early find was Jack Leonard, who sang on one of the band's big hits, 'Marie', and others included Edythe Wright, Jo Stafford, Connie Haines and Dick Haymes. The latter was the able replacement for the best singer Dorsey hired, Frank Sinatra. Although Sinatra had already begun to establish a reputation with Harry James, it was his stint with Dorsey that made him into an international singing star and helped to make the Dorsey band one of the most popular of the swing era - in many ways the band and musical sound which most aptly epitomizes this period in American popular music. Dorsey's popularity was enough to ensure his band's survival after the great days of the 40s were over, and he was one of the few to move into television. Nevertheless, the 50s were difficult times and in 1953, he was happy to be reunited with his brother, whose own outfit had folded. Tommy Dorsey gave Jimmy a featured spot and renamed his band as the Dorsey Brothers Orchestra. Despite his popularity, to say nothing of his determination to succeed and sometimes arrogant self-confidence, Dorsey was always reticent about his ability as a jazz player, although some of his early recordings display a gifted musician with a strong sense of style. Like his brother, Tommy Dorsey was an outstanding technician and brought trombone playing to new heights of perfection. His smooth playing was ideally suited to ballads and his solos on countless records were often exemplary. Even with the advent of later generations of outstanding trombone technicians, few have matched his skill and none have surpassed him in his own particular area of expertise. A noted heavy eater, Tommy Dorsey choked to death in his sleep.

● ALBUMS: *Tommy Dorsey Plays Howard Dietz* 10-inch album (Decca 1951)★★★, *In A Sentimental Mood* 10-inch album (Decca 1951)★★★★, as the Dorsey Brothers *Dixieland Jazz* 10-inch album (Decca 1951)★★★, *Tenderley* 10-inch album (Decca 1952)★★★★, *Your Invitation To Dance* 10-inch album (Decca 1952)★★★, as the Dorsey Brothers *Jazz Of The Roaring Twenties* 10-inch album (Riverside 1953)★★★★, *Tommy Dorsey Broadcasts For The American National Guard* (1953)★★★, as the Dorsey Brothers *The Dorsey Brothers With The California Ramblers* 10-inch album (Riverside 1955)★★★, *Tommy Dorsey Plays Cole Porter And Jerome Kern* (RCA Victor 1956)★★★★, as the Dorsey Brothers *A Backward Glance* (Riverside 1956)★★★, *Tommy Dorsey At The Statler Hotel* (1956)★★★, as the Dorsey Brothers *The Fabulous Dorseys In Hi-Fi Volumes 1 & 2* (Columbia 1958)★★★★.

● COMPILATIONS: with Frank Sinatra *The Dorsey/Sinatra Sessions* 1940-42 recordings (RCA 1972)★★★★, *One Night Stand With Tommy Dorsey* recorded 1940 (Sandy Hook 1979)★★★, *At The Fat Man's* 1946-48 recordings (Hep Jazz 1981)★★★, *Solid Swing* 1949-50 recordings (First Heard 1984)★★★, as the Dorsey Brothers *Spotlighting The Fabulous Dorseys* 1942-45 recordings (Giants Of Jazz 1984)★★★★, *The Indispensable Tommy Dorsey Volumes 1/2* 1935-36 recordings (RCA 1987)★★★★, *The Indispensable Tommy Dorsey Volumes 3/4* 1936-37 recordings (RCA 1987)★★★★, *The Indispensable Tommy Dorsey Volumes 5/6* 1937-38 recordings (RCA 1987)★★★★, *The Indispensable Tommy Dorsey Volumes 7/8* 1938-39 recordings (RCA 1987)★★★★, *The Legend, Volumes 1-3* (RCA 1987)★★★★, *Carnegie Hall V-Disc Session, April 1944* (Hep Jazz 1990)★★★, *The Clambake Seven: The Music Goes Round And Round* 1935-47 recordings (Bluebird 1991)★★★★, with Sinatra *The Song Is You* 5-CD box set (Columbia 1994)★★★★, *Dance With Dorsey* (Parade 1995)★★★.

● FURTHER READING: *Tommy And Jimmy: The Dorsey Years*, Herb Sanford.

● FILMS: *The Fabulous Dorseys* (1947).

DOUGHERTY, EDDIE

b. 17 July 1915, New York, USA. Dougherty first played drums as a child and quickly became highly proficient. During the 30s he was constantly on call for recording dates in New York, playing in pick up bands fronted by artists such as Taft Jordan, Mildred Bailey, Harry James, Billie Holiday, Frankie Newton and boogie-woogie pianists Pete Johnson and Meade 'Lux' Lewis. In the early 40s he played with Bud Freeman, Art Tatum, Benny Carter and others, recording piano-drum duos with James P. Johnson. His round of recording dates continued through the mid-40s, finding him accompanying Mary Lou Williams, Wilbur De Paris, Teddy Wilson and Albert Nicholas. Before the decade was out, however, Dougherty dropped out of full-time participation in music but continued to play sporadically in coming years. The quality of Dougherty's accompaniment can be measured by the company he kept; none of whom would have tolerated anyone less than a first-rate drummer. His discreetly supportive playing can be heard on many of the hundreds of recordings he made with the musicians listed.

DOUGLAS, DAVE

b. Montclair, New Jersey, USA. One of the most highly acclaimed trumpet players of the 90s *avant garde* scene, Douglas was raised in the New Jersey area, and as a talented youngster learnt to play piano, trombone and trumpet at an early age. He studied music in Barcelona and Boston, and then attended both the Berklee College Of Music and the New England Conservatory. After moving to New York City in 1984 he studied at New York University. Douglas got his first break in 1987 when he toured Europe with Horace Silver, but his trip to Switzerland the following year was to have a greater influence on his musical development, as Douglas incorporated Eastern European styles into his playing as part of a theatre troupe. Douglas has recorded extensively in the 90s as both leader and sideman, appearing on the hatART, Soul Note, New World and Arabesque labels. His bands include the Tiny Bell Trio, with drummer Jim Black and guitarist Brad Schoeppach, his String Group, with violinist Mark Feldman, cellist Erik Friedlander and bassist Mark Dresser, and his Quartet and Sextet. He has also played with John Zorn in Masada, and appeared live and on record with Don Byron, Myra Melford, Uri Caine and Anthony Braxton. On all his recordings Douglas reflects a wide range of musical elements which, allied to an outstanding technique and a highly individualistic compositional style, marks him out as one of the most distinctive talents currently working in jazz.

● ALBUMS: *Parallel Worlds* (Soul Note 1993)★★★★, *The Tiny Bell Trio* (Songlines 1994)★★★, *In Our Lifetime* (New World 1995)★★★★, *Constellations* (hatART 1995)★★★★, *Five* (Soul Note 1995)★★★★, *Sanctuary* (Avant 1996)★★★, with Tiny Bell Trio *Live In Europe* (Arabesque 1997)★★★★, *Sanctuary* (Avant 1997)★★★, *Stargazer* (Arabesque 1998)★★★★, *Charms Of The Night Sky* (Winter & Winter 1998)★★★★, *Moving Portrait* (DIW 1998)★★★★, *Magic Triangle* (Arabesque 1998)★★★★.

DOUGLAS, JIM

b. James Douglas, 13 May 1942, Gifford, East Lothian, Scotland. Playing banjo and guitar Douglas became an important figure on the traditional jazz scene in his homeland, notably as a member of the Clyde Valley Stompers. From the mid-60s he was a mainstay of the Alex Welsh band until its dissolution in 1982, touring the UK and overseas and appearing on 1971's *In Concert*. Subsequently, Douglas played in other traditional bands but throughout his career has been at ease backing mainstream musicians. On banjo he provides an urgent thrust to the bands in which he plays, but it as a subtly inventive guitarist that he has made a valuable contribution to British jazz.

DOUGLAS, TOMMY

b. 9 January 1906, Eskridge, Kansas, USA, d. 9 March 1965, Swiss Falls, South Dakota, USA. Douglas taught himself clarinet and saxophone while at school in

Tapeka, before studying at the Boston Conservatory from 1924-28. While there he was friendly with the group of Boston players with whom he was to form the core of the Duke Ellington saxophone section - Johnny Hodges, Otto Hardwicke and Harry Carney. He worked with a variety of bands in the south and midwest throughout the 30s and 40s, but settled in Kansas City. He worked with Jelly Roll Morton in Chicago in 1933 and later with Benny Moten. He also played briefly with Ellington in 1951 but usually led his own bands. His commercial records do not reflect what those who heard him describe as his more flowing, modern style. Certainly he was using some of the devises of modern jazz (like extended chords and double time) in his own music as early as 1935 and he may have had some influence on Charlie Parker, who played with his septet in 1936 at the age of 16.

DR. UMEZU

An accomplished and versatile Japanese quartet comprising Kazutoki Umezu (saxophones, piano, percussion), Hiroaki Katayama (saxophones, percussion), Takeharu Hayakawa (bass, guitar) and Takashi Kikuchi (drums), Dr. Umezu is equally entertaining whether exploring resonance and sound relationships in the style of Art Ensemble Of Chicago or in more mainstream funk-based jazz.

● ALBUMS: *Live At Moers Festival* (1983)★★★, *Eight Eyes And Eight Ears* (1985)★★★.

DRESSER, MARK

b. 26 September 1952, Los Angeles, California, USA. Dresser started on bass at the age of 10, played in rock groups in his early teens then studied music at Indiana University for one year, leaving because 'it was too straight for me, like a music factory'. Moving to San Diego, he studied with classical maestro Bertram Turetzky and also played at weekly jam sessions in LA, led by Bobby Bradford - other participants were Stanley Crouch, David Murray and James Newton. Unable to make a living playing new jazz, Dresser moved to the east coast, settling in New Haven, Connecticut, where Leo Smith, Pheeroan akLaff, Gerry Hemingway, Anthony Davis and Jay Hoggard were among his neighbours. Although he played occasional concerts in New York, often with trombonist Ray Anderson, when Dresser followed many of his New Haven colleagues and went to live in the city, he found work increasingly scarce and, disheartened, returned to California. He resumed his LA connection with Bradford and Newton, formed a trio that included Diamanda Galas (then a jazz pianist), and in 1980 toured Europe as part of the Ray Anderson Quartet (*Harrisburg Half Life*). With work still hard to find, Dresser went back to college to study music, meanwhile playing with Charles McPherson, recording with Bradford (*Lost In LA*) and Newton (*Binu*), and releasing his own solo cassette, *Bass Excursions*, in 1983. Later that year he moved to Italy to study, staying for two years, and in 1985 joined the Anthony Braxton Quartet for tours of Europe and the UK. Back in the States, he again moved to New York and has now made his mark on the city's contemporary jazz scene. He remains a member of Braxton's quartet and plays regularly too with Anderson, Tim Berne, the string trio Arcado, which he formed with Hank Roberts and violinist Mark Feldman, and the quartet Tambastics (with Robert Dick, Gerry Hemingway and Denman Maroney). He has also recorded with John Zorn (*Spy Vs Spy*) and Marilyn Crispell (*The Kitchen Concert*). A composer too, his orchestra piece *Castles For Carter* (dedicated to John Carter) was premiered at Amsterdam's October Meeting in 1991. Dresser's recent work has become deeper and emotionally rambling, in particular his excellent composition 'Bosnia', featured on *Force Green*.

● ALBUMS: *Bass Excursions* (1983)★★★, with Hank Roberts, Mark Feldman *Arcado* (1989)★★★, with Arcado *Behind The Myth* (1990)★★★, with Arcado *For Three Strings And Orchestra* (1992)★★★, *Tambastics* (1992)★★★, *The Cabinet Of Dr Caligari* (Knitting Factory 1994)★★★, *Force Green* (Soul Note 1995)★★★★, *Invocation* (Knitting Factory Works 1996)★★★, *Banquet* (Tzadik 1998)★★★★.

DREW, KENNY

b. 28 August 1928, New York City, New York, USA, d. 4 August 1993, Copenhagen, Denmark. A child prodigy, Drew studied piano and music, making his first records in 1949 with Howard McGhee. In the 50s, he was much in demand for recording and club dates by mainstream and modern musicians such as Coleman Hawkins, Lester Young and Charlie Parker. He worked regularly with Buddy De Franco and appeared on John Coltrane's seminal Blue Train. Towards the end of the 50s he worked with Buddy Rich, but by 1961 Drew was resident in Paris relocating in 1964 to Copenhagen, where he lived until his death. In his adopted city, Drew worked mainly at composing and arranging and also ran successful companies engaged in music publishing and recording. He still found time to record his own playing and regularly accompanied local luminaries, such as Niels-Henning Ørsted Pedersen, and visiting American jazz artists. In performance Drew's playing was exhilaratingly complex, but he periodically exhibited his love for the dazzling simplicity of Bud Powell's best work. His son, Kenny Drew Jnr., is a gifted pianist who plays in a style reminiscent of his father's.

● ALBUMS: *New Faces, New Sounds: Introducing The Kenny Drew Trio* 10-inch album (Blue Note 1953)★★★, *The Ideation Of Kenny Drew* 10-inch album (Norgran 1954)★★★, *Progressive Piano* reissued as *The Modernity Of Kenny Drew* (Norgran 1954)★★★, *Talkin' And Walkin' With The Kenny Drew Quartet* (Jazz West 1955)★★★★, *I Love Jerome Kern* (Riverside 1956)★★★, *Kenny Drew Trio* (Riverside 1956)★★★, *This Is New* reissued as *Hard Bop* (Original Jazz Classics 1957)★★★★, *A Harry Warren Showcase* (Judson 1957)★★★, *A Harold Arlen Showcase* (Judson 1957)★★★, *Jazz Impressions Of The Rodgers And Hart Stage And Screen Classic 'Pal Joey'* (Riverside 1957)★★★, *Undercurrent* (Blue Note 1961)★★★★, with Niels-Henning Ørsted Pedersen *Duo* (Steeple Chase 1973)★★★, *Everything I Love* (Steeple Chase 1973)★★★, with Pedersen *Duo*

2 (Steeple Chase 1974)★★★, *If You Could See Me Now* (Steeple Chase 1974)★★★, with Pedersen *Duo Live In Concert* (Steeple Chase 1974)★★★, *Morning* (Steeple Chase 1975)★★★, *The Kenny Drew Trio In Concert* (Steeple Chase 1977)★★★, *Lite Flite* (Steeple Chase 1977)★★★, *Ruby My Dear* (Steeple Chase 1977)★★★, *Home Is Where The Soul Is* (Xanadu 1978)★★★, *For Sure!* (Xanadu 1978)★★★, *Afternoon In Europe* (RCA 1980)★★★, *All The Things You Are* (1981)★★★, *It Might As Well Be Spring* (Soul Note 1981)★★★★, *Your Soft Eyes* (1981)★★★, *The Lullaby* (1982)★★★, *Moonlit Desert* (1982)★★★, *Swingin' Love* (1983)★★★, *And Far Away* (Soul Note 1983)★★★★, *Fantasia* (1983)★★★, *By Request* (RCA 1986)★★★, *Recollections* (Timeless 1989)★★★.

DREW, MARTIN

b. 11 February 1944, Northampton, Northamptonshire, England. Drew began playing drums as a child, studying under the well-known danceband drummer George Fierstone. Despite this early start, it was some time before he became a full-time professional musician; however, once his career was under way, he was soon one of the busiest drummers in the UK. He played on numerous club and recording dates, accompanying many British and American musicians during tours of the UK: these include Ronnie Scott, Oscar Peterson, Buddy Tate, Dizzy Gillespie, Gil Evans and Freddie Hubbard. He has also worked effectively with singers Ella Fitzgerald, Jimmy Witherspoon, Anita O'Day and Nina Simone. An outstanding mainstream drummer who is also comfortable playing bop, Drew is one of the most sought-after session drummers playing in the UK today, and his subtly swinging skills have enhanced numerous recording sessions.

● ALBUMS: *Red Rodney And The Bebop Preservation Society* (1975)★★★★, *The Martin Drew Band* (1977)★★★, *British Jazz Artists Volume 3* (Lee Lambert 1980)★★★.

DROOTIN, BUZZY

b. Benjamin Drootin, c.1910, Russia. Growing up in Boston, Massachusetts, USA. Drootin and his brothers, Lewis and Al, became known locally for their lively contributions to the dixieland tradition. After working with Ina Ray Hutton Drootin moved to New York where he played drums regularly with established stars and gained a solid reputation as a swinging accompanist. In the late 40s he settled into the house band at Eddie Condon's club and made many records. During the 50s he worked on a long series of traditional and mainstream record sessions with artists such as Ruby Braff and Bobby Hackett. In the 60s Drootin worked in a number of bands assembled especially for festivals, concert tours and recording dates. In the 70s he was back home in Boston working with his brothers in the Drootin Brothers Orchestra.

DUDEK, GERD

b. Gerhard Rochus Dudek, 28 September 1938, Gross Dober, Germany. Dudek emerged as a key jazz figure in the 60s with Manfred Schoof and Alexander Von Schlippenbach. He played with them over the years, as well as others, including Joachim Kuhn and Albert Mangelsdorff. In Dudek, Europe possesses arguably its most convincing exponent of mid-to-late-period John Coltrane. Dudek has been a key partner in Schlippenbach's projects - in Globe Unity, on their Jelly Roll Morton tribute, and as one of the outstanding soloists on the *Berlin Contemporary Jazz Orchestra* session. The co-operative groups the Quartet, the European Jazz Quartet, and the European Jazz Ensemble have all benefited from his hard-driving but lyrical tenor, soprano, clarinet and flute.

● ALBUMS: *Open* (1977)★★★, with RAI Big Band *Jelly Roll* (1980)★★★, with EJQ and Ernst-Ludwig Petrowsky *Interchange* (1987)★★★, with EJE *Live* (1988)★★, with BCJO *Berlin Contemporary Jazz Orchestra* (1990)★★★★.

DUDZIAK, URSZULA

b. 22 October 1943, Straconka, Poland. Although Dudziak studied piano formally for some years, she began to sing in the late 50s after hearing records by Ella Fitzgerald. Within a few years she was one of the most popular jazz artists in her native country. She met and later married Michal Urbaniak, recording with him during the 60s. In the late 60s they began to travel overseas and in the 70s settled in New York. Language barriers hold no problems for her, as she customarily eschews words in favour of a wordless vocalizing that is far more adventurous than scat. Already gifted with a remarkable five-octave range, Dudziak employs electronic devices to extend still further the possibilities of her voice. She has frequently worked with leading contemporary musicians, including Archie Shepp and Lester Bowie, and was a member of the Vocal Summit group, with Jay Clayton, Jeanne Lee, Bobby McFerrin and Lauren Newton. Although her remarkable talent is worthy of greater exposure, Dudziak's chosen style has meant that she has remained relatively unknown except to the *cognoscenti*.

● ALBUMS: with Adam Makowicz *Newborn Light* (1972)★★★★, *Urszula* (1976)★★★, *Midnight Train* (1977)★★★, *Future Talk* (1979)★★★, *Magic Lady* (In And Out 1980)★★★, *Ulla* (1982)★★★, with Vocal Summit *Sorrow Is Not Forever ... But Love Is* (1983)★★, *Warsaw Jazz Festival 1991* (Jazzmen 1993)★★★.

DUKE, GEORGE

b. 12 January 1946, San Rafael, California, USA. Duke studied the piano at school (where he ran a Les McCann-inspired Latin band) and emerged from the San Francisco Conservatory as a Bachelor of Music in 1967. From 1965-67 he was resident pianist at the Half Note, accompanying musicians such as Dizzy Gillespie and Kenny Dorham. This grounding served as a musical education for the rest of his life. He arranged for a vocal group, the Third Wave, and toured Mexico in 1968. In 1969 he began playing with French violinist Jean-Luc Ponty, using electric piano to accompany Ponty's plugged-in violin. He played on *King Kong*, an album of music Frank Zappa composed for Ponty. He then joined Zappa's group in 1970, an experience that transformed his music. As he put it, previously he had been too 'musically advanced' to play rock 'n' roll piano triplets. Zappa encouraged him to sing and joke and use electronics. Together they wrote 'Uncle Remus' for *Apostrophe* (1972), a song about black attitudes to oppression. His keyboards contributed to a great edition of the Mothers Of Invention - captured on the outstanding *Roxy & Elsewhere* (1975) - which combined fluid jazz playing with rock and *avant garde* sonorities. In 1972 he toured with Cannonball Adderley (replacing Joe Zawinul). Duke had always had a leaning towards soul jazz and after he left Zappa, he went for full-frontal funk. *I Love The Blues, She Heard My Cry* (1975) combined a retrospective look at black musical forms with warm good humour and freaky musical ideas; a duet with Johnny Guitar Watson was particularly successful. Duke started duos with fusion power-drummer Billy Cobham, and virtuoso bassist Stanley Clarke, playing quintessential 70s jazz rock - amplification and much attention to 'chops' being the order of the day. Duke always had a sense of humour: 'Dukey Stick' (1978) sounded like a Funkadelic record. The middle of the road beckoned, however, and by *Brazilian Love Affair* (1979) he was merely providing high-class background music. In 1982 *Dream On* showed him happily embracing west-coast hip easy listening. However, there has always been an unpredictable edge to Duke. The band he put together for the Wembley Nelson Mandela concert in London backed a stream of soul singers, and his arrangement of 'Backyard Ritual' on Miles Davis's *Tutu* (1986) was excellent. He collaborated with Clarke again for the funk-styled *3* and in 1992 he bounced back with the jazz fusion *Snapshot*, followed by the orchestral suite *Enchanted Forest* in 1996, and *Is Love Enough?* in 1997.

● ALBUMS: *Jazz Workshop of San Francisco* (1966)★★★, with Jean-Luc Ponty *Live In Los Angeles* (1969)★★★, *The Inner Source* (1971)★★★, *Feel* (MPS/BASF 1975)★★★, *The Aura Will Prevail* (MPS/BASF 1975)★★★, *I Love The Blues, She Heard My Cry* (MPS/BASF 1975)★★★, with Billy Cobham *Live - On Tour In Europe* (Atlantic 1976)★★★, *Liberated Fantasies* (MPS/BASF 1976)★★★, *From Me To You* (Epic 1977)★★★, *Reach For It* (Epic 1977)★★★, *Don't Let Go* (Epic 1978)★★, *Follow The Rainbow* (Epic 1979)★★, *Master Of The Game* (Epic 1979)★★, *Primal* (MPS 1979)★★★, *Secret Rendevous* (Epic 1979)★★★, *A Brazilian Love Affair* (Epic 1980)★★★, with Clarke *The Clarke/Duke Project* (Epic 1981)★★★★, *Dream On* (Epic 1982)★★, *Guardian Of The Light* (Epic 1983)★★★, with Clarke *The Clarke/Duke Project II* (Epic 1983)★★★★, *1976 Solo Keyboard Album* (Epic 1983)★★★, *Thief In The Night* (Elektra 1985)★★★, *Night After Night* (Elektra 1989)★★★, with Clarke *3* (Epic 1990)★★★, *Reach For It* (Sony 1991)★★★, *Snapshot* (Warners 1992)★★★, *Enchanted Forest: Muir Woods Suite* (Warners 1996)★★★, *Is Love Enough?* (Warners 1997)★★★★, *After Hours* (1998)★★★.

● COMPILATIONS: *The Collection* (Castle 1991)★★★.

DUKES OF DIXIELAND

Formed in 1949 by trumpeter Frank Assunto (b. 29 January 1922, New Orleans, USA, d. 25 February 1974) and his trombonist brother Fred (b. 3 December 1929, d. 21 April 1966), the Dukes got their start with bandleader Horace Heidt in his 'Youth Opportunity Programme', which toured the USA from 1948-53. Returning to their home town they were resident at the Famous Door in the Crescent City for four years, building up a big reputation in person and on Roulette and Victor records. At this time, when the original New Orleans musicians had either died or retired, the Dukes were hailed as authentic. True, they were capable enough, but no more so than any other revivalist band, including the British trad groups which proliferated in that era. However, they were fortunate both in having a contract with Audio-Fidelity Records, who recorded them with startling clarity, on superb stereo demonstration records, and, especially, on having Louis Armstrong join them temporarily. They visited Japan in 1964 along with Red Nichols and Gene Krupa in a George Wein 'Dixieland To Swing' package, with Edmond Hall as the Dukes' guest artist. The band broke up when Fred Assunto died while they were playing in Las Vegas.

● ALBUMS: *The Dukes Of Dixieland At The Jazz Band* Ball (Vik 1957)★★★★, *You've Got To Hear It To Believe It, Volume 1* (Audio Fidelity 1957)★★★, *You've Got To Hear It To Believe It, Volume 2* (Audio Fidelity 1957)★★★, *You've Got To Hear It To Believe It, Volume 3* (Audio Fidelity 1958)★★, *You've Got To Hear It To Believe It, Volume 4* (Audio Fidelity 1958)★★★, *Mardi Gras Time* (Audio Fidelity 1958)★★, *The Dukes Of Dixieland On Campus* (Audio Fidelity 1959)★★★, *Up The Mississippi* (Audio Fidelity 1959)★★, *The Dukes Of Dixieland* (RCA Victor 1960)★★★, *Breakin' It Up On Broadway* (Columbia 1962)★★★, *Struttin' At The World's Fair* (Columbia 1964)★★★, *Live At Bourbon Street* (Decca 1965)★★★, *Sunrise, Sunset* (Decca 1966)★★★, *Come To The Cabaret* (Decca 1966)★★.

● COMPILATIONS: *The Best Of The Dukes Of Dixieland* (Audio Fidelity 1961)★★★, *More Best Of The Dukes Of Dixieland* (Audio Fidelity 1962)★★★.

DULFER, CANDY

b. 19 September 1969, Amsterdam, Netherlands. Saxophonist Dulfer was bought to prominence by Prince, who introduced her on the video mix of 'Party Man' with a cry of 'when I want sax, I call for Candy'. She was bought up in a family involved in the Dutch jazz scene. Her father, Hans Dulfer, a respected tenor saxophonist, exposed his daughter to the playing of Sonny Rollins, Coleman Hawkins and Dexter Gordon. Candy's career evolved from playing with brass bands to performing on the jazz club circuit and later fronting her own band Funky Stuff, who were invited to support Madonna on part of her 1987 European tour. A similar support slot with Prince was abruptly cancelled, but the singer made amends by inviting Dufler onstage during one of his shows. The resulting recording sessions with Prince, and in particular the aforementioned 'Party Man', led to session work with Eurythmics guitarist, David A. Stewart, who gave Dulfer a joint credit on 'Lily Was Here', a UK number 6 hit in 1990. Further credits have found her working with David Gilmour, Aretha Franklin and Van Morrison. Her 1990 debut album was nominated for a Grammy and certified gold. Her subsequent albums have been pleasant enough but have broken no new ground, their R&B leanings similar in content to David Sanborn's hard-blowing work. However, she is regarded as one of Europe's leading young saxophonists.

● ALBUMS: *Saxuality* (RCA 1990)★★★, *Sax-a-Go-Go* (RCA 1991)★★★, *Big Girl* (RCA 1996)★★, *For The Love Of You* (N2K Encoded 1997)★★★.

● COMPILATIONS: *The Best Of Candy Dulfer* (N2K Encoded 1998)★★★.

Dunbar, Ted

b. Earl Theodore Dunbar, 17 January 1937, Port Arthur, Texas, USA, d. 29 May 1998. Teaching himself to play guitar and trumpet, Dunbar played in the Lincoln High School band, continuing to play music while studying pharmacy at Texas Southern University. After graduating and receiving a license to practice pharmacy he combined working at both careers. He also extended his music studies, this time with David Nathaniel Baker whose Lydian Concept of Tonal Organization influenced his subsequent work. Concentrating on guitar, Dunbar was also influenced by the playing of Wes Montgomery, for whom he sometimes subbed in Indianapolis while maintaining a day job at a pharmacy across the street from the Ebony Missile Room, a club at which Montgomery was appearing. During the 60s Dunbar continued to live this double life, for a time working with his brother, also a qualified pharmacist, in their parents' drugstore and also for the Skillern drugstore chain. This job took him to Dallas where he heard and played with David 'Fathead' Newman and Red Garland. He then moved to New York together with saxophonist Billy Harper and it was here that Dunbar was eventually able to concentrate on making music rather than making out prescriptions. In 1971 he followed John McLaughlin in Tony Williams's Lifetime. The year after this he became a faculty member at Livingston College, Rutgers, and he also wrote books on music theory and several tutors concerned with guitar technique. From time to time he played on motion picture soundtracks and also played in Broadway show pit bands. Mostly, however, he played jazz, working and frequently recording with an impressive range of top-flight musicians, including Sonny Rollins, McCoy Tyner, Gil Evans (1973's *Svengali*), Kenny Barron (1974's *Peruvian Blue* and the following year's duo set, *In Tandem*) and Charles Mingus. Dunbar's remarkable technical gifts and his fluency as soloist and improviser were never used at the expense of the form and content of his music making. He remained faithful to the core of his concept of jazz, and through his work as a teacher helped pass on to a new generation his enthusiasm and knowledge.

● ALBUMS: with Kenny Barron *In Tandem* (Muse 1975)★★★, *Opening Remarks* (Xanadu 1978)★★★, *Jazz Guitarist* (Xanadu 1982)★★★, *Gentle Time Along* (Steeplechase 1992)★★.

● FURTHER READING: *New Approaches To Jazz Guitar*, Ted Dunbar. *A System Of Tonal Convergence*, Ted Dunbar.

Duncan, Hank

b. 26 October 1894, Bowling Green, Kentucky, USA, d. 7 June 1968. In 1919, after studying piano at university, Duncan formed a small band in Louisville, Kentucky. A few years later he was in the northeast of the country before moving to New York, where he played in the popular band led by Fess Williams. He stayed with Williams for about five years, simultaneously carving out a reputation as a leading exponent of stride piano playing. After brief spells with Joe 'King' Oliver, Sidney Bechet and Tommy Ladnier, he joined Fats Waller, playing second piano. In the late 30s and early 40s he was a familiar figure on the New York club scene, playing with Zutty Singleton, Mezz Mezzrow, Bechet; recording with Gene Sedric, Snub Mosley; and also as nominal leader of a trio with Bingie Madison and Goldie Lucas. From 1947-63, with only a 15-month absence on another gig with Singleton, he was house pianist at Nick's in New York. During this period he made records with Tony Parenti. Duncan continued to play at clubs but suffered a long period of ill health before his death in June 1968.

Dunn, Johnny

b. 19 February 1897, Memphis, Tennessee, USA, d. 20 August 1937, Paris, France. Starting out in Midwest theatres, he played trumpet as a solo act before joining W.C. Handy's band with which he came to New York in 1917. He also played with singers such as Mamie Smith and Edith Wilson, recording in the early 20s. In 1923 he travelled to Europe with a band led by Will Vodery, and returned there three years later when he recorded in London, with the Plantation Orchestra, a self-titled EP released on the WRC label. He also played with Noble Sissle's band in France. During the early and mid-30s he worked steadily in Europe, being resident for some time in the Netherlands. Dunn was among the best of the musicians playing in the immediate pre-jazz years and he influenced many of his contemporaries. Overshadowed though he was by the arrival of Louis Armstrong, Dunn was still an able and gifted player, showing subtle power and using complex patterns that never descended into mere showmanship. His stylistic roots became outmoded during the 30s but his decision to remain in Europe and his early death meant that his reputation never suffered, except, perhaps, by neglect, and today he can be recognized as having been a highly accomplished trumpeter.

● COMPILATIONS: with Edith Wilson *Complete Works 1921-28, Volumes 1 & 2* (RST 1996)★★★.

Durham, Eddie

b. 19 August 1906, San Marcos, Texas, USA. As a child Durham worked in travelling shows with other musical members of his large family. In the mid-20s he worked in a number of southwest territory bands including Walter Page's Blue Devils from where he, and several others, moved to the Bennie Moten band. Up to this point Durham had been playing both guitar and trombone and now added arranging to his arsenal of skills. During the 30s he played in, and arranged for, the bands of Willie Bryant, Jimmie Lunceford and Count Basie. In the following decade he arranged for several noted swing bands including Artie Shaw's, and also worked closely with the one of the outstanding but neglected bands of the late 40s, the International Sweethearts Of Rhythm. Later in his career Durham arranged more and played less, but did return to the stage in the 70s and 80s with Eddie Barefield, Buddy Tate and other comrades from his Basie days. Durham's contributions to jazz are extensive and include helping develop and refine the electrically amplified guitar. More important still were his loosely swinging arrangements exemplified by such Basie classics as 'Moten Swing' and the popular 'In The Mood' for Glenn Miller. He was also co-composer of 'Topsy' which became an unexpected hit for Cozy Cole in 1958.

● ALBUMS: *Eddie Durham* i (1973)★★★, *Eddie Durham* ii (1974)★★, *Blue Bone* (1981)★★★.

DUTCH SWING COLLEGE BAND

This outfit's polished, cleverly arranged repertoire was still heard in concert 40 years after its formation by Peter Schilperoort (clarinet, saxophones) in 1945. Among musicians that have passed through its ranks are Wout Steenhuis (guitar), the late Jan Morks (clarinet), Kees Van Dorser (trumpet), UK's Rod Mason (cornet) and the Louis Armstrong-influenced trombonist Oscar Klein. Famous US musicians visiting Europe proudly 'sat in' with the band. Schilperoort became established as the Netherlands' foremost ambassador of trad jazz, following the foundation of his long-standing partnership with Arie Ligthart (banjo/guitar) in 1952. Yet, after embracing saxophonists and even amplification, the combo were to deviate further from the prescribed New Orleans precedent via adaptations of rock 'n' roll, country and military marches, to achieve acceptance in the generalized pop field. By the 70s, Schilperoort started his own DSC Productions record company, and was knighted by Queen Juliana of the Netherlands.

● ALBUMS: *Dixieland Goes Dutch* (Epic 1955)★★★★, *Dixie Gone Dutch* (Philips 1962)★★★★, *On Tour* (Philips 1981)★★, *Digital Dixie* (Philips 1982)★★★, *Music For The Millions* (Philips 1983)★★★, *The Bands Best* (Verve 1984)★★★, *Swing Studio Sessions* (Philips 1985)★★★, *When The Swing Comes Marching In* (Philips 1985)★★★, *40 Years 1945-1985, At Its Best* (Timeless 1986)★★★★, *Digital Anniversary* (Philips 1986)★★★, *With Guests Volume 1* (Polydor 1987)★★, *Digital Date* (Philips 1988)★★★, *Dutch Samba* (Timeless 1989)★★, *1960* (Philips 1990)★★★, *Jubilee Concert* (Philips 1991)★★★, *The Old Fashioned Way* (Jazz Hour 1993)★★★.

DUTREY, HONORE

b. 1894, New Orleans, Louisiana, USA, d. 21 July 1935. In the years preceding World War I, trombonist Dutrey worked in several New Orleans bands but during military service suffered lung damage in a shipboard accident. In the early 20s he worked with Joe 'King' Oliver in Chicago then joined Carroll Dickerson's band. During the mid-20s he led his own unit and also worked in the bands of Louis Armstrong and Johnny Dodds, but his career was truncated and he retired from active playing at the end of the decade. A sound ensemble player, Dutrey appeared on many records by his exceptional contemporaries, always lending solid support to their performances.

DUVIVIER, GEORGE

b. 17 August 1920, New York City, New York, USA, d. 11 July 1985. After formal musical education, mostly on violin, Duvivier worked with a New York symphony orchestra but soon entered the jazz world where, having recognized the limitations of the violin in that area, he switched to bass. In the early 40s he worked with several leading artists in small and large group settings, among them Coleman Hawkins and Lucky Millinder. He also began arranging and contributing many musical scores for the later Jimmie Lunceford band and the elegant but short-lived Sy Oliver big band. In the 50s he worked extensively in the studios, often accompanying singers on record, with some of whom he also collaborated on tours at home and overseas. Among these were demanding performers such as Lena Horne and Pearl Bailey. He also played with small groups, an activity he continued alongside his writing into the 60s. During this period he was with bands led by Terry Gibbs, Bud Powell, Shelly Manne, Eric Dolphy, Benny Goodman and Ben Webster. A dominant force in any rhythm section, Duvivier played with great precision and attack. He continued to play jazz dates around the world through the 70s and into the 80s, working with musicians such as Zoot Sims, Joe Venuti, Hank Jones and Warren Vaché Jnr.

● ALBUMS: *George Duvivier In Paris* (Coronet 1956)★★★, with Sonny Clark, Max Roach *Max Roach, Sonny Clark, George Duvivier* (Time 1962)★★★★.

DYANI, JOHNNY MBIZO

b. 30 November 1945, East London, South Africa, d. 25 October 1986. Dyani was a vital, emotional bass player who earned immense respect from musicians everywhere yet, not unusually for such artists, never achieved the recognition he deserved. At the 1962 Johannesburg Jazz Festival Chris McGregor invited him and four more of the best players at the Festival to form a band, and the legendary Blue Notes were created. As a mixed-race band it was impossible for them to work under apartheid and so, in 1964, while touring Europe, they decided to settle in London, where, evolving into the Chris McGregor Group, they made a huge impact on the UK jazz scene. As well as playing in the six-piece McGregor Group and the Brotherhood Of Breath (the big band which McGregor set up after disbanding the sextet), Dyani toured South America in 1966 with Steve Lacy, Enrico Rava and Louis Moholo (the quartet recording *The Forest And The Zoo* under Lacy's name in 1967), and he then worked with the Spontaneous Music Ensemble (1969) and the Musicians Co-Operative

(1971). In 1969, at the Actuel Festival organized by the French record company BYG, he took part in a jam which included Frank Zappa, Archie Shepp and Philly Joe Jones. Dyani had been growing unhappy with the direction that McGregor's band was taking, feeling that it was moving too close to free jazz and away from its African roots so, in the early 70s, he moved to Denmark, where he worked with John Tchicai, Don Cherry and Abdullah Ibrahim. He also worked with David Murray, Joseph Jarman and in the trio Detail with John Stevens and saxophonist Frode Gjerstad (they became Detail Plus when Bobby Bradford and others guested with them). After Dyani's death in 1986 several albums were dedicated to his memory including Tchicai's *Put Up The Fight*, Stevens and Dudu Pukwana's *Radebe* (*They Shoot To Kill*) and *Blue Notes For Johnny*, a searingly emotional tribute by McGregor, Pukwana and Maholo. His son, Thomas, is currently establishing a reputation as a percussionist with his own band.

● ALBUMS: with others *Music For Xaba* (1972)★★★, with Abdullah Ibrahim *Good News From Africa* (1974)★★★, *Blues Notes For Mongezi* (1976)★★★, *Blue Notes In Concert* (1978)★★★, *Witchdoctor's Son* (Steeple Chase 1978)★★★★, *Song For Biko* (Steeple Chase 1978)★★★, with Ibrahim *Echoes From Africa* (Enja 1980)★★, *Mbizo* (Steeple Chase 1981)★★★★, with Detail *Backwards And Forwards* (1983)★★★, *Angolian Cry* (Steeple Chase 1985)★★★★, with Detail Plus *Ness* (1987)★★★, with Detail Plus *Way It Goes/Dance Of The Soul* (1989)★★★.

E.S.P. - Miles Davis

Probably the best of a number of edgy and exciting albums recorded during one of Miles Davis's most creative periods, *E.S.P.* dates from 1965 and features one of his greatest bands. The daring, youthful sense of adventure that tenor saxophonist Wayne Shorter, pianist Herbie Hancock, bassist Ron Carter and drummer Tony Williams brought to Davis helped relaunch his career and put him in touch with the experimental jazz spirit of the period. The new music was looser, freer, and featured abrupt changes of direction and rhythm, as the musicians responded to each other as much as to any preset scheme.

- Tracks: *E.S.P.; Eighty One; Little One; RJ; Agitation; Iris; Mood.*
- First released 1965
- UK peak chart position: did not chart
- USA peak chart position: did not chart

Eade, Dominique

b. *c.*1959, USA. Raised in a musical environment, Eade was educated at Vassar, where she sang with a jazz group, attended Berklee College Of Music in Boston in the late 70s, studying jazz exclusively, then completed her bachelor's degree at the New England Conservatory in 1982. At the NEC she studied classical theory and composition, ethnic/world musics and jazz and in addition to her degree also received an Artist Diploma. In 1984 she was appointed to the faculty of the NEC and since then has continued to teach voice, composition and improvisation there. In addition, she has also taught and coached in various parts of the USA and in Norway and Italy. Meanwhile, she performed with various jazz groups, appeared on radio and television. In the mid-80s she worked with the Ran Blake Quartet and in 1985 and 1986 was featured at the Boston Globe Jazz Festival. She also led her own quartet which included, at different times, Alan Dawson and Bob Moses. In the late 80s she also studied privately with Blake, Moses, Dave Holland and Stanley Cowell and with soprano Nancy Armstrong. Amongst other musicians with whom she worked during this time were Stan Getz, Bill Frisell, Anthony Braxton, Mick Goodrick, Peter Leitch, Fred Hersch and Butch Morris. In the mid-80s Eade had began recording, at first on albums led by others, including Gunnar Wenneborg, in Sweden, and later with Claire Ritter. She continued to perform in and around New York and Boston and in 1991 recorded her self-produced debut album for which she composed and arranged all the music and on which her accompanists included Cowell and Dawson. She continued to perform and visited France, singing at the Toulon Jazz Festival, and also performed regularly at New York's Village Gate. Her second album was voted by *Billboard* magazine as one of the Top 10 releases of 1995. Her qualities as a teacher may be determined from the fact that of the 11 finalists of the 1994 Thelonious Monk Jazz Vocal Competition three, including the winner, were her students. *When The Wind Was Cool*, released in 1997, paid tribute to 50s singers June Christy and Chris Connor. Eade sings with a pure tone and although she favours the lower register, in which she is especially pleasing, her vocal range is wide. Her flawless technique and polished assurance allows her to deliver with flair a repertoire that is both imaginative and demanding.

- ALBUMS: *The Ruby And The Pearl* (Accurate 1991)★★★, *My Resistance Is Low* (Accurate 1995)★★★★, *When The Wind Was Cool: The Songs Of Chris Connor & June Christy* (RCA Victor 1997)★★★★.

Eadie, Irene

(see Kitchings, Irene)

Eager, Allen

b. 10 January 1927, New York City, New York, USA. Eager had formal tuition on clarinet but in 1943 received lessons on tenor saxophone from Ben Webster, a switch that marked the start of his professional career. His early experience was gained in big bands on the more lightweight side of the swing era, including those led by Bobby Sherwood and Hal McIntyre. Towards the end of 1943 he joined Woody Herman and later worked with Tommy Dorsey. In Los Angeles he played in Vine Street clubs with Barney Kessel and Zoot Sims, whom he followed into the small group led by 'Big' Sid Catlett. Around this time he heard Lester Young on records by the Count Basie band and thereafter remodelled his playing in the style of the 'Pres'. In the mid-40s Eager was mostly to be found at 52nd Street clubs, playing with Coleman Hawkins, Pete Brown and many beboppers, including Red Rodney, Stan Levey, Max Roach, Al Haig and Serge Chaloff, and sometimes leading his own small groups. He also met Charlie Parker and, although initially unimpressed, he soon became a devotee and they often worked together. In 1948 he recorded with Fats Navarro, Wardell Gray and Ernie Henry as a member of Tadd Dameron's band, taking part in the important sessions that produced 'Our Delight', 'Dameronia' and 'Early Bird'. Eager continued playing into the 50s, recording with Tony Fruscella and Danny Bank, and touring with Oscar Pettiford. In the mid-50s he spent some time living in Paris but gradually drifted out of music, preferring to spend his time pursuing other, mainly sporting, activities. In 1982 he returned to music, recording and touring both at home and overseas.

- ALBUMS: *Swingin' With Allen Eager* (1953)★★★, *Renaissance* (1982)★★★.
- COMPILATIONS: with Tadd Dameron *Anthropology* (1948)★★★.

Eardley, Jon

b. 30 September 1928, Altoona, Pennsylvania, USA, d. 4 April 1997, France. Eardley began playing trumpet when he was a child, encouraged by his musician father. His early interest in jazz came from records made by his father's generation of musicians but he soon became influenced by bop. After military service he formed his own small band, playing bop, and in the early 50s settled in New York. Here he played with Phil Woods, Gerry Mulligan, and others, touring Europe with Mulligan in 1956. He recorded with Woods, Mulligan and Chet Baker. After a spell playing in his home state he relocated to Europe, playing thereafter in studios, on radio, and in clubs in Belgium and Germany. In Europe he found a high level of admiration and recognition, and was recorded by Spotlite Records under his own name and in partnership with Al Haig. In 1989 he soloed on some tracks for Carmen McRae's *Dream Of Life*, recorded with the West German Radio Orchestra. Eardley played both trumpet and flügelhorn with a rich, burnished sound and was always a very melodic player all of which made his ballad playing especially attractive.

● ALBUMS: *Jon Eardley In Hollywood* 10-inch album (New Jazz 1954)★★★, *Hey, There* 10-inch album (Prestige 1955)★★★, *Jon Eardley Seven* (Prestige 1956)★★★, *Namely Me* (Spotlite 1977)★★★, with Al Haig *Stablemates* (Spotlite 1977)★★, *From Hollywood To New York* 1954/1955 recordings (Original Jazz Classics 1990)★★★★.

Earland, Charles

b. 24 May 1941, Philadelphia, Pennsylvania, USA. Earland began his musical career, playing saxophone, while still at school. First on alto and then tenor, he played with a number of bands and soon after graduation joined the small band led by organist Jimmy McGriff. Later, he formed a band of his own using the currently popular organ/saxophone/rhythm section format. Intent on pursuing this concept but experiencing problems with organists, he began playing the organ himself. He was hired as organist for a band led by Lou Donaldson before he resumed as a leader. Throughout the 70s, Earland's group was in great demand and he proved popular both in live performances, in clubs and at festivals, and also as a recording artist. His first album for Prestige Records, 1969's *Black Talk!*, has proved to have an enduring appeal for aficinados of the soul-jazz genre. He recorded extensively for Prestige and Muse, before releasing albums for Columbia Records and Mercury Records. He experimented with disco in collaboration with his wife, singer-songwriter Sheryl Kendrick, but her death from sickle-cell anemia in 1985 resulted in Earland's retreat from the music scene. He returned in the late 80s with two traditional soul-jazz albums for Milestone Records. In the 90s he could be heard playing not only in an updated hard bop mode but also in an earthy heavily riff-laden manner, his solidly traditional B3 sound helping him retain much of his earlier popularity. A 1995 album, featured the powerhouse modern trumpet playing of Lew Soloff, contrasting vividly with the album's musical leaning towards R&B, and was well received by audiences geared to contemporary sounds.

● ALBUMS: *Black Talk!* (Prestige 1969)★★★★, *Black Drops* (Prestige 1970)★★★, *Living Black* (Prestige 1970)★★★, *Charles 3* (Prestige 1971)★★★, *The Dynamite Brothers* (Prestige 1973)★★★, *Leaving This Planet* (Prestige 1974)★★★★, *Smokin'* (Muse 1977)★★★, *Pleaasant Afternoon* (Muse 1978)★★★, *Infant Eyes* (Muse 1978)★★★, *Coming To You Live* (Columbia 1979)★★★, *In The Pocket* (Muse 1982)★★★, *Front Burner* (Milestone 1988)★★★★, *Third Degree Burn* (Milestone 1989)★★★★, *Whip Appeal* (Muse 1990)★★★, *Unforgettable* (Muse 1992)★★★★, *I Ain't Jivin', I'm Jammin'* (Muse 1993)★★★, *Ready 'n' Able* (Muse 1995)★★★, *Slammin' And Jammin'* (Savant/City Hall 1996)★★★, *Blowing The Blues Away* (High Note 1997)★★★, *Charles Earland's Jazz Organ Summit* (Cannonball 1997)★★★.

Eastman, Madeline

b. USA. An exceptionally gifted singer, much admired among her fellow professionals for her brilliant use of scat, she works mainly on the west coast. With Kitty Margolis she is co-owner of Mad-Kat Records. Eastman's international reputation in the mid- to late 90s was slowly growing and her undoubted abilities might well lead to greater fame in the next century.

● ALBUMS: *Point Of Departure* (Mad-Kat 1991)★★★★, *Mad About Madeline* (Mad-Kat 1993)★★★, *Art Attack* (Mad-Kat 1994)★★★.

Eckstine, Billy

b. William Clarence Eckstein, 8 July 1914, Pittsburgh, Pennsylvania, USA, d. 8 March 1993, Pittsburgh, Pennsylvania, USA. Eckstine possessed one of the most distinctive voices in popular music, a deep tone with a unique vibrato. He began singing at the age of 11 but until his late teens was undecided between a career as a singer or football player. He won a sporting scholarship but soon afterwards broke his collar bone and decided that singing was less dangerous. He worked mostly in the north-eastern states in the early 30s and towards the end of the decade joined the Earl Hines band in Chicago. Although far from being a jazz singer, opting instead for a highly sophisticated form of balladry, Eckstine clearly loved working with jazz musicians and in particular the young experimenters who drifted into the Hines band in the early 40s, among them Wardell Gray, Dizzy Gillespie and Charlie Parker. While with Hines he developed into a competent trumpeter and, later, valve trombonist, having first mimed as a trumpet player in order to circumvent union rules. In 1943, acting on the advice and encouragement of Budd Johnson, Eckstine formed his own band. Although his original intention was to have a band merely to back his vocals, Eckstine gathered together an exciting group of young bebop musicians and thus found himself leader of what constituted the first true bebop big band. During the band's four-year existence its ranks were graced by Gray, Parker, Gillespie, Gene Ammons,

Dexter Gordon, Miles Davis, Kenny Dorham, Fats Navarro and Art Blakey, playing arrangements by Gillespie, Johnson, Tadd Dameron, Gil Fuller and Jerry Valentine. Eckstine also hired the Hines band's other singer, Sarah Vaughan. In 1947 the band folded but had already served as an inspiration to Gillespie, who formed his own bebop big band that year. Eckstine's commercial recordings during the life of the big band were mostly ballads which he wrapped in his deep, liquid baritone voice, and with his bandleading days behind him he continued his career as a successful solo singer. He gained a huge international reputation as a stylish balladeer. During his long career Eckstine had many hit records, including 'Jelly, Jelly', recorded in 1940 with Hines, 'Skylark', 'Everything I Have Is Yours', 'I Apologize' (stylistically covered by P.J. Proby to great success), 'Prisoner Of Love', 'Cottage For Sale', 'No One But You' (number three in the UK charts in 1954), 'Gigi' (number eight in 1959), and several duets with Vaughan, the best-known being 'Passing Strangers', which, although recorded a dozen years earlier, reached number 17 in the 1969 charts. He went on to record for Motown, Stax and A&M. In later years Eckstine recorded a new single with Ian Levine as part of his Motown revival project on the Motor City label.

● ALBUMS: *Live At Club Plantation, Los Angeles* (1945)★★★, *Billy Eckstine Sings* (National 1949)★★★, *Songs By Billy Eckstine* (MGM 1951)★★★, *Favorites* (MGM 1951)★★★, *Billy Eckstine Sings Rogers And Hammerstein* (MGM 1952)★★★★, *The Great Mr B* (King 1953)★★★, *Tenderly* (MGM 1953)★★★★, with Earl Hines *Earl Hines With Billy Eckstine* 10-inch album (RCA Victor 1953)★★★, *I Let A Song Go Out Of My Heart* (MGM 1954)★★★, *Blues For Sale* (EmArcy 1954/55)★★★★, *The Love Songs Of Mr B* (EmArcy 1954/55)★★★, *Mr B With A Beat* (MGM 1955)★★★, *Rendezvous* (MGM 1955)★★★, *I Surrender Dear* (EmArcy 1955)★★★★, *That Old Feeling* (MGM 1955)★★★★, *Prisoner Of Love* (Regent 1957)★★★, *The Duke the Blues And Me* (Regent 1957)★★★, *My Deep Blue Dream* (Regent 1957)★★★★, *You Call It Madness* (Regent 1957)★★★, *Billy Eckstine's Imagination* (EmArcy 1958)★★★★, *Billy's Best* (Mercury 1958)★★★, with Sarah Vaughan *Sarah Vaughan And Billy Eckstine Sing The Best Of Irving Berlin* (Mercury 1958)★★★★, with Vaughan *Billy And Sarah* (Lion 1959)★★★★, with Count Basie *Basie/Eckstine Inc.* (Roulette 1959)★★★★, *Golden Saxophones* (London 1960)★★★, *I Apologize* (1960)★★★★, *Mr B* (Audio Lab 1960)★★★, *Broadway Bongos And Mr B* (Mercury 1961)★★★, *No Cover No Minimum* (Mercury 1961)★★★, with Quincy Jones *Billy Eckstine & Quincy Jones At Basin St. East* (Mercury 1962)★★★, *Don't Worry 'Bout Me* (Mercury 1962)★★★, *Once More With Feeling* (Mercury 1962)★★★, *Everything I Have Is Yours* (Metro 1965)★★★, *Prime Of My Life* (Motown 1965)★★, *My Way* (Motown 1966)★★, *For Love Of Ivy* (Motown 1969)★★, *Gentle On My Mind* (Motown 1969)★★, *Feel The Warm* (1971)★★, *Stormy* (Stax 1971)★★, *If She Walked Into My Life* (Stax 1974)★★, *Something More* (Stax 1981)★★, *Billy Eckstine Sings With Benny Carter* (1986)★★★, *I'm A Singer* (Kim 1987)★★.

● COMPILATIONS: *The Best Of Billy Eckstine* (Lion 1958)★★★, *The Golden Hits Of Billy Eckstine* (Mercury 1963)★★★★, *Golden Hour: Billy Eckstine* (Golden Hour 1975)★★★★, with Sarah Vaughan (coupled with a Dinah Washington and Brook Benton collection) *Passing Strangers* (Mercury 1978)★★★, *Greatest Hits* (Polydor 1984)★★★★, *Mr B And The Band - Savoy Sessions* (Savoy 1986)★★★.

ECM Records

ECM Records - the letters stand for Edition for Contemporary Music - was launched in Munich in 1969 with Mal Waldron's *Free At Last* and, some 500 recording sessions later, is secure in its status as Europe's pre-eminent independent jazz label, despite a sometimes troubled relationship with the jazz mainstream and an open contempt for the music business. The company's musical direction reflects the taste and personality of its founder, producer Manfred Eicher (b. 1943, Lindau, Germany), who has said, 'I regard the music industry, including concert life, as a kind of environmental pollution'. Formerly a bassist, Eicher was a member of the Berlin Philharmonic Orchestra, but also played free music with Marion Brown and Leo Smith (both of whom later recorded for ECM). Experiences as a production assistant at Deutsche Grammophon prompted him to ask whether it were possible to approach jazz recording with the care that the classical companies expended. Norwegian engineer Jan Erik Kongshaug, a partner now for two decades, became an important ally. Eicher's meticulous recordings of solo piano albums by Paul Bley, Keith Jarrett, and Chick Corea were hailed by critic Allan Offstein as 'the most beautiful sound next to silence' - and a trading slogan and *leit-motif* was born. Though the audio quality of the recordings has endeared the label to two generations of hi-fi enthusiasts (and helped to sell more than two million copies of Jarrett's *The Köln Concert*), Eicher feels that technical excellence ought to be given, and is much more interested in the music. Detractors who rail against the 'ECM sound' conveniently overlook the range of the label's catalogue, which has embraced the burning, outgoing energy music of the Art Ensemble Of Chicago, Sam Rivers, and Hal Russell, the rock-influenced guitars of Terje Rypdal, Steve Tibbetts, and Pat Metheny, the straighter jazz of John Abercrombie, Kenny Wheeler, and Dave Holland, the eclectic and folklore-rooted improvisations of Egberto Gismonti, Jan Garbarek, and Collin Walcott. A classical line, the ECM New Series, provides access to the entire art music tradition from Gesualdo to Stockhausen and has introduced Estonian composer Arvo Pärt, whose pure, concentrated music at the edge of silence has proved a major influence in new composition. A New Series anthology in 1989 bore the inscription 'You wish to see; Listen. Hearing is a step towards vision', and the formula works in reverse as well. ECM album sleeve photography - landscapes, seascapes, cloudscapes, mountainscapes - has provided a powerful visual corollary for the music and gives evidence of Eicher's abiding passion for film. He has released two volumes of Eleni Karaindrou's music for the films of Theo Angelopoulos, and in 1992 issued Jean-Luc Godard's *Nouvelle Vague* on laser disc. In 1991, Eicher scripted and co-directed his first film, *Holocene*, based on a Max Frisch novel. An interest in theatre is evidenced in albums of Heiner Goebbels's music for the plays of Heiner Müller, and David Byrne's music for Robert Wilson's *Civil Wars*. ECM has also issued recordings of actor Bruno Ganz reading German poetry, and of Peter Rühmkorf's jazz and poetry fusions. It seems likely that the label will continue to move further away from 'jazz' in the years to come. Having now passed its quarter century the label has avoided ever forsaking itself for commercialism, and those artists such as Metheny who moved on to bigger sales with Geffen Records can never dispute the faith the label had in him as he developed. ECM's honesty and uncompromising route makes it one of the truly great record labels.

● COMPILATIONS: *Selected Signs I: An ECM Anthology* (ECM 1997)★★★★.

● FURTHER READING: *ECM: Sleeves Of Desire*, no editor listed.

Edelhagen, Kurt

b. 5 June 1920, Herne, Germany, d. 8 February 1982. Edelhagen first came to prominence in the years immediately following World War II. Although the prompt formation of a symphony orchestra is often cited as a notable attempt to re-establish an element of culture in post-war German society, the formation of a radio big band is rather more striking. The Berlin Philharmonic Orchestra had never really stopped playing, but dance music, especially that with a jazz-orientation, had been frowned upon by the defeated regime. In these circumstances the speed with which Edelhagen, who had been playing piano in clubs for the Allied armies, formed a big band of such a high quality was quite remarkable. His first band was in operation before the end of 1946 and thereafter he developed a series of radio big bands that continued into the early 70s. He was one of the first post-war European bandleaders to bring in foreign jazz musicians and among those who were featured in his bands were Jimmy Deuchar, Derek Humble, Dusko Goykovich and Jiggs Whigham. The various orchestras Edelhagen led featured a wide range of big-band music, with a bias towards a powerful, brassy ensemble playing that reflected his love for Stan Kenton's style.

● ALBUMS: *Big Band Jazz From Germany* (1955)★★★★, *Big Band Jazz* (1957)★★★★, *Kurt Edelhagen And His Orchestra* i (1959)★★★, *Kurt Edelhagen And His Orchestra* ii (1959)★★★, *Kurt Edelhagen And His Orchestra* iii (1964)★★★, *Live At Lucerna Hall, Prague* (1965)★★, *Swing Goodies* (1965)★★★, *Kurt Edelhagen And His Orchestra* iv (1972)★★★, *Heidelberger Jazztage 1972* (1972)★★★.

Edison, Harry 'Sweets'

b. 10 October 1915, Columbus, Ohio, USA. A trumpeter who was inspired by Louis Armstrong, Edison gained valuable early experience with a number of territory bands, including the excellent Jeter-Pillars orchestra. After a short spell with Lucky Millinder, Edison joined the Count Basie band in 1938, where he remained until Basie folded his big band in 1950. Edison then began a long career as leader of small groups, a solo artist, and studio musician; he also worked occasionally with bandleaders such as Buddy Rich. He toured with Jazz At The Philharmonic and in the 50s his work came to the attention of millions who never knew his name when he performed exquisite trumpet obligati with the Nelson Riddle orchestra behind the vocals of Frank Sinatra. In the 60s he worked occasionally with Basie again but was mostly heard as a soloist, touring extensively on the international club and festival circuit. In performance Edison often favours playing with a Harmon mute and, while he has many imitators, few have matched his laconic wit and inventiveness. Indeed, his trademark of repeated single notes is something no other trumpeter has been able to use to such good effect. On his numerous recording dates he has been teamed with most of the big names in jazz and continually defies his advancing years. In November 1989 he appeared as featured soloist with the Frank Wess-Harry Edison Orchestra at the Fujitsu-Concord Jazz Festival in Japan.

● ALBUMS: *Harry Edison Quartet* reissued as *The Inventive Harry Edison* (Pacific Jazz 1953)★★★, with Buddy Rich *Buddy And Sweets* (Norgran 1955)★★★, with Lester Young *Pres And Sweets* (Norgran 1955)★★★★, *Sweets* (Clef 1956)★★★★, *Blues For Basie* (Verve 1957)★★★★, *Gee Baby, Ain't I Good To You?* (Verve 1958)★★★, with Buck Clayton *Harry Edison Swings Buck Clayton And Vice-Versa* (Verve 1958)★★★, *The Swinger* (Verve 1958)★★★, with Roy Eldridge, Dizzy Gillespie *Tour De Force* (Verve 1958)★★★, *Mr. Swing* (Verve 1959)★★★, *Sweetenings* (Roulette 1959)★★★, with Eldridge, Young *Going For Myself* (Verve 1959)★★★★, with Eldridge, Young *Laughin' To Keep From Cryin'* (Verve 1959)★★★★, *Patented By Edison* (Roulette 1960)★★★, with Ben Webster *Ben Webster-Sweets Edison* (Columbia 1962)★★★★, with Eddie 'Lockjaw' Davis *Jawbreakers* (Riverside 1962)★★★★, *Sweets For The Taste Of Love* (Vee Jay 1964)★★★, *Sweets For The Sweet* (Sue 1965)★★★, *When Lights Are Low* (Liberty 1966)★★★, with Davis *Sweet And Lovely* (Black & Blue 1975)★★★, with Davis *Edison's Lights* (Pablo 1976)★★★, with Davis *Harry 'Sweets' Edison And Eddie 'Lockjaw' Davis, Vol. 1* (Storyville 1976)★★★, with Davis *Harry 'Sweets' Edison And Eddie 'Lockjaw' Davis, Vol. 2* (Storyville 1976)★★★, *Simply Sweets* (Pablo 1978)★★★, with Zoot Sims *Just Friends* (Pablo 1979)★★★, *'S Wonderful* (Pablo 1983)★★★, *For My Pals* (Pablo 1988)★★★, *Can't Get Out Of This Mood* (Orange Blue 1989)★★★, *Swing Summit* (Candid 1990)★★★, *Live At The Iridium* (Telarc 1998)★★★.

● COMPILATIONS: *Best Of Harry Edison* (Pablo 1982)★★★★.

● FILMS: *Jammin' The Blues* (1944).

Edwards, Eddie

b. Edwin Branford Edwards, 22 May 1891, New Orleans, Louisiana, USA, d. 9 April 1963. After playing violin in various local bands he switched to trombone which he played in Papa Jack Laine's band. In 1916 Edwards was in a band led by Johnny Stein that went to Chicago. Later that year Edwards left the band and, with Nick La Rocca, formed a new outfit named the Original Dixieland Jazz Band. Although interrupted by military service in World War I, Edwards remained more or less constantly with the ODJB until 1925. For some years he worked outside music but was back in the mid-30s playing in revivals of the ODJB and with other like-minded bands. In the 50s and 60s he performed with various groups, mostly in and around New York, and was also accompanist to the Katherine Dunham dance troupe. Edwards also composed music, including 'Tiger Rag', 'Fidgety Feet' and 'Original Dixieland One-step'. A powerful player with a strong rhythmic sense, Edwards was ideally suited for the gutsy ensemble playing that so captivated audiences attracted by the 'new-fangled' music of the ODJB. His legacy is best exemplified by the countless performances of his compositions that have echoed down the years.

EDWARDS, TEDDY

b. 26 April 1924, Jackson, Mississippi, USA. As a child Edwards played alto saxophone with local bands and continued playing this instrument when he moved to Detroit in 1940. He toured with territory bands in Michigan and Florida including those led by Ernie Fields and Stack Walton. In the Walton band he played alongside several proto-boppers including Howard McGhee, Wardell Gray and Al McKibbon. In 1944 Edwards settled in California and after playing with an R&B band led by Roy Milton he joined McGhee, switching to tenor saxophone. The McGhee band worked sporadically over the next couple of years, recording for Ross Russell's Dial Records. The resulting four sides, 'Dilated Pupils', 'Midnight At Minton's, '52nd Street Theme' and 'Up In Dodo's Room' achieved the status of minor classics and the final title alerted fans and musicians to the possibility that the tenor saxophone could go down pathways other than those previously trod by Coleman Hawkins and Lester Young. In part, Edwards's original concept arose from his youthful experience on alto and his interest at the time in the music of Charlie Parker. This was his first recording session but he quickly made up for his late start and during the next months was regularly featured on many of the best west coast record dates. In December 1947 he appeared on a Dexter Gordon date where the two tenor players duetted on 'The Duel', a fairly successful attempt to repeat the earlier success of Gordon's and Gray's 'The Chase'. In the early 50s Edwards became a weekend regular at the Lighthouse, playing with Shorty Rogers, Shelly Manne, Hampton Hawes and others. In 1954 he joined the quintet co-led by Max Roach and Clifford Brown, replacing Sonny Stitt only to be replaced himself soon afterwards by Harold Land. He also worked in San Francisco during this period but periodic bouts of ill-health, mostly related to dental problems, kept him out of the spotlight and also away from the recording studios. In 1960 he recorded for Contemporary Records as nominal leader of a co-operative quartet comprising pianist Joe Castro, Leroy Vinnegar and Billy Higgins. Their album, *Teddy's Ready*, proved popular and the following year Edwards was reunited at Contemporary with McGhee, then recovering from a bout of drug addiction. This album, *Together Again!*, was similarly successful and helped the re-establishment of Edwards as a potent voice in jazz. In the 60s he played with Benny Goodman and Milt Jackson and in the 70s worked with Jimmy Smith and singers Sarah Vaughan and Tom Waits. He also began touring internationally and continued doing so throughout the 80s. In 1991, he worked with Bill Berry and his LA Big Band for concerts at the Hollywood Bowl, having played in the band intermittently since the early 70s. In between jazz dates, Edwards has worked extensively in the studios, playing and writing for radio and television. He is the composer of many songs, including 'Sunset Eyes'. In the post-bop era, Edwards has consistently proved to be a fluent and creative performer, bringing his wide experience and imaginative mainstream concepts to bear upon music that is thoroughly contemporary while remaining deeply rooted in the great blues-influenced traditions of jazz.

● ALBUMS: *Teddy's Ready* (Comtemporary 1960)★★★, with Howard McGhee *Together Again!* (Contemporary 1961)★★★★, *Good Gravy* (Timeless 1961)★★★, *Heart And Soul* (1962)★★★, *It's Alright* (1967)★★★, *Feelin's* (1974)★★★, with Bill Berry *Hot And Happy* (1974)★★★★, *The Inimitable* (1976)★★★, with McGhee *Young At Heart* (Storyville 1979)★★★, *Out Of This World* (Steeple Chase 1980)★★★, with McGhee *Trumpet At Tempo* 1947 recordings (Spotlite 1983)★★, *Mississippi Lad* (Antilles 1991)★★★, *Blue Saxophone* (Verve 1993)★★★★, *La Villa, Live In Paris* (Verve 1994)★★, *Midnight Creeper* (HighNote 1998)★★★.

● COMPILATIONS: *Tenor Conclave* (Timeless 1992)★★★★.

EFFORD, BOB

b. London, England. Before becoming a highly accomplished reed player, especially on tenor saxophone, Efford played piano and trumpet. Drifting seemingly without design into a career in music, he played in some minor British provincial dance bands in the 40s. When one of the bands, Les Ayling's, became resident at the Lyceum Ballroom in London, Efford found his way into the local jazz scene and in 1949 joined Vic Lewis's Kenton-styled band. In the early 50s, he joined Ted Heath, touring the USA and receiving personal acclaim at the band's tour-opening concert at Carnegie Hall. He left Heath in the early 60s, thereafter mostly doing studio work which included sessions under the leadership of visiting American stars such as Benny Goodman and Harry James. In 1976 he moved to Los Angeles where he played in bands led by Dave Pell, Bob Florence, Bill Holman and the Capp-Pierce Juggernaut. In 1980 he made his debut as leader at Carmelo's, playing a bewilderingly huge range of instruments including pretty nearly the entire saxophone family as well as oboe, bassoon, flute, clarinet and cor anglais. Efford's forte remains the tenor saxophone and he is also especially adept as a baritone saxophonist which he plays with an engagingly light tone.

● ALBUMS: *Focus On Ted Heath* (1959)★★★, with Bob Florence *Trash Can City* (1986)★★.

EGAN, MARK

b. 14 January 1951, Brockton, Massachusetts, USA. Egan started playing the trumpet at the age of 10 and only turned to the double bass when he was 15. He studied at the University of Miami in the mid-70s and took lessons from Jaco Pastorius, Dave Holland and pianist Andy Laverne. Meanwhile, he was working with Ira Sullivan, the Pointer Sisters, Deodato and David Sanborn. In 1977 he started working with Pat Metheny's group with whom he stayed for three years. Egan has since worked with a variety of musicians, including Stan Getz, Gil Evans, Randy Brecker, John McLaughlin, Airto Moreira and Flora Purim. In 1982 he formed Elements with drummer Danny Gottlieb with whom he has spent some time studying ethnic music. He is an educated musician who varies the sound of his playing through his fascination for and skill in the use of electronic devices.

● ALBUMS: *Elements* (Philo 1982)★★★★, *Forward Motion* (Antilles 1984)★★★, *Mosaic* (1984)★★★, *A Touch Of Light* (GRP 1988)★★★, *Beyond Words* (Blue Beacon 1992)★★★★.

EITHER/ORCHESTRA

Based in Cambridge, Massachusetts, the eclectic Either/Orchestra was founded in the mid-80s by tenor saxophonist Russ Gershon. A 10-piece, seven-horn group that crosses the sound of a big band with the adventurousness of a small combo, members have included guitarists John Dirac, Jerry Deupree and Michael Rivard, bassist Larry Roland, drummers Syd Smart and Matt Wilson, keyboard players John Medeski and Ken Freundlich, and brass players John Carlson, Curtis Hasselbring, Russ Jewell, Charlie Kohlhase and Tom Halter, the only member, besides Gershon, who has played with the group since its inception. Gershon founded Accurate Records in 1987, on which the Either/Orchestra have released six inventive albums drawing on a vast range of material, including selections from the songbooks of Duke Ellington, Gigi Gryce, Sonny Rollins, Thelonious Monk, John Lennon and Burt Bacharach, alongside band members' originals. In 1997 the group celebrated their 10th anniversary with a celebratory concert and a 2-CD retrospective.

● ALBUMS: *Dial E For Either/Orchestra* (Accurate 1986)★★★★, *Radium* (Accurate 1988)★★★, *The Half-Life Of Desire* (Accurate 1989)★★★★, *The Calculus Of Pleasure* (Accurate 1990)★★★, *The Brunt* (Accurate 1993)★★★★, *10th Anniversary Concert* (Accurate 1997)★★★.

● COMPILATIONS: *Across The Omniverse* (Accurate 1997)★★★★.

EKYAN, ANDRÉ

b. André Echkyan, 24 October 1907, Meudon, France, d. 9 August 1972. A self-taught clarinettist and alto saxophonist, Ekyan became well known in France in the early 30s. He also played in London, with Jack Hylton, and made many recordings. The musicians with whom he worked included Django Reinhardt, recording with him in the late 30s and again in 1950. He also played with Coleman Hawkins, and Benny Carter. A secure and competent player, Ekyan was important in helping spread swing era jazz styling throughout France and other parts of Europe.

ELECTRIC BATH - DON ELLIS

A man who is criminally ignored and one who will in time surely be seen as a pioneer. The late Don Ellis was signed to CBS Records in the late 60s and marketed with Blood, Sweat And Tears, Spirit and Moby Grape, rather like selling Take That records to John Lee Hooker fans. Had Ellis been promoted properly, his standing would be much greater. This wonderful record is his best; rich full orchestration with short non-indulgent solos, this is a recording by an orchestra whose charts were painstakingly and individually worked out by Ellis. He did find success writing film themes, such as *The French Connection*.

● Tracks: *Indian Lady; Alone; Turkish Bath; Open Beauty; New Horizons.*

● First released 1968

● UK peak chart position: did not chart

● USA peak chart position: did not chart

ELDRIDGE, JOE

b. 1908, Pittsburgh, Pennsylvania, USA, d. 5 March 1952. A competent alto saxophonist, with considerable experience in territory bands, Eldridge's career was eclipsed by that of his older brother with whom he formed a band in 1933. After Roy Eldridge went on to greater things, Joe Eldridge continued working with 30s bands such as McKinney's Cotton Pickers, Blanche Calloway, Zutty Singleton and others. In the 40s he worked again with Roy and Singleton and also with Oran 'Hot Lips' Page before spending several years in Canada. Back in the USA in 1950 he played and taught a little in New York until his death in 1952.

ELDRIDGE, ROY

b. David Roy Eldridge, 30 January 1911, Pittsburgh, Pennsylvania, USA, d. 26 February 1989, Valley Stream, New York, USA. One of the chief figures in the established lineage of jazz trumpet playing, Eldridge paid his dues with territory bands in the Midwest, such as those of Speed Webb and Horace Henderson, before moving to New York in 1930. He then played with a number of bands, including that of Teddy Hill and one that he co-led with his brother, Joe Eldridge. In 1935 he joined Fletcher Henderson's orchestra, then formed his own group, which was reasonably successful but not so much so that he could afford to refuse an offer to join Gene Krupa in 1941. The engagement brought Eldridge to great prominence thanks to extensive tours of the USA and numerous recordings, notably solo features on 'Rockin' Chair', 'After You've Gone' and 'Let Me Off Uptown' (on which he partnered Anita O'Day). Despite the enormous boost to his popularity that resulted from the exposure he gained with Krupa, this was a very trying time for Eldridge who, as the only black member of the band, suffered racial harassment that brought him to the brink of a nervous breakdown. When Krupa was jailed in 1943, Eldridge briefly fronted the band before it broke up. He then formed his own band before giving a second chance to the white big band scene with Artie

Shaw and once again he encountered discrimination and abuse. After briefly trying another big band of his own, Eldridge settled on leading a small group. In the late 40s he worked again with Krupa and also joined Jazz At The Philharmonic. In the 50s he played with Benny Goodman, spent some time in Europe and continued his association with JATP. This period coincided with a personal crisis during which Eldridge began to doubt his place in jazz as the new generation of trumpeters, led by Dizzy Gillespie, forged new ideas. The stay in Europe convinced him that his place was in the mainstream of jazz, and that it was a place in which he was respected by musicians and admired by fans. In the 60s, Eldridge played with Ella Fitzgerald, Coleman Hawkins and Count Basie and co-led a band with Richie Kamuca. In 1970 he began a residency at Ryans in New York City that lasted into the second half of the decade. A fiery, combative player, Eldridge is often cited as a link between trumpeters Louis Armstrong and Dizzy Gillespie. Although there is an element of logic in this assessment, it overlooks the important role in jazz trumpet history of Henry 'Red' Allen; and it implies that Eldridge was a proto-bop trumpeter, which is far from being the truth. He was the outstanding trumpet stylist of the 40s, performing with daring aggression, his high register playing achieved with apparent ease and his verve and enthusiasm were such that he invariably brought out the best in his fellow musicians. His suggested link to bebop stems largely from a tiny handful of records which show that he was aware of the changes taking place around him and was unafraid to dabble even if he chose never to take the plunge. He was, however, undoubtedly a goad to Gillespie, with whom he played in many after-hours sessions at Minton's and other New York clubs where bebop was nurtured. In the late 50s and afterwards, having settled back into a swing-based groove, Eldridge showed his mastery of the form and of his instrument. Nicknamed 'Little Jazz', Eldridge was a giant who became an elder statesman of jazz without ever losing the fire and aggression that had always marked his playing. His career came to an end when he suffered a stroke in 1980, after which he never played again.

● ALBUMS: *Roy Eldridge In Sweden* 10-inch album (Prestige 1951)★★★, *Roy Eldridge Collates* 10-inch album (Mercury 1952)★★★★, with Sammy Price *Battle Of Jazz, Vol. 7* 10-inch album (Brunswick 1953)★★★, *Little Jazz Four: Trumpet Fantasy* 10-inch album (Dial 1953)★★★★, with Zoot Sims *Roy Eldridge With Zoot Sims* 10-inch album (Discovery 1954)★★★, *The Roy Eldridge Quintet* 10-inch album (Clef 1954)★★★, *Roy Eldridge Quartet* 10-inch album (London 1954)★★★, *The Strolling Mr. Eldridge* 10-inch album (Clef 1954)★★★, with John Simmons, Alvin Stoller, Art Tatum *The Art Tatum-Roy Eldridge-Alvin Stoller-John Simmons Quartet* (Clef 1955)★★★★, with Dizzy Gillespie *Roy And Diz* (Clef 1955)★★★★, with Gillespie *Roy And Diz, Volume 2* (Clef 1955)★★★★, with Gillespie *Trumpet Battle* (Clef 1956)★★★, with Gillespie *The Trumpet Kings* (Clef 1956)★★★, *Little Jazz* (Clef 1956)★★★★, *Rockin' Chair* 1951-1952 recordings (Clef 1956)★★★, *Dale's Wail* (Clef 1956)★★★★, *Roy's Got Rhythm* 1951 recording (EmArcy 1956)★★★, *Swing Goes Dixie* (American Recording Society 1956)★★★, with Benny Carter *The Urbane Jazz Of Roy Eldridge And Benny Carter* (American Recording Society 1957)★★★, *That Warm Feeling* (Verve 1957)★★★, with Coleman Hawkins *At The Opera House* (Verve 1957)★★★★, *The Great English Concert* (1958)★★★, with Harry 'Sweets' Edison, Gillespie *Tour De Force* (Verve 1958)★★★, with Edison, Lester Young *Going For Myself* (Verve 1959)★★★★, with Edison, Young *Laughin' To Keep From Cryin'* (Verve 1959)★★★★, *Swingin' On The Town* (Verve 1960)★★★, *Roy Eldridge Sextet* (1962)★★★, with Earl Hines *Grand Reunion, Volume 2* (Limelight 1965)★★★★, with Gillespie *Soul Mates* (Verve 1966)★★★★, *The Nifty Cat Strikes West* (Master Jazz 1966)★★★, *The Nifty Cat* (Master Jazz 1970)★★★, with Paul Gonsalves *The Mexican Bandit Meets The Pittsburgh Pirate* (Fantasy 1973)★★★★, *Little Jazz And The Jimmy Ryan All-Stars* (Pablo 1975)★★★, with Gillespie *Jazz Maturity ... Where It's Coming From* (Pablo 1975)★★★, with Gillespie *The Trumpet Kings At Montreux '75* (Pablo 1975)★★★★, *Happy Time* (Pablo 1975)★★★, *What It's All About* (Pablo 1976)★★★, *Montreux 1977* (Pablo 1977)★★★★, with Vic Dickenson *Roy Eldridge & Vic Dickenson* (Storyville 1978)★★★, *Comin' Home Baby* 1965/1966 recordings (Pumpkin 1978)★★★★, *Roy Eldridge At Jerry Newman's* (Xanadu 1983)★★★, with Count Basie *Loose Walk* 1972 recording (Pablo 1992)★★★, *Roy Eldridge In Paris* 1950 recording (Vogue 1995)★★★★.

● COMPILATIONS: *The Early Years* 1935-1949 recordings (Columbia)★★★★, *After You've Gone* 1936-1946 recordings (GRP)★★★★, with Gene Krupa, Anita O'Day *Uptown* 1941-1942 recordings (Columbia)★★★★, *All The Cats Join In* 1943-1946 recordings (MCA)★★★★, *Roy Eldridge Volume 1 Nuts* 1950 recording (Vogue 1993)★★★, *Roy Eldridge Volume 2 French Cooking* 1950-1951 recordings (Vogue 1993)★★★, *Little Jazz: The Best Of The Verve Years* (PolyGram 1994)★★★★, *Fiesta In Brass* (Le Jazz 1995)★★★, *Heckler's Hop* (Hep 1995)★★★, *Roy Eldridge 1935-1940* (Classics 1996)★★★, *Roy Eldridge 1943-1944* (Classics 1997)★★★★, *An Introduction: His Best Recordings 1935-1946* (Best Of Jazz 1998)★★★★.

ELEMENTS

When Mark Egan left Pat Metheny's group in 1981 he started playing with drummer Danny Gottlieb in the group that would, by 1983, become known as Elements. Egan is an educated musician and technically accomplished bassist who varies the sound of his playing through his fascination and skill in the use of electronic devices. Gottlieb is a skilful drummer who had wide experience playing with Eberhard Weber's Colours, the Gary Burton Quartet and Pat Metheny's band before working with Egan in Elements. Egan was already fascinated by ethnic music and had spent some time studying music from Bali, south India, Africa and Brazil but with Gottlieb he spent time in Hawaii 'playing music in nature in valleys, during very extreme weather conditions (wind, rain, etc.)'. All of these influences are reflected in the music they produced with Elements.

● ALBUMS: *Elements* (Philo 1982)★★★★, *Forward Motion* (Antilles 1984)★★★, *Far East* (1993)★★★.

Elf, Mark

b. 13 December 1949, New York City, New York, USA. A hard-working and accomplished bop guitarist, Elf has gained some long overdue recognition in the late 90s with several acclaimed recordings for his own Jen Bay label. Raised in New York, Elf attended the Berklee College Of Music from 1969 to 1971. After graduation Elf built up a reputation on the jazz scene, playing and recording with a role call of modern jazz legends including Lou Donaldson, Dizzy Gillespie, Benny Golson, Al Grey, Lionel Hampton, Jimmy Heath, Jon Hendricks, Freddie Hubbard, Branford Marsalis, Wynton Marsalis and Clark Terry. He recorded his debut between 1986 and 1987, and later decamped to Santiago, Chile for a set on the Alerce label. His second album, *The Eternal Triangle*, was recorded in 1988 but, following a series of rejections from established labels, Elf issued the set on his own Jen Bay imprint. Thanks to his own tireless self-promotion Elf's recent recordings have gained extensive airplay, introducing his fluid and melodic playing to a wider audience.

● ALBUMS: *Mark Elf Trio, Vol. 1* (Half Note 1987)★★★, *Mark Elf Trio* (Alerce 1993)★★★, *The Eternal Triangle* 1988 recording (Jen Bay 1996)★★★★, *Minor Scramble* (Jen Bay 1997)★★★★, *Trickynometry* (Jen Bay 1998)★★★★.

Elgar, Charlie

b. Charles A. Elgar, 13 June 1885, New Orleans, Louisiana, USA, d. August 1973. As a child Elgar studied violin and later extended his studies at music colleges in Wisconsin and Illinois. He played in classical music ensembles in his home-town before settling in Chicago around 1913. There, he formed his own small band and then a big band which was for many years resident at the Dreamland Café. He travelled to Europe as a member of Will Marion Cook's orchestra and then returned to Chicago for further long residencies as leader at several of the city's top nightclubs. During all this time he had been active as a teacher and at the beginning of the 30s he turned to that aspect of his career on a full-time basis. Although outside the jazz stream, his bands regularly included in their ranks top-flight early jazzmen including Manuel Perez, Lorenzo Tio, Barney Bigard and Darnell Howard. Elgar's name lives on through jazz histories rather than through a legacy of records, as he made only four sides despite his popularity and widespread activity in the 20s.

● ALBUMS: *Elgar's Creole Orchestra* (Arcadia 1926)★★.

Elgart, Larry

b. 20 March 1922, New London, Connecticut, USA. A saxophonist, in the mid-40s he played in Bobby Byrne's commercially unsuccessful band. It was while on the Byrne band that he met arranger Charlie Albertine, whose writing style he liked and whom he bore in mind when he formed his own band. Also in the mid-40s Elgart was one of the principal soloists in the band led by his brother, Les Elgart. Elgart's exuberant playing was an important feature of the band and led to the brothers deciding to part company and each lead a band of his own. For a while Larry Elgart And His Manhattan Swing Band enjoyed a measure of popularity in and around New York, usually playing top hotels and ballrooms. Business fell off in the 50s, however, and the brothers reunited in an attempt to meet current commercial demands. However, the passage of time and changes in public taste militated against their chances of survival.

● ALBUMS: *The City* (1961)★★★, *Legends* (1961)★★, as Les And Larry Elgart *Command Performance! Les And Larry Play The Great Dance Hits* (1964)★★★, as Larry Elgart And His Manhattan Swing Orchestra *Hooked On Swing* (1982)★★★★, *Hooked On Swing 2* (1983)★★★.

Elgart, Les

b. 3 August 1918, New Haven, Connecticut, USA, d. 29 July 1995. Elgart was lead trumpeter in bands headed by Bunny Berigan, Hal McIntyre, Charlie Spivak and Harry James. His brother, Larry Elgart, played lead alto saxophone with the Charlie Spivak band at the age of 17, later moving on to work with Woody Herman, Red Norvo and Freddie Slack. In 1945 the brothers formed their own band, which recorded and toured under Les's name, and used arrangements by musicians such as Nelson Riddle and Bill Finegan. Their partnership was short-lived, and they split to form their own units, without much success. They reunited in 1953, launching a 'new sound' featuring the arrangements of Charles Albertine with the emphasis on ensemble playing, no piano, and hardly any solos. Jazz fans were unimpressed, but the modern, melodic approach caught the general public's imagination and the band became prolific album sellers. Larry resumed the leadership when Les moved to California but, in 1963 they were together again for a time as joint leaders of the Les And Larry Elgart Orchestra. Les Elgart And His Manhattan Swing Orchestra charted in the US in 1982 with 'Hooked On Swing'.

● ALBUMS: as Les Elgart And His Orchestra *The Elgart Touch* (1956)★★★★, *For Dancers Only* (1957)★★★, as Les And Larry Elgart *Command Performance! Les And Larry Play The Great Dance Hits* (1964)★★★.

Elias, Eliane

b. 19 March 1960, São Paulo, Brazil. Before she reached the age of 21, Elias had attracted considerable attention, not only for her keyboard playing but also as a teacher of jazz music. In the early 80s she moved to New York, joined the Randy and Michael Brecker jazz/rock group, Steps Ahead, with whom she remained until 1984 and thereafter recorded and toured extensively. She continued to play and record with Randy Brecker, whom she married, and has also recorded with Jack DeJohnette, Nana Vasconcelos and Eddie Gomez (upon whose advice she first tried her luck in the USA). Although a gifted and interesting pianist, Elias has not completely fulfilled her early promise to become a major figure on the contemporary jazz scene.

● ALBUMS: *Illusions* (Denon 1987)★★★, *Crosscurrents* (Denon

1988)★★★, *So Far So Close* (Blue Note 1990)★★★, *Plays Jobim* (Blue Note 1990)★★★, *A Long Story* (Manhattan 1990)★★, *Fantasia* (Blue Note 1992)★★, *Paulistana* (Blue Note 1993)★★★, *Solos And Duets* (Blue Note 1995)★★, *The Three Americas* (Blue Note 1997)★★★★, *Eliane Elias Sings Jobim* (Blue Note 1998)★★★.

ELIZALDE, FRED

b. Federico Elizalde, 12 December 1907, Manila, Philippines, d. 16 January 1972. Elizalde spent his youth in the USA with his brother Manuel, and for a time led a dance band. His interest in music was a disappointment to his family, one of the richest in the Philippines, but any hopes that his education at Cambridge University in the UK might redirect his talents failed when Elizalde played his piano in a jazz-style band for the 1927 university ball. This event attracted wide media attention and he was soon in demand as a writer and composer. His work was played by Bert Ambrose and before long he was leading a professional dance band at London's Savoy Hotel which featured several leading American musicians, including some members of the California Ramblers such as Adrian Rollini and Chelsea Quealey. Although broadcast by the BBC from the Savoy, the band proved to be unpopular with hotel patrons and listeners who preferred the rather more sedate musical style of its predecessors. Later in the engagement Elizalde compromised by playing more accessible music and hiring the as-yet-unknown singer Al Bowlly, but he continued to employ American jazzmen, notably Fud Livingston and Arthur Rollini. Elizalde's policy paid off when he won the 1928 *Melody Maker* poll. Among his compositions was the unfortunately titled 'Heart Of A Nigger' (later retitled, without much improvement, 'Heart Of A Coon'), which was considered to be advanced for its time. In 1929 Elizalde folded his band after an unsuccessful tour of the UK and then led another band at a London theatre. His career changed direction in 1933 when he studied in Spain under the classical composer Manuel De Falla and thereafter he worked extensively as a symphony orchestra conductor, using his given name of Federico Elizalde.

● COMPILATIONS: *Fred Elizalde Volume 4* (1927-33)★★★★.

ELLA AND LOUIS - ELLA FITZGERALD AND LOUIS ARMSTRONG

An inspired collaboration, masterminded by producer Norman Granz. Both artists were riding high at this stage in their careers. Granz assembled a stellar quartet of Oscar Peterson (piano), Buddy Rich (drums), Herb Ellis (guitar) and Ray Brown (bass). Equally inspired was the choice of material, with the gruffness of Armstrong's voice blending like magic with Fitzgerald's stunningly silky delivery. Outstanding are Irving Berlin's 'Cheek To Cheek' and 'Isn't This A Lovely Day', and everything else works like a dream, with the golden star going to Ira and George Gershwin's 'They Can't Take That Away From Me'. Gentle and sincere, this is deserving of a place in every home.

● Tracks: *Can't We Be Friends; Isn't This A Lovely Day; Moonlight In Vermont; They Can't Take That Away From Me; Under A Blanket Of Blue; Tenderly; A Foggy Day; Stars Fell On Alabama; Cheek To Cheek; The Nearness Of You; April In Paris.*

● First released 1957

● UK peak chart position: did not chart

● USA peak chart position: 12

ELLA FITZGERALD SINGS THE COLE PORTER SONGBOOK - ELLA FITZGERALD

One of Ella Fitzgerald's great assets was also, paradoxically, one of her failings as a jazz singer. Throughout her long career her voice was that of an innocent girl. This immaturity of sound, allied as it was to consummate musical mastery, weakened her jazz performances, especially in the blues where emotional intensity is of paramount importance. As if sensing this, Norman Granz heard in Fitzgerald's voice the ideal vehicle for a selection of readings from the Great American Songbook. Her coolly detached approach to lyrics is nowhere better displayed than on this album of songs by one of the most sophisticated American songwriters.

● Tracks: *All Through The Night; Anything Goes; Miss Otis Regrets; Too Darn Hot; In The Still Of The Night; I Get A Kick Out Of You; Do I Love You; Always True To You In My Fashion; Let's Do It; Just One Of Those Things; Every Time We Say Goodbye; All Of You; Begin The Beguine; Get Out Of Turn; I Am In Love; From This Moment On; I Love Paris; You Do Something To Me; Riding High; Easy To Love; It's Alright With Me; Why Can't You Behave; What Is This Thing Called Love; You're The Top; Love For Sale; It's D'Lovely; Night And Day; Ace In The Hole; So In Love; I've Got You Under My Skin; I Concentrate On You; Don't Fence Me In.*

● First released 1956

● UK peak chart position: did not chart

● USA peak chart position: 15

ELLA FITZGERALD SINGS THE GEORGE AND IRA GERSHWIN SONGBOOK - ELLA FITZGERALD

The paradox of Ella Fitzgerald's prominence in the history of jazz singing and her lack of emotional intensity is much less apparent on this album. George Gershwin's affinity with jazz, and the corresponding delight jazz musicians take in performing his material, allow the singer to fly with the music. As for brother Ira's lyrics, they receive their due as cheerful, tender and always delightful examples of the lyricist's art. The Songbook series remains one of Ella Fitzgerald's major contributions - among many - to American popular music and this in particular is one of the best of the sizeable bunch.

● Tracks: *Including - Sam And Delilah; But Not For Me; My One And Only; Let's Call The Whole Thing Off; I've Got Beginners Luck; Lady Be Good; Nice Work If You Can Get It; Things Are Looking Up; Just Another Rhumba; How Long Has This Been Going On; S'wonderful; Man I Love; That Certain Feeling; By Strauss; Who Cares; Someone To Watch Over Me; Real American Folk Song; They*

All Laughed; Looking For A Boy; My Cousin From Milwaukee; Somebody From Somewhere; Foggy Day; Clap Yo' Hands; For You, For Me, Forever More; Stiff Upper Lip; Strike Up The Band; Soon; I've Got A Crush On You; Bidin' My Time; Aren't You Kind Of Glad We Did; Of Thee I Sing; Half It Dearie Blues; I Was Doing It Right; He Loves And She Loves; Love Is Sweeping The Country; Treat Me Rough; Love Is Here To Stay; Slap That Bass; Isn't It A Pity; Shall We Dance.

- First released 1959
- UK peak chart position: did not chart
- USA peak chart position: 111

ELLA FITZGERALD SINGS THE RODGERS AND HART SONGBOOK - ELLA FITZGERALD

Richard Rodgers' tuneful music and Lorenz Hart's wittily amusing lyrics form a very special part of American popular music. So too does Ella Fitzgerald, and their meeting - under the benign influence of Norman Granz - is a high-water mark in the story of popular singing. The singer's unworldly and ingenuous charm suits the material and transports the listener to times without care; until, that is, the occasional tartness of a Hart lyric reminds us that life is not always a song. Along with the rest of the Songbook series, this is popular vocal music at its best and sets standards never previously attained.

- Tracks: *Have You Met Miss Jones?; You Took Advantage Of Me; Ship Without A Sail; To Keep My Love Alive; Dancing On The Ceiling; The Lady Is A Tramp; With A Song In My Heart; Manhattan; Johnny One Note; I Wish I Were In Love Again; Spring Is Here; It Never Entered My Mind; This Can't Be Love; Thou Swell; My Romance; Where Or When; Little Girl Blue; Give It Back To The Indians; Ten Cents A Dance; There's A Small Hotel; I Don't Know What Time It Was; Everything I've Got; I Could Write A Book; Blue Room; My Funny Valentine; Bewitched; Mountain Greenery; Wait Till You See Her; Lover; Isn't It Romantic?; Here In My Arms; Blue Moon; My Heart Stood Still; I've Got Five Dollars.*
- First released 1957
- UK peak chart position: did not chart
- USA peak chart position: 11

ELLEFSON, ART

b. Arthur Ellefson, 17 April 1932, Moose Jaw, Canada. Ellefson began playing tenor saxophone in his mid-teens, having first played brass instruments. He played professionally in Canada but became best known after he moved to the UK in the early 50s. In London he played with a succession of leading musicians, including Carl Barriteau and Harry Hayes, then joined Vic Lewis. During the late 50s he played with modern small groups alongside musicians such as Ronnie Ross and Allan Ganley and was a member of Woody Herman's Anglo-American Herd. He then played again with Lewis and also with John Dankworth, and spent some time with the Ted Heath band. The early and mid-60s found him again with Ross and he also played with Maynard Ferguson. He then based himself for some time in Bermuda, occasionally playing in the USA and the UK. By the 90s he had settled back in his native land, playing and recording. A fluent improviser with a fine sense of bop nuances, Ellefson is a good balladeer, bringing depth and understanding to his solos. He sometimes also plays soprano saxophone.

- ALBUMS: *As If To Say* (Sackville 1992)★★★.

ELLING, KURT

b. Chicago, Illinois, USA. While still in school, Elling began singing as a chorister but at college took a serious interest in jazz. He developed a wide-ranging repertoire including ballads, standards and original material. During his formative years he also established a commanding stage presence and attracted the attention of Blue Note Records. Signed to this label, his debut album was heavily promoted and a simultaneous national tour brought Elling to a larger audience than is usually the case for new jazz singers. Elling's chief influences are instrumentalists rather than singers, notably Wayne Shorter and Keith Jarrett, although, like so many younger singers, he holds the veteran jazz singer Mark Murphy in especially high regard. The high profile enjoyed by Elling in the 90s places him in a strong position to be a major jazz artist of the twenty-first century.

- ALBUMS: *Close Your Eyes* (Blue Note 1995)★★★★, *The Messenger* (Blue Note 1997)★★★★, *This Time It's Love* (Blue Note 1998)★★★★.

ELLINGTON, DUKE

b. Edward Kennedy Ellington, 29 April 1899, Washington, DC, USA, d. 24 May 1974. Ellington began playing piano as a child but, despite some local success, took up a career as a signpainter. In his teens he continued to play piano, studied harmony, composed his first tunes and was generally active in music in Washington. Among his childhood friends were Sonny Greer, Artie Whetsol and Otto Hardwicke; from 1919 he played with them in various bands, sometimes working outside the city. In 1923 he ventured to New York to work with Elmer Snowden, and the following year formed his own band, the Washingtonians. Also in 1924, in collaboration with lyricist Joe Trent, he composed the *Chocolate Kiddies* revue. By 1927, Ellington's band had become established in east coast states and at several New York nightclubs. At the end of the year he successfully auditioned for a residency at Harlem's Cotton Club. The benefits arising from this engagement were immeasurable: regular radio broadcasts from the club ensured a widespread audience and Ellington's tours and recording sessions during the period of the residency, which ended early in 1931, built upon the band's popularity. In the early 30s the band consolidated its reputation with extended tours of the USA, appearances in films and visits to Europe, which included performances in London in 1933. Towards the end of the decade the band returned for further seasons at the Cotton Club. Throughout the 30s and early 40s the band recorded extensively and to great acclaim; they continued to tour and record with little interruption during the rest of the 40s and into the early 50s but, although the quality of the music remained high, the band became significantly less popular than had once been the case. An appearance at the 1956 Newport Jazz Festival revived their popularity, and during the rest of the 50s and the following decade Ellington toured ceaselessly, playing concerts around the world. Ellington had always been a prolific writer, composing thousands of tunes including 'It Don't Mean A Thing (If It Ain't Got That Swing)', 'Sophisticated Lady', 'In A Sentimental Mood', 'Prelude To A Kiss', 'Concert For Cootie (Do Nothin' Till You Hear From Me)', 'Cotton Tail', 'In A Mellotone', 'I Got It Bad And That Ain't Good', 'Don't Get Around Much Anymore', 'I'm Beginning To See The Light' and 'Satin Doll'. In later years he also composed film scores, among them *The Asphalt Jungle* (1950), *Anatomy Of A Murder* (1959), *Paris Blues* (1960) and *Assault On A Queen* (1966). More importantly, he began to concentrate upon extended works, composing several suites and a series of sacred music concerts, the latter mostly performed in churches and cathedrals. Over the years the personnel of Ellington's orchestra proved remarkably stable, several of his sidemen remaining with him for decades. The ceaseless touring continued into the early 70s, with Ellington making few concessions to the advancing years. After his death in 1974 the orchestra continued for a time under the direction of his son, Mercer Ellington, but despite the continuing presence of a handful of survivors, such as Harry Carney, who had been in the band virtually without a break for 47 years, the spirit and guiding light was gone. From this moment, Ellington lived on through an immense recorded legacy and in the memories of musicians and an army of fans.

Ellington was born into relatively comfortable circumstances. His father had been a butler, even working for some time at the White House. The family was deeply religious and musical, and Ellington himself was very close to his parents. He reported that he was 'pampered and spoiled rotten', and of his parents he wrote: 'My mother was beautiful but my father was only handsome.' His mother was a piano player; under her influence, Ellington had music lessons from a teacher called Mrs. Clinkscales. In later life, he whimsically commented that one of the first things she taught him was never to share the stage with Oscar Peterson. Perhaps more influential than Mrs. Clinkscales were the piano players he heard in the pool-rooms, where, like any self-respecting, under-age, sharp-suited adolescent-about-town, he found his supplementary education among a diversity of gamblers, lawyers, pickpockets, doctors and hustlers. 'At heart,' he said, 'they were all great artists.' He paid special tribute to Oliver 'Doc' Perry, a pianist who gave him lessons of a less formal but more practical nature than those of Mrs. Clinkscales - 'reading the leads and recognizing the chords'. Ellington became a professional musician in his teens. One of his first engagements was playing 'mood' music for a travelling magician and fortune teller, improvising to suit the moment, whether serious or mystical. In 1914 he wrote his first compositions: 'Soda Fountain Rag' and 'What You Gonna Do When The Bed Breaks Down?'. By the age of 18 he was leading bands in the Washington area, having learned that the bandleader, as 'Mr. Fixit', generally earned more money than the other members of the band. Thus, by the age of 20, he was pianist, composer and bandleader: the essential Duke Ellington was formed, and would later blossom into one of the most influential musicians in jazz, although with characteristic perversity, he insisted that he wrote folk music, not jazz.

By the time of the band's debut at the Cotton Club, in addition to Greer and Hardwicke, Ellington had recruited key players such as Bubber Miley, his first great 'growling' trumpet player; the trombonist Joe 'Tricky Sam' Nanton; the bassist Wellman Braud and Carney, whose baritone saxophone formed the rich and sturdy foundation of the band's reed section for its entire history. Perhaps just as crucial was Ellington's meeting with Irving Mills, who became his manager. For a black musician to survive, let alone prosper, in the America of the 20s and 30s, a tough white manager was an essential safeguard. In 1927 came the first classic recordings of 'Black And Tan Fantasy' and 'Creole Love Call', the latter with the legendary vocal line by Adelaide Hall. In these, and in up-tempo numbers such as 'Hot And Bothered', the Ellington method was fully formed. The conventional way to praise a big band was to say that they played like one man. The quality of the Ellington bands was that they always played like a bunch of highly talented and wildly disparate individuals, recalling the 'great artists' of the pool-room. The Cotton Club provided an ideal workshop and laboratory for Ellington. Situated in Harlem, its performers were exclusively black, its clientele exclusively white and in pursuit of dusky exotic pleasures. Ellington, who enjoyed being a showman, gave the audience what it wanted: music for showgirls and boys to dance to, in every tempo from the slow and sultry to the hot and hectic, coloured with so-called 'jungle sounds'. Although this was a racial slur, Ellington had the skill and wit to transcend it, creating music that met the specification but disarmingly turned it inside-out. The music winked at the audience. Moving into the 30s, the band's repertoire was enriched by pieces such as 'Rocking' In Rhythm', 'Old Man Blues', 'The Mooche' and, of course, 'Mood Indigo'. Its personnel now included Juan Tizol on trombone, Cootie Williams, de facto successor to Miley on trumpet, and the sublime Johnny Hodges on alto saxophone, whose lyricism, tempered with melancholy, became a crucial element in the Ellington palette. Hodges became the most striking example of the truism 'once an Ellingtonian, always an Ellingtonian'. Like Williams and Tizol, he would leave the band to become a leader in his own right or briefly a sideman in another band, only to return. The 30s saw the first attempts at compositions longer than the conventional three minutes (the length of a gramophone record), starting with 'Creole Rhapsody' in 1931. The period also saw, to oversimplify the situation, a move into respectability. Critics and musicians from the serious side of the tracks had begun to take notice. People as diverse as Constant

Lambert, Percy Grainger, Leopold Stokowski and Igor Stravinsky recognized the extraordinary and unique gifts of Ellington. Phrases such as 'America's greatest living composer' crept into print. Ellington continued to refer to himself, gracefully and demurely, as 'our piano player'. To be sure, his composing methods, from all accounts, were radically different from those of other title contenders. He would scribble a few notes on the back of an envelope, or memorize them, and develop the piece in rehearsal. The initial themes were often created by musicians in the band - hence the frequent shared composer credits: 'The Blues I Love To Sing' with Miley, 'Caravan' with Tizol, and 'Jeep's Blues' with Hodges. 'Bluebird Of Delhi', from the 1966 'Far East Suite', was based on a phrase sung by a bird outside Billy Strayhorn's room. Strayhorn joined the band in 1939, as arranger, composer, occasional piano player, friend and musical alter ego. A small, quiet and gentle man, he became a vital element in the Ellington success story. His arrival coincided with that of the tenor saxophone player Ben Webster, and the brilliant young bass player Jimmy Blanton, who died in 1943, aged 23. By common consent, the Webster/Blanton band produced some of the finest music in the Ellington canon, exemplified by 'Jack The Bear', with Blanton's innovative bass solo, and 'Just A-Settin' And A-Rockin', where Webster demonstrates that the quality of jazz playing lies in discretion and timing rather than vast numbers of notes to the square inch.

Duke Ellington was elegantly dismissive of analysis; too much talk, he said, stinks up the place. However, he was more than capable of sensitive examination of his own music. Of the haunting and plaintive 'Mood Indigo', he said: 'Just a story about a little girl and a little boy. They are about eight and the girl loves the boy. They never speak of it, of course, but she just likes the way he wears his hat. Every day he comes to her house at a certain time and she sits in her window and waits. Then one day he doesn't come. "Mood Indigo" just tells how she feels.' The story, and the tune it describes, are characteristically Ellingtonian: they bear the hallmark of true sophistication, which is audacious simplicity. His music is never cluttered, and travels lightly and politely.

Ellington's output as a composer was immense. The late Derek Jewell, in his indispensable biography of the man, estimated that he wrote at least 2000 pieces, but, because of his cavalier way with pieces of paper, it may have been as many as 5000. Among them were many tunes that have become popular standards - 'Sophisticated Lady', 'In A Sentimental Mood', 'Don't Get Around Much Anymore' and 'I'm Beginning To See The Light' are just a selected handful. Their significance, aside from the musical, was that their royalty income effectively subsidized the band, particularly during the post-war period when the big bands virtually disappeared under successive onslaughts from inflation, the growth of television, the decline of the dancehalls and, most significantly, the arrival of rock 'n' roll. Even Ellington was not immune to these pressures and in the early 50s, looking handsome suddenly became hard work. The turning-point came at the Newport Jazz Festival on 7 July 1956, when morale was low. The previous year had seen embarrassing attempts at cashing in on commercial trends with recordings of 'Twelfth Street Rag Mambo' and 'Bunny Hop Mambo', plus a summer season at an aquashow, with a string section and two harpists. The first set at Newport was equally embarrassing. Ellington arrived onstage to find four of his musicians missing. The band played a few numbers, then departed. They returned around midnight, at full strength, to play the 'Newport Jazz Festival Suite', composed with Strayhorn for the occasion. Then Ellington, possibly still rankled by the earlier behaviour of the band, called 'Diminuendo And Crescendo In Blue', a piece written almost 20 years earlier and by no means a regular item on their usual concert programme. In two sections, and linked by a bridge passage from, on this occasion, the tenor saxophone player Paul Gonsalves, the piece was a revelation. Gonsalves blew 27 choruses, the crowd went wild, the band played four encores, and the news travelled around the world on the jazz grapevine; it was also reported in detail in *Time* magazine, with a picture of the piano player on the cover. After Newport and until his death, Ellington's life and career became a triumphal and global procession, garlanded with awards, honorary degrees, close encounters with world leaders and, more importantly, further major compositions. 'Such Sweet Thunder', his Shakespearian suite written with Strayhorn, contains gems such as 'Lady Mac' - 'Though she was a lady of noble birth, we suspect there was a little ragtime in her soul' - and 'Madness In Great Ones', dedicated to Hamlet with the laconic remark 'in those days crazy didn't mean the same thing it means now'. Further collaborations with Strayhorn included an enchanting reworking of Tchaikovsky's 'Nutcracker Suite' and 'The Far East Suite' - still adorned with dazzling contributions from various of the now-elder statesmen in the band: Hodges, Gonsalves and Carney in the reeds, Lawrence Brown, Britt Woodman and Tizol among the trombones, and Ray Nance and Cat Anderson in the trumpet section. Astonishingly, the band that recorded the *70th Birthday Concert* in England in 1969 included Carney, Hodges and Williams 40 years after they first joined Ellington, and on the record they still sounded like a group of kids having a good night on the town. The freshness and energy of the band as it tackled material played hundreds of times before, was extraordinary.

There was another side to the story. Ellington had always been a religious man, and in his later years he turned increasingly to the writing and performance of sacred music. The origins of this can be traced back to 'Come Sunday', from the 1945 suite 'Black, Brown And Beige', and beyond that to 'Reminiscing In Tempo', written 10 years earlier, following the death of his mother, of which he said: 'My mother's death was the greatest shock. I didn't do anything but brood. The music is representative of all that. It begins with pleasant thoughts.

Then something awful gets you down. Then you snap out of it and it ends affirmatively.' From a man who was dismissive of analysis, this represented a very shrewd assessment not only of the piece in question, but of his entire output. Working within the framework of the conventional big band line-up - five reeds, four trumpets, three trombones, bass, drums and a remarkable piano player, he produced music of extraordinary diversity. His themes were startling in their simplicity, as if he had picked them off trees, and in a way, he did. The tonal qualities of the band - the unique Ellington sound - were based on a celebration of its individuals. The music might be lyrical or triumphant, elegiac or celebratory and the blues were never far away, yet it always ended affirmatively. To borrow a phrase from Philip Larkin, writing about Sidney Bechet, Duke Ellington's life and music added up to A Resounding Yes. He was a gigantic influence and one of the most important figures in the history of popular music.

● ALBUMS: *Carnegie Hall Concert* (1943)★★★★, *The Hollywood Bowl Concert Volumes 1 & 2* (1947)★★★★, *Mood Ellington* 10-inch album (Columbia 1949)★★★★, *Liberian Suite* 10-inch album (Columbia 1949)★★★, *Ellingtonia, Volume 1* 10-inch album (Brunswick 1950)★★★★, *Ellingtonia, Volume 2* 10-inch album (Brunswick 1950)★★★★, *Masterpieces By Ellington* (Columbia 1951)★★★, *Ellington Uptown* (Columbia 1951)★★★, *Duke Ellington Volumes 1-3* 10-inch albums (Jazz Panorama 1951)★★★★, *Duke Ellington* (RCA-Victor 1951)★★★★, *The Duke Is On The Air - From The Blue Note* (1952)★★★★, *This Is Duke Ellington And His Orchestra* (RCA-Victor 1952)★★★★, *Duke Ellington Plays the Blues* (RCA-Victor 1953)★★★★, *Premiered By Ellington* 10-inch album (Capitol 1953)★★★, *Ellington Plays Ellington* 10-inch album (Capitol 1953)★★★★, *Early Ellington* (Brunswick 1954)★★★, *The Music Of Duke Ellington* (Columbia 1954)★★★, *Duke Ellington Plays* 10-inch album (Allegro 1954)★★★, *Ellington '55* (Capitol 1954)★★★, *The Duke Plays Ellington* (Capitol 1954)★★★★, *Seattle Concert* (RCA-Victor 1954)★★★, *Dukes Mixture* 10-inch album (Columbia 1955)★★★, *Dance To The Duke* (Capitol 1955)★★★, *Duke And His Men* (RCA-Victor 1955)★★★, *Blue Light* (Columbia 1955)★★★★, *Here's The Duke* 10-inch album (Columbia 1956)★★★★, *Historically Speaking, The Duke* (Bethlehem 1956)★★★, *Duke Ellington Presents* (Bethlehem 1956)★★★, *Birth Of Big Band Jazz* (Riverside 1956)★★★★, *Al Hibbler With the Duke* 10-inch album (Columbia 1956)★★★, with Johnny Hodges *Ellington At Newport '56* (Columbia 1956)★★★★★, *Ellington Showcase* (Capitol 1956)★★★, *A Drum Is A Woman* (Columbia 1957)★★★, *Such Sweet Thunder* (Columbia 1957)★★★, *In A Mellotone* (RCA-Victor 1957)★★★★, *Ellington Indigos* (Columbia 1958)★★★★★, *Duke Ellington At His Very Best* (RCA-Victor 1958)★★★, *Newport 1958* (Columbia 1958)★★★★★, *Brown Black And Beige* (Columbia 1958)★★★★, *The Cosmic Scene* (Columbia 1958)★★★, *Duke Ellington At The Bal Masque* (Columbia 1959)★★★, *Duke Ellington Jazz Party* (Columbia 1959)★★★, with Hodges *Back To Back: Duke Ellington And Johnny Hodges Play The Blues* (Verve 1959)★★★★, with Hodges *Side By Side* (Verve 1959)★★★, *Festival Session* (Columbia 1959)★★★, *Ellington Moods* (SeSac 1959)★★★, *Anatomy Of A Murder* (1959), *The Ellington Suites: The Queen's Suite* (1959)★★★, *Swinging Suites By Edward E. And Edward G. (Suite Thursday/Peer Gynt)* (Columbia 1960)★★★, with Hodges *The Nutcracker Suite* (Columbia 1960)★★★, *Piano In The Background* (Columbia 1960)★★★, *Blues In Orbit* (Columbia 1960)★★★★, *Paris Blues* (1961)★★★, *The Indispensible Duke Ellington* (RCA-Victor 1961)★★★, with Count Basie *Ellington/Basie - First Time! The Count Meets The Duke* (Columbia 1962)★★★, *Afro Bossa* (Reprise 1962)★★★, with Charles Mingus, Max Roach *Money Jungle* (United Artists 1962)★★★★, *All American* (Columbia 1962)★★★, *Duke Ellington And His Orchestra Featuring Paul Gonsalves* (1962)★★★, *Midnight In Paris* (Columbia 1962)★★★, with John Coltrane *Duke Ellington And John Coltrane* (MCA/Impulse! 1962)★★★★, with Coleman Hawkins *Duke Ellington Meets Coleman Hawkins* (MCA/Impulse! 1963)★★★★, *Symphonic Ellington* (1963)★★★, *My People* (1963)★★★, *Piano In The Foreground* (Columbia 1963)★★★, with Svend Asmussen *Jazz Violin Session* (1963)★★★★, with Billy Strayhorn *Piano Duets: Great Times!* (Riverside 1963)★★★, *Duke Ellington's Concert Of Sacred Music* (RCA-Victor 1964)★★★, *The Symphonic Ellington* (Reprise 1964)★★★, *Hit's Of The 60s* (Reprise 1964)★★, *Daybreak Express* (RCA-Victor 1964)★★★, *Jumpin' Pumpkins* (RCA-Victor 1965)★★, *Johnny Come Lately* (RCA-Victor 1965)★★, *Mary Poppins* (Reprise 1965)★, *Pretty Woman* (RCA-Victor 1965)★★, *Flaming Youth* (RCA-Victor 1965)★★, *Ellington '66* (Reprise 1965)★★★, *Will Big Bands Ever Come Back?* (Reprise 1965)★★★, *Concert In The Virgin Islands* (Reprise 1965)★★★, with Boston Pops Orchestra *The Duke At Tanglewood* (RCA-Victor 1966)★★★, with Ella Fitzgerald *Ella At Duke's Place* (Verve 1966)★★★★, with Fitzgerald *The Stockholm Concert* (1966)★★★, with Fitzgerald *Ella And Duke At The Côte D'Azure* (Verve 1966)★★★, *The Popular Duke Ellington* (RCA-Victor 1966)★★★, *Concert Of Sacred Music* (RCA-Victor 1966)★★★, with Hodges *Far East Suite* (RCA-Victor 1967)★★★★, *Soul Call* (Verve 1967)★★★, *And His Mother Called Him Bill* (RCA-Victor 1968)★★★★, with Frank Sinatra *Francis A. And Edward K.* (Reprise 1968)★★★, *Second Sacred Concert* (Prestige 1968)★★★, *70th Birthday Concert* (1969)★★★, *The Latin American Suite* (Fantasy 1969)★★★, *The New Orleans Suite* (Atlantic 1970)★★★, *Afro-Eurasian Eclipse* (Fantasy 1971)★★★, with Ray Brown *This One's For Blanton* (Pablo 1972)★★★, *Third Sacred Concert* (Prestige 1973)★★★, *Eastbourne Performance* (RCA 1973)★★, *Yale Concert* (Fantasy 1973)★★★, with Teresa Brewer *It Don't Mean A Thing . . .* (Columbia 1973)★★★★, *The Duke's Big 4* (Pablo 1974)★★★★, *The Duke Ellington Carnegie Hall Concerts-January, 1943* (Prestige 1977)★★★★, *The Duke Ellington Carnegie Hall Concerts-December, 1944* (Prestige 1977)★★★★, *The Duke Ellington Carnegie Hall Concerts-January, 1946* (Prestige 1977)★★★★, *The Duke Ellington Carnegie Hall Concerts-December, 1947* (Prestige 1977)★★★★, *The Unknown Session* 1960 recording (Columbia 1979)★★★, *In Concert At The Pleyel Paris* 1958 recording (Magic 1990)★★★, *The Far East Suite: Special Mix* (Bluebird 1995)★★★★, *Berlin '65/Paris '67* (Pablo 1998)★★★.

● COMPILATIONS: *Ellington's Greatest* (RCA-Victor 1954)★★★★, *Duke Ellington Volume 1 - In The Beginning* (Decca 1958)★★★★, *Duke Ellington Volume 2 - Hot In Harlem* (Decca 1959)★★★★, *Duke Ellington Volume 3 - Rockin' In Rhythm* (Decca 1959)★★★★, *The Best Of Duke Ellington* (Capitol 1961)★★★★, *The Ellington Era Volume 1* 3-LP box set (Columbia

1963)★★★★, *The Ellington Era Volume 2* 3-LP box set (Columbia 1964)★★★★, *Duke Ellington's Greatest Hits* (Reprise 1966)★★★★, *Duke Ellington - The Pianist* 1966-74 recordings (Fantasy 1974)★★★★, *The Ellington Suites* (Pablo 1976)★★★★, *The Intimate Ellington* (Pablo 1977)★★★, *The All-Star Road Band, Volume 1* (Columbia 1983)★★★★, *The All-Star Road Band, Volume 2* (Columbia 1983)★★★★, *The Indispensable Duke Ellington Volumes 1-12* (RCA 1983-87)★★★, *The Intimacy Of The Blues* 1970 recordings (Fantasy 1986)★★★★, *The Blanton-Webster Band* (RCA Bluebird 1987)★★★★★, *Black, Brown And Beige* (RCA Bluebird 1988)★★★★, *Four Symphonic Works* (Music Master 1989)★★★★, *The Best Of Duke Ellington* (Columbia 1989)★★★, *Braggin' In Brass - The Immortal 1938 Year* (Portrait 1989)★★★★, *The Brunswick Era, Volume 1* (MCA 1990)★★★★, with Blanton and others *Solos, Duets And Trios* 1932-67 recordings (RCA Bluebird 1990)★★★★, *The OKeh Ellington* (Columbia 1991)★★★★, *Small Groups, Volume 1* (Columbia/Legacy 1991)★★★★, *The Essence Of Duke Ellington* (Columbia/Legacy 1991)★★★★★, *The Complete Capitol Recordings Of Duke Ellington* 5-CD box set (Mosaic 1996)★★★★★, *Jazz Profile* (Blue Note 1997)★★★★, *1945, Vol. 2* (Classics 1998)★★★.

● VIDEOS: *Duke Ellington* (Virgin Vision 1992), *On The Road With Duke Ellington* (Direct Cinema 1995).

● FURTHER READING: *Duke Ellington: Young Music Master*, Martha E. Schaaf. *Sweet Man, The Real Duke Ellington*, Don R. George. *Duke Ellington*, Ron Franki. *Duke Ellington*, Barry Ulanov. *The World Of Duke Ellington*, Stanley Dance. *Music Is My Mistress*, Duke Ellington. *Celebrating The Duke*, Ralph J. Gleason. *Duke: A Portrait Of Duke Ellington*, Derek Jewell. *Duke Ellington In Person*, Mercer Ellington. *Duke Ellington: His Life And Music*, Peter Gammond. *Duke Ellington: Life And Times Of A Restless Genius Of Jazz*, James Lincoln Collier. *Duke Ellington: The Early Years*, Michael Tucker. *Duke Ellington: Jazz Composer*, Ken Rattenbury. *The Duke Ellington Reader*, Mark Tucker. *Beyond Category: The Life And Genius Of Duke Ellington*, John Edward Hasse. *The Duke Ellington Primer*, Dempsey J. Travis.

ELLINGTON INDIGOS - DUKE ELLINGTON

An extraordinary man, with an equally extraordinary small group. Among the other masterful musicians are Harry Carney, Jimmy Hamilton, Johnny Hodges, Paul Gonsalves, Shorty Baker, Clark Terry and Ray Nance. This was probably his finest band since the Jimmy Blanton-Ben Webster days. They play with relaxed beauty on numbers that many of them knew how to play in their sleep. The Gonsalves solo on 'Where Or When' is beautiful, and the balance the band strike on 'Mood Indigo' is exemplary. The reissued CD comes with two additional tracks, both superb; Cole Porter's 'Night And Day' and Oscar Hammerstein and Jerome Kern's 'All The Things You Are'.

● Tracks: *Solitude; Where Or When; Mood Indigo; Night And Day; Prelude To A Kiss; All The Things You Are; Willow Weep For Me; Tenderly; Dancing In The Dark; Autumn Leaves; The Sky Fell Down.*

● First released 1958

● UK peak chart position: did not chart

● USA peak chart position: did not chart

ELLINGTON, MERCER

b. 11 March 1919, Washington, D.C., USA, d. 8 February 1996, Copenhagen, Denmark. Any son following the same career as a famous father is bound to encounter problems of recognition. For Mercer Ellington the problem was magnified through the fact that his father was Duke Ellington, who was not only one of the two or three greatest figures in jazz history but was also an acknowledged master of twentieth-century music. For all the disadvantages of having such a parent, Mercer was determined to pursue a career in music. He studied formally in Washington and New York in the 20s and formed his own band playing trumpet in the late 30s. He sometimes used musicians more usually associated with his father, among them Cat Anderson and Billy Strayhorn, but also worked with men who only later joined Duke. In addition, he used musicians who were engaged in the emerging bebop movement, including Dizzy Gillespie and Charles Mingus. In the early 40s Ellington was manager of the Cootie Williams band and also played briefly in Duke's band. He composed several tunes taken up by his father, of which the best known are 'Things Ain't What They Used To Be', 'Jumpin' Punkins' and 'Blue Serge'. Ellington spent the second half of the 50s with his father's band, mostly in an administrative capacity. He returned to the band in the mid-60s, remaining until Duke's death in 1974. Thereafter, he took over as leader of the Ellington orchestra and conducted the pit band for the Broadway show *Sophisticated Ladies* in the early 80s. His autobiography (written in collaboration with Stanley Dance) was published in 1978. Ellington continued to lead an orchestra into the 90s and, while still rooted in Duke's music, it developed a creditable musical personality of its own.

● ALBUMS: *Steppin' Into Swing Society* (Coral 1958)★★★, *Colors In Rhythm* (Coral 1959)★★★, *Continuum* (1975)★★★, *Remembering Duke's World* (1977)★★★★, *Take The Holiday Train* (1980)★★★, *Duke Ellington's Sophisticated Ladies* (1981)★★★, *Digital Duke* (GRP 1987)★★★★, *Music Is My Mistress* (Limelight 1989)★★★.

ELLINGTON, RAY

b. 1915, London, England, d. 28 February 1985. Ellington began playing drums as a teenager and by 1937 was proficient enough to replace Joe Daniels in Harry Roy's popular band. He remained with Roy for almost five years, although his personal musical taste tended more towards the new jazz styles, and soon after the end of World War II he was playing bop in London clubs. He led his own quartet at this time and made a number of records, and sometimes accompanied visiting American jazzmen. He began to incorporate comedy and novelty material into his repertoire but the group's musical base was always strongly bop-influenced. Throughout the 50s the quartet was regularly featured on *The Goon Show* on BBC Radio, usually with Ellington singing, and he also took small acting roles in the programme. By the 60s and with the passing of *The*

Goon Show, Ellington was much less in demand, but he continued playing until shortly before his death in February 1985. His son, Lance Ellington, played trombone with the National Youth Jazz Orchestra and also sang as a member of the pop duo Coffee And Cream.

● ALBUMS: *Goon Show Hits* (BBC 1958)★★★★, *You're The Talk Of The Town* (Gold Star 1975)★★.

ELLIOT, RICHARD

b. *c*.1960. It was perhaps inevitable, for a musician growing up in the 60s and early 70s, that Elliot's early taste would range through Motown and rock. However, he was also indelibly impressed by R&B. As a tenor saxophonist he found much that appealed to him in this form but he was also aware of jazz, in particular through the playing of Dexter Gordon. It was a visit to a concert by Gordon that prompted Elliot onto the jazz path, although in his case it proved to be a path with many turnings. As he honed his skills Elliot found work in the Los Angeles studios, backing artists such as Natalie Cole, Pointer Sisters and Melissa Manchester. He was a member of the Tower Of Power horns from 1982 until 1987. He began recording under his own name in 1986, and in succeeding years produced albums that displayed growing confidence. They were also increasingly successful. Fortuitously, Elliot had found that his favourite musical forms, with their jazz-inflections, R&B-base, and rock-tinges, were also popular with the record-buying public. His late 80s sessions for Manhattan Records were reissued in the early 90s by his new label, Blue Note Records, and proved to be just as popular as before. By the late 90s, Elliot was sufficiently well-established to produce *Jumpin' Off* on which he played mostly within the R&B style, a deliberate reversion to a form that had been at the height of its commercial acceptability almost two decades before Elliot was born. By this time, however, Elliot's eclecticism was stretching still further and, like many musicians of his generation, he was developing a serious interest in salsa. In addition to playing tenor, on which he produces a rich and expressive sound, Elliot is also very effective on soprano saxophone.

● ALBUMS: *Trolltown* late 80s recordings (EMD Blue Note 1991)★★, *Initial Approach* late 80s recordings (EMD Blue Note 1991)★★★★, *Take To The Skies* late 80s recordings (EMD Blue Note 1991)★★★, *What's Inside* late 80s recordings (EMD Blue Note 1991)★★, *On The Town* late 80s recordings (EMD Blue Note 1991)★★★, *Soul Embrace* late 80s recordings (EMD Blue Note 1993)★★★★, *After Dark* (Blue Note 1994)★★★, *Power Of Suggestion* (Blue Note 1996)★★★, *City Speak* (Blue Note 1996)★★★, *Jumpin' Off* (Blue Note 1998)★★★.

ELLIS, DON

b. 25 July 1934, Los Angeles, California, USA, d. 17 December 1978. Appreciation of Ellis's work has increased since his death and he is now regarded by many as an important figure in jazz. From childhood he was fascinated with brass instruments and received a trumpet at the age of two. At junior high school he had his own quartet and at Boston university he was a member of the band. His first professional work was as a member of Ray McKinley's Glenn Miller Orchestra. After his national service, Ellis formed a small group, playing coffee-houses in New York's Greenwich Village. By the late 50s he was playing with many name bands including those of Woody Herman, Lionel Hampton, Charles Mingus and Maynard Ferguson. Ellis also worked in small groups, enjoying the greater freedom of expression this allowed. In 1961/2 he was a member of George Russell's sextet. In Atlantic City, he took up a teaching fellowship and it was there that he developed and explored his interest in the complexities of Indian rhythm patterns. Ellis made a triumphant appearance at the 1966 Monterey Jazz festival with his 23-piece band. His completely original themes were scored using unbelievably complex notation. Customarily, most big band music was played at four beats to the bar but Ellis confidently and successfully experimented with 5-beat bars, then 9-, 11-, 14-, 17-, 19- and even 27-beat bars. Mixing metres created difficulties for his rhythm sections so he taught himself to play drums in order that he might properly instruct his drummers. He also experimented with brass instruments, introducing the four-valve flügelhorn and superbone. During the late 60s the Don Ellis Orchestra was promoted as part of the great CBS progressive music campaign and he found himself performing at rock festivals and concerts. His music found favour with the Woodstock generation, who could also recognize him as an exciting pioneer. His CBS albums were all successful, his work being produced by both John Hammond and Al Kooper. Dubbed the 'Father of the Time Revolution' in jazz, Ellis's music was much more than complex. It was also undeniably joyous. Tunes like the 7/4 romp 'Pussy Wiggle Stomp', 'Barnum's Revenge' (a reworking of 'Bill Bailey') and 'Scratt And Fluggs' (a passing nod to country music's Lester Flatt and Earl Scruggs), are played with zesty enthusiasm, extraordinary skill and enormous good humour. Ellis's trumpet playing was remarkable, combining dazzling technique with a hot jazz feeling that reflected his admiration for Henry 'Red' Allen. He also experimented with electronic devices, such as a Ring Modulator, which transformed his trumpet into a generator of atavistic moans and shouts. Conversely, as he showed on *Haiku*, he could play with delicate charm and often deeply moving emotion. Ellis scored the music for 10 films, including *The French Connection* (1971), for which he won a Grammy. It is, however, his brilliantly ambitious and innovative 'eastern' music, notably 'Indian Lady' and 'Turkish Bath' that makes his work as important as John Coltrane's flirtation with the music of the mystic east. He is indubitably an outstanding figure destined for future reappraisal. Ellis stated 'I am not concerned whether my music is jazz, third stream, classical or anything else, or whether it is even called music. Let it be judged as Don Ellis noise'.

● ALBUMS: *How Time Passes* (Candid 1960)★★, *New Ideas* (New Jazz 1961)★★★★, *Essence* (Pacific Jazz 1962)★★★, *Jazz Jamboree No 1* (1962)★★★, *Live At Monterey* (Pacific Jazz 1966)★★★★, *Live In 3/2/3/4 Time* (Pacific Jazz 1967)★★★,

Electric Bath (Columbia 1968)★★★★, *Shock Treatment* (Columbia 1968)★★★★, *Autumn* (Columbia 1969)★★★★, *The New Don Ellis Band Goes Underground* (Columbia 1969)★★, *Don Ellis At Fillmore* (Columbia 1970)★★★, *Tears Of Joy* (1971)★★★, *Connection* (1972)★★★, *Soaring* (1973)★★★, *Haiku* (1974)★★★★, *Star Wars* (1977)★★★, *Live At Montreux* (Atlantic 1978)★★★, *Out Of Nowhere* 1961 recordings (Candid 1989)★★★.

ELLIS, HERB

b. 4 August 1921, Farmersville, Texas, USA. In 1941 Ellis attended North Texas State College, where his fellow students included Jimmy Giuffre. After graduation, he played guitar in a number of big bands, including the Casa Loma Orchestra and the Jimmy Dorsey outfit. He was next with Soft Winds, a trio formed from the Dorsey rhythm section with John Frigo and Lou Carter, and in 1953 took Barney Kessel's place in the Oscar Peterson trio, where he remained for five years alongside Ray Brown. After leaving Peterson he accompanied Ella Fitzgerald for four years and also worked with Julie London, then spent a decade in the Los Angeles film and television studios. In the early 70s he began a succession of marvellous associations with other guitarists, including Joe Pass, Charlie Byrd and Kessel (with the latter two as the Great Guitars). In his playing, Ellis constantly reveals a deep affinity for the blues and reflects a thorough awareness of the work of Charlie Christian. As a section player he brings an earthy quality few of his peers can match, and his time with Peterson was of such a high standard that thereafter the pianist rarely used another guitarist. As a soloist his command is outstanding and the bluesy muscularity of his playing is a constant source of delight.

● ALBUMS: *Ellis In Wonderland* (Norgran 1956)★★★, *Nothing But The Blues* (Verve 1958)★★★, with Jimmy Guiffre *Herb Ellis Meets Jimmy Giuffre* (Verve1959)★★★★, *Thank You, Charlie Christian* (Verve 1960)★★★, *Softly ... But With That Feeling* (Verve 1962)★★★, *The Midnight Roll* (Epic 1962)★★, with Laurindo Almeida, Johnny Gray *Three Guitars In Bossa Nova Time* (Epic 1963)★★★, with Stuff Smith *Herb Ellis & 'Stuff' Smith Together* (Epic 1963)★★★, with Charlie Byrd *Herb Ellis & Charlie Byrd* (1963)★★★★, *Herb Ellis Guitar* (Columbia 1965)★★★, *Man With The Guitar* (Dot 1965)★★★, *Hello, Herbie* (1969)★★★, with Joe Pass *Jazz/Concord* (Concord Jazz 1973)★★★★, with Pass *Seven Come Eleven* (Concord Jazz 1973)★★★★, with Ray Brown *Soft Shoe* (Concord Jazz 1974)★★★, with Pass *Two For The Road* (Pablo 1974)★★★, *After You've Gone* (1974)★★★, as Great Guitars *Great Guitars* (Concord Jazz 1974)★★★, with Brown *Hot Tracks* (Concord Jazz 1975)★★★, with Freddie Green *Rhythm Willie* (Concord Jazz 1975)★★★, with Ross Tompkins *A Pair To Draw To* (Concord Jazz 1976)★★★★, *Windflower* (Concord Jazz 1977)★★★, *Soft And Mellow* (Concord Jazz 1978)★★, as Great Guitars *Great Guitars: Straight Tracks* (Concord Jazz 1978)★★★, *Herb Ellis At Montreux* (Concord Jazz 1979)★★★, as Great Guitars *Great Guitars At The Winery* (Concord Jazz 1980)★★★, *Herb Mix* (Concord Jazz 1981)★★★, as Great Guitars *Great Guitars At Charlie's, Georgetown* (Concord Jazz 1982)★★★★, *Sweet And Lovely* (1983)★★★, *When You're Smiling* (1983)★★★, with Red Mitchell *Doggin' Around* (Concord Jazz 1988)★★★, *Roll Call* (Justice 1992)★★, *After You've Gone* (Concord Jazz 1992)★★★, *Down-home* (Justice 1996)★★, as Great Guitars *The Return Of The Great Guitars* (Concord Jazz 1996)★★★, *An Evening With Herb Ellis* (Jazz Focus 1998)★★★.

ELLIS, SEGER

b. 4 July 1904, Houston, Texas, USA, d. 29 September 1995. A popular radio and recording entertainer of the early 30s as a pianist/vocalist, Ellis later made a laudable but doomed attempt to ring a few changes on the regimented sound of many swing era big bands. His Choirs Of Brass orchestra had the unusual instrumentation of eight brass, one clarinet, plus rhythm. Using ingenious arrangements by Stan Wrightsman and Spud Murphy and with Nate Kazebier and Irving Fazola among his personnel, he achieved a distinctive and attractive sound. The band's vocals were handled by himself and his wife, Irene Taylor, a much-underrated singer. Interesting though this approach was, it was not what the public wanted and the band folded in 1937, after which Ellis worked mostly with small groups and rarely strayed far from his home state.

● COMPILATIONS: *Choirs Of Brass* (1937)★★.

ELMAN, ZIGGY

b. Harry Finkelman, 26 May 1914, Philadelphia, Pennsylvania, USA, d. 26 June 1968. As a child Elman learned to play various brass and reed instruments, and his first professional engagement was on trombone, although his main instrument later became the trumpet. In 1936 he joined Benny Goodman and formed part of one of the best three-man trumpet sections of the swing era. With Harry James and Chris Griffin, Elman shared lead and solo duties and his dynamic, biting playing was a great asset to the band. After James left to lead his own band, Elman comfortably coped with his role as featured soloist, playing showstoppers such as 'Who'll Buy My Bublitchki' and 'And The Angels Sing', which he composed himself. After leaving Goodman, Elman worked with other big bands, including those of Joe Venuti and Tommy Dorsey. In the late 40s, as name big bands were folding all around him, Elman tried leading his own big band and met with a measure of success especially with a re-recording of 'And The Angels Sing'. In the early 50s he worked in film studios in Los Angeles but ill-health and personal problems kept him from achieving much success. In 1961 his financial situation was revealed during an alimony court hearing at which he agreed that many people thought him to be the world's greatest trumpet player, adding 'But I still can't get much work.' Six of his seven bank accounts had sums varying between $1.19 and $11.00 in them, while the seventh was overdrawn.

● ALBUMS: *One Night Stand At The Hollywood Palladium* (1947)★★★, with Jess Stacy *Tribute To Benny Goodman* (1954)★★★.

● COMPILATIONS: *And The Angels Sing* (1938-39)★★★, *Zaggin' With Zig* (1947)★★★.

Elsdon, Alan

b. 15 October 1934, London, England. Elsdon studied trumpet before turning to jazz and working with a succession of British traditional bands in the 50s. His reputation established, in the early 60s he decided to form his own band, but the musical times were changing and he failed to gain the same level of success achieved by many other traditional bands. Nevertheless, Elsdon succeeded in keeping his band afloat, working regularly at clubs and pubs and occasionally at more prestigious venues. He toured the UK with visiting American jazz and blues artists during the 60s and 70s. In the 80s, with his band still around, he also began playing with the Midnite Follies Orchestra and with other groups led by Keith Nichols. Despite his long association with the traditional jazz scene, Elsdon's virile playing style fits comfortably into the mainstream.

● ALBUMS: *Jazz Journeymen* (Black Lion 1977)★★★, *Keepers Of The Flame* (Parrot 1994)★★★.

Empyrean Isles - Herbie Hancock

The early 60s were another golden age for the Blue Note label, due, in part, to the work of a creative pool of young but conceptually advanced musicians, who constantly reappeared on each other's records, bringing an enthusiasm and creative flair each time they played. This Herbie Hancock quartet session features trumpeter Freddie Hubbard, and Hancock's regular rhythm section partners, bassist Ron Carter and drummer Tony Williams, working together so closely they might have been joined at the hip. Although best known for the popular and funky 'Cantaloupe Island', *Empyrean Isles* has its best moments on a long and free track entitled 'The Egg'.

● Tracks: *One Finger Snap; Oliloqui Valley; Cantaloupe Island; The Egg.*

● First released 1964

● UK peak chart position: did not chart

● USA peak chart position: did not chart

Ennis, Ethel

b. *c.*1935, Baltimore, Maryland, USA. A child prodigy at the piano, Ennis was playing professionally at the age of 13 but then, two years later, began singing. Although this proved to be her métier, she was unable to make a living and took secretarial classes as a back-up. However, she began to establish a reputation along the east coast and her vocation quickly became her profession. Her attractive singing style proved popular in clubs and theatres alike and by the late 50s, she was sufficiently accomplished to be hired to sing at the 1958 Brussells World's Fair with Benny Goodman and Jimmy Rushing. Despite successes such as this, and some good albums, aimed mostly at the popular market, she failed to attract the attention of the big-time promoters and for the next few years, she worked regularly but in relative obscurity, while many lesser talents rose high on a wave of pop promotion. However, perseverance paid off and in the 90s Ennis was again attracting respectful attention and headlining at places such as New York's Kennedy Center alongside more established jazz names. Stylistically, Ennis uses subtle shadings to create warm interpretations of well-known standards and less popular material alike. Her rhythmic drive is similarly understated and joyfully springy, avoiding unnecessary dramatics and allowing the full flavour of her material to emerge. Without doubt, hers is a career that deserved wider recognition, especially during the years of her prime when singers of her quality were rare.

● ALBUMS: *This Is Ethel Ennis* (RCA 1964)★★★.

● COMPILATIONS: with Benny Goodman *Live At The International World Exhibition, Brussels: The Unissued Recordings* (Magic 1958)★★★.

Ericson, Rolf

b. 29 August 1922, Stockholm, Sweden, d. 16 June 1997. Ericson had already been playing trumpet for more than two years when, in 1933, he was taken to hear Louis Armstrong during his European tour and was suitably inspired. As a young teenager Ericson was playing professionally and during the late 40s he made a number of recordings. In 1947 he moved to New York and played in several big bands, including those of Charlie Barnet, Woody Herman and Elliot Lawrence. Ericson was attracted by bebop and also played with Wardell Gray. In the early 50s he toured his homeland in company with Charlie Parker and also spent time in numerous big bands, often those assembled for one-off recording and television dates. Later in the decade and on into the 60s he divided his time between the USA and Scandinavia, playing with a wide range of musicians such as Bud Powell, Brew Moore, Kenny Dorham, Stan Kenton, Benny Goodman, Gerry Mulligan, Ernestine Anderson and Duke Ellington. During the second half of the 60s he became deeply involved in studio work, both in the USA and Germany, but found time to play with visiting American musicians. In the 80s he mostly worked from his base in Berlin, where his music would always find a receptive audience. In 1990 he was in Los Angeles and joined the Ellingtonian small band led by Bill Berry which featured Marshal Royal and Buster Cooper. In the mid-90s he was forced to relocate from his home in the USA after his German wife failed to get a green card. He spent his last years residing in Stockholm.

● ALBUMS: *Oh Pretty Little Neida* (Four Leaf Clover 1971)★★★, *Sincerely Ours* (1978)★★★, *Stockholm Sweetenin'* (Dragon 1984)★★.

Erskine, Peter

b. 5 June 1954, Somers Point, New Jersey, USA. Erskine began playing drums while still a toddler, and at the age of six was attending the Stan Kenton Stage Band Camps. He studied advanced drum techniques under Alan Dawson and then, at the age of 18, joined Kenton. He played with Kenton for three years, touring internationally and establishing a formidable reputation as a player and teacher. In 1976 he joined Maynard

Ferguson, then in a jazz-rock phase, and two years later became a member of Weather Report where he remained into the early 80s. After leaving Weather Report, Erskine worked in the studios and also made records and toured with Michael Brecker and David Sancious in the band known as Steps Ahead and with John Abercrombie. A dazzling technician, Erskine is one of the outstanding jazz-rock drummers, bringing inventiveness and rhythmic clarity to the form and playing with subtlety and swing. In the late 80s he was active as leader of his own group, a band that included Brecker and Abercrombie, playing in the tradition in which Erskine is an established master.

● ALBUMS: *Peter Erskine* (Contemporary 1982)★★★★, with John Abercrombie, Marc Johnson *Current Events* (ECM 1985)★★★★, *Transition* (Denon 1986)★★, *Motion Poet* (Denon 1988)★★★, *Big Theatre* (Ah Um 1989)★★★, with Abercrombie, Johnson *John Abercrombie, Marc Johnson & Peter Erskine* (ECM 1989)★★★★, *Sweet Soul* (RCA 1991)★★, with Jan Garbarek, Miroslav Vitous *Star* (ECM 1991)★★★, with Palle Danielsson, John Taylor *You Never Know* (ECM 1993)★★★, with Danielsson, Taylor *Time Being* (ECM 1993)★★★, with Abercrombie, Johnson, John Surman *November* (ECM 1994)★★★, *History Of The Drum* (Interworld 1995)★★★, with Danielsson, Taylor *As It Is* (ECM 1996)★★★★, with Richard Torres *From Kenton To Now* (Fuzzy Music 1998)★★★.

● VIDEOS: *The Complete Cymbal Guide For The Drumset* (DCI Music 1995).

Ervin, Booker

b. 31 October 1930, Denison, Texas, USA, d. 31 August 1970, New York City, New York, USA. As a child, Ervin played trombone but switched to tenor saxophone in the early 50s during his military service. (He led his own small group when he was stationed on Okinawa.) After returning to civilian life, Ervin studied at Berklee College Of Music under Joe Viola, then worked with Ernie Fields's R&B band and several jazz groups in the south-west. A move to New York in 1958 brought him into a long-standing if irregular association with Charles Mingus that continued into the mid-60s. He recorded extensively with Mingus and Randy Weston and also with his own groups. A powerful player, Ervin's style demonstrates his awareness of such diverse tenor saxophonists as the Texas tenor school (his father played trombone with Buddy Tate's band), Lester Young, Dexter Gordon, Sonny Rollins and John Coltrane, but he chose to follow a different star and remained very much his own man. His warm approach to ballads and searing attack on up-tempo numbers showed him to be a much hotter player than most of his contemporaries. His death in 1970 came while he was still very much in his prime.

● ALBUMS: with Roland Kirk *Soulful Saxes* (Affinity 1957)★★★★, *The Book Cooks* (Bethlehem 1960)★★★★, *Cookin'* (Savoy 1960)★★★★, *That's It!* (Candid 1961)★★★, *Exultation!* (Prestige 1963)★★★★, *The Freedom Book* (Prestige 1963)★★★★, *The Song Book* (Prestige 1964)★★★★, *The Blues Book* (Prestige 1964)★★★★, *The Space Book* (Prestige 1965)★★★★, *Lament For Booker Ervin* (Enja 1966)★★★, *Groovin' High* (Prestige 1966)★★★★, with Dexter Gordon *Settin' The Pace* (Prestige 1967)★★★, *The Trance* (Prestige 1967)★★★★, *Heavy!* (Prestige 1967)★★★, *Structurally Sound* (Pacific Jazz 1968)★★★, *Booker 'N' Brass* (Pacific Jazz 1968)★★, *The In Between* (Blue Note 1969)★★★, *Back From The Gig* 1963/1968 recordings (Blue Note 1976)★★★★.

Erwin, George 'Pee Wee'

b. 30 May 1913, Falls City, Nebraska, USA, d. 20 June 1981. A child prodigy, Erwin first attracted attention playing trumpet on the radio with the Coon-Sanders Nighthawks when he was only eight years old. After playing trumpet in local bands, including John Whetstine, with whom he toured when he was just 15, Roland Evans, Eddie Kuhn and Erwin joined the nationally popular Joe Haymes band in 1931. He followed this with a spell in the Isham Jones orchestra, the outstanding dance band of the day, was briefly with Freddy Martin, and then joined Benny Goodman at the end of 1934. After a short stay with Ray Noble (in a band formed by Glenn Miller which previewed the Miller 'sound') Erwin returned to Goodman for most of 1936 and then flitted through various bands, including Noble's again, Tommy Dorsey's, Raymond Scott's and then took temporary control of the Bunny Berigan band. From the mid-40s Erwin was often in the studios, but at the end of the decade he had become a regular at Nick's in New York. This engagement lasted through the 50s with other regular gigs at the Metropole and on numerous radio and television shows. An enormously popular man and a gifted musician, Erwin began teaching in the 60s and his qualities were imparted to many newcomers to the jazz scene, most notably Warren Vaché Jnr. In the 70s Erwin was constantly in demand for club and festival dates and in 1979 he rejoined Benny Goodman for the Playboy Jazz Festival in Hollywood. That same year his home town of Falls City nominated a 'Pee Wee Erwin Day' and presented him with the keys to the city. He worked almost until the end of his life, playing the Breda Jazz Festival in Holland in May 1981, just a few weeks before his death.

● ALBUMS: *Oh Play That Thing!* (1958)★★★, with Dick Hyman *Some Rags, Some Stomps, And A Little Blues, Pee Wee In New York* (1980)★★★★, *Pee Wee In Hollywood* (1980)★★★, *Pee Wee Erwin Memorial* (1981)★★★.

Escalator Over The Hill - Carla Bley

Escalator Over The Hill is the product of a vibrant musicians' co-operative. Arranged and composed by pianist Carla Bley, with lyrics by poet Paul Haines, it takes the form of an *avant garde* opera. Bley's innovative and imaginative score is central to this exceptional recording, but equally crucial are contributions by Don Cherry, Gato Barbieri, Roswell Rudd, Charlie Haden and Jack Bruce. Brilliant playing at the cutting edge of free jazz underscores Bruce's emphatic vocals, resulting in passages of ravaged intensity and lyrical beauty. Together they bring an urgency to a composition already charged with musical insight and adventure.

● Tracks: *Hotel Overture; This Is Here; Like Animals; Escalator Over The Hill; Stay Awake; Ginger And David; Song To Anything That Moves; Eoth Theme; Businessmen; Ginger And David Theme; Why; Detective Writer Daughter; Doctor Why; Slow Dance (Transductory Music); Smalltown Agonist; End Of Head; Over Her Head; Little Pony Soldier; Say Can You Do; Holiday In Risk; All India Radio; Rawalpindi Blues; End Of Rawalpindi; End Of Animals; . . . And It's Again.*
● First released 1971
● UK peak chart position: did not chart
● USA peak chart position: did not chart

ESCUDERO, RALPH

b. Rafael Escudero, 16 July 1898, Manati, Puerto Rico, d. 10 April 1970. After playing bass in his homeland he went to New York where he played regularly, including a spell at the famed Clef Club. He also performed in touring bands with popular shows including an out-of-town version of Eubie Blake's and Noble Sissle's *Shuffle Along*. Escudero played with bands led by Wilbur Sweatman and Fletcher Henderson, then spent around three years with McKinney's Cotton Pickers. After playing with various east coast bands, Escudero spent some time in California before deciding to continue his professional life back home in Puerto Rico where he worked with dance bands and classical orchestras. A solid and workmanlike player with excellent time, Escudero also sometimes played the brass bass (tuba), swinging mightily and soloing well with Henderson.

ETHERIDGE, JOHN

b. 12 January 1948, London, England. Etheridge is a self-taught guitarist who started playing while he was at school. He went on to Essex University and then played with jazz-rock groups in London in the early 70s before joining Soft Machine (1975-78). He is a technically gifted guitarist able to use all the effects available to an electric guitarist in his solos. He has worked with Stéphane Grappelli (1978-81) showing as much facility playing the acoustic guitar with him as he had previously done on the electric. At the same time, he formed his own group Second Vision (1980-81) and then undertook solo concerts in Australia and toured the USA with bassist Brian Torff (1982). In 1983 he toured England in a trio with Paul Rogers (bass) and Nigel Morris (drums). After spells with rock groups like Global Village Trucking Company and Darryl Way's Wolf, Etheridge played some concerts and recorded with the re-formed Soft Machine. In the mid-80s he worked with Gary Boyle (guitar) and with a quartet. In recent years he has played with Danny Thompson. He regularly teaches on guitar courses.

● ALBUMS: *First Steps* (1980)★★★, *Ash* (The Jazz Label 1993)★★★, with Andy Summers *Invisible Threads* (Mesa 1994)★★★.

ETHNIC HERITAGE ENSEMBLE

Edward Wilkerson (b. 27 July 1955, Terre Haute, Indiana, USA; reeds), Kahil El'Zabar (b. Clifton Blackburn, 11 November 1953, Chicago, Illinois, USA; percussion). The Ethnic Heritage Ensemble was formed in 1973 by Wilkerson, El'Zabar and saxophonist 'Light' Henry Huff, who stayed with the trio for their first two albums. On *Welcome*, the third member was Kalaparush Maurice McIntyre, and on *Ancestral Song*, *Hang Tuff* and *The Continuum* it was Joe Bowie. Their latest member is percussionist 'Atu' Harold Murray. A typical second-generation AACM group, the Ethnic Heritage Ensemble owe much to the example of the Art Ensemble Of Chicago, particularly in their use of 'little instruments', and even more to the general AACM emphasis on space, sound-as-texture and detailed awareness of black music history. Wilkerson attended the University of Chicago and played with Little Anthony And The Imperials and Bobby Bland in addition to studying in the AACM with players such as Roscoe Mitchell, George Lewis and Henry Threadgill. One of the most versatile of the new Chicago saxophonists, he also leads the octet 8 Bold Souls and a big band, Shadow Vignettes. Kahil El'Zabar studied at the Malcolm X School of Music and worked with Donny Hathaway and Paul Simon as well as playing in the AACM with Lester Bowie, Chico Freeman and Muhal Richard Abrams: he has also served as the organization's chairman. He performs with exquisite delicacy and startling force on a wide array of Western and ethnic percussion instruments, although his occasional wailing vocals may be an acquired taste. He also leads his own group, the Ritual, often in association with Malachi Favors: their guests on record to date have included Lester Bowie (*The Ritual*, *Sacred Love*), Billy Bang (*Another Kind Of Groove*), David Murray (*The Golden Sea*) and saxophonist Ari Brown (*Alika Rising*).

● ALBUMS: *Three Gentlemen From Chikago* (1980)★★★, *Impressions* (1981)★★★, *Welcome* (1983)★★, *Ancestral Song* (1989)★★, *Hang Tuff* (1992)★★★, *The Continuum* (Delmark 1998)★★★★, *21st Century Union March* (Silkheart 1998)★★★. Solo: Edward Wilkerson *8 Bold Souls* (1987), with Shadow Vignettes *Birth Of A Notion* (1986)★★, with Kahil El'Zabar *The Ritual* (1986)★★, *Another Kind Of Groove* (1987)★★★, *Sacred Love* (1988)★★★, *The Golden Sea* (1990)★★★, *Alika Rising* (1991)★★★.

EUBANKS, KEVIN

b. 15 November 1957, Philadelphia, Pennsylvania, USA. Eubanks comes from a very musical family: brother Robin Eubanks is a fine trombone player, Ray Bryant is his uncle and his mother, Vera, is a Doctor of Music. Kevin studied guitar at Berklee College Of Music and with Ted Dunbar. Throughout his teens he modelled his style largely on the fiery playing of John McLaughlin, but from the age of 22 he was more influenced by the gentler approach of Wes Montgomery. The Montgomery pedigree is evident in his work, but he also admires Segovia, George Benson and Oscar Peterson. From 1980-81 he was with Art Blakey's Jazz Messengers. He has also worked with Roy Haynes, Slide Hampton, Sam Rivers, Gary Thomas (*While The Gate Is Open*) and Mike Gibbs (*Big Music*). He has made a reputation and a living from smooth, well-produced contemporary fusion, but is quite capable of more challenging playing, as shown by his work on Dave Holland's highly acclaimed 1990 *Extensions*. Eubanks found his perfect niche as part of the GRP stable of artists, although he left the label in 1991 and signed with the illustrious Blue Note Records.

● ALBUMS: *Kevin Eubanks - Guitarist* (Discovery 1982)★★★, *Sundance* (GRP 1984)★★, *Opening Night* (GRP 1985)★★, *Face To Face* (GRP 1986)★★★, *The Heat Of Heat* (GRP 1988)★★★, *Shadow Prophets* (GRP 1988)★★, *The Searcher* (GRP 1989)★★★, *Promise Of Tomorrow* (GRP 1990)★★, *Turning Point* (GRP 1992)★★★, *Spirit Talk* (Blue Note 1993)★★★, *Spiritalk 2, Revelations* (Blue Note 1995)★★★, with Mino Cinelu, Dave Holland *World Trio* (Intuition 1995)★★★, *Live At Bradley's* (Blue Note 1996)★★.

EUROPE, JAMES REESE

b. 22 February 1881, Mobile, Alabama, USA, d. 9 May 1919. After a formal musical education in Washington, DC, Europe worked in New York soon after the turn of the century. He became a prominent figure in the city's musical circles, leading bands at high society balls and other prestigious functions. He was one of the founders of the Clef Club, an association to advance the cause of black musicians. In 1914 he presented the Clef Club Orchestra at Carnegie Hall, using an astonishing 125 musicians. The music played was typical of the society orchestras of the day - marches, tangos, waltzes and, because these were black musicians, a selection of so-called plantation songs. The enormous splash this concert made established Europe as the top black bandleader in the city and this led to jealousy and dissent at the Clef Club. Europe soon quit and formed a new organization, the Tempo Club. Europe became closely associated with the popular white ballroom dancers, Vernon and Irene Castle, and with them was largely responsible for popularizing the foxtrot, the dance-craze that swept the USA. In 1917, Europe enlisted in the army and formed the 369th Infantry regiment's band, the Hellfighters. This band played to army and civilian audiences in France and by the time the war was over Europe's popularity was immense. The music he played, as documented on the handful of records he made, was an intriguing combination of Sousa-like brassiness and perky ragtime. Europe's music was by no means jazz, but it did hint at his awareness of early black vernacular music and, thanks to his unprecedented popularity with white audiences, he appeared the man most likely to make this music a crossover success. It was not to be. On 9 May 1919 an altercation with one of his musicians degenerated into a brawl and Europe was stabbed to death.

● COMPILATIONS: *Jim Europe And Arthur Pryor Bands* (1907-19)★★★, *Jazz: Some Beginnings* (c.1919)★★★, *Too Much Mustard* (c.1919)★★★.

EVANS, BILL (PIANIST)

b. 16 August 1929, Plainfield, New Jersey, USA, d. 15 September 1980. One of the most important and influential of modern jazz pianists, Evans studied at Southeastern Louisiana University, while summer jobs with Mundell Lowe and Red Mitchell introduced him to the jazz scene. He was in the army from 1951-54; played with Jerry Wald in 1954-55; studied at the Mannes School of Music, New York 1955-56; then began a full-time jazz career with clarinettist Tony Scott. Through Lowe he was introduced to Riverside Records and made his recording debut as leader (of a trio) in 1956. Evans then recorded with Charles Mingus and George Russell. In 1958 he joined Miles Davis, playing a central role on the album *Kind Of Blue*, which was so influential in the development of modal jazz. Evans left Davis after less than a year to form his own trio, and favoured that format thereafter. His recordings with Scott La Faro and Paul Motian (1959-61) represent the summit of the genre (*Portrait In Jazz, Explorations*, live sessions at the Village Vanguard). The tragic loss of La Faro in a car accident deprived Evans of his most sympathetic partner, and the later recordings do not quite approach the level of those on Riverside; Eddie Gomez was the most compatible of later bassists. Evans recorded solo, most interestingly on the double-tracked *Conversations With Myself*; in duo with Jim Hall, Bob Brookmeyer and Tony Bennett; and in larger groups with such players as Lee Konitz, Zoot Sims and Freddie Hubbard. Towards the end of his life Evans was establishing a new trio with Marc Johnson and Joe LaBarbera, and playing with new-found freedom. Although he eventually kicked his heroin habit, he experienced continuing drug problems and these contributed to his early death from a stomach ulcer and other complications.

Evans' background is significant; he matured away from the bebop scene in New York. Although his earlier playing was indebted to bopper Bud Powell and more strikingly to hardbop pianist Horace Silver, as well as to Lennie Tristano, he gradually developed a more lyrical, 'impressionistic' approach, with an understated strength far removed from the aggression of bebop. His ideas were influential in the development of modal jazz and hence of the John Coltrane school, whose major pianistic voice was McCoy Tyner; however, he did not pursue that direction himself, finding it insufficiently lyrical and melodic for his needs. The softer, understated, less obviously dissonant idiom of the great trio with La Faro and Motian embodies the rival pianistic tradition to that of the eventually overbearing Tyner. Contemporary jazz piano tends towards a synthesis of the Evans and Tyner styles, but the Evans legacy is with hindsight the richer one. Technically, Evans led the way in the development of a genuinely pianistic modern jazz style. Most important was his much-imitated but completely distinctive approach to harmony, in particular to the way the notes of the chord are arranged or 'voiced'. Red Garland, who preceded Evans in the Miles Davis group, had moved away from Bud Powell's functional 'shell voicings', but it was Evans (and to a lesser extent Wynton Kelly) who first fully defined the new style of 'rootless voicings'. These retain only the essential tones of the chord (dispensing with the root itself, often played by the bassist), and form the grammatical basis of contemporary jazz piano. Evans employed a wider variety of tone-colour than is usual in jazz piano, with subtle use of the sustaining pedal and varying emphasis of notes in the chord voicing. He improvises thematically, 'rationally'; as he said, 'the science of building a line, if you can call it a science, is enough to occupy somebody for 12 lifetimes'. His influence on pianists is as considerable as that of Coltrane on saxophonists , most notably on several artists known to a wider public than he was, such as Herbie Hancock, Keith Jarrett and Chick Corea, but also on Hampton Hawes, Paul Bley and more recently Michel Petrucciani. Legions of imitators have tended to conceal from listeners the complete originality of his style as it developed in the late 50s and early 60s, and Evans' music still continues to yield new secrets.

A trio setting was Evans's ideal format, and his solo piano style is (with the exception of the double-tracked *Conversations With Myself*) less compelling. The trio with La Faro and Motian is surely one of the great combinations in jazz history. The 'collective improvisation' of this group involved rhythmic innovation, with the bass in particular escaping its standard timekeeping role. Evans commented that 'at that time nobody else was opening trio music in quite that way, letting the music move from an internalized beat, instead of laying it down all the time explicitly'. However, the apparent lassitude of Evans' mature style has led to much misunderstanding and criticism. Archie Shepp commented (incorrectly) that 'Debussy and Satie have already done those things'; Cecil Taylor found Evans 'so uninteresting, so predictable and so lacking in vitality'. As James Collier wrote, 'If Milton can write 'Il Pensero', surely Bill Evans can produce a 'Turn Out The Stars'. But Milton also wrote 'L'Allegro', and Evans is not often seen dancing in the chequer'd shade'. Melancholy is Evans' natural mood, and rhythm his greatest weakness; he does not swing powerfully, and is not interested enough in the 'groove'. Cannonball Adderley commented that when the pianist joined Davis, 'Miles changed his style from very hard to a softer approach. Bill was brilliant in other areas, but he couldn't make the real hard things come off . . . '. When Evans plays in a determined up-tempo (as on *Montreux 1968*), the result can sound merely forced and frantic, and unlike Wynton Kelly or Tommy Flanagan, he is not a first-choice accompanist. Nonetheless, he swings effectively when pushed by a drummer such as Philly Joe Jones on *Everybody Digs Bill Evans* (listen to 'Minority'), and there are many powerful swinging musicians whose music has a fraction of the interest of Evans'. In common with an unusual handful of great jazz musicians, Bill Evans was not a master of the blues. He rapidly learned to avoid straight-ahead blues settings, although his grasp of minor blues (e.g., John Carisi's wonderful 'Israel') was assured, partly because melodic minor harmony is the basis of the modern jazz sound that he helped to develop. Evans increasingly played his own compositions, which are unfailingly fine and inventive, often involving irregular phrase lengths and shifting metres, and many, incidentally, named after female friends ('Waltz For Debby', 'One for Helen', 'Show-Type Tune', 'Peri's Scope', 'Laurie', 'Turn Out The Stars', 'Blue In Green'). His originality was equally apparent in his transformations of standard songs ('Beautiful Love', 'Polka Dots And Moonbeams', 'Someday My Prince Will Come', 'My Romance', 'My Foolish Heart'). His recorded legacy is extensive.

● ALBUMS: *New Jazz Conceptions* (Riverside 1956)★★★, *Everybody Digs Bill Evans* (Riverside 1958)★★★★, *Portrait In Jazz* (Riverside 1959)★★★★, *Explorations* (Riverside 1961)★★★★, *Sunday At The Village Vanguard* (Riverside 1961)★★★★★, *Waltz For Debby* (Riverside 1961)★★★★★, *More From The Vanguard* (1961)★★★★, *Empathy* (Verve 1962)★★★, with Cannonball Adderley *Know What I Mean* (Riverside 1962)★★★★, *Moonbeams* (Riverside 1962)★★★, *How My Heart Sings* (Riverside 1962)★★★★, with Freddie Hubbard *Interplay* (Riverside 1962)★★★, *Conversations With Myself* (Verve 1963)★★★★, with Jim Hall *Undercurrent* (Blue Note 1963)★★★★, *Trio 64* (Verve 1964)★★★★, *The Bill Evans Trio Live* (1964)★★★, *At Shelly's Manne Hole* (Riverside 1964)★★★★, *Trio '65* (Verve 1965)★★★, *Bill Evans Trio With The Symphony Orchestra* (Verve 1965)★★★, *Bill Evans At Town Hall* (Verve 1966)★★★, with Hall *Intermodulation* (Verve 1966)★★★, *A Simple Matter Of Conviction* (Verve 1966)★★★, *Further Conversations With Myself* (Verve 1967)★★★★, *Polka Dots And Moonbeams* (Riverside 1967)★★★, *California Here I Come* (1967)★★★★, *Alone* (Verve 1968)★★★, *Bill Evans At The Montreux Jazz Festival* (Verve 1968)★★★, *Jazzhouse* (1969)★★★, *What's New* (Verve 1969), *Montreux* ii (1970)★★★, *You're Gonna Hear From Me* (Milestone 1970)★★★, *The Bill Evans Album* (Columbia 1971)★★★★, with George Russell *Living Time* (1972)★★★, *Live In Tokyo* (Fantasy 1972)★★★★, *Yesterday I Heard The Rain* (Bandstand 1973)★★★, *Since We Met* (Original Jazz Classics 1974)★★★, *Re: Person I Knew* (Original Jazz Classics 1974)★★★, *Intuition* (1974)★★★, *Blue Is Green* (Milestone 1974)★★★, *Jazzhouse* (Milestone 1974)★★★, *Montreux* iii (Original Jazz Classics 1975)★★★, *The Tony Bennett/Bill Evans Album* (Original Jazz Classics 1975)★★★★, with Tony Bennett *Together Again* (1976)★★★, *Alone (Again)* (Original Jazz Classics 1976)★★★, *Eloquence* (1976)★★★, with Harold Land *Quintessence* (Original Jazz Classics 1976)★★★, with Lee Konitz, Warne Marsh *Crosscurrents* (Original Jazz Classics 1977)★★★, *From The 70's* (1977)★★★, *You Must Believe In Spring* (1977)★★★, *New Conversations* (1978)★★★, with Toots Thielemans *Affinity* (1978)★★★, *I Will Say Goodbye* (Original Jazz Classics 1979)★★★, *We Will Meet Again* (1979)★★★, *The Paris Concert: Edition One* 1979 recording (1983)★★★, *The Paris Concert: Edition Two* 1979 recording (1984)★★★, *The Brilliant* 1980 recording (Timeless 1990)★★★, *Letter To Evan: Live At Ronnie Scott's* 1980 recording (Dreyfus 1996)★★★.

● COMPILATIONS: *The Complete Fantasy Recordings* box set (Fantasy 1980)★★★★, *The Complete Riverside Recordings* box set (Fantasy 1985)★★★★, *Consecration* i and ii, 1980 recording (Timeless 1990)★★★, *Turn Out The Stars: The Final Village Vanguard Recordings June, 1980* 10-LP/6-CD box set (Mosaic/Warners 1996)★★★, *The Secret Sessions, Recorded At The Village Vanguard* 8-CD box set (Milestone 1996)★★★, *The Best Of Bill Evans Live On Verve* (Verve 1997)★★★, *The Complete*

Bill Evans On Verve 18-CD box set (Verve 1998)★★★★, *The Ultimate* (Verve 1998)★★★★.
● VIDEOS: *In Oslo* (K-Jazz 1994), *The Bill Evans Trio* (Rhapsody 1995).
● FURTHER READING: *How My Heart Sings*, Peter Pettinger.

Evans, Bill (saxophonist)

b. 9 February 1958, Clarendon Hills, nr Chicago, Illinois, USA. Jazz's third famous Bill Evans (the others being the modern jazz pianist and the reedsman who changed his name to Yusef Lateef) this Evans is the fusion tenor and soprano saxophonist. A student of Dave Liebman, it was on Liebman's recommendation that he joined Miles Davis' jazz/rock band, and was thus catapulted into the spotlight. By 1983 he was recording as a leader, and when he left Davis' band a year later, he was quickly snapped up by guitarist John McLaughlin for his revived Mahavishnu Orchestra, and also began working with Herbie Hancock. A lyrical, gentler voice than is common in the action packed world of fusion, he has a soft tone, and a penchant for fast, precise tonguing in place of the more common headlong, legato style. His own recordings include *Moods Unlimited*, a fine trio session, with the veteran piano and bass team of pianist Hank Jones and bassist Red Mitchell; *The Alternative Man*, a star-studded Blue Note Records session that should appeal to fusion enthusiasts for the presence of guitarist John McLaughlin, keyboardist Mitch Forman, bassist Marcus Miller and drummers Al Foster and Danny Gottlieb; and the more recent *Push*, a funky, breakbeat-orientated session with contributions by Marcus Miller, keyboardist Bob James, pianist Bruce Hornsby and assorted rappers. *Escape* continued his flirtation with hip-hop and additionally featured Lee Ritenour and Jim Beard.
● ALBUMS: *Moods Unlimited* (Paddle Wheel 1982)★★★★, *Living In The Crest Of A Wave* (1983)★★★, *The Alternative Man* (1985)★★★, with Tony Reedus *The Far Side* (1988)★★★, with Mark Egan *A Touch Of Light* (1988)★★★, with Niels Lan Doky *Friendship* (1989)★★★, with Danny Gottlieb *Whirlwind* (1989)★★★, *Summertime* (Jazz City 1989)★★★★, *Let The Juice Loose* (1989)★★★, *The Gambler* (Jazz City 1990)★★★, with Christian Minh Doky *The Sequel* (1990)★★★, *Petite Blonde* (Lipstick 1993)★★, *Push* (Lipstick 1993)★★★★, *Live In Europe* (Lipstick 1995)★★, *Escape* (Escapade 1996)★★★★, *Starfish & The Moon* (Escapade 1998)★★★.

Evans, Doc

b. Paul Wesley Evans, 20 June 1907, Spring Valley, Minnesota, USA, d. 10 January 1977. While still at high school he played several instruments, adding cornet in the late 20s. In the early 30s, working in and around Minneapolis, he concentrated on cornet and built a good if localized reputation. During the 30s he played, composed and arranged and also worked outside music. In the 40s he played occasionally in New York and Chicago but always returned to Minneapolis. He worked with Bunk Johnson, Miff Mole, Tony Parenti, Joe Sullivan and other noted jazzmen, but mostly led his own bands. He continued an active playing career through the 50s and 60s, sometimes working with musicians like Turk Murphy but again preferring the musical backwaters of Minnesota to the richer but rougher possibilities of the big time. A fluent player of traditional jazz, an admirer of Bix Beiderbecke as evidenced by his pure tone, but with few pretensions towards originality.
● ALBUMS: *Dixieland Concert* (Soma 1953)★★★, *Classic Jazz At Carleton* (Soma 1954)★★★★, *Doc Evans And His Band Vol 1* (Audiophile 1953)★★★★, *Doc Evans And His Band Vol 2* (Audiophile 1953)★★★, with Turk Murphy *New Orleans Jazz Festival* (1955)★★★, *Dixieland Session* (Audiophile 1955)★★★★, *Traditional Jazz* (Audiophile 1955)★★★, *The Cornet Artistry Of Doc Evans* (Audiophile 1955)★★★, *Classics Of The 20s* (Audiophile 50s)★★★, *Muskrat Ramble* (Concert Disc 60s)★★★, *Reminiscing In Dixieland* (Audiophile 60s)★★★.
● COMPILATIONS: *Doc Evans And His Dixieland Jazz Band* (1947)★★★★, *Bunk Johnson And Don Ewell With Doc Evans And His Band* (1947)★★★, *Jazz Heritage Volume 1* (1949)★★★, *Blues In Dixieland* (1949)★★★.

Evans, Gil

b. Ian Ernest Gilmore Green, 13 May 1912, Toronto, Canada, d. 20 March 1988, Cuernavaca, Mexico. Although self-taught, Evans became extraordinarily proficient as a pianist and composer, though his greatest talent lay in his abilities as an arranger. He formed his first band in 1933 in California, where he was raised. He wrote most of the arrangements, a duty he retained when the band was later fronted by popular singer Skinnay Ennis. Up to this point Evans's work had followed the orthodox line demanded of commercial dancebands, but his musical ambitions lay in other areas. A long stint as chief arranger for Claude Thornhill during the 40s gave him the opportunity he needed to explore different sounds and unusual textures. Thornhill's predilection for soft and slowly shifting pastel patterns as a background for his delicate piano proved to be an interesting workshop for Evans, who would always remark on this experience as being influential upon his later work. Towards the end of his stay with Thornhill, Evans was writing for very large ensembles, creating intense moody music. However, by this time, he was eager to try something new, feeling that the music he was required to write for the band was becoming too static and sombre. During this same period, Gerry Mulligan was a member of the Thornhill band and was also writing arrangements. Both he and Evans had become fascinated by the developments of the radical new beboppers such as Charlie Parker and Miles Davis, and in 1948 the two men embarked upon a series of arrangements for Davis's nine-piece band. These records, subsequently released under the generic title *Birth Of The Cool*, proved very influential in the 50s. Despite the quality of the material Evans was creating at this point in his career, he did not meet with much commercial or critical success. Towards the end of the 50s Evans again worked with Davis, helping to create landmark albums such as *Miles Ahead* and *Sketches Of Spain*. His writing for Davis was a highly effective amalgam of the concepts developed during his Thornhill period and the needs of the increasingly restrained trumpet style Davis was adopting. Evans's use in these and later arrangements for his own band of such instruments as tubas and bass trombones broadened the range of orchestral colours at his disposal and helped him to create a highly distinctive sound and style. As with many other gifted arrangers and composers, Evans's real need was for a permanent band for the expression of his ideas, but this proved difficult to achieve. Such groups as he did form were in existence for only short periods, although some, fortunately, made records of his seminal works. He continued to write, composing many extended works, often uncertain if they would ever be performed. However, in the early 70s he was able to form a band which played regularly and the music showed his ready absorption of ideas and devices from the current pop music scene.

After a number of international tours during the 70s, his work became more widely known and his stature rose accordingly. So too did his popularity when it became apparent to audiences that his was not esoteric music but was readily accessible and showed a marked respect for the great traditions of earlier jazz. By the late 70s, the music Evans was writing had developed a harder edge than hitherto; he was making extensive use of electronics and once again was happily absorbing aspects of pop. In particular, he arranged and recorded several Jimi Hendrix compositions. His creativity showed no signs of diminishing as the 80s dawned and he continued a punishing round of concert tours, record dates, radio and television appearances, all the while writing more new material for his band. One of his final commissions was with Sting, arranging a fine version of Hendrix's 'Little Wing'.

One of the outstanding arrangers and composers in jazz, Evans was particularly adept at creating complex scores which held at their core a simple and readily understandable concept. Throughout his career, his writing showed his profound respect for the needs of jazz musicians to make their own musical statements within an otherwise formally conceived and structured work. Perhaps this is why so many notable musicians - including Steve Lacy, Elvin Jones, Lew Soloff, George Adams, Ron Carter and David Sanborn - were happy to play in his bands over the years. As a result Evans's work, even at its most sophisticated, maintained an enviable feeling of freedom and spontaneity that few other arrangers of his calibre were able to achieve.

● ALBUMS: *There Comes A Time* (RCA-Victor 1955)★★★★, *Gil Evans Plus 10* reissued as *Big Stuff* (Prestige 1957)★★★★, *New Bottles Old Wine* (Pacific Jazz 1958)★★★★, *Great Jazz Standards* (World Pacific 1959)★★★, with Johnny Coles *Out Of The Cool* (Impulse! 1960)★★★★★, *Into The Hot* (Impulse! 1961)★★★, *America's Number 1 Arranger* (Pacific Jazz 1961)★★★, *The Individualism Of Gil Evans* (Verve 1964)★★★★, with Kenny Burrell *Guitar Forms* (Verve 1965)★★★★, *Blues In Orbit* (Enja 1971)★★★, *Where Flamingos Fly* (1972)★★★, *Svengali* (Atlantic 1973)★★★, *The Gil Evans Orchestra Featuring Kenny Burrell And Phil Woods* 1963 recording (Verve 1973)★★★, *The Gil Evans Orchestra Plays The Music Of Jimi Hendrix* (Bluebird 1974)★★★★, *Montreux Jazz Festival '74* (1974)★★★, *Synthetic Evans* (1976)★★★, *Live '76* (Zeta 1976)★★★, *Priestess* (Antilles 1977)★★★, *Tokyo Concert* (West Wind 1977)★★★, *Gil Evans At The Royal Festival Hall* (1978)★★★, *The Rest Of Gil Evans At The Royal Festival Hall* (1978)★★★, *Little Wing* (DIW 1978)★★★, *Parabola* (Horo 1979)★★★, *Live At New York Public Theatre Volumes 1* and *2* (Blackhawk 1980)★★★, *The British Orchestra* (1983)★★★, *Live At Sweet Basil Volumes 1* and *2* (Electric Bird 1984)★★★, *Farewell* (Electric Bird 1987)★★★, with Helen Merrill *Helen Merrill/Gil Evans* (Emarcy 1988)★★★, with Steve Lacy *Paris Blues* (Owl 1988)★★★, *Sting And Bill Evans/ Last Session* (Jazz Door 1988)★★★, *Lunar Eclypse* 1981 recordings (New Tone 1993)★★★.

● COMPILATIONS: with Tadd Dameron *The Arrangers Touch* 1953/1956/1957 recordings (Prestige 1975)★★★★, *Jazz Masters* 1964/1965 recordings (Verve 1994)★★★★, *Giants Of Jazz: The Gil Evans Orchestra* 1957-1959 recordings (Sarabandas 1994)★★★★, with Miles Davis *Miles Davis/Gil Evans: The Complete Columbia Studio Recordings* 6-CD/11-LP box set (Columbia/Mosaic 1996)★★★★★, *Gil Evans* (GRP 1998)★★★.

● FURTHER READING: *Svengali, Or The Orchestra Called Gill Evans*, Raymond Horricks.

EVANS, HERSCHEL

b. 1909, Denton, Texas, USA, d. 9 February 1939. Tenor saxophonist Evans's early career was centred in the south-west where he worked with many of the best territory bands of the 20s and early 30s. Among the bands in which he advanced his considerable skills were those of Edgar Battle, Terrence Holder and Troy Floyd. In 1933 he joined Bennie Moten's outstanding Kansas City-based band, remaining there until 1935. He also worked with Oran 'Hot Lips' Page before deciding on stretching his geographic boundaries. After playing briefly in Chicago he wound up in Los Angeles where he became involved in the bustling Central Avenue club scene, working with the bands of Charlie Echols, Lionel Hampton and Buck Clayton. In 1936 he joined Count Basie where his robust, Coleman Hawkins-influenced style of playing formed a dramatic contrast with the light acerbic sound of his section-mate, Lester Young. Evans's career ended abruptly when he became seriously ill towards the end of 1938 while still playing with the Basie band.

EVANS, STUMP

b. Paul A. Evans, 18 October 1904, Lawrence, Kansas, USA, d. 29 August 1928. As a child Evans displayed proficiency on a variety of brass and reed instruments, finally choosing saxophones. In Chicago in the early 20s he played in bands led by Erskine Tate, Earl Hines, Joe 'King' Oliver and Carroll Dickerson and was thus regularly associated with Louis Armstrong. He recorded with several other important musicians, including Jelly Roll Morton. By the mid-20s Evans was often playing tenor saxophone, an instrument that was yet to achieve its dominant role in jazz, and was cited by Coleman Hawkins as an early influence. Evans developed tuberculosis and died in August 1928.

EVANS, SUE

b. 7 July 1951, New York, USA. Evans studied percussion with Warren Smith and Sonny Igoe before graduating from the High School of Music and Art in 1969. She worked with singer Judy Collins's backing group (1969-73) and then with Steve Kuhn; recorded with the Jazz Composers Orchestra (when it was directed by Roswell Rudd) and had a long association with Gil Evans (1969-82). She also recorded with singers James Brown, Morgana King and Tony Bennett and with Blood, Sweat And Tears. She played with singer Suzanne Vega in the late 80s. Evans's skilful, responsive playing both as percussionist and drummer has been ideal accompanying vocalists and in satisfying the very particular requirements of music as diverse as that of the Jazz Composers Orchestra and Gil Evans. She has said she does not see herself as 'a timekeeper *per se* . . . I use percussion for melody and colours'.

● ALBUMS: with Bobby Jones *The Arrival of Bobby Jones* (1972)★★, with Gil Evans *Svengali* (1973)★★★★, *The Gil Evans Orchestra Plays The Music Of Jimi Hendrix* (1974)★★★★, *There Comes A Time* (1975)★★★★.

EVIDENCE - STEVE LACY

Without doubt one of jazz's true originals, Steve Lacy was an early modern jazz disciple of the soprano saxophone - he is said to be the man who introduced it to John Coltrane, and remains one of its few practitioners to play without combining it with another instrument. He is almost as well known for his fruitful fascination with the music of Thelonious Monk, whose tunes he had continuously studied and with whom he worked in 1960. *Evidence* features four Monk compositions and two tunes by Duke Ellington, performed with the help of free jazz trumpet legend Don Cherry, bassist Carl Brown and flawless drummer Billy Higgins.

● Tracks: *The Mystery Song; Evidence; Let's Cool One; San Francisco Holiday; Something To Live For; Who Knows.*
● First released 1962
● UK peak chart position: did not chart
● USA peak chart position: did not chart

EWANS, KAI

b. Kai Peter Anthon Nielsen, 10 April 1906, Hørsholm, Denmark. After playing other instruments, Ewans chose the alto saxophone in his late teens, later also playing clarinet. He played in several bands and also formed groups under his own leadership including a big band in the mid-20s. Late in the decade he toured Europe, continuing into the 30s as a bandleader. He also played with visiting Americans including Benny Carter. His big band, one of the first in Denmark when it was formed in 1927, had continued sporadically over the years and eventually disbanded in 1947. After this Ewans worked mostly outside music, travelling to the USA where, in the early 60s, he was in the restaurant business with Carter in California. After picking up the threads of his musical career in Denmark in the late 60s, he eventually retired to the USA. A good player, Ewans was a potent force behind the development of interest in jazz, and in particular in big band, swing-era-style music in Denmark. His bands were always disciplined, well-rehearsed and enthusiastic outfits, reflecting the best qualities of the leader.

● COMPILATIONS: *Kai Ewans And His Swinging Sixteen* (Storyville 1942-43)★★★.

EWART, DOUGLAS

b. 13 September 1946, Kingston, Jamaica. Ewart moved to Chicago in 1963 and later studied music at the AACM. His early influences included Charles Mingus, Clifford Brown and Eric Dolphy, the latter's example persuading Ewart to learn bassoon and bass clarinet in addition to alto and other saxophones and flute. He has played with many of his AACM colleagues, recording with (for example) Roscoe Mitchell (*Sketches From Bamboo*), Muhal Richard Abrams (*Lifea Blinec*), Anthony Braxton (*For Trio*), Leo Smith (*Budding Of A Rose*) and Henry Threadgill, in the X-75 group. In particular, Ewart formed an association with trombonist George Lewis in 1971 that has continued through to the present: he has played on several of Lewis's projects (*Chicago Slow Dance*, *Homage To Charles Parker*) and recorded a duo album with him. Leader of a clarinet quartet (Red Hills), Ewart is also an accomplished instrument-maker, particularly renowned for his beautifully crafted Ewart flutes.

● ALBUMS: with George Lewis *Jila/Save!/Mon./The Imaginary Suite* (Black Saint 1979)★★★, *Red Hills* (1981)★★.

EWELL, DON

b. 14 November 1916, Baltimore, Maryland, USA, d. 9 August 1983, Pompano Beach, Florida, USA. Although classically trained on piano, Ewell was drawn to jazz and in particular to the music of the early jazz masters of New Orleans. This was despite the fact that by the mid-30s, which was when his career got under way, such forms were suffering a decline in popularity under the commercial pressures of the swing era. Undeterred, Ewell followed his bent, working with Bunk Johnson in the mid-40s and later in the decade with Muggsy Spanier and Sidney Bechet. Stylistically, he was influenced by pianists as different as Jelly Roll Morton, Fats Waller and Jimmy Yancey. In the mid-50s Ewell began a particularly rewarding association with Jack Teagarden, which lasted until the trombonist's death in 1964. Thereafter, Ewell toured extensively, sometimes in bands, sometimes in harness with fellow pianist Willie 'The Lion' Smith, but mostly as a soloist, until his death in 1983. Although capable of playing rousing barrelhouse style, he was also able to produce exceptionally fine and intricate playing.

● ALBUMS: *Don Ewell* 10-inch album (Windin' Ball 1953)★★★, *Don Ewell & Mama Yancey* 10-inch album (Windin' Ball 1953)★★★, *Don Ewell Plays Tunes Played By The King Oliver Band* 10-inch album (Windin' Ball 1953)★★★, *Music To Listen To Don Ewell By* (Good Time Jazz 1955)★★★, *The Man Here Plays Fine Piano* (Good Time Jazz 1956)★★★★, *Free 'n Easy* (Good Time Jazz 1956)★★★, with Willie 'The Lion' Smith *Grand Piano*

(1967)★★★★, *Jazz On A Sunday Afternoon* (Fat Cat Jazz 1969)★★★, *Live At The 100 Club* (Solo Arts 1971)★★★, *Don Ewell* (Chiaroscuro 1974)★★★, *Don Ewell In Japan* (Jazzology 1975)★★★★, *Chicago '57* 1957 recording (Stomp Off 1984)★★★, *Don Ewell Quintet* 1973/74 recording (Jazzology 1986)★★★, *Don Newell In New Orleans* 1965 recording (GHB 1986)★★★, *Yellow Dog Blues* (Jazzology 1988)★★★, *Don Ewell And His All-Stars* 1965 recording (Jazzology 1988)★★★★, *Don Ewell's Hot 4* 1966 recording (Center 1992)★★★.

● FURTHER READING: *Jazz Legacy Of Don Ewell*, John Colinson and Eugene Kramer.

FABULOUS DORSEYS, THE

The first jazz-related biopic, this 1947 film also has the dubious distinction of casting its subjects as themselves. Although both Jimmy and Tommy Dorsey managed to avoid appearing too embarrassed by the shaky plot (much of which centred on pleasing Ma and Pa Dorsey), their acting was understandably wooden. Their playing was, of course, excellent as both men, then still in their prime, were amongst the outstanding technicians on their respective instruments. For jazz fans the best moment comes in a cornily-contrived nightclub scene in which a jam session occurs. Apart from Jimmy and Tommy, the mismatched musicians include Charlie Barnet, Ray Bauduc and Ziggy Elman, all of whom get in the way of the superb Art Tatum.

FACING YOU - KEITH JARRETT

The stunning ECM Records debut that unleashed one of the greatest piano players of our time. Using jazz as an excuse, Keith Jarrett initiated and indoctrinated us with improvised solo piano, something to which listeners would become used over the next three decades. *Facing You* is boogie-woogie, country hoedown, blues, folk, rock 'n' roll-flavoured jazz, and is still an astonishing album. The music press at the time of issue were bereft of ideas about how to categorize him; it would have been much simpler just to wallow in the music. Much of Jarrett's and Manfred Eicher's future musical philosophy started out with this important record.

● Tracks: *In Front; Ritooria; Lalene; My Lady: My Child; Landscape For Future Earth; Starbright; Vapallia; Semblence.*
● First released 1972
● UK peak chart position: did not chart
● USA peak chart position: did not chart

FADDIS, JON

b. 24 July 1953, Oakland, California, USA. Faddis began playing trumpet while still a small child and at the age of 11 was introduced by his trumpet teacher, Bill Catalano, to the music of Dizzy Gillespie. At 13 years old Faddis was playing with R&B bands and in mainstream rehearsal big bands and two years later he met Gillespie, sitting in with him at a San Francisco workshop. In 1971 Faddis joined Lionel Hampton, then moved into the Thad Jones-Mel Lewis Jazz Orchestra. He was with this band on and off for the next few years, between times playing with Gil Evans, Oscar Peterson, Charles Mingus and Gillespie. It was while he was with Gillespie that Faddis first attracted widespread attention. Although he had set out deliberately to build his own playing ability through adherence to Gillespie's style, Faddis had succeeded in creating a style of his own. Nevertheless, he was deeply rooted in bebop and helped give the older man a boost at a time when he was under pressure to adapt to the current popularity of jazz-rock. The concerts and recording dates of the two trumpeters were hugely successful, both musically and commercially, and established a working pattern for Faddis for the next few years. In the early 80s Faddis was heavily committed with studio work but found time for recording sessions and tours with Jimmy Smith, Jackie McLean and McCoy Tyner. In the late 80s he joined Gillespie in a big band for a world tour but was mostly active as leader of his own bands, which included the big band Carnegie Hall Jazz Band. One of the most striking of post-bop trumpeters, Faddis blends a dazzling technique with a thorough understanding of jazz tradition. His clear, bell-like tone, is well-suited to his richly emotional playing and he has earned his place as one of the most gifted and important musicians in jazz.

● ALBUMS: *Oscar Peterson And Jon Faddis* (1975)★★★, *Youngblood* (1976)★★, *Good And Plenty* (Dunhill 1978)★★★, *Young Blood* (Pablo 1982)★★★, *Legacy* (Concord 1985), with Clark Terry *Take Double* (1986)★★★★, with Billy Harper *Jon And Billy* (Blackhawk 1987)★★, with the Carnegie Hall Jazz Band *The Carnegie Hall Jazz Band* (Blue Note 1996)★★★, *Remembrances* (Chesky 1998)★★★★.

FAGERQUIST, DON

b. 6 February 1927, Worcester, Massachusetts, USA, d. 24 January 1974. After working with the Mal Hallett band in the early 40s, Fagerquist joined Gene Krupa in 1944. He stayed with Krupa for several years, comfortably adjusting his trumpet playing to the boppish style the band adopted towards the end of the decade. After Krupa's band folded Fagerquist spent a little time with Artie Shaw before becoming a member of Woody Herman's Third Herd. He later worked with Les Brown and the Dave Pell Octet, the Brown band's small-group offshoot. A striking soloist, Fagerquist's thoughtful playing style admirably suited the west coast scene and in the 50s he played extensively and sometimes recorded with Shelly Manne, Pete Rugolo, Art Pepper and others, including the popular big band assembled for record dates by Si Zentner in the mid-60s.

FAIRWEATHER, AL

b. Alastair Fairweather, 12 June 1927, Edinburgh, Scotland, d. 21 June 1993. After a brief flirtation with the trombone, Fairweather settled on the trumpet and while still at school began playing jazz. Amongst his companions at Edinburgh Royal High School were pianist Stan Greig and clarinettist Sandy Brown, both of whom were to be important collaborators in later years. In 1953 Fairweather moved to London where he joined Cy Laurie's band and in 1954 when Brown also came to London they resumed their musical partnership. Over the next few years the Brown-Fairweather band gained in quality and strength and some of their recordings, especially *McJazz*, were widely regarded at the time to be the best to have come from a British band. Leadership of the band was at first nominally with Brown but as his non-musical interests developed Fairweather took charge. Later Brown returned, but in the mid-60s Fairweather joined Acker Bilk and in the mid-70s he began a long association with Greig's London Jazz Big Band. In 1983 he suffered a severe heart attack, thereafter played a little and also painted, eventually retiring to Edinburgh in 1987. Although his early playing recognised his admiration for Louis Armstrong, Fairweather's subtle, fluid and understated style suggested to the less discerning listener that he was the junior in his partnerships with the more forthright Brown. In fact, Fairweather's playing was deliberately couched as a perfect foil for his exuberant partner. His arrangements for their band, and for Greig's big band, reveal his deep understanding of the diverse forms of jazz. As Greig remarked, 'People didn't understand how good he was.'

● ALBUMS: with Sandy Brown unless stated *B+B+B* (1953)★★★★, *Sandy's Sidemen* (1956)★★★, *McJazz* (1957)★★★★, *Fairweather Friends* (1957)★★★, *Al And Sandy* (1959)★★★, *Al's Pals* (1959)★★, *Doctor McJazz* (1960)★★★, *The Incredible McJazz* (60s)★★★, *McJazz Lives On!* (60s)★★.

FAIRWEATHER, DIGBY

b. 25 April 1946, Rochford, Essex, England. Fairweather first played trumpet semi-professionally in and around his home town. In 1971 he formed his own small band, later playing with numerous leaders, including Eggy Ley, Dave Shepherd and Alex Welsh. His reputation established, at the beginning of 1977 Fairweather took the plunge and became a full-time musician. Subsequently, he led his own bands and played in the Midnite Follies Orchestra. He also worked in small bands including Velvet, a co-operative band with Len Skeat, Ike Isaacs and Denny Wright, a trumpet-piano duo with Stan Barker, with whom Fairweather was also involved in educational work, the Pizza Express All Stars and Brian Priestley's septet. An excellent mainstream trumpeter with a full, rich tone, Fairweather's graceful playing style is particularly well-suited to ballads. In addition to his playing, Fairweather has also turned to writing and broadcasting; his published works include some jazz-inspired short stories, a trumpet tutor, and, with Priestley and Ian Carr, a biographical directory *Jazz: The Essential Companion*, which evolved into *Jazz: The Rough Guide*.

● ALBUMS: *Dig & De Swarte* (1977)★★★, *Havin' Fun* (Black Lion 1978)★★★★, *Going Out Steppin'* (Black Lion 1979)★★★, *Velvet* (Black Lion 1979)★★★, *Songs For Sandy* (Hep Jazz 1983)★★★, with Stan Barker *Let's Duet* (1984)★★, *With Nat In Mind* (Jazzology 1994)★★★★, (Jazzology 1994), *Squeezin' The Blues Away* (Spirit Of Jazz 1996)★★★.

● COMPILATIONS: *A Portrait Of Digby Fairweather* 1979 recording (Black Lion 1994)★★★★.

FALLON, JACK

b. 13 October 1915, London, Canada. Fallon went to Britain with the Canadian Airforce and settled there in 1946. He established a professional career playing bass in the bands of Ted Heath and Jack Jackson and played with George Shearing in 1948 with whom he accompanied Duke Ellington. Jack Fallon became the staff bassist for Lansdowne Records where he recorded with a wide variety of musicians - from Josh White (vocal/guitar) through Alex Welsh and Humphrey Lyttelton to Joe Harriott. In the mid-50s Fallon had a successful sextet called In Town Tonight. It was during this period that he started his own company,Cana Agency, which later represented Kenny Ball. Fallon played regularly with light orchestral bandleaders like Frank Chacksfield and Ron Goodwin, worked as a violinist with country musicians and even recorded with the Beatles in 1968. Since then Fallon has concentrated on his agency but he did play with Lennie Felix (piano) in the 70s and later with Stan Greig (piano) and Digby Fairweather.

● ALBUMS: *The In Town Jazz Group* (1955)★★★.

FAME, GEORGIE

b. Clive Powell, 26 June 1943, Leigh, Lancashire, England. Entrepreneur Larry Parnes gave the name to this talented organist during the early 60s following a recommendation from songwriter Lionel Bart. Parnes already had a Power, a Wilde, an Eager and a Fury. All he now needed was Fame. It took a number of years before Fame and his band the Blue Flames had commercial success, although he was a major force in the popularizing of early R&B, bluebeat and ska at London's famous Flamingo club. The seminal *Rhythm And Blues At The Flamingo* was released in 1964. Chart success came later that year with a UK number 1, 'Yeh Yeh'. Fame's jazzy nasal delivery, reminiscent of Mose Allison, made this record one of the decade's classic songs. He continued with another eleven hits, including two further UK chart toppers, 'Get Away' and 'The Ballad Of Bonnie And Clyde', the latter of which was his only US Top 10 single in 1968. The former maintained his jazz feel, which continued on such striking mood pieces as 'Sunny' and 'Sitting In The Park'. Thereafter, he veered towards straight pop. His recent change of record labels had attempted to re-market him and at one stage teamed him with the Harry South Big Band. While his albums showed a more progressive style his singles became lightweight, the nadir being when he teamed up with Alan Price to produce some catchy pop songs. Fame has also played straight jazz at Ronnie Scott's club, performed a tribute to Hoagy Carmichael with singer Annie Ross, and has sung over Esso advertisements. In recent times Fame has been content touring with Van Morrison as keyboard player, given a brief cameo to perform the occasional hit. During the renaissance of the Hammond B3 organ (an instrument that Fame had originally pioneered in the London clubs) during the jazz boom of the early 90s it was announced that Georgie had recorded a new album *Cool Cat Blues*; and its subsequent release to favourable reviews and regular concert appearances indicated a new phase. The album was recorded to the highest standards and featured smooth contributions from Steve Gadd, Robben Ford, Richard Tee, Jon Hendricks and Boz Scaggs. A reggae reworking of 'Yeh Yeh' and a graceful version of Carmichael's 'Georgia' are but two outstanding tracks. Van Morrison duets with Fame on the former's classic 'Moondance'. He followed this with *The Blues And Me*, an album of a similar high standard. Tragedy struck Fame in 1994 when his wife committed suicide. Since then he has continued to work and record with Morrison as well as gigging with his latter-day version of the Blue Flames, which features his son. Fame has reached a stage in his career where he can play what he chooses, now he has reverted to his first love, jazz. He is an exemplary musician whose early and late period work is necessary for any discerning record collection.

● ALBUMS: *Rhythm And Blues At The Flamingo* (Columbia 1963)★★★★, *Fame At Last* (Columbia 1964)★★★★, *Sweet Things* (Columbia 1966)★★★, *Sound Venture* (Columbia 1966)★★★★, *Two Faces Of Fame* (Columbia 1967)★★★, *The Ballad Of Bonnie And Clyde* (Epic 1968)★★★, *The Third Face Of Fame* (Columbia 1968)★★★, *Seventh Son* (Columbia 1969)★★, *Georgie Does His Things With Strings* (Columbia 1970)★★, *Going Home* (Columbia 1971)★★, with Alan Price *Fame And Price, Price And Fame Together* (Columbia 1971)★★, *All Me Own Work* (Reprise 1972)★★, *Georgie Fame* (Island 1974)★★, *That's What Friends Are For* (1979)★★★, *Georgie Fame Right Now* (1979)★★★, *Closing The Gap* (1980)★★, with Annie Ross *Hoagland* (1981)★★★, *In Goodman's Land* (1983)★★★, *My Favourite Songs* (1984)★★, *No Worries* (1988)★★, *Cool Cat Blues* (Go Jazz 1991)★★★★, *The Blues And Me* (1994)★★★, *Three Line Whip* (1994)★★★, with Van Morrison *How Long Has This Been Going On* (Verve 1995)★★★★, with Morrison, Ben Sidran, Mose Allison *Tell Me Something: The Songs Of Mose Allison* (Verve 1996)★★.

● COMPILATIONS: *Hall Of Fame* (Columbia 1967)★★★★, *Georgie Fame* (Starline 1969)★★★★, *Fame Again* (Starline 1972)★★★★, *20 Beat Classics* (Polydor 1982)★★★★, *The First Thirty Years* (1990)★★★, *The Very Best Of Georgie Fame And The Blue Flames* (Spectrum 1998)★★★★, *The In Crowd* 3-CD set (1998)★★★★.

FARLEY AND RILEY

Although they came to prominence as members of a Red McKenzie band at the Onyx Club in 1935, neither Eddie Farley (b. 16 July 1904, Newark, New Jersey, USA; trumpet) nor Mike Riley (b. 5 January 1904, Fall River, Massachusetts, USA, d. 2 September 1984; trombone) took jazz very seriously. Their on-stage antics drove away Eddie Condon, who was also a member of the McKenzie band, but the public loved them. Farley And Riley became especially popular when they performed and recorded a song written by Red Hodgson. 'The Music Goes 'Round And 'Round', attracting non-jazz audiences to 52nd Street. Farley and Riley later capitalized upon their popularity by forming bands of their own, but their success clearly depended less on intrinsic musical qualities than on the vagaries of public taste.

FARLEY, EDDIE

(see Farley And Riley)

FARLOW, TAL

b. Talmadge Holt Farlow, 7 June 1921, Greensboro, North Carolina, USA, d. 25 July 1998, Sea Bright, New Jersey, USA. Although his father was an amateur musician, Tal Farlow did not begin playing guitar until 1942, working as a professional sign-painter for several years. Before the decade was out he had achieved a sufficiently high standard to be hired by cabaret singer Dardanelle, vibraphonist Margie Hyams and clarinettist Buddy De Franco. In 1950, by now a fleet and inventive guitarist inspired by Charlie Christian, he joined forces with another vibes player, Red Norvo, thus beginning a long-running and fruitful, if intermittent, musical partnership. The third member of this group was Charles Mingus. Although he initially struggled to keep up with Norvo's startling speed, Farlow developed a technique that in turn made him the fastest guitarist of his era. In 1953 Farlow worked with Artie Shaw, and later in the decade led his own trio on recordings for Blue Note and Verve, including work with Eddie Costa, but he drifted into retirement from music and concentrated on his career as a sign-painter. In the late 60s he made a handful of festival appearances, returning to fairly consistent public performances in the late 70s. In the 80s he resumed his working relationship with Red Norvo, touring the USA, UK and Europe and delighting audiences, many of whom had been alerted to this fine musician's talents through a 1981 television documentary, *Talmadge Farlow*. Farlow's breathtaking speed and fluent technique were highly influential, inspiring young guitarists such as John McLaughlin.

● ALBUMS: *Tal Farlow Quartet* 10-inch album (Blue Note 1954)★★★, *The Tal Farlow Album* 10-inch album (Verve 1954)★★★★, *The Artistry Of Tal Farlow* reissued as *Autumn In New York* (Norgran 1955)★★★, *The Interpretations Of Tal Farlow* (Norgran 1955)★★★, *A Recital By Tal Farlow* (Norgran 1955)★★★, *Tal* (Norgran 1956)★★★★, *The Swinging Guitar Of Tal Farlow* (Verve 1956)★★★, *Fuerst Set* (Xanadu 1956)★★★, *Second Set* (Xanadu 1956)★★★, *This Is Tal Farlow* (Verve 1958)★★★★, *The Guitar Artistry Of Tal Farlow* (Verve 1959)★★★★, *Tal Farlow Plays The Music Of Harold Arlen* (Verve 1960)★★★, *Tal Farlow Returns* (Prestige 1969)★★★, *On Stage* (Concord 1976)★★, *A Sign Of The Times* (Concord 1976)★★★, *Tal Farlow 78* (Concord 1978)★★★, *Chromatic Palette* (Concord 1981)★★★, *Cookin' On All Burners* (Concord 1982)★★★, *The Legendary Tal Farlow* (Concord 1984)★★, *Standard Recital* (FD Music 1992)★★, with Lenny Breau *Chance Meeting* 1980 recording (Guitarchives 1997)★★★.

FARMER, ADDISON

b. 21 August 1928, Council Bluffs, Iowa, USA, d. 20 February 1963. The twin brother of Art Farmer, he moved to Los Angeles in the mid-40s and was soon playing bass with noted contemporary musicians including Dexter Gordon, and also Jay McShann with both of whom he recorded. He also gigged with visiting bop stars, Charlie Parker and Miles Davis. In the early 50s he travelled to New York where he played with Stan Getz, Gigi Gryce and others. In 1959 he joined the Jazztet, a band formed by his brother and Benny Golson. The following year, Farmer left the Jazztet and subsequently played with Mose Allison. An exceptional timekeeper, Farmer's playing also revealed a rich sonority and his early death robbed jazz of one of its outstanding bass players.

● ALBUMS: with Charlie Parker *Bird With Miles And Dizzy* (Queen 1946)★★★★, *Art Farmer Quintet* (Prestige 1955)★★★★ with Art Farmer *Modern Art* (United Artists 1958)★★★★, *Meet The Jazztet* (Argo 1960)★★★, with Mose Allison *I Don't Worry About A Thing* (Atlantic 1962)★★★.

FARMER, ART

b. 21 August 1928, Council Bluffs, Iowa, USA. While still a child Farmer moved first to Phoenix, Arizona, then to Los Angeles. This was in the mid-40s, and during the next few years Farmer played trumpet in various name bands, including those led by Jay McShann and Benny Carter, and worked and recorded with musicians as diverse as Johnny Otis, Wardell Gray and Teddy Edwards. In the early 50s he was with Lionel Hampton, touring Europe and recording there (against Hampton's express orders) with fellow sideman Clifford Brown. Back in New York, where Hampton fired pretty nearly his entire band for making those now classic records, Farmer worked with many of the leading contemporary musicians resident in the city. Amongst those artists were Charles Mingus, Horace Silver, Gerry Mulligan and George Russell. At the end of the decade he and Benny Golson formed their own group which they named the Jazztet. This band also included Farmer's twin brother, Addison Farmer, who played bass. The Jazztet folded in 1962 and thereafter Farmer worked mostly as a single occasionally forming his own small groups. From the mid-60s onwards he worked extensively in Europe, spending much time in Vienna, Austria, where he was a member of the national radio big band. He also played with the Clarke-Boland Big Band. By this time he had begun favouring the fluegelhorn, especially when leading small groups which he continued to do through the 70s and 80s. In the 90s, Farmer continued to tour extensively although his work is not as well represented on record as his many admirers would wish.

A highly melodic soloist, with inventive turns of phase and a frequently elegaic approach to his music, Farmer's popularity has sometimes been overshadowed by that of his less-talented contemporaries. Study of his work over several decades reveals an artist of considerable emotional depths which he has plumbed more and more as the years have passed. In a quiet, unassuming manner, which reflects his personality, Farmer has proved hard to pigeonhole. This is a quality which has sometimes led observers to pay less attention to him than would be the case were he a more assertive man and performer.

● ALBUMS: *Art Farmer Septet* reissued as *Work Of Art* (Prestige/New Jazz 1953)★★★★, with Sonny Rollins *Art Farmer Quintet Featuring Sonny Rollins* 10-inch album (Prestige 1954)★★★★, with Gigi Gryce *Art Farmer Quintet i* 10-inch album (Prestige 1954)★★★★, *Art Farmer Quartet* 10-inch album (Prestige 1954)★★★★, with Gryce *Art Farmer Quintet ii* 10-inch album (Prestige 1955)★★★★, with Gryce *Art Farmer Quintet Featuring Gigi Gryce* reissued as *Evening In Casablanca* (Prestige/New Jazz 1956)★★★★, with Bennie Green *Bennie Green & Art Farmer* (Prestige 1956)★★★★, with Donald Byrd *Two Trumpets* (Prestige 1956)★★★, with Byrd, Idriss Suliman *Three Trumpets* (Prestige 1957)★★★★, with Gryce *When Farmer Met Gryce* 1954/1955 recordings (Prestige 1957)★★★★, *Farmer's Market* (New Jazz 1958)★★★★, *Portrait Of Art Farmer* (Contemporary 1958)★★★★, *Last Night When We Were Young* (ABC-Paramount 1958)★★★★, *Modern Art* (United Artists 1958)★★★★, *Brass Shout* (United Artists 1959)★★★★, *Aztec Suite* (United Artists 1959)★★★★, with Curtis Fuller, Benny Golson *Meet The Jazztet* (Argo 1960)★★★, *Art* (United Artists 1961)★★★, *Early Art* 1954 recordings (Prestige 1961)★★★★, with Golson *Big City Sounds* (Argo 1961)★★★, with Golson *The Jazztet And John Lewis* (Argo 1961)★★★, with Golson *The Jazztet At Birdhouse* (Argo 1961)★★★★, with Golson *Here And Now* (Mercury 1962)★★★, with Golson *Another Git Together* (Mercury 1962)★★★, with Eddie Costa *In Their Own Sweet Way* (Premier 1962)★★★, *Listen To Art Farmer & The Orchestra* (Mercury 1963)★★★★, *Interaction* (Atlantic 1963)★★★, *Live At The Half Note* (Atlantic 1964)★★★★, *Perception* 1962 recording (Argo 1964)★★★, *To Sweden With Love* (Atlantic 1964)★★★, *The Many Faces Of Art Farmer* (Scepter 1964)★★★★, shared with Art Taylor *Hard Cookin'* (Prestige 1964)★★★★, *Sing Me Softly Of The Blues* (Atlantic 1965)★★★★, *Baroque Sketches* (Columbia 1966)★★, *The Time And The Place* (Columbia 1967)★★★, *Art Farmer Plays The Great Jazz Hits* (Columbia 1967)★★★, *Art Worker* (1968)★★★★, *Art Farmer & Phil Woods* (1968)★★★, *From Vienna With Art* (MPS 1970)★★★, *Homecoming* (1971)★★★, *Gentle Eyes* (Mainstream 1972)★★, *A Sleeping Bee* (Sonet 1974)★★★, *To Duke With Love* (East Wind/Inner City 1975)★★★★, *The Summer Knows* (East Wind/Inner City 1976)★★★, *Art Farmer Quintet At Boomer's* (East Wind/Inner City 1976)★★★★, *On The Road* (Contemporary 1976)★★★, *Crawl Space* (CTI 1977)★★★★, with Jackie McLean *Art Farmer Live In Tokyo/Art Farmer Meets Jackie McLean* (1977)★★★, *Something You Got* (CTI 1977)★★★★, *Big Blues* (CTI 1978)★★★, *Yama* (CTI 1979)★★★, *Isis* (1980)★★★, *Foolish Memories* (Bellaphon 1981)★★★, *Work Of Art* (Concord Jazz 1981)★★★★, *Manhattan* (Soul Note 1982)★★★, *Mirage* (Soul Note 1982)★★★, *Warm Valley* (Concord Jazz 1982)★★★★, *Maiden Voyage* (Denon 1983)★★★, with Golson *The Jazztet: Moment To Moment* (Soul Note 1983)★★★, *In Concert* (Enja 1984)★★★, *You Make Me Smile* (Soul Note 1985)★★★, with Fuller, Golson *Back To The City* (Contemporary 1986)★★★, *Real Time* (Contemporary 1986)★★★★, *Something To Live For: The Music Of Billy Strayhorn* (Contemporary 1987)★★★★, *Azure* (Soul Note 1988)★★★, *Blame It On My Youth* (Contemporary 1988)★★★★, *Ph.D.* (Contemporary 1989)★★★, *Central Avenue Reunion* (Contemporary 1990)★★, *Soul Eyes* (Enja 1991)★★, *Live At*

Sweet Basil (Evidence 1992)★★★, *The Company I Keep* (Arabaesque 1995)★★★, *Live At The Stanford Jazz Workshop* (Monarch 1997)★★★★, *Silk Road* (Arabesque 1997)★★★, *Art In Wroclaw* (Emarcy 1998)★★★.

FARRELL, JOE

b. Joseph Carl Firrantello, 16 December 1937, Chicago Heights, Illinois, USA, d. 10 January 1986. After studying several reed instruments, Farrell concentrated on tenor saxophone from the mid-50s. At the end of the decade he joined Maynard Ferguson in New York, also playing and recording with Slide Hampton, George Russell, Charles Mingus and Jaki Byard. In the mid-60s he became a long-serving member of the Thad Jones-Mel Lewis Jazz Orchestra and also worked with Elvin Jones. Having been likened to major and various tenor stylists, such as Stan Getz, Sonny Rollins and John Coltrane, it is not surprising that Farrell's musical tastes drew him into many varied byways of jazz. He played on the Band's *Rock Of Ages*, was a member of Chick Corea's Return To Forever (Corea also played on several of Farrell's own albums). Later he was associated with Woody Shaw, Paul Horn, George Benson and JoAnne Brackeen. While still concentrating on his main instrument, Farrell also played effectively on soprano saxophone and flute. He died of bone cancer in January 1986.

● ALBUMS: *Joe Farrell Quartet* (1970)★★★, *Moon Germs* (1972)★★, *Penny Arcade* (CTI 1973)★★★, *Benson And Farrell* (1976)★★★, *Skateboard Park* (1979)★★★, *Sonic Text* (Original Jazz Classics 1979)★★★★, *Joe Farrell And Paul Horn* (1980)★★, *Vim 'n' Vigour* (Timeless 1984)★★.

FATOOL, NICK

b. 2 January 1915, Milbury, Massachusetts, USA. After starting out with the fine 30s dance band of Joe Haymes, drummer Fatool swung through a succession of top-flight big bands, notably those of Benny Goodman (appearing on the excellent Sextet sides of the late 30s and early 40s), and Artie Shaw, being unusually prominent on the original recording of 'Concerto For Clarinet'. In the early 40s Fatool settled in California, where for the next two decades he worked in the film studios but found time to play his drums in numerous bands, including those led by Les Brown, Billy Butterfield and Harry James. He also played and sometimes recorded with Bob Crosby, Louis Armstrong, Tommy Dorsey and many others, gradually moving into the field of latter-day dixieland jazz to which he brought a deftly-swinging lightness that few of his contemporaries could match. Apart from Crosby the dixieland-style bands with whom he has played include those of Charles LaVere, Matty Matlock, Pete Fountain, the Dukes Of Dixieland, Barney Bigard and the World's Greatest Jazz Band. His career continued into the 80s, with tours of the USA and Europe with the Yank Lawson-Bob Haggart band. One of the unsung heroes of jazz drumming, Fatool's self-effacing style meant that he was often overlooked by audiences accustomed to the somewhat more bombastic playing of many of his contemporaries. Conversely, his subtlety and skill were always appreciated by musicians.

● ALBUMS: with Barney Bigard *Clarinet Gumbo* (1973)★★.

FAVORS, MALACHI

b. 27 August 1937, Lexington, Mississippi, USA. Favors came from a religious family (his father preached as a pastor) who disapproved of secular music. He took up the bass at the age of 15, initially inspired by Wilbur Ware. He started playing professionally when he left school, accompanying Freddie Hubbard and Dizzy Gillespie. Moving to Chicago, he recorded with Andrew Hill in 1955 and in 1961 he played with Muhal Richard Abrams in the Experimental Band, becoming a member of the AACM at its inception in 1965. He played in groups led by Roscoe Mitchell and Lester Bowie and in 1969 joined with them and Joseph Jarman to found the Art Ensemble Of Chicago, who triumphantly carried the banner of 'Great Black Music: Ancient to the Future' into the 90s. Outside of the Art Ensemble, he has recorded on Mitchell's and Bowie's own albums, as well as with fellow AACM member Kalaparusha Maurice McIntyre, drummer Sunny Murray and gospel group From The Root To The Source. *Sightsong*, an album of duos with Abrams, was released in 1976 and two years later the solo *Natural And The Spiritual* appeared on the Art Ensemble's own AECO label. Favors, who has taken to appending Maghostut (in various spellings) to his name, typifies the AACM's interest in mysticism and once gave his biography as 'into being in this universe some 43,000 years ago. Moved around and then was ordered to this Planet Earth by the higher forces, Allah De Lawd Thank You Jesus Good God A Mighty, through the precious channels of Brother Isaac and Sister Maggie Mayfield Favors; of ten. Landed in Chicago by way of Lexington, Mississippi, for the purpose of serving my duty as a Music Messenger.' Perhaps more plausibly he has also claimed that his decision to play freely is a statement that has cost him financial rewards. As well as being a foremost exponent of free jazz upright playing, Favors is also adept at the electric bass, the African *balafon*, the zither and banjo.

● ALBUMS: with Muhal Richard Abrams *Sightsong* (1976)★★★★, *Natural And The Spiritual* (1978)★★★.

FAVRE, PIERRE

b. 2 June 1937, Le Locle, nr. Neuchatel, Switzerland. The self-taught Favre spent his formative years drumming with Philly Joe Jones, Bud Powell and Benny Bailey as well as working in a cymbal factory before developing his own style in one of the key 60s free jazz trios with Irène Schweizer on piano and, initially, George Mraz on bass. The latter was replaced by Peter Kowald who came over from Germany. The addition of Evan Parker on saxophones took the group in further new directions. Favre appeared with the other three on *European Echoes* by Manfred Schoof, but tended afterwards to avoid the more explosive areas of European new jazz. Favre's search for new voices led to his involvement with Indian and other percussionists, with the singer Tamia, and with the formation of his Drum Orchestra. A variety of bells, gongs and cymbals contribute to his percussive armoury, which has been heard to great effect in recent years on the ECM label. Favre also played with musicians such as Peter Brötzmann, John Tchicai, Don Cherry and Eje Thelin. A lasting collaboration with the French reed-player Michel Portal began in 1972. Favre's work in the 90s included his own album, *Window Steps* on which he collaborated with Kenny Wheeler (trumpet), Steve Swallow (bass) and David Darling (cello).

● ALBUMS: *Santana* (1968)★★★, *Pierre Favre Quartet* (1969)★★★, with Manfred Schoof *European Echoes* (1969)★★★, Michel Portal *à Chateauvallon* (1972)★★★★, with Gunter Hampel, Joachim Kuhn, Albert Mangelsdorff *Solo Now* (1976)★★★ with John Surman, Mal Waldron *Mal Waldron Plays The Blues* (1976)★★★★, *Drum Converstaion* (Calligraph 1979)★★★★, *Arrivederci/Le Chouartse* (1981)★★★, with Joe McPhee *Topology* (1981)★★★, with Barre Phillips *Music By ...* (1981)★★★, with Tamia *De La Nuit ... Le Jour* (ECM 1982)★★, *Such Winters Of Memory* (1983)★★★, *Singing Drums* (ECM 1984)★★★, *Window Steps* (ECM 1996)★★★★, *Portrait* (Unit 1998)★★★, *Soufflés* (Intakt 1998)★★★★.

FAWKES, WALLY

b. 21 June 1924, Vancouver, British Columbia, Canada. Fawkes moved to the UK while still very young and in the mid-40s was recruited by George Webb, leader of one of the first bands to attract popular attention during the trad-jazz boom. In 1947 he left Webb along with fellow sideman Humphrey Lyttelton to become a founder-member of the latter's new band. This musical relationship lasted until 1956 and was rewarding for musicians and fans alike. After leaving Lyttelton, Fawkes played with several other leaders, including Bruce Turner and Sandy Brown, with whom he recorded in 1954 and 1956, respectively (both sessions being reissued on a single 1989 album), and he also led his own semi-professional band, the Troglodytes, a more loosely swinging band than many of his contemporaries in the sometimes staid UK trad scene. Later, Fawkes, a gifted, Sidney Bechet-influenced clarinettist, chose to play freelance, usually showing a marked preference for obscure pubs in the London area. For several decades, Fawkes, using the byline 'Trog', drew the strip-cartoon 'Flook' in the *Daily Mail*, the script for which was written by singer George Melly. Fawkes continued his sporadic jazz career into the 80s with several excellent records, including reunions with Lyttelton and Ian Christie.

● ALBUMS: *Wally Fawkes And The Neo-Troglodytes* (Dawn 1979)★★★, with Humphrey Lyttelton *It Seems Like Yesterday* (Calligraph 1983)★★★, with Ian Christie *That's The Blues Old Man* (1984)★★★, *Wally Fawkes And The Rhythm Kings* (Stomp Off 1985)★★★, *Whatever Next!* (Stomp Off 1986)★★★, *October Song* (Calligraph 1986)★★★, with Bruce Turner, Sandy Brown *Juicy And Full Toned* 1954-56 recordings (Lake 1989)★★★★, *Fidgety Feet* (Stomp Off 1993)★★★.

● COMPILATIONS: with Lyttelton *A Tribute To Humph, Volume 1* (Dormouse 1984)★★★.

FAZOLA, IRVING

b. Irving H. Prestopnik, 10 December 1910, New Orleans, Louisiana, USA, d. 29 March 1949. In his teens and early 20s Fazola played clarinet with several noted New Orleans-based bandleaders, including Louis Prima and Joseph 'Sharkey' Bonano. Although he played frequently with dixieland-style bands, Fazola's classical training made him eligible for many of the more chart-bound big bands of the swing era. In the 30s his pugilistic nature took him on a headlong dash through numerous jobs, including work with Ben Pollack, Glenn Miller, Jimmy McPartland, Claude Thornhill, Muggsy Spanier and the band with which he attracted most attention, Bob Crosby's. His fiery, ill-tempered nature led him into several violent fights and he was also a heavy drinker and a womanizer. Despite his erratic private life, Fazola was a distinguished and polished performer and with a different nature might well have made the big time as a featured artist. But then, had his nature been different he might well have been a lesser musician. His wild lifestyle finally took its toll and he died still some way short of his 40th birthday.

FEATHER, LEONARD

b. 13 September 1914, London, England, d. 22 September 1994, Los Angeles, California, USA. After studying piano, Feather advanced his musical interests by teaching himself arranging and in the early 30s produced a number of record sessions, contributing charts and scores. Among the musicians for whom he worked in such capacities was Benny Carter and he was instrumental in persuading Henry Hall to hire Carter for the BBC Dance Orchestra. In the mid-30s Feather went to the USA and during the next decade he continued to work in record production, sometimes supplying original material for artists such as Louis Armstrong, Lionel Hampton ('Blowtop Blues') and Dinah Washington ('Evil Gal Blues'). Feather also branched into concert promotion and produced numerous recording sessions. Additionally, he continued to compose songs for artists such as Sarah Vaughan, Ella Fitzgerald, Cannonball Adderley and Sonny Stitt. Despite all these endeavours, most of his considerable efforts in the cause of jazz were gradually concentrated into writing on the subject for several magazines, including *Esquire* and *Down Beat*, and he also wrote a jazz column for the *Los Angeles Times*. He was the author of several jazz books, notably *Encyclopedia Of Jazz* and his autobiography, *The Jazz Years: Ear Witness To An Era*. He was also a frequent broadcaster on jazz on radio and television. His daughter Lorraine is an accomplished singer.

● ALBUMS: all as producer *Leonard Feather's Swinging Swedes* (1951-54)★★★, *Winter Sequence* 10-inch album (MGM 1954)★★★, *Swingin' On The Vibories* (ABC-Paramount 1956)★★, *Leonard Feather Presents Bop* reissued as *Leonard Feather Presents 52nd Street* (Mode 1957)★★★, *Hi-Fi Suite* (MGM 1957)★★★, *Oh, Captain!* (MGM 1958)★★★, *Seven Ages Of Jazz* (1958)★★★, *Swedish Punch* (1959)★★★, *Leonard Feather's Encyclopedia Of Jazz All Stars* (1967)★★★★, *Leonard Feather*

Presents (VSOP 1988)★★★, *Night Blooming* (Mainstream 1991)★★★.

● FURTHER READING: *The Jazz Years: Ear Witness To An Era*, Leonard Feather. *The Encyclopedia Of Jazz* various editions, Leonard Feather.

FEINSTEIN, MICHAEL

b. Michael Jay Feinstein, 7 September 1956, Columbus, Ohio, USA. A singer, pianist and musical archivist, Feinstein was a boy prodigy, able to play all manner of show tunes by ear. His mother was an amateur tap dancer and his father a singer and sales executive. After attending high school in Columbus he worked as a piano salesman in California, where he discovered some rare acetate recordings by Oscar Levant. He returned them to the actor/pianist's widow, who secured him a job as archivist and personal assistant to two of popular music's all-time great songwriters, Ira Gershwin and Harry Warren. In the late 70s and early 80s, as well as cataloguing their material, Feinstein unearthed several alternative Gershwin lyrics that had never been printed. Through Gershwin he met the lyricist's god-daughter, Liza Minnelli, and she opened a great many showbusiness doors for him. He also served as her accompanist, and played for other artists such as Rosemary Clooney, John Bubbles, Jessie Matthews, and Estelle Reiner. During the 80s and 90s Feinstein appeared in cabaret in Britain and America. He made his Broadway debut with *Michael Feinstein In Concert* (1988), which later toured major US cities and returned to New York in 1990. Some five years later he presented *An Evening With Michael Feinstein* at London's Comedy Theatre. He also filled the 18,000-seater Hollywood Bowl twice in July 1987. On television, Feinstein has hosted his own *Michael Feinstein And Friends* special, as well as featuring in several tributes to legendary songwriters, including George Gershwin, Irving Berlin and Jule Styne. Therefore, it was entirely appropriate that he was chosen to pay homage to Gershwin in *A Capitol Fourth*, a spectacular Independence Day celebration held in Washington, DC, in 1998 - the centenary of the composer's birth.

On his second album, *Live At The Algonquin*, Feinstein sang Raymond Jessel's 'I Wanna Hear A Show Song' ('Please don't bend my ear with punk or funk - it's junk'), which summed up his musical philosophy perfectly. One of the joys of his performances is that he includes rarely heard songs - and unfamiliar verses to more popular songs - and sings them as he believes the writers intended them to be sung. His voice has been called 'overly stylized - the high notes being rather faint, while the lower register is too loud'. Neverthless, he has a good ear for phrasing, and is recognized as a leading expert in and exponent of the American standard popular song.

● ALBUMS: *Pure Gershwin* (Parnassus 1987)★★★★, *Live At The Algonquin* (Elektra 1987)★★★, *Isn't It Romantic* (Elektra 1987)★★★, *Remember: Michael Feinstein Sings Irving Berlin Songbook* (Elektra 1987)★★★, *The MGM Album* (Elektra (1989)★★★★, *Over There: Songs Of War and Peace c.1900-1920* (EMI Angel 1989)★★★, *Sings The Burton Lane Songbook Volume One* (Elektra Nonesuch 1990)★★★★, *Sings The Burton Lane Songbook Volume Two* (Elektra Nonesuch 1992)★★★,*Sings The Jule Styne Songbook* (Elektra Nonesuch 1991)★★★, *Pure Imagination* (Elektra 1992)★★★, with Andrea Marcovicci *Just Kern* one track only (Elba 1992)★, *Forever* (Elektra 1993)★★, *Sings The Jerry Herman Songbook* (Elektra Nonesuch 1994)★★★, *Sings The Hugh Martin Songbook* (Nonesuch 1995)★★★, *Such Sweet Sorrow* (Atlantic 1995)★★★, *Nice Work If You Can Get It* (Atlantic 1996)★★★, *Michael & George: Feinstein Sings Gershwin* (Concord Jazz 1998)★★★.

● VIDEOS: *Michael Feinstein & Friends* (KulterVideo/Image Entertainment 1994).

● FURTHER READING: *Nice Work If You Can Get It: My Life In Rhythm And Rhyme*, Michael Feinstein. *The Ira Gershwin Songbook*, Michael Feinstein (ed.).

● FILMS: *Scenes From The Class Struggle In Beverly Hills* (1989).

FELD, MOREY

b. 15 August 1915, Cleveland, Ohio, USA, d. 28 March 1971. He began playing drums in his late teens, working with Ben Pollack in 1936 and then with Joe Haymes. In the early 40s he played with many bands, some of them swing era big bands, others small groups orientated towards Dixieland. The leaders for whom he played in these years include Bud Freeman, Benny Goodman, Teddy Wilson and Wild Bill Davison. In 1947 Feld began a decade-long association with Peanuts Hucko, then worked in New York studios. During the mid-50s he also played with bop musicians, including Charlie Parker with whom he recorded. During the 60s he was active in recording studios, operated a drum school, toured overseas, then moved to Colorado where he was reunited with Hucko. In 1968 he was involved with the formation of the World's Greatest Jazz Band. Feld was killed when fire destroyed his home. Technically assured and adaptable to many styles of jazz, he was a particularly gifted Dixieland drummer, bringing a lightness of touch not found by many of his contemporaries.

● ALBUMS: *Jazz Goes To Broadway* (Kapp 1956)★★★, *The World's Greatest Jazz Band* (Project 1968)★★★.

FELDMAN, VICTOR

b. 7 April 1934, London, England, d. 12 May 1987, Los Angeles, California, USA. A remarkable child prodigy, Feldman was encouraged into his professional career by his uncle, drummer Max Bacon, and was playing drums in a family trio at the age of seven, alongside his brothers Robert and Monty. When he was 10 years old he was featured at a concert with Glenn Miller's AAAF band and in his teens he worked with the bands of Ralph Sharon, Roy Fox and Ronnie Scott and like-minded spirits such as John Dankworth, Stan Tracey, Tubby Hayes and Tony Crombie. Feldman also played piano and, at the urging of Carlo Krahmer of Esquire Records, soon added the vibraphone to his armoury of instruments, gradually dropping drumming except for special features. By the mid-50s, when he emigrated to the USA, he was regarded primarily as a vibraphonist, nevertheless, he continued to play piano displaying an especially original and delicate touch. Feldman's first transatlantic job was with Woody Herman and he later became associated with the west coast scene, recording with Shelly Manne. In the late 50s Feldman extended his versatility by studying arranging with Marty Paich. In the 60s he played with diverse jazzmen such as Benny Goodman, with whom he toured Russia in 1962, and Miles Davis, for whom he wrote 'Seven Steps To Heaven'. Before hiring Feldman, Cannonball Adderley took the precaution of playing some of his records to his existing sidemen; only after they had acknowledged that here was an outstanding musical personality they would be happy to work with, did he tell them that their new companion was British, Jewish and white. Always open to new concepts, Feldman ventured into jazz-rock fusion in the 70s and 80s, working with Steely Dan and Tom Scott among many others, and recording with his own funk outfit the Generation Band. He continued to play in the mainstream of jazz, however, and in the 80s recorded with Spike Robinson, with whom he had played in London three decades earlier. He died suddenly, following an asthma attack.

● ALBUMS: *Suite Sixteen* (Contemporary 1957)★★★★, *Victor Feldman On Vibes* reissued as *With Mallets a Fore Thought* (Mode/Interlude 1957)★★★, *The Arrival Of Victor Feldman* (Contemporary 1958)★★★★, *Love Me With All Your Heart* (Vee Jay 1960)★★★★, *Merry Ole Soul* (Riverside 1961)★★★, *Stop The World, I Want To Get Off* (World Pacific 1962)★★★★, with Curtis Amy *Way Down* (Pacific Jazz 1962)★★★★, *Latinsville* 1959 recordings (Contemporary 1963)★★★, *Soviet Jazz Themes* (Ava 1963)★★, *It's A Wonderful World* (Vee Jay 1965)★★, *Everything In Sight* (1967)★★★, *The Venezuela Joropo* (1967)★★★, *Your Smile* (Choice 1973)★★★, *The Artful Dodger* (Concord Jazz 1977)★★★, *Rockavibabe* (DJM 1977)★★, with the Generation Band *Soft Shoulder* (Nautilus 1981)★★★, *Secrets Of The Andes* (Palo Alto 1982)★★★, *To Chopin With Love* (Palo Alto 1983)★★, with the Generation Band *Call Of The Wild* (Nautilus 1984)★★, *Fiesta* (Nautilus 1984)★★★, *High Visibility* (Nautilus 1985)★★★, *In My Pocket* 1977 recording (Coherent 1988)★★.

FELIX, LENNIE

b. 16 August 1920, London, England, d. 29 December 1980. Although Felix began his career in the years immediately before World War II, it was in the early post-war period that he became an established pianist on the London jazz club scene. In the 50s he played in the UK with Freddy Randall and Harry Gold, and in New York with Red Allen and Buster Bailey. Towards the end of the decade he was a member of Wally Fawkes's Troglodytes. He continued to play through the 60s and 70s, making records and radio broadcasts. At his best as a soloist or leading a trio, Felix displayed the traits of dominant musical personalities such as Fats Waller, Earl Hines and Art Tatum. Perhaps as a result of such mentors he was temperamentally unsuited to the role of accompanist and some of his musical partnerships ended disastrously. One, with visiting American cornetist Ruby Braff, a man not known for his reticence in dealing with awkward associates, ended with the visitor declaring, 'I asked for a piano player and they gave me a disease.' During the Christmas season, 1980, Felix was struck by a car as he was leaving a London jazz club and he died on 29 December that year.

● ALBUMS: *That Cat Felix!* (1958)★★★, *In His Stride* (1966)★★★★, *The Many Strides Of Lennie Felix Live at Nova Park, Zurich* (1975)★★★, *Boogie Train: Piano Solos* (1980)★★★.

FELL, SIMON

b. 13 January 1959, Dewsbury, England. Fell grew up in Batley, West Yorkshire, receiving piano lessons from an early age. He took up double bass in 1973. Although originally inspired by R&B, he took the classical path - Kirklees Youth Orchestra and the Huddersfield Philharmonic - for a number of years. Leaving school he made contact with guitarist Paul Buckton and live electronics improviser John McMillan but then moved to Cambridge, where he studied English Literature. A marked preference for emotional involvement (as against free improvisation) led him to form a jazz band called Persuasion A in the mid-80s. A self-run record label, Bruce's Fingers, released their music to critical acclaim in England and the USA in 1986. In 1989 he formed a trio with Leeds-based drummer Paul Hession and saxophonist Alan Wilkinson, characterized as 'punkjazz' for its ferocity and monumental attack. In 1991 Fell released *Compilation II*, a collage of jazz, free improvisation, serial charts and electronics that was welcomed by writer Steve Lake (*Wire*) as 'a potential classic. Brilliant.' Along with Sheffield's Martin Archer, Simon Fell is a leading composer of his generation, crossing boundaries and creating music of a passion and originality unusual in Britain.

● ALBUMS: *Compilation I* (1985)★★★★, with Persuasion A *Two Steps To Easier Breathing* (1988)★★★, *Compilation II* (1991), with Charles Wharf *M.M.* (1991)★★★, *Music For 10(0)* (Leo 1996)★★.

FERGUSON, MAYNARD

b. 4 May 1928, Montreal, Quebec, Canada. Already a bandleader in his native land by his early teenage years, trumpeter Ferguson played in the bands of Boyd Raeburn, Jimmy Dorsey and Charlie Barnet in the 40s. His breakthrough into public consciousness came in 1950 when he joined Stan Kenton, electrifying audiences with his high-note playing. Unlike many other high-note trumpeters, Ferguson proved that it was possible to actually play music up there rather than simply make noises. However, it is possible that not all his fans appreciated the skills he was demonstrating. After leaving Kenton in 1953 Ferguson worked at Paramount studios in Los Angeles before turning to bandleading, sometimes with a big band, at other times with a small group. Skilful use of arrangements often allowed the Ferguson bands to create an impression of size; the 12-piece band he led at the 1958 Newport Jazz Festival had all the power and impact of many groups twice its size. Among the many fine musicians who worked with Ferguson in the 50s and 60s were Slide Hampton, Don

Sebesky, Bill Chase, Don Ellis and Bill Berry. In the late 60s Ferguson moved to the UK, where he formed a big band with which he toured extensively. In the USA again during the 70s, he moved into jazz-rock and reached a new audience who found the music and the flamboyance with which it was presented extremely attractive. During the 80s Ferguson formed the funk band High Voltage before returning to jazz with the big band-orientated Big Bop Nouveau. Ferguson also plays several other brass instruments with considerable skill, but it is as a trumpeter that he has made his greatest impact. His technical expertise on the instrument has made him a model for many of the up-and-coming young musicians.

● ALBUMS: *Maynard Ferguson's Hollywood Party* 10-inch album (EmArcy 1954)★★★, *Dimensions* 10-inch album (EmArcy 1954)★★★★, *Jam Session Featuring Maynard Ferguson* (EmArcy 1955)★★★, *Maynard Fergsuon Octet* (EmArcy 1955)★★★★, *Around The Horn With Maynard Ferguson* (EmArcy 1956)★★★★, *Maynard Ferguson Conducts The Birdland Dream Band* (Bluebird 1956)★★★★, *Boy With Lots Of Brass* (EmArcy 1957)★★★, *A Message From Newport* (Roulette 1958)★★★★, *A Message From Birdland* (Mercury 1959)★★★★, *Maynard Ferguson Plays Jazz For Dancing* (Roulette 1959)★★★, *Newport Suite* (Roulette 1960)★★★★, *Swingin' My Way Through College* (Roulette 1960)★★★★, *Maynard '61* (Roulette 1961)★★★, with Chris Connor *Double Exposure* (Atlantic 1961)★★★, with Connor *Two's Company* (Roulette 1961)★★★, *"Straightaway" Jazz Themes* (Roulette 1961)★★★, *Maynard '62* (Roulette 1962)★★★, *Si! Si! M.F.* (Roulette 1962)★★★, *Message from Maynard* (Roulette 1963)★★★, *Maynard '64* (Roulette 1964)★★★, *The New Sound Of Maynard Ferguson* (Cameo 1964)★★★, *Color Him Wild* (Mainstream 1965)★★★, *The Blues Roar* (Mainstream 1965)★★★, *Six By Six: Maynard Ferguson And Sextet* (Mainstream 1965)★★★, *Sextet 1967* (Just A Memory 1967)★★★, *Maynard Ferguson Live At Expo '67, Montreal* (Just A Memory 1967)★★★, *Trumpet Rhapsody* (MPS 1968)★★★, *Maynard Ferguson 1969* (Prestige 1969)★★★, *M.F. Horn* (Columbia 1970)★★★, *M.F. Horn 2* (Columbia 1972)★★★, *M.F. Horn 3* (Columbia 1973)★★★, *M.F. Horn 4 + 5, Live At Jimmy's* (Columbia 1973)★★★★, *Chameleon* (Columbia 1974)★★★, *Primal Scream* (Columbia 1975)★★★, *New Vintage* (Columbia 1977)★★★, *Hot* (Columbia 1977)★★★, *Carnival* (Columbia 1978)★★, *Uncle Joe Shannon* (Columbia 1978)★★, *Conquistador* (Columbia 1978)★★, *It's My Time* (Columbia 1980)★★, *Hollywood* (Columbia 1982)★★, *Storm* (Palo Alto 1982)★★, *Live From San Francisco* (Palo Alto 1983)★★★, *Body And Soul* (Black Hawk 1986)★★★, *High Voltage* (Intima 1988)★★★, *High Voltage, Vol. 2* (Intima 1988)★★★, *Live In Italy Vols 1 & 2* (Jazz Up 1989)★★★, *Big Bop Nouveau* (Intima 1989)★★★, *Footpath Cafe* (Hot Shot 1993)★★★, with Big Bop Nouveau *These Cats Can Swing* (Concord Jazz 1995)★★★, with Big Bop Nouveau *One More Trip To Birdland* (Concord Jazz 1996)★★★, with Tito Puente *Special Delivery* (Concord Picante 1997)★★★★, with Big Bop Nouveau *Brass Attitude* (Concord Jazz 1998)★★★.

● COMPILATIONS: *Stratospheric* 1954-1956 recordings (EmArcy 1976)★★★★, *Maynard Ferguson* 1973-1979 recordings (Columbia)★★★, *The Complete Maynard Ferguson On Roulette* 10-CD box set (Mosaic)★★★★, *Verve Jazz Masters, Vol. 52* 1951-1957 recordings (Verve)★★★.

FERRELL, RACHELLE

b. *c.*1961, USA. Ferrell first attracted attention singing jazz in and around Philadelphia. Later, while teaching in New Jersey music colleges, she began developing a localized reputation as a session singer. Determined not to be pigeonholed, with the inevitable career restrictions this brings, she extended her repertoire, which had at first been dominated by standards, to encompass R&B, and gradually developed a broader, but still jazz-conscious, range. Ferrell has an astonishingly wide range, but unlike so many technically gifted singers, she uses her multi-octave potential with care and mature thought. Thanks to appearances at festivals, she has expanded her audience and is clearly a major name to watch as jazz enters its second hundred years.

● ALBUMS: *First Instrument* (Blue Note 1990)★★★, *Rachelle Ferrell* (Blue Note 1994)★★★★.

FEZA, MONGEZI

b. 1945, Queenstown, South Africa, d. 14 December 1975, London, England. Feza, nicknamed 'Mongs', began playing trumpet at the age of eight and was gigging regularly by the time he was 16. He took part in the 1962 Johannesburg Jazz Festival, where Chris McGregor invited him and four more of the best players at the Festival to form a band, the legendary Blue Notes. As a mixed race band it was impossible for them to work under apartheid and, in 1964, whilst touring Europe, they decided to settle there. After a year in Switzerland they went to London, where, evolving into the Chris McGregor Group, they made a huge impact in the UK Jazz scene. As well as McGregor's Group and the big band Brotherhood Of Breath, Feza gigged and recorded with Dudu Pukwana and Johnny Mbizo Dyani (who were both colleagues in the McGregor group), Robert Wyatt (who, like Pukwana, had Mongezi's marvellous composition 'Sonia' in his repertoire), Keith Tippett's Centipede, and Julian Sebothane Bahula. Feza's stinging, restless trumpet contributed hugely to the special edge of the McGregor Group and was a kwela-inspired counterpart to Don Cherry's folk-like melodies in the Ornette Coleman Quartet. Feza was very much affected by the lack of recognition that he and his colleagues had to contend with but, whatever his personal problems, he transformed them into an exhilarating blend of South African and free jazz traditions. His death in 1975 was a shock to his colleagues, dispiriting some of them, such as Dyani, far beyond the musical loss. The official cause of death was pneumonia, but it has been claimed that this was aggravated because Feza was left sick and unattended in a police cell after an arrest for disorderly behaviour. Shortly after his death, the remaining Blue Notes recorded the tribute *Blue Notes For Mongezi*, released in 1976.

● ALBUMS: with Chris McGregor *Very Urgent* (1968)★★★★, *Brotherhood Of Breath* (1971)★★★★, with others *Music For Xaba* (1972)★★★, with Brotherhood of Breath *Brotherhood* (1972)★★★, with Dudu Pukwana *In The Townships* (1972)★★★, with Brotherhood of Breath *Live At Willisau*

(1974)★★★, with Pukwana *Flute Music* (1975)★★★★, with Pukwana *Diamond Express* (1977)★★★.

FIELD, GREGG

b. 21 February 1956, Oakland, California, USA. Field began playing drums as a child, studying and working with local bands in California. Although he first attracted widespread attention after joining Count Basie's band in the early 80s, he had already built a formidable reputation amongst fellow musicians. In addition to appearing on television in shows such as *Saturday Night Live*, *The Merv Griffin Show* and *Frank Sinatra: A Man And His Music*, he has written many arrangements for the *Tonight Show* orchestra. He has toured or recorded with Donald Byrd, Quincy Jones, George Benson, Harry James, Herbie Hancock and Wayne Shorter and an impressive roster of singers, including Frank Sinatra, Ella Fitzgerald, Ray Charles, Sarah Vaughan, Mel Tormé, Dianne Schuur, Tony Bennett and Joe Williams. In addition to performing, Field is also a member of the faculty of the University of Southern California and is active as a record producer. His records with Basie included Grammy-award-winning albums and, following the leader's death, he has worked with all-star alumni bands, including the Frank Wess-Harry Edison all-star band which recorded at the 1989 and 1990 Fujitsu-Concord Jazz Festivals in Tokyo. In 1990 he was a member of an all-star band led by Ray Anthony for a recording session which Field also produced. In 1991, he worked with Bill Berry and his LA Big Band for concerts at the Hollywood Bowl. A superbly accomplished drummer, equipped to play in almost any setting, Field is at his considerable best playing in a mainstream big band. The enthusiastic swing of his performances ensures that a great tradition on jazz drumming continues into the closing years of the century.

FIELDS, 'KANSAS'

b. Carl Donnell Fields, 5 December 1915, Chapman, Kansas, USA. As a young teenager Fields moved to Chicago where, a few years later, he began playing drums at various clubs. Among the musicians for whom he worked during the 30s were Jimmie Noone and Horace Henderson. In 1940 he joined Roy Eldridge and then flitted through the bands of Benny Carter, Charlie Barnet, Mel Powell and others, until war service interrupted his career. After the war he was with Cab Calloway, Sidney Bechet, Eldridge again, and also ventured into modern waters with Dizzy Gillespie. Fields was, however, a mainstream drummer and was at his best in such surroundings. In the 50s and early 60s he spent much of his time in Europe working and recording with Mezz Mezzrow, Lionel Hampton and Buck Clayton. He continued working into the 80s.

FIELDS, HERBIE

b. Herbert Fields, 24 May 1919, Elizabeth, New Jersey, USA, d. 17 September 1958. Fields played clarinet and alto (occasionally tenor) saxophone in several bands in the mid- and late 30s and also studied formally at the Juilliard School of Music. Among the leaders for whom he worked were George Handy, Raymond Scott, Woody Herman and Oran 'Hot Lips' Page. In military service during World War II Fields led a service band, and after the war he joined Lionel Hampton. He led his own small and large groups during the late 40s, recorded with Miles Davis, but was unable to maintain the momentum of his career and by the following decade was mostly playing commercial music. Fields' playing was varied, perhaps even erratic at times. At his best, he could be a fluid and imaginative player, especially on clarinet. Sometimes, however, he could be undisciplined and his career appeared to lack direction.

FIFTH POWER, THE - LESTER BOWIE

Trumpeter Lester Bowie was born in St. Louis, but he remains closely associated with the jazz developments of 60s Chicago, where he relocated in 1962. Along with saxophonists Joseph Jarman and Roscoe Mitchell, and bassist Malachi Favors, musicians he had met through Chicago's Association For The Advancement Of Creative Musicians (AACM), he formed the famous Art Ensemble Of Chicago. This 1978 date was recorded in Italy, and once again features bassist Favors, as well as Chicago saxophone talent Arthur Blythe, pianist/vocalist Amina Claudine Myers and drummer Phil Wilson, playing slightly more orthodox, but no less exciting, music.

- Tracks: *Sardegna Amore (New Is Full Of Lonely People); 3 In 1 (Three In One); BBB (Duet); God Has Smiled On Me (Traditional Gospel); The 5th Power (Finale).*
- First released 1978
- UK peak chart position: did not chart
- USA peak chart position: did not chart

FINCKEL, EDDIE

b. 23 December 1917, Washington, DC, USA. After studying formally with classicist Otto Leuning, Finckel turned to jazz. In the early and mid-40s he worked as staff arranger for the bands of Boyd Raeburn and Gene Krupa. With Raeburn he helped create the distinctive qualities of this fine, progressive orchestra. Disagreements broke up the association with Raeburn, Finckel claiming sole authorship of several of the band's important numbers including 'Two Spoos In An Igloo', 'Boyd Meets Stravinsky' and 'March Of The Boyds', the last two having been credited to Raeburn and George Handy. Finckel, along with Tadd Dameron, also wrote modern, boppish arrangements for the first Buddy Rich band. In writing charts for Krupa he was faced with the unenviable task of making true the claim that the drummer's 1944 band really was 'the Band that Swings with Strings'. From this period Finckel created hits for Krupa with 'Leave Us Leap', 'Gypsy Mood', 'Starburst' and the breakneck tempoed 'Lover'. He wrote original music for the Ann Arbor Drama Festival and was founder and director of the Young Artists Chamber Orchestra of New Jersey. Finckel also wrote for the Broadway stage. In the classical field he composed a cello concerto, a clarinet concerto and a suite for cello and string orchestra. He also composed music for the ballet *Of Human Kindness*.

FINEGAN, BILL

b. 3 April 1917, Newark, New Jersey, USA. Pianist Finegan's first successes were the arrangements he wrote for the Tommy Dorsey band, but his real breakthrough came in 1938 when he became a staff arranger for Glenn Miller. Throughout the late 30s and early 40s, Finegan wrote extensively for films, but continued to provide charts for Miller, Dorsey, Horace Heidt and others. At the start of the 50s Finegan was studying at the Paris Conservatoire and began corresponding with fellow-arranger Eddie Sauter, who was then hospitalized with tuberculosis. Out of this correspondence emerged a decision to form an orchestra of their own that would play music other leaders might well regard as uncommercial. In 1952 the 21-piece Sauter-Finegan Orchestra made its appearance. With so many musicians, several of whom doubled and even trebled on other instruments, the tonal palette was huge and the two arrangers took full advantage of this. The band was hugely successful with memorable records such as 'The Doodletown Fifers' and 'Sleigh Ride' (based upon music by Prokofiev). On this latter title the sound effect of horses' hooves on hard-packed snow was created by Finegan beating his chest. Later, he wryly remarked, 'this is probably my finest effort on wax - or snow'. In the late 50s Finegan worked mostly in radio and television, but in the 70s returned to big band arranging with charts for the Glenn Miller reunion orchestra and for Mel Lewis, who continued to use his work into the 80s.

● ALBUMS: all by Sauter-Finegan Orchestra *New Directions In Music* 10-inch album (RCA-Victor 1953)★★★★, *Inside Sauter-Finegan* (RCA-Victor 1954)★★★, *The Sound Of Sauter-Finegen* (RCA-Victor 1954)★★★, *Sons Of Sauter-Finegan* (RCA-Victor 1955)★★★, *Concert Jazz* (RCA-Victor 1955)★★★, *New Directions In Music* (RCA 1956)★★★★★, *Adventure In Time* (RCA-Victor 1956)★★★, *Under Analysis* (RCA-Victor 1957)★★★★, *One Night Stand With The Sauter-Finegan Orchestra* (RCA-Victor 1957)★★★, *Straight Down The Middle* (RCA-Victor 1957)★★★, *Inside Sauter-Finegan Revisited* (RCA-Victor 1961)★★★, *Sleigh Ride* (RCA-Victor 1961)★★★★, *The Return Of The Doodletown Fifers* (Capitol 1985)★★★.

FIREHOUSE FIVE PLUS 2

The Firehouse Five Plus 2 were formed in 1949 by trombonist Walt Kimball. It was a semi-professional band whose members were drawn from the staff of Walt Disney's animation studios in Hollywood. Some members went on to full-time careers such as clarinettists Tom Sharpsteen and George Probert. The band were playing at the time of a renewal of interest in traditional jazz styles and although this was the basis of the band's music, the use of the bass saxophone, tuba and washboard encouraged their tendency towards a humorous rather frantic style which perhaps reflected their Walt Disney cartoon origins.

● ALBUMS: *Firehouse Five Plus 2 At Disneyland* (1962)★★, *Firehouse Five Plus 2 Goes To A Fire* (1964)★★.

FISCHER, CLARE

b. 22 October 1926, Durand, Michigan, USA. After formal studies at Michigan State University, Fischer became arranger and accompanist to the popular singing group, the Hi-Lo's. His arrangements, which are often in the more elaborate, left field tradition of Gil Evans and Lennie Tristano, were also used by Donald Byrd and Dizzy Gillespie, with whom he worked on the album, *A Portrait Of Duke Ellington*. In the 60s Fischer formed an occasional big band, an activity that he continued in later decades. Among the musicians attracted into his bands by his forward-thinking, swinging charts, which always leave space for soloists, were Warne Marsh, Bill Perkins, Conte Candoli and Steve Hufstetter. In recent years Fischer has worked more as a pianist, although he continues to write extensively, especially in the Latin idiom which has long been one of his chief musical interests.

● ALBUMS: *First Time Out* (1962)★★★, *Surging Ahead* (1962)★★★★, *Easy Living* (1963)★★★, *Extensions* (Discovery 1963)★★★, *One To Get Ready, Four to Go* (1963)★★★, *Fusion 2* (1964)★★, *So Danso Samba* (1964)★★, *Manteca!* (1966)★★★, *Songs For Rainy Day Lovers* (1967)★★★, *Thesaurus* (1968)★★, *Duality* (Discovery 1969)★★★, *Great White Hope!* (Revelation 1970)★★★, *The Reclamation Act Of 1972* (Revelation 1971)★★★, *Head, Heart And Hands* (1971)★★★, *Soon/T' DA-A-A-A-A* (1972)★★★, *Clare Fischer And EX-42* (1979)★★★, *The State Of His Art* (Revelation 1973)★★, *Jazz Song* (Revelation 1973)★★, *Alone Together* (Discovery 1975)★★, *Clare Declares* (1975)★★, *Salsa Picante* (Discovery 1978)★★★, *Machacha* (Discovery 1979)★★★, *Music Inspired By The Kinetic Sculpture Of Don Conrad Mobiles* (1980)★★★, *And Sometimes Voices* (Discovery 1981)★★, *Starbright* (Discovery 1982)★★, *Blues Trilogy* (Discovery 1982)★★, *Whose Woods Are These* (Discovery 1984), *Clare Fischer Plays By And With Himself* (Discovery 1986)★★★, *Crazy Bird* (Discovery 1985)★★★, *Tjaderama* (1987)★★★, *Free Fall* (Discovery 1987)★★★, 2 + 2 (Discovery 1988)★★, *By And With Myself* (1988)★★, *Waltz (Thesaurus/Duality)* (Discovery 1989)★★, *Lembrancas* (Concord 1989)★★★, *Just Me - Solo Piano Excursions* (Concord 1996)★★★, *Rockin' In Rhythm* (JMI 1997)★★★.

FITZGERALD, ELLA

b. Ella Jane Fitzgerald, 25 April 1917, Newport News, Virginia, USA, d. 15 June 1996, Beverly Hills, California, USA. Following the death of her father, Fitzgerald was taken to New York City by her mother. At school she sang with a glee club and showed early promise, but preferred dancing to singing. Even so, chronic shyness militated against her chances of succeeding as an entertainer. Nevertheless, she entered a talent contest as a dancer, but owing to last-minute nerves, she was unable to dance and was therefore forced to sing. Her unexpected success prompted her to enter other talent contests, and she began to win frequently enough to persevere with her singing. Eventually, she reached the top end of the talent show circuit, singing at the Harlem Opera House where she was heard by several influential people. In later years many claimed to have 'discovered' her, but among those most likely to have been involved in trying to establish her as a professional singer with the Fletcher Henderson band were Benny Carter and Charles Linton. These early efforts were unsuccessful, however, and she continued her round of the talent shows. An appearance at Harlem's Apollo Theatre, where she won, was the most important stepping-stone in her career. She was heard by Linton, who sang with the Chick Webb band at the Savoy Ballroom. Webb took her on, at first paying her out of his own pocket, and for the fringe audience she quickly became the band's main attraction. She recorded extensively with Webb, with a small group led by Teddy Wilson, with the Ink Spots and others, and even recorded with Benny Goodman. Her hits with Webb included 'Sing Me A Swing Song', 'Oh, Yes, Take Another Guess', 'The Dipsy Doodle', 'If Dreams Come True', 'A-Tisket, A-Tasket' (a song on which she collaborated on the lyric), 'F.D.R. Jones' and 'Undecided'. After Webb's death in 1939 she became the nominal leader of the band, a position she retained until 1942. Fitzgerald then began her solo career, recording numerous popular songs, sometimes teaming up with other artists, and in the late 40s signing with Norman Granz. It was Granz's masterly and astute control of her career that helped to establish her as one of America's leading jazz singers. She was certainly the most popular jazz singer with non-jazz audiences, and through judicious choice of repertoire, became the foremost female interpreter of the Great American Popular Song Book. With Granz she worked on the 'songbook' series, placing on record definitive performances of the work of America's leading songwriters, and she also toured extensively as part of his Jazz At The Philharmonic package.

Fitzgerald had a wide vocal range, but her voice retained a youthful, light vibrancy throughout the greater part of her career, bringing a fresh and appealing quality to most of her material, especially 'scat' singing. However, it proved less suited to the blues, a genre that, for the most part, she wisely avoided. Indeed, in her early work the most apparent musical influence was Connee Boswell. As a jazz singer, Fitzgerald performed with elegantly swinging virtuosity and her work with accompanists such as Ray Brown, to whom she was married for a time (they had an adopted son, Ray Brown Jnr, a drummer), Joe Pass and Tommy Flanagan was always immaculately conceived. However, her recordings with Louis Armstrong reveal the marked difference between Fitzgerald's approach and that of a singer for whom the material is secondary to his or her own improvisational skills. For all the enviably high quality of her jazz work, it is as a singer of superior popular songs that Fitzgerald remains most important and influential. Her respect for her material, beautifully displayed in the 'songbook' series, helped her to establish and retain her place as the finest vocalist in her chosen area of music. Due largely to deteriorating health, by the mid-80s Fitzgerald's career was at a virtual standstill, although a 1990 appearance in the UK was well received by an ecstatic audience. In April 1994 it was reported that both her legs had been amputated because of complications caused by diabetes. She lived a reclusive existence at her Beverly Hills home until her death in 1996. Her most obvious counterpart among male singers was Frank Sinatra and, with both singers now dead, questions inevitably arise about the fate of the great popular songs of the 30s and 40s. While there are still numerous excellent interpreters in the 90s, and many whose work has been strongly influenced by Fitzgerald, the social and artistic conditions that helped to create America's First Lady of Song no longer exist, and it seems highly unlikely, therefore, that we shall ever see or hear her like again.

● ALBUMS: *Ella And Ray* (1948)★★★, *The Ella Fitzgerald Set* (1949)★★★, *Souvenir Album* 10-inch album (Decca 1950)★★★, *Ella Fitzgerald Sings Gershwin Songs* 10-inch album (Decca 1950)★★★★, *Songs In A Mellow Mood* (Decca 1954)★★★★, *Lullabies Of Birdland* (Decca 1955)★★★, *Sweet And Hot* (Decca 1955)★★★, *Ella Fitzgerald Sings The Cole Porter Songbook* (Verve 1956)★★★★★, *Ella Fitzgerald Sings The Rodgers And Hart Songbook* (Verve 1956)★★★★★, with Count Basie, Joe Williams *One O' Clock Jump* (Columbia 1956)★★★★, with Louis Armstrong *Ella And Louis* (Verve 1956)★★★★★, with Armstrong *Porgy And Bess* (Verve 1956)★★★★, with Armstrong *Ella And Louis Again* (Verve 1956)★★★★★, *Like Someone In Love* (Verve 1957)★★★★★, *Ella Fitzgerald Sings The Duke Ellington Songbook* 4-LP box set (Verve 1957)★★★★★, *Ella Fitzgerald Sings The Gershwin Songbook* (Verve 1957)★★★★, *Ella Sings Gershwin* (Decca 1957)★★★★, *Ella And Her Fellas* (Decca 1957)★★★, *Ella Fitzgerald At The Opera House* (Verve 1958)★★★★, *Ella Fitzgerald Sings The Irving Berlin Songbook* (Verve 1958)★★★★★, *First Lady Of Song* (Decca 1958)★★, *Miss Ella Fitzgerald And Mr Nelson Riddle Invite You To Listen And Relax* (Decca 1958)★★★, with Billie Holiday *Ella Fitzgerald And Billie Holiday At Newport* (Verve 1958)★★★, *For Sentimental Reasons* (Decca 1958)★★★, *Ella Fitzgerald Sings The George And Ira Gershwin Songbook* 5-LP box set (Verve 1959)★★★★★, *Ella Swings Lightly* (Verve 1959)★★★★, *Ella Sings Sweet Songs For Swingers* (Verve 1959)★★★, *Hello Love* (Verve 1959)★★★, *Get Happy!* (Verve 1959)★★★★, *Mack The Knife - Ella In Berlin* (Verve 1960)★★★, *Ella Wishes You A Swinging Christmas* (Verve 1960)★★★★, *The Intimate Ella* (Decca 1960)★★★★, *Golden Favorites* (Decca 1961)★★★, *Ella Returns To Berlin* (Verve 1961)★★★, *Ella Fitzgerald Sings The Harold Arlen Songbook* (Verve 1961)★★★★★, *Clap Hands, Here Comes Charlie!* (Verve 1962)★★★, *Ella Swings Brightly With Nelson* (Verve 1962)★★★★★, *Ella Swings Gently With Nelson* (Verve 1962)★★★★★, *Rhythm Is My Business* (Verve 1962)★★★, *Ella Fitzgerald Sings The Jerome Kern Songbook* (Verve 1963)★★★★★, *These Are The Blues* (Verve 1963)★★★★, *Ella Sings Broadway* (Verve 1963)★★★, with Basie *Ella And Basie!* (Verve 1963)★★★★, *Ella At Juan-Les-Pins* (Verve 1964)★★★, *Hello, Dolly!* (Verve 1964)★★★, *Stairway To The Stars* (Decca 1964)★★★, *Early Ella* (Decca 1964)★★★, *A Tribute To Cole Porter* (Verve 1964)★★★, *Ella Fitzgerald Sings The Johnny Mercer Songbook* (Verve 1965)★★★★★, with Duke Ellington *Ella At Duke's Place* (Verve 1966)★★★★, with Ellington *The Stockholm Concert* (1966)★★★, with Ellington *Ella And Duke At The Côte D'Azure* (Verve 1966)★★★, *Ella In Hamburg* (Verve 1966)★★★, *The World Of Ella Fitzgerald* (Metro 1966)★★★, *Whisper Not*

(Verve 1966)★★★, *Brighten The Corner* (Capitol 1967)★★★, *Misty Blue* (Columbia 1968)★★★, *Ella 'Live'* (Verve 1968)★★★, *30 By Ella* (Columbia 1968)★★★, *Sunshine Of Your Love/Watch What Happens* (Prestige 1969)★★★, *Ella* (Reprise 1969)★★★, *Things Ain't What They Used To Be* (Reprise 1970)★★★, *Ella A Nice* (1971)★★★, *Ella Fitzgerald At Carnegie Hall* (Columbia 1973)★★★, with Joe Pass *Take Love Easy* (Pablo 1974)★★★, *Ella In London* (Pablo 1974)★★★, *Fine And Mellow* (Pablo 1974)★★★, *Ella - At The Montreux Jazz Festival 1975* (Pablo 1975)★★★, with Oscar Peterson *Ella And Oscar* (Pablo 1975)★★★, with Pass *Fitzgerald And Pass . . . Again* (Pablo 1976)★★★, with Tommy Flanagan *Ella Fitzgerald With The Tommy Flanagan Trio* (Pablo 1977)★★★, *Lady Time* (Pablo 1978)★★★, *Dream Dancing* (Pablo 1978)★★★, with Basie *A Classy Pair* (Pablo 1979)★★★, with Basie *A Perfect Match: Basie And Ella* (Pablo 1979)★★★, with Pass *Digital III At Montreux* (Pablo 1980)★★★, *Ella Fitzgerald Sings The Antonio Carlos Jobim Songbook* (Pablo 1981)★★★, *The Best Is Yet To Come* (Pablo 1982)★★★, with Pass *Speak Love* (Pablo 1983)★★★, *Nice Work If You Can Get It* (Pablo 1983)★★★, *Easy Living* (Pablo 1986)★★★, *All That Jazz* (Pablo 1990)★★★, *A 75th Birthday Tribute* (1993)★★★.

● COMPILATIONS: *The Best Of Ella* (Decca 1958)★★★, *The Best Of Ella Fitzgerald* (Verve 1964)★★★★, *The Best Of Ella Fitzgerald Volume 2* (Verve 1969)★★★, shared with Billie Holiday, Lena Horne and Sarah Vaughan *Billie, Ella, Lena, Sarah!* (Columbia 1980)★★★★, *The Best Of Ella Fitzgerald* (Pablo 1988)★★★★, *The Pablo Years* (Pablo 1993)★★★★, *Oh Lady Be Good! Best Of The Gershwin Songbook* (Verve 1995)★★★★, *Ella: The Legendary Decca Recordings* 4-CD box set (Decca 1995)★★★, *Ella Fitzgerald: Priceless Jazz* (GRP 1997)★★★, with Louis Armstrong *The Complete Ella Fitzgerald & Louis Armstrong On Verve* 3-CD box set (Verve 1997)★★★★★, *Unforgettable Ella* (Carlton 1998)★★★, *Ultimate Ella Fitzgerald* (Verve 1998)★★★★★.

● FURTHER READING: *Ella: The Life And Times Of Ella Fitzgerald*, Sid Colin. *Ella Fitzgerald: A Life Through Jazz*, Jim Haskins. *Ella Fitzgerald*, Stuart Nicholson. *First Lady Of Song*, Mark Fidelman.

● FILMS: *Pete Kelly's Blues* (1955), *St. Louis Blues* (1958).

FLANAGAN, TOMMY

b. 16 March 1930, Detroit, Michigan, USA. Flanagan began playing piano as a child, following a brief flirtation with the clarinet. His professional career began during his teenage while he was still living in his home town, then a thriving centre for bop. He worked with numerous visiting musicians, impressing them with his eclecticism and innate supportive gifts. In his mid-twenties he relocated to New York where he played at Birdland. From the mid-50s he continued his supportive role, working with instrumentalists and singers. The former included Miles Davis, Sonny Rollins and Coleman Hawkins. The singers included Tony Bennett and, principally, Ella Fitzgerald for whom Flanagan was accompanist for the greater part of the 60s and 70s. In the late 70s Flanagan finally made the break from his subservient role and began to make a much-deserved impact in his own right. As both small group leader and soloist, Flanagan continued to gain stature and acclaim, both popular and critical, through the 80s and into the 90s. perhaps as a result of his years in the background, perhaps through a natural diffidence and inclination towards subtly lyrical interpretations of both bop and popular standards, Flanagan's playing is often deeply introspective. His wide experience and stylistic grace have made him a major player on the internatinal stage while his bop roots and long standing admiration of Bud Powell have ensured that he remains close to the cutting edge of jazz piano.

● ALBUMS: with Kenny Burrell, John Coltrane *The Cats* (1957)★★★, *Trio Overseas/Tommy Flanagan In Stockholm* (Prestige 1957)★★★★, *Jazz ... It's Magic* (Regent 1957)★★★, with Wilbur Harden *The Music Of Rodgers And Hammerstein* (Savoy 1958)★★★, *Lonely Town* (1959)★★★, *The Tommy Flanagan Trio* (Moodsville 1960)★★★, with Ella Fitzgerald *Ella At Juan-Les-Pins* (1964)★★★, *The Tommy Flanagan Tokyo Recital* (1975)★★★, *Trinity* (Inner City 1976)★★★★, *Eclypso* (Enja 1977)★★★, with Ella Fitzgerald *Ella Fitzgerald With The Tommy Flanagan Trio* (Pablo 1977)★★★★, *I Remember Bebop* (1977)★★★, *They All Played Bebop* (1977)★★★, *Alone Too Long* (Denon 1977)★★★, with Hank Jones *Our Delights* (1978)★★★, *Something Borrowed, Something Blue* (1978)★★★, *Ballads And Blues* (1978)★★★, with Kenny Barron *Together With Kenny Barron* (Denon 1978)★★★★, *Communication* (1979)★★★, *Tommy Flanagan Plays The Music Of Harold Arlen* (1980)★★★, with Elvin Jones, Red Mitchell *Super-session* (Enja 1980)★★★, with Mitchell *You're Me* (Phontastic 1980)★★★, with Mitchell, Phil Woods *Free For All* (1981)★★★, *The Magnificent Tommy Flanagan* (Progressive 1981)★★★★, *Giant Steps* (Enja 1982)★★★, *Thelonica* (Enja 1983)★★★, *Blues In The Closet* (1983)★★★, *Nights At The Vanguard* (Uptown 1986)★★★, *Jazz Poet* (Timeless 1989)★★★★, *Beyond The Bluebird* (Timeless 1990)★★★, *Communication Live At Fat Tuesday's* (Paddle Wheel 1993)★★, *Let's Play The Music Of Thad Jones* (Enja 1993)★★★, *Lady Be Good ... For Ella* (Verve 1994)★★★, *Flanagan's Shenanigans* (Storyville 1996)★★★, *Let's* (Enja 1996)★★★, *Sea Changes* (Evidence 1997)★★★★, *Sunset And The Mockingbird: The Birthday Concert* (Blue Note 1998)★★★.

FLEAGLE, BRICK

b. Jacob Roger Fleagle, 22 August 1906, Hanover, Pennsylvania, USA. In his teens Fleagle played banjo in the south, then moved north switching to guitar. He played with numerous bands including Hal Kemp's and Joe Haymes' and began a long-running association with Rex Stewart. In the 40s he played with Jack Teagarden, J.C. Higginbotham, Buck Clayton, Stewart and others. In the 30s he had begun establishing a reputation as an arranger for big bands, writing charts for Chick Webb, Jimmie Lunceford and Duke Ellington. He continued this activity into the 40s, including writing for his own short-lived big band. In 1946 he entered fully into this aspect of music, operating his own arranging and music copying business which continued for the rest of his working life.

● ALBUMS: *One Night Stand With Brick Fleagle And His Orchestra* (Joyce 1945)★★★, *Brick Fleagle And Rex Stewart* (Black Panther/IAJRC 1945)★★★.

FLECK, BELA

b. *c*.1953, New York City, New York, USA. Fleck has been credited with expanding the parameters of the banjo by combining traditional bluegrass with jazz and classical music, similar to what David Grisman did with the mandolin. Inspired by the song 'Duelling Banjos' in the film *Deliverance*, Fleck took up the banjo at the age of 14, before moving to Boston to play with the group Tasty Licks. In 1981 he relocated to Nashville, joining the influential New Grass Revival, with whom he stayed for eight years. In 1989 he formed the Flecktones with Howard Levy (keyboards, harmonica), Victor Lamonte Wooten (bass) and Roy 'Futureman' Wooten (drumitar - a guitar wired to electric drums). The group's debut album for Warner Brothers Records sold over 50,000 copies and reached the Top 20 on the *Billboard* jazz charts. Chick Corea and Branford Marsalis have both guested on subsequent Flecktones' releases. Fleck has also collaborated with slide-player V.M. Bhatt and Chinese erhu player Jie-Bing Chen on the eclectic world music project *Tabula Rasa*, and appeared on Ginger Baker and Charlie Haden's *Falling Off The Roof*. Fleck is clearly an outstanding musician but there seems to be difficulty in establishing him beyond a jazz audience, which would seem not to be his most comfortable category - his music is more eclectic and would appeal to both rock and folk/roots audiences.

● ALBUMS: *Crossing The Tracks* (Rounder 1979)★★★, *Natural Bridge* (Rounder 1982)★★★, *Double Time* (Rounder 1984)★★★, *Drive* (Rounder 1988)★★, with the Flecktones *Bela Fleck And The Flecktones* (Warners 1990)★★★, with the Flecktones *Flight Of The Cosmic Hippo* (Warners 1991)★★★★, with Tony Trischka *Solo Banjo Works* (Rounder 1993)★★★★, with the Flecktones *UFO TOFU* (Warners 1993)★★★, *Tales From The Acoustic Planet* (Warners 1995)★★★★, with Jie Bing Chen, V.M. Bhatt *Tabula Rasa* (Water Lily Acoustics 1996)★★★, with the Flecktones *Live Art* (Warners 1997)★★★★, with the Flecktones *Left Of Cool* (Warners 1998)★★★, with Edgar Meyer, Mike Marshall *Uncommon Ritual* (Sony Classical 1998)★★★.

● COMPILATIONS: *Daybreak* (Rounder 1987)★★★★, *Places* (Rounder 1987)★★★.

● VIDEOS: *Bela Fleck Teaches Banjo Picking Styles* (Homespun Video 1996).

FLEMMING, HERB

b. Niccolaiih El-Michelle, 5 April 1900, Honolulu, Hawaii, d. 3 October 1976. Growing up in South Carolina, he studied music as a child, learning to play several brass instruments including the mellophone, the euphonium and the trombone and it was upon the latter that he became well known. He played in military bands following his enlistment and in 1917 went to France with the 369th Infantry Band which was led by James Reese Europe. After the war he returned to his studies, adding further instruments to his arsenal. In the early 20s he worked at many clubs in New York, playing with several bands including that led by Johnny Dunn with whom he recorded. In 1915 he joined Sam Wooding with whom he travelled to Europe, playing in several countries and also recording while in Berlin. Having developed a taste for travel, Flemming returned to Europe as leader of his own band, then worked again with Wooding and with Joséphine Baker before heading for South America, India, Ceylon and China. Throughout the 30s he continued to work in Europe and in 1936 acted as an interpreter for members of the US Olympic team at the Berlin games. During this period he was resident at the Sherbini Club in the city where his vocal feature, 'Summertime', customarily drew a standing ovation. Back in the USA at the start of the 40s, he played in Fats Waller's 10-piece band, then joined Noble Sissle before quitting music to work for the US government. By 1950 he was back in music, playing with Red Allen in New York before the travelbug bit again and he moved to Spain playing in Madrid in the mid-60s and also on the Costa del Sol where he played at clubs in Torremolinos and Málaga. Late in the decade he was recording in Germany and showing little sign of diminished energy or wanderlust.

● ALBUMS: *The Great Traditionalists In Europe* (MPS 1969)★★★, with The Great Traditionalists In Europe *For My Friends And Me* (Hage 1969)★★★.

FLETCHER, LIZ

b. 26 June 1959, London, England. Although she began her professional career as a dancer Fletcher soon followed in her parents' footsteps by becoming a singer. During her early years she had studied dance, singing and drama at Corona Academy and subsequently worked in the theatre and on television as a dancer, singer and actress. She began concentrating on singing, working in backing groups behind singers such as Grace Kennedy and David Grant. By the mid-90s she had begun to move towards a jazz-orientated style and a musical association with songwriter Rupert Wates proved fruitful. She has toured with the *Hot Foot From Harlem* show and confirmed her growing reputation with a very good debut album, on which she was backed by Tony Coe, Matt Wates and other artists on Malcolm Creese's label. With an appealingly mature sound and style, this is clearly a singer to watch in the twenty-first century.

● ALBUMS: *Mellow Mania* (Black Box 1997)★★★.

FLORENCE, BOB

b. 20 May 1932, Los Angeles, California, USA. Florence first attracted widespread attention amongst big band fans when he wrote elegantly crafted arrangements for Si Zentner's popular recording band in the early 60s. After leaving Zentner, with whom he sometimes played piano too, he wrote for several west coast-based musicians, including Bud Shank and Frank Capp but also varied his technique happily to accommodate blues singers Jimmy Witherspoon and Big Miller, Joanie Summers, Sue Raney and Sergio Mendes. Although an accomplished pianist, Florence's chief talents are his arranging skills and especially his ability to write for big bands. Like other arrangers he eventually realized that the only way to hear his charts (many of which were for his own compositions) played the way he wanted them was to have his own big band. First formed in the late 50s, the Florence bands continued through succeeding decades, providing object lessons in big band writing and playing. In the late 70s and 80s he was calling upon outstanding musicians such as Bob Cooper, Nick Ceroli, Bob Efford, Steve Hufstetter, Bill Perkins, Kim Richmond, Buddy Childers, Pete Christlieb and Warren Leuning. Although his roots are clearly in the post-swing era style of big band writing, Florence comfortably accommodates bebop and many latter-day fusions. In a *tour de force* on 'The Bebop Treasure Chest' (on *Trash Can City*) he demonstrated his skills by seamlessly blending phrases and quotations from 16 tunes.

● ALBUMS: *Meet The Bob Florence Trio* (Era 1957)★★★, *Bongos, Reeds And Brass* (1958)★★★, *Name Band 1959* (Carlton 1959)★★★★, with Si Zentner *Up A Lazy River* (1961)★★★★, *Big Miller With Bob Florence And His Orchestra* (1961)★★★, with Zentner *Desafinado* (1962)★★★★, with Zentner *Waltz In Jazz Time* (1962)★★★, *Here And Now* (Liberty 1964)★★★★, *Pet Project* (1968)★★, *Live At Concerts By The Sea* (Trend 1979)★★★★, with Joanie Summers *Dream* (1980)★★★, *Westlake* (Discovery 1981)★★★, *Soaring* (1982)★★★, with Sue Raney *The Music Of Johnny Mandel* (1982)★★, *Magic Time* (Trend 1983)★★★, with Raney *Ridin' High* (1984)★★★, with Raney *Flight Of Fancy - A Journey Of Alan And Marilyn Bergman* (1986)★★★, *Norwegian Radio Big Band Meets Bob Florence* (1986)★★★, *Trash Can City* (Trend 1986)★★★, *State Of The Art* (C5 1988)★★★, *Funupsmanship* (1993)★★★, with Bobby Lamb *Trinity Fair* (Hep 1996)★★★, *With All The Bells And Whistles* (Mama 1997)★★★★, *Earth* (MAMA 1997)★★★.

FLORY, CHRIS

b. 13 November 1953, New York City, New York, USA. Flory first played guitar as a child. Strongly influenced by such major guitarists as Charlie Christian and Django Reinhardt, he began playing professionally in 1974. Within a few years he had become a regular associate of Scott Hamilton, touring internationally and making records. Although he continued his links with Hamilton throughout the 80s he also played with other jazzmen including Hank Jones, Bob Wilber and Ruby Braff and for four years from 1979 was a regular member of the occasionally reformed Benny Goodman Sextet. He also played with the Goodman big band in 1985 at what proved to be the leader's final public performance. In the late 80s and early 90s Flory appeared on numerous record dates with artists such as Hamilton, Braff, Wilber, Maxine Sullivan and Rosemary Clooney. He also became a familiar and popular figure on the international circuit, sometimes in company and other times as a single. A fluent improvisor and gifted accompanist, Flory's solo work bears traces of his idols but he has steadily become a distinctive and distinguished guitarist in his own right.

● ALBUMS: *For All We Know* (Concord 1988)★★★★, *City Life* (Concord 1993)★★★, *Word On The Street* (Double-Time 1997)★★.

FLORY, MED

b. Meredith I. Flory, 27 August 1926, Logansport, Indiana, USA. Flory's early experience on alto saxophone was gained with the bands of Claude Thornhill and Woody Herman. In New York he worked mostly in small groups, some of which he led. After relocating to the west coast in 1954, he continued to play jazz in small and big bands (again sometimes as leader) but he also worked extensively in several fields other than jazz, notably as a screenwriter and an actor in films and television. While arranging for his big band in the late 50s, encouraged by Art Pepper and Joe Maini, Flory conceived the idea of arranging some of Charlie Parker's solos for a complete saxophone section. The idea was not fully developed, however, until some years later when Buddy Clark revived the concept and out of this shared interest Clark and Flory formed Supersax in 1972. Subsequently, Flory continued to lead Supersax and also played regularly with various west coast big bands.

● ALBUMS: *Med Flory And His Orchestra* (1954)★★★, *Jazz Wave* (1957)★★★, *Supersax Plays Bird* (1972)★★★★, *Supersax Plays Bird: Salt Peanuts* (1973)★★★, with Supersax *Chasin' The Bird* (1977)★★★★, *Supersax And L.A. Voices* (1984)★★★.

FOL, RAYMOND

b. 28 April 1928, Paris, France, d. 1 May 1979. In the years immediately following World War II, Fol played piano in traditional jazz bands and in bebop groups. He worked with several noted European musicians, including Boris Vian, Django Reinhardt, and his alto saxophonist older brother, Hubert Fol. In the early 50s he regularly accompanied visiting Americans and also recorded with some of them, including Roy Eldridge, Johnny Hodges, Dizzy Gillespie. Also during the 50s Fol worked in Claude Luter's band which toured with Sidney Bechet, with Guy Lafitte and Stéphane Grappelli. In the 60s he was also associated with Duke Ellington's orchestra and with various Ellingtonians including Paul Gonsalves. A deft and imaginative soloist, Fol brought to his work a considerable measure of technical virtuosity which was always at the service of the music he played.

● ALBUMS: *Les Quatres Saisons 'In Jazz'* (Philips 1965)★★★, *Echoes Of Harlem* (Blue Star 1975)★★★, *The Sky Was Blue* (Chorus 1979)★★★.

FONTANA, CARL

b. 18 July 1928, Monroe, Louisiana, USA. As a teenager Fontana played trombone in a band led by his father, then joined Woody Herman in 1952. Subsequent big band stints came with Lionel Hampton and Stan Kenton. In the late 50s he worked with Kai Winding's four-trombone band. He spent most of the 60s working in house bands in Las Vegas but returned briefly to Herman for a world tour. In the early and mid-70s he was in Supersax and was co-leader with Jake Hanna of the Hanna-Fontana Band. An enormously resourceful and inventive soloist, Fontana combines a phenomenal technique with a beautiful tone that he ably demonstrates on 'A Beautiful Friendship', recorded with Hanna at the 1975 Concord Jazz Festival. He is equally at home in a roaring big band and small groups with bebop or dixieland orientation, but is at his rhapsodic best in mainstream bands where he is given plenty of solo space.

● ALBUMS: with others *Unit From The Stan Kenton Band* (1956)★★★, with others *Colorado Jazz Party* (1971)★★★, with Jake Hanna *Live At Concord* (Concord Jazz 1975)★★★, *The Great Fontana* (Uptown 1985)★★★★, with the Bobby Shew Quintet *Heavyweights* (MAMA 1996)★★★★.

FORD, RICKY

b. 4 March 1954, Boston, Massachusetts, USA. Ford started to play drums, then changed to tenor saxophone at the age of 15, inspired by Rahsaan Roland Kirk. Ran Blake heard him playing in a Boston Club and persuaded him to study music at the New England Conservatory. (Blake later invited him to play on several albums too, including *Rapport, Short Life Of Barbara Monk* and *That Certain Feeling*). In 1974 Ford joined the Duke Ellington Orchestra under the leadership of Mercer Ellington and in 1976 he replaced George Adams in the Charles Mingus group, recording on *Three Or Four Shades of Blue* and *Me Myself An Eye*. In the late 70s and early 80s he played with Dannie Richmond, Mingus Dynasty, George Russell, Beaver Harris, Lionel Hampton and Adbullah Ibrahim's Ekaya group. However, following the release of his debut album in 1977 he has worked increasingly as a leader, often recording with Jimmy Cobb and ex-Ellington colleague James Spaulding. His latest releases also feature one of his New England Conservatory teachers, Jaki Byard. A strong, authoritative tenor player, Ford's fluency in most idioms of modern jazz has perhaps hindered the development of an individual voice, but he looks set to become a major saxophone presence in the 90s.

● ALBUMS: *Loxodonta Africana* (New World 1977)★★★, *Manhattan Plaza* (Muse 1978)★★★, *Flying Colours* (Muse 1981)★★★, *Interpretations* (Muse 1982)★★★, *Future's Gold* (Muse 1984)★★, *Shorter Ideas* (Muse 1986)★★★, *Looking Ahead* (Muse 1987)★★★★, *Saxotic Stomp* (Muse 1988)★★, *Hard Groovin* (Muse 1989)★★★, *Manhattan Blues* (Candid 1990)★★★, *Ebony Rhapsody* (Candid 1991)★★★, *Hot Brass* (Candid 1992)★★, *Tenor For The Times* (Muse 1992)★★★, *American-African Blues* (Candid 1993)★★★.

FORD, ROBBEN

b. Robben Lee Ford, 16 December 1951, Woodlake, California, USA. A jazz, blues and rock guitarist, Robben is the most celebrated member of the musical Ford family. His father Charles was a country musician, and his brothers Patrick and Mark are bluesmen, playing drums and harmonica, respectively. Inspired initially by Mike Bloomfield and Eric Clapton, Ford's first professional engagement was with Charlie Musslewhite in 1970. He formed the Charles Ford Band with his brothers in 1971, then backed Jimmy Witherspoon from 1972-74. He toured and recorded with both Joni Mitchell (as part of L.A. Express) and George Harrison in 1974, the resulting exposure bringing him a considerable amount of session work. In 1978, he formed the Yellowjackets with keyboards player Russell Ferrante and also found time to record a patchy solo debut, *Inside Story*. The early 80s saw him performing with Michael McDonald and saxophonist Sadao Watanabe; in 1986 he joined the Miles Davis band on its tour of the USA and Europe. *Talk To Your Daughter* was a triumphant return to his blues roots, and picked up a Grammy nomination in the 'Contemporary Blues' category. In 1993 he recorded with a new unit, the Blue Line featuring Roscoe Beck (bass), Bill Boublitz (keyboards) and Tom Brechtlein (drums). Ford plays cleanly in an uncluttered style (like Mike Bloomfield), but occasionally with the frantic energy of Larry Carlton.

● ALBUMS: with the Charles Ford Band *The Charles Ford Band* (1972)★★★, *Inside Story* (1978)★★★, with the Charles Ford Band *Reunion* (1982)★★★, *Talk To Your Daughter* (Warners 1988)★★★, *Mark Ford With The Robben Ford Band* (1991)★★★, *Robben Ford And The Blue Line* (1992)★★★★, with Jimmy Witherspoon *Live At The Notodden Blues Festival* (1993)★★★, with the Blue Line *Mystic Mile* (Stretch/GRP 1993)★★★, *Handful Of Blues* (Blue Thumb 1995)★★★★, *Tiger Walk* (Blue Thumb 1997)★★, *Authorized Bootleg* (GRP 1998)★★★.

● COMPILATIONS: *The Blues Collection* (Crosscut 1997)★★★★.

● VIDEOS: *Highlights* (Warner Music Video 1995).

FORMAN, BRUCE

b. *c*.1956, Springfield, Massachusetts, USA. After formal studies on piano, Forman switched to guitar and opted for the jazz scene. While playing in California he attracted the attention of Richie Cole who hired him for his small band. The spell with Cole brought Forman to the attention of a wider audience, and after leaving the band he struck out on his own. He appeared and recorded with Stanley Turrentine, Freddie Hubbard, Ray Brown, Eddie Jefferson and others. In the mid-80s he recorded a well-received album of duos with Bobby Hutcherson and George Cables. The duo format clearly appealed to Forman and in the mid- and late 90s he was often teamed with drummer Vince Lateano. Forman's playing is always eminently attractive and subtly swinging. His great technical skills are always used to enhance his performances and never at the expense of good taste.

● ALBUMS: Coast To Coast (Choice 1979), *River Journey* (Muse 1981)★★★, *20/20* (Muse 1981)★★★, *In Transit* (Muse 1982)★★★, *The Bash* (Muse 1983)★★★, *Full Circle* (Concord Jazz 1984)★★★, with George Cables *Dynamics With George Cables* (Concord Jazz 1985)★★★, *There Are Times* (Concord Jazz 1986)★★★★, *Pardon Me!* (Concord Jazz 1989)★★, *Still Of The Night* (Kamei 1991)★★★★, *Forman On The Job* (Kamei 1992)★★★.

FORMANEK, MICHAEL

b. 7 September 1958, San Francisco, California, USA. Formanek studied the bass privately in San Francisco and New York before playing with artists such as Eddie Henderson, Joe Henderson, Dave Liebman and Tony

Williams and moving to New York in the late 70s. He worked with Chet Baker, Bill Connors, Mark Murphy and Herbie Mann before moving to Germany. There he played in the Media Band and then joined Gallery with Paul McCandless, David Darling, David Samuels and Michael DiPasqua (drums). In the 90s, his collaborations with saxophonist Tim Berne are of particular note.

● ALBUMS: *Wide Open Spaces* (Enja 1990)★★★★, *Extended Animation* (Enja 1992)★★★, with Tim Berne, Jeff Hirshfield *Loose Cannon* (Soul Note 1993)★★★★, *Low Profile* (Enja 1994)★★★, *Nature Of The Beast* (Enja 1997)★★★, with Berne *Ornery People* (Little Brother 1998)★★★★, *Am I Bothering You?* (Screwgun 1998)★★★★.

FORREST, JIMMY

b. 24 January 1920, St. Louis, Missouri, USA, d. 26 August 1980. Forrest's early experience on tenor saxophone came in territory bands, including the Jeter-Pillars Orchestra, Don Albert's San Antonio-based band and the group led by Fate Marable. In 1940 he joined Jay McShann in Kansas City, where one of his section-mates was Charlie Parker. This was followed by a long period in New York with Andy Kirk, but by the end of the 40s he was back home in St. Louis. He had a huge R&B hit with 'Night Train', which actually owed more than was usually credited to a Duke Ellington composition, 'Happy-Go-Lucky Local'. At the end of the 50s he was back in New York, this time with Harry Edison, after which he led his own bands for records and club dates that lasted into the early 70s. He was then with Count Basie for a number of years and also played with the Clarke-Boland Big Band before forming a partnership with Al Grey. Together, Forrest and Grey toured the USA and Europe, playing hard-driving mainstream jazz with contrasting overtones of both R&B and bebop. Forrest's robust style echoed the Texas tenors and he proved enormously popular with audiences wherever he played.

● ALBUMS: *Night Train* (1951)★★★★, with Harry Edison *The Swinger* (1958)★★★, *All The Gin Is Gone* (1959)★★★★, *Black Forrest* (1959)★★★, *Forrest Fire* (New Jazz 1960)★★★★, *Out Of The Forrest* (Prestige 1961)★★★, *Sit Down And Relax With Jimmy Forrest* (Prestige 1961)★★, *Most Much* (Prestige 1961)★★★, *Soul Street* (New Jazz 1962)★★★★, with Count Basie *I Told You So* (1976)★★★, *Heart Of The Forrest* (1978)★★★, with Al Grey *Out Dere* (1980)★★★.

● COMPILATIONS: *The Best Of Jimmy Forrest* (Prestige 1969)★★★★.

FORTUNE, SONNY

b. Cornelius Fortune, 19 May 1939, Philadelphia, Pennsylvania, USA. An intense player on alto, tenor and soprano saxophones and flute, Fortune studied at Wurlitzers and Granoff School of Music and privately with Roland Wiggins. He started his playing career in Philadelphia R&B bands. He moved to New York in 1967 and played with Elvin Jones (1968), Mongo Santamaría (1968-70), Leon Thomas (1970), McCoy Tyner (1971-73), Roy Brooks (1973), Buddy Rich (1974) and Miles Davis (1974-75). He was with Davis when he made his highly-controversial 'heavy' album *Agartha*. Despite all the electronics Fortune frequently blisters his way to the fore during this live double album, and was showing that he had lost none of the fire in the late 80s when he toured with the Elvin Jones Jazz Machine. He has also played with George Benson, Oliver Nelson, Horace Arnold, Roy Ayers and Pharoah Sanders, but has recorded too seldom as a leader. His latest release as leader is a selection of material by Thelonious Monk, and features pianist Kirk Lightsey.

● ALBUMS: *Awakenings* (1975)★★★, *It Ain't What It Was* (1993)★★, *Laying It Down* (Konnex 1993)★★, *Monk's Mood* (Konnex 1994)★★★★, *Four In One* (Blue Note 1994)★★★★, with Gary Bartz *Alto Memories* (Verve 1995)★★★, *A Better Understanding* (Blue Note 1995)★★★, *From Now On* (Blue Note 1996)★★★.

FOSTER, AL

b. Aloysius Foster, 18 January 1944, Richmond, Virginia, USA. Given a drum kit when he was 10, Foster began playing around New York at 16, and was first recorded in 1964 (with Blue Mitchell). It was during his long residency at the Cellar Club, with the Earl May Quartet, that he was noticed by Miles Davis, resulting in three years and a worldwide tour with the Davis group (1972-75). He rejoined Davis for his comeback in 1980, staying with him for five years and recording. This highly versatile and respected drummer has also led several groups, including those with Steve Kuhn, Charlie Haden and Joe Henderson, and played in Quest with David Liebman.

● ALBUMS: with Charlie Haden, Joe Henderson *An Evening With Henderson, Haden & Foster* 1987 recording (Red 1989)★★★.

FOSTER, FRANK

b. 23 September 1928, Cincinnati, Ohio, USA. Although he began his musical career playing alto saxophone, Foster showed commendable foresight in deciding to change to tenor saxophone and flute, declaring his intention of following his own path and not the one sign-posted by Charlie Parker. In the late 40s he played with several like-minded spirits in the Detroit area, among them Wardell Gray and Snooky Young, before serving in the armed forces. In 1953 he joined Count Basie and became a significant member of the band as soloist, arranger and composer ('Shiny Stockings'). After 11 years with Basie he joined Elvin Jones, another of the musicians with whom he had played in Detroit early in his career. In the mid-60s he formed a big band which continued to play intermittently over the next decade. He also played with the Thad Jones-Mel Lewis Jazz Orchestra and co-led a small group with former Basie section-mate Frank Wess. In the mid-80s Foster began a long stint as frontman for the reactivated Basie band, with which he toured the USA and Europe. Foster's arrangements have always shown his affinity with post-war big-band writing and his work for Basie was an important factor in the success of that particular edition of the band. As a soloist, Foster's early decision to go his own way paid dividends as he developed a distinctively acerbic tone which, while reflecting an awareness of his contemporaries, was very much his own.

● ALBUMS: *Frank Foster Quintet* 10-inch album (Blue Note 1954)★★★, with Paul Quinichette *Jazz Studio 1* (Decca 1954)★★★, with Elmo Hope *Hope Meets Foster* reissued as *Wail Frank Wail* (Prestige 1956)★★★★, *Basie Is Our Boss* (Argo 1963)★★★★, *Fearless Frank Foster* (Prestige 1967)★★★, *Soul Outing!* (Prestige 1967)★★★, *Manhattan Fever* (Blue Note 1968)★★★, *The Loud Minority* (Mainstream 1974)★★★, *Giants Steps* (1975)★★★★, *Here And Now* (Catalyst 1976)★★★, *12 Shades Of Black* (Leo 1978)★★★, *Shiny Stockings* (Denon 1978)★★★★, *Roots, Branches And Dances* (1978)★★★★, *Ciquito Loco: Live At The HNITA Jazz Club* (1979)★★★, *A Blues Ain't Nothing But A Trip* (1979)★★★, *The House That Love Built* (Steeple Chase 1982)★★, *Two For The Blues* (Pablo 1983)★★★, *Frankly Speaking* (Concord Jazz 1984)★★, with James Moody *Sax Talk* (1993)★★★, *Leo Rising* (Arabesque 1997)★★★★.

FOSTER, GEORGE 'POPS'

b. 18 May 1892, McCall, Louisiana, USA, d. 30 October 1969. One of the pioneers of string bass playing, Foster began his musical career as a cellist and also occasionally played brass bass. After performing in New Orleans in the early years of the century with Kid Ory, Joe 'King' Oliver and others, he joined Fate Marable's riverboat band in 1917. He was also with the unit Ory led in California in the early 20s. Foster spent the mid-20s in the St. Louis area and by the end of the decade he was in New York working with Luis Russell. He stayed with Russell for several years, during which time the band became, in effect, the Louis Armstrong orchestra. In 1940, as the revival movement got under way, Foster was in great demand and moved on to freelance work, playing with many bands, including those led by Sidney Bechet and Jimmy Archey. He played on through the 50s and early 60s, touring the USA and Europe with Sammy Price and he also spent time in bands led by Earl Hines, at San Francisco's Hangover Club, and Elmer Snowden. Although deeply-rooted in the traditional forms of New Orleans jazz, Foster's early preference for string bass, which he played in the traditional 'slapping' manner, stood him in good stead when the inevitable musical changes occurred.

● ALBUMS: *Luis Russell And His Orchestra Volumes 1 & 2* (1926-34)★★★★, with Jimmy Archey *Jazz Dance* film soundtrack (1954)★★.

● FURTHER READING: *Pops Foster: The Autobiography Of A New Orleans Jazzman*, Pops Foster with Tom Stoddard and Ross Russell.

FOUNTAIN, PETE

b. 3 July 1930, New Orleans, Louisiana, USA. Taking up the clarinet as a small boy, Fountain was sufficiently adept to play and record before he was out of his teens. In the early 50s he worked with various bands in his home town, including the Basin Street Six. In 1954 he formed his own small band and for the next couple of years played with this group and with the Dukes Of Dixieland. In the later years of the decade he appeared as featured soloist on Lawrence Welk's networked show. Regular performances with Al Hirt ensured that he remained in demand, both in New Orleans and in the vastly different atmosphere of Las Vegas. Fountain's ability transcends the formulaic limitations of some post-revival dixieland. Although he has long been musically associated with this area of jazz, his consummate skills might more accurately place him in the mainstream. Nevertheless, he has chosen to remain in a field which has proved to be enormously popular and commercially successful and has thus, inevitably, met with critical displeasure and disregard.

● ALBUMS: with Basin Street Six *Dixieland Jazz Concert* (1951)★★★, with Dukes Of Dixieland *At The Jazz Band Ball* (1955)★★★★, *Lawrence Welk Presents Pete Fountain* (1957)★★, *Music From Dixie* (1961)★★★, *South Rampart Street Parade* (1963)★★★, with Al Hirt *Super Jazz 1* (Monument 1976)★★★★, *Alive In New Orleans* (First American 1978)★★★, *Live At The Ryman* (1988)★★, *High Society* (Bluebird 1992)★★★, *Swingin' Blues* (Start 1992)★★★, *At Piper's Opera House* (Jazzology 1993)★★★, *New Orleans All-Stars* (Tradition/Rykodisc 1997)★★★★.

FOURPLAY

A group who have earned consistent critical praise for their blend of pop and contemporary jazz, Fourplay comprise Bob James (keyboards), Lee Ritenour (guitar), Nathan East (bass) and Harvey Mason (drums). Since forming in the early 90s they have worked with a number of prominent R&B singers - including El DeBarge and Chaka Khan. Their self-titled debut album spent 31 weeks at number 1 on *Billboard*'s Contemporary Jazz Albums chart. Their second collection, *Between The Sheets*, also reached number 1 on the chart. *Elixir* featured a succession of typically smooth instrumentals and sung numbers. The styles echoed developments in pop music (particularly R&B) as well as jazz. As James told *Billboard* magazine, 'Those references to older styles are there in our roots, our training and our respect for what went before'. The album included a guest appearance from Phil Collins, with his own composition, 'Why Can't I Wait Till Morning'. The first single taken from the album, 'The Closer I Get To You', was an update of the Roberta Flack and Donny Hathaway duet, newly reinterpreted by Patti Austin and Peabo Bryson.

● ALBUMS: *Fourplay* (Warners 1991)★★★★, *Between The Sheets* (Warners 1993)★★★, *Elixir* (Warners 1995)★★★, *4* (Warner 1998)★★.

● COMPILATIONS: *The Best Of Fourplay* (Warners 1997)★★★.

FOURTH WORLD

The conception of Brazil's most famous percussionist, Airto Moreira (b. Airto Guimorva Moreira, 5 August 1941, Itaiopolis, Brazil), best known as a side man to jazz legends Chick Corea and Miles Davis, Fourth World were formed in the late 80s as his return to the traditional sounds of his youth in Curitiba, Parana State, Brazil. Before moving to the USA in 1968 he had played with a number of bossa nova groups, including the Sambalanco Trio and Quarteto Novo. Fourth World additionally includes his partner, singer Flora Purim (b. 6 March 1942, Rio de Janeiro, Brazil), José Neto (guitar) and Gary Meek (keyboards, flute, saxophone), occasionally supplemented by the central duo's daughter, Diana Moreira. Their live activities are limited somewhat by Neto's main occupation, as Harry Belafonte's musical director, but in August 1992 they travelled to England to play five weeks of engagements at Ronnie Scott's clubs in London and Birmingham. These dates provided the recordings issued on their self-titled debut album of 1992.

● ALBUMS: *Fourth World* (Ronnie Scott's Jazz House 1992)★★.

FOWLKES, CHARLIE

b. 16 February 1916, New York City, New York, USA, d. 9 February 1980. Although able to play a variety of instruments, Fowlkes appeared to recognize early on in life that he was destined to be an unsung section musician. He adopted the baritone saxophone as his chosen instrument and spells with Tiny Bradshaw and Lionel Hampton beginning in 1938 kept him busy for a decade. In the late 40s he was in Arnett Cobb's small band and then, in 1951, he became one of the most reliable members of the Count Basie band, remaining there until 1969. Six years later he was back in the band, which was where he remained until his death in 1980.

FRANCIS, DAVID 'PANAMA'

b. 21 December 1918, Miami, Florida, USA. Francis began to play drums at the age of eight, and made his first professional club appearance when he was 13 years old. Twelve months later he was on tour and in 1934 became a member of George Kelly's band. By the time he was in his late teens he was resident in New York, where he quickly found work with Tab Smith and Roy Eldridge. In 1940 he joined Lucky Millinder's big band, remaining there until 1945. Millinder's band was very popular at Harlem's Savoy Ballroom and Francis was a significant factor in that popularity. He then briefly led his own band which toured the south but met with only limited success. In 1947 he was hired by Cab Calloway for a five-year stint. Subsequently Francis worked in radio and was regularly on call as a recording session musician, backing artists such as John Lee Hooker, Eubie Blake, Ella Fitzgerald, Ray Charles and Mahalia Jackson. Francis's long absence from the jazz scene ended in the late 70s, when he returned to play with Lionel Hampton's all-star big band and, most importantly, to lead his own nine-piece band, the Savoy Sultans (named after the Al Cooper band he had played opposite at the Savoy three decades earlier). The new Sultans included Francis Williams, Norris Turney and Francis's old boss, George Kelly. A highly-accomplished drummer with an exemplary technique, Francis plays with a loosely-flowing swing that benefits any band of which he is a member.

● ALBUMS: *Panama Francis And The Dixieland Don Juans* (1959)★★★, *Panama Francis And His Orchestra* (1960)★★★★, *The Battle Of Jericho* (1962)★★★, *Tough Talk* (1963)★★★, *Panama Story* (1975)★★★, with Lionel Hampton *All Star Band At Newport '78* (1978)★★★★, *Gettin' In The Groove* (Black And Blue 1979)★★★, *Jimmy Witherspoon With Panama Francis' Savoy Sultans* (1979)★★★★, *Grooving* (Stash 1982)★★★, *Everything Swings* (Stash 1984)★★★.

● COMPILATIONS: *Get Up And Dance* (Stash 1988)★★★.

FRANKLIN, RODNEY

b. 1958, Berkeley, California, USA, Rodney Franklin was something of a child prodigy, taking piano lessons at the age of 6 at the Washington Elementary School. Upon graduation he worked extensively with John Handy in San Francisco and subsequently toured with Bill Summers, Freddie Hubbard and Marlena Shaw. In 1978 he signed with Columbia Records and recorded his debut album for the label, *In The Center*, a jazz-fusion workout that was not released in the UK. His second album, *You'll Never Know*, redressed the balance. Aided by the hit single, 'The Groove', which sparked a popular dance craze (dancers had to 'freeze' in time with the track's breaks), Rodney hit the Top 10 of the singles charts and saw *You'll Never Know* rise in the album listings. Although subsequent Columbia releases never came anywhere near repeating the extraordinary success of *You'll Never Know*, they did establish Franklin as a considerable name in the fusion market, particularly with *Marathon*. In 1988 he switched labels to BMG, recording *Diamond Inside You* which featured lead vocals by Jennifer Holliday on the single 'Gotta Give It Up'.

● ALBUMS: *In The Center* (Columbia 1978)★★★, *You'll Never Know* (Columbia 1980)★★★★, *Rodney Franklin* (Columbia 1980)★★★, *Endless Flight* (Columbia 1981)★★★, *Learning To Love* (Columbia 1982)★★, *Marathon* (Columbia 1984)★★★★, *Sky Dance* (Columbia 1985)★★★, *It Takes Two* (Columbia 1986)★★★, *Street Language* (Columbia 1986)★★★, *Diamond Inside Of You* (BMG 1988)★★★.

● COMPILATIONS: *The Best Of Rodney Franklin* (Columbia)★★★.

FRANKS, MICHAEL

b. 1944, La Jolla, California, USA. As a young teenager, Franks began singing to his own guitar accompaniment. He drew his eclectic repertoire from a broad field including folk music and aspects of the blues. He also began composing in the blues idiom, performing his own work and also hearing it picked up by other musicians. By the 70s Franks had become a well-known teacher and composer. His songs have been recorded by Mark Murphy, Carmen McRae and others. In the mid-70s he made a number of well-received records with jazzmen such as Kenny Barron and Ron Carter, and recorded with the popular Yellowjackets. Franks sings with a huskily intimate sound, interpreting lyrics with feeling and imparting a smooth swing to all his performances.

● ALBUMS: *The Art Of Tea* (1976)★★★, *Sleeping Gypsy* (1977)★★★, *Objects Of Desire* (1981)★★, *Abandoned Garden* (Warners 1995)★★★.

FRAZIER, JOSIAH 'CIÉ'

b. 23 February 1904, New Orleans, Louisiana, USA. Taught to play drums by Louis Cottrell Snr., Frazier played in several New Orleans bands in the early and mid-20s including those led by Papa Celestin and Sidney Desvigne. Working in music only part time during the 30s and the war years, Frazier worked extensively from the mid-40s, mostly in New Orleans, with bands such as that led by Percy Humphrey at Manny's Tavern as well as with Kid Howard. Later in his career, Frazier toured Europe and the UK. In a class close to that of Zutty Singleton, Frazier's springy beat and exemplary time keeping made him one of the best of the New Orleans drummers.

● ALBUMS: *Kid Howard's Vida Band* (1961)★★.

FREE JAZZ - ORNETTE COLEMAN

The revolutionary *Free Jazz* features Ornette Coleman's Double Quartet, which included Eric Dolphy (bass clarinet), trumpeters Don Cherry and Freddie Hubbard, bassists Charlie Haden and Scott La Faro, drummers Billy Higgins and Ed Blackwell and the ensemble leader on alto saxophone. Brief written parts aside, which introduced each soloist, the piece is completely improvised, without editing or overdubs. Set free to follow artistic inclinations, the musicians responded to their own imaginations, or reacted to those around them, resulting in a fervid collectivity. The ambition of the concept is rewarded with exceptional playing, at times lyrical, at others intense, but always inventive and challenging. The results were a landmark in the development of jazz.

● Tracks: *Free Jazz (Part One); Free Jazz (Part Two).*
● First released 1960
● UK peak chart position: did not chart
● USA peak chart position: did not chart

FREE MUSIC PRODUCTION

FMP has been flying the flag for uncompromising free jazz and improvisation since 1969, when a musicians' collective comprising Peter Brötzmann, Alexander von Schlippenbach, Peter Kowald, and Jost Gebers founded the company as both a record label and concert agency. Gebers was then still active as a bassist, but serious illness put paid to his performing career, and he became FMP's administrator, producer and finally its conscience. As they would say in Hollywood, Jost Gebers *is* FMP. He has produced almost 300 albums for the label and recorded virtually every minute of the twice-yearly festivals that FMP organizes in Berlin. The recordings add up to a massive archive of European improvisation, a treasure trove for musicologists of the future. FMP's original plan, to document the growth of a strictly German free jazz, was modified as the musicians formed alliances with players of other nationalities. In the early years the main dialogues were with the British and Dutch free camps. Meanwhile, the music has become truly international and one of FMP's major achievements has been the bringing together of European players with their American counterparts, including some of the Black music trailblazers who initiated free jazz: Cecil Taylor, Sunny Murray, Andrew Cyrille, Rashied Ali and Frank Wright. A festival organised around Taylor, juxtaposing the master pianist with the cream of Europe's improvisers, resulted in an 11-CD boxed set, *Cecil Taylor In Berlin '88*, which was showered in awards and nominated as the release of the year in jazz magazines throughout the world. (What makes this achievement particularly remarkable is that just a few years earlier FMP had been hit by financial crisis which almost destroyed them.) Until 1991, all FMP albums were recorded live, whether in concert or in the FMP studio, and reflected the natural ebb and flow of 'the living music' in its raw (sometimes very raw) state. But Evan Parker's *Process And Reality* departed from this tradition by using studio technology as another improvisational tool and multi-tracking the soprano saxophone. The striking results suggest fresh possibilities for free music production.

FREEMAN, BUD

b. Lawrence Freeman, 1 April 1906, Chicago, Illinois, USA; d. 15 March 1991. Freeman's early career found him in company with Jimmy McPartland, Frank Teschemacher and other members of the Austin High School Gang. Having set out playing the 'C' melody saxophone, Freeman switched to tenor in 1925 and quickly established a reputation on that instrument as one of the few genuine rivals to Coleman Hawkins. Through the late 20s and early 30s he worked in numerous bands, recording extensively and consolidating his reputation. He gravitated into big bands, playing with Joe Haymes, Ray Noble, Paul Whiteman, Tommy Dorsey, Benny Goodman and others, but he preferred a different kind of jazz and in 1939 formed his own Summa Cum Laude Orchestra which delighted audiences in New York during its brief life. From 1940 Freeman played in various bands, led his own short-lived big band, and by the middle of the decade had settled into leading a small group at Eddie Condon's New York club. For the rest of his career Freeman played as a freelance, sometimes leading, sometimes as sideman, touring the USA and Europe. A confirmed Anglophile, he lived in London in the 70s and even managed to 'look' British. In 1980 Freeman returned to live in his native Chicago but by the end of the decade his health had failed. In mid-1990 he was almost blind, hospitalized and frail, and he died early in 1991. Freeman's masterly solo on his 1933 recording of 'The Eel' displayed his qualities to the full. In later years some detractors remarked that he spent the rest of his career repeating that solo. While it is true that his playing style did not subsequently alter very much, such adverse criticism failed to recognize that like his great but very different contemporary, Coleman Hawkins, Freeman had achieved such a pinnacle of excellence that wholesale change was pointless. In fact, Freeman's later recordings show him to have an inventive mind which, allied to a fluent delivery, make all his work a delight to the listener.

● ALBUMS: *The Bud Freeman All-Stars Featuring Shorty Baker* (1960)★★★★, *Live 1960* (1960)★★, *Chicago* (1962)★★★, *Something To Remember You By* (Black Lion 1962)★★★, with the World's Greatest Jazz Band *Century Plaza* (1972)★★★★, with Bucky Pizzarelli *Bucky And Bud* (*c*.1975)★★★, *Last Night When We Were Young* (Black And Blue 1978)★★★, *Chicago* (Black Lion 1985)★★★, *Keep Smilin' At Trouble* (Affinity 1987)★★★.

● COMPILATIONS: *Chicago-Styled* (1935-40)★★, *The Commodore Years* (1938-39)★★★, *See What The Boys In The Backroom Will Have* (1940)★★★.

● FURTHER READING: *Crazeology: The Autobiography Of A Chicago Jazzman*, Bud Freeman with Robert Wolf. *You Don't Look Like A Musician*, Bud Freeman. *If You Know Of A Better Life, Please Tell Me*, Bud Freeman

FREEMAN, CHICO

b. Earl Freeman Jnr., 17 July 1949, Chicago, Illinois, USA. Freeman started out playing trumpet but while at university switched to tenor saxophone, the instrument played by his father Von Freeman. After university, where he studied music education, he played in R&B bands, before changing direction and working with Muhal Richard Abrams and the Association for the Advancement of Creative Musicians (AACM). In the mid-to late 70s he continued his studies, meanwhile working with many leading contemporary jazz artists, including Elvin Jones, Sun Ra and Don Pullen. In the early 80s he recorded two albums, *Fathers And Sons* and *Freeman And Freeman*, with his father, toured as leader of his own small group, and also appeared with Wynton Marsalis, Cecil McBee, Jack DeJohnette and others. Interestingly, Freeman's striking playing style blends the post-Coltrane tradition of long angular lines with the rougher-toned urgency of his R&B schooling into a sound which is identifiably his own. The 1979 *Spirit Sensitive* is one of the finest collections of ballads by a modern tenor player, but by the late 80s Freeman was devoting most of his time to his fusion band Brainstorm. He was also a member of the occasional supergroup, the Leaders, alongside alto saxophonist Arthur Blythe, trumpeter Lester Bowie, pianist Kirk Lightsey, drummer Famoudou Don Moye and bassist McBee.

● ALBUMS: *Morning Prayer* (India Navigation 1976)★★★, *Chico* (India Navigation 1977)★★★, *Kings Of Mali* (1978)★★★, *Beyond The Rain* (Original Jazz Classics 1978)★★★★, *Spirit Sensitive* (India Navigation 1979)★★★, *No Time Left* (Black Saint 1979)★★★★, *Peaceful Heart, Gentle Spirit* (1980)★★★, with Von Freeman *Fathers And Sons* (1981)★★★, with Von Freeman *Freeman And Freeman* (India Navigation 1981)★★, *The Outside Within* (1981)★★★, *Destiny's Dance* (Original Jazz Classics 1981)★★★★, *Tradition In Transition* (Elektra 1982)★★, *Tangents* (1984)★★★, *The Search* (India Navigation 1984)★★★, *Groovin' Late* (1986)★★★, *The Pied Piper* (Blackhawk 1986)★★★★, with the Leaders *Mudfoot* (Black Hawk 1986)★★★, with the Leaders *Out Here Like This* (Black Saint 1987)★★★, *Live At Ronnie Scott's* (Hendring 1987)★★, *You'll Know When You Get There* (Black Saint 1988)★★★, *Tales Of Ellington* (Blackhawk 1988)★★★, with the Leaders *Unforseen Blessings* (Black Saint 1989)★★★, *Brainstorm* (1989)★★★, *Luminous* (Jazz House 1989)★★★, *Up And Down* (Black Saint 1990)★★★, *The Mystical Dreamer* (In And Out 1990)★★★, with Brainstorm *Sweet Explosion* (In And Out 1990)★★★, *Threshold* (In And Out 1993)★★★, *The Unspoken Word* (Jazz House 1994)★★★★, *Focus* (Contemporary 1995)★★★★, *Still Sensitive* (India Navigation 1996)★★★★, *The Emissary* (Clarity 1997)★★★.

FREEMAN, LOUIS

b. 2 December 1893, Glasgow, Scotland, d. 9 March 1994, Glasgow, Scotland. A classically trained jazz pianist of the dance band era, Freeman's spirit was rarely contained by location or age, and up until his death at the age of 100 he would regularly employ a nurse and ambulance to conduct him to venues which were otherwise inaccessible. The progeny of the Jewish exodus from Russia following the Tsarist programs, Freeman entered the musical arena by winning the Royal Scottish Academy Of Music's Bechstein Gold Medal in 1912. Later he became the proprietor of a musical instrument shop in Glasgow's Renfield Street, where his basement was a meeting ground for local jazzers investigating the newest US imports from artists like Red Nichols and the Dorsey Brothers. Local musicians like Alan Ferguson, Billy Munn and Issy Duman were among the regular members of the congregation, the owner having already journeyed to the US, where he played vaudeville and met Al Jolson. In addition to his own Glasgow-based dance band, Freeman also acted as musical director for the Walter Donaldson Shipping Company, booking artists for their cruises (including Tommy McQuater and George Chisholm). He continued to be a respected member of the Scottish musical community up to his death.

FREEMAN, RUSS

b. Russell Donald Freeman, 28 May 1926, Chicago, Illinois, USA. Emerging onto the west coast jazz scene in the late 40s, Freeman's piano style was typically bop-orientated. He played with many important west coast musicians during the next few years including Art Pepper, Shorty Rogers and Shelly Manne. He collaborated extensively with Manne during the second half of the 50s but also accompanied important figures from other areas of jazz, amongst them Benny Goodman. As a child Freeman had studied classical music and his range and technical accomplishment allowed him to work in diverse fields of music such as film and television. In common with a growing number of musicians he also formed his own music publishing company thus giving him greater control over his own compositions. Within the jazz world Freeman's bop credentials were overlaid with an ability to accommodate other concepts. His work outside jazz has somewhat overshadowed his reputation with the wider audience but his early recordings, especially those with Manne, reveal him to have been an important contributor to a particularly creative period in the modern jazz movement.

● ALBUMS: *Russ Freeman Trio* (Pacific Jazz 1953)★★★★, with Shelly Manne *New Works* (1954)★★★★, *Shelly Manne With Russ*

Freeman (1954)★★★, with Maynard Ferguson *Dimensions* (1954)★★★, with Cy Touff *Having A Ball* (1955)★★★, *Russ Freeman, Chet Baker Quartet* (Pacific Jazz 1956)★★★★, *Trio, Russ Freeman/Richard Twardzik* (Pacific Jazz 1956)★★, *Double Play* (1957)★★★, with Manne *Boss Sounds!* (1966)v, *Trio* (Pacific Jazz 1990)★★★.

FREEMAN, VON

b. Earl Lavon Freeman, 3 October 1922, Chicago, Illinois, USA. Freeman played 'C' melody saxophone as a child, later switching to tenor. In the early 40s he played with several bands including, most notably, that of Horace Henderson. Late in the decade he was briefly with Sun Ra, and then settled into a residency at a Chicago hotel in a band which included his brothers Buzz on drums and George on guitar. Other members of the band included at different times Ahmad Jamal and Muhal Richard Abrams. The band accompanied many visiting jazzmen, notably Charlie Parker and Lester Young. In the 60s Freeman toured with a variety of artists, including several blues singers. From the 70s onwards he was again leading a jazz group, sometimes in harness with his son, Chico Freeman, with whom he recorded the albums, *Freeman And Freeman* and *Fathers And Sons*. Freeman's playing style combines the toughness of the Chicago blues scene with a plangent swing and fluent improvisation; his ballad playing is especially engaging.

● ALBUMS: *Doin' It Right Now* (Atlantic 1972)★★★, *Have No Fear* (Nessa 1975)★★★, *Serenade And Blues* (Nessa 1975)★★, *Young And Foolish* (1977)★★★, *Von Freeman* (Daybreak 1981)★★, with Chico Freeman *Fathers And Sons* (1981)★★★, with Chico Freeman *Freeman And Freeman* (India Navigation 1981)★★, *Young And Foolish* (Affinity 1988)★★★★, *Walkin' Tough!* (Southport 1989)★★★, *Never Let Me Go* (SteepleChase 1992)★★★★, *Lester Leaps In* (Steeplechase 1992)★★★★, *Dedicated To You* (Steeplechase)★★★, with Fire *Fire With Von Freeman* (Southport 1996)★★★.

FRESU, PAULO

b. 1961, Berchidda, Sardinia, Italy. An accomplished trumpet and fluegelhorn player, Fresu was self-taught and grew up playing the band music of his native island. He discovered jazz in 1980, but had to move to the mainland to practise the new-found craft. He gained a degree after studying the trumpet formally at Cagliari Conservatoire, and also attended the music faculty at Bologna. Into the early 80s and onwards, he taught at various music schools, contributed to magazines and wrote for theatres and orchestras as well as leading an excellent jazz quintet. The foundations for his own quintet were laid as a result of meeting like-minded musicians at the 1982 Sienna Jazz seminar, and the band was finally formed in late 1984. Since then it has become the most feted of the 80s Italian new wave (La Nuova Onda), with Fresu winning numerous prizes and polls. He and his band (including the excellent saxophonist Tino Tracanna) are primarily inspired by the classic Miles Davis quintets of the 50s and 60s, and play with considerable panache and conviction. Fresu has worked with Albert Mangelsdorff, Franco D'Andrea, Kenny Wheeler, Tony Oxley, John Taylor, Enrico Rava, Paul Rutherford, Dave Holland, Lee Konitz, Evan Parker, Michael Nyman, and many other jazz artists.

● ALBUMS: *Mamut* (1985)★★★, with Kenny Wheeler, John Taylor *Live In Rocella Jonica* (1985)★★★, *Ostinato* (Splasch 1985)★★★★, *Inner Voices* (Splasch 1986)★★★, *Quatro* (Splasch 1989)★★, *Live In Montpelier* (Splasch 1990)★★★, *Ensalada Mistica* (Splasch 1996)★★★★, *Wanderlust* (RCA-Victor 1997)★★★★.

FRISELL, BILL

b. 18 March 1951, Baltimore, Maryland, USA. Frisell, whose father was a tuba and string-bass player, was raised in Denver, Colorado. He began playing clarinet, then saxophone, finally settling on guitar. He also plays banjo, ukulele and bass. He majored in music at North Colorado University (1969-71) and in 1977 was awarded a diploma in arranging and composition from Berklee College Of Music, as well as winning the Harris Stanton guitar award. He took lessons from Jim Hall, Johnny Smith and Dale Bruning, and his favourite players are Hall, Wes Montgomery and Jimi Hendrix. He has played with many major contemporary figures, including Eberhard Weber, Mike Gibbs, Jan Garbarek, Charlie Haden, Carla Bley, Julius Hemphill, Gunter Hampel, and John Scofield. Since the late 80s he has appeared with Ronald Shannon Jackson and Melvin Gibbs (as Power Tools), John Zorn's harmolodic hardcore indulgence Naked City, the *News For Lulu* bebop trio with Zorn and George Lewis, the Paul Bley Quartet featuring John Surman and Paul Motian, Motian's trio with Frisell and Joe Lovano and his own band, which features the members of Naked City minus Zorn. Frisell's style makes use of electronics to produce long sustained notes with lots of vibrato and legato lines, possibly a legacy of his training as a reed player. He is equally convincing whether stitching feedback howls into the midst of violent Naked City melees or playing gentle country-influenced solo tunes, post-modern bottleneck blues or lop-sided melancholic ballads. Frisell's solo work found a wider audience with the release of *Have A Little Faith* together with a lengthy (by his standards) tour. Everchanging, in typical jazz musician style, just as he had established a first class trio (with Kermit Driscoll and Joey Barron) in 1995 he abandoned the idea for a drummerless unit of trombone, trumpet, guitar and violin. By 1996 Frisell had relocated to Seattle and was so in-demand that he was working on several projects at the same time. Recent collaborations were with Ginger Baker, Elvis Costello and Michael Shrieve. With the likes of John Scofield and Pat Metheny he is currently one of the world's leading all-round jazz guitarists. His recent work shows him riding a peak of creativity.

● ALBUMS: *In Line* (ECM 1983)★★★, with Tim Berne *Theoretically* (1984)★★★, *Rambler* (ECM 1985)★★★, with John Zorn, George Lewis *News For Lulu* (1987)★★★, with Power Tools *Strange Meeting* (1987)★★★, *Lookout For Hope* (ECM 1988)★★★, *Before We Were Born* (Elektra 1989)★★★★, *Is That*

You? (Elektra 1990)★★★, *Where In The World?* (Elektra Nonesuch 1991)★★★, with Zorn, Lewis *More News For Lulu* recorded 1989 (1992)★★★, (1992)★★★, with Don Byron *This Land* (Nonesuch 1993)★★★★, with Byron *Have A Little Faith* (Nonesuch 1993)★★★, with Ginger Baker, Charlie Haden *Going Back Home* (Atlantic 1994)★★★, *The High Sign/One Week (Music For The Films Of Buster Keaton)* (Elektra 1994)★★★, *Go West (Music For The Films Of Buster Keaton)* (Elektra 1994)★★★, with Kermit Driscoll, Joey Baron *Live* (Gramavision 1995)★★★, with Elvis Costello *Deep Dead Blue, Live At Meltdown* (Nonesuch 1995)★★★, with Victor Bruce Godsey, Brian Ales *American Blood/Safety In Numbers* (Intuition 1995)★★★, *Quartet* (Nonesuch 1996)★★★★, with Baker, Haden *Falling Off The Roof* (Atlantic 1996)★★★★, with Dave Holland, Lee Konitz, Kenny Wheeler *Angel Song* (ECM 1997)★★★★, *Nashville* (Nonesuch 1997)★★★★, *Gone, Just Like A Train* (Nonesuch 1997)★★★.

● COMPILATIONS: *Works* (ECM 1989)★★★.

FULFORD, TOMMY

b. 1912, USA, d. 16 December 1956. Fulford played piano with various territory bands in the Midwest in the early 30s and then, after a short spell with Blanche Calloway, he went to New York where he played with Snub Mosley before joining the Chick Webb band. This was in 1936 and he remained more or less continuously with the band until 1942, by which time it was under the nominal leadership of Ella Fitzgerald. Fulford then began a solo career, working in clubs and restaurants until the mid-50s when he was a member of Tony Parenti's dixieland-style band. Fulford was a good section player and a master of the difficult art of being pianist in a big band.

FULLER, CURTIS

b. 15 December 1934, Detroit, Michigan, USA. Fuller began studying trombone in his teens, eventually playing in a band during his military service in the early 50s. As the leader of the band was Cannonball Adderley, it was not surprising that, following his discharge, Fuller quickly turned to jazz. At first he worked in his home town, playing with Kenny Burrell, Yusef Lateef and others, but then moved to New York, where he worked with Dizzy Gillespie, Hampton Hawes, John Coltrane and Miles Davis, led his own small bands and was a founder-member of the Jazztet with Art Farmer and Benny Golson. In the early 60s he was a member of Art Blakey's Jazz Messengers, touring extensively with this band and also with Gillespie. In the 70s Fuller gradually incorporated jazz-rock concepts into his repertoire and worked with musicians such as Stanley Clarke. In the mid-to late 70s he was with Count Basie, Kai Winding, Lionel Hampton, Cedar Walton, Red Garland and Sal Nistico and also continued to lead his own groups. In the 80s his musical associates included Golson again and he also played in a reformed Jazztet and in the Timeless All Stars band. A major post-bop stylist on trombone, Fuller's technical facility on the instrument allows him great freedom to develop his inventive lines.

● ALBUMS: *New Trombone* (Prestige 1957)★★★, *Jazz ... It's Magic* (Regent 1957)★★★, *The Opener* (Blue Note 1957)★★★★, *Bone & Bari* (Blue Note 1957)★★★★, *Curtis Fuller, Volume 3* (Blue Note 1958)★★★, *Sliding Easy* (United Artists 1959)★★★★, *Blues-ette* (Savoy 1959)★★★, with Benny Golson *The Curtis Fuller Jazztet With Benny Golson* (Savoy 1959)★★★★, *Imagination* (Savoy 1959)★★★, with Art Farmer, Golson *Meet The Jazztet* (Argo 1960)★★★, *Images Of Curtis Fuller* (Savoy 1960)★★★, *Boss Of The Soul Stream Trombone* (Warwick 1961)★★★, *The Magnificent Trombone Of Curtis Fuller* (Epic 1961)★★★, *South American Cookin'* (Epic 1961)★★★, *Soul Trombone* (Impulse! 1962)★★★, *Cabin In The Sky* (Impulse! 1962)★★★, *Jazz Conference Abroad* (Smash 1962)★★★, with Red Garland *Curtis Fuller With Red Garland* 1957 recording (New Jazz 1962)★★★★, with Hampton Hawes *Curtis Fuller And Hampton Hawes With French Horns* 1957 recording (Status 1965)★★★, *Crankin'* (MRL 1973)★★★, *Smokin'* (Mainstream 1974)★★★, *Fire And Filigree* (Beehive 1978)★★, with Timeless All Stars *It's Timeless* (Timeless 1982)★★, with Farmer, Golson *Back To The City* (Contemporary 1986)★★★, *Four On The Outside* 1978 recording (Timeless 1986)★★★, *Curtis Fuller Meets Roma Jazz Trio* (Timeless 1988)★★★, *Bluesette Part 2* (Savoy 1993)★★★.

● COMPILATIONS: *The Complete Blue Note/UA Curtis Fuller Sessions* 5-LP/3-CD box set (Mosaic 1996)★★★★.

FULLER, GIL

b. Walter Gilbert Fuller, 14 April 1920, Los Angeles, California, USA. Although he started out in the early 40s writing for orthodox swing-era big bands such as Charlie Barnet's, Fuller's true *metier* was revealed in 1942 when he began an association with Dizzy Gillespie. In 1944 they were together in the Billy Eckstine band and continued their working relationship when Gillespie formed his 1946 bebop big band. Gillespie's interest in Latin American music was complemented by Fuller, who had previously written for Tito Puente, and his arrangements included 'Manteca'. Despite the importance of his work with Gillespie, Fuller's interest had waned by the end of the 40s. Although he wrote occasionally for Gillespie and Stan Kenton in the 50s and 60s, a new career, in engineering, occupied his time.

● ALBUMS: with Dizzy Gillespie *Gil Fuller And The Monterey Jazz Festival Orchestra With Dizzy Gillespie* (Pacific Jazz 1965)★★★, *Night Flight* (Pacific Jazz 1966)★★★.

G., Kenny

b. Kenneth Gorelick, 1959, Seattle, Washington, USA. Gorelick learned saxophone as a child and toured Europe in 1974 with the Franklin High School band. Two years later he played with Barry White's Love Unlimited Orchestra in Seattle before entering the University of Washington to study accounting. Gorelick first recorded with local funk band Cold, Bold & Together and also backed many leading artists on their Seattle shows. After graduation, he joined the Jeff Lorber Fusion, recording with the jazz-rock band for Arista Records, the label which in 1981 signed him to a solo contract. Produced by Preston Glass and Narada Michael Walden, *Duotones* was a major success and it included 'Songbird', a Top 10 hit in 1987. Like much of his other work, it featured a flawless, melodic alto saxophone solo. By now, Kenny G was in demand to play solos on albums by such singers as Whitney Houston, Natalie Cole and Aretha Franklin. Among the guest artists on *Silhouette* was Smokey Robinson who sang 'We've Saved The Best Till Last'. Like its predecessor, the album sold over three million copies worldwide. G's extraordinary success has continued into the 90s with the multi-platinum *Breathless*, and he has been acknowledged as fellow musician President Clinton's favourite saxophonist. The crossover into pop is felt to be too strong by most jazz critics, as the type of music he plays is very structured and contrived. Popular music has at least given rise to the 'great crossover debate'. Arguments aside; Kenny G. is a phenomenon, he sells albums in rock group proportions and his popularity is consistent. His *Miracles: The Holiday Album* rocketed to the top of the US pop chart, re-igniting interest in *Breathless* which, by the mid-90s had sold over 11 million copies in the USA alone and had remained at the top of the *Billboard* jazz chart for well over 18 months. It was finally toppled in October 1996 after an incredible run. The rude interloper to this was *The Moment*, the new album from . . . Kenny G.

● ALBUMS: *Kenny G* (1982)★★, *G Force* (Arista 1983)★★★, *Gravity* (Arista 1985)★★★, *Duotones* (Arista 1986)★★★, *Silhouette* (Arista 1988)★★★, *Kenny G Live* (Arista 1989)★★, *Breathless* (Arista 1992)★★★★, *Miracles: The Holiday Album.* (Arista 1994)★★, *The Moment* (Arista 1996)★★★.

● COMPILATIONS: *Greatest Hits* (Arista 1997)★★★.

Gabler, Milt

b. 20 May 1911, New York City, New York, USA. In 1926 Gabler's father opened a store, the Commodore Music Shop, at 144 East 42nd Street in New York City. When Gabler took over its operation he sold sporting goods and novelties as sidelines to the main trade, which was in sheet music, records and radio. To buy anything there, however, a customer had to like jazz: all day long Gabler played jazz records on a wind-up phonograph and soon the shop became the in-place for jazz fans to gather. In the late 30s and early 40s the habituees included several noted journalists and academics who wrote on jazz, among them Marshall Stearns, Wilder Hobson and John Hammond Jnr. Gabler's first big steps in serving the needs of jazz fans came when he persuaded several major record companies to reissue sought-after but out-of-print records even though he had to guarantee orders far in excess of likely sales. The next logical step was to make his own records, for which he hired the services of another Commodore regular, Eddie Condon. Additionally, Gabler and Condon launched weekly jam sessions at Jimmy Ryan's, a leading 52nd Street nightspot, and Gabler later opened a branch of his store across the street from Ryan's. Among the many artists recorded by Gabler for his Commodore label was Billie Holiday, who in 1939 made four sides which became classics: 'Yesterdays', 'I Gotta Right To Sing The Blues', 'Fine And Mellow' and the sombre 'Strange Fruit'. Gabler and associate Jack Crystal were responsible for assembling a series of long-playing records featuring the pick of the Commodore side, including sessions by Holiday, Lester Young, Pee Wee Russell, Don Byas, Jelly Roll Morton, Wild Bill Davison, Eddie Heywood. Gabler wound up Commodore following Crystal's death in 1963, but has since leased the masters to a succession of labels, including Mainstream, Atlantic Records, Columbia Special Products, Mosaic (who released three mammoth box sets in 1988), and, most recently, GRP Records.

● COMPILATIONS: *The Commodore Story* (Commodore 1997)★★★★★.

Gadd, Steve

b. 4 September 1945, Rochester, New York, USA. Gadd was taught the drums by an uncle from the age of three: he enjoyed Sousa marches and worked with a drum corps. He spent two years at Manhattan's School of Music before going on to Eastman College in Rochester after which he was drafted into the army and spent three years in an army band. His first professional work was with Chuck Mangione before he joined Chick Corea's Return To Forever in 1975. Corea described him as bringing 'orchestral and compositional thinking to the drum kit while at the same time having a great imagination and a great ability to swing'. Gadd worked extensively in the New York studios from the early 70s onwards and was able to provide the perfect accompaniment for a diverse series of sessions. He developed his own style of linear drumming in which no two drums are sounded at the same time. He played for many artists from Charles Mingus via George Benson to Paul Simon with whom he toured in 1991, directing the large group of percussionists on the *Rhythm Of The Saints* tour. So ubiquitous did he become that it was his sound that was sampled for the earlier drum machines. In 1976 he played in the influential funk band Stuff along with other session musicians like Eric Gale and Richard Tee. Throughout the 80s Gadd continued with a busy studio schedule but also played in the straight jazz Manhattan Jazz Quintet.

● ALBUMS: with George Benson *In Concert* (1975)★★★, *My Spanish Heart* (1976)★★★, with Carla Bley *Dinner Music* (1976)★★★, with Stuff *Stuff* (Warners 1976)★★★, *Friends* (Warners 1978)★★★, *The Mad Hatter* (1978)★★★, with Chick Corea *Three Quartets* (Warners 1981)★★★, with Al Di Meola *Electric Rendezvous* (Columbia 1982)★★, with Manhattan Jazz Quintet *Manhattan Jazz Quintet* (1986)★★★, *Gaddabout* (King 1986)★★★, *Autumn Leaves* (1986)★★★, with Paul Simon *Rhythm Of The Saints* (Warners 1989)★★.

GAILLARD, SLIM

b. Bulee Gaillard, 4 January 1916, Detroit, Michigan, USA, d. 26 February 1991. Other sources including Gaillard himself have claimed he was born on 1 January 1916 in Santa Clara, Cuba. Gaillard led an adventurous childhood. On one occasion, while travelling on board a ship on which his father was steward, he was left behind in Crete when the ship sailed. His adventures became more exciting every time he recounted his tales and include activities such as professional boxer, mortician and truck driver for bootleggers. Originally based in Detroit, Gaillard entered vaudeville in the early 30s with an act during which he played the guitar while tap-dancing. Later in the decade he moved to New York and formed a duo with bassist Slam Stewart in which Gaillard mostly played guitar and sang. Much of their repertoire was original material with lyrics conceived in Gaillard's personal version of the currently popular 'jive talk', which on his lips developed extraordinary surrealist overtones. Gaillard's language, which he named 'Vout' or 'Vout Oreenie', helped the duo achieve a number of hit records, including 'Flat Foot Floogie'. Their success led to a long-running radio series and an appearance in the film *Hellzapoppin*. In 1943 Stewart was inducted for military service and was replaced by Bam Brown. Now based in Los Angeles, Gaillard continued to write songs, often in collaboration with Brown, and had another big hit with 'Cement Mixer (Put-ti Put-ti)'. With Brown he co-authored a remarkable extended work, 'Opera in Vout', which premiered in Los Angeles in 1946. (In fact, it was not an opera and not much of it was in vout!) Another huge hit was 'Down By The Station', a song which, uniquely for a jazz artist, entered the catalogue of classic children's nursery rhymes. Contrastingly, he also recorded with bebop musicians, including Charlie Parker and Dizzy Gillespie (*Slim's Jam*). In the late 40s he continued his eccentric entertaining, which included such intriguing routines as playing piano with his hands upside-down. Not surprisingly, given his manner of performance and his private language, some people never quite understood Gaillard and one radio station banned his record 'Yep Roc Heresy', declaring it to be degenerate; in fact, the lyric was merely a recitation of the menu from an Armenian restaurant. In the late 50s and for several years thereafter, Gaillard worked mostly outside music but gradually returned to prominence by way of acting roles, (including a part in the USA television series *Roots*), festival appearances with Stewart and, in the 80s, numerous television and stage shows in the UK where he became resident in 1983. His tall, loping figure, invariably topped by a big grin and a rakish white beret, became a familiar sight in London's jazz-land. In 1989 he starred in a four-part UK BBC television series, *The World Of Slim Gaillard*. In addition to his singing and guitar playing, Gaillard also played piano, vibraphone and tenor saxophone.

● ALBUMS: with Meade Lux Lewis *Boogie Woogie At The Philharmonic* 10-inch album (Mercury 1951)★★★, *Mish Mash* 10-inch album (Clef 1953)★★★, *Opera In Vout* 10-inch album (Disc 1953)★★★, *Slim Gaillard And His Musical Aggregation Wherever They May Be* reissued as *Slim Gaillard Cavorts* (Norgran 1954), with Dizzie Gillespie *Gaillard And Gillespie* (Ultraphonic 1958)★★★, *Slim Gaillard Rides Again* (Dot 1959)★★★★, *Anytime, Anyplace, Anywhere* (1982)★★★, *Live At Billy Berg's: The Voutest!* 1946 recording (1983)★★★.

● COMPILATIONS: *Tutti Frutti* 1945 recording (1987)★★★, tribute album *The Legendary McVouty* (Hep 1993)★★★, *Slim Gaillard 1946* (Classics 1998)★★★.

GAINES, CHARLIE

b. 8 August 1900, Philadelphia, Pennsylvania, USA. He played trumpet with several east coast territory bands in the years between the ending of World War I and 1921 when he settled in New York. He remained there throughout the 20s, playing and sometimes recording with Charlie 'Fess' Johnson, Wilbur Sweatman, Fats Waller, Clarence Williams and several singers including Edith Wilson. In the early 30s Gaines was in bands led by Louis Armstrong and Williams again, but mostly played in his home-town. He stayed in Philadelphia, leading groups of all sizes from trios to big bands, for the next 40 years. An undistinguished soloist, Gaines was a solid journeyman trumpeter, reliable and with a good accompanist's ear.

● COMPILATIONS: *The Chronological Fats Waller 1929* (Classics 1929)★★★★.

GALBREATH, FRANK

b. 2 September 1913, Roberson County, North Carolina, USA, d. November 1971. Galbreath began playing trumpet as a young teenager, working in bands in Washington, DC. During the next few years he gained experience playing in bands in the south-eastern states and along the east coast until, in the early 30s, he visited Chicago and New York. During the rest of the decade he played in bands led by Fletcher Henderson, Jelly Roll Morton, Lucky Millinder, Louis Armstrong and many others, mostly in New York. After military service during World War II, Galbreath played in the bands of Willie Bryant, Tab Smith, Sy Oliver and others, then in 1948 rejoined Millinder, this time for over three years, and then was with Snub Mosley for a USO tour that brought him to the UK and Europe. Between tours he also led his own band and accompanied musicians such as Benny Goodman, and backed singers including Ray Charles, Fats Domino and Sammy Davis Jnr. During the mid-60s he was resident in Atlantic City, continuing to play until a year or so before his death. Not renowned as a soloist, Galbreath provided able backing to many more gifted musicians and was also a strong ensemble voice in the bands with which he played.

GALE, ERIC

b. 20 September 1938, Brooklyn, New York, USA, d. 25 May 1994, Baja California, Mexico. Gale studied chemistry at Niagara University. He took up the double bass when he was 12 years old and also played tenor saxophone, trombone and tuba before he chose the guitar. The basis of his style was formed on the 50s and 60s R&B circuit. He was with the Drifters, Jackie Wilson, the Flamingos and Maxine Brown, before playing in the 60s with King Curtis, Jimmy Smith, David 'Fathead' Newman, Mongo Santamaría and Aretha Franklin. In the early 70s Gale became the house guitarist with Creed Taylor's new CTI label and worked with Stanley Turrentine's band. He took four years off on his Ohio farm and went to Jamaica where he assimilated the reggae style. On his return to New York in 1976 he was a founder of the influential funk band Stuff along with artists including Steve Gadd, Cornell Dupree and Richard Tee. They played regularly at Mikell's in Manhattan with only minimal rehearsal. In the early 90s he performed as a regular band member in several US television shows. Gale thought like a frontline musician and played like a saxophonist.

● ALBUMS: *Stuff* (1977)★★★, *Ginseng Woman* (Columbia 1977)★★★, *Multiplication* (Columbia 1979)★★★, *Forecast* (Columbia 1979)★★★, *Part Of You* (Columbia 1979)★★★, *Touch Of Silk* (Columbia 1980)★★, *Blue Horizon* (Elektra 1982)★★★, *Island Breeze* (Elektra 1984)★★.

● COMPILATIONS: *The Best Of Eric Gale* (Columbia 1980)★★★.

GALLINGER, KAREN

b. USA. A powerful singer with a commanding style and a richly expressive voice, she remains little known outside the west coast environs in which she mostly works. In a branch of music that is inundated with new singers as the end of the twentieth century approaches, it is hard to forecast her future, but, given the breaks, she has the ability to carve a successful career.

● ALBUMS: *Live At The Jazz Bakery* (Sea Breeze 1994)★★.

GALLOWAY, JIM

b. 28 July 1936, Kilwinning, Scotland. After working in Glasgow while still a teenager, Galloway, a clarinettist and saxophonist, emigrated to Canada in the mid-60s where he became well known as a sideman, leader of the Metro Stompers, accompanist to visiting American jazz stars, and radio personality. Success at the 1976 Montreux Jazz Festival with a band that included Jay McShann and Buddy Tate led to worldwide recognition for this dedicated musician. Rooted in the mainstream, Galloway's playing of the many instruments on which he performs betrays his admiration for Sidney Bechet, Edmond Hall and Coleman Hawkins among others. A major work, 'Hot And Suite', was given its first performance at the 1985 Edinburgh Arts Festival.

● ALBUMS: *Metro Stompers* (Sackville 1973)★★★, *Three's Company* (Sackville 1973)★★★, *Bojangles* (Hep Jazz 1978)★★, *Featuring Jay McShann* (1981)★★★, *Thou Swell* (Sackville 1981)★★★★, with Ed Polcer *At The Ball* (Jazzology 1998)★★★.

GALPER, HAL

b. 18 April 1938, Salem, Massachusetts, USA. Galper was taught classical piano as a boy but turned to jazz and studied at the Berklee College Of Music between 1955 and 1958. He was taught privately by Jaki Byard and Herb Pomeroy. He moved to Boston in 1959 and played with Herb Pomeroy's Big Band. Then he worked with Sam Rivers, Tony Williams, Chet Baker, Stan Getz, Randy and Michael Brecker, Bobby Hutcherson and Attila Zoller. His harmonically sophisticated playing made him an an masterful accompanist to vocalists Joe Williams, Anita O'Day and Chris Connor. He played with the Cannonball Adderley Quintet between 1973 and 1975 but is said not to have enjoyed playing the electric piano. In 1981 he joined Phil Woods' Quintet with whom he has played throughout the 80s.

● ALBUMS: *Inner Journey* (Mainstream 1973)★★, *Reach Out* (Steeplechase 1976)★★, *Now Hear This* (Enja 1977)★★, *Speak With A Single Voice* (Enja 1978)★★★★, *Children Of The Night* (Double Time 1978), *Redux 1978* (Concord Jazz 1978)★★★, *Ivory Forest* (Enja 1981)★★, *Heaven* (1984)★★★, *Dreamsville* (Enja 1987)★★★, *Portrait* (Concord 1990)★★★, *Bouquet* (1989)★★★, *Invitation To A Concert* (Concord Jazz 1990)★★★, *Live At Maybeck Hall* (Concord 1991)★★, *Tippin'* (Concord 1994)★★, with Jerry Bergonzi *Rebop* (Enja 1996)★★★, *Live At Vartan Jazz* (Vartan Jazz 1997)★★★, *Fugue State* (Blue Chip 1998)★★★, *At Café Des Copains* 1990 live recording (Philology 1998)★★★.

GAMBALE, FRANK

b. 1959, Australia. A virtuoso guitarist nicknamed 'The Thunder From Down Under', Gambale has lived in Los Angeles for more than a decade and, after making his name with fusion keyboard legend Chick Corea's popular Elektric Band, is most commonly associated with America's west coast fusion/studio scene. In Australia he began his career concentrating on the pop field, singing and playing guitar in vocal-orientated bands. He became involved in Hollywood's celebrated Guitar Institute of Technology in 1982, when he moved to the US, first enrolling as a student and finally staying on as a teacher, before joining Chick Corea's group in 1986. He stayed with the outfit for seven years, soloing seldomly but blinding other guitarists with his advanced technical facility during the band's stunningly fast and intricate ensemble passages. When Corea formed his concurrent Akoustic Band, Gambale had more time on his hands to pursue his solo career, and work with other projects, including drummer Steve Smith's highly-regarded fusion quartet Vital Information. Gambale (and the virtuoso rhythm section of bassist John Pattituci and drummer Dave Weckl) left the Elektric Band in 1993, and has since concentrated on his own series of albums on the JVC label. A guitarist with perhaps more technique than he knows what to do with, Gambale plays with a rock sensibility, firing blistering, aggressive lines and more recently reverting to his old interests in singing. *Thinking Out Loud* was a change of direction with his guitar lines being replaced by smooth chords not unlike Barney Kessel or Jim Hall.

● ALBUMS: *Brave New Guitar* (1985)★★, with Chick Corea *Light Years* (1987)★★★, with Corea *Eye Of The Beholder* (1988)★★★, with Corea *Inside Out* (1990)★★★★, *Note Worker* (1991)★★, with Corea *Beneath The Mask* (1992)★★★, *The Great Explorers* (1993)★★★, *Thunder From Down Under* (1993)★★★, *Passages* (1994)★★★, *Thinking Out Loud* (JVC 1995)★★★.

GANELIN TRIO

When originally formed in 1971 this Soviet trio consisted of Vyacheslav Ganelin (b. 1944, Kraskov, USSR; keyboards, flute, percussion, guitar), Vladimir Chekasin (reeds, trombone, violin, percussion, voice), and Vladimir Tarasov (b. 1947, Archangelsk, USSR; drums, percussion). Although firmly based on composition, a recording or concert performance by the trio is a rich mix of slavonic folk, free jazz, contemporary classical music and parodies of all three traditions. Their first album, *Con Anima*, was recorded in the USSR in 1976, but the Soviet state record label, Melodiya, was highly dilatory about issuing their recordings. Leo Feigin's London-based Leo Records took on the task, though his first releases, of tapes smuggled out of the USSR, were issued with a disclaimer that the musicians bore no responsibility for their music's appearance on record. In the 80s the trio began to play outside the Soviet Union and Eastern bloc, scoring a great success at the 1980 West Berlin Jazz Festival, then visiting Italy in 1981, and the UK on a Contemporary Music Network tour in 1984, where they met with a mixed reception from jazz critics and musicians. Ganelin emigrated to Israel in 1987, where he formed a new trio, exhibiting a more severe style of music on two albums, with Victor Fonarev (bass, percussion) and Mika Markovich (drums, percussion). Tarasov and Chekasin have continued to work together.

● ALBUMS: *Con Anima* 1976 recording (Leo 1980)★★★, *Live In East Germany* 1978 recording, reissued as *Catalogue* (Leo 1980)★★★★, *Con Fuoco* 1978-1980 recordings (Leo 1981)★★★★, *Concerto Grosso* 1978 recordings (1982)★★★, *Poi Segue* (1982)★★★★, *Ancora Da Capo Part I 1980 recording* (Leo 1982)★★★★, *Ancora Da Capo Part 2* 1980 recording (Leo 1982)★★★, *New Wine* (Leo 1983)★★★, *Non Troppo* (1983)★★★, *Vide* (1983)★★★, *Strictly For Our Friends* 1978 recording (Leo 1984)★★★★, *Vide* (Leo 1984)★★★, *Baltic Triangle* 1981 recording (1985)★★★, *Con Affetto* (Leo 1985)★★★, *Non Troppo* 1980-1983 recording (hatART 1985)★★★, *Itaango...In Nickelsdorf* (1986, rec. 1985)★★★, *Great Concerts Of New Jazz Vol 1* (Leo 1987)★★★, *Poco A Poco* 1978 recording (Leo 1988)★★★★, *Jerusalem February Cantabile* (1989)★★★★, with others *Document* 1980-89 recordings 8-CD box set (1990)★★★★, *Opuses* (Leo 1990)★★★. Duo albums: Ganelin/Tarasov *Opus AZ* (1983)★★; Ganelin/Chekasin, Ganelin/Tarasov *3-1 = 3* 1980-85 recordings (1988)★★★; Chekasin/Tarasov *1-11 = 3* (1989)★★★★. *Great Concerts Of New Jazz Vol 2* (Leo 1988)★★★. Solo albums: Vyacheslav Ganelin *Con Amore* 1985 recording (Leo 1987)★★★, with Pyatras Vysniauskas, Grigory Talas *Inverso* 1984 recordings (Leo 1987)★★★, with others *Conspiracy* 1989 recording 4-CD box set (Leo 1991)★★★; Vladimir Tarasov *Atto, Vols 1-4* (1989)★★★, with Andrew Cyrille *Galaxies* (1991)★★★, *Ancora Da Capo* (Leo 1998)★★★.

● FURTHER READING: *Russian Jazz New Identity*, Leo Feigin (Ed.).

GANLEY, ALLAN

b. 11 March 1931, Tolworth, Surrey, England. A self-taught drummer, in the early 50s Ganley played in the dance band led by Bert Ambrose. In 1953 he came to prominence as a member of John Dankworth's band, then the most popular modern jazz group in the UK. Also in the 50s, he worked with pianist Derek Smith, Dizzy Reece, clarinettist Vic Ash, Ronnie Scott and several visiting American musicians. Towards the end of the decade he was co-leader with Ronnie Ross of a small group known as the Jazzmakers. In the early 60s Ganley was often with Tubby Hayes, playing with his small groups and the occasionally assembled big band. As house drummer at Scott's club he played with numerous leading American jazzmen, including Dizzy Gillespie, Stan Getz, Jim Hall, Freddie Hubbard and Raahsan Roland Kirk. In the early 70s he took time out to study at Berklee College Of Music, then returned to the UK to form and lead a big band, which he maintained sporadically for the next 10 years. Throughout the 70s and 80s Ganley could be seen and heard on countless broadcasts and recording dates, playing with jazz musicians of all styles, effortlessly slipping from traditional to post-bop to big band to mainstream, all the while swinging with great subtlety. In the 90s Ganley was as active as ever, playing club and festival dates throughout the UK with occasional overseas trips. The self-effacing nature of his playing has made him a perfect accompanist for pianists as different as Teddy Wilson and Al Haig and for singers from Carol Kidd to Blossom Dearie. Although less well known for his work as an arranger, Ganley has provided charts for many leading British jazzmen as well as for the BBC Radio Big Band, thus enhancing the enormous yet understated contribution he has made to the British jazz scene over the years.

● ALBUMS: with Tubby Hayes *Down At The Village* (1962)★★★★, with Hayes *Late Spot At Scott's* (1962)★★, with Jim Hall *Commitment* (1976)★★★, with Al Haig *Stablemates* (1977)★★★, with Carol Kidd *The Night We Called It A Day* (1990)★★★.

GARBAREK, JAN

b. 4 March 1947, Norway. Inspired by hearing John Coltrane on the radio in 1961, Garbarek taught himself to play tenor saxophone (subsequently adding soprano and bass saxophone). In 1962 he won an amateur competition, which resulted in his first professional work, and he was soon leading a group with Jon Christensen, Terje Rypdal and Arild Andersen. In 1968 he was the Norwegian representative at the European Broadcasting Union festival, and the recordings of this (notably an impressive version of Coltrane's 'Naima') brought him to wider notice when they were transmitted throughout Europe. Subsequently his style has become more severe, sometimes almost bleak, although there is a restrained warmth to his sound. Garbarek's playing is representative of the kind of music associated with Manfred Eicher's ECM Records and of a characteristically Scandinavian strand of jazz, melodic and atmospheric, which has little overt emotionalism but does not lack intensity. His writing and playing display considerable concern with tone and texture and appear to have exerted some influence on Tommy Smith and post-sabbatical Charles Lloyd (with whom he has shared colleagues Christensen, Keith Jarrett and Palle Danielsson) as well as a variety of European players such as Joakim Milder and Alberto Nacci. In the mid-70s he worked in Jarrett's 'Belonging' band with Christensen and Danielsson, recording the much-praised *Belonging* and *My Song*, and also played with Ralph Towner on *Solstice* and *Sounds And Shadows*. In the 80s his own groups have featured Eberhard Weber, Bill Frisell and John Abercrombie among others. His tours in the late 80s with a band including the remarkable percussionist Nana Vasconcelos were highly acclaimed and inspired many other musicians and bands to essay the juxtaposition of glacially imposing saxophone lines with exotic, tropical rhythm. Garbarek has also worked with Don Cherry, Chick Corea, David Torn and with George Russell during Russell's residency in Scandinavia in the late 60s - an association that resulted in a fine series of recordings featuring the young Garbarek, notably *Othello Ballet Suite*, *Trip To Prillarguri* and *Electronic Sonata For Souls Loved By Nature* (though none was released until the 80s). Garbarek has also shown an increasing interest in folk and ethnic musics that has not only coloured his own playing but led to him recording with Ravi Shankar on the 1984 *Song For Everyone* and producing an ECM album for the Norwegian folk singer Agnes Buen Gårnas, 1991's *Rosensfole*. For *Ragas & Sagas* (1993), Garbarek collaborated with the Pakistani classical singer, Usted Fateh Ali Khan and trio of musicians playing tabla and sarangi, a 39-string violin. Garbarek's melodic solos effectively complemented the traditional Pakistani instrumental sounds. In the same year, Garbarek's *Twelve Moons* concentrated once again on the Scandinavian-folk melodies he is continually exploring. The album's emphatic rhythmic 'feel' was due in no small part to the presence of drummer Manu Katche and bassist Eberhard Weber. Rather surprisingly, given his avoidance of gallery-pleasing pyrotechnics, Garbarek has steadily acquired a public following equal to his huge critical reputation. Observers of the UK Top 75 album chart in the spring of 1996 would not have been as shocked as would a jazz fan, but horror upon horror, Garbarek's *Visible World* became a hit. The highly accessible nature of the opening tracks such as 'Red Wind', 'The Creek' and the folk-inspired 'The Survivor' aided its wider appeal. World music followers would also have found a great rapport with the 12-minute mantra 'Evening Land', featuring some wonderful vocals from Marie Boine.

● ALBUMS: *Esoteric Circle* (1969)★★★, *Afric Pepperbird* (ECM 1971)★★★, *Sart* (ECM 1972)★★★, *Triptykon* (ECM 1973)★★★, with Art Lande *Red Lanta* (ECM 1974)★★★, with Babo Stenson *Witchi-Tai-To* (ECM 1974)★★★, with Stenson *Dansere* (ECM 1976)★★★, *Dis* (ECM 1977)★★★★, *Places* (ECM 1978)★★★★, *Photo With Blue Sky* (ECM 1979)★★★, with Charlie Haden, Egberto Gismonti *Magico* (1980)★★★, with Kjell Johnsen *Aftenland* (ECM 1980)★★★, with Haden, Gismonti *Folksongs* (ECM 1981)★★★★, *Eventyr* (ECM 1981)★★★, *Paths, Prints* (ECM 1982)★★★, *Wayfarer* (1983)★★★, *It's OK To Listen To The Gray Voice* (ECM 1985)★★★★, *All Those Born With Wings* (ECM 1986)★★★, *Legend Of The Seven Dreams* (ECM 1988)★★★, *I Took Up The Runes* (ECM 1990)★★★★, with Peter Erskine, Miroslav Vitous *Star* (ECM 1991)★★★, with Agnes Buen Gårnas *Rosensfole* (ECM 1991)★★★, with Usted Fateh Ali Khan and Musicians From Pakistan *Ragas & Sagas* (ECM 1992)★★★, *Twelve Moons* (ECM 1993)★★★★, with Vitous *Atmos* (ECM 1993)★★★, *Madar* (ECM 1993)★★★, with the Hilliard Ensemble *Officium* (ECM New Series 1994)★★★, *Visible World* (ECM 1996)★★★★, *Rites* (ECM 1998)★★★★.

● COMPILATIONS: *Works* (ECM 1984)★★★.

GARE, LOU

b. Leslie Arthur Gare 16 June 1939, Rugby, Warwickshire, England. A unique tenor saxophonist, deriving some elements of his playing from Sonny Rollins, Gare was a member of the early Mike Westbrook Band. He, Keith Rowe (guitar) and Lawrence Sheaff (cello/clarinet) found themselves increasingly at odds with the rest of the unit and inevitably split away. After moving to London Gare, Rowe, and drummer Eddie Prévost founded AMM. Gare's improvising typified the AMM approach, not least in his use of passages of silence, and the underpinning melodic logic of even his most abstract solos is so compelling that he gives a potent impression of phrases continuing, understood but unheard, through the gaps he leaves. During much of the 70s AMM comprised only Gare and Prévost, but Gare left the band and went to live in Exeter, Devon. For a while he led a free jazz trio but, although he occasionally plays with Prévost and others, including bassist Marcio Mattos, he has virtually given up public performing.

GARLAND, ED 'MONTUDIE'

b. 9 January 1885, New Orleans, Louisiana, USA, d. 22 January 1980. As a child, Garland played drums and brass bass, often working in marching bands in his home town. Among the early jazz stars with whom he claims to have played were Buddy Bolden (1904), Freddie Keppard (1906), and Kid Ory (1910). By 1914 he was based in Chicago, from where he toured the black vaudeville circuit, but was on hand in 1921 to help form a band, led by Joe 'King' Oliver, to play a residency at the city's newly-opened Royal Garden. When the Oliver band toured California, Garland, by now playing string bass, stayed behind in Los Angeles, working frequently with Ory. In 1927 he formed his own group in Los Angeles which lasted for a number of years. Late in 1940 he assembled a band to be led by Jelly Roll Morton for a recording date, but Morton was gravely ill and died before the session could take place. In 1944 Garland was a member of a band assembled by Orson Welles for a series of radio programmes. The 'Mercury Theatre All Stars' included Jimmy Noone, who died on the morning of the third broadcast and an impromptu performance of 'Blues For Jimmy' featured a bowed bass solo by Garland which thereafter became a permanent part of his repertoire. In 1944 he was reunited with Ory and remained with him for the next decade, their relationship ending when a misunderstanding led to a fist-fight at the Hangover club in San Francisco. From 1955 Garland freelanced with Andy Blakeney, Earl 'Fatha' Hines, Turk Murphy and others. In 1971 he returned to his birthplace for the first time in over half a century to play at the 4th New Orleans Jazz Festival. From 1973 Garland played at several festivals and toured the USA and Europe with Barry Martyn's Legends Of Jazz band. Despite failing sight and hearing, and general frailty, Garland toured until September 1977, when he was hospitalized in Germany. Back home in Los Angeles he retired, at the age of 92, but still played with the Legends Of Jazz whenever they came to town. Although he often played his instrument in the traditional 'slapping' manner, Garland had a notably light touch but he favoured using the bow, thus adding variety to his always rhythmic support.

● ALBUMS: *Kid Ory Live At The Club Hangover* (1953-54)★★★★, *Kid Ory's Creole Jazz Band* (1954)★★★.

GARLAND, HANK

b. Walter Louis Garland, 11 November 1930, Cowpens, South Carolina, USA. A professional electric guitarist at the age of 15 who played on *The Grand Ole Opry* with Paul Howard for several weeks, before Howard found out he was violating the state's child labour laws and reluctantly sent the talented youngster home. Garland returned to Nashville on his sixteenth birthday, where he quickly became one of the most popular and respected session guitarists and played on recordings by countless artists. In 1949, he made his first solo recordings for Decca Records, even including a few vocals, which clearly failed to match his instrumental talent. His recording of 'Sugarfoot Rag' not only inspired his nickname, it also firmly established him in Nashville. During the 50s, he recorded for Decca and Dot, being remembered for versions of 'E-String Rag' and 'Guitar Shuffle' and also worked with Chet Atkins. In the late 50s, Garland's playing was a prominent part of the coming of the Nashville Sound and his work extended to rockabilly and recording with Elvis Presley. In 1959, it was Garland who played the lead on Jim Reeves' recording of 'He'll Have To Go' and later on Patsy Cline's 'I Fall To Pieces'. He also became respected in other genres of music, particularly jazz, which he had always loved. He appeared at the 1960 Newport Jazz Festival and made jazz recordings with Gary Burton, Joe Benjamin and Joe Morello. On 8 September 1961, a serious car crash near Springfield, Tennessee, left him in a coma for some weeks and although he slowly recovered, the crash permanently affected his co-ordination. Considerable practice saw him managing to play a few bars but he could never remember what he was playing and his professional career ended. He left Nashville in 1963 and lived for a time in Milwaukee, but it is believed that after his wife's death in a car crash, he moved to South Carolina. It seems that in 1962, he was so respected by his fellow musicians that they often added his name to Musician Union forms indicating he should be paid for playing on sessions. Garland greatly influenced other guitarists including Willie Nelson and Albert Lee.

● ALBUMS: *Jazz Winds From A New Direction* (Columbia 1961)★★★★, *The Velvet Guitar Of Hank Garland* (Columbia 60s)★★, *The Unforgettable Guitar* (RCA 60s)★★★, with Nashville All-Stars *After The Riot At Newport* (Bear Family 1989)★★★★.

● COMPILATIONS: *Hank Garland & His Sugarfooters* covers 1949-57 recordings (Bear Family 1992)★★★★.

GARLAND, JOE

b. 15 August 1903, Norfolk, Virginia, USA, d. 21 April 1977. After studying formally and playing clarinet and saxophones in concert bands, Garland moved into danceband and jazz work under Elmer Snowden, Leon Abbey, Jelly Roll Morton, the Mills Blue Rhythm Band, Lucky Millinder and Duke Ellington. In the late 30s and through most of the 40s he freelanced with various bands, including two spells as a member of Louis Armstrong's big band where his skilled musicianship made him invaluable. In due course he became musical director of the band, a position he also held with Earl Hines in the late 40s. In the early 50s Garland ended his full-time involvement in music, turning instead to what became a very successful career in photography. Highly respected by fellow musicians, Garland is best remembered today for two of his compositions: 'Leap Frog', which was recorded by Armstrong in 1941, and became the theme tune of Les Brown and his Band Of Renown, while 'In The Mood' was Joe Loss's theme and a hit record for Glenn Miller.

GARLAND, RED

b. William M. Garland, 13 May 1923, Dallas, Texas, USA, d. 23 April 1984. Garland turned to the piano in his late teens, having earlier studied and played reed instruments. Although initially inspired by mainstream artists, he moved into bebop in the late 40s, accompanying Charlie Parker, Fats Navarro and others while still playing regularly with musicians such as Coleman Hawkins and Ben Webster. In 1955 he joined Miles Davis, remaining a member of the quintet until 1958. For the next 10 years he led his own trio, which recorded extensively, but drifted into obscurity after 1968 when he settled in Texas. Towards the end of the following decade he returned to the national and international jazz scene. As a soloist Garland was often lyrical if not especially commanding; but he made an important contribution to the powerful rhythm section (with Paul Chambers and Philly Joe Jones) of one of Davis's best bands, where his sophisticated technique, use of harmonic substitutions and block-chording set standards for many contemporary and later bop bands.

● ALBUMS: *A Garland Of Red* (Prestige 1956)★★★, *The Red Garland Trio* i (1956)★★★★, *Red Garland's Piano/The P.C. Blues* (Prestige 1957)★★★, *Groovy/Red Garland Revisited* (Prestige 1957)★★★★, *Saying Something* (1957)★★★, *All Mornin' Long* (Prestige 1957)★★★, *Soul Junction* (Prestige 1957)★★★★, *High Pressure* (Original Jazz Classics 1957)★★★, *Dig It* (Original Jazz Classics 1957)★★★★, *It's A Blue World* (1958)★★★, *Manteca* (Prestige 1958)★★★, *Rediscovered Masters* (Original Jazz Classics 1958)★★★, *Rojo* (Original Jazz Classics 1958)★★★, *The Red Garland Trio* ii (Original Jazz Classics 1958)★★★★, *All Kinds Of Weather* (Prestige 1958)★★★, *Red In Bluesville* (Prestige 1959)★★★, At The Prelude: *The Red Garland Trio* iii (Prestige 1959)★★, *The Red Garland Trio With Eddie 'Lockjaw' Davis* (Moodsville 1959)★★★, with Coleman Hawkins *Coleman Hawkins Plus The Red Garland Trio* (Swingville 1960)★★★, *Red Alone* (Moodsville 1960)★★★, *Alone With The Blues* (Moodsville 1960)★★★, *Hallello-y'all* (Prestige 1960)★★, *Bright And Breezy* (Jazzland 1961)★★, *The Nearness Of You* (Jazzland 1961)★★★, *High Pressure* (Prestige 1961)★★★★, *Solar* (Jazzland 1962)★★★, *Red's Good Groove* (Jazzland 1962)★★, *Dig It!* (Prestige 1962)★★★, *When There Are Grey Skies* (Prestige 1962)★★★★, with Curtis Fuller *Curtis Fuller With Red Garland* 1957 recording (New Jazz 1962)★★★, *Can't See For Lookin'* (Prestige 1963)★★★★, *Lil' Darlin'* (New Jazz 1963)★★★★, *High Pressure* (New Jazz 1963)★★, *Red Garland Live!* (New Jazz 1963)★★★, *Soul Burnin'* (Prestige 1964)★★★, *Red Garland Revisited* (Prestige 1969)★★, *Auf Wiedersehen* (1971)★★★, *The Quota* (1971)★★★, *Crossings* (Original Jazz Classics 1977)★★★, *Red Alert* (Original Jazz Classics 1977)★★★★, *Feelin' Red* (Muse 1978)★★★, *I Left My Heart* (1978)★★★, *Equinox* (1978)★★★, *Stepping Out* (Galaxy 1979)★★, *Strike Up The Band* (1979)★★, *Wee Small Hours* (1980)★★★, *Misty Red* (Timeless 1982)★★★.

GARNER, ERROLL

b. 15 June 1921, Pittsburgh, Pennsylvania, USA, d. 2 January 1977. A self-taught pianist, Garner played on the radio at the age of 10 and within a few more years was playing professionally in his home-town. Among the bands with which he played during this period were those led by Leroy Brown and, reputedly, Fate Marable. In 1944 Garner moved to New York and began working in nightclubs, including the Rendezvous and the Melody Bar. He became a popular and successful performer in these establishments, but also enjoyed playing at the more jazz-orientated venues along 52nd Street, such as Tondelayo's and the Three Deuces. For a short time, he worked in a trio led by Slam Stewart, but soon formed his own trio.

For the rest of his life, with only occasional exceptions, Garner worked as leader of a trio or as a soloist. Throughout the 50s, 60s and early 70s, he toured the USA, playing prestigious club and hotel engagements, appearing at festivals and on radio and television. He also visited Europe and the UK, where he appeared on television, and in 1962 he had an album in the UK charts. During these years, Garner recorded numerous albums, some of them, such as the classic *Concert By The Sea*, becoming virtual fixtures in the catalogue. Although Garner taught himself to play, he never learnt to read music, yet he contrived to create several jazz tunes, including one, 'Misty', that became a standard when Johnny Burke added a lyric. Slight echoes of the full sound of Earl 'Fatha' Hines occasionally appear in Garner's playing, as do touches that suggest he had absorbed the work of the stride piano players, yet throughout the bulk of his vast output, Garner remains unique. Playing consistently to a very high standard, he developed certain characteristics that bear few resemblances to other pianists. Notably, these include a plangent left-hand, block-chorded pulse, a dancing pattern of seemingly random ideas played with the right hand in chords or single notes, and playful introductions, which appear as independent miniature compositions, only to sweep suddenly, with apparent spontaneity and complete logic, into an entirely different song. Sumptuously romantic on ballads, and fleet and daring on up-tempo swingers, Garner's range was wide. Nicknamed 'The Elf', more, perhaps, for his diminutive stature than for the impish good humour of those introductions, Garner was the first jazz pianist since Fats Waller to appeal to the non-jazz audience, and the first jazzman ever to achieve popular acclaim from this audience without recourse to singing or clowning. Dudley Moore acknowledges much of his style to Garner, and 'swinging 60s piano jazz' owes a massive debt to him. Stylistically, Garner is in a category of which he is, so far, the only member. Since his death in January 1977, there has been no sign that any other pianist other than Keith Jarrett is following his independent path in jazz.

● ALBUMS: *Free Piano Improvisations Recorded By Baron Timme Rosenkrantz At One Of His Famous Gaslight Jazz Sessions* reissued as *Early Erroll* (Dial 1949),★★★ *Piano Moods* (Columbia 1950)★★, *Rhapsody* (Atlantic 1950)★★, *Erroll Garner Volume 1* (Dial 1950)★★★, *Erroll Garner Playing Piano Solos, Volume 1* (Savoy 1950)★★★, *Erroll Garner Playing Piano Solos, Volume 2* (Savoy 1950)★★★, *Erroll Garner Playing Piano Solos, Volume 3* (Savoy 1950)★★★, *Erroll Garner Playing Piano Solos, Volume 4* (Savoy 1951)★★★, *Gone With Garner* (Mercury 1951)★★★, *Gems* (Columbia 1951)★★, *Erroll Garner At The Piano* (Mercury 1951)★★★, *Erroll Garner At The Piano* (Atlantic 1951)★★★, *Passport To Fame* (Atlantic 1952)★★★, *Solo Flight* (Columbia 1952)★★★, *Piano Solos Volume 2* (Atlantic 1952)★★★, *Overture To Dawn Volume 1* (Blue Note 1952)★★★★, *Overture To Dawn Volume 2* (Blue Note 1952)★★★★, *Piano Stylist* reissued as *Piano*

Variations (King 1952)★★★, *Separate Keyboards* (Savoy 50s)★★, *Long Ago And Far Away* (Columbia 50s)★★★, *Erroll Garner At The Piano* (Savoy 1953)★★★, *Erroll Garner At The Piano* (Columbia 1953)★★★, *Overture To Dawn Volume 3* (Blue Note 1953)★★★, *Overture To Dawn Volume 4* (Blue Note 1953)★★★, *Overture To Dawn Volume 5* (Blue Note 1953)★★★, *Erroll Garner Plays For Dancing* (Columbia 1953)★★★, *Body And Soul* (Columbia 1953)★★★★, *Mambo Moves Garner* (Mercury 1954)★★, *Solitaire* (Mercury 1954)★★★, *Garnering* (EmArcy 1954)★★★★, *Contrasts* (EmArcy 1954)★★★, *Afternoon Of An Elf* (Mercury 1955)★★, *Garnerland* (Columbia 1955)★★★, *Penthouse Serenade* (Savoy 1955)★★★, *Serenade To Laura* (Savoy 1955)★★★, *Gone Garner Gonest* (Columbia 1955)★★★, *Erroll!* (EmArcy 1956)★★★★, *The Greatest Garner* (Atlantic 1956)★★★★, *He's Here! He's Gone! He's Garner* (Columbia 1956)★★★, *Concert By The Sea* (Columbia 1956)★★★★★, with Art Tatum *Giants Of The Piano* (Roost 1956)★★★, *Most Happy Piano* (Columbia 1957)★★★, *Other Voices* (Columbia 1957)★★, *Soliloquy* (Columbia 1957)★★★, *Erroll Garner* (Ron-lette 1958)★★★, *Encores In Hi-Fi* (Columbia 1958)★★★, *Paris Impressions* (Columbia 1958)★★★★, *Paris Impressions Volume 2* (Columbia 1958)★★★★, *Perpetual Motion* (Atlantic 1959)★★★, *The One And Only Erroll Garner* (Columbia 1960)★★★, *Swinging Solos* (Columbia 1960)★★★, *Dreamstreet* (ABC-Paramount 1961)★★★, *The Provocative Erroll Garner* (Columbia 1961)★★★★, *Closeup In Swing* (ABC-Paramount 1961)★★★, *Informal Piano Improvisations* (Baronet 1962)★★★, *Misty* (Mercury 1962)★★★★, *The Concert Garner In England* (1963)★★★★, *One World Concert* (Reprise 1963)★★★, *Seeing Is Believing* (Mercury 1964)★★★, *A Night At The Movies* (1965)★★★, *Now Playing* (MGM 1966)★★★, *Campus Concert* (MGM 1966)★★★, *That's My Kick* (MGM 1967)★★★, *Up In Erroll's Room* (MGM 1967)★★★.

● COMPILATIONS: *Historical First Recordings* (1944)★★★★, *Overture To Dawn* (1944)★★★, *Passport To Fame* (1944)★★★, *Early Erroll: 1945 Stride Volumes 1 & 2* (1945)★★★★, *Gemini* (Decca 1978)★★★, *The Great Garner* (Atlantic 1979)★★★, *Complete Savoy Sessions Volume 1* 1945-49 recordings (RCA 1986)★★★, *Yesterdays* (1945-49)★★★, *The Elf* (1945-49)★★★, *Cocktail Time* (1947)★★★, *Body & Soul* (1951-52)★★★★, *Erroll Garner Plays Gershwin And Kern* (1958-65)★★★, *Complete Savoy Sessions Volume 2* 1949 recordings (RCA 1986)★★★, *Jazz Portraits* (Jazz Portraits 1993)★★★, *Dreamstreet/One World Concert* (Telarc 1996)★★★★, *Gershwin & Kern/Magician* (Telarc 1996)★★★, *That's My Kick/Gemini* (Telarc 1996)★★★, *A Night At The Movies/Up In Erroll's Room* (Telarc 1996)★★★.

● FURTHER READING: *Erroll Garner: The Most Happy Piano*, James M. Doran.

GARRETT, DONALD RAFAEL

b. 28 February 1932, El Dorado, Arkansas, USA, d. 14 August 1989. An immensely gifted multi-instrumentalist, playing bass and several reed instruments, notably the bass clarinet, Garrett made a great impression on the hard bop scene in Chicago and elsewhere in the early and mid-60s. He played and occasionally recorded with artists such as Muhal Richard Abrams, John Coltrane and Archie Shepp. During the 70s he toured internationally and also led his own band, the Sea Ensemble, in which he was joined by his wife, Zusaan Fasteau. Garrett's ability to play a wide variety of instruments, including several ethnic wind instruments, brought an intriguingly textured atmosphere to his performances.

● ALBUMS: with Craig Harris, Joseph Jarman, Famoudou Don Moye *Earth Passage-Density* (Black Saint 1981)★★★.

GARRETT, KENNY

b. 1961, USA. It would be fair to say that Kenny Garrett was the main musical force in Miles Davis' final band, and perhaps the last truly special young musician to emerge from the Davis hot house. As the great trumpeter played less and less, he relied more and more on his sideman to fill in the gaps, and be ready to step in quickly and build something accomplished into the gaps. Garrett proved himself an incredible alto saxophone powerhouse – an intense and complex improviser with an astonishing energy and drive. Starting early at the age of 17 with a saxophone spot in Mercer Ellington's revived Ellington Orchestra, Garrett earned a complete musical education, in a series of perhaps surprisingly mainstream bands, considering his edgy and experimental, funky style. Mel Lewis' group (a traditional route for young and aspiring jazzers) followed, and a spell with veteran vibes and piano man Lionel Hampton followed that. His first recording as a leader came in 1984, and it was an assured affair, featuring the brilliant Woody Shaw on trumpet and a young, as yet unknown, Mulgrew Miller at the piano. In the following years he became involved in the Blue Note label's Out Of The Blue project, recording with the band in 1986, before continuing his extensive jazz education with a stint in Art Blakey's prestigious Jazz Messengers. A year later, in 1987, Garrett joined Miles Davis for what would be the biggest boost for his career. Garrett was given all the room he needed, and excelled in his ability to build long, escalating solos out of simple riffs and grooves, using exotic scales and sophisticated inner chord changes as the basis for an individualistic 'outside' approach. Since Davis's death, Garrett has continued to record under his own name, with variable degrees of success, as well as working on a huge array of projects by such notable leaders as Dizzy Gillespie, Donald Byrd and Freddie Hubbard. Recommended listening must include *African Exchange Student*, featuring his regular rhythm section of the time, with pianist Mulgrew Miller, bassist Charnett Moffett and, drummer Tony Reedus, as well as occasional appearances by Ron Carter and Elvin Jones. The record provides a fine example of Garrett's edgy and acidic style, on compositions that range from the Louis Armstrong anthem 'Mack The Knife' to Garrett's own raucous title track.

● ALBUMS: *Introducing Kenny Garrett* (Criss Cross 1984)★★★, *The Eternal Triangle* (Blue Note 1987)★★, *Garrett 5* (Paddle Wheel 1988)★★★, *Prisoner Of Love* (Atlantic 1989)★★★, *African Exchange Student* (Atlantic 1990)★★★★, *Black Hope* (Warners 1992)★★★★, *Trilogy* (Warners 1995)★★★, *Pursuance: The Music Of John Coltrane* (Warners 1996)★★★★, *Songbook* (Warners 1997)★★★★.

Garrick, Michael

b. 30 May 1933, Enfield, Middlesex, England. Largely self-taught as a pianist and composer, Garrick led bands during the 50s and was active in the 'jazz and poetry' movement. In the mid-60s he worked with the band co-led by Don Rendell and Ian Carr and also fronted his own small group, which often featured saxophonist Joe Harriott. A prolific composer, in the late 60s Garrick's writing reflected his beliefs and 'Jazz Praises' was performed at St Paul's Cathedral in London. In keeping with the mood of works such as this, Garrick also played the pipe organ. In the 70s he studied at Berklee College Of Music in the USA and subsequently taught extensively in the UK. In the late 70s he formed a trio with Phil Lee and Norma Winstone. The following decades saw him active with small and large bands, sometimes under his own leadership, and continuing his interest in jazz education.

● ALBUMS: *Michael Garrick* i (1963)★★, *Michael Garrick* ii (1963)★★★, *Michael Garrick* iii (1964)★★★★, *Michael Garrick* iv (1965)★★, *Michael Garrick* v (1965)★★★, *Black Marigolds* (1966)★★★, *Jazz Praises At St Paul's* (1968)★★, *Poetry And Jazz In Concert 250* (1969)★★, *Michael Garrick* (1970)★★★, *Mr Smith's Apocalypse* (1971)★★★, *Cold Mountain* (1972)★★★, *Home Stretch Blues* (1972)★★★, *Troppo* (1973)★★★, *You've Changed* (Hep Jazz 1978)★★★, *A Lady In Waiting* (Jazz Academy 1993)★★★★, *Meteors Close At Hand* (Jaza 1994)★★★, *Parting Is Such* (Jaza 1995)★★★★, *For Love Of Duke And Ronnie* (Jazz Archives 1997)★★★.

Garrison, Jimmy

b. 3 March 1934, Miami, Florida, USA, d. 7 April 1976. Garrison began playing bass in Philadelphia, where he grew up, moving to New York in the late 50s with Philly Joe Jones. By 1961 he was deeply involved with the free jazz movement, and played with Ornette Coleman at New York's Five Spot. John Coltrane sitting in with the group, was so impressed by Garrison that he invited him to join his own quartet, so beginning a five-year association in which Garrison proved 'the pivot' (to quote McCoy Tyner) of the pre-eminent modern jazz group of the era, thanks to his dynamic and forceful musical personality. In 1963 he took time out to co-lead a sextet session, *Illumination*, with his Coltrane rhythm-section partner, Elvin Jones. After leaving Coltrane in 1966 he led his own group, played with the bands of Hampton Hawes, Archie Shepp and Elvin Jones and recorded again with Ornette Coleman, 1968's *New York Is Now!* and *Love Call* supplementing a previous album, *Ornette On Tenor* (1961). Despite his career-long involvement with the *avant garde*, Garrison retained a traditional view of the role the bass should have in jazz; and although a gifted soloist, he chose to concentrate upon his instrument's rhythmic function, seeing that as the foundation of good group jazz. In the 70s Garrison taught, played with Alice Coltrane and also returned for a further spell with Elvin Jones but was troubled with ill-health. He died of lung cancer in April 1976.

● ALBUMS: *Ornette On Tenor* (1961)★★, *Coltrane* (1962)★★★, with Elvin Jones *Illumination* (1963)★★★, with John Coltrane *A Love Supreme* (1964)★★★★, with Ornette Coleman *New York Is Now!* (1968)★★★, with Jones *The Ultimate* (1968)★★★, with Jones *Puttin' It Together* (1968)★★★.

Garzone, George

b. *c.* 1951, Boston, Massachusetts, USA. A popular and highly respected tenor saxophonist, Garzone has spent a large part of his working life as a jazz educator in the Boston area. After attending music college in Boston, Garzone formed a long running trio, the Fringe, in 1972. Highlighting Garzone's adventurous tenor, the Fringe developed into one of Boston's most respected and adored groups. Away from the spotlight, Garzone built a career mentoring future jazz prodigies, including Billy Hart, Eddie Henderson and Dave Liebman, at the Berklee College Of Music and New England Conservatory. He has also recorded and toured with a diverse range of artists, including Jack DeJohnette, Joe Lovano, John Patitucci and Danilo Perez. Garzone was signed to NYC Records in 1995, debuting with *Alone*, a smooth Stan Getz homage. The follow-up, *Four's And Two's*, was a more characteristically edgy set that successfully paired Garzone with fellow tenor Lovano. Garzone has recently relocated to New York, although he still teaches and plays in Boston. He still works with the Fringe, alongside drummer and founder member Bob Gullotti and bassist John Lockwood.

● ALBUMS: *Alone* (NYC 1995)★★★, with Joe Lovano *Four's And Two's* (NYC 1996)★★★.

Gaskin, Leonard

b. 25 August 1920, New York City, New York, USA. Gaskin first entered jazz at the deep end, playing bass in the regular rhythm section at Clark Monroe's Uptown House where bebop was forged in the early 40s. Among the musicians Gaskin backed there were Charlie Parker and Dizzy Gillespie. Despite his involvement with bebop, Gaskin was also in demand by mainstream jazz artists and played with such diverse groups as those led by Eddie South and Erroll Garner. In 1953 he recorded with Miles Davis and in 1956 joined the traditional line-up led by Eddie Condon. Throughout the 60s and beyond, Gaskin's versatility ensured him a successful career in the studios, from where he regularly emerged to play with many musicians including David 'Panama' Francis and Oliver Jackson. He also became a sought-after teacher.

● ALBUMS: *Miles Davis Plays Al Cohn Compositions* (1953)★★★, with Eddie Condon *The Roaring 20s* (1957)★★★, *A Dixieland Sound Spectacular/At The Jazz Band Ball* (1961)★★★★, *At The Darktown Strutters Ball* (1962)★★★★, *Dixieland Hits* (1962)★★★, *Oliver Jackson Presents 'Le Quartet'* (1982)★★★.

Gaslini, Giorgio

b. 22 October 1929, Milan, Italy. Gaslini learnt the piano as a child and started performing when he was 13 years old, appearing with his own trio at the Florence Jazz Festival in 1947. He studied at the Milan Conservatory before a career in which he has been equally at home in jazz and classical music. He would like to bring these various skills together in what he describes as 'total music'. He composed and played the music for Antonioni's film *La Notte* (1960) and wrote a jazz opera *Colloquio Con Malcolm X* (1970). He was friends with Eric Dolphy and worked with artists including Don Cherry, Gato Barbieri, Max Roach and Roswell Rudd as well as performing as a solo pianist and with his own groups. He has been involved in music education both directly as a teacher and by taking his quartet into less usual venues like factories and hospitals.

● ALBUMS: *Nuovi Sentimenti/New Feelings* (La Voce Del Padrone 1966)★★★, *Grido* (Durium 1968)★★★, *Africa* (1969)★★★, *Colloquio Con Malcolm X* (1970)★★★★, *Fabbrica Occupata* (Produttoriassociati 1974)★★★, *Gaslini Plays Monk* (Soul Note 1980)★★★, with Anthony Braxton *Four Pieces* (1981)★★★★, *Schumann Reflections* (Soul Note 1984)★★★, *Multiple* (Soul Note 1991)★★★★, *Ayler's Wings* (Soul Note 1991)★★★, *Lampi* (Soul Note 1994)★★★★, *Jelly's Back In Town* (DDQ 1997)★★, *Mister O* (Soul Note 1997)★★.

GATEWAY

An occasional jazz trio featuring the immense talents of John Abercrombie (b. 16 December 1944, Portchester, New York, USA; guitar), Dave Holland (b. 1 October 1946, Wolverhampton, Staffordshire, England; bass) and Jack DeJohnette (b. 9 August 1942, Chicago, Illinois, USA; drums). They have recorded four excellent albums over the past three decades. It is a testament to their strength as musicians that they can reunite sporadically, and immediately ignite the same spark.

● ALBUMS: *Gateway* (ECM 1975)★★★★, *Gateway 2* (ECM 1978)★★, *Homecoming* (ECM 1995)★★★, *In The Moment* (ECM 1996)★★★★.

GAY, AL

b. 25 February 1928, London, England. After formal studies in clarinet and saxophones at the Guildhall School of Music, Gay worked in various dancebands during the mid- and late 40s. In 1953 he joined the Freddy Randall band and, after leaving three years later, he remained strongly connected with the traditional jazz scene, playing with bands led by Joe Daniels, Harry Gold and Bob Wallis. In the early 60s he became a member of Alex Welsh's band, where he remained for almost five years, returning in 1977 for a further six years. In between these stints, and on into the 80s, Gay freelanced, working in radio and as accompanist to numerous visiting jazz artists. In the late 80s and early 90s Gay could be heard leading his own band and also playing with groups such as the Pizza Express All Stars. A sound mainstream performer, Gay's work on tenor saxophone is particularly pleasing.

● ALBUMS: *At Home With Alex Welsh* (1968)★★★.

GAYNAIR, BOGEY

b. Wilton Gaynair, 11 January 1927, Kingston, Jamaica, West Indies, d. 13 February 1995. Early in his career Gaynair played tenor saxophone in reggae bands in his homeland. In the mid-50s he moved to Europe and into jazz. He played with Dizzy Reece in London, then became resident in Germany where he extended his musical understanding through the study of composition and arranging, and also played with many important German musicians as well as visiting jazz stars from the USA and UK. With Ellsworth 'Shake' Keane he was a member of Kurt Edelhagen's orchestra, and he was co-founder of Third Eye which included Kenny Wheeler and Alan Skidmore. A fluent improviser in the hard-bop mould, Gaynair continued to perform into the early 80s but in 1983, while playing with Peter Herbolzheimer, he suffered a stroke. Although much of his career was spent outside the international spotlight, Gaynair built a small but dedicated body of critical approval, including several long-time advocates such as jazz writer/photographer Val Wilmer. Gaynair played with a full-throated sound yet retained a melodic approach to his interpretations. If there were sometimes hints of John Coltrane in his playing, these were comfortably subordinated to his personal conceptions of his music.

● ALBUMS: *Blue Bogey* (Tempo/Jasmine 1959)★★★, with Horace Parlan *One For Wilton* (Ego 1980)★★★★, *Third Eye Live!* (View 1982)★★★, *Alpharian* 1982 recording (Konnex 1991)★★★.

GEBERT, BOBBY

b. John Robert Gebert, 1 April 1944, Adelaide, Australia. Gebert was classically trained on piano and studied at the London College of Music, before returning to Australia. In his teens he led jazz groups in Melbourne, Adelaide and also at the El Rocco Jazz Club, Sydney. He played with the best jazz musicians and forged a reputation as a progressive pianist and composer. In April 1961 Gebert made his recording debut with his trio, recording three originals. He also became a popular accompanist working with local musicians and many international visitors. He broadened his versatility by working in television, film and in the theatre and became musical director for *Hair* and assistant director for *Jesus Christ Superstar*. Possessing endless musical curiosity, Gebert continued his education in America, studying with Walter Davis Jnr. and working with eminent jazz musicians, Art Pepper, Freddie Hubbard and Milt Jackson. In the 90s Gebert occasionally led a successful trio and was involved in jazz education. The pop singer Delilah employed Gebert as her musical director as did Renee Geyer and her Australian tour band. He also played piano in the Dale Barlow Quartet. Although Gebert recorded with other artists including Bernie McGann (*Kindred Spirits*) and Andrew Speight (*Now's The Time*) it was not until 1994, at the age of 50, that Gebert recorded his first album under his own name. *The Sculptor* was highly regarded and consisted of originals and standards. The cohesiveness of the trio with Jonathon Zwartz (bass), Andrew Dickeson (drums), and the leader's, deft, delicate and imaginative piano playing, resulted in the album winning an ARIA award in 1995. Gebert has taken no short cuts in his stature as one of the leading jazz musicians in Australia, equally gifted with talent and integrity.

● ALBUMS: *The Sculptor* (ABC Music 1994)★★★★.

GEE, JONATHAN

b. London, England. After an early classical training between the ages of five and nine, Gee lost interest in the piano during his teens. But it was during his time at Sheffield University that he developed his love of modern jazz, and began to practise the piano again. On his return to London he attended the jazz course at the Guildhall School of Music for a short time, but soon left, disenchanted with the system of jazz education. Since then Gee has quickly earned himself a reputation on the British jazz scene. Leading a trio with Wayne Batchelor and Winston Clifford, he won the 1991 *Wire* Best Newcomer Award.

● ALBUMS: *Blah, Blah, Blah, Etc., Etc.* (1989)★★★, *Closer To* (ASC 1997)★★★★, *Your Shining Heart* (ASC 1998)★★★★.

GELLER, HERB

b. 2 November 1928, Los Angeles, California, USA. Geller's first major engagement on alto saxophone was with Joe Venuti in the mid-40s. By the end of the decade he was in New York, playing in Claude Thornhill's big band and early in the 50s he was performing with Billy May. In the mid-50s Geller worked with several leading west coast musicians, including Chet Baker, Shelly Manne, Maynard Ferguson, Shorty Rogers and Bill Holman. He was also co-leader of a small group with his wife, pianist Lorraine Walsh. After her sudden death in 1958 Geller worked with Benny Goodman and Louie Bellson, spent some time in South America and toured Europe, where he decided to settle. In 1962 he was in Berlin, playing in radio orchestras and running a nightclub. He later moved to Hamburg, where he again worked in radio and in several big bands, in between times playing and recording with his own small groups. A striking bebop player in the Charlie Parker mould, Geller's chosen pattern of work has limited his exposure to international audiences. However, the early 90s saw his return to touring with visits to the UK and elsewhere.

● ALBUMS: *Herb Geller Plays* (Emarcy 1954)★★★, *Herb Geller Sextette* (Emarcy 1955)★★★★, *The Gellers* (Emarcy 1955)★★★, *Fire In The West* (1957)★★★, *Shorty Rogers Plays Richard Rodgers* (1957)★★★, *Fire In The West* (Jubilee 1957)★★, *Stax Of Sax* (Jubilee 1958)★★★,*Shelly Manne And His Men Play Peter Gunn* (1959)★★, *Gypsy* (Atco 1959)★★★, *Herb Geller Alto Saxophone* (Josie 1963)★★★, *An American In Hamburg* (1975)★★★, *Rhyme To Reason* (Discovery 1978)vH, *Hot House* (1984)★★★, *Birdland Stomp* (Enja 1986)★★★, *A Jazz Songbook Meeting* (Enja 1989)★★★, *West Coast Scene* (Vogue 1989)★★★★, *Birdland Stomp* (Fresh Sounds 1991)★★★, *The Herb Geller Quartet* (VSOP 1994)★★★★, *Plays The Al Cohn Songbook* (Hep 1998)★★★.

GENIUS OF MODERN MUSIC VOLS. 1 & 2 - THELONIOUS MONK

Taken as a body of work these are two of the most important jazz albums of all time. Over the years Thelonious Monk's importance grows, yet when these sessions were recorded his reputation was of cult status only. Monk has given us some outstanding compositions, and many are contained here. Naturally, the most recorded jazz song of all time, 'Round Midnight', is present, but so is the evergreen 'Ruby My Dear' and 'Monk's Mood'. And so on and so on; it reads like a greatest hits package. The CD versions are indispensable as there are many additional alternate takes.

● Tracks: *Volume 1 - Round Midnight; Off Minor; Ruby My Dear; April In Paris; In Walked Bud; Thelonius; Epistrophy; Misterioso; Well You Needn't; Introspection; Humph. Volume 2 - Carolina Moon; Homin' In; Skippy; Let's Cool One; Suburban Eyes; Evonce; Straight No Chaser; Four In One; Nice Work If You Can Get It; Monk's Mood; Who Knows; Ask Me Now.*

● First Released (1947-1952 recordings)

● UK peak chart position: did not chart

● USA peak chart position: did not chart

GENTRY, CHUCK

b. Charles T. Gentry, 14 December 1911, Belgrade, Nebraska, USA, d. 1988. Starting out on clarinet, Gentry later mastered most of the saxophone family, specializing on the baritone. He began playing professionally in his mid-20s and in 1939 joined Vido Musso's big band, which soon folded; by the following year both Gentry and his former boss were working for Harry James. A year later the two men were still together, but this time with Benny Goodman. After a spell with Jimmy Dorsey, Gentry was drafted into the army and, following basic training, was transferred to the unit of musicians being assembled by Glenn Miller, where he remained until 1944. Once discharged, Gentry joined Artie Shaw and then returned for a second period with Goodman. By the late 40s, with most of the name big bands folding, Gentry was turning to studio work in Hollywood, which is where he spent most of the remainder of his career. He made numerous recordings in orchestras, backing artists such as June Christy and Nancy Wilson and performing with various leaders, including Louis Armstrong, Pete Rugolo, Woody Herman and Benny Carter. Occasionally he emerged from the studios to play dates with, for example, Stan Kenton's Los Angeles Neophonic Orchestra and with Bob Crosby at Disneyland.

● ALBUMS: with Pete Rugolo *Reeds In Hi-Fi* (1956)★★, with Stan Kenton *Wagner* (1964)★★★.

GEORGE, FATTY

b. Franz Georg Pressler, 24 April 1927, Vienna, Austria, d. 29 March 1982. In his early teens he began playing alto saxophone, later studying this and clarinet formally. At 20 he played bop, working in Austria and Germany, often leading his own band, continuing into the mid-50s when he opened a jazz club in Vienna.

Among the sidemen in his bands was Joe Zawinul who played in the Two Sounds band, a group which enjoyed a varied repertoire including bop and traditional jazz. He continued to run clubs in Vienna but spent part of the mid-60s playing in Berlin. He led bands regularly on radio and television in Austria. A gifted and hugely enthusiastic character, George moved smoothly between different styles of jazz, usually playing clarinet in traditional and mainstream swing-based settings and alto in more contemporary mode. On both instruments he revealed a smooth lyricism and was always harmonically interesting.

● ALBUMS: *Fatty 69* (Preiser 1969)★★★.

GEORGE, KARL

b. Karl Curtis George, 26 April 1913, St. Louis, Missouri, USA. Among George's early engagements was one in the early 30s when he played trumpet with McKinney's Cotton Pickers. He also worked with the Jeter-Pillars territory band, then, in 1939, joined the highly musical, if unfortunately short-lived, Teddy Wilson orchestra. After a spell with Lionel Hampton's first big band he served in the military during World War II. Immediately following the war, he played with several big bands on the west coast, including Stan Kenton and Benny Carter, and also played with small groups on recording sessions, including one led by Lucky Thompson. George occasionally formed bands for club and recording dates, often employing first-rate sidemen such as J.J. Johnson and Buddy Tate. By the 50s poor health had driven him into retirement in his home-town. Usually restricted to section work, George could play interesting solo lines, as he demonstrated with the Wilson band, often displaying a liking for the kind of linear, single-note solo adopted by Harry Edison. George's truncated career severely limited the opportunities for him to develop.

● COMPILATIONS: *The Chronological Teddy Wilson 1939-1941* (Classics 1939-41)★★★★, *Lionel Hampton 1940-1941* (Classics 1940-41)★★★★.

GERRY MULLIGAN MEETS BEN WEBSTER GERRY MULLIGAN AND BEN WEBSTER

This album combines the talents of two jazz giants. Saxophonist Ben Webster was one of the instrument's most influential exponents, primarily through his work with Duke Ellington. Gerry Mulligan, meanwhile, was an integral part of the 50s west coast movement and this set represents the confluence of two different generations. The featured quintet includes drummer Mel Lewis and bassist Leroy Vinnegar (who later played on the Doors' *The Soft Parade*), but the six tracks are noteworthy for the splendid empathy struck by Mulligan (baritone) and Webster (tenor). One of several collaborations between the former and notable guest artists, *Gerry Mulligan Meets Ben Webster* is a fine example of how two seemingly disparate musicians can perform together superbly.

● Tracks: *Chelsea Bridge; Cat Walk; Sunday; Who's Got Rhythm?; Tell Me When; Go Home.*

● First released 1960
● UK peak chart position: 15
● USA peak chart position: did not chart

GETZ, STAN

b. 2 February 1927, Philadelphia, Pennsylvania, USA, d. 6 June 1991. Getz played several reed instruments as a child, especially the alto saxophone, but he finally choosing the tenor saxophone and by the age of 15 was playing professionally. Within a year he had made his first records, playing with Jack Teagarden, who became, technically at least, Getz's guardian so that the youngster could go on the road with the band. The following year Getz worked with Stan Kenton, then with the bands of Jimmy Dorsey and Benny Goodman. Although he had already attracted attention in jazz circles during these tenures and through record dates under his own name, it was as a member of Woody Herman's 'Four Brothers' band in 1947 that he became an internationally recognized name. He was with Herman for about two years and then, during the 50s, he began leading a small group on a semi-regular basis. Spells with Kenton and Jazz At The Philharmonic were followed by an uncertain period as he sought, successfully, to throw off drug addiction. In the late 50s and early 60s he spent some time in Europe, being resident for a while in Copenhagen, Denmark. Back in the USA in the early 60s he made a milestone album, *Focus*, and worked with Charlie Byrd, developing an interest in Brazilian and other Latin American musical forms. As a result Getz made a number of Latin records that proved to be very popular, amongst them 'The Girl From Ipanema', featuring singer Astrud Gilberto, which helped to launch the bossa nova craze. Throughout the 60s and 70s Getz led small groups, whose line-ups often featured up-and-coming musicians such as Gary Burton, Chick Corea, Jimmy Raney, Al Haig, Steve Swallow, Airto Moreira and JoAnne Brackeen. Nevertheless his activity in these years was sporadic. His earlier popular success and the control he exercised over his career, including production of his own recording sessions, allowed him to work as and when he wanted. In the 80s he became more active again; in addition to playing clubs, concerts and festivals around the world he was also artist-in-residence at Stanford University. He recorded with among others Everything But The Girl. This late period saw a new surge in popularity which sadly coincided with gradual awareness that he was suffering a terminal illness: he died of cancer in June 1991.

One of the most highly-regarded tenor saxophonists in jazz history, Getz's early recording career was highlighted by his work with Herman. His playing on several records, notably 'Early Autumn', a part of Ralph Burns's 'Summer Sequence' suite, displays to great effect the featherweight and almost vibrato-free tone which hints at the admiration he had for the work of Lester Young. Getz followed the success of this recording with a string of fine albums with his own small groups, notably those he made with Haig and Raney, in the process influencing a generation of tenor saxophonists who aspired to his coolly elegant style. The remarkable *Focus* album, a suite composed and arranged by Eddie Sauter for jazz players and a string quartet, and the bossa nova recordings, which included the single, 'Desafinado', were other features of his first period. The smoothness of Getz's sound, the delicate floating effect he created, proved immensely popular with the fringe audience and led some observers to conclude that his was a detached and introspective style. In fact, during this period he had made a conscious attempt to subdue the emotional content of his playing, in order to fit in with current commercial vogues. Beneath the surface calm there was a burning, emotional quality which flared only occasionally. By the mid-60s Getz had become bored with the style he had adopted and entered a new period of brief experimentation with electronics, followed by the gradual development of a new and deeply soulful ballad style. Although he was still playing with a delicately floating sound, his rich melodic sense was given much freer rein. Towards the end of his life, when he knew he was slowly dying of cancer, Getz entered a third and in some respects even more fulfilling phase of his career. Despite, or perhaps because of, the state of his health, the emotional content of his work began to burn with a romantic fire, a glorious outpouring of which is heard on his *Anniversary* and *Serenity* albums. In retrospect it was possible to see that this romanticism had always been there, even if, at various times, it had been deliberately suppressed to accord with the musical spirit of the times. No one could doubt the emotional thrust of his late work. His sound was still smooth but now that quality was more obviously a surface patina beneath which surged a fierce desire to communicate with his audience. He succeeded in doing so, and thus helped to make those years when his life waned as his music waxed a period not of sadness but one of grateful joy for his many admirers.

● ALBUMS: *Stan Getz And The Tenor Sax Stars* (New Jazz 1950)★★★, *Stan Getz Volume 2* (New Jazz 1950)★★★★, with Lee Konitz *Stan Getz-Lee Konitz* (Prestige 1951)★★★★, *In Retrospect* (Dale 1951)★★★, with Billie Holiday *Billie And Stan* (Dale 1951)★★★, *New Sounds In Modern Music* (Savoy 1951)★★★, *Jazz At Storyville* (Roost 1952)★★★★, *Jazz At Storyville Volume 2* (Roost 1953)★★★★, *Stan Getz Plays* (Clef 1953)★★★, *The Artistry Of Stan Getz* (Clef 1953)★★★, *Jazz At Storyville Volume 3* (Roost 1954)★★★★, *Chamber Music* (Roost 1953)★★★, *Stan Plays Getz* (Verve 1954)★★★, *Split Kick* (Roost 1954)★★★, with Dizzy Gillespie *The Dizzy Gillespie-Stan Getz Sextet #1* 10-inch album (Norgran 1954)★★★★, with Gillespie *The Dizzy Gillespie-Stan Getz Sextet #2* 10-inch album (Norgran 1954)★★★★, *Interpretations By The Stan Getz Quintet Volume 1* (Norgran 1954)★★★★, *Interpretations By The Stan Getz Quintet Volume 2* (Norgran 1954)★★★★, *Interpretations By The Stan Getz Quintet Volume 3* (Norgran 1955)★★★★, *Stan Getz At The Shrine Auditorium* (1955)★★★, *At The Shrine* (Verve 1955)★★★, *West Coast Jazz* (Norgran 1955)★★★★, with Gillespie *Diz And Getz* (Verve 1955)★★★★, *Stan Getz* (American Record Society 1955)★★★, *Groovin' High* (Modern 1956)★★★, *Stan Getz' Most Famous* (Jazztone 1956)★★★, *The Sound* (Metronome 1956)★★★, with J.J. Johnson *Stan Getz & J.J. Johnson At The Opera House* (Verve 1958)★★★★, with Gerry Mulligan *Getz Meets Mulligan In Hi-Fi* (Verve 1958)★★★★, *Stan Getz And The Oscar Peterson Trio* (Verve 1958)★★★★, *At The Opera House* (Verve 1958)★★★, *Stan Getz In Denmark* (1959)★★★, *The Steamer* (Verve 1959)★★★, *The Early Days* (1959)★★★, *Award Winner* (Verve 1959)★★★, *The Soft Swing* (Verve 1959)★★★, *Imported From Europe* (Verve 1959)★★★, *Stan Getz In Europe* (1959)★★★, *Stan Getz In Poland* (1960)★★★, *Stan Getz Quintet* (Verve 1960)★★★, *At Large* (Verve 1960)★★★, *Cool Velvet: Stan Getz With Strings* (Verve 1960)★★★★, *Rhythms* (Blue Ribbon 1961)★★★, *Stan Getz Plays* (Verve 1961)★★★, *More West Coast Jazz With Stan Getz* (Verve 1961)★★★, *At The Shrine* (Verve 1961)★★★, *And The Cool Sounds* (Verve 1961)★★★, *In Stockholm* (Verve 1961)★★★, with Oscar Peterson *Stan Getz And The Oscar Peterson Trio* (Verve 1961)★★★, *Stan Meets Chet* (Verve 1961)★★★, *Focus* (Verve 1962)★★★★, with Charlie Byrd *Jazz Samba* (Verve 1962)★★★★★, *Jazz Samba Encore* (Verve 1963)★★★, *Moonlight In Vermont* (Roost 1963)★★★, *Modern World* (Roost 1963)★★★, *Reflections* (Verve 1963)★★★, *Getz Age* (Roost 1963)★★★, with Joao Gilberto *Getz/Gilberto* (Verve 1963)★★★★, *Big Band Bossa Nova* (Verve 1963)★★★★, *The Girl From Ipanema: The Bossa Nova Years* (1964)★★★★, *Getz/Gilberto 2* (Verve 1964)★★★, *The Melodic Stan Getz* (Metro 1965)★★★, *Getz Au Go Go* (Verve 1964)★★★★, with Bill Evans *Stan Getz And Bill Evans* (Verve 1965)★★★★, *A Song After Sundown* (RCA Victor 1966)★★★, with Laurindo Almeida *Stan Getz With Guest Laurindo Almeida* (Verve 1966)★★★, *Eloquence* (Verve 1966)★★★, *Another Time Another Place* (Verve 1966)★★★, *Plays Blues* (Verve 1966)★★★, *Sweet Rain* (Verve 1967)★★★, *Preservation* (Prestige 1967)★★★, *Voices* (Verve 1967)★★★, *What The World Needs Now* (Verve 1968)★★, *The Stan Getz Quartet* (1969)★★★, *Marakesh Express* (MGM 1969)★★, *Didn't We* (Verve 1969)★★★★, *Dynasty* (Verve 1971)★★★, *Portrait* (1972)★★★, *Captain Marvel* (Columbia 1972)★★, *The Peacocks* (1975)★★, *Best Of Two Worlds* (Columbia 1975)★★★, *The Master* (Columbia 1976)★★, *Live At Montmartre* (Steeple Chase 1977)★★★, *Another World* (Columbia 1978)★★★, *In Concert* (1980)★★★, *Children Of The World* (Columbia 1980)★★, *The Dolphin* (Concord 1981)★★★, *Billy Highstreet Samba* (1981)★★, *Spring Is Here* (Concord 1982)★★, *Pure Getz* (Concord 1982)★★★, with Albert Dailey *Poetry* (Elektra 1983)★★★, *Line For Lyons* (Sonet 1983)★★★, *The Stockholm Concert* (Sonet 1983)★★★, *The Voyage* (1986)★★★, *Anniversary* (Emarcy 1987)★★★, *Serenity* (Emarcy 1987)★★★, with James Moody *Tenor Contrasts* (Esquire 1988)★★★, *Apasionado* (A&M 1989)★★★, with Abbey Lincoln *You Gotta Pay The Band* (Verve 1992)★★★, with Kenny Barron *People Time* (Phonogram 1992)★★★, *Nobody Else But Me* (Verve 1994)★★★, *Blue Skies* (Concord Jazz 1996)★★★★, *Stan Getz Quartet Live In Paris* 1982 recording (Dreyfus 1996)★★★, *Yours And Mine: Live At The Glasgow International Jazz Festival 1989* (Concord Jazz 1997)★★★, *Soul Eyes* 1989 recording (Concord Jazz 1998)★★★.

● COMPILATIONS: *The Greatest Of Stan Getz* (Roost 1963)★★★*The Stan Getz Years* (Roost 1964)★★★, *The Best Of Stan Getz* (Verve 1967)★★★, *You The Night And Music* (Jazz Door 1991)★★★, *The Roost Years* (Roulette 1991)★★★, *New Collection* (Sony 1993)★★★, *Early Stan* (Original Jazz Classics 1993)★★★, *The Rare Dawn Sessions* (Biograph 1995)★★★, *A*

Life In Jazz: A Musical Biography (Verve 1996)★★★, *Best Of The West Coast Sessions* 3-CD box set (Verve 1997)★★★★, *The Complete Roost Recordings* 3-CD box set (Roost/Blue Note 1997)★★★★, *Sax Moods - The Very Best Of Stan Getz* (1998)★★★★.

● VIDEOS: *Warm Valley* (K-Jazz 1994).

● FURTHER READING: *The Stan Getz Discography*, Anne Astrup. *Stan Getz*, Richard Palmer. *Stan Getz: An Appreciation Of His Recorded Work*, Ron Kirkpatrick. *Stan Getz: A Life In Jazz*, Donald Maggin.

GIANT STEPS - JOHN COLTRANE

As influential upon contemporaries and successors as were Louis Armstrong and Charlie Parker, John Coltrane divided critical comment. For his supporters he was both high priest of contemporary jazz and prophet of what was yet to come. The ultimate statement of Coltrane's early obsession with chord progressions, this album marks the moment before he changed direction. *Giant Steps* is a vibrant demonstration of his inventive, dazzling and relentless playing of bop. Hereafter, Coltrane sought and found an avenue for his restless exploratory zeal in modal jazz. The album is therefore both a landmark and turning point and is still a textbook for many young musicians.

● Tracks: *Giant Steps; Cousin Mary; Countdown; Spiral; Syeeda's Song Flute; Mr. P.C.; Naima.*

● First released 1959

● UK peak chart position: did not chart

● USA peak chart position: did not chart

GIBBS, MIKE

b. Michael Clement Irving, 25 September 1937, Harare, Zimbabwe. One of the most individual and original composers and arrangers, Gibbs has said that he began to concentrate on writing because performing solos terrified him. He studied piano between the ages of seven and 13, then took up trombone when he was 17. He moved to Boston, Massachusetts, in 1959 to study at the Berklee College Of Music (where he played and recorded with the college band organized by Herb Pomeroy) and Boston Conservatory. He also took up a scholarship at the Lennox School of Jazz in 1961, where he studied with Gunther Schuller, George Russell and J.J. Johnson. He graduated from Berklee in 1962 and the conservatory in 1963. That same year he obtained another scholarship, this time at Tanglewood, where he studied with classical composers Xenakis, Copland, Foss and Schuller again. After this he returned to Southern Rhodesia (Zimbabwe), then in 1965 he settled in England, playing trombone for Graham Collier and John Dankworth, working in pit orchestras for pantomimes and musicals, and subsequently recording a series of highly acclaimed and influential albums featuring many of the most prominent British-based players. His concert at London's Rainbow Theatre in 1974 was significant in that it was the first time for some decades that the Musicians Union permitted Americans to play with British musicians other than as featured soloists with local rhythm sections. This came about through Gibbs's long association with Gary Burton, whose quartet integrated with Gibbs's big band for this gig. Gibbs and Burton had studied and worked together at Berklee, and Burton had been the first to record Gibbs arrangements in 1963. He returned to Berklee as a tutor and composer-in-residence from 1974-83. In 1983 he resigned from the school to freelance as an arranger and producer, and worked with Michael Mantler, Joni Mitchell, Pat Metheny, John McLaughlin, Whitney Houston, Peter Gabriel, and Sister Sledge among many others. In 1988 he made an own-name comeback with *Big Music* (composing and arranging all tracks as well as playing piano and trombone), and in 1991 toured with featured guitarist John Scofield, and appeared on Scofield's *Grace Under Pressure* in 1992. He was among the first writers to convincingly incorporate rock elements into orchestral jazz, and shared with one of his major influences, Gil Evans, the ability to organically integrate carefully arranged and scored frameworks with the most 'outside' improvisations. The list of albums below excludes those on which he only arranged or scored other people's music.

● ALBUMS: *Michael Gibbs* (Deram 1970)★★★, *Tanglewood '63* (Deram 1971)★★★★, *Just Ahead* (Polydor 1972)★★★, with Gary Burton *In The Public Interest* (Polydor 1974)★★★, *Will Power* (1974)★★★, *The Only Chrome Waterfall Orchestra* (Ah-Um 1976)★★★★, *Big Music* (Virgin 1988)★★★★, *By The Way* (Ah-Um 1993)★★★.

GIBBS, TERRY

b. Julius Gubenko, 13 October 1924, New York City, New York, USA. After all-round study of percussion, Gibbs briefly played drums professionally before and during military service. After discharge he concentrated on vibraphone, working with leaders such as Tommy Dorsey, Chubby Jackson and Buddy Rich. At the end of the 40s he achieved international prominence thanks to a two-year spell with Woody Herman followed by a brief period as a member of Benny Goodman's sextet. In the early 50s he also formed a big band and worked on television with Mel Tormé. Towards the end of the decade, by then based in California, he reformed a big band, which he led at the prestigious Monterey Jazz Festival in 1961. Gibbs's big bands became a notable annual event in Los Angeles, featuring many well-known players who clearly enjoyed taking time out from the studios to play jazz. In the early 80s Gibbs teamed up with Buddy De Franco for a highly acclaimed album. Gibbs's vibraphone style reflects the hard-driving Lionel Hampton tradition, but with slightly boppish overtones. Gibb's playing always swings and with a big band in full cry behind him, he creates some of the most exciting sounds in jazz.

● ALBUMS: *Terry Gibbs Quartet* 10-inch album (Brunswick 1954)★★★, *Terry* (Brunswick 1954)★★★, *Terry Gibbs* (EmArcy 1955)★★★, *Vibes On Velvet* (EmArcy 1956)★★★, *Mallets A-Plenty* (EmArcy 1956),★★★ *Swingin' Terry Gibbs* (EmArcy 1956)★★★, *More Vibes On Velvet* (EmArcy 1956)★★★, *A Jazz Band Ball* reissued as *Vibrations* (Mode/Interlude 1957)★★★★, with Bill Harris *The Ex-Hermanites* reissued as *Woodchoppers'*

Ball (Mode/Premier 1957)★★★★, *Terry Plays The Duke* (EmArcy 1958)★★★, *Steve Allen's All Stars* (EmArcy 1958)★★★, *Launching A New Sound In Music* (Mercury 1959)★★★, *Swing Is Here!* (Verve 1960)★★★, *The Exciting Terry Gibbs Big Band* (Verve 1960)★★★, *Music From Cole Porter's "Can Can"* (Verve 1960)★★, *Main Stem* (Contemporary 1961)★★★, *The Big Cat* (Contemporary 1961)★★★, *That Swing Thing* (Verve 1962)★★★, *Straight Ahead* (Verve 1962)★★★, *Explosion* (Mercury 1962), *Jewish Melodies In Jazztime* (Mercury 1963)★★★, *Hootenanny My Way* reissued as *It's Time We Met* (Time 1963)★★★, *El Nutto* (Limelight 1964)★★★, *Take It From Me* (Impulse! 1964)★★★, *Latino* (Roost 1965)★★★, *Reza* (Dot 1966)★★★, *Terry Gibbs Plays Arrangements By Shorty Rogers* (1966)★★★, *Bobstacle Course* (Xanadu 1974)★★★, *Live At The Lord* (1978)★★★, *Smoke 'Em Up* (1978)★★★, with Buddy De Franco *Jazz Party: First Time Together* (1981)★★★, with De Franco *My Buddy* (1982)★★★, *The Latin Connection* (1986)★★, with De Franco *Chicago Fire* (Contemporary 1987)★★★★, *Holiday For Swing* (Contemporary 1988)★★★, *Air Mail Special* 1981 recording (Contemporary 1988)★★★★, *Memories Of You* (Contemporary 1992)★★★, *Kings Of Swing* (Contemporary 1993)★★★★, *Volume 5: The Big Cat* (Contemporary 1993)★★★.

GIBSON, HARRY 'THE HIPSTER'

b. Harry Raab, 1914, New York City, New York, USA, d. May 1991. Gibson's first job was playing piano in a band which included future jazz musicians such as Joe 'Flip' Phillips and Billy Bauer. At this time he was working under his real name, but later changed it when he formed a double act with singer Ruth Gibson. In the 40s he enjoyed a brief period of fame when he caught to perfection the attitudes, language and mannerisms of a generation of zoot-suited, streetwise hipsters. Much of Gibson's nightclub act was built around his own compositions, which included gems such as 'Who Put the Benzedrine In Mrs Murphy's Ovaltine?' and 'Zoot Gibson Rides Again'. Gibson's lyrics, and the patter with which he surrounded his songs, made a marked impression upon a succeeding generation of stand-up comedians; his peers included Lord Buckley and Lenny Bruce. Gibson's troubled lifestyle was akin to that of Bruce and another friend and musical associate, Charlie Parker. Gibson was reputed to be instrumental in persuading Billy Berg to bring Parker and Dizzy Gillespie to Los Angeles for their ground-breaking engagement in 1945. Despite a frenetic life, which included periods of incarceration for drug offences, and several marriages, Gibson managed to avoid the limelight. Indeed, few jazz reference books mention him and perhaps the longest magazine article on him came in the form of Mark Gardner's obituary in *Jazz Journal International*. For all his other-worldliness, Gibson's anarchic humour had much to say that was relevant. His music, especially his piano playing, despite its boppish overtones, was firmly rooted in the older traditions of his early idols such as Fats Waller and Erroll Garner. During his later years Gibson worked sporadically, fronting a band in the 70s that included his sons in its ranks.

● ALBUMS: *Harry The Hipster Digs Christmas* (1974)★★.

● COMPILATIONS: *Boogie Woogie In Blue* 40s recordings (Musicraft 1988)★★★, *Everybody's Crazy But Me* 40s recordings (Progressive 1988)★★★★, under Slim Gaillard *McVouty* (1945-46)★★★, *Who Put The Benzedrine In Mrs Murphy's Ovaltine?* (Delmark 1996)★★★★.

● VIDEOS: *Boogie In Blue* (1992).

GIBSON, LEE

b. 5 March 1950, Watford, Hertfordshire, England. Gibson began her show business career as a singer and dancer, performing in many of the top nightspots in London's West End. These included the Talk Of The Town, where she headlined and was heard by a BBC radio producer who booked her for her first jazz broadcast. During succeeding years she made over 1,000 broadcasts for the BBC and toured with several big bands, including those led by Syd Lawrence and Don Lusher and the BBC Radio Big Band. Her parallel career as a session singer extended into films and television and she also appeared at seven Royal Command Variety Shows. She was a member of the folk-rock group Chorale, recording *Chorale* (Arista 1980), and the single, 'Riu Riu', which charted in several European countries. Meanwhile, she extended her reputation as a solo singer throughout Europe, performing at concerts and on radio and television with leading orchestras. In Finland she sang with the UMO Jazz Orchestra, in Denmark with the Danish Radio Big Band, directed by Thad Jones, in the Netherlands with the Skymasters and the Metropole Orchestra, recording *Night Songs* with the latter, and in Germany with the WDR Orchestra and the Francy Boland Band, conducted by Lalo Schifrin. She also sang the music of Andrew Lloyd Webber with the Royal Philharmonic Orchestra at a Royal Gala concert in London. Her jazz festival performances have included Munich, Sydney, Montreux, Birmingham, Cork and Grimsby, appearing at the latter with Michael Brecker. Gibson sings with elegant charm, her interpretations of lyrics being eloquent and understanding. Adjusting to the needs of the material and the nature of the performance, she can deliver the popular repertoire with warmth and enormous confidence while her jazz work is suffused with an intense yet subtle sense of swing.

● ALBUMS: *You Can See Forever* (Digital Six 1994)★★★, *The Nearness Of You* (Zephyr 1996)★★★, *The Magic Of Gershwin* (Merlin Audio 1997)★★★★, *Night Songs* (Koch 1998)★★★.

GIFFORD, GENE

b. Harold Eugene Gifford, 31 May 1908, Americus, Georgia, USA, d. 12 November 1970. Gifford began arranging music while still in high school and in the mid- to late 20s played banjo and guitar with several territory bands. In 1929 he was with Jean Goldkette's Orange Blossoms band which metamorphosed into the Casa Loma Orchestra. It was here that Gifford's arranging talent proved to be invaluable; indeed, it might well be cited as the principal reason for the band's great success. His arranging style for the band appears to owe something to that of John Nesbitt (Gunther Schuller offers compelling musical evidence to this effect in his book, *The Swing Era*); however, there is no doubt that Gifford set a pattern for numerous swing era arrangers who followed him. During the early 30s the Casa Loma band set standards by which hot dance bands were measured and laid the foundation for the coming era's commercial popularity. Although there was a slightly stiff approach in Gifford's arranging, he provided challenging, technically complex and difficult charts within which Casa Loma soloists could carve their brief moments in the spotlight. It is, however, the riff-based ensemble sound that most testifies to Gifford's ability to render the free-flowing drive of many black bands of the pre-swing period into formal arrangements accessible to many. When later bands built upon Gifford's concepts through their own arrangers, many were able to inject more swing and a greater freedom; nevertheless, his contribution to the period and to much of what followed in big band music during future decades is enormous. In 1939 Gifford left the Casa Loma band, thereafter working in radio and writing charts for other bands. In the 50s he worked in radio as an engineer and consultant. His last years were spent teaching in Memphis. Although it might be argued with reason that Gifford's work was constrained, and there are signs that long before he quit Casa Loma his ideas were drying up, the Casa Loma band, thanks to his charts, set standards by which later, better-known, if not always more technically accomplished, bands are judged.

● COMPILATIONS: *The Casa Loma Orchestra* (Jazum 1930-36)★★★★.

GILBERTO, JOÃO

b. June 1931, Juazeiro, Brazil. The Gilberto name is utterly synonymous with bossa nova: the light, melodic, samba-based musical hybrid that swept America and the rest of the world in the mid-60s. Guitarist/vocalist/composer João grew up interested in Brazilian samba, absorbing the traditional rhythms and melodies, but became seduced by jazz – the other ingredient in the bossa recipe – listening to radio stations playing American music. During the early 50s he settled in Rio De Janeiro, where the colourful cultural mix was already inspiring the brilliant guitarist/composer Antonio Carlos Jobim, with whom he soon began to collaborate. Recording toward the end of the decade, João's tune 'Bim Bom' met with considerable success, and the pair established the bossa nova sound locally; but it was not until American guitarist Charlie Byrd picked up on the craze and, with soft-toned saxophone genius Stan Getz, brought it to the USA, that the bossa nova era and Gilberto's stardom really began. Getz and Byrd's *Jazz Samba*, recorded in 1962, featured compositions by both Jobim and Gilberto, and put bossa nova squarely on the map; but it was the 1963 classic, *Getz/Gilberto*, that made the Gilberto name. The album featured both Jobim and Gilberto, and gave a receptive American audience the first taste of João's sophisticated, romantic whisper, Portuguese lyrics and mellow guitar accompaniment. The surprise hit came courtesy of João's wife Astrud Gilberto, singing the now ubiquitous 'The Girl From Ipanema' – soon a feature of every American jukebox. The bossa nova as popular American music was just a craze, but the delicate and sophisticated sound that was João Gilberto's has been absorbed into the jazz mainstream, along with a number of his and Jobim's much-loved compositions. Recommended listening from the 60s must include the original *Getz/Gilberto* album, and a live date from Carnegie Hall, recorded toward the end of 1964 when the music was at its peak of popularity. Issued as *Getz/Gilberto 2*, the album includes a series of performances by Getz with his own quartet featuring vibraphonist Gary Burton, some mellow, quiet tracks by Gilberto's trio, and a series of performances featuring everyone together, and Astrud Gilberto making a guest appearance to sing, amongst other things, the hit record of the year 'The Girl From Ipanema'.

● ALBUMS: with Stan Getz *Getz/Gilberto* (Verve 1963)★★★★, *Getz/Gilberto 2* (Verve 1964)★★.

GILLESPIE, DIZZY

b. John Birks Gillespie, 21 October 1917, Cheraw, South Carolina, USA, d. 6 January 1993, Englewood, New Jersey, USA. Born into a large family, Gillespie began playing trombone at the age of 12 and a year or so later took up the trumpet. Largely self-taught, he won a musical scholarship but preferred playing music to formal study. In 1935 he quit university and went to live in Philadelphia, where he began playing in local bands. It was during this period that he acquired the nickname by which he was to become universally known. The name Dizzy resulted from his zestful behaviour and was actually bestowed by a fellow trumpeter, Fats Palmer, whose life Gillespie saved when Palmer was overcome by fumes in a gas-filled room during a tour with the Frankie Fairfax band. Gillespie's startling technical facility attracted a great deal of attention and in 1937 he went to New York to try out for the Lucky Millinder band. He did not get the job but stayed in town and soon afterwards was hired for a European tour by Teddy Hill, in whose band he succeeded his idol, Roy Eldridge. Back in the USA in 1939, Gillespie played in various New York bands before returning to Hill, where he was joined by drummer Kenny Clarke, in whom he found a kindred spirit, who was similarly tired of big band conventions. When Hill folded his band to become booking manager for Minton's Playhouse in New York, he gave free rein to young musicians eager to experiment and among the regulars were Clarke, Thelonious Monk, Joe Guy and, a little later, Gillespie. In the meantime, Gillespie had joined the Cab Calloway Band, which was then riding high in popular esteem. While with Calloway, Gillespie began to experiment with phrasing that was out of character with what was until this time accepted jazz trumpet parlance. He also appeared on a Lionel Hampton record date, playing a solo on a tune entitled 'Hot Mallets' which many observers believe to be the first recorded example of what would later be called bebop. The following year, 1940, Gillespie met Charlie Parker in Kansas City, during a tour with the Calloway band, and established musical rapport with the man with whom he was to change the face and sound of jazz. In 1941 Gillespie was fired by Calloway following some on-stage high jinks which ended with Gillespie and his boss embroiled in a minor fracas. Gillespie returned to New York where he worked with numerous musicians, including Benny Carter, Millinder, Charlie Barnet and Earl Hines, in whose band he again met Parker and also singer Billy Eckstine.

Gillespie had begun to hang out, after hours, at Minton's and also at Clark Monroe's Uptown House. He led his own small band for club and record dates, both appealing to a small, specialized, but growing, audience. Amongst his influential recordings of the period were 'Salt Peanuts' and 'Hot House'. In 1944 Gillespie joined the big band Eckstine had just formed: originally intended as a backing group for Eckstine's new career as a solo singer, the outfit quickly became a forcing house for big band bebop. Apart from Gillespie, the sidemen Eckstine hired at various times included Gene Ammons, Sonny Stitt, Wardell Gray, Dexter Gordon, Fats Navarro, Howard McGhee and Miles Davis. Subsequently, Gillespie formed his own big band, which enjoyed only limited commercial success but which was, musically, an early peaking of the concept of big band bebop. He also began playing and recording regularly with Parker in a quintet that the two men co-led. During this period Gillespie was constantly in excellent musical company, playing with most of the major voices in bop and many of those swing era veterans who tried, with varying levels of success, to adapt to the new music. In the big band, Gillespie had employed at one time or another during its two separate periods of existence James Moody, Cecil Payne, Benny Bailey, Al McKibbon, Willie Cook, Big Nick Nicholas, John Lewis, Milt Jackson, Ray Brown and Clarke. In his small groups he recorded with Don Byas, Al Haig and others, but it was in the band he co-led with Parker that Gillespie did his most influential work. The other members of the quintet varied, but initially included Haig, Curley Russell and 'Big' Sid Catlett and, later, Haig, Jackson, Brown and Stan Levey. These small bands brought Gillespie to the fascinated attention of countless musicians; from their performances evolved the establishment of bop as a valid form of jazz, with its necessary renewal of a music which had begun to fall prey to the inroads of blandness, sanitization and formulaic repetitiveness that accompanied the commercial successes of the swing era.

Gillespie was feverishly active as a composer too. And, despite his youth he was fast becoming an *eminence grise* to beboppers. Aided by his stable private life and a disdain for the addictive stimulants increasingly favoured by a small but well-publicized coterie of bebop musicians, he was the epitome of the successful businessman. That he combined such qualities with those of musical explorer and adventurer made him one of the more dominant figures in jazz. Moreover, in his work with Chano Pozo (who joined Gillespie's orchestra in 1947) and later Machito he was one of the pioneers of US-based Latin jazz. Most important of all, his personal demeanour helped bop rise above the prevailing tide of contemptuous ignorance which, in those days, often passed for critical comment.

Gillespie's busy career continued into the 50s; he recorded with J.J. Johnson, John Coltrane, Jackson, Art Blakey, Wynton Kelly and others. Many of his record dates of this period were on his own label, Dee Gee Records. With his big band folded, Gillespie toured Europe, returning to New York in 1952 to find that his record company was on the skids. He was already undergoing some difficulties as he adjusted his playing style to accommodate new ideas and the shift from large to small band. In 1953, during a party for his wife, the members of a two-man knockabout act fell on his trumpet. The instrument was badly bent but when Gillespie tried to play it he found that, miraculously, he preferred it that way. The upward 45-degree angle of the bell allowed him to hear the notes he was playing sooner than before. In addition he found that when he was playing from a chart, and therefore was looking down, the horn was pointing outwards towards microphone or audience. He liked all these unexpected benefits and within a few weeks had arranged to have a trumpet especially constructed to incorporate them. By the end of 1953 the temporary hiatus in Gillespie's career was over. A concert in Toronto in this year featured Gillespie and Parker with Bud Powell, Charles Mingus and Max Roach in a group which was billed, and in some quarters received, as *The Quintet Of The Year*. Although all five musicians did better things at other times, collectively it was an exciting and frequently excellent session. Significantly, it was an occasion which displayed the virility of bop at a time when, elsewhere, its fire was being gently doused into something more palatable for the masses. Gillespie then began working with Norman Granz's Jazz At The Philharmonic and he also began a long series of recording dates for Granz, in which he was teamed with a rich and frequently rewarding mixture of musicians. In 1956 Gillespie's standing in jazz circles was such that Adam Clayton Powell Jnr. recommended him to President Dwight D. Eisenhower as the ideal man to lead an orchestra on a State Department-sponsored goodwill tour of Africa, the Middle East and Asia. The tour was a great success, even if Gillespie proved unwilling to play up its propagandist element, and soon after his return to the USA he was invited to make another tour, this time to South America. The all-star band assembled for these tours was maintained for a while and was also recorded by Granz. By the end of the 50s Gillespie was again leading a small group and had embarked upon a ceaseless round of club, concert, festival and recording dates that continued for the next three decades. He continued to work on prestigious projects, which included, in the early 70s, a tour with an all-star group featuring Blakey, Monk, Stitt, McKibbon and Kai Winding. Throughout the 70s and during the 80s he was the recipient of many awards, and his earlier status as an absurdly young *eminence grise* was succeeded by his later role as an elder statesman of jazz even though when the 70s began, he was still only in his early 50s. By the middle of the 70s Gillespie was once again at a point in his career where a downturn seemed rather more likely than a further climb. In the event, it was another trumpet player who gave him the nudge he needed. Jon Faddis had come into Gillespie's life as an eager fan, but in 1977 was teamed with his idol on a record date at the Montreux festival where their planned performance was abruptly altered when the scheduled rhythm section ended up in the wrong country. Hastily assembling a substitute team of Milt Jackson, Ray Brown, Monty Alexander and drummer Jimmie Smith, the two trumpeters played a highly successful set which was recorded by Norman Granz. Subsequently, Gillespie and Faddis often played together, making a great deal of memorable music, with the veteran seemingly sparked into new life. In the early 80s Gillespie recorded for television in the USA as part of the *Jazz America* project, appeared in London with a new quintet featuring Paquito D'Rivera, and played at the Nice, Knebworth and Kool festivals in duets with, respectively, such varied artists as Art Farmer, Chico Freeman and Art Blakey. He showed himself eager to experiment although sometimes, as with his less-than-wonderful teaming with Stevie Wonder, his judgement was somewhat awry. In 1987 he celebrated his 70th birthday and found himself again leading a big band, which had no shortage of engagements and some excellent players, including Faddis and Sam Rivers. He was also fêted during the JVC Festival at the Saratoga Springs Performing Arts Center, where he brilliantly matched horns with Faddis and new pretender, Wynton Marsalis. He was not always in the spotlight, however. One night in Los Angeles he went into a club where Bill Berry's LA Big Band was working and sat in, happily playing fourth trumpet. As the 90s began Gillespie was still performing, usually occupying centre stage, but also happy to sit and reminisce with old friends and new, to sit in with other musicians, and to live life pretty much the way he had done for more than half a century. It was a shock to the music world on 6 January 1993 when it was announced that Dizzy was no longer with us, perhaps we had selfishly thought that he was immortal.

In the history of the development of jazz trumpet, Gillespie's place ranked second only to that of Louis Armstrong. In the history of jazz as a whole he was firmly in the small group of major innovators who reshaped the music in a manner so profound that everything that follows has to be measured by reference, conscious or not, to their achievements. Just as Armstrong had created a new trumpet style which affected players of all instruments in the two decades following his emergence in Chicago in 1922, so did Gillespie, in 1940, redirect trumpet players and all other jazz musicians along new and undefined paths. He also reaffirmed the trumpet's vital role in jazz after a decade (the 30s) in which the saxophone had begun its inexorable rise to prominence as the instrument for change. In a wider context Gillespie's steadying hand did much to ensure that bop would survive beyond the impractical, errant genius of Parker. In much of Gillespie's earlier playing the dazzling speed of his execution frequently gave an impression of a purely technical bravura, but as time passed it became clear that there was no lack of ideas or real emotion in his playing. Throughout his career, Gillespie rarely failed to find fresh thoughts; and, beneath the spectacular high note flourishes, the raw excitement and the exuberant vitality, there was a depth of feeling akin to that of the most romantic balladeers. He earned and will forever retain his place as one of the true giants of jazz. Without his presence, the music would have been not only different but much less than it had become.

● ALBUMS: *Modern Trumpets* (Dial 1950)★★★★, with Johnny Richards *Dizzy Gillespie Plays/Johnny Richards Conducts* 10-inch album (Discovery 1950)★★★, *Dizzy Gillepsie* reissued as *School Days* (Dee Gee 1952)★★★, *Dizzy Gillespie Volume 1* 10-inch album (Atlantic 1952)★★★★, *Dizzy Gillespie Volume 2* 10-inch album (Atlantic 1952)★★★★, *Pleyel Concert 1953* (Vogue 1953)★★★, *Horn Of Plenty* 10-inch album (Blue Note 1953)★★★★, with Charlie Christian *Dizzy Gillespie With Charlie Christian* 10-inch album (Esoteric 1953)★★★★, *Dizzie Gillespie With Strings* (Clef 1953)★★★, *Dizzy In Paris* 10-inch album (Contemporary 1953)★★★★, *Dizzy Over Paris* reissued as *Concert In Paris* (Roost 1953)★★★★, *Dizzy Gillespie Orchestra* 10-inch album (Allegro 1954)★★★, *Dizzie Gillespie And His Original Big Band* 10-inch album (Gene Norman 1954)★★★, *Dizzier And Dizzier* (RCA Victor 1954)★★★, with Stan Getz *The Dizzy Gillespie-Stan Getz Sextet #1* 10-inch album (Norgran 1954)★★★★, with Getz *The Dizzy Gillespie-Stan Getz Sextet #2* 10-inch album (Norgran 1954)★★★★, *Afro* (Norgran 1954)★★★, *Dizzy Gillespie Plays* 10-inch album (Allegro 1954)★★★, *Dizzy And Strings* reissued as *Diz Big Band* (Norgran 1955)★★★, with Getz *Diz And Getz* (Verve 1955)★★★★, with Roy Eldridge *Roy And Diz* (Clef 1955)★★★★, with Eldridge *Roy And Diz, Volume 2* (Clef 1955)★★★★, *Dizzy Gillespie* (Allegro 1955)★★★, *Groovin' High* (Savoy 1955)★★★, *One Night In Washington* (1955)★★★, with Jimmy McPartland *Hot Vs. Cool* (MGM 1955)★★★★, *Dizzy Gillespie And His Orchestra* reissued as *Jazz Recital* (Norgran 1956)★★★, *Dizzy Gillespie* (American Recording Society 1956)★★★, *Big Band Jazz* (American Recording Society 1956)★★★, with Eldridge *Trumpet Battle* (Clef 1956)★★★, with Eldridge *The Trumpet Kings* (Clef 1956)★★★, *The Champ* (Savoy 1956)★★★, *The New Continent* (Limelight 1956)★★★, *For Musicians Only* (Verve 1956)★★★, *World Statesman* (Norgran 1956)★★★, *Dizzy At Home And Abroad* (Atlantic 1957)★★★★, *The Dizzy Gillespie Story* (Savoy 1957)★★★, *Dizzy In Greece* (Verve 1957)★★★, *Mantica* (Verve 1958)★★★, with Stuff Smith *Dizzy Gillespie And Stuff Smith* (Verve 1958)★★★★, with Slim Gaillard *Gaillard And Gillespie* (Ultraphonic 1958)★★★, with Harry Edison, Eldridge *Tour De Force* (Verve 1958)★★★, *Birk's Works* (Verve 1958)★★★★, *Dizzy Gillespie At Newport* (Verve 1958)★★★★, with Count Basie *Dizzy Gillespie And Count Basie At Newport* (Verve 1958)★★★★, with Sonny Rollins, Sonny Stitt *Duets* reissued as *Dizzy, Rollins & Stitt* (Verve 1958)★★★★, with Charlie Parker *Diz 'N' Bird In Concert* (Roost 1959)★★★★, *The Ebullient Mr. Gillespie* (Verve

1959)★★★, *Have Trumpet, Will Excite!* (Verve 1959)★★★★, *The Greatest Trumpet Of Them All* (Verve 1959)★★★, *A Portrait Of Duke Ellington* (Verve 1960)★★★★, *Gillespiana: The Carnegie Hall Concert* (Verve 1960)★★★★, with Basie *First Time! The Count Meets The Duke* (Columbia 1961)★★★★, *An Electrifying Evening With The Dizzy Gillespie Quintet* (Verve 1961)★★★★, *Perceptions* (Verve 1961)★★★, *Jazz Recital* (Verve 1961)★★★, with Miles Davis, Fats Navarro *Trumpet Giants* (New Jazz 1962)★★★★, *Jazz On The French Riviera* (Philips 1962)★★★, *Dateline Europe* (Reprise 1963)★★★, *New Wave!* (Philips 1963)★★★, *Something Old, Something New* (Philips 1963)★★★, *Dizzy Goes Hollywood* (Philips 1964)★★★, *Dizzy Gillespie And The Double Six Of Paris* (Philips 1964)★★★★, *The Cool World* film soundtrack (Philips 1964)★★★, *Jambo Caribe* (Limelight 1964)★★★, *The New Continent* (Limelight 1965)★★★, *The Essential Dizzy Gillespie* (Verve 1964)★★★, *Angel City* (Moon 1965)★★★, with Gil Fuller *Gil Fuller And The Monterey Jazz Festival Orchestra With Dizzy Gillespie* (Pacific Jazz 1965)★★★, with Eldridge *Soul Mates* (Verve 1966)★★★★, *A Night In Tunisia* (Verve 1966)★★★★, *Swing Low, Sweet Cadillac* (Impulse! 1967)★★★, *Reunion Big Band* (MPS 1968)★★★★, *Live At The Village Vanguard* (Solid State 1969)★★★★, *My Way* (Solid State 1969)★★, *Cornacopia* (Solid State 1969)★★★, *Portrait Of Jenny* (1970)★★★, with Dwike Mitchell, Willie Ruff *Dizzy Gillespie And The Dwike Mitchell-Willie Ruff Duo* (Mainstream 1971)★★★, *Giants Of Jazz* (Atlantic 1973)★★★★, *The Giant* (Accord 1973)★★★, *Dizzy Gillespie's Big Four* (Pablo 1974)★★★★, with Machito *Afro-Cuban Jazz Moods* (Pablo 1975)★★★★, with Eldridge *Jazz Maturity ... Where It's Coming From* (Pablo 1975)★★★, with Eldridge *The Trumpet Kings At Montreux '75* (Pablo 1975)★★★★, *Dizzy's Party* (Pablo 1976)★★★, *Free Ride* (Pablo 1977)★★★, with Count Basie *The Gifted Ones* (Pablo 1977)★★★, *Montreux '77* (Pablo 1977)★★★, *Trumpet Summit Meets Oscar Peterson Big Four* (Pablo 1980)★★★, *Digital At Montreux, 1980* (Pablo 1980)★★★, *Musician-Composer-Raconteur* (Pablo 1981)★★, with Arturo Sandoval *To A Finland Station* (Pablo 1982)★★★, *New Faces* (GRP 1984)★★★, with Arturo Sandoval *Arturo Sandoval And His Group With Dizzy Gillespie* (Egrem 1985)★★★, *Closer To The Source* (Atlantic 1985)★★, with Phil Woods *Dizzy Gillespie Meets Phil Woods Quintet* (Timeless 1987)★★★, *Live At The Royal Festival Hall* (Enja 1990)★★★, *Symphony Sessions* (Pro Arte 1990)★★, with Max Roach *Max & Dizzy - Paris 1989* (A&M 1990)★★★, *The Winter In Lisbon* film soundtrack (Milan 1990)★★, *To Diz With Love: Diamond Jubilee Recordings* (Telarc 1992)★★★, *To Bird With Love: Live At The Blue Note* (Telarc 1992)★★★, *Bird Songs: The Final Recordings* 1991 recording (Telarc 1997)★★★, the Dizzy Gillespie Alumni All-Stars *Dizzy's 80th Birthday Party!* (Shanachie 1998)★★★.

● COMPILATIONS: *Shaw Nuff* 1945-1946 recordings (Musicraft)★★★★, *One Bass Hit* 1946 recordings (Musicraft)★★★★, with Dwike Mitchell, Willie Ruff *Enduring Magic* 1970-1985 recordings (Black Hawk)★★★★, *Dizzy Gillespie 1946-1949* (RCA 1983)★★★★, *Dee Gee Days* 1951-1952 recordings (Savoy 1985)★★★, *Dizzy's Diamonds: The Best Of The Verve Years* 1950-1964 recordings (Verve 1993)★★★★, *Birk's Works: Verve Big Band Sessions* 1956-1957 recordings (Verve 1993)★★★★, *Dizzy Songs* (Vogue 1993)★★★★, *The Complete RCA Victor Recordings* 1937-1949 recordings (RCA 1996)★★★★★, *Dizzier And Dizzier* 1946-1949 recordings (RCA 1997)★★★, *Talkin' Verve* (Verve 1997)★★★, *Dizzy Gillespie 1945-6* (Classics 1998)★★★.

● VIDEOS: *Dizzy Gillespie* (1988), *Night In Havana* (1990), *Dizzy Live In London* (1993), *A Night In Chicago* (View Video 1995).

● FURTHER READING: *Dizzy: To Be Or Not To Bop*, Dizzy Gillespie and Al Fraser. *Dizzy Gillespie: His Life And Times*, Barry McRae. *Dizzy Gillespie*, M James. *The Trumpets Of Dizzy Gillespie, 1937-1943*, Jan Evensmo. *Dizzy Gillespie And The Be-Bop Revolution*, Raymond Horricks. *Waiting for Dizzy*, Gene Lees. *Dizzy: John Birks Gillespie In His 75th Year*, Lee Tanner (ed.).

GILMORE, JOHN

b. 28 September 1931, Summit, Mississippi, USA, d. 20 August 1995. Growing up in Chicago, Gilmore became fascinated by the sound of the tenor saxophone. He was given a clarinet which he learned to play, graduating to the saxophone while in the armed forces. After leaving the air force he worked for the US postal service for a while, then decided to take a chance on earning a living as a musician. Between 1948 and 1952 he was in the air force, and played clarinet and started on tenor saxophone while stationed in San Antonio, Texas. When the Harlem Globetrotters toured America in 1952, music was supplied by pianist Earl 'Fatha' Hines with John Gilmore in the band, playing tenor saxophone. In 1953 he joined Sun Ra, then leading a trio, an association that was to last many decades, interrupted only by a short spell in Art Blakey's Jazz Messengers (1964-65), when he replaced Wayne Shorter. Outside of his work with Sun Ra, Gilmore has recorded with McCoy Tyner, Dizzy Reece, Pete LaRoca, Elmo Hope, Paul Bley (on *Turns*) and with his old Chicago school-friend, pianist Andrew Hill, on two superb mid-60s Blue Note sessions, *Andrew* and *Compulsion*. Nevertheless the vast bulk of his music over the last 35 years has been with Sun Ra. Despite spending so many years in one band, Gilmore was never in danger of falling into routine. Sun Ra's musical philosophy was such that his band's repertoire was in almost constant flux. He made occasional forays outside the band, once with Miles Davis, although this project was aborted due to the trumpet player's current financial and personal problems, and toured Japan with Art Blakey. Such brief encounters aside, Gilmore's career is inextricably linked to Sun Ra and after the leader's death he struggled to keep the band together under his own leadership despite being in poor health. If Gilmore had not devoted his playing career to Sun Ra's music he would probably be listed as one of four or five most important tenor players in jazz. It is perhaps on Sun Ra's rare small group recordings, such as *New Steps*, that Gilmore is given the space he needs to really stretch out. In addition to tenor saxophone and bass clarinet, he sometimes plays percussion with the Arkestra (and is featured as a percussionist on *My Brother The Wind*) and also sings in an enthusiastic, gravelly voice - his speciality being 'East Of The Sun, West Of The Moon'. A forceful and dynamic player, Gilmore frequently drew high praise from other musicians. John Coltrane was emphatic, declaring: 'I listened to John Gilmore kind of closely before I made *Chasin' The Trane* . . . Some of the things on there are a direct influence of listening to this cat.' He died of emphysema in 1995.

● ALBUMS: co-leader with Clifford Jordan *Blowing In From Chicago* (Blue Note 1957)★★★, with Art Blakey *'S Make It* (Limelight 1965)★★★, *Dizzy Reece/John Gilmore* (Futura 1970)★★, with Sun Ra - any of the band's 150 albums.

GIRARD, ADELE

b. 1913, USA, d. 7 September 1993. By choosing the harp as her instrument, Girard severely damaged her chances of being taking seriously when she began playing jazz. Nevertheless, she persevered, working in bands such as Harry Sosnick's before coming to wider attention as a member of Joe Marsala's band at 52nd Street's Hickory House in 1938. That same year Girard and Marsala married and continued to play together during the next decade. After Marsala retired from regular performing, Girard continued her career, now as a solo act, also singing and playing piano. She worked in clubs, hotels and casinos in Los Angeles and surrounding areas, especially the popular resorts, and in the 70s appeared briefly in London with the Festival Theatre USC. By dint of her delightful melodic approach, a subtle sense of swing, allied to her perfect pitch, she became an able member of some good small jazz groups and qualified as one of the two or three - of an admittedly small number - best harpists in jazz.

● COMPILATIONS: *The Chronological Joe Marsala* (1936-1942)★★★.

GISMONTI, EGBERTO

b. 5 December 1947, Carmo, Rio de Janeiro, Brazil. Gismonti had a classical musical education starting to play the piano when he was six years old. He went to Paris in the 60s to study orchestration and analysis with Nadia Boulanger and composition with the *avant garde* composer Barraque. On his return to Brazil in 1966 he became interested in choro, which he has described as a kind of popular Brazilian funk. Gismonti successfully blends African -Brazilian forms with jazz in his compositions. He taught himself the guitar and was at first influenced by Baden Powell and Deno. His influences during the early 70s were as wide ranging as Django Reinhardt and Jimi Hendrix. In 1973 he changed to the 8-string guitar which allowed him a greater variety of chord voicings, more flexible bass lines and drones: in 1981 he moved on to the 10-string guitar on which the extra strings extended the bass. His performances on either piano or guitar are always exhilarating and tuneful. He toured the USA in 1976 with Airto Moreira and Flora Purim and in 1978/9 with Nana Vasconcelos. Gismonti's compositional and playing styles were influenced by his study in 1976 of the music of Xingu Indians. He described the resulting album as 'a walk through the jungle'. His evocative writing and playing has been used in at least 11 film scores. He has recorded regularly with members of the ECM label, Jan Garbarek, Collin Walcott, Ralph Towner, Charlie Haden, and was the orchestrator on Vasconcelos's *Suadedos* with the Stuttgart RSO.

● ALBUMS: *Danca Das Cabeças* (ECM 1976)★★★★, *Sol Do Meia Dia* (ECM 1977)★★★, *Magico* (1979)★★, with Jan Garbarek *Folk Songs* (ECM 1979)★★★★, *Circense* (Cameo 1980)★★★, with Nana Vasconcelos *Suadedas* (1980)★★★, *Sanfona* (ECM)★★★, *Duas Vozes* (1985)★★★, *Solo* (ECM 1985)★★★★, *Danca Dos Escarvos* (ECM 1989)★★★, *Arvore* (Cameo 1991)★★★, *Kuarup* (Cameo 1991)★★★, *Infancia* (ECM 1991)★★★. *Academia De Dancas* (Cameo 1992)★★★, *Trem Caipira* (Cameo 1992)★★★, *Amazonia* (Cameo 1993)★★★, *No Caipira* (Cameo 1993)★★★, *ZigZag* (ECM 1996)★★★, with the Lithuanian Symphony Orchestra *Meeting Point* (ECM 1997)★★★.

● COMPILATIONS: *Works* (ECM 1983)★★★★.

GIUFFRE, JIMMY

b. 26 April 1921, Dallas, Texas, USA. A graduate of the North Texas College in 1942, Giuffre entered the US Army where he gained professional band experience playing saxophones and clarinet. On his discharge he played in a succession of big bands, including those led by Buddy Rich, Jimmy Dorsey, Boyd Raeburn and Woody Herman. It was with Herman that he gained most attention, both as a member of the saxophone section and as the composer of 'Four Brothers', which gave that particular Herman band its tag. After leaving Herman he worked on the west coast, playing mostly in small groups, and also began to teach. He formed a trio that included Jim Hall and, later, Bob Brookmeyer plus various bassists. He appeared at the 1958 Newport Jazz Festival and in the filmed record of the event, *Jazz On A Summer's Day* (1960), playing his own composition 'The Train And The River'. He made numerous records, including dates with Lee Konitz, for which he wrote beautiful and inventive arrangements, the Modern Jazz Quartet (*At Music Inn*) and Anita O'Day, for whom he devised elegant and deceptively simple charts (*Cool Heat*). Giuffre also began to explore the world of composition, writing both film scores (*The Music Man*) and neo-classical third stream pieces, such as 'Pharoah' and 'Suspensions', both recorded by Gunther Schuller. In the 60s Giuffre became involved in free jazz, leading a trio in which he was accompanied by Paul Bley and Steve Swallow. The trio's recordings became increasingly abstract, culminating in *Free Fall*, a collection of duos and trios interspersed by totally improvised tracks on solo clarinet. *Free Fall* was deleted within a few months of release and then, in Giuffre's words, 'the doors closed' - his unique mixture of quiet, free and drummerless music proved so threatening to 'jazz' prejudices, it was nearly a decade before he was able to record again. In the 70s he was still moving with the times, introducing eastern and African sounds into his work. Later, inspired by Weather Report, he introduced electric bass and keyboards into his quartet, recording three albums for Italy's Black Saint label (*Dragonfly*, *Quasar*, *Liquid Dancers*). He also recorded a duo album with André Jaume, *Eiffel* (one of the quietest records ever made!) and in 1989 was reunited with Bley and

Swallow for two sessions released by the French Owl label. Giuffre's playing of many of the lesser-known members of the saxophone family, and especially the bass clarinet (*The Jimmy Giuffre Clarinet*), have helped to give his work unusual and frequently sombre shadings. Throughout his career, Giuffre has been an important and visionary member of the *avant garde*, yet his playing was always filled with coolly reflective tonal qualities which prove most attractive. In 1990 Giuffre, his frail appearance proving deceptive, was in fine musical form at the South Bank Jazz Festival in Grimsby, South Humberside, where he premiered a new work, 'Timeless', commissioned by the festival organizers.

● ALBUMS: *Jimmy Giuffre* (Capitol 1954)★★★, *Tangents In Jazz* (Capitol 1955)★★★, *The Jimmy Giuffre Clarinet* (Atlantic 1956)★★★★, *The Jimmy Giuffre 3* (Atlantic 1957)★★★★, *Music Man* (Atlantic 1958)★★★, *Trav'lin' Light* (Atlantic 1958)★★★, *Princess* (Fini 1958)★★★, *Four Brothers Sound* (Atlantic 1958)★★★, *Seven Pieces* (Verve 1959)★★★, with Herb Ellis *Herb Ellis Meets Jimmy Giuffre* (Verve 1959)★★★★, with Lee Konitz *Lee Konitz Meets Jimmy Giuffre* (Verve 1959)★★★★, with Anita O'Day *Cool Heat - Anita O'Day Sings Jimmy Giuffre Arrangements* (Verve 1959)★★★★, *The Easy Way* (Verve 1959)★★★★, *Ad Lib* (Verve 1960)★★★, *Western Suite* (Atlantic 1960)★★★, *The Jimmy Giuffre Quartet In Person* (Verve 1961)★★★, *Piece For Clarinet And String Orchestra* (Verve 1961)★★★, *Fusion* (Verve 1961)★★★★, *Thesis* (Verve 1961)★★★★, *Free Fall* (Columbia 1963)★★★★, *Music For People, Birds, Butterflies And Mosquitos* (1972)★★★, *River Chant/Mosquito Dance* (1975)★★★, with Paul Bley, Bill Connors *Quiet Song* (Improvising Artists 1975)★★★, *Tenors West* (GNP 1978)★★★, with Bley, Connors, Konitz *IAI Festival* (Improvising Artists 1978)★★★★, *Tangents In Jazz* (Affinity 1981)★★★, *Dragonfly* (Black Saint 1983)★★★★, *Quasar* (Black Saint 1985)★★★, *Liquid Dancers* (Black Saint 1989)★★★, with André Jaume *Eiffel* (1989)★★★, with Bley, Steve Swallow *The Diary Of A Trio: Saturday* (Owl 1990)★★★★, with Bley, Swallow *The Diary Of A Trio: Sunday* (Owl 1990)★★★, *Fly Away Little Bird* (Owl 1992)★★★, *River Station* (CELP 1992)★★★, *Emphasis, Stuttgart 1961* (1993)★★★, *The Train And The River* 1975 recording (Candid 1996)★★★, with Bley, Swallow *Conversations With A Goose* (Soul Note 1996)★★★★, with Jaume *Momentum: Willisau 1988* (hatOLOGY 1998)★★★.

● COMPILATIONS: featuring Ralph Burns, Lee Konitz, Bill Russo *Lee Konitz Meets Jimmy Giuffre* (Verve 1997)★★★★, *The Complete Capitol & Atlantic Recordings Of Jimmy Giuffre* 6-CD/10-LP box set (Mosaic 1998)★★★★.

● FILMS: *Jazz On A Summer's Day* (1960).

GLASS, PHILIP

b. 31 January 1937, Chicago, Illinois, USA. Glass was educated at the University of Chicago and the Juilliard School before going to Paris to study with Nadia Boulanger between 1963 and 1965. By this time he knew that 'playing second fiddle to Stockhausen didn't seem like a lot of fun. . . . There didn't seem to be any need to write any more of that kind of music. The only thing to do was to start somewhere else. . .' He did not know where that point was until he was hired to work on an Ornette Coleman film score. He did not want to change the music so Ravi Shankar was asked to write additional material which Glass orchestrated. As he struggled with the problem of writing this music down, Glass came to see that there was another way that music could be organized. It could be structured by rhythm. Instead of dividing the music up as he had been trying to do to write it down, the Indian musicians added to rhythmic phrases and let the music expand. With Ravi Shankar he had now also worked with a composer who was a performer. Glass travelled to North Africa and Asia before returning to New York in 1967 where he studied with the tabla player Alla Rakha. In 1968 he formed the ensemble he needed to perform the music he was now writing. This was the period of the purest minimalism with extending and contracting rhythmic figures in a stable diatonic framework performed at the kind of volume more often associated with rock music. Glass later described it as music which 'must be listened to as a pure sound event, an act without any dramatic structure.' It did not stay in that abstract world of pure sound for very long. In 1975 he had no record contract and began work with Robert Wilson on *Einstein On The Beach* which turned out to be the first of three operas on 'historical figures who changed the course of world events through the wisdom and strength of their inner vision'. *Einstein On The Beach* was premiered in Europe and reached the Metropolitan on 21 November 1976. He was signed by CBS Records in 1982 and produced the successful *Glassworks*. In 1970 he had been joined by Kurt Munkacsi, sound designer, mixer and engineer and the two explored all the potential studios and new technology on offer. The operas were produced in the studio first so that others could work with them and their final recordings were enhanced by the capabilities of the studio: 'We don't hang a mike in front of an orchestra. . . . Almost every section is extended electronically.' Although Glass's music has stayed close to the method he established in the early 70s, from *Einstein On The Beach* onwards the harmony has been richer and he has been willing to explore orchestral colour because 'the most important thing is that the music provides an emotional framework or context. It literally tells you what to feel about what you're seeing.' Much of his work since has been either for the stage or for film. This includes the two operas *Satyagraha* (1980) and *Ahknaten* (1984) and the films with Godfrey Reggio - *Koyaanisqatsi* (1983) and *Powaqqatsi* (1988).

In the late 80s and early 90s Glass also wrote film scores for *The Thin Blue Line*, *Hamburger Hill*, *Candyman*, *Compassion In Exile: The Life Of The 14th Dalai Lama* (1992). Glass's plans include a second opera with author Doris Lessing; a theatre work based on Cocteau's Orphee; a film based on Stephen Hawking's *A Brief History Of Time*, more work with Wilson and Hydrogen Jukebox; and an opera with Allen Ginsberg. Most recently, he co-operated with Brian Eno on an reappraisal of the latter's *Low* project for David Bowie and repeated the formula with *Heroes* in 1997. At the start of

1998 he gained an Oscar nomination for the score of Martin Scorcese's *Kundun*.

● ALBUMS: *Two Pages* (Folkways 1974)★★★, *Music In 12 Parts 1&2* (Cardine 1976)★★★, *Solo Music* (Shandar 1978)★★★★, *Einstein On The Beach* (Columbia 1979)★★★, *Glassworks* (Columbia 1982)★★★★, *Koyaanisqatsi* film soundtrack (Island 1983)★★★★, *Akhnaten* (1984)★★★, *Mishima* (Nonesuch 1985), *Satyagraha* (1985)★★★, *Songs From Liquid Days* (Columbia 1986)★★★, *Powaqqatsi* film soundtrack (Nonesuch 1988)★★, *North Star* (Virgin 1988)★★★, *The Photographer* (CBS 1988)★★, *1000 Airplanes On The Roof* (Venture 1989)★★★, *Solo Piano* (1989)★★★★, with Ravi Shankar *Passages* (Private Music 1990)★★★, *Low* (Philips 1993)★★★, *Hydrogen Jukebox* (1994)★★★, *Heroes* (Point 1997)★★★★, *Kundun* (Nonesuch 1998)★★★.

Glenn, Tyree

b. 23 November 1912, Corsicana, Texas, USA, d. 18 May 1974. After working in his home state on vibraphone and principally trombone, Glenn moved to the Washington DC area in the early 30s and by 1936 was in Los Angeles playing with the Charlie Echols band. He also worked with Eddie Barefield, Benny Carter, Lionel Hampton and in the band Eddie Mallory directed to accompany his wife, Ethel Waters. In 1939 Glenn was briefly with Carter again before joining Cab Calloway, with whom he remained until 1946. He next played with Don Redman and Duke Ellington, where he skilfully essayed the Joe 'Tricky Sam' Nanton trombone role, but by 1952 had turned his attention to studio work. During the next decade he occasionally acted and periodically led his own small groups, sometimes with Shorty Baker, and in 1965 joined Louis Armstrong's All Stars. After three years he again formed his own small band, but later made short return visits to Armstrong and, in the summer of 1971, to Ellington. From then until shortly before his death, in May 1974, he led his own band. A gifted musician, Glenn was an important member of any band in which he played, especially the fine big band of Cab Calloway. Too often for a man with his talent, he appeared content to take a back seat as, for example, when he was in company with Armstrong. When he did solo (other than on the Tricky Sam repertoire) he showed himself to be a robust and inventive player. An occasional composer, he wrote 'Sultry Serenade' which was recorded by Ellington and Erroll Garner (under the title 'How Could You Do A Thing Like That to Me'). Glenn's two sons are musicians, Tyree Jnr. plays tenor saxophone, Roger plays vibraphone and flute.

● ALBUMS: with Duke Ellington *The Liberian Suite* (1947)★★★★, *Masterpieces By Ellington* (1950)★★★, *Tyree Glenn And His Embers All Stars And Orchestra* (1957)★★★, *Tyree Glenn At The Roundhouse* (1958)★★, *Tyree Glenn With Strings* i (1960)★★, *Tyree Glenn With Strings* ii (1960)★★★, *Tyree Glenn At The London House* (c.1961)★★★, *Tyree Glenn With Sy Oliver And His Orchestra* (1962)★★★, with Louis Armstrong *Louis* (1964-66)★★★★.

Globe Unity Orchestra

This important European orchestra was formed in 1966 by the German free jazz pianist Alexander Von Schlippenbach, initially to perform his composition 'Globe Unity' in Berlin. Until the mid-70s the orchestra worked principally in West Germany, performing at the key festivals of improvised music, such as the Total Music Meeting, the Workshop Freie Musik in Berlin and the Free Jazz Workshop in Wuppertal. Since then it has toured worldwide, playing festivals throughout Europe, the Far East and India. Alongside Schlippenbach, regulars in its distinguished line-up include Germans Peter Brötzmann, Gerd Dudek, Paul Lovens, Albert Mangelsdorff and Manfred Schoof; Britons Derek Bailey, Evan Parker and Paul Rutherford; Canadian Kenny Wheeler and Luxembourgian Michel Pilz. Although the orchestra has its roots in the 60s free jazz tradition, its improvisations sometimes echo earlier styles of jazz as well as contemporary classical music.

● ALBUMS: *Globe Unity* (1966)★★★★, *Live In Wuppertal* (1973)★★★, *Hamburg '74* (1974)★★★, *Evidence - Vol. 1* (FMP 1976)★★★, *Into The Valley - Vol. 2* (FMP 1976)★★★★, *Pearls* (1975)★★★★, *Local Fair* (1976)★★★, *Improvisations* (1977)★★★, *Compositions* (Japo 1979)★★★, *Rumbling* reissue of *Evidence/Into The Valley* (FMP 1991)★★★, *20th Anniversary* (FMP 1987)★★★★.

Glover, Dave, Band

Northern Ireland trumpeter Dave Glover first came to prominence during the late 40s playing dixieland in Belfast. His orchestral and big band seasons included a 'show' routine, which helped spawn the showband phenomenon, which subsequently spread southwards to Eire. Glover's first showband line-up included Big Joe Clarke (vocals), Andy Wilson (trombone), Harry Mitchel (keyboards), Gerry Rice (saxophone), Harry 'Trixie' Hamilton (bass), Alex Burns (guitar) and David Martin (drums). By 1963, most of the above line-up departed to form the Witnesses, while Glover found fresh musicians. Two promising vocalists, Muriel Day and Mike Munroe were backed by Jim Gunner (guitar), Jim McDermot (saxophone), Johnny Anderson (trombone), Jackie Flavelle (bass) and Desmond McCarathy (drums). The new line-up enjoyed a modicum of success, most notably when Day represented Ireland in the 1969 Eurovision Song Contest, with the chart-topping 'Wages Of Love'. Glover's presence on the Northern Ireland dance scene was much missed when he subsequently emigrated to Canada.

Godding, Brian

b. 19 August 1945, Wales. Godding is a self-taught guitarist who started his professional career in the rock bands Blossom Toes and B.B. Blunder before John McLaughlin's *Extrapolation* 'opened the door to jazz'. He played with Magma and Dick Morrisey before performing with Keith Tippett's band Centipede in the early 70s. Since then he has played with many British musicians but has worked most regularly with Mike

Westbrook who describes him as 'one of the truly great guitarists'. His playing reflects his own eclectic taste in guitarists which ranges from John McLaughlin right through to Jeff Beck and Jimi Hendrix. He also writes songs with the singer Kevin Coyne.

● ALBUMS: with Centipede *Septober Energy* (1971)★★★★, with Mike Westbrook *Citadel/Room 315* (1974)★★★★, *The Cortege* (1982)★★★, *On Duke's Birthday* (1985)★★★, *Pier Music* (1986)★★★, *Slaughter On Shaftesbury Avenue* (1989)★★★.

GOLD, HARRY

b. 26 February 1907, Dundrum, Dublin, Eire. Gold grew up in London from the age of four. He studied music and learned to play several reed instruments, starting his professional career on alto saxophone. Later, he settled on the uncommon bass saxophone as his primary instrument. His earliest engagement was with another young musician struggling to form his first band, Joe Loss. Gold also led a small dance band which included in its ranks the young guitarist Ivor Mairants. During the 20s and 30s Gold played in several top British dance bands including those led by Jack Padbury, Roy Fox, Geraldo, Bert Firman and Oscar Rabin. It was during his stint with Rabin that he emerged as leader of a band-within-the-band; that was known as Harry Gold's Pieces Of Eight and became the basis of his own popular group. Playing a form of highly polished dixieland, the little band worked successfully during the late 40s, making its major breakthrough with an appearance at the 1947 Jazz Jamboree. Amongst his sidemen at one time or another were Norrie Paramor, Bert Weedon, Duncan Whyte and Geoff Love. The band retained its popularity during the trad jazz boom of the early 50s, even though it was never really a part of the movement. In 1956 he handed over leadership of the band to his brother, Laurie Gold, intending to concentrate on composing and arranging. However, he continued to play through the 60s and 70s, often obscurely or anonymously as a busy session musician and arranger. In the mid-70s, soon after an appearance as a member of the New Paul Whiteman Orchestra, Gold reformed his Pieces Of Eight. He continued to lead the band, still playing its own smoothed-out but very musicianly brand of jazz, into the 80s. Gold disdainfully ignored the fact that he was 80 years old in 1987 and continued playing into the 90s. In 1991, the Pieces Of Eight broke up in some acrimony, but Gold played on, guesting with many bands throughout the UK. Gold's playing of the bass saxophone is remarkably deft and the sonority of the instrument adds immeasurably to the sound of any band in which he plays. Gold has also performed in other areas of music, appearing with the Liverpool Philharmonic under André Kostelanetz in 1946 and under Charles Groves a quarter-century later. He is the composer of 'Rhapsody In Green: An Irish Rhapsody'. Late in 1991 he had begun working on his autobiography.

● ALBUMS: *Harry Gold And His Pieces Of Eight* (1960)★★★★, *Octagonal Gold* (1980)★★★★, *Bouncing Back* (1988)★★★.

GOLDBERG, STU

b. 1954, Massachusetts, USA. Goldberg played the piano from the age of 10 and took up the organ a couple of years later but continued to study classical music. At the age of 16 he played with Ray Brown's Quartet at the Monterey Jazz Festival. In 1974 he studied jazz at the University of Utah before moving to Los Angeles and joining the Mahivishnu Orchestra. He plays in the necessary virtuoso manner and is much influenced by the generation of keyboard players which includes Herbie Hancock and Joe Zawinul. When he left the Mahivishnu Orchestra he played with Miroslav Vitous, Al Di Meola and Freddie Hubbard before joining Alphonze Mouzon between 1976 and 1977. In 1978 he came to Europe as a soloist.

● ALBUMS: with Mahivishnu Orchestra *Inner Worlds* (1975)★★★, *Johnny McLaughlin, Electric Guitarist* (1978)★★★★. Solo: *Solos, Duos, Trios* (1979)★★★.

GOLDEN GATE QUARTET

This four-piece vocal group, originally titled Golden Gate Jubilee Quartet, started singing together in the mid-30s at the Booker T. Washington High School in Norfolk, Virginia, USA. The group consisted of Willie Johnson (baritone), Henry Owens (first tenor), Orlandus Wilson (bass) and William Langford (second tenor). Influenced by the sound of jazz and by the Mills Brothers, their live reputation quickly grew. In 1937 they signed to the Victor Records subsidiary Bluebird Records, and recorded several singles (often in one take), including 'Go Where I Send Thee' and 'When The Saints Go Marching In'. After Claude Riddick replaced Langford as second tenor the band moved to New York, where they recorded with the folk singer Lead Belly in June 1940. Although preominantly gospel-oriented at first, the group branched out into pop and jazz with singles including 'Stormy Weather' and 'My Prayer'. They also played at President Franklin D. Roosevelt's inauguration ceremony, the first of a series of performances at the White House.

In 1941 the group moved to OKeh Records, and enjoyed some success with a version of 'Comin' In On A Wing And A Prayer' in 1943. Wilson and Johnson saw service in the war, and Alton Bradley and Cliff Givens stepped in as replacements until 1946 (Givens then joined the Ink Spots). In 1948 they featured in the RKO musical *A Song Is Born* alongside Benny Goodman and Louis Armstrong. Other films to feature the group included *Star Spangled Rhythm*, *Hollywood Canteen* and *Hit Parade Of 1943*. Johnson left to become lead with the Jubilaires, and was replaced by Orville Brooks. Their output slowed down during the 50s, when they were joined by Caleb J.C. Ginyard of the Dixiaires, as they attempted, largely unsuccessfully, to adapt their sound to prevailing R&B trends. In 1959 they relocated to France, with the promise of a two-year residency at the Casino de Paris. Only Wilson and Riddick remained as original members in the 70s, joined by Calvin Williams (second tenor) and Paul Brembly (baritone).

● COMPILATIONS: *35 Historic Recordings* 1937-39 recordings (RCA 1983)★★★, *Negro Spirituals* (Happy Bird 1983)★★★, *Jubilee* (Ibach 1984)★★★, *The Number 1's* (Ibach 1984)★★★, *Spirituals* (EMI 1986)★★★, *Historical Recordigs From The 40s And 50s* (Columbia 1990)★★★★, *Complete Recorded Works 1937-39* (Document 1996)★★★.

GOLDINGS, LARRY

b. Lawrence Sam Goldings, 28 August 1968, Boston, Massachusetts, USA. Known primarily for his organ playing, Goldings began at the age of seven on the piano. His father, a lawyer, was a classical music enthusiast and the sound of this music took hold of the young Goldings' interest. He also developed a keen ear by listening to popular songs from the radio and learning the harmonies. At the age of 12, Goldings attended music camp in Sweden, Maine, where he studied with his first important jazz instructor, Dave Cozzolongo, who taught him about the works of Bud Powell, Art Tatum and Oscar Peterson. In his high school years, Goldings played in school bands and local rock 'n' roll groups. He also attended a high-school jazz programme at the Eastman School of Music in Rochester, New York. At this time he was very influenced by the works of Dave McKenna, Bill Evans and Wynton Kelly, along with the groups of Miles Davis and John Coltrane. He was helped in his development by some influential teachers, including Ran Blake at the New England Conservatory of Music, Peter Cassino and even Keith Jarrett, on occasion. When he graduated from high school in 1986, Goldings moved to New York City and attended the music programme of the New School for Social Research, where he studied with Fred Hersch and Jaki Byard. Goldings also led the school's weekly jam sessions, where he was heard by the great pianist Sir Roland Hanna, who invited Goldings to accompany him to an annual jazz gathering in Copenhagen, Denmark. There, Goldings performed for many great jazz artists, such as Hank Jones, Tommy Flanagan and Sarah Vaughan. After participating in a masterclass at the New School conducted by vocalist Jon Hendricks, Goldings gained his first professional experience working with the singer on a trip to Paris, France. Hendricks eventually employed the pianist for more than a year. In New York, Goldings began leading his own groups and jam sessions at clubs such as Augie's and The Village Gate, with other young musicians including Leon Parker. It was Parker who suggested that Goldings should begin to play the organ. Later, he was heard by the saxophonist Maceo Parker who asked him to join his band. Goldings established his own organ trio with his first release, *Intimacy Of The Blues* (1991). He was soon performing and recording with artists including Jim Hall, Christopher Hollyday and John Scofield. As an organist, Goldings followed the path of masters such as Jimmy Smith, Mel Rhyne, Shirley Scott and Lonnie Smith, whom he cites as his favourite. Subsequent releases with the trio - Peter Bernstein on guitar and Bill Stewart on drums - included *Light Blue* (1992) and *Caminhos Cruzados* (1994), a collection of Brazilian jazz. Goldings began to show the funkier side of his organ music with the release of *Whatever It Takes* (1995) and *Big Stuff* (1996). These included compositions by Ray Charles, Stevie Wonder and Sly Stone and allowed Goldings to express some of his pop music leanings. On his next release, *Awareness* (1997), Goldings was finally able to feature a piano trio, with Larry Grenadier on bass and former Bill Evans trio member Paul Motian on drums. Goldings is an extremely versatile performer and a very prolific composer of jazz, pop and folk music. With an eye towards the future, Goldings has become involved in writing music for films, and maintains a desire to experiment with new and developing technologies that will allow him to communicate with as large an audience as possible.

● ALBUMS: *Intimacy Of The Blues* (Verve 1991)★★★★, *Light Blue* (Minor Music 1992)★★★, *Caminhos Cruzados* (Novus 1994)★★★★, *Whatever It Takes* (Warners 1995)★★★, *Big Stuff* (Warners 1996)★★★★, *Awareness* (Warners 1997)★★★.

GOLDKETTE, JEAN

b. 18 March 1899, Valenciennes, France, d. 24 May 1962. A child prodigy, Goldkette toured as a concert pianist, spending several years in Greece and Russia and was still only 12 years old when he settled in America. Equipped with an astute business brain, Goldkette was soon working as a danceband pianist and joined the organization headed by Chicago's Edgar Benson. As director of one of the several Benson Orchestras, Goldkette expanded his knowledge of the band circuit to the point where he decided to set up his own business. He established an organization similar to Benson's and later acquired a building in Detroit which he turned into the Graystone Ballroom. With a recording contract for Victor, Goldkette soon had more work than he could handle with one band and once again followed Benson's example by forming additional bands, each labelled as a 'Jean Goldkette Orchestra'. Throughout the late 20s his bands were home to several white jazz stars, including Bix Beiderbecke, Frank Trumbauer, Joe Venuti and the Tommy and Jimmy Dorsey, and several important early big band arrangers, notably Bill Challis and Bill Rank. At the end of 1927, after a hugely successful engagement at the Roseland Ballroom in New York, the jazz nucleus of Goldkette's number one orchestra left to join Paul Whiteman. In the 30s Goldkette concentrated his energies on operating his many dancehalls and the 20-plus bands that bore his name (in none of which he ever played). Although the bands became of less importance, Jean Goldkette orchestras were still performing into the 50s. Later in his life, Goldkette returned to his first love, classical piano music. He died in March 1962, thus missing the nostalgia boom from which he would doubtless have benefitted.

● ALBUMS: *Jean Goldkette And His Orchestra* (1959)★★★★.

● COMPILATIONS: with Bix Beiderbecke *Bixology Vols 2 & 3* (1924-27 recordings)★★★★.

GOLIA, VINNY

b. 1946, New York City, New York, USA. Vinny Golia has the unique distinction of having appeared on Blue Note and ECM albums before he'd learned to play an instrument! He did it as an artist: it's his painting on the cover of Chick Corea's *Song Of Singing*, his drawing that adorns the sleeve of Dave Holland's *Music For Two Basses.* Golia graduated with a degree in fine art in 1969 and moved, by chance, into the apartment block where Corea, Holland and Dave Liebman were all living. He began to attend their concerts, drawing the musicians as they played and later turning the sketches into large, abstract canvasses. With the money he received for the *Song Of Singing* sleeve he bought a soprano saxophone and, after taking lessons from Liebman and Anthony Braxton (also an influence on his later composing), spent the next few years teaching himself to play. Then, rather than invite musicians to 'play' his paintings (as happened at one event he staged with Circle), Golia started to play them himself, before deciding he could cut out the painting and simply play. In 1973 he moved to Los Angeles and in 1977 started his own label, Nine Winds, which provided an outlet for a new generation of west coast musicians, including pianist Wayne Peet, bassist Ken Filiano, percussionist Alex Cline, guitarist Nels Cline and trombonist John Rapson. Golia's own recordings include solo, duo, trio and small-group albums (*No Reverse* and *Goin' Ahead* are outstanding) as well as three big band releases - *Compositions For Large Ensemble, Facts Of Their Own Lives* and *Pilgrimage To Obscurity* - which feature guests such as Bobby Bradford, John Carter and Tim Berne. Golia also kept practising: he now plays over 20 instruments, all self-taught - they include nearly all of the saxophone, clarinet and flute families plus piccolo, bassoon and various non-Western pieces such as conch, sho, hotchiku, shakuhachi and khee. Though he mostly leads his own groups, he has toured and/or recorded as a sideman with Berne, Braxton, George Gruntz and several of his west coast colleagues. In addition to his jazz activities, Golia's love of chamber music has prompted him to work with various classical players and to record a set of improvised duets with bass maestro Bertram Turetzky.

● ALBUMS: *Spirits In Fellowship* (1978)★★, *Openhearted* (1979)★★★, *In The Right Order* (1980)★★, *Solo* (1980)★★★, *The Gift Of Fury* (1981)★★★, *Slice Of Life* (1983)★★★, with Wayne Peet *No Reverse* (1984)★★★, *Goin' Ahead* (1985)★★★, *Compositions For Large Ensemble* 1982 recording (1986)★★★, *Facts Of Their Own Lives* 1984 recording (1987)★★, *Out For Blood* (1989)★★★, *Pilgrimage To Obscurity* 1985 recording (Nine Winds 1990)★★★★, *Worldwide And Portable* 1986 recording (Nine Winds 1990)★★★, with Bertram Turetzky *Intersections* 1986 recording (1991)★★★, *Regards From Norma Desmond* 1986 recording (Fresh Sound 1992)★★★★, *Commemoration* (Nine Winds 1993)★★★★, *Decennium Dans Axlan* (Nine Winds 1993)★★★★, *Collaboration* (Nine Winds 1995)★★★, with Ken Filiano, Joëlle Léandre *Haunting The Spirits Inside Them ...* (Music And Arts 1996)★★★★, *Against The Grain* 1993 recording (Nine Winds 1996)★★★, with Paul Smoker *Halloween '96* (CIMP 1997)★★★, ★★★ (Nine Winds 1997), ★★★ (Music And Arts 1997), *Nations Of Laws* (Nine Winds 1997)★★★★, *The Art Of Negociation* (CIMP 1997)★★, *Eleven Reasons To Begin* (Music And Arts 1997)★★, *Tutto Contare* (Nine Winds 1998)★★, *Portland 1996* (Nine Winds 1998★★★, Prataksis (Nine Winds 1998)★★★★.

GOLLA, GEORGE

b. 10 May 1935, Chorzów, Poland. While still in his teens Golla immigrated to Australia where his guitar playing attracted considerable attention. Late in the 50s he teamed up with Don Burrows, playing throughout Australia and also travelling worldwide gaining plaudits from critics and audiences alike. He also appeared on record with Burrows, on his acclaimed Sydney Opera House album, and with Stéphane Grappelli on *Steph' 'N' Us*. In the 90s he was still very active and took part in an acclaimed Martin Taylor set of duets, *Two's Company*.

● ALBUMS: with Stéphane Grappelli *Steph' 'N' Us* (Cherry Pie 1977)★★★.

GOLSON, BENNY

b. 25 January 1929, Philadelphia, Pennsylvania, USA. After receiving extensive tuition on a variety of instruments as a child, Golson began playing tenor saxophone professionally in 1951 in Bullmoose Jackson's R&B band. It was here that he first met Tadd Dameron, who had a great influence upon his writing. In the early and mid-50s he played in bands led by Dameron, Lionel Hampton and Earl Bostic, then worked for Dizzy Gillespie, playing in and arranging for the 1956-8 big band. Next, Golson became a member of Art Blakey's Jazz Messengers, for whom he composed several tunes. He later formed bands with Curtis Fuller and Art Farmer (the Jazztet), then went into the studios, writing for films and television but making occasional appearances on record dates and on jazz stages around the world. In the late 70s he returned to regular live work and toured Europe with a reunited Jazztet in 1982. The following year he recorded an acclaimed tribute album to his old Philadelphia jamming partner, John Coltrane. Golson's playing, which followed the melodic progression of late swing era stylists such as Lucky Thompson and Don Byas, was always effective. He remains best-known, however, for his writing and some of his compositions have become latterday jazz standards: 'Blues March', 'Killer Joe', 'Whisper Not' and 'I Remember Clifford'.

● ALBUMS: *Benny Golson's New York Scene* (Contemporary 1958)★★★★, *The Modern Touch Of Benny Golson* reissued as *Reunion* (Riverside/Jazzland 1958)★★★★, *The Other Side Of Benny Golson* (Riverside 1958)★★★, *Benny Golson And The Philadelphians* (United Artists 1959)★★★, with Curtis Fuller *The Curtis Fuller Jazztet With Benny Golson* (Savoy 1959)★★★, *Gone With Golson* (New Jazz 1959)★★★★, *Groovin' With Golson* (New Jazz 1959)★★★, with Farmer, Fuller *Meet The Jazztet* (Argo 1960)★★★, *Gettin' With It* (New Jazz 1960)★★★, with Farmer *Big City Sounds* (Argo 1961)★★★, with Farmer *The*

Jazztet And John Lewis (Argo 1961)★★★, with Farmer *The Jazztet At Birdhouse* (Argo 1961)★★★★, *Take A Number From 1 To 10* (Argo 1961)★★★, with Farmer *Here And Now* (Mercury 1962)★★★, with Farmer *Another Git Together* (Mercury 1962)★★★, *Pop + Jazz = Swing* (Audio Fidelity 1962)★★★, with Rahssan Roland Kirk *Roland Kirk Meets The Benny Golson Orchestra* (Mercury 1963)★★★, *Free: Benny Golson Quartet* (Argo 1963)★★★, *Just Jazz!* (Audio Fidelity 1963)★★★, *Turning Point* (Mercury 1963)★★★, *Stockholm Sojourn* (Prestige 1965)★★★, *Turn In, Turn On* (Verve 1967)★★★, *Killer Joe* (Columbia 1977)★★, *California Message* (Baystate 1980)★★★, *One More Mem'ry* (Timeless 1982)★★★, *Time Speaks* (Timeless 1983)★★★, *This Is For You, John* (Timeless 1984)★★★, with Farmer *The Jazztet: Moment To Moment* (Soul Note 1983)★★★, with Farmer, Fuller *Back To The City* (Contemporary 1986)★★★, *Benny Golson In Paris* 1958 recordings (Disques Swing 1987)★★★★, with Freddie Hubbard *Stardust* (Denon 1988)★★★★, *Live* (Dreyfus 1990)★★★, *Domingo* (Dreyfus 1992)★★★★, *I Remember Miles* (Evidence 1993)★★★★, *Up Jumped Benny* (Arkadia 1996)★★★, *Remembering Clifford* (Milestone 1998)★★★, *Free* (Chess 1998)★★★★.

GOMEZ, EDDIE

b. 4 November 1944, San Juan, Texas, USA. Gomez moved to New York as a child and took up the bass when he was 12 years old. He was at the High School of Music and Art before going on to the Juilliard School where he studied with Fred Zimmerman. He played with Marshall Brown's International Youth Band and then in the early 60s with Gary McFarland, Jim Hall, Paul Bley, Jeremy Steig (flute) and Gerry Mulligan before joining Bill Evans with whom he stayed for 10 years (1966-77). He needed his musically agile mind and technical dexterity in that trio with which he often played melodically in the upper register of the bass. During the early 80s he played in the band Steps Ahead which Mike Mainieri (vibes) kept together after a group of New York session musicians made an acclaimed tour of Japan. He has successfully played this fusion music on the amplified double bass rather than moving to bass guitar. Gomez has continued as a very much in-demand musician through the 80s playing and recording with Jack DeJohnette, Hank Jones and JoAnne Brackeen among others. In the 90s he recorded with Chick Corea.

● ALBUMS: with Paul Bley *Barrage* (1964)★★★, with Bill Evans *A Simple Matter of Conviction* (1966)★★★★, *What's New* (1969)★★★★, *Live At Tokyo* (1973)★★★, with Bob Moses *Bittersweet In The Ozone* (1975)★★★, *Crosscurrent* (1977)★★★★, with Jack DeJohnette *New Direction* (1978)★★★★, with JoAnne Brackeen *Special Identity* (1981)★★★, *Gomez* (Denon 1985)★★, *Mezgo* (Epic 1986)★★, *Down Stretch* (Blackhawk 1987)★★★, *Power Play* (Epic 1988)★★★, with Jeff Gardner *Continuum* (1990)★★★, *Streetsmart* (Epic 1990)★★★, *Live In Moscow* (B&W 1992)★★★, *Next Future* (GRP 1993)★★, with Bill Bruford, Ralph Towner*If Summer Had Its Ghosts* (Discipline 1997)★★.

GONELLA, NAT

b. Nathaniel Charles Gonella, 7 March 1908, Islington, London, England. d. 6 August 1998, Gosport, Hampshire, England. A trumpeter, vocalist, and bandleader, Gonella was a major pioneer of British jazz, and one of its best-loved personalities. After learning to play the cornet and read music while at school, Gonella worked in the tailoring trade and as an errand-boy, before buying his own cornet in 1923. A year later he switched to trumpet when joining Archie Pitt's Busby Boys in the Gracie Fields revue, *A Week's Pleasure*. During the four years that he was touring with that show and its successor, *Safety First*, Gonella began his lifelong love affair with jazz via records such as 'Wild Man Blues' and 'Cushion Foot Stomp'. These featured the musician who was to influence him most, Louis Armstrong. After leaving the Busby Boys, Gonella played in dancebands led by Bob Dryden and Archie Alexander, before being hired by Billy Cotton in 1930. The Cotton band's broadcasts from the ritzy Ciro's Club in London provided a wider audience for this sensational up-and-coming young musician who played trumpet and sang in the Armstrong style. In the same year he began recording, and appeared on Cotton sides such as 'That Rhythm Man', 'Bessie Couldn't Help It' and 'The New Tiger Rag'. In 1931, Cotton was naturally incensed when his complete brass section, Gonella, Sid Buckman and Joe Ferrie, defected overnight to the Monseigneur Band, which was fronted by one of the most successful bandleaders of the 30s, Roy Fox. One of the Monseigneur Restaurant's frequent patrons was the Prince of Wales, and he was especially keen on a Gonella speciality, 'Georgia On My Mind'. Hoagy Carmichael and Stuart Gorrell's memorable number became the musician's lifelong theme, and the title of his 1985 biography. Gonella's recording of the tune with the Fox band was made early in 1932, shortly after his highly individual version of the Negro spiritual, 'Oh! Monah!'. The latter number was adopted by Fox's pianist and arranger Lew Stone, who took over the Monseigneur band, still featuring Gonella, when Fox moved to the Café Anglais. Gonella continued to record with various ensembles and cut a few titles such as 'Rockin' Chair' and 'That's My Home' under the pseudonym Eddie Hines. On the 14 September 1932, he made 'I Can't Believe That You're In Love With Me'/'I Heard', the first record to have 'Nat Gonella and his Trumpet' on the label. A few months earlier, Gonella had met his idol for the first time, when Louis Armstrong played two weeks at the London Palladium. In later years, after they had finished their evening work, they often jammed in the early morning at clubs such as The Nest and Bag O' Nails. After working in the Netherlands with Ray Noble in 1933, in the summer of 1934, Gonella toured Variety theatres with Stone, and was featured with the Georgians, a five-piece band within a band. He also topped the bill at the Holborn Empire with violinist-singer Brian Lawrence and the Quaglino Quartette. In November 1934, Nat Gonella And His Georgians (Albert Torrence and George Evans - alto saxophones, Don Barrigo - tenor saxophone, Harold Hood - piano, Arthur Baker - guitar, Will Hemmings - string bass, Bob Dryden - drums) cut several sides for

Parlophone Records, including 'Moon Glow', 'Don't Let Your Love Go Wrong' and two 'Fox Trot Medleys' containing songs such as 'Dinah', 'Troublesome Trumpet', and 'Georgia On My Mind'. When Nat Gonella And His Georgians - 'Britain's Hottest Quintette' - finally undertook their first theatre tour in April 1935, they shrewdly mixed jazz with strong elements of comedy and crowd-pleasing numbers such as 'Tiger Rag'. In the late 30s, Gonella recorded prolifically - on one occasion accompanying George Formby on 'Doh-De-Oh-Do' - and packed theatres with shows such as *South American Joe*, which featured xylophone player Teddy Brown and singer Phyllis Robins. Another triumph came in 1938, with a summer season at Blackpool with *King Revel*, which co-starred Sandy Powell and Norman Evans. After a brief but successful spell in New York early in 1939, Gonella formed a larger band, the New Georgians, but with the advent of World War II, he was called up in the Army, and served in the Pioneer Corps and Royal Tank Regiment in North Africa. After the war, with musical tastes changing rapidly, his 13-piece outfit was quickly reduced to a quartet, and Gonella eventually went out on his own, playing holiday camps and Variety theatres. In spite of the late 50s-early 60s trad-jazz boom, bookings slumped, and he was reduced to working in a bookmaker's office for a time. Encouraged by the response to his *Salute To Satchmo* album, Gonella formed his Georgia Jazz Band, which, ironically, made its debut at the Cavern club in Liverpool in 1960. With an appearance as the subject of television's *This Is Your Life*, his comeback gathered pace for a time, and he issued *The Nat Gonella Story*. However, later in the decade he was working solo once more, and on one of his last recording dates he played the role of Fagin in the Society label's version of Lionel Bart's hit musical, *Oliver!* In the early 70s he returned to the Netherlands, and while there, he recorded 'Oh! Monah!', which reached the Top 5 in the Dutch hit parade. His subsequent retirement to Gosport in Hampshire was interrupted by occasional appearances at the local jazz club, sometimes in company with his longtime friend, supporter and fellow trumpeter, Digby Fairweather, along with ex-Georgians such as Tiny Winters, Jim Shepherd, and Pat Smuts. In the 80s there was a renewed interest in the man and his music. Fairweather embarked on a concert tour with *A Tribute To Nat Gonella*, and several collections of his work were re-released on album. In September 1994, the Gosport Borough Council named an area in the town after him: Nat Gonella Square (although one jazz-loving councillor observed that it was illogical to place the two words, 'Gonella' and 'Square' in the same sentence). Three years later, fans of contemporary music were privileged to hear just a very brief example of vintage Gonella, when computer wizard Jyoti Mishra 'sampled' part of his trumpet introduction to the 1932 Lew Stone disc, 'My Woman', and used it on his UK chart-topper, 'My Town', issued under the name of White Town. Just a week before he celebrated his 90th birthday, Gonella joined Digby Fairweather and other friends at the Pizza on the Park in London. Although he had put down the horn a long time ago, the years rolled back as this splendid, innovative musician delighted the audience with 'Shine', 'St. James Infirmary', 'When You're Smiling', and of course, 'Georgia On My Mind'.

● ALBUMS: *Runnin' Wild* (1958)★★★, *Salute To Satchmo* (Columbia 1959)★★★, *The Nat Gonella Story* (Columbia 1961)★★★★, *Nat Gonella And His Trumpet* (Ace Of Clubs 1967)★★★, *When You're Smiling* (1970)★★★★, *The Music Goes 'Round And 'Round* (1975)★★★★, *My Favourite Things* (1975)★★★, *Wishing You A Swinging Christmas* (1975)★★.

● COMPILATIONS: *Nat Gonella Story* (Note 1978)★★★, *Georgia On My Mind* 1931-46 recordings (Decca Recollections 1980)★★★★, *Mister Rhythm Man* 1945-35 recordings (EMI Retrospective 1984)★★★, *Golden Age Of Nat Gonella* (Golden Age 1985)★★★, *Nat Gonella Scrapbook* (Joy 1985)★★★, *Naturally Gonella* 1935 recordings (Happy Days 1986)★★★, *How'm I Doin'?* (Old Bean 1987)★★★, *Crazy Valves* 1934-35 recordings (Living Era 1988)★★★★, *Running Wild* (Harlequin 1988)★★★, *Yeah Man* 1935-37 recordings (Harlequin 1988)★★★, *Nat Gonella Volume One* 1934-1935 recordings (Neovox 1990)★★★, *Nat Gonella Volume Two* 1932-1935 recordings (Neovox 1990)★★★, *Hold Tight* (Memoir 1991)★★★, *The Cream Of Nat Gonella* (Flapper 1991)★★★★, *Nat Gonella - The Dance Band Years* 2-CD set (Pulse 1998)★★★, *Through The Years - 1930 To 1998* (1998).

● FURTHER READING: *Modern Style Of Trumpet Playing*, Nat Gonella. *Georgia On My Mind - The Nat Gonella Story*, Ron Brown with Cyril Brown.

● FILMS: *Pity The Poor Rich* (1935), *Sing As You Swing* (1937).

GONSALVES, PAUL

b. 12 July 1920, Boston, Massachusetts, USA, d. 15 May 1974. Gonsalves's first professional engagement in Boston was on tenor saxophone with the Sabby Lewis band, in which he played both before and after his military service during World War II. On leaving Lewis he played with Count Basie from 1946 until 1949, was briefly with Dizzy Gillespie, and then joined Duke Ellington in 1950. Gonsalves remained with Ellington for the rest of his life, his occasional absences from the band resulting from his addiction to alcohol and narcotics. Like many other would-be Ellingtonian tenor players, Gonsalves began by learning Ben Webster's 'Cottontail' solo note for note, but quickly established his own distinctive style. The circumstance which made Gonsalves's reputation was his appearance with Ellington at the 1956 Newport Jazz Festival, when his storming, 27-chorus bridge between the opening and closing sections of 'Diminuendo In Blue' and 'Crescendo In Blue' helped to focus media attention on the band and provided the basis of Ellington's 'comeback'. Thereafter, Gonsalves was obliged to play extended gallery-pleasing, up-tempo solos every night, a fact which overshadowed his enormous affinity with ballads. Gonsalves's relaxed and thoughtful approach to tunes displayed a love for melody and an ability to develop long, clean and logical solo lines. His rhapsodic playing on Ellington performances such as 'Happy Reunion', 'Chelsea Bridge', 'Solitude' and 'Mount

Harissa' from the *Far East Suite* all testify to his vulnerable, often tender sound. His playing on records made outside the Ellington aegis is usually of a similarly reflective nature. A 1970 album with Ray Nance, *Just A-Sittin' And A-Rockin'*, is a good example, including a marvellous performance of 'Don't Blame Me'. Gonsalves surpassed even this on *Love Calls*, his 1967 album of duets with Eddie 'Lockjaw' Davis, where he delivers what might well be the definitive version of this song. In such performances, the quality of the playing perhaps reflect the man himself: Gonsalves was a sensitive yet fragile human being. He succumbed to drug addiction and alcohol dependence early in life and his career was afterwards dogged by these twin perils. When he died in London, in May 1974, his employer for close on a quarter of a century was himself too ill to be told. Ellington died a few days later and the bodies of both men, and that of Tyree Glenn, lay together in the same New York funeral home.

● ALBUMS: with Duke Ellington *Ellington At Newport '56* (Columbia 1956)★★★★★, *Cookin'* (1957)★★★★, *Ellingtonia Moods And Blues* (1960)★★★★, *Gettin' Together* (Jazzland 1960)★★★★, *Duke Ellington Presents Paul Gonsalves* (1962)★★★★, *Paul Gonsalves In London I* (1963)★★★, *Rare Paul Gonsalves Sextet In Europe* (Jazz Connoisseur 1963)★★★, *Tell It The Way It Is!* (Jasmine 1963)★★★, *Salt And Pepper* (Impulse 1963)★★★★, *Cleopatra Feelin' Jazzy* (Jasmine 1963)★★★, *Paul Gonsalves In London II* (1964)★★★, *Paul Gonsalves In London III* (1965)★★★, with Ellington *Far East Suite* (1966)★★★★, with Eddie 'Lockjaw' Davis *Love Calls* (1967)★★★, *Encuentro* (1968)★★★, *Humming Bird* (1969)★★★, *Paul Gonsalves With The Four Bones* (1969)★★★, *Paul Gonsalves And His All Stars* (1970)★★, with Ray Nance *Just A-Sittin' And A-Rockin'* (Black Lion 1970)★★★, with Earl Hines *It Don't Mean A Thing* (1970-72)★★, *Meets Earl Hines* (Black Lion 1973)★★★, with Roy Eldridge *The Mexican Bandit Meets The Pittsburgh Pirate* (Fantasy 1973)★★★★, *Paul Gonsalves And Paul Quinichette* (1974)★★★.

GONZALES, BABS

b. Lee Brown Gonzales, 27 October 1919, Newark, New Jersey, USA, d. 23 January 1980. After working as a vocalist with a number of bands, including those led by Charlie Barnet and Lionel Hampton, Gonzales teamed up with Tadd Dameron and Rudy Williams. Their trio, Three Bips And A Bop, was successful in clubs and on record with a Gonzales composition, 'Oop-Pop-A-Da' being sufficiently popular to encourage a later and much more successful recording by Dizzy Gillespie. One of the few vocalists to take comfortably to bebop, Gonzales was also one of the most able of scat singers. He incorporated hip and humorous monologues into his act and was active in promoting jazz. When employment was scarce, he sought work outside music and was once chauffeur to film star Errol Flynn. A frequently surreal performer, Gonzales overcame deficiencies of poor pitch and a rough-edged voice thanks to excellent timing and a good sense of harmony. In the mid-50s he worked with, and also managed, James Moody. Gonzales continued working in the 60s and 70s although he never regained his earlier popularity. He published two volumes of memoirs, in 1967 and 1975, and died in 1980.

● ALBUMS: *The Be-Bop Story* (1957-71 recordings)★★, *Soul Stirring* (1958)★★★, *Cool Philosophy* (1959)★★★, *Babs* (c.1968)★★.

GONZALEZ, DENNIS

b. 15 August 1954, Abilene, Texas, USA. Born into a Mexican-American family, Gonzalez grew up in Mercedes, Texas, studied French, journalism and music at various institutions and is an accomplished visual artist, linguist, teacher, writer and disc jockey as well as an internationally-acclaimed trumpeter, composer and record-producer. In 1976 he settled in Dallas and two years later founded DAAGNIM (the Dallas Association for Avant Garde and Neo Impressionistic Music), setting up the similarly titled record label in 1979. His first album, *Air Light (Sleep Sailor)*, was recorded in his living room and had him playing a dozen or so instruments - at the time there were few local musicians sympathetic to his music! Later, with the help of reedsman John Purcell, he began to establish an impressive catalogue of work on Daagnim and in 1986 also started to record for the Swedish label Silkheart, releasing three albums of his own music and playing on three more by Charles Brackeen. Of these, it was his own *Stefan* and *Namesake* that really established his talent internationally. Gonzalez has worked hard to link the Dallas new music scene with like-minded communities in other areas of the USA: in particular, he has contacts with Austin, New Orleans, Los Angeles and Jackson, Mississippi, as well as with some of Chicago's AACM members - as a result his recordings feature a wide array of musicians (including Brackeen, Alvin Fielder, Ahmed Abdullah, Douglas Ewart, Malachi Favors and Kidd Jordan) in exotically-named ensembles such as New Dallasorleanssippi. He has also worked in the UK, playing and recording with Keith Tippett, Elton Dean, Louis Moholo and Marcio Mattos (*Catechism*), while two new albums from Berlin's Konnex label have him in the company of Andrew Cyrille, Alex Cline, Carlos Ward and Paul Rogers among others. A flowing, lyrical trumpeter, fond of wide intervals, Gonzalez's music sometimes shows Latin and South African influences but more often draws on the hymns of his Baptist Church upbringing: one hymn in particular, 'Holy Manna', has appeared in different guises on several of his albums. 'I found it to be a perfect link between heaven and earth, a tribute to spiritual strength,' Gonzalez has said, explaining his belief in the spiritual roots of all art. 'We are a creation, and in order to stay alive you must keep creating'. In the early 90s he worked on his first book of poems and stories, as well as recording with Fielder and Cecil Taylor.

● ALBUMS: *Air Light (Sleep Sailor)* (Daagnim 1979)★★★, *Music From Ancient Texts* (Daagnim 1981)★★★, *Kukkia* (Daagnim 1981)★★, *Stars/Air/Stripes* (Daagnim 1982)★★, *Witness* (Daagnim 1983)★★★, with John Purcell *Anthem Suite* (Daagnim 1984)★★★★, with Purcell *Little Toot* (Daagnim

1985)★★★, *Stefan* (Silkheart 1986)★★★, *Pelin Zena* (1986)★★★, *Namesake* (Silkheart 1987)★★★, *Catechism* (Daagnim 1987)★★, *Debenge-Debenge* (Silkheart 1989)★★★★, *Ya Yo Me Cure* (American Clave 1990)★★★, *The Earth And The Heart* (Konnex 1991)★★★, *Hymn For The Perfect Heart Of A Pearl* (Konnex 1991)★★★, *The River Is Deep* (Enja 1991)★★★, *Earth Dance* (Sunnyside 1991)★★★, *Obatala* (Enja 1992)★★★, *The Desert Wind* (Silkheart 1992)★★★, *Welcome To Us* (GOWI 1993)★★★.

GONZALEZ, JERRY

b. 5 June 1949, New York City, New York, USA. Multi-instrumentalist Gonzalez and his Fort Apache Band are one of the most exciting Latin jazz ensembles of the 90s, fusing the rhythms of Cal Tjader, Tito Puente and Eddie Palmieri with a fiery bebop horn section, with Gonzalez featuring on trumpet and percussion. He started off playing congas in a Latin jazz quintet alongside his bass-playing younger brother Andy, and attended the New York High School Of Music And Art and the New York City College Of Music. He joined Dizzy Gillespie's band as a percussionist, and then played for four years with Palmieri during which he was able to nurture his interest in Afro-Cuban rhythms. Gonzales left Palmieri to form the influential progressive salsa band Libre with his brother and timbales player Manny Oquendo. Gonzalez continued to develop his jazz and rumba fusion experiments with a series of informal basement sessions at his mother's house in the Bronx, attended by a stellar cast of musicians including Kenny Dorham, Woody Shaw, Alfredo de la Fé, Alfredo Rodriguez, Eddy Martinez and Wilfredo Velez. These sessions resulted in two all-star albums by the influential Grupo Folklorico y Experimental Nuyorquino. In 1979 Gonzalez was given the opportunity to transfer his fusion experiments to vinyl when he was signed to the American Clavé label as a solo artist by producer Kip Hanrahan. He made his solo debut with the notable *Ya Yo Me Curé* in 1980, backed by sidemen including trombonist Steve Turré, tenor saxophonist Mario Rivera, pianist Hilton Ruiz and singer Frankie Rodriguez on a mixture of Afro-Cuban originals and jazz standards by Wayne Shorter, Duke Ellington and Thelonious Monk (a remarkable reading of 'Evidence'). A European tour followed, with Gonzalez's ensemble hastily named the Fort Apache Band (taken from the 1981 movie *Fort Apache, The Bronx*). Gonzalez made his album debut with the Fort Apache Band on *The River Is Deep*, which was recorded at the Berlin Jazz Festival in November 1982. He left Libre at the end of the 80s to devote his energies to band leading. In 1989, he released *Obatalá* and *Rumba Para Monk*. On the latter album, an Afro-Cuban Monk tribute, Gonzalez scaled his band down to a quintet comprising his brother, pianist Larry Willis, percussionist Steve Berrios and tenor Carter Jefferson. In November 1990, the Fort Apache Band made their UK debut with an outstanding concert at London's Empire Ballroom. With the addition of alto saxophonist Joe Ford, Gonzalez's sextet recorded two more acclaimed albums on the Sunnyside label. Jefferson died in 1993 and was replaced by the experienced John Stubblefield. The current line-up of the band have released three albums on Milestone Records that have firmly established them at the forefront of Latin jazz.

● ALBUMS: *Ya Yo Me Curé* (American Clavé 1980)★★★, *The River Is Deep* (Enja 1983)★★★★, *Obatalá* (Enja 1989)★★★★, *Rumba Para Monk* (Sunnyside 1989)★★★★, *Earthdance* (Sunnyside 1991)★★★★, *Moliendo Café* (Sunnyside)★★★, *Crossroads* (Milestone 1994)★★★★, *Pensativo* (Milestone 1995)★★★, *Fire Dance* (Milestone 1996)★★★★.

GONZÁLEZ, RUBÉN

b. 1919, Santa Clara, Cuba. González became a full-time musician in 1941 having studied medicine and classical piano (he had planned to be a doctor by day and musician by night). During the 40s, while playing piano with Arsenio Rodriquez and the Orquesta De La Hermanes, he helped to shape the sound of modern Cuban music, incorporating jazz influences and developing the mambo. In the 50s he travelled to Panama and Argentina where he played with local tango musicians, subsequently returning to Havana to play in cabaret bands. He joined the band of Enrique Jorrin (the creator of the cha-cha-cha) in the early 60s, and stayed for 25 years until Jorrin's death. Following a brief and unsuccessful attempt to lead the band himself, González retired from music completely. However, in 1996 he was invited out of retirement by Juan de Marcos González of Sierra Maestra to participate in a two-week recording session involving the cream of three generations of Cuban musicians and guest guitarist Ry Cooder. Rubén González took every opportunity to play in the studio and was a key participant in both the albums planned for the session (the Afro-Cuban All Stars' *A Toda Cuba Le Gusta* and Cooder's *Buena Vista Social Club*). His playing impressed Cooder, Juan de Marcos González and co-producer Nick Gold to such an extent that time was also found to record *Introducing Ruben Gonzalez*, his debut as a bandleader. Recorded live over two days, with a small group of specially chosen musicians playing a collection of Cuban standards, some of the album is as stately and graceful as would be expected from a veteran. However, at other times he plays with a ferocious attack and improvisational inventiveness, going some way towards justifying Cooder's description of him as 'the greatest piano soloist I have ever heard in my life. He's like a Cuban cross between Thelonious Monk and Felix the Cat'.

● ALBUMS: *Introducing Rubén González* (World Circuit 1997)★★★★.

GOODE, COLERIDGE

b. 29 November 1914, St. Andrew, Jamaica, West Indies. While studying at Glasgow University, Goode began playing violin, later switching to bass. He first played professionally in 1942 and was soon working in clubs, on radio and records with noted European and UK artists such as Johnny Claes, Stéphane Grappelli, Django Reinhardt and George Shearing. In the early 40s he performed with Eric Winstone's show band and in

1944 became a member of Leslie 'Jiver' Hutchinson's all-black band, among the first of its kind in the UK. Later in the 40s he joined Ray Ellington and a decade later was a member of Joe Harriott's free-form quintet. In the 60s Goode was involved with Michael Garrick and also led his own groups which, like Harriott's, experimented with the fusion of Indian music and jazz. In the mid-70s Goode teamed up with pianist Iggy Quayle, an association which persisted for more than a decade.

● ALBUMS: all with Joe Harriott *Free Form* (1960)★★, *Abstract* (1962)★★★, *Indo-Jazz Suite* (1965)★★★★.

GOODMAN, BENNY

b. 30 May 1909, Chicago, Illinois, USA, d. 20 June 1986. Born into a large, impoverished family of immigrants, Goodman experienced hard times whilst growing up. Encouraged by his father to learn a musical instrument, Goodman and two of his brothers took lessons; as the youngest and smallest he learned to play the clarinet. These early studies took place at the Kehelah Jacob Synagogue and later at Hull House, a settlement house founded by reformer Jane Addams. From the start, Goodman displayed an exceptional talent and he received personal tuition from James Sylvester and then the renowned classicist Franz Schoepp (who also taught Buster Bailey around the same time). Before he was in his teens, Goodman had begun performing in public and was soon playing in bands with such emerging jazz artists as Jimmy McPartland, Frank Teschemacher and Dave Tough. Goodman's precocious talent allowed him to become a member of the American Federation of Musicians at the age of 14 and that same year he played with Bix Beiderbecke. By his mid-teens Goodman was already established as a leading musician, working on numerous engagements with many bands to the detriment of his formal education. In 1925 he was heard by Gil Rodin, who was then with the popular band led by Ben Pollack. Goodman was hired by Pollack, then working in California, and the following year made a triumphal return to Chicago as featured soloist with the band. Goodman remained with Pollack until 1929, when he became a much in-demand session musician in New York, making many hundreds of record and radio dates. Keenly ambitious and already a determined perfectionist, Goodman continued to develop his craft until he was perhaps the most skilled clarinet player in the country, even if he was virtually unknown to the general public.

During the late 20s and early 30s Goodman played in bands led by Red Nichols, Ben Selvin, Ted Lewis, Sam Lanin and others, sometimes for club, dance hall and theatre engagements and often on record sessions. In 1934 his ambitions led him to form a large dance band, which was successful in being hired for a residency at Billy Rose's Music Hall. After a few months, this date collapsed when Rose was replaced by someone who did not like the band but Goodman persisted and late that same year was successful in gaining one of three places for dance bands on a regular radio show broadcast by NBC. The show, entitled *Let's Dance*, ran for about six months. By this time Goodman was using arrangements by leading writers of the day such as Fletcher Henderson and Lyle 'Spud' Murphy, and including in his band musicians such as Bunny Berigan, trombonists Red Ballard and Jack Lacey, saxophonists Toots Mondello and Hymie Schertzer, and in the rhythm section George Van Eps and Frank Froeba, who were quickly replaced by Allen Reuss and Jess Stacy. Goodman's brother, Harry, was on bass, and the drummer was Stan King, who was soon replaced by the more urgent and exciting Gene Krupa. The band's singer was Helen Ward, one of the most popular band singers of the day. When the *Let's Dance* show ended, Goodman took the band on a nation-wide tour. Prompted in part by producer John Hammond Jnr. and also by his desire for the band to develop, Goodman made many changes to the personnel, something he would continue to do throughout his career as a big band leader, and by the time the tour reached Los Angeles, in August 1935, the band was in extremely good form. Despite the success of the radio show and the band's records, the tour had met with mixed fortunes and some outright failures. However, business picked up on the west coast and on 21 August 1935 the band played a dance at the Palomar Ballroom in Los Angeles. They created a sensation and the massive success that night at the Palomar is generally credited as the time and place where the show business phenomenon which became known as the 'swing era' was born.

After an extended engagement at the Palomar the band headed back east, stopping over in Chicago for another extended run, this time at the Joseph Urban Room at the Congress Hotel. Earlier, Goodman had made some trio recordings using Krupa and pianist Teddy Wilson. The records sold well and he was encouraged by Helen Oakley, later Helen Oakley Dance, to feature Wilson in the trio at the hotel. Goodman eventually was persuaded that featuring a racially mixed group in this manner was not a recipe for disaster and when the occasion passed unremarked, except for musical plaudits, he soon afterwards employed Wilson as a regular member of the featured trio. In 1936 he added Lionel Hampton to form the Benny Goodman Quartet and while this was not the first integrated group in jazz it was by far the one with the highest profile. Goodman's big band continued to attract huge and enthusiastic audiences. In the band now were leading swing era players such as Harry James, Ziggy Elman, Chris Griffin, Vernon Brown, Babe Russin and Arthur Rollini. Goodman had an especially successful date at the Paramount Theatre in New York, beginning on 3 March 1937, and his records continued to sell very well. On 16 January 1938 the band played a concert at Carnegie Hall, sealing its success and Goodman's reputation as the 'King of Swing.' Soon after the Carnegie Hall date the band's personnel underwent significant changes. Krupa left to form his own band, soon followed by Wilson and James. Goodman found replacements and carried on as before although, inevitably, the band sounded different. In the early 40s he had a particularly interesting personnel, which included Cootie Williams, 'Big' Sid Catlett, Georgie Auld and, in the small group (which was now a septet although labelled as the Benny Goodman Sextet), Charlie Christian. Other Goodman musicians of this period included Jimmy Maxwell and Mel Powell, while his singer, who had followed Ward, Martha Tilton and Helen Forrest, was Peggy Lee. With occasional fallow periods, which usually coincided with the persistent back trouble with which he was plagued, Goodman continued to the end of the 40s, dabbling with bop by way of a small group which featured musicians such as Doug Mettome, Stan Hasselgård, Wardell Gray and, fleetingly, Fats Navarro and with big bands which included Mettome, Gray, Stan Getz, Don Lamond and Jimmy Rowles.

Goodman soon ended his flirtation with bop, but the release, in 1953, of a long-playing album made from acetates cut during the 1938 Carnegie Hall concert and forgotten during the intervening years revitalized interest in him and his career. He reformed a band for a concert tour which brought together many of the old gang; but a decision to enhance the tour's chances of success by also featuring Louis Armstrong and his All Stars was an error. The two stars clashed at rehearsals and during the out-of-town warm up concert. By the time the package was ready for its opening at Carnegie Hall, Goodman was in hospital, whether for a genuine illness, or because of a sudden attack of diplomacy, no one is quite sure. In 1955 he recorded the soundtrack for a feature film, *The Benny Goodman Story*, and a soundtrack album was also released which featured Wilson, Hampton, Krupa, James, Getz and other former sidemen. During the rest of the 50s and in succeeding decades, Goodman made many appearances with small groups and with occasional big bands, but his days as a leader of a regular big band were over. Even as a small group leader, his bands tended to be one-off only affairs, although he did regularly associate with musicians for whom he had high regard, amongst them Ruby Braff and Urbie Green. In Europe he led a big band for an appearance at the 1958 World's Fair in Brussells and in 1962 took a band to the USSR for a visit sponsored by the US State Department. Later, he fronted other big bands, including two formed from British musicians for concert tours in 1969 and again in 1970. From the late 60s he began appearing at regular reunions of the quartet with Wilson, Hampton and Krupa. These reunions, along with club and television dates, occasional tours to Europe and the Far East, occupied the 70s. This decade also saw, on 16 January 1978, a Carnegie Hall date which attempted to recreate the magic of his first appearance there, 30 years before. Goodman continued to record and play concert and other dates into the early 80s. In the last few years of his life and ensconced in his apartment on west 44th, Manhattan he lived quietly and is well-remembered with great affection by the local community.

From the earliest days of his career Goodman was marked out as a hot clarinettist. Although he had an early regard for Ted Lewis, it was the playing of such musicians as Teschemacher and Jimmy Noone that most influenced him. By the start of the 30s, however, Goodman was very much his own man, playing in a highly distinctive style and beginning to influence other clarinettists. His dazzling technique, allied to his delight in playing hot jazz, made him one of the most exciting players of his day. Without question, he was the most technically proficient of all musicians regularly playing jazz clarinet. On the many records he made during this period Goodman almost always soloed, yet he rarely made an error, even on unused takes. During the swing era, despite the rising popularity of Artie Shaw and a handful of others, Goodman retained his popularity, even though his jazz style became noticeably less hot as the decade progressed. His dabblings with bop were never fully convincing, although in his playing of the 40s and later there are signs that he was aware of the changes being wrought in jazz. There are also fleeting stylistic nods towards Lester Young, whose playing he clearly admired. From the late 30s Goodman had become steadily more interested in classical music and periodically appeared and recorded in this context, often performing pieces which he had specially commissioned. The classical pursuits led him to adopt a different embouchure thus altering the sound of all his playing, and further attenuating the gap some felt had arisen between the current Goodman style and the hot jazz playing of his youth. As a musician Goodman was a perfectionist, practising every day until the end of his life (in his biography of Goodman, James Lincoln Collier reports that, at the time of his death, the clarinettist, alone at home, appeared to have been playing a Brahms Sonata). As with so many perfectionists. Goodman expected his employees to adhere to his own high standards. Many were similarly dedicated musicians, but they were also individualistic, and in some cases had egos which matched his own. Inevitably, there were many clashes; over the years a succession of Goodman stories have emerged which suggest that he was a man who was totally preoccupied with his music to the exclusion of almost everything else including social niceties.

Goodman's achievements in this particular field of American popular music are virtually matchless. He rose from poverty to become a millionaire before he was 30 years old, a real rags to riches story. He was, for a while, the best-known and most popular musician in the USA. And if the title King of Swing rankled with many musicians and was clearly inappropriate when his work is compared with that of such peers as Armstrong and Duke Ellington, Goodman's band of the late 30s was hard-driving outfit which contrasted sharply with many other white bands of the period and at its best was usually their superior. The trio and quartet brought to small group jazz a sophistication rarely heard before, and seldom matched since; but which nevertheless included much hot music, especially from the leader. It was, perhaps, in the sextet, with Christian, Williams, Auld and others that Goodman made his greatest contribution to jazz. All the tracks recorded by this group before Christian's untimely death are classics of the form. His encouragement of musicians like Christian, Wilson and Hampton not only helped Goodman to promote important careers in jazz but also did much to break down racial taboos in show business and American society. The fact that he was never an innovator means Goodman was not a great jazzman in the sense that Armstrong, Ellington, Charlie Parker and others were. Nevertheless, he was a major figure in jazz and played an important role in the history of 20th century popular music.

● ALBUMS: *Benny Goodman And Peggy Lee* (Columbia 1949)★★★, *Dance Parade* (Columbia 1949)★★★, *Goodman Sextet Session* (Columbia 1949)★★★★, *Let's Hear The Melody* (Columbia 1950)★★★, *Chicago Jazz Classics* (Brunswick 1950)★★★, *Session For Six* (Capitol 1950)★★★, *Dance Parade Vol 2* (Columbia 1950)★★★★, *Carnegie Hall Jazz Concert* (Columbia 1950)★★★★, *King Of Swing* 6-LP box set (Columbia 1950)★★★★, with Jack Teagarden *Goodman & Teagarden* 10-inch album (Jazz Panorama 1951)★★★★, *Benny Goodman* (RCA Victor 1951)★★★, *1937-38 Jazz Concert No 2* (Columbia 1952)★★★, *Easy Does It* (Capitol 1952)★★★, *Immortal Performances* (RCA Victor 1952)★★★★, *The Benny Goodman Trio* (Capitol 1952)★★★★, *The Benny Goodman Band* (Capitol 1953)★★★, *The Golden Era: Combos* (Columbia 1953)★★★★, *The Goodman Touch* (Capitol 1953)★★★★, *The Golden Era: Bands* (Columbia 1953)★★★★, *Presents Eddie Sauter Arrangements* (Columbia 1954)★★★★, *Benny Goodman 1937-1939* (RCA Victor 1954)★★★★, *Small Combo 1947* (Capitol 1954)★★★★, *Benny Goodman 1927-1934* (Brunswick 1954)★★★★, with Teagarden *Benny Goodman Featuring Jack Teagarden* 10-inch album (Jolly Rogers 1954)★★★★, *The Golden Age Of Benny Goodman* (RCA Victor 1955)★★★★, *The Benny Goodman Story* (1955)★★★★, *The Great Benny Goodman* (Columbia 1956)★★★, *Trio, Quartet, Quintet* (RCA Victor 1956)★★★★, *The Vintage Benny Goodman* (Columbia 1956)★★★★, *This Is Benny Goodman* (RCA Victor 1956)★★★★, *Benny Goodman In Brussels Vol 1* (Columbia 1958)★★★★, *Mostly Sextets* (Capitol 1958)★★★, *Benny Goodman In Brussels Vol 2* (Columbia 1958)★★★★, *The Superlative Goodman* (Verve 1958)★★★, *Happy Session* (Columbia 1959)★★★, *The Benny Goodman Tentet And Sextet* (1959)★★★, *Benny Goodman Swings Again* (Columbia 1960)★★★, *The Kingdom Of Swing* (RCA Victor 1960)★★★, *Swing Swing Swing* (Campden 1960)★★★, *Benny Goodman In Moscow* (RCA Victor 1962)★★★, *Together Again!* (RCA Victor 1963)★★★★, *Hello Benny* (Capitol 1964)★★★, with Lionel Hampton, Gene Krupa, Teddy Wilson *Together Again* (RCA Victor 1964)★★★, *The Essential Benny Goodman* (Verve 1964)★★★, *Made In Japan* (Capitol 1964)★★★★, *B.G. The Small Groups* (RCA Victor 1965)★★★, *Live In Las Vegas* (1967)★★★, *London Date* (1969)★★★, *Benny Goodman Today* (1970)★★★, *Live In Stockholm* (1970)★★★, *On Stage With Benny Goodman And His Sextet* (1972)★★★★, *Seven Come Eleven* (1975)★★★, *The King* (1978)★★★, *Carnegie Hall Reunion Concert* (1978)★★★★, *King Of Swing* (1980)★★★★, *The Famous 1938 Carnegie Hall Jazz Concert* (Columbia/Legacy 1998)★★★★.

● COMPILATIONS: have been made available of the following sessions *BG With Ben Pollack* (1926-31)★★★, *The Rare BG* (1927-29)★★★, *The Formative Years* (1927-34)★★★★, *Benny Goodman's Boys* (1928-29)★★★, *The Hotsy Totsy Gang With Benny Goodman* (1928-30)★★★, *Benny Goodman On The Side* (1929-31)★★★, *Red Nichols Featuring Benny Goodman* (1929-31)★★★, *Ben Selvin And His Orchestra Featuring Benny Goodman Vols 1, 2, 3* (1929-33)★★★, *Benny Goodman In A Melotone Manner* (1930-31)★★★, *Ted Lewis And His Band Featuring Benny Goodman* (1931-32)★★★, *Benny Goodman Accompanies The Girls* (1931-33)★★★, *Benny Goodman: The Early Years* (1931-35)★★★★, *BG With Chick Bullock And Steve Washington* (1933)★★★, *Breakfast Ball* (1934)★★★, *BG With Adrian Rollini And His Orchestra* (1933-34)★★★, *The 'Let's Dance' Broadcasts Vols 1-3* (1934-35)★★★, *The Rhythm Makers Vols 1, 2, 3* (1935)★★★, *The Indispensable Benny Goodman Vols 1/2* (1935-36)★★★★, *The Complete Small Combinations Vols 1/2* (1935-37)★★★, *This Is Benny Goodman* (1935-39)★★★★, *Benny Goodman From The Congress Hotel Vols 1-4* (1936)★★★, *The Indispensable Benny Goodman Vols 3/4* (1936-37)★★★★, *BG - The Camel Caravan Vols 1 & 2* (1937)★★★, *Benny Goodman At The Madhattan Room Vols 1-11* (1937)★★★, *Benny Goodman Trio And Quartet Live* (1937-38)★★★★, *The Complete Small Combinations Vols 3/4* (1937-39)★★★★, *Swingtime* (1938)★★★, *Solo Flight: Charlie Christian With The Benny Goodman Sextet And Orchestra* (1939-41)★★★★, *Charlie Christian With The Benny Goodman Sextet And Orchestra* (1939-41)★★★, *Benny And Sid 'Roll 'Em'* (1941)★★★, *Benny Goodman On V-Disc* (1941-46)★★★★, *The Forgotten Year* (1943)★★★, *Benny Goodman On The Fitch Bandwagon* (1944-45)★★★, *Benny Goodman Featuring Jess Stacy* (1944-47)★★★, *Live 1945 Broadcasts* (1945)★★★, *Benny Goodman In Sweden* (1950)★★★, *The Benny Goodman Yale Archives Vols-1-3* (1955-86)★★★★, *Swing Sessions* 1946 recording (Hindsight 1996)★★★★, *The Complete RCA Victor Small Group Recordings* 3-CD box set (BMG/RCA Victor 1997)★★★★.

Classical recordings include Mozart's *Clarinet Concerto KV 622*, Mozart's *Clarinet Quintet KV 581*, Weber's *Clarinet Concerto No 1 in F Minor, Op 73*, Weber's *Clarinet Concerto No 2 in E Flat, Op 74.*, *Benny Goodman's Greatest Hits* (Columbia 1966)★★★, *The Hits Of Benny Goodman* (Capitol 1961)★★★,*The Alternate Goodman Vols 1-9* (Nostalgia 1982)★★★★, *Benny Goodman* (Flapper 1991)★★★, *The Birth Of Swing 1935-36* (Bluebird 1992)★★★★, *King Of Swing (1935-5)* (Giants Of Jazz 1992)★★★★, *Air Checks 1937-1938* (Sony 1993)★★★.

● FURTHER READING: *The Kingdom Of Swing*, Benny Goodman and Irving Kolodin. *Benny Goodman: Listen To His Legacy*, D. Russell Connor. *Benny Goodman And The Swing Era*, James Lincoln Collier. *Swing, Swing, Swing: The Life And Times Of Benny Goodman*, Ross Firestone. *BG On The Record: A Bio-Discography Of Benny Goodman*, D. Russell Connor and W. Hicks Warren. *Benny, King Of Swing*, Benny Goodman. *Benny Goodman*, Bruce Crowther.

GOODWIN, HENRY

b. Henry Clay Goodwin, 2 January 1910, Columbia, South Carolina, USA, d. 2 July 1979. While still a young teenager Goodwin played several instruments with sufficient ability to secure a place in a band Claude Hopkins took to Europe. Back in the USA he played with several bands, mostly in New York, during the late 20s, by now playing the trumpet. In the early 30s he was in Europe again, this time with the Lucky Millinder band. On his return to the USA he worked with many bands including those of Cab Calloway and Sidney Bechet, then visited Scandinavia with a band that included Edgar Hayes and was led by Kenny Clarke. In the mid-40s he played with Cecil Scott, Art Hodges, Mezz Mezzrow and Bob Wilbur. The 50s found Goodwin playing with Earl 'Fatha' Hines and many other bandleaders, usually in bands specializing in the more traditional areas of jazz. An inventive soloist with a penchant for the effects created by plunger mute, he was a stalwart of the Dixieland revival without ever becoming bogged down in the repetitiveness that afflicted many of his colleagues.

● ALBUMS: *Bob Wilber And His Jazz Band* (Circle/Jazzology 1949)★★★, *Willie 'The Lion' Smith And His Band* (Urania 1957)★★★.

● COMPILATIONS: *Sidney Bechet, 1932-43: The Bluebird Sessions* (Bluebird 1932-43)★★★★, *Edgar Hayes 1937-1938* (Classics 1937-38)★★★, *The Chronological Slim Gaillard, 1939-1940* (Classics 1939-40)★★★★.

GORDON, DEXTER

b. 27 February 1923, Los Angeles, California, USA, d. 1990. Gordon began his musical career studying clarinet; by his mid-teens he had switched to tenor saxophone, on which instrument he played with Lionel Hampton in 1940. He stayed with Hampton for a little over two years, recording with the band and gaining in stature so that no less an artist than Coleman Hawkins could nominate him, in 1941, as one of his favourite tenor players. Gordon then worked with Lee Young, his own small group, Fletcher Henderson, Louis Armstrong and Billy Eckstine. By late 1944 Gordon had absorbed many of the new developments in jazz and his exposure to numerous eager beboppers in the Eckstine band soon won him over completely. In the next few years he played frequently on both the east and west coasts, comfortably ignoring the artificial but effective dividing line in the bop of the early 50s. Amongst his playing partners of this period was Wardell Gray, with whom he made several important and much-imitated records. During the rest of the 50s Gordon's career was disrupted by his addiction to narcotics, but by the 60s he was off drugs and playing better than ever. Throughout the 60s and into the 70s he toured extensively, becoming especially popular in Europe where he mostly resided. He returned to the USA in 1976 and continued to record, attracting considerable attention with his mature yet evolving style. His personal life was then in some disarray due to a second broken marriage and a drink problem. He reached a turning point in 1986 when he secured an acting role in a feature film. He had previously dabbled with acting in the early 60s, but the leading role in a major film was a very different matter. He rose to the challenge and the film, *'Round Midnight*, was widely considered an artistic and commercial success with Gordon being nominated for an Academy Award for his portrayal of an alcoholic saxophonist. One of the outstanding tenor saxophonists in jazz, Gordon's early influences gave him a deeply felt appreciation of swing. Although he was rightly regarded as a major figure in bop, his playing always displayed his awareness of the swing era cadences. In his uptempo performances, especially in his duets and duels with Gray, there is a thrusting aggression to his playing. On ballads he could be tough or tender, able to enhance any tune through his unique combination of experience and inspiration. His recordings stand as eloquent testimony to a man who influenced many musicians. Perhaps because he was not at his best in his later years (one drummer who worked with him then described the experience as 'a crash course in playing slow'), Gordon was largely ignored by record companies during the 80s, recording only the soundtrack album for *'Round Midnight* between 1982 and his death in 1990. However, in 1985 Blue Note Records, for whom he had made many of his finest records in the 60s, did release the double *Nights At The Keystone*, comprising live recordings from 1978-79, and later added more material from the same sessions to make up a three-volume CD set with the same title, which was reissued in 1990.

● ALBUMS: *Dexter Gordon Quintet* (Dial 1950)★★★★, *All Star Series - Dexter Gordon* (Savoy 1951)★★★★, *New Trends In Modern Jazz Vol. 3* (Savoy 1952)★★★★, *Daddy Plays The Horn* (Bethlehem 1955)★★★, *Dexter Blows Hot And Cool* (Dootone 1956)★★★, with Howard McGhee *The Chase* (Jazztone 1956)★★★, *Dexter Rides Again* 1945-1947 recordings (Savoy 1958)★★★, *The Resurgence Of Dexter Gordon* (Jazzland 1960)★★★, *Doin' Alright* (Blue Note 1961)★★★★, *Dexter Calling* (Blue Note 1961)★★★★, *Go* (Blue Note 1962)★★★★, *A Swingin' Affair* (Blue Note 1962)★★★★, *Cry Me A River* (Steeple Chase 1962)★★, *Our Man In Paris* (Blue Note 1963)★★★★, *One Flight Up* (Blue Note 1964)★★★★, *Cheese Cake* (Steeple Chase 1964)★★, *King Neptune* (Steeple Chase 1964)★★★, *I Want More* (Steeple Chase 1964)★★★, *It's You Or No One* (Steeple Chase 1964)★★, *Billie's Bounce* (Steeple Chase 1964)★★, *Love For Sale* (Steeple Chase 1964)★★, *Clubhouse* (Blue Note 1965)★★★, *Gettin' Around* (Blue Note 1965)★★★★, with Booker Ervin *Settin' The Pace* (Prestige 1967)★★★, *The Montmartre Collection* (1967)★★★, *Take The 'A' Train* (Black Lion 1967)★★, *Both Sides Of Midnight* (Black Lion 1967)★★★, *Body And Soul* (Black Lion 1967)★★, *Live At The Amsterdam Paradiso* (1969)★★★, *The Tower Of Power/More Power* (Prestige 1969)★★★, with Karin Krog *Some Other Spring* (1970)★★★, with Gene Ammons *The Chase!* (Prestige 1970)★★★, *At Montreaux* (Prestige 1970)★★★, *The Panther* (1970)★★, with Jackie McLean *The Meeting* (Steeple Chase 1973)★★★, with McLean *The Source* (Steeple Chase 1974)★★★, *The Apartment* (Steeple Chase 1974)★★, *Bouncin' With Dex* (Steeple Chase 1975)★★★, *Stable Mable* (Steeple Chase 1975)★★★, *Homecoming* (1976)★★, *Lullaby For A Monster* (Steeple Chase 1977)★★, *Biting The Apple* (Steeple Chase 1977)★★★, *Sophisticated Giant* (1977)★★★, *More Tha You Know* (Steeple Chase 1977)★★, *Something Different* (Steeple Chase 1977)★★★, *Midnight Dream* (West Wind 1977)★★★, *Nights At The Keystone Vol 1-3* (Blue Note 1979)★★★, *Gotham City* (1981)★★★, *American Classic* (1982)★★★, *'Round Midnight: Soundtrack* (1986)★★★, *A Gordon Cantata* recorded 1978 (West Wind 1993)★★★, *Live At Carnegie Hall: Complete*

(Columbia/Legacy 1998)★★★★, *The Squirrel* 1967 live recording (Blue Note 1998)★★★.

● COMPILATIONS: *Best Of Dexter Gordon: The Blue Note Years* (Blue Note 1988)★★★★, *Ballads* (Blue Note 1992)★★★★, *The Complete Blue Note Sixties Sessions* 6-CD box set (Blue Note 1996)★★★★, *The Art Of The Ballad* (Prestige 1998)★★★★.

● VIDEOS: *The Dexter Gordon Quartet* (Rhapsody 1995).

● FURTHER READING: *Long Tall Dexter*, Stan Britt.

GORDON, JOE

b. Joseph Henry Gordon, 15 May 1928, Boston, Massachusetts, USA, d. 4 November 1963, Santa Monica, California, USA. After taking formal tuition on trumpet, Gordon began playing jazz professionally in the late 40s. In addition to leading his own small group in and around his home town, he also gained experience through the early 50s sitting in with visiting musicians and playing in several well known bands. He subsequently worked with top-flight artists such as Georgie Auld, Lionel Hampton, Charlie 'Bird' Parker and Art Blakey, appearing on the latter's *The Jazz Messengers Featuring Art Blakey*. In the middle of the decade he toured and recorded with Dizzy Gillespie, and also recorded with Horace Silver and the Herb Pomeroy big band. After moving to Los Angeles towards the end of the 50s, Gordon again played in important company, recording with Benny Carter and Shelly Manne, appearing with the latter on 1960's *The Proper Time*. A fierce and dynamic hard bop trumpeter, Gordon's abilities were barely stretched by the time of his early death.

● ALBUMS: *Introducing Joe Gordon* (EmArcy 1955)★★★, *Lookin' Good* (Contemporary 1961)★★★.

GORDON, JOHN

b. 30 May 1939, USA. Gordon began playing trombone as a child and later studied formally at the Juilliard School Of Music in New York. He played professionally with various bands including several in the blues idiom and was also with Buddy Johnson. When he was 22 he joined Lionel Hampton where he remained for a year, then returned to his studies. For seven years he was with R&B star Lloyd Price whose musical director at the time was Slide Hampton. In 1962 he began a 20-year stint in Broadway pit bands, appearing also on many recordings on Motown Records. He found time for jazz engagements during this period, including spells with Clark Terry, Count Basie, Howard McGhee, Frank Foster and Lionel Hampton. He was a founder member of Trombones Incorporated (later known as Trombones Unlimited) and he also worked with Al Grey's Trombone Summit. In the early 90s he played in bands led by Illinois Jacquet and he also toured and recorded with a trombone trio alongside Slide Hampton and Joshua Roseman. At this time Gordon was also an occasional member of Nancy Banks's big band and of a trio which included Curtis Fuller. An extremely gifted technician, Gordon plays with drive and enthusiasm and his work with other trombonists has helped improve the instrument's following in the post-bop era after some years of neglect as a front-line jazz voice.

GOTA AND THE LOW DOG

London, England-based jazz/funk group Gota And The Low Dog are led by Japanese drummer and multi-instrumentalist Gota Yashiki. A veteran of sessions with Simply Red, Sinead O'Connor and Soul II Soul, he formed the band, originally called Gota And The Heart Of Gold, with Warren Dowd (vocals), Kenji Jammer (guitar) and Yolanda Charles (bass). *Somethin' To Think About*, their 1994 debut album, featured a pleasant blend of funk and soul influences, with a high quality of musicianship throughout. *High Wired Electro* drew its aesthetic from the 70s/80s electro hybrid of hip-hop, with several instrumentals and disorientating free-form jazz sketches similar to the more experimental work of Herbie Hancock. It included the single 'Hey Bulldog', a rare cover version of the Beatles' song from the film *Yellow Submarine*. Yashiki released his solo debut in 1997.

● ALBUMS: *Somethin' To Talk About* (RPL 1994)★★★, *Live Wired Electro* (RPL 1995)★★★, as Gota *It's So Different Here* (Instinct 1997)★★★.

GOTTLIEB, DANNY

b. Daniel Richard Gottlieb, 18 April 1953, New York City, New York, USA. Gottlieb studied percussion intensively, as a pupil of Mel Lewis and Joe Morello while still at school, and later at university. His professional career began while he was at the University of Miami, when he played with musicians such as Pat Metheny, Paul Bley and Jaco Pastorius. This was in the early 70s, and although whenever possible he worked in jazz, he also played in rock bands. In the middle of the decade he became a member of Gary Burton's quartet, recording 1976's *Passengers*, subsequently joining a band formed by fellow sideman Metheny. He remained with Metheny into the early 80s, recording albums such as *American Garage*. By the time he left, the group's popularity had helped establish Gottlieb's name around the world. Simultaneously he had begun a musical association with Mark Egan, a founder member of Metheny's group, and with him he formed a band named Elements. Overlapping his work with Egan he played with John McLaughlin (*Mahavishnu*), and Al Di Meola (*Soaring Through A Dream*). A strikingly eclectic player, Gottlieb has consistently worked in harmony with a wide range of performers, including Gil Evans, Stan Getz, Sting, the Blues Brothers, Ahmad Jamal and, in a late 90s recording session, John Abercrombie. A fleet and subtle drummer, Gottlieb is a very supportive player, ably finding appropriate backing for the many and diverse musicians with whom he works. In addition to teaching and organizing clinics, he has also appeared in instructional videos.

● ALBUMS: *Aquamarine* (Atlantic 1987)★★★, *Whirlwind* (Atlantic 1989)★★★, *Brooklyn Blues* (Big World 1991)★★★.

GOUDIE, FRANK 'BIG BOY'

b. Frank Goudie, 13 September 1899, Youngsville, Louisiana, USA, d. 9 January 1964. Goudie grew up in New Orleans, where he first played cornet and piano before switching to reed instruments, principally the tenor saxophone. He worked with numerous bands in the city, including Papa Celestin's, before touring extensively in the south-western states. In 1925 he left for Europe, where he remained for several years, playing in bands led by touring Americans who included showman-drummer Louis Mitchell, Sam Wooding, Noble Sissle, Bill Coleman and Willie Lewis. Upon the outbreak of World War II, Goudie left Europe for South America but was back in 1946. During the next few years he lived and worked in France, Germany and Switzerland, and renewed his association with Coleman. In 1957 he finally returned to America, settling in San Francisco where he worked outside music but continued to play in local clubs, especially when jazz stars visited the city. A solid, workmanlike performer, Goudie's 30 years in voluntary exile from the USA made him a marginal figure in jazz. Nevertheless, his long domicile in Europe meant that he was influential in widening the appeal of jazz in many countries.

● COMPILATIONS: *Willie Lewis And His Entertainers* (1935-37 recordings)★★★.

GOULD, TONY

b. Anthony James Gould, 2 February 1940, Melbourne, Victoria, Australia. After playing piano semi-professionally Gould began attracting notice on the Australian jazz scene in the early 60s, and later in the decade became linked with Brian Brown. Soon after this Gould entered a period during which he extended his studies, taught, engaged in lecture tours and, while retaining his interest in jazz, also performed with symphony orchestras and chamber music ensembles. In the mid-70s, he returned to the jazz audience's attention to take a significant role as performer and composer. Throughout his career, Gould's contribution to Australian jazz, especially to the stylistic cutting edge, has been invaluable.

● ALBUMS: *Gould Plays Gould* (Move 1978)★★★, *Best Of Friends* (Move 1984)★★★.

GOWANS, BRAD

b. Arthur Bradford Gowans, 3 December 1903, Billerica, Massachusetts, USA, d. 8 September 1954. A child prodigy on a wide range of brass and reed instruments, Gowans first played professionally in the early and mid-20s, happily switching back and forth between instruments. Among the bands with which he played were those led by Joe Venuti, Mal Hallett, Jimmy Durante and Red Nichols. After a spell outside music he joined Bobby Hackett in 1936 and during the next few years worked with Joe Marsala, Bud Freeman, Ray McKinley, Art Hodes and Eddie Condon. After World War II he played with Max Kaminsky, Jimmy Dorsey and Nappy Lamare, again using a variety of instruments but notably the valve-trombone. Apart from his extraordinary instrumental command, Gowans was also a good arranger, supplying charts in a range of styles for McKinley's big band, for Freeman's small group and for singer Lee Wiley.

GOYKOVICH, DUSKO

b. 14 October 1931, Jajce, Yugoslavia. After completing his formal studies at the Academy of Music in Belgrade, Goykovich played trumpet and flügelhorn in various dancebands and radio orchestras in Europe, including those of Max Greger and Kurt Edelhagen. In the late 50s he travelled to the USA, played at the Newport Jazz Festival and then pursued his studies at Berklee College Of Music. Thereafter, like many Berklee alumni, he entered the bands of Maynard Ferguson and Woody Herman. Back in Europe he played in the small group led by Sal Nistico and then joined the Clarke-Boland Big Band, where he remained for five years until 1973. In the 70s Goykovich's associates included Slide Hampton and Alvin Queen. He also worked extensively in radio and education in Europe. A fine post-bop trumpeter, Goykovich's style derives from early Miles Davis, but the inclusion of traditional melodies from his homeland in his playing makes him a distinctive soloist. In the 90s Goykovich toured European venues, both as a soloist and in tandem with Italian alto saxophonist Gianni Basso.

● ALBUMS: *Swinging Macedonia* (Enja 1965)★★★, *After Hours* (1971)★★★, *A Day In Holland* (1983)★★, *Celebration* (DIW 1987)★★★, *Soul Connection* (Enja 1994)★★★, *Bebop City* (Enja 1995)★★★, *Balkan Blue* recorded 1992/94 (Enja 1997)★★.

GOZZO, CONRAD

b. 6 February 1922, New Britain, Connecticut, USA, d. 8 October 1964. Gozzo's first notable appearance was in 1938 as a member of the trumpet section of the polished Isham Jones band. In the early 40s he played with several big bands of the swing era, including those led by Red Norvo, Claude Thornhill and Benny Goodman. While serving in the US Navy during World War II he played in the band led by Artie Shaw. After the war he returned to Goodman, played with Woody Herman, Boyd Raeburn and others, then settled in Los Angeles where he was active in the studios. During the 50s he made many record dates, some under his own name and others with leaders such as Herman, Ray Anthony, Shorty Rogers, Stan Kenton, Billy May, Cy Touff, Glen Gray's Casa Loma Orchestra and Goodman. Although he was a good soloist, Gozzo's greatest contribution to big band music lay in his talent as a lead trumpeter.

● ALBUMS: with Billy May *My Album* (1951)★★★, with Shorty Rogers *Cool And Crazy/Blues Express* (1955)★★★★, with May *Sorta May* (1954)★★, *The Benny Goodman Story* (1955)★★★★, *Cy Touff, His Octet and Quintet/Havin' A Ball* (1955)★★★, *Goz The Great* (RCA Victor 1955)★★★★, with Casa Loma *Sounds Of The Great Bands Vols 1-3* (1958-60)★★★, with May *The Girls And Boys On Broadway* (1960)★★★.

GRACE, TEDDY

b. Stella Gloria Crowson, 26 June 1905, Arcadia, Louisiana, USA, d. 4 January 1992. Born into a middle-class white family in the Deep South, Grace studied piano and guitar as a child but was fascinated by the black music which pervaded the region. While still a young teenager, her parents died and she lived for a while in Virginia before returning to Louisiana where she met and, at 19, married a local businessman named Grace (she had been nicknamed 'Teddy' from childhood). With her husband, she settled in Mongomery, Alabama, and became a member of the local country club set. One night in 1931, at a club dinner party, she responded to a 'dare' by going up to the microphone to sing with the band. The result electrified the audience and within a very short space of time she was broadcasting over local radio stations, appearing at clubs and in theatres. Owing to radio remotes she was heard widely and in 1933 was hired by Al Katz and eventually went with him to New York. There, in 1934, she was signed to sing with Mal Hallett, one of the most popular of the second-string dance bands of the pre-swing era years. With Hallett she worked extensively along the east coast. Her travelling conflicted with her husband's plans and they were divorced. Nevertheless, during 1935 the hard grind of endless one-night stands became too much for her and she left Hallett and remarried. Two years later she returned to Hallett and began her recording career with him for Decca Records. The company also recorded her under her own name, including a session with Jack Teagarden during which some serious drinking took place and the trombonist eventually passed out. As she left the studio, Grace remarked to pianist Billy Kyle, 'When that Indian wakes up tell him he's a helluva musician but he can't drink worth a damn'. Surprisingly given Decca's attitude towards jazz and blues at the time, she also made a set of 10 blues songs. These were issued as an album of 78s, *Blues Sung By Teddy Grace*, and were very well received and led many listeners to think that she was black. In September 1940 Grace also recorded with Bob Crosby's band and with Bud Freeman's Cumma Sum Lauda Orchestra. During the session she told Freeman that she was disillusioned with the music business in general and with Decca in particular and that she was quitting. When the USA entered World War II Grace, who was again divorced, joined the WACs and worked hard as a recruiter, organizing shows and touring extensively. In 1944 she was taken ill, lost her voice and was hospitalized. It was six months before her voice returned and when it did it was in such a state that, regardless of personal choice, she was unable to sing again. In 1946 she left the army, remarried and moved to the west coast and a secretarial job. In 1991, by now living in a nursing home, she was tracked down by journalist David W. McCain. The subsequent article resulted in mail from fans who thought that she was already dead. McCain's article and the response to it came only just in time to assure the singer that she was not forgotten. Grace's voice was used expressively on ballads which she sang with poise and care. When singing the blues she could be effectively growly. She is a noteworthy singer even if, due to her unusual career, she is too often overlooked.

● COMPILATIONS: *Teddy Grace* (Timeless CBC 1937-40)★★★.

GRAETTINGER, BOB

b. 31 October 1923, Ontario, Canada, d. 12 March 1957. Early in his professional career, Graettinger composed fairly orthodox material for the bands of Benny Carter, Alvino Rey and others; but in the late 40s he became associated with Stan Kenton, where his work began to explore new areas. He took a principle adopted by Duke Ellington, that of writing each part with a specific musician in mind, to extremes, creating music that was not only difficult to play but in which each part was independent of any other. He travelled with the Kenton band, listening to each musician in turn until he knew exactly what their individual capabilities were. His unusual approach to writing extended to the form his arrangements took on paper; he used colours and symbols to indicate the sound he wanted the musicians to achieve. His major works for Kenton were the suites 'City Of Glass' and 'This Modern World', both of which anticipated the atonality later explored by freeform jazz musicians.

● ALBUMS: all by Stan Kenton *City Of Glass* (Capitol 1952)★★★, *This Modern World* (Capitol 1953)★★★.

GRAHAM, KENNY

b. Kenneth Thomas Skingle, 19 July 1924, London, England, d. 17 February 1997. Graham first played professionally at the age of 15, making his debut on alto saxophone with the Nottingham-based Rube Sunshine band. He later moved to London to join Billy Smith at the Cricklewood Palais but used his spare time to good effect, by touring London clubs where he met and played with well-known British jazzmen such as Jack Parnell and Nat Gonella. He spent some time with Johnny Claes's Claepigeons, a band that included drummer Carlo Krahmer (who later founded Esquire Records). After military service during World War II he worked with a variety of bands, including Ambrose and Macari and his Dutch Serenaders and was by that point usually heard on tenor saxophone. In April 1950 Graham introduced his own band, the Afro-Cubists, who successfully fused bebop with Latin and Caribbean rhythms. The band was home to pianist Ralph Dollimore, Phil Seamen and at one time, a five-man saxophone section that included Derek Humble and Joe Temperley. The band folded in 1958 and thereafter Graham concentrated on arranging, his charts being played and recorded by jazz artists as diverse as Ted Heath and Humphrey Lyttelton. Graham proved especially adept at building interesting arrangements upon unusual tonal effects, a good example being his 'Moondog Suite', which developed the ethereal sounds of Louis Hardin, the legendary blind street musician who was recorded on the streets of New York in the early 50s. In the 80s Graham was still writing, and the incorporation of synthesizers and other electronic instruments into his work showed that he had lost none of the enthusiasm for new sounds that had marked his early career. In the 80s he had to supplement his income by taking on extra work, and in his last years he was a warden at an apartment block.

● ALBUMS: *Mango Walk* (Esquire 1953)★★★★, *Caribbean Suite/Afro Kadabra* (Esquire 1953)★★, *Moondog And Suncat Suites* (1956)★★★, *Kenny Graham And His Orchestra* (1957)★★★.

GRAINGER, GARY

b. *c.*1955, Baltimore, Maryland, USA. Grainger began playing bass with his older brother, drummer Gregory Grainger. In the late 70s the pair joined Pockets, recording for Columbia Records, and toured extensively with a package headlined by Earth, Wind And Fire. He first attracted wide attention in the late 80s, playing electric bass with John Scofield on tour and on several recording sessions, including two late 80s Gramavision albums, *Blue Matter* and *Loud Jazz*. After leaving Scofield he teamed up with the band's drummer, Dennis Chambers, forming the funk band, Graffiti. He has also recorded with Carl Filipiak and Haakon Graf. In the late 90s he began working with his brother in a fusion band, designed to display the highly empathetic nature of their musical relationship as well as Grainger's composing skills.

● ALBUMS: *Phase I* (GBM 1997)★★★.

GRANELLI, JERRY

b. Gerald John Granelli, 30 December 1940, San Francisco, California, USA. Granelli began playing drums as a small child, later studying formally and taking tuition from Joe Morello. In the early and mid-60s he played with many musicians including Vince Guaraldi, Denny Zeitlin, Jon Hendricks, Earl 'Fatha' Hines, Mose Allison, Ornette Coleman and Jimmy Witherspoon. This eclectic mix helped contribute to Granelli's questing musical style which continued into the next decade, a time which found him forming his own bands, including Visions, and also teaching, first in Denver and then in Seattle. In the 70s he retired from the jazz scene for several years, co-founding the Naropa Institute in Boulder, Colorado, with Collin Walcott and Allen Ginsberg. Returning to jazz he toured internationally, with Gary Peacock and Ralph Towner among others, and also recorded with singer Jay Clayton. Later, Granelli settled in Germany while still finding time to teach in Halifax, Nova Scotia. He also began recording as a leader, using up-and-coming young German musicians as well as established international stars such as Jane Ira Bloom, Robben Ford, Bill Frisell and Julian Priester. Perhaps as a result of the eclectic nature of his earlier years as a sideman, Granelli's records intriguingly and effectively blend aspects of hard bop, free jazz, blues, jazz-rock fusion, R&B and jazz-funk. In his bands Granelli is very much an ensemble player, adding colour, texture and atmosphere as well as providing a time base which can be fluid without ever losing contact with the reality of the music being performed by his colleagues. He currently plays with UFB, alongside guitarists Kai Brückner and Christian Kögel and bassist Andreas Walter.

● ALBUMS: *Koputai* (ITM Pacific 1989)★★, *Forces Of Flight* (ITM Pacific 1990)★★, *Another Place* (vBr 1992)★★★, *A Song I Thought I Heard Buddy Sing* (Evidence 1993)★★, with UFB *Broken Circle* (Intuition 1997)★★★, with UFB *News From The Street* (Intuition 1998)★★★.

GRANT, COOT, AND SOX WILSON

Coot Grant (b. Leola B. Pettigrew, 17 June 1893, Birmingham, Alabama, USA, d. date unk.) and Wesley Wilson (b. 1 October 1893, Jacksonville, Florida, USA, d. 10 October 1958). Pettigrew used various names including Patsy Hunter but was usually called Coot, for Cutie. She worked in vaudeville as a dancer from early childhood, touring the USA and appearing overseas, including visits to Europe and South Africa in the years before World War I. From around 1905 she sometimes worked with Wilson, a pianist and organist, who also used different names including Kid Wilson, Pigmeat Pete, Jenkins, Socks and Sox Wilson. Around 1912 they married and thereafter worked mostly as a team, usually as Grant And Wilson but occasionally using other combinations of their multiple names, such as Hunter And Jenkins. Additionally, from time to time, each worked alone. They appeared and recorded with leading bands of the day, including Fletcher Henderson's, and also with groups such as the Mezz Mezzrow-Sidney Bechet Quintet. The duo also played in musical comedies, vaudeville, travelling shows and revues, including one with Louis Armstrong. In 1933 they appeared in the film *Emperor Jones*, which starred Paul Robeson, but the 30s were generally not very successful years for the pair. In 1949 Wilson's health was such that they worked less as a team, while Grant kept going a little longer. After Wilson death, nothing more was heard about Grant and her date of death remains unknown. An engaging duo with an effective line in vaudeville and popular material, they were very popular artists of their day.

● COMPILATIONS: *The Vocal Duet* (Clifford Archives 1925-38)★★★.

GRANT, DARRELL

b. 1962, Pittsburgh, Pennsylvania, USA. Grant was raised in Denver, Colorado, and from an early age studied classical and jazz piano. As a youth he toured jazz festivals with the Pearl Street Jazz Band and at 17 took up a scholarship at the Eastman School of Music where he was awarded a BM in Piano Performance. He also attended the University of Miami before coming to New York, where he played with noted musicians including Woody Shaw, Junior Cook and Charlie Persip, and was also involved with the M-Base project. In 1986 his band, Current Events, had a brief recording contract with a major label and in 1988 he joined Betty Carter, becoming one of a succession of fine pianists whose talents were honed in the diva's service. In addition to touring with Carter, he also worked with Tony Williams, Donald Byrd, Roy Haynes and Chico Freeman. He has also played with Greg Osby, appearing on 1993's *3-D Lifestyles*. Towards the end of the 90s, Grant relocated to Toronto, Canada. A strikingly gifted pianist and composer, through his commitment and passion Grant evokes memories of Horace Silver although he is indisputably a thoroughly original performer. In common with many jazz performers, Grant has learned the lesson that theirs is an art scorned by the media. In his case, rather than resign himself to it, he has actively publicized his own engagements resulting in an growing audience base.

● ALBUMS: *Current Events* (Verve 1986)★★★, *Black Art* (Criss Cross 1994)★★★, *The New Bop* (Criss Cross 1996)★★★★, *Twilight Stories* (32 Jazz 1998)★★★.

GRANZ, NORMAN

b. 6 August 1918, Los Angeles, California, USA. A lifelong love of jazz led to Granz's early involvement in music as both film-maker and concert promoter. Together with photographer Gjon Mili, he made *Jammin' The Blues* (1944), still regarded as one of the best jazz short films ever made. Granz also promoted jazz sessions at Los Angeles clubs, insisting upon desegregated audiences. In 1944 he staged a jazz concert at the Philharmonic Auditorium in Los Angeles, an event whose title was shortened to fit the available advertising space. The abbreviated version, Jazz At The Philharmonic, or JATP, became synonymous with concert-hall jam sessions featuring the very best jazz talent. A few of the saxophonists who played at JATP in its formative years were Lester Young, Coleman Hawkins, Charlie Parker, Benny Carter, Charlie Ventura, Illinois Jacquet, Willie Smith and Joe 'Flip' Phillips. Granz insisted on desegregated audiences and first-class travel and hotel accommodation - things of which jazz musicians, especially those who were black, had previously only dreamed. From the start, Granz recorded his concerts and eventually began releasing them, often on labels he owned or controlled, among them Clef, Norgran, Verve and, more recently, Pablo. On record dates, Granz arranged for the return to the studios of several musicians who had been neglected by the major record companies. Among those whose careers were resuscitated was Art Tatum, whom Granz recorded with a wide range of musical partners and also in an extensive series of solo albums. Granz became personal manager for some of the artists he promoted, notably Ella Fitzgerald, with whom he recorded the remarkable 'Songbook' sequence of albums, and Oscar Peterson. Granz was also responsible for recording much of Billie Holiday's later work.

GRAPPELLI, STÉPHANE

b. 26 January 1908, Paris, France, d. 1 December 1997, Paris, France. After learning to play keyboard instruments, Grappelli took up the violin, later studying it formally. In the mid-20s he played in dance bands in Paris, gradually turning more to jazz. In the early 30s he met Django Reinhardt and with him formed the Quintette du Hot Club de France. Until this point in his career Grappelli had been playing piano and violin, but now concentrated on the latter instrument. Performances and especially records by the QHCF alerted the jazz world to the arrival of both an intriguing new sound and, in Reinhardt, the first authentic non-American genius of jazz. In these years Grappelli was still learning, and his early popularity was largely as a result of that of his collaborator. Shortly before the outbreak of World War II Grappelli settled in London, where he played with George Shearing. In the post-war years he worked briefly with Reinhardt again but spent the late 40s and 50s playing to diminishing audiences across Europe. In the 60s he enjoyed a revival of popularity, making records with other violinists such as Stuff Smith and Joe Venuti. In the early 70s he appeared on UK television performing duets with classical violinist Yehudi Menuhin, and the records they made together sold well. However, Grappelli's real breakthrough to the big time had come when, at the urging of Diz Disley, he made appearances at the 1973 UK Cambridge Folk Festival (accompanied by Disley and Denny Wright). Grappelli was a sensation. For the rest of the decade, throughout the 80s and into the early 90s he was on a non-stop tour of the world, playing the most prestigious venues in the UK, Europe, the USA and the Far East. In January 1994, he celebrated his 86th birthday in concert with Stanley Black at London's Barbican Hall. He made records with several backing groups, played duets with Gary Burton, Earl Hines, Martial Solal, Jean-Luc Ponty and many other leading jazzmen. He also ventured into other areas of music and, in addition to the duets with Menuhin, he has recorded with the western swing fiddler, Vassar Clements. At ease with a repertoire based upon his early career successes, Grappelli's flowing style steadily matured over the years and the occasional uncertainties of his early work with Reinhardt are long forgotten. Perhaps at odd moments in his later years he seemed to be coasting, yet some of his recorded performances are very good while several of those from the mid- and late 70s are amongst the most distinguished in the history of jazz violin. Of particular merit are *Parisian Thoroughfare*, recorded with the rhythm section of Roland Hanna, George Mraz and Mel Lewis, and a set recorded at the Queen Elizabeth Hall in London in 1973 when he was backed by Disley and Len Skeat. Grappelli's late flowering much to prompt appreciation of the old tradition of jazz violin playing. His death at the end of 1997 left a gap in music that is unlikely to ever be filled, and certainly never to be bettered.

● ALBUMS: *Improvisations* (EmArcy 1957)★★★, with Stuff Smith *Violins No End* (Original Jazz Classics 1957)★★★, *Feeling + Finesse = Jazz* (Atlantic 1962)★★★, *Django* (1962)★★★, with Svend Asmussen *Two Of A Kind* (Storyville 1965)★★★★, with Asmussen *Violin Summit* (1966)★★★★, *I Remember Django* (1969)★★★★, with Joe Venuti *Venupelli Blues* (1969)★★★★, *Stéphane Grappelli Meets Barney Kessel* (1969)★★★, *I Hear Music*

(1970)★★★, *Satin Doll* (1972)★★★, with Yehudi Menuhin *Jealousy* (1972-73)★★★, *Just One Of Those Things* (1973)★★★, *Parisian Thoroughfare* (1973)★★★★, *I Got Rhythm* (1973)★★★★, *Live At The Queen Elizabeth Hall* (1973)★★★, *Stéphane Grappelli & Jean-Luc Ponty* (1973)★★★★, *Live In London* (1973)★★★, with Earl Hines *Giants* (1974)★★★, with Slam Stewart *Steff And Slam* (1975)★★★, with George Shearing *The Reunion* (1976)★★★, *Steph' 'N' Us* (Cherry Pie 1977)★★★, *Live At Carnegie Hall* (1978)★★★★, *Young Django* (1979)★★★, with Bucky Pizzarelli *Duet* (1979)★★★, *Strictly For The Birds* (1980)★★★, with David Grisman *Live* (Warners 1980)★★★★, *At The Winery* (Concord Jazz 1980)★★★★, with Martin Taylor *We've Got The World On A String* (1980)★★★★, *Vintage 1981* (Concord Jazz 1981)★★★, *Stephanova* (Concord Jazz 1983)★★★, with Teresa Brewer *On The Road Again* (Doctor Jazz 1984)★★★, with Vassar Clements *Together At Last* (1985)★★★, *Stéphane Grappelli Plays Jerome Kern* (1987)★★★, *Stéphane Grappelli In Tokyo* (1990)★★★, *Piano My Other Love* (1990)★★★, *Live At Warsaw Jazz Festival 1991* (1993)★★★, with Marc Fosset *Looking At You* (1993)★★★, with Taylor *Reunion* 1993 recording (Honest 1995)★★★, with Michel Petrucciani *Flamingo* (Dreyfus 1996)★★★★, *Live At The Blue Note* (Telarc 1996)★★★.

● COMPILATIONS: with QHCF *Swing From Paris* (1935-39)★★★★, *Django Reinhardt And Stéphane Grappelli With The Quintet Of The Hot Club Of France* (1935-46)★★★★, with QHFC *Stéphane Grappelli 1947-1961* (1947-61)★★★★, with QHFC *Djangology* (1949)★★★.

● FURTHER READING: *Stéphane Grappelli*, Geoffrey Smith. *Stephane Grappelli, Or, The Violin With Wings*, Raymond Horricks.

GRAUSO, JOE

b. 1897, New York City, New York, USA, d. 11 June 1952. Grauso first played drums professionally while still a teenager, taking all manner of jobs in travelling shows and circuses. He also played in theatre pit bands, playing jazz gigs in-between times. After a period of poor health he returned to work in the early 40s, leading his own band and also playing with a number of jazzmen including Art Hodges, Eddie Condon and Miff Mole. He spent some time with the Muggsy Spanier band and also played drums with Billy Butterfield. A workmanlike drummer, as befits one who learned his trade in brass bands, Grauso supplied a solid foundation for the bands in which he played, although he perhaps lacked the finesse to provide the lift needed for exceptional jazz performances.

● COMPILATIONS: with Muggsy Spanier *Jam Session* (WRT 1943)★★, *Pee Wee Russell Jazz Ensemble* (Stinson 1946)★★★.

GRAVES, MILFORD

b. 20 August 1941, New York, USA. Born into a musical environment (his uncle and grandfather encouraged and coached his interest in music) Graves was playing drums at the age of three, though he had no formal teaching until he was 17. He took up congas when he was eight years old and led his own percussion ensemble and, later, workshops, while at school. He subsequently studied with George Stone in Boston and learned tabla techniques from Washantha Singh. Between 1959 and 1962 he played with dance and Latin bands around New York. He heard and was impressed by Elvin Jones with John Coltrane's group in 1961 and in 1963 decided to concentrate on his own ideas rather than stay with commercial gigs. His first recordings were all on the ESP label and included appearances with the New York Art Quartet (with John Tchicai, Archie Shepp and Lewis Warrell), pianists Lowell Davidson and Paul Bley (*Barrage*), saxophonist Giuseppi Logan and his own *Percussion Duo* with Sunny Morgan. In 1965 he and Don Pullen set up their own SRP label, later releasing three duo albums and in 1969 Graves began a long association with Andrew Cyrille, with whom he recorded *Dialogue Of The Drums* in 1974. Back in 1965 he began researching into the medical and psychological uses of music. He was also involved in the Storefront Museum, a community arts project in his home area of Jamaica, in the borough of Queens, New York City. An important figure in the 60s free jazz movement, he made an impression on a wider audience with two appearances at the 1973 Newport in New York Jazz Festival, but within two years he was forced to earn his living from teaching rather than performing. He has worked or recorded with Albert Ayler, Sonny Sharrock (*Black Woman*), Miriam Makeba, the Jazz Composer's Orchestra Association, and in a percussion trio with Cyrille and Rashied Ali and in a percussion quartet, Pieces Of Time, with Cyrille, Don Moye and Kenny Clarke (later Philly Joe Jones). Many of the musicians he worked with in the early and mid-60s have credited him with being the first drummer to provide the combination of looseness and rhythmic propulsion that the new music needed.

● ALBUMS: *Milford Graves Percussion Ensemble* (ESP 1966)★★★, with Don Pullen *Graves-Pullen Duo* (Pullen-Graves 1967)★★★, with Pullen *Nommo* (SRP 1967)★★, with Giuseppi Logan *The Guiseppi Logan Quartet* (1964)★★, with Andrew Cyrille *Dialogue Of The Drums* (1974)★★★, with David Murray *Real Deal* 1991 recording (DIW 1993)★★★★.

GRAY, WARDELL

b. 13 February 1921, Oklahoma City, Oklahoma, USA, d. 25 May 1955. Growing up in Detroit, Gray first played clarinet before switching to tenor saxophone and joining the Earl 'Fatha' Hines band in 1943. After two years he relocated on the west coast, where he became prominent among local beboppers, notably Dexter Gordon, with whom he played at Central Avenue clubs such as The Bird In The Basket. Gray made some successful recordings with Gordon, among them 'The Chase' and 'The Hunt', and also composed a number of tunes himself, including 'Twisted', which, with lyrics added, became popular with scat singers. In the late 40s and early 50s Gray worked with Benny Carter, Billy Eckstine and Count Basie, and was a member of Benny Goodman's short-lived bebop big band where he elicited a rare compliment from Goodman, who never really liked bebop: 'If Wardell Gray plays bop then it's great because he's wonderful.' He also played in a Goodman small group alongside Stan Hasselgård. Gray's tone was soft and he played light, flowing lines that reflected the influence Lester Young had upon him. Gray died on 25 May 1955 in circumstances that have never been fully resolved: his body was found in the Nevada Desert, his neck broken. The official report gave the cause of death as a drug overdose, though there was no autopsy, and rumours persisted that Gray had been murdered - either for failing to pay gambling debts or simply as a random victim of racial violence.

● ALBUMS: *Way Out Wardell* (Boplicity 1947)★★★★, with Don Lanphere *Thin Man Meets Fat Boy, Vols. 1 & 2* (c.1949-50)★★★★, with Leo Parker *Thin Man Meets Mad Lad* (c.1949-50)★★★, *Live In Hollywood* (1952)★★, *Out Of Nowhere* (1952)★★★, *Live At The Haig 1952* (Fresh Sound 1952)★★.

● COMPILATIONS: *Wardell Gray And The Big Bands* (1945-53)★★★, *One For Prez* (Black Lion 1946)★★★, *Easy Swing* (Swingtime 1946-55)★★★, *The Hunt* (1947)★★★, with Benny Goodman, Stan Hasselgård *Swedish Pastry/Benny's Bop* (1948)★★★★, *Light Gray Vol. 1* (1948-50)★★★, *Central Avenue* (1949-50)★★★, *Memorial* (1949-53)★★★★, *The Hunt* (Savoy 1979)★★★, *Central Avenue* (RCA 1979)★★★, *1947-52* (Giants Of Jazz 1987)★★★★, *Vol. 1, 1944-46* (Masters Of Jazz 1998)★★★.

GREAT GUITARS

(see Byrd, Charlie; Ellis, Herb; Kessel, Barney)

GRÉCO, JULIETTE

b. 1927, Montpelier, France. An actress and inimitable singer of the *chanson*, Gréco was born the daughter of a police chief and a Resistance worker. After spending some time in prison during the Occupation when she was 15, Gréco took acting lessons, and began to dress in men's black clothing - heavy overcoats and trousers, with polo neck sweaters. In the mid-40s she became a leading member of the philosopher Jean-Paul Sartre's intellectual Existentialist movement, which flourished in cafés such as Le Boeuf sur le Toit and Café Flore on Paris's Left Bank. Sartre encouraged her to sing, and with her slightly raw-edged voice, attractive appearance and impressive stage presence, she soon became immensely popular in the world of cabaret. Among her most memorable - and usually sad - songs are Hubert Giraud and Jean Drejec's 'Sous Le Ciel De Paris' ('Under Paris Skies'), Jacques Brel's 'J'arrive' and 'Je Suis Bien', along with several written by Joseph Kosma and Jacques Prevert, including 'Les Feuilles Mortes', which, with an English lyric by Johnny Mercer, became the wistful 'Autumn Leaves'. After appearing in a few French films from 1949 onwards, in the late 50s Gréco embarked on a brief Hollywood career sponsored by Darryl F. Zanuck, starring in *The Sun Also Rises*, *Roots Of Heaven*, *Crack In The Mirror* and *The Big Gamble*. Afterwards, she returned to her *chansons*, and has continued to sing ever since. Her popularity in Britain has waned since the 50s, but she did perform in London in 1989 for the first time in 10 years. In the previous year, Gréco married her musical director and accompanist Gérard Jouannest. Her previous husbands, Philippe Lemaire and Michel Piccoli, were both actors.

● ALBUMS: *Juliette Greco* (Philips 1954)★★★, *Gréco* (Philips 1957)★★, *Les Grandes Chansons* (Philips 1961)★★★★, *Juliette Gréco Showcase* (Philips 1962)★★★, *La Femme* (Philips 1968)★★, *Juliette Gréco* (French Decca 1972)★★★, *Je Vous Attends* (French Decca 1974)★★, *Le Disque D'Or* (Phonogram 1974)★★.

● COMPILATIONS: *Greatest Hits* (Impact 1977)★★★.

● FILMS: including *Au Royaume Des Cieux* (1949), *Orpheus* (1950), *The Green Glove* (1952), *Quand Tu Liras Cette Lettre* (1953), *Paris Does Strange Things* (1956), *The Sun Also Rises* (1957), *Bonjour Tristesse* (1958), *Naked Earth* (1958), *Roots Of Heaven* (1959), *Whirlpool* (1959), *Crack In The Mirror* (1960), *The Big Gamble* (1961), *Where The Truth Lies* (1962), *Uncle Tom's Cabin* (1965), *The Night Of The Generals* (1967).

GREEN, BENNIE

b. 16 April 1923, Chicago, Illinois, USA, d. 23 March 1977, San Diego, California, USA. After playing locally for a while during his teenage years, trombonist Green joined the bebop-orientated Earl 'Fatha' Hines band in 1942. He continued to be associated with Hines until the early 50s, his spells with the band being interrupted by military service and periods working with Charlie Ventura, the band co-led by Gene Ammons and Sonny Stitt and the small groups he led himself. In the late 60s he was briefly with Duke Ellington, then settled in Las Vegas, where he worked in various hotel and casino house bands. Green's playing ranged widely, encompassing the swing-era style prominent during his formative years; he was one of only a few trombonists to adapt comfortably to bebop, and he also played R&B.

● ALBUMS: with J.J. Johnson, Kai Winding *Jazz Workshop, Vol. 1* 10-inch album (Debut 1953)★★★, with Johnson, Winding *Jazz Workshop, Vol. 2* 10-inch album (Debut 1953)★★★, with Paul Quinchette *Blow Your Horn* (Decca 1955)★★★, *Bennie Green Blows His Horn* 10-inch album (Prestige 1955)★★★★, with Art Farmer *Bennie Green & Art Farmer* (Prestige 1956)★★★★, with Johnson, Winding *Trombone By Three* (Prestige 1956)★★★★, with Johnson, Winding *J.J. Johnson, Kai Winding, Bennie Green* (Prestige 1956)★★★★, *Walking Down* (Prestige 1956)★★★★, *Back On The Scene* (Blue Note 1958)★★★, *Soul Stirrin'* (Blue Note 1958)★★★★, *Walkin' And Talkin'* (Blue Note 1959)★★★★, *The Swingin'est* (Vee Jay 1960)★★★, *Bennie Green* (Time 1960)★★★, *Bennie Green Swings The Blues* (Enrica 1960)★★★, *Catwalk* (Bethlehem 1961)★★★, *Glidin' Along* (Jazzland 1961)★★★, *Futura* (RCA Victor 1961)★★★.

GREEN, BENNY

b. 4 April 1963, New York City, New York, USA. An exciting and hard-swinging pianist in the Bud Powell mould, Benny Green ranks alongside Mulgrew Miller and Donald Brown, as one of a number of talented hard-bop keyboard stars to have graduated from Art Blakey's Jazz Messengers training ground during America's hard-bop revival of the 80s, leading bands and establishing his own voice towards the end of the decade. A student of classical piano from the age of seven, Green developed a taste for jazz through the influence of his tenor saxophone playing father, and was keen enough as a child to start borrowing records and imitating the bebop sounds of the 40s and 50s. He played in school bands, until his keen ear and obvious commitment brought him to the attention of singer Fay Carroll, with whom he got his first real taste of a working jazz band - learning invaluable lessons about accompaniment and the blues, and gaining his first chance to play in a trio context as a way of opening the set. Still in his teens, he filled the piano chair in a quintet co-led by trumpeter Eddie Henderson and saxophonist Hadley Caliman, and a 12-piece led by bassist Chuck Israels. On finishing high-school, Green moved to the west coast and freelanced around the San Francisco Bay area, gaining experience working as a sideman. But it was with his return to New York in the Spring of 1982 that Green's career took a swift upward turn, benefiting from studies with Walter Bishop Jnr. and joining Betty Carter's band in April 1983 - the beginning of a four year stint of performing, recording and learning with jazz's most respected vocalist. The piano chair in Art Blakey's prestigious Jazz Messengers followed, and then, in 1989, a year with the Freddie Hubbard Quintet. By 1990, Green had already led a couple of blowing dates on the Criss Cross label, but it was with his Blue Note Records debut (*Lineage*) that Green really came of age, earning international respect and a reputation as one of the label's most exciting new stars. Since 1991 he has been touring with a his regular, finely tuned trio comprising bassist Christian McBride and drummer Carl Allen. He teamed up with legendary pianist Oscar Peterson for 1998's masterly *Oscar And Benny*.

● ALBUMS: *Prelude* (Criss Cross 1988)★★★★, *In This Direction* (Criss Cross 1989)★★★★, *Lineage* (Blue Note 1990)★★★★, *Furthermore* (1990)★★★, with Larry Gales *A Message From Monk* (1990)★★★, *Greens* (Blue Note 1991)★★★★, with Steve Turre *Right There* (1991)★★★, with Bob Belden *Straight To My Heart* (1991)★★★, with 29th Street Saxophone Quartet *Underground* (1991)★★★, *Testifyin' ! At The Village Vanguard* (Blue Note 1992)★★★, *That's Right!* (Blue Note 1993)★★★★, *The Place To Be* (Blue Note 1994)★★★, with Mark Murphy *Dim The Lights* 1995 recording (Millennium 1997)★★★★, *Kaleidoscope* (Blue Note 1997)★★★, with Oscar Peterson *Oscar And Benny* (Telarc 1998)★★★★.

GREEN, BUNKY

b. 23 April 1935, Milwaukee, Wisconsin, USA. Alto saxophonist Green was raised in Milwaukee, where he played with local pianist Billy Wallace. A spell in New York gave him his first big break when he was hired by Charlie Mingus as a replacement for Jackie McLean. His brief spell with the eccentric bassist made a deep impression, Mingus's sparing use of notation and his belief that there was no such thing as a wrong note having a lasting influence on Green's own style. After playing with Mingus, Green moved to Chicago where he appeared with several prominent players including Sonny Stitt, Louie Bellson, Andrew Hill, Yusef Lateef and Ira Sullivan, and recorded as leader for the Cadet and Argo labels. Despite being touted as a future star, Green gradually withdrew from the public eye to develop a career as a leading jazz educator. He taught at Chicago State University from 1972 to 1989, and in the 90s took up the directorship of the jazz studies program at the University of North Florida in Jacksonville. He has also served as president of the International Association of Jazz Educators. As a result of his educational activities Green has only released a few selective sessions since the mid 60s, including a superb spell on Vanguard Records which culminated in 1979's *Places We've Never Been*. Backed by an all-star group including trumpeter Randy Brecker, pianist Albert Dailey, bassist Eddie Gomez and drummer Freddy Waits, this recording highlighted Green's free movement in and out of chord changes, an original technique that played a significant part in shaping the style of Steve Coleman and other M-Base players in the following decade. Green's most recent release was the 1989 session *Healing The Pain*, a melodic and deeply moving recording commemorating the death of his parents.

● ALBUMS: *Testifyin' Time* (Argo 1965)★★★, *Playin' For Keeps* (Cadet 1965)★★★, *Transformations* (Vanguard 1977)★★★★, *Visions* (Vanguard 1978)★★★, *Places We've Never Been* (Vanguard 1979)★★★★, *In Love Again* (Mark 1987)★★★, *Healing The Pain* (Delos 1990)★★★★.

GREEN, CHARLIE 'BIG'

b. c.1900, Omaha, Nebraska, USA, d. February 1936. After working tent shows in the early 20s, trombonist Green joined Fletcher Henderson in 1924. He drifted in and out of the band over the next few years, in between times playing in the outfits of Benny Carter and Chick Webb. In the mid- and late 20s he played on numerous recording sessions, including those led by Louis Armstrong, Fats Waller, James P. Johnson, Zutty Singleton, Don Redman, Jimmie Noone and the Empress of the Blues, Bessie Smith. On some of his records Green's playing sounds basic but he was in fact a gifted melodic player with a delightful tone and wide-ranging ability who sometimes chose to play within fairly narrow limits. He was an exceptional accompanist and was especially sensitive when working with singers. His performances with Smith include 'Work House Blues', 'House Rent Blues', 'Trombone Cholly' and 'Shipwreck Blues', all classics, with the last title being a particularly fine example of his understanding of the singer's needs. Green died in New York in February 1936 when, on returning home from an engagement, found he couldn't gain access to his home, fell asleep on the doorstep, and froze to death.

● COMPILATIONS: with Fletcher Henderson *A Study In Frustration* (1923-38 recordings)★★★, *The Bessie Smith Story* (1925-28 recordings)★★★★.

GREEN, DAVE

b. 5 March 1942, London, England. Surprisingly for a bass player of such skill and prestige, Green is self-taught. His first important engagement as a professional musician was with the Don Rendell-Ian Carr band which he joined in the early 60s. By the end of the decade he had established himself as a major figure, having worked with musicians as diverse as Stan Tracey and Humphrey Lyttelton. He also played and recorded with many front-rank visiting Americans who counted themselves fortunate in having his solidity and flair behind them. For a while in the early 80s he led his own group, Fingers, which featured Lol Coxhill, Bruce Turner and Michael Garrick. Throughout the 80s and on into the early 90s, Green has remained at the forefront of British jazz, working with Peter King, Didier Lockwood, Spike Robinson and a host of other British and visiting jazzmen. A superb timekeeper and exceptional soloist, Green is the essence of the international jazz musician.

● ALBUMS: with Don Rendell-Ian Carr *Shades Of Blue* (1964)★★★★, *Fingers Remembers Mingus* (1980)★★★, *Spike Robinson-George Masso Play Arlen* (1991)★★★.

GREEN, FREDDIE

b. 31 March 1911, Charleston, South Carolina, USA, d. 1 March 1987. A self-taught musician who began on banjo, Green became known around New York jazz clubs in the early 30s. By 1936 he had switched to guitar and was recommended by John Hammond to Count Basie, who was looking for a replacement guitarist in his band. Green was hired in 1937 and became a member of the famous 'All-American Rhythm Section' (with Basie, Walter Page and Jo Jones). He remained there until 1950 when the big band folded and Basie organized a sextet. Unwilling to be left out of the band Green returned, uninvited. He was thus on hand when Basie reformed his big band and was still resident when Basie died in 1984. A meticulous timekeeper, Green's presence helped ensure the superb swing of the Basie band from its freewheeling Kansas City sound of the late 30s and 40s through to the metronomic accuracy of the 50s and after. On some recordings by the band, Green's contribution is virtually inaudible, but everyone who played with him insisted that his discreet beat was one of the principal factors in ensuring the band's propulsive swing. After Jones's departure Green was seldom happy with his replacements and reputedly kept a long stick by his chair with which to poke any drummer (especially Sonny Payne) who strayed off the beat. After Basie's death Green continued to work, making records with, among others, Manhattan Transfer.

● ALBUMS: *Brother John Sellers Sings Blues And Folk Songs* (1954)★★★, *Mr Rhythm* (1955)★★, with Count Basie *On My Way And Shouting Again* (1962)★★★★, with Herb Ellis *Rhythm Willie* (Concord Jazz 1975)★★★, with Basie *On The Road* (1979)★★★★.

● COMPILATIONS: with Basie *The Complete Recorded Works In Chronological Order* (1937-39 recordings)★★★★.

GREEN, GRANT

b. 6 June 1931, St Louis, Missouri, USA, d. 31 January 1979, New York City, New York, USA. Heavily influenced by Charlie Christian, guitarist Green first played professionally with Jimmy Forrest. Although noted particularly for his work in organ-guitar-drum trios in the 50s, throughout his career Green was associated with post-bop musicians and in the 60s he recorded for Blue Note Records with Stanley Turrentine, Hank Mobley, McCoy Tyner, Herbie Hancock and others. The flowing, single-line solos characteristic of Christian's early experiments in bebop were evident in much of Green's work. At home in several areas of jazz, he had a particularly strong affinity with the blues, while one album, *Feelin' The Spirit,* features gospel music. Nevertheless, he was essentially modern in his approach to music. Drug addiction severely limited his career in the 70s and he died in 1979.

● ALBUMS: *Grant's First Stand* (Blue Note 1961)★★★, *Reaching Out* (Black Lion 1961)★★★, *Green Street* (Blue Note 1961)★★★★, *Sunday Mornin'* (Blue Note 1961)★★★★, *Grantstand* (Blue Note 1961)★★★★, *Remembering* (Blue Note 1961)★★★, *Gooden's Corner* (Blue Note 1961)★★★, *Nigeria* (Blue Note 1962)★★★, *Oleo* (Blue Note 1962)★★★★, *The Latin Bit* (Blue Note 1962)★★★, *Goin' West* (Blue Note 1962)★★★, *Feelin' The Spirit* (Blue Note 1962)★★★, *Born To Be Blue* (Blue Note 1962)★★★, *Am I Blue?* (Blue Note 1963)★★★, *Idle Moments* (Blue Note 1963)★★★★, *Talkin' About!* (Blue Note 1964)★★★★, *Matador* (Blue Note 1964)★★★★, *Street Of Dreams* (Blue Note 1964)★★★, *I Want To Hold Your Hand* (Blue Note 1965)★★★, *His Majesty King Funk* (Verve 1965)★★★, *Iron City* (Muse 1967)★★★, *All The Gin Is Gone* (Delmark 1967)★★★, *Black Forrest* (Delmark 1967)★★★, *Carryin' On* (Blue Note 1969)★★★, *Green Is Beautiful* (Blue Note 1970)★★★, *Grant Green Alive!* (Blue Note 1970)★★, *Visions* (Blue Note 1971)★★★, *Shades Of Green* (Blue Note 1971)★★★, *The Final Comedown* film soundtrack (Blue Note 1972)★★, *Live At The Lighthouse* (Blue Note 1972)★★★, *The Main Attraction* (Kudu 1976)★★★, *Easy/Last Session* (1978)★★, *Solid* 1964 recording (Blue Note 1979)★★★★, *Last Session* (Atlantis 1987)★★, *Standards* 1961 recording (Blue Note 1998)★★★.

● COMPILATIONS: with Sonny Clark *The Complete Blue Note Recordings With Sonny Clark* 4-CD box set (Mosaic 1991)★★★★, *Best Of Grant Green* (Blue Note 1993)★★★, with Clark *The Complete Quartets With Sonny Clark* (Blue Note 1997)★★★★, *Jazz Profile* 1961-1965 recordings (Blue Note 1998)★★★★.

GREEN, URBIE

b. Urban Clifford Green, 8 August 1926, Mobile, Alabama, USA. Trombonist Green's first major engagement was with Gene Krupa in the late 40s; from there he joined the Woody Herman band. In the early 50s he appeared on Buck Clayton's celebrated Jam Session recordings. He then joined Benny Goodman, occasionally leading the band when Goodman was unwell. In the 60s and thereafter, Green freelanced, played in the studios, made numerous records, some of which were under his own name, gigged with Count Basie and led the reconstituted Tommy Dorsey orchestra. A masterly performer, especially in the upper register, Green has throughout his career consistently demonstrated that it is possible to blend deep jazz feeling with a seemingly perfect technique.

● ALBUMS: *Urbie Green Septet* 10-inch album (Blue Note 1954)★★★, *Urbie Green And His Band* 10-inch album (Vanguard 1954)★★★, *A Cool Yuletide* 10-inch album (X 1954)★★★, *East Coast Jazz/6* (Bethlehem 1955)★★★★, *Blues And Other Shades*

Of Green (ABC-Paramount 1956)★★★★, *All About Urbie Green* (ABC-Paramount 1956)★★★, *Let's Face The Music And Dance* (RCA Victor 1958)★★★, *Best Of The New Broadway Show Hits* (RCA Victor 1959)★★★, *The Persuasive Trombone Of Urbie Green* (Command 1963)★★★, *Urbie Green, Volume 2* (Command 1963)★★, *Urbie Green 6-Tet* (Command 1964)★★, *Urbie Green And Twenty-one Trombones i* (1968)★★★★, *Urbie Green And Twenty-one Trombones ii* (1968)★★★, *The Fox* (CTI 1976)★★, *Senor Blues* (CTI 1977)★★★★, *Live At Rick's Café Americain* (1978)★★, *The Message* (Fresh Sounds 1988)★★★, *Sea Jam Blues* 1995 recording (Chiaroscuro 1998)★★★.

GREENS - BENNY GREEN

A superbly talented young pianist of the 80s' bop revival, Benny Green always seemed like a name to watch during his stints with Betty Carter, Art Blakey's Jazz Messengers and Freddie Hubbard. He is an exciting but intelligent swinger with a clear, attractive articulation and a debt to the style of Bud Powell. On this, his second album for the Blue Note label, he is joined, in what has become a particularly productive partnership, by bassist Christian McBride and drummer Carl Allen, and plays a fine selection of standards and original tunes with panache and imagination.

● Tracks: *Greens; Bish Bash; Captain Hook; You Don't Know What Love Is; Time After Time; Battle Hymn Of The Republic; Decidedly; Soon; Cute; I See Your Face Before Me; Second Time Around; Shiny Stockings.*

● First released 1991

● UK peak chart position: did not chart

● USA peak chart position: did not chart

GREENWICH, SONNY

b. Herbert Lawrence Greenidge, 1 January 1936, Hamilton, Ontario, Canada. Greenwich began playing guitar in R&B groups but turned to jazz after working with a number of visiting American musicians. He moved into the USA, playing in bands of his own, as coleader, and also as a sideman. This was during the 60s when his musical associates included Miles Davis. He also played with John Handy, appearing with him at the *Spirituals To Swing* anniversary concert at Carnegie Hall in 1967. Shortly after this he led his own quartet at the Village Vanguard. From the 70s onwards, Greenwich's appearances on the US jazz scene became sporadic, although he frequently performed in Canada and continued to make records and festival appearances. These activities continued through succeeding decades and included dates with Kenny Wheeler, and a 1994 engagement at the Montreal Jazz Festival where an encounter with Paul Bley resulted in a studio session. By the early 90s, Greenwich was turning ever more towards composing, many of the resulting works appearing on a succession of well-received albums. On some of his 90s recordings he was accompanied by his own band, Meantime. Greenwich's playing draws interestingly from many areas of popular music, and from time to time also includes musical elements from other cultures, including Latin American. Forward thinking, and frequently displaying a penchant for out-of-tempo pieces, Greenwich has made an important contribution to Canada's position as a producer of fine jazz musicians.

● ALBUMS: *The Old Man And The Child* (CBC 1969)★★★, *Sun Song* (CBC 1974)★★★, *Evol-ution: Love's Reverse* (PM 1978)★★★, *Sonny Greenwich* (Justin Time 1986)★★★, *Bird Of Paradise* (Justin Time 1987)★★★★, *Live At Sweet Basil* (Justin Time 1988)★★, with Paul Bley *Outside In* (Justin Time 1994)★★★, *Standard Idioms* (Kleo 1994)★★★, *Hymn To The Earth* (Kleo 1995)★★★, *Welcome: Mother Earth* (Justin Time 1995)★★★, *Spirit In The Air* (Kleo 1996)★★★, with Kenny Wheeler *Live At The Montreal Bistro* (Justin Time 1997)★★★.

GREER, SONNY

b. William Alexander Greer, 13 December 1895, Long Branch, New Jersey, USA, d. 23 March 1982. After playing in New Jersey, drummer Greer appeared in Washington in 1919 where he encountered a local musician named Duke Ellington. In the early 20s the two men worked together in New York where Greer became a permanent member of the Ellington entourage. One of Duke's closest acquaintances, Greer was a subtle player who occasionally erred on the side of casualness. His timekeeping was supported initially by guitarist Freddie Guy and later by bassist Jimmy Blanton. Visually, Greer was spectacular, surrounding himself with an astonishing array of percussion instruments, including bells, gongs, timpani and xylophone. During his time with Ellington, Greer rarely went outside the band, although he did play on Lionel Hampton's famous Victor recording sessions. A smooth-talking, sharp-dressing, pool-hustler, Greer's on-stage behaviour gradually deteriorated through his inability to control his drinking. In 1951 Ellington finally asked him to leave and thereafter Greer freelanced, recording with other ex-Ellingtonians such as Johnny Hodges and Tyree Glenn and with Red Allen and J.C. Higginbotham. Despite his failings as a drummer, in retrospect it is possible to see and hear that Greer was the ideal Ellington drummer for the 30s and 40s. In the late 60s and 70s Greer led his own groups, usually a trio, appearing in concerts celebrating Ellington and proving that he was never more at ease than when playing his old boss's music.

● COMPILATIONS: with Duke Ellington *The Blanton-Webster Years* (1940-42)★★★★★, *Sonny Greer And The Duke's Men* (1944-45)★★★.

GREGER, MAX

b. 2 April 1926, Munich, Germany. After studying classical music, Greger turned to dance band work for a living. Having trained on piano and clarinet, he added accordion and tenor saxophone and in the late 40s was regularly leading his own small bands. In the mid-50s he had bigger bands, adopting a musical style that catered for popular tastes. During this period he worked with visiting American musicians, either as a sideman or leading an accompanying orchestra. He toured Europe with his band and visited Russia. In 1963 he formed a large ensemble which he led for the next two decades, appearing frequently on German radio and television and making over a hundred albums. From time to time he had ex-patriot Americans in his band, among them Benny Bailey. A good all-round instrumentalist, Greger's main contribution to popular music in Europe has been the high standard of musicianship he has demanded from members of his orchestra. If he did not break new boundaries, he certainly set standards of excellence in performance that measure up to those set anywhere else in the world.

● ALBUMS: *European Jazz Sounds* (Brunswick 1963)★★★, *Maximum* (Polydor 1965)★★★.

GREIG, STAN

b. 12 August 1930, Edinburgh, Scotland. A gifted pianist and competent drummer, Greig began playing in his home town where his school friends and fellow musicians included Al Fairweather and Sandy Brown. He played both piano and drums with Brown in the mid-to late 40s and by the mid-50s was established on the London jazz scene, working mostly in traditional jazz groups. Until the late 60s he primarily played drums but thereafter was heard more often on piano, the instrument with which he found his true, distinctive voice. Once again he stayed mostly in the traditional repertoire but also formed and led the London Jazz Big Band, in which Fairweather also played. In the late 80s he was with Humphrey Lyttelton with whom he had first played in the mid-50s. A solid, blues-based pianist, Greig is an exceptionally interesting soloist and as a band member knows few equals in his field. Rhythmically forceful, perhaps as a result of his drumming, he enhances every rhythm section in which he works.

● ALBUMS: with Sandy Brown, Al Fairweather *Fairweather Friends* (1957)★★★★, *Blues Every Time* (1985)★★★.

GREY, AL

b. 6 June 1925, Aldie, Virginia, USA. Early in his career Grey played trombone in bands in the US Navy but soon after World War II he joined Benny Carter, whom he always credited with extending his musical knowledge. After leaving Carter, Grey played in the bands of Jimmie Lunceford and Lucky Millinder. In 1948 he joined Lionel Hampton with whom he remained for five years. Briefly with Dizzy Gillespie, he then played with Count Basie for four years - a spell that gave Grey maximum exposure worldwide. When he later began touring as a single, and in a long and musically rewarding partnership with Jimmy Forrest, his success was assured. Very popular on the international club and festival circuit, Grey is an exciting and adventurous soloist, specializing in the use of the plunger mute. After Forrest's death Grey teamed up with Buddy Tate and continued touring until Tate's string of accidents and illnesses forced Grey back into solo appearances.

● ALBUMS: *The Last Of The Big Plungers* (1959)★★★, *The Thinking Man's Trombone* (1960)★★★★, *Al Grey-Billy Mitchell Sextet* (1961)★★★, *Snap Your Fingers* (1962)★★★, *Night Song* (1962)★★★, *Having A Ball* (1963)★★★★, *Boss-bone* (1964)★★★, *Al Grey And His Orchestra* (1965)★★, *The Great Concert Of Count Basie And His Orchestra* (1966)★★★★, *Al Grey And Wild Bill Davis* (1972)★★★, *Grey's Mood* (1973)★★★, *Struttin' And Shoutin'* (1976)★★★, *Al Grey All Stars Live At Travelers Lounge* (1977)★★, *Al Grey Featuring Arnett Cobb* (Black And Blue 1977)★★★, with Basie *Prime Time* (1977)★★★★, *Trombone By Five* (1977)★★★, *Al Grey-Jimmy Forrest Quintet Live At Rick's* (1978)★★★, *Get It Together: Live At The Pizza Express* (Pizza Express 1979)★★, *Truly Wonderful* (Stash 1979)★★★, *O. D.* (1980)★★★, with J.J. Johnson *Things Are Getting Better All The Time* (Original Jazz Classics 1983)★★★★, *Al Grey And The Jesper Thilo Quintet* (Storyville 1986)★★★, *The New Al Grey Quintet* (Chiarascuro 1988)★★★, *Al Meets Bjarne* (Gemini 1989)v, *Fab* (Capri 1993)★★★, *Christmas Stockin' Stuffer* (Capri 1993)★★, *Live At The Blue Note* (Telarc 1995)★★★, with Brother Jack McDuff *Me N' Jack* (Pullen 1996)★★★, *Matzoh And Grits* (Arbors 1998)★★★.

● COMPILATIONS: *Basic Grey* (Chess 1988)★★★★.

GRIFFIN, CHRIS

b. Gordon Griffin, 31 October 1915, Binghamton, New York, USA. Playing professionally from his early teens, Griffin joined Charlie Barnet's big band in 1933, where he was third trumpet to Eddie Sauter and Tutti Camarata. He then worked with several noted swing era stars, including Teddy Wilson and Benny Goodman. In the Goodman trumpet section Griffin shared lead and solo duties with Ziggy Elman and Harry James, forming one of the most powerful brass teams of the era. At the end of the 30s he was engaged mostly in studio work where, apart from occasional recording dates with Goodman and Jimmy Dorsey, he remained for the next several decades. For many years Griffin and Pee Wee Erwin ran a trumpet school. In 1974 he was reunited with Goodman at the Schaefer Music Festival in New York's Central Park and in the 80s was playing in clubs in and around New Jersey, occasionally appearing at clubs and festivals in Europe. In 1986 he took part in the Fifth Annual Floating Jazz Festival on the *SS Norway*.

● COMPILATIONS: *The Indispensable Benny Goodman Vols 1/2 and 3/4* (1936-37 recordings)★★★★, with Goodman *Carnegie Hall Jazz Concert* (1938 recordings)★★★★, *Chris Griffin, His Trumpet And Group* (1947 recordings)★★.

GRIFFIN, JOHNNY

b. 24 April 1928, Chicago, Illinois, USA. Griffin studied tenor saxophone at Du Sable High School where his tutor was Walter Dyatt, who also taught Gene Ammons and Von Freeman. In his mid-teens, Griffin joined the Lionel Hampton R&B-based big band and followed this with a spell in a similarly-oriented band led by Joe Morris. During the late 40s and early 50s he worked with numerous mainstream and bebop musicians, including Philly Joe Jones, Thelonious Monk, Bud Powell and Arnett Cobb. After military service, Griffin joined Art Blakey's Jazz Messengers in 1957, worked again with Monk, and co-led a band with Eddie 'Lockjaw' Davis - they dubbed themselves 'tough tenors', a sobriquet which has since been applied to an entire sub-genre of tenor playing. In the early 60s Griffin lived in Europe, where he often accompanied visiting American jazzmen and in 1967-68 was a member of the multi-national Clarke-Boland Big Band. In the 70s Griffin toured extensively, usually as a solo but sometimes in harness with Davis and Cobb; in the 80s he occasionally appeared with the Paris Reunion Band. A gifted and fiercely combative player, Griffin displays a seemingly endless stream of ideas, often at rapid-fire speeds. His style owes much to his bebop associates and predecessors and he was one of the best hard bop musicians of the 70s and 80s. His 90s recorded work on the Antilles label with Kenny Washington (drums) is of particular note, both fresh and rewarding.

● ALBUMS: *Introducing Johnny Griffin* (Blue Note 1956)★★★, *A Blowing Session* (Blue Note 1957)★★, *The Congregation* (Blue Note 1958)★★★, *Johnny Griffin Sextet* (Riverside 1958)★★★★, *Way Out!* (Riverside 1958)★★, *The Little Giant* (Riverside 1959)★★★, with Eddie 'Lockjaw' Davis *The Tenor Scene* reissued as *Live! The Breakfast Show* (Prestige 1960)★★★, *The Big Soul Band* (Riverside 1960)★★★, with Davis *Tough Tenors* (Jazzland 1960)★★★, *Studio Jazz Party* (Riverside 1960)★★★, *Change Of Pace* (Riverside 1961)★★★★, with Davis *Lookin' At Monk* (Jazzland 1961)★★★, with Davis *Griff & Lock* (Jazzland 1961)★★★, with Davis *Blues Up & Down* (Jazzland 1961)★★★★, *White Gardenia* (Riverside 1961)★★★, *The Kerry Dancers* (Riverside 1962)★★★, *Grab This!* (Riverside 1962)★★★, with Davis *Tough Tenor Favorites* (Jazzland 1962)★★★★, *Do Nothin' Till You Hear From Me* (Riverside 1963)★★★, with Davis *Battle Stations* (Prestige 1963)★★★, *Salt Peanuts* (Black Lion 1964)★★★, with Davis *The First Set - Recorded Live At Minton's* (Prestige 1964)★★★, with Davis *Live! The Midnight Show At Minton's Playhouse* (Prestige 1964)★★★, *Wade In The Water* (Riverside 1964)★★★★, with Mathew Gee *Soul Groove* (Atlantic 1965)★★★, with Davis *The Late Show Recorded Live!* (Prestige 1965)★★★, *The Man I Love* (Black Lion 1967)★★★, *You Leave Me Breathless* (Black Lion 1967)★★★, *A Night In Tunisia* (1967)★★★, *Night Lady* (EmArcy 1967)★★★, *Johnny Griffin Band* (1968)★★★, with Davis *Tough Tenors Again 'N Again* (MPS 1970)★★★, *Jazz Undulation* (1970)★★★, *Live At Music Inn* (1974)★★, *Live In Tokyo* (Inner City 1976)★★★, *Return Of The Griffin* (Original Jazz Classics 1978)★★, *The Jamfs Are Coming* (Timeless 1978)★★, *Bush Dance* (Galaxy 1978)★★★★, *NYC Underground* (Galaxy 1979)★★★, *To The Ladies* (Galaxy 1980)★★★, *Call It Whachawana* (Galaxy 1983)★★★, *Blues For Harvey* 1973 recording (Steeple Chase 1986)★★, *The Cat* (Antilles 1991)★★★, *3 Dances Of Passion* (Antilles 1993)★★★, *Chicago, New York, Paris* (Verve 1995)★★★, *Griff 'N' Bags* 1967-1969 recordings (Rearward 1998)★★★★, with Eddie 'Lockjaw' Davis *Tough Tenors Back Again* 1984 recording (Storyville 1998)★★★.

GRIFFITHS, MALCOLM

b. 29 September 1941, Barnet, Hertfordshire, England. In the early 60s Griffiths began a long association with Mike Westbrook, playing trombone in his band. Around this time he also studied at the London College of Music. During the years with Westbrook he also played in several other bands including a brief spell with Buddy Rich, long-lasting associations with John Surman and Stan Tracey, and he was in at the start of Chris McGregor's Brotherhood Of Breath. He also led his own bands and developed a parallel career as a studio musician. In 1994 he was reunited with Surman, appearing on Surman and John Warren's *The Brass Project*. In considerable demand for his technical skills, Griffiths has always shown himself to be eager in all that he does to push against the sometimes restricting envelope of jazz.

GRIMES, HENRY

b. 3 November 1935, Philadelphia, Pennsylvania, USA. After studying at the Juilliard School of Music, Grimes played bass in bands led by or featuring musicians such as Arnett Cobb, Lee Morgan and Al Heath. In the late 50s and early 60s he was with Gerry Mulligan, Charles Mingus, Thelonious Monk (with whom he appeared at the Newport Jazz Festival), Sonny Rollins and other leading modernists, but also played with Benny Goodman. Throughout the 60s Grimes freelanced with many leading post-bebop and free jazz players including Rollins, Albert Ayler, Archie Shepp and Don Cherry. A powerful bassist, Grimes's style changed dramatically from his earlier bebop days to the marked unconventionality of his later free-form work. Around 1967 Grimes disappeared from music.

● ALBUMS: *Henry Grimes Trio* (ESP 1965)★★★★.

GRIMES, TINY

b. Lloyd Grimes, 7 July 1916, Newport News, Virginia, USA, d. 4 March 1989, New York, USA. After playing drums and piano, Grimes turned to the guitar. Unusual among guitarists, he played a four-string instrument and was also an early experimenter with electrical amplification. In the late 30s and early 40s he worked in New York, attracting great attention when he joined Slam Stewart, succeeding Slim Gaillard. Grimes and Stewart then became accompanists to Art Tatum. In the mid-40s Grimes led several small groups, some of which dabbled in early bebop and featured artists such as Charlie Parker. In striking contrast, Grimes also played rock 'n' roll and cocktail lounge jazz to make ends meet. In the 70s and 80s he played clubs and festivals around the world.

● ALBUMS: *Blues Groove* (Prestige 1958)★★★, *Callin' The Blues* (Prestige 1958)★★★★, *Tiny In Swingville* (Swingville 1960)★★★★, *Big Time Guitar* (United Artists 1962)★★, with Kenny Burrell, Bill Jennings *Guitar Soul* (Status 1965)★★★, *Profoundly Blue* (Muse 1973)★★★, *Some Groovy Fours* (Classic Jazz 1974)★★★, *One Is Never Too Old To Swing* (Sonet 1977)★★★★.

● COMPILATIONS: *Tiny Grimes Vols 1 & 2* 1949-1955 recordings (Krazy Kat 1986)★★, *Rock The House* (Swingtime 1987)★★★, *Loch Lomond* 1947-1950 recordings (Whiskey Women & Song 1987)★★★, *Tiny Grimes And His Rockin' Highlanders* 1947-1953 recordings (Swingtime 1987)★★★, *Tiny's Boogie* 1948-1950 recordings (Oldie Blues 1988)★★★.

GROLNICK, DON

b. 23 September 1947, New York City, New York, USA, d. 1 June 1996, New York City, New York, USA.

Composer and pianist Don Grolnick split his musical career between jazz and rock and pop. However, his main calling was to jazz, which he first played as a child on an accordion. By the time he was 11 his grandparents had purchased a piano for him. He subsequently studied philosophy at New York's Tufts University, before joining the jazz-rock group Dreams in 1971. That group also included Randy and Michael Brecker. In the meantime he had become a highly-respected session musician. His fluent, elegant keyboard skills graced albums by Steely Dan (*The Royal Scam* and *Aja*), Bonnie Raitt (*Street Lights*), Linda Ronstadt (*What's New?*) and material by Bette Midler, Carly Simon, Paul Simon, Luther Vandross, Aaron Neville, Roberta Flack and James Taylor. It was with the latter artist that he was most closely identified, working as his musical director and producer in addition playing piano. Grolnick's jazz work began in earnest with a spell with Steps, a band formed by vibraphone player Mike Mainieri in 1979. Steps toured Japan and recorded two albums there in a single week. When the group learned of the existence of another group of the same name, they changed name to Steps Ahead and subsequently became one of the most influential and successful jazz groups of the 80s. Each of the members - saxophonist Michael Brecker, trumpet player Randy Brecker, bassist Eddie Gomez and drummer Steve Gadd - became celebrated players in their own right. Grolnick too was widely praised for his ensemble playing skills, but left the band in 1983 when they decided to move towards more synthesized electronic sounds. The break-up was amicable, however, and Grolnick explained the group's library to his successor, Eliane Elias. Steps Ahead also included his composition, 'Pools', on their next album. Grolnick's first solo effort, 1983's *Hearts And Numbers*, also included this piece. His former colleagues the Brecker brothers contributed to his 1989 album, *Weaver Of Dreams*, as well as 1992's *Nighttown*. By this juncture he had won his first Grammy Award for his production work on Michael Brecker's *Don't Try This At Home* set (1988). By the 90s he had become increasingly interested in Latin jazz and led such a group at his 1994 appearance at the Blue Note club in New York. The group also toured Europe but their projected debut album, *Medianoche*, had yet to be released when Grolnick died in June 1996 of complications arising from non-Hodgkin's lymphoma.

● ALBUMS: *Hearts And Numbers* (Windham Hill 1983)★★, *Weaver Of Dreams* (Blue Note 1989)★★★, *Nighttown* (Blue Note 1992)★★★, *Medianoche* (Warners 1996)★★.

GROSSMAN, STEVE

b. 18 January 1951, New York City, New York, USA. When Wayne Shorter left the Miles Davis band in 1969, his place was taken by 18 year old, Grossman. Initially the teenager was much criticized, yet his fresh approach and an emotional intensity beyond his years added much to the band. Grossman studied saxophone with his brother, starting on alto, moving to soprano and tenor by 1968. He played with a number of groups including the Jazz Samaritans, with George Cables and Lenny White before joining Davis and recording his first sessions. During the 70s Grossman played with Lonnie Liston Smith and in Elvin Jones' group and in 1975 founded the Stone Alliance with Gene Perla. His own groups have played in Europe and with particular success in Japan. A trademark of Grossman's style, and one that has gained him a new audience among younger listeners in England, is his successful adaptation of John Coltrane's inspired soprano saxophone to a jazz rock setting. *Time To Smile* featured Elvin Jones and Tom Harrell.

● ALBUMS: *Some Shapes To Come* (1973)★★★, *Perspective* (1978)★★★, *Way Out East Vol 1*(1984)★★★★, *Way Out East Vol 2* (Red 1985)★★★★, *Love Is The Thing* (Red 1985)★★★, *Steve Grossman Quartet Volume 1* (DIW 1985)★★★, *Steve Grossman Quartet Volume 2* (DIW 1985)★★★, *Standards* (DIW 1986)★★★, *Katonah* (1989)★★★, *Reflections* (Musidisc 1990)★★★, *Moon Train* (1990)★★★, *My Second Prime* 1990 recording (Red 1993)★★, *Live At Café Praga* 1990 recording (Timeless 1993)★★★, *A Small Hotel* (Dreyfus 1993)★★★★, *Do It* (Dreyfus 1994)★★, *In New York* 1991 recording (Dreyfus 1995)★★★, *Time To Smile* (Dreyfus 1995)★★, with Tyler Mitchell, Art Taylor *Bouncing With Mr A.T.* (Dreyfus 1996)★★★.

GROSZ, MARTY

b. Martin O. Grosz, 28 February 1930, Berlin, Germany. Resident in the USA since the age of three, Grosz began playing banjo and guitar in and around New York while still attending university. His musical inclinations were towards dixieland jazz, which he played with artists such as Dick Wellstood. After military service he settled in Chicago and played there for several years in local clubs, making a few records but making little impression on the national jazz scene. In the mid-70s he moved back to New York and joined Soprano Summit, the excellent small band co-led by Bob Wilber and Kenny Davern. His compositions 'Let Your Fingers Do The Walking' and 'Goody Goody' were acoustic guitar duets with Wayne Wright. In the late 70s he resumed his working relationship with Wellstood and established a new and musically-rewarding partnership with Dick Sudhalter that continued into the 80s. He also formed his own band, the Blue Angels, and, in addition to his talent for arranging and singing, proved himself to be an equally able writer on jazz topics.

● ALBUMS: *Hooray For Bix* (1957)★★★, *Marty Grosz And His Honoris Causa Band* (1957)★★, *Marty Grosz And His Gaslighters* i (1959)★★★, *Marty Grosz And His Gaslighters* ii (1959)★★, *Soprano Summit In Concert* (1976)★★, *Let Your Fingers Do The Walking* (1977)★★★, with Dick Wellstood *Take Me To The Land Of Jazz* (1978)★★★, *Goody Goody* (1978-79)★★★, *I Hope Gabriel Likes My Music* (1981)★★★, *Marty Grosz Sings Of Love And Other Matters* (1986)★★, *Keepers Of The Flame* (1987)★★★, *Swing It!* (Jazzology 1988)★★★, *Extra! The Orphan Newsboys* (Jazzology 1989)★★★, *Laughing At Life* (1990)★★★, *Unsaturated Fats* (Stomp Off 1990)★★★, *Songs I Learned At My Mother's Knee And Other Low Joints* (Jazzology 1992)★★★★, *Live At The L.A. Classic* (Jazzology 1992)★★, *Thanks* (J&M 1993)★★★, *Keep A Song In Your Soul* (Jazzology 1996)★★★★,

Ring Dem Bells (Nagel-Heyer 1996)★★★, *Rhythm For Sale* (Jazzology 1997)★★★★, *Just For Fun!* (Nagel-Heyer 1998)★★★.

GRP RECORDS

One of the most recent success stories in the recording industry has been the growth of the New York 'niche' market label, GRP Records. With a clearly defined path of MOR Jazz, the company has grown from a small production unit to a major-turnover organization. The founders were Larry Rosen and Dave Grusin, who in 1976 started ancillary production work for Patti Austin and Earl Klugh. By 1982 they had created such a reputation that they were able to start GRP. Much of their success has been due to a refusal to compromise on quality. Both were early converts to new digital technology and pioneered compact disc recordings. With a strategy aimed at the 25-50 age-group their 'all digital recordings' have been extraordinarily successful. In addition to Dave Grusin's considerable output their roster of artists is formidable and includes: Lee Ritenour, David Benoit, Diane Schuur, Special EFX, Eddie Daniels, Dave Valentin, Kevin Eubanks and the Rippingtons. Additionally they have released works by older established artists from the world of jazz like Gerry Mulligan, the Count Basie Orchestra, the Glenn Miller Orchestra, Dizzy Gillespie and Stéphane Grappelli. Still viewed as an independent company, the organization is now mainly handled by the original visionaries, Grusin and Rosen.

● VIDEOS: *GRP All-Star Big Band Live!* (GPR 1993).

GRUNTZ, GEORGE

b. 24 June 1932, Basle, Switzerland. Gruntz first attracted attention at the 1958 Newport Jazz Festival, where he appeared as a pianist with the Marshall Brown International Youth Band (which also included Dusko Goykovich). In the early 60s he worked with several leading American jazzmen, including Dexter Gordon; later in the decade he was with Phil Woods in the latter's European Rhythm Machine. In 1970 Gruntz was appointed musical director of the Zurich Schauspielhaus and since 1972 he has been artistic director of the Berlin Jazz Festival. In the early 70s he was co-founder and leader of a multi-national all-star big band, which he later led under the name of the George Gruntz Concert Jazz Band; he experimented with groups comprising multiple keyboard instruments (Piano Conclave), and played with forward-thinking jazz artists such as Don Cherry and Rahsaan Roland Kirk. More than most who have tried, Gruntz has been successful in crossing and recrossing the line between jazz and other musical forms. His compositions include symphonies, ballets and operas which stand alongside music written for all sizes of jazz groups. He has also written film scores and a jazz oratorio, 'The Holy Grail Of Jazz And Joy' (which appears on the album *Theatre*). His work always displays an inquiring and adventurous approach to jazz and has consistently chosen to push against accepted boundaries.

● ALBUMS: *Jazz Sound Track* (1962)★★★, *Jazz Goes Baroque* (1964)★★★★, *George Gruntz Et Les Swiss All Stars* (1964)★★★, *George Gruntz Ensemble* (1965)★★★, *George Gruntz With The International Peter Stuyvesant Orchestra* (1965), *Noon In Tunisia* (1967)★★, *From Sticksland With Love: Drums And Folklore* (1967)★★★, *St. Peter Power* (1968)★★★, *The Band* (MPS 1972)★★, *Monster Sticksland Meeting Two* (1974)★★★, *Eternal Baroque* (1974)★★★, *Piano Conclave* (1975)★★★, *The Band: Recorded Live At The Schauspielhaus* (MPS 1976)★★, *Trumpet Machine For Flying Out Proud* (1977)★★★, *Percussion Profiles* (1977)★★★, *Concert Jazz Band* (MPS 1978)★★★, *Live At The Quartier Latin, Berlin* (1980)★★★, *Live '82* (1982)★★★, *Theatre* (ECM 1983)★★★, *Happening Now* (hatART 1988)★★★★, *First Prize* (1989)★★★, *Beyond Another Wall: Live In China* (TCB 1995)★★★, *Mock-Lo-Motion* (TCB 1997)★★★★.

● COMPILATIONS: *25 Years ('Sins'N Wins'N Funs)* (TCB 1997)★★★, *The MPS Years* (MPS 1997)★★★.

GRUSIN, DAVE

b. 26 June 1934, Littleton, Colorado, USA. He played piano semi-professionally while studying at the University of Colorado, and almost abandoned music to become a veterinary surgeon. Grusin stated 'I'm still not sure I made the right decision, a lot of dead cows might still be alive today if I hadn't gone to music school.' His musical associates at the time included Art Pepper, Terry Gibbs and Spike Robinson, with whom he worked extensively in the early 50s. In 1959 Grusin was hired as musical director by singer Andy Williams, a role he maintained into the mid-60s. An eclectic musician, Grusin worked with mainstream artists such as Benny Goodman and Thad Jones and also worked with hard bop players. He made many recording dates, including several in the early 70s, accompanying singers amongst whom were Sarah Vaughan and Carmen McRae. Around this same time Grusin began to concentrate more and more on electric piano and keyboards, recording with Gerry Mulligan, Lee Ritenour in the jazz world and with Paul Simon and Billy Joel in pop. He has arranged and produced for the Byrds, Peggy Lee, Grover Washington Jnr., Donna Summer, Barbra Streisand, Al Jarreau, Phoebe Snow and Patti Austin. He is also co-founder and owner, with Larry Rosen, of GRP Records, a label which they founded in 1976 and has an impressive catalogue of singers, jazz and jazz-rock artists including Diane Schuur, Lee Ritenour, David Benoit, his brother Don Grusin, Michael Brecker, Chick Corea, Steve Gadd, Dave Valentin, Special EFX and Gary Burton. The success of GRP has much to do with Grusin's refusal to compromise on quality. With Rosen he pioneered an all digital recording policy, and using 'state of the art' technology their productions reach a pinnacle of recorded quality. In addition to his activities as a player and producer, Grusin has written extensively for films and television. His portfolio is most impressive; in addition to winning a Grammy in 1984 his film scores have received several Academy Award nominations, and include *Divorce Italian Style*, *The Graduate*, *The Heart Is A Lonely Hunter*, *Three Days Of The Condor*, *Heaven Can Wait*, *Reds*, *On Golden Pond*, *The Champ*, *Tootsie*, *Racing With The Moon*,

The Milagro Beanfield War, *Clara's Heart*, *Tequila Sunrise*, *A Dry White Season*, *The Fabulous Baker Boys*, *Bonfire Of The Vanities*, *Havana*, *For The Boys*, and *The Firm* (1993). Additionally one of his most evocative songs 'Mountain Dance' was the title song to *Falling In Love*. His American television credits include *St. Elsewhere*, *Maude*, *Roots*, *It Takes A Thief* and *Baretta*. Grusin is a master musical chemist - able to blend many elements of pop and jazz into uplifting intelligent and accessible music. In 1993 he appeared as a performer on the international jazz circuit and in 1997 issued a highly credible album of the music of Henry Mancini.

● ALBUMS: *Candy* soundtrack (1961)★★, *The Many Moods Of Dave Grusin* (1962)★★, *Subways Are For Sleeping* (Epic 1962)★★, *Kaleidoscope* (Columbia 1964)★★, *Don't Touch* (1964)★★★, *Discovered Again* (1976)★★, *One Of A Kind* (GRP 1977)★★★, *Dave Grusin And The GRP All Stars Live In Japan Featuring Sadao Watanabe* (GRP 1980)★★★, *Out Of The Shadows* (GRP 1982)★★★, *Mountain Dance* (GRP 1983)★★★★, *Night Lines* (GRP 1984)★★★, with Lee Ritenour *Harlequin* (GRP 1984)★★, *The NYLA Dream Band* (GRP 1988)★★★, with Don Grusin *Sticks And Stones* (GRP 1988)★★★, *Migration* (GRP 1989)★★, *The Fabulous Baker Boys* film soundtrack (GRP 1989)★★★, *Havana* (GRP 1990)★★★, *The Gershwin Collection* (GRP 1992)★★★★, *Homage To Duke* (GRP 1993)★★★, *Two For The Road: The Music Of Henry Mancini* (GRP 1997)★★★★, *Dave Grusin Presents West Side Story* (N2K 1997)★★★.

● COMPILATIONS: *Cinemagic* (1987)★★★★, *Dave Grusin Collection* (GRP 1991)★★★★.

GRUSIN, DON

b. c.1942, Littleton, Colorado, USA. Brother of Dave Grusin and a member of the successful GRP Records stable of artists. Don remains mainly in the background but has to date recorded impressive two solo albums. The music follows the formula of GRP's adult-orientated accessible jazz.

● ALBUMS: *Raven* (GRP 1985)★★★★, *Zephyr* (GRP 1987)★★★, with Dave Grusin *Sticks And Stones* (GRP1988)★★★, *Native Land* (1993)★★★.

GRYCE, GIGI

b. 28 November 1927, Pensacola, Florida, USA, d. 17 March 1983, Pensacola, Florida, USA. Alto saxophonist Gryce studied composition at Boston Conservatory and in Paris (with classicist Arthur Honegger) but then turned to jazz with spells in various bands, including that led by Tadd Dameron. In 1953 he was a member of the remarkable band with which Lionel Hampton toured Europe and which featured many other fine young musicians, notably Clifford Brown, Art Farmer, Quincy Jones and Alan Dawson. Although contractually barred from recording while on tour, most of the band were too eager to be bound by contracts and made several big band and small group records, some of which were released under Gryce's name. On their return to the USA the culprits of this breach of contract were fired by Hampton. In the mid- to late 50s Gryce worked with Lee Morgan, Oscar Pettiford, Donald Byrd (co-leading the Jazz Lab quintet with him) and also led his own small group. Gryce's playing was heavily influenced by Charlie Parker, but his writing showed great flair and inventiveness and was eagerly used by many leading post-bop artists. In the 60s Gryce began to concentrate on teaching and also extended his composing into the classical field: he is credited with three symphonies.

● ALBUMS: with Clifford Brown *Gigi Gryce-Clifford Brown Sextet* 10-inch album (Blue Note 1954)★★★, with Art Farmer *Art Farmer Quintet i* 10-inch album (Prestige 1954)★★★★, *Gigi Gryce's Jazztime Paris* 10-inch album (Blue Note 1954)★★★★, *Gigi Gryce And His Little Band, Volume 2* (Blue Note 1954)★★★, *Gigi Gryce Quintet/Sextet, Volume 3* 10-inch album (Blue Note 1954)★★★, *Gigi Gryce Quartet* reissued as *Nica's Tempo* (Signal/Savoy 1955)★★★★, with Farmer *Art Farmer Quintet ii* 10-inch album (Prestige 1955)★★★★, with Farmer *Art Farmer Quintet Featuring Gigi Gryce* reissued as *Evening In Casablanca* (Prestige/New Jazz 1956)★★★★, with Farmer *When Farmer Met Gryce* 1954/1955 recordings (Prestige 1957)★★★★, with Donald Byrd *Jazz Lab* reissued as *Gigi Gryce/Donald Byrd* (Jubilee/Josie 1957)★★★★, with Byrd *Modern Jazz Perspective/Jazz Lab, Volume 2* (Columbia 1957)★★★★, with Byrd *Gigi Gryce And The Jazz Lab Quintet* (Riverside 1957)★★★★, *Gigi Gryce* (Metrojazz 1958)★★★, *Sayin' Somethin'!* (New Jazz 1959)★★★, *The Hap'nin's* (New Jazz 1960)★★★★, *The Rat Race Blues* (New Jazz 1961)★★★★, *Reminiscin'* (Mercury 1961)★★★.

GUARALDI, VINCE

b. 17 July 1928, San Francisco, California, USA, d. 6 February 1976. Jazz pianist and latter day easy listening jazz composer Guaraldi played with Cal Tjaader in the early 50s before moving through Bill Harris' combo, and worked with Sonny Criss and George Auld. He also served as part of Woody Herman's touring band in the late 50s. It was in the 60s, however, that Guaraldi made a name for himself as a composer of light romantic jazz-influenced songs. His most famous and deservedly long-lasting classic is 'Cast Your Fate To The Wind', which was a hit for his trio in 1962 and subsequently won him a Grammy award. A surprise cover version appeared high in the UK charts at the end of 1964 by a studio-only group Sounds Orchestral. In recent years the song has been covered many times, one of the better interpretations was by David Benoit from his 1989 album *Waiting For Spring*. Less credible although also widely known is his soundtrack theme music for the Charlie Brown *Peanuts* cartoon television series. He also recorded with Conte Candoli and Frank Rosolino in the 60s. His music received an unexpected boost in the mid-90s when some of his work was reappraised during the 'space age bachelor pad music' cult boom.

● ALBUMS: *Modern Music From San Francisco* (Fantasy 1956)★★★, *Vince Guaraldi Trio* (Fantasy 1956)★★★, *A Flower Is A Lovesome Thing* (Fantasy 1958)★★★, *Cast Your Fate To The Wind; Jazz Impressions Of Black Orpheus* (Fantasy 1962)★★★, *Vince Guaraldi In Person* (Fantasy 1963)★★★, with Frank Rosolino *Vince Guaraldi/Frank Rosolino Quintet* (Premier 1963)★★★, with Conte Candoli *Vince Guaraldi/Conte Candoli Quartet* (Premier 1963)★★★, *Vince Guaraldi, Bola Sete And*

Friends (Fantasy 1963)★★★, *Tour De Force* (Fantasy 1963)★★★, *Jazz Impressions Of Charlie Brown* (Fantasy 1964)★★★, *Jazz Impressions* (Fantasy 1964)★★★, *A Boy Named Charlie Brown* (Fantasy 1964)★★, *A Charlie Brown Christmas* (Fantasy 1964)★, *The Latin Side Of Vince Guaraldi* (Fantasy 1964)★★★, *Vince Guaraldi At Grace Cathedral* (Fantasy 1965)★★★, *From All Sides* (Fantasy 1965)★★★, *Live At The El Matador* (Fantasy 1966)★★★, *Oh Good Grief!* (Warners 1968)★★★.

Guarente, Frank

b. 5 October 1893, Montemiletto, Italy, d. 21 July 1942. Arriving in the USA in his mid teens, Guarente played trumpet in several bands before joining Paul Specht's popular dance orchestra. He played hot jazz with a band-within-the-band, the Georgians, and during the mid-20s toured Europe with a similar group. After working in London for a time he returned to Specht's band in 1928. During the early and mid-30s he played in various big bands and studio orchestras, appearing on several record dates. Towards the end of his life Guarente suffered ill-health which eventually forced him into retirement.

● COMPILATIONS: *Frank Guarente And The Georgians* (1922-27 recordings)★★★.

Guarnieri, Johnny

b. 23 March 1917, New York City, New York, USA, d. 7 January 1985. Although he studied piano formally, Guarnieri's musical future was determined through meeting Fats Waller, Willie 'The Lion' Smith, James P. Johnson and Art Tatum. Johnson told him, 'After me and Fats, you're number three.' Although adept at playing stride piano, despite having remarkably small hands, Guarnieri's breakthrough into the bigtime came when he played with the swing era big bands of Benny Goodman, Artie Shaw and Tommy Dorsey. With Shaw, he played harpsichord in the band-within-the-band, the Gramercy Five. During the early 40s Guarnieri also worked extensively in the studios, making countless broadcasts, many with the Raymond Scott orchestra at CBS, and appearing on numerous record dates including sessions with Lester Young, Coleman Hawkins, Roy Eldridge, Don Byas and Louis Armstrong. Resident on the west coast from the early 60s, he occasionally toured and recorded but spent many years as the house pianist, first at the Hollywood Plaza Hotel and then at The Tail Of The Cock, a restaurant on Ventura Boulevard, Los Angeles. Night after night he played at a Hollywood-style piano-bar, tailoring his playing to suit the needs of the clientele who, too often, were there to be seen and heard rather than to listen. (Guarnieri needed the job to help pay extensive family hospital bills.) Guarnieri's solo recordings display his prodigious technique, his love of old songs, his stride beginnings and a predilection for tunes performed in 5/4 time.

● ALBUMS: *Songs Of Hudson And De Lange* (1956)★★★, *Johnny Guarnieri Quartet* i (1956)★★, *Johnny Guarnieri Quartet* ii (1956)★★★, *Johnny Guarnieri Quartet* iii (1957)★★★, *Johnny Guarnieri* (c.1967)★★★, *Johnny Guarnieri Plays Harry Warren* (1973)★★★★, *Walla Walla* (1975)★★★, *Johnny Guarnieri Plays The Music Of Walter Donaldson* (c.1975)★★★, *Breakthrough* (1976)★★★, *Superstride* (1976)★★★, *Stealin' Apples* (1978)★★★, *Johnny Garnieri Plays Fats Waller* (Taz Jazz 1979)★★★★, *Keep On Dreaming* (1979)★★★, *Originals* (1979)★★★, *Superstride* (Taz Jazz 1979)★★★, *Echoes Of Ellington* (c.1984)★★★★.

● COMPILATIONS: with Artie Shaw *The Complete Gramercy Five Sessions* (1940)★★★★.

Guercio, Jim

b. James William Guercio, 1945. A former student of classical composition at the University of Chicago, Guercio gravitated from mid-west bar bands to a spell in the backing group of Dick Clark's *Caravan Show*. He was briefly involved with the embryonic Mothers Of Invention before securing fame as a producer with the Buckinghams, whose 1966 single, 'Kind Of A Drag', topped the US charts. Guercio maintained his association with the group over the next two years and the brass sound of their later recordings anticipated the producer's work with Blood, Sweat And Tears and Chicago. Although renowned for such jazz-rock experiments, he also found artistic success with two contrasting acts, Moondog and the Illinois Speed Press. In the 70s Guercio founded James William Guercio Enterprises which included the Caribou Recording Studio. He produced, directed and scored the film *Electra Glide In Blue* (1972) and three years later became the Beach Boys' manager, as well as their in-concert bassist. Their relationship subsequently soured, and Guercio has continued to pursue his diverse business interests.

Guérin, Roger

b. 9 January 1926, Sarrebrück, France. Guérin began playing trumpet during his formative years, becoming a professional musician shortly after the end of World War II. In addition to playing in several bands led by French and other European musicians, he also accompanied numerous visiting Americans, including Rex Stewart, Kenny Clarke, Charlie Parker, Peanuts Holland, Duke Ellington, Benny Golson, Dizzy Gillespie, Woody Shaw, Slide Hampton and Louis Armstrong. His European partners included Django Reinhardt, Michel Legrand and Martial Solal; with the latter he enjoyed a fruitful musical association that lasted through the late 50s and succeeding decades. He also played with bands led by Claude Bolling and André Hodeir and was a member of the Clarke-Boland Big Band. An inventive soloist with a dazzling technique, Guérin favours intricate bebop lines but can also adapt to the special needs of section work in big bands and, as his playing list of associates indicates, is comfortable also in a mainstream small-group setting.

● ALBUMS: with Kenny Clarke *Round Midnight* (Philips 1956)★★★, co-leader with Benny Golson *I Remember Clifford* (Columbia 1958)★★★★, with Martial Solal *Suite En Ré Bémol* (Columbia 1959)★★, with André Hodeir *Bitter Ending* (Epic 1972)★★, with Solal *Coming On The Hudson* (Carlyne 1984)★★★.

GUEST STARS

This popular UK jazz-pop fusion group comprised Deidre Cartwright (b. 27 July 1956, London, England; guitar), Josefina Cupido (b. 21 July 1951, London, England; drums, vocals), Laka Daisical (b. Dorota Koch, 8 January 1953, Oxford, England; piano, vocals), Linda Da Mango (b. Linda Malone, 19 April 1951, Southampton, Hampshire, England; congas, percussion, vocals), Alison Rayner (b. 7 September 1952, Bromley, Kent, England; bass), Ruthie Smith (b. 24 November 1950, Manchester, England; saxophones, vocals). The all-women Guest Stars came together in the early 80s. Their lively mixture of Latin, African, Caribbean and jazz musics reflected their various backgrounds in groups such as Soulyard (Daisical, Da Mango, Smith), Redbrass (Cupido), Jam Today (Rayner) and Tour De Force (Cartwright - who was also co-presenter of the BBC Television series, *Rock School*). The six were also core members of the all-women big bands Sisterhood Of Spit and Lydia D'Ustebyn Swing Orchestra, and Cupido, Daisical and Smith sang with the a cappella Hipscats. Linked by their commitment to feminism and to collective working (the band organized their own tours and released their own records, with the help of administrators Deborah Dickinson and Anne Cooper), the Guest Stars did not neglect the good-time aspects of their music; their live performances were often uproarious affairs, more like parties than concerts. They toured the UK, the USA, Germany, Spain and the Middle East and released three albums before splitting up in 1989. Since then Cartwright, Daisical (with Slave To The Rhythm) and Rayner (with the Jazz Garden) have lead their own groups, while Cupido works regularly with the Grand Union big band.

● ALBUMS: *The Guest Stars* (Guest Stars 1984)★★★, *Out At Night* (Guest Stars 1985)★★★★, *Live In Berlin* (1987)★★★.

GUITAR FORMS - KENNY BURRELL

An extraordinarily varied record that moves away from jazz to encompass classical Spanish guitar, bossa nova, pop and blues. The key to its success is that the whole package is conducted and arranged by Gil Evans. He enables quite different styles to come together and sound cohesive with his remarkable vision of musical shape and form. The personnel is lengthy and includes Ron Carter (bass), Steve Lacy (saxophone), Lee Konitz (saxophone), Elvin Jones and Charlie Persip (drums) and Jimmy Cleveland (trombone). Evans mixes Burrell's lone Spanish guitar against 16 other musicians with absolute confidence and dedication, and makes it work like a dream.

● Tracks: *Greensleeves; Last Night When We Were Young; Breadwinner; Downstairs; Lotus Land; Prelude Number Two; Moon And Sand; Loie; Terrace Theme.*

● First released 1965

● UK peak chart position: did not chart

● USA peak chart position: did not chart

GULDA, FRIEDRICH

b. 16 May 1930, Vienna, Austria. After extensive studies in classical piano, Gulda began a career as a concert pianist in the mid-40s. A few years later, he was also deeply involved in jazz, playing piano and, later, flute and baritone saxophone. He performed throughout Europe, North and South America, as soloist and as orchestra leader, playing classical music and jazz, often at the same concert. He wrote much of the music played by his orchestras, writing in both classical and jazz styles. As soloists in his longer works, and as sidemen in his orchestras for concerts and recordings, he regularly employed noted American modernists including Phil Woods, Benny Bailey, Albert Heath, Art Farmer, Freddie Hubbard, Ron Carter, Mel Lewis, Cecil Taylor, Don Cherry, Dizzy Gillespie and Chick Corea. Despite a prolific career as writer and performer and his punishing schedule of concerts and extensive radio broadcasts, much of Gulda's work failed to connect with the wider audience, seemingly falling between the two stools of classical and jazz while not attracting the interest of fans of third-stream music. Gulda has also sung using the pseudonym Albert Golowin. He has presented his music on television, organized and promoted festivals, and written several books on music.

● ALBUMS: *Friedrich Gulda At Birdland* (RCA 1956)★★★, *Music For Three Soloists And Band* (Columbia 1962)★★★, *Gulda Jazz* (Amadeo 1964)★★★★, *From Vienna With Jazz* (Columbia 1964)★★★, *Ineffable* (Columbia 1965)★★★, *Music For Four Soloists And Band No 1* (Saba 1965)★★★, *Internationaler Wettbewerb Für Modernen Jazz* (Amadeo 1966)★★, *Friedrich Gulda Und Sein Eurojazz Orchester* (Preiser 1966)★★★, *Vienna Revisited* (Saba 1969)★★, *The Long Road To Freedom* (MPS 1971)★★★, *It's All One* (MPS 1971)★★★, *Anima* (MPS 1972)★★★, *Gegenwart* (ERP 1976)★★★, *Musician Of Our Time* (MPS 1977)★★★, *Concert For Ursula* (Amadeo 1982)★★, *The Master* (Amadeo 1983)★★★.

GULLIN, LARS

b. 4 May 1928, Visby, Sweden, d. 17 May 1976. After playing clarinet and alto saxophone, Gullin took up the baritone at the age of 21. From 1951-53 he worked with Arne Domnerus and Rolf Ericson, then formed his own quintet. An ardent bebopper, and influenced by Lennie Tristano, Gullin was a radical among Swedish musicians of the time; he also made an impact on the USA jazz scene, winning a *Downbeat* poll as best newcomer in 1954 (a notable achievement for a European musician). Gullin later worked chiefly as a single, playing with local rhythm sections, and recorded regularly with visiting American artists. In 1959 he toured Italy with Chet Baker. Unfortunately, his career was marred by drug addiction and he was inactive for long periods. One of the first European jazz artists to build an international reputation, Gullin's baritone playing was distinguished by his remarkable facility and by a lightness of tone that made it sound at times almost like an alto saxophone. He also wrote several distinctive jazz compositions, which reveal the influence of Swedish classical and folk musics: the tribute set *Dedicated To Lee*, has his admirer Lee Konitz playing on a selection of Gullin's tunes. The outstanding film, *Sven Klang's Kvintett* (1976), is a fictionalized account of his early career.

● ALBUMS: *Lars Gullin With The Morotone Singers* (1954)★★, *The Great Lars Gullin, Vols. 1 & 2* (1955-56)★★★★, *The Artistry Of Lars Gullin* (1958)★★★, *Portrait Of My Pals* (1964)★★, *Jazz Amour Affair* (1970)★★★, *Like Grass* (1973)★★★, *Aeros Aromatica Atomica Suite* (1976)★★, *Lars Gullin Vols 1-5 1954-60* (Dragon 1986)★★★★, *In Concert* (Storyville 1990)★★, *1955/56 Vol. 1 With Chet Baker* (1992)★★★★.

GURTU, TRILOK

b. 30 October 1951, Bombay, India. Coming from a musical family, Gurtu played tablas from the age of six and studied with Ahmed Jan Thirakwa. In 1965 he formed a percussion group with his brother. He credits John Coltrane's *Plays The Blues* (1960) with inspiring him for jazz. In 1973 he toured Europe with an Indian crossover group and stayed in Italy until 1976, when he relocated to New York and started a longterm association with alto saxophonist Charles Mariano. He also played with trumpeter Don Cherry and bassist Barre Philips. Teamed with Brazilian percussionist Nana Vasconcelos he toured Europe and recorded for the German ECM label, becoming part of a select set of musicians who fuse global music into a tastefully understated whole. After Collin Walcott's death in 1984, Gurtu took his place in Oregon. In 1988 he toured with John McLaughlin. Seated on the floor to play he has incorporated devices such as dipping resonating gongs in water (a technique invented by John Cage), always with an immaculate sense of timing and sonority. In 1988 he recorded *Usfret* with his mother Shobha Gurtu, herself an acclaimed vocalist in India. The following year they toured together. *Living Magic* in 1991 featured Nana Vasconcelos and some stellar saxophone from Jan Garbarek. Gurtu's career really blossomed in the 90s as he established a loyal following through his solo work on CMP. *Crazy Saints*, the title of his 1993 album featured Pat Metheny and Joe Zawinul and became the title of his regular band. Gurtu's rising star was confirmed when he became the No 1 percussionist in the 1994 and 1995 *Down Beat* polls. Neneh Cherry guested on 1998's *Kathak*.

● ALBUMS: with Barre Philips *Three Day Moon* (1978)★★★, with Shankar *Song For Everyone* (1984)★★★, *Usfret* (CMP 1988)★★, *Living Magic* (CMP 1991)★★★★, *Crazy Saints* (CMP 1993),★★★★ *Believe* (CMP 1994)★★, *Bad Habits Die Hard* (CMP 1995)★★★, *The Glimpse* (Silva America 1997)★★★★, *Kathak* (Escapade 1998)★★★★.

● COMPILATIONS: *The Collection* (CMP 1997)★★★.

GUY, BARRY

b. 22 April 1947, London, England. Even before he had completed his double-bass and composition studies at the Guildhall School of Music, Guy had earned a formidable reputation as a performer in jazz, improvised music and classical music. He was a member of the Howard Riley trio from 1967-70 and, also in the mid-60s, spent some time with John Stevens's Spontaneous Music Ensemble. He was a founder member of the Musicians' Co-Operative, for which he composed *Ode* for a 21-piece orchestra, that, as the London Jazz Composers' Orchestra, became a long-term project. It is still in existence today, although working more in continental Europe than in the UK. As well as being an accomplished composer, Guy is a virtuoso performer, with a stunning command of the bass through the whole range of conventional and unorthodox techniques. He is as much in demand for classical and contemporary orchestral work as for jazz gigs, and has worked in many contexts, including with Tony Oxley, Evan Parker, Mike Westbrook, Peter Kowald, Trevor Watts, Bob Downes, Dave Holdsworth, Chris McGregor and, outside jazz, with the BBC Symphony Orchestra, the London Sinfonietta, the Monteverdi Orchestra, the Academy of Ancient Music, Capricorn, the Richard Hickox Orchestra (later renamed the City of London Sinfonia) and in a duo with soprano Jane Manning. He has also been a member of the Michael Nyman Band, appearing on the soundtrack of *The Draughtsman's Contract* (1982). The selection of albums listed below omits Guy's classical work.

● ALBUMS: with London Jazz Composers Orchestra *Ode For Jazz Orchestra* (Incus 1972)★★★★, with Paul Rutherford *ISKRA 1903* (1972)★★★, *Solo Bass Improvisations* (Incus 1976)★★★★, *Statements V-XI* (1976)★★★, *Improvisations Are Forever Now* (1977)★★★★, *Endgame* (ECM 1979)★★★★, with LJCO *Stringer* 1980 recording (1983)★★★, with Evan Parker, Paul Lytton *Tracks* (1983)★★★, with Parker, Lytton, George Lewis *Hook, Drift & Shuffle* 1983 recording (1985)★★★, with Peter Kowald *Paintings* (1988)★★★, with Parker, Eddie Prevost, Keith Rowe *Supersession* (1988)★★★, with Parker *Tai Kyoku* 1985 recording (1988)★★★, *Assist* (1988)★★, with LJCO *Harmos* (1989)★★, *Arcus* (Maya 1990)★★★★, with LJCO *Double Trouble* (1990)★★★, *Elsie Jo* (Maya 1991)★★★, *Fizzles* (Maya 1992)★★★★, *Study: Witch Gong Game 11/10* (Maya 1994)★★★★, *You Forgot To Answer* (Maya 1995)★★★★, with Parker, Lytton *Breaths And Heartbeats* (Rastascan 1995)★★★, *Gryffgryffgryffs* (Music And Arts 1997)★★★, *Natives And Aliens* (Leo 1998)★★★★.

GUY, FREDDIE

b. 23 May 1897, Burkesville, Georgia, USA, d. 22 November 1971. In the early 20s Guy was active in New York, playing banjo in his own band and that of Joseph Smith before joining Duke Ellington in 1925. In the mid-30s Guy, who was one of Ellington's closest acquaintances, abandoned the banjo in favour of the guitar, continuing to supply a discreet rhythmic pulse to the orchestra. This was frequently necessary, owing to the erratic timekeeping of some of his fellow rhythm section members. The arrival of Jimmy Blanton brought great stability to the band and from that point onwards Guy's role was diminished. He left the Ellington band in 1949 and was never replaced. Retiring from active playing, Guy retained an interest in the music business through work as a dancehall manager in Chicago. He ended his own life on 22 November 1971.

● COMPILATIONS: *The Indispensable Duke Ellington Vols 1/2 and 3/4* (1927-34 recordings)★★★★.

GUY, JOE

b. 20 September 1920, Birmingham, Alabama, USA, d. early 60s. After playing trumpet in the big bands led by Teddy Hill and Coleman Hawkins in the late 30s, Guy became deeply involved in the development of bebop. He was a regular performer at Minton's Playhouse, where he often played with Thelonious Monk and Charlie Christian. In 1942 he joined the Cootie Williams big band, a group which had boppish undertones thanks to the presence at one time or another of Guy, Charlie Parker and Bud Powell. In 1944 Guy took part in the first Jazz At The Philharmonic concert staged by Norman Granz. The following year Guy began a brief personal and professional relationship with Billie Holiday, but soon afterwards drifted onto the edges of the jazz scene.

● COMPILATIONS: with Oran 'Hot Lips' Page *Trumpet Battle At Minton's* (1941)★★★, with Charlie Christian *The Origins Of Modern Jazz* (1941)★★★★, with others *Harlem Odyssey* (1941)★★★, *Jazz At The Philharmonic* (Melodisc 1944)★★★.

GWALTNEY, TOMMY

b. 28 February 1921, Norfolk, Virginia, USA. Although he played clarinet as a teenager and during military service, Gwaltney briefly turned to the vibraphone when he suffered lung damage. After the war he started to play the clarinet again, performing in and around Washington, DC, often in name bands passing through the region, including those led by Benny Goodman, Bobby Hackett and Billy Butterfield. Gwaltney was also active in concert and festival promotion and in the mid-60s opened a club in Washington, Blues Alley, at which he assisted in re-launching the career of Maxine Sullivan. In the late 60s he began a long association with the Manassas Jazz Festival, recording for impresario Fat Cat McRee's Fat Cat's Jazz label with several veteran performers, notably Wild Bill Davison, Zutty Singleton and Willie 'The Lion' Smith. Despite a sound playing technique and a deep and abiding interest in the development of early jazz, Gwaltney's work is largely unknown by the wider jazz public. Although few in number, his albums blend differing jazz talents with great skill thanks to his own intelligent arrangements.

● ALBUMS: with Bobby Hackett *Gotham Jazz Scene* (1957)★★★★, with Buck Clayton *Goin' To Kansas City* (1960)★★★★, *Tommy Gwaltney Trio* (c.1962-63)★★★, with Zutty Singleton *Zutty And The Clarinet Kings* (1967)★★★, with Wild Bill Davison *I'll Be A Friend With Pleasure* (1967)★★, *Maxine Sullivan - Queen Of Song* (c.1970)★★, with Wally Garner *Clarinets In Tandem* (1972-76 recordings)★★★, *Singin' The Blues* (1975)★★★.

GWANGWA, JONAS

b. 1941, Johannesburg, South Africa. Trombonist Gwangwa was already a leading light of the emigré South African jazz community when he teamed up with Hugh Masekela in 1971 to record *Union Of South Africa*. The band of the same name fell apart when Gwangwa was knocked down by a car on the way home from the band's debut gig at a New York club, and was hospitalized for over a year. During the late 80s, Gwangwa was musical director of a Botswanan band sponsored by the African National Congress, and renewed his links with Masekela when the latter based himself in the country to record the *Techno Bush* and *Waiting For The Rain* albums.

● ALBUMS: with Union Of South Africa *Union Of South Africa* (TML 1971)★★★.

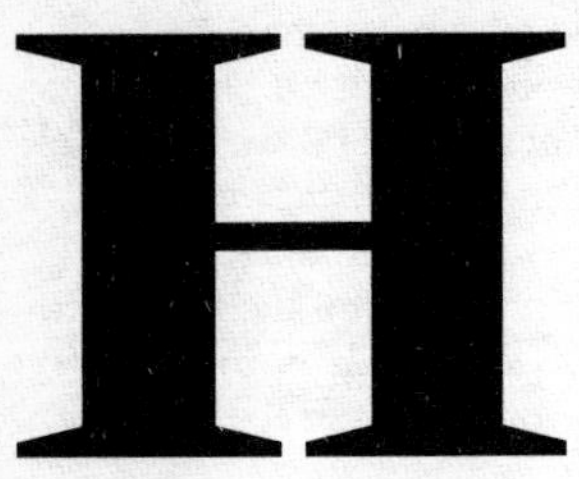

HACKETT, BOBBY

b. 31 January 1915, Providence, Rhode Island, USA, d. 7 June 1976. After learning to play a number of instruments while still at school, including cornet and guitar, Hackett became a professional musician when barely into his teens. For the first few years he played violin and guitar but by 1934 he was concentrating on cornet. In 1936 he briefly led his own band, then moved to New York where he played in the society dance bands of Meyer Davis and the Lanin brothers. In 1937 he moved towards the more jazz-oriented currently-popular big bands, working with Joe Marsala and Red McKenzie. In 1938 he was one of the guest musicians at Benny Goodman's prestigious Carnegie Hall concert. At this time Hackett was leading a band at Nick's, a prominent New York nightclub. The last few years of the 30s found him working in radio in New York, on motion pictures in Hollywood, making records and leading his own bands, big and small. In mid-summer 1941 he joined Glenn Miller, playing mostly guitar (though he was featured on cornet on the hit record 'String Of Pearls'), and then spent more time with the Marsala band, the Casa Loma Orchestra, and in staff work at NBC. He played on numerous jazz record and concert dates, including the Town Hall concert in New York that established the Louis Armstrong All Stars. At the end of the 40s and throughout the 50s he worked steadily along the east coast and in Canada and continued to make records. Many of his recordings were classics of their kind, especially his 1955 dates with Jack Teagarden and a series of mood-music albums he made for comedian Jackie Gleason. A splendid band he led at the Henry Hudson Hotel in New York during 1956/7 featured at different times Tommy Gwaltney and Bob Wilber. In the early 60s Hackett rejoined Goodman, played with Ray McKinley and then became a regular accompanist, on stage and on record, to Tony Bennett. In the late 60s and early 70s he toured the USA and Europe, playing club and festival dates often in company with Vic Dickenson. A superb cornetist with faultless taste, his delightful obligati behind singers as diverse as Bennett, Armstrong, Lee Wiley and Teresa Brewer are ample testimony to his unobtrusive skills. The mood-music albums he made for Gleason similarly demonstrate his extraordinarily graceful playing. He was equally at home both in dixieland and mainstream groups, where his straight jazz work was fiery and inventive but always elegant. Although no one could ever guess it from his cornet playing, ill health, brought on by heavy drinking, plagued Bobby Hackett for most of his life.

● ALBUMS: *Trumpet Solos* 10-inch album (Brunswick 1950)★★★, *Jazz Session* 10-inch album (Columbia 1951)★★★, *Horn A Plenty* 10-inch album (Commodore 1951)★★★, with Max Kaminsky 10-inch album *Battle Of Jazz, Vol. 5* (Brunswick 1953)★★★, *Soft Lights* 10-inch album (Capitol 1954)★★★, *In A Mellow Mood* (Capitol 1955)★★★★, *The Hackett Horn* (Epic 1955)★★★, with Jack Teagarden *Coast Concert* (Capitol 1956)★★★★, *The Bobby Hackett Horn* 10-inch album (Columbia 1956)★★★, *Rendezvous* (Rendezvous 1956)★★★, *Live From The Voyager Room Vol. 1* (Shoestring 1956)★★★★, *Gotham Jazz Scene* (Capitol 1957)★★★, with Teagarden *Jazz Ultimate* (Capitol 1958)★★★★, *Don't Take Your Love From Me* (Capitol 1958)★★★, *Live From The Voyager Room Vol. 2* (Shoestring 1958)★★★★, *Bobby Hackett At The Embers* (Capitol 1958)★★★, *Thanks, Bobby* (1958)★★★, *Blues With A Kick* (Capitol 1959)★★★★, *Bobby Hackett Quartet* (Capitol 1959)★★★, with Teagarden *Jack Teagarden And Bobby Hackett* (Commodore 1959)★★★★, *Easy Beat* (Capitol 1960)★★, *The Spirit Swings Me* (SeSac 1960)★★★, *Candlelight And Romance* (SeSac 1960)★★★, *Bobby Hackett With Johnny Seng And Glenn Osser At The Wurlitzer Pipe Organ* (1960)★★, *Bobby Hackett Quartet!* (1960)★★★, *Dream Awhile* (Columbia 1961)★★★, *The Most Beautiful Horn In The World* (Columbia 1962)★★★, *Night Love* (Columbia 1962)★★★, *Oliver* (Epic 1963)★★, *The Music Of Bert Kaempfert* (Epic 1964)★★, *Hello Louis!* (Epic 1964)★★, *Trumpet's Greatest Hits* (Epic 1965)★★★, *Bobby Hackett With Jim Cullum's Happy Jazz Band* (1966)★★, *That Midnight Touch* (1967)★★★, *Creole Cookin'* (Verve 1967)★★★, with Billy Butterfield, Luiz Henrique *Brazil* (Verve 1967)★★★, *A Time For Love* (1967)★★★, with Vic Dickenson *This Is My Bag* (1968)★★★, *Bobby Hackett, Vic Dickenson, Maxine Sullivan At The Fourth Manassas Jazz Festival* (Jazzology 1969)★★★, *Bobby Hackett's Sextet* (1970)★★★, *Live At The Roosevelt Grill Vols 1-4* (1970)★★★★, *Rare Italian Dates/Live At Louisiana Dates* (1971)★★★, with Teresa Brewer *What A Wonderful World* (1973)★★★, *Bobby Hackett-Vic Dickenson Septet* (1973)★★★, *Bobby Hackett ... Live With Ted Easton's Jazzband* (1973)★★★, *Strike Up The Band* (1974)★★★, *Butterfly Airs Vols 1 & 2* (1975)★★★, *Tin Roof Blues* (1976)★★★.

● COMPILATIONS: *At Nick's* (1944)★★★, *That Da Da Strain* rec. late 30s (1988)★★.

HADEN, CHARLIE

b. 6 August 1937, Shenandoah, Iowa, USA. Haden began his musical career when still a child, broadcasting daily on local country music radio. After formal music study he moved to Los Angeles, playing bass with Hampton Hawes, Art Pepper, Red Norvo and Paul Bley. While with Bley's trio he met Ornette Coleman and began rehearsing with him in 1958. By the following year he had moved to New York and become Coleman's regular bassist, exhibiting an exceptional understanding of the saxophonist's music. Haden stayed with Coleman until 1960, but has played with him since on several occasions, including some gigs in 1968 and 1972, where he played in tandem with one of his successors, David Izenzon. Because of drug problems, which he subsequently defeated, he was out of circulation for a while, but returned to the scene in 1964 to play with Denny

Zeitlin and Tony Scott. He returned to Coleman's group in 1966 and then joined the Jazz Composers' Orchestra Association. In 1969 he established the Liberation Music Orchestra with Carla Bley. The orchestra's first two albums, *Liberation Music Orchestra* and *Ballad Of The Fallen*, used themes from the Spanish Civil War and from Latin American resistance movements as the raw material for intense arrangements by Haden and Bley. Along with *Crisis*, a recording of a concert from a tour which Haden made with Ornette Coleman in 1969, *Liberation Music Orchestra* has the distinction of being the object of an attempt by the record companies' shareholders to withdraw it from the catalogue because of its 'anti-American' content. Both albums featured Haden's 'Song For Che' and *Crisis* also contained tunes inspired by the Vietnam conflict. Haden continued his interest in politically-motivated music in 1991 when he issued an album with Carlos Paredes, a Portuguese fado musician who had been an active anti-Fascist and also released a third Liberation Music Orchestra album, *Dream Keeper*, the title track a suite based on a poem by the African American writer Langston Hughes. During the 80s Haden widened his composing horizons, writing for a variety of instrumental combinations, collaborating with other composer-musicians such as Gavin Bryars and leading his own relatively mainstream group, Quartet West. He has also worked with Pat Metheny on a number of his albums, as well as Alice Coltrane (1968-72), Keith Jarrett (1967-75), in Old And New Dreams, virtually a reconstruction of the Ornette Coleman quartet but with Dewey Redman (an associate of Coleman during his later Blue Note period) on saxophone, in Magico (a trio with Jan Garbarek and Egberto Gismonti) and Geri Allen and Paul Motian. He also played with Chet Baker, on one of the trumpeter's last recording sessions (*Silence*), and was instrumental in introducing Cuban pianist Gonzalo Rubalcaba to a wider audience, producing and playing on his Blue Note debut, *Discovery*. In 1994 he worked with Ginger Baker on his well-received album *Going Back Home*. Through his own ventures and his contribution to the crucially important Ornette Coleman quartet, Haden carved out his place as one of the most skilful and adventurous bass-players at a time when several exponents of the instrument (including Charles Mingus and two other Coleman bassists, Scott La Faro and Izenzon) were building on the achievements of the likes of Paul Chambers, Ray Brown and Percy Heath, pushing the instrument into the spotlight with their virtuosity and range. In the 90s he was still setting standards, notably his 1997 collaboration with Pat Metheny on *Beyond The Missouri Sky (Short Stories)*.

● ALBUMS: *Liberation Music Orchestra* (Impulse! 1969)★★★, *Closeness* (Closeness 1976)★★, *The Golden Number* (1977)★★, with Hampton Hawes *As Long As There's Music* 1976 recording (Verve 1978)★★★, with Ornette Coleman *Soapsuds, Soapsuds* 1977 recordings (Artists House 1979)★★★★, with Christian Escoude *Gitane* (1979)★★★, *Duo* (Dreyfus Jazz 1979)★★★, with Jan Garbarek, Egberto Gismonti *Magico* (1980)★★★, with Garbarek, Gismonti *Folk Songs* (ECM 1981)★★★★, with Denny Zeitlin *Time Remembers One Time Once* (ECM 1983)★★★★, with Liberation Music Orchestra *The Ballad Of The Fallen* (ECM 1983)★★, *Quartet West* (Verve 1987)★★★, with Geri Allen, Paul Motian *Etudes* (1988)★★★, *Silence* 1987 recordings (Soul Note 1989)★★★, with Joe Henderson, Al Foster *An Evening With Henderson, Haden & Foster* 1987 recording (Red 1989)★★★, with Allen, Motian *In The Year Of The Dragon* (1989)★★, *In Angel City* (Verve 1989)★★★, with Allen, Motian *Segments* (1989)★★, with Allen, Motian *Live At The Village Vanguard* (1991)★★★★, with Liberation Music Orchestra *Dream Keeper* (Verve 1991)★★★, *Haunted Heart* (Verve 1991)★★★, *Dream Keeper* (Blue Note 1991)★★★, with Carlos Paredes *Dialogues* (Polydor 1991)★★, *First Song* (Soul Note 1991)★★, with Quartet West *Always Say Goodbye* (Verve 1994)★★★, *The Montreal Tapes* (Verve 1994)★★★, with Ginger Baker, Bill Frisell *Going Back Home* (Atlantic 1994)★★★, with Kenny Barron, Roy Haynes *Wanton Spirit* (1994)★★★, with Hank Jones *Steal Away Spirituals, Hymns And Folk Songs* (Verve 1995)★★★★, with Quartet West *Now Is The Hour* (Verve Gitanes 1996)★★★, with Baker, Frisell *Falling Off The Roof* (Atlantic 1996)★★★★, with Pat Metheny *Beyond The Missouri Sky (Short Stories By Charlie Haden & Pat Metheny)* (Verve 1997)★★★★, with Motian, Gonzalo Rubalcaba *The Montréal Tapes* 1989 recording (Verve 1998)★★★, with Allen, Motian *The Montréal Tapes* 1989 recording (Verve 1998)★★★, with Kenny Barron *Night And The City* (Verve 1998)★★★★, with Chris Anderson *None But The Lonely Heart* (Naim 1998)★★★★, with Lee Konitz, Brad Meldau *Alone Together* (Blue Note 1998)★★★★.

HADI, SHAFI

b. Curtis Porter, 21 September 1929, Philadelphia, USA. After playing saxophones in the Philadelphia R&B movement, Hadi studied composition at Howard University, and the University of Detroit. His legacy consists of three fortunately well recorded years with the Charles Mingus group, and the soundtrack to John Cassavetes' film *Shadows*. An emotional and blues-influenced player with enviable facility, it is a pity he was active in jazz for so short a time.

● ALBUMS: with Charles Mingus *Tijuana Moods* (1957)★★★★.

HADLEY, DARDANELLE

(see Dardanelle)

HAGANS, TIM

b. 19 August 1954, Dayton, Ohio, USA. After completing extensive formal studies at Bowling Green State University, Ohio, Hagans secured his first important professional engagement in 1974 when he joined the trumpet section of Stan Kenton's band. He remained with Kenton for a little over two years, touring, recording and teaching at the Kenton Summer Clinics. He then had a brief spell with Woody Herman before settling in Sweden. During the next few years he worked with other expatriates, including Thad Jones, Ernie Wilkins and Sahib Shihab, played in the Swedish and Danish Radio big bands, and also led his own small group which appeared at clubs and festivals. While in Sweden he continued to teach, working at various establishments including the University of Lund and the Jazz Institute of Malmö where he taught trumpet, improvisation and ensemble playing. In 1981 he returned to the USA, settling in Cincinnati, where he played in the Blue Wisp Big Band led by John Von Ohlen. He made a number of record dates with the band, on some of which his own compositions were played. He was again active in music education, teaching trumpet, improvisation and jazz history at the University of Cincinnati. In 1984 he moved to Boston, Massachusetts, taking up a teaching post at Berklee College Of Music and also playing in various groups, notably his own quintet. Three years later he moved to New York City, teaching privately and playing in various bands, including those led by Bob Belden, Bob Mintzer, Marc Copland, Vic Juris, Fred Hersch, Joe Lovano, Gary Peacock and George Russell. He made a brief return visit to Scandinavia to conduct the UMO (New Music Ensemble) in Helsinki, Finland. In 1986 and again the following year he received a grant from the National Endowment for the Arts to record and to compose a suite for a big band.

In the early 90s Hagans was still deeply involved in teaching and playing in the New York area, recording with Copland, Andy LaVerne and others. Hagans' trumpet style is rooted in bop and he plays with great drive and crackling attack on uptempo pieces. On slower tunes he develops long, logical solo lines, using his full tone to great advantage. His inherently lyrical conception is especially suited to ballads and when playing flügelhorn he creates richly atmospheric solos. Although little known outside the immediate areas in which he has played and taught, Hagans is fast developing into a major jazz voice.

● ALBUMS: with Stan Kenton *Fire, Fury And Fun* (1974)★★★★, with Kenton *Journey To Capricorn* (1976)★★★, with Thad Jones *Thad Jones' Eclipse* (1980)★★★, with Ernie Wilkins *Almost Big Band* (1980)★★★, with Blue Wisp *Butterfly* (MoPro 1982)★★★, *From The Neck Down* (1983)★★★, with Blue Wisp *Live At Carmelo's* (MoPro 1984)★★★, with Blue Wisp *Rollin' With Von Ohlen* (MoPro1984)★★, with Bob Belden *Treasure Island* (1989)★★, with Andy LaVerne *Severe Clear* (1990)★★★, with Marc Copland *All Blues At Night* (1990)★★★, *Audible Architecture* (Blue Note 1995)★★★, with Marcus Printup *Hubsongs: The Music Of Freddie Hubbard* (Blue Note 1998)★★★★.

Haggart, Bob

b. Robert Sherwood Haggart, 13 March 1914, New York City, New York, USA, d. 2 December 1998, Venice, Florida, USA. After formal tuition on guitar and informal playing of trumpet and piano, Haggart switched to bass, on which he was self-taught. After playing with various small-time dance bands, he came to national prominence when he joined the former members of the Ben Pollack unit who were planning their own co-operative band. This new outfit, under the nominal leadership of Bob Crosby, became one of the great successes of the swing era, combining as it did the currently popular dance band music with an exhilarating two-beat dixieland style. Haggart's contribution to the band's success extended far beyond his pivotal role as a member of the sprightly rhythm section. He arranged several of the band's most popular numbers, including 'South Rampart Street Parade' and 'Dogtown Blues'. Haggart was co-creator, with drummer Ray Bauduc, of a tune on which he whistled sibilantly through his front teeth, and pressed the strings of his bass while Bauduc played on them with his sticks. The unusual effect this produced created a massive hit for the duo and 'Big Noise From Winnetka' remains one of the best-known tunes from the swing era. In 1942 Haggart left the Crosby band, turning to studio work and arranging for many artists, including Louis Armstrong, but he retained his playing connections with former Crosby-band colleague Yank Lawson. In the early 50s the Lawson-Haggart Jazz band became very popular, and at the end of the 60s the two men again teamed up to create the equally acclaimed World's Greatest Jazz Band. The WGJB folded in 1978, but Haggart remained a popular figure at festivals and at reunions of the Crosby band, touring the USA and Europe as bandleader and sideman and making records, including some more with Lawson. He was also responsible for at least one other jazz standard, the ballad 'What's New?'.

● ALBUMS: with Yank Lawson *Lawson-Haggart Band Play Jelly Roll's Jazz* 10-inch album (Decca 1951)★★★, with Lawson *College Fight Song* 10-inch album (Decca 1952)★★★, with Lawson *Lawson-Haggart Band Play King Oliver's Jazz* 10-inch album (Decca 1952)★★★, with Lawson *Lawson-Haggart Band* 10-inch album (Decca 1952)★★★, with Lawson *Blues On The River* 10-inch album (Decca 1952)★★★, with Lawson *Windy City Jazz* 10-inch album (Decca 1953)★★★, with Lawson *South Of The Mason-Dixon Line* 10-inch album (Decca 1954)★★★★, with Lawson *Louis' Hot 5's And 7's* 10-inch album (Decca 1954)★★★★, with Lawson *Hold That Tiger* (Decca 1956)★★★, with Lawson *Boppin' At The Hop* (Decca 1959)★★★, with Lawson *Junior Prom* (Everest 1959)★★★, with Lawson *Dixieland Goes West* (Everest 1960)★★★, with Lawson *Live At The Roosevelt Grill* (Atlantic 1969)★★★, with Lawson *What's New?* (Atlantic 1969)★★★★, *Sentimental Journey* (1980)★★, with Lawson *Go To New Orleans* (1987)★★★, with Lawson *Yank Lawson And Bob Haggart* (Jazzology 1992)★★★★, with Bob Haggart's Swing Three *Hag Leaps In* (Arbors 1997)★★★.

● COMPILATIONS: *A Portrait Of Bix* (Jazzology 1987)★★★★.

Haig, Al

b. 22 July 1924, Newark, New Jersey, USA, d. 16 November 1982, New York City, New York, USA. One of the first bop pianists, and for a time among the very best of them, Haig spent the second half of the 40s in excellent musical company. Active in the clubs of New York, he played with Charlie Parker and Dizzy Gillespie and proved to be an outstanding accompanist. After a spell with Stan Getz, which ended in 1951, Haig drifted from the centre of the bebop stage, rarely recording and often accepting engagements which demanded little jazz playing. In the 70s he returned to the jazz scene, demonstrating on record that he had lost none of his understated skills and was also well aware of the musical developments of the intervening years. Despite his piecemeal career, Haig remains an important figure in the development of modern jazz piano playing.

● ALBUMS: with Mary Lou Williams *Piano Moderns* 10-inch album (Prestige 1953)★★★, *Al Haig Trio* reissued as *Jazz Will-O-The-Wisp* (Esoteric/Counterpoint 1954)★★★, *Al Haig Quartet* 10-inch album (Period 1954)★★★, *Al Haig Trio* 10-inch album (Pacific Jazz 1954)★★★, *Al Haig Today* (Mint 1965)★★★, *Invitation* (Spotlite 1974)★★★, *Special Brew* (Spotlite 1975)★★★, *Strings Attached* (Choice 1975)★★★★, *Chelsea Bridge* (1975)★★, *Solitaire* (Spotlite 1976)★★★, *Piano Interpretations* (Sea Breeze 1976)★★★, *Piano Time* (Sea Breeze 1976)★★★, *Interplay* (Sea Breeze 1976)★★★, *Serendipity* (1977)★★★, *A Portrait Of Bud Powell* (1977)★★, *Manhattan Memories* (Sea Breeze 1977)★★★, *Ornithology* (1977)★★★, *Reminiscence* (1977)★★★, *Al Haig In Paris* (1977)★★★, *Parisian Thoroughfare* (1977)★★★, *Al Haig Plays Dizzy Gillespie* (1977)★★★, *They All Played Bebop* (1977)★★★, *Al Haig Plays The Music Of Jerome Kern* (1978)★★★, *Expressly Ellington* (Spotlite 1979)★★★, *Al Haig Meets The Master Saxes, Vol. 1* 1948 recordings (Spotlite)★★★★, *Al Haig Meets The Master Saxes, Vol. 2* 1948 recordings (Spotlite)★★★★, *Al Haig Meets The Master Saxes, Vol. 3* 1948-1951 recordings (Spotlite)★★★.

HAINES, CONNIE

(see Dorsey, Tommy)

HAKIM, OMAR

b. c.1959, New York City, New York, USA. A graduate of the New York School of Music and Art, drummer Hakim began his career recording with various pop and soul units. When he did play with jazz musicians, his prodigious talent meant that they were artists of the calibre of Gil Evans, George Benson, and David Sanborn. In 1982 he joined Wayne Shorter and Joe Zawinul's Weather Report, in which he impressed with his ability to add complex beat divisions to funk rhythms without losing impetus. During his three years with Weather Report Hakim managed to continue recording, including a 1984 session with John Scofield, and an appearance with pop-star Sting on *Dream Of The Blue Turtles*. Playing at the major 1991 jazz festivals in a quartet completed by Shorter, Herbie Hancock, and Stanley Clarke, Hakim has already established his reputation as a major jazz artist.

● ALBUMS: *Rhythm Deep* (GRP 1989)★★.

HAKIM, SADIK

b. 15 July 1919, Duluth, Minnesota, USA, d. 20 June 1983, New York, USA. Hakim studied music with his grandfather before moving to Chicago and starting work as a professional musician. He played piano with tenor saxophonist Ben Webster in 1944-45 before playing on the Savoy sessions with Dizzy Gillespie and Charlie Parker with whom he lived for a time. Between 1946 and 1948 he worked with Lester Young. In the 50s he worked with two more tenor saxophonists - James Moody (1951-54) and Buddy Tate (1956-60). He settled in Montreal in 1966 and towards the end of his life worked in Japan (1979-80). He wrote many compositions including 'Eronel' which is sometimes credited to Thelonious Monk. He is a piano player forever associated with his work in the 40s.

● ALBUMS: *Lester Young And His Tenor Sax, Vol. 2* (1947-8 recordings)★★★★, *Sadik Hakim Plays Duke Ellington* (1974)★★, *Witches, Goblins, Etc.* (1977)★★★, *Memories* (1978)★★★.

HALCOX, PAT

b. 17 March, 1930, London, England. Playing part-time in the early 50s, trumpeter Halcox quickly established himself as a leading figure in the British trad-jazz scene. He teamed up with Chris Barber and Monty Sunshine in their co-operative band, but then decided to pursue the career of research chemist for which he had trained. The Barber band continued trumpetless for a while before engaging Ken Colyer. In 1954 a rift developed in the Barber-Colyer relationship, and Halcox was persuaded to return and become a full-time musician. He has been a member of the band ever since. The eclectic musical personality of the Barber band is an ideal setting for Halcox's wide-ranging style; he remains one of the band's greatest assets and is also one of the UK's leading traditional and mainstream trumpeters.

● ALBUMS: *Chris Barber Jubilee Album Vols 1-3* (1958-74 recordings)★★★★, *7th Avenue* (1980)★★★, *There's Yes, Yes, In Your Eyes* (Jazzology 1989)★★★, *Songs From Tin Pan Alley* (Jazzology 1991)★★★.

HALE, CORKY

b. Merylynn Hecht, *c.*1935, Illinois, USA. As a small child Hale took piano lessons but at the age of eight became enamoured of the harp. She studied the instrument, playing classical and popular music of the day but gradually developed an interest in late-swing era music. In her late teens she went to California to study, played on television and was soon finding herself overwhelmed with offers of work. Amongst these jobs was one with a pianist just starting out, Liberace. Hale's playing of the harp was of a very high order and during the 50s she was in great demand from television and film studios and worked in many bands backing popular artists of the day. Hale was offered work with several all-female bands but avoided this track as being demeaning to her skills as a musician. During the late 50s she continued to play and also ran a clothing store, then married and moved to Europe where she continued to play but only rarely. Her marriage over, she returned to the USA, tried another spell in Europe, this time in London, and eventually became relatively settled in New York. By the late 70s she was a regular at several clubs and still found time for European visits, especially to London where she enjoyed a high reputation. Hale continued to play extensively, finding opportunities to work frequent and rewarding. Unlike many other harpists, Hale brings to her playing an acute sense of the needs of jazz and thus avoids the sometimes gimmicky approach made by most others on this instrument. In her approach, Hale applies the thinking of a pianist and is thus an interesting soloist and a subtle and skilled accompanist. She is especially effective when backing singers, such as Kitty White with whom she has recorded. Like Dorothy Ashby, Hale is a true jazz player although she wryly recognizes that she is often hired because of the curiosity value of her chosen instrument.

● ALBUMS: *Kitty White-Corky Hale* (Pacifica 1954)★★★.

HALL, ADELAIDE

b. Adelaide Louisa Hall, 20 October 1901, Brooklyn, New York City, New York, USA, d. 7 November 1993, London, England. Though not a jazz singer, Hall has become one of the most famous vocalists in jazz history through her wordless vocals on such Duke Ellington recordings as 'Creole Love Call' and 'Blues I Love To Sing'. Other numbers with which she was indelibly associated, included 'Sophisticated Lady', 'Old Fashioned Love', 'Memories Of You', 'Solitude', 'Don't Get Around Much Anymore' and 'Don't Worry 'Bout Me'. Many of the songs she sang were written especially for her. Her fine soprano voice was developed by her father, a music professor. Like her friend, Lena Horne, her name will always be associated with Harlem's famous Cotton Club and the 'greats' who gathered there, such as Ellington, Fats Waller and composer Harold Arlen. Hall, a self-taught tap dancer, played in the Eubie Blake-Noble Sissle show in the early 20s, and appeared in a series of revues, including *Shuffle Along* and *Desires Of 1927*. She starred in Lew Leslie's *Blackbirds Of 1928*, in a cast which also included Bill 'Bojangles' Robinson, and Elisabeth Welch. The Dorothy Fields/Jimmy McHugh score introduced 'Diga Diga Doo', 'Doin' The New Low-Down', 'I Can't Give You Anything But Love' and a pre-Gershwin 'Porgy'. When the show transferred to the Moulin Rouge in Paris, Hall went with it, and stayed on to sing at the Lido. By this time she had married an English seaman, Bert Hicks. He opened a club for her, called La Grosse Pomme (The Big Apple), whose clientele included Django Reinhardt, Maurice Chevalier and Charles Boyer. In the early 30s she recorded with Duke Ellington and Willy Lewis in the USA, and was also accompanied by pianists Art Tatum and Joe Turner on a New York session which produced 'This Time It's Love'. During the rest of the decade she toured extensively in the USA and Europe, and by the late 30s had settled in Britain, where she lived for over 50 years. In 1938 Hall appeared at London's Theatre Royal, Drury Lane, in *The Sun Never Sets*, a musical in which she impressed audiences and critics with her version of Vivian Ellis's title song. In the same year she recorded four songs with Fats Waller in London: 'That Old Feeling', 'I Can't Give You Anything But Love', 'Smoke Dreams' and 'You Can't Have Your Cake And Eat It'. With her husband, she opened the Florida Club in Bruton Mews, but it was destroyed during a bombing raid in World War II. Later she joined an ENSA company and was one of the first artists into Germany after the liberation. After the war she worked consistently, singing in theatres throughout the country, on cruise liners, and on her own radio show, accompanied by the Joe Loss Orchestra. In 1951 she starred in the London version of Cole Porter's *Kiss Me, Kate*, and, in the following year, sang 'A Touch Of Voodoo' and 'Kind To Animals' in Jack Gray and Hugh Martin's hit musical, *Love From Judy*, at the Saville Theatre. In 1957 she was back on Broadway, with Lena Horne, in *Jamaica*, which ran for over 500 performances. In 1963, shortly after opening a new club, the Calypso, in London's Regent Street, Adelaide's husband Bert died. During the 60s and 70s, Hall was out of the limelight, but in the 80s, came a renaissance, partly sparked by the release of Francis Ford Coppola's film *The Cotton Club*. From then on she was in constant demand for cabaret at the Ritz Hotel, and other UK venues such as the Donmar Warehouse and the King's Head, Islington. In 1988, she presented her one-woman show at New York's Carnegie Hall, and three years later, was joined onstage at London's Queen Elizabeth Hall by artists such as Larry Adler, Ralph McTell and Roy Budd, in a concert to celebrate her 90th birthday.

● ALBUMS: *That Wonderful Adelaide Hall* (1969)★★★, *Hall Of Fame* (1970)★★, *Hall Of Ellington* (1976)★★★, *There Goes That Song Again* (1980)★★★, *Live At The Riverside Studios* (1989)★★★★, *I Touched A Star* (1989)★★★, *Hall Of Memories 1927-1939* (1990)★★★, *Crooning Blackbird* (1993)★★★.

HALL, AL

b. Alfred Wesley Hall, 18 March 1915, Jacksonville, Florida, USA, d. 18 January 1988. Hall was raised in Philadelphia where he began playing cello and also the tuba. By the early 30s he had switched to playing bass and worked with several bands, some of them in New York. In the late 30s he was a member of Teddy Wilson's fine sextet and, later, his short-lived big band. After Wilson's band folded in the early 40s, Hall worked with Ellis Larkins and Mary Lou Williams but was also actively pursuing the new musical trend that was bop. He recorded extensively, shifting between swing era styles and the new forms with apparent ease. He also formed his own record label, Wax, recording several bands including his own, before selling the label to Atlantic Records. During this same period, the mid-40s, he also began accompanying Erroll Garner, continuing to do so intermittently for almost two decades. During the 50s, 60s, and 70s he worked steadily, combining work in theatre pit orchestras with jazz groups. Among the jazz musicians and blues artists with whom he worked during these decades were Eubie Blake, Phil Moore, Benny Goodman, Alberta Hunter and Doc Cheatham. He continued to play until shortly before his death. A secure and reliable player with excellent time and a solid technique, Hall's appearance on countless albums was testimony to the high regard in which he was held by his fellow musicians.

● COMPILATIONS: *The Chronological Teddy Wilson 1941* (Classics 1941)★★★★.

HALL, EDMOND

b. 15 May 1901, New Orleans, Louisiana, USA, d. 11 February 1967. Hall was born into a highly musical family: his father played clarinet and four of his brothers became professional musicians, mostly on reed instruments, the best known of these being clarinettist Herbie Hall. After playing clarinet in his home town with Buddy Petit, Lee Collins, Kid Thomas Valentine and others in the early 20s, Hall headed for the north and a marked change of musical scene. From 1929 and throughout the 30s he became one of the most respected and sought-after clarinettists in jazz, playing in a manner which, while never losing the intrinsic qualities of New Orleans jazz, allowed him to play an important role in the swing era. Among the musicians with whom he worked during these years were Claude Hopkins, Lucky Millinder, Zutty Singleton and Joe Sullivan. In the early 40s Hall played in Red Allen's band, made some excellent quartet records with Charlie Christian, Israel Crosby and Meade 'Lux' Lewis (who played celeste), recorded with the De Paris Brothers Orchestra and turned down an offer to join Duke Ellington. Instead he became a member of Teddy Wilson's marvellous sextet, and after leaving Wilson in 1944, he led his own band in New York and Boston and was then a member of the house band at Eddie Condon's club. In 1955 he joined Louis Armstrong's All Stars, bringing to the band a much-needed fire and excitement at a time when it was beginning to sound a little jaded. He left Armstrong in 1958 and two years later, after living briefly in Ghana, began a sustained period of international touring which ended with his death in February 1967. A fluid and inventive soloist, Hall's playing exhibited a marvellous blend of New Orleans earthiness and Goodman-esque polish. He was one of the outstanding clarinettists of the swing era, as his recordings with his own groups testify. And those he made with the Wilson sextet, are arguably among the best ever by a small mainstream jazz combo.

● ALBUMS: *The Edmond Hall All Stars Live From The Savoy Cafe, Boston* (1949)★★, with Miff Mole *Battle Of Jazz, Vol. 4* 10-inch album (Brunswick 1953)★★★, *Edmond Hall At Club Hangover* (Storyville 1954)★★★, with Eddie Condon *Bixieland* (1955)★★★★, with Louis Armstrong *Ambassador Satch* (1956/7 recordings)★★★★, with Armstrong *A Musical Autobiography* (1956/7 recordings)★★★★, *Edmond Hall Quartet In Argentina* (1958)★★★, *Edmond Hall All Stars* (1958)★★, *Edmond Hall And His Orchestra* (1959)★★★, *Edmond Hall With The Gustav Brom Orchestra* (1960)★★★, *Edmond Hall Quartet* (1966)★★★, *Edmond Hall With Papa Bue's Viking Jazzband* (1966)★★, *Edmond Hall In Copenhagen* (Storyville 1967)★★★★, *Edmond Hall's Quartet & Quintet* (1966)★★★.

● COMPILATIONS: with others *The Complete Blue Note Sessions* (1941-52 recordings)★★★★, with Teddy Wilson *B Flat Swing* (Jazz Archives 1944 recordings)★★★★, *Rompin' In '44* (1944 recordings)★★★, *Edmond Hall 1941-57* (Giants Of Jazz 1987)★★★.

HALL, HERB

b. Herbert L. Hall, 28 March 1907, Reserve, Louisiana, USA, d. 6 March 1996, San Antonio, Florida, USA. One of the first generation of jazz clarinettists, Herb Hall and his family forebears established a tradition of excellence outside of the usual jazz melting pot of New Orleans. His father, Edward Hall Senior, had played in the Onward Brass Band at the turn of the century, and many of his eight children subsequently distinguished themselves as musicians. Edmond, the second eldest of his progeny, became the clarinet player with Louis Armstrong and earned a worldwide reputation for his skills. The success of his brothers Robert, Clarence and Herb was more limited, but between them they played with all the great names in jazz and blues from the 20s onwards. Herb initially started his musical career on the banjo, but moved to the clarinnet under the influence of his brother. Like Clarence and Robert, he was also adept at alto and baritone saxophone if the occasion demanded it. Much of his inspiration came from the Creole tradition, which included playing the Albert-system clarinet with its anachronistic fingering style. Although he had adopted the instrument after Edward, he would not see his elder brother play until he briefly visited him in New York in 1936, by which time he had established his own reputation. His first engagements had come with Kid Augustin Victor in Baton Rouge in 1926, replacing brother Clarence. From there he joined the orchestra led by Sidney Desvigne who played on Mississippi riverboats, then trumpeter Don Albert's touring group. A leading jazz orchestra of the day, they toured the southern states regularly, basing themselves in San Antonio. Here, in 1936, Hall made his first recordings, which also featured Alvin Alcorn and Louis Cottrell Jnr. Following World War II he joined his brother Edward in New York who found him regular work with trumpeter Herman Autrey and pianist Sonny White. He established a residency with Bobby Hackett and Don Ewell at Eddie Condon's club, whilst appearing regularly on recording sessions for artists such as Doc Cheatham and Sammy Price. His own recording career was less prolific, Hall always sustaining the tradition of jazz as a live event established in his youth. In the 70s he returned to San Antonio, after which his schedule gradually declined. Following his first European visit to France in 1956 he eventually reached British shores in 1981. He returned periodically thereafter, playing with the repertory band Bob Greene's World Of Jelly Roll Morton at the Newport Jazz Festival. In his later years Hall became a convert to yoga and established his own vegetable garden, in which he took as much pride as his musical achievements.

● ALBUMS: *Old Tyme Modern* (Biograph 1969)★★★.

HALL, JIM

b. 4 December 1930, Buffalo, New York, USA. While studying at the Cleveland Institute of Music, Hall made his first professional appearances playing guitar in local bands. In the mid-50s he settled on the west coast, where he continued his studies and also played with Chico Hamilton's quintet. In 1956 he became a member of Jimmy Giuffre's trio, thereafter working with Ella Fitzgerald, Bill Evans, Paul Desmond and in duo with Lee Konitz. In the early 60s he was briefly with Sonny Rollins, a stint which included two important albums, *The Bridge* and *What's New*, then teamed up with Art Farmer to co-lead a small group. In the mid-60s his career was affected by personal problems; but he soon returned to tour internationally and to make records with Evans and in duo with Ron Carter, with whom he recorded *Alone Together*. In the early 70s, he was working again with Desmond, on *Concierto*, and in duo with Red Mitchell. In the early 80s he played once more with Carter, recording *Telephone,* performed with classical violinist Itzhak Perlman and recorded *First Edition* with George Shearing. Throughout his career Hall has displayed a marked preference for working solo or in duos, and his playing is distinguished by self-effacing good taste and a clear understanding of the sensitive role demanded by partnerships such as those with Konitz, Rollins, Evans, Carter and Mitchell. Although less well known to audiences than many other guitarists of his generation, Hall's outstanding improvisational gifts and his abilities as collaborator and composer contribute towards his status as a widely respected figure within the jazz world.

● ALBUMS: with Bob Brookmeyer, Jimmy Raney *Street Swingers* reissued as *Brookmeyer And Guitars* (World Pacific/Kimberly 1957)★★★, *Jazz Guitar* (Pacific Jazz 1957)★★★, *Good Friday Blues* (Pacific Jazz 1960)★★★, with Bill Evans *Undercurrent* (United Artists 1962)★★★★, with Jimmy Raney, Zoot Sims *Two Jims And Zoot* (Mainstream 1965)★★★, with Evans *Intermodulation* (Verve 1966)★★★, *In A Sentimental Mood* reissued as *It's Nice To Be With You* (Verve1969)★★★★, *Where Would I Be?* (Original Jazz Classics 1971)★★★★, with Ron Carter *Alone Together* (Original Jazz Classics 1972)★★★, *Concierto* (CTI 1975)★★★★, *Jim Hall Live!* (Horizon 1975)★★, *Commitment* (A&M 1975)★★★, *Jim Hall Live In Tokyo* (1976)★★★, with Red Mitchell *Jim Hall And Red Mitchell* (Artists House 1978)★★★, *Concerto De Aranjuez* (Evidence 1981)★★★, *Circles* (Concord Jazz 1981)★★, *First Edition* (1982)★★★, with Carter *Telephone* (1984)★★★, *Jim Hall's Three* (Concord Jazz 1986)★★★, with Michel Petrucciani, Wayne Shorter *Power Of Three* (1987)★★★★, with Tom Harrell *These Roots* (Denon 1988)★★★, *All Across The City* (Concord Jazz 1989)★★★, *Live At Town Hall, Vol. 1* (Limelight 1991)★★★, *Live At Town Hall, Vol. 2* (Limelight 1991)★★★, *Youkali* (CTI 1992)★★★, *Subsequently* (Limelight 1992)★★★, with Carter *Live At Village West* (1993)★★★, *Something Special* (Limelight 1993)★★, *Dedications & Inspirations* (Telarc 1994)★★★★, *Dialogues* (Telarc 1995)★★, *Textures* (Telarc 1997)★★★, *Panorama: Live At The Village Vanguard* (Telarc 1997)★★★★, *By Arrangement* (Telarc 1998)★★★.

HALL, MINOR

b. 2 March 1897, Sellers, Louisiana, USA, d. 16 October 1959. The younger brother of Tubby Hall, he played in various bands in New Orleans, sometimes deputizing for his brother. He later played in Chicago before military service in World War I interrupted his career. In these early years he played with several noted musicians including Kid Ory and Sidney Bechet. After the war he joined King Oliver's band for a brief stint on the west coast, then came back to Chicago to join Jimmie Noone. In the late 20s and early 30s he was again on the coast, playing in Mutt Carey's band and then teamed up again with Ory for a long spell in San Francisco in the late 40s and early 50s. During this period he made many records and some motion pictures. A solid drummer with a foundation of basic New Orleans style overlaid with an awareness of swing drumming developments, Hall could be flashy and assertive but was generally dependable for his secure time.

● ALBUMS: with Kid Ory *Live At Club Hangover* (Dawn Club 1953-54)★★, *Kid Ory's Creole Jazz Band* (Good Time Jazz 1954)★★★.

HALL, TUBBY

b. Alfred Hall, 12 October 1895, Sellers, Louisiana, USA, d. 13 May 1946. Hall played drums with several leading New Orleans marching bands and dance orchestras before moving to Chicago in 1918. After military service in World War I he returned to Chicago, playing with many well-known jazz bands including those led by King Oliver, Jimmie Noone, Carroll Dickerson and Louis Armstrong, recording with some of them. He continued playing, mostly in Chicago, into the 40s, occasionally leading his own band at clubs. Unlike his more overt younger brother, Minor Hall, he played drums with subtlety and clearly saw his role as that of merely a discreet, supporting player.

HALLBERG, BENGT

b. 13 September 1932, Gothenberg, Sweden. Hallberg was something of a child prodigy at the piano. He made his first recording at the age of 15 and, in 1950, recorded an album with Arne Domnerus which was released in the USA. During the early 50s he would travel by train to Stockholm to play with the best Swedish musicians and was often in demand by visiting Americans of the stature of Lee Konitz, Stan Getz and Quincy Jones. In 1954 Hallberg moved to Stockholm to further his study of classical music at the Royal Academy of Music. Throughout the 50s and 60s, while establishing himself as one of Sweden's leading jazz musicians, Hallberg composed for string quartets and chamber groups and found himself much in demand as a session musician and composer of film and radio scores. Today he maintains this diverse output; his recent work as musical director of the Swedish Radio Jazz Group declare Hallberg's continuing fascination with composition.

● ALBUMS: *Stan Getz Stockholm Sessions* (1958)★★★, *Kiddin' On The Keys* (1959)★★★, *At Gyllene Cirklen* (1962)★★★, *On His Own* (Phontastic 1976)★★★, *Hallberg's Happiness* (Phontastic 1977)★★★, *The Hallberg Treasure Chest, A Bouquet From '78* (Phontastic 1979)★★, *The Hallberg Touch* (Phontastic 1980)★★★, with Ove Lind *Dialogue In Swing* (Phontastic 1982)★★★★, with Karin Krog *Two Of A Kind* (Four Leaf Clover 1982)★★★★, *Egenhandigt* (Phontastic 1982)★★★, *Hallberg's Surprise* (Phontastic 1988)★★★, *Bo Ohlgren* (Phontastic 1988)★★★, *Spring On The Air* (Phono Suecia 1988)★★★, with Kjell *Baeklelund Contrasts* (Sonet 1991)★★, *The Tapdancing Butterfly* (Aquila 1992)★★★, *Skansen In Our Hearts* (Aquila 1992)★★, *5 x 100* (Improkomp 1996)★★★, *Time On My Hands* (Improkomp 1997), *In A Mellow Tone* (Inprokomp 1997)★★★★.

HAMILTON, ANDY

b. *c.*1918, Jamaica, West Indies. Hamilton played tenor saxophone in his homeland, forming his own bands during the 30s, the first of which he named Silvershine. During the early 40s he entertained celebrities, including Errol Flynn aboard the movie star's yacht. At the end of the decade Hamilton went to the UK, settling in Birmingham where he remained and in time became a mainstay of the city's jazz scene. For more than 40 years Hamilton proved to be very popular but he was never restricted to the region's West Indian community, although he has always maintained a measure of calypso music and other Caribbean forms in his repertoire. He worked steadily if relatively obscurely, as did his musical companion, pianist Sam Brown, who worked with Hamilton for more than 40 years. Meanwhile, he built a significant reputation among visiting jazzmen. Hamilton did not make his first album until he was 72 and revealed ballad playing that is softly lyrical in tone. Other areas of his extensive repertoire, like his own compositions, vividly retain the colour and energy of his long-ago homeland.

● ALBUMS: *Silvershine* (World Circuit 1991)★★★, *Jamaica By Night* (World Circuit 1994)★★★.

HAMILTON, CHICO

b. Foreststorn Hamilton, 21 September 1921, Los Angeles, California, USA. Hamilton's future career as a drummer was well established even before he left school. By that time he had played with many other young fledgling jazz artists, including Dexter Gordon, Ernie Royal, Charles Mingus and Buddy Collette (who later became his musical partner). In 1940 he performed briefly with Lionel Hampton and Slim Gaillard, but military service interrupted his career. In the late 40s he worked with Jimmy Mundy, Count Basie and Lester Young; between 1948 and 1955 he was regular accompanist to Lena Horne. In 1952 he recorded with Gerry Mulligan's revolutionary pianoless quartet and in 1955 formed his own quartet which, with shifting personnel, remained in existence for several years. Hamilton's groups of the 50s featured several outstanding musicians - among them Collette, Fred Katz, Eric Dolphy, Ralph Pena, Dennis Budimir and Ron Carter - and experimented with unusual instrumental combinations, notably cello and flute. Their relaxed, mellow sound attracted the attention of fringe jazz audiences and their popularity was enhanced by the film, *Jazz On A Summer's Day*, which showed the group in rehearsal for their appearance at the 1958 Newport Jazz Festival. In the 60s Hamilton's group continued to perform, but changes in instrumentation and style saw the cello replaced by the trombone. In the mid-60s Hamilton was invited to write and perform advertising jingles; this proved so successful that he formed a production company, the running of which kept him from active participation in jazz for several years. In the mid-80s, however, Hamilton was back with a new 'heavy metal jazz' band, Euphoria, and had started to record again.

● ALBUMS: *Chico Hamilton Trio* 10-inch album (Pacific Jazz 1955)★★★, *Chico Hamilton Quintet With Buddy Collette* reissued as *Spectacular* (Pacific Jazz 1955)★★★★, *Chico Hamilton Quintet In Hi-Fi* (Pacific Jazz 1956)★★★, *Chico Hamilton Trio* (Pacific Jazz 1956)★★★, with Laurindo Almeida *Delightfully Modern* (Jazztone 1957)★★★★, *Chico Hamilton Plays The Music Of Fred Katz* (Pacific Jazz 1957)★★★, *South Pacific In Hi-Fi* (World Pacific 1957)★★★, *The Chico Hamilton Trio Introduces Freddie Gambrell* reissued as *Meet Chico Hamilton* (World Pacific 1958)★★★, *Chico Hamilton Quintet With Strings Attached* (Warners 1958)★★★, *Gongs East* (Warners 1958)★★★★, *Ellington Suite* (World Pacific 1959)★★★★, *The Three Faces Of Chico* (Warners 1959)★★★, *That Hamilton Man* (SeSac 1959)★★★, *The Original Chico Hamilton Quintet* (World Pacific 1960)★★★, *Selections from "Bye Bye Birdie"* (Columbia 1961)★★★, *Chico Hamilton Special* (Columbia 1961)★★★, *Drumfusion* (Columbia 1962)★★★, *Passin' Thru* (Impulse! 1962)★★★★, *A Different Journey* (Reprise 1963)★★★, *The Great Chico Hamilton Featuring Paul Horn* (Crown 1963)★★★, *Man From Two Worlds* (Impulse! 1964)★★★★, *Chic, Chic, Chico* (Impulse! 1965)★★★, *El Chico* (Impulse! 1965)★★★, *The Further Adventures Of El Chico* (Impulse! 1966)★★★, *The Dealer* (Impulse! 1966)★★, *The Gamut* (Solid State 1969)★★★, *Head Hunters* (Solid State 1969)★★★, *Easy Living* (Sunset 1969)★★★★, *El Exigente* (1970)★★★, *Chico The Master* (Ace 1974)★★★, *Peregrinations* (1975)★★★, *Chico Hamilton And The Players* (1976)★★★, *Reaching For The Top* (1978)★★★★, *Nomad* (Elektra 1979)★★★★, *Euphoria* (Discovery 1986)★★★, *Reunion* (Soul Note 1989)★★★, *Arroyo* (Soul Note 1991)★★★★, *Trio!* (Soul Note 1992)★★★, *Man From Two Worlds* (GRP 1993)★★★, *Goings East* (Discovery 1993)★★★, *My Panamanian Friend* (Soul Note 1993)★★★★, *Dancing To A Different Drummer* (Soul Note 1995)★★★.

● COMPILATIONS: *The Best Of Chico Hamilton* (Impulse! 1967)★★★★, *Chico Hamilton - His Greatest Hits* (Impulse! 1967)★★★★, *The Complete Pacific Jazz Recordings Of The Chico Hamilton Quintet* 6-CD/9-LP box set (Mosaic 1998)★★★★.

HAMILTON, ED

b. c.1967, USA. Hamilton developed his guitar playing out of an eclectic mix of influences that included Charlie Christian and rock, Latin and funk. Although he built a following during the early 90s he experienced difficulty in persuading record companies to accommodate him. As he told jazz writer Deni Kasrel, 'Since I didn't fit into any category, they didn't think they could sell it . . .' Showing remarkable tenacity, Hamilton stuck with his wide-ranging preferences and in 1996 was able to make the record he wanted. On the album he played guitar, bass and synthesizers, and also used guests Lenny White and George Howard. The diversity of approach that confounded record company executives makes it difficult to summarize Hamilton's style. The fact that the music featured on his debut album was all self-written provides the clue. It is this aspect of his work that most enables listeners to find the man inside the music.

● ALBUMS: *Planet Jazz* (Telarc 1996)★★★, *Path To The Heartland* (Telarc 1997)★★★.

HAMILTON, JEFF

b. 4 August 1953, Richmond, Indiana, USA. Hamilton began playing drums as a child and while in his early teens was a member of a trio playing at local clubs. He later studied percussion at Indiana University, where his fellow students included Peter Erskine and John Clayton. Hamilton's interest in jazz developed and he extended his studies to take tuition from John Von Ohlen. In 1974, on Clayton's recommendation, Hamilton was hired to play in the Tommy Dorsey Orchestra under the leadership of Murray McEachern. His next job was a brief stint with Lionel Hampton during 1975 and he then worked with Clayton as a member of the Monty Alexander trio. Two years later he left to play with Woody Herman. In 1978 he joined the LA Four with Ray Brown, Laurindo Almeida and Bud Shank. In the mid-80s Hamilton formed a big band in collaboration with John Clayton and his brother Jeff Clayton. He has also worked with the Philip Morris Superband. An outstanding drummer with the finesse and subtlety demanded of a small group player and the powerful swing needed for a big band, Hamilton is one of the most gifted of the younger generation of American mainstream jazz drummers.

● ALBUMS: with Monty Alexander *Live At Montreux* (c.1975)★★★★, with Woody Herman *Road Father* (1978)★★★★, with Herman *Chick, Donald, Walter And Woodrow* (1978)★★★, with LA Four *Watch What Happens* (1978)★★★, with Clayton-Hamilton *Groove Shop* (Capri 1989)★★★, with Clayton-Hamilton *Heart And Soul* (Capri 1991)★★★, *It's Hamilton Time* (Lake Street 1996)★★.

HAMILTON, JIMMY

b. 25 May 1917, Dillon, South Carolina, USA, d. 20 September 1994, St. Croix, Virgin Islands. A talented multi-instrumentalist as a child, Hamilton played baritone horn, trumpet, trombone and piano. He worked professionally in and around Philadelphia in the 30s, and after taking up tenor saxophone and clarinet, played with several name bands, including those led by Lucky Millinder, Jimmy Mundy and Teddy Wilson. In 1943 he joined Duke Ellington, playing in the saxophone section and as featured clarinet soloist. He remained with Ellington for a quarter of a century, leaving in 1968 to lead his own band briefly before going to live in the Virgin Islands. Since then Hamilton has worked as a teacher, but has also made occasional returns to the jazz scene, playing in the band for the Broadway show, *Sophisticated Ladies*, and as one of the guest soloists at the annual Ellington reunion conventions. He was also a member of the highly-regarded Clarinet Summit (with Alvin Batiste, John Carter and David Murray).Throughout his stay with Ellington, Hamilton consolidated his position as one of the most fluid and controlled of clarinettists. In contrast, his infrequent tenor solos displayed earthy vitality.

● ALBUMS: with Duke Ellington *The Cosmic Scene* (1959)★★★, with Ellington *The Nutcracker Suite* (1960)★★★★, *It's About Time* (Fantasy 1961)★★★★, *Can't Help Swingin'* (1961)★★★, with John Carter *Clarinet Summit Vol. 1* (1981)★★, with Carter *Clarinet Summit Vol. 2* (1985)★★, with Clarinet Summit *Southern Belles* (1988),★★★ *Swing Low, Sweet Clarinet* (Fresh Sounds 1988)★★★.

HAMILTON, JOHN 'BUGS'

b. 1911, St. Louis, Missouri, USA, d. 1947. A trumpet player much inspired by Louis Armstrong. He made his debut in 1931 with Chick Webb, and subsequently played with Cab Calloway, Sam Wooding, Teddy Hill and Fats Waller. With the last he can be heard on 'You're Letting The Grass Grow' (1939), 'Oh Frenchy', 'The Moon Is Low', 'You Run Your Mouth And I'll Run My Business' (1940) and 'Chant Of The Groove'.

● ALBUMS: *Fats Waller And His Rhythm - The Last Years* 1940-43 (1988)★★★★.

HAMILTON, SCOTT

b. 12 September 1954, Providence, Rhode Island, USA. As a child, Hamilton began playing clarinet, on which he had a few lessons, and piano. He then briefly played blues harmonica in a rock 'n' roll band. He took up tenor saxophone as a young teenager, teaching himself largely by listening to records in his father's collection. These records were by jazzmen of the 30s and 40s, and Hamilton appeared on the scene as an apparent throwback to those times, recreating the tenor styling of the likes of Ben Webster. As such he was rapturously received by audiences who thought players in this style were long defunct. He worked extensively in and around New York, often teaming up with Warren Vaché, similarly regarded as an important addition to the fading jazz mainstream. Hamilton's success in the late 70s led to his appearing with many leading jazzmen and performing at prestigious venues and major festivals in the USA and overseas. His ready success brought with it some personal problems and to some extent inhibited his growth as a stylist in his own right. By the early 80s, however, he had overcome all such problems and occasionally reverted to his early habit of playing in the manner of Webster, he was clearly his own man. He had also become a major figure on the international jazz stage. Most of his numerous concert and record album appearances are under his own name, but he has also appeared as a sideman in bands led by Benny Goodman, Woody Herman, Vaché, John Bunch and Bill Berry. In addition, he has been teamed up with Ruby Braff, Charlie Byrd, and on *Back To Back* and *Scott's Buddy* he duetted with veteran tenor saxophonist Buddy Tate. In the 90s Hamilton was still hugely popular on the festival circuit, appearing as leader or as principal soloist with all-star groups such as Newport Jazz Festival All-Stars and the Concord Jazz All-Stars.

● ALBUMS: *The Swinging Young Scott Hamilton* (Famous Door 1977)★★★, *Scott Hamilton Is A Good Wind Who Is Blowing Us No Ill* (Concord Jazz 1977)★★★★, *Live At Concord 1977* (Concord Jazz 1977)★★★, *Scott Hamilton 2* (Concord Jazz 1978)★★★★, *Grand Appearance* (Progressive 1978)★★★, *With Scott's Band In New York* (Concord Jazz 1978)★★★, with Buddy Tate *Back To Back* (Concord Jazz 1979)★★★★, with Warren Vaché

Skyscrapers (Concord Jazz 1979)★★★, with Dave McKenna *Tenorshoes* (Concord Jazz 1980)★★★, with Tate *Scott's Buddy* (Concord Jazz 1980)★★★★, *Apples & Oranges* (Concord Jazz 1981)★★★, with Tate, Al Cohn *Tour De Force* (Concord Jazz 1981)★★★, *Close Up* (Concord Jazz 1982)★★★, with Ruby Braff *Mr. Braff To You* (Phontastic 1983)★★★★, *Scott Hamilton Quintet In Concert* (Concord Jazz 1983)★★★, *The Second Set* (Concord Jazz 1983)★★★, *The Right Time* (Concord Jazz 1984)★★★, wih Ruby Braff *A First* (Concord Jazz 1985)★★★★, with Braff *A Sailboat In The Moonlight* (Concord Jazz 1986)★★★★, *Major League* (Concord Jazz 1986)★★★, with Charlie Byrd *It's A Wonderful World* (Concord Jazz 1988)★★★, *Scott Hamilton Plays Ballads* (Concord Jazz 1989)★★★, *Radio City* (Concord Jazz 1990)★★★, *Race Point* (Concord Jazz 1991)★★★, *Groovin' High* (Concord Jazz 1992)★★★★, *East Of The Sun* (Concord Jazz 1993)★★★, *With Strings* (Concord 1993)★★, *Organic Duke* (Concord Jazz 1994)★★★, *Live At The Brecon Jazz Festival* (Concord Jazz 1995)★★★, *My Romance* (Concord Jazz 1995)★★★, *After Hours* (Concord Jazz 1997)★★★★, *Christmas Love Song* (Concord Jazz 1997)★★, with Bucky Pizzarelli The *Red Door: Scott Hamilton & Bucky Pizzarelli Remember Zoot Sims* (Concord Jazz 1998)★★★★.

HAMMER, JAN

b. 17 April 1948, Prague, Czechoslovakia, he trained as a jazz pianist before winning a scholarship to Berklee College in Boston, Massachusetts, USA, in 1968. In 1970, he played with Elvin Jones and Sarah Vaughan. Hammer next joined the Mahavishnu Orchestra, as well as playing synthesizers on albums by Santana, Billy Cobham and others. After leader John McLaughlin temporarily disbanded the orchestra, Hammer and violinist Jerry Goodman made a 1974 album for Nemperor. This was followed by Hammer's own composition, *The First Seven Days*, a concept album based on the creation of the earth. During the late 70s, he was one of a loose aggregation of New York-based musicians creating various types of jazz-rock fusion.

Among his more important collaborations were those with Jeff Beck on *Wired* and *There And Back*. Hammer also toured with Beck. He later made a record with Journey guitarist Neil Schon and another with jazz guitarist John Abercrombie before finding a wider audience through his work in television music. Hammer was responsible for the theme to *Miami Vice*, one of the most successful police series of the 80s. Released as a single, it went to number 1 in the USA (UK number 5) in 1985. He followed it in 1987 with 'Crocketts Theme', which made number 2 in the UK yet failed completely in the USA. This new role dominated his later work - Hammer wrote the music for *Eurocops* - and in 1991 he even composed special background music for a best-selling computer game. Hammer's biggest hit was sadly tarnished during 1991 and 1992 when it was oddly used as the theme music for a major television advertising campaign for a UK bank.

● ALBUMS: *Like Children* (Nemperor 1974)★★★, *First Seven Days* (1975)★★★, *Oh Yeah* (1976)★★★, *Live With Jeff Beck* (Epic 1977), *Timeless* (1978)★★★, *Melodies* (1979)★★, *Black Sheep* (1979)★★, *Neil Schon And Jan Hammer* (1981)★★, *Untold Passion* (Columbia 1982)★★, *Night* (1984)★★, *Escape From TV* (MCA 1987)★★★, *Snapshots* (MCA 1989)★★★, *Country & Eastern Music* (1993)★★, *Behind The Mind's Eye* (1993)★★.
● COMPILATIONS: *The Early Years* (Coulmbia 1988)★★★.
● VIDEOS: *Beyond The Mind's Eye* (1982).

HAMMOND, JOHN, JNR.

b. John Henry Hammond II, 15 December 1910, New York City, USA, d. July 1987. Hammond became a jazz fan as a child and in the early 30s was a record reviewer for *Melody Maker*. He used his inherited wealth to finance recordings at a time when economic depression had made record companies unwilling to invest in jazz, and produced Billie Holiday's first session as well as tracks by Teddy Wilson, Bessie Smith, Mildred Bailey and Artie Shaw. In 1936 a chance hearing of a broadcast by Count Basie from Kansas City (Hammond was listening on his car radio outside a Chicago hotel where Benny Goodman was appearing) led him actively to promote Basie's career. In 1938/9, Hammond devised and organized the *Spirituals To Swing* concerts at New York's Carnegie Hall. These were designed to show the full breadth of black American music and featured gospel (Rosetta Tharpe), blues (Big Bill Broonzy), New Orleans jazz (Sidney Bechet) and contemporary dance music (Benny Goodman, who married Hammond's sister, Alice). In the early 40s, he worked for Columbia Records and after army service moved to Keynote, Mercury and Vanguard as a staff producer. Hammond returned to Columbia in 1958 and was chiefly responsible for signing such folk revival artists as Pete Seeger and Bob Dylan, who was known at the company as 'Hammond's folly' in the early years of his contract. Hammond was the producer of Dylan's first two albums. While chiefly involved with jazz and blues - he supervised reissues of Bessie Smith and Robert Johnson, and was a founder of the Newport Jazz Festival - Hammond continued to bring new artists to Columbia during the 60s and 70s, most notably Leonard Cohen, George Benson and Bruce Springsteen. His son, John Hammond III (often confusingly titled John Hammond Jnr. himself, which leads to his father being mistakenly identified as Hammond Snr.), is a noted white blues singer whose recording career began in the mid-60s.

HAMPEL, GUNTER

b. 31 August 1937, Gottingen, Lower Saxony, Germany. Hampel studied music from the age of 11 and by the time he was 20 was leading his own band. An accomplished vibist, he is also proficient on clarinet, flute and saxophone - perhaps taking after his grandfather, who was a multi-instrumental street musician. An early pioneer of European free improvisation, Hampel recorded *Heartplants* with Manfred Schoof and Alex von Schlippenbach in 1965, worked with Marion Brown, John McLaughlin and Jeanne Lee (later his wife) and in 1969 set up his own Birth label, on which he recorded collaborations with like-minded experimentalists such as Anthony Braxton, Willem Breuker, Sunny Murray and Enrico Rava. He also began a long term association with US clarinettist Perry Robinson. An interest in contemporary composition led to his inclusion on the 1971 project that united Don Cherry with Polish composer Krzysztof Penderecki (*Actions*). In 1972 he formed his Galaxie Dream Band, with which he has since toured Africa, Asia and South America as well as Europe and the USA. Now dividing his time between New York and Germany, Hampel remains a champion of new music, still running his label and his band and finding time for other projects, such as guesting with Cecil Taylor in the pianist's Orchestra Of Two Continents (*Winged Serpent (Sliding) Quadrants*).

● ALBUMS: with Manfred Schoof, Alex von Schlippenbach *Heartplants* (1965)★★★★, *Music From Europe* (ESP 1966)★★★, *Gunter Hampel Group Und Jeanne Lee* (1969)★★★, *The 8th July 1969* (Birth 1969)★★★, *Dances* (1969)★★★★, *Out Of New York* (1971)★★★, *Ballet Symphony No. 5* (1971)★★, *Spirits* (1971)★★★, with Anthony Braxton, Jeanne Lee *Familie* (1972)★★★★, *Broadway/Folksong* (1972)★★, with Enrico Rava *Angel* (1972)★★★, *Out From Under* (1974)★★★, *Journey To The Song Within* (1974)★★★, *Transformation* (1976)★★★, *All Is Real* (1978)★★, *Waves/Wellen* (1980)★★★★, *Cavena* (1981)★★★, *Generator* (1982)★★★, *Jubilation* (Birth 1983)★★★, *Flesh Heat: Live At Sweet Basil* (Birth 1985)★★, *Dialog, Live At The Eldena Jazz Festival 1992* (Birth 1994)★★★, *Time Is Now, Live At The Eldena Jazz Festival 1992* (Birth 1995)★★★, *Celestial Glory, Live At The Knitting Factory 1991* recording (Birth 1996)★★★★.

HAMPTON, LIONEL

b. 20 April 1909, Louisville, Kentucky, USA. After living briefly in Louisville and Birmingham, Alabama, Hampton was taken to Chicago where he lived with his grandparents. They sent him to Holy Rosary Academy at Collins, Wisconsin, where he was taught the rudiments of military band drumming by a Dominican nun. Following the death of his grandmother, Hampton, now in his early teens, went to live with his uncle, Richard Morgan. A bootlegger and friend to many showbusiness stars, Morgan encouraged his nephew in his ambition to become a musician. (Morgan later became an intimate friend of Bessie Smith and was driving the car in which she had her fatal accident.) Morgan bought Hampton his first drum kit, modelled on that of the boy's idol, Jimmy Bertrand, who played in the Erskine Tate band at the Vendome Theatre. Hampton played in the boys band organized by the *Defender*, Chicago's leading black newspaper, and by the end of the 20s had become a professional musician. He played drums in various territory bands, including those led by Curtis Mosby, Reb Spikes and Paul Howard. On the west coast in the early 30s he was drummer with Vernon Wilkins, Charlie Echols and Les Hite, who led the house band at the Los Angeles Cotton Club. When Louis Armstrong played at the club, Hite's band accompanied him in concert and also on recording sessions. On some of these dates Hampton played vibraphone, an instrument similar to the marimba on which he had become proficient.

By this time Hampton was also occasionally playing piano and singing and soon became sufficiently popular to form his own big band and small groups. In 1936, while leading his band at the Paradise Club on Central Avenue, he was joined one evening by Benny Goodman, Teddy Wilson and Gene Krupa who were passing through LA on a nationwide tour. Goodman was persuaded to visit the club by John Hammond Jnr. and was so impressed, and so much enjoyed their impromptu jam session, that he invited Hampton to attend a recording date already scheduled the following day for the Benny Goodman Trio. The resulting records, by the Benny Goodman Quartet, were so successful that a few months later Goodman asked Hampton to join his entourage. For the next few years Hampton became an integral part of Goodman's success story, recording extensively with the Quartet and, after the arrival of Charlie Christian, with the Sextet. He also occasionally played with the big band, taking over the drums after Krupa's abrupt departure in 1938. While with Goodman, Hampton was asked by Eli Oberstein of RCA Victor to make a series of small group records. The resulting dates, on which Hampton used musicians from whichever big bands happened to be in town, proved to be amongst the best small group recordings in jazz history and are classics of their kind. By the early 40s Hampton was keen to become a leader again and encouraged by his wife, Gladys, and with Goodman's approval (and financial aid), he formed his own big band in 1941. Straw boss of the first band was Marshal Royal and among his sidemen, all relatively unknown at the time, were Ernie Royal, Illinois Jacquet, Jack McVea, Irving Ashby and Milt Buckner. The band proved to be hugely successful, offering a blend of soulful ballads and all-out stomping excitement.

Building on the burgeoning popularity of R&B, Hampton developed a musical style - gutsy, riffing saxophones, powerhouse brass, a slogging back beat and raw, energetic solos - that he retained for the next half century. In the 40s and early 50s Hampton hired (and, when his patience with their antics ran out, regularly fired) outstanding artists such as Jimmy Cleveland, Al Grey, Earl Bostic, Gigi Gryce, Dexter Gordon, Arnett Cobb, Charles Mingus, Clifford Brown, Art Farmer, Fats Navarro, Quincy Jones, Joe Newman and Clark Terry. He also had an ear for singers and gave early breaks to Dinah Washington, Joe Williams and Betty Carter. From the early 50s Hampton regularly toured Europe and became very popular at international festivals, especially in France. In the mid- and late 50s Hampton recorded extensively for Norman Granz, who teamed him with jazzmen such as Stan Getz, Buddy De Franco, Oscar Peterson and Art Tatum. From the mid-60s onwards, Hampton attended many reunions of the original Benny Goodman Quartet, several of which were recorded and a few televised. Also in the 60s Lionel and Gladys Hampton became involved in urban renewal in Harlem, where they had made their home for many years. Gladys' death in 1971 was a severe blow to Hampton, who had relied upon her astute business sense and organizational ability. By the end of the 70s the first of the multi-million-dollar projects that the

Hamptons had initiated was opened: eventually two apartment buildings, the Lionel Hampton Houses and the Gladys Hampton Houses, were providing accommodation for over 700 families in the middle and lower income groups.
During this time Hampton never stopped playing; both touring with his own big band and, from the late 70s, fronting all-star orchestras specifically assembled for festivals. The 80s saw Hampton still hard at work - touring, recording only a little less frequently and, despite arthritis, playing, singing and dancing in front of his bands as if time had stood still since 1941. In 1992 he was still active, celebrating 60-plus years in the business, and showing few signs of slowing up until he suffered a 'light brain haemorrhage' during a performance in Paris. In the following year, 'fully recovered', he played UK concerts with his Golden Men Of Jazz, a group which included such luminaries as Junior Mance, Harry Edison, Benny Golson, and Al Grey. Hampton's musical personality is best, if a little superficially, described as that of a Jekyll and Hyde. He switched from introspective balladeer to outrageous swinger at the flick of a vibraphone mallet. As a drummer he was originally a solid player, as his first records with Paul Howard's Quality Serenaders testify. As a pianist he perfected a percussive, two-fingered attacking style which concealed the fact that he could also play in a modern and unusually clipped manner. As a singer he had a limited range but a pleasantly ingratiating voice. It is as a vibraphone player, however, that he made his greatest mark on jazz. Although not the first to use the instrument in jazz, he was the first to use it as anything other than a novelty and once he had mastered it he quickly became an outstanding performer (indeed, for many years he was virtually the only player of the vibraphone in jazz). After the emergence of other virtuosos, such as Milt Jackson and Gary Burton, Hampton retained his pre-eminence simply by ignoring changes in musical styles and continuing to do what he had done so successfully since the early 30s. An astonishingly long-lived and vibrant individual, Hampton's extrovert personality assured him of a prominent place in jazz. Although he was never an innovative musician, and in one sense cannot therefore be accorded a place alongside Louis Armstrong or Duke Ellington, he did become a giant of the music.

● ALBUMS: *Gene Norman Presents: Stardust* (1947)★★★, *Boogie Woogie* (Decca 1950)★★★, *Moonglow* (Decca 1951)★★★, *Just Jazz* (Decca 1952)★★★, *European Concert 1953* (1953)★★★★, *Complete Paris Sessions* (1953)★★★★, *The Hamp In Paris* (1953)★★★★, *The Lionel Hampton Quartet* i (1954)★★★★, *Lionel Hampton Quartet With Buddy De Franco* (Clef 1954)★★★★, *Lionel Hampton At The Trianon Ballroom, Chicago* (1954)★★★, *The Lionel Hampton Quartet* ii (Clef 1954)★★★★, *The Lionel Hampton Quintet* i (1954)★★★★, *The Lionel Hampton Sextet At Jazz At The Philharmonic* (1954)★★★★, *Lionel Hampton And His Orchestra: Apollo Hall Concert* (Epic 1954)★★★★, *Rockin' And Groovin'* (Blue Note 1954)★★★, *Hot Mallets* (RCA Victor 1954)★★★, *Oh Rock* (MGM 1954)★★★, *Lionel Hampton And His Orchestra: Live In Graz* (1954)★★★, *All-American Award Concert At Carnegie Hall* (Decca 1955)★★★★, *Lionel Hampton And His French Sound* (1955)★★★, *Crazy Rhythm* (EmArcy 1955)★★★, *Lionel Hampton And Stan Getz* (1955)★★★, *Jam Session In Paris* (EmArcy 1955)★★★, *The Lionel Hampton Big Band* (Clef 1955)★★★, *The Lionel Hampton Sextet* (1955)★★★, with Stan Getz *Hamp And Getz* (Norgran 1955)★★★, *Wailing At The Trianon* (Columbia 1955)★★★, with Buddy Rich, Art Tatum *The Hampton-Tatum-Rich Trio* (Clef 1956)★★★, *Lionel Hampton And His Orchestra: Live At The Olympia, Paris* (Contemporary 1956)★★★, *Lionel Hampton Meets Fatty George* (1956)★★★, *Lionel Hampton And His Rhythm* (1956)★★★, *Paris Session* (1956)★★★★, *Lionel Hampton And His Orchestra: In Madrid* (1956)★★★, *Lionel Hampton Concert Hall All Stars* (1956)★★★, *Plays Love Songs* (Clef 1956)★★★, *King Of The Vibes* (Clef 1956)★★★, *Air-Mail Special* (Clef 1956)★★★, *Flying Home* (Clef 1956)★★★, *Swingin' With Hamp* (Clef 1956)★★★, *Hamp Rides Again* (Clef 1956)★★★, with Buddy Rich, Art Tatum *The Hampton-Tatum-Rich Trio* (Clef 1956)★★★, *With The Just Jazz All-Stars* (Gene Norman 1956)★★★, *Hamp's Big Four* (Clef 1956)★★★, *Lionel Hampton And His Giants* (Norgran 1956)★★★, *Lionel Hampton And His Orchestra* i (Lion 1957)★★★, *Jazz Flamenco* (RCA Victor 1957)★★★, *Lionel* (Audio Fidelity 1957)★★★, *Open House* (Camden 1957)★★★, *Lionel Hampton And His Orchestra: In Stuttgart* (1958)★★★, *Hamp in Hi-Fi* (Harmony 1958)★★★★, *Jivin' The Vibes* (Camden 1958)★★★, *Lionel Hampton And His Orchestra: Live In Concert* (c.1958)★★★, *Lionel Hampton And His Orchestra* ii (1958)★★★, *The Genius of Lionel Hampton* (Verve 1958)★★★, *Lionel Hampton '58* (Verve 1958)★★★, *Hallelujah Hamp* (Verve 1958)★★★, *The High And The Mighty* (Verve 1958)★★★, *Lionel Hampton And His Orchestra* iii (1959)★★★, *Golden Vibes* (Columbia 1959)★★★, *Lionel Hampton Swings* (Perfect 1959)★★★, *Lionel Hampton And His Orchestra* iv (1960)★★★, *Lionel Hampton All Stars* i (1960)★★★, *Silver Vibes* (Columbia 1960)★★★, *Lionel Hampton And His Orchestra* v (1960)★★★, *Lionel Hampton And His Orchestra* vi (1961)★★★, *Travelin' Band* (Verve 1961)★★★, *Soft Vibes* (Columbia 1961)★★★, *Swing Classics* (RCA Victor1961)★★★, *Lionel Hampton And His Orchestra At The Metropole* (1961)★★★, *King Of The Vibes* (Verve 1961)★★★, *The Many Sides Of Lionel Hampton* (Glad Hamp 1961)★★★, *Lionel Hampton And His Orchestra* vii (1962)★★★, *The Exciting Hamp In Europe* (Glad Hamp 1962)★★★, *All That Twistin' Jazz* (Glad Hamp 1962)★★★, *Lionel Hampton And Charlie Teagarden* (1963)★★★, *Lionel Hampton All Stars* ii (1963)★★★, *Lionel Hampton And His Orchestra: Live In Japan* (Glad Hamp1963)★★★, *Bossa Nova Jazz* (Glad Hamp 1963)★★★, with Charlie Teagarden *The Great Hamp And Little T.* (Coral 1963)★★★, *Lionel Hampton And His Orchestra On Tour* (Glad Hamp 1964)★★★, *Lionel Hampton And His Jazz Inner Circle* i (1964)★★★, *Hamp's Portrait Of A Woman* (1964)★★, *You Better Know It* (Impulse! 1965)★★★★, *Hamp's Big Band Live At Newport* (1965)★★★, *East Meets West* (Glad Hamp 1965)★★★, *A Taste Of Hamp* (Glad Hamp 1965)★★★, *Newport Uproar* (1967)★★, *The Works* (1967)★★★, *Lionel Hampton And His Jazz Inner Circle* ii (1967)★★★, *The Lionel Hampton Quintet* ii (1968)★★★, *Lionel Hampton And His Orchestra* ix (1970)★★, *Lionel Hampton And His Orchestra* x (1970)★★, *Transition* (1974)★★, *Chameleon* (1976)★★★, *Alive And Jumping* (1977)★★★, *Lionel Hampton And His Jazz Giants* (1977)★★★★, *New York Blackout* (1977)★★★, *Giants Of Jazz*

Vols 1 & 2 (1977)★★★, *Jazz Showcase* (1977)★★, *Saturday Night Jazz Fever* (1978)★★★, *Live At The Muzeval* (1978)★★★, *50th Anniversary Album: Live At Carnegie Hall* (1978)★★★★, with Svend Asmussen *As Time Goes By* (1978)★★, *All-Star Band At Newport* (Timeless 1978)★★, *Hamp In Haarlem* (1979)★★, *Ambassador At Large* (1979)★★★, *Outrageous* (1980)★★★, *Lionel Hampton And His Orchestra At The Stadt-Casino, Basel* (1980)★★★, *Lionel Hampton And His Orchestra At The Aurex Jazz Festival '81, Tokyo* (1981)★★★, *The Boogie Woogie Album* (1982)★★★, *The Lionel Hampton Quintet* iii (1982)★★★, *Lionel Hampton Big Band In Doorwerth, Holland* (1982)★★★, *Made In Japan* (Timeless 1982)★★★, *Lionel Hampton With Orchestra Directed By Teo Macero* (c.1984)★★, *Lionel Hampton And His Orchestra Featuring Sylvia Bennett* (1985)★★★, *Mostly Blues* (Limelight 1985)★★, *Mostly Ballads* (Limelight 1990)★★, with others *Live At The Blue Note* (1991)★★★, *Two Generations* (Phontastic 1991)★★★, *Just Jazz* (Telarc 1993)★★★★, *Live At The Blue Note* (Telarc 1993)★★, *For The Love Of Music* (Mojazz 1995)★★★.

● COMPILATIONS: *Paul Howard's Quality Serenaders* (TOM 1929)★★★, with Louis Armstrong, Les Hite *Louis In Los Angeles* (1930-31)★★★, with Benny Goodman *The Complete Small Combinations* (RCA 1936-41)★★★★, *Historic Recording Sessions* (RCA 1937-41)★★★★, *Leapin' With Lionel* (1941-49)★★★.

● VIDEOS: *One Night Stand* (Video Artists International 1996).

● FURTHER READING: *Hamp: An Autobiography*, Lionel Hampton with James Haskins.

HAMPTON, SLIDE

b. Locksley Wellington Hampton, 21 April 1932, Jeannette, Pennsylvania, USA. Born into a musical family, several members of which played together for a while, trombonist Hampton joined Buddy Johnson's R&B band in the mid-50s. This engagement brought him to New York where he attracted attention not only for his playing but also for his arranging. After a brief spell with Lionel Hampton he became a member of Maynard Ferguson's band, where he played and arranged, providing exciting charts on such popular tunes as 'The Fugue', 'Three Little Foxes' and 'Slide's Derangement'. After leaving Ferguson, Hampton led his own eight-piece band, continued arranging for others, and was musical director for singer Lloyd Price. In 1968 he toured with Woody Herman, settling in Europe where he remained until the late 70s. Subsequently he worked with various jazz co-operatives including Continuum, taught, and led his own nine-trombone, three-rhythm band, World of Trombones. A masterly arranger and gifted (left-handed) trombone player, Hampton's career is among the most distinguished in jazz.

● ALBUMS: *His Horn Of Plenty* (Strand 1959)★★★★, *Sister Salvation* (Atlantic 1960)★★★, *Something Sanctified* (Atlantic 1961)★★★★, *Jazz With A Twist* (Atlantic 1962)★★★, *Explosion!* (Atlantic 1962)★★★, *Two Sides Of Slide* (Charlie Parker 1962)★★★, *Drum Suite* (Epic 1962)★★★, with Sacha Distel *Slide Hampton And Sacha Distel* (1968)★★, *The Fabulous Slide Hampton Quartet* (1969)★★★, *Slide Hampton With The Vaclav Zahradnik Big Band* (1971)★★, *Life Music* (1972)★★★★, *Interjazz 2* (1972)★★★, *Give Me A Double* (1974)★★★, *World Of Trombones* (Black Lion 1979)★★★★, with Continuum *Mad About Tadd* (1982)★★★, *Roots* (Criss Cross 1985)★★★★, *Mellow-dy* (LRC 1992)★★★, *Dedicated To Diz* (Telarc 1993)★★★, with the David Hazeltine Quartet *4 Flights Up* (Sharp Nine 1996)★★★.

HANCOCK, HERBIE

b. 12 April 1940, Chicago, Illinois, USA. Growing up in a musical household, Hancock studied piano from the age of seven and gave his first public performance just two years later. Although he played classical music at his debut Hancock's interest lay mostly in jazz. During high school and college he played in semi-professional bands and on occasion accompanied visiting jazzmen, including Donald Byrd. It was with Byrd that Hancock first played in New York, in 1961, recording with him and as leader of his own small group. Among the tunes on this later album was 'Watermelon Man', a Hancock original that appealed to more than the usual jazz audience. A version of the song, by Mongo Santamaría, reached the US Top 10.

During the early and mid-60s Hancock led bands for club engagements and record dates but the move which really boosted his career and international recognition was joining the quintet led by Miles Davis, with whom he stayed for more than five years. Towards the end of the stint with Davis, the band began its move into jazz-rock. Hancock felt comfortable in this style and in 1968 formed a sextet to pursue his own concepts. With musicians such as Julian Priester, Buster Williams and Eddie Henderson, and playing much original material composed by Hancock, the band became one of the most popular and influential of the jazz-rock movement in the early 70s.

From 1969 Hancock made extensive use of electronic piano and other electronic keyboard instruments, including synthesizers. In 1973 economic pressures compelled Hancock to cut the band to a quartet, which featured Bennie Maupin, who had also been in the bigger group. The new group's music was again fusion, but this time leaned more towards jazz-funk. Whether by good fortune or through astute observation of the music scene, Hancock's first album with the quartet, *Head Hunters*, was widely accepted in the burgeoning disco scene and achieved substantial sales. Throughout the rest of the 70s Hancock's music was concentrated in this area with occasional returns to jazz for record dates. By the end of the decade, however, his popularity in the disco market was such that he cut down still further on straight jazz performances. Certain albums he made, with Chick Corea and with his own band, V.S.O.P (a re-creation of the Davis quintet except with Freddie Hubbard in place of Miles), suggested that he retained an interest, however peripheral, in jazz. His numerous disco successes included 'You Bet Your Love', a UK Top 20 hit in 1979, and in collaboration with the group Material he recorded *Future Shock*, one track from which 'Rockit', reached the UK Top 10 in 1983 and made the top spot in the USA.

In 1986 Hancock played and acted in the film *'Round Midnight*. He also wrote the score, for which he won an Academy Award. Subsequently, he became more active in jazz, touring with Williams, Ron Carter, Michael Brecker and others. Although the career moves made by Hancock over the years have tended to alienate the hardcore jazz fans who applauded his earlier work with Davis, his popularity with the disco and related audiences has not been achieved at the expense of quality. All of his successes in this area have been executed to the highest musical and other professional standards; the pop video accompanying 'Rockit' was an award winner. In his use of synthesizers, voice-box and other state-of-the-art electronic devices, Hancock has displayed far-reaching inventiveness, setting standards for the pop industry. Where his jazz work is concerned, he has displayed an intelligent approach to his material. If the music is often cerebral, it is rarely without heart; indeed, the V.S.O.P. band's recreations have been notable for their integrity and a measure of passionate intensity that at times matches that of the original.
The New Standard was an interesting concept album. On this Hancock gave interpretations of songs by rock singer-songwriters such as Peter Gabriel, the Eagles' Don Henley, John Lennon, Paul McCartney, Stevie Wonder, Prince and lo and behold, Nirvana's Kurt Cobain. His recent tribute to George Gershwin was another excellent recording.

● ALBUMS: *Takin' Off* (Blue Note 1962)★★★★, *My Point Of View* (Blue Note 1963)★★★★, *Inventions And Dimensions* (Blue Note 1963)★★★, *Empyrean Isles* (Blue Note 1964)★★★★, *Maiden Voyage* (Blue Note 1965)★★★★, *Blow Up* (MGM 1967)★★★, *Speak Like A Child* (Blue Note 1968)★★★, *The Prisoner* (Blue Note 1969)★★★, *Mwandishi* (Warners 1971)★★★★, *Crossings* (Warners 1972)★★★★, *Sextant* (Columbia 1973)★★★★, *Head Hunters* (Columbia 1974)★★★★★, *Thrust* (Columbia 1974)★★★, *Man-Child* (Columbia 1975)★★★★, *V.S.O.P.* (Columbia 1976)★★★★, *Secrets* (Columbia 1976)★★, *V.S.O.P.: The Quintet* (Columbia 1977)★★★★, *Sunlight* (Columbia 1978)★★, with Chick Corea *An Evening With Herbie Hancock And Chick Corea* (Columbia 1979)★★★, with Corea *Homecoming: Corea And Hancock* (Polydor 1979)★★★, *Feets Don't Fail Me Now* (Columbia 1979)★★, *Mr Hands* (Columbia 1980)★★★, *Monster* (Columbia 1980)★★, *Hancock Alley* (Manhattan 1980)★★★, *Magic Windows* (Columbia 1981)★★, *Quartet* (Columbia 1982)★★★, *Lite Me Up* (Columbia 1982)★★, *Mr Hands* (Columbia 1982)★★★, *Future Shock* (Columbia 1983)★★★★, *Hot And Heavy* (Premier 1984),★★ *Herbie Hancock And The Rockit Band* (Columbia 1984)★★★,*Sound System* (Columbia 1984)★★, with Dexter Gordon *'Round Midnight* film soundtrack (Columbia 1986)★★★, with Wayne Shorter, Ron Carter, Wallace Roney, Tony Williams *A Tribute To Miles* (QWest/Reprise 1994)★★★, *Dis Is Da Drum* (Mercury 1995)★★★, *The New Standard* (Verve 1996)★★★★, with Wayne Shorter *1+1* (Verve 1997)★★★★, *Return Of The Headhunters!* (Verve/Hancock 1998)★★, with various artists *Gershwin's World* (Verve 1998)★★★★.

● COMPILATIONS: *Greatest Hits* (Columbia 1980)★★★, *A Jazz Collection* (Sony 1991)★★★, *Best Of Vol. 2* (1992)★★★, *Mwandishi: The Complete Warner Bros. Recordings* (Warners 1994)★★★, *Jazz Profile* (Blue Note 1997)★★★★, *The Complete Blue Note Sixties Sessions* 6-CD box set (Blue Note 1998)★★★★.

● VIDEOS: *Herbie Hancock And The Rockit Band* (Columbia 1984).

HANDY, 'CAPTAIN' JOHN

b. 24 June 1900, Pass Christian, Mississippi, USA, d. 12 January 1971. As a child, Handy played various instruments with members of his musical family and sat in, usually on clarinet, with noted musicians such as Kid Howard, Kid Rena and Punch Miller. By his late teens Handy was resident in New Orleans and worked there and in surroundings areas. In the late 20s Handy began playing alto saxophone, an instrument which at that time was unpopular in jazz circles, especially those in which New Orleans-style music was played.However, during the 30s he played regularly with various jazzmen, including Lee Collins and Jim Robinson. Handy's career was centred in New Orleans for many years, but in the early 60s he began to venture further afield, sometimes in company with Kid Sheik Cola and Kid Thomas Valentine. Handy's playing style was decidedly varied, ranging between hard-edged grittiness and smooth romanticism. In the late 60s, touring Europe with Barry Martyn and Sammy Rimington, and at the 1970 Newport Jazz Festival, Handy regularly confounded those who regarded the alto saxophone as an unsuitable instrument on which to play early jazz. On uptempo numbers, Handy's clipped, aggressive tone resembled that of Pete Brown and is also reflected in Rimington's playing.

● ALBUMS: *Kid Howard's Band* (1962)★★, with Kid Thomas Valentine *The December Band* (1965)★★★, *Capt. John Handy With Geoff Bull And Barry Martyn's Band* (1966)★★★, *Handyman* (1966)★★★, *Introducing Cap'n John Handy* (1967)★★★, *With The Claude Hopkins Band* (RCA 1985)★★, *All Aboard* (GHB 1986)★★★, *All Aboard With Jim Robinson* (GHB 1988)★★★, *All Aboard With Rimmington* (GHB 1988)★★★.

HANDY, GEORGE

b. 17 January 1920, New York City, New York, USA, 8 January 1997, New York City, New York, USA. After studying piano and composing at both Juilliard and New York University, Handy was tutored by Aaron Copland, the renowned American classical composer. In the early 40s he worked with Raymond Scott's orchestra at CBS studios in New York, but then turned his attention to arranging for the more progressively-minded big band leaders. Among the bands for which he wrote were those led by Alvino Rey, a popular guitarist who led an advanced and often overlooked big band in the mid-40s, and Boyd Raeburn, for whom he made his most notable contributions to jazz. It is difficult to be too precise about which of Raeburn's successes were actually written by Handy as a dispute arose between Handy and Raeburn on the one hand, and Eddie Finckel on the other over authorship of several of the band's best charts. At times Handy played piano with Raeburn, but proved an eccentric personality who was also somewhat unreliable (drummer Irving Kluger recalled that at one time Handy dyed his hair green and would occasionally lapse into unconsciousness over the keyboard). Handy made a few records of his own compositions under his own name, but by the late 40s had left the jazz scene. He reappeared briefly in the mid-50s recording and working with Zoot Sims, but drifted out of sight again. In 1964 he was writing for the New York Saxophone Quartet but this too proved to be only a temporary creative burst from an erratic individual, whose greatest failing might be that he came onto the jazz scene several years before it was ready for him.

● ALBUMS: *Handyland, U.S.A.* (X 1954)★★★, *By George! Handy Of Course* (X 1954)★★★.

HANDY, JOHN

b. 3 February 1933, Dallas, Texas, USA. When Handy's magnificent 1965 recording *Live At The Monterey Jazz Festival* hit the shops, many of the reviewers got carried away. Handy had been around for years, working with Charles Mingus from 1958-59 and again in 1964, appearing with the bassist's band at Monterey as it happened. He had also had his own band from 1959-61, but it was with the creation of the 1965 band, comprising the leader's alto, violin (Michael White), piano (Freddie Redd, replaced by the guitar of Jerry Hahn by the time of the Monterey concert), bass (Don Thompson) and drums (Terry Clarke) that the critics fastened on to him as the new Charlie Parker the jazz world had supposedly been waiting for. Handy's music was exciting, musicianly and well-crafted but it was what it was *not* that caused the excitement. Here was an outstanding alto player who was not threatening in the way that Ornette Coleman was felt to be. He deserved to be valued on more positive virtues, though. Self-taught on clarinet at the age of 13, he took up the alto saxophone at 16, finding time to win an amateur featherweight boxing title in between. He studied music formally at college, then moved to New York in 1958. After the spell with Mingus and his own group he worked in Scandinavia as a soloist, then returned to the USA as soloist with the Santa Clara Symphony Orchestra and the San Francisco State College Symphonic Band. In 1966-67 he toured with the Monterey All-Stars and performed in Gunther Schuller's opera *The Visitation*. In 1968 he began teaching jazz and black history at various colleges and conservatories on the west coast and set up a new band with Mike Nock, Ron McClure and Michael White. In 1970 he completed a *Concerto For Jazz Soloist And Orchestra*, and in 1971 began a collaboration with Ali Akbar Khan, a sarod player, in the band Rainbow. His 1976 album *Hard Work* gave his career its third wind, although this time the critics were less well-disposed, often deploring his funk/rock leanings. *Excursion In Blue* (1988) showed a return to more mainstream jazz settings. Handy also sings and plays tenor, flute and piano. He reunited his mid-60s quintet, to widespread acclaim, for the 1994 Eddie Moore Jazz Festival at Yoshi's jazz club.

● ALBUMS: *In The Ver-nac'u-lar* (Roulette 1960)★★★, *No Coast Jazz* (Roulette 1962)★★★, *John Handy Jazz* (Roulette 1964)★★★, *Quote, Unquote* (Roulette 1964)★★★, *Recorded Live At The Monterey Jazz Festival* (Columbia 1966)★★★★★, *The Second John Handy Album* (Columbia 1966)★★★, *New View* (Columbia 1967)★★★, *Projections* (Columbia 1968), with Rainbow *Karuna Supreme* (1975)★★★, *Hard Work* (Impulse! 1976)★★★★, *Carnival* (1977)★★★, *Rainbow* (1980)★★, *Right There* (Gull 1984)★★, with Lee Ritenour *Where Go The Boats* (Inak 1988)★★★, *Handy Dandy Man* (Inak 80s)★★★, *John Handy's Musical Dreamland* (Elation/Boulevard 80s)★★, *Excursion In Blue* (1988)★★★★, *Live At Yoshi's Nitespot* (Etherean 1996)★★★★.

HANNA, JAKE

b. John Hanna, 4 April 1931, Roxbury, Massachusetts, USA. Hanna began playing drums in a marching band at the age of five in Dorchester, Massachusetts. In his youth he played in and around the Boston area, a territory where many fine jazz musicians were to be found. During the late 40s and early 50s he played in bands led by Tommy Reed and Ted Weems; in the late 50s he worked with pianists Marian McPartland and Toshiko Akiyoshi, and in the big bands of Maynard Ferguson and Woody Herman. He rejoined Herman in 1962, staying for two years in the band the musicians wryly described as the 'un-Herd' and then subbed or otherwise flitted briefly through the bands of Duke Ellington, Harry James and Boston-based teacher and rehearsal band pioneer Herb Pomeroy. What Hanna has described as the best time in his life came when he played with George Wein's band at the impresario's Storyville Club in Boston. In the band were Buck Clayton, Bud Freeman, Pee Wee Russell and Vic Dickenson, with Jimmy Rushing on vocals. In 1964 Hanna became a member of the studio band for the Merv Griffin television show, then based in New York. When the show moved to California, Hanna was one of several musicians who were given the opportunity of moving with it, provided they made their minds up fast. Along with Bill Berry, Richie Kamuca and others, Hanna made the snap decision and ever since has been located on the west coast, even though the Griffin job ended in 1975. Since then he has worked with numerous bands, including Supersax and Count Basie, and co-led an occasional small group with Carl Fontana. Although highly skilled in all aspects of his work, Hanna is one of the most self-effacing drummers in jazz, happy to urge a band along with subtlety and discreet dynamics. Any band with which he plays is guaranteed to swing and to have a good time because, apart from his superb musicianship, Hanna is also a witty and gifted raconteur.

● ALBUMS: with Carl Fontana *Live At Concord* (Concord Jazz 1975)★★★★, with Mary Ann McCall *Kansas City Express* (Concord Jazz 1976)★★★, *Jake Takes Manhattan* (Concord Jazz 1976)★★★, *The Joint Is Jumpin'* (Arbors 1998)★★★.

HANNA, ROLAND, SIR

b. 10 February 1932, Detroit, Michigan, USA. Having first played informally with his father, Hanna then studied classical piano while still a child. After military service, and by now deeply interested in jazz, he continued his studies at Juilliard and Eastman College in the 50s, worked briefly with Benny Goodman, Charles Mingus and Sarah Vaughan and also led his own small groups. In 1967 he joined the Thad Jones-Mel Lewis Orchestra, remaining a regular until 1974. In the 70s Hanna was a member of the co-operative New York Jazz Sextet and Quartet. A marvellously inventive pianist, his work reflects his thorough understanding of the roots of jazz. Although eclectic, his playing vividly demonstrates his own powerful personality. He is a masterly accompanist and an excellent big band player, while his solo work is filled with clear, logical ideas delivered with considerable vitality. In the early 80s, concerned that he was getting into a rut, Hanna absented himself from the music scene in order to develop new ideas. A European tour in the late 80s, in company with Al Grey, Clark Terry and Buddy Tate, showed him to have all the fire of old and he had clearly shaken off any tendency, real or imagined, to drift into routine. His title denotes an honorary knighthood bestowed upon him by the Republic of Liberia.

● ALBUMS: *Roland Hanna Plays Harold Rome's Destry Rides Again* (Atco 1959)★★★, *Easy To Love* (Atco 1960)★★★, *Child Of Gemini* (1971)★★★, *Sir Elf* (Choice 1974)★★★★, *Perugia: Live At Montreux* (Freedom 1974)★★★★, *The New York Jazz Quartet In Concert In Japan* (1975)★★, *At Home With Friends/Time For The Dancers* (1977)★★★, *Sir Elf Plus One* (1977)★★★, *Glove* (1977)★★★, *Roland Hanna Plays The Music Of Alec Wilder* (Inner City 1978)★★★, *Orange Funk* (1978)★★★, *Bird Tracks: Remembering Charlie Parker* (Progressive 1978)★★, *A Gift From The Magi* (West 1978)★★★, *Swing Me No Waltzes* (1979)★★★, *Trinity* (1979)★★★, *Piano Soliloquy* (1979)★★★, *Impressions* (Black And Blue 1979)★★★, *Roland Hanna* (1979)★★★, *Sunrise, Sunset* (1979)★★, *A Keyboard Event* (1981)★★, *Romanesque* (1982)★★★, *Gershwin Carmichael Cats* (CTI 1983)★★, *This Time It's Real* (Storyville 1987)★★★, *Glove* (Blackhawk 1988)★★, *Time For The Dancer* (Progressive 1988)★★★, *Duke Ellington Piano Solos* (Musicmasters 1991)★★★★, *Persia My Dear* (DIW 1988)★★★, *Double Exposure* (LRC 1992)★★★, *Maybeck Recital Hall: Vol 32* (Concord Jazz 1994)★★★★, with John Burr, Bucky Pizzarelli *3 For All* (Cymekob 1996)★★★.

HANSHAW, ANNETTE

b. 18 October 1910, New York City, New York, USA, d. 12 March 1985. In 1926 Hanshaw, who had no particular ambitions to be a professional singer, was heard by an executive of Pathe Records and offered a recording contract. For the next eight years she made numerous records, radio broadcasts and film appearances before tiring of the showbusiness life. Although immensely popular, she decided to retire and married the executive, Herman Rose, who had launched her unexpected career. In 1959, by now a widow and working outside music, she was contacted by the British record enthusiasts Brian Rust and Tony Skyrme, who were eager to detail her life and arrange for the reissue of many of her long-deleted but fondly remembered records. The subsequent reappearance of these albums sparked a revival of interest in her work, particularly in the UK. Hanshaw's voice was soft and sweet, quite unlike that of the more acerbic Ruth Etting who had been her main rival in the late 20s. Although she had no pretensions to sing jazz, and indeed, never did, Hanshaw's accompanists included many of the best white jazzmen of the day. Consequently, while some fans collect her records for the nostalgic glow that her sentimental singing creates, others do so in order to hear brief solos by the likes of Jimmy and Tommy Dorsey, Eddie Lang, Red Nichols and Miff Mole.

● COMPILATIONS: *Annette Hanshaw Vols 1-3* (1926-28)★★★, *Annette Hanshaw Vol. 1: Lovable And Sweet* (c.1930)★★★, *Annette Hanshaw Vol. 2: She's Got It* (c.1930)★★★, *It Was So Beautiful* (1932-34)★★★, *The Personality Girl* (c.1934)★★★.

HARDEE, JOHN

b. 20 December 1918, Corsicana County, Texas, USA, d. 18 May 1984. A tenor saxophonist with a tone reminiscent of Chu Berry. Following his demobilization in 1945 he played in and around New York with numerous small bands. He recorded with Tiny Grimes 'Tiny's Boogie Woogie' (1946); and under his own name 'Hardee's Partee', 'Tired', 'Idaho' and 'River Edge Rock' (1946). He also recorded with Earl Bostic, Billy Kyle, Lucky Millinder and others. He continued to lead his own band until the late 70s until advancing old age slowed him down.

HARDIN, LIL

(see Armstrong, Lillian)

HARDING, BUSTER

b. Lavere Harding, 19 March 1917, Ontario, Canada, d. 14 November 1965. At the start of his teenage years, Harding was playing piano professionally in a band in Philadelphia. Before long he was leading his own unit and was much in demand as an arranger, his charts being used by the short-lived big bands of Teddy Wilson and Coleman Hawkins. In the early 40s Harding continued to arrange for swing era big bands, including those of Cab Calloway, Artie Shaw, Benny Goodman, Tommy Dorsey, Glenn Miller and Count Basie. He also played regularly, usually leading a small group. A major if frequently overlooked figure in the development of big band jazz, Harding's charts demonstrated his great gift for powerful brass-section writing and his ability to tailor his arrangements to the particular strengths of whichever band he was writing for. In the 50s he occasionally wrote for Dizzy Gillespie and was briefly musical director for Billie Holiday.

● COMPILATIONS:*The Indispensable Count Basie* (1927-50)★★★★, *The Most Important Recordings Of Cab Calloway* (1930-49)★★★.

HARDMAN, BILL, JNR.

b. 6 April 1933, Cleveland, Ohio, USA, d. 5 December 1990, Paris, France. Considering his CV, it is surprising that Hardman is not better known and more highly regarded. He spent four stints as trumpeter with the popular and influential Art Blakey's Jazz Messengers (1956-58, 1966-69, 1970 and 1975-76) as well as three with Charles Mingus (1956, 1969-70 and 1972). He also worked with Tiny Bradshaw (1953-55), Horace Silver, Lloyd Price and, from 1959 to 1966, Lou Donaldson. His style was in the mellow, lyrical tradition of Clifford Brown rather than the brasher brass masters of hard bop, and perhaps this was why he tended to be underrated. There was a dry elegance to his playing, and he contributed admirably to some fine recordings, such as the session for Atlantic when Thelonious Monk sat in with Blakey (*Blue Monk*). At least he was recognized by the *Down Beat* critics, who voted him Trumpeter Deserving Of Wider Recognition in 1973. After leading Brass Company he formed a band with Junior Cook (1979-81). Hardman died in 1990.

● ALBUMS: with Jackie McLean *Jackie's Pal - Introducing Bill Hardman* reissued as *Steeple Chase* (Prestige/New Jazz 1956)★★★, *Bill Hardman Quintet* reissued as *Saying Something* (Savoy 1961)★★★, *Home* (Muse 1978)★★★, with Junior Cook *Good Cookin'* (Muse 1979)★★★, *Focus* (Muse 1980)★★★, *Politely* (Muse 1981)★★★, *What's Up* (Steeplechase 1990)★★★★.

HARDWICKE, OTTO 'TOBY'

b. 31 May 1904, Washington, DC, USA, d. 5 August 1970. After playing the bass and C melody saxophones, Hardwicke switched to alto and began working with Duke Ellington, first in his home town and later in New York. He was with Ellington from 1923-28, then spent some time in Europe. Back in the USA, he played in the bands of Chick Webb and Elmer Snowden (with whom he had previously played in Washington in 1922) and then returned to Ellington in 1932. He stayed with the band until 1946, when he retired from music. A solid section player, Hardwicke was an undistinguished soloist. He did, however, have an ear for a melody and is accorded co-composer credit with Ellington on one of the maestro's loveliest tunes, 'Sophisticated Lady'.

HARDY, EMMETT

b. 12 June 1903, New Orleans, Louisiana, USA, d. 16 June 1925. Born into a musical family, Hardy played several instruments before settling on cornet. At the age of 14 he was good enough to work with the popular band led by Papa Jack Laine. During the next few years he played in various bands in his home state and to the north, including a spell on a riverboat. By the early 20s he was back in New Orleans, then had another riverboat engagement before travelling to Chicago to join the New Orleans Rhythm Kings. This job was short-lived and he returned to New Orleans, where he was laid low with a terminal illness. Like many other early jazzmen who made no known recordings, Hardy's reputation rests entirely upon unsubstantiated remarks passed down through the years. In Hardy's case it is suggested that he might have influenced Bix Beiderbecke. Certainly, Hardy is known to have played in Beiderbecke's home town, Davenport, Iowa, but the rest is speculation.

HARGROVE, ROY

b. 16 October 1969, Waco, Texas, USA. Hargrove's father was in the US Air Force which meant that in his early years, growing up in Mart, a small town just outside Waco, he lived with his grandparents. He started playing trumpet at the age of nine and when his father settled in Dallas, Texas, he began playing music in school thanks to the school band. At home, on records, he mostly heard R&B and soul but he had begun to hear jazz and this is what he played when he auditioned for the Dallas Arts Magnate (a school for the performing arts). At this time, despite formal tuition, he was often playing jazz by ear. The school principal played him some Clifford Brown records, broadly hinting that the rest was up to him. Later, he heard records by Lee Morgan and Freddie Hubbard and when he attended Berklee College Of Music he also heard Fats Navarro records. As he matured into his early twenties, Hargrove developed a distinctive playing style. In his own playing and in that of a band he formed, he sought to extend his jazz lines from a base in classic bop. Hargrove works mostly in a quartet setting, with regular accompaniment from alto saxophonist Antonio Hart, bassist Rodney Thomas Whitaker and drummer Greg Hutchinson, but also directs an 18-piece big band, originally formed for a performance at the 1995 Village Jazz Festival in New York. An exceptionally gifted musician, with a rich tone and inventive mind that melds Afro-Cuban rhythms with neobop, Hargrove is one of the outstanding jazz trumpeters of the 90s. His talent has been recognised commercially with strong selling albums for Verve Records and an excellent session with Jimmy Smith on *Damn!* in 1995. His recent afro-jazz experiments resulted in the formation of Cristol (Spanish for Crucible) in 1997.

● ALBUMS: *Diamond In The Rough* (Novus 1990)★★★★, *Public Eye* (Novus 1991)★★★★, with Antonio Hart *The Tokyo Sessions* (RCA 1991)★★★, *The Vibe* (Novus 1992)★★★, *Of Kindred Souls* (Novus 1993)★★★, *With The Tenors Of Our Time* (Verve 1994)★★★, *Family* (Verve 1995)★★★★, with Christian McBride, Stephen Scott *Parker's Mood* (Verve 1996)★★★, as Roy Hargrove's Crisol *Habana* (Verve 1997)★★★★.

HARLE, JOHN

b. 1958, England. Harle has long been identified more with his instrument, the saxophone, than with a genre of musical expression. Classically trained at the Royal College of Music and the Paris Conservatoire, he has played an important part in the recent expansion of the saxophone's classical repertoire. In the late 80s he established his improvising group, the John Harle Band, with whom he has since toured, and he has produced some highly respected duo work with John Lenehan. He is currently Professor of Saxophone at the Guildhall School of Music and Drama, London.

● ALBUMS: *Habanera* (Hannibal 1987)★★★, *John Harle's Saxophone* (1988)★★★, *The Shadow Of The Duke* (Blue Note 1990)★★★★.

HARMOLODICS
(see Coleman, Ornette)

HARPER, BILLY
b. 17 January 1943, Houston, Texas, USA. A child soloist in the church choir, Harper took up the tenor saxophone at the age of 12. He formed his first quintet at 14, and played in high school bands before graduating summa cum laude. At Texas State University he gained a degree in saxophone and theory, working professionally as a singer/saxophonist at the same time. He worked in R&B bands and with James Clay and Fred Smith, then moved to New York in 1966, soon beginning a decade-long musical association with Gil Evans. From 1968 to 1970 he also worked with Art Blakey, then in 1971 joined the Thad Jones-Mel Lewis Big Band until 1973. He has also worked with Lee Morgan, Elvin Jones and Max Roach. In addition to his impressive tenor, he plays flute as well as teaching and composing: his tune 'Thoroughbred' was a staple of Evans's repertoire for several years, and later Evans groups played many more Harper pieces, most notably 'Priestess'. He has taught at Livingstone College, Rutgers University, and was awarded a grant by the New Jersey Council for the Arts to teach improvisation at 15 high schools. His 1975 *Black Saint* launched the famed Italian label of that name, while the 1979 *In Europe* launched its co-label Soul Note. Although he records infrequently each release is highly worthwhile, none more so than the Coltrane-inspired *Somalia*

● ALBUMS: *Capra Black* (Strata-East 1973)★★★, *Black Saint* (Black Saint 1975)★★★★, *In Europe* (Soul Note 1979)★★, *Destiny Is Yours* (Steeple Chase 1990)★★★, *Live on Tour In The Far East Vol 1* (Steeplechase 1993)★★★★, *Live On Tour In The Far East Vol 2* (Steeplechase 1993)★★★★, *Live On Tour In The Far East Vol 3* (Steeplechase 1993)★★★★, *Somalia* (Evidence 1996)★★★★, *If Only Our Hearts Could See* (DIW 1998)★★★★.

HARRELL, TOM
b. 16 June 1946, Urbana, Illinois, USA. Harrell's family moved to San Francisco when he was five and he started playing the trumpet when he was 13. After playing with the Jazz Workshop in the late 60s, Harrell toured with the Stan Kenton and Woody Herman bands. After several years with Horace Silver during the 70s Harrell moved to New York, where he performed with Chuck Israels' National Jazz Ensemble, Azteca and Arnie Lawrence's Treasure Island. He also played with Cecil Payne, Bill Evans and Lee Konitz, and during the 80s Phil Woods expanded his quartet to a quintet with the addition of Harrell. An incisive and precise bop trumpeter with a clear, even tone, and one of music's most gifted improvisers, Harrell is much in demand for studio work. He has also recorded several sessions as a leader, with a major label recording contract exposing his compositional skills to a wider audience. His late 90s octet is a compelling mix of talent and experience, featuring trombonist Wayne Andre, tenor saxophonists Don Braden and Greg Tardy, baritone Gary Smulyan, pianist Xavier Davis, bassist Ugonna Okegwo and drummer Billy Hart.

● ALBUMS: *Aurora/Total* (Adamo 1976)★★★, *Play Of Light* (Blackhawk 1984)★★★★, *Moon Alley* (Criss Cross 1985)★★★★, *Open Air* (Contemporary 1987)★★★, *Stories* (Contemporary 1988)★★★, *Sail Away* (Contemporary 1989)★★★★, *Form* (Contemporary 1990)★★★, *Visions* (Contemporary 1991)★★★, *Passages* (Chesky 1992)★★★, *Upswing* (Chesky 1993)★★, *Labyrinth* (RCA Victor 1996)★★★★, *The Art Of Rhythm* (RCA Victor 1997)★★★★.

HARRIOTT, JOE
b. Arthurlin Harriott, 15 July 1928, Jamaica, West Indies, d. 2 January 1973. After performing in dance bands in the West Indies, Harriott emigrated to the UK in 1951 and quickly established himself as a formidable bebop player on alto and baritone saxophones. After working with Tony Kinsey, Ronnie Scott and other leading British players, Harriott formed his own group, believing that his career needed to go in a less orthodox direction than the one most beboppers were following. In the late 50s, after a protracted spell in hospital recovering from tuberculosis, a period he used to develop his musical thoughts, he formed a band with Coleridge Goode, Phil Seamen, Ellsworth 'Shake' Keane and Pat Smythe which explored Harriott's notions of 'abstract music' on three ground-breaking albums, *Free Form*, *Abstract* and *Movement*. Coincidentally, this music appeared at the same time as the free jazz of Ornette Coleman but differed markedly in its concept and realization 'of the various components comprising jazz today,' Harriott explained in his notes to *Abstract*, 'constant time signatures, a steady four-four tempo, themes and predictable harmonic variations, fixed division of the chorus by bar lines, and so on - we aim to retain at least one in each piece. But we may well - if the mood seems to us to demand it - dispense with all the others . . . (our music) is best listened to as a series of different pictures- for it is after all by definition an attempt in free improvisation to paint, as it were, freely in sound.' Ever open to the prospect of new departures, Harriott turned in the mid-60s to jazz fusion, blending his playing with that of Indian musicians in a double quintet that he co-led with violinist John Mayer. In his later years he often worked with Michael Garrick, but was obliged to abandon most of his own musical experiments in the face of uncomprehending UK audiences. Unable to finance a group, he spent his last few years touring the UK as a solo, playing bebop and standards with local rhythm sections, often living in poverty. He died of cancer in 1973. One of the most inventive and original of jazz musicians, Harriott's music was rarely fully appreciated during his lifetime, although in retrospect he can be seen as a major figure in the development of both a European Free Jazz tradition and a jazz-based fusion that incorporated elements of ethnic music. He was invariably a fine improviser too, but it is his experiments with form that have guaranteed Harriott his place in jazz history.

● ALBUMS: *Southern Horizons* (1959)★★★★, *Free Form*

(1960)★★★★, *Abstract* (1962)★★★★, *Movement* (1964)★★★, with John Mayer *Indo-Jazz Suite* (1965)★★★★, with Michael Garrick *Black Marigolds* (1966)★★★, with Mayer *Indo-Jazz Fusions* (1967)★★★★, *Swings High* (Cadillac 1967)★★, *Personal Portrait* (1967)★★, with Mayer *Indo-Jazz Fusions II* (1968)★★★, with Amancio D'Silva *Hum Dono* (1969)★★.

● COMPILATIONS: with Tony Kinsey *Jump For Me* 1954 recording (Esquire 1987)★★★.

● FURTHER READING: *Joe Harriott Memorial - A Bio-Discography*, Roger Cotterrell and Barry Tepperman.

HARRIS, ALLAN

b. 1958, New York City, New York, USA. Harris was raised in a musical atmosphere, his mother, a singer, being a friend of Clarence Williams and Louis Armstrong both of whom he met while he was still a small child. He studied classical guitar but was hooked to singing after hearing Sarah Vaughan at the famous Apollo. When he was 16 the family moved to Pittsburgh, Pennsylvania, where he began making the musical rounds, activities that continued in Atlanta, Georgia. Although early in his career Harris played guitar and only occasionally sang, he was eventually persuaded to pursue the singing at the expense of the instrument and soon began attracting widespread popular attention. In the 90s he made an impact upon European audiences, performing in a concert of Duke Ellington's sacred music alongside Jon Faddis and singer Michele Hendricks. Harris has a pleasant sounding voice, an uncluttered style, and a sometimes captivating way with a lyric. All this has helped widen his audience, appealing as he does to those who prefer smoothly sophisticated vocalizing. Although not really a jazz singer, when working with jazz musicians he edges very close to the boundary between jazz and popular singing. Thus, a session for Mons Records that produced *It's A Wonderful World*, on which he was teamed with an all-star group including Claudio Roditi, Mark Whitfield, Benny Green and Ray Brown, was well received by critics of both popular music and jazz. The same label's follow-up release, backing the singer with a 50-piece orchestra, leaned in the opposite direction but nevertheless allowed favourable references to Nat 'King' Cole, who is clearly an influence on this singer. Albums planned at the close of the 90s included appearances with other singers on tributes to Ellington, Billy Strayhorn and others.

● ALBUMS: *Setting The Standard* (Love Productions 1992)★★★, *It's A Wonderful World* (Mons 1996)★★★, *Here Comes Allan Harris And The Metropole Orchestra* (Mons 1996)★★★.

HARRIS, BARRY

b. 15 December 1929, Detroit, Michigan, USA. Harris started to play piano at a very early age and by his teens was well established in his home town, where he performed with Miles Davis, Sonny Stitt, Max Roach and other leading jazzmen. Strongly influenced by Bud Powell and Thelonious Monk, Harris in his turn made an impact upon bebop pianists through his work in Detroit and in New York, where he relocated in the early 60s. Apart from stints with Cannonball Adderley, Dexter Gordon and other leading bebop artists, Harris was also a regular accompanist to Coleman Hawkins and established a reputation as a teacher. He has recorded extensively, both under his own name and with musicians such as Al Cohn, Sonny Criss, Sam Noto, Charles McPherson and Jimmy Heath. Since the early 80s he has been deeply involved in jazz education, running the Jazz Cultural Centre in New York, and is regarded as one of the finest teachers of bebop piano. He has continued to record despite suffering a stroke in 1993.

● ALBUMS: *Breakin' It Up* (Argo 1959)★★★, *Barry Harris At The Jazz Workshop* (Riverside 1960)★★★★, *Preminado* (Riverside 1961)★★★★, *Listen To Barry Harris* (Riverside 1961)★★★, *Newer Than New* (Riverside 1962)★★★, *Chasin' The Bird* (Riverside 1962)★★★, *Luminescence* (Prestige 1967)★★★, *Bull's Eye* (Prestige 1969)★★, *Magnificent!* (Prestige 1969)★★★, *Vicissitudes* (1973)★★★, *Barry Harris Plays Tadd Dameron* (Xanadu 1975)★★★★, *Live In Tokyo* (Xanadu 1976)★★★★, *Barry Harris Plays Barry Harris* (Xanadu 1978)★★★★, *The Bird Of Red And Gold* (Xanadu 1982)★★★, *For The Moment* (Uptown 1984)★★★, *At The Jazz Workshop* (JVC 1986)★★★★, *For The Moment* (Uptown 1988)★★★, *Passing It On* (Kay Jazz 1988)★★★, *Live At Maybeck Recital Hall Vol, 12* (Concord Jazz 1991)★★★, *Confirmation* (Candid 1992)★★★, *First Time Ever* (Evidence 1996)★★★, *Live At 'DUG'* 1995 recording (Enja 1997)★★★, with Muhal Richard Abrams *Intepretations Of Monk, Vol. 1* 1981 recording (Koch 1997)★★★★.

HARRIS, BEAVER

b. William Godvin Harris, 20 April 1936, Pittsburgh, Pennsylvania, USA, d. 22 December 1991. Harris played clarinet and alto saxophone in his teens, but switched to drums while in the army. He received encouragement from Max Roach, moving to New York at the end of his national service in 1963, where he worked with Sonny Rollins, Thelonious Monk, Sonny Stitt, Dexter Gordon, Clifford Jordan, Clark Terry, Joe Henderson and Freddie Hubbard among others. By 1966 he was involved with the *avant garde* movement, joining Archie Shepp and then working with Albert Ayler in Europe. He participated in drum clinics with Roach and Kenny Clarke. At the end of the decade he formed a co-operative band, the 360 Degree Experience, with Roswell Rudd, Marion Brown and Grachan Moncur III. In 1970 he played with Shepp for productions of plays by LeRoi Jones and Aishah Rahman. He has since done studio work with Maxine Brown and Doc Cheatham and played with Pharoah Sanders, Steve Lacy, Gato Barbieri, Sheila Jordan, Vincent Herring and the Jazz Composers' Orchestra. In 1985 he toured Europe with the French Horn Connection and in a quartet with Gijs Hendricks. Not as radical as Sunny Murray or Milford Graves, he was nevertheless an important occupant of the drum chair in 60s New Thing groups.

● ALBUMS: *In Sanity* (1976)★★, *Beautiful Africa* (Soul Note 1979)★★★, *Live At Nyon* (80s)★★, *Sound Compound* (Yvp 1987)★★★, *Negcaumongus* (80s)★★★.

HARRIS, BENNY

b. 24 April 1919, New York, USA, d. 11 February 1975, San Francisco, California, USA. Harris started playing trumpet with Tiny Bradshaw's band in 1939 and in the early 40s went on to play with the big bands of Earl Hines and Boyd Raeburn. He then settled to small group work in the famous club scene of New York's 52nd Street, playing with saxophonists Coleman Hawkins and Don Byas, among others. In 1944 he was the trumpeter on an early bop session led by pianist Clyde Hart. He is better remembered as a composer who contributed a number of pieces to the bop repertoire including 'Crazeology' and 'Ornithology' for which he combined Charlie Parker's solo on 'Jumpin' Blues' with the chords of 'How High The Moon'.

● ALBUMS: some tracks with Don Byas *Savoy Jam Party* (1944-46)★★.

HARRIS, BILL

b. Willard Palmer Harris, 28 October 1916, Philadelphia, Pennsylvania, USA, d. 19 September 1973. Harris first played trombone in name bands when he was in his early twenties, having previously performed mostly in and around his home town. After deputizing with Gene Krupa and Ray McKinley he was hired by Benny Goodman, Charlie Barnet and other well-known band leaders, then in 1944 joined Woody Herman, with whom he worked intermittently for 15 years. It was while he was with Herman that his rumbustious, attacking solo style became known to big band fans. Instantly identifiable from his ripe tone and the broad humour with which he laced his solos, Harris was slightly influenced by bebop but maintained strong links with his swing era roots. Among the bands with which he worked in between his appearances with Herman were those of Boyd Raeburn, Benny Carter, Charlie Ventura, the Sauter-Finegan orchestra, and he also toured with Jazz At The Philharmonic, where his rip-roaring style fitted in well with the wilder side of these concert jam sessions. In the early 60s Harris became resident in Florida, playing with local bands and visiting jazzmen; he also worked for a spell with Charlie Teagarden and occasionally led his own groups.

● ALBUMS: *Bill Harris-Charlie Ventura Live At The Three Deuces* (1947)★★, with Ventura *Aces At The Deuces* (Phoenix 1947)★★★, *A Knight In The Village* (1947)★★★, *Bill Harris And His Orchestra* (1952)★★, with Benny Carter *New Jazz Sounds* (1954)★★★, *Bill Harris And Friends* (Original Jazz Classics 1957)★★★★, *Bill Harris And The Ex-Hermanites/Bill Harris Memorial Album* (1957)★★★, *Woody Herman Live 1957 Featuring Bill Harris Vols 1 & 2* (1957)★★★★.

● COMPILATIONS: *The Best Of Woody Herman* (1945)★★★★.

HARRIS, CRAIG

b. 10 September 1953, Hempstead, Long Island, USA. Harris emerged as a trombone player with the AACM in Chicago in the late 70s. He played for a year in the Lena Horne orchestra on Broadway and then with the Beaver Harris-Don Pullen 360 Degree Musical Experience. Having been educated at SUNY at Old Westbury (where saxophonist Pat Patrick made a great impression as a teacher) he moved to New York in 1978 and joined Sun Ra's Arkestra, the band in which Patrick played, staying for two years. In 1981 he went on a world tour with pianist Abdullah Ibrahim: Australia made a particular impression on him. He met and played with Aborigine musicians and acquired a dijeridoo, which he now plays to great effect. He later played in David Murray's first octet, participating in one of the great consolidating bands of black music in the 80s. His debut as a leader was *Aboriginal Affairs* in 1983. *Black Bone*, from the same year, had a track 'inspired by the spirit of Jimi Hendrix', while 1985's *Tributes* was dedicated to Trummy Young. *Shelter* (1987), with his new group Tailgaters Tales, was a brilliant exposition of Harris's talents as a composer and band-leader, but the follow-up *Black Out In The Square Root Of Soul* (1988) was less impressive and almost swamped by synthesizers. In 1988 he formed Cold Sweat, a band that reasserts the black tradition of funk from a non-commercial viewpoint. 1990 saw him touring with a new edition of David Murray's Octet. Craig Harris has a dark, brooding, violent trombone sound that is brightened by the warmth and directness of his musical concepts.

● ALBUMS: with Donald Rafael Garrett, Joseph Jarman, Don Moye *Earth Passage - Density* (Black Saint 1981)★★★, *Aboriginal Affairs* (1983)★★★, *Black Bone* (Soul Note 1983)★★★★, *Tributes* (1985)★★★, *Shelter* (JMT 1987)★★★, *Black Out In The Square Root Of Soul* (JMT 1988)★★, with Cold Sweat *Plays JB* (1989)★★, with Cold Sweat *Foreplay* (JMT 1991)★★★, *F-Stops* (Soul Note 1994)★★★★, with Ray Anderson, George Lewis, Gary Valente *Slideride* (hatART 1996)★★★★.

HARRIS, DON 'SUGARCANE'

b. 8 June 1938, Pasadena, California, USA. A multi-instrumentalist, trained in the classics by his mother, Sugarcane Harris came to the blues late, citing Little Walter and Jimmy Reed as inspirations. From 1957 to 1963 he and school-friend Dewey Terry led a group called the Squires. They also performed as a vocal duo, Don And Dewey, recording breathless rock 'n' roll with the same explosive energy as Specialty label-mate Little Richard. White cover artists did well out of their material. Dale And Grace sold over a million copies of their classic `Leavin' It All Up To You' and the Righteous Brothers adopted their stage act. Gradually, Harris started applying his knowledge of classical violin to improvising. Frank Zappa, long a fan (and product himself of the west coast 50s blues scene), encouraged him on the instrument, leading to the gargantuan Harris solos on *Hot Rats* and *Burnt Weenie Sandwich*. Harris had started listening to jazz - John Coltrane, Horace Silver - and he injected a raw, blues tonality into ambitious outings that were like a violinist's response to Coltrane's new intensity. 1970's *Sugarcane* included R&B, proto-funk and an astonishing classical pastiche 'Funk & Wagner'. Later work with John Mayall was less gripping, but important albums appeared under his own name and that of Pure Food And Drug Act, a group he ran with guitarist Harvey Mandel. Described by Joachim Berendt in the mid-70s as 'the dominant violinist of the contemporary world', Sugarcane's laidback attitude did not help his career. Last heard of preparing an album called *Midnight DJ* with old associate Dewey Terry (1985), it seems that of late Sugarcane has been keeping his inspired answer to blues/classical/jazz divisions to himself.

● ALBUMS: *Don & Dewey : They're Rockin Til' Midnight, Rollin Til Dawn* (Specialty 1970)★★★, (1957-60)★★★, with Johnny Otis *Cuttin' Up* (1969)★★★, with John Mayall *USA Union* (1970)★★★, *Sugarcane* (1970)★★, *Fiddler On The Rock* (1971)★★, with Jean-Luc Ponty, Michael Urbaniak *The Summit* (1971)★★★, *Flashin' Time* (1973)★★, with Pure Food And Drug Act *Choice Cuts* (Epic 1972)★★★.

HARRIS, EDDIE

b. 20 October 1936, Chicago, Illinois, USA, d. 5 November 1996, Los Angeles, California, USA. His apprenticeship was served with Gene Ammons before army service took to him to Europe. He had a surprise hit in 1961, and followed with three further hit records (in the USA), over the next decade. The most notable being 'Listen Here' in 1968. He was a daring tenor saxophone innovator, he experimented with the range of sounds that could be produced by sending a signal through an electrical effects box. At the 1970 Newport Jazz Festival he shocked audiences with his trumpet and trombone played through saxophone mouthpieces, before leaving jazz in the early 70s to play in a rock context with Steve Winwood and Jeff Beck. Because of his work outside the jazz field he was often overlooked by the cogniscenti. His work as a theme composer tended to err on the dull side, notably the background music for the Cosby Show. In the early 90s he returned to a more authentic jazz style, but still played on altered instruments. In his later years he produced some fine work with John Scofield and reunited with Les McCann, who he worked with in the early 60s.

● ALBUMS: *Exodus To Jazz* (Vee Jay 1961)★★★, *Mighty Like A Rose* (Vee Jay 1961)★★★, *Jazz For 'Breakfast At Tiffany's'* (Vee Jay 1961)★★★, *A Study In Jazz* (Vee Jay 1962)★★★, *Eddie Harris Goes To The Movies* (Vee Jay 1962)★★★, *Bossa Nova* (Vee Jay 1963)★★★, *Cool Sax, Warm Heart* (Columbia 1964), *Cool Sax From Hollywood To Broadway* (Columbia 1965)★★★, *The 'In' Sound* (Atlantic 1966)★★★, *Means Greens* (Atlantic 1966)★★★, *The Tender Storm* (Atlantic 1967)★★★, *The Electrifying Eddie Harris* (Atlantic 1967)★★★, *Silver Cycles* (Atlantic 1969)★★★, *High Voltage* (Atlantic 1969)★★★, with Les McCann *Swiss Movement* (Atlantic 1970)★★★, *Free Speech* (Atlantic 1970)★★★, with McCann *Second Movement* (Atlantic 1971)★★★, *Live At Newport* (Atlantic 1972)★★★, *Eddie Harris In The UK* (1972)★★★★, *The Electrifying Eddie Harris* (1976)★★, *Playing With Myself* (RCA 1979)★★★, *Steps Up* (Steeple Chase 1981)★★★, *Homecoming* (Spindletop 1985)★★★, *Live In Berlin* (Timeless 1988)★★★, *There Was A Time (Echo Of Harlem)* (Enja 1990)★★★, *For You, For Me, For Everyone* (Steeple Chase 1992)★★★, *Listen Here* (Enja 1993)★★★, *The Lost Album Plus The Better Half* early 60s recording (Vee Jay 1993)★★★, with Jimmy Smith *All The Way Live* 1981 recording (Milestone 1996)★★★, *Dancing By A Rainbow* (Enja 1996)★★★, *Vexatious Progressions* (Flying Heart 1996)★★★★, *The Last Concert* (ACT 1997)★★★, *Freedom Jazz Dance* (Music Masters 1997)★★★★, *The Last Concert* (ACT 1997)★★, *I Need Some Money* (Atlantic 1998)★★★, with Wendell Harrison *The Battle Of The Tenors* (Enja 1998)★★★.

● VIDEOS: with Eddie Harris *Swiss Movement* (Rhino 1997).

HARRIS, GENE

b. 1 September 1933, Benton Harbour, Michigan, USA. A self-taught pianist, Harris extended his playing ability from its original boogie-woogie base while on military service. In the mid-50s he formed The Three Sounds with drummer Bill Dowdy and bassist Andrew Simpkins. The trio played highly popular bluesy mainstream jazz and recorded prolifically for Blue Note Records throughout the 60s. After his colleagues moved on, Harris turned towards jazz-rock but returned to the mainstream in the late 70s. In subsequent decades he worked with Ernestine Anderson, Benny Carter, Scott Hamilton, Stanley Turrentine and others, was leader of the all-star Philip Morris Super Band which toured extensively, recorded several albums, and appeared at New York's Apollo backing B.B. King. A solid accompanist, for many years Harris was at his exuberant best playing in the blues idiom. More recently, he has broadened his repertoire and plays swinging, muscular mainstream to bop piano, although the blues are happily never far away.

● ALBUMS: *Gene Harris & The Three Sounds* (Blue Note 1971)★★★, *Of The Three Sounds* (Blue Note 1972)★★★, *Yesterday, Today, Tomorrow* (Blue Note 1973)★★★, *Astral Signal* (Blue Note 1974)★★★, *In A Special Way* (Blue Note 1976)★★, *Tone Tantrums* (Blue Note 1977)★★, *Gene Harris Live At Otter Crest* (Bosco 1981)★★★, *Hot Lips* (JAM 1982)★★★, *The Gene Harris Trio Plus One* (Concord Jazz 1985)★★★★, *Tribute To Count Basie* (Concord Jazz 1987)★★, *Listen Here!* (Concord Jazz 1989)★★★, *Gene Harris And The Philip Morris Superband: Live At Town Hall, New York City* (Concord Jazz 1989)★★★, *Gene Harris And The Philip Morris Superband: World Tour* (Concord Jazz 1990)★★★, with Scott Hamilton *At Last* (Concord Jazz 1990)★★★, *Black And Blue* (Concord Jazz 1991)★★★★, *Like A Lover* (Concord Jazz 1992)★★★, *Live At Maybeck Recital Hall* (Concord Jazz 1993)★★★, *Brotherhood* (Concord Jazz 1993)★★★, *A Little Piece Of Heaven* (Concord Jazz 1994)★★★, *Funky Gene's* (Concord Jazz 1994)★★★, with Frank Wess *It's The Real Soul* (Concord Jazz 1996)★★★★, *In His Hands* (Concord Jazz 1997)★★★, with Brother Jack McDuff *Down Home Blues* (Concord Jazz 1998)★★, with the Philip Morris All-Stars *Live* (Concord Jazz 1998)★★★.

HARRIS, MARILYN

b. USA. Although she has spent more than two decades in popular music, Harris remains relatively little known. Most of her work was in the anonymity of radio and television studios where she composed and arranged and also sang backing to other singers. Although pressure of work kept her from lighting her own fire, she began her own album in 1983, completing it 10 years later. Writing all the songs, either alone or in collaboration, she showed an awareness of the long tradition of pop as well as contemporary attitudes in music making. There are also occasional hints of the blues beneath her sophisticated style. Her voice is clear and melodious and she is also a gifted keyboards player, accompanying herself with skill and verve.

● ALBUMS: *Between The Lines* (Wrightwood 1993)★★★.

HARRISON, DONALD 'DUCK'

b. 23 June 1960, New Orleans, Louisiana, USA. A precociously gifted alto and soprano saxophonist, Harrison attended the New Orleans Center for the Creative Arts, studied with Ellis Marsalis, then went to Berklee College Of Music. At the start of the 80s his professional career blossomed thanks to periods in high profile hard bop bands such as those led by Roy Haynes and, most notably, Art Blakey, whom he and Terence Blanchard joined, succeeding Branford and Wynton Marsalis. The intensive education that was a standard part of any young musician's time with Blakey helped establish Harrison not only as a player, but also enhanced his abilities as a composer and arranger. Conversely, Harrison's fiery chromatic playing provided a relatively radical element within the Blakey band. Concurrently, he was able to exemplify his manifold talents through recordings with a band he co-led with Blanchard. Harrison's remarkable technical gifts and his arranging skills are coloured by his appreciation and understanding of the roots of jazz which has contributed to his accessibility to a wide range of post-bop jazz fans. In the mid-90s, Harrison became a member of Prestige Records' Chartbusters, an all-star band including Randy Brecker, Lonnie Smith and Idris Muhammad. Meanwhile, he continued his successful career as a leader.

● ALBUMS: with Terence Blanchard *New York Second Line* (George Wein Collection 1983)★★★★, with Blanchard *Discernment* (George Wein Collection 1985)★★★, with Blanchard *Nascence* (Columbia 1986)★★★, with Blanchard *Crystal Stair* (Columbia 1987)★★★, with Blanchard *Black Pearl* (Columbia 1988)★★★★, *Full Circle* (Sweet Basil 1990)★★★, *For Art's Sake* (Candid 1991)★★★, *Indian Blues* (Candid 1992)★★★, *The Power Of Cool* (CTI1993)★★★, with the Chartbusters *The Chartbusters Vol. 1* (Prestige 1995)★★★, *Nouveau Swing* (Impulse! 1997)★★★★, with the Chartbusters *Mating Call* (Prestige 1997)★★★.

HARRISON, JIMMY

b. 17 October 1900, Louisville, Kentucky, USA, d. 23 July 1931. Self-taught on trombone, Harrison played extensively in tent shows in the years after World War I. Still on the move - he was briefly in Atlantic City and Detroit among other towns - Harrison was a member of several early jazz bands, including those led by Sam Wooding and James P. Johnson; but by 1922 he had settled in New York, where he worked with various jazzmen, notably Fess Williams. A remarkably advanced and technically accomplished player, Harrison was an important influence upon other trombonists, including his great friend Jack Teagarden. Harrison's skills placed him in great demand, and later in the 20s he was hired by Duke Ellington and Fletcher Henderson. Sadly, he contracted stomach cancer, underwent surgery and after a brief attempt to resume his career with Henderson and Chick Webb, died in July 1931.

HART, BILLY

b. 29 January 1940, Washington, D.C., USA. Hart is a self-taught drummer who, by the late 90s, had established himself as an one of jazz music's most invaluable session playesr. In the early 60s he worked with Shirley Horn (vocals) and briefly with the Montgomery Brothers. In 1966 he joined Jimmy Smith and in 1968 moved on to the band of Wes Montgomery. Following Montgomery's death Hart based himself, becoming an integral part of the New York fusion and *avant-garde* scenes. Sessions with Miles Davis, Wayne Shorter, Joe Zawinul, Eddie Harris and Pharoah Sanders followed, along with long-standing commitments with the innovative Herbie Hancock sextet (1969-73) and McCoy Tyner (1973-74). Hart showed his remarkable versatility by playing mainstream jazz with Stan Getz for three years (1974-1977). His first album as a leader, *Enhance*, was a starkly *avant-garde* session recorded while Hart was still playing with Getz. In the 80s Hart played with the collectives Quest (with Dave Liebman, Richie Beirach and Ron McCLure) and Great Friends (with Billy Harper, Stanley Cowell and Reggie Workman), while continuing to record sporadically as a leader. Throughout the 80s and 90s Hart has remained a busy freelance drummer capable of providing a crisp, driving, beat or a much looser accompaniment depending on the situation. He has also played with Joe Lovano, Clark Terry, Lee Konitz, Chico Freeman, Charles Lloyd, Tom Harrell, Larry Coryell, John Handy. Since 1992 he has taught at Western Michigan University in Kalamazoo.

● ALBUMS: *Enchance* (Horizon 1977)★★★★, *Oshumare* (Gramavision 1985)★★★, *Rah* (Gramavision 1989)★★★, *Amethyst* (Arabesque Jazz 1993)★★, *Oceans Of Time* (Arabesque Jazz 1997)★★★.

HART, CLYDE

b. 1910, Baltimore, Maryland, USA, d. 19 March 1945. After working as pianist and arranger with the Jap Allen outfit, a leading territory band of the early 30s, Hart spent the second half of the decade in numerous ensembles. A solid performer with particular ability as an accompanist, Hart was in great demand and played with many of the outstanding jazz artists of the period. Among them were McKinney's Cotton Pickers, Andy Kirk, Red Allen, Billie Holiday, Stuff Smith, Roy Eldridge, Lester Young, Lionel Hampton and Frankie Newton. In the early 40s Hart was with various bandleaders, including John Kirby and Wilbur De Paris but had begun to take an interest in the new developments in jazz. He adjusted his style to accommodate the needs of bebop soloists, one of the first of the swing era pianists to do so, and subsequently played with Charlie Parker and Dizzy Gillespie, whose first studio session together was under Hart's leadership. One of the usually unsung stalwarts of jazz, whose musical personality kept him very much in the background, Hart played an important part in the transition from swing to bop. However, he was unable to build upon his important early work in this area as he fell victim to tuberculosis and died.

● COMPILATIONS: with Charlie Parker *Complete Savoy Sessions* (1944-45)★★★★, *Dizzy Gillespie With Clyde Hart's All Stars* (1945)★★★.

HARTMAN, JOHNNY

b. John Maurice Hartman, 13 July 1923, Chicago, Illinois, USA, d. 15 September 1983. Having started to sing while still at school, he went on to study at musical college. Hartman became a professional following the end of the World War II and first attracted widespread attention accompanying Earl Hines in 1947 and two years later with Errol Garner. His rich, deep baritone lent itself to a range of material and he comfortably accommodated country music alongside popular songs of the day (which meant he was able to make the breakthrough into television), although his first and lasting preference was for jazz. Within a jazz context he inclined towards modernism, performing and recording with Dizzy Gillespie, John Coltrane, and Sir Roland Hanna. He was nominated for a Grammy in 1981 for his album *Once In Every Life*. He veered from jazz to easy listening and pop in his latter years.

● ALBUMS: *Songs From The Heart* (Bethlehem 1956)★★★, *Just You Just Me* (Regent 1956)★★★, *All Of Me* (Bethlehem 1956)★★★, with John Coltrane *John Coltrane And Johnny Hartman* (Impulse! 1963)★★★★, *Dropped By To Say Hello* (Impulse! 1963)★★★, *The Voice That Is!* (Impulse! 1965)★★★, *The Unforgettable Johnny Hartman* (ABC 1966)★★, *Today* (Perception 1973)★★★, *I've Been There* (Perception 1975)★★, *Live At Sometime* (Trio 1977)★★, *Once In Every Life* (Bee Hive 1980)★★★, *This One's For Tedi* (1980)★★★, *Once In Every Life* (1981)★★★, *Thank You For Everything* 1978 recording (Audiophile 1998)★★★.

● COMPILATIONS: *The Songbook* (1947)★★★.

HARVEY, EDDIE

b. 15 November 1925, Blackpool, Lancashire, England. A fine multi-instrumentalist and arranger with a wide stylistic range, Harvey first attracted attention in traditional jazz circles. This was in the early 40s when he played trombone with George Webb's band. In the post-war years he continued to play traditional jazz, mostly with Freddy Randall, then changed direction when, in 1950, he played with Vic Lewis and was a member of the first John Dankworth Seven and Dankworth's big band. In succeeding years he played with musicians such as Tubby Hayes and Ronnie Scott, and was a member of Woody Herman's Anglo-American Herd. In the 60s he also played piano with, among others, Humphrey Lyttelton for whom he also wrote arrangements. Moving into jazz education, he worked as a teacher and also studied music education. He has also written books, including a self-education jazz guide. This all-round ability and eclectic taste has made Harvey an important member of the British jazz scene for more than half a century.

HASHIM, MICHAEL

b. 1956, Geneva, New York, USA. While attending school at Geneva in upstate New York, Hashim joined the school band programme. His first choices, drums and trombone, were ruled out and he settled instead on alto saxophone. His interest in music had been sparked when he met a fellow student, Phil Flanigan, whose father had an extensive jazz record collection. They listened to a wide range of musicians, from Sidney Bechet to Frank Zappa, by way of Lester Young and Charlie Parker. By chance, he and Flanigan met guitarist Chris Flory and with drummer Johnny Ellis they formed a quartet. By the mid-70s Hashim was working regularly, often with Flanigan and Flory. He played mostly in the New York/Rhode Island area and when Flory went into Scott Hamilton's band (where he was later joined by Flanigan), Hashim joined the Widespread Depression Orchestra of South Vermont. Later, when Widespread moved to New York, Hashim went along too, eventually taking over leadership of the band which continued to perform into the mid-90s. He has played with Muddy Waters, Benny Carter, studied with altoist Jimmy Lyons, and worked for a while in a band led by Jo Jones. He continued to work with Flory, in a trio completed by the excellent young stride pianist Judy Carmichael. He tours extensively throughout the USA and Europe and he also played in China on a US Information Service-backed tour. Although his musical interests lie in post-bop jazz, Hashim's feeling for the tradition is never far from the surface. He continues to attract attention and admiration for his warm-toned, dynamic and always inventive playing on alto and soprano saxophones.

● ALBUMS: *Lotus Blossom* (Stash 1990)★★★, *The Billy Strayhorn Project* (1990)★★★, *Guys And Dolls* (Stash 1992)★★, *A Blue Streak* (Stash 1992)★★★, *Keep A Song In Your Soul* (Hep 1996)★★★★, *Transatlantic Airs* (33 Records 1996)★★★★.

HASSELGÅRD, 'STAN' AKE

b. Ake Hasselgård, 4 October 1922, Sundsvall, Sweden, d. 23 November 1948. During the 40s Hasselgård played clarinet with several dance bands in his homeland, then moved to the USA in the mid-summer of 1947. Here he attracted considerable attention as not many American clarinettists had adapted to bebop as well as he had done. He played with a number of jazzmen, including Count Basie, Red Norvo and Barney Kessel before he came to the notice of Benny Goodman. Despite his reputation for not sharing the spotlight with any other clarinettist and also for not liking bebop, Goodman delighted in Hasselgård's playing and recorded with him and Wardell Gray, another of the tiny coterie of beboppers of whom Goodman approved. Just how far into bebop Hasselgård might have taken the clarinet can only be a matter for speculation; he died as a result of a road accident in November 1948.

● COMPILATIONS: *The Permanent Hasselgård* (Phontastic 1945-48 recordings)★★★, with Benny Goodman, Wardell Gray *Swedish Pastry* (1948)★★★★, with Goodman, Gray, others *Jammin' At Jubilee* (1948)★★★★, *At Click 1948* (Dragon, 1948 recording)★★★, *Jammin' At Jubilee* (Dragon 1986)★★★, *Young Clarinet* (Dragon 1988, 1940-48 recordings)★★★.

HASSELL, JON

b. 1937, Memphis, Tennessee, USA. Hassell acquired several university degrees including a PhD in musicology, before travelling to Cologne, Germany in 1965 to study with Karlheinz Stockhausen. While in Cologne he met and played with Irmin Schmidt and Holgar Czukay, who later went on to form Can. The trumpeter and keyboard player returned to the USA in 1967 and began to play with leading minimalist composers La Monte Young and Terry Riley. As a performer Hassell appeared on Riley's seminal minimalist piece *In C*, released in 1968 and La Monte Young's extended drone cycle *Dreamhouse*. With Young's influence Hassell became interested in Indian classical music and in 1972 he travelled to northern Indian to study Kirana tradition with master vocalist Pandit Pran Nath. From his studies Hassell created a new vocal style which he described as Fourth World - a unified primitive/futuristic sound combining features of world ethnic style with advanced electronic techniques. In 1976 he returned to the USA and recorded *Vernal Equinox*, his first attempt to integrate/expand raga studies with technological vocabulary. The record features Brazilian percussionist Nana Vasconcelos. In 1979 *Earthquake Island* was released and continued the highly influential genre of ethnic-inspired music and again featured Vasconcelos, along with Badal Roy and ex-Weather Report bassist Miroslav Vitous. In 1980 Brian Eno arrived in New York, and heard *Vernal Equinox*, and contacted Hassell about the possibility of a collaboration. The highly acclaimed *Fourth World Volume One*: *Possible Musics* released the same year pushed Hassell into the limelight and he was invited to play on the Eno-produced Talking Heads album *Remain In Light*.

Fourth World Volume Two: Dreamy Theory In Malaya was released in 1981. The recording contained playing by Eno, and engineering by Daniel Lanois, and was again received with critical acclaim. In 1982, Hassell was invited to perform at the Womad festival in Bath, England, and to participate in the prestigious Rencontres Nord-Sud Conference on World Culture in Paris. *AKA/Darbari/Java (Magic Realism)* produced by Lanois in 1983 marked a new high point for Hassell in 'techno-magic' that permit actual sound of music of various epochs and geographies to come together on the same canvas through the use of sampling and computer hardware. With the addition of percussionist J.A. Deane and keyboard player Jean-Philippe Rykiel, Hassell toured Europe and the USA. Eno produced *Powerspot*, in 1986, which contained recordings made by this group in 1983-84 and further Hassell's reputation at the forefront of burgeoning interest in hybrid and world music. In 1984, David Sylvian invited Hassell to play on his first solo album, *Brilliant Trees* and the following year to collaborate on *Alchemy - An Index Of Possibilities*. *The Surgeon Of The Night Sky Restores Dead Things By The Power Of Sound,* again was produced by Eno, released in 1987, documented the concert chemistry of the group that toured Europe in 1986. That same year, Kronos Quartet commissioned string quartet *Pano De Costa* from Hassell. It appears on their *White Man Sleeps* album. In 1987, Burkino Faso percussion ensemble Farafina invited Hassell to collaborate with them. The group played various festivals around the world, including Womad. The Eno/Lanois produced *Flash On The Spirit* documented this highly original unique blend of styles and cultures. In 1989. Hassell relocated to Los Angeles, where he formed a new group to perform live, and recorded self-produced *City: Works Of Fiction* released to critical acclaim in 1990. Despite continuous problems in locating a label for his recorded work Hassell remains an entirely unique performer with a visionary and highly original sound and style.

● ALBUMS: *Vernal Equinox* (Lovely 1977)★★★, *Earthquake Island* (Tomato 1979)★★★, with Brian Eno *Fourth World Volume One: Possible Musics* (Editions EG 1980)★★★★, *Dream Theory In Malaya/Fourth World Volume Two* (Editions EG 1981)★★, *Aka/Darbari/Java (Magic Realism)* (Editions EG 1983)★★★, *Powerspot* (ECM 1986)★★★, *The Surgeon Of The Night Sky Restores Dead Things By The Power Of Sound* (Intuition 1987)★★, with Farafina *Flash Of The Spirit* (Intuition 1988)★★★, *City: Works Of Fiction* (Land 1990)★★★.

HASTINGS, LENNIE

b. 5 January 1927, London, England, d. 14 July 1978. Although best known for his dixieland-style drumming, Hastings was well-versed in other areas of jazz. He was first noticed playing modern jazz in the late 40s, but by 1949 had joined Freddy Randall's traditional band. After five years with Randall he moved to Alex Welsh, with whom he remained until 1973. Both during and after his time with Welsh, Hastings played in rhythm sections accompanying visiting American artists such as Rex Stewart, Bill Coleman, Bob Wilber and Kenny Davern. An exuberant personality with an outrageous sense of fun, Hastings was given to wearing fright wigs in shades of vitriolic orange. His death in July 1978 left a gap in the UK jazz scene.

● ALBUMS: with Alex Welsh *Melody Maker Tribute To Louis Armstrong* (1970)★★, *Always The Best* (Dawn Club 1978)★★★.

HAUGHTON, CHAUNCEY

b. 26 February 1909, Chestertown, Maryland, USA. Coming from a musical family (his father and two brothers were professional musicians), Haughton first learned piano, then clarinet and saxophone. In the late 20s and early 30s he played in a number of minor bands but then joined Blanche Calloway, having previously worked with her brother, Elmer. He then appeared briefly with the bands of Claude Hopkins, Noble Sissle and Fletcher Henderson before joining Chick Webb.

With Webb he was featured in the Little Chicks small group, playing duets with flautist Wayman Carver. He next worked with Cab Calloway before rejoining the Webb band in 1940 which, following Webb's death, was then under the nominal leadership of Ella Fitzgerald. Haughton deputized briefly with Duke Ellington before military service during World War II. After the war he played in the Don Redman band and returned briefly to Cab Calloway but then left music. He returned for the occasional record date but otherwise remained in retirement.

HAURAND, ALI

b. 15 November 1943, Viersen, Germany. Haurand learned the double bass and percussion at school and played in amateur dixieland bands as a teenager. He studied music at Volkswangschule, Essen (1965-71) and while he was there had his own trio. In 1970 he started the group Third Eye which survived into the mid-80s despite personnel changes. In 1977 he joined the European Jazz Quintet. In 1978 with Alan Skidmore and Tony Oxley he formed SOH which is sometimes enlarged to a quartet with the addition of Kenny Wheeler or John Surman. With Oxley's propulsive drumming, Haurand's mobile, assertive bass playing combines to provide a formidable rhythm section. Between 1977 and 1980 he worked with the Hungarian clarinettist Lajos Dudas. He formed the Quintet with Joachim Kuhn and Enrico Rava in 1985.

● ALBUMS: *Ali Haurand Solo* (1974)★★★, *Third Eye Live* (1982)★★★★, *SOH Live At Neuss* (1981)★★★, with the Quartet *Dedications* (1983)★★★, *The Quartet* (1985)★★★.

HAVEN, ALAN

b. 1 April 1935, Prestwich, Manchester, Lancashire, England. Largely self-taught, Haven's first instrument was the piano and he began playing jazz while still a teenager. He played clubs and dancehall dates on the Mecca circuit and also ventured as far afield as Paris. He had been interested for some time in organists, including Jackie Davis and, in particular, a Count Basie set with the Oscar Peterson Trio on which Basie played organ. Haven acquired a Lowrey Holiday organ and taught himself to play it, this at a time when organ trios were briefly popular. Facing up to the complexities of the instrument was one thing; there were also audience (and fellow-musician) prejudices to overcome, since the organ was not highly regarded in jazz circles. He toured extensively, learning his trade with such dedication and skill that he eventually became perhaps the most skilled of all organists with his footwork. He began to enjoy a higher profile thanks to appearances on television and a popular album of songs by John Lennon and Paul McCartney. In the mid-60s Haven moved to London, persuaded Ronnie Scott to give him an opportunity at the old Gerrard Street club, and soon broke down most of the barriers of prejudice against his instrument. He played and recorded sets at Ronnie Scott's and also at Annie's Room and established a musically rewarding partnership with drummer Tony Crombie. He had hit singles with 'Image' and 'Romance On The North Sea' and topped *Melody Maker* polls for several years. He also wrote music for and played on the soundtracks of a number of films, including two James Bond films and *The Knack*. He designed and had built the Haven organ and for some years was active in the marketing and promotion of the instrument, activities that kept him from the public eye for a while. In the early 80s he was back but from the middle of the decade onwards was only rarely in the UK. Mostly, he was heard in Spain and on US-based cruise liners. In the late 90s Haven returned to the recording studios after a long absence and was working in Spain, often with the singer Karen Elle, a long-lasting partnership. Throughout his career, Haven demonstrated enormous energy, playing with drive and rhythmic vitality. His technical skills, especially his footwork, appear boundless but this is technique at the service of a master musician, not for its own sake. Although straight jazz gigs are less in evidence, the luxury liner, hotel and cabaret audience having different needs, when the opportunity presents itself, Haven admirably proves that he has lost none of the youthful fire that made his name, in the UK, synonymous with jazz organ for most of the 60s.

● ALBUMS: *Lennon And McCartney Styled By Alan Haven* (Fontana 1965)★★★★, *Thro Till Two: Live At Ronnie Scott's* (Fontana 1967)★★★★, *Live At Annie's Room* (Fontana 60s)★★★, *St Elmo's Fire* (CBS 60s)★★, with Ben Webster *Big Ben Time* (Philips 1969)★★★, *Haven For Sale* (CBS 70s)★★★, *Quiet Sounds For The Small Hours* (Fontana 70s)★★★, *Organ Magic* (Pye 70s)★★★, with John Barry *The Knack* (UA early 70s)★★, *Side By Side* (Pye early 70s)★★★, *Collector's Item* (PRT 1978)★★★★, *Organ Spectrum* (OSD 1996)★★★★.

HAVENS, BOB

b. 3 May 1930, Quincy, Illinois, USA. Havens came from a musical family and was learning violin and piano before he took up the trombone when he was aged eight. In the mid-50s he played a month's residency in New Orleans with Ralph Flanagan's orchestra and decided to settle there. He played with George Girard before joining Al Hirt in 1957 for three successful years. He followed Pete Fountain from Hirt to Lawrence Welk's band and stayed with him for 20 years. Since then he has led a band at Disneyland and continued to work in studios, always able to provide the kind of classic dixieland typified by Bob Crosby with whom he worked in 1985. He acknowledges Jack Teagarden as his principal influence. He is involved in teaching and plays with college bands.

● ALBUMS: *Bob Havens And His New Orleans All Stars* (Southland 1964)★★★, with Pete Fountain *Standing Room Only* (1965)★★★.

HAWDON, DICKIE

b. 27 August 1927, Leeds, Yorkshire, England. A remarkably eclectic musician, trumpeter Hawdon's playing career encompassed such diverse styles as traditional jazz, which he played with Chris Barber and Terry

Lightfoot, and modern jazz, with Tubby Hayes and John Dankworth. Unusually for a musician who switches styles, Hawdon did not merely make a progressive transition but comfortably moved backwards and forwards between styles. In the late 60s Hawdon entered full-time musical education, becoming head of the Light Music Department at the Leeds College of Music. At this later stage in his career he also began playing bass.

● ALBUMS: with Tubby Hayes *After Lights Out* (1956)★★★★, *Poetry And Jazz* (1976)★★★.

Hawes, Hampton

b. 13 November 1928, Los Angeles, California, USA, d. 22 May 1977. Born into a musical family (his mother played piano for the church run by his Presbyterian minister father), Hawes taught himself to play piano by listening to records of 30s jazz piano giants, among them Earl 'Fatha' Hines and Fats Waller. He began to play professionally while still attending the Polytechnic High School. In his autobiography, *Raise Up Off Me*, he recalled leaving his graduation ceremony and heading straight for a gig with the Jay McNeely band. Hawes was briefly in New York but soon returned to Los Angeles, where he became an important participant in the burgeoning 'west coast' school of jazz. He was a member of Howard McGhee's band when the trumpeter hired Charlie Parker for a gig at the Hi-De-Ho Club in Los Angeles, shortly after Parker's release from Camarillo.

Hawes's first recording date was with Dexter Gordon and Wardell Gray in 1947. He was with Shorty Rogers on his 1951 *Modern Sounds* recording session, which also featured Art Pepper. Hawes was occasionally at the Lighthouse Club during these years, working in the house rhythm section that backed all the major figures of the movement of which he had become an important part. Unfortunately, Hawes had developed a drug habit and his induction into the US Army did little to help his condition. Apart from time spent in military prison for drugs-related offences, Hawes also visited Japan where he became an early admirer and lifelong friend of Toshiko Akiyoshi. Released from the service in 1955, Hawes was recorded by Lester Koenig for his new Contemporary Records. At the same time Hawes formed a trio, with Red Mitchell and Chuck Thompson. The trio's first album was successful but not so much as subsequent albums, which included the enormously influential *All Night Session*. Recorded by a quartet, with the addition of guitarist Jim Hall, this set established Hawes as a major figure; the music on the albums, to which buzz words like 'funky' and 'soul' were applied, was suddenly the in-thing. In the mid-50s Hawes recorded with artists including Art Pepper, Bill Perkins and Charles Mingus, but an excellent 1958 record date, *For Real!*, with Harold Land, was the last for some time. Despite the urgings and advice of the late Wardell Gray, Hawes had sunk into acute drug dependency. He was imprisoned for heroin possession at a time when his musical importance and influence were at their height. Released in 1963 by order of President John F. Kennedy, Hawes returned to recording for Contemporary and other labels in the USA, Europe and Japan. In the 70s, Hawes recorded studio and festival sessions, sometimes using electric piano. A major figure in the development of modern jazz piano playing, Hawes's less successful later work has tended to overshadow the tremendously important contribution he made in his earlier years.

● ALBUMS: *The Hampton Hawes Trio* (1951)★★★, *The Hampton Hawes Memorial Album* (1952)★★★, *The Hampton Hawes Quartet* (1952)★★★★, *Piano East/West* (Original Jazz Classics 1953)★★★★, *Shorty Rogers And His Giants* (1953)★★, *Volume 1: The Trio* (Original Jazz Classics 1955)★★★★, *This Is Hampton Hawes, Vol. 2* (1955)★★★, *Everybody Likes Hampton Hawes* (1956)★★★, with Freddie Redd *Piano East Piano West* reissued as *Movin'* (Prestige/Status 1956)★★★★, *All Night Session Vols 1, 2, 3* (Original Jazz Classics 1956)★★★★, *Four!* (Original Jazz Classics 1958)★★★, *For Real* (1958)★★, *The Green Leaves Of Summer* (Original Jazz Classics 1964)★★★★, with Curtis Fuller *Curtis Fuller And Hampton Hawes With French Horns* 1957 recording (Status 1965)★★★, *Here And Now* (Original Jazz Classics 1965)★★★, *The Seance* (Original Jazz Classics 1966)★★★, *I'm All Smiles* (1966)★★, *Hampton Hawes In Europe* (1967)★★, *Piano Improvisations* (1967-68)★★★, *Spanish Steps* (Black Lion 1968)★★★, *The Challenge* (Storyville 1968)★★★, *Hampton Hawes In Tokyo* (1968)★★★, *Hamp's Piano* (1968)★★★, with Martial Solal *Key For Two* (Affinity 1969)★★, *Memory Lane* (1970)★★, *The Two Sides Of Hampton Hawes* (1970)★★, *The Hampton Hawes Trio At Montreux* (Fresh Sounds 1971)★★, *Anglo-American Jazz Phase O* (1971)★★★, *A Little Copenhagen Night Music* (Freedom 1971)★★★, *Universe* (1972)★★★, *Blues For Walls* (1973)★★, *Live At The Jazz Showcase In Chicago Vol. 1* (1973)★★, *Playin' By The Yard* (1973)★★, *Northern Windows* (1974)★★★, *This Guy's In Love With You* 1971 recording (1975)★★★ reissued as *Live At The Montmartre*), *Hampton Hawes Recorded Live At The Great American Music Hall* (1975)★★★, *Killing Me Softly With His Song/Hampton Hawes At The Piano* (Original Jazz Classics 1976)★★★, *As Long As There's Music* (Verve 1976)★★★★, *Music* 1971 recording (1978)★★, *Something Special* 1976 recordings (Contemporary 1978)★★★.

● FURTHER READING: *Raise Up Off Me*, Hampton Hawes.

Hawkins, Coleman

b. Coleman Randolph Hawkins, 21 November *c.*1901, St. Joseph, Missouri, USA, d. 19 May 1969. Coleman Hawkins (aka 'Bean' and 'Hawk') is the colossus of the tenor saxophone, and hence of modern jazz. He was the first to use the instrument as a serious means of expression and continued to be open to new developments for 40 years. Starting piano lessons at the age of five, he later learned cello and took up tenor saxophone when he was nine years old. Within a few years he was playing dances and appearing in Kansas and Chicago. He attended Washburn College in Topeka and toured as a member of Mamie Smith's Jazz Hounds in 1921. He joined Fletcher Henderson's Orchestra in 1924, a sophisticated New York dance band then coming to terms with the new jazz music - hot and improvised - that Louis Armstrong, who had also joined Henderson in 1924, had brought from New Orleans by way of Chicago. Released in 1926, 'The Stampede' featured Hawkins' first notable solo. In his ten years with the band he transformed the tenor sax - previously a novelty instrument for blues and hokum records - from rather quaint imitations of Armstrong's staccato style into a vehicle for the powerful and suave solos that were the essence of swing. 'St Louis Shuffle' (1927), 'Sugar Foot Stomp' (1931) and 'Hocus Pocus' (1934) are three brilliant sides that trace this evolution. By 1934 jazz had become a global music. Coleman Hawkins left Fletcher Henderson and travelled to Europe, where he was welcomed by the local players. He recorded with Jack Hylton in England. Excluded from a Hylton tour of Germany in 1935 by the Nazis' new racial laws, he joined Theo Masman's Ramblers Dance Orchestra and recorded with them for Decca. In 1937 he met up with Django Reinhardt and recorded some memorable music (Stéphane Grappelli was relegated to piano), and he also played with fellow exile Benny Carter. When war broke out in 1939 Hawkins returned to the USA. There his supremacy on tenor sax had been challenged by the languid yet harmonically sophisticated playing of Lester Young, but his recording of 'Body & Soul' (on 11 October 1939) was a massive hit and established him as a national figure, his confessional, tender-but-tough tenor the epitome of jazz. In 1940 he toured with his own 16-piece, appearing at premier New York jazz spots the Arcadia and the Savoy Ballroom, but the days of the big band were numbered. In December 1943 his small combo recordings - 'How Deep Is The Ocean', 'Stumpy' and an irresistible swinger called 'Voodte' - represented the apex of swing, though the sense of headlong abandon was akin to the new music of bebop. Bebop was black America's first *avant garde* art form, featuring innovations many established musicians felt moved to denounce, but Hawkins loved it. He led an early bebop recording session in February 1944 - featuring Don Byas, Dizzy Gillespie and Max Roach. In 1943 he had formed a sextet with Thelonious Monk, Don Byas and trumpeter Benny Harris and a year later gave Monk his recording debut. Most of 1944 and 1945 were spent on the west coast with a band that included Sir Charles Thompson and Howard McGhee. As featured soloist on Norman Granz's *Jazz At The Philharmonic* tours, trips to Europe followed in 1950 and 1954.

The popularity of Stan Getz's interpretation of Lester Young made Hawkins and his ripe sound unfashionable in the 50s, but his strength as a player - and his openness of mind - never left him. In 1957 Thelonious Monk repaid the compliment by inviting him to join his septet, and the application of Hawkins' big, swinging tenor to Monk's paradoxical compositions yielded wonderful results on tunes such as 'Off Minor'. Playing next to young turks such as John Coltrane, Hawkins showed that he still had something to contribute. The classic *The Hawk Flies High* (1957) showed what Hawkins could accomplish in a mainstream setting, while a reunion with his ex-Henderson colleague Henry 'Red' Allen in the same year showed he could also shine in a more traditional context. In the 60s Hawkins kept playing, recording with new tenor star Sonny Rollins. The list of his engagements in that decade is testament to the catholic taste that an established elder statesman can afford: Pee Wee Russell, Duke Ellington, Bud Powell, Tommy Flanagan, Eric Dolphy, even an appearance on Max Roach's inflammatory *We Insist! Freedom Now* suite and at a 1966 'Tenors Titan' concert that also featured Rollins, Coltrane, Zoot Sims and Yusef Lateef. He played on the last JATP tour (1967) and toured with Oscar Peterson in 1968, though by that point he was increasingly prone to bouts of depression and drinking, exacerbated by a refusal to eat. His death from pneumonia in 1969 marked the end of an era; he was a jazz master whose life-work stretched across six decades of the music's history.

● ALBUMS: *Originals With Hawkins* 10-inch album (Stinson 1950)★★★★, *Coleman Hawkins All Stars* 10-inch album (Apollo 1951)★★★, *Coleman Hawkins Favorites* 10-inch album (Advance 1951)★★★★, *King Of The Tenor Sax* reissued as *Meditations* (Commodore 1952)★★★★, *Classics In Jazz* 10-inch album (Capitol 1952)★★★★, *Tenor Sax* 10-inch album (Brunswick 1953)★★★★, *The Bean* 10-inch album (EmArcy 1954)★★★, *The Hawk Talks* 10-inch album (Savoy 1954)★★★★, *Improvisations Unlimited* (Concert Hall 1955)★★★, *Accent On The Tenor Sax* (Urania 1955)★★★, *Hawk in Flight* (RCA Victor 1955)★★★★, *The Hawk Returns* (Savoy 1955)★★★, *Coleman Hawkins And His Orchestra* (American Record Society 1956)★★★, *Coleman Hawkins: A Documentary* (Riverside 1956)★★★, *Hawk In Hi-Fi* (RCA Victor 1956)★★★, *The Hawk In Paris* (Vik 1957)★★★, *Gilded Hawk* (Capitol 1957)★★★, *The Hawk Flies High* (Riverside 1957)★★★, with Roy Eldridge *At The Opera House* (Verve 1957)★★★★, *The High And The Mighty Hawk* (Felsted 1958)★★★, *Coleman Hawkins With The Basie Sax Section* (World Wide 1958)★★★, *Soul* (Prestige 1959)★★★★, *Hawk Eyes* (Prestige 1959)★★★, with Ben Webster *Coleman Hawkins Encounters Ben Webster* (Verve 1959)★★★★, with Oscar Peterson *Coleman Hawkins And His Confreres With The Oscar Peterson Trio* (Verve 1959)★★★★, *Coleman Hawkins Plus The Red Garland Trio* (Swingville 1960)★★★, *At Ease With Colman Hawkins* (Moodsville 1960)★★★, *The Coleman Hawkins All Stars* (Swingville 1960)★★★, *Night Hawk* (Prestige 1961)★★★, *The Hawk Swings* (Crown 1961)★★★, *Things Ain't What They Used To Be* (Swingville 1961)★★★, *The Hawk Blows At Midnight* (Decca 1961)★★★, *Years Ago* (Swingville 1961)★★★, *The Hawk Relaxes* (Moodsville 1961)★★★, with Pee Wee Russell *Jazz Reunion* (Candid 1961)★★★, *Good Old Broadway* (Moodsville 1962)★★★, *The Jazz Version Of No Strings* (Moodsville 1962)★★★, *On The Bean* (Continental 1962)★★★, *In A Mellow Tone* (Original Jazz Classics 1962)★★★, *Jazz At The Metropole* (Philips 1962)★★★, with Howard McGhee, Lester Young *A Date With Greatness* (Imperial 1962)★★★★, with Duke Ellington *Duke Ellington Meets Coleman Hawkins* (MCA/Impulse! 1963)★★★★, *Desafinado: Bossa Nova & Jazz Samba* (Impulse! 1963)★★★, *Today And Now* (Impulse! 1963)★★★, *Make Someone Happy* (Moodsville 1963)★★★, *Hawkins! Alive! At The Village Gate* (Verve 1963)★★★, with Sonny Rollins *Sonny Meets Hawk!* (RCA Victor 1963)★★★★, with Clark Terry *Eddie Costa Memorial Concert* (Colpix 1963)★★★, with Earl Hines *Grand Reunion* (Limelight

1965)★★★★, *Wrapped Tight* (Impulse! 1965)★★★, with Frank Hunter *The Hawk And The Hunter* (Mira 1965)★★★, *Sirius* (1966)★★★, *Supreme* 1966 concert recording (Enja 1995)★★★.

● COMPILATIONS: with the Ramblers *The Hawk In Holland* (1935)★★★, one side only *Classic Tenors* (1943)★★★, *The Genius Of Coleman Hawkins* (Verve 1958)★★★★, *The Essential Coleman Hawkins* (Verve 1964)★★★★, *Body And Soul* (Bluebird 1988)★★★★, *1927-39* (1990)★★★★, *The Complete Recordings 1929-31* (1992)★★★★, *April In Paris* 1939-56 recordings (Bluebird 1992)★★★★, *Body And Soul* 1961 recordings (1993)★★★★, *Rainbow Mist* (1993)★★★, *Lady Be Good* (Tring 1993)★★, *The Complete Recordings 1929-1940* (Charly 1993)★★★, *A Retrospective 1929-1963* (Bluebird 1995)★★★★, *In The Groove* (Indigo 1996)★★★, *The Tenor For All Seasons* (Jazz Classics 1997)★★★★, *His Best Recordings, 1923-1945* (Best Of Jazz 1998)★★★.

● FURTHER READING: *Coleman Hawkins Volume 1 1922-44, Volume 2 1945-57*, Jean François Villetard. *The Song Of The Hawk*, John Chilton. *Coleman Hawkins*, Burnett James.

HAWKINS, ERSKINE

b. 26 July 1914, Birmingham, Alabama, USA, d. 12 November 1993, New York, USA. By the time he began playing trumpet at the age of 13, Hawkins had already mastered drums and trombone. It was on trumpet, however, that he established his name as a flamboyant player with an astonishing range. Initially an imitator of Louis Armstrong, Hawkins became leader of the 'Bama State Collegians, an orchestra that he built up into an excellent big band. In the 30s, Hawkins rivalled much bigger names in engagements all across the USA, and in particular at prestigious New York venues such as Roseland and the Savoy. He hired good section men and front-rank soloists, not least trumpeters with whom he happily shared the spotlight. Billed as the Twentieth Century Gabriel, Hawkins made a number of very successful records, including 'After Hours' and 'Tuxedo Junction', the latter a composition by Hawkins and several members of the band which became their theme tune.

Hawkins continued to lead his big band throughout the 40s, surviving the winter of 1946/7 which saw the end of many name bands. In the 50s he compromised under financial pressure and reduced the band in size, but regularly reassembled the larger unit for special events. In the 60s and 70s he led small groups at New York hotels and clubs and also made occasional appearances at festivals, including a visit to Europe in 1979. In 1986 he was on board the SS *Norway* for the Fifth Annual Floating Jazz Festival. In much the same manner as his white contemporary Harry James, Hawkins succeeded in combining a spectacular technique and an acute awareness of commercial demands with an innate feeling for good jazz.

● ALBUMS: *Erskine Hawkins Live At The Savoy Ballroom* (1940)★★★, *Sneakin' Out* (1942)★★★, *Erskine Hawkins At The Hotel Lincoln, New York* (1946)★★★★, *Live At The Apollo* (1946-47)★★★, *25 Golden Years Of Jazz Vols 1 & 2* (1962)★★★★, *Erskine Hawkins Reunion Party* (1971)★★.

● COMPILATIONS: *Complete Erskine Hawkins Vols 1/2* (RCA 1983, 1938-39 recordings)★★★★, *Original Tuxedo Junction* (Bluebird 1989)★★★★.

HAWTHORNE, VAUGHAN

One of the less-furiously hyped young alto and soprano saxophonists to emerge in the UK in the late 80s, Hawthorne's playing initially lacked the confidence of some of his better-known contemporaries. While drawing extensively upon the musical heritage of the likes of Charlie Parker and Wayne Shorter, Hawthorne regularly introduces his own compositions into his work and in some respects he is happier, certainly more forthrightly original, in such circumstances. Similarly, he displays more confidence on soprano, which he plays with a full rich and commanding tone, than on the thinner-sounding alto.

● ALBUMS: *Emanon* (1987)★★★, *The Path* (1988)★★.

HAYES, CLANCY

b. Clarence Leonard Hayes, 14 November 1908, Caney, Kansas, USA, d. 13 March 1972. Hayes played various instruments in his childhood, concentrating on banjo during his career as a singer and entertainer in vaudeville. By the late 20s he was broadcasting regularly on radio, and in the late 30s he teamed up with Lu Watters to become a leading light in the San Francisco chapter of the Revival movement. During the early 40s Hayes made many concert appearances and records with Watters and also played drums on a recording with Bunk Johnson. In the 50s he continued his Revivalist career, working with Bob Scobey. He subsequently had a successful solo career and made a number of popular albums, including *Swingin' Minstrel* which featured leading jazzmen such as Jess Stacy, Ralph Sutton and, surprisingly, Shelly Manne. Hayes's cheery singing, presented in the manner of the vaudevillean he was at heart, endeared him to a wide audience. He composed a number of novelty songs including 'Huggin' And A-Chalkin''.

● ALBUMS: *Bob Scobey's 'Frisco Band With Clancy Hayes* (1955)★★, *Scobey And Clancy* (1955)★★★, *Clancy Hayes's Dixieland Band* (1960)★★★, *Swingin' Minstrel* (1963)★★★★, *Live At Earthquake McGoon's* (1966)★★, *Clancy Hayes And The All Stars Live At Pasadena* (1968-69)★★★.

● COMPILATIONS: *Bunk Johnson And Lu Watters* (1941-44 recordings)★★★.

HAYES, EDGAR

b. 23 May 1904, Lexington, Kentucky, USA, d. 28 June 1979, San Bernadino, California, USA. Hayes's name will always be associated with his tinkling, cocktail-lounge interpretation of Hoagy Carmichael's 'Stardust', which came backed with a version of 'In The Mood', the coupling providing the piano-playing Hayes with a 1938 hit. After studying at Fisk and Wilberforce Universities, he made his debut with Fess Williams, then formed his own Blue Grass Buddies in Ohio in 1924. Throughout the 20s he worked with various bands eventually becoming pianist-arranger wth Mills Blue Rhythm Band in 1931 and retaining his place with the unit after Lucky

Millinder assumed leadership three years later. Leaving Millinder in mid-1936, he formed his own band, which debuted in early 1937, recording tracks for Varsity and Decca Records. A healthy-sounding 14-piece band, it initially featured Shelton Hemphill (trumpet), Joe Garland (tenor saxophone), Elmer James (bass) and Crawford Wetherington (alto saxophone), all of whom had partnered Hayes in the Millinder line-up. In the rhythm section was a 22-year-old drummer named Kenny Clarke, later to become one of the kingpins of bebop. Hayes toured Scandinavia in 1938, recording some tracks for the Swedish Odeon label, but neither these nor the rest of the band's Decca titles produced another 'Stardust' and the band folded in 1941. By 1942 Hayes could be found in California where he played a residency at the Somerset House, Riverside, up to 1946, after which he led a combo called the Stardusters, playing at various west coast venues through to the early 50s. During the 60s and 70s Hayes opted for a solo career, performing mainly lounge duties and frequently reprising 'Stardust' for anyone who happened to remember his bandleading days.

● COMPILATIONS: *Edgar Hayes And His Orchestra 1937-1938* (1986)★★★★.

HAYES, LOUIS

b. 31 May 1937, Detroit, Michigan, USA. Hayes began playing drums at an early age and was leading his own band in Detroit when he was in his mid-teenage years. Still in his teens, he moved to New York where he joined the Horace Silver Quintet. He was with Silver for over two years, finding time to record with John Coltrane and other leading jazz artists. Towards the end of the 50s he joined Cannonball Adderley, with whom he remained until the middle of the next decade when he became a member of Oscar Peterson's trio. After leaving Peterson, Hayes led his own bands, usually sextets, during the late 60s and early 70s, working with artists such as Freddie Hubbard, Kenny Barron, Junior Cook and Woody Shaw. With these bands Hayes toured the USA and Europe and made records. Later, he brought Joe Farrell into his band, by this time a quartet, for more successful tours and records. In the mid-80s Hayes was occasionally a member of the McCoy Tyner trio. An exceptionally gifted bop drummer, Hayes has developed a playing style which is simultaneously subtle and hard driving. His sizzling accompaniment has enhanced some fine hard bop albums and his enthusiasm regularly brings out the best in his front line companions.

● ALBUMS: *Louis Hayes* (Vee Jay 1960)★★★, *Breath Of Life* (Muse 1974)★★★, *Ichi-Ban* (Timeless 1976)★★★, *The Real Thing* (Muse 1977)★★★★, *Variety Is The Spice Of Life* (Gryphon 1979)★★★, *Light And Lively* (Steeple Chase 1989)★★★, *Una Max* (Steeple Chase 1989)★★★, *The Crawl* (Candid 1991)★★★, *Louis At Large* (Sharp Nine 1997)★★★★, with Woody Shaw Quintet *Lausanne 1977* (TCB 1997)★★.

HAYES, TUBBY

b. Edward Brian Hayes, 30 January 1935, London, England, d. 8 June 1973. Born into a musical family, Hayes studied violin as a child but took up the tenor saxophone before reaching his teens. He matured rapidly and at the age of 15 became a professional musician. In the early 50s he played with several leading jazzmen, including Kenny Baker, Vic Lewis and Jack Parnell. In the mid-50s he formed his own bop-orientated group and later in the decade was co-leader with Ronnie Scott of the Jazz Couriers. In the early 60s he continued to lead small groups for clubs, concerts, record dates and tours of the UK and USA. By this time Hayes had become adept on other instruments, including the vibraphone, flute and most of the saxophone family. He occasionally formed a big band for concerts and television dates and was active as arranger and composer. Towards the end of the 60s Hayes' health was poor and he underwent a heart operation. He returned to playing, but early in the 70s a second heart operation was deemed necessary and he died on the operating table. A virtuoso performer on tenor saxophone, Hayes was a fluent improviser, and through his energy, enthusiasm and encouragement he created a new respect for British musicians, especially in the USA. Hayes was a world-class player almost from the outset of his career, and his death in 1973, while he was still very much in his prime, was a grievous loss.

● ALBUMS: *After Lights Out* (Jasmine 1956)★★★★, *Little Giant Of Jazz* (Imperial 1957)★★★★, *Tubby Hayes With The Jazz Couriers* (1958)★★★★, *Message From Britain* (1959)★★★★, *Tubby's Groove* (Jasmine 1959)★★★★, *Tubbs In NY* (1961)★★★★, *Palladium Jazz Date* (1961)★★★★, *Introducing Tubbs* (Epic 1961)★★★★, *Tubby The Tenor* (Epic 1961)★★★★, *Almost Forgotten* (1961)★★★★, *Tubby Hayes And The All Stars: Return Visit* (1962)★★★★, *Down In The Village* (Fontana 1962)★★★★, *Tubby's Back In Town* (Smash 1962)★★★★, *A Tribute: Tubbs* (Spotlite 1963)★★★★, *Tubb's Tours* (Mole 1963)★★★★, *100% Proof* (1966)★★★★, *Mexican Green* (1967)★★★★, *The Tubby Hayes Orchestra* (1969)★★★★, *Where Am I Going To Live* (Harlequin 1986)★★★★, *New York Sessions* (Columbia 1989)★★★★, *For Members Only* recorded 1967 (Miles Music 1990)★★★★, *Live 1969* (Harlequin 1991)★★★, *200% Proof* (Mastermix 1992)★★★★, *Jazz Tete A Tete* (Progressive 1994)★★★.

HAYMER, HERBIE

b. Herbert Haymer, 24 July 1915, Jersey City, New Jersey, USA, d. 11 April 1949. Haymer played alto saxophone as a boy but switched to tenor as he left his teens. In New York in the mid- to late 30s, Haymer worked with several bands of the swing era, including those led by Red Norvo and Jimmy Dorsey. In the early 40s he was with Woody Herman, then Kay Kayser and Benny Goodman. After military service he moved to the west coast, playing with several bands and also recording. Among the important recording sessions in which he participated was one with Charlie Shavers, Nat 'King' Cole and Buddy Rich, which was released with false starts, retakes and all, offering a fascinating glimpse of the reality of improvisation in a jam session setting. He also played in studio bands and was returning from a recording session with Frank Sinatra when he died following an automobile accident. A vigorous player with a tough, sinewy sound, Haymer's early death was a great loss to the jazz world at a time when it was undergoing changes he seems likely to have navigated successfully.

● ALBUMS: *Anatomy Of A Jam Session* (Black Lion 1945)★★★.

HAYNES, ROY

13 March 1926, Roxbury, Massachusetts, USA. Haynes began his career in his home town where he played drums with Sabby Lewis's big band. In the early 40s he joined Pete Brown's jump band and later in the decade was on the road with the Luis Russell big band and also played in a small group led by Lester Young. In New York in the late 40s and early 50s, Haynes adapted readily to the demands of bebop and became a valued club gig and record session drummer for Charlie Parker, Bud Powell, Stan Getz, Wardell Gray, Miles Davis, Thelonious Monk, John Coltrane, Sarah Vaughan, Ella Fitzgerald, Billie Holiday and many other important artists. Haynes's career continued through the 60s and into the 70s with many fruitful collaborations with jazzmen such as George Shearing, Art Farmer, Kenny Burrell and Gary Burton, and in several interesting groups under his own leadership. In the early 80s Haynes recorded with Pat Metheny, Freddie Hubbard, joined Chick Corea for worldwide tours and continued to lead his own bands in New York. Haynes is a major figure in the development of bop drumming.

● ALBUMS: *Bushman's Holiday* 10-inch album (EmArcy 1954)★★★★, with Paul Chambers, Phineas Newborn *We Three* (New Jazz 1958)★★★★, *Just Us* (New Jazz 1960)★★★, *Out Of The Afternoon* (Impulse! 1962)★★★★, *Cymbalism* (New Jazz 1962)★★★, *Cracklin'* (New Jazz 1962)★★★, *People* (Pacific Jazz 1964)★★, *Hip Ensemble* (Mainstream 1971)★★★★, *Equipoise* (Mainstream 1972)★★★, *Senyah* (Mainstream 1973)★★★, *Togyu* (1973)★★★, *Booty* (1974)★★, *Jazz A Confronto 29* (1975)★★, *Thank You, Thank You* (Galaxy 1977)★★★, *Vistalite* (Galaxy 1977)★★★, *Live At The Riverbop* (EPM Musique 1979)★★★, with Chick Corea *Trio Music* (ECM 1981)★★★★, *True Or False* (Free Lance 1986)★★★, *When It's Haynes It Roars!* (Dreyfus 1993)★★★, with Kenny Clarke *Transatlantic Meetings* (Vogue 1993)★★★★, with Kenny Barron, Charlie Haden *Wanton Spirit* (1994)★★★, *Homecoming* (Evidence 1994)★★★, *Te-Vou!* (Drefus 1995)★★★★, with Hank Jones, George Mraz *Flowers For Lady Day* (Evidence 1996)★★★, *Praise* (Dreyfus 1998)★★★.

● FILMS: *The Preacher's Wife* (1996).

HAZEL, MONK

b. Arthur Hazel, 15 August 1903, Harvey, Louisiana, USA, d. 5 March 1968. During the 20s and into the early 30s Hazel played drums with many bands in New Orleans before going on the road with popular vocalist Gene Austin. After military service in World War II, he played with bands led by Santo Pecora, Sharkey Bonano and others. Although working in relatively confined and sometimes obscure areas of music and the country, Hazel was a good musician, occasionally playing cornet and mellophone as well as drums.

HEAD HUNTERS - HERBIE HANCOCK

Head Hunters has spawned a thousand copies and copyists, but is only strengthened through comparison. One of the most enduring works of the 70s' jazz/funk legacy, and surely one of Herbie Hancock's most enjoyable and infectious recordings, the album was released in the deeply groovy days of 1973, and soon became the best-selling record in jazz history. Loping along on a glorious bed of springy wah-wah and synth bass, the group used all the new technology of the time, and Hancock himself seemed to revel (as he still does) in the latest keyboard sounds available to him. Jazz/funk has never again sounded so exciting and dangerous.

● Tracks: *Chameleon; Watermelon Man; Sly; Vein Melter.*

● First released 1974

● UK peak chart position: did not chart

● USA peak chart position: 13

HEARD, J.C.

b. James Charles Heard, 8 October 1917, Dayton, Ohio, USA, d. 28 September 1988. Heard grew up in Detroit where he began his professional career at an early age, playing drums in pit bands and on the road with vaudeville shows. Encouraged by Butterbeans And Susie, two of the leading entertainers of the day, at the age of 10 Heard was drumming and dancing as 'The Child Wonder'. Influenced by drummers such as Baby Dodds, Walter Johnson, Jimmy Crawford and Chick Webb, Heard gradually turned to jazz, playing with the bands of Bill Johnson and Sammy Price. He then joined the noted territory band of Milt Larkins. In 1939 he was with Teddy Wilson's musically excellent but commercially ill-fated big band, and remained with Wilson in a small group in the early 40s. Briefly with Benny Carter and Louis Jordan, in 1942 Heard succeeded Cozy Cole in the Cab Calloway orchestra, and later deputized with Count Basie. By this time his style had moved more in line with that of Jo Jones, who became one of his closest friends. Heard also led his own small group and in the late 40s and early 50s worked as a member of Jazz At The Philharmonic with whom he travelled around the world, playing concerts in the UK and Japan. He settled for a while in Japan, where he led big and small bands made up of local musicians, and also played in Hong Kong and the Philippines. In the late 50s and early 60s he performed in many parts of the world with leaders such as Coleman Hawkins, Claude Hopkins and Red Norvo and was reunited with Price and Wilson. In the mid- to late 60s he led his own groups which, by the 70s, had developed into an excellent all-star band. He continued playing throughout the 80s, presenting a big band in a 1985 Tribute to Duke Ellington show in Detroit.

● ALBUMS: *JATP: Live At The Nichigeki Theatre, Tokyo* (1953)★★, *J.C. Heard With The Calypso Seven* (1956)★★★, *This*

Is Me, J.C. Heard (1958)★★, with Claude Hopkins *Let's Jam* (1961)★★★, *Alive And Well* (1983)★★.

● COMPILATIONS: *Jazz Off The Air Vol. 4: Cab Calloway And His Orchestra* (1943-46)★★★★.

HEARD, JOHN

b. 3 July 1938, Pittsburgh, Pennsylvania, USA. After starting out on saxophones, Heard taught himself to play bass while a teenager. He first attracted serious attention in the early and mid-60s, working with artists such as Tommy Turrentine and Al Jarreau. Towards the end of the decade he was with Sonny Rollins, then settled on the west coast where he became a long-serving member of several bands, including the Ahmad Jamal trio, Count Basie's big band and small recording groups, and Toshiko Akiyoshi's group. He was also first call bass player for the big bands occasionally assembled by Louie Bellson, with whom he visited the UK in the late 70s and early 80s. He then spent time with Oscar Peterson, Cal Tjader, George Duke, Joe Williams, Nancy Wilson, Tal Farlow and many other leading singers and jazz musicians. The quality of the company he keeps is eloquent testimony to Heard's considerable skills. Whether playing in a big band, where his powerful pulse urges along the ensemble, or subtly providing accompaniment to pianists, guitarists or singers, Heard has established an enviable reputation amongst his peers in the jazz world, although he remains relatively little known to audiences.

● ALBUMS: with Cal Tjader *Live At The Funky Quarters* (1972)★★★★, with George Duke *Faces In Reflections* (1974)★★, with Count Basie *Basie & Zoot* (1975)★★★, with Oscar Peterson *The Silent Partner* (1979)★★, with Peterson *The London Concert* (1982)★★★.

HEATH BROTHERS

James Edward (Jimmy) (b. 25 October 1926, Philadelphia, Pennsylvania, USA; composer, arranger, tenor and soprano saxophones, flute), Percy (b. 30 April 1923, Wilmington, North Carolina, USA; bass) and Albert 'Tootie' (b. 31 May 1935, Philadelphia, Pennsylvania, USA; drums). The Heath brothers have all had distinguished and prolific careers individually. They worked together as an 'official' Heath Brothers band in the late 50s and worked on the sessions for Jimmy Heath's *Swamp Seed*. The concept was revived after Jimmy and Percy appeared on Albert Heath's debut album in 1973. When the Modern Jazz Quartet, Percy's regular band for 22 years, was disbanded in 1974 the idea seemed more practicable, and in 1975 the brothers reformed with pianist Stanley Cowell. Albert left in 1978 because of a disagreement over musical direction with Jimmy and Percy, and guitarist Tony Purrone was made an official member. Extra percussion was provided by Akira Tana, but Albert returned for the brothers' final recording before their 1983 split. Apart from the odd reunion there was a long silence before the three brothers teamed up once again for 1997's *As We Were Saying...* and the following year's *Jazz Family*.

● ALBUMS: *Marchin' On* (Strata-East 1975)★★★★, *Passing Thru* (Columbia 1978)★★★, *In Motion* (Columbia 1979)★★★, *Live At The Public Theater* (Columbia 1979)★★, *Expressions Of Life* (Columbia 1980)★★, *Brotherly Love* (Island 1981)★★★★, *Brothers And Others* (Island 1983)★★★, *As We Were Saying ...* (Concord Jazz 1997)★★★, *Jazz Family* (Concord Jazz 1998)★★★.

HEATH, AL 'TOOTIE'

b. 31 May 1935, Philadelphia, Pennsylvania, USA. One of a highly talented jazz family, in the late 50s drummer Heath moved to New York where his older brothers, Percy and Jimmy, had already established their reputations. He played in a band led by J.J. Johnson and recorded with many important musicians, including John Coltrane. In the mid-60s he became resident in Scandinavia, working with Dexter Gordon and Kenny Drew (who was also resident there). Back in the USA in 1968 he played with Billy Taylor and in 1975 formed the Heath Brothers band with Percy and Jimmy. A few years later he dropped out of music but returned in the early 80s, playing with the Jazztet, Tal Farlow and others and also leading his own groups. He teamed up with his brothers on several occasions during the 80s, and appeared on 1997's reunion session *As We Were Saying* .... A subtle player with an exceptional ability as a sensitive accompanist, Heath remains one of the more interesting if lesser-known bebop drummers.

● ALBUMS: *Kawaida* (Trip 1970)★★★, *Kwanza (The First)/Oops!* (Muse 1973)★★★.

HEATH, JIMMY

b. 25 October 1926, Philadelphia, Pennsylvania, USA. The most versatile of the Heath brothers, saxophonist Jimmy joined the Howard McGhee band in 1947 with his older brother Percy. Towards the end of the 40s he worked with Dizzy Gillespie, playing alto saxophone in small and big bands. Stylistically, Heath's playing was broader and more personalized when he began playing tenor, a change which also helped him to throw off a tendency to follow too closely in the footsteps of his musical idol Charlie Parker. In the mid-50s Heath's career was interrupted by a prison sentence for drug offences. In the 60s he co-led bands with Art Farmer and in 1975 became leader of the Heath Brothers band. In the following decades Heath mostly led his own band, although the family group remained in occasional existence and reunited on record for the 1997 Concord session, *As We Were Saying* .... Despite being a good alto player and a distinctive tenorist, Heath's chief contribution has been his writing. Whether as composer, arranger or both, and whether writing for small or large ensembles, he has consistently shown himself to be interesting and resourceful. Some of his compositions have been on a grand scale, including the 'Afro-American Suite Of Evolution' while other shorter but no less impressive works have been recorded by Miles Davis, among them 'CTA' and 'Gingerbread Boy'.

● ALBUMS: *The Thumper* (Riverside 1960)★★★★, *Really Big* (Riverside 1960)★★★★, *The Quota* (Riverside 1961)★★★, *Triple Threat* (Riverside 1962)★★★★, *Swamp Seed* (Riverside

1963)★★★, *On The Trail* (Riverside 1965)★★★★, *The Gap Sealer* reissued as *Jimmy* (Cobblestone/Muse 1972)★★★, *Love And Understanding* (Xanadu 1973)★★★, *Picture Of Heath* (Xanadu 1975)★★★, *New Picture* (Landmark 1985)★★★, *Peer Pleasure* (Landmark 1987)★★★★, *Little Man, Big Band* (Verve 1993)★★★, *Time And The Place* 1974 recording (Landmark 1994)★★★, *You've Changed* (Steeple Chase 1995)★★★, *You Or Me* (Steeple Chase 1996)★★★.

HEATH, PERCY

b. 30 April 1923, Wilmington, North Carolina, USA. Growing up in Philadelphia, bassist Heath first played locally before moving to New York with his brother Jimmy to join Howard McGhee in 1947. During the next few years he played with many leading exponents of bebop, including Miles Davis, J.J. Johnson, Dizzy Gillespie, Charlie 'Bird' Parker and Thelonious Monk. In 1951 he became a member of a quartet led by Milt Jackson, which subsequently changed its name to the Modern Jazz Quartet. He played in this group for over 20 years, then in 1975 formed the Heath Brothers band with Jimmy and Al. Heath retained his connection with the Modern Jazz Quartet into the 80s, when they reformed, and also worked throughout this period with the Heath Brothers band (who reunited for a 1997 recording session on Concord Jazz). A leading bebop player, Heath has occasionally experimented with the use of the piccolo bass.

HEATH, TED

b. 30 March 1900, Wandsworth, London, England, d. 18 November 1969, Surrey, England. After playing tenor horn at the age of six, Heath later switched to trombone and throughout the 20s and 30s played with top orchestras such as Jack Hylton, Al Sarita, Sydney Lipton, and in the early 40s with Geraldo. On 7 May 1945, (VJ Day), he formed his own band, some of the early finance being provided by royalties from the songs 'That Lovely Weekend' and 'I'm Gonna Love That Guy', written by Heath and his wife Moira. Kenny Baker, Jack Parnell, Ronnie Chamberlain and Don Lusher were just some of the top musicians who played for him, plus vocalists Paul Carpenter and Beryl Davis. In 1946 the band provided the musical background for the first major British movie musical, *London Town*. Taking a big chance, Heath hired the London Palladium for a *Sunday Night Swing Session*, which proved to be so successful, that it ran for several years. The addition of singers Lita Roza, Dennis Lotis and Dickie Valentine in the early 50s gave the band more teenage appeal, and they appeared in three more films, *Dance Hall* (1950), *It's A Wonderful World* (1956) and *Jazz Boat* (1960). Their theme, 'Listen To My Music', introduced many specialities including 'Opus One', 'The Champ', 'Dragnet', 'Skin Deep', 'Hot Toddy' and 'Swingin' Shepherd Blues'. The Heath band was the first unit to go to the USA when Musicians' Union restrictions were relaxed and Anglo-American exchanges began in 1955, and subsequently toured there many times. The band compared favourably with even America's top units, and is generally accepted as the best swing band that Britain ever produced. Heath died in 1969. Many of his original personnel still play together, usually under the direction of Jack Parnell or Don Lusher. An important three-part series of biographical programmes was broadcast on BBC Radio 2 in 1993.

● ALBUMS: *Ted Heath And His Orchestra* 10-inch album (London 50s)★★★, featuring Winifred Atwell *Black And White Magic* 10-inch album (London 50s)★★★, *Tempo For Dancers* (Decca 1951)★★★, *Listen To My Music* (Decca 1952)★★★, *Selection* (Decca 1952)★★★, *At The London Palladium* (Decca 1953)★★★★, *Strike Up The Band* (Decca 1953)★★★★, *Ted Heath's Fats Waller Album* (Decca 1954)★★★, *100th London Palladium Concert* (Decca 1954)★★★★, *Gershwin For Moderns* (Decca 1954)★★★, *Kern For Moderns* (Decca 1956)★★★, *At The London Palladium Volume 4* (Decca 1956)★★★, *Rodgers For Moderns* (Decca 1956)★★★, *A Yank In Europe* (London 1956)★★★, *Spotlight On Sidemen* (London 1957)★★★, *Showcase* (London 1957)★★★, *Tribute To The Fabulous Dorseys* (London 1957)★★★, featuring Winifred Atwell *Rhapsody In Blue* (London 1957)★★★, *At Carnegie Hall* (Decca 1957)★★★★, *First American Tour* (Decca 1957)★★★, *Hits I Missed* (Decca 1958)★★★, *Olde Englyshe* (Decca 1958)★★, *Swings In Hi-Fi Stereo* (Decca 1958)★★★★, *Things To Come* (London 1958)★★★, *Shall We Dance* (London 1959)★★★, *Pop Hits From The Classics* (London 1959)★★★, *Big Band Blues* (London 1959)★★★, *Swing Session* (Decca 1959)★★★★, *Plays The Great Film Hits* (Decca 1959)★★★, *My Very Good Friends The Band Leaders* (Decca 1960)★★★, *The Big Band Dixie Sound* (London 1960)★★★, *The Hits Of The Twenties* (London 1960)★★★, *Ted Heath In Concert* (London 1960)★★★, *Songs For The Young At Heart* (London 1960)★★★, *The Hits Of The 30s* (London 1960)★★★, *Latin Swingers* (London 1961)★★, *Big Band Beat* (Richmond 60s)★★★, featuring Winifred Atwell *Ted Heath Plays Gershwin* (Richmond 60s)★★★, *Ted Heath Plays The Music Of Fats Waller* (Richmond 60s)★★★★, *Big Band Gershwin* (Richmond 60s)★★★, *Big Band Kern* (Richmond 60s)★★★, *Big Band Rodgers* (Richmond 60s)★★★, *Big Band Percussion* (Phase 4 1962)★★★, *Big Band Bash* (Phase 4 1963)★★★, *Satin Saxes And Bouncing Brass* (Phase 4 1963)★★★, *Big Band Spirituals* (Phase 4 1964)★★★, *Coast To Coast* (Phase 4 1964)★★★, *Palladium Revisited* (Phase 4 1964)★★★, with Edmundo Ros *Heath Versus Ros* (Phase 4 1964)★★★, *The Sound Of Music* (Phase 4 1965)★★, with Ros *Heath Versus Ros, Round Two* (Phase 1967)★★, *Ted Heath Recalls The Fabulous Dorseys* (Eclipse 1969)★★★★, *Fever* (Phase 4 1966)★★★, *Beatles, Bach And Bacharach* (Phase 4 1971)★★, *Salute To Glenn Miller* (Phase 4 1973)★★★★, *Big Band Themes Remembered, Volume One* (Phase 4 1974)★★★★, *Big Band Themes Remembered, Volume Two* (Phase 4 1974)★★★, *Salutes The Duke* (Phase 4 1975)★★★★, *Ted Heath At The London Palladium 1953* (Eclipse 1976)★★★★, *Salutes Benny Goodman* (Decca 1976)★★★, *Smooth 'N' Swinging* 1959-62 recordings (Decca 1981)★★★.

● COMPILATIONS: *Big Band World Of Ted Heath* (Decca 1970)★★★★, *The World Of Big Band Blues* (Decca 1972)★★★, *Swing Meets Latin* (Decca 1974)★★★, with Dennis Lotis, Lita Roza *The Ted Heath Years* (Decca 1977)★★★★, *Focus On Ted Heath* (Phase 4 1978)★★★★, *All Time Top Twelve* (Decca 1979)★★★, *Ted Heath At The BBC* (BBC 1983)★★★★, *Big Band Favourites* (Decca 1984)★★★★, *Big Band Bash, Volumes 1-4*

(Echo Jazz 1988)★★★★, *The Golden Age Of Ted Heath Volumes 1-3* (Horatio Nelson 1990)★★★★, *The Very Best Of Ted Heath Volume 1* (Horatio Nelson 1995)★★★★.

HEAVY WEATHER - WEATHER REPORT

Probably the best fusion album ever made, and the coming together of five precociously talented musicians. Joe Zawinul and Wayne Shorter assembled the unit with little knowledge that the complex music would become so accessible. Two compostions stand out; the graceful 'A Remark You Made', an evocative love song without words, and the hit single 'Birdland' (so successful it was even used by Akai for a major advertising campaign). On these two Zawinul compostions their genius bass player Jaco Pastorius gives a taste of what he was capable of. He bent the notes to make them talk, and that high octave solo on 'Birdland' is still a treasured moment.

● Tracks: *Birdland; A Remark You Made; Teen Town; Harlequin; Rumba Mama; Palladium; The Juggler; Havona.*

● First released 1977

● UK peak chart position: 43

● USA peak chart position: 30

HEBERER, THOMAS

b. 1965, Cologne, Germany. Heberer has been described by Alexander von Schlippenbach, in whose Berlin Contemporary Jazz Orchestra he plays, as 'our new young trumpet genius'. These are large claims to live up to. Heberer, a remarkably assured and daring player, knows the jazz tradition and how to apply its history to modern invention. He performs regularly in a duo with bassist Dieter Manderscheid. Their radical reinterpretations of 'Jelly Roll' Morton on *Chicago Breakdown* won critics awards in Germany.

● ALBUMS: *The Heroic Millipede* (1988)★★★, with Dieter Manderscheid *Chicago Breakdown* (1990)★★.

HECKSTALL-SMITH, DICK

b. 26 September 1934, Ludlow, Shropshire, England. After first playing soprano saxophone, Heckstall-Smith turned to the tenor saxophone. While studying at Cambridge in the early 50s he began leading the university's jazz band. Towards the end of the decade he worked in London, playing with various bands including that led by Sandy Brown. In addition to playing in jazz bands, in the late 50s and throughout the 60s he also played in bands led by blues and rock artists including the seminal R&B Organisation led by Graham Bond. He was with John Mayall on his pioneering *Bare Wires* and was a founder member of the influential Jon Hiseman's Colosseum. In the early 70s Heckstall-Smith led his own band, DHS1/Manchild, and later in the decade formed Big Chief. In the early 80s he played with Bo Diddley and thereafter freelanced extensively with jazz, jazz-rock, blues and blues-rock bands, in particular developing an interesting working relationship with John Etheridge. Unlike some musicians who have tried, Heckstall-Smith has successfully managed the interchanges necessitated by his eclectic musical tastes without any discernible loss of authenticity and commitment. In performance, his playing readily accommodates the needs of the prevailing musical format, ranging as it does from post-bop jazz to the robustness of the contemporary blues scene. In recent years Heckstall-Smith has constantly toured in Europe where his blistering and sometimes exhilarating playing is appreciated more than at home. A critical re-appraisal is long-overdue for one of Britain's leading saxophonists.

● ALBUMS: *A Story Ended* (Bronze 1972)★★★, *Woza Nasu* (Interoceter 1990)★★★★, *Live 1990* (L&R 1990)★★★, *Dick Heckstall-Smith Quartet* (L&R 1991)★★★, *Obsession Free* (R&M 1992)★★★, *Celtic Steppes* (33 Records 1996)★★★.

● FURTHER READING: *The Smallest Place In The World*, Dick Heckstall-Smith.

HEFTI, NEAL

b. 29 October 1922, Hastings, Nebraska, USA. One of the most influential big band arrangers of the 40s and 50s, Hefti's early charts were played by the Nat Towles band in the late 30s. His material was also used by Earl Hines; however, his first real taste of the big time came when he joined Charlie Barnet in 1942 and then moved into the Woody Herman band in 1944. Both engagements were as a member of the trumpet section, but his writing became steadily more important than his playing. For Herman he arranged many of the band's most popular recordings, including 'The Good Earth' and 'Wild Root', and was co-arranger with Ralph Burns of 'Caldonia'. In 1946 Hefti's charts were among those used by the ill-fated Billy Butterfield big band and by Charlie Ventura's equally short-lived band. In the late 40s he wrote for what was one of the best of Harry James's bands; in the mid-50s, along with Ernie Wilkins and Nat Pierce, he helped to give the Count Basie band the new distinctive, tighter style that led to a wholesale re-evaluation of big band music, especially in the UK. *Atomic Basie* was composed by Hefti and it features the glorious 'Lil' Darlin'' and 'Splanky'. The album remains one of Basie's finest works and Hefti's peak. Throughout the 50s and 60s Hefti was heavily involved in composing for films and television (including the theme for the US *Batman* television series), and while much of his work in these quarters was geared to the demands of the medium, there were many moments when he was able to infuse his work with echoes of his jazz heritage. Throughout those years and into the 70s Hefti periodically formed big bands either for club, concert or record dates. The tradition of precise, disciplined arranging, of which Hefti was one of the more important exponents, continues to make itself heard in the work of Sam Nestico, which has proved immensely popular with college and university bands on both sides of the Atlantic.

● ALBUMS: *Swingin' On A Coral Reef* 10-inch album (Coral 1953)★★★, *Music Of Rudolph Frimil* 10-inch album (X 1954)★★★, *Pardon My Doo-wah* (1954)★★, *Hot 'N' Hearty* (1955)★★★, *Singing Instrumentals* (Epic 1956)★★★, *Light And*

Right!! (Columbia 1960)★★, *Themes From TV's Top 12* (Reprise 1962)★★, *Boeing Boeing* film soundtrack (RCA Victor 1966)★★, *Batman Theme* (RCA Victor 1966)★★, *Hefti In Gotham City* (RCA Victor 1966)★★, *Duel At Diablo* film soundtrack (United Artists 1966)★★★, *Barefoot In The Park* film soundtrack (London 1967)★★★, *The Odd Couple* film soundtrack (Dot 1968)★★★, *Batman Theme And 19 Hefti Bat Songs* (Razor & Tie 1998)★★★.

HELIAS, MARK

b. 1 October 1950, New Brunswick, New Jersey, USA. Helias played bass professionally from the start of the 70s, studying music theory at Yale University. He also played with several musicians of diverse styles, including Anthony Braxton and Dewey Redman, and was a member of the Brahma trio with Barry Altschul and Ray Anderson. He also played in several co-operative groups, gaining much international recognition in the 80s with Nu, which included Don Cherry, Ed Blackwell and Nana Vasconcelos. He has also worked with other noted contemporary players such as Muhal Richard Abrams. In 1981 he was co-founder of the proto-funk band, Adesan, and also worked with Slickaphonics. The 80s also saw him back in occasional harness with Braxton, Redman and Altschul. In the 90s he played with Anderson and Gerry Hemingway in their trio, BassDrumBone. In his playing, especially as a leader, Helias thoughtfully explores concepts that frequently stretch the expectations of the jazz audience while allowing them to remain rooted to traditional stylistic moods. As well as composing for the jazz repertoire, Helias has written music for the theatre, films, piano, string quartets and classical orchestra.

● ALBUMS: with Ray Anderson, Gerry Hemingway *Right Down Your Alley* (Soul Note 1984)★★★, with Anderson, Hemingway *You Be* (Minor 1986)★★★, *The Current Set* (Enja 1987)★★★, *Desert Blue* (Enja 1990)★★★, *Attack The Future* (Enja 1992)★★★, *Split Image* (Enja 1994)★★★, *Loopin' The Cool* (Enja 1994)★★★★, with BassDrumBone *Hence The Reason* (Enja 1998)★★★, *Fictionary* (GMR 1998)★★★.

HELIOCENTRIC WORLDS OF SUN RA VOL. 1 - SUN RA

Cult bandleader, black activist and self-proclaimed space traveller Sun Ra left such a rich recorded legacy on planet Earth, each album with its fair share of magic, that to choose a top handful is a gruelling task. However, the records he made for the forward-thinking, musician-managed ESP Records during the 60s are surely outstanding for the concentrated and consistently powerful music they contain. Recorded before the days of the space chants and chaotic swing standards, *Heliocentric Worlds* contains long and cacophonous group improvisations, breathtaking in execution and ecstatic in conception. They also contain some of the most exciting keyboard work Sun Ra ever put to vinyl.

● Tracks: *The Sun Myth; House Of Beauty; Cosmic Chaos.*
● First released 1965
● UK peak chart position: did not chart
● USA peak chart position: did not chart

HELLBORG, JONAS

b. *c.*1958, Sweden. Classically trained as a bass player, Hellborg also listened to contemporary rock and pop and as a teenager was turned towards jazz through hearing albums by John McLaughlin's Mahavishnu Orchestra. He soon began moving more deeply into jazz during the 70s. In particular he was fascinated by the free jazz phenomenon while at the same time he explored many ethnic musical forms, especially those of the Indian sub-continent. Eventually, he joined McLaughlin's trio but left in 1989 to form his own groups. In 1982 he had formed his own record label, Day Eight Music, to allow performers 'total liberty in music creation'. Among kindred spirits with whom he has played and recorded, sometimes producing them on DEM Records, are Kenwood Dennard, Aydin Esen, Ginger Baker, Shawn Lane, Buckethead and Michael Shrieve. In addition to leading small groups, Hellborg has recorded solo bass albums, including *The Silent Life* and *Elegant Punk*.

● ALBUMS: *Adfa* (DEM late 80s)★★★, *Elegant Punk* (DEM late 80s)★★★, *Ars Moriende* (DEM late 80s)★★★, *Axis* (DEM early 90s)★★★, *Bass* (DEM early 90s)★★★, *e* (DEM early 90s)★★★, *The Silent Life* (DEM early 90s)★★★, *Jonas Hellborg Group* (DEM 1993)★★★, *Abstract Logic* (DEM 1995)★★★, *Temporal Analogues Of Paradise* (DEM 1996)★★★, *Octave Of The Holy Innocents* (DEM 1997)★★★.

HEMINGWAY, GERRY

b. 23 March 1955, New Haven, Connecticut, USA. Hemingway comes from a musical family - his grandmother was a concert pianist, his father studied composition with Paul Hindemith - and he was attracted to the drums 'from the first'. A rock fan as a teenager, he was later seduced by the jazz he heard in New York's nightclubs and, back in New Haven, began to play with Anthony Davis and George Lewis, both studying at nearby Yale, and Leo Smith, who had recently settled in the area. Hemingway attended the Berklee College Of Music but hated it, dropping out after one semester. Returning to New Haven, he formed a group, Advent, which later turned into the Anthony Davis Quartet (with Davis, Hemingway, Mark Helias and Jay Hoggard). He studied privately with Alan Dawson, attended classes in Indian and West African drumming at Yale and Wesleyan universities, played a series of solo percussion concerts and also began a long working relationship with Ray Anderson. In the late 70s Hemingway set up his own label, Auricle, released his debut *Kwambe* and then *Oahspe*, the latter also the name of the trio he formed with Anderson and Helias. In 1980 he toured Europe with Anderson's quartet, recording *Harrisburg Half Life*, and in 1981 - by now living in New York - released *Solo Works*, inspired in part by his collaborations with composer/electronic music expert/saxophonist Earl Howard. In 1983 he joined the Anthony Braxton Quartet, of which he remains a member, and has toured and recorded with the group many times, thereby establishing himself on the international stage. Oahspe, renamed on occasion the Ray Anderson Trio and BassDrumBone, continued to perform sporadically and Hemingway has also played with Davis's group Episteme (*Undine*), with Marilyn Crispell (*Circles*, *The Kitchen Concert*) and in Reggie Workman's ensemble. By the late 80s he had become well-known in Europe, following a 1985 UK tour with Derek Bailey, frequent concerts in Holland, often with cellist Ernst Reijseger (currently a member of Hemingway's own quintet) and, most recently, his work as a member of German pianist Georg Gräwe's trio (*Sonic Fiction*). He has also released three albums of his own music on European labels: one is the solo *Tubworks*, the others quintet sessions (*Outerbridge Crossing*, *Special Detail*) which reveal his love of darker sonorities. Back in New York, he works with the recently-formed quartet Tambastics (with Robert Dick, Mark Dresser and Denman Maroney), whose debut recording was released in 1992. Hemingway is expert at coaxing an incredible range of timbrel colours from his kit, even if it means using unorthodox means such as flicking the cymbals with a towel or rolling coins across his snare drum.

● ALBUMS: *Kwambe* (1979)★★, *Oahspe* (1979)★★, *Solo Works* (1981)★★★, with Ray Anderson, Mark Helias *Right Down Your Alley* (Soul Note 1984)★★★, with Anderson, Helias *You Be* (Minor 1986)★★★, *Outerbridge Crossing* 1985 recording (Sound Aspects 1987)★★, with BassDrumBone *Woofesloo* (1987)★★★, *Tubworks* (1988)★★★, *Special Detail* (hatART 1991)★★★, *Tambastics* (1992)★★★, *Down To The Wire* (hatART 1993)★★★, with Georg Graewe, Ernst Reijseger *The View From Points West* (Music & Arts 1993)★★, *Demon Chaser* (hatART 1994)★★★, *The Marmalade King* (hatART 1995)★★★, *Slamadam* (Random Acoustics 1995)★★★★, *Perfect World* (Random Acoustics 1996)★★★, with Gerry Hemingway, Fred Hersch *Thirteen Ways* (GM 1997)★★★, *Johnny's Corner Song* (Auricle 1998)★★★.

HEMPHILL, JULIUS

b. 24 January 1938, Fort Worth, Texas, USA, d. 2 April 1995. Growing up in the early 40s meant that Hemphill was surrounded by many kinds of music - swing, rural blues, R&B, gospel. He was also aware of modern jazz and was drawn towards 'cool' players like Lee Konitz. He studied harmony, clarinet and saxophone with John Carter in high school, played with a band in the US army (1964) and accompanied Ike Turner. He also attended classes at the Northern Texas State University. In 1968 he moved to St. Louis where he became a founder of BAG, the Black Artists Group, and concentrated on the alto saxophone. In 1971 he formed a group with pianist John Hicks and toured the college circuit. *Kawaida*, a multimedia event comprising music, dance and Hemphill's own lyrics, was presented at St Louis's Washington University in 1972. The same year he formed his own Mbari Records label and recorded *Dogon A.D.* (later re-issued on Arista Freedom), played in the film *The Orientation Of Sweet Willie Rollbar* and made a guest appearance on Kool And The Gang's *Hustler's Convention*. He played with Anthony Braxton in Chicago (later guesting on his debut album for Arista) and made appearances in Stockholm and Paris in 1973. The next year he played on Lester Bowie's *Fast Last*. In the mid-70s Hemphill recorded two solo double-album sets of multi-tracked alto and soprano saxophones and flute, *Blue Boyé* and the 'audiodrama' *Roi Boyé & The Gotham Minstrels*. In 1977 he became a founder member (and principal composer) of the World Saxophone Quartet, a title that was no idle boast, and they became probably his most visible showcase. A string of highly acclaimed albums and festival appearances continued until his departure from the group in 1990. His intense, earthy, nasal sound and flaring ideas mark him as one of the foremost players of his generation. He frequently appears in duets with altoist Oliver Lake and in 1980 led a big band at the Newport Festival. His small-group album *Flat-Out Jump Suite*, also from 1980, showed how he could maintain his personality on the tenor saxophone. In the next two years he recorded with old friends Baikidaa Carroll and Kalaparush Maurice McIntyre, while an appearance on Jean-Paul Bourelly's *Jungle Cowboy* (1986) showed how well his deep understanding of blues enabled him to relate to the new post-harmolodic concepts of the M-Base generation. However, his own attempts to create a populist musical fusion with his JAH Band proved less successful. In 1989 he premiered the latest version of his 'saxophone opera', *Long Tongue*, an epic combination of big band arrangements, free playing and colloquial black speech rhythms, on which he'd been working since the early 80s. Though serious injuries from a car crash in 1982 restricted his activities a little, Hemphill remained at the forefront of creative music, his long-standing interest in multi-media events fueld one of the most inventive and original composing/arranging brains in contemporary jazz. He played at the 1994 New York Jazz Festival but early the following year succumbed to complications from his diabetic condition.

● ALBUMS: *Dogon A.D.* (Mbari 1972)★★★, *Blue Boyé* (70s)★★, *Roi Boyé & The Gotham Minstrels* (1977)★★, *Raw Materials And Residuals* (Sackville 1978)★★★, with Oliver Lake *Buster Bee* (Sackville 1978)★★★, *Coon Bid'ness* (Freedom 1979)★★★, with Abdul Wadud *Live In New York* (Red Pepper 1979)★★★, *Flat-Out Jump Suite* (Black Saint 1980)★★★★, *Big Band* (Elektra 1988)★★★, *Georgie Blue* (Minor 1990)★★★, *Fat Man And The Hard Blues* (Black Saint 1992)★★★★, *Live From The New Music Cafe* (Music And Arts 1992)★★★, with Wadud *Oakland Duets* (Music & Arts Program Of America 1993)★★★, *Five Chord Stud* (Black Saint 1994)★★★★, *At Dr. King's Table* (New World 1998)★★★.

HENDERSON, BILL

b. William Randall Henderson, 19 March 1930, Chicago, Illinois, USA. He began singing as a toddler but delayed full entry into show business until he was in his early twenties. In the early 50s he sang in and around Chicago, often with Ramsey Lewis. At the end of the decade he visited New York, playing and recording with a number of leading bop musicians including Horace Silver, before returning to Chicago and Lewis. In the early 60s he had stints with Oscar Peterson and Count Basie, then relocated to Los Angeles where he began a new career as an actor. He did not abandon singing and continued to perform whenever opportunities arose, including work on television and recording. Two of his albums, *Street Of Dreams* and *Tribute To Johnny Mercer* were nominated for Grammy awards. A vibrant, blues-influenced singer with great rhythmic drive, Henderson's preference for an acting career has kept him from establishing the wide international reputation his talent deserves.

● ALBUMS: *Bill Henderson Sings* (1958)★★, *Bill Henderson With The Oscar Peterson Trio* (1963)★★, *Live At The Times* (Discovery 1975)★★★, *Street Of Dreams* (Discovery 1979)★★★★, *Tribute To Johnny Mercer* (Discovery 1984)★★★★, *'Joey' Revisited* (Monad 1996)★★★.

HENDERSON, BOBBY

b. Robert Bolden Henderson, 15 March 1910, New York, USA, d. 9 December 1969. Henderson began playing piano as a child and was soon playing gigs at various New York nightclubs. At 15 he played as the intermission act at a Fletcher Henderson engagement where he accompanied Edgar Sampson. Henderson knew Fats Waller and some sources suggest he took lessons from the master while others imply that he might have been a distant relative. By 1933 he was playing at clubs such as Pod's and Jerry's where he accompanied Billie Holiday with whom he also played at the Hot-Cha Club, the Lafayette Grill, the Jarvena Tavern And Grill and many other nightspots. Henderson's reputation as a performer was substantial and, indeed, Holiday's biographer, Stuart Nicholson, suggests that he might well have been the main attraction which resulted in the duo being booked to appear at the Apollo theatre in November 1934. Certainly, Henderson's name was spelled right on the playbills whereas Holiday's was not ('Halliday'). For all his ability, however, Henderson appears to have been somewhat feckless. He and Holiday had a love affair, perhaps her first serious relationship, but soon after the Apollo gig she ended matters, reputedly discovering that he was a bigamist. He also frequently failed to arrive up for record dates arranged by John Hammond Jnr., an admirer of his work. Later in the decade, Henderson played in various upstate towns but failed to make serious career gains. According to John Chilton, he played trumpet while in army bands during World War II. After the war he continued to play in New York state, including engagements in Albany, where he worked into the 50s. In 1957 he played at the Newport Jazz Festival, delivering a fine set of Waller's music in robust, technically skilled stride-piano style. He continued to play in and around Albany until his death.

● ALBUMS: *Handful Of Keys* (Vanguard 1956)★★★, *Call House Blues* (Vanguard 1957)★★, *A Home in The Clouds* (Chiaroscuro/Halcyon 1969)★★, *The Last Recordings* (Chiaroscuro 1969)★★.

HENDERSON, EDDIE

b. 26 October 1940, New York, USA. Henderson learned the trumpet at school and studied music at the San Francisco Conservatory of Music (1954-57). There followed three years in the Air Force. He was already playing enough music to be encouraged by Miles Davis to develop his jazz. He returned to academic study, graduating in zoology (1964) and then in medicine (1968) and has continued to work as a general practitioner and psychiatrist alongside his musical career. During summer holidays he played with John Handy and then with Handy and Philly Joe Jones when he graduated. He played with Herbie Hancock's sextet (1970-73) before spending six months with Art Blakey's Jazz Messengers. Since then he has led his own jazz-rock groups and even achieved chart success with a track from *Comin' Through* (1977).

● ALBUMS: with Herbie Hancock *Crossings* (1973)★★★, *Realisation* (1973)★★★, *Inside Out* (1973)★★★★, *Sunburst* (1975)★★★, *Heritage* (1976)★★★, *Comin' Through* (1977)★★, *Mahal* (1978)★★, *Running To Your Love* (Capitol 1979)★★★, *Phantoms* (SteepleChase 1989)★★, *Think Of Me* (Steeple Chase 1990)★★★★, *Tribute To Lee Morgan* (NYC 1995)★★, *Inspiration* (Milestone 1996)★★★, *Dark Shadows* (Milestone 1997)★★★.

HENDERSON, FLETCHER

b. 18 December 1897, Cuthbert, Georgia, USA, d. 28 December 1952. One of the most important figures in the development of big band music, in the early 30s Henderson set the standards by which early big band jazz was measured. He did this through a combination of selecting leading jazz players for his band and, together with Don Redman, creating a format for big band arrangements that was taken up by all but a handful of arrangers in the next 30 years. Yet, curiously enough, Henderson became a bandleader almost by accident, and an arranger through force of circumstance, rather than by deliberate intent. After gaining a degree in chemistry at Atlanta State University, he travelled to New York in 1920 to continue his studies. As a means of supporting himself he drifted into working as a song-plugger for the Pace-Handy Music Company. Then he became manager of Harry Pace's Black Swan Record Company, playing piano on many of the company's record dates. He next put together a band with which to accompany Ethel Waters on tour. Soon he was leading a band at the Little Club near Broadway, a popular nightspot known by its frequenters as the 'Club Alabam'. The band was really a loose-knit collection of like-minded musicians who elected Henderson as leader because, as Redman put it, 'He made a nice appearance and was well-educated and we figured all that would help in furthering our success'. This was the start of Henderson's ascendancy. Later that same year, 1924, he took his band into Roseland, one of New York's most famous ballrooms. The contract was for four years, but Henderson's connection with Roseland continued intermittently for 10 years.

In those days the route to success lay along the path

charted by Paul Whiteman, offering the public a selection of tangoes, waltzes and other popular dance tunes. Billed as 'the coloured Paul Whiteman', Henderson's was barely recognizable as a jazz group, despite the presence of outstanding jazzmen such as Coleman Hawkins. The band's musical policy underwent a marked change, however, with the arrival in its ranks of Louis Armstrong. He was there for about a year, leaving towards the end of 1925, but that brief stay forced Don Redman into completely revising the way he wrote his arrangements for the band. Redman's charts simulated the polyphonic New Orleans style of ensemble playing, pitting one section against another and giving full rein to the solo talents of the individual musicians.

By 1927 the band was the most talked-about in New York and, apart from Hawkins, included Tommy Ladnier, Jimmy Harrison, Charlie Green and Buster Bailey. Henderson was ambitious for success, even though he was not an especially astute businessman and had a pleasant unaggressive manner. However, his circumstances were about to alter in a way no one could have forecast. In mid-summer 1927 Redman left to become musical director of McKinney's Cotton Pickers. His departure meant that Henderson had to take up the bulk of the arranging duties for the band, a task he performed admirably. Unfortunately, in 1928 he was involved in a road accident and while his physical injuries were slight he underwent a change of personality. As his wife later said, 'He never had much business qualities anyhow, but after that accident, he had even less'. The most obvious effect of the change was that all ambition deserted him, leaving just an easygoing, casual individual. In the brashly commercial world of early 30s big band music this was not the way for a bandleader to achieve success.

In 1929 Henderson's lackadaisical attitude caused a mass walk-out by his star performers, but the following year he re-formed and tried again. Despite the departure of Redman, Henderson had continued to write skilful arrangements, developing ideas for saxophone voicings which, given the fact that he mostly used only a three-piece section, were remarkably intricate. The 1931 Henderson band was an astonishing array of top-flight jazzmen. The trumpets included Rex Stewart and Bobby Stark, Benny Morton was in the trombone section while the saxophones were Hawkins, Russell Procope and Edgar Sampson, himself a leading big-band arranger. The remaining years of the decade saw Henderson leading star-studded bands. In 1934 he had Red Allen and Joe Thomas in the trumpet section, while the 1936 edition included Roy Eldridge, Omer Simeon, Chu Berry, Israel Crosby and 'Big' Sid Catlett. In addition to his arrangements being played by his own band, they were also providing the basis for the successes enjoyed by others, notably Benny Goodman. However, despite the quality of the charts and the stature of the men in his band, Henderson's star was fast-waning. His indifference to commercial considerations rubbed off on his musicians and led in turn to disaffected and diminishing audiences. By 1939 Henderson had had enough of falling attendances, hassles with promoters, unrest in his own ranks and all the many pressures that came the way of big band leaders during the swing era. He folded his band and joined Goodman as staff arranger and pianist. During the 40s he continued to write for Goodman and others, and once in a while formed a band for special dates. Late in the decade he returned to his earlier role as accompanist to Ethel Waters. In 1950 he fell in the street, apparently as the result of a stroke. Partially incapacitated, he lived for a further year or so, dying on 28 December 1952.

Henderson was one of the most important figures in the development of big band music, although in abbreviated jazz history he is sometimes elevated to a degree that underplays the immense contributions made by others. Of those connected at one time or another with the Henderson band, Redman was an innovator, Sampson was a major contributor and a very talented composer and Horace Henderson, Fletcher's younger brother, was busy writing in the same vein. In other bands, the work of Charlie Dixon and Benny Carter also advanced along similar lines. Later, there would be refinements on the work of Redman and Henderson by gifted musicians such as Sy Oliver, Quincy Jones, Buster Harding, Neal Hefti and others; but until major shifts of style occurred later, the course Henderson had established remained the most significant in big band music. Even today, many big bands - including even some avant gardists such as the Sun Ra Arkestra - still trace the paths charted by a man who became a band leader by chance, whose career was blighted by an accident, and whose death came in much the same way at a time when he was all but forgotten.

● ALBUMS: *The Fletcher Henderson Septet Live In Concert* (1947)★★★★, *The Fletcher Henderson Sextet* (1950)★★★, with Rex Stewart *The Big Reunion* (Jazztone 1957)★★★★.

● COMPILATIONS: *Fletcher Henderson Volumes 1 & 2* (1923-25)★★★★, *A Study In Frustration* (1923-38)★★★, *The Indispensable Fletcher Henderson Volumes 1/2* 1927-36 recordings (Jazz Tribute 1986)★★, *Under The Harlem Moon* (Living Era 1990)★★★, *Hocus Pocus* (RCA 1990)★★★, *Fletcher Henderson And His Orchestra 1927* (Original Jazz Classics 1991)★★★★, with Louis Armstrong *Complete 1924 - 1925* (1993)★★★, *Fletcher Henderson & His Orchestra* (Tring 1993)★★★.

● FURTHER READING: *Hendersonia: The Music Of Fletcher Henderson And His Musicians*, W. Allen.

HENDERSON, JOE

b. 24 April 1937, Lima, Ohio, USA. Tenor saxophonist Henderson studied in Detroit and after army service, he moved to New York in 1962. He first made his mark with Blue Note Records recording with Kenny Dorham (*Una Mas*), Lee Morgan (*The Sidewinder*) and Andrew Hill (*Black Fire*, *Point Of Departure*), as well as leading several sessions of his own. He later worked with Horace Silver (*Song For My Father*) and towards the end of the 60s, co-led the Jazz Communicators with Freddie Hubbard before joining the Herbie Hancock sextet. In 1970 he briefly played with Blood, Sweat & Tears. In the early 70s he led his own groups, recording a rather erratic series of albums for Milestone, then moved to California, where he became involved in teaching. In the 80s he led an otherwise all-woman quartet (which included drummer Cindy Blackman) and recorded for the Italian Red label. He made the acclaimed two-volume *The State Of The Tenor*, a trio set (with Ron Carter and Al Foster) recorded live in 1985 at the Village Vanguard for Blue Note, whose co-founder Alfred Lion declared it 'one of the best ever made' for the label. He experienced a critical boom in the 90s, gaining excellent reviews for his albums of Billy Strayhorn (*Lush Life*) and Miles Davis (*So Near, So Far*) compositions. An acknowledged master of modern tenor craft, Henderson's chief influences were John Coltrane and Sonny Rollins, but he has fashioned a personal style that blends a finespun melodicism with logic, ingenuity and a dab of terse abstraction. For 1996's *Joe Henderson Big Band*, Henderson collaborated with a stellar range of players including Foster, Chick Corea, Christian McBride, Lewis Nash, Jon Faddis, Byron Stripling, Tony Kadlek, Ray Vega, Mike Mossman, Dick Oatts, Steve Wilson, Tim Ries, Charlie Pillow, Gary Smulyan, Conrad Herwig, Larry Farrell, Keith O'Quinn and Dave Taylor.

● ALBUMS: *Page One* (Blue Note 1963)★★★★, *Our Thing* (Blue Note 1963)★★★, *In 'N Out* (Blue Note 1964)★★★★, *Inner Urge* (Blue Note 1965)★★★★, *Mode For Joe* (Blue Note 1966)★★★, *The Kicker* (Milestone 1967)★★★★, *Tetragon* (Milestone 1969)★★★, *Power To The People* (Milestone 1969)★★★, *If You're Not Part Of The Problem ...* (Milestone 1970)★★★, *Live At The Lighthouse* (Milestone 1971)★★★, *In Pursuit Of Blackness* (Milestone 1971)★★★, *Joe Henderson In Japan* (Milestone 1972)★★★, *Black Is The Color* (Milestone 1972)★★★, *Multiple* (Milestone 1973)★★★★, with Alice Coltrane *The Elements* (Milestone 1973)★★★, *Canyon Lady* (Milestone 1974)★★★, *Black Narcissus* (Milestone 1975)★★★, *Barcelona* (Enja 1977)★★★, *Relaxin' At Camarillo* (Milestone 1979)★★★, with others *Mirror, Mirror* (MPS 1980)★★★, *The State Of The Tenor, Volumes 1 & 2* 1985 recording (Blue Note 1987)★★★★, with Charlie Haden, Al Foster *An Evening With Henderson, Haden & Foster* 1987 recording (Red 1989)★★★, with McCoy Tyner *New York Reunion* (Chesky 1991)★★★, *The Standard Joe* (Red 1992)★★★, *Lush Life* (Verve 1992)★★★★, *So Near, So Far (Musings For Miles)* (Verve 1993)★★★★, *Double Rainbow: The Music Of Antonio Carlos Jobim* (Verve 1995)★★★, *Shade Of Jade: Joe Henderson Big Band* (Verve 1996)★★★★, *Porgy & Bess* (Verve 1997)★★★.

● COMPILATIONS: *The Best Of Joe Henderson* (Blue Note 1985)★★★★, *The Blue Note Years* 4-CD box set (Blue Note 1994)★★★★, *The Milestone Years* (Milestone 1994)★★★★.

HENDERSON, WAYNE

b. Wayne Maurice Henderson, 24 September 1939, Houston, Texas, USA. Henderson made his first impact while still in his teens, playing trombone with a group briefly known as the Modern Jazz Sextet. The group had been formed in the early 50s, by Joe Sample, Wilton Felder and Stix Hooper, as the Swingsters. When it was expanded to accommodate Henderson, Hubert Laws and Henry Wilson it accordingly changed its name. Later name changes included the Nighthawks until they settled on the Jazz Crusaders. By the end of the 60s several of the band's members were in demand as studio musicians and Henderson was increasingly active as a record producer. The band broke up as a touring group but continued to record, making several albums for the Pacific Jazz label, including their 1961 debut *Freedom Sound*, and *Lookin' Ahead*, the latter including 'The Young Rabbits', a Henderson composition which proved to be popular in its own right. The band reformed in the early 70s, this time as the Crusaders, and Henderson stayed with them until 1975. In later years, Henderson played as a solo artist and also led bands of his own. He reunited with Felder on a 1992 recording for the Par label. The repertoire developed by the Crusaders, in all the group's forms, accommodated rock and funk into a jazz concept and attracted a wide audience among the younger set.

● ALBUMS: *Big Daddy's Place* (ABC 1977)★★★, *Living On A Dream* (Polydor 1978)★★★, *Back To The Groove* (Par 1992)★★★.

HENDRICKS, JON

b. 16 September 1921, Newark, Ohio, USA. Although he studied law, Hendricks was drawn to jazz and worked as a drummer and singer while still at college. An engagement with Charlie Parker prompted a move into full-time music. Hendricks wrote lyrics to solos created by jazzmen, a form of singing which has never been overcrowded with skilled practitioners. Collaborations with Dave Lambert and Annie Ross led to the formation of the vocal group Lambert, Hendricks And Ross, which had a number of successful records. This group continued into the mid-60s (with Ross being succeeded by Yolande Bavan for the last couple of years). Subsequently, Hendricks worked with other vocal groups and resumed his solo career. In the 70s he began performing with his wife and children and has also worked with Bobby McFerrin and Manhattan Transfer. His superb 1990 Denon release featured contributions from McFerrin, George Benson and Al Jarreau. Other outstanding Lambert releases include his 1959 debut and his most recent outing on Telarc Jazz. An outstanding writer and exponent of vocalese, Hendricks has also written longer jazz works and critical pieces for newspapers including the *San Francisco Chronicle*.

● ALBUMS: *A Good Git-Together* (World Pacific 1959)★★★★, *Evolution Of The Blues* (Columbia Special Products 1960)★★★, *Fast Livin' Blues* (Columbia 1961)★★★, *Salute To Joao Gilberto* (Reprise 1963)★★★, *Jon Hendricks Recorded In Person At The Trident* (Smash 1963)★★★★, *Cloudburst* (Enja 1972)★★★, *Tell Me The Truth* (Arista 1975)★★★, as Hendricks & Company *Love* (Muse 1982)★★★, *Freddie Freeloader* (Denon 1990)★★★★, *Boppin' At The Blue Note* (Telarc 1995)★★★★.

HENRY, HAYWOOD

b. Frank Haywood Henry, 7 January 1909, Birmingham, Alabama, USA. Haywood began playing clarinet while still a schoolboy, and at the Alabama

State Teachers College he joined the college band with classmate Dud Bascomb. This band, the 'Bama State Collegians, was also home to Erskine Hawkins, who eventually took over the band when it turned professional. This was in 1935 and Haywood stayed with the group, playing clarinet and baritone saxophone, for the next two decades. In the 50s he was often on record dates playing jazz with other leaders, including Rex Stewart, and he also played R&B. In the 60s he spent time with Wilbur De Paris and Earl Hines and in the 70s was regularly called upon as a member of bands accompanying artists such as Ella Fitzgerald. Henry was a good clarinet soloist and his baritone playing was solid and workmanlike, providing as it did a resonant foundation for the reed sections in which he appeared. He continued to perform into the 80s.

● COMPILATIONS: *The Chronological Erksine Hawkins 1939-1940* (Classics 1939-40)★★★★.

Herbolzheimer, Peter

b. 31 December 1935, Bucharest, Romania. After playing guitar early in his career, much of his subsequent playing was on trombone, although he is perhaps best known as a bandleader, composer and arranger. Throughout the 60s Herbolzheimer was frequently to be found playing in orchestras in theatres and recording and broadcasting studios. He also led his own big band in which he used many European jazzmen including Dusko Goykovich, Palle Mikkelborg, Niels-Henning Ørsted Pedersen and Alex Riel, and temporarily resident Americans such as Art Farmer and Herb Geller. In the 70s, he worked extensively in television and radio, played with Dizzy Gillespie and others, and won awards and was honoured in a number of ways, including being invited to contribute music for the 1972 Munich-based Olympic Games. Herbolzheimer's playing and writing is an intriguing mingling of jazz and rock which, while not truly classifiable as jazz-rock, contains many of the more attractive and swinging elements of both forms.

● ALBUMS: *My Kind Of Sunshine* (MPS 1971)★★, *Wide Open* (MPS 1973)★★★, *Jazz Gala Concert* (Atlantic 1976)★★★, *Jazz Gala '77 All Star Big Band* (Telefunken 1977)★★★, *Bandfire* (Panda 1981).★★★

Herfurt, Skeets

b. Arthur Herfurt, 28 May 1911, Cincinnati, Ohio, USA. As a young man Herfurt played various reed instruments, mostly in the south-west and especially in Colorado, where he grew up and was educated. His first name-band engagement was with Smith Ballew, the popular singer. This was in 1934 and in the same year he joined the Dorsey Brothers band, remaining in its ranks after the brothers split up, when the band continued under Jimmy Dorsey's name. Later in the 30s, Herfurt played with bands led by Ray Noble, George Stoll and Tommy Dorsey. Tiring of travelling, he settled in the Los Angeles area, and was briefly with the mid-40s band led by Alvino Rey before military service towards the end of World War II. After the war Herfurt worked in film studios, but had a short spell with Benny Goodman. During the 50s and beyond, he worked in studios, led his own band, and played in numerous recording studio orchestras under many different leaders and backing numerous artists of note. He had a further spell with Goodman in the early 60s and again in the middle of the decade. Herfurt's tenor saxophone and clarinet playing was of a very high standard and he was one of countless unsung stalwarts of the swing era's big bands.

● COMPILATIONS: *The Dorsey Brothers Orchestra* (MCA 1934-35)★★★★, *The Uncollected Alvino Rey* (Hindsight 1944-45)★★★.

Herman, Woody

b. Woodrow Charles Herman, 16 May 1913, Milwaukee, Wisconsin, USA, d. 29 October 1987. A child prodigy, Herman sang and tap-danced in local clubs before touring as a singer in vaudeville. To improve his act he took up the saxophone and later the clarinet, all by the age of 12. By his mid-teens he was sufficiently accomplished to play in a band, and he went on to work in a string of dance bands during the late 20s and early 30s. Last in this line was Isham Jones, Herman first being in Isham Jones's Juniors, with whom he recorded early in 1936. When Jones folded the band later that year, Herman was elected leader by a nucleus of musicians who wanted to continue. Initially a co-operative group, the band included flügelhorn player Joe Bishop, bassist Walt Yoder, drummer Frank Carlson and trombonist Neil Reid. With a positive if uncommercial view of what they wanted to achieve, they were billed as 'The Band That Plays The Blues' and gradually built a following during the swing era. The success of their recordings of 'Golden Wedding', a Jiggs Noble re-working of 'La Cinquantaine', and especially Bishop's 'At The Woodchoppers' Ball' helped the band's fortunes. During the early 40s numerous personnel changes took place, some dictated by the draft, others by a gradual shift in style. By 1944 Herman was leading the band which eventually became labelled as the First Herd. Included in this powerhouse were trumpeters Ray Wetzel, Neal Hefti and Pete Candoli, trombonist Bill Harris, tenor saxophonist Joe 'Flip' Phillips and the remarkable rhythm section of Ralph Burns, Billy Bauer, Chubby Jackson and Dave Tough, to which was added vibraphonist Margie Hyams. This band made several records which were not only musically excellent but were also big sellers, amongst them 'Apple Honey', 'Caldonia', 'Northwest Passage' and 'Goosey Gander'. During the next year or so the band's personnel remained fairly stable, although the brilliant if unreliable Tough was replaced in late 1945 by Don Lamond, and they continued to make good records, including 'Bijou', 'Your Father's Mustache', 'Wild Root' and 'Blowin' Up A Storm'. In 1946 the band still included Candoli, Harris, Phillips, Bauer, Jackson and Lamond and amongst the newcomers were trumpeters Sonny Berman, Shorty Rogers and Conrad Gozzo and vibraphonist Red Norvo. The First Herd played a concert at Carnegie Hall to great acclaim but, despite the band's continuing popularity, at the end of this same year, 1946, Herman temporarily disbanded because of economic difficulties. The following year he was back with his Second Herd, known to posterity as the 'Four Brothers' band. This band represented a particularly modern approach to big band music, playing bop-influenced charts by Jimmy Giuffre and others. Most striking, however, and the source of the band's name, was the saxophone section. With Sam Marowitz and Herbie Steward on altos, Stan Getz and Zoot Sims, tenors, and Serge Chaloff, baritone, the section was thrustingly modern; and when Steward doubled on tenor, they created a deeper-toned sound that was utterly different to any other band of the time. The concept of the reed section had originated with Gene Roland, whose rehearsal band had included Getz, Sims, Steward and Giuffre. Heard by Burns and hired by Herman, these musicians helped create a new excitement and this band was another enormously successful group. Although the modern concepts took precedence, there was still room for straight ahead swingers. The brass section at this time included Rogers, Marky Markowitz and Ernie Royal and trombonist Earl Swope. The rhythm section included Lamond and vibraphonist Terry Gibbs. The reed section was dominant, however, and when Steward was replaced by Al Cohn, it was by far the best in the land. Apart from 'Four Brothers' the band had other successful records, including 'Keen And Peachy', 'The Goof And I' and 'Early Autumn'. This last piece was written by Burns to round out a three-part suite, 'Summer Sequence', he had composed earlier and which had already been recorded. The extra part allowed the record company to release a four-sided set, and Getz's solo on 'Early Autumn' was the first example of the saxophonist's lyrical depths to make an impression upon the jazz world. Unfortunately, despite its successes, the band wasn't quite popular enough, perhaps being a little ahead of its time. Once again Herman folded, only to re-form almost at once. Numbering the Herman Herds was never easy but the leader himself named his early 50s group as the Third Herd. Although lacking the precision of the Four Brothers band and the raw excitement of the First Herd, the new band was capable of swinging superbly. As before, Herman had no difficulty in attracting top-flight musicians, including Red Rodney, Urbie Green, Kai Winding, Richie Kamuca, Bill Perkins, Monty Budwig and Jake Hanna. Of particular importance to the band at this time (and for the next few years) was Nat Pierce, who not only played piano but also wrote many fine arrangements and acted as straw boss. The times were hostile to big bands, however, and by the mid-50s Herman was working in comparative obscurity. Members of the band, who then included Bill Berry, Bobby Lamb, Kamuca, Budwig and Harris, wryly described this particular Herman group as the 'un-Herd'. Towards the end of the decade Herman was still fighting against the tide, but was doing it with some of the best available musicians: Cohn, Sims, Don Lanphere, Bob Brookmeyer, Pierce, Kamuca, Perkins and Med Flory. During the 60s and 70s Herman's bands were given various informal tags; the Swinging Herd, the Thundering Herd. Mostly they did as these names suggested, thundering and swinging through some excellent charts and with many fine sidemen many of whom were culled from the universities. Other leaders did this, of course, but Herman always ensured that he was far from being the solitary veteran on a bandstand full of beginners. He kept many older hands on board to ensure the youngsters had experienced models from whom they could draw inspiration. Among the sidemen during these years were Pierce, Hanna, Bill Chase, baritone saxophonist Nick Brignola, Sal Nistico, tenor saxophonist Carmen Leggio, John Von Ohlen, Cecil Payne, Carl Fontana, Dusko Goykovich and trombonists Henry Southall and Phil Wilson. In the late 60s Herman dabbled with jazz-rock but, although he subsequently kept a few such numbers in the band's book, it was not an area in which he was comfortable. In 1976 Herman played a major concert at Carnegie Hall, celebrating the 40th anniversary of his first appearance there. As the 80s began, Herman's health was poor and he might have had thoughts of retirement; he had, after all, been performing for a little over 60 years. Unfortunately, this was the time he discovered that his manager for many years had systematically embezzled funds set aside for taxes. Now Herman was not only flat broke and in danger of eviction from his home in the Hollywood Hills, but he also owed the IRS millions of dollars. Forced to play on, he continued to lead bands on punishing tours around the world, tours which were hugely successful but were simultaneously exacerbating his poor physical condition. In 1986 he celebrated 50 years as a bandleader with a tour that featured long-standing sideman Frank Tiberi, baritone saxophonist Mike Brignola, trumpeter Bill Byrne and bassist Lynn Seaton. The following year he was still on the road - and also on the sidewalk, when a gold star in his name was laid along Hollywood Boulevard's Walk of Fame. In March of that same year the Herman Herd, whatever number this one might be, was still thundering away at concerts, some of which fortunately, were recorded. But it could not, of course, go on forever, and Herman died in October 1987. As a clarinettist and saxophonist, sometimes playing alto, latterly soprano, Herman was never a virtuoso player in the manner of swing era contemporaries such as Benny Goodman or Artie Shaw. Unlike theirs, his playing was deeply rooted in the blues, and he brought to his music an unshakeable commitment to jazz. Despite the inevitable ups and downs of his career as a big band leader, he stuck to his principles and if he ever compromised it was always, somehow, on his own terms. He composed little, although many of the First Herd's greatest successes were head arrangements conceived and developed on the bandstand or in rehearsal. Herman's real skills lay in his ability to pick the right people for his band, to enthuse them, and to ensure that they never lost that enthusiasm. In selecting for his band he had patience and an excellent ear. He knew what he wanted and he nearly always got it. Over the many years he led a band, scores of musicians passed through the ranks, many of them amongst the finest in jazz. No one ever had a bad word to say about him.

● ALBUMS: *Sequence In Jazz* (Columbia 1949)★★★, *Dance Parade* (Columbia 1949)★★★, *And His Woodchoppers* (Columbia 1950)★★★★, *Swinging With The Woodchoppers* (Dial 1950)★★★★, *Blue Prelude* (Coral 1950)★★★★, *Souvenirs* (Coral 1950)★★★, *Live At The Hollywood Palladium* (1951)★★★★, with Charlie Parker *Bird With The Herd* (1951)★★★★, *Dance Date On Mars* (Mars 1952)★★★, *Woody Herman Goes Native* (Mars 1952)★★★, *At Carnegie Hall Vol 1 & 2* (MGM 1952)★★★★, *Classics In Jazz* (Capitol 1952)★★★, *Thundering Herd* (1953)★★★★, *The Third Herd* (MGM 1953)★★★★, *Woody's Best* (Coral 1953)★★★, *The Three Herds* (Columbia 1954)★★★★, *Woody Herman With The Erroll Garner Trio* (1954)★★★, *The Third Herd Live In Stockholm Vols 1 & 2* (1954)★★★★, *Jackpot* (1955)★★★, *Blue Flame* (MGM 1955)★★★, *The Woody Herman Band* (Capitol 1955)★★★, *Road Band* (Capitol 1955)★★★, *Music For Tired Lovers* (Columbia 1955)★★★, *12 Shades Of Blue* (Columbia 1955)★★★, *Woodchoppers Ball* (Decca 1955)★★★★, *Ridin' Herd* (Columbia 1955)★★★, *Woody* (Columbia 1956)★★★, *Hi-Fi-ing Herd* (MGM 1956)★★★★, *Jackpot* (Capitol 1956)★★★, *Blues Groove* (Capitol 1956)★★★, *Jazz The Utmost* (Clef 1956)★★★, *Woody Herman With Barney Kessel And His Orchestra* (1957)★★★, *Woody Herman And His Orchestra* i (1957)★★★★, *Woody Herman Live Featuring Bill Harris Vols 1 & 2* (1957)★★★, *Bijou* (Harmony 1957)★★★, *Early Autumn* (Verve 1957)★★★★, *Songs For Hip Lovers* (Verve 1957)★★★, *The Swinging Herman Herd* (Brunswick 1957)★★★, *Love is The Sweetest Thing Sometimes* (Verve 1958)★★★, *Live At Peacock Lake, Hollywood* (1958)★★★★, *The Herd Rides Again In Stereo* (Verve 1958)★★★, *Summer Sequence* (Harmony 1958)★★★, *Men From Mars* (Verve 1958)★★★, *58'* (Verve 1958)★★★, *Herman's Beat And Puentes Beat* (Everest 1958)★★★, *Moody Woody* (Everest 1958)★★★, *The Fourth Herd* (Jazzland 1959)★★★★, *Woody Herman's New Big Band At The Monterey Jazz Festival* (1959)★★★★, *Woody Herman Sextet At the Round Table* (Roulette 1959)★★★★, *At The Monterey Jazz Festival* (Atlantic 1960)★★★, *1960* (1960)★★★, *The Woody Herman Quartet* (1962)★★★★, *Swing Low Sweet Chariot* (Philips 1962)★★★, *Woody Herman And His Orchestra* ii (1962)★★★★, *1963* (Philips 1963)★★★, *Encore Woody Herman 1963* (Philips 1963)★★★, *Live At Basin Street West* (1963)★★★, *Encore* (1963)★★★, *The New World Of Woody Herman* (1963)★★★, *Hey! Heard The Herd* (Verve 1963)★★★, *Woody Herman At Harrah's Club* (1964)★★★, *The Swinging Herman Herd Recorded Live* (Philips 1964)★★★★, *Woody Herman 1964* (Philips 1964)★★★, *Woody's Winners* (Columbia 1965)★★★, *Woody's Big Band Goodies* (Philips 1965)★★★, *My Kind Of Broadway* (Columbia 1965)★★★, *The Jazz Swinger* (Columbia 1966)★★★, *Blowing Up A Storm* (Sunset 1966)★★★, *Woody Live East And West* (Columbia 1967)★★★, *Live In Seattle* (1967)★★★, *Light My Fire* (1968)★★★, *Heavy Exposure* (1969)★★★, *Light My Fire* (Cadet 1969)★★, *Woody* (1970)★★, *Brand New* (1971)★★★, *The Raven Speaks* (1972)★★★, *Giant Steps* (1973)★★★, *Woody Herman And His Orchestra* iii (1974)★★★★, *Herd At Montreux* (1974)★★★★, *Woody Herman With Frank Sinatra* (1974)★★★, *Children Of Lima* (1974)★★★, *King Cobra* (1975)★★★, *Woody Herman In Warsaw* (1976)★★★★, *40th Anniversary: Carnegie Hall Concert* (1976)★★★★, *Lionel Hampton Presents Woody Herman* (1977)★★★, *Road Father* (1978)★★★, *Together: Flip & Woody* (1978)★★★, *Chick, Donald, Walter & Woodrow* (1978) *Woody Herman And Friends At The Monterey Jazz Festival* (1979)★★★★, *Woody Herman Presents A Concord Jam Vol. 1* (1980)★★★, *Woody Herman Presents Four Others Vol. 2* (1981)★★★, *Live At The Concord Jazz Festival* (1981)★★★★, *Live In Chicago* (1981)★★★, *Aurex Jazz Festival '82* (1982)★★★, *Woody Herman Presents A Great American Evening* (1983)★★★, *50th Anniversary Tour* (1986)★★★, *Woody's Gold Star* (1987).

● COMPILATIONS: *The Hits Of Woody Herman* (Capitol 1961)★★★, *The Thundering Herds Vols 1-3* 3-LP box set (Columbia 1963)★★★★, *Golden Hits* (Decca 1964)★★★, *Greatest Hits* (Columbia 1966)★★★★, *The Turning Point 1943-44* (Decca 1967)★★★★, *The Band That Plays The Blues* (1937-42 recordings)★★★, *The V-Disc Years Vol. 1* (1944-45 recordings)★★★★, *The First Herd* (1945 recordings)★★★★, *The Best Of Woody Herman* (1945-47 recordings)★★★, *The V Disc Years 1944 - 46* (Hep Jazz 1993)★★★, *The Fourth Herd & The New World Of Woody Herman* (Mobile Fidelity 1995)★★★★, *Keep On Keepin' On: 1968-1970* (Universal 1998)★★★.

● FURTHER READING: *Woody Herman*, Steve Voce. *The Woodchopper's Ball*, Woody Herman with Stuart Troup. *Woody Herman: A Guide To The Big Band Recordings, 1936-87*, Dexter Morrill.

Herring, Vincent

b. 19 November, 1964, California, USA. One of the most exciting alto saxophone players working in the hard bop idiom, he idolizes Cannonball Adderley and was chosen by Cannonball's brother Nat Adderley to play in the Cannonball Adderley Legacy Band. In July 1984, when his band was playing in the Manhattan streets, Herring was approached by record-label proprietor Sam Parkins with the offer of a recording date. Since then he has gigged or recorded with many distinguished figures, including Horace Silver, Cedar Walton, Art Blakey, McCoy Tyner, Larry Coryell, Jack DeJohnette, Beaver Harris, Lionel Hampton, and David Murray. In 1988 in Paris he took part in an alto summit with Phil Woods, Frank Morgan, Bob Mover, C. Sharps and McLean. In 1990 he toured Europe with his own quintet.

● ALBUMS: *Scene One* (1989)★★★★, *American Experience* (S&R 1990)★★★, with Nat Adderley: *Talkin' About You* (1991)★★★★, with Adderley *We Remember Cannon* (1991)★★★, *Evidence* (Landmark 1991)★★★, *Secret Love* (Music Masters 1992)★★★★, *Dawnbird* (Landmark 1994)★★★, Folklore, *Live At The Village Vanguard* (Music Masters 1995)★★★★, *Don't Let It Go* (Music Masters 1995)★★★.

Hersch, Fred

b. USA. Hersch grew up in Cincinnati, Ohio, in a very musical family. Playing piano from the age of three, he turned to jazz in his high school senior year. In 1975 he attended the New England Conservatory and after two years returned to Cincinnati where he played professionally. He spent six weeks on the road with Woody Herman, then relocated to New York. During the late 70s and early 80s he played with many leading artists, including Art Farmer, Joe Henderson, Lee Konitz, Chris Connor and Jane Ira Bloom. During the middle of the decade he set up his own studios, recording several musicians, notably fellow pianists Hank Jones, Kenny Barron, Dick Hyman and Roger Kellaway. Hersch's interest in classical music has led him to arrange and perform intriguing variations on classical themes, and he has also composed extensively in both jazz and classical style, recording 'Concerto' with the intriguing combination of Toots Thielemans, a big band, and the Chamber Orchestra Of Lausanne. In 1986 Hersch was diagnosed as HIV+ and since that date has been deeply involved in work on behalf of AIDS sufferers. This has included producing and performing on recordings for Classical Action: *Last Night When We Were Young: The Ballad Album* and *Fred Hersch And Friends: The Duo Album*. The duo format is clearly one that is attractive to Hersch and he has made numerous albums of this kind, several with instrumentalists and others with singers Jay Clayton, Janis Siegel and Jeri Brown. He has also worked as a member of a trio with clarinettist Michael Moore and drummer Gerry Hemingway. Another trio is ETC, with Steve La Spina and Jeff Hirschfield, which, with the addition of Jerry Bergonzi, became ETC Plus One. His *Dancing In The Dark* and *I Never Told You* were nominated for Grammies. Hersch's technical expertise is exceptional but it is never allowed to obstruct his ability to play with great emotional depths. Hersch's delight in the work of jazz piano predecessors, such as Bill Evans and Thelonious Monk, is apparent in his work, inevitably so with his tribute albums to them. However, he is a player of great strength and integrity, and his own musical personality shines through performances such as these just as brightly as it does on his many other albums.

● ALBUMS: *Horizons* (Concord Jazz 1984)★★★, *Sarabande* (Sunnyside 1986)★★★, *ETC* (Red 1988)★★★, *Heartsongs* (Sunnyside 1989)★★★, with Janis Siegel *Short Stories* (Atlantic 1989)★★★, *Evanessence: A Tribute To Bill Evans* (Evidence 1990)★★★, *French Collection: Jazz Impressions Of French Classics* (Angel/EMI 1990)★★★, *ETC Plus One* (Red 1991)★★★, with Jeri Brown *Mirage* (Justin Time 1991)★★★, *Forward Motion* (Chesky 1992)★★★, *Red Square Blue: Jazz Impressions Of Russian Classics* (Angel/EMI 1992)★★★, with Matt Kendrick *Other Aspects* (Suitcase 1992)★★★, with Jane Ira Bloom *As One* (JMI 1992)★★★, *Dancing In The Dark* (Chesky 1993)★★★, *Live At Maybeck Recital Hall Series, Vol. 31* (Concord Jazz 1993)★★★★, *The Fred Hersch Trio Plays* (Chesky 1994)★★★, with Siegel *Slow Hot Wind* (Varese Sarabande 1994)★★★, *I Never Told You: Fred Hersch Plays Johnny Mandel* (Varese Sarabande 1994)★★★, with Jay Clayton *Beautiful Love* (Sunnyside 1994)★★★, *Point In Time* (Enja 1995)★★★, *Passion Flower: Fred Hersch Plays Billy Strayhorn* (Nonesuch 1995)★★★, *Fred Hersch Plays Rodgers & Hammerstein* (Nonesuch 1996)★★★★, with Gerry Hemingway, Michael Moore, *Thirteen Ways* (GM 1997)★★★, *Thelonious: Fred Hersch Plays Monk* (Nonesuch 1997)★★★★.

HESSION, PAUL

b. 19 September 1956, Leeds, England. Although Hession's grandfather had played the drums in a cavalry regiment, his own first musical exposure was to the guitar, a gift from his parents when he was seven years old. About the same time he started singing in a church choir, and credits choir-leader and improvising organist William Isles-Pulford with instilling in him a love of music. He began playing drums himself in 1971, a new departure which involved the usual apprenticeship in Working Men's Club rock bands. Seeing Elvin Jones at Ronnie Scott's Club in 1975 gave him 'food for thought for years'. In 1979 he formed a partnership with alto saxophonist Alan Wilkinson, which has carried on into the 90s. In 1983 they (together with guitarist Paul Buckton and live electronics improviser John McMillan) founded the Leeds Termite Club, both performing free improvised music and promoting players from the UK, Europe and the USA. In 1987 Hession proved his bop credentials by backing west coast bebop tenor saxophonist Teddy Edwards. Word of the quality of the Leeds improvisation scene reached London, and Hession played at Derek Bailey's Company Week in 1988. A partnership with Wuppertal-based tenor Hans-Peter Hiby resulted in *The Real Case* in 1988. In a trio format with Wilkinson and bassist Simon Fell, Hession toured in 1991 under the title 'October Onslaught'. His torrential polyrhythmic style and his ability to raise the stakes in formidable company establish him as a prime mover in the attempt to inject excitement and power back into total improvisation - a return to its roots in free jazz.

● ALBUMS: with Hans-Peter Hiby *The Real Case* (1988)★★★, with Simon Fell *Compilation 2* (1991)★★★.

HEYWOOD, EDDIE

b. 4 December 1915, Atlanta, Georgia, USA, d. 2 January 1989, North Miami, Florida, USA. Heywood received his first piano lessons from his father, also named Eddie, who was a well-known bandleader in the 20s. Heywood joined his father, playing piano in the pit band at an Atlanta theatre. He also accompanied singers, including Bessie Smith, and thereafter worked in various small jazz groups, including those led by Wayman Carver, Benny Carter and Don Redman. His gift for accompanying singers was displayed by his recordings with Billie Holiday and Alberta Hunter. In 1943 he took a sextet into the Cafe Society Downtown, being billed as the 'Biggest Little Band in the Land'. The type of music they played, and their billing, placed them in direct competition with John Kirby but, thanks to the presence of Doc Cheatham and Vic Dickenson, they held their own. Heywood had a hit record in 1944 with an unusual arrangement of 'Begin The Beguine' but his career was soon plagued by ill-health. Suffering partial paralysis in his hands, he worked less yet continued to write and had successes in the mid-50s with 'Canadian Sunset', 'Soft Summer Breeze' and other delightful songs. Further paralysis developed in the 60s; however he persevered and was still writing and occasionally performing throughout the 70s and into the early 80s. By this time he was working in the field of light music rather than jazz; indeed, close examination of his work, even from early in his career, shows him to have been a skilled musician with jazz associations and associates rather than a committed jazzman in his own right.

● ALBUMS: *Eight Selections* (Commodore 1950)★★★, *Piano Moods* (Columbia 1951)★★★, *It's Easy To Remember* (MGM 1952)★★★, *Eddie Heywood 45* (Brunswick 1953)★★, *The Eddie Heywood Trio* ii (MGM 1954)★★★★, *Pianorama* (MGM 1955)★★, *The Eddie Heywood Trio* At Twilight (Epic 1956)★★, *Lightly And Politely* (Decca 1956)★★★, *Swing Low Sweet Heywood* (Decca 1956)★★★, *Featuring Eddie Heywood* (Coral 1957)★★, *The Touch Of Eddie Heywood* (RCA Victor 1957)★★★, *Canadian Sunset* (RCA Victor 1957)★★★, *The Keys And I* (RCA Victor 1958)★★, *Breezin' Along With The Breeze* (Mercury 1959)★★★, *Eddie Heywood At The Piano* (Mercury 1960)★★★, *One For My Baby* (Mercury 1960)★★★, *Eddie Heywood* (Wing 1963)★★★, *The Piano Stylings Of Eddie Heywood* (Vocalion 1964)★★, *With Love And Strings* (Capitol 1967)★★★.

● COMPILATIONS: *Biggest Little Band Of The 40* (1944)★★★★, *Eddie Heywood And The Blues Singers* (Document 1996)★★★★.

HIBBLER, AL

b. 16 August 1915, Little Rock, Arkansas, USA. Blind from birth, Hibbler attended the Conservatory for the Blind in Little Rock, becoming a member of the school choir. After winning an amateur talent contest in Memphis, he worked with local bands and his own outfit before joining Jay McShann in 1942. In the following year he joined the Duke Ellington Orchestra, proving to be one of the best singers the Duke ever employed. In the 40s he sang on Ellington records such as 'Ain't Got Nothin' But The Blues', 'I'm Just a Lucky So And So', 'Pretty Woman', 'Don't Be so Mean To Baby', 'Good Woman Blues', and 'Build That Railroad' (1950). During his eight year stay with Ellington, Hibbler won the Esquire New Star Award and *Downbeat* Best Band Vocalist. He subsequently recorded with several well-known jazz musicans in his backing groups, among them Harry Carney, Billy Kyle, Count Basie and Gerald Wilson. In the 50s his recordings of songs such as 'It Shouldn't Happen To A Dream', which he had recorded with Ellington, 'The Very Thought Of You' and 'Stardust' proved popular, while his version of 'Unchained Melody' (a million-seller) was outstanding. In the 50s he also made the US Top 30 with 'He', '11th Hour Melody', 'Never Turn Back' and 'After The Lights Go Down Low'. A powerful, rich-toned baritone, Hibbler cannot be regarded as a jazz singer but as an exceptionally good interpreter of 20th-century popular songs who happened to work with some of the best jazz musicians of the time.

● ALBUMS: *Al Hibbler Sings Love Songs* (1952)★★★, *Al Hibbler Favorites* (Norgran 1954)★★★, *Sings Duke Ellington* (Norgran 1954)★★★★, *Melodies By Al Hibbler* (Marterry 1956)★★★, *After The Lights Go Down Low* (Atlantic 1956)★★★, *Sings Love Songs* (Verve 1956)★★★, *Starring Al Hibbler* (Decca 1956)★★★, *Here's Hibbler* (Decca 1957)★★, *I Surrender Dear* (Score 1957)★★, *With The Ellingtonians* (Brunswick 1957)★★★, *Torchy And Blue* (Decca 1958)★★★, *Hits By Hibbler* (Decca 1958)★★, *Remembers The Big Songs Of The Big Bands* (Decca 1958)★★★★, *Monday Every Day* (Atlantic 1961)★★★, *Early One Morning* (LMI 1964)★★★, with Rahsaan Roland Kirk *A Meeting Of The Times* (1972)★★, *For Sentimental Reasons* (1982)★★★, *Golden Greats* (MCA 1986)★★★, *Dedicated To You* (Starline 1988)★★★.

HICKS, JACQUI

b. Featherstone, Yorkshire, England. As a child, Hicks began playing on the recorder before graduating to the clarinet on which she studied classical music. She also played tenor saxophone for a while. Her musical tastes inclined towards the jazzier end of the current pop spectrum, including musicians such as George Benson and Earth, Wind And Fire. At the age of 18 Hicks attended the Leeds College of Music where she was encouraged by Bill Charleson. She sang with the college band, with Brian Layton's funk band, and with John Brown's Student Bodies. After Leeds, she went to the Guildhall School of Music in London. In 1989 she sang occasionally with the National Youth Jazz Orchestra and the following year joined the band on a regular basis. In the mid-90s she began a solo career. She has composed songs, including 'Just A Breath Away', which she recorded with NYJO. Hicks is a skilled yet un-fussy singer with charm and intelligence.

● ALBUMS: *Looking Forward/Looking Back* (1991)★★★.

HICKS, JOHN

b. 12 December 1941, Atlanta, Georgia, USA. Hicks began playing and studying piano while still a very small child, taking piano lessons from his mother. The family lived in Los Angeles, then in St. Louis, and he later attended Lincoln University in Missouri and the Berklee College Of Music. In the early 60s he went to New York where he became a member of Art Blakey's Jazz Messengers, recording *'S Make It* in the mid-60s. He followed this tough school of learning with another when he became accompanist to that most demanding of singers, Betty Carter. He probably found his next employer, Woody Herman, more easy-going although musically just as demanding. During the late 60s he also recorded with Hank Mobley. Throughout the 70s and on into the 80s, Hicks continued to tour and make records, sometimes as leader, with artists as diverse as Oliver Lake, Charles Tolliver, Lester Bowie, whom he had known since schooldays, and David Murray, with brief return trips to both Blakey and Carter. He also established fruitful musical partnerships with Curtis Lundy, Arthur Blythe, flautist Elise Wood, Vincent Herring, Bobby Watson, and made well-received duo recordings with Jay McShann and Peter Leitch. In the early 90s he made a striking solo appearance at a jazz festival in Montreal, later released on CD. He has also made several albums with the bands New York Unit and New York Rhythm Machine for PaddleWheel, Venus and Evidence Records, and recorded as the Keystone Trio with George Mraz and Idris Muhammad. Although his earlier playing was sometimes criticized for its eclecticism, as time passed Hicks has silenced his critics by developing a personal style that harmoniously blends a melodious romanticism with a buoyantly inventive dramatic flair that is especially suited to his sensitive treatment of ballads. In the late 90s, in addition to a full calendar of concerts and recording dates, Hicks was finding time to pass on his expertise through teaching at the New School for Social Research and New York University.

● ALBUMS: *Hell's Bells* (Strata-East 1975)★★★, *Steadfast* (Strata-East 1975)★★★, *After The Morning* (West 54 1979)★★★★, *Some Other Time* (Evidence 1982)★★★, *John Hicks* (Theresa 1984)★★★, *John Hicks In Concert* (Theresa 1984)★★★, *Inc. 1* (DIW 1985)★★★, *Sketches Of Tokyo* (DIW 1985)★★★, *Two Of A Kind* (Evidence 1987)★★★, *I Give You Something To Remember Me By* (Limetree 1987)★★★, *Naima's Love Song* (DIW 1988)★★★★, *East Side Blues* (DIW 1988)★★★, *Luminous* (Evidence 1988)★★★, *Rhythm-A-Ning* (Candid 1988)★★★, *Is That So?* (Timeless 1990)★★★, *Power Trio* (Novus 1990)★★★, *Live At The Maybeck Recital Hall, Vol. 7* (Concord Jazz 1990)★★★, *Newklear Music: The Songs Of Sonny Rollins* (Milestone 1990)★★★, *Crazy For You* (Red Baron 1992)★★★, *Friends Old And New* (Novus 1992)★★★, with Jay McShann *The Missouri Connection* (Reservoir 1993)★★★★, *Lover Man: Tribute To Billie Holiday* (Red Baron 1993)★★★, *Beyond Expectations* (Reservoir 1993)★★★, *Gentle Rain* (Sand Hills 1993)★★, *Duality* (Reservoir 1993)★★★, with Peter Leitch *A Special Rapport* (Reservoir 1993)★★★, *In Concert* 1984 recording (Evidence 1993)★★★, *Some Other Time* 1981 recording (Evidence 1994)★★★, with Leitch *Duality* (Reservoir 1994)★★★, *Single Petal Of A Rose* (Mapleshade 1994)★★★, *In The Mix* (Landmark 1995)★★★, *A Piece For My Peace* (Landmark 1996)★★, with the Keystone Trio *Heartbeats* (Milestone 1996)★★★, *At The Montreal International Jazz Festival* (DSM 1997)★★★, *John Hicks: Trio & Strings* (Mapleshade 1997)★★★, with the Keystone Trio *Newklear Music: The Songs Of Sonny Rollins* (Milestone 1997)★★, *Something To Live For* (HighNote 1998)★★★, *Hicks Time* (Passin Thru 1998)★★.

HIGGINBOTHAM, J.C.

b. 11 May 1906, Social Circle, Georgia, USA, d. 26 May 1973. After playing trombone with J. Neal Montgomery, an Atlanta-based territory bandleader of the early 20s, Higginbotham worked outside music for a number of years. In the middle of the decade he tried his hand at bandleading and then was briefly with the bands of Wingie Carpenter, Chick Webb and Willie Lynch before joining Luis Russell. In 1931 he moved on to Fletcher Henderson's band, worked for Benny Carter, the Mills Blue Rhythm Band, Henderson again and Louis Armstrong, who was then fronting the Russell band. Towards the end of 1940 Higginbotham shifted from big band work to play in a small group led by Red Allen, with whom he remained for about seven years. Thereafter, he played in or led small bands in New York, Boston and Cleveland, recorded extensively, appeared at the 1957 Great South Bay Jazz Festival as a member of the Fletcher Henderson reunion band, and visited Europe. In the 60s Higginbotham continued his established pattern of work, often playing in tandem with trumpeter Joe Thomas. Towards the end of the decade ill-health affected his career and he died in May 1973. A powerful, gutsy player with a solid traditional approach to his instrument overlaid with a keen appreciation of swing era styling, Higginbotham was one of the best trombone soloists in big band jazz.

● ALBUMS: with Henderson All Stars *Big Reunion* (1957)★★★, *J.C. Higginbotham All Stars* (1966)★★★.

● COMPILATIONS: with Fletcher Henderson *A Study In Frustration* (1923-38 recordings)★★★, *Higgy Comes Home* (Jazzology 1990)★★★.

HIGGINS, BILLY

b. 11 October 1936, Los Angeles, California, USA. Higgins began playing drums at the age of 12 and early in his career played with R&B bands. He was soon involved in jazz, playing with other local musicians, including Dexter Gordon. In 1957 he was in the quartet led by Red Mitchell which also included pianist Lorraine Geller and tenor saxophonist James Clay. This band recorded for Lester Koenig's Contemporary label, on what was Higgins' first record date. In New York in 1959 he appeared with Ornette Coleman at the altoist's controversial Five Spot concerts, in a band which also included Don Cherry and Charlie Haden. Later that year he joined Thelonious Monk and in 1960 was with John Coltrane. Throughout the 60s Higgins was in demand for tours, club dates and a staggering number of recording sessions, many of them for the Blue Note label. Amongst the artists with whom he played were Sonny Rollins, Steve Lacy, Donald Byrd, Gordon, Lee Morgan, Herbie Hancock and Hank Mobley. His activities increased during the 70s and he worked extensively with Cedar Walton and was also on dates with Milt Jackson and Art Pepper. In the 80s his musical companions included Coleman, Pat Metheny and Slide Hampton. Although the musical styles of Higgins' associates have latterly ranged through freeform, jazz-rock and jazz-funk, he has readily established himself as one of the two or three leading exponents of each form of drumming. He brings to his playing a remarkable subtlety and lithe swing akin to that of the best bop drummers, while readily accommodating the complex needs of the styles in which he plays.

● ALBUMS: *Presenting Red Mitchell/Red Mitchell Quartet* (1957)★★★, *Something Else! The Music Of Ornette Coleman* (1958)★★★★, with Coleman *The Shape Of Jazz To Come* (1959)★★★★, with Coleman *Free Jazz* (1960)★★★★, with Sonny Rollins *Our Man In Jazz* (1962)★★★, with Dexter Gordon *Go!* (1962)★★★★, with Hank Mobley *Dippin'* (1965)★★★, *Soweto* (Red 1979)★★★, *The Soldier* (Timeless 1980)★★★, *Mr Billy Higgins* (Evidence 1985)★★★, *Billy Higgins Quintet* 1993 recording (Evidence 1997)★★★, *3/4 For Peace* 1993 recording (Red 1997)★★★.

HILL, ANDREW

b. 30 June 1937, Chicago, Illinois, USA. Port Au Prince, Haiti, is usually given as Hill's birthplace, but he actually hails from Chicago. He studied composition privately with Paul Hindemith and Bill Russo, and played accordion and tap-danced on the streets where Earl Hines heard him. In his teens he was in Paul Williams's R&B band, played with Charlie Parker, Coleman Hawkins, Gene Ammons, Von Freeman, Johnny

Griffin, Malachi Favors and John Gilmore, and became virtually Chicago's 'house' pianist for visiting artists. Having spent some months in New York as Dinah Washington's accompanist he relocated there in 1960 whilst working with Johnny Hartman. From 1962-63 he worked in Los Angeles with Rahsaan Roland Kirk and Jimmy Woode among others. In 1963 he returned to New York to work with Joe Henderson. During the 60s he made a number of excellent albums for Blue Note Records (under his own name and with Bobby Hutcherson and Henderson), probably the best-known being *Black Fire* and the highly-acclaimed *Point Of Departure*, which featured Henderson, Eric Dolphy and Kenny Dorham. Later Blue Note sessions (several of which remain unissued) often show a dense, turbulent music that is both strikingly individual and intensely gripping; *Compulsion* has John Gilmore in ferocious form, while a set recorded with Sam Rivers (and later released under the tenorist's name as one half of the double-set *Involution*) has a moving, almost desperate, sombreness. When the contract ran out in 1970 Hill moved to upstate New York. His career during the 70s is rather a mystery and he has seemed reluctant to clarify it, but he did hold a number of academic posts, including composer-in-residence at Colgate University in New York (where he wrote pieces for string quartet and orchestra) and with the Smithsonian Institute, for whom he toured rural areas of the US, playing hospitals, prisons and introducing jazz to an entirely new audience. In 1977 he moved to Pittsburgh, California (near San Francisco), and from the early 80s his career seemed to take off again, with more record releases (most notably the 1986 recording *Shades*, with Clifford Jordan) and tours, including a season at New York's Knitting Factory, and a Contemporary Music Network tour of Britain with Howard Riley, Joachim Kühn and Jason Rebello in 1990. Now re-signed to the new Blue Note, where he has been paired with the upcoming alto saxophonist Greg Osby, Hill is a highly individual pianist and composer who is often compared with Thelonious Monk and Cecil Taylor, if only by virtue of his uniqueness. This quality has persisted through the brooding power of his 60s music to the more celebratory feel of recent releases. 'I'd say interesting . . . happy . . . warm', is how Hill responded to a 1976 request to describe his style. 'There was an angry period, but you get tired of pounding the piano. It's too good an instrument.'

● ALBUMS: *So In Love With The Sound Of Andrew Hill* (Warwick 1960)★★★, *Black Fire* (Blue Note 1963)★★★★, *Judgement!* (Blue Note 1964)★★★, *Smoke Stack* (Blue Note 1964)★★★★, *Point Of Departure* (Blue Note 1965)★★★★★, *Andrew!!! - The Music Of Andrew Hill* (Blue Note 1965)★★★, *Compulsion* (Blue Note 1965)★★★★, *Grass Roots* (Blue Note 1968)★★★★, *Lift Every Voice* (Blue Note 1969)★★★, *Invitation* (Steeple Chase 1974)★★★, *Spiral* (Freedom 1975)★★★, *Live At Montreux* (Freedom 1975)★★★, *One For One* 1969/70 recordings (Blue Note 1975)★★★, with Sam Rivers *Involution* 1966 recording (Blue Note 1975)★★★★, *Divine Revelation* (1976)★★★, *Nefertiti* (East Wind 1976)★★★★, *From California With Love* (Artists House 1979)★★★, *Dance With Death* 1968 recording (Blue Note 1980)★★★, *Strange Serenade* (Soul Note 1980)★★★, *Faces Of Hope* (Soul Note 1980)★★★, *Solo Piano* (Artists House 1981)★★★, *Shades* (Soul Note 1987)★★★, *Verona Rag* (Soul Note 1987)★★★, *Eternal Spirit* (Blue Note 1989)★★★, *Black Fire* (Blue Note 1989)★★★, *But Not Farewell* (Blue Note 1991)★★★.

● COMPILATIONS: *The Complete Blue Note Andrew Hill Sessions: 1963-1966* box set (Mosaic 1996)★★★★.

HILL, ERNEST

b 14 March 1900, Pittsburgh, Pennsylvania, USA, d. 16 September 1964. In his earlier years Hill played brass bass as well as string bass, eventually concentrating on the latter. In the early 20s he was with the orchestra led by Claude Hopkins that visited Europe as part of a show featuring Joséphine Baker. In New York he again played with Hopkins, then several other bands in the city, and in the early 30s was with Chick Webb, Benny Carter, Willie Bryant and Rex Stewart. Towards the end of the 30s he again travelled to Europe where he worked until the start of World War II. In 1940 he returned to New York, again spent time with Hopkins, then toured with Zutty Singleton, Louis Armstrong, Hopkins yet again, and Cliff Jackson. He also toured with the globe-trotting band Herbie Cowens took on USO tours. Towards the end of the 40s, Hill was again in Europe, playing with Bill Coleman, Frank 'Big Boy' Goudie and others. In the early 50s he was back in the USA, performing with several bands including that led by Happy Caldwell. As his career suggests, Hill was not only footloose but also held in high regard by bandleaders who welcomed his presence in their bands for the solidity he brought to rhythm sections.

HILL, TEDDY

b. Theodore Hill, 7 December 1909, Birmingham, Alabama, USA, d. 19 May 1978. After playing drums and trumpet, Hill switched to reed instruments and toured theatre circuits. In 1928 he joined Luis Russell as both sideman and assistant manager. In the early 30s he worked with James P. Johnson and then led his own big band, which survived until 1940. Hill's band held an occasional residency at the Savoy in Harlem and in 1937 toured Europe and the UK. During its existence, the band was home at one time or another to several outstanding jazzmen, including Chu Berry, Dicky Wells and a succession of fine trumpeters, among whom were Roy Eldridge, Bill Coleman, Shad Collins, Frankie Newton and Dizzy Gillespie. In 1940, Hill became manager of Minton's Playhouse and thus presided benevolently over the emergence of bebop, as his former sideman Gillespie joined with other revolutionaries in experimentation. While this might seem far removed from Hill's earlier role in jazz, in fact it reflected his lifelong interest in new developments. After Minton's closed, Hill continued in club management elsewhere.

● COMPILATIONS: *Teddy Hill And Cab Calloway* (1935-36 recordings, one side only)★★, *Uptown Rhapsody* (Hep Jazz 1992)★★★.

HINES, EARL 'FATHA'

b. 28 December 1903, Dusquesne, Pennsylvania, USA, d. 22 April 1983, Oakland, California, USA. An outstanding musician and a major figure in the evolution of jazz piano playing, Hines began his professional career in 1918. By that time he had already played cornet in brass bands in his home town. By 1923, the year in which he moved to Chicago, Hines had played in several bands around Pittsburgh and had been musical director for singer Lois Deppe. He performed in bands in Chicago and also toured theatre circuits based on the city. Among the bands with which he played were those led by Carroll Dickerson and Erskine Tate. In 1927 he teamed up with Louis Armstrong, playing piano, acting as musical director and, briefly, as Armstrong's partner in a nightclub (the third partner was Zutty Singleton). With Armstrong, Hines made a series of recordings in the late 20s which became and have remained classics: these were principally Hot Five, Hot Seven or Savoy Ballroom Five tracks but also included the acclaimed duet 'Weather Bird', one of the peaks of early jazz. Also in 1927 he was with Jimmy Noone's band and the following year was invited to form a band for a residency at Chicago's Grand Terrace. Although enormously popular at this engagement, the long residency, which lasted throughout the 30s, had an adverse effect upon the band's standing in big band history. Less well-known than the bands that toured the USA during the swing era, it was only through records and occasional radio broadcasts from live venues that the majority of big band fans could hear what Hines was doing. With outstanding arrangers such as Jimmy Mundy and top-flight sectionmen including Trummy Young, Darnell Howard and Omer Simeon, the band was in fact advancing musically at a speed which outstripped many of its better-known contemporaries. This was particularly so after 1937 when arranger Budd Johnson arrived, bringing an advanced approach to big band styling which foreshadowed later developments in bebop. The reason why Hines stayed at the Grand Terrace for so long is open to question, but some who were there have suggested that he had little choice: the Grand Terrace was run by mobsters and, as Jo Jones remarked, 'Earl had to play with a knife at his throat and a gun at his back the whole time he was in Chicago'.

In the early 40s Hines hired several musicians who modernized the band's sound still further, including Dizzy Gillespie, Charlie Parker and Wardell Gray, which led to Duke Ellington dubbing the band 'the incubator of bebop'. Hines also hired singers Billy Eckstine and Sarah Vaughan; but he eventually folded the big band in 1947 and the following year joined Louis Armstrong's All Stars, where he remained until 1951. He then led his own small groups, holding a long residency at the Club Hangover in San Francisco. In 1957 he toured Europe as co-leader, with Jack Teagarden, of an all-star band modelled on the Armstrong All Stars. For all this activity, however, Hines's career in the 50s and early 60s was decidedly low-profile and many thought his great days were over. A series of concerts in New York in 1964, organized by writer Stanley Dance, changed all that. A succession of fine recording dates capitalized upon the enormous success of the concerts and from that point until his death Hines toured and recorded extensively. Despite the heavy schedule he set himself the standard of his performances was seldom less than excellent and was often beyond praise. If, in later years, his accompanying musicians were of a very different calibre to their leader, his own inventiveness and command were at their peak and some of his performances from the 70s rank with his groundbreaking work from half a century before. A brilliant and dynamic player, Hines had an astonishing technique which employed a dramatic tremolo. As indicated, as a soloist his powers of invention were phenomenal. However, he was initially an ensemble player who later developed into a great solo artist, unlike many pianists who began as soloists and had to adapt their style to suit a role within a band. Hines adopted an innovative style for the piano in jazz in which he clearly articulated the melody, used single note lines played in octaves, and employed his distinctive tremolo in a manner that resembled that of a wind player's vibrato. All this helped to land his technique with the potentially misleading term, 'trumpet style'. The number of pianists Hines influenced is impossible to determine: it is not too extravagant to suggest that everyone who played jazz piano after 1927 was in some way following the paths he signposted. Certainly his playing was influential upon Nat 'King' Cole, Mary Lou Williams, Billy Kyle and even the much less flamboyant Teddy Wilson, who were themselves important innovators of the 30s. During this period, perhaps only Art Tatum can be cited as following his own star.

● ALBUMS: *Earl Hines And The All Stars* 10-inch album (Mercury 1950)★★★★, *Piano Moods* 10-inch album (Columbia 1951)★★★★, *Fats Waller Memorial Set* 10-inch album (Advance 1951)★★★★, *Earl Hines QRS Solos* 10-inch album (Atlantic 1952)★★★, *Earl Hines Trio* 10-inch album (Dial 1952)★★★, *Earl Hines All Stars* 10-inch album (Dial 1953)★★★★, with Billy Eckstine *Earl Hines With Billy Eckstine* 10-inch album (RCA Victor 1953)★★★, *Earl Hines Plays Fats Waller* 10-inch album (Brunswick 1953)★★★★, *Earl 'Fatha' Hines* 10-inch album (Nocturne 1954)★★★, *Piano Solos* 10-inch album (X 1954)★★★, *Earl Hines At Club Hangover* (1955)★★★, *After You've Gone* (1956)★★★, *'Fatha' Plays 'Fats'* (Fantasy 1956)★★★★, *Earl 'Fatha' Hines Solo* (Fantasy 1956)★★★★, *Oh, Father!* (Epic 1956)★★★, *Here Is Earl Hines* (1957)★★★, with Jack Teagarden *The Jack Teagarden-Earl Hines All Stars In England* (1957)★★★★, with Teagarden *The Jack Teagarden-Earl Hines All Stars At The Olympia Theatre, Paris* (1957)★★★, *Earl 'Fatha' Hines* (Epic 1958)★★★, *'Fatha'* reissued as *Swingin' And Singin'* (Tops 1958)★★★, *Earl's Pearls* (MGM 1960)★★★, *All Stars* (Jazz Panorama 1961)★★★, *A Monday Date* (Riverside 1961)★★★★, *Earl Hines With Ralph Carmichael And His Orchestra* (1963)★★★, *Earl 'Fatha' Hines* (Capitol 1963)★★★★, *Spontaneous Explorations* (Contact 2 1964)★★★, *The Earl Hines Trio At The Little Theatre, New York* (1964)★★★★, *The Real Earl Hines In Concert* (Focus 1965)★★★, *The New Earl Hines Trio* (Columbia 1965)★★★, *The Grand Terrace Band* (RCA Victor

1965)★★★, *Up To Date* (RCA Victor 1965)★★★, with Coleman Hawkins *Grand Reunion* (Limelight 1965)★★★★, with Roy Eldridge *Grand Reunion, Volume 2* (Limelight 1965)★★★★, *Hines '65/Tea For Two* (1965)★★★★, *Blues In Thirds* (Black Lion 1965)★★★, *Paris Session* (Ducretet Thompson 1965)★★★, *Father's Freeway* (1965)★★★, *Once Upon A Time* (Impulse! 1966)★★★, *Earl Hines At The Scandiano Di Reggio, Emilia* (1966)★★★, *Blues So Low (For Fats)* (1966)★★★★, *Dinah* (1966)★★★, *Life With Fatha* (Verve 1966)★★★, *Blues And Things* (1967)★★★, *Fatha Blows Best* (1968)★★★, *A Night At Johnnie's* (1968)★★★, *Master Jazz Piano Vols 1 & 2* (1969)★★★★, *Earl Hines At Home* (Delmark 1969)★★★★, *Boogie Woogie On St Louis Blues* i (1969)★★★, *Quintessential Recording Session* (Halcyon 1970)★★★, *Fatha And His Flock On Tour* (1970)★★★, *Earl Hines And Maxine Sullivan Live At The Overseas Press Club, New York* (1970)★★★★, *Earl Hines In Paris* (1970)★★★★, *It Don't Mean A Thing If It Ain't Got That Swing* (1970)★★★, *Master Jazz Piano Vols 3 & 4* (1971)★★★, with Jaki Byard *Duet* (1972)★★★, *Solo Walk In Tokyo* (Biograph 1972)★★★, *Tour De Force* (Black Lion 1972)★★★, *Earl Hines Plays Duke Ellington Vols 1-3* (Master Jazz 1972)★★★★, *Hines Plays Hines* (Swaggie 1972)★★★★, *My Tribute To Louis* (1973)★★★★, *Hines Does Hoagy* (Audiophile 1973)★★★★, *Hines Comes In Handy* (1973)★★★, *Back On The Street* (1973)★★★, *Live At The New School* (Chiaroscuro 1973)★★★, *Quintessential Recording Session Continued* (1973)★★★, *An Evening With Earl Hines And His Quartet* (1973)★★★, *Earl Hines Plays George Gershwin* (1973)★★★, *Swingin' Away* (1973)★★★, *Quintessential 1974* (1974)★★★, *One For My Baby* (1974)★★★, *Masters Of Jazz Vol. 2* (Storyville 1974)★★★, *Earl Hines At The New School Vol. 2* (1974)★★★, *West Side Story* (1974)★★★, *Live!* (1974)★★★, *Fireworks* (1974)★★★, *Hines '74* (1974)★★★, *At Sundown* (1974)★★★, *The Dirty Old Men* (1974)★★★, *Jazz Giants In Nice* (1974)★★★, *Piano Portraits Of Australia* (Swaggie 1974)★★★, *Concert In Argentina* (1974)★★★, *Earl Hines In New Orleans With Wallace Davenport And Orange Kellin Vols 1 & 2* (1975)★★★★, *Earl Hines Plays Duke Ellington Vol. 4* (1975)★★★, *Earl Hines At Saralee's* (1976)★★★, *Live At Buffalo* (1976)★★★, with Joe Venuti *Hot Sonatas* (Chiaroscuro 1976)★★★★, *Jazz Is His Old Lady And My Old Man* (1977)★★★, *Lionel Hampton Presents Earl 'Fatha' Hines* (1977)★★★★, *Giants Of Jazz Vol. 2* (Storyville 1977)★★★, *Earl Hines In New Orleans* (Chiaroscuro 1977)★★★, *Father Of Modern Jazz Piano/Boogie Woogie On St Louis Blues* ii (1977)★★★★, *East Of The Sun* (1977)★★★, *Texas Ruby Red* (1977)★★★, *Deep Forest* i (1977)★★★, with Harry 'Sweets' Edison *Earl Meets Harry* (1978)★★★, with Edison, Eddie 'Lockjaw' Davis *Earl Meets Sweets And Jaws* (1978)★★★★, *Fatha' Plays Hits He Missed* (M&K Real Time 1979)★★★, *Fatha's Birthday* (1981)★★★, *Deep Forest* ii (1982)★★★, *Earl Hines Live At The New School* (1983)★★★.

● COMPILATIONS: *Swingin' Down* 1932-33 recordings ()★★★, *Fatha Jumps* 1939-45 recordings (RCA)★★★★, *Harlem Lament* 1933-38 recordings (Portrait)★★★★, *Earl Hines (1937-1939)* (Classics)★★★★, *Earl Hines (1939-1940)* (Classics)★★★★, *Piano Man* 1939-1942 recordings (Bluebird)★★★★, *Giants Of Jazz* 3-LP box set (Time Life 1981)★★★★★, *The Indispensable Earl Hines* recorded 1944-66 (RCA 1983)★★★★, *Earl Hines Big Band* 1945-46 recordings ()★★★, *Father Steps In* (Tring 1993)★★★, *Another Monday Date* (Prestige 1995)★★★, *His Best Recordings, 1927-1942* (Best Of Jazz 1998)★★★.

● FURTHER READING: *The World Of Earl Hines*, Harold Courlander.

HINO, MOTOHIKO

b. 3 January 1946, Tokyo, Japan. Hino's father was a musician and dancer and Motohiko was a tap dancer when he was eight before learning the drums when he was 10. He turned professional when he was 17 and from 1972 won, yearly, the *Swing Journal* polls as Japan's top drummer. He moved to New York in 1978. There he worked with Joe Henderson, Chuck Rainey, Jean-Luc Ponty and others before joining Hugh Masekela's band in 1979. Since 1980 he has played in the trio of JoAnne Brackeen, his sharp, dynamic drumming reflecting the playing of his two favourites, Tony Williams and Elvin Jones.

● ALBUMS: *First Album* (1970)★★★, *Toko: The Motohiko Hino Quartet At Nemu Festival* (1975)★★★, *Flash* (1977)★★, *Sailing Stone* (Gramavision 1992)★★★★, *It's There* (Enja 1993)★★★★.

HINO, TERUMASA

b. 25 October 1942, Tokyo, Japan. Following, more or less literally, in the footsteps of his trumpet-playing, tap-dancing father, Hino learned to tap at the age of four, and took up the trumpet when he was nine years old. He taught himself the principles of jazz improvisation by transcribing solos by Miles Davis (from whom, no doubt, he learned his conviction about the importance of space), Louis Armstrong, John Coltrane, Clifford Brown, Lee Morgan and Freddie Hubbard. He began playing publicly in American army clubs in 1955 in Japan, then joined Hiroshi Watanabe and Takao Kusagaya, but his first major job was with the Hideo Shiraki Quintet, where he stayed from 1965-69. During 1964-65 he had led his own group, and left Shiraki at the end of the decade in order to lead his own band full-time. In 1974 he worked with Masabumi Kikuchi, then in June 1975 he went to the USA and worked with Joachim Kuhn (1975), Gil Evans, Jackie McLean and Ken McIntyre (1976), Hal Galper (1977), Carlos Garnett (1977), Sam Jones (1978), Elvin Jones (1982) and Dave Liebman, as well as continuing to lead his own group, the band which John Scofield credits as moving him from fusion to jazz. By then Hino was dividing his time equally between the USA and Japan. He plays trumpet and flugelhorn with a mellow fire, and his fame in Europe continues to grow almost matching his reputation in Japan and the USA. He toured Europe with Eddie Harris in November 1990, and was reunited with Kikuchi for a rhythmic 1996 recording date featuring alto saxophonist Greg Osby.

● ALBUMS: *Hi-Nology* (1965)★★, *Vibrations* (Enja 1971)★★★, *Taro's Mood* (Enja 1973)★★★, with Masabumi Kikuchi *East Wind* (1974)★★★★, *Speak To Loneliness* (1975)★★★, *Live In Concert* (1975)★★, *Hogiuta* (1976)★★★, *Maiden Dance* (1978)★★★, *Terumasa Hino* (Denon 1986)★★★, *Bluestruck* (Blue Note 1990)★★★★, *From The Heart* (Blue Note 1991)★★★, *Warsaw Jazz Festival 1991* (Jazzmen 1993)★★★, *Unforgettable* (Blue Note 1993)★★★★, *Spark* (Blue Note

1994)★★★★, with Kikuchi *Acoustic Boogie* (Blue Note 1996)★★★.

HINTON, MILT

b. 23 June 1910, Vicksburg, Mississippi, USA. During the 20s Hinton played bass with artists such as Boyd Atkins, Tiny Parham and Jabbo Smith. In the early 30s he established his reputation as one of the most reliable and forward-thinking contemporary bass players during engagements with Eddie South, Erskine Tate, Zutty Singleton and Fate Marable. In 1936 he began a sustained period with Cab Calloway. Not only was he a stalwart of an excellent rhythm section but he was also a featured soloist.

He left Calloway in 1951, thereafter working as a freelance session and studio musician, appearing on countless record dates. Many of these recordings were with jazzmen but his skills were such that he was in demand for sessions by pop singers too. Nicknamed 'the Judge', Hinton also toured extensively in the 70s and 80s, including one stint with Bing Crosby, appeared at jazz festivals and clubs around the world and still found time to establish himself as a teacher and jazz photographer. An important transitional figure in jazz bass playing, Hinton's career comfortably spanned the change from swing to bop, whilst his versatility ensured that so long as popular songs were being recorded he could work anywhere.

● ALBUMS: *The Milt Hinton Quartet* (1955)★★★, *Milt Hinton With Manny Albam's Orchestra* (1955)★★, *Here Swings The Judge* (1964-75)★★★, *Basically With Blue* (1976)★★, *The Trio* (1977)★★★, *Back To Bass-ics* (Progressive 1984)★★★, *We Three Live In New York* (1985)★★★, *The Judge's Decision* (Exposure 1995)★★★, *Old Man Time* (1989-90)★★★★, *Laughing At Life* (Columbia 1995)★★.

● COMPILATIONS: *Sixteen Cab Calloway Classics* (1939-41)★★★★.

● FURTHER READING: *Bass Line*, Milt Hinton and David G. Berger.

HINZE, CHRIS

b. 30 June 1938, Hilversum, The Netherlands. Hinze's father was a conductor and he learned the piano and flute as a child. He studied flute at the Royal Conservatory in The Hague and then learned arranging at the Berklee College Of Music in the USA. He won a prize for the best soloist at the Montreux Jazz Festival in 1970 and formed his jazz fusion group the Combination the following year. He founded his own record label Keytone and has often worked as a producer for other musicians. He moved to New York in 1976 but in the late 70s toured Europe with Chris Hinze And Friends and then in a duo with guitarist Sigi Schwab. In 1972 he won the Beethoven Award of the City of Bonn for a suite called *Live Music Now*. He continued to write and record symphonic works as well as presenting jazz versions of Baroque composers with his band. He recorded an album of flute solos in the Ellora Caves in India in 1979 and the following year recorded a reggae album with Peter Tosh. He has since included African and Indian musicians in the Combination.

● ALBUMS: *Stoned Flute* (1971)★★★, *Virgin Sacrifice* (1972)★★★, *Mange* (1974)★★, *Variations On Bach* (1976)★★★, *Silhouettes* (1977)★★★, *Flute And Mantras* (1979)★★★, with Peter Tosh *World Sound And Power* (1980)★★★★, *Chris Hinze/Sigi Schwab Duo* (1980)★★★, *Mirror Of Dreams* (1982)★★★, *Backstage* (1983)★★, *Saliah* (1985)★★★.

HIPP, JUTTA

b. 4 February 1925, Leipzig, Germany. Although her musical career was quite brief, Hipp made a big impression in post-war Europe. She studied piano formally as a child, taking an interest in jazz in her mid-teens. At the end of the war she formed her own small band, mostly playing bop. After playing throughout Europe, in the mid-50s she visited the USA where she led a trio that was completed by Peter Ind and Ed Thigpen. By the late 50s, however, Hipp had decided to concentrate upon being a painter. On the evidence of her few recordings, Hipp's decision to abandon professional music was purely a matter of personal choice and by no means an indication of either technical inability or lack of imaginative talent.

● ALBUMS: *Cool Europe* (MGM 1955)★★★, *New Faces-New Sounds From Germany* 10-inch album (Blue Note 1955)★★★, *At The Hickory House, Volume 1* (Blue Note 1956)★★★, *At The Hickory House, Volume 2* (Blue Note 1956)★★★, with Zoot Sims *Jutta Hipp With Zoot Sims* (Blue Note 1956)★★★★.

HIRT, AL

b. 7 November 1922, New Orleans, Louisiana, USA. After studying classical music, trumpeter Hirt divided his professional career between symphony orchestras and dance bands and still found time to play dixieland jazz in New Orleans clubs. Among the bands with which he played were those led by Tommy Dorsey and Ray McKinley, and a sideman in one of his own first bands was Pete Fountain. In the 60s an important recording contract (which resulted in albums under his own name and as accompanist to some transiently popular singers) a successful residency at his own club and a spectacular technique all helped to turn him into one of the best-known trumpeters in jazz. In the 60s, Hirt had 17 albums in the US jazz charts. As often happens, commercial success brought a measure of condemnation from jazz hardliners but Hirt was unmoved. He continued to perform in clubs and to record throughout the 70s, shrugging off a lip injury, and was still playing his high-spirited, good-humoured jazz in the 80s.

● ALBUMS: *The Greatest Horn In The World* (1961),★★★ *Al (He's The King) Hirt And his Band* (1961)★★, *Bourbon Street* (1962)★★★, *Horn-A-Plenty* (1962)★★★★, *Trumpet And Strings* (1963)★★★, *Our Man In New Orleans* (Novus 1963)★★★★, *Honey In The Horn* (1963)★★★, *Beauty And The Band* (1964)★★★, *Cotton Candy* (1964)★★, *Sugar Lips* (1964)★★★, *Pops Goes The Trumpet* (1964), *That Honey Horn Sound* (1965)★★, *Live At Carnegie Hall* (1965)★★★, *They're Playing Our Song* (1966)★★★, *The Happy Trumpet* (1966)★★★, *Music To Watch Girls Go By* (1967)★★★, *Al Hirt Plays Bert Kaempfert* (1968)★★, *Solid Gold Brass* (RCA 1982)★★★, *Al Hirt* (Audio

Fidelity 1984)★★★, *Pops Goes The Trumpet* (1985)★★★.

● COMPILATIONS: *The Best Of Al Hirt* (1965)★★★★.

HISEMAN, JON

b. 21 June 1944, Woolwich, London, England. Hiseman studied violin and piano from an early age, but only applied himself to drums when he was 13 years old. The skiffle craze resulted in Hiseman playing all kinds of blues, jazz and hokum in the early 60s. In 1964 he was a founder member of the New Jazz Orchestra. Between 1966 and 1967 he drummed for the Graham Bond Organisation and then left to join Georgie Fame in the Blue Flames. After six months with John Mayall he formed his own Colosseum in 1968, a celebrated jazz/rock band which included saxophonist Dick Heckstall-Smith and Dave Greenslade on electric piano. Colosseum attracted a lot of attention and was one of the leading jazz/rock combos of all time. Hiseman's drums were much in demand, and he recorded frequently with pianist Mike Taylor, Jack Bruce and John Surman. In 1970 Colosseum released *Daughter Of Time* with Chris Farlowe on vocals, and ambitious lyrics from Hiseman that were typical of the period. Farlowe then left to form Atomic Rooster. After a year of studio work Hiseman formed Tempest, which was not a success. In 1975 he helped to organize the United Jazz & Rock Ensemble, and also formed Colosseum II with Gary Moore of Thin Lizzy. In 1979 he joined his wife, saxophonist Barbara Thompson, in Paraphernalia, which has made sporadic tours and albums ever since. The impact of punk aligned the couple with the musical establishment; they recorded for Andrew Lloyd Webber on *Variations* and on 1982's hit musical, *Cats*. Hiseman now runs a record company, TM Records, a PA hire company and manages Thompson, plays in her band as well as maintaining a busy schedule of production and session work. He reunited with his colleagues in Colosseum in 1997.

● ALBUMS: with Colosseum *Those Who Are About To Die Salute You* (Fontana 1969)★★★★, *Valentyne Suite* (Vertigo 1969)★★★★, *The Daughter Of Time* (Vertigo 1970)★★, *Live* (Bronze 1971)★★★, *Strange New Flesh* (1976)★★, *Electric Savage* (1977)★★, *Wardance* (1977)★★.

● COMPILATIONS: *The Grass Is Greener* (Vertigo 1969)★★★, *Collector's Colosseum* (1971)★★★, *Pop Chronik* (1974)★★★, *Epitaph* (1986), *The Golden Decade Of Colosseum* (1990)★★★, with Paraphernalia *Live In Concert* (1980)★★★.

HITE, LES

b. 13 February 1903, DuQuoin, Illinois, USA, d. 6 February 1962. One of the most important figures in the southern Californian jazz scene of the 20s and early 30s, alto saxophonist Hite worked in numerous bands, often taking on responsibilities above that of sideman. In 1930 he took over leadership of Paul Howard's Quality Serenaders, which included in its ranks Lawrence Brown and Lionel Hampton. Securing a residency at Frank Sebastian's Cotton Club in Los Angeles, Hite backed many top line jazz artists, notably Fats Waller and Louis Armstrong, with whom he made some excellent recordings, and also appeared in films. Hite continued leading bands into the 40s, hiring musicians such as Dizzy Gillespie, but left the jazz scene in 1945. Thereafter, he ran a booking agency in California. Hite always demonstrated an ability to attract first-class musicians. Apart from those named above he also had George Orendorff, Joe 'King' Porter and Marshal Royal in his bands. Much less well-known outside jazz circles was another Hite sideman, trumpeter Lloyd Reese, who taught Dexter Gordon, Buddy Collette, Charles Mingus and Eric Dolphy among many others. Hite died in February 1962.

● COMPILATIONS: with Louis Armstrong *Louis In Los Angeles* (1930-31 recordings)★★★★.

HODEIR, ANDRÉ

b. 22 January 1921, Paris, France. Hodeir studied musical formally for many years but also developed a fascination for jazz. In the late 40s he frequently wrote jazz criticism, becoming chief editor of the French magazine *Jazz Hot*. He also wrote an important book, first published in the USA in 1956 under the title *Jazz: Its Evolution And Essence*. He played violin and recorded with various jazz groups, including musicians such as Django Reinhardt and Kenny Clarke. However, Hodeir was more interested in composing and writing about jazz and his playing days were thus numbered. From the mid-50s until the end of the 60s he co-led a band, Jazz Groupe De Paris, with Bobby Jaspar, a vehicle for his own compositions. In the 60s he took an interest in third stream music, composing in this hybrid medium. He was also in demand as a composer of music for the soundtracks of motion pictures. By the 80s Hodeir had abandoned composing, channelling most of his energies into writing. From recordings of his work, Hodeir's composing and arranging talents are evident, although there is much about his composing, especially in third-stream mode, that makes his work less than readily accessible to the general listener. His criticism is also interesting and perceptive although often pugnaciously argumentative and sometimes slightly wrong-headed. Nevertheless, he is always thought-provoking and some of his in-depth analyses are incisive and informed.

● ALBUMS: *Autour D'un Récif, St-Tropez* (Swing 1952)★★★, *Essais* (Swing 1954)★★★, *Le Jazz Groupe De Paris Joue André Hodeir* (Vega 1956)★★★★, as arranger *The Kenny Clarke Sextet Plays André Hodeir* (Philips 1956)★★, *Jazz Et Jazz* (Fontana 1963)★★★, *Anna Livia Plurabelle* (Epic 1966)★★★, *Bitter Ending* (Epic 1972)★★★.

HODES, ART

b. 14 November 1904, Nikoliev, Ukraine, d. 4 March 1993, Harvey, Illinois, USA. A few months after Hodes was born, his family emigrated from Russia and settled in Chicago, Illinois. He began playing piano and by his late teenage years was working in dance halls and clubs. He played with several local bands, including Wingy Manone's, but also established himself as a solo performer. For the next 10 years he was active in Chicago, but in 1938 moved to New York, where he played with jazzmen including Joe Marsala, Sidney Bechet and Mezz Mezzrow, continuing into the early 40s. During this time he had his first experience as a radio broadcaster, presenting record shows. He also began to write, and for some years was editor of *Jazz Record* magazine. He led his own bands for engagements at many clubs and restaurants in and around New York, but at the end of the 40s decided to move back to Chicago. For the next four decades he led bands, played solo piano, taught, broadcast on radio and television, all in and around Chicago. In the 60s he recorded with Truck Parham and Estelle 'Mama' Yancey. Hodes made occasional tours, including trips to Denmark, Europe and Canada, where he worked with Jim Galloway, one of their concerts being recorded and released as *Live From Toronto*. In the early 80s he appeared again in New York, but he remained true to his adopted hometown. Stylistically, Hodes was strongly rooted in the blues. His knowledge of blues piano and stride, allied to his teaching, writing and demonstration, helped keep the forms alive. In 1977 some of his earlier and perceptive writings for *Jazz Record* were published in book form.

● ALBUMS: with Albert Nicholas *The New Orleans Chicago Connection* (Delmark 1959)★★★, *Mama Yancey Sings, Art Hodes Plays Blues* (1965)★★★★, *Someone To Watch Over Me* (1981)★★★, *Art Hodes: South Side Memories* (1984)★★★, *Blues In The Night* (1987)★★, *Joy to The World - Yuletide Piano Solos* (1987)★★, with Wally Fawkes *Midnight Blue* (1987)★★★, *Live From Toronto* (1988)★★★, *The Music Of Lovie Austin* (1988)★★★, *Pagin' Mr Jelly* (Candid 1988)★★★, with Volly DeFaut *Up In Volly's Room* 50s recordings (Delmark 1993)★★, *Sessions At Blue Note* (Dormouse 1991)★★★★, *Hode's Art* 1968-1972 recordings (Delmark 1995)★★★, *Keepin' Out Of Mischief Now* (Candid/Koch 1995)★★★, *Hodes' Art* 1968 and 1972 recordings (Delmark 1996)★★★★.

● FURTHER READING: *Selections From The Gutter: Jazz Portraits From 'The Jazz Record'*, Art Hodes and Chadwick Hansen (ed.).

HODGES, JOHNNY

b. 25 July 1907, Cambridge, Massachusetts, USA, d. 11 May 1970. One of the greatest alto saxophonists in jazz, Hodges first tried other instruments before settling upon the one that would best serve his glorious romanticism. Largely self-taught, Hodges played in a number of minor bands in Boston and New York in the early 20s but also spent a little time with Willie 'The Lion' Smith, in whose band he replaced Sidney Bechet - who had given him some of the little instruction he ever received. In 1926 he joined Chick Webb, where his brother-in-law, Don Kirkpatrick, was pianist-arranger. Two years later Hodges began an association with Duke Ellington that would continue virtually uninterrupted for the rest of his life. Apart from playing on hundreds of records with Ellington, soloing magnificently on many, Hodges also originated several tunes that Ellington developed, among them 'Jeep's Blues' and 'The Jeep Is Jumpin'' ('Jeep' was one of Hodges' nicknames; others were 'Rabbit' and 'Squatty Roo'). From 1951-55 Hodges led his own band, which briefly included John Coltrane in its ranks, and had a hit record with 'Castle Rock'. In 1958 and again in 1961 he worked outside the Ellington orchestra but always in an Ellingtonian style. Although capable of playing low-down blues, Hodges was in his true element as a balladeer. The lush beauty of his playing was perfectly exhibited on compositions created for his special talents by Ellington and by Billy Strayhorn. Among the many tunes on which he played, and frequently recorded, were 'I Let A Song Go Out Of My Heart', 'Warm Valley', 'Black Butterfly', 'Isfahan' (from the 'Far East Suite') and 'Empty Ballroom Blues'. Hodges recorded several albums for Norman Granz, including a 1952 jam session that teamed him with fellow altoists Benny Carter and Charlie Parker and organist Wild Bill Davis. Despite the excellence of all his other forays, however, it is for his work with Ellington that he will be remembered. The liquid beauty of Hodges' contribution to the sound of the Ellington band, and especially to the manner in which it played ballads, was so crucial that his death in May 1970 marked the end of an era: as Ellington himself observed, 'our band will never sound the same'. Throughout his long career Hodges was indisputably among the finest alto players in jazz. Even though, after the early 40s, Charlie Parker took the alto saxophone in other directions, Hodges remains one of the giants of the instrument.

● ALBUMS: *Johnny Hodges, Volume 1* 10-inch album (Mercer 1951)★★★, *Johnny Hodges, Volume 2* 10-inch album (Mercer 1951)★★★, with Benny Carter, Charlie Parker *Norman Granz Jam Session* (1952)★★★★, *Alto Sax* 10-inch album (RCA Victor 1952)★★★, *Johnny Hodges Collates* 10-inch album (Mercury 1952)★★★, *Swing With Johnny Hodges* 10-inch album (Norgran 1954)★★★, *Memories Of Ellington* reissued as *In A Mellow Tone* (Norgran 1954)★★★, *More Of Johnny Hodges* (Norgran 1954)★★★, *Johnny Hodges Dance Bash* reissued as *Perdido* (Norgran 1955)★★★, *Creamy* (Norgran 1955)★★★, *Castle Rock* (Norgran 1955)★★★, *Hodge Podge* (Epic 1955)★★★, *Ellingtonia '56* (Norgran 1956)★★★★, with Duke Ellington *Ellington At Newport '56* (Columbia 1956)★★★★★, *In A Tender Mood* (Norgran 1956)★★★★, *Used To Be Duke* (Norgran 1956)★★★, *The Blues* (Norgran 1956)★★★, *Duke's In Bed* (Verve 1957)★★★, *The Big Sound* (Verve 1958)★★★, *The Prettiest Gershwin* (Verve 1959)★★★, with Ellington *Back To Back: Duke Ellington And Johnny Hodges Play The Blues* (Verve 1959)★★★★, with Ellington *Side By Side* (Verve 1959)★★★, *The Smooth One* (Verve 1960)★★★, *Not So Dukish* (Verve 1960)★★★, with Ellington *The Nutcracker Suite* (Columbia 1960)★★★, *Master Of Jazz* (1960)★★★, *Blues-A-Plenty* (Verve 1960)★★★★, *The Johnny Hodges All Stars/The Johnny Hodges-Harry Carney Sextet* (1961)★★★, *Johnny Hodges At The Sportspalast, Berlin* (1961)★★★, *Johnny Hodges In Scandinavia* (1961)★★★, with Wild Bill Davis *Johnny Hodges And Wild Bill Davis* (Verve 1961)★★★, with Billy Strayhorn *Johnny Hodges With Billy Strayhorn And His Orchestra* (Verve 1962)★★★★, *Johnny Hodges With Claus Ogermann's Orchestra* (1963)★★★, with Davis *Mess Of Blues* (Verve 1964)★★★★, with Davis *Blue Rabbit* (Verve 1964)★★★, *Everybody Knows Johnny Hodges* (Impulse! 1964)★★★, with Davis *Blue Pyramid* (Verve 1965)★★★★, with

Davis *Wings And Things* (Verve 1965)★★★, with Lawrence Welk *Johnny Hodges With Lawrence Welk's Orchestra* (Dot 1965)★★★, *Johnny Hodges And All The Dukesmen* (Verve 1966)★★★, *Alto Blue* (Verve 1966)★★★, with Earl Hines *Stride Right* (Verve 1966)★★★, *In A Mellotone* (Bluebird 1966)★★★★, *Things Ain't What They Used To Be* (RCA Victor 1966)★★★, with Ellington *Far East Suite* (RCA Victor 1967)★★★★, *Triple Play* (RCA Victor 1967)★★★★, *Don't Sleep In The Subway* (Verve 1967)★★★, with Hines *Swing's Our Thing* (Verve 1967)★★★★, *Rippin' And Runnin'* (Verve 1968)★★★, *3 Shades Of Blue* (1970)★★★.

● COMPILATIONS: *The Indispensable Duke Ellington Volumes 1-12* (RCA 1983-87)★★★, with Ellington *The Blanton-Webster Band* (RCA Bluebird 1987)★★★★★, *Love In Swingtime (1938-39)* (Tax 1988)★★★, *The Complete Johnny Hodges Sessions 1951-1955* 6-LP box set (1989)★★★★★, *Rarities And Private Recordings* (Suisa 1992)★★★.

HODGKINSON, COLIN

b. 14 October 1945, Peterborough, England. Hodgkinson is a self-taught bass player who turned professional with a jazz trio in 1966. In 1969 he began a long association with Alexis Korner, during which time they played in everything from a duo to a big band. In 1972 Hodgkinson and Ron Aspery (reeds) took time off in Yorkshire to write music. The two were joined by drummer Tony Hicks in the trio Back Door in which Hodgkinson had an opportunity to display his amazing technical facility. The band toured Europe and the USA and played at the Montreux Jazz Festival. In 1978 he began another long association, this time with Jan Hammer. Though he had written a lot for Back Door, with Hammer he writes lyrics more than tunes. In the late 80s he also played with Brian Auger's Blues Reunion and in the mid-90s was constantly working, touring at times with various versions of the Spencer Davis Group. Hodgkinson is one of the few people who can make the solo bass sound quite unlike any other instrument. His solo version of 'San Francisco Bay Blues' is breathtakingly original.

● ALBUMS: with Alexis Korner *New Church* (1970)★★★, with Jan Hammer *Black Sheep* (1979)★★★★, *Hammer* (1980)★★★, *Here To Stay* (1982)★★, *City Slicker* (1986)★★★.

HOGGARD, JAY

b. 24 September 1954, New York, USA. After learning to play the piano and saxophone as a child Hoggard studied vibraphone with Lynn Oliver. He went to Wesleyan University to study philosophy but transferred to ethnomusicology. In 1973 he toured Europe in a band with Jimmy Garrison (bass) and Clifford Thornton (trumpet) who were members of the faculty. He joined a group at Yale which included Anthony Davis (piano) and Leo Smith (trumpet). During a summer study in Tanzania he learned to play the balo, a West African xylophone. He returned to the USA to teach at the Educational Centre for Arts in New Haven. He moved to New York in 1977 and worked regularly with Chico Freeman, Anthony Davis, Sam Rivers, Cecil Taylor and James Newton (flute). As well as his vibraphone playing, which some find a little too mellow, he is able to bring his knowledge of and interest in ethnic music to any group with which he plays.

● ALBUMS: with Chico Freeman *Kings Of Mali* (1977)★★★★, *The Search* (1983)★★★; solo *A Solo Vibes Concert* (1978)★★★★, *Days Like These* (1979)★★★, *Rain Forest* (1980)★★★, *Mystic Winds, Tropic Breezes* (1981)★★, *Love Survives* (1983)★★★, *The Little Tiger* (1991)★★★, with James Newton *Luella* (1983)★★★, *In The Spirit* (1993)★★.

HOLDER, TERRENCE

b. c.1898. Holder's early background is extremely sketchy, but by the early 20s he was well-established as lead trumpet and principal soloist with Alphonso Trent's important territory band. In the middle of the decade he formed his own band, the Dark Clouds Of Joy, which was based in Dallas, Texas. In 1929, while undergoing financial and domestic strain, Holder resigned and the band was taken over by one of his leading sidemen, Andy Kirk. Although Kirk retained most of the original name, calling the band the Clouds Of Joy, Holder was undeterred and formed a new band with the same name as before. He continued to play into the mid-30s, employing a number of outstanding musicians who used his and other territory bands as training grounds before gaining major success elsewhere. Among the artists who played with Holder at various times were Don Byas, Budd Johnson, Herschel Evans, Earl Bostic, Carl 'Tatti' Smith and Buddy Tate. After folding his band in the late 30s Holder drifted in and out of music, never making the breakthrough into national fame. Reputedly a fine player, Holder was still working intermittently into the 60s. It must be assumed that he is now dead, although like his music, his demise has gone unrecorded.

HOLDSWORTH, ALLAN

b. 6 August 1946, Leeds, England. The professional regard for this Leeds guitarist is illustrated by the range of people with whom he has appeared, starting with Ian Carr's Nucleus in 1972. The end of Holdsworth's time with Nucleus coincided with a spell in Jon Hiseman's Tempest (in which he also played the violin). In its turn this overlapped with membership of Soft Machine. 1977 brought a brief period with Gong, prior to forming the band UK with Bill Bruford, John Wetton, and Eddie Jobson. When Bruford left to form his own outfit, Holdsworth went with him. Typically Holdsworth soon left them, rejoining Soft Machine prior to going solo in the late 70s. After a fallow period Holdsworth seems to be more active and his work in the late 80s and 90s has shown has shown his former frantic sparkle.

● ALBUMS: *Road Games* (1983)★★★, *Metal Fatigue* (JMS 1985)★★★, *IOU* (1985)★★, *Atavachron* (JMS 1986)★★★★, *Sand* (JMS 1987)★★★, *With A Heart In My Song* (JMS 1989)★★★, *Secrets* (Cream 1989)★★★, *Wardenclyffe Tower* (Cream 1993)★★★, *Hard Hat Era* (Cream 1993)★★★, *None Too Soon* (Ah/Restless 1996)★★★.

HOLIDAY, BILLIE

b. Eleanora Harris, 7 April 1915, Philadelphia, Pennsylvania, USA, d. 17 July 1959, New York, USA. Billie 'Lady Day' taught herself to sing during her early teens in Baltimore, Maryland, where she was brought up until moving to New York in 1929. Factual inaccuracies and elements of myth and exaggeration have clouded the picture of her formative years despite the best efforts of researchers to present her career story in a properly ordered manner. Not until Stuart Nicholson's immaculately researched book appeared in 1995 was a detailed and reliable account of these years made available. Nicholson's research revealed that some of the statements made by the singer in her 1956 autobiography, *Lady Sings The Blues*, were true, despite having been dismissed as exaggeration by other writers. Holidays's teenage parents, Sadie Harris (aka Fagan) and probable father, Clarence Holiday, probably never married, and it seems unlikely that they lived together for any length of time. Holiday, a banjo and guitar player is remembered principally for his work with Fletcher Henderson's band in the early 30s. He remains a somewhat shadowy figure who left his daughter in the care of Fagan or other relatives. As a musician with touring bands in the later 20s Holiday would often be away from home, and during the stay with Henderson, which lasted until 1932, the guitarist severed connections with the Fagans. However Billie proved hard to shake off after joining her mother in New York's Harlem district, and when rent on their apartment was overdue, she confronted Clarence at the Roseland Ballroom - where Henderson's orchestra enjoyed a lengthy 'residency' - and extorted money by threatening to show him up publicly.

Fragments of information about Holiday's deprived, cruelly exploited and extravagantly ill-fated early history prove she had learned how to survive extreme poverty, race prejudice and the injustice of black ghetto life by the time she was 15 or 16. Also, they hint at a more influential relationship between father and daughter (no matter how tenuous it might have been) than Holiday revealed in print. Clarence, a more than competent guitarist with a reputation for 'good time' in a rhythm section, seemed surrounded by paradox. Through the 30s, even after his barely noted death early in 1937, compilers of books which included record reviews and personnel listings employed the spellings Haliday or Halliday, and there is evidence that Billie used that name occasionally until persuaded to sing professionally as Billie Holiday. For jazz historians the interest lies in tracking down a link between her father's fine, relaxed sense of rhythm and her own astonishing command of time and swing: *laid-back* swing of a type not previously heard on records by singers. Since Holiday had very little schooling and no formal musical training, her extraordinary creative gifts were intuitive in the first place. She developed her singing in obscure New York speakeasies and Harlem nightclubs such as Pods' and Jerry's Log Cabin, the Yeah Man, Monette Moore's Supper Club, the Hot-Cha, Alabama Grill and Dickie Wells's place. She even sang at the local Elks club in order to pick up a few dollars in tips. Poverty was the spur, the initial incentive, but the dedication she then displayed to the mastering of jazzcraft is not easy to explain. No amount of theorizing will help to a real understanding of her seemingly instinctive gift for music-making. She was a perfectionist in her fashion, depending upon her excellent ear, innate taste and honesty of purpose to make up artistically for her small voice and range. This integrity, so far as vocal sound and style went, is the more baffling because of the insecurity and brutal ugliness of her early life. (She had already survived rape at age 11 and a period in care which followed this attack. In New York she endured a brief stint as a prostitute for which she and her mother were arrested in 1929. For this she served time on the notorious Ryker's Island).

It has frequently been stated that fame and success depend largely on an artist or performer being in the right place at the right time. In Holiday's case, the lucky break came when she found herself by sheer chance singing in front of the well-connected record producer and talent spotter John Hammond Jnr. Hammond had stopped off at the 133rd Street club with the intention of listening to singer Monette Moore. Instead of the blues singer, a performer who had been recording since 1923, he heard the unknown girl deputizing for Monette (absent, playing in a Broadway show) and was immediately impressed. 'She sang popular songs in a manner that made them completely her own', Hammond wrote later in his autobiography, praising her excellent memory for lyrics and sense of phrasing. He also gave Holiday the first press notice of her career. In April 1933 it appeared in the *Melody Maker*, and Hammond wrote: 'This month there has been a real find in the person of a singer called Billie Halliday' (she had by now adopted the first name of film actress Billie Dove, a childhood favourite whom she regarded as the epitome of glamour). Hammond represented a real break in Holiday's long run of bad luck because he had the power and willingness to forward the careers of those he thought worthy of special aid. The enthusiasm of his initial reaction to the promising youngster was shown in his description, 'She is incredibly beautiful and sings as well as anybody I ever heard', printed in the 1933 *Melody Maker*. Living up to his reputation, Hammond 'got into the habit of bringing people uptown to hear Billie'. Benny Goodman shared his opinion of Holiday and agreed to record with her. In the course of three sessions during November and December 1933, two songs were recorded with Goodman in charge of a nine-man studio group most of whom were strangers to the already nervous Holiday. 'Your Mother's Son-in-Law' was the first record she ever made; 'Riffin' The Scotch', a lightweight novelty concoction, was the second. Neither was successful as a showcase for her - nor, in truth, designed to be - because her role in the proceedings presented Holiday as band vocalist in a setting which stressed the instrumental prowess of Goodman, trombonist Jack Teagarden and other soloists. However, the singer managed to stamp her imprint on the vocal refrains and, for a young black performer with no experience of recording and, in her words, 'afraid to sing in the mike', came across as reasonably confident. For the Lady (she had earned that nickname on the Harlem club circuit for her regal sense of dignity, and it was amended by Lester Young who added a typically personal touch, calling her Lady Day), expecting little she was not disappointed. Royalties were not routinely paid to recording artists in those days, and Holiday remembered receiving a flat fee of about 35 dollars for her work. Having a record on the market was no great deal; she placed little value on either song, not bothering to include them in her club or stage programmes or future recording repertoire.

Holiday continued her round of club dates, as well as being heard in the film *Symphony In Black*, made with Duke Ellington and released in 1935. Her career was given a boost when she won a week's engagement at the Apollo Theatre, Harlem's most famous and, for up-and-coming artists, formidable entertainment centre. Holiday, then just 20 years old, appeared with pianist Bobbie Henderson and her notices were, at best, mildly critical. Clearly, her relaxed, seemingly lazy, behind-the-beat style did not appeal to the Apollo's often vociferous patrons. Nevertheless, when the entire show was held over for a second week, at which time she appeared with Ralph Cooper's orchestra, her notices improved thanks to her capacity to adapt. By this time, Holiday had settled on the spelling of her name (earlier, her given name, Eleanora, was also subject to variation).

By mid-July the singer had returned to the record studio and used her real name on a session organized by Hammond and directed by Teddy Wilson. In Wilson, an accomplished musician and sensitive pianist, Holiday had found the sympathetic partner she needed to reveal the full range of her talents. The four songs picked for this groundbreaking record date were above average - 'I Wished On The Moon' and 'Miss Brown To You' were film numbers - and the easygoing jam-session atmosphere suited Holiday admirably. She responded to Wilson's masterly accompaniments and solo playing, and to the brilliance of Goodman, Roy Eldridge and Ben Webster, and similar jazz aces on subsequent recordings. They in turn seemed to be spurred by the rhythmic thrust and innovative magic of her singing. Here was a rising star (since 10 July 1936 she had achieved own-name status on the Vocalion label) who could invest ordinary popular songs with the emotional kick of a first-rate blues or ballad composition. The records also paid off sufficiently well to satisfy the market men. Following appearances at a few slightly more prestigious venues than hitherto, Holiday sang with the bands of Count Basie (1937-38) and Artie Shaw (1938). She enjoyed the company of the bandsmen, and had an affair with Basie's guitarist Freddie Green. In spite of this rapport, the period with Basie was not a consistently happy one for Holiday, who encountered setbacks on the road and rejection by management people who disliked her 'way-out' style, or criticism from friends advising her to tailor her singing to the perceived requirements of the orchestra. As usual, Lady Day refused to compromise. She quit the Basie band, or was fired, in February of 1938 and, reservations about the touring life notwithstanding, joined Shaw almost at once and was on the road again, this time with a white band. She ran into trouble with racists, especially in the 'Jim Crow' Southern states, and before the end of the year had left Shaw. It was to be her final appearance as a band member: from now on she would be presented as a solo artist.

She continued making records and it seems likely that those closest to her heart were those recorded in association with Wilson, her beloved Lester Young and trumpeter Buck Clayton. And there is an emerging consensus that the inspirational partnership of Holiday and Young - musical and emotional - led to a batch of the finest vocal interpretations of her life. Undeniably, these discs and others made between 1935 and 1942 are among the finest in jazz. Early in 1939, Holiday's career took a giant step upwards. Again Hammond proffered a helping hand, as did Barney Josephson who dreamed of running a racially integrated nightclub in New York's Greenwich Village. Hammond was the one who invested in the project and, asked to advise on appropriate attractions for liberal patrons, recommended Holiday. She opened at Café Society with Frankie Newton's band that January and had her first taste of stardom at the Café whose slogan read 'The wrong place for the right people'. Holiday stayed there for nearly nine months, during which time she was given a song-poem, 'Strange Fruit', Lewis Allen's anti-lynching protest, which led her to a real hit record and new and international fame as a purveyor of socially significant ballads. The song continued to be identified with Holiday who, on 20 April 1939, made a record of this controversial title for the Commodore label, her own having refused to release it. Opinion divided sharply on the merits of 'Strange Fruit' as a jazz vehicle, and the effect it had upon her instinctive taste and artistry. Critics feared it could lead to a self-consciousness which would destroy the strangely innocent qualities of earlier days.

Unfortunately as the sound of jazz progressed into the 40s and 50s Holiday responded positively, if unwisely, to some changes in the musical and social climate. Already an eager drinker, smoker of tobacco and marijuana, eater, dresser and shopper with a sexual appetite described as 'healthy-plus', she embraced the hard-drug culture of the 40s as to the manner born. She was having troublesome love affairs, nothing new to her, but on 25 August 1941 married Jimmy Monroe. It was a union that did nothing to ease her situation, being an on-off affair which lasted until their divorce in 1957. Nobody now can say when exactly, and by whom, but Holiday was turned on to opium and then heroin. The details are unimportant; the addiction hardly affected her singing at first, although her behaviour grew increasingly unpredictable, and she gained a reputation for unreliability. At last she was earning real money, as much as $1,000 weekly, it was reported, and about half that sum was going to pay for her 'habit'. Nevertheless, she now had the public recognition she craved. In the first *Esquire* magazine poll (1943) the critics voted her best vocalist, topping Mildred Bailey and Ella Fitzgerald in second and third places respectively. Holiday was a stellar act, in spite of drug problems, and one accompanist spoke years later of her 'phenomenal musicianship.' The series of 78s - 36 titles made for Decca Records with a wide variety of more commercially acceptable accompaniments, including strings on a dozen or so sides and a vocal group on two - rank with the mature Holiday's most accomplished performances, technically speaking, although the revolutionary approach had become more calculating and mannered. To compensate, she turned up the emotional heat, depending on her imagination to deliver the right touch. Among these 78s, recorded between October 1944 and March 1950, are a number of gems of jazz singing - among them 'Lover Man', 'Porgy', 'Good Morning Heartache', 'You Better Go Now' and, as a welcome example of Lady Day back to top form as a commanding, exuberant, mistress of swing phrasing, the mid-tempo blues-drenched 'Now Or Never'. To round off this set, assembled on three *The Lady Sings* albums, she exhibits another facet of her craft by duetting comfortably with Armstrong on 'My Sweet Hunk O' Trash' and sharing space on a second Armstrong track.

At this stage of her life Holiday experienced regular bouts of depression, pain and ill-health. In 1947 she was sentenced to a long term in the Federal Reformatory, West Virginia, her arraignment coming, surprisingly, at the behest of her manager, Joe Glaser. The attendant publicity disastrously affected her confidence while drugs slowly weakened her physique. Running her own big band with husband Joe Guy in 1945 had cost Holiday a sum reckoned to be $35,000, and that blow was followed by the death of her mother. Another disappointment to Holiday's professional aspirations was her failure to secure a film break, after pinning her hopes on the part she was offered in the jazz film, *New Orleans* (1946). Both Holiday and her idol, Armstrong, had roles involving a great deal of music-making - much of it left in the cutting room - but the purported jazz story turned out to be a nonsensical fantasy; and worse, Holiday and Armstrong were cast as servants. She was quoted later as saying: 'I fought my whole life to keep from being somebody's damn maid. It was a real drag . . . to end up as a make-believe maid'. The picture failed but gave her valuable international exposure, and jazz fanciers were pleased to see and hear sequences featuring Holiday Armstrong, Kid Ory, Woody Herman and other musicians. For Holiday it was goodbye to the movies.

From the 50s on, Holiday and trouble seemed often to be inseparable, and as a consequence of her criminal record on drugs, Holiday's cabaret card was withdrawn by the New York Police Department. This prevented her appearance at any venue where liquor was on sale, and effectively ruled out New York nightclubs. In her eyes it amounted to an absolute injustice and one that diminished her out-of-town earning capacity. She appeared in England during 1954 to great acclaim, and in 1956, her outspoken autobiography (written with William Dufty) brought increased fame, or notoriety. In 1957, Holiday was still making good money but by the following year the drink and drugs crucially influenced her vocal control, and the 'hoarsely eloquent voice' had increased in hoarseness at the expense of the eloquence. However, one further segment of the Holiday discography deserves attention: the body of work on the Clef-Verve label (produced or master-minded by Norman Granz) which placed her in a jazz setting and encouraged her to shine when she and the small-group accompaniment felt right. These recordings (1952-57) include a number of satisfying performances, and several worthy of high praise. As for the final albums with the Ray Ellis Orchestra, they are, for the majority of jazz fanciers, a painfully acquired taste, although certain tracks, most notably 'You've Changed' on *Lady In Satin* are immensely moving on their own terms.

Billie Holiday paid a second and last visit to Europe late in 1958, and came to London to make a television appearance on Granada's *Chelsea At Nine* show in February 1959. Back in America, however, her condition worsened and at the end of May she was taken to hospital suffering from heart and liver disease. Harried still by the police (she had been arrested twice already for possession, in 1949 and 1956), and placed under arrest in her private room, she was charged with 'possession' and put under police guard - the final cruelty the system could inflict upon her. Thus the greatest of jazz singers died in humiliating circumstances at 3.10 am on 17 July 1959 with $750 in notes taped to one leg - an advance on a series of promised articles. Even at the end squabbles had begun between a lawyer, virtually self-appointed, and her second husband, Louis McKay, whom she had married on 28 March 1957. She did not live to rejoice in the flood of books, biographical features, critical studies, magazine essays, album booklets, discographies, reference-book entries, chapters in innumerable jazz volumes, films and television documentaries which far exceed any form of recognition she experienced in her lifetime.

In defiance of her limited vocal range, Billie Holiday's use of tonal variation and vibrato, her skill at jazz phrasing, and her unique approach to the lyrics of popular songs, were but some of the elements in the work of a truly original artist. Her clear diction, methods of manipulating pitch, improvising on a theme, the variety of emotional moods ranging from the joyously optimistic, flirtatious even, to the tough, defiant, proud, disillusioned and buoyantly barrelhouse, were not plucked out of the air, acquired without practice. Holiday paid her dues in a demanding milieu. That she survived at all is incredible; that she should become the greatest jazz singer there has ever been - virtually without predecessor or successor - borders on the miraculous. Today she is revered beyond her wildest imaginings in places which, in her lifetime, greeted her with painfully closed doors. Sadly, she would not have been surprised. As she wrote in her autobiography: 'There's no damn business like show business. You had to smile to keep from throwing up'.

● ALBUMS: *Billie Holiday, Volume 1* 10-inch album (Commodore 1950)★★★★, *Billie Holiday, Volume 2* 10-inch album (Commodore 1950)★★★, *Billie Holiday Sings* 10-inch album (Columbia 1950)★★★★, *Favorites* 10-inch album (Columbia 1951)★★★, *Lover Man* 10-inch album (Decca 1951)★★★★, *Billie Holiday Sings* 10-inch album (Mercury 1952)★★★, *Billie Holiday Sings* reissued as *Solitude - Songs By Billie Holiday* (Clef 1953)★★★, *An Evening With Billie Holiday* 10-inch album (Clef 1953)★★★, *Billie Holiday* 10-inch album (Clef 1954)★★★★, *Billie Holiday At Jazz At The Philharmonic* 10-inch album (Clef 1954)★★★, *Music For Torching* (Clef 1955)★★★, with Teddy Wilson *Lady Day* (Columbia 1955)★★★★★, *A Recital By Biliie Holiday* reissue of *An Evening With Billie Holiday* and *Billie Holiday* (Clef 1956)★★★, *The Lady Sings* (Decca 1956)★★★★, *Velvet Mood* (Clef 1956)★★★, *Lady Sings The Blues* (Clef 1956)★★★★, *Body And Soul* (Verve 1957)★★★, *Songs For Distingue' Lovers* (Verve 1958)★★★★★, *Stay With Me* (Verve 1958)★★★, *The Blues Are Brewin'* (Decca 1958)★★★★, *Lady In Satin* (Columbia 1958)★★★★, *All Or Nothing At All* (Verve 1959)★★★★★.

● COMPILATIONS: *The Unforgettable Lady Day* (Verve 1959)★★★★, *The Essential Billie Holiday* (Verve 1961)★★★★, *The Golden Years* 3-LP box set (Columbia 1962)★★★★, *Billie's Blues* (United Artists 1962)★★★★, *Rare Live Recordings* (Ric 1964)★★★, *The Commodore Recordings* (Mainstream 1965)★★★, with Teddy Wilson *Once Upon A Time* (Mainstream 1965)★★★, *Lady* (Verve 1966)★★★, *The Golden Years, Volume 2* (Columbia 1966)★★★★, *Billie Holiday's Greatest Hits* Columbia material (Columbia 1967)★★★★, *Billie Holiday's Greatest Hits* Decca material (Decca 1968)★★★, *The Billie Holiday Story* Decca material (Decca 1972)★★★★, *Strange Fruit* (Atlantic 1973)★★★, *Lady In Autumn: The Best Of The Verve Years* (Verve 1973/91)★★★★★, *The Original Recordings* (Columbia 1973)★★★★, shared with Ella Fitzgerald, Lena Horne, Sarah Vaughan *Billie, Ella, Lena, Sarah!* (Columbia 1980)★★★★, *The Silver Collection* (Verve 1984)★★★★, *Billie Holiday At Monterey 1958* (1986)★★★, *The Billie Holiday Collection* (Deja Vu 1988)★★★, *Billie's Blues* 1942, 1951, 1954 recordings (Blue Note 1988)★★★★, *The Quintessential Billie Holiday Volume 1* 1933-1935 recordings (Columbia 1991)★★★★★, *The Quintessential Billie Holiday Volume 2* 1936 recordings (Columbia 1991)★★★★★, *The Quintessential Billie Holiday Volume 3* 1936-1937 recordings (Columbia 1991)★★★★★, *The Quintessential Billie Holiday Volume 4* 1937 recordings (Columbia 1991)★★★★★, *The Quintessential Billie Holiday Volume 5* 1937-1938 recordings (Columbia 1991)★★★★★, *The Quintessential Billie Holiday Volume 6* 1938 recordings (Columbia 1991)★★★★★, *The Quintessential Billie Holiday Volume 7* 1938-1939 recordings (Columbia 1991)★★★★★, *The Quintessential Billie Holiday Volume 8* 1939-1940 recordings (Columbia 1991)★★★★★, *The Quintessential Billie Holiday Volume 9* 1940-1942 recordings (Columbia 1991)★★★★★, *Billie Holiday: The Legacy Box 1933-1958* Columbia material (Columbia 1991)★★★, *The Complete Decca Recordings* 1944-1950 recordings (Decca 1991)★★★★★, *The Essential Billie Holiday: Songs Of Lost Love* 50s material (Verve 1992)★★★★, *Billie' Best* Verve material (Verve 1992)★★★★, *The Early Classics* (Pearl Flapper 1992)★★★, *The Complete Billie Holiday On Verve 1945-1959* 10-CD box set (Verve 1993)★★★★★, *16 Most Requested Songs* Columbia material (Columbia 1993)★★★★★, *Collection* (Castle 1993)★★★, *Verve Jazz Masters 12: Billie Holiday* (Verve 1994)★★★★, *Great American Songbook* (PolyGram 1994)★★★★, *Masters Of Jazz, Volume 3* 1944-1949 recordings (Storyville)★★★★, *Greatest Hits* (MCA 1995)★★★★, *Fine And Mellow (1935-1941)* (Indigo 1995)★★★, *Lady Sings The Blues: Original Sessions 1937-1947* (Accord 1995)★★★, *Verve Jazz Masters 47: Sings Standards* 1945-1959 recordings (Verve/PolyGram 1995)★★★, *All Or Nothing At All* comprises *Distingue Lovers, Body And Soul, All Or Nothing At All* albums (Verve 1996)★★★★★, *Love Songs* Columbia material (Sony 1996)★★★★, *American Legends: Billie Holiday* Columbia/Decca material (Laserlight 1996)★★★, *This Is Jazz No. 15: Billie Holiday* Columbia material (Sony 1996)★★★★, *Billie Holiday 1935-1938* (Fat Boy 1996)★★★, *Golden Hits* (Intercontinental 1996)★★★, *Lady Day's 25 Greatest 1933-1944* (ASV/Living Era 1996)★★★, *The Complete Commodore Recordings* 1939/1944 recordings (GRP 1997)★★★★, *Priceless Jazz Collection* Decca material (GRP 1997)★★★, *Ultimate Billie Holiday* (Verve 1997)★★★★, *Gold Collection* (Fine Tune 1998)★★.

● FURTHER READING: *Billie's Blues*, John Chilton. *Lady Sings The Blues*, Billie Holiday with William Duffy, *Billie Holiday*, Stuart Nicholson.

HOLLAND, DAVE

b. 1 October 1946, Wolverhampton, Staffordshire, England. Holland plays guitar, piano, bass guitar and also composes, but it is as a bassist and cellist that he has made an international reputation. He studied at London's Guildhall School of Music and Drama from 1965-68 and was principal bassist in the college orchestra. On the London scene he worked with John Surman, Kenny Wheeler, Evan Parker, Ronnie Scott and Tubby Hayes and deputized for Johnny Mbizo Dyani with Chris McGregor's group. In 1968 Miles Davis heard him at Ronnie Scott's club and asked him to join his band in New York. Holland did so in September in time to appear on some of the tracks for *Les Filles De Kilimanjaro*. He stayed until autumn 1970, appearing on the seminal *In A Silent Way* and *Bitches Brew*, then he and Chick Corea (who had joined Davis at about the same time as Holland had) formed Circle with Anthony Braxton and Barry Altschul. Circle broke up in 1972 when Corea left, but Braxton, Altschul and Sam Rivers played on Holland's *Conference Of The Birds*. Holland also played in Rivers's and Braxton's groups in the 70s, as well as in the occasional trio Gateway (with John Abercrombie and Jack DeJohnette). The 1977 *Emerald Tears* was a solo bass album, and in 1980 Holland played at Derek Bailey's Company Festival, recording *Fables* with Bailey, George Lewis and Evan Parker. Since the early 80s, following recovery from serious illness, he has lead his own much-admired group, which has included Kenny Wheeler, Julian Priester, Marvin 'Smitty' Smith, Kevin Eubanks and Steve Coleman, and in 1984 he began a series of fine albums for ECM

Records, perhaps most notably 1990's highly-acclaimed *Extensions*. In 1986 he toured Europe in a remarkable quartet with Albert Mangelsdorff, John Surman and Elvin Jones which, regrettably, did not issue any recordings; and in the late 80s also played with the London Jazz Composers Orchestra, recording on their Zurich Concerts collaboration with his longtime associate Anthony Braxton.

● ALBUMS: with Derek Bailey *Improvisation For Cello And Guitar* (ECM 1971)★★★, with Barre Phillips *Music From Two Basses* (1971)★★★, *Conference Of The Birds* (ECM 1973)★★★★, with Sam Rivers *Sam Rivers And Dave Holland, Volume 1* (Improvising Artists 1976)★★★★, with Rivers *Sam Rivers And Dave Holland, Volume 2* (Improvising Artists 1976)★★★★, *Emerald Tears* (ECM 1977)★★★, with Company *Fables* (1980)★★★, *Life Cycle* (ECM 1983)★★★, *Jumpin' In* (ECM 1984)★★★, *Seeds Of Time* (ECM 1985)★★★, *The Razor's Edge* (ECM 1987)★★★, *Triplicate* (ECM 1988)★★★, *Extensions* (ECM 1990)★★★★, with Steve Coleman *Phase = Space* 1991 recording (DIW 1993)★★★, with Mino Cinelu, Kevin Eubanks *World Trio* (Intuition 1995)★★★, with the Dave Holland Quartet *Dream Of The Elders* (ECM 1996)★★★, *Ones All* (Intuition 1996)★★, with Bill Frisell, Lee Konitz, Kenny Wheeler *Angel Song* (ECM 1997)★★★★, *Points Of View* (ECM 1998)★★★★, with Anouar Brahem, John Surman *Thimar* (ECM 1998)★★★★, with Elvin Jones, Joe Lovano *Fascination Edition One* (Blue Note 1998)★★★★.

HOLLAND, JOOLS

b. Julian Holland, 24 January 1958, Deptford, London, England. An effervescent pianist, television host and model car collector, Holland learned the piano as a child and later came to the attention of fellow Deptford residents Glen Tilbrook and Chris Difford who invited him to join their new band Squeeze in 1974. Signed to Deptford Fun City in 1978, Squeeze began their aural assault of the pop charts at the same time as Holland had his first solo release, the *Boogie Woogie EP*. Holland left Squeeze in August 1980 after a farewell gig in their native Deptford, whereupon he was replaced by Paul Carrack. He then formed the Millionaires with Mike Paice (saxophone), Pino Palladino (bass) and Martin T. Deegan (drums). 'Bumble Boogie', their debut, trickled out in April 1981. After a few more singles with the Millionaires he went solo in 1983 with 'Crazy Over You'. Further singles followed at various junctures in his multi-media career. He can turn his hand to most styles, but would appear to favour New Orleans blues best. He became well known for his presentation of the UK television pop show *The Tube*, achieving infamy for his use of a four-letter word ('. . . all you groovy fuckers'). He rejoined Squeeze in 1985, and continued to play with them occasionally until 1990. Further television appearances with Roland Rivron preceded his return to pop presentation with the resurrected *Juke Box Jury* television programme. In 1992 he presented a BBC2 Television series, *Later With Jools Holland*, and could be seen playing piano with his band on *Don't Forget Your Toothbrush*. In 1994 he undertook touring with the ambitious, yet excellent, Jools Holland Rhythm And Blues Orchestra. *Later* has since become UK television's last hope for new and interesting music. For some, Holland's jokey persona clouds his extraordinary gift as an outstanding pianist. He has considerable dexterity as a boogie-woogie pianist and a natural ear for good music: his eclectic taste is one of his great strengths. He continues to tour with his now established orchestra.

● ALBUMS: *Jools Holland And His Millionaires* (A&M 1981)★★★, *Jools Holland Meets Rock 'A' Boogie Billy* (1984)★★★, *A World Of His Own* (IRS 1990)★★★, *The Full Complement* (IRS 1991)★★★, *The A-Z Geographer's Guide To The Piano* (1992)★★, *Jools Holland And The Rhythm And Blues Orchestra - Live Performance* (Beautiful 1994)★★★★, *Sex And Jazz And Rock And Roll* (Coliseum 1996)★★★★.

● COMPILATIONS: *The Best Of Jools Holland* (Coalition 1998)★★★★.

HOLLAND, PEANUTS

b. Herbert Lee Holland, 9 February 1910, Norfolk, Virginia, USA, d. 7 February 1979. Holland was one of several young boys to get his musical start in the Jenkins' Orphanage Band in Charleston, South Carolina, for which he played trumpet. In the late 20s and early 30s he was with Alphonso Trent's famous territory band and also worked with the Jeter-Pillars Orchestra, Willie Bryant and Jimmie Lunceford. By the end of the 30s he was based in New York, where he played in bands led by Coleman Hawkins and Fletcher Henderson and then helped to break racial restraints by becoming one of a succession of black jazzmen hired by Charlie Barnet. In 1946 he joined Don Redman for a European tour and stayed behind, first in Stockholm and later in Paris, to attain great popularity.

● ALBUMS: *Peanuts Holland With Michel Attenoux In Concert At The Salle Pleyal, Paris* (1952)★★, *Peanuts Holland In Paris* (1954)★★★★, *Peanuts Holland In Finland* (1959)★★★.

● COMPILATIONS: with Alphonso Trent, included on *Sweet And Low Blues* (1933)★★★, *Charlie Barnet In Discographical Order Vol. 16* (1942-43)★★★.

HOLLEY, MAJOR

b. 10 July 1924, Detroit, Michigan, USA, d. 26 October 1990. After starting out on violin and occasionally doubling on tuba, Holley switched to bass while serving in the US Navy. In the 40s he worked with Dexter Gordon, Earl Bostic, Coleman Hawkins and Charlie Parker and in 1950 recorded with Oscar Peterson. In the 50s he was first resident in the UK, where he worked in the studios of the BBC, then toured with Woody Herman and was a member of a small group co-led by Al Cohn and Zoot Sims. Throughout the 60s he was in great demand as a session player, recording with many leading jazz artists. Late in the decade he also taught at Berklee College Of Music. In the 70s Holley recorded and toured with many jazzmen and became a familiar and popular figure on the international festival circuit. Affectionately known as 'Mule' (a name bestowed by Clark Terry, with whom he worked in navy bands), Holley is one of a small number of bass players to effectively adopt Slam

Stewart's habit of singing in unison with his own arco playing. Although strongly identified with the post-war bebop scene, Holley was happy to play in all kinds of company and while in the UK worked with traditionally-orientated musicians such as Mick Mulligan and Chris Barber. He also played classical music with the Westchester Symphony Orchestra.

● ALBUMS: *The Good Neighbors Jazz Quartet* (1958)★★★, *Woody Herman* (1958)★★★★, with Coleman Hawkins *Today And Now* (1962)★★★, *Mule!* (Black And Blue 1974)★★★, *Excuse Me, Ludwig* (1977)★★★, *Major Step* (Timeless 1990)★★.

HOLLOWAY, RED

b. James W. Holloway, 31 May 1927, Helena, Arkansas, USA. Holloway grew up in a musical family - his father and mother were both musicians - and he initially played piano. He grew up in Chicago where he attended DuSable High School and the Conservatory of Music. While still at school, where his classmates included Von Freeman and Johnny Griffin, he took up the baritone saxophone, later switching to tenor. He played in and around Chicago, working with Gene Wright's big band for three years before entering the US Army. After his discharge he returned to Chicago, where he became deeply involved in the local jazz scene, playing with such artists as Yusef Lateef and Dexter Gordon. In 1948 he joined Roosevelt Sykes for a US tour. He remained based in Chicago throughout the 50s and early 60s, playing with many leading blues artists. In the early 60s he was resident in New York, then went back to Chicago for some time. In the mid-60s Holloway toured with Lionel Hampton and 'Brother' Jack McDuff and also led his own small groups. Towards the end of the decade he settled on the west coast. At first he worked in the studios, but eventually secured a lengthy club engagement in Los Angeles. In the early part of his career Holloway worked with many bluesmen, including Willie Dixon, Junior Parker, Bobby Bland, Lloyd Price, John Mayall, Muddy Waters, Chuck Berry and B.B. King. His jazz affiliations over the years include leading artists such as Billie Holiday, Ben Webster, Jimmy Rushing, Sonny Rollins, Red Rodney, Lester Young and Wardell Gray. He has worked with big bands, including Juggernaut, but became best known internationally after he teamed up with Sonny Stitt in 1977. During this partnership, Holloway began playing alto saxophone (at Stitt's insistence). After Stitt's death, Holloway resumed touring on his own, but occasionally worked with jazzmen such as Jay McShann and Clark Terry and jazz singer Carmen McRae.

● ALBUMS: *The Burner* (Prestige 1963)★★★, *Cookin' Together* (Prestige 1964)★★★, *Sax, Strings & Soul* (Prestige 1964)★★★, *Red Soul* (Prestige 1966)★★★, with Sonny Stitt *Just Friends* (1977)★★★, *Red Holloway And Company* (Concord Jazz 1986)★★★, with Carmen McRae *Fine And Mellow* (1987)★★★★, with Clark Terry *Locksmith Blues* (Concord Jazz 1988)★★, with Knut Riisnaes *The Gemini Twins* (1992)★★★, *Live At The 1995 Floating Jazz Festival* (Chiaroscuro 1998)★★★, with Clark Terry *Top And Bottom* (Chiaroscuro 1998)★★★★.

HOLMAN, BILL

b. Willis Leonard Holman, 21 May 1927, Olive, California, USA. After studying at Westlake College, California, in the late 40s, tenor saxophonist Holman played in Charlie Barnet's big band for three years, and then for four years with Stan Kenton. During this period Holman was not only playing but also contributing extensively to the Kenton band's book, his charts being amongst the most swinging Kenton ever played. In common with many other Kentonians of the time, Holman was also active in the various small groups experimenting on the west coast. Among the musicians with whom he worked, and sometimes recorded, were Shorty Rogers, Conte Candoli, Art Pepper and Shelly Manne (whose Blackhawk band used a Holman tune, 'A Gem From Tiffany', as their theme). He subsequently wrote for Count Basie, Louie Bellson, Maynard Ferguson, Woody Herman and Gerry Mulligan. His arrangements were also popular with the Boston-based band of Herb Pomeroy. During the late 50s he formed occasional big bands for record dates, but then came a 27-year spell during which Holman was active only in the studios. He still wrote jazz charts, however, notably for the Basie and Buddy Rich bands, and in these intervening years he often arranged for pop musicians too (e.g. 'Aquarius' by Fifth Dimension). It was not until 1975 that he reformed a big band specifically to play his own arrangements and compositions, and another 13 years elapsed before his band was eventually recorded. In 1991 Holman enhanced his reputation when he scored Natalie Cole's successful *Unforgettable*. Though he is sometimes overlooked, Holman's contribution to latterday big band music has been considerable and he is currently enjoying a creative renaissance with acclaimed releases on the JVC label.

● ALBUMS: *The Bill Holman Octet* 10-inch album (Capitol 1954)★★★, *The Fabulous Bill Holman* (Coral 1958)★★★, *In A Jazz Orbit* (Andex 1958)★★★★, *Jive For Five* (Andex 1958)★★★★, *Great Big Band* (Capitol 1960)★★★, *The Bill Holman Band* (JVC 1988)★★★★, *A View From The Side* (JVC 1995)★★★★, *Brilliant Corners: The Music Of Thelonious Monk* (JVC 1997)★★★★, *Further Adventures* (Koch 1998)★★★.

HOLMES, CHARLIE

b. 27 January 1910, Boston, Massachusetts, USA, d. 12 September 1985. Holmes started out on oboe, and gained acceptance to the Boston Civic Symphony Orchestra. Later, influenced by his childhood friend and neighbour, Johnny Hodges, he switched to alto saxophone. In 1927, in company with another friend and neighbour, Harry Carney, he went to New York. Over the next year he played with several bands, including those led by Chick Webb and Luis Russell. He spent much of the next ten years with Russell, recording with many leading jazzmen, including Joe 'King' Oliver, Red Allen and Louis Armstrong. In the early 40s Holmes played with Cootie Williams's band and later in the decade was with John Kirby and Billy Kyle. Early in the 50s he retired from music, but played occasional gigs in

New York. In the 70s he was again active in music, playing with Clyde Bernhardt and the Harlem Blues And Jazz Band.

● ALBUMS: with Clyde Bernhardt *More Blues And Jazz From Harlem* (1973)★★★, with Bernhardt *Sittin' On Top Of The World* (1975)★★★.

● COMPILATIONS: *Luis Russell And His Orchestra, 1926-1930/1930-1934* (1926-34)★★★★.

HOLMES, RICHARD 'GROOVE'

b. 2 May 1931, Camden, New Jersey, USA, d. 29 June 1991, St. Louis, Missouri, USA. A self-taught organist, early in his career Holmes worked along the east coast. A 1961 recording session with Les McCann and Ben Webster resulted in widespread interest in his work. He toured and recorded throughout the 60s, achieving widespread acceptance among mainstream and post-bop jazz audiences. Customarily working in a small group format, Holmes developed a solid working relationship with Gene Ammons, and their playing exemplified the soul-heavy, organ-tenor pairings that proliferated in the early and mid-60s. Displaying his wide-ranging interests, Holmes also played with big bands including that led by Gerald Wilson, with whom he made a fine album, and recorded with singer Dakota Staton. His powerful playing style, with its thrusting swing and booming bass notes lent itself to soul music but his playing had much more than this to offer. Later in his career Holmes's appeal to crossover audiences sometimes led to the unjustified indifference of many jazz fans. He understood the power of a simple riff and like Jimmy Smith and Jimmy McGriff, 'he had soul'.

● ALBUMS: *Richard "Groove" Holmes* (Pacific Jazz 1961)★★★★, *Groovin' With Jug* (Pacific Jazz 1961)★★★★, *Something Special* (Pacific Jazz 1962)★★, *After Hours* (Pacific Jazz 1962)★★★, *Book Of The Blues* (Warners 1964)★★★, *Tell It Like It Is* (Pacific Jazz 1966)★★★, *Soul Message* 1965 recording (Prestige 1967)★★★, *Living Soul* (Prestige 1967)★★★, *Misty* (Prestige 1967)★★, *Spicy* (Prestige 1967)★★★, *Super Cool* (Prestige 1967)★★★, *Get Up And Get It* (Prestige 1967)★★★, *Soul Power* (Prestige 1968)★★★, *The Groover!* (Prestige 1968)★★★★, *That Healin' Feelin'* (Pretige 1968)★★★, *Blues Groove* (Prestige 1968)★★★★, *Workin' On A Groovy Thing* (1969)★★★, with Gerald Wilson *You Better Believe It!* (60s)★★★, *X-77* (c.1970)★★★, *Night Glider* (Groove Merchant 1973)★★, *Comin' On Home* (c.1974)★★, *Six Million Dollar Man* (1975)★★, *I'm In The Mood For Love* (c.1975)★★★, *Shippin' Out* (Muse 1977)★★★, *Star Wars-Close Encounters* (1977)★★, *Good Vibrations* (Muse 1977)★★★, *Nobody Does It Better* (Manhattan 1980)★★, *Broadway* (Muse 1980)★★, *Swedish Lullaby* (1984)★★★, *Blues All Day Long* (Muse 1988)★★★, *Hot Tat* (Muse 1989)★★.

● COMPILATIONS: *The Best Of Richard "Groove" Holmes* (Prestige 1969)★★★.

HOMO LIBER

Vladimir Tolkachev (b. 17 June 1951, Serov, Sverdolvsk, Russia; reeds/percussion), Yuri Yukechev (b. 1954, Western Ukraine; piano/percussion). Based in Novosibirsk, Siberia, Homo Liber grew out of a trio formed in the 70s by Tolkachev, drummer Sergey Belichenko and bassist Sergey Panasenko. In 1980 Yukechev joined the group, but within a few years Homo Liber had settled into a duo of Tolkachev and Yukechev, although their first recording, *Siberian 4*, smuggled out of the USSR and released in Eurpoe and the USA by Leo Records, comprised one side by the quartet and one by the duo. The music's cool spaciousness and haunting beauty won critical acclaim around the world and was later voted one of the top 50 albums of the 80s by *Wire* magazine. A second release followed on Leo, plus three tracks on the label's eight-CD compilation *Document*, but recordings and biographical facts remain scarce. Tolkachev cites only Messaien and fellow-Sverdolvsk saxophonist Vladimir Chekasin as influences. He began to play music at the age of 12, studied accordion at the local music institute and took up the saxophone in 1969. In the early 70s he moved to the Siberian industrial centre of Novosibirsk and became involved in the contemporary jazz scene at the neighbouring 'university' town of Akademgorodok. He currently works in an orchestra. Playing music is, for him, 'an opportunity to go beyond the limits of everyday experience, to exist in another world'. Yukechev studied piano at Lutsk (1960-65) and composition at the Leningrad Conservatoire (1965-70). In addition to his improvisations in Homo Liber, he is a full-time 'classical' composer, whose works include a piano trio, a cantata for choir, a concerto for violin and 18 brass and wind instruments and an opera, *The Legend Of The People Of Taiga*. Though active in their home region, Homo Liber have rarely toured or played at festivals.

● ALBUMS: *Siberian 4* (1983)★★★★, *Untitled* (1986)★★★, with others *Document* (1990)★★★.

HOOPER, LES

b. 27 February 1940, Baton Rouge, Louisiana, USA. Although a self-taught pianist, Hooper studied composition at Louisiana State University before entering the advertising business as a writer of jingles. In Chicago in the mid-70s he formed a big band which made a fine album, *Look What They've Done*, and was beaten to a Grammy by Woody Herman. Examples of his assimilation of current musical thought can be heard on charts that he wrote for Don Ellis. Hooper's advertising career ran from the mid-60s until the late 70s, when he became a studio musician in Los Angeles. An occasional big band under Hooper's leadership has demonstrated his arranging skills with their blend of swing era principles and contemporary sounds. These charts have attracted the attention of many young musicians playing in college and university bands on both sides of the Atlantic, many of whom use Hooper's arrangements.

● ALBUMS: *Look What They've Done* (1974)★★★, *Dorian Blue* (c.1980)★★, *Hoopla* (1980)★★★, *Raisin' The Roof* (1982)★★★.

HOPE, ELMO

b. 27 June 1923, New York City, New York, USA, d. 19 May 1967, New York City, New York, USA. Influenced by Bud Powell, Hope was regarded by some as a mere imitator. However he did develop his own highly individual piano style, drawing on blues and soul for inspiration. Hope first worked with Joe Morris, touring with his orchestra from 1948 to 1951. In the 50s he recorded several sessions as a leader, with trio and quintet dates released on Blue Note Records. His playing could be just as effective in the context of hard bop with John Coltrane and Hank Mobley on 'All Star Session', or in his trio work with drummer Frank Butler. Other high profile work included sessions with Frank Foster, Lou Donaldson and Clifford Brown. Drug problems led to Hope relocating to Los Angeles in the late 50s. His later work included live dates with Lionel Hampton and Chet Baker, and recording sessions with Harold Land and the Curtis Counce Quintet. Hope returned to New York in 1961 and recorded frequent sessions up until his death in 1967.

● ALBUMS: *Elmo Hope Trio* 10-inch album (Blue Note 1953)★★★, *Elmo Hope Quintet, Volume 2* 10-inch album (Blue Note 1954)★★★, *Meditations* reissued as *The Elmo Hope Memorial Album* (Prestige 1956)★★★★, with Frank Foster *Hope Meets Foster* reissued as *Wail Frank Wail* (Prestige 1956)★★★★, *Informal Jazz* (Prestige 1956)★★★, *Elmo Hope* (HiFi Jazz 1960)★★★, *High Hopes* (Beacon 1961)★★★, *Homecoming!* (Riverside 1961)★★★, with Bertha Hope *Hope-Full* (Riverside 1962)★★★★, *Elmo Hope Trio* (Celebrity 1962)★★★, *Sounds From Riker's Island* (Audio Fidelity 1963)★★★, *The Final Sessions* 1966 recordings (Evidence 1996)★★★.

HOPE, LYNN

b. 26 September 1926, Birmingham, Alabama, USA. Tenor saxophonist Hope joined King Kolax's band upon graduation before forming his own outfit with his sister and brothers and converting to the Moslem faith, which resulted in his changing his name to Al Hajji Abdullah Rascheed Ahmed and wearing either a fez or, more usually, a turban. Seeking a recording deal, he signed an invalid contract with Miracle in 1950 and, when no recording sessions resulted, went to Premium Records where he recorded his biggest hit, the standard 'Tenderly' which was picked up by Chess Records. He recorded prolifically for Aladdin between 1951 and 1957 during which he continued his policy of bringing standards up-to-date with instrumental readings of 'September Song', 'Summertime', 'She's Funny That Way' and a re-recording of 'Tenderly' amongst others. His straight, melodic saxophone playing was derided by the musically hip - who rechristened him 'No Hope' - but his modernization of old standards was loved by the general public (in person, if not on record), and his records often harboured an exciting blues or jump tune on the b-side. Hope's last recordings were made for King in 1960, after which he seems to have disappeared from the public eye

● COMPILATIONS: *Lynn Hope And His Tenor Sax* (1983)★★★, *Morocco* (1985)★★★.

HOPKINS, CLAUDE

b. 24 August 1903, Alexandria, Virginia, USA, d. 19 February 1984. Hopkins was born into a well-educated, middle-class family, both parents being members of the faculty of Howard University. He studied formally at Howard before starting a career as a dance band pianist. In the mid-20s he visited Europe as leader of a band accompanying Joséphine Baker. Later in the decade and into the early 30s he worked in and around New York, leading bands at many prestigious dancehalls, including the Savoy and Roseland. In 1934 he began a residency at the Cotton Club, sharing headline space with the Jimmie Lunceford band, which lasted until the club closed its Harlem premises in February 1936. In the late 30s and early 40s Hopkins toured extensively but folded the band in 1942. He regularly employed first-class musicians such as Hilton Jefferson, Edmond Hall, Vic Dickenson and Jabbo Smith. After a spell outside music he returned to the scene, fronting a band in New York in 1948, and continued to appear in the city and other east coast centres, with large and small groups, into the 70s. Among the musicians with whom he performed during these years were Red Allen, Wild Bill Davison and Roy Eldridge. The bands which Hopkins led always had a relaxed, lightly swinging sound, eschewing powerhouse bravura performances.

● ALBUMS: *Yes, Indeed!* (1960)★★★, *Let's Jam* (1961)★★★, *Swing Time* (1963)★★★, with others *Master Jazz Piano Vol. 1* (1969)★★, with others *The Piano Jazz Masters* (1972)★★, *Crazy Fingers* (1972)★★★, *Soliloquy* (1972)★★★, *Safari Stomp* (1974)★★★, *Sophisticated Swing* (1974)★★.

● COMPILATIONS: *Harlem* (1935)★★★, *Claude Hopkins And His Orchestra* (1935)★★★★, *Singin' In The Rain* (1935)★★★, *Claude Hopkins 1932-34* (Original Jazz Classics 1993)★★★★, *Claude Hopkins 1934-35* (Original Jazz Classics 1993)★★★★, *Claude Hopkins 1937-40* (Original Jazz Classics 1994)★★★★.

HOPKINS, FRED

b. 11 October 1947, Chicago, Illinois, USA. Hopkins began to play double bass while a student at DuSable High School in Chicago. In the late 60s he became involved in the AACM. In 1970 he played and recorded with Kalaparush Maurice McIntyre. In 1971 he worked in a trio with altoist Henry Threadgill and drummer Steve McCall, which evolved into the group Air and remained active until the mid-80s. Gifted with a springy, propulsive rhythm and blues-drenched tone, Hopkins is the pre-eminent bass player of his generation. His scything, 'out' explorations using the bow combine folk and *avant garde* classical freedoms to devastating effect. He has contributed to the power of Threadgill's later Sextet in no small way and has supplied rhythmic bounce to the work of Oliver Lake, David Murray (recording on the seminal *Flowers For Albert* in 1977), Hamiet Bluiett, Marion Brown, Muhal Richard Abrams, and Craig Harris. In 1988 he toured in a trio with Murray and Sunny Murray, showing that the spirit of leaderless free jazz is still alive.

● ALBUMS: with David Murray *Flowers For Albert* (1976)★★★,

with Henry Threadgill *X-15 Vol I* (1979)★★★★, with Threadgill *Just The Facts And Pass The Bucket* (1983)★★★, with Craig Harris *Black Bone* (1983)★★★, with Hamiet Bluiett *Ebu* (1984)★★★★, with Threadgill *You Know The Number* (1986)★★★, with Muhal Richard Abrams *Colors In Thirty Third* (1987)★★★.

HORLER, JOHN

b. John Douglas Horler, 26 February 1947, Lymington, Hampshire, England. Horler began playing piano as a very small child, and while still a young teenager he played in a band led by his trumpeter father Ronnie Horler. In the mid-60s he studied piano and also clarinet at London's Royal Academy of Music, then began a full-time professional career. He worked with many bands, some of them jazz-orientated, including those led by Bobby Lamb-Raymond Premru, Allan Littlejohns, Tony Milliner and Tony Faulkner. In the early 70s he began a long association with the BBC, playing in many groups and musical settings. From these years onwards he was also in great demand as a session musician and accompanied many fine visiting jazzmen at London club dates. During the 70s and 80s he worked with UK and US musicians such as Art Farmer, Chet Baker, Zoot Sims, Maynard Ferguson, Tony Coe, Ronnie Ross, Pete King, Kenny Wheeler and Tommy Whittle. In the mid-80s he also began a long-term musical relationship with John Dankworth and Cleo Laine. In the 90s, although Horler continued to work in similar settings, he became better known to jazz fans thanks to some exceptionally good albums. As an accompanist, Horler's gifts are self-evident from the list of musicians he has accompanied over the years. He has also often demonstrated a flair for accompanying singers with his work with Laine and Elaine Delmar. Away from the relative anonymity of his radio work, Horler's abiding love for the playing of Bill Evans is apparent, although he never descends to merely aping his idol's style. Oddly enough, Horler has declared that he never wanted to be a jazz pianist, having had as a youth a desire to 'blow something', in particular the trombone (his older brother, Dave Horler, is a trombonist). Horler's playing demonstrates his remarkable technical gifts, which he also uses in classical work, and he is an outstanding improvisatory jazz artist. His style and repertoire, while eclectic, display a thoughtful and deeply creative musician, and his late 90s work has rightfully gained him a new and enthusiastic following.

● ALBUMS: *Lost Keys* (Mastermix 1993)★★★, with Tony Coe *Blue Jersey* (AB 1993)★★★, *Gentle Piece* (Spotlite 1996).

HORN, PAUL

b. 17 March 1930, New York, USA. Horn started to play the piano at the age of four and moved on to the saxophone when he was 12. He studied the flute at Oberlin College Conservatory during 1952 and went on to the Manhattan School of Music the following year. He played with the Sauter-Finnegan Orchestra as tenor soloist before joining Chico Hamilton's Quintet (1956-58). Then he settled to work in Hollywood's film studios. He was the main soloist in Lalo Schifrin's *Jazz Suite Of Mass Texts* in 1965 and worked with Tony Bennett the following year. During 1967 he went to India where he became a teacher of transcendental meditation. Later he toured China (1979) and the USSR (1983). In 1970 he had settled on an island near Victoria, British Colombia where he formed his own quintet, presented a weekly television show and founded his own record company called Golden Flute (1981). He wrote scores for the Canadian National Film Board and won an award for the score of *Island Eden*. His education and keen travelling encouraged and enabled him to expand his music beyond jazz into what he hoped would be 'universal music'. In 1968 he had recorded an album of solo flute pieces in the Taj Mahal making use of the half minute reverberation time; he later recorded at the Great Pyramid of Cheops near Cairo and even produced a record using the sound of whales as an accompaniment. For Horn, the term jazz merely describes the revival in this century of the art of improvisation and it is this that he continues to do either solo on a variety of flutes including the Chinese ti-tzi, or in a duo with David Friesen on bass.

● ALBUMS: with Freddy Gambrell *Mikado* (World Pacific 1959)★★★, *Inside Taj Mahal* (1968)★★★, *Inside The Great Pyramid* (Kickuck 1976)★★, with David Friesen *Heart To Heart* (1983)★★★, *Traveller* (1985)★★★, *China* (Kuckuck 1987)★★★, *Inside The Cathedral* (Kuckuck 1987)★★, *Something Blue* (Fresh Sounds 1988)★★★, *Peace Album* (Kickuck 1988)★★, *Paul Horn* (Cleo 1989)★★★★, *A Special Edition* (TM 1989)★★★, *Altitude Of The Sun* (TM 1989)★★★, *The Jazz Years* (Black Sun 1991)★★★, *Brazilian Images* (Black Sun 1992)★★★.

● FURTHER READING: *Inside Paul Horn: The Spiritual Odessey Of A Universal Traveller*, Paul Horn with Lee Underwood.

HORN, SHIRLEY

b. 1 May 1934, Washington, DC, USA. After studying piano formally, Horn continued her musical education at university. She began leading her own group in the mid-50s and made several records, often in company with front-rank bop musicians. For some years Horn spent much of her time in Europe where her cabaret-orientated performances went down especially well. Nevertheless, this absence from the USA tended to conceal her talent, something her return to the recording studios in the 80s has begun to correct. Although her piano playing is of a high order most attention is centred upon her attractive singing. Interpreting the best of the Great American Song Book in a breathily personal manner, Horn continues to perform and record. She is strikingly adept at the especially difficult task of accompanying herself on the piano. Her 1996 album *The Main Ingredient* was an interesting concept of creating a relaxed jam session atmosphere by having the musicians drop by her home. It was recorded over five days in between Horn preparing the food for her house guests it featured Charles Ables (bass, guitar), Joe Henderson (tenor saxophone), Elvin Jones (drums), Buck Hill (tenor saxophone), Steve Williams (drums), Roy Hargrove (trumpet) and Billy Hart (drums).

● ALBUMS: *Embers And Ashes* (1961)★★★, *Live At The Village Vanguard* (1961)★★★★, *Loads Of Love* (Mercury 1963)★★★, *Shirley Horn With Horns* (Mercury 1963)★★★, *Shirley Horn* (1965)★★★, *Trav'lin Light* (Impulse! 1965)★★★, *A Lazy Afternoon* (Steeple Chase 1978)★★★, *All Night Long* (Syeeplechase 1981)★★★, *Violets For Your Furs* (Steeple Chase 1981)★★★, *The Garden Of The Blues* (Steeple Chase 1984)★★★, *Softly* (Audiophile 1987)★★★, *I Thought About You* (Verve 1987)★★★, *Close Enough For Love* (Verve 1988)★★★, *You Won't Forget Me* (Verve 1990)★★★★, *Heres To Life* (Verve 1991)★★★, *Light Out Of Darkness (A Tribute To Ray Charles)* (1993)★★★★, *I Love You Paris* (Verve 1994)★★★, *The Main Ingredient* (Verve 1996)★★★, *Loving You* (Verve 1997)★★★★, *I Remember Miles* (Verve 1998)★★★★.

Horne, Lena

b. 30 June 1917, Brooklyn, New York, USA. Horne is a dynamic performer, of striking appearance and elegant style. The daughter of an actress and a hotel operator, she was brought up mainly by her paternal grandmother, Cora Calhoun Horne. She made her professional debut at the age of 16 as a singer in the chorus at Harlem's Cotton Club, learning from Duke Ellington, Cab Calloway, Billie Holiday and Harold Arlen, the composer of a future big hit, 'Stormy Weather'. From 1935-36 she was featured vocalist with the all-black Noble Sissle's Society Orchestra (the same Noble Sissle who, with Eubie Blake, wrote several hit songs including 'Shuffle Along' and 'I'm Just Wild About Harry') and later toured with the top swing band of Charlie Barnet, singing numbers such as 'Good For Nothin' Joe' and 'You're My Thrill'. Sometimes, when Barnet's Band played the southern towns, Horne had to stay in the band bus. She made her Broadway debut in 1934 as 'A Quadroon Girl' in *Dance With Your Gods*, and also appeared in Lew Leslie's *Blackbirds Of 1939*, in which she sang Mitchell Parish and Sammy Fain's 'You're So Indifferent' - but only for the show's run of nine performances.

After a spell at the Café Society Downtown in New York, she moved to Hollywood's Little Troc Club and was spotted by Roger Edens, musical supervisor for MGM Pictures, and former accompanist for Ethel Merman, who introduced her to producer Arthur Freed. In her first film for MGM, *Panama Hattie* (1942), which starred Merman, Horne sang Cole Porter's 'Just One Of Those Things', and a rhumba number called 'The Sping'. To make her skin appear lighter on film, the studio used a special make-up called 'Light Egyptian'. Horne referred to herself as 'a sepia Hedy Lamarr'. Her next two films, *Cabin In The Sky* and *Stormy Weather*, both made in 1943, are generally regarded as her best. In the remainder of her 40s and 50s movie musicals (which included *Thousands Cheer*, *Swing Fever*, *Broadway Rhythm*, *Two Girls And A Sailor*, *Ziegfeld Follies*, *Till The Clouds Roll By*, *Words And Music*, *Duchess Of Idaho* and *Meet Me In Las Vegas*), she merely performed guest shots that were easily removable, without spoiling the plot, for the benefit of southern-state distributors. Her 40s record hits included her theme song, 'Stormy Weather', and two other Arlen songs, "Deed I Do' and 'As Long As I Live'. She also recorded with several big swing era names such as Artie Shaw, Calloway and Teddy Wilson. During World War II, she became the pin-up girl for many thousands of black GIs and refused to appear on US tours unless black soldiers were admitted to the audience. In 1947 she married pianist, arranger and conductor Lennie Hayton, who also became her manager and mentor until his death in 1971. For a time during the 50s Lena Horne was blacklisted, probably for her constant involvement with the Civil Rights movement, but particularly for her friendship with alleged Communist sympathizer Paul Robeson. Ironically, she was at the peak of her powers at that time, and although she was unable to appear much on television and in films, she continued to make records and appear in nightclubs, which were regarded as her special forte. Evidence of that was displayed on *Lena Horne At The Waldorf Astoria*. The material on this classic album ranged from the sultry 'Mood Indigo', right through to the novelty 'New Fangled Tango'. *Lena At The Sands* featured a medley of songs by Richard Rodgers/Oscar Hammerstein II, Jule Styne and E.Y. 'Yip' Harburg. Other US Top 30 chart albums included *Give The Lady What She Wants* and *Porgy And Bess*, with Harry Belafonte. Horne also made the US Top 20 singles charts in 1955 with 'Love Me Or Leave Me', written by Gus Kahn and Walter Donaldson for Ruth Etting to sing in the 1928 Broadway show *Whoopee*.

In 1957 Horne had her first starring role on Broadway when she played Savannah, opposite Ricardo Montalban, in the Arlen/Harburg musical *Jamaica*. In the 60s, besides the usual round of television shows and records, she appeared in a dramatic role, with Richard Widmark, in *Death Of A Gunfighter* (1969). After Hayton's death in 1971 she worked less, but did feature in *The Wiz*, an all-black film version of *The Wizard Of Oz*, starring Diana Ross and Michael Jackson, and in 1979 she received an honorary doctorate degree from Harvard University. In May 1981, she opened on Broadway in her own autobiographical show, *Lena Horne: The Lady And Her Music*. It ran at the Nederland Theatre to full houses for 14 months, a Broadway record for a one-woman show. Horne received several awards including a special Tony Award for 'Distinguished Achievement In The Theatre', a Drama Desk Award, New York Drama Critics' Special Award, New York City's Handel Medallion, Dance Theatre of Harlem's Emergence Award, two Grammy Awards and the NAACP Springarn Award. She took the show to London in 1984, where it was also acclaimed. In 1993, after not having sung in public for several years, Lena Horne agreed to perform the songs of Billy Strayhorn at the US JVC Jazz Festival. She included several of the same composer's songs on her 1994 album *We'll Be Together Again*, and, in the same year, surprised and delighted her fans by appearing in concert at Carnegie Hall. In 1996 she won a Grammy for the best vocal jazz performance on her album *An Evening With Lena Horne*. In 1998, she sang a superb version of 'Stormy Weather' on

US television's top-rated *Rosie O'Donnell Show*, and introduced what is said to be her fortieth album, *Being Myself*.

● ALBUMS: *Lena Horne Sings* 10-inch album (MGM 1952)★★★, *This Is Lena Horne* 10-inch album 10-inch album (RCA Victor 1952)★★★★, *Moanin' Low* 10-inch album (Tops 1954)★★, *It's Love* (RCA Victor 1955)★★★, *Stormy Weather* (RCA Victor 1956)★★★★, with Ivie Anderson *Lena And Ivie* (Jazztone 1956)★★★, *Lena Horne At The Waldorf Astoria* (RCA Victor 1957)★★★★, *Jamaica* film soundtrack (RCA Victor 1957)★★, *Give The Lady What She Wants* (RCA Victor 1958)★★★, with Harry Belafonte *Porgy And Bess* film soundtrack (RCA Victor 1959)★★★★, *Songs Of Burke And Van Heusen* (RCA Victor 1959)★★★, *Lena Horne At The Sands* (RCA Victor 1961)★★★★, *Lena On The Blue Side* (RCA Victor 1962)★★★, *Lena ... Lovely And Alive* (RCA Victor 1963)★★★, *Lena Goes Latin* (RCA Victor 1963)★★★, with Gabor Szabo *Lena And Gabor* (Skye 1970)★★★, *Lena* (1974)★★★, *Lena, A New Album* (RCA 1976)★★★, *Lena Horne: The Lady And Her Music* stage cast (Qwest 1981)★★★, *A Song For You* (1992)★★★, *We'll Be Together Again* (Blue Note 1994)★★★, *An Evening With Lena Horne: Live At The Supper Club* (Blue Note 1995)★★★★, *Being Myself* (Blue Note 1998)★★★★.

● COMPILATIONS: *Twenty Golden Pieces Of Lena Horne* (Bulldog 1979)★★★, *Lena Horne* (Jazz Greats 1979)★★★, *Lena Horne And Pearl Bailey* (Jazz Greats 1979)★★★, shared with Ella Fitzgerald, Billie Holiday, Sarah Vaughan *Billie, Ella, Lena, Sarah!* (Columbia 1980)★★★★, *Lena Horne And Frank Sinatra* (Astan 1984)★★★, *The Fabulous Lena Horne* (Cambra 1985)★★★, *Being Myself* (Blue Note 1998)★★★★.

● FURTHER READING: *In Person*, Lena Horne. *Lena*, Lena Horne with Richard Schikel. *Lena: A Personal And Professional Biography*, J. Haskins and K. Benson.

● FILMS: *The Duke Is Tops* (1938), *Panama Hattie* (1942), *I Dood It* (1943), *Swing Fever* (1943), *Stormy Weather* (1943), *Thousands Cheer* (1943), *Cabin In The Sky* (1943), *Two Girls And A Sailor* (1944), *Broadway Rhythm* (1944), *Till The Clouds Roll By* (1946), *Ziegfeld Follies* (1946), *Words And Music* (1948), *Duchess Of Idaho* (1950), *Meet Me In Las Vegas* (1956), *Death Of A Gunfighter* (1969), *The Wiz* (1978).

HOT FIVES AND SEVENS 1-7, THE - LOUIS ARMSTRONG

More than seventy years on and still these recordings are breathtaking. The audacity of the virtuoso trumpeter, captured in the first full flush of his realization that he was the greatest, makes clear why Louis Armstrong in the 20s was the first true genius of jazz. An innovator, a pathfinder, not yet showman but with all the showman's qualities on tap, he surges triumphantly through a succession of masterpieces, minor and major. Above even these superlative surroundings is 'West End Blues' - endlessly imitated, never equalled. A monumental performance by a giant. Unmistakable, irreplaceable, unmissable, eternal music. At least one volume for every collection.

● Tracks: *Including - Memories Of You; You're Lucky To Me; Sweethearts On Parade; You're Drivin' Me Crazy; The Peanut Vendor; Just A Gigolo; Shine; Walkin' My Baby Back Home; I Surrender Dear; When It's Sleepytime Down South; Blue Again; Little Joe; I'll Be Glad When You're Dead; You Rascal You; Them There Eyes; When Your Lover Has Gone; Lazy River; Chinatown, My Chinatown; My Heart; (Yes!) I'm The Barrel; Gut Bucket Blues; Come Back, Sweet Papa; Georgia Grind; Heebie Jeebies; Cornet Chop Suey; Oriental Strut; You're Next; Muskrat Ramble; Don't Forget To Mess Around; I'm Gonna Gitcha; Dropppin' Shucks; Who' Sit; King Of The Zulus; Big Fat Ma And Skinny Pa; Willie The Weeper; West End Blues; Wild Man Blues; Chicago Breakdown; Alligator Crawl; Potato Head Blues; Melancholy Blues; Weary Blues; Twelfth Street Rag.*

● First Released (1925-1928 recordings)

● UK peak chart position: did not chart

● USA peak chart position: did not chart

HOTTEST NEW GROUP IN JAZZ, THE - LAMBERT, HENDRICKS & ROSS!

Hard to choose between the three fantastic albums they recorded for Columbia Records, but the great technology of the CD puts all three in one package (*Sing Ellington* and *High Flying*). Those unfamiliar with Lambert, Hendricks & Ross need to know that they sang jazz like no other, before or since. The combination of the three magnificent voices; the sweet scat of Annie Ross, the cool husky Jon Hendricks and the clean and well-pitched Dave Lambert. Fabulous renditions of 'Moanin' (written by Hendricks and Bobby Timmons) and 'Summertime' are only just beaten by Ross's classic 'Twisted' (revamped by Joni Mitchell on *Court And Spark*). The coolest, hippest jazz vocal album ever.

● Tracks: *Charleston Alley; Moanin'; Twisted; Bijou; Cloudburst; Centrepiece; Gimme That Wine; Sermonette; Summertime; Everybody's Boppin'; Cottontail; All Too Soon; Happy Anatomy; Rocks In My Bed; Main Stem; I Don't Know What Kind Of Blues I've Got; Things Ain't What They Used To Be; Midnight Indigo; What Am I Here For?; In A Mellow Tone; Caravan; Come On Home; The New ABC; Farmer's Market; Cookin' At The Continental; With Malice Toward None; Hi-Fly; Home Cookin' Halloween Spooks; Popity Pop; Blue; Mr P. C.; Walkin'; This Here (Dis Hyunh); Swingin' Till The Girls Come Home; Twist City; Just A Little Bit Of Twist; A Night In Tunisia.*

● First released 1960

● UK peak chart position: did not chart

● USA peak chart position: did not chart

HOWARD, BOB

b. Howard Joyner, 20 June 1906, Newton, Massachusetts, USA, d. 3 December 1986. Howard had begun playing piano and singing in his home state but, at the end of his teenage years, he decided to move to New York where he quickly embarked on a successful career as a hotel and nightclub act and as a recording artist. He was briefly in Europe but the mid-30s found him consolidating his popularity in New York where he added a regular radio series to his roster of achievements (no mean thing for a black musician in these years). He continued to work throughout the 40s and into the 50s, by which time he was sufficiently popular to move into television. Although he favoured New York, Howard did occasionally travel to other parts of the USA, playing residencies in Los Angeles and Las Vegas. Howard's popularity with the general public came largely as a result of his following in the footsteps of Fats Waller, his lack of originality being cloaked in skilled musicianship and easygoing rapport with audiences. From time to time Howard played and sometimes recorded with jazzmen but it is as a jazz-tinged popular singer and player that he made his mark. His singing voice varied according to material and mood, ranging from tenor to baritone, from robustness to coy meanderings. During a period when he led a band that emulated Cab Calloway's, Howard employed good musicians but habitually yelled encouragement at inappropriate moments, his exhortations getting in the way of their solos. This band is best remembered for Benny Carter's arrangements.

● COMPILATIONS: *Bob Howard* (Rarities 1935)★★.

HOWARD, DARNELL

b. 25 July c.1900, Chicago, Illinois, USA, d. 2 September 1966. Combining studying with semi-professional playing, Howard was musically active in his home town, performing on clarinet, saxophones and violin, before he entered his teens. In 1917 he visited New York to make records as a member of W.C. Handy's orchestra. In the early 20s he occasionally led his own bands and also played with Charlie Elgar, who had previously given him tuition. During the 20s Howard worked with several important bandleaders, including James P. Johnson, Carroll Dickerson, Erskine Tate and Joe 'King' Oliver. Mostly, these bands were based in and around Chicago, although the Johnson band toured Europe, playing in London, and Howard also performed in China and Japan. In the 30s he spent six years with Earl Hines, again in Chicago, and then towards the end of the decade and into the early 40s flitted through bands led by Fletcher Henderson, Coleman Hawkins and Kid Ory. Although his experience had broadened to encompass contemporary big band music, Howard's later career gravitated towards small groups that played more traditional forms of jazz. In the 50s he was with Muggsy Spanier, Jimmy Archey, Don Ewell and Hines again, but by the early 60s his health was poor. In 1966 he toured Europe but had a stroke in the middle of the year and died on 2 September. A sound saxophonist and fiddle player, Howard is perhaps best remembered for the clarinet playing of his later years when his warm, big-toned solos enhanced many club dates and record albums.

● ALBUMS: *Music To Listen To Don Ewell By* (1956)★★, with Earl Hines *A Monday Date* (1961)★★★.

HOWARD, GEORGE

b. 1956, Philadelphia, Pennsylvania, USA, d. 22 March 1998, Atlanta, Georgia, USA. Howard began learning music at the age of six, studying classical clarinet and also bassoon. In his early teens he began listening to jazz-rock and soul and was later introduced to jazz when his father played him records of Charlie 'Bird' Parker and John Coltrane. By the 70s, now predominantly playing the tenor saxophone, he was gaining a localized reputation as a session player and through his playing with bands such as Harold Melvin And The Blue Notes and Blue Magic. At the end of the decade he went on tour with Grover Washington Jnr. and early in the 80s started making records under his own name. He found that his wide musical tastes attracted a similarly wide audience, stretching into the rock fusion edges of the form. Gradually, this extended to encompass soul and it was a smooth jazz-soul mix that made his albums especially popular, a trend that was highlighted after his move to GRP Records. Howard made a number of visits to Africa, seeking to understand better the roots of his music. His dynamic playing style on tenor, alto and especially soprano saxophones found ideal expression in the potent depths of the soul style he preferred. His career was still on a distinct upswing when lymphoma cut short his life, just as the newly released *Midnight Mood* was being greeted with enthusiastic reviews.

● ALBUMS: *Asphalt Garden* (Palo Alto 1982)★★★, *Steppin' Out* (TBA 1984)★★★, *Dancing In The Sun* (TBA 1985)★★★, *Love Will Follow* (TBA 1986)★★★, *A Nice Place To Be* (MCA 1986)★★★, *Reflections* (MCA 1987)★★★, *Personal* (MCA 1989)★★, *Love And Understanding* (GRP 1991)★★, *Do I Ever Cross Your Mind?* (GRP 1992)★★★, *When Summer Comes* (GRP 1993)★★, *A Home Far Away* (GRP 1994)★★★, *Attitude Adjustment* (GRP 1996)★★★, *Midnight Mood* (GRP 1997)★★★.

● COMPILATIONS: *The Very Best Of George Howard (And Then Some)* (GRP 1997)★★★★.

HOWARD, KID

b. Avery Howard, 22 April 1908, New Orleans, Louisiana, USA, d. 28 March 1966. Howard played drums in bands in and around his home town for several years. He then switched to trumpet and by the late 20s was leading a popular local band. Although he occasionally played outside the city, New Orleans was where he was at ease and he remained there throughout the next two decades. In the 50s he ventured further afield, even visiting Europe with George Lewis. By the 60s he was back home, where he continued to play despite illness until shortly before his death, in 1966. Highly regarded by his fellow New Orleans musicians, Howard was reputed to have been a powerful player with a rich sound and fierce attack that revealed the influence of players such as Chris Kelly and Louis Armstrong. By the time of his appearances with Lewis, however, his lip was in poor shape and he was capable of only a few flashes of the power displayed on his scarce early recordings.

● ALBUMS: *George Lewis In Europe Vols. 1* and *2* (1959)★★★, *George Lewis In Europe Vol. 3/Pied Piper* (1959)★★★★, *Kid Howard And La Vida Jazzband* (Jazzology 1990)★★★★, *Heart And Bowels Of Jazz* (Jazzology 1990)★★★★, *Lavida* (American Music 1993)★★★.

HOWARD, NOAH

b. 6 April 1943, New Orleans, Louisiana, USA. Howard sang in a choir as a child, taking up trumpet and alto saxophone, his main instrument, only after his two years of national service (1960-62). After discharge from the forces he moved to California where he met Byron Allen, Sonny Simmons and Dewey Johnson. He became dissatisfied with his progress while taking trumpet lessons from Johnson and, meeting Allen at Johnson's house, he switched to taking alto saxophone lessons from him. Moving to New York City in 1965 he became involved with the *avant garde* movement, playing with Donald Ayler, Archie Shepp, Bill Dixon, Sunny Murray, and recorded a two albums for ESP. He began to lead his own groups, which included at various times Dave Burrell, Sirone, trumpeter Earl Cross and tenor saxophonist Arthur Durrell. At the end of the 60s he went to Europe for a while, recording for BYG, working with Bobby Few, Muhammad Ali (Robert Patterson) and Frank Wright, and, he has explained, being made to feel like a concert artist for the first time.

● ALBUMS: *Judson Hall Concert* (1965)★★★, *The Black Ark* (1969)★★★, *Space Dimension* (1972)★★, *Live In Europe I* (1975),★★ *Berlin Concert* (1975)★★★, *Live At The Village Vanguard* 1972 recording 1975)★★★★, *Schizophrenic Blues* (1977)★★★.

HUBBARD, FREDDIE

b. Frederick Dewayne Hubbard, 7 April 1938, Indianapolis, Indiana, USA. Hubbard began playing trumpet as a child, and in his teens worked locally with Wes and Monk Montgomery. When he was 20 he moved to New York, immediately falling in with the best of contemporary jazzmen. Amongst the musicians with whom he worked in the late 50s were Eric Dolphy (his room-mate for 18 months), Sonny Rollins, J.J. Johnson and Quincy Jones. In 1961 he joined Art Blakey's Jazz Messengers, quickly establishing himself as an important new voice in jazz. He remained with Blakey until 1966, leaving to form his own small groups, which over the next few years featured Kenny Barron and Louis Hayes. Throughout the 60s he also played in bands led by others, including Max Roach and Herbie Hancock and was featured on four classic 60s sessions: Ornette Coleman's *Free Jazz*, Oliver Nelson's *Blues And The Abstract Truth*, Eric Dolphy's *Out To Lunch* and John Coltrane's *Ascension*. Although his early 70s jazz albums *Red Clay*, *First Light* and *Straight Life* were particularly well received, this period saw Hubbard emulating Herbie Hancock and moving into jazz fusions. However, he sounded much more at ease in the hard bop context of V.S.O.P., the band which retraced an earlier quintet led by Miles Davis and brought together ex-Davis sidemen Hancock, Hayes, Wayne Shorter and Ron Carter, with Hubbard taking the Davis role. In the 80s Hubbard was again leading his own jazz group, attracting very favourable notices for his playing at concerts and festivals in the USA and Europe. He played with Woody Shaw, recording with him in 1985, and two years later recorded *Stardust* with Benny Golson. In 1988 he teamed up once more with Blakey at an engagement in Holland, from which came *Feel The Wind*. In 1990 he appeared in Japan headlining an American-Japanese concert package which also featured Elvin Jones, Sonny Fortune, pianists George Duke and Benny Green, bassists Carter and Rufus Reid and singer Salena Jones.

An exceptionally talented virtuoso performer, Hubbard's rich full tone is never lost, even when he plays dazzlingly fast passages. As one of the greatest of hard bop trumpeters, he contrives to create impassioned blues lines without losing the contemporary context within which he plays. Although his periodic shifts into jazz-rock have widened his audience, he is at his best playing jazz. He continues to mature, gradually leaving behind the spectacular displays of his early years, replacing them with a more deeply committed jazz. His 1995 Music Masters session, *MMTC*, highlights this maturity with new recordings of the music of four giants: Thelonious Monk, Miles, Coltrane and Cannonball Adderly.

● ALBUMS: *Open Sesame* (Blue Note 1960)★★★★, *Goin' Up* (Blue Note 1960)★★★★, *Hub Cap* (Blue Note 1961)★★★, with Willie Wilson *Minor Mishap* (Blue Note/Black Lion 1961)★★★★, *Ready For Freddie* (Blue Note 1961)★★★★, *The Artistry Of Freddie Hubbard* (Impulse! 1962)★★★★, *Hub-Tones* (Blue Note 1962)★★★★, *Here To Stay* (Blue Note 1963)★★★, *The Body And Soul Of Freddie Hubbard* (Impulse! 1963)★★★★★, *Breaking Point* (Blue Note 1964)★★★★, *Blue Spirits* (Blue Note 1965)★★★★, *The Night Of The Cookers - Live At Club La Marchal, Vol. 1* (Blue Note 1965)★★★, *The Night Of The Cookers - Live At Club La Marchal, Vol. 2* (Blue Note 1965)★★★, *Backlash* (Atlantic 1967)★★★★, *High Pressure Blues* (Atlantic 1968)★★★, *The Black Angel* (Atlantic 1969)★★★, *The Hub Of Hubbard* (MPS 1970)★★★★, *Red Clay* (CTI 1970)★★★★★, *Straight Life* (CTI 1970)★★★★, *Sing Me A Song Of Songmy* (Atlantic 1971)★★★, *First Light* (CTI 1972)★★★★, *Sky Dive* (CTI 1973)★★★, *In Concert, Vol. 1* (CTI 1973)★★★, *In Concert, Vol. 2* (CTI 1973)★★★, *Keep Your Soul Together* (CTI 1974)★★★, *Polar AC* (CTI 1974)★★★, *High Energy* (Columbia 1974)★★★, *Liquid Love* (Columbia 1975)★★, *Gleam* (Sony 1975)★★★, *Windjammer* (Columbia 1976)★★, *Bundle Of Joy* (Columbia 1977)★★, *Super Blue* (Columbia 1978)★★★, *Here To Stay* 1961/1962 recordings (Blue Note 1979)★★★★, *The Love Connection* (Columbia 1979)★★, *Skagly* (Columbia 1980)★★, *Live At The North Sea Jazz Festival* (Pablo 1980)★★★★, *Mistral* (Liberty 1980)★★, *Outpost* (Enja 1981)★★★, *Splash* (Fantasy 1981)★, *Rollin'* (MPS 1981)★★★, *Keystone Bop* (Prestige 1982)★★★, *Keystone Bop: Sunday Night* (Prestige 1982)★★★, *Born To Be Blue* (Pablo 1982)★★★★, *Face To Face* (Pablo 1982)★★★, *Back To Birdland* (Real Time 1983)★★★★, *Sweet Return* (Atlantic 1983)★★★, with Woody Shaw *Double Take* (Blue Note 1985)★★, with Shaw *The Eternal Triangle* (Note 1987)★★★, with Benny Golson *Stardust* (Denon 1987)★★★★, *Life Flight* (Blue Note 1987)★★★, with Art Blakey *Feel The Wind* (Timeless 1988)★★★, *Times 'Are Changin'* (Blue Note 1989)★★, *Topsy: Standard Book* (Triloka 1990)★★, *Bolivia* (Music Masters 1991)★★★, *Live At Fat Tuesday's* (Music Masters 1992)★★★★, *Live At The Warsaw Jazz Festival* (Jazzmen 1992)★★, *MMTC* (Music Masters 1995)★★★, *Blues For Miles* 1992 recording (Evidence 1996)★★★.

● COMPILATIONS: *The Best Of Freddie Hubbard* 1970-1973 recordings (Columbia 1990)★★★★, *Ballads* 1960-1964 recordings (Blue Note 1997)★★★★.

HUBBLE, EDDIE

b. 6 April 1928, Santa Barbara, California, USA. Hubble's father played trombone, composed and arranged for a radio station staff band in Los Angeles. Hubble was thus encouraged to pursue a career in music and at the age of 12 was playing trombone in the LA County Band. In 1944 the family moved to New York, where he continued his schooling in company with Bob Wilber. Heavily influenced by Jack Teagarden and Miff Mole, Hubble's first full-time professional job was with Red McKenzie in 1947 and around this time he also made his first records, substituting for George Brunis on a Doc Evans date. After a brief spell with the Alvino Rey band Hubble joined Buddy Rich, with whom he remained for about three years. Throughout the 50s he worked steadily, sometimes leading his own group, and in 1966 joined the Dukes Of Dixieland. In 1968 he was a member of the newly-formed World's Greatest Jazz Band - led by Bob Haggart and Yank Lawson. In the early 70s Hubble worked with musicians such as Flip Phillips, Pee Wee Erwin and Bernie Privin. A road accident in 1979 interrupted his career, but he was soon back on the bandstand again. He worked with Jim Cullum in Texas and continued to tour into the 80.

● ALBUMS: with World's Greatest Jazz Band *Century Plaza* (1972)★★★★, *Pee Wee Erwin Memorial* (1981)★★★.

HUCKO, PEANUTS

b. Michael Andrew Hucko, 7 April 1918, Syracuse, New York, USA. Between his arrival in New York in 1939 and his induction into the US Army Air Force in 1942, Hucko had played in several bands, usually on tenor saxophone. They included outfits led by Jack Jenney, Will Bradley, Joe Marsala, Charlie Spivak and Bob Chester. In the army, Hucko switched over to clarinet as the tenor was not an easy instrument to play while marching. He was recommended to Glenn Miller by Ray McKinley and Zeke Zarchy and, after several delays resulting from typical military 'snafus', he finally made the AAF band. Eventually settled in with the band, as lead alto saxophonist doubling on clarinet, Hucko became noted for his version of 'Stealin' Apples', a tune with which he has subsequently remained associated. After the war Hucko worked with Benny Goodman (on tenor) and McKinley, spent time in radio bands, and also played dixieland with Jack Teagarden, Eddie Condon and others. He was a member of the Teagarden-Earl Hines band that toured Europe in 1957 and the following year he joined Louis Armstrong's All Stars. In the 60s he was employed mostly in studio work at CBS, NBC and ABC, where, for 15 years, he played lead clarinet in their light orchestra and second clarinet in the classical orchestra.

In between these engagements, he found time to play in jazz clubs with Condon and squeeze in solo tours around the world. In the 70s he played for Lawrence Welk, continued to tour, sometimes as leader of the Glenn Miller Orchestra, and also led his own band, which featured his wife, Louise Tobin, on vocals. In the 80s he was still touring, sometimes as a single, sometimes with his band, the Pied Pipers. Late in 1991 he toured Europe and the UK, leading a small band which included Glenn Zottola and Roy Williams in its Anglo-American ranks.

● ALBUMS: *Peanuts Hucko And His Orchestra* i (1953)★★★, *Peanuts Hucko And His Orchestra* ii (1956)★★★, *Peanuts Hucko And His Orchestra* iii (1957)★★★, *The Jack Teagarden Earl Hines All Stars In England* (1957)★★★, *Peanuts Hucko And His Roman New Orleans Jazz Band* (1959)★★★★, *Live At Eddie Condon's* (1960-61)★★★★, with Eddie Condon *Midnight In Moscow* (1962)★★★, with Red Norvo *Live In Pasadena* (1970-72)★★★, *Peanuts...* (1975)★★★, *Peanuts Hucko With His Pied Piper Quintet* (1978)★★★★ *Peanuts In Everybody's Bag* (1980)★★★, *Stealin' Apples* (1982)★★★, *Tribute To Louis Armstrong* (Timeless 1983)★★★★, *Tribute To Benny Goodman* (Timeless 1983)★★★★.

● COMPILATIONS: with Glenn Miller *Rare Performances* (1943-44)★★★★ *Jam With Peanuts* (1947-48)★★★★, *The Sounds Of The Jazz Greats* (Zodiac 1981)★★★, *Jam With Peanuts* (Swing House 1984)★★★★.

HUFSTETTER, STEVE

b. 7 February 1936, Monroe, Michigan, USA. Hufstetter began his musical career as a teenager, playing trumpet in Phoenix, Arizona, where he was raised. In 1959 he moved to Los Angeles, California, where he joined Stan Kenton's orchestra. He remained with Kenton for a year, then in the early 60s played in bands led by Si Zentner, Les Brown and others. In the mid-60s he worked with the band led by Louie Bellson to accompany Pearl Bailey and was also briefly with Ray Charles. He then played in the band led by Preston Love for Motown shows. At the end of the decade he played with Clare Fischer and in the studio band for the Donald O'Connor television show. In 1970 he began a working relationship with Willie Bobo which lasted, on and off, for a decade. Another long-lasting musical relationship began in 1973, when he became an important member of the big band co-led by Toshiko Akiyoshi and Lew Tabackin. Also during the 70s, Hufstetter played with Bob Florence, whom he had first met in the Zentner band, making many concert and record dates. Throughout the 80s Hufstetter worked with Florence, Gordon Brisker, Bellson, Dave Pell, Bill Berry and Poncho Sanchez, all the while being much in demand for studio work. Towards the end of the decade and into the 90s his busy schedule included tours with Akiyoshi, Benny Carter and Supersax, and concert appearances with a Kenton reunion band formed for a 1991 engagement at Newport Beach, sponsored by KLON, which also featured Bill Holman and Shorty Rogers. Although comfortably at home with all kinds and sizes of bands, much of Hufstetter's best work comes when he is with a contemporary big band. Combining fiery, powerful trumpet playing with a warm and intimate ballad style on flügelhorn, Hufstetter is one of the outstanding talents of the day. The facts that much of his work has been concentrated in the Los Angeles area and that many of his recordings have been made as a sideman have tended to keep his name from the wider jazz audience.

● ALBUMS: with Stan Kenton *Two Much* (1960)★★★★, with Kenton *Stan Kenton's Christmas* (1961)★★, with Clare Fischer *Thesaurus* (1969)★★★, with Akiyoshi-Tabackin *Road Time* (1976)★★★, with A-T *Insights* (1976)★★, with A-T *Live At Newport '77* (1977)★★★, with Bob Florence *Live At Concerts By The Sea* (1979)★★★, with Florence *Westlake* (1981)★★, with A-T *Tanuki's Night Out* (1981)★★★, with Florence *Trash Can City* (1986)★★★, with Gordon Brisker *New Beginning* (1987)★★★, with Florence *State Of The Art* (1989)★★★, *Circles* (1990)★★★.

HUG, ARMAND

b. 6 December 1910, New Orleans, Louisiana, USA, d. 19 March 1977. Taught to play piano by his mother, Hug worked for a while as a pianist in silent movie theatres before starting to play in a dance band. Still only in his early teens, he quickly built a solid reputation in his home town. In the mid-30s he recorded with Sharkey Bonano but by the end of the decade had decided upon a career as a soloist. He played several long club residencies in New Orleans culminating, in 1967, in a lifetime contract at a leading Cresent City hotel. In later years, Hug occasionally returned to playing in bands, including those led by Bonano and Johnny Wiggs, but was at his best as a single. His repertoire mixed traditional New Orleans music with the popular songs of his hey-days. Solid, reliable, with a stirring left hand, Hug was a thorough professional and throughout his career ably continued the great tradition of New Orleans jazz pianists.

● ALBUMS: *Armand Hug Plays Armand Piron* (1953)★★★, *Piano Solos* (Nola 1968)★★, *Armand Hug Of New Orleans: 1971* (Swaggie 1971)★★★, *Armand Hug Of New Orleans: 1974* (Swaggie 1974)★★★, *In New Orleans On Sunday Afternoon* (1974-75)★★★, *Armand Hug Plays Jelly Roll Morton* (Swaggie 1976)★★★★, *New Orleans Piano* (unk. date)★★★, *Huggin' The Keys* (Swaggie 1983)★★★, with Eddie Miller *New Orleans Dixielanders And Rhythm Pals* (Southland 1988)★★.

HUGHES, SPIKE

b. Patrick C. Hughes, 19 October 1908, London, England, d. 2 February 1987. In the early and mid-30s bassist Hughes was active in UK dance band and light music circles, playing and composing in a wide range of musical styles. Some of his compositions attempted to blend jazz with classical music - for example, his 'A Harlem Symphony' and 'High Yellow', a jazz ballet. After making some jazz-oriented records in the UK, Hughes visited New York where he led a recording date with a band organized for him by Benny Carter, playing several of his own compositions and arrangements. These records, on which outstanding musicians such as Coleman Hawkins, Red Allen, Chu Berry, Dicky Wells and Sid Catlett appeared, proved that Hughes had fully assimilated what was still, for many Europeans, an alien musical concept. These 1933 recordings became, and remain, classics of big band music. As if aware that he had achieved a peak he could never surpass, Hughes played little after this, concentrating instead on journalism. He was for many years 'Mike' of *Melody Maker* and also wrote extensively on classical music as well as publishing two volumes of autobiography.

● COMPILATIONS: *Spike Hughes And His Decca-dents* (1930)★★★★, *Spike Hughes And His All-American Orchestra* (1933)★★★★.

● FURTHER READING: *Opening Bars*, Spike Hughes. *Second Movement*, Spike Hughes.

HUMAIR, DANIEL

b. 23 May 1938, Geneva, Switzerland. Humair played clarinet and drums from the age of seven and won a competition for jazz playing in his teens. Paris has traditionally provided a Mecca for exiled jazz musicians: by the time he was 20 Humair was accompanying these visiting heroes from the drums. Most celebrated was a season with tenor saxophonist Lucky Thompson at a club called Le Chat Qui Pèche. Humair became the drummer American musicians would ask to work with (despite a gig with the Swingle Singers in the early 60s). In 1967 he played on violinist Jean-Luc Ponty's debut *Sunday Walk* (also contributing the title track). When alto saxophonist Phil Woods emigrated to Paris in 1968 it was natural that Humair should be the drummer in what Woods called the European Rhythm Machine.

In 1969 he won the *Downbeat* critics' poll as Talent Deserving Wider Recognition. Humair was so in demand that his job-sheet for the 70s reads like a list of the pre-eminent names in jazz: Herbie Mann, Roy Eldridge, Stéphane Grappelli and Anthony Braxton all availed themselves of his graceful, incisive drums. He played with Gato Barbieri on the soundtrack to *Last Tango In Paris* in 1972. *Welcome* on Soul Note in 1986, a record which listed all members of the quartet as leaders, was a perfect demonstration of his warmth and responsiveness as a drummer. Cited by Nat Hentoff as a European 'who long ago destroyed the notion that European drummers can't swing' and also active as a painter, Humair continued to top drum polls in France into the 90s. In 1991 *Surrounded* documented a selection of his work from 1964-87, including tracks with legends such as Eric Dolphy, Gerry Mulligan and Johnny Griffin - a neat way of giving Humair centre-stage and celebrating the breadth of his involvement with jazz history.

● ALBUMS: with Gordon Beck, Ron Mathewson *All In The Morning* (1971)★★★, with Claudio Fasoli, Kenny Wheeler, J-F Jenny Clarke *Welcome* (1986)★★★, *Pépites* (CELP 1987)★★★★, *9-11 PM, Town Hall* (Label Bleu (1989)★★★★, *Surrounded* (1991)★★★, *Up Date 3.3* (Label Bleu 1991)★★, *Edges* (Label Bleu 1992)★★.

HUMBLE, DEREK

b. 1931, Livingston, Durham, England, d. 22 February 1971. Humble began playing alto saxophone as a child, becoming a professional musician in his mid-teens. In the early 50s he played in bands led by Vic Lewis, Kathy Stobart and others, working alongside Peter King. In 1953 he joined Ronnie Scott where he remained for the next few years during which he recorded extensively with Vic Feldman, Jimmy Deuchar, Tony Crombie and other leading British modernists. In 1957 he went to Germany where he began a long association with Kurt Edelhagen and, a few years later, with the Clarke-Boland Big Band with whom he made several records. In 1970 he began a stint with Phil Seamen but his health, never good owing to his lifestyle, deteriorated sharply following a mugging. A gifted player with a direct, passionate solo style, Humble was one of the outstanding alto saxophonists of his generation. His long periods in Europe kept him from attracting the international status he warranted and his early death has helped make him one of the forgotten men of UK jazz.

● ALBUMS: with Clarke-Boland *More Smiles* (1968)★★★.

HUMES, HELEN

b. 23 June 1913, Louisville, Kentucky, USA, d. 13 September 1981. Coming from a happy, close-knit, musical family, Humes learned to play trumpet and piano. As a child she sang with the local Sunday school band, which boasted future jazz stars such as Dicky Wells and Jonah Jones. In 1927 she made her first records for the OKeh label in St. Louis. Humes then went to New York where she recorded again, this time accompanied by James P. Johnson, and worked for several years with the orchestra led by Vernon Andrade, star of Harlem's Renaissance Ballroom. She also recorded with Harry James. In 1937 she was offered a job by Count Basie but turned it down because the pay was too meagre. The following year she changed her mind and signed up, replacing Billie Holiday. Her recordings with Basie mixed attractive performances of poor-quality songs and marvellous versions of the better material she was given. She left Basie in 1941 to freelance, and by 1944 was working on the west coast; she had moved into the then popular R&B field. Humes had a big hit with 'Be-Baba-Leba', recorded with Bill Doggett. On a 1947 session in New York, supervised by John Hammond Jnr., she made some excellent mainstream jazz records with Buck Clayton and Teddy Wilson. By the 50s, despite another big hit with 'Million Dollar Secret', her career was in the doldrums as the R&B tag she had acquired proved somewhat limiting. This hiatus continued into the late 60s, at which time she retired to care for ailing members of her family. In 1973 the writer and record producer Stanley Dance persuaded her out of retirement and into an appearance with Basie at the Newport Jazz Festival. This date was a great success and Humes returned to full-time singing. Equally at home with ballads, to which she brought faultless jazz phrasing, blues shouting and R&B rockers, Humes was one of the outstanding singers of her day. Her light, clear voice retained its youthful sound even into her 60s, and late-period recordings were among the best she ever made.

● ALBUMS: including *T'ain't Nobody's Biz-ness If I Do* (Contemporary 1959)★★★★, *Helen Humes* (Contemporary 1959)★★★, *Songs I Like To Sing* (Contemporary 1960)★★★★, *Swingin' With Humes* (Contemporary 1961)★★★★, *Helen Comes Back* (1973)★★★, *Helen Humes* (1974)★★★, *On The Sunny Side Of The Street* (Black Lion 1974)★★★, with Gerard Badini *Sneaking Around* (Black And Blue 1974)★★★, *The Incomparable Helen Humes* (1974)★★★, *Talk Of The Town* (1975)★★★, *Helen Humes And The Muse All Stars* (Muse 1979)★★★, *Helen* (Muse 1980)★★★, *The New Years Eve* (Le Chant Du Monde 1980)★★★, *Live At The Aurex Jazz Festival, Tokyo, '81* (1980)★★, *Let The Good Times Roll* (Black And Blue 1983)★★★, *Swing With Helen Humes And Wynton Kelly* (Contemporary 1983)★★★★, *Helen Humes With The Connie Berry Trio* (Audiophile 1988)★★★, *New Million Dollar Secret* (Whiskey Women And Song 1988)★★★, *Deed I Do* (Contemporary 1995)★★★.

● COMPILATIONS: *Be-Baba-Leba* rec. 1944-52 (Whiskey Women And Song 1991)★★★.

HUMPHREY, PERCY

b. 1905, New Orleans, Louisiana, USA, d. 22 July 1995, New Orleans, Louisiana, USA. Humphrey enjoyed a long career as a trumpeter and bandleader in the pre-war dixieland dance band scene. Having played in or around New Orleans with the Louisiana Jazz Hounds, Sweet Emma Barret, the Eureka Brass Band, George Lewis And The Crescent City Joy Makers, he founded his own band in 1925. In the 30s Humphrey toured with Bessie Smith, but turned down the chance of national fame to remain with his family in New Orleans. He remained active on the local scene there, and in 1961 he founded the Preservation Hall. He continued to appear with the Preservation Hall Jazz Band regularly, until his elder brother, Willie Humphrey, died in 1994. His last performance came as the closing act at the annual New Orleans Jazz and Heritage Festival jazz tent, an honour he had been afforded over several years for his contribution to the local music community. He was still an active musician when he died of heart failure in 1995, aged 90.

HUMPHREY, WILLIE

b. 29 December 1900, New Orleans, Louisiana, USA, d. 7 June 1994. A member of a highly musical family, Humphrey started out on violin before switching to clarinet. His brothers Earl and Percy Humphrey played trombone and trumpet respectively. After playing in local bands and on riverboats, Humphrey moved to Chicago in 1919, playing briefly in bands led by Freddie Keppard and Joe 'King' Oliver. Between 1920 and the early 30s he played in New Orleans and St Louis. After a short spell in Lucky Millinder's big band, Humphrey settled in New Orleans where, war service and an occasional tour apart, he remained. Over the years he played in several bands including those led by Paul Barbarin, Sweet Emma Barrett and De De Pierce. Playing in a forceful manner, deeply rooted in the New Orleans tradition, Humphrey remained a vigorous and enthusiastic performer into his old age.

● ALBUMS: *Billie And De De Pierce In Scandanavia* (1967)★★★, *New Orleans Clarinet* (1974)★★★★, *New Orleans Jazz* (GHB 1989)★★★, *Two Clarinets On The Porch* (GHB 1992)★★★.

Hunt, Fred

b. 21 September 1923, London, England, d. 25 April 1986. A self-taught pianist, Hunt began playing jazz in the 40s. In the next decade he emerged as a significant figure in traditional jazz when, after stints with Mike Daniels and Cy Laurie, he joined Alex Welsh. Throughout the 50s and 60s, Hunt could be heard with Welsh where he was a featured soloist as well as a stalwart member of the robustly swinging rhythm section. His work with Welsh did not prevent him from accompanying visiting Americans, including recording with the four-tenor group, Tenor Of Jazz, featuring Ben Webster and Eddie 'Lockjaw' Davis, which toured in the late 60s. In the mid-70s Hunt left the UK, residing successively in South Africa, Denmark and Germany. At the end of the decade he returned to the UK but soon afterwards retired through ill health. Although remembered primarily for his long association with Welsh, Hunt's eclectic, strong style made him a sought-after and thoroughly dependable player in both traditional and mainstream settings.

● ALBUMS: with Alex Welsh *The Melrose Folio* (1958)★★, with Welsh *Echoes Of Chicago* (1962)★★★, *Pearls On Velvet* (1968)★★★.

Hunt, Pee Wee

b. Walter Hunt, 10 May 1907, Mt. Healthy, Ohio, USA, d. 22 June 1979, Plymouth, Massachusetts, USA. A bandleader since the mid-40s, Pee Wee Hunt came from a musical family, his father being a violinist and his mother a banjoist. Hunt also started playing banjo during his teen years and after graduating from Cincinnati Conservatory of Music and Ohio State University, he began playing with local bands. He played both banjo and trombone before becoming trombonist with Jean Goldkette's Orchestra in 1928. A year later he joined Glen Gray's Orange Blossoms, a Detroit band that eventually became known as the Casa Loma Orchestra, and remained a heavily featured member of that unit for many years, providing not only a solid line in trombone choruses but also a large portion of likeable vocals. Hunt eventually left the Casa Loma in 1943, and became a Hollywood radio disc jockey for a while before spending the closing period of the war as a member of the Merchant Marine. He returned to the west coast music scene again in 1946, forming his own dixieland outfit and playing the Hollywood Palladium, where audience reaction to his pure hokum version of '12th Street Rag' was so enthusiastic that Hunt decided to record the number at one of the band's Capitol sessions. The result was a hit that topped the US charts for eight weeks in 1948. Five years later, Hunt was in the charts again with a cornball version of 'Oh!', an evergreen song from 1919. Like '12th Street Rag' it became a million-seller and charted for nearly six months. This proved to be Hunt's last major record and the trombonist dropped from the limelight, but still continued playing his happy music until his death in June 1979.

● ALBUMS: *Plays And Sings Dixie* (1958)★★★, *Cole Porter A La Dixie* (1958)★★★★, *Blues A La Dixie* (1959)★★★★, *Dixieland Kickoff!* (1959)★★★, *Dance Party* (1960)★★★, *Saturday Night Dancing Party* (1961)★★★.

● COMPILATIONS: *Masters Of Dixieland, Volume Six* (1975)★★★.

Hunter, Alberta

b. 1 April 1895, Memphis, Tennessee, USA, d. 17 October 1984. Growing up in Chicago, Hunter began her remarkable career singing at Dago Frank's, one of the city's least salubrious whorehouses. There she sang for the girls, the pimps and the customers, earning both their admiration and good money from tips. Later, she moved on and marginally upwards to a job singing in Hugh Hoskins' saloon. She continued to move through Chicago's saloons and bars, gradually developing a following. She entered the big time with an engagement at the Dreamland Cafe, where she sang with Joe 'King' Oliver's band. Among the songs she sang was 'Down Hearted Blues', which she composed in collaboration with Lovie Austin and which was recorded in 1923 by Bessie Smith. Early in her career she sometimes performed and occasionally recorded under different names, including May Alix and Josephine Beaty. During the 20s and early 30s Hunter often worked in New York, singing and recording with many leading jazzmen of the day, among them Louis Armstrong, Sidney Bechet, Eubie Blake, Fletcher Henderson and Fats Waller. She also appeared in various shows on and off Broadway. A visit to London prompted so much interest that she was offered the role of Queenie in *Show Boat* at the Drury Lane Theatre, playing opposite Paul Robeson in the 1928/9 season. During the 30s she frequently returned to London to appear at hotels and restaurants, including an engagement at the Dorchester Hotel with Jack Jackson's popular band. She also appeared in the UK musical film *Radio Parade Of 1935*. The 30s saw her in Paris and Copenhagen too, consistently meeting with enormous success. In the 40s she continued to appear at New York clubs and to make records, notably with Eddie Heywood. These recordings include two of her own compositions, 'My Castle's Rockin'' and 'The Love I Have For You'. In the war years she toured extensively to perform for US troops. In the early 50s she visited the UK with Snub Mosley and again toured with the USO, this time to Korea. She played a number of club dates, but, due to increasingly hard times, in 1954 she retired from showbusiness. At that time, aged 60, she began a new career as a nurse. In 1961 writer and record producer Chris Alberston persuaded her to record two albums, but she continued to concentrate on her new profession. Then, in 1977, her employers belatedly realized that diminutive Nurse Hunter was 82 and insisted that she should retire. Having already lived a remarkably full life she could have been forgiven for calling it a day, but she was a tough and spirited lady. She supplied the score for the film *Remember My Name* (1978) and, invited to sing at Barney Josephson's club, The Cookery in Greenwich Village, New York, she was a smash hit and began her singing career anew. She made numerous club and concert appearances, made more records and appeared on several television shows. Hunter sang with power and conviction, her contralto voice having a distinct but attractive vibrato. Inimitably interpreting every nuance of the lyrics, especially when they were her own, she made many fine recordings. Even late in her career, she ably controlled her audiences with a delicate but firm hand, all the time displaying a sparkling wit and a subtle way with a risqué lyric. It is hard to think of any singer who has improved upon her performances of certain songs, notably 'The Love I Have For You' and 'Someday, Sweetheart'.

● COMPILATIONS: including *Alberta Hunter With Lovie Austin And Her Blues Serenaders* (1961)★★★, *Amtrak Blues* (*c.*1980)★★★, *Classic Alberta Hunter: The Thirties* recorded 1935-40 (Stash 1981)★★★★, *The Legendary* (DRG 1983)★★★, *The Glory Of* (Columbia 1986)★★★, *Complete Works 1921-46, Volumes 1-4* 4-CD set(Document 1996)★★★.

● VIDEOS: *My Castle's Rockin'* (Virgin Vision 1992).

HUNTER, ALFONZO

b. *c.*1973, USA. Despite starting his musical career as a jazz alto saxophonist, Alfonzo Hunter was subsequently driven to find work outside of a declining live scene in Chicago, Illinois. His determination was rewarded when he built a new audience for his singing capabilities. He auditioned as a back-up musician for R&B star R. Kelly, but Kelly opted to use him as a full-time backing singer instead of a saxophonist. His debut vocal set combined the spaciousness of hip hop grooves with more complex jazz songwriting conventions and ideas. Nine of the 13 tracks were produced by Erick Sermon (EPMD) in his role as founder of the label and production team, Def Squad. Much of the recording was tailored to Sermon's preference for spontaneous performances in the studio. This imbued *Blacka Da Berry* with an engaging freshness, accentuated by Hunter's evident talents as a vocalist.

● ALBUMS: *Blacka Da Berry* (Def Squad/EMI 1996)★★★.

HUNTER, CHARLIE

b. 1968, Rhode Island, USA. Hunter grew up in Berkeley, California, where his mother repaired guitars for a living. He had his own first guitar at 12 and took lessons from Joe Sotriani, but although he attended the same school as Joshua Redman and Benny Green he chose not to participate in the music programme. His musical interests were varied but heavily pop-orientated: blues, rockabilly, soul, funk. He first listened seriously to jazz at the age of 18, in particular to records by Weather Report and Wes Montgomery, but found neither especially to his taste. As he acknowledged later, in the latter's case he had inadvertently stumbled across an album with strings that missed the essence of the man. Hunter then heard Charlie 'Bird' Parker, John Coltrane and Charlie Christian and was now wholly turned on to jazz. He also found the sound of Jimmy Smith and others organists fascinating. He spent some time in Europe, mostly busking in the streets of various cities, then returned to the Bay Area where he linked up with poet-rapper Michael Franti to form a duo. In 1993 he toured with Franti's Disposable Heroes Of Hiphoprisy, opening the show on a U2 package. He began moving more towards jazz, teaming next with tenor saxophonist Dave Ellis and Jay Lane, formerly drummer with Primus. This group, the Charlie Hunter Trio, attracted attention with its first album and was signed by Blue Note Records. Later, Lane was succeeded by Scott Amendola. Hunter also formed a quartet, James T. Kirk, the band assembling its name from the artists whose repertoire it played: James Brown, Thelonious Monk and Rahsaan Roland Kirk. Although formed for fun, this band was sufficiently successful to be signed by Warner Brothers Records at which point Paramount Pictures stepped in, requesting a change of name to avoid disrespecting the fictional commander of the Starship *Enterprise*. Promptly renamed TJ Kirk, the band continued to boldly go on attracting audiences. After disbanding in 1997, Hunter formed a new group, adding and replacing musicians along the way, allowing the music to adjust to accommodate the creativity of new arrivals such as Canadian alto saxophonist Calder Spanier, tenor saxophonist Kenny Brooks, and vibraphonist Stefon Harris. In that same year, Hunter relocated to New York and in its then current format his band was named Pound For Pound. Hunter's playing is remarkable for its fluency and the manner in which he effortlessly evokes the essence of early bop and beyond to the multiple roots of jazz. When Hunter was tagged with the imprecise and marketing-man label of acid jazz he expressed his displeasure with the term by labelling his music as antacid jazz. Nevertheless, Hunter is a fusionist, although he might accurately be labelled as someone whose playing attracts an audience who think they do not like fusion. In some of his recordings there are hints that he has heard and likes the music of John Scofield, and he certainly admires and respects him, but for the most part Hunter's playing stems from his own creativity. Perhaps drawing upon his awareness as a child of his mother's guitar repairing skills, he designed his own guitar which had seven strings and some years later added an eighth, bass, string to an instrument built for him by Ralph Novak. This instrument allows Hunter to develop a heady, rhythmically propulsive sound somewhat reminiscent of the organled trios that had fascinated him in his formative years.

● ALBUMS: *The Charlie Hunter Trio* (Mammoth 1993)★★★, *Bing, Bing, Bing!* (Blue Note 1995)★★★, *Ready, Set ... Shango!* (Blue Note 1996)★★, *Natty Dread* (Blue Note 1997)★★★, with Pound For Pound *Return Of The Candy Man* (Blue Note 1997)★★★★.

HUNTER, CHRIS

b. 21 February 1957, London, England. Hunter took up the saxophone at the age of 12 and later studied improvisation with Don Rendell. Between 1976 and 1978 he played with the New York Jazz Orchestra with whom he toured Europe and the USSR. During the late 70s he worked extensively with Mike Westbrook's Brass Band

and became involved in studio work where his excellent technique and committed soloing were much in demand. In 1983 he played with Gil Evans' British Orchestra and in the following year moved to New York where he continued to work and tour with Evans. He also worked with the Michel Camilo Sextet and then back in Europe as soloist on projects with the Metropole Orchestra, Holland and with Mike Gibbs and the Cologne Radio Orchestra.

● ALBUMS: with Mike Westbrook *Mama Chicago* (1979)★★★, *The Cortège* (1982)★★★★; *Early Days* (1980)★★★, *The Warriors* (1981)★★; with Gil Evans *The British Orchestra* (1983)★★★★, *Gil Evans And The Monday Night Orchestra Live At Sweet Basil* (1984)★★★★; with Michel Camilo *The Michel Camilo Sextet* (1985)★★★.

HUSBAND, GARY

b. 14 June 1960, Leeds, England. A drummer who comes from a musical family (his father played flute and composed, his mother danced), Husband started on piano lessons at the age of seven, then took up drums in 1970. An infant prodigy, he created a stir in the local jazz clubs with his precision and fire. Drawn towards jazz-rock and its older protagonists, he gravitated to London in the late 70s, playing and recording with Gordon Beck, Barbara Thompson and Allan Holdsworth.

● ALBUMS: *Allan Holdsworth IOU* (1982)★★★, *Metal Fatigue* (1984)★★★, with John Themis *Ulysses & the Cyclops* (1984)★★.

HUTCHENRIDER, CLARENCE

b. Clarence Behrens Hutchenrider, 13 June 1908, Waco, Texas, USA. After playing clarinet and saxophones as a teenage schoolboy, Hutchenrider began playing professionally with bands in south-eastern states. He continued working in territory bands throughout the late 20s and into the 30s and then, in 1931, joined the Casa Loma Orchestra. Despite a sometimes shaky early technique, Hutchenrider quickly became one of the band's most popular soloists, playing hot jazz clarinet on records such as 'Clarinet Marmalade' and 'Dixie Lee'. He also played good solos on tenor saxophone, 'No Name Jive', and on baritone, 'I Got Rhythm'. As the 30s advanced and Benny Goodman's popularity grew, Hutchenrider adapted some aspects of his sound and style, finding a somewhat richer texture than the occasionally slightly reedy, but hard-swinging, sound of his earlier years. Hutchenrider remained with the Casa Lomans until 1943 when his career was interrupted by illness. He then joined a band led by fellow-clarinettist Jimmy Lytell which played mostly on radio in New York. Further illness with a lung condition followed, but he continued playing in the early 50s, sometimes leading a small group for club and hotel lounge work in New York. He continued to play into the late 70s, often with bands formed to recapture the musical sounds of the 20s and early 30s, Hutchenrider's glory days when his clarinet solos were an important feature in the success of the Casa Loma band.

● COMPILATIONS: *The Casa Loma Orchestra* (1930-36)★★★★.

HUTCHERSON, BOBBY

b. 27 January 1941, Los Angeles, California, USA. After formal tuition on piano, Hutcherson switched to playing jazz vibraphone when he heard records by Milt Jackson. He worked briefly on the west coast then, in 1961, moved to New York, where he established himself as an inventive, forward-thinking musician. He played with many of the outstanding artists of the 60s, among them Archie Shepp, Eric Dolphy, Herbie Hancock, Andrew Hill and McCoy Tyner. Hutcherson made many records, sometimes as sideman (including the important *Out To Lunch* album with Dolphy), but regularly led his own groups, which often featured tenor saxophonist Harold Land, with whom he co-led a quintet from 1968-71. By now back on the west coast, Hutcherson played with Gerald Wilson and remained in San Francisco through the 70s, though he also toured around the world. In the late 80s, often playing in all-star bebop revival groups, Hutcherson continued to make numerous records, bringing his superb technique to bear upon an eclectic choice of material that demonstrated his awareness of his jazz roots. Despite this late flurry of activity, Hutcherson undeservedly remains one of the lesser-known of contemporary jazzmen.

● ALBUMS: *Dialogue* (Blue Note 1965)★★★, *Components* (Blue Note 1965)★★★, *Happenings* (Blue Note 1966)★★★, *Stick Up!* (Blue Note 1966)★★★★, *Total Eclipse* (Blue Note 1967)★★★, *Oblique* (Blue Note 1967)★★★, *Bobby Hutcherson* (1968)★★★, *Patterns* (1968)★★★, *Spiral* (1968)★★★, *Bobby Hutcherson Now* (Blue Note 1969)★★, *Medina* (Blue Note 1969)★★, *San Francisco* (Blue Note 1971)★★★, *Head On* (1971)★★★, *Natural Illusions* (Blue Note 1972)★★★, *Live At Montreux* (1973)★★★★, *Cirrus* (Blue Note 1974)★★★, *Linger Lane* (1974)★★, *Montara* (1975)★★★, *Waiting* (1976)★★★, *The View From The Inside* (1976)★★★★, *Knucklebean* (Blue Note 1977)★★★, *For Bobby Hutcherson/Blue Note Meets The Los Angeles Philharmonic* (1977)★★★, *Highway One* (Columbia 1978)★★★, *Conception: The Gift Of Love* (1979)★★★, *Un Poco Loco* (Columbia 1979)★★★, *Bobby Hutcherson Solo/Quartet* (Contemporary 1981)★★★★, *Farewell To Keystone* (Evidence 1982)★★★, *Four Seasons* (Timeless 1984)★★★, *Good Bait* (Landmark 1984)★★★, *Color Schemes* (Landmark 1985)★★★, *In The Vanguard* (Landmark 1987)★★★, *Cruisin' The Bird* (Landmark 1988)★★★, *Ambos Mundos: Both Worlds* (Landmark 1989)★★★, *Mirage* (Landmark 1992)★★, *Farewell Keystone* (1993)★★★★, *Components* (Connoisseur 1994)★★★, with McCoy Tyner *Manhattan Moods* (Blue Note 1994)★★★.

HUTCHINSON, DOLLY

(see Jones, Dolly)

HUTCHINSON, LESLIE 'JIVER'

b. 18 March 1906, Crossroads, St. Andrews, Jamaica, d. 22 November 1959. Schooled on the trumpet in Jamaica's West India Regiment army band, Hutchinson appeared in London with them at the 1924 Empire Exhibition, Wembley. Fellow WIR bandsman Louis Stephenson had moved to England in 1935 with saxophonist Bertie King and pianist Yorke de Souza, and in

1936 Hutchinson followed, joining them in drummer Happy Blake's band at Soho's Cuba Club. He played with trumpeter Leslie Thompson's Emperors Of Jazz, who were fronted by dancer Ken 'Snakehips' Johnson, then recorded and performed intermittently with Johnson's West Indian Dance Orchestra when the dancer took over the leadership. At Mayfair's Florida Club he played with Nigerian pianist Fela Sowande and led the same band in the Rialto film *Traitor Spy* (1939). During the war he played with leading dance bands, attaining prominence as star soloist with Geraldo and broadcasting frequently. He formed his own band with former Johnson sidemen and, until his death in a road accident in 1959, struggled to remain a bandleader and, in particular, to maintain a visible black presence on the UK jazz scene. His musicians included pre-war Jamaican settlers Joe Appleton (saxophone), Coleridge Goode (bass), Clinton Maxwell (drums), and later arrivals George Tyndale (saxophone), Peter Pitterson, Bushy Thompson and Frank Williams (trumpets) as well as UK-born black singers Cab Kaye and Marion Williams. He appeared in the film *The Captain's Paradise* (1953), worked with American pianist Mary Lou Williams during her extended London sojourn and recorded with his own band in Czechoslovakia ('I Can't Get Started', 1947) and accompanying Jamaican vocalists Tony Johnson (1958) and the distinguished folklorist Louise Bennett (1950). He was also the father of singer Elaine Delmar. (This artist should not be confused with the pianist Leslie 'Hutch' Hutchinson who played in London during the same period.)

HUTTON, INA RAY

b. Odessa Cowan, 13 March 1916, Chicago, USA, d. 19 February 1984. As a child Hutton tap-danced in a Gus Edwards revue and later worked for other leading impresarios of the period, among them George White and Flo Ziegfeld. In 1934 Hutton was hired by Irving Mills to front an all-female band he was organizing. This was at a time when the concept of women playing big band music was briefly a commercial proposition and one which the astute Mills decided to exploit. The band, Ina Ray Hutton And Her Melodears, benefited from the Mills organization's publicity machine and became hugely popular. Hutton played no instrument but waved a baton colourfully. Dressed-to-kill, and labelled 'the Blonde Bombshell of Rhythm', Hutton exuded extravagant sex-appeal and her eye-catching outfits and on-stage antics helped the band's commercial success. The band had some fine musicians, notably multi-instrumentalist Alyse Wells, tenor saxophonist Betty Sattley and pianist Betty Roudebush. From 1936 the band's repertoire was in the hands of Eddie Durham, which greatly enhanced its musical qualities. Hutton led her band in several Hollywood films and they also made some records. By 1939, Hutton had severed her connection with Mills and led an all-male band but then drifted from the scene. In the late 40s and again in 1956 she appeared on television with an all-woman band and made another film but shortly afterwards went into married retirement from show business. Although by far the best known of the all-woman big bands, Hutton's Melodears were musically outclassed by the International Sweethearts Of Rhythm; they were, nevertheless, a far better outfit than their glitzy, showbiz trappings might suggest.

● COMPILATIONS: with others *Jazz Women: A Feminist Retrospective* (c.1936 recordings)★★★.

HUTTON, JUNE

b. 11 August *c*.1920, Chicago, Illinois, USA, d. 2 May 1973, Encinio, California, USA. A popular band vocalist during the 40s swing era, Hutton was the half-sister of Ina Ray Hutton, and sang with her fine all-female band in the late 30s. From 1941-43 she was a member of Charlie Spivak's vocal group, the Stardusters, and appeared with the Spivak outfit in the 1944 movie, *Pin Up Girl*, which starred Betty Grable. In that same year, Hutton replaced Jo Stafford in Tommy Dorsey's renowned Pied Pipers, and stayed with the group after it left Dorsey. She was on Pipers hits such as 'Dream', 'Lily Belle', 'Aren't You Glad You're You?', 'Mam'selle', and 'Ok'l Baby Dok'l'. In 1950 she went solo, and during the next few years had US hits with 'Say You're Mine Again', 'No Stone Unturned' and 'For The First Time (In A Long Time)', all of which featured orchestral accompaniment by her husband, arranger-conductor Axel Stordahl. Along with other artists of her kind, she suffered with the arrival of rock 'n' roll, and by the end of the 50s her career was in decline.

● ALBUM: *Johnny Mercer And The Pied Pipers* (40s material)★★★.

HUTTON, MARION

(see Miller, Glenn)

HYAMS, MARGIE

b. 1923, New York City, New York, USA. Hyams's brother was the pianist Mike Hyams and she also played piano, but it was on vibraphone that she first attracted serious attention in the jazz world. While working in Atlantic City she was heard by Woody Herman, who hired her. From 1944 until 1945 she was a member of the First Herd, but left to play in the small group setting she favoured. Her trio was popular for the next few years and appeared regularly at the Hickory House on New York's 52nd Street. She also appeared in an all-woman trio led by Mary Lou Williams at a 1947 Carnegie Hall concert. In 1949 she joined George Shearing, appearing on several of his records, including the big hit 'September In The Rain'. In 1950 Hyams married Rolf Ericson and decided to leave a business which, while giving her pleasure and success, had brought more than its share of problems. Like so many women in jazz, she had grown tired of the pressures created by musicians who refused to take her very real talents seriously.

● COMPILATIONS: *Woody Herman's Greatest Hits* (1945)★★★, with others *Women In Jazz Vol. 1* (1948)★★★★, *The George Shearing Quintet: Lullaby Of Birdland* (1949-50)★★★.

HYDER, KEN

b. 29 June 1946, Dundee, Scotland. Hyder took up the drums at the age of 15 and began playing bebop in Edinburgh and Dundee. He soon switched to free jazz, inspired by the music of John Coltrane and Albert Ayler - and, in particular, by their drummers Elvin Jones and Sunny Murray. At the end of the 60s Hyder moved to London and in 1970 set up his group Talisker to explore and combine his interest in free jazz and Celtic folk musics. He guided Talisker through two decades and various personnel changes (though saxophonists John Rangecroft and Davie Webster play on most of the albums), and has provided a blueprint for the increasing number of European musicians who have been incorporating elements of folk music into their jazz. Hyder's own interest in Scottish and Irish traditional musics had led to collaborations with Dick Gaughan, Irish uillean piper Tomas Lynch and Scottish bagpipes player Dave Brooks. A more recent fascination with shamanic singing has taken him on research trips to Canada and Siberia and brought projects with vocalists Valentina Ponomareva, Sainkho Namchilak and Anatoly Kokov. Back in the 70s, Hyder played with Julian Bahula's Jo'burg Hawk and in the 80s was busy on the UK improvised music scene, co-founding the occasional Orchestra Of Lights, recording *Under The Influence* with his octet, Big Team (which included Chris Biscoe, Elton Dean and Paul Rogers), and the duo Shams with ex-Henry Cow member Tim Hodgkinson. His latest group is the leftfield, 'polytempic' One Time, with members of B-Shops For The Poor and the Honkies.

● ALBUMS: with Talisker *Dreaming Of Glenisla* (1975)★★★, with Talisker *Land Of Stone* (1977)★★★, with Talisker *The Last Battle* (1978)★★★, with Talisker *The White Light* (1980)★★, *Under The Influence* (1984)★★★, with Dick Gaughan *Fanfare For Tomorrow* (1985)★★, with Talisker *Humanity* (1986)★★★, with Tim Hodgkinson *Shams* (1987)★★★, with Hodgkinson, Valentina Ponomareva *The Goose* (1992)★★.

HYMAN, DICK

b. 8 March 1927, New York City, New York, USA. After studying classical music, Hyman broadened his interests to encompass jazz and many other areas of music. In the late 40s he played piano in and around his hometown, working with leading bop musicians, including founding fathers Charlie Parker and Dizzy Gillespie. Early in the 50s he began a long career as a studio musician, playing piano, arranging, composing and leading orchestras. His work in the studios did not keep him from actively participating in jazz dates, many of which he himself organized. He also became deeply interested in the history of jazz and especially the development of jazz piano. He demonstrated his interest in radio broadcasts and concert performances. His enormously eclectic taste allowed him to range from ragtime to freeform with complete confidence. Through performances and recordings with the New York Jazz Repertory Company, he encouraged interest in the music of Jelly Roll Morton, Fats Waller, James P. Johnson and Louis Armstrong. He also formed a small group, the Perfect Jazz Repertory Quintet. During his freeform period he played electric piano and later added the organ to the instruments at his command, recording *Cincinnati Fats, New School Concert* and other duo albums with Ruby Braff. Later still, Hyman recorded with Braff using, however improbably in a jazz context, a Wurlitzer organ. Unusual though it might have been, *A Pipe Organ Recital Plus One* was a critical and popular success. As a composer, Hyman has written for large and small ensembles and composed the score for the film *Scott Joplin* in 1976. A master of jazz piano, his performances not only display his extraordinary virtuoso technique but also demonstrate his deep understanding and abiding love for the great traditions of the music.

● ALBUMS: *60 Great All Time Songs, Volume 3* (MGM 1957)★★★, *Electrodynamics* (Command 1963)★★★, *Fabulous* (Command 1964)★★★, *Mirrors - Reflections Of Today* (Command 1968)★★★, *Moog -The Electric Eclectics Of Dick Hyman* (Command 1969)★★★, *The Age Of Electronicus* (Command 1969)★★★, *The Happy Breed* (1972)★★★, *Genius At Play* (1973)★★★, *Some Rags, Some Stomps And A Little Blues* (Columbia 1974)★★★★, with NYJRC *Satchmo Remembered* (Atlantic 1974)★★★, *Scott Joplin: The Complete Works For Piano* (1975)★★★★, *A Waltz Dressed In Blue* (1977)★★★, *Charleston* (Columbia 1977)★★, *Sliding By* (1977)★★★, *Ragtime, Stomp And Stride* (1977)★★★, *Themes And Variations On 'A Child Is Born'* (Chiaroscuro 1978)★★, with NYJRC *The Music Of Jelly Roll Morton* (Smithsonian 1978)★★★, *Dick Hyman And The Perfect Jazz Repertory Quintet Plays Irving Berlin* (World Jazz 1979)★★★, *Dick Hyman Piano Solos* (Monmouth 1979)★★★, with Ruby Braff *Cincinnati Fats* (1981)★★★★, with Braff *A Pipe Organ Recital Plus One* (1982)★★★, *The New School Concert 1983* (1983)★★★, *Kitten On The Keys: The Music Of Zez Confrey* (1983)★★, with Dick Wellstood *I Wish I Were Twins* (Swingtime 1983)★★★, with Braff *The New School Concert 1983* (1983)★★★, *Eubie* (1984)★★★, with Braff *Manhattan Jazz* (Music Masters 1985)★★★, *Blues In The Night* (Music Masters 1990)★★★, *Plays Fats Waller* (Reference 1990)★★★, with Braff *Younger Than Swingtime* (1990)★★★, *Running Ragged* (Pro Arte)★★★, *Stride Piano Summit* (Milestone 1992)★★★, *Swing Is Here* (Reference 1996)★★★, with Braff *Ruby Braff & Dick Hyman Play Nice Tunes* (Arbors 1996)★★★, *Cheek To Cheek* (Arbors 1997)★★★, with Bob Wilber *A Perfect Match* (Arbors 1998)★★★, *In Recital* (Reference 1998)★★★★.

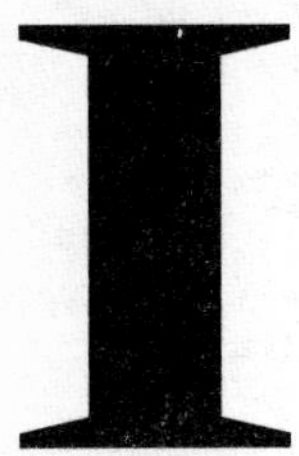

I Got My Mojo Workin' - Jimmy Smith

Nobody, but nobody, has ever made the Hammond organ work so hard as Smith. He is the undisputed king of jazz organ, and defined the sound of 'soul jazz' throughout the 60s. His work with arrangers such as *Oliver Nelson* represents the commercial peak of his long career. This album is one of many on the Verve label that it was cool to tuck under your arm and say that you owned. Smooth covers of 'C-Jam Blues', 'Satisfaction' and 'Hi Heel Sneakers' complement the originals as another entirely different way of playing them. The CD reissue has the complete *Hoochie Coochie Man* as an excellent bonus.

● Tracks: *Hi-Heel Sneakers; (I Can't Get No) Satisfaction; 1-2-3; Mustard Greens; Got My Mojo Working; Johnny Come Lately; C-Jam Blues; Hobson's Hop; I'm Your Hoochie Coochie Man; One Mint Julip; Ain't That Just Like A Woman; Boom Boom; Blues And The Abstract Truth; TNT; (I Can't Get No) Satisfaction (alternate take).*

● First released 1966

● UK peak chart position: 19 & did not chart

● USA peak chart position: 28 & 77

Ibrahim, Abdullah

b. Adolph Johannes Brand, 9 October 1934, Cape Town, South Africa. Ibrahim began playing piano as a small child, learning church music and hearing many other forms, including jazz, from radio and records. Known initially by the name Dollar Brand, he began his professional career in the mid-50s playing popular music of the day, but by the end of the decade had formed a band that included Hugh Masakela and concentrated on jazz. In the early 60s his political activities drew the attention of the authorities and he embarked upon a protracted visit to Europe with singer Sathima Bea Benjamin, whom he married. In Switzerland they attracted the much more benign and welcome attention of Duke Ellington, who helped arrange a recording date and opened other doors that led to appearances in the USA in the mid-60s. Later resident in New York City, Ibrahim played with leading exponents of free-form music, amongst them John Coltrane, Don Cherry and Ornette Coleman. He also continued to develop his involvement in politics and religion and in the late 60s he converted to Islam, subsequently adopting the name by which he has since been known. The banning of the African National Congress made it difficult for Ibrahim to retain close personal ties with his homeland but he returned there occasionally for recording dates. Despite the enforced separation from his roots he continued to explore African music and the manner in which it could be blended with contemporary American jazz. As a consequence, his extensive performing and recording dates, often of his own compositions, are shot through with rare intensity. In the early 80s Ibrahim expanded his musical horizons with the composition of an opera, *Kalahari Liberation*, which was performed throughout Europe to great acclaim.

From the mid-80s his seven-piece band, Ekaya, has recorded and performed in concert and at festivals. As a performer, Ibrahim's playing of the piano (he also plays cello, flute and soprano saxophone) is vigorously rhythmic, intriguingly mixing bop with the music of his homeland and overlaid with touches of Ellington and Thelonious Monk. As a composer Ibrahim has ably and convincingly mixed the music of two cultures creating a distinctive style through which his highly motivated political and religious beliefs can be spread to a wide, mixed audience.

● ALBUMS: *Jazz Epistles: Verse I* (1960)★★★, *Duke Ellington Presents The Dollar Brand Trio* (1964)★★★★, *Anatomy Of A South African Village* (1965)★★★, *The Dream* (1965)★★, with Gato Barbieri *Hamba Khale* (1968 recording)★★, *This Is Dollar Brand* 1965 recording (1973)★★★, *African Piano* 1969 recording (1973)★★★, *Sangoma* (1973)★★, *African Portraits* (1973)★★★, *Ode To Duke Ellington* (West Wind 1973)★★★, *African Sketchbook* (Enja 1974)★★★★, *African Space Program* (Enja 1974)★★★, with Johnny Dyani *Good News From Africa* (1974)★★★, *Ancient Africa* (1974)★★★★, *The Children Of Africa* (Enja 1976)★★★★, *African Herbs* (1976)★★★, *Blues For A Hip King* (1976)★★★, *Black Lightning* (1976)★★★, with Buddy Tate *Buddy Tate Meets Dollar Brand* (Chiaroscuro 1977)★★★, *The Journey* (1978)★★★, with Max Roach *Streams Of Consciousness* (1978)★★★, *Soweto* (Bellaphon 1978)★★★★, *Africa - Tears And Laughter* (1979),★★★ with Dyani *Echoes From Africa* (Enja 1980)★★★, *Memories* (1980)★★★, *African Market Place* (1980)★★★, *At Montreux* (Enja 1980)★★, *Matsidiso* (1981)★★★, *South African Sunshine* (1982)★★★, *Duke's Memories* (1982)★★, *African Dawn* (Enja 1982)★★★, *Mannenberg - Is Where It's Happening* (1983)★★★, *Zimbabwe* (1983)★★★, *The Mountain* (Kaz 1983)★★, *Autobiography* 1978 recording (1983)★★★, *Ekaya* (Blackhawk 1984)★★★, with Carlos Ward *Live At Sweet Basil Vol. 1* (Blackhawk 1984)★★★, *Water From An Ancient Well* (Tiptoe 1986)★★★, *Mindiff* (Enja 1988)★★★, *African River* (Enja 1990)★★★★, *Mantra Mode* (Tiptoe 1991)★★★★, *Desert Flowers* (Enja 1993)★★★, *Fats, Duke & Monk* (Sackville 1993)★★★★, *S'En Fout La Mort* (1993)★★, *Knysna Blue* (Enja/Tip Toe 1994)★★★, *Yarona* (Enja/Tip Toe 1995)★★★★, *Cape Town Flowers* (Enja 1997)★★★.

Icebreaker

A British band formed in 1988 by several young musicians with an interest in a diverse range of music, from Dutch minimalism, through rock to jazz, all directed by flautist James Poke. Icebreaker's main inspiration was Louis Andriessen: the band was put together specifically for a performance of Andriessen's 'Hoketus' and first played in public at the festival of new Dutch music in York, England during April 1988. Andriessen was very impressed and has subsequently given the band much encouragement. Their repertoire includes compositions by established figures like Andriessen, Steve Reich and Michael Nyman as well as new writers such as Peter Garvey and band members Poke and Damian Le Gassick. Their non-compartmentalized attitude, shared by others of Andriessen's followers, has led to an exciting and viable fusion of contemporary classical genres like minimalism, musique concrete and electro-acoustic music with their rock descendants, scratch, techno-pop and hip-hop. At the time of writing they have not issued any recordings but have made several enthusiastically received tours, including concerts at London's Purcell Room and Shaw Theatre, and a Contemporary Music Network tour at the end of 1991.

Idle Moments - Grant Green

Guitarist Grant Green's bright but bluesy sound and infectious swing have been featured on a huge number of Blue Note albums. During the label's soul-jazz trend, Green was a true stalwart, touching each session with a certain spirited brilliance. Probably his best date, *Idle Moments* is marked by a more serious, introspective quality, and features vibraphone by Bobby Hutcherson, tenor saxophone by a young but already undeniably exceptional Joe Henderson and underrated pianist and composer Duke Pearson. The long, intimate title track is a particular highlight, and deserves to be played again and again.

- Tracks: *Idle Moments; Jean De Fleur; Django; Nomad.*
- First released 1963
- UK peak chart position: did not chart
- USA peak chart position: did not chart

If

This ambitious, multi-instrumentalist jazz-rock ensemble made its recording debut in 1970. Leader Dick Morrissey (saxophones, flute) was already a well-established figure in UK jazz circles, having led a quartet that included Phil Seaman and Harry South. Having flirted with pop and rock through an association with the Animals and Georgie Fame, Morrissey formed this new venture with guitarist Terry Smith, J.W. Hodgkinson (vocals), Dave Quincy (alto saxophone), John Mealing (keyboards), Jim Richardson (bass) and Dennis Elliott (drums) completing the initial line-up. They recorded four powerful, if commercially moribund, albums before internal pressures undermined progress. Mealing, Richardson and Elliott - the latter of whom later joined Foreigner - abandoned the group in 1972, while by the release of If's final album in 1975 only Morrissey remained from the founding septet. Although popular in Europe, the group was never able to achieve consistent commercial success, though the saxophonist subsequently enjoyed a fruitful partnership with guitarist Jim Mullen as Morrissey/Mullen.

- ALBUMS: *If* (Capitol 1970)★★★★, *If2* (Capitol 1970)★★★★, *If3* (Capitol 1971)★★, *If4* aka *Waterfall* (Capitol 1972)★★, *Double Diamond* (Capitol 1973)★★★, *Not Just Another Bunch Of Pretty Faces* (Capitol 1974)★★★, *Tea Break Is Over, Back On Your Heads* (Gull 1975)★★★.
- COMPILATIONS: *This Is If* (Capitol 1973)★★, *God Rock* (1974)★★, *Forgotten Roads: The Best Of If* (Sequel 1995)★★★.

Impressions - John Coltrane

So this is the source of the Byrds' 'Eight Miles High'? (Yes, listen to 'India'.) Coltrane continued to influence and break barriers both within his own highly fickle *cognoscenti* and outside in the rock world during the mid-60s, as his contemporaries cited his massive influence. Four exquisite excursions with McCoy Tyner (piano), Jimmy Garrison and Reggie Workman (bass), Elvin Jones and Roy Haynes (drums) and Eric Dolphy playing some extraordinary bass clarinet on the aforementioned 'India'. The other *tour de force* is the similarly explorative 'Impressions'. Not easy, but absolutely worthwhile.

- Tracks: *India; Up Against The Wall; Impressions; After The Rain.*
- First released 1963
- UK peak chart position: did not chart
- USA peak chart position: did not chart

Impulse! Records

Founded in 1960 to record currently developing areas of jazz, the Impulse! label was a division of ABC-Paramount. Under the supervision first of Creed Taylor and later Bob Thiele, Impulse! rapidly became synonymous with the new wave. Amongst the artists recorded in the 60s were Albert Ayler, John Coltrane, Pharoah Sanders and Archie Shepp. The producers were, however, alert to the continuing interest in bop and recorded several major jazzmen including Art Blakey, Freddie Hubbard and Max Roach. Simultaneously, the company's catalogue was broadened and commercially strengthened by recordings of musicians playing in older traditions: Benny Carter, Duke Ellington, Terry Gibbs, Paul Gonsalves and Coleman Hawkins. Following Coltrane's death in 1967 Impulse! gradually adopted a more commercial approach. A major reissue programme in the 80s saw much of the company's back catalogue on the shelves again, sometimes under licence to other companies, at other times under the original label and using the original distinctive fold-out sleeve format.

In A Silent Way - Miles Davis

Miles Davis's hushed masterpiece *In A Silent Way* was pieced together in the studio from a series of long stretches of quiet and intense collective improvisation. Masterfully demonstrating to the jazz world that rock's electric instruments were not necessarily harsh and noisy creatures, he again proved his creative and conceptual genius, fashioning the sound of fusion with the aid of Herbie Hancock, Chick Corea and Joe Zawinul on electric pianos and organ, John McLaughlin on electric guitar, Wayne Shorter on soprano saxophone, British bassist Dave Holland and drummer Tony

Williams. This is a delicate and beautiful thing that has rarely been repeated.

- Tracks: *Shhh; Peaceful; In A Silent Way; It's About That Time.*
- First released 1969
- UK peak chart position: did not chart
- USA peak chart position: 134

Ind, Peter

b. 20 July 1928, Uxbridge, Middlesex, England. After studying piano and composition formally, Ind began playing bass at the age of 19 and was soon hired to play in a band working on transatlantic liners. In 1951 he settled in New York where over the next few years he played with many noted jazz artists, including Lee Konitz, Warne Marsh and Buddy Rich. He also continued his studies under Lennie Tristano. In the early 60s he relocated to California, then returned to the UK. By performing and recording unaccompanied, Ind has greatly extended acceptance of the bass as a solo instrument. He has also worked in bass duos with Bernie Cash. In addition to his playing, Ind operates his own record company, Wave, and until the mid-90s ran his own London club, The Bass Clef.

- ALBUMS: with Lennie Tristano *Descent Into The Maelstrom* (1951)★★★, with Lee Konitz *Timespan* (1954-76)★★★★, *Warne Marsh New York* (1960)★★★, *Looking Out* (Wave 1957-61)★★★, *Improvisation* (Wave 1968)★★★, with Sal Mosca *At The Den* 1959 recording (1969)★★★, *No Kidding* (1974)★★★, *Peter Ind Sextet* (Wave 1975)★★, with Bernie Cash *Çontrabach* (1975)★★★★, with Konitz, Marsh *London Concert* (1976)★★★, *At The Den* (Wave 1979)★★★, with Martin Taylor *Triple Libra* (1981)★★★, with Taylor *Jazz Bass Baroque* (1987)★★★.

Infascelli, Silvia

b. 16 February 1956, Akron, Ohio, USA. A singer, composer and multi-instrumentalist, Ingram moved to Los Angeles in the early 70s where he played keyboards for Leon Haywood, and formed his own group, Revelation Funk. He also served as demo singer for various publishing companies, an occupation that led to his meeting and working with Quincy Jones. Ingram's vocals were featured on 'Just Once' and 'One Hundred Ways' from *The Dude* (1981), one of Jones's last albums for A&M Records. Both tracks made the US Top 20. Signed to Jones's own Qwest label, Ingram had a US number 1 in 1982, duetting with Patti Austin on 'Baby, Come To Me', which became the theme for the popular television soap *General Hospital*. In the same year, he released *It's Your Night*, an album that eventually spawned the hit single 'Ya Mo B There' (1984), on which he was joined by singer-songwriter Michael McDonald, and made the US Top 20 again when he teamed with Kenny Rogers and Kim Carnes for 'What About Me?'. Ingram's subsequent albums, *Never Felt So Good*, produced by Keith Diamond, and *It's Real*, on which he worked with Michael Powell and Gene Griffin, failed to live up to the promise of his earlier work, although he continued to feature in the singles chart with 'Somewhere Out There', a duet with Linda Ronstadt from Steven Spielberg's animated movie *An American Tail*, and 'I Don't Have The Heart', which topped the US chart in 1990. Also in that year, Ingram was featured, along with Al B. Sure!, El DeBarge and Barry White, on 'The Secret Garden (Sweet Seduction Suite)', from Quincy Jones's album *Back On The Block*. Ingram has also served as a backing singer for several other big-name artists, such as Luther Vandross and the Brothers Johnson. His compositions include 'P.Y.T. (Pretty Young Thing)', which he wrote in collaboration with Quincy Jones for Michael Jackson's 1982 smash hit album *Thriller*.

- ALBUMS: *It's Your Night* (Qwest 1983)★★, *Never Felt So Good* (Qwest 1986)★★, *It's Real* (Qwest 1989)★★, *Always You* (Qwest 1993)★★.
- COMPILATIONS: *The Power Of Great Music* (Qwest 1991)★★★.

Ingham, Keith

b. 5 February 1942, London, England. Ingham is a self-taught jazz pianist who turned professional in 1964. He played with artists including Sandy Brown and Bruce Turner. In 1974 he recorded in London with Bob Wilber and Bud Freeman and recorded two solo albums for EMI. In 1978 he moved to New York where he played with Benny Goodman and the World's Greatest Jazz Band. He became musical director and record producer for Susannah McCorkle as well as recording with Maxine Sullivan. He works with guitarist Marty Grosz in various bands including the Orphan Newsboys in which they perform some of the lesser-known music of the 30s and 40s.

- ALBUMS: with Bud Freeman *Superbud* (1977)★★, with Dick Sudhalter *Get Out And Get Under The Moon* (1989)★★★★, with Marty Grosz *Unsaturated Fats* (1990)★★★, *The Music Of Victor Young* (Jump 1991), with the Orphan Newsboys *Laughing At Life* (1990)★★★, *Out Of The Past* (Stomp Off 1992)★★★, *My Little Brown Book* (Progressive 1995)★★★★, *The Intimacy Of The Blues* (Progressive 1995)★★★, *Music From The Mauve Decades* (Sackville 1996)★★★★, *Just Imagine* (Stomp Off 1996)★★★, *New York Nine Vol 1* (Jump 1997)★★, *New York Nine Vol 2* (Jump 1997)★★, *The Back Room Romp* (Sackville 1997)★★★, *Donaldson Redux* 1991 recording (Stomp Off 1996)★★★★.

International Sweethearts Of Rhythm

In 1937, Laurence Clifton Jones, administrator of a school for poor and orphaned children at Piney Woods, Mississippi, USA, decided to form a band. At first his enterprise was only mildly successful, but by the end of the decade it had achieved a high standard of musicianship and was growing in reputation. In 1941 the band came under new management and hired Eddie Durham as arranger and musical director. Soon afterwards, Durham was replaced by Jesse Stone, a noted Kansas City bandleader and arranger. Although mostly using black female musicians, a few white women were hired but, given the existence of segregation, these often had to 'pass' for black. At the end of World War II the Sweethearts toured American bases in Europe, played the Olympia Theatre in Paris, and broadcast on the Armed Forces Radio service. In 1949 the band folded but their leader for many years, Ann Mae Winburn, formed a new group. By the mid-50s, however, this band too had ceased to exist. All but forgotten, memories of the band were revived largely through the efforts of record producer Rosetta Reitz, who released an album of the Sweethearts' AFRS broadcasts. Reminiscences by former members of the band were recorded in books on women jazz players by Sally Placksin (*Jazz Women*), Linda Dahl (*Stormy Weather*) and others, and in a television documentary which included footage of the band in performance. At its peak, in the early 40s, the Sweethearts were an excellent, swinging band with a style and power similar to that of bands such as Lucky Millinder's. Although the band led by Ina Ray Hutton was more popular with the general public, the Sweethearts were more accomplished musicians; unfortunately they were ignored in certain important areas of showbusiness, such as the motion-picture industry, because they were black. Among the long-serving members of the band were several excellent musicians, particularly trumpeter Ray Carter and alto saxophonist Roz Cron. The band's outstanding players were another trumpeter, Ernestine 'Tiny' Davis, Pauline Braddy and Vi Burnside. Davis was a fine jazz player who also sang; Braddy was a superb, driving drummer whose advisers and admirers included Big Sid Catlett and Jo Jones. The solo playing of Burnside, a tenor saxophonist (one of whose high-school classmates was Sonny Rollins) shows her to have been a player who, had she been male, would have been ranked alongside the best of the day. Her breathy sound resembled that of Ben Webster, but there was never any suggestion that she was merely a copyist. Burnside was a major jazz talent and the International Sweethearts Of Rhythm were one of the best big bands of the swing era. The fact that they are so often overlooked is a sad reflection on the male-dominated world in which they strove to make their mark.

● COMPILATIONS: *The International Sweethearts Of Rhythm* (Rosetta 1945-46)★★★, with others *Women In Jazz Vol. 1* (1945-46)★★★.

IRVIS, CHARLIE

b. *c.*1899, possibly New York City, New York, USA, d. *c.*1939. After playing in a youth band in which his companions included Bubber Miley, trombonist Irvis accompanied blues singer Lucille Hegamin and also worked with Willie 'The Lion' Smith. During the early and mid-20s he was with Duke Ellington and also appeared on numerous recording dates, often under the leadership of Clarence Williams. In the late 20s he played with bands led by Charlie 'Fess' Johnson and Jelly Roll Morton and in 1931 performed briefly with his old school friend Miley. Although he drifted into obscurity as the decade progressed, Irvis left a number of recordings on which his distinctive muted playing can be heard, notably those made with Fats Waller.

● COMPILATIONS: *The Real Fats Waller* (1929)★★★.

ISAACS, IKE

b. 1 December 1919, Rangoon, Burma. Until the end of World War II Isaacs lived in India and Burma, where he occasionally played guitar but mostly worked as a chemist. In the UK in the late 40s he freelanced, playing radio shows and leading his own small groups. Among the musicians with whom he played and sometimes recorded during the 40s and 50s were Ted Heath, Ralph Sharon and George Chisholm. A busy session musician, very active in studio work and playing in all manner of musical styles, Isaacs' first love was for jazz and through the 60s, 70s and 80s he played with leading jazz musicians, including Barney Kessel, Stéphane Grappelli, Digby Fairweather and Martin Taylor. A notable player on both acoustic and electric guitars, Isaacs has written extensively on his craft and in the 80s taught music at the Sydney Guitar School in Australia. This artist should not be confused with the similarly named American bass player, Charles Edward 'Ike' Isaacs.

● ALBUMS: *Ike Isaacs* (1966)★★★, *The Latin Guitars Of Ike Isaacs* (1978)★★★★, with Martin Taylor *After Hours* (1979)★★★.

ISAACS, MARK

b. 22 June 1958, London, England. Isaacs's family emigrated to Australia in 1963. He was taught harmony and theory by his jazz musician father and at the age of 12 Mark had written a woodwind suite. During his schooling he was an after-hours student at the Sydney Conservatorium, studying piano and theory with the eminent Peter Sculthorpe. By the age of 18, Isaacs was developing a simultaneous career as a classical and jazz musician. In 1979 his first jazz solo album was released containing original compositions. In the early 80s he went to America to play and continue his studies, where he completed his Master Of Music degree at the Eastman School of Music. His second album, *Preludes*, was recorded in Australia in 1988. Returning to America, Isaacs witnessed his work, *So It Does*, performed at Carnegie Hall by the Australian Ensemble. In New York in 1988, Isaacs, together with jazz veterans Dave Holland and Roy Haynes, recorded *Encounters*, an impromptu album of jazz originals. The album was a major breakthrough for Isaacs and heralded him as a major talent. He then formed a trio with Adam Armstrong (bass) and Andrew Gander (drums), which toured Europe. This unit captured Isaacs at his peak of creative flair and technical virtuosity and in 1993 they toured Russia playing 24 concerts in 17 cities. Isaacs also performed his own piano concerto with the St. Petersburg State Symphony Orchestra. 'Playing the same piano that Rachmaninov and Shostakovich played was quite an experience', says Isaacs, who completed his Russian tour with five trio concerts in Moscow. In 1995 ABC Music released a four-album set of originals, *Air*, *Earth*, *Fire* and *Water*, collectively entitled *The Elements*. The work featured an introspective Isaacs at the piano and his response to the transcendent and spiritual potential of music. In 1996 he was arranging for the Australian Art Orchestra, working with his trio and contemplating writing an opera. An admirable jazz piano player and composer, Isaacs personifies a fertile and creative period of Australian improvised music. His uncle is the guitarist Ike Isaacs.

● ALBUMS: *Originals* (ABC 1979)★★★, *Preludes* (1988)★★★★, *Encounters* (ABC 1988)★★★, *So It Does* (ABC 1989)★★★, *For Sure* (ABC 1993)★★★, *The Elements* (ABC 1995)★★★★.

ISHAM, MARK

b. *c*.50s, New York City, New York, USA. Born into a musical family that encouraged him to learn the piano, violin and trumpet at an early age, Mark Isham began studying the jazz trumpet while at high school and then explored electronic music while in his early 20s. For a time he pursued parallel careers as a classical, jazz and rock musician, performing, for instance, with the San Francisco Opera, the Beach Boys and Pharoah Sanders, but by he early 70s, he concentrated his efforts on jazz. As co-leader of pianist Art Lande's Rubisa Patrol, he recorded two albums on ECM Records in the late 70s, continuing his partnership with Lande through to the late 80s. Together with guitarist Peter Mannu, Synthesizer player Patrick O'Hearn and drummer Terry Bozzio, he set up the Group 87 ensemble in 1979, releasing a self-titled debut album in 1981. At the same time, Isham continued his links with rock music, recording and touring as part of Van Morrison's band, where his trumpet and flugelhorn set off the saxophone of Pee Wee Ellis to good effect. During the 80s, Isham developed his compositional skills, using a synthesis of brass, electronics and his own plaintive trumpet to produce a very visual, narrative form of music. He recalls that 'my mother once told me that, as a kid, even before I really played music, I tried to tell stories with music. So, whether it's in the vocabulary of heavy metal or Stravinsky, the thread has to do with images.' Isham has taken that thread into film music, scoring the Academy winning documentary *The Life and Times Of Harvey Milk*, the film *Mrs Soffel* (both recorded on *Film Music*), and writing music to accompany children's fairy tales. His feature credits include *Trouble In Mind*, *Everybody Wins*, *Reversal Of Fortune*, *Billy Bathgate*, *Little Man Tate*, *Cool World*, *Of Mice And Men*, *Sketch Artist*, *The Public Eye*, *A River Runs Through It*, *Nowhere To Run*, *Fire In The Sky*, *A Midnight Clear*, *Made In America*, *Romeo Is Bleeding*, *Short Cuts*, *Quiz Show*, *The Getaway*, *The Moderns*, *The Browning Version*, *Timecop*, *Mrs. Parker And The Vicious Circle*, *Nell*, *Quiz Show* (1994) and *Gotti* (1996). Throughout his career, Isham has remained a prolific session man, whose work encompasses recordings with artists as varied as saxophonist David Liebman, guitarist David Torn, and singers Suzanne Vega, Tanita Tikaram and Marianne Faithfull. Isham is blessed with an instantly memorable trumpet sound, one that is burnished, resonant, in places lush but which can, at times, be bleakly powerful, relying on minimalist fragments to achieve its subdued effect.

● ALBUMS: with Art Lande *Rubisia Patrol* (ECM 1976)★★, with Lande *Desert Marauders* (ECM 1978)★★★, *Group 87* (1981)★★, *Vapour Drawings* (Windham Hill 1983)★★★★, *A Career In Dada Processing* (1984)★★★, with Lande *We Begin* (1987)★★★, *Film Music* (Windham Hill 1987)★★★★, *Fire In The Sky* (1993)★★★, *Blue Sun* (Columbia 1995)★★★, *Afterglow* (Columbia 1998)★★★★.

ISOLA, FRANK

b. 20 February 1925, Detroit, Michigan, USA. When Isola was 11 years old he was taken to see the Benny Goodman band with Gene Krupa on drums and was inspired to take up drumming. Six years later he won a local heat of a national Gene Krupa Drum Contest but was later disqualified as being already technically a professional. (The eventual national winner was Louie Bellson whom he met a few years later when doing basic training following induction into the armed services during World War II.) After the war, Isola studied formally in California, then joined successively the bands of Earle Spencer and Johnny Bothwell. In the late 40s and on into the early 50s he gigged in New York and also sat in on countless informal jam sessions, playing with Stan Getz, Charlie Parker, Warne Marsh and many others. Some of the sessions with Parker were privately recorded and released many years later. In 1952 he joined Getz and for the next five years was a frequent member of his quintet. During this period Isola also played with Gerry Mulligan. When Mose Allison joined Getz the two hit if off and Isola was hired by the pianist when he recorded *Back Country Suite*. This was in 1957 and proved to be Isola's last recording date. By the time the 60s were over Isola's career as a jazz musician was virtually finished, although he continued to play occasionally in Detroit to where he returned. As Gordon Jack reported in *Jazz Journal International*, for many years Isola lived in a hotel from where he could see the building in which he first took drum lessons, then in 1992 he moved to an apartment from which he could see the Fox Theatre where he had seen Gene Krupa back in 1936. A self-effacing, undemonstrative drummer, Isola always regarded himself as 'just a timekeeper' but, as his recordings with Getz, Bob Brookmeyer, Mulligan and others clearly demonstrate, his understated skills were a major contribution to some outstanding jazz sessions.

● ALBUMS: with Charlie Parker *Apartment Sessions* (Spotlite 1950)★★★★, with Stan Getz *At The Shrine Auditorium* (1954)★★★, with Gerry Mulligan *Paris Concert* (Vogue 1954)★★★★, with Mose Allison *Back Country Suite* (Original Jazz Classics 1957)★★★.

ISOTOPE

Led by former session guitarist Gary Boyle (b. 24 November 1941, Patna, India), Isotope was a highly-regarded UK jazz-rock band of the 70s. Boyle had previously played with Brian Auger, Keith Tippett, and Stomu Yamash'ta when he formed this progressive jazz/rock fusion band in 1974 with Jeff Clyne (b. 29 January 1947, London, England; bass), Brian Miller (b. 28 April 1947, St. Neots, Cambridgeshire, England; keyboards) and Nigel Norris (b. 20 June 1948, Dalston, London, England; drums). They signed to the newly formed Gull label but after a US tour in 1974 Clyne and Miller returned to the orthodox jazz scene. They were replaced for the second album with ex-Soft Machine stalwart Hugh Hopper (bass) and Lawrence Scott (keyboards). Vocalist Zoe Kronberger appeared on the final album and guested on *The Dancer* (1977), the first of two solo albums made by Boyle for Gull after Isotope disbanded in 1976.

● ALBUMS: *Isotope* (Gull 1974)★★★★, *Illusion* (Gull 1974)★★★, *Deep End* (1976)★★★.

● COMPILATIONS: *The Best Of Isotope* (1979)★★★★.

ISRAELS, CHUCK

b. Charles H. Israels, 10 October 1936, New York City, New York, USA. After extensive studies in the USA and France, Israels began playing bass with various leading jazzmen in the mid-50s. He recorded with Cecil Taylor, John Coltrane, George Russell and Eric Dolphy. In 1961 he joined the Bill Evans trio, taking over from Scott La Faro. He remained with Evans for five years, concurrently recording with several other artists including Herbie Hancock, Stan Getz and Hampton Hawes. In the early 70s Israels was instrumental in establishing the National Jazz Ensemble, a big band which brought contemporary ideas and techniques to the music of early jazzmen, such as Jelly Roll Morton and Louis Armstrong, while simultaneously developing for big band the creations of Thelonious Monk and other leading bop musicians. After the dissolution of the NJE in 1978 Israels performed less, although he did make occasional record dates in the early 80s.

● ALBUMS: with Bill Evans *How My Heart Sings!* (1962)★★★★, with Evans *The Second Trio* (1962)★★★, *National Jazz Ensemble* (1975-76)★★★, with Metropole Orchestra, Claudio Roditi *Endhoven Concert* (Azica 1998)★★★.

IZENZON, DAVID

b. 17 May 1932, Pittsburgh, Pennsylvania, USA, d. 8 October 1979. Izenzon sang in the local synagogue as a child, and did not begin studying bass until 1956. After working with Bill Dixon, Archie Shepp, Paul Bley and Sonny Rollins he joined the Ornette Coleman trio from 1962-66, recording on important releases such as *Town Hall Concert*, *An Evening With Ornette Coleman*, the two volumes of *At The Golden Circle* and the film soundtracks *Chappaqua Suite* and *Who's Crazy?*. Izenzon was later re-united with Coleman for some gigs in 1968, 1972 and 1973 by a two bass quartet where he played in tandem with one of his predecessors, Charlie Haden. During Coleman's 1965-66 European tour Izenzon settled in London, recording a number of tracks which have never been publicly issued. Back in New York in 1967 he played with Coleman at the funeral of John Coltrane, and also worked with Jaki Byard (*Sunshine Of My Soul*) and Perry Robinson. From 1968-71 he taught at Bronx Community College, New York. After his second stint with Coleman he formed a quintet with Carlos Ward, Gato Barbieri, Karl Berger and Art Lewis, and an all-bass band called Bass Revolution. In 1972 Izenzon gave up performing to spend more time with his son, who was born with serious brain-damage, and to study for a PhD in psychotherapy at Indiana Northwestern University. He set up in practice as a therapist in New York and published a book, *Emotions*. Although he restricted his playing he continued to compose during this time, one piece being a jazz opera, *How Music Can Save The World*. He was a highly individual and influential player, especially because of his remarkable arco (bowed) playing.

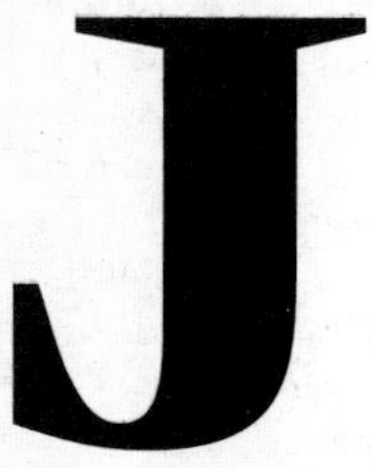

Jackie And Roy

(see Kral, Roy)

Jackson, Chubby

b. Greig Stewart Jackson, 25 October 1918, New York City, New York, USA. As a youth Jackson started out playing clarinet but switched to bass in the mid-30s. In 1937 he began playing professionally, working in a number of minor dance bands. In 1942 he joined the Charlie Barnet band and, the following year, was a member of Woody Herman's First Herd, where he played alongside Ralph Burns, Billy Bauer and Dave Tough in one of the most exciting rhythm sections in the history of big band jazz. After leaving Herman in 1946 Jackson freelanced, playing with various bands for record dates, including those led by Charlie Ventura and Herman. He also led a bop-orientated small group, featuring Conte Candoli, Terry Gibbs, Frank Socolow, Lou Levy, Denzil Best and others, with which he toured Scandinavia. In the late 40s and early 50s Jackson was active in the studios, led his own big band and made numerous record dates with artists including Bill Harris, Zoot Sims and Gerry Mulligan. Jackson was also a member of the Charlie Ventura Big Four with Marty Napoleon and Buddy Rich. In the 60s Jackson worked in television, hosting a programme for children. He intermittently led bands during these years and also freelanced, playing in bands led by Harold Baker and Bill Coleman. To a great extent, however, Jackson was largely forgotten by the jazz world other than through his earlier records. Then, in the late 70s, he reappeared as a member of the all-star band which Lionel Hampton led on a tour of festivals in the USA, UK and Europe. One of the most overtly enthusiastic musicians in jazz, Jackson's forceful, attacking style was particularly suited to the bands of Herman, Ventura and Hampton. His son is Duffy Jackson, drummer with Count Basie and Hampton. In the late 80s Jackson was still around the jazz scene, lending his exhilarating support to a variety of bands.

● ALBUMS: with Charlie Ventura *The Big Four* (1951)★★★, *Chubby's Back!* (1957)★★★, with Lionel Hampton *All Star Band At Newport '78* (1978)★★★★.

● COMPILATIONS: *The Best Of Woody Herman* (1945-47)★★★★, with Woody Herman *Carnegie Hall Concert* (1946)★★★★, *Jam Session* (1947)★★★, *Choice Cuts* (Esquire 1986)★★★, *The Happy Monster* (Cool 'n' Blue 1993, recordings 1944-1947)★★★★.

Jackson, Cliff

b. 19 July 1902, Culpeper, Virginia, USA, d. 24 May 1970, New York City, New York, USA. After studying piano formally Jackson turned to jazz, working in various east coast cities before coming to New York in the early 20s. During the rest of the decade he played in several minor bands, eventually joining one led by Elmer Snowden. Jackson later formed his own small group for club engagements. In the 30s he worked mostly as a soloist but also accompanied singers. In the 40s he was with Sidney Bechet, Eddie Condon and others, appearing regularly throughout this and the following decade at New York's top jazz clubs, including Nick's Cafe Society (Downtown) and Jimmy Ryan's. Also in the 60s he worked with his wife, Maxine Sullivan. He was resident at the RX Room from 1968 until the night before his death in May 1970. His widow later turned their home into a museum, the 'House That Jazz Built'. A vigorous performer, early in his career Jackson was a leading stride pianist, greatly feared in cutting contests where he would happily take on much bigger names.

● ALBUMS: *Cliff Jackson's Washboard Wanderers* (1961)★★★, with Dick Wellstood *Uptown And Downtown* (Swingville 1961)★★★, *Hot Piano* (1965)★★★, *Parlor Social Piano* (Fat Cat Jazz 1968)★★★, *Cliff Jackson And His Crazy Cats* 1930 recordings (Fountain 1981)★★★, *Carolina Shout!* 1961/1962 recordings (Black Lion)★★★★.

Jackson, Dewey

b. 21 June 1900, St. Louis, Missouri, USA. Jackson began playing trumpet as a child and was still only in his mid-teens when he was playing professionally with several bands in his home-town. In 1919 he became a regular on the Mississippi riverboats plying out of St. Louis, where his musical companions included Charlie Creath and, a few years later, Fate Marable. He continued to work the riverboats with Creath and Marable during the 20s and into the late 30s, although he spent a few months in New York playing in Andy Preer's band at the Cotton Club in 1926. In the early 40s he was still based in St. Louis, but now playing hotels, before he drifted from music for a while, returning in the 50s to play with fellow townsman Singleton Palmer's popular local orchestra. Jackson continued to play sporadically through the 50s and 60s but became steadily less active as the years passed. A sound player in an early jazz style, Jackson's career choices kept him from the big city limelight, but doubtless also offered him a more reliable career than the much more competitive New York scene. Although his rather ornamental style now sounds a little dated, he played with considerable command and fluency. His playing with his own Peacock Orchestra, a band he led on the riverboat *SS Capitol*, and which made a tiny handful of records, shows a fine sense of the polyphonic drive of post-New Orleans music.

JACKSON, DUFFY

b. USA. A dynamic and skilful drummer, he is the son of Chubby Jackson and displays a similarly exuberant sense of swing and enthusiasm. He has worked with many musicians, playing in a wide range of styles, including an appearance on a mid-90s Harry Allen session for the Nagel-Heyer release, *The King*. It is clear that Jackson is at his happiest and best working with mainstreamers such as Allen.

● ALBUMS: *Swing! Swing! Swing!* (Milestone 1995)★★★.

JACKSON, J.J.

b. Bronx, New York City, New York, USA. Jackson first attracted attention as an arranger for jazz organist Brother Jack McDuff and blues singer Jimmy Witherspoon. He subsequently formed a songwriting partnership with Sid Barnes and enjoyed success with compositions for Inez And Charlie Foxx and Mary Wells. Jackson's performing career began in earnest in 1966. The ebullient 'But It's Alright' was recorded in London with a backing band which featured saxophonists Dick Morrissey and John Marshall. Subsequent releases included the energetic 'Come See Me', later recorded by the Pretty Things, as well as a version of Robbie Robertson's 'The Stones I Throw'. Jackson continued recording into the 70s and his voice was featured in the soundtrack to the film *Car Wash*. He has since become a respected disc jockey and, more recently, a 'video jockey' on the MTV channel.

● ALBUMS: *J.J.* (1966)★★, *But It's Alright/I Dig Girls* (1967)★★★, *J.J. Jackson With The Greatest Little Soul Band* (Strike 1967)★★★, *The Great J.J. Jackson* (1968)★★★, *The Greatest Little Soul Band In The World* (MCA 1969)★★★, *J.J.'s Dilemma* (RCA Victor 1970)★★.

JACKSON, MILT 'BAGS'

b. 1 January 1923, Detroit, Michigan, USA. Jackson's first professional engagement, at the age of 16, was in his hometown, playing the vibraphone alongside tenor saxophonist Lucky Thompson (one year his junior). Jackson benefited from the 40s loose attitude towards band personnel, spending six years accompanying visiting musicians, as well as studying at Michigan State University. In 1945 Dizzy Gillespie heard him and invited him to join his band for a west coast tour. Later moving to New York, the brilliant young vibes player found himself much in demand, playing and recording with Howard McGhee and Thelonious Monk (including Monk's classic 1951 session for Blue Note). A spell with Woody Herman (1949-50) and more work with Gillespie established him as the pre-eminent player on his instrument. Jackson's recording debut as a leader was for Gillespie's Dee Gee label in 1951. He also had the depth of experience to play with both Ben Webster and Charlie Parker. In 1954 the Milt Jackson Quartet transformed itself into the Modern Jazz Quartet, with pianist John Lewis becoming musical director. For the next 20 years, Milt Jackson led a Dr Jeckyll and Mr Hyde existence, playing the consummately sophisticated music of the MJQ, all dressed in their famous tuxedoes, and leading his own dates in the swinging company of Coleman Hawkins, Lucky Thompson or Horace Silver. In 1961 Jackson accompanied Ray Charles on *Soul Meeting*, on which the soul singer restricted himself to electric piano and alto saxophone. Sleevenote writers loved to debate how happy Jackson could be with the MJQ's starchy charts. Certainly when he broke up the group in 1974, it was due to what he considered its financial exploitation rather than musical antagonism. Before Jackson, the vibes were an instrument associated with the hot, swinging proto-R&B of big band leaders Lionel Hampton and Johnny Otis. By slowing the vibrato and giving the right-hand mallet sweeping lines like a saxophone, Jackson gave the instrument sensuality and soul. Not until the appearance of Bobby Hutcherson in the mid-60s did anyone come up with an alternative modern approach to playing it. Jackson's harmonic sense was unerringly inventive and he also kept his ears open for new talent. He championed guitarist Wes Montgomery and recorded with him for Riverside Records (*Bags Meets Wes*, 1961). Jackson was a strong force in the reintegration of bebop with swing values and musicians, the very definition of what came to be known as 'mainstream' jazz. His own quintets included players such as Cedar Walton, Jimmy Heath and James Moody. The 70s were a hard period for jazz players, but even in the dated arrangements of Bob James on a record like *Olinga* (recorded in 1974 for CTI) his caressing, ebullient vibes playing shines through. The 80s jazz revival was reflected by the MJQ reforming and appearing at countless jazz festivals. In 1985 Jackson toured Europe under his own name. Pablo Records continued to document his music into the 90s.

● ALBUMS: *In The Beginning* 1948 recordings (Original Jazz Classics)★★★, *Milt Jackson* 10-inch album (Dee Gee 1952)★★★, *Wizard Of The Vibes* reissued as *Milt Jackson* (Blue Note 1952)★★★★, *Milt Jackson* reissued as *Meet Milt Jackson* (Savoy 1954)★★★★, *Milt Jackson Quintet* 10-inch album (Prestige 1954)★★★★, *Milt Jackson* reissued as *Soul Pioneers* (Prestige 1955)★★★★, *Opus De Jazz* (Savoy 1955)★★★, *Roll Em Bags* (Savoy 1955)★★★, *The Jazz Skyline* (Savoy 1956)★★★, *Jackson's-ville* (Savoy 1956)★★★, *Ballads & Blues* (Atlantic 1956)★★★★, *Plenty, Plenty Soul* (Atlantic 1957)★★★★, *Bags & Flutes* (Atlantic 1958)★★★, with Ray Charles *Soul Brothers* (Atlantic 1958)★★★★, *Bean Bags* (Atlantic 1959)★★★★, *Bags' Opus* (United Artists 1959)★★★★, *Ballad Artistry* (Atlantic 1960)★★★, with John Coltrane *Bags And Trane* (Atlantic 1961)★★★★, with Charles *Soul Meeting* (Atlantic 1961)★★★★, with Wes Montgomery *Bags Meets Wes* (Riverside 1962)★★★★, *Statements* (Impulse! 1962)★★★, *Big Bags* (Riverside 1962)★★★★, *Invitation* (Riverside 1963)★★★★, *Jazz n' Samba* (Impulse! 1964)★★★, *In A New Setting* (Limelight 1964)★★★, *At The Museum Of Modern Art* (Limelight 1965)★★★★, *Born Free* (Limelight 1966)★★★, *For Someone I Love* (Riverside 1966)★★★, *'Live' At The Village Gate* (Riverside 1967)★★★, *Memphis Jackson* (Impulse! 1967)★★★, *Bags And Brass* (Riverside 1968)★★★, *Milt Jackson And The Hip String Quartet* (Verve 1969)★★★, *Sunflower* (CTI 1973)★★★, *Goodbye* (CTI 1973)★★★, *Olinga* (CTI 1974)★★, *Montreux '75* (Pablo

1975)★★★, *The Big 3* (Pablo 1975)★★★, *Feelings* (Pablo 1976)★★★, *Soul Fusion* (Pablo 1977)★★★★, *Montreux '77* (Pablo 1977)★★★, *Milt Jackson + Count Basie + The Big Band, Vols 1 and 2* (Pablo 1978)★★★, *Soul Believer* (Pablo 1978)★★, *All Too Soon: The Duke Ellington Album* (Pablo 1980)★★★, *Night Mist* (Pablo 1980)★★★, *Big Mouth* (Pablo 1981)★★★, *Ain't But A Few Of Us Left* (Pablo 1982)★★★, *Jackson, Johnson, Brown & Company* (Pablo 1983)★★★, *Soul Route* (Pablo 1984)★★, *It Don't Mean A Thing If You Can't Tap Your Foot To It* (Pablo 1985)★★★, *Brother Jim* (Pablo 1986)★★, *A London Bridge* 1982 recording (Pablo 1986)★★★, *Bebop* (East West 1988)★★★, *Mostly Duke* 1982 recording (Pablo 1991)★★★, *Memories Of Thelonious Sphere Monk* 1982 recording (Pablo 1991)★★★, *The Harem* (Music Masters 1991)★★★, *Reverence And Compassion* (Qwest 1993)★★★, *The Prophet Speaks* (Qwest 1994)★★★, *Burnin' In The Woodhouse* (Qwest 1995)★★★, *Sa Va Bella (For Lady Legends)* (Qwest 1997)★★.

● COMPILATIONS: *The Complete Milt Jackson* (Prestige 1969)★★★★, *The Best Of Milt Jackson* (Pablo 1982)★★★★.

JACKSON, OLIVER

b. 28 April 1933, Detroit, Michigan, USA, d. 29 May 1994, New York, USA. In the mid-40s drummer Jackson was active among Detroit R&B and bebop musicians, picking up the nickname 'Bops Jnr.' in the process. Among the artists with whom he worked during his formative years were Barry Harris, Donald Byrd and Tommy Flanagan, as well as the equally young and inexperienced John Coltrane. Jackson established a reputation as a sensitive accompanist to pianists and later in the decade played in trios with Flanagan and Dorothy Donegan. Then, in collaboration with fellow drummer Eddie Locke, Jackson formed a tap-dancing duo, Bops And Locke, which met with considerable success. Throughout the 50s he played with a variety of jazzmen, shifting comfortably between exponents of traditional and of modern music such as Red Allen and Yusef Lateef. In the early 60s he worked with Charlie Shavers, Buck Clayton, Benny Goodman and Lionel Hampton and then spent the rest of the decade with Earl Hines. In 1969 he formed the JPJ Quartet (with Budd Johnson, Bill Pemberton and Dill Jones), which played extensively in the USA. In the 70s and 80s Jackson appeared with Sy Oliver, Hampton again, Oscar Peterson, Doc Cheatham, Vic Dickenson, Buddy Tate, a band he co-led with Haywood Henry, and with his own groups, which featured Irving Stokes, Norris Turney and his bass-playing brother, Ali Jackson (who died in 1987). During this period Oliver became a familiar and popular figure at jazz festivals in the USA and Europe. Jackson's playing ranged over the full spectrum of jazz and he made an important contribution to many excellent concert and recording sessions.

● ALBUMS: *The Oliver Jackson-Jack Sels Quartet* (1961)★★★, with Buck Clayton *Olympia Concert* (1961)★★★★, *Coleman Hawkins And The Earl Hines Trio* (1965)★★★, with Doc Cheatham *Jive At Five* (1975)★★★, with Haywood Henry *Real Jazz Express* (1977)★★, *The Oliver Jackson Trio* (1979)★★★, *Oliver Jackson Presents Le Quartet* (1982)★★, *Billie's Bounce* (Black And Blue 1984)★★★.

JACKSON, PRESTON

b. 3 January 1902, New Orleans, Louisiana, USA, d. 12 November 1983. From his early teens Jackson lived in Chicago, where he learned the trombone in 1920. He played with several local bands throughout the 20s and in the early 30s was in demand by prominent local bandleaders such as Dave Peyton and Erskine Tate. In 1926 he recorded with Luis Russell and with a band led by clarinettist Arthur Sims; he also fronted his own pick-up group on a 1928 date. In 1931 he joined Louis Armstrong, then worked with Frankie Jaxon, recording with him in 1933, Carroll Dickerson, Jimmie Noone, Zilner Randolph, Walter Barnes and others, mostly touring the mid-western and south-west states by the end of the decade. However, Jackson was musically active only on a part-time basis. During the 40s and 50s he was involved in musicians' union work, but occasionally formed bands for club and record dates and also worked briefly with Richard M. Jones, Johnny Dodds, Lillian Armstrong and others. He continued this sporadic activity into the next decade, towards the end of which he worked with Little Brother Montgomery. In the 70s he toured with Kid Thomas and, resident once more in New Orleans, played with the Preservation Hall Jazz Band. During his playing career Jackson's style moved with the times. Although his occupation began in Chicago, he based his early playing on that of other relocated New Orleans jazzmen. In mid-career he incorporated swing era developments into his repertoire, then late in life returned to his roots but with a sophisticated stylistic patina. Deeply interested in the history of jazz, Jackson wrote extensively for magazines over a 40-year period.

● ALBUMS: with Kid Thomas *The New Orleans Joymakers* (1973)★★★.

● COMPILATIONS: *Louis Armstrong And His Orchestra Vol. 9* (1931)★★★★.

JACKSON, QUENTIN

b. 13 January 1909, Springfield, Ohio, USA, d. 2 October 1976. As a child Jackson had learned to play piano, organ and violin, but in his late teens he took up the trombone. He received tuition from his brother-in-law, Claude Jones, who played in McKinney's Cotton Pickers; after a couple of years of intensive touring with various territory bands, in 1930 Jackson, too, joined McKinney. Two years later he switched to the band formed by the McKinney band's musical director, Don Redman. During his long stay with Redman he picked up the nickname, 'Butter', and attracted considerable attention from other trombone players and bandleaders. In 1939 he joined Cab Calloway, with whom he remained for eight years, then moved on to the Duke Ellington orchestra for an even longer period, eventually leaving in 1959. In the early 60s Jackson was briefly with Quincy Jones and Count Basie, Ellington again, and recorded important albums with Charles Mingus. Jackson then settled into a combination of studio work and appearances with big bands led by Louie Bellson and Gerald Wilson and in the early 70s was in the Thad Jones-Mel Lewis Jazz Orchestra. A strong and reliable section player, Jackson was also an excellent soloist with a rich, emotional tone.

● ALBUMS: *Ellington '55* (1953-54)★★★★, with Ellington *Such Sweet Thunder* (1957)★★★, *Mingus, Mingus, Mingus, Mingus* (1963)★★★★, with Thad Jones-Mel Lewis *Suite For Pops* (1972)★★★.

JACKSON, RONALD SHANNON

b. 12 January 1940, Fort Worth, Texas, USA. Jackson studied piano at the age of five, taking up clarinet and drums at school. He began professional work when he was 15, gigging regularly in Dallas with James Clay and Leroy Cooper who were then in the Ray Charles's band. He studied history and sociology before gaining a music scholarship in New York, where he worked with artists including Albert Ayler, Charles Tyler, Betty Carter, Charles Mingus and Stanley Turrentine. From 1975-79 Jackson played alongside James 'Blood' Ulmer in the Ornette Coleman Sextet which evolved into Prime Time, and also worked with Cecil Taylor. Jackson joined Ulmer's band until setting up his own innovative and highly acclaimed Decoding Society in 1981. Although continuing to be based in Coleman's theory of harmolodics, the music of the Decoding Society changed its sound and direction with each album during the late 80s, often radically changing its instrumental line-up too. However, the foundation was always Jackson's thunderous, supple percussion. In 1986 he set up Last Exit with Peter Brötzmann, Sonny Sharrock and Bill Laswell, and in 1987 formed the trio Power Tools with Bill Frisell and Melvin Gibbs. In the late 80s and early 90s Jackson was re-united with Ulmer on record and in tours with a blues/funk-based power trio.

● ALBUMS: *Eye On You* (1981)★★★, *Nasty* (1981)★★★★, *Man Dance* (1982)★★, *Barbecue Dog* (Antilles 1984)★★★, *Decode Yourself* (Island 1985)★★★, *When Colors Play* (1987)★★★, with Power Tools *Strange Meeting* (1987)★★★, *When Colours Play* (Caravan Of Dreams 1987)★★★, *Live At The Caravan Of Dreams* (1987)★★, *Texas* (1989)★★★, *Taboo* (Virgin 1990)★★★, *Red Warrior* (Axiom 1991)★★, *Raven Roc* (DIW 1992)★★★.

JACKSON, TONY

b. 5 June 1876, New Orleans, Louisiana, USA, d. 20 April 1920. An entertainer of great repute, Jackson played piano and sang in New Orleans saloons and brothels in the early 1900s. His repertoire included popular songs of the day, emergent blues and operatic arias, but it was as a ragtime pianist that he had most influence upon his contemporaries. As with Buddy Bolden in the field of jazz, Jackson's fame rests on stories told about him by other musicians because, like Bolden, he never recorded. In 1912 Jackson moved to Chicago, where he played in the city's leading nightclubs, usually as a solo act. Billed as 'the 'world's greatest single-handed entertainer', Jackson's private life was troubled. He was an alcoholic and his sexual activities left him disease-ridden. However, his musical ability was such that Jelly Roll Morton, who rarely praised anyone but himself, spoke very highly of him. Jackson seldom bothered to have his own compositions published, believing that the pittance which music publishers of the day would pay him would not be worth the effort involved. Among his songs were such delights as 'Some Sweet Day' and 'Pretty Baby'.

JACQUET, ILLINOIS

b. Jean Baptiste Illinois Jacquet, 31 October 1922, Boussard, Louisiana, USA. Raised in Texas, Jacquet started out on drums, later switching to alto and soprano saxophones. He worked in the popular territory band led by Milt Larkins and after stints with other units ended up on the west coast, where he was invited to join Lionel Hampton's new band. In fact, Hampton had wanted Jacquet's section-mate in the Larkins band, tenor saxophonist Arnett Cobb, but when Cobb refused to leave, Hampton took Jacquet on condition he switch instruments. Jacquet took the plunge and his solo on Hampton's 1942 recording of 'Flying Home' established him as a major figure in jazz. Indeed, his solo was eventually integrated into subsequent performances of the tune. At the end of 1942, when Cobb finally agreed to leave Larkins and join Hampton, Jacquet moved on first to Cab Calloway and then to Count Basie. Also in the early 40s, he was involved with Norman Granz, appearing in the short film, *Jammin The Blues* (1944), and appearing with Granz's Jazz At The Philharmonic. From the mid-40s and on through the 50s Jacquet combined leading his own bands with JATP tours. In the 50s and 60s he became a popular figure at international festivals, leading his own groups, working in all-star ensembles and periodically appearing with Hampton. In the 80s Jacquet continued to record, and late in the decade formed a fine big band for occasional concerts and recording sessions. In June 1993 he took part in a jam session at the White House, appearing with President Bill Clinton. An important if often overlooked transitional figure in the development of the tenor saxophone, Jacquet has made a significant contribution to the mainstream of jazz while retaining a strong affinity for the blues of his adopted state. This blues feeling, superbly realized on his first recording of 'Flying Home', helped immeasurably in giving rise and substance to the Texas tenor style. His reputation as a wild man of the tenor, based in part upon his time with JATP, is ill-deserved. Indeed, although his high-note playing in the uptempo flagwavers was a demonstration of his incredible technical ability, almost any concert performance or recording date will attest that Jacquet is also a consummate interpreter of ballads.

● ALBUMS: *Illinois Jacquet Jam Session* 10-inch album (Apollo 1951)★★★★, *Illinois Jacquet Collates* 10-inch album (Mercury 1952)★★★★, *Illinois Jacquet Collates #2* 10-inch album (Clef 1953)★★★, *Tenor Sax* 10-inch album (Savoy 1953)★★★, with Lester Young *Battle Of The Saxes* (Aladdin 1953)★★★★, *Illinois Jacquet And His Tenor Sax* 10-inch album (Aladdin 1954)★★★, *Jazz By Jacquet* 10-inch album (Clef 1954)★★★, *Illinois Jacquet Septet* reissued as *Illinois Jacquet And His Orchestra* (Clef/Verve 1955)★★★, with Ben Webster *"The Kid" And "The Brute"* (Clef

1955)★★★★, with Rex Stewart *Rex Stewart Plays Duke/Uptown Jazz* (Grand Award 1955)★★★, *Jazz Moods By Illinois Jacquet* (Clef 1956)★★★, *Port Of Rico* (Clef 1956)★★★, *Groovin' With Jacquet* (Clef 1956)★★★★, *Swing's The Thing* (Clef 1956)★★★, *Illinois Jacquet Flies Again* (Roulette 1959)★★★, *Illinois Jacquet* (Epic 1962)★★★, *Flying Home* (Imperial 1962)★★★★, *Message* (Argo 1963)★★★, *Desert Winds* (Argo 1964)★★★, *Illinois Jacquet Plays Cole Porter* (Argo 1964)★★★, *Spectrum* (Argo 1965)★★★, *Go Power* (Cadet 1966)★★★, *Illinois Jacquet On Prestige! Bottoms Up* (Prestige 1968)★★★★, *The King!* (Prestige 1968)★★★, *The Soul Explosion* (Prestige 1969)★★★, *The Blues - That's Me!* (Prestige 1969)★★★★, *The Comeback* (Black Lion 1971)★★★, *Genius At Work* (Black Lion 1971)★★★, with Wild Bill Davis *Illinois Jacquet With Wild Bill Davis* (Black & Blue/Classic Jazz 1973)★★★★, *Blues From Louisiana* (Black & Blue/Classic Jazz 1973)★★★, *Jacquet's Street* (Black & Blue/Classic Jazz 1976)★★★, *Midnight Slows Volume 8* (Black & Blue 1978)★★★, *Jacquet's Got It!* (Atlantic 1988)★★★★.

● COMPILATIONS: *The Black Velvet Band* 1947-1967 recording (Bluebird 1988)★★★★, *Flying Home: The Best Of The Verve Years* (Bluebird 1992)★★★★, *The Complete Illinois Jacquet Sessions, 1945-50* 4-CD/6-LP box set (Mosiac 1996)★★★★.

JAMAL, AHMAD

b. Fritz Jones, 2 July 1930, Pittsburgh, Pennsylvania, USA. A professional pianist from before his teenage years, Jamal (who changed his name in the early 50s) managed to break through to a wider audience than most jazz artists. His trio work produced many excellent recordings and his accompanists included Israel Crosby. The most influential of his advocates was Miles Davis, who recognized Jamal's interesting rhythmic concepts as being something which he could incorporate into his own work. Jamal worked extensively in the USA throughout the 60s, 70s and 80s, usually in trio format but occasionally with larger backing for record dates, and also appeared with Gary Burton. Jamal is an important figure among mainstream pianists and their post-bop successors. A lyrical, gently swinging musician, his playing is a constant delight.

● ALBUMS: *Chamber Music Of The New Jazz* (Creative/Argo 1956)★★★, *The Ahmad Jamal Trio* i (Epic 1956)★★★, *Count 'Em 88* (Argo 1956)★★★, *But Not For Me/Ahmad Jamal At The Pershing* (Argo 1958)★★★★, *Ahmad's Blues* (Impulse! 1958)★★★★, *Ahmad Jamal, Volume IV* (Argo 1958)★★★, *The Ahmad Jamal Trio* ii (Epic 1959)★★★, *Jamal At The Penthouse* (Argo 1959)★★★, *Happy Mood* (Argo 1960)★★★, *Ahmad Jamal At The Pershing, Volume 2* (Argo 1961)★★★, *Listen To Ahmad Jamal* (Argo 1960)★★★, *Ahmad Jamal's Alhambra* (Argo 1961)★★★, *Ahmad Jamal At The Blackhawk* (Argo 1961)★★★★, *Macanudo* (Argo 1962)★★★, *Poin'ci-an'a* (Argo 1963)★★★, *'Naked City' Theme* (Argo 1964)★★★, *The Roar Of The Greasepaint, The Smell Of The Crowd* (Argo 1965)★★★★, *Extensions* (Argo 1965)★★★, *Ahmad Jamal With String* (1965)★★★, *Rhapsody* (Cadet 1966)★★★, *Heat Wave* (Cadet 1966)★★★, *Standard Eyes* (Cadet 1967)★★★, *Cry Young* (Cadet 1967)★★★, *The Bright, The Blue And The Beautiful* (Cadet 1968)★★★, *Tranquillity* (ABC 1968)★★, *Jamal At The Top/Poinciana Revisited* (Impulse! 1969)★★★, *The Awakening* (MCA 1970)★★, *Free Flight Vol. 1* (1971)★★★, *Outertimeinnerspace* (Impulse! 1972)★★★, *Jamal Plays Jamal* (1974)★★★ *Live At Oil Can Harry's* (1976)★★, *Prelude To A Kiss* (1976-8)★★★, *Steppin' Out With A Dream* (c.1977)★★★, *Intervals* (c.1979)★★★, *Ahmad Jamal Live At Bubba's* (Kingdom Jazz 1980)★★★, *Night Song* (Motown 1980)★★★, *Ahmad Jamal In Concert* (1981)★★, *American Classical Music* (1982)★★★, *Digital Works* (Atlantic 1985)★★★★, *Rossiter Road* (Atlantic 1985)★★★, *Live At The Montreaux Jazz Festival* (Atlantic 1986)★★★★, *Goodbye Mr Ecans* (Black Lion 1988)★★★, *Crystal* (WEA 1993)★★★, *Chicago Revisited* (Telarc 1993)★★★, *Live In Paris 92* (Birdology 1993)★★★, *I Remember Duke, Hoagy & Strayhorn* (Telarc 1995)★★★, *The Essence Part 1* (Verve 1996)★★★, *Big Byrd: The Essence Part 2* (Verve 1997)★★★, *Ahmad Jamal With The Assai Quartet* (Roesch 1997)★★★, *Nature* (Atlantic 1998)★★★.

● COMPILATIONS: *Genetic Walk* (20th Century 1980)★★★, *Cross Country Tour 1958-1961* (Chess 1998)★★★★.

JAMES, BOB

b. 25 December 1939, Marshall, Missouri, USA. James played the piano from the age of four and eventually gained an MA in Composition from the University of Michigan in 1962. He worked as musical director and accompanist with vocalist Sarah Vaughan until 1968. In 1973 Quincy Jones introduced him to Creed Taylor who was forming his CTI label. James became his arranger and producer working on albums with Dionne Warwick, Roberta Flack, Eric Gale, Grover Washington and Quincy Jones, as well as producing four solo works. In 1976 he moved to CBS Records as Director of Progressive A&R and worked with musicians as diverse as Joanne Brackeen and Santamaria. In 1986 James worked with saxophonist David Sanborn on *Double Vision*. James has also written musical scores for Broadway and for films including *The Selling Of The President* and *Serpico*. The television series *Taxi* used 'Angela' from 1978's *Touchdown* as its theme. His success in the 90s has been as a member of the fusion group Fourplay.

● ALBUMS: *Bold Conceptions* (Mercury 1963)★★★, *Explosions* (ESP 1965)★★★, *One* (CTI 1974)★★★, *Two* (CTI 1975)★★★, *Three* (CTI 1976)★★, *BJ4* (CTI 1977)★★, *Heads* (Tappan Zee 1977)★★, *Touchdown* (Tappan Zee 1978)★★★, *Lucky Seven* (Tappan Zee 1979)★★★, with Earl Klugh *One On One* (Tappan Zee 1979)★★★, *H* (Tappan Zee 1980)★★★, *All Around The Town* (Tappan Zee 1981)★★★, *Sign Of The Times* (Tappan Zee 1981)★★★, *Hands Down* (Tappan Zee 1982)★★★, with Klugh *Two Of A Kind* (Capitol 1982)★★★, *The Genie (Themes & Variations From The TV Series 'Taxi')* (Columbia 1983)★★, *Foxie* (Tappan Zee 1983)★★★, *12* (Tappan Zee 1984)★★★, *The Swan* (Warners 1985)★★★, with David Sanborn *Double Vision* (Warners 1986)★★★, *Obsession* (Warners 1986)★★, *Ivory Coast* (Warners 1988)★★★, *Grand Piano Canyon* (Warners 1990)★★★★, with Klugh *Cool* (Warners 1992)★★, *Chicago Revisited* (Telarc 1993)★★★★, *Restless* (Warners 1994)★★★, with Kirk Whalum *Joined At The Hip* (Warners 1996)★★★, *The Essence Part 1* (Birdology 1996)★★, *The Essence Part 2: Big Byrd* (Bydology 1996)★★, *Straight Up* (Warners 1996)★★★, *Playin' Hooky* (Warners 1997)★★★★.

JAMES, BONEY

b. Lowell, Massachusetts, USA. A Grover Washington Jnr.-inspired saxophonist, James has released several smooth jazz records that have established him as one of contemporary jazz's most popular recording artists. Raised in New Rochelle, New York, James started out on the clarinet before switching to saxophone at the age of ten. He took up keyboards in his teens, playing in a fusion band while studying at Berkley. James transferred to UCLA where he graduated in history, and then played with several bands in the LA area, initially as a keyboard player with Morris Day's band. Stints with Ray Parker Jnr., Randy Crawford, Teena Marie and the Isley Brothers followed before James began a solo career. He released his 1992 debut album on the small Spindletop label, but moved to Warner Brothers Records for the follow-up, *Backbone*, which reached number five on the contemporary jazz charts in 1994. His most consistent set to date is the seasonal *Boney's Funky Christmas*, recorded with James's long-time producer Paul Brown.

● ALBUMS: *Trust* (Spindletop 1992)★★★, *Backbone* (Warners 1994)★★, *Seduction* (Warners 1995)★★★, *Boney's Funky Christmas* (Warners 1996)★, *Sweet Thing* (Warners 1997)★★★.

JAMES, GEORGE

b. 7 December 1906, Beggs, Oklahoma, USA. After moving to St. Louis, Missouri, as a youth, James began playing clarinet and various saxophones with popular local bands, including some of those organized by band contractor Charlie Creath for work in hotels and on riverboats. In the late 20s James tried his luck in Chicago where he played with Jimmie Noone and also led his own small outfit. In 1931 he joined Louis Armstrong for several months, then played in a number of New York bands including the Savoy Bearcats, Fats Waller, James P. Johnson, Benny Carter, and Teddy Wilson. After a spell with Lucky Millinder he led his own bands in New York and other eastern cities during the early 40s. In the mid-40s he was with Claude Hopkins, Noble Sissle and others before forming a band of his own which he continued to lead intermittently during the next two decades. During the 70s and early 80s he became well known internationally through tours as a member of Clyde Bernhardt's Harlem Blues And Jazz Band. James was a competent sideman and could also deliver good solos when the opportunity or need arose. Indeed, his alto playing is one of the highlights of Armstrong's 1931 recordings with what was otherwise a rather inferior band.

● ALBUMS: *Harlem Blues & Jazz Band 1973-1980* (Barron 1973-80)★★★.

● COMPILATIONS: *The Chronological Louis Armstrong 1931-1932* (Classics 1931-32)★★★★.

JAMES, HARRY

b. 15 March 1916, Albany, Georgia, USA, d. 5 July 1983, Las Vegas, Nevada, USA. Harry James's father played trumpet in the band of a touring circus, and at first Harry played the drums, but then he, too, took up the trumpet and at the age of nine was also playing in the circus band. He showed such enormous promise that his father had soon taught him everything he knew. Harry left the circus and played with various bands in Texas before joining Ben Pollack in 1935. Early in 1937 James was hired by Benny Goodman, an engagement which gave him maximum exposure to swing era audiences. Heavily featured with Goodman and, with Ziggy Elman and Chris Griffin, forming part of a powerful and exciting trumpet section, James quickly became a household name. He remained with Goodman a little under two years, leaving to form his own big band. James popularity increased and his public image, aided by his marriage to film star Betty Grable, reached remarkable heights for a musician. The band's popularity was achieved largely through James own solos, but a small part of its success may be attributed to his singers, Louise Tobin, to whom he was briefly married before Grable, Frank Sinatra, who soon left to join Tommy Dorsey, Dick Haymes and Kitty Kallen. James maintained his band throughout the 40s and into the early 50s, establishing a solid reputation thanks to distinguished sidemen such as Willie Smith, Buddy Rich, Corky Corcoran and Juan Tizol. Owing chiefly to the recorded repertoire, much of which featured James playing florid trumpet solos on tunes such as 'The Flight Of The Bumble Bee', 'The Carnival of Venice', 'I Cried For You' and 'You Made Me Love You', his band was at times less than popular with hardcore jazz fans. This view should have altered when, in the mid-50s, after a period of re-evaluation, James formed a band to play charts by Ernie Wilkins and Neal Hefti. One of the outstanding big bands, this particular group is often and very unfairly regarded as a copy of Count Basie's, a point of view which completely disregards chronology. In fact, James band can be seen to have pre-empted the slightly later but much more widely recognized middle-period band led by Basie, which also used Wilkins's and Hefti's charts. James continued leading into the 60s and 70s, dividing his time between extended residencies at major hotel and casino venues, mostly in Las Vegas, Nevada, and touring internationally. Amongst the first-rate musicians James used in these years were Willie Smith again, a succession of fine drummers (including Rich, Sonny Payne and Louie Bellson) and lead trumpeter Nick Buono, who had joined in December 1939 and showed no signs of relinquishing his chair and would, indeed, remain until the end. In his early years James was a brashly exciting player, attacking solos and abetting ensembles with a rich tone and what was at times an overwhelmingly powerful sound. With his own band he exploited his virtuoso technique, performing with great conviction the ballads and trumpet spectaculars that so disconcerted his jazz followers but which delighted the wider audience at whom they were aimed. Over the years James appeared in several movies - with his band in *Private Buckaroo* (1942), *Springtime In The Rockies, Best Foot Forward, Bathing Beauty, Two Girls And A Sailor, Do You Love Me?, If I'm*

Lucky, *Carnegie Hall*, and *I'll Get By* (1950) - and as a solo artist in *Syncopation* (1942) and *The Benny Goodman Story* (1956). He also played trumpet on the soundtrack of *Young Man With A Horn* (1950). Later in his career, James work combined the best of both worlds - jazz and the more flashy style - and shed many of its excesses. He remained popular into the 80s and never lost his enthusiasm, despite suffering from cancer, which eventually claimed him in 1983.

● ALBUMS: *All Time Favorites* (Columbia 1950)★★★★, *Trumpet Time* (Columbia 1950)★★★, *Dance Parade* (Columbia 1950)★★★★, *Your Dance Date* (Columbia 1950)★★★★, *Soft Lights And Sweet Trumpet* (Columbia 1952)★★★, *One Night Stand* (Columbia 1953)★★★★, *At The Hollywood Palladium* (Columbia 1954)★★★★, *Trumpet After Midnight* (Columbia 1954)★★★, *Juke Box Jamboree* (Columbia 1955)★★★, *Man With The Horn* (Columbia 1995)★★★, *Harry James In Hi-Fi* (Capitol 1955)★★★★, *More Harry James In Hi-Fi* (Capitol 1956)★★, *Wild About Harry* (Capitol 1957)★★★, *The New James* (1958)★★★, *Harry's Choice!* (Capitol 1958)★★★, *Harry James And His New Swingin' Bands* (1959)★★★, *Harry James Today* (MGM 1960)★★★, *The Spectacular Sound Of Harry James* (1961)★★★, *Harry James Plays Neal Hefti* (1961)★★★★, *The Solid Trumpet Of Harry James* (1962)★★★, *Double Dixie* (MGM/Verve 1962)★★★, *On Tour In '64* (1964)★★★, *Harry James Live At The Riverboat* (1966)★★★, *Live From Clearwater, Florida Vols 1-3* (1970)★★★★, *Live In London* (1971)★★★, *King James Version* (1976)★★★, *Still Harry After All These Years* (1979)★★★.

● FILMS: *The Big Beat* (1957).

JAMMIN' THE BLUES

Held by many movie buffs to be the finest jazz short ever filmed, and with considerable justification. The film, released in 1944, features superbly evocative photography by Gjon Mili, who also directed, and was supervised by Norman Granz. The musicians include Red Callender, Big Sid Catlett, Harry Edison, Illinois Jacquet, Jo Jones, Barney Kessel and the magnificent Lester Young. Timeless music by these assembled giants, allied to moody, smoky chiaroscuro makes this a must for any self-respecting jazz fan.

● VIDEOS: *Swing! Swing! Swing!* (1997).

JANNAH, DENISE

b. 1956, Surinam. Before she reached her first birthday Jannah's family had moved to the Netherlands, although they returned to South America a few years later. The family permanently relocated to the Netherlands when she was 15. She began singing professionally when she was 20 but was also intent on a legal career. However, in 1982 she abandoned her law studies and began studying music at Hilversum Conservatory. Her professional career was varied, she would happily sing rock and jazz and pop, and she had a minor pop hit in Germany in 1985. Two years later, however, she was teaching jazz singing at the Conservatory of Rotterdam. Her first album, a jazz set, was heard by the eminent American writer-critic, Gary Giddins, whose praise helped bring her to the attention of a wider audience. In 1995 Giddins was invited to produce Jannah's Blue Note Records debut on which she sang with a big band arranged and conducted by Bob Belden. Jannah's singing voice is richly expressive and her interpretation of lyrics is especially fine, betraying no hint that the American English in which they are written is not her native tongue.

● ALBUMS: *Take It From The Top* (Timeless 1993)★★★, *Heart Full Of Music* (Timeless 1993)★★★★, *I Was Born In Love With You* (Blue Note 1995)★★★.

JARMAN, JOSEPH

b. 14 September 1937, Pine Bluff, Arkansas, USA. When he was a child Jarman's family moved to Chicago, where he studied drums at high school. While in the army he played saxophone and clarinet; after demobilisation he travelled until settling back in Chicago in 1961. He joined the AACM in 1965, leading various groups and playing in Richard Muhal Abrams's The Experimental Band. During that year he also collaborated with controversial classical composer John Cage on a multi-media event. A poet himself, Jarman's concerts would often include poets or dancers, his taste for the theatrical having been developed when he studied drama at the Second City Theatre School and the Art Institute of Chicago School. In 1969, dispirited by the death of Charles Clark and Chris Gaddy, two of his regular sidemen, he disbanded his own group and joined the Art Ensemble Of Chicago, with whom the bulk of his work was done until his departure in the mid-90s. Like his partners in the Ensemble (Lester Bowie, Roscoe Mitchell, Malachi Favors and Famoudou Don Moye) Jarman plays a dazzling number of instruments, the primary ones being sopranino, soprano, alto, tenor and bass saxophones, bassoon, oboe, flutes and clarinets as well as various percussion and 'little instruments'. If Jarman is the dramatist of the Ensemble to Mitchell's purer musician, he has nonetheless written a number of rigorous compositions for large groups. Regrettably, little of his work away from the AEC has been recorded during the 70s and 80s; that which has is mostly in small groups which he co-leads with Moye, though he sometimes guests with other bands - playing, for example, with the Reggie Workman Ensemble in the late 80s and recording with Leroy Jenkins.

● ALBUMS: *Song For* (Delmark 1966)★★★★, *As If It Were The Seasons* (Delmark 1968)★★★★, with Anthony Braxton *Together Alone* 1972 recording (Delmark 1974)★★★, *Sunbound* (1976)★★★, with Don Moye *Egwu-Anwu* (India Navigation 1978)★★★, with Moye, Don Pullen *The Magic Triangle* (Black Saint 1979)★★★★, with Moye *Black Paladins* (Black Saint 1980)★★★, with Donald Rafael Garrett, Craig Harris, Don Moye *Earth Passage - Density* (Black Saint 1981)★★★, *Calypso's Smile* (AECO 1985)★★★, *Connecting Spirits* (Music & Arts 1996)★★★, with Leroy Jenkins *Out Of The Mist* (Ocean 1998)★★★.

JARREAU, AL

b. 12 March 1940, Milwaukee, Wisconsin, USA. Although Jarreau sang from childhood, it was many years before he decided to make singing his full-time occupation. Working outside music for most of the 60s, he began to sing in small west coast clubs and eventually achieved enough success to change careers. By the mid-70s he was becoming well known in the USA, and, via records and a European tour, greatly extended his audience. Singing a highly sophisticated form of vocalese, Jarreau's style displays many influences. Some of these come from within the world of jazz, notably the work of Jon Hendricks, while others are external. He customarily uses vocal sounds that include the clicks of African song and the plosives common in oriental speech and singing patterns. This range of influences makes him both hard to classify and more accessible to the wider audience for crossover music. More commercially successful than most jazz singers, Jarreau's work in the 70s and 80s consistently appealed to young audiences attuned to fusions in popular music. By the early 90s, when he was entering his 50s, his kinship with youth culture was clearly diminishing, but his reputation was by this time firmly established.

● ALBUMS: *1965* (1965)★★, *We Got By* (Reprise 1975)★★★, *Glow* (Reprise 1976)★★, *Look To The Rainbow: Live In Europe* (Warners 1977)★★, *All Fly Home* (Warners 1978)★★, *This Time* (Warners 1980)★★★, *Breakin' Away* (Warners 1981)★★★, *Jarreau* (Warners 1983)★★★, *Spirits And Feelings* (Happy Bird 1984)★★★, *Ain't No Sunshine* (Blue Moon 1984)★★★, *High Crime* (Warners 1984)★★, *Al Jarreau In London* (Warners 1984)★★, *You* (Platinum 1985)★★★, *L Is For Lover* (Warners 1986)★★★, *Hearts Horizon* (Reprise 1988)★★★, *Manifesto* (Masters 1988)★★★, *Heaven And Earth* (Reprise 1992)★★★, *Tenderness* (Warners 1994)★★★.

● COMPILATIONS: *Best Of Al Jarreau* (Warners 1996)★★★★.

● FILMS: *Breakdance - The Movie* (1984).

JARRETT, KEITH

b. 8 May 1945, Allentown, Pennsylvania, USA. Growing up in a highly musical family, Jarrett displayed startling precocity and was playing piano from the age of three. From a very early age he also composed music and long before he entered his teens was touring as a professional musician, playing classical music and his own compositions. He continued with his studies at Berklee College Of Music in the early 60s but was soon leading his own small group. From the mid-60s he was based in New York where he was heard by Art Blakey who invited him to join his band. Jarrett stayed with Blakey for only a few months but it was enough to raise his previously low profile. In 1966 he joined Charles Lloyd's quartet which made his name known internationally, thanks to extensive tours of Europe and visits to the Soviet Union and the Far East. It was with this quartet that he befriended Jack DeJohnette. During his childhood Jarrett had also played vibraphone, saxophone, flute and percussion instruments, and he resumed performing on some of these instruments in the late 60s. In 1969 he joined Miles Davis, playing organ for a while, before turning to electric piano. This was during the jazz/fusion period and although the best music from this group was never recorded they released *Live At The Fillmore* and *Live-Evil*. By now, word was out that Jarrett was one of the most exciting new talents in the history of jazz piano. During his two years with Davis he also found time to record under his own name, enhancing his reputation with a succession of fine albums with Charlie Haden, Dewey Redman, Paul Motian and others. After leaving Davis he resumed playing acoustic piano and established a substantial following for his music, which he has described as 'universal folk music'. *Facing You* in 1971 created a considerable response and was a brilliant demonstration of speed, dynamics and emotion. The now familiar Jarrett characteristic of brilliantly adding styles was first aired on this album. Country, folk, classical, blues and rock were given brief cameos, this was a remarkable solo debut.

Subsequently, Jarrett has become a major figure not only in furthering his own music but in 'showing the way' for contemporary jazz and in particular the growth of ECM Records and the work of Manfred Eicher. Eicher and Jarrett complement each other like no other business partnership. Jarrett's success with huge sales of his albums enabled ECM to expand. Eicher in turn will record and release anything Jarrett wishes, such is their trust in each other. He has often worked and recorded with artists including Jan Garbarek, Gary Burton, Palle Danielsson and Jon Christensen. It is with DeJohnette and bassist Gary Peacock, he regularly returns to playing with. Known as the 'standards trio', there can be few units currently working that have such intuition and emotional feeling of each others musical talent. Albums such as *Changes*, *Standards Vol. 1* and *Vol. 2*, *Live Standards* and *The Cure* represent the finest possibilities of an acoustic jazz trio. Jarrett's greatest achievement, however, is as the master of improvised solo piano. It is in this role that Jarrett has arguably created a musical genre. His outstanding improvisational skills have led to his ability to present solo concerts during which he might play works of such a length that as few as two pieces will comprise an entire evening's music. His pivotal and often breathtaking *Solo Concerts: Bremen and Lausanne* released in 1973, received numerous accolades in the USA and Europe. Similarly in 1975 *The Koln Concert* was a huge success becoming a million plus seller. It remains his biggest selling work and is a must for any discerning music collection, even though it was recorded on a badly tuned piano. In Ian Carr's biography, Jarrett explains that in addition to feeling unwell on the day of the concert the right piano did not arrive in time. Instead he had to make do by restricting his improvisation to the middle keys as the top end was shot and the bass end had no resonance. Additionally the ambitious multi-album set*The Sun Bear Concerts* are rich journeys into the improvisational unknown. Jarrett's solo improvised work has not resulted in his turning his back on composing and he has written and recorded music for piano and string orchestra resulting in albums such as *In The Light* and *The Celestial Hawk*. His interest in this form of music has added to his concert repertoire and during the 80s, in addition to solo and continuing small group jazz concerts he also played and recorded classical works. Jarrett's continuing association with ECM Records has helped advance his constantly maturing musical persona. Technically flawless, Jarrett's playing style draws upon many sources reaching into all areas of jazz while simultaneously displaying a thorough understanding of and deep feeling for the western classical form. Unquestionably one of the most dazzling improvising talents the world of music has ever known, Jarrett is also remarkable for having achieved recognition from the whole musical establishment as well as the jazz audience while also enjoying considerable commercial success.

● ALBUMS: *Life Between The Exit Signs* (Vortex 1967)★★, *Restoration Ruin* (Vortex 1968)★★, *Somewhere Before* (Atlantic 1968)★★, with Gary Burton *Gary Burton And Keith Jarrett* (Atlantic 1970)★★★, *The Mourning Of A Star* (Atlantic 1971)★★, *Facing You* (ECM 1971)★★★★★, *Expectations* (Columbia 1972)★★★, with Jack DeJohnette *Rutya And Daitya* (ECM 1973)★★★, *Fort Yawuh* (Impulse! 1973)★★, *In The Light* (ECM 1973)★★★, *Solo Concerts: Bremen And Lausanne* (ECM 1973)★★★★★, *Treasure Island* (Impulse! 1974)★★★, with Jan Garbarek *Belonging* (ECM 1974)★★★★, with Garbarek *Luminessence* (ECM 1974)★★★, *Death And The Flower* (Impulse! 1975)★★★, *Arbour Zena* (ECM 1975)★★★, *The Köln Concert* (ECM 1975)★★★★★, *Sun Bear Concerts* (ECM 1976)★★★★, *Mysteries* (Impulse! 1976)★★★, *The Survivor's Suite* (ECM 1976)★★★★, *Silence* (Impulse! 1976)★★★, *Shades* (Impulse! 1976)★★★, *Byablue* (Impulse! 1977)★★★, *My Song* (ECM 1977)★★★★, *Nude Ants* (ECM 1979)★★★★, *Personal Mountains* (ECM 1979)★★★, *Expectations* (Columbia 1979)★★★, *The Moth And The Flame* (ECM 1980)★★★, *The Celestial Hawk* (ECM 1980)★★, *Invocations* (ECM 1980)★★★, *Concerts Bregenz And München* (ECM 1981)★★★★, *Concerts (Bregenz)* (ECM 1982)★★★★, *Bop-Be* (Impulse! 1982)★★, *Standards Volume 1* (ECM 1983)★★★★, *Changes* (ECM 1983)★★★★, *Backhand* (Impulse! 1983)★★★, *Eyes Of The Heart* (ECM 1985)★★, *Spirits* (ECM 1985)★★, *Standards Live* (ECM 1985)★★★★, *Sacred Hymns* (ECM 1985)★★★, *Staircase* (1985)★★★★, *Still Live* (ECM 1986)★★★, *Book Of Ways* (ECM 1986)★★★, *Hymns Spheres* (ECM 1986)★★, *Dark Intervals* (ECM 1988)★★★, *Standards Volume 2* (ECM 1988)★★★★, *The Well Tempered Clavier Book* (ECM 1988)★★, *J.S. Bach Das Wohitemperierte Klavier Buch 1* (ECM 1988)★★★, *Changeless* (ECM 1989)★★★, *Treasure Island* (Impulse! 1989)★★, *Paris Concert* (ECM 1990)★★★★, *J.S. Bach Das Wohitemperierte Klavier Buch 2* (ECM 1991)★★★★, *Tribute* (ECM 1991)★★★★, *The Cure* (ECM 1992)★★★★, *Vienna Concert* (ECM 1992)★★★★, *Bye Bye Blackbird* (ECM 1993)★★★★, with Gary Peacock, Paul Motian *At The Deer Head Inn* (ECM 1994)★★★, *Standards In Norway* (ECM 1995)★★★, with the Stuttgart Chamber Orchestra *W.A. Mozart Piano Concertos Nos. 21, 23, 17. Masonic Funeral Music* (ECM 1996)★★★, *La Scala* 1995 recording (ECM 1997)★★★★, with Jack DeJohnette, Gary Peacock *Tokyo '96* (ECM 1998)★★★★.

● COMPILATIONS: *Best Of Keith Jarrett* (Impulse! 1979)★★, *Works* (ECM 1989)★★★, *Keith Jarrett At The Blue Note: The Complete Recordings* 6-CD box set (ECM 1995)★★★★, *The Impulse! Years 1973-74* 5-CD box set (Impulse! 1997)★★★.

● FURTHER READING: *Keith Jarrett: The Man And His Music* Ian Carr.

JARVIS, CLIFFORD

b. Clifford Osbourne Jarvis, 26 August 1941, Boston, Massachusetts, USA. One of the most significant alumni of Sun Ra's Arkestras, Jarvis was prominent for much of the 60s and periodically thereafter. Barry Harris, Yusef Lateef and Grant Green were among his other employers. Jarvis's hard-hitting, supportive drumming can be heard on several Sun Ra classics. *Nothing Is* and *Pictures Of Infinity* both contain several excellent examples of his playing. Jarvis has been less well-represented on record in recent years. During the 80s he moved to England.

● ALBUMS: with Jackie McLean *Right Now* (1965)★★★★, with Sun Ra *Nothing Is* (1966)★★★, with Pharoah Sanders *Deaf, Dumb, Blind* (1971)★★★.

JASPAR, BOBBY

b. 20 February 1926, Liege, Belgium, d. 28 February 1963. Jaspar came from a family of musicians, and studied piano between the ages of 11 and 13. In 1939 he adopted the clarinet and played jazz at US army bases in Germany. In 1950 he relocated to Paris, where he played tenor sax and flute with Henri Renaud and Bernard Peiffer. In the mid-50s he led a quartet at the Club St. Germain, backing visiting Americans such as Chet Baker and Jimmy Raney. He married the singer Blossom Dearie and moved to New York in April 1956. Jaspar had no difficulty in making contacts, as he had been voted 'New Star' in the *Down Beat* critics' poll, and recorded some sterling hard bop with Elvin Jones and Tommy Flanagan in November of that year. A tour with J.J. Johnson followed, then a brief stint with Miles Davis in 1957 and six months with Donald Byrd. Returning to Paris he held court for five months at the Chat Qui Peche club in 1958, then went back to New York to work with pianist Bill Evans (1959) and singer Chris Connor (1960). In 1962 he toured Europe with guitarist Rene Thomas. Involvement with heroin took its toll. Hospitalized in September 1962, he died aged 37 after heart surgery. His relaxed, authentic version of the Stan Getz sound hardened up and became more individual after his move to New York. Jaspar remains one of a handful of Europeans who managed to feel at ease in straight-ahead jazz while creating their own individual niche.

● ALBUMS: *Bobby Jaspar And His All Stars* (EmArcy 1957)★★★, *Bobby Jaspar* (Riverside 1956)★★★, with Rene Thomas *Live At Ronnie Scott's* (1962)★★★.

JAY, BARBARA

b. England. Growing up in a jazz-loving family, her father playing trumpet in various bands, Jay began singing as a child. During the 60s she sang with many leading British jazz musicians, including Ronnie Scott, George Chisholm and Tommy Whittle. In 1970 she sang with the orchestra Benny Goodman led on a long European tour. She also sang in New York, appearing at the Carnegie Tavern where she was accompanied by Ellis Larkins. Jay has performed extensively on radio and television in the UK and at many European festivals including Nice and Cork. She sings with a true, clear voice, warmly interpreting the great standards of the popular and jazz repertoires. Her phrasing is elegant and her diction superb. Consistently working with outstanding British jazz musicians, she is married to Whittle with whom she regularly appears.

● ALBUMS: *The Nearness Of You* (Tee-Jay 80s)★★★, *Memories Of You* (Tee-Jay 90s)★★★★.

JAZZ AT THE PHILHARMONIC

In 1944 the tyro jazz impresario Norman Granz began a series of jazz concerts at the Philharmonic Auditorium in Los Angeles, USA. Reputedly, the name by which these concerts became known, JATP, arose from an abbreviation of the foregoing. The form, style and content of the concerts caught the jazz public's imagination and they continued through the rest of the decade and into the 50s, gradually becoming bigger and more spectacular musical packages. Fortunately, Granz had the foresight and acumen to record all his concerts. The release, on the new long-playing records, of these extended jam session performances proved commercially profitable and helped to establish Granz as a leading record producer. From 1957 onwards JATP tours were confined to Europe and in 1967, after a farewell tour of the USA, the concept was largely abandoned, although Granz continued to tour artists under the generic banner. Indeed, in some measure it might be claimed that his concept is mirrored in many latterday festival packages. Although often criticized for their showier aspects, JATP concerts included a wealth of fine playing by a succession of outstanding mainstream and bebop performers. Among the musicians who appeared with JATP over the years have been trumpeters Joe Guy, Howard McGhee, Buck Clayton, Charlie Shavers, Dizzy Gillespie and Roy Eldridge, trombonists J.J. Johnson, Bill Harris and Tommy Turk, saxophonists Charlie Parker, Willie Smith, Benny Carter, Lester Young, Coleman Hawkins, Illinois Jacquet, Flip Phillips and Stan Getz, pianists Oscar Peterson, Nat 'King' Cole, Hank Jones and Kenny Kersey, and drummers Gene Krupa, Buddy Rich, J.C. Heard, Jo Jones and Louie Bellson. Granz also included the entire Count Basie and Duke Ellington orchestras in some of his more ambitious packages, and Ella Fitzgerald was a mainstay for many years.

● ALBUMS: *In London 1969* (Pablo 1969)★★★, *At The Montreux Festival* (Pablo 1975)★★★★, *The First Concert* 1944 recording (Verve 1977)★★★★, *Bird And Pres: The '46 Concerts* 1946 recordings (Verve 1977)★★★★, *Return To Happiness, Tokyo 1983* (Pablo 1983)★★★, *The Rarest Concerts* 1946-1953 recordings (PolyGram 1983)★★★, *Bird & Pres* 1949 recording (PolyGram 1983)★★★★★, *Norgran Blues* 1950 recording (PolyGram 1983)★★★, *The Trumpet Battle* 1952 recording (PolyGram 1983)★★★, *Gene Krupa & Buddy Rich* 1952/1954 recordings (PolyGram 1983)★★★, *One O'Clock Jump* 1953 recording (PolyGram 1983)★★★★, *The Challenges* 1954 recording (PolyGram 1983)★★★★, *Blues In Chicago* 1955 recording (PolyGram 1983)★★★, *Frankfurt 1952* 1952 recording (Pablo 1984)★★★, *Hartford, 1953* 1953 recording (Pablo 1984)★★★, *Tokyo: Live At The ...* 1953 recording (Pablo 1984)★★★, *The Exciting Battle: Stockholm '55* 1955 recording (Pablo 1984)★★★.

● COMPILATIONS: *The Complete Recordings On Verve: 1944-1949* 10-CD box set (Verve 1999)★★★★.

JAZZ COMPOSER'S ORCHESTRA ASSOCIATION

The Jazz Composer's Orchestra grew out of the Jazz Composer's Guild, a co-operative formed in 1964 by Cecil Taylor, Bill Dixon, Archie Shepp, Roswell Rudd, John Tchicai, Sun Ra, Paul Bley, Carla Bley, Michael Mantler and Burton Greene, with the intention of finding new performance outlets for the New Jazz. In practice, Guild members spent as much time arguing with each other as with the powers that controlled the concert world and the airwaves, and the co-operative collapsed within a year - but not before Mantler and Carla Bley had initiated the Jazz Composer's Guild Orchestra. In 1966, Mantler, taking the idea further, established the Jazz Composer's Orchestra Association (JCOA) as a non-profit, tax-exempt organization to support an orchestra committed to New Jazz, release the orchestra's music on its own label, and operate the New Music Distribution Service, an alternative distribution network for independent labels. In the first decade JCOA gave many concerts and workshops, and released fine albums by Mantler, Bley, Don Cherry, Rudd, Clifford Thornton, Grachan Moncur III, and Leroy Jenkins, but funding was always problematic. By the late 70s, the orchestra folded. The New Music Distribution Service lasted until the early 90s.

● ALBUMS: *Communication* (Fontana 1965)★★★, *The Jazz Composer's Orchestra* (JCOA 1968)★★★.

JAZZ FESTIVALS

In its early years, jazz music was tightly bound to such social activities as drinking, dancing and 'goodtiming' of all kinds. Most jazz was heard in small, intimate clubs, and the larger venues were usually dance halls which still provided a kind of intimacy, even if it took a slightly different form. By the mid-50s, however, the mass audience for jazz frequently had to settle for somewhat strait-laced concert-hall performances. When they became a major feature of the jazz life, festivals sometimes managed to combine large-scale performances with a kind of intimacy, this became one of their great strengths. The intimacy came from the free and easy manner in which artists and customers might meet between sets at outdoor venues. This, together with the fact that they offer an unrivalled opportunity for many people to see and hear more jazz in a few tightly-packed days than they usually hear in the rest of the year, gave the festival scene an unrivalled attractiveness. Outdoor concerts had been given in the USA in the late 30s, notably at Randall's Island, New York City, but the palm for the first real festival goes to Australia and the 1946 Australian Jazz Convention which was founded by Harry Stein and band leader Graeme Bell. It was, however, the first Nice Jazz Festival, held in 1948 at which

Louis Armstrong was the main attraction, that spread the word that a festival could work both artistically and financially. The following year, the French tried their hand again, this time with the Festival International de Jazz in Paris, featuring such strikingly different musical styles as those of Sidney Bechet, soon to make France his home, and Charlie Parker and Miles Davis. During the early 50s the notion that jazz festivals were a sound proposition prompted a string of such events and by the early 90s jazz festivals were the dominating force in live jazz around the world.

For all their worldwide popularity, the majority of festivals are held in the USA where the early starters included two which quickly established themselves amongst the most prestigious events on the jazz calendar: the Newport Jazz Festival and the Monterey Jazz Festival. Among the estimated 1,000 jazz festivals held annually around the word in the 90s are some which concentrate upon certain clearly-defined stylistic or thematic areas of jazz. For example, Sacramento, California holds an annual Dixieland Jubilee, the Bix Beiderbecke memorial festival takes place in his hometown of Davenport, Iowa. Jazz women, so often lightly regarded in jazz circles except as singers, were given their due at the Women's Jazz Festival, in Kansas City, Missouri, between 1978 and 1985. One of the most important impresarios in jazz, George Wein, has a hand in numerous festivals including those held at Saratoga Springs, New York; Jacksonville, Florida; Boston, Massachusetts, among many other venues throughout the USA and elsewhere around the world of jazz. Festivals can range from intimate affairs in small towns or quiet rural areas to major events in cities. Among the former are the annual Colorado Jazz Party held in Denver by Dick Gibson, and every April, in Oregon, high on cliffs overlooking the Pacific Ocean, jazz musicians and fans gather at the Inn at Otter Crest for a relaxed weekend during which audience and performers mingle on easy and equal terms. Important city festivals include that held in New Orleans. The annual Heritage festival, begun in the early 60s, brings in a flood of visitors eager to sample a wide range of music, from old-time marching bands to hard bop groups. Among UK festivals is another excellent city-based event, Peter Boizot's Soho Jazz Festival, held in London for 10 days at the end of September. Another increasingly important British festival, which 'takes over' a town as its venue, is that held at Brecon in Wales.

Among other important events around the world is the Montreux International Jazz Festival, the Aurex Jazz Festival in Japan and the International Jazz Festival of Japan, held over 15 days in February in eight cities. Every July since 1976 the North Sea Festival, at The Hague in The Netherlands, has offered a package to daunt even the most ardent fan. Ten stages are in simultaneous use for very nearly 24 hours on each of its three days, extended to four in 1991. In Eire, for four days every October, there is the Cork Jazz Festival. Begun in the late 70s, and sponsored by Guinness since 1982, this is rapidly rising in the estimation of audiences and performers, offering as it does an atmosphere befitting a nation which prides itself on greeting its visitors with a thousand welcomes. Other important, popular and musically excellent festivals include the JVC/Capital Radio Jazz Parade in London, Montauban in France and Kongsberg in Norway which began in the mid-60s. There are jazz festivals in Italy, Spain, Gemany, Poland and several other countries which formed what was once the eastern bloc. Then there are the floating festivals, jazz cruises of which the S.S. *Norway*, sailing out of Miami and Caribbean bound on a seven-day jaunt, is an outstanding example. The word 'festival' is commonly defined as 'a musical entertainment on a large scale, usually periodical', a definition which prompts the thought that not all organizers of jazz events have read their dictionaries lately. Some so-called festivals are little more than a series of concerts strung together but the jazz festival looks set to remain the means by which live jazz will continue to reach the biggest audiences. Importantly, many festivals are recorded and even filmed and, perhaps most significant of all, they have become the principal means by which many jazz fans have a chance to see and hear their idols - and, perhaps, discover new ones.

Jazz Giant - Benny Carter

One of a very small number of jazz musicians to have enjoyed successful careers playing both trumpet and saxophone, Benny Carter was already firmly established as an important swing name when, in 1958, he recorded this superb small-group album. Accompanied by tenor saxophone legend Ben Webster, trombonist Frank Rosolino, pianists André Previn and Jimmie Rowles, swinging west coast guitarist Barney Kessel, bassist Leroy Vinnegar and top west coast drummer Shelly Manne, Carter proves he was as great a jazz improviser as big band composer and arranger, on a selection of standards and two original compositions.

- Tracks: *Old Fashioned Love; I'm Coming Virginia; A Walkin' Thing; Blue Lou; Ain't She Sweet; How Can You Lose; Blues My Naughty Sweetie Gives To Me.*
- First released 1958
- UK peak chart position: did not chart
- USA peak chart position: did not chart

Jazz In Silhouette - Sun Ra

This 1957 Sun Ra album is perhaps surprisingly orthodox for what we have come to expect of an Arkestra outing. Speaking a language grounded in bop, a superb 10-piece of Sun Ra's finest players work through some inspired tunes and arrangements with an unusual flair and consistency – baritone saxophonist Pat Patrick and tenor genius John Gilmore soloing with particular strength. Breaking the mould, and in many ways a glimpse of what was to come, 'Ancient Aiethopia' is a mesmerizing percussion-based composition with chanting, displaying an unusual freedom and featuring superbly compelling solo contributions by trumpeter Hobart Dotson and pianist Ra himself.

- Tracks: *Enlightenment; Saturn; Velvet; Ancient Aiethopia; Hours*

After; Horoscope; Images; Blues At Midnight.
- First released 1959
- UK peak chart position: did not chart
- USA peak chart position: did not chart

JAZZ JAMAICA

Jazz Jamaica was the brainchild of Gary Crosby, who in 1991, inspired by the rhythms of traditional Jamaican music and the largely improvisational nature of jazz, turned his concept into a reality. He enrolled a number of talented young jazz musicians from the jazz and reggae circuits, including himself on double bass, Clifton 'Bigga' Morrison (keyboards), Alan Weekes (guitar), Kenrick Rowe (drums), Tony Uter (percussion) and a horn section featuring the legendary Rico Rodriguez (trombone), Eddie 'Tan Tan' Thornton (trumpet), and Michael 'Bammi' Rose (alto saxophone, flute). The group toured extensively, playing worldwide festivals from 1993 to the present day. In 1993 the Roots and Reminiscence Tour included performances from Crosby's uncle, Ernest Ranglin, and Marjorie Whylie, who played the piano, provided vocals and followed in the tradition of an African griot as the storyteller. Also featured on the tour was Lord Tanamo who performed in his own distinctive style. Following the tour the band set up workshops specifically for elderly Caribbean expatriates, although these were, in fact, attended by a cosmopolitan audience encompassing all ages and races. In 1994 the band played the St. Lucia Jazz Festival, where they proved so successful that the great George Benson had to wait in the wings until the band played an encore. The band also released *Skaravan*, initially through the Japanese Quattro label. Tracks included ska versions of 'Peanut Vendor', Charlie Parker's 'Barbados', Don Drummond's 'Don Cosmic' and 'Confucius', the Skatalites' 'Green Island' and Rodriguez's 'Africa'. By the autumn of 1994 the group secured a Japanese-based major label contract. The release of *The Jamaican Beat - Blue Note Blue Beat Volume One* found the musicians playing alongside Courtney Pine, Brian Edwards, Cleveland Watkiss and Julie Dexter. The album leant heavily towards jazz while remaining faithful to the initial concept of a ska fusion. In 1995, sponsored by the British Council, the group toured Senegal and Nigeria, featuring a performance at the British Embassy in Senegal, and a live jamming session with the Nigerian ensemble Fran And Tunde Kuboye And The Extended Family Band, who supported Jazz Jamaica on their UK tour in October. As well as the constant touring, the band's recording sessions included Dennis Rollins, Denys Baptiste, Tony Kofi, Byron Wallen, Kevin Robinson, and the sublime vocals of lovers rock singer Carroll Thompson. In addition to his Jazz Jamaica commitments, Crosby also leads a jazz ensemble known as Gary Crosby's Nu Troop. In 1997 the group contributed a competent skazz version of 'Wrapped Around Your Finger' to the Police tribute album.

- ALBUMS: *Skaravan* (Skazz/Rykodisc 1994)★★★, *The Jamaican Beat - Blue Note Blue Beat Volume One* (Toshiba EMI 1994)★★★★, *The Jamaican Beat - Blue Note Blue Beat Volume Two* (Toshiba EMI 1995)★★★.

JAZZ LAB

(see Byrd, Donald; Gryce, Gigi)

JAZZ MESSENGERS

In 1947 Art Blakey formed a short-lived big band which he named the 17 Messengers. He also recorded with a smaller group which he called the Jazz Messengers. In 1954 Blakey was a member of a co-operative band with Kenny Dorham, Hank Mobley, Doug Watkins and Horace Silver. This band recorded in 1955 as the Jazz Messengers with Silver as nominal leader. With minor personnel changes the group remained together until 1956. Subsequently, Blakey formed his own band, calling it the Jazz Messengers, a name he retained for all his bands until his death in 1990.

- ALBUMS: *The Legacy Of Art Blakey* (Telarc 1998)★★★.

JAZZ ON A SUMMER'S DAY

From its opening moments, depicting reflected sailboats while Jimmy Giuffre's 'The Train And The River' bubbles on the soundtrack, this film sets out to create an unforgettable record of the 1958 Newport Jazz Festival. Directed by Bert Stern in 1960, repeated viewing might make some of the 60s photo-gimmickry a little trying and there are certainly too many audience cutaways during performances, but, overall, the concept is very well-realized. And the music is magnificent. Amongst the assembled giants are Louis Armstrong, Bob Brookmeyer, Ben Webster, Thelonious Monk, Roy Haynes, Rex Stewart, Sonny Stitt, Dinah Washington singing superbly and also clowning very musically on vibes with Terry Gibbs, Max Roach, Gerry Mulligan, Art Farmer, Chico Hamilton seen in rehearsal, Eric Dolphy, George Shearing, Jack Teagarden, Buck Clayton and Jo Jones. Mahalia Jackson brings the show to a sacred finale but for most people the outstanding moment is the considerably less-sacred sight of Anita O'Day, in high heels, cartwheel hat, gloves, and tight dress, struggling up onto the stage where she memorably recomposes 'Sweet Georgia Brown' and 'Tea For Two' in her own image. The video of this film should be on every jazz fan's shelf.

JAZZ PASSENGERS

Formed as an alternative to the more stoic traditions of jazz, this New York ensemble took influence instead from the music's renegades, be they Thelonious Monk, Sun Ra or Charlie Mingus. Evolving in 1987 out of the Knitting Factory in Lower Manhattan, a popular art scene, the group specialised in a free-flowing form of bop-inspired jazz. However, their range also took in Latin dance, jazz rap and film dialogue. The principals behind the Jazz Passengers were Roy Nathanson and Curtis Fowlkes, who first met when working in the pit band for the Big Apple Circus. They subsequently moved to John Lurie's Lounge Lizards, with the intention of recording a duo album together. However, along the way they picked up a whole host of additional musicians who would make up the Jazz Passengers, in particular E.J. Rodriguez (percussion), Brad Jones (bass; also an accompanist to Elvin Jones and Muhal Richard Abrams), Bill Ware (vibraphone; has also worked with Steely Dan) and Marc Ribot (guitar; also recorded with Tom Waits and Elvis Costello). After releasing some five albums on small and obscure labels, including *Implement Yourself* using a grant from the Lila Wallace/Reader's Digest Fund, the group made its major label debut in 1994 with *Jazz Passengers In Love*, produced by Hal Willner. A collection of 12 originals, the guest vocalists featured included Jimmy Scott, Debbie Harry, Mavis Staples, Freedy Johnston and Jeff Buckley. Other personnel involved were lyricist Arto Lindsay, singer Bob Dorough, playwright Ray Dobbins and David Cale, a performance artist. They collaborated with 70s new wave icon Deborah Harry in 1997 for *Individually Twisted* which featured a new version of her Blondie hit 'The Tide Is High'.

● ALBUMS: *Broken Night/Red Light* (Crépescule 1987)★★★, *Deranged And Decomposed* (Crépescule 1988)★★★★, *Implement Yourself* (New World 1990)★★★, *Live At The Knitting Factory* (Knitting Factory 1991)★★, *Plain Old Joe* (Knitting Factory 1993)★★★, *Jazz Passengers In Love* (High Street 1994)★★, with Deborah Harry *Individually Twisted* (32 Records 1997)★★★.

JAZZ SAMBA - STAN GETZ

The album that launched Antonio Carlos Jobim's now classic 'Desafinado', *Jazz Samba* was released in 1962, in the early days of America's bossa nova craze and before the music lost its charm to cliché. Joined by fellow Latin jazz pioneer Charlie Byrd on classical guitar, and a discreet bass and drums team, tenor saxophonist Getz makes light and elegant music out of a collection of catchy bossas and sambas. His virtuosity, bluesy drive and smooth, soft tone make the music cook like bossa jazz rarely has since. There are still enough surprises to make this record more than just a period piece, and it stands as a fine example of Stan Getz's lyrical genius.

● Tracks: *Desafinado; Samba Dees Days; O Pato; Samba Triste; Samba De Uma Nota So; E Luxo So; Baia.*

● First released 1962

● UK peak chart position: 15

● USA peak chart position: 1

JAZZ WARRIORS

Formed in London in the mid-80s, largely through the efforts of Courtney Pine and Gail Thompson, the Jazz Warriors drew musicians from the growing group of young black musicians who were active in the UK during the 80s. Initially the band was around 20 pieces and made extensive use of Afro-Caribbean percussive patterns overlaid with powerhouse brass. Many of the band's early soloists demonstrated their enthusiasm for John Coltrane, but in later years a wider range of influences was evident. The freedom from stylization that the Warriors displayed in their approach to big band music allowed the introduction of disparate musical forms, and proved a heady mixture which attracted many fans from the fringes of jazz. This freedom also extended into the band's public performances, which were sometimes undisciplined and disorganized. At their best, however, and with excellent soloists such as Pine, Phillip Bent, Orphy Robinson and singer Cleveland Watkiss, the Warriors offered an interesting concept of how big band music might evolve. In the late 80s, the Warriors worked with guest American leaders Henry Threadgill and Craig Harris, while another, home-grown, project was a suite in tribute to Joe Harriott. By the early 90s the lack of discipline and commitment displayed by some of its members allowed the band to drift and led to the defection of some elder statesmen, such as Harry Beckett. Sad though this was, several of the individual members retained a measure of their initial popularity and embarked upon successful solo careers.

● ALBUMS: *Out Of Many, One People* (Antilles 1987)★★★.

JAZZ WRITING

Newspaper and magazine articles apart, and most of them ill-informed and derogatory, very little was written about jazz during the music's formative years. In the late 30s and early 40s, however, a more informed coterie of writers emerged, some of whom launched what was to become an ongoing list of formal histories. Amongst the earlier works were *Aux Frontières Du Jazz* (1932) and *Jazz From The Congo To The Metropolitan* (1946) (alt. title: *Jazz: From Congo To Swing*) by Robert Goffin, *American Jazz Music* (1939) by Wilder Hobson, *Shining Trumpets: A History Of Jazz* (1946) by Rudi Blesh, *Jazz: A People's Music* (1948) by Sidney Finkelstein and *Introduction À La Musique De Jazz* (1948) and *Jazz: Its Evolution And Essence* (1956) by André Hodeir. Several of these histories were the work of Europeans, detached by time, distance and culture from their subject matter. For all such distancing, some of these early books provided an interesting, frequently perceptive and often undeniably worthy basis for an understanding of the music's origins. Unfortunately, by the 40s and 50s, when these books were written, many of the music's pioneers and early innovators were dead often leaving behind only sketchy evidence of their roles in jazz. Through this and other factors created by the passage of time misconceptions crept in to some of these histories and were given an aura of authenticity. In part, these frequently understandable errors resulted from the historians concerned having to form opinions upon the evidence of recorded jazz. Although this is a legitimate means of research, it can and did lead to misjudgements on such important matters as chains of influence. Later jazz historians were able to bring into their deliberations clearer views of the chronology of the music's development together with an understanding of the social context and the significance of jazz in the black experience and of black culture in American society. Nevertheless, only a small percentage of jazz writers and historians are of African-American origin and to some extent certain important aspects of jazz as a cultural phenomenon remain less than fully explored to this day. Among later jazz histories are James Lincoln Collier's *The Making Of Jazz: A Comprehensive History* (1978), John Chilton's *Jazz* (1979) and Joachim Berendt's *The Jazz Book: From Ragtime To Fusion And Beyond* (1982). Gunther Schuller's *Early Jazz: Its Roots And Musical Development* (1968) and *The Swing Era: The Development Of Jazz 1930-1945* (1989), two volumes which form part of a projected trilogy, already displays the qualities necessary to make this, on its completion, the most thorough and best-researched history of jazz. Many other histories of jazz exist, of course, some dealing with the subject as a whole, others dealing in close detail with specific areas or periods or concise themes. Amongst these latter volumes are *Jazz Style In Kansas City And The Southwest* (1971) by Ross Russell, *Big Band Jazz* (1974) by Albert McCarthy, *Jazz: A History Of The New York Scene* (1981) by Samuel B. Charters and Leonard Kunstadt, *Swing To Bop: An Oral History* (1985) by Ira Gitler, *The Jazz Cataclysm* (1967) by Barry McRae, *The Freedom Principle: Jazz After 1958* (1985) by John Litweiler and *American Women In Jazz: 1900 To The Present* (1982) by Sally Placksin.

An important source of information on jazz lies in the many biographies and autobiographies of musicians. In some cases, these works need to be viewed with caution. Some biographers approach their subjects in awe, treating them almost as idols and taking for granted utterances that need an element of discernment. Some musicians, writing of their own lives - whether directly or through a 'ghost' - also require to be considered with a cautiously critical eye. This is not to suggest that any musician deliberately sets out to deceive but there are those who choose not to let accuracy hinder their love for a good story. Important artists who have attracted biographers include Louis Armstrong: *Louis: The Louis Armstrong Story 1900-1971* (1971) by John Chilton and Max Jones, the contentious *Louis Armstrong: An American Genius* (1983) by James Lincoln Collier, and Gary Giddins's *Satchmo* (1988). Books on Duke Ellington include *Beyond Category, The Life And Genius Of Duke Ellington* by John Edward Hasse (1993), *The Duke Ellington Reader*, edited by Mark Tucker (1993), *Duke* (1977) by Derek Jewell and *Duke Ellington* (1987), another contentious volume by James Lincoln Collier. Charlie Parker's life was explored by Robert Reisner in *Bird: The Legend Of Charlie Parker* (1962), Ross Russell in *Bird Lives!: The High Life And Hard Times Of Charlie 'Yardbird' Parker* (1973), and Gary Giddins in *Celebrating Bird: The Triumph Of Charlie Parker* (1986). John Chilton's books include several on noted jazz artists including *Billie's Blues: A Survey Of Billie Holiday's Career 1933-1959* (1975), *Sidney Bechet: The Wizard Of Jazz* (1987), and *Song Of The Hawk: The Life And Recordings Of Coleman Hawkins* (1990). Ian Carr is the author of *Miles Davis: A Critical Biography* (1982), Dave Gelly and Lewis Porter have both written books entitled *Lester Young* (respectively in 1984 and '85), and the story of Bessie Smith was told by Chris Albertson in *Bessie* (1972). Recently an excellent book on the life of Bill Evans has appeared, and this is destined to become the standard biography for this artist; *How My Heart Sings* by Peter Pettinger.

Musicians' autobiographies which also project a vivid picture of the jazz life include *A Life In Jazz* (1986) by Danny Barker, *Treat It Gentle* (1960) by Sidney Bechet, *Buck Clayton's Jazz World* (1986), *We Called It Music* (1948) by Eddie Condon, *Dizzy, To Be Or Not To Bop: The Autobiography Of Dizzy Gillespie* (1979), *Beneath The Underdog* (1971) by Charles Mingus and *Straight Life: The Story Of Art Pepper* (1979). Books by lesser musicians abound and some of these can often provide interesting reading and cast light on overlooked areas of jazz. Mezz Mezzrow's *Really The Blues* (1946) is an example of the workings of a particularly extravagant if highly entertaining imagination.

A highly valuable source of information are interviews, sometimes conducted for magazines or radio shows, many of which have found their way into book form. Noted interviewers include Max Jones and Whitney Balliett. Both have an enviable ability to put their subjects at ease and to draw from them revealing and insightful commentaries upon their lives and music. For all such similarities, Jones and Balliett differ in their prose style, Jones opting for a spare yet discerning approach, Balliett for a sometimes lavish yet usually appropriate approach which includes a remarkable ability to convey through words striking visual and aural images. Jones's interviews have been collected in book form as *Talking Jazz* (1987) while Balliett's appear in several volumes including *The Sound Of Surprise* (1959), *Dinosaurs In The Morning* (1962), *Such Sweet Thunder* (1966), *Improvising: Sixteen Jazz Musicians And Their Art* (1977) and *Jelly Roll, Jabbo And Fats* (1983). Other important volumes of interviews are *Hear Me Talkin' To Ya: The Story Of Jazz By The Men Who Made It* (1955) edited by Nat Shapiro and Nat Hentoff and *Notes And Tones* (1983) by Arthur Taylor.

Books that mingle interviews with essays on a wide range of topics and artists include Gary Giddins's *Riding On A Blue Note: Jazz And American Pop* (1981) and *Rhythm-a-ning: Jazz Tradition And Innovation In The '80s* (1985), Stanley Dance's *The World Of Duke Ellington* (1970), *The World Of Earl Hines* (1977) and *The World Of Count Basie* (1980), *Jam Session: An Anthology Of Jazz* (1958) edited by Ralph Gleason, *Jazzmen* (1958) edited by Frederic Ramsey Jnr. and Charles Edward Smith, *A Handbook Of Jazz* by Barry Ulanov, *Jazz* (1977) edited by Nat Hentoff and Albert McCarthy, and *The Art Of Jazz: Ragtime To Bebop* (1981) by Martin Williams. Among many others who have written on jazz with wit, insight, a perceptive critical eye and ear, and occasionally with a touch of contentiousness, are Francis Davis, Richard Hadlock, Philip Larkin, Gene Lees, Humphrey Lyttelton, Leroy Ostransky and Val Wilmer.

Important vehicles for jazz writing are the jazz magazines. Amongst many magazines, some of which have proved impossible to keep afloat despite the determination of their editors and proprietors, are *Le Jazz Hot* (1935-), edited for several years by André Hodeir, *Jazz Journal International* (1948-), whose editors have included Sinclair Traill, Mike Hennessey and, currently, Eddie Cook, *Coda* (1958-), *Crescendo International* (1962-) and *Cadence* (1976-). These magazines may be broadly identified with mainstream to bop while traditional and New Orleans jazz has been served by *Storyville* (1965-) and *Footnote* (1969-). More recent developments in jazz and music beyond have been closely followed by *Wire* (1986-), particularly under the original editorship of Richard Cook. Cook and Brian Morton have established themselves with the *Penguin Guide To Jazz On CD*. Although they are frustratingly dismissive of certain artists and highly opinionated about others, it is, without doubt, the best guide of it's kind. They write honestly and from the heart.

At certain times, some popular music magazines have had strong leanings towards jazz. Amongst American magazines in this category are *Metronome* (1885-1961) which was strongly jazz-orientated between the mid-30s and the mid-50s, the period when George T. Simon held senior editorial posts, and *Down Beat* (1934-), especially during the late 30s, 40s and 50s. In the UK, *Melody Maker* (1926-) was an important jazz organ in the 40s and 50s, especially during the tenure as editor of Max Jones. In recent years *Jazz Times* (1970-), has become a reliable source, and to a slightly lesser degree *Jazziz*, although fusion has always been given a strong presence since it started in 1984

Other sources of often valuable comment which should not be overlooked are sleeve notes. Although the sleeve of a record album is customarily a part of the marketing package, the notes on jazz albums have often escaped becoming merely a part of the sales pitch. Writers with perception and style who frequently appear in this form include Alun Morgan, author of *Count Basie* (1984) and co-author of *Modern Jazz: 1945-1970 The Essential Records*, and Dan Morgenstern, who also edited *Metronome*, *Jazz* and *Down Beat* in the 60s, has been director of the Institute Of Jazz Studies at Rutgers University since the mid-70s, and whose books include *Jazz People* (1976).

Jazz encyclopedias which set out to provide in capsule form data on numerous artists have also become a familiar part of the literature of jazz. An early venture was Hugues Panassie's *Dictionary Of Jazz* (1954), a volume sometimes too readily maligned because of its author's dismissal of any of the music's developments after 1940 (Panassie chose to regard bop as being something other than jazz). For all such eccentricties, Panassie's book is frequently perceptive even if much of its content has been overtaken by later research. Later encycloppedias include Leonard Feather's *The Encyclopedia Of Jazz* (1955), *The Encyclopedia Of Jazz In The '60s* (1966) and *The Encyclopedia Of Jazz In The '70s* (1976), *The Illustrated Encyclopedia Of Jazz* (1986) by Brian Case, Stan Britt and Chrissie Murray, John Chilton's *Who's Who Of Jazz* (1985), *Jazz: The Essential Companion* by Ian Carr, Digby Fairweather and Brian Priestley (1987), has now mutated into *Jazz: The Rough Guide*, and *The New Grove Dictionary of Jazz* (1988) by Barry Kernfeld and others. The latter is highly authoritative, but the stodgy typographical presentatation makes it a trial to read rather than a pleasure.

Some of the most assiduous of the many researchers into jazz are the discographers. The sheer volume of work involved in accumulating the necessary data would daunt even the most dedicated enthusiasts and, indeed, some discographies have suddenly stopped in mid-alphabet, never to be resumed. There exist numerous discographies on individual artists with few major figures being without a volume. Comprehensive discographies (or at least those that seek to be comprehensive) include Charles Delauney's pathfinding *Hot Discography*, which first appeared in 1936, Dave Carey and Albert McCarthy's *Jazz Directory* (1949-1957), which fizzled out around the letter 'k', and Brian Rust's *Jazz Records: A-Z, 1897-1942* (1978). The major discograhies are those prepared by Jorgen Grunnet Jepsen and Walter Bruyninckx, both of which appear in multiple volumes.

Although not directly relevant to the subject of jazz writing, the work of many jazz photographers continually illuminate magazines, books and album sleeves, to say nothing of sometimes appearing in exhibitions. Amongst the best known in the field are K. Abé, *Jazz Giants: A Visual Retrospective* (1986), Ole Brask, in Morgenstern's *Jazz People*, and David Redfern, *David Redfern's Jazz Album* (1980). Other skilled photographers of jazz musicians include Ray Avery, William Claxton, William Gottlieb, Tim Motion, Bob Parent, Charles 'Chuck' Stewart, Val Wilmer and some, like Colin Priestley, Lee Richardson and Sue Storey, perhaps less well known but whose work is often at least on par with more noted figures.

Jazz writing is now a long established subject. Important newer artists will almost certainly warrent some serious biographical documentation, although it is debatable if the jazz greats can produce yet another bibliographer with anything fresh to say. In 1998 two exceptional books on jazz writing were published, and they now form the core recommendation to anyone wanting to immerse themself in the subject. *Reading Jazz: A Gathering Of Autobiography, Reportage And Criticism From 1919 To Now*, edited by Robert Gottlieb and *Visions Of Jazz: The First Century* by Gary Giddins. Both these books are eclectic and neither set out to preach. They are both worthy additions to 'great' books about jazz.

JAZZTET

(see Farmer, Art; Golson, Benny)

JEFFERSON, EDDIE

b. 3 August 1918, Detroit, Michigan, USA, d. 9 May 1979, Detroit, Michigan, USA. Beginning his show business career as a dancer and occasional singer, Jefferson gradually concentrated on his latter talent. After achieving limited success, as a scat singer in the mid- to late 40s, Jefferson was largely responsible for the creation of so-called 'vocalese', devising lyrics to fit solos originally improvised by leading jazz musicians. Among the solos to which Jefferson wrote words was that played on 'Body And Soul' by Coleman Hawkins (with whom he had briefly worked in the early 40s), 'Parker's Mood' by Charlie Parker and James Moody's version of 'I'm In The Mood For Love'. This tune, variously retitled but usually known as 'Moody's Mood For Love' was recorded by King Pleasure, and achieved considerable success, thus opening doors for its adaptor. Jefferson subsequently worked with Moody's small group as both singer and manager, an association which lasted for almost 20 years. He continued to adapt solos by important musicians, including Miles Davis and Horace Silver. In the early 70s Jefferson sang with Richie Cole but on 9 May 1979, during an engagement at the Showcase in Detroit and within days of being filmed in performance there, he was fatally shot in the street outside the club.

● ALBUMS: *The Jazz Singer* (Evidence 1962)★★★, *Hipper Than Thou* (Zu Zazz)★★★★, with James Moody *Letter From Home* (Original Jazz Classics 1962)★★★★, *Moody's Mood/Moody/Hi-Fi Party* (1962)★★★, *Body And Soul* (Original Jazz Classics 1968)★★★★, *Come Along With Me* (Original Jazz Classics 1969)★★★★, *Things Are Getting Better* (1974)★★★, *Still On The Planet* (1976)★★★, *The Live-liest* (1976)★★, *Godfather Of Vocalese* (Muse 1977)★★★, *The Main Man* (1977)★★★, *There I Go Again* (Prestige 1984)★★★.

JEFFERSON, HILTON

b. 30 July 1903, Danbury, Connecticut, USA, d. 14 November 1968. After playing banjo in various outfits in the north-eastern states, Jefferson switched to alto saxophone and by 1926 had graduated to the Claude Hopkins band in New York. During the next few years he played briefly with ensembles led by King Oliver (recording on 'Shake It And Break It'), Benny Carter, McKinney's Cotton Pickers and Fletcher Henderson ('You Can Take It' and 'Harlem Madness') but was mainly in the Chick Webb and Hopkins bands. After these years of restlessness he joined Cab Calloway, staying as lead alto saxophonist for nine years. With Calloway he was featured only occasionally but used such moments to great advantage, placing on record some of his gorgeously lyrical performances as, for example, on 'Willow Weep For Me'. He left Calloway in 1949, returned in 1951 and then worked with Duke Ellington and Don Redman (accompanying Pearl Bailey). In 1953 Jefferson left music to work as a bank guard, but frequently turned up at club sessions, reunions and on recording dates, including the magnificent *Big Reunion* by former members of the Fletcher Henderson orchestra.

● ALBUMS: with Fletcher Henderson All Stars *The Big Reunion* (1957)★★★.

● COMPILATIONS: with Henderson *A Study In Frustration* (1923-38)★★★, *Cab Calloway's Sixteen Classics* (1939-41)★★★★.

JEFFERSON, THOMAS

b. 19 June 1921, Chicago, Illinois, USA. Raised in New Orleans, Jefferson learned to play trumpet as a child. His first professional job came when he was 13 years old. He worked with De De Pierce, George Lewis and others. In the mid-50s Jefferson was caught up in the resurgence of interest in New Orleans music and became a regular member of Lewis's band, recording and touring with him. In the 60s he was a regular at the Paddock Lounge, continuing to preserve the musical traditions of jazzmen a generation older than himself. A vigorous player, Jefferson continued his career into the 70s and 80s, often teaming up with outstanding musicians from other contries, including Sammy Rimington.

●ALBUMS: *If I Could Be With You* (unk. date), *International New Orleans Jazz Band* (unk. date), *New Orleans At Midnight* (unk. date), *Thomas Jefferson And His Dixieland All Stars* (unk. date).

JEFFREY, PAUL H.

b. 8 April 1933, New York, USA. In the 50s Jeffrey had worked throughout the USA with R&B/Blues artists including Wynonie Harris, Big Maybelle and B.B. King before returning to New York to study music at Ithaca College. Jeffrey worked with Illinois Jacquet, Sadik Hakim and Howard McGhee before touring Europe in 1968 with Dizzy Gillespie. In the 70s, after a brief spell with the Count Basie Orchestra, Jeffrey worked on and off with Thelonious Monk as well as conducting a concert of his music at the Newport Jazz Festival in 1974. Later he arranged and conducted Charles Mingus's music on his last albums. Jeffrey has also been head of Jazz Studies at Rutgers University since the early 80s.

● ALBUMS: *Electrifying Sounds* (1968)★★★.

JEFFRIES, HERB

b. 24 September 1916, Detroit, Michigan, USA. Early in his career Jeffries sang with the Erskine Tate band, for many years one of the most popular bands residing in Chicago. In 1931 he joined Earl Hines and was then briefly with Blanche Calloway. A tall, striking-looking man, in the late 30s Jeffries appeared in a number of films made by black producer-director Oscar Micheaux. In *The Bronze Buckaroo* and similar tales, Jeffries appeared as a black equivalent to the then popular white singing cowboys such as Gene Autry. In the early 40s Jeffries sang with Duke Ellington and his recording of 'Flamingo' was hugely successful. In the 50s Jeffries sang in clubs, often on the west coast, recording with artists including Lucky Thompson and Bobby Hackett. A re-recording of 'Flamingo', this time with Les Brown, was also successful. In the 70s and 80s Jeffries continued performing as a singer and actor, operated his own record label, United National, and appeared, exuding charm, bonhomie and good humour, as singer and master of ceremonies at several of the Ellington reunion conventions in the USA and UK. At one such reunion in Los Angeles in the summer of 1991, Jeffries received excellent notices for his performance in a revival of Ellington's *Jump For Joy*, half a century after his first appearance in the show.

● ALBUMS: *Calypso Joe* (1957)★★★, *Flamingo* (c.1957)★★, *Say It Isn't So* (1957)★★★, *If I Were A King* (c.1960)★★★, *I Remember Bing* (c.1960)★★.

● COMPILATIONS: with Earl Hines *Swingin' Down* (1932-

33)★★★, with Duke Ellington *The Blanton-Webster Band* (1940-42)★★★★★, *The Bronze Buckaroo Rides Again* (Warner Western 1995)★★★.

JENKINS, BILLY

b. 5 July 1956, Bromley, Kent, England. Jenkins started to play the violin when he was seven years old and sang in a Parish church choir until the age of 12, graduating to special choirs at Westminster and St. Paul's Cathedral. Piano and viola lessons started when he was 11, providing a theoretical background to self-taught guitar, which he began the following year. The formation of Burlesque in 1972 began a 10-year partnership with saxophonist Ian Trimmer. Burlesque's derisory attitude - musicians would crowd round drummer Kevin Currie during his solos, gasping with amazement - was not deemed saleable until the birth of punk in 1977, when the band signed to Arista Records. The humour did not translate well to record, though it is obvious that Jenkins's guitar is something special. Burlesque folded and Trimmer and Jenkins started working as a duo, performing at the Comic Strip alongside alternative comedians such as Alexei Sayle and Rik Mayall. In 1981 the band toured with maverick master-drummer Ginger Baker as his 'Nutters'. Jenkins had the musical training to take his absurdist-punk viewpoint into the web of his music, as was demonstrated by *Greenwich*, the first release with his group Voice Of God Collective. His prolific ideas demanded more regular release, so he started his own label Wood Wharf (later VOTP Records). *Piano Sketches*, outlined compositions that later became fully fledged suites. Despite his onstage clowning, Jenkins has always managed to attract the best young players, frequently forcing them to produce better playing than they achieved in more self-regarding circumstances. Roy Dodds, drummer with Fairground Attraction, provided his music with a firm rhythmic base; Loose Tubes members Dai Pritchard (bass clarinet) and Iain Ballamy (tenor) provided brilliant solos on *Uncommerciality* and *Motorway At Night*. In 1991 Jenkins formed an alliance with free-improvising drummer Steve Noble, releasing *Tumba La Casa!* and engaging him in a sparring match at the 1991 Crawley Outside In Festival (complete with referee and five-minute rounds!). In 1996 he turned to the blues with the Blues Collective and released the excellent *S.A.D.*The unsettling humour and parodic bossa novas of Jenkins' often brilliant music bring life (and audiences) to advanced improvisation: a Willem Breuker figure the UK jazz scene badly needs. Like bassist Danny Thompson and the late Frank Zappa (to whom he is often compared), if Jenkins were unable to play any longer he could become a stand up comedian with natural ease.

● ALBUMS: *Burlesque* (1977)★★★, with Ian Trimmer *Live At The Comic Strip* (1981)★★★, *Sounds Like Bromley* (1982)★★★, *Piano Sketches 1973-1984* (1984)★★★★, *Beyond E Major* (1985)★★★, *Greenwich* (1985)★★, *Uncommerciality* (1986)★★★★, *Scratches Of Spain* (Babel 1987)★★★★, *In The Nude* (1987)★★★, *Wiesen '87* (1987)★★, *Motorway At Night* (1988)★★★, *Jazz Cafe Concerts Vols 1 & 2* (1989)★★★, *Tumba La Casa!* (1990)★★★, *Blue Moon In a Function Room* (1990)★★★, *First Aural Exhibition* (1992),★★★ *Entertainment USA* (Babel 1994)★★★★, *Mayfest '94* (Babel 1995)★★, *S.A.D.* (Babel 1996)★★★.

JENKINS, FREDDIE

b. 10 October 1906, New York City, New York, USA, d. 1978. A student at Wilberforce University, trumpeter Jenkins played in the band directed by Horace Henderson, that later turned professional. Jenkins's light, airy style, coupled with an outgoing musical personality, attracted the attention of Duke Ellington, who hired him in 1928. Jenkins's health deteriorated, however, and six years later he had to leave the band because of respiratory problems. He continued to play intermittently, recording with his own band and playing in the bands of Luis Russell and Ellington again, but retired from music in 1938.

● ALBUMS: *The Indispensable Duke Ellington Vols 1/2 & 3/4* (RCA 1929-34)★★★★.

JENKINS, LEROY

b. 11 March 1932, Chicago, Illinois, USA. Jenkins began playing violin as a small child and, although he later tried other instruments, it was as a violinist that he became known in local jazz circles. In the early 60s he taught music in Alabama and back in Chicago, which is where, in 1965, he became involved with Muhal Richard Abrams in the AACM. He joined Anthony Braxton's first group with Leo Smith, and moved to Paris in 1969. The unit added drummer Steve McColl, recorded several albums, became known as the Creative Construction Company, but then broke up and Jenkins returned to the USA. In 1971, the Creative Construction played a reunion concert with guests Abrams and Richard Davis, which was recorded and later released in two parts by Muse Records. In 1971 Jenkins formed the Revolutionary Ensemble, a trio with bassist Sirone and drummer Jerome Cooper. After the Revolutionary Ensemble folded in the late 70s, Jenkins was associated with the New York-based Composer's Forum and also recorded with both upcoming musicians such as Anthony Davis, George Lewis and James Newton and veterans Muhal Richard Abrams and Andrew Cyrille. In his playing style Jenkins ignored the conventions of the European classical violin. Although a jazz predecessor, Stuff Smith, had used the instrument in a manner which also ignored preconceptions, scraping the strings and striking the box to create whatever sounds his imagination demanded, Jenkins went much further. In his hands the violin became many instruments; it could be a richly lyrical singer of ballads, it could be used to deliver harsh and sometimes raucous counterpoint, it could be a means to play driving rhythmic patterns. In freeing the instrument from previous constraints, Jenkins has established himself as a major figure in contemporary music. He has also occasionally recorded on viola. The 80s saw him devoting much of his time to composing, though he also led a blues-inspired band, Sting, which featured a front-line of violins and two guitars. In the 90s he recorded with Joseph Jarman.

● ALBUMS: with Creative Construction Company *Creative Construction Company, Vols 1 And 2* 1971 recording (1975)★★★, *George Lewis* (Black Saint 1978)★★★★, *For Players Only* (1975)★★★, *Solo Concert* (India Navigation 1977)★★★★, *The Legend Of Ai Glatson* (Black Saint 1978)★★★, *Space Minds, New Worlds, Survival Of America* (Tomato 1979)★★★, with Muhal Richard Abrams *Lifelong Ambitions* 1977 recording (Black Saint 1981)★★★, *Revolutionary Ensemble* (Enja 1982)★★★★, *Mixed Quintet* 1979 recording (1983)★★★, with Sting *Urban Blues* (Black Saint 1984)★★★★, *Live!* (Black Saint 1993)★★, with Joseph Jarman *Out Of The Mist* (Ocean 1998)★★★.

JENNEY, JACK

b. Truman Elliot Jenney, 12 May 1910, Mason City, Indiana, USA, d. 16 December 1945. After performing in a band directed by his father, a music teacher, Jenney debutted with Austin Wylie but then played trombone in various bands, including one led by Mal Hallett and a junior edition of the high-class Isham Jones band. In the late 30s Jenney became a studio musician but also recordedand played with Richard Himber, Phil Harris, Lenny hayton, Andre Kostelanetz, Freddy Rich, Red Norvo, Johnny Williams and Glenn Miller. In 1939 he briefly led his own big band, and worked together with vocalists including Louise Tobin, Bonnie Lake and Meredith Blake, but when this band collapsed he joined Artie Shaw. In the early 40s he resumed studio work, then tried leading again, including taking over the Bobby Byrne band and recorded with his wife, singer Kay Thompson; soon afterwards he was inducted into the US Navy. On his discharge he returned to the studios after relocating to the west coast and worked in radio (notably with Dick Haymes), but died in a Hollywood hospital during December 1945 after surgery for appendicitis. A polished stylist, Jenney is still highly regarded by musicians for his flawless technique.

● ALBUMS: *Jack Jenney And His Orchestra* (1938-40)★★★.

JENSEN, PAPA BUE

b. Arne Jensen, c.1928, Denmark. After becoming hugely popular in his own country during the late 50s and early 60s, trombonist Jensen's reputation spread as his band was used to accompany many visiting American jazz artists. Although these performances were usually restricted to Scandinavian countries, recordings with the visitors helped to give the band and its leader a following elsewhere. In more recent years Jensen has capitalized upon this popularity by travelling the international festival circuit. The mostly traditional musicians with whom he has played, sometimes on record, have included Wild Bill Davison, George Lewis, Edmond Hall, Wingy Manone and Albert Nicholas.

● ALBUMS: *Papa Bue's Viking Jazz Band: The Anniversary Album* (1956-66)★★★★, *Papa Bue's Viking Jazz Band* (1958)★★★★, *George Lewis With Papa Bue's Viking Jazz Band* (1959)★★★, *Papa Bue's Viking Jazz Band With Wingy Manone And Edmond Hall* (1966)★★★, *Down By The Riverside* (1968)★★★, *Wild Bill Davison With Papa Bue's Viking Jazz Band* (1974-75)★★★★.

JENSON, JOYA

b. Australia. Jenson's highly successful career as a singer was paralleled by a steadily burgeoning career as a writer, broadcaster and tireless spokesperson for jazz in her homeland. For many years she was jazz critic for *The Sydney Morning Herald* and in 1998 she celebrated the 30th anniversary of her weekly radio show, *The Joy-a-Jazz*, on 2MBS-FM, with a concert featuring many luminaries of Australian jazz. Her own career as a performer made her extremely popular in Australia and elsewhere.

JEROME, JERRY

b. 19 June 1912, New York City, New York, USA. In 1935, after playing tenor saxophone part-time in dance bands as a means of paying his way through medical school, Jerome opted for a career in music. The following year he was in Glenn Miller's short-lived band, then played with Red Norvo and Artie Shaw and in 1938 became a member of Benny Goodman's highly-popular band. In 1940 he was back with Shaw, but freelanced on record dates with Lionel Hampton. Two years later he was mostly working in studios, occasionally playing on record dates and carrying out executive duties with record companies. By the end of the 40s he was fully immersed in broadcasting, as a conductor, composer, arranger and musical director. Highly regarded by the bandleaders for whom he worked, and to whose performances he contributed many fine jazz solos, Jerome eventually retired from his formal work in music, but continued to play for pleasure into the 80s.

● ALBUMS: *The Jerry Jerome Trio* (1985)★★★, *Something Old, Something New* (Arbors 1998)★★★.

● COMPILATIONS: *Jerry Jerome And His Cats And Jammers* (1944)★★★★.

JETER-PILLARS ORCHESTRA

When the popular territory band led by Alphonso Trent broke up in 1933, two of the saxophonists decided to form their own small band. These musicians, friends from boyhood, were alto saxophonist James Jeter and tenor saxophonist Hayes Pillars. Taking their example from Trent, they set very high standards of musicianship and owing to careful choice of sidemen and the development of a popular repertoire, they became very successful on the dancehall circuits of the mid and south-western states. Based for many years at the Plantation Club, St. Louis, Missouri, the band played sophisticated danceband charts with considerable elan. Although it was never a jazz orchestra, over the years future jazz stars such as Art Blakey, Jimmy Blanton, Sid Catlett, Charlie Christian, Kenny Clarke, Harry Edison, Jimmy Forrest, Jo Jones and Walter Page were in the ranks. The band played on into the late 40s before disbanding. The Jeter-Pillars Orchestra had only one recording date, cutting four sides in 1937 during a period when none of its future stars was in the band. These records were unexceptional and the band's considerable reputation rests therefore upon the recollections of those who heard it in person or on the air, and for the many fine musicians who graced its ranks.

● ALBUMS: *The Territory Bands* (1937 recordings, one track only)★.

JEUNEMANN, MARGEURITE

b. USA. Raised in a musical family, Jeunemann studied classical piano and clarinet, picked up guitar and banjo, and also began singing in folk music groups. Her decision to work within a group rather than as a soloist was prompted by shyness not a lack of belief in her abilities. She gradually branched into jazz while still maintaining a wide interest in many other musical forms. In 1978 she formed the vocal group, Rare Silk, based in Colorado and originally a female trio. In 1979 Rare Silk toured the Far East and the following year achieved considerable prominence touring the USA and Japan with Benny Goodman. In 1983 Jeunemann left the group and moved to New York working now as a single. In 1988 she joined the faculty of the University of Maine as Director of the Vocal Jazz department and has continued to successfully mix careers as a teacher and performing artist. She has worked in duos with bassists Ed Schuller, in 1983, and Richard Davis, in 1994. She has also sung in reunions with Rare Silk. An exceptionally gifted singer with a thorough understanding of the form and substance of jazz singing, Jeunemann's exceptional skills and talent are worth seeking out.

● ALBUMS: with Benny Goodman, Rare Silk *Live At The Aurex Jazz Festival* (East Wind 1980)★★★, with Rare Silk *New Weave* (Polygram 1982)★★, *By Whose Standards* (Jeunetunes 1994)★★★.

JOBIM, ANTONIO CARLOS

b. Antonio Carlos Brasileiro de Almeida Jobim, 25 January 1927, Rio de Janiero, Brazil, d. 8 December 1994. Jobim can rightfully claim to have started the bossa nova movement when, as director of Odeon Records, he gave his friend João Gilberto his own composition 'Chega De Saudade'. The influence of the resulting record soon spread to the USA, where Stan Getz and Charlie Byrd made his compositions hugely popular. Although Jobim did record, and performed at Carnegie Hall with Getz, Byrd, and Dizzy Gillespie in 1962, it is as a composer that Jobim's influence remains huge, with tunes including 'Desafinado', 'How Insensitive', 'The Girl From Ipanema', 'One Note Samba' and 'Wave' still jazz standards. Enigmatic and cruelly underrated, his praises have been sung for many years by Frank Sinatra, and in recent times the mantle has fallen to Lee Ritenour.

● ALBUMS: *Black Orpheus* film soundtrack (1958)★★★, *The Composer Of 'Desafinado' Plays* (Verve 1963)★★★, *Wave* (A&M 1967)★★★, with Frank Sinatra *Francis Albert Sinatra And Antonio Carlos Jobim* (Reprise 1967)★★★★, *Elis And Tom* (Verve 1974)★★★, *Terra Brasilis* (Warners 1980)★★★, *The Wonderful World* (Discovery 1986)★★★, *Passarim* (Verve 1987)★★★, *Stone Flower* (1992)★★★, *Compact Jazz* (Verve 1993)★★★★, *A Certain Mr Jobim* (1993)★★★, *Verve Jazz Masters Vol. 13* (Verve 1995)★★★, *Antonio Carlos Jobim And Friends* (Verve 1996)★★★★.

● COMPILATIONS: various artists *A Twist Of Jobim* (I.E. 1997)★★★.

JOHANSSON, JAN

b. 16 September 1931, Söderhamn, Sweden, d. 9 November 1968, Stockholm, Sweden. Johansson was a pianist, composer and arranger who became known to European audiences as a member of Stan Getz's quartet touring with Norman Granz's JATP concerts in 1960. The following year he joined Arne Domnérus's band, and also the Swedish Radio Jazz Group, in 1967, composing and arranging for both. Johansson also wrote for film, theatre, ballet (e.g. *Rörelser*) and television (e.g. the Pippi Långströmpa tune). He reached a broad audience with sensitive renditions of Swedish folk songs. His considerable talents as composer and arranger were especially apparent in his experimental writing for the Radio Jazz Group, which fused and reinterpreted European art music, folk and jazz in ways that went beyond the Count Basie or Stan Kenton formats for big band jazz (*Den Korta Fristen*). As a jazz pianist in a trio context, Johansson adopted a swinging Wynton Kelly-like style, but his skill in fully exploring the potentialities of a song far exceeded the American musician (e.g. 'Willow Weep For Me' on *8 Bitar*). Not to be confused with Jan Johansson, the guitarist and music teacher.

● ALBUMS: *Rörelser* (Megafon, 1963)★★★, *Jazz På Svenska* (Megafon 1964), *Younger Than Springtime* (Artist 1972)★★★★, *8 Bitar/Innertrio* (Megafon 1989)★★★, *Jan Johansson & Radiojazzgruppen: Den Korte Fristen* (Megafon 1991)★★★, *300.000 Km/h* (Heptagon 1994)★★★★, *Musik Genom Fyra Sekler Med Jan Johansson* (Heptagon 1994)★★★, *Jan Johansson Spelar Musik På Sitt Eget Vis* (Heptagon 1995)★★★, *En Resa I Jazz Och Folkton* (Heptagon 1995)★★★, *Jazz På Ungerska/In Pleno* (Heptagon 1996)★★★.

JOHNSON, ALPHONZO

b. 2 February 1951, Philadelphia, USA. Johnson learned the double bass and trombone as a child but turned to the bass guitar in 1968. He played with the bands of Woody Herman, pianist Horace Silver and trumpeters Chuck Mangione and Chet Baker. It was with Weather Report between 1974 and 1976 that Johnson established his reputation. He is a technically accomplished musician whose punchy syncopated ostinatos were a characteristic of the band's playing during that period and contributed much to the wide appeal of Weather Report's music. Since leaving the band he has played with saxophonists Cannonball Adderly and Arthur Blythe, trumpeter Eddie Henderson, drummer Billy Cobham, vocalist Flora Purim, the Crusaders, the band co-led by Freddie Hubbard and Joe Henderson, and the band of guitarist Carlos Santana.

JOHNSON, BILL

b. 10 August 1872, New Orleans, USA, d. unknown. Johnson was the earliest of the first great bass players in jazz. He first took up the harmonica and then the guitar. A member of all the best known bands, Johnson left New Orleans at the beginning of the 20th century. He also helped found the Original Creole Band with which he toured California. A possibly apocryphal story relates how Johnson, who originally used a bowed bass, broke his bow in the course of a gig and had to continue by plucking the strings and thus established the tradition of playing jazz bass pizzicato that has continued ever since. From 1918-24 he worked with Joe Oliver and laid the foundation of the style which Pops Foster did so much to develop.

● ALBUMS: featured on *The Complete Johnny Dodds* (c.1900)★★★.

JOHNSON, BUDD

b. Albert J. Johnson, 14 December 1910, Dallas, Texas, USA, d. 20 October 1984, Kansas City, Missouri, USA. Before taking up the tenor saxophone Johnson had earlier played piano and drums. In his teens he performed in a number of territory bands in the midwest and in Texas, including those led by Terrence Holder, Jesse Stone and George E. Lee. In the mid-30s he worked in Chicago, playing in several bands, most notably, Louis Armstrong's, but was most often with Earl Hines. In the 40s he played in units led by Hines, Don Redman, Al Sears, Sy Oliver and Dizzy Gillespie. During these years Johnson was also a busy arranger, providing charts for the bands of Georgie Auld, Woody Herman, Buddy Rich and Boyd Raeburn. Johnson was deeply involved in the early days of bebop, writing for numerous small groups and acting as musical director for Billy Eckstine's big band. During the 50s Johnson often led his own small groups for club and record dates, and was also active in music publishing and as a recording company executive. In the late 50s and early 60s he played with Benny Goodman, Count Basie, Quincy Jones, Gerald Wilson, Hines and Jimmy Rushing. In 1969, after yet another stint with Hines, Johnson formed the JPJ Trio with Dill Jones, Bill Pemberton and Oliver Jackson. After the dissolution of JPJ in 1975 Johnson worked with the New York Jazz Repertory Orchestra, appeared at numerous international festivals and managed to fit in time as a teacher. It was as an arranger and contributor to bop that Johnson made his most lasting mark on jazz. Although he never approached the extraordinary improvisational flights of men like Gillespie and Charlie Parker, he was one of the musicians who helped give the new form coherence and structure. In his later playing career Johnson's style - on tenor, alto, soprano and clarinet - had thoroughly absorbed the influences of the beboppers with whom he had worked but he remained strongly identified with the jazz mainstream in which he had spent so much of his life. (NB: this artist should not be confused with Buddy Johnson.)

● ALBUMS: *Rock 'n' Roll Stage Show* (Mercury 1955)★★★, *Blues A La Mode* (Riverside 1958)★★★★, *Budd Johnson And The Four Brass Giants* (Riverside 1960)★★★★, *Let's Swing* (Prestige 1960)★★★, *Ya! Ya!* (Argo 1964)★★★, with Earl Hines, Jimmy Rushing *Blues And Things* (1967)★★★, *Ya! Ya! ii* (1970)★★★, *JPJ Quartet* (1973)★★, *In Memory Of A Very Dear Friend* (1978)★★★★, with Phil Woods *The Ole Dude And The Fundance Kid* (Uptown 1984)★★★.

● FURTHER READING: *The Tenor Saxophones Of Budd Johnson, Cecil Scott, Elmer Williams, Dick Wilson*, Jan Evensmo.

● FILMS: *Last Of The Blue Devils* (1979).

JOHNSON, BUDDY

b. Woodrow Johnson, 10 January 1915, Darlington, South Carolina, USA, d. 9 February 1977. Pianist in several dance bands of the 30s, Johnson visited Europe with the Cotton Club Revue and later formed his own big band. Although popular with dancers at Harlem's Savoy Ballroom Johnson's band was not especially jazz-oriented and neither did it become well-known to white audiences. In the mid-40s Johnson adapted his style to suit changes in public taste and had several hit records in the R&B field, notably 'Please, Mr Johnson' which was sung by his wife, Ella Johnson. (NB: this artist should not be confused with Budd Johnson.)

● ALBUMS: *Buddy Johnson Wails* (1957)★★★, *Go Ahead And Rock* (1958)★★★★.

● COMPILATIONS: *Buddy Johnson And His Orchestra* (1944-52 recordings)★★★, *Buddy Johnson At The Savoy Ballroom* (1945-46 recordings)★★★, *Rock 'N' Roll* (1953-55 recordings)★★★, *Walkin'* (1952-56 recordings)★★★, *Walk Em* (Ace 1996)★★★★.

JOHNSON, BUNK

b. William Geary Johnson, 27 December 1889, New Orleans, Louisiana, USA, d. 7 July 1949. Johnson's early career has only recently been unravelled, and then only partly, thanks to his own, often inaccurate testimony. Until his enforced retirement from music in 1934 Johnson was certainly an active musician, playing in numerous New Orleans-based bands. He claimed to have worked with Buddy Bolden and Jelly Roll Morton; however as has been determined by recent researchers such as Christopher Hillman, these associations were unlikely given Johnson's age (he had, for years, claimed to be 10 years older than he was). He certainly played in some of the best New Orleans brass and marching bands, including the Superior and the Eagle bands. Johnson also claimed to have been an important influence upon and teacher of Louis Armstrong, but this assertion too should be treated with caution. Undoubtedly, Johnson was an important musician in New Orleans during the early years of jazz; yet he was a somewhat wayward character, whose presence in a band was not always a guarantee of musical excellence. Around 1914 Johnson moved to Alexandria, Louisiana and, from then until the late 20s, he played in scores of bands in many towns and cities of the 'Deep South'. By the early 30s, however, Johnson's career was in disarray and the loss of his front teeth had made playing difficult to the point of impossibility. In 1938 research by jazz writers Frederic Ramsey Jnr. and Charles Edward Smith located Johnson, who was then living at New Iberia, Louisiana. During correspondence with the writers Johnson insisted that, if he could be given money with which to buy false teeth and a trumpet, he could play again. The money was raised and Johnson duly returned to active performing. His return to the jazz public's consciousness came in 1940 and from that point until his death he made a tremendous impact upon that area of the early jazz scene currently enjoying a resurgence of interest. Johnson toured, playing concerts and making broadcasts, and made several records; all the while enhancing his new-found and self-perpetuated reputation as one of the originators of jazz. The quality of the playing which Johnson demonstrated on the records he made in these years shows him to have been a good player of the blues and suggests that in his hey-day he must have been a better-than-average trumpeter. There are also strong hints that he possessed a measure of musical sophistication which, had his career not foundered when he was approaching his prime, would have made him an important figure in the mainstream. As it was, Johnson's reappearance on the jazz scene, which helped to cement the Revival Movement of the early 40s, tied him firmly to a musical style that, as his biographer Hillman observes, he had probably outgrown. Instead, Johnson, together with his near contemporary George Lewis, was responsible for resurrecting an interest in early jazz that has remained strong until the present day.

● ALBUMS: *Bunk Johnson And His Superior Jazz Band* (Good Time Jazz, 1942 recordings)★★★, *Bunk Johnson In San Francisco* (American Music, 1944 recordings)★★★, *Bunk And Lou* (Good Time Jazz, 1944 recordings)★★★, *Old New Orleans Jazz* (1942)★★★★, *Spicy Advice* (1944)★★★, *The American Music Recordings* (1944)★★★, *Bunk Johnson & Lu Watters* 1944 recordings (Contemporary 1983)★★★★, *The King Of The Blues* (American Music, 1944-45 recordings)★★★, *Bunk Johnson: The Last Testament* (1947)★★★.

● FURTHER READING: *Bunk Johnson: His Life And Times*, Christopher Hillman. *Willie Geary Bunk 'Johnson'*, Austin H. Sonnier.

JOHNSON, CHARLIE

b. 21 November 1891, Philadelphia, Pennsylvania, USA, d. 13 December 1959. After playing trombone in the New York area Charlie 'Fess' Johnson switched to piano and moved to Atlantic City around the end of World War I. He led his own small band, at various times, which featured Benny Carter, Sidney De Paris, Roy Eldridge and Edgar Sampson. In 1925 Johnson was engaged for a residency at Small's Paradise in New York and remained at the club well into the following decade. By 1938, however, Johnson's bandleading days were over. He continued playing piano in and around New York but his health deteriorated and most of his final years were spent in enforced retirement. Despite the band's long stint at one of Harlem's most important nightspots, they made only few recordings and were poorly promoted.

● ALBUMS: *Jazz Classics In Digital Stereo: New York* (1929)★★★★, *The Complete Charlie Johnson Sessions* 1925-1929 recordings (Hot 'n Sweet)★★★★.

JOHNSON, ELLEN

b. USA. After studying for a masters' degree in music while at San Diego State University, Johnson decided to sing professionally. She quickly developed an enthusiastic, if localized, following for her work, which ranges across standards and the contemporary popular songbook but generally features a very high proportion of jazz songs. In particular, she favours the music of Duke Ellington and Bill Evans, while she has also composed lyrics to some of the music of Charles Mingus, including 'Peggy Blue Skylight'. Johnson's singing voice is a true, clear soprano and she sings with rare poise and subtle awareness of the music's intrinsic properties.

● ALBUMS: *Too Good To Title* (Nine Winds 1993)★★★.

JOHNSON, FRANK

b. Francis Walter Johnson, 22 May 1927, Melbourne, Victoria, Australia. Among the pioneers of traditional jazz in Australia in the years after World War II, Johnson played vigorous trumpet in several bands before forming his own. The band's popularity with audiences for live appearances, on radio and in record sales continued into the 50s. By the middle of the decade, however, like so many bands of its kind in Australia and elsewhere, it was severely challenged by changing tastes in popular music. Johnson folded the band but continued to play whenever opportunities presented themselves during succeeding decades.

JOHNSON, GINGER

b. *c*.1920, Nigeria, d. 1972, Lagos, Nigeria. Percussionist Johnson emigrated to London in the late 40s, where one of his first performances was with the orchestra led by Edmundo Ros. As well as being widely respected within the expatriate African community, both as a drummer and herbalist, Johnson was a well-known figure in London's counter culture during the late 60s, as leader of Ginger Johnson's African Drummers (who played alongside the Rolling Stones during the famous Hyde Park Concert) and manager of the Iroko Club. He returned to Nigeria in the early 70s, but died of a heart attack within a few months.

JOHNSON, GUS

b. 15 November 1913, Tyler, Texas, USA. Active in music from about the age of 10, Johnson played piano, bass, drums and sang in a vocal quartet. Choosing drums, he played in a number of territory bands, then in 1938 joined the Jay McShann band in Kansas City. This was the unit that included the young Charlie Parker. Johnson stayed with McShann until entering the US Army in 1943. After the war he played with several bands, including those led by Earl Hines and Cootie Williams, and in 1949 joined Count Basie, with whom he remained until 1954, playing in both the sextet Basie briefly led during hard times and the powerful new-style big band that heralded a change in the leader's fortũnes. Later, Johnson worked as a freelance accompanying singers including Lena Horne and Ella Fitzgerald and playing on numerous club dates, concert and recording sessions with Buck Clayton, Jimmy Rushing, Woody Herman and the World's Greatest Jazz Band. An exemplary drummer, Johnson's style combined fluid grace with skilful dynamics and he was just as happy discreetly supporting singers and soloists as explosively driving a big band. By the early 70s he was living in semi-retirement in Denver, Colorado.

● ALBUMS: with Jay McShann *Early Bird* (1940-43)★★★, *Count Basie Octet* (1950)★★★, with Count Basie *Sixteen Men Swinging* (1953)★★★★, with World's Greatest Jazz Band *Century Plaza* (1971)★★★.

JOHNSON, HOWARD

b. 7 August 1941, Montgomery, Alabama, USA. Johnson taught himself baritone saxophone in 1954, then learned tuba a year later. He moved to New York in February 1963 - at a time when the tuba was not a fashionable instrument (outside of dixieland bass-line chores, the only visible player was Ray Draper), but Charles Mingus welcomed him into his workshop in 1964. In 1965 he toured with soul jazz altoist Hank Crawford, playing baritone, but returned to the Workshop for a year from July 1965. In 1966 he played in the Archie Shepp band for some months and appeared with him at the Newport Jazz Festival in 1968. Gil Evans used his multi-instrumental capacity at various points between 1966 and 1970. Active on the west coast in the mid-60s, Johnson played with Buddy Rich, Gerald Wilson and Oliver Nelson. In 1968 he played on Michael Mantler's *The Jazz Composers Orchestra*, an epic combination of scores and extreme performances from Cecil Taylor, Pharoah Sanders and Larry Coryell. The late 60s also saw him forming a tuba ensemble named Substructure. He supplied the tuba solo on a version of Jimi Hendrix's 'Little Wing' in 1974 (one of Gil Evans's more bizarre inspirations). Johnson's career makes nonsense of the so-called divisions between commercial and *avant garde*, and he even peformed a stint as the conductor of the *Saturday Night Live* band in the late 70s. He also arranged for Taj Mahal, B.B. King and Paul Butterfield and played on the Band's *Rock Of Ages*. In 1982 he played on Bob Moses's *When Elephants Dream Of Music*, and later formed a second tuba band, Gravity, who have released two acclaimed late-90s sessions for Verve Records.

● ALBUMS: *Arrival* (Verve 1995)★★★, with Gravity *Gravity!!!* (Verve 1997)★★★, with Gravity, Taj Mahal *Right Now!* (Verve 1998)★★★.

JOHNSON, J.J.

b. James Louis Johnson, 22 January 1924, Indianapolis, Indiana, USA. Johnson began playing trombone at the age of 14; by the time he was 18 years old, he had performed professionally with various bands culminating in that led by Benny Carter. Johnson was with Carter for three years during which period he also worked with Jazz At The Philharmonic. In the mid-40s he was briefly with Count Basie and for the rest of the decade was active in small bebop groups in New York. In the early 50s he joined Oscar Pettiford but then was forced to earn a living outside music. In 1954 he returned to the jazz scene and immediately attracted widespread attention through the band he co-led with Kai Winding. This band, Jay And Kai, remained together for two years, by which time Johnson was re-established and now both leading small jazz groups and composing extended works that encompassed jazz and classical forms. In the early 60s he played with Miles Davis and toured with his own groups, and at the end of the decade was also involved in studio work. The 70s saw Johnson writing for films and television but finding time to play too in a variety of settings. In the 80s he began to devote more of his time to playing, demonstrating in the process that his ability had not diminished in the slightest. Tours of Japan with JATP groups led to a brief association on record with another trombone player, Al Grey. A major figure in jazz trombone, Johnson was one of very few players of that instrument to succeed in bebop. In his earlier years, especially when playing in bebop groups with artists such as Charlie Parker, Dizzy Gillespie, Fats Navarro and Max Roach, his extraordinary technique often dominated the content of his solos; however, in later years the content matured and expanded while his technique showed no signs of faltering. Johnson remains one of the major trombonists in modern mainstream jazz.

● ALBUMS: with Kai Winding *Modern Jazz Trombones, Volume 1* 10-inch album (Prestige 1951)★★★★, with Bennie Green *Modern Jazz Trombones, Volume 2* 10-inch album (Prestige 1952)★★★, *Jay Jay All Stars* 10-inch album (Blue Note 1953)★★★, with Green, Winding *Jazz Workshop, Vol. 1* 10-inch album (Debut 1953)★★★, with Green, Winding *Jazz Workshop, Vol. 2* 10-inch album (Debut 1953)★★★, with Winding *Jay And Kai* i 10-inch album (Prestige 1954)★★★★, with Winding *Jay And Kai* i 10-inch album (Savoy 1954)★★★★, *The Eminent Jay Jay Johnson, Volume 2* 10-inch album (Blue Note 1955)★★★★, *Jay Jay Johnson, Volume 3* 10-inch album (Blue Note 1955)★★★★, with Winding *Jay And Kai, Volume 2* 10-inch album (Savoy 1955)★★★★, with Winding *Jay And Kai, Volume 3* 10-inch album (Savoy 1955)★★★★, with Winding *An Afternoon At Birdland* (Vik 1955)★★★★, with Winding *Kai Winding & J.J. Johnson* (Bethlehem 1955)★★★, with Winding *Trombone For Two* (Columbia 1956)★★★, with Winding *Kai + J.J.* 10-inch album (Columbia 1956)★★★, with Winding *J.J. Johnson/Kai Winding + Six* (Columbia 1956)★★★, with Green, Winding *Trombone By Three* (Prestige 1956)★★★★, with Green, Winding *J.J. Johnson, Kai Winding, Bennie Green* (Prestige 1956)★★★★, *'J' Is For Jazz* (Columbia 1956)★★★, *First Place* (Columbia 1956)★★★, shared with Dave Brubeck *American Jazz Festival At Newport '56* (Columbia 1956)★★★, *Live At The Café Bohemia* (Fresh Sound 1957)★★★★, with Stan Getz *Stan Getz & J.J. Johnson At The Opera House* (Verve 1958)★★★★, *Dial J.J. 5* (Columbia 1957)★★★, *J.J. In Person* (Columbia 1958)★★★, *Really Livin'* (Columbia 1959)★★★, *Trombone & Voices* (Columbia 1960)★★★, *J.J., Inc.* (Columbia 1961)★★★, with André Previn *André Previn And J.J. Johnson Play Mack The Knife And Bilbao Song* (Columbia 1961)★★★, with Winding *The Great*

Kai & J.J. (Impulse! 1961)★★★★, *A Touch Of Satin* (Columbia 1962)★★★, *J.J.'s Broadway* (Verve 1963)★★★, with Winding *Looking Back* (Prestige 1963)★★★, *J.J.!* (RCA Victor 1965)★★, *Proof Positive* (Impulse! 1965)★★★, *Goodies* (RCA Victor 1965)★★★, *Broadway Express* (RCA Victor 1966)★★★, *The Total J.J. Johnson* (RCA Victor 1967)★★★, with Winding *Israel* (A&M 1968)★★★, with Winding *Betwixt And Between* (A&M 1969)★★★, with Winding *Stonebone* (A&M 1970)★★★★, *The Yokohama Concert* (Pablo 1977)★★★, *Pinnacles* (Milestone 1979)★★★, *Concepts In Blue* (Original Jazz Classics 1980)★★★, with Milt Jackson *A Date In New York* (Inner City 1980)★★★, with Al Grey *Things Are Getting Better All The Time* (Original Jazz Classics 1983)★★★★, *Quintergy: Live At The Village Vanguard* (Antilles 1988)★★★★, *Standards: Live At The Village Vanguard* (Emarcy 1988)★★★★, *Vivian* (Concord Jazz 1992)★★★, *Let's Hang Out* (Verve 1993)★★★, with the Robert Farnon Orchestra *Tangence* (Verve Gitanes 1994)★★★, *The Brass Orchestra* (Verve 1997)★★★★.

● COMPILATIONS: *Jay Jay Johnson's Quintets/Mad Be Bop* 1949-1954 recordings (Savoy 1985)★★★★,*The Eminent J. J. Johnson Vols 1* and *2* (Blue Note 1989)★★★★, *The Complete Columbia J.J. Johnson Small Group Sessions* 11-LP/7-CD box set (Mosaic 1997)★★★★.

JOHNSON, JAMES P.

b. 1 February 1894, New Brunswick, New Jersey, USA, d. 17 November 1955. Taught piano by his mother, Johnson assimilated a wide range of musical styles. In the years following his family's relocation to New York, he continued his studies and by his late teens was working in clubs in the Hell's Kitchen district. Johnson was adept in ragtime, blues, and all the popular musical forms of the day. He was also a capable performer of classical music. By the early 20s Johnson was a leading light on New Yorks burgeoning jazz scene and was already known for his compositions, including 'Carolina Shout', which demanded virtuoso technical ability. During this period Johnson became the acknowledged master of stride piano. He also attracted the attention of Broadway producers and in 1923 composed the musical *Runnin' Wild*, in which he introduced his composition 'The Charleston'. He also engaged the admiration of emerging pianists; the young Fats Waller was an eager pupil. In the mid-20s and especially during the 30s, Johnson's interest in classical music surfaced in his own work; he composed several long pieces, including 'Yamekraw', a piano rhapsody, 'Harlem Symphony', 'Jassamine', a piano concerto, 'Spirit Of America' a string quartet, and a blues opera, 'De Organizer'. Unfortunately, many of his scores have since been lost. (An album of piano arrangements of some of the surviving pieces, performed by William Albright, was issued in 1983 under the somewhat misleading title, *The Symphonic Jazz Of James P. Johnson*.) Although Johnson continued to play in the 40s, often in small groups with companions such as Eddie Condon, Albert Nicholas and Wild Bill Davison, ill-health damaged his career. A series of strokes culminated in a severe attack in 1951, which left him bedridden and he died in November 1955. As a pianist Johnson was outstanding, not only for his dazzling technique but also for the construction of his solos. However intricate they might be, his solos were logical, non-repetitive and effectively incorporated much of his catholic musical background. Records by Johnson include transcriptions from some early piano rolls and even in this form his music generates excitement. As a composer, the manner in which his work has lasted testifies to its inherent timelessness. Apart from the excitement of 'The Charleston', 'Carolina Shout' and 'Runnin' Wild', there were reflective melodic delights such as 'Old Fashioned Love', 'If I Could Be With You One Hour Tonight' and 'Just Before Daybreak'. Apart from Waller, Johnson influenced most of the pianists working in New York in the 20s and 30s, which means almost everyone of importance. Among the older players were Count Basie, Duke Ellington, Art Tatum and Teddy Wilson, while the younger group included Erroll Garner, Johnny Guarnieri and Thelonious Monk. In the history of jazz piano, Johnson's contribution is of paramount importance.

● ALBUMS: *James P. Johnson* (1921-26)★★, *James P. Johnson* (1921-39)★★, *The Original James P. Johnson* (1943-45)★★, *Yamekraw* (1962)★★★, *A Flat Dream* 1939-45 recordings (1980)★★★, *From Ragtime To Jazz: The Complete Piano Solos 1921-1939* (1985)★★★★, with others *The Complete Edmond Hall/James P. Johnson/Sidney De Paris/Vic Dickenson Blue Note Sessions* 1943-44 recordings, 6-LP box set (1985)★★★, *Ain'cha Got Music* (Pumpkin 1986)★★★, *Carolina Shout* (Biograph 1991)★★★, *Snowy Morning Blues* (GRP 1991)★★, *The Original James P. Johnson: 1942-1945 Piano Solos* (Smithsonian Folkways 1996)★★★, *1944* (Classics 1996)★★★, *Runnin Wild* 1921-1926 recordings (Tradition/Rykodisc 1997)★★★.

● FURTHER READING: *James P. Johnson: A Case Of Mistaken Identity*, Scott E. Brown. *James P. Johnson: Father Of The Stride Piano*, Frank H. Trolle.

JOHNSON, KEG

b. Frederic H. Johnson, 19 November 1908, Dallas, Texas, USA, d. 8 November 1967. Born into a musical family (Johnson's father played cornet and his younger brother was tenor saxophonist Budd Johnson), he began playing trombone as his principal instrument when in his late teens. With his brother, he performed in local bands before they moved to Kansas City, playing there with Jesse Stone and George E. Lee, then to Chicago where, in the early 30s, they played with various bands including the Zilner Randolph-organized band fronted by Louis Armstrong. In 1933 Johnson moved to New York where he played briefly with Benny Carter and Fletcher Henderson before joining Cab Calloway with whom he remained for almost 15 years. In the early 50s he played with several bands, usually for short periods, sometimes deputizing for regular sidemen, and also sometimes playing guitar. This was mostly on the west coat but he eventually returned to New York where he played with Gil Evans, then joined Ray Charles' touring band where he remained until his death. A fluid, light-toned player with a great feeling for the blues, Johnson's solos show imagination allied to unforced technique.

JOHNSON, KEN 'SNAKEHIPS'

b. Kenrick Reginald Hymans Johnson, 10 September 1914, Georgetown, British Guiana (now known as Guyana), d. 8 March 1941. Son of a Guyanese doctor and Surinamese mother, Johnson played piano and violin as a child. On completing his schooling in England, he began dancing, making an early appearance in the provinces on the variety circuit. Studying with the African-American choreographer Clarence 'Buddy' Bradley, he gained professional confidence and contacts in the USA. These brought him film work in New York and cabaret in Hollywood, and the chance to observe black American practitioners of jazz and dance at firsthand. On the same trip he made a series of Caribbean appearances; these inspired a host of imitators with the belief that a West Indian could become part of the British showbusiness establishment and were responsible for launching several noteworthy careers. In London he persuaded Jamaican trumpeter Leslie Thompson to form a band for him to front; this, later known as the West Indian Dance Orchestra, was the first regular black band of any size in Britain. It included musicians from the Caribbean, such as clarinettist Carl Barriteau, as well as local instrumentalists of African descent, among them Welsh-born guitar-playing brothers Joe and Frank Deniz, and the latter's wife, pianist Clare Deniz. By the start of the war the 'West Indians' were broadcasting regularly and featured artists such as Barbadian trumpeter/vocalist Dave Wilkins and Welsh-born vocalist Don Johnson, whose father came from Barbuda, became household names. To many listeners, the Johnson band was the first local unit to 'swing' in the American manner, but the prominence of local black musicians ended when the leader was killed in an air-raid while on stage at London's exclusive Café de Paris in 1941.

● ALBUMS: with others *And The Bands Played On* (1938)★★★, with others *Swing Classics From Europe* (1938)★★★, with others *Al Bowlly - The Big Swoon Of The Thirties* (1940)★★.

JOHNSON, LEM

b. Lemuel Charles Johnson, 6 August 1909, Oklahoma City, Oklahoma, USA, d. 1 April 1989. While still at school, Johnson began playing clarinet and worked with local bands. In his late teens he added the tenor saxophone to his instrumental abilities and played with Walter Page's Blue Devils, then with Sammy Price. After playing with several other territory bands in the Midwest he played with Earl 'Fatha' Hines and then moved to New York. There he played in bands led by Fess Williams, Louis Jordan and others, occasionally led his own small groups, and in the early 40s was with Buster Harding, Edgar Hayes, Sidney Bechet and others. During 1942/3 he frequently played with Claude Hopkins on a part-time basis while working in defence industry factories. In the late 40s and on through the 50s he mostly led his own bands in the north-east, occasionally touring overseas, and making record dates with several leaders including Oran 'Hot Lips' Page. Gradually, Johnson's musical career became part-time although he continued to perform into the 60s. A relaxed and subtly swinging player, especially on tenor, Johnson's career sometimes seemed to lack direction and drive. On the evidence of his recorded work, this must be seen as a loss to jazz.

● COMPILATIONS: *Sidney Bechet, 1932-43: The Bluebird Sessions* (Bluebird 1932-43)★★★★, *Louis Jordan And His Tympany Five* (MCA/Charly 1939-40),★★★★ *Classics In Swing: Buck Clayton-Jonah Jones-Hot Lips Page* (Commodore 1944)★★★★.

JOHNSON, MANZIE

b. Manzie Isham Johnson, 19 August 1906, Putnam, Connecticut, USA, d. 9 April 1971. As a very small child Johnson went to New York where he learned to play violin and piano before turning to the drums. While still a teenager and then into his early twenties, he played with bands led by, among many others, Willie Gant, June Clark, Elmer Snowden and Horace Henderson. In 1931 he joined Don Redman for a six-year spell after which he played with Willie Bryant before forming his own band, then rejoined Redman. During the 30s he played on numerous record dates with leaders including Henry 'Red' Allen, Lillian Armstrong and Mezz Mezzrow, including an appearance on the famous sessions co-led by Mezzrow and Tommy Ladnier. In the 40s Johnson continued to record and play with several bands including Frankie Newton, Fletcher Henderson, Horace Henderson again, and Ovie Alston; another spell with Redman preceded military service and after the war he was again leading his own groups and playing with Alston. In the 50s Johnson gradually drifted into only occasional playing. He remained a part-time musician for the rest of his life, performing with Happy Caldwell, Lem Johnson and others. A sure timekeeper with a good sense of swing overlying a clear understanding of the more traditional role of the drummer in jazz, Johnson's playing was usually discreet and always at the service of the soloist and ensembles with which he performed.

● COMPILATIONS: *The Chronological Don Redman 1931-1933* (Classics 1931-33)★★★★, with Mezz Mezzrow, Tommy Ladnier, Sidney Bechet *The Panassie Sessions* (RCA 1938-39)★★★★, *The Fabulous Sidney Bechet* (Blue Note 1951)★★★★.

JOHNSON, MARC

b. 21 October 1953, Omaha, Nebraska, USA. After studying at North Texas State University Johnson spent the greater part of a year on the road playing bass with Woody Herman's big band. After this intensive learning experience, he auditioned in early 1978 as replacement for Eddie Gomez with the Bill Evans trio. Securing this job not only brought Johnson fulfilment of a dream he had nurtured since his days as a student, but also presented him on the world stage with a major jazz artist. After two years with Evans, Johnson played with Stan Getz, then led his own groups, including Bass Desires and the Right Brain Patrol trio, which featured guitarist Ben Monder and percussionist Arto Tuncboyaci. He also played with several South American musicians, including bandoneon player Dino Saluzzi and pianists Enrico Peranunzi and Eliane Elias, recording with the latter on 1997's *The Three Americas*. Apart from his own small bands, Johnson has also sought the company of leading guitarists for recording sessions, obviously finding this particular combination of stringed instruments, bass and guitar, very much to his taste. On a 1985 album he teamed up with John Scofield and Bill Frisell, then in the late 90s celebrated his signing to Verve Records by recording with Frisell and Pat Metheny. Built upon a solid foundation of training and deep understanding of the music he plays, Johnson has been able to work comfortably outside the customary envelope of jazz, in particular embracing South American concepts, yet he retains a firm belief in the roots of contemporary jazz. His solos indicate a fine intelligence at work and his support of other soloists and ensemble playing demonstrates that he has the technical mastery to match an extensive imagination. In addition to his exceptional playing, Johnson is also a composer of merit.

● ALBUMS: with John Abercrombie, Peter Erskine *Current Events* (ECM 1985)★★★★, with Bass Desires *Bass Desires* (ECM 1985)★★★★, with Bass Desires *Second Sight* (ECM 1987)★★★, *2x4* (Verve 1989)★★★, with Abercrombie, Erskine *John Abercrombie, Marc Johnson & Peter Erskine* (ECM 1989)★★★★, with Right Brain Control *Right Brain Control* (JMT 1991)★★, with Abercrombie, Erskine, John Surman *November* (ECM 1994)★★★★, *Magic Labyrinth* (JMT 1996)★★★, *The Sound Of Summer Running* (Verve 1998)★★★★.

JOHNSON, MONEY

b. Harold Johnson, 23 February 1918, Tyler, Texas, USA, d. 28 March 1978. He began playing trumpet as a young teenager and in his late teens was living in Oklahoma City where his musical companions included Charlie Christian. In 1937 he joined Nat Towles' famous territory band, remaining there until 1942 when the band effectively transferred to the leadership of Horace Henderson. He stayed with Henderson until 1944, then played with various leaders including Count Basie, Cootie Williams and Lucky Millinder. In the 50s Johnson was with Louis Jordan, Buddy Johnson and others, continuing into the 60s as a much in-demand session player. In the 60s he played with Earl Hines, Duke Ellington and others, returning to Ellington in the early 70s where he remained until the leader's death in 1974. He then played in New York, working with Buck Clayton and others towards the end of his life. A solid technician with a nice but somewhat underused talent for fluid and interesting solos, Johnson's long career with important bands indicates the high regard in which he was held.

● ALBUMS: *Reuben Phillips And His Orchestra* (Ascot 1961)★★, with Duke Ellington *Second Sacred Concert* (Prestige 1968)★★★, with Houston Person *Houston Express* (Prestige 1971)★★★, with Buck Clayton *Jam Session* (Chiaroscuro 1975)★★★★.

JOHNSON, OLIVER

b. 28 October 1892, Biloxi, Missouri, USA, d. 29 November 1954, Portland, Oregon, USA. Johnson, (aka Dink), played the piano, clarinet and drums. He learned the piano playing around Storyville in the years before World War I. Although he never achieved great technical proficiency he played in a rough and ready way with a great deal of humour. In 1913 he went to California and joined the Original Creole Band playing drums. He only stayed with the band for a year but when he left them he remained in California recording on drums with his brother-in-law, pianist Jelly Roll Morton and later on clarinet with Kid Ory. During the 20s he led a band called the Five Hounds Of Jazz which became the Los Angeles Six for a residency in Chicago in 1924. He returned to California to play around clubs and eventually settled in Las Vegas playing the piano in his sister's bar. Although he ceased performing in the 40s he continued to record.

JOHNSON, PETE

b. 25 March 1904, Kansas City, Missouri, USA, d. 23 March 1967. After playing drums when a teenager, Johnson switched to piano in 1926 and swiftly became a leading exponent of the blues. He was also an excellent accompanist to blues singers; especially Joe Turner, with whom he established a partnership that lasted for the rest of his life. In 1936 the ubiquitous John Hammond Jnr. brought Johnson and Turner to New York where they played at the Famous Door. Two years later Johnson played at one of Hammond's Spirituals To Swing concerts at Carnegie Hall and later performed and recorded with Albert Ammons and Meade 'Lux' Lewis as the Boogie Woogie Trio. During the 40s, Johnson continued his solo career, interspersed with engagements with Ammons and, often, Joe Turner. In the 50s Johnson toured the USA and Europe and made several records with Turner and with Jimmy Rushing. As a blues and boogie-woogie pianist, Johnson was superb and his thunderous left hand was always a joy to hear. In the recordings he made with Turner he invariably rose above himself, delivering both forceful solos and lifting the singer to some of his best work. Shortly after playing at the Newport Jazz Festival in 1958 Johnson suffered a stroke which incapacitated him. He did venture back to the recording studios in 1960 but did not appear again in public until 1967, when he was helped onstage to receive an ovation from the audience at the Spirituals To Swing 30th Anniversary concert. He took a bow and was being led off when the band swung into his best-known composition, 'Roll 'Em Pete', and his old companion, Joe Turner, prepared to sing. Johnson sat down at the piano alongside Ray Bryant and began picking uncertainly at the keys. Then, gradually, with Bryant laying down a solid left hand, Johnson showed that there was still music inside him. It was a long way from great piano playing but given the circumstances it was a highly emotional moment. It was made more so when, two months later, in March 1967, Johnson died.

● ALBUMS: with others *Spirituals To Swing* (1938-39)★★★, with Pete Johnson *8 To The Bar* 10-inch album (RCA Victor 50s)★★★★, *The Essential Jimmy Rushing* (1955)★★★, with Joe

Turner *The Boss Of The Blues* (1956)★★★★, with others *Spirituals To Swing 30th Anniversary Concert* (1967)★★★.

● COMPILATIONS: *Master Of Blues And Boogie Woogie Volumes 1-2* (1939-49)★★★, *The Boogie King* (1940-44)★★★, *The Rarest Pete Johnson Volumes 1-2* (1947-54)★★★★, *Classics 1939-41* (Original Jazz Classics 1992)★★★★, *Central Avenue Boogie* 1947 recordings (Delmark 1993)★★★.

● FURTHER READING: *The Pete Johnson Story*, Hans J. Mauerer.

JOHNSON, PLAS

b. 21 July 1931, Donaldsonville, Louisiana, USA. After being taught soprano saxophone by his father, Johnson took up the tenor as well. Resident on the west coast in the 50s he worked in the studios but played jazz dates with artists including Benny Carter. His film and television work increased and his work (though not his name) became known to millions when he was featured playing the main title theme on the soundtrack of *The Pink Panther* (1963). He continued to make infrequent jazz appearances, playing on record dates and at clubs and the occasional festival. Among the musicians with whom he worked in the 70s and 80s were Bill Berry, Herb Ellis, Carl Fontana, Jake Hanna, Dave McKenna and the Capp-Pierce Juggernaut. A highly melodic player with an effortlessly graceful ballad style, Johnson's choice of career has meant that he is often overlooked by jazz audiences.

● ALBUMS: *This Must Be Plas* (1959)★★★, under pseudonym Johnny Beecher *Sax Fifth Avenue* (1962)★★★, with Jake Hanna, Carl Fontana *Live At The Concord Festival* (1975)★★, *The Blues* (Concord 1975)★★★★, *Positively* (1976)★★★, *Rockin' With The Plas* (Capitol 1983)★★★, *LA 55* (1983)★★, *Hot Blue And Saxy* (Carell 1989)★★★.

JOHNSON, SY

b. 15 April 1930, New Haven, Conneticut, USA. Johnson studied music and the piano while he played jazz in high school bands and in the Air Force. When he was discharged he went to Los Angeles where he earned a living writing arrangements while involved in the *avant garde* jazz scene which centred around musicians such as Ornette Coleman and Paul Bley. In the 60s Johnson went to New York where he played briefly with Charles Mingus, with the Rod Levitt Octet and singer Yolande Bavan and led his own trio. From the 70s Johnson worked increasingly arranging commercial music but did arrangements for a variety of Mingus groups (1971-78) and for the Lee Konitz Nonet among others. In 1984 Johnson was involved in work on the film *The Cotton Club* the score of which sought to recreate the sound of Duke Ellington's classic band of the late 20s and early 30s. Johnson is also an acute jazz journalist and photographer.

● ALBUMS: with Charles Mingus *Let My Children Hear Music* (1971)★★★★.

JOHNSTON, RANDY

b. *c*.1957, Detroit, Michigan, USA. Johnston was raised in Richmond, Virginia, taking up the guitar as a young child after seeing the Beatles on television. His musical interests quickly spread, encompassing Eric Clapton, Jimi Hendrix, B.B. King and John McLaughlin's Mahavishnu Orchestra. He began playing professionally when he was 14, by which time he was already leaning strongly towards jazz. By the time he had completed his education at the University of Miami he had decided upon a career in jazz and soon became known as a highly proficient, blues-influenced performer. In 1982 he settled in New York where he found work with Warne Marsh. He has also played with musicians such as Ira Sullivan, Houston Person and Lou Donaldson and in the late 90s with Johnny Griffin. In the spectrum of bop guitarists, Johnston is firmly in the Wes Montgomery line of influence and there are also hints in his playing that he has heard and approves of Kenny Burrell. There is, however, a strong personal flavour to his music whether he is playing in a low-down funky mode or in a fleet and intellectually inventive manner. Johnston's solos display a fast-thinking mind backed up by a formidable technique which allows him to fully realize his conceptions. In the mid-90s Johnston made some critically acclaimed albums for Muse Records and their successor, HighNote Records, sometimes using organist Joey DeFrancesco, young tenor saxophonist Eric Alexander, and veteran drummer Mickey Roker. These sets show an intriguing blending of the leader's melodic guitar with a thrusting organ sound that evokes without imitating the organ-led combos popular several decades before. In addition to performing, Johnston also teaches at the Hartt College of Music, West Hartford, Connecticut.

● ALBUMS: *In-A-Chord* (Muse 1994)★★★, *Wonder Why* (Muse 1995)★★★, *Somewhere In The Night* (HighNote 1996)★★★.

JOLLY, PETE

b. 5 June 1932, New Haven, Connecticut, USA. As a small child Jolly became adept on both accordion and piano. From the early 50s he was resident in Los Angeles, where he became a much in-demand pianist for many of the recording sessions that helped to establish the so-called west coast school of bebop. Among the dates on which Jolly appeared were those for *The Swinging Mr Rogers* with Shorty Rogers And His Giants in 1955, when he joined Jimmy Giuffre, Curtis Counce and Shelly Manne and played a fine solo on 'Michele's Meditation'. Also in 1955 he recorded with the Cy Touff Quintet and the following year played with the Chet Baker-Art Pepper Sextet on *Playboys*. During the late 50s and most of the 60s Jolly led his own small groups but spent much of his time in film and television studio work. In the 80s he again recorded with Pepper and occasionally deputized with west coast big bands, including that led by Bill Berry. Jolly's playing was always of high quality and he made an important contribution to the west coast jazz of the 50s. Some authorities hold his accordion playing in high regard, although this instrument has yet to make a serious impact in the jazz world.

● ALBUMS: *Jolly Jumps In* (1955)★★★, *The Pete Jolly Duo, Trio*

And Quartet (Fresh Sounds 1955)★★★★, with Shorty Rogers *The Swinging Mr Rogers* (1955)★★, *Cy Touff, His Octet And Quintet* (1955)★★★, with Chet Baker, Art Pepper *Playboys* (1956)★★★★, *The Pete Jolly Trio* i (1956)★★★, with Ralph Pena *The Pete Jolly Duo* (1959)★★★, with Pepper *Smack Up!* (1960)★★★, *5 O'Clock Shadows* (1962)★★★, *Little Bird* (1963)★★★, *Sweet September* (1963)★★★, *The Sensational Pete Jolly Gasses Everybody* (1963)★★★, *Hello, Jolly* (1964)★★, *The Pete Jolly Trio* ii (1965)★★★, *Pete Jolly With Marty Paich And His Orchestra* (1968)★★, *Give A Damn* (1969)★★★, *Sessions, Live* (1969)★★★, *Strike Up The Band* (1980)★★★, *The Five* (Fresh Sounds 1988)★★★★, *Gems* (1990)★★★, *Yeah!* (VSOP 1996)★★.

JONES, ALBENNIE

b. 29 November 1914, Gulfport, Mississippi, USA, d. 24 June 1989, Bronx, New York, USA. Jones arrived in New York in 1932, her only singing experience at the Mt. Holy Baptists Church in Gulfport. Her first professional engagement was at the Elk's Rendezvous Club, which proved so successful that she was retained for nine months. Other nightclubs she sang in included the Club Harlem, the Village Vanguard and Murrains Cafe. Her first recordings for National in 1944/5 featured jazz musicians Dizzy Gillespie, Don Byas, Edmond Hall, Sammy Price and Cliff Jackson. She toured the south and Midwest with Blanche Calloway and Eddie 'Cleanhead' Vinson, and worked alongside Gillespie and Tiny Bradshaw with the Erskine Hawkins Orchestra. After the war, she recorded three sessions for Decca, backed by Price's group. In the early 50s she fell over on stage, suffering an injury that forced her to use a crutch at club dates. Because of this, she retired from music shortly afterwards and eventually succumbed to leukemia.

● ALBUMS: *Ladies Sing The Blues* (Savoy 1980)★★★.

JONES, BOBBY

b. 30 October 1928, Louisville, Kentucky, USA, d. 6 March 1980, Munich, Germany. In the immediate post-swing era years, Jones played tenor saxophone and clarinet in the reed sections of a few surviving big bands and also played in other forms of popular music. In the early 60s he had spells with Woody Herman and Jack Teagarden, but then came off the road for a while to teach. In the early 70s he displayed the diversity of his repertoire by joining Charles Mingus, with whom he toured and recorded, appearing on albums including 1971's *Let My Children Hear Music*. Subsequently, Jones settled in Europe where poor health led him to abandon playing in favour of writing arrangements. Although adept in the bop idiom, as shown by his work with Mingus, Jones always displayed an affection for earlier musical styles, with some of his solos indicating a strong affinity with the blues.

● ALBUMS: *The Arrival Of Bobby Jones* (Cobblestone 1972)★★★, *Hill Country Suite* (Enja 1974)★★★.

JONES, CARMELL

b. 19 July 1936, Kansas City, Kansas, USA, d. 7 November 1996. After attracting favourable attention for his trumpet playing in bands in the Kansas City area, Jones moved to Los Angeles in 1961, where he joined Bud Shank for an engagement at the Drift Inn, Malibu. He recorded with this group and later worked with Gerald Wilson and the Red Mitchell-Harold Land Quintet with whom he also recorded. Most of 1965 was spent touring with Horace Silver and by the end of the year Jones had become resident in Germany. He played regularly as a member of radio and studio orchestras, mainly in Berlin, and also worked with his old high-school friend, Nathan Davis. In the music he recorded in the 60s Jones displayed an affinity with Clifford Brown and his return to the US jazz scene in the early 80s showed that in maturity he had developed into an accomplished player, who deserved a wide audience.

● ALBUMS: *The Remarkable Carmell Jones* (1961)★★★★, with Bud Shank *New Groove* (1961)★★★, *Brass Bag* (1962)★★, *Business Meetin'* (1962)★★★, *Jay Hawk Talk* (1965)★★★, *Carmell Jones In Europe* (1965)★★★, with Nathan Davis *Happy Girl* (1965)★★★, *Carmell Jones Returns* (1982)★★★★.

JONES, CLAUDE

b. 11 February 1901, Boley, Oklahoma, USA, d. 17 January 1962. After playing various instruments in school, Jones had opted for trombone by the time he attended Wilberforce College. In 1922 he moved to Springfield, Ohio, where he became a member of the band which eventually metamorphosed into McKinney's Cotton Pickers. In 1929 he left for a job with the Fletcher Henderson band and during the early 30s switched several times between Henderson, Chick Webb and Don Redman. In 1934 he settled into the Cab Calloway band, where he remained until 1940; then moved through a number of bands, working with Coleman Hawkins, Joe Sullivan, Henderson again, Benny Carter, Redman, Calloway, until, in 1944, he joined Duke Ellington. He was with Ellington until 1948, when he played briefly with Machito, Henderson and Ellington again and then finally his itchy feet led him to leave music and go to sea. He died on board the S.S. *United States*, on which he was a chief steward, in January 1962. An inventive and melodic soloist, Jones was an important influence in the pre-war era for helping to shift perceptions of the trombone's role from a purely rhythmic instrument to one on which melody lines and solos could be played.

● ALBUMS: *McKinney's Cotton Pickers* (1928-29)★★★, with Fletcher Henderson *Swing's The Thing* (1931-34)★★★★.

JONES, DAVEY

b. c.1888, Lutcher, Louisiana, USA. Jones was well-known in the early days of jazz and played mainly in St. Louis and on the Mississippi riverboats. It is thought that he played a C tenor saxophone. He was an early inspiration to many musicians including Gene Sedric and Happy Caldwell. Jones formed the Jones And Collins Astoria Eight with trumpeter Lee Collins and recorded four titles for Victor in 1929 including 'Astoria Strut' and 'Damp Weather' both being recognized as classic examples of New Orleans jazz, with fine ensembles receiving the lead from Collins trumpet.

JONES, DILL

b. Dillwyn O. Jones, 19 August 1923, Newcastle Emlyn, Wales, England, d. 22 June 1984. After formal studies at London's Trinity College of Music, Jones began associating with the younger jazzmen who were playing bebop. He had already played jazz while serving in the navy and his fluent, inventive style quickly made him a welcome addition to the London scene. In 1948 he performed at the first Nice Jazz Festival and was regularly heard in company with musicians including Humphrey Lyttelton, Ronnie Scott, Joe Harriott and Bruce Turner. Jones visited the USA during the 50s while working on a transatlantic liner, and in the early 60s he settled in New York. During the next few years he played with several noted American jazz stars, including Roy Eldridge and Gene Krupa. In 1969 he became a member of the JPJ Quartet with Budd Johnson, Bill Pemberton and Oliver Jackson. His fine soloing, whether in subtly developed ballads or on roof-raising spectaculars such as his version of 'Little Rock Getaway', showed his wide stylistic range.

● ALBUMS: *The Dill Jones Trio* i (1955)★★★, *The Dill Jones Trio* ii (1956)★★★, *The Dill Jones Quintet* (1959)★★, *Jones The Jazz* (1961)★★★, with others *Jazz Piano Masters* (1972)★★, *Up Jumped You With Love* (1972)★★★, *The Music Of Bix Beiderbecke* (c.1972)★★★, *The Welsh Connection* (1982)★★★.

JONES, DOLLY

b. *c.*1907, USA, d. late 70s. The fact that her mother, Dyer Jones, was also a noted jazz trumpeter probably makes Jones unique in jazz. Although she learned initially from her mother, she was largely self-taught. According to musicians who knew her, she was completely dedicated to her instrument, studying and practising when she was not playing. In Chicago in the early 30s she performed in Irene Eadie's band and with Lillian Armstrong's Harlem Harlicans. Jones also played in a trio with saxophonist George James and in Eddie Durham's All-Star Girl Orchestra. In Chicago, she was often to be found in after-hours clubs jamming with other musicians and earning their respect. Roy Eldridge and Doc Cheatham were amongst trumpeters who publicly praised her talent. Jones continued to play whenever she could, working intermittently into the 70s. Her role model was Louis Armstrong and throughout her career worked hard to maintain the higher-than-high standards needed by any woman trying to succeed in jazz in her era. She made only one record 'Creole Blues', but did appear in the Oscar Micheaux film, *Swing* (1937), playing 'China Boy' and 'I May Be Wrong'. Jones was sometimes billed as Dolly Hutchinson and also as Dolly (Doli) Armenra.

JONES, DYER

b. *c.*1890, USA, d. unk. Jones played trumpet in pre-jazz and early jazz bands and had already built a reputation before moving to New York in the late 20s. She was presented as a featured attraction with Sammy Stewart and his band at the Arcadia Ballroom. In addition to Jones the band included Charlie 'Big' Green, 'Big' Sid Catlett and Johnny Dunn. Even in distinguished surroundings such as these she more than held her own. Jones appears to have given music lessons and Valaida Snow might have studied trumpet with her. And Jones certainly helped her daughter, Dolly Jones, when she, too, began playing trumpet. Tommy Benford told Sally Placksin, '. . . she was wonderful . . . Man, she was something else . . . and Dolly was right behind her'. Jones appears not to have made records.

JONES, EDDIE

b. Edward Jones, 1 March 1929, Red Bank, New Jersey, USA, d. 31 May 1997, Hartford, Connecticut, USA. For 10 years a member of the Count Basie band, bass player Eddie Jones grew up in a house just two doors away from Basie's home. As an undergraduate at the local Howard University, Jones studied musical education, and collaborated with Frank Wess and Bill Hugham (later members of the Basie band) and composer Benny Golson. After graduation he also toured with Sarah Vaughan and worked as a teacher. Jones eventually joined Basie's band in 1953, although competition for places was hot: 'You couldn't afford to get sick in that band - if you didn't show up you disappeared.' The bass player's mellifluous style, and deep, resonant tone, proved a perfect accompaniment to drummer Sonny Payne in the Basie group, and he soon found himself in demand as a session player. Among the famous bandleaders with whom he recorded were Milt Jackson, Ray Charles, Joe Newman, Coleman Hawkins, Ben Webster and Thad Jones. However, it was his contributions to the 'New Testament' version of Basie's band that made his name. He eventually left Basie in 1963 after a disagreement over wages. He attempted to break into the New York studio scene but was disconcerted by the racism that stood in the way of black musicians attempting to work on commercial projects. Instead, he became an executive with IBM Records. He toured with various jazz aggregations in his holidays, even during his stint as an insurance salesman in Hartford, Connecticut, where he died in 1997.

JONES, ELVIN

b. 9 September 1927, Pontiac, Michigan, USA. The youngest of the remarkable Jones brothers (see also Thad Jones and Hank Jones), Elvin grew up in a musical atmosphere. He played drums with local bands before and after military service and by the early 50s was playing regularly with Billy Mitchell's small group. In the middle of the decade Jones relocated in New York, rapidly establishing himself as a leading exponent of bop drumming. He worked with several notable musicians including J.J. Johnson, Donald Byrd and Sonny Rollins, and in 1960 became a member of John Coltrane's quartet. He played with Coltrane for five years during which period he grew into one of the outstanding drummers in jazz history. The role he occupied in this period was of considerable importance in the development of post-bop drumming. Jones's career after Coltrane was mainly as a leader of small groups, where he was able to exercise full control over the musical policy (although he was briefly, in 1966, with Duke Ellington). In the late 60s and on through the 70s and 80s Jones toured ceaselessly, playing clubs, concerts and festivals around the world. His sidemen have included Joe Farrell, George Coleman and Wilbur Little. In 1979 he recorded *Very R.A.R.E.* with Art Pepper and that same year saw the release of a documentary film, *Different Drummer: Elvin Jones*. Jones extended the scope of the work done by proto-bop drummers such as Max Roach and Art Blakey. Although associated with free jazz, in which context his example was an incentive to later occupants of *avant garde* drum chairs, his own playing was always closely linked to what had gone before. Nevertheless, in his expansion of the role of the post-bop jazz drummer, Jones was responsible for a major stylistic shift: he integrated the drums so thoroughly with the improvisations of the front line musicians that the drummer now became their partner on equal terms not merely the accompanist or pulse provider of previous eras. Through his example and his astonishing technical mastery, Jones has become one of the master drummers of jazz and is currently seeing something of a revival in his fortunes with a spate of recently recorded albums.

● ALBUMS: *Thad Jones-Billy Mitchell Quintet* (1953)★★★, with Sonny Rollins *A Night At The Village Vanguard* (Enja 1957)★★★, *Together* (1961)★★★, *Elvin* (Riverside 1962)★★★, *Dear John C* (Impulse! 1965)★★★, *And Then Again* (Atlantic 1965)★★★, *Midnight Walk* (Atlantic 1967)★★, *Heavy Sounds* (Impulse! 1967)★★, *Puttin' It Together* (Blue Note 1968)★★★, *Poly-Currents* (Blue Note 1969)★★★, *The Ultimate Elvin Jones* (Blue Note 1969)★★★, *Coalition* (1970)★★★, *Genesis* (1971)★★, *Live At The Lighthouse* (1972)★★★, *Mr Thunder* (1974)★★★, *New Agenda* (1975)★★, *Summit Meeting* (1976)★★★, with Oregon *Oregon/Jones Together* (Vanguard 1976)★★★, *Time Capsule* (1977)★★★, *Remembrance* (1978)★★★, *Very R.A.R.E.* (1979)★★★, with Tommy Flanagan, Red Mitchell *Super-session* (Enja 1980)★★★, *Brother John* (1982)★★★, *Earth Jones* (1982)★★★, *The Elvin Jones Jazz Machine In Europe* (Enja 1992)★★★, *Live In Japan* (Konnex 1992)★★★, with Takehisa Tanaka *When I Was At Aso-Mountain* (Enja 1993)★★★, *Youngblood (Enja 1993)*★★, Live At The Pit Inn, Tokyo (Columbia 1993)★★★★, *Going Home* (Enja 1994)★★★, *It Don't Mean A Thing* (Enja 1994)★★★, as Elvin Jones' 'Special' Quartet *Tribute To John Coltrane: A Love Supreme* (Columbia 1997)★★★, with Dave Holland, Joe Lovano *Fascination Edition One* (Blue Note 1998)★★★★.

JONES, ETTA

b. 25 November 1928, Aiken, South Carolina, USA. By the time she began singing professionally, she was living in New York. She worked with Buddy Johnson, then Pete Johnson, J.C. Heard and Earl Hines. From the early 50s she often worked as a single, recording for Prestige Records and winning an award for *Don't Go With Strangers*. Although her early singing, with Buddy Johnson, had been angled towards the R&B market, by the 70s she was sufficiently eclectic to work with mainstream artists such as Billy Taylor and she began a long-running partnership with her husband Houston Person, touring and recording extensively. A lively, strong-voiced singer with a rich, bluesy tone, Jones has enjoyed a successful career despite being little known outside the jazz world and even within this arena she is sometimes overlooked in favour of less talented but better hyped singers. On *At Last* her voice sounded richer in texture and her versions of classic popular songs, such as 'God Bless The Child' were a triumph. In particular, pianist Benny Green added some exquisite piano.

● ALBUMS: *The Jones Girl ... Etta* reissued as *Etta Jones Sings* (King 1958)★★★, *Don't Go With Strangers* (Prestige 1960)★★★★, *Something Nice* (Prestige 1961)★★★, *So Warm - Etta Jones & Strings* (Prestige 1961)★★★, *From The Heart* (Prestige 1961)★★★★, *Lonely And Blue* (Prestige 1962)★★★★, *Love Shout* (Prestige 1963)★★★, *Hollar!* (Prestige 1963)★★★, *Ms. Jones To You* (Muse 1976)★★★★, *My Mother's Eyes* (Muse 1977)★★★, *Love Me With All Your Heart* (Muse 1983)★★★, *Fine And Mellow* (Muse 1987)★★★★, *I'll Be Seeing You* (Muse 1988)★★★★, *Sugar* (Muse 1990)★★★★, *Christmas With Etta Jones* (Muse 1990)★★, *Reverse The Charges* (Muse 1991)★★★, *At Last* (Muse 1995)★★★★, *My Gentleman Friend* (Muse 1996)★★★★, *The Melody Lingers On* (Highnote 1997)★★★★, *My Buddy* (Highnote 1998)★★★.

● COMPILATIONS: *Etta Jones' Greatest Hits* (Prestige 1967)★★★★.

JONES, HANK

b. Henry Jones, 31 July 1918, Vicksburg, Mississippi, USA. Eldest of three remarkable brothers in jazz (Thad Jones and Elvin Jones), Hank Jones was raised in Pontiac, Michigan and by the beginning of his teenage years played piano professionally in local bands. In 1944 he went to New York where he joined the Oran 'Hot Lips' Page band. Although Jones had previously been in the mainstream of jazz, he was an eager student and fully aware of the changes currently taking place in the music. He incorporated bebop into his repertoire but remained an eclectic player, happily adapting to suit the needs of the artists he accompanied (who ranged from Coleman Hawkins to Charlie Parker). Jones freelanced extensively throughout the 50s, working with Jazz At The Philharmonic, Benny Goodman and Milt Jackson among many, and ended the decade by becoming a staff musician at CBS Records where he remained until the mid-70s. During this long period of studio activity, Jones accompanied countless performers outside jazz and continued to record with numerous names in jazz. Since the mid-70s he has continued to work in various jazz contexts, as soloist, as duettist with Tommy Flanagan, George Shearing and other pianists, as accompanist to singers and instrumentalists, and as leader of his own small groups. A masterly musician, adept in most aspects of the jazz repertoire, Jones has been an important influence, as much for his professionalism as for the immense sweep of his talent.

● ALBUMS: *Hank Jones Piano* (Mercury 1950)★★★, *The Jazz Trio Of Hank Jones* (Savoy 1955)★★★★, *Bluebird* (Savoy 1955)★★★★, *Have You Met Hank Jones* (Savoy 1956)★★★, *Urbanity - Piano Solos By Hank Jones* (Clef 1956)★★★★, *The Hank Jones Quartet/Quintet* (Savoy 1956)★★★★, *The Trio* (Savoy 1956)★★★, *Relaxin' At Camarillo* (Savoy 1956)★★★, *Hank Jones Swings Songs From Gigi* (Golden Crest 1958)★★, *The Talented Touch Of Hank Jones* (Capitol 1958)★★★, *Porgy And Bess: Swinging Impressions By Hank Jones* (Capitol 1959)★★★, *Arrival Time* (RCA Victor 1962)★★★, *Here's Love* (Argo 1963)★★, *This Is Ragtime Now* (ABC 1964)★★, *The Hank Jones Trio ii* (1964)★★★, with Oliver Nelson *Hank Jones With Oliver Nelson And His Orchestra* (1966)★★★, *Hanky Panky* (1975)★★★, *Satin Doll* (1976)★★★, *Love For Sale* (1976)★★, *Hank* (All Art 1976)★★★, *Jones-Brown-Smith* (Concord 1976)★★★, *Arigato* (1976)★★★, with John Lewis *John Lewis Solo/Duo With Hank Jones* (1976)★★★, *Bop Redux* (Muse 1977)★★★★, *The Great Jazz Trio At The Village Vanguard Vols 1 & 2* (1977)★★★, *Just For Fun* (Original Jazz Classics 1977)★★★★, *Tiptoe Tapdance* (Original Jazz Classics 1977)★★★, *I Remember You* (Black And Blue 1977)★★★, *Have You Met This Jones?* (1977)★★★, *Kindness, Joy, Love And Happiness* (1977)★★★, *Direct From L.A.* (1977)★★★, *The Trio* (1977)★★★, *Groovin' High* (1978)★★★, *Milestones* (1978),★★★ *Compassion* (1978)★★★, *Ain't Misbehavin'* (1978)★★, with Tommy Flanagan *Our Delights* (1978)★★★, *Easy To Love* (1979)★★★, *Live In Japan* (Jazz Alliance 1979)★★★, with Lewis *An Evening With Two Grand Pianos* (Little David 1979)★★★★, with Lewis *Piano Playhouse* (1979)★★★, *Bluesette* (Black And Blue 1979)★★★, *The Great Jazz Trio* (1980)★★★, *Chapter II* (1980)★★, *The Incredible Hank Jones* (Stash 1980)★★★, *The Great Jazz Trio Revisited At The Village Vanguard Vols 1 & 2* (1980)★★★★, *The Great Jazz Trio And Friends At The Aurex Jazz Festival, Tokyo '81* (1981)★★★, *Threesome* (1982)★★★, *The Club New Yorker* (1983)★★★, with Flanagan *I'm All Smiles* (MPS 1983)★★★, *Monk's Moods* (1984)★★★, with George Shearing *The Spirit Of 176* (1988)★★, *Duo* (Timeless 1988)★★★, *Lazy Afternoon* (Concord 1989)★★★, *The Oracle* (Emarcy 1990)★★★, *Essence* (DMP 1991)★★★, *Live At the Maybank Recital Hall, Vol 16* (Concord 1991)★★, *Jazzpar 91 Project* (Storyville 1991)★★★, *Handful Of Keys* (Emarcy 1992)★★★, *Upon Reflection* (Verve 1993)★★★, with Charlie Haden *Steal Away* (Verve 1995)★★★★, with Cheick-Tidiane Seck, the Mandinkas *Sarala* (Verve 1996)★★★, with Roy Haynes, George Mraz *Flowers For Lady Day* (Evidence 1996)★★★, *Favors* (Verve 1997)★★★.

JONES, ISHAM

b. 31 January 1894, Coalton, Ohio, USA, d. 19 October 1956. A multi-instrumentalist, Jones was leading his own band by his late teens. He played mostly in the Chicago area until the early 20s, when he moved to New York. After a brief visit to the UK in 1924, he returned to form a new band, which by the end of the decade he had developed into an outstanding dance orchestra. The band enjoyed enormous popularity with audiences. A 1930 recording of Hoagy Carmichael's 'Stardust', arranged as a ballad, was a huge hit and changed perceptions of how this song might be performed. Arrangements were by Jones, together with Gordon Jenkins and Victor Young, and created a relaxed, melodic style unusual among bands of this type. Fine musicians who played in the band at one time or another included Jack Jenney and Pee Wee Erwin. In 1936, with the swing era freshly launched and big bands fast becoming popular, Jones went against all logic and decided to fold his band. Some of the more jazz-orientated members decided to go ahead with their own outfit under the leadership of one of the saxophone players, Woody Herman. In the late 30s Jones concentrated on composing and arranging, but by the 40s he was working mostly outside music. A possibly apocryphal tale recounts that when his wife bought him a new piano for his 30th birthday, he was so worried at the expense she had incurred, he sat up all night at his birthday gift and by morning had composed three tunes to help restore the family fortunes: 'It Had To Be You', 'Spain' and 'The One I Love Belongs To Somebody Else'.

● ALBUMS: *Isham Jones And His Orchestra* 1920-1924 recordings (Fountain 1979)★★★, *Isham Jones And His Orchestra* (1929-30)★★★, *Isham Jones And His Orchestra Featuring Woody Herman* (1936)★★★★.

JONES, JIMMY

b. 30 December 1918, Memphis, Tennessee, USA, d. 29 April 1982. Jones started out on guitar while growing up in Chicago but later switched to piano. In the early and mid-40s he played with several prominent jazzmen including Stuff Smith, Don Byas and Coleman Hawkins. Later in the decade he also played on many recording sessions with such Ellingtonians as Ben Webster, Johnny Hodges and Paul Gonsalves. In 1947 he began accompanying Sarah Vaughan with whom he established a great musical rapport. Apart from a two-year break, he remained with Vaughan until 1958. Throughout the 60s Jones was deeply involved with arranging and composing, often working with Duke Ellington although he did tour Europe in 1966 as musical director for Ella Fitzgerald. An adept and elegant accompanist, Jones chose to follow a musical path which frequently led to his working almost anonymously with brighter stars. For all this apparently deliberate avoidance of the spotlight, his solo work, when heard, displays a musician with orderly thoughts and a lightly swinging touch.

● ALBUMS: *The Jimmy Jones Trio* (1954)★★★, with George Wallington *Trios* (Vogue 1993)★★★.

JONES, JO

b. Jonathan Jones, 7 October 1911, Chicago, Illinois, USA, d. 3 September 1985. While he was still a child Jones became adept on several instruments, including trumpet and piano. In his teens he worked as a singer and dancer, taking up drums along the way. By the late 20s he was drumming in territory bands, eventually settling in Kansas City in the early 30s. It was here that he met Count Basie, at the time still plain Bill Basie, and worked with him on a number of occasions before joining the band full-time in 1936. Here Jones became a member of the magnificent 'All-American Rhythm

Section' with Basie, Freddie Green and Walter Page. The flowing, rhythmic pulse of the band was aided enormously by Jones's changes to previous conceptions of jazz drumming. He shifted the dominant role among the instruments at his disposal from the bass drum to the hi-hat cymbal, thus creating an enviable looseness in which he was free to punctuate the ensemble and 'goose' the soloists with accented bass, snare and tom-tom beats. Although Jones always gave credit for such innovations to others, there is no doubt that he popularized and refined this way of playing himself. After his innovations, the way was open for the further changes in the drummer's role that occurred in bebop. The sleek power of the Basie rhythm section, and Jones's part in its success, made him the envy of and model for numerous other drummers, even if swing era audiences tended to prefer more extrovert, busier and showboating percussionists. Jones left the Basie band when he was inducted into the US Army in 1944; after the war he freelanced with numerous major jazz stars, among them Lester Young, Teddy Wilson and Roy Eldridge, worked with Jazz At The Philharmonic and led his own groups on record and for club engagements. In his later years Jones worked the international festival circuits, playing with wit, polish and always that extraordinary subtle swing that had led Don Lamond to describe him as the man who played like the wind. A highly perceptive and articulate man, Jones also grew steadily more and more disillusioned with the jazz life, which occasionally created stars out of musical nonentities and lavished attention upon individuals whose talent was minuscule in comparison to his own. His knowledge and understanding of jazz drumming was extensive and, although he preferred to accompany rather than play solo, in his later years he would sometimes enliven his performances by demonstrating the techniques and idiosyncrasies of fellow drummers, often appearing to play even more like them than they did themselves.

● ALBUMS: *Jo Jones Special* (1955)★★★, with Lester Young, Teddy Wilson *Prez And Teddy* (1956)★★★★, *The Jo Jones Special* (Vanguard 1956)★★★, *Jo Jones Plus Two* (Vanguard 1958)★★★, *The Jo Jones Trio* (Fresh Sounds 1959)★★★★, *The Jo Jones Quintet* (1960)★★★, with Milt Hinton *The Jo Jones Duo* (1960)★★★, with Willie 'The Lion' Smith *The Drums* (1973)★★★, *Caravan* (1974)★★★, *The Main Man* (1976)★★, *Papa Jo And His Friends* (1977)★★, *Our Man, Papa Jo* (1977)★★.

● COMPILATIONS: *Count Basie: Complete Recorded Works In Chronological Order* (1937-39)★★★★, *Count Basie At The Chatterbox* (1937)★★★★.

JONES, JONAH

b. Robert Elliott Jones, 31 October, 1909, Louisville, Kentucky, USA. As a youth Jones played trumpet with numerous local and territory bands before joining Horace Henderson in 1928. After drifting through various other minor bands, he joined Jimmie Lunceford and then in Buffalo, in 1932, began a highly profitable musical partnership with Stuff Smith. Although he found time for excursions with Lillian Armstrong and McKinney's Cotton Pickers, he was still with Smith when they took their little band into New York and a residency at the Onyx Club in early 1936. For the next four years the band captivated audiences with their hot music, eccentric appearance and crazy clowning. In 1940 Jones left to work with the big bands of Benny Carter, Fletcher Henderson and then spent a decade with Cab Calloway. He next played with Earl Hines but from the mid-50s led his own small band, which attained great popularity with the fringe jazz audience. Musically, this and the later bands Jones fronted offered a repertoire that was a long way from the rough and ready excitement of the group he had co-led with Smith. Indeed, as the years passed, it was often seen to be unadventurous, predictable and a little bland, concentrating on straightforward arrangements of show tunes and popular songs of the day. It was easy-listening jazz for the masses, although Jones's playing was always skilful and consistently showed that he had not forgotten the roots of his music. He continued playing throughout the 60s, 70s and into the 80s, proving remarkably durable and, latterly, still to be capable of a few surprises.

● ALBUMS: *Jonah Jones Sextet* 10-inch album (Bethlehem 1954)★★★★, *Jonah Wails - 1st Blast* 10-inch album (Angel 1954)★★★★, *Jonah Wails - 2nd Wind* 10-inch album (Angel 1954)★★★, *Jonah Jones At The Embers* (Groove 1956)★★★, *Muted Jazz* (Capitol 1957)★★★★, *Swingin' On Broadway* (Capitol 1958)★★★, *Jumpin' With Jonah* (Capitol 1958)★★★★, *Swingin' At The Cinema* (Capitol 1958)★★★, *Jonah Jumps Again* (Capitol 1959)★★★, *I Dig Chicks* (Capitol 1959)★★★, *Swingin' 'Round The World* (Capitol 1959)★★★, with Jack Teagarden *Dixieland* (Bethlehem 1959)★★★, with Charlie Shavers *Sounds Of The Trumpets* (Bethlehem 1959)★★★, *Hit Me Again!* (Capitol 1960)★★★, *A Touch Of Blue* (Capitol 1960)★★★, *The Unsinkable Molly Brown* (Capitol 1961)★★★, *Greatest Instrumental Hits Styled By Jonah Jones* (Capitol 1961)★★★, *Broadway Swings Again* (Capitol 1961)★★★, with Glen Gray *Jonah Jones/Glen Gray* (Capitol 1961)★★★, *Jazz Bonus* (Capitol 1962)★★★, *And Now, In Person - Jonah Jones* (Capitol 1963)★★★, *Blowin' Up A Storm* (Capitol 1964)★★★, *Hello Broadway* (Decca 1965)★★★, *On The Sunny Side Of The Street* (Decca 1966)★★★, *Confessin'* (1978)★★★.

● COMPILATIONS: *Butterflies In The Rain* 1944 recordings (Circle 1987)★★★, *Harlem Jump And Swing* (Affinity 1983)★★★.

JONES, LEROY

b. 20 February 1958, New Orleans, Louisiana, USA. As a small child Jones began playing guitar and took lessons from veteran jazzman Danny Barker. Soon, he became interested in brass instruments, first trying the cornet, then moving on to trumpet and fluegelhorn. He continued studying, taking lessons from a trumpet-playing nun at a Catholic school he attended. Mostly, however, he learned from listening to jazz musicians on record, especially Louis Armstrong. His listening was, nevertheless, decidedly eclectic. As he told Derek Ansell in an interview for *Jazz Journal International*, he was influenced also by Hugh Masakela, Shorty Rogers and

Freddie Hubbard amongst several trumpeters of note. Later, he heard records by Clifford Brown and Lee Morgan. Despite all these influences, Jones steadily matured his own style while still remaining attuned to other young musicians such as Wynton Marsalis. His early professional experience included playing in R&B bands and with the Louisiana Repertory Ensemble. In the early 90s he began playing regularly with the band backing popular singer Harry Connick Jnr., an engagement which brought him worldwide exposure. Rich and melodic, his trumpet playing happily blends most of the traditional ingredients of jazz from the blues, through New Orleans and gospel to bop and beyond. His example and dedication should make him one of the keepers of the flame for the 21st century.

● ALBUMS: *Mo' Cream From The Crop* (Columbia 1994)★★★, *Props For Pops* (Columbia 1997)★★★.

JONES, OLIVER

b. 11 September, 1934, Montreal, Canada. Jones's parents were immigrants from Barbados. As a child he learned classical piano starting at the age of 2. At 5 he played for his local church and later he studied with Oscar Peterson's sister who lived near by. After establishing himself in Canada he began touring internationally in the early 60s as accompanist to pop singers Kenny Hamilton and Terry Malone. In the early 80s he concentrated on playing jazz, initially resident at Biddle's, a club in Montreal. After a succession of eye operations he once again toured but this time in his own right. A highly accomplished technician, Jones's playing style indicates the influences of gifted performers such as Peterson and Art Tatum. He has also acknowledged his debt to Bill Evans, Herbie Hancock and other pianists of a later school. By the late 80s and early 90s, Jones was no longer under the shadow of his mentor even if, inevitably, critics often referred to Peterson in attempting to describe Jones's technical gifts. His work with Clark Terry, Herb Ellis and Red Mitchell, with whom he toured the UK late in 1991, revealed him to be a jazz piano player of considerable stature in his own right. In the mid-90s at the age he decided to ease back from his busy touring schedule and released one of his best ever albums (albeit with Oscar Peterson tracks) *From Lush To Lively*.

● ALBUMS: *Speak Low, Swing Hard* (1985)★★★★, *Requestfully Yours* (1985)★★★, *The Many Moods Of Oliver Jones* (c.1986)★★, *Jazz And Ribs Live At Biddle's* (1986)★★, *Cookin' At Sweet Basil* (1987)★★, with Clark Terry *Just Friends* (1989)★★★, *Northern Summit* (Enya 1990)★★★, *A Class Act* (Enya 1991)★★★, *From Lush To Lively* (Justin Time 1995)★★★★, *Have Fingers ... Will Travel* (Justin Time 1997)★★★.

JONES, PHILLY JOE

b. Joseph R. Jones, 15 July 1923, Philadelphia, Pennsylvania, USA, d. 30 August 1985. Jones began his drumming career in his home town, later moving to New York where he worked with many leading bebop musicians. Despite this early exposure to Charlie Parker, Dizzy Gillespie and other innovators, Jones was able to adapt to the stylistic needs of any group in which he played. Although proficient in bands led by mainstreamers such as Ben Webster and Lionel Hampton he was happiest in his many fruitful associations with modernists, among whom were Tadd Dameron, John Coltrane and Miles Davis. His tenure with Davis occupied a substantial slice of the 50s; in the following decade he played and recorded with Gil Evans, Bill Evans and led his own groups. In the late 60s he lived briefly in the UK, playing with musicians such as Kenny Wheeler and Pete King and also teaching. In the early 80s Jones formed the band Dameronia, with which to play the music of his former associate. Whether subtly encouraging or with sustained power, often working with a minimal, scaled-down drum kit, Jones was able to adjust his playing style to accommodate any group or individual.

● ALBUMS: *Blues For Dracula* (Riverside 1958)★★★, *Drums Around The World* (Riverside 1959)★★★, *Showcase* (Riverside 1959)★★★, *Philly Joe's Beat* (Atlantic 1960)★★★, *Trailways Express* (Black Lion 1968)★★, *'Round Midnight* (1969)★★★, *Mo' Jo* (Black Lion 1969)★★★, *Mean What You Say* (Sonet 1977)★★, *Philly Mignon* (1977)★★★, *Drum Song* (Galaxy 1978)★★, *Advance!* (1978)★★, *To Tadd With Love* (1982)★★★, *Dameronia* (Uptown 1983)★★★, *Look, Stop And Listen* (Uptown 1983)★★★, *Filet De Sole* (Marge 1992)★★★.

JONES, QUINCY

b. Quincy Delight Jones Jnr., 14 March 1933, Chicago, Illinois, USA. Jones began playing trumpet as a child and also developed an early interest in arranging, studying at the Berklee College Of Music. When he joined Lionel Hampton in 1951 it was as both performer and writer. With Hampton he visited Europe in a remarkable group that included rising stars Clifford Brown, Art Farmer, Gigi Gryce and Alan Dawson. Leaving Hampton in 1953, Jones wrote arrangements for many musicians, including some of his former colleagues and Ray Anthony, Count Basie and Tommy Dorsey. He mostly worked as a freelance but had a stint in the mid-50s as musical director for Dizzy Gillespie, one result of which was the 1956 album *World Statesman*. Later in the 50s and into the 60s Jones wrote charts and directed the orchestras for concerts and record sessions by several singers, including Frank Sinatra, Billy Eckstine, Brook Benton, Dinah Washington (an association that included the 1956 album *The Swingin' Miss 'D'*), Johnny Mathis and Ray Charles, whom he had known since childhood. He continued to write big band charts, composing and arranging albums for Basie, *One More Time* (1958-59) and *Li'l Ol' Groovemaker...Basie* (1963). By this time, Jones was fast becoming a major force in American popular music. In addition to playing he was busy writing and arranging, and was increasingly active as a record producer. In the late 60s and 70s he composed scores for around 40 feature films and hundreds of television shows. Among the former were *The Pawnbroker* (1965), *In Cold Blood* (1967) and *In The Heat Of The Night* (1967), while the latter included the long-running

Ironside series and *Roots*. Other credits for television programmes include *The Bill Cosby Show*, *NBC Mystery Series*, *The Jesse Jackson Series*, *In The House* and *Mad TV*. He continued to produce records featuring his own music played by specially assembled orchestras. As a record producer Jones had originally worked for Mercury's Paris-based subsidiary Barclay, but later became the first black vice-president of the company's New York division. Later, he spent a dozen years with A&M Records before starting up his own label, Qwest. Despite suffering two brain aneurysms in 1974 he showed no signs of reducing his high level of activity. In the 70s and 80s, in addition to many film soundtracks, he produced successful albums for Aretha Franklin, George Benson, Michael Jackson, the Brothers Johnston and other popular artists. With Benson he produced *Give Me The Night*, while for Jackson he helped to create *Off The Wall* and *Thriller*, the latter proving to be one of the bestselling albums of all time. He was also producer of the 1985 number 1 charity single 'We Are The World'. Latterly, Jones has been involved in film and television production, not necessarily in a musical context. As a player, Jones was an unexceptional soloist; as an arranger, his attributes are sometimes overlooked by the jazz audience, perhaps because of the manner in which he has consistently sought to create a smooth and wholly sophisticated entity, even at the expense of eliminating the essential characteristics of the artists concerned (as some of his work for Basie exemplifies). Nevertheless, with considerable subtlety he has fused elements of the blues and its many offshoots into mainstream jazz, and has found ways to bring soul to latter-day pop in a manner that adds to the latter without diminishing the former. His example has been followed by many although few have achieved such a level of success. A major film documentary, *Listen Up: The Lives Of Quincy Jones*, was released in 1990, and five years later Jones received the Jean Hersholt Humanitarian Award at the Academy Awards ceremony in Los Angeles. This coincided with *Q's Jook Joint*, a celebration of his 50 years in the music business with re-recordings of selections from his extraordinarily varied catalogue. The album lodged itself at the top of the *Billboard* jazz album chart for over four months. The film *Austin Powers* prompted a release of his 60s classic 'Soul Bossa Nova' in 1998.

● ALBUMS: *Quincy Jones With The Swedish/U.S. All Stars* (Prestige 1953)★★★, *This Is How I Feel About Jazz* (ABC-Paramount 1957)★★, *Go West Man* (ABC-Paramount 1957)★★★, *The Birth Of A Band* (Mercury 1959)★★★, *The Great Wide World Of Quincy Jones* (Mercury 1960)★★, *Quincy Jones At Newport '61* (Mercury 1961)★★★★, *I Dig Dancers* (Mercury 1961)★★★, *Around The World* (Mercury 1961)★★★, *The Quintessence* (Impulse! 1961)★★★, with Billy Eckstine *Billy Eckstine & Quincy Jones At Basin St. East* (Mercury 1962)★★★, *Big Band Bossa Nova* (Mercury 1962)★★★, *Quincy Jones Plays Hip Hits* (Mercury 1963)★★, *The Boy In The Tree* (1963)★★★, *Quincy's Got A Brand New Bag* (Mercury 1964)★★, *Quincy Jones Explores The Music Of Henry Mancini* (Mercury 1964)★★★, *Golden Boy* (Mercury 1964)★★★, *The Pawnbroker* (Mercury 1964)★★★, *Quincy Plays For Pussycats* (Mercury 1965)★★★, *Walk Don't Run* (Mainstream 1966)★★, *The Slender Thread* (Mercury 1966)★★★, *The Deadly Affair* (Verve 1967)★★★, *Enter Laughing* (Liberty 1967)★★★, *In The Heat Of The Night* film soundtrack (United Artists 1967)★★★★, *In Cold Blood* film soundtrack (Colgems 1967)★★★, *Banning* (1968)★★★, *For The Love Of Ivy* (ABC 1968)★★, *The Split* (1968)★★★, *Jigsaw* (1968)★★★, *A Dandy In Aspic* (1968)★★★, *The Hell With Heroes* (1968)★★★, *MacKennas Gold* (RCA 1969)★★★, *The Italian Job* film soundtrack (Paramount 1969)★★★★, *The Lost Man* (1969)★★★, *Bob & Carol & Ted & Alice* (Bell 1969)★★★, *John And Mary* (A&M 1969)★★★, *Walking In Space* (A&M 1969)★★, *Gula Matari* (A&M 1970)★★★, *The Out Of Towners* (United Artists 1970)★★★, *Cactus Flower* (Bell 1970)★★★, *The Last Of The Hot Shots* (1970)★★★, *Sheila* (1970)★★, *They Call Me Mr Tibbs* (United Artists 1970)★★★, *Smackwater Jack* (A&M 1971)★★★, *The Anderson Tapes* (1971)★★★★, *Dollars* (1971)★★★, *Man And Boy* (1971)★★★, *The Hot Rock* (Prophesy 1972)★★★, *Ndeda* (Mercury 1972)★★★, *The New Centurians* (1972)★★★, with Donny Hathaway *Come Back Charleston Blue* film soundtrack (Atco 1972)★★, *You've Got It Bad Girl* (A&M 1973)★★, *Body Heat* (A&M 1974)★★★★, *This Is How I Feel About Jazz* (Impulse! 1974)★★★, *Mellow Madness* (A&M 1975)★★★, *I Heard That!* (A&M 1976)★★★, *Roots* (A&M 1977)★★★, *Sounds ... And Stuff Like That* (A&M 1978)★★, *The Wiz* (MCA 1978)★★★, *The Dude* (A&M 1981)★★★, *The Color Purple* film soundtrack (Qwest 1985)★★★★, *Back On The Block* (Qwest 1989)★★★, *Listen Up, The Lives Of Quincy Jones* (Qwest 1990)★★★, with Miles Davis *Live At Montreux* recorded 1991 (Reprise 1993)★★★★, *Q's Jook Joint* (Qwest 1995)★★★★.

● COMPILATIONS: *Compact Jazz: Quincy Jones* (Phillips/PolyGram 1989)★★★★, *Best Of Quincy Jones* (Spectrum 1998)★★★.

● VIDEOS: *Miles Davis And Quincy Jones: Live At Montreux* (1993).

● FURTHER READING: *Quincy Jones*, Raymond Horricks.

● FILMS: *Listen Up: The Lives Of Quincy Jones* (1990).

JONES, REUNALD

b. 22 December 1910, Indianapolis, Indiana, USA, d. 1989. Jones came from a musical family; his father and two brothers were professional musicians and he was a cousin of Roy Eldridge. Jones played trumpet with various bands around Minneapolis in the late 20s; joined Speed Webb's noted territory band in 1930, and thereafter swung through many leading bands of the 30s and early 40s, notably those of Don Redman, Claude Hopkins, Chick Webb, Jimmie Lunceford and Duke Ellington. In 1952 he joined Count Basie, playing lead trumpet until 1957. He subsequently played with Woody Herman and spent several years working in studio bands, a period which included stints backing Nat 'King' Cole on television and playing with Gene Ammons. A strikingly good lead trumpeter, Jones seldom attracted attention, unless it was as a result of a calculatedly casual habit he adopted while with Basie of playing with one hand in his pocket. Reunald Jones's few recorded solos included some with Chick Webb, 'Let's Get Together' and 'When Dreams Come True', and 'Swingin' With The Fat Man' with Don Redman.

● ALBUMS: with Count Basie *Sixteen Men Swinging* (1953)★★★★.
● COMPILATIONS: *The Chronological Chick Webb* (1929-34)★★★★.

JONES, RICHARD M.

b. 13 June c.1889, Donaldsonville, Louisiana, USA, d. 8 December 1945. Although Jones had learned piano from an early age, as a teenager he played on various wind instruments in dancebands and marching bands in his home town. Later, he reverted to piano, playing solo and as a bandleader. He worked with a number of leading New Orleans musicians before moving to Chicago in 1918. He performed in several bands, but was also active in music publishing and as an executive with OKeh Records. During the 20s he recorded with his own pick-up bands and also played with many other recording artists of the day, notably Louis Armstrong. He continued playing and occasionally recording during the 30s and early 40s. His compositions include 'Lonesome Nobody Cares', popularized by Sophie Tucker, 'Riverside Blues' and, best known of all, 'Trouble In Mind'. He died in 1945.
● COMPILATIONS: included on *Jazz Sounds Of The 20s, Volume 4: The Blues Singers* (1923-31 recordings)★★, *Complete Works 1923-36, Volumes 1 & 2* (RST 1996)★★★★, *Richard M. Jones And The Blues Singers* (Document 1996)★★★.

JONES, RODNEY

b. 30 August 1956, New Haven, Conneticut, USA. Jones was raised in a musical family and plays bass and drums as well as guitar. He studied improvization with John Lewis at the City College of New York and guitar with a variety of teachers. He became a regular studio musician before playing with the Music Complex Orchestra led by pianist Jaki Byard (1975). In the late 70s Jones worked with the groups of Chico Hamilton and Dizzy Gillespie as well as forming his own quartet. He toured the world with the Subtle Sounds jazz group in the early 80s before joining vocalist Lena Horne. He is a meticulous musician whose aim is 'to make each note have a meaning'. He has won a Certificate of Merit from New Orleans (1977) and a recording grant from the National Endowment for the Arts (1983).
● ALBUMS: *Articulation* (1978)★★★, *When You Feel The Love* (1980)★★★, *Friends* (1981)★★, *My Funny Valentine* (1981)★★★.

JONES, SALENA

b. Joan Elizabeth Shaw, 29 January 1944, Newport News, Virginia, USA. Jones's first stage name was Joan Temple. After starting to sing in her home-town she tried her luck in New York. Like so many other singers of note, Jones won a talent contest at Harlem's Apollo theatre, singing 'September Song', and was soon appearing professionally at the Village Vanguard. In the mid-60s she left the USA for Europe, singing in Paris and London, where she appeared at Ronnie Scott's club attracting considerable praise. She appeared on television and had success with 'A Walk In The Black Forest'. In 1978 she made her first visit to Japan, which proved to be her destiny for almost two decades. Hugely popular in the Far East, she made numerous albums, including 20 for JVC alone. In the mid-90s she renewed her following in the UK with appearances at London's Pizza on the Park and she also appeared at European festivals and in the USA. She worked on the Concord Fujitsu jazz tour in 1995, backed by Benny Green, Ray Brown and Scott Hamilton. The following year she made her first album outside the Far East for 18 years with the Save the Children fund release, *It Amazes Me*. That same year, she began recording in London for Jay/Ter and also toured the USA with a band that included Alan Barnes. A distinctive smoky sound lends itself well to Jones's ballad interpretations and when backed by jazz musicians she comfortably accommodates the rhythmic aspects of the music without becoming a full-fledged jazz singer. As a headliner for over 30 years, Jones has a very large following and in the late 90s those of her fans who reside in Europe or the USA were at last able to see and hear her in person and to obtain her records with comparative ease, thus catching up with what the Japanese have been enjoying all along.
● ALBUMS: *It Amazes Me* (HMV 1995)★★, *On Broadway - Only Love* (Ter 1996)★★, *In Hollywood - Making Love* (Ter 1996)★★★, *Salena Jones Meets Kenny Burrell & Richie Cole* (Vinegate 1997)★★★★.

JONES, SAM

b. 12 November 1924, Jacksonville, Florida, USA, d. 15 December 1981. A dependable bass-player, cellist and composer of some fine tunes, Jones never achieved the kind of critical esteem which was accorded other players whose reputations were built during the 50s. The under-estimation of Jones's talent is surprising in view of his contribution to a number of excellent bands, including those of Cannonball Adderley (1955-56 and 1959-66), Oscar Peterson (1966-69) and Cedar Walton from 1971. His partnerships with Billy Higgins (in Walton's trio) and Louis Hayes (with Adderley and Peterson) were models of the imaginative support that a good modern, mainstream rhythm section should provide. Jones also worked with Tiny Bradshaw, Illinois Jacquet, Kenny Dorham, Thelonoious Monk, Clark Terry, Bill Evans, and Johnny Hodges. In the 10 years before his death he freelanced and led a big band.
● ALBUMS: *The Soul Society* (1960)★★★, *The Chant* (1961)★★★, *Down Home* (1962)★★★, *Seven Minds* (1974)★★, *Cello Again* (1976)★★, *Changes And Things* (1977)★★★, *Something In Common* (1977)★★★, *Visitation* (1978)★★★, *The Bassist* (1979)★★★, *Something New* (1979)★★.

JONES, SLICK

b. Wilmore Jones, 13 April 1907, Roanoke, Virginia, USA, d. 2 November 1969. Jones began playing drums as a child in Virginia where his father and brother were also musicians. While still in his teens he moved to New York to study and then began playing with Fletcher Henderson's band. In 1936 he began a long association with Fats Waller, appearing on numerous recording dates. After Waller's death he played with small bands led by Stuff Smith, Una Mae Carlisle, Eddie South and others. He was also with Claude Hopkins, Don Redman, Gene Sedric, Wilbur De Paris, Doc Cheatham and Eddie Durham through into the early 60s when poor health interfered with his career. Particularly adept with brushes, Jones's drumming had a sprightliness that helped lift the musicians he backed.

● ALBUMS: *Fats Waller Live At the Yacht Club* (Giants of Jazz 1938)★★★.

JONES, THAD

b. Thaddeus Joseph Jones, 28 March 1923, Pontiac, Michigan, USA, d. 20 August 1986, Copenhagen, Denmark. A self-taught trumpet player, Jones began playing with a band led by his older brother, Hank Jones, in his early teens. He developed his technique and advanced his musical knowledge during military service and in several dancebands. In the early 50s he played in a band led by Billy Mitchell, which also included his younger brother, Elvin Jones. In 1954 Thad was with Charles Mingus; the same year he also joined Count Basie, an engagement that lasted until 1963. In the mid-60s Jones formed The Jazz Orchestra, which he co-led with Mel Lewis. During this period he extended his writing activities, composing and arranging the bulk of this remarkable band's outstanding book. In 1979 Jones quit The Jazz Orchestra and emigrated to Denmark, where he wrote for and performed with the Danish Radio Big Band, often playing valve trombone (which he had taken up following a lip injury). He also appeared with the Swedish Radio Big Band and formed a band of his own, Eclipse. In 1985 he took on the leadership of the Count Basie Orchestra, leaving in February the following year, some six months before his death. A lyrical player, especially on the slightly mellower flügelhorn, Jones was a superbly inventive, bebop-influenced soloist with a crisp tone. Despite such gifts, however, Jones's major contribution to jazz was his extensive library of compositions and arrangements for big bands. In these he ranged widely, experimenting with meters not usually adopted by jazz orchestras, and comfortably incorporating various popular fads and fancies into jazz with a skill that ensured their survival long after fashions had changed.

● ALBUMS: *The Fabulous Thad Jones* reissued as *Thad Jones* (Debut 1954)★★★★, with Charles Mingus *Jazz Collaborations* 10-inch album (Debut 1954)★★★★, *Mad Thad* (Period 1956)★★★★, *Detroit-New York Junction* (Blue Note 1956)★★★★, *The Magnificient Thad Jones* (Blue Note 1956)★★★★★, *The Magnificent Thad Jones, Volume 3* (Blue Note 1957)★★★, *After Hours* (Prestige 1957)★★★★, *Motor City Scene* (United Artists 1959)★★★★, with Pepper Adams *Mean What You Say* (Milestone 1966)★★★★, with Mel Lewis *Presenting Thad Jones-Mel Lewis & The Jazz Orchestra* (Solid State 1966)★★★★, with Lewis *Thad Jones Live At The Village Vanguard* (Solid State 1967)★★★★, with Sonny Rollins *Sonny Rollins With Guest Artist Thad Jones* (Archive Of Folk And Jazz 1968)★★★, with Lewis *The Big Band Sound Of Thad Jones & Mel Lewis* (Solid State 1968)★★★★, with Lewis *Thad Jones & Mel Lewis Featuring Miss Ruth Brown* (Solid State 1969)★★★★, with Lewis *Monday Night* (Solid State 1969)★★★★, with Lewis *Central Park North* (Solid State 1969)★★★★, with Lewis *Consummation* (Blue Note 1970)★★★★★, with Lewis *Suite For Pops* (Horizon 1972)★★★, with Lewis *Potpourri* (Philadelphia International 1974)★★★, with Swedish Radio Big Band *Greetings And Salutations* (Passport 1975)★★★, with Lewis *New Life: Dedicated To Max Gordon* (A&M 1975)★★, with Lewis *Live In Munich* (A&M 1976)★★★, with Lewis *Thad Jones With Mel Lewis, Manuel Desica And The Jazz Orchestra* (Pausa 1977)★★★, with Lewis *Thad Jones And The Mel Lewis Quartet* (A&M 1977)★★★★, *By Jones, I Think We've Got It* (1978)★★, with Danish Radio Big Band *Live At Montmartre, Copenhagen* (Storyville 1978)★★★, *Eclipse* (Storyville 1979)★★★, *Jazzhus Slukefter* (1980)★★, *Three And One* (Steeple Chase 1985)★★, with Lewis *Basie, 1969* 1969 recording (TOB 1995)★★★★.

● COMPILATIONS: with Lewis *The Complete Solid State Recordings Of The Thad Jones/Mel Lewis Orchestra* 1966-1970 recordings, 5-CD box set (Mosaic)★★★★, *The Complete Blue Note/UA/Roulette Recordings Of Thad Jones* 3-CD/5-LP box set (Mosaic 1997)★★★★.

JONES, VINCE

b. Vincent Hugh Jones, 24 March 1954, Paisley, Scotland. In 1955 Jones's family emigrated to Australia and lived in Wolloongong, New South Wales. The son of a musician, he was exposed to the jazz greats at an early age and he began to play trumpet in local bands. As an admirer of cool jazz he was especially influenced by Chet Baker and Miles Davis. In 1974 Jones began many years of playing and singing on the New South Wales club and jazz circuit. In 1982 he recorded his debut, *Watch What Happens*, which featured standards and some original material. The success of the album enabled him to form a sextet that played and toured extensively. More recordings followed, and Jones became a popular festival and cabaret attraction. In 1990 he accepted an acting role in the ABC period series, *Come In Spinner*. The subsequent album soundtrack of standards, with Jones and Grace Knight, became a milestone in the Australian recording industry as the biggest selling Australian jazz album ever, with sales in excess of 200,000. Jones rejected the commercial and celebrity opportunities that beckoned, preferring to concentrate on his own musicality and he released and produced new albums each year. Standards became less obvious in his repertoire and originals, written by himself or band members, became more prominent. In 1992, he toured Europe with his sextet which included Barney McAll, Lloyd Swanton and Andrew Gander. There were concerts in The Netherlands, Germany, England and at the Montreux International Jazz Festival. An effective concert and cabaret performer, Jones's sensitive, almost tortured persona, complimented the melancholic nature of his music, which became increasingly more introspective. In 1992 after the release of *Trustworthy Little Sweethearts*, the Jones band toured Europe to considerable success. When he returned to Australia Jones retreated to his isolated farm in rural Victoria to compose new material. The 1993 album, *Future Girl*, contained original material, much of it inspired by his passion for the environment and conservation. Jones maintains full control in all aspects of his recordings and performs only when inclined, but his fierce independence and dedication to his art has resulted in a highly original and important body of work. By the mid-90s he had developed more as a vocalist who occasionally played the trumpet. His singing is individual and eloquent, containing sensitive phrasing and sincerity. In 1996 Jones worked on a compilation release with EMI Records and once again toured Europe.

● ALBUMS: *Watch What Happens* (EMI 1982)★★★, *Spell* (EMI 1983)★★, *For All Colours* (EMI 1984)★★★, *On The Brink Of It* (EMI 1985)★★★, *It All Ends Up In Tears* (EMI 1987)★★★, *Trustworthy Little Sweethearts* (Intuition 1988)★★★★, *One Day Spent* (Intuition 1990)★★★, *Come In Spinner* (Intuition 1990)★★★★, *Future Girl* (IntuitionI 1993)★★★, *Here's To The Miracles* (Intuition 1995)★★★.

JOOS, HERBERT

b. 21 March 1940, Karlsruhe, Germany. Joos studied fluegelhorn, trumpet and bass, but also plays baritone-horn and alphorn. In the first half of the 70s he was a member of Modern Jazz Quintet, New Jazz Ensemble and the Fourmenonly group. During this period he also worked with different bands at Free Jazz Meeting in Baden-Baden, Free Jazz Day in Frankfurt and in a fluegelhorn workshop together with Kenny Wheeler, Ian Carr, Harry Beckett and Ack van Rooyen. During the Blow project he collaborated with Bernd Konrad and Wolfgang Czelusta. He had also led his own quartet and orchestra. The most acknowledged of his assignments has been the one with the Vienna Art Orchestra. His warm and big tone and the romantic-impressionistic influences combined with the affinity of free improvisation gives him a strong and personal profile within the European jazz community.

● ALBUMS: *The Philosophy Of The Fluegelhorn* (1973)★★★, *Daybreak* (Japo 1976)★★★★, *Blow* (1977)★★★, *Mel-An-Cho* (1981)★★★, *Still Life* (1983)★★★, with Hans Koller And The International Brass Company *The Horses* (1980)★★, *Live At The Jazz Festival Frankfurt* (1981)★★, with Part Of Art *Son Sauvage* (1983)★★★, with Harry Pepl, Jon Christensen *Cracked Mirrors* (ECM 1987)★★★, with Vienna Art Choir *Five Old Songs* (1984)★★, with Vienna Art Orchestra *Tango From Obango* (1979)★★★, *Concerto Piccolo* (1981)★★★, *Suite For The Green Eighties* (1982)★★★, *From No Time To Rag Time* (1983)★★★, *Perpetuum Mobile* (1945)★★, *Nightride Of A Lonely Saxophoneplayer* (1985)★★★, *Jazzbuhne Berlin '85* (1985)★★★, *Two Little Animals* (1987)★★★, *Inside Out* (1988)★★★, *Blues For Brahms* (1989)★★★, *Innocence Of Clichés* (1989)★★★, with Eberhard Weber *Eberhard Weber Orchestra* (1988)★★★, *Plays Billie Holiday Songs* (Emarcy 1994)★★★★.

JOPLIN, SCOTT

b. 24 November 1868, Texarkana, Texas, USA, d. 1 April 1917. Joplin's father was born into slavery, becoming a freeman with Emancipation in 1863. A musical individual, he encouraged the musical aspirations of his sons and daughters. Scott Joplin, who was originally self-taught, moved to St. Louis while still in his teens, by which time he was an accomplished pianist. Although adept in various styles, including that of contemporary classicists such as Louis M. Gottschalk, Joplin excelled in the currently popular ragtime music. In 1894 he was in Sedalia and soon afterwards began committing to paper many of the rags he had heard played by ragtime 'professors' and tunes he had himself composed. One of the latter, 'Maple Leaf Rag', was hugely successful and this recognition encouraged him to turn his attention to extended works in a quasi-classical style. His efforts at ragtime ballets and ragtime operas proved disappointingly uncommercial but his straightforward ragtime tunes continued to be very popular. A failed marriage, the death of his child and the fast decline of his health as he succumbed to a debilitating venereal disease, allied to his losing battle to be accepted as a classical composer, created a desperately sad atmosphere for his declining years. Despite his problems, however, Joplin completed another ragtime opera, *Treemonisha*. Unable to interest anyone in staging the opera, he paid for a run-through performance in 1915 only to see it, too, fail. The following year his illness entered its final stages, he was hospitalized and died some months later in April 1917. In the early 70s ragtime suddenly became popular again and its use and success on the soundtrack of a successful film, *The Sting* (1973), brought Joplin to the attention of a new audience. His tunes including 'The Entertainer', 'Elite Syncopations', 'Solace I', 'Solace II' and 'Chrysanthemum' were heard everywhere, often in rather stately recreations by Joshua Rifkin and other classically-trained pianists. Such versions would doubtless have pleased their composer as they avoided jazz inflections, but also failed to reflect much of their lively and sometimes earthy origins. Joplin's belated recognition as a pioneer of Third Stream Music was confirmed by an acclaimed staging and recording of *Treemonisha* by Gunther Schuller and the Houston Grand Opera, performed and released in the mid-70s. Unfortunately most of Joplin's other scores for extended compositions have been lost. In 1997 his music was combined with that of Irving Berlin, another great composer from the early golden era, in a new musical *The Tin Pan Alley Rag*, which had its world premiere at the Pasadena Playhouse, California.

● FURTHER READING: *Scott Joplin and the Ragtime Era*, Peter Gammond. *The Life And Works Of Scott Joplin*, A.W. Reed.

JORDAN, CLIFFORD

b. 2 September 1931, Chicago, Illinois, USA, d. 27 March 1993, New York City, New York, USA. Jordan began his professional career playing tenor saxophone in R&B bands in the Chicago area. In 1957 he moved to New York, made the album *Blowin' In From Chicago* with fellow tenor saxophonist John Gilmore and then spent time in groups led by Max Roach and Horace Silver. In the 60s he played with artists including J.J. Johnson, Charles Mingus, Kenny Dorham, Julian Priester and also led his own bands, touring extensively. In 1965 he released a tribute to Leadbelly, *These Are My Roots*, and in the late 60s began to record for the Strata East label: outstanding releases include *In The World* and *Glass Bead Game*. In the 70s he worked with Cedar Walton, often in a quartet context with Sam Jones and Billy Higgins (known as the Magic Triangle), recording some distinctive large ensemble albums for Muse (*Remembering Me-Me*, *Inward Fire*), and he also established a reputation as a teacher. In the 80s Jordan continued to record regularly, both as a guest with leaders such as Slide Hampton (*Roots*) and in various small groups of his own, where his associates have included Walton again (*Half Note*), Barry Harris (*Repetition*) and Junior Cook (*Two Tenor Winner*). With his roots in blues and the bebop mainstream tempered by work with modernists such as Mingus, Eric Dolphy and Don Cherry, Jordan was both an accessible, adventurous player and an impressive, underrated composer/arranger.

● ALBUMS: with John Gilmore *Blowing In From Chicago* (Blue Note 1957)★★★★, *Clifford Jordan All Stars* (Blue Note 1957)★★★★, *Cliff Craft* (Blue Note 1957)★★★, *Spellbound* (Blue Note 1960)★★★★, with Sonny Red *A Story Tale* (Jazzland 1961)★★, *Starting Time* (Jazzland 1961)★★★, *Bearcat* (Jazzland 1962)★★, *These Are My Roots* (Atlantic 1965)★★★, *Clifford Jordan And His Orchestra* (1966)★★, *In The World* (1969)★★★, *Glass Bead Game* (Strata East 1973)★★★, *The Highest Mountain* (Steeple Chase 1975)★★★, *Night Of The Mark VII* (1975)★★★, *On Stage Vols 1-3* (Steeple Chase 1975)★★, *Firm Roots* (Steeple Chase 1975)★★★, *The Highest Mountain* (1975)★★★, *Remembering Me-Me* (1976)★★, *Inward Fire* (1977)★★★, *The Adventurer* (1978)★★★, *Hello Hank Jones* (1978)★★★, *Adventurer* (Muse 1981)★★, with Jaki Byard *Dr Chicago* (1984)★★★, *Repetition* (Soul Note 1984)★★★, with Junior Cook *Two Tenor Winner!* (Criss Cross 1984)★★★, *Half Note* (1985)★★★, *Royal Ballads* (Criss Cross 1986)★★, *Masters From Different Worlds* (Mapleshade 1990)★★★★, *Down Through The Years* (Milestone 1992)★★★, *Play What You Feel* (Mapleshade 1997)★★, *The Mellow Side* (Mapleshade 1998)★★★.

JORDAN, DUKE

b. Irving Sidney Jordan, 1 April 1922, New York City, New York, USA. After studying classical music, Jordan played piano in a number of swing era bands, including Al Cooper's Savoy Sultans. In the mid-40s, he became involved in bebop, playing with Charlie Parker and others. Later in the decade and in the early 50s Jordan played in bands led by Sonny Stitt and Stan Getz and thereafter led his own units. Also in the early 50s, he married the singer Sheila Jordan, but they later split up. Jordan's career drifted for a while in the late 60s, but from 1972 onwards he was very active, playing in many parts of the world, especially in Scandinavia, and since 1978 he has lived in Denmark, recording extensively for the Copenhagen label Steeplechase. A lyrically inventive player, Jordan has also composed a number of tunes, one of which, 'Jordu', became a bebop classic.

● ALBUMS: *Jordu* (New Jazz 1953)★★★★, *The Duke Jordan Trio* (Savoy 1954)★★★★, *Do It Yourself Jazz* (Savoy 1955)★★★, *The Street Swingers* (1955)★★★, *The Duke Jordan Quintet* (1955)★★, *Flight To Jordan* (Blue Note 1955)★★★★, *Les Liaisons Dangereuses* (1962)★★★, *East And West Of Jazz* (Charlie Parker 1962)★★★, *Brooklyn Brothers* (1973)★★★, *The Murray Hill Caper* (1973)★★★★, *Flight To Denmark* (Steeple Chase 1973)★★★, *Two Loves* (Steeple Chase 1973)★★★, *Truth* (1975)★★★, *Duke's Delight* (1975)★★, *Misty Thursday* (Steeple Chase 1975)★★★, *Lover Man* (1975)★★, *The Duke Jordan Trio Live In Japan* (Steeple Chase 1976)★★, *Osaka Concert: Vols 1* and *2* (Steeple Chase 1976)★★★, *Flight To Japan* (1976)★★★, *I Remember Bebop* (1977)★★★, with others *They All Played Bebop* (1977)★★, *Duke's Artistry* (Steeple Chase 1978)★★, *The Great Session* (Steeple Chase 1978)★★★, *Midnight Moonlight* (1979)★★★, *Tivoli One* (Steeple Chase 1979)★★★, *Wait And See* (Steeple Chase 1979)★★★, *Solo Masterpieces* (Steeple Chase 1979)★★, *Lover Man* (1979)★★★, *Change A Pace* (1979)★★★, *Thinking Of You* (Steeple Chase 1979)★★★, *Blue Duke* (RCA 1983)★★★, *As Time Goes By* (Steeple Chase 1986)★★★★, *Time On My Hands* (Steeple Chase 1986)★★★, *One For The Library* (Storyville 1994)★★, *Tivoli Two* (Steeple Chase 1995)★★★.

JORDAN, LOUIS

b. Louis Thomas Jordan, 8 July 1908, Brinkley, Arkansas, USA, d. 4 February 1975, Los Angeles, California, USA. Saxophonist and singer, Jordan began touring as a teenager with the Rabbit Foot Minstrels, and supported classic blues singers Ma Rainey, Ida Cox and Bessie Smith. In the 30s, after relocating to New York City, he played in the bands of Louis Armstrong, Clarence Williams, Chick Webb and Ella Fitzgerald, appearing with these orchestras on records for RCA Victor, Vocalion and Decca, and making his vocal debut with Webb's band on novelty songs such as 'Gee, But You're Swell' and 'Rusty Hinge'. In 1938 Jordan formed his first combo, the Elks Rendez-Vous Band (after the club at which he had secured a residency), and signed an exclusive deal with Decca. While he had been with Webb, he had often been brought to the front to perform a blues or novelty swing number. These spots had been so well-received that, from the start of his own band, Jordan had decided to promote himself as a wacky musical comedian with a smart line in humorous jive. In early 1939, in line with this image, he changed the band's name to the Tympany Five and enjoyed steady, if unspectacular, success with recordings of 'T-Bone Blues' (1941), 'Knock Me A Kiss' and 'I'm Gonna Move To The Outskirts Of Town' (1942), 'What's The Use Of Gettin' Sober (When You Gonna Get Drunk Again)' and 'Five Guys Named Moe' (1943). After World War II, the Tympany Five really hit their stride with a string of million-selling records, including 'Is You Is Or Is You Ain't My Baby?' (1944), 'Caldonia (Boogie)' (1945), '(Beware, Brother) Beware!', 'Choo Choo Ch'boogie' (1946) and 'Saturday Night Fish Fry' (1949). Other hits which were not so commercially successful, but which are inextricably linked with Jordan's name nevertheless include 'G.I. Jive', 'Buzz Me', 'Ain't Nobody Here But Us Chickens', 'Let The Good Times Roll', 'Reet, Petite And Gone', 'Open The Door, Richard', 'School Days', and 'Blue Light Boogie'. Jordan remained with Decca until 1954, when he switched briefly to Aladdin (1954), RCA's

'X' subsidiary (1955) and Mercury (1956-57) but, sadly, his reign was coming to an end; the new generation wanted 'fast and loud' not 'smooth and wry', and Jordan, dogged by ill-health, could not compete against rock 'n' roll artists such as Little Richard and Chuck Berry, even though his songs were being recycled by these very performers. Chuck Berry ('Run Joe' and 'Ain't That Just Like A Woman') and B.B. King 'Do You Call That A Buddy?', 'Early In The Morning', 'Just Like A Woman', 'How Blue Can You Get?', 'Buzz Me', 'Let The Good Times Roll' and 'Jordan For President!' in particular, have been successful with Jordan covers. Surprisingly, his performances were taken to the heart of many Chicago blues artists with songs like 'Somebody Done Hoodooed The Hoodoo Man', 'Never Let Your Left Hand Know What Your Right Hand's Doin'' and 'Blue Light Boogie'; even Bill Haley would often admit that his 'revolutionary' musical style was simply a copy of the Tympany Five's shuffles and jumps that had been recorded the previous decade in the same Decca studios.

Owing to his fluctuating health Louis Jordan spent the 60s and 70s working when he could, filling summer season engagements and recording occasionally for small companies owned by old friends including Ray Charles (Tangerine Records), Paul Gayten (Pzazz) and Johnny Otis (Blues Spectrum). His last recordings were as a guest on trumpeter Wallace Davenport's *Sweet Georgia Brown*, after which he suffered eight months of inactivity due to his deteriorating health, and a fatal heart-attack on 4 February 1975. The main factor that set Jordan apart from most of the competition was that he was at once a fine comedian and a superb saxophonist whose novelty value was never allowed to obscure either his musicianship or that of his sidemen, who at one time or another included trumpeters Idrees Sulieman and Freddie Webster (both major influences on boppers like Miles Davis and Dizzy Gillespie), tenor saxophonists Paul Quinichette, Maxwell Davis and Count Hastings, drummer Shadow Wilson, and pianists Wild Bill Davis and Bill Doggett. In 1990 a musical by Clarke Peters entitled *Five Guys Named Moe*, which featured 'music written or originally performed by Louis Jordan', opened in London. Four years later it overtook *Irma La Douce* to become the longest-running musical ever at the Lyric Theatre. After initially lukewarm revues, another production enjoyed a decent run on Broadway. That Louis Jordan influenced all who came after him, and continues to be a prime source of material for films, theatre, television advertising, R&B bands and bluesmen, 40 or 50 years after his heyday, is a testament to his originality and talent.

● ALBUMS: *Go! Blow Your Horn* (Score 1957)★★★★, *Somebody Up There Digs Me* (Mercury 1957)★★★★, *Man, We're Wailin'* (Mercury 1958)★★★★, *Let The Good Times Roll* (Decca 1958)★★★★, *Hallelujah ... Louis Jordan Is Back* (1964)★★★★, *One Sided Love* (1969)★★★★, *Louis Jordan's Greatest Hits* (1969)★★★★, *Louis Jordan* (1971)★★★★, *Great R&B Oldies* (1972)★★★★, *I Believe In Music* (1974)★★★★, *In Memoriam* (1975)★★★★, *Louis Jordan's Greatest Hits Volume 2* (1975)★★★★, *The Best Of Louis Jordan* (1975)★★★★, *Louis Jordan With The Chris Barber Band* (1976)★★★, *Three Hot Big Band Sessions In 1951* (1976)★★★★, *More Stuff* (1976)★★★★, *Some Other Stuff* (1977)★★★★, *Louis Jordan And His Tympany Five* i (1977)★★★★, *Come On ... Get It ...* (1978)★★★★, *Prime Cuts* (1978)★★★★, *Collates* (1979)★★★★, *Good Times* (1980)★★★★, *The Best Of Louis Jordan* (1981)★★★★, with Oran 'Hot Lips' Page *Jumpin' Stuff* (1981)★★★★, *Louis Jordan And His Tympany Five* ii (1982)★★★★, *The Last Swinger, The First Rocker* (1982)★★★★, *Choo Choo Ch'boogie* (1982)★★★★, *G.I. Jive* (1983)★★★★, *Cole Slaw* (1983)★★★★, *Look Out!...It's Louis Jordan And The Tympany Five* (1983)★★★★, *Louis Jordan And His Tympany Five, 1944-1945* (1983)★★★★, *Louis Jordan On Film - Reet, Petite And Gone* (1983)★★★★, *Louis Jordan On Film - Look Out Sister* (1983)★★★★, *Go! Blow Your Horn - Part 2* (1983)★★★★, *Jump 'N' Jive With Louis Jordan* (1984)★★★★, *Louis Jordan And Friends* (1984)★★★★, *Jivin' With Jordan* (1985)★★★★, *Hoodoo Man 1938-1940* (1986)★★★★, *Knock Me Out 1940-1942* (1986)★★★★, *Somebody Done Hoodooed The Hoodoo Man* (1986)★★★★, *Louis Jordan And His Tympany Five, More 1944-1945* (1986)★★★★, *Rock And Roll Call* (1986)★★★★, *Rockin' And Jivin', Volume 1* (1986)★★★★, *Rockin' And Jivin', Volume 2* (1986)★★★★, *Louis Jordan And His Tympany Five* (1986)★★★★, *Out Of Print* (1988)★★★★, *Greatest Hits* (1989)★★★★, *The V-Discs* (1989)★★★★, *Hits And Rarities* (1989)★★★★, *More Hits, More Rarities* (1990)★★★★, *Rock 'N' Roll* (1990)★★★★, *The Complete Aladdin Sessions* (1991)★★★★, *The Complete Recordings 1938 - 1941* (1992)★★★★.

● FURTHER READING: *Let The Good Times Roll: A Biography Of Louis Jordan*, John Chilton.

JORDAN, RONNY

b. England. Described by some as 'the quintessential acid-jazz guitarist', Jordan has an intimate and readily accessible musical demeanour which has endeared him to many. By the mid-90s he had begun to disassociate himself with the acid-jazz movement, commenting that 'the way I see acid-jazz, it's more of a fashion statement and I'm not really about that'. Nevertheless, the high profile of the genre had served him well. After signing to Island Records subsidiary 4th And Broadway Records in 1991, Jordan released two acclaimed albums and participated in a number of collaborative projects. *Light To Dark* (1996) was a more restrained, mature collection, designed to appeal to jazz purists for the first time. A link with the past was maintained in its rhythms - Jordan favouring pummelling beats informed by a love of good hip-hop - while the melodies belonged to an earlier era. 'It's You', the first single to be taken from the album, typified this marriage of the new and the old.

● ALBUMS: *The Antidote* (4th & Broadway/Island 1991)★★★★, *The Quiet Revolution* (4th & Broadway/Island 1993)★★★, *Light To Dark* (4th & Broadway/Island 1996)★★.

JORDAN, SHEILA

b. Sheila Jeanette Dawson, 18 November 1928, Detroit, Michigan, USA. Raised in poverty in Pennsylvania's coal-mining country, Jordan began singing as a child and by the time she was in her early teens was working semi-professionally in Detroit clubs. Her first great influence was Charlie Parker and, indeed, most of her influences have been instrumentalists rather than singers. Working chiefly with black musicians, she met with disapproval from the white community but persisted with her career. She was a member of a vocal trio, Skeeter, Mitch And Jean (she was Jean), who sang versions of Parker's solos in a manner akin to that of the later Lambert, Hendricks And Ross. After moving to New York in the early 50s, she married Parker's pianist, Duke Jordan, and studied with Charles Mingus and Lennie Tristano, but it was not until the early 60s that she made her first recordings. One of these was under her own name, the other was *The Outer View* with George Russell, which featured a famous 10-minute version of 'You Are My Sunshine'. In the mid-60s her work encompassed jazz liturgies sung in churches and extensive club work, but her appeal was narrow even within the confines of jazz. By the late 70s jazz audiences had begun to understand her uncompromising style a little more and her popularity increased - as did her appearances on record, which included albums with pianist Steve Kuhn, whose quartet she joined, and an album, *Home*, comprising a selection of Robert Creeley's poems set to music and arranged by Steve Swallow. A 1983 duo set with bassist Harvie Swartz, *Old Time Feeling*, comprises several of the standards Jordan regularly features in her live repertoire, while 1990's *Lost And Found* pays tribute to her bebop roots. Both sets display her unique musical trademarks, such as the frequent and unexpected sweeping changes of pitch which still tend to confound an uninitiated audience. Entirely non-derivative, Jordan is one of only a tiny handful of jazz singers who fully deserve the appellation and for whom no other term will do.

● ALBUMS: with George Russell *The Outer View* (1962)★★★, *Portrait Of Sheila* (Blue Note 1962)★★★★, *Confirmation* (1975)vH, *Grapevine Discovery* (1976)★★★, *Sheila* (Steeple Chase 1977)★★★, with others *Lennie Tristano Memorial Concert* (1979)★★, *Playground* (1979)★★★, with Harvie Swartz *Old Time Feeling* (Palo Alto 1982)★★, *The Crossing* (Blackhawk 1984)★★★★, *Songs From Within* (MA Recordings 1989)★★★, *Lost And Found* (Muse 1990)★★★, *The Very Thought Of You* (MA Recordings 1993), with Mark Murphy *One For Junior* (Muse 1994)★★★★.

JORDAN, STANLEY

b. 31 July 1959, Chicago, Illinois, USA. Having absorbed a certain amount of theory from an early training on the piano, Jordan taught himself the guitar while in his teens, and performed with the numerous pop and soul groups working around Chicago in the mid-70s. However, winning a prize at the 1976 Reno Jazz Festival inspired Jordan to devote some time to a serious study of music. Studying electronic music, theory, and composition at Princeton University, his reputation quickly spread and he soon found himself playing with Dizzy Gillespie and Benny Carter. In 1982 he recorded his first album: *Touch Sensitive* was a relatively uninspiring solo collection which registered poor sales. But three years later, Jordan's second album *Magic Touch* was a huge commercial success. Produced by Al Di Meola, it featured Onaje Allen Gumbs, Charnett Moffett, and Omar Hakim, while retaining some unaccompanied tracks. Since *Magic Touch*, Jordan's band has become a regular feature of the major international jazz festivals. He is commonly known for his development of a complex technique of 'hammering-on' which has enabled him to accompany himself with bass lines and chords.

● ALBUMS: *Touch Sensitive* (1982)★★, *Magic Touch* (Blue Note 1985)★★★★, *Standards* (Blue Note 1986)★★★, *Flying Home* (EMI Manhattan 1988)★★★, *Cornucopia* (Blue Note 1990)★★★, *Stolen Moments* (Blue Note 1991)★★★★, *Bolero* (Arista 1994)★★★.

JORDAN, STEVE

b. 15 January 1919, New York, USA, d. 13 September 1993, Alexandria, Virginia, USA. Jordan studied guitar with Allan Reuss who had played with Benny Goodman's band. Steve performed with the big bands of Will Bradley and Artie Shaw before the war took him off for service in the navy. On his return he played in a series of big bands - the Casa Loma Orchestra, Stan Kenton, Jimmy Dorsey and Boyd Raeburn. In the early 50s Jordan became a member of the NBC production staff as well as providing the guitar in the rhythm section on many of the sessions produced by John Hammond. Given his role and ability as rhythm guitarist, he has often been compared to guitarist Freddie Green with Count Basie's Orchestra. After completing three years with Benny Goodman in the mid-50s he worked more regularly as a tailor. It was only in 1965 he returned to full-time music with the band of Tommy Gwaltney at Blues Alley in Washington.

● ALBUMS: with Vic Dickenson *Showcase* (1953)★★, *Here Comes Mr Jordan* (1972)★★★, *The Many Sounds Of Steve Jordan* (1993)★★★.

JORDAN, TAFT

b. James Jordan, 15 February 1915, Florence, South Carolina, USA, d. 1 December 1981. Jordan began playing trumpet professionally in 1929 and within four years had achieved such a standard that he was hired by Chick Webb. Apart from a few weeks with Willie Bryant, Jordan stayed with the band until Webb's death and then continued until 1941 during the period when the band was nominally led by Ella Fitzgerald. After briefly leading his own outfit he joined Duke Ellington in 1943. From 1947 he worked with various bands, some of which were relatively obscure. In the mid-50s he led his own bands and also played with Benny Goodman. In the 60s he was active in the studios and theatre-land, occasionally playing in clubs. In the 70s he worked with the New York Jazz Repertory Company and played with Earle Warren. Although the influence of Louis Armstrong affected some of his earlier work, both as a trumpeter and a singer, Jordan was a fiery and often inventive player whose solos could ignite a band.

● ALBUMS: *Taft Jordan* (1960)★★★, *Taft Jordan With George Rhodes And His Orchestra* (1960)★★, *Mood Indigo* (1961)★★★.

● COMPILATIONS: *Taft Jordan And The Mob* (1935)★★★, *The*

Chronological Chick Webb (1935-39)★★★★, *The Indispensable Duke Ellington Vols 11/12* (1944-46)★★★★.

JOSEPH, JULIAN

b. 1967, England. Pianist and bandleader Joseph has been at the forefront of attempts to break down barriers between jazz and classical traditions in the 90s. His 20-piece All Star Big Band certainly includes some of the most prominent musicians in both genres, including Tony Remy, Jean Toussaint and Andy Sheppard. His records have received excellent reviews from several quarters, yet Joseph treats them as little more than an adjunct to his live performances: 'Recording is just a documentation of where you are creatively. Live is where you move on and do other things.' His concerts, at venues including the Proms at the Royal Albert Hall and the Barbican in London, the Montreal Jazz Festival and the Wigmore Hall, have captured a wide range of supporters. The successful marriage of disparate forms arose as the result of his studies in classical composition at the Berklee College Of Music in Boston, Massachusetts, USA, where he would blend the required listening of Prokofiev and Beethoven with jazz influences such as Miles Davis and Herbie Hancock. His third album, meanwhile, documented his set at the Wigmore Hall auditorium, with a set featuring Alec Dankworth, Eddie Daniels, Jason Rebello and Johnny Griffin. In the same year he also performed Gershwin's Piano Concerto In F, live on BBC television, as well as a duet with Bheki Mseleku. Afterwards he began a fourth album, this time a studio affair with the aid of drummer Mark Mondesir and bass player Reginald Veal.

● ALBUMS: *The Language Of Truth* (East West 1991)★★★, *Reality* (East West 1993)★★★, *Julian Joseph In Concert At The Wigmore Hall* (East West 1995)★★★★, *Universal Traveller* (East West 1996)★★★.

JURGENS, DICK

b. 9 November 1911, Sacramento, California, USA. Jurgens, was an accomplished trumpeter by the age of 14. He and his brother Will formed their first band for summer camps at Lake Tahoe, working as rubbish collectors when not playing. Within three years the unit had been booked for a residency local hotel staying until offered a spot at the St. Francis Hotel in San Francisco in 1934. They developed into a polished band with a rich ensemble sound that was ideal for hotel and ballroom work, and vocals by guitarist Eddy Howard, an old friend from Sacramento. Jurgens was resident at the Aragon Ballroom, Chicago, the Elitch Gardens in Denver, and the Avalon Ballroom on Catalina Island, according to the season. He recorded for Decca, ARC, Vocalion, OKeh and Columbia and did many radio transcriptions, issued on Hindsight in the 70s. Jurgens also composed evergreens like 'Careless', 'If I Knew Then', 'Elmer's Tune', 'A Million Dreams Ago' and 'One Dozen Roses', which, as well as being covered by other artists, gave his band hit records without reaching the million-sellers. During World War II service in the US Marine Corps, Dick and Will formed an entertainment unit to tour the South Pacific war areas. Back in civilian life Jurgens returned to the Aragon and Trianon Ballrooms in Chicago until 1956, when he went into business outside the profession. After a break of 13 years he was asked to form a band for the Willowbrook Club outside Chicago, and continued playing there till his retirement in 1976. Singer Don Ring bought the rights to the band's name and library in 1986, and the New Dick Jurgens Orchestra now plays permanently at Ring's Pla Mor Ballroom in Wisconsin.

● ALBUMS: *Radio Years (1937-39)* (1979)★★★, *The Uncollected Dick Jurgens And His Orchestra Vol. 2 (1937-38)* (1979)★★★★.

JURIS, VIC

b. 1953, Parsippany, New Jersey, USA. His guitar playing first began to attract attention in the early and mid-70s thanks to appearances and recordings with Lyn Christie and Eric Kloss. These performances showed Juris to be adept in the wide range of styles covered by these leaders: jazz, rock, funk, pop. Subsequently, he stayed in a jazz-rock groove by joining Barry Miles but also played with Richie Cole which took him into hard-bop. Juris's ability to move between styles without loss of integrity ensured popular acceptance and records sold well. In the late 70s he worked in various small groups, some of them organ combos, and he also teamed up with other guitarists including Bireli Lagrene, on record in 1985, and John Abercrombie, in concert in New York in 1998. In the mid-90s he led a quartet that toured extensively and recorded in Denmark in 1996 (released as *Moonscape* two years later). Juris plays with fluent lyricism, choosing to seduce his listeners with subtle phrasing and engaging romanticism. Not surprisingly, therefore, his playing of ballads is particularly attractive, allowing the romantic element to blossom. In addition to his inventive playing, Juris has also composed many songs, some of which he has performed on record.

● ALBUMS: *Roadsong* (Muse 1977)★★★, *Horizon Drive* (Muse 1979)★★★, *Bleecker Street* (Muse 1981)★★★, *Night Tripper* (Steeple Chase 1994)★★★★ *Pastels* (Steeple Chase 1996)★★★, *Music Of Alec Wilder* (Double-Time 1996)★★★★, *Moonscape* 1996 recording (Steeple Chase 1998)★★★.

Kahn, Roger Wolfe

b. 19 October 1907, Morristown, New Jersey, USA, d. 12 July 1962, New York City, New York, USA. Scion of a very rich New York family, Kahn had money enough to indulge his whims, one of which was to lead a dance-band. For a decade he played exclusive venues frequented by New York's top set and occasionally recorded. Always, Kahn had fun; when the band was playing especially well he used to throw himself onto the floor and wave his legs in the air. For his recording dates he would augment his regular band with renowned jazz artists, including Jack Teagarden and Gene Krupa. In 1933, he folded his band in order to follow another whim; this time he became a test pilot.

● COMPILATIONS: *Roger Wolfe Kahn* (1925-29 recordings)★★★.

Kahn, Tiny

b. Norman Kahn, c.1923, New York City, New York, USA, d. 19 August 1953. After learning to play drums while in school, Kahn performed with a number of important and progressively-minded big bands of the late 40s - including those of Boyd Raeburn, Georgie Auld and Charlie Barnet. While with these bands Kahn began writing, and his arrangements for Chubby Jackson's band were especially successful. This aspect of his talent was also employed by Elliot Lawrence in the early 50s. Kahn's writing was an influence upon other young arrangers of the period, including Al Cohn and Johnny Mandel. Extremely overweight (his nickname was ironical), Kahn died of cardiac problems in August 1953.

● ALBUMS: with Stan Getz *Jazz At Storyville* (1951)★★★★, *Elliot Lawrence Plays Kahn And Mandel* (1956)★★★.

Kaiser, Henry

b. Oakland, California, USA. Experimental, *avant garde* guitarist Henry Kaiser is a prolific musician whose work has run the gamut from free improvisation, to San Francisco-style 60s psychedelia to country music. Kaiser began playing guitar in 1971, influenced by Captain Beefheart's music, and live concerts by San Francisco groups such as Quicksilver Messenger Service and the Grateful Dead. He has recorded numerous solo and group albums for labels such as SST Records and his own Metalanguage, and has collaborated on two albums with guitarists Richard Thompson and Fred Frith, along with former Beefheart drummer John French. The 1990 album, *Heart's Desire*, included keyboards from early Grateful Dead member Tom Constanten and he has recorded with musicians such as John Zorn, Eugene Chadbourne, the Golden Palominos and Herbie Hancock. As a session player he had appeared on over 100 hundred albums by the mid-90s.

● ALBUMS: with ROVA *Daredevils* (1979)★★★★, *Protocol* (1979), with Fred Frith *With Friends Like These* (1980)★★★, *Alloha* (1980)★★★, *Outside Pleasure* (1980)★★★★, with others *The Metalanguage Festival Of Improvised Music, Volume One: The Social Set* (1981)★★, *Volume Two: The Science Set* (1981)★★★, as French, Frith, Kaiser And Thompson *Live, Love, Larf And Loaf* (Demon 1987)★★★, *Crazy Backwards Alphabet* (1987)★★★, *Those Who Know History Are Doomed To Repeat It* (1989)★★★, as French, Frith, Kaiser And Thompson *Invisible Means* (Demon 1990)★★★, *Heart's Desire* (1990)★★★★, *Hope You Like Our New Direction* (1991)★★★, with Derek Bailey *Wireforks* (Shanachie 1995)★★★★, with Wadada Leo Smith *Yo Miles!* (Shanachie 1998)★★★★.

Kallen, Kitty

(see Shaw, Artie)

Kaminsky, Max

b. 7 September 1908, Brockton, Massachusetts, USA, d. 6 September 1994, Castle Point, New York, USA. Kaminsky was a trumpet player with a vigorous style, who played briefly with some big bands, including Tommy Dorsey and Artie Shaw, but was mainly associated with white Chicago-style small groups. Kaminsky started out with bands in Boston around 1924. In the late 20s, he played with George Wettling and Bud Freeman in New York, and toured with Red Nichols. During the 30s and early 40s he worked for several bandleaders, including Leo Reisman, Joe Venuti, Pee Wee Russell, Tony Pastor, Tommy Dorsey, Alvino Rey and Joe Marsala. Between 1942 and 1943, he played for Artie Shaw's famous Navy Band. After his discharge, he led his own popular combo in New York and Boston clubs until 1946, when he resumed freelancing with dixieland groups with artists such as Eddie Condon and Art Hodes.

In 1957, he toured Europe with a Jack Teagarden-Earl Hines All Star group, and the following year travelled to Asia with Teagarden. From then on, he was generally based in New York, mainly freelancing, but sometimes leading small groups at venues such as the Gaslight Club, and at Jimmy Ryan's, where he was still appearing occasionally until 1983. He appeared on several US television jazz programmes, including a 1973 Timex Special. His few recordings as leader included 'Love Nest', 'Everybody Loves My Baby', 'Dippermouth Blues', 'Someday Sweetheart' plus the albums *Chicago Style*, *Ambassador Of Jazz* and *Dixieland Horn*. He recorded prolifically with other groups including George Brunis ('I Used To Love You', 'I'm Gonna Sit Right Down And Write Myself A Letter' and 'In The Shade Of The Old Apple Tree'); Bud Freeman ('China Boy' and 'The Eel'), Art Hodes ('Sweet Georgia Brown' and 'Sugar Foot Stomp'), Willie 'The Lion' Smith ('Muskrat Ramble' and 'Bugle Call Rag'), Tommy Dorsey

('Maple Leaf Rag', 'That's A Plenty' and 'Keepin' Out Of Mischief Now').

● ALBUMS: with Jack Teagarden 10-inch album *Battle Of Jazz, Vol. 5* (Brunswick 1953)★★★, with various artists *Art Ford's Jazz Party, 1958* (Jazz Connoisseur 1987)★★★★.

● FURTHER READING: *My Life In Jazz*, Max Kaminsky.

KAMUCA, RICHIE

b. 23 July 1930, Philadelphia, Pennsylvania, USA, d. 22 July 1977, Los Angeles, California, USA. After working in groups in and around his home town, Kamuca joined the Stan Kenton Orchestra on tenor saxophone in 1952. Two years later he was in Woody Herman's band and then settled on the west coast, where he played and recorded with, among others, Shelly Manne and Shorty Rogers. Kamuca was also on the 1955 Cy Touff Octet and Quintet sessions for Pacific Jazz which featured Harry Edison and used charts by Johnny Mandel. The following year Kamuca was again on dates for Pacific, as a member of the Chet Baker-Art Pepper Sextet and also on a Bill Perkins album that included Pepper. In 1959, he again recorded with Pepper and was also featured on the highly successful live recordings made by Manne at the Black Hawk club in San Francisco. In the early 60s, Kamuca moved to New York, where he worked in a small group with Roy Eldridge, where he can be heard to particular effect on the mid-60s *Comin' Home Baby* sessions (released in 1978 on the Pumpkin label). He also became a member of the studio orchestra for the Merv Griffin television show. He was a founder member of Bill Berry's rehearsal band, which comprised mostly musicians from the studio orchestra, and when the Griffin show abruptly moved to Los Angeles, Kamuca went too. There, he worked with Berry in his re-formed big band, recording with him and under his own name for the Concord label. A fine player of ballads, with a warm and impassioned style, Kamuca's indebtedness to Lester Young is apparent, but he never slavishly followed his idol. One of his final 1977 recordings for the Concord label was dedicated to Charlie Parker, and throughout his later years he can be heard developing original ideas and gradually changing his style as he matured.

● ALBUMS: with Al Cohn, Bill Perkins *The Brothers!* (RCA Victor 1955)★★★★, with Art Pepper, Bill Perkins *Just Friends* (Pacific Jazz 1956)★★★, with Perkins *Tenors Head-On* (Liberty 1957)★★★★, *The Richie Kamuca Quartet* (Mode 1957)★★★★, *Jazz Erotica* reissued as *West Coast Jazz In Hifi* (Hifi Jazz 1959)★★★★, *Drop Me Off In Harlem* (Concord Jazz 1977)★★★★, *Richie* (Concord Jazz 1977)★★★, *Charlie* (Concord Jazz 1977)★★★.

KANSAS CITY JAZZ

During the late 20s and throughout the 30s Kansas City, Missouri, was an important centre for bands touring the southwest and mid-western states. Thanks to the corrupt political machine of city boss Tom Pendergast, with its benign tolerance of the seamier aspects of after-hours drinking and gambling joints, Kansas City became legendary as a place for jam sessions. Musicians with reputations earned elsewhere found themselves up against their peers, likewise passing through, and also confronted by strikingly talented unknowns. In time, these unknowns moved on, some into obscurity, others to become legends of jazz. Amongst the bands based in Kansas City, pride of place is generally granted to Bennie Moten's, although the leader's early death opened the way for others to attain positions of influence. Other leading bands of the region were Alphonso Trent, the Jeter-Pillars Orchestra, George E. Lee, Andy Kirk, Jap Allen, Harlan Leonard, Jesse Stone, George Morrison, Thamon Hayes, Clarence Love, Terrence T. Holder, Jay McShann and Count Basie, who took over the reins of the Moten band. Individual musicians who built or consolidated reputations in Kansas City included some who were local while others were from out of town, notably from Texas. These included Mary Lou Williams, Pete Johnson, Big Joe Turner, Walter Page, Jesse Price, A.G. Godley, Jo Jones, Ben Thigpen, Gus Johnson, Oran 'Hot Lips' Page, Harry Edison, Carl 'Tatti' Smith, Peanuts Holland, Buck Clayton, Buddy Anderson, Dickie Wells, Snub Mosely and Fred Beckett. The roster of saxophonists is especially notable and includes out-of-towners Buster Smith, Herschel Evans, Buddy Tate, Budd Johnson, Arnett Cobb, Dick Wilson, Eddie Barefield, Earle Warren, Tab Smith, Henry Bridges and Lester Young. Kansas City residents added to the list of saxophonists with Ben Webster and Charlie Parker. Stylistically, Kansas City jazz differed from the music developing simultaneously elsewhere in the USA. Bands in Kansas City and the southwest drew more heavily upon the blues and used looser arrangements, many of which were 'heads' created in rehearsal or on the stand by the musicians themselves. These arrangements had plenty of solo space and were backed by a subtle, free-flowing rhythmic drive. The music associated with the city, and exemplified by the early Basie band, eventually entered the public's consciousness by way of the swing era. In time, the style and many of its leading exponents became identified with what writer Stanley Dance would later term the 'mainstream' of jazz.

● FURTHER READING: *Jazz Style In Kansas City And The Southwest*, Ross Russell. *Jazz City: The Impact Of Our Cities On The Development Of Jazz*, Leroy Ostransky.

KASPERSEN, JAN

b. 22 April 1948, Copenhagen, Denmark. Composer and pianist Kaspersen's wry, quirky tunes reveal the influences of Thelonious Monk, Horace Silver and Abdullah Ibrahim, who, under the name of Dollar Brand, played regularly at the jazzhouse Montmartre in Copenhagen 1963/4. All have strong roots in Black church music and this may account for Kaspersen's attraction to the funky aspects of American jazz. Kaspersen's composition and playing never descend to mere pastiche or antiquarian seriousness but display a touch of ironic humour that appeals to both head and feet. Kaspersen has written for the Radio Big Band, for theatre, and performed with poets. He regularly records with his own ensemble, large or small.

● ALBUMS: *Bizarre Ballet* (Storyville 1983)★★★, *Puzzle In Four* (Olufsen 1985)★★★★, *Memories Of Monk* (Olufsen 1986)★★★, *Erik Satie-3 Gymnopedies* (Olufsen 1986)★★★★, *Love Eyes* (Olufsen 1987)★★★, *Space And Rhythm Jazz* (Olufsen 1987)★★★, *Ten By Two* (Olufsen 1987)★★★, *Special Occasion* (Olufsen 1990)★★★, *Live In Sofie's Cellar* (Olufsen 1991)★★★, *Heavy Smoke* (Olufsen 1992)★★★★, with Horace Parlan *Joinin' Forces* (Olufsen 1993)★★, *Live In Copenhagen Jazzhouse* (Olufsen 1994)★★, *Portrait In Space And Rhythm* (Olufsen 1997)★★★.

KAWAGUCHI, GEORGE

b. 15 June 1917, Fukakusa, Japan. As a child he was raised in Dairen, Manchuria, returning to Japan after World War II. In the late 40s he first played drums professionally, turning naturally to the newly popular jazz that came with the American occupation. During the 50s and afterwards, Kawaguchi played most often with his own bands, including the Big Four and the Big Two. He also accompanied visiting American musicians including fellow drummers Art Blakey, in 1981, and Elvin Jones, in the early 90s. His penchant for working with other drummers included recording sessions with countryman Motohiko Hino. A very strong player with a commanding technique, Kawaguchi enjoys extended solo excursions often with crowd-pleasing results. In the right company, however, and with his enthusiasm under control, he applies his considerable technique to the services of the band with great effect.

● ALBUMS: *Jazz At The Toris* (King 1957)★★★, *Yesterdays 1: The Original Big Four* (King 1959)★★★, *The Drum Battle: George Kawaguchi vs Motohiko Hino* (Teichiku 1975)★★, *The Original Big Four Live* (Philips 1977)★★★, *Super Drums* (Paddle Wheel 1979)★★★★, *African Hot Dance* (Electric Bird 1980)★★★, with Art Blakey *Killer Joe* (Union 1980)★★★, *Big 2 With Lionel Hampton* (Paddle Wheel 1982)★★.

KAWASAKI, RYO

b. 25 February 1947, Tokyo, Japan. Kawasaki chose a career as a guitarist after spending some years studying as a scientist. During the 60s he played with various Japanese jazz groups and also formed his own bands. In the early 70s he came to New York where he settled and found steady work in very distinguished company, including the bands of Gil Evans, Elvin Jones and JoAnne Brackeen. In the mid-80s, Kawasaki drifted out of performing music in favour of writing music software programmes for computers. He also produced several techno dance singles, forming his own company, Satellites Records, for their release. In 1991 he returned to jazz and proved to be as skilled and adept as ever on albums recorded for a Japanese label but marketed in the USA by his own company. Thanks to his long and wide experience, Kawasaki is able to switch with apparent ease between hard bop and jazz-rock. His playing is notable for its fluency and a sometimes hard-hitting style.

● ALBUMS: *Prism* (East Wind 1975)★★★, *Ryo* (Philips 1981)★★★, *Lucky Lady* (Teichiku-Continental 1982)★★★, *Here, There And Everywhere* (One Voice-Satellites 1991)★★★, *My Reverie* (One Voice-Satellites 1993)★★★, *Love Within The Universe* (One Voice-Satellites 1994)★★★, *Sweet Life* (One Voice-Satellites 1996)★★★, *Mirror Of My Mind* 1979 recording (One Voice-Satellites 1997)★★★, *Live* 1980 recording (One Voice-Satellites 1997)★★★, *Little Tree* 1980 recording (One Voice-Satellites 1997)★★★.

KAY, CONNIE

b. Conrad Henry Kirnon, 27 April 1927, Tuckahoe, New York, USA, d. 30 November 1994, New York City, New York, USA. A self-taught drummer, in his late teens Kay played with leading bop musicians, including Miles Davis. He gained big band experience with Cat Anderson late in the decade. In the early 50s, he was playing R&B in studio backing bands - but was mostly playing in small modern jazz groups with Lester Young, Stan Getz, Davis, Charlie Parker and others. In 1955, he took over from Kenny Clarke in the Modern Jazz Quartet, remaining with the group for the next 20 years. During these years he also performed with other artists on record dates, amongst them Chet Baker, Paul Desmond, Cannonball Adderley and fellow MJQ member John Lewis. He played on rock singer Van Morrison's 1968 masterpiece *Astral Weeks*. After the MJQ disbanded in 1974 Kay worked with Lewis and other jazzmen, including Benny Goodman in whose band he played at the Carnegie Hall 40th Anniversary Concert. In the late 70s he was mostly working in New York playing jazz-club dates which included several years in the house band at Eddie Condon's. In 1981, he was again a member of the MJQ when the group reformed. Despite his wide experience in several areas of jazz, Kay was understandably best known for his highly sophisticated work with the MJQ in which context he played with great subtlety and deftly understated swing.

KAZEBIER, NATE

b. Nathan Forrest Kazebier, 13 August 1912, Lawrence, Kansas, USA, d. 22 October 1996. Kazebier began playing trumpet as a small child and became a professional musician while still in his teens. His first name band was Jan Garber's which he joined in 1931, and in the middle of the decade he spent over a year with Benny Goodman. Later in the 30s he played in a succession of bands, including those led by Ray Noble and Seger Ellis, then joined Gene Krupa with whom he had recorded in 1935 on some outstanding small group sides. In 1940 he went into the Jimmy Dorsey band where he remained for more than three years. After a mid-40s spell in west coast film studios, Kazebier rejoined Goodman for a year, then returned to studio work. He continued to work in the studios with occasional jazz gigs for some years, although John Chilton indicates that for a while he worked as a golf professional in Reno. A well-rounded, trained musician, Kazebier often played lead trumpet in the bands with which he worked and was thus less well known than his soloing colleagues.

Nevertheless, he played an important role in the success of the bands with which he worked.

KEANE, ELLSWORTH 'SHAKE'

b. Ellsworth McGranahan Keane, 30 May 1927, St. Vincent, West Indies, d. 10 November 1997. Although taught music by his father as a child, Keane did not turn to the trumpet as a career until the mid-50s. Originally a teacher in St. Vincent, he came to England in 1952 to study English literature. He was already an accomplished poet - his nickname is short for 'Shakespeare' - with two collections of verse published, but could find no work in London except as a musician. For several years he played as a sideman in nightclubs and on recording sessions, performing calypso and Latin music as well as blues and jazz. One regular employer was calypso king Lord Kitchener, while a selection of tracks Keane originally made for the west African market with Guyanese pianist Mick McKenzie was reissued on the compilation *Caribbean Connections: Black Music In Britain In The Early 50s, Volume 2*. From 1959-65, Keane was a member of the Joe Harriott Quintet, which pioneered freeform and abstract jazz in the UK. Keane played on all their classic recordings, notably *Free Form*, *Abstract* and *Movement*. When the group disbanded in the mid-60s he moved to Germany, becoming a featured soloist with Kurt Edelhagen's Radio Band. In the 70s he returned to St. Vincent where he was Minister of Culture for several years, and published prize-winning books of poetry. In the early 80s, he settled in New York, where he occasionally played reggae and soca but spent most of his time writing poetry. In 1989, however, he toured the UK with the Joe Harriott Memorial Quintet, which also included original members Coleridge Goode and Bobby Orr. A documentary film was made in 1992 covering his early years in London at the Sunset Club. Equipped with flawless technique and brilliant invention, Keane - equally adept at calypso and bebop, freeform and classical - was recognized as one of the outstanding trumpeters of his generation. He died of cancer in November 1997. His son Roland Ramanan is a trumpeter and writer on jazz.

● ALBUMS: with Joe Harriott *Free Form* (1960)★★★, *In My Condition* (1961)★★★, with Harriott *Abstract* (1962)★★★, *Shake Keane And The Boss Men* (1962)★★, *The Shake Keane And Michael Garrick Quartet* (1963)★★, with Harriott *Movement* (1963)★★★, with Harriott *High Spirits* (1964)★★★, *Shake Keane And The Keating Sound* (1965)★★★, with Harriott *Indo-Jazz Fusions* (1966)★★★★, *Shake Keane And His Orchestra* i (1966)★★★, *Shake Keane And His Orchestra* ii (1968)★★★.

● FURTHER READING: *The Volcano Suite* (1979), *One A Week With Water*.

KELLAWAY, ROGER

b. 1 November 1939, Waban, Massachusetts, USA. Kellaway was initially attracted to jazz by the piano playing of George Shearing. He switched from piano to double bass and studied at the New England Conservatory (1957-59). He played the bass with Jimmy McPartland before returning to work full-time at the piano. In the mid-60s he played with the bands of Kai Winding, Al Cohn and Zoot Sims, and Clark Terry/Bob Brookmeyer, as well as working in the studios with musicians as varied as Ben Webster, Wes Montgomery and Sonny Rollins. In 1966, he moved to Los Angeles and played with the Don Ellis band. Since the late 60s he has worked as musical director for Bobby Darin (1967-69) and concentrated on studio work with musicians as diverse as Joni Mitchell and Jimmy Knepper. He has written numerous film scores including *The Paper Lion* (1968), *A Star Is Born* (1976) and *Breathless* (1983), as well as writing a ballet *PAMTGG* (1971), commissioned by George Balanchine and *Portraits Of Time* (1983), commissioned by the Los Angeles Philharmonic Orchestra. In 1984, he returned to New York to studio work and a duo with Dick Hyman. In the mid-90s he recorded an interesting album with cornetist Ruby Braff.

● ALBUMS: *Portrait Of Roger Kellaway* (Regina 1963)★★★★, *Roger Kellaway Trio* (Prestige 1965)★★★★, *Stride* (World Pacific 1967)★★★★, *Spirit Feel* (Pacific Jazz 1967)★★★, *Cello Quartet* (1971)★★★, *Come To The Meadow* (1974)★★★, *Nostalgia Suite* (1978)★★★, *Say That Again* (1978)★★, *Fifty-Fifty* (Natasha 1987)★★★, with Red Mitchell *Alone Together* (Dragon 1989)★★, *In Japan* (All Art Jazz 1987)★★, with Red Mitchell *Life's A Take* (Concord Jazz 1982)★★★★, *Live At the Maybank Recital Hall Vol II* (Concord Jazz 1991)★★★, with Gene Bertoncini, Michael Moore *Roger Kellaway Meets The Duo* (Chiaroscuro 1996)★★★, with Ruby Braff *Inside And Out* (Concord Jazz 1996)★★★.

KELLEY, PECK

b. John Dickson Kelley, 1898, Houston, Texas, USA, d. 26 December 1980. In the early 20s pianist Kelley led a band, Peck's Bad Boys, which featured several excellent musicians who were then beginning their careers. They included Jack Teagarden and Pee Wee Russell. Although he made occasional trips to mid-western cities and also to New Orleans, Kelley concentrated his career on his home town. He resisted offers to join important bands such as those of Paul Whiteman and both Tommy and Jimmy Dorsey, and continued playing in self-imposed obscurity. His reputation among fellow musicians was very high, but his first formal recordings were not made until he was almost 60 and partially blind. Even allowing for the ravages of time and health, these records support the view that in his prime he must have been a formidable talent. Further evidence emerged with the release, in 1987, of an album containing earlier recordings. Home-made and with some reminiscing by Kelley, but with astonishing bursts of bravura piano-playing, they go a long way to proving that this time, at least, the legend was right. Kelley eventually became totally blind and died in December 1980, in the obscurity he had sought during his lifetime.

● ALBUMS: with the Dick Shannon Quartet *Peck Kelley Jam, Volumes 1 & 2 (1957)* (1987)★★★.

KELLIN, ORANGE

b. Örjan Kjellin, 21 July 1944, Ljungby, Sweden. Kellin began playing clarinet at the age of 15 and two years later formed his first band in partnership with pianist Lars Edegran. The band played music in the New Orleans manner. Kellin made his first records in his native Sweden at the age of 17. In 1966, he moved to New Orleans where he became a regular performer at several leading jazz venues including the Preservation Hall. In 1968 he was a founder member of the New Orleans Ragtime Orchestra. He also led his own bands in the city including, in 1970, a band which held a residency at the Maison Bourbon Club. Two years later he formed the New Orleans Joymakers. Kellin recorded with several veteran New Orleans musicians including Josiah 'Cié' Frazier, Preston Jackson, Jim Robinson, Jabbo Smith, Zutty Singleton and Kid Thomas Valentine. In 1978, Kellin played with the NORO for the soundtrack of the film *Pretty Baby*. The following year he appeared in New York with the stage musical *One Mo' Time* for which he was musical director and co-arranger in addition to playing in the onstage band. In the early 80s he appeared with the same show during its long and successful run in London's West End. Kellin has toured extensively with his own bands and with bands formed largely from New Orleans veterans. In 1992 he made his first solo tour of the UK. A gifted and highly musicianly clarinettist, Kellin's dedication to the music of New Orleans has contributed greatly to the preservation of the style. He has an excellent technique and solos with flair and eloquence. As an admirable ensemble player, he lends authority to any group of which he is a member.

● ALBUMS: *Orange Kellin In New Orleans* i (1967)★★★, *Orange Kellin In New Orleans* ii (1967)★★, *Scandanavians In New Orleans* (c.1971)★★★, *New Orleans Ragtime Orchestra* (1971)★★★, *Pretty Baby* film soundtrack (1978)★★.

KELLY, CHRIS

b. 18 October c.1890, Deer Range Plantation, Louisiana, USA, d. 19 August 1929. Resident in New Orleans from around 1915, Kelly began playing cornet and eventually led his own bands. His reputation rests entirely upon hearsay for he never recorded. Reports suggest that he was an exciting player who could, when occasion demanded, play with deep feeling. His most popular number was 'Careless Love'. Kelly led a riotous life, drank heavily, and died young. Amongst the musicians with whom he worked, and from whom stem most of what is known of this legendary character of early jazz, were George Lewis and Kid Howard. The latter reputedly adopted many facets of Kelly's style.

KELLY, GEORGE

b. 31 July 1915, Miami, Florida, USA, d. 24 May 1998. Kelly began playing tenor saxophone in childhood and was a bandleader in his home state while still in his teenage years. After playing with several territory bands during the late 30s he joined Al Cooper's Savoy Sultans in New York. After leaving the Sultans, he played in and around New York for the rest of the 40s and on through the 50s. He also worked as a commercial arranger and songwriter, with his songs covered by artists including Sarah Vaughan. After playing with drummer William 'Cozy' Cole's quintet for a lengthy period, Kelly switched to piano as accompanist for the Ink Spots from 1970-76. Occasional visits further afield attracted a small amount of attention, but it was not until the late 70s that he made an impact on the jazz world's consciousness. In 1979, David 'Panama' Francis, who had played in Kelly's Florida band, formed a new version of the Savoy Sultans and invited Kelly into the group. Thanks to successful records and hugely popular appearances at festivals around the world, Kelly's qualities were widely recognized. During the 80s and into the early 90s he worked with Francis and led his own bands for tours and record dates, amongst which was a set paying tribute to Don Redman on which Kelly was joined by Glenn Zottola. A fine tenor saxophonist with a relaxed style, Kelly was also an accomplished arranger and entertaining singer.

● ALBUMS: *Stealin' Apples* (1976)★★★, *George Kelly In Cimiez* (1979)★★★, with David 'Panama' Francis *Gettin' In The Groove* (1979)★★, *Fine And Dandy* (1982)★★★★, *Live At The West End Cafe* (1982)★★, *The Cotton Club* (1983)★★★, *George Kelly Plays The Music Of Don Redman* (Stash 1984)★★★.

KELLY, PAULA

b. 1920, USA, d. 2 April 1992, Costa Mesa, California, USA. An excellent band and ensemble singer with a vivacious personality, Kelly began her career in 1937 with top saxophonist Dick Stabile's band, and then spent two years with Al Donahue. She joined Glenn Miller in 1941 as a featured singer with the Modernaires vocal group; her husband, Hal Dickinson, was founder-leader. Early in 1941 Kelly appeared in the first Glenn Miller movie, *Sun Valley Serenade*, in which the Modernaires sang classics such as 'Chattanooga Choo Choo' and 'I Know Why'. Later in the year she left Miller when former vocalist Marion Hutton rejoined the band. For a while Kelly sang with Artie Shaw, and then for Bob Allen's band. In the mid-40s she rejoined the Modernaires when the group expanded to five. In the 50s they appeared in clubs and theatres, toured with Bob Crosby, and sang on his radio and television shows. They also featured with Crosby, Frankie Laine and Billy Daniels in the movie *When You're Smiling* (1950), and in *The Glenn Miller Story* (1954). After Dickinson died on 18 November 1970, Kelly and the Modernaires worked with ex-Miller sideman Tex Beneke's band and Miller's original boy vocalist, Ray Eberle, riding on the nostalgia boom of the 70s. Kelly's records with the Modernaires included 'Jukebox Saturday Night', 'There, I've Said It Again', 'You Belong To My Heart', 'Goody Goody', 'Margie' and 'Stop, Look And Listen'. With Dick Stabile she recorded 'Lost And Found' and 'My Heart Is Taking Lessons'; with Al Donahue, 'Jeepers Creepers', 'Moon Love', 'The Lambeth Walk', 'Stairway To The Stars' and 'South American Way'; and with Artie Shaw, 'Someone's

Rocking My Dreamboat' and 'I Don't Want To Walk Without You'. Kelly retired in 1978, and in the late 80s her daughter, Paula Kelly Jnr., was reported to be singing an updated version of 'Jukebox Saturday Night' with the Modernaires, accompanied by a 15-piece band led by the same Tex Beneke.

KELLY, WYNTON

b. 2 December 1931, Jamaica, West Indies, d. 12 April 1971. Raised in New York, Kelly first played piano professionally with various R&B bands, where his musical associates included Eddie 'Lockjaw' Davis. In the early 50s, he played with Dizzy Gillespie, Dinah Washington and Lester Young. In 1954, after military service, he rejoined both Gillespie and Washington for brief stints and later played with many important contemporary musicians, notably Charles Mingus and Miles Davis, with whom he worked from 1959-63. Kelly also led his own trio, using the bass (Paul Chambers) and drums (Jimmy Cobb) from Davis' band, and also recorded successfully with a variety of artists such as Wes Montgomery, Freddie Hubbard and George Coleman. A subtle and inventive player, Kelly's style was individual even if his work denotes his awareness both of his contemporaries and the piano masters of an earlier generation. Throughout his records there is a constant sense of freshness and an expanding maturity of talent, which made his death, in 1971, following an epileptic fit, all the more tragic.

● ALBUMS: *Piano Interpretations By Wynton Kelly* 10-inch album (Blue Note 1953)★★★, *Wynton Kelly Piano* reissued as *Whisper Not* (Riverside 1957)★★★, with Steve Lacy *Soprano Today* reissued as *With Wynton Kelly* (Prestige 1958)★★★★, *Autumn Leaves* (1959)★★★, *Kelly Blue* (Riverside 1959)★★★★★, *Kelly Great!* (Vee Jay 1960)★★★, *Kelly At Midnight* (Vee Jay 1960)★★★, *Wynton Kelly* (Vee Jay 1961)★★★, *The Best Of Wynton Kelly* (Vee Jay 1963)★★★, *Comin' In The Back Door* (Verve 1964)★★★, *It's All Right* (Verve 1964)★★★★, *Undiluted* (Verve 1965)★★★, with Wes Montgomery *Smokin' At The Half Note* (Verve 1965)★★★, *Blues On Purpose* (Xanadu 1965)★★★, *Full View* (Milestone 1968)★★★★, *Wynton Kelly And George Coleman In Concert* (1968)★★★, *In Concert* (Affinity 1981)★★★, *Live In Baltimore* (Affinity 1984)★★★, *Wrinkles* (Affinity 1986)★★★, *Last Trio Session* (Delmark 1988)★★★, *Takin' Charge* 1961 recording (Charly 1993)★★★★.

KELLY BLUE - WYNTON KELLY TRIO & SEXTET

From the opening flute played by Bobby Jasper, the listener is immediately hooked and welcomed; Kelly's piano floats in, his fingers landing like a butterfly. The title track opens this album, and although all the other tracks are excellent, the album is worth the price of this one piece. The cool support in addition to Jasper comes from Nat Adderley (cornet), Benny Golson (tenor), Paul Chambers (bass) and Jimmy Cobb (drums). This is an amaxingly relaxed album with Kelly at times seemingly only breathing on the keys. The CD reissue has the bonus of the third take of 'Keep It Moving': only serious buffs will notice the difference. An essential album, often overlooked by the populist vote.

● Tracks: *Kelly Blue; Soflty, As In A Morning Sunrise; Do Nothin' Till You Hear From Me; On Green Dolphin Street; Willow Weep For Me; Keep It Moving (take four); Keep It Moving (take three); Old Clothes.*

● First released 1960

● UK peak chart position: did not chart

● USA peak chart position: did not chart

KENNEDY, JESSE 'TINY'

b. 20 December 1925, probably Chattanooga, Tennessee, USA. Blues shouter Kennedy first came to prominence in Kansas City in November 1949, where he recorded a session for Capitol Records with Jay McShann's Quintet. In 1951, he joined Tiny Bradshaw's Orchestra as vocalist, recording two unusual tracks with Bradshaw's band for King Records; the tracks were curious in that the two risqué blues feature Kennedy duetting with himself as both deep-voiced macho male and shrill female! While touring with the orchestra in the south in 1951-52, Kennedy made some recordings under his own name with local musicians for Trumpet Records at Sam Phillips' Sun studio in Memphis, including the successful 'Strange Kind Of Feelin'', which was later covered by Elmore James. Gotham Records' 20th Century subsidiary leased the hit for the northern market, and Trumpet Records tried unsuccessfully to record another hit by Kennedy in New York City in 1953. Nevertheless, he recorded a fine session for RCA-Victor's Groove subsidiary in April 1955 as the contradictory 'Big Tiny Kennedy'; the recordings included a remake of his Trumpet hit, after which he seems to have drifted into obscurity.

● ALBUMS: with Clayton Love, Jerry 'Boogie' McCain *Strange Kind Of Feelin'* (1990)★★★.

KENNEY, BEVERLY

b. USA. Although her name is not very well known outside the USA or, indeed, in more recent years, in the late 50s and early 60s Kenney made several very good albums. Among these were sessions with top-flight musicians such as Ralph Burns, Ellis Larkins, and a Jimmy Jones-led band featuring several ex-Count Basie band stalwarts including Joe Newman, Freddie Green and Jo Jones. Her rich voice and eloquent phrasing made her singer of quality and the reissue of several of her albums on CD brought her to the attention of aficionados of the great standards.

● ALBUMS: *Beverly Kenney Sings For Jimmy Smith* (Roost/Fresh Sounds 1956)★★★, *Come Swing With Me* (Roost 1956)★★★★, *Beverly Kenney With Jimmy Jones And The Basie-ites* (Roost/Fresh Sounds 1956)★★★, *Beverly Kenney Sings For Playboys* (Decca/Fresh Sounds 1958)★★★ *Born To Be Blue* (Decca 1959)★★★★, *Like Yesterday* (Decca 1960)★★★.

KENT, STACEY

b. 27 March 1968, USA. Starting to sing as a child, Kent never thought of singing as a career, treating it only as a hobby. She took a degree in comparative literature, also studying languages. After graduation she visited

England, 'just to get away', and while in London decided to take a post-graduate course in jazz. This brought her into contact with musicians and she began singing and soon found offers of work coming in. She was soon working at prestigious venues including Ronnie Scott's, the Purcell Room, Pizza On The Park, the 100 Club and the Barbican, appearing with the Vile Bodies Swing Orchestra, resident at London's Ritz Hotel from 1991-95, and also with her own group which features saxophonist Jim Tomlinson to whom she is married. Kent has toured the UK and appeared in and sung on the soundtrack of the 1995 film, *Richard III*. A self-taught singer, 'I just listened a lot', Kent was influenced before she knew she would be a singer by a wide range of artists including Louis Armstrong, Ella Fitzgerald, Frank Sinatra and Billie Holiday, together with instrumentalists Stan Getz, Duke Ellington, Ben Webster, Charlie Christian and Django Reinhardt. Her repertoire is eclectic but draws heavily upon the Great American Song Book to which she is devoted. Kent sings expressively, displays great understanding of and emotional involvement with her material, and she swings. Casual though her drift into jazz singing was, she is clearly a serious talent.

● ALBUMS: *Stacey Kent Sings* (SK 1995)★★★, *Close Your Eyes* (Candid 1997)★★★, *Love Is ... The Tender Trap* (Candid 1998)★★★★.

KENTON, STAN

b. 15 December 1911, Wichita, Kansas, USA, d. 25 August 1979. After playing piano in various dance bands, including those of Everett Hoagland and Vido Musso, mostly on the west coast, Kenton decided to form his own band in 1941. Although geared partially to the commercial needs of the dancehall circuit of the time, Kenton's band, which he termed the 'Artistry In Rhythm' orchestra, also featured powerful brass section work and imaginative saxophone voicings, unlike those of his more orthodox competitors. The band developed a substantial following among the younger elements of the audience who liked their music brash and loud. During the remainder of the 40s Kenton's popularity increased dramatically, seemingly immune to the declining fortunes that affected other bands. A succession of exciting young jazz musicians came into the band, among them Buddy Childers, Art Pepper, Kai Winding, Shelly Manne, Bob Cooper and Laurindo Almeida, playing arrangements by Kenton, Gene Roland and Pete Rugolo. His singers included Anita O'Day, June Christy and Chris Connor. In the 50s, his enthusiasm undimmed, Kenton introduced a 43-piece band, his 'Innovations In Modern Music' orchestra, again featuring Pepper and Manne as well as newcomers such as Maynard Ferguson and Bud Shank. Complex, quasi-classical arrangements by Bob Graettinger and others proved less appealing, but a 1953 tour of Europe ensured Kenton's international reputation. Reduced to a more manageable 19-piece, his New Concepts In Artistry In Rhythm band continued playing concerts and recording, using arrangements by Roland, Gerry Mulligan and Johnny Richards. Always eager to try new ideas, and to clearly label them, in the 60s Kenton introduced his 'New Era In Modern Music' orchestra, a 23-piece band using mellophoniums, and the 'Neophonic' orchestra, five pieces larger and tempting fate with neo-classical music. In the 70s, he embraced rock rhythms and looked as if he might go on forever. By 1977, however, his health had begun to deteriorate and although he returned from hospitalization to lead his band until August 1978, his bandleading days were almost over. He died in August 1979.

More than most bandleaders, Kenton polarized jazz fans, inspiring either love or hatred and only rarely meeting with indifference. Almost half a century after the event it is hard to understand what all the fuss was about. Certainly the band did not swing with the grace of, for example, the Jimmie Lunceford band, but it was equally wrong to declare, as many critics did, that Kenton never swung at all. Although some of the arrangements were too monolithic for effective jazz performances, the abilities of his key soloists were seldom buried for long. Kenton's band was important in bringing together many excellent musicians and for allowing arrangers free rein to experiment in big band concepts, a practice that few other leaders of the period would tolerate.

● ALBUMS: *Stan Kenton At The Hollywood Palladium* (1945)★★★, *Progressive Jazz* (1946-47)★★★, *One Night Stand With Nat 'King' Cole And Stan Kenton* (1947)★★★, *One Night Stand At The Commodore* (1947)★★★, *Stan Kenton And His Orchestra With June Christy* (1949)★★★★, *Encores* 10-inch album (Capitol 1950)★★★, *Innovations In Modern Music* 10-inch album (Capitol 1950)★★★★, *Milestones* 10-inch album (Capitol 1950)★★★, *Artistry In Rhythm* 10-inch album (Capitol 1950)★★★★, *A Presentation Of Progressive Jazz* 10-inch album (Capitol 1950)★★★, *One Night Stand With Stan Kenton* i (1950)★★★, *Stan Kenton Presents* 10-inch album (Capitol 1950)★★★★, *Nineteen Fifty-One* (1951)★★★, *One Night Stand With Stan Kenton* ii (1951)★★★, *Carnegie* (1951)★★★★, with Charlie Parker *Kenton And Bird* (1951-54)★★★, *Artistry In Tango* (1951-52)★★★, *Concert In Miniature* (1952)★★★, *Classics* 10-inch album (Capitol 1952)★★★, *City Of Glass* 10-inch album (Capitol 1952)★★★★, *Concert In Miniature No 9 And 10* (1952)★★★, *Concert In Miniature No 11 And 12* (1952)★★★, *Concert In Miniature No 13 And 14* (1952)★★★, *New Concepts Of Artistry In Rhythm* (Capitol 1953)★★★★, *Concert Encores* (1953)★★★, *Prologue This Is An Orchestra* 10-inch album (Capitol 1953)★★★, *Popular Favorites* 10-inch album (Capitol 1953)★★★, *The Definitive Stan Kenton With Charlie Parker And Dizzy Gillespie* (1953-54)★★★, *Stan Kenton In Berlin* (1953)★★★, *Europe Fifty Three Part One and Two* (1953)★★★, *Paris, 1953* (1953)★★★, *Sketches On Standards* 10-inch album (Capitol 1953)★★★, *This Modern World* 10-inch album (Capitol 1953)★★★, *Stan Kenton Radio Transcriptions* 10-inch album (MacGregor 1953)★★★, *Portraits Of Standards* 10-inch album (Capitol 1953)★★★, *Artistry In Kenton* (1954)★★★, *Kenton Showcase - The Music Of Bill Russo* 10-inch album (Capitol 1954)★★★, *Kenton Showcase - The Music Of Bill Holman* 10-inch album (Capitol 1954)★★★, *Stan Kenton Festival* (1954)★★★, with June Christy *Duet* (Capitol 1955)★★★★, *Contemporary*

Concepts (Capitol 1955)★★★, *Stan Kenton In Hi-Fi* (Capitol 1956)★★★★, *Kenton In Concert* (1956)★★★, *Kenton In Stereo* (1956)★★★, *In Stockholm* (1956)★★★, *Cuban Fire!* (Capitol 1956)★★★★, *Kenton '56* (1956)★★★, *Rendez-vous With Kenton/At The Rendezvous Volume 1* (Capitol 1957)★★★, *Kenton With Voices* (Capitol 1957)★★★, *Back To Balboa* (Capitol 1958)★★★, *Lush Interlude* (Capitol 1958)★★★, *The Stage Door Swings* (Capitol 1958)★★★, *On The Road* (1958)★★★, *The Kenton Touch* (Capitol 1958)★★★, *The Ballad Style Of Stan Kenton* (Capitol 1958)★★★, *Stan Kenton At The Tropicana* (Capitol 1959)★★★, *In New Jersey* (1959)★★★, *At Ukiah* (1959)★★★, *Viva Kenton* (Capitol 1959)★★★, with Christy *The Road Show, Volumes 1 & 2* (Capitol 1960)★★★, with Ann Richards *Two Much* (1960)★★★, with Christy *Together Again* (Capitol 1960)★★★, *Standards In Silhouette* (Capitol 1960)★★★, *Stan Kenton's Christmas* (1961)★★, *The Romantic Approach* (Capitol 1961)★★★, *Stan Kenton's West Side Story* (Capitol 1961)★★★★, *Mellophonium Magic* (1961)★★★, *Sophisticated Approach* (1961)★★★, *Adventures In Standards* (1961)★★★, *Adventures In Blues* (Capitol 1961)★★★, *Adventures In Jazz* (Capitol 1961)★★★, *The Sound Of Sixty-Two* (1962)★★★, *Adventures In Time* (Capitol 1962)★★★, *Stan Kenton's Mellophonium Band* (Capitol 1962)★★★, *Artistry In Bossa Nova* (Capitol 1963)★★★, *Artistry In Voices And Brass* (Capitol 1963)★★★, *The Best Of Brant Inn* (1963)★★, *Kenton In England* (1963)★★★, *Wagner* (1964)★★★, *Stan Kenton Conducts The Los Angeles Neophonic Orchestra* (Capitol 1965)★★★, *Rhapsody In Blue* (1965)★★★, *Stan Kenton Conducts The Jazz Compositions Of Dee Barton* (Capitol 1968)★★★, *Live At Redlands University* (Creative World 1970)★★, *Live At Brigham Young University* (Creative World 1971)★★, *Live At Fairfield Hall, Croydon* (1972)★★, *Live At Butler University* (Creative World 1972)★★, *National Anthems Of The World* (1972)★★, *Stan Kenton Today* (London Philharmonic 1972)★★★, *Birthday In Britain* (Creative World 1973)★★, *7.5 On The Richter Scale* (Creative World 1973)★★, *Solo: Stan Kenton Without His Orchestra* (1973)★★, *Stan Kenton Plays Chicago* (Creative World 1974)★★, *Fire, Fury And Fun* (Creative World 1974)★★, *Kenton 1976* (Creative World 1976)★★, *Journey Into Capricorn* (Creative World 1976)★★, *Stan(dard) Kenton: Stan Kenton In Warsaw* (1976)★★★, *Stan Kenton In Europe* (1976)★★★, *Live At Sunset Ridge Country Club Chicago* (Magic 1977)★★, *Live In Cologne 1976 Vols. 1 and 2* (Magic 1977)★★, *Street Of Dreams* (Creative World 1977)★★, *Tunes And Topics* 1970 live recording (Tantara 1998)★★★.

● COMPILATIONS: *The Kenton Era (1940-53)* (Capitol 1955)★★★★, *Stan Kenton's Greatest Hits* (Capitol 1965)★★★★, *Stan Kenton's Greatest Hits (1943-51)* (1983)★★★★, *The Christy Years (1945-47)* (Creative World 1985)★★★★, *The Fabulous Alumni Of Stan Kenton (1945-56)* (Creative World 1985)★★★★, *Collection: 20 Golden Greats* (Deja Vu 1986)★★★★, *Retrospective 1943-1968* 4-CD box set (Capitol 1992)★★★★, *Best Of* (Capitol 1995)★★★★, *The Complete Capitol Studio Recordings Of Stan Kenton 1943-47* 7-CD/10-LP box set (Mosaic 1996)★★★★, *Broadcast Transcriptions (1941-1945)* (Music And Arts 1996)★★★.

● VIDEOS: *Stan Kenton And Frank Rosolino* (Kay Jazz 1988), *Stan Kenton And His Orchestra* (Kay Jazz 1988).

● FURTHER READING: *Straight Ahead: The Story Of Stan Kenton*, Carol Easton. *Stan Kenton: Artistry In Rhythm*, William F. Lee. *Stan Kenton: The Man And His Music*, Lillian Arganian.

KENYON, CAROL

b. *c.*1960, London, England. As a child Kenyon was encouraged to sing and dance, taking lessons and entering arts festival contests; she also played piano and listened to her father's collection of jazz records. While singing with a school choir at a music festival in Harrow she was heard by Guy Barker, a young musician who was also appearing there. With his encouragement she began moving towards a serious and focused interest in singing. With Barker, she joined Steam Heat, a local jazz-rock band, and was then encouraged by him to attend an engagement by the National Youth Jazz Orchestra. There, she sang 'Summertime' with the band and to such good effect that NYJO took her on as its first regular band singer, at the age of only 14. With a repertoire of quality songs, many of them written especially for her by Bill Ashton and others, Kenyon quickly became an integral part of the band's performances, singing with the ensemble in addition to performing solos. With NYJO she toured extensively, appeared on television and record, and at the Royal Command Variety Performance in 1978. On leaving NYJO, Kenyon sang with Car Park, an outfit formed from NYJO members, with the band led by Dick Morrissey and Jim Mullen, and frequently appeared on television in support of better-known artists. She also toured internationally with some of them, including Mick Jagger. She then joined Heaven 17, who in 1983 charted at number 2 in the UK with 'Temptation'. Signed to A&M Records and relaunched as the 'Warrior Woman', complete with gimmicky black leather gear and a live hawk, she made more records. She was then with Go West, and in 1986 teamed with Paul Hardcastle for further chart successes, particularly with 'Don't Waste My Time', which reached number 5. She continued to work on television and also sang on motion picture soundtracks, and in 1995 appeared again at the Royal Command Variety Performance, this time opening the show. Always singing with superb control and great flair, Kenyon's stylistic range appears unlimited. In addition to straight pop and the jazz-inflected ballads she sang with NYJO, she has also sung in a classical vein, performing memorably on NYJO's 'The Sherwood Forest Suite', composed by Paul Hart, and a 1996 album aimed at the elusive classical crossover market. An enormously versatile singer with a secure musical foundation, Kenyon seems well-placed to continue expanding her growing audience well into the twenty-first century.

● ALBUMS: with NYJO *Return Trip* (NYJO 1976)★★★, with NYJO *To Russia With Jazz* (NYJO 1977)★★★, *Go West* (Chrysalis 1986)★★.

KEPPARD, FREDDIE

b. 27 February 1890, New Orleans, Louisiana, USA, d. 15 July 1933, Chicago, Illinois, USA. Before choosing to play the cornet, Keppard experimented with various other instruments, none of which was especially suitable for performing jazz. In the years before World War I he played with the Olympia Orchestra in New Orleans and several other parade and concert bands. He was leader of the Original Creole Orchestra which toured California and the east coast, and also worked in Chicago. After the war Keppard settled in Chicago, where he worked with Joe 'King' Oliver, Jimmie Noone and other luminaries of the city's jazz scene. In the early 20s he played in various bands, sometimes leading his own, almost always in or around Chicago. Among the last bands with which he worked were those of Erskine Tate and Charlie Elgar. He seldom played after 1928 and died in July 1933. Keppard's few recordings barely support his status as a leading hornman of early jazz and a direct link to the legendary playing of Buddy Bolden. Nevertheless, there are suggestions of his qualities and it is hard to question the reputation he enjoyed among fellow musicians such as Sidney Bechet and Milt Hinton. Along with Edward 'Kid' Ory, Keppard was important in helping to spread jazz into areas of the west coast not previously familiar with the music.

● COMPILATIONS: *The Legend Of Freddie Keppard (1923-27)* (1973)★★★, *Freddie Keppard (1923-28)* (Jazz Treasury 1988)★★★★, *Complete Freddie Keppard 1923-1927* (King Jazz 1993)★★★★★.

KERR, TRUDY

b. 3 January 1963, Brisbane, Queensland, Australia. Singing from an early age, Kerr began her professional career in her homeland and among the Pacific Islands. In addition to playing clubs and festivals, she gained experience recording advertising jingles for radio and television. Set upon a career in jazz, she moved to London where she was accepted into the Guildhall School of Music and Drama on a post-graduate jazz course. This was in 1994, and the following year she was heard by Ronnie Scott who booked her for an engagement at his club. Other London club dates included the Pizza Express and the 606 Club, and she also toured throughout Europe. She works mostly with the younger generation of jazz musicians, including Dave O'Higgins and Mornington Lockett, but on a 1998 record date she was agreeably joined not only by Lockett but also by veteran Acker Bilk. Kerr's repertoire blends the great song standards with the best of contemporary compositions and she brings to them all originality of thought and interpretation. She sings with a mature sound, swings with subtlety, and develops her melodic and lyrical concepts with impeccable taste and great sensitivity.

● ALBUMS: *Sweet Surprise* (FMR 1997)★★★, *Trudy* (Jazzizit 1998)★★★.

KESSEL, BARNEY

b. 17 October 1923, Muskogee, Oklahoma, USA. After playing in various bands (including one led by Chico, the piano-playing Marx brother), Kessel began to establish a name for himself on the west coast. He appeared in the Norman Granz-produced short film *Jammin' The Blues* (1944), then played in various big bands of the late swing era. From the mid-40s he was in great demand for studio work, jazz record sessions, club and concert dates, and on tours with Jazz At The Philharmonic. Among the artists with whom he performed and recorded over the next 20 years were Charlie Parker, Oscar Peterson, Billie Holiday and Harry Edison. By the mid-60s he was one of the best-known and most-recorded guitarists in jazz. He continued to tour and record in groups and as a solo artist. In the early 70s, he teamed up with Herb Ellis and Charlie Byrd to perform as the group Great Guitars. This project continued to tour into the 80s, which saw Kessel as active as ever. An exceptionally gifted musician with a very wide range, Kessel's versatility has ensured that he is always in demand. In a jazz context he plays in a boppish, post-Charlie Christian style, but has his own distinctive flavour. In the context of Great Guitars, he ably fills the mid-ground between Byrd's latent classicism and Ellis's blues-tinged swing. In person, Kessel has a swift and waspish sense of humour, a characteristic which often appears in his music. He was incapacitated by a stroke in 1992.

● ALBUMS: *Barney Kessel Vol 1* (Contemporary 1953)★★★, *Barney Kessel Vol 2* (Contemporary 1954)★★★, *To Swing Or Not To Swing* (Contemporary 1955)★★★, *Plays Standards* (Contemporary 1955)★★★★, *Easy Like* (1956)★★★, *Sessions, Live* (1956)★★★, *Let's Cook* (1957)★★★, *Music To Listen To Barney Kessel By* (Contemporary 1957)★★★, with Holiday *Body And Soul* (1957)★★★★, *The Poll Winners* (Contemporary 1958)★★★★, *The Poll Winners Ride Again* (Contemporary (1959)★★★, *Some Like It Hot* (Contemporary 1959)★★★, *Plays Carmen* (Contemporary 1959)★★, *Workin' Out* (Contemporary 1961)★★★, *Breakfast At Tiffany's* (Reprise 1961)★★, *Bossa Nova Plus Big Band* (Reprise 1962)★★★, *Let's Cook* (Contemporary 1962)★★★, *Swingin' Party* (Contemporary 1963)★★★, *Kessel Jazz* (Reprise 1963)★★, *Feelin' Free* (Contemporary 1965)★★★, *On Fire* (Emerald 1965)★★★, *Swinging Easy* (1968)★★★, *Kessel's Kit* (1969)★★, with others *Limehouse Blues* (Black Lion 1969)★★★, *Autumn Leaves* (Black Lion 1970)★★★, *Just Friends* (Sonet 1973)★★★, with Ken Baldcock *Summertime In Montreux* (1973)★★★, *Yesterday* (Black Lion 1974)★★★★, as Great Guitars *Great Guitars* (Concord Jazz 1974)★★★, *Two-Way Conversation* (1975)★★★, *Three Guitars* (Concord 1975)★★★, *Plays Barney Kessel* (Concord 1975)★★, *Soaring* (Concord 1977)★★★, as Great Guitars *Great Guitars: Straight Tracks* (Concord Jazz 1978)★★★, *Live At Sometime* (Storyville 1978)★★★, as Great Guitars *Great Guitars At The Winery* (Concord Jazz 1980)★★★, *Jelly Beans* (Concord 1981)★★★, as Great Guitars *Great Guitars At Charlie's, Georgetown* (Concord 1982)★★★, *Solo* (Concord 1983)★★★★, *Spontaneous Combustion* (JVC 1987)★★★, *Kessel Plays Standards* (Contemporary 1989)★★★, *Red Hot And Blues* (Contemporary 1988)★★★★.

● COMPILATIONS: *The Artistry Of Barney Kessel* (Fantasy 1987)★★★.

KHAN, STEVE

b. 28 April 1947, Los Angeles, California, USA. Khan is the son of lyricist Sammy Cahn and learned to play the piano and drums as a child. He was the drummer with the surf group the Chantays (1962-63) and only turned to the guitar when he was 20. After graduating in music from UCLA in 1969, he settled in New York where he became a prolific session musician recording with artists as varied as George Benson, Hubert Laws, Maynard Ferguson, Billy Joel and Steely Dan. In 1977, he worked with Larry Coryell and Randy and Michael Brecker before touring Japan with the CBS All Stars. In 1978, he published a transcription of solos by Wes Montgomery. He has continued to develop his skills as a composer as can be seen in his tribute to pianist Thelonious Monk on *Evidence*. In 1981, he formed Eyewitness with Manolo Badrena, Anthony Jackson and Steve Jordan.

● ALBUMS: with Larry Coryell *Two For The Road* (1977)★★★★, *Tightrope* (1977)★★★★, *Evidence* (Arista 1980),★★★★ with Eyewitness *Eyewitness* (Antilles 1981)★★, with Eyewitness *Casa Loco* (1983)★★, *Local Colour* (Denon 1988)★★★, *Public Access* (GRP 1990)★★★, *Let's Call This* (Polydor 1991)★★★, *Headline* (Polydor 1993)★★, *Crossings* (Verve 1994)★★★, *Got My Mental* (Evidence 1997)★★★★.

● COMPILATIONS: *Best Of Steve Khan* (CBS 1980)★★★.

Kibbey, Sue

b. England. Singing as a child in school opened her mind to the joys of music. Although Kibbey sang in a school choir, she really wanted to be in the Music and Movement class and she had herself deliberately relegated there by singing out of tune: 'I knew enough at that age to know how to sing out of tune on purpose'. As a teenager she sang in choirs and at folk festivals. She also spent many years training as a dancer and became a qualified teacher of dance. As an adult she continued to sing, mostly pop with some jazz, but was diverted into marriage and children. After her fourth child and a divorce she sang on, gradually dropping all but jazz from her repertoire and gaining a reputation. In 1987 she studied jazz and rock at the Guildhall School of Music and Drama and in the 90s was teaching at the Royal Academy of Music. Kibbey has worked with many noted jazz musicians ranging stylistically from Acker Bilk and Bud Freeman to Harry Beckett and Tony Coe. In 1991 she was featured singer in a jazz suite composed by Michael Garrick. She has played jazz festivals in the USA, Europe and in the UK, including appearance at Sacramento, Köln and Ascona. Kibbey has also been featured at arts festivals including those at Bradford on Avon and Bath where, in 1994, she performed a one-woman show. She has also held residencies in Sweden and Japan. Kibbey's repertoire ranges widely across traditional and modern jazz and encompasses the best of popular songs. Her vocal range is similarly wide and she sings with great dramatic flair and has a commanding stage presence.

Kidd, Carol

b. 19 October 1945, Glasgow, Scotland. Kidd began her career singing in and around Glasgow in the early 60s, entering numerous talent shows where one of her regular fellow contestants was Marie McDonald, later to find fame as pop singer Lulu. At the age of 15, Kidd was singing with a traditional jazz band; two years later she married the trombone player and started a family, then spent a further five years with another trad band. By this time she was developing an appreciation of the finer aspects of popular music. Unfortunately, her options were limited, trad and rock being the only commercially viable choices. Frustrated at not being able to sing how and what she wanted, she retired from the music scene for four years, returning only when a Glasgow-based quartet asked her to join them for a Saturday morning session. She stayed for 11 years, the quartet evolving into a trio with which she worked regularly until early 1990. This long relationship proved invaluable in allowing Kidd to develop an extensive and well-honed repertoire that has at its centre a fine selection of standards. Her record albums, appearances at Ronnie Scott's and an annual engagement at the prestigious Edinburgh Festival helped to expand her audience. A series of concert appearances in 1989 and 1990 with Humphrey Lyttelton's band also opened new doors. Midway through 1990, with different accompanists, including the excellent pianist David Newton, and a wholesale change in her repertoire, Kidd re-launched her career. An invitation to open at a Frank Sinatra concert and an appearance at London's Queen Elizabeth Hall, in November 1990, helped to raise her career profile. Although she has still to achieve her ambition to appeal to more than a specialist jazz audience, there seems little chance that her rich talent will go unrecognized in the larger public arena through another decade. She was awarded an MBE in the Queen's Birthday Honours List in 1998.

● ALBUMS: *Carol Kidd* (Linn 1984)★★, *All My Tomorrows* (Linn 1985)★★★, *Nice Work (If You Can Get It)* (Linn 1987)★★★★, *Night We Called It A Day* (Linn 1990)★★★, *I'm Glad We Met* (Linn 1992)★★★, *When I Dream* (1992)★★★.

Kikuchi, Masabumi

b. 19 October 1939, Tokyo, Japan. Kikuchi took piano lessons from the age of five and studied music at Tokyo University (1955-58). He led his own trio in the early 60s when his playing displayed the influence of Thelonious Monk. He toured Japan with Lionel Hampton, recorded with Charlie Mariano and then toured with Sonny Rollins. In 1968 he went to the Berklee College Of Music in Boston, Massachusetts on a *Down Beat* magazine scholarship. The following year he returned to Japan where he led a trio with Gary Peacock and worked with visiting American musicians. He recorded an album with Gil Evans conducting a band of Japanese musicians. In the early 70s, he worked with Elvin Jones and, briefly, with McCoy Tyner. After 1974, he again worked regularly with Sonny Rollins as well as with the trumpet player, Terumasa Hino.

● ALBUMS: *Masabumi Kikuchi/Gil Evans* (1972)★★★, with Terumasa Hino *East Wind* (1974)★★★★, *Reconfirmation* (1970),★★★ *Doo Sun* (1970)★★★, *Dancing Mist* (1970)★★★★, *But Not For Me* (1978),★★★ *Susoto* (1980)★★★, *One Way Traveller* (1980)★★★, *Poesy* (Philips 1981)★★★, with Hino *Acoustic Boogie* (Blue Note 1996)★★★.

KILGORE, REBECCA

b. USA. Raised in New England, Kilgore played guitar and sang as a child. In 1979 she moved to Portland, Oregon, where she sang with a wide range of groups in many different musical styles, including a big band, a western swing group, and her own sextet, Beck-a-Roo. This group mostly performed country music hits from the 60s. Her jazz credentials were greatly enhanced through engagements with Dave Frishberg with whom she worked as a duo. She has also recorded with a mainstream band, Dan Barrett's Celestial Six. Kilgore sings with lithe swing and has a breathily engaging tone. Her repertoire ranges through the great song standards which she interprets with charm and felicity.

● ALBUMS: with Dan Barrett's Celestial Six *I Saw Stars* (Arbors 1996)★★★, with Dave Frishberg *Not A Care In The World* (Arbors 1997)★★★.

KILLIAN, AL

b. Albert Killian, 15 October 1916, Birmingham, Alabama, USA, d. 5 September 1950. Killian began playing trumpet as a child and in his late teens was regularly in New York. He worked with several bands in the late 30s including those of Teddy Hill and Don Redman and in 1940 joined Count Basie. During the 40s he had spells with Lionel Hampton, Charlie Barnet, Basie, Billy Eckstine, and also led his own band. He was also with Jazz At The Philharmonic and in the closing years of the decade was briefly with Boyd Raeburn and Duke Ellington, visiting Europe with the latter. A strong player with a distinctively aggressive style, he was alert to bop but was rooted in swing era concepts. He was murdered in 1950.

● ALBUMS: *Lester Young And Charlie Christian 1939-1940* (Jazz Archives 1939-40)★★★★, *Jazz Concert West Coast* (Regent 1947)★★★, *Duke Ellington Carnegie Hall Concert, December 1947* (Prestige 1947)★★★★.

KINCAIDE, DEANE

b. 18 March 1911, Houston, Texas, USA, d. 14 August 1992, St. Cloud, Florida, USA. Although he played saxophone in the Ben Pollack band of the early 30s and its successor, the highly successful Bob Crosby band, Kincaide's main talent was his arranging. Indeed, his charts were a principal factor in creating the distinctive two-beat style of the Crosby band. He later worked for Woody Herman and Tommy Dorsey as both arranger and musician. In the 40s Kincaide freelanced, his arrangements finding their way into the repertoire of several bands, including Glenn Miller's. After World War II, Kincaide continued much as before, writing for the Glenn Miller Orchestra and for films and television.

● ALBUMS: *The Solid South* (1959)★★.

KIND OF BLUE - MILES DAVIS

Advocates from the many corners of jazz will argue their points, some with bigoted passion and self-righteousness - a trait that has been known to follow some jazz buffs. When you find jazzers, rock and popular music followers unanimously united over one record, then you know something must be right. This album contains only five tracks, with musicians Julian Adderley (alto), John Coltrane (tenor), Bill Evans (piano), Paul Chambers (bass), James Cobb (drums) and Miles on trumpet. It is played with absolute cool perfection, not a drop of sweat or cigarette ash. There can be no debate, this is the greatest jazz album in the world ever; so what, just accept it.

● Tracks: *So What; Freddie Freeloader; Blue In Green; Al Blues; Flamenco Sketches.*

● First released 1960

● UK peak chart position: did not chart

● USA peak chart position: did not chart

KING OF JAZZ, THE

The title of this lavish and spectacular musical revue which was released by Universal in 1930 refers, of course, to Paul Whiteman, who led the most popular orchestra of his time. Although not a jazzman himself, he did promote that brand of music by employing many fine jazz musicians over the years, such as Joe Venuti, Eddie Lang, and Frankie Trumbauer. That trio are all featured prominently in this film along with Whiteman's most famous vocalist, Bing Crosby and his fellow Rhythm Boys Harry Barris and Al Rinker, plus a host of other artists including John Boles, Jeannie Lang, the Brox Sisters, William Kent, Grace Hayes, Stanley Smith, Jeanette Loff, Walter Brennan, Laura La Plante, and Slim Summerville. Inevitably the spotlight is very firmly on Paul Whiteman And His Orchestra throughout, from the opening 'Rhapsody In Blue' (George Gershwin), during which the entire orchestra seated inside - and at the keyboard - of a gigantic grand piano, through to the breathtaking finalé when, beginning with 'D'Ye Ken John Peel' and 'Santa Lucia', the music from various countries around the world is symbolically blended together in 'The Melting Pot Of Music'. In between those two amazing sequences, and introduced every time by a caption card giving song title and performer details, were well over 50 musical items ranging from folk and classical pieces to popular songs such as 'Mississippi Mud' (Harry Barris-James Cavanaugh), 'It Happened In Monterey' (Mabel Wayne-Billy Rose), 'So The Bluebirds And The Blackbirds Got Together' (Barris-Billy Moll), 'Ragamuffin Romeo' (Wayne-Harry DeCosta); and 'A Bench In The Park', 'Happy Feet', 'Music Hath Charms', and 'Song Of The Dawn' (all by Milton Ager and Jack Yellen). As well as conducting the orchestra, Whiteman appeared at other times in a variety of costumes (including baby clothes, complete with feeding bottle), mugging to the camera and looking not unlike Oliver Hardy *sans* Stan Laurel. Russell Markert staged the dances, and the sketches were written by John Murray Anderson who had enjoyed a great deal of success on Broadway with several editions of the *Greenwich Village Follies*, and his own *John Murray Anderson's Almanac*. He was also the director, the man responsible for assembling this whole marvellously original concept, parts of which eventually influenced many a future screen musical. Hal Mohr, Jerome Ash and Ray Rennahan photographed the film in two-colour Technicolor which gave the film a charm of its own, and contributed to the desire to watch it over again, if only to catch some of the details and bits of business missed the first time around.

KING, NORAH LEE

b. USA. King became quite well known in the 30s and early 40s, mostly singing the blues with flair, and developed an easy-going rapport with audiences. In the mid-40s she recorded with Mary Lou Williams but most of her later records found her in harness with her husband, Lawrence Lucie. In her early years, King performed and often recorded under a bewildering array of pseudonyms, including Lenore King, Lenore Kinsey, Susan King and Susan Lenore King.

● ALBUMS: all with Lawrence Lucie *Travellin' Guitars* (Request 50s)★★★, *Cool And Warm Guitar* (Toy 50s)★★★, *Mixed Emotions* (Toy 50s)★★★, *Sophisticated Lady/After Sundown* (Toy 50s)★★.

● COMPILATIONS: with Mary Lou Williams *The Asch Recordings, 1944-47* (Folkways 1944-47)★★★★.

KING, PETER

b. 11 August 1940, Kingston-upon-Thames, Surrey, England. Self-taught on several reed instruments, by the late 50s King had established himself as an important and exciting alto saxophonist on the UK jazz scene. Over the next few years he worked with John Dankworth, Tubby Hayes, Stan Tracey and other leading British musicians. He also worked with numerous visiting American artists, ranging stylistically from Ray Charles to Red Rodney, from Jimmy Witherspoon to Hampton Hawes. By the 70s King's stature had grown until he was on the verge of becoming a major international figure. During the 80s he consolidated his gains and amply fulfilled his potential. In the early 90s King was one of the world's outstanding hard bop alto saxophonists. Playing with a hard-edged brilliant tone, his remarkable agility and technical virtuosity are at the command of an exceptionally fast mind. Although his remarkable imagination and improvisational ability are best displayed on up-tempo tunes he is also a lyrical balladeer. His latest release, an attempt to reach a wider audience, was co-produced by Everything But The Girl's Ben Watt.

● ALBUMS: *My Kind Of Country* (Tank 1977)★★, *New Beginning* (Spotlite 1982)★★★, *East 34th Street* (Spotlite 1983)★★★, *Hi Fly* (Spotlite 1984)★★★, *90% Of 1%* (Spotlite 1985)★★★, *Live At The Bull* (1987)★★, with Guy Barker *Brother Bernard* (Miles 1988)★★★, *Blues For Buddy* (1988)★★★, *Crusade* (Blanco Y Negro 1989)★★★, *New Years' Morning '89* (1989)★★★.

KING, SANDRA

b. 12 October 1950, London, England. King's family background included singers and other performing artists and by the age of nine she knew that she was to be a singer. At 16 years old she was heard by Mark Murphy who recommended her to Ronnie Scott who in turn booked her into his club. In the late 60s she sang with the National Youth Jazz Orchestra, touring eastern Europe. She continued to work in the UK and Europe for some years, receiving accolades from many distinguished musicians including Henry Mancini ('an extraordinary artist for her age, in fact, for any age'). In 1981 while at Ronnie Scott's she was asked by Stan Getz to sing with him. For many years her musical mentor was Pat Smythe who accompanied her in 1985 when she sang at the Corcoran Gallery of Art in Washington, DC, performing a concert of songs by Vernon Duke. The concert won a rave review from John S. Wilson in the New York *Times* and the subsequent release of an album recorded at the concert was a major breakthrough. She made more dates, for Audiophile Records including a set of Jimmy Van Heusen songs with Richard Rodney Bennett, and continued to work in the USA, where she was based mostly from 1986-93. Nevertheless, she found time during this period for appearances in Copenhagen in 1988 with the Thad Jones big band and in 1994 in The Netherlands with Robert Farnon. In the mid-90s King has worked in the UK and Europe, with more US visits and albums planned for the late 90s. Quite clearly, her career is still on an upward curve. King has a deep, richly expressive voice and sings with enormous charm, skill and integrity.

● ALBUMS: *Warm And Swingin: The Songs Of Henry Mancini* (Avenue 1970)★★★, *The Sentimental Touch Of Albert Van Dam* (RCA 1984)★★, *Sandra King In A Concert Of Vernon Duke* (Audiophile 1985)★★★, *Magic Window: The Songs Of Jimmy Van Heusen* (Audiophile 1988)★★★★.

KING, STAN

b. 1900, Hartford, Connecticut, USA, d. 19 November 1949. King played drums part-time for a number of years before heading for New York and a full-time career in music. He worked with several leading dance bands, including those led by Roger Wolfe Kahn and Paul Whiteman and he also played jazz with the California Ramblers. By the early 30s he had become a respected and sought-after studio musician in New York and he also played in the bands of Benny Goodman and Joe Haymes. King performed in jazz groups supporting leading artists such as Jack Teagarden and Louis Armstrong. He was an exceptionally good dance band drummer with meticulous time; however, his jazz work always left something to be desired. Listening to, for example, Goodman's recordings in late 1934 will reveal how King's playing never lifts the band in the way Gene Krupa did when he took over as drummer in December that year. In his own field, however, that of dance music, King was always a very good drummer.

KINSEY, TONY

b. 11 October 1927, Sutton Coldfield, West Midlands, England. Kinsey was a key drummer in the London jazz scene of the 50s, having studied formally in the UK and USA before joining the John Dankworth Seven in 1950. He later formed his own groups, working with many leading jazz musicians, including Joe Harriott, Peter King and a succession of visiting American stars. Kinsey's early musical studies had extended into composition, and he has written many longer works for jazz orchestra and for classical groups. He has also written for films and television, but in the late 80s was still leading his small jazz groups around London clubs. As a skilful technician, Kinsey is comfortable playing in bebop or mainstream settings and is an outstanding jazz drummer.

● ALBUMS: *Starboard Bow* (1955)★★★, *Jazz At The Flamingo* (1956)★★★★, *The Tony Kinsey Quartet* (1957)★★★★, *The Tony Kinsey Quintet* i (1957)★★★, *The Tony Kinsey Quintet* ii (1958)★★★, *The Tony Kinsey Quintet* iii (1959)★★, *Foursome* (1959)★★, *The Tony Kinsey Quintet* iv (1961)★★★, *How To Succeed In Business* (1963)★★, *The Thames Suite* (Spotlite 1976)★★★.

KIRBY, JOHN

b. 31 December 1908, Baltimore, Maryland, USA, d. 14 June 1952. Kirby's career began in New York but suffered a hiatus when his first instrument, a trombone, was stolen. Replacing this with a tuba, he resumed his musical career, joining Fletcher Henderson in 1930. Soon after this he began using a string bass, at first alternating between the two instruments. He spent about two years with Chick Webb, then rejoined Henderson, but in 1937 decided to form his own band. Securing a residency at New York's Onyx Club, Kirby set about melding his group into a smooth, thoroughly rehearsed and musicianly outfit. Although this was the height of the big band-dominated swing era, he settled on a six-piece band and within a year saw his judgement pay off. The John Kirby Sextet, billed as 'The Biggest Little Band In The Land', became the yardstick by which nearly all sophisticated small jazz groups were measured. For most of the band's four-year existence the personnel was stable; Charlie Shavers, Buster Bailey, Russell Procope, Billy Kyle and drummer O'Neill Spencer. The addition of Kirby's wife, Maxine Sullivan, did the group's popularity no harm at all. The group disbanded with the onset of World War II and, although Kirby re-formed after the war, he never again achieved either the quality or the popularity of his first band. He was planning a comeback when he died in June 1952.

● ALBUMS: *John Kirby* (Atlantic 1986)★★★, *The Biggest Little Band In The Land (1938-41)* (Giants Of Jazz 1987)★★★, *John Kirby And His Orchestra, With Maxine Sullivan* (1988)★★★, *More* (Circle 1988)★★, *John Kirby And Onyx Club Boys Volumes 1-4* (Collectors Classics 1988)★★★, *John Kirby And His Orchestra* (Circle 1988), *Biggest Little Band* (Columbia 1993)★★★★.

KIRK, ANDY

b. 28 May 1898, Newport, Kentucky, USA, d. 11 December 1992, New York, USA. Raised in Colorado, Kirk dabbled in music as a child, learning to play several instruments. He studied assiduously, one of his tutors being Wilberforce Whiteman, father of Paul Whiteman. Kirk played in several bands in and around Denver, in particular that led by George Morrison which played popular music of the day mixed with a smattering of light classics. It was a solid musical apprenticeship for the young man, but he was cautious about his career and all the while kept other regular employment. In 1927, he moved to Dallas, Texas, where he joined Terrence Holder's band, the Dark Clouds Of Joy. By this time Kirk was mostly playing tuba, doubling on baritone and bass saxophones. In 1929, Holder, an erratic individual with his own ideas on how to run the band's finances, was persuaded to quit and Kirk took over leadership. The band's name underwent various minor changes but thereafter was mostly known as Andy Kirk And His Clouds Of Joy. At the instigation of George E. Lee, the band auditioned for and obtained an engagement at Kansas City's prestigious Pla-Mor Restaurant. During their stay at the Pla-Mor the band auditioned again, this time for a recording contract. When Marion Jackson, the regular pianist, could not make the date, Kirk brought in Mary Lou Williams. In addition to playing on the date, Williams also supplied several arrangements, some of which were of her own compositions. She so impressed the record company's executives, Jack Kapp and Dick Voynow, that they insisted she appear on all the band's record dates. Soon afterwards, Jackson tired of this implied slur, quit the band. Williams joined the band full-time and quickly became one of its most important and influential members. The band's personnel was relatively stable over the years and included many excellent musicians such as Buddy Tate (tenor saxophone), Edgar Battle (trumpet), Claude Williams (violin), Ben Thigpen (drums), Pha Terrell (vocals) and Mary Lou's husband, John Williams (alto saxophone). A subtly swinging band, epitomizing the best of the more commercial end of the Kansas City Jazz sound, the Clouds Of Joy enjoyed several years of success. There were difficult moments, not least in early 1931 when the band had to take engagements and record dates under the nominal leadership of Blanche Calloway, but they survived into the late 40s. The size of the band, usually ranging between 11-13 pieces, meant that it was smaller than the average swing era big band and this, allied to Mary Lou Williams's skilful charts, gave it an enviable cohesion. Mary Lou Williams left in 1942 to develop her remarkable career. Williams apart, the band's outstanding soloist was tenor saxophonist Dick Wilson. A light-toned player with a sound, if not style, akin to that of Lester Young, he contributed many memorable moments to the band's recorded output. Wilson's death, in 1941 at the age of 30, was a great loss. For all the enormous talents of Williams and Wilson as far as the non-jazz public was concerned, the band's greatest asset for many years was singer Pha Terrell. He had a light tenor voice with little or no jazz feeling but had several hit records, of which the best known was 'Until The Real Thing Comes Along'. One of the few territory bands to gain a national reputation, the Clouds Of Joy folded in 1948. Thereafter, Kirk played only occasionally but eventually left of music to take up hotel management. In the 60s, he was occasionally active in music, then dabbled in real estate. In the 80s he took a further job with the local New York American Federation of Musicians, where he continued to put in appearances until long after retirement age.

● COMPILATIONS: *Walking And Swinging (1936-42)* (Affinity 1983)★★★★, *Andy's Jive (1944-45)* (Swing House 1984)★★★, *Cloudy (1929)* (Hep Jazz 1984)★★★★, *All Out For Hicksville (1931)* (Hep Jazz 1988)★★★, with Mary Lou Williams *Mary's Idea* (GRP 1993), *Mellow Bit Of Rhythm* (RCA 1993)★★★, *Kansas City Bounce* 1936-1940 recordings (Black And Blue 1993)★★★, *An Introduction To Andy Kirk* 1926-46 recordings (Best Of Jazz 1998)★★★.

● FURTHER READING: *Twenty Years On Wheels*, Andy Kirk as told to Amy Lee.

KIRK, MARY

b. Mary Colston, *c.*1900, Denver, Colorado, USA. As a child at school, Kirk had the good fortune to grow up in a region which benefited from a progressive outlook on musical education. Head of the schools' music department was Wilberforce Whiteman, father of Paul Whiteman, through whose hands passed many future professional musicians. Kirk had begun playing piano at home, copying lessons being given to her sister until she excelled and was actively encouraged by her parents. At school she extended her studies and also took private lessons. Taught classical music and the popular music of the early years of the twentieth century, her repertoire was extremely wide. In the early 20s she was hired as one of two pianists in a show band led by George Morrison which was extremely popular in the mid-western states. Another member of the band was Andy Kirk who greatly admired her playing. The couple were married in 1925 and for a time both played in bands directed by Morrison until Kirk moved on, eventually to lead his own band. His wife played less after this time, instead bringing up a child. Her professional career was over although she continued to take an interest in music and would still play either privately or in church.

KIRK, RAHSAAN ROLAND

b. 7 August 1936, Columbus, Ohio, USA, d. 5 December 1977, Bloomington, Indiana, USA. Originally named 'Ronald', Kirk changed it to 'Roland' and added 'Rahsaan' after a dream visitation by spirits who 'told him to'. Blinded soon after his birth, Kirk became one of the most prodigious multi-instrumentalists to work in jazz, with a career that spanned R&B, bop and the 'New Thing' jazz style. According to Joe Goldberg's sleevenotes for *Kirk's Work* (1961), Kirk took up trumpet at the age of nine after hearing the bugle boy at a summer camp where his parents acted as counsellors. He played trumpet in the school band, but a doctor advised against the strain trumpet-playing imposes on the eyes. At the Ohio State School for the Blind, he took up saxophone and clarinet from 1948. By 1951 he was well-known as a player and was leading his own dance band in the locality. Kirk's ability to play three instruments simultaneously gained him notoriety. Looking through the 'scraps' in the basement of a music store, Kirk found two horns believed to have been put together from different instruments, but which possibly dated from late 19th century Spanish military bands. The manzello was basically an alto sax with a 'large, fat, ungainly' bell. The strich resembled 'a larger, more cumbersome soprano'. He found a method of playing both, plus his tenor, producing a wild, untempered 'ethnic' sound ideal for late-60s radical jazz. He also soloed on all three separately and added flute, siren and clavietta (similar to the melodica used by Augustus Pablo and the Gang Of Four) to his armoury. With all three horns strung around his neck, and sporting dark glasses and a battered top hat, Kirk made quite a spectacle. The real point was that, although he loved to dally with simple R&B and ballads, he could unleash break-neck solos that sounded like a bridge between bebop dexterity and *avant garde* 'outness'. His debut for a properly distributed label - recorded for Cadet Records in Chicago in June 1960 at the behest of Ramsey Lewis - provoked controversy, some deriding the three-horn-trick as a gimmick, others applauding the fire of his playing. In 1961, he joined the Charles Mingus Workshop for four months, toured California and played on *Oh Yeah!*. He also played the Essen Jazz Festival in Germany. In 1963, he began the first of several historic residencies at Ronnie Scott's club in London. Despite later guest recordings with Jaki Byard (who had played on his *Rip Rig & Panic*) and Mingus (at the 1974 Carnegie Hall concert), Kirk's main focus of activity was his own group, the Vibration Society, with whom he toured the world until he suffered his first stroke in November 1975, which paralysed his right side. With characteristic single-mindedness, he taught himself to play with his left hand only and started touring again. A second stroke in 1977 caused his death.

Long before the 80s 'consolidation' period for jazz, Kirk presented a music fully cognizant of black American music, from Jelly Roll Morton and Louis Armstrong on through Duke Ellington and John Coltrane; he also paid tribute to the gospel and soul heritage, notably on *Blacknuss*, which featured songs by Marvin Gaye, Smokey Robinson and Bill Withers. Several of his tunes - 'The Inflated Tear', 'Bright Moments', 'Let Me Shake Your Tree', 'No Tonic Pres' - have become jazz standards. His recorded legacy is uneven, but it contains some of the most fiery and exciting music to be heard.

● ALBUMS: *Triple Threat* (King 1956)★★★, with Booker Ervin *Soulful Saxes* (Affinity 1957)★★★★, *Introducing Roland Kirk* (Argo 1960)★★★, *Kirk's Work* (Prestige 1961)★★★★, *We Free Kings* (Mercury 1962)★★★★, *Domino* (Mercury 1962)★★★, *Reeds And Deeds* (Mercury 1963)★★★, with Benny Golson *Roland Kirk Meets The Benny Golson Orchestra* (Mercury 1963)★★★, *Kirk In Copenhagen* (Mercury 1963)★★★, *Gifts And Messages* (Mercury 1964)★★★, *I Talk With The Spirits* (Limelight 1964)★★★, *Rip Rig & Panic* (Limelight 1965)★★★★, *Slightly Latin* (Limelight 1966)★★★, *Now Please Don't You Cry, Beautiful Edith* (Verve 1967)★★★, *Funk Underneath* (Prestige

1967)★★★, *Here Comes The Whistle Man* (Atlantic 1967)★★★, *The Inflated Tear* (Atlantic 1968)★★★★, *Left And Right* (Atlantic 1969)★★★, *Volunteer Slavery* (Atlantic 1969)★★★★, *Rahsaan, Rahsaan* (Atlantic 1970)★★★, *Natural Black Inventions: Root Strata* (Atlantic 1971)★★★, *Blacknuss* (Atlantic 1972)★★★★, *A Meeting Of The Times* (Atlantic 1972)★★★, *Bright Moments* (Atlantic 1973)★★★, *Prepare Thyself To Deal With A Miracle* (Atlantic 1974)★★★, *The Case Of The Three Sided Dream In Audio Colour* (Atlantic 1975)★★★, *The Return Of The 5000 Lb. Man* (Warners 1975)★★★, *Kirkatron* (Warners 1976)★★★, *Other Folks' Music* (Warners 1976)★★★, *Boogie-Woogie String Along For Real* (Warners 1977)★★, *Vibration Society* (Stash 1987)★★★, *Paris 1976* (1990)★★★, *Soul Station* (Affinity 1993)★★★, *I, Eye, Aye Live At Montreux 1972* (Rhino 1996)★★★.

● COMPILATIONS: *The Art Of Rahsaan Roland Kirk (1966-71)* (1973)★★★★, *The Man Who Cried Fire* 1973-1977 recordings (Night/Virgin 1990)★★★★, *Rahsaan: Complete Recordings Of Roland Kirk* 10-CD box set (Mercury 1991)★★★★, *Talkin' Verve: Roots Of Acid Jazz* 1961-1967 recordings (Verve 1997)★★★, *Does Your House Have Lions: The Rahsaan Roland Kirk Anthology* 1961-1976 recordings (Rhino 90s)★★★★, *Dog Years In The Fourth Ring* 1965-1975 recordings (32 Jazz 90s)★★★, *Simmer, Reduce, Garnish & Serve* 1976/1977 recordings (Warners 90s)★★★, *Aces Back To Back* 4-CD set (32 Jazz 1998)★★★.

● VIDEOS: *The One Man Twins* (Rhino 1997).

KIRKLAND, KENNY

b. 28 September 1955, New York City, New York, USA, d. 12 November 1998, New York City, New York, USA. After graduating from the Manhattan School of Music in 1977, Kirkland taught classical music for a period. His friendship with Herbie Hancock led to a growing interest in fusion He toured with violinist Michal Urbaniak in 1977, and joined Miroslav Vitous (ex-Weather Report) in 1979. Stints with drummer Elvin Jones and Japanese trumpeter Terumasa Hino followed, but it was with Wynton Marsalis (1981-85) that Kirkland gained his reputation as a skilful Hancock-influenced pianist, and led to him being in demand from a host of bandleaders including Branford Marsalis and Chico Freeman. He left Wynton Marsalis to work with the rock singer/bassist Sting, and his work on 1985's *The Dream Of The Blue Turtles* was of particular note. He toured with Sting on several occasions, helping to widen the audience for his exquisite keyboard work. Kirkland only recorded one session as a leader before his untimely death in 1998.

● ALBUMS: *Kenny Kirkland* (GRP 1991)★★★.

KIRKLAND, LEROY

b. 10 February 1906, South Carolina, USA, d. 6 April 1988, New York, USA. Raised in Jacksonville, Florida, Kirkland was a butcher before he moved to New York in 1942. He became an arranger whose career spanned the eras of big band jazz, R&B, rock 'n' roll and soul. Kirkland played guitar in southern jazz bands in the 20s and during the 30s worked as arranger and songwriter for Erskine Hawkins. He joined Tommy and Jimmy Dorsey in the 40s and later in that decade began arranging music at Savoy Records in New York. He continued to arrange R&B artists for OKeh Records, Mercury Records and other companies, working with such groups as the Five Satins, the Ravens and the Everly Brothers. He managed Ruby And The Romantics during the 60s, and in the last few years of his life concentrated on gospel music.

KIRKPATRICK, DON

b. 17 June 1905, Charlotte, North Carolina, USA, d. 13 May 1956. After playing piano with bands in and around Baltimore, Kirkpatrick journeyed to New York in 1926 and the following year began a long association with Chick Webb. He played piano in Webb's band and also wrote arrangements during its early years. In the early 30s he worked with Don Redman and also played piano in bands led by Henry 'Red' Allen and Coleman Hawkins. During these and succeeding years Kirkpatrick was very active as a freelance arranger, writing charts for Webb, Count Basie, Benny Goodman, Alvino Rey and 'Cootie' Williams. In the mid-40s he was once again to be found playing piano, generally working in amongst traditional musicians, including Mezz Mezzrow and Bunk Johnson, although stylistically he was more attuned to swing. In the 50s, he played with Sidney Bechet and Wilbur De Paris, and also worked as a solo artist up to his death in 1956.

● COMPILATIONS: *The Chronological Chick Webb And His Orchestra* (1929-34)★★★★, *The Fabulous Sidney Bechet And His Hot Six With Sidney De Paris* (1951)★★★★, *Wilbur De Paris And His Rampart Street Paraders* (1952)★★★.

KITAMURA, EIJI

b. 8 April 1929, Tokyo, Japan. Kitamura began playing clarinet while still a student and was a professional musician from his twenties onwards. He often played with visiting American jazzmen, including Benny Goodman (never renowned for his eagerness to share the bandstand with another clarinettist) in the 50s, and Teddy Wilson and Woody Herman in the 70s. From the late 70s Kitamura began making regular appearances in the USA, mostly on the west coast. Through the late 80s and into the mid-90s he was frequently associated with Bill Berry, sharing stages and bandleading duties in festivals such as the Pacific International Jazz Party. Kitamura is a highly accomplished technician with a subtle sense of swing. He has helped inspire a succeeding generation of Japanese musicians with his skill and dedication to his craft and art.

● ALBUMS: with Teddy Wilson *Teddy Wilson Meets Eiji Kitamura* (Storyville 1970)★★★, *Kitamura Eiji vs Suzuki Shoji* (Teichiku 1976)★★★, *Because Of You* (Audio Lab 1976)★★★★, *My Monday Date* (Victor 1977)★★★, *Memories Of You* (RCA 1978)★★★★, *April Date* (Sony 1979),★★★ *3 Degrees North* (Sony 1980)★★★, *Seven Stars* (Toshiba/EMI 1981),★★★ *We With Woody Herman* (Toshiba/EMI 1983)★★★, with Bill Berry *Jazz Party* (Jazz Cook 1998)★★★.

KITCHINGS, IRENE

b. Irene Eadie, *c.*1910, Marietta, Ohio, USA, d. *c.*1975. After taking piano lessons from her piano-teacher mother, Kitchings moved to Chicago and in her late teens was working as a solo pianist in jazz clubs and sitting-in at after-hours sessions. She formed her own jazz groups, mostly with all-male personnel, and was very popular especially with the club-owning gangsters of late-20s Chicago. In addition to playing piano, she also wrote music but at this time playing came first. At the start of the 30s she met and married Teddy Wilson and for a while their careers ran in parallel. When Wilson moved to New York, however, she went with him, abandoning her playing career. In the mid-30s, Wilson was a highly popular member of the Benny Goodman organization and the marriage foundered. She was encouraged by Benny Carter to turn to her composing as a means of lifting her from the depression the breakdown in her marriage had caused. Billie Holiday, who had become friendly with her when recording with Wilson, effected an introduction to lyricist Arthur Herzog Jnr. Their first collaboration, 'Some Other Spring', was recorded by Holiday, and for the next few years the partnership produced some fine songs, the last of which was 'I'm Pulling Through', also recorded by Holiday. At this time, the early 40s, Kitchings was unwell and had gone to Cleveland where she was cared for by an aunt. Here she met and married Elden Kitchings. Her later years were largely inactive in musical terms, although happy ones. Such musical activity as there was centred upon the church where she sang and played the organ. She suffered from an eye disease which made her final years difficult. Kitchings' reputation as a pianist was restricted largely to musicians with whom she played in Chicago but within this group she was highly praised. As a composer her reputation is even higher. Sally Placksin quotes her collaborator Herzog as saying, 'Anything she wrote, I could put words to, and that doesn't happen very often'. Helen Oakley Dance said, 'Her musical streak came out in composition'. Kitchings and Dance were good friends and another of their group, who was encouraged by both, was Carmen McRae, then a teenager starting out. But for the hiatus in her career during her marriage to Wilson, there seems little doubt that Kitchings would be remembered today as an exceptionally good pianist and leader. As it is, her name lives on with her songs, some of which became standards and paradigms of the songwriter's art.

KLEIN, MANNY

b. Emmanuel Klein, 4 February 1908, New York City, New York, USA. Although he spent most of his long working life as a studio musician, Klein played the trumpet in many of the leading white bands of the late 20s and 30s, making countless records. At one time or another, his powerful lead trumpet sparked the bands of Benny Goodman, Jimmy and Tommy Dorsey, Frank Trumbauer and Red Nichols. His studio work included soundtrack appearances in many feature films, most notably ghosting for Montgomery Clift in the 1953 film *From Here To Eternity*. He also played most of the trumpet solos in *The Benny Goodman Story* (1955), regardless of who might be seen performing on the screen. A stroke in 1973 barely made him pause, and he continued to play with enormous skill and enthusiasm.

● ALBUMS: *Manny Klein And His Sextet* (1956)★★★, with Tutti Camarata *Tutti's Trumpets* (1957)★★★.

● COMPILATIONS: with Benny Goodman *Breakfast Ball (1934)* (1988)★★★★.

KLEMMER, JOHN

b. 3 July 1946, Chicago, Illinois, USA. After trying guitar and alto saxophone in early childhood, Klemmer settled on tenor saxophone in his early teens. He studied extensively, playing in school and other youth bands, then played professionally with several name dancebands of the early 60s, including those led by Les Elgart and Ralph Marterie. In the late 60s he made his first records and then joined Don Ellis's formidable big band. During these years he also played in small groups led by Oliver Nelson and Alice Coltrane. During this time he led his own groups, making jazz and jazz-fusion records. He experimented with electronics and fusion and some of his 1969 recordings slightly pre-date Miles Davis's *Bitches Brew*. Sometimes Klemmer used electronic enhancements to allow him to record complex solo saxophone albums. He continued to develop these electronic concepts throughout the 70s and into the 80s. Playing with a diamond-hard tone, Klemmer's solos are filled with daring lines and imaginative ideas, often tossed out almost casually. On ballads, at which he excels, he introduces a breathy quality which aids the sometimes light and airy feeling he imparts. Many of his recordings feature his own compositions. Musically, his interest in areas on the fringes of jazz has tended to keep him from acceptance by the jazz world at large.

● ALBUMS: with Don Ellis *Autumn* (CBS 1968)★★★★, with Oliver Nelson *Black, Brown And Beautiful* (1969)★★★, *Eruptions* (1969)★★★, *All The Children Cried* (1969)★★★, *Blowin' Gold (Eruptions/All The Children Cried)* (Chess 1969)★★★, *Constant Throb* (1971)★★★, *Solo Saxophone I: Cry* (1975)★★★, *Arabesque* (1977)★★★, *Nexus For Duo And Trio* (1978)★★★, *Nexus One (For Trane)* (1979)★★★, *Straight From The Heart* (1979)★★★, *Hush* (Elektra 1981)★★★, *Finesse* (Elektra 1983)★★, *Solo Saxophone II: Life* (1985)★★, *Barefoot Ballet* (MCA 1987)★★, *Music* (MCA 1989)★★★, *Waterfalls* (Impulse! 1990)★★★, with Oscar Castro-Neves *Simpatico* (JVC 1997)★★★.

KLINK, AL

b. 28 December 1915, Danbury, Connecticut, USA, d. 8 March 1991. One of the many unsung heroes of the swing era, Klink's career took him through the bands of Benny Goodman and Tommy Dorsey and he was a mainstay of the Glenn Miller Orchestra during its most successful period. Although an excellent soloist on both saxophones and clarinet, Klink was usually overshadowed either by soloing leaders or other more favoured sidemen. After World War II he worked mostly in the studios, recording with Billie Holiday, the Sauter-Finegan Orchestra and Ruby Braff. In the late 70s and early 80s he joined fellow veterans Bob Haggart and Yank Lawson in their World's Greatest Jazz Band and also freelanced with several other jazz groups.

● ALBUMS: *The Al Klink Quintet* one side only (1955)★★, with Bob Alexander *Progressive Jazz* (Grand Award 1956)★★★, *The World's Greatest Jazz Band Of Yank Lawson And Bob Haggart On Tour* (1975)★★★★.

KLUGER, IRVING

b. 9 July 1921, New York City, New York, USA. In the early 40s, after studying music at high school and while still at university, Kluger drifted into New York's bebop scene. He played drums in Georgie Auld's modernistic band and also worked with Dizzy Gillespie, appearing with him on a 1945 recording date which produced the hugely popular 'Salt Peanuts' and 'Good Bait'. Kluger then moved on to the adventurous Boyd Raeburn band and also worked with Stan Kenton and Artie Shaw in the late 40s. In the 50s and subsequently, Kluger played in studio, as well as in theatre and casino orchestras, across the country, eventually settling on the west coast. In the early 80s he was an executive of the American Federation of Musicians in Las Vegas and talked of returning to drumming in his 'retirement', and, time permitting, also of writing his memoirs.

● ALBUMS: *Boyd Raeburn: On The Air Vol. 2* (1945-47)★★★, with Milt Bernhardt *Modern Brass* (1955)★★★.

● COMPILATIONS: with Stan Kenton *The Kenton Era* (1940-55 recordings)★★★★.

KLUGH, EARL

b. 16 September 1953, Detroit, Michigan, USA. Jazz guitarist Klugh has an unorthodox style in that when he sits down he rests the guitar on his right knee instead of the left. After studying piano and nylon string guitar as a child, Klugh settled on the latter instrument. While still in his mid-teens he recorded with Yusef Lateef and George Benson, with whom he also toured. He continued to work with Benson and briefly with Return To Forever and, in the mid-70s, he also led his own groups for a solo career. Influenced by a wide range of guitarists including Benson (jazz), Chet Atkins (country) and folk, Klugh's style contains elements of all, yet is presented with a strong feeling for the great tradition of post-Charlie Christian jazz guitar through which his own personality constantly shines.

● ALBUMS: with Yusef Lateef *Suite 16* (1970)★★★★, with George Benson *White Rabbit* (1971)★★★, *Earl Klugh* (1976)★★, *Living Inside Your Love* (Liberty 1976)★★★, *Finger Paintings* (Liberty 1977)★★★, *Magic In Your Eyes* (United Artists 1978)★★★, *Heart String* (United Artists 1979)★★, with Bob James *One On One* (Tappan Zee 1979)★★★, *Dream Come True* (EMI 1980)★★, with Hubert Laws *How To Beat The High Cost Of Living* film soundtrack (1980)★★, *Late Night Guitar* (United Artists 1980)★★★, *Crazy For You* (Liberty 1981)★★★, with James *Two Of A Kind* (Capitol 1982)★★, *Low Ride* (Capitol 1983)★★★, with Hiroki Miyano *Hotel California* (Mercury 1984)★★, *Wishful Thinking* (Capitol 1984)★★★, *Nightsongs* (Capitol 1983)★★★, *Soda Fountain Shuffle* (WEA 1985)★★★, *Life Stories* (WEA 1986)★★★, with Benson *Collaboration* (1987)★★★★, *A Time For Love* (Capitol 1988)★★★, *Solo Guitar* (WEA 1989)★★★, with James *Cool* (Warners 1992)★★★★, *Sounds And Visions* (1993)★★★, *Sudden Burst Of Energy* (Warners 1996)★★★, *The Journey* (Warners 1997)★★★.

● COMPILATIONS: *The Best Of Earl Klugh (1977-84)* (Blue Note 1985)★★★★, *World Star* (1985)★★★, *The Best Of Earl Klugh Volume 2* (Blue Note 1993)★★★★.

KNEPPER, JIMMY

b. 22 November 1927, Los Angeles, California, USA. Knepper learned to play trombone as a small child, later studying intensively. In the early 40s he played in local dance bands, playing jazz with various small groups. From the late 40s and into the early 50s he played with numerous name bands, including those led by Freddie Slack, Roy Porter, Charlie Spivak, Charlie Barnet, Woody Herman and Claude Thornhill. Later in the 50s Knepper worked extensively with Charles Mingus and also with Art Pepper and Stan Kenton. During the 60s he was with Mingus again, Benny Goodman and he also began a long-lasting if intermittent association with Gil Evans. Towards the end of the 60s he began another long-term musical relationship, this time with the Thad Jones-Mel Lewis Jazz Orchestra. In the 70s he was a member of the nine-piece band led by Lee Konitz and also worked with Mingus Dynasty. He made several records under his own name, including *Cunningbird* which featured such distinguished jazz musicians as Al Cohn, Roland Hanna and Richard Davis. A virtuoso performer, Knepper's bop-influenced style is technically on a par with that of J.J. Johnson, one of the few other trombonists to adapt wholly to bop. Nevertheless, Knepper's style is very much his own, with few obvious direct influences. His remarkable technical dexterity allows him to develop solo lines of startling ingenuity and imagination. In the 80s, Knepper was active on both sides of the Atlantic, renewing interest among older fans and finding a new audience for his exceptional skills and talent.

● ALBUMS: *A Swinging Introduction To Jimmy Knepper* (Bethlehem 1957)★★★, with Pepper Adams *The Pepper-Knepper Quintet* (Metrojazz 1958)★★★, with Tony Scott *Free Blown Jazz* (Carlton 1959)★★★, *Cunningbird* (Steeple Chase 1976)★★★★, *Jimmy Knepper In L.A.* (Inner City 1977)★★★★, *Primrose Path* (Hep 1982)★★★★, *First Place* (Black Hawk 1982)★★★★, *I Dream Too Much* (Soul Note 1984)★★★, *Dream Dancing* (Criss Cross 1987)★★★, *Muted Joys* (Affinity 1989)★★★.

KNOWLES, PAMELA

b. *c.*1950, Australia. After studying drama at the American Conservatory Theater and at London's Academy of Music and Dramatic Art, Knowles spent some time working in the theatre in New York before deciding to concentrate on singing. She played clubs in New York, Paris, where she worked with Claude Bolling's big band, and London, appearing at Ronnie Scott's club. She has also sung in her native Australia and in New Zealand, sometimes with classical orchestras such as the Christchurch Symphony, and at jazz festivals. Her rich, contralto voice lends itself admirably to ballads and show tunes but her repertoire extends beyond these to incorporate Latin and contemporary pop. Her dramatic flair and big voice, allied to a great stage presence, have considerable audience appeal and she is at her best in live settings that allow her to develop this enviable rapport.

● ALBUMS: *Love Dance* (Larrikin 1993)★★★.

KNUDSEN, KENNETH

b. 28 September 1946, Copenhagen, Denmark. Knudsen is a keyboardist and composer who during the 70s co-led, with alto saxophonist and composer Karsten Vogel, two of the best Danish jazz-rock groups, Secret Oyster and Birds Of Beauty. In 1976 Knudsen joined Palle Mikkelborg's Entrance band inspired by Weather Report. Knudsen's keyboards provides an ambience of tonal colouration that works best in slow, sparse minimalist settings. Close to ECM Records's sound Knudsen's music successfully avoids any new age saccharine mellowness.

● ALBUMS: with Karsten Vogel *Birds Of Beauty* (1976)★★★, with Niels-Henning Ørsted Pedersen *Pictures* (1977)★★★, *Anima* (Kong Pære 1979)★★★, with Ørsted Pedersen, Palle Mikkelborg *Heart To Heart* (1986)★★★, *I Me Him* (1987)★★★★, *Bombay Hotel* (1989),★★ *Sounds And Silence* (1993)★★★, *Nordic Frames* (1994)★★★.

KOGLMANN, FRANZ

b. 22 May 1947, Vienna, Austria. Koglmann took up the trumpet after seeing a Louis Armstrong concert at the age of 13. Despite this epiphany, he studied exclusively classical trumpet at the Vienna Conservatory and his interest in jazz was reawakened only in 1968, this time by an encounter with Miles Davis. Koglmann, trumpeter, flügelhorn player and composer, is serious about 'roots' and the influence of countrymen Schubert, Berg and Krenek is to be discerned in his music, tempering and shaping the nature of the jazz, and giving new credence to the maligned ideas of Third Stream Music. Though *A White Line*, specifically setting out to celebrate the (under-recognized) achievements of white jazz musicians, prompted predictable sermonizing from (white) critics, other Koglmann recordings draw upon the music of Thelonious Monk and Dizzy Gillespie, and the list of distinguished soloists who have played with Koglmann's band includes Bill Dixon and Alan Silva, as well as Paul Bley, Ran Blake and Steve Lacy. Most of Koglmann's music is written for his 10-12 piece band, the Pipetet, launched in 1973. The prevalent mood is one of melancholy, the compositional structures are labyrinthine, the execution is consistently brilliant.

● ALBUMS: with Steve Lacy *Flaps* (Pipe 1973)★★★, with Bill Dixon *Opium/For Franz* (Pipe 1976)★★★, *Schlaf Schlemmer, Schlaf Magritte* (hatART 1984)★★★★, *Good Night* (1985)★★★, *Ich, Franz Koglmann* (hatART 1986)★★★★, *About Yesterday's Ezzthetics* (hatART 1988)★★★, *Orte Der Geometrie* (hatART 1988)★★★, *A White Line* (hatART 1989)★★★, *The Use Of Memory* (hatART 1990)★★★, *L'Heure Bleue* (hatART 1991)★★★, *Cantos I-IV* (hatART 1993)★★★★, with Paul Bley, Gary Peacock *Annette* (1993)★★, with Lee Konitz *We Thought About Duke* (hatART 1997)★★★.

KOLLER, HANS

b. 12 February 1921, Vienna, Austria. Koller studied clarinet at the Academy of Music in Vienna (1936-39) before doing wartime service in the army. After the war he played in the group of the Hot Club of Vienna and became its leader in 1947. He moved to Germany in 1950 and formed an influential modern group with Albert Mangelsdorff. He played with many visiting Americans including Dizzy Gillespie, Lee Konitz and Benny Goodman. Koller continued to lead a quartet in the late 50s while he was working in Hamburg as musical director of Norddeutscher Rundfunk jazz workshops (1958-65) and at Deutsches Schauspielhaus (1968). In 1970, he returned to Vienna where he founded the band Free Sounds and in the late 70s occasionally led the International Brass Company. He has a duo with Fritz Pauer. Koller has also performed with Warne Marsh who had been a member of pianist Lennie Tristano's group which had been the biggest influence on the young Koller, though he later tried to absorb the music of John Coltrane. Since the late 50s he has been an exhibiting abstract painter.

● ALBUMS: *Hans Is Hip* (1952)★★★, *Exclusive* (1963)★★, *Zoller-Koller-Solal* (1965)★★★, *Relax With My Horns* (1966)★★★, *New York City* (1968)★★, *Phoenix* (1972)★★, *Out On The Rim* 1984 and 1991 recordings (In + Out)★★★.

KÖLN CONCERT, THE - KEITH JARRETT

Albums that sell vast quantities are not always to be recommended. This exceptional example of solo piano is the biggest selling record in the 25 year history of the pioneering jazz label ECM Records. It is an almost perfect recording of the art of piano dynamics, full of emotion, and throughout the hour or so duration the listener is never bored. Jarrett has repeated his concerts of improvisation hundreds of times. Many have been recorded, and presumably, many routes of his spontaneity have led to blind alleys of jazz doodling. This is the best recorded example of the art, unlikely to be bettered.

● Tracks: *Part I; Part II a; Part II b; Part II c.*
● First released 1975
● UK peak chart position: did not chart
● USA peak chart position: did not chart

KOMEDA, KRZYSZTOF

Long before western Europe enthused over Zbigniew Namyslowski and the Ganelin Trio, pianist and composer Komeda showed that Warsaw Pact countries, especially Poland, were capable of producing fine jazz. He composed the music for Roman Polanski's films *Two Men And A Wardrobe*, *When Angels Fall*, *The Fat And The Lean*, *Knife In The Water*, *Cul-De-Sac*, *Dance Of The Vampires* and *Rosemary's Baby*. The score for *Knife In The Water*, featuring fast and freewheeling themes for saxophone and rhythm, demonstrated that he had kept abreast of modern jazz developments, and his album *Astigmatism*, taking up the directions pointed out by

Miles Davis's mid-60s Quintet and featuring Namyslowski, has just been re-issued by the Polish state record label. His band included tenor saxist Bernt Rosengren and trumpeter Tomasz Stanko. His last work was on Buzz Kulik's film *Riot* in 1968. In April 1969, he died from an illness resulting from a head injury sustained in November 1968.

● ALBUMS: *Knife In The Water* (1962)★★★, *Polish Jazz Volume 3* (Polskie Nagrania Muza 1960, 1961, (1965)★★★, *Live In Copenhagen* (Polonia 1965)★★, *Astigmatic* (Power Bros 1967)★★★★, *Rosemary's Baby* (1968)★★★.

KÖNER, THOMAS

b. Dortmund, Germany. A minimalist *avant garde* composer with a distinctive ethos, Köner bases much of his output on the concept of cold - and the gradual acceleration of global warming. More precisely he has described it as 'Asthetik Der Untergang', a term originally coined by Einsturzende Neubaten, meaning the 'aesthetic of decline'. He claims that no picture exists of him in the company of another human being. Though his music would be anathema to creators of dance records, he feels a kinship with techno and ambient artists working in that field. His debut, *Nunatak Gonamur*, took as its theme the final moments of Scott's polar expedition. Its sources included gongs scraped and rubbed, before electronic 'layering'. Its successor, *Teimo*, explored the process of cooling which takes place in the molecular structure of humans and animals after death. This time the musical imagery was dominated by circular movements frequently ending in silence. *Permafrost*, as the title suggested, took the permanently frozen Arctic subsoil as its text. As Köner explained, 'In a cold environment, everything slows down, and everything is going towards a stop event. And that is my favourite area in sound - just before it stops. It's an interesting border.' 1996's *Aubrite*, which explored other concepts, still maintained the link to his previous albums with the track 'Nuuk', titled after the capital of Greenland.

● ALBUMS: *Nunatak Gonamur* (Barooni 1990)★★★, *Teimo* (Barooni 1992)★★, *Permafrost* (Barooni 1994)★★, *Aubrite* (Barooni 1996)★★★.

KONITZ, LEE

b. 13 October 1927, Chicago, Illinois, USA. Konitz began on clarinet, studying in the classical form, later switching to alto saxophone. In the mid-late 40s he played in the bands of Jerry Wald and Claude Thornhill, appeared on jazz dates with Miles Davis and was simultaneously studying with Lennie Tristano, with whom he also recorded. In the early 50s he worked for a while with Stan Kenton and although he left the band before the end of 1953, he had established his name and an international reputation. From the mid-50s onwards Konitz generally led his own bands, recording and playing publicly, and made a brief return visit to work with Tristano. He also became involved in teaching. During the following years Konitz's interest in teaching developed and soon he was running clinics and workshops, giving private tuition and also conducting worldwide correspondence courses. In the mid-70s he recorded several albums with Warne Marsh, all finding immediate critical and commercial popularity. He also formed a nine-piece band modelled upon the one led by Davis in which he had played 30 years earlier. One of very few alto saxophonists of his generation not to have been influenced by Charlie Parker, Konitz managed to avoid being cast in any mould other than that which he created himself. Unlike many of his peers, he has proved to be flexible and capable of continually growing to accommodate new concepts. In performance his sound has changed over the years. Originally he played with a deliberately thin sound but he thickened this during his time with Kenton, a necessity to avoid being drowned by the volume of the band. ('It was not easy playing alto in that band. Next time around, I'd rather be the drummer.') Deeply interested in and committed to jazz education, Konitz encourages his students to respect their material and through his courses strives to teach solo improvisation, something he regards as being just as much a measurable discipline as ensemble playing. His own playing remains exemplary of that strain of contemporary music which emphasizes thoughtfulness rather than instinctive responses.

● ALBUMS: *Lee Konitz - The New Sounds* 10-inch album (Prestige 1951)★★★★, with Gerry Mulligan *Konitz Meets Mulligan* 10-inch album (Pacific Jazz 1953)★★★★, *Originalee* 10-inch album (Roost 1953), *Lee Konitz At Storyville* 10-inch album (Storyville 1954)★★★★, *Konitz* (Storyville 1954)★★★, *Lee Konitz In Harvard Square* 10-inch album (Storyville 1955)★★★, with Warne Marsh *Lee Konitz With Warne Marsh* (Atlantic 1955)★★★, with Lennie Tristano *Lee Konitz Groups* reissued as *Subconsciouslee* (Prestige 1955)★★★★, *Inside Hi-Fi* (Atlantic 1957)★★★★, *The Real Lee Konitz* (Atlantic 1957)★★★, *Very Cool* (Verve 1958)★★★★, *Tranquility* (Verve 1958)★★★★, with Bill Russo *An Image - Lee Konitz With Strings* (Verve 1958)★★★, with Jimmy Guiffre *Lee Konitz Meets Jimmy Guiffre* (Verve 1959)★★★★, *You And Lee* (Verve 1960)★★★, *Motion* (Verve 1961)★★★★, with Teddy Charles, Miles Davis *Ezz-Thetic* (New Jazz 1962)★★★, *Together Again* (Moon 1966)★★★, *Lee Konitz Duets* (Milestone 1968)★★★★, with Albert Mangelsdorff, Attila Zoller *ZO-KO-MA* (MPS 1968)★★★★, with Alto Summit *Alto Summit* (Verve 1968)★★★★, *Peacemeal* (Milestone 1969)★★★, *Spirits* (Milestone 1971)★★★, *Satori* (Milestone 1974)★★★, with Red Mitchell *I Concentrate On You* (Steeple Chase 1974)★★★★, *Lone-Lee* (Steeple Chase 1974)★★★, *Oleo* (Sonet 1975)★★★, *Jazz A Juan* (Steeple Chase 1975)★★★★, with Marsh *Warne Marsh & Lee Konitz (Live At Club Montmartre)* (Storyville 1976)★★★, *Figure And Spirit* (Progressive 1976)★★★, *The Lee Konitz Nonet* (Chiaroscuro 1977)★★★, *Windows* (Steeple Chase 1977)★★★, *Pyramid* (Improvising Artists 1977)★★★, *Yes, Yes, Nonet* (Steeple Chase 1979)★★★, *Seasons Change* (Circle 1980)★★★★, *Live At Laren* (Soul Note 1980)★★★, *Toot Sweet* (Owl 1982)★★★, *Dovetail* (1984)★★★, *Stereokonitz* (RCA 1985)★★★, *Ideal Scene* (Soul Note 1986)★★★, *Medium Rare* (Label Blue 1986)★★, *Wild As Springtime* (GFM 1987)★★, *Blew* (Philology 1988)★★★, *Shades Of Kenton* (Hep Jazz 1988)★★★, *Songs Of The Stars* (1988)★★★, *The New York Album* (Soul Note 1988)★★★★, *Spirits* (Milestone 1988)★★★,

12 Gershwin In 12 Keys (Philology 1989)★★★, *Round And Round* (Limelight 1989)★★★, *Frank-Lee Speaking* (West Wind 1990)★★★, *In Rio* (MA Music 1990)★★, *Once Upon A Live* (Musidisc 1991)★★★, *Zounds* (Soul Note 1991)★★★, *S'Nice* (Nabel 1991)★★★, with Peggy Stern *Lunasea* (Soul Note 1992)★★, *So Many Stars* (Philology 1993)★★★, *Free With Lee* (Philology 1994)★★, *A Venezia* (Philology 1994)★★★, *Haiku* (Nabel 1995)★★, *Rhapsody II* (Evidence 1996)★★★, with Don Friedman, Attila Zoller *Thingin* (hatART 1996)★★★, *Strings For Holiday: A Tribute To Billie Holiday* (Enja 1997)★★★, with Bill Frisell, Dave Holland, Kenny Wheeler *Angel Song* (ECM 1997)★★★★, *Dig Dug Dog* (Sony Jazz 1997)★★★, *Dearly Beloved* (Steeplechase 1997)★★★★, *Out Of Nowhere* (Steeplechase 1997)★★★★, *Unaccompanied In Yokohama* (1997)★★★, *Self Portrait* (Philology 1997)★★★, with Harold Danko *Wild As Springtime* (Candid 1997)★★★, with Franz Koglmann *We Thought About Duke* (hatART 1997)★★★, with Charlie Haden, Brad Meldau *Alone Together* (Blue Note 1998)★★★★, *Saxophone Dreams* (Koch Jazz 1998)★★★, with Martial Solal *Star Eyes: Hamburg 1983* (hatOLOGY 1998)★★★, with Franco D'Andrea *Inside Cole Porter* (NelJazz 1998)★★★.

● COMPILATIONS: *Timespan* 1954-1961 recordings (Wave 1977)★★★, *From Newport To Nice* 1955-1980 recordings (Philology 1992)★★★★, *First Sessions (1949-1950)* (Prestige)★★★, featuring Ralph Burns, Jimmy Giuffre, Bill Russo *Lee Konitz Meets Jimmy Giuffre* (Verve 1997)★★★★, with Warne Marsh, Lennie Tristano *The Complete Atlantic Recordings Of Lennie Tristano, Lee Konitz & Warne Marsh* 6-CD box set (Mosaic 1997)★★★★.

KOTICK, TEDDY

b. 4 June 1928, Haverill, Massachusetts, USA, d. 17 April 1986. Kotick started playing the guitar when he was six years old and only took up the double bass in high school. He moved to New York in 1948 and played with Buddy Rich, Buddy De Franco and Artie Shaw. Throughout his career Kotick played interesting lines with perfect timing, secure pitch and a full tone. In the early 50s he played with Charlie Parker and Stan Getz. Later Kotick played on Bill Evans' debut album and then toured with the Horace Silver Quintet (1957-58). After a break in his career he settled in Massachusetts and recorded again with Allen Eager and J.R. Monterose.

● ALBUMS: with Stan Getz *Jazz At Storyville* (1951)★★★, *Charlie Parker Plays Cole Porter* (1954)★★★★, with Bill Evans *New Jazz Conceptions* (1956)★★★★, with Horace Silver *Further Explorations* (1958)★★★★, with J.R. Monterose *Live In Albany* (1979)★★★★.

KOWALD, PETER

b. 21 April 1944, Masserberg, Germany. Kowald, who plays bass, tuba and alphorn, is one of the key figures in the development of European improvisation. Before he became a professional musician he was a translator, and his multilingual abilities have stood him in good stead on his travels. Kowald opened up the contacts between the German free-jazzers and their British counterparts, and played with the Spontaneous Music Ensemble in London in 1967. He was responsible for bringing Peter Brötzmann and Dutch drummer Han Bennink together, and that there exists a Greek free-jazz scene at all has much to do with his endeavours. Kowald was also one of the first of his generation of players to journey to the USA and Japan. He was also instrumental in the revival of Globe Unity in 1973 and for five years co-led this free orchestra with Alexander Von Schlippenbach. Globe Unity's *Jahrmarkt/Local Fair* (1977), on which the improvisers encounter a Greek folk group and 25 Wuppertal accordion players, is a typically Utopian Kowald project.

● ALBUMS: *Peter Kowald Quintet* (1972)★★★, with Michel Pilz, Paul Lovens *Carpathes* (1976)★★★, with Barre Phillips *Die Jungen: Random Generators* (1979)★★, with Leo Smith, Günter Sommer *Touch The Earth* (FMP 1980)★★★, with Smith, Sommer *Break The Shells* (1981)★★★, with Barry Guy *Paintings* (1982)★★★, with Maarten Altena *Two Making A Triangle* (1982)★★★, with Frank Wright, A.R. Penck *Run With The Cowboys* (1987)★★★, with Danny Davis, Takehisa Kosugi *Global Village Suite* (1988)★★★★, *Open Secrets* (1988)★★★★, *Duos Europa/USA/Japan* 1984-1990 recording (FMP 1992)★★★, *When The Sun Is Out You Don't See The Stars* (FMP 1992)★★★, *Was Da Ist* (FMP 1994)★★★★.

KOZ, DAVE

b. Los Angeles, California, USA. Saxophonist Dave Koz is one of a small number of modern jazz players to have found significant contemporary success without necessarily obtaining critical approval for their efforts. His repertoire, like that of both Kenny G. and Najee, incorporates instrumental treatments of familiar pop fare, as well as extended solo spots. His technique may not bear comparison with the greats of jazz, but within his limitations he is an accomplished performer. His debut album was a continual presence on the *Billboard* Contemporary Jazz charts in that year (charting for 25 weeks). Singles drawn from it included 'Nothing But The Radio On' and 'Castle Of Dreams', both of which also sold well. He secured widespread fame by appearing regularly on the *Arsenio Hall* television show as part of the 'Posse', and also appeared and performed on *Family Matters* and *General Hospital*. The latter chose his song, 'Faces Of The Heart', as their new theme song - the first such revision in 30 years of transmission. 1993's *Lucky Man* was similarly successful and led to him being hailed as 'a prince of multi-media'. It was promoted with widespread television and concert appearances alongside artists such as Michael Bolton and Kenny Loggins. Spending over two years in the Contemporary Jazz chart, by 1995 the album had earned a gold award for sales of over half a million. Further prestige bookings followed, including one for the Inaugural Celebration at the Lincoln Memorial alongside Grover Washington Jnr., David Sanborn and Gerry Mulligan. He also began to host his own radio show - *Personal Notes With Dave Koz* - a two hour contemporary jazz programme. While continuing to work as a session musician with artists including Jonathon Butler, Stevie Nicks and Julio Iglesias, Koz also composed themes for television shows *Late Night With Greg*

Kinnear and *Jones Vs. Jury*. He also regularly hosts the United Cerebral Palsy telethon.

● ALBUMS: *Dave Koz* (Capitol 1990)★★★, *Lucky Man* (Capitol 1993)★★★★, *Off The Beaten Path* (Capitol 1996)★★★, *December Makes Me Feel That Way* (Capitol 1997)★★.

KRAL, IRENE

b. 18 January 1932, Chicago, Illinois, USA, d. 15 August 1978. Taking heed of the success of her older brother, Roy Kral, she began singing while still a teenager. She gained valuable on-the-road experience with bands led by Woody Herman and former Herman bassist Chubby Jackson before spending some time with a vocal group. In the late 50s she was with Maynard Ferguson's band and during the next few years sang with units led by Stan Kenton and ex-Kenton drummer Shelly Manne. Kral then took off on a solo career which lasted until shortly before her early death. An elegantly poised ballad singer, she acknowledged Carmen McRae as one of her musical guides. Not surprisingly, given the time in which she was an up-and-coming singer, Kral was comfortable in a boppish setting and her up-tempo work was free-flowing and distinctive. She also had a jaunty way with Latin-flavoured songs.

● ALBUMS: with Maynard Ferguson *Boy With Lots Of Brass* (EmArcy 1957)★★★, with Herb Pomeroy *Detour Ahead* (UA 1958)★★★, *Steveireneo* (UA 1959)★★★, *Better Than Anything* (DRG 1963)★★★★, with Laurindo Almeida *Guitar From Ipanema* (Capitol 1964)★★★, *Wonderful Life* (Mainstream 1965)★★★.

KRAL, ROY

b. 10 October 1921, Chicago, Illinois, USA. Kral played piano and sang alone and in small groups until, in the mid-40s, he met singer Jackie Cain (b. 22 May 1928, Milwaukee, Wisconsin, USA). Together, Kral and Cain became very popular, working as Jackie And Roy. They joined Charlie Ventura's 'Bop for the People' band for which Kral also played piano and contributed arrangements. In 1949, Kral and Cain quit Ventura, were married, and continued to perform as a duo throughout the 50s. In the 60s Kral was active in the studios but they frequently performed together, recording on into the late 80s. Apart from interesting and duly deferential interpretations of the great standards, Kral and Cain are noted for their vibrant enthusiasm, the sparkling audacity of their bop styling and their use of vocalese. Kral also performs with his sister, the singer Irene Kral.

● ALBUMS: *Jackie Cain And Roy Kral* (1954)★★★, *Spring Can Really Hang You Up The Most* (1955)★★★★, *Free And Easy* (1957)★★★, *Like Sing* (1962)★★★, *Lovesick* (1966)★★★, *Time And Love* (1972)★★, *Concerts By The Sea* (1976)★★★, *Star Sounds* (1979)★★★, *East Of Suez* (1980)★★, *High Standards* (1982)★★★, *A Stephen Sondheim Collection* (1982)★★, *We've Got It: The Music Of Cy Coleman* (1984)★★★, *Bogie* (1986)★★★, *One More Rose* (1987)★★★, *Full Circle* (1988)★★★.

● COMPILATIONS: *Jackie & Roy With Charlie Ventura And His Orchestra* (1948)★★★, as Jackie And Roy *Forever* (Music Masters 1995)★★, as Jackie And Roy *The ABC-Paramount Years* (Koch 1997)★★★.

KRALL, DIANA

b. Nanaimo, British Columbia, Canada. Raised in a musical family, and hearing in particular Fats Waller records, as a child Krall tried to learn all his tunes and to play and sing at the same time. She studied classical piano at school but played jazz piano in a school band. Her first professional gig was at the age of 15 and she has not stopped since. She won a Vancouver Jazz Festival scholarship to Berklee College Of Music in the USA but later returned to her hometown where she continued to play professionally. Amongst her musical associates were visiting Americans Ray Brown and Jeff Hamilton. The visitors were deeply impressed and convinced Krall to go to Los Angeles which she did with help from a Canadian Arts Council grant. In Los Angeles, she studied with Jimmy Rowles who persuaded her to sing more. Although she had sung from the start she had always entertained reservations about this aspect of her work. Nevertheless, the inclusion of singing into her performances led to more engagements than had been the case as a pianist. In 1984 she returned to Canada from Los Angeles, this time settling in Toronto and she appeared in New York in 1990. She continued to attract respectful admiration from other musicians, including John Clayton and he and Hamilton accompanied her on her first album. By the mid-90s Krall was also attracting the attention of jazz fans and even featured in articles in the non-jazz media. Her accompanists on later records have included Brown, Stanley Turrentine and Christian McBride, and her regular working band colleagues, Russell Malone, guitar, and Paul Keller, bass. Krall's piano playing is crisp, deft and swinging. Her singing style is relaxed and intimate and she interprets ballads with warmth and persuasive charm. Although forward thinking and alert to contemporary musical thought in jazz, Krall's heritage is such that she brings echoes of earlier swinging simplicity to her work. The fact that her first album for Impulse! Records, in 1995, was a tribute to Nat 'King' Cole was highly appropriate to her musical direction. The follow up, 1997's *Love Scenes*, rose above the Cole allusions thanks to the power of Krall's personality. Her interpretation of Gershwin's 'They Can't Take That Away From Me' is particularly inspired, and features some sensitive stand-up bass from McBride.

● ALBUMS: *Steppin' Out* (Justin Time 1993)★★★, *Only Trust Your Heart* (GRP 1994)★★★, *All For You (A Dedication To The Nat King Cole Trio)* (Impulse! 1995)★★★, *Love Scenes* (Impulse! 1997)★★★★.

KRESS, CARL

b. 20 October 1907, Newark, New Jersey, USA, d. 10 June 1965. An outstanding and highly-respected guitarist, Kress was active throughout the 20s and 30s, making numerous recordings. Often he worked in company with other guitarists, including Eddie Lang and Dick McDonough, with whom he recorded duets. In the 40s and 50s Kress retained his earlier unusual chordal style and preference for the acoustic instrument, despite changes generated by Charlie Christian and others. He continued to work into the 60s, frequently in partnership with George Barnes, and was performing with him in Reno, Nevada, when he collapsed and died in June 1965.

● ALBUMS: *Carl Kress* (1958)★★, with George Barnes *Two Guitars* (Stash 1962)★★★, with Barnes *Guitars Anyone?* (1963)★★★, with Barnes *Town Hall Concert* (1963)★★.

● COMPILATIONS: shared with Eddie Lang, Dick McDonough *Pioneers Of Jazz Guitars* 1927-1938 recordings (Challenge 1998)★★★★.

KRIEGEL, VOLKER

b. 24 December 1943, Darmstadt, Germany. Kriegel taught himself guitar at the age of 15 and started his own trio when he was 18. Both he and the trio won awards at the 1963 German Amateur Jazz Festival. While studying social science and psychology at Frankfurt University he met Emil and Albert Mangelsdorff and continued to develop his jazz interests. An offer to join the new band being set up by American expatriate vibes-player Dave Pike led him to give up his studies to become a full-time musician. He stayed with the Dave Pike Set until the leader returned to the USA, at which point Kriegel and Eberhard Weber founded Spectrum. When Weber left in 1976 Kriegel started the Mild Maniac Orchestra. In the meantime, in 1975, he had been a co-founder of the United Jazz And Rock Ensemble. In 1977 he co-founded Mood Records. As well as his musical activities, he is a distinguished cartoonist (both for journals and record sleeves), animator and broadcaster.

● ALBUMS: *Spectrum* (1971)★★★, *Missing Link* (1972)★★★, *Topical Harvest* (1975)★★★, *Octember Variations* (1976)★★★, *Elastic Menu* (1977)★★★, *Houseboat* (MPS 1978)★★★, *Long Distance* (MPS 1979)★★★, *Missing Link* (MPS 1981)★★, *Journal* (1981)★★★, *Star Edition* (MPS 1981)★★, *Schone Aussichten* (1983)★★★, *Palazzo Blue* (1987)★★★; with the United Jazz And Rock Ensemble: *Live In Schutzenhaus* (1977)★★, *Teamwork* (1978)★★★, *The Break Even Point* (1980)★★★, *Live In Berlin* (1981)★★, *United Live Opus Sechs* (1984)★★★.

KRIVDA, ERNIE

b. 1945, Cleveland, Ohio, USA. Having turned down an offer to play in Miles Davis's band in the mid-70s, tenor saxophonist Ernie Krivda spent the early part of his career performing around the Cleveland area before moving to New York in his mid-thirties. By then he was a veteran of work with Quincy Jones, but he had left that band due to dissatisfaction with Jones' increasing orientation towards pop music. However, Krivda found the pace of life in New York unsatisfying, and subsequently returned to Cleveland to concentrate on his own more idiosyncratic and jazz-based compositions. Throughout this period he recorded and collaborated widely, though it was not until he signed a new deal with Koch Records in the 90s that he began to attract more widespread attention. In 1995 he released an album with pianist Bill Dobbins, director of the West German Radio Orchestra in Cologne. This highlighted Krivda's unusual style, of which Harvey Pekar noted in *Down Beat* magazine that 'he tongues faster and more often than the vast majority of tenor players, and, like trumpeters, makes wide interval leaps into the upper register. And sometimes he uses a fast, violin-like vibrato'.

● ALBUMS: *Ernie Krivda Jazz* (Cadence 1992)★★★★, *So Nice To Meet You* (Cadence 1994)★★★, with Bill Dobbins*The Art Of The Ballad* (Koch 1995)★★★★, *Sarah's Theme* (CIMP 1996)★★★★, with Dan Wall *Golden Moments* (Koch 1997)★★, and Fat Tuesday Big Band *Perdido* (Koch 1998)★★★★.

KROG, KARIN

b. 15 May 1937, Oslo, Norway. Although she had already worked extensively in Scandinavia with players such as Jan Garbarek and Arild Andersen, vocalist Krog's first impact on the international jazz scene came in 1964 with her appearance at the Antibes Jazz Festival. She subsequently toured Europe and the USA, frequently working with some of the more progressive musicians. In the late 60s she performed, and sometimes recorded, with Don Ellis and Clare Fischer and during the following decade she extended her reputation through sessions with Warne Marsh, Dexter Gordon, Archie Shepp, Red Mitchell and Bengt Hallberg. In the 80s and 90s she recorded and toured with John Surman, with whom she had first performed in the early 70s. An effortless singer, with a good vocal range and excellent taste in material, Krog's penchant for more modern music has tended to restrict her popularity to the hardcore jazz audience, although her repertoire does incorporate the sophisticated songs of Dave Frishberg alongside standards and jazz classics. By the mid-80s her repertoire had extended still further to encompass African click rhythms and Indian Alap music, which she performs with absolute confidence and considerable charm. She is also an experienced television producer and has made several programmes on jazz, which have been broadcast in Norway.

● ALBUMS: *By Myself* (1964)★★★, *Jazz Moments* (1966)★★★, *Eleven Around Karin* (1967)★★★★, with Jan Garbarek, Arild Andersen *Joy* (1968)★★★★, *Blue Eyes* (1969)★★★, with others *Gittin' To Know Y'all* (1969)★★★, *Different Days, Different Ways* (1970)★★★, with Dexter Gordon *Some Other Spring* (Storyville 1970)★★★★, *My Workshop Songbook* (1970)★★★, *Karin Krog* (1973)★★★★, *You Must Believe In Spring* (1974)★★★, *Jazz Jamboree '75 Vol. 2* (1975)★★★, with Archie Shepp *Hi-Fly* (Meantime 1976)★★, *The Malmö Sessions* (1976)★★★, with Bengt Hallberg *A Song For You* (Phontastic 1977)★★★, with Red Mitchell *Three's A Crowd* (1977)★★★, with John Surman *Cloud Line Blue* (1978)★★★, *With Malice Toward None* (1980)★★, with Warne Marsh, Mitchell *I Remember You* (Spotlite 1980)★★★, *Swingin' Arrival* (1980)★★, with Hallberg *Two Of A Kind* (1982)★★★, with Surman *Such Winters Of Memory* (ECM 1983)★★★★, *Freestyle* (Odin 1985)★★★★, *Something Borrowed...Something New* (Meantime 1989)★★★, *Gershwin With Karin Krog* (Meantime 1993)★★★★, *Jubilee: The Best Of 30 Years* (Verve 1994)★★★★, with Surman, Terje Rypdal *Nordic Quartet* (ECM 1995)★★★.

Kroner, Erling

b. 16 April 1943, Copenhagen, Denmark. Composer and trombonist who began playing dixieland music in the early 60s, but soon also participated in 'free' jazz groups with John Tchicai and others. Kroner participated in George Russell's 'Electronic Sonata For Souls Loved By Nature' performed by Russell with the Danish Radio Big Band in 1969. At the end of that year a *Down Beat* stipend enabled him to study at the Berklee College Of Music. A gifted composer and arranger Kroner has successfully adopted Charles Mingus's improvisational method of writing and arranging in changing moods, metres and tempos for soloists in a 10-piece band that employs unusual textures and voicings, e.g. a tuba in the brass section. In the 80s Kroner co-led with drummer Leif Johansson a band, which with similar music and orchestration, extended complex compositions for quasi-operatic or dramatic stagings. Kroner's long-standing fascination with Argentinian culture and music, in particular the tango, is reflected in several compositions dedicated to Astor Piazzolla and Dino Saluzzi. Kroner has also visited and worked with musicians in Argentina.

● ALBUMS: *Music Book* (Spectator 1970)★★★, *The Forgotten Art* (Storyville 1977)★★★, with Leif Johansson *Jo-Jo* (Metronome 1979)★★★★, *Entre Dos Cielos* (Music Mecca 1983)★★★, *Vølvens Spådom* (Olufsen 1985)★★★, *Beowulf Suite/Nijinsky Suite* (Music Mecca 1985-86)★★, *From The Dark Side* (Music Mecca 1987)★★★, *The Erling Kroner Dark Side Orchestra* (Olufsen 1992)★★★, with Lars Beijbom *Live In Copenhagen* (Four Leaf Clover 1996)★★.

Kronos Quartet

David Harrington (first violin), John Sherba (second violin), Joan Jeanrenaud (cello) and Hank Dutt (viola) formed Kronos in San Francisco, California, USA, in 1978. Although classically trained, all of the members had catholic musical upbringings and felt that the gap between classical and popular music was becoming increasingly irrelevant. Led by the charismatic Harrington, whose idols are Bessie Smith and Beethoven, they crossed musical barriers by performing chamber music with the spirit and energy of rock, and refused to dress in the formal garb of the classical establishment. They also established a unique musical identity in several ways: by commissioning new works for the group by modern composers (Philip Glass, Terry Riley, Alfred Schnittke and John Zorn); by working with musicians form other cultures, notably on *Pieces Of Africa*, where every cut is written by African musicians; by transforming popular music (Jimi Hendrix, Willie Dixon, Ornette Coleman) into string quartet arrangements. Their weekly US Public Radio show, *Radio Kronos*, ensured that they reached the widest possible audience on a regular basis.

● ALBUMS: *White Man Sleeps* (1985)★★★, *Kronos* (1987)★★★, *Music Of Sculthorpe, Hendrix, Sallinen, Glass And Nancarrow* (Nonesuch 1987)★★★★, *Winter Was Hard* (1988)★★★, *Black Angels* (1991)★★★, *Information* (Reference 1991)★★★, *Pieces Of Africa* (Nonesuch 1992)★★★, *Short Stories* (Nonesuch 1993)★★★, *Monk Suite* (Landmark 1993)★★★, *Kronos Quartet Performs Phillip Glass* (Nonesuch 1995)★★★★, *Howl, USA* (Nonesuch 1996)★★★, *Early Music* (Nonesuch 1997)★★★.

● COMPILATIONS: *Released 1985-1995* (Nonesuch 1996)★★★, *The Complete Landmark Sessions: Music Of Monk And Evans* (32 CD 1997)★★★.

Krupa, Gene

b. 15 January 1909, Chicago, Illinois, USA, d. 16 October 1973. Krupa began playing drums as a child and after his mother failed to persuade him to become a priest, most of his large family actively encouraged his career in music. He studied formally, his most important teacher being Roy C. Knapp. However, growing up in Chicago in the 20s meant that he was inevitably drawn to jazz. He listened to relocated New Orleans masters such as Baby Dodds, Zutty Singleton and Tubby Hall. In his teens he played in several local dancebands, among them those led by Al Gale, Joe Kayser, Thelma Terry and Mezz Mezzrow and the Benson Orchestra. In 1927, Krupa made his first records in a band nominally fronted by visitor Red McKenzie but actually organized by Eddie Condon whose record debut this also was. This date is reputed to be the first on which a drummer used a bass drum and tom-toms (engineers feared the resonance would cause the needle to lift off the wax). The records were successful and when, in 1929, Krupa and Condon decided to move to New York, their reputation had preceded them. Although highly regarded in the jazz world the new arrivals found the going tough. Mostly, Krupa worked in theatre pit bands, including some directed by Red Nichols, in which he played alongside Benny Goodman and Glenn Miller. In the early 30s, Krupa played in dance bands led by Russ Columbo, Mal Hallett and Buddy Rogers. Late in 1934, he joined Goodman's recently-formed big band. Krupa was the most enthusiastic of sidemen, urging the band along as if it were his own and helping to establish the distinctive sound of the Goodman band. After the band's breakthrough in August 1935 Krupa quickly became a household name. His fame and popularity with the fans built upon his highly visual playing style and film-star good looks, eventually irritated Goodman, although Krupa's frequent alteration of the tempos the leader set did not help their relationship. Soon after the band's Carnegie Hall concert in 1938 Krupa and Goodman had a public quarrel and Krupa quit. He formed his own band, which swiftly became one of the most popular of the swing era.

In 1941, after he had hired Roy Eldridge and Anita O'Day, the band also became one of the best. Success was short-lived, however, and in 1943 it folded after Krupa was jailed following a drugs bust in San Francisco. By the time that he was released on bail pending an appeal against his 1-6 years sentence, he believed his career was over. He returned to New York, planning to spend his time studying and writing music, but was persuaded by Goodman to join a band with which he was touring east coast US Army bases. When

Goodman prepared to extend the tour across the USA, Krupa opted to stay behind. He was convinced that audiences would react against him and instead joined Tommy Dorsey, believing that the comparative anonymity of working in a band based at a New York movie theatre would be best for him. In fact, his appearance, unannounced, at the Paramount Theatre was greeted with rapturous applause and proved to be a remarkably emotional milestone in his rehabilitation. He went on tour with Dorsey and when the charges against him were deemed to have been improper, he decided to form a new band of his own. He maintained a band throughout the rest of the 40s, adapting to bop by incorporating musicians such as Charlie Ventura, Red Rodney and Don Fagerquist and playing charts by Gerry Mulligan, even though Krupa himself was never able to adapt his own playing style which, since his arrival in New York at the end of the 20s, had been closely modelled upon that of Chick Webb. Krupa managed to keep the band working until 1951 and thereafter continued playing with a small group, usually a quartet, touring with Jazz At The Philharmonic and, for a while, operating a drum school with William 'Cozy' Cole. During the 60s he began to appear at occasional reunions of the Benny Goodman Quartet (with Teddy Wilson and Lionel Hampton). The 60s also saw his health deteriorate, first with heart trouble and later with leukaemia. By the early 70s, he was limited to working around New York and most public performances, usually now with Goodman, Wilson and Hampton, had to be preceded by a blood transfusion. He died in October 1973.

Stylistically, Krupa was usually a heavier-handed version of Webb, the man he always acknowledged as his greatest influence and for whom he had genuine admiration and respect. There can be little doubt that Krupa was a major contributor to the powerful attack of the pre-1939 Goodman band. Apart from the 1943 stint with Goodman, when he came close to the standards set by Webb, his big band playing never had the subtlety and swing of his mentor or other contemporaries such as Jo Jones. His spectacular visual style, adored by the fans, tended to alienate critics, though another great contemporary, 'Big' Sid Catlett, was even more flamboyant. Krupa's best playing came in his performances with the Goodman trio and quartet. On these recordings, usually playing only with brushes, he performs with subtlety, skill and great verve. Krupa made the jazz drummer into a highly visible and extremely well-paid member of the band. His countless imitators usually supplied the flash and spectacle without the content, but thanks to his example and encouragement many fine swing style drummers continued to play in the decades following his death.

● ALBUMS: *Gene Krupa* (Columbia 1949)★★★, *Dance Parade* (Columbia 1949)★★★★, *Drum Boogie* (1952)★★★★, *The Exciting Gene Krupa* (1953)★★★★, *The Gene Krupa Sextet/Driving Gene* (1953)★★★, *Gene Krupa Trio* (Mercury 1953)★★★, *Sing, Sing, Sing* (Clef 1953)★★★★, *The Gene Krupa Trio At JATP* (Mercury 1953)★★★, *The Jazz Rhythms Of Gene Krupa* (1954)★★★★, *Gene Krupa Sextet Number 1* (Clef 1954)★★★★, *Gene Krupa Sextet Number 2* (Clef 1954)★★★★, *Gene Krupa's Sidekicks* (Columbia 1955)★★★, *Drummin' Man* (Columbia 1955)★★★, *Selections From The Benny Goodman Story* (Clef 1956)★★★★, with Buddy Rich *Krupa And Rich* (Clef 1956)★★★★, *The Big Band Sound Of Gene Krupa* (1956)★★★★, *Hey, Here's Gene Krupa* (1957)★★★, *Gene Krupa Plays Gerry Mulligan* (Verve 1958)★★★★, *Krupa Rocks* (Verve 1958)★★★★, *The Gene Krupa Story/Drum Crazy* (1959)★★★★, *Hey Here's Gene Krupa* (Verve 1959)★★★, *Big Noise From Winnetka: Gene Krupa At The London House* (Verve 1959)★★★, *The Gene Krupa Sory In Music* (Harmony 1960)★★★, with Buddy Rich *Drum Battle* (Verve 1960)★★★★, *Percussion King* (1961)★★★, *Drummer Man: Gene Krupa In Highest-Fi* (Verve 1961)★★★, *Gene Krupa Trio* (Verve 1961)★★★, *Classics In Percussion* (1961)★★★, *Drum Boogie* (Verve 1961)★★★★, *The Driving Gene Krupa* (Verve 1961)★★★, *The Jazz Rhythms Of Gene Krupa* (Verve 1961)★★★, *Percussion King* (Verve 1961)★★★, with Rich *Burnin' Beat* (Verve 1962)★★★★, *Perdido* (1962)★★★★, with Louie Bellson *The Mighty Two* (Roulette 1963)★★★, with Goodman *Together Again!* (1963)★★★★, *The Great New Gene Krupa Quartet Featuring Charlie Ventura* (Verve 1964)★★★, *The Swingin' Gene Krupa Quartet* (1965)★★★, *That Drummer's Band* (Verve 1966)★★★, with Eddie Condon *Jazz At The New School* (Chiaroscuro 1971)★★★, *In Concert* 1971 recording (DBK 1998)★★★★.

● COMPILATIONS: with Roy Eldridge, Anita O'Day *Uptown* 1941-1942 recordings (Columbia)★★★★, *The Essential Gene Krupa: Let Me Off Uptown* (Verve 1964)★★★★, *Gene Krupa, Volumes 1-14 (1935-41)* (Ajax 1979)★★★★, *The Gene Krupa Collection - 20 Golden Greats* (1987)★★★★, *Gene Krupa - On The Air (1944-46)* (1988)★★★, *The Drummer* (Flapper 1993)★★★.

● FURTHER READING: *Gene Krupa: His Life & Times*, Bruce Crowther.

KUBIS, TOM

b. 1951, Los Angeles, California, USA. After studying, Kubis began playing also, tenor and soprano saxophones with various bands. He also played piano for Bobby Vinton. However, Kubis's chief interest was in writing and his arrangements were in much demand, especially from big band leaders. He formed his own big band expressly to play his charts and this attracted the attention of Jack Sheldon who became an informal co-leader of the band. Apart from writing for the band, Kubis continues to provide charts for others, including Bill Watrous, the BBC Radio Big Band, and his work is also performed by youth and college bands in the USA and UK. His writing is always lively and entertaining, often difficult but never simply for the sake of being hard to play. His own recording career has been relatively meagre, beginning with Dimitri Pagalidis and only relatively recently has his own big band been heard and appreciated by fans of contemporary big band music around the world.

● ALBUMS: with Dimitri Pagalidis *Silverware* (Mark 56 70s)★★, with Pagalidis *Another Place Setting* (Mark 56 1970)★★★, *Slightly Off The Ground* (Sea Breeze 90s)★★★★, *At Last* (Cexton 90s)★★★★, *Keep Swingin'* (Sea Breeze 1998)★★★, *Fast Cars And Fascinating Women* (Sea Breeze 1998)★★.

KÜHN, JOACHIM

b. 15 March 1944, Leipzig, Germany. Between the ages of five to his mid-teens, Kühn took lessons in classical piano and composing, then became a professional jazz musician. He set up his own trio in 1962, which lasted until 1966, when he established a quartet with his brother, clarinettist Rolf Kühn. When this band ended in 1969 he led his own group in Paris, until joining the Jean-Luc Ponty Experience in 1971. He left Ponty in 1972 to co-lead a group with Eje Thelin. Since then he has frequently worked solo, but has also been a member of the acclaimed Tony Oxley Quintet. While he has done work which might be categorized as 'new age' in the mid-90s, recent concerts have shown that he can still play in tougher fashion.

● ALBUMS: *Boldmusic* (1969)★★★, *Piano* (1971)★★★★, *Solos* (Futura 1971)★★★★, *This Way Out* (1973),★★★ with Rolf Kuhn *Connection 74* (1973)★★, with Rolf Kuhn *Transfiguration* (70s)★★★, *Open Strings* (70s)★★★, *Spring Fever* (Atlantic 1977)★★★, Distance (CMP 1984)★★★★, *Wandlungen Transformations* (CMP 1987)★★★, *Ambiance* (AMB 1988)★★★, *Get Up Early* (AMB 1991)★★★, with Ray Lema *Euro African Suite* (1993)★★★, *Abstracts* (Label Bleu 1996)★★, with Ornette Coleman *Colors Live From Leipzig* (Verve 1997)★★★★.

KÜHN, ROLF

b. 29 September 1929, Cologne, Germany. After playing piano, Kühn turned to the clarinet and during the 40s and early 50s worked with numerous dance bands. His frequent broadcasts, often as leader, led to widespread popularity. In the mid-50s he was encouraged to visit the USA where he attracted attention, not least when he deputized for an incapacitated Benny Goodman in the latter's own band. He played with several other bands, including those led by Urbie Green and Toshiko Akiyoshi. Back in Germany from the early 60s, he resumed regular broadcasting and also played concerts and recording dates with various bands and in a startlingly wide range of styles including bop, free jazz, and jazz-rock fusion. Technically, Kühn is wholly assured and in complete command of his instrument and repertoire. A virtuoso player, unafraid to explore beyond the artificial limitations imposed upon clarinettists in the jazz world since the arrival of bop, Kühn has done much to liberate other players of this instrument. His younger brother is pianist Joachim Kühn.

● ALBUMS: *Streamline* (Vanguard 1956)★★★, *Impressions Of New York* (Impulse! 1967)★★★★, *Going To The Rainbow* (1970)★★★, *The Day After* (MPS 1972),★★ *Cinemascope* (MPS 1974)★★★, *Total Space* (MPS 1975)★★, *Symphonic Swampfire* (MPS 1978)★★, *Don't Split* (L+R 1982)★★★, *As Time Goes By* (Blue Flame 1989)★★★★, *Big Band Connection* (Miramar 1996)★★★.

KUHN, STEVE

b. 24 March 1938, New York, USA. Kuhn began playing the piano when he was five and was studying with Serge Chaloff's mother when he was 12. He first played professionally at the age of 13. He graduated from Harvard in 1959 and worked with Kenny Dorham before spending two months with John Coltrane. He joined Stan Getz in 1961 and stayed right through the bossa nova craze. After two years with trumpeter Art Farmer, he settled in Stockholm, Sweden in 1966, working with his own trio throughout Europe. Since his return to New York in 1971, he has worked extensively in the world of commercial music. He has also performed with his own quartet which includes Sheila Jordan and has become an ECM Records solo artist. Kuhn is an accomplished musician whose playing and compositions have developed from standard post-bop to include increasingly dissonant harmony and unusual time signatures and phrase lengths. Kuhn's favourites range from Fats Waller to Bill Evans.

● ALBUMS: *Stan Getz/Bob Brookmeyer* (1961)★★★★, *Ecstasy* (1974),★★★ *Trance* (1974)★★★, *Mobility* (1977)★★, *Non Fiction* (1978)★★★, *Last Year's Waltz* (ECM 1981)★★★, *Life's Magic* (Blackhawk 1986)★★, *The Vanguard Date* (Owl 1986)★★, *Mostly Ballads* (New World 1987)★★★, *Raindrops Live In My* (Muse 1988)★★★, *Porgy* (Jazz City 1988)★★, *Oceans In The Sky* (Owl 1990)★★★, *Looking Back* (Concord Jazz 1991)★★★, *Live At The Maybank Recital Hall Vol. 13* (Concord Jazz 1991)★★, *Years Later* (Concord Jazz 1993)★★★, *Seasons Of Romance* (Postcards 1995)★★★, *Remembering Tomorrow* (ECM 1996)★★★★, *Dedication* (Reservoir 1998)★★★.

KURYOKHIN, SERGEY

b. 16 June 1954, Murmansk, Russia, d. 9 July 1996 St. Petersburg, Russia. Kuryokhin started to play piano at the age of four and when his family settled in Leningrad in 1971 he attended the Leningrad Conservatory and later the Institute of Culture, but was expelled from both for failing to attend classes. After playing in rock groups at school, he was attracted to jazz by McCoy Tyner's playing on the John Coltrane records he heard broadcast on 'Voice Of America' radio programmes. Later piano influences included Cecil Taylor, Muhal Richard Abrams and Alex Von Schlippenbach, though he said that his chief inspirations were contemporary saxophonists such as Anthony Braxton, Evan Parker and, particularly, his compatriots Vladimir Chekasin and Anatoly Vapirov. He first came to notice playing with Vapirov in 1977 and later worked in groups with Chekasin and Boris Grebenshikov (with whom he co-led the rock group Aquarium) as well as forming his own Crazy Music Orchestra. The tapes of his first record, the solo *The Ways Of Freedom*, were smuggled out of the USSR and released by the London-based Leo Records in 1981. The album established him as a virtuoso technician, but many critics considered there was more style than substance to his music. Later releases on Leo included sessions with Chekasin (*Exercises*), Vapirov (*Sentenced To Silence, Invocations, De Profundis*) and Grebenshchikov (*Subway Culture* and the minimalist organ/guitar duo, *Mad Nightingales In The Russian Forest*) as well as further solos (*Popular Zoological Elements, Some Combinations Of Fingers And Passion*) and concerts with Pop Mechanics, the name he gave to all his ensembles from 1984 onwards. Increasingly eclectic in style and anarchic in spirit, Pop Mechanics became a major presence in the Russian musical underground; their one UK appearance, in Liverpool in 1989, featured massed electric guitars, bagpipes, African drummers, gospel singers, the Bootle Concertina Band and the brass section of the Liverpool Philharmonic, as well as theatrical elements such as onstage karate fights, Kuryokhin eating flowers and brief appearances by assorted cows and goats! The same year he toured the USA, playing with a range of musicians from John Zorn to Henry Kaiser to Boz Scaggs and recording for the Nonesuch label. The first international celebrity to emerge from the Russian jazz scene, Kuryokhin was as much a performance artist as a pianist and was also in demand as a composer, collaborating on projects with both Alfred Schnittke and the Kronos Quartet.

● ALBUMS: *The Ways Of Freedom* (Leo 1981)★★★, with Anatoly Vapirov *Sentenced To Silence* 1981 recording (1983)★★★, with Boris Grebenshchikov *Subway Culture* (Leo 1986)★★★★, *Introduction In Pop Mechanics* (Leo 1987)★★★★, *Popular Zoological Elements* (Leo 1987),★★★ *Pop Mechanics No 17 Live In Novosibirsk 1983* (Leo 1988)★★★, with Grebenshchikov *Mad Nightingales In The Russian Forest* (Leo 1989)★★★, with others *Document* 8-CD box-set (1990)★★★★, *Some Combinations Of Fingers And Passion* (Leo 1992)★★★★.

KYLE, BILLY

b. 14 July 1914, Philadelphia, Pennsylvania, USA, d. 23 February 1966. Kyle began playing piano semi-professionally while still at school and in the mid-30s was accompanying the popular singer Bon Bon Tunnell. Later in the decade he played with Tiny Bradshaw and Lucky Millinder and in 1938 joined John Kirby's band, where he remained until drafted for military service in 1942. After the war, Kyle rejoined Kirby for a while, then worked with Sy Oliver and also led his own small groups. Studio and theatre work occupied him for the next few years until, in 1953, he joined Louis Armstrong's All Stars. He remained with the All Stars until his death in February 1966. Although a highly-accomplished technician, Kyle preferred the accompanist's role, content to lend rhythmic support to his front-line colleagues. His delicate touch fitted superbly into the Kirby band and, although somewhat at odds with the flamboyance of the Armstrong band (he succeeded Earl 'Fatha' Hines), there were times when he appeared to be its most musicianly member.

● ALBUMS: *Louis Armstrong Plays W.C. Handy* (1954)★★★★.

● COMPILATIONS: with John Kirby *The Greatest Little Band In The Land (1939-42)* (1987)★★★★, *Finishing Up A Date 1939-46* (Collectors Item 1988)★★★.

KYNER, SONNY RED

b. Sylvester Kyner, 17 December 1932, Detroit, Michigan, USA, d. 20 March 1981, Detroit, Michigan, USA. Kyner made his first impact while still in his teens, playing alto saxophone with Barry Harris. This engagement spanned the end of the 40s and early 50s, and Kyner then spent a little while playing tenor saxophone before reverting to his first love, the alto. During the 50s he worked with several leading jazz musicians, including Frank Rosolino, Art Blakey, Curtis Fuller and Paul Quinichette. He recorded with some of these musicians and also under his own name. In succeeding decades he continued to work with bop musicians, including Donald Byrd, Kenny Dorham and Howard McGhee. A vigorous soloist with an inventive flair, Kyner's recordings suggest that his reputation deserves reevaluation.

● ALBUMS: with Art Pepper *Two Altos* reissued as *Art Pepper-Sonny Redd* (Regent/Savoy 1959)★★★, *Out Of The Blue* (Blue Note 1960)★★★★, *Breezin'* (Jazzland 1960)★★★, *The Mode* (Jazzland 1961)★★★, *Images* (Jazzland 1962)★★★.

L'Aventure Du Jazz

An outstanding film documentary produced and directed in 1969 by Louis and Claudine Panassie, this film features numerous leading mainstream musicians including, Eddie Barefield, Buck Clayton, William 'Cozy' Cole, Jimmy Crawford, Vic Dickenson, Sister Rosetta Tharpe, Milt Hinton, Pat Jenkins, Budd Johnson, Jo Jones, Eli Robinson, Zutty Singleton, Willie 'The Lion' Smith, Tiny Grimes, Buddy Tate and Dick Vance. Also on hand are blues singers John Lee Hooker and Memphis Slim and the exciting dance team, Lou Parks' Lindy Hoppers. Rarely seen, this film is a major achievement and worth a place on the shelf of any collector lucky enough to come across a copy. Soundtrack excerpts were issued as a double album on the Jazz Odyssey label.

La Faro, Scott

b. 3 April 1936, Newark, New Jersey, USA, d. 6 July 1961. After playing clarinet and saxophones in his early teens, La Faro switched to bass when he was 17 years old. Despite this late start, it was only a couple of years before he was good enough to join the Buddy Morrow band. Alerted to contemporary developments in jazz bass playing by listening to Percy Heath and Paul Chambers on records, La Faro quit Morrow late in 1956 while the band was in Los Angeles. During the next two years he played with several prominent west coast musicians, including Chet Baker, Buddy De Franco, Sonny Rollins and Herb Geller. In 1958, La Faro recorded with Harold Land and Hampton Hawes, and the following year joined Paul Motian and Bill Evans to form the Bill Evans Trio. This group played an important role in reshaping ideas on how the bass should function in a piano/bass/drums line-up. From being merely a supportive instrument which had only briefly enjoyed front-line status, after La Faro's work with Evans the bass became a major instrumental voice in its own right with considerable harmonic freedom. In 1959, La Faro worked with Thelonious Monk and the following year recorded with Ornette Coleman. La Faro's exceptional technique was facilitated by modifications he made to his instrument to accommodate his remarkably fast fingering. La Faro's death, in a road accident, came when he was 25 years of age. His influence on bass playing in jazz was akin to that of Jimmy Blanton who, with sad coincidence, also died in his early twenties.

● ALBUMS: *Joe Gordon And Scott La Faro* reissue (1993)★★, with Joe Gordon *West Coast Days* (Fresh Sounds 1994)★★★.

La Roca, Pete

b. Peter Sims, 7 April 1938, New York City, New York, USA. Although classically trained, drummer La Roca's early professional work was with Latin bands (hence his adopted name). Before he was out of his teens he was playing jazz with some of the music's leading exponents, including Sonny Rollins with whom he worked for two years. La Roca can be heard on Rollins' classic 1957 Blue Note Records date documented on *A Night At The Village Vanguard*. In the late 50s and early 60s La Roca played with Jackie McLean, Slide Hampton and John Coltrane. Later, he worked with, among others, Art Farmer, Mose Allison and Freddie Hubbard, and led his own quartet featuring Joe Henderson, Steve Swallow and Steve Kuhn. Disenchanted with the music scene of the mid-60s, he retired in 1968 to practice law. Subsequent returns to music proved only fleeting until he returned with an all-star band for a sublime 1997 major label session. La Roca is a vigorous exponent of the complex free-time school of jazz, a concept that defies all preconceptions of the drummer's role.

● ALBUMS: *Basra* (Blue Note 1965)★★★★, *Bliss!/Turkish Women At The Baths* (Douglas 1967)★★★, *Swingtime* (Blue Note 1997)★★★★.

La Velle

b. La Velle McKinnie, 22 May 1944, Kankakee, Illinois, USA. Born into a musical family, McKinnie was a child prodigy, singing at the age of three, taking piano lessons from four, and at five was a member of the Little Black Angels gospel group with whom she appeared on *The Ed Sullivan Show*. Six years later she was studying at Chicago's American Conservatory of Music. As a young teenager, she sang classical music including oratorios and opera, appearing in productions of Handel's *Messiah*, Verdi's *Tosca*, Puccini's *Madame Butterfly*, and Bizet's *Carmen*. Earning a living in music, however, thrust her onto the nightclub and hotel lounge circuit with engagements in Chicago, Dallas and Las Vegas. She visited Europe, becoming very popular in France and decided to base herself in Paris. Her repertoire had by now encompassed the great standards of popular song with touches of jazz, the blues and gospel. She ventured into a rock-funk mode for a time, but her career faltered a little, reviving in the late 80s by which time she was based in Geneva, Switzerland. She recorded with Ray Brown, Guy Lafitte, and others, and returned to Paris for a 1992 engagement with Archie Shepp, playing in *Black Ballad* at the Casino de Paris. She also made a hit at the 1994 Marciac jazz festival. She has worked extensively on radio and television both on-screen and on advertising jingles. Among her single recordings have been winners of the Disques D'or Européen (1980 and 1983) while her album appearances include guest spots on the rock operas *Deamonia* and *Nostradamus*, and backing to Dee Dee Bridgewater and Ray Charles. Her albums under her own name clearly demonstrate her highly developed sense of style. Always musical, she ranges through her repertoire with flair and great zest. Her piano-playing is sure and sound as befits one with her background. Although her name remains little known outside France and Switzerland, her reputation is gradually spreading throughout Europe.

● ALBUMS: with Bessie Griffin *Gospel* (1974)★★★, *Right Now* (1980)★★★, *Brand New Start* (1983)★★★, with Psalms *Psalms* (1987)★★, with Steve Lacy *Festival De Jazz De Besançon* (1989)★★★, *Hot Brass Club* (1989)★★, *Straight Singing'* (OMD 1991)★★★.

LaBarbera, Joe

b. 22 February 1948, Mount Morris, New York, USA. The youngest of three musically active brothers, LaBarbera was taught to play drums by his father before moving on to Berklee College Of Music. In the late 60s he worked and recorded with a number of jazz musicians, including his brother Pat LaBarbera, and also showed a special aptitude for accompanying singers. After a brief stint with Woody Herman in the 70s he joined Chuck Mangione with whom he remained for four years. He then joined Bill Evans for two years and for much of the 80s was with singer Tony Bennett. A highly sophisticated, stylish and subtle player, his work with singers is light, uncluttered and always propulsive. As an accompanist to instrumentalists, he is similarly swinging and supportive.

● ALBUMS: with Chuck Mangione *Land Of Make Believe* (Mercury 1973)★★★, with Bill Evans *The Paris Concert: Edition One* (Elektra 1979)★★★★, with Norma Winstone *Well Kept Secret* (Hot House 1993)★★★.

LaBarbera, Pat

b. Pascel LaBarbera, 7 April 1944, Warsaw, New York, USA. Older brother of John and Joe LaBarbera, he, too, was first taught by his father. He later studied at Berklee College Of Music from where he went into Buddy Rich's band as featured tenor saxophone soloist. In the mid-70s he moved to Canada and then joined Elvin Jones. A powerful player with a style rooted in post-John Coltrane tenor thinking, his talent is such that he has not fallen into the self-induced trap which befell so many others. His energy and improvisational skills are linked to an engaging romantic flavour which he displays on several other instruments in the saxophone family and also the flute.

Lacy, Steve

b. Steven Lackritz, 23 July 1934, New York City, New York, USA. Few modern jazzmen have chosen the soprano saxophone as their main instrument; Steve Lacy is probably unique in choosing it as his only one. Reputed to be the player who inspired John Coltrane to take up the soprano (after which, thousands followed!), he is ultimately responsible for the renaissance and current popularity of the straight horn. He may also be unique for a career that has taken him through virtually every genre of jazz, from dixieland to bebop, free-form and total improvisation. As a child he started piano lessons, then changed to clarinet and finally soprano saxophone. Inspired initially by Sidney Bechet, he began his career playing dixieland (two 1954 dates led by trumpeter Dick Sutton were reissued under Lacy's name as *The Complete Jaguar Sessions* in 1986). Then, in an extraordinary switch, he spent the mid-50s working with *avant garde* pioneer Cecil Taylor (*In Transition*) and by the end of the decade had also played with Gil Evans (*Pacific Standard Time*), Jimmy Giuffre and Sonny Rollins. His own 1957 debut, *Soprano Saxophone*, featured Wynton Kelly and the follow-up, *Reflections: Steve Lacy Plays The Music Of Thelonious Monk*, marked the beginning of a long, and continuing association with Mal Waldron. Both albums also included several tracks by Thelonious Monk, by whose music Lacy had become increasingly beguiled. In 1960, he persuaded Monk to hire him as a sideman for 16 weeks, and between 1961 and 1965 he and Roswell Rudd co-led a group that played only Monk tunes - 'to find out why they were so beautiful'. (This fascination has remained with him - *School Days*, *Epistrophy*, *Eronel*, *Only Monk* and *More Monk* are all devoted to further exploring, in group and solo context, the great man's compositions.) In 1965, Lacy moved to Europe, where he worked with Carla Bley in the Jazz Realities project and co-led a group with Enrico Rava, with whom he also toured South America in 1966. In this period, influenced in part by earlier collaborations with Don Cherry, Lacy was playing mostly free jazz (*Sortie* and *The Forest And The Zoo*). The focus of his attention would later shift back towards jazz compositions, especially after the mid-60s when he completed his first major piece, 'The Way', a suite based on text from the ancient Chinese *Tao Te Ching*; he has maintained an occasional involvement with total improvisation, most notably on records with Derek Bailey (*Company 4*) and Evan Parker (*Chirps*). In 1966, he revisited New York and played in a quintet with Karl Berger and Paul Motian but, finding work scarce, he returned to Europe in 1967, settling in Rome with his Swiss wife, Irene Aebi, who sings and plays cello and violin on many of his albums. Three years later, he relocated to Paris, which became his home base until a move to Berlin in 1997. Leading his own group (usually a sextet), he has in the last two decades built up one of the most impressive and diverse recording catalogues in jazz, hitting a peak in the 80s with a series of albums - *Prospectus, Furturities*, *The Gleam* and *Momentum* - which show the group honing to perfection the intricate dialogues and seamless blends of invention and discipline so typical of their music. Important group members over the years have included Steve Potts (saxophone), Kent Carter and Jean-Jacques Avenal (both bass), Bobby Few (piano), Oliver Johnson (drums), guest George Lewis (trombone) and - perhaps most crucially - Aebi, for whose severe, lieder-style vocals Lacy created what is virtually a new concept of jazz songwriting. He has often set texts by modern writers - *Sons* is a collaboration with Brion Gysin, *Futurities* a series of poems by Robert Creely - but *Tips* is more unusual still, with Lacy shaping his tunes around extracts from the notebooks of painter Georges

Braque. Outside of his regular group (currently one of the most adventurous in jazz), Lacy's projects have included duos with Potts, Ran Blake, Mal Waldron and Gil Evans; plus tributes to Monk and Herbie Nichols (*Regenerations*, *Change Of Season* and *The ICP Orchestra Performs Nichols - Monk*) in the company of Misha Mengelberg and Han Bennink, who also collaborated on the *Dutch Masters* recording. Lacy is also one of today's outstanding practitioners of solo saxophone music. Inspired by hearing the solo work of Anthony Braxton, he began to develop his own soprano saxophone repertoire in the early 70s and has since developed this over a succession of solo concerts and recordings, the latter including such notable examples of the genre as *Hocus Pocus*, *The Kiss* and *Remains*. Incredibly prolific, Lacy has released over 80 albums under his own name and probably appeared on as many again as a sideman: paradoxically, 1991's *Itinerary* was his first-ever release as leader of a big band. A brilliant composer and improviser, Lacy can be counted one of the most significant jazz figures of the era, his music sure to stand as an enduring treasure. He is, as well, simply an enchanting player. To quote Graham Lock's 1983 comment: 'There are few sounds as distinctive or as lovely as Lacy's soprano, with its comet-trails of bare bones lyricism.'

● ALBUMS: *Soprano Today* reissued as *Wynton Kelly With Steve Lacy* (Prestige 1958)★★★★, *Reflections: Steve Lacy Plays Thelonious Monk* (New Jazz 1959)★★★, *The Straight Horn Of Steve Lacy* (Candid 1961)★★★, with Don Cherry *Evidence* (New Jazz 1962)★★★★, *Disposability* (Vik/RCA Italia 1966)★★★, *Sortie* (GTA 1966)★★★, *The Forest And The Zoo* (ESP 1967)★★★, *Moon* (BYG 1969)★★★, *Epistrophy* (BYG 1969)★★★, *Roba* 1969 recording (Saravah 1971)★★★, *Wordless* (Futura 1971)★★★, *Lapis* (Saravah 1971)★★★★, with Mal Waldron *Journey Without End* (Victor 1971)★★★, *Estilhaços (Chips) - Live In Lisbon* (Sassetti 1972)★★★, with Waldron *Mal Waldron With The Steve Lacy Quintet* (America 1972)★★★, *The Gap* (America 1972)★★★, with Franz Koglmann *Flaps* (Pipe 1973)★★★, *Concert Solo* 1972 recording (Emanem 1974)★★★, *Scraps* (Saravah 1974)★★★, *Flakes* (RCA-Vista 1975)★★★, *The Crust* 1973 recording (Emanem 1975)★★★, *School Days* 1963 recordings (Emanem 1975)★★★★, *Stalks* (Columbia Japan 1975)★★★, *Dreams* (Saravah 1975)★★★, *Solo At Mandara* (Aim 1975)★★★, *Saxophone Special* 1974 recording (Emanem 1976)★★★, *Distant Voices* (Columbia Japan 1976)★★★, *Stabs* (FMP 1976)★★★, with Andrea Centazzo *Clangs* (Ictus 1976)★★★, *Trickles* (Black Saint 1976)★★★, *The Wire* (Denon Jazz 1977)★★★, with Michael Smith *Sidelines* (Improvising Artists 1977)★★★, *Straws* (Cramps 1977)★★★, with Centazzo, Kent Carter *Trio Live* 1976 recording (Ictus 1977)★★★★, *Raps* (Adelphi Jazz 1977)★★★, *Threads* (Horo 1977)★★, *Lumps* 1974 recordings (ICP 1978)★★★, *Follies* (FMP 1978)★★★, *The Owl* (Saravah 1978)★★★, *Axieme Volumes 1 & 2* 1975 recordings (Red 1978)★★★, *Clinkers* (hatART 1978)★★★, with Carter *Catch* (Horo 1978)★★★, *Points* (Chant Du Monde 1978)★★★, *Shots* 1977 recording (Musica 1979)★★★★, *Torments (Solo In Kyoto)* 1975 recording (Morgue 1979)★★★, *Crops/The Woe* 1973/1976 recordings, reissued as *Weal & Woe* (Quark 1979)★★★, *Stamps* 1977/1978 recordings (hatART 1979)★★★, with Maarten Altena *High, Low And Order* (Claxon 1979)★★★, *Eronel* (Horo 1979)★★★, *Troubles* (Black Saint 1979)★★★, *The Way* (hatART 1980)★★★★, with Walter Zuber Armstrong *Alter Ego* (World Artists 1980)★★★, with Armstrong *Call Notes* (World Artists 1980)★★★, *Capers* 1979 recording (hatART 1981)★★★, with Steve Potts, Irene Aebi *Tips* 1979 recording (hatART 1981)★★★, with various artists *Amarcord Nino Rota* (Hannibal 1981)★★★, with Brion Gysin *Songs* (hatART 1981)★★★★, *Ballets* 1980/1981 recordings (hatART 1982)★★★, *The Flame* (Soul Note 1982)★★★, with Mal Waldron *Snake Out* (hatART 1982)★★★, with Waldron *Herbe De L'Oubli* 1981 recording (hatART 1983)★★★, with Masahiko Togashi *Eternal Duo* 1981 recording (Paddle Wheel/King 1983)★★★, *Blinks* (hatART 1984)★★★, with various artists *That's The Way I Feel Now* (A&M 1984)★★★, *Prospectus* (hatART 1984)★★★, with Han Bennink, Arjen Gorter, George Lewis, Misha Mengelberg *Change Of Season (Music Of Herbie Nichols)* (Soul Note 1985)★★★, *Futurities* (hatART 1985)★★★, with Evan Parker *Chirps* (FMP 1985)★★★, *Outings* (ISMEZ 1986)★★★, *The Condor* (Soul Note 1986)★★★★, with Waldron *Let's Call This* 1981 recordings (hatART 1986)★★★, *Hocus-Pocus* (Crepuscule 1986)★★★, *Solo* Japanese limited edition (no label 1986)★★★, with Ulrich Gumpert *Deadline* 1985 recording (Sound Aspects 1987)★★★, *Only Monk* 1985 recordings (Soul Note 1987)★★★★, with Waldron *Sempre Amore* (Soul Note 1987)★★★★, *The Kiss* (Lunatic 1987)★★★, *The Gleam* (Silkheart 1987)★★★, *One Fell Swoop* (Silkheart 1987)★★★, *Momentum* (Novus 1987)★★★, with Waldron *Live At Sweet Basil* (King 1987)★★★, *The Complete Jaguar Sessions* 1954 recordings (Fresco 1988)★★★, with Subroto Roy Chowdhury *Explorations* (Jazz Point 1988)★★★, *The Window* (Soul Note 1988)★★★, with Potts *Live In Budapest* (West Wind 1988)★★★, with John Lindberg, Eric Watson*The Amiens Concert* (Label Bleu 1988)★★★, with Gil Evans *Paris Blues* (Owl 1988)★★★, with Steve Argüelles *Image* 1987 recording (Ah-Um 1989)★★★, with Jean-Jacques Avenel, Togashi *Voices* (NEC Avenue/Pan 1989)★★★, *The Door* (Novus 1989)★★★, *Morning Joy* 1986 recording (hatART 1990)★★★★, *Anthem* (Novus/RCA 1990)★★★, *Rushes: 10 Songs From Russia* (New Sound Planet 1990)★★★★, *Steve Lacy Solo* 1985 recording (In Situ 1991)★★★, with Bennink, Lewis, Mengelberg, Ernst Reyseger *Dutch Masters* 1987 recording (Soul Note 1991)★★★, *More Monk* 1989 recordings (Soul Note 1991)★★★, with Potts *Flim-Flam* 1986 recording (hatART 1991)★★★, with Waldron *Hot House* (Novus 1991)★★★★, as Steve Lacy + 16 *Itinerary* (hatART 1991)★★★, *Remains* (hatART 1992)★★★, *Live At Sweet Basil* (Novus 1992)★★★, with Togashi *Twilight* (Nippon Crown 1992)★★★, with Watson *Spirit Of Mingus* (Freelance 1992)★★★, as Steve Lacy 6 *We See* (hatART 1993)★★★★, with Waldron *Lets Call This ... Esteem* (Slam 1993)★★★, as Steve Lacy Octet *Vespers* (Soul Note 1993)★★★★, as Steve Lacy Double Sextet *Clangs* (hatART 1993)★★★, as Antonyms 1 *Established Mode Of Speech* (Sub Rosa 1994)★★★, with others *Interpretations Of Monk* 4-CD box set (DIW 1994)★★★, with Potts *Steve Lacy Meets Steve Potts* (Soul Note 1994)★★★, with Lol Coxhill, Evan Parker *Three Blokes* 1992 recordings (FMP 1994)★★★, with Keptorchestra *Sweet Sixteen* (Caligola 1994)★★★, *Findings* (CMAP/Outre Mesure 1995)★★★, with Barry Wedgle *The Rendezvous* (Exit 1995)★★★, as Steve Lacy Quartet *Revenue* 1993 recordings (Soul Note 1995)★★★★,

Packet (New Albion 1995)★★★, *Actuality* (Cavity Search 1995)★★★★, with Waldron *Live At The Dreher, Paris 1981: Round Midnight Vol. 1* (hatART 1996)★★★★, *Bye-Ya* (Freelance 1996)★★★, with Waldron *I Remember Thelonious* 1992 recording (Nel Jazz 1996)★★★, *Five Facings* (FMP 1996)★★★★, *Associates* (Musica Jazz 1996)★★★, *Blues For Aida* (Egg Farm 1996)★★★, with Togashi *Eternal Duo 95* (Take One 1996)★★★, with Waldron *Communiqué* 1994 recordings (Soul Note 1997)★★★, *5 x Monk 5 x Lacy* 1994 recording (Silkheart 1997)★★★★, with Waldron *Live At The Dreher, Paris 1981: The Peak Vol. 2* (hatART 1997)★★★★, *Two, Five & Six Blinks* (hatART 1997)★★★, *Live At Unity Temple* (Wobbly Rail 1998)★★.

● COMPILATIONS: *Giants Of Jazz* 1957/1961/1963 recordings (Sarabandas 1996)★★★★.

● FURTHER READING: *Findings: My Experience With The Soprano Saxophone*, Steve Lacy.

LADNIER, TOMMY

b. 28 May 1900, Florenceville, Louisiana, USA, d. 4 June 1939. As a child Ladnier played trumpet locally, as well as in nearby Mandeville where he was heard by George Lewis and Bunk Johnson. Later, during Johnson's renaissance, he claimed to have taught Ladnier. In 1917, Ladnier travelled to Chicago where he played in several bands, culminating, in 1924, with the band led by his idol, Joe 'King' Oliver. Early in 1925, Ladnier was hired by Sam Wooding with whom he visited Europe. During the next few years Ladnier played in Germany, Poland, France and other European countries with, among others, Wooding, Benny Peyton, Louis Douglas, Noble Sissle and also played engagements back in the USA, mainly with Fletcher Henderson. In the early 30s, Ladnier teamed up with Sidney Bechet to co-lead a band they named the New Orleans Feetwarmers. In 1933, Ladnier and Bechet continued their partnership but on a non-musical basis, jointly running a tailor's shop in New York. In the mid-30s, Ladnier led his own small groups in comparative obscurity, but in 1938 he played with Bechet on recording dates for the French jazz writer Hugues Panassie. The two musical partners also played at a Carnegie Hall concert, *Spirituals To Swing*, organized by John Hammond Jnr. Ladnier's playing style was a simple and direct exposition of the blues and as an accompanist to blues singers, like Ma Rainey and Ida Cox, he displayed considerable empathy.

● ALBUMS: with Ida Cox *Ida Cox With Tommy Ladnier* 10-inch album (Riverside 1953)★★★, *Early Ladnier* 10-inch album (Riverside 1954)★★★, *Tommy Ladnier Plays The Blues* 10-inch album (Riverside 1954)★★★, *Tommy Ladnier* (X 1955)★★★.

LADY IN AUTUMN - BILLIE HOLIDAY

Without question the greatest jazz singer there has ever been (or will ever be), Billie Holiday's unmistakable sound, her inimitable phrasing, her faultless sense of what was right, helped mould an artist unique in the history of popular music. In the early years her joyous, youthful voice was backed by soloists of the calibre of Buck Clayton, her close friend Lester Young, and her ideal arranger, pianist Teddy Wilson. Towards the end of her life her voice was a flaking, fractured caricature of itself but her commanding artistry and musical integrity lent dignity and poignancy to her recordings.

● Tracks: *Body And Soul; Strange Fruit; Trav'lin' Light; All Of Me; (There Is) No Greater Love; I Cover The Waterfront; These Foolish Things (Remind Me Of You); Tenderly; Autumn In New York; My Man; Stormy Weather; Yesterdays; (I Got A Man, Crazy For Me) He's Funny That Way; What A Little Moonlight Can Do; I Cried For You (Now It's Your Turn To Cry Over Me); Too Marvelous For Words; I Wished On The Moon; I Don't Want To Cry Anymore; Prelude To A Kiss; Nice Work If You Can Get It; Come Rain Or Come Shine; What's New?; God Bless The Child; Do Nothin' Till You Hear From Me; April In Paris; Lady Sings The Blues; Don't Explain; Fine And Mellow; I Didn't Know What Time It Was; Stars Fell On Alabama; One For My Baby (And One More For The Road); Gee Baby, Ain't I Good To You; Lover Man (Oh, Where Can You Be?); All The Way; Don't Worry 'bout Me.*

● First released 1973

● UK peak chart position: did not chart

● USA peak chart position: did not chart

LADY IN SATIN - BILLIE HOLIDAY

This was Billie Holiday's penultimate album, recorded when her body was telling her enough was enough. During the sessions with arranger Ray Ellis she was drinking vodka neat, as if it were tap water. Yet, for all her ravaged voice (the sweetness had long gone) she was still an incredible singer. The feeling and tension she manages to put into almost every track sets this album as one of her finest achievements. 'You've Changed' and 'I Get Along Without You Very Well' are high art performances from the singer who saw life from the bottom upwards. The CD reissue masterminded by Phil Shaap is absolutely indispensable.

● Tracks: *I'm A Fool To Want You; For Heaven's Sake; You Don't Know What Love Is; I Get Along Without You Very Well; For All We Know; Violets For Your Furs; You've Changed; It's Easy To Remember; But Beautiful; Glad To Be Unhappy; I'll Be Around; The End Of A Love Affair; I'm A Fool To Want You (Alternate tracks); The End Of A Love Affair (Alternate tracks); Pause Track.*

● First released 1958

● UK peak chart position: did not chart

● USA peak chart position: did not chart

LAFITTE, GUY

b. 12 January 1927, St. Gaudens, France, d. 10 June 1998. Lafitte took up the tenor saxophone in his early 20s, having earlier played clarinet with gypsy bands in the Toulouse area. He later led his own bands in Paris and worked extensively with visiting American jazz and blues artists, including Big Bill Broonzy, Mezz Mezzrow, Bill Coleman and Buck Clayton. This was in the early 50s and by the end of the decade he had also played with Lionel Hampton and Arnett Cobb, and appeared in the film *Paris Blues* (1961), in which Louis Armstrong and Duke Ellington also featured. Although capable of powerful, earthy playing, Lafitte is at his best as a balladeer where the early influence of Coleman Hawkins gleams through his solos.

● ALBUMS: *Club Sessions No. 2* (1954)★★★, *Blue And*

Sentimental (1954)★★★, *Guy Lafitte Et Son Orchestre* (1954)★★★, *Guy Lafitte, Son Saxo-ténor Et Son Orchestre* (1954)★★★★, *Guy Lafitte Et Son Quartette* (1955)★★★, *Guy Lafitte Avec Frank Pourcel Et Son Orchestre* (1955)★★★, *Les Classiques Du Jazz Vol. 1* (1955)★★★, *Do Not Disturb* (1956)★★★, *Guy Lafitte Quartet i* (1956)★★★, *Guy Lafitte Et Son Grand Orchestre* (1957)★★, *Classiques Du Jazz Vol. 2* (1957)★★★, *Guy Lafitte Et Son Grand Orchestre, Sextet Et Quartet* (1959)★★★, *Guy Lafitte Quartet ii* (1960)★★★, *10 Sax Succes* (1960)★★★, *Guy Lafitte* (1961)★★★, *Guy Lafitte Jazz Sextet* (1962)★★, *Love In Hi-Fi* (1962)★★★, *Jambo!* (1963)★★, *Guy Lafitte Quintet* (1964)★★★, *Blues* (1969)★★★★, *Blues In Summertime* (1970)★★★, *Sugar And Spice* (1972)★★★, with Bill Coleman *Mainstream At Montreux* (1973)★★★, *Guy Lafitte Joue Charles Trenet* (1977-84)★★★, *Corps Et Ame* (1978)★★, *Happy!* (1979)★★★, *Three Men On A Beat* (1983)★★★, with Wild Bill Davis *Lotus Blossom* (Black And Blue 1983)★★★★, *The Things We Did Last Summer* (Black And Blue 1990)★★★.

LAGRENE, BIRELI

b. 4 September 1966. Saverne, Alsace, France. The son of Fiso Lagrene, a popular guitarist in pre-war France, Lagrene displayed a prodigious talent as a very young child. Born into a gypsy community, his origins and his fleet, inventive playing style inevitably generated comparisons with Django Reinhardt. In 1978, he won a prize at a festival at Strasbourg and subsequently made a big impact during a televised gypsy festival. In his early teenage years Lagrene toured extensively playing concerts and festivals across Europe, often accompanied by distinguished jazz artists such as Benny Carter, Benny Goodman, Stéphane Grappelli and Niels-Henning Ørsted Pedersen. He also made his first record *Routes To Django*, which helped to prove that early estimates of his capabilities were not excessive. An outstanding technician, Lagrene has revealed influences other than Reinhardt, happily incorporating bebop phraseology, rock rhythms and Brazilian music into his work. By the late 80s he had moved substantially from his early Reinhardt-style to fully embrace jazz-rock and other electronically-aided fusions, a shift which, while extending his popularity to a wider audience, tended to lower his standing among jazz purists. In mid-summer 1991, he was one of several leading guitarists featured at the International Guitar Festival in Seville, Spain.

● ALBUMS: *Routes To Django: Live At The Krokodil* (Jazzpoint 1980)★★★★, *Bireli Swing '81* (Jazzpoint 1981)★★★, with Joseph Bowie Concert *And Space* (Sackville 1981)★★, *15* (Antilles 1982)★★★, *Down In Town* (Antilles 1983)★★★, *Musique Tzigane/Manouch* (1984)★★, *Erster Tango* (1985)★★★, *Bireli Lagrene Ensemble Live Featuring Vic Juris* (1985)★★★, *Stuttgart Aria* (Jazzpoint 1986)★★★, *Special Guests Freitag 2 Mai, Samstag 3 Mai, Mühle Hunziken* (1986)★★★, *Foreign Affairs* (1986)★★, *Inferno* (Blue Note 1987)★★★★, with Larry Coryell, Miroslav Vitous *Bireli Lagrene* (1988)★★★, *Acoustic Moments* (Blue Note 1990)★★★, *Standards* (Blue Note 1992)★★★, *Live In Marciac* (Dreyfus 1996)★★★, *Blue Eyes* (Dreyfus 1998)★★★.

LAI, FRANCIS

b. 1932, Nice, France. A composer and conductor for films from the early 60s. After scoring *Circle Of Love*, Roger Vadim's re-make of Ophuls' classic *La Ronde*, starring Jane Fonda, Lai won an Academy Award for his music to director Claud Lelouch's classic love story *A Man And A Woman* (1966). He also scored Lelouch's follow-up, *Live For Life*, before going on to something lighter with the comedy-drama, *I'll Never Forget What's 'Is Name*; followed by others in the late 60s such as *Three Into Two Won't Go*, *Mayerling* and *Hannibal Brooks*. In 1970, Lai won his second Oscar for *Love Story*, one of the most popular movies of the decade. The soundtrack album stayed at number 2 in the US album chart for six weeks, and the film's theme, 'Where Do I Begin?' (lyric by Carl Sigman), was a singles hit in the USA for Andy Williams, Henry Mancini and Lai himself; and in the UK for Williams and Shirley Bassey. In the same year, Lai, with his Orchestra, had a big hit in Japan with the title music for the film *Le Passager De La Pluie (Rider Of The Rain)*. During the 70s, Lai's cosmopolitan career included several more films for Lelouch, such as *The Crook*, *Money, Money, Money*, *Happy New Year*, *Cat And Mouse*, *Child Under A Leaf*, *Emmanuelle II* and *Another Man, Another Chance*; and others, such as *. . . And Hope To Die*, *Visit To A Chief's Son*, *And Now My Love*, *International Velvet* and the sequel to *Love Story*, *Oliver's Story* (1979) (music written with Lee Holdridge). In the 80s and early 90s the majority of Lai's music continued to be for French productions, and the Lelouch connection was maintained through films such as *Bolero* (in conjunction with Michel LeGrand), *Edith And Marcel*, *Bandits*, *La Belle Histoire (The Beautiful Story)* (co-composer Philippe Servain) and *Les Cles Du Paradis (The Keys To Paradise)* (1992). His work for other directors included *Beyond The Reef*, *Marie*; *A Man And A Woman: 20 Years Later* and *My New Partner II*. Besides his scores for feature films, Lai also contributed music to television programmes such as *Berlin Affair* and *Sins* (mini-series). Recordings include: *Great Film Themes*; *A Man, A Woman And A Love Story*; and the soundtracks, *Bilitis* and *Dark Eyes*.

LAINE, CLEO

b. Clementina Dinah Campbell, 28 October 1927, Southall, Middlesex, England. Her earliest performance was as an extra in the film, *The Thief Of Bagdad* (1940). Laine's singing career started with husband John Dankworth's big band in the early 50s working with some of the best modern jazz musicians available. She married Dankworth in 1958 and since then they have become one of the UK's best-known partnerships, although they have clearly developed additional separate careers. Throughout the 60s, Laine began extending her repertoire adding to the usual items like 'Riding High', 'I Got Rhythm' and 'Happiness Is Just A Thing Called Joe', arrangements of lyrics by literary figures like Eliot, Hardy, Auden and Shakespeare (*Word Songs*). Her varied repertoire also includes Kurt Weill and

Schoenberg's 'Pierrot Lunaire'. She possesses a quite unique voice which spans a number of octaves from a smokey, husky deep whisper to a shrill but incredibly delicate high register. Her scat-singing matches the all time greats including Ella Fitzgerald and Sarah Vaughan. In 1976, she recorded 'Porgy And Bess' with Ray Charles in a non-classical version, which is in the same vein as the earlier Ella Fitzgerald and Louis Armstrong interpretation. She has recorded, with great success, duets with flautist James Galway and guitarist John Williams. Laine is also an accomplished actress having appeared in a number of films and stage productions. In addition to her incredible vocal range and technique she has done much, through her numerous television appearances, to broaden the public's acceptance of different styles of music in a jazz setting, and in doing so she has broken many barriers. In 1997 she was made a Dame in the New Year's Honours List.

● ALBUMS: *Cleo Laine* (Esquire 1955)★★★, *Cleo's Choice* (Pye 1958)★★★, *She's The Tops* (MGM 1958)★★★, *All About Me* (Fontana 1962)★★★, *Woman Talk* (Fontana 1966)★★★, *Cleo Laine Live At Carnegie Hall,* (RCA 1973)★★★★, *Day By Day* (Buddah 1974)★★★, *A Beautiful Thing* (RCA 1974)★★★, *Born On A Friday* (RCA 1976)★★★, with Ray Charles *Porgy And Bess* (RCA 1976)★★★★, *A Lover And His Lass* (1976)★★★★, *Feel The Warm* (1976)★★★, with John Williams *Best Friends* (RCA 1978)★★★★, *Cleo* (Arcade 1978)★★★, *Word Songs* (1978)★★★, *Return To Carnegie* (RCA 1979)★★★★, *I Am A Song* (RCA 1979)★★★, with James Galway *Sometimes When We Touch* (RCA 1980)★★★, *The Incomparable Cleo Laine* (1980)★★★, *Gonna Get Through* (1980)★★★, *This Is Cleo Laine* (1981)★★★, *Smilin' Through* (1982)★★★, *Let The Music Take You* (1983)★★★, *Off The Record* (1984)★★★, *Themes* (1985)★★★, *That Old Feeling* (Music Collection 1987)★★★, *Cleo Sings Sondheim* (1987)★★★★, *Shakespeare And All That Jazz* (Affinity 1988)★★★★, *Woman To Woman* (RCA 1989)★★★, with Mel Tormé *Nothing Without You* (1993)★★★, *Blue And Sentimental* (1993)★★★.

● COMPILATIONS: *Platinum Collection* (Cube 1981)★★★★, *The Essential Collection* (1987)★★★★, *Cleo's Choice* (1988)★★★★, *Unforgettable Cleo Laine* (PRT 1988)★★★★, *Portrait Of A Song Stylist* (Masterpiece 1989)★★★★, *The Very Best Of Cleo Laine: 34 Classic Hits* (BMG 1997)★★★★.

● FURTHER READING: *Cleo*, Cleo Laine. *Cleo And John*, Graham Collier (ed.).

LAINE, PAPA JACK

b. 21 September 1873, New Orleans, Louisiana, USA, d. 1 June 1966. Towards the end of the 19th century, drummer and alto horn player Laine formed ragtime and marching bands in his home town. The marching band, which Laine named the Reliance Brass Band, became very popular and he continued to lead it, and also to run other bands under the same banner up until his retirement in 1917. Many of the best-known white musicians in New Orleans played in one or another of Laine's bands, among them Nick La Rocca and Joseph 'Sharkey' Bonano. Although he did not record as a musician, Laine did record his reminiscences while some of his former sidemen recorded as Papa Laine's Children.

LAIRD, RICK

b. 5 February 1941, Dublin, Eire. Laird started playing the piano when he was aged five and turned to the double bass when he was 18. The family had moved to New Zealand but he went on to Australia where he played with Mike Nock before coming to England where he studied at the Guildhall School of Music in the early 60s. He accompanied vocalists Lambert, Hendricks And Ross, joined the house band at Ronnie Scott's club (1964-66) and played with Sonny Rollins on the soundtrack of the film *Alfie* (1965). In 1966, he went to the Berklee College Of Music in Boston, USA and in 1968 started playing bass guitar. He toured with Buddy Rich (1969-71) and then played with the Mahivishnu Orchestra (1971-73). While the double bass remains his favourite instrument it was on bass guitar that he played with the Orchestra combining with drummer Billy Cobham to provide its massive rhythmic punch. Since leaving the Orchestra he has worked primarily in the New York studios with artists such as Chick Corea and tenor saxophonists Stan Getz and Joe Henderson.

LAKE, OLIVER

b. 14 September 1942, Marianna, Arkansas, USA. Lake's family moved to St. Louis, Missouri in 1943. He played in high school, but only applied himself seriously to alto saxophone at the age of 20. Lake worked in R&B and soul bands with Lester Bowie, then formed his own group with Floyd LeFlore (trumpet) and Leonard Smith (drums). In 1968, he received a BA in music education from Lincoln University and taught music in St. Louis schools for three years. During this time he became a founder member of the Black Artists Group (BAG) and co-ordinated exchange concerts with Chicago's AACM. He studied arrangement and composition with Oliver Nelson and bassist Ron Carter. In 1972, he joined other BAG members in Paris, played with Anthony Braxton and explored electronic music. He relocated to New York in September 1973, but returned to Paris to record *Passing Thru*, a solo alto saxophone record with a sax/synthesizer dialogue called 'Whap', in May 1974. Braxton used his position at Arista Records to get Lake a record contract and wrote a sleevenote for *Heavy Spirits* (1975). The album was a masterpiece of chilled modernity, including three tracks of improvised alto against scored strings. Lake subsequently lightened his approach, to mixed results. A band with Michael Gregory Jackson (guitar) and Paul Maddox (drums, later Pheeroan akLaff) played startlingly original music (1976-8), spiky *avant garde* classical sonorities threaded with pliant saxophone. *Prophet*, recorded in 1980 for the Black Saint label, was a tribute to Lake's idol Eric Dolphy, while the next year's *Clevont Fitzhubert*, was classic free-bop. Later signed to Gramavision, Lake attempted to come on as a pop band (*Jump Up*), but despite spirited playing they never seemed to quite get the hang of the reggae rhythms they attempted to use. Lake had played in a saxophone quartet brought together by Braxton for his *New York, Fall 1974* and in 1977, with David Murray replacing Braxton, they called themselves the World Saxophone Quartet. By the mid-80s the group were firm favourites at international jazz festivals. Lake meanwhile led small groups that often included Geri Allen, akLaff and Fred Hopkins, producing shining, incisive music that brought together all the diverse threads of his career. In the late 80s he was also playing with Reggie Workman in the bassist's own Ensemble and in the collective Trio Transition, and he can also be heard in electrifying form on Marilyn Crispell's live 1991 *Circles*.

● ALBUMS: *Passing Thru* (1974)★★★, *Heavy Spirits* (Arista 1975)★★★★, *NTU: Point From Which Creation Begins* 1971 recording (Arista 1976)★★★★, *Holding Together* (Black Saint 1976)★★★, *Buster Bee* (Sackville 1978)★★★, *Shine!* (Novus 1978)★★★, *Prophet* (Black Saint 1981)★★★★, *Clevont Fitzhubert* (Black Saint 1981)★★★★, *Jump Up* (Gramavision 1982)★★, *Plug It* (Gramavision 1983)★★★, *Expandable Language* (Black Saint 1985)★★★, *Gallery* (Gramavision 1986)★★★, *Impala* (1987)★★★, *Otherside* (Gramavision 1988)★★★, *Trio Transition With Oliver Lake* (1989)★★★, *Again And Again* (Gramavision 1991)★★★, *Zaki* (hatART 1992)★★★★, *Prophet* 1980 recording (1993)★★★, with Donai Leonellis Fox *Boston Duets* (Music And Arts 1992)★★, *Virtual Reality (Total Escapism)* (1993)★★★, Edge-ing (Black Saint)★★, *Dedicated To Dolphy* (Black Saint 1996)★★★, with Andrew Cyrille, Reggie Workman *Live In Willisau* (Dizim 1998)★★★.

● COMPILATIONS: *Compilation* 1982-1988 recordings (1990)★★★.

LAMARE, HILTON 'NAPPY'

b. Hilton Napoleon Lamare, 14 June 1907, New Orleans, Louisiana, USA, d. 9 May 1988. Guitarist and banjo player Lamare's early career was spent in his home town where he played with a number of leading bands of the 20s including those of Johnny Bayersdorffer, Johnny Wiggs and Sharkey Bonano. In 1930, he joined Ben Pollack's nationally-popular band and stayed in the group when it evolved into the Bob Crosby band. As a member of Crosby's sprightly rhythm section Lamare, who also sang occasionally, became a well-known performer on record, on the dancehall circuit and in films. In 1942, he left Crosby with other sidemen for the Eddie Miller Orchestra. During the 40s he regularly led his own bands and helped run the Club 47 in Los Angeles of which he was co-owner. In subsequent decades he worked with various like-minded musicians, including Joe Darensbourg. Lamare also appeared in a number of Crosby reunion bands and led his own band, the Straw Hat Strutters, on a television show, *Dixie Showboat*, and, with Ray Bauduc, another old comrade from the Crosby band, he co-led the Riverboat Dandies.

● ALBUMS: with Ray Bauduc *Riverboat Dandies* (Capitol 1957)★★★, with Bauduc *On A Swinging Date* (Mercury 1960)★★★.

● COMPILATIONS: *Masters Of Dixieland, Volume 4* (1975).

LAMB, BOBBY

b. Robert Lamb, 11 February 1931, Cork, Eire. During his musical education Lamb played wind instruments before finally specializing on the trombone. While still a teenager he led his own band, playing on radio in his homeland. After moving to London to continue his studies he played trombone in a succession of fine dance and jazz bands including those led by Teddy Foster, Jack Parnell and Ted Heath. He then went to the USA, where he studied in New York and played with several bands, including Charlie Barnet's, before joining Woody Herman's outfit for two years. He spent the 60s back in London where he became a BBC studio musician, continued his studies, and also extended his burgeoning parallel career as a composer. His first major work, 'The Children Of Lir', was recorded in 1970. Throughout the 70s and beyond he continued to work as a freelance musician and also formed the Bobby Lamb-Raymond Premru Orchestra, a big band specializing in playing Lamb's concert jazz scores. He also played with Buddy Rich and Louie Bellson, the London Trombone Ensemble, formed to play his jazz scores, and led his own band, Keyman. With various orchestras, and sometimes as leader, he has made more than 6,000 radio broadcasts, played on soundtracks of over 200 films, and worked on innumerable television shows in Ireland, the UK and Germany. He has worked as composer and/or conductor with several symphony orchestras throughout Europe. His composing credits are similarly extensive and include film scores, concertos and orchestral suites, including the 'Dublin City Suite' which was subsequently developed as a film shot to music. He has also composed his 'Symphony No. 1' for orchestra and large jazz band and 'Symphony No. 2'. In 1982 he was appointed Director of Jazz Studies at Trinity College of Music in London and took up a similar post in 1994 at Detmold in Germany, continuing to hold both positions to the present day. The Trinity College Big Band. in particular, is an excellent showcase for highly talented young musicians coached and encouraged by Lamb. The orchestra, which has made numerous public appearances and several albums, also showcases Lamb's talents as a composer for the jazz orchestra. Over the decades, Lamb has consistently displayed an immense and varied talent as performer, composer and educator. Through his enthusiasm he has communicated his love for and deep understanding of jazz and many other musical forms to a new generation of musicians. In 1998, an Irish television company, RTE, completed a documentary film on Lamb's life and career.

● ALBUMS: with Raymond Premru *Live At Ronnie Scott's* (BBC 1971)★★★, *Conversations* (EMI 70s)★★★, with the Trinity College Big Band *Say No More* (Trinity 1985)★★★, with the Trinity College Big Band *Porgy And Bess* (Trinity 1992)★★★, with the Trinity College Big Band *Trinity Fair* (Hep 1993)★★★.

LAMBE, JEANIE

b. *c*.1949, Scotland. Lambe sang at the age of 17 with the Clyde Valley Stompers and then for many years she worked in the London area with a variety of bands including Kenny Ball, Chris Barber, Acker Bilk and Alex Welsh. Gradually, her fame spread, partly owing to appearances at many international jazz festivals where she often sang with small groups led by her husband Danny Moss. With him, she spent time in Australia, residing there at the start of the 90s but continuing to tour annually either in America or Europe. During her career Lambe has sung with modern and mainstream jazz musicians including Monty Alexander, Ben Webster, Budd Johnson, Oscar Peterson, Wild Bill Davison, Kenny Davern, Joe Pass and Buddy Tate. Over the years, Lambe's voice has subtly darkened, adding greater texture to an already fluid musical instrument.

● ALBUMS: *Jeanie Lambe With The Danny Moss Quartet* (Flyright 1980)★★★, *Blues And All That Jazz* (Zodiac 1982)★★★, *The Midnight Sun* (Zodiac 1983)★★★★, *My Man* (Zodiac 1988)★★★, *Happy Birthday Jazz Welle Plus* (Nagel-Heyer 1994)★★★, *Three Great Concerts Jeanie Lambe And The Danny Moss Quartet Live In Hamburg* (Nagel-Heyer 1996)★★★★.

Lambert, Dave

(see Lambert, Hendricks And Ross)

Lambert, Donald

b. c.1904, Princeton, New Jersey, USA, d. 8 May 1962. Taught initially by his mother, Lambert developed into a leading exponent of the stride piano style. During the late 20s he was much in demand as a solo pianist in clubs and at 'rent parties' in Harlem. From the early 30s he worked mostly in and around New York, spending many years in long residencies at a small number of clubs. Consequently, Lambert's fame was largely localized although he was highly-regarded by fellow pianists. He made a handful of well-received records in the early 40s and a few more in the years just prior to his death in 1962.

● COMPILATIONS: *Harlem Stride Classics 1960-62* (1979)★★★★, *Piano Giant - Stride* (1979)★★★★, *Classics In Stride* (1988)★★★★.

Lambert, Hendricks And Ross

In the late 50s a group of singers began informal 'vocalese' jam sessions at the New York apartment of Dave Lambert (b. 19 June 1917, Boston, Massachusetts, USA, d. 3 October 1966). At these sessions singers would improvise vocal lines in much the same manner as jazz instrumentalists. Ten years previously, Lambert had worked as arranger and singer in Gene Krupa's band, recording 'What's This?', an early example of a bop vocal. In 1955, Lambert teamed up with Jon Hendricks (b. 16 September 1921, Newark, Ohio, USA) to record a vocalized version of 'Four Brothers'. In 1958, Lambert and Hendricks added to their duo the highly distinctive singer Annie Ross (b. Annabelle Short Lynch, 25 July 1930, Mitcham, Surrey, England) to record the album *Sing A Song Of Basie*. The concept of the Lambert, Hendricks And Ross recordings was simple, although highly complex in execution. The singers performed wordless vocal lines, matching the brass and reed section parts of the Count Basie band's popular recordings. With this formula they enjoyed great success in the late 50s and early 60s. In 1962, Ross left the trio and was replaced by Yolanda Bavan (b. 1 June 1940, Colombo, Ceylon). Two years later Lambert also left and soon thereafter the trio concept was abandoned. Subsequently, Lambert worked briefly as a studio arranger before his death in 1966. Nobody has ever matched this incredible style of vocalese. They had grace and style and made complicated singing sound effortless.

● ALBUMS: *Sing A Song Of Basie* (ABC-Paramount 1958)★★★★, *Sing Along With Basie* (Roulette 1958)★★★★, with Zoot Sims *The Swingers!* (Affinity 1959)★★★, *The Hottest New Group In Jazz* (Columbia 1959)★★★★★, *Lambert, Hendricks & Ross Sing Ellington* (Columbia 1960)★★★★, *High Flying* (Columbia 1961)★★★★. As Lambert, Hendricks And Bavan: *Live At Basin Street East* (RCA Victor 1963)★★★, *Lambert, Hendricks & Bavan At Newport* (RCA Victor 1963)★★★, *Lambert, Hendricks & Bavan At The Village Gate* (RCA 1964)★★★.

● COMPILATIONS: *Twisted: The Best Of Lambert , Hendricks And Ross* (Rhino 1992)★★★★.

Lamond, Don

b. 18 August 1920, Oklahoma City, Oklahoma, USA. Lamond's early drumming career was spent in and around Washington, DC, where he was raised, and later in Baltimore, Maryland. In the early 40s he played in Sonny Dunham's dance band and in the forward-looking big band of Boyd Raeburn. In 1945, he joined Woody Herman's First Herd where he had the unenviable task of replacing the excellent if unstable Dave Tough. Lamond stood up well to the test and became an important member of Herman's band, playing in the Second Herd in the late 40s. Lamond also made records with several small bebop groups of the period, including those led by Charlie Parker and by fellow Herdsman Serge Chaloff. Lamond's abilities are such that he proved a welcome addition to bands covering a wide range of jazz, from bebop to dixieland by way of big and small mainstream groups. Always swinging, he played with Benny Goodman, Zoot Sims, Sonny Stitt, Quincy Jones, Johnny Guarnieri and the Sauter-Finegan Orchestra. In the 60s, Lamond toured extensively, visiting Europe and the following decade began leading a big band formed from eager young musicians in Florida where he had become resident.

● ALBUMS: as Don Lamond And His Big Band *Extraordinary* (Progressive 1983)★★★.

Lancaster, Byard

b. 6 August 1942, Philadelphia, Pennsylvania, USA. Multi-instrumentalist Lancaster (alto, tenor and soprano saxophones, flutes, clarinets, piano) was, with Sonny Sharrock, Dave Burrell and Eric Gravatt, part of a second generation of African-American 'new jazz' players who viewed themselves as John Coltrane's spiritual heirs or 'John's Children' as the title of an early Lancaster band song (written by Sharrock) insisted, committed to the same 'healing' energies inherent in the jubilant scream. Lancaster identified with secular screams, hence the motto on his business cards: *From A Love Supreme To The Sex Machine And All In Between.* In the 80s, following the demise of the French Palm label, which had championed his solo work, Lancaster was heard often as a star guest musician, playing loud and proud with Ronald Shannon Jackson's Decoding Society, Kip Hanrahan and Garrett List.

● ALBUMS: *It's Not Up To Us* (Vortex 1967)★★★, *Live At McAlester College '72* (1972)★★★, *Sounds Of Liberation - New Horizons* (1972)★★★, *Us* (1974)★★★, *Exactement* (1974)★★★, *Funny Funky* (1975)★★★, *Exodus* (1977)★★★, *Documentation: The End Of A Decade* (1980)★★, *Personal Testimony* (1980)★★★.

LAND, HAROLD

b. 18 December 1928, Houston, Texas, USA. Resident in California from early childhood, tenor saxophonist Land practised extensively with Eric Dolphy, holding informal, all-day sessions at Dolphy's home. Arising from the local fame these sessions engendered, Land was hired as replacement for Teddy Edwards in the Max Roach-Clifford Brown Sextet. This was in 1954, and by the time he left the band in November of the following year, Land's name and reputation were thoroughly established. In 1956, he became a member of Curtis Counce's influential group, made numerous important record dates with many leading west coast musicians, led his own groups and also co-led a fine band with Red Mitchell. An exceptionally gifted player, Land developed his own distinctive style early in his career although he later acknowledged John Coltrane by incorporating some of the latter's stylistic patterns into his own highly original work.

● ALBUMS: *Harold In The Land Of Hi Fi* reissued as *Grooveyard* (Contemporary 1958)★★★★, *The Fox* (Hifijazz/Contemporary 1960)★★★, *West Coast Blues!* (Jazzland 1960)★★★, *Eastward Ho! Harold Land In New York* (Jazzland 1961)★★★★, with Red Mitchell *Hear Ye!* (Atlantic 1961)★★★, *Jazz Impressions Of Folk Music* (Imperial 1963)★★★, *The Peace-maker* (Cadet 1968)★★★, *Choma* (Mainstream 1971)★★★, *Damisi* (Mainstream 1974)★★★, with Blue Mitchell *Mapenzi* (Concord Jazz 1977)★★★★, with Blue Mitchell *Best Of The West* (Concord Jazz 1977)★★★, *Live At Junk* (1980)★★, *Xocia's Dance (Sue-Sha's Dance)* (Muse 1981)★★★, *A Lazy Afternoon* 1994 recording (Postcards 1997)★★★★.

LANDSCAPE

Formed in 1975, this English jazz-funk instrumental group comprised Richard James Burgess (vocals/computer/drums), Andy Pask (bass), Christopher Heaton (keyboards), Peter Thomas (trombone/synthesizer) and John Walters (computer programming/wind synthesizers). They built up a loyal following by continuously touring and after a couple of years formed their own independent record label. Their album debut came in 1979 when they signed to RCA. However, the record sold badly, this was a surprise considering the reputation they had gained as a live act. In 1980, 'European Man' revealed the band going in a new direction. The easy-going jazz-funk had been replaced by advanced technology, computer programming, synthesizers and vocals. The single became a dancefloor favourite and just missed a national chart position. In 1981, the group finally made an impact with the commercial 'anti-war' track 'Einstein A Go-Go'. Complete with a simple catchy hookline, it reached number 5 in the UK and Top 10s all over Europe. The follow-up, 'Norman Bates', a tribute to the classic Hitchcock movie *Psycho*, also reached the UK Top 40. The line-up survived another album and a handful of singles, but by 1983 they had been reduced to a trio renamed Landscape 3. By the time the final split came in 1984 Burgess was already making a name for himself by producing acts including Spandau Ballet and Living In A Box.

● ALBUMS: *Landscape* (1979)★★★, *From The Tea Rooms Of Mars...To The Hell Holes Of Uranus* (1981)★★★, *Manhattan Boogie Woogie* (1982)★★.

LANG, EDDIE

b. Salvatore Massaro, 25 October 1902, Philadelphia, Pennsylvania, USA, d. 26 March 1933, New York City, New York, USA. The first truly significant guitarist in jazz, Lang began his career playing violin but was familiar with what was to become his main instrument through his father's work as a guitar maker. As a youth, Lang became acquainted with Joe Venuti, forming a musical partnership of exceptional quality. After working in bands in his home town and Atlantic City he joined the Mound City Blue Blowers, visiting London with the band in 1924. Later, Lang played in a band led by Venuti and then the pair joined Roger Wolfe Kahn, Adrian Rollini, led their own band, then were hired by Paul Whiteman. During their stint with Whiteman, Lang recorded with Bing Crosby and appeared in the films, *The King Of Jazz* (1930) and *The Big Broadcast* (1932). After leaving Whiteman, Lang accompanied Crosby, who had a clause in his recording contract stipulating that the guitarist should always be present on his record dates. During this time, Lang continued to record with Venuti. Lang's playing was notable for his single-string solos and his deft accompaniments. Until his emergence the guitar had been thought of as little more than a rhythm instrument, but his work opened the way for it as an effective solo voice. During his brief career he made numerous records including superb duets with Lonnie Johnson and sessions with Crosby and Joe 'King' Oliver, but is best-remembered for those with Venuti which remain classics of their kind. Lang died in March 1933 while undergoing a tonsillectomy.

● COMPILATIONS: with Joe Venuti *Joe Venuti And Eddie Lang* (X 1955)★★★, with Venuti *The Golden Days Of Jazz: Stringing The Blues* 1926-1933 recordings (Columbia 1976)★★★★, with Venuti *Joe Venuti And Eddie Lang* 1926-1928 recordings (JSP 1983)★★★★, with Venuti *Joe Venuti And Eddie Lang* 1928-1931 recordings (JSP 1983)★★★★, *Jazz Guitar Virtuoso* 1925-1932 recordings (Yazoo 1988)★★★★, *A Handful Of Riffs* 1927-1928 recordings (ASV/Living Era 1989)★★★, *Jazz Guitar Rarities* (Recording Arts 1993)★★★, shared with Carl Kress, Dick McDonough *Pioneers Of Jazz Guitars* 1927-1938 recordings (Challenge 1998)★★★★, with Venuti *Joe Venuti And Eddie Lang* 1926-1933 recordings (ABC)★★★★, with Venuti *Joe Venuti And*

Eddie Lang 1926-1930 (Swaggie)★★★★, with Venuti *Joe Venuti And Eddie Lang 1930-1933* (Swaggie)★★★★.
● FILMS: *The King Of Jazz* (1930), *The Big Broadcast* (1932).

LANPHERE, DON

b. 26 June 1928, Wenatchee, Washington, USA. Lanphere first played tenor saxophone professionally at 13, having already played in public as a guest with visiting bands. At the age of 17 he guested with the Jimmie Lunceford Orchestra when they played a gig in his home town. After studying music at Northwestern University, Illinois, Lanphere recorded in New York under his own name with, among others, Fats Navarro and Max Roach. In 1949, he joined Woody Herman and the following year was with Artie Shaw. In 1951, he was in Sonny Dunham's band which was touring with Bob Hope. It was then that addiction to narcotics interrupted his career but he straightened out and made brief appearances in bands led by Herman, Charlie Barnet, Billy May, Herb Pomeroy and others during the period 1958-61. Further personal problems, with alcohol and drugs, then arose and little was heard of him until the early 80s. Thoroughly straight this time, actively supported by his wife, Midge, and encouraged by UK record producer Alastair Robertson, Lanphere subsequently toured extensively and made many fine records. Originally a Coleman Hawkins disciple, Lanphere later absorbed the work of Lester Young and Charlie Parker, but was able to retain his own strikingly individual approach to jazz. In addition to tenor, Lanphere also plays alto and, since his return, has proved to be an especially adept and interesting player on soprano saxophone and, in turn, exhilaratingly inventive on fast numbers and lyrical on ballads.
● ALBUMS: *Don Lanphere Quartet With Fats Navarro* (1949)★★, *Woody Herman's Big New Herd* (1959)★★★★, *Out Of Nowhere* (Hep Jazz 1982)★★★, *Into Somewhere* (Hep Jazz 1983)★★★, *Stop* (Hep Jazz 1983)★★★, *Don Loves Midge* (Hep Jazz 1984)★★, *Go Again* (Hep Jazz 1988)★★★, with Larry Coryell *Lanphere/Coryell* (Hep Jazz 1990)★★★★, *Jazz Worship: A Closer Walk* (1993)★★★, *Don Still Loves Midge* (Hep Jazz 1998)★★★.

LARKINS, ELLIS

b. 15 May 1923, Baltimore, Maryland, USA. A child prodigy, Larkins performed on the piano in public at the age of seven, playing Mozart. He attended the Paebody Conservatory of Music in Baltimore, then the Juilliard School of Music where he was one of only a few black musicians at that time. To support himself while studying he played clubs in New York and was heard by John Hammond while with the Billy Moore Trio. Hammond booked the trio for the Cafe Society Uptown, with the proviso that Larkins was in the group. During the next two decades Larkins became a regular on the New York club and recording scene, but remained discreetly in the background as he developed into one of the finest accompanists to singers. Among those who have enjoyed his supportive playing are Mildred Bailey, Georgia Gibbs and Ella Fitzgerald. His recordings with Fitzgerald, reputedly unrehearsed, remain among the best the First Lady made. Larkins also played on record in numerous pick-up groups, but made only occasional albums as soloist or as leader of his own trio. In the 70s, during a period when he was accompanist to Rod McKuen, a series of records corrected this imbalance in Larkins's recorded output. He appeared on record again with Ruby Braff, with whom he had first recorded in the mid-50s. One of the most musicianly pianists to grace jazz, Larkins has been content to remain in the shadows, unobtrusively using his enormous yet delicate gifts to the benefit of others.
● ALBUMS: *Blues In The Night* 10-inch album (Decca 1952)★★★, *Perfume And Rain* 10-inch album (Storyville 1955)★★★★, with Ruby Braff *Inventions In Jazz - Volume 1* 10-inch album (Vanguard 1955)★★★★, with Braff *Inventions In Jazz - Volume 2* 10-inch album (Vanguard 1955)★★★★, with Braff *Two By Two* (Vanguard 1956)★★★, *Do Nothing Till You Hear From Me* (Storyville 1956)★★★, *Pocketful Of Dreams* reissue of *Inventions In Jazz* (Vanguard 1957)★★★★, *Manhattan At Midnight* (Decca 1956)★★★, *The Soft Touch* (Decca 1958)★★★, *Blue And Sentimental* (Decca 1958)★★★, *Ellis Larkins Plays The Bacharach & McKuen Songbook* (1972)★★, with Braff *The Grand Reunion* (1972)★★★, *Concert In Argentina* (1974)★★, *A Smooth One* (Black & Blue 1977)★★★, *Swingin' For Hamp* (1979)★★★, *The Ellis Larkins Trio* (1980)★★★, *At Maybeck Recital Hall* (Concord 1993)★★★★, with Braff *Calling Berlin: Vol. 2* (Arbors 1997)★★★★.

LASHLEY, BARBARA

b. *c.*1938, New York City, New York, USA. Lashley grew up in a musical family (in their youth her parents danced at the Savoy Ballroom in Harlem) and was constantly hearing singers on record. While still a child, she moved to Washington, DC, and with her brother and parents she sang to records, often R&B hits of the day. Although her brother began singing semi-professionally with a group, Lashley did not and eventually married, had four children, was divorced; which made a career in music out of the question. It was not until 1974, when she moved to San Francisco, that she began to consider the possibility. She was working as a freelance film editor and decided to study part-time at the University of California, Berkeley, reading for a degree in Afro-American Studies. This focused her interest in black music and eventually she began visiting local jazz clubs, encouraged in this by the director of the chorus of the Berkeley Community Chorus and orchestra of which she was a member. She began singing with local jazz groups, sitting in at jam sessions and the like, and was coached in this by bass player Billy Cayou. Gradually, her confidence grew and her reputation spread as her talent blossomed. She sang with several bands including those led by Manny Funk, Rex Allen and a big band she helped organize for Earl Hines in 1981, during a lecturing engagement the veteran pianist had undertaken at Berkeley. Later in the 80s, Lashley moved further afield, singing at international festivals, including those at Rimini, where she worked with Merrill Hoover, and Breda, where she sang with Dick Hyman and also met and was encouraged by Maxine

Sullivan. She also visited Japan with the Royal Street Jazz Members Band. In the USA, she has worked at the Walnut Creek Jazz Festival both singing and organizing concerts. Much influenced by singers of the 30s and 40s, such as Ivie Anderson, Billie Holiday, Lee Wiley, Mildred Bailey and, especially, Ethel Waters, Lashley has developed a wide-ranging repertoire and a good, if so far limited, following. Considering that she began singing professionally at the age of 40, her ability and reputation are remarkable. Her voice and style are finely crafted and her love for the music she performs gleams through every song.

● ALBUMS: *How Long Has This Been Going On?* (Shoestring 1983)★★★★, *Sweet And Lowdown* (Stomp Off 1986)★★★.

LAST EXIT

Last Exit is a high-power, high-intensity band that came together by chance when its members happened to be playing in the same city (Zurich) in early 1986 and has since become something of a cult institution. Comprising Peter Brötzmann (b. 6 March 1941, Remscheid, Germany; reeds), Sonny Sharrock (b. 27 August 1940, Ossining, New York, USA; guitar), Bill Laswell (bass) and Ronald Shannon Jackson (b. 12 January 1940, Fort Worth, Texas, USA; drums/vocals), their music is passionate and visceral, mixing elements of free jazz, blues, metal, hardcore, R&B and even the occasional quote from Wordsworth surreally interjected by Jackson. Last Exit, though largely a musical law unto itself, is flexible enough to have incorporated other musicians in live sessions, including Diamanda Galas, Akira Sakata and Herbie Hancock, who Laswell worked with on his *Future Shock* album which produced the hit single 'Rockit'. Their earliest (and probably wildest) recording, a tape of a concert in Cologne, was held up by legal difficulties until 1990, when it became available on compact disc in some European countries. It is now on general issue.

● ALBUMS: *Last Exit* (1986)★★★, *The Noise Of Trouble* (1987)★★★, *Cassette Recordings 1987* (1988)★★, *Iron Path* (1989)★★★, *Koln* 1986 recording (1990)★★★★, *Live In Europe - Headfirst Into The Flames* (1993)★★★.

LAST OF THE BLUE DEVILS, THE

A superior USA film documentary, worth its place in any collection, this film celebrates the remarkable contribution to jazz provided by Kansas City-based musicians. Extensive interviews and live performances filmed especially for the documentary mingle effectively with archive film clips. Amongst the artists displaying their considerable talents are Count Basie, Jimmy Forrest, Dizzy Gillespie, Budd Johnson, Gus Johnson, Jo Jones, Jay McShann, Charlie Parker, Jesse Price, Buster Smith, Joe Turner and Lester Young.

LASWELL, BILL

b. 14 February 1950. Laswell started playing guitar but later switched to bass. He was, he has said, more interested in being in a band than in playing music, but in the 70s he became more committed and has since organized some of the most challenging bands in recent popular music, including Material, Curlew (with Tom Cora, Nicky Skopelitis and George Cartwright), Arcana (with Derek Bailey and Tony Williams) and Last Exit (with Sonny Sharrock, Peter Brötzmann and Ronald Shannon Jackson). He also established OAO and Celluloid, two adventurous record labels. For the latest Material album, *Third Power*, he assembled a band including Shabba Ranks, the Jungle Brothers, Herbie Hancock, Sly And Robbie and Fred Wesley. Laswell and Hancock had already worked together, in Last Exit (on *The Noise Of Trouble*) and on two Hancock albums which he produced: on *Future Shock* in particular the 'backing band' was effectively Material. In the late 90s, Laswell has begun to explore drum 'n' bass, including the trance dub vehicle Sacred System. The list of albums below includes only those that Laswell has made under his own name; in addition he has produced for a wide range of people, including Iggy Pop, Motörhead, Laurie Anderson, Fela Kuti, Gil Scott-Heron, Yellowman, Afrika Bambaataa, Yoko Ono, Public Image Limited, Mick Jagger, Nona Hendryx, James 'Blood' Ulmer and Manu Dibango.

● ALBUMS: *Baselines* (Rough Trade 1984)★★★, with John Zorn *Points Blank/Metlable Snaps* (No Mans Land 1986),★★★ with Peter Brötzmann *Low Life* (1987)★★★, *Hear No Evil* (Venture 1988)★★★, *Outer Dark* (Fax 1994)★★★, with Pete Namlook *Outland* (Fax 1994)★★★, with Klaus Schulze, Pete Namlook *Dark Side Of The Moog IV* (Fax 1996)★★, as Arcana *The Last Wave* (DIW 1996)★★★, as Sacred System *Chapter One - Book Of Entrance* (ROIR 1996)★★★, *Oscillations 2* (Sub Rose 1998)★★★.

● COMPILATIONS: *The Best Of Bill Laswell* (Celluloid 1985)★★★, *Panthalassa: The Music Of Miles Davis 1969-1974* (Columbia 1998)★★★★.

LATEEF, YUSEF

b. William Evans, 9 October 1920, Chattanooga, Tennessee, USA. Raised in Detroit, Michigan, Lateef began playing tenor saxophone in his late teens. In New York in the mid-40s he played in bands led by Lucky Millinder, Roy Eldridge and other leading jazz musicians of the swing era, but later in the decade, in Chicago, he played with Dizzy Gillespie. Thereafter, his work was consciously modern in style. In the mid-50s he adopted the Muslim faith and took the name by which he is now known. He led several small bands during this period and also began to play flute. At the end of the decade he was again in New York, this time working with leading modernists amongst whom were Charles Mingus and Cannonball Adderley. He also led his own groups for public performance and record dates. In the 70s and 80s Lateef extended the number of instruments upon which he performed, now including the oboe and bassoon and also a wide range of similar Asian and African reeds. He revealed himself as a gifted performer on all these instruments and later recordings showed an increasing interest in various ethnic musical forms, sometimes - not always - fused with jazz, and crossing over into new age mood music. In addition to his performing career in music he has also taught music and has lately become proficient as a writer and painter. He currently records on his own YAL label.

● ALBUMS: *The Sounds Of Yusef* (Prestige 1957)★★★, *Jazz Mood* (Savoy 1957)★★★★, *Jazz For The Thinker* (Savoy 1957)★★★★, *Prayer To The East* (Savoy 1957)★★★★, *Jazz And The Sound Of Nature* (Savoy 1957)★★★, *The Dreamer* (Savoy 1958)★★★, *The Fabric Of Jazz* (Savoy 1958)★★★, *Before Dawn* (Verve 1958)★★★, *Live At Cranbrook* (Argo 1959)★★★, *Other Sounds* reissued as *Expressions* (New Jazz/Prestige 1959)★★★★, *Cry! Tender* (New Jazz 1960)★★★★, *Three Faces Of Yusef Lateef* (Riverside 1960)★★★★, *The Centaur And The Phoenix* (Riverside 1960)★★★★, *Eastern Sounds* (Moodsville 1961)★★★★, *Into Something* (New Jazz 1962)★★★★, *Lost In Sound* (Charlie Parker 1962)★★★, *Jazz Around The World* (Impulse! 1963)★★★★, *Live At Pep's* (Impulse! 1964)★★★★, *1984* (Impulse! 1965)★★★★, *Yusel!* (Delmark 1965)★★★, *Psychicemotus* (Impuse! 1966)★★★, *A Flat, G Flat And C* (Impuse! 1966)★★★, *The Golden Flute* (Impulse! 1966)★★★★, *Yusef Lateef Plays For Lovers* (Prestige 1967)★★★, *The Complete Yusef Lateef* (Atlantic 1968)★★★★, *The Blue Lateef* (Atlantic 1969)★★★, *Yusef Lateef's Detroit* (Atlantic 1969)★★, *The Diverse Yusef Lateef* (Atlantic 1970)★★★, *Suite 16* (Atlantic 1971)★★★, *Part Of The Search* (Atlantic 1972)★★★, *The Gentle Giant* (Atlantic 1974)★★★, *Ten Years Hence* (Atlantic 1975)★★★★, *The Doctor Is In...And Out* (Atlantic 1976)★★, *Autophysiopsychic* (CTI 1976)★★★, *The Live Session* 1964 recording (ABC/Impulse! 1978)★★★★, *In A Temple Garden* (1979)★★★, *In Nigeria* (Landmark 1984)★★★, *Yusuf Lateef's Little Symphony* (Atlantic 1988)★★★, *Concerto For Yusef Lateef* (Atlantic 1988)★★, *Nocturnes* (Atlantic 1989)★★★, *Meditations* (Atlantic 1990)★★, *Heart Vision* (YAL 1992)★★★, *Tenors Of Yusef Lateef & Von Freeman* (YAL 1992)★★★, *Yusef Lateef Plays Ballads* (YAL 1993)★★★, *Yusef Lateef Tenors Featuring Rene McLean* (YAL 1993)★★★, *Woodwinds* (YAL 1993)★★★, *Metamorphosis* (YAL 1994)★★, *Claiming Open Spaces* (YAL 1994)★★, *Tenors Of Yusef Lateef & Ricky Ford* (YAL 1994)★★★, *Cantata* (YAL 1994)★★★, *Suite Life* (YAL 1995)★★, *Full Circle* (YAL 1996)★★, *Earth And Sky* (YAL 1997)★★, *CHNOPS Gold And Soul* (YAL 1997)★★, with Adam Rudolph *The World At Peace* (YAL/Meta 1997)★★★, *The Man With The Big Front Yard* (32 Jazz 1998)★★★.

● COMPILATIONS: *Every Village Has A Song* 1949-1976 recordings (Rhino/Atlantic)★★★★, *Re-Evaluations: The Impulse! Years* 1963-1966 recordings (Impulse!)★★★★.

● FURTHER READING: *The Pleasures of Jazz: Leading Performers On Their Lives, Their Music, Their Contemporaries*, Leonard Feather.

Laurence, Chris

b. 6 January 1949, London, England. Laurence was born into a musical family and studied at the Royal Junior College of Music and the Guildhall School of Music. He started playing the bass professionally at the end of the 60s as one of a remarkable wave of new British jazz musicians. He worked with the bands of Mike Westbrook, Mike Pyne, John Surman, John Taylor and Kenny Wheeler. The breadth of his musicianship has made him one of the most dependable bass players in any rhythm section. During the 80s he played in the Orchestra of the Academy of St. Martins in the Fields and the London Bach Orchestra as well as in trios with Tony Oxley, Alan Skidmore and Tony Coe as well as continuing to appear in the various bands of John Surman.

● ALBUMS: with Frank Ricotti *Our Point Of View* (1969)★★★, with the London Jazz Composers Orchestra *Ode* (1972)★★★, with John Surman *Morning Glory* (1973)★★★, with Tony Coe, Tony Oxley *Nutty On Willisau* (1983)★★, *Aspects Of Paragonne* (1985)★★★★.

Laurie, Cy

b. 20 April 1926, London, England. A leading figure in the post-war traditional jazz boom in the UK, clarinettist Laurie led his own band in the late 40s and early 50s. He also played with the band led by Mike Daniels. Dividing his time between playing and running a popular London jazz club, Laurie became a seemingly immovable fixture on the scene but in 1960 dropped out of music. In the early 70s he was back and by the end of the decade had re-established his following. In the 80s he was a very popular figure on the UK traditional jazz scene, recording and playing concerts with fellow-veteran performers Ken Colyer and Max Collie. Although rooted in the playing of Johnny Dodds, Laurie's performances display an acute ear for changing musical fashions and there are often hints that his range could in fact be much wider than either he or his fans have ever allowed.

● ALBUMS: *Cy Laurie Blows Blue-Hot* (1956)★★★, *Cy Laurie And Les Jowett* (1957)★★, *Shades Of Cy* (Suntan 1984)★★★, with Max Collie, Ken Colyer *New Orleans Mardi Gras* (1985)★★★, *That Rhythm Man* (1989)★★, *Delving Back With Cy* (Esquire 1986)★★★.

Laurin, Anna-Lena

b. Sweden. Laurin began playing piano as a child, studying classical music. Then she played alto saxophone before finally settling on singing. Her first musical experience as a professional was in rock and she also sang Irish folk and Balkan music amongst many other forms. Declaring herself to be unsatisfied at the time with what she was singing, she moved to Malmö in 1987 and discovered that jazz was her métier. She sings with several Malmö-based groups including Con Brio and, especially Fee-Fi-Fo-Fum, a band comprising Anders Bergcrantz (trumpet, flügelhorn), Rolf Nilsson (guitar), Hans Andersson (bass), Kristofer Johnansson (drums). While including standards in her jazz repertoire, Laurin writes a great deal of her own material, words and music, and writes her own arrangements. In performance, she sings as an ensemble member rather than as a featured singer. She is also interested in Brazilian music and some of her own work reflects this with its Latin nuances.

● ALBUMS: *Dance In Music* (Dragon 1994)★★★.

LaVere, Charles

b. Charles LaVere Johnson, 18 July 1910, Salina, Kansas, USA, d. 28 April 1983. A talented multi-instrumentalist, he mostly played piano, working with an array of fine early jazzmen, including Wingy Manon, Jack

Teagarden and Zutty Singleton. LaVere worked with several bandleaders, among them Paul Whiteman and Ben Pollack and was for a while with the Casa Loma Orchestra. During the 40s he began regularly to lead his own bands, often hiring top-flight jazz musicians especially for recording dates, such as Joe Venuti and Matty Matlock. He had a hit record as a singer in 1947, 'Maybe You'll Be There', accompanied by Gordon Jenkins. He also made many recording dates, including a 1950 session with Jenkins to accompany Billie Holiday. During the second half of the 50s LaVere was resident at Disneyland playing a somewhat denaturalized Dixieland for the mass audience. He continued to lead bands through the 60s, 70s and into the 80s. He composed several pieces including 'Cuban Boogie Woogie', which he recorded with Charlie Barnet in 1939. LaVere was an accomplished player with an abiding enthusiasm for music. Many of his bands, although often overlooked, were solid jazz groups with very good soloists.

LaVerne, Andy

b. 4 December 1947, New York City, New York, USA. Playing the piano from an early age, LaVerne studied extensively including periods, sometimes brief, at the Berklee College Of Music, the Juilliard School of Music, and the New England Conservatory of Music. After considering other musical forms, in the early 70s he committed to jazz and joined Woody Herman's big band. He also played and sometimes recorded in jazz, post-bop and jazz-rock groups with many musicians including John Abercrombie and Lee Konitz. Already gaining an international reputation, he underscored his presence on the world stage with a spell in the late 70s as a member of Stan Getz's group. During the following decade he continued to play an eclectic repertoire, working with musicians from all parts of the jazz spectrum. In the early 90s he became better known as leader of his own small groups, recording with musicians such as Joe Lovano. He also continued his ongoing musical relationship with Abercrombie. In part, LaVerne's playing is deeply rooted in bop, and his tribute albums to Bud Powell and Tadd Dameron demonstrate how fully he has embraced the form while still managing to retain a large measure of his own post-bop sensibilities. His playing style, while constantly displaying thoughtful undertones, is vigorous and fluently inventive. LaVerne is also a composer of merit, having written material in classic style for Getz and a number of shorter pieces for his own performances.

● ALBUMS: *Another World* (Steeple Chase 1977)★★★, *Liquid Silver* (DMP 1984)★★★, *Jazz Piano Lineage* (DMP 1988)★★★★, *Frozen Music* (Steeple Chase 1989)★★★, *Fountainhead* (Steeple Chase 1989)★★★, *Severe Clear* (Steeple Chase 1990)★★★, *Standard Eyes* (Steeple Chase 1991)★★★, *Pleasure Seekers* (Triloka 1991)★★★★, *Buy One Get One Free* (Steeple Chase 1992)★★★, *Universal Mind* (Steeple Chase 1993)★★★, *Double Standard* (Triloka 1993)★★★, *In The Mood For A Classic: Andy LaVerne Plays Bud Powell* (Steeple Chase 1993)★★★, *Live At Maybeck Recital Hall Series, Vol. 28* (Concord Jazz 1993)★★★★, *Serenade To Silver* (Steeple Chase 1994)★★★★, *Time Well Spent* (Concord Jazz 1995)★★★, *Tadd's Delight* (Steeple Chase 1995)★★★★, *Bud's Beautiful* (Steeple Chase 1996)★★★, with John Abercrombie *Where We Were* (Double-Time 1996)★★★, *Four Miles* (Triloka 1997)★★★.

● VIDEOS: *Jazz Piano Standards* (Homespun Video 1998).

Lawrence, Denise

b. England. An established singer on the British jazz and jazz-fringe scene for many years, Lawrence has a wide-ranging repertoire. Comfortably at home with standards, blues and gospel, she has a warm, clear voice and always presents her material with an easy-flowing swing. She often works with the Storeyville Tickle Bands, based in Reading, Berkshire, and led by her husband, pianist Tony Lawrence.

● ALBUMS: *Let It Shine* (Lake 1994)★★, *Can't Help Lovin' Those Men Of Mine* (Lake 1995)★★★.

Lawrence, Elliot

b. Elliot Lawrence Broza, 14 February 1925, Philadelphia, Pennsylvania, USA. A precociously talented pianist, at the age of four Lawrence participated in his father's children's shows on the radio and in his teens he led an orchestra of children for a local broadcast. He continued to be active in music during his university days, and his early professional work was in dance bands and with radio orchestras, some of which he led himself. Lawrence wrote many arrangements for his own bands, accommodating, but without wholly embracing, contemporary shifts in jazz. He also used arrangements by other young men who were testing the boundaries of big band music, notably Gerry Mulligan, Al Cohn and Tiny Kahn. As times became harder for big bands, Lawrence eventually abandoned his full-time bandleading career, but occasionally reformed the group for special engagements and record dates. On such sessions his choice of musicians reflected his determination to look ahead, and soloists included Cohn, Red Rodney, Zoot Sims and Urbie Green. Subsequently, Lawrence's career took him into television and theatrical work.

● ALBUMS: *One Night Stand With Elliot Lawrence* (1947)★★, *Elevation* (1947)★★, *College Prom* 10-inch album (Decca 1950)★★, *Moonlight On The Campus* 10-inch album (Decca 1950)★★, *Elliot Lawrence Plays Tiny Kahn And Johnny Mandel Arrangements* (Fantasy 1956)★★★, *Dream* (Fantasy 1956)★★★, *Swinging At The Steel Pier* (Fantasy 1956)★★★, *The Four Brothers Together Again!* (Fantasy 1957)★★★, *Plays For Swinging Dancers* (Fantasy 1957)★★★, *Elliot Lawrence And His Orchestra* (Fantasy 1957)★★, *Dream On Dance On* (Fantasy 1958)★★★, *Jazz Goes Broadway* (Vik 1958)★★★, *Music For Trapping, Tender, That Is* (Top Rank 1958)★★★, *Big Band Sound* (Fantasy 1959)★★, *Big Band Modern* (Jazztone 1960)★★, *Jump Steady* (SeSac 1960)★★.

Laws, Hubert

b. 10 November 1939, Houston, Texas, USA. The brother of saxophonist Ronnie Laws, flautist Hubert has enjoyed successful careers in both classical and jazz contexts. In the 60s and 70s he recorded for Atlantic

Records and Creed Taylor's CTI label, enjoying particular commercial success with crossover albums such as *Afro Classic* and *The Rite Of Spring*. Like most of his early 70s albums they featured Laws performing on Don Sebesky's arrangements of classical themes. He played in the New York Jazz Sextet while retaining a place in the New York Metropolitan Opera House and the New York Philharmonic Orchestra. Despite several disappointing albums with Columbia Records and a quiet period during the 80s, Laws returned with two accomplished sets for the Music Masters label in the mid-90s. Laws also performed a series of concerts with classical flautist Jean-Pierre Rampal. Having played with Gunther Schuller, James Moody, Clark Terry and many others, Laws' virtuosity has done much to increase the flute's credibility in the jazz world.

● ALBUMS: *The Laws Of Jazz* (Atlantic 1965)★★★★, *Flute By-Laws* (Atlantic 1966)★★★, *Laws Cause* (Atlantic 1969)★★★, *Crying Song* (CTI 1970)★★★, *Afro Classic* (CTI 1971)★★★★, *The Rite Of Spring* (CTI 1972), *Morning Star* (CTI 1973), *At Carnegie Hall* (CTI 1973)★★, *In The Beginning* (CTI 1974)★★★★, *Chicago Theme* (CTI 1975)★★★, *The San Francisco Concert* (CTI 1976)★★★, *Romeo And Juliet* (Columbia 1976)★★, *Land Of Passion* (Columbia 1978)★★, *How To Beat The High Cost Of Living* film soundtrack (Columbia 1980)★★★, *My Time Will Come* (Music Masters 1992)★★★, *Storm Then The Calm* (Music Masters 1994)★★★.

LAWS, RONNIE

b. Ronald Laws, 3 October 1950, Houston, Texas, USA. Laws played the saxophone from the age of 12, growing up with the musicians who were to become the Crusaders - the band with which his brother Hubert played. Ronnie studied flute at the Stephen F. Austin State University and then at Texas Southern University. When he was 21 he moved to Los Angeles, where he worked with Von Ryan's Express, Quincy Jones, pianist Walter Bishop Jnr. and Kenny Burrell. After playing with Earth, Wind And Fire for 18 months, during the period when they recorded *Last Days In Time* (1972), he worked with Hugh Masekela and Ujima. His solo career in the late 70s and early 80s saw him achieve popularity with a smooth jazz style similar to that of Bob James, Earl Klugh, Lonnie Liston Smith and Grover Washington.

● ALBUMS: with Pressure *Pressure Sensitive* (EMI 1975)★★★, *Fever* (Blue Note 1976)★★★★, *Friends And Strangers* (EMI 1977)★★, *Flame* (United Artists 1978)★★★, *Every Generation* (United Artists 1980)★★★, *Solid Ground* (Liberty 1981)★★★, *Mr. Nice Guy* (Capitol 1983)★★★, *Mirror Town* (Columbia 1986)★★★, *All Day Rhythm* (Columbia 1987)★★, *Identity* (New Note 1992)★★★, *Deep Soul* (Par 1992)★★★, *True Spirit* (Par 1993)★★★, *Brotherhood* (101 South 1993)★★★, *Natural Laws* (Capitol 1995)★★, *Tribute To The Legendary Eddie Harris* (Blue Note 1997)★★★, *Harvest For The World* (Blue Note 1998)★★★.

● COMPILATIONS: *Ronnie Laws* (1987)★★★, *Classic Masters* (1988)★★★★, *The Best Of Ronnie Laws* (Blue Note 1992)★★★★.

LAWSON, HUGH

b. Richard Hugh Jerome Lawson, 12 March 1935, Detroit, Michigan, USA, d. 17 March 1997, New York City, New York, USA. Lawson's fine piano playing first came to wide attention when he played in small groups led by Yusef Lateef in the late 50s. He played mostly in New York for a number of years, recording with various leaders, including Harry 'Sweets' Edison and Roy Brooks, and also developing a parallel career as a composer and arranger. In 1972 he helped form the Piano Choir, composing for and recording with this seven-piano ensemble. Among their recordings are two albums with the same title, *Handscapes* (Strata-East 1972 and 1974). During the mid-70s he began touring with Charles Mingus, continuing to do so for the next few years. In between tours he recorded with Charlie Rouse and George Adams and under his own name. Lawson also gained an excellent reputation as a teacher. A remarkable improviser, he remained much less well known among audiences than should have been the case for a musician of his calibre.

● ALBUMS: *Prime Time* (Storyville 1977)★★★★, *Colour* (Soul Note 1983)★★★.

LAWSON, YANK

b. John Rhea Lawson, 3 May 1911, Trenton, Missouri, USA, d. 18 Febraury 1995. After playing the trumpet in various local bands, in 1933 Lawson joined Ben Pollack's popular band. When this group developed into the co-operative Bob Crosby band Lawson was one of its dominant musical voices. He later played in the bands of Tommy Dorsey and Benny Goodman and then spent a quarter of a century, on and off, in the studios, making occasional jazz club and record dates. Reunions with other veterans of the Crosby band eventually led to a partnership with Bob Haggart. Their co-led band eventually evolved into the World's Greatest Jazz Band and when this group folded in the late 70s Lawson and Haggart continued to perform together well into the 80s. A striking and aggressive player, Lawson dominated any of the dixieland-orientated jazz bands with which he played and drew admiration from such leading jazz artists as Louis Armstrong, with whom he appeared on record.

● ALBUMS: with Bob Haggart *Lawson-Haggart Band Play Jelly Roll's Jazz* 10-inch album (Decca 1951)★★★★, with Haggart *College Fight Song* 10-inch album (Decca 1952)★★★, with Haggart *Lawson-Haggart Band Play King Oliver's Jazz* 10-inch album (Decca 1952)★★★★, with Haggart *Lawson-Haggart Band* 10-inch album (Decca 1952)★★★, with Haggart *Blues On The River* 10-inch album (Decca 1952)★★★, with Haggart *Windy City Jazz* 10-inch album (Decca 1953)★★★, with Haggart *South Of The Mason-Dixon Line* 10-inch album (Decca 1954)★★★, with Haggart *Louis' Hot 5's And 7's* 10-inch album (Decca 1954)★★★, *Yank Lawson's Dixieland Jazz* 10-inch album (Riverside 1954)★★★, with Haggart *Hold That Tiger* (Decca 1956)★★★, with Haggart *Boppin' At The Hop* (Decca 1959)★★★, with Haggart *Junior Prom* (Everest 1959)★★★, *The Best Of Broadway* (1959)★★★★, with Haggart *Dixieland Goes*

West (Everest 1960)★★★, *Ole Dixie* (1966)★★★, with Haggart *Live At The Roosevelt Grill* (Atlantic 1969)★★★, with Haggart *What's New?* (Atlantic 1969)★★★, *Live At Louisiana Jazz Club* (1979)★★, *Century Plaza* (World Jazz 1979)★★★, with Haggart *Best Of Jazz At The Troc* (World Jazz 1981)★★★, *Plays Mostly Blues* (Audiophile 1987)★★★, *Something Old, Something New, Something Borrowed, Something Blue* (Audiophile 1988)★★★★, *Easy To Remember* (Flyright 1989)★★★, with Haggart *Yank Lawson And Bob Haggart* (Jazzology 1992)★★★★.

LE SAGE, BILL

b. 20 January 1927, London, England. From the mid-40s Le Sage was a popular figure on the London jazz scene, leading his own group and also playing in the John Dankworth Seven. At this point in his career Le Sage played piano, on which he was self-taught. In the early 50s he began playing vibraphone, the instrument he later became associated with. During the 50s and 60s he played with bands led by Tony Kinsey, Ronnie Ross and also led his own groups. In 1970, he formed his Bebop Preservation Society band which remained in existence until midway through the following decade. During this period he also worked with many of the UK's leading contemporary jazz artists including Barbara Thompson and Martin Drew. Alongside his playing career, Le Sage has also written music for a number of television shows.

● ALBUMS: *The Bill Le Sage-Ronnie Ross Quartet* (1963)★★★, *Directions In Jazz* (1964)★★★, *Road To Ellingtonia* (1965)★★, *Martin Drew And His Band* (1977)★★★, with John Dankworth *Gone Hitchin'* (1983)★★.

LEA, BARBARA

b. Barbara LeCoq, 4 October 1929, Detroit, Michigan, USA. Her family name was changed to Leacock and she shortened this when she took up a career as a singer. Her higher education took place at Wellesley College where she majored in Music Theory. She sang in the college choir and in the late 40s sang jazz and with dance bands in the north eastern states. She also worked as a jazz disc jockey, wrote a jazz column for the college newspaper, sang and taught classical music and jazz. When Lea graduated she began working professionally as a singer almost at once, singing mostly in Boston and in New Jersey but occasionally picked up engagements at swish New York venues. During the 50s she worked extensively in the north-east and in Canada and also made records, including sets with trumpeter Johnny Windhurst. Her early recordings were very well received and in 1956 was voted *Down Beat*'s Best New Singer. She then moved into acting, mostly on the stage, performing in musical and straight drama. Her theatrical life, which included supporting and leading roles in works from William Shakespeare to Stephen Sondheim, extended from off-Broadway productions to touring companies. In the late 70s she was invited to join the radio series, *American Popular Music With Alex Wilder And Friends*. Lea then returned to performing in clubs, in New York, Washington, Los Angeles, sang at festivals and jazz parties and also recorded for Audiophile from 1978 into the mid-90s. She is a great admirer of Lee Wiley and is highly knowledgeable about her work. In 1996 she was showing no signs of slowing up, having been booked to appear at the Kool-JVC Jazz Festival in New York and had just recorded her latest album. she sings in a deep, rich-toned voice with a pleasingly astringent sound which is especially effective in her meaningful interpretation of ballads.

● ALBUMS: *A Woman In Love* (Riverside/Audiophile 1955)★★★, *Barbara Lea* (Prestige/Fantasy/OJC 1956)★★★★, *Lea In Love* (Prestige/Fantasy/OJC 1957)★★★, *The Devil Is Afraid Of Music* (Audiophile 1979)★★★, *Remembering Lee Wiley* (Audiophile 1979)★★★, *Do It Again* (Audiophile 1983)★★★, *Hoagy's Children* (Audiophile 1983)★★★★, *You're The Cats* (Audiophile 1989)★★★, *Sweet And Slow* (Audiophile 1990)★★★, *At The Atlanta Jazz Party* (Jazzology 1993)★★★, *Pousse Cafe* (Audiophile 1993)★★, *Hoagy's Children Vols 1* and *2* (Audiophile 1994)★★★★, *Fine And Dandy* (Challenge 1996)★★★.

LEADERS

(see Blythe, Arthur; Bowie, Lester; Freeman, Chico; Lightsey, Kirk; McBee, Cecil; Moye, Famoudou Don)

LÉANDRE, JOËLLE

b. 12 September 1951, Aix-en-Provence, France. One of Europe's most gifted and versatile young bassists, Léandre is equally at home performing scores by *avant garde* composers such as Giacinto Scelsi or playing total improvisation with the likes of Maggie Nicols and Irène Schweizer. She studied both double bass and piano as a child; later graduated from the Conservatoire National Superieur de Musique de Paris; played with Pierre Boulez's Ensemble Intercontemporain and studied in the USA with John Cage. Her 1981 debut, *Contrebassiste*, featured mostly her own composed music, but also included vocals, overdubbing and pre-recorded tapes (of taxi-drivers refusing to take her bass in their cabs!) - intimations of the invention and droll humour that have become hallmarks of her improvisations (along with her *bravura* technique). The recording of *Live At The Bastille* in 1982, with Nicols and Lindsay Cooper, was completely improvised and this has been the dominant mode on most of her subsequent recordings (the exceptions being *Contrebasse Et Voix*, which includes pieces by Scelsi and Cage and the recent *All Scelsi*). *Sincerely* was another solo, while other releases feature duos and trios with leading European improvizers, such as Schweizer, Derek Bailey, Barre Phillips, Peter Kowald, the Portuguese violinist Carlos Zingaro, plus US trombonist George Lewis and violinist Jon Rose; the latter of whom she recorded a duo album of 'domestic' noises, including pieces for television set, fridge, bathroom, creaking door and pet dog! In 1983, Léandre joined Schweizer's European Women's Improvising Group and played with her at the 1986 Canaille Festival of Women's Improvised Music in Zurich, as well as appearing on the pianist's *Live At Taktlos* and *The Storming Of The Winter Palace*, and recording the duo *Cordial Gratin* with her. In 1988, Léandre played at

Canada's Victoriaville Festival, recording with Anthony Braxton on his *Ensemble (Victoriaville) 1988*: a duo project with Braxton released in late 1992 as is an album by her current Canvas Trio with Zingaro and reedman/accordionist Rüdiger Carl.

● ALBUMS: *Contrabassiste* 1981 recording (1983)★★★, with Maggie Nicols, Lindsay Cooper *Live At The Bastille* 1982 recording (1984)★★★, *Les Douze Sons* (Nato 1984)★★★, *Sincerely* (1985)★★★, with Irène Schweizer *Cordial Gratin* (1987)★★★★, *Paris Quartet* 1985 recording (1989)★★★★, *Contrebasse Et Voix* 1987 recording (1989)★★★, *Urban Bass* (Adda 1990)★★★, with Jon Rose *Les Domestiques* 1987 recording (1990)★★★, with Carlos Zingaro *Ecritures* (Adda 1990)★★★, with others *Unlike* (1990)★★★, with Eric Watson *Palimpeste* (hatART 1992)★★★, *Canvas Trio* (1992)★★★, *All Scelsi* (1992)★★★, *L'Histoire De Mme Tasco* (hatART 1993)★★, *Blue Goo Park* (FMP 1993)★★★★, with Giacinto Scelsi *Okanagon* (1993)★★, with Ken Filiano, Vinny Golia *Haunting The Spirits Inside Them ...* (Music And Arts 1996)★★★★, with Fritz Hauser, Urs Leimgruber *No Try No Fail* (hatOLOGY 1998)★★★.

Lee, Dave

b. 12 August 1930, London, England. After winning a *Melody Maker* poll for his jazz piano playing while still in his mid-teens, Lee joined Johnny Dankworth's band, later winning another poll in the same magazine. From the mid-50s and throughout the 60s, Lee was active in jazz, the musical theatre, television and films, contributing scores for several well-known films. In the early 80s Lee was sufficiently active on the jazz scene to be elected BBC Jazz Society Musician of the year, but begun to plan a 'jazz-only' radio station which, while not unusual in the USA, was unheard of in the UK. Against the odds and all expectations, Lee was successful, and in 1990, Jazz FM was on the air. Broadcasting to the Greater London area, Jazz FM made an important contribution to the hopes and aspirations of jazz musicians and broadcasters until financial pressures forced policy and other changes, after which Lee moved on to other ventures.

● ALBUMS: *Jazz Improvisations Of 'Our Man Crichton'* (1965)★★★.

Lee, George E.

(see Lee, Julia; Kansas City Jazz)

Lee, Jeanne

b. 29 January 1939, New York City, New York, USA. Lee studied modern dance at Bard College (1956-60), where she met Ran Blake. They began to work as a duo, with Lee improvising on vocals, recording together in 1961 (*The Newest Sound Around*) and toured Europe in 1963. In 1964, she moved to California and married the sound-poet David Hazelton. Returning to Europe in 1967, she began a long association with Gunter Hampel, recording with him on his Birth label on numerous occasions over the next two decades (*The 9th July 1969*, *Spirits* in 1971, *Journey To The Song Within* in 1974, *Fresh Heat* in 1985), including one entirely improvised session with him and Anthony Braxton in 1972. Although a striking singer in conventional terms, with a strong, husky voice, Lee developed a new, inventive approach to vocals, often improvising wordlessly and using lip, throat and mouth sounds rather than standard pitches. In the 60s and 70s she was a prominent member of the jazz *avant garde*, working with fellow pioneers Archie Shepp (*Blasé*), Marion Brown (*Afternoon Of A Georgia Faun*), Braxton again (*Town Hall 1972*) and Enrico Rava, as well as recording her own *Conspiracy* and, later, in a trio with Andrew Cyrille and Jimmy Lyons. In the 80s and 90s she has worked with the group Vocal Summit (with Bobby McFerrin, Lauren Newton, Urszula Dudziak and Jay Clayton) and with the Reggie Workman Ensemble (*Images*), but has concentrated more on writing her own material. Her works include a five-part suite, *Emergence*, and a ten-act oratorio, *A Prayer For Our Time*. In 1990, she again recorded a duo album with Blake, with whom she has been teaching in the Third Stream department of the New England Conservatory of Music since 1976.

● ALBUMS: with Ran Blake *The Newest Sound Around* (1961)★★★, *The Gunter Hampel Group Und Jeanne Lee* (1969)★★★★, with Hampel, Anthony Braxton *Familie* (1972)★★★★, *Conspiracy* (1974)★★★, with Andrew Cyrille, Jimmy Lyons *Nuba* (1979)★★★, with Vocal Summit *Sorrow Is Not Forever - Love Is* (1983)★★★, with Blake *You Stepped Out Of A Cloud* (1990)★★★, *Natural Affinities* (Owl 1992)★★★.

Lee, John

b. John Arthur Lee, 24 May 1915, Mt. Willing, Alabama, USA. Few post-war country blues tracks merit the description 'masterpiece', but John Lee's July 1951 recording of 'Down At The Depot' deserves the accolade. In essence a standard train blues, it is elevated by his propulsive slide guitar playing and keening vocal. Lee came from a musical family, in which all seven brothers, a sister and both parents played guitar. However, the significant influence on his playing was Uncle Ellie Lee, renowned in Evergreen, Alabama, as its finest exponent of slide technique, using a knife rather than a bottleneck. Both 'Down At The Depot' and the equally impressive 'Blind Blues' bear witness to his tutelage. Lee was also influenced by Brewton musician Levi Kelley. He supplemented practical instruction with the records of Blind Blake, Blind Lemon Jefferson and Leroy Carr. Moving to Montgomery in 1945, he soon had, by his own estimation, 'the town sewed up' when it came to playing at house parties and suppers. In 1951 he heard talent scout Ralph Bass advertise for talent on WMGY radio; four of the six songs he recorded were released on two Federal singles, representing some of the last instances of country blues being issued on a major label. Lee retired from active performance in 1960. He was rediscovered in 1973 after a three-year search and recorded sessions in Montgomery and Cambridge, Massachusetts, at which he revealed an equally individual piano style.

● ALBUMS: *Down At The Depot* (Rounder 1974)★★★.

Lee, Julia

b. 13 October 1903, Booneville, Missouri, USA, d. 8 December 1958. Beginning her career as a pianist and singer while in her early teens, Lee joined a band led by her brother, George E. Lee (1896-1958), a popular vocalist whose 'Novelty Singing Orchestra' played extensively in and around Kansas City. Despite the musical advances being made by other Kansas City Jazz bands of the time, notably the Lees' great rival, Bennie Moten, they retained their popularity into the mid-30s. After her brother's retirement, Julia Lee continued her career as a solo artist, enjoying a resurgence of popularity during the blues revival of the early and mid-40s. Her recordings of these and the following few years feature leading jazz musicians, including Benny Carter and Red Norvo. An effective if sometimes unprofound performer of the blues, and a disarming singer of popular songs of the day, Lee was well-placed to adapt to the growing public interest in R&B. However, her decision to spend most of her career in Kansas City rather than New York or Los Angeles, where R&B really took off, meant that she was far more unfamiliar to the wider public than many less talented singer-pianists of her generation.

● COMPILATIONS: *Tonight's The Night (1944-52)* (1982)★★★★, *Party Time (1946-52)* (1983)★★★★, *Ugly Papa (1945-52)* (1987)★★★★, *Snatch And Grab It* (1987)★★★, *A Porter's Love Songs* (1988)★★★, *Of Lions And Lambs* (1988)★★★.

Lee, Peggy

b. Norma Deloris Egstrom, 26 May 1920, Jamestown, North Dakota, USA. Lee is of Scandinavian descent, her grandparents being Swedish and Norwegian immigrants. She endured a difficult childhood and her mother died when she was four; when her father remarried she experienced a decidedly unpleasant relationship with her stepmother. Her father took to drink, and at the age of 14 she found herself carrying out his duties at the local railroad depot. Despite these and other hardships, she sang frequently and appeared on a local radio station. She took a job as a waitress in Fargo, where the manager of the radio station changed her name to Peggy Lee. In 1937, she took a trip to California to try her luck there but soon returned to Fargo. Another California visit was equally unsuccessful and she then tried Chicago where, in 1941, as a member of a vocal group, The Four Of Us, she was hired to sing at the Ambassador West Hotel. During this engagement she was heard by Mel Powell, who invited Benny Goodman to hear her. Goodman's regular singer, Helen Forrest, was about to leave and Lee was hired as her replacement. She joined the band for an engagement at the College Inn and within a few days sang on a record date. A song from this period, 'Elmer's Tune', was a huge success. Among other popular recordings she made with Goodman were 'How Deep Is The Ocean?', 'How Long Has This Been Going On?', 'My Old Flame' and 'Why Don't You Do Right?'. Later, Lee married Goodman's guitarist, Dave Barbour. After she left Goodman's band in 1943, she had more successful records, including 'That Old Feeling' and three songs of which she was co-composer with Barbour, 'It's A Good Day', 'Don't Know Enough About You' and 'Mañana'. She also performed on radio with Bing Crosby. In the 50s she made several popular recordings for Capitol Records, the orchestral backings for many of which were arranged and conducted by Barbour, with whom she maintained a good relationship despite their divorce in 1952. Her 1958 hit single 'Fever' was also a collaboration with Barbour. Her *Black Coffee* album of 1953 was particularly successful, as was *Beauty And The Beat* a few years later. On these and other albums of the period, Lee was often accompanied by jazz musicians, including Jimmy Rowles, Marty Paich and George Shearing. During the 50s Lee was also active in films, performing the title song of *Johnny Guitar* (1954), and writing songs for others including *Tom Thumb* (1958). She also made a number of on-screen appearances in acting roles, including *The Jazz Singer* (1953), and for one, *Pete Kelly's Blues* (1955), she was nominated for an Academy Award as Best Supporting Actress. However, her most lasting fame in films lies in her off-screen work on Walt Disney's *Lady And The Tramp* (1955), for which Lee wrote the song 'He's A Tramp' and provided the voice for the characters of 'Peg', the Siamese cats, and one other screen feline. Her recording successes continued throughout this period even if, on some occasions, she had to fight to persuade Capitol to record them. One such argument surrounded 'Lover', which executives felt would compete directly with the label's then popular version by Les Paul. Lee won out and her performance of her own arrangement, played by a studio orchestra under the direction of Gordon Jenkins, was a sensation. Towards the end of the 50s, the intense level of work began to take its toll and she suffered a period of illness. Throughout the 60s and succeeding decades Lee performed extensively, singing at concerts and on television and, of course, making records, despite being frequently plagued with poor health. Her voice is light with a delicate huskiness, offering intriguing contrasts with the large orchestral accompaniment that is usually a part of a Lee performance. Over the years her repeated use of previously successful settings for songs has tended to make her shows predictable but she remains a dedicated perfectionist in everything that she does. In the early 80s she attempted a stage show, *Peg*, but it proved unpopular and closed quickly. In the late 80s she again suffered ill health and on some of her live performances her voice was starting to betray the ravages of time. For her many fans, it did not seem to matter: to paraphrase the title of one of her songs, they just loved being there with Peg. In 1992, wheelchair-bound for the previous two years, Lee was persisting in a lawsuit, begun in 1987, against the Walt Disney Corporation for her share of the video profits from *Lady And The Tramp*. A year later, dissatisfied with the 'paltry' £2 million settlement for her six songs (written with Sonny Burke) and character voices, she was preparing to write a book about the whole affair. Meanwhile, she continued to make occasional cabaret appearances at New York venues such as Club 53. In 1993 she recorded a duet with Gilbert O'Sullivan for his album *Sounds Of The Loop*. Lee is one of the greatest 'classy' vocalists of the century, alongside such stellar artists such as Ella Fitzgerald, Billie Holiday, Sarah Vaughan and Betty Carter.

● ALBUMS: with Benny Goodman *Benny Goodman And Peggy Lee* (Columbia 1949)★★★, *Rendezvous* (Capitol 1952)★★★, *My Best To You* (Capitol 1952)★★★, *Song In Intimate Style* (Decca 1953)★★★, *Black Coffee* (Decca 1953)★★★★★, *White Christmas* film soundtrack (Decca 1954)★★★★, *Lady And The Tramp* film soundtrack (Decca 1955)★★★★, with Ella Fitzgerald *Songs From Pete Kelly's Blues* film soundtrack (Decca 1955)★★★, *Dream Street* (Decca 1956)★★★, *The Man I Love* (Capitol 1957)★★★★, *Jump For Joy* (Capitol 1958)★★★, *Sea Shells* (Decca 1958)★★★, *Things Are Swingin'* (Capitol 1958)★★★★, with George Shearing *Beauty And The Beat* (Capitol 1959)★★★★, *I Like Men!* (Capitol 1959)★★★, *Miss Wonderful* (Capitol 1959)★★★, *Pretty Eyes* (Capitol 1960)★★★, *Alright, Okay, You Win* (Capitol 1960)★★★, *Latin A La Lee!* (Capitol 1960)★★★, *All Aglow Again* (Capitol 1960)★★★, *Olé A La Lee* (Capitol 1960)★★★, *Christmas Carousel* (Capitol 1960)★★, *At Basin Street East* (Capitol 1960)★★★, *Blues Cross Country* (Capitol 1961)★★★, *If You Go* (Capitol 1961)★★★, *Sugar 'N' Spice* (Capitol 1962)★★★, *I'm A Woman* (Capitol 1963)★★★, *Mink Jazz* (Capitol 1963)★★★, *In Love Again* (Capitol 1963)★★★, *Lover* (Decca 1964)★★★, *In The Name Of Love* (Capitol 1964)★★★, *Pass Me By* (Capitol 1965)★★★, *That Was Then, This Is Now* (Capitol 1965)★★★, *Big Spender* (Capitol 1966)★★★, *Extra Special* (Capitol 1967)★★★, *Guitars A La Lee* (Capitol 1967)★★★, *Is That All There Is?* (Capitol 1969)★★★, *Bridge Over Troubled Water* (Capitol 1970)★★★, *Make It With You* (Capitol 1970)★★★, *Let's Love* (Atlantic 1974)★★★, *Mirrors* (A&M 1976)★★★, *Close Enough For Love* (DRG 1979)★★★, *Miss Peggy Lee Sings The Blues* (Music Masters 1988)★★★, *The Peggy Lee Songbook: There'll Be Another Spring* (Musicmasters 1990)★★★, with Quincy Jones *P'S & Q'S* (1992)★★★, *Love Held Lightly* (1993)★★★, *Moments Like This* (1993)★★★, *If I Could Be With You* 1951-52 recordings (1993)★★★.

● COMPILATIONS: *Bewitching-Lee!* (Capitol 1962)★★★★, *The Best Of Peggy Lee* (MCA 1980)★★★★, *Peggy Lee Sings With Benny Goodman (1941-43)* (Columbia 1984)★★★★, *The Peggy Lee Collection - 20 Golden Greats* (MCA 1985)★★★★, *Unforgettable: Peggy Lee* (Unforgettable/Castle 1987)★★★, *The Capitol Years* (Capitol 1988)★★★★, *Capitol Collectors Series: The Early Years* (Capitol 1990)★★★, *All-Time Greatest Hits* (Curb 1990)★★★, *Peggy Lee - Fever* (1992)★★★★, *The Best Of* (1993)★★★★, with Bing Crosby *It's A Good Day* (1993)★★★, *The Best Of Peggy Lee, 1952-1956* (Music Club 1994)★★★★, *EMI Presents The Magic Of Peggy Lee* (EMI 1997)★★★★, *Black Coffee: The Best Of The Decca Years* (Half Moon 1998)★★★★, *Miss Peggy Lee* 4-CD box set (Capitol 1998)★★★★.

● VIDEOS: *Quintessential* (Hendring 1989).

● FURTHER READING: *Miss Peggy Lee*, Peggy Lee.

LEE, PHIL

b. 8 April 1943, London, England. Lee's parents were musical, but he is a self-taught guitarist. He was a member of the group that Ivor Mairants (guitar) took to the Antibes Jazz Festival in the mid-60s, and worked with the John Williams Big Band. He first came to prominence with the Graham Collier Septet. He became coleader with Tony Coe (reeds) of Axel while freelancing with musicians like Henry Thomas Lowther, Michael Garrick and Jeff Clyne. He played in and wrote for the band Paz formed by Dick Crouch (vibes) in 1972. Later he toured with Michel Legrand's Quartet (1979) and Gordon Beck's Nonet (1983). In 1991, he played with Michael Garrick's Big Band in performances of Garrick's suite Hardy Country.

● ALBUMS: with Graham Collier *Deep Dark Blue Centre* (1967)★★, with Tony Coe *Zeitgeist* (1976)★★★★, with Gilgamesh *Gilgamesh* (1975)★★★, *Another Fine Tune I've Got You Into* (1978)★★★, with Andres Boiarsky *Play South Of The Border* (1980)★★★, *Twice Upon A Time* (Cadillac 1987)★★★★.

LEE, RANEE

b. Canada. A gifted singer with a growing maturity of style and purpose, Lee first attracted international attention when she played the 1992 Nice Jazz Festival. Until that time, her performances were sometimes overly energetic with a deliberately tough and raunchy manner. That same year, she appeared in the Canadian film *Giant Steps*. During the early 90s, Lee's style displayed much greater subtlety and an acute awareness of the needs of the music. Her voice is full and mellow, with delicate shadings on ballads and an easy sense of swing on mid- and up-tempo songs. She has recorded with a number of leading jazzmen including Ray Brown, Pat LaBarbera and Ed Thigpen.

● ALBUMS: *Live At Le Bijou* (Justin Time 1983)★★★, *You Must Believe In Swing* (Justin Time 1996)★★★★, *Seasons Of Love* (Justin Time 1997)★★★.

LEE, WILL

b. 8 September 1950, San Antonio, Texas, USA. Lee studied jazz at the University of Miami before coming to New York. He played bass with Randy and Michael Brecker in Billy Cobham's band Dreams (1971). From 1973 he has worked in the studios with an enormous variety of musicians including Larry Coryell, David Sanborn, Herbie Mann, George Benson and Maynard Ferguson.

LEEMAN, CLIFF

b. 10 September 1913, Portland, Maine, USA, d. 26 April 1986. After playing in the percussion section of a local symphony orchestra, Leeman turned to danceband and jazz drumming as a career. In 1936, he joined Artie Shaw, playing an important role in the band's swing era success story. After leaving Shaw, he played in several leading big bands, including those led by Tommy Dorsey, Charlie Barnet and Woody Herman. In the late 40s, as the big bands became fewer, Leeman played in many small groups along New York's 52nd Street, returning briefly to big band work whenever opportunities were offered. In the 50s he worked in the studios but continued to play in jazz groups, usually those with a traditional bent. During this and the following decade he worked with Big Joe Turner, (appearing on the singer's classic *Boss Of The Blues*), Eddie Condon, Ralph Sutton (with whom he recorded a duo album, *I Got Rhythm*), Wild Bill Davison, Yank Lawson and Bob Haggart. In the 70s he toured extensively, including a trip to Japan with Condon and an all-star band that featured Buck Clayton, Pee Wee Russell and Jimmy Rushing. Leeman also recorded with Bobby Hackett, Bud Freeman, Don Ewell, Joe Venuti, Zoot Sims and Lawson and Haggart's group, the World's Greatest Jazz Band. A powerful yet self-effacing big band drummer and a subtly encouraging small group player, Leeman's work was always exemplary. In the dixieland bands, with which he spent many of his later years, he played with zesty enthusiasm. In all of these settings his playing maintained a standard which should have eclipsed many of his better-known contemporaries. Sadly, he was the one who was often overshadowed and he remains one of the unsung heroes of jazz drumming.

● ALBUMS: *I Got Rhythm* (1953),★★★ with Joe Turner *The Boss Of The Blues* (1956)★★★★, *Eddie Condon In Japan* (1964)★★★, with Bobby Hackett *String Of Pearls* (1970)★★★★, with Hackett *Live At The Roosevelt Grill Vols. 1-4* (1970)★★★, with Joe Venuti, Zoot Sims *Joe And Zoot* (1974★★★, with Bud Freeman *The Joy Of Sax* (1974)★★★.

● COMPILATIONS: *The Indispensable Artie Shaw Vols. 1/2 (1938-39)* (RCA 1986)★★★.

LEES, GENE

b. 8 February 1928, Hamilton, Ontario, Canada. After studying music at Hamilton and the Berklee College Of Music in Boston, Massachusetts, Lees developed his writing talent, working in journalism, often as music critic, in both Canada and the USA. Lees has also written many song lyrics, some, like 'Quiet Nights On Quiet Stars' and 'Yesterday I Heard The Rain', were originals while others, for bossa nova songs by Antonio Carlos Jobim, he translated from Portuguese. In addition to his work as journalist and lyricist, Lees has also been active in musical education. His journal, *Jazzletter*, is widely read and respected and such books as *Singers And The Song* reveal an abiding interest in lyric writing and such diverse jazz artists as Sarah Vaughan and the Clarke-Boland Big Band, all of which is communicated with an able command of language.

● FURTHER READING: *Waiting For Dizzy*, Gene Lees.

LEGRAND, MICHEL

b. 24 February 1932, Paris, France. Legrand grew up in a musical environment - his father was an orchestra leader and film composer - and studied formally at the Paris Conservatoire. In the 50s he was an active pianist but was most successful as an arranger. Later in the decade he moved to New York and continued to arrange, but now with a strong orientation towards the contemporary jazz scene, for leading artists such as Miles Davis and John Coltrane. In France he had occasionally led his own bands and did so again in the USA. In these years he was also a prolific composer, writing material performed by Stan Getz, Phil Woods and others, and occasionally playing with jazzmen such as Shelly Manne. He had begun to compose music for French films in 1953, and, in the 60s, developed this area of his work on productions such as *Lola*; *Cleo From 5 To 7*, which he also appeared in, and *My Life To Live*. In 1964 he received the first of his many Academy Award nominations, for the score to *The Umbrellas Of Cherbourg*, which contained 'I Will Wait For You' and 'Watch What Happens' (English lyrics by Norman Gimbel). His second Oscar came for his work on the follow-up, *The Young Ladies Of Rochefort* (1968). In the late 60s he began to compose for US and British films. His score for one of the first of these, *The Thomas Crown Affair*, included 'The Windmills Of Your Mind' (lyric by Alan and Marilyn Bergman), which became popular for Noel Harrison (son of actor Rex) and Dusty Springfield, and won an Academy Award in 1968. Another collaboration with Alan and Marilyn Bergman produced 'What Are You Doing The Rest Of Your Life?', from *The Happy Ending* (1969). Throughout the 70s, Legrand continued to write prolifically for films such as *The Go-Between*, *Wuthering Heights*, *Summer Of 42* (another Oscar), *Lady Sings The Blues*, *One Is A Lonely Number* and *The Three Musketeers*. He teamed with the Bergmans yet again for Barbra Streisand's film *Yentl* (1983). Two of their 12 songs, 'Papa, Can You Hear Me?' and 'The Way He Makes Me Feel' were nominated, and the complete score won an Academy Award. Legrand's other film music included *Never Say Never Again*, Sean Connery's eagerly awaited return to the role of James Bond; *Secret Places* (title song written with Alan Jay Lerner); the amusing *Switching Channels* (theme written with Neil Diamond), *Fate* and *The Burning Shore*, and *Pret-A-Porter* (1994). In 1991 Legrand was back to his jazz roots for the score to *Dingo*, which he wrote with Miles Davis. Davis also gave an impressive performance in the movie. At his best with lyrical and sometimes sentimental themes, Legrand's writing for films remains his major contribution to popular music. Besides his feature film credits, Legrand also worked extensively in television, contributing music to *Brian's Song*, *The Adventures Of Don Quixote*, *It's Good To Be Alive*, *Cage Without A Key*, *A Woman Called Golda*, *The Jesse Owens Story*, *Promises To Keep*, *Sins* (mini-series), *Crossings*, *Casanova* and *Not A Penny More, Not A Penny Less*.

● ALBUMS: *Legrand Jazz* (Philips 1958)★★★★, *At Shelly's Manne Hole* (1968)★★★★, *Michel Legrand Recorded Live At Jimmy's* (1973)★★, *Themes And Variations* (1973)★★★, *After The Rain* (1982)★★★, *Live At Fat Tuesday's* (Verve 1985)★★★★, ★★★ (Verve 1993), *Douce France* (Verve 1997)★★★, and film soundtracks.

LEIGHTON, VICTORIA

b. 6 September 1962, Glasgow, Scotland. Leighton began her singing career performing in clubs and pubs in her home town and in other parts of the country. Her repertoire at the time was mainly R&B songs. After moving to London she worked as a session singer, but also made concert and club appearances and sang at jazz and blues festivals. She was persuaded by Glasgow-based DJ and impresario Jim Waugh to redirect her repertoire, and in the mid-90s began singing jazz. Performing in various parts of the UK she has shared bills with jazz notables, including Martin Taylor, and made a well-received debut album. Working with guitarist and composer Nigel Clark, she has appeared on BBC radio and also on television. In the late 90s she was centering her career on London and also seeking to expand her vocal boundaries beyond the confining envelope of jazz. Leighton's singing voice is warm and mature and she swings with subtlety. Her treatment of ballads is especially pleasing, and she possesses excellent interpretative skills.

● ALBUMS: *Speak Low* (Blu Jazz 1997)★★★.

LEIGHTON-THOMAS, NICKI

b. 11 October 1967, Bath, Somerset, England. Educated in England and Mauritius, her father is Welsh and her mother Mauritian. She began singing and acting at an early age, and while at school in Mauritius formed a jazz trio that performed in hotels. After living in Paris for two years, she then attended the Birmingham School of Speech and Drama in England continuing to sing although now with pop bands. Based in London from 1991 she worked in the theatre before deciding that her future lay in music and singing rather than in acting. She played the London club and pub scene where she was heard by pianist-composer Simon Wallace. He was currently working with the distinguished American poet and lyricist Fran Landesman, and he recognized in Leighton-Thomas's voice the qualities needed to suitably interpret Landesman's darkly wise and witty lyrics. This three-way collaboration began in the mid-90s and resulted in a succession of fine performances both live and, latterly, on record. By the late 90s Leighton-Thomas was performing at the top level of London venues including the Barbican, Pizza on the Park and the Vortex. Leighton-Thomas's voice is fluid, sensuous and perfectly geared to the needs of her repertoire, which extends beyond Landesman to incorporate all that is stylish, witty and intellectually demanding in the pantheon of superior popular music. At the beginning of 1999 she was recording and touring with a group led by Gary Husband and featuring fellow-vocalists Georgie Fame and Jack Bruce. She was also planning her own second and third albums, one of standards and the other with more latterday gems from Wallace and Landesman.

● ALBUMS: *Damned If I Do* (Babeldown 1998)★★★.

LEMER, PEPI

b. 25 May 1944, Ilfracombe, Devon, England. Lemer was born into a musical family and had classical singing lessons from the age of five. She went on to stage school and has worked in cabaret and the theatre both in the UK and abroad. Lemer was able to cover all sorts of singing styles from the most abstract improvisation to popular song and has done session work with Alan Price and Mike Oldfield. In the 60s and early 70s she worked with John Stevens' Spontaneous Music Ensemble, Peter Lemer's E, Keith Tippett's Centipede, Mike Gibbs and Barbara Thompson's Paraphernalia. Then with Jeff Clyne she led the band Turning Point, which undertook an Arts Council UK tour in 1971 with guests Allan Holdsworth and Neil Ardley, who later wrote 'The Harmony Of The Spheres' for a 9-piece ensemble with her voice and that of Norma Winstone.

● ALBUMS: *Will Power* (1974)★★★★, with Turning Point *Creatures Of The Night* (1977)★★★, with Neil Ardley *The Harmony Of The Spheres* (1978)★★★★, *Silent Promise* (1979)★★★.

LEMER, PETER

b. Peter Naphtali Lemer, 14 June 1942, London, England. Lemer studied piano extensively, both privately and at London's Royal Academy of Music. For the most part this was directed towards the classical repertoire, but he also pursued a growing interest in jazz through lessons with Paul Bley and others. In the early 60s he played in a trio with Jeff Clyne and Tony Crombie and led several bands of his own, many performing free jazz although his interests and abilities allowed him to play jazz-rock and straight jazz with equal confidence and credibility. Apart from playing with his own bands, Lemer has worked for numerous leaders including Don Rendell, Barbara Thompson, Jon Hiseman, Mike Westbrook and John Surman. Throughout this period, Lemer also developed a level of skill as a composer comparable to his distinction as a performer.

● ALBUMS: *Local Colour* (ESP 1966)★★★.

LEMON, BRIAN

b. 11 February 1937, Nottingham, England. After playing piano in and around his home town, Lemon moved to London in the mid-50s where he joined the Freddy Randall band. During the late 50s and early 60s he played with several bands ranging from those of a traditional bent through to the mainstream and into post-bop. Amongst the leaders with whom he has worked are Betty Smith, Al Fairweather, Sandy Brown, Dave Shepherd, Danny Moss, George Chisholm and Alex Welsh. A regular member of the house band at leading London venues such as the Pizza Express and Ronnie Scott's, he has also backed several visiting American jazz musicians, including Benny Goodman, Ben Webster, Milt Jackson and Buddy Tate. Always displaying considerable flair and switching styles with rare ease, by the 70s Lemon had become a familiar and popular figure on the UK jazz scene, a role he maintained throughout the 80s and into the late 90s. He is also in demand as a session musician on radio, performing and writing music within and beyond the framework of jazz.

● ALBUMS: *Our Kind Of Music* (Hep Jazz 1970)★★★, *Piano Summit* (1975)★★★★, *But Beautiful* (Zephyr 1995)★★★, *A Beautiful Friendship* (Zephyr 1996)★★, *How Long Has This Been Going On* (Zephyr 1996)★★★★, *Lemon Looks Back Just For Fun* (Zephyr 1997)★★★.

LEO RECORDS

Founded in London, England, in 1980 by Russian expatriate Leo Feigin (b. 1 February 1938, St. Petersburg, Russia), Leo Records is the label that brought new Russian jazz to the west. Several of its first releases were of tapes smuggled out of Russia (formerly the USSR) and the sleeves bore the dramatic disclaimer: 'The musicians do not bear any responsibility for publishing these tapes.' Sometimes (of necessity) poorly recorded, these early albums met with a decidedly mixed critical reception, but Feigin proved an indefatiguable champion of Russian jazz, gradually building up an impressive catalogue on only minimal resources. In addition to the Ganelin Trio, the first and best-known of the Russian groups on Leo, the label introduced numerous other artists from the then-USSR, including Sergey Kuryokhin, Anatoly Vapirov, Valentina Ponomareva, Jazz Group Archangelsk and the Siberian Homo Liber. Feigin also released many albums of west European and American jazz, usually from the more *avant garde* end of the spectrum: notable among these are releases by Anthony Braxton, Marilyn Crispell, Amina Claudine Myers, Sun Ra and Cecil Taylor, whose sound-poetry was first released on the Leo album *Chinampas* and whose *Live In Bologna* on Leo was voted record of the year in the 1988 *Wire* magazine critics' poll. Nevertheless, it is for its stalwart support of Russian new music that the label is best known - arguably its finest achievement. The realization of a dream for Feigin - who still runs the label on a shoestring from his front room - was the 1990 *Document*, a lavishly-presented eight-CD boxed-set that traced the development of Russia's contemporary jazz through the 80s. (This label should not be confused with the Finnish Leo label, run by Edward Vesala.)

● COMPILATIONS: *Document* 8-CD box set (Leo 1990)★★★★.

● FURTHER READING: *Russian Jazz New Identity*, Leo Feigin (ed.).

LEONARD, HARLAN

b. 2 July 1905, Kansas City, Missouri, USA, d. 1983. After working in various bands in and around Kansas City, including that led by George E. Lee, in 1923, saxophonist Leonard joined Bennie Moten for a lengthy stay. In 1931, he co-led a band with Thamon Hayes that they named the Kansas City Skyrockets, which, by 1934, had relocated to Chicago, becoming Harlan Leonard And His Rockets. In 1937, the band folded, but Leonard reformed it in 1938, this time keeping the band together until the mid-40s. Despite some important engagements at such venues as the Savoy Ballroom in Harlem and the Hollywood Club in Los Angeles, the Rockets remained relatively little known among jazz fans. Thanks to the handful of records they made it is possible to see that the band had many important qualities. Notably, it was an early testing ground for arranger Tadd Dameron whose arrangements for 'A La Bridges' and 'Dameron Stomp', recorded in 1940, were ahead of their time. There were also some sidemen of merit; in addition to drummer Jesse Price, tenor saxophonists Jimmy Keith and Henry Bridges stood out, both composing and soloing on 'A La Bridges'. This same track also features the band's outstanding soloist, trombonist Fred Beckett, who later joined Lionel Hampton. In the mid-40s Leonard left music to work for the US Internal Revenue Service.

● COMPILATIONS: *Harlan Leonard Volumes1/2* (1939-40 recordings)★★★★, *Harlan Leonard And His Rockets 1940* (Original Jazz Classics 1992)★★★★.

LEONARD, JACK

(see Dorsey, Tommy)

LES JAZZ MODES

(see Rouse, Charlie; Watkins, Julius)

LESBERG, JACK

b. 14 February 1920, Boston, Massachusetts, USA. After playing bass in a number of jazz clubs in and around his home town in his late teens, Lesberg moved to New York. From 1945, he spent three years doubling with the New York Symphony Orchestra and at Eddie Condon's club. During the 50s and 60s Lesberg concentrated on playing jazz, working with numerous top-flight traditional and mainstream musicians including Sarah Vaughan, Benny Goodman, Louis Armstrong, Jack Teagarden, Earl Hines, Sidney Bechet, Tommy Dorsey, Billy Butterfield, Ruby Braff and Joe Venuti. Solid, reliable and obviously highly respected by his fellow musicians, in the early 70s Lesberg was resident in Australia and later in the decade resumed his extensive gigging with artists such as Kenny Davern, Howard Alden, Yank Lawson and Keith Ingham.

● ALBUMS: *Hollywood Swing* (1977)★★★, with Howard Alden *No Amps Allowed* (1990)★★.

LETMAN, JOHNNY

b. 6 September 1917, McCormick, South Carolina, USA. Growing up in Chicago, Letman played trumpet in various youth bands including the first band organized by Nat 'King' Cole. After leaving Cole in 1934 he continued to play in the Chicago area, appearing with leaders such as 'Scat Man' Carruthers, Delbert Bright, Horace Henderson and Red Saunders. In the early 40s he moved to New York and during the rest of the decade played in numerous bands including those of Cab Calloway and Lucky Millinder. In the 50s he was active in the studios and also played in theatre bands along Broadway, but found time for gigs with Count Basie, Stuff Smith, Chubby Jackson and many others, as well as leading his own bands for club and record dates. In the 60s and 70s he continued much as before but also visited Europe, playing with Milt Buckner, Tiny Grimes, Lionel Hampton and Earl Hines. In the 80s he was often on tour, playing festivals throughout Europe.

● ALBUMS: *Cascade Of Quartets* (50s)★★★, *The Many Angles Of Johnny Letman* (1960)★★.

LEVALLET, DIDIER

b. 19 July 1944, Arcy sur Cure, France. Levallet is largely a self-taught bass player who studied journalism at L'Ecole Superieure de Journalisme de Lille (1963-66) and went on for a short time to study bass at Lille Conservatory. He moved to Paris in 1969 and played with a wide range of local and visiting musicians including Ted Curson, Hank Mobley, Mal Waldron and Johnny Griffin. He worked with the free-jazz quartet Perception through the 70s and worked in the USA with tenor saxophonist Byard Lancaster (1974-76). He also led Confluence, a group based on strings and percussion only. In the early 80s he played with Frank Lowe, Archie Shepp, Mike Westbrook's Concert Band and Chris McGregor's Brotherhood Of Breath as well as the Double Quartet with Tony Oxley. Levallet is a prolific composer who can combine free-improvisation and structure coherently. He works within four bands - the Quintet, a 12-piece band, Swing Strings System (which utilises seven string players plus drums) and a trio with Pifarely (violin) and Marais (guitar). In 1976, he founded ADMI (Association pour la Developement de la Musique Improvise) which acts as a pressure group and concert organizer. He teaches jazz at L'Ecole National de Musique in Angouleme.

● ALBUMS: *Perception* (1976)★★★, *Swing String System* (1978)★★★★, *Ostinato* (1981)★★★, *Instants Cavires* (1982)★★, *Scoop* (In And Out 1983)★★★, *Quiet Days* (1985)★★★.

LEVEY, STAN

b. 5 April 1925, Philadelphia, Pennsylvania, USA. After working as a professional heavyweight boxer and part-time drummer in his home town, Levey moved to New York while still in his teens. Abandoning boxing and concentrating on drumming, he was soon in great demand. He had already gigged with Dizzy Gillespie in Philadelphia and worked with him again, also playing in bebop bands such as those led by Oscar Pettiford, Charlie Parker, Coleman Hawkins and George Shearing. In 1945, he was a member of the remarkable band co-led by Gillespie and Parker, of which the other members were Al Haig and Ray Brown (and sometimes Milt Jackson and Eli 'Lucky' Thompson), which took the bebop message around the USA. Perhaps the most notable point on the tour was Billy Berg's nightclub in Los Angeles, an engagement which proved to be the catalyst for the creation of the west coast school of bebop. In the late 40s Levey played in a number of big bands including those of Georgie Auld and Woody Herman and in 1952 joined Stan Kenton. After leaving Kenton in 1954, Levey became resident in Los Angeles, working with Howard Rumsey's Lighthouse All Stars, where he replaced Max Roach, and recording extensively, often under his own name, with musicians such as Conte Candoli, Frank Rosolino, Lou Levy, Richie Kamuca, Art Pepper and Dexter Gordon. In such company, Levey appeared on several of the best albums made by the west coast beboppers. He also played in the Shorty Rogers big band assembled for a record date in 1956. Subsequently, Levey worked in film and television studio bands and appeared on many recording dates, occasionally playing jazz gigs. One of the best of the early bebop drummers, Levey's playing was marked by his clean, precise attack which was at its most striking at fast tempos.

● ALBUMS: with Dizzy Gillespie *The Development Of An American Artist* (1945)★★★, *Stan Levey Plays Bill Holman, Jimmy Giuffre* (1954)★★★★, *This Time The Drum's On Me/Stanley The Steamer* (1955)★★★, *Grand Stan* (1956)★★★, with Shorty Rogers *Blues Express* (1956)★★★, with the Lighthouse All Stars *Double Or Nothin'* (1957)★★, *The Stan Levey Quintet* (VSOP 1957)★★★, with Max Roach *Drummin' The Blues* (Liberty 1957)★★★.

LEVIEV, MILCHO

b. 19 December 1937, Plovdiv, Bulgaria. Leviev studied formally at the Bulgarian State Music Academy, and by the early 60s was playing piano and directing orchestras on radio and television. He was also active as a composer, experimenting with music to be played by classical and jazz ensembles. In the early 70s he was in Germany and soon moved to the USA, where he began a fruitful association with Don Ellis. In addition to playing with Ellis he also composed and arranged, finding considerable rapport with Ellis's imaginative use of complex time signatures and incorporation of ethnic concepts. Also in the 70s, Leviev played in small groups led by, amongst others, John Klemmer and Billy Cobham. In the early 80s, Leviev worked with Art Pepper, with whom he appeared at Ronnie Scott's, an occasion recorded on *Blues For The Fisherman* and *True Blues*. He also worked with Al Jarreau and led his own small band, Free Flight. Although Free Flight was a jazz-rock fusion band, Leviev continued to associate with big bands, working with Gerald Wilson and others. In the mid-80s he formed a duo with Charlie Haden and later in the decade was involved in a number of US west coast-based small groups. In addition to the valuable contribution he has made through his writing, Leviev consistently demonstrates his skills as a keyboard player, bringing his classical training to bear upon the complexities of the advanced musical style in which he frequently chooses to work.

● ALBUMS: *Jazz Focus 65* (1967)★★★★, *Piano Lesson* (1977)★★★, *Music For Big Band And Symphony Orchestra* (1981)★★★★, *Blues For The Fisherman* (1981)★★★★, *What's New?* (1980)★★★, *True Blues* (1982)★★★, *Milcho Leviev Plays The Music Of Irving Berlin* (1983)★★★.

LEVINE, HENRY 'HOT LIPS'

b. 26 November 1907, London, England. Levine's family emigrated to the USA early in 1908. In 1917, Levine heard Nick La Rocca playing with the Original Dixieland Jazz Band, an event which determined his future career. He learned to play trumpet and turned professional in 1925; by extraordinary coincidence his first job was with the ODJB, by then much-changed from the line-up Levine had seen as a child. Levine played in several studio bands of the mid-20s, recording with Nat Shilkret, Vincent Lopez and others, but in 1927 was hired by British bandleader Bert Ambrose. He opened with Ambrose at the Mayfair Hotel in London in March and in June made records with the band. The following month he recorded under the leadership of Fred Elizalde. Towards the end of the year, he returned to New York where, for the next few years, he played in bands led by Cass Hagan, Rudy Vallee and other popular entertainers of the period. He then returned to studio work, among other things leading NBC's Chamber Music Society of Lower Basin Street jazz group. After World War II Levine directed radio, television and hotel orchestras in various parts of the USA, settling in Las Vegas in 1961 where he played in numerous hotel and casino bands. He retired in 1982. A fine lead trumpeter and an effective soloist, Levine remains little known among jazz fans despite his long and active career.

● ALBUMS: *Chamber Music Society Of Lower Basin Street* (1940-41 recordings)★★★.

LEVITT, ROD

b. 16 September 1929, Portland, Oregon, USA. A regular trombone player in studio orchestras, Levitt first attracted attention in the jazz world through a job with Dizzy Gillespie, with whose big band he played in 1956. Apart from Gillespie, he also recorded with big bands led by Ernie Wilkins, Sy Oliver and Gil Evans. In the early 60s, he recorded with his own octet which included Bill Berry and Rolf Ericson but was most often heard on big band sessions under leaders such as Quincy Jones, Oliver Nelson and the Chuck Israels's National Jazz Ensemble. Apart from his sound playing ability, Levitt is also a gifted arranger.

● ALBUMS: *Dynamic Sound Patterns* (1963)★★★, *Insight* (1964)★★, *Solid Ground* (1965)★★★, *42nd Street* (1966)★★★.

LEVY, HANK

b. Henry J. Levy, 27 September 1927, Baltimore, Maryland, USA. After an extensive period of formal study, baritone saxophonist Levy joined Stan Kenton in 1953. By the 60s Levy was mostly writing, arranging and, in many instances, composing original material for Kenton, Don Ellis and other bands. Towards the end of the decade Levy entered musical education on a full-time basis. His work with students at Towson State University has generated considerable interest and enthusiasm, and many of his graduates found work in latter-day 'name' bands.

● ALBUMS: by Don Ellis *Live At Monterey* (1966)★★★★, by Ellis *Connection* (1972)★★★, by Stan Kenton *Journey To Capricorn* (1976)★★★.

LEVY, LOU

b. 5 March 1928, Chicago, Illinois, USA. Among Levy's early piano jobs were stints in the late 40s with the big bands of Georgie Auld and Woody Herman. He also accompanied Sarah Vaughan in 1947, the first of many singers with whom he worked over the years. Others included Ella Fitzgerald, Anita O'Day, Nancy Wilson and Peggy Lee, whom he accompanied sporadically for 18 years from 1955. Among the bands with which he has played are those led by Terry Gibbs, Benny Goodman and Stan Getz. He also worked with Supersax, Conte Candoli, Shelly Manne, Zoot Sims and Al Cohn. Influenced by Bud Powell but with his own forthright style and a distinctive soloist and superb accompanist, Levy remains an important if sometimes overlooked jazz pianist.

● ALBUMS: *The Lou Levy Trio* (Nocturne 1954)★★, with Conte Candoli *West Coast Wailers* (Atlantic 1955)★★★★, *Solo Scene* (RCA Victor 1956)★★★, *Jazz In Four Colors* (RCA Victor 1956)★★★★, *A Most Musical Fella* (RCA Victor 1956)★★★, *Piano Playhouse* (1957)★★★, *Lou Levy Plays Baby Grand Jazz* (Jubilee 1958)★★, *The Hymn* (Philips 1963)★★★, *The Kid's Got Ears* (1982)★★★.

LEWIS, ED

b. Edwards Lewis, 22 January 1909, Eagle City, Oklahoma, USA, d. 18 September 1985. After briefly playing baritone horn in a marching band in Kansas City, where he was raised, Lewis switched to trumpet. He worked with a number of territory bands, notably Bennie Moten's, during the 20s and early 30s. Other leaders included Thamon Hayes, Harlan Leonard and Jay 'Hootie' McShann. In 1937 he joined Count Basie, coincidentally auditioning on the same day as Billie Holiday. After spending more than a decade with Basie he dropped out of music for a while, returning in the mid-50s to lead his own band. He continued to play for the rest of his life, visiting Europe with the Countsmen the year before his death. Although best known as a capable and often inspiring lead trumpet, Lewis was a good soloist and played with a light, airy sound. He also composed several tunes.

LEWIS, GEORGE (CLARINETTIST)

b. George Louis Francis Zeno, 13 July 1900, New Orleans, Louisiana, USA, d. 31 December 1968, New Orleans, Louisiana, USA. Lewis began playing clarinet in his early teens and between 1917 and the early 20s had worked alongside many leading New Orleans musicians including Buddy Petit and Edward 'Kid' Ory. Through the 20s and 30s, Lewis chose to play mostly in and around his home town, thus missing the attention paid to many early jazz musicians who visited Chicago, New York and other urban centres outside the south. In the early 40s Lewis benefited from the resurgence of interest in New Orleans jazz and began recording extensively, sometimes in partnership with Bunk Johnson. By the middle of the decade, however, Lewis was back in New Orleans, but the 50s found him touring all over the USA and to Europe. Although he lacked the sophisticated grace of, say, an Edmond Hall, Lewis's playing was marked by an often delightful simplicity and his fans were happy to overlook occasional musical inconsistencies in order to enjoy what they regarded as his authentic style. At his best, especially on some of the records made by William Russell in his American Music series, Lewis played with a charming distinction, which went a long way to deter criticism of his occasionally out-of-tune performances. On those records cited, and others where he was in complete control of the style in which his accompanists played, Lewis's work gives a taste of how some facets of early jazz might well have been and, as such, should be heard by anyone interested in the origins of the music. Plagued by ill-health during the 60s, Lewis continued playing almost to the end of his life.

● ALBUMS: *George Lewis At Herbert Otto's Party* (1949)★★★, *Jazz At The Ohio Union* (Disc Jockey 1950)★★★, *George Lewis And His New Orleans All Stars* (Circle 1951)★★, *George Lewis Band In The French Quarter* (American Music 1951)★★★, *George Lewis* (Paradox 1951)★★, *George Lewis' New Orleans Stompers Vol 1* (Blue Note 1951)★★★★, *George Lewis' New Orleans Stompers Vol 2* (Blue Note 1951)★★★★,*George Lewis With Kid Shots Madison* (American Music 1952)★★★, *George Lewis' New Orleans Stompers Vol 3* (Blue Note 1954)★★★,*George Lewis' New Orleans Stompers Vol 4* (Blue Note 1954)★★★, *New Orleans Music* (Jazzman 1954)★★★, *George Lewis* (Southland 1955)★★, *George Lewis Concert* (Blue Note 1955)★★★, *George Lewis With Guest Artist Red Allen* (Riverside 1955)★★★★, *George Lewis In Hi-Fi* (Cavalier 1956)★★, *Spirituals In Ragtime* (Empirical 1956)★★★, *Jazz In The Classic New Orleans Tradition* (Riverside 1956)★★★, *Jazz At Vespers* (Riverside 1957)★★★, *Blues From The Bayou* (Verve 1957)★★, *Doctor Jazz* (Verve 1957)★★★, *Hot Time In The Old Town Tonight* (Verve 1957)★★★★, *George Lewis' Dixieland Band* (Verve 1957)★★★, with Mark Murphy *George Lewis And Mark Murphy At Newport* (Verve 1957)★★★, *A Very Good Year* (1957)★★, *The Perennial George Lewis* (Verve 1958)★★★, *On Stage, George Lewis Concert Vol 1* (Verve 1959)★★★, *On Stage, George Lewis Concert Vol 2* (Verve 1959)★★★, *Oh Didn't He Ramble* (Verve 1959)★★, *George Lewis In Japan, 1 In Osaka* (1963)★★, *George Lewis In Japan, 2 In Tokyo* (1965)★★, *George Lewis In Japan, 3 In Kokura* (1965)★★, *George Lewis And The Moustache Stompers* (1965)★★★.

● COMPILATIONS: *The Oxford Series Volume 1* (1952)★★★★, *On Parade* (1953)★★★, *George Lewis Memorial Album* (1953)★★★, *New Orleans Stompers, Volumes 1 & 2* (1974)★★★★, *Pied Piper, Volumes 1-3 (1959)* (1981)★★★, *George Lewis Authentic New Orleans Ragtime Jazz Band* (1981)★★★, *Live At The Club Hangover (1953-54)* (1986)★★★, *In Japan Volumes 1-3* (GHB 1986)★★, *In New Orleans* (Ace 1993)★★★.

● FURTHER READING: *Call Him George*, Jay Alison Stuart (Dorothy Tait). *George Lewis: A Jazzman from New Orleans*, Tom Bethell.

LEWIS, GEORGE (TROMBONIST)

b. 14 July 1952, Chicago, Illinois, USA. By chance George Lewis went to school with Ray Anderson, the other leading trombonist to emerge in the late 70s. Lewis took up trombone at the age of nine and taught himself by copying Lester Young's tenor saxophone solos from records. He studied philosophy at Yale, playing there with pianist Anthony Davis and percussionist Gerry Hemingway. In 1971, he returned to Chicago where the AACM was active: he studied with Muhal Richard Abrams and began a long association with reeds player Douglas Ewart. He developed a virtuoso technique, combining tailgate bluster with bebop agility - something he attributes to listening to saxophonists and practising from Eddie Harris's exercise books. He then studied music at Yale, graduating with a BA in 1974. In 1976, he spent two months with Count Basie. In 1976, he started working with Anthony Braxton, recording duo, quartet and orchestra pieces with him (*Elements Of Surprise*, *Quartet (Dortmund) 1976*, *Creative Orchestra Music 1976*); later he became an international figure of the *avant garde*, playing with Richard Teitelbaum of Musica Elettronica Viva and free-improvisers Derek Bailey and Dave Holland. He also played in the Gil Evans Orchestra, with pianist Randy Weston, recorded regularly with Abrams and worked with Steve Lacy (*Prospectus*, *Futurities* and the Herbie Nichols tribute *Change Of Season*). Lewis appeared in several of Bailey's Company line-ups and with leading European improvisers such as Joëlle Léandre and Irène Schweizer. He also recorded again with Braxton, both on the saxophonist's own *Four Compositions (Quartet)* 1983 and with him on Teitelbaum's extraordinary *Concerto Grosso*. In 1987, he recorded *News For Lulu*, a retrospective of hard bop tunes, with John Zorn and Bill Frisell, showing a stunning combination of bebop chops and free-improvising imagination. From the early 80s Lewis began to develop an interest in electronics, amazing people with improvised duets with programmed computers, and in recent years much of his time has been devoted to this project. From 1980-82 he was also the director of the New York radical theatre and music venue, The Kitchen.

● ALBUMS: with Anthony Braxton *Creative Orchestra Music 1976* (Bluebird 1976)★★★★, with Braxton *Elements Of Surprise* (1976)★★★★, *Jazz At Ohio Union* (1976)★★★, *The George Lewis Solo Trombone Record* (Sackville 1977)★★, *Monads/Triple Slow Mix/Cycle/Shadowgraph 5* (Black Saint 1978)★★★, with Douglas Ewart *Jila/Save!/Mon./The Imaginary Suite* (Black Saint 1979)★★★, *Homage To Charles Parker* (Black Saint 1979)★★★★, *Chicago Slow Dance* recorded 1977 (Lovely/Vital1979)★★★, with Muhal Richard Abrams *Spihumonesty* (Black Saint 1979)★★★, with Abrams *Mama And Daddy* (Black Saint 1980)★★★, with Evan Parker *From Saxophone & Trombone* (1980)★★★★, with Company *Fables* (1980)★★★, with Derek Bailey, John Zorn *Yankees* (Celluloid 1983)★★★★, with Parker *Hook, Drift & Shuffle* (1985)★★★, with various *Change Of Season* (1985)★★★, with Zorn, Bill Frisell *News For Lulu* (hat Art 1987)★★★★, with Braxton *Ensemble (Victoriaville) 1988* (Victo 1989)★★★★, with Braxton *Dortmund (Quartet) 1976* (hat Art 1991)★★★★, with Zorn, Frisell *More News For Lulu* (hat Art 1992)★★★, with Ray Anderson, Craig Harris, Gary Valente *Slideride* (hat Art 1996)★★★★, *Changing With The Times* (New World 1996)★★★, with Roscoe Mitchell *Voyager* (Avant 1996)★★★.

LEWIS, HERBIE

b. *c*.1941, Pasadena, California, USA. Set on a career in music, Lewis first planned to be an opera singer, then took up the trombone and tried the baritone horn before settling on the bass. He was a childhood friend of Bobby Hutcherson whom he encouraged to take up the vibraphone so that they could emulate the music of the

Modern Jazz Quartet. During the late 50s Lewis played bass with a number of small jazz groups on the west coast, including that led by Les McCann, and he also made some records, notably with Harold Land on his 1959 recording *The Fox*. In the 60s Lewis spent some time in New York, again playing with McCann and musicians such as Chico Hamilton and Jackie McLean, appearing on sessions for the latter's *Let Freedom Ring*. During the rest of the decade he moved between coasts, playing once more with McCann and also with Gerald Wilson, Cannonball Adderley, Sam Rivers, the Crusaders, Freddie Hubbard and McCoy Tyner. Lewis recorded with several of these leaders, but disenchantment with the music industry led to spells working in a flower shop and a museum, and studying psychology. In the early 80s Lewis moved to San Francisco and became deeply involved in education, writing books on educational theory and bass technique, and he was eventually appointed director of the music department of the New College of California. He continued to perform, including appearances at the Keystone Korner in 1981 as a member of the rhythm section, alongside Cedar Walton and Billy Higgins, backing Sonny Stitt for a session belatedly released in 1998 by 32 Jazz as *Just In Case You Forgot How Bad He Really Was*. In the late 80s and early 90s he played with a small group led by trumpeter Jerry Rusch, appearing on 1990's *Native L.A.* and later recording with Rusch as a duo. A secure performer with a solid sense of time, Lewis displays a fluent ability to adapt between modern jazz styles and soul and funk fusions.

● ALBUMS: with Jerry Rusch *Duo* (Jeru 1995)★★★.

LEWIS, JOHN

b. 3 May 1920, La Grange, Illinois, USA. A formally trained pianist from a very early age, Lewis first took an interest in jazz after meeting Kenny Clarke. In 1946, both men joined Dizzy Gillespie's big band with Lewis writing charts in addition to his rhythm section duties. In the late 40s and early 50s, Lewis continued his musical studies and also accompanied numerous important jazz artists including Charlie Parker, Miles Davis and Milt Jackson. His association with Jackson continued with their group taking the name, the Modern Jazz Quartet. The MJQ stayed in existence until 1974 after which Lewis turned to teaching. In the 80s the MJQ reformed and Lewis also worked with his own sextet and as musical director of the American Jazz Orchestra, a group especially dedicated to the performance of big band music and which played and recorded such important pieces as Benny Carter's 'Central City Sketches'. Although he began his jazz career in bebop, a style that is always apparent in his playing, Lewis's classical training and extensive musical studies emerge in many of his compositions, which use 18th and 19th century European musical forms. In the 80s Lewis was also musical director of the Monterey Jazz Festival, a role he gave up as his long-lived playing career continued to blossom.

● ALBUMS: with Bill Perkins *Grand Encounter: 2 East 3 West* (Pacific Jazz 1956)★★★★, with Sacha Distel *Afternoon In Paris* (Atlantic 1957)★★★, *European Windows* (RCA Victor 1958)★★★, *The John Lewis Piano* (Atlantic 1958)★★★★, *Improvised Meditations & Excursions* (Atlantic 1959)★★★★, *The Golden Striker* (Atlantic 1960)★★★, *John Lewis Presents Jazz Abstractions* (Atlantic 1961)★★★★, *Original Sin* (Atlantic 1961)★★★, *The Wonderful World Of Jazz* (Atlantic 1961)★★★★, with Svend Asmussen *European Encounter* (Atlantic 1962)★★★★, *A Milanese Story* film soundtrack (Atlantic 1962)★★★, *Animal Dance* (Atlantic 1963)★★★, *Essence* (Atlantic 1964)★★★, *P.O.V.* (Columbia 1975)★★★, with Hank Jones *John Lewis Solo/Duo With Hank Jones* (1976)★★★, *I Remember Bebop* (1977)★★★, *Mirjana* (1978)★★, with Jones *An Evening With Two Grand Pianos* (Little David 1979)★★★★, with Jones *Piano Playhouse* (1979)★★★, *The John Lewis Album With Putte Wickman And Red Mitchell* (1981)★★★, *Kansas City Breaks* (DRG 1982)★★★, *Slavic Smile* (1982)★★, *J.S. Bach Preludes And Fugues From The Well-Tempered Clavier, Book 1* (1984)★★, *The Bridge Game* (Philips 1984)★★★, with the American Jazz Orchestra *Central City Sketches* (1987)★★★, *Delaunay's Delemma* (EmArcy 1988)★★★, *Midnight In Paris* (EmArcy 1989)★★★★, *Private Concert* (EmArcy 1991)★★★.

LEWIS, MEADE 'LUX'

b. 4 September 1905, Chicago, Illinois, USA, d. 7 June 1964. Although he was popular in Chicago bars in the 20s, Lewis was little known elsewhere and made his living running a taxicab firm with fellow-pianist Albert Ammons. A record he made in 1927, 'Honky Tonk Train Blues', but which was not released until 1929, eventually came to the attention of John Hammond Jnr. some half-dozen years later. Encouraged by Hammond and the enormous success of 'Honky Tonk Train Blues', which he re-recorded in 1936 (and later), Lewis became one of the most popular and successful of the pianists to enjoy fleeting fame during the boogie-woogie craze. With Ammons and Pete Johnson, billed as the 'Boogie Woogie Trio', he played at Hammond's Carnegie Hall 'Spirituals to Swing' concert and at many top New York clubs. Later resident in Los Angeles, Lewis continued to tour and make records. From the mid-30s onwards, Lewis often played celeste and records such as those he made in the early 40s with Edmond Hall's Celeste Quartet, where the remaining members of the group were Israel Crosby and Charlie Christian, showed him to be much more versatile than his mass audience appeared to assume. Lewis died following a road accident in 1964.

● ALBUMS: *Meade Lux Lewis* (Mercury 1951)★★★★, *Boogie Woogie Classics* (Blue Note 1952)★★★★, *Boogie Woogie Interpretations* (Atlantic 1952)★★★, *Meade Lux Lewis At The Philharmonic* (Disc 1953)★★, with Louis Bellson *Boogie Woogie Piano And Drums* (Clef 1954)★★, *Yancey's Last Ride* (Down Home 1955)★★★, *Cat House Piano* (Down Home 1955)★★★★, *Barrel House Piano* (1956)★★★★, *The Meade 'Lux' Lewis Trio* (1956)★★★, *Out Of The Roaring 20s* (ABC Paramount 1957)★★★, *The Blues Artistry Of Meade 'Lux' Lewis* (Riverside 1961)★★★★, *Boogie Woogie House Party* (1962)★★★★.

● COMPILATIONS: with Albert Ammons *The Complete Blue Note Recordings Of Albert Ammons And Meade Lux Lewis* (Mosaic

1983)★★★★, *Honky Tonk Piano* (Classic Jazz Masters 1988)★★★, with others *Meade Lux Lewis Volume 1 (1927-39)* (1988)★★★★, *Tell Your Story* (1989)★★★, *Meade Lux Lewis 1927-1939* (Original Jazz Classics 1993)★★★★.

LEWIS, MEL

b. Melvin Sokoloff, 10 May 1929, Buffalo, New York, USA, d. 3 February 1990, New York City, New York, USA. Following in the footsteps of his father, Lewis took up drumming as a child and was playing professionally by his early teens. In 1948, he joined Boyd Raeburn's modern big band, then played in a number of well-known dance bands of the late swing era, including those of Ray Anthony and Tex Beneke. In 1954, he was hired by Stan Kenton and then worked in the west coast film studios, with the big bands of Bill Holman and Woody Herman, later performing with various small jazz groups until the end of the decade. In the 60s, he played with numerous bands, including those led by Gerry Mulligan, Benny Goodman and Dizzy Gillespie. Settling in New York, Lewis established a musical partnership with Thad Jones, which in 1965 resulted in the formation of the Jazz Orchestra, a big band formed from the many fine jazz players living in the city and earning their living in non-jazz work in radio and television orchestras. The Thad Jones-Mel Lewis Jazz Orchestra, with a regular weekly gig at the Village Vanguard and a series of fine recordings, became a byword for the best in contemporary big band music. National and international tours helped spread the word and by the time the Jones-Lewis partnership was dissolved, in 1978, there were few comparable units left in existence. With Jones gone, Lewis decided to continue with the band (as someone was to remark, 'Mel and Thad got divorced, Mel got the kids') and with Bob Brookmeyer providing new arrangements to augment the magnificent library Jones had created, the band was still a big attraction. A skilled and always swinging drummer, equally at home subtly urging a small group or punching along a powerful big band, Lewis was a master of his craft and greatly respected among his peers.

● ALBUMS: with The Five *The Five* (RCA Victor 1955)★★★, *Got 'Cha* (San Francisco 1957)★★★, *Mel Lewis Sextet* (Mode 1957)★★★★, *Gettin' Together* (Vee Jay 1963)★★★, with Thad Jones *Presenting Thad Jones-Mel Lewis & The Jazz Orchestra* (Solid State 1966)★★★★, with Jones *Thad Jones Live At The Village Vanguard* (Solid State 1967)★★★★, with Jones *The Big Band Sound Of Thad Jones & Mel Lewis* (Solid State 1968)★★★★, with Ruth Brown, Jones *Thad Jones & Mel Lewis Featuring Miss Ruth Brown* (Solid State 1969)★★★★, with Jones *Monday Night* (Solid State 1969)★★★★, with Jones *Central Park North* (Solid State 1969)★★★★, with Jones *Consummation* (Blue Note 1970)★★★★, with Jones *Suite For Pops* (Horizon 1972)★★★, with Jones *Potpourri* (Philadelphia International 1974)★★★, with Jones *New Life: Dedicated To Max Gordon* (A&M 1975)★★, with Jones *Live In Munich* (A&M 1976)★★★, *Mel Lewis And Friends* (Horizon 1976)★★★, with Jones *Thad Jones With Mel Lewis, Manuel Desica And The Jazz Orchestra* (Pausa 1977)★★★, with Jones *Thad Jones And The Mel Lewis Quartet* (A&M 1977)★★★★, *Naturally* (Telarc 1979)★★★, *Live At Village Vanguard* (Gryphon 1980)★★★★, *Mel Lewis Plays Herbie Hancock: Live In Montreux* (MPS 1980)★★★, *Mellifluous* (Landmark 1982)★★★, *Mel Lewis & The Jazz Orchestra* (Finesse 1982)★★★, *20 Years At The Village Vanguard* (Atlantic 1985)★★★, *The Definitive Thad Jones, Vol. 1* (Music Masters 1988)★★★, *The Definitive Thad Jones, Vol. 2* (Music Masters 1988)★★★, *Soft Lights And Hot Music* (Music Masters 1988)★★★, *The Lost Art* (Music Masters 1989)★★★, with Jones *Basie, 1969* 1969 recording (TOB 1995)★★★★.

● COMPILATIONS:, *Jazz At The Smithsonian Volume 3* (Parkfield 1990)★★★, with Jones *The Complete Solid State Recordings Of The Thad Jones/Mel Lewis Orchestra* 1966-1970 recordings, 5-CD box set (Mosaic)★★★★.

LEWIS, RAMSEY

b. 27 May 1935, Chicago, Illinois, USA. Lewis started playing piano at the age of six. He graduated from school in 1948, after winning both the American Legion Award as an outstanding scholar and a special award for piano services at the Edward Jenner Elementary School. He began his career as an accompanist at the Zion Hill Baptist Church, an experience of gospel that never left him. He later studied music at Chicago Music College with the idea of becoming a concert pianist, but left at the age of 18 to marry. He found a job working in a record shop and joined the Clefs, a seven-piece dance band. In 1956, he formed a jazz trio with the Clefs' rhythm section (whom he had known since high school) - bassist Eldee Young and drummer Isaac 'Red' Holt. Lewis made his debut recordings with the Argo record label, which later became Chess. He also had record dates with prestigious names such as Sonny Stitt, Clark Terry and Max Roach. In 1959, he played at Birdland in New York City and at the Randall's Island Festival. In 1964, 'Something You Got' was a minor hit, but it was 'The In Crowd', an instrumental cover version of Dobie Gray's hit, that made him famous, reaching number 5 in the US charts and selling over a million copies by the end of 1965. Lewis insisted on a live sound, complete with handclaps and exclamations, an infectious translation of a black church feel into pop. His follow-up, 'Hang On Sloopy', reached number 11 and sold another million. These hits set the agenda for his career. Earnings for club dates increased tenfold. His classic 'Wade In The Water' was a major hit in 1966, and became a long-standing encore number for Graham Bond. The rhythm section of Eldee Young and Redd Holt left and resurfaced as a funk outfit in the mid-70s, variously known as Redd Holt Unlimited and Young-Holt Unlimited. Lewis had an astute ear for hip, commercial sounds: his replacement drummer Maurice White left in 1971 to found the platinum mega-sellers Earth, Wind And Fire. Lewis never recaptured this commercial peak; he attempted to woo his audience by using synthesizers and disco rhythms, and continued securing *Billboard* Top 100 hits well into the 70s. His album success was a remarkable achievement, with over 30 of his albums making the *Billboard* Top 200 listings. *The In Crowd* stayed on the list for almost a year, narrowly missing the top spot. *Mother Nature's Son* was a tribute to the Beatles, while the *Newly Recorded Hits* in 1973 was a mistake: the originals were far superior. By the 80s he was producing middle-of-the-road instrumental albums and accompanying singers, most notably Nancy Wilson. Nevertheless, it is his 60s hits - simple, infectious and funky - that will long endure.

● ALBUMS: *Down To Earth* (EmArcy 1958)★★★, *Gentleman Of Swing* (Argo 1958)★★★, *Gentlemen Of Jazz* (Argo 1958)★★★, *An Hour With The Ramsey Lewis Trio* (Argo 1959)★★★, *Stretching Out* (Argo 1960)★★★, *The Ramsey Lewis Trio In Chicago* (Argo 1961)★★★, *More Music From The Soil* (Argo 1961)★★★, *Sound Of Christmas* (Argo 1961)★★★, *The Sound Of Spring* (Argo 1962)★★★, *Country Meets The Blues* (Argo 1962)★★★, *Bossa Nova* (Argo 1962)★★★, *Pot Luck* (Argo 1962)★★★, *Barefoot Sunday Blues* (Argo 1963)★★★, *The Ramsey Lewis Trio At The Bohemian Caverns* (Argo 1964)★★★, *Bach To The Blues* (Argo 1964)★★★, *More Sounds Of Christmas* (Argo 1964)★★★, *You Better Believe It* (Argo 1965)★★★★, *The In Crowd* (Argo 1965)★★★★, *Hang On Ramsey!* (Cadet 1965)★★★★, *Swingin'* (Cadet 1966)★★★★, *Wade In The Water* (Cadet 1966)★★★★, *Goin' Latin* (Cadet 1967)★★, *The Movie Album* (Cadet 1967)★★, *Dancing In The Street* (Cadet 1967)★★★, *Up Pops Ramsey Lewis* (Cadet 1968)★★★, *Maiden Voyage* (Cadet 1968)★★★, *Mother Nature's Son* (Cadet 1969)★★, *Another Voyage* (Cadet 1969)★★, *Ramsey Lewis: The Piano Player* (Cadet 1970)★★★, *Them Changes* (Cadet 1970)★★★, *Back To The Roots* (Cadet 1971)★★★, *Upendo Ni Pamoja* (Columbia 1972)★★★, *Funky Serenity* (Columbia 1973)★★, *Sun Goddess* (Columbia 1974)★★★, *Don't It Feel Good* (Columbia 1975)★★★, *Salongo* (Columbia 1976)★★★, *Love Notes* (Columbia 1977)★★★, *Tequila Mockingbird* (Columbia 1977)★★★, *Legacy* (Columbia 1978)★★★, *Routes* (Columbia 1980)★★★, *Three Piece Suite* (Columbia 1981)★★★, *Live At The Savoy* (Columbia 1982)★★★, *Les Fleurs* (1983)★★, *Chance Encounter* (Columbia 1983)★★, with Nancy Wilson *The Two Of Us* (Columbia 1984)★★★, *Reunion* (Columbia 1984)★★★, *Fantasy* (1986)★★, *Keys To The City* (Columbia 1987)★★, *Classic Encounter* (Columbia 1988)★★, with Billy Taylor *We Meet Again* (Columbia 1989)★★★, *Urban Renewal* (Columbia 1989)★★★, *Electric Collection* (Columbia 1991)★★★, *Ivory Pyramid* (GRP 1992)★★, with King Curtis *Instrumental Soul Hits* (1993)★★, *Between The Keys* (GRP 1996)★★, *Dance Of the Soul* (GRP 1998)★★★.

● COMPILATIONS: *Choice! The Best Of The Ramsey Lewis Trio* (Cadet 1965)★★★, *The Best Of Ramsey Lewis* (Cadet 1970)★★★, *Ramsey Lewis' Newly Recorded All-Time, Non-Stop Golden Hits* (Columbia 1973)★★★, *The Greatest Hits Of Ramsey Lewis* (Chess 1988)★★★★, *20 Greatest Hits* (1992)★★★, *Collection* (More Music 1995)★★★, *The Ramsey Lewis Trio In Person 1960-1967* (Chess 1998)★★★★, *Priceless Jazz Collection* (GRP 1998)★★★.

● FILMS: *Gonks Go Beat* (1965).

LEWIS, SABBY

b. William Sebastien Lewis, 1 November 1914, Middleburg, North Carolina, USA. Pianist Sabby Lewis entered the jazz world in the early 30s in Boston, Massachusetts, becoming leader of his own band in 1936. Although he rarely strayed far from Boston during the rest of his career, Lewis's small groups and big bands were highly regarded among musicians. Many visiting bandleaders, among them Woody Herman, Benny Goodman and Stan Kenton, were eager to sit in with Lewis at such Boston nightspots as the Savoy Cafe whenever they were in town. Lewis's bands were proving grounds for a number of youngsters who went on to become big names in their own right. Saxophonists Paul Gonsalves and Sonny Stitt, trumpeters Cat Anderson, Joe Gordon and Freddie Webster, drummers Alan Dawson, Jimmy Crawford and Roy Haynes are just a few who played for Lewis, usually early in their careers. Despite a hit record with 'Bottoms Up', which reworked Illinois Jacquet's version of 'Flying Home', Lewis never made the national big-time, nor appeared to feel the need to do so. He continued to lead a big band well into the 50s and thereafter led smaller groups until the late 70s.

● COMPILATIONS: *Sabby Lewis Orchestra And Quartet (1946)* (1981)★★★, *Boston Bounce (1944-47)* (1988)★★★.

LEWIS, VIC

b. 29 July 1919, London, England. Lewis began playing a four-string banjo while still a child, later switching to guitar. In his teens he formed his own quartet, having developed an interest in jazz through listening to records. His quartet appeared on a talent show and soon obtained radio work on the BBC and Radio Luxembourg and also in London theatres. In the London jazz clubs Lewis met and played with artists such as Django Reinhardt, Stéphane Grappelli, George Shearing and George Chisholm. In 1938, he visited New York where he played with Joe Marsala, Marty Marsala, Joe Bushkin, Buddy Rich, Pee Wee Russell, Bobby Hackett and other noted jazzmen, even sitting in with Tommy Dorsey, Jack Teagarden and Louis Armstrong. He also made a handful of records during this trip with Hackett, Eddie Condon and Zutty Singleton in the band. He returned to England and with the outbreak of war served in the RAF where he played in a band whenever the opportunity presented itself. After the war, Lewis formed a new unit, teaming up with Jack Parnell to co-lead a small group. When Parnell moved on, Lewis continued to lead the band, which proved very popular and broadcast frequently on the BBC. In the late 40s Lewis formed a big band, employing musicians such as Ronnie Chamberlain, Bob Efford and Gordon Langhorn, that emulated the music of Stan Kenton. He also formed an orchestra that backed visiting American artists including Armstrong and Johnny Ray. On occasion, Lewis sat in with Armstrong and Kenton, playing trombone. In the 60s, Lewis switched tracks, becoming a manager and agent, handling tours by Count Basie, whom he had met in New York in 1938, Dudley Moore (his first client), Judy Garland, Carmen McRae, Johnny Mathis, Andy Williams and Nina Simone. Lewis was also deeply involved with NEMS Enterprises, working with Brian Epstein, the Beatles and Cilla Black. Lewis's activities in these areas continued through the 70s when he organized tours for Shirley Bassey and Elton

John. He retained his jazz links, however, recording a bossa nova album in 1963, half in the USA with several Kenton alumni and half in London with a band featuring Tubby Hayes and Ronnie Scott. In the early 80s he began to form occasional big bands for jazz dates. He recruited visiting American stars such as Shorty Rogers and Bud Shank to perform on a series of records. As a bandleader and promoter, Lewis has been active for many decades and has brought to the UK jazz scene a great deal of enthusiasm; his activities on the pop scene were also of much value. For all that, as his autobiography hints, he would probably have given away his entire musical career for a chance to play cricket for England.

● ALBUMS: *Mulligan's Music And At The Royal Festival Hall* (1955)★★★★, *Vic Lewis And His Bossa Nova All Stars* (1963)★★★★, *Vic Lewis At The Beaulieu Jazz Festival* (1965)★★★, *Vic Lewis Plays The Music Of Donovan Leith* (1968)★★, *Vic Lewis With Maynard Ferguson* (1969)★★★, *Don't Cry For Me Argentina* (1974)★★, *Vic Lewis And R.P.O.* (RCA 1977)★★★, *Back Again* (1984)★★★, *Vic Lewis Big Bands* (1985)★★★, *Tea Break* (1985)★★★, *Vic Lewis And The West Coast All Stars* (1989)★★★★, *Know It Today, Know It Tomorrow* (1993)★★★, *Shake Down The Stars* (Candid 1993)★★★, *Play Bill Holman* (Candid 1994)★★★, *A Celebration Of West Coast Jazz* (Candid 1996)★★★★.

● COMPILATIONS: *My Life, My Way* 4-LP box set (1975)★★★, *New York, 1938* (Esquire 1986)★★★, *Vic Lewis Jam Sessions, Volumes 1-6 (1938-49)* (Harlequin 1986)★★★, *Vic Lewis Plays Stan Kenton (1948-54)* (Harlequin 1987)★★★★, *The EMI Years* (EMI 1991)★★★★.

● FURTHER READING: *Music And Maiden Overs: My Show Business Life*, Vic Lewis with Tony Barrow.

LEWIS, WILLIE

b. 10 June 1905, Cleburne, Texas, USA, d. 13 January 1971. Lewis's first important job was as a clarinettist and saxophonist in the band led by Will Marion Cook, one of the leading black musicians in New York in the first quarter of the century. In the mid-20s Lewis joined another popular New York-based bandleader, Sam Wooding, with whom he toured Europe. In 1931, Lewis decided to stay in Europe and formed his own band for a residency at a Parisian nightclub. By the end of the decade, Lewis had built-up a big name for himself and his band, which featured a number of visiting American jazz musicians including Benny Carter and Bill Coleman. In 1941, Lewis was forced to fold the band and left Europe for his homeland. Back in New York, he drifted on the edges of music for a while but then worked outside the business for the rest of his life.

● COMPILATIONS: *Willie Lewis In Paris* (1925-37) (1988)★★★.

LEY, EGGY

b. Derek Ley, 4 November 1928, London, England, d. 20 December 1995. Beginning as a drummer and pianist when he was 13 years old, Ley took up soprano saxophone and by the early 50s was playing professionally. Among the bands with which he played were those led by Eric Silk, Mick Mulligan and Ron Simpson. In 1955, Ley took his own band to Germany for a two-week tour but stayed seven years, visiting Scandinavia and building a formidable reputation as a powerful exponent of latter-day dixieland jazz. Throughout the 60s he led bands in the UK and Europe, but at the end of the decade began working in radio as a producer, first with Radio Luxembourg and then the British Forces Broadcasting Service. He continued performing, however, and in 1980 began playing alto saxophone. In 1983, he returned to bandleading, once again dividing his time between the UK and engagements in Europe. Enormously popular on the continent, even if he is much less known in his homeland, Ley appeared at many festivals including those at Frankfurt, Breda and Cork. Stylistically, Ley is rooted in the great tradition of soprano saxophonists of which Sidney Bechet is the grand master while Ley's work on alto recalls Pete Brown. His singing may have been something of an acquired taste, but it is always rhythmically infectious.

● ALBUMS: with Benny Waters *Live At The Esplanade* (1981)★★★, *Come And Get It* (1985)★★★, *Eggy Ley's Hotshots* (1986)★★.

LIEBMAN, DAVE

b. 4 September 1946, New York City, New York, USA. After studying theory and composition with Lennie Tristiano, and saxophone and flute with Charles Lloyd, Liebman's first important job was with Elvin Jones in 1971. When he joined Miles Davis in 1974, he was simultaneously running Lookout Farm, one of many groups that have tried to fuse jazz and Indian music. Touring with Chick Corea and leading a highly successful quintet in the late 70s, featuring Terumass Hino, John Scofield, Ron McLure and Adam Nussbaum. Liebman was already one of the leading saxophonists playing improvised fusion. In the 80s he co-led Quest, and is today very active in jazz education. His recent output has been extraordinary, 20 albums this decade so far., including the smooth (by his standards) *Setting The Standard.*

● ALBUMS: *Doin' It Again* (Timeless 1980),★★★ *If They Only Knew* (Timeless 1980)★★★★, *Pendulum* (Artists House 1981)★★★, *Opal Heart* (Enja 1982)★★★, *Spirit Renewed* (Owl 1983)★★★, *The Loneliness Of The Long Distance Runner* (CMP 1985)★★, *One Of A Kind* (Core 1985)★★★★, *Double Edge* (Storyville 1985)★★★, *Homage To John Coltrane* (Owl 1987)★★, *Trio + One* (Owl 1989)★★★, *The Tree* (Soul Note 1990)★★★, *Time Line* (Owl 1990)★★★, *Chant* (CMP 1990)★★★★, *Nine Again* (Red 1990)★★, *The Blessing Of The Old Long Sound* (Neuva 1991)★★★, *Dedications* (CMP 1991)★★★, *First Visit* (West Wind 1991)★★, *West Side Story (Today)* (Owl 1991)★★, *Classic Ballads* (Candid 1992)★★★, *Classique* (Owl 1992)★★★, *Joy* (Candid 1993)★★★, *Setting The Standard* (Red 1993)★★★, *The Seasons* (Soul Note 1994)★★, *Besame Mucho* (Red 1994)★★, *Songs For My Daughter* (Soul Note 1996)★★, *Return Of The Tenor Standards* (Double-Time 1996)★★★★, *Miles Away* (Owl 1996)★★★★, *New Vista* (Arkadia 1997)★★★, *John Coltrane's Meditations* (Arkadia 1998)★★★.

LIFETIME

Led by former Miles Davis drummer Tony Williams and named after his 1965 solo debut, the Lifetime appellation has been used and abandoned at the whim of its creator. It was first applied with reference to a group on the pulsating *Emergency*, but is best recalled for the exciting jazz-rock quartet formed in 1970. Here Williams was joined by guitarist John McLaughlin, keyboard player Larry Young and former Cream bassist Jack Bruce in what was, potentially, one of the genre's most impressive line-ups. *Turn It Over* showcased its loud, dexterous talents, but personality clashes doomed the group to a premature end. Bruce resumed his solo career and while Young joined McLaughlin for the latter's propulsive *Devotion*, Williams forged a less intensive musical path. In 1976, the drummer resurrected the Lifetime name for *Believe It*, but the new unit lacked the purpose and commitment of its predecessor.

● ALBUMS: as Lifetime *Emergency* (Verve 1969)★★★★, *One Word/Two Worlds* (Polydor 1970)★★★, *Turn It Over* (Verve 1970)★★, *Ego* (Polydor 1971)★★.

● COMPILATIONS: *Lifetime* (1975)★★★. As Tony Williams' New Lifetime *Believe It* (1976)★★★, *Million Dollar Legs* (1976)★★.

LIGHTFOOT, TERRY

b. 21 May 1935, Potters Bar, Middlesex, England. Lightfoot made his first appearance on the UK jazz scene as a clarinettist in the early 50s. After leading his own band throughout the 50s, he maintained a band into the next decade, having established a reputation strong enough to shrug off the decline in popularity of his brand of music. During the trad boom of the early 60s he appeared in the film *It's Trad Dad*. Apart from a brief spell in Kenny Ball's band he continued to lead into the 70s only stepping sideways into hotel management towards the end of the decade. He continued to play however, and by the mid-80s was back in full-time music. Amongst the most polished of British traditional clarinettists, Lightfoot achieved and maintained high standards of performance not only from himself but also from the many fine musicians he employed over the years.

● ALBUMS: *Jazz Gumbo Volume 1* (Nixa 1956)★★★★, *Tradition In Colour* (Columbia 1958)★★★★, *Trad Parade* (Columbia 1961)★★★, *King Kong* (1961)★★★, *Lightfoot At Lansdowne* (Columbia 1962)★★★★, *Alleycat* (Columbia 1965)★★★, *Personal Appearance* (1975)★★★, *Terry Lightfoot In Concert* (Black Lion 1979)★★, *Clear Round* (Plant Life 1981)★★★, *As Time Goes By* (PRT 1986)★★★, *At The Jazzband Ball* (Bold Reprive 1988)★★, *Stardust* (Upbeat 1990)★★★, *New Orleans Jazzmen* (Hanover 1990)★★★, *When The Saints* (See For Miles 1991)★★★★, *Down On Bourbon Street* (Timeless 1994)★★.

LIGHTHOUSE ALL-STARS

(see Rumsey, Howard)

LIGHTSEY, KIRK

b. 15 February 1937, Detroit, Michigan, USA. A gifted modern jazz pianist, and a competent if occasional singer, Lightsey has not yet received the attention his talents deserve, despite a career that has included sessions with some of America's finest modern jazz instrumentalists, and a series of enjoyable recordings under his own name. He began working in jazz in the mid-50s, largely accompanying vocalists, first in New York and then, in the early 60s, on the west coast. He recorded with the great bebop saxophonist Sonny Stitt in 1965, and began an association with the subtle west coast singer/trumpeter Chet Baker, that resulted in five fine album recordings. At the beginning of the 80s, his career received a boost when he joined the popular saxophonist Dexter Gordon's band for four years. He has since worked with individualistic trumpeter Don Cherry, guitarist Jimmy Raney and brilliant tenor saxophonists Clifford Jordan and James Moody, as well as touring and recording with the Leaders, a daring, Chicago-orientated group featuring trumpeter Lester Bowie, alto saxophonist Arthur Blythe, tenor saxophonist Chico Freeman, bassist Cecil McBee and drummer Famoudou Don Moye. He has earned a reputation as a fine solo performer, visiting the UK regularly. Recommended recordings include *Isotope*, a lively trio plus percussion date from 1983, and *Everything Happens To Me*, a subtle date under Chet Baker's deft, romantic leadership.

● ALBUMS: *Lightsey 1* (Sunnyside 1982)★★★, *Lightsey 2* (Sunnyside 1982)★★★, *Isotope* (Criss Cross 1983)★★★★, *Shorter By Two* (Sunnyside 1983)★★★, *Lightsey Live* (Sunnyside 1985)★★★, *Everything Is Changed* (Sunnyside 1986)★★★★, with Marcus Belgrave *Kirk'n'Marcus* (Criss Cross 1986)★★★, with the Leaders *Out Here Like This* (Black Saint 1987)★★★, with the Leaders Trio *Heaven Dance* (Sunnyside 1988)★★★, with the Leaders *Unforseen Blessings* (Black Saint 1989)★★★, *From Kirk To Nat* (Criss Cross 1990)★★★, *Goodbye Mr Evans* (Evidence 1997)★★★★.

LIKE SOMEONE IN LOVE - ELLA FITZGERALD

An album of sensitive arrangements by the underrated Frank DeVol, this collection was staple diet for 50s lounge romantics. Perched with a martini and a cherry in one of those triangular glasses, this is immaculate music. Ella Fitzgerald stepped outside the pattern of recording the *Songbook* series and used some lesser-known writers. Both 'Hurry Home', by Meyer, Emmerick and Bernier, and 'Night Wind', by Rothberg and Pollock, are strong tracks. She later re-recorded 'How Long Has This Been Going On', while the title track is so perfect it could never be done again. The CD reissue has four bonus tracks to make this a collection by which to propose marriage.

● Tracks: *There's A Lull In My Life; More Than You Know; What Will I Tell My Heart; I Never Had A Chance; Close Your Eyes; We'll Be Together Again; Then I'll Be Tired Of You; Like Someone In Love; Midnight Sun; I Thought About You; You're Blase; Night*

Wind; What's New; Hurry Home; How Long Has This Been Going On; I'll Never Be The Same; Lost In A Fog; Everything Happens To Me; So Rare.

- First released 1958
- UK peak chart position: did not chart
- USA peak chart position: did not chart

LINCOLN, ABBEY

b. Gaby Wooldridge, 6 August 1930, Chicago, Illinois, USA. Lincoln began singing publicly in the early 50s, working in Chicago nightclubs and using a variety of pseudonyms, including Anna Marie and Gaby Lee, as well as her real name. By the middle of the decade she was using the name by which she has since been largely known. She appeared successfully at the Moulin Rouge in Los Angeles and also made her first records, with Benny Carter, but was soon associating with bop musicians including Thelonious Monk, Mal Waldron and Max Roach. Her style changed during these years and following her marriage to Roach in 1962 she also became more politically aware. She wrote some of her own material, much of it stressing the rising tide of black consciousness in the USA. She collaborated with Roach on some important works, including *We Insist!*, *Freedom Now Suite* and *Straight Ahead*. In the 60s Lincoln had a simultaneous career as an actress, co-starring in the films *Nothing But A Man* (1964) and *For Love Of Ivy* (1968), for both of which she received excellent notices. Following a tour of Africa in the mid-70s, she adopted the name Aminata Moseka (her marriage to Roach had ended in 1970) and some subsequent albums were released under this name. With a deeply emotional singing voice, she has always made a close connection with her audiences. Her style veers between powerful versions of ballads from her early years and the sometimes bitter polemic of her middle period. By the late 80s her repertoire was once again featuring love songs and more accessible material akin to that of her youth, and her work for Verve Records in the 90s has proved to be an admirable showcase for her suitably mature vocal talents. Nevertheless, it is probable that her politically motivated material will prove to be her most lasting contribution to black American culture.

- ALBUMS: *Abbey Lincoln's Affair ... A Story Of A Girl In Love* (Liberty 1956)★★★, *That's Him!* (Riverside 1957)★★★★, *It's Magic* (Riverside 1958)★★★★, *Abbey Is Blue* (Riverside 1959)★★★★, *Straight Ahead* (Candid 1961)★★★★, *People In Me* (Inner City 1973)★★★, *Golden Lady* (Inner City 1980)★★, *Talking To The Sun* (Enja 1983)★★★, *Thats Him* (Riverside 1984)★★★, *A Tribute To Billie Holiday* (Enja 1987)★★★, *Abbey Sings Billie Vol. 2* (Enja 1987)★★★, *The World Is Falling Down* (Verve 1991)★★★, with Stan Getz *You Gotta Pay The Band* (Verve 1992)★★★, *Devil's Got Your Tongue* (Verve 1992)★★★, *When There Is Love* (Verve 1993)★★★, *A Turtle's Dream* (Verve 1995)★★★★, *Who Used To Dance* (Verve 1997)★★★★.
- FILMS: *The Girl Can't Help It* (1956).

LINCOLN, ABE

b. Abraham Lincoln, 29 March 1907, Lancaster, Pennsylvania, USA. Lincoln took up the trombone as a small child and by his late teens was proficient enough to follow Tommy Dorsey into the California Ramblers. He played in various other bands and in the 20s was with those led by Roger Wolfe Kahn and Paul Whiteman. During the late 30s he was with Ozzie Nelson's popular dance band. During the 40s he was active in film studio work but made occasional record dates with singers and a handful of jazz musicians. In the 50s he made rather more jazz dates, including sessions with the Rampart Street Paraders, Pete Fountain, Matty Matlock and Bob Scobey. In the 60s, he played club and festival dates with several bands including brief stints with Wild Bill Davison and Fountain. Although Lincoln was capable of playing in the legato style achieved by such notable contemporaries as Dorsey and Jack Teagarden, it is as a bristling dixieland player that he has made his greatest mark.

- ALBUMS: with the Rampant Street Preachers, *Jam Session Coast To Coast* (1953)★★★.

LIND, OVE

b. 29 June 1926, Stockholm, Sweden, d. 16 April 1991. After playing clarinet for some years he became a professional musician in the mid-40s, quickly becoming well known in his homeland. He was co-leader of the co-operative band the Swinging Swedes, and of a quartet which also featured Bengt Hallberg. In the early 60s Lind worked in popular music but retained his interest in swing era jazz and was therefore in a good position to capitalize on a revival of interest in this form in Sweden in the late 60s. An accomplished technician, Lind plays with a clean flowing and swinging style, delivering inventive solos with great aplomb.

- ALBUMS: *Who's Harry Warren? Evergreen!* (Phontastic 1975)★★★★, *Swinging Down The Lane* (Phontastic 1977)★★★★, *One Morning In May* (Phontastic 1977)★★★★, *Summer Night* (Phontastic 1978)★★★★.

LINDSAY, ERICA

b. 5 June 1955, San Francisco, California, USA. Lindsay spent her childhood in Europe, her parents being teachers in American schools there. She took up clarinet at high school, then alto and tenor saxophones. At this time she was studying with Mal Waldron. In 1973, she went to the Berklee College Of Music in Boston for a year, then returned to Europe to tour with her own quartet and to freelance as soloist, composer and arranger. She came back to New York in 1980, composing for television, video and ballet, and playing with Melba Liston, Clifford Jordan, Ted Curson and McCoy Tyner. As a composer of well-crafted and atmospheric tunes, her influences include Waldron, Gene Ammons, Johnny Griffin, Dexter Gordon, Wayne Shorter, John Coltrane and Miles Davis.

- ALBUMS: *Dreamer* (1989)★★★.

LISTON, MELBA

b. 13 January 1926, Kansas City, Missouri, USA. Although she was born and spent her childhood in Kansas City during its hottest jazz years, Liston's entry into music began in Los Angeles where her family moved when she was 11 years old. At the age of 16, she joined the pit band, playing trombone, at the Lincoln Theatre and the following year, 1943, joined Gerald Wilson's orchestra. With Wilson's guidance and encouragement, she began arranging but remained an active performer, appearing on record with an old school friend, Dexter Gordon. When the Wilson band folded while on a tour of the east coast, Liston was hired by Dizzy Gillespie. This was in 1948 and the following year she toured briefly with Wilson who was leading a band accompanying Billie Holiday. The tour was a disaster and the experience led to Liston quitting music for a while. She worked as an educational administrator in California, played occasionally in clubs, and also worked as an extra in films. In 1956, and again in 1957, she returned to Gillespie for his State Department tours of the Middle East, Asia and South America. She then began a musical association with Quincy Jones, writing scores for his band and working on the show *Free And Easy* with which they toured Europe. In the 60s, she wrote extensively for Randy Weston and occasionally for Duke Ellington, Solomon Burke and Tony Bennett. Her arrangements were used on Johnny Griffin's *White Gardenia*. In the 70s she was involved in a number of jazz educational projects, especially in Jamaica where, for almost six years, she ran the pop and jazz division of the country's School of Music. She continued to write charts for the bands of Ellington and Count Basie and singers such as Abbey Lincoln and Diana Ross. At the end of the 70s she was persuaded to return to the USA as the headline attraction at the first Kansas City Women's Jazz Festival. There, she led her own band, with an all-woman line-up, and made a great impact. Her successful return to playing led to a revitalisation of her performing career and although her band later developed into a 'mixed' group, she has continued to play an important role in furthering the role of women in jazz. A sound section player whose ballad solos are particularly effective, Liston is one of the best latter-day arrangers in jazz. Unfortunately, the male domination of so many aspects of the jazz life has resulted in this enormously talented artist remaining little-known.

● ALBUMS: with Dexter Gordon *The Chase* (1947)★★★, *Melba Liston And Her Orchestra* (1958)★★★, with Randy Weston *Uhuru Afrika* (Roulette 1960)★★★★, with Weston *Volcano Blues* (Verve 1993)★★★, with Liston *Earth Birth* (Verve 1997)★★★★.

LITTLE PATTIE

b. Patricia Amphlett, *c.*1950, Sydney, New South Wales, Australia. Amphlett began singing while still a young schoolgirl and had a surprise hit in 1963 with 'He's My Blonde Headed Stompie Wompie Real Gone Surfer Boy'. Later, she moved into other realms of music and built a successful and long-lasting singing career. In the mid-90s she recorded with jazz musicians including Errol Buddle, David Seidel and Lawrie Thompson. Her singing voice as a mature artist is fluid and she eloquently interprets the great standards. In 1998 a 45-cent Australian postage stamp, issued as part of a series recalling highlights of rock 'n' roll, commemorated her 60s hit.

● ALBUMS: *Moments Like This* (La Brava 1995)★★★.

LITTLE, BOOKER

b. 2 April 1938, Memphis, Tennessee, USA, d. 5 October, 1961. One of the most promising of all trumpeters in the second bebop wave of the 50s, Booker Little was equipped with a superb technique, crystal clarity of intonation and rhythmic originality. His imagination extended beyond the strict harmonic disciplines of bop however, and hinted at the vision of Ornette Coleman or Miles Davis, but an early death from uraemia consigned such promise to the realm of speculation. Little was born into a musical family, and played clarinet before taking up the trumpet at the age of 12. He was involved in Memphis jam sessions with local pianist Phineas Newborn Jnr. in his teens, but moved to Chicago in 1957 to enrol at the city's Conservatory. During this period Little worked with Johnny Griffin's band, but his most significant engagement of the period was with Max Roach, replacing another gifted trumpeter, Clifford Brown. His recordings with Roach include *Deeds Not Words*, *We Insist!*, *Freedom Now Suite* and *Percussion Bitter Sweet*. Little's originality quickly marked him out, as did his flexibility about non-bop settings, and he collaborated with Eric Dolphy on *Far Cry* and *Live At The Five Spot* (reissued as *The Great Concert Of Eric Dolphy*) and John Coltrane on the *Africa/Brass* recording. Little's own recordings featured some outstanding players, including Roach, Dolphy (*Out Front*), Booker Ervin and the 'legendary quartet' of Scott La Faro, Roy Haynes and both Wynton Kelly and Tommy Flanagan taking turns on piano. He worked too with Donald Byrd (*The Third World*), Abbey Lincoln (*Straight Ahead*) and Frank Strozier. By the time of his death Little was balancing tonality and dissonance with an insight that suggested his influence on jazz directions in general might have been even more substantial.

● ALBUMS: *Booker Little 4 And Max Roach* (Blue Note 1959)★★★★, *Booker Little* (Time 1960)★★★, *In New York* (Jazz View 1960)★★★, *The Legendary Quartet Album* (1960)★★★★, *Out Front* (Candid 1961)★★★, with Booker Ervin *Sounds Of The Inner City* (1961)★★★, *Victory And Sorrow* (Affinity 1961)★★★.

LIVINGSTON, FUD

b. Joseph Anthony Livingston, Charleston, South Carolina, USA, d. 25 March 1957. After learning to play piano, Livingston turned to tenor saxophone and clarinet and while still in his teens was working regularly with several bands including that led by Ben Pollack. He also played with the California Ramblers, Jean Goldkette, Nat Shilkret, Jan Garber and others. In demand as a studio sideman on record dates, he also arranged, and by the 30s was active in this field for Paul

Whiteman and Pollack. In the late 30s he joined Jimmy Dorsey's reed section, then turned again to arranging. Later in his career he was working in film studios in California but his career gradually went awry through personal problems, and he eked a living playing bar-room piano. Livingston's playing sets him apart from most of his contemporaries. He played with a quirky distinctiveness and his thinking often appears to have been far ahead of his more orthodox musical companions.

● COMPILATIONS: *Ben Pollack* (RCA 1926)★★★, *Benny Goodman's Boys And The Whoopee Makers* (Sunbeam 1928)★★★.

LIVINGSTON, ULYSSES

b. 29 January 1912, Bristol, Tennessee, USA. As a young man Livingston played guitar in a college band and also gained on-the-road experience with Horace Henderson, although in a non-musical capacity. After working around the country as a guitarist, he went to New York in the mid-30s where he played with several leaders of small bands including Lillian Armstrong, Stuff Smith and Frankie Newton. He then spent some time in Benny Carter's band before joining Ella Fitzgerald. After military service during World War II, he played with a number of west coast bands including the Spirits Of Rhythm, Illinois Jacquet and Rex Stewart. He also appeared with Norman Granz's Jazz At The Philharmonic. From the 50s onwards, Livingston worked mostly outside music but continued to make occasional record dates and club appearances. A fluid player with imagination and rhythmic solidity, Livingston had much more talent than his relatively short full-time career would suggest.

● ALBUMS: with JATP *The Beginning* (Charly 1945)★★, with Jack McVea *Nothin' But Jazz* (77 Records 1962)★★★.

LLOYD, CHARLES

b. 15 March 1939, Memphis, Tennessee. Lloyd was self-taught on tenor saxophone, which he played in his high school band. He gained a Masters Degree at the University of Southern California and became a music teacher at Dorsey High in Los Angeles. In October 1960, he joined the Chico Hamilton Quintet, where he played flute, alto and clarinet as well as tenor, and soon became the band's musical director. In January 1964, he joined the Cannonball Adderley Sextet, where he stayed until forming his own quartet with guitarist Gabor Szabo, bassist Ron Carter and drummer Tony Williams in July 1965. Soon Szabo was replaced by pianist Keith Jarrett and Carter and Williams returned to the Miles Davis group. At the start of 1966 Cecil McBee came in on bass (he was replaced by Ron McClure in 1967), Jack DeJohnette took the drum chair and the stage was set for a jazz phenomenon. Manager George Avakian decided to market the band in the same way he would a rock group, and the tactic paid off. In modern jazz terms the Quartet was hugely successful, playing to massive rock audiences at the Fillmore Stadium in San Francisco and becoming the first American band to appear in a Soviet festival. While the public and musicians such as Miles Davis and Ian Carr admired the band, the critics were predictably cynical, criticizing the musicians' clothes, hair styles and hippy attitudes but ignoring the basic virtues of the music itself, which included rhythmic vitality and a sound foundation in bop and the blues. In due course his public looked elsewhere and, eventually, Lloyd left music to pursue his interest in philosophy and meditation, although during this period he did work and record with the Beach Boys (*Surf's Up*) as a result of his friendship with Mike Love. His solo on 'Feel Flows' is partic-ul;arly memorable. In the early 80s he edged back onto the jazz scene, notably with a Montreux Festival performance featuring Michel Petrucciani, and he began to tour again with a quartet containing Palle Danielson and Jon Christensen. In the 90s he hit another peak with some excellent recordings for ECM Records. During his semi-retirement his flute playing had become stronger whilst his tenor took on some of the ethereal quality his flute formerly had.

● ALBUMS: *Discovery!* (Columbia 1964)★★★, *Of Course Of Course* (Columbia 1965)★★★, *Dream Weaver* (Atlantic 1966)★★★★, *Live At Antibes* (1966)★★★, *Forest Flower* (Atlantic 1966)★★★★, *Charles Lloyd In Europe* (Atlantic 1967)★★★, *Love-In At The Fillmore* (Atlantic 1967)★★★, *Live In The Soviet Union* (Atlantic 1967)★★★, *Nirvana* (Columbia 1968)★★★, *Journey Within* (Atlantic 1968)★★★, *Moon Man* (1970)★★★, *The Flowering Of The Original Charles Lloyd Quartet* (1971)★★★, *Warm Waters* (1971)★★★, *Geeta* (1972)★★★, *Waves* (1972)★★★, *Weavings* (1978)★★★, *Big Sur Tapestry* (1979)★★★, *Montreux '82* (Elektra Musician 1982)★★★, *A Night In Copenhagen* (Blue Note 1989)★★★, *Fish Out Of Water* (ECM 1990)★★★★, *Notes From Big Sur* (ECM 1992)★★★★, *The Call* (ECM 1994)★★, *All My Relations* (ECM 1995)★★★★, *Canto* (ECM 1997)★★★★.

LLOYD, JON

b. 20 October 1958, Stratford-upon-Avon, Warwickshire, England. Lloyd dabbled with piano at the age of 12, and then taught himself tenor saxophone at 23. His first public appearances were with a pop/soul band in the mid-80s and with an ECM-inspired duo, Confluence. His first professional job was with a duo playing standards on the restaurant/wine-bar/pub circuit. Despite his relatively late start on saxophone he has developed an individual style of music that is exhibited to especially good advantage on his first, privately-produced recording. His influences include Jan Garbarek, John Surman, Trevor Charles Watts and, 'more for affirmation than emulation', Eric Dolphy, Evan Parker, Jimmy Lyons, Anthony Braxton and Arthur Blythe. He has also been inspired by composers Olivier Messiaen (who has influenced several non-classical figures, notably Mike Ratledge of the Soft Machine and Mike Gibbs) and Benjamin Britten. He has organized several worthy attempts at regular venues for improvised music, including the 'Sun Sessions' in Clapham, south London. Apart from his own trio and quartet he has worked with Dave Fowler and in duos with Evan Shaw Parker and

Phil Wachsmann, and organizes Anacrusis, a nine-piece improvising group containing several major names.

● ALBUMS: *Pentimento* (1988)★★, *Syzygy* (Leo 1990)★★★, with Dave Fowler *As It Was* (1990)★★★, *Head* (Leo 1993)★★★★, *By Confusion* (hatART 1997)★★★, *Praxis* (FMR 1997)★★★.

Lockwood, Didier

b. 11 February 1956, Calais, France. Lockwood studied classical violin at the Conservatoire de Musique de Paris, but exposure to the blues of Johnny Winter and John Mayall persuaded him to cut short formal study in 1972 and form a jazz-rock group with his brother, Francis. A three-year stint with Magma followed, but Lockwood was more excited by the improvising of Jean-Luc Ponty, whom he heard on Frank Zappa's 'King Kong'. He listened to other jazz violinists, particularly the Pole, Zbigniew Seifert and the veteran Stéphane Grappelli. The latter quickly realised the talent in Lockwood and played with him whenever possible. During the late 70s Lockwood played and recorded with many major European and American artists including Tony Williams, Gordon Beck, John Etheridge, Daniel Humair and Michal Urbaniak. In 1981, Lockwood recorded *Fusion*, which typified the approach he followed throughout the 80s: a solid rock-based rhythm with plenty of soloing room for lightning improvisations on his 160-year-old violin.

● ALBUMS: *Fusion* (1981)★★★, *New World* (1984)★★★★, *Out Of The Blue* (JMS 1986)★★, *1,2,3,4* (JMS 1987)★★★, *Pheonix 90* (1990)★★, *DLG* (JMS 1993)★★, *Martial Solal* (JMS 1993)★★★, *New York Rendevous* (JMS 19960★★★★, *Storyboard* (Dreyfus 1997)★★★.

Loeb, Chuck

b. Charles Samuel Loeb, 12 July 1955, Suffern, New York, USA. Raised in Nyack, New York, Loeb began playing guitar at the age of 11. He played in various local bands until going to the Berklee College Of Music. After leaving Berklee in 1976 he toured with Chico Hamilton, Hubert Laws and Ray Barretto, making his breakthrough in 1979 when he joined Stan Getz. He stayed with Getz for two years, touring Europe and playing at the Jazz Yatra Festival in India. In 1985 he joined Michael Brecker's Steps Ahead, where he doubled on guitar synthesizer. Subsequently, he has appeared on over 1,000 recordings as a session musician and composed underscores for numerous television soaps and documentaries. He has regularly led his own bands, co-led others, and also worked extensively with the groups Metro, the Fantasy Band, and Petite Blonde. During the 80s he became deeply involved in record producing, continuing in this role into the late 90s although, by then, he had determined to divide his time equally between this activity and performing. As a record producer, he has worked with numerous pop and jazz artists including Gary Burton, Earl Klugh, Jim Hall, Carly Simon, Eddie Daniels, and, in the late 90s, Larry Coryell, Donald Harrison, Warren Bernhardt, Gato Barbieri and Spyro Gyra. In 1998, a single, 'Just Us', from the *Billboard* charting *The Moon, The Stars And The Setting Sun*, reached number 1 on the *Gavin* and NAC/Jazz Radio charts.

● ALBUMS: *My Shining Hour* (Jazz City 1988)★★★, *Life Colors* (DMP 1990)★★★, *Magic Fingers* (DMP 1990), *Balance* (DMP 1991)★★★, *Mediterranean* (DMP 1993)★★★, *Simple Things* (DMP 1994)★★★, *Memory Lane* (DMP 1996)★★★, *The Music Inside* (Shanachie 1996)★★★, *The Moon, The Stars And The Setting Sun* (Shanachie 1998)★★★.

Loftus, Caroline

b. 1970, Sydney, New South Wales, Australia. After studying Jazz Fundamentals, acting and voice, with Bill Pepper, at the New South Wales Conservatorium of Music, Loftus began singing professionally in her home town in 1990. She quickly became known in Australia and soon extended her experience and her audience in the far east with performances in Hong Kong and elsewhere. In 1994 she came to Europe and the following year settled in London. Since then she has established a considerable reputation, appearing at many nightclubs, including Ronnie Scott's, and building a new audience through engagements such as these and well-received albums. Loftus, who has declared her first musical influence to be Nina Simone, judiciously allows her training and performances as an actor to enhance her singing. Mostly, however, her clear voice, which she sometimes uses in a deliberate and skilful bluesy manner, is well suited to the needs of a jazz singer. She is also a composer and lyricist of merit. By the time of her second album, this singer's fast-growing talent was proving to be a valued asset to the London jazz scene. However, she was already chafing at the occasionally confining boundaries of the jazz world and in 1998 was planning a pop album.

● ALBUMS: *Sugar* (Larrikin 1992)★★★, *Close Your Eyes* (Torch 1997)★★★.

London Jazz Composers Orchestra

(see Guy, Barry)

Longo, Pat

b. 11 September 1929, Passaic, New Jersey, USA. Adept on several reed instruments, Longo concentrated on alto saxophone and clarinet. During military service he played in the band of the 2nd Marine Airwing and following his discharge studied music full-time. Although intent on a career in music, throughout the 60s and into the early 70s Longo found it necessary to support himself by working in a bank. However, in 1974 and resident in Los Angeles, he decided the time was right to give up banking and just play music. He joined the Harry James band but had ambitions to lead his own big band. In 1979, he achieved his goal and formed a big band which quickly gained regular bookings in and around LA. In the late 70s and early 80s Longo's Super Big Band successfully blended the more traditional aspects of big band music with currently popular jazz-rock funkiness. His line-ups usually featured many of the best west coast session men and a useful handful of talented jazzmen, including Gordon Brisker, Lanny Morgan, Bob Efford, Buddy Childers, Frank Szabo and Nick Ceroli. Intent on developing other areas of exposure for the band, Longo has recently been involved in a television series.

● ALBUMS: *Crocodile Tears* (1980)★★★, *Billy May For President* (1982)★★★, *Chain Reaction* (1983)★★.

Loose Tubes

Appearing on the London scene in 1984 this big (20-piece plus) band appealed to (and reflected) the new, smart young audience jazz was attracting at the time, and seemed likely to prove a considerable 'crossover' success. It was run as a collective, although trombonist Ashley Slater acted as 'frontman' and Django Bates (b. Leon Bates, 2 October 1960, Beckenham, Kent, England) emerged as a main writer for the band. Characterized by clever arrangements, technically slick soloing and an urbane stage-presence, Loose Tubes was acclaimed by many critics and created interest in jazz among sections of the public which had not previously paid the genre any attention. It spawned several other successful units, which indulged in various styles (funk, African, soca, bebop and so on), including Human Chain, Pig Head Son, Lift, the Iain Ballamy Quartet, the Steve Berry Trio, the Tim Whitehead Band, Parker Bates Stubbs and the Julian Argüelles Quartet. By the early 90s the parent group had disbanded - although reunions should never be ruled out.

● ALBUMS: *Loose Tubes* (Loose Tubes 1986)★★★★, *Delightful Precipice* (Loose Tubes 1986)★★★, *Open Letter* (Editions EG 1988)★★★.

Lorber, Jeff

b. 4 November 1952, Philadelphia, USA. Lorber started playing the piano when he was four and played in local R&B bands while he was still at school. While studying at the Berklee College Of Music in Boston he came under the influence of Herbie Hancock and his contemporaries. When he left Berklee he studied privately with Ran Blake. In 1979, he moved to Portland, Oregon and taught improvisation at Lewis and Clark College. In 1977, he had recorded *Jeff Lorber Fusion* and in 1979 he was able to form a band of the same name. Lorber's compositions are characterized by syncopated, chromatic melody and modal writing which facilitated a funk style. In the early 80s he started singing on record and playing the guitar and his music incorporated increasing pop elements.

● ALBUMS: *Jeff Lorber Fusion* (1977)★★★★, *Soft Space* (1978)★★★, *Water Sign* (1978)★★★, *Jeff Lorber Fusion* (1979)★★★★, *Wizard Island* (1979)★★★, *Galaxian* (1980)★★★, *Its A Fact* (1981)★★, *In The Heat Of The Night* (1983)★★, *Step By Step* (1984)★★, *Worth Waiting For* (1993)★★★, *State Of Grace* (Verve 1996)★★, *Midnight* (Zebra 1998)★★★.

Lost And Found - Sheila Jordan

Sheila Jordan is commonly regarded as the finest contemporary singer working within the jazz field. With a musical grounding in the bebop language of the late 40s, she single-mindedly developed her own demanding and complex style of improvisation, based on what she learned from Charlie Parker, but with a freer and more dramatic edge that suits the vocalist's art. This highly acclaimed 1990 date features the fabulous piano of Kenny Barron, her long-standing musical partner Harvie Swartz on bass and ex-Thelonious Monk drummer Ben Riley, and helped put Jordan back firmly in the limelight.

● Tracks: *Good Morning Heartache; Anthropology; I Concentrate On You; The Water Is Wide; Alone Together; The Very Thought Of You; Lost In The Stars; My Shining Hour/We'll Be Together Again*

● First released 1990

● UK peak chart position: did not chart

● USA peak chart position: did not chart

Lost Jockey

(see Man Jumping)

Louis Armstrong Story 1-7, The - Louis Armstrong

Legendary New Orleans trumpeter and vocalist Louis Armstrong was jazz's first instrumentalist soloist. An immensely gifted technician with a profoundly lyrical melodic conception and ringing, celebratory tone, he broke away from the entirely polyphonic New Orleans tradition to play a music that shifted the emphasis onto his (and sometimes others') individual solos. This skilfully compiled seven-volume set starts in November 1925 and ends in March 1931, and features his celebrated Hot Fives and Hot Sevens recordings, his brilliant early big band work, and the start of the concurrent interest in his extraordinary vocals.

● Tracks: *Including - When You're Smiling; Some Of These Days; On The Sunny Side Of The Street; Solitude; When The Saints Go Marching In; Ain't Misbehavin'; Jeepers Creepers; I Want A Little Girl; Someday You'll Be Sorry; Lazy River; I Love Jazz; Mack The Knife; Muskat Ramble; Tiger Rag; When It's Sleepy Time Down South; Cabaret; Volare; Indiana; A Kiss To Build A Dream On; Hello Dolly; Blueberry Hill; St. James Infirmary; Tenderly; You'll Never Walk Alone; Mop Mop.*

● First released 1988 (1925-1931 recordings)

● UK peak chart position: did not chart

● USA peak chart position: did not chart

Louiss, Eddy

b. Edouard Louise, 2 May 1941, Paris, France. Born into a musical family, his father was a trumpet player, and he studied several musical instruments, including trumpet and piano. In his early teenage years Louiss played in his father's band. In the early 60s he was playing piano in various Paris nightclubs and continuing with his studies. He also sang with the French vocal group Double Six, other members of which included Roger Guérin, Ward Swingle and Christiane Legrand, the sister of Michel Legrand. Adding the organ to his array of instrumental ability, Louiss played with various jazzmen in the 60s, among them Johnny Griffin, Art Taylor, Dizzy Gillespie, Jean-Luc Ponty and Stan

Getz. In the late 60s he was with a trio led by Kenny Clarke and he also recorded with Barney Kessell. Louiss continued to play extensively throughout Europe during the 70s and into the 80s when he formed an adventurous big band, Multicolor Feeling. In the 90s he was also heard in duo with Michel Petrucciani. A very melodic player on both piano and organ, Louiss also has an intense rhythmic undercurrent to his work which adds excitement especially on mid- and up-tempo numbers.

● ALBUMS: *Our Kind Of Sabi* (Verve 1958)★★★, *Les Double-six* (Columbia 1961-62)★★, *Dizzy Gillespie Et Les Double Six* (Philips 1963)★★★, with Jean-Luc Ponty *Jazz Long Playing* (Philips 1964)★★★★, with Ponty, Daniel Humair Trio *HLP* (Columbia 1968)★★★, *Barney Kessel* (Mercury 1969)★★★, with Stéphane Grappelli *Satin Doll* (Festival 1972)★★★, *Eddy Louiss Orgue* (America 1972)★★, with Michel Petrucciani *Conference De Presse* (Dreyfus 1994)★★★, *Trio* 1968 recording (Dreyfus 1997)★★★.

LOUNGE LIZARDS

(see Lurie, Evan)

LOUSSIER, JACQUES

b. 26 October 1934, Angers, France. A classically taught pianist, Loussier found a career in commercial popular music more lucrative. Then, in 1959, he hit upon the idea of performing the classical piano works of Johann Sebastian Bach in a quasi-jazz style. Together with Pierre Michelot and Christian Garros, the trio had enormous international success with the wider public. The concept, the low-key detached style, and possibly the huge commercial success, failed to endear the group to the hardcore jazz audience. In the mainstream, his interpretation of Bach is better known as the long-running music accompanying the award winning Benson & Hedges film and television advertisements of the 60s and 70s.

● ALBUMS: *Play Bach* i (Decca 1960)★★★★, *Play Bach* ii (Decca 1961)★★★★, *Play Bach* iii (Decca 1962)★★★, *Play Bach* iv (London 1963)★★★, *The World Of Jacques Loussier - Live* (Decca 70s)★★★★, *Bach To The Future* (State Of The Art 70s)★★★, *The Jacques Loussier Trio In Concert At The Royal Festival Hall* (Philips 70s)★★★, *Jacques Loussier Plays Bach* (Telarc 1996)★★★, *The Four Seasons* (Telarc 1997)★★★, *Satie* (Telarc 1998)★★★.

● COMPILATIONS: *The Best Of Play Bach* (Start 1985)★★★.

LOVANO, JOE

b. 29 December 1952, Cleveland, Ohio, USA. Lovano grew up to the sounds of jazz, thanks to a father who played tenor saxophone professionally and also owned a large record collection. In 1971, he went to the Berklee College Of Music, where he studied with Gary Burton and first met with future collaborators Bill Frisell and John Scofield. Returning to Ohio in the mid-70s, he played tenor saxophone with Lonnie Liston Smith, making his recording debut with him on 1974's *Aphrodisiac For A Groove Merchant*, and later toured with another organist, Brother Jack McDuff. Lovano moved to New York in 1976 and, after work with Albert Dailey and Chet Baker, played with the Woody Herman band until 1979.

The following year he joined the Mel Lewis big band (with which he still works on occasion) and a little later met up with Paul Motian, in whose groups he has played and recorded for the last decade, renewing his acquaintance with Frisell in the process. (Motian and Frisell also play on Lovano's own *Worlds*.) In 1987, he toured Europe with Elvin Jones and in the late 80s worked with Charlie Haden's Liberation Music Orchestra (*Dream Keeper*) and recorded a duo album with drummer Aldo Romano. Reuniting with Scofield, he played on the guitarist's highly-acclaimed Blue Note Records debut *Time On My Hands* together with the follow-up *What We Do*, and was signed by the label himself, his *Landmarks* appearing in 1991. Lovano's third album on Blue Note, *Universal Language*, comprised a line-up of Jack DeJohnette, Charlie Haden, Steve Swallow, Tim Hagans, Scott Lee, Kenny Werner and Judi Silverman.

An admirer of Hank Mobley, Sonny Stitt, John Coltrane and Sonny Rollins, Lovano's own saxophone playing is distinguished by a lovely tone, fluent line and lucid sense of time - still showcased to best advantage, perhaps, in the company of Motian and Frisell on recordings such as *One Time Out*, *On Broadway* and *Bill Evans* (all under the drummer's name). Lovano's output with Blue Note during the early 90s is particularly inspiring especially *From The Soul* and *Rush Hour* (Orchestrated by Gunther Schuller). He performed the excellent 'Joe Lovano Tango' on Dave Brubeck's *Young Lions & Old Tigers* and recorded with his Wind Ensemble (Bill Frisell, Gary Valente, Henri Texier, Paul Motian, Judi Silvano, Tim Hagens in 1995 He now stands in the very top league of tenor players, already rated by many amongst the finest jazz saxophonist of the century.

● ALBUMS: *Tones, Shapes And Colours* (Soul Note 1986)★★★, *One Time Out* (Soul Note 1988)★★★★, *Village Rhythm* (Soul Note 1989)★★★★, with Aldo Romano *Ten Tales* (Owl 1989)★★★★, *Worlds* (1990)★★★, *Landmarks* (Blue Note 1991)★★★★, *Sounds Of Joy* (Enja 1991)★★★★, with Paul Motian, Bill Frisell *Motian In Tokyo* (1992)★★★, *From The Soul* (Blue Note 1992)★★★★, *Universal Language* (Blue Note 1993)★★★, *Tenor Legacy* (Blue Note 1994)★★★★, *Rush Hour* (Blue Note 1995)★★★★, *Quartets: Live At The Village Vanguard* (Blue Note 1996)★★★★, with the Wind Ensemble *Worlds* 1989 recording (Evidence 1996)★★, with George Garzone *Four's And Two's* (NYC 1996)★★★, *Celebrating Sinatra* (Blue Note 1997)★★★★, with Gonzalo Rubalcaba *Flying Colors* (Blue Note 1998)★★★★, with Dave Holland, Elvin Jones *Trio Fascination Edition One* (Blue Note 1998)★★★★.

LOVE, PRESTON

b. 26 April 1921, Omaha, Nabraska, USA. He inherited an alto saxophone from his older brother 'Dude' and obtained his first professional job in 1940, after which he took lessons from Illinois Jacquet's brother Julius. Inspired further by Count Basie's Earle Warren, Love played with Lloyd Hunter, Nat Towles and Snub Mosely before replacing Warren in Basie's band briefly in 1943. He worked with Lucky Millinder in 1944 and rejoined Basie for a longer spell from 1945-47, after which he played on-and-off in the band of his friend, Johnny Otis. Love also led his own orchestra (recording for his own Spin label and Federal Records) until 1962. Moving to California in 1962, he became a top session-player until he joined Ray Charles' band in 1966, going on to become the west coast house bandleader at Motown. Today, he lectures in African-American music at colleges and writes for local newspapers while maintaining a healthy touring schedule, including frequent trips to Europe.

● ALBUMS: *Omaha Barbeque* (60s)★★, *Strictly Cash* (1982)★★★.

Lovens, Paul

b. 6 June 1949, Aachen, Germany. Self-taught Lovens grew up listening to his sister's Elvis Presley records and BFR hit parades. While at school he played drums in dixieland and dance groups. His earliest jazz influences included Chris Barber, Art Blakey and Thelonious Monk. In 1969, he met German improvisers Manfred Schoof and Alexander von Schlippenbach. Thereafter, he established himself as one of the leading percussionists in improvised music. Lovens has toured worldwide, making numerous collaborations and recordings; most notably with Schlippenbach's trio, quartet and Globe Unity Orchestra, and duos with Paul Lytton, Toshinori Kondo, Urs Voerkel and the influential pianist, Cecil Taylor. In 1976, he founded the Po Torch label with Lytton. His playing is likely to veer, without a moment's notice, from unrestrained tumult to the most delicate use of a horsehair bow drawn across tiny cymbals.

● ALBUMS: with the Globe Unity Orchestra *Live In Wuppertal* (1973)★★★★, with Paul Lytton *The Fetch* (1980)★★, with Toshinori Kondo *The Last Supper* (1980)★★★, with the Alexander von Schlippenbach Trio *Detta Fra Di Noi* (1981)★★★★, with Cecil Taylor *Regalia* (1988)★★★, with Urs Voerkel *Goldberg* (1989)★★★.

Lowe, Frank

b. 24 June 1943, Memphis, Tennessee, USA. Although originally categorized as a 'new thing' (the US 60s free-jazz movement) player, Lowe has grown into one of the most distinctive and thoughtful of contemporary tenor saxophonists. Growing up in Memphis, one of his first jobs was at the Satellite record shop and its offshoot label, Stax Records. A liking for the records of Gene Ammons developed into a fascination with the newer musics of John Coltrane, Ornette Coleman and the AACM. He attended the University of Kansas, then moved to San Francisco and studied with Rafael Garrett, Sonny Simmons and Bert Wilson. Moving to New York in the mid-60s, he worked with Sun Ra then, after a spell at the San Francisco Conservatory, he settled in New York, playing with numerous musicians from the jazz *avant garde*, including Rashied Ali (*Duo Exchanges*), Alice Coltrane (*World Galaxy*) and Don Cherry (*Relativity Suite*, *Brown Rice*), while his own debut as leader - *Black Beings* - had Joseph Jarman guesting. In the mid-70s he formed a group with Joe Bowie and Charles 'Bobo' Shaw, recording *Fresh* (which also featured Lester Bowie) and *The Flam* (with Leo Smith). While in San Francisco, he had met Lawrence 'Butch' Morris, who has become one of his most frequent collaborators (*Current Trends In Racism In Modern America*), as has Billy Bang, with whom he plays in the collective quartet Jazz Doctors (*Intensive Case*) and in the violinist's own group (*Valve No 10*). Always open to new ideas, Lowe has played with leftfield rock musicians such as Eugene Chadbourne and seems as comfortable with New York's 80s *avant garde* downtown scene as he does with 60s jazzers such as Cherry and Charles Moffett: indeed, his own recordings feature a diverse array of artists, from John Zorn (*Lowe And Behold*) to Geri Allen and Grachan Moncur III (*Decision In Paradise*). He also plays with James Carter, Michael Marcus and Cassius Richmond in SaxEmble. As he told *Cadence* magazine, 'I've always tried to go in *and* out', though adding that even when playing in, he likes to 'experiment with time and colours'.

● ALBUMS: *Black Beings* (ESP 1973)★★★, *Fresh* (Freedom 1975)★★★, *The Flam* (Black Saint 1976)★★★★, *Lowe And Behold* (1977)★★★, *The Other Side* (1977)★★★, *Tricks Of The Trade* (1977)★★★★, *Doctor Too-Much* (1977)★★★, *Don't Punk Out* (1977)★★, *Skizoke* (1981)★★★, *Exotic Heartbreak* (Soul Note 1982)★★★, with the Jazz Doctors *Intensive Care* (1984)★★, *Decision In Paradise* (Soul Note 1985)★★★, *Inappropriate Choices* (ITM Pacific 1991)★★★, with SaxEmble *SaxEmble* (Warners 1996)★★★, *Bodies And Soul* (CIMP 1996)★★★★, *Vision Blue* (CIMP 1997)★★★.

Lowe, Mundell

b. 21 April 1922, Laurel, Mississippi, USA. Guitarist Lowe began playing at the age of six and seven years later, left home and headed for New Orleans, Louisiana. He listened and learned at many of the city's clubs before he was found by his Baptist minister father and taken back home. He soon made another try for an early career in music, this time visiting Nashville where he played in the Pee Wee King band. Taken home again he graduated from school in 1940 and promptly joined the Jan Savitt band. Drafted for military service, Lowe was posted to a camp near New Orleans. At a nearby camp the entertainments officer was John Hammond Jnr. and their meeting helped Lowe establish his career after the war. Hammond introduced him to Ray McKinley who was leading the postwar Glenn Miller band and thereafter the guitarist worked with Benny Goodman, Wardell Gray, Fats Navarro and Red Norvo among many leading jazz musicians. During the late 40s and early 50s, Lowe worked mostly in New York, playing club dates and recording sessions with a remarkable array of top-flight artists, including Lester Young, Buck Clayton, Charlie Parker and Billie Holiday. During the 50s Lowe played in the NBC studio orchestra, was musical director on the *Today* show on television, acted on and off Broadway and continued to play and record with such well-known jazz musicians as Georgie Auld, Ruby Braff, Ben Webster, Carmen McRae and Harold Ashby.

Since 1965, Lowe has been based in Los Angeles, again working in television and radio and also establishing himself as a writer of scores for films and television. He also became active as an educator but despite his busy schedule found time to continue his recording career, accompanying such musically diverse artists as Sammy Davis Jnr., Tony Bennett, Bill Berry, Richie Kamuca and many others. In the early 80s he formed a small band he named TransitWest, in which he was joined by Sam Most, Monty Budwig and Nick Ceroli, which made its first major appearance at the 1983 Monterey Jazz Festival. A quietly elegant player with a cool but surging swing, Lowe's playing style, with its deceptively sparse exploration of the often-overlooked subtleties of many standards from the jazz and popular song repertoires, is in the great tradition of jazz guitar. Nevertheless, his experimentations with 12-tone compositions have also put him in the forefront of jazz-guitar thinking.

● ALBUMS: *The Mundell Lowe Quartet* (Original Jazz Classics 1955)★★★★, *Guitar Moods* (Riverside 1956)★★★★, *The Mundell Lowe Trio* (1956)★★, *New Music Of Alec Wilder* (Riverside 1956)★★★, *A Grand Night For Swinging* (Riverside 1957)★★, *Porgy And Bess* (RCA 1958)★★, with Donald Byrd and others *TV Themes* (Camden 1959)★, with Billy Taylor and Gene Quill *Low-Down Guitar* (Jazzland 1960)★★★, *The Mundell Lowe All Stars* (1960)★★★, *Tacit For Neurotics* (Offbeat 1960)★★★, *Mundell Lowe And His Orchestra* (1961),★★★ *Blues For A Stripper* (Charlie Parker 1962), ★★★, *California Guitar* (1974)★★, *Guitar Player* (1976)★★★, with Richie Kamuca *Richie* (Concord 1977)★★, with Bill Berry *Shortcake* (Concord 1978)★★★, *TransitWest* (1983)★★★, *Souvenirs A Tribute To Nick Carroll* (Jazz Alliance 1992)★★, as Great Guitars *The Return Of The Great Guitars* (Concord Jazz 1996)★★★.

Lowther, Henry

b. 11 July 1941, Leicester, England. As a child Lowther learned trumpet from his father and took private violin lessons before going on to study with Manoug Parakian at London's Royal Academy of Music. From the mid-60s on he worked with Mike Westbrook, the New Jazz Orchestra, Keef Hartley, John Mayall, Manfred Mann, Michael Garrick, Norma Winstone (in *Edge Of Time*), John Dankworth, Art Themen, Alan Jackson (in the superb *Kinkade*), Barbara Thompson (*Jubiaba*), John Stevens, Kenny Wheeler, Mike Gibbs, Tony Coe, John Surman, Gordon Beck, Gil Evans, John Taylor, the BBC Symphony Orchestra and the London Brass Virtuosi as well as his own groups, Quarternity and Group Sounds Five. That list is in itself a testimony to his versatility and craftsmanship. As well as playing trumpet, flügelhorn, cornet and violin he has composed for jazz and orchestral groups. Influenced by sources as varied as Indian music, Karlheinz Stockhausen, Joe 'King' Oliver, Weather Report and the Average White Band, Lowther is still playing with as much freshness and directness as ever, touring in the early 90s with Kenny Wheeler and Barry Guy's London Jazz Composers Orchestra. A rare solo album was completed and issued in 1998. It was a fruitful collaboration with Julian Arguelles.

● ALBUMS: see also Keef Hartley Band; *Child Song* (Deram 1970)★★★★, *Henry Lowther's Stillwaters* (Village Life 1998)★★★★.

Lubinsky, Herman

b. 30 August 1896, USA, d. 16 March 1974. Lubinsky formed Savoy Records in 1942 in Market Street, Newark, New Jersey after running a record shop on the site for many years. He had previously been responsible for operating New Jersey's first radio station in 1924. Savoy scored a number 1 hit from its first recording session and, bolstered by this success, went on to build a peerless jazz, gospel and R&B roster in the late 40s with top-selling records by such artists as, on the jazz roster: Charlie Parker, Lester Young, Dexter Gordon, Erroll Garner, J.J. Johnson, Fats Navarro, Miles Davis, Leo Parker, Eddie 'Lockjaw' Davis; gospel: the Kings Of Harmony and the Deep Tones (on the King Solomon subsidiary); and R&B: Dusty Fletcher, Paul Williams, Wild Bill Moore, Hal Singer and Brownie McGhee. In 1948, Savoy opened a successful west coast office under Ralph Bass who continued in Savoy's excellent tradition of recording the finest R&B and bebop, having big hits with Johnny Otis/Little Esther Phillips and Big Jay McNeely. In the 50s, Savoy largely eschewed rock 'n' roll, concentrating on its jazz and ever-expanding gospel catalogue - the latter of which now included Clara Ward, the Drinkard Singers, the Davis Sisters, the Selah Jubilee Singers and, later, Alex Bradford and Jimmy Cleveland. This catalogue would prove to be the company's 'bread and butter' through the 60s and 70s. However, they continued to enjoy R&B success with Nappy Brown, Big Maybelle and Varetta Dillard, as well as making several brilliant territorial forays into the Atlanta and New Orleans musical communities and purchasing important smaller independents labels such as National. Lubinsky remained a strong character, fronting Savoy until just a few months before his death from cancer in March 1974. Savoy Records was purchased by Arista in 1975, and a large-scale reissue programme was commenced.

Lucas, Al

b. Albert B. Lucas, Windsor, Ontario, Canada, d. 19 June 1983. Born into a musical family, he was taught first by his mother and also took advice from his bass-playing father. Before he was in his teens he had chosen the bass as his principal instrument and while still only in his mid-teens he was living and playing in New York. He spent almost a decade with the Sunset Royal Orchestra and then joined Coleman Hawkins. Between 1943 and the end of the 40s he played with numerous front-rank jazz musicians including Oran 'Hot Lips' Page, Duke Ellington, Eddie South, Erroll Garner, Mary Lou Williams and Illinois Jacquet. He had also played with Eddie Heywood during this period and rejoined him for a long spell in the 50s, playing also with

Hawkins, Williams, Jacquet, Teddy Wilson, Ruby Braff and Charlie Byrd. Lucas continued to play jazz gigs in the 60s and 70s but was mostly to be found engaged in studio work. A strong and rhythmic player, Lucas extracted a full, rich sound from his instrument adding pleasing texture to the ensembles of which he was a member.

LUNCEFORD, JIMMIE

b. 6 June 1902, Fulton, Mississippi, USA, d. 12 July 1947. At school in Denver, Colorado, Lunceford studied under Wilberforce Whiteman, father of Paul Whiteman. He later read for a degree in music at Fisk University, where his studies included composition, orchestration and musical theory and he also developed his precocious ability as a performer on many instruments although he preferred alto saxophone. After leaving Fisk, he worked briefly in New York in bands led by Elmer Snowden and others before taking up a teaching post at Manassas High School in Memphis, Tennessee. He formed a band at the school which included Moses Allen (bass) and Jimmy Crawford (drums). Later, Willie Smith and pianist Eddie Wilcox were added before Lunceford took the band on tour. They became very popular and after several such tours Lunceford decided in 1929 to make the band his full-time activity. For the next few years, with the same nucleus of musicians, he toured and broadcast throughout the mid-west. In 1933, the band reached New York and quickly established a reputation. More broadcasts, national tours and, eventually, some successful records made Lunceford's one of the most popular black bands of the swing era. The band's arrangers were originally Wilcox and Smith but later additions were Eddie Durham and Sy Oliver. It was the arrival of Oliver that set the seal on Lunceford's greatest period. Thanks to excellent charts, brilliantly performed by a meticulously rehearsed reed section (credit due largely to Smith), biting brass and a powerful rhythm section sparked by Crawford, the band became one of the best of the period. In addition to the band's sound they also looked good on stage. The Lunceford band was chiefly responsible for the showmanship which crept into many subsequent big band performances, but although many copied, none ever equalled the *élan* of Lunceford's band, especially the members of the trumpet section who would toss their horns high into the air, catching them on the beat. Apart from Smith, the band had good soloists in tenor saxophonist Joe Thomas and trombonist Trummy Young who gave the band a hit recording with his own composition, 'Tain't What You Do (It's The Way That You Do It'. Oliver's departure in mid-summer 1939 to join Tommy Dorsey was a blow but the band continued to use his arrangements. How long this state of affairs could have continued is debatable because the band's days were numbered. Lunceford's personal behaviour was distressing many of his long-serving sidemen. Their dismay at the manner in which he spent money (on buying airplanes for example), while refusing to meet what they saw as reasonable pay demands led, in 1942, to a mass walk-out. The band continued with replacements but the flair and excitement had gone. Although recordings over the next few years show a new promise any further improvement was forestalled when Lunceford died suddenly in July 1947. Although often overlooked in surveys of swing era big bands, during its glory days Lunceford's was one of the best in its precision playing of superbly professional arrangements, it had no betters and very few equals.

● ALBUMS: *Lunceford Special* (Columbia 1950)★★★★, *For Dancers Only* (Decca 1952)★★★, *Jimmie Lunceford And His Orchestra* (Decca 1954)★★★★, *Jimmie Lunceford And His Chicksaw Syncopaters* (Decca 1954)★★, *Rhythm Is Our Business* (Decca 1958)★★★, *Harlem Shout* (Decca 1958)★★★★.

● COMPILATIONS: *Jimmie Lunceford And Louis Prima 1945* (1979)★★★★, *The Golden Swing Years* (1981)★★★★, *Jimmie Lunceford (1935-41)* (1982)★★★, *Strictly Lunceford* (Jasmine 1983)★★★, *The Complete Jimmie Lunceford (1935-41)* (Jasmine 1986)★★★★, *Oh Boy* (Happy Days 1987)★★★, *Runnin' A Temperature* (Affinity 1986)★★, *Oh Boy!* (1987)★★, *Stomp It Off Vol 1 1934-1935* (Decca 1992)★★★★, *Jimmie Lunceford And His Orchestra Vol. 1 1934 - 1939* (Black And Blue 1993)★★★★, *For Dancers Only* (Charly 1993)★★★, *Swingsation* (GRP 1998)★★★★.

LURIE, EVAN

Lurie was a part of a group of young New York musicians, including his brother, John Lurie (saxophone) plus Arto Lindsay and Henry Kaiser (guitars), and Anton Fier (drums). They were unwilling to recognize the boundaries between different forms of popular and not-so-popular music and so happily mixed *avant garde* techniques with pop music and jazz. Lurie became the keyboard player with the Lounge Lizards, a band led by his brother John, which was one of the first New York bands to play jazz with a pop sensibility and present it in that adaptation of 50s style which became fashionable in the 80s. The black-and-white cover on the band's first album showed them in a picture reminiscent of the 50s and this was typical of the approach. Lurie is a technically able pianist who is able to adapt his playing to the very varied repertoire encompassed by the band, everything from 'Harlem Nocturne' to Thelonious Monk pieces like 'Epistrophy'. Lurie also wrote music for the band.

● ALBUMS: with the Lounge Lizards *The Lounge Lizards* (Editions EG 1981)★★★, *Live From The Drunken Boat* (1983)★★★, *Live In Berlin 1991 Vol. II* (Intuition 1993)★★★★, *Queen Of All Ears* (Strange And Beautiful Music 1998)★★★; solo *Pieces Of Bandoneon* (1989)★★★, *Selling Water By The Side Of The River* (1990)★★★.

LUSHER, DON

b. 6 November 1923, Peterborough, Cambridgeshire, England. Lusher grew up in a musical family, his grandfather, father and mother playing and singing in Salvation Army bands. Lusher learned to play trombone and pursued his musical interests at school. At the age of 18, he went into the army but contrived to keep up his playing by joining Salvation Army bands in any town he happened to be near. A visit to a camp he was at by Geraldo And His Orchestra, in whose trombone section was Ted Heath, convinced Lusher that once the war was over that was how he would make his career. In 1947, he left the army, bought a secondhand trombone, and joined a band led by an army friend in Tenby, Wales. He then joined Joe Daniels And His Hot Shots, but only a few weeks later the band folded. Lusher's next professional engagement was with Lou Preager at London's leading dancehall, the Hammersmith Palais. He then worked in a band led by Maurice Winnick at Ciro's Club, following this with important and career-moulding engagements with the Squadronaires and the Ted Heath band, with which he visited the USA. By the 60s Lusher was one of the UK's best-known trombonists, touring extensively with prominent artists, such as Frank Sinatra. Subsequently, Lusher led big bands for special television and radio appearances and for limited concert work, activities which continued into the early 90s. He also established a reputation as an educator, working in this capacity in the USA, Japan and Australia as well as in the UK. Despite his international fame, Lusher has never lost contact with his musical origins and regularly performs and records with brass bands. An outstanding technician, Lusher's flowing, precisely articulated playing style remains an object lesson to fellow trombonists in all areas of music.

● ALBUMS: *Lusher & Lusher & Lusher* (1972)★★★, *Collection* (1976)★★★, *Don Lusher Big Band* (1981)★★★, *Don Lusher Pays Tribute To The Great Bands* (1986)★★★, *Don Lusher Pays Tribute To The Great Bands, Volume 2* (1988)★★, with Maurice Murphy *Just Good Friends* (1993)★★.

● FURTHER READING: *The Don Lusher Book*, Don Lusher.

LYNNE, GLORIA

b. 23 November 1930 or 1931, New York City, New York, USA. Lynne began singing as a very small child in the local Mother African Methodist Episcopal Zion Church, but she was also interested in secular music. She entered numerous amateur talent contests, including one at the famed Apollo Theatre, which she won, and these helped to attract attention. Although she studied music for five years, much of her learning was gained through gigging with jazz musicians including Quincy Jones, Bobby Timmons, Philly Joe Jones and Harry 'Sweets' Edison. She began making records and in the early 60s had minor hits with 'June Night', 'Love I Found You' and a big one with 'I Wish You Love', a recording that did much to establish her career. She toured as supporting artist to many other singers, such as Ray Charles, Ella Fitzgerald and Billy Eckstine. Nevertheless, after the hits and some moderately successful albums, limelight work became harder to find. The late 60s and 70s were leaner years, although Lynne never stopped singing, continuing to develop her personal style and keep her voice in good order. Perseverance paid off and in the 90s an earlier recording of hers, 'Speaking Of Happiness', was used in the film *Seven*, and was also taken up for a television commercial for the Ford Motor Company both in the USA and the UK. This helped to reawaken interest and her appearances became higher in profile; a new recording in 1997 drew the attention of audiences who had lost touch or who had missed her earlier heyday. Lynne's voice is strong and authoritative and even as she approached her late 60s, she displayed no loss of power and few of the inevitable signs of ageing to which singers are prey. Lynne has also written songs, among other things supplying lyrics to the jazz instrumentals 'Watermelon Man' by Herbie Hancock, and Kenny Burrell's 'All Day Long'.

● ALBUMS: *Miss Gloria Lynne* (Evidence 1958)★★★, *I Don't Know How To Love Him* (ABC 1975)★★★, *This One's On Me* (HighNote 1997)★★★★.

LYONS, JAMES L.

b. 18 November 1916, USA, d. 10 April 1994. One of the greatest of jazz's promotors and impressarios, Lyons was first employed in 1941 as a publicity agent for a dance hall venue offering Stan Kenton's 'Artistry In Rhythm Orchestra'. Already a jazz enthusiast, and impressed by Kenton's craft, he took a DJ job in California, where he persuaded the management to give Kenton a live spot. This helped bring the bandleader to the public's attention, and Lyons too was well served by his success, graduating to NBC where he worked as a presenter and producer, notably on New York's *The Jubilee Show* for Armed Forces Radio. Post-war, Lyons returned to his native California, hosting the NBC show *Discapades*, where he proved a major influence on the jazz scene's transition from dixieland to bebop (the Gerry Mulligan/Chet Baker group famously paying tribute in 'Line For Lyons'). Lyons also played a crucial role in bringing to light the talents of Dave Brubeck and his octet, when everybody else was turning a deaf ear. However, Lyons greatest triumph still lay ahead of him. In 1958 he programmed the first line-up of the Monterey Festival, boasting the discovery of vibraharpist and drummer Cal Tjader in addition to new work from Duke Ellington. Other artists included Billie Holiday and Dizzy Gillespie. Lyons remained the captain of the Monterey event up until the early 90s, when he was forced to retire after being criticised for his conservative and intransient booking policies. Whilst this was perhaps true, the sniping should not rob him of his status as a vital component in the emergence of the west coast jazz scene.

LYONS, JIMMY

b. 1 December 1933, Jersey City, New Jersey, USA, d. 19 May 1986. A self-taught alto saxophone player, Lyons was encouraged while still in his early teens by such leading jazzmen as Buster Bailey, Bud Powell and Thelonious Monk. He first worked with Cecil Taylor in 1960 and through this association became known as a leading exponent of free-jazz. In the early 70s he was actively engaged in musical education while simultaneously pursuing his own studies. This period saw him broadening his musical base but he retained his links with Taylor, touring with him in various parts of the world. In the early 80s Lyons formed a quartet with Andrew Cyrille, Joseph Jarman and Don Moye. Soon thereafter his health began to fail and he died of cancer in May 1986.

● ALBUMS: *Other Afternoons* (Affinity 1969)★★★, *Push Pull* (1978)★★★, *Jump It Up* (hatART 1981)★★★, *Something In Return* (Black Saint 1981)★★★, *Wee Sneezawee* (Black Saint 1983)★★★, *Give It Up* (Black Saint 1985)★★★, with Andrew Cyrille *Burnt Offering* (Black Saint 1991)★★★.

LYSIS

(see Dean, Roger)

LYTELL, JIMMY

b. James Sarrapede, 1 December 1904, d. 28 November 1972. Lytell began playing clarinet as a child, quickly taking an interest in jazz and achieving a sufficient level of expertise to be called upon occasionally to deputize for Larry Shields with the Original Dixieland Jazz Band. In 1922 he became a member of the Original Memphis Five, playing and recording with the group until 1925. During the late 20s and on into the following decade he worked as a freelance studio musician, playing popular classics as well as contemporary dance and popular music. Although still active in jazz (he was host of the popular radio show *The Chamber Music Society Of Lower Basin Street*), his main occupation in these years was as a musical director with NBC. Occasionally, Lytell played in reunions of the OMF and also led his own small bands into the early 70s. A fluent soloist with a strikingly assured technique, Lytell was influential in bringing traditional forms of jazz to a wide audience through both his playing and his broadcasting.

LYTLE, JOHNNY

b. John Dillard Lytle, 13 October 1932, Springfield, Ohio, USA. A gifted percussionist, Lytle has played drums and, most notably, vibraphone with several well-known leaders. His early engagements included spells with Ray Charles and Gene Ammons and he later led his own bluesy small groups, often using top-flight jazzmen, such as Frank Wess and Ron Carter. During the 60s Lytle followed a current stylistic trend for small organ combos which proved popular. In addition to performing, Lytle has also taught and composed music. Although his career has been relatively low-key, Lytle's skill as a vibraphone player is high and his albums worth hunting out.

● ALBUMS: *Blue Vibes* (Jazzland 1960)★★★, *Happy Ground* (Jazzland 1961)★★★, *Nice And Easy* (Jazzland 1962)★★, *Moon Child* (Jazzland 1962)★★, *Got That Feeling* (Riverside 1963)★★★, *Happy Ground* (Riverside 1964)★★★, *The Village Caller* (Riverside 1965)★★★, *The Loop* (1965)★★★★, *New And Groovy* (1965)★★★★, *A Groove* (Riverside 1967)★★★, *Be Proud* (Solid State 1969)★★★, *The Soulful Rebel* (Milestone 1971)★★★, *Everything Must Change* (Muse 1977)★★★, *Fast Hands* (Muse 1978)★★★, *Good Vibes* (Muse 1985)★★★, *Happy Grand* (Muse 1985)★★★.

LYTTELTON, HUMPHREY

b. 23 May 1921, Eton, Buckinghamshire, England. Raised in an academic atmosphere (his father was a Housemaster at Eton College), he taught himself to play a variety of instruments including the banjolele. His prodigious talent was spotted early and he was given formal lessons on piano and, a little later, in military band drumming. Eventually, his education took him back to Eton College, this time as a pupil. He joined the school orchestra as a timpanist but after a while drifted away from the orchestra and the instrument. At the age of 15 he discovered jazz, thanks to records by trumpeters Nat Gonella and, decisively, Louis Armstrong. By this time Lyttelton had switched to playing the mouth-organ, but, realizing the instrument's limitations, he acquired a trumpet, which he taught himself to play. Forming his own small jazz band at the college, he developed his playing ability and his consuming interest in jazz. With the outbreak of World War II he joined the Grenadier Guards, continuing to play whenever possible. After the war he resumed playing, this time professionally, and in 1947 became a member of George Webb's Dixielanders. The following year he formed his own band and quickly became an important figure in the British revivalist movement. In the late 40s and through to the mid-50s Lyttelton's stature in British jazz increased. Significantly, his deep interest in virtually all aspects of jazz meant that he was constantly listening to other musicians, many of whom played different forms of the music. Although he was never to lose his admiration for Armstrong, he refused to remain rooted in the revivalist tradition. His acceptance and absorption of music from the jazz mainstream ensured that when the trad boom fizzled out, Lyttelton continued to find an audience. In the mid-50s he added alto saxophonist Bruce Turner to his band, outraging some reactionary elements in British jazz circles, and a few years later added Tony Coe, Joe Temperley and other outstanding and forward-thinking musicians.

In the early 60s Lyttelton's reputation spread far beyond the UK and he also developed another important and long-term admiration for a trumpet player, this time, Buck Clayton. By this time, however, Lyttelton's personal style had matured and he was very much his own man. He was also heavily involved in many areas outside the performance of music. In 1954, he had published his first autobiographical volume and in the 60s he began to spread his writing wings as an essayist, journalist and critic. He also broadcast on radio and television, sometimes as a performer but also as a speaker and presenter. These multiple activities continued throughout the next two decades, his UK BBC Radio 2 series, *The Best Of Jazz*, running for many years. His writings included further autobiographical work and his ready wit found outlets in seemingly unlikely settings, such as his role as quizmaster on the long-running radio comedy-panel series, *I'm Sorry I Haven't A Clue*. During this time he continued to lead a band, employing first-rate musicians with whom he toured and made numerous records. Among the sidemen of the 70s and 80s were Dave Green, Mick Pyne, John Surman, John Barnes, Roy Williams and Adrian Macintosh. He also toured and recorded with singers Helen Shapiro, Carol Kidd and Lillian Boutté. Back in the late 40s Lyttelton had recorded with Sidney Bechet and in the 70s and 80s he occasionally made albums with other American jazz stars, including Buddy Tate on *Kansas City Woman*, and Kenny Davern on *Scatterbrains* and *This Old Gang Of Ours*. In the early 80s Lyttelton formed his own recording company, Calligraph, and by the end of the decade numerous new albums were available. In addition to these came others, mostly on the Dormouse label, which reissued his earlier recordings and were eagerly snapped up by fans of all ages. Although he has chosen to spend most of his career in the UK, Lyttelton's reputation elsewhere is extremely high and thoroughly deserved. As a trumpet player and bandleader, and occasional clarinettist, he has ranged from echoing early jazz to near-domination of the British mainstream. For more than 40 years he has succeeded in maintaining the highest musical standards, all the time conducting himself with dignity, charm and good humour. In the early 90s, touring with Kathy Stobart, he showed no signs of letting up and barely acknowledged the fact that he had sailed past his 70th birthday.

● ALBUMS: *Jazz Concert* (Parlophone 1953)★★★★, *Humph At The Conway* (Parlophone 1954)★★★★, *Jazz At The Royal Festival Hall* (Parlophone 1955)★★★★, *Jazz Session With Humph* (Parlophone 1956)★★★★, *Humph Swings Out* (Parlophone 1956)★★★★, *Here's Humph* (Parlophone 1957)★★★★, *I Play As I Please* (Decca 1958)★★★★, with Kathy Stobart *Kath Meets Humph* (Parlophone 1958)★★★★, *Humph In Perspective* (Parlophone 1958)★★★, *Triple Exposure* (Parlophone 1959)★★★, *Triple Exposure* (Parlophone 1959)★★★, *Back To The 60s* 1960-1963 recordings (Philips 60s)★★★, *Humphrey Lyttelton And His Band 1960-63* (Philips 60s)★★★★, with Buck Clayton *With Humphrey Lyttelton And His Band* (Harlequin 1965)★★★, *21 Years On* (1969)★★★, *South Bank Swing Session* (1973)★★★, with Buddy Tate *Kansas City Woman* (Black Lion 1974)★★★, *Spreadin' Joy* (Black Lion 1978)★★★, *One Day I Met An African* (Black Lion 1980)★★★, *In Canada* (Sackville 1980)★★★, *It Seems Like Yesterday* (Calligraph 1983)★★★, *Movin' And Groovin'* (Black Lion 1983)★★★, with Kenny Davern *Scatterbrains* (Stomp Off 1984)★★★, *Humph At The Bull's Head* (Calligraph 1985)★★★★, with Davern ... *This Old Gang Of Ours* ... (Calligraph 1985)★★★, with Helen Shapiro *Echoes Of The Duke* (Calligraph 1985)★★★★, *Gonna Call My Children Home: The World Of Buddy Bolden* (Calligraph 1986)★★★, *Gigs* (Calligraph 1987)★★★, *Doggin Around* (Wam 1987)★★★, *The Dazzling Lillian Boutté* (1988)★★★, *The Beano Boogie* (Calligraph 1989)★★★, with Shapiro *I Can't Get Started* (Calligraph 1990)★★★★, *Rock Me Gently* (Calligraph 1991)★★★, *Hook Line And Sinker* (Angel 1991)★★★, *At Sundown* (Calligraph 1992)★★★, *Rent Party* (Stomp Off 1992)★★★, *Movin' And Groovin'* (1993)★★★, *Hear Me Talkin' To Ya* (Calligraph 1994)★★★★, *Three In The Morning* (Calligraph 1995)★★★★, *Lay Em Straight* (Calligraph 1997)★★★.

● COMPILATIONS: *Delving Back And Forth With Humph* 1948-86 recordings (Esquire 1979)★★★, *Bad Penny Blues: The Best Of Humph* 1949-1956 recordings (Cube 1983)★★★★, *Tribute To Humph Vols 1-8* 1949-1956 recordings (Dormouse 1984-1988)★★★, *The Parlophone Years* 1949-1956 recordings (Dormouse 1989)★★★★, *Jazz At The Royal Festival Hall & Jazz At The Conway Hall* 1951-1954 recordings (Dormouse 1991)★★★★, *Dixie Gold* 1960-1963 recordings (1991)★★★.

● FURTHER READING: *I Play As I Please*, Humphrey Lyttelton. *Second Chorus*, Humphrey Lyttelton. *Take It From The Top*, Humphrey Lyttelton. *Humph*, Julian Purser.

M-BASE
(see Coleman, Steve; Wilson, Cassandra)

MACDONALD, RALPH
b. 15 March 1944, New York City, New York, USA. MacDonald learnt the conga while listening to his father's band playing in Harlem. His own playing reflects interests in both African and West Indian music. When he was 17, he joined Harry Belafonte's band and stayed with him for 10 years (1961-71). After that he played with Roberta Flack before leading his own band right through to the 80s. His main work was as a producer in his own studio (Rosebud Recording Studio), with a team of writers that included William Salter and William Eaton. Donny Hathaway had a huge hit with their 'Where Is the Love', which sold 10 million copies. MacDonald went on to write songs on eight million-selling records and produced seven gold records, including Grover Washington's *Mr. Magic* and Rod Stewart's *Trade Winds*. He has also worked with saxophonists Roland Kirk, Paul Desmond, David Sanborn and Randy and Michael Brecker.

● ALBUMS: *Sound Of A Drum* (1977), *The Path* (1978).

MACEO AND THE KING'S MEN
This group was formed in 1970 by Maceo Parker (b. 14 February 1943, Kinston, North Carolina, USA; tenor saxophone) and Melvin Parker (b. Kinston, North Carolina, USA; drums). Former members of various high school bands, the brothers joined the James Brown revue in 1964, and were featured on several of the artist's seminal recordings before embarking on an independent career in March 1970. The new group, Maceo And The King's Men, was completed by other defecting members of Brown's troupe. Richard 'Kush' Griffiths (trumpet), Joseph 'Joe' Davis (trumpet), L.D. 'Eldee' Williams (tenor saxophone), Jimmy 'Chank' Nolen (guitar), Alphonso 'Country' Kellum (guitar) and Bernard Odum (bass) were all serving members of the James Brown Orchestra, and similarities between both groups' music were thus inevitable. Despite this, however, neither of the King's Men albums sold well, and several musicians drifted back to their former employer. Both Maceo and Melvin also rejoined Brown, but in deference to their obvious frustration, he wrote, arranged and produced several tracks for a spin-off project, Maceo And The Macks. Two singles, 'Party - Part 1' and 'Soul Power 74 - Part 1', reached the R&B Top 30, before an album entitled *Us*, credited solely to Maceo, was released in 1974. The brothers left the fold again in 1976, whereupon the saxophonist joined George Clinton's Funkadelic empire. Maceo did, however, rejoin Brown briefly in the 80s. 'Cross The Track (We Better Go Back)', a track by Maceo And The Macs, was reissued in 1987 and reached number 54 in the UK chart. In the early 90s Maceo Parker joined with fellow Brown alumni, tenor saxophonist Pee Wee Ellis and trombonist Fred Wesley, to make the well-received *Roots Revisited* and *Mo' Roots*.

● ALBUMS: as Maceo And The King's Men *Doing Their Own Thing* (House Of Fox 1970)★★★, *Funky Music Machine* (People 1974)★★. As Maceo *Us* (Polydor 1974)★★★★. As Maceo Parker *For All The King's Men* (4th & Broadway 1989)★★★, *Roots Revisited* (Verve 1990)★★★★, *Mo' Roots* (Verve 1991)★★★, *Life On Planet Groove* (1992)★★★, *Southern Exposure* (1993)★★★. Solo, *Funk Overload* (What Are Records 1998)★★.

MACERO, TEO
b. Attilio Joseph Macero, 30 October 1925, Glens Fall, New York, USA. A member of the first Charles Mingus Jazz Composers' Workshop in 1953, Macero's keen interest in composition led to an involvement in the Third Stream Music and Guggenheim Awards for composition in 1957 and 1958. It was arguably after he joined CBS Records as a producer in 1957 that Macero had his greatest influence. Working on many of Miles Davis's finest albums, he played a particularly important role on *In A Silent Way* and *Bitches Brew*, where his editing gave the albums their form. He continues to perform on the saxophone.

● ALBUMS: *Explorations* (1953)★★★, *Teo Macero With The Prestige Jazz Quartet* (1957)★★★★, *Impressions Of Charles Mingus* (1983)★★.

MACHINE GUN - PETER BRÖTZMAN
Perhaps the most savage and brutal recording in jazz history, *Machine Gun* is a landmark in the European *avant garde*. The reasoning behind the record's title becomes brutally clear within the first five seconds, as the three-saxophone front line of leader Peter Brötzmann, Willem Breuker and Evan Parker ruthlessly fires off round after round of thunderous musical ammunition, accompanied by pianist Fred Van Hove, bassists Buschi Niebergall and Peter Kowald and drummers Han Bennink and Sven Ake Johansson. Bordering on the unbearable, there is an acute sense of both the emotional and technical extremes, which constitutes a curiously addictive, if draining, experience.

● Tracks: *Machine Gun (second take); Machine Gun (third take); Responsible (first take); Responsible (second take); Music For Man Bennick 1 (first take).*

● First released 1968

● UK peak chart position: did not chart

● USA peak chart position: did not chart

MACHITO
b. Frank Raul Grillo, 16 February 1912, Tampa, Florida, USA, d. 15 April 1984. Raised in Cuba, Machito became a singer and maracas player, working with many of the best-known bands on the island. After arriving in New

York in the late 30s, he became similarly well known as an accomplished player in various Latin-American dance bands. In 1941 he formed his own unit, the Afro-Cubans, and the following year his brother-in-law, Mario Bauza, until then lead trumpeter with Chick Webb, joined him. Under Bauza's watchful eye, the Afro-Cubans became one of the leading exponents of their particular form of Latin-American music. In the late 40s, and throughout the 50s, Machito's band regularly teamed up with leading jazz musicians, especially beboppers, for recording sessions, some of the earliest of which were produced by Norman Granz. These artists included Charlie Parker, Dizzy Gillespie, Joe 'Flip' Phillips, Buddy Rich and Howard McGhee. His music appealed greatly to Stan Kenton, helping to prompt Kenton's long-lasting love affair with Latin rhythms. Machito played percussion instruments on some of Kenton's recordings, including the original version of 'Peanut Vendor'. Machito had a number of successful records during the mambo craze of the 60s, but it was the increasing popularity of salsa that helped to keep him in the front rank of popular entertainment until his death in April 1984, which occurred during an engagement in London.

● ALBUMS: *Machito's Afro-Cuban* 10-inch album (Decca 1949)★★★★, *Jungle Drums* 10-inch album (Mercury 1950)★★★, *Rhumbas* 10-inch album (Mercury 1950)★★★, *Afro-Cuban Jazz Suite* 10-inch album (Mercury 1951)★★★, *Machito Jazz With Flip &Bird* 10-inch album (Mercury 1952)★★★★, *Latin Soul Plus Jazz* (1957)★★★★, *Kenya* (Roulette 1958)★★, *With Flute To Boot* (Roulette 1958)★★★, *Machito At The Crescendo* (GNP 1959)★★★, *The World's Greatest Latin Band* (GNP 1962)★★★, *Soul Source* (Verve 1966)★★★★, *Fireworks* (1973)★★★, with Dizzy Gillespie *Afro-Cuban Jazz Moods* (Pablo 1975)★★★★, *Machito And His Salsa Big Band 1982* (Impulse! 1982)★★★, *Live At North Sea '82* (Timeless 1982)★★, *Machito!* (Timeless 1983)★★★.

MACINTOSH, ADRIAN

b. 7 March 1942, Tadcaster, Yorkshire, England. Macintosh began playing drums as a child and worked with various bands locally before moving to London in the mid-60s. He played with several small, mainstream bands but attracted most attention during a stint with Alan Elsdon's more traditionally orientated group. He gained further experience backing visiting American jazz musicians at various London clubs, and in 1982 joined Humphrey Lyttelton. His work with Lyttelton drew widespread attention to his fine musicianship and subtle swing. His playing on the band's many concert and recording sessions of the late 80s helped to consolidate critical and audience opinion that Macintosh was the best of all the drummers to accompany Lyttelton over the years.

MACKEL, BILLY

b. John William Mackel, 28 December 1912, Baltimore, Maryland, USA. After playing banjo in and around Baltimore, he switched to guitar and also tried his hand at bandleading. In 1944, however, he joined Lionel Hampton's big band where he remained more or less continuously for more than three decades. With Hampton, Mackel's duties were primarily those of a rhythm player, a role at which he excelled. When solo opportunities did present themselves he took them eagerly, displaying a freewheeling style with a strong underpinning that gave colouring to his blues performances and R&B. Constrastingly, his occasional arrangements for the Hampton band show a good and confident ear for the nuances of bop.

● ALBUMS: with Lionel Hampton *Hamp* (GRP/Decca 1942-63)★★★★, with Hampton *The Complete Paris Sessions* (Vogue 1953)★★★★.

MACKNESS, VANESSA

b. Christchurch, Hampshire, England. Mackness grew up in Ipswich, Suffolk, and studied painting in the late 70s at the celebrated Camberwell School of Art, London. She later shared a studio with Maggie Nicols and met Phil Minton (then singing with Mike Westbrook, but also exploring freely improvised vocals), who gave Mackness the idea of using her voice. She asked Minton for lessons, some of which were conducted under bridges to gain greater resonance. She later studied with the Hungarian mezzo-soprano Julianna Bethlen and the French composer/singer Gilles Petit; another influence was Indian classical music, through Imrat Khan and the teachings of Pandit Ravi Shankar. The London free improvisation scene embraced her wide-ranging vocal palette and sensitivity. In 1990 and 1991, she sang at Company Week and also broadcast a 'Music In Our Time' programme organized by Derek Bailey for the BBC's Radio 3. Duos with bassist and composer Barry Guy (formed in 1989), violinist Phil Wachsmann, pianist Keith Tippett and saxophonist John Butcher have produced astonishingly varied and powerful music. Mackness remains open to a wide variety of vocal styles and musics - she declares she has an 'endless preoccupation with sound in all contexts, including everyday sounds' - and her cornucopia of vocalism has attracted much attention. In 1991, she initiated a duet with Alexander Balanescu, leader of one of the pre-eminent contemporary classical quartets.

● ALBUMS: *Respiritus* (Incus 1995)★★★★.

MACPHERSON, FRASER

b. John Fraser MacPherson, 10 April, 1928, Winnipeg, Manitoba, Canada, d. 28 September 1993, Vancouver, Canada. Although his later fame rested on his playing of the tenor saxophone, MacPherson began his musical career on the clarinet. This was at the St. Louis College in Victoria, before he started at the University of British Columbia on a business studies course. He quickly abandoned business in favour of a career playing in clubs and as a studio musician with the Canadian Broadcasting Company. In 1951 he was playing clarinet, alto saxophone and flute, and he pursued this career for the next quarter of a century before turning to playing jazz full time and simultaneously switching to the tenor saxophone. From this point onwards he gained worldwide attention, playing in Russia and the USA, where he also recorded. MacPherson's melodic playing style owed much to his appreciation of the elegance of Lester Young, while hints of the more robust style of Zoot Sims and Al Cohn emerged through his full-bodied sound.

● ALBUMS: *Live At The Planetarium* 1975 recording (Concord Jazz 1979)★★★★, *I Didn't Know About You* (Sackville 1981)★★★, *Indian Summer* (Concord Jazz 1983)★★★, *Jazz Prose* (Concord Jazz 1984)★★★★, *Ellington '87* (Sackville 1987)★★★, *Honey And Spice* (Justin Time 1987)★★★, *Encore* (Justin Time 1990)★★★, *In The Tradition* (Concord Jazz 1991)★★★★.

MADISON, BINGIE

b. Bingie S. Madison, 1902, Des Moines, Iowa, USA, d. 1978. In his late teens and early twenties, he played piano in his home-town and in California, but later took up clarinet and saxophones. He played with numerous bands and in the late 20s and early 30s briefly led his own band. In 1931 he joined Luis Russell and was in the unit when it backed Louis Armstrong for tours and records. During his tenure with the band, Madison occasionally wrote very effective arrangements. From 1940 he began another round of bands; usually these were second-rankers but he had brief spells with Edgar Hayes and Ovie Alston. Madison's playing was sometimes less than perfect but he was an able section player. His arranging talents were very good but underused, although he did write a number of charts for Earl Hines' big band in its later years.

MADISON, KID SHOTS

b. Louis Madison, 19 February 1899, New Orleans, Louisiana, USA, d. September 1948. He began playing trumpet, having first played drums in the waifs' home band that saw the musical beginnings of Louis Armstrong and Kid Rena. As he gained proficiency as a trumpet player, Madison worked with several New Orleans brass and marching bands. He continued these activities through the 30s and in the early 40s played in bands led by Bunk Johnson. Like so many of his generation of New Orleans musicians, Madison was able to play music only as a sideline to full-time work in other things. He played with drive and vigorous attack.

MADRIGUERA, ENRIC

b. 17 February 1904, Barcelona, Spain, d. 7 September 1975. A child prodigy on violin, Madriguera played concerts in Spain and France before studying music with Leopold Auer at Barcelona Conservatory. After emigrating to the USA, he played as soloist with the Boston and Chicago Symphony Orchestras and, while still in his 20s, became conductor of the Cuban Philharmonic, later joining NBC in New York as concertmaster. While visiting Colombia he worked as musical director for the Columbia Records' subsidiary there; as a result Madriguera became interested in dance music, forming his first band for the Havana Casino. Back in New York, he recorded with the group for the parent Columbia company. Madriguera's occupation for the eight years of his popular career was as leading violinist of a society band, which debuted in 1932 at the Commodore, Biltmore and Weylin hotels in New York. Helen Ward was his vocalist in her pre-Benny Goodman days; her place was later taken by Patricia Gilmore, who subsequently married Madriguera. In 1940, his musical policy became almost exclusively Latin-American for recording contracts with RCA Records and Brunswick as well as for the usual Columbia releases, so much so that he was known as 'Musical Ambassador Of The Americas'. Madriguera compositions include a stage musical *The Moor And The Gipsy*, a ballet *Follies Of Spain*, and many popular songs including 'Adios' and 'The Minute Samba'. When the band business had no more to offer, Mr. and Mrs. Madriguera retired to an old inn and country house in Connecticut where they continued to entertain visitors until his death in 1975.

MAGUIRE, ALEX

b. 6 January 1959, Croydon, Surrey, England. Maguire remembers improvising at the piano before he received any lessons, which began at the age of eight. He studied music at the University of London and gained a BA degree; he also took lessons from Wanda Jeziorska, Andrew Ball and Howard Riley. He names as his inspiration a number of respected figures in the free improvising scene, such as Tony Oxley and Evan Parker, as well as jazz players Cecil Taylor and Eric Dolphy. McGuire says he is interested in 'pre-literate music, anything original rather than imitative (irrespective of idiom)'. He has studied with classical composers John Cage and Michael Finnissy and his arsenal of techniques and figures, which stretch from *avant garde* classical piano to jazz, from kwela to R&B, has made him much in demand. His sympathy as an accompanist is only matched by his imagination, perverse and frequently humorous. He formed a partnership with drummer Steve Noble and played with him at Company Week 1989. He is also a member of Tony Oxley's Celebration Orchestra and plays with Sean Bergin's MOB groups. In 1989, he toured with his own nine-piece, the Cat O' Nine Tails, which featured drummer Louis Moholo and saxophonist Alan Wilkinson.

● ALBUMS: with Steve Noble *Live At Oscars* (1987)★★, with Cat O'Nine Tails *Hoki Poki* (1990)★★★, with Luc Houtcomp, Willie Kellers *HKM* (1990)★★★.

MAHAVISHNU ORCHESTRA

Led by guitarist John McLaughlin, (b. 4 January 1942, Yorkshire, England), between 1972 and 1976 the Mahavishnu Orchestra played a leading part in the creation of jazz/rock fusion music. Mahavishnu was the name given to McLaughlin by his Hindu guru Snr i Chimnoy, and the group's early work showed the influence of Indian ragas. The first line-up included several musicians who had played on McLaughlin's previous solo album, *The Inner Mounting Flame*. The high-energy electric music created by keyboardist Jan Hammer, ex-Flock violinist Jerry Goodman, bassist Rick Laird and drummer Billy Cobham made *Birds Of Fire* a Top 20 hit in the USA. After releasing the live *Between Nothingness And Eternity*, whose lengthy 'Dreams' sequence featured spectacular duetting between the guitarist and Cobham, McLaughlin split the group. A year later he re-formed Mahavishnu with an entirely new personnel. Jean-Luc Ponty replaced Goodman, Narada Michael Walden took over on drums, with Gayle Moran on keyboards and vocals, and there was also a four-piece string section. This line-up made *Apocalypse* with producer George Martin. In 1975, Ponty left and keyboardist Stu Goldberg played on the final albums. McLaughlin next decided to pursue classical Indian music more rigorously in the acoustic quartet Shakti, but Cobham and Hammer in particular carried on the Mahavishnu approach to jazz/rock in their later work. Moran played with Chick Corea's Return To Forever while Walden became a noted soul music producer in the 80s.

● ALBUMS: *The Inner Mounting Flame* (Columbia 1972)★★★★, *Birds Of Fire* (Columbia 1973)★★★★, *Between Nothingness And Eternity* (Columbia 1973)★★★, *Apocalypse* (Columbia 1974)★★, *Visions Of The Emerald Beyond* (Columbia 1975)★★★, *Inner Worlds* (Columbia 1976)★★★, *Adventures In Radioland* (Relativity 1987)★★★.

MAHOGANY, KEVIN

b. 30 July 1958, Kansas City, Missouri, USA. Mahogany studied music as a child and at the age of 12 played baritone saxophone in Eddie Baker's New Breed Jazz Orchestra while studying in Kansas City. He sang in a choir while in high school and entered and won a church singing scholarship open to baritone singers, not saxophonists. While studying at Baker University he formed a jazz choir. Later, after postgraduate studies, he began singing in Midwestern towns with a trio and was eventually heard by a producer who signed him to Enja Records. The Baronial Baritone, as he was dubbed by jazz writer Whitney Balliett, has a rich melodic voice, singing standards with eloquent ease. His debut for Warner Brothers Records, 1996's *Kevin Mahogany*, concentrated on pop standards to the annoyance of some jazz purists. However, Mahogany's bold versions of songs such as Stevie Wonder's 'I Never Dreamed You'd Leave In Summer', the Fats Domino standard 'I'm Walkin'', and James Carr's 'Dark End Of The Street', demonstrated that he is one of the finest jazz singers of his generation.

● ALBUMS: *Double Rainbow* (Enja 1993)★★★, *Songs And Moments* (Enja 1994)★★★★, *You Got What It Takes* (Enja 1995)★★★, *Kevin Mahogany* (Warners 1996)★★★, *Another Time Another Place* (Warners 1998)★★★★, *My Romance* (Warners 1998)★★★.

MAIDEN VOYAGE - HERBIE HANCOCK

Probably the best in Herbie Hancock's series of fine Blue Note albums from the 60s, *Maiden Voyage* finds him in what is basically the Miles Davis band of the time, with Davis replaced by the young Freddie Hubbard. Hancock has always been a fine composer, but *Maiden Voyage* contains two classic compositions in particular - the beautiful 'Dolphin Dance', and the atmospheric and popular title track. Saxophonist George Coleman, bassist Ron Carter and drummer Tony Williams play as well throughout as they have ever played, and the whole record is marked with a timeless freshness and sense of creative tension.

● Tracks: *Maiden Voyage; The Eye Of The Hurricane; Little One; Survival Of The Fittest; Dolphin Dance.*

● First released 1964

● UK peak chart position: did not chart

● USA peak chart position: did not chart

MAINI, JOE

b. 8 February 1930, Providence, Rhode Island, USA, d. 8 May 1964. Maini began playing alto saxophone as a child, encouraged by his musical family, and as a teenager toured with the bands of Alvino Rey and Johnny Bothwell. In the early 50s he settled in Los Angeles, playing with musicians such as Max Roach and Clifford Brown, recording with the latter on the 1954 recordings issued as *Best Coast Jazz* and *Clifford Brown All-Stars*. He also worked and sometimes recorded with Bill Holman, Jack Sheldon, Shelly Manne, Jimmy Knepper and others. He worked as a session musician in film studios, playing alto and tenor saxophones, and was on the soundtrack of *I Want To Live* (1958). He also appeared on-screen in the 14-minute short, *Birth Of A Band* (1955), and in two 25-minute shorts in the *Frankly Jazz* series, with Shorty Rogers and his Giants and an all-star orchestra directed by Gerald Wilson (both 1962). A strong and inventive bop player, Maini's career was still not fully realized when his life ended abruptly during a 'game' of Russian roulette.

MAINIERI, MIKE

b. 24 July 1938, New York City, New York, USA. Born in the Bronx, Mainieri was playing the vibraphone by the time he was 10 years old and performing publicly at 14. He studied at the Juilliard School and then joined the Paul Whiteman Band before touring with the Buddy Rich Orchestra (1956-62). He left Rich to become a session musician in New York. During the 70s he wrote music for television and films. He played with Jeremy Steig's band Jeremy And The Satyrs at the Café A Go Go, formed a 16-piece rock band and led his own quartet with Steve Gadd on drums. He invented the synthivibe, which not only allowed him to treat the sound of the vibes electronically but also to be heard in high-volume situations. In 1979, he brought together a group of session musicians to tour Japan. The unit included Gadd (later replaced by Peter Erskine), Michael Brecker, Don Grolnick (piano), and Eddie Gomez. They were named Steps, later to be Steps Ahead, and were described as 'a contemporary bebop band'.

● ALBUMS: *Free Smiles* (1978)★★★, *Wanderlust* (NYC 1981)★★★★, *Steps Ahead* (1983)★★★★, *Modern Times* (1984)★★★, *Magnetic Love* (1986)★★★, *Come Together* (NYC 1993)★★★.

● VIDEOS: *Mike Mainieri Quintet* (Kay Jazz 1988).

Mairants, Ivor

b. 8 July 1908, Rypin, Poland, d. 20 February 1998, London, England. An influential guitarist, composer, teacher and author, Mairants moved to England with his parents in 1914, just prior to the outbreak of World War I. His father was a Talmudic scholar, and his mother ran a tobacconist's shop in London's East End. Young Mairants' fascination with dance-band music began when he heard radio broadcasts by the Savoy Orpheans on a primitive crystal set. He saved enough money to buy a banjo, and by his mid-teens was playing in groups such as the Magnetic Dance Band (later the Florentine Dance Band), Fred Anderson's Cabaret Band, and the Valencians. Soon he was doubling banjo and guitar, and it was on the latter instrument that he excelled. He subsequently worked with big-name bands led by Roy Fox, Jack Harris, Lew Stone, Ambrose, Mantovani and Ted Heath. From 1940-52 Mairants served as the featured guitarist with Geraldo, and composed several guitar solos and pieces for the innovative Geraldo Swing Septet, which he led. These included 'Russian Salad', which was inspired by the Russians entering the war in June 1941. For most of his time with Geraldo, Mairants topped the guitar section of the annual *Melody Maker* poll, and made regular broadcasts with his own quintet on the BBC's *Guitar Club*. In 1950, he established the Central School of Dance Music in London, and later opened the Ivor Mairants Musicentre. During his long and active life, he published many works for guitar, both jazz and classical. Mairants had a million-seller with his recording of the beautiful adagio from Joaquin Rodrigo's 'Concerto De Aranjuez', and, at the behest of Thomas Beecham, he played the mandolin for Ezio Pinza in the renowned 1938/9 production of *Don Giovanni* at Covent Garden. As a teacher, he coached two of Britain's top comedians, Benny Hill and Eric Sykes, and appeared on both their television shows. Mairants' acclaimed tutor on flamenco sold consistently over the years. Towards the end of his life he composed 'Jazz Sonatas For Solo Guitar', and was made a Freeman of the City of London. In 1997, the Ivor Mairants Guitar Award was inaugurated, under the auspices of the Worshipful Company of Musicians, of which he was a Liveryman.

● ALBUMS: with Albert Harris *The Ivor Mairants Swing Years - 1935-54* (Zodiac 1992)★★★.

● FURTHER READING: *My Fifty Fretting Years. Great Jazz Guitarists*, Ivor Mairants.

Major Surgery

A four-piece outfit based in Croydon, Surrey, England, during the latter part of the 70s, Major Surgery comprised Don Weller, Tony Marsh (drums), Bruce Collcutt (bass guitar) and Jimmy Roche (guitar). Roche had a blues background, having been a brief member of an early Colosseum line-up; he subsequently joined East Of Eden, where he played with Weller. This pair also played together in Boris prior to forming Major Surgery. Thus, Major Surgery drew on the blues, rock, and *avant garde* music, reconstituting them as a muscular blend of intellectual electric jazz.

● ALBUMS: *First Cut* (1977)★★★.

Makeba, Miriam

b. 4 March 1932, Johannesburg, South Africa. The vocalist who first put African music on the international map in the 60s, Makeba began her professional career in 1950, when she joined Johannesburg group the Cuban Brothers. She came to national prominence during the mid-50s as a member of leading touring group the Manhattan Brothers, an 11-piece close harmony group modelled on African-American line-ups such as the Mills Brothers. She performed widely with the outfit in South Africa, Rhodesia and the Congo until 1957, when she was recruited as a star attraction in the touring package show African Jazz And Variety. She remained with the troupe for two years, again touring South Africa and neighbouring countries, before leaving to join the cast of the 'township musical' *King Kong*, which also featured such future international stars as Hugh Masekela and Jonas Gwangwa. By now one of South Africa's most successful performers, Makeba was nonetheless receiving just a few dollars for each recording session, with no additional provision for royalties, and was increasingly keen to settle in the USA. The opportunity came following her starring role in American film-maker Lionel Rogosin's documentary *Come Back Africa*, shot in South Africa. When the Italian government invited Makeba to attend the film's premiere at the Venice Film Festival in spring 1959, she privately decided not to return home. Shortly afterwards, furious at the international furore created by the film's powerful exposé of apartheid, her South African passport was withdrawn. In London after the Venice Festival, Makeba met Harry Belafonte, who offered to help her gain an entry visa and work permit to the USA. Arriving in New York in autumn 1959, Belafonte further assisted Makeba by securing her a guest spot on the popular *Steve Allen Show* and an engagement at the prestigious Manhattan jazz club, the Village Vanguard. As a consequence of this exposure, Makeba became a nationally feted performer within a few months of arriving in the USA, combining her musical activities - major chart hits such as 'Patha Patha', 'The Click Song' and 'Malaika' - with outspoken denunciations of apartheid. In 1963, after an impassioned testimony before the United Nations Committee Against Apartheid, all her records were banned from South Africa. Married for a few years to fellow South African emigré Masekela, in 1968 Makeba divorced him in order to marry the Black Panther activist Stokeley Carmichael - a liaison that severely damaged her following amongst older white American record buyers. Promoters were no longer interested, and tours and record contracts were cancelled. Consequently, she and Carmichael, from whom she is now divorced, moved to Guinea in West Africa. Fortunately, Makeba continued to find work outside the USA, and during the 70s and 80s spent most of her time on the international club circuit, primarily in Europe, South America and Africa. She has also been a regular attraction at world jazz events such as the Montreux Jazz Festival, the Berlin Jazz Festival and the Northsea Jazz Festival. In 1977, she was the unofficial South African representative at the pan-African festival of arts and culture, FESTAC, in Lagos, Nigeria. In 1982, she was reunited with Masekela at a historic concert in Botswana. As was previously the case in the USA, Makeba combined her professional commitments with political activity, and served as a Guinean delegate to the United Nations. In 1986, she was awarded the Dag Hammarskjold Peace Prize in recognition of this work. In 1987, Makeba was invited to appear as a guest artist on Paul Simon's *Graceland* tour, which included emotional returns to the USA and Zimbabwe (she had been banned from the country, then known as Rhodesia, in 1960). While some anti-apartheid activists, mostly white Westerners, criticized her for allegedly breaking the African National Congress's cultural boycott by working with Paul Simon (whose *Graceland* album had been part-recorded in South Africa), Makeba convincingly maintained that the *Graceland* package was substantially helping the anti-apartheid movement by drawing attention to the culture and plight of black South Africans.

● ALBUMS: *Miriam Makeba* (RCA 1960)★★★★, *The World Of Miriam Makeba* (RCA 1962)★★★, *Makeba* (RCA 1963)★★★, with Harry Belafonte *An Evening With Belafonte/Makeba* (RCA Victor 1965)★★★★, *The Click Song* (RCA 1965), *A Promise* (Les Disques Esperance 1974)★★★, *Country Girl* (Les Disques Esperance 1975)★★, *Pata Pata* (Les Disques Esperance 1977)★★, *Sangoma* (WEA 1988)★★★, *Welela* (Mercury 1989)★★★, *Sing Me A Song* (Sonodisc 1993)★★★, *Live From Paris & Conakry* (DRG 1998)★★★.

● COMPILATIONS: *Africa* 1960-65 recordings (Novus 1991)★★★, *The Best Of Miriam Makeba And The Sklarks* (1993)★★★, *The Best Of Miriam Makeba & The Skylarks* 1956-59 recordings (Camden 1998)★★★★.

● FURTHER READING: *Makeba: My Story*, Miriam Makeba with James Hall.

MAKOWICZ, ADAM

b. 18 August 1940, Czechoslovakia. Makowicz's piano teacher mother taught him to play. He studied classical music at the Fryderyck Chopin School in Kracow, but left when he became interested in jazz. His first work was with Tomasz Stanko (trumpet) in one of the first European groups to be influenced by the free style of Ornette Coleman. In 1965, he moved to Warsaw, where he had his own trio and played with Zbigniew Namyslowski (alto) with whom he toured worldwide. Makowicz's interest in composition grew during this period and he became involved with electric keyboards. In 1970, he joined Michal Urbaniak in his new group Constellation and recorded an album with Urbaniak's wife, Urszula Dudziak. Between 1973 and 1976 he played in a group called Unit with Stanko and played the piano with the Duke Ellington Orchestra at a concert in Prague (1976). In 1977 he went to the USA as a solo performer, playing in a style that reflected his interest in Art Tatum, Keith Jarrett and romantic piano music. He settled in New York in 1977 and became an American citizen in 1986.

● ALBUMS: with Urszula Dudziak *Newborn Light* (1972)★★★★, *Adam* (Columbia 1977)★★★, with George Mraz *Classic Jazz Duets* (Stash 1979)★★★★, *The Name Is Makowicz* (Sheffield Lab 1983)★★★★, *Moonray* (Novus 1986)★★★, *Interface* (Gazell 1987)★★★, *Naughty Baby* (Novus 1987)★★★★, *Adam In Stockholm* (Verve 1987)★★★, *Adam Makowicz Plays Irving Berlin* (VWC 1992)★★★, *Live At Maybeck Recital Hall Series, Vol. 24* (Concord Jazz 1992)★★★, *The Music Of Jerome Kern* (Concord Jazz 1993)★★★, with Mraz *Adam Makowicz/George Mraz* (Concord Jazz 1993)★★★, *My Favorite Things: The Music Of Richard Rogers* (Concord Jazz 1994)★★★, *Tribute To Art Tatum* (VWC 1997)★★★.

MALLORY, EDDIE

b. *c.*1905, Chicago, Illinois, USA, d. 20 March 1961. An all-round journeyman musician, he played trumpet and occasionally saxophones, arranged, led bands and worked in various non-playing areas of the music business. In the late 20s and through into the early 30s he played in bands such as the Alabamians, Tiny Parham's and, in New York, played in and occasionally led the Mills Blue Rhythm Band. He also played in a band led by Benny Carter and then, in 1934, formed a band to accompany Ethel Waters to whom he was married at the time. He toured and recorded with Waters throughout the 30s. In the 40s he led bands for club and hotel work, often in his home-town. From the late 40s onwards he worked mostly as an agent and also outside showbusiness. The band Mallory used on some of his wife's recordings included top-flight musicians such as Shirley Clay, Tyree Glenn, Carter and Milt Hinton.

● COMPILATIONS: *An Introduction To Ethel Waters* (Best Of Jazz 1921-40)★★★.

MALOMBO JAZZ

Formed in Pretoria, South Africa, in 1962, the original - and definitive - Malombo Jazz was a three-piece comprising guitarist Philip Tabane (b. Riverside, near Pretoria, South Africa), flautist Abe Cindi and traditional drummer and percussionist Julian Bahula. The group's repertoire drew heavily on the ancient folk music of South Africa's Venda and Pedi peoples, but was also used as an appropriate backdrop for Tabane's exquisite jazz-based improvisations, which were capable of moving through every emotional area from the loud and lascivious to the pastoral and delicate. In a country long racked by tribal rivalries, jazz had served since the 30s to unite various ethnic groups, and Malombo achieved much the same success in the 60s. In 1964, the band won first prize at the prestigious Castle Lager Jazz Festival. Bahula and Cindi left Malombo in the late 60s to base themselves in London, where they formed the short-lived Malombo Jazzmen prior to Bahula setting up his own band, Jabula. Malombo's line-up underwent numerous personnel changes in subsequent years, as Tabane strove to recapture the magic of the original trio. His first replacement for Bahula was Gabriel Thobejani, who later left to join fusion outfit Sakhile. In 1981, Cindi briefly rejoined the band. In 1986, Thobejani returned. In the late 80s, Tabane began leading an occasional big band, the Homeland Symphony Orchestra, reinterpreting Venda and Pedi folk music in jazz-influenced orchestral style. Sadly, the project remains unrecorded.

● ALBUMS: *Castle Lager Jazz Festival 1964* (N 1964)★★, *The Indigenous Afro-Jazz Sounds Of Philip Tabane And His Malombo Jazzmen* (AYC 1968)★★★★, *Sangoma* (ATH 1972)★★★, *Pele Pele* (ATC 1974)★★★, *Malombo* (KAYA 1984)★★★, *Man Phily* (PAM 1986)★★★.

MALTBY, RICHARD

b. 26 June 1914, Chicago, Illinois, USA, d. 19 August 1991, Santa Monica, California, USA. Maltby started playing cornet in his school band, going on to Northwest University Music School, before his first professional experience with 'Little' Jack Little and his band. He was musical director for CBS radio in Chicago (1940-45), and during this period he wrote 'Six Flats Unfurnished' for the Benny Goodman band, and then spent 10 years working as musical associate for Paul Whiteman at ABC radio in New York. During 1950-65, Maltby was also musical director for SESAC Jazz Classics, recording radio transcriptions with a big band which he took on the road from 1955, encouraged by the success of his 'St Louis Blues Mambo' which had charted the previous year, followed in 1956 by 'The Man With The Golden Arm'. The band recorded prolifically for various RCA labels and Columbia during the 50s, and Maltby was active on many different labels, directing backings for artists Peggy Lee, Giselle Mackenzie, Sarah Vaughan, Gordon MacRae, Johnnie Ray, Vic Damone and Ethel Merman. *Downbeat* voted his unit 'Best New Swing Band', but, the swing era having long since passed, he found more financial reward, if less musical satisfaction, as Lawrence Welk's arranger and conductor on records and television. Maltby's original compositions (mostly for the SESAC transcriptions) for his own orchestra and big band must number in the hundreds, although few measured up to the commercial success of his first Goodman hit and its successor, 'Five Flats Unfurnished', for Sy Oliver. Maltby's only venture into 'serious music' was his threnody 'Requiem For John Fitzgerald Kennedy'. He suffered from ill-health in the 80s, enduring five bouts of open-heart surgery before his death in 1991. His son, Richard Maltby Jnr., is a Broadway director and lyricist.

● ALBUMS: *Manhattan Bandstand* (Viking 50s)★★, *Hello, Young Lovers* (Columbia 1959)★★★★, *A Bow To The Big Name Bands* (Camden 1959)★★★, *Swings For Dancers* (Roulette 50s)★★★, *Mr Lucky* (Camden 1960)★★★, *Swingin' Down The Lane* (Columbia 1961)★★★★, *Swings Folk Songs* (Roulette 1961)★★★, *Most Requested* (1962)★★★, *Music From Mr. Lucky* (Camden 60s)★★★.

MAN JUMPING

Once described by Brian Eno as the most interesting band in the world, Man Jumping evolved out of the co-operative band, Lost Jockey. Lost Jockey had been set up in 1980 to perform the music of American Minimalist/Systems composers (Steve Reich, Philip Glass, Terry Riley), together with works by members of the ensemble, such as Andrew Poppy and Orlando Gough. Growing to over 30 musicians, it became unmanageable and collapsed in 1983 after producing two excellent albums: *Hoovering The Beach* (1981) and the 10-inch *Lost Jockey* (1982). Saxophonist Andy Blake, bassist and keyboardist John Lunn and Gough, Schaun Tozer, Charlie Seaward and Glyn Perrin (all keyboards) decided to pull a more viable unit out of the ashes, planning a more varied repertoire with the emphasis on original pieces. Martin Ditcham came in on drums (replaced in 1986 by Simon Limbrick, from the Lumiere Theatre Company). They had problems getting their recordings promulgated (A&R people liked their mix of Systems, funk, jazz, Afro and the 'classical' *avant garde*, but did not know how to label or market it) and the band started doing live gigs in late 1985. The following summer they opened the Covent Garden Music Festival with a free open-air concert, and took part in the Summerscope season at London's South Bank Centre. The band and individual members have also done much fine work with dance companies such as Second Stride (e.g., Weighing The Heart) and the London Contemporary Dance Theatre (e.g., *Unfolding Field*).

● ALBUMS: *Jump Cut* (1984)★★★★, *World Service* (1987)★★.

MANCE, JUNIOR

b. Julian Clifford Mance, Jnr., 10 October 1928, Chicago, Illinois, USA. Taught piano by his father, a professional jazz musician, Mance was playing professionally long before he entered his teenage years. In the late 40s, still in his teens, he joined a band led by Gene Ammons and in 1950 worked with Lester Young. After military service he gained a residency at a Chicago jazz club before becoming Dinah Washington's accompanist. In the mid-60s he played with Cannonball and Nat Adderley, whom he had first met in an army band, then joined Dizzy Gillespie. By the early 60s, Mance had decided on a career as leader and from then onwards worked clubs throughout the USA. Although primarily known for his work in bop and post-bop groups, Mance's playing reveals echoes of his father's early instruction which drew heavily upon the blues piano tradition. A gifted player with a fluent technique and subtle touch, Mance's reputation worldwide is somewhat less than his talent deserves.

● ALBUMS: *The Soulful Piano Of Junior Mance* (1960)★★★, with Eddie 'Lockjaw' Davis, Johnny Griffin *Tough Tenors* (1960)★★★, *Junior Mance Trio At The Village Vanguard* (Carrere 1961)★★★, with Buddy Guy, Junior Wells *Buddy And The Juniors* (Blue Thumb 1970)★★★★, *Holy Mama* (1976)★★★, *Smokey Blues* (JSP 1980)★★★, *Deep* (JSP 1982)★★, with Martin Rivera *For Dancers Only* (1983)★★, with Rivera *The Tender Touch Of* (Niva 1984)★★★, *Junior Mance Special* (Sackville 1989)★★★, *Plays The Music Of Dizzy Gillespie* (Sackville 1993)★★, *At Town Hall - Vol. 1* (Enja 1996)★★★, *Softly As In A Morning Sunrise* 1994 recording (Enja 1996)★★★★.

Mandingo Griot Society

Formed in Chicago, USA, in 1977 by the Gambian kora player Foday Musa Suso, the Mandingo Griot Society were a flexible line-up of like-minded African, Caribbean and American musicians who played a fusion of rock, funk, reggae and traditional Gambian styles, and who did much to foster the spirit of stylistic eclecticism and multicultural collision then emerging amongst *avant garde* Western musicians and audiences. Their music was both lyrical and irresistibly danceable and, unlike so many subsequent fusion attempts, retained the rough edges of its many constituent styles rather than attempting to make them blandly acceptable to mainstream listeners. In addition to the Western instruments of bass, guitar and kit drums, the group employed a wide range of ethnic instruments, including the West African dusungoni (seven-stringed hunter's harp), bala (xylophone), djembe (hand drum), bolon (three-stringed warrior's harp), dundungo (bass drum), tamo (talking drum) and, of course, Suso's kora (21-stringed harp). North Indian tabla drums and Afro-Cuban timbales, bongos and congas were also employed from time to time.

Aside from Suso, key members of the group included percussionist Adam Rudolph, who had previously played with numerous jazz, Latin and new music ensembles, including Chevere, Streetdancer, Eternal Wind and Detroit's Contemporary Jazz Quintet. He had also performed in Europe and the USA with trumpeter Don Cherry. Drummer Hamid Drake had been an important part of numerous Chicago jazz and R&B groups, working with Muhal Richard Adams, Douglas Ewart and George Lewis. He had also toured Europe and West Africa with Don Cherry. Bassist Joseph Thomas and guitarist John Markiss had previously worked together in bands led by Sun Ra, Lonnie Liston Smith and Peter Tosh, and in Tower Of Power and Earth Wind And Fire. Mandingo Griot Society recorded two outstanding albums before disbanding in 1983. Suso then moved to New York to work with Bill Laswell and Herbie Hancock, while the other members subsequently pursued solo and guest artist careers on the Chicago jazz and R&B scenes.

● ALBUMS: *Mandingo Griot Society* (1978)★★★, *Mighty Rhythm* (1981)★★.

Mangelsdorff, Albert

b. 5 September 1928, Frankfurt-Am-Main, Germany. From a musical family, Mangelsdorff and his brother, saxophonist Emil, learned about jazz from secret meetings of the Frankfurt Hot Club, since jazz was banned by the Nazis. He has subsequently become one of the most important and distinctive European jazz players. After playing violin and danceband guitar, he took up the trombone at the age of 20 and extended its range with the use of multiphonics (playing more than one note at a time) through his technique of humming and growling while playing, so that the brass-generated note is augmented by the vocal sound. He won awards in Germany in 1954, and in 1958 gained attention in the USA as a member of the Newport International Band. In 1962 he recorded with John Lewis. In 1964 he toured Asia with his own band and at that time began to move towards free jazz. He also recorded an album with Ravi Shankar. In the late 60s he joined the Globe Unity Orchestra. In 1975, he joined the United Jazz And Rock Ensemble. From 1976-82 Mangelsdorff worked with Michel Portal, and in 1981 he co-founded the French/German Jazz Ensemble with J.F. Jenny-Clark. In the mid-70s he augmented John Surman's The Trio (with Barre Phillips and Stu Martin) to create MUMPS. In 1986 he and Surman joined with Elvin Jones and Dave Holland for a tour of Europe.

● ALBUMS: with John Lewis *Animal Dance* (Atlantic 1962)★★★★, *Tension* (1963)★★★, *New Jazz Ramwong* (L+R 1964)★★★, with Lee Konitz, Attila Zoller *ZO-KO-MA* (MPS 1967)★★★★, *And His Friends* (1967)★★★, *Wild Goose* (1969)★★★, *Never Let It End* (1970)★★★, *Live In Tokyo* (Enja 1971)★★, *Spontaneous* (Enja 1971)★★★, *Birds Of Underground* (1972)★★★, *Trombirds* (1973)★★★, *The Wide Point* (MPS 1975)★★★, *Solo Now* (1976)★★, *Tromboneliness* (1976)★★★, with Alphonse Mouzon, Jaco Pastorious *Trilogue-Live* (1976)★★★★, with MUMPS *A Matter Of Taste* (1977)★★★, *A Jazz Tune I Hope* (1978)★★★, *Albert Live In Montreux* (1980)★★★★, *Eternal Rhythm* (MPS 1981)★★★, *Three Originals* (MPS 1981)★★★, *Triple Entente* (1983)★★★, with Wolfgang Dauner *Two Is Company* (1983)★★, with Peter Brötzmann, Günter Sommer Pica *Pica* (1983)★★★, *Hot Hut* (1985)★★★, with Konitz *The Art Of The Duo* 1983 recording (1988)★★, *Internationales Jazzfestival Munster* (Tutu 1989)★★★, with John Surman *Room 1220* 1970 recording (Konnek 1993)★★★★, *Lanaya* (Plainisphare 1994)★★★★.

Mangione, Chuck

b. Charles Frank Mangione, 29 November 1940, Rochester, New York, USA. Mangione began playing trumpet as a child, studying formally at the Eastman School of Music. He gained experience accompanying visiting jazzmen, then in 1960 went to New York where he formed a band with his brother, pianist Gap Mangione. The band, the Jazz Brothers, remained in existence for five years, playing hard bop. In 1965, Mangione played in the trumpet sections of the Woody Herman and Maynard Ferguson bands and later that year he joined Art Blakey, with whom he remained until 1967. After leaving Blakey, Mangione taught at his old school and again formed his own small band. He began making albums with which he achieved considerable popular success. He had started to dabble on flügelhorn and eventually abandoned the trumpet altogether in favour of the more mellow-sounding instrument. Throughout the 70s and into the 80s Mangione continued to capitalize upon his successful recordings, appearing widely in concert and making more records that again appealed to a wide audience. To a great extent, Mangione achieved his popular success by offering melodic and uncluttered music, sometimes with interesting hints of Latin influence. Although much of his popular material failed to excite the hardcore jazz audience, there can be little doubt that he helped to introduce the music to many who might otherwise have passed it by. His compositions have appealed to a wide range of musicians, being played by artists as diverse as Percy Faith and Cannonball Adderley. Perhaps the best-known of his compositions is 'Land Of Make Believe', which has frequently been recorded. Additionally, Mangione has written for films, notably *The Children Of Sanchez* (1978).

● ALBUMS: *The Jazz Brothers* (Milestone 1960)★★★, *Hey Baby!* (Original Jazz Classics 1961)★★★★, *Spring Fever* (Original Jazz Classics 1961)★★★★, *Recuerdo* (Original Jazz Classics 1963)★★★★, with Art Blakey *Buttercorn Lady* (1966)★★, *Land Of Make Believe* (1972)★★★, *Bellavia* (1975)★★★, *Feels So Good* (A&M 1977)★★★, *The Children Of Sanchez* (1978)★★★, *An Evening Of Magic* (A&M 1979)★★★, *Tarentella* (A&M 1981)★★, *Love Notes* (Columbia 1982)★★★, *Journey To A Rainbow* (CBS 1983)★★★, *Disguise* (1984)★★, *Save Tonight For Me* (CBS 1987)★★, *Eyes Of The Veiled Temptress* (CBS 1988)★★★.

● COMPILATIONS: *The Best Of Chuck Mangione* (Mercury 1983)★★★★, *Compact Jazz* (Mercury 1984)★★★★.

MANHATTAN TRANSFER

The original band was formed in 1969, performing good-time, jugband music. By 1972, the only surviving member was Tim Hauser (b. 1940, Troy, New York, USA; vocals), accompanied by Laurel Masse (b. 1954, USA; vocals) Alan Paul (b. 1949, Newark, New Jersey, USA; vocals) and Janis Siegel (b. 1953, Brooklyn, New York, USA; vocals). Although they covered a variety of styles, their trademark was their use of exquisite vocal harmony. Like their Atlantic Records stablemate, Bette Midler, they were selling nostalgia, and they were popular on the New York cabaret circuit. An unlikely pop act, they nonetheless charted on both sides of the Atlantic. It was symptomatic of their lack of crossover appeal that the hits were different in the UK and the USA, and indeed their versatility splintered their audience. Fans of the emotive ballad, 'Chanson D'Amour', were unlikely to go for the brash gospel song 'Operator', or a jazz tune like 'Tuxedo Junction'. In 1979, Cheryl Bentyne replaced Masse without noticeably affecting the vocal sound. Arguably their greatest moment remains 1985's Grammy award-winning *Vocalese*, featuring the lyrics of vocal master Jon Hendricks. The power of Manhattan Transfer is in their sometimes breathtaking vocal abilities, strong musicianship and slick live shows. Their stunning version of Weather Report's 'Birdland' remains a modern classic.

● ALBUMS: *Jukin'* (Capitol 1971/75)★★, *Manhattan Transfer* (Atlantic 1975)★★★★, *Coming Out* (Atlantic 1976)★★★, *Pastiche* (Atlantic 1978)★★★, *Live* (Atlantic 1978)★★, *Extensions* (Atlantic 1979)★★★, *Mecca For Moderns* (Atlantic 1981)★★★, *Bodies And Souls* (Atlantic 1983)★★★, *Bop Doo-Wop* (Atlantic 1985)★★★, *Vocalese* (Atlantic 1985)★★★★, *Live In Tokyo* (Atlantic 1987)★★★, *Brasil* (Atlantic 1987)★★, *The Offbeat Of Avenues* (Columbia 1991)★★★, *Tonin'* (Atlantic 1995)★★★, *Swing* (Atlantic 1997)★★★.

Solo: Janis Siegel *Experiment In White* (1982)★★.

● COMPILATIONS: *Best Of Manhattan Transfer* (Atlantic 1981)★★★, *The Christmas Album* (Columbia 1992)★★, *The Very Best Of ...* (Rhino 1993)★★★★.

MANLY, GILL

b. England. A gifted post-bop singer with an eclectic style and repertoire, Manly has attracted much praise in her, thus far, short career. She is particularly admired by Mark Murphy who has drawn attention to 'her rapidly developing gifts'. Like so many young women caught up in the jazz singing explosion of the late 80s and 90s, Manly has yet to establish the widespread following that might well be her due.

● ALBUMS: *Detour Ahead* (Parrot 1994)★★★.

MANN, HERBIE

b. 16 April 1930, New York City, New York, USA. After learning to play the clarinet while still a small child, Mann took up the flute. He developed his musical experience during military service. After leaving the US army, he was active in film and television studios as both performer and composer. He played in several small jazz groups during the late 50s, including his own Afro-Jazz Sextet with which he toured internationally. Early in the 60s, his interest in Brazilian music led to a series of profitable recordings, notably 'Coming Home Baby'. Although rooted in bop and recording with leading jazzmen such as Bill Evans, by the late 60s, Mann's writing and playing had broadened to include musical influences from many lands - especially those of the Middle East. He was also open-minded about rock and by the early 70s was a leading figure in jazz-rock fusion. Indeed, his wide acceptance of areas of popular music outside jazz created some difficulties of categorization, especially when he embraced, however briefly, reggae and disco-pop. He has become one of the widest-known flautists in jazz, gaining a considerable measure of credibility for an instrument that has always had an uncertain status in jazz circles. In addition to his performing and writing, Mann has also been active as a record producer, running his own label, Embryo, under the Atlantic Records aegis for a decade. Subsequently, he formed his own independent label, Herbie Mann Music.

● ALBUMS: *East Coast Jazz 4* (Bethlehem 1954)★★★, *Flamingo My Goodness: Four Flutes Volume 2* (Bethlehem 1955)★★★, *Herbie Mann Plays* (Bethlehem 1956)★★★, *Love And The Weather* (Bethlehem 1956)★★★, with Sam Most *The Herbie Mann-Sam Most Quintet* (Bethlehem 1956)★★★, *Mann In The Morning* (1956)★★★, *Salute To The Flute* (Epic 1957)★★★, *Mann Alone* (Savoy 1957)★★★, *Flute Suite* (Savoy 1957)★★★, *Sultry Serenade* (Riverside 1957)★★★, *Great Ideas Of Western Mann* (Riverside 1957)★★★, *Yardbird Suite* (Savoy 1957)★★★, with Buddy Collette *Flute Fraternity* (Mode 1957)★★★, *Flute Souffle* (Prestige 1957)★★★, *Flute Flight* (Prestige 1957)★★★, *Just Wailin'* (1958)★★★, *The Mann With The Most* (Bethlehem 1958)★★★, *Herbie Mann With The Licken Trio* (Epic 1958)★★★, *The Magic Flute Of Herbie Mann* (Verve 1958)★★★, *Just Wailin'* (New Jazz 1958)★★★, *Mann In The Morning* (Prestige 1958)★★★, *African Suite* (United Artists 1959)★★★, *Flautista! Herbie Mann Plays Afro-Cuban Jazz* (Verve 1959)★★★, *The*

Common Ground (Atlantic 1960)★★★, *Flute, Brass, Vibes And Percussion* (Verve 1960)★★★, *Herbie Mann Quintet* (Jazzland 1960)★★★, *Epitome Of Jazz* (Bethlehem 1961)★★★, *The Family Of Mann* (Atlantic 1961)★★★, with Bill Evans *Brasil Bossa Nova And Blue* (United Artists 1962)★★★, *St Thomas* (United Artists 1962)★★★, *Herbie Mann At The Village Gate* (Atlantic 1962)★★★★, *Right Now* (Atlantic 1962)★★★, *Do The Bossa Nova With Herbie Mann* (Atlantic 1962)★★★, *Sound Of Herbie* (Verve 1963)★★★, with Machito *Afro-Jazziac* (Roulette 1963)★★★, *Herbie Mann Returns To The Village Gate* (Atlantic 1963)★★★, *Live At Newport* (Atlantic 1963)★★★★, *Nirvana* (Atlantic 1964)★★★, *Latin Fever* (Atlantic 1964)★★★, *My Kinda Groove* (Atlantic 1965)★★★, *The Roar Of The Greasepaint The Smell Of The Crowd* (Atlantic 1965)★★, *Latin Mann* (Columbia 1965)★★★, with Joao Gilberto *Herbie Mann And Joao Gilberto With Antonio Carlos Jobim* (Atlantic 1965)★★★, *Standing Ovation At Newport* (Atlantic 1966)★★★, *Herbie Mann Today* (Atlantic 1966)★★★, *Monday Night At The Village Gate* (Atlantic 1966)★★★★, *Our Mann Flute* (Atlantic 1966)★★★, *Bongo Conga And Flute* (Verve 1966)★★★, *Big Band Mann* (Verve 1966)★★★, *Big Band* (Surrey 1966)★★★, *New Mann At Newport* (Atlantic 1967)★★★, *Impressions Of The Middle East* (Atlantic 1967)★★★★, *The Beat Goes On* (Atlantic 1967)★★★★, *Mann And A Woman* (Atlantic 1967)★★★, *Glory Of Love* (A&M 1967)★★★, *The Herbie Mann String Album* (Atlantic 1968)★★★, *Moody Mann* (Riverside 1968)★★★, *Jazz Impressions Of Brazil* (Solid State 1968)★★★, *Wailing Dervishes* (Atlantic 1968)★★★, *Memphis Underground* (Atlantic 1968)★★★, *Free For All* (Atlantic 1968)★★★, *Windows Open* (Atlantic 1969)★★★, *Herbie Mann In Sweden* (Prestige 1969)★★★, *Inspiration I Feel* (Atlantic 1969)★★★, *Concerto Grosso In D Blues* (Atlantic 1969)★★★, *Stone Flute* (Polydor 1970)★★★, *Memphis Two Step* (Atco 1971)★★★, *Muscle Shoals Nitty Gritty* (Atco 1971)★★★, *Push Push* (Atlantic 1972)★★★, *Mississippi Gambler* (Atlantic 1972)★★★, *London Underground* (Atlantic 1973)★★★, *Reggae* (Atlantic 1973)★★★, *Hold On I'm Coming* (Atlantic 1973)★★★, *Evolution Of Mann* (Atlantic 1973)★★★, *Turtle Bay* (Atlantic 1974)★★★, *Gagaku And Beyond* (1974)★★★, *Discotheque* (Atlantic 75)★★★, *Water Bed* (Atlantic 1975)★★★, *Surprises* (Atlantic 1976)★★★, *Brazil - Once Again* (1978)★★★, *Astral Island* (1983)★★★, *Opalescence* (Kokopelli 1989)★★★, *Caminho De Casa* (Chesky 1990)★★★, *The Jazz We Heard Last Summer* (Savoy 1993)★★★, with Bobby Jaspar *Deep Pocket* (Kokopelli 1994)★★★, *Peace Pieces* (Kokopelli 1995)★★★, *Celebration* (Lightyear 1997)★★★, *America/Brasil* (Lightyear 1998)★★★★★.

● COMPILATIONS: *Nirvana* (Atlantic 1961-62)★★★, *The Best Of Herbie Mann* (Prestige 1965)★★★, *Best Of Herbie Mann* (WEA 1993).

MANNE, SHELLY

b. Sheldon Manne, 11 June 1920, New York City, New York, USA, d. 26 September 1984. After switching to drums from saxophone, Manne worked with a number of dance and swing bands of the late 30s and early 40s, including Joe Marsala's big band. He was also active in small groups in New York, accompanying Coleman Hawkins as well as some of the up-and-coming bebop artists. He first attracted widespread attention in 1946, the year he joined Stan Kenton. On and off, he was with Kenton until 1952, finding time in between stints to work in bands led by George Shearing, Woody Herman and others. From the early 50s, he was resident in Los Angeles, working in the studios by day and gradually becoming one of the most important musicians in the rising west coast school of jazz. In 1951, he had recorded with Shorty Rogers and become a member of the house band at Howard Rumsey's Lighthouse Cafe at Hermosa Beach. During the next few years he took part in many fine record sessions, notably for Contemporary, with Teddy Edwards, Jimmy Giuffre, Art Pepper, Lennie Niehaus, Bud Shank, Bob Cooper, Maynard Ferguson, Hampton Hawes and most of the other west coast stars. Among the most successful of these recordings were those made with Rogers in 1951 and 1955/6, a set he recorded with Russ Freeman and Chet Baker, and an album of tunes from the Broadway Show, *My Fair Lady*, which he recorded with Leroy Vinnegar and André Previn. This set, the first ever complete album of jazz versions of tunes from a single show, was particularly successful. Almost as popular was another album made by the same trio with visiting guest Sonny Rollins. Although recording with many different musicians, Manne retained a fairly constant personnel for his regular working band, and towards the end of 1959 was booked into the Blackhawk in San Francisco. The band comprised trumpeter Joe Gordon, Richie Kamuca, Monty Budwig, who had recently taken over from Vinnegar, and Freeman's replacement, Vic Feldman. It was immediately apparent to Manne that the band he had assembled for this two-week engagement was something special, and he persuaded Les Koenig of Contemporary to travel to San Francisco to record them. The resulting four albums became some of the most successful in Contemporary's catalogue and an outstanding example of the west coast's so-called 'cool' sounds at their smokiest. In 1960, Manne opened his own nightclub, Shelly's Manne-Hole, which remained in existence until the middle of the following decade. In the 60s he recorded with Bill Evans and in 1974 was a founder-member of the LA Four, with Shank, Ray Brown and Laurindo Almeida. By the late 70s Manne was a familiar figure on the international jazz festival circuit, appearing at the 1980 Aurex festival in Japan with Benny Carter's Gentlemen of Swing. Although deeply rooted in the swinging tradition of drumming, Manne's sensitive, explorative playing made him an ideal accompanist in almost any setting and one of the finest drummers of the post-war period.

● ALBUMS: with Shorty Rogers *Modern Sounds* (1951)★★★, *Here's That Manne* (DeeGee 1952)★★★, with Rogers *Cool And Crazy* (1953)★★★, *And His Men* (Contemporary 1953)★★★, *And His Men Volume 2* (Contemporary 1954)★★★★, *The Three And The Two* (Contemporary 1954)★★★, with Lennie Niehaus *The Quintet* (1954)★★★, *The Shelly Manne-Russ Freeman Duo* (1954)★★★, with Rogers *The Swinging Mr Rogers* (1955)★★★, *Concerto For Clarinet And Combo* (Contemporary 1955)★★★, *The West Coast Sound* (Contemporary 1955)★★★, with Rogers *Martians Come Back!* (1955)★★★, with Rogers *Big Band Express/Blues Express* (1956)★★★, *Swinging Sounds Volume 4*

(Contemporary 1956)★★★, *Quartet: Russ Freeman And Chet Baker* (1956)★★★, *Shelly Manne And His Friends* (Contemporary 1956)★★★★, *More Swinging Sounds Volume 5* (Contemporary 1956)★★★, *My Fair Lady* (Contemporary 1957)★★★, *Lil' Abner* (Contemporary 1957)★★★, *The Gambit* (Contemporary 1957)★★★, with Sonny Rollins *Way Out West* (1957)★★★★, *The Bells Are Ringing* (Contemporary 1958)★★★, *Shelly Manne And His Men Play Peter Gunn* (Contemporary 1959)★★★, *Son Of Gunn* (Contemporary 1959)★★★, *Shelly Manne And His Men At The Blackhawk Volumes 1-4* (Contemporary 1959)★★★★, *Swinging Sounds In Stereo* (Contemporary 1959)★★★★, *The Proper Time* (Contemporary 1960)★★★, *West Coast Jazz In England* (1960)★★★, *Shelly Manne And His Men Live At The Manne-Hole Volumes 1* and *2* (Contemporary 1961)★★★★, *Checkmate* (Contemporary 1961)★★★, *Sounds Unheard Of* (Contemporary 1962)★★★, *2,3,4* (Impulse! 1962)★★★, with Bill Evans *Empathy* (1962)★★★, *My Son, The Jazz Drummer* (Contemporary 1962)★★★, with Art Pepper *Pepper/Manne* (Charlie Parker 1963)★★★, *Shelly Manne And His Orchestra* i (1964)★★★★, *My Fair Lady With Un-Original Cast* (Capitol 1964)★★★, *Shelly Manne And His Orchestra* ii (1965)★★★, *Manne - That's Gershwin!* (Capitol 1965)★★★★, *Shelly Manne Sounds* (Capitol 1966)★★★, *Perk Up* (1967)★★★, *Shelly Manne And His Orchestra* iii (1967)★★★, *Boss Sounds* (Atlantic 1967)★★★, *Jazz Gun* (Atlantic 1968)★★★, *Daktari* (Atlantic 1968)★★, *Outside* (Contemporary 1968)★★★, *Alive In London* (Contemporary 1970)★★★, *A Night On The Coast* 1969-70 recordings (Moon 70s)★★★, *Mannekind* (Original Master Recordings 1972)★★★, *Hot Coles* (1975)★★★, *The LA Four Scores!* (1975)★★★, *Rex - Shelly Manne Plays Richard Rodgers* (1976)★★★, *Essence* (Galaxy 1977)★★, *French Concert* (1977)★★★, *Jazz Crystallizations* (1978)★★, *The Manne We Love* (1978)★★, *Interpretations Of Bach And Mozart* (Trend 1980)★★★, *In Concert At Carmelo's/Double Piano Jazz Quartet Volume 1* (Trend 1980)★★★, *Double Piano Jazz Quartet Volume 2* (Trend 1980)★★★, with Benny Carter *The Gentlemen Of Swing* (1980)★★★, *Hollywood Jam* (1981)★★★, *Fingering* (1981)★★★, *Remember* (1984)★★★, *In Concert At Carmelo's Volumes 1 & 2* (Trend 1986)★★★.

MANONE, WINGY

b. Joseph Manone, 13 February 1900, New Orleans, Louisiana, USA, d. 9 July 1982. Manone lost his right arm in a road accident while still a child, but took up trumpet playing, turning professional in his mid-teens. The 20s were hectic times for Manone. He worked with many riverboat and territory bands, visited St. Louis where he made his first records in 1924, moved on to New York in 1929 to record with Benny Goodman, and settled in Chicago. He led his own band at nightclubs, then took it to New York for a string of successful engagements which were enhanced by the popularity of his recording of 'The Isle Of Capri'. By the early 40s he was in California, appearing in films and becoming a regular on Bing Crosby's radio show, visiting New York and other centres for concerts and record dates with, for example, Sidney Bechet. In the mid-50s Manone moved to Las Vegas, playing there for several years but making occasional trips to New York and visiting Europe for festivals and tours of clubs. Manone's vocal style, although popular with audiences, was filled with rather forced humour. Contrastingly, he played trumpet with a forthright, honest style that compounded his love for the playing of Louis Armstrong with the New Orleans tradition he heard in his childhood. His early recordings are solidly entertaining.

● ALBUMS: *Wingy Manone And His Band* i (X LVA 1954)★★★★, *Wingy Manone And His Band* ii (Decca 1957)★★★, *Wingy Manone And His Band* iii (1957)★★★, *Wingy Manone And His Band* iv (1959-60)★★★, *Wingy Manone And His Band* v (1960)★★★, with Papa Bue Jensen *A Tribute To Wingy Manone* (1966)★★, *Jazz From Italy* (1975)★★.

● COMPILATIONS: *Wingy Manone Vol. 1* (1928-34)★★★, *Wingy Manone Vol. 2* (1934-35)★★★★, *Wingy Manone/Sidney Bechet - Together at Town Hall, 1947* (1947)★★★★, *Collection Vols 1-3* (Collectors Classics 1989)★★★★.

MANTLER, MICHAEL

b. 10 August 1943, Vienna, Austria. Mantler took up trumpet at the age of 12, and from 14 worked in dance bands, playing stock arrangements with little opportunity for creative jazz. He found more musical freedom after moving to the USA in 1962. After what he regarded as educationally barren years at the Berklee College Of Music in Boston, he moved to New York in 1964 and immediately became involved with musicians such as Paul Bley, Carla Bley (whom he would later marry) and Cecil Taylor. In 1965-66 he toured Europe with Carla Bley and Steve Lacy in the Jazz Realities quintet. In more recent times, he has toured with Carla Bley's Sextet and Charlie Haden's Liberation Music Orchestra, and has recorded several albums of his own pieces. Although a striking trumpet player, he concentrates most of his energy on organizing, producing and composing (often setting the words of Samuel Beckett, Harold Pinter and Edward Gorey to music). He was a co-founder of the Jazz Composers' Guild and the Jazz Composers' Orchestra Association. He also set up two record labels with Carla Bley: Watt, for their own recordings, and JCOA Records, to promote the work of others.

● ALBUMS: with Carla Bley, Kent Carter, Steve Lacy, Aldo Romano *Jazz Realities* (Fontana 1966)★★★, *No Answer* (1974)★★, with Bley *13 & 3/4* (1975)★★★, *The Hapless Child* (Watt 1976)★★★★, *Silence* (1977)★★★, *Movies* (1978)★★★★, *More Movies* (1980)★★★, *Something There* (ECM 1982)★★★, *Alien* (Watt 1985)★★★, *Live* (Watt 1987)★★, *Many Have No Speech* (Watt 1988)★★★, *Folly Seeing All This* (ECM 1993)★★★, *Cerco Un Paese Innocente* (ECM 1996)★★★, *The School Of Understanding* (ECM 1997)★★★★.

MARCUS, STEVE

b. 18 September 1939, New York, USA. Marcus studied at the Berklee College Of Music in Boston (1959-61) before joining Stan Kenton's Orchestra in 1963. From 1967-70 he played with the Herbie Mann Group as well as for diverse bands including those of Woody Herman and the Jazz Composers Orchestra. In the early 70s, he played with Larry Coryell (1971-73) before forming his own Count's Rock Band (1973-75). He joined Buddy Rich in 1975, and played with him regularly over the next 10 years. His tenor playing blends R&B stylings with the influence of John Coltrane in much the way Sal Nistico, another Rich tenor, does: it is a style that can punch its way through the ebullient backings of the big band in full swing.

● ALBUMS: *Count's Rock Band* (1974)★★★, *Buddy Rich Plays And Plays And Plays* (1975)★★, *Lionel Hampton Presents Buddy Rich* (1977)★★★★, *201* (Red Baron 1992)★★★.

Mares, Paul

b. Paul Joseph Mares, 15 June 1900, New Orleans, Louisiana, USA, d. 18 August 1949. Mares began playing trumpet as a boy and although self-taught, he quickly gained sufficient expertise to work with musicians such as Leon Roppolo and Tom Brown. Shortly after the end of World War I he moved to Chicago, playing in several bands and then helping to form the Friars Society Orchestra. The Friars included Georg Brunis, Elmer Schoebel and Roppolo and quickly became popular both in clubs and on record. In 1923 the band was renamed the New Orleans Rhythm Kings, a name reused by Mares and Roppolo in 1925 in New Orleans. Mares recorded in later years, again using the NORK name; however, from the mid-20s onwards he played only part-time. Through his short-lived popularity alone, Mares helped to spread the jazz word to audiences and also to fellow trumpeters who took heed of his crisp playing.

● COMPILATIONS: *The New Orleans Rhythm Kings* (Swaggie 1922-23)★★★★.

Margolis, Kitty

b. California, USA. Raised in San Francisco's Bay Area, Margolis was surrounded by music from early childhood. At the age of 12 she taught herself to play guitar and played and sang in folk-rock and blues groups through high school. She studied at Harvard University and San Francisco State where she turned to jazz under the tutelage of saxophonist John Handy II. She formed her own groups and often performed at San Francisco's Keystone Korner, playing and singing with numerous visiting jazzmen including Stan Getz, Dexter Gordon, Art Blakey and Cedar Walton. In the early 90s, Margolis formed her own recording company in collaboration with fellow singer Madeline Eastman and her first releases alerted the jazz world to the arrival of an important new vocalist on the scene. Margolis's second album reached the Top 10 on US radio jazz charts and features guest saxophonist Joe Henderson. Her third set features Roy Hargrove and R&B veteran Charles Brown. Singing with great zest and vitality, Margolis brings to her work a well-defined sense of purpose and a total commitment to jazz. Her voice is a rich contralto and she uses it with warmth and wit, intelligently interpreting lyrics and sensitively observing the intentions of the songwriters. She has also written a number of lyrics, including those for Walton's 'Firm Roots' and Wayne Shorter's 'Ancient Footprints'. She frequently writes her own arrangements, drawing from the jazz and standards repertoires. Widely praised by critics and fellow musicians, including Jon Hendricks and Lionel Hampton, Margolis is an important singer for the 90s.

● ALBUMS: *Live At The Jazz Workshop* (Mad-Kat 1992)★★★, *Evolution* (Mad-Kat 1994)★★, *Straight Up (With A Twist)* (Mad-Kat 1996)★★★.

Mariano, Charlie

b. 12 November 1923, Boston, Massachusetts, USA. One of many fine students to emerge from Boston's Berklee College Of Music, Mariano gained most of his early experience in and around his home-town. Among the musicians with whom he played in the formative years of the late 40s and early 50s were Herb Pomeroy, Nat Pierce, Gigi Gryce, Quincy Jones and Jackie Byard. In 1953, he joined Stan Kenton for a two-year spell and then worked in Los Angeles with Shelly Manne. By 1958 he was back in Boston, this time teaching at Berklee College Of Music. The following year he was briefly with Kenton again, then met, married and formed a band with Toshiko Akiyoshi. This association lasted into the mid-60s, with part of that time spent in Japan. During the 60s Mariano also played with Charles Mingus, spent more time teaching at Berklee, travelled extensively in the Far East, and led his own jazz-rock group. In the 70s and 80s Mariano lived mostly in Europe, leading bands with Philip Catherine and others, continuing to explore eastern music and playing many kinds of fusion music with, among other groups, the United Jazz And Rock Ensemble and Eberhard Weber's Colours. Throughout his career, Mariano has displayed a striking ability to encompass many diverse musical forms and incorporate them into jazz without losing the emotional intensity of his early bebop-orientated playing style. Through his continued exploration of ethnic musical forms, particularly those of eastern origin, Mariano has established a secure and significant place as a truly international jazz artist.

● ALBUMS: *Charlie Mariano With His Jazz Group* (1950-51)★★★, *The Modern Saxophone Stylings Of Charlie Mariano* (1950-51)★★★, *Charlie Mariano* Vol 1 (Imperial 1952)★★★, *Charlie Mariano Boston All Stars* (Original Jazz Classics 1953)★★★, *Charlie Mariano* Vol 2 (Imperial 1953)★★★, *Swinging With Mariano* (Affinity 1954)★★★, *Charlie Mariano Plays* (Fresh Sound 1954)★★★★, *Alto Sax For Young Moderns/Johnny One-note* (Affinity 1954)★★★★, with Stan Kenton *Contemporary Concepts* (1955)★★★★, *Charlie Mariano* (1957)★★★, with Jerry Dodgion *Beauties Of 1918* (World Pacific 1958)★★, *Toshiko-Mariano Quartet* i (1960)★★★, with Charles Mingus *The Black Saint And The Sinner Lady* (1963)★★★★★, *Toshiko-Mariano Quartet* ii (1963)★★, *A Jazz Portrait Of Charlie Mariano* (Regina 1963)★★★, *Folk Soul* (1967)★★, with Sadao Watanabe *Iberian Waltz* (1967-68)★★★, *Charlie Mariano And His Orchestra* (1970)★★★, *Cascade* (1974)★★★★, *Reflektions* (1974)★★★, *Jazz Confronto 15/JaC's Group Featuring Charlie Mariano* (1975)★★, *The Door Is Open/Pork Pie* (1975)★★★, *Helen 12 Trees* (1976)★★, *October* (1977)★★★, with United Jazz And Rock Ensemble *Teamwork* (1978)★★★, *Crystal Bells* (1979)★★, *Tea For Four* (1980)★★★, *Some Kind Of Changes*

(1982)★★★, *Jyothi* (ECM 1983)★★★, *The Charlie Mariano Group* (1985)★★★, *Mariano* (Intuition 1987)★★, *Charlie Mariano And The Karnataka College Of Percussion: Live* (1989)★★, *Live* (Verabra 1990)★★, *It's Standard Time* (Fresh Sound 1990)★★★, *Innuendo* (Lipstick 1992)★★★, *Adagio* (Lipstick 1995)★★★★.

MARIANO, TORCUATO

b. 1963, Buenos Aires, Argentina. A powerful and talented advocate of Brazilian instrumental jazz, Mariano moved to that country from his native Argentina at the age of 14. By this time already a fluent, self-taught performer, under the tutelage of guitarist Claudio Gabis he studied music theory and harmony. By 1980 he was a regular at various night clubs, performing alongside bossa nova legends including Johnny Alt. However, his other influences were drawn from a wide musical vocabulary, and he delighted in mixing his South American heritage with the rock, blues, jazz and funk traditions of the USA. Numbering Santana, Pat Metheny, Jeff Beck, Ivan Luis and Djavan among his primary influences, he was pleased to oblige when the opportunity arose to accompany the last-named pair in the studio. They were impressed enough by his emerging technique to invite Mariano to join their respective touring bands. Further sessions in Brazil's music capital, Rio de Janeiro, confirmed his new-found status, and brought him into harness with names such as Sergio Mendez, Xuxa, Cal Costa and Leo Gandelman. The first to use his own compositions was saxophonist Gandelman, before he teamed up with lyricist Claudio Rabello to produce a powerful songwriting partnership, benefiting the careers of Xuxa, Angelica, Rosana and others. These successes awoke the interest of VISOM Records, and they duly released a debut solo album, *Paradise Station*. Written, arranged and co-produced by Mariano, it became a welcome addition to the artist's growing legacy and furthered Brazil's discourse with other musical forms and countries. His growing professionalism in producing and composing material with Brazil's major record companies was reflected on *Last Look*. The most poignant track, 'Everything I Couldn't Say With Words', saw him combine his guitar with the flute of Marcelo Martins. Just as affecting was the hip hop-based 'In The Rhythm Of My Heart'.

● ALBUMS: *Paradise Station* (VISOM 1993)★★★, *Last Look* (Windham Hill 1995)★★.

MARMAROSA, DODO

b. Michael Marmarosa, 12 December 1925, Pittsburgh, Pennsylvania, USA. After formal studies and gigging with local bands, Marmarosa played piano with a succession of name big bands of the early and mid-40s, including those of Gene Krupa, Tommy Dorsey and Artie Shaw. In 1946, he settled in Los Angeles, playing and recording with several leading jazz musicians, including Barney Kessel, Lester Young and Charlie Parker. His affinity with bebop made him, briefly, one of the outstanding exponents of the form, but ill-health drove him from the scene around 1948. Marmarosa returned to music in 1961, recording alone and with Gene Ammons. Within a couple of years he was again forced into retirement.

● ALBUMS: *Dodo's Back!/The Return Of Dodo Marmarosa* (1961)★★, with Gene Ammons *Jug And Dodo* (Prestige 1962)★★★, *The Chicago Sessions* 1961-62 recordings (Affinity 1989)★★★, *Pittsburgh, 1958* (Uptown 1998)★★★.

● COMPILATIONS: with Barney Kessel, others *Central Avenue Breakdown Volumes 1 & 2* (1945-46)★★★★, *The Dial Masters* (1946)★★★★, *Piano Man* 1946 recording (Phoenix 1981)★★★, *A 'Live Dodo'* 1947 recording (Swing House 1979)★★, *Experiment In Bop* (Raretone 1989)★★★.

MARRERO, LAWRENCE

b. Laurence Henry Marrero, 24 October 1900, New Orleans, Louisiana, USA, d. 6 June 1959. Marrero was born into a highly musical family. His father and two brothers played bass and another brother played banjo, the instruments he settled upon. He first played professionally in a dance band in which his father also played. Later he worked with several leading New Orleans dance and early jazz bands including those led by Chris Kelly, Kid Rena, John Robichaux and, in the late 30s, George Lewis. He played regularly with Lewis, helping to provide a steady foundation for the band that brought late fame to Lewis during the Revival. After leaving Lewis he worked mostly in his home-town, sometimes leading his own small band. A solid player with an ability to produce a clear, bell-like tone from his instrument, Marrero was a master of a tradition that faltered in the face of advances by the guitar.

● ALBUMS: with George Lewis *Ragtime Band* (Delmark 1953)★★★.

MARSALA, JOE

b. 4 January 1907, Chicago, Illinois, USA, d. 4 March 1978. After playing locally, Marsala's first name-band job was with Wingy Manone in 1929. In the early 30s he gigged in Chicago and elsewhere, returning several times to Manone, with whom he appeared at a number of leading New York nightspots. In 1935, he played and recorded with Adrian Rollini's Tap Room Gang before yet another spell with Manone, this time at the Hickory House. Taking over the band on Manone's departure in 1936, Marsala became one of the first bandleaders on 52nd Street to regularly front a racially mixed band, which included Red Allen. The Hickory House engagement was another long-running affair, extending into the mid-40s, but interspersed with leading bands on cruise ships he also briefly led a big band that played charts commissioned from Don Redman. In some of these bands, Marsala was joined by his brother, trumpeter Marty Marsala. In 1938, Marsala married harpist Adele Girard with whom he recorded and later collaborated on the composition of a number of songs, including such popular hits as 'Little Sir Echo' and 'Don't Cry, Joe'. During the early 40s, the bands Marsala led at the Hickory House included not only swing era veterans but also several younger musicians in transition to bebop and the mainstream, among them Buddy Rich,

Charlie Byrd and Shelly Manne. He was also instrumental in giving an early career boost to Frankie Laine. The Hickory House job finally ended in 1947; thereafter, Marsala redirected his career to songwriting and administrative work in music publishing and related businesses. During the 60s, he sometimes played on recording sessions, on one occasion teaming up with Bobby Hackett to accompany Tony Bennett. Although he deliberately ended his full-time playing career while still at his peak, Marsala left some very good recordings featuring his Jimmie Noone-inspired clarinet playing.

● COMPILATIONS: *Joe Marsala And His Orchestra Featuring Adele Girard* 1942 recording (Aircheck 1979)★★★, *Joe Marsala And His Band* 1944 recording (Jazzology 1986)★★★, *Hickory House Jazz* (Affinity 1991)★★★.

MARSALA, MARTY

b. Mario Salvatore Marsala, 2 April 1909, Chicago, Illinois, USA, d. 27 April 1975. As a young man Marsala first played drums but then switched to trumpet. He played this instrument in various bands in and around Chicago in the late 20s and early 30s. In the middle of the decade he came to New York to team up with his brother, Joe Marsala, who led a band there. With side visits to other bands, he stayed with his brother into the early 40s, then joined Chico Marx and also led a band of his own before military service intervened. After the war he was briefly back with his brother and also played in bands led by Miff Mole and others, but mainly led his own bands into the middle of the next decade. On the west coast he played occasionally with Kid Ory and Earl 'Fatha' Hines and also led his own bands through to the 60s. From this time onwards Marsala's career was constantly interrupted by illness. Marsala played with a rich, gutsy tone, delivering pungent solos with wit and fire. His long periods spent in Chicago and San Francisco, allied to his latter-day poor health, kept him in undeserved obscurity.

● ALBUMS: with Earl 'Fatha' Hines *At The Club Hangover Vol. 5* (Storyville 1955)★★★.

MARSALIS, BRANFORD

b. 26 August 1960, Breaux Bridge, Louisiana, USA. With their father, Ellis Marsalis, a bop pianist, composer and teacher, it is not surprising that his sons Branford, Delfeayo and Wynton Marsalis all took up music in childhood. Branford Marsalis's first instrument was the alto saxophone, which he played during his formative years and while studying at Berklee College Of Music. In 1981, he played in Art Blakey's Jazz Messengers and the following year began a spell with a small band led by Wynton. During this period Marsalis switched instruments, taking up both soprano and tenor saxophones. He also played on record dates with leading jazzmen such as Miles Davis and Dizzy Gillespie. After three years in his brother's band, he began a period of musical searching. Like many young musicians of his era, Marsalis often played in jazz-rock bands, including that led by Sting. He also formed his own small group with which he toured and recorded. By the late 80s he had established a reputation as a leading post-bop jazz saxophonist, but also enjoyed status in fusion and even classical circles (*Romances For Saxophone*). Marsalis drew early inspiration from the work John Coltrane, Ben Webster, Wayne Shorter, Ornette Coleman and especially Sonny Rollins. In some of his recordings these influences have surfaced, leading to criticisms that he has failed to develop a personal style. Closer attention reveals that these stylistic acknowledgements are merely that and not an integral part of his musical make-up. His recent work, including 1993's *I Heard You Twice The First Time* and 1997's *The Dark Keys*, has shown a strong leaning towards the blues, with both John Lee Hooker and B.B. King featured on the former. Perhaps of more significance to Marsalis's development as a musician is the fact that his career appears fated to be constantly compared to and contrasted with that of his virtuoso brother Wynton. This has often resulted in his being overshadowed, which is unfortunate because Branford Marsalis had proved himself to be an inventive soloist with considerable warmth. His best work contains many moments of powerful emotional commitment. In the mid-90s he relocated to Hollywood for a spell on Jay Leno's *The Tonight Show*.

● ALBUMS: *Scenes In The City* (Columbia 1983)★★★★, with Dizzy Gillespie *New Faces* (1984)★★★, with Wynton Marsalis *Black Codes (From The Underground)* (Columbia 1985)★★★, with Sting *Bring On The Night* (A&M 1986)★★★, *Royal Garden Blues* (Columbia 1986)★★★, *Random Abstract* (Columbia 1987)★★★★, *Renaissance* (Columbia 1987)★★★, *Trio Jeepy* (Columbia 1988)★★★★, *Crazy People Music* (Columbia 1990)★★★★, *The Beautyful Ones Are Not Yet Born* (Columbia 1992)★★★★, *I Heard You Twice The First Time* (Columbia 1993)★★★, *Bloomington* (Columbia 1993)★★★, *Spike Lee's Mo Better Blues* (1993)★★★, *Buckshot La Fonque* (Columbia 1994)★★★★, with Ellis Marsalis *Loved Ones* (Columbia 1996)★★★, *The Dark Keys* (Columbia 1996)★★★★.

● VIDEOS: *Steep* (1989), *The Music Tells You* (1993).

MARSALIS, DELFEAYO

b. *c.*1963, New Orleans, Louisiana, USA. The third of four musician sons of pianist Ellis Marsalis, he began studying trombone when he was 12 years old, then went to Berklee College Of Music. His professional career as a performer was delayed because he took up record production, working on albums by his father, his brothers Wynton and Branford Marsalis and Courtney Pine. An eclectic taste incorporates classical music and many areas of jazz. While he has expressed admiration for trombonists Tommy Dorsey and Jack Teagarden, his instrumental idol is J.J. Johnson. Marsalis's playing experience has all been at a very high level, including spells with bands led by Ray Charles, Fats Domino, Abdullah Ibrahim and Art Blakey. As he explained to Derek Ansell in an interview for *Jazz Journal International*, he is eager to develop his own playing style and to expand his own career which has hitherto been overshadowed by his more famous brothers.

● ALBUMS: *Pontius Pilate's Decision* (RCA Novus 1992)★★★, *Musashi* (Evidence 1997)★★★.

MARSALIS, ELLIS

b. 14 November, 1934, New Orleans, Louisiana, USA. Although he has never really been a revolutionary band-leader or pianist, Ellis Marsalis's influence on the American mainstream jazz scene cannot be overestimated. As an inspirational figure to a new generation of artists, and an educator and spokesman, this New Orleans-born pianist is unrivalled. Marsalis's professional music career began on tenor saxophone while still in high school, but he changed to piano a few years later, performing with such New Orleans-based modern jazz luminaries as clarinettist Alvin Batiste and drummer Ed Blackwell. He spent a brief spell on the west coast (he accompanied Blackwell out there, who was going out to meet up with Ornette Coleman), before signing up for military service with the marines in the mid-50s. His musical career was hardly interrupted by the services, and he soon found himself accompanying singers on CBS television, on the marine-sponsored *Dress Blues* show. Back in New Orleans during the early 60s, Marsalis's reputation as a sensitive and versatile accompanist led to a job fronting the house trio at the Playboy Club, where he accompanied star vocalists such as Ernestine Anderson and Jimmy Rushing. He joined trumpeter Al Hirt's showboating trad band during the late 60s, and appeared with the group on many popular American television shows, before leaving to join Bob French's Storyville Jazz Band in 1970, continuing the all-round jazz education and understanding that has made him such a unique figure on the current scene. He went on to lead his own highly successful modern jazz band with drummer James Black, enjoying a residency at one of New Orleans' premier jazz clubs for a year and a half. In the mid-70s, Marsalis began to turn his attention towards furthering his involvement in education. He had been teaching since the mid-50s, but now he began working in earnest on a jazz curriculum, and was taken on by the New Orleans Centre for the Creative Arts (NOCCA) in 1975. As a teacher, Marsalis's students have included many of the new generation of New Orleans-based modern jazz stars, including Victor Goines (saxophone), Reginald Veal (bass), Kent Jordan (flute), Terence Blanchard (trumpet), Harry Connick Jnr. (piano/vocals) and, of course, his progeny Wynton Marsalis (trumpet), Branford Marsalis (saxophones), Delfeayo Marsalis (trombone) and Jason Marsalis (drums), who have affected the US jazz scene permanently, with their emphasis on craftsmanship and learning. Ellis Marsalis is head of jazz studies at the University of New Orleans and a panellist, grant evaluator and board member for the National Endowment for the Arts and the Southern Arts Federation.

● ALBUMS: *Piano In E* (Rounder 1984)★★★, *Ellis Marsalis Trio* (Blue Note 1990)★★★★, *Heart Of Gold* (Columbia 1991)★★★, *The Classic Marsalis* (Boplicity 1993)★★★★, with Wynton Marsalis *Joe Cool's Blues* (Columbia 1995)★★★, *A Night At Snug Harbor, New Orleans* (Evidence 1995)★★★★, with Branford Marsalis *Loved Ones* (Columbia 1996)★★★, *Twelve's It* (Columbia 1998)★★★.

MARSALIS, WYNTON

b. 18 October 1961, New Orleans, Louisiana, USA. Marsalis took up the trumpet at the age of six, encouraged by his father, Ellis Marsalis, a pianist, composer and teacher. His brothers, Delfeayo and Branford Marsalis are also musicians. Before entering his teenage years he was already studying formally, but had simultaneously developed an interest in jazz. The range of his playing included performing with a New Orleans marching band led by Danny Barker, and playing trumpet concertos with the New Orleans Philharmonic Orchestra. Marsalis later extended his studies at two of the USA's most prestigious musical education establishments, Berkshire Music Center at Tanglewood and the Juilliard School of Music in New York City. By the age of 19, he was already a virtuoso trumpeter, a voracious student of jazz music, history and culture, and clearly destined for great things. It was then that he joined Art Blakey's Jazz Messengers, perhaps the best of all finishing schools for post-bop jazzmen. During the next two years he matured considerably as a player, touring and recording with Blakey and also with other leading jazzmen, including Herbie Hancock and Ron Carter. He also made records under his own name and, encouraged by his success, decided to form his own permanent group. In this he was joined by his brother Branford. During 1983, he again worked with Hancock. The following year he recorded in London with Raymond Leppard and the National Philharmonic Orchestra, playing concertos by Haydn, Hummell and Leopold Mozart - a side-step that led to his becoming the unprecedented recipient of Grammy Awards for both jazz and classical albums. He next toured Japan and Europe, appearing at many festivals, on television and making many recording sessions. By 1991, and still only just turned 30, he had become one of the best-known figures on the international musical stage. Insofar as his classical work is concerned, Marsalis has been spoken of in most glowing terms. In his jazz work his sublime technical ability places him on a plateau he shares with very few others. Nevertheless, despite such extraordinary virtuosity, the emotional content of Marsalis's work often hints only lightly at the possibilities inherent in jazz. Sometimes, the undeniable skill and craftsmanship are displayed at the expense of vitality. If compared to, for instance, Jon Faddis, eight years his senior, or Clifford Brown, who died at the age of only 26, then there is clearly some distance to go in his development as a player of emotional profundity.

● ALBUMS: with Art Blakey *Recorded Live At Bubba's* (1980)★★★, with Blakey *Straight Ahead* (1981)★★★, *Wynton Marsalis* (Columbia 1981)★★★★, *Think Of One* (Columbia 1982)★★★★, with Branford and Ellis Marsalis *Fathers And Sons* (Columbia 1982)★★★, with Blakey *Keystone 3* (1982)★★★, *Think Of Me* (Columbnia 1983)★★★, *Hot House Flowers* (Columbia 1984)★★★★, *Black Codes (From The Underground)* (Columbia 1985)★★★★, *J Mood* (Columbia 1986)★★★★, *Live At Blues Alley* (Columbia 1987)★★★★, *Marsalis Standard Time* (Columbia 1987)★★★★, *The Majesty Of The Blues* (Columbia

1988)★★★, *Crescent City Christmas Card* (1989)★★★, *Marsalis Standard Time Volume 2* (Columbia 1991)★★★, *Marsalis Standard Time Volume 3* (Columbia 1991)★★★, *Thick In The South* (Columbia 1991)★★★, *Uptown Ruler* (Columbia 1991)★★★, *Levee Low Moan* (Columbia 1991)★★★, *Tune In Tomorrow* (Columbia 1991)★★★, *Blue Interlude* (Columbia 1992)★★★, *Citi Movement* 2-CD set (Columbia 1993)★★★, *Resolution To Swing* (Columbia 1993)★★★, *In This House, On This Morning* (Columbia 1994)★★★, with the Lincoln Center Jazz Orchestra *Blood On The Fields* (Columbia 1997)★★★★, *Jump Start & Jazz* (Sony Classical 1997)★★★★, *The Midnight Blues Standard Time Vol. 5* (Columbia 1998)★★★.

● VIDEOS: *The London Concert* (Sony Classical 1994), *Marsalis On Music* (Sony 1995).

MARSH, TINA

b. USA. Based in Texas, Marsh is often associated with a contemporary big band, the Creative Opportunity Orchestra, which was formed in 1979 and which records in Austin. In addition to singing with the band, she also composes original material and is responsible for many of their adventurous arrangements.

● ALBUMS: *Songs And Moments* (1994)★★★.

MARSH, WARNE

b. 26 October 1927, Los Angeles, California, USA, d. 18 December 1987, Los Angeles, California, USA. Tenor saxophonist Marsh first played professionally in the early 40s with the Hollywood Canteen Kids, later working with Hoagy Carmichael's Teenagers. By the end of the decade, he had spent time in Buddy Rich's band and had also begun an important association as student and sideman of Lennie Tristano. In the late 40s and early 50s, he made a number of milestone recordings with temporary musical partners such as Lee Konitz, among them 'Wow', 'Crosscurrent' and 'Marshmallow'. The 50s and 60s saw Marsh active mainly in teaching and there were only occasional forays into playing and recording with, among others, Art Pepper and Joe Albany. In the 70s he became rather more prominent, working with Supersax, Lew Tabackin and Konitz. He also toured overseas, attracting considerable attention from the more discerning members of his audiences as well as from among his fellow musicians who held him in highest regard. Also in the 70s, he recorded rather more extensively, including material from an especially successful engagement in London with Konitz. A meticulously accurate yet free-flowing improviser, Marsh was comfortable in most bebop-orientated settings. His ballad playing was especially attractive, replete with clean and highly individual phrasing which constantly and consistently demonstrated his total command of instrument and genre. He died onstage at Donte's, a Los Angeles jazz club, in December 1987.

● ALBUMS: *Live In Hollywood* (Xanadu 1952)★★, with Lee Konitz *Lee Konitz With Warne Marsh* (Atlantic 1955)★★★, *Jazz Of Two Cities* (Imperial 1956)★★★, *Winds Of Marsh* (Imperial 1956)★★★, with Art Pepper *The Way It Was!* (1957)★★★★, *Music For Prancing* (Mode 1957)★★★★, *Warne Marsh* (Atlantic 1958)★★★, *The Art Of Improvising Vols 1 & 2* (Revelation 1959)★★★★, *Jazz From The East Village* (Wave 1960)★★★, *Live At The Montmartre Club* (Storyville 1965)★★, *Ne Plus Ultra* (hatART 1969)★★★, *Warne Marsh Quintet* (Storyville 1975)★★★, *All Music* (Nessa 1976)★★★, with Konitz *Warne Marsh & Lee Konitz (Live At Club Montmartre)* (Storyville 1976)★★★, with Lew Tabackin *Tenor Gladness* (1977)★★★, *Warne Out* (1977)★★★, *How Deep/How High* (Discovery 1979)★★★, *Star Highs* (Criss Cross 1982)★★★, *A Ballad Album* (Criss Cross 1983)★★★★, *In Norway/Sax Of A Kind* (1983)★★★, *Posthumous* (Interplay 1985)★★★, *Back Home* (Criss Cross 1986)★★★, *Two Days In The Life Of...* (Storyville 1987)★★, *Music For Prancing* (Criss Cross 1988)★★★, *Noteworth* (Discovery 1988)★★★, *For The Time Being* (1987)★★★, *Newly Warne* (Storyville 1990)★★★.

● COMPILATIONS: with Lee Konitz, Lennie Tristano *The Complete Atlantic Recordings Of Lennie Tristano, Lee Konitz & Warne Marsh* 6-CD box set (Mosaic 1997)★★★★.

MARSHALL, JOHN

b. 28 August 1941, London, England. Marshall is one of the most impressive drummers Britain has produced, equally powerful, flexible and reliable in rock, jazz or fusion. He played at school, but became more heavily involved with music while reading psychology at university. He studied drums privately with Allan Ganley and Philly Joe Jones, and worked with Alexis Korner's Blues Incorporated (1964), Graham Collier (1965-70), Nucleus (of which he was a founder-member with Ian Carr in 1969, and to which he returned in 1982), Mike Gibbs, Jack Bruce (1971-72), and, in February 1972, he began his long-term membership of Soft Machine. On leaving the band he joined Eberhard Weber's Colours (1977-81). He has been a regular associate of John Surman over many years, and has also worked with Michael Garrick, Keith Tippett, Chris McGregor, John McLaughlin, John Taylor, Graham Bond, Mike Westbrook, Tubby Hayes, Jaspar Van't Hof, Kenny Wheeler, Gil Evans, Alan Skidmore, Ronnie Scott and many others, including those in the contemporary classical field and in session work.

MARSHALL, KAISER

b. Joseph Marshall, 11 June 1899, Savannah, Georgia, USA, d. 3 January 1948. While he was still a child Marshall's family moved to Boston, Massachusetts, where he began playing drums, tutored by George L. Stone. In 1923, by now in New York, he joined Fletcher Henderson's band during its rise to fame and prominence but left in 1930 just as Henderson entered his headiest period. In the late 20s, Marshall made some landmark recordings with Louis Armstrong's small studio groups. A solid reliable drummer, in the late 30s and early 40s he found regular work, playing and recording with many leading figures of the jazz world including Duke Ellington, Cab Calloway, Wild Bill Davison, Art Hodes, Sidney Bechet and Bunk Johnson. Marshall's work was sufficiently highly regarded for him to be called upon to deputize for Chick Webb when the more famous drummer was too sick to play all night with his own band.

MARSHALL, WENDELL

b. 24 October 1920, St. Louis, Missouri, USA. He took up the bass thanks to the example of his cousin, Jimmy Blanton, who was also his first tutor. Although Marshall played regularly in his younger years, including brief stints with Lionel Hampton, Stuff Smith and others, he did not fully enter the big-time until the late 40s when he moved to New York. Briefly with Mercer Ellington, he joined Duke Ellington in 1948 with whom he remained until 1955. During the rest of the 50s he worked with many important jazz artists including Carmen McRae, Hank Jones and Art Blakey. By the end of the decade, however, he was turning more and more to work in New York theatre pit bands where he remained until his retirement from regular playing in the late 60s. A gifted soloist with a full tone, Marshall's solid rhythmic playing and adaptable style made him a valuable member of any band in which he played.

● ALBUMS: with Duke Ellington *Seattle Concert* (1952)★★★, *Duke Ellington Plays Duke Ellington* (1953)★★★★, *Wendell Marshall With The Billy Byers Orchestra* (1955)★★★, with Mary Lou Williams *A Keyboard History* (1955)★★★, with Carmen McRae *By Special Request* (1955)★★★.

MARTERIE, RALPH

b. Ralph Martin, 24 December 1914, Accerra, near Naples, Italy, d. 10 October 1978, Dayton, Ohio, USA. While Marterie was still a child his parents emigrated to the USA, where his father joined the orchestra of the Chicago Civic Opera. Ralph was still a teenager when he started playing trumpet with Dan Russo's Otriole Orchestra. He went on to play in local theatres and with other bands in Chicago, which was at that time the country's largest musical centre outside New York. Consequently, Marterie never had to leave the city to find work, joining the NBC staff orchestra where he played under conductors such as Percy Faith and André Kostelanetz. During World War II Marterie led a US Navy band, then after the war he returned to Chicago as a leader with ABC radio. In 1949 he started recording for Mercury with his own band, which featured his brassy open trumpet. He did not achieve instant success but in 1952 the band spent 10 weeks in the US charts with 'Caravan', earning a second Gold Disc the following year with 'Pretend'. His album and singles output varied between swing standards, novelties and pop instrumentals that highlighted his trademark of trumpet and guitar voiced together (compare his temporary partnership with guitarist/musical director Al Caiola on a cover version of 'Acapulco 22'). There were moderate hits with 'Guaglione', 'Skokiaan' and 'Tequila', which were successful enough to maintain his reputation and keep him working through changing fashions in pop music. Marterie was still touring with a band until his death in Dayton, where he had just played a one-nighter in October 1978.

MARTIN, ANDY

b. 10 August 1960, Provo, Utah, USA. Martin was born into a highly musical family in which his father played trumpet and two brothers, Stan and Scott, played trumpet and saxophones respectively. He took up the trombone and while still a youth with his siblings formed a band, the Martin Brothers. At Golden West College he studied with saxophonist-bandleader Tom Kubis and he also attended California State University, Long Beach. His professional career began in earnest playing in a dixieland band at Disneyland, and at 18 he recorded with Dick Berk and two years later toured with Lou Rawls. Two years after that he was regularly playing with Los Angeles big bands, and he also toured with various artists including Paul Anka, Poncho Sanchez, Joe Walsh and Les Brown. By the start of the 90s he was in demand as a concert and recording artist by many bandleaders, including Vic Lewis, Dave Grusin, Horace Silver, Clare Fischer, Louie Bellson, Jack Sheldon, Frank Capp, Matt Catingub, Bill Berry and Bill Holman, appearing on the latter's late-90s releases, *A View From The Side* and *Brilliant Corners*. He also appeared with pop artists such as Prince, Neil Diamond and Lionel Richie. An immensely talented musician with a remarkable technique, a flowing style and an abundance of creative ideas, Martin is one of the outstanding trombone talents of his generation. However, he has never allowed his technical mastery and intellectual commitment to overpower the emotional expressiveness that marks all great jazz musicians. At the end of the 90s, with his reputation spreading around the world, he is one of the artists best placed to carry the creative flame of jazz into the new century.

● ALBUMS: *Andy Martin With The Metropole Orchestra* (Mons 1996)★★★★, *Andy Martin Leading Off* (RM 1998)★★★★, *Bill Liston-Andy Martin Express: Walkin' The Walk* (Chartmaker 1998)★★★, *Pete Christlieb-Andy Martin* (Woofy 1999)★★★, *Carl Fontana-Andy Martin* (Woofy 1999)★★★.

MARTIN, CLAIRE

b. 6 September 1967, Wimbledon, London, England. In 1982, after spending 10 years at stage school, Martin became resident singer at the Savoy Hotel in Bournemouth. In 1987 she sang on cruise liners for Cunard, including the *QE2*. In 1990 she visited the USA where she studied with Marilyn J. Johnson in New York. In 1991 she returned to the UK to form her own band, playing many prestigious London jazz venues including Ronnie Scott's, the 100 Club and the Pizza On The Park, and also toured extensively. In 1992 she played a return engagement at Ronnie Scott's and also appeared at the Glasgow and Sheffield Jazz Festivals. In addition to leading her own band, Martin also works regularly with Mick Hutton's group, Straight Face, which includes Steve Argüelles and Iain Ballamy, with Ray Gelato's Giants Of Jive, and with a free-music band led by John Stevens. She has also recorded with Bobby Wellins. A remarkably versatile singer, Martin's repertoire ranges happily from R&B to free music, incorporating along the way the great standards of which she is an accomplished interpreter. Despite her youth, Martin's work displays exceptional maturity which, allied to her warm, sensual sound, makes her performances a constant delight. Her choice of musical associates (her own group comprises pianist Jonathan Gee, bassist Arnie Somogyi and Clark Tracey) reveals her commitment to jazz. Although still at the beginning of her career, Martin has already made it clear that she is one of the most important new singers to emerge on the jazz scene in recent years.

● ALBUMS: *The Waiting Game* (Linn 1991)★★, with Bobby Wellins *Remember Me* (1992)★★★, *Devil May Care* (Linn 1993)★★★, *Old Boyfriends* (Linn 1994)★★★★, *Offbeat* (Linn 1996)★★★, *Make This City Ours* (Honest 1998)★★★★.

Martino, Pat

b. Pat Azzara, 25 April 1944, Philadelphia, Pennsylvania, USA. Martino's singer father encouraged him to play guitar and he received some instruction from his cousin. He was a professional guitarist by the age of 15, playing with saxophonists Gator Jackson and Red Holloway. He played in all the leading organ combos of the 60s: with Don Patterson, Jimmy Smith, Brother Jack McDuff, Richard 'Groove' Holmes and Jimmy McGriff. In 1966, after four months with Sonny Stitt's band, he worked with John Handy's rather more *avant garde* quintet. In the late 60s, Martino had his own bands with Cedar Walton, Richard Davis (bass) and Billy Hart. The main influences on Martino were Wes Montgomery and eastern music, but during the 70s he became interested in the music of composers such as Stockhausen and Elliott Carter (he also taught and published a book called *Linear Expressions* with T. Baruso in 1983). He also formed the fusion group Joyous Lake, featuring keyboardist Delmar Brown and drummer Kenwood Dennard, who recorded an eponymous album in 1976. Martino suffered a seizure in 1980 which led to a temporary loss of memory, but he recovered and returned to playing in 1984, although he did not record again until 1987's *The Return*. He has since released several albums, including 1997's guitar showcase *All Sides Now*, which matched Martino with fellow players Charlie Hunter and Joe Satriani. The following year Martino teamed up with Brown and Dennard in a resurrected Joyous Lake. Martino's playing is characterized by fleet fingerwork and virtuoso flourishes, while his improvisations involve passages in octaves like Wes Montgomery, and are often influenced by his choice of the 12-string guitar. The trick of his dark and chunky sound is that he tunes the treble strings down and the bass strings up.

● ALBUMS: *El Hombre* (Fantasy 1966)★★★, *Strings* (Fantasy 1967)★★★, *East!* (Fantasy 1968)★★★★, *Baiyina (The Clear Evidence)* (Fantasy 1968)★★★, *Desperado* (Fantasy 1970)★★★★, *Footprints* (Cobblestone 1972)★★★★, *Exit* (Muse 1972)★★★, *Consciousness* (Muse 1974)★★★, *Exit* (Muse 1976)★★★, *We'll Be Together Again* (Muse 1976)★★★, *Starbright* (Warners 1976)★★, with Joyous Lake *Joyous Lake* (Warners 1976)★★★, *The Return* (Muse 1987)★★★, *The Maker* (Evidence 1994)★★★, *All Sides Now* (Blue Note 1997)★★★★, with Joyous Lake *Stone Blue* (Blue Note 1998)★★★★, *Firedance* (Mythos 1998)★★★.

● COMPILATIONS: *Head And Heart* 70s recordings (32 1998)★★★.

Martyn, Barry

b. Barry Martin Godfrey, 23 February 1941, London, England. Martyn began playing drums in his early teens and was soon leading his own band and making records. Playing in the New Orleans tradition, Martyn's musical interest led him to visit New Orleans in the early 60s where he studied with Josiah 'Cié' Frazier. Martyn recorded in New Orleans with many leading local jazzmen and also organized and led international tours by major figures such as George Lewis and Albert Nicholas. Resident in the USA since the early 70s, Martyn has continued to play and record New Orleans jazz to a very high standard with the likes of Barney Bigard and the Eagle Brass Band. In addition to bands under his own name Martyn was also leader of the Legends Of Jazz, a group of elderly but still musically active New Orleans jazzmen. Deeply committed to preserving the great tradition of New Orleans jazz, over the years Martyn has done much more than play and record. He formed his own recording company, writes extensively, and, perhaps most importantly, has recorded for archive purposes numerous interviews with New Orleans jazz survivors.

● ALBUMS: *Barney Bigard And The Pelican Trio* (1976)★★★, with the Eagle Brass Band *Last Of The Line* (1983)★★.

Masekela, Hugh

b. Hugh Rampolo Masekela, 4 April 1939, Witbank, Johannesburg, South Africa. South Africa's leading *émigré* trumpeter and bandleader was born into a musical family which boasted one of the largest jazz record collections in the city. One of Masekela's earliest memories is of winding up the household gramophone for his parents; by the age of 10, he was familiar with most of the 78s issued by Duke Ellington, Count Basie, Cab Calloway and Glenn Miller. Other early influences were the traditional musics of the Swazis, Zulus, Sutus and Shangaan, all of which he heard at weekend musical gatherings in the township and neighbouring countryside. A difficult and rebellious schoolboy, Masekela was frequently given to playing truant. On one such occasion, he saw Kirk Douglas in the Bix Beiderbecke biopic *Young Man With A Horn* - and decided there and then that he wanted to become a trumpeter and bandleader when he grew up. His teacher, the anti-apartheid activist and Anglican priest Trevor Huddlestone, welcomed this enthusiasm and gave Masekela his first trumpet, a battered old instrument owned by a local bandleader. A year later, in 1955, Huddlestone was expelled from South Africa. In New York, he met Louis Armstrong, and enthused to him about Masekela's talents and persuaded Armstrong to send a trumpet over to Johannesburg for the boy. With trombonist Jonas Gwangwa, Masekela dropped out of school in 1955 to form his first group, the Merry Makers. His main influences at this time were the African-American bop trumpeters Dizzy Gillespie and Clifford Brown and by 1956, the Merry Makers were playing nothing but bop. By 1958, apartheid had tightened up to the extent that it was very difficult for black bands to make a living - they were banned from the government-controlled radio and were not allowed to travel freely from one town to another. Masekela was obliged to leave the Merry Makers and join the African Jazz and Variety package tour (which also included his future wife, Miriam Makeba). Operated by a white man, Alfred Herbert, the troupe was able to circumvent some of the travel restrictions imposed on blacks and continued to tour the country. In 1959, with Makeba, Masekela left Herbert to join the cast of the 'township musical', *King Kong.* The same year, he formed the pioneering band, the Jazz Epistles, with Gwangwa and pianist Dollar Brand (now Abdullah Ibrahim). They became the first black band in South Africa to record an album, all previous releases having been 78s.

In 1960, the year of the Sharpeville massacre, the government extended the Group Areas Act to ban black musicians from working in inner city (that is, white) clubs. The move effectively ended the Jazz Epistles' ability to make a living, and Masekela decided the time had come to emigrate to the USA. With the help of Trevor Huddlestone and Harry Belafonte in New York, he obtained a passport and, after a brief period in London at the Guildhall School of Music, won a scholarship to New York's Manhattan School of Music. Initially aspiring to become a sideman with Art Blakey, Masekela was instead persuaded by the drummer to form his own band, and put together a quartet which debuted at the Village Gate club in 1961. A year later, he recorded his first album, *Trumpet Africa,* a considerable critical success. In 1964, Masekela married Miriam Makeba, another of Belafonte's protégées (who divorced him a few years later to marry Black Panther activist Stokeley Carmichael). Continuing to lead his own band, Masekela also wrote arrangements for Makeba and toured with her backing group. Husband and wife became prominent critics of the South African regime, and donated part of their touring income to fund scholarships that enabled black musicians to leave South Africa. In 1964, Masekela also released his second solo album, *The Americanization Of Ooga Booga,* and appeared at the first Watts, Los Angeles, California Jazz Festival. In 1966, he linked up with old Manhattan School of Music classmate Stewart Levine to form the production company Chisa. The original idea was for Levine to be the artist and Masekela the producer, but the success of Chisa's debut release, an album called *The Emancipation Of Hugh Masekela,* led to a role-reversal. (The Levine-Masekela partnership continued throughout the 60s, 70s and 80s.)

In 1967, Masekela appeared at the legendary Monterey Jazz Festival and released two more albums, *Promise Of A Future* and *Coincidence*. Unable to find top-quality South African musicians with whom to work in the USA, Masekela became drawn into the lucrative area of lightweight jazz/pop. His first chart success in the genre was an instrumental version of 'Up Up And Away' in 1967, which reached number 71 in the US charts. In 1968, he had a number 1 hit with 'Grazin' In The Grass', selling four million copies. The follow-up, 'Puffin' On Down The Track', disappointingly only reached number 71. Not surprisingly, given the mood of the times, the latter two singles were widely perceived to carry pro-marijuana statements in their titles and, in autumn 1968, Masekela was arrested at his home in Malibu and charged with possession of the drug. Despite the urging of the record business, Masekela refused to capitalize on the success of 'Grazin' In The Grass' with a lightweight album in the same vein, and instead recorded the protest album *Masekela,* which included track titles such as 'Fuzz' and 'Riot'.

In 1970, Masekela signed with Motown Records, who released the album *Reconstruction.* Also that year, he formed the Union of South Africa band with fellow *émigrés* Gwangwa and Caiphus Semenya. The band was short-lived, however, following the lengthy hospitalization of Gwangwa from injuries sustained in a car crash. Frustrated in his attempt to launch an American-based, South African line-up, Masekela visited London to record the album *Home Is Where The Music Is* with exiled South African saxophonist Dudu Pukwana. Deciding to reimmerse himself in his African roots, Masekela set off in late 1972 on a 'pilgrimage' to Senegal, Liberia, Zaire and other countries. He worked for a year in Guinea (where his ex-wife Makeba was now living) as a music teacher, and spent some months in Lagos, Nigeria, playing in Fela Anikulapo Kuti's band. He finally ended up in Ghana, where he joined the young highlife-meets-funk band Hedzolleh Soundz. Between 1974 and 1976, Masekela released five albums with the group - *Your Mama Told You Not To Worry, I Am Not Afraid, The Boys Doin' It, The African Connection* and *Colonial Man.* By 1975, however, leader and band had fallen out, with Hedzolleh accusing Masekela of financial mistreatment. In fact, the cost of supporting Hedzolleh in the USA during loss-making tours had drained Masekela's resources, and in 1976, he and Levine were obliged to wind up Chisa. Short of money, Masekela signed to A&M Records, where he recorded two lightweight albums with label boss Herb Alpert - *The Main Event* and *Herb Alpert/Hugh Masekela.*

In 1980, with Makeba, Masekela headlined a massive Goin' Home outdoor concert in Lesotho. In 1982, in a similar venture, they appeared in neighbouring Botswana. Both concerts were attended by large numbers of black and white South Africans, who gave the duo heroes' welcomes. Masekela decided to settle in Botswana, 20 miles from the South African border, and signed to the UK label Jive, who flew over to him in a state-of-the-art mobile studio. The sessions resulted in the albums *Technobush* and *Waiting For The Rain.* In 1983, he made his first live appearance in London for over 20 years, at the African Sounds for Mandela concert at Alexandra Palace. In 1986, Masekela severed his links with Jive and returned to the USA, where he signed with Warner Brothers Records, releasing the album *Tomorrow*, and joining label-mate Paul Simon's Graceland world tour. In 1989, he co-wrote the music for the Broadway show *Sarafina*, set in a Soweto school during a state of emergency, and released the album *Up Township*.

● ALBUMS: *Jazz Epistles* (1959)★★★, *Trumpet Afnca* (1962)★★★★, *The Americanization Of Ooga Booga* (1964)★★★, *The Emancipation Of Hugh Masekela* (1966)★★★, *Promise Of A Future* (1967)★★★, *Coincidence* (1967)★★★, *Hugh Masekela* (Fontana 1968)★★★, *Alive And Well At The Whiskey* (Uni 1968)★★★, *Reconstruction* (Motown 1970)★★★, *And The Union Of South Africa* (Rare Earth 1971)★★★, with Dudu Pukwana *Home Is Where The Music Is* (1972)★★★★, Your *Mama Told You Not To Worry* (1974)★★★, *I Am Not Afraid* (1974)★★★, *The Boys Doin' It* (1975)★★★, *The African Connection* (1975)★★★, *Colonial Man* (1976)★★★, with Herb Alpert *The Main Event* (A&M 1978)★★, *Herb Alpert/Hugh Masekela* (A&M 1979)★★, *Home* (1982)★★★, *Dollar Bill* (1983)★★★, *Technobush* (Jive 1984)★★★, *Waiting For The Rain* (Jive 1985)★★★, *Tomorrow* (Warners 1987)★★★, *Up Township* (Novus 1989)★★★, *Hope* (Triloka 1994)★★★, *Notes Of Life* (Sony 1996)★★★, *Black To The Future* (Columbia 1997)★★★★.

● COMPILATIONS: *Liberation* (Jive 1988)★★★.

● VIDEOS: *Notice To Quit (A Portrait Of South Africa)* (Hendring 1986), *Vukani* (BMG 1990).

Maslak, Keshavan

b. 26 February 1947, Detroit, Michigan, USA, into a Ukrainian family. As a child, Keshavan 'spoke Ukrainian around the house, and Russian and Polish to the neighbours' and was regularly beaten up by his all-American contemporaries at elementary school for being different. He started playing saxophone at the age of eight. An early enthusiasm for polkas and mazurkas was soon replaced by an obsession with John Coltrane's music, and some of Coltrane's yearning, burning passions infuse Maslak's best work (e.g., *Big Time*). The saxophonist has been a stylistic jack-of-all-trades, having performed with Philip Glass, the Temptations, and Sam Rivers, and rechristening himself Kenny Millions in a futile attempt to crack the punk/rock market. He has toured and performed extensively in Eastern Europe and Russia: 'I'm like Mick Jagger over there, I'm telling you.'

● ALBUMS: *Buddha's Hand* (1979)★★, *Maslak One Thousand* (1979)★★, *Mayhem In Our Streets* (1980)★★, *Humanplexity* (Leo 1980)★★★, *Loved By Millions* (Leo 1981)★★★, with Charles Moffett *Blaster Master* (Black Saint 1981)★★★, *Big Time* (Affinity 1981)★★★★, *Better And Better* (Leo 1987), *Get The Money Whatever It Takes* (Leo 1990)★★★, *Mother Russia* (Leo 1990)★★★, with Paul Bley *Not To Be A Star* (Black Saint 1993)★★★, with Bley *Romance In The City* (Leo 1993)★★★★, Excuse Me Mr Satie (Leo 1995)★★★.

Mason, Harvey

b. 22 February 1947, Atlantic City, New Jersey, USA. Mason began playing the drums when he was four years old. He studied at the Berklee College Of Music in Boston and later gained a degree in education at New England Conservatory. He worked with pianists Errol Garner, George Shearing and Jan Hammer before moving to Los Angeles in 1971, where he worked as a studio musician covering music such as jazz, pop/rock and orchestral. He played with a wide range of bandleaders and musicians, including Duke Ellington, Quincy Jones, Gunther Schuller, Donald Byrd, Gerry Mulligan, Grover Washington, George Benson and Lee Ritenour. His clear, strong rhythm playing was perfect for Herbie Hancock's *Headhunters* in 1973, which also highlighted several of Mason's expert arrangements. He is now drummer of the highly successful fusion group Fourplay.

● ALBUMS: *World Class* (1981)★★★, *Ratamacue* (Atlantic 1996)★★★.

Mason, Rod

b. 28 September 1940, Plymouth, Devon, England. Mason worked first in 1959 with Cy Laurie before spending four years (1962-66) with the band of Monty Sunshine. When he contracted Bell's palsy, he had to adjust his embouchure which, fortunately for him, improved his range. In 1970, he joined Acker Bilk's band, but in the late 70s, was leading his own ensemble and playing all over Europe. He spent some time with the Dutch Swing College Band in the early 80s, but resumed leading his own outfit in 1985. His wide range and exceptional stamina make him a natural lead trumpeter who seems effortlessly to recreate the sound of Louis Armstrong in the 30s.

● ALBUMS: *Rod Mason/Ian Wheeler Band* (1974)★★★, *Great Having You Around* (1978)★★★, *Six For Two* (1979)★★★.

Massey, Cal

b. 11 January 1928, Philadelphia, USA, d. 25 October 1972, New York City, New York, USA. Despite having played trumpet in the big bands of Jay McShann and Jimmy Heath, Massey's interests were firmly in the field of composition by the mid-50s. Between 1956 and 1958, he led a group of distinguished musicians, including McCoy Tyner, Jimmy Garrison, and Al Heath, playing solely his own compositions. His tunes have since been recorded by countless musicians from Philly Joe Jones to Archie Shepp. When he died, Massey had just completed a musical play about Billie Holiday.

● ALBUMS: compositions featured on John Coltrane *Coltrane* (1957)★★★★, Freddie Hubbard *Here To Stay* (1962)★★★★.

Masso, George

b. 17 November 1926, Cranston, Rhode Island, USA. Coming from a musical background, Masso began on trumpet, then became a competent multi-instrumentalist, playing piano and vibraphone. However, it was hearing a Lou McGarity trombone solo on Benny Goodman's recording of 'Yours' that determined his final choice of instrument. Despite his background, and a two-year stint with Jimmy Dorsey in the late 40s, Masso opted for a career as a teacher of music. In 1973, with his family grown up, he decided to return to playing after persistent needling from Bobby Hackett. He spent a year and a half with Goodman's Sextet, played with the World's Greatest Jazz Band and on some of Buck Clayton's later Jam Sessions. Since then, Masso has toured extensively, usually as a single, sometimes in harness with Scott Hamilton, Warren Vaché, Spike Robinson, Bobby Rosengarden and other mainstream artists, playing clubs and festivals around the world.

● ALBUMS: *Choice NYC 'Bone* (1978)★★★, *Dialogue At Condon's* (1979)★★★, *A Swinging Case Of Masso-Ism* (Famous Door 1980)★★★, *Pieces Of Eight* (Dreamstreet 1982)★★★★, *No Frills, Just Music* (Famous Door 1984)★★★, *Just For A Thrill* (Sackville 1990)★★★, *The Wonderful World Of George Gershwin* (Nagel-Heyer 1993)★★★★, with Dan Barrett *Let's Be Buddies* (Arbors 1994)★★★, *Trombone Artistry* (Nagel-Heyer 1995)★★★★, *That Old Gang Of Mine* (Arbors 1998)★★★, *Shakin' The Blues Away* 1995-1996 recordings (Zephyr 1998)★★★★.

MASTREN, CARMEN

b. Carmine Niccolo Mastandrea, 6 October 1913, Cohoes, New York, USA, d. 31 March 1981. As a child he learned to play violin before becoming adept on banjo and finally guitar. For several years he played in the family band alongside four musician brothers, the best-known being trombonist Al Mastren. In the early 30s he began to make a name for himself outside the family fold and by the middle of the decade was a mainstay of the Tommy Dorsey band. He stayed with Dorsey until 1940, along the way becoming a poll-topper in US music magazines, then joined Joe Marsala and also played in orchestras at NBC in New York. During military service in World War II he played in Glenn Miller's orchestra. In the late 40s he was on call in New York for session work, playing, conducting and arranging. In 1953 he returned to studio work at NBC, remaining there for almost 20 years. In later years he worked in jingle mills and also played with Dick Hyman's New York Jazz Repertory Company. In these years he also sometimes renewed his early acquaintance with the banjo, proving to be something of a virtuoso performer. As a guitarist, Mastren was a secure section player, his playing helping to provide the swinging bedrock of the Dorsey band and the Miller Army-Air Force band. When called upon to solo, as with the Sidney Bechet-Muggsy Spanier Big Four, he showed rich ideas, although often couched in the older tradition of the instrument.

● COMPILATIONS: *The Sidney Bechet - Muggsy Spanier Big Four: A Jam Session* (Swaggie 1940)★★★★.

MATERIAL

One of Bill Laswell's projects, Material was mixing jazz, funk and punk with hip-hop and scratch before the terms were invented; the result was stunning and powerful music. With a core membership comprising Michael Beinhorn, Fred Maher and Laswell, Material has also included Fred Frith, Sonny Sharrock, Shankar, George Lewis, Henry Threadgill and Olu Daru. Laswell and Beinhorn also recorded with Afrika Bambaataa as Shango, releasing the *Funk Thelogy* album in 1984. After a long hiatus in its career, Material reappeared in 1989 with *Seven Souls*, when it seemed to be evolving into a 'new age' band. However, on *Third Power*, Laswell assembled a new, back-on-the-block version that included Shabba Ranks, the Jungle Brothers, Herbie Hancock, Sly And Robbie and Fred Wesley.

● ALBUMS: *Temporary Music 1 & 2* aka *Secret Life* (1979)★★, *Memory Serves* (Restless/Metrotone 1981)★★★, *One Down* (Restless/Metrotone 1983)★★★, *Seven Souls* (Virgin 1989)★★, *Third Power* (Axiom 1991)★★★, *Hallucination Engine* (Axiom 1994)★★★.

● COMPILATIONS: *The Best Of Material* (Charly 1998)★★★.

MATHENY, DMITRI

b. *c.*1966, Nashville, Tennessee, USA. Based in San Francisco, California, USA, flügelhorn player Dmitri Matheny made his debut with the 1996 release of *Red Reflections*. Raised in Tucson, Arizona, Matheny was first drawn to jazz when he heard his father playing Miles Davis's *Kind Of Blue*. Inspired, Matheny took up the trumpet in an attempt to emulate his hero, but found the sound was too 'brash and edgy'. Eventually he chose the flügelhorn, preferring its warm, rich tones. He trained at the Interlochen (Michigan) Arts Academy and the Berklee College Of Music, alternating between flügelhorn and trumpet. When he came to write his own compositions, however, the flügelhorn proved more suited to the emotive textures he wished to produce. After training under Art Farmer, Matheny graduated from Berklee in 1989 and moved to San Francisco. There he formed the SOMA Ensemble, featuring John Heller (guitar), Rob Scheps (tenor saxophone), Bill Douglass (bass), Alan Jones (drums), Trevor Dunn (bass) and two members of the Charlie Hunter Trio, Scott Amdendola (drums) and Davis Ellis (tenor saxophone). All contributed to his 1996 debut album, *Red Reflections*, which included cover versions of Horace Silver's 'The Outlaws' and Michael Brecker's 'Take A Walk'. Matheny's own compositions included 'Myth Of The Rainy Night', part of a series of pieces concerning author Jack Kerouac, which Matheny described as a 'tone poem'.

● ALBUMS: *Red Reflections* (Monarch 1996)★★★, *Penumbra: The Moon Sessions* (Monarch 1997)★★★.

MATHEWS, MAT

b. Matthieu Schwartz, 18 June 1924, The Hague, The Netherlands. Mathews began playing accordion as a young man, establishing his name in his homeland before extending his reputation in the 50s in New York. However unlikely the concept might appear on paper, Mathews took the accordion into bop with remarkably effective results. His fellow musicians, with several of whom he recorded, included influential figures such as Kenny Clarke and Oscar Pettiford. He also accompanied singers including fellow-countrywoman Rita Reyes and Carmen McRae, appearing with her on 1955's Decca Records session *By Special Request*, leading a band with Clarke, Dick Katz, Wendell Marshall and Herbie Mann. He gained experience as a session musician and, when he returned to the Netherlands in the mid-60s, it was this aspect of his career that he pursued as both performer and arranger.

● ALBUMS: *Mat Mathews Quintet* (Brunswick 1953)★★★, *Accordion Solos* (Brunswick 1956)★★★, *The Modern Art Of Jazz By Mat Mathews* (Dawn 1956)★★★, *Bob Stewart Sings With The Mat Mathews Quintet* 1956 recording (Dawn 1998)★★★.

● COMPILATIONS: *The Modern Art Of Jazz* 50s recordings (Dawn 1998)★★★, *The Gentle Art Of Love* 50s recordings (Dawn 1998)★★★.

Matlock, Matty

b. Julian Clifton Matlock, 27 April 1907, Paducah, Kentucky, USA, d. 14 June 1978, Los Angeles, California, USA. Matlock began playing clarinet as a child, in Tennessee, and played with several local and territory bands before, in 1929, joining Ben Pollack as replacement for Benny Goodman. Five years later, with Pollack's departure, this band metamorphosed into the Bob Crosby orchestra. As the new band's popularity rose during the 30s Matlock began spending more time arranging than playing and when an adequate replacement on clarinet was eventually found, in Irving Fazola, he concentrated on writing. At the outset of World War II and the band's demise, Matlock became a studio musician in Los Angeles, but continued to play jazz with musicians such as Bobby Hackett and Rex Stewart, sometimes leading his own group, the Paducah Patrol. He also played with and arranged for several bands, including the continuing Crosby band under Eddie Miller, and the all-star Rampart Street Paraders. He often worked with Paul Weston, a great admirer, and his arrangements were also used by Billy May and Harry James, the latter for the 1962 Verve Records session that produced *Double Dixie*. Matlock often appeared on and wrote arrangements for radio, especially during long spells with Bing Crosby and on the popular series *Pete Kelly's Blues*. This series later moved onto television and was made into a film in 1955, all featuring Matlock's arrangements. In succeeding decades Matlock was active in many areas of music, not least as a member of various Crosby reunions. Matlock was a fluent clarinettist with a joyous, singing sound, but he made his chief impression as an immensely talented arranger. It was he, along with Bob Haggart, who best captured the freewheeling essence of dixieland that formed the core of the Crosby band's repertoire and was such an important part of its success.

● ALBUMS: *Sports Parade* 10-inch album (X 1955)★★★, *Pete Kelly's Blues* (Columbia 1955)★★★, *Pete Kelly At Home* (RCA Victor 1957)★★★, *Dixieland* (Tops 1957)★★★, *The Dixieland Story, Vol. 1* (Warners 1958)★★★★, *The Dixieland Story, Vol. 2* (Warners 1958)★★★★, *And They Called It Dixieland* (Warners 1959)★★★★, *Four-Button Dixie* (Warners 1959)★★★, *Gold Diggers In Dixieland* (Warners 1960)★★★.

Matthews, Dave

b. 6 June 1911, Chagrin Falls, Ohio, USA. As a young man Matthews studied music in Oklahoma and Chicago. He became proficient on alto and tenor saxophones and also developed skills as an arranger. Caught up in the swing era, he played (mostly alto) with Ben Pollack, Jimmy Dorsey and Benny Goodman. In 1939 he left Goodman to go with Harry James who had formed a new band. Matthews contributed some fine swinging charts for the band and over the next few years continued to write for and also play with (now mostly on tenor) bands led by Hal McIntyre, Woody Herman, Stan Kenton and Charlie Barnet. With the latter, his admiration for the stylings of Duke Ellington were allowed to go unfettered. From time to time he led his own bands but it was as an arranger that he became best known during the 50s. Skilled though he was as a player, and with original thoughts on the occasions when he performed solos, Matthews was usually content to remain an anonymous sideman in the bands in which he played and that he helped to achieve popularity through his writing. (This artist should not be confused with the similarly named pianist, arranger and bandleader active in New York in the mid-70s.)

Matthews, George

b. 23 September 1912, Dominica, West Indies, d. 28 June 1982. Matthews settled in New York with his family while he was still a small child. He studied music formally and began playing trombone professionally in the late 20s. In the early 30s he played and recorded with Tiny Bradshaw, then moved on through the bands of Willie Bryant and Louis Armstrong, ending up in Chick Webb's band in 1938. He remained with the band after Webb's death, when it was led nominally by Ella Fitzgerald. In the 40s he was briefly with Lucky Millinder before joining Count Basie for a four-year stint. In 1950 he joined Erksine Hawkins, then played in a variety of bands both in jazz and on its fringes. A section man at heart, in his early years Matthews played with a rough-hewn sound, ripping into blues-inflected solos with great delight.

Matthewson, Ron

b. Rognuald Andrew Matthewson, 19 February 1944, Lerwick, Shetland Isles, Scotland. Matthewson began playing piano at the age of three, but switched to bass at 16. The first band with which he played was a local quartet in which he was teamed with a violinist, pianist and an accordionist playing reels and old-time dances. His first jazz enthusiasm was for trad stars Acker Bilk and Chris Barber, and his first engagements with a well-known band were with the Clyde Valley Stompers, with whom he moved to London in 1962. After a spell back in the Shetlands working for the Herring Industry Board, he returned to London to work with Alex Welsh in 1964. He began to work in a modern jazz context with John Stevens, then returned to Welsh's band for a while before spending time with John Cox, Tubby Hayes, the Kenny Clarke/Francy Boland Big Band, Philly Joe Jones, Phil Woods' European Rhythm Machine, Gordon Beck's Gyroscope, Stan Sulzmann, Kenny Wheeler and a long spell with Ronnie Scott's Quintet. There was also a duo with bassist Ron Rubin.

● ALBUMS: *All In The Morning* (1972)★★.

MAUPIN, BENNIE

b. 29 August 1940, Detroit, Michigan, USA. Maupin played saxophone in high school before studying music at the Detroit Institute for Music and Art. He came to New York in 1963, making his living from commercial music while playing with saxophonists Marion Brown and Pharoah Sanders. In 1966, he played with Roy Haynes and in 1968 joined the Horace Silver Quintet. By 1969, drummer Jack DeJohnette had introduced him to Miles Davis who made his bass clarinet improvisations an integral part of *Bitches Brew*. He went on to play with pianists Chick Corea and Andrew Hill before joining Herbie Hancock's sextet in 1970. He played with the band that recorded the influential *Headhunters*, and continued with Hancock when the sextet became the funk band. He settled in Los Angeles where he has worked ever since.

● ALBUMS: with Miles Davis *Bitches Brew* (1969)★★★★, with Chick Corea *Sundance* (1969)★★★, with Andrew Hill *One For One* (1970)★★★, with Herbie Hancock *Mwandishi* (1971)★★★, *Crossings* (1972)★★★, *Sextant* (1973)★★★, *Headhunters* (1973)★★★★, *The Jewel In The Lotus* (1974)★★★, *VSOP* (1976)★★★, *Slow Traffic To The Right* (1977)★★★.

MAURO, TURK

b. Mauro Turso, 11 June 1944, New York City, New York, USA. Mauro began playing clarinet while still in school and was largely self-taught. By the age of 15, he was proficient enough both on this instrument and the alto saxophone to obtain his union card. In 1960, he joined Red Allen's quartet, playing at clubs in Queens and Harlem. After graduation, Mauro decided to become a professional musician and around this time switched to tenor saxophone. Not surprisingly for a musician of his generation, he was attracted to jazz-rock, though between these gigs he would sit in at the Half Note club with jazzmen such as Zoot Sims, Al Cohn, Nat Pierce and Dave Frishberg. In the late 60s, he played at holiday resorts in upstate New York - originally as a sideman - but later leading a dance band playing Latin American music. Subsequently, he led a small group at the Half Note, then worked with Richie Cole before becoming resident at Sonny's Place, a club on Long Island where he remained for more than a dozen years. He found time, however, for appearances with the bands of Dizzy Gillespie, Buddy Rich and others. Of greater long-term significance were some appearances with Billy Mitchell, for whom he had to play baritone saxophone. Gradually, over the years, Mauro became steadily more proficient on the baritone until it eventually became his principal instrument. In the early 80s, he worked solo in New York and also toured Europe, both as a single performer and with Cole. He appeared in Paris and London and also at various festivals. Back in New York in the mid-80s, he had to take work outside of music to help make ends meet; however, in 1987, he decided to return to Europe and settle in Paris. Although of an age to have come under more modern influences, Mauro's chief musical mentors are great mainstreamers such as tenor saxophonists Ben Webster, Coleman Hawkins, Lester Young, Stan Getz and Dexter Gordon - though he also acknowledges debts to Sims, Cohn, Mitchell, Gene Ammons and others with whom he has worked. As such a list indicates, Mauro still thinks of himself as a tenor player. Perhaps this is what has allowed him to develop an interesting and highly distinctive baritone style. His playing is forceful, fiery and committed, and his occasional vocal excursions show a tough, no-nonsense approach and considerable rhythmic vitality.

● ALBUMS: *The Underdog* (Storyville 1978)★★★, *The Heavyweight* (Phoenix 1980)★★★, *Live In Paris* (Bloomdido 1987)★★, *Jazz Party* (Bloomdido 1993)★★★, *Plays Love Songs* (Bloomdido 1993)★★, *Hittin' The Jug* (Milestone 1996)★★★, *The Truth* (Milestone 1997)★★.

MAXEY, LEROY

b. 6 June 1904, Kansas City, Missouri, USA. Maxey played drums with various territory bands in the 20s, including that led by Bennie Moten. In 1923 he joined a band in St. Louis, the Syncopators, which went to New York for an appearance at the Cotton Club. The band changed its name to the Missourians and then became the Cab Calloway Orchestra. In 1938, Maxey was obliged through poor health to leave the band, retiring from full-time playing. Maxey was a skilful, dynamic player, creating an urgent, rhythmic attack on many of the recordings he made with the orchestra during his career. His drumming on some of the Missourians' records, and later with Calloway, are especially impressive and have greater fluidity than the work of his better-known and technically superior successor with Calloway, Cozy Cole. Had circumstances not driven him from music at the height of the swing era Maxey might well have made a more lasting mark.

MAXWELL, JIMMY

b. 9 January 1917, Stockton, California, USA. After extensive studies in all aspects of brass playing, Maxwell established himself as a major-league trumpet player. Among his first professional engagements was one in the early 30s with Gil Evans, who was raised in Maxwell's home-town. By the end of the decade he had played in the trumpet sections of several leading dance and swing bands, including those of Jimmy Dorsey and Benny Goodman. His stint with Goodman lasted from 1939-43, when he joined CBS. During the 30 years this job lasted, he found time to work with Woody Herman, Count Basie, Gerry Mulligan, Duke Ellington, Quincy Jones and others. Among his Ellington engagements was an informal appearance on stage at the famous Newport concert in 1956, when Willie Cook was late returning to the stand. In the 70s he played with the New York Jazz Repertory Company under Dick Hyman, with Lionel Hampton's All-Star Big Band and with Chuck Israels' National Jazz Ensemble. After Ellington's death, he also played in the band that continued for a while under Mercer Ellington. Since the late 70s, Maxwell has employed his early training and subsequent breadth of playing experience to good effect as a teacher. He has also published a trumpet manual.

● ALBUMS: with Benny Goodman *Benny And Sid 'Roll 'Em'* (1941)★★★★, with Chuck Israels *National Jazz Ensemble* (1976)★★★, *Strong Trumpet* (1977)★★★, *Let's Fall In Love* (1980)★★.

May, Tina

b. England. Encouraged by her piano-playing parents, who 'just assumed she would be musical', she began training as a singer at 16, first thinking of a career as a classical singer. Then, to use her expression, 'jazz chose her'. She developed as a fine performing singer, became popular on the UK club circuit and also began teaching. A skilled improviser, she builds her repertoire with a careful eye for melody, lyric and mood. For most of the 90s she customarily worked with a piano-bass-drums trio that usually includes her husband Clark Tracey and David Newton.

● ALBUMS: *It Ain't Necessarily So* (33 Records 1994)★★, *So Nice* (33 Records 1995)★★★, *Time Will Tell* (33 Records 1996)★★★.

Mays, Bill

b. William Allen Mays, 5 February 1944, Sacramento, California, USA. Mays studied piano formally for a number of years into his twenties. In the early 70s his proficiency and growing reputation was such that he was hired as accompanist to Sarah Vaughan and then Al Jarreau. In the mid-70s he led his own small band and also worked with many other leaders including Bobby Shew and Bud Shank. In the 80s he was with Shelly Manne, Benny Golson, Mark Murphy and Red Mitchell. Later in the decade, he played with Tom Harrell in his own group, with Murphy, and also with Gerry Mulligan. A talented pianist with the special skills needed by an accompanist allied to those of an imaginative soloist (by no means a common combination), Mays also composes and arranges much of the material he plays.

● ALBUMS: with Bob Magnusson *Road Work Ahead* (Discovery 1980)★★, *Tha's Delight* (Trend 1983)★★★, *Kaleidoscope* (Jazz Alliance 1990)★★, *At Maybeck* (Concord 1993)★★★★, *An Ellington Affair* (Concord 1995)★★★★, *Mays In Manhattan* (Concord Jazz 1997)★★★.

Mays, Lyle

b. 27 November 1953, Wausaukie, Wisconsin, USA. The varied keyboard talents of Mays are regularly heard together with Pat Metheny. They met in 1975, and have since forged a musical partnership built upon respect and admiration for each other's work. While it is Metheny who rightly takes the limelight, the integral backbone of the music has much to do with May's fluid keyboard playing, thoughtful arrangements and superb composing ability. In addition to sharing the credits on *As Falls Wichita, So Falls Wichita Falls*, he has played on virtually all of Metheny's impressive catalogue. He contributed to Eberhard Weber's *Later That Evening*, and has so far released two critically acclaimed solo albums. The 'Alaskan Suite', in particular, shows the vast range of capabilities from this dedicated musician.

● ALBUMS: *Lyle Mays* (Geffen 1986)★★★, *Street Dreams* (Geffen 1988)★★★★, with John DeJohnette, Marc Johnson *Fictionary* (Geffen 1993)★★★.

McAll, Barney

b. 1968, Melbourne, Australia. In his childhood, McAll was exposed to all forms of jazz. His father was a traditional jazz lover, while elder brother John introduced him to more recent and contemporary artists such as Bud Powell and Bill Evans. McAll played in the Melbourne jazz scene in the mid-80s and in 1986 was chosen as pianist for Vince Jones. He was featured on the subsequent Jones albums, *It All Ends Up In Tears* (1987) and *Trustworthy Little Sweethearts* (1988). In 1989 McAll worked with American alto saxophonist Vincent Herring, who encouraged him to write more original compositions. A year later McAll won the inaugural AMP Jazz Piano Award at the Wangaratta Festival Of Jazz and he spent the prize money travelling to New York, USA, to study and perform. In 1992 he rejoined the Vince Jones group as pianist and musical director. After touring Europe a year later, McAll shared the APRA award for Best Jazz Composition Of The Year with Jones for their work on *Future Girl*. In late 1994, he toured with saxophonist Dewey Redman and in early 1995, with drummer Cindy Blackman. The same year McAll released his debut, *Exit*. It featured the best of Australia's young jazz musicians and visiting Americans including Herring and Jimmy Cobb and contained seven originals played with impressive swing and vitality. Barney McAll is a versatile performer with a striving, melodic style and his debut album heralded the arrival of a mature, creative talent.

● ALBUMS: *Exit* (ABC 1995)★★★★.

McBee, Cecil

b. 19 May 1935, Tulsa, Oklahoma, USA. A full-toned bassist who creates rich, singing phrases in a wide range of contemporary jazz contexts, McBee studied clarinet at school, but switched to bass at the age of 17, playing in local nightclubs. He gained a degree in music from Ohio Central State University, then spent two years in the army, conducting the band at Fort Knox. Moving to Detroit in 1962, he worked with Paul Winter (1963-64), then went to New York and played with Jackie McLean (1964), Wayne Shorter (1965-66), Charles Lloyd (1966), Yusef Lateef (1967-69) and Alice Coltrane (1969-72). He established his own group in 1975, but, as one of the most in-demand sidemen in jazz, has continued to work with others, including Freddie Hubbard, Grachan Moncur III, Miles Davis, Bobby Hutcherson, Charles Tolliver, Pharoah Sanders, Lonnie Liston Smith, Sonny Rollins, Michael White, JoAnne Brackeen, Horace Tapscott, Anthony Braxton, Abdullah Ibrahim, Buddy Tate and Harry 'Sweets' Edison. During the 80s he also worked with the *avant-garde* supergroup, the Leaders, alongside trumpeter Lester Bowie, alto saxophonist Arthur Blythe, tenor saxophonist Chico Freeman, pianist Kirt Lightsey and drummer Famoudou Don Moye.

● ALBUMS: *Mutima* (Strata East 1975)★★★★, *Music From The*

Source (Enja 1977)★★★, *Compassion* (Enja 1977)★★★, *Alternate Spaces* (India Navigation 1979)★★★★, *Flying Out* (India Navigation 1982)★★★, with the Leaders *Mudfoot* (Black Hawk 1986)★★★, with the Leaders *Out Here Like This* (Black Saint 1987)★★★, with the Leaders Trio *Heaven Dance* (Sunnyside 1988)★★★, with the Leaders *Unforseen Blessings* (Black Saint 1989)★★★, *Unspoken* (Palmetto 1997)★★★.

McBride, Christian

b. 21 May 1972, Philadelphia, Pennsylvania, USA. McBride began taking bass lessons at the age of 11, and at 17 attended the Juilliard School of Music where he studied and played the classical repertoire. Soon after his arrival there, however, he began playing in clubs with Bobby Watson's band alongside fellow student Roy Hargrove. When Hargrove formed his own group McBride was on board, and during the same school year he also played with Benny Golson and Freddie Hubbard. With characteristic understatement, McBride remarked to *Jazz Journal International*'s Derek Ansell, 'That was a hard year.' In 1991 McBride met Ray Brown and two years later the veteran invited the newcomer to partner him at Pittsburgh's 'Ray Brown Day'. Although very much attuned to contemporary happenings in jazz, McBride has expressed a particular delight in playing bop, while at the same time he retains a deep awareness of the traditions of the jazz form. During the relatively short span of his career he has played with a remarkable parade of leading jazz musicians, including Benny Green, Joshua Redman, Steve Turré, Chick Corea, Kenny Barron and Jack DeJohnette, with most of whom he has recorded, sometimes under his own name.

In the mid-90s he began a series of intriguing trio recordings with Hargrove and others. McBride's startling technical accomplishment, allied as it is to a gorgeous full tone, has led to his being spoken of in the same awed breath as Jimmy Blanton and Brown, and there is little doubt that he continues the tradition of virtuoso bassists in jazz. McBride also writes many originals for his own groups. He was a key member of Diana Krall's best-selling *Love Scenes* in 1998.

● ALBUMS: *Getting' To It* (Verve 1994)★★★, *Number Two Express* (Verve 1996)★★★, with Roy Hargrove, Stephen Scott *Parker's Mood* (Verve 1996)★★★, with Ray Brown, John Clayton *Super Bass* (Telarc 1997)★★★★, with Nicholas Payton, Mark Whitfield *Fingerpainting: The Music Of Herbie Hancock* (Verve 1997)★★★★, *A Family Affair* (Verve 1998)★★★.

McCall, Mary Ann

b. 4 May 1919, Philadelphia, Pennsylvania, USA, d. 14 December 1994, Los Angeles, California, USA. McCall's early career was spent singing with the bands of Buddy Morrow, Tommy Dorsey, Woody Herman and Charlie Barnet. During this period, which ended in 1940, she was regarded as an average big band singer. Her return to the spotlight, when she rejoined Herman in 1946, saw her maturing and by the time she left the band in 1950, she was an able, original and forthright jazz singer. She recorded with several leading beboppers in the late 40s and early 50s, including Howard McGhee, Dexter Gordon, Charlie Ventura and her then husband, Al Cohn. During the next three decades, McCall worked extensively as a soloist, making occasional records with jazz musicians such as Jake Hanna and Nat Pierce and singing in jazz clubs and at festivals.

● ALBUMS: *Mary Ann McCall Sings* 10-inch album (Discovery 1950)★★★, with Charlie Ventura *An Evening With Mary Ann McCall & Charlie Ventura* (Norgran 1954)★★★★, with Ventura *Another Evening With Charlie Ventura & Mary Ann McCall* (Norgran 1954)★★★, *Easy Living* (Regent 1957)★★★, *Detour To The Moon* (Jubilee 1958)★★★, *Melancholy Baby* (Coral 1959)★★★, with Jake Hanna *Kansas City Express* (Concord Jazz 1976)★★★, with Nat Pierce *5400 North ... In Concert With Mary Ann McCall* (Hep 1978)★★★.

McCall, Steve

b. 30 September 1933, Chicago, Illinois, USA, d. 25 May 1989. McCall studied music at conservatory and university, though his first professional gig was drumming with blues singer Lucky Carmichael. In 1964, he recorded with soul/jazz pianist Ramsey Lewis. McCall was not only a founder-member of the AACM, but also a member of its predecessor, the legendary Experimental Band. He brought to both years of experience with blues, dance and show bands, having worked with Gene Ammons, Dexter Gordon and Arthur Prysock. His incisive, precise drumming always had the ability to boil up when necessary. In Chicago, he played with Muhal Richard Abrams and Joseph Jarman. Between 1967 and 1970 he lived in Paris, where he played and recorded with Anthony Braxton on his recordings for the BYG label. When the Chicago musicians played in New York in 1971 under the name of Creative Construction Company, McCall again played drums, relating to the established New York bassist Richard Davis with no problems at all. McCall's most visible gig after that was with Henry Threadgill and Fred Hopkins in the trio Air, a group that rapidly became festival favourites. McCall supplied magically sensitive percussion to the group, so important to their collective sound that when he left in 1982 - to be replaced by Pheeroan akLaff - they changed their name to New Air. He worked, too, with Marion Brown, Chico Freeman, Arthur Blythe and David Murray's Octet: McCall's creative drumming, with its irreverent enthusiasm for past styles, was the ideal accompaniment for Murray's great 'jazz consolidation' band of the 80s. He returned to Chicago later in the 80s, giving solo concerts and leading his own sextet.

● ALBUMS: with Anthony Braxton *B-X/N-O-1-47A* (1969)★★★★, with Marion Brown *Geechee Recollections* (1973)★★★, with Brown *Sweet Flying Earth* (1974)★★★, with Creative Construction Company *CCC* 1970 recording (1975)★★★★, with CCC *CCC Vol II* 1970 recording (1976)★★★, with Muhal Richard Abrams *I-OQA + 19* (1979)★★★, with David Murray Octet *Ming* (1980)★★★★, with Murray Octet *Home* (1981)★★★, with Murray *Murray's Steps* (1982)★★★.

McCandless, Paul

b. 24 March 1947, Indiana, Pennsylvania, USA. The distinctive, curling sound of Paul McCandless on English horn, oboe, saxophones, flute, clarinet, musette (a French bagpipe from the last century) and wind-driven synthesizers has done much to define the fusion music of Oregon. The nucleus of the group, Ralph Towner, Collin Walcott, and McCandless, came together as members of the influential Paul Winter Consort. Just as the part-time nature of Oregon has enabled its members to undertake other projects, so, too, has McCandless taken that opportunity to work with Art Lande and David Samuels; he also reunited with ex-Consort cellist David Darling in the Gallery project, and played with Eberhard Weber.

● ALBUMS: *All The Mornings Bring* (Elektra 1979)★★★, *Navigator* (Landslide 1981)★★★★, *Heresay* (Windham Hill 1988)★★★, *Premonition* (Windham Hill 1992)★★★, *Skylight* (ECM 1996)★★★.

McCann, Les

b. Leslie Coleman McCann, 23 September 1935, Lexington, Kentucky, USA, d. November 1996. 'There is no end to the possibilities (and fun) in music. So, why don't we get on in there and get it?' McCann's comment highlights two distinctive elements of his music: an interest in innovation, particularly in new technology, and a preference for the dance-based rhythms of jazz, gospel and funk. Self-taught as a pianist, he played and sang in school bands and in the navy, where a talent contest won him a spot on the *Ed Sullivan Show*. Moving to California in the late 50s, he played with Gene McDaniels before forming a successful trio with which he first recorded in 1960. A series of popular jazz piano albums followed, and in the late 60s, McCann had two hit singles with the protest song 'Compared To What' and the ballad 'With These Hands'. *Swiss Movement*, his Montreux live duet album with saxophonist Eddie Harris, was also a best-seller. The early 70s saw the pianist exploring electronic keyboards and synthesizers and, while still recording, he performed in films such as *Soul To Soul* and shows such as the all-star *Black Music Show* from 1972-74. McCann also practised as a photographer, exhibiting on a number of occasions, and worked as a volunteer teacher with his wife in Mexico. His recording diminished in the late 70s, following an unsuccessful foray into soul and R&B. He bounced back in the late 80s and continued in the jazz funk field. Despite a stroke in January 1995, McCann kept recording until his death the following year.

● ALBUMS: *Les McCann Plays the Truth* (Pacific Jazz 1960)★★★, *The Shout* (Pacific Jazz 1960)★★★, *Les McCann In San Francisco* (Pacific Jazz 1961)★★★★, *Pretty Lady* (Pacific Jazz 1961)★★★, *Les McCann Sings* (Pacific Jazz 1961)★★, *Les McCann In New York* (Pacific Jazz 1961)★★★, *Les McCann On Time* (Pacific Jazz 1962)★★★★, *Les McCann Plays The Shampoo At The Village* (Pacific Jazz 1962)★★★, *The Gospel Truth* (Pacific Jazz 1963)★★★, *Soul Hits* (Pacific Jazz 1963)★★★★, *Jazz Waltz* (Pacific Jazz 1964)★★★, *McCanna* (Pacific Jazz 1964)★★★, with Gerald Wilson *McCann Wilson* (Pacific Jazz 1965)★★, *But Not Really* (Limelight 1965)★★★, *Poo Boo* (Limelight 1965)★★★, *Beaux J. Pooboo* (Limelight 1966)★★, *Live At Shelly's Manne-Hole* (Limelight 1966)★★★, *Les McCann Plays The Hits* (Limelight 1966)★★, *Spanish Onions* (Pacific Jazz 1966)★★★, *Bucket Of Grease* (Limelight 1967)★★★, *Les McCann Live At The Bohemian Cafe* (Limelight 1967)★★, *More Of Les McCann* (World Pacific 1967)★★★, *Much Les* (Atlantic 1969)★★★, *Django* (Sunset 1969)★★★, with Eddie Harris *Swiss Movement* (Atlantic 1970)★★★, with Harris *Second Movement* (Atlantic 1971)★★, *Invitation To Openness* (Atlantic 1972)★★★, *Talk To The People* (Atlantic 1972)★★★★, *Another Beginning* (Atlantic 1975)★★★, *Hustle To Survive* (Atlantic 1975)★★★, *The Man* (A&M 1978)★★★, *Music Box* (Paladin 1988)★★★, *On The Soul Side* (Music Masters)★★★, with Marian McPartland *Marian McPartland's Piano Jazz With Guest Les McCann* (The Jazz Alliance 1996)★★★, *Listen Up!* (Music Masters 1996)★★★.

● COMPILATIONS: *The Les McCann Anthology* (Rhino/Atlantic)★★★★.

● VIDEOS: with Eddie Harris *Swiss Movement* (Rhino 1997).

McClure, Ron

b. 22. November 1941, New Haven, Connecticut, USA. McClure started playing the accordion when he was five years old, and played the piano at high school. He studied the bass at the Julius Hartt Conservatory in Hartford, and when he left in 1963 went on to study composition with Hall Overton and Don Sebesky. By the time he joined Charles Lloyd in 1967, he had played with Buddy Rich, Herbie Mann and Wynton Kelly backing Wes Montgomery. Lloyd's enormously successful group took McClure on worldwide tours before he returned to San Francisco, where he was a founder-member of the fusion group Fourth Way. Later on, he played with the group Blood, Sweat And Tears before settling to studio work in New York. McClure played with musicians as diverse as vocalists Tony Bennett, Dionne Warwick and the Pointer Sisters, and instrumentalists Thelonious Monk, Gary Burton and Joe Henderson. In 1985, he joined the group of Al Di Meola and then worked with Michel Petrucciani and George Russell. His firm bass lines are characterized by rhythmic fills on open strings against the fretboard. He has taught at the Berklee College Of Music (1971) and Long Island University (1983-85).

● ALBUMS: with Fourth Way *Sun And Moon* (1969)★★★, with Joe Henderson *In Pursuit Of Blackness* (1971)★★★, *McJolt* (Steeplechase 1991)★★★, Strikezone (Steeplechase 1991)★★★★, *Never Forget* (Steeplechase 1991)★★★★, *For Tonite Only* (Steeplechase 1992)★★, *Sunburst* (Steeplechase 1992)★★★★, *Descendants* (Ken Music 1992)★★, *Yesterday's Tomorrow* (EMP 1992)★★★, *Inner Account* (Steeplechase 1994)★★★★, *Never Always* (Steeplechase 1994)★★★★, *Concrete Canyons* (Steeplechase 1996)★★, *Closer To Your Tears* (Steeplechase 1997)★★★, *Pink Cloud* (Naxos Jazz 1997)★★★.

McConnell, Rob

b. 14 February 1935, London, Ontario, Canada. After playing valve trombone in various bands in his homeland during the mid- and late 50s, McConnell joined fellow-Canadian Maynard Ferguson's New York Band in 1964. Despite the attention he attracted there, he returned to Canada to work with the Phil Nimmons band; he also played in studio orchestras and wrote many arrangements. Towards the end of the 60s he formed a band, the Boss Brass, playing his own charts of currently popular music for a 15-piece brass and rhythm group. In the early 70s McConnell added a reed section and, with the band's musical policy slanted strongly towards jazz, he made a series of outstanding albums. Among the musicians in the band were Sam Noto, Guido Basso, Don Thompson and Ed Bickert. Apart from its own albums, the band also made records with Singers Unlimited, the Hi-Lo's, Phil Woods and Mel Tormé. He also made *Old Friends/New Music*, using a sextet drawn from the big band. Despite the popularity of the Boss Brass and the success of its albums, by the late 80s McConnell decided it was time to make changes. He accepted a teaching post at the Dick Grove Music School in Los Angeles, where he relocated at the end of 1988.

In the early 90s, he was active in the southern California jazz scene, playing with various rehearsal bands and seriously considering the re-formation of his own big band. An excellent arranger with a real affection for hard-swinging, contemporary, big band jazz, McConnell has made an outstanding contribution to the development of this area of music. His decision to enter teaching should ensure that a future generation of musicians will develop some of the theories he has already put into practice.

● ALBUMS: *The Rob McConnell-Guido Basso Quintet* (1963)★★, *Rob McConnell And His Orchestra* (1965)★★, *The Boss Brass* i (1968)★★★, *The Boss Brass* ii (1972)★★★, *The Best Damn Band In The Land* (1974)★★★, *Satin Sheets* (1975)★★★, *The Jazz Album* (Pausa 1976)★★★★, *Big Band Jazz, Vol. 1* (Pausa 1977)★★★, *The Boss Brass Again!, Vol. 1* (Pausa 1978)★★★, *The Boss Brass Again!, Vol. 2* (Pausa 1978)★★★, *Present Perfect* (Pausa 1979)★★★, *Live In Digital* (Sea Breeze 1980)★★★, *Tribute* (Pausa 1981)★★★, *All In Good Time* (Innovation 1982)★★★, *Atras Da Porta* (Innovation 1983)★★★, with Ed Bickert *Mutual Street* (Innovation 1984)★★★, *Old Friends, New Music* (Unison 1984)★★★, with Phil Woods *Boss Brass And Woods* (MCA 1985)★★★, *Boss Of The Boss Brass* (1988)★★★, *The Rob McConnell Jive Five* (Concord Jazz 1990)★★★, *The Brass Is Back* (Concord Jazz 1991)★★, *Live At The 1990 Concord Jazz Festival* (Concord Jazz 1991)★★★, *Brassy And Sassy* (Concord Jazz 1992)★★★, *Our 25th Year* (Concord Jazz 1993)★★★★, *Trio Sketches* (Concord Jazz 1993)★★★, *Overtime* (Concord Jazz 1994)★★★, *Don't Get Around Much Anymore* Concord 1995)★★, *Even Canadians Get The Blues* (Concord Jazz 1996)★★★, with Bickert, Don Thompson *Three For The Road* (Concord Picante 1997)★★, *Play The Jazz Classics* (Concord Jazz 1997)★★★.

McCord, Castor

b. 17 May 1907, Birmingham, Alabama, USA, d. 14 February 1963. Together with his twin brother, Ted (Theodore Jobetus), McCord played clarinet and saxophones in the Edgar Hayes band in the early 20s (Ted also playing similar instruments). McCord moved on to the band of Horace Henderson when it was still a student group at Wilberforce University, and remained with the band when it became a professional group. At the end of the decade he was with the Mills Blue Rhythm Band, and also played with Louis Armstrong and others. Following a trip to Europe in 1934 he remained in France for some time and also travelled to India and the Netherlands. During this period he again played with Armstrong and also with Coleman Hawkins. In the late 30s he was back in the USA where he joined Benny Carter and then played with Eddie Mallory and Claude Hopkins before retiring from music in the mid-40s.

● ALBUMS: with Mills Blue Rhythm Band *Blue Rhythm* (Hep 1930-31)★★★, *Benny Carter And His Orchestra* (Tax 1939)★★★★.

McCorkle, Susannah

b. 1 January 1949, Berkeley, California, USA. In the late 60s, McCorkle lived for a while in Paris. It was during this sojourn that she heard Billie Holiday on records and decided to take up singing. Multilingual, she lived for a time in Italy, working as a translator and taking any singing jobs she could find. In 1972, she moved to the UK, singing in clubs and pubs and learning about what she had determined would be her future career. She also made two albums which, although well received, enjoyed only limited circulation. In the late 70s, McCorkle returned to the USA and settled in New York, where a five-month engagement at the Cookery in Greenwich Village brought her to wider public attention and elicited rave reviews from critics. She continued to record during the 80s, and her maturing style and the darkening timbre of her voice greatly enhanced her performances. By the early 90s, with the release by Concord Records of *No More Blues* and *Sabia*, two enormously successful albums, McCorkle was poised to make her name known to the wider world. Indeed, her linguistic abilities, skills that enabled her to translate lyrics, notably the Brazilian songs on *Sabia*, make her a likely candidate for international success. In the meantime, she is consolidating her status in jazz with awards, including the 1989 New York Music Award, and is being recorded by the Smithsonian Institute, the youngest singer ever to be included in their popular music series. A graduate of the University of California at Berkeley, McCorkle has also had several short stories published and, in 1991, was working on her first novel.

● ALBUMS: *The Music Of Harry Warren* (1976)★★★, *There Will Never Be Another You* (Retrospect 1976)★★★, *The Quality Of Mercer* (Black Lion 1977)★★★★, *Over The Rainbow - The Songs Of E.Y. Harburg* (1980)★★★, *The People That You Never Get To Love* (1982)★★★, *How Do You Keep The Music Playing?* (1982)★★★, *Thanks For The Memory - Songs Of Leo Robin* (1986)★★, *As Time Goes By* (1987)★★★, *Dream* (1987)★★★, *No More Blues* (Concord Jazz 1989)★★★, *Sabia* (Concord Jazz 1990)★★★, *I'll Take Romance* (Concord Jazz 1992)★★★, *From Bessie To Brazil* (Concord Jazz 1993)★★, *Easy To Love: The Songs Of Cole Porter* (Concord Jazz 1996)★★★★, *Let's Face The Music:*

The Songs Of Irving Berlin (Concord Jazz 1997)★★★★, *Someone To Watch Over Me: The Songs Of George Gershwin* (Concord Jazz 1998)★★★.

McCoy, Clyde

b. 29 December 1903, Ashland, Kentucky, USA, d. 1 June 1990, Memphis, Tennessee, USA. McCoy grew up in Portsmouth, Ohio, bought his first trumpet at the age of nine and taught himself to play. While in his teens he formed his own small group, and by the late 20s, led a full orchestra, playing clubs and ballrooms. Using a mute, he developed a distinctive hiccuping, growling, 'wah-wah' trumpet sound, exemplified by his first big hit in 1931, 'Sugar Blues'. This first McCoy recording of the number on Columbia Records (he re-recorded it several times) reputedly sold several million copies and became his theme tune. His other hits during the 30s included Glen Gray's signature tune 'Smoke Rings', 'In The Cool Of The Night', 'Wah Wah Lament', 'The Goona Goo' and 'Sugar Blues', this time on Decca. In 1937, McCoy added a female vocal group, the Bennett Sisters, and later married the lead singer. During World War II McCoy took his band and vocalists into the Navy's Special Services as a complete unit. He regrouped after the war and during the 50s had an especially successful band, working major clubs, ballrooms and concert halls throughout the USA and Canada. In later years he often led a small Dixieland outfit, and was still performing up to the mid-80s.

● ALBUMS: *Sammy Kaye And His Orchestra With Clyde McCoy And His Orchestra* (1987)★★★.

McCracken, Bob

b. 23 November 1904, Dallas, Texas, USA, d. 4 July 1972, Los Angeles, California, USA. McCracken's early clarinet playing included work in Doc Ross's band with Jack Teagarden. He worked in Chicago and New York with Willard Robison's Band in the late 20s before returning to Texas. It was only in 1939 that he settled in Chicago and worked with various artists including trumpeters Jimmy McPartland and Wingy Manone. His elegant playing fitted well with the Louis Armstrong All Stars with whom he played in the early 50s, touring Europe in 1952-53. He played with Kid Ory's Band before settling in California, where he continued playing with Ben Pollack (drums), Pete Dailey (cornet), Jack Teagarden and Wild Bill Davison.

● ALBUMS: *Henry 'Red' Allen And The Kid* (1959)★★★.

McDonough, Dick

b. 1904, USA, d. 25 May 1938. Guitarist McDonough began on banjo and by the mid-20s was in great demand on record sessions by jazz groups, popular singers and dance bands of the day. Among the artists with whom he recorded were Red Nichols, Red McKenzie, Connee Boswell, Benny Goodman, Mildred Bailey and Glenn Miller. His career continued into the 30s, which saw a particularly fruitful musical partnership with fellow-guitarist Carl Kress. McDonough's high-pressure musical life was matched by equally high living, and his health finally gave out. He died in May 1938. Although often overlooked, McDonough was an important figure in the development of jazz guitar and his recorded work, especially that with Kress, is worthy of study.

● COMPILATIONS: *The Guitar Genius Of Dick McDonough And Carl Kress In The Thirties* (1934-37)★★★, shared with Carl Kress, Eddie Lang *Pioneers Of Jazz Guitars* 1927-1938 recordings (Challenge 1998)★★★★.

McDuff, Brother Jack

b. Eugene McDuff, 17 September 1926, Champaign, Illinois, USA. McDuff adopted a professional name that reflected the racial consciousness of the 60s. Self-taught on piano, he became adept on the Hammond organ, an instrument associated with the church and hence with black music at its most heated. He took time out from touring to study music in Cincinnati, Ohio. He toured with various R&B bands from 1948, then formed his own jazz group in 1954, playing in the Midwest. In 1957, he broke up the group and left music, but returned in 1958 as a bass player. This was an ideal introduction to the Hammond, on which the organist supplies bass with foot pedals. In 1961, he recorded an album with Roland Kirk, *Kirk's Works*. In that year he also worked with guitarist Grant Green and, from 1962 to 1965, with superstar-to-be George Benson. 1964's *The Dynamic Jack McDuff* was a highly successful meeting of organ and big band, featuring arrangements by Benny Golson.

In the 80s McDuff started playing electric piano and working with vocalists, but he reverted to the soul jazz organ sound of the 60s when the acid jazz movement revitalized the instrument during the 90s.

● ALBUMS: *Brother Jack* (Prestige 1960)★★★★, *Tough 'Duff* (Prestige 1960)★★★★, *The Honeydripper* (Prestige 1961)★★★★, *Goodnight, It's Time To Go* (Prestige 1961)★★★, with Gene Ammons *Mellow Gravy - Brother Jack Meets The Boss* (Prestige 1962)★★★★, with Ammons, Sonny Stitt *Soul Summit* (Prestige 1962)★★★, *Screamin'* (Prestige 1963)★★★★, *Somethin' Slick!* (Prestige 1963)★★★, *Brother Jack McDuff Live!* (Prestige 1963)★★★★, *Live! At The Jazz Workshop* (Prestige 1963)★★★, *The Dynamic Jack McDuff* (Prestige 1964)★★★, *Prelude* (Prestige 1964)★★★, *The Concert McDuff Recorded Live!* (Prestige 1965)★★★, *Silk And Soul* (Prestige 1965)★★★, *Hot Barbeque* (Prestige 1966)★★★, *A Change Is Gonna Come* (Atlantic 1966)★★, with Willis Jackson *Together Again!* (Prestige 1966)★★★, *Walk On By* (Prestige 1967)★★★, *Hallelujah Time!* (Prestige 1967)★★, *Tobacco Road* (Atlantic 1967)★★, *The Midnight Sun* (Prestige 1967)★★★, *Getting Our Thing Together* (1968)★★★, *Soul Circle* (Prestige 1968)★★, *Jack McDuff Plays For Beautiful People* (Prestige 1969)★★★, *I Got A Woman* (Prestige 1969)★★★, *Steppin' Out* (Prestige 1969)★★★, *Live, The Best Of Brother Jack McDuff* (Prestige 1969)★★★, *Down Home Style* (Blue Note 1969)★★★, *Moon Rappin'* (Blue Note 1969)★★★, *The Fourth Dimension* (1974)★★★, *Heatin' System* (1975)★★★, *The Re-Entry* (Muse 1989)★★★★, *Colour Me Blue* (Concord 1992)★★★, *Another Real Good'un* (Muse 1992)★★★★, *Write On Cap'n* (Concord 1994)★★, *The Heatin' System* (Concord Jazz 1995)★★★★, with Joey DeFrancesco *It's About Time* (Concord Jazz 1996)★★★, with Al Grey *Me N' Jack*

(Pullen 1996)★★★, *That's The Way I Feel About It* (Concord Jazz 1997)★★★.

● COMPILATIONS: *Brother Jack McDuff's Greatest Hits* (Prestige 1967)★★★.

McEACHERN, MURRAY

b. 16 August 1915, Toronto, Canada, d. 28 April 1982. After learning to play a wide range of musical instruments, McEachern began playing in dance bands during the early 30s. In 1936, he joined the Benny Goodman Orchestra, where he played trombone. After Goodman he was with the Casa Loma Orchestra, playing trombone and alto saxophone; following this there was a short spell with Paul Whiteman. By 1942 McEachern was settled on the west coast and for much of the next three decades he was active in film and television studio work. In 1972, he took the lead alto chair when Bill Berry re-formed his big band on moving to Los Angeles, but soon afterwards, McEachern went on the road as leader of the re-formed Tommy Dorsey band - this time, naturally enough, playing trombone. A remarkably polished player on trombone with a contrastingly strong and gutsy saxophone style, McEachern was one of the outstanding sidemen in the history of big band music.

● COMPILATIONS: *The Indispensable Benny Goodman Vols. 1/2* (RCA 1935-36)★★★★, *The Indispensable Benny Goodman Vols. 3/4* (RCA 1936-37)★★★★.

McFARLAND, GARY

b. 23 October 1933, Los Angeles, California, USA, d. 3 November 1971, New York City, New York, USA. McFarland was a vibraphonist, arranger and orchestra leader. He moved to Grants Pass in Oregon when he was 15 years old, and became interested in jazz while studying at the University of Oregon. He began to play the vibes during a stint in the US Army at Fort Sill, Oklahoma, in 1954, and, three years later, joined a group led by Santiago Gonzalez. Encouraged by musicians such as John Lewis, Buddy Montgomery and fellow vibes player Cal Tjader, McFarland won scholarships to the School of Jazz in Lennox and the Berklee College Of Music in Boston (1959). In the early 60s he blossomed into a fine young jazz writer, contributing arrangements and compositions to albums including those of the Modern Jazz Quintet, Gerry Mulligan, and John Lewis. He also wrote all the charts, and conducted the orchestra for Anita O'Day's *All The Sad Young Men* - although, according to O'Day, she sang to pre-recorded tapes, and did not meet McFarland until four or five years after the record had been released! Presumably he did become personally involved when working on albums with Stan Getz, Bill Evans and other leading musicians.

In 1961, he recorded his own jazz version of the Frank Loesser-Abe Burrows Broadway Musical, *How To Succeed In Business Without Really Trying*, and subsequent releases included *Soft Samba*, *Point Of Departure*, *Profiles*, *Simpatico*, *Tijuana Jazz* and *America The Beautiful* and *Does The Sun Real, Shine On The Moon?* for the Skye Label, of which he was the co-founder. During the mid-60s, McFarland toured with his own quintet, and, in 1966, wrote the score for the Deborah Kerr-David Niven thriller movie, *Eye Of The Devil*. His last film music was for another 'whodunnit', *Who Killed Mary What's'ername?*, in 1971. He died in November of that year. The cause of death was given as a heart attack, although it is rumoured that methadone, a synthetic drug similar to morphine, was put in his drink by a 'joker'.

● ALBUMS: *Does The Sun Really Shine On The Moon?* (DCC 1998)★★★.

McFERRIN, BOBBY

b. 11 March 1950, New York City, New York, USA. To call Bobby McFerrin a jazz vocalist is hardly to do him justice, for when McFerrin performs - he usually appears solo in lengthy concerts - he uses his entire body as a sound-box, beating noises out of his slender frame while emitting a constant accompaniment of guttural noises, clicks and popping sounds. To all this he adds a vocal technique that owes a slight debt to the bop vocalist Betty Carter and her daring swoops and scat vocals. McFerrin was brought up in a musical family - both his parents are opera singers, his father performing on the film soundtrack of *Porgy And Bess* in 1959 - but his main jazz influence came from Miles Davis's *Bitches Brew*. Training as a pianist at the Juilliard School and later at Sacramento State College, he worked first as an accompanist, then as a pianist and singer during the 70s. He came to public notice in 1979, when he performed in New York with the singer Jon Hendricks, but it was his unaccompanied appearance at the 1981 Kool Jazz Festival that brought him widespread acclaim. By 1983, he had perfected his solo style of wordless, vocal improvisations. His debut album contained a dramatic reworking of Van Morrison's 'Moondance', while *The Voice* mixed his fondness for pop classics - this time, the Beatles' 'Blackbird' - with more adventurous pieces, notably the self-descriptive 'I'm My Own Walkman'. The 1988 album *Simple Pleasures* shows off his wide range with its mixture of pop classics and self-composed material. The highlight of the album was his idiosyncratic version of Cream's 'Sunshine Of Your Love', complete with a vocal electric guitar. That recording also spawned a huge hit single, 'Don't Worry Be Happy', which was featured in the popular movie *Cocktail*. It reached number 1 in the USA and number 2 in the UK. Further success came when Cadbury's chocolate used 'Thinkin' About Your Body' in a major advertising campaign (substituting the word 'chocolate' for 'body'). This moved him away from a jazz audience although *Paper Music* was an impressive venture, with McFerrin attempting the music of Bach, Mozart and Mendelssohn. He moved back to his jazz roots when he joined forces with Yellowjackets on *Bang!Zoom*, arguably his finest album to date. McFerrin is a true original, blessed with a remarkable vocal ability that goes beyond the usual limitations of the human voice.

● ALBUMS: *Bobby McFerrin* (Elektra Musician 1982)★★★, *The*

Voice (Elektra Musician 1984)★★★, *Spontaneous Inventions* (Blue Note 1986)★★★, *Simple Pleasures* (EMI Manhattan 1988)★★★, *Medicine Music* (EMI Manhattan 1990)★★★, with Chick Corea *Play* (Blue Note 1992)★★★, *Paper Music* (Sony 1995)★★★, *Bang!Zoom* (Blue Note 1996)★★★, *Circle Songs* (Sony 1997)★★★.

McGann, Bernie

b. 22 June 1937, Sydney, New South Wales, Australia. Arguably Australia's premier saxophonist, McGann began on drums, taking lessons from his father, who was a professional musician. He switched to alto saxophone in 1955, initially inspired by Paul Desmond, though later influences were Sonny Rollins and *avant garde* players such as Ornette Coleman and Albert Ayler. In the late 50s, McGann began a long association with drummer John Pochée, and in 1964, joined him in a group called the Heads, which also featured pianist Dave MacRae. McGann played regularly at Sydney's El Roco club, but when it closed in 1969, he found jazz gigs extremely scarce and for a while worked as a postman. From 1975, he played in Pochée's group, the Last Straw, and also led his own trio into the 80s, recording with Sonny Stitt on the latter's 1981 Australian tour. He has worked with other visiting Americans, notably Dewey Redman and Red Rodney, continues to perform both with the Last Straw and Pochée's big band, Ten Part Invention, and still leads his own small groups, which usually feature Pochée and bassist Lloyd Swanton. Although active since the 50s and a striking soloist, whose lines have the gnarled beauty of a truly original talent, McGann has rarely recorded. *At Long Last*, on the Emanem label, was his first album as leader after 30 years on the scene and remains his best to date - a twisting, eloquent bebop spiced with modernity.

● ALBUMS: *With The Ted Vining Trio* 1983 recording (1986)★★★, *At Long Last* 1983 recording (1987)★★★, *Kindred Spirits* (1987)★★, *The Last Straw* 1987 recording (1991)★★★★, *Ten Part Invention* 1987 recording (1991)★★★, *Ugly Beauty* (Spiral Scratch 1992)★★★, *McGann McGann* (Rufus 1995)★★★★, *Playground* (Rufus 1995)★★★★.

McGarity, Lou

b. 22 July 1917, Athens, Georgia, USA, d. 28 August 1971. After playing in dance bands in and around Atlanta, Georgia, trombonist McGarity moved north. In 1938, he joined Ben Bernie's popular recording unit and, two years later, became a member of the Benny Goodman band. After military service in World War II, McGarity again played with Goodman, then divided his time between west coast studio work and playing in small jazz groups, often those under the nominal leadership of Eddie Condon, Yank Lawson and Bob Haggart. In the 60s, he played with Bob Crosby And The Bobcats and was with Lawson and Haggart in the World's Greatest Jazz Band. His warm sound and sometimes aggressive style made McGarity a welcome member of any Dixieland-orientated jazz band. He worked until the day of his death in August 1971.

● ALBUMS: with Lawson-Haggart *Jelly Roll's Jazz* (1951)★★★, with Eddie Condon *Jammin' At Condon's* (1954)★★★★, *Blue Lou* (1959)★★★, *Jazz Master* (1970)★★★, *In Celebration* (IAJRC 1989)★★★.

McGhee, Howard

b. 6 March 1918, Tulsa, Oklahoma, USA, d. 17 July 1987, New York City, New York, USA. During the late 30s, McGhee played trumpet in several territory bands in the Midwest before moving to Detroit, where he became well known in that city's lively jazz scene. He first enjoyed major success with Lionel Hampton in 1941; however, he quickly moved on, joining Andy Kirk, for whom he wrote arrangements and was featured soloist. Although he was to work in other big bands of the early 40s, including Charlie Barnet's and Georgie Auld's, McGhee soon became most closely associated with bebop. From the mid-40s he could be heard playing in clubs and on records with Charlie Parker, Fats Navarro and others. He was present on the notorious Parker recording date for Dial that produced 'Lover Man' and was, in fact, largely responsible for salvaging the session from potential disaster when Parker broke down. During the 50s, McGhee's career was damaged by drug addiction and his private life was blighted by some of the worst excesses of racism: his marriage to a white woman resulted in his wife being beaten up and he himself was framed on drugs-related charges. However, he survived and, in the early 60s, was making records with Teddy Edwards, George Coleman and others and later returned to regular playing. A big band he formed at this time and a 1969 appearance at the Newport Jazz Festival with Buddy Tate helped to prove that he still had talent to spare. One of the most melodic of bebop trumpeters, McGhee was an important influence on two major figures, Navarro and Clifford Brown, both of whom, ironically, were to die many years before him.

● ALBUMS: *Night Music* 10-inch album (Dial 1951)★★★, *Jazz Goes To The Battlefront, Volume 1* 10-inch album (Hi Lo 1952)★★★, *Jazz Goes To The Battlefront, Volume 2* 10-inch album (Hi Lo 1952)★★★, *Howard McGhee's All Stars/Howard McGhee-Fats Navarro Sextet* 10-inch album (Blue Note 1952)★★★★, *Howard McGhee, Volume 2* 10-inch album (Blue Note 1953)★★★★, *Howard McGhee And Milt Jackson* (Savoy 1955)★★★★, *The Return Of Howard McGhee* (Bethlehem 1956)★★★, *Life Is Just A Bowl Of Cherries* (Bethlehem 1956)★★★, with Dexter Gordon *The Chase* (Jazztone 1956)★★★, *Dusty Blue* (Bethlehem 1961)★★★, *The Bop Master* (Affinity 1961)★★★, *Maggie's Back In Town* (Contemporary 1961)★★★★, with Teddy Edwards *Together Again* (Contemporary 1961)★★★★, *Shades Of Blue/Sharp Edge* (Black Lion 1961)★★★, *House Warmin'!* (Argo 1962)★★★, with Coleman Hawkins, Lester Young *A Date With Greatness* (Imperial 1962)★★★★, *Nobody Knows You When You're Down & Out* (United Artists 1963)★★★, *Cookin' Time* (Hep Jazz 1966)★★★, *Here Comes Freddy* (Sonet 1976)★★★, *Just Be There* (Steeple Chase 1977)★★★, with Charlie Rouse *Jazzbrothers* (Storyville 1977)★★★, *Live At Emerson's* (Zim 1978)★★★, *Home Run* (Storyville 1978)★★★, with Edwards *Young At Heart* (Storyville 1979)★★★, *Wise In Time* (Storyville 1980)★★★, with Edwards *Trumpet At Tempo* 1947 recordings (Spotlite 1983)★★★★.

McGlohon, Loonis

b. 29 September 1921, Ayden, North Carolina, USA. After graduating from East Carolina University, he turned his piano-playing talents into a professional career, but was interrupted by military service between 1942 and 1945, during which time he worked as a pianist-arranger in the US Army Air Force. In 1949 he joined Jimmy Dorsey's orchestra and was also briefly with Ray McKinley and Jack Teagarden, but from 1950 he was deeply involved in radio and television as a producer and presenter, although he continued to play frequently and also to write music. He formed his own trio for club and concert engagements and with the group has appeared all across the USA, including three appearances at Carnegie Hall, and also in Japan, China, Singapore, France, Italy and the UK. He has accompanied several singers including Helen O'Connell, Judy Garland, in 1964 and 1966, and was musical director for the legendary Mabel Mercer, 1978-80, and Eileen Farrell, 1981-96. His compositions include operas, musicals, revues, a children's cantata, *A Child's Christmas*, which was recorded and released in 1974, and numerous songs, among which are 'Blackberry Winter', in collaboration with Alec Wilder, which has been recorded by numerous singers including Mark Murphy, Mike Campbell, Teddi King, Vic Juris and Marlene VerPlanck, 'A Long Night' and 'South To A Warmer Place', both also with Wilder and which were recorded by Frank Sinatra, and 'Songbird', recorded more than 30 times by artists such as George Shearing and Robert Farnon, Jackie Cain, VerPlanck, Farrell and Weslia Whitfield. In addition to Wilder, his songwriting collaborators have included Billy VerPlanck, Hugh Martin and Marian McPartland. For several years, McGlohon served as Program Director for WBT Radio Station in Charlotte, North Carolina. On a regular radio show for National Public Radio he introduced many fine singers and instrumentalists and collaborated with Wilder on a series based on the latter's book, *The American Popular Song*, and a subsequent series, *American Popular Singers*, hosted by Eileen Farrell. This show featured artists such as Carrie Smith, Anita Ellis, Johnny Hartman, VerPlanck, Barbara Lea, King, Mercer, Hugh Shannon and Thelma Carpenter. Virtually the house pianist for Audiophile Records, he has accompanied many singers, including albums by Dick Haymes, David Allyn, Margaret Whiting, Smith, Lea, Dardanelle, Maxine Sullivan, Farrell, Campbell, Joyce Breach, Daryle Ryce and VerPlanck, and he has recorded with Farnon and the London Philharmonic Orchestra. With the latter, he recorded a particularly fine set of Wilder songs and also *You'd Better Love Me*, which featured music by Hugh Martin and Ralph Blane. In a liner note for this album, which was made in 1976, VerPlanck wrote of her first encounter with McGlohon the pianist, 'beautiful chords, beautiful technique, and lovely soulful playing.' McGlohon has founded a number of scholarships and a school of music and a theatre bear his name. Appreciation of McGlohon both inside and outside the world of popular music is evidenced by numerous honours, including four doctorates, nomination to the National Academy of Television and Science Hall of Fame, and the scheduling for August 1998 of a tribute at New York's Lincoln Center at which many of the artists who have played with him and sung his songs were eager to appear.

● ALBUMS: *Loonis And London* 1981 recordings (Audiophile 1996)★★★.

McGregor, Chris

b. 24 December 1936, Somerset West, South Africa, d. 27 May 1990. In his early years in the Transkei, McGregor studied classical piano music, but was more significantly affected by the hymns in his father's Church of Scotland mission and the music of the Xhosa people. At the 1962 Johannesburg Jazz Festival, he selected five of the best players (Mongezi Feza, Dudu Pukwana, Nick Moyake, Johnny Dyani and Louis Moholo) and invited them to join him in a new band. Thus, the legendary Blue Notes were created. Apartheid made it impossible for them, as a mixed-race band, to work legally in South Africa, and so, while touring Europe in 1964, they decided not to return home. After a year in Switzerland, they settled in London, where, evolving into the Chris McGregor Group (with Ronnie Beer replacing Moyake on tenor), they made a huge impact with their exhilarating mixture of free jazz and kwela, the South African Township dance music. During that period McGregor established a big band for gigs at Ronnie Scott's Old Place and, in 1970, he formed a regular big band, the Brotherhood Of Breath. He moved to Aquitaine, France, in 1974, often playing solo gigs, although from time to time he revived the Brotherhood. McGregor was an exciting piano player whose style encompassed the power of Cecil Taylor and the gentleness of African folk melodies, but it was as leader of a series of joyful, powerful bands that he made his main reputation. He once told Valerie Wilmer, 'Real musical freedom is the ability to look inside your own personal experience and select from it at will.' He died of lung cancer in May 1990.

● ALBUMS: *The African Sound* (Gallojazz 1963)★★★, *Very Urgent* (Polydor 1968)★★★, *Brotherhood Of Breath* (RCA Neon 1971)★★★★, *Brotherhood* (RCA 1972)★★★★, *Live At Willisau* (1975)★★★, *Blue Notes For Mongezi* (1976)★★★, *Piano Song Volumes 1 & 2* (1977)★★★, *Procession* (Ogun 1977)★★★, *Blue Notes In Concert* (1978)★★★, *In His Good Time* (Ogun 1979)★★★, with Brian Abrahams *Yes Please* (1982)★★★, *Blue Notes For Johnny* (Ogun 1987)★★★, *Country Cooking* (Venture 1990)★★★, *Grandmother's Teaching* (ITM 1991)★★★.

● FURTHER READING: *Chris McGregor & The Brotherhood Of Breath*, Maxine McGregor.

McGriff, Jimmy

b. James Herrell, 3 April 1936, Philadelphia, Pennsylvania, USA. Encouraged by a musical home environment (both his parents were pianists), by the time he left school, McGriff played not only piano but bass, vibes, drums and saxophone. He played with Archie Shepp, Reggie Workman, Charles Earland and Donald Bailey in his youth, but after two years as an military policeman in the Korean War, he decided to take up law enforcement rather than music as a career. This did not satisfy him in the event, and he began moonlighting as a bassist, backing blues stars such as Big Maybelle. He left the police force and studied organ at Combe College, Philadelphia, and New York's Juilliard. He also took private lessons with Jimmy Smith, Richard 'Groove' Holmes and Milt Buckner, as well as from classical organist Sonny Gatewood. His career first took off with the single 'I Got A Woman' in 1962, and he had a string of hits released through the legendary Sue label. During this decade McGriff was arguably the crown prince of the soul jazz organ movement (the undisputed King being Jimmy Smith). His stabbing style and shrill tone was much copied, particularly in the UK with the rise of the 60s beat R&B scene. Georgie Fame and Brian Auger were greatly influenced by McGriff. His memorable 'All About My Girl' remains one of his finest compositions, and has become a minor classic. Also in the 60s, his version of Thelonious Monk's 'Round Midnight' became the nightly closing down theme for the legendary UK Pirate ship, Radio London. In the late 80s he experienced a revival in his commercial success, collaborating with Hank Crawford on record and in concert. He tours for most of the year, still concentrating on Hammond organ, but also using synthesizers. A fine, bluesy player, he helped to popularize a jazz-flavoured style of R&B that is still gathering adherents in the 90s.

● ALBUMS: *I've Got A Woman* (Sue 1962)★★★, *One Of Mine* (Sue 1963)★★★, *Jimmy McGriff At The Apollo* (Sue 1963)★★★, *Jimmy McGriff At The Organ* (Sue 1963)★★★★, *Topkapi* (Sue 1964)★★★, *One Of Mine* (Sue 1964)★★★, *Blues For Mister Jimmy* (Sue 1965)★★★★, *The Big Band Of Jimmy McGriff* (Solid State 1966)★★★★, *A Bag Full Of Soul* (Solid State 1966)★★★★, *Cherry* (Solid State 1967)★★★, *Honey* (Solid State 1968)★★★, *The Worm* (Solid State 1968)★★★★, *A Thing To Come By* (Solid State 1969)★★, *Electric Funk* (Blue Note 1969)★★, *Groove Grease* (Groove Merchant 1971)★★★, *Black And Blues* (Groove Merchant 1971)★★★, *Let's Stay Together* (Simitar 1972)★★★, *Fly Dude* (Groove Merchant 1972)★★★, *Come Together* (Groove Merchant 1973)★★★, *Main Squeeze* (Groove Merchant 1974)★★★, *City Lights* (Jazz America 1981)★★, *Movin' Upside The Blues* (Jazz America 1982)★★★, *The Countdown* (Milestone 1983)★★★, *Skywalk* (Milestone 1985)★★★, *State Of The Art* (Milestone 1986)★★★, with Hank Crawford *Soul Survivors* (Milestone 1986)★★★★, *The Starting Five* (Milestone 1987)★★★, *Blue To The Bone* (Milestone 1988)★★, *On The Blue Side* (Milestone 1990)★★★, *You Ought To Think About Me* (Headfirst 1990)★★★, *In A Blue Mood* (Headfirst 1991)★★, with Crawford *Blues Groove* (Telarc 1996)★★★, *The Dream Team* (Milestone 1997)★★★★.

● COMPILATIONS: *A Toast To Jimmy McGriff's Golden Classics* (Collectable 1989)★★★, *Georgia On My Mind* (LRC 1990)★★★★, *The Funkiest Little Band In The Land* (LRC 1992)★★★, *Pullin' Out The Stops! The Best Of Jimmy McGriff* (Blue Note 1994)★★★★.

McHargue, Rosy

b. James Eugene McHargue, 6 April 1902, Danville, Illinois, USA. After being taught music by his mother, McHargue began playing clarinet and C melody saxophone, settling on the former as his principal instrument largely through the inspiration of Larry Shields. He first played professionally in 1917 with the Novelty Syncopaters where he was featured as vocalist on the song 'When Rosie Riccoola Do The Hoola Ma Boola', which led to his nickname. In 1924 he hoped to join the Wolverines but when the job went to Jimmy Lord, he took over Lord's empty chair in the Sig Meyer band in Chicago. Later, he played with the Seattle Harmony Kings in Atlantic City and recorded with them on alto and baritone saxophones. During the 30s and early 40s McHargue played in the bands of Kay Kayser, Ted Weems and Benny Goodman and was also with Eddie Miller. In the mid-40s he played in several Dixieland bands including those led by Pete Daily, Red Nichols and Pee Wee Hunt. With the latter he played on '12th Street Rag', his burlesqued clarinet solo helping greatly in the record's startling success with the fringe and non-jazz audience. McHargue eventually settled on the west coast where he continued to play and frequently lead his own bands through succeeding decades. In April 1992 he celebrated his 90th birthday at a West Hollywood club, playing and singing with all his old verve and enthusiasm. Despite being little known even within the jazz community, McHargue consistently set an example to all through his ability, dedication and demeanour.

● ALBUMS: *Memphis Five* (Jump 1947)★★★, *Ragtimers* (Jump 1952)★★, *Oh, How He Can Sing!* (Stomp Off 1992)★★★.

McIntyre, 'Kalaparush' Maurice

b. 24 March 1936, Clarksville, Arkansas, USA. McIntyre's family moved to Chicago when he was six weeks old, and he grew up on the city's south side. He began to play drums at the age of seven, and clarinet two years later, but he did not really study music seriously until his mid-teens, when he concentrated on tenor saxophone. After a drugs problems in the early 60s, he worked on the Chicago blues scene - performing with Little Milton, recording with J.B. Hutto - and also joined Muhal Richard Abrams's Experimental Band, becoming one of the first members of the AACM in 1965. He played with Roscoe Mitchell's sextet (*Sound*) and with Abrams (*Levels And Degrees Of Light*) before forming his own group, the Light, and recording his first session as leader in 1969 (*Humility In The Light Of The Creator*). That same year he underwent a form of spiritual conversion and changed his name to Kalaparush (or Kalaparusha) Ahrah Difda (or Defda), though subsequent recordings have usually been credited to Kalaparush(a) Maurice McIntyre. He later spent time in New York, recording there for the *Wildflower* series of compilations (volume 1), but he was mostly based in Chicago throughout the 70s and 80s, during which time he played with a variety of artists, including Abrams again, Julius Hemphill, Jerome Cooper, Warren Smith, Roland Alexander, Sonelius Smith and Wilbur Morris. In 1982, he replaced 'Light' Henry Huff in the Ethnic Heritage Ensemble, recording with them on *Welcome* (but did not play on the later *Ancestral Song*). A robust, inventive tenor saxophonist, McIntyre cites his chief influences as Sonny Rollins, Charlie Parker, John Coltrane and Sam Rivers, but he has evolved a personal, rhythmically assured style, bristling with authority on his own *Ram's Run*, waxing more tenderly on *Welcome*. Regrettably, he is one of several AACM stalwarts who have not been recorded as frequently as their talent deserves.

● ALBUMS: *Humility In The Light Of The Creator* (Delmark 1969)★★★★, *Forces And Feelings* (1972)★★★, *Peace And Blessings* (Black Saint 1979)★★★★, *Ram's Run* (Cadence 1982)★★★.

McIntyre, Ken

b. 7 September 1931, Boston, Massachusetts, USA. McIntyre was born into a musical family (his father played mandolin) and took lessons in classical piano between 1940 and 1945. At the age of 19 he began alto saxophone lessons with Andrew McGhee, Gigi Gryce and Charlie Mariano. In 1954, he attended the Boston Conservatory, and after graduating with an MA in composition, he studied at Brandeis University for two years. He formed his own group in Boston and recorded his debut, *Stone Blues*, for the Prestige label in 1959. In 1960, he moved to New York and met Eric Dolphy, who played on his *Looking Ahead* in June of that year. Discouraged by the poor financial returns of the jazz life, McIntyre decided to make teaching his full-time profession. However, he continued to record, releasing *The Years Of The Iron Sheep* and *Way, Way Out* (the latter featuring his own flute, oboe, bass-clarinet and alto sax plus his arrangements for strings). In 1964, McIntyre recorded with the Bill Dixon Septet, and in 1965, he played with the Jazz Composers Guild Orchestra. He was also in the Cecil Taylor group that recorded *Unit Structures* in 1966, a monumental work of intricate jazz modernism. Having taught in schools in New York, he obtained a post at Wilberforce University in Ohio between 1967 and 1969, and taught at the Wesleyan University for two years after that. Since 1971, he has been director of the African-American Music and Dance Department at Old Westbury. The Danish label Steeplechase documented his playing and compositions on a series of five albums in the 70s, since when he has played with Charlie Haden's Liberation Music Orchestra, but made only one more recording under his own name (taken from a 1990 tribute concert to Dolphy, with French reeds player Thierry Bruneau). Although a less innovative talent than Eric Dolphy or Ornette Coleman, McIntyre's work represents an equally valid extension of the music of Charlie Parker and often includes elements of African-Caribbean musics in recognition of the West Indian cultural heritage.

● ALBUMS: *Stone Blues* (New Jazz 1959)★★★★, *Looking Ahead* (New Jazz 1960)★★★★, *The Years Of The Iron Sheep* (United Artists 1962)★★, *Way, Way Out* (United Artists 1963)★★★, *Hindsight* (1974)★★, *Home* (1975)★★, *Open Horizon* (1976)★★★, *Introducing The Vibrations* (Steeple Chase 1977)★★★, *Chasing The Sun* (1979)★★★★, with Thierry Bruneau *Tribute* (Serene 1991)★★★.

● COMPILATIONS: *The Complete United Artists Sessions* 1962/1963 recordings (Blue Note 1998)★★★★.

McKendrick, 'Big Mike'

b. Reuben Michael McKendrick, 1901, Paris, Tennessee, USA, d. 22 March 1965. In the 20s he played banjo and guitar with various bands including one of those led by Edgar Hayes and also with Dave Peyton. In the early 30s he was on the road with Louis Armstrong, in a playing and managerial capacity, led his own band and also played with Erskine Tate and others. He regularly accompanied singer-pianist Cleo Brown. Through the 40s and 50s he continued playing in bands including Franz Jackson's Original Jass All Stars. A solid, if occasionally erratic, player with an agreeable singing voice, McKendrick's career ran parallel to and sometimes intersected with that of his younger brother, 'Little Mike' McKendrick, with whom he is sometimes confused.

McKendrick, 'Little Mike'

b. Gilbert Michael McKendrick, *c.*1903, Paris, Tennessee, USA, d. 1961. McKendrick was born into a very musical family; his father and four brothers were all musicians. In the 20s he played guitar and banjo and also sometimes sang with various bands including Doc Cook's. In the late 20s he worked with Eddie South, visiting Europe where he remained for several years, mostly leading his own band. He returned to the USA shortly before the outbreak of World War II, playing in several bands in New York and Chicago and also leading his own trio, activities he kept up through the 40s and 50s. A good accompanist with a fine sense of rhythm, McKendrick's long years in Europe kept him from wider appreciation in his homeland. One of his brothers played similar instruments and worked as 'Big Mike' McKendrick.

McKenna, Dave

b. 30 May 1930, Woonsocket, Rhode Island, USA. By his late teens, McKenna was active in and around Boston, playing piano with Boots Mussulli's band. In 1949, he joined Charlie Ventura, then worked with Woody Herman until drafted during the Korean War. From 1953 until well into the 60s he was mostly engaged in small group work, playing with Ventura again and with several major artists, including Gene Krupa, Stan Getz and Zoot Sims. From the late 60s until the end of the 70s, he played long residencies at bars and restaurants in the Boston and Cape Cod areas of Massachusetts. His return to the national and international scene happened on several fronts, with record dates, tours and festival appearances with Bob Wilber, Scott Hamilton, Warren Vaché Jnr and many other musicians associated with Concord Records. An exceptionally accomplished pianist whether playing solo, as accompanist or in an ensemble role, McKenna's range is wide - although he is clearly happiest playing ballads to which he brings a delightfully melodic touch. Chuck Berg, writing in *Jazz Times*, stated: 'If Bach had played jazz, he just might have sounded like Dave McKenna', meaning that he makes every single note and space count.

● ALBUMS: *Solo Piano* (ABC-Paramount 1956)★★★, *Dave McKenna* (Epic 1959)★★★, *This Is The Moment* (Portrait 1963)★★★, with Hall Overton *Dual Piano Jazz* (Bethlehem 1960)★★★, *Cookin' At Michael's Pub* (1973)★★, *Both Sides Of Dave McKenna* (1973)★★★, with Zoot Sims *The Dave McKenna Quartet Featuring Zoot Sims* (Chiaroscuro 1975)★★★, *By Myself* (1976)★★★, *Dave 'Fingers' McKenna* (1977)★★, *No Holds Barred* (1977)★★★, with Joe Venuti *Alone At The Palace* (Chiaroscuro 1977)★★★★, *This Is New* (1977)★★★, *No Bass Hit* (Concord Jazz 1979)★★★, *Giant Strides* (Concord Jazz 1979)★★★★, *Oil And Viegar* (Honeydew 1979)★★★, with Scott Hamilton *Tenorshoes* (Concord Jazz 1980)★★★, *Left Handed Complement* (Concord Jazz 1980)★★★, *Piano Mover* (Concord Jazz 1980)★★★, *Dave McKenna Trio Plays The Music Of Harry Warren* (Concord Jazz 1981)★★★, *A Celebration Of Hoagy Carmichael* (Concord Jazz 1983)★★★★, *The Keyman* (Concord Jazz 1985)★★★, *Dancing In The Dark And Other Music Of Arthur Schwarz* (Concord Jazz 1985)★★★, *My Friend The Piano* (Concord Jazz 1986)★★★, *No More Ouzo For Puzo* (Concord Jazz 1988)★★, *Live At Maybeck Recital Hall - Vol. 2* (Concord Jazz 1989)★★, *Shadows 'N Dreams* (Concord Jazz 1990)★★★, *Hanging Out* (Concord Jazz 1992)★★★, with Gary Sargeant *Concord Duo Series Vol. 2* (Concord Jazz 1993)★★, *Easy Street* (Concord Jazz 1995)★★★, with Joe Temperley *Sunbeam And Thundercloud* (Concord Jazz 1996)★★★, *The Piano Scene Of* 1955 recordings (Koch Jazz 1996)★★★★, with Buddy De Franco *You Must Believe In Swing* (Concord Jazz 1997)★★★, *Christmas Ivory* (Concord Jazz 1997)★★★.

McKenzie, Red

b. William McKenzie, 14 October 1899, St. Louis, Missouri, USA, d. 7 February 1948. Very much a Jazz Age figure, McKenzie was an ordinary singer and something of a hustler. His principal contribution to jazz lay in his associations with several leading jazzmen of his day for whom he worked tirelessly, promoting record dates and gigs often in the face of reluctance and indifference. In the early 20s, he formed the Mound City Blue Blowers, a group that became enormously popular with the fringe audience. McKenzie's singing and playing of an improvised comb-and-paper instrument, together with other instrumentation such as the kazoo, sometimes militated against a true jazz feel, but among the musicians he hired to augment the band for record dates were some of the best available. The results included two tracks featuring Coleman Hawkins, 'Hello Lola' and 'If I Could Be With You One Hour Tonight', which became classics. A later band, the Rhythm Kings, featured Bunny Berigan. A close associate of McKenzie's was Eddie Condon, for whom he arranged a record date, Condon's first, which helped show the outside world what was happening in the white jazz scene in Chicago. By the early 30s, McKenzie's star had waned, but he returned to limited prominence in the mid-40s, playing at Condon's club and making a handful of records.

● COMPILATIONS: with the Rhythm Kings *Bunny And Red* (1935-36)★★★, with Eddie Condon *Chicagoans* (Jazzology 1988)★★★★.

McKibbon, Al

b. Alfred Benjamin McKibbon, 1 January 1919, Chicago, Illinois, USA. After playing bass in various Midwest bands in the late 30s and early 40s, McKibbon moved to New York where he established a solid reputation with leaders of large and small bands, such as Lucky Millinder and Coleman Hawkins. His musical interests were, however, moving away from such late swing era stylists and from the late 40s he became a prominent member of important bop groups including Dizzy Gillespie's big band and the studio band assembled for the Miles Davis-Gil Evans *Birth Of The Cool* sessions. He also worked with Thelonious Monk but maintained his connection with the mainstream and in 1951 joined George Shearing's quintet for a seven-year stint. Throughout the 60s and succeeding decades, McKibbon played and recorded with leading jazzmen, including Monk, Benny Carter and Gillespie. A meticulous sense of time, allied to a robust style has made McKibbon a much sought-after session musician, able to adapt readily to mainstream and bop demands.

McKinley, Ray

b. 18 June 1910, Fort Worth, Texas, USA, d. 7 May 1995, Largo, Florida, USA. After drumming in the dance band led by fellow Texan, singer Smith Ballew, McKinley joined the Dorsey Brothers orchestra in 1934. When the band became Jimmy Dorsey's, after his brother Tommy walked out, McKinley remained in the drum chair until 1939. In the autumn of that year he formed a band which he co-led with Will Bradley. A string of successful novelty songs, and the use of orchestral arrangements that capitalized on the current boogie-woogie craze, helped the band to become very popular. In 1942, he briefly led a band on his own but was then drafted into the US Army Air Force. He became a key member of Glenn Miller's USAAF band and, following Miller's death, took over leadership of the dance-band unit. After the war, McKinley led his own outfit for a number of years, then formed a Miller-style unit which he led until 1966. Thereafter he continued to lead bands, large and small, often geared to Miller's music, until the late 70s. He was still active, playing at Miller reunion sessions, into the mid-80s. A fine, swinging drummer, equally at home in big bands and small groups, playing four-beat or two-beat with consummate ease, and an engaging singer, McKinley made a substantial contribution to American dance music.

● ALBUMS: *One Night Stand With Ray McKinley* (1948-49)★★★, *The Swingin' 30s* (1955)★★★★, *Ray McKinley's Greatest Hits* (1956)★★★, *Glenn Miller Time* (1965)★★★★.

● COMPILATIONS: The *Will Bradley-Ray McKinley Orchestra*

(1940-41)★★★, *Howdy Friends* (1946)★★, *Ray McKinley And His Musicians 1946-1949* (1946-49)★★★★, *Blue Skies* (1948)★★★, *Ray McKinley And His Orchestra Play The Arrangements And Compositions Of Eddie Sauter* (1949)★★★★, *Ray McKinley And His Orchestra* (1949)★★★, *A Legend* (1949)★★★.

McKinney's Cotton Pickers

Originally formed shortly after the end of World War I by drummer Bill McKinney (b. 17 September 1895, d. 14 October 1969), the band adopted their name in 1926. By this time McKinney was manager, having hired Cuba Austin to replace himself on the drums. Although geared towards harmless hokum, novelty songs and other aspects of currently popular entertainment, the arrival in 1927 of arranger Don Redman turned the band onto a jazz course. Among the many fine musicians who played in the band in its earlier years were Joe Smith, Doc Cheatham, Claude Jones and Fats Waller. Resident for several years at Detroit's Graystone Ballroom, promoter Jean Goldkette's flagship venue, the unit made a huge impression upon other bands and their arrangers. In 1931, Redman left, forming his own outfit from a nucleus of McKinney musicians. This was a blow from which the band never fully recovered. Even though several important jazzmen played in later editions, among them Benny Carter, who became its musical director, the glory days were over. Indeed, the band made no more records even though it stayed in existence for a few more years. McKinney managed to continue leading a band into the early 40s, but by then it was a shadow of what had gone before. During the four years of its supremacy, the Cotton Pickers established new standards towards which all later big bands would strive. Although history would later credit the period Don Redman spent with the Fletcher Henderson Orchestra as being the start of big band music as it is known today, the arranger's work with this earlier band should not be overlooked. In particular, the lively, skilful manner in which they played Redman's arrangements suggest a band well ahead of its time and place in the story of big band jazz. McKinney himself remained only sporadically active in music for the rest of his life. A year or two after his death in 1969, a number of musicians from Detroit formed the New McKinney's Cotton Pickers, using Redman's and Carter's old scores for successful engagements at jazz festivals in America and Europe.

● COMPILATIONS: *The Complete McKinney's Cotton Pickers Volumes 1/2, 3/4, 5* 1928-31 recordings (RCA 1983)★★★★, *The Band Don Redman Built* 1928-30 recordings (Bluebird 1990)★★★★, *McKinney's Cotton Pickers* (Zeta 1991)★★★.

● FURTHER READING: *McKinney's Music: A Bio-discography Of McKinney's Cotton Pickers*, John Chilton.

McKinney, Bill

(see McKinney's Cotton Pickers)

McLaughlin, John

b. 4 January 1942, Yorkshire, England. Born into a musical family - his mother played violin - McLaughlin studied piano from the age of nine. He then took up the guitar because, like so many of his generation, he was inspired by the blues. By the time he was 14 years old, he had developed an interest in flamenco - the technical guitarist's most testing genre - and later started listening to jazz. He moved to London and his first professional gigs were as part of the early 60s blues boom, playing with Alexis Korner, Georgie Fame and Graham Bond. As the 60s progressed, McLaughlin became interested in more abstract forms, working and recording with John Surman and Dave Holland. He also spent some time in Germany playing free jazz with Gunter Hampel. His *Extrapolation*, recorded in 1969, with Surman and drummer Tony Oxley, was a landmark in British music. The rock music of the Beatles and the Rolling Stones seemed to be adding something to R&B that the Americans had not considered, so when Tony Williams - the drummer who had played on Eric Dolphy's *Out To Lunch* - formed his own band, Lifetime, it seemed natural to invite the young English guitarist aboard. McLaughlin flew to New York in 1969, but left the band the following year. His own *My Goal's Beyond* (1970) flanked his guitar with the bass of Charlie Haden and the percussion of Airto Moreira. Meanwhile, ever conscious of new directions, Miles Davis had used McLaughlin on *In A Silent Way*, music to a rock beat that loosened rhythmic integration (a nod towards what Dolphy and Ornette Coleman were doing). However, it was McLaughlin's playing on the seminal *Bitches Brew* (1970) that set the jazz world alight: it seemed to be the ideal mixture of jazz chops and rock excitement. Nearly everyone involved went off to form fusion outfits, and McLaughlin was no exception. His Mahavishnu Orchestra broke new boundaries in jazz in terms of volume, brash virtuosity and multifaceted complexity. The colossal drums of Billy Cobham steered McLaughlin, ex-Flock violinist Jerry Goodman and keyboard player Jan Hammer into an explosive creativity bordering on chaos. McLaughlin sported a custom-built electric guitar with two fretboards. By this time, too, his early interest in Theosophy had developed into a serious fascination with Eastern mysticism: McLaughlin announced his allegiance to guru Snr i Chinmoy and started wearing white clothes. When Cobham and Hammer left to form their own bands, a second Mahavishnu Orchestra formed, with ex-Frank Zappa violinist Jean-Luc Ponty and drummer Narada Michael Walden. This group never quite recaptured the over-the-top glory of the first Orchestra, and compositional coherence proved a problem. In the mid-70s, McLaughlin renounced electricity and formed Shakti with Indian violinist L. Shankar and tabla-player Zakir Hussain. This time McLaughlin's customized guitar had raised frets, allowing him to approximate sitar-like drone sounds. In 1978, McLaughlin made another foray into the world of electricity with the One Truth Band, but punk had made the excesses of jazz-rock seem old-fashioned and the band did not last long. In 1978, he teamed up with Larry Coryell and Paco De Lucia as a virtuosic guitar trio. Guitar experts were astonished, but critics noted a rather dry precision in his acoustic playing: McLaughlin seemed to need electricity and volume to spark him. After two solo albums (*Belo Horizonte*, *Music Spoken Here*), he played on Miles Davis's *You're Under Arrest* in 1984. In November 1985, he performed a guitar concerto written for him and the LA Philharmonic by Mike Gibbs. The same year he joined forces with Cobham again to create a violin-less Mahavishnu that featured saxophonist Bill Evans as an alternate solo voice. In 1986, they were joined by keyboardist Jim Beard. Two years later, McLaughlin toured with Trilok Gurtu, a percussionist trained in Indian classical music, and was again playing acoustic guitar; a 1989 trio concert (with Gurtu) at London's Royal Festival Hall was later released on record. McLaughlin was back in the UK in 1990, premiering his *Mediterranean Concerto* with the Scottish National Orchestra at the Glasgow Jazz Festival. *After The Rain* proved to be his most successful album for many years in 1995.

● ALBUMS: *Extrapolation* (Polydor/Marmalade 1969)★★★★, *Devotion* (Douglas 1970)★★★★, *My Goal's Beyond* (Douglas 1971)★★★, *Where Fortune Smiles* (Dawn 1971)★★★★, with the Mahavishnu Orchestra *The Inner Mounting Flame* (Columbia 1972)★★★★, with the Mahavishnu Orchestra *Birds Of Fire* (Columbia 1973)★★★★, with the Mahavishnu Orchestra *Between Nothingness And Eternity* (Columbia 1973)★★★, with Devadip Carlos Santana *Love, Devotion, Surrender* (Columbia 1973)★★★, with the Mahavishnu Orchestra *Apocalypse* (Columiba 1974)★★, with the Mahavishnu Orchestra *Visions Of The Emerald Beyond* (Columbia 1975)★★★, *Shakti With John McLaughlin* (Columbia 1975)★★★, with the Mahavishnu Orchestra *Inner Worlds* (Columbia 1976)★★★, *A Handful Of Beauty* (Columbia 1976)★★★, with Shakti *Natural Elements* (Columbia 1977)★★★, *Johnny McLaughlin, Electric Guitarist* (Columbia 1978)★★★★, with Al Di Meola, Paco De Lucia *Friday Night In San Francisco* (Columbia 1978)★★★, *Electric Dreams Electric Sighs* (Columbia 1979)★★★, *Belo Horizonte* (Warners 1982)★★★, *Music Spoken Here* (Warners 1982)★★★, with Di Meola, De Lucia *Passion Grace And Fire* (Mercury 1983)★★★, *Mahavishnu* (Warners 1985)★★★, *Inner Worlds* (Columbia 1987)★★★, with the Mahavishnu Orchestra *Adventures In Radioland* (PolyGram 1987)★★, *Mediterranean Concert/Duos For Guitar And Piano* (Columbia 1990)★★★, *Live At The Royal Festival Hall* (Mercury 1990)★★★, *Que Alegria* (Verve 1992)★★★★, *Time Remembered: John McLaughlin Plays Bill Evans* (1993)★★★, *Tokyo Live* (Verve 1994)★★★, *After The Rain* (Verve 1995)★★★, *The Promise* (Verve 1996)★★★★, with De Lucia, Di Meola *Paco De Lucia, Al Di Meola, John McLaughlin* (Verve 1996)★★★, *The Heart Of Things* (Verve 1998)★★★.

● COMPILATIONS: *The Best Of* (Columbia 1981)★★★★, *Compact Jazz* (Verve 1989)★★★, *The Collection* (Castle 1991)★★★, *Greatest Hits* (Columbia 1991)★★★, *Where Fortune Smiles* (Beat Goes On 1993)★★★.

● FURTHER READING: *John McLaughlin And The Mahavishnu Orchestra*, John McLaughlin.

McLawler, Sarah

b. *c.*1928, Louisville, Kentucky, USA. McLawler began playing piano by ear at the age of seven, quickly graduating to playing at the church of which her father was minister. She then took lessons and later won a scholarship to a music conservatory where she studied pipe organ and developed her wide musical knowledge. In the early 40s she was living in Chicago and her interest in jazz, already aroused by hearing touring bands elsewhere, was accelerated thanks to hearing Earl 'Fatha' Hines at a hotel where her brother-in-law was working. McLawler continued to study, this time at Fisk University, and was also starting to play in public. Her first important engagements were in Chicago clubs where she played piano as a single and also teamed up with two other young female musicians to form a trio. She continued to work in small female groups and also as a single, sometimes leading a small band, such as the Syncoettes which she led for five years in the late 40s and early 50s. During this period McLawler also occasionally sing and had a minor hit record. Eventually, the band reached New York but finally McLawler folded the group. Around this time she was encouraged by Wild Bill Davis to take up the organ and, equipped with a Hammond B3, she formed a trio that played a residency in Brooklyn. The engagement quickly became noticed in jazz circles and many leading musicians sometimes sat in. While there, McLawler was introduced to violinist Richard Ott and they teamed up musically and then matrimonially. With the addition of a drummer the group became very popular, playing the Apollo Theatre in Harlem and also making records. As McLawler told Sally Placksin, 'I reached a new plateau when I met Richard Ott. The organ and the violin was a very unusual thing . . . We were always experimenting with sound'. Mostly in duo with Ott but sometimes with drums, McLawler played throughout the 60s and into the 70s. Ott died in 1979 but McLawler played on, appearing at jazz festivals, mostly in and around New York, and appearing with the Big Apple Jazzwomen. An exceptionally gifted musician, McLawler's organ playing is perhaps her most popular form but her piano playing has a controlled flair, while her singing justifies her authentic labelling as an all-round entertainer.

● ALBUMS: *We Bring You Love* (1954)★★★, *We Bring You Swing* (1956)★★★.

McLean, Jackie

b. 17 May 1932, New York City, New York, USA. Coming as he did from a musical background (McLean's father played guitar with the Tiny Bradshaw band), Jackie was encouraged by family friends who included Bud Powell. It was through Powell that alto saxophonist McLean came to the attention of Miles Davis, with whom he played in 1951, having previously gigged with Sonny Rollins. Throughout the 50s McLean performed and recorded with numerous leading jazzmen, among them Charles Mingus and Art Blakey. He also led his own groups, touring internationally, and from the early 70s became active in musical education. In the late 70s, he had a surprising entry in the UK pop charts with his 'Dr Jackyll And Mr Funk', a disco favourite, which reached number 53. Strongly influenced by Charlie Parker and Ornette Coleman, McLean's forceful and highly personal playing style reflects his interest in several schools of modern jazz. McLean's son, Rene, is a jazz saxophonist. A fresh wave of albums in the early 90s gave McLean an Indian summer after a number of years of recording inactivity. The recent crop easily matches the best of his work during his vintage Blue Note Records period in the 60s.

● ALBUMS: *The Jackie McLean Quintet* (Adlib 1955)★★★, *Lights Out!* (Prestige 1956)★★★★, *4, 5 And 6* (Prestige 1956)★★★★, with Bill Hardman *Jackie's Pal - Introducing Bill Hardman* reissued as *Steeple Chase* (Prestige/New Jazz 1956)★★★, *McLean's Scene* (New Jazz 1957)★★★★, *Jackie McLean & Co* (Prestige 1957)★★★, *Strange Blues* (Prestige 1957)★★★, with John Jenkins *Alto Madness* (Prestige 1957)★★★, *Jackie McLean Plays Fat Jazz* (Jubilee 1958)★★★, with Gene Quill, Jenkins, Hal McKusick, Phil Woods *Bird Feathers* (New Jazz 1958)★★★, *New Soil* (Blue Note 1959)★★★★, *Swing, Swang, Swingin'* (Blue Note 1959)★★★, *Makin' The Changes* (New Jazz 1960)★★★, *Capuchin Swing* (Blue Note 1960)★★★, *Jackie's Bag* (Blue Note 1960)★★★★, *A Long Drink Of The Blues* (New Jazz 1961)★★★, *Bluesnik* (Blue Note 1961)★★★★, *Let Freedom Ring* (Blue Note 1962)★★★★, *Tippin' The Scales* (Blue Note 1962)★★★, *A Fickle Sonance* (Blue Note 1963)★★★, *Jackie McLean Sextet* (Josie 1963)★★★, *One Step Beyond* (Blue Note 1963)★★★★★, *Destination ... Out!* (Blue Note 1963)★★★★, *It's Time!* (Blue Note 1964)★★★★, *Right Now!* (Blue Note 1965)★★★★, *Action Action Action* (Blue Note 1965)★★★★, *High Frequency* (Blue Note 1966)★★★★, *Dr. Jackle* (Steeple Chase 1967)★★★★, *Tune Up* (Steeple Chase 1967)★★★★, with Ornette Coleman *New And Old Gospel* (Blue Note 1967)★★★, *'Bout Soul* (Blue Note 1968)★★★★, *Demon's Dance* (Blue Note 1969)★★★, *Live At Montmartre* (Steeple Chase 1972)★★★★, *A Ghetto Lullaby* (Inner City 1973)★★★, with Gary Bartz *Ode To Super* (Steeple Chase 1973)★★★★, with Dexter Gordon *The Meeting* (Steeple Chase 1973)★★★, with Gordon *The Source* (Steeple Chase 1974)★★★, *Antiquity* (Steeple Chases 1975)★★★, *New York Calling* (Steeple Chase 1975)★★★, *Jacknife* 1966 recording (Blue Note 1975)★★★, with Mal Waldron *Like Old Times* (1976)★★★, with Art Farmer *Art Farmer Live In Tokyo/Art Farmer Meets Jackie McLean* (1977)★★★, *Hipnosis* 1962/1967 recordings (Blue Note 1978)★★★, *New Wine, Old Bottles* (East Wind/Inner City 1978)★★★, *Monuments* (RCA 1979)★★, *Consequences* 1965 recording (Blue Note 1979)★★★, *Vertigo* 1959-1963 recordings (Blue Note 1980)★★★, *Contour* (Prestige 1980)★★★, with McCoy Tyner *It's About Time* (Blue Note 1985)★★★, with Waldron *Left Alone '86* (Evidence 1987)★★★★, *Fat Jazz* (Fresh Sounds 1988)★★★, *Dynasty* (Triloka 1990)★★★★, *Rites Of Passage* (Triloka 1991)★★★★, *Rhythm Of The Earth* (Birdology 1992)★★★★, *The Jackie Mac Attack Live* (Birdology 1993)★★★★, *Hat Trick* (Blue Note 1996)★★★, *Fire & Love* (Blue Note 1998)★★★★.

● COMPILATIONS: *The Complete Blue Note 1964-1966* 4-CD box set (Mosaic)★★★★, the Essence All Stars *Jackies Blues Bag: A Tribute To Jackie McLean* (Hip Bop Essence 1997)★★★.

McLeod, David

b. 5 January 1960, Sydney, New South Wales, Australia. In his early years McLeod showed many signs of artistic talent and studied at art school. He subsequently developed as painter, actor, pianist, singer, and, later, songwriter. As a singer-pianist he spent several years in the late 70s in 'the abyss of the piano bar circuit . . . where musicians have been known to disappear – at times forever!' The experience was invaluable, however, and in the 80s he was sufficiently developed and proficient to work as a straight pop singer, as a studio vocalist, singing advertising jingles, and as backing singer for other artists. In 1988 he formed his own band, McLeod Nine, a jazz/blues quintet. His acting career continued alongside his music and he appeared in a 1990 staging of *Chess – The Musical* at Sydney's Theatre Royal, and in 1992 was in *Godspell* at the Sydney Opera House, appearing on the subsequent cast recording. McLeod's singing draws upon several admitted influences in the worlds of jazz, pop and R&B. His singing voice is persuasive and he admirably textures his interpretation of lyrics. His own compositions offer intriguing hints of his continuing interest in the musical and lyrical aspects of nature.

● ALBUMS: *Am I Blue* (La Brava 1995)★★★.

McLin, Jimmy

b. James A. McLin, 27 June 1908, Brookesville, Florida, USA, d. 15 December 1983. After learning piano as a small child he began playing banjo, then guitar. On the latter instruments he played with several bands throughout the 20s, then moved to New York where he played with James P. Johnson and others during the 30s. In the early 40s he was with Claude Hopkins. Throughout his New York years he was frequently on call for recording sessions, including dates with Willie 'The Lion' Smith and Billie Holiday. He was in the US Navy during World War II, playing in a service band. After the war he returned to Hopkins, playing with the band into the early 50s, although he undertook extensive musical studies during these years. Always in demand for recording dates, McLin continued to work through succeeding decades, spending many years with the Ink Spots vocal group. Essentially a rhythm section player, rather than a soloist of note, McLin supplied discreet and subtly encouraging accompaniment to numerous artists on countless recording dates.

● COMPILATIONS: *The Chronological Willie 'The Lion' Smith* (Classics 1937-38)★★★★.

McMurray, David

b. *c.*1963, USA. McMurray began playing tenor saxophone in his youth and gained much experience playing in Detroit clubs. He was influenced by recordings of John Coltrane and Cannonball Adderley, among others, and also by Detroit veteran Willie Metcalf. He gained further experience on the road with blues guitarist Albert Collins and also played with pop, funk and rap artists. It is this eclectic mixture of influences and interests that have helped McMurray develop a following among the younger audience of the late 90s. His blending of jazz and rap caught the imaginations of many, with McMurray averring to jazz writer Deni Kasrel that his concept for this fusing of styles predated the appearance of Miles Davis's posthumous *Doo Bop*.

● ALBUMS: *The Dave McMurray Show* (Warners 1996)★★★.

McNair, Harold

b. 5 November 1931, Kingston, Jamaica, West Indies, d. 7 March 1971. After playing in the relative obscurity of his homeland, McNair went to Europe in the late 50s where he played with musicians such as Kenny Clarke and Quincy Jones and also led his own small group. For a while he commuted between Europe and the USA, eventually making London his base in the mid-60s. From then until his death he worked with British and American mainstream and modern musicians, and was also active in the studios.

● ALBUMS: *Affectionate Fink* (Island 1965)★★★.

McNulty, Chris

b. 23 December 1953, Melbourne, Victoria, Australia. Starting to sing professionally when she was aged 15, McNulty quickly developed a reputation in and around Melbourne. In the early 70s, while still singing in clubs and hotels, she studied musical theory. Tours of Australia and South-East Asia extended her experience and popularity and in 1975 she helped to form a jazz group that performed in the jazz-funk idiom. Simultaneously, McNulty was also in growing demand as a studio singer, working on radio and television. In 1980 she moved to Sydney where she formed a new jazz group that was highly successful during the next few years. In 1985 she visited New York where she sang at the Bluenote club. By the late 80s McNulty was back in New York, this time gaining a contract to record for Trend/Discovery. She has continued to sing in the New York area, working with such leading musicians as Peter Leitch, Cecil McBee, George Mraz and Kenny Washington. McNulty's repertoire ranges over the great standards and modern jazz classics. She has also written lyrics for various songs including Miles Davis's 'A Kind Of Blue'. Singing in a rich contralto with a pleasing hint of toughness, McNulty ably interprets the lyrics she sings while giving full rein to her ability to phrase imaginatively in the jazz idiom.

● ALBUMS: *Waltz For Debby* (1990)★★★★.

McPartland, Jimmy

b. 15 March 1907, Chicago, Illinois, USA, d. 13 March 1991. McPartland began playing cornet while still at Austin High School in Chicago, and became a founding member of both the Austin High School Gang (not all of whom were pupils there) and the Blue Friars. At the age of 17, he replaced Bix Beiderbecke in the Wolverines, and two years later was with Art Kassell's Castles In The Air band. In 1927, he joined Ben Pollack for a two-year stint, then freelanced with numerous bands, small and large, playing on many record dates, until World War II. While still on active service, he married British pianist Marian Turner (see Marian McPartland). After the war he returned to playing in small Dixieland-orientated bands, toured many countries, and was still entertaining audiences in the mid-80s with appearances at prestigious events such as the Nice Jazz Festival. A fiery, exuberant player, McPartland was also capable of playing with a wistful elegance that recalled his earliest and greatest influence, Bix Beiderbecke.

● ALBUMS: *Shades Of Bix* (1953)★★★, with Dizzy Gillespie *Hot Vs. Cool* (MGM 1955)★★★★, *Jimmy McPartland's Dixieland* (1957)★★★★, *Meet Me In Chicago* (1959)★★★★, with Marian McPartland *The McPartlands Live At The Monticello* (1972)★★★.

● COMPILATIONS: *One Night Stand* (Jazzology 1987)★★★★, *On Stage* (Jazzology 1990)★★★.

McPartland, Marian

b. Marian Margaret Turner, 20 March 1920, Windsor, Berkshire, England. Prior to World War II, McPartland played British music halls as a member of a four-piano group led by Billy Mayer. While touring with ENSA (the British equivalent of America's USO), she met and married Jimmy McPartland. At the end of the war she went to the USA with her husband, quickly establishing a reputation in her own right. During the late 40s and throughout the following decade, she worked steadily, usually leading a trio, holding down several long residencies, notably an eight-year spell at the Hickory House. During the 60s and 70s she developed a long-lasting interest in education, established her own recording company, Halcyon Records, performed extensively in clubs and at festivals and also began parallel careers as a writer and broadcaster on jazz. A very gifted pianist, rhythmically near-perfect and with a seemingly endless capacity for intelligent improvising, her long-running radio show, *Piano Jazz*, has helped to establish her as one of the best-known jazz artists in America. Although divorced from her husband Jimmy, she has latterly made occasional concert appearances with him. McPartland has also worked successfully in duos with Joe Venuti, and with fellow pianists Teddy Wilson and George Shearing. In addition to her other many activities, she has also made a successful crossover into classical music, performing such works as the Grieg Piano Concerto, George Gershwin's 'Rhapsody in Blue', and a series of popular songs arranged for piano and orchestra by Robert Farnon. Although relatively little known in the country of her birth, McPartland continues to prove herself to be one of the outstanding pianists in jazz. A collection of her articles on jazz, *All In Good Time*, was published in 1987.

● ALBUMS: *Jazz At Storyville* (1951)★★★★, *Moods Vol. 2* (1952)★★★, *The Magnificent Marian McPartland At The Piano* (1952)★★★★, *Great Britons* one side only (1952)★★, *Lullaby Of Birdland* (1953)★★★★, *Jazz At The Hickory House* i (Savoy 1953)★★★, *Jazz At The Hickory House* ii (Savoy 1954)★★★, *The Marian McPartland Trio* i (1955)★★★, *The Marian McPartland Trio* ii (1956)★★★, *With You In My Mind* (1957)★★★, *At The London House* (1958)★★★, *The Music Of Leonard Bernstein*

(1960)★★★★, *The Marian McPartland Quintet* (1963)★★★, *Marian McPartland And Her Orchestra/Marian McPartland January 6th & 8th 1964* (1964)★★, *The Marian McPartland Trio iii* (1968)★★★, *Interplay* (1969)★★, *Ambiance* (1970),★★ *A Delicate Balance* (1972)★★★, with Teddy Wilson *Elegant Piano* (1972)★★★, with Jimmy McPartland *The McPartlands Live At The Monticello* (1972)★★★, *Marian McPartland Plays The Music Of Alec Wilder* (Jazz Alliance 1973)★★★, *Marian Remembers Teddi* (1973)★★, *Swingin'* (1973)★★★, *Solo Concert At Haverford* (1974)★★★, *Concert In Argentina* one side only (1974)★★, with Joe Venuti *The Maestro And Friend* (Halcyon 1974)★★★, *Send In The Clowns* (1976)★★, *Wanted!* (1977)★★, *Make Magnificent Music* (1977)★★, *Now's The Time* (1977)★★, *From This Moment On* (Concord 1978)★★★, *Portrait Of Marian McPartland* (Concord 1979)★★★★, *At The Festival* (1979)★★★, *Live At The Carlyle* (1979)★★★, *Alone Together* (1981)★★★, *Personal Choice* (Concord 1982)★★★, *Willow Creek And Other Ballads* (Concord 1985)★★, *Marian McPartland Plays The Music Of Billy Strayhorn* (Concord 1987)★★★★, *Marian McPartland Plays The Benny Carter Songbook* (Concord 1990)★★★, *Live At Maybeck Recital Hall* (Concord 1991)★★★, *Marian McPartland's Piano Jazz With Guest Dave Brubeck* (Bellaphon 1993)★★★, *With Rosemary Clooney* (The Jazz Alliance 1993)★★★★, *In My Life* (Concord Jazz 1993)★★★, *Marian McPartland's Piano Jazz With Henry Mancini* (The Jazz Alliance 1995)★★★, *Marian McPartland's Piano Jazz With Roy Eldridge* (The Jazz Alliance 1995)★★★, with Stanley Cowell *Marian McPartland's Piano Jazz With Guest Stanley Cowell* 1981 recording (Concord Jazz 1995)★★★, *Piano Jazz With Joe Williams* (Concord Jazz 1996)★★★, *Live At Yoshi's Nightspot* (Concord Jazz 1996)★★★, with Les McCann *Marian McPartland's Piano Jazz With Guest Les McCann* (The Jazz Alliance 1996)★★★, with Charles Brown *Marian McPartland's Piano Jazz With Guest Charles Brown* (The Jazz Alliance 1996)★★★★, *Silent Pool* (Concord Jazz 1997)★★★, with various artists *Just Friends* (Concord Jazz 1998)★★★★.

● FURTHER READING: *All In Good Time*, Marian McPartland.

McPhee, Joe

b. 3 January 1939, Miami, Florida, USA. McPhee played the trumpet in his school band and studied music theory and harmony in his Division Band while he was with the army in Germany (1964-65). His first recording was with fellow trumpeter Clifford Thornton in 1967. While he was playing with the Matt Jordan Orchestra in the late 60s, he took up the saxophone as he became interested in free jazz. He gave a lecture course entitled 'The Revolution In Sound' when he taught at Vassar College (1969-71). McPhee has sought to extend the tonal range of the saxophone, introducing grainy effects into his playing and extending his phrasing by using circular breathing. The freedom he seeks is often clearly tied to melody. Though his first recording on saxophone was with Shakey Jake (vocal/harmonica) in 1972, he soon moved to New York to work with trumpeter Don Cherry, Thornton and the Jazz Composers Orchestra. In the mid-70s he worked in Europe with Steve Lacy, among others.

● ALBUMS: *Black Magic Man* (hatART 1970)★★★, *The Willisau Concert* (hatART 1976)★★★, *Graphics* (hatART 1977)★★★, *Variations On A Blue Line ' Round Midnight* (hatART 1978)★★★, *Old Eyes And Mysteries* (hatART 1979)★★★, *Topology* (hatART 1981)★★★, *Po Music: Oleo* (hatART 1982)★★★, with the Bill Smith Ensemble *Visitation* 1983 recording (Sackville 1987)★★★★, *Linear B* (hatART 1990)★★★, with André Jaume, Raymond Boni *Impressions Of Jimmy Giuffre* (1993)★★, with Lisle Ellis, Paul Plimley *Sweet Freedom: Now What?* (hatART 1995)★★★, *Joe McPhee & Survival Unit II At WBAI's Free Music Store* 1971 recording (hatART 1996)★★★★, with Rashied Ali, Borah Bergman, Wilber Morris *The October Revolution* 1994 recording (Evidence 1997)★★★, with David Prentice *Inside Out* (CIMP 1997)★★★★, with Michael Bisio *Fingers Wigglers* (CIMP 1997)★★★, *Legend Street One* (CIMP 1997)★★★★, *A Meeting In Chicago* (Okkadisk (1997)★★★★, *As Serious As Your Life* (hatOLOGY 1998)★★★.

McPherson, Charles

b. 24 July 1939, Joplin, Missouri, USA. Often dismissed as a Charlie Parker copyist, McPherson is in fact more than a simple revivalist. While the style in which he plays, bebop, is now outmoded, it is one with which he grew up, and he plays it with fire and conviction. His family moved to Detroit when he was aged nine, and it was at high school, a few years later, that he started playing trumpet and flügelhorn. McPherson took up alto saxophone in his early teens (although he had wanted to play tenor), but his vocation for alto was confirmed, however, when he heard Parker. While in Detroit he spent some time studying with Barry Harris, and then, after moving to New York, he worked in Greenwich Village with Lonnie Hillyer in the early 60s. Fellow Detroit saxophonist Yusef Lateef suggested to Charles Mingus that he should hear McPherson when he was looking for a replacement for Eric Dolphy, and thus McPherson began the first of his stints with Mingus's band, garnering some critical plaudits for his work with one of the more adventurous bop-based leaders. Almost a forgotten man until the late 80s, he deservedly came back into the limelight as a result of a couple of successful European tours. He also played on part of the soundtrack for Clint Eastwood's biopic of Parker, *Bird*.

● ALBUMS: *Bebop Revisited!* (Prestige 1965)★★★★, *Con Alma!* (Prestige 1966)★★★, *The Charles McPherson Quintet Live!* (Prestige 1967)★★★★, *From This Moment On* (Prestige 1968)★★★, *Horizons* (Prestige 1969)★★★, *McPherson's Mood* (1969)★★★, *Siku Ya Bibi* (Mainstream 1972)★★★, *Beautiful* (Xanadu 1975)★★, *Live In Tokyo* (Xanadu 1976)★★★, *New Horizons* (Xanadu 1977)★★★, *Free Bop!* (Xanadu 1978)★★★, *The Prophet* (Discovery 1983)★★★, *First Flight Out* (Arabesque 1994)★★★★, *Live At Vartan Jazz* (Vartan Jazz 1997)★★★, *Manhattan Nocturne* (Arabesque 1998)★★★★.

McQuater, Tommy

b. Thomas Mossie, 4 September 1914, Maybole, Ayrshire, Scotland. A self-taught trumpeter, he gained wide professional experience in the mid-30s playing in many leading British dance bands. These included Jack Payne, Lew Stone and Ambrose. During World War II he was in the Royal Force's noted dance band, the Squadronaires. In the late 40s and for the next four decades, he worked extensively in theatre, radio and television bands. A highly accomplished lead trumpeter, McQuater's solo work in a jazz context was fiery and exhilarating and he played and recorded with many notable leaders including George Chisholm, John Dankworth and visiting Americans such as Benny Carter in the 30s and Benny Goodman in the 60s. In 1995 he was still enjoying life and helping fellow octogenarian Chisholm celebrate his birthday. McQuater's enthusiasm and skills as a teacher brought him the respect of many younger musicians and his pupils include distinguished trumpeters such as Ian Carr and Digby Fairweather.

● COMPILATIONS: *Swing' Britain: The Thirties* (Deccas 1935-38)★★★.

McRae, Carmen

b. 8 April 1920, New York City, New York, USA, d. 10 November 1994, Beverly Hills, California, USA. One of the best American jazz singers, McRae was also an accomplished pianist and songwriter. Early in her career she sang with bands led by Benny Carter, Mercer Ellington, Charlie Barnet and Count Basie (sometimes under the name of Carmen Clarke, from her brief marriage to Kenny Clarke). Although a familiar figure on the New York jazz club scene, including a spell in the early 50s as intermission pianist at Minton's Playhouse, her reputation did not spread far outside the jazz community. In the 60s and 70s she toured internationally and continued to record - usually accompanied by a small group - but she was joined on one occasion by the Clarke-Boland Big Band. By the 80s, she was one of only a tiny handful of major jazz singers whose work had not been diluted by commercial pressures. One of her early songs, 'Dream Of Life', written when she was just 16 years old, was recorded in 1939 by Billie Holiday. Although very much her own woman, McRae occasionally demonstrated the influence of Holiday through her ability to project a lyric with bittersweet intimacy. She also sang with remarkable rhythmic ease and her deft turns-of-phrase helped to conceal a relatively limited range, while her ballad singing revealed enormous emotional depths. Her repertoire included many popular items from the Great American Songbook, but her jazz background ensured that she rarely strayed outside the idiom. Relaxed and unpretentious in performance and dedicated to her craft, McRae secured a place in the history of jazz singing.

● ALBUMS: *Carmen McRae* i 10-inch album (Bethlehem 1954)★★★, *By Special Request* (Decca 1955)★★★, *Torchy!* (Decca 1956)★★★, *Blue Moon* (Decca 1956)★★★, *After Glow* (Decca 1957)★★★, *Carmen For Cool Ones* (Decca 1957)★★★★, *Mad About The Man* (Decca 1957)★★★★, with Sammy Davis Jnr. *Boy Meets Girl* (1957)★★★, *Book Of Ballads* (Kapp 1958)★★★★, *Birds Of A Feather* (Decca 1958)★★★, *When You're Away* (Kapp 1958)★★★, *Something To Swing About* (Kapp 1959)★★★★, *Carmen McRae Live At Sugar Hill* (Time 1960)★★★, *Carmen McRae Sings Lover Man And Other Billie Holiday Classics* (Columbia 1961)★★★★, *Carmen McRae Live At The Flamingo Club, London* (1961)★★★, *Carmen McRae* iii (Vocalion 1962)★★★, *Something Wonderful* (Columbia 1962)★★★, *Carmen McRae* ii (Vocalion 1963)★★★, *In Person* (1963)★★★, *Bittersweet* (Focus 1964)★★★, *Woman Talk: Carmen McRae Live At The Village Gate* (Mainstream 1965)★★★★, *Second To None* (Mainstream 1965)★★★, *Live And Doin' It* (1965)★★★, *Haven't We Met?* (Mainstream 1965)★★★, *Alfie* (Mainstream 1966)★★★, *Portrait Of Carmen* (Atlantic 1967)★★★, *This Is Carmen McRae* (Kapp 1967)★★★★, *For Once In My Life* (Atlantic 1967)★★★, *Yesterday* (Harmony 1968)★★★, with Kenny Clarke, Francy Boland *November Girl* (1970)★★★, *Just A Little Lovin'* (1970)★★★, *The Great American Songbook* (1971)★★★, *As Time Goes By* (1973)★★★, *It Takes A Whole Lot Of Human Feeling* (1973)★★★, *Carmen McRae And Zoot Sims* (1973)★★★, *I Am Music* (1975)★★★, *Can't Hide Love* (Blue Note 1976)★★, *Carmen McRae At The Great American Music Hall* (1976)★★★, *Live At The Roxy* (1976)★★★, *Ronnie Scott Presents Carmen McRae 'Live'* (Pye/Ronnie Scott 1977)★★★, *For Carmen McRae* (1977)★★★, *I'm Coming Home Again* (1978)★★★, with George Shearing *Two For The Road* (Concord Jazz 1980)★★★, *Recorded Live At Bubba's* (1981)★★★, *Heat Wave* (Concord Jazz 1982)★★★, *You're Lookin' At Me (A Collection Of Nat 'King' Cole Songs)* (Concord Jazz 1983)★★★, *Any Old Time* (Denon 1986)★★★, *Fine And Mellow: Live At Birdland West* (Concord Jazz 1987)★★★, *Velvet Soul* 1973 recording (Denon 1988)★★★, *Carmen Sings Monk* (Novus 1989)★★★, *Sarah Dedicated To You* (Novus 1991)★★★, *Dream Of Life* 1989 recording (Qwest 1998)★★★★.

● COMPILATIONS: *The Ultimate Carmen McRae* (Mainstream 1991)★★★★, *Sings Great American Songwriters* 1955-59 recordings (GRP 1994)★★★★.

● VIDEOS: Live (Verve Video 1990).

McRae, Teddy

b. Theodore McRae, 22 January 1908, Philadelphia, Pennsylvania, USA. He first played in a family band that included his brothers Bobby and Dave. Playing tenor saxophone, he worked with various bands in the 20s and also led his own. John Chilton records that he also studied medicine before settling on music as his career. In New York in the early 30s, he played with Chick Webb, Elmer Snowden, Benny Morton, Stuff Smith and others, then rejoined Webb, remaining in the band after it was taken over by Ella Fitzgerald who was its nominal leader, McRae being the straw boss. During the 40s he played in several big bands including those led by Cab Calloway, Jimmie Lunceford and Lionel Hampton. By this time, McRae was also established as an arranger and he worked in this capacity for Artie Shaw, arranging for the band his own compositions 'Traffic Jam' and 'Back Bay Shuffle', among others. In 1944 he became musical director of the last big band Louis Armstrong led. Thereafter, McRae concentrated on writing and also ran his own record company in partnership with pianist Eddie Wilcox. A robust-toned player in the Coleman Hawkins tradition, McRae's playing often reveals great imagination and a subtle understanding of the chiaroscuro effects possible with his instruments (he also sometimes played alto). His abilities as a composer and arranger were also extremely good although the sometimes derivative sounds of the swing era big bands offered little scope for free flights of imagination.

● COMPILATIONS: as arranger *The Indispensable Artie Shaw Vols. 1 & 2* (RCA 1938-39)★★★★, *The Chronological Chick Webb* (Classics 1935-38)★★★★.

McShann, Jay 'Hootie'

b. 12 January 1909, Muskogee, Oklahoma, USA. After playing in many territory bands in the south-west and Midwest, pianist McShann settled in Kansas City in the mid-30s, playing in Buster Smith's band, which also included Charlie Parker, in 1937. The following year, McShann formed his own unit which included Gene Ramey and Gus Johnson as well as Parker. By 1941, with the departure from Kansas City of Harlan Leonard, McShann's became the city's top band, Count Basie having moved on to greater things a few years earlier. The most popular member of the band was singer Walter Brown, who was featured on a handful of hit records, although McShann was himself an above-average blues shouter. In retrospect, the 1941 band is regarded as the most interesting of those McShann led because the saxophone section included the fast-developing and revolutionary talent of Parker. In fact, all McShann's bands had the virtues common to most Kansas City bands, those of lithely swinging, blues-based, exciting jazz. In 1944, McShann folded the band to enter the armed forces, regrouping in 1945 on the west coast. Once again he showed himself to have a good ear for singers by hiring Jimmy Witherspoon. During the 50s and 60s, McShann was active, sometimes leading small groups, sometimes working as a solo act, but the jazz world was largely indifferent. By the 70s, however, he had become a popular figure on the international festival circuit, playing piano and singing the blues with flair and vigour. His recording career was also revitalized, and the 70s and 80s saw a steady stream of fine recordings, many of which were in the authentic tradition of the blues. The remarkable McShann was still performing at Blues Festivals in the mid-90s.

● ALBUMS: *Kansas City Memories* (Decca 1954)★★★★, *McShann's Piano* (1966)★★★, *Confessin' The Blues* (1969)★★★, *Live In France* (1969)★★★, *Roll 'Em* (1969-77)★★★, *With Kansas City In Mind* (Swaggie 1969-72 recordings)★★★, *Jumpin' The Blues* (1970)★★★, *The Man From Muskogee* (1972)★★★★, *Going To Kansas City* (1972)★★★, *Kansas City Memories* (Black And Blue 1973)★★★, *Vine Street Boogie* (1974)★★★, *Kansas City Joys* (1976)★★, *Crazy Legs And Friday Strut* (1976)★★★, *Live At Istres* (1977)★★, *Kansas City On My Mind* (1977)★★★, *After Hours* (1977)★, *The Last Of The Blue Devils* (1977)★★★, *Blues And Boogie* (1978)★★★, *Kansas City Hustle* (1978)★★★, *A Tribute To Fats Waller* (1978)★★★, *The Big Apple Bash* (1978)★★, *Tuxedo Junction* (1980)★★, with Al Casey *Best Of Friends* (JSP 1982)★★★, *Swingmatism* (Sackville 1982), *Just A Lucky So And So* (1983), *At The Cafe Des Copains* (Sackville 1983-89)★★★, *Magical Jazz* (1984)★★★, *Airmail Special* (Sackville 1985)★★★, *A Tribute To Charlie Parker* (S&R 1991)★★, *Some Blues* (Chiaroscuro 1993)★★★, with John Hicks *The Missouri Connection* (Reervoir 1993)★★★, *Some Blues* (Chiaroscuro 1994)★★★, *My Baby With The Black Dress On* 1991 live recording (Chiaroscuro 1998)★★, *Havin' Fun* 1986 live recording (Sackville 1998)★★.

● COMPILATIONS: *Hootie's KC Blues* (1941-42)★★★, *Blues From Kansas City* (MCA 1941-43 recordings)★★★★, *The Band That Jumps The Blues* (1947-49)★★★★.

● VIDEOS: *Roosevelt Sykes/Jay 'Hootie' McShann* (1992).

McVea, Jack

b. 5 November 1914, Los Angeles, California, USA. Starting out on banjo, McVea played in his father's band before he reached his teenage years. In the late 20s, he began playing reed instruments, eventually concentrating on tenor saxophone. In the early 30s, after graduating from high school, he turned professional and worked with a number of bands, including that led by Charlie Echols. In 1936, he was with Eddie Barefield and, after a brief spell leading his own unit, joined Lionel Hampton in 1940. With Hampton he mostly played baritone saxophone. After a short stint with Snub Mosley, he became interested in new developments in jazz and worked with Dizzy Gillespie and Charlie Parker. McVea was also featured at an early Jazz At The Philharmonic concert. Despite his interest in bop, McVea appreciated current popular tastes, and his R&B single, 'Open The Door, Richard', a massive hit in 1946, brought him international attention. This celebrity allowed him to maintain a small R&B band for the next several years, playing clubs, hotels, casinos and concerts in various parts of the USA. In the late 50s he also played in bands led by Benny Carter among others. In the mid-60s McVea led a trio at Disneyland, a gig he retained into the 80s.

● ALBUMS: *Nothin' But Jazz* (Harlequin 1962)★★★.

● COMPILATIONS: *Open The Door, Richard* 40s recordings (Jukebox Lil 1985), *Come Blow Your Horn* (Ace 1985)★★★★, *Two Timin' Baby* (Jukebox Lil 1986)★★★, *New Deal* (Jukebox Lil 1989)★★★.

Medeski, Martin And Wood

(see MMW)

Meditations - John Coltrane

One of John Coltrane's classic religious suites, *Meditations* is a long and complex work from a period late in his career, when he was beginning to break his ties with the classic quartet, and augment the band with new members. Pianist McCoy Tyner, bassist Jimmy Garrison and drummer Elvin Jones are joined by tenor saxophonist Pharoah Sanders on the front line and drummer Rashied Ali. In five parts, joined by long improvised linking passages, *Meditations* is an intense, emotional and difficult work, and signalled the beginning of a fiercely challenging final period for Coltrane.

● Tracks: *Love; Consequences; Serenity; The Father And The Son And The Holy Ghost; Compassion.*

● First released 1966

● UK peak chart position: did not chart

● USA peak chart position: did not chart

Mehldau, Brad

b. 1970, USA. Contemporary jazz pianist Brad Mehldau has built an enviable reputation in his early career for his use of spacious phrasing and single-note figures and phrases. He chose this approach because 'it helps to bring more expression to the playing, more depth, particularly with ballads.' Others have analogized this technique as 'meditative'. He made his debut for Warner Brothers Records in 1995 with *Introducing Brad Mehldau*. Mainly comprising standards such as Duke Ellington's 'Prelude To A Kiss', this album also featured his own compositions such as 'Angst', which betrayed a stylistic debt to idols such as Art Tatum, Oscar Peterson and Herbie Hancock. Previously Mehldau had worked on recordings by Joshua Redman, Peter Bernstein and Christopher Hollyday. He has also toured with tenor saxophonist David Sanchez.

● ALBUMS: *Introducing Brad Mehldau* (Warners 1995)★★★, *The Art Of The Trio Volume One* (Warners 1996)★★★★, *The Art Of The Trio Volume Two* (Warners 1998)★★★★, *Songs: The Art Of The Trio Volume Three* (Warners 1998)★★★★.

Melly, George

b. 17 August 1926, Liverpool, Lancashire, England. Deeply involved in the UK trad scene of the late 40s and 50s, Melly sang with Mick Mulligan's band. In the 60s he switched careers, exploiting his interest in and knowledge of both music and art to become one of the UK's most ubiquitous critics and writers. He also became a popular television personality, and published the first volume in a series of three autobiographical works. In the early 70s Melly returned to music, performing regularly with John Chilton's band. He has continued to sing with Chilton, touring extensively and entertaining audiences with his broadly based repertoire which encompasses early blues, popular songs of 20s and 30s vaudeville, and a smattering of later material, some of it written especially by Chilton, which suits Melly's highly personal, orotund singing style.

● ALBUMS: *George Melly With Mick Mulligan's Band* (1957)★★★★, *George Melly* (1961)★★★, *Nuts* (WEA 1971)★★★, *Son Of Nuts* (WEA 1972)★★, *At It Again* (1976)★★★, *Melly Sings Hoagy* (1978)★★★, *Ain't Misbehavin'* (1979)★★★★, *It's George* (1980)★★★, *Let's Do It* (PRT 1981)★★★, *Like Sherry Wine* (1981)★★, *Makin' Whoopee* (1982)★★★, *The Many Moods Of Melly* (1984)★★★★, *16 Golden Classics* (Unforgettable 1986)★★★★, *Running Wild/Hometown* (1986)★★★, *Anything Goes* (PRT 1988)★★★, *George Melly And Mates* (One-Up 1991)★★★, *Best Of George Melly* (Kaz 1992)★★★★, *Frankie And Johnny* (D-Sharp 1992)★★★.

● FURTHER READING: *Owning Up*, George Melly. *Rum, Bum And Concertina*, George Melly. *Scouse Mouse*, George Melly. *Mellymobile, 1970-1981*, George Melly. *Scouse Mouse*, George Melly. *Revolt Into Style*, George Melly.

Memphis Jug Band

Perhaps the most important and certainly the most popular of the jug bands, the Memphis Jug Band flourished on record between 1927 and 1934, during which time they recorded some 80 tracks - first for Victor then later for Columbia/OKeh Records. On one occasion they moonlighted for Champion using the name the Picaninny Jug Band. Their repertoire covered just about every kind of music that anybody could wish to hear, and their personal appearances ran from fish-frys to bar mitzvahs. Recording for their own people, they restricted themselves to ballads, dance tunes (including waltzes), novelty numbers and blues. Usually a knockabout conglomeration, they could produce blues of feeling and beauty when required. The group had an ever-changing personnel that revolved around the nucleus of Charlie Burse and Will Shade. Other members included some of the stars of the Memphis blues scene such as Memphis Minnie, Casey Bill Weldon, Jab Jones, Milton Robey, Vol Stevens, Ben Ramey, Charlie Polk and Hattie Hart. Basically a string band augmented by such 'semi-legitimate' instruments as harmonicas, kazoos, washboards and jugs blown to supply a bass, the MJB had a constantly shifting line-up featuring violins, pianos, mandolins, banjos and guitars in different combinations. This, coupled with ever-changing vocalists, lent their music a freshness, vitality and variety that enables it to charm, entertain or move the listener as much today as it did during the great days of Beale Street. Although they ceased to record in 1934, this loose aggregation of musicians continued to work around Memphis until well into the 40s; some of its members were recorded again by researchers in the 60s.

● COMPILATIONS: *The Memphis Jug Band 1927-1934* (Matchbox 1986)★★★, *The Memphis Jug Band: Volume 1 (1927-28)* (Roots 1988)★★★, *Volume 2 (1928-29)* (Roots 1988)★★★, *Volume 3 (1930)* (Roots 1988)★★★, *Volume 5 (1932-34)* (Roots 1988)★★★, *The Memphis Jug Band - Alternate Takes And Associates* (1991)★★★.

Mendoza, Vince

b. Connecticut, USA. A highly skilled arranger with multicultural influences, Mendoza has become very well known in Europe, thanks in large part to a spell as arranger and conductor with the German WDR Big Band, based in Cologne. Performances with this band have often featured visiting American jazzmen, among them Charlie Mariano, Peter Erskine, Dave Liebman and Michael Brecker, and British trombonist Dave Horler. In 1992 he released the twice-Grammy-nominated *Jazzpaña*, co-leading the WDR Big Band with Arif Mardin. *Sketches* was premiered at the 1993 Berlin Jazz Festival, and showcased Liebman's soprano work. Currently resident in West Los Angeles, Mendoza still makes regular trips to Europe, and has recently collaborated with the Dutch Metropole Orchestra. His writing incorporates classical music influences together with shades of Latin American music. His jazz influences evolve from a deep awareness of the music of Gil Evans and Miles Davis.

● ALBUMS: *Jazzpaña* (ACT/Atlantic 1992)★★★★, *Sketches* (ACT/Blue Jackel 1994)★★★★.

MENGELBERG, MISHA

b. 5 April 1935, Kiev, Ukraine. Mengelberg was raised in Holland where, for 30 years, he has personified the Dutch *avant garde*. He characterizes himself as 'a rotten piano player' - if that is the case, wittier use has rarely been made of limitations. Mengelberg has consistently aligned himself with iconoclastic and provocative musicians, from straight music's Zen terrorists David Tudor and John Cage in the early 60s, to Eric Dolphy in 1963, to the members of the Dutch Instant Composers Pool, with whom he still works. Together with his long-standing ICP collaborator Han Bennink, he has been one of the main instigators behind three albums that have paid tribute to pianist Herbie Nichols - two with a small group that also featured Steve Lacy, and one with the ICP Orchestra. As an improviser, Mengelberg holds out for the 'responsibility to be different every day' and is against the jazzman's obsession with personal style and touch. All the same, his compositions reveal an identifiable preoccupation with irony, some pieces, in fact, dripping with sarcasm. The ICP Orchestra is currently the main outlet for his writing, but he also composes for the Berlin Contemporary Jazz Orchestra.

● ALBUMS: *Misha Mengelberg Trio* (1960)★★★, *Kwartet* (1966)★★, *Driekusman Total Loss* (1966)★★★, with John Tchicai, Han Bennink *Instant Composers Pool* (1968)★★★, *Groupcomposing* (1970)★★, with Tchicai, Bennink, Derek Bailey *Instant Composers Pool 1970* (1971)★★★★, *Misha Mengelberg/Han Bennink* (1971)★★★, with Bennink *Het Scharrebroekse* (1972)★★★, with Bennink *Einepartietischtennis* (1974)★★★★, with Bennink *Coincidents* (1975)★★★, with Bennink *Untitled Album* (1975)★★★, *Tenterett* (1977)★★, with Bennink *Midwoud* (1977)★★★, *Pech Onderweg* (1978)★★★, with Dudu Pukwana, Bennink *Yi Yole* (1978)★★★, *ICP Tentet In Berlin* (1978)★★★, *Mengelberg-Bennink* (1979)★★, with Paul Rutherford, Mario Schiano, Bennink *A European Proposal* (1979)★★★, with Peter Brötzmann, Bennink *Three Points And A Mountain* (1980)★★★★, *ICP Orchestra Live In Soncino* (1980)★★★, *Japan Japon* (1982)★★★, with Bennink, Arjen Gorter, Steve Lacy, George Lewis *Change Of Season (Music Of Herbie Nichols)* (Soul Note 1985)★★★, *Impromptus* (FMP 1986)★★★, *Two Programs: ICP Performs Nichols/Monk* (1986)★★, with Pino Minafra *Tropic Of The Mounted Sea Chicken* (1990)★★★, with Bennink, Lacy, Lewis, Ernst Reyseger *Dutch Masters* 1987 recording (Soul Note 1991)★★★, *The Root Of The Problem* (hatOLOGY 1998)★★★★, *No Idea* (DIW 1998)★★★★.

● FURTHER READING: *New Dutch Swing*, Kevin Whitehead.

MENZA, DON

b. 22 April 1936, Buffalo, New York, USA. In 1960, after military service, during which he had become adept as both an instrumentalist and an arranger, tenor saxophonist Menza joined the Maynard Ferguson band. He was then briefly with Stan Kenton but opted to return to his home-town, showing a preference for small-group work. In the mid-60s, he lived and worked in Germany. In 1968, he returned to the USA, playing in the Buddy Rich big band. Resident in Los Angeles throughout the next decade, Menza developed his writing, both as arranger and composer. In particular, he wrote for Louie Bellson, with whom he also played and recorded. In the 80s, he played with several Los Angeles-based big bands, including that led by Bill Berry, and also led his own big bands and small groups. He toured extensively, at home and overseas, usually appearing as a single. His thorough musical background and eclectic tastes - he admires and has studied the work of many classical composers - have also allowed him to work in non-jazz contexts. A fiery, aggressive performer, Menza's writing shows his bebop leanings, which he brings even into his big band work.

● ALBUMS: with Stan Kenton *Adventures In Time* (1962)★★★, *Menza In Munich* (1965)★★★, with Buddy Rich *Mercy, Mercy* (1968)★★★★, with Rich *Channel One Suite* (1968)★★★, with Louie Bellson *150 MPH* (1974)★★★, *Horn Of Plenty* (1979)★★★, *Burnin'* (1980)★★★, *Hip Pocket* (Palo Alto 1981)★★★, with Bellson *East Side Suite* (1987)★★, *Ballads* (Fresh Sounds 1988)★★★, with Bellson *Jazz Giants* (1989)★★★★.

MERRILL, HELEN

b. 21 June 1929, New York City, New York, USA. Merrill's early career found her singing in exalted bebop company. Among the major artists with whom she sang in the late 40s were Charlie Parker, Miles Davis and Bud Powell. She spent part of the 50s outside music, but continued to make a few records with notable figures such as Clifford Brown; by the end of the decade, she was resident in Italy and a familiar figure at European festivals. In the early 60s, she returned to the USA but had difficulty in attracting the attention of either radio and television networks or the major record companies. She did make a handful of records backed by leading musicians such as Thad Jones, Ron Carter, Richard Davis, Elvin Jones and Jim Hall. By the late 60s, Merrill was again resident outside the USA, this time in Japan, where her talents were much appreciated. Back in the USA in the mid-70s, she was still largely overlooked but was periodically recorded, again with excellent jazz backing from the likes of Teddy Wilson, John Lewis and Pepper Adams. In November 1994, Merrill reappeared on the scene, promoting a new album and planning a UK and European tour for 1995. One of the most musical of singers, Merrill customarily explores the emotional depths of the lyrics of songs, imbuing them with great passion.

● ALBUMS: *Helen Merrill Featuring Clifford Brown* (Emarcy 1954)★★★★, *Helen Merrill With Hal Mooney And His Orchestra* i (1955)★★★, *Helen Merrill With Gil Evans And His Orchestra* (1956)★★★★, *Dream Of You* (Emarcy 1956)★★★, *Helen Merrill With Hal Mooney And His Orchestra* ii (1957)★★★, *Merrill At Midnight* (Emarcy 1957)★★★★, *Helen Merrill* i (Philips 1957)★★★, *The Nearness Of You* (Emarcy 1958)★★★★, *You've Got A Date With The Blues* (Metrojazz 1958)★★★, *American Country Songs* (Atco 1959)★★, *Helen Merrill* ii (1959)★★★, *Helen Merrill With Quincy Jones And His Orchestra* (1959)★★★★, *Helen Merrill In Italy* (Liuto 1959-62 recordings)★★, *Helen Merrill* iii (1964)★★★, *The Artistry Of Helen Merrill* (Mainstream 1965)★★★★, *Autumn Love* (1967)★★★,

The Feeling Is Mutual (Milestone 1967)★★★★, *A Shade Of Difference* (Spotlite 1968)★★★, *Helen Merrill In Tokyo* (1969)★★, with Teddy Wilson *Helen Sings, Teddy Swings* (1970)★★★, *Sposin'* (1971), *Helen Merrill/John Lewis* (1977)★★★, *Chasin' The Bird* (1979)★★★, *Case Forte* (1980)★★, *The Rodgers & Hammerstein Album* (DRG 1982)★★★, *No Tears...No Goodbyes* (Owl 1984)★★★, *Music Makers* (Owl 1986)★★★, with Gil Evans *Helen Merrill/Gil Evans* (Emarcy 1988)★★★★, *Just Friends* (Emarcy 1989)★★★★, *Dream Of You* 1956 recording (Emarcy 1993)★★, *Clear Out Of This World* (Emarcy 1992)★★★, *Brownie: Tribute To Clifford Brown* (Verve 1994)★★★.

● COMPILATIONS: *Blossom Of Stars* (1954-92 recordings)★★★★.

MERTZ, PAUL

b. Paul Madeira Mertz, 1 September 1904, Reading, Pennsylvania, USA. Mertz played piano in various local bands while a student and in 1922 he joined Tommy and Jimmy Dorsey's first band, the Wild Canaries. Later that year he played in Detroit while completing his studies at the city's university. For the greater part of the 20s Mertz worked with several of band contractor Jean Goldkette's orchestras, playing piano and also arranging. He also took part in many recording sessions including some with Bix Beiderbecke and Frank Trumbauer. He had a short spell with Fred Waring, during which he visited Europe. Although he occasionally played in and recorded with jazz groups in the 30s, his main activity in the decade was playing and composing in film studios in Hollywood. He worked successively for Paramount, Columbia and MGM, then continued his film work into the 60s as a freelance. A thoroughly skilled musician, Mertz's early interest in jazz was only a passing phase, his film studio work proving to be much more consistent and financially rewarding.

METCALF, LOUIS

b. 28 February 1905, Webster Groves, Missouri, USA, d. 27 October 1981. Metcalf was playing trumpet professionally by his early teenage years and spent some five years with Charlie Creath. The 20s were Metcalf's finest decade. Based in New York, he worked and sometimes recorded with blues singers and a galaxy of important jazz artists, including Sidney Bechet, Duke Ellington, J.C. Higginbotham, James P. Johnson, Albert Nicholas, Luis Russell, Jelly Roll Morton and King Oliver. In the 30s and 40s, Metcalf sometimes moved away from New York, frequently visiting Canada as a bandleader. Although his career profile was now much lower he still played with leading figures, including Lester Young and Billie Holiday. He played on through the 50s and 60s, often working at clubs in New York; but Metcalf's later years were overshadowed by his earlier successes. A gifted, blues-orientated trumpeter, with a precisely articulated style, Metcalf's was an original talent whose recorded work offers only tantalizing glimpses of a major jazz artist.

● ALBUMS: *Louis Metcalf At The Ali Baba* (1966)★★★.

METHENY, PAT

b. 12 August 1954, Kansas City, Missouri, USA. Although classed as a jazz guitarist, Metheny has bridged the gap between jazz and rock music in the same way that Miles Davis did in the late 60s and early 70s. Additionally, he has played a major part in the growth of jazz with the younger generation of the 80s. His first musical instrument was a French horn, and surprisingly he did not begin with the guitar until he was a teenager. His outstanding virtuosity soon had him teaching the instrument at the University Of Miami and the Berklee College Of Music in Boston. He joined Gary Burton in 1974, and throughout his three-album stay, he contributed some fluid Wes Montgomery-influenced guitar patterns. Manfred Eicher of ECM Records saw the potential and initiated a partnership that lasted for 10 superlative albums. He became, along with Keith Jarrett, ECM's biggest-selling artist, and his albums regularly topped the jazz record charts. Metheny is one of the few artists to make regular appearances in the pop album charts, such is the accessibility of his music. Both *Bright Size Life*, featuring the late Jaco Pastorious, and *Watercolours*, though excellent albums, still showed a man who was feeling his way. His own individualistic style matured with *Pat Metheny Group* in 1978.
Together with his musical partner (and arguably, his right arm), the brilliant keyboardist Lyle Mays, he initiated a rock group format that produced album after album of melodious jazz/rock. Following a major tour with Joni Mitchell and Pastorious (*Shadows And Light*), Metheny released *New Chautauqua* and demonstrated an amazing dexterity on 12-string guitar and, against the fashion of the times, made the US Top 50. He returned to the electric band format for *American Garage*, which contained his country-influenced '(Cross The) Heartland'. The double set *80/81* featured Michael Brecker, Jack DeJohnette, Charlie Haden and Dewey Redman, and was more of a typical jazz album, featuring in particular the moderately *avant garde* 'Two Folk Songs'. Nevertheless, the record still climbed the popular charts. During this time, Metheny constantly won jazz and guitarist polls. Mays' keyboards featured prominently in the group structure, and he received co-authorship credit for the suite *As Falls Wichita, So Falls Wichita Falls*. Metheny had by now become fascinated by the musical possibilities of the guitar synthesizer or synclavier. He used this to startling effect on *Offramp*, notably on the wonderfully contagious and arresting 'Are You Going With Me?'. The double set *Travels* showed a band at the peak of its powers, playing some familiar titles with a new freshness. The short piece 'Travels' stands as one of his finest compositions, the low-level recording offers such subtle emotion that it becomes joyously funereal. *Rejoicing* was a modern jazz album demonstrating his sensitive interpretations of music by Horace Silver and Ornette Coleman. *First Circle* maintained the standard and showed a greater leaning towards Latin-based music, still with Metheny's brilliant ear for melody; additionally, the track 'If I

Could' displayed the same sparse subtlety of *Travels*. In 1985, he composed the film score for *The Falcon And The Snowman* which led to him recording 'This Is Not America' with David Bowie. The resulting Top 40 US hit (number 12 in the UK), brought Metheny many new young admirers. The concert halls found audiences bedecked in striped rugby shirts, in the style of their new hero.
Ironically, at the same time, following a break with ECM, Metheny turned his back on possible rock stardom and produced his most perplexing work, *Song X*, with free-jazz exponent Ornette Coleman. Reactions were mixed in reviewing this difficult album - ultimately the general consensus was that it was brilliantly unlistenable. He returned to more familiar ground with *Still Life (Talking)* and *Letter From Home*, although both showed a greater move towards Latin melody and rhythm. In 1990, *Reunion* was released, a superb meeting with his former boss Gary Burton and a few months later together with Dave Holland and Roy Haynes he made *Question And Answer*. Additionally he was heavily featured, along with Herbie Hancock, on the excellent Jack DeJohnette album, *Parallel Realities*. He continued into the 90s with *Secret Story*, an album of breathtaking beauty. Although the album may have made jazz purists cringe, it was a realization of all Metheny's musical influences. His second live album, *The Road To You*, did not have the emotion of *Travels*. It was something to keep the fans quiet before he unleashed an exciting recording with John Scofield, both guitarists having been sharing the honours at the tops of jazz polls for the past few years. *Zero Tolerence For Silence* can only be described as astonishing - for many this wall-of-sound guitar was a self-indulgent mess. After repeated play, the music does not get any easier, but at least we can understand his motives more and appreciate what a bold move this thrash metal outing was. Metheny found himself reviewed in the Heavy Metal press for the first (and last) time. *We Live Here* was a return to familiar ground, and a familiar position at the top of the jazz charts. It won a Grammy in 1996 for the best contemporary jazz album. He has an extraordinary sense of melody and his work neither rambles nor becomes self-indulgent; much credit must also be given to the like-minded Lyle Mays, whose quiet presence at the side of the stage is the backbone for much of Metheny's music.

● ALBUMS: *Bright Size Life* (ECM 1976)★★★★, *Watercolours* (ECM 1977)★★★, *Pat Metheny Group* (ECM 1978)★★★★, *New Chautauqua* (ECM 1979)★★★★, *American Garage* (ECM 1979)★★★★, *80/81* (ECM 1980)★★★, *As Falls Wichita, So Falls Wichita Falls* (ECM 1981)★★★★, *Offramp* (ECM 1982)★★★★, *Travels* (ECM 1983)★★★★, with Charlie Haden and Billy Higgins *Rejoicing* (ECM 1983)★★★, *First Circle* (ECM 1984)★★★, *The Falcon And The Snowman* film soundtrack (EMI America 1985)★★, with Ornette Coleman *Song X* (Geffen 1986)★★★, *Still Life (Talking)* (Geffen 1987)★★★★, *Letter From Home* (Geffen 1989)★★★★, with Gary Burton *Reunion* (Geffen 1990), *Question And Answer* (Geffen 1990)★★★★, with Jack DeJohnette *Parallel Realities* (MCA 1990)★★★, *Secret Story* (Geffen 1992)★★★★, *The Road To You - Recorded Live In Europe* (Geffen 1993)★★★, with John Scofield *I Can See Your House From Here* (Blue Note 1994)★★★, *Zero Tolerance For Silence* (Geffen 1994)★★, *We Live Here* (Geffen 1995)★★★, *"Quartet"* (Geffen 1997)★★★, with Charlie Haden *Beyond The Missouri Sky (Short Stories By Charlie Haden & Pat Metheny)* (Verve 1997)★★★★, *Imaginary Day* (Warners 1997)★★★★, with Derek Bailey, Gregg Bendian, Paul Wertico *The Sign Of 4* 3-CD set (Knitting Factory Works 1997)★★★★.

● COMPILATIONS: *Works* (ECM 1983)★★★★, *Works 2* (ECM 1988)★★★★.

● VIDEOS: *More Travels* (1993).

MEYER, JON

b. *c*.1938, New York City, New York, USA. Meyer's professional career caught fire in the late 50s when he played piano with Jackie McLean and John Coltrane. During the following decade he moved into free jazz but was uncomfortable with the form. During this period he had personal problems which eventually drove him from the scene for a long while. By the mid-90s he was well and truly back in business, and from a base in Los Angeles had begun to re-establish himself as a musician of consequence and a pianist of fire and flair.

● ALBUMS: *Round Up The Usual Suspects* (Pullen 1995)★★★.

MEZZOFORTE

Until the arrival of the Sugarcubes, jazz-fusion band Mezzoforte were Iceland's best-known musical export. The group was formed in 1977 at a Rekjavik high school by Fridrik Karlsson (guitar), Eythor Gunnarsson (keyboards), Johann Asmundsson (bass), Gunnlaugur Briem (drums) and Kristin Svararsson (saxophone). They signed a recording contract with local label Steinar and the second album contained the exuberant 'Garden Party' which was a Top 20 hit in the UK in 1983. The tune was covered in the USA by Herb Alpert who performed it at half-speed, reportedly because he had learned the piece from a 45 rpm single accidentally played at 33. The follow-up, 'Rockall', was only a minor hit but it was adopted as a signature tune by radio chart shows in the Netherlands and UK. For a brief period, the group was based in London and in the mid-80s Mezzoforte played the European jazz festival circuit with vocalists Chris Cameron and Noel McCalla, formerly with Moon and Mike Rutherford's group. In 1990, Karlsson formed a jazz/funk band Point Blank featuring singer Ellen Kristjansdottor and members of Mezzoforte.

● ALBUMS: *Mezzoforte* (Steinar 1981)★★★, *I Hakanum* (Steinar 1982)★★★, *Thvilkt Og Annadeins* (1983)★★★, *Catching Up With Mezzoforte* (Steinar 1983)★★, *Surprise Surprise* (Steinar 1983)★★, *Observations* (Steinar 1984)★★★, *Rising* (Steinar 1984)★★, *No Limit* (Steinar 1987)★★★, *Playing For Time* (Steinar 1989)★★★.

MEZZROW, MEZZ

b. Milton Mesirow, 9 November 1899, Chicago, Illinois, USA, d. 5 August 1972. After playing club dates in and around his home-town during the 20s, clarinettist

Mezzrow moved to New York where he became a popular figure, partly owing to his other career as a supplier of marijuana. In the 30s he recorded with Sidney Bechet and Tommy Ladnier on the famous sessions organized by French critic Hugues Panassie, and in the 40s formed his own King Jazz record label to record Bechet and other important jazz artists. In the 50s, he moved to France, touring from a Paris base with visiting musicians (who included Lionel Hampton, Lee Collins and Zutty Singleton), recording and enjoying a level of adulation he had never achieved in his own country. A vehement anti-segregationist, Mezzrow wholly identified with black music and musicians, even to the extent of occasionally 'passing' for black in order to play with his idols. Much written about, critically by Eddie Condon and hyperbolically by himself, Mezzrow's image suffered and he was often dismissed by jazz commentators. In fact, despite the often outrageous claims he made in his racily extravagant autobiography, Mezzrow did much to foster jazz. In his early years in Chicago he encouraged many young musicians, even if later he claimed to have taught them how to play. He was tireless in setting up record dates and he boldly formed multiracial bands during a period when such groups were rarely seen or heard. Mezzrow's clarinet style was earthy and at times elementary, but among the many records he made are flashes of a genuine feeling for the blues. His autobiography is witty, anecdotal and a classic of its kind.

● ALBUMS: *Mezz Mezzrow And His Band* (Blue Note 1952)★★★, with Lionel Hampton *The Hamp In Paris* (1953)★★★★, *Mezz Mezzrow's Swing Session* (X LVA 1954)★★★★, *Mezz Mezzrow* (X LVA 1954)★★★, *Mezzin Around* (RCA Victor 1954)★★★★, with Lee Collins *Clarinet Marmalade* (1955)★★★, *A La Schola Cantorum* (London 1956)★★.

● COMPILATIONS: with Sidney Bechet *The Panassie Sessions* (1938-39)★★★, with Bechet *Out Of The Galleon* (1945)★★★, with Bechet *Really The Blues* (1945)★★★★, with Bechet *King Of Jazz Vols 1-5* (Storyville 1986)★★★★, *The Chronological Mezz Mezzrow 1928-1936* (Original Jazz Classics)★★★★.

● FURTHER READING: *Really The Blues*, Mezz Mezzrow.

MICHELOT, PIERRE

b. 3 March 1928, Saint Denis, France. Michelot studied classical bass from the age of 16, but it was the playing of Jimmy Blanton and Oscar Pettiford that attracted him to jazz. He played with Rex Stewart in 1948, toured Europe with Kenny Clarke and recorded with Coleman Hawkins. Although such experience must have sharpened his playing, he only gained the chance because he was already an accurate, melodic player who could provide a band with a springy rhythm. Throughout the 50s he worked in Paris clubs with Django Reinhardt, tenor players Lester Young, Don Byas, Dexter Gordon, Zoot Sims and Stan Getz. Among his recordings were sessions with Miles Davis in 1956/7, and pianist Bud Powell in the early 60s. Meanwhile, he was writing arrangements for trumpeter Chet Baker, Kenny Clarke and for session work. For 15 years, from 1959, he worked with Jacques Loussier's Play Bach Trio. He took part in the filming of Tavernier's *Round Midnight* in 1986.

● ALBUMS: with Django Reinhardt *Blues For Ike* (1953)★★★, with Bud Powell *A Portrait Of Thelonious* (1961)★★, with Dexter Gordon *Our Man In Paris* (1963)★★★★, *Round About A Bass* (1963)★★★.

MICUS, STEPHAN

b. 19 January 1953, Stuttgart, Germany. Micus made his first overseas trip to Morocco at the age of 16. Since then he has travelled all over the world, studying traditional wind and string instruments, including the Japanese shakuhachi and sho, the Indian sitar and dilruba, as well as a range of percussion instruments from China, Korea, Bali, Java, Tibet and Ireland. For *East Of The Night* he designed a new type of 10- and 14-string guitar with resonant strings like that of the sitar. He has given concerts in Europe (including one in Düsseldorf with Oregon), the USA, Japan, Taiwan, Israel and Afghanistan. In 1977, his ballet, *Koan*, received its premiere in Cologne. Further performances included London, Paris and New York. *The Music Of Stones*, his compositions for the resonating stone sculptures of Elmar Daucher, were recorded in the atmospheric ambience of Ulm Cathedral and proved to be among his most inspired work. In the recording studio Micus has preferred to work as a soloist, making sensitive use of multi-track playback techniques. His compositions, which are often based on improvisation and always difficult to classify, have been widely acclaimed for their meditative and spiritual qualities. Micus's expressed intention is not to play traditional music, but to search for fresh possibilities by using traditional instruments in unconventional combinations. On this subject the jazz writer Joachim E. Berendt has written: 'He plays them with a profound internationalization of their tradition and spirituality, uniting their sounds in a musical river which makes the stream of inner consciousness audible'.

● ALBUMS: *Implosions* (ECM 1977)★★★★, *Koan* (ECM 1981)★★★, *East Of The Night* (ECM 1985)★★★, *Ocean* (ECM 1986)★★★★, *Twilight Fields* (ECM 1987)★★★, *Wings Over Water* (ECM 1988)★★★, *The Music Of Stones* (ECM 1989)★★★★, *Darkness And Light* (ECM 1990)★★★, *Behind Eleven Deserts* (Verabra 1990)★★★, *To The Evening Child* (ECM 1992)★★★, *Till The End Of Time* (ECM 1993)★★★, *Listen To The Rain* (ECM 1993)★★★.

MIDNIGHT BLUE - KENNY BURRELL

From the first sight of Reid Miles' brilliant typography on the cover you know what you are getting. Smooth smootchy jazz guitar played at the pace of a slow loris - quite magnificent in its sparing qualities. Kenny Burrell, together with Grant Green and Wes Montgomery, defined this style. 'Chitlins Con Carne' is a late-night feast while 'Midnight Blue' is smokey and soulful, and yes, Van Morrison did borrow the intro for 'Moondance'. There is subtle support from Major Holley (bass), Bill English (drums), Ray Barretto (conga) and lustrous understated tenor from Stanley Turrentine.

- Tracks: *Chitlins Con Carne; Mule; Soul Lament; Midnight Blue; Wavy Gravy; Gee Baby Ain't I Good To You; Saturday Night Blues.*
- First released 1963
- UK peak chart position: did not chart
- USA peak chart position: did not chart

MIDNITE FOLLIES ORCHESTRA

The Orchestra was formed in the UK during 1978 by pianist Keith Nichols and arranger Alan Cohen to specialize in the repertoire of the 20s and 30s, and to play originals written in a similar style. After a memorable first night at London's 100 Club, the band were signed to EMI for whom they have recorded since, using the cream of British mainstream musicians - Alan Elsdon, Digby Fairweather, Pete Strange (trombone), John Barnes, Olaf Vas and Randolphe Colville (saxophones). The orchestra regularly plays on radio and television, and in tribute concerts for artists including Louis Armstrong, Fats Waller and Duke Ellington.

- ALBUMS: *Hotter Than Hades* (1978)★★★, *Jungle Nights In Harlem* (1981)★★★★.

MIKKELBORG, PALLE

b. 6 March 1941, Copenhagen, Denmark. Mikkelborg is a self-taught trumpeter who studied conducting at the Royal Music Conservatory, Copenhagen. After turning professional in 1960, he joined Danish Radiojazzgruppen (1963), of which he was the leader from 1967-72. He was also a member of Radioens Big Band from 1964-71. For both of these, he would write, arrange and conduct as well as play trumpet. In 1966, he formed a quintet with drummer Alex Riel that won first prize at the Montreux Jazz Festival and played at the Newport Jazz Festival (1968). Then he led an octet called V8 (1970-75) and an outfit called Entrance (1975-85). Mikkelborg has also worked with bandleaders George Russell, Gil Evans, George Gruntz, Mike Gibbs and Maynard Ferguson and a wide variety of musicians, including Jan Garbarek, Terje Rypdal, Don Cherry, Abdullah Ibrahim and Charlie Mariano. His trumpet playing is characterized by a clear, firm sound, a huge range and the successful incorporation of a variety of electronic effects. He has written many pieces for his various bands as well as a series of extended pieces for larger ensembles. In 1984, he wrote and later recorded *Aura*, a tribute to Miles Davis, for big band and soloists, featuring Davis himself.

- ALBUMS: *Ashoka Suite* (1970)★★★, with Entrance *Entrance* (1977)★★, with Terje Rypdal *Waves* (1977)★★★★, *Descendre* (1978)★★★, *Live As Well* (1978)★★★, with Shankar, Jan Garbarek *Visions* (1983)★★★★, with George Gruntz *Theatre* (1984)★★★, *Journey To...* (1985)★★★, *Aura* (1985)★★★, *Heart To Heart* (Storyville 1986)★★★, with Niels-Henning Ørsted Pederson *Once Upon A Time* (1992)★★★★.

MILES, BUTCH

b. Charles Thornton, 4 July 1944, Ironton, Ohio, USA. After playing the drums as a small child, Miles later studied music in college. As a teenager, he played with a rock band, but his admiration for Gene Krupa inclined him towards jazz drumming. Resident in Charleston, West Virginia, he began playing with small jazz groups and in 1972 became Mel Torme's regular drummer. In 1975, he left Torme and offered his services to Count Basie. When Basie's drummer, Ray Porello, was injured in a road accident, Miles deputized for a week and stayed for four and a half years. In 1979, he joined Dave Brubeck, and the following year was backing Tony Bennett. In the 80s Miles worked extensively with small groups, sometimes as leader, accompanying such artists as Gerry Mulligan, Al Cohn, Buddy Tate, Bucky Pizzarelli, Glenn Zottola, Scott Hamilton and Bob Wilber. Miles also sings occasionally, proving an engaging if uninspired vocalist with a limited range. As a drummer, he is a gifted performer with an eclectic style that revealed his admiration for such big band drummers as Krupa, Chick Webb and Buddy Rich. In a small group setting he is a self-effacing and supportive player but, stylistically, he seems better suited for big band work, where he ably continues the great tradition set by his idols.

- ALBUMS: with Mel Torme *Live At The Maisonette* (1974)★★★, with Count Basie *Montreux '77* (1977)★★★★, *Basie In Europe* (1977)★★★★, *Miles And Miles Of Swing* (1977)★★★, *Butch's Encore* (1977-78)★★★, *Lady Be Good* (1978)★★★, with Dave Brubeck *Back Home* (1979)★★★, *Butch Miles Salutes Chick Webb* (1979)★★★, *Butch Miles Salutes Gene Krupa* (1982)★★★, *Hail To The Chief! Butch Miles Salutes Basie* (1982)★★★, *More Miles . . . More Standards* (1985)★★, *Jazz Express* (1986)★★★.

MILES, LIZZIE

b. Elizabeth Mary Pajaud, née Landreaux, 31 March 1895, New Orleans, Louisiana, USA, d. 17 March 1963. As a teenager, Miles sang with outstanding early jazzmen from the age of 16, including Joe 'King' Oliver, Freddie Keppard, Kid Ory and Bunk Johnson. By the early 20s, she had established a reputation in Chicago and New York and toured Europe in the middle of the decade. The late 20s found her resident in New York, singing in clubs and recording with Oliver and Jelly Roll Morton. Illness kept her out of the business for a few years, but she returned to work in New York and Chicago in the late 30s and early 40s. Miles then abandoned her career, but she returned to nightclub work in the 50s, made records and re-established her reputation in the wake of the Dixieland revival, singing with Bob Scobey, Sharkey Bonano and George Lewis. She retired in 1959, turning her back on music to embrace religion. Often singing in Louisiana Creole patois, Miles had a robust and earthy style that made her a distinctive performer, despite a rather narrow vocal range. Miles was an all-round entertainer, applying her powerful delivery impartially to blues, pop songs, ballads, Creole songs, and improbable Creolized (French language) versions of 'Bill Bailey' and 'A Good Man Is Hard To Find'.

- ALBUMS: *George Lewis Live At The Hangover Club* (1953-54)★★★, *Moans And Blues* (1954)★★★, with Red Camp *Torch Lullabies My Mother Sang Me* (1955)★★.
- COMPILATIONS: *Complete Recordings 1922-29, Volumes 1-3* (Document 1996)★★★★.

MILES SMILES - MILES DAVIS

This was the last Miles Davis album before his next plateau (or his next album), an occurrence that happened throughout his career. This is the quintet that moved into electronic music with *Bitches Brew*, Herbie Hancock, Wayne Shorter, Tony Williams, Ron Carter, an astonishing line-up and surely Miles's best post-Coltrane group. This is like music for the last supper; they all knew that Fender Rhodes pianos and Precision basses were coming and this is a superb farewell to acoustic jazz. All six tracks are rewarding, all different, yet the sound is the same. Much more appreciated today than when it was first released.

- Tracks: *Orbits; Circle; Footprints; Dolores; Freedom Jazz Dance; Ginger Bread Boy.*
- First released 1966
- UK peak chart position: did not chart
- USA peak chart position: did not chart

MILESTONES - MILES DAVIS

An album that has matured with age. Featuring the classic sextet with the personnel of John Coltrane, Cannonball Adderley, Red Garland, Philly Joe Jones and Paul Chambers, it hints at what was to come with the phenomenal *Kind Of Blue* the following year. The modal jazz period was germinated here, particularly with 'Sid's Ahead', featuring one of Davis's finest solos, a tribute to late-night New York disc jockey Symphony Sid. Elsewhere the pace is swing and cool, with a unique drum sound on 'Billy Boy' and it closes with a superior reading of Thelonious Monk's 'Straight No Chaser'.

- Tracks: *Doctor Jekyll; Sid's Ahead; Two Bass Hits; Miles; Billy Boy; Straight No Chaser.*
- First released 1958
- UK peak chart position: did not chart
- USA peak chart position: did not chart

MILEY, BUBBER

b. James Wesley Miley, 3 April 1903, Aiken, South Carolina, USA, d. 20 May 1932. By his late teens, trumpeter Miley was working extensively in clubs in Chicago and New York and was on the road with Mamie Smith. In 1923, he became a member of Elmer Snowden's band, staying on when Duke Ellington took over as leader. His heavy drinking made him unreliable and erratic, and he left the band in 1929, touring Europe that year with Noble Sissle. He briefly led his own band but was stricken with tuberculosis and died in May 1932. As a formative member of Ellington's orchestra, Miley's influence remained long after his departure. His dramatic use of the plunger mute, together with growls and other unusual sounds, helped to create many of the so-called 'jungle' effects that became an integral part of Ellington's music.

MILLER, BIG

b. Clarence Horatio Miller, 18 December 1922, Sioux City, Iowa, USA, d. 9 June 1992. Miller's parents were Henry Miller, a Sioux, who was a preacher, and Nora Epperson, a descendant of slaves. His first influence in music came from his father's church but he also heard the blues sung by men working on the railroad. In the 30s, while still a student, he formed a band, but with the outbreak of World War II he joined the army. After serving in the Pacific and in Europe, he began entertaining his fellow soldiers. In 1949 he joined Lionel Hampton's band, then had a five-year spell with Jay McShann. Miller's abiding interest in the blues was such that writer-poet Langston Hughes wrote a series of songs especially for him and he also performed at Carnegie Hall in *The Evolution Of The Blues Song* with Jon Hendricks and Miriam Makeba, the recording of which won the Grand Prix Du Disque. In 1963 Miller moved to Australia, then to Hawaii. In 1967 he toured with The Evolution Of The Blues Song and was stranded in Vancouver. Taking a liking to Canada, he settled in Alberta and became a respected performer and educator, teaching at the Banff School of Fine Arts and the Grant MacEwan Community College. He was also the recipient of an Honorary Doctorate from Athabasca University. In 1981 the Canadian National Film Board produced a biographical film, *Big And The Blues*. Miller had a commanding style and his rich voice lent itself especially well to the material he favoured. His influences in the blues were Joe Turner, Jimmy Rushing, 'T-Bone' Walker and Jimmy Witherspoon, whom he followed into the McShann band. He also admired the ballad style of Billy Eckstine. Miller's chosen lifestyle was such that he has left behind considerably fewer recordings than his undoubted talent deserves.

- COMPILATIONS: *The Last Of The Blues Shouters* (Southland 1990)★★★.

MILLER, CLARENCE 'BIG'

b. 18 December 1922, Sioux City, Iowa, USA, d. 9 June 1992, Edmonton, Alberta, Canada. Miller moved to Kansas City as a child and his style is in that city's tradition of big-voiced, sophisticated blues singing. In the late 40s and early 50s, he worked with the big bands of Jay 'Hootie' McShann, Lionel Hampton, Duke Ellington and others. Miller began recording in 1957 for the Savoy label, and continued to record and tour internationally, primarily in a jazz context, until his death in 1992.

MILLER, EDDIE

b. Edward Raymond Müller, 23 June 1911, New Orleans, Louisiana, USA, d. 6 April 1991, Los Angeles, California, USA. Miller began playing clarinet as a child and in his early teens played in street bands. Before he was 17 years old he was on his way to New York where he played with several bands, including that led by Julie Wintz which had the unenviable task of playing opposite Fletcher Henderson at the Roseland Ballroom. While on this engagement, Miller met Henderson's star tenor saxophonist, Coleman Hawkins, with whom he formed a lifelong friendship. By this time Miller had also taken up the tenor and in 1930, at the age of 19, joined Ben Pollack's band where he remained until its break-up in 1934. A founder-member of the co-operative group that became known as the Bob Crosby Orchestra, Miller was one of the leading soloists of the band and played an important part in its huge success. He was composer of 'Slow Mood', a hit for the band. In 1943, he briefly led his own unit before entering the US army. On his discharge, following illness, he re-formed a band, but by the mid-40s he had become a studio musician in Hollywood where he remained for the next 10 years. Miller appeared in the film *Pete Kelly's Blues* (1955) and its television spin-off series, but by the late 50s was back on the jazz circuit. In the 60s, he played dates across the USA as a single and was also a member of the band led by Pete Fountain as well as that run by his former Crosby soulmates Yank Lawson and Bob Haggart, the World's Greatest Jazz Band. During the 70s and 80s Miller continued his career, touring as a single and working with the WGJB and its later version, the Lawson-Haggart Jazz Band. Among his associates in the band was pianist Lou Stein, with whom he recorded a duo album, *Lazy Mood For Two*. He also appeared at several Crosby reunions. He was still active when, while with the Lawson-Haggart band in 1988, he suffered a disabling stroke that ended his playing career. A later stroke was even more damaging and he eventually died in April 1991. A fluid player with a relaxed and smoothly elegant style, Miller was at his best on ballads, although his up-tempo excursions with Crosby, especially on the numbers performed by the Bobcats, the band-within-the-band, lent weight to his status as one of the best white tenor players of his generation.

● ALBUMS: *Tenor Of Jazz* (1967)★★★★, *A Portrait Of Eddie* (1971)★★★, *Live At Capolinea* (1976)★★★, with Lou Stein *Lazy Mood For Two* (1978)★★★, *It's Miller Time* (1979)★★, *Street Of Dreams* (1983)★★★.

● COMPILATIONS: with Bob Crosby *South Rampart Street Parade* (MCA 1935-42)★★★, with Crosby *Big Noise From Winnetka* (MCA 1937-42)★★★★, *Soft Jive* (1943-44)★★★, *Live At Michele's Silver Stope* (Audiophile 1988)★★★, *Piano Blues 1929-34* (Blues Document 1989)★★★.

● FURTHER READING: *Stomp Off, Let's Go!: The Story Of Bob Crosby's Bob Cats & Big Band*, John Chilton.

MILLER, ERNEST 'PUNCH'

b. Ernest Burden, 10 June 1894, Raceland, Louisiana, USA. d. 2 December 1971. Miller began playing cornet as a child, playing with local dance and early jazz bands. Shortly after World War I he settled in New Orleans for a while before joining the northward migration. Resident in Chicago from the mid-20s, he played with many bands including those led by Freddie Keppard and Jelly Roll Morton. From the mid-40s he was often in New York where he recorded with Jimmy Archey, Ed Hall, Ralph Sutton and others and also appeared on Rudi Blesh's *This Is Jazz* radio show. By the middle of the following decade, however, he had returned to New Orleans. In the early 60s he toured with George Lewis. A technically proficient trumpeter, Miller's playing mingled the New Orleans tradition with a deep feeling for the blues. His solos were often pungent and moving. He sang in a casual yet engaging manner, in this department, at least, displaying the influence of Louis Armstrong. In 1971 he was the subject of an exceptionally fine film documentary, *'Til The Butcher Cuts Him Down*.

● ALBUMS: *Punch Miller And His Jazz Band* (1960)★★, *Punch Miller's Hongo Fongo Players* (1961)★★★, *Punch Miller's Bunch And George Lewis* (1962)★★★, *Punch's Delegates Of Pleasure* (1962)★★★, *Preservation Hall* (1962)★★, *The River's In Mourning* (1962)★★, *George Lewis And His New Orleans All Stars In Tokyo* (1963)★★★, *Oh! Lady Be Good* (1967)★★★.

● COMPILATIONS: *Kid Punch Miller: Jazz Rarities* (1929-30)★★★, *The Wild Horns* (1941)★★★, *Punch Miller And His All Star Band, New York 1947* (1947)★★★★, with Jimmy Archey, Mutt Carey *Jazz New Orleans* (1947)★★★★, *Delegates Of Pleasure* (Jazzology 1990)★★★.

MILLER, GLENN

b. 1 March 1905, Clarinda, Iowa, USA, d. 15 December 1944. Miller was the first artist to be credited with a million-selling disc (for 'Chattanooga Choo Choo'), and was the toast of North American popular music during World War II for his uniformed orchestra's fusion of sober virtuosity, infectious dance rhythms and varied intonation of brass and woodwind. In Miller's hands, close harmony vocals - often wordless - were almost incidental in a slick repertoire that embraced Tin Pan Alley standards ('April In Paris', Hoagy Carmichael's 'The Nearness Of You'), jump blues ('St. Louis Blues', Jelly Roll Morton's 'King Porter Stomp'), western swing ('Blueberry Hill', once sung by Gene Autry) and mainstream jazz ('Jersey Bounce', 'Tuxedo Junction'), also exemplified by the 'hotter' big bands of Artie Shaw and Jimmy Dorsey. After his family moved to North Platts, Nebraska, Miller's trombone skills earned him places in bands operational within his Fort Morgan high school, and afterwards at the University of Colorado. On becoming a professional musician, he found work on the west coast and in New York as both a player and arranger - notably for Victor Young, whose Los Angeles studio orchestra accompanied Judy Garland and Bing Crosby. Other prestigious feathers in Miller's cap were his supervision of Britain's Ray Noble And The New Mayfair Orchestra's first USA tour and a scoring commission for Columbia Records. His earnings were ploughed back into the organization and rehearsal of his own band which, despite setbacks such as his wife's long illness in 1938, built up a huge following in New York, through dogged rounds of one-night-stands and record-breaking residencies in venues such as Pompton Turnpike roadhouse and the celebrated Glen Island Casino.

Signed to RCA Records in 1939, Miller proved a sound investment with immediate consecutive bestsellers in evocative classics such as 'Little Brown Jug' (written in 1869), 'In The Mood' and 'Sunrise Serenade'. The latter was coupled with 'Moonlight Serenade' - a strikingly effective extrapolation of a trombone exercise that became Miller's signature tune. As synonymous with him, too, was 1940's 'Chattanooga Choo Choo' with a chorus (by Tex Beneke, Marion Hutton and the Modernaires) atypically to the fore. This novelty was also among highlights of *Sun Valley Serenade* (1941), the orchestra's first movie (co-starring Norwegian ice-skating champion, Sonja Henie). Other Miller classics included the irresistible 'Pennsylvania 6-5000' and the haunting 'Tuxedo Junction'. At Miller's commercial peak the next year, *Orchestra Wives* (1942, with Ann Rutherford and Cesar Romero), enveloped a similarly vacuous plot with musical interludes that included another smash in '(I've Got A Gal In) Kalamazoo'. The enduring lyric brilliantly used the alphabet; 'a b c d e f g h I got a gal in Kalamazoo'. That same year also brought both Miller's lively hit arrangement of 'American Patrol' and his enlistment into the US Army. Even though he was too old for combat he still volunteered out of patriotism, was elevated to the rank of captain and sent out to entertain the Allied forces. He was promoted to major in August 1944. Following a visit to Britain, his aircraft disappeared over the English Channel on 15 December 1944, although a recent report alleges that Miller actually died of a heart attack in a French brothel. His death was an assumption that some devotees found too grievous to bear, and rumours of his survival persisted. In any case, his orchestra lived on - even if the economics of staying on the road, combined with the rise of rock 'n' roll, finished off lesser rivals. Universal Pictures produced the immensely successful 1954 biopic, *The Glenn Miller Story* (with James Stewart in the title role). An Oscar-nominated soundtrack album (directed by Henry Mancini) was released, and a reissued 'Moonlight Serenade' reached number 12 in the UK singles charts. Miller's habit of preserving many of his radio broadcasts on private discs enabled the issue of another album, *Marvellous Miller Moods*. Also reaching the US chart in the late 50s was a 1939 Carnegie Hall concert recording and *The New Glenn Miller Orchestra In Hi-Fi*.

Miller's original arrangements were regarded as definitive by those multitudes who continued to put repackagings such as *The Real Glenn Miller And His Orchestra* high into the international charts as late as 1977. The sound was recreated so precisely by the Syd Lawrence Orchestra that it was employed in a 1969 television documentary of the late bandleader whose UK fan club booked Lawrence regularly for its annual tribute shows. Among the best tributes paid were those by Manhattan Transfer in a 1976 version of 'Tuxedo Junction', and Jive Bunny And The Mastermixers, whose 1989 medley, 'Swing The Mood' - a UK number 1 - was sandwiched between excerpts of 'In The Mood', sampled from Miller's 1938 recording. The arranging style perfected by Miller's staff arrangers, notably Jerry Gray, continued to influence several middle-of-the-road writers and bandleaders during the next two or three decades. Curiously enough, for a musician whose work is now preserved eternally in its 40s style, Miller was always eager to move on. Shortly before his death he remarked to McKinley that the style that had made him famous was no longer of interest to him, 'I've gone as far as I can go with the saxophone sound. I've got to have something new'. The enduring quality of Miller's work is most forcibly underlined by the realization that his tunes have become part of the instant musical vocabulary of listeners young and old. In 1995, just over 50 years after Miller's death, a set of recordings made by the American Band of the AEF at the Abbey Road studios in London late in 1944, was released as a two-CD set.

● ALBUMS: *Glenn Miller Concert Vol. 1* (RCA Victor 1951)★★★★, *Glenn Miller Concert Vol. 2* (RCA Victor 1951)★★★★, *Glenn Miller* (RCA Victor 1951)★★★, *Glenn Miller Concert Vol. 3* (RCA Victor 1951)★★★★, *This Is Glenn Miller* (RCA Victor 1951)★★★, *This Is Glenn Miller Vol 2* (RCA Victor 1951)★★★, *Sunrise Serenade* (RCA Victor 1951)★★★, *The Glenn Miller Story* (1954)★★★★, *Marvelous Miller Moods* (RCA Victor 1957)★★★, *The New Glenn Miller Orchestra In Hi Fi* (RCA Victor 1957)★★★, *The Glenn Miller Carnegie Hall Concert* (RCA Victor 1957)★★★, *Something Old, New, Borrowed And Blue* (RCA Victor 1958)★★★, *The Miller Sound* (RCA Victor 1959)★★★, *Marvelous Miller Medleys* (RCA Victor 1959)★★★, *The Great Dance Bands Of The 30s And 40s* (RCA Victor 1959)★★★, *On Tour With The New Glenn Miller Orchestra* (RCA Victor 1959)★★★, *Dance Anyone?* (RCA Victor 1960)★★★, *The Authentic Sound Of The New Glenn Miller Orchestra Today* (RCA Victor 1961)★★★, *Glenn Miller Time* (RCA Victor 1961)★★★, *Echoes Of Glenn Miller* (RCA Victor 1962)★★★, *On The Air* 3-LP box set (RCA Victor 1963)★★★, *The Best Of Glenn Miller Vols. 1-3* (RCA Victor 1963)★★★★, *Blue Moonlight* (RCA Victor 1966)★★★, *In The Mood* (RCA Victor 1967)★★★, *The Chesterfield Broadcasts Vol 1* (RCA Victor 1967)★★★, *Under The Direction Of Buddy DeFranco Returns To The Glen Island Casino* (RCA Victor 1967)★★★, *The Chesterfield Broadcasts Vol. 2* (RCA Victor 1968)★★★, *The Nearness Of You* (1969)★★★, *A Memorial 1944-1969* (1970)★★★, *The Real Glenn Miller And His Orchestra Play The Original Music From The Film 'The Glenn Miller Story' And Other Hits* (1971)★★★, *A Legendary Performer* (1975)★★★, *A Legendary Performer Vol.2* (1976)★★★, *The Unforgettable Glenn Miller* (1977)★★★, *Glenn Miller Army Air Force Band (1943-44)* (1981)★★★, *Chesterfield Shows 1941-42* (1984)★★★, *Chesterfield Shows - Chicago 1940* (1984)★★★, *Chesterfield Shows - New York City 1940* (1984)★★★, *Glenn Miller Airforce Orchestra, June 10, 1944* (1984)★★★, *April 3, 1940 Chesterfield Show* (1989)★★★, *The Glenn Miller Gold Collection* (1993)★★★★, *The Ultimate Glenn Miller* (RCA Bluebird 1993)★★★★★, *Live At The Café Rouge* (1994)★★★, *The Lost Recordings* 2-CD set (RCA Victor 1995)★★★, *The Secret Broadcasts* 3-CD set (RCA Victor 1996)★★★, *Candlelight Miller* (BMG 1998)★★★, *The Very Best Of Glenn Miller* (Camden 1997)★★★, *The Unforgettable* (RCA 1998)★★★.

● FURTHER READING: *Next To A Letter From Home - Major Glenn Miller's Wartime Band*, Geoffrey Butcher. *Glen Miller & His Orchestra*, George Thomas Simon.

MILLER, HARRY

b. 21 April 1941, Johannesburg, South Africa, d. 16 December 1983. A highly impressive and emotional bass player, Miller played R&B (with Manfred Mann) in South Africa. He moved to the UK in 1961, and then worked in bands on transatlantic liners, so that he heard New York jazz at first hand. Settling back in London, he made a reputation playing with John Surman, Keith Tippett (Ovary Lodge and Centipede), Dudu Pukwana (Spear), Elton Dean (Ninesense and Just Us), Stan Tracey (Tentacles and the Octet), Alan Skidmore (part of the quintet that won the 1969 Press prize at Montreux), Louis Moholo, Kenneth Terroade, Chris McGregor, Mike Westbrook and Mike Osborne, forming, with Louis Moholo, the superb Mike Osborne Trio for several years. He also worked in a trio with Moholo and Peter Brötzmann. He also led bands of his own, notably the ferocious and all-star Isipingo, and the Quartette A Tête, which he co-founded with Tippet, Radu Malfatti and Paul Lytton. He co-founded the Lambeth New Music Society and Ogun records, both of which showcased many of the best UK-based musicians. He also ran regular gigs through his Grass Roots agency. He died as a result of a road accident in 1983. His widow, Hazel, continues to make an important contribution to the scene through Ogun, and by the intermittent, tenacious organization of benefits and other gigs.

● ALBUMS: *Children At Play* (1974)★★, with Isipingo *Family Affair* (1977)★★★, *In Conference* (1978)★★★★, with Radu Malfatti *Bracknell Breakdown* (1978)★★, with Peter Brötzmann, Louis Moholo *The Nearer The Bone The Sweeter The Meat* (1980)★★★★, with Brötzmann, Moholo *Opened, But Hardly Touched* (1981)★★★, with Malfatti *Zwecknagel* (1981)★★★.

MILLER, MARCUS

b. 14 June 1959, New York City, New York, USA. Taking up the electric bass in his teens, Miller's early musical experience came from the New York soul scene. Flautist Bobbi Humphrey gave him his first serious work in the jazz idiom in 1977, which was quickly followed by a tour with Lenny White's group. Becoming competent on an impressive number of instruments, Miller's reputation grew in the New York studio world. By 1980, he had recorded for Bob James, Grover Washington Jnr., Roberta Flack, and Aretha Franklin. In 1980, he joined Miles Davis, but left after two years for the financial lure of session work, producing and playing on several albums for David Sanborn. The second and more important period of Miller's relationship with Miles Davis began in 1986, when he played almost every instrument and wrote most of the music for *Tutu*, Davis's first album for Warner Brothers Records. Davis had never before given away so much artistic control, but must have been pleased with the result, for Miller worked just as closely with him on his *Siesta* and *Amandlia* albums. He continues to work as one of New York's top studio musicians.

● ALBUMS: with Miles Davis *The Man With The Horn* (1981)★★★, with Davis *We Want Miles* (1981)★★★, with Davis *Tutu* (1986)★★★★, with Davis *Siesta* (1988)★★★, with Davis *Amandlia* (1989)★★★, *The Sun Don't Lie* (Dreyfus Jazz Line 1993)★★★, *Tales* (Dreyfus 1995)★★, *Live & More* (Dreyfus 1998)★★★.

MILLER, MULGREW

b. 13 April 1955, Greenwood, Massachusetts, USA. Miller learnt the piano while a child and studied music at university, at the same time playing in local gospel and R&B groups. After playing with Mercer Ellington's Orchestra in the late 70s, he joined vocalist Betty Carter before moving on to the quintet of Woody Shaw and Art Blakey's Jazz Messengers (1983-86). He has added all the innovations of recent piano playing to this solid background, and fused them with a brilliant technique. In the late 80s he continued with his prolific studio career and played with the quintet of Tony Williams and Joe Lovano. His own trio became a priority in the 90s as he recorded a number of stylish albums. His trio features Kareen Riggins and Richie Goods (bass).

● ALBUMS: with Art Blakey *Blue Night* (1985)★★★, *Keys To The City* (1985)★★★, *Live At Sweet Basil's* (1985)★★★★, *Work!* (1986)★★★, with James Spalding *Gotshabe A Better Way* (1988)★★, with Benny Golson *Benny Golson Quartet* (1990)★★★, with Kenny Garrett *African Exchange Student* (1990)★★★, *Time And Again* (1992)★★★, *Hand In Hand* (Novus 1993)★★★, *Getting To Know You* (Novus 1995)★★★★.

MILLIAN, BAKER

b. 1908, Crowley, Louisiana, USA. As a youth and young man he played various instruments, including piano and several members of the saxophone family before settling on the tenor. He first worked in several Louisiana bands, including Chris Kelly's in New Orleans, before moving to Texas where he played in territory bands such as Chester Boone's and Boots Douglas's. At the end of the 30s he relocated to California and thereafter worked mostly outside music, although he regularly took up his instrument to play with visiting musicians such as Bunk Johnson. A competent player, his work with Douglas's band Boots And His Buddies, displays an interesting, if sometimes derivative, style, suggesting his fondness for the playing of Coleman Hawkins, although in later years he accommodated the new sound of Lester Young. In some respects, Millian can be seen as an early manifestation of the tough-Texas-tenor school of playing.

● COMPILATIONS: *Boots And His Buddies: San Antonio Jazz* (Tax 30s)★★★.

MILLINDER, LUCKY

b. Lucius Millinder, 8 August 1900, Anniston, Alabama, USA, d. 28 September 1966, New York, USA. Growing up in Chicago, Millinder worked in clubs and theatres in the late 20s as a dancer and master of ceremonies. His engaging personality resulted in his being appointed leader of several bands in Chicago, New York, and on tour. In 1933, he brought a band to Europe, playing as part of an all-black revue. The following year he was appointed leader of the Mills Blue Rhythm Band, fronting it at the Cotton Club in Harlem. Beginning in 1938, he had a few bad years, part of the time leading the Bill Doggett band but mostly suffering acute financial embarrassment. In 1940, he formed a new band of his own, hiring some high-quality musicians - including, at one time or another in the first few years, trumpeters Dizzy Gillespie, Joe Guy and Freddie Webster, saxophonists Tab Smith, Eddie 'Lockjaw' Davis and Sam 'The Man' Taylor, and in the rhythm section Doggett, Trevor Bacon and David 'Panama' Francis. Millinder also had Sister Rosetta Tharpe in the band for a while. He enjoyed considerable success, playing dance dates, often at the Savoy Ballroom in Harlem, broadcasting and touring, with occasional recording dates for good measure. Despite the changing times, Millinder kept the band afloat throughout the 40s, eventually calling it a day in 1952. Thereafter, he earned his living outside music, but formed occasional bands for special concerts. Although he was not a musician and could not read music, Millinder was an exceptional frontman, conducting his bands with flair and showmanship. Given the fact that many of the arrangements used by his bands over the years were complex, he clearly had a good ear and was able to create the effect of leading when in reality he was following the musicians under his baton. Although it might be said with some justification that the Mills Blue Rhythm Band and his own band of the early 40s owed little to him musically, there can be little doubt that they owed him much for the success they enjoyed.

● COMPILATIONS: *Big Bands Uptown!* (1931-43)★★★, *Lucky Millinder And His Orchestra 1941-1943* (1941-43)★★★★, *Apollo Jump* (Affinity 1983)★★★★, *Let It Roll Again* (Jukebox Lil 1985)★★★, *Shorty's Got To Go* (Jukebox Lil 1985)★★★★, *Lucky Millinder And His Orchestra* (Hindsight 1987)★★★, *Ram-Bunk-Shush* (Sing 1988)★★★, *Stompin' At The Savoy 1943-44* (Bandstand 1988)★★★★, *Lucky Millinder 1941-42* (Original Jazz Classics 1993)★★★★.

Mills Blue Rhythm Band

Late in 1929, a group of New York musicians, under the nominal leadership of drummer Willie Lynch, formed a big band that they named the Blue Rhythm Band. A succession of front men, who included pianist Edgar Hayes and singer Cab Calloway, led the band, but despite high musical standards, it failed to attract a large following. In 1931, Irving Mills took over management of the band and appended his name. The Mills Blue Rhythm Band became third string in Mills's stable, behind the bands of Duke Ellington and Calloway. Later conducted by Jimmy Ferguson ('Baron Lee') and then Lucky Millinder, the band made many fine records. Subsequently billed as the Instrumental Gentlemen From Harlem, the band eventually folded in 1938. During its existence, several top-flight musicians played in its ranks, among them trumpeters Henry 'Red' Allen, Shelton Hemphill, Charlie Shavers, Harry Edison and Edward Anderson, trombonist J.C. Higginbotham, saxophonists Charlie Holmes, Caster and Ted McCord, and clarinettist Buster Bailey. Especially in its middle and later years, the band was musically outstanding, playing fine arrangements by Tab Smith, Joe Garland and others. Regrettably, the band's lack of a charismatic frontman seemed to carry more weight with the public than its musical excellence, and the Mills Blue Rhythm Band sank into undeserved latter-day obscurity. In the late 40s, the band was briefly re-formed for record dates.

● COMPILATIONS: *Henry 'Red' Allen And The Mills Blue Rhythm Band* (1934-35)★★★, *Big Bands* (1947)★★★, *Blue Rhythm* 1930-31 recordings (Hep Jazz 1986)★★★, *1937* (CJM 1987)★★★, *Rhythms Splash* (Hep Jazz 1987)★★★, *Savage Rhythm* 1931-32 recordings (Hep Jazz 1987)★★★★, *Rhythm Spasm* 1932-33 recordings (Hep Jazz 1993)★★★★.

Mills Brothers

The three permanent members of the group comprised Herbert Mills (b. 2 April 1912, d. April 1989, Las Vegas, Nevada, USA), Harry Mills (b. 9 August 1913, d. 28 June 1982) and Donald Mills (b. 29 April 1915). John Mills Jnr. (b. 11 February 1911, d. 1935), added vocal notes in string bass form and played guitar. All the brothers were born in Piqua, Ohio, USA, sons of a barber who had been a successful concert singer. By the mid-20s, they were singing in sweet, close harmony in local vaudeville, providing their own backing by accurately imitating saxophones, trumpets, trombones and bass. With the main trio still teenagers, they had their own show on Cincinnati radio before moving to New York in 1930. The brothers signed to Brunswick Records and had a hit in 1931 with their first disc, 'Tiger Rag', which they also sang in the movie *The Big Broadcast*, featuring Bing Crosby and many other stars of US radio. They appeared in several other musical montage movies such as *Twenty Million Sweethearts* (1934), *Broadway Gondolier* (1935) and *Reveille With Beverly* (1943), *Rhythm Parade* (1943), *Cowboy Canteen* (1944) and *When You're Smiling* (1950). In the early 30s, Crosby featured on several of the brothers' record hits, including 'Dinah'/'Can't We Talk It Over', 'Shine' and 'Gems From George White's Scandals', which also included the Boswell Sisters. On later tracks, the Mills Brothers were also joined by Louis Armstrong, Ella Fitzgerald and Cab Calloway. Their early records were labelled: 'No musical instruments or mechanical devices used on this recording other than one guitar'. Other 30s hits included 'You Rascal, You', 'I Heard', 'Good-Bye, Blues', 'Rockin' Chair', 'St. Louis Blues', 'Sweet Sue', 'Bugle Call Rag', 'It Don't Mean A Thing (If It Ain't Got That Swing)', 'Swing It Sister', 'Sleepy Head' and 'Sixty Seconds Together'.

In 1935, John Mills died suddenly and the brothers' father, John Snr., took over as bass singer, and ex-bandleader Bernard Addison joined the group on guitar. During the late 30s, the Mills Brothers toured the USA and abroad, appearing in two UK Royal Command Performances. Their popularity peaked in 1943 with the record 'Paper Doll', which sold over six million copies. They had consistent chart success throughout the 40s with titles on the Decca label such as 'You Always Hurt The One You Love', 'Til Then', 'I Wish', 'I Don't Know Enough About You', 'Across The Alley From The Alamo', 'I Love You So Much It Hurts', 'I've Got My Love To Keep Me Warm', 'Someday (You'll Want Me To

Want You)' and 'Put Another Chair At The Table'. By 1950, the instrumental impressions having generally been discarded, the brothers were accompanied by ex-Tommy Dorsey arranger Sy Oliver's orchestra on their hit 'Nevertheless (I'm In Love With You)' and again in 1952 on 'Be My Life's Companion'. That same year, 'The Glow Worm', gave them another blockbuster. This was a 1908 song from the German operetta *Lysistrata*, with a new lyric by Johnny Mercer. Other 50s favourites from the brothers included Sy Oliver's own composition 'Opus Number One', 'Say 'Si-Si'', 'Lazy River' and 'Smack Dab In The Middle'. In 1956, John Snr. retired, and the brothers continued as a trio. Their last hit on Decca was 'Queen Of The Senior Prom' in 1957. The switch to the Dot label gave them two US Top 30 entries, 'Get A Job' and their final chart success, 'Cab Driver', in 1968. After Harry Mills' death in 1982, Herbert and Donald continued to perform their brand of highly polished, humorous entertainment with a substitute singer. However, when Herbert died seven years later, Donald, now walking with a cane, gained excellent reviews and favourable audience reaction when he played nightclubs with his son John, using mainly the old Mills Brothers catalogue, but with additional new material.

● ALBUMS: *Barber Shop Ballads* (Decca 1950)★★★★, *Souvenir Album* (Decca 1950)★★★, *Wonderful Words* (Decca 1951)★★★, *Meet The Mills Brothers* (Decca 1954)★★★★, *Louis Armstrong And The Mills Brothers* (Decca 1954)★★★★, *Four Boys And A Guitar* (Decca 1954)★★★, *Singin' And Swingin'* (Decca 1956)★★★, *Memory Lane* (Decca 1956)★★★★, *One Dozen Roses* (Decca 1957)★★★, *The Mills Brothers In Hi-Fi* (Decca 1958)★★★★, *Glow With The Mills Brothers* (Decca 1959)★★★, *Barbershop Harmony* (Decca 1959)★★★, *Harmonizing With The Mills Brothers* (Decca 1959)★★★, *Mmmm, The Mills Brothers* (Dot 1958)★★★, *Great Barbershop Hits* (Dot 1959)★★★, *Merry Christmas* (Dot 1959)★★★, *The Mills Brothers Sing* (Dot 1960)★★★, *Yellow Bird* (1961)★★★, *San Antonio Rose* (London 1961)★★★, *Great Hawaiian Hits* (1961)★★, *The Beer Barrel Polka And Other Hits* (London 1962)★★, *Sing 'The End Of The World' & Other Great Hits* (London 1963)★★, *Gems By The Mills Brothers* (1964)★★, *Hymns We Love* (1964)★★, *Say Si Si, And Other Great Latin Hits* (1964)★★, *The Mills Brothers Sing For You* (1964)★★★, *These Are The Mills Brothers* (1966)★★★, *That Country Feelin'* (1966)★★, *The Mills Brothers Live* (1967)★★, *Fortuosity* (Dot 1968)★★★, with Count Basie *The Board Of Directors* (Dot 1968)★★★, *My Shy Violet* (Dot 1968)★★★, *Dream* (Dot 1969)★★★.

● COMPILATIONS: *The Mills Brothers Greatest Hits* (Dot 1958)★★★, *Ten Years Of Hits 1954-1964* (1965)★★★, *Greatest Hits* (MCA 1987)★★, *The Very Best Of The Mills Brothers* (Half Moon 1998)★★★, in addition, there are a great many compilations available.

● FILMS: *The Big Beat* (1957).

MINCE, JOHNNY

b. 8 July 1912, Chicago Heights, Illinois, USA, d. 23 December 1994. A highly accomplished clarinettist, Mince's early career saw him playing with several of the most sophisticated bands of the early swing era. At the age of 17, he was with Joe Haymes's excellent danceband, and during the 30s, Mince moved on to Ray Noble, Bob Crosby and Tommy Dorsey. During the spell with Noble, Mince played an important part in helping to establish the 'sound' of Glenn Miller's arrangements, a sound that Miller later developed with his own band. After military service, Mince was mostly active in studio work, but he returned occasionally to play jazz dates in clubs and on record. In later years, Mince became a familiar and popular figure at international jazz festivals, touring extensively with a variety of musicians, such as the Kings Of Jazz, and with the bands of Dixieland veterans led by Yank Lawson and Bob Haggart and by British trumpeter Keith Smith. On all such forays, Mince attracted the favourable attention of a new generation of fans through his superb technique and distinctive style.

● ALBUMS: *Summer Of '79* (1979)★★★, *The Master Comes Home* i (1980)★★★, *I Can't Give You Anything But Love* (1982)★★★★, with others *Swingin' The Forties With The Great Eight* (1983)★★★, *The Master Comes Home* ii (1983)★★★.

● COMPILATIONS: with Tommy Dorsey *The Sentimental Gentleman* (1941-42)★★★★.

MING - DAVID MURRAY OCTET

Albert Ayler-influenced tenor saxophonist and bass clarinettist David Murray has earned a reputation for releasing more albums in a year than other important jazz musicians manage to issue in a decade. However, *Ming*, recorded in 1980, holds a special place in the Murray canon, for the huge enthusiasm with which it was received by fans and critics alike, and the attention it brought to Murray's superb compositional skills. Its star cast includes saxophonist Henry Threadgill, cornettist Butch Morris and trombonist George Lewis, blasting through Murray's intricate but daring arrangements and playing some intense, memorable solos. Check out the beautiful title track, and the chaotic 'Dewey's Circle'.

● Tracks: *Fast Life; The Hill; Ming; Jasvan; Dewey's Circle.*

● First released 1981

● UK peak chart position: did not chart

● USA peak chart position: did not chart

MINGUS

Like its subject, this documentary film made in 1968 is unflinching and at times uncomfortably honest. Charles Mingus was being evicted from his home during the making of the film and these events are depicted as is the artist at work composing, rehearsing and performing. Amongst other musicians involved are Charles McPherson and Dannie Richmond.

MINGUS AH UM - CHARLES MINGUS

One of the five essential Charles Mingus albums to own, and even if you are not a jazz fan this is still worthy of being in any comprehensive collection. The opening track, 'Better Git It In Your Soul', rushes along at a furious pace and then there is a wonderful change of tempo into an *a cappella* and handclap pause. It rolls on, of course, but the nature of this track reflects the nature of Mingus who never failed to experiment (even though sometimes he failed). The personnel comprises John Handy III, Shafi Hadi and Booker Ervin (saxophones), Horace Parlan Jr (piano), Willie Dennis and James Knepper (trombones) and Charles Richmond (drums). Mingus whoops, shouts and holds it all together and then turns the pace majestically on numbers such as 'Goodbye Pork Pie Hat'.

● Tracks: *Better Git It In Your Soul; Goodbye Pork Pie Hat; Boogie Stop Shuffle; Self-Portrait In Three Colours; Open Letter To Duke; Bird Calls; Fables Of Faubus; Pussy Cat Dues; Jelly Roll*

● First released 1960

● UK peak chart position: did not chart

● USA peak chart position: did not chart

MINGUS BIG BAND

Formed to represent the music of Charles Mingus to the world this conglomerate was organized by his widow Sue, originally to play a tribute concert at Carnegie Hall in 1979, the year of the bassist's death. That line-up used four horns and a rhythm section, but since the mid-90s a 14-piece band has played weekly at New York's Time Cafe and performed on the European festival circuit. Drawing on over 100 musicians, the band includes regular players such as Randy Brecker, Frank Lacy, Ku-Umba, Kenny Drew Jr., Ryan Kisor, John Stubblefield (an original Mingus alumni), and musical directors Andy McKee and Steve Slagle.

● ALBUMS: *Nostalgia In Times Square* (Dreyfus 1993)★★★, *GunSlinging Birds* (Dreyfus 1995)★★★, *Live In Time* (Dreyfus 1997)★★★★, *¡Que Viva Mingus!* (Dreyfus 1998)★★★.

MINGUS MINGUS MINGUS MINGUS MINGUS - CHARLES MINGUS

While Charles Mingus is rightly revered by the jazz world, he is yet to receive the universal blessing of the rock audience in the way that John Coltrane and Miles Davis have. This album is perfect for a Mingus primer. It is fat, gorgeous, accessible and often breathtaking. Suddenly, the swinging orchestra will pause its riff completely and a few notes of Mingus's growling bass will sneak in. For once the sleeve-note is right: 'he jolts with the unexpected'. 'II B.S.' is a stunning opener and from then on the listener can settle into a comfortable half-hour. A brilliant record.

● Tracks: *II B.S.; I X Love; Celia; Mood Indigo; Better Get Hit In Yo' Soul; Theme For Lester Young; Hora Decubitus.*

● First released 1963

● UK peak chart position: did not chart

● USA peak chart position: did not chart

MINGUS, CHARLES

b. 22 April 1922, Nogales, Arizona, USA, d. 5 January 1979, Cuernavaca, Mexico. Mingus was never allowed the luxury of the feeling of belonging. Reactions to his mixed ancestry (he had British-born, Chinese, Swedish and African-American grandparents) produced strong feelings of anger and reinforced his sense of persecution. However, this alienation, coupled with his own deep sensitivity and tendency to dramatize his experiences, provided substantial fuel for an artistic career of heroic turmoil and brilliance. Formative musical experiences included both the strictures of European classical music and the uninhibited outpourings of the congregation of the local Holiness Church, which he attended with his stepmother. There he heard all manner of bluesy vocal techniques, moaning, audience-preacher responses, wild vibrato and melismatic improvisation, along with the accompaniment of cymbals and trombones - all of it melding into an early gospel precursor of big band that heavily influenced Mingus's mature compositional and performance style. Other influences were hearing Duke Ellington's band, and recordings of Richard Strauss's tone poems and works by Debussy, Ravel, Bach and Beethoven. Thwarted in his early attempts to learn trombone, Mingus switched from cello to double bass at high school. He studied composition with Lloyd Reese and was encouraged by Red Callender to study bass with Herman Rheimschagen of the New York Philharmonic. He developed a virtuoso bass technique and began to think of the bass finger-board as similar to a piano keyboard. His first professional dates as a bassist included gigs with New Orleans players Kid Ory and Barney Bigard, and then stints with the Louis Armstrong Orchestra (1943-45) and Lionel Hampton (1947), but it was with the Red Norvo Trio (1950) that he first gained national recognition for his virtuosity. Work with other great pioneers of his generation such as Charlie Parker, Miles Davis, Thelonious Monk, Bud Powell, Sonny Stitt, Stan Getz, Lee Konitz, Dizzy Gillespie, Quincy Jones and Teddy Charles continued throughout the 50s. He joined Duke Ellington's band briefly in 1953, but a more artistically profitable association with his hero occurred with the trio album *Money Jungle*, which they made with Max Roach in 1962. Mingus was a pioneer of black management and artist-led record labels, forming Debut in 1953, and the Charles Mingus label in 1964. His early compositions were varying in success, often due to the difficulty of developing and maintaining an ensemble to realize his complex ideas.

He contributed works to the Jazz Composers' Workshop from 1953 until the foundation of his own workshop ensemble in 1955. Here, he was able to make sparing use of notation, transmitting his intentions from verbal and musical instructions sketched at the piano or on the bass. Mingus's originality as a composer first began to flourish under these circumstances, and with players such as Dannie Richmond, Rahsaan Roland Kirk, Jaki Byard, Jimmy Knepper and Booker Ervin he developed a number of highly evolved works. Crucial among his many innovations in jazz was the use of non-standard chorus structures, contrasting sections of quasi-'classical' composed material with passages of freeform and group improvisations, often of varying tempos and modes, in complex pieces knitted together by subtly evolving musical motifs. He developed a 'conversational' mode of interactive improvisation, and pioneered melodic bass playing. Such pieces as *The Black Saint*

And The Sinner Lady (1963) show enormous vitality and a great depth of immersion in all jazz styles, from New Orleans and gospel to bebop and free jazz. Another multi-sectional piece, 'Meditations For A Pair Of Wire Cutters', from the album *Portrait* (1964), is one of many that evolved gradually under various titles. Sections from it can be heard on *Mingus Plays Piano* (1963), there called 'Myself When I Am Real'. It was renamed 'Praying With Eric' after the tragic death of Eric Dolphy, who made magnificent contributions to many Mingus compositions, but especially to this intensely moving piece.

In the mid-60s, financial and psychological problems began to take their toll, as poignantly recorded in Thomas Reichman's 1968 film *Mingus*. He toured extensively during this period, presenting a group of ensemble works. In 1971, Mingus was much encouraged by the receipt of a Guggenheim fellowship in composition, and the publication of his astonishing autobiography, *Beneath The Underdog*. The book opens with a session conducted by a psychiatrist, and the work reveals Mingus's self-insight, intelligence, sensitivity and tendency for self-dramatization. Touring continued until the gradual paralysis brought by the incurable disease Amyotrophic Lateral Sclerosis prevented him doing anything more than presiding over recordings. His piece 'Revelations' was performed in 1978 by the New York Philharmonic under the direction of Gunther Schuller, who also resurrected *Epitaph* in 1989. Also in 1978, Mingus was honoured at the White House by Jimmy Carter and an all-star jazz concert. News of his death, aged 56, in Mexico was marked by many tributes from artists of all fields. Posthumously, the ensemble Mingus Dynasty continued to perform his works.

Mingus summed up the preoccupations of his time in a way that transcended racial and cultural divisions, while simultaneously highlighting racial and social injustices. Introducing the first 1964 performance of *Meditations*, Mingus told the audience: 'This next composition was written when Eric Dolphy told me there was something similar to the concentration camps down South, [. . .] where they separated [. . .] the green from the red, or something like that; and the only difference between the electric barbed wire is that they don't have gas chambers and hot stoves to cook us in yet. So I wrote a piece called *Meditations* as to how to get some wire cutters before someone else gets some guns to us.' Off-mike, he can be heard saying to fellow musicians: 'They're gonna burn us; they'll try.' In the turmoil of his life and artistic achievements, and in his painful demise, Mingus became his own artistic creation. A desperate, passionate icon for the mid-twentieth century to which all can relate in some way, he articulated the emotional currents of his time in a way superior to that of almost any other contemporary jazz musician.

● ALBUMS: *Red Norvo Jazz Trio* (1951)★★★, with Spaulding Givens *Strings And Keys* (Decca 1951)★★★, *The Red Norvo - Charles Mingus - Tal Farlow Trio* (1951)★★★, *Autobiography In Jazz* (1953)★★★, *Strings And Keys* (Debut 1953)★★★★, with others *Quintet Of The Year/Jazz At Massey Hall* (1953)★★★, with Thad Jones *Jazz Collaborations* 10-inch album (Debut 1954)★★★★, *Jazz Composers Workshop* (Savoy 1954)★★★★, *Jazz Experiments* (Jazztone 1954)★★★, *Charles Mingus And Thad Jones* (1955)★★★, *Jazzical Moods, Volume 1* (Period 1955)★★★, *Jazzical Moods Volume 2* (Period 1955)★★★, *Jazz Composers Workshop No 2* (Savoy 1956)★★★, *Mingus At The Bohemia* (Debut 1955)★★★, *Charlie Mingus* (Savoy 1955)★★★, with Max Roach *The Charles Mingus Quintet And Max Roach* (Debut 1956)★★★, *Pithecanthropus Erectus* (Atlantic 1956)★★★★, *The Clown* aka *Reincarnation Of A Lovebird* (Atlantic 1957)★★★, with Gunther Schuller, George Russell *Adventures In Sound* (1957)★★★, *Jazz Experiment* (Jazztone 1957)★★★, *Jazz Workshop Presents: Jimmy Knepper* (1957)★★★, *The Jazz Experiments Of Charles Mingus* (Jazztone 1957)★★★, *The Clown* (Atlantic 1957)★★★, *Mingus Three* (Jubilee 1957)★★★, *East Coasting* (Bethlehem 1958)★★★, *A Modern Jazz Symposium Of Music And Poetry* (Bethlehem 1958)★★★, with Langston Hughes *Weary Blues* (1958)★★★, with Billie Holiday, etc. *Easy To Remember* (1958)★★★, *East Coasting* (Bethlehem 1958)★★★, *Duke's Choice* aka *A Modern Jazz Symposium Of Music And Poetry* (Bethlehem 1958)★★★, *Wonderland* (United Artists 1959)★★★, *Jazz Portraits* (United Artists 1959)★★★, *Blues And Roots* (Atlantic 1959)★★★★, *Mingus Ah-Um* (Columbia 1959)★★★★★, *Nostalgia In Times Square* (1959)★★★, *Mingus Dynasty* (Columbia 1960)★★★, *Pre-Bird* aka *Mingus Revisited* (Emarcy 1960)★★★, *Mingus At Antibes* (1960)★★★★, *Charles Mingus Presents Charles Mingus!* (Candid 1960)★★★★, *Mingus* (Candid 1960)★★★★, *The Jazz Life* (1960)★★★, *Newport Rebels* (1960)★★★, with Tubby Hayes *All Night Long* (1960)★★★★, *Oh Yeah!* (Atlantic 1961)★★★★, *Pre Bird* (Mercury 1961)★★★, *Tonight At Noon* (Atlantic 1961)★★★, *Hooray For Charles Mingus* (1962)★★★, *J-For-Jazz Presents Charles Mingus* (1962)★★★, with Duke Ellington, Max Roach *Money Jungle* (United Artists 1962)★★★★, *Town Hall Concert* (United Artists 1962)★★★, *Chazz!* (Fantasy 1962)★★★, *The Black Saint And The Sinner Lady* (Impulse! 1963)★★★★★, *Mingus Mingus Mingus Mingus Mingus* (Impulse! 1963)★★★★, *Tijuana Moods* 1957 recording (RCA 1964)★★★★, *Town Hall Concert (Portrait)* (Original Jazz Classics 1964)★★★, *Live in Oslo* 1964 recording (60s)★★★, *Charles Mingus Sextet Live In Europe Volumes 1, 2 & 3* (1964)★★★, *The Great Concert Of Charles Mingus* (1964)★★★, *Mingus In Europe Volumes 1 & 2* (1964)★★★, *Charles Mingus In Amsterdam* (1964)★★★, *Mingus In Stuttgart Volumes 1 & 2* (1964)★★★, *Right Now! Live At The Jazz Workshop* (Fantasy 1964)★★★, *Charles Mingus In Europe* (Enja 1964)★★★, *Mingus At Monterey* (Prestige 1964)★★★, *Music Written For Monterey 1965, But Not Heard* (1965)★★★, *My Favourite Quintet* (1965)★★★, *Statements* (1970)★★★, *Charles Mingus In Paris* (DIW 1970)★★★, *Pithy Canthropus Erectus* aka *Blue Bird* (1970)★★★, *Charles Mingus In Berlin* (1970)★★★, *Charles Mingus And The New Herd* (1971)★★★, *Let My Children Hear Music* (Columbia 1971)★★★, *Charles Mingus And Friends In Concert* (1972)★★★, *Jazz Jamboree* (1972)★★★, *Charles Mingus Meets Cat Anderson* (1972)★★★, *Mingus Mingus* (1973)★★★, *Mingus At Carnegie Hall* (1974)★★★, *Cumbria And Jazz Fusion* (Atlantic 1977)★★★, *Three Or Four Shades Of Blue* (1977)★★★, *Lionel Hampton Presents: The Music Of Charles Mingus* aka *His Final Works* (1977)★★★, *Me Myself An Eye* (1978)★★★, *Something Like A Bird* (1978)★★★, *The Charles Mingus Memorial Album* (1978)★★★, with Joni Mitchell *Joni*

Mitchell - Mingus (Geffen 1979)★★★.

● COMPILATIONS: *The Mingus Connection* 1951-53 recordings (1957)★★★, *The Debut Recordings* (1951-57)★★★★, *Vital Savage Horizons* (1952, 1961-62)★★★, *The Atlantic Years* (1956-78)★★★★, *Better Git It In Your Soul* (1959)★★★★, *The Complete Candid Recordings Of Charles Mingus* (1960)★★★, *Charles Mingus/Cecil Taylor: Rare Broadcast Performances* (1962, 1966)★★★, *The Impulse! Years* (1963)★★★★, *Portrait* (1964)★★★, *Re-Evaluation: The Impulse! Years* 1963-64 recordings (1973)★★★, *The Art Of Charles Mingus* (1974)★★★, *Passions Of A Man* 1956-61, 1973, 1977 recordings (1979)★★★, *Nostalgia In Times Square* 1959 recordings (1979)★★★, *Great Moments With Charles Mingus* 1963-64 recordings (1981)★★★, *Mingus, The Collection* 50s recordings (1985)★★★★, *Charles Mingus - New York Sketchbook* 50s recordings (1986)★★★★, *Charles Mingus - Shoes Of The Fisherman's Wife* 1959, 1971 recordings (1988)★★★★, *Abstractions* 1954, 1957 recordings (1989)★★★, *Charles Mingus - Mysterious Blues* 1960 recording (1989)★★★, *Charles Mingus 1955-1957* (1990)★★★, *Charles Mingus* (1991)★★★, *Charles Mingus - The Complete Debut Recordings* 50s recordings, 12-CD box set (Debut 1991)★★★★, *Meditations On Integration* 1964 recording (1992)★★★, *Thirteen Pictures: The Charles Mingus Anthology* 1956-1977 recordings (Rhino 1993)★★★★★, *The Legendary Paris Concerts* 1964 recording (Revenge 1996)★★★, *Passions Of A Man - The Complete Atlantic Recordings 1956-1961* 6-CD box set (Rhino/Atlantic 1998)★★★★★, *The Complete 1959 Columbia Sessions* 3-CD box set (Columbia/Legacy 1998)★★★★.

● VIDEOS: *Charles Mingus Sextet 1964* (1994), *Triumph Of The Underdog* (Academy Video 1998).

● FURTHER READING: *Beneath The Underdog*, Charles Mingus. *Mingus: A Critical Biography*, Brian Priestley. *Revelations*, Charles Mingus. *Charles Mingus, Sein Leben, Seine Musik, Seine Schallplatten*, Horst Weber. *Mingus/Mingus*, Janet Coleman.

MINTZER, BOB

b. 27 January 1953, New Rochelle, Westchester, New York, USA. Interested in music from childhood, he began serious studies shortly before he left high school. He went to Interlochen Arts Academy in Michigan, by which time he was becoming adept on tenor saxophone and was also taking an interest in arranging. Fellow students at Interlochen included Peter Erskine and two sons of Dave Brubeck. Mintzer then studied and played, mostly clarinet, at Hart College of Music in Hartford, Connecticut, then went to the Manhattan School of Music in New York. However, the active New York music scene proved to be a greater attraction and in 1974 he went on the road with Eumir Deodato and the following year began a two-year stint with Buddy Rich where his arranging talents blossomed. After leaving Rich he worked regularly with the Thad Jones-Mel Lewis Jazz Orchestra.

He continued to develop as an arranger and preferred the context of a big band, playing with Stone Alliance, and the big bands of Sam Jones and Jaco Pastorius. In 1984 he formed his own big band before becoming a regular member of the popular Yellowjackets. In his playing, Mintzer acknowledges the influence of most of the leading tenor saxophone stylists of jazz, from Coleman Hawkins through to John Coltrane, but has developed his own powerful and distinctive style. As an arranger he happily uses latter-day musical movements, such as rock and post-rock, without ever losing the tradition of big band jazz. His arrangements, especially when played by his own band, are finely crafted, tight and urgent.

● ALBUMS: with Stone Alliance *Heads Up* (PM 1980)★★, *Papa Lips* (Sony 1984)★★★, *Incredible Journey* (DMP 1985)★★★, *Camouflage* (DMP 1986)★★, *Spectrum* (DMP 1987)★★★, *Urban Contours* (DMP 1988)★★★, *Art Of The Big Band* (DMP 1989)★★★, with Peter Erskine *Sweet Soul* (BMG 1991)★★★★, *One Music* (DMP 1991)★★★, *I Remember Jaco* (BMG 1991)★★★★, *Departure* (DMP 1992)★★★, *Only In New York* (DMP 1994)★★★, *Big Band Trane* (DMP 1996)★★★★, *Latin From Manhattan* (DMP 1998)★★★, *Quality Time* (TVT 1998)★★★.

MISSISSIPPI SHEIKS

This musical combination flourished between 1930 and 1935, during which time they recorded more than 80 tracks for various 'race' labels. The Sheiks was a string band made up of members and friends of the Chatman family, and included Lonnie Chatman (guitar, violin), Sam Chatman (guitar), Walter Vincson (guitar, violin), Bo (Carter) Chatman (guitar), and Charlie McCoy (banjo, mandolin). Vocal chores were handled by all the members. Most of these individuals pursued independent musical careers either at this time or later. The instrumental abilities of all members were extremely high and their repertoire covered all ground between popular waltzes to salacious party songs, with a fair quantity of high-quality blues thrown in. Their work also appeared under the names the Mississippi Mud Steppers, the Down South Boys and also the Carter Brothers.

● COMPILATIONS: *Sitting On Top Of The World* (1972)★★★, *Stop And Listen Blues* (1973)★★★, *The Mississippi Sheiks* (1984)★★★.

MISSOURIANS

In the early 20s, St. Louis-based violinist Wilson Robinson formed a band that he named the Syncopaters. By 1924, the band was in New York and, now directed by another violinist, they were engaged as the house band at the Cotton Club. Incorporating the club's name in its title, the band was known as Andy Preer And His Cotton Club Orchestra. When the band was replaced at the club by Duke Ellington, Preer's group changed its name yet again, this time calling itself the Missourians. After Preer's death, the band secured another prestigious New York engagement, this time at the Savoy Ballroom under the leadership of George Scott.

The band retained a good measure of popularity with dancers at the Savoy, playing with a propulsive, free-flowing swing that reflected its now-distant Midwestern origins. Early in 1930, the band backed singer Cab Calloway on record dates, and soon thereafter became his permanent band, changing their name to the Cab Calloway Orchestra. In its early years at the Cotton Club, the band did much to foster the type of music that was associated with that venue and which Ellington later refined. The band had a number of fine soloists, among them trumpeter R.Q. Dickerson, whose use of the plunger mute helped to establish the so-called 'jungle' music with which the Cotton Club show bands were associated.

● COMPILATIONS: *The Missourians* (1929-30 recordings)★★★.

MITCHELL, BILLY

b. 3 November 1926, Kansas City, Missouri, USA. Mitchell studied in Detroit and played tenor saxophone with Nat Towles' band in the late 40s before moving to New York with Lucky Millinder's Orchestra. He spent a couple of months in Woody Herman's Second Herd, and then led his own bop quintet back in Detroit, which included Thad Jones on trumpet and Elvin Jones on drums (1950-53). In the mid-50s, after a couple of years with Dizzy Gillespie, he recorded with Ray Charles and joined Count Basie's Orchestra. He co-led a sextet with ex-Basie trombonist Al Grey, and worked as musical director for Stevie Wonder in the mid-60s, before rejoining Basie (1966-67). He uses a tough, bluesy tone to construct fluent solo lines. In the 70s Mitchell settled in New York and undertook studio work, as well as teaching and performing with the Xanadu All Stars.

● ALBUMS: with Ray Charles *Soul Brothers* (1957)★★★, with Count Basie *One More Time* (1958)★★★★, *Al Grey With Billy Mitchell* (1961)★★★, *Little Juicy* (1963)★★★, with Xanadu *Xanadu At Montreux* (1978)★★, with Paul Lingle *Vintage Piano Vol 3* (Euphonic 1979)★★, *De Lawd's Blues* (1980)★★★, *Faces* (Optimism 1987)★★★, *In Focus* (Optimism 1989)★★★.

MITCHELL, BLUE

b. Richard Allen Mitchell, 13 March 1930, Miami, Florida, USA, d. 21 May 1979, Los Angeles, California, USA. Mitchell's early professional career found him playing trumpet in a number of R&B bands, including that led in the mid-50s by Earl Bostic. Later in the decade he worked briefly with Cannonball Adderley in New York, and then joined Horace Silver's band, an engagement that established Mitchell's reputation. When Silver disbanded in 1963, Mitchell formed his own group, employing most of his fellow musicians, with Silver's place being taken by Chick Corea. This band continued until the end of the decade, at which time Mitchell joined the band that was backing Ray Charles. During the early 70s, Mitchell played with a number of artists in fields outside jazz, notably bluesman John Mayall and popular singers such as Tony Bennett and Lena Horne. Resident in Los Angeles from the mid-70s, Mitchell played in both small and big bands, including those led by Harold Land, Louis Bellson and Bill Berry. A gifted, soulful player with a full, rich tone, Mitchell's frequent excursions into areas of music outside jazz never caused him to lower his standards. Indeed, he enhanced every record date, concert or club engagement on which he played with the sincerity of his playing and the beautiful sound he drew from his instrument.

● ALBUMS: *Big 6* (Riverside 1958)★★★★, *Out Of The Blue* (Riverside 1958)★★★★, *Blue Soul* (Riverside 1959)★★★★, *Blues On My Mind* (Riverside 1959)★★★, *Blue's Moods* (Riverside 1960)★★★, *Smooth As The Wind* (Riverside 1960)★★★, *A Sure Thing* (Riverside 1962)★★★, *The Cup Bearers* (Riverside 1963)★★★★, *Step Lightly* (Blue Note 1963)★★★, *The Thing To Do* (Blue Note 1964)★★★, *Down With It* (Blue Note 1965)★★★, *Bring It Home To Me* (Blue Note 1966)★★★, *After This Message* (Atlantic 1966)★★★, *Boss Horn* (Blue Note 1967)★★★, *Heads Up!* (Blue Note 1968)★★★, *Collision In Black* (Blue Note 1968)★★★, *Bantu Village* (Blue Note 1969)★★★, *Blue Mitchell* (1971)★★★, *Vital Blue* (1971)★★★, *Blue's Blues* (Mainstream 1974)★★★, *Graffiti Blues* (Audio Fidelity 1974)★★★, *Many Shades Of Blue* (1974)★★, *Stratosonic Nuances* (1975)★★★, *Funktion Junction* (1976)★★★, with Harold Land *Mapenzi* (Concord Jazz 1977)★★★★, with Land *Best Of The West* (Concord Jazz 1977)★★★, *Last Dance* (1977)★★, *African Violet* (1977)★★, *Summer Soft* (1977)★★★.

● COMPILATIONS: *The Complete Blue Mitchell Blue Note Sessions (1963-67)* 4-CD/6-LP box set (Mosaic 1998)★★★★.

MITCHELL, DWIKE

(see Mitchell-Ruff Duo)

MITCHELL, GEORGE

b. 8 March 1899, Louisville, Kentucky, USA, d. 27 May 1972. Mitchell began playing trumpet while still a child and was soon of a standard that allowed him to play with bands touring during the school holidays. By his late teens he had switched to cornet and he left Louisville, touring with various groups and also with minstrel shows. Towards the end of 1919 he settled for a spell in Chicago, playing in theatre and dancehall bands, and he also played with the celebrated ragtime pianist Tony Jackson. During the 20s he worked in the Midwest, toured Canada, and played in Chicago. Among the leaders for whom he played were Carroll Dickerson, Doc Cook, Jimmie Noone, Lillian Armstrong, Jelly Roll Morton and Earl 'Fatha' Hines. From the beginning of the 30s, Mitchell played only part-time and by the end of the decade, for all practical purposes, his playing days were over. An important early jazz player, Mitchell's work was in the early mould of Louis Armstrong and Joe Oliver and, like them, he sometimes played interesting two-cornet duets. Among these are performances with Natty Dominique, in a recording band led by Johnny Dodds, and with Shirley Clay in a recording by Hines' band of an Alex Hill arrangement of 'Beau Koo Jack', which updated to 1929 the earlier Oliver-Armstrong duets. Mitchell's playing was forceful and imaginative and although clearly in the classic tradition of New Orleans-style cornetists, he is never slavish to the famous advances made by Armstrong and Oliver during their partnership. Mitchell's work, long overdue for revaluation, has been overlooked, perhaps a side effect of his early departure from the jazz scene.

● COMPILATIONS: *The Chronological Jelly Roll Morton 1926-*

1928 (Classics 1926-28)★★★★, *The Chronological Johnny Dodds 1927* (Classics 1927)★★★★, *The Chronological Earl Hines 1928-1932* (Classics 1928-32)★★★★.

MITCHELL, LOUIS

b. Louis A. Mitchell, 1885, Philadelphia, Pennsylvania, USA, d. 2 December 1957. A showman drummer, adept on numerous percussion instruments, Mitchell played in vaudeville from the turn of the century. He was popular in New York and attracted a great deal of attention on a visit to London in 1914. He returned to London the following year, appearing as a solo variety act on the stages of UK music halls. He went back to Europe in 1918 with a band labelled Mitchell's Jazz Kings with which he toured extensively and held a long residency in Paris. During the 30s, Mitchell was still often in Europe but increasingly worked in capacities other than as a musician. His playing revealed often startling dexterity and it is easy to understand his appeal to audiences of the era in which he played. His playing in a jazz context was less secure but his band did much to spread the word 'jazz' throughout the UK and continental Europe in this period.

MITCHELL, MALCOLM

b. 9 November 1926, London, England, d. 9 March 1998, Bognor Regis, Sussex, England. The guitarist leader of the Malcolm Mitchell Trio, a popular rhythm outfit on the UK Variety circuit and in radio programmes during the 50s, Mitchell was originally taught to play his instrument by an erudite survivor of the 30s dance bands, Ivor Mairants. Thereafter, he worked for various bands led by the likes of George Evans and Felix Mendelssohn, before joining the Jack Fallon Trio. This ensemble, with Fallon on bass, and Tony Crombie playing drums, accompanied the legendary Duke Ellington on a tour of Britain in 1949. In October 1949, the Malcolm Mitchell Trio was formed, with Johnny Pearson (piano) and Teddy Broughton (bass). After making their first appearance at a local church hall, the Trio were offered a booking in the south of France. Having spent all their funds on a one-way ticket, they found police had closed the club, so had to find work elsewhere. Broadcasting stints on Radio Monte Carlo were followed in March 1949 by an important residency at the Grand National Hotel in Lucerne, Switzerland, and the group also performed in other European locations, including Paris, before returning to London to take up an engagement at Ciro's nightclub. Early in 1950, they continued to 'double' at various West End clubs while also appearing in the Jack Buchanan revue *Castle In The Air* at the Adelphi Theatre. In 1952, they were signed by Ambrose for a major road tour with trumpet star Eddie Calvert, but two years later Mitchell disbanded the Trio and formed an all-star modern jazz orchestra for one-night bookings and recordings for Decca. Johnny Pearson subsequently went on to a distinguished career as a composer, arranger, instrumentalist and conductor. The strain of running the large band adversely affected Mitchell's health, and he dissolved it in 1956, losing a good deal of money. He re-formed the Trio in 1957, and also continued to appear as a soloist in cabaret, and accompany visiting stars from abroad. In 1961, the Trio appeared with the immensely popular vocal duo Nina And Frederik on the *Royal Variety Performance*. A year later, Mitchell joined with Henry Howard and comedian-scriptwriter Bob Monkhouse to set up Mitchell, Monkhouse Associates in order to write and produce television commercials. From then on he was responsible for numerous background scores for projects such as *That Kind Of Girl* and *Yellow Teddy Bears*, as well as composing hundreds of jingles, and the music for *Mad Movies* and *Golden Silents*. Mitchell, Monkhouse was also a pioneer company in the corporate conference field. Mitchell himself re-formed the Trio in 1997 for the *Ellington '97 Conference* in Leeds, England.

MITCHELL, RED

b. Keith Moore Mitchell, 20 September 1927, New York City, New York, USA, d. 8 November 1992, Salem, Oregon, USA. After studying piano and alto saxophone, Mitchell took up the bass while serving in the armed forces. In the late 40s he played in bands led by Jackie Paris, Mundell Lowe, Chubby Jackson (with whom he played piano) and Charlie Ventura. He spent two years with Woody Herman, but was hospitalized with tuberculosis in 1951. In the early 50s he worked with Red Norvo and Gerry Mulligan, opting to stay in California when Mulligan headed back to New York. Resident in Los Angeles from 1954, Mitchell became an important figure on the west coast scene, accompanying and sometimes leading artists such as Chet Baker, Bill Perkins, André Previn, Mel Lewis, Hampton Hawes, Don Cherry, Ornette Coleman and Harold Land. In the late 60s, Mitchell moved to Sweden, remaining in Europe for 10 years, accompanying visiting American musicians and leading his own groups, which included Communication. During the 80s, Mitchell divided his time between Europe and the USA, playing and recording extensively with jazzmen including Lee Konitz, Warne Marsh, Art Pepper and Jimmy Rowles. Mitchell's playing in the 50s was advanced for its time, and in some of his technical developments he opened the way for artists such as Scott La Faro. His clean articulation made his solo work of particular interest and an unaccompanied album, *Home Suite*, clearly revealed his remarkable talent. (His brother Whitey Mitchell, also a bass player, was active in the 50s and 60s, but later left the jazz scene.)

● ALBUMS: *Happy Minors* 10-inch album (Bethlehem 1955)★★★, *Jam For Your Bread* (Affinity 1955)★★, *Some Hot, Some Sweet, Some Wild* (Bethlehem 1957)★★★, *Presenting Red Mitchell* (Contemporary 1957)★★★, *Red Mitchell At The Renaissance* (1960)★★★, with Frank Butler *Rejoice* (Pacific Jazz 1961)★★★, with Harold Land *Hear Ye!* (Atlantic 1961)★★★, *The Red Mitchell Trio* (1969)★★★, *The Red Mitchell Quartet* (1972)★★★, with Lee Konitz *I Concentrate On You* (Steeple Chase 1974)★★★★, *Communication* (1974)★★, *Red Mitchell Meets Guido Manusardi* (1974)★★, *Blues For A Crushed Soul*

(Sonet 1976)★★★, *Chocolate Cadillac* (1976)★★★, *Red Mitchell And Friends* (1978)★★★, *Jim Hall/Red Mitchell* (1978)★★★, with Jimmy Rowles *Red 'N' Me* (1978)★★★, *Red Mitchell Plays Piano And Sings* (1979)★★★, with Art Pepper *Straight Life* (1979)★★★★, *Empathy* (1980)★★★, with Tommy Flanagan, Red Mitchell *Super-session* (Enja 1980)★★★, with Flanagan *You're Me* (Phontastic 1980)★★★, *Home Cookin'* (1980)★★★★, with Flanagan, Phil Woods *Free For All* (1981)★★★, *Soft And Warm And Swinging* (1982)★★★, *When I'm Singing* (1982), *Holiday For Monica* (1983), with Rowles *Jimmy Rowles With The Red Mitchell Trio* (Contemporary 1985)★★★, *Home Suite* (1985)★★★, with Clark Terry *To Duke And Basie* (Rhino 1986)★★★★, with Kenny Barron *The Red Barron Duo* (Storyville 1986)★★★, with Terry *Jive At Five* (Enja 1988)★★★★, with Herb Ellis *Doggin' Around* (Concord Jazz 1988)★★★, with Putte Wickman *The Very Thought Of You* (1988)★★★, with Roger Kellaway *Alone Together* (Dragon 1988)★★★, with Barron, Ben Riley *Talking* (Capri 1989)★★★, *Evolution* (1990)★★★.

MITCHELL, ROSCOE

b. 3 August 1940, Chicago, Illinois, USA. As a child Mitchell enjoyed listening to Nat 'King' Cole, Lester Young and Charlie Parker. He studied clarinet and baritone saxophone in high school, taking up alto saxophone in his senior year and continuing with it while in the army. He went to Europe with an army band, where he heard Albert Ayler, who was also playing in a military band. After demobilization, he played bop in an outfit with Henry Threadgill, but Ayler's music had been a revelation to him. Back in Chicago, he jammed with Threadgill, Malachi Favors, Jack DeJohnette, and Muhal Richard Abrams. Abrams was even more of an influence than Ayler. In 1965 Mitchell was made a charter member of the AACM, having played in the Experimental Band (organized by Abrams, the AACM President, inspirer and prime mover) since 1961. His debut, *Sound*, was the first and one of the most famous recordings to come out of the AACM, characterizing the Chicagoan's new emphasis on sound-as-texture and the importance of the relationship between sound and silence. On these tracks, wrote critic John Litweiller, 'Music is the tension of sounds in the free space of silence'. For a while Mitchell led his own groups, and it was from one of these (a quartet including Lester Bowie, Favors and Phillip Wilson) that the Art Ensemble Of Chicago grew. He once explained: 'It was my band, but I couldn't afford to pay those guys what they deserved, so everybody was shouldering an equal amount of responsibility. We became a co-operative unit in order to remain committed to one another and in order to survive.' Since co-founding the Art Ensemble in 1969, most of his work has been accomplished with them, but he has continued to lead bands of his own, including Space (a trio with saxophonist Gerald Oshita and vocalist Tom Buckner) and Sound (a quintet with trumpet, guitar, bass and percussion). He has also worked with Byron Austin, Scotty Holt and DeJohnette; and has assembled an impressive body of solo saxophone music. Like his partners in the Art Ensemble, Mitchell plays a dazzling number of instruments, the primary ones being soprano, alto, tenor and bass saxophones, oboe, flute, piccolo and clarinet as well as various percussion and 'little instruments'. He and Joseph Jarman represent the two poles of the Ensemble's art: Jarman brings the bulk of the theatrical impulse, while Mitchell - the one member of the group who does not habitually wear facepaint or costume - is the musical structuralist who, despite the apparent freedom of the Ensemble's music, worries about how true an improviser will be to the composer's intention. As a composer he has been an influence on Anthony Braxton and Leo Smith. There is an ascetic streak to his art, and it is not insignificant that as soon as he was able, he went to live on a 365-acre farm in Wisconsin, dissatisfied with the lifestyle necessitated by constant touring. Recent projects have included *Songs In The Wind*, which features Steve Sylvester on 'bull roarers and wind wands', a meeting with the Stockholm-based Brus Trio (*After Fallen Leaves*), and *Four Compositions*, which shows Mitchell evolving into an impressive writer of classical chamber music.

● ALBUMS: *Sound* (Delmark 1966)★★★★, *The Roscoe Mitchell Solo Saxophone Concerts* (Sackville 1974)★★★, *The Roscoe Mitchell Quartet* (Sackville 1975)★★★, *Old/Quartet* 1967 recording (1975)★★★, *Nonaah* (1977)★★★, *L-R-G/The Maze/S II Examples* (Nessa 1978)★★★, with Anthony Braxton *Duets With Anthony Braxton* (Sackville 1978)★★★★, *Congliptious* (Nessa 1978)★★★, *Roscoe Mitchell* (Chief 1979)★★★, *Sketches From Bamboo* (Moers 1979)★★★, with Tom Buckner, Gerald Oshita *New Music For Woodwinds And Voice* (1981)★★★, *3x4 Eye* (Black Saint 1981)★★★, *More Cutouts* (Cecma 1981)★★★, *Snurdy McGurdy And Her Dancin' Shoes* (Nessa 1981)★★★, *Concert Toronto 4/5 October 1975* (Sackville 1981)★★★, with Space *An Interesting Breakfast Conversation* (1984)★★★★, *Roscoe Mitchell And The Sound And Space Ensembles* (Black Saint 1984)★★★, *Live At The Muhle Hunziken* (1986)★★★, *The Flow Of Things* (Black Saint 1987)★★★, *Four Compositions* (1987)★★★, *Live In Detroit* (1989)★★, *Songs In The Wind* (Victo 1990)★★★, with Brus Trio *After Fallen Leaves* 1989 recording (Silkheart 1992)★★★, *Live At The Knitting Factory* 1987 recording (Black Saint 1992)★★★★, with Muhal Richard Abrams *Solos And Duets At Merkin Hall* (Black Saint 1992)★★★★, *This Dance Is For Steve McCall* (Black Saint 1993)★★★, *Hey Donald* (Delmark 1995)★★★, with George Lewis *Voyager* (Avant 1996)★★★, with Matthew Shipp *2-Z* (2.13.61/Thirsty Ear 1997)★★★, *The Day And The Night* (Dizim 1998)★★★, *Sound Songs* 1994-1997 recordings (Delmark 1998)★★★.

MITCHELL-RUFF DUO

Dwike Mitchell (b. 14 February 1930, Dunedin, Florida, USA; piano) and Willie Ruff (b. 1 September 1931, Sheffield, Alabama, USA; French horn, bass) first met while they were in the army, and afterwards played together in Lionel Hampton's band. Mitchell has a formidable technique, and though Ruff sometimes solos on the horn, he usually plays bass. He is an academic musician who became a professor of music at Yale. They formed the duo in 1955, and were the first jazz musicians to appear in the USSR when they performed impromptu concerts during a tour with the Yale Russian Chorus in 1959. During the 60s they played regularly at their own club in New Haven, Connecticut, or at the Hickory House in New York - usually with the addition of a drummer, either Charlie Smith or Helicio Milito. In 1966, they were the first jazz musicians to be used by the State Department on a goodwill tour when they went to Mexico City with President Johnson. In 1967, they made a film in Brazil tracing the African roots of Brazilian music. They have continued performing together and toured China in 1981.

● ALBUMS: *The Mitchell-Ruff Duo* (Epic 1956)★★★, *Campus Concert* (Epic 1956)★★★, *Appearing Nightly* (Roulette 1957)★★★, *The Mitchell-Ruff Duo Plus Strings & Brass* (Roulette 1958)★★★, *Jazz For Juniors* (Roulette 1959)★★★, *Jazz Mission To Moscow* (Roulette 1959)★★★, *The Sound Of Music* (Roulette 1960)★★★, *The Catbird Seat* (Atlantic 1961)★★★, *After This Message* (Atlantic 1966)★★★, *Brazilian Trip* (1966)★★, with Dizzy Gillespie *Dizzy Gillespie And The Dwike Mitchell-Willie Ruff Duo* (Mainstream 1971)★★★, *Virtuoso Elegance In Jazz* (1984)★★.

● COMPILATIONS: with Dizzy Gillespie *Enduring Magic* 1970-1985 recordings (Black Hawk)★★★★.

MMW

Progressive jazz fusionists MMW, an acronym for Medeski, Martin and Wood, were formed in New York City, New York, USA, in the early 90s. At the beginning their shows together were regarded as part of a 'connoisseur's scene' at clubs such as the Knitting Factory. From their inception, the participants' jazz skills were tempered by soul, funk and rock embellishments. Their national tours soon won them a much broader cross-section of supporters, as the band deliberately attempted to secure a young, open-minded audience. John Medeski (keyboards), Billy Martin (drums/percussion) and Chris Wood (bass) could boast of previous stints in such celebrated underground acts as the Either/Orchestra and the Lounge Lizards. As Medeski told the press, 'Our deal is to try to take improvised music - an elevated art form - and bring it down to earth. And if the kids dig it, then maybe we can help turn them on to Miles or Coltrane or Mingus. That'd be cool.' As a testament to the group's wide-ranging appeal, they were invited to support Phish - a rock band but one nevertheless similarly committed to improvised live performance - at their sold-out New Orleans date at the State Theater in 1995. MMW have also supported artists as diverse as Los Lobos and Morphine, while members have contributed to studio projects by Biz Markie and Rickie Lee Jones. Phish guitarist Trey Anastasio subsequently joined MMW onstage for later shows, while Medeski contributed to his solo album, *Surrender To The Air*. A series of albums for Gramavision have cemented MMW's rise and confirmed the viability of their intentions to popularize contemporary jazz. *Friday Afternoon In The Universe* was arguably the best of these. It included 'Chubb Sub', which was featured on the soundtrack to the hit movie, *Get Shorty*.

● ALBUMS: *Notes From The Underground* (Accurate 1992)★★★, *It's A Jungle In Here* (Gramavision/Rykodisc 1993)★★★★, *Friday Afternoon In The Universe* (Gramavision/Rykodisc 1995)★★★, *Shack-man* (Gramavision/Rykodisc 1996)★★★, *Combustication* (Blue Note 1998)★★★.

Mobley, Hank

b. Henry Mobley, 7 July 1930, Eastman, Georgia, USA, d. 30 May 1986, Philadelphia, Pennsylvania, USA. Tenor saxophonist Mobley began his professional career with an R&B band in 1950. The following year, he was attracting the attention of such important beboppers as Max Roach and Dizzy Gillespie, and by 1954 his stature was such that he was invited to become a founder-member of Horace Silver's Jazz Messengers. When Silver re-formed a band under his own name, bequeathing the Messengers to Art Blakey, Mobley went along, too. In the late 50s he was briefly with Blakey, then worked with Dizzy Reece and, in 1961, spent a short but memorable time with Miles Davis. Throughout the 60s, Mobley worked with many distinguished musicians, among them Lee Morgan, Barry Harris and Billy Higgins, often leading the bands, and recording several outstanding sessions for Blue Note Records. In the 70s, Mobley was dogged by poor health, but he worked sporadically, including a stint as co-leader of a group with Cedar Walton. Mobley played even less frequently in the 80s, but shortly before his death in 1986, he worked with Duke Jordan. The seemingly casual ease with which Mobley performed, comfortably encompassing complex rhythmical innovations, and the long period spent on the sidelines have tended to obscure the fact that his was a remarkable talent. Also militating against widespread appeal was his sometimes detached, dry and intimate sound, which contrasted sharply with the more aggressively robust style adopted by many of his contemporaries.

● ALBUMS: with Max Roach *Max Roach Quartet Featuring Hank Mobley* 10-inch album (Debut 1954)★★★, *Hank Mobley Quartet* 10-inch album (Blue Note 1955)★★★★, *The Jazz Message Of Hank Mobley* (Savoy 1956)★★★★, *Jazz Message #2* (Savoy 1956)★★★★, *Mobley's Message* reissued as *52nd Street Theme* (Prestige/Status 1956)★★★★, *Mobley's 2nd Message* (Prestige 1957)★★★, with Donald Byrd, Lee Morgan *Hank Mobley With Donald Byrd And Lee Morgan* (Blue Note 1957)★★★, *Hank Mobley* i (Blue Note 1957)★★★★, *Hank Mobley And His All Stars* (Blue Note 1957)★★★★, *Hank* (Blue Note 1957)★★★★, *Hank Mobley* ii (Blue Note 1957)★★★★, *Peckin' Time* (Blue Note 1958)★★★★, *Soul Station* (Blue Note 1960)★★★★, *Roll Call* (Blue Note 1961)★★★★, *Workout* (Blue Note 1961)★★★★, *No Room For Squares* (Blue Note 1963)★★★, *The Turnaround!* (Blue Note 1965)★★★★, *Dippin'* (Blue Note 1965)★★★, with Kenny Burrell, Byrd *Donald Byrd, Hank Mobley & Kenny Burrell* (Status 1965)★★★, *A Caddy For Daddy* (Blue Note 1966)★★★, *Far Away Lands* (Blue Note 1967)★★★, *Hi Voltage* (Blue Note 1968)★★★, *Reach Out!* (Blue Note 1968)★★★, *The Flip* (Blue Note 1969)★★★, *Curtain Call* 1957 recording (Blue Note 1979)★★★, *A Slice Of The Top* 1966 recording (Blue Note 1979)★★★, *Poppin'* 1957 recording (Blue Note 1980)★★★, *Third Season* 1967 recording (Blue Note 1980)★★★, *Thinking Of Home* 1970 recording (Blue Note 1980)★★★, *Another Workout*

1961 recordings (Blue Note 1985)★★★★, *Straight No Filter* 1963/1965 recordings (Blue Note 1985)★★★, various artists *Tenor Conclave: A Tribute To Hank Mobley* (Evidence 1997)★★★.
● COMPILATIONS: *The Complete Blue Note Hank Mobley Fifties Sessions* 6-CD/10-LP box set (Mosaic 1998)★★★★.

MODERN ART - ART FARMER

Trumpet and flugelhorn player Art Farmer is a warm and lyrical improviser, capable of creating stunningly original and carefully structured solos. This fascinating 1958 Blue Note Records date brings Farmer together with the highly regarded swing-led tenor saxophonist Benny Golson (and prolific jazz composer, most notably of 'I Remember Clifford') a year before they went on to form the enduringly popular Jazztet. The amazing Bill Evans, on loan at the time from Miles Davis's Sextet, fills the piano chair, while Art's twin brother Addison Farmer plays bass, and Dave Bailey is on drums. This is swinging and melodic modern mainstream jazz at its very best.
● Tracks: *Mox Nix; Fair Weather; Darn That Dream; The Touch Of Your Lips; Jubilation; Like Someone In Love; I Love You; Cold Breeze.*
● First released 1958
● UK peak chart position: did not chart
● USA peak chart position: did not chart

MODERN JAZZ QUARTET

In 1951, four musicians who had previously played together in the Dizzy Gillespie big band formed a small recording group. Known as the Milt Jackson Quartet, the group consisted of Jackson (vibraphone), John Lewis (piano), Ray Brown (bass), and Kenny Clarke (drums). Brown's place was soon taken by Percy Heath, and by the following year, the group had adopted the name Modern Jazz Quartet. Although initially only a recording group, they then began playing concert engagements. In 1955, Clarke dropped out to be replaced by Connie Kay. The new line-up of Jackson, Lewis, Heath and Kay continued performing as a full-time ensemble for the next few years, later reducing their collective commitments to several months each year. Seen as both a black response to the intellectualism of the Dave Brubeck quartet and New York's answer to west coast cool jazz, the MJQ were both very popular and very controversial, their detractors claiming that their music was too delicate and too cerebral. Whatever the case, there was certainly no denying that the group brought the dignity and professionalism of a classical quartet to their jazz performances. In 1974, the MJQ was disbanded, but re-formed once more in 1981 for a concert tour of Japan. The success of this comeback convinced the members to reunite on a semi-permanent basis, which they did in the following year. Since 1982 they have continued to play concert and festival dates. Among the most sophisticated of all bop ensembles, the MJQ's directing influence has always been Lewis, whose sober performing and composing style was never more apparent than in this context. Lewis's interest in classical music has also been influential in MJQ performances, thus placing the group occasionally, and possibly misleadingly, on the fringes of third-stream jazz. The playing of Heath and Kay in this, as in most other settings in which they work, is distinguished by its subtle swing. Of the four, Jackson is the most musically volatile, and the restraints placed upon him in the MJQ create intriguing formal tensions which are, in jazz terms, one of the most exciting aspects of the group's immaculately played, quietly serious music.
● ALBUMS: *Modern Jazz Quartet With Milt Jackson* (Prestige 1953)★★★★, *Modern Jazz Quartet Vol 2* (Prestige 1953)★★★, *Django* (1953)★★★★, *Concorde* (Prestige 1955)★★★★, *Modern Jazz Quartet* (Savoy 1955)★★★, *The Artistry Of* (Prestige 1956)★★★★, *The MJQ At Music Inn* (Atlantic 1956)★★★, *Django* (Prestige 1956)★★★★, *Fontessa* (Atlantic 1956)★★★★, *Live* (Jazz Anthology 1956)★★★, *One Never Knows* (1957)★★★, *MJQ* (Atlantic 1957)★★★★, *Concorde* (Original Jazz Classics 1957)★★★, *Live At The Lighthouse* (Atlantic 1957)★★★★, *At Music Inn: Vol 2* (Atlantic 1958)★★★, *Odds Against Tomorrow* (1959)★★★, *Longing For The Continent* (LRC 1959)★★★, *European Concert* (Atlantic 1960)★★★, *Patterns* (United Artists 1960)★★★, *Third Stream Music: MJQ And Guests* (Atlantic 1960)★★★, *Pyramid* (Atlantic 1960)★★★★, *MJQ And Orchestra* (Atlantic 1961)★★, *Lonely Woman* (Atlantic 1962)★★★, *The Comedy* (Atlantic 1962)★★★, *The Sheriff* (Atlantic 1964)★★★, with Laurindo Almeida *Collaboration* (Atlantic 1964)★★★, *A Quartet Is A Quartet Is A Quartet* (Atlantic 1964)★★★, *Plays Gershwin's Porgy And Bess* (Atlantic 1965)★★★, *Play For Lovers* (Prestige 1966)★★★, *Plays Jazz Classics* (Prestige 1966)★★★, *Jazz Dialogue* (Atlantic 1966)★★★, *Blues At Carnegie Hall* (Atlantic 1967)★★★, *Live At The Lighthouse* (Atlantic 1967)★★★, *Under The Jasmine Tree* (Apple 1968)★★, *Space* (Apple 1969)★★, *Plastic Dreams* (Atlantic 1971)★★, *The Legendary Profile* (Atlantic 1972)★★★, *Blues On Bach* (Atlantic 1974)★★★★, *The Complete Last Concert* (Atlantic 1974)★★★★, *Plus* 1957-71 recordings (70s)★★★, *In Memoriam* (1977)★★★, *Together Again!* (Pablo 1982)★★★, *Together Again!: Echoes* (Pablo 1984)★★★, *The Best Of The MJQ* 1984-85 recordings (80s)★★★, *Three Windows* (Atlantic 1987)★★★, *For Ellington* (East West 1988)★★★, *MJQ & Friends* (Atlantic 1994)★★★, *A Celebration* (Atlantic 1994)★★★, *In A Crowd* 1963 live rcording (Douglas Music 1998)★★★.
● COMPILATIONS: *MJQ 40* 4-CD box set (Atlantic 1992)★★★★.
● VIDEOS: *40 Years Of MJQ* (View Video 1995).

MODERN MANDOLIN QUARTET

America's Modern Mandolin Quartet were co-founded by producer Mike Marshall, a native of Florida, whose early interests in bluegrass music were later qualified by his experiences as second mandolin player in the eclectic David Grisman Quartet, before he experienced full-blooded modern jazz first-hand with Montreaux. This circuitous passage was further complicated by a growing awareness of classical structures, which led in turn to him adapting string quartet literature to different musical forms. The MMQ was thus formed with Dana Rath in 1985. Rath's second mandolin was augmented by Paul Binkley on mandola and John Imholz on mandocello. The latter pair adopted responsibility for arranging the group's material. Binkley had previously performed on classical guitar with the San Francisco Symphony, Opera and Ballet. Marshall's intention was explicitly to 'take a folk instrument, and by tackling classical music bring the mandolin into the concert hall'. By 1988 they were sufficiently prepared to announce their self-titled debut. It was followed two years later by *Intermezzo*, featuring pieces drawn from the repertoires of Shostakovich, Ravel, Brahms and Bach. Continuing this thread, 1991's *Nutcracker Suite* became one of the top 35 Christmas releases in the US *Billboard* charts. The group's fourth album for Windham Hill Records was arguably their most audacious. *Pan-American Journeys: 20th Century Music Of The Americas, Vol. 1*, was exactly what its title suggested. Rather grandly, it invited the ensemble to adapt pieces drawing on the musical history of their continent, in an attempt to produce a patchwork map of classical music's evolution from ethnic forms. The featured writers included George Gershwin, Argentinean Astor Piazzolla, famous for his demonstrative tangos (his contribution, 'Four For Tango', was originally written for the Kronos Quartet), and Brazilian composer Heitor Villa-Lobos. Other contemporary writers consulted included Tully Cathey, whose 'Elements IV: Water', was inspired by the Colorado River, which runs by his home. The set opened with 'Redonda', specially composed for the quartet by former Montreaux drummer Tom Miller, and climaxed in an adaptation of a Cuban folk song, 'Ojos Brujos' ('Eye Of The Sorceror').

● ALBUMS: *Modern Mandolin Quartet* (Lost Lake Arts/Windham Hill 1988)★★★, *Intermezzo* (Windham Hill 1990)★★★★, *The Nutcracker Suite* (Windham Hill 1991)★★★, *Pan-American Journeys: 20th Century Music Of The Americas, Vol. 1* (Windham Hill 1994)★★★.

MODERNAIRES

Originally called the Three Weary Willies, this vocal trio was formed in 1935 at Lafayette High School in Buffalo, New York, USA. Consisting of Hal Dickinson (lead and second tenor), Bill Conway (baritone) and Chuck Goldstein (first tenor), they became residents on local radio station WGR. They became Don Juan And Two And Three when they moved to New York, where they began to feature on CBS radio. At this point Ralph Brewster joined as first tenor and Goldstein moved to baritone while Conway took over on bass. After a brief time backing Ray Noble in 1939 they switched allegiance to Glenn Miller's new outfit (Miller had been trombonist with Noble during the trio's residency with Noble). They became the Modernaires, and their debut release, 'Perfidia', was as backing to Miller's singer Paula Kelly. A number 11 hit, it presaged a further 10 chart records in 1941, the most popular of which included 'The Booglie Wooglie Piggy' (with Tex Beneke) and 'I Guess I'll Have To Dream The Rest' and 'Elmer's Tune', with Ray Eberle, which rose to number 1 in the *Billboard* charts. Other hits included collaborations with Beneke again and Ernie Caceras. They also sang on the Glenn Miller Orchestra's signature tune, 'Chattanooga Choo Choo'. Further number 1s with Miller came in 1942 with 'Don't Sit Under The Apple Tree', '(I've Got A Gal In) Kalamazoo' and 'Moonlight Cocktails'. When Miller was enlisted in the air force during the war, the Modernaires produced another number 1 in 1943 with 'That Old Black Magic', with Miller's orchestra and Skip Nelson, which was included in the propaganda film *Star Spangled Rhythm*. With Miller missing in action, the Modernaires moved to Columbia Records in 1944 and began to record for the first time without an orchestra. Their second single was 'Tribute To Glenn Miller', a medley of his most popular moments. The rest of the 40s saw numerous line-up changes with Alan Copeland, Vernon Polk and Tommy Treynor all joining at some point. In 1949 the Modernaires recorded 'The Old Master Painter' with Frank Sinatra, and this was followed in 1950 by four further singles with Sinatra for Columbia. The early part of the 50s was less successful for the Modernaires, who had to wait until 1953 and a new contract with Coral Records for their next success, an update of 'Jukebox Saturday Night', which had previously been a staple of their work with Miller. However, though they continued to release records until 1958, it was to diminishing returns, and by the end of the decade they were no longer releasing new material.

MOFFETT, CHARLES

b. 1 September 1929, Fort Worth, Texas, USA, d. 14 February 1997. Moffett began his career playing trumpet with local R&B groups, and in the same high school band as Ornette Coleman, but at the age of 16 he began to study percussion. In 1953 he gained a BA in music and went on to teach in Texas for eight years. Coleman had been best man at Moffett's wedding in 1952; in 1961 they met again, Moffett taking the drummer's stool in Coleman's band. During Coleman's hiatus from performance in the early 60s, Moffett returned to teaching, but he was ready when the group re-formed to tour Europe in 1965. In 1970, Moffett moved to California, where he resumed his teaching while playing with local players such as Steve Turré, Frank Lowe, Keshavan Maslak and Prince Lasha. He also formed groups with his students and with members of his family (the Moffettes). During the 80s Moffett moved back to New York, where he taught mentally retarded children and continued to play. Moffett's easy swing and perfect sense of time often appeared to owe much to earlier styles while remaining a perfect foil for the *avant garde* musicians he most often accompanied.

● ALBUMS: *The Gift* (Savoy 1969)★★★★, *Family* (LRS 1974)★★★.

MOFFETT, CHARNETT

b. 10 June 1967, New York City, New York, USA. The bass-playing son of the noted free jazz drummer Charles Moffett, and the younger brother of singer Charisse, drummer Cody, trumpeter Mondre and tenor saxophonist Charles Jnr. Charnett started playing bass in the Moffett family band at the age of seven, appearing on their 1974 LRS session. Charnett studied at Julliard and was a member of trumpeter Wynton Marsalis' quintet at the age of sixteen. Heavily in demand as a session musician, he has since played with a diverse range of musicians, including Charles Lowe, Arturo Sandoval, Slide Hampton, Mulgrew Miller, Sonny Sharrock, David Sanborn, Bette Midler and Anita Baker. He joined Ornette Coleman's quartet in 1993, emulating his father who played a prominent part in the altoist's mid-60s trio (Charnett's name is a contraction of his father and Coleman's first names). Moffett has released several sessions as a leader, utilising synthesizers and electronic basses, although his potential was only fully realised on *Planet Home*. This 1994 recording closed with a powerful and electronically enhanced solo bass rendition of 'The Star Spangled Banner', in tribute to Jimi Hendrix's Woodstock showstopper.

● ALBUMS: *Net Man* (Blue Note 1986)★★★, *Beauty Within* (Blue Note 1987)★★, *Nettwork* (Manhattan 1991)★★, *Planet Home* (Evidence 1995)★★★★, *Still Life* (Evidence 1997)★★★.

Mohamed, Pops

b. Ismail Mohamed-jan, 10 December 1949, Bemoni, South Africa. Mohamed founded and played guitar with his first band, the Valients, in the mid-60s. Their repertoire was made up of soul, Latin and local kwela music. Following the break-up of the Valients, he formed Children's Society, predominantly a covers band who, nevertheless, had a big local hit with the self-penned 'I'm A Married Man'. In the 70s Mohamed teamed up with Basil Coetzee and Sipho Gumede, bassist with Sakhile, and made four albums that became huge hits in the townships of South Africa. The 80s saw him working behind the scenes as a producer and recording engineer while also mastering the mbira (a South African thumb piano). In the early 90s he released two solo jazz albums for the local market only, *Kalamazoo* in 1991 and *Sophiatown* a year later. Both sold well and received lavish critical praise. Having produced and played on the *Outernational Meltdown* recording sessions in 1994, he released *Ancestral Healing*, his international debut, a year later. Subtitled 'From New York To Jo'burg', it was recorded in New York and featured local musicians, such as Valerie Naranjo (vibraphonist, percussionist, ex-Caribali), along with South African players and Mohamed himself playing piano, penny whistle, mbira and percussion. The album successfully melded traditional styles with the South African jazz sound made internationally popular by artists such as Abdullah Ibrahim and the African Jazz Pioneers. At the time of the release of *Ancestral Healing*, Mohamed was in the Kalahari Desert recording the chants and music of the Khoisian bushmen. Tapes of these recordings were used as the basis for a recording session featuring Mohamed and a group of young British jazz musicians including Chris Bowden and Roland Sutherland. The result, released as *How Far Have We Come*, featured funky South African-style jazz, with the tribal elements integrated more effectively on some tracks than on others.

● ALBUMS: *Ancestral Healing* (B&W Music 1995)★★★★, *How Far Have We Come* (M.E.L.T. 2000 1997)★★★.

Moholo, Louis

b. 10 March 1940, Cape Town, South Africa. Moholo is simply one of the great drummers, regardless of genre. In common with Ed Blackwell and Billy Higgins, both alumni of Ornette Coleman's Quartet, he has developed a sharp, clean, agile style, and shares with Higgins a remarkable ability to play with considerable dynamic restraint without losing strength and momentum. He is equally capable of thunderous, breakneck playing, which commands attention as much through its constant inventiveness as through its inexorable power. He grew up in a musical environment (his father a pianist, his mother and sister, singers). At the age of 16 he co-founded the Cordettes big band. In 1962, he won the Best Drummer award at the Johannesburg Jazz Festival and, together with four more of the best players at the Festival, he was invited by Chris McGregor to form a band. Thus, the legendary Blue Notes were created. As a mixed-race band it was impossible for them to work under apartheid and so, in 1964, while touring Europe, they decided to stay in Switzerland. After a year there they settled in London, where, ultimately evolving into the Chris McGregor Group, they made a huge impact. As well as playing in the six-piece McGregor Group and the Brotherhood Of Breath big band, Moholo put his stamp on many fine bands, including Elton Dean's Ninesense, the Mike Osborne Trio, and Keith Tippett's extra-big band, Ark. In 1966, he toured South America with Steve Lacy, Enrico Rava and Johnny Dyani. In the 70s and 80s he often worked in Europe, particularly in trios with Irène Schweizer and Rudiger Carl, and Peter Brötzmann and Harry Miller, and recorded a duo concert with Schweizer in 1986. Moholo has also worked in duos with Tippett and Andrew Cyrille, and organized the African Drum Ensemble. He currently leads Viva La Black as well as a trio with Gary Curzon and Paul Rogers (recalling the classic Osborne trio) and plays in a percussion duo with Thebe Lipere.

● ALBUMS: with Irène Schweizer, Rudiger Carl *Messer* (1975)★★★, *Blue Notes For Mongezi* (1976)★★★, with Schweizer, Carl *Tuned Boots* (1977)★★★, *Blue Notes In Concert Volume I* (1978)★★★★, *Spirits Rejoice* (1978)★★★★, with Peter Brötzmann, Harry Miller *The Nearer The Bone, The Sweeter The Meat* (1980)★★★, with Keith Tippett *No Gossip* (1980)★★★, with Brötzmann, Miller *Opened, But Hardly Touched* (1981)★★★★, with Tippett, Larry Stabbins *Tern* (1982)★★, *Irène Schweizer/Louis Moholo* (1987)★★, *Blue Notes For Johnny* (1987)★★★, *Viva La Black* (1988)★★★, with Cecil Taylor *Remembrance* (1989)★★★★, *Exile* (Ogun 1991)★★★, with Derek Bailey, Thebe Lipere *Village Life* (Incus 1992)★★★, *Freedom Tour - Live In South Afrika 1993* (Ogun 1995)★★.

Mole, Miff

b. Irving Milfred Mole, 11 March 1898, Roosevelt, Long Island, New York, USA, d. 29 April 1961, New York City, New York, USA. A youthful multi-instrumentalist, Mole had settled on the trombone by his mid-teenage years.

Gigging extensively in and around New York, he worked with many small early jazz bands, including one led by pianist-turned-comedian Jimmy Durante, and was also a member of the Original Memphis Five, led by Phil Napoleon. In the mid-20s he became a close friend and musical associate of Red Nichols; they made many records together and generally encouraged one another's development. After a stint with Roger Wolfe Kahn's popular society band, Mole began a long period of studio work, and in 1938 joined Paul Whiteman. In the early 40s Mole began teaching, worked briefly with Benny Goodman, and led his own small bands at nightspots in New York and Chicago. Ill-health restricted his career in the 50s. Although subsequently overshadowed by outstanding contemporaries such as Jack Teagarden and Tommy Dorsey, Mole played an important role in the development of jazz trombone. He was a major influence in elevating the instrument from its slightly jokey status as a purveyor of unusual sounds, ably demonstrating that it could be a tasteful, melodic vehicle on which to play effective jazz solos. His exceptional technique also provided a standard by which trombonists could be measured, at least until the arrival on the scene of latter-day technical wizards.

● ALBUMS: with Edmond Hall *Battle Of Jazz, Vol. 4* 10-inch album (Brunswick 1953)★★★, *The Immortal Miff Mole* (Jazzology 1959)★★★, *Miff Mole's Molers 1927* (Swaggie 1983)★★★★, *Miff Mole's Molers 1928/30* (Swaggie 1983)★★★★, *And His "World Jam Session" Band - 1944* (Jazzology)★★★★.

Moncur, Grachan, III

b. 3 June 1937, New York City, New York, USA. An early starter (his father played bass with Al Cooper's Savoy Sultans), Moncur had already mastered several other instruments when, at the age of 11, he turned to the trombone. In his teens, Moncur worked with local bands and also studied music. In the early 60s he was with Ray Charles, and was a member of the Art Farmer-Benny Golson Jazztet. He also worked with Jackie McLean and Sonny Rollins, recorded for Blue Note and, by the late 60s, was a leading figure of the free jazz movement, playing with Archie Shepp in the USA and Europe. In the 70s, Moncur worked with the Jazz Composers' Orchestra, and in the 80s, with Frank Lowe, among others. In the last decade or so, his experience has also been applied to teaching and to several major compositions in musical areas ranging from jazz to ballet. An accomplished performer, Moncur's fluid style has helped to make his playing more readily accessible than that of many other free jazz trombonists. Through his teaching and recording he continues to exercise considerable influence upon the rising generation of musicians.

● ALBUMS: *Evolution* (Blue Note 1963)★★★★, *Some Other Stuff* (1964)★★★, *New Africa* (Affinity 1969)★★★, with Jazz Composers Orchestra *Echoes Of Prayer* (1974)★★★.

Mondello, Toots

b. Nuncio M. Mondello, 1912, Boston, Massachusetts, USA, d. 15 November 1992. Mondello began playing saxophone as a youth, as did his brother, both becoming professional musicians. His first name-band job was with Mal Hallett's popular dance band where he remained fairly consistently for five years, playing alto. He then went into a number of bands including those led by Buddy Rogers, Benny Goodman and Ray Noble before turning to studio work. He broadcast and recorded with many diverse musicians including André Kostelanetz, Chick Bullock, Bunny Berigan, Larry Clinton, Louis Armstrong and Lionel Hampton. In 1939 he rejoined Goodman after a spell leading his own band. He recorded with the Metronome All Stars in 1940/1 before being inducted into the US Army. After the war he resumed freelance recording work, playing on sessions with Sarah Vaughan, Billie Holiday and others in the 40s and with Billy Butterfield, Artie Shaw and Goodman in the 50s and 60s. A highly skilled musician with the necessary qualities for playing lead alto in big bands, Mondell's occasional recorded solos display proficiency and intelligence. In later years he continued his studio work.

● COMPILATIONS: *Benny Goodman And His Music Hall Orchestra* (Saville 1934)★★★, with Lionel Hampton *Historic Recording Sessions* (RCA 1937-41)★★★★.

Money Jungle - Duke Ellington

Although this excellent album is listed as a Duke Ellington recording, equal billing should be given to the participation of Charles Mingus and Max Roach. The remastered CD is outstanding, having been cleaned up from the original master tape. The CD also has the addition of six extra tracks, including four unheard Ellington originals: 'Very Special', 'Rem Blues', 'Switch Blade' and 'Backward Country Boy Blues'. He is as at home in the setting of a trio as he is with a wailing bigband, and as usual, he allows the other musicians to play. The trio version of 'Caravan' is exceptional, raucous and swinging.

● Tracks: *Very Special; A Little Max (Parfait); A Little Max (Parfait) Alternate Take; Fleurette Africaine (African Flower); Rem Blues; Wig Wise; Switch Blade; Caravan; Money Jungle; Solitude (Alternate Take); Solitude; Warm Valley; Backward Country Boy Blues.*

● First released 1963

● UK peak chart position: did not chart

● USA peak chart position: did not chart

Monk, Meredith

b. 20 November 1943, Lima, Peru. In 1964, Monk graduated in performing arts from Sarah Lawrence College where she had been encouraged to mix the arts in a variety of projects. She saw herself as an 'orchestrator of music and image and movement', someone making 'live movies'. She first appeared in New York at Washington Square Gallery and was one of a group of artists, including painter Robert Rauschenberg, creating mixed-media pieces like Duet For Cat's Scream And Locomotive at Judson Church. She presented her theatre piece, *Juice*, at New York's Guggenheim Museum in 1969, and brought her group the House to Liverpool in

1972 to perform *The Vessel*. In the same year, she received a *Village Voice* Award for Outstanding Achievement in the Off-Broadway Theatre. She also performed solo vocal pieces such as 'Raw Recital', from which 'a definite American Indian quality emerged'. She sees herself as performing ethnic music from a culture she has herself created. In 1978, she formed the Vocal Ensemble to perform compositions that consisted of simple, often modal melodies or melodic cells, which are repeated with small variations and contrasted with different material. These performances are sometimes accompanied by repetitive keyboard parts reminiscent of the minimalist movement, and usually depend on extended vocal techniques. The success of *Dolmen Music* and *Turtle Dreams* has brought the Ensemble to an international audience.

● ALBUMS: *Our Lady Of Late* (1973)★★★, *Key: An Album Of Invisible Theatre* (Lovely 1977)★★★, *Songs From The Hill* (1979)★★★★, *Dolmen Music* (1980)★★★, *Dolmen Music* (ECM 1981)★★★, *Turtle Dreams* (ECM 1983)★★★, *Do You Be* (ECM 1987)★★★, *Book Of Days* (ECM 1990)★★★★, with Robert Een *Facing North* (1992)★★, *Atlas* (ECM 1993)★★★, *Volcano Songs* (ECM 1997)★★★.

MONK, T.S.

b. Thelonious Sphere Monk Jnr., 27 December 1949, New York City, New York, USA. Inevitably, Monk grew up in a musically aware household. His father and his father's friends, who included Max Roach, Dizzy Gillespie, Miles Davis and John Coltrane, were all prime movers in the development of jazz in the 50s and 60s. At school he ran into problems with music teachers who could not understand his father's music and hence resented his fame. Determined to build a career of his own in music, Monk sought tuition outside school, gradually turning to drums as his instrument. When he was 16 years old he was given lessons by Roach and at age 20 joined his father, with whom he played until 1975. He then moved into R&B, forming the band Circles, which included singers Yvonne Fletcher and his sister, Barbara. In the early 80s both young women died and he subsequently helped form the Thelonious Monk Foundation (later the TM Institute of Jazz) and gradually returned to the jazz fold. In 1989 he joined Roach in a series of school clinics, sat in with various leading jazzmen including Gillespie and Clark Terry, played with Clifford Jordan's big band, and then, in 1991, formed his own jazz group. Fiercely determined to have a first-class band, he ensured that its members were skilled, well-rehearsed and as committed as himself. With the help and support of George Wein, who booked him internationally, and with a recording contract with Blue Note Records, he was soon on his way to considerable fame. No longer in the shadow of his famous father as an instrumentalist and bandleader, Monk also writes music for his band, a talent that will present him with another hurdle to surmount. An exceptionally gifted drummer and dedicated to his craft, he is ensuring that the family name lives on at the cutting edge of jazz.

● ALBUMS: *Take One* (Blue Note 1991)★★, *A Changing Of The Guard* (Blue Note 1993)★★★, *Monk On Monk* (N2K 1997)★★★★.

MONK, THELONIOUS

b. 11 October 1917, Rocky Mount, North Carolina, USA, d. 17 February 1982. Monk's family moved to New York when he was five years old. He started playing piano a year later, receiving formal tuition from the age of 11 onwards. At Stuyvesant High School he excelled at physics and maths, and also found time to play organ in church. In the late 30s he toured with a gospel group, then began playing in the clubs and became pianist in Kenny Clarke's house band at Minton's Playhouse between 1941 and 1942. He played with Lucky Millinder's orchestra in 1942, the Coleman Hawkins Sextet between 1943 and 1945, the Dizzy Gillespie Big Band in 1946 and started leading his own outfits from 1947. It was Hawkins who provided him with his recording debut, and enthusiasts noted a fine solo on 'Flyin' Hawk' (October 1944). However, it was the Blue Note sessions of 1947 (subsequently issued on album and CD as *Genius Of Modern Music*) that established him as a major figure. With Art Blakey on drums, these recordings have operated as capsule lessons in music for subsequent generations of musicians. An infectious groove makes complex harmonic puzzles sound attractive, with Monk's unique dissonances and rhythmic sense adding to their charm. They were actually a distillation of a decade's work. ''Round Midnight' immediately became a popular tune and others - 'Ruby My Dear', 'Well You Needn't', 'In Walked Bud' - have become jazz standards since. In his book *Bebop*, Leonard Feather recognized Monk's genius at composition, but claimed his playing lacked technique (a slight for which he later apologized). Monk certainly played with flat fingers (anathema to academy pianists), but his bare-bones style was the result of a modern sensibility rather than an inability to achieve the torrents of Art Tatum or Oscar Peterson. For Monk, the blues had enough romance without an influx of European romanticism, and enough emotion without the sometimes overheated blowing of bebop. His own improvisations are at once witty, terse and thought-provoking.

A trumped-up charge for possession of drugs deprived Monk of his New York performer's licence in 1951, and a subsequent six-year ban from playing live in the city damaged his career. He played in Paris in June 1954 (recorded by Vogue Records). Riverside Records was supportive, and he found sympathetic musicians with whom to record - both under his own name and guesting with players such as Miles Davis, Sonny Rollins and Clark Terry. *Plays Duke Ellington* (1955) was a fascinating look at Duke Ellington's compositions, with a nonpareil rhythm section in bassist Oscar Pettiford and drummer Clarke. *Brilliant Corners* in 1956 showcased some dazzling new compositions and featured Sonny Rollins on tenor saxophone. Regaining his work permit in 1957, Monk assembled a mighty quintet for a residency at the Five Spot club, including Shadow Wilson (drums), Wilbur Ware (bass) and John Coltrane (tenor).

Coltrane always spoke of the fine education he received during his brief stay with the band - although the group was never recorded live, the studio albums that resulted (*Thelonious Monk With John Coltrane, Monk's Music*) were classics. Monk repaid Coleman Hawkins' earlier compliment, and featured the tenorman on these records: history and future shook hands over Monk's keyboard. Previously considered too 'way out' for mass consumption, Monk's career finally began to blossom. In 1957, he recorded with Gerry Mulligan, which helped to expose him to a wider audience, and worked with classical composer Hall Overton to present his music orchestrally (*At Town Hall*, 1959). He toured Europe for the first time (1961) and also Japan (1964). He formed a stable quartet in the early 60s with Charlie Rouse on tenor, John Ore (later Butch Warren or Larry Gales) on bass and Frankie Dunlop (later Ben Riley) on drums. Critics tend to prefer his work with other saxophonists, such as Harold Land (1960) or Johnny Griffin (the late 50s), but overlook the fact that Rouse truly understood Monk's tunes. He may not have been the greatest soloist, but his raw, angular tone fitted the compositions like a glove.

In the early 70s, Monk played with Pat Patrick (Sun Ra's alto player), using son T.S. Monk on drums. Illness increasingly restricted his activity, but he toured with the Giants Of Jazz (1971-72) and presented a big band at the Newport Festival in 1974. Two albums recorded for the English Black Lion label in 1971 - *Something In Blue* and *The Man I Love* - presented him in a trio context with Al McKibbon on bass and Blakey on drums: these were stunning examples of the empathy between drummer and pianist - two of Monk's best records. When he died from a stroke in 1982, at Englewood, New Jersey, leaving his wife (for whom he had written 'Crepuscule With Nellie') and son, he had not performed in public for six years. Monk's influence, if anything, increased during the 80s. Buell Neidlinger formed a band, String Jazz, to play only Monk and Ellington tunes; Steve Lacy, who in the early 60s had spent a period playing exclusively Monk tunes, recorded two solo discs of his music; and tribute albums by Arthur Blythe (*Light Blue*, 1983), Anthony Braxton (*Six Monk's Compositions*, 1987), Paul Motian (*Monk In Motian*, 1988) and Hal Wilner (*That's The Way I Feel Now*, 1984, in which artists as diverse as the Fowler Brothers, John Zorn, Dr. John, Eugene Chadbourne, and Peter Frampton celebrated his tunes) prove that Monk's compositions are still teaching artists new tricks. His son, T.S. Monk, is a gifted drummer who continues a tradition by encouraging young musicians through membership of his band. One of the most brilliant and original performers in jazz, Thelonious Monk was also one of the century's outstanding composers. ''Round Midnight' is probably the most recorded jazz song of all time. His unique ability to weld intricate, surprising harmonic shifts and rhythmic quirks into appealing, funky riffs means that something special happens when they are played: his compositions exact more incisive improvising than anybody else's. In terms of jazz, that is the highest praise of all.

● ALBUMS: *Genius Of Modern Music, Volume 1* (Blue Note 1951)★★★★★, *Genius Of Modern Music Volume 2* (Blue Note 1952)★★★★★, *Thelonious Monk Trio* (Prestige 1953)★★★, *And Sonny Rollins* (Prestige 1954)★★★★, *Thelonious Monk Quintet* (Prestige 1954), *Pure Monk* (1954)★★★★, *Solo 1954* (Vogue 1955)★★★★, *Plays Duke Ellington* (Riverside 1955)★★★, *The Unique* (Riverside 1956)★★★★, *Brilliant Corners* (Riverside 1957)★★★★, *Thelonious Himself* (Riverside 1957)★★★, *With John Coltrane* (Jazzland 1957)★★★★, with Gerry Mulligan *Mulligan Meets Monk* (Riverside 1957)★★★★, with Clark Terry *In Orbit* reissued as *C.T. Meets Monk* (Riverside 1958)★★★★, *Art Blakey/Thelonious Monk* (1958)★★★, *Monk's Music* (Riverside 1958)★★★★, *Thelonious In Action* (Riverside 1958)★★★★, *Misterioso* (Riverside 1958)★★★★★, *The Thelonious Monk Orchestra At Town Hall* (Riverside 1959)★★★, *Five By Monk By Five* (Riverside 1959)★★★, *Thelonious Alone In San Francisco* (Riverside 1960)★★★★, *At The Blackhawk* (Riverside 1960)★★★★, *Two Hours With Thelonious* (1961)★★★, *Criss Cross* (Columbia 1963)★★★, *Monk's Dream* (Columbia 1963)★★, *April In Paris* (Riverside 1963)★★★★, *Thelonious Monk In Italy* (Riverside 1963)★★★, *Big Band And Quartet In Concert* (Columbia 1964)★★★, with Miles Davis *Miles & Monk At Newport* (Columbia 1964)★★★, *It's Monk's Time* (Columbia 1964)★★★, *Monk* (Columbia 1965)★★★, *Solo Monk* (Columbia 1965)★★★, *The Thelonious Monk Story Vol. 1* (Riverside 1965)★★★, *The Thelonious Monk Story Vol. 2* (Riverside 1965)★★★, *Monk In France* (Riverside 1965)★★★, *Straight, No Chaser* (Columbia 1966)★★★★, *Underground* (Columbia 1967)★★★, *Monk's Blues* (Columbia 1968)★★★, *Epistrophy* (1971)★★★, *Something In Blue* (1972)★★★, *The Man I Love* (1972)★★★, *Always Know* 1963 recording (Columbia 1979)★★★, *Sphere* (1979)★★★, *April In Paris/Live* (1981)★★★, *Live At The It Club* 1964 recording (Columbia 1982,)★★★, *Live At The Jazz Workshop* 1964 recording (Columbia 1982)★★★, *Tokyo Concerts* 1963 recording (1983)★★★, *The Great Canadian Concert Of Thelonious Monk* 1965 recording (1984)★★★, *1963 - In Japan* (1984)★★★, *Live In Stockholm 1961* (1987)★★★, *Solo 1954* (1993)★★★, *The Nonet Live* 1967 recording (Charly 1993)★★★, *Live At The It Club: Complete* 1964 recording (Columbia/Legacy 1998)★★★★.

● COMPILATIONS: *Thelonious Monk's Greatest Hits* (Riverside 1962)★★★★, *Mighty Monk* (Riverside 1967)★★★, *Best Of Thelonious Monk* (Riverside 1969)★★★, *Always Know* 1962-1968 recordings (1979)★★★, *Memorial Album* 1954-1960 recordings (1982)★★★★, *The Complete Blue Note Recordings Of Thelonious Monk* 1947-1952 recordings, 4-LP box set (Blue Note 1983)★★★★★, *The Complete Black Lion And Vogue Recordings Of Thelonious Monk* 4-LP box set (1986)★★★★, *The Composer* (Giants Of Jazz 1987)★★★, *Monk Alone: The Complete Columbia Solo Studio Recordings Of Thelonious Monk 1962-1968* (Columbia 1998)★★★, *The Art Of The Ballad* (Prestige 1998)★★★★.

● VIDEOS: *American Composer* (1993), *Thelonious Monk: Live In Oslo* (1993).

● FURTHER READING: *Thelonious Monk: His Life And Music*, Thomas Fitterling. *Monk On Records: A Discography Of Thelonious Monk*, L. Bijl and F. Canté. *Straight, No Chaser: The Life And Genius Of Thelonious Monk*, Leslie Gourse. *Monk*, Laurent De Wilde.

Monsbourgh, Ade

b. Adrian Herbert Monsbourgh, 17 February 1917, Melbourne, Victoria, Australia. During childhood and his early teens Monsbourgh took up a wide range of instruments, including piano, brass and several reeds, notably the alto saxophone. It was on clarinet and saxophones that he became best known, especially during the many years he spent in Graeme Bell's band in the 30s and 40s. With Bell, and later as a freelance, he played in Europe, visiting England on a number of occasions to play with fellow spirits during the trad jazz boom of the 50s. In London in 1951 he recorded a handful of sides, leading a band that included Bell and Humphrey Lyttelton. In his homeland he played with numerous other bands, and for almost 30 years regularly formed his own bands for concerts, club dates and recording sessions. During his long and highly active career 'Lazy Ade' worked with many of Australia's best jazzmen, among them Bob and Len Barnard and Dave Dallwitz. A vigorous player with an engaging capacity for creating musical surprises (for example playing the recorder in a jazzy context), Monsbourgh has made an inestimable contribution to traditional jazz in Australia.

● ALBUMS: *Recorder In Ragtime* (Swaggie 1956)★★★, *Lazy Ade And His Late Hour Boys* (Swaggie 1956)★★★, *Wild Life* (Swaggie 60s)★★★, *The Odds Are Against Me* (Swaggie 1971)★★★, *All Steamed Up* (Swaggie 1983)★★★, *The Jazz Parade* (Swaggie 1984)★★★.

Monterey Jazz Festival

Founded in 1958 by Jimmy Lyons and Ralph J. Gleason, the festival has been held every year since its inception and has become one of the most prestigious and popular of all jazz events in the USA. Lyons, a missionary's son born in Peking, China, was a DJ in Southern California in the early 40s and introduced many of the early broadcasts by the Stan Kenton band. During his army service in and after World War II he produced many 'Jubilee' shows for the Armed Forces Radio Service, including sessions with Dizzy Gillespie, Charlie Parker and Milt Jackson. He was also involved in recording the first Jazz At The Philharmonic concert staged by Norman Granz. After his military service was over Lyons became a DJ in San Diego, then was a publicist for the Woody Herman Four Brothers band. He settled in San Francisco in 1948, working again as a radio DJ, presenting a late-night show with a strong orientation towards modern jazz. Lyons developed an ambition to establish a west coast jazz festival along the lines of those being staged in the east by George Wein. He had discussed this with jazz writer Gleason and, in 1953, when Lyons moved south of San Francisco to Big Sur, he decided that Monterey was the place in which to realize his ambition. With Gleason as advisor and Lyons as the enthusiastic generator of support from local businessmen, the festival was eventually underway. After the success of the first festival, which included Louis Armstrong, Gillespie, John Lewis, Max Roach, Gerry Mulligan, Dave Brubeck, Harry James, Benny Carter and Billie Holiday, Gleason recommended that Lewis should be appointed permanent musical director. Lewis retained the post until 1983, missing only occasional years when major tours clashed with the festival's regular late September date. For a few years after Lewis the musical director was Mundell Lowe, who was later replaced by Bill Berry. Among other artists who played the festival are Chris Barber, George Lewis, Earl Hines, Herman, Coleman Hawkins, Ornette Coleman, Count Basie, Duke Ellington, Modern Jazz Quartet, Charles Mingus, Anita O'Day, Don Ellis, Gil Evans, Johnny Otis, Cannonball Adderley, Hampton Hawes, Sonny Stitt, Sarah Vaughan, Big Joe Turner, Art Blakey, Betty Carter, Tito Puente, Horace Silver, Jay McShann, JoAnne Brackeen, Cal Tjader, Billy Eckstine, Herbie Mann, Freddie Hubbard. Several major musical works have been premiered at Monterey and the festival has also become a major showcase for emerging talent with regular appearances of all-star Californian high school bands. Much of the material played over each of the three-day festivals has been recorded and issued. Lyons was due to retire in 1991, but the festival he created looks set to continue for many more years.

● COMPILATIONS: *Monterey Jazz Festival: 40 Legendary Years* 3-CD set (Warners 1997)★★★★.

● FURTHER READING: *Dizzy, Duke, the Count and Me: The Story Of The Monterey Jazz Festival*, Jimmy Lyons with Ira Kamin. *Monterey Jazz Festival: Forty Legendary Years*, William Minor.

Monterose, J.R.

b. Frank Anthony Monterose, 19 January 1927, Detroit, Michigan, USA, d. 26 September 1993, Utica, New York, USA. After gaining experience playing tenor saxophone in a number of Midwestern bands of the 40s, he joined Buddy Rich in the early 50s. He became known on the New York bebop scene, playing and recording with a wide range of musicians, including Charles Mingus and Kenny Dorham. Although he has worked elsewhere, including a spell of some three years in Belgium, Monterose has chosen to spend much of his career in and around New York and Albany, thus limiting his international reputation. A soft-spoken, introverted individual, Monterose plays with a rich and warm sound and in an intensely melodic style.

● ALBUMS: *J. R. Monterose* (1956)★★, *Straight Ahead* (1960)★★★★, *In Action* (Studio 4 1964)★★★, *Live In Albany* (Uptown 1979)★★★, *Luan* (1979)★★, with Tommy Flanagan *...And A Little Pleasure* (Uptown 1981)★★★, *Bebop Loose And Live* (1981)★★★, *The Message* (Fresh Sounds 1993)★★★.

Montgomery, Marian

b. 17 November 1934, Natchez, Mississippi, USA. Montgomery quit school to sing on television in Atlanta, Georgia. After working in advertising and publishing, performing in plays and singing in strip joints and jazz clubs, she became an established cabaret performer. She moved to the UK in 1965 to sing at a new London club, the Cool Elephant, with the John Dankworth Band. That same year she married composer and musical director Laurie Holloway. Possessing a voice that has been likened to 'having a long, cool glass of mint julep on a Savannah balcony', she expanded her career with a starring role in the 1969 West End revival of *Anything Goes*, and frequent appearances on radio and television, as well as concerts and cabaret in the UK and abroad. Her one-woman show was televised by the BBC in 1975. Besides her musical association with Holloway, she successfully collaborated with classical composer/pianist Richard Rodney Bennett on several projects, including *Puttin' On The Ritz*, *Surprise Surprise* and *Town And Country*. With an instantly recognizable, relaxed and intimate style, she has become one of a handful of American artists to take up permanent residence in the UK.

● ALBUMS: *Swings For Winners And Losers* (Capitol 1963)★★★, *Let There Be Marian Montgomery* (Capitol 1963)★★★, *What's New* (Decca 1965)★★★, *Lovin' Is Livin'* (1965)★★★, *Marian Montgomery On Stage* (1979)★★★, with Richard Rodney Bennett *Town And Country* (1978)★★★, with Bennett *Surprise Surprise* (1981)★★★, with Bennett *Puttin' On The Ritz* (1984)★★★, *I Gotta Right To Sing* (1988)★★★, *Sometimes In The Night* (1989)★★★, *Nice And Easy* (1989)★★★.

MONTGOMERY, MONK

b. William Howard Montgomery, 10 October 1921, Indianapolis, Indiana, USA, d. 20 May 1982, Las Vegas, Nevada, USA. One of three musical brothers, Montgomery began playing relatively late in life. After first taking up the acoustic bass he switched to the electric bass guitar in 1951. He toured with Lionel Hampton, recording in Paris in 1953, then became a member of the Montgomery-Johnson Quintet, which included his brothers Buddy, a pianist and vibraphonist, and guitarist Wes Montgomery, alongside tenor saxophonist Alonzo Johnson and drummer Robert Johnson. In the mid-50s he settled in Seattle, frequently working with Buddy in the Mastersounds, and with both brothers in the Montgomery Brothers group. Montgomery continued playing throughout the 60s and 70s with leaders such as Cal Tjader, Hampton Hawes and Red Norvo. In the late 70s and early 80s he worked in Las Vegas, Nevada, as a studio and show band musician, as a radio disc jockey and as the founder and organizer of the Las Vegas Jazz Society.

● ALBUMS: with The Montgomery Brothers *The Montgomery Brothers And Five Others* reissued as *Wes, Buddy & Monk Montgomery* (World Pacific/Pacific Jazz 1957)★★★, with The Montgomery Brothers *Montgomeryland* (Pacific Jazz 1959)★★★, with The Montgomery Brothers *The Montgomery Brothers* (Fantasy 1960)★★★, with The Montgomery Brothers *The Montgomery Brothers In Canada* (Fantasy 1961)★★★, with The Montgomery Brothers *Groove Yard* (Riverside 1961)★★★, with George Shearing *Love Walked In* (Jazzland 1961)★★★, with The Montgomery Brothers *Wes' Best* (Fantasy 1967)★★★, *It's Never Too Late* (Mojazz 1969)★★★, *Reality* (Philadelphia International 1974)★★★.

MONTGOMERY, WES

b. John Leslie Montgomery, 6 March 1923, Indianapolis, Indiana, USA, d. 15 June 1968, Indianapolis, Indiana, USA. Montgomery was inspired to take up the guitar after hearing records by Charlie Christian. Nearly 20 years old at the time, he taught himself to play by adapting what he heard on records to what he could accomplish himself. Guided in part by Christian's example, but also by the need to find a way of playing that did not alienate his neighbours, he evolved a uniquely quiet style. Using the soft part of his thumb instead of a plectrum or the fingers, and playing the melody line simultaneously in two registers, Montgomery was already a distinctive stylist by the time he began to work with local bands. In 1948 he joined Lionel Hampton, touring and recording. In the early 50s he returned to Indianapolis and began playing with his brothers Buddy and Monk Montgomery in the Montgomery-Johnson Quintet (the other members being Alonzo and Robert Johnson). During an after-hours session at a local club, the visiting Cannonball Adderley asked him if he would like a record date. On Adderley's recommendation, Montgomery was recorded by Riverside Records in a series of trio albums that featured artists such as Hank Jones and Ron Carter. These albums attracted considerable attention and Montgomery quickly became one of the most talked about and respected guitarists in jazz. In the early 60s he worked with his brothers in northern California and also played with John Coltrane. Further recordings, this time with a large string orchestra, broadened Montgomery's horizons and appealed to the non-jazz public. However, despite such commercially successful albums as *Movin' Wes*, *Bumpin'*, *Goin' Out Of My Head* and *A Day In The Life*, he continued to play jazz in small groups with his brothers and with Wynton Kelly, Herb Alpert, Harold Mabern and others. In 1965 he visited Europe, playing club and festival dates in England, Spain and elsewhere. His career was at its height when he died suddenly in June 1968. An outstanding guitarist with an enormous influence upon his contemporaries and countless successors, Montgomery's highly personal style was developed deliberately from Christian, and unwittingly shadowed earlier conceptions by musicians such as Django Reinhardt. In Montgomery's case he stumbled upon these methods not with deliberate intent but through what jazz writer Alun Morgan has described as 'a combination of naïvety and good neighbourliness'.

● ALBUMS: with The Montgomery Brothers *The Montgomery Brothers And Five Others* reissued as *Wes, Buddy & Monk Montgomery* (World Pacific/Pacific Jazz 1957)★★★, with the Mastersounds *Kismet* (World Pacific 1958)★★★, with The Montgomery Brothers *Montgomeryland* (Pacific Jazz 1959)★★★, *New Concepts In Jazz Guitar* (Riverside 1959)★★★★, *The Incredible Jazz Guitar Of Wes Montgomery* (Riverside 1960)★★★★★, *Movin' Along* (Riverside 1960)★★★★, with The Montgomery Brothers *The Montgomery Brothers* (Fantasy 1960)★★★, with The Montgomery Brothers

The Montgomery Brothers In Canada (Fantasy 1961)★★★, with The Montgomery Brothers *Groove Yard* (Riverside 1961)★★★, with George Shearing *Love Walked In* (Jazzland 1961)★★★, *So Much Guitar!* (Riverside 1961)★★★★, *Far Wes* (Pacific 1961)★★★, *Full House Recorded 'Live' At Tsubo-Berkley, California* (Riverside 1962)★★★, with Milt Jackson *Bags Meets Wes* (Riverside 1962)★★★★, *Boss Guitar* reissued as *This Is Wes Montgomery* (Riverside 1963)★★★★, *Fusion! Wes Montgomery With Strings* reissued as *In The Wee Small Hours* (Riverside 1964)★★★, *Portrait Of Wes* (Riverside 1964)★★★★, *Guitar On The Go* (Riverside 1965)★★★, *Movin' Wes* (Verve 1965)★★★★, *Bumpin'* (Verve 1965)★★★★, *Smokin' At The Half Note* (Verve 1965)★★★★, *Tequila* (Verve 1966)★★★, *Goin' Out Of My Head* (Verve 1966)★★★, *California Dreaming* (Verve 1966)★★★, with Jimmy Smith *Jimmy & Wes The Dynamic Duo* (Verve 1966)★★★★, with Smith *Further Adventures Of Jimmy And Wes* (Verve 1966)★★★★, *Easy Groove* (Pacific Jazz 1966)★★★, with The Montgomery Brothers *Wes' Best* (Fantasy 1967)★★★, *A Day In The Life* (A&M 1967)★★★, *Down Here On The Ground* (A&M 1968)★★, *Road Song* (A&M 1968)★★, *Willow Weep For Me* 1965 recording (Verve 1969)★★★, *Eulogy* (Verve 1969)★★★, *Mood I'm In* (Sunset 1969)★★, *Just Walkin'* 1965/1966 recordings (Verve 1971)★★★, *Impressions* 1965 recording (Affinity 1978)★★★★, *Solitude* 1965 recording (Affinity 1978)★★★★, *Recorded Live At Jorgies Jazz Club* 1961 recording (VGM 1985)★★★, *Live At Jorgies And More* 1961/1968 recordings (VGM 1985)★★★, *Live In Paris* 1965 recording (France Concert 1988)★★★★.

● COMPILATIONS: *The Best Of Wes Montgomery* (Verve 1967)★★★★, *March 6, 1925 - June 15, 1968* (Riverside 1968)★★★★, *Portrait* (Pacific Jazz 1968)★★★★, *Panorama* (Riverside 1969)★★★★, *The Best Of Wes Montgomery, Volume 2* (Verve 1969)★★★★, *The Silver Collection* (PolyGram 1984)★★★★, *Wes Montgomery Plays The Blues* (Verve 1988)★★★, *Verve Jazz Masters 14: Wes Montgomery* (Verve 1990)★★★★, *Classics, Vol. 22: Wes Montgomery* (A&M 1991)★★★, *Talkin' Verve: Roots Of Acid Jazz* (Verve 1996)★★★★, *Ultimate Wes Montgomery* (Verve 1998)★★★, *Impressions: The Verve Jazz Sessions* (Verve)★★★★, *The Complete Riverside Recordings* 12-CD box set (Fantasy)★★★★, *Encores, Vol. 1: Body And Soul* 1960/1961 recordings (Fantasy)★★★★, *Encores, Vol. 2: Blues 'n' Boogie* 1962/1963 recordings (Fantasy)★★★★, *The Alternative Wes Montgomery* 1960-1963 recordings (Fantasy)★★★★.

● FURTHER READING: *Wes Montgomery*, Adrian Ingram.

MONTOLIU, TETE

b. Vincente Montoliu y Massana, 28 February 1933, Barcelona, Spain, d. 24 August 1997, Barcelona, Spain. Blind from birth, pianist Montoliu studied classical music as a child, but in his early teens started listening to the American jazz records issued by the La Vos de su Amo label, in particular the challenging work of artists such as Art Tatum, Earl Hines and Bud Powell. His own playing developed into a European interpretation of these American greats. He began playing with the American tenor Don Byas when he was 13, while still studying at the Barcelona Conservatory. By the mid-50s he was regularly sitting in with visiting American artists, including Lionel Hampton. By the end of the decade he had ventured north to play at a number of important European jazz festivals and had also played in Scandinavia. Montoliu's own recording career began in 1958, and he was to prove a prolific recording artist. In the late 60s he played in New York, thereafter establishing an international reputation as a gifted soloist with enormous technical skills that never obstructed his ability to generate a powerful swing. Among the musicians with whom he worked are Ben Webster, Anthony Braxton, Roland Kirk and Dexter Gordon. He led a series of talented trios from the mid-70s onwards, including bassists George Mraz and Niels-Henning Ørsted Pedersen, and drummers Al 'Tootie' Heath and Al Foster. He was active up until his death from lung cancer in 1997.

● ALBUMS: *The Tete Montoliu Trio* (1965)★★★, *Blues For Nuria* (1968)★★★, *Ben Webster Meets Don Byas In The Black Forest* (1968)★★★★, *Interpreta A Serrat* (1969)★★★, *Ricordando A Line* (1971)★★, *Songs For Love* (Enja 1971)★★★, *That's All* (Steeple Chase 1971)★★★, *Body And Soul* (1971)★★★★, *Lush Life* (Steeple Chase 1971)★★★, *Temi Latino Americani* (1973)★★★, *Temi Brasiliani* (1973)★★, *Music For Perla* (Steeple Chase 1974)★★★, *Catalonian Fire* (Steeple Chase 1974)★★★, *Tete* (Steeple Chase 1974)★★★, *Vampyria* (1974)★★★, *Tete A Tete* (Steeple Chase 1976)★★★, *Tootie's Tempo* (Steeple Chase 1976)★★, *Words Of Love* (1976)★★, *Blues For Myself* (1977)★★★★, *Yellow Dolphin Street* (Timeless 1977)★★★, *Secret Love* (1977)★★★, *Boleros* (1977)★★★, *Catalonian Folksongs* (Timeless 1977)★★, *Al Palau* (1979)★★★, *Live At The Keystone Corner* (Timeless 1979)★★, *Lunch In LA* (1980)★★, *Catalonian Nights Vols 1-2* (Steeple Chase 1980)★★★★, *Boston Concert* (Steeple Chase 1980)★★★, *I Wanna Talk About You* (1980)★★★, *Face To Face* (1982)★★★, *Carmina* (1984)★★★, *The Music I Like To Play Vols 1-2* (Soul Note 1986)★★★, with Peter King *New Year's Morning '89* (1989)★★★★ , *Sweet N' Lovely Vols 1-2* (Fresh Sound 1990)★★★, *The Man From Barcelona* (Timeless 1991)★★★, *A Spanish Treasure* (Concord 1992)★★★, *Music For Anna* (Mas I Mas 1993)★★.

MONTREUX INTERNATIONAL JAZZ FESTIVAL

Held at the Montreux Casino over 17 days in July, since its opening in 1967 the Montreux Jazz Festival has become one of the leading European festivals. Attracting large audiences and a host of major artists, the festival has benefited through close association with record companies, notably Pablo, and regular filming for transmission over television networks in many countries. Among the recorded results have been masterly sets by the likes of Dizzy Gillespie, Monty Alexander and Benny Carter. More fusion-orientated than most jazz festivals, at times Montreux has proved less than wholly attractive to hardcore jazz fans but high standards of performance and presentation have helped it to maintain its rightful place as a major venue.

MOODY, JAMES

b. 26 February 1925, Savannah, Georgia, USA. Beginning to play saxophones in his mid-teens, Moody developed his abilities as an instrumentalist during a spell in the American armed forces. Discharged in 1946, he joined Dizzy Gillespie's big band (on tenor saxophone), later touring Europe (mostly playing alto saxophone). His 1949 recording of 'I'm In The Mood For Love' became a hit three years later and greatly enhanced his reputation at home and abroad. During the 50s he led a number of small groups, some of which were R&B-orientated, and recorded several sessions for Argo Records. In the 50s he also began to play the flute. By the 60s he had become a major figure on the US club scene and the international festival circuit, and played in a three tenor band with Sonny Stitt and Gene 'Jug' Ammons. He played with Gillespie again between 1963 and 1968, and occasionally thereafter. An able and melodic soloist on all three of his instruments, Moody is especially effective on ballads. He has continued to release excellent sessions into the 90s on the Novus label.

● ALBUMS: *James Moody-His Saxophone And His Band* 10-inch album (Dial 1950)★★★, *James Moody In France* 10-inch album (Roost 1951)★★★, *James Moody Favorites, No. 1* 10-inch album (Prestige 1951)★★★★, *James Moody Favorites, No. 2* 10-inch album (Prestige 1952)★★★★, *James Moody With Strings* 10-inch album (Blue Note 1952)★★★, *James Moody And His Modernists* 10-inch album (Blue Note 1952)★★★, *Sax Talk* (Vogue 1952)★★★, *James Moody, Volume 3* 10-inch album (Prestige 1953)★★★, *Moody In France* 10-inch album (Prestige 1953)★★★★, *Moody's Mood* reissued as *Moody* (Prestige 1954)★★★, *James Moody And His Band* reissued as *James Moody's Moods* (Prestige 1954)★★★, *The Moody Story* 10-inch album (EmArcy 1954)★★★★, *Moodsville* 10-inch album (EmArcy 1954)★★★, *Hi-Fi Party* (Prestige 1955)★★★★, *Wail Moody Wail* (Prestige 1955)★★★★, *Flute 'N Blues* (Creative/Argo 1956)★★★, *Moody's Mood For Blues* (Prestige 1956)★★★★, *Moody's Mood For Love* (Argo 1957)★★★, *Last Train From Overbrook* (Argo 1958)★★★, *James Moody* i (Argo 1959)★★★, *Hey! It's James Moody* (Argo 1959)★★★, *Moody's Workshop* (Prestige 1960)★★★, *Moody With Strings* (Argo 1961)★★, *Another Bag* (Argo 1962)★★★, *Great Day* (Argo 1963)★★★, *Comin' On Strong* (Argo 1963)★★, *Running The Gamut* (Scepter 1964)★★, *Group Therapy* (1964)★★, *Cookin' The Blues* (Argo 1965)★★★, *The Blues And Other Colours* (1967)★★★, *Brass Figures* (Milestone 1968)★★★, *Don't Look Away Now!* (Prestige 1969)★★★, *The Beginning And End Of Bop* (Blue Note 1969)★★★, *Heritage Hum* (1971)★★, *Lush Life* (1971)★★★, *Too Heavy For Words* (PA 1971)★★★, with Gene Ammons *Chicago Concert* (1971)★★★, *Never Again!* (1972)★★★, *Everything You've Always Wanted To Know About Sax* (Cadet 1972)★★★, *Feelin' It Together* (1973)★★★, *Beyond This World* (1977)★★★, *Something Special* (Novus 1987)★★★, with Stan Getz *Tenor Contrasts* (Esquire 1988)★★★, *Moving Forward* (Novus 1988)★★★, *Sweet And Lovely* (Novus 1990)★★★, *Honey* (Jive/Novus 1991)★★★, *Live At The Blue Note* (Telarc 1995)★★★, *Young At Heart* (Warners 1996)★★★, *Feelin' It Together* (32 Records 1998)★★, *Moody Plays Mancini* (Warners 1997)★★★, *At The Jazz Workshop* 1961 recording (Chess 1998)★★★★.

● COMPILATIONS: *James Moody's Greatest Hits* (Prestige 1967)★★★, *James Moody's Greatest Hits, Volume 2* (Prestige 1967)★★★.

MOONDOC, JEMEEL

b. 5 August 1951, Chicago, Illinois, USA. Despite being a creative musician from Chicago, saxophonist Moondoc was never involved with the AACM - by the time he was looking for people with whom to play in the late 60s, Anthony Braxton, Leroy Jenkins and the Art Ensemble Of Chicago had left for Paris and New York. Turning down a career as an architect in the early 70s he studied music with Ran Blake in Boston, where he also played in the James Tatum Blues Band, and then followed Cecil Taylor to Wisconsin University and Antioch College, playing alto and soprano saxophones in Taylor's student orchestras. He moved to New York in 1972, where he met and played with *avant garde* luminaries such as bassist William Parker and trumpeter Roy Campbell, and also formed his Ensemble Munta, which lasted for nearly 10 years. In 1981 he toured Poland and recorded *The Intrepid* for the Poljazz label. In 1984 he formed the Jus Grew Orchestra, a wild 15-piece that had a residency at the Neither/Nor club on the Lower East Side. He says, 'I try to speak through the horn - it's something I learned from Jimmy Lyons and Ornette Coleman', and he often plays deliberately sharp, like a free version of Jackie McLean. Moondoc's approach, which combines the looseness of bar-room blues with post-Coleman multi-key valency, found a willing accomplice in guitarist Bern Nix from Coleman's harmolodic outfit Prime Time. Their band - with Parker on bass and Dennis Charles on drums - provided a tipsy, dislocated jazz that was excellently captured on *Nostalgia In Times Square*. Moondoc remains a strikingly individual musical mind in a jazz scene too often willing to conform to the standards of the past.

● ALBUMS: *First Feeding* (1977)★★★, *The Evening Of The Blue Men* (1979)★★★, *New York Live* (1981)★★, *Konstanze's Delight* (Soul Note 1981)★★★, *The Intrepid Live In Poland* (1981)★★, *The Athens Concert* (1982)★★, *Judy's Bounce* (Soul Note 1982)★★★, *Nostalgia In Times Square* (Soul Note 1985)★★★.

MOONDOG

b. Louis Hardin, 26 May 1916, Marysville, Kansas, USA. This idiosyncratic composer lost his sight at the age of 16 following an accident with a dynamite cap. He was introduced to classical music at the Iowa School for the Blind, studying violin, viola and piano, but having moved to New York, opted for a life as a 'street musician'. He took the name Moondog in 1947 and established a pitch on the city's fabled Times Square. Such was his notoriety, Hardin successfully retained this sobriquet after issuing legal proceedings against disc jockey Alan Freed, who had claimed the 'Moondog' name for his radio show.

In a manner similar to fellow maverick Harry Partch, Moondog constructed his own instruments, claiming conventional scales could not reproduce the sounds heard in his head. This was immediately apparent on his first release, *On The Streets Of New York* (1953), a 45 rpm EP issued by Epic and London/American. Percussive devices, named the 'oo' and 'trimba', were at the fore of albums recorded for the Prestige label, notably *More Moondog* and *The Story Of Moondog*, although a distinctive jazz influence can also be detected. Further releases ensued, including *Moondog And His Honking Geese*, which the composer financed and distributed. Hardin also arranged an album of Mother Goose songs for singer Julie Andrews. During the 60s Moondog continued to perform and beg on the city's streets, but his unconventional lifestyle and appearance - he wrapped himself in army surplus blankets and wore a Viking-styled helmet - found succour in the emergent counter-culture. He performed with anti-establishment comedian Lenny Bruce and eccentric singer Tiny Tim, while several groups, including Big Brother and the Holding Company and the Insect Trust, recorded his distinctive musical rounds. In 1969, James Guercio, producer of the highly successful Chicago, introduced Moondog to CBS Records. Buoyed by a full orchestra, *Moondog* encapsulates 20 years of compositions, showing musical references to such diverse figures as Stravinsky and Charlie Parker, the latter of whom often conversed with Moondog. One particular selection, 'The Witch Of Endor', stands as one of his finest pieces. *Moondog 2* was a collection of rounds, inspired by the recognition afforded the composer by the hip cognoscenti. In 1974 Moondog undertook a tour of Germany where he opted to settle. 'I am a European at heart', he later stated. A further series of albums maintained his unique musical vision, but although he then ceased recording for over twenty years, interest in this fascinating individual continued to flourish.

● ALBUMS: *Moondog And His Friends* 10-inch album (Epic 1954)★★★, *Moondog* (Prestige 1955)★★★, *More Moondog* (Prestige 1956)★★★, *The Story Of Moondog* (Prestige 1957)★★★, *Moondog* (Columbia 1969)★★★★, *Moondog 2* (Columbia 1970)★★★, *Moondog In Europe* (1978)★★★, *H'Art Songs* (1979)★★★, *A New Sound Of An Old Instrument* (1980)★★★, *Selected Works* (1980)★★★, *Big Band* (Trimba 1996)★★★, with the London Saxophonic *Sax Pax For A Sax* (Atlantic 1998)★★★.

MOORE, ALTON

b. 7 October 1908, Selma, Alabama, USA, d. 1978. After being taught formally on baritone horn, Alton 'Slim' Moore took up the trombone and in his late teens was playing professionally with tent and other travelling shows. He played in several territory bands including those led by Gene Coy, Jesse Stone and Jap Allen before joining Blanche Calloway in 1931. He remained with this band for three years, then settled in New York where he played and sometimes recorded with many leading jazz artists of the late 30s and early 40s, among them Oran 'Hot Lips' Page, Fats Waller, Coleman Hawkins, Ella Fitzgerald and Louis Armstrong. In this same period he also visited the west coast, appearing in the film *Stormy Weather* (1943) with Waller, Zutty Singleton, Benny Carter and others. After leaving Armstrong's big band in 1947 he worked with Herbie Fields, then spent a few years with less well-known bands before leaving full-time music in 1952. A solid section player with a sympathetic ear for the needs of the ensemble and of soloists, Moore's contribution to the bands in which he played was substantial even if his work sometimes went underestimated by audiences. Although in semi-retirement in the 50s and 60s he returned from time to time, most notably in the Fletcher Henderson reunion band in 1957.

MOORE, BILLY

b. William Moore Jnr., 7 December 1917, Parkersberg, West Virginia, USA, d. 28 February 1989. Although he was a competent pianist, it was as an arranger that Moore made his greatest mark on jazz. An important contributor to the development of big band arranging in the 30s, his talents were often overlooked, sometimes deliberately so. As he told documentary film-maker John Jeremy, he started writing music in 1937, offered some material to Chick Webb, and was told they needed an arrangement. He taught himself arranging, in the meantime working outside music. In his non-musical capacity he met Sy Oliver but chose not to prevail upon the acquaintanceship until Oliver accidentally learned of his abiding interest. Coincidentally, Moore was with Oliver soon after he had left Jimmie Lunceford for Tommy Dorsey. When Lunceford asked for some new charts, Oliver promptly recommended Moore. In addition to arranging for the Lunceford band, Moore also wrote for Charlie Barnet. He formed his own music publishing company in order to combat the then prevalent habit of bandleaders taking credit for the work of their arrangers and composers - Moore's actions thus predated the commonplace practice among present-day musicians by almost half a century. The struggle to be granted the credit that was his due eventually disillusioned Moore and in the early 50s he abandoned his career in the USA and emigrated to Denmark, where he remained for the rest of his life. Amongst his uncredited works is the famous countermelody to Barnet's million-selling hit 'Skyliner'. In his later years Moore was administrator in Denmark of the music foundation established in Ben Webster's name and for whom he also worked as a business aide. He was also manager to and musical director for the European tours of the Peters Sisters.

MOORE, BREW

b. Milton Aubrey Moore, 26 March 1924, Indianola, Mississippi, USA, d. 19 August 1973. After learning to play a range of instruments, Moore concentrated on tenor saxophone and in his teens sought work in various parts of the USA. A melodic player with a liquid ballad style, Moore's roots were in the style of the early Lester Young, and the advent of bebop restricted his progress. Nevertheless, he made many records in the 50s, then in 1961 became resident in Europe where, apart from a three-year return to the USA (1967-70), he remained for the rest of his life. Although his decision to stay away from America for so many years, allied to his refusal to move with the times, kept him out of the spotlight, it is now generally acknowledged that the quality of Moore's ballad playing was of the very highest order. His early death from a fall, attributed to his dependence upon alcohol, silenced a player whose talent, if not his career, was comparable to that of near-contemporaries such as Stan Getz and Zoot Sims.

● ALBUMS: *Brewer's Brew* (1950)★★★, *Fru And Brew* (1953)★★★, *The Brew Moore Quintet* (1956)★★★, *Danish Brew* (1959)★★★★, *The Brew Moore Quartet* i (1962)★★★★, *Svinget 14* (Black Lion 1963)★★★, *If I Had You* (1965)★★★, *I Should Care* (Speeplechase 1965)★★★, *Brew's Stockholm Dew* (1971)★★★, *No More Brew* (Storyville 1971)★★★.

MOORE, DUDLEY

b. 19 April 1935, Dagenham, Essex, England. Although severely hampered by having a deformed foot and spending a great deal of his childhood in hospital, this did not deter Moore from becoming passionately interested in music from an early age. The young Dudley played piano in a local youth club and organ at his church. He wore an old brown boot strapped over his normal shoe to give his bad foot extra length to touch the pedals easily. As a young teenager Moore played semi-professionally in various jazz clubs. He studied music at Oxford University, graduating in the late 50s and thereafter playing with Vic Lewis. Early in the following decade he worked with John Dankworth before forming his own trio with Pete McGurk (bass) and Chris Karan (drums). For a while he successfully performed jazz while concurrently appearing in *Beyond The Fringe* in London and New York. During this time he forged a partnership with comedian Peter Cook. With the trio, he also made records and appeared on television in the seminal *Not Only But Also* (with Cook). By the mid-60s Moore's acting career had begun to take precedence over his jazz work and he later moved to Hollywood. His musical interests continued with the writing of scores for feature films including *The Wrong Box* (1966), *30 Is A Dangerous Age Cynthia* (1967), *Inadmissible Evidence* (1968), *Bedazzled* (1968) and *Staircase* (1969), and also for stage shows, plays and ballet. His own acting career took off to such an extent that 'Cuddly Dudley' became a huge Hollywood star in such films as *10* (1979), *Wholly Moses* (1980), *Arthur* (1981), *Six Weeks* (1982), *Lovesick* (1983), *Best Defence* (1984), *Micki And Maude* (1984) and *Santa Claus* (1985). Additionally, he made three hilarious albums with Cook of pure filth and bad language as Derek And Clive. Moore has cited Erroll Garner and Oscar Peterson as two of his main influences. His jazz playing is notable for his lightness of touch and deft right-hand filigrees although his eclecticism, allied to his absorption with other interests, has inhibited the development of a truly identifiable personal style. In recent years, having achieved everything as a 'movie star', Moore has returned to recording and performing, and has resurrected the definitive Dudley Moore Trio. In a revealing biography published in 1997 Moore disclosed a troubled soul who has seemingly succeeded at everything, but remains deeply unfulfilled. Leaving behind him a trail of broken marriages and a number of critically slammed films during the 80s and 90s, Dudley Moore has always returned to music in times of stress. His brilliance as both jazz and classical pianist has been constantly undermined by his personal life.

● ALBUMS: *Beyond The Fringe* (Parlophone 1961)★★★, *Theme From Beyond The Fringe And All That Jazz* (Atlantic 1962)★★★, *Beyond The Fringe; Original Broadway Cast* (Capitol 1962)★★★, *The Other Side Of The Dudley Moore Trio* (Decca 1965)★★★★, *Genuine Dud* (Decca 1966)★★★★, *Bedazzled* soundtrack (Decca 1968)★★★, *The Dudley Moore Trio* (Decca 1968)★★★★, *The Music Of Dudley Moore* (Decca 1969)★★★, *Today With The Dudley Moore Trio* (Atlantic 1971)★★★, *Dudley Moore At The Wavendon Festival* (Black Lion 1976)★★★, *The Dudley Moore Trio* (Warners 1978)★★★, *Dudley Down Under* (1978)★★★, *Smilin' Through* (Finesse 1982)★★★, *Orchestra* (Decca 1991)★★★, *Songs Without Words* (GRP 1991)★★★, *Concerto!* (RCA Victor 1992)★★★, *Grieg Piano Concerto In A Minor* (EMI 1995)★★★.

● FURTHER READING: *Dudley*, Paul Donovan. *Off Beat: Dudley Moore's Book Of Musical Anecdotes*, Dudley Moore. *Dudley Moore: The Authorized Biography*, Barbra Paskin.

MOORE, FREDDIE

b. 20 August 1900, Washington, North Carolina, USA, d. 3 November 1992, New York, USA. He began playing drums as a child and was soon working in tent shows, travelling throughout southern states. After playing with Charlie Creath and leading his own band, he moved to New York, joining Wilbur Sweatman, then toured with King Oliver and once again led his own band. During the 40s and 50s he was constantly in demand, mostly in New York but also for tours as far afield as Europe, and played in bands led by, amongst others, John Kirby, Sidney Bechet, Wilbur De Paris, Bob Wilber, Mezz Mezzrow, Sammy Price and Emmett Berry. In the 60s and 70s he was still playing, with musicians such as Tony Parenti and Roy Eldridge, but by the mid-80s had slowed down a little and mostly played washboard. A robust drummer steeped in the solid timekeeping tradition of early jazz, he took naturally to the mainstream and provided steady, fluid support to the front-line horns with which he played.

● ALBUMS: *Emmett Berry And His Orchestra* (Columbia 1956)★★★.

MOORE, GLEN

b. 28 October 1941, Portland, Oregon, USA. It was on sets with Tim Hardin and Cyrus that Moore came to public notice. However, upon uniting with Ralph Towner, Paul McCandless, and Collin Walcott within the fluid context of Oregon, Moore's bass style was best showcased. Like his co-members he revealed an easy command of classical, folk, Eastern, and jazz overtones. Since Oregon was formed in 1970, Moore's distinctive upright bass sound has distinguished each of their albums, wherein he has also been known to play viola and flute. The intermittent development of Oregon has allowed Moore the freedom to pursue a parallel career in sessions.

● ALBUMS: For ratings see individual artist entries. With Tim

Hardin *Bird On A Wire* (1970), with Annette Peacock *Bley/Peacock Synthesizer Show* (1971), with Cyrus *Cyrus* (1971), with Peacock *I'm The One* (1972), with Oregon *Music Of Another Present Era* (1973), with Oregon *Distant Hills* (1974), with Oregon *Winter Light* (1974), with Larry Coryell *Restful Mind* (1975), with Oregon *In Concert* (1975), with Ralph Towner *Trios/Solos* (1975), with Oregon *Friends* (1975), with Oregon *Together* (1977), with Oregon *Violin* (1978), with Oregon *Out Of The Woods* (1978), with Oregon *Roots In The Sky* (1979), with Zbigniew Seifert *We'll Remember Zbiggy* (1980), with Oregon *In Performance* (1980), *Oregon* (1983), with Oregon *Crossing* (1984), with Oregon *Ecotopia* (1987), with Oregon *45th Parallel* (1989), with Oregon *Always, Never And Forever* (1991).

MOORE, MARILYN

b. 16 June 1931, Oklahoma City, Oklahoma, USA, d. March 1992. Born into a showbusiness family, Moore began performing at the age of three, singing and dancing in the finale of her family's vaudeville act. As a teenager, she decided to concentrate on singing and soon turned to jazz, working in clubs in Oklahoma City and Chicago. In 1949 she sang with Woody Herman, then with Charlie Ventura and by the early 50s had settled in New York. She sang with various groups, including those led by Ray McKinley, Boyd Raeburn and Al Cohn, whom she married in 1953. They had two children, Lisa and Joe Cohn (now a leading jazz guitarist), and Moore's life became focused upon her home and family. In 1957, however, she was invited to record for Bethlehem and the resulting album, on which she is backed by Cohn, Joe Wilder, Don Abney, Barry Galbraith and other leading jazzmen, attracted a great deal of interest. The following year, she was cast in a jazz show, *Oh Captain!*, recorded by MGM Records in which Coleman Hawkins, Art Farmer, Oscar Pettiford and Harry 'Sweets' Edison also appeared. Soon afterwards, Moore and Cohn were divorced and once again she was tied to home-making and family-raising. Despite a deep desire to go back to professional singing and make more records, she never returned. A warm and sensitive voice marked Moore's work and in her phrasing and overall style there is evidence of her affinity for Billie Holiday. Overlooked and under-recorded (the MGM album was swiftly deleted and never reissued), the quality of Moore's singing on her first album, reissued on CD in 1990, marks her out as one of the great losses to the world of jazz.

● ALBUMS: *Moody Marilyn Moore* (Affinity 1957)★★★, with others *Oh Captain!* (MGM 1958)★★.

MOORE, MICHAEL

b. Michael Watson Moore, 16 May, 1923, Glen Este, Ohio, USA. While in his early teens Moore began playing bass, and worked semi-professionally while studying music. In the mid-60s he attracted worldwide attention thanks to a spell touring with Woody Herman. After this he settled in New York, quickly finding himself in great demand for studio and club dates. During the late 60s and into the next decade he played with many leading mainstream and contemporary jazz musicians, including Marian McPartland, Freddie Hubbard, Benny Goodman, Ruby Braff and Lee Konitz. He spent several years in a fruitful partnership with Gene Bertoncini and also recorded with artists such as Zoot Sims, Michal Urbaniak, Carol Sloane and Marvin Stamm. He is expert with the bow, and in some of his playing evokes intriguing aural images of the cello. Moore's melodic and richly inventive style makes him not only a valued and much sought-after accompanist but also a bass soloist of great presence.

● ALBUMS: with Gene Bertoncini *Close Ties* (Omnisound 1984)★★★, *The Michael Moore Trio Plays Gershwin* (Master Mix 1993)★★★, with Bill Charlap *Concord Duo Series: Volume Nine* (Concord Jazz 1995)★★★, *Chicoutimi* (Ramboy 1994)★★★★, with Bertoncini, Roger Kellaway *Roger Kellaway Meets The Duo* (Chiaroscuro 1996)★★★, with Rufus Reid *DoubleBass Delights* (Double-Time 1996)★★★, *Tunes For Horn Guys* (Ramboy 1996)★★★★, with Gerry Hemingway, Fred Hersch *Thirteen Ways* (GM 1997)★★★, *Bering* (Ramboy 1998)★★★.

MOORE, OSCAR

b. 25 December 1912, Austin, Texas, USA, d. 8 October 1981. Moore formed his first band with his brother Johnny (who was also a guitarist), while still in his mid-teens. In 1937 he became a founder-member of the Nat 'King' Cole Trio, and for the next few years was an important element in the group's success. In 1947 Moore joined the Three Blazers, a group led by his brother, and also led his own groups for recording sessions. In the mid-50s he dropped out of music, but returned occasionally to gig and make recording dates as a sideman. An outstanding guitarist in the mould of Charlie Christian, Moore was an exceptionally gifted soloist and an accompanist of rare distinction. The quicksilver exchanges between him and Cole on their early records provide eloquent testimony to his talent and make his long and presumably self-determined absence from the scene a matter of considerable regret.

● ALBUMS: *The Oscar Moore Trio* (Skylark 1954), *Gallivantin' Guitar* (Tampa 1957), *Tribute To Nat King Cole* (1965).

● COMPILATIONS: *The Complete Capitol Recordings Of The Nat 'King' Cole Trio* 18-CD box set (Mosaic 1990)★★★★★.

MOORE, RALPH

b. 1956, London, England. So assured, so steeped in the post-bop language and sensibility is Ralph Moore that it can come as a surprise that he is actually a British-born saxophonist (he has an English mother and an American father). He began learning the trumpet when he was 14, but was gradually seduced by the tenor saxophone. He moved to the USA at 15, settling on the west coast and served his apprenticeship in America's jazz hothouse environment until he reached a standard that enabled him to study at the prestigious Berklee College Of Music in Boston. Leaving after a couple of years, his innate ability and solid, raspy tone led to a period with the great drummer Roy Haynes, and then three years with the legendary hard-bop pianist and leader Horace Silver. With enough of a reputation to make it on the world's most competitive jazz scene, he moved to New York, and continued working with the greats, including John Hicks, Dizzy Gillespie, Gene Harris and Freddie Hubbard, as well as leading his own groups with some of the new wave of gifted, young hard-bop players, including trumpeter Brian Lynch, guitarist Kevin Eubanks and pianists Dave Kikoski, Benny Green and Mulgrew Miller. Ralph Moore's tenor work is characterized by an attractive, throaty tone, a little reminiscent of Charlie Rouse, and solid, self-assured phrasing. Hardly unorthodox but always creative and confident, he is undoubtedly one of the most promising of the new generation of bop saxophonists.

● ALBUMS: *Round Trip* (Reservoir 1985)★★★, *623 C Street* (Criss Cross Criss 1987)★★★★, with Marvin 'Smitty' Smith *Keeper Of The Drums* (Concord 1987)★★, with Bobby Hutcherson *Cruisin' The 'Bird* (Landmark 1988)★★★, *Rejuvenate!* (Criss Cross Criss 1988)★★★, *Furthermore* (Landmark 1990)★★★, with Freddie Hubbard *Bolivia* (Musicmasters/Limelight 1991)★★.

Moore, Russell 'Big Chief'

b. 13 August 1912, nr. Sacaton, Arizona, USA, d. 15 December 1983. A Native American of the Pima tribe, Moore began playing trombone in the Chicago area before settling in the mid-30s in Southern California, where he played in one of Lionel Hampton's first bands. By the end of the decade he had moved to New Orleans, where he became a regular musical associate of many of the older generation of traditional jazzmen. In 1944 he joined Louis Armstrong for a three-year spell, then worked in and around New York with Sidney Bechet, Eddie Condon, Buck Clayton, Red Allen, Oran 'Hot Lips' Page, Pee Wee Russell and many others. Occasional trips to Europe brought him to the attention of a wider range of fans and a short period with Armstrong's All Stars, beginning in 1964, further enhanced his reputation. He spent part of the 60s in Canada and led his own bands, recording occasionally on into the 70s. In the early 80s he was again on tour in Europe but died in 1983. Moore's style was well suited to the ensemble playing of the traditional New Orleans-style band, but his soloing had much to commend it.

● ALBUMS: *Russell 'Big Chief' Moore* (1953-74)★★★, *Russell 'Big Chief' Moore's Pow Wow Jazz Band* (1973)★★★.

Morand, Herb

b. 1905, New Orleans, Louisiana, USA. d. 23 February 1952. Beginning to play trumpet as a youth, Morand became a professional musician at the age of 18. He worked in bands led by Nat Towles, Chris Kelly and others, often in and around his home-town. In Chicago from the late 20s, he played and recorded with many musicians, including Johnny Dodds, Rosetta Howard, and the Harlem Hamfats. In the early 40s he returned to New Orleans where he led his own bands, later joining George Lewis. A competent player raised in the New Orleans tradition, during his career Morand's playing took on characteristics of other styles of jazz. He remained a good ensemble player, his solo work seldom having the dash and fire of many of his contemporaries.

● ALBUMS: *Herb Morand And His New Orleans Band* (1950)★★★.

Moreira, Airto

b. 5 August 1941, Itaiopolis, Brazil. Moreira moved to Rio de Janeiro when he was 16 years old. In the 60s he played in a quartet with the pianist/flautist Hermeto Pascal, travelling the length and breadth of Brazil collecting and using over 120 percussion instruments. He moved to Los Angeles in 1968 and then to New York in 1970. He was a musician who managed to be in the right place at the right time; jazz was being opened up to the kind of extra rhythmic subtlety a second percussionist could offer. Moreira describes how 'you look and listen for your own place in the music - your own space - and then you start to make sounds . . . music is like a picture; it's not just sound'. He worked with Miles Davis in 1970 as he sought to establish the changes announced in *Bitches Brew*. He played percussion on the Weather Report debut album in 1971 and then worked with Chick Corea's Return To Forever. Since then he has worked with musicians ranging from tenor saxophonists Stan Getz and Gato Barbieri to the Grateful Dead's drummer Mickey Hart with whom he recorded the percussion soundtrack for Francis Ford Coppola's film *Apocalypse Now*. He worked most regularly with his wife Flora Purim. In the mid-80s he played with the Al Di Meola Project, with which he toured Europe. Moreira also began to lean towards world music, including his own native Brazilian traditions, recording with Hart, Zakir, Hussain, Babatunde Olatunji and T.H. Vinyakram as Planet Drum (whose album won a Grammy Award) and as part of the highly regarded Fourth World. He also released his successful solo album, *The Other Side Of This*, for Rykodisc, which again paired him with Hussain. The central appeal of this was the unfettered approach to improvising songs, all of which were unrehearsed. The sparkling, spontaneous performances of songs such as 'Dom Um' provided a further career highlight.

● ALBUMS: with Miles Davis *At Fillmore* (1970)★★★, *Black Beauty* (1970)★★, *Live - Evil* (1970)★★★★; *Weather Report* (1971)★★★, with Chick Corea *Return To Forever* (1972)★★★★, *Fingers* (1973)★★★, with Stan Getz *Captain Marvel* (1975)★★★, with Mickey Hart *Rhythm Devils Play River Music* (1980)★★★, with Flora Purim *Colours Of Life* (In & Out 1988)★★★★, *Struck By Lightning* (Virgin 1989)★★★, *The Other Side Of This* (Rykodisc 1992)★★★, with Fourth World *Fourth World* (Ronnie Scott's Jazz House 1992)★★, with the Gods Of Jazz *Killer Bees* (B&W 1993)★★★, with David Friesen, Gary Barone *Ancient Kings* (Shamrock 1998)★★★.

Morello, Joe

b. 17 July 1928, Springfield, Massachusetts, USA. After studying violin Morello turned to playing drums while still at school. He played locally, accompanying fellow high school student Phil Woods among others. In the early 50s he moved to New York, performing with many bands in a wide variety of musical settings, including the big band of Stan Kenton. He was, however, most often to be found playing in small groups, notably those led by guitarists Johnny Smith, Tal Farlow, Sal Salvador and Jimmy Raney, pianist Marian McPartland and singers Jackie Cain and Roy Kral. He first attracted wide attention when he joined the Dave Brubeck Quartet in 1956. He remained with Brubeck for 12 years and, Paul Desmond apart, was that band's most accomplished jazzman. Indeed, Morello's playing with Brubeck was exemplary in its unassertive precision which, allied to a remarkably delicate swing, provided object lessons during a period when jazz drumming was notable for its aggression. After leaving Brubeck in 1967, Morello, who was partially sighted from childhood, was involved mostly in teaching. He occasionally led small groups in the 70s and also made a handful of records with Brubeck, McPartland and Salvador. An outstanding small group drummer, Morello's long stint with Brubeck, while giving him a highly visible presence, resulted in a considerable loss to the wider world of jazz.

● ALBUMS: with Red Norvo, Art Pepper *Joe Morello Sextet* reissued as *The Art Pepper-Red Norvo Sextet* (Intro/Score 1957)★★★★, *It's About Time* (RCA Victor 1961)★★★.

● FURTHER READING: *All In Good Time*, Marian McPartland.

Morgan, Al

b. Albert Morgan, 19 August 1908, New Orleans, Louisiana, USA, d. 14 April 1974. The youngest of four Morgan brothers who all became professional musicians, he first played clarinet and drums before settling on the bass. Among his early engagements was one with his bandleading brother Isaiah (although he never worked with his more famous brother, Sam Morgan). He also played with Lee Collins and Davey Jones, and spent some time on riverboats under the leadership of Fate Marable. At the end of the 20s he went to New York where he recorded with Fats Waller, continuing to gig in the city for the next few years. During this period he played on the justly celebrated sides recorded by an all-star group under the nominal leadership of Billy Banks. The same year, 1932, he joined Cab Calloway, making records and films, then settled in Los Angeles where he played in bands led by Eddie Barefield and Les Hite and he also worked with Louis Armstrong. In the early 40s he played with Sabby Lewis for a couple of years, then with Louis Jordan, before returning to Lewis's band in Boston where he remained until the late 50s. Morgan then returned to the west coast, playing in several small groups including one led by Joe Darensbourg. A strong, highly rhythmic player in his younger days, Morgan's early style owed much to the post-New Orleans tradition of bass playing which he later adapted into a more fluid, subtle style.

Morgan, Frank

b. 23 December 1933, Minneapolis, Minnesota, USA. The west coast bebop altoist Frank Morgan's career was obscured for over 30 years by prison sentences for narcotics offences and it is only in recent times that his talents and imagination have been more widely displayed or discussed. Morgan began playing guitar under the tuition of his guitarist father, and then, after moving to Los Angeles in 1947, learned alto saxophone at Los Angeles' Jefferson High from the same teacher who taught Dexter Gordon, Wardell Gray and Don Cherry. He began on saxophone as a Charlie Parker admirer, then grew closer to the interpretation of his west coast contemporary, Art Pepper, whom he resembles in his sharply accented sounds, fragmented figures and blurted, episodic delivery. Morgan once told the American critic Francis Davis, 'for me, prowess isn't as important as rapport', and he has always spaced out his statements with patience, artifice, a wide tonal palette and an avoidance of fireworks. At the age of 15 he won a television talent contest, which eventually led to a place in Lionel Hampton's band. He also recorded as a sideman with Ray Charles, Teddy Charles, Kenny Clarke and others before releasing his debut as leader, *Introducing Frank Morgan*, in 1955.

Since 1953 Morgan's drug problems have resulted in several prison sentences, and although largely absent from the jazz scene he did continue to play (mostly inside prison). Morgan returned to the outside jazz world in the mid-80s to startle audiences with his exhilarating Parker-inspired style. Morgan was over 50 before he made his second record, *Easy Living*, which introduced his sparkling bebop to a new generation of admirers. With further releases and tours to his credit, he is now recognized as one of the premier bebop altoists of the day. Interviewed in 1988 by Stan Woolley for *Jazz Journal International*, Morgan declared that he was 'one of the old purists and proud of it.' New albums and appearances on the international circuit have brought his strikingly inventive playing to the attention of a new and admiring audience. His recovery from the problems that beset him over more than half his lifetime is fortunate and he appears to be well aware of how much he has lost. In the same interview he spoke of the present and future, remarking, 'I just want to take time and absorb everything.'

● ALBUMS: *Introducing Frank Morgan* (Gene Norman 1955)★★★, *Easy Living* (1985)★★★, *Lament* (Contemporary 1986)★★, *Double Image* (Contemporary 1987)★★★, *Bebop Lives!* (JVC 1987)★★★★, *Quiet Fire* (Contemporary 1987)★★★★, *Major Changes* (Contemporary 1987)★★★, *Yardbird Suite* (Contemporary 1989)★★★★, *Reflections* (Contemporary 1989)★★★, *Mood Indigo* (Antilles 1989)★★★, *A Lovesome Thing* (Antilles 1991)★★★, *You Must Believe In Spring* (Antilles 1992)★★★, *Listen To The Dawn* (Antilles 1994)★★★, *Love, Lost & Found* (Telarc 1995)★★★, *Bop!* (Telarc 1997)★★★★.

Morgan, Lanny

b. Harold Lansford Morgan, 30 March 1934, Des Moines, Iowa, USA. As a child he played violin before taking up the alto saxophone. When he was 10 his family moved to Los Angeles and he continued his studies. As a young man he played in big bands including those led by Charlie Barnet, Terry Gibbs and Bob Florence, then settled for a while in New York where he worked with

Maynard Ferguson. Back on the west coast he played and recorded with several bands including Supersax and that led by Bill Berry. In addition to performing, Morgan also developed a reputation as a teacher. Since the mid-80s he had played mostly in small groups and has toured Europe and the UK as a single. A hard-blowing saxophonist, with a crisply incisive tone, Morgan is a commanding musician and is much respected by his peers.

● ALBUMS: *Maynard Ferguson Sextet* (1965)★★★★, with Bill Berry *Hello Rev* (Concord 1976)★★★, with Supersax *Dynamite!* (1978)★★★★, *It's About Time* (Pausa 1981)★★★, with Jeff Hamilton *Indiana* (1982)★★★, *Pacific Standard* (Contemporary 1997)★★★★.

Morgan, Lee

b. 10 July 1938, Philadelphia, Pennsylvania, USA, d. 19 February 1972, New York City, New York, USA. Prodigiously talented, Morgan played trumpet professionally at the age of 15 and three years later joined Dizzy Gillespie's big band. During this same period he recorded with John Coltrane, Hank Mobley and others. In 1958 the Gillespie band folded and Morgan joined Art Blakey's Jazz Messengers where he made a tremendous impact not only nationally but around the world, thanks to the group's recordings. In the early 60s Morgan returned to his home-town, where he played in comparative obscurity, but by 1963 he was back in New York, leading his own groups and also working for a while with Blakey in 1964. Morgan's popularity was enhanced by the success of a recording of his own composition, the irresistibly catchy 'The Sidewinder' which helped to spark a jazz/funk mini-boom and has remained a dance floor favourite ever since. Morgan's trumpet style was marked by his full-blooded vitality, aided by the richness of his tone. Playing with the strictly controlled Blakey band impacted his natural enthusiasm and the resulting tensions created some of the best hard-bop trumpet playing of the period. Indeed, despite the passage of time and the many fine trumpeters to have entered jazz in his wake, only a handful have attained Morgan's remarkable standards of emotional virtuosity. In the late 60s, Morgan's career was damaged for a while by personal problems, but a female friend helped him to recover. Unfortunately, this same woman became jealous of a new relationship he had formed and on 19 February 1972, she shot and killed him at the New York nightclub where his quintet was performing.

● ALBUMS: *Introducing Lee Morgan* (Savoy 1956)★★★, *Lee Morgan Indeed!* (Blue Note 1957)★★★, *Lee Morgan, Volume 2* (Blue Note 1957)★★★, *Lee Morgan, Volume 3* (Blue Note 1957)★★★★, with Donald Byrd, Hank Mobley *Hank Mobley With Donald Byrd And Lee Morgan* (Blue Note 1957)★★★, *City Lights* (Blue Note 1958)★★★★, *The Cooker* (Blue Note 1958)★★★★, *Candy* (Blue Note 1959)★★★★, *Lee-Way* (Blue Note 1960)★★★, *Here's Lee Morgan* (Vee Jay 1960)★★★, *Expoobident* (Vee Jay 1960)★★★, *Indestructible Lee* (Affinity 1960)★★★, *Take Twelve* (Jazzland 1962)★★★, *The Sidewinder* (Blue Note 1963)★★★★★, *Search For The New Land* (Blue Note 1964)★★★, *Tom Cat* (Blue Note 1964)★★★, *Cornbread* (Blue Note 1965)★★★★, *The Rumproller* (Blue Note 1965)★★★★, *Lee Morgan Quintet* (Vee Jay 1965)★★★, *The Gigolo* (Blue Note 1965)★★★★, *Cornbread* (Blue Note 1965)★★★, *Delightfulee Morgan* (Blue Note 1966)★★★, *Charisma* (Blue Note 1966)★★★, *The Rajah* (Blue Note 1966)★★★, *The Procrastinator* (Blue Note 1967)★★★★, *Caramba* (Blue Note 1968)★★★, *The Sixth Sense* (Blue Note 1969), *Live At The Lighthouse* (Fresh Sound 1970)★★★★, *Capra Beach* (1971)★★★, *Lee Morgan* (Blue Note 1972)★★★, *We Remember You* (Fresh Sound 1972)★★★, *Live At The Lighthouse* 3-CD reissue (Blue Note 1996)★★★★, *Standards* 1967 recording (Blue Note 1998)★★★.

● COMPILATIONS: *The Complete Fifties Blue Note Lee Morgan Sessions* 4-CD/6-LP box set (Mosaic 1996)★★★★★, *Jazz Profile* (Blue Note 1997)★★★★.

Morgan, Sam

b. 1887, Bertrandville, Louisiana, USA, d. 25 February 1936. Immensely popular in and around New Orleans, trumpeter Morgan's career was dogged by ill-health. Nevertheless, he achieved lasting fame thanks to some classic recordings made in 1927 that showed his to be a band of great style and attack, playing in the New Orleans manner. The band survived changing fashions but, following Morgan's second stroke, broke up in 1933. Morgan had two musical brothers: Isiah, who also played trumpet, and Al, who played bass with numerous bands including those of Cab Calloway, Fats Waller and Les Hite, and also worked with Louis Armstrong, Louis Jordan and Sabby Lewis.

● COMPILATIONS: with others *The Sound Of New Orleans* (1925-45)★★★★, *The Get Happy Band* (1927)★★★★, *Papa Celestin And Sam Morgan* (Azure 90s)★★★★.

Morris, Audrey

b. 12 November 1928, Chicago, Illinois, USA. Raised in Chicago, Morris studied piano as a child and would listen to the radio when she was supposed to be sleeping, hearing artists such as Fats Waller when he broadcast from the city's Sherman House Hotel. Her studies were at the American Conservatory of Music in Chicago, and she also studied with Mildred Davis. Although her piano playing was of a very high standard, she was sometimes cajoled into singing. Her initial reluctance to sing was eventually overcome and a significant part in this was played by Gene Gifford, who was writing arrangements for a band with which she was working. He insisted that she should sing and wrote an arrangement especially for her of a song made popular by Peggy Lee, 'What More Can A Woman Do?'. After her marriage to reed player Stu Genovese she abandoned band work and thereafter appeared on her own, singing and playing the piano. In the late 50s Morris appeared on Bobby Troup's television show, *Stars Of Jazz*, but was mainly active and very much in demand in Chicago's upper echelon supper clubs, including the London House. Her skills were also admired by musicians and she became friendly with Billy Strayhorn when the Duke Ellington band played the Cloister Inn in Chicago. In the mid-80s she sang on George Shearing's New York radio show. A 1996 engagement at Eighty-Eights in

Greenwich Village, where she initiated a series of evening performances paying homage to singer-pianist composers, led to her recording *Look At Me Now*. An outstanding interpreter of the great American Song Book, Morris sings with seemingly effortless command of music and lyric, her voice ageing with grace. Her self-accompaniment, a difficult art in itself, is highly accomplished. Although Morris is reluctant to place too much emphasis on influences, when pressed she has cited Lee in particular, but also Billie Holiday, Carmen McRae and Lee Wiley. As is apparent from her repertoire, which is replete with the great standards, Morris believes that lyrics are the most important thing in a song. However, she does not ignore latter-day songs, declaring, 'I don't agree that good songs are not being written nowadays, it's just that there aren't too many of them.'

● ALBUMS: *Bistro Ballads* (RCA 1954)★★★, *The Voice Of Audrey Morris* (Bethlehem 1956)★★★, *Afterthoughts* (Fancy Faire 1985)★★★, *Film Noir* (Fancy Faire 1989)★★★, *Look At Me Now* (Audiophile 1996)★★★★, *Roundabout* (Fancy Faire 1998)★★★.

MORRIS, BUTCH

b. Lawrence Morris, 10 February 1947, Long Beach, California, USA. Playing cornet on the west coast, Morris worked with bop tenor saxophonist J.R. Monterose, bassist George Morrow and *avant garde* players Frank Lowe and Don Moye as well as studying with well-known west coast mentors, Horace Tapscott and Bobby Bradford (which is where he first met his long-time associate David Murray). In 1975 he relocated to New York, playing free jazz in the Loft scene. From 1976-77 he lived in Paris, working with Lowe and bassist Alan Silva. In 1977 he joined Murray's seminal Octet, recording on *Ming*, *Home* and *Murray's Steps*. Morris developed what he called 'conduction', a method of leading improvisers with visual instructions, conducting the David Murray Big Band at Sweet Basil in 1984 (recorded for Black Saint). Meanwhile, Morris had also been recording his own music: *In Touch ... But Out Of Reach* was a 1978 live concert with a sextet that included trombonist Grachan Moncur III and drummer Steve McCall; *The New York City Artists' Collective Plays Butch Morris* had him conducting an eight-piece group, which featured vocalist Ellen Christi, through a set of his own pieces. In 1985 he recorded a free-improvisation record with guitarist Bill Horvitz (*Trios*) and 1988 saw the appearance of two albums featuring a trio of Morris, Wayne Horvitz and Robert Previte (*Nine Below*, *Todos Santos*), the latter album showcasing the compositions of pianist/singer Robin Halcomb. In 1986 he released *Current Trends In Racism In Modern America*, an innovative record in which he led 10 musicians (including Lowe, John Zorn, harpist Zeena Parkins and drummer Thurman Barker) through poignant, desolate and highly charged 'free-improvisations'. *Homeing* (1987) and *Dust To Dust* (1991) continued his search for a new method of assembling musicians drawn from both the black *avant garde* and white avant-rock circles. In a period where conservatism has become the normal approach, Morris has bravely taken steps to provide a part of the future.

● ALBUMS: *In Touch ... But Out Of Reach* 1978 recording (1982)★★★, with Wayne Horvitz and William Parker *Some Order Long Understood* (1982)★★★, *The New York City Artists' Collective Plays Butch Morris* (1984)★★★, with Bill Horvitz, J.A. Deane *Trios* (1985)★★, *Current Trends In Racism In Modern America* (Sound Aspects 1986)★★, *Homeing* (Sound Aspect 1988)★★★, with Robert Previte, Wayne Horvitz *Nine Below* (1988)★★★, with Previte, Wayne Horvitz *Todos Santos* (1988)★★, *Dust To Dust* (New World 1991)★★★, *Burning Cloud* (FMP 1993)★★★.

● COMPILATIONS: *Testament: A Conduction Collection* CD box set (New World/Cross Currents 1997)★★★★.

MORRIS, JOE

b. 1922, Montgomery, Alabama, USA, d. November 1958, Phoenix, Arizona, USA. Morris studied music at Alabama State Teachers' College, and toured with the college band led by the Trenier Twins. Heard by Lionel Hampton in Florida in 1942, Morris joined Hampton's Orchestra, where he became a valued writer/arranger as well as a trumpeter. He remained with Hampton until 1946, when he briefly joined Buddy Rich's band. After forming his own band towards the end of 1946, Morris went on to record for Manor, Atlantic, Decca and Herald, introducing new jazz and R&B stars such as Johnny Griffin, Elmo Hope, Matthew Gee, Percy Heath, Philly Joe Jones, Laurie Tate and Faye Adams. On the strength of his 'Blues Cavalcade', one of the first self-contained, touring R&B package shows, Morris had several hits including 'Any Time, Any Place, Anywhere' and 'Don't Take Your Love From Me' on Atlantic and, most notably, 'Shake A Hand' and 'I'll Be True' on Herald.

● ALBUMS: *Lowdown Baby* (1985)★★★, with Johnny Griffin *Fly Mister Fly* (1985)★★★, *You Be Me* (Soul Note 1997)★★★.

MORRIS, JOE

b. 1922, Montgomery, Alabama, USA, d. November 1958, Phoenix, Arizona, USA. Morris studied music at Alabama State Teachers' College, and toured with the college band led by the Trenier Twins. Heard by Lionel Hampton in Florida in 1942, Morris joined Hampton's Orchestra, where he became a valued writer/arranger as well as a trumpeter. He remained with Hampton until 1946, when he briefly joined Buddy Rich's band. After forming his own band towards the end of 1946, Morris went on to record for Manor, Atlantic, Decca and Herald, introducing new jazz and R&B stars such as Johnny Griffin, Elmo Hope, Matthew Gee, Percy Heath, Philly Joe Jones, Laurie Tate and Faye Adams. On the strength of his 'Blues Cavalcade', one of the first self-contained, touring R&B package shows, Morris had several hits including 'Any Time, Any Place, Anywhere' and 'Don't Take Your Love From Me' on Atlantic and, most notably, 'Shake A Hand' and 'I'll Be True' on Herald.

● ALBUMS: *Lowdown Baby* (1985)★★★, with Johnny Griffin *Fly Mister Fly* (1985)★★★, *You Be Me* (Soul Note 1997)★★★.

MORRIS, MARLOWE

b. 16 May 1915, New York, USA, d. *c*.1977. Morris became proficient on several instruments before settling on piano. In the mid- to late 30s he played with June Clark, then joined Coleman Hawkins in the early 40s. He was briefly in the army at the start of the US involvement in World War II, then returned to the New York scene where he was active with several leaders including Al Sears and Sid Catlett, performing in the latter's quartet with Ben Webster. He appeared in the short film *Jammin' The Blues* in 1944, and was briefly with Tiny Grimes before forming his own small group. By the end of 1946, however, he had dropped out of full-time music, returning at the end of the decade when he began to make a mark as an organist. He continued to play this instrument for most of the remaining years of his career. A good soloist and worthy accompanist, Morris played in a swing-rooted style, but his later work displayed an awareness of, if not a direct involvement in, the changes in jazz brought about by the advent of bop.

● ALBUMS: with Jimmy Rushing *If This Ain't The Blues* (Vanguard 1957)★★★, *Play The Thing* (Columbia 1961)★★★.

MORRISON, BARBARA

b. Ypsilanti, Michigan, USA. Raised in a suburb of Detroit, Morrison sang as a child, mostly in church. Success in a talent contest was rewarded with a scholarship to Eastern Michigan University. She continued to sing, gaining confidence with maturity and in 1973 moved to Southern California, teaming up with Eddie 'Cleanhead' Vinson with whose band she remained for a few years. Later, she toured the USA and Europe and also recorded with R&B legend Johnny Otis. In 1987 Morrison went solo, dividing her time between Los Angeles and Europe, where she developed a following thanks in part to her recordings made for the company owned by German jazz drummer Thilo Berg. In the mid-90s she was continuing this roving career, attracting the attention of a growing number of fans who include singer Dionne Warwick. Morrison sings in a ringing soul-inflected jazz style and her striking and exuberant personality shines through her voice.

● ALBUMS: *Doing All Right* (Mons 1992)★★★, *Blues For Ella* (Mons 1993)★★★★, *I'm Getting 'Long All Right* (Chartmaker 1997)★★★.

MORRISON, JAMES

b. James Lloyd Morrison, 11 November 1962, Sydney, Australia. Morrison was born into a musical family and at the age of seven started to play the cornet at school and in church. Within a year he was also playing other instruments, including trombone, tuba and saxophone. In 1971, with his brother John, he formed a band that played at local shopping centres. Morrison progressed to performing in various bands and in 1975 entered the New South Wales Conservatorium. A meeting with Don Burrows proved to be a decisive moment in Morrison's fledgling career. Burrows encouraged him to join his quartet, which was about to tour Australia and Asia. At the age of 17 Morrison made his debut American performance at the Monterey Jazz Festival. In 1982 he became Lecturer Of Jazz Studies at the NSW Conservatorium. The following year, with Burrows, Morrison made his featured recording debut on *At The Winery*. This displayed Morrison's technical virtuosity and personal flamboyance as a trumpet and trombone player. Another project, the Morrison Brothers Big Band, featured James and John with some of Sydney's most talented young musicians, they recorded an album and were featured in an ABC television special. With a flair for publicity, Morrison became a national television celebrity, performing instrumental theatrics, playing a dozen instruments, mountain climbing while playing his trumpet, car racing and playing trombone while flying an aircraft. Serious musical events included a 1986 Royal Command Performance and a five-month association with veteran trumpet player, Red Rodney. A well-received album, *Swiss Encounter - Live At The Montreux Jazz Festival*, enhanced Morrison's ever increasing international profile. In 1989 he played the trombone in the all-star international Philip Morris Superband. The following year Morrison's prodigious talents and fame inspired a feature film entitled *The Wizard Of Oz*. He also began touring with the veteran bass player Ray Brown and his trio. The outfit recorded *Snappy Doo* and the title tune became a successful single. In 1992 Morrison expanded his musical activities by performing in Brisbane with opera singer Joan Carden and the Queensland Symphony Orchestra. There was also an encore performance at the Royal Opera House in London's Covent Garden. The following year he recorded a Christmas album in the Berlin Opera House with the 70-piece RIAS Radio Orchestra and the Ray Brown Trio. In Australia, Morrison enjoyed the position of a national celebrity as a regular on television and radio; he also became an ubiquitous performer on the jazz and cabaret circuit with groups ranging from trios to big bands, always with an ever increasing arsenal of musical instruments. In October 1996 he travelled to Davenport, Iowa, USA, to perform a new work by Lalo Schifrin dedicated to Bix Beiderbecke. Playing Beiderbecke's own cornet, Morrison performed *A Rhapsody For Bix*, with the Quad Symphony Orchestra. Within a week of returning to Australia, he was recording a live album at Brisbane's Bass Note Restaurant. James Morrison is Australia's most popular and talented Australian jazz musician. He is virtuoso on trumpet and trombone, an excellent euphonium and tuba player and competent on piano and alto saxophone.

● ALBUMS: *A Night In Tunisia* (ABC 1984)★★★★, *James Morrison At The Winery* (ABC 1985)★★★, *Postcards From Down Under* (WEA 1988)★★★, *Swiss Encounter* (WEA 1988)★★★, *Snappy Doo* (WEA 1990)★★, *Two In The Max* (WEA 1991)★★★, *This Is Christmas* (WEA 1993)★★, *James Morrison And The Hot Horn Happening - Live In Paris.*(WEA 1994)★★★, *Live At The Sydney Opera House* (WEA 1995)★★★.

MORRISSEY, DICK

b. 9 May 1940, Horley, Surrey, England. A self-taught tenor saxophonist who is also adept on clarinet, flute and soprano saxophone, Morrissey became a professional musician at the end of his teens. In 1960 he played in a band led by Harry South and soon afterwards formed his own quartet with South, Phil Bates and Phil Seamen. He maintained a small band throughout the 60s, playing club engagements in the UK, backing visiting American jazzmen (including Jimmy Witherspoon) and making records. In the 70s Morrissey was deeply involved in jazz-rock, co-leading the highly respected band If, working with Herbie Mann, and recording with the Average White Band. The most important of the bands in this idiom with which he was associated was the excellent Morrissey-Mullen band he co-led with Jim Mullen. The band became one of the UK's best-known jazz-rock bands and remained in existence into the mid-80s, after which Morrissey returned to leading a more mainstream jazz-orientated group until cancer drastically curtailed his appearances.

● ALBUMS: *It's Morrissey, Man!* (1961)★★★, *Have You Heard?* (1963)★★★, *Jimmy Witherspoon At The Bull's Head* (1966)★★, *Storm Warning* (Mercury 1967)★★★★, *After Dark* (Coda 1983)★★★, *Resurrection Ritual* (Miles 1988)★★★, *Souliloquy* (Coda 1988)★★★. As Morrissey-Mullen *Up* (1977)★★★, *Cape Wrath* (Harvest 1979)★★★★, *Badness* (1981)★★★, *Life On The Wire* (1982)★★★, *It's About Time* (1983)★★★, *This Must Be The Place* (1985)★★★, *Happy Hour* (1988)★★★.

MORRISSEY-MULLEN

(see Morrissey, Dick; Mullen, Jim)

MORROW, BUDDY

b. Muni Zudecoff, 8 February 1919, New Haven, USA. Morrow, after graduating from Juilliard, began his prolific career as a sideman with the hotel bands of Eddy Duchin and Vincent Lopez. He developed into a jazzman in Vocalion sessions with Sharkey Bonano's Sharks Of Rhythm, a 1936 Eddie Condon Dixieland group. He reached swing band status with Artie Shaw the same year, under his real name then later as Muni Morrow (his adopted name). He joined Tommy Dorsey's trombone section in 1938 for 'Boogie Woogie' and 'Hawaiian War Chant', the next year playing with Paul Whiteman's Concert Orchestra in their Decca/Brunswick recording of Gershwin's 'Concerto In F'. He joined Tony Pastor in 1940 on his way to replacing Ray Conniff with the Bob Crosby band (1941). (The next year saw him in the US Navy, with a one-off Red McKenzie jazz session for Commodore producing, among others, 'Sweet Lorraine' and 'Talk Of The Town'). On demob Morrow played with Jimmy Dorsey for a while ('Jumping Jehosaphat') then moved into radio; conducting in the studios gave him a taste for leading, and RCA Victor decided to back him with his own band in 1951. His first minor hit was a crossover into R&B with 'Night Train', taken from Duke Ellington's 'Happy Go Lucky Local' by Jimmy Forrest, who had his own hit on United. There was little room for big bands in subsequent years, on singles at least, and after more minor hits with 'Man With The Golden Arm' and 'Dragnet', Morrow concentrated in the late 50s and early 60s on albums of standards for Mercury, Victor and Camden, not all of which were issued in the UK. He returned to studio work, emerging on occasion to front revivals of the Dorsey and Miller bands.

MORROW, GEORGE

b. George Washington Morrow, 15 August 1925, Pasadena, California, USA, d. 26 May 1992. Starting out on violin as a child, Morrow moved up in size of instrument as he grew up, passing through the cello and ending as a bass player. He studied formally and in the immediate post-war years, while resident in Los Angeles, played with many leading bop musicians. Among those jazzmen were Charlie Parker, Hampton Hawes and Teddy Edwards. In the late 40s, now settled in San Francisco, he accompanied many visiting artists including Billie Holiday and Dexter Gordon. He then became a member of the famed Clifford Brown-Max Roach quintet with whom he made several records, including 1954's *Brown And Roach Incorporated* and the following year's *A Study In Brown*, both released on the EmArcy label. He also recorded with Roach and Ray Bryant, as members of the Sonny Rollins Quartet. After Brown's death he stayed on with Roach's reformed band, then became a longtime accompanist to Anita O'Day. In the mid-70s he relocated to Florida, working at Disney World and accompanying visiting musicians. A strong player with a secure sense of time and great swing, Morrow's contribution to the bands in which he played is sometimes overlooked. However, the list of artists with whom he has played, of whom those named above are just a very small sample, indicate clearly the high regard in which he was held by his fellow musicians.

MORSE, ELLA MAE

b. 12 September, 1924, Mansfield, Texas, USA. A singer with an appealing jazz/blues style, Morse first sang with a band organized by her pianist mother and her father who was a drummer. At the age of 12 she was heard at a Houston Jam session by Jimmy Dorsey, who hired her as replacement for June Richmond. Her stay with Dorsey was a brief one, and she returned to Texas and sang with local bands. Subsequently she was heard singing in a San Diego club by Freddie Slack, who had been the pianist when she was with the Dorsey band. He signed her as the vocalist on his first Capitol recording session in 1942, which resulted in 'Cow Cow Boogie'. The record became a million-seller, and Morse had further hits in the 40s with 'Mr. Five By Five', 'Shoo Shoo Baby', 'Tess's Torch Song (If I Had A Man)', 'Milkman, Keep Those Bottles Quiet', 'The Patty Cake Man', 'Captain Kidd', 'Buzz Me', and 'House Of Blue Lights' (1946). She also appeared in a few minor films such as *Reveille With Beverly*, *Ghost Catchers*, *South Of Dixie*, and *How Do You Do It?* Morse retired for a time, but made a spectacular comeback in 1952 with another enormous hit, 'Blacksmith Blues', on which she was accompanied by Nelson Riddle and his orchestra. She continued to perform over the years, and was spotted in 1987 at Michael's Pub in New York with another 40s survivor, Nellie Lutcher.

● COMPILATIONS: *The Morse Code* (1957)★★★, *Sensational* 1951-57 recordings (Capitol 1986)★★★, *Barrel House, Boogie And The Blues* (Pathé Marconi 1984)★★★, *The Hits Of* (Pathé Marconi 1984)★★★, *Capitol Collectors* (Capitol 1992)★★★, *The Very Best Of* (Collectables 1998)★★★★.

MORTON, BENNY

b. 31 January 1907, New York City, New York, USA, d. 28 December 1985. Largely self-taught, Morton played trombone in bands in and around New York during his teenage years and by 1926 was sufficiently advanced to be hired by Fletcher Henderson. He subsequently played in bands led by Chick Webb, Don Redman and Count Basie; in 1940 he became a member of Teddy Wilson's superb sextet. He also made record dates with Billie Holiday. In 1943 he joined Edmond Hall's small group, then led his own band for a few years before becoming active in theatre pit bands in New York. In the 50s and 60s he was also busy in radio and recording studio bands, but occasionally turned up on record dates with artists such as Buck Clayton and Ruby Braff, and by the end of the 60s was mostly back on the jazz scene. He toured widely, playing in various bands including the Saints And Sinners package and outfits led by Wild Bill Davison, Bobby Hackett and Sy Oliver. A smooth and polished player with a relaxed and elegant style, Morton was one of the unsung heroes of the swing era.

● ALBUMS: with Buck Clayton, Ruby Braff *Buck Meets Ruby* (1954)★★★.

MORTON, JELLY ROLL

b. Ferdinand Joseph Lemott, 20 October 1890, New Orleans, Louisiana, USA, d. 10 July 1941, Los Angeles, California, USA. A gifted musician, Morton played various instruments before deciding to concentrate on piano. In the early years of the 20th century he was a popular figure on the seamier side of New Orleans nightlife. He played in brothels, hustled pool and generally lived the high-life. His reputation spread extensively, owing to tours and theatrical work in various parts of the Deep South and visits to Kansas City, Chicago, Los Angeles and other important urban centres. He also worked in Canada, Alaska and Mexico. From 1923 he spent five years based in Chicago, touring and recording with various bands, including the New Orleans Rhythm Kings and his own band, the Red Hot Peppers. He later worked with Fate Marable and W.C. Handy, and by the end of the 20s had moved to New York for residencies and more recording sessions. He also formed a big band, with which he toured throughout the east coast states. Various business ventures played a part in his life, often with disastrous financial consequences, but he remained musically active throughout the 30s, even though he was on the margins of the commercial success which many jazzmen enjoyed in that decade. During the 30s Morton moved to Washington, DC, where he made many recordings, also playing and reminiscing for Alan Lomax Snr. of the US Library of Congress. By 1940 his health was failing and he moved to Los Angeles, where he died in July 1941.

One of the major figures in jazz history and a significant musical conceptualist, in particular the role of the arranger, Morton's penchant for self-promotion worked against him and for many years critical perceptions of his true worth were blighted. Many of the recordings that he made during his stay in Chicago have proved to be classics, not least for the construction of those songs he composed and the manner in which they were arranged. Although some thought that carefully arranged music went contrary to the spirit of improvisation that was inherent in jazz, Morton's arrangements, to which he insisted his musicians should strictly adhere, inhibited neither soloists nor the ability of the ensembles to swing mightily. In his arrangements of the mid-20s, Morton foreshadowed many of the musical trends that only emerged fully a decade later as big band jazz became popular. Curiously, Morton failed to grasp the possibilities then open to him and preferred to concentrate on small group work at a time when popular trends were moving in the opposite direction. His compositions include many jazz standards, among them 'The Pearls', 'Sidewalk Blues', 'King Porter Stomp', 'Dead Man Blues', 'Grandpa's Spells', 'Doctor Jazz', 'Wolverine Blues', 'Black Bottom Stomp' and 'Mister Jelly Lord'. As a pianist, Morton's early work was ragtime-orientated, but unlike many of his contemporaries, he was able to expand the rather rigid concept of ragtime to incorporate emerging jazz ideas, and his later playing style shows a vital and often exhilarating grasp of many styles. It was, however, as an arranger that Morton made his greatest contribution and he can be regarded as the first significant arranger in jazz. Morton himself certainly never underestimated his own importance; quite the opposite, in fact, since he billed himself as the Originator of Jazz, Stomps and Blues. Shortly before his death he became involved in a mildly embarrassing public wrangle over the origins of the music, denying (rightly, of course) that W.C. Handy was the 'originator of jazz and the blues' and counterclaiming that he had created jazz in 1902. This outburst of self-aggrandizement was ridiculed and created an atmosphere in which few fans, critics or fellow musicians took his work seriously. By the early 50s, however, some more perceptive individuals began to reassess his contribution to jazz and this reappraisal gradually swelled into a tidal wave of critical acclaim. By the 70s musicians were eager to play Morton's music, and through into the 90s many concerts and recordings in the USA and UK have been dedicated to his achievements.

● ALBUMS: *New Orleans Memories* (Commodore 1950)★★★, *Peppers* (Jazz Panorama 1951)★★★, *The Saga Of Mr Jelly Lord*

Volumes 1-12 (Circle 1951)★★★, *Immortal Performances* (RCA Victor 1952)★★★, *Rediscovered Solos* (Riverside 1953)★★★, *First Recordings* (Riverside 1954)★★★, *Classic Jazz Piano Volumes 1 & 2* (Riverside 1954)★★★★, *Classic Piano Solos* (Riverside 1955)★★★, *The Incomparable Jelly Roll Morton* (Riverside 1956)★★★, *Mr Jelly Lord* (Riverside 1956)★★★, *Plays And Sings* (Riverside 1956)★★★, *Rags And Blues* (Riverside 1956)★★★, *Library Of Congress Recordings Volumes 1-12* (Riverside 1956)★★★★, *Mr Jelly Lord* (RCA Victor 1956)★★★, *Stomps And Joys* (RCA Victor 1965)★★★, *Jelly Roll Morton* (Mainstream 1965)★★★, *I Thought I Heard Buddy Bolden Say* (RCA Victor 1966)★★★, *Jelly Roll Morton Centennial: His Complete Victor Recordings* 1926-1939 recordings (Bluebird 1990)★★★★, *Rarities And Alternatives* 1923-1940 recordings (Suisa 1991)★★★, *Mr Jelly Lord* (Pickwick 1992)★★★, *Jelly Roll Morton: The Piano Rolls* (Nonesuch 1997)★★★★, *Last Sessions: The Complete General Recordings* (Commodore 1997)★★★★.

● FURTHER READING: *Mister Jelly Roll: The Fortunes Of Jelly Roll Morton, New Orleans Creole And 'Inventor Of Jazz'*, Alan Lomax. *Jelly Roll Morton*, M. Williams. *Jelly Roll, Jabbo, And Fats*, Whitney Balliett. *Jelly Roll Morton's Last Night At The Jungle Inn*, Samuel B. Charters.

Mosca, Sal

b. Salvatore Joseph Mosca, 27 April 1927, Mount Vernon, New York, USA. A student, disciple and close friend of Lennie Tristano, pianist Mosca has followed his mentor's example by recording and touring only rarely. In the 50s he did play on several Lee Konitz albums, and some sessions with Peter Ind later appeared on the bassist's Wave label. In the 70s Mosca again worked with Konitz and with Warne Marsh, toured Europe as a solo artist and played at the Lennie Tristano Memorial Concert in 1979. In the 80s he was seldom heard as a performer, but remained active as a teacher. A remarkably subtle player, with the sophisticated harmonic ear characteristic of Tristanoites, Mosca can disguise the chord changes of the best-known standard so cleverly that he makes it virtually unrecognizable, creating an entirely new tune in the process.

● ALBUMS: With Peter Ind *At The Den* 1959 recording (1969)★★★, *On Piano* 1955-59 recordings (1969)★★★★, *Sal Mosca Music* (1977)★★, *For You* (1979)★★, with others *Lennie Tristano Memorial Concert* (1979)★★★★, with Warne Marsh *How Deep, How High* 1977-79 recordings (1980)★★★, *Sal Mosca And Warne Marsh Quartet Vol 1* (Zinnia 1981)★★, *Sal Mosca And Wayne Marsh Quartet Vol 2* (Zinnia 1981)★★, *A Concert* 1979 recording (Jazz Records 1990)★★.

Moses, Bob

b. 28 January 1948, New York, USA. Moses grew up surrounded by musicians such as Charlie Mingus, for whom his father was press agent. Largely self-taught, he started to play drums when he was 10 years old and also played vibes in local Latin bands in his teens. He appeared with Rahsaan Roland Kirk in the mid-60s and formed Free Spirits with Larry Coryell, one of the first jazz-rock bands. After a short stay with Dave Liebman's Open Sky he joined Gary Burton. In the early 70s he formed Compost with Harold Vick (tenor) and Jack DeJohnette and toured the UK with the Mike Gibbs Orchestra before returning to the groups of Gary Burton and Pat Metheny. At this stage he was also writing for large ensembles and formed his own label - Mozown Records - to release the results. The music was recorded by all-star line-ups of New York musicians and was accorded great critical acclaim. In the 80s he played with the Steve Kuhn/Sheila Jordan Band (1979-82), George Gruntz Big Band and his own quintet. He is the author of the drum method *Drum Wisdom*. Moses makes personal use of a wide range of influences to create colourful, complex yet swinging music.

● ALBUMS: *Bittersweet In The Ozone* (Mozown 1975)★★★, *Home* (1979)★★★, *Family* (Sutra 1980)★★★, *When Elephants Dream Of Music* (Gramavision 1982)★★★, *Visits With The Great Spirit* (Gramavision 1983)★★★, *Wheels Of Coloured Light* (Open Minds 1983)★★★, *Story Of Moses* (Gala 1989)★★★, *Devotion* 1979 recording (Soul Note 1997)★★★.

Moses, J.C.

b. John Curtis Moses, 18 October 1936, Pittsburgh, Pennsylvania, USA, d. 1977. Moses began as a percussionist, learning congas and bongos, with drummer Paula Roberts. Between 1958 and 1960 he played with Walt Harper, then relocated to New York. His accurate, expansive timekeeping was embraced by the progressive jazz community, most notably Eric Dolphy, who used him on the sessions that produced the little-known masterpieces *Conversations* and *Iron Man* (1964). Other musical associates included pianists Cedar Walton and Herbie Hancock and bebop trumpeter Kenny Dorham. In 1963 he left for Europe with the short-lived New York Contemporary Five and later appeared on fellow-Fiver Archie Shepp's *Fire Music* (1965) and *On This Night* (1966). Between 1965 and 1967 he drummed with Roland Rahsaan Kirk. For the next two years he freelanced, playing with John Coltrane, Sonny Stitt, Jackie McLean, Hal Singer and singer Nancy Wilson. In 1969 he left for Denmark and became house drummer at the famous Cafe Montmartre in Copenhagen. As well as working with fellow expatriates Dexter Gordon and Kenny Drew, he accompanied Coleman Hawkins, Ben Webster, Ted Curson and Tete Monteliou, and also recorded with John Tchicai's Cadentia Nova Danica orchestra (*Afrodisiaca*, 1969). After 1970, problems with his kidneys limited his activities and he returned to Pittsburgh, where he played with Nathan Davis and Eric Kloss. His death in 1977, aged 41, deprived the world of a drummer who could relate both to New Thing iconoclasts and swing veterans.

● ALBUMS: with Eric Dolphy *Conversations* (1964)★★★, with Dolphy *Iron Man* (1964)★★★, *Archie Shepp & The New York Contemporary Five* (1963)★★.

Mosley, Snub

b. Lawrence L. Mosley, 29 December 1905, Little Rock, Arkansas, USA, d. 21 July 1981. Starting out on trombone, in the 20s Mosley joined in the popular territory band led by Alphonso Trent. Noted for his aggressive, attacking style, Mosley was dissatisfied with what he saw as the limitations of the trombone and invented his own instrument. This was a slide saxophone, which he thereafter preferred to a more orthodox instrument, although he still continued to play trombone. Leaving Trent in 1933, Mosley worked with some of the best-known bands of the period, including those led by Claude Hopkins, Fats Waller and Louis Armstrong. He also tried his hand at bandleading, but while he worked steadily throughout the 40s and into the 50s, accommodating shifts in musical tastes by playing and singing R&B, he never made the breakthrough to nationwide success. In the late 70s he became a popular figure on the international club and festival scene.

● ALBUMS: *Snub Mosley Live At The Pizza Express* (1978)★★★.

Moss, Danny

b. 16 August 1927, Redhill, Surrey, England. By the late 40s tenor saxophonist Moss had established a reputation as an outstanding musician and was hired by many of the leading UK jazz and dance bands of the day, including those of Ted Heath, Oscar Rabin, Vic Lewis, John Dankworth and Humphrey Lyttelton. From the early 60s Moss led his own small groups, touring the UK and sometimes working with fellow UK musicians such as Sandy Brown and Dave Shepherd. Additionally, he was in great demand as an accompanist and featured soloist with visiting American artists, most notably with a succession of leading singers that included Ella Fitzgerald, Sarah Vaughan and Rosemary Clooney. In 1990 Moss, whose wife is singer Jeannie Lambe, took up residence in Australia. In the summer of the same year he was awarded an MBE in the Queen's Birthday Honours List. A committed jazzman, Moss's distinctive playing style shows him to be at ease whether on up-tempo swingers, where his full-bodied sound is a delight, or on soulful ballads to which he brings great emotional depth.

● ALBUMS: *Danny Moss Quintet With Strings* (1966)★★★, *The Good Life* (1968)★★★, *Straighten Up And Fly Right* (1979)★★, *Danny Moss Quartet With Geoff Simkins* (1979)★★★, *Jeannie Lambe* (1980)★★★★, with Lambe *Blues And All That Jazz* (1982)★★★, with Simpkins *Danny Moss And Geoff Simpkins Vol 2* (Flyright 1982)★★★, with Lambe *The Midnight Sun* (1984)★★★, *Weaver Of Dreams* (Nagel-Heyer 1995)★★★★, with Buddha's Gamblers *A Swingin' Affair* (Nagel-Heyer 1998)★★★, *Three Great Concerts* 1995 recordings (Nagel-Heyer 1998)★★.

Moten, Bennie

b. 13 November 1894, Kansas City, Missouri, USA, d. 2 April 1935. In his youth, Moten gained a substantial reputation in and around his home-town as a pianist; by 1920 he had become an established and respected bandleader. His unit, originally a small outfit, gradually expanded until it was a big band ready to take advantage of the upsurge in interest in this kind of ensemble. As a pianist and an accomplished arranger, Moten deftly blended New Orleans concepts into the freewheeling style popular in the Midwest. Beginning its recording career in 1923, the band built a reputation far afield, and residencies in New York followed. Moten attracted many excellent musicians until his was the outstanding band of the region. Some of the best men were poached from Walter Page's Blue Devils, among them Bill (not yet Count) Basie, Oran 'Hot Lips' Page, Eddie Durham and Jimmy Rushing. Eventually, Walter Page went along, too. Later additions to the band included Ben Webster, Herschel Evans, Eddie Barefield and Lester Young. By the mid-30s the band was not merely the finest in the region, but was superior to many of the headline bands in the east and elsewhere. In 1935 the unit visited Chicago to audition for a residency at the Grand Terrace Ballroom. When they headed for home Moten remained behind for a tonsillectomy and died when the surgeon's knife slipped and severed his jugular vein. The band subsequently broke up, but later, many of the musicians regrouped under the leadership of Buster Smith and Basie, and later still the band became Basie's. As the leader of an outstanding band, Moten occupies an important position in the history of Kansas City jazz, even if he was understandably overshadowed by his musical legatees.

● COMPILATIONS: with Count Basie *Count Basie In Kansas City* 1929-1932 recordings (Camden 1959)★★★★, *The Complete Bennie Moten Vols 1/2, 3/4, 5/6* (RCA 1923-32 recordings)★★★★.

Mother Earth

Matt Deighton (vocals, guitar), Neil Corcoran (bass guitar), Chris White (drums), Bryn Barklam (Hammond organ). The UK's 'acid jazz' craze gained momentum in the mid-80s, when the original Acid Jazz label began to capitalize on the swelling interest in jazz, by encouraging a series of crossover bands who were mixing the music with funk and creating a danceable but harmonically rich, essentially live sound. As more and more London musicians began looking to the 70s, and projects led by Herbie Hancock, Billy Cobham or Lonnie Liston Smith, for inspiration, Mother Earth came together in 1990, originally as a six-piece, with additional vocalists Shauna Greene and Bunny. Their first recordings – '5th Quadrant' and 'Riot On 103rd Street' on the *Totally Wired 6* and *Totally Wired 7* Acid Jazz compilations – swiftly gained the group a cult popularity and a contract with the label. A funky, Hammond organ-led affair very much in the jazz funk mould, *Stoned Woman* was released in 1992, and the band quickly followed up with a hectic tour schedule, establishing a trendy, retro stage image heavy on flared trousers and sheepskin. If *Stoned Woman* suffered from an occasional blandness and lack of musical direction, Mother Earth tightened things up in 1994, with the release of *The People Tree*. Harder and funkier, with catchier tunes, *The People Tree* featured guest appearances by Paul Weller and popular Acid Jazz percussionist Snowboy, and represented a significant change in direction for the band, who were now looking towards 70s funk rock for a tougher, Santana-influenced sound. Deighton released a wistful solo set, *Villager*, before

Mother Earth bowed out with another strong collection, *You Have Been Watching*. One of Acid Jazz's more interesting acts, Mother Earth's vocalist Deighton can now be found playing guitar in Paul Weller's touring band.

● ALBUMS: *Stoned Woman* (Acid Jazz 1992)★★★, *The People Tree* (Acid Jazz 1994)★★★★, *You Have Been Watching* (Focus 1995)★★★★.

MOTIAN, PAUL

b. 25 March 1931, Providence, Rhode Island, USA. Motian played guitar in Providence in his teens, then served a term in the US army. On his discharge in 1954 he went to New York to study music at the Manhattan School. By 1956 he was playing drums for George Wallington and Russell Jacquet. Between 1956 and 1958 he worked with Tony Scott, with whom he met the pianist Bill Evans. His work in the Evans trio (1959-64) has since achieved legendary status for its delicacy and balance. Motian also played with Oscar Pettiford, Zoot Sims and Lennie Tristano in the late 50s. In the mid-60s he worked with singers Mose Allison and Arlo Guthrie and was part of the Paul Bley trio in 1964. Motian had met Ornette Coleman's bassist Charlie Haden in 1959 and had a chance to work with him in Keith Jarrett's band with Dewey Redman (1967-76); he also joined Haden's Liberation Music Orchestra for its debut recording in 1969 and toured with the re-formed Orchestra in the 80s. In the 70s he was active in the Jazz Composers' Orchestra and played on Carla Bley's *Escalator Over The Hill* in 1972. He emerged as a leader in 1974, since which time he has released an impressive series of albums on the ECM, Soul Note and JMT labels that have confirmed his stature as a drummer and composer. *Tribute* (1974) featured Carlos Ward on alto, while *Dance* and *Le Voyage* from the late 70s boast rare appearances by saxophonist Charles Brackeen. In the 80s he began long-term associations with guitarist Bill Frisell, whose arching, tremulous interpretations of Motian's melodies are particularly sympathetic, and the inventive tenorist Joe Lovano. In the late 80s he renewed his acquaintance with Paul Bley on a marvellous album of improvised duets (*Notes*), and joined with Haden and pianist Geri Allen to form one of the most thoughtful of contemporary piano trios; a guest appearance with Marilyn Crispell's trio (*Live In Zurich*, 1991) proved he was also at home in more exploratory modes. Motian's examination of Thelonious Monk (*Monk In Motian*), standards (*Motian On Broadway*) and his pianoless tribute to Bill Evans (1991) show a questing musical mind, still working as keenly as ever. He recorded with his Electric Bebop band in the 90s, which included Steve Swallow and Don Alias.

● ALBUMS: *Conception Vessel* (ECM 1974)★★★, *Tribute* (ECM 1974)★★★, *Dance* (1977)★★★, *Le Voyage* (ECM 1979)★★★★, *Psalm* (ECM 1982)★★★★, *The Story Of Maryam* (ECM 1984)★★★, *It Should've Happened A Long Time Ago* (ECM 1985)★★★★, *Jack Of Clubs* (ECM 1985)★★★, *Misterioso* (Soul Note 1986)★★★★, with Paul Bley *Notes* (1987)★★★★, with Geri Allen, Charlie Haden *Etudes* (1988)★★★, *Monk In Motian* (JMT 1988)v, *Paul Motian On Broadway Vol 1* (JMT 1989)★★★, with Allen, Haden *In The Year Of The Dragon* (1989)★★★, with Allen, Haden *Segments* (1989)★★★, *One Time Out* (Soul Note 1990)★★★, *Paul Motian On Broadway Vol 2* (JMT 1990)★★, *Motian In Motian* (JMT 1989)★★★★, *Bill Evans* (JMT 1991)★★★, with Allen, Haden *Live At The Village Vanguard* (1991)★★★★, *Motian In Tokyo* (JMT 1992)★★★, *On Broadway Vol. 3* (JMT 1992)★★★, *And The Electric Bebop Band* (JMT 1992)★★★, with Keith Jarrett, Gary Peacock *At The Deer Head Inn* (ECM 1994)★★★, *Trioism* (JMT 1994)★★★, *Reincarnation Of A Love Bird* (JMT 1995)★★★, *At The Village Vanguard* (Verve 1996)★★★★, with Marilyn Crispell, Gary Peacock *Nothing Ever Was, Anyway: Music Of Annette Peacock* (ECM 1997)★★★★, *Sound Of Love* (Winter & Winter 1998)★★★, *2000 + One* (Edel 1998)★★★★, *You Took The Words Right Out Of My Heart* 1995 recording (JMT 1998)★★★★, with Gary Peacock, Martial Solal *Just Friends* (Dreyfus 1998)★★★★.

MOTLEY, FRANK

b. 30 December 1923, Cheraw, South Carolina, USA. Motley learned the rudiments of trumpet playing from Dizzy Gillespie and soon developed a novelty technique of playing two trumpets simultaneously, thereafter being known by the nicknames of 'Dual Trumpet' and 'Two Horn' Motley. After navy service, he studied music at Chicago and Washington, DC, and formed his own band in 1949. The Motley Crewe included drummer T.N.T. Tribble and recorded for Lilian Claiborne who placed masters with Gotham, RCA Victor, Specialty, Gem, DC, Big Town, Hollywood and many small labels. In the mid-50s, with the advent of rock 'n' roll, Motley married and moved north to Toronto, Canada, where he continued to play and perform until 1984 when he retired to Durham, North Carolina.

● ALBUMS: *Frank Motley* (1986)★★★, with T.N.T. Tribble *The Best Of Washington D.C. R&B* (1991)★★★.

MOUND CITY BLUE BLOWERS

Formed in 1924 by Red McKenzie as a novelty group, the Mound City Blue Blowers expanded to include Eddie Lang, with whom they visited London in the mid-20s. Later the band became a more orthodox, and often much larger, Dixieland outfit under McKenzie's leadership. In its bigger form the band was occasionally home in the late 20s to leading musicians such as Eddie Condon, Gene Krupa, Glenn Miller and Jack Teagarden. McKenzie continued to record under this collective title into the mid-30s, using artists including Yank Lawson, Bob Haggart, Dave Tough and Bunny Berigan. Although the band's first record, 'Arkansas Blues', in 1924, was its biggest seller, the finest jazz performance came at a 1929 session featuring Coleman Hawkins, which included 'Hello Lola' and the classic '(If I Could Be With You) One Hour (Tonight)'.

● COMPILATIONS: *Mound City Blue Blowers 1935-1937* (Timeless 1996)★★★★.

MOUZON, ALPHONSE

b. 21 November 1948, Charleston, South Carolina, USA. Mouzon started playing when he was four years old and was taught drums at high school. He relocated to New

York when he was 17 and in 1969 played in the Broadway musical *Promises, Promises*. He released his first record in the same year, with Gil Evans. He freelanced for a time before playing with Weather Report in 1971, McCoy Tyner (1972-73), Larry Coryell's Eleventh House (1973-75) and in a trio with Albert Mangelsdorff and Jaco Pastorius. After that Mouzon again freelanced until he joined Herbie Hancock in the late 70s. Later recordings such as *Early Spring* (1988) and *The Survivor* (1992) edged towards smooth mainstream jazz, alienating some fans and critics. In 1996 he released a new album and landed a small part in the Tom Hanks movie *That Thing You Do*. Mouzon tries to bring 'jazz polyrhythms to a rock pulse' and in this he succeeds, with his furiously propulsive drumming which is as welcome in a rock setting as in straight jazz.

● ALBUMS: *Gil Evans* (1969)★★★, *Funky Snakefoot* (1973)★★★, *Mind Transplant* (RPM 1975)★★, with Albert Mangelsdorff, Jaco Pastorius *Trilogue-Live* (1976)★★★★, *In Search Of A Dream* (MPS 1981)★★★, *Back To Jazz* (L&R 1986)★★★, *Early Spring* (1988)★★★, *The Survivor* (1992)★★, *The Night Is Still Young* (Tenacious 1996)★★★.

● COMPILATIONS: *Best Of Alphonse Mouzon* (Black Sun 1989)★★★★.

● FILMS: *That Thing You Do* (1996).

Moye, Famoudou Don

b. 23 May 1946, Rochester, New York, USA. Moye studied at Wayne State University, Detroit, and, with trumpeter Charles Moore, participated in the Detroit Free Jazz Artists' Workshop, where he met Joseph Jarman. In 1968 Moye began touring Europe and Morocco with Detroit Free Jazz, playing also with Steve Lacy in Rome, North Africa and Paris, where he joined the Art Ensemble Of Chicago in 1969. Since then most of his work has been with the Ensemble, and with the group he co-leads with Jarman, and with the Leaders, an all-star post-bop group featuring alto saxophonist Arthur Blythe, trumpeter Lester Bowie, tenor saxophonist Chico Freeman, pianist Kirk Lightsey and bassist Cecil McBee. He has also worked with the Gospel Messenger Singers, Sonny Sharrock, Dave Burrell, Gato Barbieri, Pharoah Sanders, Randy Weston and Alan Shorter, and in 1989 replaced Phil Wilson in Lester Bowie's Brass Fantasy.

● ALBUMS: *Sun Percussion* (AECO 1975)★★★★, with Joseph Jarman *Egwu-Anwu* (India Navigation 1978)★★★, with Jarman, Don Pullen *The Magic Triangle* (Black Saint 1979)★★★★, with Jarman *Black Paladins* (Black Saint 1980)★★★, with Donald Rafael Garrett, Craig Harris, Jarman *Earth Passage - Density* (Black Saint 1981)★★★, with the Leaders *Mudfoot* (Black Hawk 1986)★★★, with the Leaders *Out Here Like This* (Black Saint 1987)★★, with the Leaders Trio *Heaven Dance* (Sunnyside 1988)★★, with the Leaders *Unforseen Blessings* (Black Saint 1989)★★★, *Jam For Your Life* 1983-1991 recordings (AECO 1997)★★★★.

Mraz, George

b. Jiří Mraz, 9 September 1944, Písek, Czechoslovakia. A gifted musician as a child, Mraz studied formally at the music conservatory in Prague. Although skilled on several instruments, he settled eventually on the bass. He worked in his homeland and in Germany, then in 1968 emigrated to the USA. He entered Berklee College Of Music for further studies, after which he played with Dizzy Gillespie, Oscar Peterson and other leading jazzmen. In New York in the mid-70s he became a member of the Thad Jones-Mel Lewis Jazz Orchestra and also recorded with Stan Getz, Pepper Adams, Zoot Sims, Charles Mingus, Stéphane Grappelli and in duos with Walter Norris and his fellow Jones-Lewis rhythm section-mate, Roland Hanna. Towards the end of the decade he worked with the New York Jazz Quartet and with John Abercrombie. By the 80s Mraz, who became an American citizen in 1973, was established as a major force among jazz bass players. Constantly in demand, Mraz has supported Hank Jones and Joe Henderson on recent tours. In 1995 he found the time to record his first US release as a leader, the aptly named *Jazz*., featuring pianist Richie Beirach and drummer Billy Hart.

● ALBUMS: with Adam Makowicz *Classic Jazz Duets* (Stash 1979)★★★★, *Catching Up* (Alfa 1991)★★★, with Makowicz *Adam Makowicz/George Mraz* (Concord Jazz 1993)★★★, *Jazz* (Milestone 1995)★★★★, with the Keystone Trio *Heartbeats* (Milestone 1996)★★★, with Roy Haynes, Hank Jones *Flowers For Lady Day* (Evidence 1996)★★★, *My Foolish Heart* (Milestone 1997)★★★, *Bottom Lines* (Milestone 1997)★★★★, with the Keystone Trio *Newklear Music: The Songs Of Sonny Rollins* (Milestone 1997)★★★.

Mseleku, Bheki

b. 1955, Durban, South Africa. Proper recognition of this fine multi-instrumentalist's (piano, composer, vocals, saxophone, guitar) jazz talents seemed long overdue, but since 1991 this modest and dignified performer has been very much in the limelight, touring internationally and releasing an album annually. One of a number of supremely talented improvising musicians who have left South Africa and its oppressive apartheid system to take up residence in London, Mseleku made the move relatively recently, touring out of South Africa in the late 70s, moving to Sweden in 1980 and finally settling in London in 1985. A Ronnie Scott's club debut in 1987, with some of the more prominent figures from London's jazz revival, including Courtney Pine and Cleveland Watkiss, did much to bring his talents to the notice of the local scene, and helped pave the way for *Celebration* - a star-studded, major label debut featuring London-based musicians Pine, Steve Williamson, Eddie Parker and Jean Toussaint and a high-power American rhythm section comprising Michael Bowie and Marvin 'Smitty' Smith. A lively and enthusiastic record, it mixed gentle, township-inspired compositions with modal, post-John Coltrane burnouts, and was marked by a hectic touring campaign and a deserved nomination for British Mercury Music Prize for Album Of The Year. After the media furore had died down, Mseleku resumed the solo performances in which he excels, accompanying overtly spiritual and dedicatory vocal-lines with gently rocking, township-inspired piano voicings, and punctuating the whole with sparkling, McCoy Tyner-style runs and one-handed riffs on the tenor saxophone. *Meditations*, a live recording from the Bath International Music Festival, captured this absorbing style on two long tracks. Signing to the Verve/PolyGram label at the end of 1993, Mseleku's *Timelessness* found him in the company of some top American heavyweights, including Joe Henderson, Pharoah Sanders, Abbey Lincoln and Elvin Jones, and was accompanied by more media furore.

● ALBUMS: *Celebration* (World Circuit 1992)★★★, *Meditations* (1993)★★★★, *Timelessness* (Verve 1994)★★★, *Star Seeding* (Verve 1996)★★★, *Beauty Of Sunrise* (Verve 1997)★★★★.

Muhammad, Idris

b. Leo Morris, 13 November 1939, New Orleans, Louisiana, USA. Immaculate, imaginative and equally at home on contemporary jazz and more popular funk and soul sessions, Idris Muhammad is one of America's most impressive and swinging drummers. Playing since the age of eight, he began working professionally in the soul scene in the early 60s, accompanying vocalists Jerry Butler, Sam Cooke and the Impressions. The gifted bebop alto saxophonist Lou Donaldson hired Muhammad for his soul-jazz group in 1965, and work with guitarist George Benson followed. In the early 70s, Muhammad became house drummer for the Prestige label, again playing mainly an unadventurous soul/jazz that offered him little room to stretch out and take advantage of his talents. Spells with Roberta Flack followed, but by the end of the 70s, Muhammad was able to put together his own band and started concentrating on modern jazz. Toward the end of the decade he joined hard-bop tenor saxophonist Johnny Griffin, and then began a celebrated spell with another tenor saxophonist, Pharoah Sanders. He continues to work intermittently with Sanders, and recently toured internationally and recorded with an all-star saxophone-orientated band that included Chico Freeman, Arthur Blythe, Sam Rivers and pianist Don Pullen. He also records as the Keystone Trio with John Hicks and George Mraz.

● ALBUMS: *Black Rhythm Revolution* (Prestige 1971)★★, *Peace And Rhythm* (Prestige 1971)★★★, *Power Of Soul* (Kudu 1975)★★★, *Kabsha* (Theresa 1980)★★★★, *My Turn* (Lipstick 1993)★★, with the Keystone Trio *Heartbeats* (Milestone 1996)★★★, with the Keystone Trio *Newklear Music: The Songs Of Sonny Rollins* (Milestone 1997)★★★, *Right Now* (Cannonball 1998)★★★★.

Mujician

(see Levin, Tony; Rogers, Paul; Tippett, Keith)

Mullen, Jim

b. 26 November 1945, Glasgow, Scotland. After starting out on guitar while he was still a small child, Mullen switched to bass in his early teens. He played in various dance bands in his home-town before forming his own trio and reverting to guitar. At the end of the 60s he relocated to London and moved into R&B. In the early 70s he was frequently associated with jazz-rock and other fusion bands including Paz, the Average White Band, Kokomo (UK) and Herbie Mann's group. He also formed a group with Dick Morrissey, Morrissey-Mullen, which became one of the best-known jazz-rock bands in the UK. The band remained in existence until 1985, after which Mullen led his own small bands. Towards the end of the decade he occasionally appeared again with Morrissey, performing at jazz festivals throughout the UK. A dynamic and forceful player, Mullen's years in jazz-rock and his deep affinity with the blues give his music a quality of earthy excitement.

● ALBUMS: *Thumbs Up* (Coda 1984)★★★, *Into The 90s* (Castle 1990)★★★, *Soundbites* (EFZ 1993)★★★. As Morrissey-Mullen *Up* (1977)★★★★, *Cape Wrath* (Harvest 1979)★★★★, *Badness* (1981)★★★, *Life On The Wire* (1982)★★★, *It's About Time* (1983)★★★, *This Must Be The Place* (1985)★★★, *Happy Hour* (1988)★★★.

Mulligan, Gerry

b. 6 April 1927, New York City, New York, USA, d. 19 January 1996, Darien, Connecticut, USA. Raised in Philadelphia, Mulligan started out on piano before concentrating on arranging. He also took up the saxophone, first the alto and a few years later the baritone. Among the name bands that used his arrangements were those led by Gene Krupa and Claude Thornhill and he occasionally played in their reed sections. While writing for Thornhill he met and began a musical association with fellow-arranger Gil Evans. In New York in 1948 Mulligan joined Evans and Miles Davis, for whom he wrote and played, by now almost exclusively on baritone. In the early 50s Mulligan led his own groups but continued to arrange on a freelance basis. In this capacity his work was performed by Stan Kenton (these charts also being performed in the UK by Vic Lewis). In 1952 Mulligan began a musical association that not only attracted critical acclaim but also brought him widespread popularity with audiences. This came about through the formation with Chet Baker of a quartet that was unusual for the absence of a piano. When Baker quit in 1953, Mulligan subsequently led other quartets, notably with Bob Brookmeyer in the mid-50s. Although the quartet format dominated Mulligan's work during this part of his career he occasionally formed larger groups and early in the 60s formed his Concert Jazz Band. This band was periodically revived during the decade and beyond. He interspersed this with periods of leading groups of various sizes, working and recording with other leaders, including Dave Brubeck, in frequently rewarding partnerships with musicians such as Paul Desmond, Stan Getz, Johnny Hodges, Zoot Sims and Thelonious Monk, and writing arrangements on a freelance basis. In the early 70s Mulligan led big bands, some of which used the name Age Of Steam, and small groups for worldwide concert tours, recording sessions and radio and television appearances. The 80s and early 90s saw him following a similar pattern, sometimes expanding the size of the big band, sometimes content to work in the intimate setting of a quartet or quintet. As an arranger, Mulligan was among the first to attempt to adapt the language of bop for big band and achieved a measure of success with both Krupa (who recalled for George T. Simon that Mulligan was 'a kind of temperamental guy who wanted to expound a lot of his ideas'), and Thornhill. For all the variety of his later work, in many ways his music, as writer and performer, retains the colours and effects of his 50s quartets. In these groups Mulligan explored the possibilities of scoring and improvising jazz in a low-key, seemingly subdued manner. In fact, he thoroughly exploited the possibilities of creating interesting and complex lines that always retained a rich, melodic approach. His classic compositions from the 50s, including 'Night At The Turntable', 'Walkin' Shoes', 'Venus De Milo', 'Soft Shoe' and 'Jeru', and his superb arrangements for 'Bernie's Tune', 'Godchild' and others, helped to establish the sound and style of the so-called 'cool school'. The intimate styling favoured in such settings was retained in his big-band work and his concert band recordings from the 60s retained interest not only for their own sake, but also for the manner in which they contrasted with most other big-band writing of the same and other periods. As a player, the lightness of touch Mulligan used in his writing was uniquely brought to the baritone saxophone, an instrument that in other, not always lesser, hands sometimes overpowers the fragility of some areas of jazz. It is hard to see in Mulligan's work, whether as writer or performer, a clearly discernible influence. Similarly, despite the enormous popularity he enjoyed over more than five decades, few, if any, writers or players seem to have adopted him as a role model. At the least, this must be something to regret and maybe in time his contribution to jazz, especially in the pioneering decade of the 50s will be seen as 'great'.

● ALBUMS: *Gerry Mulligan* 10-inch album (Prestige 1951)★★★★, *Mulligan Plays Mulligan* (Prestige 1951)★★★★, *Jazz Superstars* (1952)★★★, *The Gerry Mulligan Quartet With Chet Baker* (Pacific 1952-53)★★★★, with Lee Konitz *Konitz Meets Mulligan* 10-inch album (Pacific Jazz 1953)★★★, *Gerry Mulligan And His Ten-tette* 10-inch album (Capitol 1953)★★★, *The Fabulous Gerry Mulligan Quartet: Paris Concert 1954* (Vogue 1954)★★★★, *Gerry Mulligan And His Quartet, Featuring Guests Zoot Sims And Bob Brookmeyer: California Concerts* (World Pacific 1954)★★★, *California Concerts Vols 1 & 2* (Pacific Jazz 1955)★★★, *Presenting The Gerry Mulligan Sextet* (EmArcy 1955)★★★★, *Gerry Mulligan Live In Stockholm* (1955)★★★, *The Original Gerry Mulligan Quartet* (Pacific Jazz 1955)★★★★, *Mainstream Of Jazz* (EmArcy 1955)★★★, *The Vibes Are On* (Chazzer 1955)★★★, *Paris Concert* (Pacific Jazz 1956)★★★★, *Recorded Live In Boston At Storyville* (Pacific Jazz 1956)★★★, *Lee Konitz With The Gerry Mulligan Quartet* (Pacific Jazz 1956)★★★★, with Paul Desmond *Gerry Mulligan Quartet/Paul Desmond Quintet* (Fantasy 1956)★★★★, *Gerry Mulligan, The Arranger* (Columbia 1957)★★★, *Quartet Live In Stockholm* (Moon 1957)★★★, *The Mulligan Songbook* (World Pacific 1957)★★★, with Desmond *Blues In Time* (Fantasy 1957)★★★★, with Thelonious Monk *Mulligan Meets Monk* (Riverside 1957)★★★★, with Monk *Alternate Takes* (1957)★★★, *Gerry Mulligan With Vinnie Burke's String Jazz Quartet* (Pacific Jazz 1957)★★★, *At Storyville* (Pacific Jazz 1957)★★★★, with Chet Baker *Reunion With Baker* (Pacific Jazz 1957)★★★, with Teddy Wilson *The Teddy Wilson Trio And The Gerry Mulligan Quartet At Newport* (Verve 1958)★★★★, *I Want To Live* (United Artists 1958)★★★, with Desmond *The Gerry Mulligan-Paul Desmond Quartet* (Verve 1958)★★★★, with Annie Ross *Annie Ross Sings A Song With Mulligan!* (World Pacific 1958)★★★, with Stan Getz *Getz Meets Gerry Mulligan In Hi-Fi* (Verve 1958)★★★★, *What Is There To Say?* (Columbia 1959)★★★★★, with Ben Webster *Gerry Mulligan Meets Ben Webster* (Verve 1959)★★★★★, *A Profile Of Gerry Mulligan* (Mercury 1959)★★★, *The Subterraneans: Original Soundtrack* (MGM 1959)★★★, *Gerry Mulligan And The Concert Band On Tour* (1960)★★★, *New York-December 1960* (Jazz Anthology 1960)★★★, *Gerry Mulligan And The Concert Jazz Band* (Verve 1960)★★★, *Nightwatch* (United Artists 1960)★★★, *Mulligan* Columbia 1960)★★★, with Johnny Hodges *Gerry Mulligan Meets Johnny Hodges* (Verve 1960)★★★, *Gerry Mulligan Presents A Concert In Jazz* (Verve 1961)★★★, *Gerry Mulligan And The Concert Jazz Band Live At The Village Vanguard* (Verve 1961)★★★★, with Judy Holliday *Holliday With Mulligan* (DRG 1961)★★★, *The Gerry Mulligan Quartet* (Verve 1962)★★★, *Jeru* (Columbia 1962)★★★★, *Gerry Mulligan And The Concert Jazz Band Presents A Concert In Jazz* (Verve 1962)★★★, with Paul Desmond *Two Of A Mind* (RCA Victor 1962)★★★★★, *Gerry Mulligan And The Concert Jazz Band On Tour With Guest Soloist Zoot Sims* (Verve 1962)★★★, *Blues In Time* (Verve 1962)★★★, *Historically Speaking* (Prestige 1963)★★★, *Timeless* (Pacific Jazz 1963)★★★, *Gerry Mulligan '63-The Concert Jazz Band* (Verve 1963)★★★, *Spring Is Sprung* (Philips 1963)★★★, *Night Lights* (Philips 1963)★★★, *The Essential Gerry Mulligan* (Verve 1964)★★★, *Butterfly With Hiccups* (Limelight 1964)★★★, *If You Can't Beat 'Em, Join Em'* (Limelight 1965)★★★, with Kai Winding and Red Rodney *Broadway* (Status 1965)★★★, *The Gerry Mulligan Quintet* (1965)★★★, *Feelin' Good* (Limelight 1965)★★★, *Gerry Mulligan Meets Zoot Sims* (1966)★★★, *Gerry's Time* (Verve 1966)★★★, *Something Borrowed Something Blue* (Limelight 1966)★★★, *Concert Days* (Sunset 1966)★★★, *Gerry Mulligan With The Dave Brubeck Quartet* (1968)★★★, *Live In New Orleans* (1968)★★★, *The Age Of Steam* (A&M 1971)★★★★, *The Shadow Of Your Smile* (Moon 1971)★★★★, *Summit* (1974)★★★, *Astor Piazzolla Summit Tango Nuevo* (Atlantic 1974)★★★, *Carnegie Hall Concert* (CTI 1974)★★★, *Gerry Mulligan Meets Enrico Intra* (Pausa 1975)★★★, *Idle Gossip* (Chiaroscuro 1976)★★★, *Lionel Hampton Presents Gerry Mulligan* (1977)★★★, *Mulligan* (LRC 1977)★★★, with Benny Carter *Benny Carter/Gerry Mulligan* (LRC 1977)★★★, with Judy Holliday *Holliday With Mulligan* 1961 recording (DRG 1980)★★★★, *Walk On The Water* (DRG 1980)★★★, *LA Menace* film soundtrack (DRG 1982)★★★, *Little Big Horn* (GRP 1983)★★★, with Barry Manilow *2 am Paradise Cafe* (Arista 1984)★★★, with Scott Hamilton *Soft Lights & Sweet Music* (Concord 1986)★★★, *Symphonic Dream* (Sion 1988)★★★, *Lonesome Boulevard* (A&M 1990)★★★, *Re-Birth Of The Cool* (GRP 1992)★★★★, *Dream A Little Dream* (Telarc 1995)★★★, *Dragonfly* (Telarc 1995)★★★★, *Symphonic Dreams* (Sion 1997)★★★.

● COMPILATIONS: with Chet Baker *Gerry Mulligan And Chet Baker* 1951-65 recordings (GNP Crescendo 1988)★★★★, with Baker *The Best Of The Gerry Mulligan Quartet With Chet Baker*

1952-57 recordings (Pacific Jazz 1991)★★★★, with Baker *The Complete Pacific Jazz Recordings Of The Gerry Mulligan Quartet With Chet Baker* 4-CD box set (Pacific Jazz 1996)★★★★, *Legacy* (Encoded Jazz 1997)★★★★, *Jazz Profile* (Blue Note 1997)★★★★.

● VIDEOS: *A Master Class On Jazz And Its Legendary Players* (1996).

● FURTHER READING: *Gerry Mulligan's Ark*, Raymond Horricks. *Listen: Gerry Mulligan: An Aural Narrative In Jazz*, Jerome Klinkowitz.

● FILMS: *The Subterraneans* (1959), *The Fortune Cookie* (1966).

MULLIGAN, MICK

b. 24 January 1928, Harrow, Middlesex, England. Mulligan taught himself to play trumpet during the early jazz revival of the 40s. Ignoring the fact that he was practically a raw beginner, he promptly formed his own group which he named the Magnolia Jazz Band. With the enthusiastic support of sidemen such as Bob Dawbarn, Roy Crimmins, Archie Semple, Ian Christie and singer George Melly, the band became very popular. With radio broadcasts, occasional appearances on television and endless one-night stands at clubs, pubs and theatres throughout the UK, the band established itself as a driving force of the British trad boom. Later renamed Mick Mulligan's Jazz Band, the group continued until the early 60s before folding in the face of a new kind of popular music. Mulligan stayed on in music for a short time before retiring. A forceful player, Mulligan has left behind only a few records but his band's often hilarious exploits have been extensively recounted in books by Melly and the band's manager, Jim Godbolt. Although in its early days the Mulligan band was noted more for enthusiasm than skill, towards the end it had become one of the finest examples of UK trad even if, probably deliberately, it always remained engagingly unpolished.

● ALBUMS: *George Melly With Mick Mulligan's Band* (1957)★★★★.reissued as *Meet Mick Mulligan And George Melly* (Lake).

● FURTHER READING: *Owning Up*, George Melly. *All This And Many A Dog*, Jim Godbolt.

MUNDY, JIMMY

b. 28 June 1907, Cincinnati, Ohio, USA, d. 24 April 1983. Formally taught as a classical musician, Mundy began to concentrate on arranging for big bands in the late 20s and by the beginning of the next decade was well placed to take advantage of their popularity. During the 30s he wrote for the bands of Earl Hines ('Cavernism'), Benny Goodman ('Madhouse', 'Sing, Sing, Sing', 'Solo Flight') and Gene Krupa. His inclination towards medium and up-tempo swingers with impressively orchestrated riffs attracted the interest of Count Basie ('Feather Merchant'), for whom he arranged throughout the 40s. Late in the decade he also wrote for Dizzy Gillespie. Inevitably, Mundy's tenor saxophone-playing career suffered from his emphasis on his arranging, but he did make some records and briefly led his own band. During the 50s he drifted out of jazz, continuing to arrange for large studio orchestras. He died in 1983.

● ALBUMS: *Jimmy Mundy And His Orchestra* i (1958)★★★, *Jimmy Mundy And His Orchestra* ii (1959)★★★.

● COMPILATIONS: *Groovin' High* (1946)★★★.

MUNN, BILLY

b. 12 May 1911, Glasgow, Scotland. His father led a local amateur orchestra and at the age of seven Munn began formal piano studies at the Athenaeum School of Music. Four years later, while still at school, he was playing piano at silent movie theatres in Glasgow. He graduated to playing with an orchestra and at 14 played in a dance band. Eventually, he and a friend, Andy Lothian, became regulars at Glasgow's Kings Café where they were heard by a local theatrical impresario. Munn moved on to larger venues and at 17 was ready for the big-time. In London he played with Arthur Rosebery then returned to Glasgow to audition for Jack Hylton's band, which happened to be appearing in Scotland. From 1930 he played with Hylton throughout the UK, Europe and also visited the USA. When Hylton remained in the USA, Munn led the band in London for a while, then joined Sydney Lipton. During World War II Munn played whenever he could and after the war continued playing in various London nightspots and also in Brittany. He broadcast on the BBC's *Jazz Club* but was then hired to lead a band at Torquay's Imperial Hotel, where he remained for the next 30 years. In the early 90s Munn was still playing in shows at theatres along England's south coast.

MUNRO, CHARLIE

b. Charles Robert Munro, 22 May 1917, Christchurch, New Zealand, d. 9 December 1985. Establishing himself as a good player of several members of the saxophone family while still in his teens, Munro moved to Australia where he began a long career as a respected studio musician. Although much of this career was spent working in the commercial surroundings of dance bands and music for the theatre, Munro's wide-ranging musical interests led him into effective contact with free jazz. He also drew inspiration from music of other cultures, studied and played the cello, and was an able accompanist to singers.

● ALBUMS: *Eastern Horizons* (Philips 1967)★★★, *Count Down* (Columbia 1969)★★★, *Integration* (Larrikin 70s)★★★.

MURANYI, JOE

b. 14 July 1928, Martin's Ferry, Ohio, USA. Muranyi is of Hungarian descent and first played in a balalaika ensemble. He studied for three years with Lennie Tristano and played in New York with a variety of Dixieland groups as well as joining the Red Onion Jazz Band (1952-54). He worked as a producer and sleevenote writer for major record labels while playing with trumpeters Max Kaminsky, Yank Lawson and Jimmy McPartland. Between 1967 and 1971 he played with Louis Armstrong's All Stars, providing just the kind of elegant support Armstrong then required. Since Armstrong's death he has played with Roy Eldridge, the

World's Greatest Jazz Band (1975) and the Classic Jazz Quartet (1983) as well as continuing his career as a record producer.

● ALBUMS: *Clarinet Wobble* (1970)★★★, *Classic Jazz Quartet* (1984)★★★, with Keith Ingham *Unsaturated Fats* (1990)★★★.

Murphy, Lyle 'Spud'

b. 19 August 1908, Salt Lake City, Utah, USA. During his schooldays Murphy became proficient on several brass and reed instruments. He played saxophones and clarinet in several dance bands, along the way teaching himself arranging. By the late 20s he was secure enough to graduate from playing in territory bands to work in playing and arranging capacities in several leading dance bands, including those of Jan Garber, Mal Hallett and Joe Haymes. He then became a staff arranger for Benny Goodman during the mid-30s, a period when he was also active writing charts for the Casa Loma Orchestra and for the Tommy Dorsey band. Specializing in driving, up-tempo charts, Murphy's contribution to the early success of Goodman and Dorsey was considerable. Late in the decade, he formed his own band, writing for it and playing alto saxophone. In the 40s Murphy's interest was sparked by new developments in jazz, and his writing, and the playing of occasionally formed bands, showed an acute awareness of the musical advances being made. In later years, Murphy experimented in third-stream music.

● COMPILATIONS: as arranger *Benny Goodman On The Air* (Sunbeam 1935)★★★★, as arranger *The Chronological Tommy Dorsey* (Classics 1935)★★★★.

Murphy, Mark

b. 14 March 1932, Syracuse, New York, USA. Murphy began singing as a child and in his mid-teens was performing with a band led by his brother. He worked in many parts of the USA, and had built a small reputation for himself in New York when the appearance of several albums in the late 50s announced that the jazz world had a new and important singer in its midst. During the 60s he continued to tour, visiting Europe and making more fine records with Al Cohn (*That's How I Love The Blues*) and a group drawn from the Clarke-Boland Big Band (*Midnight Mood*). In the middle of the decade he decided to settle in Europe and worked extensively on the Continent (including dates with the Dutch Metropole Orchestra), with occasional visits to the UK. In the early 70s he returned to the USA, where he recorded with Michael and Randy Brecker on *Bridging A Gap* and the later *Satisfaction Guaranteed*, and continued to attract new audiences. Murphy's repertoire is extensive and draws upon sources as diverse as Big Joe Turner and Jon Hendricks. An accomplished stylist who sings with panache, good humour and great vocal dexterity, Murphy has remained dedicated to jazz. This commitment has been unswayed by the fact that his warm voice and highly personable stage presentation would almost certainly have guaranteed him a successful and much more lucrative career in other areas of popular music. In the early 90s Murphy was still on tour, still pleasing his old audience, and still, remarkably, pulling in newcomers attracted by the acid jazz revival of Murphy's version of 'Milestones'.

● ALBUMS: *Meet Mark Murphy* (Decca 1956)★★★★, *Let Yourself Go* (Decca 1957)★★★, *This Could be The Start Of Something* (Capitol 1959)★★★, *Hit Parade* (Capitol 1960)★★★, *Playing The Field* (Capitol 1960)★★★, *Rah!* (Riverside 1961)★★★★, *That's How I Love The Blues!* (Riverside 1962)★★★, *Mark Time* (Fontana 1964)★★★, *A Swingin' Singin' Affair* (Fontana 1965)★★★, *Who Can I Turn To* (Immediate 1966)★★★, *Midnight Mood* (1967)★★★, *Bridging A Gap* (1972)★★★, *Mark II* (1973)★★★, *Red Clay: Mark Murphy Sings* (Muse 1975)★★★, *Mark Murphy Sings Dorothy Fields And Cy Coleman* (Audiophile 1977)★★★, *Stolen Moments* (Muse 1978)★★★, *Satisfaction Guaranteed* (Muse 1979)★★★, *Bop For Kerouac* (Muse 1981)★★★★, *Mark Murphy Sings The Nat 'King' Cole Songbook, Volumes 1 & 2* (Muse 1983)★★★, *Beauty And The Beast* (Muse 1986)★★★, *Night Mood* (Milestone 1987)★★★, *September Ballads* (Milestone 1988)★★★, *Kerouac: Then And Now* (Muse 1989)★★★, *What A Way To Go* (Muse 1992)★★★, *Very Early* (West And East 1993)★★★, *I'll Close My Eyes* (Muse 1994)★★★, with Sheila Jordan *One For Junior* (Muse 1994)★★★, *Song For The Geese* 1995 recording (RCA Victor 1997)★★★, with Benny Green *Dim The Lights* 1995 recording (Millennium 1997)★★★★, *Sings Mostly Dorothy Fields And Cy Coleman* 1979, 1998 recordings (Audiophile 1998)★★★.

● COMPILATIONS: *The Dream: Mark Murphy & Metropole Orchestra* (Jive 1995)★★★★, *Stolen ... And Other Moments* (32 Jazz 1998)★★★★.

Murphy, Turk

b. Melvin Murphy, 16 December 1915, Palermo, California, USA, d. 30 May 1987. Murphy's early career was as a trombonist in popular dance bands such as that led by Mal Hallett, but in the late 30s he joined the revivalist band led by Lu Watters and remained there for most of the next decade. After leaving Watters he formed his own band, gaining just as much fame and popularity as Watters had, and a similarly high level of critical disdain. Murphy opened his own club, Earthquake McGoon's, in San Francisco and continued to lead his band there and around the world until shortly before his death in 1987. An earthy, sometimes raucous but always entertaining player, Murphy was one of the key figures in retaining public interest in traditional jazz during a period, and in a place (the west coast) that saw most critical attention directed to other styles of music.

● ALBUMS: *Turk Murphy's Jazz Band Favourites* (Good Time Jazz 1949-51 recordings)★★★, *The Music Of Jelly Roll Morton* (1953)★★★★, *Music For Losers* (1957)★★★, *Turk Murphy At The Newport Jazz Festival 1957* (1957)★★★, *Turk Murphy In Concert Vols 1 & 2* (1972)★★, *Southern Stomps* (1980-86)★★★, *San Francisco Memories* (1986)★★★, *Concert In The Park* (Merry Makers 1986)★★★, with Jim Cullum *Turk At Carnegie Hall* (1987)★★★.

● COMPILATIONS: *San Francisco Jazz, Volume 1* (1949-50 recordings)★★★★, *San Francisco Jazz, Volume 2* (1950-52 recordings)★★★★, *Live At Easy Street Volumes 1-3* (Dawn Club 1979)★★, *The Best Of Turk Murphy* (Merry Makers 1993)★★★.

MURRAY, DAVID

b. 19 February 1955, Oakland, California, USA. Murray is regarded by many critics as the most important tenor saxophonist of his generation. While he was still an infant his family moved from the Oakland ghetto to integrated Berkeley. He learnt music from his mother, a church pianist, and took up the tenor saxophone at the age of nine, learning the fingering from his clarinet-playing older brother. Three years later he was leading R&B bands. On the day that Martin Luther King was assassinated he was asked, as president of the student body at his junior high school, to address his fellow students. He led the soul revue, the Notations Of Soul, in a two-hour session that helped to avert violence in response to Dr. King's murder. He continued formal study at Pomona College, Los Angeles, where he was taught by Stanley Crouch and Margaret Kohn. He and Crouch later worked together as part of Black Music Infinity and in Murray's 1975 Trio. It was with this unit that Murray relocated to New York, becoming involved with the loft circuit of experimental musicians. He linked up with three of these (Hamiet Bluiett, Oliver Lake, and Julius Hemphill) to form the World Saxophone Quartet in 1977. In the early 80s he joined the comparable Clarinet Summit, led by John Carter. He also worked with Curtis Clarke, Billy Bang, Fred Hopkins, Phil Wilson, Sunny Murray, Jack DeJohnette (in duo and in the drummer's group Special Edition) and James 'Blood' Ulmer (with whom he also played in Music Revelation Ensemble), and, while still in California, he had played with Bobby Bradford, James Newton, Arthur Blythe and Butch Morris, the latter still supplying him with many of the tunes he records. In 1978 he established a big band, out of which distilled the more economically and logistically viable Octet.

Throughout the 80s he led a quartet as well as the octet and, when feasible, the big band. Each of these units has been highly praised throughout the world. Murray's bands offer well-crafted, distinctive writing and adventurous, though equally well-crafted, solos. His own playing on tenor, soprano, bass-clarinet and flute welds traces of his R&B and gospel background, the freedom of Albert Ayler (one of his early heroes) and the classic quality of players such as Paul Gonsalves into an individualist whole. He told Francis Davis: 'When I first came to New York I was playing more melodically, almost the way I play now. If you listen to my records chronologically you'll hear me gradually laying off the overblown notes, but I still use energy techniques as a kind of capper to my solos.' He is both a polished and a passionate improviser, whose other influences include Coleman Hawkins, Ben Webster and Duke Ellington. To date, the best of his work can be found among the many albums he recorded for Black Saint during the 80s (notably *Ming*, *Morning Song*, *Children*, *The Hill* and *I Want To Talk About You*) together with *Ming's Samba* on the Portrait label, and the set of four 1988 quartet records released by DIW: *Deep River*, *Lovers*, *Spirituals* and *Ballads*. His 90s output is (so far) considerable and to a continuing high standard. Highly recommended are *Death Of A Sideman*, *Fast Life*, *Real Deal* and *Tenors*. Quite how many more albums he will have issued by the end of the century is mind-expanding.

● ALBUMS: *Low Class Conspiracy* (Adelphi 1976)★★★, *Flowers For Albert* (India Navigation 1976)★★★★, with Synthesis *Sentiments* (1976)★★, with James Newton *Solomon's Sons* (Circle 5 1977)★★★, *And Low Class Conspiracy Volume 1: Penthouse Jazz* (1977)★★, *And Low Class Conspiracy Volume 2: Holy Siege On Intrigue* (1977)★★, *Live At The Lower Manhattan Ocean Club - Vols. 1 & 2* (India Navigation 1978)★★★, *Last Of The Hipmen* (1978)★★★, *Let The Music Take You* (1978)★★★, *Sur-Real Saxophone* (1978)★★, *Conceptual Saxophone* (1978)★★★, *Organic Saxophone* (1978)★★★, *Interboogieology* (Black Saint 1978)★★★, *The London Concert* (1979)★★, *Murray's 3D Family* (hatART 1979)★★★, *Sweet Lovely* (Black Saint 1980)★★★, *Solo Live Vols. 1 & 2* (Cecma 1980)★★★, with Music Revelation Ensemble *No Wave* (1980)★★★, *Ming* (Black Saint 1980)★★★★, *Home* (Black Saint 1982)★★★, *Murray's Steps* (Black Saint 1983)★★★, with Wilber Morris *Wilber Force* (1983)★★★, *Morning Song* (Black Saint 1984)★★★★, *Live At Sweet Basil Volume 1* (Black Saint 1985)★★, *Children* (Black Saint 1985)★★★★, with Clarinet Summit *Concert At The Public Theater Volume 2* 1982 recording (Black Saint 1985)★★★, *Live At Sweet Basil Volume 2* (Black Saint 1986)★★★, *David Murray* (1986)★★★★, with Jack DeJohnette *In Our Style* (DIW 1986)★★★, *New Life* (1987)★★★, with Randy Weston *The Healers* (Black Saint 1987)★★★, *The Hill* 1986 recording (Black Saint 1988)★★★★, with others *A Tribute To John Coltrane: Blues For Coltrane* (1988)★★★, *Lovers* (1988)★★★★, with Clarinet Summit *Southern Belles* (1988)★★★, *Music Revelation Ensemble* (1988)★★★, *The People's Choice* (1988)★★★, *I Want To Talk About You* 1986 recording (Black Saint 1989)★★★★, *Deep River* (DIW 1989)★★★★, *Ming's Samba* (Portrait 1989)★★★★, with Kahil El' Zabar *Golden Sea* (1989)★★★, with others *Lucky Four* (Tutu 1990)★★★, *Ballads* 1988 recording (DIW 1990)★★★★, *Spirituals* 1988 recording (DIW 1990)★★★★, with Music Revelation Ensemble *Elec. Jazz* (1990)★★★, *Hope Scope* 1987 recording (Black Saint 1991)★★★, *Special Quartet* (Columbia 1991)★★★★, *Live At The Peace Church* 1976 recording (1991)★★, *Remembrances* (DIW 1992)★★★, *Shakill's Warrior* (DIW 1992)★★★, *Big Band* (Columbia 1992)★★★, *A Sanctuary Within* (Black Saint 1992)★★★, with Music Revelation Ensemble *After Dark* (1992)★★★, with Dave Burrell *In Concert* (Victo 1992)★★★, *Fast Life* (DIW 1993)★★★★, with Milford Graves *Real Deal* 1991 recording (DIW 1993)★★★★, *Death Of A Sideman* 1991 recording (DIW 1993)★★★★, *The Jazzpar Prize* (Enja 1993)★★★, *Tea For Two* 1990 recording (Fresh Sound 1993)★★★, *Black And Black* (Red Baron 1993)★★★, *MX* (Red Baron 1993)★★★, *Ballads For Bass Clarinet* (DIW 1993)★★★, *Live '93 Acoustic Octfunk* (Sound Hills 1994)★★★, *Tenors* (DIW 1994)★★★★, *Picasso* (DIW 1994)★★★, *Body And Soul* (Black Saint 1994)★★★, *Saxmen* (Red Baron 1994)★★★, *Jazzosaurus Rex* (Red Baron 1994)★★★, *The Tip* (DIW 1996)★★★★, *Dark Star (The Music Of The Grateful Dead)* (Astor Place 1996)★★★★, with Burrell *Windward Passages* 1993 recording (Black Saint 1997)★★★, *Fo Deuk Revue* (Justin Time 1997)★★★★, *Creole* (Justin Time 1998)★★★, *South Of The Border* (DIW 1998)★★★, *For Deuk Revue* (Justin Time 1998)★★, *Long Goodbye* (DIW 1998)★★★★.

MURRAY, SUNNY

b. James Marcellus Arthur Murray, 21 September 1937, Idabel, Oklahoma, USA. Murray is probably the most influential and certainly the most controversial drummer to emerge from the 60s new wave. He began to teach himself drums at the age of nine, subsequently flirting briefly with trumpet and trombone. In 1956 he moved to New York and worked with figures as diverse as Henry 'Red' Allen, Willie 'The Lion' Smith, Jackie McLean, Rocky Boyd, Ted Curson and Cecil Taylor. In 1963 he went with Taylor and Jimmy Lyons to Europe, where he joined Albert Ayler in the legendary trio that produced *Ghosts* and *Spiritual Unity*. He later played on several more Ayler albums, including *New York Eye And Ear Control*, *Bells* and *Spirits Rejoice*, while Ayler guested on Murray's debut, *Sunny's Time Now*. He lived in France from 1968-71, then moved to Philadelphia, Pennsylvania, USA, where he worked with an equally influential drummer from the hard bop era, Philly Joe Jones. In the 70s and 80s Murray remained extremely active, co-leading the Untouchable Factor, running a trio (that included tenor tyro David Murray - no relation) and recording with pianists Don Pullen (*Applecores*) and Alex Von Schlippenbach (on the duo *Smoke*) as well as renewing his old association with Cecil Taylor (*It Is In The Brewing Luminous*) and Jimmy Lyons. A player with an abstract and oblique approach to the beat, paying at least as much attention to the cymbals as the drums, Murray nevertheless creates a strong feeling of pulse for the music. He has played with most of the major figures of *avant garde* jazz, including Archie Shepp, Ornette Coleman, Don Cherry, John Coltrane, John Tchicai, Roswell Rudd, and Grachan Moncur III.

● ALBUMS: *Sunny's Time Now* (1966)★★★, *Sunny Murray Quintet* (1966)★★★, *Sunny Murray* (ESP 1969)★★★, *Big Chief* (1969)★★, *Homage To Africa* (1969)★★★, *Sunshine* (1969)★★, *An Even Break (Never Gives A Sucker)* (Affinity 1970)★★★, *New American Music Vol. 1* (1973)★★★, with others *Wildflowers Vols. 1 & 5* (1977)★★, with Untouchable Factor *Charred Earth* (1977)★★, *Applecores* (Philly Jazz 1978), *Live At Moers Festival* (Moers Music 1979), *African Magic* (1979)★★★, with Jimmy Lyons *Jump Up/What To Do About* (1981)★★★, *Indelicacy* (West Wind 1987)★★★, with Alex Von Schlippenbach *Smoke* (1990)★★★★, *Illuminators* (Audible Hiss 1996)★★★.

MURSAL, MARYAM

b. 1 January 1950, Mogadishu, Somalia. Mursal began singing professionally at 16, performing the mix of blues, soul African and Arabic influences known locally as Somali jazz. Her warm, deep voice initially drew comparisons with American singers such as Etta James. As well as solo performances, she also sang with Waaberi, the 300-strong music and dance troupe associated with the Somalian National Theatre. However, growing political unrest in Somalia led many of the members of Waaberi into exile in different parts of the world. Mursal herself was forced to work as a taxi driver following a national ban on her music, resulting from a song she had written criticizing the government. With the break-out of full-scale civil war, Mursal, fearing for the safety of her family, fled the country with her five young children. Having walked for an incredible seven months, they eventually arrived in Djibouti, where they were given asylum by the Danish Embassy. In Denmark Mursal was reunited with members of Waaberi, who had already settled there, and with whom she recorded *New Dawn*. It featured Mursal and other vocalists backed by percussion and oud (Arabic lute), performing a mixture of Somalian folk songs and modern material, some of it written by Mursal. The group toured throughout Europe to promote the album in 1997, including a support slot for Nina Simone at London's Barbican Theatre. *The Journey*, Mursal's international solo debut, was released a year later. A collection of songs relating to her seven-month trek across the Horn of Africa, it featured backing vocals from Peter Gabriel and was produced by Simon Emmerson. On the record, the latter developed the fusion of progressive dance music and traditional influences he had previously explored in his work with Baaba Maal and the Afro-Celt Sound System, while at the same time retaining the essential personality of Mursal's music.

● ALBUMS: with Waaberi *New Dawn* (Real World 1997)★★★, *The Journey* (Real World 1998)★★★★.

MUSIC REVELATION ENSEMBLE

(see Jackson, Ronald Shannon; Murray, David; Ulmer, James 'Blood')

MUSSO, VIDO

b. 13 January 1913, Carrini, Sicily, d. 9 January 1982. Musso's family emigrated to the USA in 1920, settling in Detroit, where he began playing clarinet. Relocating to Los Angeles in 1930, he became friendly with Stan Kenton and the two men worked together in various bands, including one led by Musso and one they co-led. In the mid-30s Musso, by now playing tenor saxophone, joined Benny Goodman and thereafter played in the big bands of Gene Krupa, Harry James, Tommy Dorsey and others, rejoining Kenton in 1946. He stayed only a year and then formed another band of his own, continuing to lead jazz-orientated dancebands until the mid-50s. An entirely untutored musician, Musso's powerful, buzzing sound and aggressive solo style inclined him to the more extrovert areas of jazz and big band music. Untouched by the changes that took place in jazz in the 40s, Musso became something of an anachronism and for the rest of his career he played in relatively obscure settings, often in Las Vegas showbands.

● ALBUMS: *Vido Musso And His Orchestra* i (1954)★★★, *Vido Musso And His Orchestra* ii (*c.*1955)★★★, *One Night Stand With Vido Musso* (Savoy 1982, 1947 recording)★★★.

● COMPILATIONS: *The Indispensable Benny Goodman Vols 3/4* (RCA 1936-37 recordings)★★★★, *Stan Kenton's Greatest Hits* (1943-51 recordings)★★★★, *Vido Musso's All Stars* (1946 recordings), *Loaded* (Savoy 1993)★★★.

MUSSOLINI, ROMANO

b. Full Mussolini, 26 September 1927, Carpena, Forli, Italy. The son of the fascist dictator Benito Mussolini, who was executed by partisans at the end of World War II, he played piano under a pseudonym in his early years. By the early 50s he was becoming known outside Italy thanks to festival appearances and his work as an accompanist to visiting jazzmen. Among the visitors were Lars Gullin and Chet Baker (reportedly, Baker, worried over how to handle his first meeting with Mussolini, stuck out his hand and blurted out, 'Sorry to hear about your Dad!'). Mussolini regularly led his own small groups, usually playing in a boppish mode; he also developed a technically accomplished solo style.

● ALBUMS: *Topsy* (RCA 1957)★★★.

MY FAVORITE THINGS - JOHN COLTRANE

One of John Coltrane's (many) extraordinary talents was his ability to drastically transcend the material he chose to play, and often infuse the trivial or frivolous with something altogether very profound. Under the spell of the quartet (with pianist McCoy Tyner, temporary bassist Steve Davis and drummer Elvin Jones), 'My Favorite Things' becomes an almost religious celebration of life, brought to a series of ecstatic climaxes by Coltrane's nasal, Eastern-sounding soprano saxophone and Jones's propulsive, 6/8 clatter. This popular album also contains 'But Not For Me', a breakneck version of 'Summertime' and a beautiful 'Every Time We Say Goodbye'.

● Tracks: *My Favorite Things; Every Time We Say Goodbye; Summertime; But Not For Me.*

● First released 1960

● UK peak chart position: did not chart

● USA peak chart position: did not chart

MY FUNNY VALENTINE - MILES DAVIS

One of the finest live albums in the history of jazz, *My Funny Valentine* presents the Miles Davis Quintet live at the Lincoln Centre's Philharmonic Hall in 1964. Surrounded by the vibrant and youthful rhythm section of Herbie Hancock (piano), Ron Carter (bass) and Tony Williams (drums), Davis was enjoying a strong new surge of creativity, and played with a stunning level of invention and passion throughout. The resonance of the long title track - one of those flawless performances that happens only very occasionally - dominates the record. Front-line partner George Coleman (tenor saxophone) chose a good evening to play some of the most beautiful solos of his life.

● Tracks: *My Funny Valentine; All Of You; Stella By Starlight; All Blues; I Thought About You.*

● First released 1964

● UK peak chart position: did not chart

● USA peak chart position: 138

MYERS, AMINA CLAUDINE

b. 21 March 1942, Blackwell, Arkansas, USA. As a young woman, Myers played piano and sang in church. In the mid-60s she moved to Chicago, became a member of the AACM and over the next 10 years or so worked frequently with fellow-members such as Kalaparush Maurice McIntyre (*Humility In The Light Of The Creator*), Muhal Richard Abrams, Henry Threadgill and Lester Bowie (*African Children, The 5th Power*). In the early 70s she also played with Gene Ammons, Sonny Stitt and Little Milton as well as leading her own trio. She moved to New York in the mid-70s and spent some time in Europe in the early 80s, recording there with Frank Lowe (*Exotic Heartbreak*) and with Martha and Fontella Bass and David Peason on the highly praised gospel set, *From The Root To The Source*. Her first recording as leader, for London's Leo Records, featured her on piano, organ and vocals, and presented powerful, even stark, evocations of her blues and gospel roots. Inexplicably, later recordings - particularly an ill-judged couple of fusion-based albums for Novus - largely failed to capture the outstanding talents that have won her a high standing among her peers. From the mid-80s she has been playing with Charlie Haden's Liberation Music Orchestra, recording with them on *Dream Keeper*.

● ALBUMS: *Song For Mother E* (Leo 1980)★★★, *Salutes Bessie Smith* (Leo 1980)★★★★, *Poems For Piano: The Music Of Marion Brown* (1980)★★, with Muhal Richard Abrams *Duet* (Black Saint 1981)★★, *The Circle Of Time* (1983)★★★, *Jumping In The Sugar Bowl* (Minor 1984)★★★, *Country Girl* (Minor 1986)★★, *Amina* (Novus 1988)★★★, *In Touch* (Novus 1989)★★★, *Jumping In The Sugar Bowl* (Digital Stereo 1995)★★★.

MYERS, BUMPS

b. Hubert Maxwell Myers, 22 August 1912, Clarksburg, West Virginia, USA, d. 9 April 1968. While still a small boy, Myers moved to the west coast and when he began playing tenor saxophone it was there that he made his debut. Among early engagements were spells with Curtis Mosby, Charlie Echols and Buck Clayton, all of whom led bands in Los Angeles. With Clayton, he travelled to China, playing a residency at Shanghai's Canidrome Ballroom. Back in Los Angeles, he played with bands led by Lionel Hampton and Les Hite, then joined a small group co-led by Lee and Lester Young. He visited New York, playing with Jimmie Lunceford, the Youngs, then returned to the west coast, served in the US Army, and subsequently resumed his round of short spells in various bands, including those led by Benny Carter, Lunceford and 'Big' Sid Catlett. He spent the 50s and early 60s freelancing on the west coast, sometimes working with Carter, and he was also with Horace Henderson's band. Myers played with conviction, soloing with imagination and flair and providing sterling backing to the artists with whom he worked. His later years were largely inactive due to poor health.

● COMPILATIONS: *Benny Carter And His Orchestra* (Joyce 1945)★★★★, *Mel Powell Quintet* (Pausa 1947)★★★, *Russell Jacquet And His Bopper Band* (King 1949)★★★.

Naked City

Formed in 1990, this radical act revolves around alto saxophonist/composer John Zorn (b. 2 September 1953, New York City, New York, USA). A leading figurehead of the 'downtown' *avant garde* enclave, centred on New York's Lower East Side, Zorn drew increasing parallels between free jazz and sonic extremists Napalm Death, whom he consistently championed. His radical versions of Ornette Coleman compositions unveiled on *Spy Vs Spy* (1989) bore the legend 'Fucking hardcore rules' and set the tone for the founding of Naked City. Fred Frith (bass), formerly of Henry Cow, Bill Frisell (guitar), Wayne Horvitz (keyboards) and Joey Baron (drums) joined Zorn for the group's self-titled album debut. Jazz, surf and noise gelled perfectly on this impressive collection, which merged original compositions with 'The James Bond Theme' and sundry film music, each of which was viciously deconstructed. Guest vocalist Yamatsuka Eye, from Japanese hardcore act the Boredoms was billed as special guest, although he later became a full-time member. The sense of adventure on *Naked City* was maintained on the equally compulsive *Torture Garden*, after which Zorn undertook an offshoot project, Painkiller (*The Guts Of A Virgin*, 1991), with Frisell and Napalm Death drummer Mick Harris. A film soundtrack, *Heretic - Jeux Des Dames Cruelles*, released on the Japanese Avant label, maintained Naked City's uncompromising stance; track titles including 'Copraphagist Rituals' merely heightened the controversy. A second Avant disc, *Grand Guignol*, proved even more challenging, combining Debussy's 'La Cathedrale Engloutie' and Charles Ives' 'The Cage' with 32 virulent blasts of freeform noise, only three of which lasted more than one minute. Zorn and Naked City remain at the cutting edge of adventurous music.

● ALBUMS: *Naked City* (Elektra/Nonesuch 1990)★★★★, *Torture Garden* (Earache 1990)★★★★, *Heretic - Jeux Des Dames Cruelles* (Avant 1992)★★★, *Grand Guignol* (Avant 1993)★★★, *Radio* (Avant 1993)★★, *Absinthe* (Avant 1994)★★, *Avenue Blue* (Bluemoon 1995)★★★.

Namyslowski, Zbigniew

b. 9 September 1939, Warsaw, Poland. Namyslowski's *Lola*, recorded during his visit to the UK in 1964, caused quite a stir, since few people in the West were aware of the state of the jazz art in Soviet bloc countries (formerly). However, it was not simply the surprise of Eastern European musicians playing modern, post-bop jazz at all that impressed: Namyslowski was very good indeed, with a hard, emotional tone and considerable facility on the alto saxophone. He had begun his musical studies on piano at the age of six, switching to the cello at 12. He also plays soprano saxophone, flute and trombone. He studied music theory at the Warsaw High School of Music and began his career playing trombone with a trad band and 'cello with a modern group. Concentrating on alto, he set up his quartet in 1963 and toured Europe, Asia and Australasia as well as the USSR. He plays with the kind of intensely personal passion one associates with Jackie McLean and Mike Osborne, weaving in strong strands of Polish folk music in both his writing and improvising. In the late 70s and early 80s he moved away from the more *avant garde* side of his style and, without losing his individuality, used rock-fusion elements. There was also an adventurous album, *Zbigniew Namyslowski*, for orchestra and large jazz group. By the late 80s, he was back in the hard-bop mainstream, sounding a little less dangerous than in his early days, but just as sincere and inventive. He has also worked with Krzysztof Komeda and Air Condition, the fine Polish fusion band that he led in the early 80s.

● ALBUMS: *Lola* (1965)★★★, *Zbigniew Namyslowski Quartet* (1966)★★, with Krzysztof Komeda *Astigmation* (1967)★★★★, *Winobranie* (1973)★★★, *All Stars After Hours* (1974)★★★, *Kujaviek Goes Funky* (1975)★★★, with Michael J. Smith *Geomusic III* (1975)★★★, *Namyslowski* (1977)★★★, *Zbigniew Namyslowski* (1980)★★★★, with Air Condition *Follow Your Kite* (1980)★★★, *Air Condition* (Affinity 1982)★★★, *Polish Jazz Vol 4:* (Polskie Nagrania 1966-87 recordings)★★★★, *Open* (1988)★★★, *The Last Concert* (Polonia 1992)★★★.

Nance, Ray

b. Willis Nance, 10 December 1913, Chicago, Illinois, USA, d. 28 January 1976. A gifted multi-instrumentalist, Nance studied formally for several years and played in various small bands, mostly in the Chicago area. By the early 30s he was a popular local entertainer, leading his own bands and playing several instruments, including trumpet and violin, as well as singing, dancing and performing engaging comedy routines. The 30s also saw him playing in the Chicago big bands led by Earl 'Fatha' Hines and Horace Henderson. He joined Duke Ellington in 1940 and quickly became an integral, valued and much-loved part of the organization. He left Ellington for a short spell in the mid-40s to lead his own band, but returned at the end of 1945; this time he remained virtually without a break, until 1963. From 1964 until his death he led his own small bands but returned regularly to guest with the Ellington band. Whether playing trumpet - later cornet - or violin, Nance's contributions to the Ellington band's recordings are many and marvellous. His violin playing on 'Moon Mist' and his trumpet solo on the 1941 version of 'Take The 'A' Train' are fine examples of his work. Outside the Ellington band he made some excellent recordings with ex-Ellingtonians Paul Gonsalves and Johnny Hodges, while a 1971 Jimmy Rushing recording includes a moving violin solo on 'When I Grow Too Old To Dream'.

● ALBUMS: *Duke Ellington Presents* (1956)★★★, with Johnny

Hodges *Duke's In Bed* (1956)★★★, with Duke Ellington *Black, Brown And Beige* (1958)★★★★, *Body And Soul* (1969)★★★★, with Paul Gonsalves *Just A-Sittin' And A-Rockin'* (1970)★★★, with Jimmy Rushing *The You And Me That Used To Be* (1971)★★★, *Huffin' 'N' Puffin'* (1971)★★★, *Ray Nance Quartet And Sextet* (Unique 1986)★★★.

● COMPILATIONS: with Ellington *The Blanton-Webster Years (1940-42)* (Bluebird 1987)★★★★.

NANTON, JOE 'TRICKY SAM'

b. Joseph N. Irish, 1 February 1904, New York City, New York, USA, d. 20 July 1946. After playing trombone with a number of small bands in the early and mid-20s, including two stints with Cliff Jackson, Nanton joined Elmer Snowden and by 1926 was in the re-formed band led by Duke Ellington. Along with Bubber Miley, Nanton was a major force in creating the distinctive 'jungle' sound of Ellington's early work. Although occasionally beset by illness, Nanton remained with Ellington until he suffered a stroke in 1945. An inventive soloist capable of producing fascinating excursions within a narrow range, and with a marked penchant for creating sounds that resembled the human voice, Nanton helped to establish a role for the trombone in the Ellington band which, thereafter, had to be followed, more or less faithfully, by most of his successors.

● COMPILATIONS: *The Indispensable Duke Ellington Vols. 1/2, 3/4, 5/6 (1927-40)* (RCA 1983)★★★★, with Duke Ellington *The Blanton-Webster Years (1940-42)* (Bluebird 1986)★★★★.

NAPOLEON, MARTY

b. 2 June 1921, New York City, New York, USA. A member of a musical family (his father was a professional musician, as were several uncles of whom the most famous is Phil Napoleon), Marty played piano in several second-string big bands of the 40s, including those led by Lee Castle and Joe Venuti. Later, he joined Charlie Barnet and also spent a brief spell with Gene Krupa. In the 50s, Napoleon began playing with his uncle Phil's revived Original Memphis Five and then showed his versatility by becoming a member of Charlie Ventura's Big Four. He next spent periods with Louis Armstrong's All Stars, as well as bands led by his brother Teddy (who was also a professional musician), Coleman Hawkins, Ruby Braff and others. Since the beginning of the 60s he has worked mostly as a solo artist, but has made occasional appearances with small groups, which have included Red Allen, and also played return stints with Armstrong and Krupa. Napoleon's wide stylistic range, which has taken him from Dixieland to the edges of bop, has tended to limit appreciation of his talent among those members of the jazz public who like to label musicians.

● ALBUMS: *Trio* (1955)★★★, with Ruby Braff *Little Big Horn* (1955)★★★★, with Red Allen *Ride, Red, Ride In Hi-Fi* (1957)★★★, with Louis Armstrong *Louis* (1966)★★★.

NAPOLEON, PHIL

b. 2 September 1901, Boston, Massachusetts, USA, d. 30 September 1990, Miami, Florida, USA. A child prodigy, Napoleon came from a musical family, two of his nephews being Marty and Teddy Napoleon. He played trumpet in public at the age of five and made his first records 10 years later. In 1922 he was a founder-member of the Original Memphis Five, an exceptionally good Dixieland band that made numerous records, many of which sold very well. By the end of the 20s, however, Napoleon had folded the band and gone into studio work where he remained for a decade or more. At the end of the 30s, after an unsuccessful attempt to run a big band, he stopped playing for some years. In the early 50s he returned to the music scene, reviving the Memphis Five and thereafter leading a succession of Dixieland bands. He continued to play well into the 80s, often at his own club, Napoleon's Retreat, in Miami, Florida. A fiery player with an attacking style, Napoleon was never on a par with such near-contemporaries as Bix Beiderbecke, although he claimed to have been influential on Beiderbecke and Red Nichols. Nevertheless, his many records show him to have been a distinctive and clear-toned trumpeter. These records, together with his remarkably long playing career, made him an important figure in the spread of jazz throughout the world.

● ALBUMS: with Pete Daily *Pete Daily/Phil Napoleon* 10-inch album (Decca 1950)★★★, *Dixieland Classics* 10-inch album (Mercury 1953)★★★★, *Dixieland Classics #1* 10-inch album (EmArcy 1954)★★★★, *Dixieland Classics #2* 10-inch album (EmArcy 1954)★★★★, *Dixieland By Phil Napoleon* 10-inch album (Jolly Roger 1954)★★★, *Two-Beat* 10-inch album (Columbia 1955)★★★, *Phil Napoleon And The Memphis Five* (Capitol 1960)★★★★, *In The Land Of Dixie* (Capitol 1960)★★★.

● COMPILATIONS: *From 1950s Broadcasts* (Take Two 1978)★★★, *Live At Nick's NYC* 1949-1950 recordings (Jazzology 1996)★★★, *Featuring The Original Memphis Five* 1926-1929 recordings (IAJRC)★★★★, *1929-1931* (Old Masters)★★★★.

NAPOLEON, TEDDY

b. 23 June 1914, New York City, New York, USA, d. 5 July 1964. Older brother of Marty Napoleon and nephew of Phil Napoleon, Teddy played piano in a band led by Lee Castle in the early 30s. After touring extensively with minor bands he arrived in New York at the end of that decade. He played in yet more minor dance bands but then, in 1944, joined Gene Krupa. Featured not only in the big band but also in Krupa's band-within-a-band, a trio that was often rounded out by Charlie Ventura, Napoleon continued this association even after Krupa had folded the big band. He toured the world with Krupa's trio in the 50s, making concert, club and festival appearances and several records. He also played and sometimes recorded with Flip Phillips, Bill Harris and his brother Marty.

● ALBUMS: with Gene Krupa *The Rocking Mr Krupa* (1953)★★★★, with Krupa *Krupa Rocks* (1957)★★★.

● COMPILATIONS: *Drummin' Man Vol. 2 (1945-49)* (1987)★★★★.

NASCIMENTO, MILTON

b. 26 October 1942, Rio de Janeiro, Brazil. Singer-songwriter Nascimento draws much of his inspiration from Brazil's Portuguese heritage, where even the jolliest tune can be counted on to contain more than a frisson of melancholy. His biggest successes, both at home and abroad, came in the 70s with *Milagre Dos Peixes* (1973, re-released in the UK in 1990) and *Milton* (1977), the latter featuring contributions from Herbie Hancock, Wayne Shorter, Airto Moreira, Roberto Silva and Laudir De Oliviera. First teaming with Shorter on his 1975 album *Native Dancer*, Nascimento was widely taken up by the Los Angeles music fraternity over the next few years, most notably guesting on albums by Flora Purim, Deodato and Charlie Rouse.

● ALBUMS: *Milagre Dos Peixes* (1973)★★★, with Flora Purim *500 Miles High* (1976)★★★, *Milton* (1977)★★★★, *Travessia* (Sign 1986)★★★, *Meetings And Farewells* (Polydor 1986)★★★, *Ship Of Lovers* (Verve 1987)★★★★, *Yauarete* (CBS 1988)★★★, *Txai* (Columbia 1991)★★★, *Planeta Blue Estrada Do Sol* (1992)★★★, *Noticias Do Brasil* (Tropical 1993)★★★, *Angelus* (Warners 1994)★★, *Nascimento* (Warners 1997)★★★★.

NASH, DICK

b. Richard Taylor Nash, 26 January 1928, Somerville, Massachusetts, USA. Born into a musical family (his older brother is Ted Nash Snr.) Nash played trombone from an early age. In the years immediately following World War II he played in bands led by Sam Donahue, Tex Beneke, and others, then played in army bands during the Korean conflict. From the mid-50s onwards he was a studio musician in Los Angeles, also playing in dance bands and jazz groups. He played on several records, such as the extensive *Time-Life* series of big band recreations, helping to recapture the music of the swing era. Nash is a superb technician and his mellifluous playing on ballads is always a joy to hear.

● ALBUMS: *Ken Hanna And His Orchestra* (Trend 1954)★★★, with Ted Nash *The Brothers Nash* (Liberty 1956)★★★.

NASH, TED, JNR.

b. 28 December 1959, Hollywood, California, USA. Born into a highly musical family (his father is Dick Nash and his uncle is Ted Nash Snr.) Ted took up the tenor saxophone as a youth. He played with Louie Bellson in the 70s, and also toured and recorded with Don Ellis in 1977. While occasionally displaying the influence of John Coltrane in his earlier work, Nash has a strong personal sound and constantly and consistently displays elegant lyricism in his playing of ballads.

● ALBUMS: *Out Of This World* (Mapleshade 1994)★★★.

NASH, TED, SNR.

b. Theodore Malcolm Nash, 31 October 1922, Somerville, Massachusetts, USA. Nash began playing saxophone as a child, taking up tenor and alto. In the mid-40s, now mostly playing tenor, he was with Les Brown's Band Of Renown, touring and recording. He also played with Jerry Gray, one of a handful of late swing era bands that survived into the early 50s, albeit mostly as a recording outfit. During the 50s Nash was in considerable demand from similarly-minded bandleaders, playing with Billy May and Ray Anthony among many, and also leading his own band with which he recorded. Throughout succeeding decades Nash was active in the studios, playing for radio and films but mainly for television. A strikingly good technician, Nash has written tutors and by example alone has set high standards of performance. His younger brother is Dick Nash.

● ALBUMS: *Ted Nash* 10-inch album (Starlite 1954)★★★, with Dick Nash *The Brothers Nash* (Liberty 1956)★★★, *Star Eyes* (Columbia 1957)★★★.

NATAL, NANETTE

b. 6 October 1945, New York City, New York, USA. She began performing in her mid-teens, acting and playing classical music. In the 60s she became a singer, working with rock and blues bands and also playing guitar and writing songs. During this period Natal worked extensively in New York's Greenwich village music scene, performed on radio and television and also toured the university campus circuit. In 1968 she was signed by Vanguard Records which brought her a great deal of exposure and promotion. In the late 70s she began singing jazz, developing as an improviser, performing mostly in New York and headlining at the Tin Palace for over a year. In 1980 she formed her own production company and jazz record label, Benyo Music. Around the same time, Natal also began teaching, eventually building a thriving private practice. In the early 90s she was contributing a regular feature on singing technique to the magazine *The Music Paper*. In addition to her performing and teaching roles, Natal is also a gifted composer, having written many of the songs she performs, and planned to record her own jazz opera, *Street Opera*, in 1997. She simultaneously worked on a theatrical production, a one-woman show, *Too Much Jazz*. Natal's inventiveness as composer and performer is reflected in her recordings, which are lively, polished and vibrant with enthusiasm. Her singing style is poised and rhythmic and she displays elegant control in all that she does. Her vast knowledge of technique, which she ably imparts to her students, both in lessons and magazine articles, is never allowed to come between her and the songs she sings. Instead, she employs her skills, over which she has superb command, to enable her to give insightful interpretations of her wide-ranging repertoire.

● ALBUMS: *Yesterday, Today, Tomorrow* (Vanguard 1969)★★★, *The Beginning* (Evolution 1972)★★★, *My Song Of Something* (Benyo 1986)★★, *Stairway To The Stars* (Benyo 1992)★★★.

NATIONAL JAZZ ENSEMBLE

(see Israels, Chuck)

NATIONAL YOUTH JAZZ ORCHESTRA

In 1965 Bill Ashton, a teacher at a London school, formed the London Schools Jazz Orchestra. This was an organization in which youngsters could pursue musical ambitions in a setting that related to music which interested them, rather than forms imposed upon them by the educational hierarchy. Thanks to Ashton's persistence in the face of establishment hostility the orchestra survived, later becoming known as the London Youth Jazz Orchestra and, eventually, the National Youth Jazz Orchestra. In 1974 NYJO became a fully professional organization and remains the UK's only full-time professional big band playing jazz. Although Ashton's conception was to create an atmosphere in which young musicians could develop their craft, NYJO has long since passed the stage of being either a training ground or even a 'youth' orchestra. The extraordinarily high standard of musicianship demanded by the band means that newcomers to its ranks must have already achieved a very high standard of technical competence before auditioning. Ashton's leadership is a mixture of democracy and benign autocracy. The band's members choose the music, which varies from the brand-new to charts originally played by editions of NYJO that were on the road when present members were barely walking, and Ashton organizes the musicians' choices into an entertaining programme. Although the nature of the orchestra means that it is in an almost constant state of flux, NYJO has developed an identifiable sound. Much of the music that is played by the band is original, often written by members, and everything is especially arranged. While many arrangements are 'in-house', others come from outside. Among the arrangers are Paul Higgs, David Lindup, Brian Priestley, Chris Smith, Terry Catharine, Bill Charleson, Neil Ardley, Alec Gould and Ashton. Many exceptional talents have passed through NYJO's ranks over the years, including Steve and Julian Argüelles, Chris Hunter, Lance Ellington, Paul Hart, David O'Higgins, Phil Todd, Mark and Andy Nightingale, Stan Sulzmann, Chris Laurence, Richard Symons, Gerard Presencer and Guy Barker. Ashton's interest in songwriting has ensured a succession of good singers with the band, including Carol Kenyon, Helen Sorrell and Litsa Davies. Over the years NYJO has travelled extensively, appearing in various European countries and also visiting the USA. The band's many albums have proved successful and help spread the sound of a remarkable orchestra that, although effectively the creation of one man, has come to represent the best in big band jazz and consistently denies its name by being both international and fully mature.

● ALBUMS: *Return Trip* (1976)★★★, *Eleven Plus: Live At LWT* (1976)★★★, *In Camra* (1977)★★★★, *The Sherwood Forest Suite* (1977)★★★★, *To Russia With Jazz* (1977)★★★, *Mary Rose* (1979)★★, *Down Under* (1980)★★, *Why Don't They Write Songs Like This Any More?* (1982)★★★, *Playing Turkey* (1983)★★★, *Born Again* (1983)★★★, *Full Score* (1985)★★★, *Concrete Cows* (1986)★★★, *With An Open Mind* (1986)★★★, *Shades Of Blue And Green* (1987)★★★★, *Big Band Christmas* (1989)★★, *Maltese Cross* (NYJO 1989)★★★, *Rememberance* (NYJO 1990)★★★, *Cookin' With Gas* (NYJO 1990)★★★, *Looking Forward Looking Back* (NYJO 1992)★★★, *These Are The Jokes* (Jazz House 1992)★★★, *Merry Christmas And A Happy New Year* (NYJO 1993)★, *In Control* (Jazz House 1994)★★, *Cottoning On* (NYJO 1995)★★★, *A View From The Hill* (Jazz House 1995)★★, *Algarhythms* (NYJO 1996)★★★, *Unison In All Things* (NYJO 1996)★★★, *This Time Live At The Club* (Jazz House 1997)★★★.

Naura, Michael

b. 19 August 1934, Memel, Lithuania. Naura is a self-taught pianist and flautist who studied philosophy, sociology and graphic arts in Berlin. In the 50s he and Wolfgang Schluter (vibes) started a band that sought to mix blues, bebop and European *avant garde* and became one of the leading German bands of the 60s. Since 1971, he has worked as the Head of the Norddeutscher Rundfunk Jazz Department. He continues occasional work with bands and regularly accompanies Peter Ruhmkorf in poetry-jazz recitals. He is also president of Performers and Artists for Nuclear Disarmament (PANDA) in Germany.

● ALBUMS: with Peter Ruhmkorf *Kein Apolloprogramm Fur Lyrik* (1976)★★★, *Country Children* (1977)★★★.

Navarro, Fats

b. Theodore Navarro, 24 September 1923, Key West, Florida, USA, d. 7 July 1950. After starting to learn the tenor saxophone and piano, Navarro opted for trumpet and by his mid-teens was playing professionally. In 1943 he joined the Andy Kirk band, working alongside Howard McGhee, and two years later was in the trumpet section of Billy Eckstine's bebop-orientated big band. He later settled in New York, where he played with leading beboppers such as Kenny Clarke, Ernie Henry, Howard McGhee, Tadd Dameron, Bud Powell, Charlie Parker, Leo Parker, Sonny Rollins and Dizzy Gillespie, the last of whom he had replaced in the Eckstine band. Navarro also played with mainstreamers such as Coleman Hawkins and Eddie 'Lockjaw' Davis. Most of these musical associations resulted in a legacy of fine recordings, with the Dameron sessions proving to be especially fruitful. During his short life Navarro displayed a precocious talent, his rich, full tone contrasting with the thin sound adopted by many of the other young bebop trumpeters of the day. In this respect his sound resembled that of an earlier generation of trumpeters who were considered somewhat *passé* by the late 40s. His last years were dogged by ill-health, exacerbated by an addiction to heroin, and he died in 1950. Despite his brief life, Navarro proved to be one of the most accessible of the early bop trumpeters and was an influence on another similarly short-lived talent, Clifford Brown.

● ALBUMS: with Billy Eckstine *Together!* (1947)★★★★, with Charlie Parker *One Night In Birdland* (Savoy 1950)★★★★, *New Sounds In Modern Music* (Savoy 1952)★★★★, *New Trends In Jazz* (Savoy 1952)★★★★, *Memorial Album* (Blue Note 1952)★★★★, *Fats Navarro Memorial* (Savoy 1955)★★★★, *The Fabulous Fats Navarro Vols. 1 & 2 (1947-49)* (Blue Note 1955)★★★★, *Nostalgia* (Savoy 1958)★★★★, with Miles Davis, Dizzy Gillespie *Trumpet Giants* (New Jazz 1962)★★★★, *The Tadd Dameron Band 1948,*

Vols. 1 & 2 (1948) (1976)★★★★, *Fat Girl - The Savoy Sessions (1947)* (1985)★★★★, *Memorial* (Savoy 1992)★★★★.

NEIDLINGER, BUELL

b. 2 March 1936, Westport, Connecticut, USA. After studying piano, trumpet and bass, Neidlinger concentrated on teaching himself the latter instrument more extensively. He led bands in high school, then attended Yale for a year, ending up as a disc jockey. In 1955 he relocated to New York, where he gigged with Coleman Hawkins, Tony Scott and Zoot Sims. He made his name with Cecil Taylor, negotiating the pianist's difficult compositions with astonishing aptitude; he was part of Taylor's famous residency at the Five Spot in 1957 and played with him in a 1960 staging of *The Connection*. Always one for a surprising career move, Neidlinger then worked in singer Tony Bennett's band for six months. Subsequent work included stints with Gil Evans and Steve Lacy. He studied music at Buffalo State University (1964-66), played with the Budapest Quartet at Tanglewood in 1965 and gave several recitals of works for solo bass by Sylvano Bussotti and Mauricio Kagel. In the late 60s he became a member of the Boston Symphony Orchestra. In 1970 Neidlinger played bass on Frank Zappa's suite for violinist Jean-Luc Ponty, 'Music For Electric Violin And Low Budget Orchestra', brought in, according to Zappa, 'because he's the only man I could think of who could play the bass part'. In 1971 he became professor of music at the California Institute of the Arts and was also busy in the Hollywood recording studios. Neidlinger's ability to relate to different kinds of music is only equalled by his interest in them: at various times he has played with Willie 'The Lion' Smith, Roy Orbison, Barbra Streisand and Archie Shepp. He has several bands; Buellgrass provides a unique blend of country and jazz: an updated western swing; Thelonious plays Thelonious Monk tunes exclusively; String Jazz interprets Duke Ellington and Monk on saxophone, drums and various string instruments. Most of his releases are on the K2B2 label, which he co-runs with tenor saxophonist Marty Krystall, a playing associate of his for over 20 years. A caustic interviewee, Neidlinger has continually involved himself with the cutting edge of jazz and has an inimitable sound on his instrument.

● ALBUMS: with Cecil Taylor *New York City R&B* 1961 recording (Barnaby 1971)★★★★, with Taylor *Cecil Taylor All Stars Featuring Buell Neidlinger* 1961 recording (Candid/Victor 1977)★★★★, *Ready For The 90s* (1980)★★★, *Our Night Together* (1981)★★★, *Big Day At Ojai* (1982)★★, with Taylor *Jumpin' Punkins* 1961 recordings (Candid 1987)★★★★, with String Jazz *Locomotive* (Soul Note 1988)★★★, with Taylor *Cecil* 1961 recordings (Maestri Del Jazz 1991)★★★★, *Big Drum* (KB Records 1991)★★★★.

● COMPILATIONS: *The Complete Candid Recordings Of Cecil Taylor And Buell Neidlinger* 6-LP/4-CD box set (Mosaic 1989)★★★★, *Rear View Mirror* 1979-86 recordings (KB Records 1991)★★★★, *Blue Chopsticks: A Portrait Of Herbie Nichols* (KB Records 1995)★★★.

NELSON, 'BIG EYE' LOUIS

b. 28 January *c.*1885, New Orleans, Louisiana, USA, d. 20 August 1949. Nelson settled on playing the clarinet after experimenting with a wide range of instruments. Throughout his career he rarely played outside his home-town, choosing to work in the emerging jazz bands and the traditional New Orleans marching and brass bands. Nelson is reputed to have played on bass in Buddy Bolden's band, and he also worked with leading New Orleans jazzmen such as John Robichaux, Joe 'King' Oliver and Jelly Roll Morton. Nelson made few records - a handful of tracks with Kid Rena in 1940, and a few more in 1949 with 'Wooden' Joe Nicholas and as leader, using the name Louis DeLisle, under which he sometimes worked. From these recordings it is possible to understand the high regard in which Nelson was held by musicians such as Baby Dodds and Sidney Bechet, whom Nelson tutored for a while. He played with a full sound and employed a facile technique. His records with Rena provide interesting testimony to the skill and stylistic devices of the earliest New Orleans jazz musicians.

● ALBUMS: with Wooden Joe Nicholas *Wooden Joe's New Orleans Band* (1945-49)★★★, *Louis Delisle's Band* (1949)★★★.

NELSON, LOUIS

b. 17 September 1902, New Orleans, Louisiana, USA, d. 5 April 1990. Nelson grew up in a cultured family; his mother was a graduate of the Boston Conservatory of Music, his father was a physician. After starting out on alto horn, he switched to trombone in the 20s. Working mostly with bands in and around New Orleans, including those led by Oscar 'Papa' Celestin and Kid Rena, he built a sound reputation during the 30s. During this period he also frequently worked with the popular big band led by Sidney Desvigne. In the early 40s he joined Kid Thomas and in the 50s was a regular member of the band led by George Lewis, with whom he toured extensively. In the 60s Nelson also worked with the New Orleans Joymakers, the Legends Of Jazz, Kid Thomas, Peter Bocage, Sammy Rimington and other leading New Orleans-style musicians. For many years he was a frequent performer at Preservation Hall in his home-town. Although best known for his New Orleans playing, Nelson's style incorporated many elements foreign to the form - an attribute that is due, most observers believe, to the time spent with Desvigne. This gave him a somewhat different approach to music than that followed by stalwarts of the tradition, such as Jim Robinson. Indeed, many keen followers of Nelson's work consider his sophisticated trombone playing to be more akin to that of Tommy Dorsey rather than that of the earthier New Orleanians. Nelson could still be heard at Preservation Hall in the late 80s and into early 1990, when, in April, he was the victim of a hit-and-run accident. He continued working for a few days, but one night on the bandstand he complained of feeling unwell and collapsed. He died the following day.

● ALBUMS: *Kid Thomas At Moulin Rouge* (1955)★★★, *George*

Lewis And His New Orleans All Stars (1963)★★★★, *Peter Bocage At San Jacinto Hall* (1964)★★★, *Louis Nelson's Big Four Vols 1 & 2* (1964)★★★★, *Skater's Waltz* (1966)★★★, *Louis Nelson's New Orleans Band* (1970)★★★, *New Orleans Tradition* (1971)★★★, with Kid Thomas *Preservation Of Jazz Vol. 2* (1973)★★★, *Everybody's Talkin' Bout The* (GHB 1986)★★★, *Louis Nelson All Stars Live In Japan* (1987)★★, *April In New Orleans* (GHB 1989)★★★, *New Orleans Portraits Vol 3* (Storyville 1990)★★★.

NELSON, OLIVER

b. 4 June 1932, St. Louis, Missouri, USA, d. 28 October 1975, Los Angeles, California, USA. After studying piano and alto saxophone, he settled on playing the latter instrument, paying his dues in various territory bands. In the late 40s he was with the popular Jeter-Pillars Orchestra as well as that led by Nat Towles. Early in the 50s he was briefly with Louis Jordan but then resumed his studies at universities in Washington, DC, and Missouri, also taking lessons from the respected composer Elliott Carter. In New York in the late 50s, he worked in bands led by Erskine Hawkins and Louie Bellson, then moved on to the bands of Duke Ellington and Quincy Jones. He was writing extensively at this time, both as arranger and composer, and made several records under his own name, the best-known with a small group that often featured leading jazz soloists such as Eric Dolphy and Freddie Hubbard. He later turned more to big band work, recording with numerous soloists who included Johnny Hodges and Pee Wee Russell. By the mid-60s Nelson was in great demand as a teacher and arranger and he was also called upon to write scores for films and television. His classy arrangements with Jimmy Smith during this period were particularly fertile, and included orchestrations of *Bashin'* and *The Dymanic Duo* (with Wes Montgomery). He played much less frequently in these years but did lead a small band from time to time and also formed all-star big bands for festival appearances. Nelson's work ranged widely, covering R&B and modal jazz, and he also composed pieces in the classical form. Much of his writing suggests considerable facility, though very occasionally slipping a little into being merely facile. Nevertheless his recordings as a performer, especially the majestic *Blues And The Abstract Truth*, on which he is joined by Dolphy and Hubbard, are extremely rewarding. 'Stolen Moments' from this album is an unsung jazz classic. Many of the other albums he made as composer-leader, such as the excellent *Sound Pieces*, are interesting for their unstinting professionalism. He died from a heart attack in 1975.

● ALBUMS: *Meet Oliver Nelson* (New Jazz 1959)★★★★, *Takin' Care Of Business* (New Jazz 1960)★★★★, *Screamin' The Blues* (New Jazz 1960)★★★★, *Soul Battle* (New Jazz 1960)★★★, *Nocturne* (Moodsville 1960)★★★, *Blues And The Abstract Truth* (Impulse! 1961)★★★★★, *Main Stem* (Prestige 1961)★★★, *Straight Ahead* (New Jazz 1961)★★★★, *Afro-American Sketches* (Prestige 1962)★★★, *Main Stem* (Prestige 1962)★★★, *Impressions Of Phaedra* (United Artists 1962)★★★, *Full Nelson* (Verve 1963)★★★, *Fantabulous* (Argo 1964)★★★, *More Blues And The Abstract Truth* (Impulse! 1965)★★, *Michelle* (Prestige 1966)★★, *Sound Pieces* (Impulse! 1966)★★★★, *Live From Los Angeles* (Prestige 1967)★★★, *Happenings* (Impulse! 1967)★★★, *Musical Tribute To JFK: The Kennedy Dream* (Impulse! 1967)★★★, with Pee Wee Russell *The Spirit Of '67* (Impulse! 1967)★★★, *Soulful Brass* (Impulse! 1968)★★★, *Leonard Feather Presents The Sound Of Feeling And The Sound Of Oliver Nelson* (Verve 1968)★★★, *Black, Brown And Beautiful* (RCA 1970)★★★, *Berlin Dialogue For Orchestra* (Flying Dutchman 1970)★★★★, *Swiss Suite* (Flying Dutchman 1971)★★★, *Oliver Nelson With Oily Rags* (Flying Dutchman 1974)★★, *Skull Session* (Flying Dutchman 1975)★★★, *Stolen Moments* (Inner City 1975)★★★★.

NESBITT, JOHN

b. *c.*1900, Norfolk, West Virginia, USA, d. 1935. In the early 20s Nesbitt played trumpet with various bands before joining the band led by Bill McKinney, which eventually evolved into McKinney's Cotton Pickers. He stayed with the band for several years, playing and writing arrangements. In the early 30s he was resident in New York, playing in the bands of Fletcher Henderson and Luis Russell, before returning to territory bands, including those of Zack Whyte and Speed Webb.

● COMPILATIONS: *McKinney's Cotton Pickers (1928-29)* (1983).

● FURTHER READING: *McKinney's Music: A Bio-discography Of McKinney's Cotton Pickers*, John Chilton.

NESTICO, SAMMY

b. 6 February 1924, Pittsburgh, Pennsylvania, USA. Nestico studied music after completing military service, although by this time he had already gained experience playing trombone in a radio orchestra. During the 50s and 60s he worked as staff arranger for various military bands. In the late 60s he began writing for Count Basie and subsequently wrote for films and television. He is also a teacher and many of his arrangements have been written with college and university bands in mind. He is a cousin of the arranger Sal Nistico.

● ALBUMS: *Swingphonic (With Time Out For Seven)* (70s)★★, by Count Basie *Basie Big Band* (1975)★★★★, by Basie *Warm Breeze* (1981)★★★, *Dark Orchid* (1982)★★★, *Night Flight* (1985)★★★★, with Frank Capp Juggernaut *'Play It Again Sam'* (Concord Jazz 1997)★★★.

NEW BIRTH BRASS BAND

A New Orleans, Louisiana, USA-based sextet, the New Birth Brass Band have done much to revive the city's marching brass band jazz tradition. Led by trumpeter and lead vocalist James Andrews, the group does not, however, intend simply to imitate that tradition. 'The old cats used to play a lot of sacred dirges and church hymns and traditional standards, and we just got a new spin with our new music and a new beat', Andrews told *Billboard* magazine at the time of the release of their debut album. The rest of the group is comprised of Derrick Shezbie (trumpet), Kerwin James (tuba), Kerry Hunter (snare drum), Cayetano Hingle (bass drums) and Reginald Steward (trombone). It is Andrews' trumpet-playing that has been the main focus of attention in jazz circles - leading to him being saddled with a

'Satchmo of the Ghetto' moniker. By the time he assembled the New Birth Brass Band, Andrews was already a veteran of groups such as the Danny Barker Band, the Junior Olympia Brass Band, the All Star Brass Band, and the Treme Brass Band. It was for the latter that he composed 'Gimme My Money Back', already considered a Mardi Gras classic. Andrews has also toured alongside artists including Michelle Shocked, Wynton Marsalis, Quincy Jones and Dizzy Gillespie. Traditional material on *D-Boy*, the group's 1997 debut, included the marching standards 'Whoopin' Blues', 'Jesus On The Main Line' and 'Li'l Liza Jane', alongside Andrews originals such as the title track.

● ALBUMS: *D-Boy* (NYNO 1997)★★★.

NEW CONCEPTS OF ARTISTRY IN RHYTHM - STAN KENTON

When west coast big band leader Stan Kenton recorded this 1952 masterpiece, his powerful and versatile 21-piece featured bebop trumpet virtuoso and high note specialist Maynard Ferguson, trombonists Frank Rosolino and Bill Russo, the brilliant and advanced alto saxophonist Lee Konitz, Sal Salvador on guitar and the subtle swing of drummer Stan Levey. It is a typically dramatic production – dissonant and experimental, and thunderous in a similar way to the Hollywood film music of the time. Highlights include a fascinating introduction ('This Is An Orchestra') featuring Kenton as narrator and, among the CD's extra tracks, a brilliantly 'out' rearrangement of 'You Go To My Head'.

● Tracks: *Prologue (This Is An Orchestra!); Portrait Of A Count; Young Blood; Frank Seaking; 23 Degrees North - 82 Degrees West; Taboo; Lonesome Train; Invention For Guitar And Trumpet; My Lady; Swing House; Improvisation; You Go To My Head.*

● First released 1952

● UK peak chart position: did not chart

● USA peak chart position: did not chart

NEW TIJUANA MOODS - CHARLES MINGUS

The original sessions for this album were held in 1957 and released as *Tijuana Moods*; the bonus of the CD age gives us additional alternate versions that benefit from digital remastering. It is glorious fare, with Mingus leading strong musicians on his personal favourite recording. Mingus acts like a kindly father allowing his offspring to shine, without taking over or showing off; this alone is a sure sign of his greatness as a musician and band leader.

● Tracks: *Dizzy Moods; Ysabel's Table Dance; Tijuana Gift Shop; Los Mariachis; Flamingo; Dizzy Moods; Tijuana Gift Shop; Los Mariachis II; Flamingo.*

● First released 1986 (1957 recordings)

● UK peak chart position: did not chart

● USA peak chart position: did not chart

NEW JAZZ ORCHESTRA

The New Jazz Orchestra was founded in 1963 by Clive Burrows and resurrected and directed by Neil Ardley between 1964 and 1968. It provided the up-and-coming generation of British jazz musicians with the experience of working with a large jazz orchestra, its personnel including Harry Beckett, Henry Lowther and Ian Carr (trumpets), Paul Rutherford and Mike Gibbs (trombones), Don Rendell, Trevor Watts, Dick Heckstall-Smith and Barbara Thompson (saxophones), Michael Garrick (piano), Jack Bruce (bass) and Jon Hiseman (drums). It is not surprising that with such high-quality musicians *The Times* critic, Miles Kington, would write that the NJO 'makes most big bands sound like trained elephants with two tricks'. It was not the only purpose of the NJO to provide such invaluable big band experience for these musicians; it also fostered a workshop atmosphere to provide its arrangers with a chance to try out scores. Among those who wrote for the orchestra were Ardley, Alan Cohen, Gibbs, Rutherford, Garrick and Mike Taylor. 'I learnt by my mistakes', Ardley said later, and by the time he had become the leader he was producing major scores including 'Shades Of Blue' from the first album and 'Dejeuner Sur L'Herbe' from the second. All the material in the latter is derived from two/four-bar motifs in the main theme. There are no repeated chord sequences or scales; rather, the piece grows organically in the manner of classical music. This is not merely a third-stream piece but an attempt to write jazz in new way. It was the kind of experiment the NJO was formed to encourage and a score Ardley would have been lucky to have performed anywhere else. The NJO gave some concerts in London and at festivals. They also had a fruitful pairing with Colosseum. Despite what a contemporary described as its 'fiercely swinging rhythm, first class solos and brilliant ensemble', it gained no recognition abroad, though in time many of its members have become very well known on the continent.

● ALBUMS: *Western Reunion* (1965)★★★, *Le Dejeuner Sur L'Herbe* (1969)★★★★.

NEW ORLEANS RHYTHM KINGS

After the hugely popular Original Dixieland Jazz Band created a storm of interest in Chicago in the early 20s, other musicians decided to try their luck at the new jazz music. Among them were Georg Brunis, Jack Pettis, Arnold Loyacano, Louis Black, Elmer Schoebel and Frank Snyder. They formed a band they named the New Orleans Rhythm Kings for an engagement at the Friars Inn. With the ODJB safely on their way to international fame in New York and London, the NORK became Chicago's top jazz band. They recorded in 1922 and looked set to become one of the mainstays of the suddenly vital white jazz scene. With a few personnel changes the band was strengthened, but by 1925 they had folded, leaving behind a handful of records and a lasting impression upon the next generation of musicians who would form the basis of Chicago-style jazz.

● COMPILATIONS: *The New Orleans Rhythm Kings 1922-23* (Swaggie 1988)★★★★, *The New Orleans Rhythm Kings* 1923 recordings (Swaggie 1988)★★★, *The New Orleans Rhythm Kings Vol. 1* (King Jazz 1992)★★★★, *The New Orleans Rhythm Kings Vol. 2* (Village Jazz 1992)★★★★.

NEW YORK JAZZ REPERTORY ORCHESTRA

(see Hyman, Dick)

NEWBORN, PHINEAS, JNR.

b. 14 December 1931, Whiteville, Tennessee, USA, d. 26 May 1989. In the late 40s and early 50s Newborn, a gifted multi-instrumentalist who had studied extensively, played piano in a number of R&B and blues bands in and around Memphis, Tennessee. He had two brief spells with Lionel Hampton before military service interrupted his career. Subsequently, he led his own small group in New York, played with Charles Mingus, Oscar Pettiford and Kenny Clarke among others, made several records and appeared in the John Cassavetes film *Shadows* (1960). Relocated in Los Angeles in the 60s, he continued to record with artists such as Howard McGhee, Teddy Edwards, Ray Brown and Elvin Jones. His career then faltered, largely through a nervous breakdown and an injury to his hands, but the mid-70s saw his return to public performances. Newborn's early records were marked by displays of his phenomenal technique, while those made later suggested a growing maturity. Unfortunately, the interruptions to his career did not allow his potential full rein, and further illness prevented him from working for most of the 80s. Doctors discovered a lung tumour in 1988; he died the following year. The last years of his life are movingly recounted in a chapter of Stanley Booth's book on Memphis musicians, *Rhythm Oil*.

● ALBUMS: *Here Is Phineas* (Atlantic 1956)★★★, *Phineas Rainbow* (RCA Victor 1956)★★★, *Phineas Newborn With Dennis Farnon Orchestra* (1957)★★, *While The Lady Sleeps* (RCA Victor 1957), *Phineas Newborn And His Orchestra Plays Jamaica* (RCA Victor 1957)★★★, *Fabulous Phineas* (RCA Victor 1958)★★, with Paul Chambers, Roy Haynes *We Three* (New Jazz 1958)★★★★, *Stockholm Jam Session Vol 1* and 2 (Steeple Chase 1958 recording)★★★★, *Phineas Newborn Plays Again* (1959)★★★, *Piano Portraits* (Roulette 1959)★★, *Newborn Piano* (1959)★★★, *I Love A Piano* (Roulette 1960)★★★, *The World Of Piano* (Contemporary 1961)★★★★, *The Great Jazz Piano Of Phineas Newborn* (Contemporary 1962)★★★★, *The Newborn Touch* (Contemporary 1964)★★★★, *Please Send Me Someone To Love* (Contemporary 1969)★★★★, *Harlem Blues* (Original Jazz Classics 1969)★★★★, *Solo Piano* (Atlantic 1974)★★★, *Solo* (1975)★★★, *Look Out...Phineas Is Back* (Pablo 1976)★★★, *Phineas Is Genius* (1977)★★★, *Tivoli Encounter* 1979 live recording (Storyville 1998)★★★.

NEWMAN, DAVID 'FATHEAD'

b. 24 February 1933, Dallas, Texas, USA. Newman is a tenor/baritone/soprano saxophone player and flautist, whose work contains elements of both jazz and R&B. In the early 50s he toured with Texan blues guitarist 'T-Bone' Walker and recorded the classic 'Reconsider Baby' with Lowell Fulson in 1954. For the next 10 years Newman was part of Ray Charles's orchestra, appearing on landmark recordings such as 'I Got A Woman', 'What'd I Say' and 'Lonely Avenue'. Other tenures have included the saxophone position in Herbie Mann's Family Of Mann (1972-74). He has recorded some two dozen albums as a leader since 1958, most tending towards mainstream and post-bop jazz with a funk edge, and has worked extensively as an accompanist in the blues, rock and jazz fields. He worked on Natalie Cole's bestselling *Unforgettable* (1990), and enjoyed much acclaim for his involvement in the *Bluesiana Triangle* benefit projects in aid of the homeless. *Blue Greens And Beans* was a collection of bop standards also featuring another Texan player, Marchel Ivery.

● ALBUMS: *Ray Charles Presents David 'Fathead' Newman* (Atlantic 1959)★★★★, *Straight Ahead* (Atlantic 1961)★★★★, *Fathead Comes On* (Atlantic 1962)★★★, *House Of David* (Atlantic 1968)★★, *Lonely Avenue* (1971)★★★, *Mr. Fathead* (1976)★★★, *Fire! Live At the Village Vanguard* (Atlantic 1989)★★★, *Blue Greens And Beans* (Timeless 1991)★★★, *Blue Head* (Candid 1991)★★★, with Art Blakey, Dr. John *Bluesiana Triangle* (1990)★★★, *Return To The Wide Open Spaces* (Meteor 1993)★★★.

● COMPILATIONS: *Back To Basics* (1990)★★★.

NEWMAN, JOE

b. 7 September 1922, New Orleans, Louisiana, USA, d. 4 July 1992, New York, USA. After playing with and leading a college band, trumpeter Newman joined Lionel Hampton in 1941. Two years later he joined Count Basie at the start of a long association. In the late 40s and early 50s he spent some time in bands led by Illinois Jacquet and J.C. Heard and also led his own bands for club and record dates. By 1952 he was back in the Basie fold and he remained with the band, handling most of the trumpet solos, until 1961. Subsequently, he toured worldwide, usually as a solo act, but occasionally in specially formed bands such as those led by Benny Goodman and Hampton. He also became active in jazz education. This pattern of work continued throughout the 80s and into the early 90s. A powerful player with a wide repertoire, Newman's style acknowledged latter-day developments in jazz trumpet while remaining rooted in the concepts of his great idol, Louis Armstrong.

● ALBUMS: *Joe Newman And His Band* (Vanguard 1954)★★★, *Joe Newman And The Boys In The Band* (Storyville 1954)★★★, *The Joe Newman Sextet* (1954)★★★, *All I Wanna Do Is Swing* (RCA Victor 1955)★★, *The Count's Men* (Jazztone 1955)★★★★, *I'm Still Swinging* (RCA Victor 1955)★★★, *I Feel Like A Newman* (Storyville 1956)★★★, *Salute To Satch* (RCA Victor 1956)★★, *The Joe Newman-Frank Wess Septet* (1956)★★★, *New Sounds In Swing* (Jazztone 1956)★★★★, *Jazz For Playboys* (Savoy 1957)★★★, *The Happy Cats* (Coral 1957)★★★, *Midgets* (Vik 1957)★★, *The Joe Newman-Zoot Sims Quartet* (1957)★★★, *Swing Lightly* (Jazztone 1957)★★★★, *Locking Horns* (Roulette 1958)★★★★, *Soft Swingin' Jazz* (Coral 1958)★★★, *Joe Newman And His Orchestra With Woodwinds* (Roulette 1958)★★★, *Joe Newman And Count Basie's All Stars* (1958)★★★★, *Jive At Five* (Swingville 1960)★★★★, *Countin'* (World Pacific 1960)★★★, *Good 'N' Groovy* (Swingville 1961)★★★, *Joe's Hap'nin's* (Swingville 1961)★★★★, *The Joe Newman-Oliver Nelson Quintet* (1961)★★★★, *In A Mellow Mood* (1962)★★★, *Shiny Stockings*

(1965)★★★★, *Way Down Blues* (1965)★★★, with Lionel Hampton *Newport Uproar!* (1967)★★★, *I Love My Baby* (1978)★★★, *Joe Newman-Jimmy Rowles Duets* (1979)★★★, *At The Atlantic* (Phontastic 1978)★★★, *Similar Souls* (Vogue 1983)★★★, with Joe Wilder *Hangin' Out* (Concord 1984)★★★.

NEWPORT JAZZ FESTIVAL

Newport, Rhode Island, USA is not the kind of venue normally associated with music that began as low-life entertainment, but the jazz festival, begun in 1954, blended comfortably into Newport's somewhat refined surroundings with considerable ease. The nature of the event, which was founded by two of Newport's top set, Louis and Elaine Lorillard and directed by George Wein, was exposed to the world at large thanks to a marvellous, if occasionally visually overwrought, evocation of the 1958 festival filmed by Bert Stern and released in 1960 under the title *Jazz On A Summer's Day*. The artists at Newport that year included Louis Armstrong, Gerry Mulligan, Dinah Washington, Thelonious Monk, gospel singer Mahalia Jackson and, perhaps the most visually arresting sight of the festival, Anita O'Day in hip-hugging dress, gloves and cartwheel hat. Following crowd trouble in 1960, the 1961 festival was cancelled, but it was back the following year. However, more unsavoury events in 1971 caused it be moved permanently to New York City. Still under Wein's benignly autocratic direction, the festival gained in strength and has never lost its early importance. New York is where it remains, with events taking place over 10 days in June in venues ranging from Carnegie Hall to small intimate clubs, and even onto the streets of the city. Over the years the festival's name has changed slightly to accommodate different sponsors but most recently, in deference to the Japanese Victor Corporation, it has been known as the JVC Jazz Festival New York. Since 1984 Newport has once again had its own festival, with George Wein presenting a two-day show in August at Fort Adams State Park, again under the patronage of JVC.

NEWTON, DAVID

b. 2 February 1958, Glasgow, Scotland. As a child he took lessons on piano, clarinet and bassoon, but while studying at the Leeds College of Music he decided to concentrate on piano. After playing in various bands as a semi-pro, he secured his first professional engagement leading a trio at a restaurant in Bradford, Yorkshire, in 1978. Around this time he also played in numerous other bands, ranging musically from traditional jazz to funk, from strict-tempo dance bands to classical. In the early 80s he worked extensively in the theatre, especially with Scarborough-based playwright Alan Ayckbourn. Newton then returned to Scotland, and from a base in Edinburgh quickly established himself as a rising star of the jazz world. He played in backing groups for many visiting jazzmen, including Art Farmer, Bud Shank, Shorty Rogers and Nat Adderley. He also recorded with Buddy De Franco. By the late 80s he had settled in London, recording with Alan Barnes, the Jazz Renegades, Martin Taylor, with whom he toured India, and also playing club dates with Andy Cleyndert, Don Weller, Spike Robinson and others. At the end of the decade he became accompanist and musical director to Carol Kidd, recording with her and making numerous concert appearances. An outstanding talent, Newton's wide-ranging experience has ensured that he is at home in most musical settings. Despite his eclecticism he has developed a distinctive and distinguished personal style. As he matures he appears likely to become one of Europe's leading jazz musicians, well-equipped to take the music into the 21st century.

● ALBUMS: with Alan Barnes *Affiliation* (1987)★★★, *Given Time* (GFM 1988)★★★, *Victim Of Circumstance* (Linn 1991)★★★★, *Eye Witness* (Linn 1991)★★★, *Return Journey* (Linn 1993)★★★, with Barnes *Like Minds* (Fret 1993)★★★, *12th Of The 12th* (Candid 1997)★★★★, DNA (Candid 1998)★★★★.

NEWTON, FRANKIE

b. 4 January 1906, Emory, Virginia, USA, d. 11 March 1954. In the late 20s and early 30s Newton played trumpet in a number of leading New York bands, including those led by Charlie 'Fess' Johnson, Sam Wooding and Chick Webb. He later joined Charlie Barnet and was briefly with Andy Kirk. The 40s saw him playing in various bands on the verge of the big-time, including those led by Lucky Millinder and Pete Brown. Apparently without direction, his career drifted and he worked mostly in clubs in New York and Boston, sometimes in company with James P. Johnson, 'Big' Sid Catlett and Edmond Hall. By the 50s he was playing only rarely. A gifted player with a full, burnished sound, Newton was especially attuned to the needs of singers and played on a number of memorable vocal recordings, including Bessie Smith's last date, plus Maxine Sullivan's 'Loch Lomond', and Billie Holiday's 'Strange Fruit' session. Newton's briefly shining talent promised much, but his lack of ambition steadfastly countered any chance of popular success. However, the easy-going life he led was perhaps what he really wanted.

● COMPILATIONS: *At The Onyx Club 1937-1939* (Tax 1987)★★★, *Frankie's Jump* (Affinity 1993)★★★★.

NEWTON, JAMES

b. 1 May 1953, Los Angeles, California, USA. Already playing a host of reed instruments, Newton took up the flute when he was 17 years old. After three years in Stanley Crouch's Black Music Infinity (1972-75), playing saxophones alongside Arthur Blythe and David Murray, Newton moved to New York in 1978. By now working only on flute, he led groups with Anthony Davis, an important association that continues. He also played with Cecil Taylor and began recording as a leader. As well as experimenting with unusual flute techniques found in modern classical music, Newton has developed the art of humming and playing simultaneously to the degree of producing contrapuntal lines. Newton taught at the University of California, Irvine during the 90s, and is currently composer-in-residence at the Societa Italiana Par Lo Studio Della Musica Afro

Americana in Pescara, Italy. His extensive collaborations have resulted in live and recorded sessions with artists as diverse as drummer Andrew Cyrille, saxophonist David Murray, flautist Yacouba Alzouma and Chinese erhu player Chen Jie-Bing. His 1997 trio session with Indian alto saxophonist Kadri Gopalnath and mridangam drummer P. Svinivasan was a mesmerising fusion of jazz and raga rhythms.

● ALBUMS: with David Murray *Solomon's Sons* (Circle 5 1977)★★★, *From Inside* (BV Haast 1978)★★★, *Crystal Texts* (Moers 1979)★★★, *Paseo Del Mar* (India Navigation 1978)★★★, *Mystery School* (India Navigation 1979)★★★, with Anthony Davis *Hidden Voices* (India Navigation 1980)★★★, *Axum* (ECM 1981)★★★, *James Newton* (Gramavision 1983)★★★★, *Luella* (Gramavision 1984)★★★★, *Echo Canyon* (Celestial Harmonies 1985)★★★, *Water Mystery* (Gramavision 1985)★★★, *The African Flower* (Blue Note 1986)★★★★, *Romance And Revolution* (Blue Note 1987)★★★, *In Venice* (1988)★★★, *Suite For Frida Kahlo* (Audioquest 1995)★★★, *Above Is Above All* (Contour 1997)★★★★, with Kadri Gopalnath, P. Svinivasan *Southern Brothers* (Water Lily Acoustics 1997)★★★★, with Chen Jie-Bing *Yellow River Blue* (Water Lily Acoustics 1997)★★★, *Suite For Frida Kahlo* 1994 recording (Audioquest 1997)★★★.

● FURTHER READING: *Improvising Flute*, James Newton.

NICE JAZZ FESTIVAL

The first jazz festival held in Nice, in the south of France, took place in 1948, when it was headlined by Louis Armstrong. Although it was in some ways the touch-paper that lit the fire of enthusiasm for jazz festivals, it was not until 1974 that the Nice Jazz Festival became a regular and important event on the international jazz calendar. Today the Grande Parade du Jazz, held in July at the Jardins des Arénes de Cimiez, and presented by George Wein, is a major event attracting audiences approaching 75,000. It also draws leading artists from the USA, UK and the rest of the world.

NICHOLAS, 'WOODEN' JOE

b. 23 September 1883, New Orleans, Louisiana, USA, d. 17 November 1957. A well-known figure in his native city, Nicholas started out on clarinet but took up the cornet under the influence of Buddy Bolden and Joe 'King' Oliver. He worked in marching bands, forming his own, the Camelia Band, in 1918. A powerful player with an earthy, basic style, Nicholas embodied the traditions of the music but never managed to achieve the panache of his idols and mentors. His nephew was the distinguished clarinettist Albert Nicholas.

● ALBUMS: with others *Echoes From New Orleans (1945)* (1988)★★★, *Echoes From New Orleans Vol. 2 (1949-51)* (1988)★★★.

NICHOLAS, ALBERT

b. 27 May 1900, New Orleans, Louisiana, USA, d. 3 September 1973. After taking lessons from Lorenzo Tio, the young Nicholas, a nephew of 'Wooden' Joe Nicholas, played the clarinet in bands led by several of his home-town's leading musicians, who included Buddy Petit, Joe 'King' Oliver and Manuel Perez. Service in the US Navy during World War I interrupted his career, but after the war he returned to working in various New Orleans-based bands, some of which he led. Late in 1924 he joined Oliver in Chicago, leaving again in the autumn of 1926 to work in Shanghai, China. On the way back home he played in Cairo, Egypt, and Paris, France. Back in the USA at the end of 1928 he joined Luis Russell for a five-year stint. He then played with Chick Webb, Sam Wooding, John Kirby, Louis Armstrong, Zutty Singleton and others, mostly in and around New York. In the early 40s he dropped out of music, but returned in mid-decade to work with Bunk Johnson, Kid Ory and others who were benefiting from the resurgence of interest in traditional jazz. In the early 50s he toured Europe, settling in France for the rest of his life, making occasional trips to the USA. One of the best of the New Orleans clarinettists, Nicholas played with a rich, full sound, favouring the chalumeau end of the instrument's range and liberally imbuing his solos with a strong feeling for the blues.

● ALBUMS: with Art Hodes *The New Orleans Chicago Connection* (Delmark 1959)★★★, *Tribute To Jelly Roll Morton* (60s)★★, *Memorial* (60s)★★★, *Albert Nicholas And The John Defferary Jazztet* (60s)★★★.

● COMPILATIONS: with Joe 'King' Oliver *Snag It Vol. 1* (1926-27)★★★★, *The Luis Russell Story* (1929-30)★★★, with Jelly Roll Morton *Last Band Dates* (1940)★★★, with Baby Dodds *Jazz A La Creole* (1946)★★★.

NICHOLAS, BIG NICK

b. George Walker Nicholas, 2 August 1922, Lansing, Michigan, USA, d. 29 October 1997, New York City, New York, USA. Nicholas took up the tenor saxophone during his teenage years, having earlier studied piano and clarinet. Among his teenage colleagues were Hank and Thad Jones. In the early 40s Nicholas worked in some well-known and important bands, including those led by Earl Hines and Tiny Bradshaw. He was also active in the early experimental days of bop, playing at Mintons. In the late 40s he played in the bands of Sabby Lewis and Lucky Millinder, and was a member of Dizzy Gillespie's big band, with which he recorded in 1947, soloing on 'Manteca'. In the 50s Nicholas played regularly in New York, often as leader of small groups, but by the end of the decade his career was in the doldrums, a situation that persisted through to the end of the 60s. In the early 70s he began attracting more attention both as a performer and teacher, and later began touring internationally, although it would be 1983 before he made his first album under his own name. Nicholas's later years were spent largely in and around New York, playing club engagements. Nicholas played with a warm, rich sound in which could be heard echoes of his admiration for Coleman Hawkins. He also composed, his best-known work being 'Big Nick', a tune recorded by John Coltrane on a 1962 album with Duke Ellington. Nicholas's few albums as leader, allied to occasional solo spots on records with Millinder, Gillespie, Oran 'Hot Lips' Page, with whom he had a long professional association in the late 40s and early

50s, show him to have been a player worthy of much greater prominence than was accorded him during his lifetime.

● ALBUMS: *Big And Warm* (India Navigation 1983)★★★, *Big Nick* (India Navigation 1984)★★★.

Nichols, Herbie

b. 3 December 1919, New York City, New York, USA, d. 12 April 1963. In the late 30s and early 40s Nichols played piano with numerous bands in a wide variety of styles. The bands included those of Herman Autrey, Illinois Jacquet, Lucky Thompson, Edgar Sampson and Arnett Cobb, while the styles ranged across small-group swing, Dixieland and R&B. A remarkably original and talented musician, Nichols developed a personal music that owed a debt to bebop, particularly to its more idiosyncratic practitioners such as Thelonious Monk, but for much of his life the only gigs he could secure were playing Dixieland music, which he came to dislike intensely. In the early 60s, he was able to work occasionally with modern musicians closer to his advanced thinking, among them Roswell Rudd and Archie Shepp, but by then he was terminally ill with leukaemia (though Rudd also blamed 'a broken heart' brought on by 'years of frustration, neglect and disillusionment'). In recent years Nichols' reputation has grown rapidly and there have been several tribute albums that feature his compositions, notably two on the Soul Note label and one each by Holland's Instant Composers Pool Orchestra and New York's Jazz Composers Collective. Nichols' own recorded legacy, though small, is of outstanding quality: two Blue Note trio sessions, reissued as the double album *The Third World*, feature sympathetic support from Art Blakey and Max Roach. A later trio set for Bethlehem has George Duvivier and Dannie Richmond. These records mostly feature his own distinctive and delightful compositions, some of which - '2300 Skiddoo', 'Shuffle Montgomery', 'House Party Starting', 'Hangover Triangle' - look like becoming established standards in the 90s. 'There is charm and interest all around you', Rudd wrote of Nichols' music, 'from bright ripples on down to heavy undercurrents. What a beautiful sense of space! What incredible lyricism! What soulfullness! What grace! What an expansive palette of sonorities!. Wit, taste, discretion, subtleties, nuances . . . and all so personal and individual.'

● ALBUMS: *The Prophetic Herbie Nichols Volume 1* 10-inch album (Blue Note 1955)★★★★, *The Prophetic Herbie Nichols Volume 2* 10-inch album (Blue Note 1955)★★★★, *The Third World* (Blue Note 1955)★★★★, *The Herbie Nichols Trio* (Blue Note 1956)★★★, *Out Of The Shadows* (Affinity 1957)★★★★, *Love, Gloom, Cash And Love* (Bethlehem 1957)★★★, the Herbie Nichols Project *Love Is Proximity* (Soul Note 1997)★★★★.

● COMPILATIONS: *The Complete Blue Note Recordings* 5-LP/3-CD box set (Mosaic/Blue Note 1997)★★★★.

● FURTHER READING: *Four Lives In The Bebop Business*, A.B. Spellman.

Nichols, Keith

b. 13 February 1945, Ilford, Essex, England. Although he was playing the trombone and leading the band at school Nichols also became All-Britain junior accordion champion. He can now play most of the instruments in the bands he leads but excels on piano and trombone. He played with Dick Sudhalter's Anglo-American Alliance (1969) before leading bands of his own, such as the New Sedalia, in the early 70s. He led the Ragtime Orchestra which played scholarly versions of the repertoire, before going to the USA to record with the New Paul Whiteman Orchestra. He wrote arrangements for the New York Jazz Repertory Company, for Dick Hyman and for the Pasadena Roof Orchestra. By 1978 he was well equipped to found the Midnite Follies Orchestra with Alan Cohen. Their aim was to play the music of the 20s and 30s and original pieces in a similar vein. Nichols is an authority on ragtime and earlier styles of jazz, and he works ceaselessly to keep them being performed. In the mid-80s he played with Harry Gold (bass saxophone) and led the Paramount Theatre Orchestra. He now leads his own Cotton Club Band.

● ALBUMS: *Ragtime Rules OK?* (1976)★★★, *Hotter Than Hades* (1978)★★★, *Jungle Nights In Harlem* (1981)★★★, *Shakin' The Blues Away* (Stomp Off 1988)★★★, *Doctors Jazz* (Stomp Off 1988)★★, *Chitterlin' Strut* (Stomp Off 1989)★★★, *Syncopated Jamboree* (Stomp Off 1992)★★★, *Keith Nichols* (Stomp Off 1992)★★★, *I Like To Do Things For You* (Stomp Off 1993)★★★, Henderson Stomp (Stomp Off 1994)★★★, *Harlem's Arabian Nights* (Stomp Off 1997)★★★★.

Nichols, Red

b. Ernest Loring Nichols, 8 May 1905, Ogden, Utah, USA, d. 28 June 1965, Las Vegas, Nevada, USA. Taught by his father, cornetist Nichols quickly became a highly accomplished performer. Strongly influenced by early white jazz bands, and in particular by Bix Beiderbecke, he moved to New York in the early 20s and was soon one of the busiest musicians in town. He recorded hundreds of tracks, using a bewildering array of names for his bands, but favouring the Five Pennies, a group that was usually eight pieces or more in size. In these bands Nichols used the cream of the white jazzmen of the day, including one of his closest friends, Miff Mole, plus Jimmy Dorsey, Joe Venuti, Eddie Lang, Pee Wee Russell, Benny Goodman and Jack Teagarden. Although his sharp business sense and desire for formality and respect alienated him from hard-living contemporaries such as Eddie Condon, Nichols remained enormously successful, continuing to lead bands and record until the outbreak of World War II. After a brief spell outside music Nichols returned to performing with a short stint with Glen Gray, and then resumed his bandleading career from his new base in California. A sentimental Hollywood biopic, *The Five Pennies* (1959), starring Danny Kaye, gave his career a boost and during the last few years of his life he was as busy as he had ever been in the 20s. A polished player with a silvery tone and a bold, attacking style that reflected his admiration for

Beiderbecke, Nichols at his best came close to matching his idol. As a bandleader he left an important recorded legacy of the best of 20s' white jazz.

● ALBUMS: *Jazz Time* (Capitol 1950)★★★★, *Red Nichols Vol 1* (Brunswick 1950)★★★, *Red Nichols Vol 2* (Brunswick 1950)★★★, *Red Nichols Vol 3* (Brunswick 1951)★★★, *Syncopated Chamber Music* Vols 1 And 2 (Audiophile 1953)★★★, *Red Nichols And Band* (Audiophile 1953)★★★★, *For Collectors Only* (Brunswick 1954)★★, *The Red Nichols Story* (Brunswick 1955)★★★★, *Hot Pennies* (Capitol 1956)★★★★, with the Charleston Chasers *Thesaurus Of Classic Jazz, Vol. 3* (1961)★★★.

● COMPILATIONS: *Class Of '39 - Radio Transcriptions* (1979)★★★, with Miff Mole *Red And Miff, 1925-31* (Village 1982)★★★★, *Rhythm Of The Day* (ASV 1983)★★★, *Feelin' No Pain (1920s-30s)* (Affinity 1987)★★★★, *Great Original Performances 1925-30* (1988)★★★, *Red Nichols And Other Radio Transcriptions* (Meritt 1988)★★★★, *Red Nichols And The Five Pennies Vols 1-5* (Swaggie 1989)★★★★.

NICHOLSON, J.D.

b. James David Nicholson, 12 April 1917, Monroe, Louisiana, USA, d. 27 July 1991, Los Angeles, California, USA. Nicholson learned to play the piano in church from the age of five. He later emigrated to the west coast where, influenced by the popular black recording artists of the day, he built up a solo act and travelled and performed all over California. In the mid-40s he teamed up with Jimmy McCracklin and they made their first recordings together; Nicholson played, McCracklin sang and both their styles were very much in the mould of Walter Davis. Over the next decade, Nicholson accompanied a number of well-known artists, such as Lowell Fulson and Ray Agee, and also made some records under his own name. Later in the 50s, Nicholson joined Jimmy Reed's band, and also played with Little Walter. He made a few more records in the 60s.

● COMPILATIONS: *Mr. Fullbright's Blues Vol. 2* (1990)★★★.

NICOLS, MAGGIE

b. 24 February 1948, Edinburgh, Scotland. Nicols is a renowned vocalist in UK jazz and has worked at the roots of experimental jazz since the mid-60s. She started her career in song and dance as a child by enrolling at the Italia Conti Stage School in London's Soho. By the age of 15 she was dancing and singing at the Windmill Theatre and at 16 was singing in cabaret in a Manchester, subsequently appearing at the Moulin Rouge in Paris after undergoing a dancing tour of Europe. By the mid-60s Nicols had turned her attention to jazz and had become a member of the Spontaneous Music Ensemble; she was also involved in inaugurating a free-jazz workshop in south London that included therapy work with mental patients, using jazz vocal expression as an emotional outlet. She was responsible for the instigation of several groups including the quartet Voice, which featured Julie Tippetts and Phil Minton and utilized Nicols' own experimental 'scat' language. Her involvement with the Feminist Improvising Group (and its European counterpart, the EWIG) found her working with the *avant garde* bassist Joëlle Léandre and the former Henry Cow multi-instrumentalist Lindsay Cooper, as well as the free-jazz pianist Irène Schweizer. In 1982 she collaborated with Léandre and Cooper to record the completely improvised *Live At The Bastille*. That same year, Nicols collaborated with Tippetts again on *Sweet And S'ours*. On this set there featured an example of the duo's idiosyncratic technique, with the use of vacuum-cleaner tubes (on 'Whailing'). 1985's joint effort with Peter Nu was released on Leo Records and was funded by the London Arts Council. Nicols has since continued to work in fringe theatre and various groups on the UK jazz scene.

● ALBUMS: with Voice *Voice* (1977)★★★, with Julie Tippetts *Sweet And S'ours* (1982)★★, with Joëlle Léandre, Lindsay Cooper *Live At The Bastille* 1982 recording (1984)★★, with Peter Nu *Nicols 'N' Nu* (1985)★★★, with Irène Schweizer, Paul Lovens, Léandre, Cooper *Live At Taklos* (1986)★★★, with Keith Tippett, Julie Tippetts *Mr. Invisible And The Drunken Sheilas* 1987 recording (1989)★★★.

NIEHAUS, LENNIE

b. 11 June 1929, St. Louis, Missouri, USA. After completing his studies at university in California, to where his family had moved when he was seven years old, alto saxophonist Niehaus joined Jerry Wald and then Stan Kenton in 1951. Apart from a spell away in the army, he remained with the Kenton band until 1960. During this period Niehaus also recorded under his own name and played and recorded with other small groups, including that led by Shorty Rogers. From the 60s onwards Niehaus was active in film and television studios, writing scores for a number of films including two, *City Heat* (1984) and *Pale Rider* (1985), that starred Clint Eastwood. When Eastwood came to make his film about Charlie Parker, *Bird* (1988), he invited Niehaus to handle the complex musical problems, which included writing the score and 'engineering' Parker's solos so that they could be re-recorded with new accompaniments. The skill and integrity with which Niehaus accomplished this difficult task represent one of the highlights of the film. A brilliant technician, playing with a hard-edged sound, Niehaus sometimes fails to engage the emotions of his listeners, but for the most part overcomes this failing through an extraordinary rush of exciting ideas.

● ALBUMS: *Lennie Niehaus Vol. 1: The Quintet* (1954-56)★★★, *Lennie Niehaus Vol. 2: The Octet/Zounds!* (1954-56)★★★, *Lennie Niehaus Vol. 3* (1955)★★, *The Lennie Niehaus Quintet With Strings* (1955)★★, *The Lennie Niehaus Sextet* (1956)★★★, *Lennie Niehaus* (1957)★★★, *Patterns* (Fresh Sound 1990)★★★★.

NIEMACK, JUDY

b. USA. A deep and richly textured singing voice allows Niemack to bring warmth and understanding to ballads and modern jazz standards alike. Her interpretations of songs indicate her awareness of the intentions of composers and lyricists and her performances always display originality and freshness of thought and approach.

On *Heart's Desire* she worked with Kenny Barron in what was clearly a meeting of minds.

● ALBUMS: *Blue Bop* (Freelance 1989)★★★, *Long As You're Living* (Freelance 1991)★★★, *Heart's Desire* (Stash 1992)★★★★, *Straight Up* (Freelance 1993)★★★, *Mingus Monk And Mal* (Freelance 1993)★★★.

Nimitz, Jack

b. Jerome Nimitz, 11 January 1930, Washington DC, USA. As a child Nimitz took up the clarinet and later played alto, but when he was in his early twenties he took over the baritone saxophone chair with Woody Herman. Two years later he moved into the Stan Kenton band, appearing on 1956's *Stan Kenton In Hi-Fi*, and after that began freelancing as a session musician. During the late 50s and on through the 60s he alternated between film studio work and jazz gigs, appearing with Kenton again and with various editions of Terry Gibbs's Dream Band, recording several times, including the 1961 recordings for Contemporary Records issued as *Main Stem* and *The Big Cat*. He also co-led a band with Bill Hood. In the 70s he continued his double life, appearing on the original line-up of Buddy Clark and Med Flory's Supersax and working with the big bands of Gerald Wilson and Bill Berry. Associations and activities such as these continued through the 80s and 90s with numerous sessions at clubs, festivals and always the 'day job' in the studios. In 1995 he finally got to record as leader, heading a quartet comprising pianist Lou Levy, bassist Dave Carpenter and drummer Joe LaBarbera on an accomplished Fresh Sound session. Enormously respected among musicians, Nimitz's playing of the baritone is flexible and swinging, and although he is best known for his solid section work he is an able bop-influenced soloist when let off the leash. On his own club dates he also regularly plays many of the other members of the saxophone family.

● ALBUMS: *Confirmation* (Fresh Sound 1995)★★★★, with Bill Berry *Live At Capozzoli's* (Woofy 1997)★★★.

Nistico, Sal

b. Salvatore Nistico, 12 April 1940, Syracuse, New York, USA, d. 3 March 1991. Nistico started out on alto saxophone, later switching to tenor and joining an R&B band. In the late 50s he joined the Jazz Brothers, a band led by Gap and Chuck Mangione. In 1962 he became a member of the Woody Herman band, to which he returned frequently during the next two decades. Also in the 60s he spent some time in the band of Count Basie and early in the 70s he was with Don Ellis. In the next few years he worked with Buddy Rich and Slide Hampton, with whom he visited Europe. Eventually he settled in Europe, working there through the 80s. A bristling, aggressive player in the post-bop tradition, Nistico's live and recorded performances are filled with excitement and a vitality that made his sudden death in 1991 all the more tragic.

● ALBUMS: with Chuck Mangione *Hey Baby!* (1961)★★★, *Heavyweights* (1961)★★★, *Comin' On Up* (1962)★★★, *Woody Herman, 1963* (1963)★★★★, *Encore* (1963)★★★, with Herman *Woody's Winners* (1965)★★★, *The Buddy Rich Septet* (1974)★★★★, *Just For Fun* (1976)★★, *East Of Isar* (1978)★★★, *Neo/Nistico* (1978)★★★.

Noa

b. Achinoam Nini, Israel. Of Yemenite origin, Noa was transplanted to New York, USA, at the age of one. She subsequently studied at the High School of Performing Arts. She then abandoned her studies to return to Israel to 'establish her identity' and complete her military service, at which time she also began her professional singing career. She regularly performed on makeshift stages to troops stationed throughout Israel as a member of the entertainment corps. However, it was in France that she initially found favour. Her self-titled debut album was produced by Pat Metheny (her instructor at Boston's Berklee School Of Music) and Steve Rodby, and released on Geffen Records. It quickly earned gold certification (100,000 sales) through Noa's frequent television and radio appearances. These included her performance of 'I Don't Know' on the Europe 1 *Top Live* programme, and the same song on television programme *Velvet Jungle* (plus a rendition of 'Ave Maria' with French duo Native). A further appearance on the *Taratata* television programme pushed the album higher up the French charts. Her second album, *Calling*, was recorded alongside long-time collaborator Gil Dor (co-founder of the Rimon School of Jazz and Contemporary Music, where Noa also studied) as well as Rupert Hine, who had previously produced for Tina Turner and Kate Bush. The resulting album explored themes as diverse as war ('Mark Of Cain'), female oppression ('Camilla') and seduction ('By The Light Of The Moon').

● ALBUMS: *Noa* (Geffen 1995)★★★★, *Calling* (Geffen 1996)★★★.

Noble, Steve

b. 16 March 1960, Streatley, Berkshire, England. Noble studied with the Nigerian master-drummer Elkan Ogunde. His first professional engagement was with the *avant garde* jazz-pop group, Rip Rig And Panic, touring England and Europe and playing on *I'm Cold* (1982) and *Attitude* (1983). His precision and invention as a percussionist made it natural for him to gravitate towards free improvisation. In 1985 he appeared at the Thessalonika Jazz Festival with Derek Bailey and later took part in the Company Weeks of 1987, 1989 and 1990. In 1987 he toured Holland with Tristan Honsinger. In the late 80s, he was part of the Alan Wilkinson Trio and a member of Kahondo Style. A long-standing partnership with pianist Alex Maguire produced countless gigs and *Live At Oscars*. Noble, along with Louis Moholo, provided percussion for Maguire's Cat O' Nine Tails in 1989. Other collaborations include Katie Duck, Group O and the Bow Gamelan Ensemble. In 1991 he provided drums both for the rock band CC Sagar and an improvising trio with tenor saxophonist Tony Bevan and bassist Paul Rogers; he also recorded an improvised duo with up-and-coming reedsman Alex

Ward. Noble's lightning responses, wit and catholic taste promise a lot for the future.

● ALBUMS: with Company *Once* (1987)★★★, with Alex Maguire *Live At Oscars* (1987)★★★★, with Kahondo Style *Green Tea & Crocodiles* (1988)★★★, with Alex Ward *Ya Boo, Reel & Rumble* (1991)★★★, with Tony Bevan, Paul Rogers *Bigshots* (1992)★★★.

NOCK, MIKE

b. 27 September 1940, Christchurch, New Zealand. Nock is largely a self-taught pianist who was able to work professionally when he was only 15 years old. When he was 18 he went to Australia playing in a hard bop trio before moving on to England. He did not settle but went to the Berklee College Of Music in Boston, Massachusetts, on a scholarship in 1961. In the early 60s he was the house pianist in a Boston Club before joining Yusef Lateef for three years. In 1968 he moved to San Francisco and formed the jazz-rock group Fourth Way, which was extremely successful until disbanding in 1971. Nock became involved in electronic music and composed numerous film scores. In 1985 he returned to Australia where he spent most of his time composing, though he also taught improvisation at the New South Wales Conservatorium in Sydney.

● ALBUMS: with Yusef Lateef *Live At Peps* (1964)★★★, with John Handy *Projections* (1968)★★★, with Fourth Way *The Fourth Way* (1969)★★★, with Fourth Way *The Sun And The Moon Have Come Together* (1969)★★, with Fourth Way *Werewolf* (1970)★★, *Magic Mansions* (1977)★★★, *Piano Solos* (1978)★★, *Talismen* (1978)★★★, *Ondas* (ECM 1982)★★★, *Dark And Curious* (Verabra 1990)★★, *Touch* (Birdland 1994)★★★, *Not We But One* (Naxos Jazz 1998)★★★.

NOONE, JIMMIE

b. 23 April 1895, Cut Off, Louisiana, USA, d. 19 April 1944. One of numerous students of Lorenzo Tio, Noone turned to the clarinet after first playing guitar. In the years immediately prior to World War I he played in bands led by notable New Orleans musicians such as Freddie Keppard and Buddy Petit. In 1918 he worked with Joe 'King' Oliver in Chicago and two years later was with Doc Cooke, remaining there for five years. In 1926 Noone took his own band into Chicago's Apex Club, thus beginning a remarkable period of sustained creativity during which he became the idol of countless up-and-coming young musicians, black and white, clarinettists and all. During part of its existence, the Apex Club band included Earl 'Fatha' Hines. Noone had made records during his stints with Oliver and Cooke, but now embarked on another series of recordings, including his theme, 'Sweet Lorraine', which remain classics of their kind. In the early 40s he moved to Los Angeles where he worked with Kid Ory, led his own band and appeared as a member of the New Orleans All Stars on Orson Welles' weekly radio show, as well as playing with the Capitol Jazzmen. Noone appeared well poised to capitalize upon the upsurge of interest in traditional music heralded by the Revival movement, but he died suddenly in April 1944. One of the most important of the New Orleans clarinettists, he had a remarkable technique and exercised full control of his instrument. Playing with a deep appreciation of the blues, his records stand as significant milestones in the history of jazz. His son, Jimmie Noone Jnr. (b. James Fleming, 21 April 1938, Chicago, Illinois, USA, d. 1991), also played clarinet and from the 80s enjoyed a successful international career.

● COMPILATIONS: *Jimmie Noone And His Apex Club Orchestra Vol. 1* (1979)★★★★, *Jimmie Noone (1931-40)* (Queendisc 1981)★★★★, *King Of New Orleans* (Jazz Bird 1982)★★★, *With The Apex Club Orchestra 1928* (Swaggie 1992)★★★★, *Collection Vol 1* (Collectors Classics 1992)★★★, *The Complete Recordings Vol 1* (Affinity 1992)★★★★.

NORRIS, WALTER

b. 27 December 1927, Little Rock, Arkansas, USA. Norris studied piano formally as a child, then began playing professionally in his home-town while still in his early teens. In the early 50s he played in various parts of the country, sometimes as sideman, sometimes as leader of his own small group. In 1954 he settled for a time on the west coast, working with an array of leading jazz musicians including Jack Sheldon, Frank Rosolino and Ornette Coleman. In the early 60s he moved to New York, taking up a post as musical director at the Playboy Club and also studying at the Manhattan School of Music.

In the early 70s he occasionally played with the Thad Jones-Mel Lewis Jazz Orchestra. He toured internationally with this band, then continued to work overseas as a single and also with small bands accompanying Red Mitchell, Dexter Gordon, Red Rodney and others. Back in New York in 1976 he played with Charles Mingus, then went to Europe where he became resident in Germany, playing with German orchestras and also teaching. He has continued to work in Europe although he periodically visits the USA. An outstanding technician, Norris's highly adventurous musical mind has taken him from bop beginnings through most subsequent developments in jazz, notably free jazz and third-stream.

● ALBUMS: *Something Else!!!! The Music Of Ornette Coleman* (Contemporary 1958)★★★★, *Drifting* (Enja 1974)★★★, *Synchronicity* (Enja 1978)★★★, *Stepping On Cracks* (Progressive 1978)★★★, *Live At The Berklee Performance Center* (Shiah 1985)★★.

NORVO, RED

b. Kenneth Norville, 31 March 1908, Beardstown, Illinois, USA. After playing in a marimba band, Norvo was hired by Paul Whiteman in the late 20s. With this band he played xylophone and was called upon largely to deliver novelty effects. While with Whiteman he met and married one of the band's singers, Mildred Bailey; in 1933 they went to New York and embarked upon a career that culminated with them being billed as 'Mr and Mrs Swing'. During the 30s Norvo played and recorded with many leading jazz musicians of the day and remained in demand into the mid-40s, at which time he joined Benny Goodman and switched to vibraphone. During the 40s Norvo worked with leading bop musicians such as Dizzy Gillespie and Charlie Parker, and in 1945 became a member of Woody Herman's First Herd. In the early 50s he was resident in California (his marriage to Bailey had ended in 1945), working in a trio he formed with Tal Farlow and Charles Mingus. He continued to play throughout the 60s and on into the mid-70s, when he decided to retire. This decision proved to be only temporary and the 80s saw him engaged in a series of worldwide tours as a solo artist, performing with Benny Carter, and in a reunion with Farlow. Norvo's vibraphone style retains the sound and feel of his earlier xylophone work, a fact that ensures a rhythmic urgency to much of his playing and which might well be the motive behind his long-standing preference for working in groups without a drummer. The assurance with which he incorporated bop phrasing into his work makes him unusual among musicians of his generation and brings an added quality to his work that ensures that it is always interesting.

● ALBUMS: *Red Norvo Trio* 10-inch album (Discovery 1950)★★★★, *Red Norvo Trio, Volume 1* (Discovery 1951)★★★★, *Fabulous Jazz Session* (Dial 1951)★★★★, *Red Norvo Trio* 10-inch album (Discovery 1952)★★★★, *Town Hall Concert, Volume 1* 10-inch album (Commodore 1952)★★★, *Town Hall Concert, Volume 2* 10-inch album (Commodore 1952)★★★, *Dancing On The Ceiling* 10-inch album (Decca 1953)★★★, *Red Norvo Trio* reissued as *The Red Norvo Trios* (Fantasy 1953)★★★★, with Henry 'Red' Allen *Battle Of Jazz, Vol. 6* 10-inch album (Brunswick 1953)★★★, *Improvisation* 10-inch album (EmArcy 1954)★★★, *Red's Blue Room* (X 1955)★★★, *Classics In Jazz* (Capitol 1955)★★★, *Red Norvo And His All Stars* (Epic 1955)★★★★, *Red Norvo Trio* (Fantasy 1955)★★★★, *Red Norvo With Strings* (Fantasy 1956)★★★, *Move!* (Savoy 1956)★★★★, *Midnight On Cloud 69* (Savoy 1956)★★★, *Vibe-rations In Hi-Fi* (Liberty 1956)★★★, *Red Norvo Quintet* reissued as *Norvo Naturally* (Rave/Tampa 1957)★★★, *Ad-Lib* (Liberty 1957)★★★, with Joe Morello, Art Pepper *Joe Morello Sextet* reissued as *The Art Pepper-Red Norvo Sextet* (Intro/Score 1957)★★★★, *Music To Listen To Red Norvo By* (Contemporary 1957)★★★, *Hi Five* (RCA Victor 1957)★★★, *Some Of My Favorites* (RCA Victor 1957)★★★, *Red Norvo In Stereo* (RCA Victor 1958)★★★, *Red Plays The Blues* (RCA Victor 1958)★★★, *Red Norvo Trio* (Rondolette 1958)★★★, *Windjammer City Style* film soundtrack (Dot 1958)★★, with Dinah Shore *Dinah Sings Some Blues With Red* (Capitol 1960)★★★★, *Mainstream Jazz* (Continental 1962)★★★, *Pretty Is The Only Way To Fly* (Charlie Parker 1962)★★★, *Red Norvo Quintet* (Studio West 1962)★★★, *Swing That Music* (Affinity 1969)★★★★, *Vibes À La Red* (Famous Door 1975)★★★, *The Second Time Around* (Famous Door 1975)★★★, *Red In New York* (Famous Door 1977)★★★★, *Live At Rick's Cafe Americain* (Flying Fish 1978)★★★, with Ross Tompkins *Red & Ross* (Concord Jazz 1979)★★★★, with Bucky Pizzarelli *Just Friends* (Stash 1983)★★★, with Nat Adderley, Benny Carter *Benny Carter All Stars, Featuring Nat Adderley & Red Norvo* (Sonet 1985)★★★, *The Forward Look* 1957 recording (Reference Recordings 1991)★★★, *Red Norvo Orchestra Live From The Blue Gardens* 1942 recording (Music Masters 1992)★★★★, with Frank Sinatra *Live In Australia, 1959* (Blue Note 1997)★★★, *Red Norvo And Mildred Bailey* 1938 recording (Circle)★★★.

● COMPILATIONS: *Red Norvo* 1933-1957 recordings (Time-Life)★★★, *Dance Of The Octopus* 1933-1936 recordings (Hep)★★★★, *Red Norvo And His Big Band Featuring Mildred Bailey* 1936-1942 recordings (Sounds Of Swing)★★★★, *Red Norvo, Featuring Mildred Bailey* 1937-1938 recordings (Portrait)★★★★, *Red Norvo, Vol. 1: The Legendary V-Disc Masters* 1943-1944 recordings (Vintage Jazz)★★★★, *Legendary Trio, Vol. 2: The Norvo-Mingus-Farlow Trio* 1943/1949/1950 recordings (Vintage Jazz)★★★★, *Just A Mood* 1954-1957 recordings (Bluebird)★★★★.

Noto, Sam

b. 17 April 1930, Buffalo, New York, USA. After playing trumpet in a number of leading 50s big bands, including that led by Stan Kenton, Noto worked in small groups until joining Count Basie for two spells in the mid- and late 60s. He then returned to small group format, co-leading a band with Joe Romano. After spending part of the 70s in show bands in Las Vegas, Noto moved to Canada where he worked with Rob McConnell, playing and arranging for the latter's big band. During the late 70s and throughout the 80s Noto played on the international festival circuit and also worked in clubs in his home-town and in Canada. A fluent improviser, Noto's composing and arranging reveal an exceptional talent although his chosen locations for much of his best work have unfortunately kept him hidden from the attention of audiences.

● ALBUMS: *Entrance!* (Xanadu 1975)★★★, *Act One* (Xanadu 1975)★★★★, with Rob McConnell *The Jazz Album* (1976)★★★, *Notes To You* (Xanadu 1977)★★★, *Noto-riety* (Xanadu 1978)★★★, *2-4-5* (Unisson 1988)★★.

Nottingham, Jimmy

b. 15 December 1925, New York City, New York, USA. After a brief apprenticeship with Cecil Payne, trumpeter Nottingham served in the US Navy, where he was a member of a band directed by Willie Smith. After World War II, he joined Lionel Hampton and during the late 40s also worked in the big bands led by Lucky Millinder and Charlie Barnet. Then he joined Count Basie's Orchestra, where he remained until 1950. In the 50s he played mostly in small groups and was also with bands specializing in Latin-American dance music. From the mid-50s until the mid-70s he was a staff musician with CBS Records, but continued to play jazz with artists such as Dizzy Gillespie, Edgar Sampson, Quincy Jones and Benny Goodman. From 1966 until the end of the decade, his Monday evenings were spent at the Village Vanguard as a member of the Thad Jones-Mel Lewis band. A powerful lead trumpeter with a searing high register, Nottingham's skill and versatility make him a notable member of any band in which he plays.

● ALBUMS: with Edgar Sampson *Swing Softly Sweet Sampson* (1956)★★★, with Thad Jones *Mel Lewis Live At The Village Vanguard* (1957)★★★★, with Lionel Hampton *Newport Uproar!* (1967)★★★★, with Jones-Lewis *Central Park North* (1969)★★★.

NUCLEUS

The doyen of British jazz-rock groups, Nucleus was formed in 1969 by trumpeter Ian Carr. He was joined by Chris Spedding (guitar, ex-Battered Ornaments), John Marshall (drums) and Karl Jenkins (keyboards). The quartet was signed to the distinctive progressive outlet, Vertigo, and their debut, *Elastic Rock*, is arguably their exemplary work. The same line-up completed *We'll Talk About It Later*, but Spedding's subsequent departure heralded a bewildering succession of changes that undermined the group's potential. Carr nonetheless remained its driving force, a factor reinforced when *Solar Plexus*, a collection the trumpeter had intended as a solo release, became the unit's third album. In 1972 both Jenkins and Marshall left the group to join fellow fusion act Soft Machine, and Nucleus became an inadvertent nursery for this 'rival' ensemble. Later members Roy Babbington and Alan Holdsworth also defected, although Carr was able to maintain an individuality despite such damaging interruptions. Subsequent albums, however, lacked the innovatory purpose of those first releases and Nucleus was dissolved during the early 80s. Nucleus took the jazz/rock genre further into jazz territory with skill, melody and a tremendous standard of musicianship. Their first three albums are vital in any comprehensive rock or jazz collection.

● ALBUMS: *Elastic Rock* (Vertigo 1970)★★★★, *We'll Talk About It later* (Vertigo 1970)★★★, *Solar Plexus* (Vertigo 1971)★★★★, *Belladonna* (Vertigo 1972)★★★, *Labyrinth* (Vertigo 1973)★★★, *Roots* (Vertigo 1973)★★★, *Under The Sun* (Vertigo 1974)★★★, *Snake Hips Etcetera* (Vertigo 1975)★★★, *Direct Hits* (Vertigo 1976)★★★, *In Flagrante Delicto* (1978)★★★, *Out Of The Long Dark* (1979)★★, *Awakening* (1980)★★, *Live At The Theaterhaus* (1985)★★★.

NUEVA MANTECA

Led by pianist Jan Laurenz Hartong (b. *c*.1941, Netherlands), eight-piece band Nueva Manteca are a Dutch-based Latin jazz outfit who produce a highly authentic distillation of Latin music and also embrace traditions such as Arabic, classical, Dutch Antillean and salsa. As Hartong told the press in 1996, 'It's the same situation as hearing a Korean violinist playing a Beethoven concerto. It's already accepted in the jazz world. In the whole world music development, a lot of people are digging into all kinds of cultures.' Hartong began playing Dixieland piano at the age of 12, before progressing to bebop by 15, at which time he began to work professionally. He played alongside Jan Hammer and Joachim Kühn in a 1966 international jazz festival judged by Cannonball and Nat Adderley where he won a medal. A fan of Latin music since his childhood, Hartong formed a 10-piece salsa band in Rotterdam in 1983. He also visited the music's home in Cuba in 1984 and 1987, which led to him switching to a Latin jazz style and changing his group's name from Manteca to Neuva Manteca. For the first three years of the group's existence he was joined by highly respected New York timbales player Nicky Marrero. The group won its live reputation playing festivals throughout Europe, also performing alongside guest artists including Giovanni Hidalgo, Juanito Torres, Orestes Vilato, Armando Peraza and Bobby Sanabria as part of the state-sponsored Nueva Manteca Meets The Legends series. The group also toured the USA in 1995, preparing for the release of *Let's Face The Music And Dance*. Dedicated to Vernon Boggs, the late New York professor who championed salsa in Scandinavia, it featured Latin-flavoured treatments of material by Duke Ellington ('Caravan'), Miles Davis ('All Blues') and an Irving Berlin medley. Previous albums included *Porgy & Bess*, a revision of the George Gershwin opera set to a Latin tempo.

● ALBUMS: *Porgy & Bess* (Lucho 1993)★★★, *Let's Face The Music And Dance* (Blue Note 1996)★★★★.

NUNEZ, ALCIDE 'YELLOW'

b. 17 March 1884, New Orleans, Louisiana, USA, d. 2 September 1934. One of his home-town's most noted musicians, Nunez's career was dogged by bad luck and poor timing. After playing clarinet with several famous marching and brass bands, including Papa Laine's, Nunez visited Chicago, where he teamed up with Nick La Rocca and others to form a band. He fell out with La Rocca, however, and quit to work in vaudeville with a music and comedy act. Meanwhile, La Rocca and the band, calling themselves the Original Dixieland Jazz Band, went on to international fame and fortune. After working with obscure bands in Chicago, Nunez returned to New Orleans in 1927 and remained there for the rest of his life. Although an enormously skilled musician, Nunez displayed a penchant for the shrill, jokey, barnyard effects popular with audiences in the early years of this century. As a result, his few records have received attention more for their curiosity value than for their musical content.

NUSSBAUM, ADAM

b. 29 November 1955, New York, USA. Nussbaum had initially learnt to play the piano and alto saxophone, then switched to studying drums with Charlie Persip and majoring in music at the Davis Centre, City College of New York. After freelancing in New York he played through the late 70s and 80s with the bands of John Scofield, Dave Liebman, Stan Getz, Gil Evans, Randy Brecker, George Gruntz and Gary Burton. Nussbaum has attained a wide knowledge of the history of jazz drumming. He has a bright, swinging style that he has been able to adapt to all these differing contexts.

● ALBUMS: with Dave Liebman *If Only They Knew* (1980)★★★★, with John Scofield *Shinola* (1981)★★★, *Out Like A Light* (1981)★★★, with Bill Evans *Living On The Crest Of A Wave* (1983)★★★, with Gil Evans *Live At Sweet Basil* (1984)★★★★, with John Abercrombie, Dan Wall *Tactics* (ECM 1997)★★★.

O'Brien, Floyd

b. 7 May 1904, Chicago, Illinois, USA, d. 26 November 1968. Throughout the 20s and early 30s trombonist O'Brien worked regularly, playing in numerous bands, mostly in Chicago. In the mid-30s he also played in New York, appearing on record with the Chocolate Dandies, Fats Waller, Eddie Condon, George Wettling and other leading jazz groups. He spent the second half of the 30s in the orchestra led by popular singer-comedian Phil Harris, then joined successively Gene Krupa and Bob Crosby. During the 40s he played mostly in Dixieland and New Orleans-style bands, some of which he led. This pattern continued into the 50s, when he recorded with Albert Nicholas and also established a reputation as a brass teacher. Although not as well known as some of his contemporaries, O'Brien was a gifted trombonist and an often vital and exciting exponent of Chicago-style.

● ALBUMS: with Albert Nicholas *All Star Stompers* (1959)★★★.

● COMPILATIONS: with George Wettling *Chicago Jazz* (1939-40)★★★, with Bob Crosby *South Rampart Street Parade* (1935-42)★★★.

O'Connell, Helen

(see Dorsey, Jimmy)

O'Day, Anita

b. Anita Belle Colton, 18 October 1919, Kansas City, Missouri, USA. As Anita Colton, in her early teens she scraped a living as a professional Walkathon contestant (marathon dancer). During this period she changed her surname to O'Day. Along with other contestants she was encouraged to sing and during one Walkathon was accompanied by Erskine Tate's orchestra, an event that made her think that singing might be a better route to showbusiness fame than dancing. By her late teens she had switched to singing and was told by Gene Krupa, who heard her at a Chicago club, that if he ever had a slot for her he would call. In the meantime, she failed an audition with Benny Goodman, who complained that she did not stick to the melody, and upset Raymond Scott, who disliked her scatting - actually, she had momentarily forgotten the words of the song. Eventually Krupa called and O'Day joined the band early in 1941, just a few weeks before Roy Eldridge was also hired. The combination of Krupa, Eldridge and O'Day was potent and the band, already popular, quickly became one of the best of the later swing era. O'Day helped to give the band some of its hit records, notably 'Let Me Off Uptown' (also a feature for Eldridge), 'Alreet', 'Kick It' and 'Bolero At The Savoy'. After Krupa folded in 1943, O'Day went with Stan Kenton, recording hits with 'And Her Tears Flowed Like Wine' and 'The Lady In Red'. In 1945 she was back with the re-formed Krupa band for more hit records, including 'Opus No. 1'. In 1946 she went solo and thereafter remained a headliner. She made a number of fine albums in the 50s, including a set with Ralph Burns in 1952, and made a memorable appearance at the 1958 Newport Jazz Festival. This performance, at which she sang 'Tea For Two' and 'Sweet Georgia Brown', resplendent in cartwheel hat, gloves, and stoned out of her mind, was captured on film in *Jazz On A Summer's Day* (1958). Drug addiction severely damaged O'Day's life for many years, although she continued to turn out excellent albums, including *Cool Heat* with Jimmy Giuffre, *Trav'lin' Light* with Johnny Mandel and Barney Kessel and *Time For Two* with Cal Tjader. Extensive touring, high living and a punishing lifestyle (not to mention a dozen years of heroin addiction) eventually brought collapse, and she almost died in 1966. Eventually clear of drugs, O'Day continued to tour, playing clubs, concerts and festivals around the world. She recorded less frequently, but thanks to forming her own record company, Emily, in the early 70s, many of the albums that she did make were entirely under her control. In 1985 she played Carnegie Hall in celebration of 50 years in the business, and towards the end of the decade appeared in the UK at Ronnie Scott's club and at the Leeds Castle Jazz Festival in Kent.

O'Day's singing voice is throaty and she sings with great rhythmic drive. Her scat singing and the liberties she takes on songs, especially when singing up-tempo, result in some remarkable vocal creations. In her heydays her diction was exceptional and even at the fastest tempos she articulated clearly and precisely. On ballads she is assured and distinctive, and although very much her own woman, her phrasing suggests the influence of Billie Holiday. On stage she displays enormous rapport with musicians and audience, factors that make some of her studio recordings rather less rewarding than those made in concert. Late in her career some of her performances were marred by problems of pitch but, live at least, she compensated for such difficulties through the sheer force of her personality. O'Day's autobiography makes for compulsive reading.

● ALBUMS: *Anita O'Day Specials* reissued as *Singin' And Swingin'* (Advance/Coral 1951)★★★★, *Anita O'Day Collates* reissued as *Anita O'Day* and *The Lady Is A Tramp* (Clef/Norgran/Verve 1953)★★★, *Songs By Anita O'Day* reissued as *An Evening With Anita O'Day* (Norgran 1954)★★★★, *Anita* reissued as *This Is Anita* (Verve 1956)★★★★, *Pick Yourself Up With Anita O'Day* (Verve 1957)★★★, *For Oscar* (American Recording Society 1957)★★★, *Anita O'Day At Mr. Kelly's* (Verve 1958)★★★, *Anita Sings The Most* (Verve 1958)★★★★, *Anita O'Day Sings The Winners* (Verve 1958)★★★★, with Jimmy Guiffre *Cool Heat - Anita O'Day Sings Jimmy Guiffre Arrangements* (Verve 1959)★★★★, *Anita O'Day Swings Cole Porter* (Verve 1959)★★★★, *Anita O'Day And Billy May Swing*

Rodgers And Hart (Verve 1960)★★★★, *Waiter, Make Mine Blues* (Verve 1960)★★★, *Trav'lin' Light* (Verve 1960)★★★★, *All The Sad Young Men* (Verve 1962)★★★★, with Cal Tjader *Time For Two* (Verve 1962)★★★★, with the Three Sounds *Anita O'Day & The Three Sounds* (Verve 1963)★★★, *Incomparable! Anita O'Day* (Verve 1964)★★★★, *Recorded Live At The Berlin Jazz Festival* (MPS 1970)★★★, *I Get A Kick Out Of You* (Emily 1975)★★★, *My Ship* (Emily 1975)★★★, *Live At Mingo's* (Emily 1976)★★★, *Once Upon A Summertime* 1963-1976 recordings (Glendale 1976)★★★, *Angel Eyes* (Emily 1978)★★★, *Mello' Day* (GNP 1979)★★★, *Live At The City* (Emily 1979)★★, *A Song For You* (Emily 1984)★★★, *In A Mellow Tone* (DRG 1989)★★★, *At Vine St.: Live* (DRG 1992)★★, *Anita O'Day Live* 1976 recording (Star Line 1993)★★★, *Rules Of The Road* (Pablo 1994)★★.

● COMPILATIONS: with Roy Eldridge, Gene Krupa *Uptown* 1941-1942 recordings (Columbia)★★★★, *Hi Ho Trailus Boot Whip* 1947 recordings (Flying Dutchman)★★★, *Anita O'Day 1949-1950* (Tono)★★★★, *Verve Jazz Masters 49* (PolyGram 1995)★★★★★.

● FURTHER READING: *High Times Hard Times*, Anita O'Day with George Eells.

O'Farrill, Chico

b. Arturo O'Farrill, 28 October 1921, Havana, Cuba. After playing trumpet in several Cuban-based bands throughout the 40s, O'Farrill moved to the USA where he concentrated on arranging. During the 50s his work was played and recorded by Benny Goodman, Stan Kenton and Dizzy Gillespie among others, and he also collaborated with Machito on albums featuring such leading American jazzmen as Charlie Parker and Joe 'Flip' Phillips. O'Farrill also toured and recorded with his own band. He spent the early 60s in Mexico, then returned to the USA, taking up a staff post with CBS Records, but retained his jazz links by arranging for Count Basie. In the 70s and 80s O'Farrill continued to be active but his jazz work gradually diminished. He made a striking return in 1995 with a big band date for Milestone Records, his first recording session as a leader in over 25 years. An outstanding exponent of Latin-American music, O'Farrill's arrangements consistently demonstrate his comprehensive grasp of the music's potential and are often far more imaginative than others who work in this field.

● ALBUMS: *Afro-Cuban* 10-inch album (Clef 1953)★★★★, *Chico O'Farrill Jazz* reissued as *Jazz North Of The Border And South Of The Border* (Clef/Verve 1953)★★★★, *The Second Afro-Cuban Jazz Suite* 10-inch album (Norgran 1954)★★★★, *Mambo Dance Sessions* 10-inch album (Norgran 1954)★★★, *Latino Dance Sessions* 10-inch album (Norgran 1954)★★★, *Chico O'Farrill* 10-inch album (Norgran 1955)★★★, *Music From South America* (Verve 1956)★★★, *Nine Flags* (Impulse! 1967)★★★, *Pure Emotion* (Milestone 1995)★★★★.

● COMPILATIONS: *Cuban Blues: The Chico O'Farrill Sessions* 1950-1954 recordings (Verve 1997)★★★★.

O'Flynn, Bridget

b. 1923, Berkely, California, USA. O'Flynn taught herself to play drums as a small child, eventually taking lessons while attending school. Fighting against the automatic resistance towards women in jazz, especially as a drummer, she eventually joined an all-female band led by Sally Banning. This was in 1939 and she later played in an otherwise all-male band co-led by Sally and George Banning. O'Flynn then formed her own all-male big band, which she led until the USA's entry into World War II. After the war, and by that time based in New York, she played in various clubs, eventually becoming a member of a trio led by Mary Lou Williams that also included June Rotenberg. In the mid-50s O'Flynn became progressively more discouraged with the entrenched attitudes that militated against her as a woman in jazz, and also when racism affected the mixed-race bands with whom she sometimes worked. Early in the following decade, she quit the business. In the early 80s, however, she reportedly told Sally Placksin that she was tempted to return. A fine, supportive drummer with a fine ear for those she is accompanying, O'Flynn always preferred brushes, providing a discreet and subtle rhythmic underpinning to the bands in which she worked.

● COMPILATIONS: included on *Café Society* (Onyx 1948)★★★.

Obiedo, Ray

b. San Francisco, California, USA. Contemporary jazz composer and guitarist Obiedo had an eclectic musical background during his youth, spent in the Bay Area of San Francisco. Here the sounds of Miles Davis, Henry Mancini, Antonio Jobim and the imported soul and pop of Motown Records influenced his early musical persona. Probably the greatest influence on his embryonic career, however, was the James Brown revue, whose funky, percussive guitar sound was the platform on which Obiedo built his technique. In the early 80s his reputation grew as one of California's finest exponents of jazz, pop and fusion. He joined organist Johnny 'Hammond' Smith on tour, then ECM trombonist Julian Priester. His own fusion band, Kick, included Sheila E. on drums and Sonny Rollins associate Mark Soskin on keyboards. His other outlet during this time was the pop-rock vehicle Rhythmus 21, wherein he worked with other prominent session musicians from the Bay Area. His own session/touring experience is considerable, having partnered artists including Herbie Hancock, George Duke, Lou Rawls, Rodney Franklin and Marc Russo. His solo compositions also attracted acclaim, and saw interpretations from Sheila E., saxophonist Alex Murzyn, guitarist Bruce Forman and percussionist Pete Escovedo. Parts of this work have appeared on film soundtracks, most notably Michael Caine's *A Shock To The System* and Richard Gere's *Internal Affairs*, and he also collaborated with Teresa Tull on *Claire Of The Moon*. Such notoriety co-existed with Obiedo's rising status as a solo artist, recording a clutch of 90s albums for Windham Hill Records while leading the Ray Obiedo group on club dates and concerts. *Sticks And Stones* peaked at number 7 on *Billboard*'s Contemporary Jazz chart, while *Zulaya* continued his exploration of Latin and Brazilian influences. Sheila E. was on hand to provide percussion, while the backing vocals of Claytoven

Richardson, Annie Stocking, Sandy Griffith and Jenny Meltzer lent the compositions a new emotive depth and identity. It was the first album to be produced solely by the artist, ensuring a clarity of vision to match the pristine musical performances.

● ALBUMS: *Perfect Crime* (Windham Hill 1989)★★★, *Iguana* (Windham Hill 1991)★★★, *Sticks & Stones* (Windham Hill 1993)★★★, *Zulaya* (Windham Hill 1995)★★★★.

Offramp - Pat Metheny Group

Opening with some beautiful synclavier and Lyle Mays' exquisite soaring synths on 'Barcarole', this is an atmosphere album. It moves from delicacy to beauty and is arguably the most complete album of his incredible career. The delightful 'James' (a tribute to James Taylor, listen to the guitar inflections) is complemented by the awesome 'Au Lait'; and if that was not enough, this contains surely Pat Metheny's finest moment, 'Are You Going With Me', a song that builds and builds over the most fabulous rhythm, and even after nearly nine minutes it leaves you begging for more. A stunning piece of music that is neither jazz nor rock.

● Tracks: *Barcarole; Are You Going With Me?; Au Lait; Eighteen; Offramp; James; The Bat Part II.*

● First released 1983

● UK peak chart position: did not chart

● USA peak chart position: 50

Okoshi, Tiger

b. 21 March 1950, Ashita, Japan. An accomplished composer and trumpet player, Tiger Okoshi moved to the USA in 1972 and has since played with artists including Gary Burton, Bob Moses and George Russell's Living Time Orchestra. He also records regularly with his own groups, playing what he calls 'Baku music' - a Baku is a mythical creature that eats bad dreams. Okoshi's recording sessions concentrate on a jazz-rock fusion derived from the music Miles Davis played in the late 60s, although his Louis Armstrong tribute *Echoes Of A Note* created modern versions of Dixieland standards.

● ALBUMS: *Tiger's Baku* (JVC 1981)★★★★, *Face To Face* (JVC 1989)★★★, *That Was Then, This Is Now* (JVC 1990)★★★, *Echoes Of A Note (A Tribute To Louis 'Pops' Armstrong)* (JVC 1993)★★★, *Two Sides To Every Story* (JVC 1994)★★★★.

Old And New Dreams

This group formed in 1976 and featured Ornette Coleman alumni Dewey Redman, Don Cherry, Charlie Haden and Ed Blackwell. They came together to play music, particularly that of the early acoustic bands. By the mid-70s Coleman had become committed to expressing his musical theory of harmolodics through the medium of his electric band, Prime Time. Old And New Dreams set out to play in the spirit of, rather than recreate, the earlier acoustic groups by reworking compositions of the period as well as composing new numbers within the parameters of the Coleman style. The group experienced a great deal of success, particularly on the European festival circuit, indicating the enduring quality of Coleman's early musical output.

● ALBUMS: *Old And New Dreams* i (ECM 1977)★★★★, *Old And New Dreams* ii (ECM 1979)★★★★, *Playing* (ECM 1980)★★★★, *One For Blackwell* (Black Saint 1988)★★★.

Oliver, Joe 'King'

b. 11 May 1885, Louisiana, USA, d. 10 April 1938. Raised in New Orleans, cornetist Oliver became well known through appearances with local marching and cabaret bands during the early years of this century. After playing with such notable early jazzmen as Kid Ory and Richard M. Jones in 1918, he left for Chicago and two years later was leading his own band. After a brief trip to California, Oliver returned to Chicago and performed an engagement at the Lincoln Gardens. This was in 1922 and his band then included such outstanding musicians as Johnny and Baby Dodds, Lil Hardin and Honore Dutrey. Not content with being merely the best jazz band in town, Oliver sent word to New Orleans and brought in the fast-rising young cornetist Louis Armstrong. His motives in hiring Armstrong might have been questionable. Hardin, who later married Armstrong, reported that Oliver openly stated that his intention was to ensure that by having the newcomer playing second cornet in his band he need not fear him as a competitor. Whatever the reason, the Oliver band with Armstrong was a sensation. Musicians flocked to hear the band, marvelling at the seemingly telepathic communication between the two men. The band's glory days did not last long; by 1924 the Dodds brothers had gone, dissatisfied with their financial arrangements, and Armstrong had been taken by his new wife on the first stage of his transition to international star. Oliver continued leading a band but he quickly discovered that his example had been followed by many, and that even if his imitators were often musically inferior, they had made it harder for him to obtain good jobs. His own judgement was also sometimes at fault; he turned down an offer to lead a band at New York's Cotton Club because the money was not good enough and lived to see Duke Ellington take the job and the radio exposure that went with it. In the early 30s Oliver led a succession of territory bands with a measure of local success but he rarely played. He was suffering from a disease of the gums and playing the cornet was, at best, a painful exercise. By 1936 he had quit the business of which he had once been king and took a job as a janitor in Savannah, Georgia, where he died in 1938. An outstanding exponent of New Orleans-style cornet playing, Oliver was one of the most important musicians in spreading jazz through his 1923-24 recordings, even if these did not gain their internationally accepted status as classic milestones until after his death. His role in the advancement of Armstrong's career is also of significance, although, clearly, nothing would have stopped the younger man from achieving his later fame. Stylistically, Oliver's influence on Armstrong was important, although the pupil quickly outstripped his tutor in technique, imagination and inventiveness. Setting aside the role he played in Armstrong's life, and the corresponding reflected glory Armstrong threw upon him, Oliver can be seen and heard to have been a striking soloist and a massively self-confident ensemble leader. He was also a sensitive accompanist, making several fine records with popular blues singers of the day.

● COMPILATIONS: *King Oliver* (Brunswick 1950)★★★★, *King Oliver Plays The Blues* (Riverside 1953)★★★, *King Oliver's Uptown Jazz* (X 1954)★★★, *King Oliver Featuring Louis Armstrong* (Epic 1956)★★★★, *King Oliver And His Orchestra* (Epic 1960)★★★★, *King Oliver In New York* (RCA Victor 1965)★★★, *Complete Vocalion/Brunswick Recordings 1926 - 1931* (1992)★★★★.

● FURTHER READING: *King Joe Oliver*, Walter C. Allen and Brian A.L. Rust. *'King' Oliver*, Laurie Wright. *King Oliver And Kings Of Jazz*, M. Williams.

OLIVER, SY

b. Melvin James Oliver, 17 December 1910, Battle Creek, Michigan, USA, d. 28 May 1988, New York City, New York, USA. Born into a family in which both parents were music teachers, Oliver played trumpet as a child and at the age of 17 was a member of the popular territory band led by Zack Whyte. During this stint he began arranging, primarily to prove to his older and supposedly wiser fellow sidemen that his theories about harmony were sound. After the Whyte band, Oliver played in another important territory band, led by Alphonso Trent. Then, after some of his arrangements had been accepted by Jimmie Lunceford, Oliver took a job with his band, playing in the trumpet section, singing and arranging. Lunceford had already enjoyed the benefits of good arrangers in Eddie Durham and, especially, Eddie Wilcox; but, more than anyone, it was Oliver who shaped the sound of the Lunceford band from 1933 until 1939, the period of its greatest commercial and aesthetic success. Oliver's use of two-beat rhythm, stop-time breaks, intricate saxophone choruses and ear-splitting brass explosions, brilliantly executed by Lunceford's musicians, in particular drummer Jimmy Crawford and lead alto saxophonist Willie Smith, not only sealed Lunceford's success but created a style of big band music that proved widely influential. Oliver's arranging style was especially suitable to the more commercial aspects of the swing era and was taken up and adapted by many of his contemporaries and successors. Although employed by Lunceford, Oliver did arrange for other bands too, including Benny Goodman's, and his reputation in the business was enviable. Tiring of his work with Lunceford, Oliver decided to quit music and study law, but Tommy Dorsey made him an offer he could not refuse: $5,000 a year more than he'd earned with Lunceford. Oliver's arrangements for Dorsey propelled the band into a new era of success, which transcended what had gone before for both arranger and leader. 'Swing High', 'Well, Git It!', 'Sunny Side Of the Street' and 'Opus No. 1' were all massively popular and the records became big sellers. After military service during World War II, Oliver briefly led his own musically excellent but commercially unsuccessful big band and worked as a freelance arranger, his charts being used by Dorsey and by studios for recording orchestras' dates with singers such as Ella Fitzgerald and Frank Sinatra. In the 60s he once again tried bandleading, but as before was not prepared to bow to commercial pressures. In the late 60s and 70s he toured extensively, resumed trumpet playing and undertook several club residencies in New York, a pattern that persisted into the 80s. A major figure in the development of jazz arranging, Oliver was almost single-handedly responsible for the creation of what later became definable as mainstream big band music. His use of attacking brass and clean ensemble passages was picked up and modified, sometimes simplified, but rarely if ever improved.

● ALBUMS: *Sy Oliver And His Orchestra* i (1954)★★★, *Sy Oliver And His Orchestra* ii (1957)★★★, *Sy Oliver And His Orchestra* iii (1958)★★★★, *Sy Oliver And His Orchestra* iv (1958)★★★, *Back Stage* (1959)★★★, *77 Sunset Strip* (1959)★★, *Just A Minute* (1960), *Annie Laurie* (1960)★★★, *Four Roses Dance Party* (1961)★★★, *Easy Walker* (1962)★★★, *Take Me Back* (1972)★★★★, *Yes, Indeed!* (1973)★★★, *Sy Oliver And His Orchestra Play The Famous Rainbow Room* (1976)★★★.

ON THE ROAD WITH DUKE ELLINGTON

A remarkable film record, made originally in 1967 and updated after Duke Ellington's death in 1974. In addition to Ellington talking about his life there are sequences showing him receiving honorary doctorates, rehearsing and recording his orchestra, playing the piano and, most intriguing of all, composing and arranging. If anything, the casual manner in which he does this simply adds to the mystique. Sprawled out on a couch, feet up, he and Billy Strayhorn put together a piece of music with such deceptive ease as to make even a Hollywood songwriter biopic seem forced. Apart from the Maestro, musicians such as Harry Carney, Jimmy Hamilton, Johnny Hodges, Paul Gonsalves and Louis Armstrong also make appearances.

OPEN SESAME - FREDDIE HUBBARD

Trumpeter Freddie Hubbard had an amazing gift for being around at just the right time, appearing on countless modern jazz classics, and recording some of the Blue Note label's greatest albums of the 60s. *Open Sesame* was his very first Blue Note release as leader, and features bluesy tenor saxophonist Tina Brooks, pianist McCoy Tyner (who had recently joined John Coltrane), bassist Sam Jones and drummer Clifford Jarvis. A fiery, but superbly controlled, trumpeter who never, even at this stage in his career, sounds stretched or short of an idea, Hubbard would become one of the most profound trumpet talents in post-war jazz.

● Tracks: *Open Sesame; But Beautiful; Gypsy Blue; All Or Nothing At All; One Mint Julep; Hub's Nub.*

● First released 1960

● UK peak chart position: did not chart

● USA peak chart position: did not chart

OREGON

This inventive and influential progressive jazz chamber group was formed in 1970 from the nucleus of the Paul Winter Consort, an aggregation led by Paul Winter. Oregon comprised Ralph Towner (b. 1 March 1940, Chehalis, Washington, USA; guitar, keyboards), Collin Walcott (b. 24 April 1945, New York City, USA, d. 8 November 1984, Magdeburg, Germany; percussion, sitar, tabla, clarinet), Glen Moore (b. 28 October 1941, Portland, Oregon, USA; bass, violin, piano, flute) and Paul McCandless (b. 24 March 1947, Indiana, Pennsylvania, USA; alto saxophone, oboe, bass clarinet). Walcott's death from a car accident in 1984 seemed a fatal blow to the band, but after a year in mourning they returned. The recruitment of Walcott's friend Trilok Gurtu (b. 30 October 1951, Bombay, India; tabla, drums, percussion) gave them a fresh incentive. Their debut on ECM Records in 1983 was an eclectic, part-electric album. Oregon explore the boundaries of jazz, using uniquely disparate influences of classical, folk, Indian and other ethnic music. Their chamber-like approach encourages hushed auditoriums and intense concentration, which is required to derive maximum benefit from their weaving style. Occasionally they will burst into a song of regular form and pattern, as if to reward a child with a treat. One such number is the evocatively rolling 'Crossing' from the same album. Another outstanding piece from their immense catalogue is 'Leather Cats'. Their refusal to compromise leaves them a lone innovative force and one of the most important jazz-based conglomerations of the past three decades. Their 1997 Intuition date featured percussionists Arto Tuncboyaciyan and Mark Walker.

● ALBUMS: *Our First Record* (Vanguard 1970)★★★, *Music Of Another Present Era* (Vanguard 1972)★★★, *Distant Hills* (Vanguard 1973)★★★, *Winter Light* (Vanguard 1974)★★★★, *In Concert* (Vanguard 1975)★★★, with Elvin Jones *Oregon/Jones Together* (Vanguard 1976)★★★, *Violin* (Vanguard 1977)★★★, *Out Of The Woods* (Elektra 1978)★★★★, *Roots In The Sky* (Elektra 1979)★★★★, *Moon And Mind* (Vanguard 1979)★★★, *Oregon In Performance* (Elektra 1980)★★★, *Oregon* (ECM 1983)★★★, *Crossing* (ECM 1985)★★★★, *Ecotopia* (ECM 1987)★★★, *45th Parallel* (Verabra 1989)★★, *Always, Never, And Forever* (Verabra 1991)★★★, *Beyond Words* (Chesky 1995)★★★, *Northwest Passage* (Intuition 1997)★★★★.

ORENDORFF, GEORGE

b. George Robert Ordendorff, 18 March 1906, Atlanta, Georgia, USA, d. 1984. Orendorff learned to play guitar and cornet as a child, working professionally from his mid-teens. This was in Chicago where his family had settled and he attracted the attention of many bandleaders; by this time he was mostly playing trumpet. In California in the mid- and late 20s he worked in several bands including Paul Howard's Quality Serenaders and Les Hite's Sebastian Cotton Club Orchestra. In both these bands he was with Lionel Hampton whom he had known in Chicago. With Hite he recorded with Louis Armstrong, and also appeared in films. He spent some years from 1939 with guitarist Ceele Burke, then entered the armed forces during World War II. During the 50s and 60s he sporadically played in and around Los Angeles on a casual basis. He also made appearances in films in these years and John Chilton records that he has published poetry. A good section player, Orendorff could also play driving solos when opportunities arose. Backing Armstrong, he sometimes played discreet obbligati behind vocals, and even as early as his recordings with Howard, he displays startlingly progressive ideas.

● COMPILATIONS: *Paul Howard's Quality Serenaders* (TOM 1929)★★★, with Louis Armstrong, Les Hite *Louis In Los Angeles* (1930-31)★★★★.

ORGAN GRINDER SWING - JIMMY SMITH

Using the monicker 'Incredible' was no flash banner, it was true. Jimmy Smith defined the Hammond organ as a jazz instrument and milked and bled it to its limit. The sub-credit for guitarist Kenny Burrell and drummer Grady Tate is also well deserved. This is the ultimate groovy, smokey jazz trio record that Smith made. The title track has been used for countless radio trailers over the years, while the often covered Duke Ellington classic, 'Satin Doll', is given extra special effort. Burrell has worked with Smith more than any other musician. His mellow tone and Smith's treble notes blend like cucumber and salmon.

● Tracks: *The Organ Grinder's Swing; Oh, No, Babe; Blues For J; Greensleeves; I'll Close My Eyes; Satin Doll.*

● First released 1965

● UK peak chart position: did not chart

● USA peak chart position: 15

ORIGINAL AMERICAN DECCA RECORDINGS, THE - COUNT BASIE

These recordings capture all the fire, energy and raw excitement of the Count Basie band as it roared out of Kansas City to startle the jazz world. Talented players occupy every chair, many of them awesome soloists: Buck Clayton, Harry 'Sweets' Edison, Dicky Wells, Earle Warren, Herschel Evans, and the sublime and trend-setting Lester Young; all were buoyed and spurred along by the All-American Rhythm Section of Basie, Freddie Green, Walter Page and Jo Jones. If this were not enough, the band singer was the great Jimmy Rushing. Not surprisingly, after this, big band jazz was never quite the same again. Indeed, it might even be argued that later Basie bands never recaptured this early magic.

● Tracks: *Including - Honeysuckle Rose; Pennies From Heaven; Swinging At The Daisy Chain; Roseland Shuffle; Exactly Like You; Boo Hoo; Glory Of Love; Boogie Woogie (I May Be Wrong); Smarty (You Know It All); One O'clock Jump; Listen My Children And You Shall Hear; Jon's Idea; Goodmorning Blues (1st take); Goodmorning Blues (2nd take); Our Love Was Meant To Be; Time Out; Topsy; I Keep Remembering; Out Of The Window; Don't You Miss Your Baby; Let Me Dream; Georgianna; Blues In The Dark; Sent For You Yesterday; Every Tub; Now Will You Be Good?; Swingin' The Blues;*

Mama Don't Want No Peas 'N' Rice 'N' Coconut Oil; Blue And Sentimental; Doggin' Around; Stop Beatin' Around The Mulberry Bush (1st take); Stop Beatin' Around The Mulberry Bush (2nd take); London Bridge Is Falling Down; Texas Shuffle.

- First released (1937-1939 recordings)
- UK peak chart position: did not chart
- USA peak chart position: did not chart

ORIGINAL DIXIELAND JAZZ BAND

In May 1916 several young white New Orleans musicians were working in Chicago, often appearing in the same bands. After a few changes the musicians settled down as a permanent band, with the personnel consisting of Nick La Rocca (b. 11 April 1889, d. 22 February 1961; cornet) Eddie Edwards (b. 22 May 1891, New Orleans, Louisiana, USA, d. 9 April 1963; trombone), Larry Shields (b. 13 September 1893, d. 21 November 1953; clarinet), pianist Henry Ragas (b. 1891, d. 18 February 1919) - his successor at the piano, J. Russell Robinson (b. 8 July 1892, d. 30 September 1963) and Tony Sbarbaro (Spargo) (b. 27 June 1897, New Orleans, Louisiana, USA, d. 30 October 1969; drums). Under its somewhat hyperbolic and misleading title, the Original Dixieland Jazz Band, aided by widespread publicity, became known as the creators of jazz. Despite this hopelessly inaccurate and unfair description, the ODJB's 1917 recordings of 'Livery Stable Blues' and 'Dixie Jass Band One-Step' succeeded in bringing the emergent music to the attention of millions. They were also able to make far more prestigious public appearances than would have been possible had they been black. First at Resenweber's restaurant in New York and later at London's Palladium theatre, the ODJB offered audiences a mixture of vaudeville eccentricity and good jazz (rather more of the former than the latter) and helped to boost the music from its limited origins into worldwide popularity. Synonymous with the Jazz Age, and sometimes having just as little to do with real jazz as that loose term for a sociological and cultural phenomenon, the ODJB quickly became legendary and thereafter did not need to live up to the usually unfulfilled promise their name evokes. By the mid-20s, with the rise of artists such as Paul Whiteman and the New Orleans Rhythm Kings, the ODJB were quickly deemed passé and broke up in 1925, re-forming in 1936 for a brief and not too successful tour. The founding five had variable success after their ODJB days with Sbarbaro being perhaps the most active. Several ODJB alumni, including Sbarbaro, trombonist Eddie Daniels and pianist Frank Signorelli, recorded a 1943 session with multi-instrumentalist Brad Gowans. In the late 50s trumpeter Don Fowler and clarinetist George Phillips recorded a note-for-note ODJB tribute album for Paramount.

- ALBUMS: *Original Dixieland Jazz In Hi-Fi* (Paramount 1957)★★★, *1943* (GHB)★★★.
- COMPILATIONS: *Sensation!* 1917-1920 recordings (ASV/Living Era 1983)★★★, *In England* 1917-1924 recordings (EMI Pathe)★★★, *The Complete Original Dixieland Jazz Band* 1917-1936 recordings (RCA)★★★★.

ORIGINAL MEMPHIS FIVE

Formed by a group of white musicians who were based in New York, the Original Memphis Five became hugely popular during the 20s. Founder-members were trumpeter Phil Napoleon (b. 2 September 1901, Boston, Massachusetts, USA, d. 30 September 1990, Miami, Florida, USA), pianist Frank Signorelli (b. 24 May 1901, New York City, USA, d. 9 December 1975), trombonist Miff Mole (b. Irving Milfred Mole, 11 March 1898, Roosevelt, Long Island, New York, USA, d. 29 April 1961, New York City, New York, USA), clarinetist Jimmy Lytell (b. James Sarrapede, 1 December 1904, d. 28 November 1972) and drummer Jack Roth. The band filled an engagement at the Balconnades Ballroom in New York, USA, and then stayed together for a number of years and made many popular records, sometimes using other names. Later, other musicians including trombonist Charles Panelli, cornetist Red Nichols, drummer Ray Bauduc and the Dorsey brothers graced the band's ranks but, by the end of the 20s, the band, which had been the inspiration for many young white jazzmen, broke up. Towards the end of the 40s Napoleon re-formed the band, and some time later Signorelli also formed a band that used the same name and included Mole and Lytell. Reunions and re-formations continued during the 50s. Specializing in snappily played Dixieland jazz, the band did much to popularize jazz in the early years of its development. Napoleon and Mole made notable individual contributions to the music, gaining many emulators.

- COMPILATIONS: *Collection, Vol. 1: 1922-1923* (Collector's Classics)★★★★.

ØRSTED PEDERSEN, NIELS-HENNING

b. 27 May 1946, Osted, Denmark. Ørsted Pedersen first learned to play piano but took up the bass as his friend Ole Kock Hansen was also a pianist and they wanted to play duets together. He achieved an amazing facility on his new instrument while still in his mid-teens, making his first record at the age of 14. Playing regularly at the noted Montmartre Club in Copenhagen from early in 1961, he accompanied and occasionally recorded with visiting and expatriate American jazz stars, including Brew Moore, Yusef Lateef, Sonny Rollins, Bud Powell and Bill Evans (with whom he toured in the early 60s, having earlier refused an invitation to join Count Basie). He recorded frequently in the 60s, 70s and 80s, happily ranging from mainstream through bop to free jazz with artists such as Don Byas, Ben Webster, Tete Montoliu, Kenny Dorham, Dexter Gordon, Anthony Braxton and Albert Ayler. By the end of the 70s he had sealed his international reputation, thanks in part to a long stint with Oscar Peterson that continued well into the 80s. He has made a number of fine duo albums with Kenny Drew (*Duo*), Joe Pass (*Chops*) and Archie Shepp (*Looking At Bird*). A superbly accomplished technician, his brilliant virtuosity is underpinned with a great sense of time and dynamics. His solos are always interesting and display his awareness of the roots of jazz bass while acknowledging the advances made in more recent years.

● ALBUMS: *Oscar Peterson Big Six At The Montreux Jazz Festival 1975* (1975)★★★★, *Jay Walkin'* (Steeple Chase 1975)★★★, *Double Bass* (Steeple Chase 1976)★★★★, with Oscar Peterson *The Paris Concert* (1978)★★★, with Joe Pass *Chops* (1978)★★, *Dancing On The Tables* (Steeple Chase 1979)★★★, *Just The Way You Are* (1980)★★★, with Archie Shepp *Looking At Bird* (1980)★★, with Count Basie *Kansas City Six* (1981)★★★, *The Viking* (1983)★★★, with Palle Mikkelborg *Once Upon A Time* (1992)★★, *Friends Forever* (Milestone 1997)★★★, *Those Who Were* (Verve 1998)★★★★, *This Is All I Ask* (Verve 1998)★★★★.

Ory, Edward 'Kid'

b. 25 December 1886, La Place, Louisiana, USA, d. 23 January 1973, Honolulu, Hawaii, USA. A gifted, hard-blowing trombonist and a competitive musician, Ory came to New Orleans when in his mid-20s and he quickly established a fearsome reputation. An aggressive music maker and a tireless self-promoter, he was determined to be successful and very quickly was. By 1919 he was one of the city's most popular musicians and bandleaders but he left town on medical advice. Taking up residence in California, he became just as popular in Los Angeles and San Francisco as he had been in New Orleans. In 1922 Ory became the first black New Orleans musician to make records and the success of these extended his fame still further. In 1925 he travelled to Chicago, playing and recording with Joe 'King' Oliver, Jelly Roll Morton and Louis Armstrong, with whom he made many classic Hot Five and Hot Seven sides. In 1930 he was back in Los Angeles, joining Mutt Carey, who had taken over leadership of the Ory band. By 1933, however, Ory had tired of the business and the lack of success he was enjoying compared to that of his earlier days and quit music. He returned in the early 40s, sometimes playing alto saxophone or bass. Encouraged by some prestigious radio dates, he was soon bandleading again and playing trombone and was thus well placed to take advantage of the boom in popularity of traditional jazz that swept the USA. Throughout the 50s and into the early 60s he played successfully in San Francisco and Los Angeles, where he had his own club, touring nationally and overseas. He retired to Hawaii in 1966. A strong soloist and powerful ensemble player, Ory's work, while redolent of New Orleans-style jazz, demonstrated that his was a much richer and more sophisticated ability than that of many early trombonists. His compositions included 'Ory's Creole Trombone' and 'Muskrat Ramble', which became a jazz standard.

● ALBUMS: *Kid Ory & His Creole Dixieland Band* 10-inch album (Columbia 1950)★★★★, *Kid Ory's Creole Jazz Band, 1953* (Good Time 1954)★★★, *Kid Ory's Creole Jazz Band, 1954* (Good Time 1954)★★★★, with Johnny Wittwer *Kid Ory's Creole Band/Johnny Wittwer Trio* 10-inch album (Jazz Man 1954)★★★, *Kid Ory's Creole Jazz Band, 1955* (Good Time 1955)★★★, *The Legendary Kid* (Good Time 1955)★★★★, *Kid Ory's Creole Jazz Band, 1944-45* (Good Time 1955)★★★★, *Kid Ory's Favorites!* (Good Time 1956)★★★★, *This Kid's The Greatest!* (Good Time 1956)★★★★, with Johnny Dodds *Johnny Dodds And Kid Ory* (Epic 1956)★★★★, *Song Of The Wanderer* (Verve 1957)★★★, *The Kid From New Orleans* (Verve 1957)★★★, *Kid Ory Plays W.C. Handy* (Verve 1957)★★★, *Dance With Kid Ory Or Just Listen* (Verve 1957)★★★, *The Original Jazz* (Verve 1957)★★★, *Dixieland Marching Songs* (Verve 1957)★★★, with Henry 'Red' Allen *Henry 'Red' Allen Meets Kid Ory* (Verve 1957)★★★★, with Allen *We've Got Rhythm* (Verve 1957)★★★★, with Allen, Jack Teagarden *Red Allen, Jack Teagarden & Kid Ory At Newport* (Verve 1958)★★★★, *Kid Ory In Europe* (Verve 1958)★★★, *Storyville Nights* (Verve 1962)★★★, *Kid Ory At The Green Room, Vol. 1* 1947 recording (American Music)★★★, *Kid Ory At The Green Room, Vol. 2* 1947 recording (American Music)★★★, *King Of The Tailgate Trombone* 1948/1949 recordings (American Music)★★★.

Osborne, Mary

b 17 July 1921, Minot, North Dakota, USA, d. 4 March 1992, Bakersfield, California, USA. As a child Osborne studied various string instruments, including the banjo and violin, but from the age of nine she began to concentrate upon the guitar. She played in one or another of several bands led by her father, playing ragtime and country dances. By the time she was 12 Osborne had begun to appear on radio, singing to her own guitar accompaniment, and also joined a female trio. Around 1938 she heard the Alphonso Trent band at a dance, having been urged by friends to pay attention to the guitar player, Charlie Christian. This event changed her direction and she switched from acoustic to electric guitar and even sat in with Christian. By the early 40s Osborne had married; her husband, a trumpet player named Ralph Scaffidi, actively encouraged her playing, and she worked in a number of well-known if lesser big bands, including those led by Dick Stabile and Bob Chester. The 40s were busy times for Osborne - she played in an all-female band, with Joe Venuti, and in the closing years of the decade was active in New York, playing clubs and making records. In the 50s she was busier than ever, working in television and radio and also finding time to extend her studies. She continued an active career into the late 70s, forming a small band that included her husband and her son on bass. A fine, inventive soloist and a gifted accompanist, Osborne played and recorded with many of the great names of jazz, amongst them Mary Lou Williams, Coleman Hawkins and Charlie Shavers. Her enthusiasm and skill never flagged.

● ALBUMS: *A Girl And Her Guitar* (Warwick 1960)★★★★, *Now And Then* 1959/1981 recordings (Stash 1981)★★★★.

Osborne, Mike

b. 28 September 1941, Hereford, England. Osborne played violin in the school orchestra, but when he went to the Guildhall School it was to study clarinet. He could play piano too, but since turning professional his main instrument has always been alto saxophone. His favourite players are Phil Woods, Joe Henderson and Jackie McLean, with whom he shares a sharp-edged, slightly distressed-sounding tone, but he is often compared with Ornette Coleman for the urgency of his sound and his ability to create long, intense, graceful skeins of free melody. He first came to notice with the Mike Westbrook Concert Band when it re-formed after Westbrook's move to London from Plymouth. 'Ossie' sat in for a couple of gigs and was asked to join permanently in early 1963, when he was one of only two professional musicians in the orchestra. Over the next few years he was an important constituent of several fine bands, including the Michael Gibbs Band, Chris McGregor's Brotherhood Of Breath, Harry Miller's Isipingo and the group, ranging from a quartet to an octet, that he co-led with John Surman during 1968 and 1969. He also worked with John Warren, Alan Skidmore, Kenneth Terroade, Rik Colbeck, and Humphrey Lyttelton. In 1969 he established his own exceptionally exciting trio with Harry Miller and Louis Moholo, which, apart from many fine public gigs, recorded several superb sessions for BBC Radio's Jazz Club. In the early 70s he began a fruitful association with Stan Tracey in wholly improvised duets, which brought Tracey back from the brink of retirement through disillusion with the music business. In 1973 he co-founded S.O.S., probably the first regular all-saxophone band, with Alan Skidmore and John Surman. He was voted best alto saxophonist in the *Melody Maker* poll every year from 1969-73. During the late 70s he became increasingly ill and has been unable to play since 1980. His relatively small recorded oeuvre does show the range of his playing, from deeply moving but unsentimental ballad interpretations with Westbrook to scorchingly intense free explorations with Isipingo or the trio.

● ALBUMS: *Outback* (Future Music 1970)★★★★, with Stan Tracey *Original* (1972)★★★★, *Border Crossing* (Ogun 1975)★★★, *All Night Long* (Ogun 1975)★★, *SOS* (1975)★★★, with Tracey *Tandem* (1976)★★★, *Marcel's Muse* (Ogun 1977)★★, *Gold Hearted Girl* (Crosscut 1988)★★★, *A Case For The Blues* (Crosscut 1993)★★★.

OSBY, GREG

b. 3 August 1960, St. Louis, Missouri, USA. Osby is a New York-based saxophonist who has attracted criticism for his attempts to attach jazz's cool to a militant hip-hop beat. Osby began life as an R&B musician, only discovering jazz when he began attending Howard University in 1978. He also studied at Berklee College Of Music, and appeared on the East Coast with Woody Shaw, Jon Faddis, Ron Carter, Dizzy Gillespie and Jack DeJohnette's Special Edition. Osby also worked with the M-Base project, a self-help organization founded by saxophonist Steve Coleman and singer Cassandra Wilson, that attempted to integrate all forms of black music into a new ecumenical style. Following several releases for JMT, Osby recorded the free-ranging hip-hop album, *3-D Lifestyles*, on his new label, Blue Note Records: 'The purpose was to function as an 'either/or', meaning that it could rest solely as a hardcore hip-hop record without any jazz or musicians at all, and that it also would be a strong musical statement without breakbeats or anything. I wanted it to bridge the gap'. Alongside jazz musicians including Geri Allen and Darrell Grant, he enlisted the aid of hip-hop producers Ali Shaheed Muhammed (A Tribe Called Quest) and Street Element, and a variety of rappers. Following this muted experiment, subsequent albums concentrated on acoustic jazz.

● ALBUMS: *Greg Osby And Sound Theater* (JMT 1987)★★★, *Mind Games* (JMT 1988)★★★, *Season Of Renewal* (JMT 1989)★★, *Man-Talk For Moderns, Vol. X* (Blue Note 1991)★★, *3-D Lifestyles* (Blue Note 1993)★★, *Black Book* (Blue Note 1995)★★★, *Art Forum* (Blue Note 1996)★★★★, *Further Ado* (Blue Note 1997)★★★, *Zero* (Blue Note 1998)★★★.

OUR MAN IN PARIS - DEXTER GORDON

One of the most successful of Blue Note Records' 'blue' period and an album that remains Dexter Gordon's finest work. Although his tenor sax occasionally grates, this is a brilliant example of late bebop. Supported by Bud Powell (piano), Kenny Clarke (drums) and Pierre Michelot (bass), the simple quartet sound coolly in control. 'Willow Weep For Me' is played with great beauty and 'A Night in Tunisia' is yet another well-crafted version. The bonus of 'Our Love Is Here To Stay' and 'Like Someone In Love' (from Powell's *Alternate Takes*) on the CD reissue puts this album in the first division.

● Tracks: *Scrapple From The Apple; Willow Weep For Me; Stairway To The Stairs; A Night In Tunisia; Our Love Is Here To Stay; Like Someone In Love; Broadway.*

● First released 1963

● UK peak chart position: did not chart

● USA peak chart position: did not chart

OUT OF THE COOL - GIL EVANS

A much admired and loved man, of all the many brilliant orchestration projects this was his finest in his own right. He teases us with the opening of 'La Nevada' until the gorgeous repeated four-bar riff finally bursts on our ears with orgasmic delight. There are wonderful brass solos from John Coles, Tony Studd and Budd Johnson and a bass showcase for Ron Carter. As the opening track peters out after 15 minutes the listener enjoys the smug realization that there are a further four outstanding pieces to come. Too much of Evans's fame came through Miles Davis and Jimi Hendrix.

● Tracks: *La Nevada; Where Flamingoes Fly; Bilbao Song; Stratusphunk; Sunken Treasure.*

● First released 1960

● UK peak chart position: did not chart

● USA peak chart position: did not chart

OUT TO LUNCH! - ERIC DOLPHY

Although a difficult album for those not seeped in jazz, *Out To Lunch!* is still regarded as a milestone recording. Featuring Freddie Hubbard (trumpet), Bobby Hutcherson (vibes), Tony Williams (drums) and Richard Davis (bass), this recording shows a unit hell-bent on pushing forward the perimeters of jazz, with extraordinary success. Dolphy's various saxophones, flute and chilling bass clarinet are literally all over the place without ever detracting from the quite outstanding performances from his supporting musicians. Although it won't be played as often as *Kind Of Blue* your collection would be all the poorer without it.

● Tracks: *Hat And Beard; Something Sweet, Something Tender; Gazzelloni; Out To Lunch; Straight Up And Down.*
● First released 1964
● UK peak chart position: did not chart
● USA peak chart position: did not chart

Owens, Jimmy

b. 9 December 1943, New York City, New York, USA. Owens went to the High School of Music and Art in New York when he was aged 14. He studied composition with Henry Bryant and trumpet with Donald Byrd. In the 60s, after appearing with Marshall Brown's Newport Youth Band, he played with the bands of Slide Hampton, Lionel Hampton, Maynard Ferguson, Gerry Mulligan, Charles Mingus and Herbie Mann. Owens worked briefly with Duke Ellington and Count Basie and was a member of the Thad Jones-Mel Lewis band. During the early 70s he played with drummer Billy Cobham as well as in Billy Taylor's band on the *Frost Show*, and continued the work he had started with Collective Black Artists Inc. (1969) and Jazzmobile. He has been on the music panel of the New York State Council on the Arts and was musical director of the New York Jazz Repertory Company (1974). Owens has written many extended pieces for the Brooklyn Philharmonic Orchestra. A gifted hard bop player, the foundation of Owens' music remains in the blues, and he plays with a prodigious technique and clear, ringing tone.

Oxley, Tony

b. 15 June 1938, Sheffield, Yorkshire, England. Oxley began to teach himself piano at the age of eight, and did not pursue the drums seriously until he was 17. During his National Service (1957-60) he studied drums and theory and for the following four years he led his own group in Sheffield. From 1963-67 he worked with Derek Bailey and bassist/composer Gavin Bryars in developing an abstract, freely improvised genre. In 1966 he moved to London, and was for some years in the house band at Ronnie Scott's club, backing many famous visiting musicians. He was also in Scott's octet, the Band, and worked with Howard Riley, Gordon Beck, Alan Skidmore, Mike Pyne and Barry Guy's London Jazz Composers Orchestra (LJCO). In 1970 he co-founded Incus Records with Evan Parker and Bailey and was a founder-member of the London Musicians' Co-operative, and from 1973 was an organizing tutor at the Barry Summer School in Wales. In the mid-70s he led his own band, Angular Apron, which included Riley, Guy and Dave Holdsworth. In 1978 he moved to East Germany, then (clandestinely) to West Germany in 1981, but has returned to the UK for concerts. He also plays in the trio SOH (with Skidmore and Ali Havrand), with Didier Levallet and in the Quartet. Since the late 80s he has been a regular associate of Cecil Taylor, playing in the pianist's Feel Trio and recording the *Leaf Palm Hand* duo with him at FMP's special Taylor festival in Berlin in 1988. His Celebration Orchestra comprised four brass players, six strings, piano and five drummers, but he enjoys small-group improvising best: witness the excellence of the trio Coe, Oxley & Co. (with Tony Coe and Chris Laurence). Oxley is a highly skilled and versatile drummer whose fierce dedication to his music has gained him a reputation for being a difficult person to deal with. His playing is, however, that of a responsive and supportive colleague.

● ALBUMS: *The Baptised Traveller* (1969)★★★, *Four Compositions For Sextet* (1970)★★★, *Ichnos* (1971)★★★, with Alan Davie *Duo* (1974)★★★, *Tony Oxley* (Incus 1975)★★★★, *February Papers* (1977)★★★, *Nutty (On) Willisau* (1984)★★, with Phil Wachsmann *The Glider And The Grinder* (1987)★★, *Tomorrow Is Here* (1988)★★★, with Cecil Taylor *Leaf Palm Hand* (1989)★★★, *The Tony Oxley Quartet* (Incus 1993)★★★★, with the Celebration Orchestra featuring Bill Dixon *The Enchanted Messenger: Live From The Berlin Jazz Festival* (Soul Note 1997)★★★, with Paul Bley, Furio Di Castri *Chaos* (Soul Note 1998)★★★.

Ozone, Makoto

b. 25 March 1961, Kobe, Japan. Makoto is the son of one of Japan's best jazz pianists, Minoru Ozone, and has a prodigious technique and a wide knowledge of jazz piano styles. He started on the organ at the age of four, but took up the piano in his teens after hearing Oscar Peterson. In 1980 he went to the USA to study composing and arranging at the Berklee College Of Music, and played a Carnegie Hall recital to open the Kool Jazz Festival of 1983. On Ozone's arrival at Berklee he immediately impressed Gary Burton and was playing regularly with his quartet in 1985 when he was also playing in a duo with Michel Petrucciani. Alongside his jazz activities he has extensively studied classical piano playing. John Scofield joined Makoto's regular cohorts Kiyoshi Kitagawa and Clarence Penn on three tracks for 1997's *The Trio*.

● ALBUMS: *Makoto Ozone* (Columbia 1984)★★★, *After* (Columbia 1986)★★★, *Now You Know* (Columbia 1987)★★★, *Starlight* (JVC 1990)★★★, *Breakout* (Verve 1996)★★★, *The Trio* (Verve 1997)★★★.

P

PAGE, ORAN 'HOT LIPS'

b. 27 January 1908, Dallas, Texas, USA, d. 5 November 1954. In the 20s Page played trumpet mostly in his home state but also toured in bands accompanying some of the best of the day's blues singers, among them Ma Rainey, Bessie Smith and Ida Cox. Towards the end of the 20s Page joined Walter Page's Blue Devils, a band formed in Oklahoma City out of the remnants of a touring band in which the trumpeter had worked. With the Blue Devils Page built a reputation as a powerful lead and solo trumpet, an emotional blues player and singer, and an inspirational sideman. In 1931 he was one of several Blue Devils enticed into Bennie Moten's band, where he remained until Moten's death in 1935. The following year he joined Count Basie in Kansas City where he was heard by Louis Armstrong's manager, Joe Glaser, who signed him up. Glaser's motives have been much-speculated upon. At the time Armstrong was suffering lip trouble and Glaser certainly needed a trumpeter/singer. However, the neglect displayed by the manager towards his new signing once Armstrong was back suggests that he might well have seen Page as a competitor to be neutralized. In the late 30s Page led bands large and small, mostly in and around New York and appeared at numerous after-hours sessions and on many record dates, including Ida Cox's comeback date after her retirement. At the start of the 40s he was briefly in Artie Shaw's band, with which he made a superb recording of 'St James Infirmary'. The rest of this decade was spent much as he had spent the late 30s, playing and recording in a succession of bands mostly in the New York area. He also featured on several record dates, including the excellent 1944 V-Disc sides. At the end of the 40s he made another hit record, this time 'Baby, It's Cold Outside' coupled with 'The Hucklebuck' with Pearl Bailey, a record that helped to establish her stardom. In the early 50s Page often played in Europe until his death in 1954. Although he was strongly influenced by Armstrong during part of his career, Page was in fact an inventive and exceptionally interesting blues-orientated trumpet player in his own right as well as an excellent singer of the blues. Whatever the reason, Page's career was partially overshadowed by Armstrong and during his lifetime he was rarely granted the critical appraisal his talents deserved. Almost four decades after his death, his re-evaluation remains incomplete.

● ALBUMS: *Hot Lips Page In Sweden* (1951)★★★, *Hot Lips Page* (1952-53)★★★★, *Hot Lips Page 1951* (Jazz Society 1989)★★★.

● COMPILATIONS: *Hot Lips Page 1938-1940* (Official 1989)★★★★, *Oran 'Hot Lips' Page Vols 1/2* (1942-53)★★★★, with others *Midnight At V-Disc* (Pumpkin 1944)★★★, *Play The Blues In B* (Jazz Archives 1993)★★★, *1940-1944* (Classics 1995)★★★★, *1944-1946* (Classics 1998)★★★.

PAGE, WALTER

b. 9 February 1900, Gallatin, Missouri, USA, d. 20 December 1957. Page was one of many pupils of Major N. Clark Smith who gained fame in jazz circles. In the early 20s, Page played bass with Bennie Moten in Kansas City. In 1925 Page was stranded in Oklahoma City when a band he was playing in folded. He decided to form his own group out of the wreckage and this band became the legendary Blue Devils. One of the outstanding territory bands of the south-west and instrumental in helping to form the musical concept that eventually became known as Kansas City style, Page gathered many fine musicians into his band. Among them were Oran 'Hot Lips' Page, Jimmy Rushing, Lester Young and Bill Basie (in the days before he was ennobled). After Moten headhunted some of his best sidemen Page kept going for a while but eventually gave up the struggle and he too joined Moten. He later played in Basie's band where he became one quarter of the fabled All American Rhythm Section (with Basie, Freddie Green and Jo Jones). Leaving Basie in 1942 he played with several leading territory bands, including those led by Nat Towles and Jesse Price, and in the middle of the decade was back with Basie. Later, he played in various pick-up groups, often in New York but with occasional tours, a pattern of work that continued into the mid-50s. He died in 1957. A solid player with an impeccable sense of time, Page is generally credited as one of the originators of the 'walking bass', a style of playing in which the bassist plays passing notes, up or down the scale, in addition to the three or four root notes of the chord, thus creating a flowing line.

● COMPILATIONS: *Kansas City Hot Jazz* (1926-30)★★★, incl. on *Sweet And Low Blues, Big Bands And Territory Bands Of The 20s* (1929)★★★, with Count Basie *Swinging the Blues* (1937-39)★★★★, *Hot Lips Page 1938-1940* (Classics 90s)★★★★, *Hot Lips Page 1940-1944* (Classics 90s)★★★★.

PALMER, EARL

b. 25 October 1924, New Orleans, Louisiana, USA. Palmer's mother was a vaudeville performer, and from an early age he began entertaining as a singer and dancer. Playing drums in his school band, he started listening to jazz drummers such as Big Sid Catlett and Panama Francis, and joined Dave Bartholomew's band in 1947. He recorded with the Bartholomew band and went on to play on many of his productions for Imperial Records, notably Fats Domino's classic records. Palmer is probably featured on virtually every other Crescent City classic, including those Specialty rockers by Little Richard and Lloyd Price, but in 1956 Aladdin Records hired him as a session arranger to handle their New Orleans sessions. In February 1957, he moved out to Los Angeles to work for Aladdin until the company was liquidated. He remained one of the busiest session drummers on the west coast throughout the 60s and 70s, recording with everyone from Lightnin' Hopkins to Marvin Gaye and subsequently wrote film scores and advertising jingles.

Palmer, Holly

b. USA. Holly Palmer grew up in Santa Monica, California, and Seattle, Washington, where she regularly sang Sarah Vaughan and Nancy Wilson standards in high school. By the time she attended the Berklee College Of Music in Boston on a scholarship, she had rediscovered her love of pop music and spent many evenings playing at impromptu rock gigs. After Berklee she continued to play irregularly in rock bands in New York, though she still returned to jazz standards when the occasion arose. She signed a development deal with Island Records in 1993 but this failed to produce a full contract. However, she eventually came to the attention of Sue Drew at Reprise Records, resulting in the release of her self-titled debut album in 1996. As she later told Billboard magazine, she never set out to prove herself the easiest of people to work with: 'Because of my experiences before with industry types, there were certain things that I wanted. I wanted to co-produce the album, and I didn't want anyone telling me what to sound like.' The record was indeed co-produced, with Kenny White (Shawn Colvin, Marc Cohn). *Holly Palmer* featured Me'Shell Ndegé Ocello (bass) on its strongest track, 'Lickerish Man', as well as guitarists Bill Frisell and John Leventhal.

● ALBUMS: *Different Languages* (Reprise 1996)★★★.

Palmer, Roy

b. *c.*1892, New Orleans, Louisiana, USA, d. 22 December 1963. Early in his career Palmer played guitar and trumpet but eventually settled on trombone. In the early years of the century he worked mostly in his home-town. By 1920 he had moved to Chicago where he recorded with, amongst others, Jelly Roll Morton, Johnny Dodds and Jimmy Blythe. In the early 30s he quit full-time music but, according to jazz musician and writer John Chilton, he continued to teach into the 50s.

Papa Bue

(see Jensen, Papa Bue)

Papadimitriou, Sakis

b. 1 May 1940, Kavala, Greece. Pianist, broadcaster, promoter, novelist and journalist Papadimitriou has been one of the moving forces behind the still-small Greek jazz scene. His radio programmes and articles in the magazine *TZAZ* helped to build an informed audience for jazz at its most experimental. Papadimitriou's duo with Floros Floridis (saxophone, clarinet) was Greece's first free music group. Unfortunately, 'musical and personal differences' made it a short-lived one. Although Papadimitriou periodically works with other Greek musicians, his discography is composed almost entirely of solo piano recordings. Particularly striking is his use - alternately subtle and dramatic - of the piano's interior: plucking, strumming and striking the strings of the instrument.

● ALBUMS: with Floros Floridis *Improvisation At Barakos* (1979)★★★, *Piano Contacts* (1980)★★★, *Piano Plays* (1983)★★★★, *First Move* (1985)★★★, *Piano Oracles* (1989)★★, *Piano Cellules* 1986 recording (1991)★★★.

Parenti, Tony

b. 6 August 1900, New Orleans, Louisiana, USA, d. 17 April 1972. By his early teenage years, Parenti was playing clarinet in various local bands that performed an incipient style of jazz. While still in his teens he formed his own band and made some records. In the late 20s he tried his luck in New York, playing with several popular dance bands including those of Meyer Davis, Ben Pollack and Freddy Rich. He worked in the studios for many years in the 30s, but at the end of the decade joined Ted Lewis for a five-year stint. In the late 40s he played at several clubs in New York and Chicago. He spent the early 50s in Florida playing with local bands before returning to New York to lead bands for residencies that extended throughout the 60s at clubs such as Eddie Condon's and Jimmy Ryan's. A fluent player in the Dixieland tradition, Parenti deserves rather more attention than he has gained. His neglect results largely from his long periods in New York's clubland and a relatively small recorded output.

● ALBUMS: *Jazz, That's All* (1955)★★, *Tony Parenti's Talking Records* (1958)★★★.

Parham, Tiny

b. Hartzell S. Parham, 25 February 1900, Winnipeg, Manitoba, Canada, d. 4 April 1943. Raised in Kansas City, pianist and organ player Parham played in a number of lesser-known territory bands in the early 20s. During the later years of the decade he recorded with blues singers and such jazzmen as Johnny Dodds. In the late 20s and early 30s he led his own small and big bands in and around Kansas City, but by 1936 abandoned bandleading in favour of a career as a solo organist, mostly in Chicago.

● COMPILATIONS: *Tiny Parham And His Musicians* (1928-29)★★★, *Tiny Parham 1928-1929* (Swaggie 1988)★★★★, *Tiny Parham 1929-1930,* (Neovox 1993)★★★, *Tiny Parham And His Musicians 1929-1940* (Classic Jazz Masters 1993)★★★★.

Paris Blues

For a few moments at the beginning, hopes are raised that this is a film that will take seriously the problems of racial intolerance. Soon, however, jazz musicians Paul Newman and Sidney Poitier drift into stereotypes and there is little left for the audience to do except enjoy the scenes of Paris and the music. Fortunately, much of the latter, including the film's score, is in the hands of Duke Ellington, which almost makes up for the disappointment in the dramatics. Apart from Ellington And His Orchestra, which includes Cat Anderson, Willie Cook, Johnny Hodges, Ray Nance, Clark Terry and Sam Woodyard, other musicians include Max Roach, Philly Joe Jones and local boys Joseph Reinhardt and Guy Lafitte. Louis Armstrong puts in an appearance and locks horns with the Ellington ensemble in a rowdy nightclub sequence. The playing of Newman and Poitier was dubbed, respectively, by Murray McEachern and Paul Gonsalves. Directed by Martin Ritt, this 1961 film was based upon the novel by Harold Flender that did not dodge the issues and in which the black musician was the sole protagonist, his white sidekick being very much a minor character.

PARIS, BARBARA

b. Barbara Perea, 2 October 1954, Denver, Colorado, USA. Although growing up in a jazz atmosphere (Paris's father introduced her to jazz on record and she worked in a non-musical capacity in a jazz club while still a teenager), it was some years before she settled into a career as a singer. In her mid-twenties she met and was encouraged by saxophonist Eddie Shu. Building upon her experience singing in choirs and childhood piano lessons, she turned to singing with flair and a natural accomplishment. While remaining based in Colorado, with numerous engagements in Boulder and her hometown, she has also sung in Los Angeles and New York and in Paris, France. Her warm voice and clear diction lend themselves admirably to ballads, while on mid- and up-tempo songs she swings with subtlety. Her repertoire is very wide, ranging through popular songs of the past and present, Latin, and jazz standards. She has broadcast extensively and has sung with many visiting jazz musicians including Ellyn Rucker, Joe Pass, Barry Harris, Freddie Hubbard and, while in Paris, Claude Bolling. The simplicity and discreet soulfulness of her style is sometimes at odds with the clamorous demands of a pop music industry based upon flash and drama.

● ALBUMS: *Where Butterflies Play* (Perea 1993)★★★, *Happy Talk* (Perea 1994)★★★, *Day By Day* (Perea 1997)★★★.

PARIS, JACKIE

b. 20 September 1926, Nutley, New Jersey, USA. From the early 40s Paris was active in New York as a singer and guitarist. He worked mostly with bop groups and his singing soon became his primary activity. He achieved a considerable measure of critical acclaim but failed to attract a popular following amongst the jazz audience. During the 50s and 60s he worked steadily but mostly in clubs and resort hotels, although he did record with jazzmen such as Donald Byrd, Gigi Gryce and Charles Mingus. Paris sings with an urgent attack, his voice throaty and rhythmically infectious. At his best on up-tempo boppish numbers, he can also bring qualities of understanding and depth to ballads. His wife is singer Anne Marie Moss.

● ALBUMS: with Donald Byrd, Gigi Gryce *Modern Jazz Perspectives* (1957)★★★★, *Jackie Paris* (Audiophile 1988)★★★, *Nobody Else But Me* (Audiophile 1988)★★★, with Marc Johnson, Carlos Franzetti *Jackie Paris/Marc Johnson/Carlos Franzetti* (Audiophile 1994)★★★.

PARKER, CHARLIE 'BIRD'

b. 29 August 1920, Kansas City, Kansas, USA, d. 12 March 1955. Although he was born on the Kansas side of the state line, Parker was actually raised across the Kaw River in Kansas City, Missouri. His nickname was originally 'Yardbird' due to his propensity for eating fried chicken - later this was shortened to the more poetic 'Bird'. Musicians talk of first hearing his alto saxophone as if it were a religious conversion. Charles Christopher Parker changed the face of jazz and shaped the course of 20th-century music. Kansas City saxophonists were a competitive bunch. Ben Webster and Herschel Evans both came from Kansas. Before they became national celebrities they would challenge visiting sax stars to 'blowing matches'. It is this artistically fruitful sense of competition that provided Charlie Parker with his aesthetic. Live music could be heard at all hours of the night, a situation resulting from lax application of prohibition laws by the Democrat Tom Pendergast (city boss from 1928-39). While in the Crispus Attucks high school Parker took up the baritone. His mother gave him an alto in 1931. He dropped out of school at the age of 14 and devoted himself to the instrument. A premature appearance at the High Hat Club - when he dried up mid-solo on 'Body & Soul' - led to him abandoning the instrument for three months; the humiliation was repeated in 1937 when veteran drummer Jo Jones threw a cymbal at his feet to indicate he was to leave the stage (this time Parker just went on practising harder). Playing in bands led by Tommy Douglas (1936-37) and Buster Smith (1937-38) gave him necessary experience. A tour with George E. Lee and instructions in harmony from the pianist Carrie Powell were helpful. His first real professional break was with the Jay McShann band in 1938, a sizzling swing unit (with whom Parker made his first recordings in 1941). Parker's solos on 'Sepian Bounce', 'Jumpin' Blues' and 'Lonely Boy Blues' made people sit up and take notice: he was taking hip liberties with the chords. Brief spells in the Earl 'Fatha' Hines (1942-43) and Billy Eckstine (1944) big bands introduced him to Dizzy Gillespie, another young black player with innovative musical ideas and a rebellious stance. Wartime austerities, though, meant that the days of the big bands were numbered. Parker took his experience of big band saxophone sections with him to Harlem, New York. There he found the equivalent of the Kansas City 'cutting contests' in the clubs of 52nd Street, especially in the 'afterhours' sessions at Minton's Playhouse. Together with Dizzy and drummers Kenny Clarke and Max Roach, and with the essential harmonic contributions of Charlie Christian and Thelonious Monk, he pioneered a new music. Furious tempos and intricate heads played in unison inhibited lesser talents from joining in. Instead of keeping time with bass and snare drums, Clarke and Roach kept up a beat on the cymbal, using bass and snare for accents, whipping up soloists to greater heights. And Parker played *high*: that is, he created his solo lines from the top notes of the underlying chord sequences - 9ths, 11ths, 13ths - so extending the previous harmonic language of jazz. Parker made his recording debut as a small combo player in Tiny Grimes' band in September 1944.

In 1945 Savoy Records - and some more obscure labels including Guild, Manor and Comet - began releasing 78s of this music, which the press called 'bebop'. It became a national fad, Dizzy's trademark goatee and beret supplying the visual element. It was a proud declaration of bohemian recklessness from a black community that, due to wartime full employment, was feeling especially confident. Charlie Parker's astonishing alto - so fluent and abrupt, bluesy and joyous - was the definition of everything that was modern and hip. 'Koko', 'Shaw Nuff', 'Now's The Time': the very titles announced the dawning of a new era. A trip to the west coast and a residency at Billy Berg's helped to spread the message.

There were problems, however. Parker's addiction to heroin was causing erratic behaviour and the proprietor was not impressed at the small audiences of hipsters the music attracted (apart from a historic opening night). In January 1946 Norman Granz promoted Charlie Parker at the LA Philharmonic and the same year saw him begin a series of famous recordings for Ross Russell's Dial label, with a variety of players that included Howard McGhee, Lucky Thompson, Wardell Gray and Dodo Marmarosa. However, Parker's heroin-related health problems came to a head following the notorious 'Loverman' session of July 1946 when, after setting his hotel-room on fire, the saxophonist was incarcerated in the psychiatric wing of the LA County Jail and then spent six months in a rehabilitation centre (commemorated in 'Relaxin' At Camarillo', 1947). When he emerged he recorded two superb sessions for Dial, one of them featuring Erroll Garner. On returning to New York he formed a band with Miles Davis and Max Roach and cut some classic sides in November 1947, including 'Scrapple From The Apple' and 'Klactoveeseds-tene'. Parker toured abroad for the first time in 1949, when he played at a jazz festival in Paris. In November 1950 he visited Scandinavia. He felt that his music would be taken more seriously if he was associated with classical instrumentation. The 'With Strings' albums now sound hopelessly dated, but they were commercially successful at the time. Fans reported that Parker's playing, though consummate, needed the spark of improvisers of his stature to really lift off on the bandstand. A more fruitful direction was suggested by his interest in the music of Edgard Varese, whom he saw on the streets of Manhattan, but Parker's untimely death ruled out any collaborations with the *avant garde* composer. His health had continued to give him problems: ulcers and cirrhosis of the liver. According to Leonard Feather, his playing at the Town Hall months before his death in March 1955 was 'as great as any period in his career'. His last public appearance was on 4 March 1955, at Birdland, the club named after him: it was a fiasco - Parker and pianist Bud Powell rowed onstage, the latter storming off followed shortly by bassist Charles Mingus. Disillusioned, obese and racked by illness, Parker died eight days later in the hotel suite of Baroness Pannonica de Koenigswarter, a wealthy aristocrat and stalwart bebop fan. His influence was immense. Lennie Tristano said, 'If Charlie wanted to invoke plagiarism laws, he could sue almost everybody who's made a record in the last ten years.' In pursuing his art with such disregard for reward and security, Charlie Parker was black music's first existential hero. After him, jazz could not avoid the trials and tribulations that beset the *avant garde*.

● ALBUMS: *The Bird Blows The Blues* (Dial 1949)★★★★, *The Charlie Parker Story* 1945 recording (Savoy 40s)★★★★, *Charlie Parker Quintet* (Dial 1949)★★★★, with Lester Young *Bird & Pres Carnegie Hall 1949* (1949)★★★★, *Dance Of The Infidels* (1949)★★★★, *Sextet* (Dial 1950)★★★★, *With Strings* (Mercury 1950)★★★★, *With Strings Volume 2* (Mercury 1950)★★★★, *Broadcasts* (1950)★★★★, *Bird At St Nick's* (1950)★★★★, *Just Friends* (1950)★★★★, *Apartment Sessions* (1950)★★★★, *One Night In Chicago* (1950)★★★★, *At The Pershing Ballroom* (1950)★★★, *Bird In Sweden* (1950)★★★, *Charlie Parker Volume 1* (Savoy 1950)★★★★, *Charlie Parker Volume 2* (Savoy 1951)★★★★, *Alternate Masters* (Dial 1951)★★★, *The Mingus Connection* (1951)★★★, *Norman Granz Jam Session* (1952)★★★★, *Inglewood Jam* (1952)★★★, *Charlie Parker Volume 3* (Savoy 1952)★★★★, with Dizzy Gillespie *Bird And Diz* (Mercury 1952)★★★★, *Charlie Parker Volume 4* (Savoy 1952)★★★★, *South Of The Border* (Mercury 1952)★★★, *Live At Rockland Palace* (1952)★★★, *New Bird Vols 1 & 2* (1952-53)★★★★, *Yardbird* (1953)★★★★, *Jazz At Massey Hall* reissued as part of *The Greatest Jazz Concert Ever* (1953)★★★★, *Birdland All Stars At Carnegie Hall* (1954)★★★★, *Charlie Parker* (Clef 1954)★★★★, *Charlie Parker Big Band* (Clef 1954)★★★★, *Charlie Parker Memorial Volume Vol 1* (Savoy 1955)★★★★, *The Immortal Charlie Parker* (Savoy 1955)★★★★, *The Magnificent Charlie Parker* (Clef 1955)★★★★, with Dizzy Gillespie *Diz 'N' Bird In Concert* (Roost 1959)★★★★, *An Evening At Home With The Bird* (Savoy 1959)★★★, *The Bird Returns* (Savoy 1962)★★★★, *Newly Discovered Sides By The Immortal Charlie Parker* (Savoy 1964)★★★, *One Night At Birdland* 1950 recording (1977)★★★, *One Night In Washington* 1953 recording (1982)★★★, *Charlie Parker At Storyville* 1953 recording (1985)★★★★, *Newly Discovered Sides By The Immortal Charlie Parker* 1948-1949 recordings (1996)★★★.

● COMPILATIONS: *Charlie Parker Story Volumes 1-3* (Verve 1957)★★★★, *The Genius Of Charlie Parker Volumes 1-8* (Verve 1957)★★★★, *Les Jazz Cool Vols 1-3* (Les Jazz Cool 1960)★★★, *Charlie Parker On Dial, Vols. 1-6* 1945-47 recordings (1974)★★★★, *Bird With Strings* 1950-52 recordings (1977)★★★★, *Summit Meeting At Birdland* 1951-53 recordings (1977)★★★★, *The Complete Savoy Studio Sessions* 1944-48 recordings, 5-LP box set (1978)★★★★, *The Complete Charlie Parker On Verve* 1950-1954 recordings, 10-CD box set (Verve 1989)★★★★★, *The Savoy Master Takes* 1944-48 recordings (1989)★★★★★, *The Legendary Dial Masters, Vols. 1 & 2* 1946-47 recordings (1989)★★★★★, *Bird At The Roost, Vols. 1-4* 1948-49 recordings (1990)★★★★★, *The Complete Dean Benedetti Recordings Of Charlie Parker* late 40s recordings, 7-CD box set (Mosaic 1991)★★★★, *Gold Collection* (1993)★★★, *The Complete Dial Sessions* (Spotlight 1993)★★★★, *Yardbird Suite: The*

Ultimate Charlie Parker Collection (Rhino 1997)★★★★, *Charlie Parker* (Verve 1998)★★★★.

● VIDEOS: *The Bird* (1994).

● FURTHER READING: *Bird Lives! The High Life & Hard Times Of Charlie (Yardbird) Parker*, Ross Russell. *Bird: The Legend Of Charlie Parker*, Robert Reisner. *Cool Blues*, Mark Miller. *Discography Of Charlie Parker*, Jorgen Grunnet Jepsen. *Charlie Parker*, M. Harrison. *Bird Lives: The High Life And Hard Times Of Charlie (Yardbird) Parker*, Ross Russell. *To Bird With Love*, C. Parker and F. Paudras. *Charlie Parker*, Brian Priestley. *Charlie Parker*, Stuart Isacoff. *Celebrating Bird: The Triumph Of Charlie Parker*, Gary Giddins. *From One Charlie To Another*, Charlie Watts. *Charlie Parker: His Music And Life*, Carl Woideck.

PARKER, EVAN

b. Evan Shaw Parker, 5 April 1944, Bristol, Avon, England. Soprano and tenor saxophonist Parker has one of the most awesome techniques in any field of music. When playing solo he combines circular breathing, multiphonics and tonguing tricks to build up complex, contrapuntal masses of sound that are credible only to those who have heard him live and can testify that there is no overdubbing involved. (However, with his 1991 album, *Process And Reality*, he began to experiment with multi-tracking techniques, but not simply to mimic his solo feats: the overdubbed tracks found him producing more lyrical, though equally complex interweaving lines.) He is also to be heard from time to time in conventional big band contexts (such as Orchestra UK led by Kenny Wheeler at the start of the 90s) and at all points between there and total abstract improvisation. He has also occasionally worked in the pop field, with Scott Walker and Annette Peacock, and with contemporary classical composers Michael Nyman and Gavin Bryars. While he has created a unique style and sound-world, which would seem to exclude other players, he can glory in any type of jam, digging in for the gritty blues with the best of them, sparking off players including Annie Whitehead, Dudu Pukwana, Mark Sanders, Paul Rogers and John Stevens so that he and they play at their best. His mother, an amateur pianist, introduced him to jazz in the shape of Fats Waller. He studied saxophone with James Knott from 1958 until 1962 when he went to Birmingham University to study botany. He left to concentrate on music, playing with Howard Riley from time to time and developing his taste for free improvisation. In 1966 he moved to London to play with Stevens's Spontaneous Music Ensemble and with Derek Bailey, with whom he cofounded the Music Improvisation Company in 1968 and the Incus Records label in 1970. As well as some remarkable solo concerts and albums, Parker has gigged or recorded with Chris McGregor, Tony Oxley, Barry Guy, Paul Lytton, George Lewis, the Globe Unity Orchestra, Steve Lacy, Peter Brötzmann, several Company line-ups, electronics expert Walter Prati and, with Paul Lovens, has long been a member of the regular trio led by Alex Von Schlippenbach. He currently leads his own trio too, with Paul Rogers on bass and Mark Sanders on drums, participates in Jon Lloyd's Anacrusis and continues to develop his singular solo saxophone improvisations.

● ALBUMS: with Derek Bailey, Han Bennink *The Topography Of The Lungs* (1970)★★★, *Music Improvisation Company* (1971)★★★, *The Music Improvisation Company 1968-71* (1971)★★★★, with Paul Lytton *Collective Calls (Urban) (Two Microphones)* (1972)★★★, with Lytton *At The Unity Theatre* (1975)★★, with Bailey *The London Concert* (1975)★★★, *Saxophone Solos* (1975)★★★★, with others *Company 1* (1976)★★★, with Bailey, Anthony Braxton *Company 2* (1976)★★★, with Lytton *RA 1+2* (1976)★★★, with John Stevens *The Longest Night Vols 1 & 2* (1977)★★★, with Alvin Curran, Andrea Centazzo *Real Time* (1977)★★★, *Monoceros* (1978)★★, with Greg Goodman *Abracadabra* (1978)★★★, *At The Finger Palace* (1978)★★★, with others *Four Four Four* (1980)★★★, with Company *Fables* (1980)★★★, with George Lewis *From Saxophone & Trombone* (1980)★★★, *Six Of One* (1980)★★★, with Barry Guy *Incision* (1981)★★★, *Zanzou* (1982)★★★★, with Guy, Lytton *Tracks* (1983)★★★, with Lewis, Guy, Lytton *Hook Drift & Shuffle* (1983)★★★, with Company *Trios* (1983)★★★, with Bailey *Compatibles* (Incus 1985)★★★, with Guy *Tai Kyoku* (1985)★★★, with Steve Lacy *Chirps* (FMP 1985)★★★, *The Snake Decides* (1986)★★★, with others *Supersession* 1985 recording (1988)★★★, with others *The Ericle Of Dolphi* (1989)★★★★, with Cecil Taylor, Tristan Honsinger *The Hearth* (1989)★★★★, with Guy *Duo Improvisations* (1990)★★★, with others *Dithyrambisch* (1990)★★★, *Atlanta* (Impulse! 1990)★★★★, with Walter Prati *Hall Of Mirrors* (1990)★★★, *Hall Of Mirrors* (MMT 1991)★★★, *Process And Reality* (FMP 1991)★★★, *Conic Sections* 1989 recordings (Ah-Um 1993)★★★★, *Corner To Corner* (Ogun 1994)★★★★, *50th Birthday Concert* (Leo 1994)★★★, *Imaginary Values* (Maya 1994)★★★★, with Lol Coxhill, Steve Lacy *Three Blokes* 1992 recordings (FMP 1994)★★★, with Barry Guy, Paul Lytton *Breaths And Heartbeats* (Ratascan 1995)★★★, *Ghost In The Machine Featuring Evan Parker* (Leo 1995)★★★★, *Obliquities* (Maya 1995)★★★★, with Paul Bley, Barre Phillips *Time Will Tell* (ECM 1996)★★★★, *The Redwood Sessions* (CIMP 1996)★★★, *Chicago Solo* (Okkadisk 1997)★★★, *Tempranillo* (New Contemporary 1997)★★★, *Towards The Margins* (ECM 1998)★★★★, *At The Vortex 1996* (Emanem 1998)★★★★, *Most Material* (Matchless 1998)★★★, *Live At Les Instants Chavires* (Leo 1998)★★★★, with Marilyn Crispell *Natives And Aliens* (Leo 1998)★★★★, with Ned Rothenberg *Monkey Puzzle* (Leo 1998)★★★, with John Russell, John Edwards and Mark Sanders *London Air Lift* (FMP 1998)★★★★.

● COMPILATIONS: *Collected Solos* (1989)★★★★.

PARKER, JOHN 'KNOCKY'

b. 8 August 1918, Palmer, Texas, USA, d. 3 September 1986. During the 30s Parker played piano in several Texas bands, some of which were only on the edges of jazz. In the mid-40s he was working on the west coast with leading traditional jazz musicians such as Albert Nicholas. Parker later went into education, teaching at colleges and universities, but still found time to play with Omer Simeon, Tony Parenti and others during the 50s and 60s. In the early 60s he undertook an extensive recording programme of ragtime music, notably including the works of Scott Joplin and James Scott. A few years later he turned his attention to early jazz piano with a set of music by Jelly Roll Morton. In the early 80s he recorded a fine album with Big Joe Turner.

● ALBUMS: *The Complete Piano Works Of Scott Joplin* (1960)★★★, *The Complete Piano Works Of James Scott* (1962)★★, *Golden Treasury Of Ragtime* (1968)★★★★, *The Complete Piano Works Of Jelly Roll Morton* (1970)★★★★, *Big Joe Turner With Knocky Parker And His Houserockers* (1983)★★★★, *From Cakewalk To Ragtime* (Jazzology 1986)★★★, *Texas Swing - And The Blues* (1987)★★★, *Texas Swing - Boogie Woogie* (1987)★★★★, *Texas Swing - The Barrel-House* (1987)★★★, *Knocky Parker And Galvanised Washboard Band* (GHB 1994)★★★.

PARKER, JOHNNY

b. 6 November 1929, Beckenham, Kent, England. Parker is a self-taught pianist with a great talent for solo ragtime and boogie woogie but who can fit easily into a band's rhythm section. In the early 50s he worked with Mick Mulligan and Humphrey Lyttelton playing the catchy boogie woogie on the latter's 'Bad Penny Blues' hit in 1956. He later played with Monty Sunshine and Kenny Ball but also with Alexis Korner's Blues Incorporated to which he made an important contribution as the 60s blues boom got underway. His own bands at this time reflected his love of the music of Sidney Bechet and Eddie Condon. Latterly he has presented his own one-man show, worked regularly with vocalist Beryl Bryden and provided the backing for the vocal group Sweet Substitute.

● ALBUMS: with Alexis Korner *R&B From The Marquee* (Ace Of Clubs 1962)★★★★, with Korner *Alexis Korner's Blues Inc.* (1963)★★★, *Johnny Parker's Boogie Woogie* (1979)★★★.

PARKER, LEO

b. 18 April 1925, Washington, DC, USA, d. 11 February 1962. Starting out on alto saxophone, an instrument on which he recorded with Coleman Hawkins, Parker switched to baritone in 1944 when he joined the bebop-orientated big band led by Billy Eckstine. For the next year or so he was a member of the band's so-called 'unholy four'. Fellow saxophonists in the band included Dexter Gordon, Sonny Stitt and Gene Ammons but it was another Eckstine alumnus, his namesake Charlie Parker, who appears to have exercised most musical influence upon him. After leaving Eckstine, Parker played in New York with Dizzy Gillespie and Fats Navarro before joining Illinois Jacquet's popular band. A record date with Sir Charles Thompson featured Parker on a tune entitled 'Mad Lad' and this became his nickname. Despite several other fine record dates with Gordon, and club sessions with Stitt, Ammons, Teddy Edwards, Wardell Gray and others, at all of which he more than held his own, Parker's career proved short-lived. By 1947 drug addiction was severely affecting his health. He played on into the 50s, but only intermittently, making occasional record dates, on some of which he rallied sufficiently to play superbly. One of the major baritone saxophonists in jazz, he died in 1962.

● ALBUMS: *Leo Parker's All Stars* (1947)★★★, *Leo Parker's Sextette/Quintette* (1948)★★★★, *Leo Parker And His Mad Lads* i (1950)★★★, *Leo Parker And His Mad Lads* ii (1950)★★★, *The Leo Parker Quintet* (1951)★★★★, *The Leo Parker Quartet* (1953)★★★, *Let Me Tell You 'Bout It* (Blue Note 1961)★★★★, *Rollin' With Leo* (Blue Note 1961)★★★.

PARKER, LEON

Raised in White Plains, New York, Parker was influenced by his grandfather, Milford Tucker, a swing-era drummer. Parker played drums in church before joining a local youth jazz band, and was studying classical percussion at the age of 17. He moved to New York City where he became involved with Barry Harris' Jazz Workshop. Regular work at Augie's bar in Manhattan followed, with Parker gradually reducing his drum set, often playing gigs with a single cymbal. Recording and touring dates with Harvie Swartz, Shelia Jordan, Dewey Redman, Kenny Barron raised his profile, before Parker enjoyed a fruitful period as part of the Jacky Terrasson trio. Parker came to the attention of producer Joel Dorn, who produced his debut for the Epicure label. Subsequent sets for Columbia Records have demonstrated Parker's ability to create mesmeric music from his minimal set-up (cymbal, snare and floor tom), creating a rhythmic fusion of diverse styles. Musicians appearing on Parker's albums have included highly regarded contemporaries such as soprano David Sanchez, altoist Steve Wilson, tenor Mark Turner, trumpeter Tom Harrell, trombonist Steve Davis and bassist Ugonna Okegwo.

● ALBUMS: *Above And Below* (Epicure 1994)★★★, *Belief* (Columbia 1996)★★★★, *Awakening* (Columbia 1998)★★★.

PARKER, WILLIAM

b. 10 January 1952, New York City, New York, USA. Parker played cello in junior school and acquired a bass in the last year of high school. He remembers being sent with 99 cents to the store to buy Duke Ellington records for his father. He found a cut-price record by Ornette Coleman and rapidly became interested in the New Thing: John Coltrane, Albert Ayler and Archie Shepp. He attended sessions at Studio We in the early 70s, playing with Sam Rivers and Frank Lowe amongst others, and was involved with a Cecil Taylor big band at Carnegie Hall in 1973. Parker married in 1974 and worked at his day-job for the housing authority for a short time, then quit to play the Five Spot with Don Cherry. He next played with drummer Rashid Baker in Jemeel Moondoc's band and in 1980 also joined Taylor, with whom he has continued to work regularly throughout the 80s and early 90s in a variety of settings, including the pianist's recent Feel Trio. Other long-term associates - in addition to Taylor and Moondoc - have included Peter Kuhn, Billy Bang and Bill Dixon, and Parker is also much in demand in New York's *avant garde* scene, appearing with experimenters such as Wayne Horvitz, Butch Morris and Ellen Christi. In 1989 Parker started a trio with Peter Brötzmann (saxophone) and Milford Graves (drums) and in 1990 recorded with drummer Dennis Charles in a trio led by up-and-coming saxophonist Rob Brown (*Breath Rhyme*). Parker released three discs as leader in 1996, his first since his late 70s debut. *Testimony* was his first solo-bass outing; *In Order To Survive* a group date with Brown, Charles and trombonist Grachan Moncur III; and *Flowers Grow In My Room* a session with his large but never unwieldy Little Huey Creative Music Orchestra. Parker has a warm sound, and whether he is setting up simple vamps or responding to the torrential Taylor, his playing is always strong and creative.

● ALBUMS: *Through Acceptance Of The Mystery Peace* (1979)★★★, with Wayne Horvitz, Butch Morris *Some Order Long Understood* (Black Saint 1982)★★★, *Testimony* (Zero In 1996)★★★★, *In Order To Survive* (Black Saint 1996)★★★, *Flowers Grow In My Room* (Centering 1996)★★★, with the Little Huey Creative Music Orchestra *Sunrise In The Tone World* (AUM Fidelity 1998)★★★★, with Joe Morris *Invisible Weave* (No More 1998)★★★★.

PARLAN, HORACE

b. 19 January 1931, Pittsburgh, Pennsylvania, USA. Parlan played piano from an early age, his first professional work being in R&B bands during the early and mid-50s. In 1957 he joined Charles Mingus in New York, later playing with Lou Donaldson, Booker Ervin, Eddie 'Lockjaw' Davis, Johnny Griffin, Roland Kirk and others. In the early 70s he settled in Denmark, playing with local and visiting musicians including Dexter Gordon, Archie Shepp and Michal Urbaniak. As a result of contracting polio as a child, Parlan suffered limitations in the use of his right hand; to compensate, he developed a powerful left hand and evolved a distinctive style in which echoes of bop and the blues blend comfortably and to great effect. Although he is always an interesting soloist, it is in the interplay with other musicians that he displays his talents to the full: a fine example is the set of two duo albums - one of blues, one of spirituals - that he recorded with Shepp.

● ALBUMS: *Movin' And Groovin'* (Blue Note 1960)★★★, *Headin' South* (Blue Note 1960)★★★, *Us Three* (Blue Note 1960)★★★★, *Speakin' My Piece* (Blue Note 1960)★★★★, *Up And Down* (1961)★★★, *On The Spur Of The Moment* (Blue Note 1961)★★★★, *Happy Frame Of Mind* (Blue Note 1963)★★★, *Back From The Gig* (1963)★★★★, *Arrival* (Steeple Chase 1973)★★, *No Blues* (Steeple Chase 1975)★★★, *Blue Parlan* (Steeple Chase 1975)★★★★, *Frank-ly Speaking* (1977)★★★, with Archie Shepp *Goin' Home* (1977)★★★, *Hi-Fly* (1978)★★★, *Musically Yours* (Steeple Chase 1979)★★★, *The Maestro* (1979)★★★, with Bogey Gaynair *One For Wilton* (Ego 1980)★★★, with Shepp *Trouble In Mind* (1980)★★★, *Pannonica* (Enja 1981)★★★, *Glad I Found You* (Steeple Chase 1984)★★★, with Shepp *Reunion* (1987)★★, *Splashes* (1987)★★★, *Little Esther* (Soul Note 1987)★★★.

PARNELL, JACK

b. 6 August 1923, London, England. One of the best known and most popular of post-World War II British jazzmen, Parnell was at his most prominent during a long stint with Ted Heath's big band. Before then, however, he had already made a mark on the UK jazz scene. While still on military service he became a member of Buddy Featherstonehaugh's Radio Rhythm Club Sextet, playing alongside Vic Lewis and other jazz-minded servicemen. Between 1944 and 1946 Parnell also recorded with Lewis, and the Lewis-Parnell Jazzmen's version of 'Ugly Child' sold extremely well (50,000 78 rpm discs would probably have made it a hit had there been such a thing as a hit parade in those days). The Lewis-Parnell band played in clubs and also made a number of theatrical appearances. Following a minor disagreement over billing, Lewis took over sole leadership of the band while Parnell joined Heath, where he became one of the band's most popular figures. With the band he also sang, displaying an engaging voice and an attractive stage personality. Leaving Heath after seven years, Parnell became musical director of ATV, directing the pit band for the popular *Sunday Night At The London Palladium*, throughout the 60s. Among his later television credits, he was musical director for *The Muppet Show*. In the late 70s, after two decades in television, Parnell returned to the UK jazz scene. He has continued to play in clubs and at festivals, sometimes backing visiting American jazzmen, at other times working with leading British stars. During his early days with the Heath band Parnell had an image of gum-chewing showman drummer, an image that in fact concealed a skilful, swinging and often underrated artist. His later work, with the need for an image no longer necessary, reveals his subtle and propulsive playing. In 1994, Parnell took over as leader of the newly formed London Big Band, 'the largest band in Britain', consisting of the 'cream' of the UK music business.

● ALBUMS: *Jack Parnell Quartet* (Decca 1952)★★★★, *Trip To Mars* (Parlophone 1958)★★★★, *Big Band Show* (1976)★★★★, *Big Band Stereo Spectacular* (1981)★★★, *Plays Music Of The Giants* (1975)★★★, *The Portrait Of Charlie Gilbraith* (1977)★★★, *Braziliana* (1977)★★★, *50 Big Band Favourites* (1984)★★★.

PARRISH, AVERY

b. 24 January 1917, Birmingham, Alabama, USA, d. 10 December 1959. Parrish began playing piano as a child and while attending college became a member of the 'Bama State Collegians band. In 1934 the band, under the leadership of Erskine Hawkins, visited New York and became professional; Parrish stayed on, recording with them his own composition, 'After Hours'. He remained with the band until 1941, continuing to play piano in Los Angeles. In 1942 he was severely injured in a fight and never played again. John Chilton records that his death, in New York, was in 'mysterious circumstances'. Although remembered largely for his famous composition, long a jazz standard, Parrish's own playing was of a very high order and the manner in which his career ended was clearly a tragedy for jazz.

● COMPILATIONS: *The Chronological Erskine Hawkins* (Classics 1940)★★★.

Pärt, Arvo

b. Tallinn, Estonia. A renowned but reclusive *avant garde* composer, Arvo Pärt initially followed his native '12-tone' tradition before expanding his musical vocabulary to encompass jazz and ambient as well as classical music. A good example is his early composition 'Für Alina', which utilized a single piano chord as an experiment in stark minimalism. A former radio engineer and film composer, his work found a champion in Manfred Eicher, founder and director of ECM Records, who has subsequently released a number of Pärt's albums. The first of these, *Tabula Rosa*, drew comparisons to John Cage, not least in its use of the 'prepared' piano. Other records have pursued specific themes. *Passio* (1988) is noteworthy in this respect, being a setting for episodes drawn from the New Testament. As a committed member of the Russian Orthodox Church, Pärt set out his intention with such music - to imitate the church's Easter services where a long, melancholic atmosphere is produced before the eventual salvation/epiphany. Cryptic and enchanting, despite the monotony of many of his passages, Pärt's music provided a vital bridge between classical music and what has been termed 'mystic minimalism', typified by the growth of Gregorian chants and medieval structures in the 90s.

● ALBUMS: *Tabula Rasa* (ECM 1984)★★★★, *Arbos* (ECM 1987)★★★, *Passio* (ECM 1988)★★★★, *Symphonies 1-3, Pro Et Contra* (BIS 1989)★★★, *Miserere* (ECM 1991)★★★, *Trivium* (ECM 1992)★★★, *Collage* (Chandos 1993)★★★, *Te Deum* (ECM 1993)★★, *Arvo Pärt* (EMI 1994)★★★, *Fratres* (EMI 1995)★★★, *Litany* (ECM 1996)★★★, *Kanon Pokajanen* (ECM 1998)★★★.

Pasadena Roof Orchestra

Britain's most commercially successful traditional jazz-based act of the 70s was formed in the mid-60s by baker John Arthey (bass) as a larger, slicker recreation of a 20s ragtime band than that of the Temperance Seven. Among its mainstays were John Parry (vocals), arranger Keith Nichols (piano), Mac White (clarinet) and trumpeters Clive Baker, Enrico Tomasino and Mike Henry. Transient members included Viv Stanshall (euphonium). Despite much interest from London's music press - especially the *Melody Maker* - the Orchestra had no major record hits, but their albums did brisk business in foyers on the European college circuit and at the more prestigious jazz festivals.

● ALBUMS: *The Show Must Go On* (1977)★★★, *A Talking Picture* (Columbia 1978)★★★, *Night Out* (Columbia 1979)★★★, *Puttin' On The Ritz* (Spot 1983)★★★★, *Fifteen Years On* (Pasadena Roof Orchestra 1985)★★★, *Good News* (Transatlantic 1987)★★★, *On Tour* (Transatlantic 1987)★★★, *Happy Feet* (Pasadena Roof Orchestra 1988)★★★★.

● COMPILATIONS: *Anthology* (Transatlantic 1978)★★★, *Everythin' Stops For Tea* (Cambra 1984)★★★, *C'mon Along And Listen To* (Conifer 1986)★★★, *Isn't It Romantic* (Transatlantic 1987)★★★, *Collection* (Castle 1987)★★★, *Top Hat, White Tie And Tails* (Ditto 1988)★★★, *16 Greatest Hits* (Fun 1988)★★★, *Sentimental Journey* (1993)★★★.

Pasquall, Don

b. Jerome Don Pasquall, 20 September 1902, Fulton, Kentucky, USA, d. 18 October 1971. Pasquall was raised in St. Louis, Missouri, where he learned to play mellophone and worked in brass bands. During military service in World War I, he switched to playing clarinet and after his return to St. Louis he played in several bands including those led by Charlie Creath and Fate Marable. In 1921 he moved to Chicago where he studied music and also played regularly with noted local bandleaders including Doc Cook. With Cook's band he played tenor saxophone; late in the decade he moved to New York where he played alto saxophone with Fletcher Henderson's band for a short spell before returning to Chicago. In the early 30s he played in many bands, among them those led by Freddie Keppard and Jabbo Smith. He also visited Europe in 1934, then returned briefly to Henderson before settling in to the Noble Sissle orchestra for several years. From the mid-40s he freelanced in New York. Pasquall's extensive studies in Chicago made him a reliable and sought-after musician. In addition to his playing of several reed instruments, he also arranged for many of the bands with which he played.

● COMPILATIONS: *The Chronological Fletcher Henderson 1927* (Classics 1927)★★★.

Pass, Joe

b. Joseph Anthony Passalaqua, 13 January 1929, New Brunswick, New Jersey, USA, d. 23 May 1994, Los Angeles, California, USA. In his mid- and late teens guitarist Pass worked with a number of name bands, including those led by Tony Pastor and Charlie Barnet. From the early 50s until the beginning of the following decade, Pass dwelt in self-imposed obscurity playing when and where he could in order to sustain a drug habit for which he also served a prison sentence. The 60s saw his rehabilitation and revealed an astonishing talent. Following his internment at the Synanon Foundation in Santa Monica, a self-help regime that allowed him to break his habit, Pass was returned to the outside world as a reformed character, and a media-worthy example of the powers of Synanon healing (since largely discredited).

The new profile brought engagements with artists as diverse as Julie London and Richard 'Groove' Holmes. Through the patronage of Norman Granz of Pablo he moved on to work with jazz's biggest names, including duos with leading artists such as Oscar Peterson (winning a Grammy for his album with the latter and bassist Niels-Henning Ørsted Pedersen), Jimmy Rowles and Zoot Sims, or in small groups including Count Basie's re-formed Kansas City Six. He proved especially gifted as accompanist to singers, particularly Ella Fitzgerald. It was as a solo performer, however, that he most ably displayed his mastery of guitar, but despite the virtuoso standard of his playing his work never degenerated into a mere display of technical accomplishment. His phenomenal technique, coupled as it was with an intense jazz feel, made him welcome in almost any setting.

● ALBUMS: with Arnold Ross *Sounds Of Synanon* (Pacific Jazz 1962)★★★, *The Complete 'Catch Me' Sessions* (Pacific Jazz 1963)★★★, *Joe Pass-John Pisano Quartet* (1963)★★★, *Joy Spring* (1964)★★★, *For Django* (Pacific Jazz 1964)★★★★, *A Sign Of The Times* (World Pacific 1966)★★★, *The Stones Jazz* (World Pacific 1967)★★★, *Simplicity* (World Pacific 1967)★★★, *The Living Legends* one side only (1969)★★, *Intercontinental* (1970)★★★, *Virtuoso* (Pablo 1973)★★★★, with Herb Ellis *Jazz/Concord* (Concord Jazz 1973)★★★★, with Ellis *Seven Come Eleven* (Concord Jazz 1973)★★★★, with Ella Fitzgerald *Take Love Easy* (Pablo 1974)★★★, with Ellis *Two For The Road* (Pablo 1974)★★★, *Portraits Of Duke Ellington* (Pablo 1974)★★★, *Joe Pass At The Montreux Jazz Festival* (1975)★★★, with Fitzgerald *Fitzgerald And Pass . . . Again* (Pablo 1976)★★★, with Oscar Peterson *Porgy And Bess* (1976)★★★★, *Virtuoso Vol. 2* (Pablo 1976)★★★★, *Guitar Player* (1976)★★★, *Quadrant* (1977)★★★, *Virtuoso Vol. 3* (Pablo 1977)★★★, *Live At Montreux '77* (Pablo 1977)★★★, *Guitar Interludes* (1977), *Tudo Bem!* (Pablo 1978)★★★, *Chops* (Pablo 1978)★★★★, *I Remember Charlie Parker* (Pablo 1979)★★, *Northsea Nights* (1979)★★★, with Fitzgerald *Digital III At Montreux* (Pablo 1980)★★★, *Quadrant Toasts Duke Ellington - All Too Soon* (1980)★★★, with Jimmy Rowles *Checkmate* (1981)★★★, *Ira, George And Joe/Joe Pass Loves Gershwin* (1981)★★★, with Zoot Sims *Blues For Two* (Pablo 1982)★★★★, *Eximious* (1982)★★★, with Fitzgerald *Speak Love* (Pablo 1983)★★★, *Live At Long Beach City College* (1984)★★, *We'll Be Together Again* (1985)★★★, *Whitestone* (Pablo 1985)★★★, *University Of Akron Concert* (Pablo 1985)★★, *Blues For Fred* (Pablo 1988)★★★, *One For My Baby* (Pablo 1988)★★★★, *Summer Nights* (Pablo 1990)★★★, *Appassionato* (Pablo 1990)★★★, *Virtuoso Live!* (Pablo 1991)★★★, *Live At Yoshi's* (Pablo 1992)★★★, *My Song* (Telarc 1993)★★★, with Roy Clark *Play Hank Williams* 1994 recording (Ranwood 1996)★★, *Joe Pass In Hamburg* 1992 recording (ACT 1997)★★★★.

PASTORIUS, JACO

b. John Francis Pastorius, 1 December 1951, Norristown, Pennsylvania, USA, d. 12 September 1987, Fort Lauderdale, Florida, USA. Encouraged by his father, a drummer and vocalist, to pursue a career in music, Pastorius learned to play bass, drums, guitar, piano and saxophone while in his teens. As a result of a football injury to his arm, his ambitions were mainly orientated towards the drums, but he soon found work playing bass for visiting pop and soul acts. After backing the Temptations and the Supremes, he developed a cult following, and his reputation spread. In 1975, Bobby Colomby, drummer with Blood, Sweat And Tears, was impressed enough to arrange the recording of Pastorius's first album, and a year later Pat Metheny asked him to play bass on his own first album for ECM Records, additionally he worked with Joni Mitchell. However, the most important stage in Pastorius's career came in 1976: joining Weather Report to record the highly influential *Heavy Weather*, his astonishing technique on the fretless bass and his flamboyant behaviour on stage consolidated the band's popularity and boosted his own image to star status. He established his own band, Word Of Mouth, in 1980, and they enjoyed three years of successful tours, while Pastorius himself recorded intermittently with some of the top musicians in jazz. However, Pastorius suffered from alcoholism and manic depression. In 1987, after increasing bouts of inactivity, he suffered fatal injuries in a brawl outside the Midnight Club in his home town of Fort Lauderdale. Pastorius was one of the most influential bass players since Charles Mingus, and extended the possibilities of the electric bass as a melodic instrument in a way that has affected many bassists since.

● ALBUMS: *Jaco* (DIW 1974)★★★★, *Jaco Pastorius* (Epic 1975)★★★★, with Weather Report *Heavy Weather* (Columbia 1976)★★★★, *Word Of Mouth* (Warners 1980)★★, *Invitation* (1982)★★, *Punk Jazz* (Big World 1986)★★, *PDB* (DIW 1987)★★, *Honestly* (Jazzpoint 1986)★★, *Heavy N' Jazz* (Jazzpoint 1987)★★, *Jazz Street* (Timeless 1987)★★★, *Live In Italy* 1986 recording (Jazzpoint 1991)★★★, *Holiday For Pans* 1980-82 recording (Sound Hills 1993)★★★★, *The Birthday Concert* (Warners 1995)★★★.

● FURTHER READING: *Jaco: The Extraordinary And Tragic Life Of Jaco Pastorius*, Bill Milkowski.

PATITUCCI, JOHN

b. 22 December 1959, Brooklyn, New York, USA. Patitucci is a technically gifted bassist best known for his work on both the electric and acoustic instruments for fusion keyboard legend Chick Corea. After playing some pop and rock in his brother's band in New York, he moved with his family to America's west coast, the home of a fearsome tradition for jazz/rock fusion virtuosi, in 1972, and was introduced to the jazz tradition by bass teacher Chris Poehler. Studying the acoustic work of Ron Carter, Dave Holland, Charlie Haden and Eddie Gomez, and the electric bass techniques of Larry Graham, Marcus Miller, Stanley Clarke and, particularly, bass hero Jaco Pastorius, he developed quickly, working with pianist Gap Mangione (brother of Chuck Mangione), and veteran British-born vibesman Victor Feldman. It was with Feldman that Chick Corea came across him, and asked him to join the newly formed Elektric Band. Patitucci stayed with the Elektric Band throughout its life, recording five albums, and played an important part in the Akoustic Band trio. Since the late 80s he has also been working as a leader on GRP Records and Stretch – Corea's own subsidiary of the GRP label. An incredible technician on both acoustic and six-string electric basses, Patitucci has unfortunately allowed his output to be dominated by material that works primarily as a means to demonstrate his technique. One of his best records is *Sketchbook*, featuring drummer Peter Erskine, tenor saxophonist Michael Brecker and guitarist John Scofield.

● ALBUMS: *John Patitucci* (GRP 1988)★★★, *On The Corner* (GRP 1989)★★★, *Sketchbook* (GRP 1990)★★★★, *Heart Of The Bass* (Stretch 1991)★★★, *Another World* (GRP 1993)★★★, *Mistura Fina* (GRP 1994)★★★, *One More Angel* (Concord Jazz 1997)★★★, *Now* (Concord Jazz 1998)★★★★.

PATRICK, PAT

b. November 1929, the Midwest, USA. Like most of Sun Ra's long-term associates, Pat Patrick's origins are shrouded in mystery. He studied piano and drums as a child and received trumpet lessons from his father and from Clark Terry. At DuSable High School in Chicago he met tenor saxophonists John Gilmore and Clifford Jordan and bassist Richard Davis. Patrick began playing alto and baritone saxophones and clarinet. Having worked with some of the pre-eminent shakers of American music - Muddy Waters, Lillian Armstrong, Nat 'King' Cole and Cab Calloway - he joined Sun Ra in 1953. His strong technique and expansive imagination were perfect for Sun Ra's mind-bending compositions and he stayed with him until the mid-80s. In 1961 he contributed baritone to John Coltrane's *Africa/Brass* album. In the early 70s he played in Thelonious Monk's group, joined the Jazz Composers Orchestra, recording with them on projects led by Grachan Moncur III (*Echoes Of A Prayer*) and Clifford Thornton (*The Gardens Of Harlem*), and also worked for Quincy Jones and Duke Ellington. In 1978 he recorded on Jordan's *Inward Fire*, which also featured Davis and fellow Chicagoan Muhal Richard Abrams. In 1990 Patrick was reported to be living in Chicago and concentrating on playing tenor saxophone.

PATTERSON, ANN

b. *c.*1950, Texas, USA. As a child Patterson learned to play piano, then switched to oboe, before moving to the saxophone family. Directed in part by parental pressure and partly because of the prejudice against women in music, she studied to be a teacher of music. After attending North Texas University and the University of Illinois, she began teaching. She married around this time and moved with her husband to California. She continued to teach but was unhappy both with this role and in her marriage. After her divorce she began to look more towards playing, not teaching, and while on the west coast worked in various bands including one led by Don Ellis. She established a high reputation as a player who could be called upon for commercial work and to play jazz, preferably with a bebop slant. In time, Patterson started to play with an all-female band despite her awareness that the nature of such bands is sometimes limiting. Impressed by the quality and seriousness of the musicians with whom she was now working, she continued for a while, appearing at the Kansas City Women's Jazz Festival, and on television on the *Johnny Carson Show*. Subsequently, she left the band and formed her own female big band, Maiden Voyage, aiming to develop a commercial 'dance date' band, but one that could also play original and demanding music in order to employ fully and extend the skills and abilities of its members. Influenced on alto saxophone by Charlie Parker and Phil Woods, Patterson is a forward-thinking musician with a keen sense of the nature and roots of jazz but with a realistic attitude towards the prejudices against women. Her personal attributes and the great respect afforded to Maiden Voyage have done much to break down these prejudices, especially amongst male jazz musicians in California.

PATTERSON, OTTILIE

b. Anna-Ottilie Patterson, 31 January 1932, Comber, County Down, Northern Ireland. Patterson is perhaps best known for her long-time association with Chris Barber, her husband, in the 50s and 60s. With Barber she sang jazz and blues but she was also an accomplished folk-singer. Ranging outside popular fields, she has also composed music to accompany poetry. For some years she was obliged through ill-health to abandon her singing career, but later returned to the stage to the delight of her many fans. An engaging singer, with a strong, earthy delivery that lends itself well to the blues and some aspects of the jazz songbook, for her folk-singing she was always able to adjust to a more pensive approach. A bright and bubbling personality, she is at her best in live performances and has been captured in splendid form on a number of live albums by the Barber band.

● ALBUMS: with Chris Barber *Chris Barber At The London Palladium* (Columbia 1961)★★★★.

● COMPILATIONS: with Barber *40 Years Jubilee Volumes 1* and *2* (Timeless 1990)★★★★.

PATTON, 'BIG' JOHN

b. 12 July 1935, Kansas City, Missouri, USA. Unusually for a Hammond organ supremo, Patton does not come from Philadelphia. His mother played piano in church, and Patton took it up in 1948. He played in the Lloyd Price band from 1954-59, quitting just as Price topped his 1952 hit 'Lawdy Miss Clawdy' with a string of three million-sellers. Patton moved to New York and switched to organ. He was signed to Blue Note Records on the recommendation of Lou Donaldson, debuting with *Along Came John* in 1963, which featured Grant Green on guitar. In the late 60s he worked with tenor saxophonist Clifford Jordon and guitarist James 'Blood' Ulmer, as well as sitting in with Sun Ra's musicians. In the 70s he moved to East Orange, New Jersey. John Zorn's use of him on a track of *The Big Gundown* in 1985 rekindled interest in his career, and in the 90s when the Hammond B3 was experiencing another comeback, Patton's work was rightly compared to the leaders of the genre, Jimmy Smith and Jimmy McGriff.

● ALBUMS: *Along Came John* (Blue Note 1963)★★★★, *The Way I Feel* (1964)★★★, *Blue John* (Blue Note 1964)★★★★, *Oh Baby!* (Blue Note 1964)★★★★, *Got A Good Thing Goin'* (Blue Note 1965)★★★, *Let 'Em Roll* (Blue Note 1966)★★★★, *That Certain Feeling* (Blue Note 1968)★★★, *Understanding* (Blue Note 1968)★★★, *Accent On The Blues* (Blue Note 1969)★★★, *Soul Connection* (Nilva 1984)★★★, *Blue Planet Man* (Paddlewheel 1993)★★★, *Memphis To New York Spirit* 1969/70 recordings (Blue Note 1996)★★★.

● COMPILATIONS: *The Organization!: The Best Of Big John Patton* (Blue Note 1994)★★★★.

PAVAGEAU, ALCIDE 'SLOW DRAG'

b. 7 March 1888, New Orleans, Louisiana, USA, d. 19 January 1969. During his early years Pavageau became known as a competent guitarist and an excellent dancer and he was almost 40 years old before he took up the bass. On this instrument he played with a number of leading New Orleans bands of the day, including Buddy Petit's. His fame did not spread, however, until 1943, when he joined George Lewis. He toured and recorded with Lewis throughout the 40s and also worked with Bunk Johnson. His association with Lewis continued through the 50s and on into the early 60s. Despite his late start, Pavageau became one of the best-known New Orleans-style bass players and if much of that fame rested on his long-term relationship with Lewis he was certainly an above-average player. Late in life he became a popular figure, leading street parades in his home-town. For all that fame, it was on one of the city's streets that he was attacked and robbed, dying soon afterwards on 19 January 1969.

● ALBUMS: with George Lewis *Jazz At Vespers* (1954)★★★.

● COMPILATIONS: *American Music By George Lewis* (1944-45 recordings)★★★.

PAYNE, CECIL

b. 14 December 1922, New York City, New York, USA. After first learning guitar, alto saxophone and clarinet, Payne took up the baritone saxophone. In 1946, a year in which he played and recorded with J.J. Johnson and Roy Eldridge, he joined Dizzy Gillespie's big band for a three-year stint. Leaving Gillespie in 1949 he joined Tadd Dameron's band, following this with appearances with James Moody and Illinois Jacquet. In the mid-50s he played with Randy Weston, John Coltrane and Duke Jordan. During the 60s he was with Machito, Lionel Hampton, Woody Herman, Count Basie and Gillespie again. In the 70s he worked again for Basie and also formed a double-act with his vocalist sister, Cavril. In the 80s he played in a trio with Bill Hardman and led by Richard Wyand. An accomplished player with a special affinity for bebop, Payne's technical command is on a par with that of many better-known players, whose greater charisma has kept them more in the public eye.

● ALBUMS: with Randy Weston *Jazz A La Bohemia* reissued as *Greenwich Village Jazz* (Riverside 1957)★★★★, *Bird's Night* (1957)★★★, *Patterns Of Jazz* (Savoy 1957)★★★, *Cool Blues* (1961)★★★★, *The Connection* (Jazz Reactivation 1962)★★★, *Brookfield Andante* (Spotlite 1966)★★★, *The Cecil Payne Quintet* (1970)★★★, *Brooklyn Brothers* (1973)★★★, *Bird Gets The Worm* (Muse 1976)★★★, *Bright Moments* (Spotlite 1979)★★, *Casbah* (Stash 1985)★★, *Zodiac* (Strata East 1993)★★★, *Cerupa* (Delmark 1995)★★★, with Eric Alexander *Two Of A Kind* (Criss Cross 1997)★★.

PAYNE, JACK

b. 22 August,1899, Leamington Spa, England, d. 4 December 1969, London, England. A leading bandleader in the UK during the 20s and 30s, Payne learnt to play the piano as a child, then joined the Royal Flying Corps. in 1917 and qualified as a pilot. He formed a small band for the officers' mess and decided on music as a career on demobilisation. After six years of insignificant dates in the Midlands he became leader of a band at London's Hotel Cecil where he stayed for four years, broadcasting regularly from the hotel, recording for Regal and Zonophone before they amalgamated, and playing his first stage show at the Holborn Empire. In 1928 he took over the BBC Dance Orchestra and his daily broadcasts at 5.15 pm were so popular that when he left the BBC four years later he was a great success on stage, being a natural showman second only to the great Jack Hylton. Two films were built around the band, *Say It With Music* (1932) scored by Ray Noble, and *Sunshine Ahead* (1933). Although a great show band, Payne's was never regarded as the musical equal of those led by Noble, Hylton, Ambrose, Lew Stone and Carroll Gibbons, for example, *vide* the paucity of reissues from the era. He went back to radio during the early war years, but by then his top-heavy orchestrations did not compare with the new modern styles of Geraldo and Ted Heath. During the 30s he had been recording variously for Columbia, Imperial, Rex and Decca, and recorded a few wartime recordings for HMV. After the war, Payne disbanded to become a theatrical agent and impresario and then a BBC disc jockey. He left the music business and endured many financial setbacks and bouts of ill-health, before his death in 1969.

● COMPILATIONS: *Radio Nights 1928-31* (1983)★★★, *The Golden Age Of Jack Payne* (1985)★★★★, *Rhythmitis* (1986)★★★, *I'll String Along With You* (1988)★★★, *The Imperial Days* (1988)★★★.

● FURTHER READING: *Signature Tune*, Jack Payne. *This Is Jack Payne*, Jack Payne.

PAYNE, SONNY

b. Percival Payne, 4 May 1926, New York City, New York, USA, d. 29 January 1979. Payne began studying drums at an early age, encouraged by the fact that his father, Chris Columbus, was a jazz drummer. Payne's first jobs included spells with Oran 'Hot Lips' Page, Earl Bostic and Tiny Grimes. In 1950 he joined the Erskine Hawkins band, where he spent three years, then led his own band for a couple of years before joining Count Basie. He was with Basie for over 10 years, leaving to form his own small group and working as staff drummer for Frank Sinatra. In 1966 he began another long engagement with a big band, this time led by Harry James. In 1973 he was back with Basie, then played with, among others, Illinois Jacquet during the mid-70s. An aggressive, showman-drummer, Payne was an indifferent timekeeper but brought a sense of sustained excitement to any band in which he played. Even the Basie band, accustomed to such immaculate timekeepers as Jo Jones and Gus Johnson, was given a lift by Payne when he was at his best and, even when he was at his worst, audiences loved him.

● ALBUMS: all with Count Basie *The Atomic Mr Basie* (1957)★★★★★, *Basie - Chairman Of The Board* (1959)★★★, *On My Way And Shoutin' Again* (1962)★★★★.

PAYTON, NICHOLAS

b. 26 September 1973, New Orleans, Louisiana, USA. Born into a musical family, Payton took up the trumpet at the age of four. Encouraged by his pianist-singer mother and his bass-playing father, he swiftly reached a level of proficiency that enabled him, at the age of nine, to play alongside his father in the Young Tuxedo Brass Band. At 12 he was a member of the All Star Jazz Band, playing with this group both locally and at European festivals. Encouraged by Wynton Marsalis he played semi-professionally throughout his school years, then enrolled at the New Orleans Centre for Creative Arts where he studied the trumpet, music theory and also undertook classical training. He next attended the University of New Orleans where he studied with Ellis Marsalis. During the early 90s Payton played throughout the USA and also in Europe with many leading jazz musicians. These artists included Clark Terry, on a *S.S.* Norway Jazz Cruise in 1990, and Marcus Roberts in 1992. The following year he toured with Jazz Futures II, the year after that with Elvin Jones, and he joined the Rising Star circuit tour of Europe in 1996. He also recorded with Roberts and Jones and with Jesse Davis, Teresa Brewer, the Joe Henderson big band, Manhattan Projects, the New Orleans Collective, Courtney Pine, Joshua Redman, the Kansas City Band, in a trio with Christian McBride and Mark Whitfield, and with fellow trumpeters Roy Hargrove and Marsalis. He appeared on the soundtrack album for the 1996 movie *Kansas City*. Memorably, he appeared at club engagements with the veteran trumpeter Doc Cheatham, the pair recording shortly before Cheatham's death in 1997. Payton's technical mastery is remarkable and he plays with a clear, ringing sound that brings added depths to the bop styling in which he appears most comfortable. Clearly, his is a talent that is developing confidently as he matures.

● ALBUMS: *From This Moment* (Verve 1995)★★★, *Gumbo Nouveau* (Verve 1996)★★★, with Christian McBride, Mark Whitfield *Fingerpainting: The Music Of Herbie Hancock* (Verve 1997)★★★★, with Doc Cheatham *Doc Cheatham And Nicholas Payton* (Verve 1997)★★★★, *Payton's Place* (Verve 1998)★★★★.

PAZ

This UK Latin-jazz band was formed in 1972 by vibraphone player Dick Crouch. They have been very popular on the club circuit and recorded a series of exciting albums, the first of which was issued on an independent label and sold more than 2,000 copies in the first week. This was remarkable for a unit of such specialist interest. Musicians who have played with the band include Lol Coxhill and Brian Smith (saxophones), Ray Warleigh (saxophone, flute), Geoff Castle (piano, synthesizer), Phil Lee and Jim Mullen (guitar), Simon Morton and Chris Fletcher (percussion), Ron Matthewson (bass). The lively arrangements used by the band have been provided by Lee, Castle and Crouch, who describe the music as 'today's form of bop'.

● ALBUMS: *Kandeen Love Song* (1977)★★★★, *Paz Are Back* (1980)★★★, *Look Inside* (1983)★★★, *Always There* (1986)★★★, *The Message* (1989)★★.

PEACOCK, ANNETTE

b. New York, USA. A highly individual and challenging songwriter with a distinctive voice, Peacock was in the centre of the Milbrook, New York psychedelic scene in the 60s, having been 'discovered' by Timothy Leary. Her mother was a classical musician, and she was brought up on chamber music. She discovered jazz for herself at an early age but came into contact with the *avant garde* after she eloped to New York City with Gary Peacock, who was then the bass-player with Albert Ayler. Gary then joined the trio of Paul Bley, who began to use her compositions as well as those of Carla Bley. Paul Bley's 1967 *Ballads* used Annette Peacock's tunes exclusively. Her compositions include such beautiful modern classics as 'Open, To Love' and 'Nothing Ever Was, Anyway'. Touring as the Annette And Paul Bley Synthesizer Show at the start of the 70s, they used what was then state-of-the-art hardware: machines the size of a Welsh Dresser, with wiring like a telephone exchange, which took 10 minutes to 'tune' and programme between numbers. Moogs were then intended only for studio use. Certainly, on the road, the results were primitive and rough by today's standards, but this was real pioneering work. Annette used the technology in her own solo, somewhat more rock-inclined, work to process her voice or, often, used her voice to generate electronic sounds through the synthesizer, as on *I'm The One*, an album that led David Bowie to ask her to record and tour with him (she told him to learn the synthesizer himself). So pioneering was her work in this field that recently an electronics expert tried to tell her that the processes she was using were impossible given the technology of the time. Her songs are raw and personal, with an unblinking frankness about emotions and human relationships, and as well as keyboards she plays vibes and electric bass. She set up her own label, Ironic, in 1978. She has worked with Bill Bruford over a number of years and has also played with controversial composer Karlheinz Stockhausen.

● ALBUMS: as the Annette And Paul Bley Synthesizer Show *Dual Unity* (1970)★★, with the Synthesizer Show *Improvisie* (1970)★★★, *Revenge* (1970)★★★, *I'm The One* (1972)★★★★, *X-Dreams* (1978)★★★, with Bill Bruford *Feels Good To Me* (1978)★★★, *Perfect Release* (1979)★★★, *Sky Skating* (1982)★★, *Been In The Streets Too Long* 1975 recording (1983)★★, *I Have No Feelings* (1986)★★★, *Abstract Contact* (1988)★★★.

PEACOCK, GARY

b. 12 May 1935, Barley, Idaho, USA. Peacock went to Germany in the late 50s playing the piano in a US Army band. During this period he took up the bass and when he left the army he stayed in Germany playing with local musicians including Albert Mangelsdorff and Attila Zoller and visiting Americans such as saxophonists Bud Shank and Bob Cooper. In 1958 he moved to California where he played with a wide range of musicians including Shorty Rogers, Paul Horn and Paul Bley.

He continued to work with Bley when he moved to New York in 1962 and became involved in the burgeoning *avant garde* scene. He played with Bill Evans, Rahsaan Roland Kirk, George Russell, Roswell Rudd, Steve Lacy and Albert Ayler with whom he worked in Europe (1964). He is technically an excellent musician with a very full tone able to create appropriate lines in many contexts. In the mid-60s he studied Eastern philosophy and medicine. He later had a brief stint with Miles Davis and played again with Paul Bley before he went to study in Japan, returning to Washington University in 1972 to study biology. In the mid-70s he once again worked with Bley and also in a trio with pianist Keith Jarrett and drummer Jack DeJohnette. In the 80s he taught at Cornish Institute of the Allied Arts in Seattle, Washington. His playing continues to delight, he is one of the most evocative bassists of the modern contemporary era.

● ALBUMS: with Bill Evans *Trio '64* (1963)★★★★, with Albert Ayler *New York Eye And Ear Control* (1964)★★★, with Paul Bley *Ballads* (1967)★★★★, *Tales Of Another* (ECM 1977)★★★, *December Poems* (ECM 1979)★★★, *Shift In The Wind* (ECM 1980)★★★★, *Voice From The Past* (ECM 1981)★★★, with Keith Jarrett *Standards* i (ECM 1983)★★★★, with Jarrett *Changes* (ECM 1984)★★★, with Jarrett *Standards* ii (ECM 1985)★★★★, *Guamba* (ECM 1987)★★★, *Partners* (Owl 1990), with Barry Altschul, Paul Bley *Virtuosi* (Al 1992)★★★, with Bley, Franz Koglmann *Annette* (1993)★★★, with Jarrett, Paul Motian *At The Deer Head Inn* (ECM 1994)★★★, *Oracle* (ECM 1995)★★★★, with Marilyn Crispell, Motian *Nothing Ever Was, Anyway: Music Of Annette Peacock* (ECM 1997)★★★★, with Ralph Towner *A Closer View* (ECM 1998)★★★, with Jack DeJohnette, Keith Jarrett *Tokyo '96* (ECM 1998)★★★, with Paul Bley *Mindset* (Soul Note 1998)★★★★, with Motian, Martial Solal *Just Friends* (Dreyfus 1998)★★★★.

PEARCE, DICK

b. 19 April 1951, London, England. A fine, clear-toned, lyrical trumpeter and flugelhorn-player, Pearce has shown his consistency and imagination over 10 years with Ronnie Scott's band, playing regularly at Scott's club and on the road. He took trumpet lessons at the age of 13, but taught himself theory. From 1968-71 he was in the army, where he played in the band, and on discharge he joined Graham Collier, with whom he worked from 1971-72. As well as Scott's quintet he has played with Mike Westbrook, Keith Tippett, Dudu Pukwana, Chris Biscoe, Brian Abrahams, and Gil Evans' UK Band. In September 1990 he was injured in a motorcycle accident, and was out of action for some months, but by the end of 1991 he was back leading his own quartet.

● ALBUMS: with Graham Collier *Portraits* (1972)★★★, with Mike Westbrook *The Cortege* (1982)★★★★.

PEARSON, DUKE

b. Columbus C. Pearson, 17 August 1932, Atlanta, Georgia, USA, d. 4 August 1980. After studying piano and trumpet, Pearson opted for the former and played professionally in various parts of the USA before settling in New York at the end of the 50s. Working as both performer and composer, he associated with several leading musicians, including Donald Byrd, Art Farmer, Benny Golson and Pepper Adams. In 1963 he succeeded Ike Quebec as A&R director of Blue Note Records, a post he held until 1971. During the late 60s Pearson formed a strikingly good big band from New York-based session musicians and jazzmen. The band, designed to perform his own music, made some excellent albums, notably *Now Hear This*. In the 70s Pearson divided his time between performing, accompanying singers such as Carmen McRae and Nancy Wilson, directing his big band and fighting against the onset of multiple sclerosis.

● ALBUMS: *Profile* (1959)★★★, *Dedication* (1961)★★, *Wahoo* (1964)★★, *Sweet Honey Bee* (Blue Note 1966)★★★★, *The Right Touch* (Blue Note 1967)★★★★, *Introducing Duke Pearson's Big Band* (1967)★★★, *The Phantom* (1968)★★★, *Now Hear This* (1968)★★★, *How Insensitive* (Blue Note 1969)★★★, *Merry Ole Soul* (1969)★★, *It Could Only Happen To You* (1970)★★★, *Bags Groove* 1961 recording (Black Lion 1991)★★★.

PEART, NEIL

b. 12 September 1952, Hamilton, Ontario, Canada. Beginning with piano lessons at the age of seven, Peart always had a keen interest in popular music. Inspired by the film *The Gene Krupa Story* and by banging out rhythms on pots and pans, he began drum lessons when he was 13. After participating in many church and high-school shows, and eventually playing in local Toronto bands, in an effort to pursue a career as a professional musician, he moved to London, England, at the age of 18. Disillusioned with a dead-end job working in souvenir shops on Carnaby Street, Peart returned home to Canada to work for his father in his farm equipment business. In 1974, in a chance meeting with the manager of the Canadian rock band Rush, Peart learned that the band was looking for a new drummer and was asked to audition. Upon meeting the band, it seemed that his drumming style meshed perfectly with the group members' own musical complexities and prog rock ambitions. A fan of writers such as Ayn Rand, C.S. Lewis, J.R.R. Tolkien and F. Scott Fitzgerald, Peart also became the chief lyricist of the group and began a journey that would make Rush Canada's most famous rock trio for more than 20 years. Inspired by other complex drummers such as Bill Bruford, Carl Palmer and Keith Moon, Peart was acclaimed for his intricate time-keeping patterns, double bass drum work and classically inspired use of percussion. Equally, Peart's lyric writing, which used science fiction themes and epic adventures, helped to distinguish Rush as one of the most literate rock groups.

The band's popularity, which had formerly been considered a cult following, reached a peak in the early 80s, and around this time, Peart began using electronic drums and sounds in addition to his acoustic set, to further enhance his artistic palette. In 1994 Peart took a break from his duties with Rush to produce a tribute to the late drummer Buddy Rich. The series, *Burning For*

Buddy Volumes 1 and *2*, contained performances by many of the world's most respected drummers, such as Steve Gadd, Joe Morello, Steve Smith and Dave Weckl, as well as Peart himself, playing with Rich's big band on some of their classic songs. Before rejoining his band-mates in Rush, Peart took time to re-evaluate his drumming and began studies with the renowned drum teacher Fred Gruber. Gruber's philosophies of fluidity and circularity of motion enabled Peart to develop a more ergonomic way of approaching his instrument. Peart remains at the head of his field of rock drummers, with a unique style that combines elements of big band jazz and classical percussion as well as heavy-hitting rock and roll.

● ALBUMS: *Burning For Buddy Volume 1* (Atlantic 1994)★★★★, *Burning For Buddy Volume 2* (Atlantic 1997)★★★★.

PEAVEY, DORIS

b. Doris Yenney, 1895, Oskaloosa, Iowa, USA, d. 26 December 1973. Peavey learned to played piano as a child and for a while entertained hopes of a career as a concert pianist. However, there was a living to be earned as a popular musician and she began working in hotels and restaurants in the years before World War I. In 1919 she joined a band led by tenor saxophonist Hollis M. Peavey, who had first heard her play a few years earlier, and in 1920 they were married. Soon, the Peaveys heard jazz for the first time and began to incline their music that way. She played piano with her husband and also in silent movie theatres and heard and was influenced by Peck Kelly and Jess Stacy. In 1922, back in Iowa, the Peaveys formed their own jazz band, Hollis Peavey's Jazz Bandits, a member of which was Eddie Condon. Although the band did not record, contemporary accounts rate it highly and Doris Peavey most highly of all its personnel. Condon attested to her playing ability and that she taught him much about music. The band played extensively in the northern states and Canada throughout the 20s, eventually moving to California where the Peaveys settled. The band continued to play as a unit until 1960. Thereafter, Doris Peavey performed in churches and privately. A strong, gifted pianist with a commanding attack, she later played Hammond organ.

PECORA, SANTO

b. 31 March 1902, New Orleans, Louisiana, USA, d. 29 May 1984. Pecora's first important job was with the New Orleans Rhythm Kings, with whom he played trombone from 1924-25. In the late 20s and during the following decade Pecora's early formal studies helped him to obtain work with several theatre orchestras and in such pre-swing era big bands as that led by Ben Pollack. In the mid- to late 30s he was often found in Dixieland bands, playing with Sharkey Bonano and others. He went back to his home-town in the early 40s and thereafter led bands in and around the city, with occasional trips to Chicago, and sometimes joining forces with Bonano. Pecora's musical training gave him a broader range than he customarily chose to use and he was happy to be heard playing in a dixieland style.

● ALBUMS: *Recorded Live In New Orleans* (1956)★★★.

PEDDLERS

Though short of 'teen appeal', this seated, short-haired jazz-styled combo was appreciated by other artists for their stylistic tenacity and exacting technical standards. For much of 1964, the polished jazz-pop concoctions of ex-Tornados Tab Martin (b. 24 December 1944, Liverpool, England; bass), ex-Faron's Flamingos Trevor Morais (b. 16 October 1943, Liverpool, England; drums) and the Dowlands' former backing guitarist Roy Phillips (b. 5 May 1943, Parkstone, Poole, Dorset, England; Hammond organ/vocals) were heard nightly at London's exclusive Scotch of St. James's club - and, the following January, their arrangement of Teddy Randazzo's 'Let The Sunshine In', delivered by Phillips in a blues-tinged snort, slipped fleetingly into the UK Top 50. It took over four years for the three to come up trumps again when an invigorating CBS Records contract launched *Freewheelers* into the album chart. This was the harbinger of a Top 10 strike with the self-penned 'Birth', a stunningly innovative composition. The follow-up, 'Girlie', was a minor success and the Peddlers fared well in the album lists with *Birthday*. The long-term benefits of this commercial Indian summer included the broadening of the group's work spectrum - notably in providing musical interludes for television chat-shows - and the command of larger fees for their stock-in-trade cabaret bookings. When the trio split in the mid-70s, Martin found employment as a session player, Phillips emigrated to Australasia and Morais joined Quantum Jump.

● ALBUMS: *The Fantastic Peddlers* (1966)★★★, *Live At The Pickwick* (Philips 1967)★★★, *Freewheelers* (Columbia 1968)★★★★, *Three in A Cell* (Columbia)★★★, *Birthday* (Columbia 1970)★★★, *Three For All* (Philips 1970)★★★, *Georgia On My Mind* (Philips 1971)★★★, *Suite London* (Philips 1972)★★.

● COMPILATIONS: *The Best Of The Peddlers* (1974)★★★, *Part One* (Sony 1997).

PEIFFER, BERNARD

b. 23 October 1922, Epinal, France, d. 7 September 1976. Following intensive training as a classical pianist, Peiffer began playing jazz in distinguished company. While still a young man he played with Django Reinhardt, Hubert Rostaing and other European jazzmen and also with visiting Americans such as Rex Stewart, Don Byas and Sidney Bechet. By the end of the 40s he had become very well known in his native land, leading small groups and also working alone. Persuaded to visit the USA, he moved there in the mid-50s and thereafter commuted between the USA and Europe. An accomplished technician, Peiffer's solo playing was rich and sometimes florid. He was forward-thinking in his style, despite the swing era resonances of his early associations. He also composed much of his repertoire.

● ALBUMS: *Bernie's Tunes* (EmArcy 1956)★★★, *Modern Jazz For People Who Like Original Music* (Laurie 1960)★★★.

PEMBERTON, BILL

b. William McLane Pemberton, 5 March 1918, New York, USA, d. 13 December 1984. After first playing violin, he switched to bass in his late teens. In the early and mid-40s he played in bands led by Frankie Newton and Herman Chittison, also finding time to play with Mercer Ellington, Billy Kyle and others. In the 50s he worked with Art Tatum and Rex Stewart, the latter association being with the acclaimed Fletcher Henderson reunion band. In the mid- to late 60s he had a long spell with Earl 'Fatha' Hines and then formed the JPJ Quartet with Budd Johnson, Oliver Jackson and Dill Jones. This band was active until the mid-70s but Pemberton also played and sometimes recorded with many other musicians, including Ruby Braff and Vic Dickenson. He continued freelancing during the late 70s, then joined David 'Panama' Francis And The Savoy Sultans. He stayed with this band until shortly before his death, his last formal recording date being with Doc Cheatham. A secure and dynamic player, Pemberton displayed a strong rhythmic approach to his instrument. His rich sound added texture to the rhythm sections of the bands in which he played.

● ALBUMS: with Fletcher Henderson *All Stars The Big Reunion* (Jazztone 1957)★★★, with the JPJ Quartet *Montreux '71* (MJR 1971)★★★, with David 'Panama' Francis *Gettin' In The Groove* (Black And Blue 1979)★★★, with Doc Cheatham *The Fabulous Doc Cheatham* (Parkwood 1983)★★★.

PEPLOWSKI, KEN

b. 23 May 1959, Cleveland, Ohio, USA. Peplowski took up the clarinet as a child and played his first professional engagement at the age of 10. He studied formally and played both classical music and jazz, appearing on radio and television in and around his home-town. In 1978 his quartet played opposite the Tommy Dorsey Orchestra, at the time under the direction of Buddy Morrow, and he was promptly offered a job. Peplowski toured extensively with the band, including a visit to Europe. During this period he met and briefly studied with Sonny Stitt. After two and a half years with the orchestra he decided to settle in New York. He obtained work in many areas of music, playing with a touring company of the show *Annie*, in symphony orchestras, in studio bands for films and records, and with jazz groups that ranged from traditional to the *avant garde*. Among these engagements, the most prestigious was a television date and two albums with Benny Goodman. During the 80s his reputation spread and he appeared at several festivals, making a great impression at the 1990 Nice Jazz Festival.

He has also made records with singers such as Mel Tormé, Peggy Lee and Rosemary Clooney and jazzmen Hank Jones, George Shearing, Dan Barrett, Scott Hamilton and Howard Alden. A highly gifted clarinettist who plays alto and tenor saxophones too, Peplowski is strongly rooted in the mainstream. The quality of his playing is such that he is one of a small number of musicians who are helping to restore the fortunes of the clarinet in jazz as well as the more popular tenor saxophone.

● ALBUMS: *Double Exposure* (Concord Jazz 1987)★★★, *Sonny Side* (Concord Jazz 1989)★★★, *Mr. Gentle And Mr. Cool* (Concord Jazz 1990)★★★, *Illuminations* (Concord Jazz 1990)★★★★, *The Natural Touch* (Concord Jazz 1992)★★★★, with Howard Alden *Concord Duo Series Vol. 3* (Concord Jazz 1993)★★★★, *Steppin' With Peps* (Concord Jazz 1993)★★★, *Live At Ambassador Auditorium* (Concord Jazz 1994)★★★, *It's A Lonesome Old Town* (Concord Jazz 1995)★★★, with Allan Vaché, Antti Sarpilå *Summit Meeting* (Nagel-Heyer 1995)★★★★, *A Good Reed* (Concord Jazz 1997)★★★, *The Other Portrait* (Concord Jazz 1997)★★★★, *Grenadilla* (Concord Jazz 1998)★★★.

PEPPER, ART

b. 1 September 1925, Gardena, Los Angeles, California, USA, d. 15 June 1982, Panorama City, California, USA. Pepper started out on clarinet at the age of nine, switching to alto saxophone four years later. After appearing in school groups, he first played professionally with Gus Arnheim's band. During his mid-teens he developed his jazz style sitting in with otherwise all-black bands along Los Angeles's Central Avenue. After leaving Arnheim he worked with Dexter Gordon in Lee Young's band at the Club Alabam. He then joined Benny Carter, playing alongside artists such as Gerald Wilson, Freddie Webster and J.J. Johnson. In 1943 Pepper joined Stan Kenton but soon afterwards was drafted into the US Army, spending most of his wartime service in England. In 1946 he rejoined Kenton, staying with the band until 1951. That year he also recorded with Shorty Rogers, playing a marvellous version of 'Over The Rainbow', a tune he would regularly play over the years. Later, he appeared on Rogers' *Cool And Crazy* album. Pepper subsequently freelanced around Los Angeles, performing many record dates, some under his own name, and usually playing extremely well. Nevertheless, his career in the 50s and 60s was marred by his drug addiction and interrupted by several prison sentences. At the end of the 60s Pepper began a slow, uphill fight against his addiction, a struggle that was eventually successful and heralded his re-emergence in the mid-70s as a major figure on the international jazz scene. In the last years of his life, he produced a rich crop of recordings, including *Winter Moon*, an album with strings (a long-held ambition of Pepper's), the three-album set *Live At The Village Vanguard* (a fourth volume appeared posthumously) and two records recorded live in London under the name of pianist Milcho Leviev, *Blues For The Fisherman* and *True Blues*. Early in his career Pepper played with a light airy tone, through which burned a rare intensity of emotion that reflected his admiration for Charlie Parker and the lessons he learned playing with Carter. After his rehabilitation and a period playing tenor saxophone, on which instrument he showed both the influence of Lester Young and an awareness of John Coltrane, Pepper developed a strong, bop-rooted alto style that retained much of the richly melodic elements of his earlier playing. Pepper's life story was memorably recounted in his candid autobiography and a subsequent film, *Art Pepper: Notes From A Jazz Survivor*, which offered a potent and harshly unsentimental lesson for any young musician contemplating the use of addictive drugs.

● ALBUMS: *Art Pepper Quartet* 10-inch album (Discovery 1952)★★★, *Art Pepper Quintet* reissued as *Surf Ride* (Discovery/Savoy 1954)★★★★, with Richie Kamuca, Bill Perkins *Just Friends* (Pacific Jazz 1956)★★★, *The Return Of Art Pepper* (Jazz: West 1956)★★★, *The Route* (Pacific Jazz 1956)★★★, with Joe Morello, Red Norvo *Joe Morello Sextet* reissued as *The Art Pepper-Red Norvo Sextet* (Intro/Score 1957)★★★★, with Chet Baker *Playboys* reissued as *Picture Of Health* (Pacific Jazz 1957)★★★, *The Artistry Of Pepper* (Pacific 1957)★★★★, *Modern Art* (Intro 1957)★★★★, *The Art Of Pepper* (Blue Note 1957)★★★★, *Art Pepper Meets The Rhythm Section* (Contemporary 1957)★★★★★, *The Art Pepper Quartet* (Tampa 1958)★★★, *Art Pepper + Eleven: Modern Jazz Classics* (Contemporary 1959)★★★★★, with Sonny Red *Two Altos* reissued as *Art Pepper-Sonny Redd* (Regent/Savoy 1959)★★★, *Gettin' Together!* (Contemporary 1960)★★★★, *Smack Up!* (Contemporary 1961)★★★★, *Intensity* 1960 recording (Contemporary 1963)★★★★, with Shelly Manne *Pepper/Manne* (Charlie Parker 1963)★★★, *The Art Pepper Quartet In San Francisco* (Fresh Sound 1964)★★★, *The Way It Was!* (Contemporary 1966)★★★★, *I'll Remember April: Live At Foothill College* (Storyville 1975)★★★, *Living Legend* (Storyville 1976)★★★★, *The Trip* (Storyville 1977)★★★, *A Night In Tunisia* (Storyville 1977)★★★, *No Limit* (Storyville 1978)★★★★, *Among Friends* (Discovery 1978)★★★, *Live In Japan, Vol. 1* (Storyville 1978)★★★, *Live In Japan, Vol. 2* (Storyville 1978)★★★, *Art Pepper Today* (Galaxy 1979)★★★, *Landscape* (Galaxy 1979)★★★, *Straight Life* (Galaxy 1979)★★★★, *Omega Alpha* 1957 recording (Blue Note 1980)★★★, *So In Love* (Artists House 1980)★★★, *Thursday Night At The Village Vanguard* 1977 recording (Contemporary 1981)★★★★, *Friday Night At The Village Vanguard* 1977 recording (Contemporary 1981)★★★★, *Saturday Night At The Village Vanguard* 1977 recording (Contemporary 1981)★★★★, *More For Less* 1977 recording (Contemporary 1981)★★★★, *Winter Moon* (Galaxy 1981)★★★, *Besame Mucho* 1979 recording (1981)★★★, *One September Afternoon* (Galaxy 1981)★★★, *Road Game* (Galaxy 1982)★★★, *Darn That Dream* (Galaxy 1982)★★★, *Goin' Home* (Galaxy 1982)★★★, *Art Lives* 1981 recording (Galaxy 1983)★★★, *Art Works* 1979 recording (Galaxy 1984)★★★, *Tokyo Debut* 1977 recording (Galaxy 1995)★★★★, with Zoot Sims *Art 'N' Zoot* 1981 recording (Pablo 1995)★★★★.

● COMPILATIONS: *Early Art* 1956/1957 recordings (Blue Note 1976)★★★★, *Discoveries* 1952-1954 recordings (Muse 1985)★★★★, *Rediscoveries* 1952-1954 recordings (Muse 1986)★★★★, *Artistry In Jazz* (JVC 1987)★★★, *The Complete Galaxy Recordings* 16-CD box set (Galaxy 1989)★★★★, *Memorial Collection Vols. 1-4* (Storyville 1990)★★★, *The Best Of Art Pepper* (Blue Note 1993)★★★★, *The Complete Village Vanguard Sessions* 9-CD box set (Contemporary 1995)★★★★, *Laurie's Choice* 1978-1981 recordings (Laserlight)★★★, *The Complete Pacific Jazz Small Group Recordings Of Art Pepper* 3-LP box set (Mosaic)★★★★, *The Return Of Art Pepper: The Complete Art Pepper Aladdin Recordings* 1956/1957 recordings (Blue Note)★★★, *The Art Of The Ballad* (Prestige 1998)★★★★.

● FURTHER READING: *Straight Life: The Story Of Art Pepper*, Art and Laurie Pepper.

● FILMS: *Art Pepper: Notes From A Jazz Survivor* (1982).

PEREZ, MANUEL

b. 28 December 1871, New Orleans, Louisiana, USA, d. 1946. One of the Crescent City's legendary figures, Perez was a respected cornet player, bandleader and teacher. He rarely played anywhere else, working in dancehalls and leading the Onward Brass Band in street parades. He made few trips outside his home-town, playing in Chicago in 1915 and again in 1928. Fellow musicians thought highly of him, suggesting that his technique and command were at least on a par with his better-known contemporaries. By the 40s he was inactive through ill-health and died in 1946.

PERFECT JAZZ REPETORY QUINTET

(see Hyman, Dick)

PERKINS, BILL

b. 22 July 1924, San Francisco, California, USA. Having started out on a career as an electrical engineer, tenor saxophonist Perkins was in his mid-20s before he made an appearance in Jerry Wald's band in 1950. The following year he was with Woody Herman's Third Herd and by 1953 was in Stan Kenton's band. The rest of the 50s were spent alternating between Herman and Kenton during which time his reputation as a subtly inventive soloist grew steadily. His playing at this time was derived from Lester Young by way of Stan Getz, although he was also influenced by Richie Kamuca, who was with him in both the Herman and Kenton bands. His light, relaxed style made him a natural for the currently active west coast school of music. In 1956 he recorded with John Lewis, Richie Kamuca, Art Pepper and others and in 1959 was on Pepper's highly successful *Plus Eleven*. In the 60s he chose to turn his back on life on the road, taking a job with Pacific Jazz Records, but was active in the studios and playing occasional jazz gigs, a pattern that continued into the 70s. By the 80s he was touring widely, and appeared in the UK where he showed that he had lost none of his earlier inventiveness. A relaxed style and an elegant, dry-toned sound characterize his playing.

● ALBUMS: with Al Cohn, Richie Kamuca *The Brothers!* (RCA Victor 1955)★★★★, *The Bill Perkins Octet On Stage* (Pacific Jazz 1956)★★★★, with Kamuca, Art Pepper *Just Friends* (Pacific Jazz 1956)★★★, with John Lewis *Grand Encounter: 2 East 3 West* (Pacific Jazz 1956)★★★★, with Kamuca *Tenors Head-On* (Liberty 1957)★★★★, *Bossa Nova* (Liberty 1963)★★★, *Quietly There* 1966 recording (Riverside 1969)★★★★, with Pepper Adams *Front Line* (Storyville 1979)★★★★, *Many Ways To Go* (Sea Breeze 1980)★★★, *Journey To The East* (Contemporary 1984)★★★, *The Right Chemistry* (Jazz Mark 1988)★★★★, *I Wished On The Moon* (Candid 1991)★★★, *Remembrance Of Dino's* (Interplay 1991)★★★★, *Our Man Woody* (Jazz Mark 1991)★★★, *Frame Of Mind* (Interplay 1994)★★★★, *Perk Plays Prez* (Fresh Sound 1995)★★★.

PERKINS, CARL

b. 16 August 1928, Indianapolis, Indiana, USA, d. 17 March 1958. Perkins was a self-taught pianist who, after playing in R&B bands, including those led by Tiny Bradshaw and Big Jay McNeely, settled in California in the late 40s. At this time he changed his musical direction, working in the 50s in jazz mainstream with Illinois Jacquet and Oscar Moore and in bebop with Miles Davis. In the mid-50s he became one of the most active figures on the west coast scene, playing and recording extensively with artists such as Wardell Gray, Dexter Gordon, Jim Hall, Pepper Adams, Mel Lewis, Jack Sheldon and Art Pepper. He was also a member, briefly, of the Max Roach-Clifford Brown group and of the Curtis Counce group. Although physically impaired through contracting polio as a child, Perkins developed a strong sound and his style showed him to be an endlessly inventive musician. As a rhythm section member he made a substantial contribution to jazz in the 50s, playing on many classic west coast albums.

● ALBUMS: *Introducing Carl Perkins* (Boplicity 1955)★★★★.

PERRSON, BENT

b. 6 September 1947, Blekinge, Sweden. Perrson's powerful trumpet and cornet playing made him the star of Swedish bands such as Maggie's Blue Five and Bent's Blue Rhythm Band throughout the 70s. During this time he was recording a four-volume set of Louis Armstrong's *Fifty Hot Choruses* which had been transcribed from cylinder recordings now lost, but published by the Melrose Brothers in 1927. These accurate-sounding recordings add significantly to what is available of Armstrong's early playing. In the 80s Perrson continued to perform in the re-creative style he favours. He has formed the Weatherbird Jazzband, worked with Tomas Ornberg (reeds) and recorded with vocalist Maxine Sullivan.

● ALBUMS: *Louis Armstrong's Fifty Hot Choruses For Cornet As Re-created By Bent Perrson, Vols 1-4* (1974-79)★★★.

PERRY, OLIVER 'KING'

b. 1920, Gary, Indiana, USA. Starting with the violin, Perry learned a variety of instruments in his youth, including bass, trumpet, drums, piano and clarinet, before the alto saxophone after seeing Johnny Hodges with Duke Ellington's Orchestra. Perry ended up in Los Angeles, in 1945, after a tour with his small band and stayed, recording for Melodisc Records in July of that year. They went on to have records released on Excelsior/United Artists (not the well-known label from recent years) - finding success on the R&B charts with his 'Keep A Dollar In Your Pocket', which was covered by Roy Milton. He also recorded for DeLuxe, Specialty (with whom he had his only other substantial hit, 'Blue And Lonesome'), Dot, RPM, Lucky, Hollywood, Trilyte, Look and Unique through to the late 50s. He turned to selling real estate when work was scarce, but returned to music in 1967 and resumed his recording career on Accent in 1975. He continues to perform around the Bakersfield area and runs his own record company (Octive) and publishing company (Royal Attractions).

● ALBUMS: *King Perry* (1986)★★★.

PERSIANY, ANDRÉ

b. André Paul Stephane Persiani, 19 November 1927, Paris, France. Persiany began playing piano as a child and by his early twenties was an accomplished leader of small groups playing swing-style jazz. He worked with numerous touring American jazz artists including Bill Coleman, Buck Clayton and Lionel Hampton through the late 40s and early 50s. In the mid-50s he moved to New York where he played with several bands before becoming a member of the Jonah Jones quartet in 1961. He remained with Jones for most of the decade before returning to his homeland. In the 70s he again played with visiting Americans, including Milt Buckner in whose playing style Persiany found qualities he liked and chose to emulate. He plays with a strong rhythmic pulse and a clear preference for the swing era style of jazz piano.

● ALBUMS: *Swinging Here And There* (Pathé 1956-58)★★★.

PERSIP, CHARLIE

b. 26 July 1929, Morristown, New Jersey, USA. After taking up drums as a child Persip began playing bop, moving to New York where he worked with Tadd Dameron in the early 50s. From 1953 he was associated with Dizzy Gillespie, playing in small groups and big bands. He also recorded with Lee Morgan, Zoot Sims and Dinah Washington. In 1960 he formed his own band with Freddie Hubbard but continued to record with such artists as Gil Evans, Roland Kirk, Don Ellis and Gene Ammons. In the late 60s he began a long association with Billy Eckstine, playing drums and conducting the touring orchestra. In the early 70s Persip teamed up with several other leading jazzmen to work with Jazzmobile in New York City, teaching and performing. In the mid- to late 70s he recorded with Archie Shepp, Kirk and others and also led his own big band. Hard driving and technically assured, Persip is an excellent bop drummer whose skills are best represented by his superb big band work.

● ALBUMS: with Dizzy Gillespie *World Statesman* (1956)★★★, with Gil Evans *Out Of The Cool* (1960)★★★★, with Don Ellis *How Time Passes* (1960)★★★★, *The Charlie Persip Sextet* (1960)★★★, with Ellis *New Ideas* (1961)★★★★, with Rahsaan Roland Kirk *We Free Kings* (1961)★★★★, *Charlie Persip and Gary La Furn's 17-Piece Superband* (1980)★★★, *In Case You Missed It* (Soul Note 1984)★★★, *No Dummies Allowed* (Soul Note 1988)★★★.

PERSON, HOUSTON

b. 10 November 1934, Florence, South Carolina, USA. A late starter, Person took up the tenor saxophone in his late teenage years and gained considerable experience in bands during his military service. In the 60s he was sometimes sideman, sometimes leader of small groups cashing in on the organ-tenor fad, and was a member of Johnny Hammond's group from 1963 until 1966. Late in the decade he began a long-lasting association with his wife, singer Etta Jones. Although his playing style is rooted in earthy R&B, he has also played with forward-thinking musicians such as Ran Blake.

● ALBUMS: *Underground Soul* (Prestige 1967)★★★★, *Goodness!* (Prestige 1969)★★★★, *The Truth!* (Prestige 1970)★★★, *Person To Person!* (Prestige 1970)★★★★, *Houston Express* (Prestige 1970)★★★, *Stolen Sweets* (Muse 1976)★★★, *The Big Horn* (Muse 1976)★★★, *Wildflower* (Muse 1977)★★★, *The Nearness Of Houston Person* (Muse 1978)★★★, *Suspicions* (Muse 1980)★★★, *Very Personal* (Muse 1981)★★★, *The Talk Of The Town* (Muse 1987)★★★★, *Basics* (Muse 1988)★★★, *Something In Common* (Muse 1989)★★★, *The Party* (Muse 1990)★★★★, *Now's The Time* (Muse 1990)★★★, *Why Not!* (Muse 1991)★★★★, *The Lion And His Pride* (Muse 1995)★★★, *The Opening Round* (Savant 1998)★★★.

● COMPILATIONS: *Island Episode* 1971-73 recordings (Prestige 1997)★★★, *Lost & Found* 1977/1993 recordings (32 Jazz 1997)★★★.

PERSSON, ÅKE

b. 25 February 1932, Stockholm, Sweden, d. 5 February 1975. From his teens Persson was active and respected in his own country, playing trombone with fellow Scandinavians such as Arne Domnerus, Lars Guillin, Bengt Hallberg and Harry Arnold. While a member of Arnold's popular big band Persson was heard by several Americans who played with the band during visits to Sweden. These included Benny Bailey and Quincy Jones and he made records with them and with Roy Haynes. He played briefly in one of the orchestras Jones led in Europe before becoming a member of a radio band in Germany, where he remained for 15 years. During this period he was also a founder-member of the Clarke-Boland Big Band, occasionally joining touring big bands for brief spells. In this way he played with Count Basie and Duke Ellington. An outstanding soloist whose flow of ideas and inventiveness was enhanced by an exceptionally good technique, Persson was a major figure on the European jazz scene.

● ALBUMS: with Harry Arnold *Big Band Classics* (1958)★★★, *Aake Persson-Benny Bailey-Joe Harris* (1959)★★★, with the Clarke-Boland Big Band *Jazz Is Universal* (1961)★★★★.

PETE KELLY'S BLUES

A marvellous opening sequence, depicting the funeral of a New Orleans jazz musician, is the best moment in what is otherwise a fairly predictable movie tale of jazzmen and gangsters in the 20s. Other bright spots are appearances by singers Peggy Lee and Ella Fitzgerald. Teddy Buckner plays in the opening scene and elsewhere can be heard the likes of Nick Fatool, Matty Matlock, Eddie Miller, George Van Eps and Joe Venuti. The role of Pete Kelly is played by Jack Webb, who also directed, and his trumpet playing was dubbed by Dick Cathcart. Lee Marvin made the most unlikely-looking clarinettist in jazz history, with the possible exception of Pee Wee Russell. Four years later, in 1959, a television spin-off lasted 13 episodes.

PETERSON, MARVIN 'HANNIBAL'

b. 11 November 1948, Smithville, Texas, USA. One of many fine musicians to graduate from North Texas State University, Peterson settled on trumpet having previously played cornet and drums. After graduation he moved to New York where he played with Rahsaan Roland Kirk, Elvin Jones, Archie Shepp and other leading jazzmen, notably Gil Evans with whom he formed a lasting musical relationship. Throughout the 60s he toured and recorded with these and other musicians, sometimes leading his own band. He continued performing in similar settings through the 70s, working again with Evans and Jones and also with Pharoah Sanders and Roy Haynes. In the 80s he was touring internationally. For a while in the mid- to late 70s Peterson played free jazz with Roswell Rudd, but his best work comes in bop and post-bop settings. A sparkling virtuoso trumpeter, Peterson's brilliant technique allows him to do pretty much anything he sets his mind upon; as his playing and writing testify, this ranges over the entire spectrum of jazz.

● ALBUMS: with Pharoah Sanders *Black Unity* (1971)★★★★, with Gil Evans *Svengali* (1973)★★★★, *Children Of Fire* (1974)★★★, *Hannibal* (1975)★★★, *Hannibal In Berlin* (1976)★★, *Gil Evans Live At New York Public Theater* (1980)★★★★, *The Angels Of Atlanta* (1981)★★★, *Hannibal In Antibes* (Enja 1982)★★★, *Poem Song* (Mole 1983)★★★, *Kiss On The Bridge* (Ear Rational 1990)★★★.

PETERSON, OSCAR

b. Oscar Emmanuel Peterson, 15 August 1925, Montreal, Canada. Blessed with an attractive stage personality, this behemoth of mainstream jazz's fluid technique was influenced by Art Tatum, Errol Garner and, later, George Shearing. After studying trumpet, illness redirected him to the piano. His enthusiasm resulted in endless hours of practice that helped to mould his remarkable technique. In his mid-teens, after winning a local talent contest in 1940, Peterson was heard regularly on radio in Canada and beyond. By 1944, he was the featured pianist with the nationally famous Johnny Holmes Orchestra before leading his own trio. Peterson was unusual in not serving an apprenticeship as an older player's sideman. Although early recordings were disappointing, he received lucrative offers to appear in the USA but these were resisted until a debut at New York's Carnegie Hall with Norman Granz's Jazz At The Philharmonic in September 1949. Louis Armstrong, Billie Holiday, Count Basie, Dizzy Gillespie, Zoot Sims, Ella Fitzgerald and Stan Getz have been among Peterson's collaborators during a career that has encompassed hundreds of studio and concert recordings. With 1963's *Affinity* as his biggest seller, Peterson's output has ranged from albums drawn from the songbooks of Cole Porter and Duke Ellington, to a Verve single of Jimmy Forrest's perennial 'Night Train', and 1964's self-written *Canadiana Suite.* Although he introduced a modicum of Nat 'King' Cole-type vocals into his repertoire in the mid-50s, he has maintained a certain steady consistency of style that has withstood the buffeting of fashion. Since 1970, he has worked with no fixed group, often performing alone, although at the end of the 70s Peterson had a long stint with bass player Niels-Henning Ørsted Pedersen, which continued well into the 80s. The soundtrack to the movie *Play It Again Sam*, the hosting of a television chat show, a 1974 tour of Soviet Russia, and 1981's *A Royal Wedding Suite* (conducted by Russ Garcia) have been more recent commercial high points of a fulfilling and distinguished professional life. While musicians as diverse as Steve Winwood, Dudley Moore and Weather Report's Joe Zawinul absorbed much from Peterson discs, younger admirers have been advantaged by his subsequent publication of primers such as *Jazz Exercises And Pieces* and *Peterson's New Piano Solos*. Peterson's dazzling technique and unflagging swing have helped to make him one of the most highly regarded and instantly identifiable pianists in jazz. Although the technical qualities of his work have sometimes cooled the emotional heart of his material, Peterson's commitment to jazz is undeniable. The high standard of his work over the years is testimony to his dedication and to the care that he and his mentor, Granz, have exercised over the pianist's career. Throughout this time, Peterson has displayed through his eclecticism an acute awareness of the history of jazz piano, ranging from stride to bop, from James P. Johnson to Bill Evans, but always with Art Tatum as an abiding influence. However, this influence is one that Peterson has been careful to control. Tatum may colour Peterson's work but he has never shaped it. Thus, for all his influences, Peterson is very much his own man. Yet, for all the admiration he draws from other pianists, there is little evidence that he has many followers. He may well prove to be the last in the line of master musicians in the history of jazz piano.

● ALBUMS: *Oscar Peterson Piano Solos* (Mercury 1950)★★★, *Oscar Peterson At Carnegie Hall* (Mercury 1951)★★★★, *Oscar Peterson Collates* (Mercury 1952)★★★, *The Oscar Peterson Quartet* (Mercury 1952)★★★, *Oscar Peterson Plays Pretty* (Mercury 1952)★★★, *This Is Oscar Peterson* (RCA Victor 1952)★★★, *In Concert* (1952)★★★, *Jazz At The Philharmonic, Hartford 1953* (Pablo 1953)★★★, *Oscar Peterson Plays Cole Porter* (Mercury 1953)★★★, *Oscar Peterson Plays Irving Berlin* (Mercury 1953)★★★, *Oscar Peterson Plays George Gershwin* (Mercury 1953)★★★, *Oscar Peterson Plays Duke Ellington* (Mercury 1953)★★★, *Oscar Peterson Collates No. 2* (Clef 1953)★★★, *1953 Live* (Jazz Band Records)★★★, *Oscar Peterson Plays Pretty No. 2* (Clef 1954)★★★, *The Oscar Peterson Quartet No. 2* (Clef 1954)★★★, *Oscar Peterson Plays Jerome Kern* (Clef 1954)★★★, *Oscar Peterson Plays Richard Rogers* (Clef 1954)★★★, *Oscar Peterson Plays Vincent Youmans* (Clef 1954)★★★, with Lester Young *Lester Young With The Oscar Peterson Trio* i (Norgran 1954)★★★★, with Young *Lester Young With The Oscar Peterson Trio* ii (Norgran 1954)★★★★, *At Zardi's* 1955 recording (Pablo)★★★, *Oscar Peterson Plays Harry Warren* (Clef 1955)★★★, *Oscar Peterson Plays Harold Arlen* (Clef 1955)★★★, *Oscar Peterson Plays Jimmy McHugh* (Clef 1955)★★★, with Young *The Pres-ident Plays With The Oscar Peterson Trio* (Norgran 1955)★★★★, *Recital By Oscar Peterson* (Clef 1956)★★★, *Nostalgic Memories By Oscar Peterson* (Clef 1956)★★★, *An Evening With Oscar Peterson Duo/Quartet* (Clef 1956)★★★, *Oscar Peterson Plays Count Basie* (Clef 1956)★★★, *In A Romantic Mood - Oscar Peterson With Strings* (Verve 1956)★★★, *Pastel Moods By Oscar Peterson* (Verve 1956)★★★, *Romance - The Vocal Styling Of Oscar Peterson* (Verve 1956)★★★, *Soft Sands* (Verve 1957)★★★, *The Oscar Peterson Trio At The Stratford Shakesperean Festival* (Verve 1957)★★★★, *Keyboard Music By Oscar Peterson* (Verve 1957)★★★, *Oscar Peterson Trio With Sonny Stitt, Roy Eldridge And Jo Jo Jones At Newport* (Verve 1958)★★★★, *Oscar Peterson Trio At The Concertgebouw* (Verve 1958)★★★, *Oscar Peterson Trio With The Modern Jazz Quartet At The Opera House* (Verve 1958)★★★, *A Night On The Town* (Verve 1958)★★★, *Oscar Peterson Plays My Fair Lady* (Verve 1958)★★★, *The Oscar Peterson Trio With David Rose* (Verve 1958)★★★, with Ben Webster *Ben Webster Meets Oscar Peterson* (Verve 1959)★★★★, *Songs For A Swingin' Affair - A Jazz Portrait Of Frank Sinatra* (Verve 1959)★★, with Louis Armstrong *Louis Armstrong Meets Oscar Peterson* (Verve 1959)★★★, *The Jazz And Soul Of Oscar Peterson* (Verve 1959)★★★, *Swinging Brass With The Oscar Peterson Trio* (Verve 1959)★★★, with Coleman Hawkins *Coleman Hawkins And His Confreres With The Oscar Peterson Trio* (Verve 1959)★★★★, *Plays The Cole Porter Songbook* (Verve 1960)★★★★, *Plays Porgy And Bess* (Verve 1960)★★★, *The Music From Fiorello* (Verve 1960)★★★, *The Oscar Peterson Trio At J.A.T.P.* (Verve 1960)★★★, *The Trio Live From Chicago* (Verve 1961)★★★, *Very Tall* (Verve 1962)★★★, *West Side Story* (Verve 1962)★★, *Bursting Out With The All Star Big Band!* (Verve 1962)★★★, *The Sound Of The Trio* (Verve 1962)★★★, *Night Train* (Verve 1963)★★★★, *Affinity* (Verve 1963)★★★, with Nelson Riddle *The Oscar Peterson Trio With Nelson Riddle* (Verve 1963)★★★, with Gerry Mulligan *The Oscar Peterson Trio And The Gerry Mulligan Four At Newport* (Verve 1963)★★★, *Exclusively For My Friends* (1964)★★★, *Oscar Peterson Trio + One* (Mercury 1964)★★★, *Canadian Suite* (Limelight 1964)★★★, *We Get Requests* (Verve 1965)★★, *Eloquence* (Limelight 1965)★★★, *With Respect To Nat* (Limelight 1965)★★★, *Blues Etude* (Limelight 1966)★★★, *Put On A Happy Face* (Verve 1966)★★★, *Something Warm* (Verve 1966)★★★, *Stage Right* (Verve 1966)★★★, *Thoroughly Modern 20s* (Verve 1967)★★, *Night Train Volume 2* (Verve 1967)★★★, *Soul-O!* (Prestige 1968)★★★, *My Favourite Instrument* (1968)★★★, *The Vienna Concert* (Philology 1969)★★★, *Oscar's Oscar Peterson Plays The Academy Awards* (Verve 1969)★★★, *Motion's And Emotions* (MPS 1969)★★★, *Hello Herbie* (MPS 1969)★★★, *The Great Oscar Peterson On Prestige* (Prestige 1969)★★★, *Oscar Peterson Plays For Lovers* (Prestige 1969)★★★, *Easy Walker* (Prestige 1969)★★★, *Tristeza On Piano* (MPS 1970)★★★, *Three Originals* (MPS 1970)★★★, *Tracks* (1970)★★★, *Reunion Blues* (MPS 1972)★★★, *Terry's Tune* (1974)★★★, *The Trio* (Pablo 1975)★★★, *The Good Life* (Fantasy 1975)★★★, with Sonny Stitt *Sittin' In* (1975)★★★, with Dizzy Gillespie *Oscar Peterson And Dizzy Gillespie* (Pablo 1975)★★★, with Roy Eldridge *Oscar Peterson And Roy Eldridge* (Pablo 1975)★★★, with Ella Fitzgerald *Ella And Oscar* (Pablo 1975)★★★, with Count Basie *Satch And Josh* (Pablo 1975)★★★, *At The Montreux Jazz Festival* (Pablo 1976)★★★, *Again* (1977)★★★, *Oscar Peterson Jam* (1977)★★★, *The Vocal Styling Of Oscar Peterson* (1977)★★★, with Basie *Satch And Josh ... Again* (Pablo 1977)★★★, with Basie *Yessir, That's My Baby* (Pablo 1978)★★★, with Basie *Night*

Rider (Pablo 1978)★★★, with Basie *The Timekeepers* (Pablo 1978)★★★, *Montreux '77 i* (Pablo 1978)★★★, *Montreux '77 ii* (Pablo 1978)★★★, *The Silent Partner* (1979)★★★, *The Paris Concert* (Pablo 1979)★★★, *Skol* (Pablo 1980)★★★, *The Personal Touch* (Pablo 1981)★★★, *A Royal Wedding Suite* (Pablo 1981)★★, *Live At The Northsea Jazz Festival* (Pablo 1981)★★, *Nigerian Marketplace* (Pablo 1982)★★★, *Romance* (1982)★★★, with Stéphane Grappelli, Joe Pass, Mickey Roker, Niels-Henning Ørsted Pedersen *Skol* (1982)★★★, *In Russia* (Pablo 1982)★★★, *Oscar Peterson & Harry Edison* (Pablo 1982)★★★, *Carioca* (Happy Bird 1983)★★★, *A Tribute To My Friends* (Pablo 1984)★★★, *Time After Time* (Pablo 1984)★★★, *If You Could See Me Now* (Pablo 1984)★★★, *Live!* (Pablo 1987)★★★, *The Legendary Oscar Peterson Trio: Saturday Night At the Blue Note* (Telarc 1991)★★★, *... Last Call At The Blue Note* (Telarc 1992)★★★, *The More I See You* (Telarc 1995)★★★, *An Oscar Peterson Christmas* (Telarc 1995)★★, *Oscar Peterson Meets Roy Hargrove And Ralph Moore With Niels-Henning Ørsted Pedersen And Lewis Nash* (Telarc 1996)★★★, *The London House Sessions* 5-CD box set (Verve 1996)★★★★, *Oscar In Paris: Live At The Salle Pleyel* (Telarc 1997)★★★, with various artists *A Tribute To Oscar Peterson: Live At The Town Hall* (Telarc 1997)★★★, *The Trio* (Verve 1998)★★★★, *Live At CBC Studios, 1960* (Just A Memory 1998)★★★, with Bennie Green *Oscar And Benny* (Telarc 1998)★★★★, *Oscar In Paris* (Telarc 1998)★★★.

● COMPILATIONS: *History Of An Artist* (Pablo 1982)★★★, *History Of An Artist, Volume 2* (Pablo 1987)★★★, *Compact Jazz: Oscar Peterson And Friends* (Verve 1988)★★★★, *Compact Jazz: Plays Jazz Standards* (Verve 1988)★★★★, *Exclusively For My Friends* 4-CD box set (MPS/Verve 1992)★★★★, *Exclusively For My Friends: The Lost Tapes* 1963-1968 recordings (Verve 1997)★★★★, *Ultimate Oscar Peterson* (Verve 1998)★★★.

● VIDEOS: *Music In The Key Of Oscar* (View Video 1995), *The Life Of A Legend* (View Video 1996).

● FURTHER READING: *Oscar Peterson Highlights Jazz Piano*, Oscar Peterson. *Oscar Peterson: The Will To Swing*, Gene Lees.

PETIT, BUDDY

b. Joseph Crawford, *c*.1897, White Castle, Louisiana, USA, d. 4 July 1931. By his early teens Petit was well known in New Orleans and by 1916 was co-leading a band with Jimmie Noone. The following year he was in California with Jelly Roll Morton. By 1918, however, he was back in his home state and, apart from another brief trip to California, he lived and worked in New Orleans and its environs for the rest of his life. Petit's reputation rests upon the acclaim of fellow musicians - he never recorded - and if they are to be believed he was an outstanding trumpet player with a reputation second only to that of Louis Armstrong. He died after 'over-indulging' in food and drink at an Independence Day celebration in 1931.

PETRUCCIANI, MICHEL

b. 28 December 1962, Orange, France, d. 6 January 1999, New York, USA. Born into a musical family, Petrucianni played drums and piano as a child. He gave his first solo concert at the age of 13, at the Cliousclat Festival. After playing with Kenny Clarke and Clark Terry at the age of 15, Petrucciani moved to Paris, recorded his first album, and formed a successful duo with Lee Konitz just two years later. Moving to California in 1982, he joined Charles Lloyd's new quartet. However, it was a solo performance at Carnegie Hall as part of the Kool Jazz Festival that resulted in widespread critical acclaim. In 1986 Petrucciani became the first French musician to sign a contract with Blue Note Records. *Michel Plays Petrucciani* featured all his own compositions and included some sparkling guitar work from John Abercrombie. Of the dozens of Duke Ellington tributes recorded over the years, Petrucciani's *Promenade With Duke* oozed respect for the master. During a productive career, Petrucciani also worked with organist Eddy Louiss, his childhood idol Stéphane Grappelli, and Wayne Shorter in Manhattan Project. A melodic and thoughtful piano player, Petrucciani was one of the most striking virtuosi of recent years.

● ALBUMS: *Michel Petrucciani Trio* (Owl 1982)★★★, *Estate* (IRD 19 1983)★★★, *Oracles's Destiny* (Owl 1983)★★★, *100 Hearts* (Concord Jazz 1983)★★★★, *Note'n Notes* (Owl 1985)★★★, *Live At The Village Vanguard* (Concord Jazz 1985)★★★★, *Pianism* (Blue Note 1986)★★★★, *Power Of Three* (Blue Note 1986)★★★★, *Cold Blues* (Concord Jazz 1986)★★★, *Michel Plays Petrucciani* (Blue Note 1988)★★★★, *Music* (Blue Note 1989)★★★, *Playground* (Blue Note 1991)★★★, *Live* (1991)★★★★, *Promenade With Duke* (1993)★★★★, *Marvellous* (Dreyfus 1994)★★★, with Eddy Louiss *Conference De Presse* (Dreyfus 1994)★★★, *Au Théâtre Des Champs-Élysées* (Dreyfus 1995)★★★★, with Louiss *Eddy Louiss/Michel Petrucianni* (Dreyfus 1995)★★★, with Stéphane Grappelli *Flamingo* (Dreyfus 1996)★★★★, *Both Worlds* (Dreyfus 1997)★★★.

PETTIFORD, OSCAR

b. 30 September 1922, Okmulgee, Oklahoma, USA, d. 8 September 1960. Coming from a musical background, Pettiford was competent on several instruments, settling for bass in the early 40s. He played with Charlie Barnet, Roy Eldridge, Coleman Hawkins, Ben Webster and others; then in the middle of the decade, was active among the New York beboppers. He briefly co-led a band with Dizzy Gillespie, and later led his own groups. From 1945 he was with Duke Ellington, moving on in 1948 to the Woody Herman band. During the 50s he played in several bands, big and small, often leading his own groups, and was usually in the company of important musicians such as Thelonious Monk, Lucky Thompson and Art Blakey. In 1958 he toured Europe with a jazz concert package, remaining behind to take up residence in Denmark where he died in 1960. A major influence upon bop bass players, Pettiford played with a superb tone and clarity. Nevertheless, he was frequently dissatisfied with his own work and also played cello, an instrument that gave him an opportunity to develop ideas sometimes inhibited by the physical limitations of the bass.

● ALBUMS: *The Oscar Pettiford Memorial Album* (1954)★★★★, *Oscar Pettiford Sextet* (Debut 1954)★★★, *Basically Duke* (Bethlehem 1954)★★★, *Bohemia After Dark* (Affinity 1955)★★★★, *Discoveries* (Savoy 1952-57 recordings)★★★★,

The Oscar Pettiford Orchestra In Hi-Fi (ABC Paramount 1957)★★★, *O.P.Js Jazz Men Oscar Pettiford Orchestra In Hi-Fi Vol 2* (ABC Paramount 1958)★★★, *The Legendary Oscar Pettiford* (Black Lion 1959)★★★★, *Radio Tapes* (Jazzline 1958-60 recordings)★★★, *Blue Brothers* (Black Lion 1960)★★★, *Last Recordings By The Late Great Bassist* (Jazzland 1962)★★, *Monmartre Blues* (Black Lion 1959-60)★★★, *My Little Cello* (Fantasy 1964)★★, *The Essen Jazz Festival* (Fantasy 1964)★★★, *Live At Jilly's* (Atlantic 1965)★★★.

● COMPILATIONS: *Oscar Rides Again* (Affinity 1986)★★★★.

PEYROUX, MADELEINE

b. *c.*1974, France. A precocious contemporary jazz singer, Madeleine Peyroux was first spotted singing in a Greenwich Village bar in New York, USA, by Atlantic Records Vice President of A&R, Yves Beauvais, in the early 90s. By the advent of her debut album in 1996, Peyroux had already spent much of her young life as a performer, working principally in Paris and Amsterdam with the Great Lost Wandering Blues And Jazz Band. By this time her uncanny similarity in phrasing and technique to Billie Holiday had already been widely commented upon. This led to Beauvais' advice to Peyroux that, for someone with a voice so similar to Holiday's, a straight jazz debut could prove injurious to her career. Instead, *Dreamland* was more obviously themed around blues and roots music. As Beauvais told *Billboard* magazine in 1996: 'I don't even consider *Dreamland* a jazz record, just a very eclectic bunch of songs in a variety of settings.' The final selection of tracks included 'Walkin' After Midnight' (Patsy Cline), 'La Vie En Rose' (Edith Piaf) and 'Reckless Blues' (Bessie Smith). The musicians involved ranged from mainstream jazz figures to representatives of other traditions, including James Carter (saxophone), Cyrus Chestnut (piano) and Marc Ribot (guitar). The producer was Greg Cohen, well known within the music industry for his work with Lou Reed, Laurie Anderson and John Zorn.

● ALBUMS: *Dreamland* (Atlantic 1996)★★★.

PHALANX

(see Ali, Rashied)

PHILLIPS, BARRE

b. 27 October 1934, San Francisco, California, USA. At the age of three Barre Phillips was giving solo song recitals. He studied romance languages at Berkeley and then moved to New York where he received double bass lessons from Frederick Zimmermann in the early 60s. In March and April 1963 he played with Eric Dolphy at Carnegie Hall, part of Gunther Schuller's Twentieth-Century Innovations series, and from 1964 he was a member of Jimmy Giuffre's revolutionary drumless trio. He worked with Hungarian guitarist Attila Zoller between 1965 and 1967 and also with Archie Shepp, playing on Shepp's side of the famous *New Thing At Newport* and on one track of his classic *On This Night*. In 1969 he played in an orchestral project led by John Lennon and Yoko Ono, with the improvising band Gong (*Magick Brother*) and with Mike Westbrook. Increasingly involved with the European scene, he played with Rolf and Joachim Kuhn (1969) and with English saxophonist John Surman and fellow-expatriate drummer Stu Martin as the Trio (1969-71). In 1971, in conjunction with Dave Holland, he led a whole band of bass players. In 1976 he began recording for ECM Records (*Mountainscapes*), an arrangement that lasted until 1983. In the latter year he played and recorded with the classical ensemble Accroche Note and in 1988 with Derek Bailey and Company. 1989 saw him involved with several of British bassist Barry John Guy's projects. Possessed of an acute rhythmic intelligence, Barre Philips is an important link between the free jazz of 60s America and the European free improvisation scene.

● ALBUMS: *Unaccompanied Barre* (1968)★★★, with John Surman, Stu Martin *The Trio* (1970)★★★★, *Alors!!!* (1970)★★★, with Dave Holland *Music From Two Basses* (1971)★★★, *Mountainscapes* (ECM 1976)★★★★, *Three Day Moon* (ECM 1978)★★★★, *Journal Violine II* (ECM 1980)★★★, *Music By* (1981)★★★, *Call Me When You Get There* (1983)★★★, with Accroche Note *En Concert* (1983)★★★, with the Trio *By Contact* 1971 recording (1987)★★★, with Derek Bailey *Figuring* (Incus 1988)★★★, with Company *Once* (1988)★★★, *Camouflage* (Victo 1989)★★★★, *Naxos* (1990)★★★, with Jon Rose *Violin Music For Restaurants* (1991)★★★, *Aquarian Rain* (Philips 1992)★★★, *Uzu* (PSF 1996)★★★, with Paul Bley and Evan Parker *Time Will Tell* (ECM 1996)★★★★.

PHILLIPS, FLIP

b. 26 March 1915, New York City, New York, USA. After playing in small groups in the New York area, Joe 'Flip' Phillips joined Woody Herman's First Herd in 1944. By the time he left the band, Phillips' reputation as a tenor saxophonist was established nationally and on record. He then became a member of Norman Granz's touring package, Jazz At The Philharmonic, a move that raised his international profile. He remained with JATP until the late 50s, toured Europe with Benny Goodman and then opted for working outside music by day and leading a small group by night in Florida. This lifestyle continued for 15 years, then, in 1975, Phillips moved to New York and became more active in jazz, touring Europe into the late 80s. A magnificent ballad player, early in his career Phillips was often obliged to play uptempo rabble-rousers, which he did with enormous vitality. In later years, in control of his repertoire, he developed the ballad side of his playing and proved himself to be an outstanding interpreter of great songs.

● ALBUMS: *Flip* (1949)★★★, *Flip Phillips Quintet i* (1951)★★★, *Flip Phillips Trio* (1952)★★★, with JATP *Live At The Nichigeki Theatre Tokyo* (1953)★★, *Flip Phillips Quintet* ii (1954)★★★, *Your Place Or Mine?* (1963)★★★, *Phillips' Head* (1975)★★★, *Together* (1978)★★★, *Flipenstein* (1981)★★, *Flip Phillips And His Swedish Friends* (1982)★★★, *A Melody From The Sky* (Doctor Jazz 1986)★★★, *A Real Swinger* (Concord 1988)★★★, *A Sound Investement* (Concord 1988)★★★, *The Claw* (Chiaroscuro 1988)★★★, *Try A Little Tenderness* (Chiaroscuro 1993)★★★.

● COMPILATIONS: *Flip Wails: The Best Of The Verve Years* (Verve 1994)★★★★.

PHILLIPS, SID

b. 14 June 1902, London, England, d. 23 May 1973. Deeply involved in the music business from childhood, Phillips played clarinet in various bands, including one led by his brothers, and also worked in music publishing and for record companies. In the early 30s he was staff arranger for the popular band led by Bert Ambrose and later became a member of the band. He also began leading his own small group in the 30s, but it was the bands he led from 1949 onwards that built his reputation. Broadcasting regularly on the radio, Phillips also recorded, and his band became one of the best-known Dixieland groups in the UK. Among the many fine musicians he employed at one time or another were George Shearing, Kenny Ball and Tommy Whittle. A gutsy, full-toned clarinettist, Phillips was also a skilful arranger and composed jazz-orientated dance tunes and several classical works. Changes in popular taste meant that from the 60s onwards his music was not in great demand, but he continued working until his death in 1973.

● ALBUMS: *Sid Phillips And His Band* i (1960)★★★★, *Stardust* (60s)★★★, *Sid Phillips And His Band* ii (1962)★★★★, *Sid Phillips And His Band* iii (1964)★★★, *Rhythm Is Our Business* (1970)★★★, *Clarinet Marmalade* (Rediffusion 1975)★★★, *Sid Phillips And His Great Band Play Stomps, Rags And Blues* (Rediffusion 1975)★★★, *Sid Phillips Plays Barrelhouse Piano* (Rediffusion 1975)★★★.

● COMPILATIONS: *Golden Hour Presents Sid Phillips H'ors D'Ouvres* (Golden Hour 1976)★★★, *Anthology, Volume 1 - Chicago* (Gold Star 1976)★★★★, *Anthology, Volume 2 - Lonesome Road* (Gold Star 1977)★★★, *Anthology, Volume 3 - Way Down Yonder In New Orleans* (Gold Star 1978)★★★, *The Best Of Sid Phillips* (EMI 1977)★★★★.

PHILLIPS, WOOLF

b. *c.*1920, London, England. At the age of 14 Phillips worked in the arranging department of music publisher Lawrence Wright, then went to Campbell Connolly where his older brother, Sid Phillips, was also arranging. Among the bands for whom the brothers arranged was one led by Bert Ambrose. Phillips began playing trombone and eventually joined Ambrose. Soon, he moved to the Joe Loss band, playing trombone and writing arrangements, played with other less well-known bands, then joined Jack Hylton. During World War II Phillips played in the band of the Royal Army Medical Corps and also performed with and arranged for Harry Roy. Phillips was a member of the original Ted Heath band on radio and records. After the war he played with Ambrose again and with Geraldo, formed his own big band, and was also leader of the Skyrockets at the London Palladium. Phillips continued to play and arrange in a variety of musical styles and settings. In 1967 he moved to the USA, continuing to arrange and also compose symphonic music. He has also conducted the Camarillo symphony orchestra.

PIAZZOLLA, ASTOR

b. 30 January 1921, Mar de Plata, Argentina, d. 5 July 1992. An immensely innovative player of the Argentinian bandonean (a close relation of the accordion), Piazolla successfully took the instrument - and tango music in general - on to the international concert stage, without diluting its roots in the working-class dancehalls and dockland nightclubs of Buenos Aires. He moved to New York as a child, and at the age of 13 he was hired by Carlos Gardél (the undisputed king of classical tango) to play in the film, *El Did Que Me Quieras*. He then returned to Argentina to play in the band led by Anibal Tróila. When Tróila died, Piazzolla began his solo career, achieving massive success throughout the 50s and 60s. By this time he had won a government scholarship to study under Nadia Boulanger in Paris. Boulanger encouraged him to discover the possibilities of his own, native music, and he duly turned his attention to the tango. Updating it for new generations, his vivacious style ('nuevo tango') soon attracted a massive South American audience (and opposition from tango traditionalists). In the 70s he was forced to leave Argentina for Paris, because of the volatile political climate, but his influence continued to spread. His international breakthrough came in the early 80s with his Quinteto Tango Nuevo (formed in 1976) featuring Fernando Suarez Paz (violin), Pablo Ziegler (piano), Horacio Malvicino (guitar) and Hector Console (bass) - and two albums recorded with the American producer Kip Hanrahan: *Tango Zero Hour* and *The Rough Dancer And The Cyclical Night*. Both are essential parts of any representative world music collection, as is the harder to find but outstanding live album *Concert A Vienne*.

● ALBUMS: *Essencia Musica* (1978)★★★, *Concert A Vienne* (Messidor 1983)★★★★, *Tango Zero Hour* (American Clave 1986)★★★★, *The Rough Dancer And The Cyclical Night* (American Clave 1988)★★★★, *Maria De Buenos Aires* (Milan 1991)★★★, *Tanguedia De Amor* (Tropical Storm 1992)★★★, *The Lausanne Concert* (1993)★★, *Tango* (EPM 1996)★★★, *Concerto For Bandoneon* (Harmonia Mundi 1996)★★★.

● COMPILATIONS: *The Late Masterpieces* 3-CD set (American Clave 1993)★★★★, *Adios Nonino* (Milan 1995)★★★.

PICARD, JOHN

b. 17 May 1934, Wood Green, London, England. Picard is a self-taught trombonist whose shouting style was a part of Humphrey Lyttelton's classic traditional band (1954-61). Picard's interests broadened in the 60s and he played with the bands of Sandy Brown, Bruce Turner and Tony Coe. Although Picard became semi-professional in later years his taste became ever more catholic. He recorded with pianist Brian Lemon and played in a septet that was equally at home with Charles Mingus-style pieces as with Duke Ellington compositions. He was the lead trombone with the London Jazz Big Band (1975-83) for whom he wrote some very modern arrangements. He has played with Rocket 88, the band featuring Alexis Korner and boogie pianist Ian Stewart, as well as with Charlie Watts' Big Band.

● ALBUMS: with Humphrey Lyttelton *Swing Out* (1959)★★★, with Lyttelton *Triple Exposure* (1959)★★★, with Brian Lemon *Our Kind Of Music* (1970)★★, with Charlie Watts' Big Band *The Live Album* (1986)★★★★.

PICHON, WALTER 'FATS'

b. 3 April 1906, New Orleans, Louisiana, USA, d. 25 February 1967, Chicago, Illinois, USA. Pichon spent his musical career in the area between jazz, blues and pop, leading his own bands occasionally, and working as a pianist for artists including Luis Russell, Fess Williams, Ted Lewis, Mamie Smith, Elmer Snowden and Armand Piron. He recorded a few hokum vocals for Russell under his own name; the accompanists on the latter included Hawaiian guitarist King Benny Nawahi, for whom Pichon returned the compliment. In the 40s he began a long residency at the Absinthe House, New Orleans, also working in New York and the Caribbean. He was still active in the 60s, although treatment for failing eyesight interrupted his playing for long periods.

PICKERING, TOM

b. Thomas Mansergh Pickering, 8 August 1921, Burra, South Australia, Australia. After learning to play various reed instruments, in particular the clarinet, Pickering played traditional jazz in various parts of Australia during the late 30s and 40s. He continued working throughout succeeding decades, continuing his preference for older styles but also playing effective tenor saxophone in mainstream settings. His playing and recording career continued apace into the 80s, and his contribution to the musical life of his country has been rewarded with a number of honours.

● ALBUMS: *Good Time Jazz* (Swaggie 1970)★★★, *Red Hot & Blue* (Candle 1983)★★★.

PICOU, ALPHONSE

b. 19 October 1878, New Orleans, Louisiana, USA, d. 4 February 1961. An enormously popular musician in his home-town, clarinettist Picou worked in numerous bands playing dance music, jazz or military marches. It was his adaptation of a piccolo descant in a military band piece for use in a performance of a jazz number, 'High Society', that ensured Picou's immortality. That descant became a part of 'High Society' and ever afterwards the skills of New Orleans and Dixieland clarinettists were measured by the way they played his variation. Relatively inactive in the 30s, Picou returned to the jazz scene during the Revival Movement, recording with Kid Rena in 1940. He worked on through the 40s and 50s, dying in 1961. A skilful player, Picou's work suggests that for all his fame he was much less committed to jazz than many of his fellow townsmen. Nevertheless, as long as Dixieland jazz is played, clarinettists the world over will have to prove themselves by performing Picou's 'test piece'.

● ALBUMS: with Kid Rena *Down On The Delta* (1940)★★, *Alphonse Picou And His Paddock Jazz Band* (1953)★★★.

PIED PIPER, THE - CHICO FREEMAN

One of the more talented and interesting of America's younger(ish) crop of saxophonists, Chico Freeman combines a Coltrane-influenced intensity on up-tempo tunes, with a lush, romantic feel for ballads. Joined on the front line here by fellow reedsman John Purcell, the pair utilize a vast array of instruments, including oboe, sopranino saxophone, flute and piccolo, to create a good range of sounds and textures. The title track is a complex but catchy composition combining two time signatures, and the rest of the material includes a jaunty blues, and a fast and exciting 'Softly, As In A Morning Sunrise'.

● Tracks: *The Pied Piper; The Rose Tattoo; Blues On The Bottom; Monk 2000; Softly, As In A Morning Sunrise; Amor Soña Dor.*

● First released 1984

● UK peak chart position: did not chart

● USA peak chart position: did not chart

PIERCE, DE DE

b. Joseph De Lacrois, 18 February 1904, New Orleans, Louisiana, USA, d. 23 November 1973. For many years, playing the cornet was only a secondary occupation to Pierce, in common with many of the older generation of New Orleans musicians who traditionally and rightly regarded music as an unreliable business. In Pierce's case, however, he kept up a 'day job' rather longer than most and not until after his marriage in 1935 to singer-pianist Billie Goodson (see Billie Pierce) did he devote himself to a musical career. The husband-and-wife duo worked regularly, although still within a restricted area, until Pierce retired temporarily in the 50s through ill-health and failing eyesight. The duo made a comeback in the mid-60s achieving international fame with a succession of concert tours and records and, inevitably perhaps, regular appearances at Preservation Hall, where they entertained the tourists of New Orleans.

● ALBUMS: *New Orleans Jazz* (1959)★★★, *Blues In The Classic Tradition* (1961)★★★, *Jazz At Preservation Hall* (1962)★★★, *Billie And De De* (1966)★★★, *De De Pierce's New Orleans Stompers* (1966)★★★, *New Orleans* (1992)★★.

PIERCE, NAT

b. 16 July 1925, Somerville, Massachusetts, USA, d. 10 June 1992, Los Angeles, California, USA. After studying and playing in local bands in his home state, Pierce worked with a handful of name bands, including Larry Clinton's, then briefly led his own band in 1949-51, instigating what is commonly regarded among fellow musicians as being the birth of the so-called 'rehearsal band' concept. In 1951 he joined Woody Herman, in whose band he played piano, arranged, and acted as straw boss until 1955. Thereafter, he arranged for several bands and singers, including Count Basie and Ella Fitzgerald. In great demand as a session musician, he made countless record dates, on which he played with almost everyone who was anyone in the upper echelons of jazz. In 1957 he appeared in the television programme *The Sound Of Jazz*, on which he was responsible for several of the arrangements, including the classic performance of 'Dickie's Dream' that featured Basie, Roy Eldridge, Coleman Hawkins, Ben Webster, Joe Newman, Vic Dickenson and Gerry Mulligan among many others. In the late 50s he led a band that included Buck Clayton and that had the dubious honour of being the last band to play at Harlem's 'Home of Happy Feet', the Savoy Ballroom, before it closed forever. Also in the late 50s he worked with Pee Wee Russell, Quincy Jones, Fitzgerald, Hawkins and others. In 1960 he returned to Herman for a brief spell as road manager and was back again the following year, this time in his former capacities, remaining until 1966. In the early 70s Pierce relocated to the west coast where he played in several bands, including those led by Louie Bellson and Bill Berry.

In 1975 he joined Frank Capp as co-leader of a big band that mostly played his arrangements, many of which were in the Basie/Kansas City tradition. This band, which became known as Juggernaut, continued to play through the 80s and on into the 90s. Pierce also continued to write for other musicians and to appear on record dates. He toured extensively, appearing in the UK and Europe with several Basie-alumni bands and other concert packages. A superb pianist in his own right, Pierce's eclecticism was such that at various times he appeared at the piano as substitute for three of the best-known piano-playing bandleaders in big band history: Basie, Duke Ellington and Stan Kenton. In small groups he proved the lynchpin of the rhythm section, swinging with unflagging enthusiasm. As an arranger, especially for big bands, Pierce made an invaluable contribution to jazz, effortlessly creating swinging charts that underscored the 60s success stories of both Herman and Basie. Apart from his performing and arranging, Pierce was also a major source of information on many aspects of jazz history, a history that, through his personal dedication and extensive contributions, he helped to create.

● ALBUMS: *The Nat Pierce-Dick Collins Nonet* 10-inch album (Fantasy 1954)★★★, *Nat Pierce Bandstand* 10-inch album (Vanguard 1955)★★★, *Kansas City Memories* (Coral 1956)★★★, *The Nat Pierce Octet And Tentette* (Keynote 1957)★★★, *The Nat Pierce Big Band At The Savoy Ballroom* (RCA Victor 1957)★★★, with various artists *The Real Sound Of Jazz* television soundtrack (1957)★★★★, *The Ballad Of Jazz Street* (Hep 1961)★★★★, *Juggernaut* (Concord 1977)★★★★, *Juggernaut Live At Century Plaza* (Concord 1978)★★, with Mary Ann McCall *5400 North ... In Concert With Mary Ann McCall* (Hep 1978)★★★, *Juggernaut Strikes Again* (Concord 1981)★★★, *Boston Bustout* (Hep Jazz 1981)★★★, *Juggernaut Live At The Alleycat* (Concord 1986)★★★★.

PIIRPAUKE

A jazz/rock band from Finland that take tunes from anywhere in the world and adapt them to their own style. Arguably, they predated the whole world music movement, and, because of their locality, benefited little from it. Sakari Kukko (saxophone) still leads this excellent, but somewhat obscure, group.

● ALBUMS: *Algazara* (1987)★★★.

● COMPILATIONS: *Metamorphosis: Live 1977-1995* (RockAdillo 1996)★★★★.

PIKE, DAVE

b. 23 March 1938, Detroit, Michigan, USA. Pike started playing drums when he was eight and is self-taught on vibes, inspired by the playing of Lionel Hampton and Milt Jackson. He moved to Los Angeles in 1953 and played with musicians including Elmo Hope and the saxophonists Harold Land and Dexter Gordon. He played for two years with Paul Bley. In 1960 he moved to New York and started to experiment with ways of amplifying the vibraphone when he played with flautist Herbie Mann (1961-65). After playing at the 1968 Berlin Jazz Festival and recording with the Clarke-Boland Big Band he stayed on in Germany and formed the Dave Pike Set with local musicians. In the early 70s the Set twice toured South America for the Goethe Institute. Pike returned to California in 1973 and led a quartet at Hungry Joe's Club in Huntingdon Beach.

● ALBUMS: *Pike's Peak* (1962)★★★, with Herbie Mann *Live At Newport* (1963)★★★, *Noisy Silence, Gentle Noise* (1969)★★★, *The Four Reasons* (1969)★★★, *Infra Red* (1969)★★★, *Live At The Philharmonic* (1970)★★★, *Album* (1971)★★★, *Salamao* (1973)★★, *Times Out Of Mind* (1975)★★, *Let The Minstrels Play On* (1979)★★★, *Moa Bird* (1981)★★★, *Pike's Groove* (Criss Cross 1986)★★★, *Bluebird* (Timeless 1989)★★★, *Bophead* (Ubiquity Jazz 1998)★★★.

PINE, COURTNEY

b. 18 March 1964, London, England. Like many of his generation of young, black, UK jazz musicians, Pine came from a reggae and funk background. Pine is a dazzling performer on many instruments, notably saxophone, clarinet, flute and keyboards. He had been a member of Dwarf Steps, a hard-bop band consisting of Berklee College Of Music graduates, before joining reggae stars Clint Eastwood and General Saint. His interest in jazz was fostered when he participated in workshops run by John Stevens. In 1986 he deputized for Sonny Fortune in Elvin Jones's band, and was involved in setting up the Jazz Warriors. He came to wider public notice as a result of playing with Charlie Watts' Orchestra, George Russell's European touring band and with Art Blakey at the Camden Jazz Festival. Blakey invited him to join the Messengers, but he decided to stay in Britain. In 1987 he played at the Bath Festival with the Orchestre National de Jazz. By that time his reputation had spread far beyond jazz circles, and his first album was a massive seller by jazz standards. He appeared before a huge worldwide audience at the Nelson Mandela 70th Birthday Concert at Wembley, backing dancers IDJ, and was the main subject of a number of television arts programmes about jazz in the late 80s, his smart image and articulate seriousness about his music enabling him to communicate with many people who had never before given jazz a hearing. He became much in demand for film and television, and appeared, for example, on the soundtrack of Alan Parker's *Angel Heart* and over the titles of BBC Television's *Juke Box Jury*. His quartet was comprised of young American luminaries Kenny Kirkland (piano), Charnett Moffett (bass) and Marvin 'Smitty' Smith (drums). Many of his admirers feel that in some ways his high media profile has hindered his development, but his talent, dedication and level-headedness have ensured that he has never been diverted by the hype, and his most recent work illustrates an emotional depth matching his undoubted technical brilliance. He has also continued to play in reggae and other pop contexts (*Closer To Home*), and is a frequent collaborator with UK soul singer Mica Paris. *Modern Day Jazz Stories* showed a strong rap/hip-hop influence and featured a funky support trio of Ronnie Burrage (drums), Charnett Moffett (bass) and Geri Allen (piano). *Underground* delved further into hip-hop rhythms with support from DJs Sparky and Pogo.

● ALBUMS: *Journey To The Urge Within* (Island 1986)★★, *Destiny's Song And The Image Of Pursuance* (Island 1988)★★, *The Vision's Tale* (Island 1989)★★★, *Within The Realms Of Our Dreams* (Island 1991)★★★, *Closer To Home* (Island 1992)★★★, *To The Eyes Of Creation* (Island 1992)★★★★, *Modern Day Jazz Stories* (Antilles 1996)★★, *Underground* (Talkin' Loud 1997)★★★, *Another Story* (Talkin' Loud 1998)★★.

PINSKI ZOO

Like a more user-friendly Last Exit, the loud and joyful Pinski Zoo has combined the free jazz of the 60s, the funk-fusion beat of the 70s and the technology of the 80s to produce a powerful, accessible brand of harmolodics. Head-keeper Jan Kopinski claims Yma Sumac, Jimi Hendrix and John Coltrane as his seminal influences, though clearly Albert Ayler and Ornette Coleman's Prime Time have also been inspirations. The band, one of the most lively and exhilarating working units around, originated in Nottingham, like Kopinski and fellow-founder member Steve Iliffe. Earlier editions included Tim Bullock (drums), Tim Nolan (bass) and Mick Nolan (percussion, vocals), but by the early 90s the personnel comprised Kopinski (soprano and tenor saxophones), Iliffe (keyboards), Karl Wesley Bingham (electric bass) and Steve Harris (drums). The unit won the best small group title in the 1990 *Wire/Guardian* readers' poll, and their albums *Rare Breeds* and *East Rail* were highly acclaimed by UK jazz critics. Kopinski and Bingham are two of the most exciting and individual talents in contemporary jazz.

● ALBUMS: *Introduce Me To The Doctor* (1981)★★★★, *The Dizzy Dance Record* (1982)★★★, *The City Can't Have It Back* (1983)★★★, *Speak* (1984)★★★★, *Live In Warsaw* (1985)★★, *Rare Breeds* (JCR 1988)★★★, *East Rail East* (JCR 1990), *De-Icer* (Slam 1994)★★★.

PIRON, ARMAND

b. Armand John Piron, 16 August 1888, New Orleans, Louisiana, USA, d. 17 February 1943. As a child he was taught violin by his music teacher father. In turn-of-the-century New Orleans he played in various dance bands, including one led by his father, eventually becoming leader of the Olympia Orchestra. In taking this role, he replaced Freddie Keppard, the orchestra's founder. During this engagement, Piron formed an alliance with another band member, Clarence Williams. Their jointly owned publishing company was successful, many of their published songs being compositions of Piron's, including 'I Wish I Could Shimmy Like My Sister Kate' and 'The Purple Rose Of Cairo'. Later, Piron formed his own orchestra, which became very popular with dancers in New Orleans, especially among members of the city's high society. In the mid-20s Piron took his band to New York and late in the decade began leading bands on riverboats and in New Orleans.

PIZZARELLI, BUCKY

b. 9 January 1926, Paterson, New Jersey, USA. Although a self-taught guitarist, Pizzarelli quickly showed a comprehensive grasp of the guitar's potential. He played in large dance bands and small combos, worked as a studio musician, and as accompanist to singers, and even ventured into the classical field. He became a regular sideman with the later bands formed by Benny Goodman and in the 70s also appeared with Soprano Summit, the fine small band co-led by Bob Wilber and Kenny Davern, sometimes playing banjo. The 70s also saw him working with fellow guitarist George Barnes and with Zoot Sims, Bud Freeman and Stéphane Grappelli. He has also toured as a solo and in the 80s formed a duo with his son, John Pizzarelli, also a gifted guitarist, with whom he recorded the album *Swinging Sevens*. One of the finest of the mainstream guitarists in jazz, Pizzarelli remains rather less well known than many of his fellows, a state of affairs that seems likely to change in the 90s thanks to the continued high standard of his performances.

● ALBUMS: *Midnite Mood* (1960)★★★, *Green Guitar Blues* (1972)★★★, *Bucky Plays Bix: Bix Beiderbecke Arrangements By Bill Challis* (1973)★★★, *Soprano Summit II* (1977)★★★, with Zoot Sims *Zoot Sims With Bucky Pizzarelli* (Classic Jazz 1977)★★★, *Bucky's Bunch* (1977)★★★★, *2 x 7 = Pizzarelli* (1980)★★★★, *New York, New York/Sounds Of The Apple* (1980)★★★, *Love Songs* (1981)★★★★, *The Cafe Pierre Trio* (1982)★★★, with Red Norvo *Just Friends* (Stash 1983)★★★, with John Pizzarelli *I'm Hip* (1983)★★★, with John Pizzarelli *Swinging Sevens* (1984)★★★, with John Pizzarelli *Hit That Jive, Jack* (1985)★★★, *Solo Flight* (1986)★★★, *The Complete Guitar Duos (The Stash Sessions)* (Stash 1985)★★★★, with John Pizzarelli *My Blue Heaven* (1990)★★★, with John Burr, Sir Roland Hanna *3 For All* (Cymekob 1996)★★★, with John Pizzarelli 1986 recording *Live At The Vineyard* (Challenge 1997)★★★★, with Scott Hamilton *The Red Door: Scott Hamilton & Bucky Pizzarelli Remember Zoot Sims* (Concord Jazz 1998)★★★★.

PIZZARELLI, JOHN

b. John Paul Pizzarelli, 6 April 1960, Paterson, New Jersey, USA. One of four sons of jazz guitarist Bucky Pizzarelli, he took up the same instrument as his father and by his late teens they were regularly appearing together. During the 80s he worked extensively in the New York area, and at the end of the decade was established internationally. By the 90s Pizzarelli had begun singing regularly, and in some of his recordings was leaning heavily towards vocals, using the model of Nat 'King' Cole as his guide. In the late 90s, he led a trio in a Broadway show, *Dream*, a tribute to Johnny Mercer. His recordings often find him in good company with players such as his father, Stéphane Grappelli, Benny Green and Christian McBride. One of his brothers, Martin, regularly plays bass in his groups. A 1998 album found him working with a big band, playing charts by Don Sebesky. Not surprisingly, Pizzarelli credits his father with directing his guitar playing into jazz and the result is a combination of great technical skill and thorough understanding of the form. He plays with delicacy on ballads and crisp attack on up-tempo pieces. He solos inventively and is also a sound supportive player when accompanying other soloists. His singing broadened his musical horizons and increased his audience and, while entertaining, displays qualities that are somewhat less distinctive than are those of his instrumental work.

● ALBUMS: *My Blue Heaven* (Novus 1990)★★★, *All Of Me* (Novus 1991)★★★, *Naturally* (Novus 1993)★★★, *New Standards* (Novus 1994)★★★, *Dear Mr. Cole* (Novus 1994)★★★, *After Hours* (Chesky 1996)★★★★, with Bucky Pizzarelli *Live At The Vineyard* 1986 recording (Challenge 1997)★★★★, *One Night With You: The John Pizzarelli Collection* (Chesky 1997)★★★, *Our Love Is Here To Stay* (RCA 1998)★★★.

PLANET JAZZ

Tom Kubli (b. Heidelberg, Germany) employed the Planet Jazz sobriquet in the mid-90s to release ambient dance records that drew heavily on Herbie Hancock and Miles Davis. Previously Kubli had played keyboards and bass in a variety of musical conglomerations, including both punk and gospel groups. However, after discovering techno and house music he elected to work solo, establishing a studio in his own converted warehouse home in Frankfurt. Hosting parties from there gave him the impetus to start recording his own work as Planet Jazz. These releases included two singles for Sven Vath's acclaimed Harthouse Records, 'Monster' and 'Yellow Agents', as well as a project with Eden 123 credited to True Frequencies.

PLATER, BOBBY

b. Robert Plater, 13 May 1914, Newark, New Jersey, USA, d. 20 November 1982. Plater began playing alto saxophone while still a child and in his early teens was talented enough to work with several noted musicians, including Don Lambert. He became a full-time professional musician in the late 30s, working with Tiny Bradshaw and others. After military service during World War II, he returned to gigging but then joined Lionel Hampton in 1946 where he remained until 1964. With Hampton, Plater played lead alto and was also an important soloist. He also wrote arrangements for the band, showing a special aptitude for writing for singers, notably Sonny Parker. He had also taken the time to teach some basic principles to Dinah Washington during her first major professional engagement with Hampton. After leaving Hampton, Plater moved into the Count Basie band, becoming lead alto there, too, and musical director of the band. A highly skilled instrumentalist with a wide musical knowledge, Plater's sound was rich and creamy, suggesting an influence of Johnny Hodges but overlaid with a slightly acerbic touch that gave his solos added poignancy. He was co-composer of 'Jersey Bounce', a 40s hit.

● ALBUMS: with Lionel Hampton *Lionel Hampton And His Orchestra: Apollo Hall Concert* (Epic 1954)★★★★, with Count Basie *Basie Big Band* (Pablo 1975)★★★, with Basie *Farmer's Market Barbecue* (Pablo 1982)★★★.

PLAXICO, LONNIE

b. Lonnie Luvell Plaxico, 4 September 1960, Chicago, Illinois, USA. Plaxico studied the bass and in his early twenties was a highly accomplished player, finding work with notable jazzmen including Sonny Stitt and Chet Baker. At the start of the 80s he played in Wynton Marsalis's band, then joined Marsalis's former boss, Art Blakey, with whom he toured and made records, including 1985's Timeless Records set *Blue Night*. After this he worked in the band co-led by two other Blakey alumni, Terence Blanchard and Donald Harrison, and also played with Dizzy Gillespie and other leading performers. In 1998 he toured internationally with Ravi Coltrane. As his engagements suggest, Plaxico commands great respect among musicians. He is a skilled player with a strong sense of time allied to an urgent attack that can galvanize any rhythm section of which he is a member.

● ALBUMS: *Plaxico* (Muse 1990)★★★★, *Iridescence* (Muse 1991)★★★, *Short Takes* (Muse 1992)★★★, *With All Your Heart* (Muse 1993)★★★.

PLETCHER, STEW

b. 1907, d. 29 November 1978, USA. While he studied at Yale University, Pletcher was a trumpeter and vocalist with the Yale Collegians. In the early 30s he led his own bands and recorded with Ben Pollack (1934), but his swinging, melodic trumpet playing came to prominence in the time he spent in vibes player Red Norvo's band (1936-37). He continued to work professionally as a musician and later played with Jack Teagarden (in 1945 and 1955) and with Hilton 'Nappy' Lamare (in 1949).

POINDEXTER, PONY

b. Norwood Poindexter, 8 February 1926, New Orleans, Louisiana, USA, d. 14 April 1988. While still a youngster Poindexter learned to play several reed instruments including clarinet and alto saxophone, the instrument upon which he was later recognized as a strong and distinctive performer. He gained experience working in his home town and then in several bands including that led by Lionel Hampton. He also established a reputation for ably accompanying singers, including Billy

Eckstine, Jon Hendricks (appearing on his 1959 World Pacific session, *A Good Git-Together*), and Lambert, Hendricks And Ross, with whom he often played during the early 60s. He recorded *Pony's Express* on which he was joined by Eric Dolphy, Jimmy Heath, Pepper Adams, Sonny Red Kyner and Elvin Jones. Poindexter spent about 15 years in Europe, playing in many countries, including Spain where he worked with the young Norwegian guitarist and singer, Magni Wentzel, then at the start of her career. He also appeared with Lee Konitz's Alto Summit, rubbing shoulders with Phil Woods and Leo Wright, and playing on the 1968 Verve Records sessions for *Alto Summit*. After his return to the USA Poindexter began working as a singer, his saxophone playing career having been halted through illness. Throughout his performances, Poindexter displayed a wide appreciation of various aspects of the jazz form, in particular bop.

● ALBUMS: *Pony's Express* (Epic 1962)★★★, *Pony Poindexter Plays The Big Ones* (New Jazz 1962)★★★, *Gumbo!* (Prestige 1964)★★★.

POLCER, ED

b. 10 February 1937, Paterson, New Jersey, USA. Polcer first displayed his musical talents at the age of six when he played the xylophone. He began playing cornet semi-professionally while studying engineering at university. The band there, Princeton's very own Stan Rubin's Tigertown Five, had the distinction of playing both at Carnegie Hall and at the 1956 wedding of Prince Rainier and Grace Kelly in Monaco. In the 50s Polcer played in New York's clubland, returning there permanently after military service in the early 60s. Although gigging regularly at Jimmy Ryan's, the Metropole and other clubs, he remained a semi-pro, continuing his simultaneous business career. Throughout the 70s and into the mid-80s he was steadily more active in jazz, becoming a full-time musician in 1975 and taking on co-ownership of Eddie Condon's club. Apart from co-leading the house band (with Red Balaban, who was also co-owner of the club), he worked with a number of other bands, including recordings with Dick Wellstood and a spell in 1973 with Benny Goodman. In 1975 he toured the USA and Canada with Bob Greene's *World Of Jelly Roll Morton* show. In 1982 Polcer became president of the New York International Art of Jazz Organization, which promotes community and corporate involvement in jazz education and performance. Latterly, he has toured extensively, playing cornet and occasionally adding vibraphone too.

● ALBUMS: with Dick Wellstood, Jane Harvey *You Fats ... Me Jane* (1975)★★★, with Red Balaban *A Night At The New Eddie Condon's* (1975)★★★, *Coast To Coast Swingin' Jazz* (Jazzology 1990)★★★★, with Jim Galloway *At The Ball* (Jazzology 1998)★★★.

POLLACK, BEN

b. 22 June 1903, Chicago, Illinois, USA, d. 7 June 1971, Palm Springs, California, USA. After playing drums with the New Orleans Rhythm Kings in the early 20s, Pollack formed his own band, which he proceeded to stock with the best of the up-and-coming young white jazz and dance-band musicians of the day. Among the future stars who played in Pollack's bands in the late 20s were Benny Goodman, Glenn Miller and Jack Teagarden. Despite this interest in fostering emerging jazz talent, Pollack was primarily concerned with commercial success and this led to a number of disputes that often ended with one or another of the musicians quitting. By the mid-30s, Pollack had largely given up drumming to direct the band and concern himself with business affairs, the drum chair being taken over by Ray Bauduc. In his band at this time were Yank Lawson, Gil Rodin and Eddie Miller; when another argument broke out the bulk of the band left to form a co-operative unit, at the head of which they placed Bob Crosby. Pollack formed a new band, featuring another rising star, Harry James, who quit in 1936 to join another former Pollack sideman, Goodman, who was by now the country's most famous bandleader. The years of accumulated resentments propelled Pollack into suing everyone in sight: Goodman, Crosby, Victor Records, Goodman's sponsors, the Camel Cigarette Co., and a motion picture company. The exact reason for some of this litigation is obscure but was presumably directed at recovering some of the financial benefits that had accrued to his protégés. For a while Pollack stopped performing regularly, although he remained in the music business, spending the 40s running a record company and acting as an agent. He also ran a restaurant and occasionally returned to bandleading, achieving a modest success in all these activities. His depression over what he saw as his rightful heritage going to others never fully lifted, however, and he took his own life, hanging himself on 7 June 1971.

● COMPILATIONS: *Ben Pollack And His Orchestra (1933-34)* (1979)★★★★, *Futuristic Rhythm (1928-29)* (Saville 1983)★★★★.

POLLOCK, MARILYN MIDDLETON

b. 25 October 1947, Chicago, Illinois, USA. While still at college and university in Chicago, Pollock began singing with folk groups. In the late 60s she continued to sing folk locally and also performed with rock bands. In the early 70s her career encompassed radio and television commercials, tours of the USA with the rock bands Hurricane, Thunder and others, and continued activity as a folk-singer. In the early 80s Pollock visited Ireland, where she sang with the Chicago-based folk band the Irish Ramblers. She continued to mix folk and rock performances in her repertoire, then, in 1985, she relocated to Glasgow, Scotland. Her folk album, *Nobody Knows You*, won the British Music Retailers Association Award for Excellence in 1989. That same year she began singing jazz, appearing on *Yonder Come The Blues*. In 1990, she consolidated her acceptance as a jazz singer with an appearance at the Bude Festival and the following year joined the Max Collie band. Since then, although still active as a folk-singer, Pollock's career has moved increasingly towards jazz. She has recorded several albums and has appeared at numerous festivals including the Edinburgh International Festival and the Burnley Blues Festival, at both of which she performed her one-woman show, *Those Women Of The Vaudeville Blues*. In 1992, in addition to recording and touring clubs and festivals, both as a single and with Collie, she produced a new one-woman vaudeville blues show, *Jazz Me Blues*. A powerful and dynamic singer with great style and stage presence, Pollock's deep interest in and knowledge of the folk, blues and vaudeville traditions lend her repertoire considerable depth. Her vibrant voice, ranging through sensitivity to raunchiness, is well suited to the breadth and content of her repertoire and since her move to the UK she has established herself as a major contributor to the international jazz scene. In addition to singing, she has also taught herself to play several instruments including guitar and flute.

● ALBUMS: *Nobody Knows You* (Fellside 1988)★★★★, *Yonder Come The Blues* (1989)★★, *Those Women Of The Blues* (Lake 1990)★★★, *Max Collie's Mardi Gras Vol. 2* (1991)★★, *A Doll's House* (Fellside 1992)★★★, *With The Lake Records All-Star Jazzband* (Lake 1993)★★★.

POLO, DANNY

b. 22 December 1901, Toluca, Illinois, USA, d. 11 July 1949. After playing clarinet in bands in various parts of the Midwest, Polo joined Elmer Schoebel in Chicago in 1923. Throughout the 20s he was very active, playing in numerous bands in various parts of the USA and also visiting Europe, where he played in and sometimes led bands in Paris, Berlin and London. His European visit lasted from 1927 until 1935 and included a spell with Bert Ambrose. He then returned to the USA but made another visit to Paris and London before World War II. In the early 40s he worked with Jack Teagarden and Claude Thornhill, with whom he had first worked when both were still youngsters. Polo's recordings, whether with the likes of Coleman Hawkins and Benny Carter in New York or with Tommy McQuater in London, display a musicianly clarinettist with coolly understated gifts.

● COMPILATIONS: *Danny Polo And His Swing Stars* (1937-39 recordings)★★★.

POMEROY, HERB

b. 15 April 1930, Gloucester, Massachusetts, USA. After extensive studies at what later became known as the Berklee College Of Music in Boston, Massachusetts, Pomeroy joined the faculty to become one of the most respected teachers of the trumpet in jazz. His experience as a performer included work with the big bands of Lionel Hampton and Stan Kenton and, although he also played in small groups with Charlie Parker and others, it is in a big band context that he has made his greatest mark. Numerous contemporary jazz stars have graduated from Berklee, many of them paying tribute to Pomeroy's contribution to their musical education. His big bands, usually formed from college students and graduates, maintain an enviably high standard of musicianship. Unlike many of the college and university bands, Pomeroy's are not merely showcases for exceptional musical ability but also display an awareness of the underlying emotional qualities of jazz. The fact that his students demonstrate a greater involvement in the music they play is a tribute to his dedication to pursuing aims that transcend the simple imparting of knowledge. Pomeroy has also taught at the Massachusetts Institute of Technology, the Lenox School of Jazz and was, in 1962, employed by the US State Department to direct the house orchestra at Radio Malaya.

● ALBUMS: *Jazz In A Stable* (1955)★★★, *Life Is A Many Splendoured Gig* (Fresh Sounds 1957)★★, *Band In Boston* (United Artists 1958)★★★, *Herb Pomeroy And His Orchestra* (1958)★★★, *Pramlatta's Hips: Live At The El Morocco* (Shiah 1980)★★★.

PONCE, DANIEL

b. 21 July 1953, Havana, Cuba. Percussionist and bandleader Ponce - who first gained international recognition with his contributions to Herbie Hancock's *Future Shock* - received his early musical education from his grandfather, a renowned player of the bata drum. At the age of 11, he was playing cowbell with a group called Los Brilliantes in the Callo Weso district of Havana. During his mid-teens he moved over to conga drums, with Comparso Federacion Estuniantil Universitario. Ponce arrived in the USA, at Key West, Florida in 1980, and within a few months had settled in New York. Invited to sit in at the Village Gate with brothers Andy and Jerry Gonzalez, he met the Cuban saxophonist Paquito D'Rivera, for whom he guested on two albums. He also did sessions for Eddie Palmieri. Ponce's career really took off, however, when he met bass guitarist and avant-funk and jazz producer Bill Laswell in 1983, who secured him the *Future Shock* sessions and went on to involve him in a multiplicity of productions for the Celluloid and OAO labels. In 1984, Ponce released the self-produced *New York Now* - a *tour de force* through the roots of traditional Cuban percussion-based music, which also included contributions from D'Rivera and Laswell. He went on to lead two New York-based bands: New York Now and Jazzbata.

● ALBUMS: *New York Now* (1984)★★★★.

PONOMAREV, VALERY

b. 20 January 1943, Moscow, former USSR. After studying music in Moscow and achieving great proficiency on trumpet, he turned to jazz, playing with various groups of young musicians. Mostly playing hard bop, he appeared at clubs and festivals in the USSR until the mid-70s when he defected. Within a year or so he achieved worldwide fame as a member of Art Blakey's Jazz Messengers. He toured extensively with the band, playing in the Far East, South America and Europe, with appearances at many festivals including the 1978 Middlesborough Jazz Festival in the north of England. A sparkling player with great verve and enthusiasm, Ponomarev's talent was finely honed thanks to his sojourn with Blakey, and after leaving the Messengers he usually led his own groups, which included Universal Language.

● ALBUMS: *Means Of Identification* (Reservoir 1985)★★★, *Trip*

To Moscow (Reservoir 1985)★★★, *Profile* (Reservoir 1991)★★★★, *Live At Sweet Basil* (Reservoir 1994)★★★★, *Live At Vartan Jazz* (Vartan 1996)★★, *A Star For You* (Reservoir 1998)★★★.

Ponsford, Jan

b. 1954, England. As a child she somehow managed to sidestep Beatlemania and began singing along with records and the radio to music that was often instrumental rather than vocal. She would improvise lyrics or scat to anything from classics to rock. While attending the Reading Jazz And Blues Festival she heard George Melly with John Chilton's Feetwarmers. 'It sounded so happy and alive and acoustic in comparison to what else was going on.' Thus diverted, her interest in jazz proved to be just as eclectic as her other musical interests, turning from Melly to Archie Shepp with ease. She began listening to singers as diverse as Ella Fitzgerald and Helen Merrill and Joni Mitchell. She also listened to bands such as Count Basie's and folk groups like Pentangle. She began singing professionally with Big Chief, a jazz-rock fusion band which included Dick Heckstall-Smith in its ranks. Her listening tastes continued to be angled towards modern jazz, with particular favourites being Charlie Parker and Thelonious Monk, and singers including Stevie Wonder and Roberta Flack. The wide range of Ponsford's musical interests and her searching stylistic endeavours led inevitably to her forming her own group, Vocal Chords, which in the mid-90s had a line-up that bespeaks the very best in contemporary vocal talent: Norma Winstone, Ian Shaw, Winston Clifford, Liane Carroll, Jill Francis, Clare Foster and Anton Browne. Outspoken in her likes and dislikes, and positive in her career plans, Ponsford, who also teaches, is clearly a voice - singing and speaking - to listen out for in the future.

● ALBUMS: *Vocal Chords* (ASC 1995)★★★.

Ponty, Jean-Luc

b. 29 September 1940, Avranches, France. Ponty grew up in an intensely musical home environment. His father ran a local music school, teaching violin, and his mother taught piano. He was a proficient pianist and violinist while still very young and at the age of 11 he added clarinet to his instrumental arsenal. After studying classical violin at the Paris Conservatoire, he became a professional musician but also developed an interest in jazz. For a while he divided his musical loyalty between the classical violin and jazz clarinet and tenor saxophone. However, he began to play jazz on violin, making this his chief activity from the mid-60s. He played with numerous European musicians (recording with Stuff Smith), sometimes as leader (in HLP). He visited the USA and UK, recording with Frank Zappa on the jazz-rock album *Hot Rats* ('It Must Be A Camel') and thereafter joined George Duke. Zappa later produced Ponty's *King Kong* in 1970. In the early 70s he experimented with free jazz, played again with Zappa on *Overnite Sensation*, as a member of the Mothers, and with John McLaughlin's Mahavishnu Orchestra, *Visions Of The Emerald Beyond* (1974). Subsequently, he led his own band playing jazz-rock and gaining a substantial international following. In the 80s he also recorded with other artists including Cleo Laine and Stéphane Grappelli. A master technician, Ponty was not the first violinist in jazz to use electronic enhancement but he was the first to integrate electronics fully into his playing style. Rather than settle merely for the greater volume, which had been enough for his predecessors, Ponty used electronics in a complex and advanced way. He uses a fully electric violin, not just an electronically amplified instrument, and incorporates numerous devices to create effects. By switching from bop to rock to free jazz and back to bop again with ease, he continues to prove himself a musician of many styles and for all seasons of jazz fashion. In 1995 he formed Rite Of Strings with bassist Stanley Clarke and guitarist Al Di Meola.

● ALBUMS: with Stuff Smith *Violin Summit* (1966)★★★, *Sunday Walk* (1967)★★★, *Electric Connection* (1968)★★★, with George Duke *The Jean-Luc Experience* (1969)★★★★, *King Kong* aka *Cantaloupe Island* (Blue Note 1970)★★★, *Astrorama* (1970)★★★, *Open Strings* (1972)★★★, *Live In Montreux* (1972)★★★, *Portrait* (1972)★★★, *Upon The Wings Of Music* (1975)★★, *Aurora* (Atlantic 1975)★★★★, *Imaginary Voyage* (Atlantic 1976)★★, *Enigmatic Ocean* (Atlantic 1977)★★, *Cosmic Messenger* (Atlantic 1978)★★★, *A Taste For Passion* (1979)★★★, *Jean-Luc Ponty Live* (1979)★★★, *Sonata Erotica* (Atmosphere 1979)★★, *Civilized Evil* (1980)★★, *Mystical Adventures* (Atlantic 1981), *Individual Choice* (Atlantic 1983)★★, with George Benson, Chick Corea *Open Mind* (Atlantic 1984)★★, *Fables* (Atlantic 1985)★★, *The Gift Of Time* (Columbia 1987)★★★, *No Absolute Time* (Fnac 1993)★★★, with Stanley Clarke, Al Di Meola *The Rite Of Strings* (IRS 1995)★★★, *Live At Chene Park* (Atlantic 1997)★★.

● COMPILATIONS: *Le Voyage* 2-CD set 1975-85 (Rhino 1996)★★★★.

● FURTHER READING: *The Musical Styles Of Jean-Luc Ponty*, Jean-Luc Ponty.

Pop Mechanics

(see Kuryokhin, Sergey)

Porcino, Al

b. 14 May 1925, New York City, New York, USA. While still in his teenage years, Porcino joined the Louis Prima band where his high-note trumpet playing attracted excited attention. In the 40s he played in many of the leading big bands of the day, including those led by Tommy Dorsey, Gene Krupa, Stan Kenton and Woody Herman. In the 50s he again worked with Kenton and Herman among others such as Charlie Parker, Count Basie and Elliot Lawrence before settling in Los Angeles, where he did studio work and also made regular appearances in jazz groups, usually big bands, including Terry Gibbs' 'dream bands'. He made many record dates with singers including Frank Sinatra, Sarah Vaughan, Ella Fitzgerald, Judy Garland and Ray Charles. He was co-leader with Med Flory of the Jazz Wave Orchestra. In the 60s he continued to play in big bands, adding Buddy Rich and the Thad Jones-Mel Lewis Jazz Orchestra to his list of credits. He rejoined Herman again and also formed his own band, with which he accompanied Mel Tormé. His career continued along similar lines in the 70s and then, in 1977, he settled in Munich, Germany, where he worked with radio bands and led his own big band. During the 80s he made many concert appearances with his big band, some of which were recorded, often in company with visiting American jazzmen such as Al Cohn. One of the outstanding lead trumpeters in big band history, Porcino set remarkably high standards of performance for himself and for his section mates and any band in which he played was assured of a first-rate trumpet section. His German band of the late 80s clearly benefits from his remarkable leadership.

● ALBUMS: with Stan Kenton *Contemporary Concepts* (1955)★★★, with Med Flory *The Jazz Wave Orchestra* (1957)★★★, with Terry Gibbs *Dream Band* (1959)★★★, with Gibbs *Live At The Summit* (1961)★★★, with Buddy Rich *Mercy, Mercy* (1968)★★★★, with Jones-Lewis *Consummation* (1969)★★★, with Woody Herman *The Raven Speaks* (1972)★★★, with Mel Tormé *Live At The Maisonette* (1974)★★★★, with Jones-Lewis *New Life* (1975)★★★, with Jones-Lewis *Live In Munich* (1976)★★, with Al Cohn *In Oblivion* (Jazz Mark 1986)★★★, with Cohn *The Final Performance* (Red Baron 1987)★★★.

PORTAL, MICHEL

b. 27 November 1935, Bayonne, France. Portal was as comfortable playing a Mozart clarinet concerto as he was performing a Stockhausen intuitive piece, or scoring a film on bandoneon as playing free jazz on various reeds - Portal has always surprised. Francois Tusques, Sunny Murray, Joachim Kuhn and John Surman are just some of the artists who have made use of his talents in a jazz context. Although accused by some of being over-clinical as a soloist, he has produced a number of remarkable recordings with editions of his ever-changing unit. Many leading French and Swiss players have passed through the ranks, while his *Men's Land* from 1987 includes Jack DeJohnette and Dave Liebman.

● ALBUMS: *No, No, But It May Be* (1974)★★★, *Men's Land* (1987)★★★.

PORTER, ART

b. 1961, Little Rock, Arkansas, USA, d. 23 November 1996, Sai Yok, Kanchanburi, Thailand. Jazz saxophonist Art Porter grew up in a musical family. His father, Art Porter Snr., played in his own band and that of John Stubblefield, and also accompanied singer Carmen McRae in a long career as a professional pianist. At the age of 15 Porter Jnr. joined his father's band in Little Rock, but he was arrested and charged for working under-age in a nightclub. However, state attorney general and fellow saxophonist Bill Clinton intervened on his behalf. Clinton launched a new state law that allowed under-age musicians to perform in adult venues as long as they were accompanied by a legal guardian. That act became widely known as the 'Art Porter Bill'. Porter subsequently studied at the Berklee College Of Music, and the Virginia Commonwealth University. He studied piano with Ellis Marsalis and, after moving to Chicago in the mid-80s, tenor saxophone with Von Freeman. He also worked professionally in groups such as the Pharaoh Sanders and Jack McDuff bands. Although his principal influence remained Charlie Parker, he eschewed the more radical routes pioneered by other neo-classicist bebop devotees, always preferring to adopt the role of jazz popularizer. During the 90s he developed an interest in the rhythms of R&B and, to a lesser extent, hip-hop, incorporating these elements into his shows. He was scheduled to appear at the 1996 Thailand International Jazz Festival when he was drowned in a local reservoir when his boat overturned.

● ALBUMS: *Pocket City* (Verve Forecast 1991)★★★, *Straight To The Point* (Verve Forecast 1993)★★★★, *Undercover* (Verve Forecast 1994)★★★, *Lay Your Hands On Me* (Verve Forecast 1996)★★, *For Art's Sake* (Verve Forecast 1998)★★★.

PORTER, GENE

b. Eugene Porter, 7 June 1910, Pocahontas, Mississippi, USA. Raised in a musical family atmosphere, he tried brass instruments before settling, mainly, on reed instruments. From his late teens he lived in Chicago for a few years, working with various bands, some of which toured into the 'deep south'. After a spell in Jackson, Mississippi, close to his birthplace, he moved to New Orleans, playing there with bands led by Oscar 'Papa' Celestin and Joseph Robichaux. By this time, Porter was playing mostly alto saxophone and clarinet, having taken lessons on the latter instrument from Omer Simeon. In the 30s he played with various bands including the Jeter-Pillars Orchestra and that led by Don Redman, with whom he also played tenor. In the early 40s he was with Jimmie Lunceford, then worked with Benny Carter in Hollywood, working on, and also in, several motion pictures. In the mid-40s he accompanied a varied selection of jazz artists, including Dinah Washington and Charles Mingus, before joining Walter Fuller's band where he remained for more than a decade. In the 60s Porter led his own bands, playing most of the reed instruments, flute and percussion instruments, and also singing.

● COMPILATIONS: *Don Redman* (CBS 1932-37)★★★.

PORTER, ROY

b. 30 July 1923, Walsenburg, Colorado, USA, d. 25 January 1998. Porter began playing drums in his youth and was briefly a member of the territory band led by Milt Larkin. Later, settled in Los Angeles, he played with several small bands, including that led by Howard McGhee. By the late 40s, Porter was embracing bop and he was called upon to record with Charlie 'Bird' Parker on the famous sessions for Dial Records. He continued his association with leading bop musicians, including Teddy Edwards and Dexter Gordon. At the end of the 40s he led his own short-lived big band which included

Eric Dolphy, Art Farmer, Jimmy Knepper and Joe Maini. In the 50s he played mostly on the west coast, in clubs and on record dates, then drifted into a long spell as a session musician. His career was affected by personal problems but in the 70s he was active again in jazz, leading his own band for club and record dates. However, by the end of the decade ill health had driven him out of music. His autobiography is *There And Back*.

● COMPILATIONS: Roy Porter Big Band and others *Black California* 1949 recordings (Savoy 1970)★★★.

● FURTHER READING: *There And Back*, Roy Porter.

PORTER, YANK

b. Allen Porter, *c*.1895, Norfolk, Virginia, USA, d. 22 March 1944. Porter played drums in touring bands with tent shows and the like until he was aged about 30. He then moved to New York where, through the late 20s and early 30s, he played in groups led by musicians such as Cliff Jackson, Louis Armstrong and James P. Johnson. In the middle of the decade he became more widely known thanks to his association with Fats Waller, during which time he played on many recording sessions. In the early 40s he played with a number of musicians for both club and record dates, among them Teddy Wilson, Benny Carter, Joe Sullivan and Art Tatum. Briefly, he led a band of his own but died in his prime. Although Porter's early playing style was robust, he gradually adopted a subtly flowing style which was much favoured by his employers, perhaps accounting for the large percentage of pianists for whom he worked.

PORTRAIT OF SHEILA - SHEILA JORDAN

One of a (perhaps disappointingly small) number of jazz vocalists to break out of the cabaret ghetto and make a real contribution to jazz and the vocalist's art, Sheila Jordan was influenced as much by instrumentalists, and Charlie Parker in particular, as by vocalists. Her sparse, understated style and empathy for the musicians who work with her have resulted in collaborations with some of the most original and striking contemporary jazz players around. *Portrait Of Sheila* features guitarist Barry Galbraith, bassist Steve Swallow and drummer Denzil Best, in 1962 making subtle, interesting music.

● Tracks: *Falling In Love With Love; If You Could See Me Now; Am I Blue?; Dat Dere; When The World Was Young; Let's Face The Music And Dance; Laugh Clown Laugh; Who Can I Turn To Now; Baltimore Oricle; I'm A Fool To Want You; Hum Drum Blues; Willow Weep For Me.*

● First released 1962

● UK peak chart position: did not chart

● USA peak chart position: did not chart

POTTER, CHRIS

b. 1 January 1971, Chicago, Illinois, USA. A highly-gifted and forward looking player, Potter was raised in Columbia, South Carolina where he played piano before taking up both the tenor and alto saxophone. He began playing the local clubs when he was only 13, before moving to New York in 1989. Potter spent four years playing saxophone, and occasional piano, in Red Rodney's quintet, and graduated from the Manhattan School of Music in 1993. During his time with Rodney Potter played in a heavily bebop-influenced style, but following the trumpeter's death in 1994 he has expanded his musical horizons, demonstrating a refreshing sense of adventure in his exploration of harmony and odd melodic structures on several sessions as a leader. Potter has also recorded with the Mingus Big Band, Marian McPartland, Paul Motian, John Patitucci and Steely Dan, and as part of The Jazz Mentality alongside pianist Steve Elmer, bassist Ralph Hamperian and drummer Myles Weinstein.

● ALBUMS: *Presenting Chris Potter* (Criss Cross 1993)★★★★, *Concentric Circles* (Concord Jazz 1994)★★★★, *Pure* (Concord Jazz 1994)★★★, with The Jazz Mentality *Show Business Is My Life* (Koch 1995)★★★, *Sundiatta* (Criss Cross 1996)★★★, with Kenny Werner *Chris Potter/Kenny Werner* (Concord Jazz 1996)★★★, *Moving In* (Concord Jazz 1996)★★★★, *Unspoken* (Concord Jazz 1997)★★★★, *Vertigo* (Concord Jazz 1998)★★★★.

POTTER, TOMMY

b. 21 September 1918, Philadelphia, Pennsylvania, USA, d. March 1988. After taking up the bass in his early 20s, having previously mastered piano and guitar, Potter was soon involved in early bebop. He played in the bebop-orientated big band led by Billy Eckstine in the mid-40s, then joined Charlie Parker. He recorded with Parker and many other leading bebop musicians, including Fats Navarro, Max Roach and Bud Powell. In the 50s and early 60s he worked with a broader range of musicians, such as Stan Getz, Sonny Rollins, Miles Davis, Artie Shaw and Harry Edison, before retiring from full-time playing in the mid-60s. One of the leading bass players of bebop, Potter set a high standard of performance with clearly articulated lines and impeccable timekeeping.

● ALBUMS: *The Sonny Rollins Quartet* (1954)★★★, *The Tommy Potter Sextet In Sweden* (1956)★★★★.

● COMPILATIONS: with Charlie Parker *The Legendary Dial Masters, Volume 4 (1946-47)* (1983)★★★★, with Parker *The Complete Savoy Sessions, Volume 3 (1947)* (1985)★★★★.

POURCEL, FRANCK

With the violin his chosen instrument, Pourcel found playing in downtime jazz combos a liberating change from his studies at the Paris Conservatoire. He became an admirer of Stéphane Grappelli whose mainstream style he emulated before assuming leadership of the French Fiddlers in the late 40s. Signed to Pathe-Marconi, the orchestra adjusted to the popular forum and was rewarded with encouraging sales for 1952's 'Blue Tango'. Seven years later, a novel instrumental version of the Platters' 'Only You' - attributed to Franck Pourcel And His Rockin' Strings - represented the commercial peak of Pourcel's career as it scaled the US Top 10. It also anticipated the early 60s 'Stringbeat' that proved beneficial to John Barry and Adam Faith. Collectively, the Fiddlers - under whatever name they called themselves - had sold 15 million records by the early 70s with comparatively few chart placings. In Britain, for example, only *This Is Pourcel* registered in the album list. Nevertheless, its perpetrator continued to cut a suave, dapper figure at international award ceremonies when nominated for his lush film scores and easy-listening arrangements.

● ALBUMS: *Latino Americano* (1966)★★★, *Magnifique* (1966)★★★, *The Sound Of Magic* (1967)★★★, *Pourcel Today* (1968)★★★, *The Franck Pourcel Sound* (1968)★★★, *The Importance Of Your Love* (1968)★★★, *Rhapsody In Blue* (1968)★★★, *The Versatile Franck Pourcel* (1969)★★, *Dancing In The Sun* (Studio 2 1970)★★★, *Impressions* (1970)★★★, with the Paris Concert Orchestra *The World's Favourite Classics* (1970)★★, *This Is Pourcel* (1971)★★★, *Franck Pourcel Meets The Beatles* (1972)★, *Western* (1973)★★★, *And Now ... Pourcel* (Studio 2 1974)★★★, *Franck Pourcel Plays Abba* (1979)★★, *Classical Favourites In Digital* (1980)★★★, with the London Symphony Orchestra *A Digital Experience* (1981)★★★, *New Sound Tangos* (1983)★★★, *Nostalgia Mood* (1984)★★★, *Les Hits Classiques* (1986)★★★.

● COMPILATIONS: *The Very Best Of Franck Pourcel* (1976)★★★★.

POWELL, BUD

b. Earl Powell, 27 September 1924, New York City, New York, USA, d. 1 August 1966. After learning to play the piano in the classical tradition while still a child, Powell began working around New York's Coney Island, where he played in a band featuring Valaida Snow around 1940. During the next couple of years he became a regular visitor to Minton's Playhouse, where he heard the first stirrings of bebop. In particular, he was influenced by Thelonious Monk's harmonic innovations but quickly developed his own style. Despite his leanings towards the new music, he was hired by Cootie Williams for his big band. During his stay with Williams he was arrested in Philadelphia and reportedly badly beaten by police officers, an event usually cited as the beginning of the mental problems that were to dog him for the rest of his life. He retained his links with events on 52nd Street and was soon one of the most striking of the bebop pianists. By 1945, however, he was displaying the first overt signs of acute mental instability and was hospitalized - the first of many incarcerations in mental hospitals, during some of which he was given electro-convulsive therapy.

Throughout the 50s he worked regularly, appearing with all the leading figures of bebop, including Charlie Parker, Dizzy Gillespie and Max Roach. During this same period his mental instability increased, the sudden death in 1956 of his brother Richie Powell adding to his problems. Additionally, his mental and physical health were being gravely damaged by his growing dependence on narcotics and alcohol. At the end of the decade he left New York for Paris, where he spent three years of popular success but was still plagued by his mental and addiction troubles. Back in New York in 1964, his performances became fewer and were frequently fraught with emotional and technical breakdowns. He died on 1 August 1966. At his performing peak, Powell's playing style displayed a startling brilliance, with remarkable ideas being executed with absolute technical mastery, often at extraordinary speeds. By the late 50s his personal problems were such that he rarely played at his best, although the flow of ideas continued, as can be deduced from some of his compositions from these years. He was a major figure in bebop and an influence, both directly and indirectly, upon most pianists in jazz since the 50s.

● ALBUMS: *Bud Powell Trio* (Roost 1950)★★★, *Bud Powell Piano* (Mercury 1950)★★★, with Charlie Parker *One Night In Birdland* (1950)★★★, *Piano Solos* (Mercury 1951)★★★★, *Piano Solos Volume 2* (Mercury 1952)★★★, with Parker *Jazz At Massey Hall: The Quintet Of The Year* (1953)★★★★, *Broadcast Performances Volumes 1 & 2* (1953)★★★, *Inner Fires* (1953)★★★, *Bud Powells Moods* (Mercury 1953)★★★, *The Bud Powell Trio: The Verve Sessions* (1955)★★★★, *Jazz Original* (Norgran 1955)★★★, *Bouncing With Bud* (Storyville 1955)★★★, *The Lonely One* (Verve 1956)★★★, *Blues In The Closet* (Verve 1956)★★★, *Strictly Powell* (1956)★★★, *Swinging With Bud* (1957)★★★, *The Bud* (Blue Note 1957)★★★★, *The Time Waits* (Blue Note 1959)★★★, *Bud Powell In Paris* i (1960)★★★, *Bud Powell In Concert* (1960)★★★, *Oscar Pettiford Memorial* (1960)★★★, *Bud Powell In Europe* (1961)★★★, *A Portrait Of Thelonious* (CBS 1961)★★★, *The Genius Of Bud Powell* (Verve 1961)★★★★, *Jazz Giant* (Verve 1961)★★★, *Moods* (Verve 1961)★★★, *The Bud Powell Trio At The Golden Circle Volumes 1 & 2* (1962)★★★★, *The Bud Powell Trio In Copenhagen* (1962)★★★, *Bud Powell '62* (1962)★★★, *Bud Powell In Paris* ii (1963)★★★, *Blues For Bouffemont/The Invisible Cage* (1964)★★★, *The Bud Powell Quartet* (1964)★★★, *The Bud Powell Trio* (1964)★★★, *Salt Peanuts* (Black Lion 1964)★★★, *Ups 'N' Downs* (1965)★★★, *The Return Of Bud Powell* (1965)★★★, *At The Blue Note Cafe, 1961* (1981)★★★★, *The Complete Essen Jazz Festival Concert* 1960 recording (1988)★★★.

● COMPILATIONS: *The Genius Of Bud Powell* 1950-51 recordings (Verve 1978)★★★★, *The Best Years* (1978)★★★★, *The Amazing Bud Powell, Volumes 1 & 2 (1949-53)* (Blue Note 1982)★★★★, *The Amazing Bud Powell, Volume 3 (1949-53)* (Blue Note 1984)★★★★, *Jazz Profile* (Blue Note 1997)★★★★, *Ultimate Bud Powell* (Verve 1998)★★★★.

● FURTHER READING: *The Glass Enclosure: The Life Of Bud Powell*, Alan Groves with Alyn Shipton. *Bud Powell*, Clifford Jay Safane (ed.). *Dance Of The Infidels: A Portrait Of Bud Powell*, Francis Paudras.

POWELL, JESSE

b. 27 February 1924, Fort Worth, Texas, USA. Powell studied music at Hampton University, where he became inspired by Count Basie's Lester Young and Herschel Evans, and played his tenor saxophone with the bands of Oran 'Hot Lips' Page (1942-43), Louis Armstrong (1943-44), and Luis Russell (1944-45). In 1946 he accepted an offer from Count Basie to replace Illinois Jacquet in the reed section. After briefly leading his own band in 1948 and being featured at that year's Paris Jazz Festival, he joined Dizzy Gillespie's Orchestra

(1949-50), but the R&B era found him with copious session work and, again, his own unit, which recorded for Federal (the infamous 'Walkin' Blues' sung by Fluffy Hunter) and Jubilee.

POWELL, MEL

b. Melvin Epstein, 12 February 1923, New York City, New York, USA, d. 24 April 1998, Los Angeles, California, USA. As a teenager Powell played piano at Nick's in New York City and soon thereafter joined Muggsy Spanier. His exceptional and at the time eclectic gifts attracted the attention of Benny Goodman, whom he joined in 1941. During his stint with Goodman he wrote several interesting charts, sometimes for his own compositions, which included 'The Earl', 'Clarinet A La King' and 'Mission To Moscow'. Powell was then briefly on the staff at CBS Records before military service threatened to disrupt his career. In fact, his army service had the opposite effect and he was soon a member of Glenn Miller's Army Air Force band, playing in the dance band and in the small jazz group, the Uptown Hall Gang. After the war Powell made a few jazz records in Los Angeles, then in the early 50s recorded again with Ruby Braff and Paul Quinichette; he also appeared with Goodman around this same time, but that was the last the jazz world heard of him until the mid-80s. Powell had turned to classical music and studied with Paul Hindemith and eventually took over his place as professor of composition at Yale, and later became head of the California Institute of the Arts. During this same period Powell's health deteriorated and his movements were severely limited. However, his playing ability was unimpaired and his return to the jazz scene, with appearances on the Caribbean jazz cruise ship, the *SS Norway*, and new recordings, showed that he had lost none of his skill in performing inventive solos. In 1990 Powell was awarded a Pulitzer Prize for *Duplicates*, a concerto for two pianos and orchestra. He died of liver cancer in 1998.

● ALBUMS: *The Mel Powell Septet* 10-inch album (Vanguard 1953)★★★, *Bandstand* 10-inch album (Vanguard 1954)★★★, *Borderline* (Vanguard 1954)★★★, *Thigamagig* (Vanguard 1954)★★★★, *Out On A Limb* (Vanguard 1955)★★★, *Easy Swing* (Vanguard 1955)★★★★, *Classics In Jazz* (Capitol 1955)★★★, *Bouquet* (Vogue 1980)★★★, *Piano Forte* (1986)★★★, *The Return Of Mel Powell* (Chiaroscuro 1989)★★★, *Unavailable Mel Powell* 1947 recordings (Pausa)★★★.

POWELL, RICHIE

b. 5 September 1931, New York City, New York, USA, d. 26 June 1956. After studying at college and with Mary Lou Williams, Powell emulated his older brother, Bud Powell, and embarked on a career in jazz. He played with Jackie McLean, a friend and neighbour, then joined Johnny Hodges. Attracted to bebop, Powell became a member of the Max Roach-Clifford Brown quintet in 1954. This engagement was an opportunity to begin a potentially interesting development, but before Richie Powell attained his full musical maturity he was killed in a road accident, with Brown, in 1956.

● ALBUMS: *Clifford Brown With Max Roach* (1955)★★, with Clifford Brown, Max Roach *Study In Brown* (1955)★★★, *Sonny Rollins Plus Four* (1956)★★★.

● COMPILATIONS: *More Of Johnny Hodges* (1951-54)★★★.

POWELL, RUDY

b. Everard Stephen Powell, 28 October 1907, New York City, New York, USA, d. 30 October 1976. Born and raised in a tough district of New York, Powell was one of a number of young men from the same neighbourhood who turned to music and enjoyed distinguished careers (among others was Benny Carter). Taking up clarinet and alto saxophone, Powell worked extensively in the vibrant New York club scene of the late 20s and early 30s including stints with Cliff Jackson, Rex Stewart, Red Allen and, most notably, Fats Waller. In the late 30s and early 40s, Powell's skilful musicianship meant that he was in demand as a sideman in several big bands, including those led by Claude Hopkins, Fletcher Henderson and Don Redman. In the late 40s he was with Cab Calloway and in the 50s and 60s he worked with several small groups and also with singers Jimmy Rushing and Ray Charles. In the mid-60s he played with the Saints And Sinners band and then played around his home-town until the end of his life. An exciting, hot clarinet player, Powell's playing made a distinctive contribution to many Waller recordings.

● ALBUMS: *Saints And Sinners In Europe* (1968)★★.

POWELL, SELDON

b. 15 November 1928, Lawrenceville, Virginia, USA, d. 25 January 1997. Studying and working mostly in New York, tenor saxophonist Powell played and recorded extensively throughout the 50s. His musical associates were many and varied, including Lucky Millinder, Sy Oliver, Neal Hefti, Johnny Richards, Billy VerPlanck and Benny Goodman. Aided by his early training in classical music and his ability to play other instruments, especially the flute, Powell found work in the studios throughout the 60s and 70s. Nevertheless, he was active in jazz, recording with musicians such as Buddy Rich, Louie Bellson, Richard 'Groove' Holmes, Gato Barbieri, Dizzy Gillespie and Anthony Braxton. Powell's early training had allowed him to develop twin careers but within the framework of largely mainstream jazz he established a sound reputation. As an improvisatory soloist, his work was perhaps less impressive than when he worked within a tightly orchestrated framework where he excelled.

● ALBUMS: *Seldon Powell Plays* (1955)★★★, *Seldon Powell Sextet* (1956)★★★, with Billy VerPlanck *Jazz For Play Girls* (1957)★★, with others *We Paid Our Dues* (1961)★★★.

POWELL, TEDDY

b. 1 March 1906, Oakland, California, USA. As a boy Powell studied violin and music theory privately, then attended the San Francisco Conservatory of Music. In 1927 he was playing guitar and banjo with Abe Lyman's band, staying with them until 1935 when he became a radio producer for an advertising agency. He also branched out as a songwriter, with hits such as 'Take Me Back To My Boots And Saddle', 'All I Need Is You', 'Snake Charmer' and 'March Winds And April Showers'. Royalties from these and other songs helped to finance a big band in 1939, which included some key personnel from the Tommy Dorsey and Benny Goodman bands and had Ray Conniff contributing some arrangements. At first recording for Decca, some of the band's tracks appeared in the UK on Brunswick (Conniff's 'Feather Merchant's Ball'/'Teddy Bear Boogie' by Powell). After a year Powell moved to the Bluebird label, and Regal-Zonophone issued only four tracks in the UK: 'Straight Eight Boogie'/'Ode To Spring' and 'Sans Culottes'/'In Pinetops' Footsteps', all the work of new arranger Bob Mersey. The band opened at New York's Famous Door club to local acclaim but had less success further afield and, returning to Manhattan, Powell bought the club as a showcase for the group. It was a good, clean-sounding outfit with imaginative scores by Mersey and Conniff, and the leader maintained his policy of using jazzmen in key positions no matter how commercial the band's output. Peggy Mann and Gene Barry were the band's vocalists. After the swing era Powell adopted a more commercial policy for hotel work and eventually left the band business to return to songwriting and publishing.

POWERS, OLLIE

b. Oliver Powell, *c.*1890, Louisville, Kentucky, USA, d. 14 April 1928. Powers played drums and sang with various small groups, favouring working in duos, as with pianist-composer Shelton Brooks and novelty singer May Alix. In Chicago in the early 20s, where he had lived and worked since about 1914, he played with artists such as these and also in bands led by, among others, Jimmie Noone, with whom he played for the last year and a half of his life. According to John Chilton, his early death was a result of diabetes and mellitus.

● COMPILATIONS: *The Chronological Jimmie Noone 1923-1928* (Classics 1923-28)★★★★.

POZO, CHANO

b. Luciano Pozo y Gonzales, 7 June 1915, Havana, Cuba, d. 2 December 1948, New York, USA. Drummer and vocalist Pozo's first appearance in the USA was at a Carnegie Hall concert in September 1947, at which he played with Dizzy Gillespie. Thereafter he worked regularly with Gillespie, making a number of records that were enormously influential on many jazzmen who responded to the intriguing Latin-American rhythms he used. In December 1948, before the two men could fully exploit what was clearly a potentially exciting musical relationship, Pozo was murdered, shot in a Harlem bar.

● COMPILATIONS: all with Dizzy Gillespie *Dizzy Gillespie Big Band* (1947-49 recordings)★★★, *Afro Cuban Suite* (1948 recordings)★★★, *Melodic Revolution* (1948 recordings)★★★, with Arsenio Rodriguez, Machito *Legendary Sessions* (Fresh Sounds 1993)★★★.

PREVIN, ANDRÉ

b. 6 April 1929, Berlin, Germany. After studying music in Berlin and Paris, Previn moved to the USA in 1938 when his family emigrated. Resident in Los Angeles, he continued his studies and while still at school worked as a jazz pianist and as an arranger in the film studios. From the mid-40s he made records with some measure of success, but it was in the middle of the following decade that he achieved his greatest renown. The breakthrough came with a series of jazz albums with Shelly Manne, the first of which featured music from the popular show *My Fair Lady*. Previn recorded with lyricist Dory Langdon, whom he later married. The marriage broke up in 1965 and was controversially chronicled in Dory Previn's later solo recordings. In the 60s Previn continued to divide his time between jazz and studio work but gradually his interest in classical music overtook these other fields. By the 70s he was established as one of the world's leading classical conductors. His term as conductor for the London Symphony Orchestra saw him emerge as a popular personality, which involved him television advertising and making celebrated cameo appearances for light-entertainers such as Morecambe And Wise. He became conductor of the Pittsburg Symphony Orchestra in 1976 and later the London Philharmonic and the Los Angeles Philharmonica. He continues to involve himself in many facets of music throughout the 80s and into the 90s - one of his most recent projects, in 1992, was a jazz album with opera singer Dame Kiri Te Kanawa and jazz bass player Ray Brown. In 1993, Previn took up his appointment as conductor-laureate of the London Symphony Orchestra, while the stage musical *Rough Crossing*, for which he has written the music to playwright Tom Stoppard's book and lyrics, had its US regional premiere. In 1995, Previn toured the UK with his jazz trio, and a year later he was awarded an honorary knighthood by the Queen for his 'outstanding contribution to Anglo-American cultural relations and the musical life of Britain'.

● ALBUMS: *All Star Jazz* (Monarch 1952)★★★, *André Previn Plays Duke* (Monarch 1952)★★★, *André Previn Plays Harry Warren* (RCA Victor 1952)★★★, *André Previn Plays Fats Waller* (1953)★★★, *Gershwin* (RCA Victor 1955)★★★, *Let's Get Away From It All* (Decca 1955)★★★, *But Beautiful* (1956)★★★, with Shelly Manne *My Fair Lady* i (1956)★★★, *André Previn And His Friends: Li'l Abner* (1957)★★★, *André And Dory Previn* (1957)★★★, with Russ Freeman *Double Play!* (Contemporary 1957)★★★, *Hollywood At Midnight* (Decca 1957)★★★, *Pal Joey* (Contemporary 1957)★★★★, *Gigi* (Contemporary 1958)★★★, *Sessions, Live* (1958)★★★, *André Previn Plays Songs By Vernon Duke* (Contemporary 1958)★★★, *Jazz King Size* (Contemporary 1959)★★★, *André Previn Plays Songs By Jerome Kern* (Contemporary 1959)★★★★, *West Side Story* (Contemporary 1959)★★★★, with the David Rose Orchestra *Secret Songs For Young Lovers* (MGM 1959)★★★, *The Previn Scene* (1959)★★★, *The Magic Moods Of André Previn* (60s)★★★, *Like Love* (Columbia 1960)★★★, *André Previn Plays Harold Arlen* (Contemporary 1960)★★★★, *André Previn* (1960)★★★, *Give*

My Regards To Broadway (Columbia 1960)★★★, *Thinking Of You* (Columbia 1960)★★★, *Music From Camelot* (Columbia 1961)★★★★, *A Touch Of Elegance* (Columbia 1961)★★★, *Thinking Of You* (Columbia 1961), *André Previn And J.J. Johnson Play Mack The Knife And Bilbao Song* (Columbia 1961)★★★, *Mack The Knife & Other Kurt Weill Music* (Columbia 1962)★★★, *Two For The See-saw* (1962)★★★, *Faraway Part Of Town* (Columbia 1962)★★★, *The Light Fantastic* (Columbia 1962)★★★, *The Word's Most Honored Pianist* (PRI 1962)★★★, *Sittin' On A Rainbow* (1962)★★★, *The Light Fantastic: A Tribute To Fred Astaire* (Columbia 1962)★★★, with Herb Ellis, Shelly Manne, Ray Brown *4 To Go!* (1963)★★★, *The Essential André Previn* (Verve 1963)★★★, *André Previn In Hollywood* (Columbia 1963)★★★★, *Soft And Swinging* (1964)★★★, *Sound Stage* (1964)★★★, *My Fair Lady* ii (Columbia 1964)★★★★, *Previn At Sunset* (1975)★★★, with Itzhak Perlman *A Different Kind Of Blues* (Angel 1981)★★★★, with Perlman *It's A Breeze* (Angel 1981)★★★, *Uptown* (Telarc 1994)★★★, *André Previn And Friends Play Show Boat* (Deutsche Grammophon 1995)★★★, *Jazz At The Musikverein* (Verve 1998)★★★★, with David Finck *We Got Rhythm: A Gershwin Songbook* (Deutsche Grammophon 1998)★★★.

● FURTHER READING: *André Previn*, Michael Freedland. *Music Face To Face*, André Previn. *Orchestra*, André Previn. *André Previn's Guide To The Orchestra*, André Previn. *No Minor Chords: My Days In Hollywood*, André Previn.

PREVITE, BOBBY

b. 16 July 1957, Niagara Falls, New York, USA. Previte studied at Buffalo University and was playing drums from an early age. He quickly established himself as a remarkable technician with a wide ranging view of what constitutes the jazz repertoire. Granted equal time alongside post-bop jazz in his thinking is rock, funk, Latin, and elements of free jazz. His drumming is dextrous, pliant, exciting and he is always eager to experiment. The charts played by his bands are ingenious, difficult and sometimes apparently limiting. However, this impression of forcing back the explosive energies of his musicians does not repress; rather it generates in performance an atmosphere of repressed drama, like steam awaiting an opportunity to escape. Alongside his continually growing skills as a performer Previte demonstrates equally remarkable gifts as a composer, and just as he was making international tours as a leader he was simultaneously in great demand as a composer. In 1989 he wrote for the string trio, Relache, and in 1991 he composed music for the New York appearance of the Moscow Circus. This music was recorded as a suite and vividly captures the laughter, danger and excitement of the circus it so ably depicts. Indeed, many of Previte's compositions are compelling studies that are often operatic in scope. In 1992 he composed for the International Puppet Festival in New York, and in the same year toured Japan. He was again in the far east in 1993. He visited Europe the same year, and in 1994 toured the UK. His bands often bear the name of current albums, names that are also applied to the tours following upon their release. In 1997 he formed his own label, Depth Of Field Records, the first release being a duo set with John Zorn. Previte's striking skills as a performer and writer make him one of the most challenging and exhilarating musicians on the late 90s jazz scene and, as the title of one of his early albums suggests, he is constantly seeking to push to its limits the often constraining envelope of jazz.

● ALBUMS: *Bump The Renaissance* (Sound Aspects 1986)★★★, *Pushing The Envelope* (Gramavision 1987)★★★, *Claude's Late Morning* (Gramavision 1988)★★★, *Empty Suits* (Gramavision 1990)★★★, *Weather Clear, Track Fast* (Enja 1991)★★★★, *Music Of The Moscow Circus* (Gramavision 1991)★★★, with Weather Clear, Track Fast *Hue And Cry* (Enja 1994)★★★, *Slay The Suitors* (Avant 1994)★★★, *Too Close To The Pole* (Enja 1996)★★★, *Dull Bang, Gushing Sound, Human Shriek* 1987 recording, film soundtrack (Koch 1996)★★★, *My Man In Sydney* (Enja 1997)★★★, with John Zorn *Euclid's Nightmare* (Depth Of Field 1997)★★★★, with Latin For Travelers *My Man In Sydney* (Enja 1998)★★★★.

PRÉVOST, EDDIE

b. 22 June 1942, Hitchin, Hertfordshire, England. As a teenager Prévost drummed for various trad and skiffle bands and later played jazz. In 1965 he, along with saxophonist Leslie Gare and guitarist Keith Rowe, formed AMM, an *avant garde*, improvising chamber group that remains as radical, uncompromising and *sui generis* in 1992 as it was at its inception. AMM has been one of Prévost's major projects for most of the last 30 years. Very active in all kinds of free improvisation, Prévost frequently draws attention to the political resonances of playing free music - he also gives lectures and writes articles. His quartet, with Larry Stabbins (tenor saxophone), Veryan Weston (piano) and Marcio Mattos (bass), performed throughout the 70s and 80s and Prévost has also recorded with the collective groups Supersession, Resoundings and the Free Jazz Quartet, releasing their (and his) albums on his own label, Matchless Records. A 1987 album, *Flayed*, on the Californian Silent label, featured Prévost on one side only playing solo. In 1990, with AMM colleagues Gare and Rowe, Prévost formed The Masters Of Disorientation; in 1991 he undertook a brief UK tour in a duo with pianist Marilyn Crispell. An expert percussionist in every mode of improvisation, Prévost cites Max Roach and Ed Blackwell as the jazz drummers he most admires.

● ALBUMS: *Now-Here-This-Then* (Spotlite 1977)★★★, *Live, Volumes 1 & 2* (Matchless 1979)★★★★, *Continuum* (Matchless 1985)★★★, with Resoundings *Resound* (1986)★★★, *Supersession* 1984 recording (Matchless 1988)★★★, with Organum *Flayed* (1987)★★★, with the Free Jazz Quartet *Premonitions* (1989)★★★, with Marilyn Crispell *Band On The Wall* (Matchless 1994)★★, *Loci Of Change, Sound And Sensibility* (Matchless 1998)★★★, *Touch, The Weight, Measure And Feel Of Things* (Matchless 1998)★★★★.

PRICE, JESSE

b. 1 May 1909, Memphis, Tennessee, USA, d. 19 April 1974. After playing drums locally, Price toured with blues singers (including Ida Cox) and tent shows until

1934, when he settled in Kansas City. There he worked in several territory bands and helped to establish the free-flowing rhythmic pulse that is at the heart of the Kansas City style of jazz. He led his own band, was a familiar figure at after-hours jam sessions and then joined Harlan Leonard's Rockets. In the early 40s he worked briefly with Ella Fitzgerald and with the big bands of Louis Armstrong, Stan Kenton, Count Basie and Benny Carter. Despite his importance in the early development of the style refined and polished by such peers as Jo Jones, Price worked in comparative obscurity during his later years and by the end of the 60s was in semi-retirement. In 1971 he appeared at the Monterey Jazz Festival as part of the 'Kansas City Revisited' set, leading a band that included Harry Edison, Jimmy Forrest and Big Joe Turner.

● COMPILATIONS: *Harlan Leonard Vol. 2* (RCA 1940 recordings)★★★, *Stan Kenton's Greatest Hits* (Capitol 1943-51 recordings)★★★★.

PRICE, RAY

b. 20 November 1921, Sydney, New South Wales, Australia. Price first made a mark on the Australian traditional jazz scene, playing banjo and guitar in various bands in the 40s by which time he had been playing, at least on a semi-professional level, for several years. He also played bass with studio and symphony orchestras, and often appeared with the Port Jackson Jazz Band. For several decades he was well known for his jazz work as both a touring musician and an educator. His vigorous and rhythmic playing enhanced many traditional jazz bands, including those led by John Sangster and Bob Barnard.

● ALBUMS: *Jazz Part No. 1* (Dixie 1975)★★★.

PRICE, SAMMY

b. 6 October 1908, Honey Grove, Texas, USA, d. 14 April 1992, New York, USA. After studying alto horn and piano at schools in Texas, Price won a dancing contest. Arising from this he was invited to tour with the Alphonso Trent band. Back in Texas he accompanied singers on record dates, playing occasional club gigs. He also formed a band of his own, then toured with a succession of popular entertainers. By 1930 he was becoming known in and around Kansas City, but by 1937 was resident in New York where he became house pianist for Decca, playing on countless record dates, mostly with singers. The 40s saw him working as a solo act, leading his own small band, the Bluesicians, and working with Sidney Bechet. Price also found time for a brief European tour in 1948. During the 50s he divided his time between Texas and New York, playing clubs and recording with artists such as Henry 'Red' Allen. In the 60s he was active in New York and once again toured Europe, a pattern of work that continued through the following decade and into the 80s, sometimes in company with other veterans such as Doc Cheatham. Price was an effective singer and his blues piano playing was of a very high standard.

● ALBUMS: *Blues And Boogie* (1955)★★★, *Sammy Price: Concert In Fontainebleau/The Price Is Right* (1956)★★★, *Piano Solo* (1956)★★★, *Sidney Bechet With Sammy Price's Bluesicians Live In Paris* (1956)★★, *Sammy Price And Doc Cheatham* (1958)★★★, *Rib Joint* (1959)★★★, *Sammy Price And His All Stars* (1959)★★★, *Sammy Price And His Bluesicians* (Circle 1961)★★★, *Midnight Boogie* (Black & Blue 1969)★★, *Barrelhouse And Blues* (Black Lion 1969)★★★★, *Blues On My Mind* (1969)★★★, *Texas And Louisiana Piano* one side only (1969)★★, *Fire* (Black & Blue 1975)★★, *Rockin' Boogie* (1975)★★★, *Boogie And Jazz Classics* (Black & Blue 1975)★★★, *The New Sammy Price* (1975)★★★, *Sammy Price With Fessor's Big City Band* (1975)★★★, with Torben Petersen *The Boogie Woogie Twins* (1975)★★★, *Just Right* (1977)★★★, *Blues And Boogie-Woogie* (1978)★★★, with Cheatham *Black Beauty: A Tribute To Black American Songwriters* (1979)★★, *Sweet Substitute* (1979)★★★, *Play It Again, Sam* (Whiskey Women And Song 1983)★★★, *King Of The Boogie Woogie* (Storyville 1996)★★★.

● FURTHER READING: *What Do They Want? A Jazz Autobiography*, Sammy Price and Caroline Richmond (ed.).

PRIESTER, JULIAN

b. 29 June 1935, Chicago, Illinois, USA. Trombonist Priester began his professional career with Muddy Waters and Bo Diddley; he then changed direction to join Sun Ra And His Arkestra. In the late 50s Priester was with Lionel Hampton, Dinah Washington and Max Roach. Most of the 60s were spent in studio work in New York, with a brief spell with Duke Ellington at the end of the decade. In the early 70s he played with Herbie Hancock, then moved to San Francisco (along the way adopting the name Pepo Mtoto). In the late 70s he worked and recorded with Stanley Cowell and Red Garland and in the 80s was featured with the George Gruntz big band and in the Dave Holland quintet. A powerful player with an inquiring mind, Priester's 70s work, which included explorations of electronics and other artificially created musical sounds, took him from the centre of the jazz scene and into the world of contemporary composers such as John Cage. He worked with Jane Ira Bloom in the mid-90s.

● ALBUMS: *Spiritsville* (1958)★★★, *Love, Love* (1973)★★★, *Polarization* (1977)★★, with Jane Ira Bloom *The Nearness* (Arabesque 1996)★★★, with Sam Rivers *Hints On Light And Shadow* (Postcards 1997)★★.

PRIESTLEY, BRIAN

b. 10 July 1946, Manchester, England. Priestley studied piano as a child, later playing in bands whilst studying at university. In the early 70s he wrote arrangements for the National Youth Jazz Orchestra and played in various small groups. Later he was co-leader with Dave Gelly of Stylus. He worked with Alan Cohen on the music of Duke Ellington, recording 'Black, Brown, And Beige' in 1972 and making a public performance at the 1988 Ellington Convention. In the late 80s and early 90s, he led his own group, the Special Septet, recording both a tribute album to Ellington and a live concert with ex-Ellington musician Bill Berry. In addition to his playing and arranging, Priestley was for many years a regular broadcaster on BBC Radio London. He has also written several books, including works on Charles Mingus, Charlie Parker and John Coltrane, and has contributed articles to several leading music magazines. With Ian Carr and Digby Fairweather he is co-author of *Jazz: The Essential Companion*.

● ALBUMS: with Alan Cohen *Black, Brown, And Beige* (1972)★★★, with Bill Berry *Live At The Pizza Express* (1987)★★, *Love You Gladly* (Cadillac 1989)★★★, with Berry *Bilberry Jam* (1990)★★★★, *You Taught My Heart To Sing* (Spirit Of Jazz 1995)★★★.

PRIMA, LOUIS

b. 7 December 1911, New Orleans, Louisiana, USA, d. 24 August 1978, New Orleans, Louisiana, USA. A trumpeter, bandleader, singer and composer, Prima was the son of Italian immigrant parents. He was educated at Jesuit High School, and studied the violin for several years under Hemmersback, before switching to the trumpet. At the age of 17, inspired by jazz greats such as Louis Armstrong and King Oliver, he gained his first job as a singer/trumpeter in a New Orleans theatre - his elder brother, Leon, also played trumpet at a local nightspot. For a time in the early 30s Prima worked with Red Nichols, before forming his own seven-piece New Orleans Gang, with its signature tune, 'Way Down Yonder In New Orleans', who recorded more than 70 titles in New York for various labels from 1934-39. Several of them made the US Hit Parade, including 'The Lady In Red', 'In A Little Gypsy Tea Room' and 'The Goose Hangs High'. His sidemen during this period included Georg Brunis (trombone), Claude Thornhill (piano), George Van Eps (guitar), Artie Shapiro (bass), Eddie Miller (reeds), Ray Bauduc (drums), Sidney Arodin (clarinet), Frank Pinero (piano), Frank Frederico (guitar), Oscar Bradley (drums), and Pee Wee Russell (clarinet). By this stage, Prima was also composing songs, and one of them, 'Sing, Sing, Sing', when developed by Benny Goodman, became a smash hit for the 'King Of Swing', and remains a Swing Era classic. Over the years, Prima wrote or co-wrote many other numbers, including 'Robin Hood', which was successful for Les Brown in 1945, and the 1947 Jo Stafford hit, 'A Sunday Kind Of Love', along with 'Alone', 'Little Boy Blew His Top', 'Marguerita', 'New Aulins', 'Angelina', 'Where Have We Met Before?', 'Brooklyn Boogie', 'Boogie In The Bronx', 'Bridget O'Brien', 'Boogie In Chicago', 'It's The Rhythm In Me', 'Sing A Spell', 'It's A Southern Holiday' and 'Rhythm On The Radio'. His collaborators included Jack Loman, Dave Franklin, Milton Kabak, Bob Miketta, Barbara Belle, Anita Leonard, and Stan Rhodes. After making an good impression on his feature film debut in the Bing Crosby movie musical *Rhythm On The Range* (1936), Prima continued to have relatively small, but telling roles in a number of other movies, notably *Rose Of Washington Square* (1939), in which he enhanced Alice Faye's rendering of 'I'm Just Wild About Harry' with his ebullient and exciting trumpet accompaniment. By this time he had his own big band which he fronted with great showmanship and panache. It had 40s hits with 'Angelina', 'Bell-Bottom Trousers' (vocal: Lily Ann Carol), and 'Civilization (Bongo, Bongo, Bongo)', an amusing novelty from the 1947 Broadway revue *Angel In The Wings*. In 1948, Prima began working with the poker-faced singer Keely Smith, and, after having a US hit in 1950 with their joint composition, 'Oh, Babe!', they were married two years later. During the next decade they were recognized as one of the hottest nightclub acts in the USA, and became known as 'The Wildest Show In Las Vegas'. Prima's inspired clowning and zany vocals delivered in a fractured Italian dialect, coupled with Smith's cool image and classy singing, were augmented by tenor saxophonist Sam Butera and his group, the Witnesses. A typical performance was filmed at Lake Tahoe in 1957, and released under the title of *The Wildest*, and they reassembled in 1959 for the feature *Hey Boy! Hey Girl!* Prima and Smith were awarded Grammys in 1958 for their inimitable reading of the Harold Arlen-Johnny Mercer standard, 'That Old Black Magic'. In 1958 Prima was briefly in the UK Top 30 with Carl Sigman and Peter de Rose's likeable 'Buona Sera', and two years later made the US singles and albums charts with the instrumental 'Wonderland By Night'. Other Top 40 albums included *Las Vegas-Prima Style* and *Hey Boy!, Hey Girl!* In 1961, while still at the height of their fame - and having recently signed a multi-million dollar contract with the Desert Inn, Las Vegas - the couple were divorced. Prima and Butera subsequently attempted to cash in on the then-popular dance fad by appearing in the movie *Twist All Night*, which sank without a trace, in spite (or because) of items such as 'When The Saints Go Twistin' In'. Far more lasting was Prima's contribution in 1967 to The Jungle Book, the Walt Disney Studio's first cartoon feature for four years, which went on to gross around $26 million. Prima provided the voice of hip orang-utan King Louie, and sang the film's hit song, 'I Wanna Be Like You'. In later years he mostly confined himself to performing with a small group at venues such as the Sands Hotel, Las Vegas, and in 1975 underwent surgery for the removal of a brain tumour. He never recovered from the operation, and remained in a coma until his death nearly three years later in a New Orleans nursing home.

● ALBUMS: *A Nite On 42nd Street* (50s)★★★, *One Night Stand With Louis Prima Volumes 1 & 2* (50s)★★★, *Louis Prima At Frank Dailey's Terrace Room* (Mercury 1953)★★, *Swings* (Capitol 1955)★★★, *The Wildest* (Capitol 1956)★★★, *Call Of The Wildest* (Capitol 1957)★★★, *The Wildest Show At Tahoe* (Capitol 1957)★★★, with Keely Smith *Las Vegas-Prima Style* (Capitol 1958)★★★★, *Jump, Jive An' Wail* (Capitol 1958)★★★, with Smith *Hey Boy! Hey Girl!* film soundtrack (Capitol 1959)★★★★, with Smith *Louis And Keely!* (Dot 1959)★★★, *Strictly Prima* (Capitol 1959)★★★, with Smith *Senior Prom* (1959)★★★, with Sam Butera *The Continental Twist* (Capitol 60s)★★★, with Smith *Together* (Dot 1960)★★★, *Plays Pretty Music Prima Style* (Dot 1960)★★★, with Smith *On Stage* (Dot 1960)★★★, *Wonderland By Night* (Dot 1961)★★★★, *Blue Moon* (Dot 1961)★★★, with Smith *Return Of The Wildest* (Dot 1961)★★★, *The Wildest Comes Home* (Capitol 1962)★★★, *Doin' The Twist*

(Dot 1962)★★★, *Lake Tahoe Prima Style* (Capitol 1963)★★★, *Plays Pretty For The People* (1964)★★★, *Plays And Sings* (Hamilton 1965)★★★, *On Broadway* (United Artists 1967)★★, with Jimmie Lunceford *Lunceford And Prima-1945* (Aircheck 1979)★★★, *Live From Las Vegas* (Jazz Band 1988)★★, *Angelina* (Big Band Era 1989)★★★.

● COMPILATIONS: *His Greatest Hits* (Dot 1960)★★★★, with Keely Smith *Hits* (Capitol 1961)★★★★, *Best Of Louis Prima* (MFP 1985)★★★, *Just A Gigolo 1945-50* (Bandstand 1988)★★★, *Capitol Collectors Series* (Capitol 1991)★★★★.

● FILMS: *Rhythm On The Range* (1936), *The Star Reporter In Hollywood* (1936), *Swing It* (1936), *Vitaphone Varieté* (1936), *You Can't Have Everything* (1937), *Manhattan Merry-Go-Round* (1937), *Start Cheering* (1938), *Swing Cat's Jamboree* (1938), *Rose Of Washington Square* (1939), *New Orleans Blues* (1943), *Rhythm Masters* (1948), *The Wildest* (1957), *Senior Prom* (1958), *Hey Boy! Hey Girl!* (1959), *Twist All Night* (1961), voice only *The Man Called Flintstone* (1966), voice only *The Jungle Book* (1967), *Rafferty And The Gold Dust Twins* (1974).

PRIME TIME

(see Coleman, Ornette)

PRINTUP, MARCUS

b. 1967, Conyers, Georgia, USA. Beginning life in a small southern town, Printup grew up around the music of the church. His formal musical education began with marching, concert and jazz bands at high school. Staying close to home, Printup attended Georgia State University in Atlanta, where he became a featured soloist with the school's jazz band, as well as participating in the wind ensemble and brass groups. Printup soon outgrew the local college, however, and transferred to the University of North Florida in Jacksonville, Florida. The school's music programme at that time was led by jazz baritonist Rich Matteson. While there, Printup won honours in several national competitions, including the National Collegiate Jazz Competition and the 1991 Thelonious Monk International Trumpet Competition. The great young pianist Marcus Roberts visited the school and recognized Printup's potential, employing the young trumpeter initially as his road manager on a solo piano tour in 1992. During the tour, Printup accompanied his new mentor on selected tunes each night, and soon became a member of Roberts' working band. After this first big break, employment by such artists as Carl Allen, Betty Carter and Bob Belden followed. Printup's connection with Roberts led to an association with fellow trumpeter Wynton Marsalis. As the music director for the Jazz At Lincoln Center programme, Marsalis recruited Printup to play in his prestigious orchestra. He subsequently recorded as leader for Blue Note Records, and his first release, *Song For A Beautiful Woman* (1995), was greeted with much critical acclaim. The album showcased Printup's affinity for the hard bop school of trumpet playing, influenced by legends such as Booker Little and Fats Navarro.

The trumpeter's compositional skills also displayed a maturity beyond his years. Printup's second release, *UNveiled* (1996), continued in this vein and served to strengthen his presence as a significant artist. His eloquence of style and his ability to express his own unique voice are characteristics that distinguish Printup from many young musicians of his generation.

● ALBUMS: *Song For A Beautiful Woman* (Blue Note 1995)★★★★, *Unveiled* (Blue Note 1996)★★★, with Tim Hagans *Hub Songs: The Music Of Freddie Hubbard* (Blue Note 1997)★★★.

PRIVIN, BERNIE

b. 12 February 1919, New York City, New York, USA. A self-taught musician, by his late teens Privin was playing trumpet professionally in dance bands and quickly graduated to some of the best big bands of the swing era, including those of Bunny Berigan, Tommy Dorsey and Artie Shaw (with whom he was featured soloist). In the early 40s he was with Charlie Barnet and Benny Goodman and during World War II played in Glenn Miller's Army Air Force band. After the war he made a brief return to Goodman but then entered studio work, where he remained until the late 60s. In later years he worked in Europe, seizing many opportunities to prove that, despite his advancing years, he retained much of the biting tone that had characterized his earlier work.

● ALBUMS: *Bernie Privin And His Orchestra* (1956)★★★, *The Bernie Privin Quintet In Sweden* (1969)★★★.

● COMPILATIONS: with Artie Shaw *Deux Grandes Annees - In The Blue Room/In The Cafe Rouge (1938-39)* (1983)★★★.

PROCOPE, RUSSELL

b. 11 August 1908, New York City, New York, USA, d. 21 January 1981. A neighbour of Benny Carter, Rudy Powell and Bobby Stark, Procope played clarinet and alto saxophone in New York clubs in his late teens and when he was 20 years old recorded with Jelly Roll Morton. A year later he was a member of Carter's big band, then was successively with Chick Webb, Fletcher Henderson, Tiny Bradshaw, Teddy Hill and Andy Kirk. His apprenticeship well and truly served, Procope had to wait until the end of World War II and his army discharge before entering the post for which he had been unconsciously grooming himself. From 1946 until 1974 he was a member of the Duke Ellington orchestra, with only a brief aside in the Wilbur De Paris band in 1961. After Ellington's death, Procope worked in a number of Ellington-inspired small groups and also in the pit band for the show *Ain't Misbehavin'*. His long spell with Ellington was unspectacular; he was a section man rather than a soloist and as such provided the kind of solid base the Ellington band sometimes lacked when its less reliable members had other things on their minds. When he did solo, on such features as 'Mood Indigo', he revealed a warm and full-toned clarinet style that recalled New Orleans rather than New York.

● ALBUMS: with Duke Ellington *Masterpieces* (1950)★★★, *Russell Procope And His Orchestra* (1956)★★★★, *Duke Ellington's Seventieth Birthday Concert* (1969)★★★.

● COMPILATIONS: *John Kirby And His Orchestra (1941-42)* (1988)★★.

PROFIT, CLARENCE

b. 26 June 1912, New York City, New York, USA, d. 22 October 1944. By his late teenage years, Profit had played piano with several bands, small and large, performed with Edgar Sampson, a schoolfriend, and formed his own big band. In 1930 he joined Teddy Bunn, touring and playing residencies in various Caribbean locations, but by the middle of the decade was resident in New York as leader of a trio. It was a format that best suited his powerful stride piano style and the next few years saw him achieve a substantial measure of popularity. Before he could take full advantage of the public's liking for his piano-bass-guitar line-up, he died in 1944.

● COMPILATIONS: *Complete 1939-40* (Meritt 1988)★★★, *Solo And Trio Sides* (Memoir 1993)★★★.

PRYSOCK, ARTHUR

b. 2 January 1929, Spartanburg, South Carolina, USA, d. 14 June 1997, Hamilton, Bermuda. After singing with a number of small bands, in 1945 Prysock joined Buddy Johnson, with whom he appeared at many Harlem clubs and ballrooms. Subsequently, he worked as a soloist, signing to Decca Records in 1952 and achieving chart success with a version of the standard 'I Couldn't Sleep A Wink Last Night'. After recording for numerous small labels he signed a long-term contract with Hy Weiss's Old Town Records and, in 1964, broke into the big time via a recording contract with Verve and record dates with Count Basie's orchestra. He had some success thereafter, performing at Carnegie Hall in 1966 and hosting his own television show. He also appeared on labels including Mercury, MGM, Polydor and King Records. Although not a jazz singer in the real sense, Prysock had a broad vocal sound and his deep voice sometimes resembled Billy Eckstine, some of whose hits he covered. He also sang R&B ('When Love Is New' was a Top 10 R&B hit in 1976) and it might well be that his eclecticism harmed his wider acceptance. He also gained wide exposure as the voice on the Lowenbraü beer 'Here's To Good Friends' jingle. While recording for Milestone Records in the late 80s he received Grammy nominations in 1987 and 1988 for best jazz performance by a group or duo ('Teach Me Tonight') and best jazz vocal ('This Guy's In Love With You'). He also taught vocal jazz at Five Towns College as part of an artists in residence programme in his later years.

● ALBUMS: *I Worry About You* (Old Town 1962)★★★, *Arthur Prysock Sings Only For You* (Old Town 1962)★★★, *Coast To Coast* (Old Town 1963)★★★, *Everlasting Songs For Everlasting Lovers* (Old Town 1964)★★★★, *Intimately Yours* (Old Town 1964)★★★, *A Double Header With Arthur Prysock* (Old Town 1965)★★★, *In A Mood* (Old Town 1965)★★★, *Strictly Sentimental* (Decca 1965)★★★, *Showcase* (Decca 1965)★★★, with Count Basie *Arthur Prysock/Count Basie* (Verve 1965)★★★, *Art & Soul* (Verve 1966)★★★, *A Portrait Of Arthur Prysock* (Verve 1967)★★★, *Mister Prysock* (Verve 1967)★★★, *Love Me* (Verve 1968)★★, *To Love Or Not To Love* (Verve 1968)★★★, *I Must Be Doing Something Right/Funny Thing* (Verve 1968)★★★, *This Is My Beloved* (Verve 1969)★★, *Where The Soul Trees Grow* (Verve 1969)★★★, *Arthur Prysock* (Verve 1970)★★★, *All My Life* (Polydor 1977)★★★, *. . . Does It Again* (Polydor 1978)★★★, *A Rockin' Good Way* (Milestone 1985)★★★, *This Guy's In Love With You* (Milestone 1986)★★★.

● COMPILATIONS: *A Portrait Of Arthur Prysock* (Old Town 1963)★★★★, *The Best Of Arthur Prysock* (Verve 1967)★★★, *The Best Of Arthur Prysock, Volume 2* (Verve 1968)★★★, *24 Karat Hits* (Verve 1969)★★★.

PRYSOCK, WILBERT 'RED'

b. 2 February 1926, Greensboro, North Carolina, USA, d. 19 February 1993. After attempting to learn piano, organ, clarinet and trumpet, Prysock received a tenor saxophone from his sister for his 17th birthday. He learned to play the instrument during his military service in World War II. Prysock turned professional upon his demobilization in 1947 and joined Tiny Grimes' Rocking Highlanders, with whom he recorded for the fledgling Atlantic Records. He left them in 1950 to join Roy Milton's Solid Senders before finding fame with Tiny Bradshaw's band and such recordings as 'Soft', 'Off And On' and 'Free For All' (which became known as 'Go, Red, Go') on King Records. Prysock formed his own band in 1953, after experimenting with three releases on Bobby Robinson's Red Robin label, and was signed by Mercury the following year, for whom he notched up many big sellers, among them 'Hand Clappin'', 'Jump, Red, Jump' and 'Finger Tips'. He played with the Alan Freed Big Band, backing all the top rock 'n' roll artists of the 50s, and was able to switch styles with the advent of soul music in the 60s, recording for King and Chess and supporting many of the era's big names. In 1971, Red teamed up with his famous elder brother, Arthur Prysock, and toured and performed together - the sax and the voice.

● ALBUMS: *Rock 'N' Roll* (Mercury 1956)★★★★, *Cryin' My Heart Out* (1983)★★★, *Rock 'n' Roll: The Best Of Red Prysock* (Avi 1996)★★★★.

PUENTE, TITO

b. Ernesto Antonio Puente Jnr., 20 April 1923, Harlem Hospital, New York City, New York, USA. Born of Puerto Rican parentage, Tito began piano lessons when he was seven years old and around the age of 10 he started tuition in drums and percussion, which became his forte. Around 1936, Puente commenced his professional career as a drummer with the orchestra of Noro Morales. In 1941 he played with the Machito band. World War II intervened and Tito was drafted into the US Navy for three years' service. After his discharge he took courses at New York's Juilliard School of Music and did stints with the bands of José Curbelo and Fernando Alvarez between 1946 and 1947. With Curbelo, Puente performed alongside Tito Rodríguez, who later became his arch-rival. Tito's reputation as a sizzling arranger quickly grew and led to numerous assignments from prominent bandleaders. Even Rodríguez hired him to write the charts for four numbers he recorded with his Mambo Devils on Gabriel Oller's SMC (Spanish Music

Center) label. In the late 40s, while Tito was performing the roles of contractor, arranger and timbales player with Pupi Campo's orchestra, he organized a group that promoter Federico Pagani dubbed the Picadilly Boys ('Picadillo' meaning: beef or pork hash) after being impressed by their performance of the latin jam style (descarga). With them, Puente recorded a number of sides for SMC. Shortly afterwards, he renamed his aggregation Tito Puente And His Orchestra. Tito used two lead vocalists, Angel Rosa and then Paquito Sosa, before settling for Cuban Vicentico Valdés as his resident lead singer.

In late 1949, Puente organized a line-up of four trumpets, three trombones, four saxophones and a full rhythm section for a recording session for Tico Records. One recording from this session, leaving out the trombones and saxophones, resulted in a fiery version of 'Abaniquito'. With the help of English translation by disc jockey Dick 'Ricardo' Sugar, the song became one of the first crossover mambo hits. Between the late 40s and mid-50s, Puente issued recordings on Tico. During a suspension of recording by the company in 1950 - due to a wrangle between the co-founders, George Goldner and Art 'Pancho' Raymond - Puente recorded for the Seeco, Verne and RCA labels. Along with Tito Rodríguez and Machito, Puente became one of the kings of the 50s mambo era. His consistent top billing at New York's Palladium Ballroom, the famed 'Home of the Mambo', became one of the areas of friction between himself and Rodríguez. Puente switched to RCA Victor Records and between 1956 and 1960 he released a string of albums on the label, including the notable *Cuban Carnival* and his all-time bestseller, *Dance Mania*. The album marked the debut of Santos Colón (b. 1 November, Mayagüez, Puerto Rico) as Puente's new lead singer. Colón arrived in New York in 1950 and performed with the bands of Jorge Lopés, Tony Novos and José Curbelo before joining Tito. He remained with Puente until 1970, when he departed to pursue a solo career and released a series of albums on Fania Records.

Several of Puente's Tico and RCA Victor releases between the mid- to late 50s were entirely devoted to the cha cha chá rhythm, which was enjoying considerable popularity at the time. At the beginning of the 60s, the pachanga style took over. One of the prime-movers of the dance craze was Afro-Cuban singer Rolando La Serie's 1960 smash hit recording of 'La Pachanga' with the Bebo Valdés band. The following year, while the fad was still raging at full force, Puente teamed up with La Serie to make *Pachanga In New York* for Gema Records. In 1960, Tito and His Orchestra journeyed to the west coast of America to record *Exciting Band In Hollywood* (aka *Puente Now!*) for GNP Records. Upon his arrival, Puente contacted Los Angeles-based flautist Rolando Lozano (b. José Calazan Lozano, 27 August 1931, Cienfuegos, Santa Clara Province, Cuba), an alumnus of Orquesta Aragón, Orquesta América, Orquesta Nuevo Ritmo, Mongo Santamaría and Cal Tjader. Puente rejoined Tico Records (and remained with them until the mid-80s) to make *Pachanga Con Puente*, which yielded the big hit 'Caramelos'. 1962's *El Rey Bravo* was essentially a descarga set: an untypical Puente album, it stands as one of his strongest recordings. The disc featured Cuban violinist/flautist Pupi Legarreta and spawned the original version of Puente's perennial classic 'Oye Como Va', which was given a latin-rock treatment by Santana in 1970. Around 1965, Tito linked up with Alegre Records for *Y Parece Bobo*, which was produced by the label's founder, Al Santiago, and featured Chivirico Dávila on lead vocals. Santiago also co-produced *Cuba Y Puerto Rico Son...* on Tico, Puente's first in a series of collaborations with the 'Queen of Salsa' Celia Cruz. Tito also recorded a string of successful albums with La Lupe between 1965 and 1967, and made a couple of albums with Beny Moré's widow, Noraida, at the beginning of the 70s. On his late 60s releases, *20th Anniversary* and *The King Tito Puente*, Tito was obliged to bow to the overwhelming popularity of the R&B/Latin fusion form called boogaloo. 'The Boogaloo meant nothing to me. It stunk', he said forthrightly in 1977. 'It hurt the established bandleaders. It was a dance Eddie Palmieri, I and other bandleaders didn't want to record but had to in order to keep up with the times' (quote from *Latin Times*).

Panamanian vocalist Miguel 'Meñique' Barcasnegras, who worked previously with Kako and Willie Rosario, did a brief stint with Puente's band in the early 70s. After performing on Tito's *Pa'Lante!/Straight!* and *Para Los Rumberos*, Meñique departed to work as a solo artist (Puente arranged and directed his 1972 solo debut *Meñique*) and with Santos Colón, Charlie Palmieri, Charanga Sensación de Rolando Valdés and Conjunto Chaney. In 1977, Tito and Santos Colón reunited on *The Legend*, the title track of which was written by Rubén Blades. The album, which was nominated for a Grammy Award, was produced by 'The Genius of Salsa', Louie Ramírez. The following year, Puente's first tribute album to Beny Moré (in a series of three volumes) won a Grammy Award. The trio of albums featured a galaxy of vocalists from the Fania Records stable, including Cruz, Colón, Cheo Feliciano, Ismael 'Pat' Quintana, Adalberto Santiago, Héctor Lavoe, Pete 'El Conde' Rodríguez, Ismael Miranda and Justo Betancourt. In 1979 and 1980, Puente toured Europe and recorded with the Latin Percussion Jazz Ensemble (LPJE), members of which included Argentinian pianist Jorge Dalto (1948-87), violinist Alfredo De La Fé and conga player Carlos 'Patato' Valdez. This group was a precursor of his own Latin jazz outfit, which debuted on the Concord Picante label in 1983 with *Tito Puente And His Latin Ensemble On Broadway*. He garnered another Grammy Award for the album. Tito released a further seven albums with his Latin Ensemble on Concord Picante between 1984 and 1991, two of which - *Mambo Diablo* and *Goza Mí Timbal* - received Grammys. However, Puente's work with his Latin Ensemble woefully sank into tired recycling of his earlier material. At concerts Tito and his high-calibre musicians often appeared just to be 'going through the motions'. For 1991's *The Mambo*

King: 100th LP on RMM Records, Tito returned to a full big band line-up to back an assortment of the label's vocalists (including Oscar D'León, Tito Nieves, Tony Vega, José Alberto and Domingo Quiñones) plus Santos Colón and Celia Cruz. Although the album is purported to be his 100th, the actual total of his recordings in 1992 exceeded that figure. In addition to those mentioned, Puente has recorded with an array of Latin music and jazz names, including the Tico All-Stars, Fania All Stars, Bobby Capó, Ray Barretto, Camilo Azuquita, Gilberto Monroig, Sophy, Myrta Silva, Manny Roman, Doc Severinsen, Woody Herman, Buddy Morrow, Cal Tjader, Terry Gibbs, George Shearing, Phil Woods, Pete Escovedo and Sheila E. (Escovedo's daughter).

● ALBUMS: *Cha Cha Chá For Lovers* (1954)★★★★, *Dance The Cha Cha Chá* (1955)★★★★, *Cuban Carnival* (1956)★★★★, *Puente Goes Jazz* (1956)★★★, *Mambo On Broadway* (1957)★★★, *Let's Cha-Cha With Puente* (1957)★★★, *Night Beat* (RCA Victor 1957)★★★★, *Mucho Puente* (1957)★★★★, *Top Percussion* (1958)★★★, *Dance Mania* (1958)★★★, with Vicentico Valdés *Tito Puente Swings, Vicentico Valdés Sings* (1958)★★★, *Puente In Love* (1959)★★★, with Woody Herman *Herman's Heat & Puente's Beat* (1959)★★★, *Dancing Under Latin Skies* (1959)★★★, *Mucho Cha-Cha* (1959)★★★, *Cha Cha With Tito Puente At Grossinger's* (1960)★★, *Tambo* (1960)★★★★, with Rolando La Serie *Pachanga In New York* (1961)★★★, *The Most Exciting Band In Hollywood* aka *Puente Now!* (1961)★★★, *Pachanga Con Puente* (1961)★★★★, *Vaya Puente* (1961)★★★, *El Rey Bravo* (1962)★★★, *Bossa Nova By Puente* (1962)★★★, *Tito Puente In Puerto Rico - Recorded Live* (1962)★★★, *Bailables* (1963)★★★, *More Dance Mania* 1959 recording (1963)★★★, *Excitante Ritmo de Tito Puente/The Exciting Rhythm Of Tito Puente* (1964)★★★, Puente's rhythm section, featuring Mongo Santamaría, Willie Bobo, Carlos 'Patato' Valdez *Puente In Percussion* (1964)★★, *Mucho Puente* (1964)★★★, with La Lupe *La Excitante Lupe Canta Con El Maestro Tito Puente /Tito Puente Swings, The Exciting Lupe Sings* (1965)★★★, with La Lupe *Tú y Yo/You 'N' Me* (1965)★★★, *My Fair Lady Goes Latin* (1965)★★, *Carnaval En Harlem* (1965)★★★, with Chivirico Dávila *Y Parece Bobo* (1965)★★★, with La Lupe *Homenaje A Rafael Hernández* (1966)★★★, with Tico All-Stars *Descargas At The Village Gate-Live, Volumes 1-3* (1966)★★★, with Celia Cruz *Cuba Y Puerto Rico Son...* (1966)★★★, *20th Anniversary* (1967)★★★★, with La Lupe *The King And I//El Rey y Yo* (1967)★★★, *The King Tito Puente/El Rey Tito Puente* (1968)★★★, *En El Puente/On The Bridge* (1969)★★★, with Cruz *Quimbo Quimbumbia* (1969)★★★, *Pa'Lante!/Straight!* (1971)★★★, with Cruz *Alma Con Alma/The Heart And Soul Of Celia Cruz* (1971)★★★★, with Noraida *Tito Puente Presents Noraida: La Barbara del Mundo Latino* (1971)★★★, with Cruz *Celia Cruz y Tito Puente en España* (1971)★★★★, with Noraida *Me Voy A Desquitar* (1971)★★★, *Para Los Rumberos* (1972)★★★★, with Cruz *Algo Especial Para Recordar/Something Special To Remember* (1972)★★★, *Tito Puente And His Concert Orchestra* (1973)★★★, *Tito Unlimited* (1974)★★★, *The Tico-Alegre All Stars Recorded Live At Carnegie Hall, Volume 1* (1974)★★★★, with Cal Tjader *Primo* (1974)★★★, *The Legend* (1977)★★★, *Homenaje A Beny* (1978)★★★, with La Lupe *La Pareja* (1979)★★★, *Homenaje A Beny, Volume 2* (1979)★★★, with the Latin Percussion Jazz Ensemble (LPJE)★★★, *Just Like Magic* (1979)★★★, *LPJE Live At The Montreux Jazz Festival 1980* (1980)★★★, with Frankie Figueroa *Dancemania 80's* (1980)★★★, with Camilo Azuquita *Ce' Magnifique* (1981)★★★, *Tito Puente And His Latin Ensemble On Broadway* (1983)★★★, *El Rey* (1984)★★★, with various artists *Super All Star* (1984)★★★, with George Shearing *Mambo Diablo* (1985)★★★, with Cruz *Homenaje A Beny Moré Volume 3* (1985)★★★, with Terry Gibbs *Sensación* (1986)★★★, *Un Poco Loco* (1987)★★★, with guest Phil Woods *Salsa Meets Jazz* (1988)★★, *Goza Mí Timbal* (1989)★★★, with Sheila E., Pete Escovedo *Latina Familia* (1989)★★★, *Out Of This World* (1991)★★★, *The Mambo King: 100th LP* (1991)★★★, *Mambo Gozon* (1993)★★★, with His Jazz Allstars *Master Timabelero* (Concord 1994)★★★, with His Golden Jazz Allstars *In Session* (Bellaphon 1994)★★★, *Tito's Idea* (Tropi 1995)★★★, with the Count Basie Orchestra, India *Jazzin'* (Tropijazz 1996)★★★, featuring Maynard Ferguson *Special Delivery* (Concord Picante 1997)★★★, with TropiJazz All Stars *TropiJazz All Stars* (TropiJazz 1997)★★★.

● COMPILATIONS: *The Latin World Of Tito Puente* (1965)★★★, *No Hay Mejor - There Is No Better* (1975)★★★★, *The Best Of The Sixties* (1988)★★★, *Rumbas And Mambos* (1991)★★★★, *Mamborama!* (1990)★★★, *Royal 'T'* (1993)★★★, *50 Years Of Swing* 3-CD box set (Tropijazz 1997)★★★★.

PUKWANA, DUDU

b. Mtutuzel Pukwana, 2 September 1941, Port Elizabeth, South Africa, d. 29 June 1990, London, England. Although for the majority of his career Pukwana specialized in the alto saxophone, playing a wild, passionate style influenced by South African township mbaqanga, sax jive, Charlie Parker and King Curtis, the first instrument he played was the piano which he learned as a 10-year-old from his father. Moving to Cape Town, and still playing piano, he joined his first band, Tete Mbambisa's Four Yanks, in 1957. It was around this time that he began playing saxophone, learning the rudiments from friend and fellow sideman Nick Moyake, and spending a lot of time listening to imported records by King Curtis, Charlie Parker, Louis Jordan, Sonny Rollins and Ben Webster. In Cape Town, he became friends with the white jazz pianist and bandleader Chris McGregor, who in 1960 invited Pukwana to join his Blue Notes band as saxophonist. He spent the next three years touring South Africa with the Blue Notes, under increasingly difficult conditions, until apartheid legislation made it practically impossible for a mixed race band to appear in public. The group's opportunity to leave the country came in 1963, when they were invited to appear at the annual jazz festival held in Antibes, France. Once the festival was over, the band spent a few months working in Switzerland, until, with the help of London musician and club owner Ronnie Scott, they were able to acquire work permits and entry visas for the UK. Pukwana remained with McGregor until 1969 (by which time the Blue Notes had been renamed the Brotherhood Of Breath), when he took up an offer to join Hugh Masekela's fledgling Union Of South Africa in the USA. When that band fell apart in 1970, he returned to London and formed his own band, Spear, shortly afterwards renamed Assegai.

Pukwana also performed and recorded with, variously, Keith Tippett's Centipede, Jonas Gwangwa, Traffic, the Incredible String Band, Gwigwi Mrwebi, Sebothane Bahula's Jabula, Harry Miller's Isipingo and the Louis Moholo Unit. He made memorable contributions to John and Beverly Martyn's *Road To Ruin* in 1970, and the same year co-led a sax jive/kwela album, *Kwela*, with fellow South African saxophonist Gwigwi Mrwebi. With Assegai, he recorded two albums - *Assegai* and *Assegai Zimbabwe* - before launching the second Spear in 1972. That year, he was also a featured artist on Masekela's London-recorded album *Home Is Where The Music Is*. The new Spear included in its line-up fellow ex-Blue Notes Mongezi Feza (trumpet) and Louis Moholo (drums), along with South Africans Harry Miller (bass) and Bixo Mngqikana (tenor saxophone). Their first album was *In The Townships*, in 1973, which, like its follow-up, *Flute Music*, took the mbaqanga/sax jive/jazz fusion into previously uncharted depths of emotional and creative intensity. In 1978, Pukwana disbanded Spear to form the larger band Zila, a horns- and percussion-dominated outfit whose debut was *Diamond Express*. He continued leading Zila, recording the occasional album and working the UK and European jazz club and festival circuit, until his death from liver failure in 1990 deprived the jazz and African music scene of one of its most consistently inventive players.

● ALBUMS: *Spear: In The Townships* (Virgin 1971)★★★★, *Flute Music* (1974)★★★★, with Assegai *Zimbabwe* (1974)★★★, *Blue Notes For Mongezi* (1976)★★★, *Diamond Express* (1977)★★, *Blue Notes In Concert* (1978)★★★, with Zila *Sounds - Live At The 100 Club* (Jika 1981)★★★, with Zila *Live At Bracknell & Willisau* (Jika 1984)★★★, *Zila '86* (Jika 1986)★★, with John Stevens *Radebe - They Shoot To Kill* (Affinity 1987)★★★, *Blue Notes For Johnny* (1987)★★★, with Zila *Cosmics Chapter 90* (Ah-Um 1990)★★★.

Pullen, Don

b. 25 December 1941, Roanoke, Virginia, USA, d. 22 April 1995. After playing piano in church, accompanying gospel singers, Pullen worked in various R&B bands before turning to jazz. In the early 60s he studied with Muhal Richard Abrams, and Giuseppe Logan, with whom he made his recording debut in 1964. Pullen also continued to work in R&B and related fields, occasionally working with Albert Ayler and saxophonist Sil Austin but usually as accompanist to singers, often playing organ, and in 1970 he joined Nina Simone for a year. In the meantime, he led his own small bands and formed a long-standing partnership with Milford Graves, recording with him on the SRP label they ran together. In the early 70s he joined Charles Mingus, appearing on *Mingus At Carnegie Hall* and *Changes*, and played briefly with Art Blakey. Later in the decade he played with Sam Rivers and the Art Ensemble Of Chicago. Towards the end of the 70s he formed a lasting musical partnership with George Adams, with whom he co-led as the Pullen/George Adams Quartet, which additionally featured Cameron Brown (bass) and Dannie Richmond (drums), and also worked with Mingus Dynasty. A vibrant, eclectic and usually exciting pianist that often resulted in bruised and blistered knuckles, Pullen possessed the technique to match his questing imagination and his playing, whether as soloist or as accompanist, was always interesting. In particular, his interplay with Adams displayed his talent to the full. In recent times he formed the African Brazilian Connection but lost his battle with cancer in 1995. The tracks for *Sacred Common Ground* were recorded a few weeks before his death.

● ALBUMS: with Milford Graves *Graves-Pullen Duo* (Pullen-Graves 1967)★★★, with Graves *Nommo* (SRP 1968)★★, *Jazz A Confonto* (Horo 1975)★★★, *Five To Go* (1976)★★★, *Capricorn Rising* (Black Saint 1976)★★★, *Healing Force* (1976)★★★, *Montreux Concert* (Atlantic 1978)★★★, with Joseph Jarman, Famoudou Don Moye *The Magic Triangle* (Black Saint 1979)★★★★, with Mingus Dynasty *Chair In The Sky* (1979)★★★, *Warriors* (Black Saint 1979)★★★, with George Adams *Don't Lose Control* (Soul Note 1979)★★★★, *Milano Strut* (Black Saint 1979), with Adams *Lifeline* (Timeless 1981)★★★, with Adams *Earth Beams* (Timeless 1981)★★★, with Adams *Melodic Excursions* (Timeless 1982)★★★★, with Adams *Live At The Village Vanguard, Volume 1* (Soul Note 1983)★★★★, with Adams *Live At The Village Vanguard, Volume 2* (Soul Note 1983)★★★★, *Evidence Of Things Unseen* (Black Saint 1983)★★★, with Adams *City Gates* (Timeless 1983)★★★, with Adams *Decisions* (Timeless 1984)★★★, *Plays Monk* (Paddle Wheel 1985)★★★, *The Sixth Sense* (Black Saint 1985)★★★★, with Adams *Live At Montmartre* (Timeless 1985)★★★, with Adams *Breakthrough* (Blue Note 1986)★★★, with Adams *Song Everlasting* (Blue Note 1987)★★★, *New Beginnings* (Blue Note 1988)★★★, with Jane Bunnett *New York Duets* (Music & Arts 1989)★★★★, *Random Thoughts* (Blue Note 1990)★★★, *Kele Mou Bana* (Blue Note 1992)★★★, *Ode To Life* (Blue Note 1993)★★★, *Live ... Again* (Blue Note 1995)★★★, *Sacred Common Ground* (Blue Note 1996)★★.

Purbrook, Colin

b. Colin Thomas Purbrook, 26 February 1936, Seaford, Sussex, England. A gifted pianist, Purbrook's highly active career hit its stride in the late 50s when he played with Sandy Brown's band. During the next few years he worked with a succession of leading musicians, confidently moving from traditional jazz, with Kenny Ball, to modern, with Tubby Hayes, Ronnie Scott and others. In the early 60s he often worked with Tony Coe and he also played in the band led by Don Rendell and Ian Carr, recording with them on 1964's Columbia Records' session, *Shades Of Blue*. In the early 60s he showed his adaptability and broad musicianship by playing bass with the Dudley Moore trio. Purbrook also led his own small bands for club and radio work, appeared on television and in films, and during the 70s and 80s was a stalwart accompanist for many of the American jazz artists who visited the UK, among them Benny Carter and Buddy Tate. His skills were also in demand in the theatre and he served as musical director for several shows, including *One Mo' Time*. He continued his dual role of accompanist and leader into the 90s, working clubs and festivals throughout the UK. A stylish and sensitive player when in a supporting role, Purbrook's solos are filled with invention and great drive. He has contributed immeasurably to numerous recordings by many artists.

PURDIE, BERNARD 'PRETTY'

b. 11 June 1939, Elkton, Maryland, USA. Purdie, the eleventh of 15 children, began to learn drums at the age of six. During the 60s he became a highly respected session drummer, and played on numerous releases ranging from Nina Simone to Tim Rose and Jack Jones. He is, however, better remembered for his work in the New York-based house band put together for the Atlantic label by saxophonist King Curtis. Purdie was thus present on several of Aretha Franklin's finest recordings. The self-proclaimed 'world's greatest drummer' also played on numerous jazz sessions, including Albert Ayler's controversial *New Grass*. Such work anticipated the direction Purdie took when he embarked on a solo career. One of his most recent studio sessions was with Jimmy Smith on 1995's *Damn!*.

● ALBUMS: *Soul Drums* (Direction 1968)★★★, *Soul Fingers* (1968)★★, *Stand By Me* (1971)★★★, *Purdie Good* (1971)★★★, *Soul Is ... Pretty Purdie* (1972)★★, *Shaft* (1974)★★★, *Delights Of The Garden* (1975)★★★, *Soul To Jazz II* (ACT 1997)★★★.

PURIM, FLORA

b. 6 March 1942, Rio de Janeiro, Brazil. Purim was raised in a musical atmosphere (her parents were classical musicians) and she played several instruments before settling on a career as a singer. While studying percussion she met and later married Airto Moreira. After moving to the USA in the late 60s she worked with musicians including Stan Getz, Duke Pearson, Gil Evans and George Duke before becoming a member of Chick Corea's Return To Forever unit, which also included Moreira. In the early and mid-70s Purim and Moreira had their own band; the singer also made several solo albums, which broadened her appeal into more popular areas of music. In the late 70s and early 80s Purim recorded with David Sanborn and a few years later was again working with Moreira. Purim scats interestingly, and frequently vocalizes wordlessly, her light, captivating voice floating over the improvisations of the accompanying musicians. Her sister, Yana Purim, is also a singer and worked with her mother and father on 1992's Fourth World project.

● ALBUMS: *Milestone Memories* (1972)★★, *Butterfly Dreams* (Original Jazz Classics 1973)★★★★, *Stories To Tell* (1974)★★★, *Open Your Eyes You Can Fly* (1976)★★★, *500 Miles High At Montreux* 1974 recording (1976)★★, *Nothing Will Be As It Was...Tomorrow* (1977)★★★, *Encounter* (1977)★★★, *That's What She Said* (1977)★★★, *Everyday, Everynight* (1978)★★★, *Humble People* (1985)★★★, *The Magicians* (Crossover 1986)★★★, *Love Reborn* (Fantasy 1986)★★★, with Airto Moreira *The Colours Of Life* (1987)★★★★, *The Midnight Sun* (Venture 1988)★★★, *The Sun Is Out* (Crossover 1989)★★, *Speed Of Light* (B&W 1995)★★★.

PURNELL, ALTON

b. 16 April 1911, New Orleans, Louisiana, USA, d. 14 January 1987. Starting out as a singer, Purnell took up piano in his youth and became a professional musician in his mid-teens. He worked with a number of well-known bands in his home-town, including those led by Alphonse Picou and Big Eye Louis Nelson, before moving to New York in the mid-40s, where he played in various bands, including those led by Bunk Johnson and George Lewis. In the mid-50s he moved out to the west coast where he played with many leading New Orleans and Dixieland jazzmen such as Kid Ory, Teddy Buckner, Ben Pollack and Barney Bigard. From the mid-60s onwards, Purnell toured extensively, sometimes in bands such as the Legends of Jazz, the Young Men Of New Orleans and Kid Thomas's band. He also toured as a soloist. A strong player who ably blended the traditional New Orleans style of piano playing with elements of Harlem stride, Purnell proved very popular in the later years of his career. His singing was always engaging and entertaining.

● ALBUMS: with George Lewis *New Orleans Stompers* (1955)★★★, *Alton Purnell Quartet* (1958)★★★, *Live With Keith Smith's Climax Jazz Band* (1965)★★★, *Tribute To Louis* (1971)★★, *Kid Thomas* (1975)★★★, *In Japan* (GHB 1977)★★, *Alton Purnell Meets Houlind* (Nathan 1988)★★★, *Alton Purnell Live* (CSA 1989)★★★.

PURNELL, KEG

b. William Purnell, 7 January 1915, Charleston, West Virginia, USA, d. 25 June 1965. Purnell began playing drums while still at school, working in college bands into the early 30s. In 1934 he joined King Oliver's band, then briefly led his own small group in New York. In the last year or so of the decade, he played with a number of leading musicians of the day, including Benny Carter, and also with rising young stars, among them Thelonious Monk. In the early 40s he was with Claude Hopkins, then joined Eddie Heywood for a time. In the mid-50s he played with various artists, mostly in the New York area, such as Willie 'The Lion' Smith and Snub Mosley. He remained with the latter's band until shortly before his death.

● COMPILATIONS: *The Chronological Benny Carter 1939-1940* (Classics 1939-40)★★★★.

PURTILL, MOE

b. Maurice Purtill, 4 May 1916, Huntington, New York, USA. After playing drums with a number of bands in the New York area, Purtill joined Red Norvo in 1936. Playing in the exceptional small band Norvo led at this time, which built its repertoire upon the arranging skills of Eddie Sauter, Purtill attracted attention from other musicians for his subtly swinging work. He then played briefly with Glenn Miller before joining Tommy Dorsey early in 1938. Here, too, he made a marked difference to the band's sound, swinging the Dorsey dance music-orientated swing band with effortless ease. When he was replaced, in 1939, by the more extrovert Buddy

Rich, Purtill returned to Miller, who was at that time searching for a secure and swinging drummer who would fulfill the leader's ideals for his big band. Purtill filled the bill admirably, providing the Miller band with a flowing swing it previously never had and would also later lack. Purtill remained with Miller until the latter entered the US Army. Purtill then joined Kay Kayser's dance band, again providing a lift and swing not usually associated with a novelty band of this kind. He was then drafted into the US Navy and after service resumed playing, for a while with the Miller-style band led by Tex Beneke. He was then with the strict tempo dance band of Richard Himber before taking his considerable skills into the radio and recording studios where he played for the next few decades. Purtill's playing style in rhythm sections was subtle and swinging, displaying his fondness for the style of Jo Jones, one of two drummers he clearly admired. The other was Gene Krupa, and something of this drummer's flamboyance can be heard in Purtill's solos, as on 'Anvil Chorus' and 'Bugle Call Rag', both recorded with Miller. He also appeared with Miller's band in the films *Sun Valley Serenade* (1941) and *Orchestra Wives* (1942), soloing in the latter. Although jazz fans are sometimes dismissive of Miller's band, and sometimes with cause, it could and often did swing, and in its pre-war incarnation that quality was largely due to Purtill's exemplary and all-too-often unsung contribution.

● COMPILATIONS: *Red Norvo And His All Stars* (Philips 1933-38)★★★, *The Indispensable Tommy Dorsey Vols. 5 & 6* (RCA 1938-39)★★★★, with Glenn Miller *Jazz Archives Masterpieces 4* (Jazz Archives 1939-42)★★★.

PURVIS, JACK

b. 11 December 1906, Kokomo, Indiana, USA, d. 30 March 1962. In the early 20s Purvis played trumpet and trombone with the Original Kentucky Night Hawks, then began a life that, as jazz musician and writer Digby Fairweather has observed, 'makes a ripping jazz yarn' - even if only a tenth of it is true. In the late 20s Purvis played in various bands, made records, including a remarkable take-off of Louis Armstrong, and sat in with Fletcher Henderson's band. In the 30s he made more records with the likes of Coleman Hawkins and J.C. Higginbotham, played the harp with Fred Waring, arranged music for motion pictures, became a smuggler in his own small aircraft, fought as a mercenary and was a hotel chef. By the end of the decade he was reputedly playing in a Texas prison band while serving time for robbery. He served 10 years, vanishing from sight on his release but was later believed to be serving time again for second-degree murder.

He died in 1962, his body being found in a gas-filled room. Whether he killed himself - at the time of his death he was an unemployed radio repairman - or died accidentally was made uncertain when an autopsy showed a substantial level of alcohol in his blood. Highly regarded by fellow musicians, Purvis's few records suggest an enormously talented trumpet player with a flamboyant and sometimes erratic style.

● COMPILATIONS: with Louis Armstrong *Satchmo Style (1929-30)* (1988)★★★★.

PYNE, CHRIS

b. 14 February 1939, Bridlington, Yorkshire, England, d. 12 April 1995. Pyne was a self-taught trombonist whose initial band experience was with a Royal Air Force band during his National Service (1960-61). He later appeared in a succession of units throughout the 60s, which included John Cox's band, Alexis Korner's Blues Incorporated, Humphrey Lyttelton, John Dankworth, Ronnie Scott, Tubby Hayes and Maynard Ferguson. Pyne was a consummately professional studio musician who recorded with Ella Fitzgerald and Tony Bennett and played on many of Frank Sinatra's UK tours. Pyne had a polished, accurate playing style that reflected an early liking for J.J. Johnson. During the 70s and 80s he worked with, among others, John Taylor, Mike Gibbs, Kenny Wheeler, Gordon Beck and John Surman. Pyne's brother, Mike Pyne, was also a jazz musician.

● ALBUMS: with Alexis Korner *Blues Incorporated* (1967)★★★★, with John Dankworth *Million Dollar Collection* (1967)★★★, with John Stevens' SME *The Source* (1970)★★★★, with John Taylor *Pause And Think Again* (1971)★★★, with Pete Hurt *Lost For Words* (1984)★★★, with Kenny Wheeler *Music For Large And Small Ensembles* (1990)★★★★.

PYNE, MIKE

b. 2 September 1940, Thornton-le-Dale, Yorkshire, England, d. 24 May 1995. Pyne's father was a pianist and he encouraged him to play from the age of three. He came to London in 1961 and played piano regularly in a succession of bands - with drummer Tony Kinsey, Alexis Korner's Blues Incorporated, Tubby Hayes and Humphrey Lyttelton. Pyne sometimes had the chance to play his second instrument, the trumpet, but more regularly contributed his strong solo lines or accompaniments on piano. He worked with Philly Joe Jones, saxophonists Stan Getz, Rahsaan Roland Kirk, Dexter Gordon and Ronnie Scott, with the Mike Gibbs Orchestra and the Cecil Payne Quintet. In the 80s he also played with Georgie Fame's Stardust Road show and Keith Smith's Hefty Jazz. Pyne's brother, Chris Pyne, was also a jazz musician and tragically, died just one month before his brother.

● ALBUMS: with Philly Joe Jones *Trailways Express* (1968)★★★, with John Stevens' SME *The Source* (1970)★★★★, with Humphrey Lyttelton *21 Years On* (1969)★★★, with Lyttelton *Once In A While* (Black Lion 1976)★★★, with Lyttelton *Alone Together* (Spotlite 1977)★★★, with Jon Eardley *Two Of A Kind* (1977)★★★, with Tubby Hayes *Mexican Green* (1981)★★★★, with Lyttelton *Humph At The Bull's Head* (1984)★★★, with Tommy Whittle *Straight Eight* (1985)★★★, *A Little Blue* (Miles Music 1988)★★★.

QUEALEY, CHELSEA

b. 1905, Hartford, Connecticut, USA, d. 6 May 1950. After a brief flirtation with the saxophone, Quealey chose the trumpet and while still a young man, worked in well-known bands such as Jan Garber's and the California Ramblers. In the late 20s he played in London with Fred Elizalde, then returned to the USA and engagements with the Ramblers, Paul Whiteman and Ben Pollack. In the 30s he played in a succession of good bands including those led by Isham Jones, Fred McKenzie, Joe Marsala and Frank Trumbauer. He rounded off the decade with a spell in Bob Zurke's short-lived big band. In the 40s he was often to be heard in New York nightspots playing in the company of traditional musicians such as Georg Brunis and Miff Mole. Towards the end of the decade he played in bands in California and Nevada hotels and casinos.

● COMPILATIONS: *California Ramblers With Adrian Rollini* (Village 1923-27), *Adrian Rollini Groups 1924-27* (Village 1924-27), *The Chronological Mezz Mezzrow, 1928-1936* (Classics 1928-36), with Benny Carter *All Of Me* (Bluebird 1934-59), *Bob Zurke And His Delta Rhythm Band* (Meritt 1939).

QUEBEC, IKE

b. 17 August 1918, Newark, New Jersey, USA, d. 16 January 1963. Quebec played piano at first, then took up the tenor saxophone in 1940. He worked in several well-known bands, including outfits led by Benny Carter, Coleman Hawkins, Roy Eldridge and, later, Cab Calloway, with whom he stayed from 1944-51. He also led his own small groups in the 40s, recording several sessions for Blue Note, the first of which produced the hit 'Blue Harlem'. A close friend of the label's co-founder, Alfred Lion, Quebec advised Blue Note on the bebop scene, recommending that they record both Thelonious Monk and Bud Powell. For much of the 50s, Quebec struggled against heroin addiction and worked various day jobs, including a stint as a taxi driver. He returned to the music business in 1959, becoming an A&R man for Blue Note and also recording for them again - first making several juke-box singles, then a series of albums that showcased his expertise at slow blues and soulful ballads. He also guested on albums by Sonny Clark, Grant Green, Jimmy Smith and vocalist Dodo Green. In January 1963, he died of lung cancer, and, for many years, appeared to be one of the forgotten men of jazz. Then, in the 80s, Blue Note issued some previously unreleased sessions, while Mosaic Records produced lavishly packaged compilations both of his 40s Blue Note recordings and the later juke-box singles. The appearance of this material sparked a new interest in, and welcome re-evaluation of, Quebec's shapely, affecting, big-toned tenor playing.

● ALBUMS: *Heavy Soul* (Blue Note 1958)★★★, *Blue And Sentimental* (Blue Note 1961)★★★★, *It Might As Well Be Spring* (Blue Note 1962)★★★, *Bossa Nova Soul Samba* (Blue Note 1962)★★★, *Easy Living* (Blue Note 1962)★★★, *With A Song In My Heart* 1962 recording (1980)★★, *Congo Lament* 1962 recording (1981)★★.

● COMPILATIONS: *The Complete Blue Note Forties Recordings Of Ike Quebec And John Hardee* 4-LP box-set (Blue Note 1987)★★★, *The Complete Blue Note 45 Sessions Of Ike Quebec* 1959-62 recordings, 3-LP box-set (Blue Note 1987)★★★★.

QUEST

This US jazz group emerged in 1978 and have since diminished to a quartet consisting of Dave Liebman (saxophone, flute), Richie Beirach (piano), Ron McClure (bass) and Billy Hart (drums). Earlier versions of the group included George Mraz (bass) and Al Foster (drums) as substitutes in the rhythm section. The group's music is primarily centred on Liebman and Beirach. Since the early 70s they have worked together, both as instrumentalists and composers. Liebman's approach is clearly influenced by John Coltrane, but he has a strong and easily recognized style of his own. Beirach can be equally powerful in this region, but also shows influences from classical music. The rhythm section is as competent and creates the rhythmic drive that this group's music requires. These different influences give the group a wide range of expressive possibilities that include hard swinging up-tempo jazz, more introspective tone-painting pastiches and occasionally free improvisation.

● ALBUMS: *Quest* (Palo Alto 1982)★★★, *Quest II* (Storyville 1986)★★, *Midpoint, Quest III Live At The Montmartre Copenhagen Denmark* (Storyville 1988)★★, *Natural Selection* (Pathfinder 1988)★★★, *Of One Mind* (CMP 1990)★★★.

QUINICHETTE, PAUL

b. 17 May 1916, Denver, Colorado, USA, d. 25 May 1983, New York City, New York, USA. After formally studying clarinet and alto saxophone, Quinichette switched to tenor saxophone. He played in a number of local and territory bands, notably that led by Nat Towles. Amongst the outfits with which he played in the early 40s were those led by Jay McShann, Benny Carter and Johnny Otis. Later in the decade he was active in New York, playing and recording with Louis Jordan, Dinah Washington, Lucky Millinder and others, and in the early 50s he worked with Count Basie. Included in his recordings of this period are concert performances with Washington released as *The Jazz Sides* (1954-58). In the mid-50s Quinichette played briefly with Benny Goodman, John Coltrane and Nat Pierce but then drifted out of music for several years. In the 70s he was back on the jazz scene but, plagued by poor health, he made little impact. During the late 40s and early 50s Quinichette attracted attention because of similarities in tone and style to Lester Young, even picking up the nickname 'Vice-Pres'. The resemblance was deliberate and when he was at his best was more than merely superficial. Nevertheless, such comparisons were damaging to Quinichette's career and he rarely overcame the link for long enough to establish a strong personal identity. In retrospect he can be seen as a fine, lyrical and always swinging player; had he not suffered a hiatus in his career, he might well have been able to overcome the disadvantage of following so closely upon Young's unique path.

● ALBUMS: *The Vice 'Pres'* 10-inch album (EmArcy 1954)★★★, *Sequel* (EmArcy 1954)★★★, with Frank Foster *Jazz Studio 1* (Decca 1954)★★★, *Moods* (EmArcy 1955)★★★, with Bennie Green *Blow Your Horn* (Decca 1955)★★★, *The Kid From Denver* (Dawn 1956)★★★, with Gene Roland *Jazzville* (Dawn 1957)★★★, *On The Sunny Side* (Prestige 1957)★★★★, *For Basie* (Prestige 1957)★★★, with Charlie Rouse *The Chase Is On* (Bethlehem 1958)★★★, *Basie Reunion* (Prestige 1958)★★★, with John Coltrane *Cattin' With John Coltrane And Paul Quinichette* (Prestige 1959)★★★, *Like Basie* (United Artists 1959)★★★, *Like Who?* (United Artists 1959)★★★, *Paul Quinichette* (United Artists 1960)★★★.

QUINTETTE DU HOT CLUB DU FRANCE

(see Reinhardt, Django; Grappelli, Stéphane)

RAEBURN, BOYD

b. 27 October 1913, Faith, South Dakota, USA, d. 2 August 1966, Layfayette, Indiana, USA. Raeburn attended the University of Chicago, where he led a campus band, before becoming a professional musician leading a small, light music band, but in the 30s turned his attention to swing. In 1944 he formed a high-class band that featured some fine young musicians including Dizzy Gillespie, Sonny Berman (trumpets), Earl Swope, Tommy Pederson (trombones), Al Cohn, Johnny Bothwell (saxophones), while older stars such as Roy Eldridge and Trummy Young played with the band that recorded for the V Disc label. Raeburn was unlucky - a fire at New Jersey's Palisades Amusement Park destroyed the band's library together with many of its instruments. Undeterred, Raeburn put together an astonishing outfit that seemed, in 1945, years ahead of its time. It played numbers such as 'Dalvatore Sally', 'Yerxa' and 'Boyd Meets Stravinsky', and the music was as impressionistic as the titles suggest. Vocalists David Allyn and Raeburn's wife Ginny Powell found their songs placed in Debussy-like settings and although the critics loved it all, the public did not take to a band that played non-danceable music. In 1947, although signed to Atlantic Records, Raeburn broke up the band. The man who fronted the band holding an ungainly bass saxophone had become disenchanted with the scene, and moved on to part ownership of a Fifth Avenue shop, later moving to Nassau in the Bahamas for more business interests. He died of a heart attack in 1966, having outlived his wife Ginny by seven years.

● ALBUMS: *Innovations By Boyd Raeburn, Volume 1* 10-inch album (Savoy 1951)★★★, *Innovations By Boyd Raeburn, Volume 2* 10-inch album (Savoy 1951)★★★, *Innovations By Boyd Raeburn, Volume 3* 10-inch album (Savoy 1951)★★★, *Man With The Horn* (Savoy 1955)★★★, *Boyd Meets Stravinsky* (Savoy 1955)★★★, *Dance Spectacular* (Columbia 1956)★★★, *Teen Rock* (Columbia 1957)★★★, *Boyd Raeburn And His Orchestra* 1944 recordings (Circle)★★★, *Boyd Raeburn And His Orchestra* 1944/1945 recordings (Circle)★★★, *Rhythms By Raeburn* 1945 recordings (Aircheck)★★★, *The Unissued Boyd Raeburn* 1945 recordings (Joyce)★★★, *Experiments In Big Band Jazz* 1945 recordings (Musicraft)★★★, *Where You At* 1945-1948 recordings (Hep)★★★, *Jubilee Broadcasts: 1946* (Hep)★★★, *Boyd Raeburn Orchestra - On The Air, Volume One* (1981)★★★, *Memphis In June* 1945-1947 recording (Hep)★★★★, *Jewels* 1945-1949 recordings (Savoy)★★★★, *Airshots 1944-1946* (IAJRC 1990)★★★, *Hep Boyds* 1945-1947 recordings (Hep)★★★.

RAGLIN, JUNIOR

b. Alvin Redrick Raglin, 16 March 1917, Omaha, Nebraska, USA, d. 10 November 1955. Raglin played guitar and bass, eventually settling on the latter, in various territory bands in the south-eastern states. In 1941 he was in Los Angeles and was hired by Duke Ellington as second bassist to back up the ailing Jimmy Blanton. After Blanton's hospitalization and death in mid-summer 1942, Raglin stayed with Ellington. In 1945 he moved on, playing in several small bands, but returned to Ellington in 1946 for less than a year. After this he was forced into semi-retirement through illness, although he did play again with Ellington before his death. During the 40s, in addition to his work with Ellington, Raglin also played on record dates with artists such as Edmond Hall, Ella Fitzgerald and a clutch of ex-Ellingtonians including Rex Stewart, Ray Nance and Al Hibbler. Although Raglin's time with Ellington was during a period when the leader was using two bassists (during his second spell Raglin shared duties with Oscar Pettiford), he was a secure and highly competent player with a firm beat and a ringing tone. His small group work showed him to be a player of subtlety and swing.

● ALBUMS: with Duke Ellington *Carnegie Hall Concert* (Jazz Panorama 1943)★★★.

● COMPILATIONS: *The Chronological Duke Ellington 1942-1944* (Classics 1942-44)★★★★, *The Chronological Edmond Hall 1944-1945* (Classics 1944-45)★★★.

RAMEY, GENE

b. 4 April 1913, Austin, Texas, USA, d. 8 December 1984. A student of Walter Page, bass player Ramey briefly led his own band in Kansas City before joining Jay McShann. This was in 1938 and he remained with McShann until the band broke up in 1943. During the rest of the 40s Ramey became a regular at numerous club and recording dates in New York, playing with top-flight swing and bop stars including Charlie Parker, Coleman Hawkins and Lester Young. In the 50s he freelanced with mainstreamers and beboppers, comfortably fitting in with the musical concepts of Buck Clayton and Art Blakey while also making the transition to dixieland with Muggsy Spanier. Ramey's skills were highly regarded and his musical range meant that he was in demand throughout his musical career and appeared on countless albums with musicians as diverse as Thelonious Monk, Teddy Wilson, Horace Silver, Lennie Tristano, Count Basie and Stan Getz. In the 60s he retired to become a bank security guard but later returned to the jazz scene to play at international festivals with his old comrade McShann. He retired in 1975, moving to Texas to run a smallholding.

● ALBUMS: *The Count Basie Sextet* (1952)★★★.

RAMIREZ, RAM

b. Roger Ramirez, 15 September 1913, Puerto Rico, d. 11 January 1994, New York, USA. Raised in New York City, Ramirez displayed a prodigious talent as a pianist and at the age of 13 became a member of the American Federation of Musicians. During the mid- and late 30s he worked with various artists, including Monette Moore, the Spirits Of Rhythm, Putney Dandridge, Stew Pletcher and Willie Bryant. He recorded with Dandridge and Bryant in 1936. Mostly working in the New York area, he occasionally led small groups in the early 40s, but was also with Ella Fitzgerald in 1940, in the band she took over after the death of Chick Webb. He next played in bands led by Frankie Newton and Ike Quebec, appearing with the latter on some early Blue Note records. In the mid-40s he was with John Kirby, playing and recording with his re-formed sextet. Ramirez also recorded under his own name in 1946, leading a trio with guitarist Jimmy Shirley and bassist Al Hall. In 1944 Billie Holiday recorded Ramirez's composition, 'Lover Man', a song that subsequently became a jazz standard. In the late 40s and early 50s he continued to play in and around New York, and towards the end of this period began to play organ. In the 60s he worked with 'T-Bone' Walker, and the following decade was with the Harlem Blues And Jazz Band. He continued to make appearances with this group into the early 80s. A blues-orientated pianist and organist, Ramirez is perhaps less well known than his skills warrant. Although he visited Europe in 1937 and toured with the Harlem Blues And Jazz band, his decision to spend much of his career in a small geographical area has meant that his international reputation rests largely upon numerous recordings of his most famous composition.

● ALBUMS: *Lover Man* (1966-67)★★★, *Rampant Ram* (1973-74)★★★, *Harlem Blues And Jazz Band, 1973-80* (1973-80)★★★★.

RANDALL, FREDDY

b. 6 May 1921, London, England. Randall began playing trumpet in the late 30s and led his own small band in 1939. By the mid-40s he was one of the most respected Dixieland trumpeters in the UK, appearing on radio and at clubs and concerts. He was therefore well placed to take advantage of the trad boom that swept the UK from the late 40s and on through the 50s. Randall's band became one of the most popular of the era and he also toured the USA. Ill-health forced his retirement in the late 50s but he was back, part-time, in 1963, and thereafter continued to make occasional and usually unscheduled appearances at London clubs and pubs. These gigs found him playing as well as ever and delighting an army of fans that seemed to grow stronger and more numerous as the years passed. A band he formed in the early 70s in collaboration with Dave Shepherd played at international festivals to great acclaim. Reissues of his earlier records confirmed that his qualities were not the result of nostalgic glow. Randall played hard-driving Chicago-style jazz with verve and great skill, and the many fine musicians who played in his band at one time or another responded to his enthusiastic lead.

● ALBUMS: *His Great Sixteen* (1951-56)★★★, *Something Borrowed, Something Blue* 50s recordings (Alamo 1978)★★, *Wild Bill Davison With Freddy Randall's Band* (1965)★★★, *Freddy Randall-Dave Shepherd All Stars* (1972)★★★, *Freddy Randall-Dave Shepherd All Stars 'Live' At Montreux Jazz Festival* (1973)★★, *Freddie Randall And His Band* (Dormouse 1986)★★★.

RANDOLPH, MOUSE

b. Irving Randolph, 22 January 1909, St. Louis, Missouri, USA. After serving a long apprenticeship in numerous territory bands including those led by Fate Marable and Alphonso Trent, trumpeter Randolph joined Andy Kirk in 1931. After leaving Kirk in 1934 he played in big bands led by Fletcher Henderson, Benny Carter, Luis Russell and Cab Calloway, the former Chick Webb band under the nominal leadership of Ella Fitzgerald and Don Redman. During this period he also recorded with pick-up groups, including Teddy Wilson's band, and after leaving Redman in 1943 he then began a round of small groups, including the sextet led by Edmond Hall. Throughout the 50s and 60s he worked for long periods in relatively unknown and undistinguished orchestras, occasionally recording with jazz groups. He later drifted into retirement. Highly regarded by fellow musicians, Randolph's career, although taking him into many fine swing era bands, suggests that he lacked the ambition that brought fame and fortune to lesser musicians.

● ALBUMS: *The Chronological Teddy Wilson And His Orchestra 1936-1937* (1936-37)★★★★.

RANDOLPH, ZILNER

b. Zilner Trenton Randolph, 28 January 1899, Dermott, Arkansas, USA. During the early 20s he played trumpet in bands in and around St. Louis, Missouri, before joining a territory band in Wisconsin. Randolph also studied extensively, becoming a skilled arranger. In the early 30s he moved to Chicago where he played in a band led by Louis Armstrong, also writing arrangements and organizing and rehearsing the bands Armstrong fronted during these years. He was also composer of the song 'Old Man Mose', which Armstrong recorded. In 1935 he formed a big band of his own, but the late 30s mostly found him active as an arranger for many of the popular swing era bands, including Woody Herman, Duke Ellington and Fletcher Henderson. In the 40s he formed a small band and also worked in a musical act featuring his children. Randolph also taught music, and in the 50s played piano.

RANEY, JIMMY

b. 20 August 1927, Louisville, Kentucky, USA, d. 10 May 1995, Louisville, Kentucky, USA. After working in the New York and Chicago areas, in bands led by Jerry Wald and Lou Levy, guitarist Raney joined Woody Herman in 1948. Thereafter he played and recorded with a number of leading swing era veterans and up-and-coming stars including Artie Shaw, Stan Getz, Terry Gibbs and Red Norvo. Throughout the 60s he worked in studios, making occasional jazz club appearances. This pattern continued into the 70s with the bias gradually swinging towards jazz work. A relaxed and highly proficient technician, Raney's solo work displayed a cool, lambent style which is much admired, although his attraction was often cerebral rather than emotional. His son, Doug, also plays guitar.

● ALBUMS: *Jimmy Raney Quartet Featuring Hall Overton* 10-inch album (New Jazz 1953)★★★, *Jimmy Raney Ensemble Introducing Phil Woods* 10-inch album (New Jazz 1953)★★★, *Jimmy Raney Plays* 10-inch album (Prestige 1953)★★★★, *Jimmy Raney In Sweden* 10-inch album (Prestige 1954)★★★, *Jimmy Raney Quintet* 10-inch album (Prestige 1954)★★★★, *Jimmy Raney Featuring Bob Brookmeyer* (ABC-Paramount 1956)★★★, *Jimmy Raney/A* (Prestige 1957)★★★★, *Jimmy Raney In Three Attitudes* (ABC-Paramount 1957)★★★, with Bob Brookmeyer, Jim Hall *Street Swingers* reissued as *Brookmeyer And Guitars* (World Pacific/Kimberly 1957)★★★, with Kenny Burrell *Two Guitars* (Prestige 1957)★★★★, *Jimmy Raney Visits Paris* (Dawn 1958)★★★, with George Wallington *Swingin' In Sweden* (EmArcy 1958)★★★, with Jim Hall, Zoot Sims *Two Jims And Zoot* (Mainstream 1965)★★★, *Momentum* (1974)★★★, *The Influence* (1975)★★★, *Live In Tokyo* (Xanadu 1976)★★★, with Doug Raney *Stolen Moments* (Steeple Chase 1979)★★★, with Doug Raney *Duets* (Steeple Chase 1979)★★★, *Here's That Raney Day* (Black And Blue 1980)★★★, with Doug Raney *Raney '81* (Criss Cross 1981)★★★, *The Master* (Criss Cross 1983)★★★★, with Doug Raney *Nardis* (1983)★★★, *Visits Paris* (Fresh Sounds 1988)★★★, *Wisteria* (Criss Cross 1990)★★★★, *But Beautiful* (Criss Cross 1993)★★★.

RANEY, SUE

b. Raelene Claire Claussen, 18 June 1940, McPherson, Kansas, USA. Raised in New Mexico, as a small child Raney was trained by her mother, a professional singer and music teacher. Raney began singing at the age of four and at age eight was singing professionally. Four years on, she had regular radio and television spots including appearances with country singer Glen Campbell. Her early singing idols were in the popular field, although some were jazz-inflected, but by her mid-teens had begun to direct her style more firmly into jazz. She gained some valuable early experience working with the Ray Anthony band. In the early 60s she sang with Nelson Riddle in the UK and made several albums that were critically successful but failed to find a wide audience. She continued to perform, her career remaining regrettably low-key, although musical partnerships with Stan Kenton, Michel Legrand, Henry Mancini and others continued to attract critical favour. Further fine albums in the mid-80s and an outstanding 1990 release, *In Good Company*, on which she was backed by jazzmen such as Conte Candoli, Bob Cooper, Bill Watrous and Alan Broadbent, attracted wider attention. Raney is also an accomplished songwriter, contributing lyrics to several songs including 'Statue Of Snow'. Singing with a finely textured voice, beautifully pitched, always displaying impeccable timing and taste, and with effortless swing, Raney is an exceptionally gifted performer. She is one of the finest living interpreters of the great standards and is an excellent jazz singer. Sadly, even following her most recent albums, she remains relatively little known outside a small circle of justifiably devoted admirers. Her husband is flügelhorn player Carmen Falzone.

● ALBUMS: *Sue Raney Sings The Music Of Johnny Mandel* (Discovery 1982)★★★, with Bob Florence *Ridin' High* (Discovery 1984)★★, *Flight Of Fancy* (Discovery 1985)★★★, with Florence *Quietly There* (Discovery 1988)★★, *In Good Company* (Discovery 1990)★★★, *Breathless!* (Studio West 1998)★★★.

RANGELL, NELSON

b. Denver, Colorado, USA. One of the more distinctive voices working in the oversubscribed pop/jazz firmament, Rangell first picked up the flute at the age of 15. Six months later he found himself studying at the Interlochen Arts Academy, before travelling to the New England Conservatory Of Music in Boston, Massachusetts, to study with renowned saxophone tutor Joe Allard. Immersed in the work of Charlie Parker, Sonny Stitt and Cannonball Adderley, he headed to New York in 1984 to pursue his calling to jazz. The next three years were spent playing with top players including Hiram Bullock, Eric Gale, Richard Tee, David Sanborn and others. He also found occasional employment with the Gil Evans Monday Night Orchestra. Rangell's debut album was released for Gramavision/Gaia Records before he found a more satisfying environment at GRP Records. A succession of albums followed, beginning with 1989's *Playing For Keeps*. His stated ambition throughout these endeavours has been to surmount the 'challenge for an artist to do music that's accessible but also has musical merit. I try to deliver emotions and share experiences that people can recognise and relate to in themselves in a form that has real musical substance.' His musical armoury encompassing flute, piccolo, alto, tenor and soprano saxophone, he was well equipped to fulfil this desire, with 1994's *Yes, Then Yes* confirming his talent in its vibrant evocation of moods and feelings.

● ALBUMS: *Nelson Rangell* (Gramavision/Gaia 1987)★★★, *Playing For Keeps* (GRP 1989)★★★, *Nelson Rangell* (GRP 1990)★★★, *In Every Moment* (GRP 1991)★★, *Truest Heart* (GRP 1992)★★★, *Yes, Then Yes* (GRP 1994)★★★.

RANGLIN, ERNEST

b. 1932, Manchester, Jamaica, West Indies. Ranglin had two uncles who played guitar and ukulele, and as a child he would pick up their instruments and try to imitate their playing. He was also influenced by the recordings of Charlie Christian, and by Cecil Hawkins, an unrecorded local guitarist. At the age of 15, Ranglin joined his first group, the Val Bennett band, and subsequently played with Eric Deans and Count Boysie. By the early 50s, he had developed into a proficient jazz guitarist, and started to tour overseas. Around 1959, he joined bassist Cluett Johnson in a studio group called Clue J And His Blues Blasters, who recorded several instrumentals for Coxsone Dodd at JBC studio. The first of these recordings, 'Shuffling Jug', is widely regarded as one of the first ska recordings. Ranglin's beautiful, versatile guitar playing ensured that he was in demand as a session musician throughout the ska era, and he provided the musical accompaniment for Millie's worldwide smash, 'My Boy Lollipop'. In the mid-60s he recorded two jazz albums for the Merritone label, *Wranglin* (1964) and *Reflections* (1965). Around this time, Duke Reid employed him as musical director at his Treasure Isle recording studio, where he worked for several years. From the late 60s and all through the 70s he worked as a studio musician and arranger for many of the island's top producers, such as Coxsone Dodd, Lee Perry and Clancy Eccles. His other albums have included *Ranglin Roots* (1977) and *From Kingston JA To Miami USA* (1982). He continues to record, but spends most of his time playing live, both locally and abroad. In 1996 Ranglin and his musical colleague Monty Alexander were the first to have albums issued on the Jamaica Jazz label, under the Island imprint. *In Search Of The Lost Riddim* was the first release on Blackwell's new label, Palm Pictures.

● ALBUMS: *Wranglin* (Island 1964)★★★, *Reflections* (Island 1965)★★★★, *Ranglin Roots* (Water Lily 1977)★★, *From Kingston JA To Miami USA* (1982)★★★, *Below The Bassline* (Island Jamaica Jazz 1996)★★★, *In Search Of The Lost Riddim* (Palm Pictures 1998)★★★★, *Memories Of Barber Mack* (Island Jamaica Jazz 1998)★★.

RANK, BILL

b. 8 June 1904, Lafayette, Indiana, USA, d. 20 May 1979. During the mid-20s trombonist and arranger Rank played with Jean Goldkette alongside Bix Beiderbecke. In 1928 he was one of several former Goldkette sidemen who joined Paul Whiteman where he led the trombone section and was for a while featured soloist. Respected by fellow musicians, Rank's career was frequently overshadowed by other trombone luminaries such as Jack Teagarden, with whom he played in the Whiteman band and who took over solo duties. In the late 30s he began working in film studios and thereafter divided his time between playing, mostly in Cincinnati where he led his own band, and non-musical activities.

● ALBUMS: *Bix Beiderbecke And His Gang* (1927-28)★★★★.

RANKIN, KENNY

b. *c*.1945, New York City, New York, USA. Rankin was raised in New York and was introduced to music by his mother who sang at home and for friends. Early in his career he developed as a singer-songwriter, and developed a considerable following during the 70s with a steady flow of albums, three of which broke into the Top 100 of the *Billboard* Album Chart. His liking for jazz was evident from an early age but the times were such that in order to survive his career had to take a more pop-oriented course. By the 90s, however, he was able to angle his repertoire to accommodate his own musical preferences and to please a new audience while still keeping faith with the faithful. Rankin's warm singing style and his soft, nylon-stringed guitar sound might suggest an artist more attuned to the supper-club circuit than the jazz arena, but his work contains many touches that appeal to the jazz audience. His accompanists might include Alan Broadbent, Mike Wofford and Bill Watrous, and on such occasions the mood slips easily into a jazz groove. His compositions have been performed by artists such as Mel Tormé and Carmen McRae, while Stan Getz said of him that he was 'a horn with a heartbeat'. Rankin is deeply interested in Brazilian music and his *Here In My Heart*, on which he used jazz guests including Michael Brecker and Ernie Watts, was recorded mostly in Rio De Janeiro.

● ALBUMS: *Mind Dusters* (1967)★★★, *Like A Seed* (Little David 1972)★★★, *Silver Morning* (Little David 1974)★★★, *Inside* (Little David 1975)★★★, *The Kenny Rankins Album* (Little David 1977)★★★, *After The Roses* (Atlantic 1980)★★★, *Hiding In Myself* (1991)★★★, *Because Of You* (Chesky 1991)★★★, *Professional Dreamer* (Private Music/Windham Hill 1995)★★★★, *Here In My Heart* (Private Music/Windham Hill 1997)★★★.

RAT RACE, THE

Better than its original reception suggests, this downbeat tale of a jazz musician and his dancehall girl has a quirky charm. Directed by Robert Mulligan and staring Tony Curtis and Debbie Reynolds, this 1960 film was based upon the stage play by Garson Kanin who also wrote the screenplay. In the forefront of the jazz musicians taking part is Gerry Mulligan.

RAVA, ENRICO

b. 20 August 1943, Trieste, Italy. Rava's mother was a classical pianist, but he began on trombone in bands playing New Orleans jazz and then graduated to trumpet. He studied with Carmine Caruso in New York and joined Gato Barbieri's quintet in 1964. Between 1965 and 1968 he toured with Steve Lacy, then left to join trombonist Roswell Rudd, with whom he worked until 1972 (also fitting in stints with the Jazz Composers Orchestra and Bill Dixon). Later in the 70s he worked with Abdullah Ibrahim, Giorgio Gaslini and the Globe Unity Orchestra amongst others. In 1975 he formed a group with guitarist John Abercrombie and has led his own groups ever since (Rudd played in his quartet in 1978-79). In 1980 he collaborated with classical composer Morton Feldman and visual artist Michelangelo Pistoletto for a project in Atlanta, Georgia. In 1982 he played with Gil Evans and he toured with Cecil Taylor's Segments II big band in 1984. In 1984 and 1985 he worked with English drummer Tony Oxley and in 1988 renewed his acquaintance with Taylor, playing in the European Orchestra assembled in Berlin by FMP to perform with the pianist. Enrico Rava's name has become synonymous with Italian jazz, though he is now increasingly involved in straight composing and has also written the score for Bertolucci's film *Oggetti Smarriti*.

● ALBUMS: *Il Giro Del Giorno In 80 Mondi* (1972)★★★, *Katcharpari Rava* (1973)★★★, *Pupa O Crisalide* (1974)★★★★, *Quotation Marks* (1974)★★★, *Jazz A Confronto* (1974)★★★★, with John Abercrombie *The Pilgrim And The Stars* (ECM

1975)★★★★, *The Plot* (ECM 1976)★★★, *Enrico Rava Quartet* (ECM 1978)★★, *AH* (1979)★★★, *Opening Night* (1982)★★★, *Andanada* (1983)★★★, with Augusto Manchinelli *Rava String Band* (Soul Note 1984)★★★, *Secrets* (Soul Note 1986)★★★, *Volver* (ECM 1988)★★, *Electric Five* (Soul Note 1996)★★, *Bella* 1990 recording (Philology 1998)★★★, *Noir* 1996 recording (Label Bleu 1998)★★★.

RAY, CARLINE

b. 1925, New York City, New York, USA. Although her father was a gifted musician he had been unable to find steady employment in music. Even so, he played with James Reese Europe's band and was also offered work with the New York Philharmonic. Carline herself sang and played piano, and at the age of 16 entered the Juilliard School of Music, from which her father had graduated in 1925. While at Juilliard, Ray studied composition and she also first played jazz, joining Edna Smith, a fellow student and bass player, gradually becoming adept on this instrument. In 1946, upon graduating from Juilliard, she and Smith joined the International Sweethearts Of Rhythm. In addition to playing guitar with the band, Ray also sang. In 1948, after the Sweethearts disbanded, Ray joined Erskine Hawkins And His Orchestra as a singer but also played guitar rather than simply sitting idle between vocal numbers. After the Hawkins engagement, Ray and Smith teamed up with fellow Sweetheart Pauline Braddy to form a trio that played in New York clubs, including one managed by Luis Russell, whom Ray married in 1956. At this time, Ray added the Fender bass to her growing arsenal of instruments and she and Smith would sometimes switch instruments. In addition to working with the trio, Ray also played with various other bands, in particular a Latin band led by pianist Frank Anderson. She continued to study, gaining a master's degree in voice in 1956. Throughout the next two decades Ray worked constantly, singing and playing all the instruments upon which she was proficient, in a wide variety of musical settings. In 1981 she was awarded a grant to study the acoustic bass under renowned jazzman Major Holley. Comfortably adapting to the differing demands of jazz, popular music, classics, and choral works, Ray is a complete professional, finding in music a lifetime of challenge and fulfilment. Nevertheless, she has met her share of the prejudice that greets women in jazz. As she remarked to Sally Placksin, ' . . . I would rather be taken seriously as a musician, and the fact that I'm female - I just happen to be female, that's all'.

RAZAF, ANDY

b. Andrea Menentania Razafinkeriefo, 16 December 1895, Washington, DC, USA, d. 3 February 1973, Hollywood, California, USA. Related to the Queen of Madagascar but raised in the USA, Razaf was lyricist to several leading ragtime and jazz pianists of the late 20s and early 30s. Among his collaborations were those with Eubie Blake and James P. Johnson, although he is best remembered for his work with Fats Waller. On the Broadway show *Keep Shufflin'* (1928), Razaf was co-lyricist with Henry Creamer, and the music was by Waller and Johnson. Among the Razaf-Waller songs from this show was 'Willow Tree', and in 1928 the duo wrote 'Honeysuckle Rose' and 'My Fate Is In Your Hands'. In the following year Razaf contributed to *Hot Chocolates*, again with Waller, who this time was teamed with Harry Brooks. The hit of the show was 'Ain't Misbehavin'', which was taken up by Louis Armstrong, who joined the cast during its early days. Another song from the show, 'What Did I Do To Be So Black And Blue?', was also popular. Aside from this show, 1929 also saw another Razaf hit, 'I've Got A Feeling I'm Falling' (music by Waller and Harry Link). With Blake, Razaf wrote 'Memories Of You' for *Blackbirds Of 1930*. He also wrote lyrics for 'In The Mood', the popular instrumental hit by Joe Garland, collaborated with Paul Denniker on 'S'posin'', and wrote a seldom-heard lyric for the Edgar Sampson composition 'Stompin' At The Savoy'. Apart from his song lyrics, Razaf also wrote and published poetry. From the 50s onwards he lived in California but worked less and less in music.

● FURTHER READING: *Black And Blue: The Life And Lyrics Of Andy Razaf*, Barry Singer.

REARDON, CASPAR

b. 15 April 1907, Little Falls, New York, USA, d. 9 March 1941. One of only a handful of harpists to make any impact on the jazz scene (the others being Adele Girard, Corky Hale and Dave Snell), Reardon was a classically trained musician who played with the Philadelphia and Cincinnati Symphony Orchestras. In the early 30s he made some records with Paul Whiteman and Jack Teagarden, the latter being the most interesting. Any aspirations he might have had to enhance the peripheral role his chosen instrument had in jazz ended with his premature death in 1941.

● ALBUMS: with Jack Teagarden *A Hundred Years From Today* (1931-34 recordings)★★★.

REBELLO, JASON

b. 1969, London, England; of mixed Indian-Portuguese and English ancestry. In 1988, pianist Rebello was one of the most talked-about young musicians on the London jazz scene, having just won the Pat Smythe Award for the most promising young player of that year. Unlike a purely bebop-based performer, Rebello's technique was as strong in either hand, and he was as liable to play snatches of boogie and stride as in a fast, linear improvising style. Rebello's interests as a piano student lay equally in classical music and jazz, but the earliest music he heard was by Jimi Hendrix and the Beatles, and in his mid-teens, exposure to Herbie Hancock's pop-funk Rockit band turned him on to dance music with a strong improvisational flavour. Through Hancock's antecedents, Rebello discovered the jazz piano tradition, went to London's Guildhall School of Music to pursue it, and was soon working with younger UK jazz celebrities such as Courtney Pine, Jean Toussaint, Steve Williamson and Cleveland

Watkiss. In the late 80s he was a member of Tommy Smith's group and in 1990 he released his first album as leader, with Wayne Shorter producing and has since built a considerable following, aware of his extraordinarily mature style. In the summer of 1995 he played at the Festival Hall, London, after which he spent some time in a monastery.

● ALBUMS: *A Clearer View* (Novus 1990)★★★, *Permanent Love* (1993)★★★, *Keeping Time* (Novus 1993)★★★★, *Make It Real* (RCA 1994)★★★.

Red, Sonny

(see Kyner, Sonny Red)

Redbone, Leon

Believed to have been born in Canada, this enigmatic, gravelly voiced singer ('I am a performer, but only in the metaphysical sense') resolutely declines to divulge his origins. He was first heard of in Toronto during the early 70s, and achieved some popularity on the US television show *Saturday Night Live*. Even then he maintained an air of strict privacy, so much so that the contact number he gave to the legendary jazz and rock producer John Hammond Jnr. turned out to be a 'Dial-A-Joke' line. With his trademark fedora, dark glasses, and Groucho Marx moustache, Redbone celebrates a pre-World War II era of ragtime, jazz, blues, and minstrel shows, resurrecting the work of his heroes, who include 'Jelly Roll' Morton, Lonnie Johnson, Joe Venuti, the young Bing Crosby, and vaudeville performer Emmett Miller. Jazz violinist Venuti was featured on Redbone's *On The Track* in 1976, along with Don McLean, who played the banjo. The album is said to have sold more than 100,000 copies, and his next release, *Double Time*, made the US Top 40. Redbone is joined by well-known musical personalities on most of his albums, and for *Whistling In The Wind*, he duetted with Merle Haggard on 'Settin' By The Fire' and Ringo Starr on 'My Little Grass Shack'. Joe Venuti was present too, and the other tracks on this varied and entertaining set included 'Bouquet Of Roses', 'If I Could Be With You', 'Love Letters In The Sand', and 'I'm Crazy 'Bout My Baby' Redbone's distinctive baritone became familiar to UK television viewers in the late 80s/early 90s when he sang 'Relax', 'Sleepy Time', and 'Untwist Again' in a series of commercials with nostalgic themes for British Rail's Inter-City service.

● ALBUMS: *On The Track* (Warners 1976)★★★★, *Double Time* (Warners 1977)★★★, *Champagne Charlie* (Warners 1978)★★, *From Branch To Branch* (ATCO/Emerald 1981)★★★, *Red To Blue* (August 1986)★★★, *No Regrets* (Sugar Hill 1988)★★★, *Christmas Island* (Private Music 1990)★★★, *Sugar* (Private Music 1990)★★★, *Up A Lazy River* (Private Music 1992)★★★, *Whistling In The Wind* (Private Music 1994)★★★.

Redd, Freddie

b. 29 May 1928, New York City, New York, USA. A self-taught pianist, Redd worked semi-professionally for a number of years, then led his own small groups in and around his home town. In the early 50s he began working with established leaders including Tiny Grimes, Cootie Williams and Charles Mingus. During the rest of the decade he played with jump bands, including a precursor of soul-jazz, Gene Ammons, and also with mainstream and bop musicians, including Art Farmer and Gigi Gryce. He also visited Europe, playing and recording with Ernestine Anderson, Rolf Ericson and others. In the late 50s and early 60s he again played with Mingus, but found temporary fame when he appeared in and wrote the music for the play *The Connection*, appearing in New York, London and Paris and in the 1961 film version. The soundtrack, released on Blue Note Records, featured Redd leading a quartet that included alto saxophonist Jackie McLean. For most of the next dozen years, Redd, who had composed several pieces, lived and worked outside the USA but returned there in the mid-70s, gradually drifting onto the edges of the music business. Redd's career choices, which have mingled bop and the R&B impregnated jump style, helped create an intriguing and vigorous playing style worthy of wider appreciation.

● ALBUMS: *Introducing The Freddie Redd Trio* 10-inch album (Prestige 1954)★★★, with Hampton Hawes *Piano East Piano West* reissued as *Movin'* (Prestige/Status 1956)★★★★, *San Francisco Suite For Jazz Trio* (Riverside 1957)★★★★, *Shades Of Redd* (Blue Note 1960)★★★★, *Music From 'The Connection'* (Blue Note 1960)★★★★, *Under Paris Skies* (Futura Swing 1971)★★★, *Straight Ahead!* (Interplay 1978)★★★, *Extemporaneous* (Interplay 1979)★★★★, *Lonely City* (Uptown 1985)★★★, *Live At The Studio Grill* (Triloka 1988)★★★★, *Everybody Loves A Winner* (Milestone 1990)★★★.

● COMPILATIONS: *The Complete Blue Note Freddie Redd* 2-CD/3-LP box set (Mosaic)★★★★.

Redd, Vi

b. Elvira Redd, 10 September 1928, Los Angeles, California, USA. As a child, Redd took up the saxophone and was directed into jazz through the influence of her father, professional jazz drummer Alton Redd. Concentrating on the alto but also playing soprano and singing, Redd's career moved slowly at first but she blossomed in the 60s, appearing nationally and internationally with Earl 'Fatha' Hines, Max Roach, Dizzy Gillespie and other distinguished jazz stars. At the end of the decade she turned to teaching but throughout the 70s and 80s continued to make occasional appearances as a performer. Like most alto saxophonists of her generation, she was deeply influenced by Charlie Parker and, like her idol, her playing is redolent with a strong feeling for the blues, as is her singing.

● ALBUMS: *Bird Call* (1962)★★★, with Al Grey *Shades Of Grey* (1965)★★★★, with Gene Ammons, Dexter Gordon *The Chase!* (1973)★★★, with Marian McPartland *Now's The Time!* (1977)★★★.

Redman, Dewey

b. 17 May 1931, Fort Worth, Texas, USA. After first playing clarinet at school, where one of his musical companions was Ornette Coleman, Redman turned to alto saxophone, and later still, took up the tenor. One of many well-versed students at North Texas State University, Redman became a professional musician on graduation. In the late 60s and through into the mid-70s he played and recorded with Coleman, Charlie Haden, Roswell Rudd, Keith Jarrett and Carla Bley. In 1976 he formed Old And New Dreams, a quartet completed by Don Cherry, Ed Blackwell and Haden, touring and recording into the mid-80s. An eclectic musician, seamlessly linking the blues with freeform music over a hard bop base, Redman's playing style constantly demonstrates his technical mastery of his instruments, which sometimes include the Arabian musette. He also composes and arranges much of the material he performs and records, drawing inspiration from eastern music as well as that of his own heritage.

● ALBUMS: *Look For The Black Star* (Freedom 1966)★★★★, *Tarik* (Affinity 1970)★★★, *The Ear Of The Behearer* (Impulse! 1973)★★★★, *Coincide* (Impulse! 1975)★★★, *Musics* (Galaxy 1979)★★★, with Ed Blackwell *Redman And Blackwell In Willisau* (Black Saint 1980)★★★, *The Struggle Continues* (ECM 1982)★★★, *Living On The Edge* (Black Saint 1989)★★★★, *Choices* (Enja 1992)★★★★, with Harald Haerter *Mostly Live* (Enja 1997)★★★, *Dewey Redman In London* 1996 recording (Palmetto 1998)★★★★.

Redman, Don

b. 29 July 1900, Piedmont, West Virginia, USA, d. 30 November 1964. A gifted child, alto saxophonist Redman studied extensively and by his graduation had mastered most of the wind instruments and was also adept at arranging. He then joined a territory band based in Pittsburgh, Pennsylvania, with whom he visited New York. This was in 1923 and by the following year he had begun a musical relationship with Fletcher Henderson that was to alter perceptions of big band jazz. In 1927 he took over leadership of McKinney's Cotton Pickers, continuing to develop the arranging style with which he had experimented while with Henderson. In 1931 Redman formed his own band which remained in existence for almost a decade. During this period Redman wrote charts for numerous other big bands and after his own unit folded he pursued this aspect of his career, writing for Jimmy Dorsey, Count Basie, Jimmie Lunceford, Harry James and many others. In 1946 he formed a new band, taking it to Europe and subsequently worked in radio and television. For several years he was musical director for Pearl Bailey, occasionally recording and dedicating what time he could spare to composing. Originally inspired by the creative genius of Louis Armstrong, who joined the Henderson band while he was arranger, Redman went on to lay down many of the ground rules for much of what is today regarded as 'big band music'. In his work for Henderson, the Cotton Pickers and his own band he consistently demonstrated his confident grasp of all arranging techniques in use up to his time, extending them to prove that an arranged format need not lose the spontaneity of an improvised performance and, indeed, could enhance the work of a good jazz soloist. In particular, his writing for the reed and brass sections, in which he set up call-and-response passages, while polished to perfection by such successors as Sy Oliver, has rarely been improved upon.

● ALBUMS: *For Europeans Only* (1946)★★★, *Don Redman's Park Avenue Patters* (Golden Crest 1957)★★★, *July 22nd And 26th, 1957* (1957)★★, *Don Redman And The Knights Of The Round Table* (1959)★★★, *Dixieland In High Society* (Roulette 1960)★★★, *Master Of The Big Band* (RCA Victor 1965)★★★, *Shakin' The African* (Hep Jazz 1986)★★★.

● COMPILATIONS: *Don Redman And His Orchestra 1931-1933* (1931-33)★★★, *Doin' The New Low Down* 1932-33 recordings (Hep Jazz 1984)★★★★, *Redman's Red Book* (1932-36)★★★, *Smoke Rings* (Nostalgia 1988)★★★, *Don Redman* (1932-37)★★★, *1936-1939* (Classics 1991)★★★★, *Doin' What I Please* (1993)★★★.

Redman, Joshua

b. 1 February 1969, Berkeley, California, USA. The latest in a long line of intensively marketed young jazz musicians, Joshua Redman saw his star rise dramatically in 1991, when he burst suddenly into the international arena in his (very) early 20s with all the right credentials: a hard bop-influenced style, good looks, a Harvard education, a famous saxophone-playing father (see Dewey Redman) and a compelling fluency and originality that captured the imagination of the older generation of jazz musicians. Despite the inevitable media tag lines, Redman was influenced less by his famous father, whom he saw infrequently, than by his mother, who always encouraged an awareness of music, and enrolled him at Berkeley's Centre For World Music at the age of five, to study Indian and Indonesian music. Whilst his flair for music was obvious, his flair for practice was less clear, and although he played in the jazz big band and combo while at school, he displayed little genuine commitment. Concentrating, instead, on a glittering academic career, he won a place at Harvard to study social sciences. It was there that he began to listen to jazz in earnest, studying records by the post-war master saxophonists, and spending summer breaks in Boston with the Berklee College Of Music jazz students. Graduating in 1991 (with highly distinguished grades), he accepted a place at Yale Law School, but took a year off to dabble in the New York music scene. He began attending jam sessions and playing the occasional sideman gig, and then, in the autumn of 1991, won the Thelonious Monk International Saxophone Competition. This prestigious award threw Redman into the limelight, and he soon found himself working with a host of jazz legends, including Elvin Jones, Jack DeJohnette, Red Rodney, Paul Motian, Roy Hargrove and John Hicks, and winning *Jazz Times* readers' poll Best New Jazz Artist in 1992, *Rolling Stone*'s Hot Jazz Artist Of 1993 and *Down Beat*'s critics' poll's Number 1 Tenor Saxophonist Deserving Of Wider Recognition (1993). Signed to Warner Brothers, his eponymous debut album was released in March 1993 to widespread critical acclaim, but never reached the UK. *Wish*, his all-star second featuring Pat Metheny, Charlie Haden and Billy Higgins, helped to spread the word to the UK, and serves as a good introduction to his warm and swinging style. In 1994 he joined older saxophone star Joe Lovano on a lively and extrovert two tenor date for the Blue Note label. *Timeless Tales (For Changing Times)* represented a departure for Redman, with ten cover versions ranging from Gershwin ('Summertime') to the Beatles ('Eleanor Rigby') and Bob Dylan ('The Times They Are A Changin'').

● ALBUMS: *Joshua Redman* (Warners 1993)★★★★, *Wish* (Warners 1993)★★★★, with Joe Lovano *Tenor Legacy* (Blue Note 1994)★★★, *Mood Swings* (Warners 1994)★★★★, *Spirit Of The Moment Live At The Village Vanguard* (Warners 1995)★★★★, *Freedom In The Groove* (Warners 1996)★★★★, *Timeless Tales (For Changing Times)* (Atlantic 1998)★★★★.

Reece, Dizzy

b. Alphonso Reece, 5 January 1931, Kingston, Jamaica. After playing in Jamaica as a young teenager, trumpeter Reece moved to the UK in 1948. Over the next few years he established a reputation in the UK and throughout Europe, working mostly with bop musicians like Kenny Graham, Victor Feldman and Tubby Hayes. Reece also occasionally played with such leading swing era figures as Don Byas. At the end of the 50s, an especially active period of creative work, Reece settled in the USA. There he played with Duke Jordan, Philly Joe Jones and others, and made occasional and usually well-spaced return trips to Europe with bands such as that led by Dizzy Gillespie and the Paris Reunion Band. A technically gifted player with an eclectic yet distinctive playing style, Reece has not been recorded as frequently or as well as his talent deserves.

● ALBUMS: *Progress Report* (Jasmine 1956)★★★, *Victor Feldman In London* (1956)★★★, *Blues In Trinity* (Blue Note 1958)★★★★, *Star Bright* (1959)★★★, *Soundin' Off* (1960)★★★, *Asia Minor* (Original Jazz Classics 1962)★★★★, *From In To Out* (1970)★, *Possession, Exorcism, Peace* (Honeydew 1972)★★, *Manhattan Project* (Beehive 1978)★★★, *Moose The Mooche* (Discovery 1978)★★★, *Blowin' Away* (Interplay 1979)★★★.

Reed, Lucy

b. *c.*1924, Marshfield, Wisconsin, USA, d. 1 July 1998. While attending high school in St. Paul, Minnesota, Reed began singing with a girls' quartet formed by her singing teacher, Cleste Burns. Taught the basic techniques of singing, together with the skills of arranging, the group was soon singing regularly on a St. Paul radio show on Station KSTP. This lasted for two years and Reed then moved to Iron Mountain, Michigan, where she sang at Saturday night dances with Jerry Salone And His Band from the Land of the Sky Blue Water. She married the band's drummer and they had a child but her husband was killed during World War II. Two years later, she began singing again, then moved to Duluth, Minnesota, where she was heard by Woody Herman who hired her for a tour of Canada. After that she joined Charlie Ventura's big band for a year, then moved to Chicago, Illinois, where she began singing in clubs. She established a good local reputation and was invited to join Duke Ellington but she regretfully turned down the offer because she needed a stable home life for her young son. Nevertheless, she decided to try New York and took up an offer of an engagement at the Village Vanguard. She also made her first record album, with Bill Evans, for Fantasy Records. This was in 1955 but after a year, living expenses drove her back to Chicago where work was more plentiful. She also made another album for Fantasy and later remarried and had two more sons. During the next decade she performed only occasionally, turning down an offer from Benny Goodman to tour Russia. She could earn $650 a week in Chicago and asked for the same, 'Benny smiled and said, "I was thinking more like $125." I thanked him and stayed home.' During the 70s and 80s she continued to work intimate clubs and small concert rooms, attracting a solid following in Chicago. She returned to the recording studios in 1989/90 for an album on which she was backed by Larry Novack, Herb Ellis and Ray Brown. A highly accomplished singer of the standard repertoire, Reed's clear, accurately pitched voice brought out the melodic and lyrical best of the material she sang. Her voice had barely darkened at all in the period between her records of the 50s and her 90s return to the studios. In live performance, although not on record, she loved to scat, especially with an instrumentalist or another singer: 'Excitement builds up with this kind of jamming that's very contagious. I love it.' Owing in part to her decades-long residence in Chicago, and also to the scandalously few records she had made, Reed remained a little-known figure in jazz and popular singing.

● ALBUMS: *The Singing Reed* (Fantasy 1955)★★★, *This Is Lucy Reed* (Fantasy 1957)★★★, *Basic Reeding* (Audiophile 1990)★★.

Reeves, Dianne

b. 1956, Detroit, Michigan, USA. A vocalist with an international reputation and following, Dianne Reeves made her name in the late 80s, when she was discovered by Blue Note Records during a worldwide revival of interest in jazz. A gifted technician with a genuine swing feel, Reeves' career has tended to reflect the difficult fortunes of the singer trying to find a voice in contemporary jazz, without succumbing to the financially dominant worlds of soul or R&B. Born in Detroit but raised from the age of two in Denver, Reeves was still in high school, singing with the high-school big band, when she was spotted by swing trumpeter Clark Terry at the National Association of Jazz Educators Conference in Chicago. Terry's encouragement and advice led her to study at the University of Colorado, where she was able to perform with him, and later to move to California and pursue music full-time. In Los Angeles in the mid-70s, Reeves' range and rich, expressive natural voice, led her quickly into the west coast's famous studio scene, where she became very much in demand, recording for drummer Lenny White, saxophonist Stanley Turrentine and drummer Alphonzo Johnson. Between 1978 and 1980, she worked full-time with Los Angeles-based pianist Billy Childs, whom Reeves still credits for giving her a chance to experiment and grow, while working almost nightly. Still studying (under vocal coach Phil Moore), she gained her first big international exposure in 1981, touring with Sergio Mendes. Reeves recorded her first album a year later. *Welcome To My Love*, co-produced by Childs and released on Palo Alto Jazz, set the trend for the original material that helped to distinguish much of Reeves' work in later years. However, it was in 1987 that she had her biggest break, when Blue Note Records president Bruce Lundvall spotted her at an Echoes Of Ellington concert in Los Angeles, and wasted no time in setting up her first major session. The resulting *Dianne Reeves* featured George Duke, Freddie Hubbard, Herbie Hancock, Tony Williams, Stanley Clarke and her old friend Billy Childs, and rocketed Reeves onto the international festival circuit. Despite a long-running flirtation with R&B and soul (her discography is split almost exactly down the middle), Reeves has managed to retain her jazz credibility, in 1995 releasing *Quiet After The Storm*, a superb world music-influenced jazz record with guest contributions by saxophonist Joshua Redman, trumpeter Roy Hargrove, flautist Hubert Laws, guitarist Kevin Eubanks and percussionist Airto Moreira.

● ALBUMS: *Welcome To My Love* (Palo Alto Jazz 1982)★★★, *For Every Heart* (Palo Alto Jazz 1985)★★★, *Dianne Reeves* (Blue Note 1987)★★★, *Never Too Far* (EMI 1989)★★★, *I Remember* (EMI 1990)★★★, *Art And Survival* (EMI 1994)★★★, *Quiet After The Storm* (Blue Note 1995)★★★★, *The Grand Encounter* (Blue Note 1996)★★★★, *That Day* (Blue Note 1997)★★.

● COMPILATIONS: *The Palo Alto Sessions* (Blue Note 1996)★★★.

REEVES, REUBEN

b. 25 October 1905, Evansville, Indiana, USA, d. September 1975. Reeves played trumpet in various small bands in the area where he was born, but in his later teenage years he moved to New York. Ostensibly, this was to study for a career outside music, but the city's teeming musical life drew him in and he was soon playing in clubs and elsewhere. In 1925 he moved to Chicago to join Erskine Tate's popular orchestra and he also played with Dave Peyton's band. At this time, he resumed studying, although now it was music. At the start of the 30s he was briefly with Cab Calloway, but was also active in Chicago as leader of his own band. In the late 30s he joined the US National Guard, playing in various bands during the subsequent war years. After the war he played for a short time with Harry Dial but by the early 50s he was working only part-time in music. John Chilton records that at this time he served as a bank guard, but continued to play occasionally with Dial. Although much of his career went unrecorded, Reeves was a good technician and a reliable sideman.

● COMPILATIONS: *The Chronological Cab Calloway 1931-1932* (Classics 1931-32)★★★★.

REICH, STEVE

b. 3 October 1936, New York City, USA. Reich studied philosophy at Cornell University and composition at Juilliard School of Music and, moving to California, at Mills College with *avant garde* composers Luciano Berio and Darius Milhaud. He supported himself while at college by working as a drummer, but declined to follow an academic career and became a taxi-driver in 1963. In 1966 he formed a group, Steve Reich And Musicians, to play his compositions. In the 70s he studied African drumming in Ghana and gamelan music and Hebrew cantillation in the USA. One of the founders of the Minimalist/Systems/Process/Repetitive (choose your own label) school, his music is deeply rooted in African, Balinese and Baroque music, having less overt connections with (and less influence on) rock and new age than, say, Terry Riley, Louis Andriessen or Philip Glass. However, his astonishing early tape works, *My Name Is*, *Come Out* and *It's Gonna Rain*, anticipated by a good 15 years techniques now in common use in scratch and hip-hop, as well as using them in ways with which rock has never caught up. His work has ranged from the most minimalist (*Clapping Music*, which is just that, two people clapping, working through a pre-determined rhythmic process, and *Pendulum Music*, for microphones that are set swinging over amplifiers until the feedback pulses resolve into a continuous tone) to *The Four Sections*, a concerto for orchestra, and *The Desert Music* for orchestra and choir, which examines the premise that humankind has only survived because it has been unable to realize its ambitions: now that it is able to do so it must change its ambitions or perish. Desert Music characterized Reich's move towards a fuller, more conventional orchestration, a development that meant that performances of his music would have to involve resources beyond those of his own ensemble. (In fact, Reich had never restricted the use of his scores in the way that Philip Glass had done.) However, he still composed for small forces as well, and in 1988 he wrote *Electric Counterpoint* for jazz guitarist Pat Metheny. This was coupled on record with *Different Trains*, a remarkable work reflecting on the Holocaust and devised for live string quartet, pre-recorded string quartet and sampled voices. He recently completed a music theatre piece about the prophet Abraham, important to Judaism, Christianity and Islam, called *The Cave*, which incorporated a video film by his wife, Beryl Corot.

● ALBUMS: *Drumming* (Nonesuch 1970)★★★★, *Music For 18 Musicians* (Nonesuch 1978)★★★, *Octet - Music For A Large Ensemble - Violin Phase* (ECM 1980)★★★, *Tehillim* (ECM 1982)★★★, *Eight Lines -Vermont Counterpoint* (1985)★★★★, *The Desert Music* (Elektra 1986)★★★★, *Six Marimbas* (Nonesuch 1987)★★★, *Early Works* (Nonesuch 1987)★★, *Different Trains - Electric Counterpoint* (Nonesuch 1989)★★★★, *The Four Sections* (1990)★★★, *The Cave* (Nonesuch 1996)★★★, *Music For 18 Musicians* 1996 recording (Nonesuch 1998)★★★.

● COMPILATIONS: *Works* 10-CD box set (1997)★★★★.

REICHEL, HANS

b. 10 May 1949, Hagen, Germany. Reichel has described himself as the cuckoo's egg in the catalogue of Berlin's FMP label. In between all the hard-core free jazz, much of it a cheerfully barbaric yawp, Reichel's records nestle: albums of glittering, pretty, fragile electric guitar music in which silence has a role to play. Trained as a classical musician - he still occasionally reverts to violin or cello - Reichel took to rock in the 60s until contact with the music of Derek Bailey changed his thinking totally; henceforth he was a free improviser and instrument builder. Multi-necked guitars became a speciality and on these he developed a technique of two-handed tapping long before Stanley Jordan appeared on the jazz scene. Recent Reichel innovations have included the development of a new bowed instrument, the daxophon. Because his music, with its subtleties and nuances, needs space for its proper development, Reichel has mostly worked as a solo performer or in duo settings. However, the formation in 1987 of the X-Communication band ('spiritual leader': Butch Morris) showed that the guitarist's individualism could function profitably inside a carefully controlled group context.

● ALBUMS: *Wichlinghauser Blues* (1973)★★★, *Bonobo* (1976)★★★★, with Derek Bailey, Fred Frith *Guitar Solos* (1976)★★★, with Achim Knispel *Erdmännchen* (1977)★★★, *The Death Of The Rare Bird Ymir* (FMP 1979)★★★★, with Rüdiger Carl *Buben* (1980)★★★, *Bonobo Beach* (FMP 1981)★★★★, with Eroc *Kino* (1985)★★, *The Dawn Of Dachsman* (FMP 1987)★★★, *Coco Bolo Nights* (FMP 1989)★★★★, with Tom Cora *Angel Carver* (FMP 1990)★★★, with Butch Morris, Shelley Hirsch and others *X-Communication* (1991)★★★, with Wädi Gysi *Show-Down* (1991)★★★, with Frith, Kazuhisha Uchihashi *Stop Complaining/Sundown* (1991)★★★, *Lower Lurum* (1994)★★★.

● COMPILATIONS: with Eroc *The Return Of Onkel Boskopp* (Repertoire 1997)★★.

REID, IRENE

b. *c.*1930, Savannah, Georgia, USA. Beginning her singing career in church choirs, Reid tried her luck, in her late teens, at New York's famed Apollo theatre. This was in 1948 and she won the amateur talent contest there four weeks in a row. This resulted in a job with Dick Vance's band, then resident at the Savoy Ballroom on 125th Street in Harlem. She stayed with the band for two years, then struck out as a single. Her lamp burned steadily but low until 1961 when she joined Count Basie. She stayed with Basie for a year, touring Europe and appearing on some of the band's live concert albums. It was both an enjoyable and a learning experience. 'Singing with a big band, when the arrangements get behind you and the adrenaline is there, it's wonderful'. After Basie she continued her solo career, often working with an organ-guitar-drums trio billed as Irene Reid And Company. Once again, however, although work was steady, the widespread recognition that was so clearly due to her failed to materialize. In the late 80s, Reid was still singing every opportunity she had ('I just love to sing, it's a gift God gave me') and visited Europe again, where, among a number of high-profile engagements, she appeared at Ronnie Scott's club in London. It was in London, in 1989, that she recorded her first album under her own name, with organist Mike Carr, Dick Morrissey, Jim Mullen, and drummer Mark Taylor. Reid has a powerful singing style, her voice echoing the ethos of the gospel tradition that marked her formative years. There is a bittersweet element to her sound that particularly suits her ballad interpretations, but when the mood is upon her she can belt the blues with enormous authority. She swings mightily, whatever and wherever she performs.

● ALBUMS: with Count Basie *Basie In Sweden* (Roulette 1962)★★★★, *The Lady From Savannah* (Birdland 1989)★★★, *Million Dollar Secret* (Savant 1998)★★★.

REID, RUFUS

b. 10 February 1944, Sacramento, California, USA. After starting out on trumpet, Reid switched to playing bass during his miltary service. He played and studied in California for some years, often working in company with leading bop musicians. He also played in Chicago, toured internationally and, in the mid-70s, settled in New York. During the 80s Reid was active as a teacher and writer of tutors. Throughout his professional career Reid has appeared on numerous record dates, playing with musicians such as Kenny Burrell, Art Farmer, Jack DeJohnette, Dexter Gordon, Jimmy Heath, Lee Konitz, Thad Jones-Mel Lewis and Howard McGhee. An outstandingly talented bass player, Reid has begun to attract wider attention since forming a successful and superbly swinging hard bop band, TanaReid, with drummer Akira Tana.

● ALBUMS: *Perpetual Stroll* (1980)★★★, *Seven Minds* (1984)★★★, with TanaReid *Yours And Mine* (1990)★★, with Michael Moore *DoubleBass Delights* (Double-Time 1996)★★★.

REINHARDT, DJANGO

b. Jean Baptiste Reinhardt, 23 January 1910, Liberchies, near Luttre, Belgium, d. 16 May 1953. Reinhardt first played violin but later took up the guitar. Living a nomadic life with his gypsy family, he played in a touring show before he was in his teens. Following serious injuries which he suffered in a caravan fire in 1928 he lost the use of two fingers on his left hand. To overcome this handicap, he devised a unique method of fingering and soon embarked on a solo career in Parisian clubs. He was hired as accompanist to the popular French singing star, Jean Sablon, and in 1934 teamed up with Stéphane Grappelli to form a band they named the Quintette Du Hot Club De France. Reinhardt was a popular sitter-in with visiting American jazzmen, recording with Eddie South, Benny Carter, Coleman Hawkins and others. It was, however, the recordings by the Quintet that made him an international name. His remarkable playing caused a sensation and it is not an exaggeration to state that he was the first non-American to make an impact upon jazz and become an important influence upon the development of the music. His distinctive, flowing lines were filled with inventive ideas and couched in a deeply romantic yet intensely rhythmic style. Above all, Reinhardt's was an original talent, revealing few if any precedents but becoming a major influence upon other jazz guitarists of the 30s.

With the outbreak of war in 1939, the Quintet folded and Reinhardt returned to his nomadic life, playing in various parts of Europe and ensuring that he kept well clear of the German army. At the end of the war (by which time he had switched from acoustic to electric guitar), Reinhardt was invited by Duke Ellington to visit the USA and duly arrived in New York. The visit was less than successful, however. Some reports of the time suggest that Reinhardt was eager to pursue the new concepts of jazz created by the bebop revolution: musically, however, the guitarist's gloriously romantic style fitted uneasily into the new music and his efforts in this field were overshadowed by those of another guitarist, the late Charlie Christian. Back in Europe he led his own small band and was occasionally reunited with Grappelli in a re-formed Quintet. He continued to tour and record during the late 40s and early 50s, simultaneously pursuing a career as a composer. Reinhardt remains one of the outstanding figures in jazz, and although Christian ultimately became the more profound influence, echoes of Reinhardt's style can be heard today in many musicians, some of whom were born after his death. His brother, Joseph, was also a guitarist and his two sons, Lousson and Babik, are also gifted players of the instrument. In the early 90s Babik Reinhardt was featured at an international jazz and gypsy guitar festival in France.

● ALBUMS: *The Great Artistry Of Django Reinhardt* (Mercury 1953)★★★★, *Django Reinhardt* (Jay 1954)★★★★, *Le Jazz Hot* (Angel 1954)★★★★, *Nuages* (Felsted 1954)★★★★, *Django Reinhardt Memorial Volumes 1-3* (Period/Vogue 1954)★★★★, *Django's Guitar* (Angel 1955)★★★★, *Swing From Paris* (London 1955)★★★★, *Django Reinhardt* (RCA Victor 1955)★★★★, *Django Reinhardt Memorial Album Vols 1-3* (Period 1956)★★★★, *The Best Of Django Reinhardt* (Period 1956)★★★★, *The Art Of Django* (HMV 1960)★★★★, *The Unforgettable* (HMV 1960)★★★★, *The Best Of Django Reinhardt* (Capitol 1960)★★★★, *Djangology* (RCA Victor 1961)★★★★, *The Immortal Django Reinhardt* (Reprise 1963)★★★★, *Django Reinhardt And His Guitar* (Sutton 1966)★★★★, *Django Reinhardt* (Archive Of Folk 1968)★★★★, *Django Reinhardt Vol 2* (Archive Of Folk 1969)★★★★, *Djangology Vols 1-20* (EMI 1983)★★★★, *Swing In Paris 1936-1940* (Affinity 1991)★★★★, *Rare Recordings* (1993)★★★★, *Jazz Portraits* (Jazz Portraits 1993)★★★★, *Djangologie/USA* 1936-1938 recordings (Disques Swing 1996)★★★★, *Django/Django In Rome 1949-50* (BGO 1998)★★★★, *Nuages* (Arkadia 1998)★★★★, *Quintet Of The Hot Club Of France* (Prestige 1998)★★★, *Django And His American Friends* 3-CD set (DRG 1998)★★★★.

● FURTHER READING: *Django Reinhardt*, Charles Delauney. *La Tristesse De Saint Louis: Swing Under The Nazis*, Mike Zwerin. *The Book Of Django*, M. Abrams. *Django's Gypsies: The Mystique Of Django Reinhardt*, Ian Cruickshank (ed.).

Remler, Emily

b. 18 September 1957, New York City, New York, USA, d. 4 May 1990, Australia. Emily Remler began playing guitar as a small child and her early preference for rock was superseded by jazz while studying at Berklee College Of Music. After leaving Berklee in 1976 she began performing professionally, playing club, concert and festival engagements across the USA. A residency in New Orleans attracted attention when she was called upon to accompany important visiting instrumentalists and singers. She was heard by Herb Ellis, who actively encouraged her career, helping her to obtain her first recording date, for Concord, and an appearance at the Concord Jazz Festival. She continued to tour, particularly with Astrud Gilberto, and made a fine duo album, *Together*, with Larry Coryell. Other guitarists with whom she worked were Barney Kessel and Charlie Byrd. A strikingly gifted performer with eclectic musical tastes, she played with flair and her dazzling technique was built upon a deep knowledge and understanding of all forms of jazz. Appealing alike to audiences, critics and her fellow musicians, she rapidly gained respect and admiration for her dedication, enthusiasm and remarkable skills. That someone as gifted as this should have died so young (she was addicted to heroin) was a major loss to the jazz world. Her death, at the age of 32, came while she was on tour in Australia. Remler had played on David Benoit's *Waiting For Spring* and he wrote the beautiful 'Six String Poet' in her memory on his *Inner Motion*.

● ALBUMS: *The Firefly* (Concord 1981)★★, *Take Two* (Concord 1982)★★, *Transitions* (Concord 1983)★★★, *Catwalk* (Concord 1985), with Larry Coryell *Together* (1985)★★★, *East To Wes* (Concord 1988)★★★★.

● COMPILATIONS: *Retrospective Vols 1 & 2* (Concord 1989)★★★★, various artists *Just Friends: A Gathering In Tribute To Emily Remler Vol. 2* (1992)★★★, *This Is Me* (Justice 1992)★★★.

Rena, Kid

b. Henry René, 30 August 1898, New Orleans, Louisiana, USA, d. 25 April 1949. Like Louis Armstrong, trumpeter Rena was a 'graduate' of Joseph Jones's Colored Waifs' Home band. In 1919 he succeeded Armstrong in the Kid Ory band, quitting in 1921 to form his own group. Thereafter, he mostly led his own bands but also played in a number of marching bands. He made his first and only records in 1940 but was unable to participate fully in the Revival because ill-health forced him into early retirement. According to the testimony of other musicians, in his prime Rena was a forceful player with a remarkably wide range and melodious style. Unfortunately, his recordings display only the vestiges of his talent, affected as they are by his fast-deteriorating physical condition.

● ALBUMS: *Down On The Delta* (1940)★★★.

Rendell, Don

b. 4 March 1926, Plymouth, Devon, England. Rendell began playing alto saxophone as a child but later switched to tenor. He played in a number of dance bands during the late 40s, and in 1950 became a member of John Dankworth's septet. After leaving Dankworth in 1953 he formed his own small group but also worked with bands led by Tony Crombie, Ted Heath and others. In 1956 he joined Stan Kenton for a European tour, appearing on *Live At The Albert Hall*. In the late 50s he played with Woody Herman. During the

60s Rendell was again leading his own bands, featuring musicians such as Graham Bond, Michael Garrick and Ian Carr, with whom he was co-leader of a successful band. Rendell has also recorded with Stan Tracey (*The Latin American Caper*), and Neil Ardley (*Greek Variations*). A fluent improviser, with hints of post-bop styling overlaying a deep admiration for the earlier work of Lester Young, Rendell has long been one of the most admired of British jazz artists. For many years he has been tireless in the promotion of jazz through his activities as a sought-after teacher.

● ALBUMS: *Meet Don Rendell* (Tempo 1955)★★★, *Recontre A Paris* (Vogue 1955)★★★★, *Presents The Jazz Six* (Nixa 1957)★★★, *Playtime* (Decca 1958)★★★, *Roarin'* (Jazzland 1962)★★★, with Ian Carr *Shades Of Blue* (Columbia 1964)★★★★, with Carr *Phase III* (Columbia 1968)★★★, with Carr *Live* (Columbia 1968)★★★, with Carr *Change Is 1* (Columbia 1969)★★★, with Carr *Dusk Fire* (Columbia 1970)★★★, *Spacewalk* (Columbia 1971)★★★, *Live At The Avgarde Gallery, Manchester* (1973)★★★, *Just Music* (1974)★★★, *Earth Music* (1979)★★★.

RETURN TO FOREVER

This jazz group featured Chick Corea (b. 12 June 1941, Chelsea, Massachusetts, USA; keyboards), Joe Farrell (b. 16 December 1937, Chicago Heights, Illinois, USA, d. 10 January 1986; soprano saxophone, flute), Flora Purim (b. 6 March 1942, Rio de Janeiro, Brazil; vocals), Stanley Clarke (b. 30 June 1951, Philadelphia, USA; bass, electric bass), and Airto Moreira (b. 5 August 1941, Itaiopolis, Brazil; percussion). Formed by Chick Corea in 1971, Return To Forever began as a Latin-influenced fusion band, mixing the wild vocals of Purim with the tight, funk-edged slapping bass of Clarke to create a new sound. The group toured and made two commercially successful albums before disbanding in 1973. Keeping Clarke, Corea immediately put together the second of what was to be three successive Return To Forever bands. Hiring Bill Connors to play electric guitar (soon replaced by Earl Klugh and then Al Di Meola), and drummer Lenny White, the second band was much more of a rock-orientated outfit. Producing a harder overall sound, and aided by Corea's adoption of various electronic keyboard gadgetry, the new band achieved massive popularity, particularly with rock audiences, and its 1976 *Romantic Warrior* quickly became its best-selling album. The third and final Return To Forever was a huge but not altogether successful departure from what had come before. Corea put together a 13-piece band that included small string and brass sections, as well as Clarke and Farrell from the original band. A soft, unchallenging music resulted, and Return To Forever refined itself out of existence in 1980. Corea, Clarke, Di Meola, and White joined up for a single tour in 1983.

● ALBUMS: *Light As A Feather* (Polydor 1972)★★★★, *Return To Forever* (ECM 1973)★★★★, *Hymn Of The Seventh Galaxy* (Polydor 1973)★★★★, *Where Have I Known You Before* (Polydor 1974)★★★, *No Mystery* (Polydor 1975)★★, *The Leprechaun* (Polydor 1976)★★★★, *Romantic Warrior* (Columbia 1976)★★★, *Music Magic* (Columbia 1977)★★★, *Live: The Complete Concert* 4-LP box set (Columbia 1978)★★★, *Light As A Feather* 2-CD re-release (Verve 1998)★★★★.

● COMPILATIONS: *The Best Of Return To Forever* (Columbia 1980)★★★★, *Return To The 7th Galaxy: The Return To Forever Anthology Featuring Chick Corea* (Chronicles/Verve 1996)★★★★, *Musicmagic* (Columbia 1997)★★★.

RETURN TO FOREVER - CHICK COREA

'Return To Forever' became the name keyboardist Chick Corea gave to a series of three different fusion projects during the 70s. Coined here in 1972, it was a stunning Latin-influenced jazz/rock quintet, featuring the now celebrated vocals and percussion team of Flora Purim and Airto Moreira, flautist/saxophonist Joe Farrell and virtuoso bassist Stanley Clarke. The eerie and distinctly 'trippy' title track that opens the album is a breathtaking lesson for fusion rhythm sections, as Corea, Clarke and Moreira surge forward on something close to telepathy, while Purim adds mesmeric and disturbing shrieks and cries across the top. This is a fusion classic and 45 minutes of genius.

● Tracks: *Return To Forever; Crystal Silence; What Game Shall We Play Today; Sometime Ago - La Fiesta.*

● First released 1972

● UK peak chart position: did not chart

● USA peak chart position: did not chart

REVEILLE WITH BEVERLY

A fluffy but engaging US wartime musical film, made in 1943, about a radio station DJ, Ann Miller, who plays swing music for the boys in local army camps. Several leading musicians of the era appear, including the orchestras of Count Basie, Bob Crosby and Duke Ellington. Amongst the singers on hand are the Mills Brothers, Ella Mae Morse, Betty Roché and Frank Sinatra.

REVIVAL MOVEMENT

Around 1940, at the height of the swing era when commercialism was affecting jazz, adversely so by most standards, many musicians sought alternative forms of expression. Strikingly, this produced two massively dissimilar views. One, bebop, looked forward and wrought fundamental changes to jazz; the other looked back and revived interest in New Orleans-style jazz. Heading this latter movement in the USA were Lu Watters, with his Yerba Buena Jazz Band, and his colleagues Bob Scobey and Turk Murphy. Amongst the forgotten masters who rose again to public acclaim were Bunk Johnson and George Lewis. Musicians were not the only people who generated new interest in this early jazz. Many writers helped to bring the movement to the attention of the jazz audience, and sometimes general public, among them Frederic Ramsey, Rudi Blesh and William Russell. In the UK the revivalist movement made its first major impact in the closing years of World War II. One of the most influential of the bandleaders active at this time was George Webb and his example was followed by Humphrey Lyttelton, Wally Fawkes (both of whom played in Webb's band), Chris Barber, Freddy Randall and a succession of others, many of whom followed a significantly more commercial path, unlike Ken Colyer, who remained utterly dedicated to the first principles of New Orleans jazz. All these musicians found audiences and their once-removed pioneering efforts found their reward in the continuation around the world, but notably in the UK, of a persistent strain of Dixieland. Many of these Dixieland bands owed more to early Chicago music than that of New Orleans, while even more missed the point of revivalism by basing themselves upon the style and format of the Louis Armstrong All Stars of the late 40s and 50s. Despite these dilutions of revivalist principles, the standards set by New Orleans advocates such as Watters and Colyer helped to retain interest in early forms of jazz and their records demonstrate that imitation can be more than sincere flattery and retain much of the enthusiasm and skills of the music's progenitors.

Revolution Will Not Be Televised - Gil Scott-Heron

Unconsciously, Gil Scott-Heron was one of the first rappers. The title track is a strong attack on the way the racist media can manipulate and distort. Cutting and humorous, he gets to the heart of the matter and his literate delivery explains why he wrote his first book at the age of 12. What is not often addressed is his fabulous voice, a cross between Mark Murphy and Jackie Wilson, full of soul, especially emotive on 'The Get Out Of The Ghetto Blues'. He has chosen to use his voice to educate, and his crystal-clear diction (he is a regular public performer of his work at poetry readings) makes listening wholly pleasurable.

● Tracks: *The Revolution Will Be Televised; Sex Education-Ghetto Style; The Get Out Of The Ghetto Blues; No Knock; Lady Day And John Coltrane; Pieces Of A Man; Home Is Where The Hatred Is; Brother; Save The Children; Whitey On The Moon; Did You Hear What They Said; When You Are Who You Are; I Think I'll Call It Morning; A Sign Of The Ages; Or Down You Fall; The Needle's Eye; The Prisoner.*

● First released 1974 (1970-1972 recordings)

● UK peak chart position: did not chart

● USA peak chart position: did not chart

Revolutionary Ensemble

Leroy Jenkins, Sirone and Jerome Cooper. Violinist Leroy Jenkins was dispatched to New York in 1970 as a representative for Chicago's AACM. On the east coast, the musicians, by and large, still viewed performance in the competitive terms of the 'cutting contest' and 'fighting for your space'. Chicago's music had been geared toward collective endeavour; to convey this message effectively, Jenkins needed a band. The Revolutionary Ensemble explored chamber-music textures in an unstuffy way, was often the most subtle band in the new music, used multi-instrumentation undemonstratively, and juxtaposed broken-time nerve-pulse playing with drummer/pianist Cooper's often tribal-sounding rhythms, while Jenkins's acid-edged violin skirled on and on. Bassist Sirone saw the group as 'interpreters of Nature's Music. We find that everything on the earth contributes to its harmony.' The group's example was a big influence on the 'Loft movement' of the mid-70s but, by 1978, the Ensemble players were pulling in different directions and the group disbanded. At Sirone's instigation, the Revolutionary Ensemble re-formed for a one-off appearance at the Nickelsdorf Festival in Austria in 1990.

● ALBUMS: *Vietnam I & II* (1972)★★★, *Manhattan Cycles* (1974)★★★★, *The Psyche* (1975)★★★, *The People's Republic* (1976)★★★, *Revolutionary Ensemble* (1978)★★.

Rey, Alvino

b. Al McBurney, 1 July 1911, Cleveland, Ohio, USA. An accomplished guitarist, Rey played with various dance-bands, including those of Phil Spitalney, Russ Morgan, Freddy Martin and Horace Heidt, before forming his own band in the winter of 1938/9. With Heidt, Rey had been featured on the steel Hawaiian guitar and also on an early form of electronically amplified guitar. He continued to play guitar in his own band, and also brought from Heidt the vocal group the King Sisters, one of whom, Louise, he married. Rey toured extensively in the early 40s and eventually became popular with dancers across the USA. The band featured comedy, lots of vocals and highly competent musicianship. All this, allied to the unusual effect Rey created by miking Louise King's vocals through the guitar amplifier, helped to build a following for the band. Towards the end of 1942, however, Rey changed to a more jazz-orientated policy, commissioning arrangements from Billy May, Johnny Mandel, Neal Hefti and others. He also hired top flight musicians, including at one time or another saxophonists Zoot Sims, Al Cohn and Herbie Steward and a succession of excellent drummers, amongst whom were Nick Fatool, Mel Lewis, Dave Tough and Don Lamond. During the early years of World War II, Rey managed to keep the band going while also engaging himself and his sidemen in factory work for the war effort. The band eventually folded in 1944 and Rey entered the US Navy where he led a band. In the post-war years Rey formed a new band, even more strongly committed to playing jazz, but his attempts to sustain a big band met with increasing difficulties. By the 50s he was leading a small group and in the following decade drifted into television as a producer and occasional performer. One of the shows with which he was associated was *The King Family Show*, which featured his wife and her sisters. By the 70s, Rey was in semi-retirement.

● ALBUMS: *The Uncollected Alvino Rey Vols 1-3* (1940-46)★★★, *Alvino Rey And His Orchestra 1946* (1946)★★★.

Rhemi, T.J.

b. 5 May 1961, Pakistan. Rhemi moved to England at a young age, and initially worked as a session guitarist, including a stint with Andy Hamilton's group (1981-82). In the late 80s he formed Saaz, his own jazz-fusion band. He also began producing local bhangra artists.

During the early 90s he continued to work as a producer as well as playing in a group that mixed Indian influences with jazz. In 1996 Rhemi signed to London-based Nation Records and released two well-received EPs, *The Fusionist* and *Skrutinizer*, both of which demonstrated his ability to mix a broad range of musical influences (dub, Indian classical, jazz, drum 'n' bass and bhangra), creating a diverse but distinctive sound. He contributed the track 'Mind Filter' to *Outcaste Untouchable Beats* (1997), a highly acclaimed compilation of underground Anglo-Asian dance music. *Mind Filter*, his debut album, featured tracks from his EPs alongside other old and new recordings. Ranging in style from live Indo-jazz experimentation to hard, tabla-infused drum 'n' bass.

● ALBUMS: *Mind Filter* (Nation 1998)★★★★.

Rich, Buddy

b. Bernard Rich, 30 September 1917, New York City, New York, USA, d. 2 April 1987, Los Angeles, California, USA. In showbusiness from the age of two, Rich achieved considerable fame as a drummer and tap dancer, performing on Broadway when he was four years old as a member of his parents' act. Two years later he was touring as a solo artist, playing the US vaudeville circuit and also visiting Australia. At the age of 11 he formed his own band and within a few more years was attracting attention sitting in with bands in New York clubs. In 1937 he was hired by Joe Marsala and soon thereafter began to rise in critical estimation and public popularity. In quick succession he played in several important bands of the swing era, including those of Bunny Berigan, Harry James, Artie Shaw and Tommy Dorsey. After military service he again played with Dorsey, then formed his own big band which survived for a few years in the late 40s. He next worked with Les Brown and also became a regular with Jazz At The Philharmonic. In the early 50s he led his own briefly re-formed big band and also became a member of the Big Four, led by Charlie Ventura. He also recorded extensively for Norman Granz, not only with the impresario's JATP but also with Art Tatum, Lionel Hampton, Ray Brown, Oscar Peterson, Flip Phillips, Dizzy Gillespie, Roy Eldridge, Louis Armstrong, Lester Young, Gene Krupa and many others.

Return stints with James and Dorsey followed, but by the late 50s, despite a heart attack, he was appearing as a singer and leading his own small bands. He continued to make records with, amongst others, Max Roach. In the early 60s, Rich was once more with James, but by 1966 had decided to try again with his own big band. He continued to lead a big band for the next dozen years, spent a while leading a small group, then re-formed a big band in the 80s, continuing to lead this band for the rest of his life. His later bands frequently featured young, recently graduated musicians, towards whom he displayed an attitude that resembled that of a feudal lord. Nevertheless, whether through awareness of these musicians' interests or the demands of audiences, the repertoire of many of Rich's 60s and 70s bands contained elements of rock without ever becoming a true fusion band. Rich's playing was characterized by his phenomenal speed and astonishing technical dexterity. His precision and clarity were legendary even if, at times, the band's charts were specifically designed to display his remarkable skills. During his bandleading years, Rich continued to make records in many settings; in these he would usually revert to the drummer's traditional role of supporting player. In such contexts Rich was a subtle accompanist, adept with brushes but always swinging and propulsive. Early in his career Rich was notorious for his short temper, and during his stint with Dorsey frequently clashed with the band's singer, Frank Sinatra, a similarly short-fused artist. A caustically witty man, later in his life Rich became popular on television chat shows, where his put-downs of ill-equipped pop singers often bordered upon the slanderous. In person he was particularly unpleasant to Dusty Springfield, although she returned the abuse. Rich came back frequently from illness and accident (once playing one-handed when his other arm was in a sling, without any noticeable diminution of his ability) but was finally diagnosed as having a brain tumour. Even during his final illness, his wit did not desert him. When a nurse preparing him for surgery asked if there was anything to which he was allergic, he told her, 'Only country music.'

● ALBUMS: *One Night Stand* 1946 recording (Bandstand)★★★, *Buddy Rich And His Legendary '47-'48 Orchestra* 1945-1948 recordings (Hep)★★★, with Nat 'King' Cole, Lester Young *The Lester Young Trio* 10-inch album (Mercury 1951)★★★★, with Cole, Young *The Lester Young Trio* ii (Clef 1953)★★★★, *Buddy Rich Swinging* 10-inch album (Norgran 1954)★★★★, *Sing And Swing With Buddy Rich* (Norgran 1955)★★★★, with Harry 'Sweets' Edison *Buddy And Sweets* (Norgran 1955)★★★, with Lionel Hampton, Art Tatum *The Hampton-Tatum-Rich Trio* (Clef 1956)★★★, with Gene Krupa *Krupa And Rich* (Clef 1956)★★★★, with Cole, Young *Lester Young-Nat 'King' Cole-Buddy Rich Trio* (Norgran 1956)★★★★, *Buddy Rich Sings Johnny Mercer* (Verve 1956)★★, *The Wailing Buddy Rich* (Norgran 1956)★★★, *This One's For Basie* reissued as *Big Band Shout* (Norgran 1956)★★★★, *Buddy Just Sings* (Verve 1957)★, *The Buddy Rich Quartet In Miami* (Verve 1957)★★★, with Max Roach *Rich Versus Roach* (Mercury 1959)★★★★, *Richcraft* (Mercury 1959)★★★, *The Voice Is Rich* (Mercury 1959)★★, *Playtime* (Argo 1961)★★, *Blues Caravan* (Verve 1962)★★★★, with Krupa *Burnin' Beat* (Verve 1962)★★★★, *Swingin' New Big Band* (Pacific Jazz 1966)★★★, *Big Swing Face* (Pacific Jazz 1967)★★★★, *The New One!* (Pacific Jazz 1967)★★★★, *Mercy, Mercy* (World Pacific 1968)★★★★, *Buddy & Soul* (World Pacific 1969)★★★★, *Rich A La Rakha* (World Pacific 1969)★★★, *Super Rich* (Verve 1969)★★★, *Keep The Customer Satisfied* (1970)★★★, *A Different Drummer* (RCA 1971)★★★, *Buddy Rich-Louie Bellson-Kenny Clare With The Bobby Lamb-Ray Premru Orchestra* (1971)★★★, *Rich In London* (RCA 1971)★★★, *Time Being* (RCA 1972)★★★, *Stick It* (1972)★★★, *The Roar Of '74* (1973)★★★, *Buddy Rich And His Orchestra* (Laserlight 1973)★★★, *Ease On Down The Road* (LRC 1974)★★★, *The Last Blues Album Vol. 1* (1974)★★★, *Speak No Evil* (1976)★★★, *Buddy Rich Plays And Plays* (1977)★★★, *Killing Me Forcefully* (1977)★★★, *Jam Session* (1977)★★★, *Giants Of Jazz Vol. 1*

(1977)★★★, *Class Of '78* (RCA 1977)★★★, *Lionel Hampton Presents Buddy Rich* (Kingdom Gate 1977)★★★, *The Man From Planet Jazz* (1980)★★★, *Rich And Famous* (c.1980)★★★, *The Legendary Buddy Rich* (1982)★★★, *The Magic Of Buddy Rich* (1984)★★★, *Tuff Dude* (LRC 1984)★★★, *Live At King Street Cafe* (Pacific Jazz 1985)★★★, *The Cinch* (1985)★★★.

● COMPILATIONS: *Buddy Rich And His Greatest Band* 1946-47 recordings (First Heard 1977)★★★, *Rich Riot* (First Heard 1979)★★★, *Illusion* 3-CD set (Sequel)★★★★, *No Jive* (Novus 1992)★★★, *The Collection* (Beat Goes On 1998)★★★.

● VIDEOS: *The Making Of Burning For Buddy, Parts One And Two* (DCI 1997).

● FURTHER READING: *Improvising*, Whitney Balliett.

RICH, FREDDY

b. 3 January 1898, Warsaw, Poland, d. 8 September 1956. A leader of successful dancebands from the early 20s, Rich toured Europe late in the decade. In the 30s and early 40s he was active in radio and films, appearing in such musical shorts as *Song Hits On Parade* (1936) leading a band that featured Bunny Berigan and Adrian Rollini. His studio work continued into the 50s despite partial paralysis following an accident. Although he was primarily a very commercial leader, Rich made several interesting records and radio broadcasts, some of which were recorded, on which he augmented his regular band with leading jazz performers such as Berigan, Benny Goodman, Joe Venuti, Eddie Lang, Manny Klein, Jimmy and Tommy Dorsey, Roy Eldridge and Benny Carter.

● ALBUMS: *Freddy Rich On The Air Vol. 1* (1931)★★★, *Freddy Rich On The Air Vol. 2* (1931)★★★.

● COMPILATIONS: *Dance The Depression Away* (1929-31)★★★★, *Freddy Rich And His Orchestra Vols 1 & 2* (1931)★★★★.

RICHARDS, EMIL

b. Emilio Joseph Radocchia, 2 September 1932, Hartford, Connecticut, USA. After playing the xylophone as a small child Richards attended the Julius Hart School of Music, the Hartford School of Music, and Hilliard College, developing his skills as a percussionist. His early professional career included performances with symphony orchestras and studio bands and he also worked with Bobby Hackett and Flip Phillips. After military service in 1952/3 he moved to New York where he played with Charles Mingus and others, and in 1955 began a four-year spell with George Shearing. From 1959 he worked in Los Angeles with Paul Horn and Shorty Rogers and was on numerous studio dates with Nelson Riddle, Frank Sinatra, Ella Fitzgerald, Sarah Vaughan and others. In 1962 he toured internationally with Sinatra on a round of benefit concerts for underprivileged children instigated by President John F. Kennedy. Throughout the 60s he worked mostly in Hollywood with a host of artists including Quincy Jones, Dave Grusin and Shelly Manne and also joined Don Ellis studying and playing Indian rhythms. Like Ellis, he was interested in playing unusual time signatures. During 1968-9 he was in Stan Kenton's Neophonic Orchestra. In the 70s he was again in great demand in the studios and he recorded with Louie Bellson on his 1977 Pablo Records session, *Ecué - Ritmos Cubanos*. His film credits listing is huge and it is this activity that kept him busy through the 80s and 90s, although he always strove to keep in touch with the jazz world, sitting in at clubs whenever the opportunity arose. An enormously talented percussionist, Richards' playing style intriguingly builds a rich display of multi-cultural forms upon the swing era base of his formative years. Richards has long been an avid collector of percussion instruments from all around the world and in 1972 published *World Of Percussion*, a catalogue of 300 musical instruments with photographs by fellow drummer Stan Levey. By the late 90s his collection had grown to more than 650 items.

● ALBUMS: *New Time Element* (Uni 1967)★★★, *New Sound* (Uni 1967)★★★ *Spirit Of '76* (Impulse! 1968)★★★, *Journey To Bliss* (Impulse! 1968)★★★, *The Wonderful World Of Percussion* (Interworld 1996)★★★, *Luntana* (Interworld 1996)★★★.

● COMPILATIONS: *Yazz Per Favore* 60s recordings (Del-Fi 1995)★★★.

RICHARDS, JOHNNY

b. John Cascales, 2 November 1911, Schenectady, New York, USA, d. 7 October 1968. This most progressive of modern jazz arrangers began his musical career at the age of 10 playing trumpet, violin and banjo in a vaudeville act called 'The Seven Wonders Of The World'. Taking up the saxophone when 17 years old, he was in London in 1931 working in films, then went to Hollywood as an arranger. Forming a big band in the 40s, he had trouble finding musicians who could cope with his involved scores, so he gave it up to write for Boyd Raeburn's forward-looking band. Oddly enough, considering the reputations of both men, Richards' contributions to the Raeburn library were pretty, romantic, woodwind scores for *inter alia*, 'Prelude To The Dawn', 'Love Tales' and 'Man With The Horn'. He scored and conducted the first *Dizzy Gillespie With Strings* album, and in a more commercial vein wrote (with Carolyn Leigh) 'Young At Heart' for the Frank Sinatra film (1954). He later joined the Stan Kenton arranging staff, which gave scope for his progressive writing (e.g., 1957's *Cuban Fire!* album). That year he formed a new band for recording, resulting in several albums for Capitol Records, Roulette Records, Coral Records and Bethlehem Records. Hardly a commercial success, Richards was nevertheless a musical, if sometimes misused asset to any employer.

● ALBUMS: with Dizzy Gillespie *Dizzy Gillespie Plays/Johnny Richards Conducts* 10-inch album (Discovery 1950)★★★, *Something Else By Johnny Richards* (Bethlehem 1957)★★★, *Wide Range* (Capitol 1957)★★★, *I'm Shooting High* (Capitol 1957)★★★, *Experiments In Sound* (Capitol 1958)★★★, *The Rites Of Diablo* (Roulette 1958)★★★, *Walk Softly/Run Wild* (Coral 1959)★★★, *My Fair Lady* (Roulette 1964)★★★.

Richards, Red

b. Charles Coleridge Richards, 19 October 1912, Brooklyn, New York City, New York, USA, d. 12 March 1998, New York City, New York, USA. After playing classical piano as a child, Richards was moved to turn to jazz after hearing Fats Waller. He played in and around the city of his birth for several years as both soloist and band pianist. In the late 40s and early 50s he worked with several leading jazz musicians including periods in bands led by Tab Smith and Sidney Bechet. During the 50s he worked in the USA and in Europe, playing with diverse artists including Mezz Mezzrow and Frank Sinatra, but spent most of this decade in Muggsy Spanier's band. After a brief stint with Wild Bill Davison he teamed up with Vic Dickenson to form a band they named the Saints And Sinners. This band remained in existence until the early 70s, after which Richards returned to New York where he worked in various clubs as soloist and leader of small groups. Towards the end of the decade he began touring internationally, an activity he continued throughout the 80s, sometimes as soloist but also as a member of the Savoy Sultans led by Panama Francis. Richards' best work has always been heard in his role as a band player where he adds swing and drive to any rhythm section. He collapsed and died on stage in New York in March 1998.

● ALBUMS: *Saints And Sinners In Europe* (1968)★★★, *Soft Buns* (1978)★★★, *In A Mellow Tone* (1979)★★.

Richardson, Jerome

b. 15 November 1920, Sealy, Texas, USA. Raised in California, Richardson began playing alto saxophone in local bands in his early teens. In 1941 he was briefly with the Jimmie Lunceford band, then, after military service during World War II, he played in bands led by Marshal Royal, Lionel Hampton and Earl 'Fatha' Hines. In 1953 he relocated to New York City, working at Minton's Playhouse with his own group. Later in the decade he worked with such leading swing and bop musicians as Lucky Millinder, Kenny Burrell, Gerry Mulligan and Oscar Pettiford. In 1959 he began an association with Quincy Jones and also accompanied several leading song stylists. In 1965 he was a founder-member of the Thad Jones-Mel Lewis big band at New York's Village Vanguard. In 1971 he settled in Los Angeles, working mostly in film studios but also appearing with Quincy Jones, Art Pepper, Bill Berry and others. In later decades he continued to combine studio work with jazz gigs, the former paying the rent while the latter consistently demonstrated his great versatility and talent as both soloist and section musician.

● ALBUMS: *Jerome Richardson Sextet* (New Jazz 1958)★★★, *Roamin' With Jerome Richardson* (New Jazz 1959)★★★, *Going To The Movies* (United Artists 1962)★★★★, *Groove Merchant* (Verve 1967)★★★, *Jazz Station Runaway* (TCB 1997)★★★.

Richman, Boomie

b. Abraham S. Richards, 2 April 1921, Brockton, Massachusetts, USA. In the early and mid-40s Richman played tenor saxophone in bands led by Jerry Wald, Muggsy Spanier and Tommy Dorsey. This last engagement lasted five years and was followed by a long spell of studio work, during which he also played and recorded with Benny Goodman, Neal Hefti, Ruby Braff, the Sauter-Finegan Orchestra, Red Allen and Cootie Williams. By the 60s his studio work considerably outweighed his jazz appearances, a trend that did not alter over succeeding decades. As the quality of his musical leaders indicates, Richman is a sound player with considerable versatility and a great sense of swing.

● ALBUMS: with Benny Goodman *B.G. In Hi-fi* (1954)★★★★, *Muggsy Spanier* (1954)★★★.

Richmond, Dannie

b. 15 December 1935, New York City, New York, USA, d. 15 March 1988, New York City, New York, USA. After starting out as an R&B tenor saxophonist, Richmond switched to drums and changed musical direction in the early 50s. His success was such that by 1956 he was a member of Charles Mingus's band, a role he maintained until 1970. After a spell working in rock bands, backing Joe Cocker and Elton John, Richmond returned to Mingus. After Mingus's death in 1979 he became a founder-member of the Mingus Dynasty. He also worked in small groups with George Rufus Adams and Don Pullen. A powerful drummer with a playing style that allowed him to range widely in music, from jazz to jazz-rock fusion and straight rock, Richmond's long service with Mingus led to his appearing on many seminal recording dates.

● ALBUMS: *In Jazz For The Culture Set* (Impulse! 1965)★★★, *Ode To Mingus* (Soul Note 1979)★★★★, with Jack Walrath *Dannie Richmond Plays Charles Mingus* (Timeless 1980)★★★.

Richmond, June

b. 9 July 1915, Chicago, Illinois, USA, d. 14 August 1962. Richmond's early years are somewhat obscure, but in the mid-30s she was in California singing with Les Hite's popular band. In 1938 she became one of the first black singers to join an all-white band when she was signed by Jimmy Dorsey. The following year she moved to Andy Kirk's band where her talent blossomed. She remained closely associated with Kirk until 1942 and thereafter was mostly to be heard as a single. By the end of the 40s she had to move to Europe to find steady work, singing in France and Scandinavia and making records, usually with local bands such as that led by Eddy Mers, but also worked with Quincy Jones. She was still in Europe, in Gothenburg, Sweden, when she suffered a fatal heart attack. Although of heavy build, Richmond had a light-toned, clear voice, which she used with great verve. Her phrasing was subtle and distinctly jazz-influenced. Some of her European recordings were in languages other than her own, but she handled them with ease.

● ALBUMS: *June Richmond* (Gala Klubben 1955)★★★.

● COMPILATIONS: *Andy Kirk At The Trianon* (Jazz Society 30s-40s)★★★.

RICOTTI, FRANK

b. 31 January 1949, London, England. Ricotti was born into a musical family and followed in his drummer-father's footsteps by taking up percussion. Educational facilities were limited but fortunately Ricotti came to the attention of Bill Ashton, then a teacher in London. With Ashton's encouragement, Ricotti was able to extend his studies (and, inspired by Ricotti, Ashton embarked on a project that eventually became the National Youth Jazz Orchestra). Although adept on most percussion instruments, Ricotti concentrated upon the vibraphone and also developed his talents as a composer and arranger. In the late 60s and early 70s Ricotti played and recorded with Neil Ardley, Dave Gelly, Graham Collier, Mike Gibbs, Stan Tracey and Gordon Beck. By the late 70s Ricotti had become established as a studio musician; during the following decade he was deeply involved in the soundtrack music for a succession of popular British television series by Alan Plater, including *The Beiderbecke Affair*. Also in the 80s he was co-leader, with Chris Laurence and John Taylor, of Paragonne.

● ALBUMS: *Aspects Of Paragonne* (1985)★★★, *The Beiderbecke Collection* (1986-88)★★★★.

RIEL, ALEX

b. 13 September 1940, Copenhagen, Denmark. After drum lessons in his teens, Riel started playing with local trad jazz bands in the 50s. He soon moved on to modern jazz and became the house drummer at the Montmatre Jazzhus, Copenhagen (1963-65). He spent a short time at the Berklee College Of Music in 1966. Although he was playing with Danish Radiojazzgruppen (1965-68), he had become very committed to free jazz and worked with saxophonists John Tchicai and Archie Shepp and bassist Gary Peacock. He formed a quintet with Palle Mikkelborg, which won first prize at the Montreux Jazz Festival (1968), and then played Newport. Meanwhile, he was playing with rock group Savage Roses (1968-72). In the 70s he co-led a group called V8 with Mikkelborg and has since freelanced throughout Europe.

● ALBUMS: *Alex Riel Trio* (1965)★★★, *Unriel* (Stunt 1998)★★★.

RIFKIN, JOSHUA

b. 22 April 1944, New York, USA. A pianist, musicologist, arranger and conductor, Rifkin was instrumental in reviving interest in the important composer of ragtime music, Scott Joplin. During the 60s, Rifkin studied at the Juilliard School of Music, New York University, Gottingen University and Princeton; and worked on composition with Karl-Heinz Stockhausen in Darmstadt. At the same time, he played ragtime and piano jazz, and recorded for Elektra as a member of the Even Dozen Jug Band. Also for Elektra, he conducted *The Baroque Beatles*, classical-style versions of John Lennon and Paul McCartney songs. He also arranged and conducted *Wildflowers*, and other recordings for Judy Collins. In 1970 he was appointed Professor of Music at Brandeis University in Massachusetts, and musical director of the Elektra ancillary, Nonesuch Records. The following year, the Lincoln Centre produced the highly successful *An Evening With Scott Joplin*, at which Rifkin was a featured artist. From 1970-74, he released a series of three *Piano Rags By Scott Joplin*, which won *Stereo Review* and *Billboard* awards as records of the year, and coincided with the release of the film *The Sting* (1973), whose soundtrack featured 'The Entertainer' and several other Joplin tunes, arranged by another Juilliard 'old boy', Marvin Hamlisch. The film won seven Academy Awards, and, together with Rifkin's albums, sparked off a nationwide revival of Joplin's works. Subsequently, Rifkin worked a good deal in the classical field, conducting concerts and releasing several albums. He was also at the forefront of the move to revitalize vintage recordings of ragtime music by the digital process.

● ALBUMS: *The Baroque Beatles Book* (Elektra 1965)★★★★, *Piano Rags By Scott Joplin, Volumes 1 & 2* (Nonesuch 1974)★★★, *Piano Rags By Scott Joplin, Volume 3* (Nonesuch 1974)★★★, *Digital Ragtime* (EMI 1980)★★.

RILEY, BEN

b. Benjamin A. Riley, 17 July 1933, Savannah, Georgia, USA. After playing drums with various bands during his teenage years, Riley began playing with front-rank jazzmen in the mid-50s and over the next dozen years appeared with an impressive roster of leaders. These included Stan Getz, Woody Herman, Eddie 'Lockjaw' Davis, Ahmad Jamal and Ray Bryant. In 1964 he joined Thelonious Monk with whom he toured extensively and played on several Columbia Records album sessions, including 1964's *It's Monk's Time* and 1967's *Underground*. Subsequently he played with several more important figures including, through the 70s and into the 80s, Ron Carter, Milt Jackson, the New York Saxophone Quartet, Abdullah Ibrahim and Maria Muldaur. In the early 80s Riley formed the band Sphere, with Charlie Rouse, Kenny Barron and Buster Williams, to pay musical tribute to Monk. A fluent, tasteful and thinking drummer, Riley's playing is always inventive and highly supportive of the musicians he accompanies.

● ALBUMS: all with Sphere *Four In One* (Elektra Musician 1982)★★★★, *Flight Path* (Elektra Musician 1983)★★★, *Sphere On Tour* (Red 1985)★★★, *Four For All* (Verve 1987)★★★, *Bird Songs* (Verve 1988)★★★★, *Sphere* (Verve 1998)★★★.

RILEY, HOWARD

b. John Howard Riley, 16 February 1943, Huddersfield, Yorkshire, England. Riley began playing piano at the age of six, although it was another 10 years before he began to play jazz. At university he studied under Bernard Rands at Bangor, North Wales (1961-66) gaining BA and MA degrees, then with David Baker at Indiana, adding M.Mus to his name in 1967. From 1967-70 he studied for his PhD at York University under Wilfred Mellers, who wrote a piece (Yeibichai) for symphony orchestra, scat singer and jazz trio that was performed by the BBC Symphony Orchestra, Frank Holder and Riley's trio at the 1969 Proms. Riley had led a trio at Bangor, and later joined Evan Parker's quartet. On his return from Indiana he formed a trio with Barry Guy (and sometimes Ron Rubin) and Jon Hiseman (also Tony Oxley and, later, Alan Jackson) and began writing for bands including the Spontaneous Music Ensemble and the Don Rendell-Ian Carr Quintet. At this time he also began to have his chamber and orchestral pieces performed in concert, and was a founder-member of the Musicians' Co-Operative. He has composed for Barry Guy's London Jazz Composers' Orchestra and the New Jazz Orchestra and played with Keith Tippett, John McLaughlin (who had also occasionally sat in with the late 60s trio), Jaki Byard, Elton Dean, the LJCO (being the featured soloist on their *Double Trouble*), Barbara Thompson, Tony Oxley and many others. He has also taught at the Guildhall and Goldsmith's schools of music in London and at the Center Of The Creative And Performing Arts in Buffalo. In the late 80s he began to release both old and new recordings on his own cassette label, Falcon Tapes. In 1990 he and Elton Dean co-led a quartet of improvisers on a set of jazz standards, *All The Tradition*.

● ALBUMS: *Discussions* (1967)★★, *Angle* (1969)★★, *The Day Will Come* (1970)★★★, *Flight* (Future Music 1971)★★★★, *Synopsis* (1976)★★★, *Singleness* (1976)★★★, *Interwine* (1977)★★★, *Shaped* (Mosaic 1977)★★★, *Toronto Concert* 1976 recording (1979)★★★, *Facets* 3-LP box set (Impetus 1981)★★★★, *Duality* (1982)★★★, *The Other Side* (1983)★★★, *For Four On Two Two* (Affinity 1984)★★★, with Keith Tippett *In Focus* (Affinity 1985)★★★, with Jaki Byard *Live At The Royal Festival Hall* 1984 recording (1987)★★★, with Elton Dean *All The Tradition* (1990)★★★★, *Procession* (Wondrous 1991)★★★★, *The Heat Of Moments* (Wondrous 1993)★★★, with Tippett *The Bern Concert* (Future Music 1994)★★★, *Beyond Category* (Wondrous 1993)★★★, *Wishing On The Moon* (Future Music 1995)★★★★, *Descending Circles* (Blueprint 1996)★★★★, *Inner Minor* (ASC 1997)★★★, *Classics Live* (Slam 1998)★★★★, *Making Noises* (Slam 1998)★★★.

RILEY, MIKE

(see Farley And Riley)

RILEY, TERRY

b. 24 June 1935, Colfax, California, USA. A former ragtime pianist on San Francisco's Barbary Coast, Riley forged an exceptional, *avant garde* minimalist style while performing in Europe. Having studied with fellow radical LaMonte Young, he completed his revolutionary piece, 'In C', in 1964. Here, Riley's piano part, the pulse, strikes a uniform tempo as an ensemble plays 53 separate figures. Each musician moves at his/her own pace and the composition is only complete when every player reaches figure 53. Riley found a more widespread audience with *A Rainbow In Curved Air*, which comprised two lengthy compositions, the title track and 'Poppy Nogood And The Phantom Band'. Electric organ and electric harpsichord ebb and flow in cyclical patterns, creating a mood adopted by the Soft Machine, Brian Eno, Philip Glass and a host of new age practitioners. *Church Of Anthrax*, a joint effort with John Cale, which for the most part was a unsatisfying collaboration, brought Riley a small degree of commercial success, but he preferred to pursue an irregular release schedule rather than capitalize on any newfound fame. Indeed, it was 1980 before he recorded for the American market, although intermediate releases had been undertaken for European outlets. Riley has since garnered plaudits and his work has been interpreted successfully by the acclaimed Kronos Quartet.

● ALBUMS: *Reed Streams* (Columbia 1967)★★, *In C* (Columbia 1968)★★★, *A Rainbow In Curved Air* (Columbia 1969)★★★★, with John Cale *Church Of Anthrax* (1971)★★★★, *Persian Surgery Dervishes* (Shandar 1972)★★★, *Happy Ending* (1973)★★, *Le Secret De La Vie* (1974)★★, *Ten Voices Of The Two Prophets* (70s)★★★, *Shri Camel* (1980)★★★, *Descending Moonshine Dervishes* (1982)★★★, *The Ethereal Time Shadow* (1985)★★★, *No Man's Land* (1990)★★, *Chanting The Light Of Foresight* (New Albion 1996)★★★★.

RIMINGTON, SAMMY

b. 29 April 1942, London, England. Rimington began playing clarinet and alto saxophone professionally in his mid-teens as a member of Barry Martyn's band and by 1960 was with Ken Colyer where he remained for four years. In 1965 he visited the USA, playing in New Orleans with several leading veterans including George Lewis and Zutty Singleton. In the late 60s he was back in the UK working with Martyn and touring Americans, such as Kid Thomas and John Handy, but was also experimenting with jazz rock. He was, however, most at home in New Orleans-style music and since the mid-70s has played with many leading exponents of traditional jazz, including George Webb, Keith Smith and Chris Barber. On clarinet, Rimington is an exceptionally fine performer in the tradition originating in the style of Lewis, whom he clearly admires, and he has great flair on this instrument. Like Barber, Rimington has constantly sought to expand the boundaries of his chosen area of jazz and this is most apparent when he plays alto saxophone. On this instrument he plays with great emotional depth, creating fascinating and rhythmic solos using a quirky distinctive style that faintly echoes the sound of Pete Brown. Despite his comparative youthfulness, Rimington is one of the outstanding exponents of New Orleans jazz playing today, and owing to his broad-based musical outlook he can appeal to a wider audience than this might at first suggest.

● ALBUMS: with Kid Thomas *The December Band* (1965)★★★, with Zutty Singleton *Zutty And The Clarinet Kings* (1967)★★★, with Keith Smith *Way Down Yonder In New Orleans, Then And Now* (1977)★★★, *And Red Beans* (1977)★★, *Sammy Rimington And His New Orleans Quartet* (1977)★★★, *Reed All About It* (Hefty Jazz 1978)★★★, *The Sammy Rimington Band* (1980)★★★, *Exciting Sax* (Progressive 1986-91)★★★, *In Town With Sam Lee* (GHB 1988)★★, *A New Orleans Session With* (GHB 1989)★★★, *One Swiss Night* (Music Mecca 1993)★★★, *More Exciting Sax Of Sammy Rimmington* (Progressive 1995)★★, *Watering The Roots* (Jazz Crusade 1996)★★★.

RIP RIG AND PANIC

Evolving out of Bristol's the Pop Group, Rip Rig And Panic was formed in 1981 as a conceptual musicians' collective, taking its name from an album by Roland Kirk. The group's prime movers were multi-instrumentalist and songwriter Gareth Sager, jazz trumpeter Don Cherry's step-daughter Neneh Cherry (b. Neneh Mariann Karlsson, 10 March 1964, Stockholm, Sweden; vocals), Cherry's partner and drummer Bruce Smith, Sean Oliver (d. March 1990; bass) and Mark Springer (piano). Powerful and disturbing live, their playful, anarchic jazz-funk was well captured on the irreverent 1981 debut album *God*, which appeared as two 45rpm discs, but was too radical for daytime airplay or significant sales. They performed at the first WOMAD festival in 1982 shortly before Cherry returned to Sweden to have her first baby. Sean Oliver's sister Andrea temporarily took over vocals, and Louis Moholo joined on drums. The equally experimental second album, *I Am Cold*, appeared in 1982, followed by the more accessible *Attitude* in 1983. Unwilling to compromise further, but feeling the strain of constant innovation, they split in 1985, only to realign as the smaller outfit Float Up CP, and, briefly, God Mother And Country, before Cherry went on to a successful solo career, with Andrea Oliver contributing to some of her songs. Sean Oliver, who went on to co-write Terence Trent D'Arby's 'Wishing Well', died of sickle-cell anaemia in 1990. Sager formed Head, while Springer released a solo album before going on to work on film and television soundtracks. He returned to solo recording with 1998's *Eye*.

● ALBUMS: *God* (Virgin 1981)★★★, *I Am Cold* (Virgin 1982)★★★, *Attitude* (Virgin 1983)★★★. As Float Up CP *Kill Me In The Morning* (Upside 1985)★★.

Solo: Mark Springer *Piano* (Illuminated 1984)★★, *Eye* (Exit 1998)★★★.

RIPPINGTONS

Russ Freeman (b. 11 February 1960, Nashville, Tennessee, USA; guitar), Kenny G. (b. Kenneth Gorelick, 1959, Seattle, Washington, USA; saxophone) and David Benoit (b. 1953, Bakersfield, California, USA; keyboards). The man generally recognized as the founder of the Rippingtons, Russ Freeman discovered the guitar with the kind of inevitability that comes from growing up in Nashville. In fact, it was a studio guitarist friend of Freeman's father that gave him his initial encouragement. He studied at Cal Arts and at UCLA, developing the essential studio skills, releasing a debut album (*Nocturnal Playground*) in 1985. *Moonlighting* came the following year, after Freeman got together with Kenny G., David Benoit and a group of friends, to record some of his own new compositions, in an unambitious project he lightheartedly called the Rippingtons, and the record was an instant hit. One of the GRP label's most coveted acts, the band specializes in a smooth instrumental pop fusion, featuring elements of Latin music and R&B.

● ALBUMS: *Moonlighting* (Passport 1987)★★★, *Kilimanjaro* (Passport 1988)★★★, *Tourist In Paradise* (GRP 1989)★★★, *Welcome To The St. James' Club* (GRP 1992)★★★, *Curves Ahead* (GRP 1991)★★★, *Weekend In Monaco* (GRP 1992)★★★, *Live In L.A.* (GRP 1993)★★★, *Sahara* (GRP 1995)★★★, *Brave New World* (GRP 1996)★★★, *Black Diamond: The Rippingtons Featuring Russ Freeman* (Windham Hill 1997)★★★★.

● COMPILATIONS: *The Best Of The Rippingtons* (GRP 1997)★★★★.

RITENOUR, LEE

b. 1 November 1953, Los Angeles, California, USA. The prolific Ritenour has established himself as one of the world's leading jazz fusion guitarists with a series of accessible albums over the past two decades. Known as 'Captain Fingers', Ritenour became a sought-after session player in the mid-70s and, like Larry Carlton (both regularly play a Gibson 335), has developed his own solo career. Although heavily influenced in his early days by the relaxed styles of Wes Montgomery, Joe Pass and Barney Kessel, he now has his own distinctive sound and fluid style. His list of session work is awesome, but some of his notable performances were with Herbie Hancock, Steely Dan and Stanley Clarke. Since the mid-80s Ritenour has been strongly influenced by Brazilian music. He joined GRP Records around this time, having worked with stablemate Don Grusin in the band Friendship. He recorded the magnificent *Harlequin* with GRP co-owner Dave Grusin in 1985. In the early 90s Ritenour teamed up with Bob James, Harvey Mason and bassist Nathan East under the name of Fourplay, who have released a number of soul/jazz/funk fusion albums for Warner Brothers. In 1993 Ritenour topped the *Billboard* jazz chart with his accomplished tribute to Wes Montgomery, *Wes Bound*, and followed it in 1995 with an excellent joint album with Larry Carlton. He founded his own record label I.E. Music, in 1998

● ALBUMS: *First Course* (Epic 1974)★★, *Guitar Player* (Epic 1975)★★, *Captain Fingers* (Epic 1977)★★★, *The Captain's Journey* (Elektra 1978)★★★, *Gentle Thoughts* (JVC 1978)★★, with Kazume Watanbe *Sugarloaf Express* (Elite 1978)★★, *Feel The Night* (1979)★★★, *Friendship* (JVC 1979)★★★, *Rit* (Asylum 1981)★★★, *Rio* (GRP 1982)★★★, *Rit 2* (GRP 1983)★★★, *Banded Together* (1983)★★★, *On The Line* (GRP 1984)★★★, with Dave Grusin *Harlequin* (GRP 1985)★★★, *American Flyers* (1986)★★★, *Earth Run* (GRP 1986)★★★, *Portrait* (GRP 1987)★★, *Festival* (GRP 1988)★★, with John Handy *Where Go The Boats* (Inak 1988)★★★, *Color Rit* (GRP 1989)★★★, *Stolen Moments* (GRP 1990)★★★, *Wes Bound* (GRP 1993)★★★★, with Larry Carlton *Larry And Lee* (GRP 1995)★★★★, *Alive In L.A.* (GRP 1997)★★, *This Is Love* (I.E. Music 1998)★★★.

● COMPILATIONS: *The Collection* (GRP 1991)★★★.

RIVERS, MAVIS

b. *c.*1930, Apia, Upolu, Western Samoa. As a child Rivers sang with a small band led by her father, entertaining US troops based on Samoa during World War II. After the war her family moved to New Zealand where she worked in clubs and on radio, and for three years from 1949, she was voted the country's most popular singer.

In 1954 she moved to the USA where her first album, *Take A Number*, was nominated for a Grammy. She continued to record and in 1962 became the regular singer with Red Norvo's small group. Thereafter, she sang with various small bands including those led by Terry Gibbs and Page Cavanaugh. She has also performed in concert and recorded with her son, Matt Catingub. A tuneful singer with a light, airy vocal sound, Rivers is most at ease in a small group setting.

● ALBUMS: *Take A Number* (1959)★★★★, *Hooray For Love* (1960)★★★, *Mavis Rivers Sings About The Simple Life* (1960)★★, *Mavis Rivers* i (1961)★★★, *Sing Along With Mavis* (1961)★★★, *Mavis Rivers* ii (1962)★★★, *Mavis Rivers* iii (1962)★★★, *Mavis Rivers* iv (1964)★★★, with Matt Catingub *It's A Good Day* (1983)★★★, with Catingub *My Mommy And Me* (1983)★★★.

RIVERS, SAM

b. 25 September 1930, El Reno, Oklahoma, USA. Alto, soprano and tenor saxophone, flute and piano player and composer. After extensive studies, Rivers began playing in and around Boston, Massachusetts, in the late 40s. (His first professional engagement had been with Jimmy Witherspoon during his military service.) During the next few years he played mostly in the Boston area with Jaki Byard, Nat Pierce, Herb Pomeroy and the very young Tony Williams. He also worked in Florida in a band led by Don Wilkerson. It was not until 1964 that he achieved prominence when he joined Miles Davis thanks to the recommendation of Williams, then a member of Davis's band. In the mid-60s he worked in New York, recording for Blue Note Records with Williams, Byard, Ron Carter and others. In the late 60s he continued recording with such artists as Donald Byrd, Bobby Hutcherson and Julian Priester. Around this time he also began teaching and established a five-year association with Cecil Taylor with whom he visited Europe. Since that time he has continued to teach, compose and perform with a wide variety of musical groups, including the San Francisco Symphony Orchestra, his own small groups and has had a lasting relationship with Dave Holland. A highly acclaimed musician, Rivers' concentration on teaching and on developing original musical concepts has tended to make him less accessible to the wider audience. Those who have persevered with his music have found it rewarding in its imaginative blending of many jazz styles, ranging from blues to the *avant garde*. Rivers is particularly effective on flute and soprano, instruments on which he displays a light, dancing style. Whether as performer or composer, it is his remarkably sustained inventiveness that characterizes his work.

● ALBUMS: *Fuchsia Swing Song* (Blue Note 1964)★★★, *Contours* (Blue Note 1965)★★★★, *A New Conception* (Blue Note 1966)★★★★, *Streams - Live At Montreux* (MCA 1973)★★★, *Crystals* (Impulse! 1974)★★★, *Sizzle* (Impulse! 1975)★★★★, *Dimensions & Extensions* released on Andrew Hill's *Involution* (Blue Note 1975)★★★★, with Dave Holland *Sam Rivers And Dave Holland, Volume 1* (Improvising Artists 1976)★★★★, with Holland *Sam Rivers And Dave Holland, Volume 2* (Improvising Artists 1976)★★★★, *Paragon* (Fluid 1977)★★★, *Waves* (Tomato 1978)★★★★, *Colours* (Black Saint 1983)★★★, *Lazuli* (Timeless 1990)★★★, with Julian Priester *Hints On Light And Shadow* (Postcards 1997)★★, *Portrait* (FMP 1997)★★, *Configuration* (Pelican Sound 1998)★★★, *Concepts* (RivBea 1998)★★★.

● COMPILATIONS: *The Complete Blue Note Sam Rivers Sessions* 5-LP/3-CD box set (Mosaic 1996)★★★★.

RIVERSIDE RECORDS

Beginning life as an important US label for traditional jazz, Riverside later became a major presenter of modern jazz. Founded in 1953 by Bill Grauer and Orrin Keepnews, early Riverside albums provided long-playing compilations of many classic early jazz labels, including Gennett, HRS, QRS and Circle. The following year Riverside tested current waters with an album by Randy Weston and soon added Thelonious Monk, Bill Evans and Cannonball Adderley to its roster. Later, Wes Montgomery signed and, in the early 60s, Barry Harris. The early interest in traditional jazz was not forgotten and new recordings were made, also in the 60s by Kid Thomas Valentine, Peter Bocage and, before his rediscovery and promotion as a mainstream giant, Earl 'Fatha' Hines. Soon after Graner's death at the end of 1963, Riverside folded, but the following decade saw many of the company's best albums reissued by Fantasy on their Milestone and OJC (Original Jazz Classics) labels.

● COMPILATIONS: *The Riverside Records Story* 4-CD box set (Riverside/Fantasy 1998)★★★★.

ROACH, MAX

b. 10 January 1924, New Land, North Carolina, USA. Learning to play drums in his pre-teenage years, Roach later studied in New York and by 1942 was active in the bebop revolution. As a member of the house rhythm section at Monroe's Uptown House and a regular at Minton's Playhouse, he backed all the leading practitioners of the new art. Along with Kenny Clarke he established a new drummers' vocabulary, and his work with Charlie Parker and Dizzy Gillespie from this period demonstrates his inventiveness and masterly technique. In addition to playing bebop, the 40s also found him working in small and big bands led by such swing era veterans as Coleman Hawkins and Benny Carter. Towards the end of the decade, however, he abandoned the older style and was henceforth one of bebop's major voices. He was with Miles Davis for two years from 1948, participating in the seminal *Birth Of The Cool* recording dates. In 1954 Roach formed a quintet with Clifford Brown, a band that was one of the most musically inventive of the period. Brown's accidental death in 1956 was a devastating loss to Roach and it took many years for him fully to shake off the traumatic effect it had upon him. From the late 50s Roach began to take a political stance and was active in many black cultural projects. Inevitably, his work of this period took on elements of his commitment to Civil Rights issues. His compositions included the *We Insist! Freedom Now Suite*. He also experimented with unusual line-ups, sometimes abandoning conventional time structures. In these respects he was in line with concurrent developments in free jazz, but was never a true part of that movement. His own small groups saw an impressive array of talented musical partners including Freddie Hubbard, Sonny Rollins, George Coleman and Stanley Turrentine. He also worked with a variety of singers and vocal groups, including performances with his wife Abbey Lincoln. In the 70s, although he was by then becoming an elder statesman of jazz, Roach continued to associate with musicians of the *avant garde*, recording duo albums with Abdullah Ibrahim, Archie Shepp, Cecil Taylor and Anthony Braxton. One of few drummers to perform and record extended solo works, Roach achieved a remarkably high standard of performance and overcame the customary negative critical response to such works. Throughout the 80s and into the early 90s, Roach continued to perform, and compose, finding time to teach at the University Of Massachusetts and to maintain his activism in black politics. One of the most technically gifted musicians in jazz, Roach has long been a major figure in the development of the music and his consistently high standard of performance has never faltered. As a drummer, he is a master of all aspects of his work, a mastery that he demonstrated during his 1990 tour by playing as an encore a thoroughly absorbing 10-minute solo using only the hi-hat cymbal. If there is another jazz drummer capable of such feats he has yet to appear in public. In 1995 he worked with Ginger Baker and Tony Williams in the percussion band M'Boom. One of his most ambitious projects was in 1996 with a 50-piece orchestra, which crossed over into the classical market.

● ALBUMS: with Hank Mobley *Max Roach Quartet Featuring Hank Mobley* 10-inch album (Debut 1954)★★★, with Clifford Brown *Clifford Brown & Max Roach* 10-inch album (EmArcy 1954)★★★★, with Brown *Brown And Roach Incorporated* (EmArcy 1954)★★★★, with Brown *A Study In Brown* (EmArcy 1955)★★★★, with Brown *Clifford Brown & Max Roach At Basin Street* (EmArcy 1956)★★★★, with Brown, Sonny Rollins *Sonny Rollins Plus Four* reissued as *Three Giants* (Prestige 1956)★★★★, *Max Roach + Four* (EmArcy 1957)★★★★, *Jazz In 3/4 Time* (EmArcy 1957)★★★★, with Stan Levey *Drummin' The Blues* (Liberty 1957)★★★, *The Max Roach 4 Plays Charlie Parker* (EmArcy 1958)★★★, *Max Roach Plus 4 On The Chicago Scene* (EmArcy 1958)★★★, *Max* (Argo 1958)★★★, *Max Roach Plus Four At Newport* (EmArcy 1958)★★★★, *Max Roach With The Boston Percussion Ensemble* (EmArcy 1958)★★★, *Deeds, Not Words* (Riverside 1959)★★★★, with Buddy Rich *Rich Versus Roach* (Mercury 1959)★★★★, *The Many Sides Of Max Roach* (Mercury 1959)★★★, *Award-Winning Drummer* reissued as *Max Roach* (Time 1959)★★★, *Quiet As It's Kept* (Mercury 1959)★★★, *We Insist! Freedom Now Suite* (Candid 1960)★★★, *Moon Faced And Starry-Eyed* (Mercury 1960)★★★, *Percussion Bitter Suite* (Impulse! 1961)★★★★, *It's Time* (Impulse! 1962)★★★★, *Parisian Sketches* (Mercury 1962)★★★★, with Sonny Clark, George Duvivier *Max Roach, Sonny Clark, George Duvivier* (Time 1962)★★★★, with Duke Ellington, Charles Mingus *Money Jungle* (United Artists 1962)★★★★, *Speak Brother, Speak* (Fantasy 1963)★★★★, *The Many Sides Of Max* (Mercury 1964)★★★, *Max Roach Trio Featuring The Legendary Hasaan* (Atlantic 1964)★★★★, *Drums Unlimited* (Atlantic 1966)★★★, *Members Don't Get Weary* (Atlantic 1968)★★★, *Lift Every Voice And Sing* (1971)★★★, with Archie Shepp *Force-Sweet Mao-Suid Afrika '76* (BASE 1976)★★★★, *Max Roach Quartet Live In Tokyo Volumes 1 & 2* (1977)★★★, *The Loadstar* (Horo 1977)★★★, *Live In Amsterdam* (1977)★★★, *Solos* (1977)★★★, *Confirmation* (1978)★★★, *Birth And Rebirth* (Black Saint 1978)★★★, with Shepp *The Long March* (hatART 1979)★★★★, *One In Two-Two In One* (hatART 1979)★★★, *Pictures In A Frame* (Soul Note 1979)★★★, *Sounds As A Roach* 1968 recording (Joker/Lotus 1980)★★★, *Chattahoochee Red* (1981)★★★, *Swish* (1982)★★★, *In The Light* (Soul Note 1982)★★★, with Brown, Rollins *Pure Genius* 1956 recording (Elektra 1982)★★★★, *Live At Vielharmonie, Munich* (Soul Note 1983)★★★, with Cecil Taylor *Historic Concerts* 1979 recording (Soul Note 1984)★★★★, *Scott Free* (Soul Note 1984)★★★, *Survivors* (Soul Note 1984)★★★, *Easy Winners* (Soul Note 1985)★★★, *Bright Moments* (Soul Note 1987)★★★★, with Dizzy Gillespie *Max & Dizzy - Paris 1989* (A&M 1990)★★★, *To The Max!* (Blue Moon 1992)★★★, *It's Christmas Again* (Soul Note 1995)★★, *Max Roach With The New Orchestra Of Boston And The So What Brass Quintet* (Blue Note 1996)★★★.

Roadside Picnic

This UK group is comprised of Dave O'Higgins (tenor saxophone, soprano saxophone, EWI), John Smith (piano, keyboards), Mario Castronari (bass), and Mike Bradley (drums, percussion). Despite the considerable press coverage given to the saxophonist O'Higgins, it was the compositional and conceptual strength of Castronari that gave Roadside Picnic its initial impetus. Formed during the British jazz boom of the mid-80s, it is a strong four-piece fusion band featuring some of the young UK talent presently securing a niche in the jazz scene. Their popular debut, *Roadside Picnic*, was recorded in 1988 and released to an enthusiastic reception. In 1990 they followed up with their concept set *For Mad Men Only*. Intended as a musical representation of scenes from Herman Hesse's novel *Steppenwolf*, it was accompanied by another burst of media attention. The group's repertoire consists of carefully arranged original material. Smith's futuristic keyboard sounds are played over complex rhythmic patterns and shifting time signatures, leaving a fairly strict framework for O'Higgins' Michael Brecker-influenced saxophone solos.

● ALBUMS: *Roadside Picnic* (1988)★★★, *For Mad Men Only* (1990)★★★.

Robert, Yves

b. 17 January 1958, Clermont-Ferrand, France. Robert received a classical training at the Conservatoire de Vichy where he studied the flute before concentrating on the trombone. In 1981 he joined the Lyon-based experimental music collective ARFI (Association à la recherche d'un folklore imaginaire) and was particularly influenced by its co-founder, the eclectic jazz saxophonist and clarinettist Louis Sclavis. During the 80s he worked with Sclavis's quartet, the Didier Levallet Quintet, Chris McGregor's afro-free jazz ensemble, the

Brotherhood Of Breath, Steve Lacy's music-dance project Futurities and La Marmite Infernale big band. He also led his own improvising quartet and gave solo trombone concerts. In 1991 he made an impressive debut at Derek Bailey's Company Week festival of improvised music in London. Robert is a versatile and highly inventive trombone player with a strong sense of timing and a Tatiesque eye for humour, should the opportunity arise.

● ALBUMS: with La Marmite Infernale *Moralité Surprise* (1983)★★★, *Yves Robert Trombone Solo* (1983)★★★, with Didier Levallet Quintet *Quiet Days* (1985)★★★, *Tout Court* (Deux Z 1992)★★★★.

ROBERTS, HANK

b. 1954, Terre Haute, Indiana, USA. Cellist - and until recently, professional chef - Roberts has become one of the busiest musicians in New York's 'downtown' scene. His music is wide-open experimental and heedless of idiomatic boundaries. It acknowledges his hillbilly roots with a comic barn dance or two, but moves out towards sleek rock, free sound exploration, anything and everything. First heard amongst the massed strings of Michael Mantler's Orchestra on *13* (1975), Roberts began to attract rave notices for his work with guitarist Bill Frisell. The cellist leads his own group Birds Of Prey and co-leads two others - Miniature (with Tim Berne and Joey Baron) and Arcado, a string trio with Mark Dresser and Mark Feldman. Roberts is also a distinctive singer, his vocals having an ethereal quality that has prompted critics to make comparisons with Milton Nascimento and Robert Wyatt. Often doctoring his voice with echo and tape-delay, Roberts uses it to expand the sound of his cello, 'to make the chords bigger'.

● ALBUMS: *Black Pastels* (JMT 1988)★★, *Miniature* (1988)★★★, *Arcado* (1989)★★★, *Hank Robert & Birds Of Prey* (JMT 1990)★★, with Arcado *Behind The Myth* (1990)★★★, with Miniature *I Can't Put My Finger On It* (1991)★★★, with Arcado *For Three Strings And Orchestra* (1992)★★★, *Little Motor People* (JMT 1993)★★★★.

ROBERTS, HOWARD

b. Howard Mancel Roberts, 2 October 1929, Phoenix, Arizona, USA, d. 28 June 1992, Seattle, Washington, USA. After intensive studies on guitar and in music theory, Roberts became a very busy studio musician in Los Angeles. Through the 50s and 60s he played on countless records, mostly pop and rock, but he also featured on several jazz dates. During these years he played in jazz groups for club sessions, sometimes as leader. When let loose from studio restrictions on a true jazz date, as on an especially exhilarating set by his so-called Magic Band, recorded live at Donte's in 1968 with musicians including Pete Christlieb, Dave Grusin and Chuck Berghofer, he could be an exceptionally creative and exciting player. In the early 70s he added to his busy schedule by starting to teach and write instructional material for music publications. In the middle of the decade he was a founder member of the Guitar Institute of Technology, which subsequently became the Musicians Institute, in Hollywood. In his bop-styled guitar work, Roberts often displayed his early classical training and his continuing interest in contemporary classical music. Although much less well known to the general public than his talent merited, Roberts's work as player, teacher and theorist made him into a quietly influential figure.

● ALBUMS: *Mr. Roberts Plays Guitar* (Verve 1957)★★★, *Good Pickin's* (Verve 1959)★★★, *Color Him Funky* (Capitol 1963)★★★, *H.R. Is A Dirty Guitar Player* (Capitol 1963)★★★, *Something's Cookin'* (Capitol 1965)★★, *Goodies* (Capitol 1965)★★, *Whatever's Fair* (Capitol 1966)★★, *All-Time Great Instrumental Hits* (Capitol 1966)★★, *Velvet Groove* (Verve 1966)★★★, *The Movin' Man* (Verve 1966)★★★, *Jaunty-Jolly* (Capitol 1967)★★, *Guilty* (Capitol 1967)★★, *Out Of Sight-But In Mind* (Capitol 1968)★★, *Antelope Freeway* (Impulse! 1969)★★★, *The Real Howard Roberts* (Concord Jazz 1977)★★★★, *Turning To Spring* (Discovery 1980)★★★, *The Magic Band II* 1968 recording (VSOP 1998)★★★.

ROBERTS, LUCKEY

b. Charles Luckyeth, 7 August 1887, Philadelphia, Pennsylvania, USA, d. 5 February 1968. After working in vaudeville as a child, Roberts moved to New York where he established a minor reputation as a composer and a major one as a performer of rags and, later, stride piano. In the years between the wars, Roberts' composing talents were recognized more and several of his musical shows were produced. During the 40s and early 50s he owned and regularly played at a Harlem bar. Roberts made few records and most of these were early piano rolls, while his later records were made after he had suffered strokes and injuries in a road accident. Nevertheless, it is possible to understand the awe felt by such pianists as Fats Waller, James P. Johnson and Willie 'The Lion' Smith at his astonishing technique, a technique that was greatly facilitated by his remarkably large hands.

● ALBUMS: *Happy Go Luckey* (Period 1956)★★, with Willie 'The Lion' Smith *Harlem Piano Solos* (Good Time Jazz 1958)★★★.

ROBERTS, MARCUS

b. 7 August 1963, Jacksonville, Florida, USA. If Thelonious Monk frequently pursued improvisation through harmonic as well as (or sometimes instead of) melodic routes, pianist Roberts is an appropriate inheritor of the method. Like Wynton Marsalis (later to be his employer) Roberts is a dedicated and outspoken respecter of earlier jazz traditions, and his technique comfortably encompasses stride, many variations of blues, and bebop. Blind since childhood, Roberts took up the instrument early after exposure to a mixture of classical and gospel music, and studied piano at Florida State, winning competitions on the instrument by the mid-80s. Roberts' vitality, knowledge, technique and admiration for his keyboard predecessors brought him a place in the Wynton Marsalis group by 1985 and - as with Marsalis - a series of albums as leader took him further back into the archives, albeit with a continuing grace and swing. Roberts' commercial standing was also confirmed when his first three albums all reached number 1 on the *Billboard* jazz chart. *Alone With Three Giants* demonstrated Roberts' single-minded determination to subjugate self-expression to interpretation of classic works, including pieces by Jelly Roll Morton and Monk. The simultaneous release of *Portraits In Blue* and *Time And Circumstance* in 1996 juxtaposed Roberts' radical take on George Gershwin with a set of original trio compositions. The following year's *Blues For The New Millennium* was a tribute to the blues that covered Robert Johnson alongside Morton.

● ALBUMS: *The Truth Is Spoken Here* (Novus 1989)★★★, *Deep In The Shed* (Novus 1990)★★★, *Alone With Three Giants* (Novus 1990)★★★★, *Prayer For Peace* (Novus 1991)★★★, *As Serenity Approaches* (Novus 1992)★★★, *If I Could Be With You* (Novus 1993)★★★, *Gershwin For Lovers* (Columbia 1994)★★★, *Portraits In Blue* (Columbia 1996)★★★★, *Time And Circumstance* (Columbia 1996)★★★, *Blues For The New Millennium* (Columbia 1997)★★★★, *The Joy Of Joplin* (Sony Classical 1998)★★★★.

Robertson, Dick

b. 3 July 1903, New York City, New York, USA, d. date unknown. Although he had sung in his youth, singer Dick Robertson did not begin to attract attention as a soloist until he was in his mid-twenties. He made many records, often singing to the accompaniment of leading jazz musicians of the day, including Ben Pollack, Duke Ellington and Benny Goodman. By the mid-30s Robertson was an important recording artist and was sometimes featured as nominal leader of the bands that accompanied him. Changing times and public taste in singers began to leave him behind and by the mid-40s he had virtually abandoned singing as a career. However, he had long had a second string to his bow and now concentrated on composing popular songs. One of the best known of his compositions is 'I'm A Little On The Lonely Side'.

Robertson, Zue

b. C. Alvin Robertson, 7 March 1891, New Orleans, Louisiana, USA, d. 1943. After learning to play piano, Robertson switched to trombone and first played professionally in his early teenage years. He worked with such leading New Orleans musicians as Manuel Perez, John Robichaux and Richard M. Jones. He was also a member of the band accompanying a touring Wild West show, which featured frontiersman Kit Carson. Dividing his time between New Orleans and Chicago, Robertson became a proficient performer and by the early 20s had recorded with Jelly Roll Morton and King Oliver. After spending most of the 20s on the road he settled in New York where he reverted to piano and also played organ, giving up the trombone entirely. He played on through the 30s, relocating in California, and took up yet another instrument, the bass.

Robichaux, John

b. 16 January 1886, Thibodaux, Louisiana, USA, d. 1939. Resident in New Orleans from the last years of the 19th century, violinist and drummer Robichaux formed a dance orchestra in 1893 and thereafter continuously led a band until his death. He worked with many noted New Orleans musicians including Lorenzo Tio and Manuel Perez. Although he was active during the birth and early development of jazz, Robichaux mostly, apart from this musical trend, concentrated instead on providing dance music for the wider audiences of the day. His nephews include Joseph Robichaux and John Robichaux, a drummer, who worked on into the 70s.

Robichaux, Joseph

b. 8 March 1900, New Orleans, Louisiana, USA, d 17 January 1965. A nephew of John Robichaux, he played piano in New Orleans and Chicago in the years immediately after World War I. In the early 20s he was a member of the Black Eagle Band and also worked with the Davey Jones-Lee Collins Astoria Hot Eight. In the early 30s he played with Kid Rena and also formed his own band, the New Orleans Rhythm Boys, which stayed in existence until 1939. During the 40s Robichaux worked as a soloist in New York. In the 50s he was accompanist to Lizzie Miles and then joined the George Lewis band, touring internationally and recording. He remained with Lewis until 1964, then returned to New Orleans where he died in 1965. He was a solid ensemble pianist with a lively solo style.

● ALBUMS: *Joe Robichaux And His New Orleans Boys* (1933)★★★, with George Lewis *The Perennial George Lewis* (1958)★★★, *The Perennial George Lewis* (1958)★★★★.

● COMPILATIONS: *Joe Robichaux And His New Orleans Boys* (1933)★★★, *1933* (Classic Jazz Masters 1986)★★★, *The Complete* (Blu-Disc 1988)★★★★.

Robinson, 'Banjo' Ikey

b. 28 July 1904, Dublin, Virginia, USA. Despite a brief stint with Jelly Roll Morton, recording with Clarence Williams, and providing superb single-string guitar on the records of Georgia White, most of Robinson's work was on the borderline between jazz and popular music. He worked for Wilbur Sweatman and Noble Sissle in New York, and was a member of the Hokum Boys. In Chicago, he played with Carroll Dickerson and Erskine Tate before forming his own band in the 40s. He has continued to be active in music, though on a diminishing scale. Robinson's guitar and banjo work is fast, precise and elaborate, and his singing is likewise clearly enunciated. An all-round entertainer, Robinson, though black, is reminiscent of such black-influenced white musicians as Ukulele Ike (Cliff Edwards).

● ALBUMS: *Banjo Ikey Robinson* (1986)★★★, *'Banjo' Ikey Robinson* (RST 1996)★★★.

ROBINSON, ELI

b. 23 June 1908, Greenville, Georgia, USA, d. 24 December 1972. Robinson began playing trombone in his mid-teens while at school in Charleston, West Virginia. He played in school bands and also with local groups, and after leaving school moved to Detroit, where he began a long spell in various territory bands, mostly centred upon Cincinnati. Among the bands in which he played between 1930 and 1936 were those of Speed Webb, Zack Whyte and Blanche Calloway and he was also with McKinney's Cotton Pickers. He spent most of the second half of the decade in New York, working in the Mills Blue Rhythm Band, and in bands led by Willie Bryant and Teddy Hill. In the early 40s he joined Count Basie, remaining in the band until 1947. He then played in a variety of bands until settling in for a long stint with Buck Clayton. He remained intermittently with Clayton from 1954 until shortly before his death. Robinson played in a crisp, attacking manner and brought a high standard of musicianship to his work, which included arranging.

● ALBUMS: with Count Basie *The Jubilee Alternatives* (Hep 1943-44)★★★★, with Buddy Tate *Swinging Like Tate* (Felstead 1958)★★★.

ROBINSON, JANICE

b. 1951, Clairton, Pennsylvania, USA. Robinson began playing piano as a small child, and also took some music lessons. In school, she joined a band and took up the trumpet. Later she was asked to switch to the trombone, upon which she became remarkably proficient. Studying intensively, she developed her early skills and eventually attended the Eastman School of Music where her talent fully blossomed. She played and wrote with jazz orchestras and also sang and studied classical music, specifically Gregorian chants, and met many visiting musicians, one of whom, Mary Lou Williams, promptly advised her to leave Eastman and use her talent in the outside world. In fact, even before Eastman, Robinson had played her instrument on a television spectacular hosted by Bill Cosby. After graduating in 1973 she played with many types of musical group and in Los Angeles worked in bands led by musicians such as Oliver Nelson and in New York spent some time and recorded with the Thad Jones-Mel Lewis Jazz Orchestra. She also recorded and toured with Clark Terry and his Big B.A.D. Band. She became widely known for her skills and consistency and played with Gil Evans, Slide Hampton's World Of Trombones and the Jazz Composer's Orchestra. She also formed a group with pianist Sharon Freeman as co-leader, mostly playing bop. She also led her own small group, which included bassist Buster Williams and pianist Kenny Kirkland. During this same period, Robinson extended her interests in composing, and amongst the results are 'Crying To Be Me', 'Soul Music', and 'The Sound Of Light'. Deeply aware of the conflict and tensions of being a woman in jazz and the pressures that militate against a 'normal' family life, she seeks to blend all aspects of her life. As she observed to Sally Placksin, ' . . . everything that happens in life is reflected in the music, in what I play or what I write. To me, it's not separate'. A superb technician with a deep and abiding commitment to jazz and, indeed, to all forms of musical expression, Robinson is one of the outstanding jazz trombonists.

● ALBUMS: with Thad Jones-Mel Lewis *Suite For Pops* (A&M 1975)★★★, with Frank Foster *Twelve Shades Of Black: For All Intents And Purposes* (Leo 1978)★★★.

ROBINSON, JIM

b. 25 December 1890, Deer Range, Louisiana, USA, d. 4 May 1976. After playing guitar for a number of years, Robinson took up the trombone while serving in the US Army during World War I. In the immediate post-war years he played regularly in New Orleans, and was good enough to be hired by such leading New Orleans musicians as Kid Rena and Sam Morgan. He later played in the bands of John Handy and Kid Howard but, like many other New Orleans jazzmen, he retained his 'day job'. In his case he worked as a longshoreman well into the 30s. The Revival Movement persuaded him that he could make his living playing jazz and in the 40s he played with Bunk Johnson and in the 50s was a regular member of George Lewis's band. He toured extensively in the 60s, with Billie and De De Pierce, Percy Humphrey and the Preservation Hall Jazz Band. An outstanding ensemble player, Robinson played with great attack and brought drive and enthusiasm to any band of which he was a member.

● ALBUMS: *George Lewis At The San Jacinto Hall* (1964)★★★, *Robinson's Jacinto Ballroom Orchestra* (1964)★★, with Percy Humphrey *Climax Rag* (1965)★★★, *Economy Hall Breakdown* (1965)★★★, *Jim Robinson And Tony Fougerat* (1967)★★, *Birthday Memorial Session* (GHB 1973)★★★, *Living New Orleans Jazz* (1976)★★★.

● COMPILATIONS: *Bunk Johnson With George Lewis* (1944)★★★★, *Jim Robinson And His New Orleans Band* (Center 1992)★★★, *Classic New Orleans Jazz Vol 2* (Biograph 1993)★★★★.

ROBINSON, PERRY

b. 17 August 1938, New York City, New York, USA. Robinson grew up in a musical family, his father Earl being a well-known film-score composer. He started playing clarinet at the age of eight, and graduated from the New York High School Of Music and Art in 1956. From there he went to the School of Jazz at Lennox in Massachusetts (1959), to the Manhattan School of Music between 1961 and 1962, and then studied clarinet with Kalman Black (first clarinettist with the Los Angeles Philharmonic) and Eric Simon (at the Mannes Music School). He toured Spain in 1959-60, where he met and played with Tete Montoliu. Returning to New York, he formed a trio with Paul Bley and Sunny Murray in 1962, although his debut recording, *Funk Dumpling*, from the same year, featured Kenny Barron, Henry Grimes and Paul Motian. Robinson next played with Bill Dixon and Archie Shepp, recording on the latter's classic *Mama*

Too Tight (1967), then he joined Roswell Rudd's Primordial Quartet in 1968. He also appeared in a trio with bassist David Izenzon and drummer Randy Kaye. He was a member of Charlie Haden's Liberation Music Orchestra, recording on their 1969 debut album and, as an occasional member of the Jazz Composer's Orchestra, he played on Carla Bley's *Escalator Over The Hill* in 1974. In 1973 he played with Dave Brubeck and also performed regularly with German vibes player Gunter Hampel and his Galaxie Dream Band (1972-78). In 1978 he recorded *Kundalini* with Brazilian percussionist Nana Vasconcelos and Indian tabla-player Badal Roy, a particularly successful encounter between jazz dexterity and world music textures. Robinson is the missing link between the clarinet playing of Pee Wee Russell and new bloods like Don Byron.

● ALBUMS: *Funk Dumpling* (1962)★★★, with Archie Shepp *Mama Too Tight* (1967)★★★, with Gunter Hampel *Cosmic Dancer* (1975)★★★, *The Traveller* (1977)★★, with Badal Roy, Nana Vasconcelos *Kundalini* (1978)★★★.

Robinson, Prince

b. 7 June 1907, Portsmouth, Virginia, USA, d. 23 July 1960. An exceptionally gifted tenor saxophonist, Robinson was a close contemporary of Coleman Hawkins and was consequently overshadowed for much of his career. Doubling on clarinet, Robinson played with several bands in New York in the 20s, including those led by Elmer Snowden and Duke Ellington before joining McKinney's Cotton Pickers where he remained, with a short break, for seven years. In the late 30s and early 40s he worked in a succession of bands including those of Blanche Calloway, Roy Eldridge, Louis Armstrong, Willie Bryant and Lucky Millinder. He also played in one of Teddy Wilson's bands accompanying Billie Holiday on a 1937 record date. From the mid-40s until 1952 he was with the Claude Hopkins band. Thereafter he led his own groups and also played with Red Allen. A gifted player on both instruments, with an especially robust and exciting tenor style, Robinson has had only limited opportunities to play solos on his many record dates. He died in 1960.

● ALBUMS: *McKinney's Cotton Pickers Vols 1/2* (1928-29)★★★★, *The Chronological Teddy Wilson And His Orchestra 1936-1937* (1936-37)★★★, *Roy Eldridge At The Arcadia Ballroom, August/September 1939* (1939)★★★.

Robinson, Spike

b. Henry Berthold Robinson, 16 January 1930, Kenosha, Wisconsin, USA. Beginning on alto saxophone in his early teenage years, Robinson soon discovered that it was hard to make a living playing the kind of music he wanted to play. In 1948 he joined the US Navy as a musician and by 1950 was based in the UK. He was soon regularly jamming at London's Club Eleven, Downbeat Club and Studio 51 with leading UK beboppers, including Tommy Pollard and Victor Feldman. He made a few records for Carlo Krahmer's Esquire label but eventually was transferred home and demobilized. Unhappy with the music scene in the Chicago area, he took advantage of the GI Bill to study electronic engineering at university. For most of the next 30 years he lived and worked in Colorado, eventually taking up music again, this time playing tenor saxophone and working nights at local clubs. A constant musical companion of these times was Dave Grusin. In 1981 Robinson recorded for the first time since his London sessions, in a band led by Feldman. Encouraged to visit the UK by a British fan, in 1984 Robinson began a series of tours that were so successful that he took early retirement from his engineering job to turn to a full-time career in music. Throughout the rest of the 80s and into the early 90s, he has played at clubs and festivals throughout the UK, Europe and in various parts of the USA, making his New York debut at Christmas 1990. A succession of superb record albums, most as leader but some with artists such as Louis Stewart, Harry Edison, Al Cohn, Roy Williams and Claude Tissendier, have attracted high critical and public praise. Despite his bebop beginnings, the mature musician who emerged in the 80s from self-imposed exile is a consummate ballad player who eagerly explores the endless archives of the Great American Song Book. His rhapsodic, breathy style is instantly identifiable and the effortless loping swing of everything he plays has helped to make Robinson into one of the outstanding tenor saxophonists of his generation. In the early 90s Robinson was touring extensively from a UK base, recording many albums and headlining at clubs and festivals in Europe and the USA.

● ALBUMS: *The Guv'nor* (1951)★★★★, with Victor Feldman *The Music Of Harry Warren* (1981)★★, *Spike Robinson At Chesters Vols 1 & 2* (Hep 1984)★★★, *London Reprise* (1984)★★★, with Roy Williams *It's A Wonderful World* (1985)★★★, *The Gershwin Collection* (1987)★★★★, with Al Cohn *Henry B. Meets Alvin G.* (1987)★★★, *In Town* (Hep 1987)★★★, *The Odd Couple* (Capri 1988)★★★, with Louis Stewart *Three For The Road* (Hep 1989)★★★★, with Harry Edison *Jusa Bit O' Blues Vols 1 & 2* (Capri 1989)★★★, with Claude Tissendier *Saxomania Presenting Spike Robinson* (OMD 1989)★★★, *Stairway To The Stars* (Hep 1990)★★★, *One Man In His Time* (1991)★★★, *Spike Robinson And George Masso Play Arlen* (Hep 1992)★★★, *Reminiscin'* (Capri 1993)★★★★, *A Real Corker* (Capri 1993)★★★, *Plays Harry Warren* (Hep 1994)★★★★, Tenor Madness (Essential Jazz 1997)★★★.

Roché, Betty

b. 9 January 1920, Wilmington, Delaware, USA. After winning an amateur talent contest in the early 40s, Roché sang with Al Cooper's Savoy Sultans. Joining Duke Ellington in 1943 she appeared at Carnegie Hall, then, after a brief spell with the Earl Hines band, she drifted out of the big time. In 1952 she was back with Ellington, appearing at clubs and concerts and also broadcasting with the band. A further period out of the spotlight followed, although she made several albums under her own name in the late 50s and early 60s. After this she again returned to obscurity. An attractive song stylist, Roché was one of the best to work for Ellington, who, after Ivie Anderson, was notoriously casual with his choice of vocalists.

● ALBUMS: with Duke Ellington *Carnegie Hall Concert: January 1943* (1943)★★★★, with Ellington *The Duke Is On The Air* (1952)★★★, *Take The 'A' Train* (1956)★★★★, *Singing' And Swingin'* (Original Jazz Classics 1961)★★★★, *Lightly And Politely* (Original Jazz Classics 1961)★★★★.

Rock Workshop

Formed in 1970, this fluid but short-lived jazz/rock group featured several of the UK's leading young jazz musicians, and originally included Harry Beckett, Bob Downes (saxophone), Bud Parkes and Tony Roberts (woodwind), Derek Wadsworth, Alan Greed and Brian Miller (keyboards), Ray Russell (guitar), Daryl Runswick (bass), Alan Rushton and Robin Jones (drums). Several were involved in other, simultaneous projects, notably solo albums by Downes and Russell and session appearances for Jack Bruce, Keef Hartley and Alex Harvey. Wadsworth and Parkes appeared on the latter's solo album, *Roman Wall Blues*, and Harvey reciprocated by singing on *Rock Workshop*. *For The Very Last Time* featured percussionists Phil Wainman and Tony Uter in place of Jones, while Ginger Harper was added on vocals. The individual members then went their separate ways. *Rock Workshop* in particular remains an underrated gem, featuring Russell's frantic 'Spoin Kop' and the evocative and brassy 'Primrose Hill'. Although both albums have long since been deleted, they represent a bold attempt at fusing what would be termed rock/jazz as opposed to jazz/rock.

● ALBUMS: *Rock Workshop* (CBS 1970)★★★★, *For The Very Last Time* (CBS 1971)★★★.

Roderick, Stan

b. 1919, Barrow-in-Furness, Westmorland, England, d. 26 March 1994. Although Roderick studied piano while still a small child, he was soon intent on playing the trumpet. From the mid-30s he was resident in London playing mostly in dance bands, but he also sat in with visiting American jazz artists including Coleman Hawkins and Benny Carter. During World War II, after being invalided out of the army, he resumed his dance band work, playing with many of the most popular bands of the day, including those led by Harry Roy and Geraldo, and he also played with the Harry Hayes Sextet. He then joined the newly-formed band of Ted Heath, remaining there until 1951. From this point onwards, Roderick worked mostly as a freelance session musician in London, often playing in orchestras formed to accompany important visiting artists such as Ella Fitzgerald and Frank Sinatra. Throughout most of his career, Roderick played lead trumpet in the bands in which he worked and was thus not well represented on record as a soloist. However, listening to the bite and power of the Heath band's trumpet section, for example, gives some indication of his value to the British music scene.

Rodin, Gil

b. Gilbert A. Rodin, 9 December 1909, Russia, d. 17 June 1974. Raised in Chicago, Rodin played clarinet and saxophones in a number of local dance bands before moving to California. In 1927 he became a member of the Ben Pollack band. He quickly became a key figure in the band as both player and administrator. He also wrote a number of arrangements. In 1935, following disagreements with Pollack, Rodin was one of the founders of a new co-operative band that was eventually fronted by Bob Crosby. Once again, Rodin assumed multiple roles, one of which was as president of the Crosby corporation, and was the mastermind of the band's huge popularity. After World War II he worked with another ex-Crosby sideman, Ray Bauduc, and in a reconstituted Crosby band. At the end of the 40s he moved out of music and into radio and television where he worked as a programme producer.

● ALBUMS: with Bob Crosby *South Rampart Street Parade* (MCA 1935-42)★★★.

Roditi, Claudio

b. 28 May 1946, Rio De Janeiro, Brazil. Roditi began playing piano as a child and studied formally for a while but although he continued to play piano, including it when he composes, he turned to the trumpet at the age of 12. He played in a school band and gradually, through records by Harry James, Louis Armstrong, Red Nichols and others, he began playing jazz alongside the music of his native land. During the 60s the Brazilian music scene was very lively, thanks in great part to the universal popularity of the bossa nova. Roditi worked extensively but in 1970 went to the USA to study at the Berklee College Of Music. For the next six years he played in the north-eastern states, eventually moving to New York. He continued to play Brazilian music, recording *Cinnamon Flower* with Bob Mover, on which he was joined by Charlie Rouse. Subsequent albums under his own name have been in the jazz idiom but his Brazilian musical roots often emerge. A strikingly proficient technician, Roditi brings enormous zest and fire to his playing. His eclecticism was put to good use during his work with the United Nations Orchestra, a band originating through Dizzy Gillespie. He has also worked with Slide Hampton's Jazz Masters. Roditi will continue to blend the two musical forms he loves. As he told Stan Woolley in *Jazz Journal International*, 'I am a Gemini. I was born in one country and live in another but I love them both - and both kinds of music, too'.

● ALBUMS: *Gemini Man* (Milestone 1988)★★★, *Slow Fire* (Milestone 1989), *Two Of Swords* (Candid 1990)★★, *Milestones* (Candid 1990)★★★, *Jazz Turns Samba* (Groovin' High 1993)★★, *Free Wheelin'* (Reservoir 1994)★★★★, *Samba Manhatten Style* (Reservoir 1995)★★★★, *Double Standards* (Reservoir 1997)★★★, *Mind Games - Live* (Summit 1998)★★★.

Rodney, Red

b. Robert Chudnick, 27 September 1927, Philadelphia, Pennsylvania, USA, d. 27 May 1994, Boynton Beach,

Florida, USA. Within a few years of taking up the trumpet (first presented to him by a great aunt at his bar mitzvah), Rodney was hired by dance band leader Jerry Wald. While still in his teens he also played with Jimmy Dorsey, Elliot Lawrence and Benny Goodman. By 1946, when he joined Gene Krupa, Rodney was a highly experienced big band trumpeter but was already experimenting with bebop. These inclinations were encouraged by Krupa, Claude Thornhill and Woody Herman, with whom he also played in the late 40s. In 1949, with his reputation as a rising bop star fast gaining ground, he joined the Charlie Parker quintet (via an introduction from Dizzy Gillespie). For the next two years he was acclaimed as one of the best bebop trumpeters around and was certainly among the first white players to gain credibility and acceptance in the field (he would go on to help to record the soundtrack to Clint Eastwood's film tribute to Parker, *Bird*). Among the anecdotes to emerge from this time was the tale of Parker telling his agent that Rodney was in fact an albino, in order to ensure he was not barred from a tour of the South. Ill-health and drug addiction nevertheless damaged his career and the 50s and 60s were bleak periods - despite arranging an elaborate fraud whereby he impersonated the similar-looking General Arnold T. MacIntyre in order to obtain money by deception. During the early 70s Rodney returned to the centre of the jazz stage, playing better than ever and displaying inventiveness and thorough mastery of his instrument in all bop and post-bop settings. He continued to be in demand playing in festivals, concerts and clubs around the world until his death, from lung cancer, in 1994.

● ALBUMS: *Georgie Auld/Red Rodney On The Air* (1947)★★★, with Charlie Parker *Live At Carnegie Hall* (1949)★★★★, *The New Sounds* (1951)★★★, *Red Rodney* (Prestige 1952)★★★, *Modern Music From Chicago* (Fantasy 1956)★★★, *Red Rodney 1957* (Signal 1957)★★★★, reissued as *Fiery*, *Red Arrow* (1957)★★★, *The Red Rodney Quintet* (1958)★★★, *Red Rodney Returns* (Argo 1959)★★★, *Bird Lives!* (Muse 1973)★★★★, *Superbop* (Muse 1974)★★★★, *Red Rodney With The Bebop Preservation Society* (1975)★★★, *Red Rodney With The Danish Jazz Army* (1975)★★★, *The Red Tornado* (Muse 1975)★★★★, *Yard's Pad* (Sonet 1976)★★★, *Red, White And Blues* (Muse 1976)★★★★, *Home Free* (Muse 1977)★★★, *The Three Rs* (1979)★★★, *Hi Jinx At The Village Vanguard* (Muse 1980)★★★, *Live At The Village Vanguard* (1980)★★★★, *Spirit Within* (1981)★★★, *Night And Day* (1981)★★★, *Sprint* (1982)★★★, *Red Giant* (Steeple Chase 1988)★★★, *No Turn On Red* (Denon 1988)★★★, *One For Bird* (Steeple Chase 1988)★★★, *Red Snapper* (Steeple Chase 1988)★★★, *Red Alert!* (Continuum 1991)★★★, *Then And Now* (Chesky 1992)★★★, with Greg Abate *Bird Lives! Tribute To Bird: Live At Town Hall* 90s recording (Muse 1998)★★★.

ROGERS, PAUL

b. 1956, Luton, Bedfordshire, England. Bassist Rogers moved to London in 1974. A versatile player, he has worked with Paul Rutherford, Art Themen, Keith Tippett, John Stevens, Elton Dean, Mike Osborne, Stan Tracey, Louis Moholo, Alan Skidmore's Tenor Tonic, and 7 RPM (with Tony Marsh and Simon Picard). Among European musicians, those he worked with include Alexander von Schlippenbach and Joachim Kuhn. In 1981 he played on the British debut recording of Brazilian saxophonist Andres Boiarsky (*Plays South Of The Border*). He took part in two notable foreign tours by British musicians: Harry Beckett (touring the Middle East in 1984) and Evan Parker (Rumania, Yugoslavia and Greece in 1985). Since the late 80s he has been working frequently with drummer Mark Sanders, and together they have provided a powerful and flexible engine for Atlas (with pianist John Law), Parker, Dennis Gonzalez, and the Elton Dean/Howard Riley Quartet (*All The Tradition*). Recently he has also been a member of Tippett's intense quartet Mujician and the Louis Moholo trio. An Arts Council grant led to the composition of a suite (*Anglo American Sketches*) for three saxophonists, flute, bass and drums, which was well received when it was toured nationally in 1990. In the same year Rogers also toured in a trio with Andrew Cyrille.

● ALBUMS: with Mujician *Mujician* (1982)★★★, with Mujician *Mujician II* (FMP 1987)★★★★, with Atlas *Trio Improvisations* (1989)★★★, *Heron Moon* (Rare Music)★★★★, with Mujician *Birdman* (Cuneiform Rune 1996)★★★★.

ROGERS, SHORTY

b. Milton Rajonsky, 14 April 1924, Great Barrington, Massachusetts, USA, d. 7 November 1994, Los Angeles, California, USA. After studying in New York, Rogers played trumpet in the bands of Will Bradley, where he first met Shelly Manne, and Red Norvo. Military service interrupted his career, but in 1945 he joined Woody Herman for a spell, during which he also wrote a number of bop-flavoured big band charts. After Herman, he played with and arranged for the Stan Kenton band, thus increasing his public exposure still more. While with Kenton he also composed a number of features for fellow sidemen such as Art Pepper and Maynard Ferguson. During the 50s Rogers worked mostly in California, still writing hard-swinging charts for Kenton but trying to find work locally. He worked in films, appearing on-screen and on the soundtrack of *The Man With The Golden Arm* (1955). He also recorded with his own big band, effectively 'borrowing' most of the Kenton band, but he was most often in a succession of important small groups. Rogers' involvement in the west coast scene was intense and he, more than any other single musician, is most readily identifiable as a prime mover in the movement's success. The first small group record date Rogers organized was in October 1951 and resulted in the influential *Modern Sounds*, on which he was joined by Manne, Pepper, Jimmy Giuffre, Hampton Hawes and others. He also appeared on the *Lighthouse All Stars*, then led his own groups through a succession of fine recordings, including the big band *Cool And Crazy*, on which he used Kenton's men. On these and his many other albums of the 50s, including *The Swinging Mr Rogers* and *Martians Come Back*, Rogers ably demonstrates his arranging gifts and magnificently showcases the musicians hired for the occasion. This use of several young veterans of the swing era tradition to play music that drew heavily upon the newer vocabularies of bebop created a perfect blending of all that was best of both forms. There was little or no evidence of the clichés which were, by then, adversely affecting the performances of many of the surviving big bands. While the Rogers brand of west coast jazz did not have the aggressive urgency of its east coast counterpart, it always swung lithely. Rogers was constantly on the look-out for new and unusual sounds and styles and was an early jazz experimenter with 12-tone writing. He continued playing and writing throughout the 60s, 70s and 80s, touring extensively and always eager to work with young musicians in the USA or UK and with old friends like Bud Shank and Vic Lewis. In the early 90s he most frequently played flügelhorn, the warmer, denser sound admirably suiting his expressive playing style.

● ALBUMS: *Modern Sounds* (Affinity 1951)★★★, *Popo* (1951)★★, *Cool And Crazy* (1953)★★★★, *Short Snort* (1953)★★★, *Blues Express* (RCA 1953-56)★★★★, *Shorty Rogers Courts The Count* (1953)★★★, *Shorty Rogers And His Giants* (1954)★★★, *The Swinging Mr Rogers/Martians Stay Home* (Atlantic 1955)★★★★, *Martians Come Back/Way Up There* (1955)★★★, *Clickin' With Clax* (Atlantic 1956)★★★, *Wherever The Five Winds Blow* (1956)★★★, *Shorty Rogers Plays Richard Rodgers* (1957)★★★, *Portrait Of Shorty* (1957)★★★, *Gigi In Jazz* (1958)★★★, *Afro-Cuban Jazz Inc.* (1958)★★★, *Chances Are, It Swings* (1958)★★★, *Wizard Of Oz* (1959)★★★, *Shorty Rogers Meets Tarzan* (1959)★★, *The Swinging Nutcracker* (1960)★★, *Fourth Dimension* (1961)★★★, *Bossa Nova* (1962)★★, *Jazz Waltz* (Discovery 1962)★★★, *Gospel Mission* (1963)★★, *West Coast Jazz* (Atlantic 1976)★★★, *Re-entry* (1983)★★★, *Yesterday, Today And Forever* (Concord 1983)★★★, *Shorty Rogers And The West Coast Giants* (1983)★★★★, with Vic Lewis, Bud Shank *Back Again* (Concept 1984)★★★, *Shorty Rogers And Bud Shank Live At The Concorde Club, Southampton* (1984)★★★, *California Concert* (1985)★★★, with Shank *America The Beautiful* (Candid 1991)★★★, *Eight Brothers* (Candid 1992)★★★.

ROKER, MICKEY

b. 3 September 1932, Miami, Florida, USA. Raised in Philadelphia, Pennsylvania, Roker played drums with R&B bands but was attracted to jazz. He worked briefly with such visiting and local jazzmen as Jimmy Heath, Lee Morgan and McCoy Tyner and it was not until the end of the 50s that he went to New York. During the next few years he played in bands led by Gigi Gryce, Ray Bryant, Duke Pearson, Art Farmer, Sonny Rollins, Milt Jackson, Clifford Jordan and Morgan. He was for a while in the house band at Blue Note Records and played on many dates. In 1971 he began a long association with Dizzy Gillespie that lasted through the rest of the decade. Freelancing in the 80s has brought him into groups led by Oscar Peterson, Ray Bryant, Zoot Sims, Jackson and Ray Brown. A forceful, dynamic drummer, Roker's style is rooted in swing but has the urgent attack of the best of the beboppers.

● ALBUMS: with Gigi Gryce *Rat Race Blues* (1960)★★★, with Duke Pearson *Wahoo!* (1964)★★★, with Lee Morgan *Live at The Lighthouse* (1970)★★★, *Dizzy Gillespie's Big 4* (1974)★★★, with Gillespie *Dizzy's Party* (1976)★★, with Ray Bryant *Potpourri* (1980)★★★.

ROLAND, GENE

b. 15 September 1921, New York City, New York, USA, d. 11 August 1982. In the early 40s many of Roland's arrangements played an important part in establishing the success of the Stan Kenton band. Among his arrangements was the June Christy hit, 'Tampico'. During this period he sometimes played trumpet in the band, later switching to trombone. Generally credited with Jimmy Giuffre as co-creator of the 'Four Brothers' sound of the Woody Herman band, Roland arranged for and played piano with Stan Getz, Giuffre (with whom he had studied at North Texas State Teachers' College, forerunner of NTSU), Herbie Steward and Zoot Sims in a small group that was heard by Herman in 1947. Later in the 40s Roland played in the bands of Georgie Auld, Count Basie, Charlie Barnet and Lucky Millinder, sometimes on trumpet, at other times on trombone. He tried his hand at bandleading in 1950 with an adventurous but ill-fated bebop big band which featured Charlie Parker, Don Fagerquist, Red Rodney, Jimmy Knepper, Sims and Al Cohn. In the 50s he again wrote for Kenton and Herman, helping to create the former's 'mellophonium band'. During the 60s Roland worked in Scandinavia, writing and directing a radio orchestra, and in the 70s, back in the USA, he continued to write challenging big band charts and to play on a variety of instruments.

● ALBUMS: *The Band That Never Was* (1950)★★★, *A Swinging Introduction To Jimmy Knepper* (1957)★★, with Paul Quinichette *Jazzville* (Dawn 1957)★★★, with Stan Kenton *Adventures In Blues* (1961)★★★★, *Swinging Friends* (1963)★★★.

ROLLINI, ADRIAN

b. 28 June 1904, New York City, New York, USA, d. 15 May 1956. After starting out on piano and xylophone, Rollini switched to bass saxophone in the early 20s. As a member of the California Ramblers he played with many leading jazzmen of the day including Bix Beiderbecke, Frank Trumbauer and Red Nichols. His younger brother, Arthur Rollini, was also a sometime member of the Ramblers. Rollini had a great influence upon many young white jazzmen in the USA and UK, where he worked towards the end of the decade as a member of Fred Elizalde's band. In the mid-30s and 40s he was mostly in New York where he held several long hotel residencies, at the time adding the vibraphone to the list of instruments he played. He continued playing into the 50s but in Florida where he had moved to run his own hotel. Despite the cumbersome nature of the bass saxophone, Rollini always played with great flair and swing and few other musicians in jazz have matched him on this instrument. He influenced Harry Gold and baritone saxophonist Harry Carney.

● ALBUMS: *The Adrian Rollini Quartet And Trio* (1938-40 recordings)★★★★.

Rollini, Arthur

b. 13 February 1912, New York City, New York, USA. By his late teens, Rollini was playing tenor saxophone with various bands including the California Ramblers, where a fellow musician was his older brother, Adrian Rollini. He also played with Adrian in London in the Fred Elizalde band. In the 30s he worked mostly in New York, often in company with his brother. In 1934 he joined Benny Goodman, staying on through the early years of struggle to the successes of the swing era. He left Goodman in 1939 and thereafter played mostly as a freelance and studio musician, recording with Brad Gowans and others. By the 60s he had virtually stopped playing. A very musicianly player with a coolly elegant solo style, Rollini's jazz dates were tantalizingly infrequent. His autobiography was published in 1987.

● COMPILATIONS: with Benny Goodman *Breakfast Ball* (1934)★★★, *Brad Gowans And His New York Nine* (1946)★★★.

● FURTHER READING: *Thirty Years With The Big Bands*, Arthur Rollini.

Rollins, Sonny

b. Theodore Walter Rollins, 7 September 1929, New York, USA. Although an older brother played violin and, at the age of nine, he took piano lessons, Rollins was destined for the saxophone. In 1944 he played alto saxophone in high school and when he left in 1947 he began gigging round New York on tenor. His first inspiration was Coleman Hawkins, but he was well aware of the beboppers, many of whom lived in his neighbourhood. His first recording date was with scat-singer Babs Gonzales for Capitol Records in 1948. Soon he was recording with Bud Powell, Fats Navarro and J.J. Johnson, who recorded his first composition, 'Audubon'. Rollins' assured version of Charlie Parker on tenor was embraced by the top jazz artists: in 1949 he played with Art Blakey, in 1950 with Tadd Dameron, in 1951 with Miles Davis and in 1953 with Thelonious Monk. In 1954 Davis recorded with Rollins, including in the set three important Rollins compositions: 'Airegin' (Nigeria backwards - a salute to the newly independent African state), 'Oleo' and 'Doxy'. However, Rollins left for Chicago and Davis chose John Coltrane when he formed his new quintet. In January 1956, when the Clifford Brown/Max Roach quintet lost its tenor (Harold Land) in Chicago, Rollins stepped in, and played with them for 18 months. After that, Rollins began leading his own groups. In May 1956 he recorded *Tenor Madness* for Prestige, with the Paul Chambers/Philly Joe Jones rhythm team from Coltrane's group. The title track consisted of a mighty 'tenor battle' with Coltrane himself, Rollins's melodious expansion contrasting with Coltrane's pressure-cooker angularity.

In April 1956 Rollins recorded *Saxophone Colossus*, generally regarded as his first masterpiece. However, the advent of Ornette Coleman caused a deal of self-reflection and he retired for two years (1959-60), amid rumours that he was practising on Williamsburg Bridge. In 1961 he re-emerged to work with Jim Hall and then with two musicians associated with Coleman: trumpeter Don Cherry and drummer Billy Higgins. *Our Man In Jazz* shows him taking on the new freedoms with confidence and passion; the 20-minute 'Oleo' was a *tour de force*. He then toured as a soloist, using local rhythm sections (European tours in 1965, 1966 and 1967). In 1966 he recorded *East Broadway Rundown* with the Jimmy Garrison/Elvin Jones rhythm section from Coltrane's classic quartet. The music, with its blistering title track and tremulous version of 'We Kiss In A Shadow', was superb, but it was indicative of Rollins' problems that it was a one-off group. Rollins found it difficult to deal with the possibilities opened up by the assaults on form of the *avant garde*. He again took a two-year sabbatical (1968-71), this time studying in India and Japan.

In 1973 he recorded *Horn Culture* using electric accompaniment. On electric bass Bob Cranshaw lacked the fire he had shown on *Our Man In Jazz* and despite Rollins' self-overdubs and characteristically ambitious solos, he seemed to be mired in pedestrian jazz-rock. *The Cutting Edge* (1974) had a bravura *a cappella* rendition of 'To A Wild Rose' but a similarly subdued band. In 1978 he toured with the Milestone All Stars. Here, a band of the stature of McCoy Tyner, Ron Carter and Al Foster could not fail to spark him, but these musicians were all leaders in their own right and could not work with him regularly. At this point Rollins refused all further nightclub performances and resolved to play festivals and concert halls exclusively. In 1985 Rollins attempted to do without rhythm sections altogether in *The Solo Album* and then toured Europe with a band featuring ex-Weather Report bassist Victor Bailey and drummer Tommy Campbell.

In 1986 his *Concerto For Saxophone And Orchestra* was premiered in Japan. 1988 saw him linking up with some of the new names of the jazz revival: Marvin 'Smitty' Smith provided him with ferociously good drumming at live appearances. However, a rather tight and commercial sound made *Dancing In The Dark* unsatisfactory. Rollins is a soloist *par excellence*. His indecision about the form of his music - whether it is to be free/electric/acoustic - reflects the general quandary of jazz in the 80s. He is still capable of the solo flights that caused Davis to vote for him as 'greatest tenor ever' in a poll conducted by Leonard Feather at the end of the 60s.

● ALBUMS: *Sonny Rollins Quartet* 10-inch album (Prestige 1952)★★★, *Sonny Rollins Quintet* 10-inch album (Prestige 1954)★★★, *Sonny Rollins* 10-inch album (Prestige 1954)★★★, with Art Farmer *Art Farmer Quintet Featuring Sonny Rollins* 10-inch album (Prestige 1954)★★★★, *Work Time* (Prestige 1954)★★★★, *Sonny Rollins With The Modern Jazz Quartet* reissued as *Sonny And The Stars* (Prestige 1956)★★★★, with Clifford Brown, Max Roach *Sonny Rollins Plus Four* reissued as *Three Giants* (Prestige 1956)★★★★, *Tenor Madness* (Prestige 1956)★★★★, *Moving Out* reissued as *Sonny Rollins Plays Jazz Classics* (Prestige 1956)★★★, with Jimmy Cleveland *Sonny Rollins Plays/Jimmy Cleveland Plays* (Period 1956)★★★, *Saxophone Colossus* (Prestige 1956)★★★★★, *Sonny Rollins* (Blue

Note 1956)★★★★, *Rollins Plays For Bird* (Prestige 1957)★★★, *Tour De Force* (Prestige 1957)★★★, *Sonny Rollins, Volume Two* (Blue Note 1957)★★★★, *The Sound Of Sonny* reissued as *Sonny's Time* (Riverside 1957)★★★, *Way Out West* (Contemporary 1957)★★★★, *A Night At The Village Vanguard Vol 1* (Blue Note 1958)★★★★, *A Night At The Village Vanguard Volume 2* (Blue Note 1958)★★★★, *Newk's Time* (Blue Note 1958)★★★★★, *Freedom Suite* reissued as *Shadow Waltz* (Riverside 1958)★★★★, with Dizzy Gillespie, Sonny Stitt *Duets* reissued as *Dizzy, Rollins & Stitt* (Verve 1958)★★★★, *Sonny Rollins And The Big Brass* reissued as *Sonny Rollins Brass/Sonny Rollins Trio* (Metrojazz 1958)★★★, *Sonny Rollins At Music Inn* reissued as *Tender Titan* (Metrojazz 1958)★★★, *Sonny Rollins & The Contemporary Leaders* (Contemporary 1959)★★★, *Sonny Boy* (Prestige 1961)★★★, *The Bridge* (RCA Victor 1962)★★★★, *What's New?* (RCA Victor 1962)★★★, *Our Man In Jazz* (RCA Victor 1962)★★★★, with Coleman Hawkins *Sonny Meets Hawk!* (RCA Victor 1963)★★★★, shared with Gary Burton, Clark Terry *3 In Jazz* (RCA Victor 1963)★★★, *All The Things You Are* (RCA Victor 1964)★★★, *Now's The Time* (RCA Victor 1964)★★★, *The Standard Sonny Rollins* (RCA Victor 1965)★★★, *Sonny Rollins On Impulse!* (Impulse! 1965)★★★★, *Sonny Rollins Plays Alfie* (Impulse! 1966)★★★, *East Broadway Run Down* (Impulse! 1967)★★★, *There Will Never Be Another You* (1967)★★★, with Thad Jones *Sonny Rollins With Guest Artist Thad Jones* (Archive Of Folk And Jazz 1968)★★★, *Next Album* (Milestone 1972)★★★★, *Horn Culture* (Original Jazz Classics 1973)★★★, *In Japan* (JVC 1974)★★★, *The Cutting Edge* (Milestone 1974)★★★, *Nucleus* (Milestone 1975)★★★, *More From The Vanguard* 1957 recording (1975)★★★, *The Way I Feel* (Original Jazz Classics 1976)★★★, *Easy Living* (1977)★★★, *Don't Stop The Carnival* (Milestone 1978)★★★★, with others *Milestone Jazz Stars In Concert* (Milestone 1978)★★★, *Don't Ask* (1979)★★★, *Love At First Sight* (1980)★★★, *The Alternative Rollins* 1964 recording (1981)★★★, *No Problem* (1982)★★★, with Brown, Roach *Pure Genius* 1956 recording (Elektra 1982)★★★★, *Reel Life* (1982)★★★, *St Thomas: In Stockholm 1959* (1984)★★★, *Sunny Days, Starry Nights* (Milestone 1984)★★★, *In Paris* 60s recording (1984)★★★, *The Solo Album* (Milestone 1985)★★★, *Alternate Takes* 1957-58 recording (1986)★★★, *Plays G-Man* (Milestone 1986)★★★, *Dancing In The Dark* (Milestone 1988)★★, *Falling In Love With Jazz* (Milestone 1990)★★, *Here's To The People* (Milestone 1991)★★★, *Old Flames* (Milestone 1994)★★★, *Sonny Rollins And Co. 1964* (Bluebird 1995)★★★★, *Sonny Rollins + 3* (Milestone 1996)★★★★, *Global Warming* (Milestone 1998)★★★.

● COMPILATIONS: *Complete Prestige Recordings* 7-CD box set (Prestige)★★★★★, *Silver City: A Celebration Of 25 Years On Milestone* (Milestone 1996)★★★★, *The Complete Sonny Rollins RCA Victor Recordings* 6-CD box set (RCA Victor 1997)★★★★.

● VIDEOS: *Saxophone Colossus* (Rhapsody 1995).

● FURTHER READING: *Sonny Rollins*, Charley Gerard (ed.). *Sonny Rollins: The Journey Of A Jazzman*, Charles Clement Blancq.

ROMANO, ALDO

b. 16 January 1941, Belluno, Italy. Moving to France as a child, Romano studied guitar before teaching himself drums. Employment with the local modern groups Barney Wilen and Michel Portal led to Romano playing with visiting Americans including Jackie McLean, Bud Powell and Stan Getz, but it was playing with the Don Cherry group in 1963 that convinced him that free jazz was to be his chosen path. During the late 60s Romano drummed for Carla Bley, Gato Barbieri and Steve Lacy, Joachim Kuhn and Jean-Luc Ponty, whose bands featured Romano at the turn of the decade, were both experimenting with jazz rock, and in 1971 Romano formed his own rock group in which he sang and played guitar. The 70s saw him with fusioneers, Pork Pie, and recording with Francois Jeanneau and Enrico Rava. During the 80s Romano has looked back to his earlier style, to the small-group free music of the 60s. He expressed his fondness for this music in a recent sleevenote: 'I have said a number of times that if Ornette (Coleman) had been Italian, he would have composed *La Traviata*'.

● ALBUMS: with Pork Pie *Transitory* (1973)★★★, *Il Piacere* (1978)★★★, *To Be Ornette To Be* (1989)★★★, *Non Dimenticar* (1994)★★, *Prosodie* (Verve 1995)★★★.

ROMANO, JOE

b. 17 April 1932, Rochester, New York, USA. After playing alto and tenor saxophones with various bands in the north-eastern states, Romano joined Woody Herman in 1956. Subsequently, he worked with Chuck Mangione, Gus Mancuso, Sam Noto and others, returning frequently to Herman. In the late 60s and early 70s he played in bands led by Buddy Rich and Les Brown. In the mid-70s he was a member of Chuck Israel's National Jazz Ensemble and in 1978 joined the Louie Bellson band which played in the USA and UK. He has also played with the Thad Jones-Mel Lewis band and has recorded with Bill Watrous and Don Menza. An aggressive, bebop-influenced player, Romano's career has rarely been settled for long periods, making it difficult to form an accurate assessment of his status in the jazz world. Nevertheless, the regularity with which important leaders have called upon his services is an indicator of his standing among fellow musicians. The power and dynamism of his section work is particularly impressive and his solos display fiery urgency and an impressive flow of ideas.

● ALBUMS: with Sam Noto *Act One* (1975)★★★, with Noto *Notes To You* (1977)★★★, with Bill Watrous *Watrous In Hollywood* (1978)★★★, with Louie Bellson *Matterhorn* (1978)★★, *Louie Bellson's Big Band Explosion Live At Ronnie Scott's* (1979)★★★, with Bellson *London Scene* (1980)★★★, with Don Menza *Burnin'* (1980)★★, *And Finally Romano* (Fresh Sounds 1988)★★★.

ROMAO, DOM UM

b. 3 August 1925, Rio de Janeiro, Brazil. Romao's father was a drummer and Dom started playing in his youth. In the early 60s he joined the Bossa Rio Sextet with Sergio Mendes. After recording with saxophonist Cannonball Adderley at the Carnegie Hall in 1962 he settled in the USA and worked in Chicago with vocalist Oscar Brown Jnr. (1965). After moving to Los Angeles in 1966 he toured with Sergio Mendes before replacing Airto Moreira in Weather Report (1971-74). During the early 70s he established his own rehearsal studio in New York - Black Beans Studio. In 1976 he recorded with George Gruntz's Band in Zurich and has since spent a lot of time in Europe with the Swiss band Om.

● ALBUMS: *Dom Um Romao* (1972)★★★, *Spirit Of The Times* (1973)★★★, with Weather Report *I Sing The Body Electric* (1972)★★★★, with Weather Report *Sweetnighter* (1973)★★★, with Collin Walcott *Grazing Dreams* (1977)★★★★.

Roney, Antoine

b. USA. A talented multi-instrumentalist, Roney has played tenor and soprano saxophones with drummer Lenny White, Ricky Ford, Cindy Blackman and extensively with the group led by his brother Wallace Roney, with whom he has also recorded. His playing on saxophones and also on bass clarinet is fluent and filled with flair and conviction. Playing mostly in the post-bop mode, he is an inventive soloist.

● ALBUMS: *Traveller* (Muse 1994)★★★, *Whirling* (Muse 1996)★★★.

Roney, Wallace

b. 25 May 1960, Philadelphia, Pennsylvania, USA. Roney began playing trumpet at the age of seven and six years later was given some informal but invaluable tuition by Clark Terry. Later he studied briefly at both Howard University and Berklee College Of Music. In 1981 he was hired by Art Blakey and during the 80s he also met Miles Davis, whom he greatly admired, but did not have the chance to play with him until 1991, a few months before Davis's death. His recording career has included appearances with Tony Williams, Dizzy Gillespie and Gerry Mulligan. From the late 80s and on into the 90s he has made several well-received albums as leader. A fluent, melodic improviser, Roney's playing consistently displays imagination and it is self-evident why his fellow musicians hold him in such high regard.

● ALBUMS: *Verses* (Muse 1988)★★★★, *Intuition* (Muse 1989)★★★★, *The Standard Bearer* (Muse 1990)★★★, *Obsession* (Muse 1991)★★★★, *Seth Air* (Muse 1992)★★★, *Crunchin'* (Muse 1993)★★★, *Misterios* (Warners 1994)★★★, *Munchin'* (Muse 1995)★★★★, *The Wallace Ronay Quintet* (Warners 1996)★★★, *Village* (Warners 1997)★★★★.

Roppolo, Leon

b. 16 March 1902, Lutcher, Louisiana, USA, d. 14 October 1943. After being taught clarinet by his father, Roppolo began playing in bands in and around New Orleans, including those led by George Brunis and Santo Pecora. After playing on riverboats he made his way to Chicago where, in 1921, he became a member of the Friars' Inn Society Orchestra. This band, led by Paul Mares and which included Brunis, later evolved into the New Orleans Rhythm Kings. In 1923 Roppolo and Mares quit and went to New York and the following year Roppolo was in Texas playing with Peck Kelley's Bad Boys. In 1925 he was back in New Orleans and was once again teamed with Mares in a re-formed NORK. By this time Roppolo's lifestyle (he was a heavy drinker and used marijuana), allied to ill-health, had begun to take its toll. That same year he suffered a severe mental breakdown and was committed to a state asylum. Apparently he continued to play while in the institution, taking up the tenor saxophone. He was released in 1940 and died in 1943. Roppolo played clarinet with a full, rich tone and was always experimenting with technique and phrasing. His imaginative work influenced many of his contemporaries and the younger musicians who heard him.

● ALBUMS: with NORK incl. on *Jazz Sounds Of The Twenties* (1922-25)★★★.

Rosengarden, Bobby

b. 23 April 1924, Elgin, Illinois, USA. After starting to play drums while still a child, Rosengarden studied at university and played in military bands during his army service. In 1945 he played in a New York dance band with Henry Busse and during the next two decades played drums and percussion with many bands in a wide range of styles including jazz with Miles Davis and Benny Goodman, television studio bands, and symphony orchestras. In the 70s he was with the World's Greatest Jazz Band and the Bob Wilber-Kenny Davern group, Soprano Summit. With Davern and Dick Wellstood he formed the Blue Three and he also played with Dick Hyman's New York Jazz Repertory Company and at Dick Gibson's Colorado Jazz Parties. He has also played with Gerry Mulligan and led his own bands. A driving, enthusiastic drummer, Rosengarden's broad-based technique allows him to feel at home in most settings especially those with a traditional to mainstream bias. His deep interest in Brazilian music also makes its presence felt in his work.

● ALBUMS: *Colorado Jazz Party* (1971)★★★, with the Blue Three *The Blue Three Live At Hanratty's* (1981)★★★★, *By Request* (Statiras 1987)★★★.

● COMPILATIONS: with Kenny Davern, Dick Wellstood *Dick Wellstood And His Famous Orchestra Featuring Kenny Davern* 1973-1981 recordings (Chiaruscuro 1981)★★★★.

Rosengren, Bernt

b. 24 December 1937, Stockholm, Sweden. Rosengren had already played the tenor saxophone professionally with the Swedish hard bop group Jazz Club '57 when he became a member of Marshall Brown's International Youth Band in 1958. His earthy tenor playing was later influenced by the early sound of John Coltrane. In the early 60s he moved to Poland where he played the tenor solos on the soundtrack of Roman Polanski's 1962 film *Knife In The Water*. The music had been written by Krzysztof Komeda with whom Rosengren had appeared at 1961's Polish Jazz Jamboree. After he returned to Sweden he worked and recorded with George Russell, Don Cherry and Lars Gullin (baritone saxophone) in the early 70s, and has since led his own groups.

● ALBUMS: *Live In Stockholm* (1974)★★, *Big Band* (1979)★★★, *Summit Meeting* (1984)★★★, with Tomasz Stanko *Latania* (ECM 1997)★★.

ROSEWOMAN, MICHELE

b. 19 March 1953, Oakland, California, USA. Rosewoman comes from a musical family: her parents ran a record shop and her elder brother is a musician, so she was exposed to jazz and world music at an early age. She began playing piano at the age of six and when she was 17 years old she met pianist Edwin Kelly, who introduced her to hard bop and the music of Thelonious Monk and John Coltrane and gave her lessons. She also studied Cuban percussion with Orlando 'Puntilla' Rios and Shona (Zimbabwean) and Yoruba (Nigerian) traditional music. San Francisco's Keystone Korner was a centre for jazz, where she heard Cecil Taylor. She met trumpeter Baikida Carrol and altoist Oliver Lake from BAG (Black Artists Group) in St. Louis and also members of the AACM. In 1978 she relocated to New York - her first appearance was with Lake at Carnegie Hall. Since then she has performed regularly as sidewoman and leader. In 1981 she played on Billy Bang's *Rainbow Gladiator*. She also worked with a number of Cuban groups, notably Los Kimy, with whom she recorded. Her interest in Afro-Cuban music led her to form the 15-piece New Yor-Uba: in December 1983 she premiered 'New Yor-Uba, A Musical Celebration Of Cuba In America' at the Public Theatre in New York to great acclaim. She made her recording debut as a leader in 1985 with *The Source* for Soul Note. In 1986 she formed a quintet, Quintessence, which has released *Quintessence* and *Contrast High*. In summer 1991 she toured with Carlos Ward. 1991's *Occasion To Rise* was a trio recording with Rufus Reid on bass and Ralph Peterson Jnr. on drums. Michele Rosewoman's broad musical vision, welcome in a period of jazz neo-conservatism, is matched by the strength of her compositions and the energy of her playing.

● ALBUMS: *The Source* (Soul Note 1985)★★★, *Quintessence* (Enja 1987)★★★★, *Contrast High* (Enja 1989)★★★, *Occasion To Rise* (Evidence 1991)★★★, *Harvest* (Enja 1993)★★★, *Spirit* 1994 recording (Blue Note 1996)★★★.

ROSOLINO, FRANK

b. 20 August 1926, Detroit, Michigan, USA, d. 26 November 1978. After dabbling with guitar, Rosolino took up the trombone while in his teens. After military service during World War II he played in a succession of big bands, including those of Bob Chester and Glen Gray. In 1948 he was one of several bebop-influenced musicians playing in Gene Krupa's big band (contributing the scat vocalizing on the band's hit record of 'Leon Drop'). After playing in several other dance bands he briefly led his own group before joining Stan Kenton in 1952. Two years later he left the band and settled in California, where he divided his time between studio and jazz work. He recorded with Dexter Gordon, Stan Levey, Conte Candoli and many of the musicians who frequented the Lighthouse. In the mid-70s Rosolino again worked with Candoli, visiting Europe, and he also played several times with Benny Carter, who was one of the trombonist's greatest admirers. Also in the 70s he played in Med Flory's band, Supersax, and with Quincy Jones. A brilliant technician with a precisely articulated attacking style, Rosolino was one of the finest trombonists of his time and one of few practitioners on the instrument to adapt fully to bebop. His later work showed him to be a consummate section player whether in big bands or small groups. He died in 1978 in acutely tragic circumstances, shooting both of his children (one of whom survived) before shooting himself.

● ALBUMS: with Stan Kenton *New Concepts Of Artistry In Rhythm* (1952)★★★★, one side only *The Trombone Album/Swing Not Spring* (1952)★, *Stan Kenton Presents: Frank Rosolino Sextet* (1954)★★★, *Frankly Speaking* (1955)★★★, with Stan Levey *This Time The Drum's On Me* (1955)★★★, with Levey *Grand Stan* (1956)★★★, *I Play Trombone* (1956)★★, with Lighthouse All Stars *Double Or Nothin'* (1957)★★★, *The Most Happy Fella* (1957)★★★, with Benny Carter *Aspects* (1959)★★★, *Turn Me Loose!* (1961)★★★, *Conversations* (1975)★★★, *Just Friends* (1975)★★★, *Thinking About You* (1976)★★★, *In Denmark* (1978)★★.

● COMPILATIONS: *Fond Memories Of* ... 1973/1975 recordings (Double-Time 1997)★★★.

ROSS, ANNIE

b. Annabelle Short Lynch, 25 July 1930, Mitcham, Surrey, England. After working as a child actress in Hollywood, she then toured internationally as a singer. She sang with both Tony Crombie and Jack Parnell during the 50s. Ross had recorded successful wordless jazz vocals before becoming a member of the brilliant vocalese trio, Lambert, Hendricks And Ross from 1958-62. Her song 'Twisted', written with Wardell Gray, was expertly covered by Joni Mitchell, among others. In the mid-60s Ross operated Annie's Room, a jazz club in London, and in later years worked in films and television as both actress and singer, at one point being briefly reunited with Jon Hendricks. Personal problems affected the continuity of Ross's career but despite the resulting irregularity of her public performances she maintained an enviably high standard of singing. In the early 80s she found a compatible musical partner in Georgie Fame with whom she toured and recorded.

● ALBUMS: *Annie Ross Sings* (Original Jazz Classics 1953)★★★★, *Annie By Candlelight* (Pye 1956)★★★★, with Gerry Mulligan *Annie Ross Sings A Song With Mulligan* (World Pacific 1958)★★★★, *Gypsy* (World Pacific 1959)★★★, with Zoot Sims *A Gasser* (Pacific Jazz 1959)★★★★, *You And Me Baby* (1964)★★★, *Annie Ross And Pony Poindexter With The Berlin All Stars* (1966)★★★, with Tony Kinsey *With The Tony Kinsey Quartet* (Extra 1966)★★★★, *Fill My Heart With Song* (Decca 1967)★★★, with Georgie Fame *In Hoagland '81* (Bald Eagle 1981)★★★★, *Sings A Handful Of Songs* (Fresh Sounds 1988)★★★.

ROSS, RONNIE

b. 2 October 1933, Calcutta, India, d. 12 December 1991. Ross came to England in his early teens where he first took up the tenor saxophone. In the mid-50s he joined Don Rendell who persuaded him to change to baritone.

Thereafter, Ross built a reputation as an outstanding player of the instrument, working in bands led by Ted Heath, Marshall Brown and Woody Herman. He was also co-leader with Allan Ganley of the Jazzmakers. In the early 60s he was leader of his own small band and also participated in numerous recording sessions, including some with John Dankworth. The 60s also saw him spending time in Europe where he played with the Clarke-Boland Big Band. Ross continued leading his own groups and recording under various leaders during the 70s and into the 80s, including an appearance on rock singer Lou Reed's hit single 'Walk On The Wild Side'. A forceful player, Ross's baritone has long been one of the treasures of the British jazz scene although he seldom achieved the recognition his talent deserves.

● ALBUMS: *The Ronnie Ross Quintet* (1958)★★★, *Swinging Sounds Of The Jazz Makers* (1959)★★★, *Beatle Music By The Session Men* (1967)★, *Cleopatra's Needle* (1968)★★.

Rostaing, Hubert

b. 17 September 1918, Lyons, France. He played several reed instruments, working mostly in provincial bands until 1939 when he came to Paris. In the capital he attracted a great deal of attention, capturing an even wider audience thanks to records made with the Quintette Du Hot Club De France. Rostaing was with the Quintette for most of the 40s, a period during which he also played in big bands with Django Reinhardt and led his own small groups. As the war ended he began to take note of developments in bop. Simultaneously with his career as a jazz instrumentalist, playing mostly clarinet, Rostaing also composed music for films and played classical music. His technical facility is noteworthy but he played with an uncomplicated charm on small group jazz performances.

● COMPILATIONS: with Django Reinhardt *Django's Music* (Hep 1940-43)★★★.

Rotenberg, June

b. *c*.1926, Philadelphia, Pennsylvania, USA. Encouraged in her interest in music, she was thought to be taking piano lessons but was, in fact, taking lessons on the bass. By the time her ruse was detected she had gained enough proficiency to stay with the instrument, becoming one of very few female bass players in any kind of music. In fact, although trained in classical music, and later a jazz player of distinction, Rotenberg played in many musical forms, including classical, throughout her career. In New York from the early 40s, she met and sat in with many fine jazz musicians including Ben Webster, Lester Young and Mary Lou Williams. She played and recorded in a trio led by Williams, with Bridget O'Flynn on drums. She also played in a trio with O'Flynn led by Beryl Booker. In the mid- to late 40s Rotenberg was splitting her musical time between long spells with the St. Louis Symphony Orchestra and after-hours sessions with Art Tatum. During the 50s she spent some time in Europe, mostly playing classical music but with the occasional jazz session in Parisian clubs. She played at festivals centred upon the playing of the renowned classical cellist Pablo Casals. Eventually, Rotenberg began spending most of her time in New York, playing in studios and in Broadway pit orchestras. Despite her status, she still found it necessary to prove herself; she told Sally Placksin, 'to be treated as an equal, you better be very good.'

Rotondo, Nunzio

b. 1924, Palestrina, Italy. A gifted child, Rotondo studied music, first playing piano, then trumpet. In the late 40s he was leader of a small jazz group and in those years and into the early 50s regularly supported visiting American jazzmen including Louis Armstrong. He also played with Bill Coleman, Roy Eldridge and others from the jazz mainstream, but by the early 50s he was taking heed of bop, leading and co-leading several boppish bands in company with fellow nationals such as Gil Cuppini and Romano Mussolini. During the 60s he was active with many forward-thinking musicians, among them Albert Mangelsdorff, Gato Barbieri and Mal Waldron. In the early 70s he was co-leader of a band with Franco D'Andrea. After a period outside music he resumed performing in the early 80s. A lyrical player with a strong melodic sense, Rotondo also composes in a contemporary style.

● ALBUMS: with others *IIIrd Festival Del Jazz Del San Remo* (Carish 1958)★★.

Round About Midnight - Miles Davis

An important album that saw Miles Davis and the his best ever quintet (John Coltrane, Red Garland, Philly Joe Jones and Paul Chambers) move to the mighty Columbia Records. It was while at Columbia that he grew to be the biggest name in jazz, and with their marketing, even made the pop chart. This debut is also musically very fine; with production by George Avakian, the quintet breeze through six tracks that include excellent readings of 'Tadd's Delight' and, from his Charlie Parker apprenticeship, the familiar 'Ah-Leu-Cha'. The title track is just a shade too dry, but nevertheless credible. This album started a 30-year relationship with Columbia.

● Tracks: *Round Midnight; Ah-Leu-Cha; All Of You; Bye Bye Blackbird; Tadd's Delight; Dear Old Stockholm.*

● First released 1957

● UK peak chart position: did not chart

● USA peak chart position: did not chart

Rouse, Charlie

b. 6 April 1924, Washington, DC, USA, d. 30 November 1988, Seattle, Washington, USA. After learning to play clarinet, Rouse took up the tenor saxophone; by the end of his teens he was proficient enough to be hired by Billy Eckstine for his bebop-orientated big band. Thereafter, Rouse played with Dizzy Gillespie, Tadd Dameron and Fats Navarro. At the end of the 40s he worked in an R&B band but also subbed with Duke Ellington and Count Basie. In the early 50s he played and recorded with a number of important small groups, including those led by Clifford Brown, Art Farmer, Paul Quinichette and Oscar Pettiford. In the second half of the decade he co-led Les Jazz Modes with Julius Watkins, was briefly with Buddy Rich and the Gerry Mulligan Concert Band and then, at the end of 1958, began a long and fruitful association with Thelonious Monk that lasted until 1970. During this period he made records with others, including Donald Byrd and Benny Carter, appearing on the latter's fine *Further Definitions*. Throughout the 70s and 80s he freelanced, touring as a single or playing as accompanist. In 1982 he formed the Monk tribute group Sphere alongside Kenny Barron, Ben Riley and Buster Williams. A distinctively quirky player, Rouse's long musical partnership with Monk had the advantage of bringing his work to a very wide audience, and the disadvantages of linking him with an often overpowering personality, and enclosing him in a very specific, fairly limited area of bop.

● ALBUMS: with Les Jazz Modes *Jazzville* (Dawn 1956)★★★, with Les Jazz Modes *Les Jazz Modes* (Dawn 1956)★★★, with Les Jazz Modes *Mood In Scarlet* reissued as *Smart Jazz For The Smart Set* (Dawn 1957)★★★, with Les Jazz Modes *The Most Happy Fella* (Atlantic 1958)★★★, with Paul Quinichette *The Chase Is On* (Bethlehem 1958)★★★, *Takin' Care Of Business* (Jazzland 1960)★★★★, *We Paid Our Dues* (Epic 1961)★★★, *Yeah!* (Epic 1960)★★★, *Bossa Nova Bacchanal* (Blue Note 1962)★★★, *Two Is One* (Strata-East 1974)★★★★, *Cinnamon Flower* (Rykodisc 1976)★★★, *Moment's Notice* (Storyville 1977)★★★, with Howard McGhee *Jazzbrothers* (Storyville 1977)★★★, *The Upper Manhattan Jazz Society* (Enja 1981)★★★, with Sphere *Four In One* (Elektra Musician 1982)★★★★, with Sphere *Flight Path* (Elektra Musician 1983)★★★, *Social Call* (Uptown 1984)★★★, with Sphere *Sphere On Tour* (Red 1985)★★★, with Sphere *Four For All* (Verve 1987)★★★, *Epistrophy* (Landmark 1988)★★★, with Les Jazz Modes *Les Jazz Modes* 1956 recordings (Biograph)★★★★, *Unsung Hero* 1960/1961 recordings (Columbia)★★★.

ROVA Saxophone Quartet

Jon Raskin (baritone, alto and soprano saxophones, B flat clarinet), Larry Ochs (b. 3 May 1949, New York City, New York, USA; tenor, alto and sopranino saxophones), Andrew Voigt (alto, soprano, sopranino saxophones, flute), Bruce Ackley (E flat alto and B flat clarinets, soprano saxophone). Formed on America's west coast in 1977, ROVA soon established itself as the *avant garde* representative on the saxophone quartet front, seeking to link the new, improvised saxophone languages of players such as Anthony Braxton and Steve Lacy with both the world of contemporary composition (from Ives to Stockhausen) and extremely left-field rock (Fred Frith, Henry Kaiser). ROVA recorded at first on Kaiser's Metalanguage label, but later releases have been on European labels such as Black Saint, Hat Hut and Sound Aspects. In 1983 and 1989 they toured the Soviet Union (the former visit documented on *Saxophone Diplomacy*, the latter on *This Time We Are Both*, while other projects have included albums with Braxton (*The Aggregate*) and electronics expert Alvin Curran (*Electric Rags II*) plus a record of Lacy tunes (*Favorite Street*). In 1986 they initiated a special concert series, PreEchoes, in the San Francisco area, in which the group commissioned and collaborated on pieces by composers from all genres of contemporary music: participants to date have included Braxton, Curran, Frith, Kaiser, Butch Morris, Terry Riley, Richard Teitelbaum and John Zorn. Although essentially an improvising group, ROVA's music is densely textured and closely integrates composition with freer modes. Their music has often been influenced by literary sources - for example, the title track of their double-set *The Crowd* takes its name from Elias Canetti's book *Crowds And Power*, and a continuing series of pieces is called *Trobas Clus* after a spontaneous form of poetry sung by the medieval troubadours of southern France. In 1989 Steve Adams replaced Andrew Voigt in the quartet. Voigt has since recorded a duo album with Braxton (*Kol Nidre*) and Larry Ochs guested on Chris Brown's *The Room*.

● ALBUMS: *Cinema Rovaté* (1978)★★★, with Henry Kaiser *Daredevils* (1979)★★★★, *The Removal Of Secrecy* (1979)★★★, with Andrea Centazzo *The Bay* (1979)★★★, *This, This, This, This* (1981)★★★, *As Was* (1981)★★★, with others *The Metalanguage Festival Of Improvised Music, Volume One: The Social Set* (1981)★★★, *Invisible Frames* (1982)★★★, *Favorite Street* (Black Saint 1984)★★★★, *Saxophone Diplomacy* 1983 recording (hatART 1985)★★★★, *The Crowd* (1986)★★★, *Beat Kennel* (Black Saint 1987)★★★, with Anthony Braxton *The Aggregate* (1989)★★★★, with Alvin Curran *Electric Rags II* (1990)★★★, *Long On Logic* (Sound Aspects 1990)★★★★, *This Time We Are Both* (1991)★★★, *For The Bureau Of Both* (Black Saint 1993)★★★★, *Ptow!!* (Victo 1996)★★★, *The Works (Volume 2)* (Black Saint 1997)★★★, *Bingo* (Victo 1998)★★★.

Solo: Andrew Voigt with Braxton *Kol Nidre* (1990)★★★.

Rowland, Dennis

b. *c*.1950, Detroit, Michigan, USA. Growing up in a musical family, Rowland began singing as a child. Inevitably influenced by Motown Records, he also heard and greatly admired the singing of Joe Williams, whose hit record of 'Every Day I Have The Blues', with Count Basie, was popular in the mid-50s. Nurturing ambitions to be a singer and an actor, Rowland patiently developed his crafts and in 1977 was rewarded when he was engaged to sing with the Basie band. The engagement lasted until Basie's death, in 1984. During this period he toured worldwide, describing these years as 'an awesome experience. I felt like a kid in a candy store'. In 1980 he sang on the band's Grammy Award-winning *On The Road*. After leaving the band, Rowland was able to spend more time with his other passion and acted in *Jesus Christ Superstar*, *Big River*, *The Seven Deadly Sins*, which also featured Cleo Laine, and, in the mid-90s, *Blues In The Night*. Based in Phoenix, Arizona, Rowland continues to sing as well as act and in 1995 was signed by Concord Records, making an album with former Count Basie drummer Gregg Field and which also features Snooky Young, Pete Chrieslieb, Joe Sample and Eric Marienthal. Dennis Rowland's strong baritone is ideally suited to ballads which he sings with warmth and expressiveness. On mid- to up-tempo songs he swings as befits a singer with his background.

● ALBUMS: *Rhyme, Rhythm And Reason* (Concord Jazz 1995)★★★, *Get Here* (Concord Vista 1996)★★★, *Now Dig This! A Vocal Celebration Of Miles Davis* (Concord Jazz 1997)★★★★.

ROWLES, JIMMY

b. James George Hunter, 19 August 1918, Spokane, Washington, USA, d. 28 May 1996, Los Angeles, California, USA. A self-taught pianist, Rowles first attracted wide attention in Southern California in the early 40s as a member of small groups led by Slim Gaillard, Lester Young and others. It was at this time that he struck up a friendship with Ben Webster that was to last for many years. Later in the decade he was with big bands led by Benny Goodman, Tommy Dorsey, Les Brown and Woody Herman, and was also in great demand as accompanist to singers. His reputation in this latter respect was enhanced by his work with Peggy Lee, Webster, Billie Holiday, Sarah Vaughan, Carmen McRae and Ella Fitzgerald (although he stated that he detested his work with Fitzgerald). His long years as a studio musician in Hollywood, and later in New York, failed to dampen either his own talent or the regard in which he was held by musicians. He has recorded with George Mraz, Al Cohn, Zoot Sims, Stan Getz, Dexter Gordon, Herbie Harper, Pepper Adams and Mel Lewis among many others. His work with Getz and his accompaniment to Lee were particularly inspiring. He was a highly gifted player, with a deft touch and a seemingly endless store of ideas, which he imparted with acerbic wit and skill. He was also a talented artist and highly skilled as a tennis player. This combination made Rowles one of the best mainstream pianists in jazz. As an accompanist to singers he had few, if any, superiors. His many record albums are ample testimony to his talent, yet he remains one of the least known of jazz players. His daughter Stacy (b. 11 September 1955) is an accomplished jazz trumpeter, and the Rowleses worked together in Los Angeles during the early 80s, later recording *Tell It Like It Is* in 1984. He was plagued with ill-health in his later years.

● ALBUMS: *Rare, But Well Done* (Liberty 1955)★★, *Let's Get Acquainted With Jazz ... For People Who Hate Jazz* reissued as *Upper Classmen* (Tampa 1957)★★★, *Weather In A Jazz Vane* (Andex 1958)★★★, *Fiorello Uptown, Mary Sunshine Downtown* (Signature 1960)★★★, *Kinda Groovy!* (Capitol 1963)★★★, *Some Other Spring* (1970)★★, *Jazz Is A Fleeting Moment* (1974)★★★, *The Special Magic Of Jimmy Rowles* (Halcyon 1974)★★★, with Sarah Vaughan *Sarah Vaughan And The Jimmy Rowles Quintet* (Mainstream 1975)★★★, *Music's The Only Thing That's On My Mind* (1976)★★★, *Grandpaws* (Choice 1976)★★★, *Paws That Refresh* (1976)★★★, with Stan Getz *The Peacocks* (Columbia 1977)★★★, *If I'm Lucky* (1977)★★★, *I Remember Bebop* (1977)★★★, with Al Cohn *Heavy Love* (Xanadu 1977)★★★, *Isfahan* (Sonet 1978)★★, with Zoot Sims *If I'm Lucky* (Pablo 1978)★★★, *Scarab* (1978)★★★, *As Good As It Gets* (1978)★★★, *We Could Make Such Beautiful Music Together* (Xanadu 1978)★★★, *Nature Boy* (1978)★★★, with Red Mitchell *Red 'N' Me* (1978)★★★, *My Mother's Love* (1979)★★★, *Jimmy Rowles At The Philharmonic, Warsaw* (1979)★★, *Jimmy Rowles Plays Duke Ellington And Billy Strayhorn* (Columbia 1981)★★★, *In Paris* (Columbia 1981)★★, *Profile* (Columbia 1982)★★★, with Stacy Rowles *Tell It Like It Is* (Concord Jazz 1984)★★★, with Mitchell *Jimmy Rowles With The Red Mitchell Trio* (Contemporary 1985)★★★, *Jimmy Rowles, Vol. 2* (Contemporary 1985)★★★, *Looking Back* (Delos 1989)★★, *Remember When* (Mastermix 1989)★★★, with Sims *For Lady Day* 1978 recording (Pablo 1990)★★★★, *Plus 2 Plus 3 Plus 4* (JVC 1990)★★★★, *Trio* (Capri 1991)★★★, *Lilac Time* (Kokopelli 1994)★★★, *Weather In A Jazz Vane* (VSOP 1998)★★★★.

ROYAL CROWN REVUE

An engrossing amalgamation of such disparate musical styles as swing, jive, blues and hip-hop, Royal Crown Revue further established a growing reputation with the release of their 1996 debut album. *Mugzy's Move*, a Ted Templeman production, showcased the group's intricate musicianship and seemingly limitless depth of energy. The group had come to prominence at 'swing-dancing' engagements in their native Los Angeles, California, USA, including a two-year weekly run at the Derby club, centrepoint of the whole scene. Their popularity eventually caught the attention of industry executives, with Warner Brothers Records winning the race to sign them. The group's baritone saxophone player, writer and arranger, Bill Ungerman, described their appeal thus: 'We do everything from 30s to 50s styles, and we throw it in a blender and mix it up. We don't stay in one era or genre, but we're not trying to be a copy band. We want to do something new', he told *Billboard* magazine. Other members of the septet include James Achor (guitar), Scott Steen (trumpet) and Eddie Nichols (vocals). *Mugzy's Move* included revisions of Bobby Darin's 'Beyond The Sea' and Willie Dixon's 'Honey Child'. However, their best-known early recording was 'Hey Pachuco!', featured in the mainstream film release, *The Mask*. The song was also reprised in front of millions of Americans when figure skater Kurt Browning used it as the musical accompaniment to his programme in 1996. Further evidence of the group's potential for crossover appeal came later that year with the announcement of support dates for bills headed by Jerry Lee Lewis and Porno For Pyros.

● ALBUMS: *Mugzy's Move* (Warners 1996)★★★.

ROYAL, ERNIE

b. 6 February 1921, Los Angeles, California, USA, d. 16 March 1983. Royal began playing trumpet as a child and while at Jefferson High School numbered among his fellow pupils future jazz artists such as Dexter Gordon, Chico Hamilton, Vi Redd, Jackie Kelso and Melba Liston. He played in a number of bands in Southern California in the late 30s and early 40s, including those led by Les Hite and Lionel Hampton, in both of which he followed in the footsteps of his older brother, Marshal Royal. In the post-war years he was with Count Basie, Woody Herman and, briefly, Duke Ellington. After a spell in Europe in the early 50s he returned to his home-town and played in small groups with Wardell Gray, Gerry Mulligan, Sonny Criss, Sonny Rollins,

Cannonball Adderley, Jimmy Rowles, Hamilton, Red Mitchell and others. He also played in Stan Kenton's big band. From the late 50s to the early 70s he worked mostly in studios in New York but took time out to play with Gil Evans, Quincy Jones, Oliver Nelson and others on record dates and for special tours. An experienced musician with often underused melodic gifts, Royal died in 1983.

● ALBUMS: *Accent On Trumpet* (1954)★★★, with Sonny Rollins *Brass/Trio* (1958)★★★, with Quincy Jones *The Birth Of A Band!* (1959)★★★★, with Gil Evans *Blues In Orbit* (1969)★★★★.

ROYAL, MARSHAL

b. 5 December 1912, Sapulpa, Oklahoma, USA, d. 9 May 1995, Los Angeles, California, USA. Royal learned several instruments as a child, finally concentrating on alto saxophone in his teenage years. In the 30s he moved to Los Angeles and played there in several bands, including a long spell with Les Hite. Among his fellow musicians in this band were his brother, Ernie Royal, and Lionel Hampton. When Hampton formed his own band in 1940 Royal joined and became the band's straw boss, ruthlessly drilling the younger musicians. One of them, Dexter Gordon, later paid tribute to Royal as being largely responsible for teaching him to breathe and phrase correctly. After military service in World War II, he played briefly in New York before returning to Los Angeles and work in the studios. In 1951 he joined Count Basie's small group, and when Basie re-formed his big band Royal took on similar duties to those he had carried out for Hampton. Under his watchful eye, the Basie band became a crisp and efficient outfit. He remained in the band for 20 years, touring the world several times, but then, while absent due to ill-health, he was quietly replaced. Resident once more in Los Angeles, Royal became lead alto with the big bands of Bill Berry and Frank Capp-Nat Pierce. He also played many club and festival dates, recording with Dave Frishberg, Snooky Young and others. In 1989 he returned to Europe to play club and festival dates, sometimes alone, at other times with Berry and Buster Cooper. Also in 1989, Royal visited Japan with the Basie-style big band co-led by Frank Wess and Harry Edison, receiving a rapturous welcome from audiences who revelled in his soaring romanticism. Although Royal's main contribution to jazz may well have been his important, if relatively anonymous, work as lead alto in a succession of fine bands, for the fans it was the rich flowing solos, especially on romantic ballads, that made him universally popular.

● ALBUMS: with Count Basie *Basie* (1957)★★★★, *Marshal Royal With Gordon Jenkins And His Orchestra* (1960)★★★, *Back To Basie* (1962)★★★, with Bill Berry *Hot & Happy* (1974)★★★★, with Berry *Hello Rev* (1976)★★★, with Frank Capp-Nat Pierce *Juggernaut* (1976)★★★★, with Dave Frishberg *Getting Some Fun Out Of Life* (1977)★★★, with Snooky Young *Snooky And Marshal's Album* (1978)★★★, with Berry *Shortcake* (1978)★★★, *First Chair* (1978)★★★, *Royal Blue* (1980)★, with Capp-Pierce *Juggernaut Strikes Again!* (1981)★★★★, with Frank Wess-Harry Edison *Dear Mr Basie* (1989)★★★.

RUBIN, VANESSA

b. USA. Jazz singer Vanessa Rubin has built her reputation on a gruelling schedule of live appearances that have seen her tour from coast to coast in America. However, despite a strong following and a popular back catalogue, in 1997 her record label, RCA Records, attempted to launch her in the mainstream market. *New Horizons* featured some jazz standards, including a version of Phyllis Hyman's classic 'Here's That Rainy Day', but also included contemporary pop and R&B tracks. As Rubin herself admitted, this was part of a process of 'getting some of my other voices out.' She described the transition from working in jazz to working on more contemporary material as difficult: 'It was like having a vocabulary of 1,000, then going in and using only 400 words'. The album was produced by Andre Fischer, and was promoted by further touring with long-standing musical collaborators Harvey Mason, Patrice Rushen and Dave Carpenter.

● ALBUMS: *New Horizons* (RCA 1997)★★★.

RUCKER, ELLYN

b. 29 July 1937, Des Moines, Iowa, USA. Coming from a very musical family, Rucker first took an interest in piano when she was eight years old. Later, she studied classical piano but by the age of 13 her brother had persuaded her to listen to jazz. She began playing clubs and hotels in her home-town area, but it was 1979 before she became a full-time professional musician. By this stage in her career, she had also begun to sing occasionally to her own accompaniment. She spent several years working in Denver, Colorado, where she was heard by Mark Murphy who advised her to try for the 'big time'. Although essentially a solo player, sometimes working with a rhythm section, she has occasionally worked with visiting jazzmen, including Roy Eldridge, James Moody, Clark Terry, Richie Cole and Buddy Tate. In 1986 she played at the Northsea Jazz Festival in Holland and in subsequent years toured Europe and the UK. Latterly, Rucker has continued to concentrate on solo tours but has also worked with Spike Robinson on a number of occasions. Her accompanists on records have included Robinson, Pete Christlieb and John Clayton. An eclectic pianist, with a wide-ranging repertoire, Rucker is gradually becoming accepted as an inventive and skilled jazz musician. Her playing style can be elegantly poised or dynamically forceful depending upon the material or the mood that she is in. Her singing, although less strongly promoted than her piano playing, is easy and natural.

● ALBUMS: with Spike Robinson *Nice Work* (Capri 1985)★★★★, *Ellyn* (Capri 1987)★★★, *This Heart Of Mine* (Capri 1988)★★★, *Thoughts Of You* (Capri 1997)★★.

RUDD, ROSWELL

b. 17 November 1935, Sharon, Connecticut, USA. Rudd studied singing and French horn at college and theory at Harvard (1954-58). Like several other members of the 60s *avant garde* he began his jazz career playing

Dixieland, a fact that points up the line of evolution between the New Orleans roots and the New Thing, and his big, fulsome trombone sound strongly recalls the early 'tailgate' players, even when he is working in the most abstract surroundings. Rudd moved to New York in 1954 and played in various traditional bands. He began to work in a modern context with Herbie Nichols (1960-62) and in 1961 he joined Steve Lacy (who also started out playing traditional jazz). His conversion to free-form jazz began as a result of meeting Bill Dixon. In 1964 he formed the New York Art Quartet with John Tchicai, to whom he had been introduced by Dixon (*Mohawk, New York Art Quartet*). When the Quartet disbanded in 1965 he became a member of Archie Shepp's highly influential group until 1967 (*Four For Tranc, Mama Too Tight*). In 1968 he formed the Primordial Quintet (which ended up as a nine-piece band) with Lee Konitz. During the late 70s and 80s he toured extensively with his own groups, and in 1982 was reunited with Lacy in the Monk Project with Misha Mengelberg. He has also worked with Cecil Taylor, Jazz Composers Orchestra (who, in 1973, commissioned the *Numatik Swing Band* from him), Albert Ayler, Karl Berger, Enrico Rava, Perry Robinson, Gato Barbieri, Robin Kenyatta and Charlie Haden's Liberation Music Orchestra, and in 1961 he appeared in the film *The Hustler*. He has also worked with Alan Lomax, and became professor of Music Ethnology at the University of Maine. He has tried to show the connections between jazz, so-called ethnic music and the European classical tradition in his compositions. In the early 90s he was reportedly playing Dixieland again in upstate New York.

● ALBUMS: *Roswell Rudd Quartet* (1965)★★★, *Everywhere* (1966)★★★, *Numatik Swing Band* (1973)★★★★, *Flexible Flyer* (1974)★★★, with Steve Lacy *School Days* 1963 recordings (Emanem 1975)★★★★, *Inside Job* (Freedom 1976)★★★, *Maxine* (1976)★★★, with Giorgio Gaslini *Sharing* (1978)★★★, *Blown-Bone* 1976 recording (Philips Japan 1979)★★★, *The Definitive Roswell Rudd* (1979)★★, *Regeneration* (Soul Note 1983)★★★, *The Unheard Herbie Nichols Vol. 1* (CIMP 1997)★★.

RÜEGG, MATTHIAS

b. 8 December 1952, Zurich, Switzerland. During the 70s Rüegg played piano with a variety of bands while studying composition and arranging in Graz and Vienna, where he eventually settled and formed the Vienna Art Orchestra (1977) and later the Vienna Art Choir (1983). Notable members of the Orchestra have included Wolfgang Puschnig, Roman Schwaller, Lauren Newton and Wolfgang Reisinger, and in the early 80s they won several big band awards and released acclaimed albums for the hatART label. Rüegg continues to play the piano with the Orchestra in a competent modern style, and in 1997 celebrated its 20th anniversary with an extensive European tour and a box set release. Rüegg is acclaimed for the music he has written and arranged for the orchestra. He has taken themes from the whole history of jazz and even produced a double album of arrangements of the music of Eric Satie. In his arrangements he fulfils his hopes that he has 'arranged, orchestrated, altered and alienated . . . added some parts, extended phrases, and exposed striking solos, always . . . following the sense of the composition and the composer's intention'.

● ALBUMS: *Tango From Obango* (hatART 1979)★★★, *Suite For The Green Eighties* (hatART 1981)★★★, *From No Time To Rag Time* (hatART 1982)★★★, *The Minimalism Of Eric Satie* (hatART 1983)★★★★, *Perpetuum Mobile* (hatART 1985)★★★.

● COMPILATIONS: with the Vienna Art Orchestra *20th Anniversary* 3-CD box set (Amadeo/Verve 1997)★★★★.

● FURTHER READING: *Vienna Art Orchestra 1977-1997.*

RUFF, WILLIE

(see Mitchell-Ruff Duo)

RUGOLO, PETE

b. 25 December 1915, San Piero, Sicily. After studying composing and arranging under classicist Darius Milhaud, Rugolo began writing arrangements for Stan Kenton. Many of Kenton's most successful recordings of the late 40s were Rugolo charts and of these a high proportion were also his compositions. After his full-time collaboration with Kenton ended in 1949, Rugolo produced a number of recording sessions for Capitol Records including some with Miles Davis, Mel Tormé, Peggy Lee and Nat 'King' Cole. He also recorded with a studio band under his own name. The period with Capitol also saw him writing additional material for Kenton and his Innovations in Modern Music Orchestra, and he was arranger and musical director for June Christy's *Something Cool* album. In the 50s he joined Columbia Records and in the late 50s was with Mercury Records, writing for Sarah Vaughan, Billy Eckstine and others. From the 60s into the early 80s he worked in film and television studios, eventually retiring in 1985. Heavily influenced by Kenton, Rugolo's arrangements demonstrate his interest in developing ideas for the modern orchestra often as displays of technical virtuosity.

● ALBUMS: *Music For Hi-Fi Bugs* (1956)★★★, *Out On A Limb* (1956)★★★, *Pete Rugolo And His Orchestra* i (1956)★★, *Pete Rugolo And His Orchestra* ii (1958)★★, *Pete Rugolo And His Orchestra* iii (1958)★★, *The Music From Richard Diamond* (1959)★★★, *Pete Rugolo And His Orchestra* iv (1959)★★, *The Thriller* (1960)★★★, *Pete Rugolo And His Orchestra* v (1960)★★★, *Ten Trumpets And Two Guitars* (1961)★★★, *The Diamonds Meet Pete Rugolo* (1961)★★, *TV Themes* (1962)★★.

● COMPILATIONS: by Stan Kenton *The Kenton Era* (1940-53)★★★★, *Rugolomania* (Fresh Sounds 1988)★★★★.

RUIZ, HILTON

b. 29 May 1952, New York City, New York, USA. Ruiz studied piano from an early age, performing public recitals as a small child. In the mid- to late 60s he worked as a professional musician in bands playing Latin American music. In the early 70s he turned to jazz, studying with Mary Lou Williams. Later in the decade he played on numerous club, concert and recording dates with Joe Newman, Freddie Hubbard, Clark Terry, Charles Mingus, Rahsaan Roland Kirk (with whom he recorded *Return Of The 5000lb Man*), Chico Freeman (on *Beyond The Rain*), Betty Carter and Archie Shepp. He continued an active career in the 80s, appearing with Terry's all-star big band at festivals and on television and making records, including some as a member of Marion Brown's group. A strikingly inventive pianist, Ruiz's jazz style incorporates many elements from his continuing interest in Latin music.

● ALBUMS: *Piano Man* (Steeple Chase 1975)★★★★, *Excitation* (1977)★★★, *New York Hilton* (1977)★★, *Fantasia* (1978)★★★, *The Hilton Ruiz Trio* (1978)★★★, *Cross Currents* (1984)★★★, *Vibration Society: The Music Of Rahsaan Roland Kirk* (1986)★★, *El Camino* (1987)★★★, *Strut* (Novus 1988)★★★★, *Cross Currents* (Stash 1987)★★★★, *Doin' It Right* (Novus 1989)★★★, *A Moment's Notice* (Novus 1991)★★★, *Live At Birdland* (Candid 1993)★★★, *Manhattan Mambo* (Telarc 1993)★★★★, *Island Eyes* (Tropijazz/RRM 1997)★★★.

RUMSEY, HOWARD

b. 7 November 1917, Brawley, California, USA. After briefly playing piano and drums, Rumsey took up the bass while still at school. In the late 30s he played in the Vido Musso band alongside Stan Kenton and went with the pianist when he formed his own band in 1941. From 1943 he mostly freelanced but played in the bands of Freddie Slack and Charlie Barnet. At the end of the decade he was directly responsible for establishing a jazz club at the Lighthouse Café at Hermosa Beach, a venue that became the focus of the west coast jazz scene. He was himself a member of the Lighthouse All-Stars, the house band at the Lighthouse. Throughout the 50s Rumsey played at the Lighthouse, eventually taking over the running of the Café. During this period he played and recorded with many of the outstanding musicians of the day, among them Teddy Edwards, Sonny Criss, Hampton Hawes, Shorty Rogers, Jimmy Giuffre, Conte Candoli, Rolf Ericson, Frank Rosolino, Bob Cooper, Art Pepper and Shelly Manne. He continued his activities into the 60s but eventually ceased playing and severed his connection with the Lighthouse. In the early 70s he returned to the scene by opening another club, Concerts By the Sea. A solid player with a good ear for the best in musical talent, Rumsey's greatest achievement in jazz remains the fact that he provided a setting and format that gave great encouragement to one of the most important areas of jazz in the 50s.

● ALBUMS: *Sunday Jazz A La Lighthouse* 10-inch album (Contemporary 1953)★★★★, *Howard Rumsey's Lighthouse All-Stars* 10-inch album (Contemporary 1953)★★★, *Howard Rumsey's Lighthouse All-Stars* reissued as *Howard Rumsey's Lighthouse All-Stars, Vol. 4: Oboe/Flute* (Contemporary 1954)★★★, *Howard Rumsey's Lighthouse All-Stars, Volume 1: The Quintet* 10-inch album (Contemporary 1954)★★★, *Howard Rumsey's Lighthouse All-Stars, Volume 2: The Octet* 10-inch album (Contemporary 1954)★★★, *Lighthouse At Laguna* (Contemporary 1955)★★★, *In The Solo Spotlight* (Contemporary 1956)★★★★, *Music For Lighthousekeeping* (Contemporary 1957)★★★, *Double Or Nothin'* (Liberty 1957)★★★, *Jazz Rolls-Royce* (Lighthouse 1957)★★★, with Max Roach *Drummin' The Blues* (1957)★★★, *Jazz Structures* (Philips 1957)★★★.

● COMPILATIONS: *Mexican Passport* 1952-56 recordings (Contemporary 1996)★★★★.

RUSHEN, PATRICE

b. 30 September 1954, Los Angeles, California, USA. Rushen grew up in Los Angeles and attended the University of Southern California. She started learning classical piano when she was three, and turned to jazz in her teens. A group with which she was playing won an award for young musicians at Monterey in 1972. She played with a host of artists, including Abbey Lincoln, Donald Byrd and Sonny Rollins, before joining Lee Ritenour's group in 1977. Her career as a solo singing artist, which commenced in the late 70s as a pop/soul artist, bore fruit on the Elektra label. The US R&B Top 20 hit 'Hang It Up' (1978) was followed by 'Haven't You Heard' (US R&B number 7/US pop Top 30, 1979). The latter, plus 'Never Gonna Give You Up (Won't Let You Be)', were minor UK hits in the early 80s, but were eclipsed by the Top 10 'Forget Me Nots'. Despite a tailing-off in UK/US pop chart action from that point, Rushen continued to appear regularly on the US R&B/soul charts. She gained notable chart success with 'Feel So Real (Won't Let Go)' (number 3, 1984) and 'Watch Out (number 9, 1987). After a period of label change, to Arista Records, she has focused increased attention on her singing, and her predominantly bop-based playing has given way to fusion and urban R&B styles. In 1988 she played with the Wayne Shorter/Carlos Santana group.

● ALBUMS: *Prelusion* (1974)★★★, *Before The Dawn* (1975)★★★, with Sonny Rollins *The Way I Feel* (Original Jazz Classics 1976)★★★, *Shout It Out* (Prestige 1977)★★★, with Lee Ritenour *Sugarloaf Express* (Elite 1978)★★, with John McLaughlin *Johnny McLaughlin, Electric Guitarist* (Columbia 1978)★★★★, *Patrice* (Elektra 1979)★★★, *Pizzazz* (Elektra 1979)★★★, *Let There Be Funk* (Elektra 1980)★★★, *Posh* (Elektra 1980)★★★, *Straight From The Heart* (Elektra 1982)★★★, *Now* (Elektra 1984)★★★, *Breaking All The Rules* (1986)★★★, *Watch Out!* (Arista 1987)★★★, *Signature* (Discovery 1997)★★★.

● COMPILATIONS: *The Best Of Patrice Rushen* (Rhino 1996)★★★★.

RUSHING, JIMMY

b. 26 August 1902, Oklahoma City, Oklahoma, USA, d. 8 June 1972. Rushing began singing while still studying music at school in his home-town. By 1923 he was a full-time professional singer, working in California with, among others, Jelly Roll Morton and Paul Howard. Back home in the mid-20s he teamed up with Walter Page and then joined Bennie Moten, and by 1935 was a member of the Count Basie band. He remained with Basie until 1948 and then worked as a solo, sometimes leading a small band. During these later years he regularly worked with leading jazz artists including Benny Goodman, Buck Clayton, Basie, and, during tours of the UK, with Humphrey Lyttelton. Rushing's voice was a slightly nasal high tenor that carried comfortably over the sound of a big band in full cry. The fact that he sang at a somewhat higher pitch than most other male blues singers gave his performances a keening, plaintive quality. In fact, his singing style and repertoire made him far more than merely a blues singer and he was at ease with romantic ballads. Nevertheless, he tinged everything he sang, from love songs to up-tempo swingers, with the qualities of the blues. Despite his extensive repertoire, in later years he favoured certain songs, including 'Going To Chicago', 'Every Day I Have The Blues' and 'Exactly Like You', but even repeated performances at clubs, concerts and record dates were infused with such infectious enthusiasm that he never palled. Known because of his build as 'Mr Five By Five', Rushing was at his best in front of a big band or a Kansas City-style small group, but even when he stepped out of character, as on his final formal record date, he could enchant listeners. By the early 70s, and his last date, his voice was showing signs of decades of wear and tear, but he retained his unflagging swing and brought to unusual material such as 'When I Grow Too Old To Dream' and 'I Surrender Dear', great emotional depth and a sharp awareness of the demands of both music and lyrics.

● ALBUMS: *Sings The Blues* (Vanguard 1954)★★★★, *Goin' To Chicago* (1954)★★★★, *Listen To The Blues* (Vanguard 1955)★★★★, *The Jazz Odyssey Of James Rushing Esq* (Columbia 1957)★★★, *If This Ain't The Blues* (Vanguard 1957)★★★, *Listen To The Blues* (Fontana 1957)★★★, *Showcase* (Vanguard 1957)★★★, with Ada Moore, Buck Clayton *Cat Meets Chick* (Philips 1957)★★★, *Little Jimmy Rushing And The Big Brass* (Columbia 1958)★★★, with Clayton *Copenhagen Concert* (1959)★★★, *Rushing Lullabies* (Columbia 1959)★★★, *Two Shades Of Blue* (Audio Lab 1959)★★★, *The Smith Girls* (Columbia 1961)★★★, *Five Feet Of Soul* (Colpix 1963)★★★, *Blues I Love To Sing* (Ace Of Hearts 1966)★★★, *Gee, Baby, Ain't I Good To You* (1967)★★★, *Who Was It Sang That Song* (1967)★★★, *Every Day I Have The Blues* (Bluesway 1967)★★★, *Livin' The Blues* (Bluesway 1968)★★★, *The You And Me That Used To Be* (Bluebird 1971)★★★.

● COMPILATIONS: *The Essential Jimmy Rushing* (Vanguard 1978)★★★★, *Mister Five By Five* (Columbia 1980)★★★★, *The Classic Count* (Intermedia 1982)★★★.

RUSHTON, JOE

b. 7 November 1907, Evanston, Illinois, USA, d. 2. March 1964, San Francisco, California, USA. Rushton learned to play the drums, clarinet and saxophone but had settled on the bass saxophone by the time he was playing with the California Ramblers in the late 20s. He moved to Chicago in the 30s and though he later worked in the aircraft industry he had spells with Jimmy McPartland and Bud Freeman before returning to California. He worked with Benny Goodman and Horace Heidt in the mid-40s and in 1947 recorded with Louis Armstrong. In the same year he joined cornetist Red Nichols (1947) with whom he stayed until his death. His booming, rhythmically swinging bass saxophone parts make an important contribution to the success of the Five Pennies' later recordings. Rushton toured Europe with Nichols and took part in the film *The Five Pennies* (1958).

● ALBUMS: *Rampart Street Paraders* (1954)★★★, *Meet The Five Pennies* (1959)★★★.

RUSSELL, CURLEY

b. 19 March 1917, Trinidad, d. 3 July 1986. After playing bass in several big bands of the early 40s, Russell directed his attention towards bop. As a member of the quintet led by Dizzy Gillespie and Charlie Parker in 1945, he attracted considerable attention and thereafter was much in demand for club and recording dates. In the late 40s and early 50s he played in bands led by Tadd Dameron, Bud Powell, Horace Silver, Art Blakey, Thelonious Monk and others. Despite his popularity with beboppers and his undoubted skills in this area of jazz, Russell appeared to be impervious to changing needs within later rhythm sections and by the end of the 50s he was playing in R&B bands. He died in 1986.

● ALBUMS: with Art Blakey *A Night At Birdland* (1954)★★★★, *Thelonious Monk Quintet* (1954)★★★.

● COMPILATIONS: with Dizzy Gillespie and others *The Small Groups 1945-46* (1945-46)★★★, *The Bud Powell Trio Plays* (1947)★★★★.

RUSSELL, GEORGE

b. 23 June 1923, Cincinnati, Ohio, USA. One of modern jazz's leading composers, Russell started out as a drummer with Benny Carter, but first came to prominence in the mid-40s writing for Dizzy Gillespie, notably 'Cubano Be, Cubano Bop'. He also wrote for Artie Shaw and Claude Thornhill and his 'A Bird In Igor's Yard', combining elements of Charlie Parker and Stravinsky, was recorded by the Buddy De Franco big band in 1949. Periods of hospitalization for tuberculosis led to him developing his theoretical *The Lydian Chromatic Concept Of Tonal Organization*, first published in 1953 and a crucial influence on the later modal jazz of Miles Davis and John Coltrane. In the 50s Russell wrote 'All About Rosie' on a commission from Brandeis University and taught both privately and at the School of Jazz in Lennox, Massachusetts: his students, then and later, included Carla Bley, Rahsaan Roland Kirk, Don Ellis and Steve Swallow (the latter pair also recording with him). In the early 60s he led a sextet and made several celebrated recordings, often featuring *avant garde* artists such as Sheila Jordan ('You Are My Sunshine'), Eric Dolphy (*Ezz-Thetics*) and Don Cherry (*At Beethoven Hall*). In the mid- to late 60s, Russell was based in Sweden, where he experimented with electronic music and worked with up-and-coming players, such as Jan Garbarek, Terje Rypdal and Palle Mikkelborg. In 1969 he returned to the USA to teach at the New England Conservatory, but still continued to record in Sweden. (Many of the recordings he made in Scandinavia in the 60s and 70s have since reappeared on the Soul Note label in the 80s.) From the late 70s he began playing and recording regularly in the USA, often working with a big band. He was one of the first artists signed up by the reactivated Blue Note label, and in the mid- to late 80s he toured the UK with bands that included several well-known British players, for example, Chris Biscoe, Ian Carr, Andy Sheppard and Kenny Wheeler. Russell has continued with his theoretical work, completing a second volume of his *Lydian Chromatic Concept* in 1978. This stands as one of the central texts of modern jazz theory. A complex work, its basic premise is that traditional jazz structures, such as chord sequences, can be overlaid with scales or modes that introduce a degree of pan-tonality and so allow the player more choices for improvising.

● ALBUMS: *George Russell Octets* (MGM 1955)★★★★, *The Jazz Workshop* (RCA Victor 1956)★★★, *New York, NY* (Decca 1959)★★★, with David Nathaniel Baker Jnr *Jazz In The Space Age*, (Decca 1958)★★★, *At The Five Spot* (Decca 1960)★★★★, *In Kansas City* (1960)★★, with Baker *Stratosphunk* (Riverside 1960)★★★, with Baker *Ezz-thetics* (Riverside 1961)★★★★, *The Outer View* (Riverside 1962)★★★★, *At The Beethoven Hall Volumes 1 & 2* (1965)★★★, with Bill Evans *Living Time* (1972)★★★, *Electronic Sonata For Souls Loved By Nature 1980* (Soul Note 1980)★★★★, with Jan Garbarek *Othello Ballet Suite* 1967 recording (Soul Note 1981)★★★, with Garbarek *Trip To Prillarguri* 1970 recording (Soul Note 1982)★★, *New York Big Band* 1978 recording (Soul Note 1982)★★★, *Listen To The Silence* 1972 recording (1983)★★★, *The Essence Of George Russell* 1966-70 recordings (1983)★★★, *Live In An American Time Spiral* (Soul Note 1983)★★★, *The African Game* 1983 recording (1985)★★★★, *So What* (Blue Note 1986)★★★★, *Time Space* (PolyGram 1988)★★★, *The London Concert Volumes 1-2* (Stash 1990)★★★.

● FURTHER READING: *The Lydian Chromatic Concept Of Tonal Organization*, George Russell.

RUSSELL, HAL

b. Harold Russell Luttenbacher, 28 August 1926, Detroit, Michigan, USA, d. 5 September 1992. Russell grew up in Chicago and first became involved in music by playing drums. He attended the University of Illinois, receiving both bachelor and masters degrees in musical education. Although he had learned the trumpet as part of his degree course, he abandoned it for 30 years while he worked in jazz groups as a drummer and vibraphonist. In 1950 he played with Miles Davis and later in the decade performed with many leading jazz artists, such as Sonny Rollins, Duke Ellington, Billie Holiday, Erroll Garner and Sarah Vaughan. From 1961 he played drums in the Joe Daley Trio, one of Chicago's first free jazz groups, then in the late 60s, inspired by the high-energy music of *avant gardists*, such as Albert Ayler and Sunny Murray, he began to lead his own groups. From the late 70s Russell headed a quintet and a trio in what he called NRG Ensembles, and was perhaps most creative in the freedom granted him by the latter format. The incompetence of the group's original saxophonist led Russell to take up saxophone himself - at the age of 50 - and he became an enthusiastic performer on tenor and soprano. 'I thought God, what a fool I am! I should have been playing saxophone all along! I shouldn't have played drums at all!' In 1990 he released *Hal On Earth*, with an unusual quintet consisting of two saxophones, two basses and drums - with three members of the ensemble doubling on didjeridoo! Russell stated: 'I find that the more popular you become the less you like the music you are playing. This makes you search for new forms and ways of musical expression'. In 1991 ECM Records recognized what had previously been underground success by releasing the live *Finnish-Swiss Tour* by an NRG Ensemble that comprised Russell and long-time associates Mars Williams (best known for his work with the Psychedelic Furs), Steve Hunt, Brian Sandstrom and Kent Kessler. In the summer of 1992 Russell became ill and was rushed into hospital for heart bypass surgery. The operation was considered a success, but he died three weeks later.

● ALBUMS: *The Hal Russell NRG Ensemble* (1981)★★★, with Mars Williams *EFT Soons* (1981)★★★, with Charles Tyler *Generation* (Chief 1982)★★★, *Conserving NRG* (Principally Jazz 1984)★★★, *Hal On Earth* (1990)★★★★, *The Finnish-Swiss Tour* (ECM 1991)★★★★, *Naked Colours* (Silkheart 1991)★★★★, *Hal's Bells* (ECM 1992)★★★★, *The Hal Russell Story* (ECM 1993)★★★★.

RUSSELL, LUIS

b. 6 August 1902, Careening Clay, Bocas Del Toro, Panama, d. 11 December 1963. After playing various instruments in his homeland, Russell moved to New Orleans in 1919 and thereafter played piano in local saloons and clubs. In the early 20s he played with Albert Nicholas among others, and also led bands. He played with King Oliver in Chicago in 1925 and in 1927 became leader of a band in New York. For the next few years he led his band in the city and on tours, often backing Louis Armstrong. In 1935 the band became known as Armstrong's but Russell stayed on until the early 40s, when he formed a new band for touring. From the late 40s he ran a business outside music but continued to lead small bands for club dates. Russell's bands never had the impact on the jazz public achieved by many of his contemporaries. Nevertheless, he was a dedicated musician and made serious attempts to integrate some of the fundamental concepts of the New Orleans style into big band music.

● ALBUMS: with others *Gut Bucket Blues And Stomps - Chicago* (1926-28)★★★★, *New York Jazz* (1928-33)★★★, *1930-1934* (VJM 1986)★★★, *Luis Russell And His Orchestra 1929-30* (Swaggie 1988)★★★★, *Savoy Shout* (JSP 1989)★★★.

RUSSELL, PEE WEE

b. Charles Ellsworth Russell, 27 March 1906, Maple Wood, Missouri, USA, d. 15 February 1969, Alexandria. Russell began playing clarinet in the early 20s and by 1927, the year he came to New York, had already worked with luminaries such as Jack Teagarden, Frank Trumbauer and Bix Beiderbecke. In the late 20s and throughout the 30s and 40s, Russell played with numerous jazzmen working in the traditional sphere, among them Bobby Hackett, Wild Bill Davison, Louis Prima, Billy Butterfield, Muggsy Spanier, George Wettling and Art Hodes. He also enjoyed a long association with

Eddie Condon, although enjoyed is perhaps an inappropriate term for what Russell later described as a time of sadness - thanks to his hangdog expression and idiosyncratic style of playing, he was often treated as a clown. In the 50s Russell's health was suspect - he suffered from alcoholism - but by the 60s he was back playing at clubs, concerts and festivals around the world. One of the most endearing eccentrics in jazz, Russell's playing style was unique and on first and sometimes even second hearing might be thought primitive. Nevertheless, the sometimes grating sounds he produced on his instrument and the seemingly indecisive placing of notes during solo and ensemble passages had a cumulative effect that demonstrated the existence of an inquiring and adventurous musical mind. This became more overtly apparent when he blended easily with such diverse musical associates as Thelonious Monk, Henry 'Red' Allen and Coleman Hawkins. In the 60s he played in a pianoless quartet with Marshall Brown and on a big band album with Oliver Nelson, as well as working again in more traditional contexts. A totally original and often brilliant clarinettist, he inspired writer George Frazier to enthuse about 'the bliss and the sadness and the compassion and the humility that are there in the notes he plays'. Finally, the liver condition that had almost killed him in the 50s returned to finish the job, and he died in February 1969.

● ALBUMS: *Pee Wee Russell All Stars* 10-inch album (Atlantic1952)★★★, *Pee Wee Russell* 10-inch album (Storyville 1954)★★★, with Jack Teagarden *Jack Teagarden's Big Eight/Pee Wee Russell's Rhythmakers* 1938/1940 recordings (Riverside 1956)★★★, *We're In The Money* (Storyville 1956)★★★★, *Portrait Of Pee Wee Russell* (Counterpoint 1957)★★★★, with Buck Clayton *A Salute To Newport* (Dot 1959)★★★★, with Clayton *Memorial Album* (Prestige 1960)★★★, with Coleman Hawkins *Jazz Reunion* (Candid 1961)★★★, *New Groove* (Columbia 1963)★★★, *Hot Licorice* (Honey Dew 1964)★★★, *Gumbo* (Honey Dew 1964)★★★, *Ask Me Now!* (Impulse! 1966)★★★★, with Henry 'Red' Allen *The College Concert Of Pee Wee Russell And Henry Red* (Impulse! 1967)★★★, with Oliver Nelson *The Spirit Of '67* (Impulse! 1967)★★★.

● COMPILATIONS: *Giants Of Jazz* 3-LP box set (Time-Life)★★★, *A Chronological Remembrance* 1927-1965 recordings (IAJRC)★★★★, *The Pied Piper Of Jazz* 1944 recording (Commodore)★★★★, *The Individualism Of* (Savoy 1985)★★★★, *Portrait Of Pee Wee* (Fresh Sounds 1991)★★★★, *Jazz Original* 1938-1944 recordings (Commodore 1997)★★★.

● FURTHER READING: *Pee Wee Speaks: A Discography Of Pee Wee Russell*, Robert Hilbert with David Niven. *Pee Wee Russell: The Life Of A Jazzman*, Robert Hilbert.

RUSSIN, BABE

b. Irving Russin, 18 June 1911, Pittsburgh, Pennsylvania, USA, d. 4 August 1984. Russin began playing tenor saxophone and other reed instruments while still a young man, sometimes in company with his brother and sister, both pianists. He played in many jazz and dance bands of the late 20s and early 30s, including the California Ramblers, Smith Ballew, Ben Pollack, Red Nichols and Russ Colombo, before a spell of studio work. He then joined Benny Goodman and Tommy Dorsey, led his own band, was then with Jimmy Dorsey, and in 1944, entered the US Army where he continued to play in bands. After the war he returned to studio work, often Hollywood, where he played on-screen in musical biopics based on the lives of Goodman and Glenn Miller. A much-valued sideman with the leading bands with which he played during the swing era, Russin's tenor playing showed a keen awareness of developments in the instrument's changing role in jazz.

● ALBUMS: *Benny Goodman At Carnegie Hall* (Columbia 1938)★★★★.

RUSSO, BILL

b. 25 June 1928, Chicago, Illinois, USA. After extensive studies in arranging, Russo wrote for Lennie Tristano and also occasionally played trombone. One of the earliest musicians to lead a rehearsal band, his experimental style came to the attention of Stan Kenton in the early 50s. In the mid-50s he concentrated on performing with a small group but by the end of the decade was again deeply involved in writing for larger jazz ensembles. He was also active as a teacher and this combination of work continued on throughout the 60s and early 70s. After spending some time in film and television work he returned to teaching in the 80s. He remains one of the more interesting writers for the large modern jazz orchestra.

● ALBUMS: *A Recital In New American Music* 10-inch album (Dee Gee 1952)★★, with Shelly Manne *Deep People* (Savoy 1955)★★★, *Bill Russo Plus The Hans Koller Ensemble* (1955)★★, *Bill Russo And The New Jazz Group, Hanover* (1955)★★★★, *The World Of Alcina* (Atlantic 1956)★★★, with Lee Konitz *An Image - Lee Konitz With Strings* (Verve 1958)★★★, *School Of Rebellion* (Roulette 1960)★★★, *The Seven Deadly Sins* (Roulette 1960)★★, *Suite No. 1 Opus 5 & Suite No. 2 Opus 8* (1962)★★★, *Bill Russo On The Air In London* (1963)★★★, *Bill Russo And The London Jazz Orchestra* (1964)★★★.

RUTHERFORD, PAUL

b. 29 February 1940, Greenwich, London, England. Rutherford began to play saxophone in the mid-50s, then changed to trombone, which he played in RAF bands from 1958-63. While in the RAF he met John Stevens and Trevor Watts, with whom he founded the Spontaneous Music Ensemble in 1965. From 1964-68 he studied at London's Guildhall School of Music in the day and played free jazz in The Little Theatre Club at night. In 1967 be began to work regularly in Mike Westbrook's bands. In the early 70s he formed his own Iskra 1903 group, with Derek Bailey and Barry Guy, and also worked with the London Jazz Composers Orchestra the Globe Unity Orchestra and the Tony Oxley septet as well as with other freelance improvisers, such as Evan Parker and Paul Lovens. A major figure on the European improvising scene, Rutherford's major contribution is probably the new language for solo trombone that he began to develop in the early 70s and best demonstrated on the 1976 classic *Gentle Harm*

Of The Bourgeoisie. *Neuph*, from 1978, also showed his skills as a composer and euphonium player. In the 80s he formed a new line-up of Iskra 1903, with Guy and Phil Wachsmann, continued to work with LJCO, played in the Free Jazz Quartet with Eddie Prevost and recorded a set of solos and duos with baritone saxophonist George Haslam. A virtuoso trombonist, his commitment to experimental and improvised music has earned him the respect of players all over the world.

● ALBUMS: *Iskra 1903* (1972)★★★★, *Iskra 1903* (Maya 1974)★★★★, *Gentle Harm Of The Bourgeoisie* 1974 recording (1976)★★★, *Old Moers Almanac* (1976)★★★, with Paul Lovens *And When I Say Slowly...*(1977)★★★, *Neuph* (1978)★★★, with Evan Parker, Barry Guy, John Stevens *Four Four Four* (1979)★★★, with others *The Ericle Of Dolphi* 1985-87 recordings (1989)★★★, with George Haslam *1989 And All That* (1989)★★★, with free Jazz Quarter *Premonitions* (1989)★★, *Rogues* (Emanem 1989)★★★★.

RUTHERFORD, RUDY

b. Elman Rutherford, 1912, Detroit, Michigan, USA. Rutherford played alto and baritone saxophones and clarinet in various local bands until joining Lionel Hampton in 1943. He played baritone in the band and also with Count Basie, whom he joined in 1944. He went into this band as replacement for baritone saxophonist Jack Washington, and when Washington returned he stayed on, switching to alto. In 1947 he left to play with Teddy Buckner and thereafter played in several bands, including a return spell with Basie, and also led his own groups. The return to Basie coincided with the leader's brief period with a small band in the early 50s, with Rutherford again playing baritone and doubling on his other instruments. In the 50s he was with Wilbur De Paris and Roger 'Ram' Ramirez and also worked with Chuck Berry. In the 60s he was with Buddy Tate and during the early 70s he played with Earl 'Fatha' Hines. As a section player, Rutherford's work was solid without being especially notable. As a clarinet soloist, however, he played with verve and distinction while his baritone playing had a lightness of touch and fluidity not always apparent with players of this instrument.

● ALBUMS: with Count Basie *The Jubilee Alternatives* (Hep 1943-44)★★★★, with Wilbur De Paris *Over And Over Again* (Atlantic 1959-60)★★★, with Earl 'Fatha' Hines *Swingin' Away* (Black Lion 1973)★★★.

RYCE, DARYLE

b. *c*.1954, Spartanburg, South Carolina, USA. After taking piano lessons as a child, Ryce tried various other instruments but it was as a singer that she entered the music business. She first worked professionally in Toledo, Ohio, singing to her own piano and guitar accompaniment. She worked on the Midwest club circuit for some years and while in Charlotte, North Carolina, was heard by pianist-arranger-composer-broadcaster Loonis McGlohon. Guided by McGlohon, Ryce refined her vocal style and began recording. Although Ryce consciously avoids stylistic influences, she admires singers such as Ella Fitzgerald, Betty Carter and Cleo Laine, while the writing and playing of James Taylor and Joni Mitchell have also made their mark. With a strong and liquid vocal sound, Ryce's performances of slow and medium tempo ballads are particularly attractive, and she always sings with an underlying swing.

● ALBUMS: *I Walk With Music* (Audiophile 1980)★★★, *Unless It's You* (Audiophile 1995)★★.

RYPDAL, TERJE

b. 23 August 1947, Oslo, Norway. The son of a nationally famous conductor, Rypdal had piano lessons as a child, but taught himself the electric guitar. Studying composition at Oslo University, he also studied George Russell's theories of improvisation with Russell himself, and then played in his big band and sextet. In the late 60s he began to collaborate with Jan Garbarek, and played on Garbarek's first two albums for ECM Records; but he received more exposure in the 1969 German Free Jazz Festival, playing with musicians from the burgeoning Chicago free jazz scene in a band led by Lester Bowie. Forming Odyssey in the 70s, Rypdal, now recording, also began touring, which he has continued strenuously ever since. Odyssey made a highly successful tour that included the USA, and since then he has made annual appearances at the major European jazz festivals, leading a trio in the mid-80s with Bjorn Kjellemyr and Audun Kleive, and performing with Palle Mikkelborg in Norway. Rypdal is making an important contribution to the European genre. Writing for orchestra as well as jazz ensemble, he is noted for his system of bowing the guitar in the manner of violin. On *If Mountains Could Sing* the violin is featured strongly, not by the guitarist but by Terje Tonnesen, Lars Anders Tomter and Oystein Birkland. It is, however, in rolling and uplifting pieces such as 'The Return Of Per Ulv' that Rypdal is renowned.

● ALBUMS: *What Comes After* (ECM 1974)★★, with Jan Garbarek *Afric Pepperbird* (ECM 1974)★★★, *Odyssey* (ECM 1975)★★★, *Whenever I Seem To Be Far Away* (ECM 1975)★★★, *After The Rain* (ECM 1976)★★★, *Waves* (ECM 1978)★★★, *To Be Continued* (ECM 1981)★★★, *Eos* (ECM 1984)★★★, *Chaser* (ECM 1985)★★★, *Sunrise* (1985)★★★, *Terje Rypdal/Miroslav Vitous/Jack DeJohnette* (ECM 1985)★★★★, *Descendre* (ECM 1986)★★★, *Blue* (ECM 1987)★★★, *The Singles Collection* (ECM 1989)★★★, *Undisonus* (1990)★★★, *Q.E.D.* (1993)★★★, *If Mountains Could Sing* (ECM 1995)★★★★, *Skywards* (ECM 1997)★★★★.

● COMPILATIONS: *Works* (ECM 1989)★★★.

S.O.S.
(see Skidmore, Alan; Osborne, Mike; Surman, John)

SAFRANSKI, EDDIE
b. 25 December 1918, Pittsburgh, Pennsylvania, USA, d. 10 January 1974. Safranski first played bass in high school but was in his early 20s before he joined a name band, that led by Hal McIntyre, with whom he played for four years, departing in 1945 to join a small group led by Miff Mole. Later that year he joined Stan Kenton and, from 1948, spent about a year with Charlie Barnet. From then onwards, a handful of jazz engagements apart, Safranski was mostly engaged in studio work in New York, teaching and working for a company that manufactured musical instruments. A powerful player with a good sense of the swing style, his bass playing with Kenton's band was exemplary.

● ALBUMS: with Stan Kenton *The Kenton Era (1940-53)* (1955)★★★★, *Stan Kenton's Greatest Hits (1943-51)* (1983)★★★★, *Loaded* (1946)★★★.

SALUZZI, DINO
b. Timoteo Saluzzi, 20 May 1935, Campo Santa, Argentina. Saluzzi was born into a family of folk musicians, and was taught bandoneon by his father. A bandoneon is an accordian used primarily for playing the tango, a style in which he is widely acknowledged as the leader. Despite subsequent classical training and forays into *avant garde* composition, 'Dino' Saluzzi insists that these folk roots are the most crucial ingredient in his music, his particular variety of impressionistic tango frequently making use of chants and percussive effects. At home, he is best known as the leader of his experimental chamber music group Musica Creativa, while in Europe his reputation is based upon his solo concerts and his collaborations with jazz musicians. Saluzzi has worked with Gato Barbieri, Enrico Rava, Louis Sclavis, Charlie Haden, the George Gruntz Concert Jazz Band, and Edward Vesala's Sound & Fury.

● ALBUMS: *Kultrum* (ECM 1983)★★, *Once Upon A Time - Far Away In The South* (ECM1986)★★★, *Andina* (ECM 1988)★★★, *Cité De La Musique* (ECM 1997)★★★★.

SALVADOR, SAL
b. 21 November 1925, Monson, Massachusetts, USA. Like so many other guitarists, Salvador was inspired by Charlie Christian and, by the late 40s, was making an impact on the New York scene. Briefly working with Stan Kenton in the early 50s, Salvador then worked mostly in small groups but formed a big band of his own late in the decade. After spending many years working in studios and teaching, with only occasional recording dates, Salvador returned to the jazz scene in the late 70s, making records with artists such as Billy Taylor, Mel Lewis and Eddie Bert and leading his own band.

● ALBUMS: *The Sal Salvador Quartet/Quintet* (1953)★★★, *Boo Boo Be Doop* (1954)★★★★, *The Sal Salvador Quartet* (1956)★★★, *A Tribute To The Greats* (1957)★★, *Colors In Sound* (1958)★★★, *Sal Salvador And His Orchestra* (1960)★★, *The Sal Salvador Quartet* ii (1963)★★★, *Starfingers* (1978)★★★, *Parallelogram* (1978)★★★, *Juicy Lucy* (1978)★★★, *In Your Own Sweet Way* (1982)★★★, *The World's Greatest Jazz Standards* (1983)★★, *Sal Salvador Plays Gerry Mulligan/Bernie's Tune* (1984)★★★, *Sal Salvador And Crystal Image* (1989)★★★.

SALVATORE, SERGIO
b. 3 March 1981, Ringwood, New Jersey, USA. Taught piano by his father, Luciano Salvatore, a music teacher who had studied at the Berklee College Of Music with Gary Burton, Sergio Salvatore began performing in public at the age of four. Influenced by jazzmen such as Chick Corea and Keith Jarrett, he quickly attracted attention with his mainstream-orientated style. Soon, however, his interests expanded into contemporary areas of jazz and other forms of popular music. On *Point Of Presence*, on which he was joined by Michael Brecker, Bob Mintzer, Steve Gadd and others, elements of classic rock were rubbing shoulders, not always comfortably, with jazz. Making value judgements on an artist of his age is always speculative, but his precocious talent, allied as it is to a developing commitment to composing original material, suggests that Salvatore is here to stay. Certainly, his solo performances display intelligence and a powerful musical personality.

● ALBUMS: *Sergio Salvatore* (GRP 1993)★★★, *Tune Up* (GRP 1994)★★★, *Always A Beginning* (Concord Jazz 1996)★★★, *Point Of Presence* (N2K Encoded Music 1997)★★★.

SAMPLE, JOE
b. 1 February 1939, Houston, Texas, USA. While still at high school, Sample co-founded a group that would dominate his working life. Known from 1960 as the Jazz Crusaders, the band, with its core of Sample on piano, Wayne Henderson, Wilton Felder and Nesbert 'Stix' Hooper, produced a series of popular albums that helped to define the term 'soul jazz'. A change of name, to the Crusaders, led to a change of direction in 1972, with increasing emphasis on a soul and funk repertoire. Sample stayed with the group throughout the 70s and, in a number of re-formations, into the 80s, but throughout these periods, Sample and the other group members have maintained independent careers. Sample worked as an accompanist with the Bobby Hutcherson/Harold Land quintet in 1967 and during the late 60s became a regular Motown session musician, working with artists such as Diana Ross and the Jackson Five. Further session work in Hollywood studio bands followed until, in the early 70s, Sample joined Tom Scott's group LA Express, an experience that led to

more session work for many pop and folk musicians, notably Joni Mitchell. Recent interest in jazz funk of the early 70s has introduced the Crusaders to a new audience in the mid-90s, and Sample continues to produce solo works with great success. As a writer Sample's partnership with Will Jennings has been particularly fruitful. Together they wrote 'Street Life' and 'One Day I'll Fly Away' for Randy Crawford, and further collaborations have produced three albums of material for B.B. King.

● ALBUMS: as the Joe Sample Trio *Fancy Dance* (Gazell 1969)★★★, *Rainbow Seeker* (MCA 1978)★★★, *Carmel* (MCA 1979)★★, *Fancy Dance* (Sonet 1979)★★, *Voices In The Rain* (MCA 1981)★★, with David T Walker *Swing Street Cafe* (MCA 1982)★★★, *The Hunter* (MCA 1983)★★★, *Oasis* (MCA 1985)★★★, *Spellbound* (Warners 1989)★★★, *Ashes To Ashes* (Warners 1990)★★★, *Roles* (MCA 1992)★★★, *Invitation* (Warners 1993)★★★, *Did You Feel That?* (Warners 1994)★★, *Old Places Old Faces* (Warners 1996)★★★, *Sample This* (Warners 1997)★★★.

● COMPILATIONS: *Joe Sample Collection* (GRP 1991)★★★.

SAMPSON, EDGAR

b. 31 August 1907, New York City, New York, USA, d. 16 January 1973. One of the outstanding arrangers in big band jazz, Sampson played alto saxophone and violin in a number of bands during the 20s and 30s, including those led by Duke Ellington, Rex Stewart and Fletcher Henderson, but his most notable period was a two-year spell with Chick Webb that began in 1934. Apart from writing many excellent arrangements of popular songs for the Webb band he also composed several tunes that became jazz standards, among them 'Stompin' At The Savoy', 'Don't Be That Way' (later adopted by Benny Goodman as his theme tune), 'If Dreams Come True' and 'Blue Lou'. After leaving Webb he continued to write for him and several other bandleaders, including Goodman, Artie Shaw and Teddy Wilson. He also resumed playing occasionally, sometimes on alto and also on tenor and baritone saxophones. He briefly led his own big band in the late 40s and early 50s, forming small groups thereafter. Although often overlooked in accounts of the development of big band arranging, Sampson's work was always of the very highest standard and bears favourable comparison with that of the better-known arrangers of the period. In the 50s and early 60s he showed his versatility by writing for Tito Puente and several other currently popular Latin bands.

● ALBUMS: *Swing Softly Sweet Sampson* (Jasmine 1956)★★★.

SAMUELS, DAVE

b. 9 October 1948, Waukegan, Illinois, USA. Samuels played the drums from the age of six. While pursuing a degree in psychology at Boston University in 1971, he studied vibes with Gary Burton and went on to teach at the Berklee College of Music (1971-74). He moved to New York in 1974 and worked with Gerry Mulligan for three years as well as starting the group Timepiece. In the late 70s he worked and recorded with Frank Zappa and the group Double Image, with which he toured Europe. He taught workshops at the Manhattan School of Music and played in a group called Gallery with Michael DiPasqua, Paul McCandless and David Darling. Throughout this period he had an increasing involvement with Spyro Gyra, becoming a full member in 1986 and staying until the mid-90s. Samuels has released several sessions as leader, and currently works with clarinetist Paquito D'Rivera and steel drummer Andy Narrell as co-leader of the Carribean Jazz Project.

● ALBUMS: with Double Image *Double Image* (Enja 1977)★★★, with Gallery *Gallery* (1981)★★, *Ten Degrees North* (MCA 1989)★★, *Natural Selection* (GRP 1991)★★★, *Del Sol* (GRP 1992)★★★, *Tjader-Ized: A Cal Tjader Tribute* (Verve 1998)★★★.

SANBORN, DAVID

b. 30 July 1945, Tampa, Florida, USA. Sanborn's virtuosity has now spanned four decades, taking him from being a band member (with the seminal Paul Butterfield) to a leading session player for artists such as David Bowie, James Taylor and Stevie Wonder. His is the alto saxophone solo on Bowie's 'Young Americans'. He grew up in St. Louis and played with some of the finest Chicago school bluesmen, including Albert King. Nowadays, under his own name, Sanborn records and performs regularly. His blistering alto saxophone style competes somewhere between Junior Walker and Dick Heckstall-Smith. and is all the more remarkable because for many years as a child he suffered from polio and had breathing difficulties. Sanborn does not flirt with his instrument; he blows it hard. His solo debut was in 1975 with *Taking Off*. Over the next decade he produced a series of albums that were all successful, and won a Grammy for *Voyeur*. In 1985, *A Change Of Heart* proved to be a big hit in the jazz charts, although much of it was in the rock style, notably the unrelenting and powerful 'Tintin' along with the pure funk of 'High Roller'. *Close Up* featured a sensitive (though raucous) reading of the Diana Ross and Marvin Gaye hit 'You Are Everything'. In 1991 Sanborn made his first ever 'pure jazz album' and achieved the esteem of the jazz reviewers. *Another Hand* and more recently *Pearls* have lifted Sanborn to the peak of his already lengthy career. The latter album was lodged at the top of the *Billboard* Jazz chart for many weeks in 1995.

● ALBUMS: *Taking Off* (Warners 1975)★★, *Sanborn* (Warners 1976)★★, *David Sanborn Band* (1977)★★★, *Heart To Heart* (Warners 1978)★★★, *Hideaway* (Warners 1980)★★★, *Voyeur* (Warners 1981)★★★, *As We Speak* (Warners 1982)★★★, *Backstreet* (Warners 1983)★★★, *Let It Speak* (Warners 1984)★★★, *Love And Happiness* (1984)★★★, *Straight To The Heart* (Warners 1985)★★★★, with Bob James *Double Vision* (Warners 1986)★★★, *A Change Of Heart* (Warners 1987)★★★, *Close Up* (Reprise 1988)★★★, *Another Hand* (Elektra 1991)★★★★, *Upfront* (Elektra 1992)★★★, *Hearsay* (Elektra 1993)★★★, *Pearls* (Elektra Musician 1995)★★★★, *Love Songs* (Warners 1995)★★★, *Songs From The Night Before* (Warners 1996)★★★.

● COMPILATIONS: *The Best Of David Sanborn* (Warners 1996)★★★★.

SANCHEZ, DAVID

b. 1969, Puerto Rico. Starting out as a percussionist in a Latin band with his brother, Sanchez took up the saxophone at the age of 12. By the time he was 15 he had begun taking the tenor saxophone more seriously and was also hearing jazz, on record, and liking it. He listened to Miles Davis, Dexter Gordon and Sonny Rollins. When Sanchez was 16 he visited New York on holiday, buying more records, and eventually reached a standard in his own playing to allow him to join Kenny Burrell's quartet. From there he moved to Dizzy Gillespie's small group, then his big band. Sanchez's Latin music background, which includes working with musicians such as Claudio Roditi, Charlie Sepulveda and Eddie Palmieri, allied to the Latin-influenced jazz of Gillespie, has ensured that this rising young musician has been able to retain the musical traditions of his national heritage and to incorporate them with insight and integrity into jazz. In his listening he has extended backwards, to Lester Young, Don Byas and others, and forward to musicians of his own generation. He is also writing much of his own music, drawing from many sources. As he told *Jazz Journal International*'s Derek Ansell, 'What I have in mind is trying to develop in composition and working in the two cultures (jazz and Latin).' From its origins, jazz has regularly drawn from Latin music and with Sanchez it is clear that the influence will continue in the twenty-first century.

● ALBUMS: *The Departure* (Columbia 1994)★★★, *Sketches Of Dreams* (Columbia 1995)★★, *Street Scenes* (Columbia 1996)★★★, *Obsession* (Columbia 1998)★★★★.

SANDERS, MARK

b. 31 August 1960, Beckenham, Kent, England. A self-taught drummer who combines power with agility and precision, Sanders began his career playing with a disco band at UK American Air Force bases. He turned to jazz in 1984, studying with Will Evans who, along with Elvin Jones and Tony Oxley, was a major influence. His first jazz engagements were with Lyn Dobson, Stu Brown, Pete Nu and Elton Dean. In 1987 he joined Mervyn Afrika's Kaap Finale and formed a duo with Phil Durrant. Since 1988 he has played in duos and trios with Evan Parker, and has often worked with bassist Paul Rogers. He and Rogers have provided an intense and versatile rhythm section for Atlas (with John Law on piano), Parker, Dennis Gonzalez and the Elton Dean Trio. He has recently been working with Jon Lloyd and Spirit Level, and was part of the Paul Rogers Sextet which toured Britain in 1990 with the Arts Council-commissioned Anglo American Sketches. He has also played with Dreamtime (with Nick Evans), Dick Heckstall-Smith's DHSS, and in a quartet with Peter Cusack, Clive Bell and Dean Broderick.

● ALBUMS: with Atlas *Trio Improvisations* (1989)★★★, with Spirit Level *New Year* (1990)★★★, with Elton Dean/Howard Riley Quartet *All The Tradition* (1991)★★★★, with Jon Lloyd *Syzygy* (1991)★★★, with John Adams, Paul Dunmall *Ghostly Thoughts* (hatOLOGY 1997)★★★.

SANDERS, PHAROAH

b. 13 October 1940, Little Rock, Arkansas, USA. By the time he left high school Sanders was proficient on several instruments, but eventually chose the tenor saxophone. After working in R&B bands he settled in New York in the early 60s where he became a frequent musical associate of Don Cherry, Albert Ayler and others active in the 'free jazz' movement and worked for a while in the Sun Ra Arkestra. For a couple of years beginning in 1965, he worked frequently with John Coltrane, playing on several influential recording dates during the period when Coltrane was extending the boundaries he had previously breached with his music. Sanders' playing with Coltrane was marked by a ferocious tone which sometimes growled, sometimes screeched and, within a limited range, he shaped intriguing and often adventurous phrases. In 1968, he played with the Jazz Composer's Orchestra led by Michael Mantler and Carla Bley.

In his mid-career Sanders rarely extended the format of his earlier popular success and many of his 70s and 80s records were curious and unsuccessful mixtures of jazz, strings and vocals that offered fairly banal paeans to peace and love. In the late 80s, he reverted to a more purely instrumental jazz and was later a familiar figure at international festivals, playing in a style that displayed a clear understanding of bebop and hinted only occasionally at his earlier espousal of the sometimes less accessible aspects of the freedom principle. His two records for Verve Records were produced by Bill Laswell.

● ALBUMS: *Pharoah's First* (ESP 1965)★★★, *Tauhid* (Impulse! 1967)★★★, *Karma* (MCA 1968)★★★, *Izipho Zam* (Strata-East 1969)★★★, *Jewels Of Thought* (Impulse! 1969)★★★, *Sumnen, Bukmen, Umyun* (Impulse! 1970)★★★, *Thembi* (Impulse! 1972)★★★, *Black Unity* (Impulse! 1972)★★★, *Love In Us All* (ASD 1974)★★★, *Beyond A Dream* (Arista 1978)★★★, *Rejoice* (Evidence 1981)★★★, *Pharoah Sanders Live* (1982)★★, *Heart Is A Melody* (Evidence 1982)★★★, *Oh Lord Let Me Do No Wrong* (Doctor Jazz 1987)★★★, *Quartet Africa* (Timeless 1987)★★★, *A Prayer Before Dawn* (Evidence 1989)★★, *Moon Child* (Timeless 1989)★★★, *Welcome To Love* (Timeless 1990)★★★, *Shukuru* (Evidence 1992)★★★, *Ed Kelly & Pharoah Sanders* (1993)★★★, *Crescent With Love* (Evidence 1993)★★★★, *Message From Home* (Verve 1996)★★★, *Save Our Children* (Verve 1998)★★★.

SANDKE, RANDY

b. *c.*1955, Chicago, Illinois, USA. Sandke took an early interest in jazz and began playing trumpet, studying under Frank Tirro at a small private school in Chicago. He played in the school band which at the time included trombonists George Lewis and Ray Anderson. Sandke also wrote music which stood him in good stead when he suffered serious throat problems necessitating surgery. He continued to work in music, employed by ASCAP and also played guitar and piano. In 1980 he was persuaded to resume playing trumpet and he also returned to studying, taking more care with his technique in order to avoid a recurrence of his throat problems. In the early 80s he toured extensively, including playing in bands led by Peanuts Hucko and Bob Wilber. As a child he had been attracted to the jazz of Louis Armstrong and Bix Beiderbecke but by the time of his resumption he was intrigued by trumpeters such as Clifford Brown. Sandke's repertoire has expanded to incorporate these wide-ranging musical forms and he happily teams up with Ken Peplowski or Michael Brecker, Anderson or Danny Moss. Sandke is also interested in classical music and has written in this form but with jazz overtones. Among his works in this hybrid idiom are 'The Mystic Trumpeter', a suite in seven parts, 'When Worlds Collide', 'Symphony For Six' and 'Fugue State'. His jazz heritage allows him to integrate himself and his playing fully into the ethos of the past while retaining a firm sense of the present. In addition to Wilber's Bechet Legacy band he has also worked in the Buck Clayton Legacy band, and is perhaps at his best and happiest-sounding when working with musicians from the mainstream, especially those of his own generation such as Harry Allen, Antti Sarpilâ and Dan Barrett.

● ALBUMS: *The Sandke Brothers* (Stash 1986), *The Stampede* (Jazzology 1990)★★★, *I Hear Music* (Concord 1992)★★★, *Get Happy* (Concord 1993)★★★, *The Bix Beiderbecke Era* (Nagel-Heyer 1993)★★, *The Chase* (Concord 1994)★★★, *Wild Cats* (Jazzology 1994)★★, *Broadway* (Nagel-Heyer 1994)★★★, *I Hear Music* (Concord 1994)★★★, *Get Happy* (Concord 1995)★★★★, *Calling All Cats* (Concord Jazz 1996)★★★, with Harry Allen *The Music Of The Trumpet Kings* (Nagel-Heyer 1998)★★★, *The Awakening* (Concord 1998)★★★★.

Sandoval, Arturo

b. 6 November 1949, Artemisa, Havana, Cuba. Starting out as a student of classical trumpet, Sandoval quickly turned to jazz and during the 70s attracted worldwide attention not only for the technical brilliance of his playing but also through the exhilarating Latin influence of his work. He was a founding member of the Cuban Orchestra Of Modern Music, which evolved into Irakere. This band performed to great acclaim, winning a Grammy in 1979. After leaving Irakere in 1981, Sandoval led his own bands and appeared as a soloist at festivals and major venues around the world. In July 1990 he defected to America during a European tour. Although mostly engaged in jazz he has also pursued his early interest in the classical form through performances with symphony orchestras in the USA, UK, France and Russia, recording his own 'Concerto For Trumpet' with the London Symphony Orchestra for BMG/RCA Records in 1994. He has also appeared with pop artists, including Celine Dion, Tony Bennett, Patti LaBelle, Frank Sinatra, Paul Anka and Johnny Mathis. Apart from performing at concerts and festivals, Sandoval has long been deeply involved in education. He conducts classes and clinics at universities and colleges, including Florida International University. He serves on several committees, including the Chicago Symphony Orchestra Educational Committee and is active in the Grammy in the Schools Program. He has also been involved in the publication of trumpet tutors. His jazz work has included spells with Dizzy Gillespie's United Nations Orchestra and appearances with many leading jazz artists, including Woody Herman, Stan Getz, Woody Shaw, Billy Cobham and Herbie Hancock. His jazz albums have been applauded by critics and public alike, winning a Grammy for *Danzón*. This album and the subsequent *The Latin Train* also won *Billboard* Awards. As can happen with virtuoso musicians, Sandoval's astonishing technique and his sometimes spectacular playing has occasionally caused less perceptive critics to overlook his deep rooted commitment to the importance of earlier jazz musicians and, in particular, the trumpet giants. Indeed, even when playing at extravagantly fast tempos the clear articulation of his solo lines demonstrates an artist in complete command of his physical, mental and emotional capacities. Although much of his jazz work is developed out of the hard bop school, the older traditions of the form are seldom far from the surface and his love for and understanding of Latin music adds colour and excitement to performances already vivid and exhilarating. In addition to the trumpet Sandoval also plays the flügelhorn and is an excellent pianist, an instrument to which he brings an understated lyricism that contrasts starkly with his bravura brass playing. In addition to composing jazz, Latin and classical music he has also written scores for motion pictures.

● ALBUMS: *Breaking The Sound Barrier* (Chicago Caribbean Art 1985)★★★, with Dizzy Gillespie *Arturo Sandoval And His Group With Dizzy Gillespie* (Egrem 1985)★★★, *Tumbaito* (Messidor 1986)★★★, *No Problem* (Ronnie Scott's Jazz House 1987)★★★, *Arturo Sandoval Plays For The Pandas* (Cocoral 1987)★★★, *Arturo Sandoval En Concierto Vols. 1 & 2* (Egrem 1987)★★★, *Songs From Europe* (Cocoral 1988)★★★, with Chucho Valdes *Straight Ahead* (Ronnie Scott's Jazz House 1988)★★★★, *Flight To Freedom* (GRP 1991)★★★★, *I Remember Clifford* (GRP 1992)★★★★, *Dream Come True* (GRP 1993)★★★, *Danzón (Dance On)* (GRP 1994)★★★★, *The Latin Train* (GRP 1995)★★★★, *Swingin'* (GRP 1996)★★★★, *Just Music* 1988 recording (Jazz House 1996)★★★ *Hot House* (N2K 1997)★★★.

Sangster, John

b. 17 November 1928, Melbourne, Australia. Sangster started off playing the trombone but switched to trumpet when he appeared in trad bands in 1948. In 1950, he learned enough about drumming to be able to tour overseas with Graeme Bell's band. His interests have become increasingly progressive and he worked with Don Banks in the 60s playing at the Expos in Montreal and Tokyo. He now plays the vibraphone and marimbaphone and sees himself principally as a composer. *The Hobbit Suite* is typical of his eclectic style, mixing hummable tunes with highly abstract or impressionistic passages. It has been followed by an eight-album set, *Lord Of The Rings*, as well as tribute works to Bix Beiderbecke and Duke Ellington. Film producers have been attracted by his colourful style and he has written numerous film scores including *Fluteman* (1982).

● ALBUMS: *Conjurman* (1967)★★★, *Australia & All That Jazz* (1971)★★, *The Hobbit Suite* (1973)★★★, *Lord Of The Rings* (1974)★★★★.

SANTAMARÍA, MONGO

b. Ramón Santamaría, 7 April 1927, Jesús María district, Havana, Cuba. 'Mongo stands for integrity, both personal and musical, throughout almost half a century in a mad, bad and dangerous to blow business. He, as much as any other individual, is responsible for whatever wider familiarity with the music exists today. Mambo, charanga, salsafunk, jazzlatino - he has brought taste, swing and sass to them all, his modesty alone denying the widest acclaim' (Tomek). Santamaría arrived in New York at the end of the 40s. There he performed with the first charanga (flute, violins, rhythm section and voices band) to be organized in the city, led by Gilberto Valdés (b. Matanzas Province, Cuba; multi-instrumentalist, composer), Pérez Prado (for a brief stint) and Tito Puente (between 1951 and 1957). In 1955 Mongo recorded *Changó* (aka *Drums And Chants*), an album of roots Afro Cuban music featuring the Cuban percussionists Silvestre Méndez (b. Jesús María district, Havana, Cuba; bongo, composer), Carlos 'Patato' Valdez and Julito Collazo. In 1991, Mongo commented: '*Changó* is the best album recorded in the USA, within that genre, and much better than *Yambú* and other albums which I recorded later for Fantasy Records' (quote from an interview with Luis Tamargo published in *Latin Beat* magazine). As Puente's conguero, Santamaría enjoyed celebrity status in the Latino community. However, in 1957 he and two other Puente sidemen, percussionist Willie Bobo and bassist Bobby Rodríguez, provoked the bandleader's wrath when they were credited as performers on *Más Ritmo Caliente* by Latin jazz vibes player Cal Tjader. Hurt by Puente's response, Mongo and Bobo informed Tjader of their intention to leave. Cal could not believe his luck, and offered to hire them. Early the following year, they both joined him in San Francisco. During their three-year tenure, Santamaría and Bobo contributed significantly to Tjader's sound on a string of classic albums recorded for Fantasy Records, and through their association with Cal, they attained more widespread fame.

Santamaría was still with Tjader when he recorded the Afro Cuban sets *Yambú* and *Mongo* on Fantasy. The second contained his hit composition 'Afro Blue', which became a much covered jazz standard. In 1960, Mongo and Willie took time out to visit Cuba, where they recorded the progressive típico album *Our Man In Havana* with local musicians, including the legendary tres guitarist, arranger and composer Niño Rivera and teenage pianist Paquito Echavarría. The latter relocated to Miami and worked there with bassist Israel 'Cachao' López. In 1961, Santamaría left Tjader (taking Bobo with him) to inherit former personnel from Armando Sánchez's Chicago-based charanga Orquesta Nuevo Ritmo (whose only album was 1960's *The Heart Of Cuba*), including violinist and composer Pupi Legarreta, flautist and composer Rolando Lozano, pianist René 'El Flaco' Hernández, vocalist and composer Rudy Calzado and bassist Victor Venegas (a good friend of Mongo who remained with him until the late 60s). Santamaría added the incredible violinist and tenor saxophonist José 'Chombo' Silva and others to form his own charanga, which debuted on the excellent *Sabroso!*. On this and his other charanga releases on Fantasy, including one with pianist Joe Loco, Mongo successfully managed to infuse the traditional Cuban flute and strings framework with jazz idioms.

In 1962, Santamaría returned to New York, leaving Bobo in San Francicso (however, Willie rejoined him later on for a brief spell). Mongo put together a Latin fusion (although this nomenclature did not exist then) group with a view to securing a contract with Riverside Records. He succeeded and debuted on the label with *Go, Mongo!*. At the end of 1962, Santamaría recorded the crowd-pleaser 'Watermelon Man', written by keyboardist Herbie Hancock, who performed with Mongo's group that year. With negligible promotion, the single became a Top 10 hit in 1963. The song's R&B/jazz/Latin cocktail pretty much set Santamaría's stylistic compass for the rest of his career. After a few more albums on Riverside, he continued in the Latin fusion vein into the 90s with a string of releases on the Columbia, Atlantic, Vaya, Pablo, Roulette, Tropical Budda and Concord Picante labels. 1977's *Dawn (Amanecer)*, his sixth release on Vaya, won a Grammy Award, becoming the first album from the Fania Records stable to receive the accolade.

From the mid-60s, Santamaría only rarely diverted from his fusion path to record typical Latin albums such as *El Bravo* and the Justo Betancourt collaboration *Ubane*. During his career as a bandleader, Mongo hired and developed such notable artists as Chick Corea, La Lupe, Hubert Laws, Marty Sheller and others. Sheller began his long association with Santamaría as a trumpeter on 1963's *Watermelon Man*. He switched to percussion because of a problem with his lower lip, then increasingly concentrated on arranging, composing, musical direction and production. Marty worked with various salsa names, including Willie Colón, Tito Puente, Conjunto Libre, Louie Ramírez, Roberto Torres and Conjunto Clásico.

● ALBUMS: with Tito Puente's rhythm section, featuring Willie Bobo, Carlos 'Patato' Valdez *Puente In Percussion* (1955)★★★★, *Changó* (1955)★★★★, reissued as *Drums And Chants* in 1978, with Cal Tjader *Más Ritmo Caliente* (1957)★★★★, *Yambú* (1958)★★★, with Tjader *Cal Tjader's Latin Concert* (1958)★★★, *A Night At The Blackhawk* (1959)★★★, with Tjader *Tjader Goes Latin* (1959)★★★★, *Mongo* (1959)★★★, with Tjader *Concert By The Sea, Volumes 1 & 2* (1959)★★★★, reissued as *Monterey Concerts*, *Concert On The Campus* (1960)★★★, *Our Man In Havana* (1960)★★, with Tjader *Demasiado Caliente* (1960)★★★, *Live And Direct* (1960))★★★, with Joe Loco *Pachanga con Joe Loco*, *Arriba! La Pachanga* (1962)★★★, *Más Sabroso* (1962)★★★, *Viva Mongo!* (1962)★★★, *Go, Mongo!* (1962)★★★, *Watermelon Man* (1963)★★★★, with La Lupe *Mongo Introduces La Lupe* (1963)★★★, aka *Mongo y La Lupe*, *Mongo At The Village Gate* (1963)★★★, *Mongo Explodes* (1964)★★★, *El Pussy Cat*

(1965)★★, *La Bamba* (1965)★★★★, *Hey! Let's Party* (1966)★★★, *El Bravo!* (1966)★★★, *Mongo Santamaría Explodes At The Village Gate* (1967)★★, *Soul Bag* (1968)★★★, *Stone Soul* (1969)★★★, *Workin' On A Groovy Thing* (1969)★★★, *Feelin' Alright* (1970)★★, *Mongo '70* (1970)★★, *Mongo At Montreux* (Atlantic 1971)★★★★, *Mongo Santamaría At Yankee Stadium* (1974)★★★, with the Fania All Stars *Latin-Soul-Rock* (1974)★★★, *Live At Yankee Stadium, Voume. 2* (1975)★★, with Justo Betancourt *Ubane* (1976)★★★, *Dawn (Amanacer)* (1977)★★★, with Bob James, Charlie Palmieri *Red Hot* (1979)★★, with Dizzy Gillespie, Toots Thielemans *'Summertime' Digital At Montreux* 1980 (1981)★★, the Ensemble of Latin Music Legends featuring Palmieri, José 'Chombo' Silva, Barry Rogers, Johnny 'Dandy' Rodriguez, Nicky Marrero *Mambo Show* (1990)★★★★, *Live At Jazz Alley* (1990)★★★, *Mongo Returns* (Milestone 1995)★★★, *Brazilian Sunset* (Candid 1996)★★★, with Poncho Sanchez *Conga Blue* (Concord Picante 1996)★★★, *Afro Blue* (Concord Picante 1998)★★★★.

● COMPILATIONS: with Tjader *Latino* (1965)★★★★, *Mongo's Greatest Hits* (1987)★★★★, *Mongo's Groove* (1987)★★★, *Mongo Santamaría's Greatest Hits, Mongo Mongo* (1978)★★★★, *Afro Roots* (1972)★★★★, combined *Yambú* and *Mongo, The Watermelon Man* (1973)★★★★, combined *Watermelon Man* and *Mongo At The Village Gate, Skins* (1976)★★★★, combined *Go, Mongo!* and *Mongo Explodes*.

SARGENT, KENNY

(see Casa Loma Orchestra; Steele, Blue)

SARMANTO, HEIKKI

b. 22 June 1939, Helsinki, Finland. Sarmanto studied languages and music at Helsinki University and Sibelius Academy before going on to the Berklee College of Music (1968-71). He was named the best pianist at Montreux in 1971. He led his own bands from 1962 and in 1976 a workshop group he ran became the big band UMO. He has written *New Hope Jazz Mass*, a jazz ballet and a jazz opera, and was chosen by saxophonist Sonny Rollins to arrange and orchestrate his *Saxophone Concerto* (1986). He continues to write vocal, orchestral and theatre works in a most assured style.

● ALBUMS: *Suomi* (1983)★★★.

SARPILÅ, ANTTI

b. Sweden. A brilliantly gifted clarinettist and saxophonist, Sarpilå has established a strong reputation throughout Europe. He made a great impact with his appearance at the 1988 Duke Ellington Convention, held that year in England, where he appeared as a soloist and section member in the orchestra directed by Bob Wilber. Sarpilå plays in the clarinet tradition of which Benny Goodman was the founding father and he blends technical mastery with a strong feeling for the music of the swing era. His solo style is fluid, demanding and always filled with interesting, flawlessly executed ideas.

● ALBUMS: *Hot Time In Umeå: A Tribute To Benny Goodman* (1993)★★★, with Allan Vaché *Swing Is Here* (Nagel-Heyer 1995)★★★, with Ken Peplowski, Vaché *Summit Meeting* (Nagel-Heyer 1995)★★★★.

SATCHMO THE GREAT

Made for television by Ed Murrow, this 1956 film follows Louis Armstrong on a tour of Europe and Africa. Intercut with scenes of live performance by Armstrong And His All Stars, and their reception, often by tens of thousands of well-wishers, at airports, are interviews with Armstrong. Although one of the finest and most respected journalists of his, or any other, era, Murrow's questions are sometimes a shade naïve, but Armstrong takes it all in his stride. The film ends with a New York concert performance of 'St Louis Blues' in which Armstrong and his men are joined by Leonard Bernstein and the New York Philharmonic to play to a capacity audience that includes W.C. Handy. One moving moment shows Handy, then over 80, removing his hat to take his handkerchief from his head to mop a tear from his blind eyes. The All Stars featured are Trummy Young, Edmond Hall, Billy Kyle, Jack Lesberg and Barrett Deems with singer Velma Middleton.

SATO, MASAHIKO

b. 6 October 1941, Tokyo, Japan. A child prodigy on violin and piano, Sato played piano with George Kawaguchi while a student, and then, in the mid-60s, pursued his studies in the USA at the Berklee College Of Music. Back in Japan in the late 60s, he led his own small groups, displaying his great virtuosity as player and composer. He also played with visiting American artists including Charles Mingus and Helen Merrill, who was resident in Japan for a number of years during the early 70s. Sato also toured internationally, becoming especially popular in Germany where he played with leading local musicians including Albert Mangelsdorff, and other noted Europeans, such as Attila Zoller. He continued to play at home and abroad through the 80s, with musicians such as Steve Gadd and Art Farmer, and he also continued to develop as a progressive composer and arranger.

● ALBUMS: *Palladium* (Toshiba Express 1969)★★★★, *Samardhi: Masahiko Meets Gary Peacock* (Toshiba Express 1971)★★★, *Kanzigai* (Columbia 1976)★★★, *Brink* (Continental 1983)★★★, with Art Farmer *Maiden Voyage* (Interface 1983)★★★, with John Zorn *Ganryu Island* (Yukon 1985)★★★.

SAUTER, EDDIE

b. 2 December 1914, New York City, New York, USA, d. 21 April 1981. After studying arranging and composition at the Juilliard School of Music, Sauter became staff arranger for Red Norvo. In 1939, after four years with Norvo, he freelanced, writing charts for several prominent big bands, including Artie Shaw's, Woody Herman's and Tommy Dorsey's. He made his greatest impact with Benny Goodman, for whom he wrote 'Clarinet A La King' in the early 40s. He later worked for Ray McKinley where, unusually for an arranger at that time (or any other), he was given prominent billing. While hospitalized with tuberculosis Sauter began corresponding with Bill Finegan and in 1952 the two arrangers formed their own orchestra. The resulting 21-

piece band was conceived as a studio band, but its records, which included the joyous 'The Doodletown Fifers' and the irresistible 'Midnight Sleigh Ride', were so popular that they took it on the road. In 1957, Sauter became musical director of the South-West German Radio Big Band in Baden-Baden. He later worked with Stan Getz, the New York Saxophone Quartet and in films and television.

● ALBUMS: all by Sauter-Finegan Orchestra *New Directions In Music* 10-inch album (RCA Victor 1953)★★★★, *Inside Sauter-Finegan* (RCA Victor 1954)★★★, *The Sound Of Sauter-Finegen* (RCA Victor 1954)★★★, *Sons Of Sauter-Finegan* (RCA Victor 1955)★★★, *Concert Jazz* (RCA Victor 1955)★★★, *New Directions In Music* (RCA Victor 1956)★★★★★, *Adventure In Time* (RCA Victor 1956)★★★, *Under Analysis* (RCA Victor 1957)★★★★, *One Night Stand With The Sauter-Finegan Orchestra* (RCA Victor 1957)★★★, *Straight Down The Middle* (RCA Victor 1957)★★★, *Inside Sauter-Finegan Revisited* (RCA Victor 1961)★★★, *Sleigh Ride* (RCA Victor 1961)★★★★, *The Return Of The Doodletown Fifers* (Capitol 1985)★★★.

Sauter-Finegan Orchestra

(see Sauter, Eddie; Finegan, Bill)

Savoy Records

(see Lubinsky, Herman)

Savoy Sultans

The Savoy Sultans were a highly accomplished US small band (usually nine pieces) led by alto saxophonist/clarinettist Al Cooper. They were formed originally out of a band in which Cooper and trumpeter Pat Jenkins had played at New York's 101 Club and New Jersey's Harlem-on-the-Hudson. The band was heard by John Hammond and Willie Bryant who recommended them to Charles Buchanan, manager of the Savoy Ballroom in New York's Harlem. The band opened at the Savoy on Labor Day 1937, and was an instant success with the Savoy's hyper-critical dancers. The Sultans had excellent soloists in Sam Massenberg (trumpet), George Kelly (tenor saxophone) and Rudy Williams (alto saxophone), and had a fine rhythm section in pianist Cyril Haynes (piano), Grachan Moncur (bass, also Cooper's half-brother and father of trombonist Grachan Moncur III) and Razz Mitchell (drums). Despite its relatively small size and its occasionally rather rudimentary arrangements, the Sultans swung mightily and maintained their popularity, and a remarkably stable personnel, until they broke up in 1946. Stylistically, the Sultans' brand of swinging dance music was slightly aside from that offered by most big bands of the day and had greater affinity with the small jump bands of the same period.

In 1974, David 'Panama' Francis, who had played drums with the Lucky Millinder band in the early 40s, formed a small band modelled on the original Sultans. From the late 70s and on into the 90s, Panama Francis And His Savoy Sultans, which regularly included Kelly in its ranks, revived the spirit of the original band while offering its own exciting brand of swinging jazz music.

Saxophone Colossus - Sonny Rollins

A truly flawless album representing bop at its best, *Saxophone Colossus* is a quartet recording from 1956 led by the great Sonny Rollins on tenor saxophone and featuring pianist Tommy Flanagan, bassist Doug Watkins and drummer Max Roach. The record opens with the original, catchy and rousing version of Rollins' much-loved Caribbean-flavoured standard, 'St. Thomas', and includes a richly emotional 'You Don't Know What Love Is' and a superbly angular, side-long blues entitled 'Blue Seven'. Few musicians ever spoke the bebop language with such consistent inspiration and flair.

● Tracks: *Moritat; Blue Seven; Strode Rode; St. Thomas; You Don't Know What Love Is.*

● First released 1956

● UK peak chart position: did not chart

● USA peak chart position: did not chart

Sayles, Emmanuel

b. Emanuel René Sayles, 31 January 1907, Donaldsonville, Louisiana, USA, d. 5 October 1986. A self-taught player of the banjo and guitar, Sayles had earlier studied formally on violin. He played with various bands in the south and south-east of the USA before moving to New Orleans, where he played with a number of bands, including those led by Fate Marable, Davey Jones-Lee Collins, Armand Piron and Sidney Desvigne. He played in the city through the 30s, then spent the 40s in Chicago, playing in many bands and also leading his own. He returned to New Orleans for most of the 50s and in the 60s travelled widely, playing throughout the USA and in Europe and the Far East with musicians such as George Lewis and Sweet Emma Barrett. He continued to divide his time between New Orleans and international tours during the 70s and into the early 80s, working with numerous leaders including Ernest 'Punch' Miller, Kid Thomas Valentine and Earl 'Fatha' Hines. A drivingly rhythmic player on both instruments. Sayles had a light touch with the banjo and was a delightfully uncomplicated soloist on guitar.

● ALBUMS: with Louis Cottrell Jnr. *Bourbon Street Parade* (Riverside 1961)★★★.

Sbarbaro, Tony

b. 27 June 1897, New Orleans, Louisiana, USA, d. 30 October 1969. After playing drums in several local bands in his home-town, Sbarbaro moved to Chicago where, in 1916, he became a member of the Original Dixieland Jazz Band. In 1925 he took over leadership of the band and was involved in various ODJB recreations and re-formations for much of the next three decades, often playing kazoo as well as drums. Although he did not have the polished jazz technique of his black counterparts from New Orleans, or indeed of some of the better white Dixieland drummers, Sbarbaro (who frequently used the name Tony Spargo) was a lively drummer who brought great enthusiasm to his performances.

SCALA, PRIMO

Primo Scala was a bestseller on Rex records with his Accordion Band but he did not really exist. The name was a pseudonym for musical director/producer Harry Bidgood (b. 1898, London, England, d. 1955), who recorded much anonymous dance music in the 20s and 30s. He was pianist with De Groot's salon orchestra at the Piccadilly Hotel, and recorded on HMV with its offshoot, the Piccadilly Dance Band. When De Groot left the hotel, his light music was replaced by an orthodox dance band with Bidgood as pianist. After visiting Berlin in 1924, where the band recorded for Vox, Bidgood resigned, going to Vocalion Records as recording manager and musical director. He made records with his house band, releasing them on the various Vocalion labels (Aco, Beltona, Guardsman, Broadcast, Coliseum, etc.) under names such as the Midnight Merrymakers, Riverside Dance Band and Kentucky Revellers. In the late 20s his regular pool of musicians included Ted Heath, who played for him at the Ritz Hotel and Ciro's Club. Vocalion dropped all their other labels and concentrated on Broadcast, a more expensive product with a retail price of 2/- (10p). In 1932 the company was taken over by Crystalate, who inaugurated the Imperial, Rex and Eclipse labels, the latter sold by Woolworth's at 6d each (two-and-a-half pence). Bidgood built up an all-accordion band for Imperial as Roma's Accordion Band, whose records were also issued on Eclipse under the name of Don Porto. When he decided Rex too should have some of this music, it was released under the name of Primo Scala's Accordion Band; then Crystalate discontinued Eclipse Records and introduced Crown, another 6d record label, on which Bidgood/Porto/Scala/Roma became Rossini's Accordion Band. Though they were all the same band it was Scala on whom Bidgood concentrated his efforts, taking the band on radio and music-hall tours. In a more musically ambitious and challenging vein he spent part of the World War II years conducting the London Symphony Orchestra in film music in his capacity as Musical director for British Columbia Pictures. He disappeared from the music scene soon afterwards.

● ALBUMS: *Primo Scala And His Accordion Band* (1981)★★★★, *Strike Up The Band* (1983)★★★, *Shoe Shine Boy* (1988)★★★★.

SCATMAN JOHN

b. John Larkin, *c.*1942, USA. One of the more unlikely success stories of the mid-90s, Scatman John is a side-project for jazz singer and pianist John Larkin. Based in Los Angeles, California, USA, he performed widely at festivals and at piano bars throughout the world. Despite his prolific work in jazz, however, it was within the house music tradition that he eventually became a star. He was discovered by Manfred Zähringer, owner of Danish label Iceberg Records, in Frankfurt, Germany, in 1994. Larkin passed him some tapes of his 'bebop poetry' renditions, which impressed the label owner greatly. However, no record label he approached would take seriously the prospect of a 50-year-old jazz pianist improvising scat vocals over a pop dance rhythm. Eventually he found a sympathetic home at BMG Ariola Hamburg and Axel Alexander. He paired Larkin with producers Tony Catania and Ingo Kays, with whom he recorded a single, 'Scatman'. Though sales were slow initially, the single earned repeated plays on mainstream radio and eventually became a massive Europe-wide hit. A remix version was produced by disc jockey Alex Christensen to ensure that the record also appealed to dance club audiences. 'Scatman' eventually sold over 600,000 copies in Germany alone, reaching number 2 in the national charts. It also topped charts in Scandinavia, Austria, Switzerland, France, Belgium, Netherlands, Italy, Spain and Turkey. It peaked at number 3 in the UK charts. A second single, 'Scatman's World', also sold heavily in Europe and preceded the release of a debut album of the same title, by which time the attraction was wearing a little thin for some.

● ALBUMS: *Scatman's World* (BMG 1995)★★★★.

SCHERTZER, HYMIE

(see Shertzer, Hymie)

SCHIFRIN, LALO

b. 21 June 1932, Buenos Aires, Argentina. Schifrin was taught classical piano from the age of six but later studied sociology and law at university. He won a scholarship to the Paris Conservatoire where he studied with Olivier Messiaen. In 1955 he represented Argentina in the Third International Jazz Festival in Paris. He met Dizzy Gillespie first in 1956 when the trumpeter was touring South America. Schifrin had founded the first Argentine big band in the Count Basie tradition and in 1957 wrote his first film music. He moved to New York in 1958 and toured Europe in 1960 with a Jazz At The Philharmonic ensemble, which included Gillespie, with whom he played between 1960 and 1962. He had become increasingly interested in large-scale compositions and wrote two suites for Gillespie - *Gillespiana* and *New Continent*. He worked with Quincy Jones when he left Gillespie, but became more and more involved in scoring for television and feature films including *The Cincinatti Kid* (1965), *Bullitt* (1968), *Dirty Harry* (1971), and the distinctive theme from the television series *Mission Impossible*. His more than 150 scores over a period of nearly 30 years have also included *The Liquidator*, *Cool Hand Luke*, *The Fox*, *Coogan's Bluff*, *Kelly's Heros*, *Hit!*, *Magnum Force*, *Voyage Of The Damned*, *The Eagle Has Landed*, *Rollercoaster*, *The Amityville Horror*, *The Competition*, *The Sting II*, *Hollywood Wives* (television mini-series), *The Fourth Protocol*, *F/X2 - The Deadly Art Of Illusion*, *The Dead Pool*, *Return From The River Kwai*, *A Woman Called Jackie* (1992 television series), and *The Beverly Hillbillies* (1993). He lectured in composition at the University of California, Los Angeles (1968-71), and has spent a good deal of his career searching for common ground between jazz and classical music.

In 1995, he conducted the London Philharmonic Orchestra at London's Festival Hall, in *Jazz Meets The*

Symphony, 'an evening of jazz-symphonic fusion'.

● ALBUMS: *Bossa Nova - New Brazilian Jazz* (Audio Fidelity 1962)★★★, *New Fantasy* (Verve 1966)★★★, *The Dissection And Reconstruction Of Music From The Past As Performed By The Inmates Of Lalo Schiffrin's Demented Ensemble As A Tribute To The Memory Of The Marquis De Sade* (Verve 1966)★★★, *Music From 'Mission: Impossible'* (1967)★★★, *Insensatez* (Verve 1968)★★★, *Towering Toccata* (1977)★★, *Black Widow* (CTI 1976)★★★, *Free Ride* (1979)★★, *Guitar Concerto* (1985)★★, *Anno Domini* (1986)★★, with Jimmy Smith *The Cat Strikes Again* (Verve 1986)★★★, *Jazz Meets The Symphony* (Atlantic 1993)★★★★, *More Jazz Meets The Symphony* (Atlantic 1994)★★★ *Firebird* (Four Winds 1996)★★★, *Gillespiana* (Aleph 1998)★★.

● COMPILATIONS: *Mission: Impossible . . . And More! The Best Of Lalo Schifrin 1962-1972* (Motor 1997)★★★★.

SCHNEIDER, MARIA

b. 27 November 1960, Windom, Minnesota, USA. A highly acclaimed composer, arranger and conductor, Schneider is viewed as a natural successor to Gil Evans and Bob Brookmeyer, two men who played an extensive role in promoting her career. Schneider studied classical theory and composition at the University of Minnesota, before furthering her education at the Eastman School of Music and the University of Miami. Schneider moved to New York in 1985 when she received a National Endowment for the Arts grant to study with Brookmeyer, who helped her to further develop her already extensive writing skills. During this period, Schneider also gained valuable experience as a writer for the Thad Jones-Mel Lewis orchestra. Following her stint with Brookmeyer she was assistant to Evans, working on reorchestration and arranging cues for his soundtrack to the movie *The Color Of Money*. After Evans' death Schneider made her debut as a leader of the Maria Schneider Jazz Orchestra with the melancholy and densely-layered *Evanescence*. Comprising nine original compositions, the Grammy-nominated album featured strong contributions from pianist Kenny Werner, trumpeter Tim Hagans, tenor saxophonists Rick Margitza and Rich Perry and altoist Tim Ries. Schneider followed up with another difficult and multi-layered avant classical recording, *Coming About*, built around the disturbing three part composition 'Scenes From Childhood'. Despite the acclaim she has received for her Jazz Orchestra, Schneider's commission work as a composer and conductor have proved far more lucrative. She has written for the Danish Radio Orchestra, the Dutch Metropole Orchestra and the Orchestre National de Jazz in Paris, and appeared as guest conductor with several leading European and American orchestras.

● ALBUMS: *Evanescence* (Enja 1994)★★★★, *Coming About* (Enja 1996)★★★★.

SCHOEBEL, ELMER

b. 8 September 1896, East St. Louis, Illinois, USA, d. 14 December 1970. His first professional work was as a pianist in silent-movie theatres. By the early 20s he was well known in Chicago where he worked with the New Orleans Rhythm Kings and also led his own band. In New York later in the 20s he played in the Isham Jones band but was also busy as an arranger and composer. He then settled into studio work until the mid-40s when he became active as a pianist in clubs and also continued to write. His compositions and co-compositions include 'Nobody's Sweetheart', 'Prince Of Wails' and two jazz standards, 'Farewell Blues' and 'Bugle Call Rag'.

SCHOOF, MANFRED

b. 6 April 1936, Madgeburg, Germany. This innovative jazz trumpet and flügelhorn player wrote his first arrangements for his school band. From 1955-58 he studied at the Musikakademie at Kassel and from 1958-63 at the Cologne Musikhochschule where he took a course in jazz run by the West German bandleader Kurt Edelhagen. After writing arrangements for Edelhagen's Radio Big Band and touring with Gunter Hampel, he led his own pioneering free jazz quintet in 1965, which included Alex Von Schlippenbach and Gerd Dudek. The quintet later formed the nucleus of the Manfred Schoof Orchestra in 1969, which brought together some of the leading exponents of European improvised music, such as Evan Parker, Derek Bailey, Peter Brötzmann, Irène Schweizer and Han Bennink. Schoof was also a member of George Russell's orchestra from 1969-71. During the 70s and 80s he toured throughout Europe, recording with the New Jazz Trio, the Globe Unity Orchestra, Jasper Van't Hof, Albert Mangelsdorff and others. In 1987, he performed and recorded with the George Gruntz Concert Jazz band in Fort Worth, Texas. Schoof has also composed in a contemporary classical vein, most notably for the Berlin Philharmonic.

● ALBUMS: *The Early Quintet* (1966)★★★, *European Echoes* (1969)★★★, with New Jazz Trio *Alternate Takes* (1970)★★★, with the Globe Unity Orchestra *Pearls* (1975)★★, *Scales* (1977)★★★, *Light Lines* (1977)★★★, with Peter Brötzmann a.o. *In A State Of Undress* (1989)★★★★, *Shadows And Smiles* (Wergo 1989)★★★.

SCHROEDER, GENE

b. 5 February 1915, Madison, Wisconsin, USA, d. 16 February 1975. Schroeder's parents were musicians and, growing up in a musical atmosphere, he learned to play piano at an early age. He continued his studies through high school and university before turning professional. In the late 30s he arrived in New York, where he led his own small bands and also worked with leading jazzmen such as Joe Marsala and Wild Bill Davison. By the early 40s he was a familiar figure at several clubs in Boston, Chicago and New York; this is how he met Eddie Condon, with whom he formed a long-lasting musical friendship. He played in the house band at Condon's club for 17 years, occasionally touring with them too. In the 50s he appeared on a number of essential recording dates with Condon and with Bobby Hackett and Jack Teagarden. Eventually, Schroeder left Condon to join the Dukes Of Dixieland. Late in the 60s he was briefly with Tony Parenti, but ill-health curtailed his career and he was musically inactive during the last years of his life. Schroeder was an unspectacular, rock-solid supportive player, ideally suited to the role in which he was cast by Condon.

● ALBUMS: with Eddie Condon *At The Jazz Band Ball* (1955)★★★, with Bobby Hackett and Jack Teagarden *Jazz Ultimate* (1957)★★★.

SCHULLER, GUNTHER

b. 22 November 1925, New York City, New York, USA. After studying several instruments together with arranging and composition and music theory, Schuller played in several symphony orchestras before turning to jazz. He recorded with Miles Davis in the late 40s and early 50s and subsequently was a prime mover in what he termed 'third stream' music, a form that sought to blend jazz with appropriate aspects of western classical music. Schuller continued to combine his interests in classical music and jazz in his playing, composing and teaching career. Among the jazz musicians for whom he has written special pieces, and in some cases has recorded with, are Ornette Coleman, Eric Dolphy, Bill Evans and John Lewis. His teaching has included spells at the Lennox School of Jazz, of which he was a co-founder, and the New England Conservatory. He has also been active in music publishing and recording, forming his own companies in both fields. He has also written extensively on jazz and, apart from numerous magazine articles, he is the author of an important trilogy of which the first two volumes are *Early Jazz: Its Roots And Musical Development* (1968) and *The Swing Era: The Development Of Jazz, 1930-1945* (1989).

● ALBUMS: *Three Little Feelings* (1956)★★★, *The Gunther Schuller Orchestra* i (1957)★★★, *Jazz Abstractions* (1960)★★★, *The Gunther Schuller Orchestra* ii (*c*.1966)★★★, *Ellington's Symphony In Black* (1980)★★★★, *Vintage Dolphy* (1986)★★.

● FURTHER READING: *Early Jazz: Its Roots And Musical Development*, Gunther Schuller. *The Swing Era: The Development Of Jazz 1930-1945*, Gunther Schuller.

SCHUTT, ARTHUR

b. 21 November 1902, Reading, Pennsylvania, USA, d. 28 January 1965. After playing piano in silent-movie theatres, Schutt joined a band led by Paul Specht. During the 20s Schutt played piano in several of the more popular society bands, including those of Specht, Roger Wolfe Kahn and Freddy Rich. Towards the end of the decade he was involved in recording sessions with several of the leading white jazzmen of the day, notably Bix Beiderbecke, Red Nichols, Frank Trumbauer and Benny Goodman. Throughout the 30s and early 40s he was mostly active in the studios but found time for occasional club dates in New York. Later in the 40s and on through the 50s he continued with studio work but was now based in Hollywood, where he played clubs only rarely.

SCHUUR, DIANE

b. Tacoma, Washington, USA. Schuur is a top-selling GRP Records artist of long standing, and one of jazz's most popular vocalists. Born in Tacuma, but growing up in Auburn, she took to jazz with prodigious enthusiasm, learning Dinah Washington's repertoire at the age of three and four, and listening to her mother's Duke Ellington records and her father at the piano. Astonishingly, she was singing professionally at the age of nine, and began performing her own tunes at 16. In 1975, she won a place in drummer Ed Shaughnessy's big band (of *Late Show* fame), and travelled with the group to the Monterey Jazz Festival, where she met and jammed with the great Dizzy Gillespie. Her biggest break, however, came at the same festival four years later, when she was discovered by an enthusiastic Stan Getz, who began to spread the word about Schuur's obvious talent, and even invited her to perform with him at the White House in 1982. Two years later, she was invited back by Nancy Reagan, and the broadcast recording of this concert won her a contract with the GRP label. She has been with GRP ever since, winning Grammys in 1986 and 1987, and releasing nearly one album per year ever since, some of them featuring other top jazz and blues stars, including B.B. King and the Count Basie Orchestra. Schuur has a pleasant, musical voice, but tends to follow the GRP label style of jazz/pop rather than her own heart.

● ALBUMS: *Deedles* (GRP 1984)★★★, *Schuur Thing* (GRP 1985)★★★, *Timeless* (GRP 1986)★★, *Deedles And Basie: Diane Schuur & The Count Basie Orchestra* (GRP 1987)★★★, *Talkin' Bout You* (GRP 1988)★★★, *Pure Schuur* (GRP 1990)★★★, *In Tribute* (GRP 1992)★★★, *Love Songs* (GRP 1993)★★★★, with B.B. King *Heart To Heart* (GRP 1994)★★, *Love Walked In* (GRP 1996)★★★, *Blues For Schuur* (GRP 1997)★★★.

● COMPILATIONS: *Diane Schuur Collection* (GRP 1989)★★★, *The Best Of* (GRP 1998)★★★.

● VIDEOS: *Diane Schuur And The Count Basie Orchestra* (GRP 1992).

SCHWEIZER, IRÈNE

b. 2 June 1941, Schaffhausen, Switzerland. Her interest in music sparked by the dance bands who played in her parents' restaurant, Schweizer began to play folk songs on the accordion at the age of eight and took up the piano four years later. By her late teens she was playing hard bop in a student band, but a brief stay in England in the early 60s alerted her to the more modern approaches of Joe Harriott and Tubby Hayes. Settling in Zurich she formed a trio, whose recordings show that her music was still relatively conservative - Junior Mance and Bill Evans were early heroes - but by the time she recorded with Pierre Favre's groups in the late 60s (*Santana, This Is Free Jazz*) she was investigating the freer music that has since remained her chief focus of interest (and was partly inspired by hearing Cecil Taylor in the mid-60s). One of the first members of Berlin's FMP organization, Schweizer released most of her recordings on their label for the next 15 years, many featuring her in partnership with saxophonist Rüdiger Carl, though other associates included Manfred Schoof, John Martin Tchicai and Louis Moholo, plus a guest appearance with the group Henry Cow (*Western*

Culture). In 1978, Lindsay Cooper invited her to join the newly formed Feminist Improvising Group (FIG) and in 1983 Schweizer set up the European Women's Improvising Group (EWIG); she has remained a committed advocate for women's music, helping to organize the Canaille Festival of Women's Improvised Music in Zurich in 1986. In the mid-80s, with FMP in financial crisis, she was instrumental in setting up Switzerland's annual, three-city Taktlos Festival of improvised music, plus its associated label, Intakt, on which many of her own recent releases have appeared. Prominent among these have been two CD releases of solo music and a series of duets - with drummers Moholo, Günter Sommer and Andrew Cyrille (Schweizer herself is a capable drummer), plus bassist Joëlle Léandre (a frequent collaborator) and pianist Marilyn Crispell. One of Europe's premier improvisers, Schweizer can play the entire gamut of piano, from dynamic, percussive attack to delicate and humorous interplay. Her latest UK tour was in 1991 with the London Jazz Composers' Orchestra, whose leader Barry Guy wrote 'Theoria' for her, a 'kind of piano concerto' to celebrate her 50th birthday.

● ALBUMS: *Jubilation* (1962)★★★, *Brandy* (1964)★★★, *Willem's Fun Feast* (1973)★★★, *Ramifications* 1973 recording (1975)★★★, with Rüdiger Carl *Goose Pannee* (1975)★★★, with Carl, Louis Moholo *Messer* (1976)★★★, with John Tchicai *Willi The Pig* (1976)★★★, *Wilde Señoritas* (1976)★★★, *Hohe Ufer Konzerte* (1977)★★, *Early Tapes* 1967 recording (1978)★★★, *Hexensabbat* (1978)★★★, with Carl, Moholo *Tuned Boots* (1978)★★★, with Carl *The Very Centre Of Middle Europe* (1979)★★★, with Carl *Die V-Mann Suite* (1981)★★, *Live At Taktlos* 1984 recording (1986)★★, with Joëlle Léandre *Cordial Gratin* (1987)★★★, *Irène Schweizer - Louis Moholo* (1987)★★, with others *Canaille* 1986 recording (1988)★★★, *The Storming Of The Winter Palace* (1988)★★★, *Irène Schweizer - Günter Sommer* (1988)★★★, *Irène Schweizer - Andrew Cyrille* (1989)★★★, *Piano Solo Volume One* (Intakt 1991)★★★★, *Irene Schweizer And Pierre Favre* (Intakt 1990)★★★★, *Piano Solo Volume Two* (Intakt 1991)★★★★, with Marilyn Crispell *Overlapping Hands: Eight Segments* (1991)★★, *Les Diaboliques* (Intakt 1994)★★, *Irène Schweizer - Han Bennink* (Intakt 1996★★★★, *Many And One Direction* (Intakt 1997)★★★.

SCLAVIS, LOUIS

b. 2 February 1953, Lyon, France. Louis Sclavis specializes in soprano saxophone, clarinet and bass clarinet; when he plays the clarinets, in particular, he does so with an authority very few modern jazz players can even approximate. Sclavis first came to attention with the group Workshop de Lyon, with whom he recorded five albums between 1975 and 1985. In 1976, he was a founder-member of the Association à la Récherce d'un Folklore Imaginaire which proposed (among other things) that, rather than being constrained by musical 'roots', a group of musicians should be free to dream up their own culture. Correspondingly, Sclavis's own recordings cover a wide and colourful terrain. Still much in demand as a sideman, Sclavis has played with Anthony Braxton, Cecil Taylor, Chris McGregor's Brotherhood Of Breath and others. On *Alms/Tiergarten (Spree)* by the Cecil Taylor European Orchestra, Sclavis emerges as one of the most powerful voices in a power-packed band.

● ALBUMS: with Jean Bolcato *Champ De Frigg* (1975)★★★, *Ad Augusta Per Angustia* (Nato 1981)★★★, *Rencontres* (Nato 1985)★★★, *Clarinettes* (IDA 1985)★★★, *Chine* (IDA 1987)★★★, *Chamber Music* (IDA 1989)★★★★, with André Ricros *Le Partage Des Eaux* (1989)★★, with Evan Parker, Hans Koch, Wolfgang Fuchs *Duets (Dithyrambische)* (1990)★★★★, *Rouge* (ECM 1992)★★★★, *Ellington On The Air* (Ida 1993)★★★, *Acoustic Quartet* (ECM 1993)★★★, *Les Violences De Rameau* (ECM 1996)★★★.

SCOBEY, BOB

b. 9 December 1916, Tucumcari, New Mexico, USA, d. 12 June 1963. In the 30s Scobey played trumpet in several dance bands, mostly in California where he grew up. In 1938, he began a long-lasting musical association with Lu Watters, which brought him to the forefront of the jazz revival movement. During the 50s, he led his own traditional band, which attained a level of popularity similar to those of Watters and Turk Murphy, another companion in the west coast Dixieland revival. In the 60s Scobey ran his own club in Chicago and remained a popular figure at festivals of traditional jazz. A sound, if unspectacular, trumpet player, Scobey's great enthusiasm for his music rubbed off on the sidemen in any band of which he was a member.

● ALBUMS: *Bob Scobey's Alexander's Jazz Band* 1946-47 recordings (Dawn Club 1986)★★★, *Bob Scobey's Frisco Band Vol. 1* (1950-51)★★★, *Bob Scobey's Frisco Band Vol. 2* (1952-53)★★, *Direct From San Francisco* (Good Time 1993)★★★.

SCOFIELD, JOHN

b. 26 December 1951, Ohio, USA. From an early background of playing with local R&B groups, guitarist Scofield attended the renowned Berklee College Of Music in Boston during the early 70s. He recorded with Gerry Mulligan and Chet Baker and eventually received an invitation to join Billy Cobham as replacement for John Abercrombie. Following a two-year stint he played with Charles Mingus, Gary Burton, and Dave Liebman. His early solo work built slowly and steadily into a style that is uniquely his. *Shinola* was recorded live and is a mellow album, bordering on the lethargic, and features the bass playing of Scofield's acknowledged mentor, Steve Swallow. Between 1983 and 1985 Scofield was an integral part of Miles Davis's band, playing on a number of recordings including *Decoy* and *You're Under Arrest*. Following this exposure, Scofield had accumulated a considerable following. During the mid-80s he played with McCoy Tyner, Marc Johnson and the French National Orchestra. *Electric Outlet* showed that Scofield had now created his own uniquely rich and creamy sound, and *Still Warm* capitalized on this burst of creativity and became the first of a series of outstanding albums on Gramavision. Great excitement preceded its release, following a giveaway record in *Guitar Player* magazine. The album became a big seller and was a flawless work. He continued in a similar funky, though less jazzy, vein for *Blue Matter* and *Loud Jazz*, the former featuring some impressive drum work from Dennis Chambers. *Flat Out* featured diverse and interesting arrangements of standards such as Sammy Fain/Paul Francis Webster's 'Secret Love' and Jerome Kern/Oscar Hammerstein II's 'All The Things You Are'. A live offering, *Pick Hits*, brilliantly encapsulated the best of Scofield's recent work, and demonstrated his growing importance as a class player. *Time On My Hands* was a critics' favourite and another strong seller. For many, it was the jazz album of 1990. Scofield's playing had now reached a point where he was regarded as one of the world's top guitarists. His compositional skills continued to blossom; his interplay with Charlie Haden and Jack DeJohnette was imaginative and uplifting. Maintaining an extraordinarily prolific musical peak, he delivered another exciting record in the shape of *Meant To Be* and toured with the Mike Gibbs Orchestra during 1991, where his accessible and rich jazz guitar blended harmoniously with Gibbs' innovative compositions. *Grace Under Pressure* and *What We Do* continued his run of first-rate and highly popular albums, still showing Scofield full of fresh ideas. *Hand Jive* was his return to funk and soul/jazz with some excellent contributions from the saxophone of Eddie Harris. *Groove Elation* continued that theme and featured Idris Muhammad, Don Alias, Steve Turre and Randy Brecker. Following his work on Herbie Hancock's *The New Standard*, Scofield released his Verve Records' debut, *Quiet*, which was his unplugged album (using an amplified nylon string guitar). It reached breathtaking heights, continuing a roll of superlative albums that Scofield has been releasing for some years. Jim Ferguson, writing in *Guitar Player*, perceptively stated that Scofield's solos are 'like the chase scene in *The French Connection* - incredibly exciting, intense and constantly flirting with disaster, but rarely out of control'. Scofield is unquestionably one of the most original and talented jazz guitarists currently playing.

● ALBUMS: *John Scofield Live* (Enja 1977)★★★, *Rough House* (Enja 1979)★★★, *Who's Who* (Novus 1979)★★★, *Bar Talk* (Enja 1980)★★★, *Shinola* (Enja 1981)★★★, *Out Like A Light* (Enja 1981)★★★, *Electric Outlet* (Gramavision 1984)★★★, *Still Warm* (Gramavision 1987)★★★★★, *Blue Matter* (Gramavision 1987)★★★★, *Loud Jazz* (Gramavision 1988)★★★, *Pick Hits Live* (Gramavision 1989)★★★, *Flat Out* (Gramavision 1989)★★★, *Time On My Hands* (Blue Note 1990)★★★★, *Slo Sco* (Gramavision 1990), *Meant To Be* (Blue Note 1991)★★★★, *Grace Under Pressure* (Blue Note 1992)★★★★, *What We Do* (Blue Note 1993)★★★★, with Pat Metheny *I Can See Your House From Here* (Blue Note 1994)★★★, *Hand Jive* (Blue Note 1994)★★★★, *Groove Elation* (Blue Note 1995)★★★★, *Quiet* (Verve 1996)★★★★, *A Go Go* (Verve 1998)★★★★.

SCOTT, BOBBY

b. 29 January 1937, New York City, New York, USA, d. 5 November 1990, New York City, New York, USA. Scott was a pianist, singer, composer, arranger, teacher and record producer. He also played several other instruments such as cello, bass, vibes, accordion and clarinet, but was mainly known for his jazz piano work and vocals. He attended Dorothea Anderson Follette's School of Music, and then in 1949 studied composition with Edward Moritz, a former pupil of Claude Debussy. Despite his early classical training, Scott turned to jazz in his teens, and played with small bands led by the likes of Louis Prima, Tony Scott and Gene Krupa, with whom he cut some sides for Verve Records. From 1954, he recorded under his own name for labels such as Bethlehem, Savoy, Atlantic and ABC, and in 1956 had a US Top 20 hit with 'Chain Gang', written by Sol Quasha and Hank Yakus (not the Sam Cooke song). In 1960, Scott wrote the title theme for Shelagh Delaney's play *A Taste Of Honey*, which became popular for pianist Martin Denny and, when Ric Marlow added a lyric, for Tony Bennett. It was also included on the Beatles' first album (UK). The song won a Grammy in 1962, and three more when Herb Alpert took it into the US Top 10 in 1965. In the early 60s Scott was the musical director for Dick Haymes for a time, and, as a pianist, arranger and record producer for Mercury Records, also maintained a close working relationship with Quincy Jones. Scott played piano on most of Jones's Mercury albums, and accompanied Tania Vega and John Lee Hooker on Jones's soundtrack music for the film *The Color Purple* (1986). As a producer, Scott supervised sessions for important artists such as Aretha Franklin, Marvin Gaye, Bobby Darin, Harry Belafonte and Sarah Vaughan. He discovered and recorded guitarist/vocalist Perry Miller, who changed his name to Jesse Colin Young, and he is also credited with taking singer Bobby Hebb back to Mercury, although Scott left the label before Hebb released his biggest hit, 'Sunny', in 1966. Scott's compositions included 'He Ain't Heavy, He's My Brother' (written with Bob Russell), a hit for Neil Diamond in 1970 and a UK number 1 for the Hollies that same year and later in 1988, when it featured impressively in a UK television commercial for Miller Lite Lager; 'Where Are You Going?' (with Danny Meehan), sung by Joe Butler in the film *Joe* (1970); and 'Slaves (Don't You Know My Name?)', performed by Dionne Warwick in the movie *Slaves* (1969). Scott also composed incidental music for the play *Dinny And The Witches*, and several pieces for harp and string trios, including 'The Giacometti Variations', so-called because it was part-used as a radio advertisement for the Giacometti Exhibition held at the New York Museum of Modern Art. His compositions for guitar included 'Solitude Book' and 'The Book Of Hours', the latter recorded with Brazilian guitarist Carlos Barbosa-Lima. *For Sentimental Reasons* displayed Scott simply as an accomplished pianist, who also sang. He died of lung cancer in the year of its release.

● ALBUMS: *The Jazz Keyboard Of Bobby Scott* (1953)★★★, *Great Scott* 10-inch album (Bethlehem 1954)★★★, *The Compositions Of Bobby Scott, Volume 1* 10-inch album (Bethlehem 1954)★★, *The Compositions Of Bobby Scott, Volume 2* 10-inch album (Bethlehem 1954)★★, *The Compositions Of Bobby Scott* (Bethlehem 1955)★★, *Scott Free* (ABC-Paramount 1956)★★★,

Bobby Scott And Two Horns (ABC-Paramount 1957)★★★, *Bobby Scott Sings The Best Of Lerner And Loewe* (Verve 1958)★★★, *Serenade - Bobby Scott, Pianist* (Verve 1959)★★★, *Bobby Scott Plays The Music Of Leonard Bernstein* (Verve 1959)★★★, *Bobby Scott With Friends* (1960)★★★, *The Complete Musician* (Atlantic 1960)★★★, *A Taste Of Honey* (Atlantic 1960)★★, *Joyful Noises* (Mercury 1962)★★★, *When The Feeling Hits You* (Mercury 1963)★★★, *108 Pounds Of Heartache* (Mercury 1963)★★, *I Had A Ball* (Mercury 1964)★★★, *For Sentimental Reasons* (Music Masters 1990)★★★.

SCOTT, CECIL

b. 22 November 1905, Springfield, Ohio, USA, d. 5 January 1964. Scott began playing clarinet and saxophones as a child and had his own band while still a teenager. His bandleading career lasted throughout the 20s and by the end of that decade he was resident in New York, where he made a big impression on audiences and rival bands. His sidemen included his brother, drummer Lloyd Scott, plus Dicky Wells, Johnny Hodges, Chu Berry and a succession of distinguished trumpeters, such as Bill Coleman, Joe Thomas, Frankie Newton and Roy Eldridge. Scott continued to lead a band until the early 30s, when a bad leg injury interrupted his career. From the mid-30s into the early 40s he played with various small groups, mostly in the New York and Chicago areas. In 1942, he returned to leading a big band and subsequently a series of small groups, activities that continued throughout the 50s and into the early 60s. During this late period he worked with Willie 'The Lion' Smith and was recorded with the encouragement of Chris Barber. A driving, gutsy player on clarinet and tenor saxophone, Scott was a forceful leader who demanded and received enthusiastic support from his sidemen. At its peak his band was one of the best of the New York-based black bands and had it not been for his enforced lay-off just as the swing era was getting underway, he might well have achieved greater recognition.

● ALBUMS: *Chris Barber Presents Harlem Washboard: Cecil Scott And His Washboard Band* (1959)★★★.

SCOTT, HAZEL

b. Hazel Dorothy Scott, 11 June 1920, Port of Spain, Trinidad, d. 2 October 1981. Scott was brought up and educated in New York where she studied classical piano. Later, she turned to jazz and began earning a living in the city's nightclubs. She became very popular and played at Café Society, a favourite haunt of the in-crowd. She had her own radio show and also appeared in films, usually in a nightclub scene, among them Mae West's *The Heat's On* (also known as *Tropicana*), Red Skelton's *I Dood It (By Hook Or By Crook)*, *Something To Shout About* (all 1943), *Broadway Rhythm* (1944) and *Rhapsody In Blue* (1945), the George Gershwin biopic. She married the prominent black politician, Adam Clayton Powell Jnr. Later, her career drifted somewhat but she appeared briefly in a French film, *Le Désordre Et La Nuit* (*Night Affair*) in 1958. Scott's piano playing was of a high order, reflecting her childhood training. She was also adept at playing boogie-woogie. Indeed, she had popular records of jazzed-up classical pieces. Her singing was pleasantly engaging and her stage presentation was finely honed. Although she continued to perform through the 60s and 70s, she never attained the high profile of her early years.

SCOTT, LITTLE JIMMY

b. James Victor Scott, 17 July 1925, Cleveland, Ohio, USA. An influential figure to popular singers as stylistically diverse as Nancy Wilson, Ray Charles, and Frankie Valli, the highly acclaimed balladeer 'Little' Jimmy Scott nevertheless found it extremely difficult to transcend his enduring cult status. Revered by only the most knowledgeable of jazz aficionados, it was not until quite recently that Scott was able to mount a successful comeback after suffering decades of undeserved obscurity. His wavering, ethereal contralto vocal range, much closer in pitch to that of a woman than a man, was a result of a rare hereditary condition called Kallmann's Syndrome, which restricted Scott's height to 4 feet 11 inches until he was in his mid-30s (when he suddenly grew to an unprecendented 5 feet 7 inches), blocked his sexual development, and stopped his voice from lowering into a conventional masculine register - thereby creating one of the most unusual and stunning vocal deliveries in post-war music history. He was one of 10 children, all of whom sang along heartily to their mother Justine's spirited piano playing at Hagar's Universal Spiritual Church in Cleveland. After her death (she was struck down while pushing her daughter out of the way of a speeding car), Scott was raised in various foster homes from the age of 13. While in his teens, he ushered at Cleveland's Metropolitan Theater, where he heard the bands of Buddy Johnson, Erskine Hawkins and Lucky Millinder. He received his first chance to sing in front of an audience in Meadsville, Pennsylvania, in the mid-40s, backed by jazz saxophone legends Ben Webster and Lester Young. Scott toured from 1945 to 1949 with shake dancer Estelle 'Caledonia' Young. Comedian Redd Foxx, actor Ralph Cooper, and heavyweight boxing champion Joe Louis helped the promising young singer to gain a job in 1948 at the Baby Grand nightclub on 125th Street in New York City. Scott joined Lionel Hampton's band the next year, with whom he made his debut recordings. In 1950, he sang the hit 'Everybody's Somebody's Fool' on Decca Records as Hampton's featured vocalist (the song reached number 6 on *Billboard*'s R&B charts). Scott was also spotlighted vocally on 'I Wish I Knew', a popular but non-charting 1950 Decca side credited to the Lionel Hampton Quintet that featured Doug Duke's organ accompaniment, and 'I've Been A Fool'. Scott soon left Hampton's band to join forces with New Orleans R&B mainstay Paul Gayten's band (which also featured vocalist Annie Laurie) in 1951. Scott made some live recordings for Fred Mendelsohn's Regal label that year with Gayten's band (trumpeter John Hunt, tenor saxophonist Ray Abrams, baritone saxophonist Pee Wee Numa-Moore, pianist Teddy Brannon, bassist Thomas

Legange, and drummer Wesley Landis) that were captured for posterity at Rip's Playhouse, a New Orleans nightspot. Those long-buried tapes belatedly saw the light of day in 1991 on a Specialty Records disc. Mendelsohn sold Scott's contract to Teddy Reig and Jack Hook's Roost Records, where he recorded 16 further tracks under his own name (including his first classic rendition of 'The Masquerade Is Over') before signing with Herman Lubinsky's larger Savoy label in 1955. Four ballad-heavy sessions were held that year for Savoy, surrounding Scott with top-notch bandsmen including pianist/arranger Howard Biggs, saxophonist Budd Johnson, guitarists Mundell Lowe, George Barnes, and Everett Barksdale, bassist Charles Mingus, and drummer Kenny Clarke. Scott was unhappy with the skimpy financial rewards he received while under contract to the Newark, New Jersey-based Savoy (more dates ensued in 1956 and 1958). Nevertheless, under Mendelsohn's astute supervision, Scott did manage to create numerous classic ballads for the company despite the fiscal discord. 'When Did You Leave Heaven', 'Imagination', and the bluesy 'Don't Cry Baby' are among Scott's finest performances for Savoy. Although his early years were artistically enriching, Scott's offstage existence was apparently another matter. The singer endured multiple divorces and suffered from a reported drinking problem. Scott temporarily switched over to Sydney Nathan's King Records in 1957 for a dozen sides supervised by Henry Glover before returning to Savoy in 1960 for one more session. Finally, in 1962, Scott received what appeared to be his big break: a contract with Ray Charles's fledgling Tangerine label. With Marty Paich and Gerald Wilson supplying lush arrangements and Charles himself deftly handling the keyboards, the resulting album, *Falling in Love is Wonderful*, would have most likely boosted Scott's national profile considerably. Unfortunately, Lubinsky quashed the set's distribution shortly after its release, claiming that Scott remained under contract to Savoy. In 1969, Atlantic Records producer Joel Dorn recorded an album with Scott, *The Source*, with arrangements by Arif Mardin and sporting a varied set that included 'Day By Day', 'This Love Of Mine', and 'Exodus', but it failed to further Scott's fortunes. He returned to Savoy one last time in 1975 for a Mendelsohn-produced album that made little impact. For a lengthy period prior to his triumphant return to live performance in 1985 (which was spurred by the urging of his fourth wife, Earlene), Scott toiled as a shipping clerk at Cleveland's Sheraton Hotel, forgotten by all but his most loyal fans. Scott has engineered quite an amazing comeback in the years since. In 1992, his Blue Horizon album *All The Way* (listed as being by Jimmy Scott, with no reference to his height) found him backed by an all-star jazz aggregation that included saxophonist David 'Fathead' Newman, pianist Kenny Barron, bassist Ron Carter, and drummer Grady Tate and string arrangements by Johnny Mandel. Scott followed it in 1994 with another set for Sire/Blue Horizon, *Dream*. Jimmy Scott's reputation as a unique vocal master is assured, but his status definitely has not come easily.

● ALBUMS: *Very Truly Yours* (Savoy 1955)★★★, *The Fabulous Little Jimmy Scott* reissued as *The Fabulous Songs Of Jimmy Scott* (Savoy 1959)★★★★, *Falling In Love Is Wonderful* (Tangerine 1962)★★★, *If You Only Knew* (Savoy 1963)★★★, *The Source* (Atlantic 1969)★★, *Can't We Begin Again* (Savoy 1975)★★, *Little Jimmy Scott* (Savoy Jazz 1984)★★★, *All Over Again* (Savoy Jazz 1985)★★★, *Regal Records: Live In New Orleans!* (Specialty 1991)★★★, *All The Way* (Blue Horizon 1992)★★★, *Lost And Found* (Rhino/Atlantic 1993)★★★, *Dream* (Sire/Blue Horizon 1994)★★★, *All Over Again* (Denon/Savoy Jazz 1994)★★★, *Heaven* (Warners 1996)★★★, *Holding Back The Years* (Artists Only! 1998)★★★★.

SCOTT, RONNIE

b. 28 January 1927, London, England, d. 23 December 1996, London, England. Scott began playing on the soprano saxophone but switched to tenor in his early teens. After playing informally in clubs he joined the Johnny Claes band in 1944, before spells with Ted Heath, Bert Ambrose and other popular British dance bands. Scott also played on transatlantic liners in order to visit the USA and hear bebop at first hand. By the late 40s he was a key figure in the London bop scene, playing at the Club Eleven, of which he was a co-founder. During the 50s he led his own band and was also co-leader with Tubby Hayes of the Jazz Couriers. In 1959, he opened his own club in Gerrard Street, London, later moving to Frith Street. During the 60s he divided his time between leading his own small group and running the club, but also found time to play with the Clarke-Boland Big Band. The decade of the 60s was a milestone for popular music; for high-quality jazz there was only one place in London to visit - Ronnie's. In the 70s and 80s he continued to lead small bands, usually a quartet, occasionally touring but most often playing as the interval band between sessions by the modern American jazz musicians he brought to the club. As a player, Scott comfortably straddles the mainstream and modern aspects of jazz. His big tone lends itself to a slightly aggressive approach, although in his ballad playing he displays the warmth that characterized the work of Zoot Sims and late-period Stan Getz, musicians he admires, but does not imitate. Although a gifted player, Scott's greatest contribution to jazz was in his tireless promotion of fine British musicians and in his establishment of his club, booking the best American talent. His venue has become renowned throughout the world for the excellence of its setting and the artists on display. In 1981, Scott was awarded an OBE in recognition of his services to music. Following a bout of depression he was found dead at his London flat in December 1996.

● ALBUMS: *Battle Royal* (Esquire 1951)★★★, *The Ronnie Scott Jazz Group* i (Esquire 1952)★★★★, *The Ronnie Scott Jazz Group* ii (Esquire 1953)★★★, *The Ronnie Scott Jazz Group* iii (Esquire 1954)★★★, *The Ronnie Scott Jazz Group* iv (Esquire 1954)★★★, *At The Royal Festival Hall* (Decca 1956)★★★, *Presenting The Ronnie Scott Sextet* (Philips 1957)★★★, *The Jazz Couriers In Concert* (1958)★★★, *The Last Word* (1959)★★★, *The Night Is*

Scott And You're So Swingable (Fontana 1966)★★★, *Live At Ronnie's* (1968)★★★★, *Scott At Ronnie's* (1973)★★★, *Serious Gold* (1977)★★★, *Great Scott* (1979)★★★, with various artists *Ronnie Scott's 20th Anniversary Album* (1979)★★★, *Never Pat A Burning Dog* (Jazz House 1990)★★★, *When I Want Your Opinion* (Ronnie Scott's Jazz House 1998)★★★★, with Sonny Stitt *The Night Has A Thousand Eyes* (Ronnie Scott's Jazz House 1998)★★★.

● FURTHER READING: *Jazz At Ronnie Scott's*, Kitty Grime (ed.). *Let's Join Hands And Contact The Living*, John Fordham. *Jazz Man: The Amazing Story Of Ronnie Scott And His Club*, John Fordham.

SCOTT, SHIRLEY

b. 14 March 1934, Philadelphia, Pennsylvania, USA. Although she had studied both piano and trumpet as a child, Scott's breakthrough occurred when she switched to organ in the mid-50s. Mostly working in small groups with a saxophone leader and a drummer, she became very popular. Her musical associates have included such outstanding jazzmen as Eddie 'Lockjaw' Davis, Stanley Turrentine (to whom she was married for a while), Jimmy Forrest and Dexter Gordon. A gifted player with an eclectic style that encompasses the blues and bebop, Scott is one of only a handful of organists to satisfactorily fit a potentially unsuitable instrument into a jazz setting. Her career received a boost in the 90s when the Hammond organ became fashionable once more.

● ALBUMS: *Great Scott!* (Prestige 1958)★★★, *Shirley's Sounds* (Prestige 1958)★★★, with Eddie 'Lockjaw' Davis *The Eddie 'Lockjaw' Davis Cookbook* (Prestige 1958)★★★★, with Davis *Jaws* (Prestige 1959)★★★, *Scottie* (Prestige 1959)★★★★, *Scottie Plays Duke* (Prestige 1959)★★★, with Davis *Jaws In Orbit* (Prestige 1959)★★★, with Davis *Bacalao* (Prestige 1960)★★★, with Davis *Eddie 'Lockjaw' Davis With Shirley Scott* (Moodsville 1960)★★★, *Soul Searching* (Prestige 1960)★★★, *Mucho, Mucho* (Prestige 1960)★★★, *Shirley Scott Trio* (Moodsville 1960)★★★, *Like Cozy* (Moodsville 1960)★★★, *Shirley's Sounds* (Prestige 1961)★★★, *Hip Soul* (Prestige 1961)★★, *Hip Twist* (Prestige 1961)★★, *Shirley Scott Plays Horace Silver* (Prestige 1961)★★★, with Davis *The Eddie 'Lockjaw' Davis Cookbook, Vol. 3* (Prestige 1961)★★★★, *Happy Talk* reissued as *Sweet Soul* (Prestige 1963)★★★, *The Soul Is Willing* (Prestige 1963)★★★, *Satin Doll* (Prestige 1963)★★★, *Drag 'Em Out* (Prestige 1963)★★★, with Davis *Misty* (Moodsville 1963)★★★, *For Members Only* (Impulse! 1963)★★★★, *Soul Shoutin'* (Prestige 1964)★★★, *Travellin' Light* (Prestige 1964)★★★, with Davis *Smokin'* (Prestige 1964)★★★★, *Great Scott!* (Impulse! 1964)★★★, *Everybody Loves A Lover* (Impulse! 1964)★★★, *Blue Flames* (Prestige 1965)★★★, *Blue Seven* (Prestige 1965)★★★, *Soul Sisters* (Prestige 1965)★★★, *Queen Of The Organ* (Impulse! 1965)★★★, *Latin Shadows* (Impulse! 1965)★★★, *Workin'* (Prestige 1966)★★★, *The Night Is Scott And You're So Swingable* (Fontana 1966)★★★, *Roll Em* (Impulse! 1966)★★★, *On A Clear Day* (Impulse! 1966)★★★, *Now's The Time* (Prestige 1967)★★★, *Stompin'* (Prestige 1967)★★★, with Clark Terry *Soul Duo* (Impulse! 1967)★★★, *Girl Talk* (Impulse! 1967)★★★, *Soul Song* (Atlantic 1969)★★★, *Shirley Scott And The Soul Saxes* (Atlantic 1969)★★★, *The Shirley Scott Quintet* (1972)★★★, *One For Me* (Strata East 1975)★★★, *Oasis* (Muse 1990)★★★, *Blues Everywhere* (Candid 1993)★★★, *A Walking Thing* (Candid 1996)★★★.

● COMPILATIONS: with Stanley Turrentine *The Best Of Shirley Scott And Stanley Turrentine* (Prestige 1969)★★★, with Eddie 'Lockjaw' Davis *The Best Of Eddie Davis And Shirley Scott* (Prestige 1969)★★★★.

SCOTT, TOM

b. 19 May 1948, Los Angeles, California, USA. Scott's mother - Margery Wright - was a pianist, his father - Nathan Scott - a film and television composer. Scott played clarinet in high school and won a teenage competition with his Neoteric Trio at the Hollywood Bowl in 1965. He learned all the saxophones and played in the studios for TV shows such as *Ironside*. He performed on Roger Kellaway's *Spirit Feel* in 1967, playing fluent alto and soprano over a proto-fusion encounter of hard bop and rock music. As a member of Spontaneous Combustion in 1969, he played on *Come And Stick Your Head In*, an experimental record in the jazz-rock idiom. His own records - *Honeysuckle Breeze* (1967) and *Rural Still Life* (1968) - presented a tight, forceful jazz funk. From his early 20s he wrote prolifically for television and films (including *Conquest Of The Planet Of The Apes*), his sound becoming the blueprint for LA copshow soundtracks: urgent, funky, streamlined. His band, the LA Express, became one of the most successful fusion bands of the 70s. Joni Mitchell used them as her backing band on *Miles Of Aisles* (and guested on 1975's *Tom Cat*) and George Harrison played slide guitar on *New York Connection*. 1987's *Streamlines* showed that Scott had not lost his sound, but an interest in samples of ethnic instruments had given his music a more world-music feel.

● ALBUMS: *Honeysuckle Breeze* (1967)★★★, *Rural Still Life* (1968)★★★, with Spontaneous Combustion *Come And Stick Your Head In* (1969)★★★, *Tom Scott & The LA Express* (Ode 1974)★★★, *Tom Cat* (Ode 1975)★★, *New York Connection* (Ode 1975)★★, *Blow It Out* (Epic 1977)★★, *Apple Juice* (1981), *Desire* (Elektra 1982), *Streamlines* (GRP 1987)★★★, *Target* (1993), *Night Creatures* (GRP 1994)★★★.

● FILMS: *Americation* (1979).

SCOTT, TONY

b. Anthony Sciacca, 17 June 1921, Morristown, New Jersey, USA. Scott learned to play clarinet as a child, later studying formally at the Juilliard School in Manhattan. During the late 40s and beyond, he made his living playing in big bands and as a sideman in mainstream groups, sometimes playing tenor saxophone. Fascinated by the new jazz sounds emerging from Minton's Playhouse and other New York venues, he became a strongly committed bop musician. Unfortunately for the development of his career, bop and the clarinet were uneasy bedfellows, although Scott was one of the tiny number of clarinettists to achieve some recognition, building a reputation through the 50s as one of the best new players on his instrument. He was also active as an arranger and musical director for several singers, including Harry Belafonte, Billie Holiday and Sarah Vaughan. In 1959 he recorded the remarkably forward-looking *Sung Heroes*, with Bill Evans, Scott La Faro and Paul Motian, but the same year left America, tired of music business racism and despairing of the fact that so many of his close friends - Oran 'Hot Lips' Page, Charlie Parker, Art Tatum, Sid Catlett, Lester Young, Billie Holiday - had recently died. Scott spent six years travelling, both in Europe and (mostly) the Far East, and began to incorporate into his repertoire elements of ethnic music, especially from India and the Orient, creating a personal precedent for world music long before the genre was acknowledged. The records he made in the mid-60s as aids to meditation proved to be popular and consistent sellers - 'a godsend' he said of them in 1988, claiming that their royalties were still his main source of income. In the early 70s Scott settled in Italy, playing at festivals and touring, often to the Far East, making occasional records and as often as not anticipating trends and fashions in music - even if, as so often happens with pioneers, his work has been overshadowed by that of other less talented musicians. One recent project was a double album consisting entirely of different versions of Billy Strayhorn's standard, 'Lush Life'. 'No one has sung it right yet', Scott told *Wire* magazine in 1988, 'including Nat 'King' Cole, Sarah Vaughan, everybody - they all goof it'.

● ALBUMS: *Music After Midnight* 10-inch album (Brunswick 1953)★★★, *Tony Scott Quartet* 10-inch album (Brunswick 1954)★★★, *Jazz For GI's* 10-inch album (Brunswick 1954)★★★, *Scott's Fling* (RCA Victor 1955)★★★, *The Touch Of Tony Scott* (RCA Victor 1956)★★★★, *Tony Scott In Hi Fi* (Brunswick 1957)★★★, *Tony Scott Quartet* (Brunswick 1957)★★★, *The Complete Tony Scott* (RCA Victor 1957)★★★★, *A Day In New York* (Fresh Sound 1958)★★★, *52nd Street Scene* (Coral 1958)★★★, *South Pacific Jazz* (ABC-Paramount 1958)★★, *Gypsy* (Signature 1959)★★★, *The Modern Art Of Jazz* (Seeco 1959)★★★★, *Hi Fi Land Of Jazz* (Seeco 1959)★★★, with Jimmy Knepper *Free Blown Jazz* (Carlton 1959)★★★, *Sung Heroes* (Sunnyside 1959)★★★, *My Kind Of Jazz* (Perfect 1960)★★★, with Herman 'Trigger' Alpert, Al Cohn, Zoot Sims *East Coast Sounds* (Jazzland 1960)★★★, *Music For Zen Meditation* (Verve 1965)★★★, *Music For Yoga Meditation & Other Joys* (Verve 1967)★★★, *Homage To Lord Krishna* (Verve 1969)★★, *Prism* (1977)★★, *Boomerang* (1977)★★, *African Bird: Come Back! Mother Africa* (Soul Note 1984)★★★, *Lush Life Vols. 1 and 2* (Core 1989)★★★, *Astral Meditation: Voyage Into A Black Hole 1-3* (Core 1989)★★★, *The Clarinet Album* (Philology 1993)★★★.

Scott-Heron, Gil

b. 1 April 1949, Chicago, Illinois, USA. Raised in Jackson, Tennessee, by his grandmother, Scott-Heron moved to New York at the age of 13 and had published two novels (*The Vulture* and *The Nigger Factory*) plus a book of poems by the time he was 12. His estranged father played football for Glasgow Celtic. He met musician Brian Jackson when both were students at Lincoln University, Pennsylvania, and in 1972 they formed the Midnight Band to play their original blend of jazz, soul and prototype rap music. *Small Talk At 125th And Lenox* was mostly an album of poems (from his book of the same name), but later albums showed Scott-Heron developing into a skilled songwriter whose work was soon covered by other artists: for example, Labelle recorded his 'The Revolution Will Not Be Televised' and Esther Phillips made a gripping version of 'Home Is Where The Hatred Is'. In 1973 he had a minor hit with 'The Bottle'. *Winter In America* and *The First Minute Of A New Day*, for new label Arista Records, were both heavily jazz-influenced, but later sets saw Scott-Heron exploring more pop-orientated formats, and in 1976 he scored a hit with the disco-based protest single, 'Johannesburg'. One of his best records of the 80s, *Reflections*, featured a fine version of Marvin Gaye's 'Inner City Blues'; however, his strongest songs were generally his own barbed political diatribes, in which he confronted issues such as nuclear power, apartheid and poverty and made a series of scathing attacks on American politicians. Richard Nixon, Gerald Ford, Barry Goldwater and Jimmy Carter were all targets of his trenchant satire, and his anti-Reagan rap, 'B-Movie', gave him another small hit in 1982. An important forerunner of today's rap artists, Scott-Heron once described Jackson (who left the band in 1980) and himself as 'interpreters of the black experience'. However, by the 90s his view of the development of rap had become more jaundiced: 'They need to study music. I played in several bands before I began my career as a poet. There's a big difference between putting words over some music, and blending those same words into the music. There's not a lot of humour. They use a lot of slang and colloquialisms, and you don't really see inside the person. Instead, you just get a lot of posturing'. In 1994 he released his first album for ten years, *Spirits*, which began with 'Message To The Messenger', an address to today's rap artists: '. . . Young rappers, one more suggestion before I get out of your way, But I appreciate the respect you give me and what you got to say, I'm sayin' protect your community and spread that respect around, Tell brothers and sisters they got to calm that bullshit down, 'Cause we're terrorizin' our old folks and we brought fear into our homes'.

● ALBUMS: *Small Talk At 125th And Lenox* (Flying Dutchman 1972)★★★, *Free Will* (Flying Dutchman 1972)★★★, *Pieces Of A Man* (Flying Dutchman 1973)★★★, *Winter In America* (Strata East 1974)★★★, *The First Minute Of A New Day* (Arista 1975)★★★, *From South Africa To South Carolina* (Arista 1975)★★★, *It's Your World* (Arista 1976)★★★, *Bridges* (Arista 1977)★★★, *Secrets* (Arista 1978)★★★, *1980* (Arista 1980)★★★, *Real Eyes* (Arista 1980)★★★, *Reflections* (Arista 1981)★★★, *Moving Target* (Arista 1982)★★★, *Spirits* (TVT Records 1994)★★★.

● COMPILATIONS: *The Revolution Will Not Be Televised* (Flying Dutchman 1974)★★★★, *The Mind Of Gil Scott-Heron* (Arista 1979)★★★, *The Best Of Gil Scott-Heron* (Arista 1984)★★★★, *Tales Of Gil* double album (Essential 1990)★★★, *Glory: The Gil Scott-Heron Collection* (Arista 1990)★★★.

● VIDEOS: *Tales Of Gil* (1990).

SEAMEN, PHIL

b. 28 August 1928, Burton-on-Trent, Staffordshire, England, d. 13 October 1972. Seamen first attracted attention when he played drums with post-war British dance bands, including those led by Nat Gonella and Joe Loss. By the early 50s he was a key figure in the nascent London bop scene, working with Ronnie Scott, Tubby Hayes, Joe Harriott and other leading musicians. Later in the decade he recorded with Stan Tracey, on *Little Klunk* (1959) and the following year with Harriott, on the saxophonist's *Free Form*. In the early 60s Seamen tried his hand in blues bands, including those of Georgie Fame and Alexis Korner. In the late 60s he was back with Scott but also played in rock bands, including Air Force which was led by one of his students, Ginger Baker. The range of Seamen's musical interests is apparent from the company he kept, and he brought to everything he did enormous enthusiasm and vitality. His dynamic playing enhanced countless club and pub sessions in and around London, a handful being captured on record. Sadly, for all his skills, Seamen's career and ultimately his life were blighted by drug addiction. Seamen's virtuosity was remarkable: his work with Harriott was noteworthy for the manner in which he adapted to free jazz, and he coped admirably with the very different demands required by his performances in rock and blues bands. Despite such performances, however, it is a bop drummer that he made his most notable mark on the British jazz scene.

● ALBUMS: *Third Festival Of British Jazz* (1956)★★, *Now!...Live!* (1968)★★★, *Phil On Drums! A Jam Session At The Hideaway* (1971)★★, *Phil Talks And Plays/The Phil Seamen Story* (1972)★★★.

SEARS, AL

b. 21 February 1910, Macomb, Illinois, USA, d. 23 March 1990. After playing alto and baritone saxophones in various bands in the north-eastern states, Sears switched to tenor saxophone and moved to New York, where he was soon in demand. In the late 20s he was with Chick Webb and Zack Whyte, then briefly played with Elmer Snowden before forming his own band. In 1941 he folded his band and joined Andy Kirk, then Lionel Hampton, and, in 1944, succeeded Ben Webster in the Duke Ellington band. Sears remained with Ellington until 1949 and soon thereafter joined Johnny Hodges' band, which had a successful record with Sears' composition 'Castle Rock'. Sears subsequently ran his own music publishing business in partnership with Budd Johnson, playing occasionally in R&B bands and using the name Big Al Sears. A forceful player with enormous drive and energy, Sears needed only a slight coarsening of his naturally rasping tone to adapt readily into the R&B fold. Despite such later manifestations, however, his recorded solos with Ellington indicate a musician of considerable sophistication, and his recordings, which include 'Hiawatha' from Ellington's 'The Beautiful Indians', frequently offer fine examples of his craft.

● ALBUMS: *Duke Ellington At Carnegie Hall* (1946)★★★★, *Duke Ellington And His Orchestra 1946* (1946)★★★★, with Ellington *Liberian Suite* (1947)★★★★, with Johnny Hodges *Rabbit On Verve Vol. 1* (1951)★★★, *Al Sears And His Orchestra* (1960)★★★, *Swing's The Thing* (1960)★★★, *Sear-iously* (Bear Family 1992)★★.

SEATON, LYNN

b. 18 July 1957, Tulsa, Oklahoma, USA. Seaton first played guitar but switched to bass at the age of nine. While still at school he won numerous prizes for his playing. He studied music at the University of Oklahoma and simultaneously played with jazz groups in various clubs statewide. Late in 1980 he settled in Cincinnati, Ohio, where he became a regular member of pianist Steve Schmidt's Trio and of the big band led by John Von Ohlen at the city's Blue Wisp jazz club. The Schmidt group accompanied visiting jazzmen at the Blue Wisp, among them Al Cohn, Scott Hamilton, Mark Murphy, Maxine Sullivan, Carol Sloane and Teddy Wilson. In 1981 he took advantage of a National Endowment of the Arts Jazz Studies Fellowship to study in New York with Rufus Reid. In late 1984 he joined Woody Herman's Young Thundering Herd and in July the following year began a two-year spell with the Count Basie Orchestra. He later worked with George Shearing and also with Tony Bennett. In the early 90s he spent some time with Monty Alexander, but in 1993 turned to freelancing, playing with a dazzling array of musicians throughout the USA and also at many overseas jazz festivals. Among the artists he has accompanied are Ernestine Anderson, Clark Terry, Howard Alden and Frank Wess. He also played as a regular member of Jeff Hamilton's trio. By this time, Seaton had become a respected teacher, working in this capacity at the State University of New York and various Jamey Aebersold Jazz Camps, and he is also in demand as a private tutor. By the late 90s, Seaton had already clocked up appearances on some 100 albums accompanying many musicians, including Diane Schuur, Tim Hagans, Kenny Drew Jnr., Bucky and John Pizzarelli and John Colliani. He has also played and recorded popular classical music with the Cincinnati Pops Orchestra. A strikingly gifted bass player with a brilliant technique, Seaton's mastery of all aspects of the bass player's role in jazz is evidenced by the range of topics covered by the seminars he conducts, which include improvisation, accompaniment, solo playing, business matters, phrasing and dynamics, and rhythm section playing. His standing with fellow bass players is high, veteran Milt Hinton listing him as one of his favourite five on the instrument. He has a lightly dancing approach where appropriate and fierce drive when needed. He is also a virtuoso player with the bow.

● ALBUMS: with Woody Herman *50th Anniversary Tour* (Concord 1986)★★★, with Frank Wess *Live At The 1990 Concord Jazz Festival: Second Set* (Concord 1990)★★★, as leader *Bassman's Basement* (Timeless 90s)★★.

SECOND CHORUS

This 1940 film is an enjoyable piece of hokum about two swing band trumpeters, Fred Astaire and Burgess Meredith, vying for the affections of Paulette Goddard. The musicians play with Artie Shaw's band and there are some excellent musical sequences featuring the leader's clarinet, backed in a performance of 'Concerto For Clarinet' by Nick Fatool's drums, and the trumpets of Bobby Hackett and Billy Butterfield ghosting for Astaire and Meredith.

SEDRIC, GENE

b. 17 June 1907, St. Louis, Missouri, USA, d. 3 April 1963. Sedric began playing clarinet in local bands, later taking up the tenor saxophone. His first important jobs were with Charlie Creath, Fate Marable and other bandleaders playing in the region and on the riverboats. In the early 20s he arrived in New York with a touring band and there joined Sam Wooding, with whom he visited Europe. In 1934, he became a member of Fats Waller's small group, remaining there until the leader's death in 1943. Subsequently he led his own small bands, also playing and recording with other leaders. In the early 50s he again visited Europe, playing with Mezz Mezzrow, Buck Clayton and others. In 1953 he joined a band led by Conrad Janis and at the end of the decade freelanced until ill-health forced him into retirement. Although he was not an exceptional performer on either instrument, he fitted well into the cheerful music that Waller's accompanists offered. Thanks to this association Sedric enjoyed a long and successful career.

SEGURE, ROGER

b. 22 May 1905, Brooklyn, New York, USA. Segure studied at university in Nevada and California. He worked as a pianist on boats to the East and played in both China and Japan in the 30s. He settled in New York in the late 30s doing arrangements for the bands of Louis Armstrong, Andy Kirk, John Kirby and Jimmy Lunceford, whose full-time arranger he became between 1940 and 1942. He wrote the score for the film *Blues In The Night* for Lunceford. Segure was an influential arranger who wrote several very forward-looking pieces. In the late 40s he moved to Los Angeles and in time became the musical director for various television shows. He spent some time teaching before retiring.

SEIDEL, JANET

b. 28 May 1955, Cummins, South Australia, Australia. Raised on the family dairy farm, Seidel began playing piano as a child and also performed while at school. After graduating from the University of Adelaide with a BM degree she began working as a high school music teacher. She extended her performing career, as pianist and singer, working extensively in her homeland and also visiting Europe. This was in the early 80s and she later formed her own trio with her brother, David Seidel, on bass and Billy Ross on drums. Based in Sydney, she began attracting a dedicated audience and also started her recording career. Her style comfortably accommodates a jazz-tinged popular repertoire, befitting a superior supper club entertainer, and the fully realized jazz book demanded by appearances at prestigious venues such as Japan's Kobe festival where she has sung on three occasions. In the late 90s her records were receiving deserved attention in Europe and the USA. She and her brother David are co-owners of La Brava Records, a label which features many distinguished Australian musicians. Seidel's singing voice is clear, subtly swinging and elegantly poised. She is a highly accomplished interpreter of lyrics, bringing to them warmth, understanding and illumination.

● ALBUMS: *Little Jazz Bird* (La Brava 1992)★★★, *Winter Moon* (La Brava 1994)★★★, *Doodlin'* (La Brava 1995)★★★, *The Art Of Lounge* (La Brava 90s)★★★, *The Way You Wear Your Hat* (La Brava 1998)★★★, *Chaise Lounge* (La Brava 1998)★★★.

SEIFERT, ZBIGNIEW

b. 6 June 1946, Cracow, Poland, d. 15 February 1979, Munich, Germany. Seifert studied violin from the age of six and took up the alto saxophone in his teens. He studied music at the Chopin School of Music in Cracow and graduated from the Higher School of Music in 1970. In 1965 he had started his own quartet modelled on the style of John Coltrane's classic quartet. By the time he played with Tomasz Stanko's band (1969-73) he was playing a freer form of jazz, gradually incorporating more violin and dropping the alto altogether in 1971. The free style was well served by his passionate, tough and technically adept playing which measured up to his desire to 'play as Coltrane would if he played the violin'. He moved to Germany in 1973 and worked with Hans Koller's Free Sound (1974-75) and appeared at the Montreux Jazz Festival with John Lewis in 1976. Hamburg Radio commissioned a large-scale piece from him and he played and recorded with Oregon. He died from cancer at the age of 32.

● ALBUMS: with Tomasz Stanko *Purple Sun* (1973)★★★, *Man Of The Light* (1976)★★★, with Oregon *Violin* (1977)★★, with Charlie Mariano *Helen 12 Trees* (1977)★★★, *Passion* (1978)★★★.

SEMPLE, ARCHIE

b. 1 March 1928, Edinburgh, Scotland, d. 26 January 1974. After first playing clarinet in bands in his homeland, Semple moved to London in the early 50s. There he became an important voice in the burgeoning traditional jazz scene, playing with the bands of Mick Mulligan, Freddy Randall and Alex Welsh, with whom he remained until the early 60s. During that decade he played with various bands, led his own small groups and made many records, despite the fast-encroaching effects of a severe drinking problem. A very distinctive player with a rich and quirky musical imagination, Semple was one of the most strikingly individualistic musicians to emerge from the sometimes predictable British trad scene. His presence in the already formidable Welsh band helped to create memorable music.

● ALBUMS: *The Clarinet Of Archie Semple* (1957-58)★★★, with Welsh *It's Right Here For You* (1960)★★★★, *The Archie Semple Trio* (1960)★★★, *Archie Semple And His Orchestra* (1962)★★, *The Archie Semple Quartet* (1963)★★★.

SENFLUK, JERRY

b. 17 March 1946, Prague, Bohemia (Czechoslovakia). His pianist mother and cellist father encouraged his musical interests and upon taking up the clarinet he received private tuition from the principal clarinettist with the Czech Philharmonic Orchestra. His tutor was an admirer of Benny Goodman and his father brought home many jazz records from overseas tours; as a result he developed a deep interest in jazz and, in particular, swing era styles. When he was 12 years old he heard Edmond Hall during the veteran clarinettist's tour of Czechoslovakia. Four years later Senfluk made his first public appearance, playing in a jam session at the International Jazz Festival in Prague. Senfluk continued with his studies, graduating from the Conservatoire of Prague in 1967. By this time he had gained valuable experience playing with the Cats Jazz Band and the Jazz Fiddlers. In 1968 he began playing on Czechoslovak Radio and also became assistant editor of the popular music magazine *Melodie*. In 1969 he worked in both jazz and classical music, playing at the jazz festival in San Sebastien, Spain, and with the Orchestra Of The State Theatre in Aussig, Northern Bohemia. At the end of that year he moved to Berlin and toured Germany with a band supporting Albert Nicholas. In the early 70s he played in Germany, began teaching clarinet at the Steglitz School of Music, Berlin, and toured Germany and Switzerland with a traditional jazz band. He also visited London where he played with many noted jazzmen, including Fred Hunt. In 1974, together with his wife, Georgina, he opened the Coppelia Ballet School in Berlin. From the mid-70s he was active in Germany and the UK, mostly playing jazz but also developing an interest in the music of Brazil. At the end of the decade and on into the early 80s he led the Hallmark Swingtet in Berlin and worked extensively on radio and television in Germany. During the second half of the 80s he was frequently to be heard in London and also began travelling further afield and, as a result, built an international reputation. He also played with Al Casey and Max Collie, and wrote arrangements for Eggy Ley's show, *Prohibition And All That Jazz*. In 1991 he formed his Capital Swing band in London, with Mick Pyne, guitarist Nils Solberg, bassist John Rees-Jones and drummer Rex Bennett. During the mid-90s he continued to work extensively with this band, Martin Litton replacing Pyne after the latter's death. He also played residencies in Switzerland and appeared at festivals in the UK, Spain and Germany. Senfluk continues to divide his time between the UK and continental Europe, and balances his repertoire between jazz, which is the dominant form, and other areas of music. Technically assured and possessing enormous flair, Senfluk's clarinet playing is rooted firmly in the instrument's great jazz tradition, but he is clearly a musician who listens to and learns from a rich and ever-widening range of music.

● ALBUMS: with the Revival Jazz Band Of Prague *From East To West* (Amayana 1974)★★★, *We Swing - Take It From Me* (Loose Tie/Parrot 1994)★★★, with the Spirituál Quintet *Na Káre* (Pupava 1997)★★★.

SEVERINSEN, DOC

b. Carl Hilding Severinsen, 7 July 1927, Arlington, Oregon, USA. After playing trumpet in several name bands during the late years of the swing era (including the Tommy Dorsey, Charlie Barnet and Benny Goodman bands). Severinsen began a long career as a studio musician in New York in 1949, becoming assistant leader of Johnny Carson's *Tonight Show* orchestra in 1962. Following Lyle 'Skitch' Henderson's sudden departure in 1967, he became the orchestra's leader. In addition to leading the band and playing trumpet, he frequently wisecracked with host Carson, all of which helped to make him one of the best-known musicians in the USA. A sound, if occasionally over-spectacular, trumpeter, Severinsen's later work on the west coast displayed an interest in jazz-rock. When Carson retired in 1992, Severinsen and his orchestra were replaced by the band brought in by new host Jay Leno.

● ALBUMS: *Tempestuous Trumpet* (1960)★★★, *Doc Severinson And His Orchestra* i (Amherst 1965)★★★, *Doc Severinson And His Orchestra* ii (Amherst 1965)★★★, *Doc Severinson And His Orchestra* iii (Amherst 1966)★★★, *Night Journey* (1975)★★, *The Tonight Show Orchestra With Doc Severinson* (1986)★★, *Good Medicine* (1992)★★★.

SHAKATAK

This UK group were one of the original benefactors of the early 80s UK jazz/funk boom (alongside contemporaries Level 42). The group comprised Bill Sharpe (keyboards), George Anderson (bass), Keith Winter (guitar), Roger Odell (drums), Nigel Wright (keyboards, synthesizers) and Gil Seward (vocals). Between 1980 and 1987, Shakatak had 14 UK chart singles. Since their chart debut with 'Feels Like The First Time' on Polydor Records (a long-standing partnership), other notable hits have been 'Easier Said Than Done' (1981), 'Night Birds' (UK Top 10 - 1982), 'Dark Is The Night' (1983) and 'Down On The Street' (UK Top 10 - 1984). This understated group proved their reputation as one of the finest purveyors of classy jazz/funk with the successful K-Tel compilation *The Coolest Cuts*. The latter half of the 80s showed Shakatak leaving behind the demands of instant pop chart hits and allowing themselves to mature, honing their jazz influences - most evidently on the 1989 set *Turn The Music Up*, their first studio effort in almost five years. In addition to releasing a solo album in 1988, Sharpe collaborated with Gary Numan on the one-off single 'Change Your Mind', in 1985. On reaching the UK Top 20, it was not until four years later that the duo released a full album, *Automatic*. Sharpe also collaborated with producer Don Grusin on the Latin-jazz project *State Of The Heart*, a 1998 release that featured saxophonist/flautist Gerald

Albright, bassists Abe Laboriel and Brian Bromberg, drummer Alex Acuna, and vocalists Jeffrey Osborne and Pauline Wilson.

● ALBUMS: *Drivin' Hard* (Polydor 1981)★★★, *Nightbirds* (Polydor 1982)★★★, *Invitations* (Polydor 1982)★★★, *Out Of This World* (Polydor 1983)★★★, *Down On The Street* (Polydor 1984)★★★, *Live!* (Polydor 1985)★★, *Turn The Music Up* (Polydor 1989)★★★, *Bitter Sweet* (Polydor 1991)★★★, *Street Level* (1993)★★, *Live At Ronnie Scott's Club* (Indigo 1998)★★★, *Shinin' On* (Instinct 1998)★★★.

Solo: Bill Sharpe *Famous People* (Polydor 1988)★★, with Gary Numan *Automatic* (Polydor 1989)★★, *State Of The Heart* (Passion 1998)★★★.

● COMPILATIONS: *The Coolest Cuts* (K-Tel 1988)★★★, *The Remix Best Album* (1992)★★.

SHANK, BUD

b. Clifford Everett Jnr., 27 May 1926, Dayton, Ohio, USA. After studying and gigging on most of the reed instruments, Shank concentrated on alto saxophone, later doubling on flute and baritone saxophone. From 1947 he was resident on the west coast, playing in the big bands of Charlie Barnet, Alvino Rey, Art Mooney and Stan Kenton but making his greatest impact in small groups. With Shorty Rogers, Milt Bernhardt, Bob Cooper, Art Pepper and Shelly Manne, he was one of the tightly knit group of Los Angeles-based musicians who formed the nucleus of the white west coast jazz scene of the 50s. As a member of the Lighthouse All-Stars and groups recording under the names of one or another of the leaders of the movement, Shank built a substantial reputation. He also recorded with Laurindo Almeida, beginning an association that was renewed several years later with the formation of the LA Four. Although active in the film and television studios during the 50s and 60s, Shank continued to make jazz dates, and with increasing frequency. In 1974 he was a founder-member of the LA Four. In the early 80s, by then wholly engaged in jazz, he toured as a single and also with Rogers, appearing in the UK with the Vic Lewis big band and recording with the Royal Philharmonic Orchestra. Shank's extensive recorded output over four decades allows an interesting examination of his development as a musician. His early alto playing was derivative of Charlie Parker and Art Pepper, while his flute playing, taken up during his stint with Kenton, was highly original and greatly advanced the use of the instrument in bebop settings. In later years his alto style became highly personalized and no longer showed influences outside of his own creative impulse. Indeed, by the mid-80s he had reputedly abandoned his other instruments in order to concentrate fully on alto.

● ALBUMS: *Compositions Of Shorty Rogers* 10-inch album (Nocturne 1954)★★★, *Bud Shank And Three Trombones* 10-inch album (Pacific Jazz 1954)★★, with Laurindo Almeida *The Laurindo Almeida Quartet Featuring Bud Shank* aka *Brazilliance, Volume 1* (Pacific Jazz 1955)★★★, *Bud Shank And Bob Brookmeyer* 10-inch album (Pacific Jazz 1955)★★★, with Bob Cooper *Jazz At Cal-Tech* (Pacific Jazz 1956)★★★, with Cooper *Flute 'N Oboe* (Pacific Jazz 1957)★★★, with Claude Williamson *The Bud Shank Quartet* (Pacific Jazz 1957)★★★, with Cooper *The Swing's To TV* (Pacific Jazz 1957)★★, *I'll Take Romance* (World Pacific 1958)★★★, *Misty Eyes* (West Wind 1958)★★, *Holiday In Brazil* (World Pacific 1959)★★★, *Latin Contrasts* (World Pacific 1959)★★★, *Flute 'N Alto* (World Pacific 1960)★★★, *Koto 'N Flute* (World Pacific 1960)★★★, *Bud Shank Plays Tenor* (Pacific Jazz 1960)★★★, *New Groove* (Pacific Jazz 1961)★★★, *Improvisations* (World Pacific 1962)★★★, with Almeida *Brazilliance, Volume 2* (World Pacific 1962)★★★, with Almeida *Brazilliance, Volume 3* 1953 recordings (World Pacific 1962)★★★, *Bossa Nova Jazz Samba* (Pacific Jazz 1962)★★★, *Brasamba Bossa Nova* (Pacific Jazz 1963)★★★, *Bud Shank And His Brazilian Friends* (Pacific Jazz 1965)★★, *Bud Shank And The Sax Section* (Pacific Jazz 1966)★★★, *Folk 'N Flute* (World Pacific 1966)★★★, *Flute, Oboe And Strings* (World Pacific 1966)★★★, with Chet Baker *Michelle* (World Pacific 1966)★★★, *California Dreaming* (World Pacific 1966)★★★, *Girl In Love* (World Pacific 1967)★★★, *Brazil! Brazil! Brazil!* (World Pacific 1967)★★★, *A Spoonful Of Jazz* (World Pacific 1967)★★★, *Magical Mystery* (World Pacific 1967)★★★, *The Windmills Of Your Mind* (1969)★★, *Bud Shank And The Bob Alcivar Singers* (1970)★★, *The LA Four Scores!* (1975)★★★, *Sunshine Express* (Concord 1976)★★★, *Heritage* (1977)★★★, with LA Four *Watch What Happens* (1978)★★, *Crystal Comments* (Concord 1979)★★★, *Explorations 1980* (Concord 1979)★★★, *Shades Of Dring* (1981)★★, with Almeida *Selected Classical Works For Guitar And Flute* (1982)★★★, with Rogers *Yesterday, Today, And Forever* (1983)★★★, with Rogers, Vic Lewis *Back Again* (1984)★★★, *This Bud's For You* (Muse 1984)★★★★, *California Concert* (1985)★★★, *That Old Feeling* (Contemporary 1986)★★★, *Concert For Alto Saxophone And Symphony Orchestra* (1987)★★★, *Serious Swingers* (Contemporary 1987)★★★, *Tomorrow's Rainbow* (Contemporary 1987)★★★, *At Jazz Alley* (Contemporary 1987)★★★, *Tales Of The Pilot* (1989)★★★, *Lost In The Stars* (Fresh Sound 1991)★★★, *The Doctor Is In* (Candid 1992)★★★, with Almeida *Baa-Too-Kee* (1993)★★★, *I Told You So* (Candid 1994)★★★, *New Gold!* (Candid 1995)★★★, *Plays Harold Arlen* (1996)★★★★, *By Request* (Milestone 1998)★★★.

● COMPILATIONS: *The Pacific Jazz Bud Shank Studio Sessions* 5-CD/7-LP box set (Mosaic 1998)★★★★.

SHANKAR, LAKSHMINARAYANA

b. 26 April 1950, Madras, India. The son of noted violinist, V. Lakshminarayana, Shankar was taught to sing ragas at the age of two and began studying violin with his father at five. At his father's insistence he also studied a South Indian drum, the mridangam. It was his father, too, who encouraged him to learn from the North Indian (Hindustani) as well as his native South Indian (Carnatic) tradition. In 1969 he moved to the USA to take a PhD in ethnomusicology at the Wesleyan University. Subsequently, while working at the university, he began to meet jazz and rock musicians such as Ornette Coleman, Jimmy Garrison and John McLaughlin. From 1973 he and McLaughlin studied together and between 1975 and 1978 they co-led Shakti, an acoustic fusion of free jazz and Indian music, which grew out of Turyanandha Sangeeth, a duo with McLaughlin. He has continued to lead bands which cross the boundaries of music, including Peshkar,

Shankar and the less adventurous, rock-based Epidemics. In 1988 the Epidemics took part in a world tour for human rights along with Sting, Tracy Chapman, Bruce Springsteen and Peter Gabriel. A remarkable, compelling musician who can carry an audience with him through Hindustani, Carnatic and jazz-based music in a single concert, Shankar plays an impressive-looking and -sounding 10-string double-necked violin that he designed himself. He is much in demand for rock sessions requiring his unique sound, and can be heard (sometimes very briefly) on albums by Gabriel, Lou Reed, Talking Heads, Frank Zappa, Phil Collins, Echo And The Bunnymen and the Pretenders. He also played on the soundtrack of Martin Scorcese's *The Last Temptation Of Christ* and joined Bill Laswell's band, Material, for its 'comeback', *Seven Souls*.

● ALBUMS: with Shakti *Shakti* (1975)★★★★, *A Handful Of Beauty* (1976)★★★, *Natural Elements* (1977)★★★, *Touch Me There* (1979)★★★, with the Epidemics *The Epidemics, Who's To Know* (ECM 1981)★★★★, *Song For Everyone* (ECM 1984)★★★, with the Epidemics *Vision, Caroline* (1986)★★★, with Material *Seven Souls* (1989)★★★, *Nobody Told Me* (ECM 1990)★★★★, *Pancha Nadai Pallavi* (1990)★★★★, *Soul Searcher* (Axiom 1991)★★★, *Les Heures Et Les Saisons* (Occora 1993)★★★.

SHAPE OF JAZZ TO COME, THE - ORNETTE COLEMAN

As the 50s ended, Ornette Coleman became the new herald of the future of jazz, surpassing for a time, even John Coltrane. Intent on feeling and with often scant regard for technique, he plunged headlong into a musical form that defied categorization and dismayed orthodox musicologists. Especially aware of the blues, Coleman eschewed a rigid structure in the music and favoured instead explorations of its poetic content. Free jazz to Coleman and his followers was jazz freed not only from musical restraints but also from sociological and cultural parameters. This album demonstrates his radicalism and his awareness of both past and future jazz.

● Tracks: *Lonely Woman; Eventually; Peace; Focus On Sanity; Congeniality Chronology.*

● First released 1960

● UK peak chart position: did not chart

● USA peak chart position: did not chart

SHAPIRO, ARTIE

b. Arthur Shapiro, 15 January 1916, Denver, Colorado, USA. As a small child Shapiro went to New York with his family where he became interested in music, playing trumpet before settling on the bass. He played with several well-known jazzmen of the mid-30s, including Gil Rodin, Wingy Manone and Joe Marsala. From the end of the 30s onwards, interrupted only by military service during World War II, he was active as a studio musician. In this capacity he played on numerous jazz recording sessions with a host of leading names, among them Sharkey Bonano, Red McKenzie, Bud Freeman, Eddie Condon and Chu Berry. He also spent some time with Paul Whiteman's orchestra. Shapiro subsequently moved to the west coast where he continued to divide his time between studio work and jazz recording dates, now with musicians such as Jack Teagarden, Artie Shaw and Benny Goodman. He was often on call for recording dates by popular singers, among them Bing Crosby and Frank Sinatra. Shapiro's excellent time and his outstanding musicianship kept him extremely active for more than five decades.

● ALBUMS: with Jess Stacy *A Tribute To Benny Goodman* (Atlantic 1955)★★★.

SHAPIRO, HELEN

b. 28 September 1946, Bethnal Green, London, England. Helen Shapiro drew considerable attention when, as a 14-year-old schoolgirl, she scored a UK Top 3 hit with 'Don't Treat Me Like A Child'. A deep intonation belied her youth, and by the end of 1961 the singer had scored two chart-topping singles with 'You Don't Know' and 'Walkin' Back To Happiness'. This success was maintained the following year with 'Tell Me What He Said' (number 2) and 'Little Miss Lonely' (number 8), as Shapiro won concurrent polls as 'Best British Female Singer' and was voted 'Best Newcomer' by the Variety Club of Great Britain. However, having recorded the original version of 'It's My Party' during an artistically fruitful session in Nashville, Helen was disappointed when an acetate reached Lesley Gore, who enjoyed a massive international hit using a similar arrangement. Shapiro's producer, Norrie Paramor, also vetoed the opportunity to record 'Misery', composed with Shapiro in mind by John Lennon and Paul McCartney. Indeed the advent of the Beatles helped to undermine the singer's career. Despite being younger than many beat group members, Shapiro was perceived as belonging to a now outmoded era and despite a series of excellent singles, was eclipsed by 'newcomers' Cilla Black and Dusty Springfield. The late 60s proved more fallow still and, barring one pseudonymous release, Shapiro did not record at all between 1970 and 1975. A Russ Ballard song, 'Can't Break The Habit', became a minor hit in Europe during 1977 and in turn engendered *All For The Love Of The Music*, a set sadly denied a UK release. Six years later Shapiro resurfaced on writer Charlie Gillett's Oval label. *Straighten Up And Fly Right* showed the singer had lost none of her early power and this excellent collection of standards was rightly acclaimed. An equally confident collaboration with jazz musician Humphrey Lyttelton ensued, since which Shapiro has maintained a high profile through radio, television and live appearances, singing jazz-influenced big band material and gospel songs. She also made an impressive London cabaret debut at the Café Royal in 1995.

● ALBUMS: *Tops With Me* (Columbia 1962)★★★★, *Helen's Sixteen* (Columbia 1963)★★★★, *Helen In Nashville* (Columbia 1963)★★, *Helen Hits Out* (Columbia 1964)★★★, *All For The Love Of The Music* (1977)★★★, *Straighten Up And Fly Right* (Oval 1983)★★★, *Echoes Of The Duke* (1985)★★★, *The Quality Of Mercer* (Calligraph 1987)★★★★, *Nothing But The Best* (1995)★★★.

● COMPILATIONS: *Twelve Hits And A Miss Shapiro* (Encore

1967)★★★, *The Very Best Of Helen Shapiro* (Columbia 1974)★★★★, *The 25th Anniversary Album* (MFP 1986)★★★★, *The EP Collection* (See For Miles 1989)★★★★, *Sensational! The Uncollected Helen Shapiro* (RPM 1995)★★★.

● FURTHER READING: *Walking Back To Happiness*, Helen Shapiro. *Helen Shapiro: Pop Princess*, John S. Janson.

● FILMS: *It's Trad, Dad* aka *Ring-A-Ding Rhythm* (1962).

SHARON, RALPH

b. 17 September 1923, London, England. Sharon came to prominence as pianist with the Ted Heath band in the years immediately following World War II. He also played, and sometimes recorded, with British bop musicians of the late 40s, including Ronnie Scott and Victor Feldman. In the early 50s he moved to the USA, became an American citizen, and continued to play piano in a variety of settings, frequently in distinguished company. He also established a reputation as a sympathetic accompanist to singers, notably Tony Bennett and Chris Connor. On one of his albums with Bennett, Sharon wrote arrangements for the Count Basie band, playing piano on most tracks, while on another album, three decades later, he arranged songs by Irving Berlin for his own small group, with added guests who included George Benson, Dexter Gordon and Dizzy Gillespie. Sharon's habitual diffidence has kept him hidden from the spotlight he clearly deserves. Among his early American recordings were some with his wife, the singer Sue Ryan. In the mid-90s he was regularly on the world's stages accompanying Tony Bennett.

● ALBUMS: *The Ralph Sharon Sextet i* (1955)★★★, *The Ralph Sharon Trio* (Bethlehem 1956)★★★, *Mr & Mrs Jazz* (Fresh Sounds 1956)★★, *The Ralph Sharon Sextet ii* (1957)★★★, *The Ralph Sharon Quartet* (1958)★★★, *Ralph Sharon With The Rolena Carter Chorale* (1962)★★★, *Do I Hear A Waltz* (Columbia 1965)★★★, *The Magic Of George Gershwin* (Horatio Nelson 1988)★★★★, *The Magic Of Irving Berlin* (Horatio Nelson 1989)★★★★, *The Magic Of Cole Porter* (Horatio Nelson 1989)★★★★, *Portrait Of Harold* (DRG 1996)★★★.

SHARPE, BILL

(see Shakatak)

SHARROCK, SONNY

b. Warren Harding Sharrock, 27 August 1940, Ossining, New York, USA, d. 26 May 1994, Ossining, New York, USA. Now regarded as one of the most remarkable guitarists in contemporary jazz, Sharrock was a late starter, teaching himself the instrument at the age of 20. Before that he sang in a doo-wop group, the Echoes. He recorded with them for Alan Freed but the tracks were never released. When he was 21 he spent a few months studying formally at Berklee College Of Music. Starting in 1965 he worked with a succession of major names in the *avant garde* (including Pharoah Sanders, Don Cherry, Sunny Murray and Olatunji, John Gilmore and Byard Lancaster) then from 1967-73 provided the 'outside' element in Herbie Mann's band. In 1970 he contributed to 'Yesternow', the second part of Miles Davis's *Jack Johnson*. In 1973 he formed a band with his then wife, Linda Sharrock (Chambers), but was relatively quiet until he emerged in 1982 to record with Bill Laswell's Material. In 1986, he played with Laswell, Peter Brötzmann, and Ronald Shannon Jackson in Last Exit. After a fascinating and innovative solo album, *Guitar*, he established a more conventional band which toured successfully with packages organized by New York's Knitting Factory club. In 1991 he released *Ask The Ages*, with an all-star quartet containing Sanders, Charnett Moffett and Elvin Jones. Sharrock died of a heart attack in May 1994.

● ALBUMS: *Black Woman* (Vortex 1969)★★★, *Monkie Pockie Boo* (Affinity 1974)★★★, *Paradise* (1974)★★★, *Guitar* (Enemy 1986)★★★★, *Live In New York* (Enemy 1990)★★★, *Highlife* (Enemy 1991)★★★, with Nicky Skopelitis *Faith Moves* (1991)★★★★, *Ask The Ages* (Axiom 1991)★★★★.

● COMPILATIONS: *Into Another Light* (Enemy 1996)★★.

SHAVERS, CHARLIE

b. 3 August 1917, New York City, New York, USA, d. 8 July 1971, New York, USA. Shavers took up trumpet in his teens and played with various minor bands before joining Tiny Bradshaw in 1937. In the same year he played with Lucky Millinder, Jimmie Noone and John Kirby. The Kirby sextet proved an ideal setting for him, both as trumpeter and arranger, and he stayed for seven years. Among his compositions written during his time with Kirby are 'Pastel Blue', which with lyrics added became 'Why Begin Again', and 'Undecided', which became a jazz standard in its own right and with added lyrics a hit for Ella Fitzgerald. In 1944 he left Kirby for the Tommy Dorsey orchestra, where for a decade he was featured soloist. He made records throughout these years with various leaders, including a session under the nominal guidance of Herbie Haymer that featured Nat 'King' Cole and Buddy Rich. This set was issued, fluffs, retakes, off-microphone comments and all, under the title *Anatomy Of A Jam Session*. Another admirable date from this period was a Gene Norman concert at Pasadena, California, issued under Lionel Hampton's name. In the 50s and 60s Shavers played mostly in small groups, often as leader, touring extensively as a single and with Jazz At The Philharmonic. A masterly musician, Shavers was capable of adapting to almost any mainstream setting. In the right company he would produce emotionally powerful playing; with Kirby he played with the elegance and finesse this group demanded, and in his later years with JATP he would deliver wildly exciting bravura solos, all with remarkable ease and overt good humour.

● ALBUMS: with Nat 'King' Cole and Buddy Rich *Anatomy Of A Jam Session* (1945)★★★, with Lionel Hampton *Stardust* (1945)★★★, *Jazz At The Philharmonic: Hartford 1953* (1953)★★★★, *Horn O'Plenty* 10-inch album (Bethlehem 1954)★★★★, with Maxine Sullivan *Flow Gently, Sweet Rhythm* 10-inch album (Period 1955)★★★, *The Most Intimate Charlie Shavers* 10-inch album (Bethlehem 1955)★★★, *Gershwin, Shavers And Strings* (Bethlehem 1955)★★★, *We Dig Cole!* (1958)★★, with Jonah Jones *Sounds Of The Trumpets* (Bethlehem 1959)★★★, *Charlie Digs Paree* (MGM 1959)★★★,

Charlie Digs Dixie (MGM 1960)★★★, *Girl Of My Dreams* (Everest 1960)★★★★, *Here Comes Charlie* (Everest 1960)★★★, *Like Charlie* (Everest 1961)★★★, *The Charlie Shavers-Wild Bill Davis Combo* (1961)★★★, *A Man And His Music* (1962)★★★, *Live At The London House* (1962)★★, *Live From Chicago* (1962)★★★, *Excitement Unlimited* (Capitol 1963)★★, *Charlie Shavers At Le Crazy Horse Saloon In Paris* (Everest 1964)★★★, *The Last Session* (1970)★★★, *Live!* (Black And Blue 1970)★★★.
● COMPILATIONS: *November 1961 & March 1962* (1980)★★★, *Trumpet Man (1944-58)* (1981)★★★.

Shaw, Artie

b. Arthur Jacob Arshawsky, 23 May 1910, New York City, New York, USA. Shaw took up the alto saxophone at the age of 12 and a few years later was playing in a Connecticut dance band. In 1926, he switched to clarinet and spent the next three years working in Cleveland, Ohio, as arranger and musical director for Austin Wylie. He also played in Irving Aaronson's popular band, doubling on tenor saxophone. In New York from the end of 1929, Shaw became a regular at after-hours sessions, sitting in with leading jazzmen and establishing a reputation as a technically brilliant clarinettist. He made numerous record dates with dance bands and jazz musicians including Teddy Wilson, with whom he appeared on some of Billie Holiday's sessions. In 1936, Shaw formed a band which included strings for a concert and, with the addition of regular dance band instruments, secured a recording contract. The band did not last long and in April 1937 he formed a conventional big band that was an immediate success, thanks in part to melodic arrangements by Jerry Gray. The band made several records including 'Begin The Beguine', which was a huge popular success. Musically, Shaw's band was one of the best of the period and, during the first couple of years of its existence, included Johnny Best, Cliff Leeman, Les Robinson, Georgie Auld, Tony Pastor and Buddy Rich. During 1938 Shaw briefly had Holiday as the band's singer, but racial discrimination in New York hotels and on the band's radio shows led to a succession of disagreeable confrontations that eventually compelled the singer to quit. Other singers Shaw used were Kitty Kallen and Helen Forrest. Always uneasy with publicity and the demands of the public, Shaw abruptly folded the band late in 1939, but a featured role in the 1940 Fred Astaire-Paulette Goddard film, *Second Chorus*, brought another hit, 'Frenesi', and he quickly re-formed a band. The new band included a string section and a band-within-a-band, the Gramercy Five. The big band included Billy Butterfield, Jack Jenney, Nick Fatool and Johnny Guarnieri. In the small group, Guarnieri switched from piano to harpsichord to create a highly distinctive sound. More successful records followed, including 'Concert For Clarinet', 'Summit Ridge Drive' and 'Special Delivery Stomp'. Shaw's dislike of celebrity caused him to disband once again, but he soon regrouped, only to be forced to fold when the USA entered the war. In 1942 he headed a band in the US Navy that included several leading jazzmen. After the war he formed a new band that featured Roy Eldridge, Dodo Marmarosa, Barney Kessel, Chuck Gentry, Stan Fishelson and other top musicians. This band, like all the others, was short-lived and during the rest of the 40s Shaw periodically formed bands only to break them up again within a few months. At the same time he also studied classical guitar and began to develop a secondary career as a writer. By the mid-50s he had retired from music and spent much of his time writing. He lived for a number of years in Spain but in the late 60s returned to the USA, where he continued to expand his writing career. In the 80s he reassembled a band, under the direction of Dick Johnson, and performed at special concerts. In 1985 a film documentary, *Time Is All You've Got*, traced his career in detail. In June 1992 he appeared in London at a concert performance where Bob Wilber recreated some of his music.

During the late 30s and early 40s Shaw was set up as a rival to Benny Goodman, but the antagonism was a creation of publicists; in reality, the two men were amicable towards one another. Nevertheless, fans of the pair were divided, heatedly arguing the merits of their respective idol. Stylistically, Shaw's playing was perhaps slightly cooler than Goodman's, although his jazz sense was no less refined. Like Goodman, Shaw was a technical marvel, playing with remarkable precision, yet always swinging. His erratic bandleading career, allied as it was to a full private life - among his eight wives were some of Hollywood's most glamorous stars - militated against his ever achieving the same level of success as Goodman or many other bandleading contemporaries. Nevertheless, his bands were always musicianly and his frequent hiring of black musicians, including Holiday, Eldridge and Oran 'Hot Lips' Page, helped to break down racial barriers in music.

● ALBUMS: *Modern Music For Clarinet* (Columbia 1950)★★★, *Artie Shaw Plays Cole Porter* 10-inch album (MGM 1950)★★★, *Artie Shaw Dance Program* 10-inch album (Decca 1950)★★★, *Speak To Me Of Love* 10-inch album (Decca 1950)★★★, *Artie Shaw Favorites* 10-inch album (RCA Victor 1952)★★★, *Four Star Favorites* 10-inch album (RCA Victor 1952)★★★, *This Is Artie Shaw* 10-inch album (RCA Victor 1952)★★★, *Artie Shaw With Strings* 10-inch album (Epic 1954)★★★, *Non-Stop Flight* 10-inch album (Epic 1954)★★★, *Artie Shaw And His Grammercy Five, Volumes 1-4* (Clef 1955)★★★★, *An Hour With Artie Shaw* (Allegro 1955)★★★, *Artie Shaw* 10-inch album (Epic 1955)★★★, *Artie Shaw And His Orchestra* (Epic 1955)★★★, *My Concerto* (RCA Victor 1955)★★★, *Both Feet In The Groove* (RCA Victor 1956)★★★, *Back Bay Shuffle* (RCA Victor 1956)★★★, *Did Someone Say Party?* (Decca 1956)★★★, *Artie Shaw And His Gramercy Five* (RCA Victor 1956)★★★, *Sequence In Music* (Verve 1956)★★★, *Moonglow* (RCA Victor 1956)★★★, *Any Old Time* (RCA Victor 1957)★★★, *A Man And His Dream* (RCA Victor 1957)★★★, *Plays Irving Berlin And Cole Porter* (Lion 1958)★★★, *One Night Stand* (Camden 1959)★★★.

● COMPILATIONS: *Artie Shaw Recreates His Great '38 Band* (1963)★★★, *The 1938 Band In Hi-Fi (1938)* (Fanfare 1979)★★★★, *Swinging Big Bands, 1938-45, Volumes 1 & 2* (Joker 1981)★★★, *Melody And Madness Volumes 1-5 (1938-39)* (Nostalgia/Mainline 1982)★★★, *This Is Artie Shaw* (RCA

1983)★★★, *Traffic Jam* (Big Band Era/Mainline 1985)★★★, *The Indispensable Artie Shaw Volumes 1/2 (1938-39)* (RCA 1986)★★★★, *The Indispensable Artie Shaw Volumes 3/4 (1940-42)* (RCA 1986)★★★★, *The Rhythmakers Volumes 1-8 (1937-38)* (Bluebird 1987)★★★, *Thou Swell (1936-37)* (Living Era/ASV 1988)★★★, *Gloomy Sunday* (Pickwick 1992)★★★, *Frenesi* (Bluebird 1992)★★★, *The Last Recordings: Rare & Unreleased* (S&R 1992)★★, *More Last Recordings: The Final Sessions* (Music Masters)★★★, *Personal Best* (Bluebird 1992)★★★★, *Lets Go For Shaw* (Avid 1993)★★★.

● FURTHER READING: *The Trouble With Cinderella: An Outline Of Identity*, Artie Shaw.

Shaw, Arvell

b. 15 September 1923, St. Louis, Missouri, USA. Although he had previously studied other instruments, Shaw began playing bass while working with the Fate Marable band in the early 40s. Shortly after this, military service interrupted his career but soon after World War II ended he joined Louis Armstrong, a job that, on and off, lasted for a quarter of a century. First, he was with Armstrong's big band; he rejoined when the All Stars were formed in 1945, staying until 1953 (with a short break to study in Switzerland). In the mid- to late 50s and in the 60s he made frequent return visits to Armstrong but found time for appearances with Benny Goodman, Teddy Wilson and others. After Armstrong's death in 1971, Shaw worked with a number of mainstream jazz artists, including Buddy Tate, Dorothy Donegan and Earl Hines, freelanced in the USA and Europe and then, in the 80s, re-entered the Armstrong fold by joining Keith Smith's *Wonderful World Of Louis Armstrong* concert package. A solid and thoroughly dependable member of the rhythm section, Shaw is also an energetic and accomplished soloist whose playing always commands attention.

Shaw, Charles 'Bobo'

b. 15 September 1947, Pope, Mississippi, USA. Shaw studied with a string of drummers and also learned bass and trombone with Frank Mokuss. He played drums in R&B bands, backing soul saxophonist Oliver Sain, singers Ike And Tina Turner and bluesman Albert King. He moved to St. Louis, Missouri, and was a founder of BAG (Black Artists Group). There he met and played with altoist Oliver Lake as well as playing in the St. Louis Symphony Orchestra. In the early 70s he moved with other BAG members to Europe, where he played with Anthony Braxton, Steve Lacy, Frank Wright and Alan Silva. He calls his bands the Human Arts Ensemble or (more recently) the Red, Black & Green Solidarity Unit. In 1972 the Human Arts Ensemble made its debut recording with *Whisper Of Dharma*, followed a year later by *Under The Sun*, which featured Lake and Lester Bowie as guest artists. In 1974 Shaw moved to New York, and in the next few years recorded with Frank Lowe (*Fresh*, *The Flam*), Bowie (*Fast Last*, *Rope-A-Dope*) and Lake (*Heavy Spirits*). In 1977 he recorded a duo album with Bowie (*Bugle Boy Bop*), although this was not released until 1983. He also teamed up with Bowie's trombonist brother, Joseph Bowie, in a new line-up of the Human Arts Ensemble and in the next two years released *P'nk J'zz*; *Trio Performances Vol 1*, which featured guitarist James Emery (from String Trio Of New York), *Vol 2*, which featured Luther Thomas on alto and John Lindberg (also from STONY) on bass, and *Junk Trap*, which combined all five players. Shaw also played on two Human Arts Ensemble dates led by Thomas (*Funky Donkey Vol 1*, *Poem Of Gratitude*) and as a member of the St Louis Creative Ensemble, which played Europe in 1979 and recorded *I Can't Figure Out*. Since this burst of activity little has been heard from him, apart from appearances with Marion Brown and Bowie's punk-funk group Defunkt.

● ALBUMS: with the Human Arts Ensemble *Whisper Of Dharma* (1973)★★★, *Streets Of St Louis* (1974)★★, with HAE *Under The Sun* 1973 recording (1975)★★★, with Luther Thomas/HAE *Poem Of Gratitude* (70s)★★★, with Luther Thomas/HAE *Funky Donkey Vol 1* (1977)★★★, with HAE *P'nk J'zz* (1977)★★, with HAE *Trio Performances Vols 1* and *2* (1978)★★★, with HAE *Junk Trap* (1978)★★★★, with St Louis Creative Ensemble *I Can't Figure Out* (1979)★★★, with Lester Bowie *Bugle Boy Bop* 1977 recording (Muse 1983)★★★★.

Shaw, Ian

b. 2 June 1962, St. Asaph, North Wales. Shaw studied piano and music theory at Kings College, London, where he gained a Bachelor of Music in 1983. He later encountered Mel Tormé in Amsterdam, a stimulus that still informs his performances. In 1987 he returned to London, forming the soul/rock band Brave New World with keyboard player Adrian York. He appeared at Ronnie Scott's, and toured Europe with virtuoso blues and jazz vocalist Carol Grimes. This association yielded 1990's *Lazy Blue Eyes*. He won a Perrier Award, was nominated Best British Jazz Singer by the *Guardian*, and guested on Fairground Attraction's *First Of A Million Kisses*. In 1992 he released *Ghostsongs*, recorded at Ronnie Scott's. The set showcased Shaw's catholic taste, from Duke Ellington to Charles Mingus, including a haunting interpretation of 'Danny Boy'. It captured his astounding vocal range, dipping into scat and occasionally applied as an additional instrument. Touring to promote the album, Shaw guested with Kenny Wheeler and John Taylor, and contributed to Yello's *Zebra*. He became a staple of the London jazz scene, sometimes playing alone at the piano, sometimes with full backing band. *Taking It To Hart*, a tribute to Richard Rodgers and Lorenz Hart, featured appearances by Guy Barker, Mari Wilson, Iain Ballamy and Carol Grimes.

● ALBUMS: with Carol Grimes *Lazy Blue Eyes* (1990)★★, *Ghostsongs* (1992)★★★, *Taking It To Hart* (Jazz House 1995)★★★.

Shaw, Marlena

b. Marlina Burgess, 1944, New Rochelle, New York, USA. Shaw was a cocktail lounge-type jazz singer who occasionally ventured onto the soul music charts. She began her career in 1963, and was discovered by Chess

Records in 1966 while singing on the Playboy lounge circuit. On Chess's Cadet subsidiary, under the aegis of producer Richard Evans, she performed vocal counterparts of jazz hits such as 'Mercy Mercy Mercy' (number 33 R&B, number 58 pop) by Cannonball Adderley and 'Wade In The Water' by Ramsey Lewis Trio. Chess released two albums and a series of singles before Shaw left the company in 1968. For the next five years she performed periodically with Count Basie, and after signing with Blue Note Records in 1972 built a solidly based jazz recording career. Her most popular album for the company was *Who Is This Bitch, Anyway?*, but her last Blue Note release in 1976, *Just A Matter Of Time*, saw a more disco-driven result that yielded a modest chart single, 'It's Better Than Walkin' Out' (number 74 R&B). A move to Columbia Records in 1977 resulted in her biggest chart success with *Sweet Beginnings* and a hit single, 'Go Away Little Boy' (number 21 R&B), a remake of Steve Lawrence's 'Go Away Little Girl'. From an album for South Bay, *Let Me In Your Life*, she achieved her last chart single, 'Never Give Up On You' (number 91 R&B), but has remained active in the 90s, recently signing to the Concord label.

● ALBUMS: *Out Of Different Bags* (Cadet 1967)★★★, *The Spice Of Life* (Cadet 1968)★★★, *From The Depths Of My Soul* (Blue Note 1973)★★★, *Live At Montreaux* (Blue Note 1974)★★★, *Who Is This Bitch Anyway?* (Blue Note 1975)★★★, *Just A Matter Of Time* (Blue Note 1976)★★, *Sweet Beginnings* (Columbia 1977)★★★, *Acting Up* (Columbia 1978)★★★, *Take A Bite* (Columbia 1979)★★★, *Let Me In Your Life* (South Bay 1983)★★★, *Love Is In Flight* (Polydor 1988)★★, *Dangerous* (Concord Jazz 1996)★★★, *Elemental Soul* (Concord Jazz 1997)★★★.

SHAW, WOODY

b. Herman Shaw II, 24 December 1944, Laurinburg, North Carolina, USA, d. 11 May 1989. Shaw was raised in Newark, New Jersey, where his father sang in a gospel group. Taking up the trumpet at the age of 11, he quickly attained a level of proficiency that allowed him to sit in with visiting jazzmen. He left school when he was 16 years old to work in New York with Willie Bobo in whose band he played alongside Chick Corea and Joe Farrell. He also met Eric Dolphy, recording with him on 1963's *Iron Man*. The following year Dolphy invited Shaw to join his European tour, but died before the trumpeter had arrived. Shaw decided to go to Europe anyway, and stayed for a while in France, playing with Kenny Clarke, Bud Powell and others. Back in the USA in the mid-60s he joined Horace Silver, recording *The Cape Verdean Blues* (1965) and *The Jody Grind* (1966) and also worked with McCoy Tyner and Art Blakey. In the late 60s and early 70s he was busy as a studio musician and to some extent his jazz reputation suffered through his absence from the scene. He began recording for the Muse label in 1974 and this heralded a revival of interest in his work. He again played with Corea and Blakey and his group backed Dexter Gordon on his return to the USA, recording *The Homecoming* (1976). In the early 80s Shaw's band was in constant flux and amongst the musicians he used were Terri Lyne Carrington and Larry Willis. In 1984 he was featured with the Paris Reunion Band, appearing on two fine albums, *French Cooking* and *For Klook*. Shaw suffered periods of severe illness, mostly induced through problems of drug addiction. He was going blind when, early in 1989, he visited the Village Vanguard to hear Max Roach. On the way home, he appeared to stumble down the steps at a New York subway station and fell under an approaching train, severing an arm. Though rushed to hospital, he remained in a coma and died three months later. Shaw's playing was filled with the crackling brilliance of a post-Dizzy Gillespie trumpeter and yet he had the warmth that characterized musicians such as Clifford Brown and Freddie Hubbard, in whose shadow he laboured. Given a slight shift in time, and a major change in his personal habits, Shaw could well have been one of the great names of contemporary jazz.

● ALBUMS: *Blackstone Legacy* (Contemporary 1971)★★★, *Cassandranite* (Muse 1972)★★★★, *Song Of Songs* (1973)★★★, *Moontrane* (Muse 1974)★★★★, *Love Dance* (Muse 1976)★★★, *The Woody Shaw Concert Ensemble At The Berliner Jazztage* (Muse 1977)★★★, *Little Red's Fantasy* (Muse 1978)★★★★, *Stepping Stones* (Columbia 1978)★★★, *Rosewood* (Columbia 1978)★★★★, *Woody III* (Columbia 1979)★★, *The Iron Men* 1977 recording (Muse 1981)★★★, *United* (1981)★★★, *Lotus Flower* (Enja 1982)★★, *Master Of The Art* (Elektra Musician 1982)★★★, *Time Is Right* (Red 1983)★★, *Night Music* (Elektra 1984)★★★, *Setting Standards* (1985)★★★, with Freddie Hubbard *Double Take* (Blue Note 1985)★★, *Woody Shaw With The Tone Jansa Quartet* (Timeless 1986)★★★, *Imagination* (Muse 1987)★★★, *Solid* (Muse 1987)★★★, with Hubbard *The Eternal Triangle* (Blue Note 1987)★★★, *In My Own Sweet Way* (In And Out 1989)★★★★, *Bemsha Swing* 1986 recording (Blue Note 1998)★★★.

SHEARING, GEORGE

b. 13 August 1919, London, England. Shearing was born blind but started to learn piano at the age of three. After limited training and extensive listening to recorded jazz, he began playing at hotels, clubs and pubs in the London area, sometimes as a single, occasionally with dance bands. In 1940 he joined Harry Parry's popular band and also played with Stéphane Grappelli. Shortly after visiting the USA in 1946, Shearing decided to settle there. Although at this time in his career he was influenced by bop pianists, notably Bud Powell, it was a complete break with this style that launched his career as a major star. Developing the locked-hands technique of playing block-chords, and accompanied by a discreet rhythm section of guitar, bass, drums and vibraphone, he had a succession of hugely popular records including 'September In The Rain' and his own composition, 'Lullaby Of Birdland'. With shifting personnel, which over the years included Cal Tjader, Margie Hyams, Denzil Best, Israel Crosby, Joe Pass and Gary Burton, the Shearing quintet remained popular until 1967. Later, Shearing played with a trio, as a solo and increasingly in duo. Among his collaborations have been sets with the Montgomery Brothers, Marian McPartland, Brian Torff, Jim Hall, Hank Jones and Kenny Davern (on a rather polite Dixieland selection). Over the years he has worked fruitfully with singers including Peggy Lee, Ernestine Anderson, Carmen McRae, and, especially, Mel Tormé, with whom he performed frequently in the late 80s and early 90s at festivals, on radio and record dates. Shearing's interest in classical music resulted in some performances with concert orchestras in the 50s and 60s, and his solos frequently touch upon the musical patterns of Claude Debussy and, particularly, Erik Satie. Indeed, Shearing's delicate touch and whimsical nature make him an ideal interpreter of Satie's work. As a jazz player Shearing has sometimes been the victim of critical indifference and even hostility. Mostly, reactions such as these centre upon the long period when he led his quintet. It might well be that the quality of the music was often rather lightweight but a second factor was the inability of some commentators on the jazz scene to accept an artist who had achieved wide public acceptance and financial success. That critical disregard should follow Shearing into his post-quintet years is inexplicable and unforgivable. Many of his late performances, especially his solo albums and those with Torff, bassist Neil Swainson, and Tormé, are superb examples of a pianist at the height of his powers. Inventive and melodic, his improvisations are unblushingly romantic but there is usually a hint of whimsy that happily reflects the warmth and offbeat humour of the man himself.

● ALBUMS: *George Shearing Quintet* 10-inch album (Discovery 1949)★★★, *Piano Solo* 10-inch album (Savoy 1950)★★★, *Souvenirs* 10-inch album (London 1951)★★★, *You're Hearing The George Shearing Quartet* 10-inch album (MGM 1950)★★★, *Touch Of Genius* 10-inch album (MGM 1951)★★★, *I Hear Music* 10-inch album (MGM 1952)★★★, *When Lights Are Low* 10-inch album (MGM 1953)★★★, *An Evening With George Shearing* 10-inch album (MGM 1954)★★★, *Shearing In Hi-Fi* (MGM 1955)★★★★, *The Shearing Spell* (Capitol 1955)★★★, *By Request* (London 1956)★★★, *Latin Escapade* (Capitol 1956)★★★, *Velvet Carpet* (Capitol 1956)★★★, *Black Satin* (Capitol 1957)★★★, *Shearing Piano* (Capitol 1957)★★★, *Burnished Brass* (Capitol 1958)★★★, *Latin Lace* (Capitol 1958)★★★, with Peggy Lee *Americana Hotel* (1959)★★★★, *Blue Chiffon* (Capitol 1959)★★★, *Shearing On Stage* (Capitol 1959)★★★, *Latin Affair* (Capitol 1959)★★★, *White Satin* (Capitol 1960)★★★, *On The Sunny Side Of The Strip* (Capitol 1960)★★★, *San Francisco Scene* (Capitol 1960)★★★, *The Shearing Touch* (Capitol 1960)★★★, with the Montgomery Brothers *Love Walked In* (Jazzland 1961)★★★, *Mood Latino* (Capitol 1961)★★★, *Satin Affair* (Capitol 1961)★★★, *Nat 'King' Cole Sings/George Shearing Plays* (Capitol 1962)★★★★, *Soft And Silky* (MGM 1962)★★★, *Jazz Moments* (Capitol 1963)★★★, *Jazz Concert* (Capitol 1963)★★★, *Bossa Nova* (Capitol 1963)★★★, *Deep Velvet* (Capitol 1964)★★★, *Rare Form* (Capitol 1965)★★★, *Out Of The Woods* (Capitol 1965)★★★, *Classic Shearing* (Verve 1966)★★★, *That Fresh Feeling* (Capitol 1966)★★★, *George Shearing Today* (Capitol 1968)★★★, *Fool On The Hill* (Capitol 1969)★★★, *My Ship* (Polydor 1974)★★★, *Light, Airy And Swinging* (1974)★★★, *The Way We Are* (1974)★★★, *Continental Experience* (1975)★★★, with Stéphane Grappelli *The Reunion* (PA 1976)★★★, *The Many Facets Of George Shearing* (1976)★★★, *500 Miles High* (MPS 1977)★★★, *Windows* (1977)★★★, *On Target* (1979)★★, with Brian Torff *Blues Alley Jazz* (Concord 1979)★★★, *Getting In The Swing Of Things* (1979)★★★, *On A Clear Day* (Concord 1980)★★★, with Carmen McRae *Two For The Road* (Concord 1980)★★★, with Marian McPartland *Alone Together* (Concord 1981)★★★★, with Jim Hall *First Edition* (Concord 1981)★★★, *An Evening With Mel Tormé And George Shearing* (1982)★★★, with Mel Tormé *Top Drawer* (Concord 1983)★★★, *Bright Dimensions* (1984)★★★, *Live At The Cafe Carlyle* (Concord 1984)★★★, *Grand Piano* (Concord 1985)★★★, with Tormé *An Elegant Evening* (1985)★★★, *George Shearing And Barry Treadwell Play The Music Of Cole Porter* (Concord 1986)★★★, *More Grand Piano* (Concord 1986)★★★, *Breakin' Out* (Concord 1987)★★★★, *Dexterity* (Concord 1987)★★★, *A Vintage Year* (1987)★★★, with Ernestine Anderson *A Perfect Match* (Concord 1988)★★★, with Hank Jones *The Spirit Of '76* (Concord 1988)★★★, *Piano* (Concord 1989)★★★, *George Shearing In Dixieland* (Concord 1989)★★, with Tormé *Mel And George 'Do' World War II* (1990)★★★, *I Hear A Rhapsody - Live At The Blue Note* (Telarc 1992)★★★, *Walkin'* (Telarc 1995)★★★, *Paper Moon: Music Of Nat King Cole* (Telarc 1996)★★★, *Favorite Things* (Telarc 1997)★★★.

● COMPILATIONS: *The Young George Shearing (1939-44)* (Archive 1961)★★★, *The Best Of George Shearing* (MFP 1983)★★★, *White Satin - Black Satin* (Capitol 1991)★★★, *The Capitol Years* (Capitol 1991)★★★★.

● FILMS: *The Big Beat* (1957).

SHELDON, JACK

b. 30 November 1931, Jacksonville, Florida, USA. After studying trumpet as a child, Sheldon played professionally while still in his early teens. In the late 40s, now relocated in the Los Angeles area, he played with many leading west coast musicians, including Art Pepper, Dexter Gordon and Wardell Gray. He was also closely associated with comedian Lenny Bruce. In 1955 he was one of the first of the west coast school to record for the Pacific Jazz label. In the mid-50s he recorded with the Curtis Counce group, which included Harold Land, and later in the decade with Dave Pell and Pepper. He also toured with Gray, Stan Kenton and Benny Goodman. In the 60s Sheldon's natural wit brought him work as a stand-up comedian and he also took up acting, playing the lead in a US television series, *What Makes Sammy Run?*

In the 70s he worked with various bands, big and small, including Goodman's, Woody Herman's and Bill Berry's, and also led his own small bands for club and record dates. Sheldon's trumpet playing is deeply rooted in bebop but he ably adapts it to the mainstream settings in which he often works. His live appearances always include examples of his engaging singing style and his sparkling, frequently abrasive wit. Much less well known internationally than his talent deserves, Sheldon has survived many problems, including drug addiction and alcoholism, that would have ended the careers of less durable men.

● ALBUMS: *Get Out Of Town* 10-inch album (Jazz: West

1955)★★★, *The Jack Sheldon Quintet* 10-inch album (Jazz: West 1955)★★★, *Jack's Groove* (Gene Norman 1961)★★★, *A Jazz Profile Of Ray Charles* (Reprise 1961)★★★, *Out!* (Capitol 1963)★★★, *Play Buddy, Play!* (Capitol 1966)★★★, *Jack Sheldon With Orchestra Conducted By Don Sebesky* (1968)★★, *Singular* (1980)★★★, *Angel Wings* (1980)★★★, *Playin' It Straight* (1980)★★★, *Stand By For The Jack Sheldon Quartet* (Concord Jazz 1983)★★★★, *Blues In The Night* (Phontastic 1984)★★, *Hollywood Heroes* (Concord Jazz 1988)★★, with Ross Tomkins *On My Own* (Concord Jazz 1992)★★★, *Jack Sheldon Sings* (Butterfly 1996)★★★, *Jack Is Back!* (Butterfly 1996)★★★, with Ross Tompkins *Class Act* (Butterfly 1997)★★★.
● VIDEOS: *In New Orleans* (Hendring Music Video 1990).

SHEPHERD, DAVE

b. 7 February 1929, London, England. In the years following World War II, Shepherd took up the clarinet and quickly developed into one of the UK's most respected and admired musicians. An eclectic performer, ranging from Dixieland through most aspects of the mainstream to the fringes of bop, he has played with many British and American musicians. These include artists as diverse as Freddy Randall and Billie Holiday. Despite a short spell in the USA in the mid-50s and appearances at international festivals, Shepherd's career has centred on the UK and he works regularly with the Pizza Express All Stars, with Digby Fairweather, Roy Williams, Len Skeat and others. A superbly professional musician, Shepherd's ability to recreate the immaculate styling of Benny Goodman has led to an unfair tendency to narrow the focus of critical attention. In fact, when allowed free rein to his talent, he consistently demonstrates unfailing swing and a quality of musical elegance conspicuously absent in many better-known players.
● ALBUMS: *Shepherd's Delight* (1969)★★★, *Freddy Randall/Dave Shepherd Live At Montreux* (1973)★★★, *Benny Goodman Classics* (1975)★★★, *Dixieland Classics* (1976)★★★★, *Airmal Special* (Chevron 1984)★★, *Tribute To Benny Goodman* (Music Masters 1992)★★★.

SHEPP, ARCHIE

b. 24 May 1937, Fort Lauderdale, Florida, USA. Shepp was raised in Philadelphia. While studying dramatic literature at college he began playing on various instruments including the alto saxophone. His first professional engagement was on clarinet and he later played tenor saxophone with R&B bands. Settling in New York he tried to find work as an actor but was obliged to make a living in music, playing in Latin bands. He also played jazz with Cecil Taylor, Bill Dixon, Don Cherry, John Tchicai and others during the early 60s. With Cherry and Tchicai he was co-leader of the New York Contemporary Five. Shepp's musically questing nature drew him into the orbit of John Coltrane, with whom he established a fruitful musical relationship. Through Coltrane, Shepp was introduced to Bob Thiele of Impulse! Records and began recording under his own name for the label. Shepp's collaborations with Coltrane included an appearance at the 1965 *Down Beat* Festival in Chicago. That same year he appeared at the Newport Festival and had a play staged in New York. Although closely associated with the free jazz movement of the 60s, Shepp's music always included elements that were identifiably rooted in earlier forms of jazz and blues and he was very conscious of the importance of the music's roots. In an article in *Down Beat*, he wrote of the *avant garde*, 'It is not a movement, but a state of mind. It is a thorough denial of technological precision and a reaffirmation of *das Volk*.' With his name and reputation established by 1965, Shepp embarked upon a period of successful tours and recordings. He was busily writing music and occasionally stage plays, many of which carried evidence of his political convictions and concern over civil rights issues. At the end of the 60s he played at the Pan African Festival in Algiers, recorded several albums during a brief stop-over in Paris, then returned to the USA, where he became deeply involved in education, teaching music and literature, and was eventually appointed an associate professor at the University of Massachusetts. Over the next decade Shepp expanded his repertoire, incorporating aspects of jazz far removed from his earlier freeform preferences, amongst them R&B, rock, blues and bop. Some of his recordings from the late 70s and early 80s give an indication of his range: they include improvised duo albums with Max Roach, sets of spirituals and blues with Horace Parlan and tribute albums to Charlie Parker and Sidney Bechet. In the 80s Shepp had matured into an all-round jazz player, impossible to pigeonhole but capable of appealing to a wide audience through the heart and the mind. Although he has added the soprano saxophone to his instrumental arsenal, Shepp still concentrates on tenor, playing with a richly passionate tone and developing commanding solos shot through with vigorous declamatory phrases that emphasize his dramatic approach.
● ALBUMS: with Bill Dixon *The Archie Shepp-Bill Dixon Quartet* (Savoy 1962)★★★, *Archie Shepp And The New York Contemporary Five* (Impulse! 1963)★★★★, *Four For Trane* (Impulse! 1964)★★★★, with Dixon *Archie Shepp & The New Contemporary 5/The Bill Dixon 7-Tette* (Savoy 1964)★★★, *Fire Music* (Impulse! 1965)★★★, *On This Night* (Impulse! 1965)★★★, with John Coltrane *New Thing At Newport* (Impulse! 1965)★★★, *Archie Shepp Live In San Francisco* (Impulse! 1966)★★★★, *Mama Too Tight* (Impulse! 1967)★★★, *Magic Of Ju-Ju* (Impulse! 1968)★★★, *Freedom* (JMY 1968)★★★, *The Way Ahead* (1968)★★★, *Yasmina & Poem For Malcolm* (Affinity 1969)★★★, *Blase* (Charly 1970)★★, *Attica Blues* (Impulse! 1972)★★★, *Kwanza* (Impulse! 1974)★★★, *Montreux One/Two* (Arista 1975)★★★, *There's A Trumpet In My Soul* (Freedom 1975)★★★, *A Sea Of Faces* (1975)★★★, with Max Roach *Force-Sweet Mao-Suid Afrika '76* (BASE 1976)★★★★, *Steam* (Enja 1976)★★★★, *Montreaux One* (Freedom 1976)★★★, *Hi Fly* (1976)★★★, *Ballads For Trane* (Denon 1977)★★★, *On Green Dolphin Street* (Denon 1977)★★★★, *Goin' Home* (Steeple Chase 1977)★★★, *Day Dream* (Denon 1978)★★★, with Abdullah Ibrahim *Duet* (Denon 1978)★★★, *Perfect Passions* (West Wind 1978)★★, with Roach *Sweet Mao* (1979)★★★, *Lady Bird* (Denon 1979)★★★, *Bird Fire* (West Wind 1979)★★, with

Roach *The Long March* (hatART 1979)★★★★, *Trouble In Mind* (Steeple Chase 1980)★★★, *Tray Of Silver* (Denon 1980)★★★, *I Know About The Life* (1981)★★★, *My Man* (1981)★★★, *Looking At Bird* (Steeple Chase 1981)★★★★, *Soul Song* (Enja 1982)★★★, *Mama Rose* (Steeple Chase 1982)★★★, *African Moods* (1984)★★★★, *I Know About the Life* (Sackville 1984)★★★, *Down Home In New York* (Soul Note 1984)★★★, *Live On Broadway* (Soul Note 1985)★★, *The Fifth Of May* (1987)★★★, *Reunion* (L&R 1988)★★★, with Chet Baker *In Memory Of* (1988)★★, *First Set* (52 Rue Est 1988)★★★, *Second Set* (52 Rue Est 1988)★★★, *Splashes (Tribute To Wilbur Little)* (L&R 1988)★★★, *Lover Man* (Timeless 1988)★★★, *In Memory Of First And Last Meeting 1988* (L&R 1989)★★★, *Art Of The Duo* (Enja 1990)★★★, *I Didn't Know About You* (Timeless 1991)★★★, *Black Ballad* (Timeless 1993)★★★, *Something To Live For* (Timeless 1997)★★★.

SHEPPARD, ANDY

b. 20 January 1957, Bristol, Avon, England. Sheppard attempted to learn saxophone at school, but was told he would have to take up clarinet first. In disgust he bought a guitar instead, but began on tenor saxophone after hearing John Coltrane. He also played the flute and sang solo in the choir while at school. He later discovered that he had perfect pitch, and only learned to read music in his late 20s. He took up the soprano under the influences of Steve Lacy and alcohol, having sold his tenor to a friend when drunk. Before moving to London Sheppard played with Sphere (not to be confused with the US band of the same name). He also played in Klaunstance, then spent two years in Paris working with Laurent Cugny's big band, Lumiere, and Urban Sax. Returning to the UK he played with Paul Dunmall and Keith Tippett. In early 1987 Sheppard formed his own small band, recording two acclaimed albums and undertaking several successful tours. He also became a regular performer in bands led by Carla Bley, Gil Evans and George Russell. In 1990 he set up the Soft On The Inside big band, which produced an album and a video, and he also recorded an acclaimed set of duo improvisations with Tippett. Since early 1991 Sheppard has run an electric small group, In Co-Motion (featuring the fine trumpeter Claude Deppa), alongside the big band, and he recently composed a piece for ice-dancers Torville and Dean. He also played in an occasional trio with Bley and Steve Swallow (producer on most of his albums). After being dropped by Blue Note Records he moved to Colin Towns's Provocateur label for 1998's *Learning To Wave*. Sheppard is one of the most assured and versatile (and least flashy) saxophonists on the scene today.

● ALBUMS: *Andy Sheppard* (Antilles 1987)★★★, with Sphere *Sphere* (Cadillac 1988)★★★, with Sphere *Present Tense* (Cadillac 1988)★★★, *Introductions In The Dark* (Antilles 1989)★★, *Soft On The Inside* (Antilles 1990)★★★, with Keith Tippett *66 Shades Of Lipstick* (Editions EG 1990)★★, *In Co-Motion* (Antilles 1991)★★★★, *Rhythm Method* (Blue Note 1993)★★★, *Delivery Suite* (Blue Note 1994)★★★, *Inclassifiable* (Label Bleu 1995)★★★, with Steve Lodder *Moving Image* (Verve 1996)★★★, *Learning To Wave* (Provocateur 1998)★★★★.

SHERMAN, DARYL

b. 14 June 1950, Woonsocket, Rhode Island, USA. At the age of five she was picking out tunes on the piano, and soon began singing along with her trombone-playing father, a local bandleader. By her teenage years she was singing professionally with her father's band. She widened her base a little, singing also in the Boston area, until, in 1974, she moved to New York. There, she played various clubs, usually singing with jazz trios. When Artie Shaw formed a band, after 25 years in retirement, he asked Sherman to join him as the band singer. The inevitable publicity attending this venture benefited Sherman, and long engagements at the Fortune Garden and the Sheraton Center consolidated her impact. She appeared with many noted jazz musicians, including George Duvivier, Mel Lewis and Marian McPartland, on whose famed *Piano Jazz* radio show she was featured. In the early and mid-90s Sherman worked at many prestigious hotel and club venues in New York, Washington, Los Angeles, Monterey, and elsewhere, and also appeared at festivals and other gatherings including the Atlanta Jazz Festival, the March of Jazz, in Clearwater, Florida, in Toronto, Canada, and with Dick Hyman, at the Jazz Society of Sarasota in Florida. Her love of good songs and fine interpretations of lyrics have made her a popular choice for gatherings and recordings that celebrate such arts: a Rex Reed tribute to Ira Gershwin, for example. A 1996 album celebrating the talent of a singer of an earlier generation, Mildred Bailey, with vibraphone player John Cocuzzi, superbly demonstrated this gifted singer's huge talent. Her voice, light and fluid, commands attention and her subtle sense of swing and adept phrasing is a constant joy.

● ALBUMS: *I'm A Dreamer, Aren't We All* (Tropical Belt 1983)★★★, *She's A Great Girl* (Tono 1987)★★, with Sudhalter and others as Mr. Tram And Company *Getting Some Fun Out Of Life* (Audiophile 1989)★★, *I've Got My Fingers Crossed: A Celebration Of Jimmy McHugh* (Audiophile 1991)★★★, *Look What I Found* (Arbors 1995)★★★, *Celebrating Mildred Bailey And Red Norvo* (Audiophile 1996)★★★.

SHEROCK, SHORTY

b. Clarence F. Cherock, 17 November 1915, Minneapolis, Minnesota, USA, d. 19 February 1980. As a child Sherock played cornet, later switching to trumpet when he worked in local bands. In 1936 he was hired by Ben Pollack and subsequently played in numerous bands, including those important units led by Seger Ellis, Jimmy Dorsey, Bob Crosby, Gene Krupa, Tommy Dorsey and Alvino Rey. Immediately following World War II he formed and led his own band and played with Jazz At The Philharmonic. He then worked in film studios for much of his remaining career, although he did play with Georgie Auld and Matty Matlock in the 50s and with Benny Carter during the 60s. A skilful, highly respected musician, Sherock was able to communicate his enthusiasm to his fellows and in his earlier years frequently played exciting solos.

SHERTZER, HYMIE

b. Herman Schertzer, 2 April 1909, New York City, New York, USA, d. 22 March 1977. After playing alto saxophone in a number of bands around the New York area, Shertzer (whose family name was Schertzer) became lead alto for Benny Goodman. In 1938 he joined Tommy Dorsey, switching a number of times back and forth between the two bands. In the 40s he played in the band led by Bunny Berigan and also appeared on a number of record dates with such luminaries as Lionel Hampton and Billie Holiday. In the mid-40s he went into studio work where he remained for the next 30 years, making numerous record dates with such artists as Ella Fitzgerald and Louis Armstrong. Shertzer was one of the unsung heroes of the swing era, soloing only rarely, but his solid and skilful playing made him one of the most sought-after lead altos of his time.

● ALBUMS: *Hymie Shertzer* (1957)★★.

SHEW, BOBBY

b. 4 March 1941, Albuquerque, New Mexico, USA. Shew taught himself to play trumpet and was playing semi-professionally as he entered his teens. During military service he decided to make music his career and in 1964, soon after his discharge, became a member of the Tommy Dorsey Orchestra. The following year he moved on to Woody Herman, then Buddy Rich, and thereafter took a succession of jobs with bands in hotels and casinos in Las Vegas. In the early 70s he settled in Los Angeles, playing in the studios but also working jazz gigs, including a sustained period with the Toshiko Akiyoshi-Lew Tabackin big band. His spell with the band produced many fine albums, notably *Kogun* (1974), *Tales Of A Courtesan* (1975) and *Insights* (1976). Also during the 70s he played in many Los Angeles-based rehearsal bands, including Don Menza's and Juggernaut. He played, too, in small groups, as well as teaching privately and directing clinics and workshops. In the late 70s he toured Europe and the UK with Louie Bellson's big band, appearing on some of the live recordings, including *Dynamite!* (1979) and *London Scene* (1980). During these tours he expanded his teaching activities wherever he went. In the 80s Shew's playing was mostly in small groups, as both sideman and leader, but he made occasional appearances with youth bands including the UK's Wigan Youth Jazz Orchestra, with whom he recorded *Aim For The Heart* in 1987. In the late 80s and early 90s Shew's teaching role developed still further and he remains in great demand around the world. The soft, warm sound Shew creates from his instrument is especially suitable for ballads and lends a distinctive quality to any trumpet section in which he appears. An important influence through his teaching activities, Shew is ensuring that, in a period when dazzling technical proficiency is becoming almost commonplace, the emotional qualities of jazz are not forgotten.

● ALBUMS: *Telepathy* (1978)★★★, *Outstanding In His Field* (1979)★★★, *Class Reunion* (1980)★★★★, *Parallel 37* (1980)★★★, *Play Song* (1981)★★★, *Trumpets No End* (1983)★★★, *Breakfast Wine* (1984)★★★, with Wigan Youth Jazz Orchestra *Aim For The Heart* (1987)★★★★, with Carl Fontana *Heavyweights* (MAMA 1996)★★★★, *Playing With Fire* 1986 recording (MAMA 1997)★★★★, *Salsa Caliente* (MAMA 1998)★★★.

SHIHAB, SAHIB

b. Edmund Gregory, 23 June 1925, Savannah, Georgia, USA, d. 24 October 1989, USA. After learning to play several reed instruments, Shihab concentrated on alto saxophone and played professionally while still in his early teens. At the age of 19 he was lead alto with Fletcher Henderson and also played in Roy Eldridge's big band. After 1947, the year in which he adopted the Muslim faith and changed his name, Shihab played with several of the leading bop musicians, including Thelonious Monk, with whom he made the first recording of ''Round Midnight', Tadd Dameron, Art Blakey (playing in the first of the drummer's Jazz Messengers groups to record), Dizzy Gillespie and John Coltrane, the last performing on the tenorman's first recording date as leader. In the 50s Shihab began to play baritone saxophone and at the end of the decade travelled to Europe with Quincy Jones. He remained on the Continent for several years, playing with the Clarke-Boland Big Band for almost a decade. During this period he added soprano saxophone and flute to his instrumental armoury, and in 1965 he composed a jazz ballet based on Hans Christian Andersen's *The Red Shoes*. In the early 70s Shihab returned to the USA to work in film studios, but was frequently back in Europe during the remaining part of the decade and into the early 80s. He finally settled in the USA in 1986. Over the years, Shihab's inventiveness when playing flute and soprano surpassed his earlier work on alto. It was, however, on baritone that he made his most distinctive contribution, weaving thoughtfully agile solos with a light sound.

● ALBUMS: *Jazz Sahib* (Savoy 1957)★★★, *The Jazz We Heard Last Summer* (1957)★★★, *Jazz-Sahib* (1957)★★★, with Gene Quill, Hal Stein, Phil Woods *Four Altos* (Prestige 1957)★★★, *Companionship* (1965)★★★, *Sahib Shihab And The Danish Radio Jazz Group* (1965)★★, *Seeds* (1968)★★★, *Sentiments* (Storyville 1971)★★★, *Sahib Shihab And The Jef Gilson Unit* (1972)★★★, with others *Flute Summit* (1973)★★, *Conversations* (1992)★★★, *And All Those Cats* (Rearward 1998)★★★.

SHORE, DINAH

b. Frances Rose Shore, 1 March 1917, Winchester, Tennessee, USA, d. 24 February 1994, Los Angeles, California, USA. One of her country's most enduring all-round entertainers, Shore staked her first claim to fame while still at school, on Nashville radio. Further broadcasting and theatre engagements in New York soon followed. She recorded with Xaviar Cugat and Ben Bernie, and sang on some of Cugat's early 40s hits, such as 'The Breeze And I', 'Whatever Happened To You?', 'The Rhumba-Cardi' and 'Quierme Mucho (Yours)', initially under the name Dinah Shaw. Shore was one of the first vocalists to break free from the big bands (she had been rejected at auditions for Benny Goodman and Tommy Dorsey) and become a star in her own right. She became extremely popular on radio, and made her solo recording debut in 1939. Her smoky, low-pitched voice was especially attractive on slow ballads, and from 1940-57 she had a string of some 80 US chart hits, including 'Yes, My Darling Daughter', 'Jim', 'Blues In The Night', 'Skylark', 'You'd Be So Nice To Come Home To', 'Murder, He Says', 'Candy', 'Laughing On The Outside (Crying On The Inside)', 'All That Glitters Is Not Gold', 'Doin' What Comes Natur'lly', 'You Keep Coming Back Like A Song', 'I Wish I Didn't Love You So', 'You Do', 'Baby, It's Cold Outside' (with Buddy Clark), 'Dear Hearts And Gentle People', 'My Heart Cries For You', 'A Penny A Kiss', 'Sweet Violets', and number 1s with 'I'll Walk Alone', 'The Gypsy', 'Anniversary Song' and 'Buttons And Bows'. She made a number of film appearances, including *Thank Your Lucky Stars* (1943), *Up In Arms* (1944), *Follow The Boys* (1944), *Belle Of The Yukon* (1945), *Till The Clouds Roll By* (1946) and *Aaron Slick From Punkin Crick* (1952). She also lent her voice to two Walt Disney animated features, *Make Mine Music* (1946) and *Fun And Fancy Free* (1957), and was last seen on the big screen in the George Burns comedy *Oh God!* (1977), and Robert Altman's quirky political satire *H.E.A.L.T.H.* (1979). In 1951 Shore began appearing regularly on television, making several spectaculars. Later, it was her continuing success on the small screen that brought about a career change when she became host on a highly rated daytime talk show, a role she maintained into the 80s. Her popularity on television barely declined throughout this period, and she won no less than 10 Emmys in all. The late 80s saw her performing on stage once more, though she returned to the television format for *Conversation With Dinah*, which ran from 1989-91.

● ALBUMS: *Dinah Shore Sings* 10-inch album (Columbia 1949)★★★, *Reminiscing* 10-inch album (Columbia 1949)★★★, *Bongo/Land Of The Lost* (Columbia 1950)★★, *Call Me Madam* 10-inch album (RCA Victor 1950)★★, *The King And I* 10-inch album (RCA Victor 1951)★★★, *Two Tickets To Broadway* 10-inch album (RCA Victor 1951)★★★, *Aaron Slick From Punkin Crick* film soundtrack (RCA Victor 1952)★★, *Dinah Shore Sings The Blues* 10-inch album (RCA Victor 1953)★★★, with Buddy Clark *'SWonderful* (1953)★★★★, *The Dinah Shore TV Show* 10-inch album (RCA Victor 1954)★★, *Holding Hands At Midnight* (RCA Victor 1955)★★★, *Bouquet Of Blues* (RCA Victor 1956)★★★, *Moments Like These* (RCA Victor 1957)★★★, *Buttons And Bows* (1959)★★★★, *Dinah, Yes Indeed!* (Capitol 1959)★★★, with André Previn *Dinah Sings, Previn Plays* (Capitol 1960)★★★, *Lavender Blue* (Capitol 1960)★★★, with Red Norvo *Dinah Sings Some Blues With Red* (Capitol 1960)★★★★, *Dinah, Down Home!* (Capitol 1962)★★★, *Fabulous Hits Newly Recorded* (Capitol 1962)★★★, *Lower Basin St. Revisted* (1965)★★★, *Make The World Go Away* (1987)★★★, *Oh Lonesome Me* (1988)★★★.

● COMPILATIONS: *Best Of Dinah Shore* (RCA 1981)★★★, *'Deed I Do (1942-1952)* (Hep Jazz 1988)★★★, *Dinah Shore's Greatest Hits* (Capitol 1988)★★★★, *The Capitol Years* (Capitol 1989)★★★★.

● FILMS: *Thank Your Lucky Stars* (1943), *Up In Arms* (1944), *Follow The Boys* (1944), *Belle Of The Yukon* (1945), *Till The Clouds Roll By* (1946), *Make Mine Music* (1946), *Aaron Slick From Punkin Crick* (1952), *Fun And Fancy Free* (1957), *Oh God!* (1977), *H.E.A.L.T.H.* (1979).

● FURTHER READING: *Dinah!*, B. Cassidy.

SHORT, BOBBY

b. Robert Waltrip, 15 September 1926, Danville, Illinois, USA. A self-taught pianist, Short worked in vaudeville as a child and sang in clubs and on radio in Chicago. In mid-1937 he went to New York where he played and sang for audiences unprepared for smart-suited sophistication from a pre-teenager. Short went back to school, but, influenced by the stylish performances of such nightclub artistes as Hildegarde, he continued to hone his act. When he returned to showbusiness he toured extensively, eventually spending some time on the west coast. By the early 50s he had matured into a sophisticated singer-pianist. Whether in Los Angeles, New York or Paris, he played the most exclusive nightclubs, establishing a reputation as a witty purveyor of songs. His vocal range is limited, and accordingly he sings with engaging restraint. His club appearances over the years at such places as the Café Carlyle and 21 have earned him a loyal following.

● ALBUMS: *Bobby Short Loves Cole Porter* (Atlantic 1952)★★★, *Songs By Bobby Short* (Atlantic 1955)★★★, *Bobby Short* (Atlantic 1956)★★★, *Speaking Of Love* (Atlantic 1958)★★★, *Sing Me A Swing Song* (Atlantic 1958)★★★, *The Mad Twenties* (Atlantic 1959)★★, *On The East Side* (Atlantic 1960)★★, *Songs Of New York Live At The Cafe Carlyle* (Telarc 1995)★★★★, *Celebrating 40 Years At The Café Carlyle* (Telarc 1997)★★★.

● FURTHER READING: *Black And White Baby*, Bobby Short. *The Life And Times Of A Saloon Slinger*, Bobby Short with Robert Mackintosh.

SHORTER, WAYNE

b. 25 August 1933, Newark, New Jersey, USA. Shorter first played clarinet, taking up the tenor saxophone during his late teens. He studied music at New York University during the mid-50s before serving in the US army for two years. During his student days he had played with various bands, including that led by Horace Silver, and on his discharge encountered John Coltrane, with whom he developed many theoretical views on music. He was also briefly with Maynard Ferguson. In 1959 he became a member of Art Blakey's Jazz Messengers, remaining with the band until 1963. The following year he joined Miles Davis, staying until 1970. Late that year he teamed up with Joe Zawinul, whom he had first met in the Ferguson band, to form Weather Report. During his stints with Blakey and Davis Shorter had written extensively and his compositions had also formed the basis of several increasingly experimental record sessions under his own name for the Blue Note label. He continued to write for the new band and also for further dates under his own name and with V.S.O.P., with whom he worked in the mid- and late 70s.

In the mid-80s he was leading his own band and also recording and touring with other musicians, thus reducing his activities with Weather Report.As a player, Shorter developed through his period with Blakey into a leading proponent of hard bop. His fiery, tough-toned and dramatically angular playing was well suited to the aggressive nature of the Blakey band. During his time with Davis, another side to his musical personality emerged, in which a more tender approach greatly enhanced his playing. This side had made its appearance earlier, on *Wayning Moments*, but was given greater scope with Davis. On Davis's *Bitches Brew*, Shorter also played soprano saxophone: two weeks later he employed this instrument throughout on his own *Super Nova*, playing with exotic enthusiasm. The years with Zawinul broadened his range still further, highlighting his appreciation of freer forms and giving rein to his delight in musical exotica. Although laying ground rules for many later fusion bands, Weather Report's distinction lay in the way the group allowed the two principals to retain their powerful musical personalities. Later, as the band began to sound more like other fusion bands, Shorter's exploratory nature found greater scope in the bands he formed away from Weather Report. As a composer, Shorter was responsible for some of the best work of the Blakey band of his era and also for many of Davis's stronger pieces of the late 60s. A major innovator and influence on hard boppers and fusionists alike, Shorter remains one of the most imaginative musicians in jazz, constantly seeking new horizons but - thanks to his broad musical knowledge - retaining identifiable links with the past.

● ALBUMS: *The Vee Jay Years* (Affinity 1959)★★★★, *Introducing Wayne Shorter* (Vee Jay 1960)★★★★, *Wayne Shorter* (1959-62)★★★★, *Wayning Moments* (Vee Jay 1962)★★★, *Second Genesis* (Vee Jay 1963)★★★, *Night Dreamer* (Blue Note 1964)★★★★, *Juju* (Blue Note 1964)★★★★, *Speak No Evil* (Blue Note 1964)★★★★, *Night Dreamer* (Blue Note 1964)★★★, *The Soothsayer* (1965)★★★, *The All-Seeing Eye* (Blue Note 1965)★★★★, *Etcetera* (Blue Note 1965)★★★, *Adam's Apple* (Blue Note 1966)★★★, *Schizophrenia* (Blue Note 1967)★★★, *Super Nova* (Blue Note 1969)★★★★, *Odyssey Of Iska* (Blue Note 1970)★★★, *Moto Grosso Feio* (1971)★★★, *Native Dancer* (Columbia 1974)★★★, *Atlantis* (Columbia 1985)★★★, *Endangered Species* (1985)★★, *Phantom Navigator* (Columbia 1987)★★, *Joy Ryder* (Columbia 1987)★★★, with Herbie Hancock, Ron Carter, Wallace Roney, Tony Williams *A Tribute To Miles* (QWest/Reprise 1994)★★★, *All Seeing Eye* (Connoisseur 1994)★★★, *High Life* (Verve 1995)★★★, with Herbie Hancock *1+1* (Verve 1997)★★★★.

● COMPILATIONS: *The Best Of Wayne Shorter* (Blue Note)★★★★.

SHRIEVE, MICHAEL

b. USA. Shrieve was the original drummer with Santana, whom he joined at the age of 19. With that band he became the youngest musician to appear at Woodstock, helping to write and produce eight studio albums with the group. His engagements since then have included recording credits with Mick Jagger, the Rolling Stones, Pete Townshend, Steve Winwood and jazz musicians Freddie Hubbard, John McLaughlin and Jaco Pastorious. He has also collaborated with Japanese composer Stomu Yamash'ta and worked with Klaus Schulze, a founding member of Tangerine Dream. His film credits include *The Tempest* and *The Bedroom Window*, as well as varied television work. He launched his solo career in 1994 with a triple album for CMP Records. Together with guitarist Bill Frisell and organist Wayne Horvitz, *Fascination* was an adventurous album that received glowing reviews for the tonal quality of its music. 1996's *Two Doors* was a double disc set featuring two distinct sides of Shrieve's music. The second CD, *Flying Polly*, included out-takes from his previous work for *Fascination*, while the first, *Deep Umbra*, featured a new trio comprising bass player Jonas Hellborg and guitarist Shawn Lane. Few critics welcomed the new development, however, with Lane's brash guitar displays incurring particular derision.

● ALBUMS: *Fascination* (CMP 1994)★★★, *Two Doors* (CMP 1996)★★★.

SIDEWINDER, THE - LEE MORGAN

Simple and direct and somewhat of a runt album in the history of jazz. The solo on Art Blakey's recording of Bobby Timmons' 'Moanin' is by Morgan, as is that on 'A Night In Tunisia'. By the time he came to record this album he had simplified his style, which appealed to the soul/jazz lovers of the 60s. To use the ultimate cliché, this is groovin' music; it rolls, it bops, it makes you feel good and its success is that it is refreshingly uncomplicated. Supported by Joe Henderson (tenor), Billy Higgins (drums), Barry Harris (piano) and Bob Cranshaw (bass).

● Tracks: *The Sidewinder; Totem Pole; Gary's Notebook; Boy, What A Night!; Hocus Pocus.*

● First released 1964

● UK peak chart position: did not chart

● USA peak chart position: 25

SIDRAN, BEN

b. 14 August 1943, Chicago, Illinois, USA. A PhD in musicology and philosophy, Sidran became embroiled in rock music upon joining the Ardells, a popular attraction at the University of Wisconsin that also featured Steve Miller and Boz Scaggs. Sidran later travelled to London to complete a doctoral thesis on the development of black music in America. This was published as *Black Talk* in 1971. Here he became reacquainted with Miller during the recording of the latter's *Brave New World*, an album marked by Sidran's memorable piano work and compositional skills. He remained an associate member of Miller's band, contributing to *Your Saving Grace* and *Number 5* before making numerous session appearances. The artist's solo career began in 1971 with the release of *Feel Your Groove*; he has since pursued an idiosyncratic, jazz-based path, eschewing commercially minded motives in favour of a relaxed, almost casual, approach. His best work, captured on *Puttin' In Time On Planet Earth* (1973) and *The Doctor Is In* (1977), reveals a laconic wit redolent of Mose Allison, but elsewhere Sidran's underachievements suggest lethargy rather than control. He nonetheless remains a highly respected musician and is best known in the UK as host of *On The Live Side*, a perennial favourite of late-night television. In 1991 he released *Cool Paradise* to favourable reviews and helped to relaunch the career of Georgie Fame, now a stablemate on the new jazz label Go Jazz. A further successful collaboration with Fame, together with Van Morrison and Mose Allison, resulted in a tribute album to the latter in 1996.

● ALBUMS: *Feel Your Groove* (Capitol 1971)★★, *I Lead A Life* (Blue Thumb 1972)★★★, *Puttin' In Time On Planet Earth* (Blue Thumb 1973)★★, *Don't Let Go* (Blue Thumb 1974)★★★, *Free In America* (Arista 1976)★★, *The Doctor Is In* (Arista 1977)★★★, *A Little Kiss In The Night* (Arista 1978)★★, *The Cat And The Hat* (A&M 1979)★★, *Live At Montreaux* (Arista 1979)★★, *Old Songs For The New Depression* (Antilles 1982)★★★, *Bop City* (Antilles 1984)★★★, *On The Live Side* (Windham Hill 1987)★★, *Too Hot To Touch* (Windham Hill 1988)★★, *Cool Paradise* (Go Jazz 1991)★★★, *Enivre D'Amour* (Go Jazz 1992)★★★, *Heat Wave* (Go Jazz 1992)★★★, *A Good Travel Agent* (Go Jazz 1992)★★★, *Life's A Lesson* (Go Jazz 1993)★★★, with Van Morrison, Georgie Fame and Mose Allison *Tell Me Something: The Songs Of Mose Allison* (Verve 1996)★★.

● COMPILATIONS: *That's Life I Guess* (1988)★★★.

● FURTHER READING: *Black Talk*, Ben Sidran.

SIGNATURES

Formed in 1954 at the Servicemen's Center in Seattle, Washington, USA, the Signatures featured Cathi Hayes (lead), Lee Humes (tenor), Ruth Alcivar (alto), Jerry Hayes (baritone) and Bob Alcivar (bass). Their style, as well as being made notable by the presence of two female singers, was distinguished by a pronounced lean towards jazz as well as doo-wop. They were also proficient on several instruments: Cathi Hayes (vibes), Ruth Alcivar (drums), Humes (bass), Bob Alcivar (piano) and Jerry Hayes (guitar). Their first major performance came in front of a big-band jazz ensemble created by local disc jockey Norm Bobrow, and thereafter, they continued to feature prominently on the jazz circuit. After a year of such pursuits the Hayes siblings were replaced by Bunny Phillips on lead, and multi-instrumentalist and former Four Freshmen member Hal Kratzsch as bass singer. Their recording debut came in July 1956, when an album was recorded for Whippet Records. The resulting collection sold steadily, as did the accompanying single 'Julie Is Her Name'. Engagements at prestigious New York jazz nightclubs followed, where Count Basie became a fan. He encouraged Morris Levy of Roulette Records to sign the still young band, but they stayed instead with an earlier mentor, Stan Kenton, who brought them to Warner Brothers Records. A second album attracted further good notices, and was used as the launch pad for coast-to-coast tours playing with prestigious jazz artists including Dizzy Gillespie. Phillips was replaced on lead by Dottie Dunn just as the album was released, and Don Purdy also stepped in for Humes. Their next project was a tribute album to Duke Ellington and Billy Strayhorn, but this was never completed. Instead, they issued *Prepared To Flip* before appearing at the Playboy Jazz Festival in Chicago. However, the advent of rock 'n' roll in the 60s proved to be their nemesis, and after several more tours they finally folded. Most of the ex-members retired to day jobs, though Cathi Hayes recorded a solo jazz album. Bob Alcivar and his wife Ruth moved to Los Angeles where he still works as a film composer and she as a painter.

● ALBUMS: *The Signatures, Their Voices And Instruments* (Whippet 1956)★★★, *The Signatures Sign In* (Warners 1959)★★★, *The Signatures - Prepared To Flip* (Warners 1959)★★★.

SIGNORELLI, FRANK

b. 24 May 1901, New York City, USA, d. 9 December 1975. Playing piano from childhood, Signorelli became a founder-member of the Original Memphis Five while still a teenager. He also played with the Original Dixieland Jazz Band and during the 20s was ceaselessly active. During this decade he worked with Joe Venuti, Eddie Lang, Adrian Rollini, Bix Beiderbecke and a host of leading white jazzmen of the day. He also played with Paul Whiteman, but he remained most closely associated with Phil Napoleon, a friend and musical companion from his youth. During the 30s he resumed his connection with the ODJB and in the 50s with the OMF, recording with them and with Connee Boswell. A sound if unexceptional pianist, Signorelli also composed a number of tunes that became standards, amongst which are 'I'll Never Be The Same' and 'Stairway To The Stars'.

● ALBUMS: *Piano Mood* (Davis 1951)★★★, with George Wettling *Ragtime Duo* (Kapp 1955)★★★.

SILVA, ALAN

b. 22 January 1939, Bermuda. Silva grew up in New York, studying piano and violin from the age of 10. He also took trumpet lessons from Donald Byrd for three years. He only started playing double bass at the age of 23. His acute musical ear and interest in new sounds made him ideal for some of Cecil Taylor's most demanding music: he played on the classic Blue Note Records releases of 1966, *Unit Structures* and *Conquistador!*, and played with Taylor until 1969. Together with Burton Greene he formed the Free Form Improvisation Ensemble, and also worked for other key innovators, including Sun Ra (1965-70), Albert Ayler (1966-70), Sunny Murray (1969) and Archie Shepp (1969). In 1970 he moved to France and formed the Celestial Communication Orchestra to play free jazz with various instrumentations. He also played in smaller groups with tenor saxophonist Frank Wright, pianist Bobby Few and drummer Muhammad Ali. From the mid-70s he lived and taught in both New York and Paris, recording with Taylor, trumpeter Bill Dixon and pianist Andrew Hill. In 1982 he recorded with the Globe Unity Orchestra. In the mid-80s he dropped out of performance, declaring that the scene had become sterile (though 1986's *Take Some Risks* makes one question that judgement). In 1990 he returned to performance with the pioneering British percussionist Roger Turner and tenor saxophonist Gary Todd, playing at the Crawley Outside In Festival in 1990 and touring in 1991. On this last tour he played only keyboards - a Roland U-20 - declaring that he found his bass playing no longer surprised him. An intensely involving and visual performer, Silva is a great educationalist and communicator. He needs to be witnessed live to appreciate the energy and passion of his playing.

● ALBUMS: *Lunar Surface* (1969)★★★, with the Celestial Communication Orchestra *Seasons* 1970 recording (BYG 1972)★★★, *Desert Mirage* (1973)★★★, with Bobby Few, Frank Wright *Solos, Duos* (1975)★★★, with Roger Turner *Take Some Risks* (1986)★★, with the Celestial Communication Orchestra *My Country* 1971 recording (Leo 1989)★★★.

SILVER, HORACE

b. 2 September 1928, Norwalk, Connecticut, USA. Silver studied piano and tenor saxophone at school, settling on the former instrument for his professional career. Early influences included Portuguese folk music (from his father), blues and bop. He formed a trio for local gigs which included backing visiting musicians. One such visitor, Stan Getz, was sufficiently impressed to take the trio on the road with him in 1950. The following year Silver settled in New York, playing regularly at Birdland and other leading venues. In 1952 he began a long-lasting association with Blue Note, recording under his own name and with other leaders. In 1953 he formed a band named the Jazz Messengers with Art Blakey, who later adopted the name for all his own groups. By 1956 Silver was leading his own quintet, exploring the reaches of bop and becoming a founding father of the hard bop movement. Silver's line-up - trumpet, tenor saxophone, piano, bass and drums - was subject to many changes over the years, but the calibre of musicians he hired was always very high. Among his sidemen were Donald Byrd, Art Farmer, Michael and Randy Brecker, Woody Shaw, Blue Mitchell, Hank Mobley and Joe Henderson. He continued to lead fine bands, touring and recording extensively during the following decades, and in the late 80s and early 90s could still be heard at concerts around the world performing to an impressively high standard. As a pianist Silver is a powerful, thrusting player with a rhythmic pulse. As a composer, his early musical interests have constantly reappeared in his work and his incorporation into hard bop of elements of gospel and R&B have ensured that for all the overall complexities of sound his music remains highly accessible. Several of his pieces have become modern standards, among them 'Opus de Funk', 'Doodlin'', 'Nica's Dream' and 'The Preacher'. The introduction on Steely Dan's 'Ricki Don't Lose That Number' was strongly influenced by Silver's memorable 'Song For My Father'. During the 70s Silver experimented with compositions and recordings that set his piano-playing and the standard quintet against larger orchestral backing, often achieving far more success than others who have written and performed in this way.

● ALBUMS: *Introducing The Horace Silver Trio* 10-inch album (Blue Note 1953)★★★, *Horace Silver Trio* (Blue Note 1954)★★★, *Horace Silver Quintet Vol.1* 10-inch album (Blue Note 1955)★★★, *Horace Silver Quintet, Vol. 2* 10-inch album (Blue Note 1955)★★★, *Horace Silver And The Jazz Messengers* (Blue Note 1956)★★★, *Silver's Blue* (Epic 1956)★★★, *6 Pieces Of Silver* (Blue Note 1957)★★★★, *The Stylings Of Silver* (Blue Note 1957)★★★, *Further Explorations* (Blue Note 1958)★★★, *Finger Poppin'* (Blue Note 1959)★★★★, *Blowin' The Blues Away* (Blue Note 1959)★★★, *Horace-Scope* (Blue Note 1960)★★★, *Doin' The Thing: The Horace Silver Quintet At The Village Gate* (Blue Note 1961)★★★★, *The Tokyo Blues* (Blue Note 1962)★★★, *Silver's Serenade* (Blue Note 1963)★★★★, *Song For My Father* (Blue Note 1964)★★★★★, *Horace Silver Live - 1964* (Emerald 1964)★★★, *Cape Verdean Blues* (Blue Note 1965)★★★★, *The Jody Grind* (Blue Note 1966)★★★★★, *Serenade To A Soul Sister* (Blue Note 1968)★★★, *You Gotta Take A Little Love* (Blue Note 1969)★★★, *That Healin' Feelin' (The United States Of Mind, Phase I)* (Blue Note 1970)★★★, *Total Response (Phase II)* (1971)★★, *All (Phase III)* (1972)★★★, *In Pursuit Of The 27th Man* (Blue Note 1973)★★★, *Silver 'n Brass* (Blue Note 1975)★★★, *Silver 'n Wood* (Blue Note 1976)★★★, *Silver 'n Voices* (Blue Note 1976)★★★, *Silver 'n Percussion* (Blue Note 1977)★★★, *Silver 'n Strings Play The Music Of The Spheres* (1978)★★★, *Guides To Growing Up* (1981)★★★, *Spiritualizing The Senses* (Silveto 1983)★★★, *There's No Need To Struggle* (Silveto 1983)★★★, *It's Got To Be Funky* (Columbia 1993)★★, *Pencil Packin' Papa* (Columbia 1994)★★, *The Hardbop Grandpop* (Impulse! 1996)★★★, *A Prescription For The Blues* (Impulse! 1997)★★★.

● COMPILATIONS: *The Best Of Horace Silver* (Blue Note 1969)★★★★, *The Best Of Horace Silver - The Blue Note Years* (Blue Note 1988)★★★★.

SIMEON, OMER

b. 21 July 1902, New Orleans, Louisiana, USA, d. 17 September 1959. Although taught clarinet by fellow New Orleanian Lorenzo Tio, Simeon's musical education took place in Chicago where he lived from 1914. After playing in various bands he joined Charlie Elgar's popular Chicago-based dance band, where he remained for several years. During his stint with Elgar he appeared on a number of record dates with Jelly Roll Morton and also left the band for a short engagement with Joe 'King' Oliver. In the late 20s he played with Luis Russell in New York and then resumed his association with Morton. Back in Chicago in 1928 he spent a couple of years with Erskine Tate and then joined Earl 'Fatha' Hines for a six-year spell at the Royal Gardens. In the 40s he played with various bands, including Jimmie Lunceford's, and he spent most of the 50s with Wilbur De Paris in New York. A bold and imaginative clarinettist, Simeon's long periods in big bands afforded him only limited opportunities to solo, although his recordings with small groups give frequent, if tantalizing, hints of a gifted musician.

● COMPILATIONS: *Omer Simeon 1926-29* (Hot n' Sweet 1993)★★★.

SIMMONS, JOHN

b. 14 June 1918, Haskell, Oklahoma, USA, d. 19 September 1979. While living in California, Simmons took up the bass when a sporting injury affected his trumpet playing. He advanced quickly on his new instrument and worked with Nat 'King' Cole and Teddy Wilson in the mid- to late 30s. In the early 40s he moved to Chicago, playing with Roy Eldridge, Benny Goodman, Louis Armstrong and other leading jazzmen. In the remaining years of the decade he appeared on countless small group recording dates, backing distinguished artists such as Hot Lips Page, Ben Webster, Billie Holiday, Erroll Garner, Coleman Hawkins, Benny Carter and Ella Fitzgerald. Although essentially a mainstream musician with a robust sound and unflagging swing, Simmons also coped comfortably with the demands of playing with beboppers, who included Thelonious Monk. In the 50s he toured and recorded with Harry Edison, Tadd Dameron, Phineas Newborn Jnr. and others, but these and his later years were dogged by poor health. He died in 1979.

● ALBUMS: with Roy Eldridge, Alvin Stoller, Art Tatum *The Art Tatum-Roy Eldridge-Alvin Stoller-John Simmons Quartet* (Clef 1955)★★★, with Phineas Newborn *I Love A Piano* (1959)★★★.

SIMMONS, NORMAN

b. 6 October 1929, Chicago, USA. Simmons studied piano at the Chicago School of Music (1945-49) and then worked as house pianist in various Chicago clubs - the BeeHive (1953-56) and the C&C Lounge (1957-59). In the late 50s he became the accompanist to vocalists Dakota Staton and Ernestine Anderson and then settled in New York. He worked as an arranger for Riverside Records. He recorded with Johnny Griffin and worked with the Eddie 'Lockjaw' Davis/Johnny Griffin Quintet. He rarely solos but is an accomplished accompanist who worked with Carmen McRae throughout the 60s and with Joe Williams ever since. He has also played with vocalists Anita O'Day, Helen Humes and Betty Carter and with Roy Eldridge and Scott Hamilton and Warren Vaché. He taught for Jazzmobile (1974) and joined the faculty of Paterson State College in 1982.

● ALBUMS: *Interpolations* reissued as *Norman Simmons Trio* (Creative/Argo 1956)★★★, *Ramira The Dancer* (1976)★★★, *Midnight Creeper* (1981)★★★, *13th Moon* (1986)★★★, *I Am The Blues* (1988)★★★★.

SIMMONS, SONNY

b. Huey Simmons, 4 August 1933, Sicily Island, Louisiana, USA. Simmons' family moved to Oakland, California, when he was eight years old. Though he was interested in music, his parents could not afford to pay for lessons for him, and it was not until 1950 that he was able to buy his own alto saxophone. A few years later he met flautist Prince Lasha and worked with him for a decade. In 1960 they appeared on television together in Sacramento, and in 1962 Simmons made his recording debut as part of Lasha's quintet, appearing on sessions for *The Cry* on the west coast label Contemporary Records. Initially inspired by Charlie Parker, Simmons found that Ornette Coleman's freedom from the chord changes 'worked out' for him. Following stints with Elvin Jones and Eric Dolphy Simmons married the trumpeter Barbara Donald, with the couple subsequently appearing together at numerous dates. In 1966 he cut *Staying On The Watch* for ESP Records, a masterpiece of new jazz. In the late 60s Simmons and Donald moved to Woodstock, New York, where they started the Woodstock Music Festival and in 1969, made a movie. In 1970 they returned to California. Despite formidable playing skill and a strong set of compositions - including 'City Of David', 'Interplanetary Travellers', 'Dolphy's Days' and 'Burning Spirits' - Simmons dropped out of sight in the 70s. He and Donald separated towards the end of that decade. Still based in San Francisco, Simmons continued to play but fell on hard times. He suprisingly re-emerged in 1994 on the Qwest label with the adventurous *Ancient Ritual*, and has subsequently recorded several acclaimed sessions for CIMP.

● ALBUMS: *Staying On The Watch* (ESP 1966)★★★★, *Rumasuma* (Contemporary 1966)★★★, *Music Of The Spheres* (ESP 1967)★★★★, *Manhattan Egos* (Arhoolie 1969)★★★, *Burning Spirits* (Contemporary 1971)★★★★, *American Jungle* 1995 recording (Qwest 1997)★★★, *Transcendence* (CIMP 1997)★★★, *Judgment Day* (CIMP 1997)★★★★.

SIMONE, NINA

b. Eunice Waymon, 21 February 1933, Tyron, North Carolina, USA. An accomplished pianist as a child, Simone later studied at New York's Juilliard School Of Music. Her jazz credentials were established in 1959 when she secured a hit with an emotive interpretation of George Gershwin's 'I Loves You Porgy'. Her influential 60s work included 'Gin House Blues', 'Forbidden Fruit' and 'I Put A Spell On You', while another of her singles, 'Don't Let Me Be Misunderstood', was later covered by the Animals. The singer's popular fortune flourished upon her signing with RCA. 'Ain't Got No - I Got Life', a song lifted from the mock-hippie musical *Hair*, was a UK number 2, while her searing version of the Bee Gees' 'To Love Somebody' reached number 5. In America, her own composition, 'To Be Young, Gifted And Black', dedicated to her late friend, the playwright Lorraine Hansberry, reflected Simone's growing militancy. Releases then grew infrequent as her political activism increased.

A commanding, if taciturn, live performer, Simone's appearances were increasingly focused on benefits and rallies, although a fluke UK hit, 'My Baby Just Cares For Me', a resurrected 50s master, pushed the singer, momentarily, into the commercial spotlight when it reached number 5 in 1987. Tired of an America she perceived as uncaring, Simone has settled in France where her work continues to flourish. An uncompromising personality, Nina Simone's interpretations of soul, jazz, blues and standards are both compulsive and unique.

● ALBUMS: *Little Girl Blue* (Bethlehem 1959)★★, *Nina Simone And Her Friends* expanded reissue of first album (Bethlehem

1959)★★, *The Amazing Nina Simone* (Colpix 1959)★★★★, *Nina Simone At The Town Hall* (Colpix 1959)★★★, *Nina Simone At Newport* (Colpix 1960)★★★★, *Forbidden Fruit* (Colpix 1961)★★★, *Nina Simone At The Village Gate* (Colpix 1961)★★★, *Nina Simone Sings Ellington* (Colpix 1962)★★★, *Nina's Choice* (Colpix 1963)★★★, *Nina Simone At Carnegie Hall* (Colpix 1963)★★★★, *Folksy Nina* (Colpix 1964)★★★, *Nina Simone In Concert* (Philips 1964)★★★, *Broadway ... Blues ... Ballads* (Philips 1964)★★★, *I Put A Spell On You* (Philips 1965)★★★, *Tell Me More* (Philips 1965)★★★, *Pastel Blues* (Philips 1965)★★★, *Let It All Out* (Philips 1966)★★★, *Wild Is The Wind* (Philips 1966)★★★, *Nina With Strings* (Colpix 1966)★★★, *This Is* (1966)★★★, *High Priestess Of Soul* (Philips 1966)★★★★, *Nina Simone Sings The Blues* (RCA Victor 1967)★★★★, *Sweet 'N' Swinging* (1967)★★★, *Silk And Soul* (RCA Victor 1967)★★★, *'Nuff Said* (RCA Victor 1968)★★★, *And Piano!* (1969)★★★, *To Love Somebody* (1969)★★★, *Black Gold* (RCA 1970)★★★, *Here Comes The Sun* (RCA 1971)★★★, *Heart And Soul* (1971)★★★, *Emergency Ward* (RCA 1972)★★★, *It Is Finished* (RCA 1972)★★★, *Gifted And Black* (Mojo 1974)★★★, *I Loves You Porgy* (1977)★★★, *Baltimore* (CTI 1978)★★★, *Cry Before I Go* (Manhattan 1980)★★★, *Nina Simone* (Dakota 1982)★★★, *Fodder On My Wings* (IMS 1982)★★★, *Nina's Back* (VPI 1985)★★★, *Live At Vine Street* (Verve 1987)★★★, *Live At Ronnie Scott's* (Windham Hill 1988)★★★, *Live* (Zeta 1990)★★, *The Blues* (Novus/RCA 1991)★★★, *In Concert* (1992)★★★, *A Single Woman* (Elektra 1993)★★, *The Great Show Of Nina Simone: Live In Paris* (Accord 1996)★★.

● COMPILATIONS: *The Best Of Nina Simone* (Philips 1966)★★★★, *The Best Of Nina Simone* (RCA 1970)★★★★, *Fine And Mellow* (Golden Hour 1975)★★★, *The Artistry Of Nina Simone* (RCA 1982)★★★, *Music For The Millions* (Phillips 1983)★★★, *My Baby Just Cares For Me* (Charly 1984)★★★★, *Lady Midnight* (Connoisseur 1987)★★★, *The Nina Simone Collection* (Deja Vu 1988)★★★★, *The Nina Simone Story* (Deja Vu 1989)★★★, *16 Greatest Hits* (1993)★★★★, *Anthology: The Colpix Years* (Rhino 1997)★★★★, *Saga Of The Good Life And The Hard Times* 1968 sessions (RCA 1997)★★★★, *The Great Nina Simone* (Music Club 1997)★★★, *Ultimate Nina Simone* (Verve 1997)★★★★, *Blue For You: The Very Best Of Nina Simone* (Global 1998)★★★★, *Sugar In My Bowl: The Very Best Of 1967-1972* (RCA 1998)★★★★.

● VIDEOS: *Live At Ronnie Scott's* (Hendring Music Video 1988).

● FURTHER READING: *I Put A Spell On You: The Autobiography Of Nina Simone*, Nina Simone with Stephen Cleary.

SIMS, PETE

(see La Roca, Pete)

SIMS, ZOOT

b. John Haley Sims, 29 October 1925, Inglewood, California, USA, d. 23 March 1985, New York City, New York, USA. Sims played clarinet in grade school but took up the tenor saxophone to work with singer Kenny Baker in 1941. He played with Bobby Sherwood from 1942-43, Sonny Durham in 1943 and the Benny Goodman big band in 1944. His recording debut was with Joe Bushkin's small group in 1944. The years 1944-46 were spent in the army. On discharge Sims rejoined Goodman, playing alongside his brother Ray until 1947 when he joined Woody Herman, becoming famous as one of the 'Four Brothers' (the other saxophonists were Stan Getz, Herbie Steward and Serge Chaloff). He left to play with Artie Shaw from 1949-50, then toured Europe with Goodman at regular intervals (1950, 1958, 1972 and 1976) and also toured with Stan Kenton and Gerry Mulligan. In the early 70s Sims started playing soprano saxophone as well as tenor, and later in the decade embarked on a prolific period of recording for Norman Granz's Pablo label, making approximately 15 albums between 1975 and 1984. In 1972 and 1978 he took part in reunion concerts with Herman. He also liked to free-lance, especially in company with tenor saxophonist Al Cohn, with whom he had first worked in the early 50s. Sims was the first American to play a residency at Ronnie Scott's following the lifting of the embargo on visiting musicians in 1961, and he returned there many times, his last visit being in 1982. He toured Scandinavia in 1984, but the doctors had diagnosed terminal cancer, of which he died in 1985. Zoot Sims was a redoubtable exponent of the tenor style developed by Lester Young and contributed swinging, lithe solos to countless big band arrangements.

● ALBUMS: *The Zoot Sims Quartet In Paris* 10-inch album (Discovery 1951)★★★★, *Swingin' With Zoot Sims* 10-inch album (Prestige 1951)★★★, *Tenor Sax Favorites* 10-inch album (Prestige 1951)★★★, *Zoot Sims All Stars* 10-inch album (Prestige 1953)★★★★, with Roy Eldridge *Roy Eldridge With Zoot Sims* 10-inch album (Discovery 1954)★★★, *Zoot Sims In Hollywood* reissued as *Good Old Zoot* (New Jazz 1954)★★★, *Tenorly* (Vogue 1954)★★★, *Zoot Sims Quartets* (Prestige 1956)★★★, *Zoot* (Argo 1956)★★★★, *The Modern Art Of Jazz* (Dawn 1956)★★★★, with Bob Brookmeyer *Tonight's Jazz Today* (Storyville 1956)★★★, with Brookmeyer *Whoo-eeee!* (Storyville 1956)★★★, with Jutta Hipp *Jutta Hipp With Zoot Sims* (Blue Note 1956)★★★★, with Al Cohn *From A To Z* (RCA Victor 1956)★★★★, *Zoot Sims Goes To Jazzville* (Dawn 1957)★★★, *Zoot!* (Riverside 1957)★★★★, *Morning Fun* (Black Lion 1957)★★★, *Zoot Sims Plays Alto, Tenor And Baritone* (ABC-Paramount 1957)★★★, *Zoot Sims Plays Four Altos* (ABC-Paramount 1957)★★★, with Cohn *Al And Zoot* (Coral 1958)★★★, with Serge Chaloff, Cohn, Herbie Steward *The Four Brothers: Together Again* (RCA 1957)★★★★, *A Night At The Half Note* (United Artists 1959)★★★, *Down Home* (Bethlehem 1960)★★★★, with Cohn *Either Way* (Abundance 1960)★★★, with Cohn *You 'N Me* (Mercury 1960)★★★, with Herman 'Trigger' Alpert, Al Cohn, Tony Scott *East Coast Sounds* (Jazzland 1960)★★★, *Choice* (Pacific Jazz 1961)★★★, *Cookin'!* (Fontana 1961)★★★, *New Beat Bossa Nova* (Colpix 1962)★★★, *New Beat Bossa Nova, Volume 2* (Colpix 1962)★★★, *Either Way* (Evidence 1962)★★★, *Zoot Sims In Paris* (United Artists 1962)★★★, *Trotting* (Prestige 1963)★★★, *Koo Koo* (Status 1965)★★★, with Jim Hall, Jimmy Raney *Two Jims And Zoot* (Mainstream 1965)★★★, *The Waiting Game* (Impulse! 1967)★★★, with Pepper Adams *Encounter!* (Prestige 1969)★★★★, with Cohn *Motoring Along* (Sonet 1974)★★★, *Zoot Sims Party* (Choice 1974)★★★, with Joe Venuti *Joe And Zoot* (Chiaroscuro 1974)★★★★, with Venuti *The Joe Venuti Blue Four* (Chiaroscuro 1974)★★★★, with Venuti *Joe Venuti And Zoot Sims* (Chiaroscuro 1975)★★★★, with Dave McKenna *The Dave McKenna Quartet Featuring Zoot Sims* (Chiaroscuro 1975)★★★, with Count Basie *Basie And Zoot* (Pablo 1975)★★★★, *Zoot Plays Soprano* (Pablo 1976)★★★, *Zoot Sims And The Gershwin Brothers* (Pablo 1976)★★★★, with Bucky Pizzarelli *Zoot Sims With Bucky Pizzarelli* (Classic Jazz 1977)★★★, *Hawthorne Nights* (Pablo 1977)★★★, with Jimmy Rowles *If I'm Lucky* (Pablo 1978)★★★, *Warm Tenor* (Pablo 1979)★★★, with Harry 'Sweets' Edison *Just Friends* (Pablo 1979)★★★, *Passion Flower* (Pablo 1980)★★★, *The Swinger* (Pablo 1980)★★★, *I Wish I Were Twins* (Pablo 1981)★★★, with Joe Pass *Blues For Two* (Pablo 1982)★★★★, *Innocent Years* (Pablo 1982)★★★, with Cohn *Zoot Case* (Sonet 1983)★★★, *Suddenly Its Spring* (Pablo 1984)★★★, *Quietly There: Zoot Sims Plays Johnny Mandel* (Pablo 1984)★★★, *In A Sentimental Mood* (Sonet 1984)★★★, *Happy Over There* 1957/1958 recordings (Jass 1987)★★★, with Rowles *For Lady Day* 1978 recording (Pablo 1990)★★★★, *On The Korner* 1983 recording (Pablo 1994)★★★, with Art Pepper *Art 'N' Zoot* 1981 recording (Pablo 1995)★★★★, *Live In Copenhagen* 1978 recording (Storyville 1995)★★★★.

● COMPILATIONS: *The Best Of Zoot Sims* (Pablo 1982)★★★★.

● FURTHER READING: *The John Haley Sims (Zoot Sims) Discography*, Arne Astrup. *The John Haley Sims (Zoot Sims) Discography Supplement*, Arne Astrup.

SINGER, HAROLD 'HAL'

b. 8 October 1919, Tulsa, Oklahoma, USA. After beginning his musical tuition on the violin at the age of eight, Singer switched to clarinet and, finally, tenor saxophone which he played with various big bands in the 40s - notably Ernie Fields and Tommy Douglas (both 1941), Nat Towles (1942), Jay McShann (1942-43), Roy Eldridge (1944) and Lucky Millinder and Oran 'Hot Lips' Page (both 1947). After appearing on various jazz and R&B records in the late 40s - he played tenor on Wynonie Harris's 'Good Rocking Tonight' - he was recommended to Savoy Records by his close friend, Don Byas, and began a run of instrumental hits in 1948 with a tune that would furnish him with a lifelong nickname - 'Cornbread'. He later went to Mercury (1950), Coral (1951-52), returning to Savoy in 1952 to play as both session musician and to usher in the new musical era with his own 'Rock & Roll' and 'Hot Rod'. In the late 50s he recorded R&B for Time, DeLuxe and King and blues and jazz for Prestige and in the 60s recorded a jazz album for Strand before moving to France, where he maintained a steady, if unexciting, living recording for French Polydor, Black & Blue and Futura. In the 80s, Hal made a comeback with guest spots on records by Booker T. Laury, Jimmy Witherspoon, and Rocket 88, as well his own excellent *Swing On It*, on England's JSP Records.

● ALBUMS: with Charlie Shavers *Blue Stompin'* (1959)★★★, *Shades Of Blue* (1963)★★★★, with Milt Buckner *Milt And Hal* (1966)★★★, *Paris Soul Food* (1969)★★★, *Blues And News* (1971)★★★, with Paul Williams, Big Jay McNeely, Sam 'The Man' Taylor and Lee Allen *Honkers & Screamers - Roots Of Rock 'N' Roll Volume 6* (1979)★★, *Swing On It* (1981)★★★, *Rent Party* (1984)★★★★, *No Rush* (1993)★★★.

SINGLETON, MARGIE CREATH

b. Marjorie Creath, *c.*1900, Ironton, Missouri, USA, d. 5 January 1982. She was born into a musical family with her sister Pauline playing piano and her older brother Charlie Creath a popular cornetist and bandleader. She took piano lessons and showed remarkable aptitude in both classical and popular forms. She would later state that she never particularly wanted to be a professional pianist but simply enjoyed playing and hearing piano music. In and around St. Louis, she became known and would sometimes play in her brother's band although not on his recordings. She had an excellent ear and would advise other pianists on their style and shortcomings. Later, she met Zutty Singleton and when he went to Chicago she followed him and they were married. She continued to advise on musical matters but from this point onwards, the mid-30s, she was mostly engaged in administering her husband's business affairs but would sit in if a piano player failed to show up. In Chicago for some years, then in Los Angeles throughout the 40s, she continued her life as wife and business manager and did so in later years in New York. During the final years of her husband's life she nursed him and afterwards resisted persuasion to return to her playing. Those who heard her play insisted that she was an exceptionally good blues and ragtime pianist and during her spell with her brother's band in St. Louis she was effectively the leader, rehearsing and directing the band and helping it retain its status as one of the city's finest and most popular jazz groups.

SINGLETON, ZUTTY

b. Arthur James Singleton, 14 May 1898, Bunkie, Louisiana, USA, d. 14 July 1975. Playing drums from his early childhood, Singleton first worked professionally in 1915. After military service in World War I he played in several leading New Orleans bands, including those of Oscar 'Papa' Celestin and Louis Nelson, then worked the riverboats with Fate Marable in the early 20s. After spending time in New Orleans and St Louis, where he played with Charlie Creath (whose sister he married), Singleton moved to Chicago where he played in bands led by Dave Peyton and Jimmie Noone, then teamed up with Louis Armstrong and Earl 'Fatha' Hines for record dates and a brief spell as co-owners of a club. As a member of the Carroll Dickerson band he went to New York, where he subsequently played with many leading jazzmen of the day. He also led his own band, securing residencies at several clubs and recording extensively throughout the 30s with musicians such as Roy Eldridge, Mezz Mezzrow and Sidney Bechet. In the 40s he worked in bands that played in a startlingly wide range of styles, accompanying musicians as diverse as T-Bone Walker and Charlie Parker, Wingy Manone and Dizzy Gillespie. In the 50s he toured Europe, teaming up with Bill Coleman, Oran 'Hot Lips' Page, Mezzrow again and also leading his own bands. He recorded extensively in this period and throughout the 60s. A stroke in 1970 effectively ended his playing career, but he remained a father-figure in the jazz community, especially in New York where he and his wife made their home. Although Singleton had all the fundamental skills displayed by Baby Dodds, generally regarded as the master of New Orleans drummers, he was far more flexible, as the range of his musical companions demonstrates. His joyously springy playing style enhanced numerous recording sessions and his solo excursions managed the usually impossible task of being highly musical, even melodious, while being compellingly rhythmic. He appeared in several films, including *Stormy Weather* (1943) and *L'Aventure Du Jazz* (1969).

● ALBUMS: *Zutty And The Clarinet Kings* (1967)★★★, *L'Aventure Du Jazz* film soundtrack (1969)★★.

SIRONE

b. Norris Jones, 28 September 1940, Atlanta, Georgia, USA. Master bassist and occasional trombonist Sirone (more or less 'Norris' backwards) has one of the most exceptional resumés of any New Jazz musician, having played with John Coltrane, Cecil Taylor, Ornette Coleman, Albert Ayler, Sun Ra, and Bill Dixon - i.e., *all* of the most important innovators. In the 70s he commuted between the Cecil Taylor Unit and the Revolutionary Ensemble and was the pivot of innumerable New York 'loft scene' sessions but, by the mid-80s, work opportunities had reduced greatly. (Even improvisation has its fashion cycles.) Since 1986, Sirone's major gig has been with the group Phalanx, an all-star aggregate also featuring James 'Blood' Ulmer, George Adams and Rashied Ali.

● ALBUMS: *Artistry* (1978)★★★, *Live* (1980)★★, with Phalanx *Original Phalanx* (DIW 1987)★★★, with Phalanx *In Touch* (DIW 1988)★★★.

SKETCHES OF SPAIN - MILES DAVIS

The third collaboration between Miles Davis and Gil Evans was another work of two men who were musically plugged into each other. The orchestral score by Evans is both haunting and breathtaking when it bursts into life, while the understated playing from Davis is the parmesan on the pasta. The 16-minute 'Concierto De Aranjuez' is a stunning opening track. Many people stop the record at this point because there is so much to take in, and often one track will suffice. It sounds somewhat insulting to say that this album is the perfect background music for a dinner party. Conversation can continue, but it is the magnificent music that really captures the ears of the guests.

● Tracks: *Concierto De Aranjuez; Will O' The Wisp; The Pan Piper; Saeta; Solea.*
● First released 1960
● UK peak chart position: did not chart
● USA peak chart position: did not chart

SKIDMORE, ALAN

b. 21 April 1942, Kingston-on-Thames, London, England. 'Skid' plays soprano and tenor saxophones, flutes and drums. He is the son of Jimmy Skidmore, who gave him a discarded tenor that Alan ignored until he was about 15. At that time he decided to teach himself to play. A muscular and versatile player himself, the musicians he particularly admires include Sonny Rollins, Dexter Gordon, Michael Brecker, Ronnie Scott, Andy Sheppard and, above all, John Coltrane. Skid began playing professionally in 1958, and did various commercial engagements, including tours with comedian Tony Hancock and singer Matt Monro and five years in the house band at London's Talk Of The Town nightclub. In 1961 he made the first of many appearances on BBC Radio's *Jazz Club*, and also met his idol, Coltrane. In the following years Skidmore worked with numerous important and/or successful bands, including Eric Delaney, where he replaced his father when Jimmy decided to leave (in 1963), Alexis Korner (1964), John Mayall's Blues Breakers (1964), Ronnie Scott (1965), Georgie Fame And The Blue Flames (1970), Mike Westbrook (1970-71), Michael Gibbs (1970-71), and Chris McGregor's Brotherhood Of Breath (1971). In 1969 he had formed his own quintet, with which he won the best soloist and best band awards at the Montreux Jazz Festival and gained a scholarship to Berklee, though he did not take this up. In 1973 he co-founded S.O.S., probably the first all-saxophone band, with Mike Osborne and John Surman. He has subsequently had various small groups of his own, including El Skid (co-led with Elton Dean), SOH, and Tenor Tonic, and has worked with the George Gruntz Concert Band, the Elvin Jones Jazz Machine, the Charlie Watts Orchestra, Stan Tracey, Van Morrison, Georgie Fame again, and with the West German Radio Band as featured soloist from 1981-84. In April 1991 he was reunited with Surman when they played as a duo at a benefit for Osborne.

● ALBUMS: *Once Upon A Time* (1969)★★★★, with Mike Westbrook *Marching Song* (1969)★★★★, *TCB* (1970)★★★★, with Michael Gibbs *Michael Gibbs* (1970)★★★★, *Tanglewood 63* (1971)★★★★, with Chris McGregor *Brotherhood Of Breath* (1971)★★★★, *S.O.S.* (1975)★★★, *El Skid* (1977)★★★, *SOH* (Ego 1979)★★★, *SOH Live* (1981)★★, with Charlie Watts *Live At Fulham Town Hall* (1986)★★, *Tribute To Trane* (Miles Music 1988)★★★, with Peter King *Brother Bernard* (1988)★★★, *From East To West* (Miles Music 1993)★★★, *After The Rain* (Miles Music 1998)★★★★.

● COMPILATIONS: *Jazz In Britain 68-69* (1971)★★, *Alexis Korner And... 1961-72* (1986)★★.

SKIDMORE, JIMMY

b. 8 February 1916, London, England, d. 22 April 1998, Welwyn, Hertfordshire, England. After teaching himself to play tenor saxophone when he was 20, Skidmore played with Harry Parry, George Shearing and others, becoming especially active in the years immediately following World War II. He attracted attention as a member of the Vic Lewis Jazzmen and in the 50s played with Kenny Baker and Humphrey Lyttelton, forming part of the latter's non-traditionalist saxophone line-up alongside Tony Coe and Joe Temperley. During the 60s and 70s he continued to appear in clubs but with diminishing frequency. A combination of changing musical times and his own casual approach to his music militated against the success his talent deserved. In fact, it was his son Alan Skidmore who gained the lion's share of public attention from the mid-60s onwards. In the mid-80s he still played in the London area and apparently took the jazz world a little more seriously than he had in the past. He celebrated his 80th birthday by appearing alongside his son.

● ALBUMS: *Humphrey Lyttelton Plays Standards* (1960)★★★, *Skid Marks!* (1975)★★★.

SKY

A UK instrumental group founded in 1979 and devoted to fusing classical, jazz and rock music, Sky was led by virtuoso classical guitarist John Williams (b. 24 April 1941, Melbourne, Victoria, Australia). Having already played concerts at Ronnie Scott's jazz club, Williams formed the group with rock guitarist Kevin Peek, classical percussionist Tristram Fry, ex-Curved Air keyboards player Francis Monkman and Herbie Flowers, a versatile session bass player and composer of the novelty UK number 1 'Grandad'. In 1981, Monkman was replaced by Steve Gray. The group made an instant impact in Britain. Mixing original compositions with inventive adaptations of classical pieces, each of the first four albums reached the UK Top 10. *Sky 2* even headed the UK chart in 1980, aided by 'Toccata', a hit single taken from a theme by Bach. European and Japanese concert tours were equally successful. *Cadmium* was more pop-orientated, containing the Alan Tarney compositions 'The Girl In Winter' and 'Return to Me'. After its release, Williams left the group which continued to record sporadically until 1987 when it folded.

● ALBUMS: *Sky* (Ariola 1979)★★★, *Sky 2* (Ariola 1980)★★, *Sky 3* (Ariola 1981)★★★, *Forthcoming* (Ariola 1982)★★, *Sky 5 Live* (Ariola 1983)★★, *Cadmium* (Ariola 1983)★★, *The Great Balloon Race* (Epic 1985)★★, *Mozart* (1987)★★.

● COMPILATIONS: *Masterpieces - The Very Best Of Sky* (Telstar 1984)★★★, *The Best Of ...* (Music Club 1995)★★★.

SLINGSBY, XERO

b. Matthew Coe, 23 November 1957, Skipton, Yorkshire, England, d. 16 August 1988. Coe's name change came in the mid-70s when punk rock made colourful stage-names *de rigeur*. He grew up in Bradford, where an accident at the age of 10 damaged his left hand: he took up the bass guitar as an alternative to therapeutic rubber-ball squeezing. He fell in with a motorbike crowd and played electric bass in numerous heavy rock bands. Sick of endless guitar indulgence, Ornette Coleman's *New York Is Now!* was a revelation to him. He sold his Fender and Marshall amps and bought a double bass. He also acquired an alto saxophone. After spells as a grave-digger and tractor-driver for Bradford Council, he attended a two-year course at Harrogate Music School, supplemented by gigs with tenor player Richard Ward. In 1979 Xero played in Ghent, the first of many visits to the more receptive European audiences. After a long apprenticeship playing Monk standards and free jazz, he formed a band called Xero Slingsby And The Works with bassist Louis Colan and drummer Gene Velocette. The idea was to present free jazz with punk-type brevity and was remarkably successful: the Works became part of the 'punkjazz' flowering in England that included Blurt, Rip, Rig And Panic and Pigbag. Baritone saxophonist Alan Wilkinson and drummer Paul Hession readily acknowledge their debt to Xero's inspirational belief in musical communication. After fighting brain cancer for three years - probably caused by his childhood accident - he died in 1988. The obituary in *The Wire* concluded: 'As jazz at the end of the 80s faces the twin temptations of purist pessimism or commercial betrayal, Xero's scorched alto sound, his booting lines and clamorous compositions, as well as his understanding of music as event and spectacle, could well become the crucial lessons.'

● ALBUMS: *Shove It* (1985)★★★, *Up Down* (1986)★★★★.

SLOANE, CAROL

b. 1937, Providence, Rhode Island, USA. While still only 14 years old, Sloane sang with a local dance band, Ed Drew's, thanks to the active encouragement of her piano- and saxophone-playing Uncle Joe. By her late teens she had gained sufficient experience to be hired by the popular dance band led by the brothers Les And Larry Elgart. In 1960 she briefly deputized for Annie Ross with Lambert, Hendricks And Ross, and the following year sang at the Newport Jazz Festival. This event opened many doors for her. She made her first record album and appeared at a succession of New York nightclubs, including many that were on the stand-up comic circuit, which thus found her singing talents providing contrast with artists such as Woody Allen, Bill Cosby and Lenny Bruce. She also made a number of television appearances singing with the Lyle 'Skitch' Henderson band on Johnny Carson's *Tonight Show*. The end of the 60s found Sloane in much less demand, her very real and intensely musical talent being somewhat out of step with audience demands. She moved to Raleigh, North Carolina, taking employment as a legal secretary: 'I lived a different life (in the South), among sweet wonderful people, and I spent good, productive years there, even if the rest of the world didn't know it.' In the late 70s she returned to New York where she worked with the pianist Jimmy Rowles, one of the outstanding accompanists of jazz singers of his and any other day. By the early 80s she was working in radio, again in North Carolina, but then moved to Boston, Massachusetts, where she sang in clubs, hosted a radio show, and was married (to club owner Buck Spurr). Her recording career had been sporadic, although it included a fine 1978 album with Rowles, but in the early 90s it went into high gear with a succession of albums for Concord Records. All were very good indeed, with her 1995 tribute to her good friend Carmen McRae, on which she was joined by alto saxophonist Phil Woods, being one of the outstanding vocal albums of the year, if not the decade. Sloane is a regular visitor to Japan where she appears at festivals. A consummate interpreter of ballads, Sloane draws her extensive repertoire from many areas of the field, happily mixing standards with jazz classics and the more arcane reaches of the popular songwriters' canon. In all her work there is poise and distinction and when she moves to mid- and up-tempo tunes she swings with flair and great drive. In an age where subtlety and finesse are either largely absent or, if present, widely misunderstood, Sloane's name is by no means as well known as she deserves. She is one of the great exponents in a long tradition of fine vocal artists in jazz and popular music.

● ALBUMS: *Out Of The Blue* (Columbia 1961)★★★★, *Carol Sings* (Audiophile 1978)★★★★, *Love You Madly* (Contemporary 1989)★★★★, *The Real Thing* (Contemporary 1991)★★★, *Heart's Desire* (Concord 1992)★★★, *Sweet & Slow* (Concord 1993)★★★, *When I Look In Your Eyes* (Concord 1994)★★★★, *The Songs Carmen Sang* (Concord 1995)★★★, *The Songs Sinatra Sang* (Concord Jazz 1996)★★★★, with Clark Terry *The Songs Ella & Louis Sang* (Concord Jazz 1998)★★.

SMALLS, CLIFF

b. 3. March 1918, Charleston, South Carolina, USA. Smalls graduated from Kansas Conservatory and worked for seven years with the Carolina Cotton Pickers before joining Earl Hines' band (1942-46). In 1948 he worked as accompanist/musical director for Billy Eckstine and has over the years worked with many vocalists, often on the R&B circuit he knew from his time with Earl Bostic in the early 50s. These vocalists have included Clyde McPhatter, Brook Benton and Smokey Robinson and the Miracles in the 60s. Since the 70s he has done more work in jazz with musicians like Sy Oliver and the New York Jazz Repertory Company, Paul Gonsalves and Roy Eldridge, Buddy Tate and the Oliver Jackson Trio.

● ALBUMS: with Sy Oliver *Yes Indeed* (1973)★★★, with Buddy Tate *The Texas Twister* (1975)★★★, with Oliver Jackson *Le Quartet* (1982)★★, *Swing And Things* (1976)★★, *Cliff Smalls* (1978)★★★.

SMIETANA, JAROSLAW

b. 29 March 1951, Kraców, Poland. Smietana studied jazz guitar formally while playing as a professional musician. By the mid-70s he was well known in his homeland as the leader of a popular jazz-rock band. His reputation spread thanks to a succession of appearances at international festivals including some dates in the USA. In the middle of the following decade he had shifted the balance towards jazz although he continued to use elements of rock in his performances. He was also now experimenting with larger ensembles for which he wrote most of the music. He continued to gain plaudits in his homeland, and to appear at festivals, such as the 1993 Poznan Jazz Fair. Smietana's technique is remarkable and allows him to fully realize his forward thinking attitude towards his music.

● ALBUMS: *Birthday* (Muza 1976)★★★, *Go Ahead* (Muza 1979)★★★, *Mosquito* (Poljazz 1981)★★★, *Talking Guitar* (Muza 1983)★★★, *From One To Four* (Poljazz 1987)★★★, *Sound Colors* (Muza 1987)★★★.

SMITH, BETTY

b. 6 July 1929, Sileby, Lincolnshire, England. After studying piano and tenor saxophone as a child, Smith concentrated on the latter instrument at the start of her professional career. In the early 50s she played in Freddy Randall's popular traditional band, but her real forte was in the mainstream. From the late 50s she regularly led her own small group and also played and sang with the Ted Heath band. Her solo career continued through the next two decades and in the 70s she was one of the highlights of the touring package 'The Best Of British Jazz'. In the 80s she was still active and playing as well as ever. An outstanding performer, Smith is one of only a few women of her generation to overcome successfully the offensive yet seemingly immovable prejudice against women instrumentalists in jazz. The quality of her playing and the high standards she has set herself reveal the absurdity of such prejudices.

● ALBUMS: with others *The Best Of British Jazz* (1981)★★, with others *The Very Best Of British Jazz* (1984)★★.

SMITH, BILL

b. 12 May 1938, Bristol, England. A jazz fan from childhood, Smith began to learn trumpet and drums, turning to soprano saxophone only in 1966, three years after he had moved to Toronto. Influenced by 60s free jazz and by the new music from Chicago's AACM, Smith played a prominent role in Canada's contemporary jazz scene of the 70s, working with various ensembles such as the All Time Sound Effects Orchestra, the *avant garde* Jazz Revival Band, the CCMC and Air Raid. In 1976 he recorded a set of duos with pianist Stuart Broomer, then in the late 70s formed a trio with David Lee (bass, cello) and David Prentice (violin). Originally called the New Art Music Ensemble (NAME), they later became the Bill Smith Ensemble, recording two albums themselves and one each with guests Leo Smith and Joe McPhee. Also a well-known photographer and writer, Smith has long been co-publisher and editor of *Coda*, since the 60s one of the world's leading jazz magazines; is co-owner of Sackville Recordings; and was a founder of the Onari label (named after his wife, who co-runs it with him). He is also the originator of *Imagine The Sound* - a series of five (to date) projects that have included two photographic exhibitions, a set of jazz postcards, a film (featuring Paul Bley, Bill Dixon, Archie Shepp and Cecil Taylor) and a book of his photographs and writings. In 1988, he toured and recorded with the international saxophone sextet, Six Winds, but was not with them on their second album. (This artist should not be confused with the US saxophonist/clarinettist Bill Smith, best known for his work with Dave Brubeck.)

● ALBUMS: with Stuart Broomer *Conversation Pieces* (1976)★★★, *Pick A Number* (1980)★★★, *The Subtle Deceit Of The Quick Gloved Hand* (1981)★★★, with Leo Smith *Rastafari* (Sackville 1983)★★★, with Joe McPhee *Visitation* (Sackville 1987)★★★, with Six Winds *Elephants Can Dance* (1988)★★★.

● FURTHER READING: *Imagine The Sound*, Bill Smith.

SMITH, BRIAN

b. 3 January 1939, Wellington, New Zealand. Smith is a self-taught saxophonist. He played in rock, dance and jazz bands at home and in Australia before coming to England in 1964, when he first played with Alexis Korner's Blues Incorporated (1964-65). In the late 60s he worked with the big bands of Tubby Hayes and Maynard Ferguson, with whom he stayed until 1974. He also worked with the bands of Graham Collier, Gordon Beck, Mike Westbrook, Mike Gibbs, Keith Tippett and John Stevens. In 1969 he was a founder-member of the successful band Nucleus with whom he stayed until he returned home to New Zealand in 1982. Since then he has played with his own quartet and won the Australian Jazz Record of the Year Award with *Southern Excursions* in 1984. He is a player with a formidable technique and the ability to fit into any music from rock and blues right through to free improvisation.

● ALBUMS: with Nucleus *Elastic Rock* (Vertigo 1970)★★★, with Ian Carr *Belladonna* (1972)★★★, *Roots* (1973)★★, *Awakening* (1980)★★★, with Neil Ardley *Kaleidoscope Of Colours* (1976)★★★★, *Southern Excursions* (1984)★★★.

SMITH, BUSTER

b. Henry Smith, 24 August 1904, Aldorf, Texas, USA, d. 10 August 1991. Smith first taught himself to play clarinet, working professionally in Texas in the early 20s. He then added alto saxophone and in 1925 joined Walter Page's Blue Devils in Oklahoma City. Smith was one of several Blue Devils who left *en masse* to join Bennie Moten in Kansas City and briefly led this band after Moten's sudden death. He then co-led a band with Count Basie, but bowed out when the band left the familiar surroundings of Kansas City. Whatever the motive behind his decision to stay in Kansas City, when the band he had helped to form went on to greatness, his career thereafter achieved less than earlier potential had promised. Forming a new band in 1937, Smith employed Jay McShann, the excellent if almost forgotten trombonist Fred Beckett, and a teenage saxophonist named Charlie Parker. During his career Smith had also written many arrangements for the bands in which he worked and also for other leaders. In the late 30s and early 40s his bandleading activities suffered when his attempts to break into the New York scene failed, a circumstance that diverted him more and more to arranging. In the early 40s he returned to his home state, settling in Dallas and leading small bands there for the greater part of the next four decades. Generally credited as being a major influence on Parker, Smith's own playing career has thus been overshadowed and his few recordings do little to confirm his legendary status.

● ALBUMS: *The Legendary Buster Smith* (1959)★★★.

● COMPILATIONS: with others *Kansas City 1926 To 1930* (1926-30)★★★, with others *Original Boogie Woogie Piano Giants* (1938-41)★★★★, with others *Kansas City Jazz* (1940-41)★★★.

SMITH, CARL 'TATTI'

b. *c*.1908, Marshall, Texas, USA. He began playing trumpet in territory bands in the late 20s, among them the famed Terrence Holder band. He also played for a while with Gene Coy, then joined Count Basie, making important small group records with a Basie sextet billed as Jones-Smith Inc. In 1937 Smith quit the Basie band, working then with the Gentlemen Of Swing, Oran 'Hot Lips' Page, Leon Abbey, Benny Carter and others. He then played with a band led by Chris Columbus (drummer and adoptive father of Sonny Payne). In the late 40s Smith moved to South America where he continued to play into the following decade. Smith's decision to spend a substantial part of his playing life outside of the USA makes an accurate assessment of his abilities difficult, but on the basis of his Jones-Smith session, he was a trumpeter of originality and great ability.

● COMPILATIONS: *Jones-Smith Inc.* (Tax 1936)★★★.

SMITH, CARRIE

b. 25 August 1941, Fort Gaines, Georgia, USA. Smith appeared at the 1957 Newport Jazz Festival as a member of a New Jersey church choir, but her solo professional career did not take off until the early 70s. An appearance with Dick Hyman and the New York Jazz Repertory Company at Carnegie Hall in 1974 should have alerted audiences to her exceptional qualities, but for the rest of the decade she was much better received in Europe than in the USA. Her tours of festivals and concert halls were sometimes as a single, but also in company with NYJRC, Tyree Glenn, the World's Greatest Jazz Band and others. Smith's style is rooted in the blues and gospel but her repertoire is wide, encompassing many areas of twentieth-century popular music. Her voice is deep and powerful and she is especially effective in live performances. Although her reputation has grown throughout the 80s, she remains far less well known than her considerable talent warrants.

● ALBUMS: with Dick Hyman *Satchmo Remembered* (1974)★★★★, *Do Your Duty* (1976)★★★, *When You're Down And Out* (1977)★★★, *Carrie Smith* (1978)★★, with others *Highlights In Jazz Anniversary Concert* (1985)★★★.

SMITH, CARSON

b. Carson Raymond Smith, 9 January 1931, San Francisco, California, USA, d. 2 November 1997, Las Vegas, USA. Smith's family moved to Los Angeles while he was still a child, but, after completing his schooling, he first tried working in the New York area. Although he was a good bass player, work was scarce and in 1952 he returned to Los Angeles, where he promptly found work in Gerry Mulligan's legendary quartet alongside Chet Baker. Mulligan not only used his playing abilities but also recorded some of his compositions, and later acknowledged that some of Smith's ideas helped to shape the sound and style of the group. The absence of a piano, in particular, made his bass a central part of the quartet's sound. The band broke up in 1953 soon after 'My Funny Valentine' had provided them with a big hit, and during the remainder of the 50s Smith worked in small bands led by Russ Freeman and Chico Hamilton; he also worked with Charlie Parker, Clifford Brown, Billie Holiday and Dick Twardzik. At the end of the decade he was briefly with Stan Kenton before relocating to Las Vegas, where he worked with Charlie Teagarden's band, Buddy Rich, Georgie Auld, with whom he toured Japan, Lew Tabackin, Zoot Sims and many others, including a Los Angeles reunion concert with Mulligan. Dizzy Gillespie remarked of Smith in the 80s that he had not heard a bass player like him since Oscar Pettiford. Smith's brother, Putter Smith, is also a well-known west coast-based bass player.

Smith, Clarence 'Pine Top'

b. 11 January 1904, Troy, Alabama, USA, d. 15 March 1929, Chicago, Illinois, USA. Often considered to be the founder of the boogie-woogie style of piano playing, 'Pine Top' Smith was actually a vaudeville performer. From his mid-teens, Smith toured tent shows and theatres as a pianist and dancer. He gradually concentrated on piano and, encouraged by Charles 'Cow Cow' Davenport, made a handful of records. Smith's style was largely in the mould of humorous songs backed up by vigorous two-handed playing. His small list of recordings also included blues, but his fame rests, more than anything, on his recording of 'Pine Top's Boogie Woogie' (1928). This song possibly represents the first documented use of the term. His work on the circuits took him all over the south in the company of such artists as Butterbeans And Susie and Ma Rainey, but it was in Chicago that his promising career was cut short when he was accidentally shot by a man named David Bell during a skirmish in a dancehall. He was 25 and left a wife and two children. His work has been covered by many artists over the years, and 'Pine Top's Boogie Woogie' remains as satisfying today as it was in 1928 when it made its initial impact.

● COMPILATIONS: *Compilation 1928-29-30* (Oldie Blues 1986)★★★, *Pine Top Smith And Romeo Nelson* (Oldie Blues 1987)★★★, *Compilation 1929-30* (Oldie Blues 1988)★★★.

Smith, Derek

b. 17 August 1931, London, England, England. After starting to play piano as a tiny child, Smith quickly developed until he was playing professionally at the age of 14. He began playing jazz and in the early 50s worked with Kenny Graham, John Dankworth, Kenny Baker and other leading British bands. In the mid-50s he moved to New York where he was soon in demand as a session musician, playing in studio orchestras and on record dates. However, he also played jazz with Benny Goodman, Connie Kay and others. During the 60s, Smith's career followed similar lines, mixing studio work with jazz, and towards the end of the decade he became a long-serving member of the *Tonight* show orchestra. In the 70s he again played with Goodman, touring overseas, and also worked with Scott Hamilton and in bands led by Nick Brignola, Arnett Cobb and others. As the 80s progressed Smith became steadily more active on the international jazz festival circuit, sometimes as soloist, at other times in a trio with Milt Hinton and Bobby Rosengarden. A stylish player with a wide-ranging repertoire and a gift for elegantly presenting a constant fund of ideas, Smith is very much a musician's musician but by the early 90s was deservedly becoming better known to audiences.

● ALBUMS: *Love For Sale* (Progressive 1978)★★★, *The Man I Love* (Progressive 1978)★★★, *Plays The Music Of Jerome Kern* (Progressive 1981)★★, *Dark Eyes* (East Wind 1985)★★★, *Plays Passionate Piano* (Hindsight 1992)★★.

Smith, Huey 'Piano'

b. 26 January 1934, New Orleans, Louisiana, USA. Pianist Smith drew his pulsating style from a variety of musical sources, including the boogie-woogie of Albert Ammons and jazz of Jelly Roll Morton. Having served in bands led by Earl King and Eddie 'Guitar Slim' Jones, Smith became a respected session musician before embarking on an independent recording career. Leading his own group, the Clowns, which at its peak included Gerry Hall, Eugene Francis, Billy Roosevelt and vocalist Bobby Marchan, he achieved two million-selling singles in 1957 with 'Rockin' Pneumonia And The Boogie Woogie Flu' and 'Don't You Just Know It'. Both releases showcased classic New Orleans rhythms as well as the leader's vibrant, percussive technique. The pianist was also featured on 'Sea Cruise', a 1959 smash for Frankie Ford, whose speeded-up vocal was overdubbed onto an existing Clowns tape. However, despite other excellent releases, Huey Smith did not enjoy another substantial hit and, having become a Jehovah's Witness, forsook music in favour of preaching.

● ALBUMS: *Having A Good Time* (Imperial 1959)★★★, *For Dancing* (Imperial 1961)★★, *T'was The Night Before Christmas* (Imperial 1962)★★, *Rock 'N' Roll Revival* (Imperial 1963)★★★.

● COMPILATIONS: *Rockin' Pneumonia And The Boogie Woogie Flu* (1965)★★★, *Huey 'Piano' Smith's Rock And Roll Revival* (1974)★★★, *Rockin' Pneumonia And The Boogie Woogie Flu* (Ace 1979)★★★, *Rockin' And Jivin'* (Charly 1981)★★★, *The Imperial Sides 1960/1961* (Pathe Marconi 1984)★★★, *Somewhere There's Honey For The Grizzly* (Ace 1984)★★★, *Serious Clownin' - The History Of Huey 'Piano' Smith And The Clowns* (Rhino 1986)★★★★, *Pitta Pattin'* (Charly 1987)★★★.

Smith, Jabbo

b. Cladys Smith, 24 December 1908, Pembroke, Georgia, USA, d. 16 January 1991. Smith was taught trumpet and trombone while still a small child and later toured with a youth band. At the age of 16 he was working professionally as a trumpeter (although he would periodically play trombone in later years). In New York from about 1925 he played with Charlie 'Fess' Johnson, Duke Ellington, James P. Johnson and others. Stranded in Chicago when a show in which he was playing folded, he worked in bands led by Carroll Dickerson, Earl 'Fatha' Hines, Erskine Tate and Charlie Elgar. During the 30s he played with Fess Williams, Dickerson, led his own band, then returned to New York with Claude

Hopkins and also played with Sidney Bechet. By the mid-40s, reputedly exhausted through high-living, he was leading his own band in the comparative musical backwater of Milwaukee and for the next dozen years mostly played in that city. He also worked outside music, for a car rental company, into the late 50s. Thereafter, he played less and less until he was brought to New York in 1975 to receive an award at Carnegie Hall. This event prompted him to begin practising again and he was soon touring internationally, playing and singing with Sammy Rimington, Orange Kellin and others. In the early 80s he suffered a series of heart attacks but kept on playing, often working in harness with seemingly unlikely musical companions such as Don Cherry. In these later years he increasingly turned to composing, writing music for the Mel Lewis orchestra, often in collaboration with Keith Ingham. Despite his remarkable durability and longevity, Smith remains a little-known figure in jazz and, given the extremely high regard in which he is held by fellow musicians, he is also very much under-recorded. In his youth he was often considered to be a potential rival to Louis Armstrong and although he has none of Armstrong's creative genius, his recordings display many flashes of spectacular brilliance.

● COMPILATIONS: *Jabbo Smith Vols 1 & 2* (1927-29)★★★, *Jabbo Smith Vols 1 & 2* (1928-38)★★★★, *The Ace Of Rhythm* (1929)★★★, *Jabbo Smith And The Hot Antic Band* (1982)★★★, *Sweet 'N' Lowdown* 1927-29 recordings (Affinity 1986)★★★, *Jabbo Smith Vol 1 1928-29* (Retrieval 1990)★★★, *Complete 1928-38 Sessions* (Jazz Archives 1993)★★★★.

SMITH, JIMMY

b. James Oscar Smith, 8 December 1925, Norristown, Pennsylvania, USA. The sound of the Hammond Organ in jazz was popularized by Smith, often using the prefix 'the incredible' or 'the amazing'. Smith has become the most famous jazz organist of all times and arguably the most influential. Brought up by musical parents, he was formally trained on piano and bass and combined the two skills with the Hammond while leading his own trio. He was heavily influenced by Wild Bill Davis. By the mid-50s Smith had refined his own brand of smoky soul jazz, which epitomized laid-back 'late night' blues-based music. His vast output for the 'soul jazz' era of Blue Note Records led the genre and resulted in a number of other Hammond B3 maestros' appearing, notably, Jimmy McGriff, 'Brother' Jack McDuff, 'Big' John Patten, Richard 'Groove' Holmes and 'Baby Face' Willette. Smith was superbly complemented by outstanding musicians. Although Art Blakey played with Smith, Donald Bailey remains the definitive Smith drummer, while Smith tackled the bass notes on the Hammond. The guitar was featured prominently throughout the Blue Note years and Smith used the talents of Eddie McFadden, Quentin Warren and Kenny Burrell. Further immaculate playing came from Stanley Turrentine (tenor saxophone), Lee Morgan (trumpet) and Lou Donaldson (alto saxophone). Two classic albums from the late 50s were *The Sermon* and *Houseparty*. On the title track of the former, Smith and his musicians stretch out with majestic 'cool' over 20 minutes, allowing each soloist ample time. In 1962 Jimmy moved to Verve Records where he became the undisputed king, regularly crossing over into the pop bestsellers and the singles charts with memorable titles such as 'Walk On The Wild Side', 'Hobo Flats' and 'Who's Afraid Of Virginia Woolf'. These hits were notable for their superb orchestral arrangements by Oliver Nelson, although they tended to bury Smith's sound. However, the public continued to put him into the charts with 'The Cat', 'The Organ Grinder's Swing' and, with Smith on growling vocals, 'Got My Mojo Working'. His albums at this time also made the best-seller lists, and between 1963 and 1966 Smith was virtually ever-present in the album charts with a total of 12 albums, many making the US Top 20. Smith's popularity had much to do with the R&B boom in Britain during the early 60s. His strong influence was found in the early work of Steve Winwood, Georgie Fame, Zoot Money, Graham Bond and John Mayall. Smith's two albums with Wes Montgomery were also well received; both allowed each other creative space with no ego involved. As the 60s ended Smith's music became more MOR and he pursued a soul/funk path during the 70s, using a synthesizer on occasion. Organ jazz was in the doldrums for many years and although Smith remained its leading exponent, he was leader of an unfashionable style. After a series of low-key and largely unremarkable recordings during the 80s, Smith delivered the underrated *Off The Top* in 1982. Later in the decade the Hammond organ began to come back into favour in the UK with the James Taylor Quartet and the Tommy Chase Band, and in Germany with Barbara Dennerlein. Much of Smith's seminal work has been remastered and reissued on compact disc since the end of the 80s, almost as vindication for a genre that went so far out of fashion, it disappeared. A reunion with Kenny Burrell produced a fine live album, *The Master*, featuring reworkings of classic trio tracks; further renewed interest in his career came in 1995 when he returned to Verve for *Damn!*, the home of of his most commercial work. On this album he was joined by some of the finest young jazz players, many of whom were barely born at the time of Smith's 60s heyday. The stellar line-up on this, one of the finest albums of his career, comprises Roy Hargrove (b. 16 October 1969, Waco, Texas, USA; trumpet), Mark Turner (b. 10 November 1965, Wright Patterson Air Force Base, Ohio, USA; saxophone), Ron Blake (b. 7 September 1965, St. Thomas, Virgin Islands; saxophone), Nicholas Payton (b. 26 September 1973, New Orleans, Louisiana, USA; trumpet), Abraham Burton (17 March 1971, New York City, New York, USA; saxophone), Art Taylor (b. 6 April 1929, New York City, New York, USA, d. 6 February 1995; drums), Tim Warfield (b. 2 July 1965, York, Pennsylvania, USA; saxophone), Mark Whitfield (b. 6 October 1966, Lindehurst, New York, USA; guitar), Bernard Purdie (b. 11 June 1939, Elkton, Maryland, USA; drums), Christian McBride (b. 31 May 1972,

Philadelphia, Pennsylvania, USA; bass). Smith continues to enjoy a major renaissance during the 90s, and he is, the Frank Sinatra of the jazz organ, as both the instruments greatest ambassador and interpreter.

● ALBUMS: *Jimmy Smith At The Organ Volume 1* (Blue Note 1956)★★★★, *Jimmy Smith At The Organ Volume 2* (Blue Note 1956)★★★★, *The Incredible Jimmy Smith At The Organ Volume 3* (Blue Note 1956)★★★, *The Incredible Jimmy Smith At Club Baby Grand Volume 1* (Blue Note 1956)★★★, *The Incredible Jimmy Smith At Club Baby Grand Volume 2* (Blue Note 1956)★★★, *The Champ* (Blue Note 1956)★★★, *A Date With Jimmy Smith Volume 1* (Blue Note 1957)★★★, *A Date With Jimmy Smith Volume 2* (Blue Note 1957)★★★, *The Sounds Of Jimmy Smith* (Blue Note 1957)★★★, *Plays Pretty Just For You* (Blue Note 1957)★★★, *House Party* (Blue Note 1957)★★★★, *Groovin' At Small's Paradise Volume 1* (Blue Note 1958)★★★, *Groovin' At Small's Paradise Volume 2* (Blue Note 1958)★★★, *The Sermon* (Blue Note 1958)★★★★, *Cool Blues* (Blue Note 1958)★★★★, *Home Cookin'* (Blue Note 1958)★★★★, *Crazy! Baby* (Blue Note 1960)★★★★, *Midnight Special* (Blue Note 1960)★★★★, *Open House* (Blue Note 1960)★★★★, *Back At The Chicken Shack* (Blue Note 1960)★★★★, *Jimmy Smith Plays Fats Waller* (Blue Note 1962)★★★, *Bashin': The Unpredictable Jimmy Smith* (Verve 1962)★★★★, *Hobo Flats* (Verve 1963)★★★, *I'm Movin' On* (Blue Note 1963)★★★★, *Rockin' The Boat* (Blue Note 1963)★★★, *Any Number Can Win* (Verve 1963)★★★, with Kenny Burrell *Blue Bash* (Verve 1963)★★★★, *Prayer Meetin'* (Blue Note 1964)★★★★, *Who's Afraid Of Virginia Woolf* (Verve 1964)★★★★, *The Cat* (Verve 1964)★★★★, *Christmas '64* (Blue Note 1964)★★★, *Organ Grinder's Swing* (Verve 1965)★★★★★, *Softly As A Summer Breeze* (Blue Note 1965)★★★, *Monster* (Verve 1965)★★, *'Bucket'!* (Blue Note 1966)★★★★, *Got My Mojo Workin'* (Verve 1966)★★★★, *Hoochie Coochie Man* (Verve 1966)★★★★, *Peter And The Wolf* (Verve 1966)★★★, with Wes Montgomery, *Jimmy & Wes The Dynamic Duo* (Verve 1966)★★★★, with Montgomery *Further Adventures Of Jimmy And Wes* (Verve 1966)★★★★, *Christmas Cookin'* (Verve 1966)★★★, *Respect* (Verve 1967)★★★, *Stay Loose* (Verve 1968)★★★, *Livin' It Up* (Verve 1968)★★★, featuring George Benson *The Boss* (Verve 1969)★★★, *Groove Drops* (Verve 1970)★★★, *Root Down* (Verve 1972)★★★, *Bluesmith* (Verve 1972)★★★★, *Portugese Soul* (Verve 1973)★★★, *I'm Gonna Git Myself Together* (MGM 1973)★★, *Other Side Of Jimmy Smith* (MGM 1973)★★, *It's Necessary* (Mercury 1977)★★★, *Confirmation* 1957/1958 recordings (Blue Note 1979)★★★, *The Cat Strikes Again* (Laserlight 1980)★★★, *On The Sunny Side* 1958 recording (Blue Note 1981)★★★, *Off The Top* (Elektra Musician 1982)★★★, *Keep On Comin'* (Elektra Musician 1983)★★★, *Lonesome Road* 1957 recording (Blue Note)★★★★, *Go For Whatcha Know* (Blue Note 1986)★★★, *Prime Time* (Milestone 1990)★★★, *Fourmost* (Milestone 1991)★★★, *Sum Serious Blues* (Milestone 1993)★★★, *The Master* (Somethin' Else/Blue Note 1994)★★★, *The Master II* (Somethin' Else/Blue Note 1997)★★, *Damn!* (Verve 1995)★★★★, with Eddie Harris *All The Way Live* 1981 recording (Milestone 1996)★★★, *Jimmy Smith And His Trio* 1965 recording (RTE 1996)★★★, *Angel Eyes - Ballads & Slow Jams* (Verve 1996)★★★★, *Standards* 1958 recordings (Blue Note 1998)★★★.

● COMPILATIONS: *Best Of Jimmy Smith* (Verve 1967)★★★★, *Best Of Jimmy Smith II* (Verve 1967)★★★, *Jimmy Smith's Greatest Hits* 1956-1963 recordings (Blue Note 1968)★★★★, *The Best Of Jimmy Smith* (Blue Note 1988)★★★★, *Compact Jazz: Jimmy Smith Plays The Blues* (Verve 1988)★★★★, *Walk On The Wild Side: The Best Of The Verve Years* 1962-1973 recordings (Verve 1995)★★★★, *The Complete February 1957 Jimmy Smith Blue Note Sessions* 5-LP/3-CD box set (Mosaic)★★★★, *Jazz 'Round Midnight* 1963-1972 recordings (Blue Note)★★★, *Talkin' Verve: Roots Of Acid Jazz* 1963-1972 recordings (Verve 1996)★★★★, *A New Sound, A New Star: Jimmy Smith At The Organ, Vols. 1-2* 1956 recordings (Capitol 1997)★★★★.

SMITH, JOHNNY

b. John Henry Smith Jnr., 25 June 1922, Birmingham, Alabama, USA. After first playing trumpet and violin, Smith took up the guitar, on which he became best known, although he continued to play trumpet in later years. In New York in the 40s Smith maintained steady employment as a studio musician, but also took part in after-hours bop sessions. In the early 50s a recording under his own name of 'Moonlight In Vermont', with Stan Getz, was greeted with great popular and critical acclaim. He also recorded with Bennie Green, Kenny Clarke and others on *Jazz Studio*, using the pseudonym Sir Jonathan Gasser, and made albums under his own name. In the 60s Smith moved west, remaining active in music as a teacher and occasional performer.

● ALBUMS: *A Three Dimension Sound Recording Of Jazz At NBC With The Johnny Smith Quintet* 10-inch album (Roost 1953)★★★★, *Johnny Smith Quintet* 10-inch album (Roost 1953)★★★★, *In A Mellow Mood* reissued as *Moods* (Roost 1954)★★★, *In A Sentimental Mood* 10-inch album (Roost 1954)★★★, *Annotations Of The Muses* 10-inch album (Legende 1955)★★★, *Johnny Smith Plays Jimmy Van Heusen* (Roost 1955)★★★, *Johnny Smith Quartet* (Roost 1955)★★★, *Moonlight In Vermont* (Roost 1956)★★★★, *New Quartet* (Roost 1956)★★★★, *Johnny Smith Foursome, Volume 1* (Roost 1956)★★★, *Johnny Smith Foursome, Volume 2* (Roost 1956)★★★, *Flower Drum Song* (Roost 1958)★★★, with Jeri Southern *Jeri Southern Meets Jimmy Smith* (Roulette 1958)★★★, *Easy Listening* (Roost 1959)★★★, *Favorites* (Roost 1959)★★★, *Designed For You* (Roost 1960)★★★, *Dear Little Sweetheart* (Roost 1960)★★★, *Guitar And Strings* (Roost 1960)★★★, *Johnny Smith Plus The Trio* (Roost 1960)★★★, *The Sound Of The Johnny Smith Guitar* (Roost 1961)★★★, *Man With The Blue Guitar* (Roost 1962)★★★.

SMITH, JOHNNY 'HAMMOND'

b. John Robert Smith, 16 December 1933, Louisville, Kentucky USA, 4 June 1997, Chicago, Illinois, USA. Not be confused with the legendary swing promoter and talent spotter John Hammond Jnr., Johnny 'Hammond' Smith (sometimes known simply as Johnny Hammond) is one of the giants of the soul jazz Hammond organ. Born the year the instrument was invented, he studied piano, trying to emulate the intricate jazz styles of Art Tatum and Bud Powell, before devoting himself to the Hammond during the 50s. His naturally funky approach and feel for the instrument established him as one of the leaders in a movement of bluesy, soul jazz organists who were mixing the sound of church gospel and hard-bop; and he began recording sessions under his own name for the Prestige (throughout the 60s) and, later, Kudu labels. Later in his career he added a range of synthesised and electronic sounds to his palette, but he remains most associated with the original Hammond. Recent years witnessed a resurgence in popularity for the Hammond in jazz, and the soul jazz genre in general, and Smith became in demand in the studio and on the international jazz circuit. He died of cancer in June 1997.

● ALBUMS: *All Soul* (New Jazz 1959)★★★, *That Good Feelin'* (New Jazz 1959)★★★, *Talk That Talk* (New Jazz 1960)★★★, *Stimulation* (Prestige 1961)★★★, *Gettin' The Message* (Prestige 1961)★★★★, *Look Out!* (New Jazz 1962)★★★★, with Willis 'Gator Tail' Jackson *Johnny 'Hammond' Cooks With Gator Tail* (Prestige 1962)★★★, *Black Coffee* (Riverside 1963)★★★★, *Mr. Wonderful* (Riverside 1963)★★★, *Open House!* (Riverside 1965)★★★★, *A Little Taste* (Riverside 1965)★★★, *The Stinger* (Prestige 1965)★★★, *Opus De Funk* (Prestige 1966)★★★, *The Stinger Meets The Golden Thrush* (Prestige 1967)★★★, *Love Potion #9* (Prestige 1967)★★, *Ebb Tide* (Prestige 1967)★★, *Nasty* (Prestige 1968)★★★, *Dirty Grape* (Prestige 1968)★★★, *Soul Flowers* (Prestige 1968)★★, *Soul Talk* (Prestige 1969)★★★, *Black Feeling* (Prestige 1969)★★★, *Wild Horses Rock Steady* (Kudu 1971)★★★, with Hank Crawford *Portrait* (Milestone 1990)★★★.

● COMPILATIONS: *The Best Of Johnny 'Hammond' Smith* (Prestige 1969)★★★★.

Smith, Keith

b. 19 March 1940, London, England. Taking up the trumpet in 1957, Smith originally favoured the New Orleans style and established a considerable reputation in this field. In the late 50s and through to the mid-60s he played with several bands, leading his own in Europe and in the USA from 1964, where he performed and recorded with George Lewis and 'Captain' John Handy. He relocated in New Orleans and became known as the 'Albino Kid' after managing to get enrolled into the black musician's union in the days of segregation. To subsidise his income as a musician he went into business running a fish and chip shop, but became a victim of the protection racket and decided to 'get out of town'. Smith was also a member of the New Orleans All Stars, a package of mostly American musicians who toured Europe in the 60s. After spells in California and Chicago he moved to Denmark with Papa Bue Jensen's band in the early 70s, he again formed his own band in the UK when he returned in 1981. He named the band Hefty Jazz, a name he also gave to his own record company and booking agency, and established a practice of touring with well-conceived thematic package shows. Among these were 'The Wonderful World Of Louis Armstrong', for which he hired such ex-Louis Armstrong sidemen as Arvell Shaw and Barrett Deems, '100 Years Of Dixieland Jazz' and 'The Stardust Road', a tribute to the music of Hoagy Carmichael, which was headlined by Georgie Fame. As a personal record he completed 1000 concert appearances highlighting the music of Gershwin and Hoagy Carmichael. A dedicated musician who also combines effective business and entrepreneurial skills, Smith remains at the forefront of the UK's traditional jazz scene in the 90s.

● ALBUMS: *Keith Smith's American All Stars In Europe* (1966)★★, *Way Down Yonder In New Orleans, Then And Now* (1977)★★★, *Ball Of Fire* (Hefty Jazz 1978)★★★, *Up Jumped The Blues* (Hefty Jazz 1978)★★★, *Keith Smith's Hefty Jazz* (Jazzology 1988)★★★, *A Portrait Of Keith Smith Vols 1-4* (Let's Do It 1994)★★★★.

Smith, Leo

b. 18 December 1941, Leland, Mississippi, USA. Smith's stepfather was blues guitarist Alex 'Little Bill' Wallace and in his early teens Smith led his own blues band. He was already proficient on trumpet, which he later studied in college and continued to play in various army bands. In 1967 he moved to Chicago, where he joined the AACM, recording with Muhal Richard Abrams and 'Kalaparusha' Maurice McIntyre and becoming a member of Anthony Braxton's trio. In 1969, the group moved to Paris, but broke up a year later. Smith returned to the USA and settled in Connecticut. He recorded again with Abrams and Braxton in the Creative Construction Company and also worked with Marion Brown in the Creative Improvisation Ensemble and in a duo format. Smith continued to play occasionally with AACM colleagues such as Braxton and Roscoe Mitchell ('L-R-G') during the 70s, but his chief focus of interest now was his own music. He set up a label, Kabell, formed a group, New Dalta Ahkri, and also began to develop his solo music in a series of concerts and records (*Creative Music-1, Solo Music/Ahkreanvention*). New Dalta Ahkri, whose members included Anthony Davis, Oliver Lake and Wes Brown, made a handful of albums renowned for their spacious, abstract beauty, as did Smith's trio (with Bobby Naughton and Dwight Andrews). *Divine Love* also featured guest artists Lester Bowie, Charlie Haden and Kenny Wheeler, while *Spirit Catcher* had one track ('The Burning Of Stones') on which Smith played with a trio of harpists. Smith's trumpet style blended the terseness of Miles Davis with the lyricism of Booker Little (his two chief influences), while his music was based on the innovatory concepts of 'ahkreanvention' and 'rhythm units', alternative methods of structuring improvisation that he had been refining since the late 60s. A writer too, his *Notes (8 Pieces)* set out his views on African American music history and included scathing attacks on jazz journalism and the mainstream music business. The late 70s found him making several trips to Europe, playing at Derek Bailey's Company Week (*Company 5, 6, 7*) and in 1979 recording both the big band *Budding Of A Rose* and the first of two trio discs with Peter Kowald and drummer Gunter Sommer. In 1983 he recorded *Procession Of The Great Ancestry*, with Naughton and Kahil El'Zabar among the players ('a music of ritual and blues, of space and light', enthused *Wire*). The same year he visited Canada to record *Rastafari* with the Bill Smith trio, the title signalling a conversion to Rastafarianism that led him, on later albums, to explore more popular forms, including reggae (*Jah Music, Human Rights* - though the latter also has one side of free improvisation with Kowald and Sommer from 1982). He also changed his name to Wadada Leo Smith. At the end of the 80s Smith was still playing in the New York area, but was also working as a teacher and had released no new recordings for several years. Hailed by Braxton as 'a genius' and by Anthony Davis as 'one of the unsung heroes of American music', the belated appearance of his *Procession Of The Great Ancestry* in 1990 prompted many to lament his long absence from the recording studio: as writer Graham Lock put it, 'such a silence hurts us all'. He has broken his silence in the 90s with two richly ambitious sets, *Kulture Jazz* on ECM Records and *Tao-Nija* on John Zorn's Tzadik label.

● ALBUMS: *Creative Music-1* (1972)★★★★, with Marion Brown *Duets* 1970 recording (Freedom 1973)★★★★, *Reflectativity* (1975)★★★, with Anthony Braxton *Trio And Duet* (1975)★★★★, with Creative Construction Company *CCC Volume One* 1970 recording (1975)★★★, with Creative Construction Company *CCC Volume Two* 1970 recording (1976)★★★, *Song Of Humanity* (1977)★★★, *Mass On The World* (Moers 1978)★★★★, *Divine Love* (ECM 1979)★★★, *Solo Music/Ahkreanvention* (1979)★★★, *Spirit Catcher* (Nessa 1979)★★★, *Budding Of A Rose* (Moers 1980)★★★, with Peter Kowald, Günter Sommer *Touch The Earth* (FMP 1980)★★★, with Kowald, Sommer *Break The Shells* (1982)★★★, *Go In Numbers* 1980 recording (Black Saint 1982)★★★, with Bill Smith Trio *Rastafari* (Sackville 1983)★★★, *Jah Music* 1984 recording (1986)★★, *Human Rights* 1982-85 recordings (Gramm 1986)★★★, *Procession Of The Great Ancestry* 1983 recording (Chief 1990)★★★, *Kulture Jazz* (ECM 1993)★★★★, *Tao-Njia* (Tzadik 1997)★★★★, with Henry Kaiser *Yo Miles!* (Shanachie 1998)★★★★.

● FURTHER READING: *Notes (8 Pieces)*, Leo Smith.

SMITH, LONNIE LISTON

b. 28 December 1940, Richmond, Virginia, USA. Not to be confused with the soul/jazz organist Lonnie Smith. Born into a very musical family, Smith seemed destined from a very early age to make music his career. His father and two brothers were all vocalists, but it was the keyboard that attracted Lonnie. After studying at Morgan State University, he moved to New York and immersed himself in the city's thriving jazz scene. Accompanying Betty Carter for a year in 1963, Smith soon became a highly sought-after pianist, working with successive jazz stars, from Rahsaan Roland Kirk (1964-65), Art Blakey (1966-67), and Joe Williams (1967-68), through to Pharoah Sanders (1969-71), Gato Barbieri (1971-73), and finally Miles Davis (1972-73). In 1974, Smith formed the Cosmic Echoes with his brother Donald as vocalist. Playing a very popular soft fusion, they recorded a highly successful album in 1975, and remained popular throughout the decade. In 1991, after some time out of the spotlight, Smith recorded a high-quality album, *Magic Lady*, and embarked on a European tour (including the UK).

● ALBUMS: *Astral Traveling* (Flying Dutchman 1973), with the Cosmic Echoes *Expansions* (Flying Dutchman 1975)★★, with the Cosmic Echoes *Visions Of A New World* (Flying Dutchman 1975)★★★, with the Cosmic Echoes *Reflections Of A Golden Dream* (Flying Dutchman 1976)★★★★, with the Cosmic Echoes *Renaissance* (RCA 1976)★★★, *Live!* (RCA 1977)★★★, *Loveland* (Columbia 1978)★★★, *Exotic Mysteries* (Columbia 1979)★★★, *Dreams Of Tomorrow* (Doctor Jazz 1983)★★★, *Silhouettes* (Doctor Jazz 1984)★★★, *Rejuvenation* (Doctor Jazz 1986), *Magic Lady* (1991)★★★, *Foxy Lady* (Music Masters 1997)★★★, *Afro Blue* (Music Masters 1998)★★★.

● COMPILATIONS: *The Best Of Lonnie Liston Smith* (Columbia 1981)★★★★.

SMITH, RUSSELL

b. 1890, Ripley, Ohio, USA, d. 27 March 1966, Los Angeles, California, USA. The Smiths were a musical family, although the two trumpeters Joe and Russell could scarcely have been less similar. Russell was a sober, ordered man who long outlived his more volatile brother. Russell became a professional musician in 1906 and moved to New York in 1910. He first played in Army Bands and then in reviews. He joined Fletcher Henderson's band in 1925 and stayed for 15 years. He was very much the straight musician willing to leave the jazz to others and perfectly suited to playing lead in a big band. After Henderson he played with Cab Calloway (1941-46) and then with Noble Sissle (1946-50) before retiring to California in the 50s.

● ALBUMS: with Fletcher Henderson *A Study In Frustration* (1923-38).

SMITH, STUFF

b. Hezekiah Leroy Gordon Smith, 14 August 1909, Portsmouth, Ohio, USA, d. 25 September 1967. Smith began playing violin as a child; he had some formal tuition but left home at the age of 15 to make his way as a professional musician. In 1926 he became a member of the popular Alphonso Trent band, where he remained, with side trips to other bands, for four years. In 1930 he settled in Buffalo, where he formed his own group, and in 1936 he went to New York for a long and highly successful residency at the Onyx Club. This band, which included Jonah Jones and Cozy Cole, established Smith's reputation as a forceful, hard-swinging jazzman with an anarchic sense of humour (he performed wearing a battered top hat and with a stuffed parrot on his shoulder). Offstage he was an aggressive and disorganized individual, and in the late 30s he was forced to disband because of trouble with his sidemen, bookers, club owners and the union. Following Fats Waller's death in 1943, Smith took over the band but this too was a short-lived affair.

By the late 40s his career was in decline, but a series of recordings for Norman Granz in the late 50s, in which he was teamed, improbably but successfully, with Dizzy Gillespie, brought him back into the spotlight. He began to tour, especially in Europe where he was extremely popular, settled in Denmark and continued to record. Perhaps the most exciting and dynamic of all the jazz fiddlers, Smith concentrated on swinging, attacking his instrument with wild fervour and producing a rough-edged, almost violent sound. His performance of 'Bugle Call Rag' at a New York Town Hall concert in 1945 vividly demonstrates his all-stops-out approach to jazz and is a remarkable bravura display. Despite his swing era roots, Smith's recordings with Gillespie are filled with interesting explorations and he never seems ill at ease. A hard-drinker, Smith's later years were beset by hospitalizations, during which parts of his stomach and liver were removed. A visit to a Paris hospital resulted in his being declared a 'medical museum' and he was placed on the critical list, but within a few days he was back on the concert platform. He died in September 1967.

● ALBUMS: *Swingin' Stuff* (1956)★★★★, *Have Violin, Will Swing* (1957)★★★, *Soft Winds* (1957)★★★, with Dizzy Gillespie *Dizzy Gillespie And Stuff Smith* (Verve 1958)★★★★, with Stéphane Grappelli *Violins No End* (Original Jazz Classics 1957)★★★, *Sessions, Live* (1958)★★, *Stuff Smith* (1959)★★, *Cat On A Hot Fiddle* (1959)★★★, with Herb Ellis *Herb Ellis & 'Stuff' Smith Together* (Epic 1963)★★★, *Blues In G* (1965)★★★, with Grappelli *Stuff And Steff* (1965)★★★, with Grappelli, Jean-Luc Ponty *Violin Summit* (1966)★★★★, *Black Violin* (1967)★★★.

● COMPILATIONS: *Stuff Smith And His Onyx Club Orchestra* (1936)★★★, *The Varsity Sessions* (1938-40)★★★, with others *Town Hall Concert Volume 2* (1945)★★.

● FURTHER READING: *Stuff Smith: Pure At Heart*, Anthony Barnett and Evan Logager. *Desert Sands: The Recordings And Performances Of Stuff Smith*, Anthony Barnett.

SMITH, TAB

b. Talmadge Smith, 11 January 1909, Kinston, North Carolina, USA, d. 17 August 1971. After learning to play piano and C melody saxophone, Smith settled on alto and soprano saxophones. It was on alto that he made his name, working in bands led by Fate Marable, Lucky Millinder and Frankie Newton during the 30s. He also played in Teddy Wilson's ill-fated big band, at this time often playing tenor. In 1939 and into the early 40s he was in great demand, recording with Billie Holiday, Earl 'Fatha' Hines, Charlie Shavers, Coleman Hawkins, playing with Count Basie and Millinder again, and also leading his own band. In the late 40s and early 50s he played only part-time but, after making some popular R&B recordings, he was soon back leading a band, which he continued to do throughout most of the 50s. Late in the decade he again dropped out of full-time music, ending his career playing organ in a St. Louis restaurant. Smith was a forceful player on both alto and soprano, his solos having an attractively restless urgency. His sound was burred and possessed a surging intensity that helped him to make the transition into R&B. Under-recorded in his lifetime and largely overlooked since his death, Smith's contribution to jazz was inevitably if unjustly overshadowed by better-known contemporaries such as Benny Carter, Willie Smith and, perhaps his closest musical counterpart, Pete Brown.

● ALBUMS: *Tab Smith* i (1959)★★★, *Tab Smith* ii (1960)★★★.

● COMPILATIONS: *I Don't Want To Play In Your Kitchen* (Saxophonograph 1987)★★★, *Jump Time 1951-52* (Delmark 1987)★★★★, *Joy At The Savoy* (Saxophonograph 1987)★★★, *Because Of You* (Delmark 1989)★★★, *Worlds Greatest Altoist - These Foolish Things* (Saxophonograph 1989)★★★★, *Aces High* (Delmark 1992)★★★, *Top 'N' Bottom* 1951-57 recordings (Delmark 1998)★★★.

SMITH, TOMMY

b. 27 April 1967, Luton, Bedfordshire, England. Smith grew up in Edinburgh and started playing saxophone at the age of 12. He wowed the jazz clubs with his precocious brilliance and appeared on television in 1982, backed by pianist Gordon Beck and bassist Niels-Henning Ørsted Pedersen. The next year, aged only 16, he recorded *Giant Strides* for Glasgow's GFM Records. It was an astonishing debut. The young tenor made mistakes, but the stark recording revealed his major assets: a full, burnished tone and a firm idea of the overall shape of his solos. It shone out of the British jazz of the time like a beacon, a herald of the 'jazz revival' among younger players. In 1983 he played the Leverkusen Jazz Festival in Germany. The Scottish jazz scene helped to raise the money to send him to Berklee College Of Music, where he enrolled in January 1984. Jaco Pastorius invited him to join his group for club dates, as did vibist Gary Burton.

In 1985 Smith formed Forward Motion, with Laszlo Gardonyi (piano), Terje Gewelt (bass) and Ian Froman (drums), and began international tours, playing a spacious, reflective jazz. It was no surprise when ECM Records' Manfred Eicher asked him to play on Burton's *Whiz Kids* in 1986, as Smith was sounding more and more like the label's established saxophone maestro, Jan Garbarek. In 1988 he toured under his own name with Froman from Forward Motion, pianist John Taylor and bassist Chris Laurence. In 1989 he introduced a series of 10 jazz television broadcasts and in 1990 worked with pop band Hue And Cry. In May 1990 he premiered a concerto for saxophone and string ensemble commissioned by the Scottish Ensemble. Signed to Blue Note Records in the late 80s, he released three albums before a move to the audiophile label Linn.

● ALBUMS: *Giant Strides* (GFM 1983)★★★, with Forward Motion *Progressions* (1985)★★★, with Forward Motion *The Berklee Tapes* (1985)★★★, *Step By Step* (Step By Step 1989)★★★★, *Peeping Tom* (Blue Note 1990)★★★★, *Standards* (Blue Note 1991)★★★★, *Paris* (Blue Note 1992)★★★, *Reminiscence* (Linn 1994)★★★, *Misty Morning & No Time* (Linn 1995)★★★, *Beasts Of Scotland* (Linn 1996)★★★, *Azure* (Linn 1997)★★★, *The Sound Of Love* (Linn 1998)★★★.

SMITH, WILLIE

b. 25 November 1910, Charleston, South Carolina, USA, d. 7 March 1967. Smith began playing clarinet while still at school, performing professionally in his mid-teens. While at Fisk University he met Jimmie Lunceford, joining him in an orchestra there that eventually became a full-time professional organization. By now playing alto saxophone, Smith became a key member of the Lunceford band, meticulously drilling the saxophone section into perfection. He was with Lunceford until 1942, shortly before entering the US

Navy, where he directed a band. After the war he joined Harry James, bringing with him a level of commitment and dedication similar to that he had brought to Lunceford's band. He was with James until 1951, then played briefly with Duke Ellington and Billy May, then joined Jazz At The Philharmonic, touring internationally. During the remainder of the 50s he was with the ill-fated Benny Goodman/Louis Armstrong all-star package, followed by James and May again, then he did film studio work while battling with a drink problem. In the early 60s Smith worked in various minor show bands in Los Angeles, Las Vegas and, briefly, led his own band in New York. Before the arrival of Charlie Parker, Smith, along with Benny Carter and Johnny Hodges, was one of the three major alto saxophonists in jazz. As a section leader he was outstanding, as almost any record by the Lunceford band will testify. As a soloist he had a sinuously beautiful tone, marked by a definitive hard edge that prevented him from ever slipping into sentimentality.

● ALBUMS: *Jazz At The Philharmonic* (1944-46)★★★, *Jazz At The Philharmonic 1946 Vol. 2* (1946)★★★, *Jazz History Volume 12: Harry James* (1959-62)★★★, *Alto Saxophonist Supreme* (1965)★★★.

SMITH, WILLIE 'THE LION'

b. William Henry Joseph Bonaparte Bertholoff, 25 November 1897, Goshen, New York, USA, d. 18 April 1973. Smith began playing piano at the age of six, encouraged by his mother. He continued with his informal musical education and by his mid-teenage years had established a formidable reputation in New York as a ragtime pianist. During World War I Smith acquired his nickname, apparently through acts of great heroism. In the post-war years he quickly developed into one of Harlem's best-known and feared stride pianists. Despite his popularity in Harlem and the respect of his fellow musicians, including Fats Waller, James P. Johnson and Duke Ellington, he made few records and remained virtually unknown outside the New York area. In the 40s he travelled further afield, and during the 50s and 60s gradually extended his audience, playing and reminiscing at the keyboard, and recording albums that demonstrated his commanding style.

● ALBUMS: *The Lion Roars* (1957)★★★★, *Music On My Mind* (1966)★★, *Pork And Beans* (Black Lion 1966)★★★, *The Memoirs* (1967)★★★, *Live At Blues Alley* (1970)★★, *The Lion's In Town* 1959 recordings (Vogue 1993)★★★.

● COMPILATIONS: *The Original 14 Plus Two* (1938-39)★★★, *Tea For Two* (Jazz Live 1981)★★★, *Memoirs Of Willie The Lion* (RCA 1983)★★★★, *Memorial* 1949-50 recordings (Vogue 1988)★★★★, *Reminiscing The Piano Greats* (1950)★★★.

● FURTHER READING: *Music On My Mind*, Willie 'The Lion' Smith and George Hoefer (ed.).

SMYTHE, PAT

b. 2. May 1923, Edinburgh, Scotland, d. 6. May 1983, London, England. Smythe practised as a lawyer in Edinburgh before moving to London in the late 50s. He played with trumpeter Dizzy Reece before joining Joe Harriott's Quintet (1960-64). Harriott was developing the beginnings of a European free jazz quite unlike Ornette Coleman's American form. Smythe was able to help both as pianist in the band and with suggestions to organize the new ideas. He stayed on with Harriott in the Indo Jazz Fusions, which organized improvization along new lines. Throughout the 70s he worked in a variety of contexts with Kenny Wheeler. He was a skilled accompanist of singers including Anita O'Day, Blossom Dearie, Tony Bennett, Annie Ross, Elaine Delmar and Mark Murphy. So respected a musician was he that after his death the Pat Smythe Memorial Trust and Award was established in his memory.

● ALBUMS: with Joe Harriott *Free Form* (1960)★★★, *Abstract* (1961-62)★★, *Movement* (1963)★★★, *High Spirits* (1964)★★★, *Indo Jazz Suite* (1966)★★★, *Indo Jazz Fusions* (1966)★★★★, *Personal Portrait* (1967)★★★, *Sandra King In A Concert Of Vernon Duke* (Audiophile 1982)★★★.

SNOW, VALAIDA

b. 2 June 1905, Chattanooga, Tennessee, USA, d. 30 May 1956. Born into an intensely musical family, Snow was taught by her mother to play cello, bass, violin, banjo, mandolin, harp, accordion, clarinet, saxophone and trumpet. She also sang and danced. By the time she was 15 years old she was entertaining professionally and had decided to concentrate on trumpet and vocals. Her sisters Lavaida, Alvaida and Hattie were also professional singers, as was a brother, Arthur Bush. In 1924 Snow was attracting favourable attention in New York in the Noble Sissle and Eubie Blake show, *In Bamville (The Chocolate Dandies)*. Soon thereafter she was in London with *Blackbirds*, recording with Johnny Claes, Derek Neville, Freddy Gardner and others. She then worked in China for a time; on her return to the USA she headlined in Chicago and Los Angeles, then rejoined the cast of *Blackbirds*, this time in Paris. Tireless, she played in *Liza* across Europe and in Russia. In the early 30s she was performing in, and involved with the production of, the Ethel Waters show, *Rhapsody In Black*, in New York. In the mid-30s she returned to London and then to Hollywood, where she made films with her husband Ananais Berry, one of the famed Berry Brothers dancing troupe. After playing New York's Apollo Theatre she revisited Europe for more shows and films, then toured the Far East. In 1939 she was in Scandinavia, where she was arrested by the invading Germans and interned in a concentration camp at Wester-Faengle. After 18 months she was released as an exchange prisoner and returned to New York. Her experiences had severely damaged her both physically and psychologically, but she began performing again, remarried, and played several prestigious engagements. Sadly, the spark and vitality that had made her one of the outstanding American entertainers of the 30s had begun to dim. Snow played and sang the blues with deep feeling and could more than hold her own on up-tempo swingers. She had perfect pitch and was also a skilled transcriber and arranger. In short, she was a phenomenal musician yet, because she was a woman, in the jazz world of the 30s and 40s she was regarded as something of a curiosity. Fortunately, Rosetta Records' owner Rosetta Reitz has recently instigated a comprehensive reissue programme of Snow's excellent recorded legacy, and this clearly shows that as a trumpet player she was at least the equal of many of her more famous male contemporaries.

● ALBUMS: with others *Harlem Comes To London* (1929-38)★★, *Valaida: Swing Is The Thing* (1936-37)★★★, *Hot Snow: Valaida Snow* (1937-50)★★★★.

Snowden, Elmer

b. 9 October 1900, Baltimore, Maryland, USA, d. 14 May 1973. Snowden was playing banjo professionally in the Washington, DC area while still in his teens and in 1919 teamed up with Duke Ellington in a trio. Some time later, in New York, Snowden needed a piano player and sent for Ellington. Soon thereafter the rest of the band, the Washingtonians, parted company with Snowden, forming the nucleus of the orchestra Ellington was to lead with such success. Snowden formed a new band, and also began acting as a band contractor and musicians' agent. Through the late 20s and early 30s he was a popular bandleader in the New York area, employing many fine jazzmen. After a brief hiatus owing to union problems he resumed bandleading, continuing to do so into the early 60s when he also taught and briefly enjoyed some success on the jazz festival circuit. During this period he played and sometimes recorded with Turk Murphy, Lonnie Johnson and Darnell Howard. Snowden died in May 1973.

● ALBUMS: *Harlem Banjo* (1960)★★★★, with Lonnie Johnson *Blues And Ballads* (1960)★★★.

Soft Machine

Founded in 1966, the original line-up was Robert Wyatt (b. 28 January 1945, Bristol, Avon, England; drums, vocals), Kevin Ayers (b. 16 August 1945, Herne Bay, Kent, England; vocals), Daevid Allen, Mike Ratledge and, very briefly, guitarist Larry Nolan. By autumn 1967 the classic line-up of the Soft Machine's art-rock period (Ayers, Wyatt and Ratledge) had settled in. They toured with Jimi Hendrix, who, along with his producer, ex-Animals member Chas Chandler, encouraged them and facilitated the recording of their first album. (There had been earlier demos for Giorgio Gomelsky's Marmalade label, but these were not issued until later, and then kept reappearing in different configurations under various titles.) From the end of 1968, when Ayers left, until February 1970, the personnel was in a state of flux (Lyn Dobson, Marc Charig and Nick Evans were members for a while), and the music was evolving into a distinctive brand jazz-rock. Arguably, *Volume Two* and *Third* contain their most intriguing and exciting performances. Highlighted by Wyatt's very English spoken/sung vocals, the group had still managed to inject some humour into their work. The finest example is Wyatt's mercurial 'Moon In June'. By mid-1970 the second definitive line-up (Ratledge, Wyatt, Hugh Hopper and Elton Dean) was finally in place. It was this band that Tim Souster showcased when he was allowed a free hand to organize a late-night Promenade Concert in August 1970. In autumn 1971, Wyatt left to form Matching Mole (a clever pun on the French translation of Soft Machine; Machine Molle), and Phil Howard came in on drums until John Marshall became the permanent drummer. For the next few years, through a number of personnel changes (farewell Dean and Hopper, welcome Roy Babbington, Karl Jenkins) the Soft Machine were, for many listeners, the standard against which all jazz-rock fusions, including most of the big American names, had to be measured. However, with Ratledge's departure in January 1976 the group began to sound like a legion of other guitar-led fusion bands, competent and craftsmanlike, but, despite the virtuosity of Allan Holdsworth and John Etheridge, without the edge of earlier incarnations, and certainly without the dadaist elements of Wyatt's time. In 1984, Jenkins and Marshall brought together a new edition of the band (featuring Dave Macrae, Ray Warleigh and a number of new Jenkins compositions) for a season at Ronnie Scott's club. Jenkins moved into a highly successful career composing advertising jingles, including work for Renault, Levi's and Jaguar cars. His composition for Delta Airlines, 'Adiemus', was released as a single and became a hit in Germany. Soft Machine's first three albums contain the best of their work, clearly showing they were one of the most adventurous and important progressive bands of the late 60s, one that gently led their followers to understand and appreciate jazz.

● ALBUMS: *Soft Machine* (Probe 1968)★★★, *Soft Machine Volume Two* (Probe 1969)★★★★, *Third* (Columbia 1970)★★★★, *Fourth* (Columbia 1971)★★★, *Fifth* (Columbia 1972)★★★, *Six* (Columbia 1973)★★, *Seven* (Columbia 1973)★★, *Bundles* (Harvest 1975)★★★, *Softs* (Harvest 1976)★★, *Triple Echo* (Harvest 1977)★★, *Alive And Well* (Harvest 1978)★★, *Live At The Proms 1970* (1988)★★, *The Peel Sessions* (Strange Fruit 1990)★★★★, *The Untouchable* (1990)★★★, *As If ...* (1991)★★, *Rubber Riff* (Voiceprint 1995)★★, *Spaced* 1968 recording (Cuneiform 1996)★★★, *Live 1970* (Voiceprint 1998)★★.

Solo: Hugh Hopper *1984* (1973)★★★.

● FURTHER READING: *Gong Dreaming*, Daevid Allen.

Solal, Martial

b. 23 August 1927, Algiers, Algeria. Solal was taught to play the piano from the age of seven by his opera-singing mother. He worked with local bands in Algiers before moving to Paris in 1950. There he played with all the prominent French musicians as well as the visiting Americans - Don Byas, Lucky Thompson, Sidney Bechet. In 1968, he began a long association with alto saxophonist Lee Konitz. He occasionally leads a big band. Solal has a prodigious technique at the piano and an extensive harmonic knowledge. He has often worked as a solo performer, when he rarely plays in a constant tempo and his melodic improvisation can be at its most remote. He wrote the score for Jean-Luc Godard's film *Breathless* (1959) and has scored over 20 further screenplays. *Triangle* in 1996 was a particularly impressive recording, aided, embellished and improved by Pete Erskine and Marc Johnson.

● ALBUMS: *French Modern Sounds* (Contemporary 1954)★★★, *Martial Solal* (Capitol 1960)★★★, *Vive La France! Viva La Jazz! Vive Solal!* (Capitol 1961)★★, *Martial Solal In Concert* (Liberty 1963)★★, *Martial Solal At Newport* (1963)★★★★, *Solal!* (Milestone 1963)★★★, *Impressive Rome* (1968)★★★, *On Home Ground* (Milestone 1969)★★★, *Suite For Trio* (1970)★★★, *Jazz A Gareau* (1970)★★, *Nothing But Piano* (1975)★★, with Lee Konitz *Duplicity* (1977)★★★, with Stéphane Grappelli *Happy Reunion* (1980)★★★, *Big Band* (1981)★★★, *Bluesine* (1983)★★★, *Martial Solal Plays Andre Hoideir* (1984)★★, with Pete Erskine, Marc Johnson *Triangle* (JMS 1996)★★★, with Lee Konitz *Star Eyes: Hamburg 1983* (hatOLOGY 1998)★★★, with Paul Motian, Gary Peacock *Just Friends* (Dreyfus 1998)★★★★.

Soloff, Lew

b. Lewis Michael Soloff, 20 January 1944, New York City, New York, USA. After studying piano, trumpet and music theory at several colleges of music, Soloff played jazz trumpet with several leaders, notably Maynard Ferguson and Gil Evans and the Latin groups of Machito, Tito Puente and Chuck Mangione. In the late 60s he moved into jazz/rock, joining Blood, Sweat And Tears with whom he remained for five years. During this same period he also played jazz, recording with the Thad Jones-Mel Lewis band and Clark Terry's big band. Throughout the 70s and early 80s, Soloff continued to mix pop and jazz work, playing and recording with musicians as diverse as Evans, Sonny Stitt, George Russell, Jon Faddis and with Spyro Gyra. He also demonstrated his versatility by playing classical music. A fiery, gutsy player, Soloff's broad repertoire has caused some jazz fans to overlook his work. He is, nevertheless, a musician of considerable depth, integrity and flair.

● ALBUMS: *Yesterdays* (Paddle Wheel 1986)★★★, *But Beautiful* (Paddle Wheel 1988)★★★, *My Romance* (Paddle Wheel 1989)★★★, *Little Wing* (Sweet Basil 1992)★★.

Someday My Prince Will Come - Miles Davis

Quintessential Miles Davis, laid-back, confident and spacious, together with, for many, his best musical unit of John Coltrane, Wynton Kelly, Paul Chambers and Philly Joe Jones, further augmented by Hank Mobley (tenor) and Jimmy Cobb. Although Coltrane was only guesting, his strong spirit is felt and his vignettes are faultless. The title track builds beautifully until a wonderful drone-like, booming bass line closes it. The other stand-out tracks are 'Pfrancing', with some glorious light fingers from Kelly and on 'Teo' the groove is very much in the *Kind Of Blue* mould. This is an exceptional Miles Davis album that often gets overlooked.

● Tracks: *Someday My Prince Will Come; Old Folks; Pfrancing; Drad-Dog; Teo; I Thought About You.*

● First released 1961

● UK peak chart position: did not chart

● USA peak chart position: did not chart

Song For My Father - Horace Silver Quintet

Yet another jazz steal; this time, Steely Dan borrowed the title track for 'Rikki Don't Lose That Number'. Horace Silver should take heart, this is his most successful album and one that finds its way onto many recommended lists, not just for the jazz fraternity. Its strength is its accessibility, and in keeping with many piano leader albums Silver does not seek to dominate. The quintet is completed by Carmell Jones (trumpet), Joe Henderson (tenor), Teddy Smith (bass) and Roger Humphries (drums). The reissued CD version contains four extra tracks from the same 1963/1964 sessions.

● Tracks: *Song For My Father; The Natives Are Restless Tonight; Calcutta Cutie; Que Pasa; Kicker; Lonely Woman.*

● First released 1965

● UK peak chart position: did not chart

● USA peak chart position: 95

Sonny Rollins Vol. 2 - Sonny Rollins

The famous Harold Feinstein cover borrowed by Joe Jackson ('how dare he', said the purists) for *Body And Soul* also announces 'Monaural' Sonny Rollins. Did we ever have a 'Stereophonic' Charlie Parker; do we care? This is a blisteringly good album that never once loses pace. The formidable line-up is Jay Jay Johnson (trombone), Horace Silver and Thelonious Monk (piano), Art Blakey (drums) and Paul Chambers (bass). Wonderful versions of Thelonious Monk's 'Misterioso' and 'Reflections' are included, plus Rollins' own 'Why Don't I' and 'Wail March'. The finest 'monaural' record Rollins ever made.

● Tracks: *Why Don't I; Wail March; Misterioso; Reflections; You Stepped Out Of A Dream; Poor Butterfly.*

● First released 1957

● UK peak chart position: did not chart

● USA peak chart position: did not chart

Soprano Sax - Steve Lacy

Soprano specialist Steve Lacy remains one of jazz's instantly recognizable soloists. His big, steady tone, matter-of-fact phrasing and lean, angular melodic conception make up a truly unique and refreshing sound. Originally inspired by Sidney Bechet, and playing predominantly New Orleans jazz, he quickly propelled himself forward, becoming obsessed with the compositions of Thelonious Monk, working with piano rebel Cecil Taylor and eventually experimenting with jazz-and-spoken-word recordings. *Soprano Sax* dates from 1957, and features sparkling, exuberant pianist Wynton Kelly, and Cecil Taylor alumni Buell Neidlinger on bass and Dennis Charles on drums.

● Tracks: *Day Dream; Alone Together; Work; Rockin' In Rhythm; Little Girl Your Daddy Is Calling You; Easy To Love.*

● First released 1957

● UK peak chart position: did not chart

● USA peak chart position: did not chart

SOPRANO SUMMIT

(see Davern, Kenny; Wilber, Bob)

SOUL - COLEMAN HAWKINS

The opening track starts with a typical Ray Bryant piano boogie roll, akin to 'Little Susie'. The groove starts and is joined by the familiar tone of Kenny Burrell's guitar. Coleman Hawkins comes in late and takes control with some of his sweetest ever tenor playing. We are still discussing the first track 'Soul Blues', but in reality this is the benchmark for the whole session. 'Groovin' highlights the ease and rapport the musicians have with each other. Wendell Marshall on bass and Osie Johnson on drums never dominate, they merely embellish.

- Tracks: *Soul Blues; I Hadn't Anyone Till You; Groovin'; Greensleeves; Sunday Mornin'; Until The Real Thing Comes Along; Sweetnin'.*
- First released 1959
- UK peak chart position: did not chart
- USA peak chart position: did not chart

SOUL NOTE RECORDS

(see Black Saint And Soul Note Records)

SOULVILLE - BEN WEBSTER

Ben Webster's breathy and romantic tenor saxophone tone was one of the best-loved and most widely imitated sounds in all of jazz. This flawless 1957 date features pianist Oscar Peterson's celebrated trio as the rhythm section, with guitarist Herb Ellis and bassist Ray Brown, as well as Stan Levey on drums. The title track is a slow, mellow blues number, but the record's highlight is probably the short but breathtakingly beautiful 'Time On My Hands' - one of Webster's wonderful ballad performances. Interestingly, the CD reissue ends with three tracks of Webster playing an exuberant and appealingly clumsy stride piano - the only surviving examples of him at the keyboard.

- Tracks: *Soulville; Late Date; Time On My Hands; Lover Come Back To Me; Where Are You; Makin' Whoopee; Ill Wind.*
- First released 1958
- UK peak chart position: did not chart
- USA peak chart position: did not chart

SOUND OF JAZZ, THE

An outstanding achievement in the presentation of jazz on US television, this 1957 film was conceived and produced by Robert Herridge with the advice of jazz writers Nat Hentoff and Whitney Balliett. Directed by Jack Smight, the film shows the musicians playing in an atmosphere of complete relaxation and achieving an exceptionally high standard of performance. Regardless of who the musicians might have been, the concept and format would have been commendable. The fact that the musicians on display are some of the greatest figures in the history of jazz make this an hour of continuous joy. The all-star bands led by Count Basie and Red Allen feature Doc Cheatham, Freddie Green, Coleman Hawkins, Jo Jones, Roy Eldridge, Joe Newman, Gerry Mulligan, Rex Stewart, Earle Warren, Dicky Wells, Ben Webster, Lester Young, singer Jimmy Rushing, Vic Dickenson, Danny Barker, Milt Hinton, Nat Pierce (who also contributed the arrangements played by the Basie-led band) and Pee Wee Russell. Also on hand is the Jimmy Giuffre trio with Jim Hall and Jim Atlas playing 'The Train And The River', and Thelonious Monk plays 'Blue Monk' accompanied by Ahmed Abdul-Malik and Osie Johnson. If all this were not enough there is Billie Holiday accompanied by Mal Waldron. She sings her own composition, 'Fine And Mellow', in what must be this song's definitive performance, backed by many of the listed musicians, with Lester Young contributing a poignant solo. Four decades after its making, this film remains a high-water mark in jazz and its standards remain those to which all other film-makers aspire.

SOUND OF MILES DAVIS, THE

Produced and directed by the same team responsible for *The Sound Of Jazz* (Robert Herridge and Jack Smight), this 1959 film was originally entitled *Theater For A Song*. Davis is presented with his quintet (John Coltrane, Wynton Kelly, Paul Chambers and Jimmy Cobb) and also with Gil Evans And His Orchestra. The performance captures Davis in eloquent form and the contributions from the other musicians on hand help to make this an important filmed record of one of the music's most important figures.

SOUTH, EDDIE

b. 27 November 1904, Louisiana, Missouri, USA, d. 25 April 1962, Chicago, Illinois, USA. Taught violin as a child, South was educated for a career as a classical musician. Sadly, this goal proved overly optimistic; in the USA in the 20s there was no place on concert stages for black performers. Inevitably, therefore, he became a dance-band musician, mainly in Chicago, at first working with artists such as Jimmy Wade, Charlie Elgar and Erskine Tate. In the late 20s he teamed up with Mike McKendrick and then led his own band, the Alabamanians, recording with both. In 1928 he visited Europe, proving extremely popular, and during a visit to Budapest he resumed his studies and also established an interest in eastern-European gypsy music that remained with him for the rest of his life. In the early 30s he was again leading a band in Chicago, but did not enjoy the popular success of many of his contemporaries. In 1937 he returned to Europe to play at the International Exhibition in Paris. During this visit he recorded some outstanding sides with Django Reinhardt.

From 1938 onwards he worked in the USA, mostly in a small group context but briefly led a big band. He played clubs and radio dates throughout the 40s and 50s, usually as leader but also with artists such as Earl Hines. He had his own radio show for a while and also appeared on television. The most stylish and melodic of all the jazz violinists, South's classical training is evident on all his recorded work. Nevertheless, he played with a powerful swing and the neglect shown by record companies in the years since his death in April 1962 is regrettable.

● ALBUMS: *The Dark Angel Of The Fiddle* (Trip 1958)★★.

● COMPILATIONS: *No More Blues* (RCA 1927-33)★★★, *Django Reinhardt And His American Friends* (1937-38)★★★, *Earl 'Fatha' Hines* (1947)★★★★, *1923-1937* (Classics 1998)★★★.

SOUTHERN, JERI

b. Genevieve Hering, 5 August 1926, Royal, Nebraska, USA, d. 4 August 1991, Los Angeles, California, USA. A warm, 'smokey' voiced, jazz-influenced singer/pianist, Southern studied at the Notre Dame Academy, Omaha, and later played piano at the local Blackstone Hotel. After touring with a US Navy recruiting show, where she began singing, she worked at several venues in Chicago in the late 40s. These included the Hi Note Club, where she supported stars such as Anita O'Day. After obtaining a nightly spot on television, Southern was signed to Decca Records and had US Top 30 hits with 'You Better Go Now' (1951) and 'Joey' (1954). Her wistful version of 'When I Fall In Love' established her as a favourite in the UK, where she also had a Top 30 hit with 'Fire Down Below' (1957). She then switched to the Capitol label and made the highly acclaimed *Jeri Southern Meets Cole Porter*, which featured a set of humorous arrangements by Billy May, including a 20s setting of 'Don't Look At Me That Way'. One of her many album releases, *When I Fall In Love*, which was released by MCA Records in 1984, contained several numbers closely identified with Southern including 'An Occasional Man'. She retired from performing in the mid-60s to become a vocal and piano coach for professional artists. She subsequently moved to Hollywood, and worked on arrangements with the film music composer Hugo Wilhelm Friedhofer, and later, cared for him. She also published a book, *Interpreting Popular Music At The Keyboard*. In 1991, her last public performance was at the Vine Street Bar And Grill in Los Angeles, where she was persuaded by Anita O'Day to emerge from the audience and play a medley of Jerome Kern songs. She died of pneumonia six months later.

● ALBUMS: *Intimate Songs* 10-inch album (Decca 1954)★★★, *Southern Style* (Decca 1955)★★★, *You Better Go Now* (Decca 1956)★★★, *When Your Heart's On Fire* (Decca 1956)★★★, *Jeri Southern Gently Jumps* (Decca 1957)★★★, *Prelude To A Kiss* (Decca 1958)★★★, *Southern Breeze* (Roulette 1958)★★★, *Southern Hospitality* (Decca 1958)★★★, with Johnny Smith *Jeri Southern Meets Johnny Smith* (Roulette 1959)★★★, *Jeri Southern Meets Cole Porter* (Capitol 1959)★★★★, *Coffee, Cigarettes And Memories* (Capitol 1959)★★★, *At The Crescendo* (Capitol 1960)★★, *You Better Go Now* (Official 1989)★★★.

● COMPILATIONS: *When I Fall In Love* (MCA 1984)★★★.

● FURTHER READING: *Interpreting Popular Music At The Keyboard*, Jeri Southern.

SPANIER, MUGGSY

b. Francis Joseph Spanier, 9 November 1901, Chicago, Illinois, USA, d. 12 February 1967, Sausalito, California, USA. Spanier began playing cornet while barely in his teens and within a couple of years was a professional musician. His first job was with Elmer Schoebel. By the end of the 20s he had established a reputation mostly in and around Chicago and had been hired by Ted Lewis for his popular band. He remained with Lewis until the mid-30s, then joined Ben Pollack. After a short period of serious illness he formed his own band, the Ragtimers, for a hotel residency in 1938 and also recorded with the band the following year. Although short-lived, the Ragtimers made an enormous impact on the public. During the 40s Spanier combined leading his own bands with working for other artists such as Bob Crosby, Pee Wee Russell, Art Hodes and Miff Mole. In the 50s he worked frequently with Earl Hines, playing at numerous hotels, clubs and festivals all across the USA. Highly regarded by his fellow musicians, as much for his personal qualities as for his playing, Spanier's style was simple and direct, akin in these respects to that of earlier jazzmen. In spirit, however, he was very much a product of his home-town. The 16 tracks recorded by Spanier's Ragtimers in 1939 are classics of a kind of jazz that retains its popularity, even if his successors rarely match their quality. Spanier's last years were dogged by poor health; he was forced to retire in 1964, and died three years later.

● ALBUMS: *Spanier's Ragtimers* (Commodore 1950)★★★, *Muggsy Spanier And His Dixieland Band* (Mercury 1953)★★★, *Muggsy Spanier And Frank Teschemacher* (Riverside 1953)★★★★, *Muggsy Spanier And His Bucktown Five* (Riverside 1954)★★★★, *Dynamic Dixie* (Weathers 1954)★★, *Hot Horn* (Decca 1957)★★★, *The Great 16* (RCA Victor 1956)★★★★, *Spanier In Chicago* (1958)★★★★.

● COMPILATIONS: *Francis Joseph Muggsy Spanier* (1926-29)★★★, with Pee Wee Russell *Muggsy And Pee Wee* (1941-57)★★★★, *Muggsy Spanier And His V-Disc All Stars* (1944)★★★★.

SPANN, LES

b. Leslie L. Spann Jnr., 23 May 1932, Pine Bluff, Arkansas, USA. Playing both guitar and flute, Spann was already becoming an accomplished performer when he began studying at Tennessee State University. In the late 50s, now concentrating on guitar, he played professionally with Phineas Newborn and Dizzy Gillespie, recording on the 1959 Verve Records session for *The Ebullient Mr. Gillespie*. In contrast, he also recorded with artists from different spheres, including Katie Bell Nubin on *Soul Searching* (Verve 1960), a set that had in the backing band Nubin's mother, Sister Rosetta Tharpe, bowing to Spann and playing piano instead of her usual guitar. He made several tours of the USA and Europe, recording there with Quincy Jones, and he appeared on a number of recording dates with artists such as Ben Webster, Johnny Hodges and Duke Ellington, playing on the latter pair's 1959 Verve session *Back To Back*, Benny Bailey, Randy Weston, Charlie Shavers, Charles Mingus and Sonny Stitt among many. He also occasionally led small bands of his own. Adept equally in mainstream and hard bop settings, Spann's guitar playing demonstrates a sound technique.

● ALBUMS: *Gemini* (Jazzland 1961)★★★.

Spargo, Tony

(see Sbarbaro, Tony)

Spaulding, James

b. 30 July 1937, Indianapolis, Indiana, USA. In the mid-50s Spaulding studied at Chicago's Cosmopolitan School of Music, specializing in alto saxophone and flute, and also played in Sun Ra's Arkestra and in Sonny Thompson's R&B group. In 1962, Spaulding moved to New York and came to prominence playing as a sideman on numerous Blue Note Records releases, particularly on dates led by Freddie Hubbard (*Hubtones* and *Breaking Point*) but also on albums by Stanley Turrentine, Horace Silver and Wayne Shorter. Later work saw him playing with many leading post-bop artists, among them Max Roach, Woody Shaw and Randy Weston. In the 70s he played in the Duke Ellington Orchestra under Mercer Ellington and his debut as a leader was a tribute to Duke. Astonishingly, Spaulding has only made a handful of albums in his own name in over 30 years as a player. His second, *Brilliant Corners*, was also a tribute - this time to Thelonious Monk. In the 80s he worked with Ricky Ford and later joined the David Murray Octet, touring and recording *Hopescope* with them. *Gotstabe A Better Way*, comprises tunes from a longer, ongoing project called 'The Courage Suite'.

● ALBUMS: *James Spaulding Plays The Legacy Of Duke Ellington* (Storyville 1977)★★★★, *Brilliant Corners* (Muse 1989)★★★★, *Songs Of Courage* (Muse 1992)★★★, *Blues Nexus* (Muse 1993)★★★, *Smile Of The Snake* (High Note 1997)★★★.

Spear

(see Pukwana, Dudu)

Special EFX

Formed in New York in 1982 by George Jinda (b. 4 June, Hungary; drums, percussion) and Chieli Minucci (b. 17 April; guitar), Special EFX blend African and Latin rhythms and produce a mixture of light rock and MOR jazz. Their music is perfect for the GRP label and consequently their output is prolific. They employ additional musicians to give them a rich and, in keeping with GRP's policy, state-of-the-art recording sound. Session players include Mark Egan, McCoy Tyner, Dave Grusin and Omar Hakim. All the albums up to *Just Like Magic* were basically the same sensitive mixture of accessible jazz/pop. The latter album is more acoustic and Jinda's electronic percussion was replaced by 'wooden world music'.

● ALBUMS: *Modern Manners* (1985)★★★, *Slice Of Life* (GRP 1986)★★★, *Mystique* (GRP 1987)★★, *Double Feature* (GRP 1988)★★, *Confidential* (1989)★★★, *Just Like Magic* (1990)★★, *Peace Of The World* (1991)★★, *Play* (1993)★★★. George Jinda solo. *Between Dreams* (Shanachie 1996)★★★. Chieli Minucci solo *Renaissance* (JVC 1996)★★, *It's Gonna Be Good* (JMI 1998)★★★.

Spencer, J.

A 90s hip-hop/jazz fusion saxophone player, Spencer (b. *c.*1971, Oakland, California, USA) originally emerged via Motown Records' MoJazz subsidiary imprint as a talented harbinger of a 'new age in jazz and rap'. The result was 'A little bit of hip-hop/A little bit of jazz', as one track on his debut album, *Chimera Vol. 1*, suggested. Writing credits included several for his friend, Elijah Baker (Tony! Toni! Tone!), alongside his own compositions. He was joined on sessions for the project by Derrick Hall (bass), John 'Jubu' Smith (guitar) and Tommy Bradford (drums). The additional rapping personnel included Mike D, P. Funk and Vitamin C, all fellow natives of Oakland, plus the 'Flat Lip Horns' brass section. The follow-up collection, *Blue Moon*, was released at the end of 1995 and peaked at number 49 in the *Billboard* R&B charts.

● ALBUMS: *Chimera Vol. 1* (MoJazz 1993)★★★, *Blue Moon* (MoJazz 1995)★★★.

Sphere

(see Barron, Kenny; Riley, Ben; Rouse, Charlie; Williams, Buster; Bartz, Gary).

This loose unit were formed primarily as a tribute band to Thelonious Monk. Charlie Rouse died in 1988 and when the unit reconvened Gary Bartz replaced him.

● ALBUMS: *Flight Path* (Elektra 1983)★★★, *Sphere On Tour* (Red 1985)★★★, *Pumpkin's Delight* (Red 1986)★★★★, *Four For All* (Verve 1987)★★★★, *Bird Songs* (Verve 1988)★★★★, *Sphere* (Verve 1998)★★★.

Spirit Of Django - Martin Taylor

Something about this album captured more than just the core of jazz buffs and fans of Martin Taylor's exquisite acoustic jazz guitar. It sold remarkably well and was universally applauded. Taylor is supported by Alec Dankworth (bass), Jack Emblow (accordion) and guitarist John Goldie. The concept of paying homage by playing in Django Reinhardt's style, but not necessarily following his songs, is highly original. To choose to Djangoize George Gershwin's 'Lady Be Good' and Cole Porter's 'Night And Day was clever. To Djangoize Robert Palmer's 'Johnny And Mary' and Pat Metheny's James Taylor tribute, 'James', was inspiring.

● Tracks: *Chez Fernand; Minor Swing; Night And Day; Nuages; James; Double Top; Django's Dream; Swing; Lady Be Good; Honeysuckle Rose; Johnny And Mary.*

● First released 1994

● UK peak chart position: did not chart

● USA peak chart position: did not chart

Spirit Level

Spirit Level was a British jazz quartet formed in the early 80s. Playing excellent, fiery, free-ranging music, they were unfortunately not young enough - and lacked the requisite designer appearance - to benefit from the 80s jazz revival. The members were Paul Dunmall (tenor saxophone), a powerful player often cited as one of the cream of British saxophonists and whose experience includes spells with Alice Coltrane and Johnny 'Guitar' Watson, Tim Richards (piano), Paul Anstey (bass) and Tony Orrell (drums). For albums, they would often invite along a guest trumpeter: *Proud Owners* had Dave Holdsworth; *Killer Bunnies* featured Jack Walrath. In 1989, Paul Dunmall left to form Mujician with pianist Keith Tippett and Tony Orrell dropped out to form the delightful improvising trio MOR, with altoist Pete McPhail and bassist Paul Rogers. Reconstituted as Tim Richards' Spirit Level, the group now comprised a quartet of pianist Richards, Jerry Underwood (tenor saxophone), Ernest Mothle (bass) and Mark Sanders (drums), and released *New Year* in 1991.

● ALBUMS: *Mice In The Wallet* (1983)★★★, *Proud Owners* (1984)★★★, *Killer Bunnies* (1986)★★, *The Swiss Radio Tapes* (1989)★★★, as Tim Richards' Spirit Level *New Year* (1991)★★★.

Spirits Of Rhythm

First formed in the late 20s by the brothers Wilbur and Douglas Daniels, the group performed under various names. By 1930 the band was making its way in New York City, having added Leo Watson to its ranks. In 1932, with Teddy Bunn on hand, the name was changed from the Five Cousins to the Spirits Of Rhythm and the group quickly established a reputation for highly entertaining performances. The instrumentation of the group was unusual. The Daniels brothers and Watson all sang and played the tiple - a stringed instrument, rather like a small guitar, of South American origin which has 10 strings with pairs and triples tuned in octaves. The instrument has an interesting and melodious sound not unlike a rather classy mandolin. Bunn played guitar and drummer Virgil Scroggins used whisk brooms on a paper-wrapped suitcase. Despite the apparent eccentricity such a line-up implies, they were a fine rhythmic band, with Bunn and Watson its outstanding members. In addition to a residency at the Onyx Club, the band also enjoyed success in Los Angeles and its records were immensely popular. With occasional changes in personnel the Spirits Of Rhythm remained together until 1946. Latter-day reissues of their records underline the fact that they were far more than an easily forgotten novelty band.

● ALBUMS: *Rhythm Personified - 1933-34* (1985)★★★.

Spirits Rejoice - Albert Ayler

Recorded on the musician-controlled ESP (short for Esperanto) label in 1965, *Spirits Rejoice* is a free jazz masterpiece – a riotous, hugely emotional and astonishingly creative celebration of the urge to make noise, recorded when the 'new thing' was still genuinely new. This is Albert Ayler at his very best - playing his gospel-soaked themes with a poignant dignity, and a sad introspection that is liable at any time to tumble into chaotic aggression, before being saved by a beautiful, if mournful, resolution. He is joined by saxophonist Charles Tyler, bassists Henry Grimes and Gary Peacock, harpsichordist Call Cobbs and drummer Sunny Murray.

● Tracks: *Spirits Rejoice; Holy Family; D.C.; Angels; Prophet.*
● First released 1965
● UK peak chart position: did not chart
● USA peak chart position: did not chart

Spivak, Charlie

b. 17 February 1907, Kiev, Ukraine, d. 1 March 1982, Greenville, North Carolina, USA. Spivak learned to play trumpet as a small child growing up in the USA. In his mid-teens he joined Paul Specht's orchestra where he remained until 1930, moving on to the Ben Pollack band. Later, he was with the Dorsey Brothers orchestra, artists such as Ray Noble, Raymond Scott, Bob Crosby and Jack Teagarden, and also played in the New York studios. In 1939 he formed his own big band which, after a shaky start, became very successful. Thereafter, with only a short break through illness, he led the band for much of the next four decades. A skilled trumpeter, on the sweeter side of the swing era, Spivak's musical longevity owes much to his ability to see what the public wanted and then make sure that he delivered. His last residency, in Greenville, South Carolina, began in 1967 and continued until shortly before his death in 1982.

● ALBUMS: *Charlie Spivak And His Orchestra* i (1958)★★★, *Charlie Spivak And His Orchestra* ii (1962)★★, *Charlie Spivak And His Orchestra* iii (1967)★★★, *Charlie Spivak And His Orchestra* iv (1968)★★★, *Charlie Spivak And His Orchestra* v (1972)★★★, *1n9o8w1! (Now!)* (1981)★★★.

● COMPILATIONS: *Charlie Spivak And Jimmy Joy (1945)* (1979)★★★, *One Way Passage* (1979)★★, *Charlie Spivak 1942* (1988)★★★, *Charlie Spivak And His Orchestra (1943-46)* (1988)★★★★.

Spontaneous Music Ensemble

Formed in 1965 by drummer John Stevens (b. 10 June 1940, Brentford, Middlesex, England, d. 13 September 1994, London, England), SME was a group dedicated to free interplay between musicians. Early members included Trevor Watts, Kenny Wheeler, Dave Holland, and Derek Bailey, with guest appearances from artists such as Paul Rutherford (*Challenge*), Evan Parker (*Karyobin*), Johnny Dyani (*Oliv*) and Bobby Bradford. Rather like Company with Bailey, SME became a name for any improvised music project in which John Stevens became involved (though, unlike Bailey, Stevens also had other group names for 'less spontaneous' music: the Septet, Splinters, Away, Freebop, etc.). In 1970 Stevens formed the Spontaneous Music Orchestra to explore improvisation in larger groups, and SME became a core quartet of Stevens, Watts, singer Julie Tippetts and bassist Ron Herman (*Birds Of A Feather, 1, 2, Albert Ayler*). The *SME For CND* album featured Stevens and Watts with a workshop group, while *Bobby Bradford Plus SME* initiated a long association between Stevens and the west coast trumpeter. *Face To Face* was a particularly successful duo encounter between Stevens' drums and the soprano saxophone of Watts. As his interest turned to more structured musics, Stevens' SME projects became less frequent, but the group was still playing on an occasional basis into the early 90s, until their leader's death in 1994. Stevens seemed to have little time for the 'no leader' aspect of many freely improvised encounters: unlike Company, whatever the line-up of SME, the instigator was always very much in charge.

● ALBUMS: *Challenge* (1966)★★★, *Karyobin* (Chronoscope 1968)★★★, *Oliv* (1969)★★★, *The Source* (Tangent 1971)★★, *SME For CND For Peace And You To Share* (1971)★★★, *Birds Of A Feather* (1971)★★★, *So What Do You Think?* (Tangent 1971)★★★★, *Bobby Bradford Plus SME* (1971)★★★, *Face To Face* (1975)★★★, with SMO *"+ ="* (1975)★★★★, *Biosystem* (Incus 1977)★★★, *Live - Big Band And Quartet* recorded 1977 (1979)★★, *1,2, Albert Ayler* recorded 1971 (1982)★★★★, *85 Minutes, Parts 1 & 2* recorded 1974 (Emanem 1986)★★★, *Live At Notre Dame Hall* (Sweet Folk All 1987)★★, *Withdrawal (1966-7)* (Emanem 1997)★★★, *A New Distance* (Acta 1996)★★★.

SPRING, BRYAN

b. 24 August 1945, London, England. Spring was one of a handful of young drummers (others included Bobby Orr and Phil Seamen) who emerged in the 50s to give the lie to the cliché 'English rhythm sections don't swing'. Initially self-taught since the age of six, Spring also studied with Philly Joe Jones. After freelancing through the early 60s, he began a fruitful collaboration with Stan Tracey, playing and recording with the pianist's bands for eight years. In the late 60s and early 70s Spring played with Frank Ricotti and Klaus Doldinger's band, Passport, as well as spending several months with the group Nucleus. In 1975 the drummer formed his own band, co-led by saxophonist Don Weller, an association that lasted into the 80s. Great energy and drive linked to a fine technique have made Spring the perfect drummer in many different settings, from big band to duet, and often the drummer of choice for visiting Americans of the stature of George Coleman and Charlie Rouse.

● ALBUMS: with Weller *Commit No Nuisance* (1979)★★★.

SPYRO GYRA

Formed in 1975 by saxophonist Jay Beckenstein and pianist Jeremy Wall, the original Spyro Gyra comprised Chet Catallo (electric guitar), David Wolford (electric bass), Eli Konikoff (drums), and Gerardo Velez (percussion). After a modest start in Buffalo, New York, and an album on a small independent label, Beckenstein's hard work and commitment through countless changes of personnel resulted in appearances at major international jazz festivals in the 80s, and several gold albums. In addition to having numerous hits in the USA, the band found considerable success in the UK with the infectious 'Morning Dance'. The band's mainstream treatment of a mixture of funk, Latin, and jazz remains popular today. They remain, however, an enigma; their following is considerable and stays stable after more than 20 years together. In terms of their music, they have never challenged the jazz world to take them seriously. Similarly, they are too clever musically to be taken into the mainstream of easy listening. They fit well into the GRP Records family with its high standard of technical excellence and accessible music. The line-up in 1997 comprised Julio Fernandez (guitar), Tom Schuman (keyboards), Joel Rosenblatt (drums), Scott Ambush (bass), in addition to the guiding force, Beckenstein.

● ALBUMS: *Spyro Gyra* (Infinity 1978)★★, *Morning Dance* (Infinity 1979)★★★★, *Catching The Sun* (MCA 1980)★★, *Carnival* (MCA 1980)★★★, *Freetime* (MCA 1981)★★, *Incognito* (MCA 1982)★★, *City Kids* (MCA 1983)★★, *Access All Areas* (MCA 1984)★★, *Alternating Currents* (GRP 1985)★★, *Breakout* (MCA 1986)★★, *Stories Without Words* (MCA 1987)★★, *Rites Of Summer* (GRP 1988)★★, *Point Of View* (MCA 1989)★★★, *Fast Forward* (GRP 1990)★★, *Three Wishes* (GRP 1992)★★, *Dreams Beyond Control* (GRP 1993)★★★, *Love And Other Obsessions* (GRP 1994)★★, *Heart Of The Night* (GRP 1996)★★, *20/20* (GRP 1997)★★★, *Road Scholars* (GRP 1998)★★.

● COMPILATIONS: *The Collection* (GRP 1991)★★★.

● VIDEOS: *Graffiti* (GRP 1992).

SQUIRES, ROSEMARY

b. Joan Rosemary Yarrow, 7 December 1928, Bristol, Avon, England. This civil servant's daughter took vocal, piano and guitar lessons before and during study at Salisbury's St Edmund's Girls School. In 1940, a broadcast on the BBC Home Service's *Children's Hour* created demand for her in local venues that embraced US army bases. With an endearing west country burr, she sang in various combos formed within these camps, as well as in the Polish Military Band while employed in an antique bookshop and then an office. After becoming a professional performer, she was employed by Ted Heath, Geraldo, Cyril Stapleton and other big band conductors as well as smaller jazz bands led by Max Harris, Kenny Baker and Alan Clare - with whose trio she appeared at a BBC Festival of Jazz at the Royal Albert Hall. She has long been known to Britain at large, having been omnipresent since the late 40s on BBC Radio light entertainment programmes - including *Melody Time*, *Workers' Playtime* and many of her own series. In 1962, she hovered just outside the UK chart with a version of 'The Gypsy Rover'. Currently reported to be living again in Salisbury, she remains an active musician, with Tibetan culture among her extra-mural interests. She was secretary of Britain's Tibet Society from 1972-75. In 1991, she surprised her friends (and herself) by marrying for the first time, although it was far from being the first occasion on which she has changed her name. She recorded one of her most successful titles, 'Frankfurter Sandwiches', under the *nom de plume* of Joanne And The Streamliners, and in the 90s she still continues with her 'second career' - singing for television jingles. She is also DJ on her own Sunday afternoon programme on Radio Wiltshire.

● ALBUMS: *My One And Only* (C5 1989)★★, *A Time For Rosemary* (1993)★★★.

SQUIRREL NUT ZIPPERS

A throwback to the world of big band jazz and swing bands, the Squirrel Nut Zippers are a seven-piece group formed in Chapel Hill, North Carolina, USA. The group comprises Jim 'Jimbo' Mathus (vocals, guitar, trombone), Katharine Whalen (vocals, banjo), Ken Mosher (guitar, reeds), Chris Phillips (drums), Tom Maxwell (vocals, guitar, saxophone), Stu Cole (bass) and Je Widenhouse (trumpet). Taking their name from a peanut-flavour candy manufacturer from Massachusetts, the group began life in 1992 entertaining a wide range of audiences with their mix of swing, hot jazz and calypso. Their bookings have included everything from nightclub sets to festivals, weddings, wine-tastings and even a fireman's ball. They subsequently signed with Mammoth Records, making their debut with *The Inevitable* in 1995. Though this sold less than 20,000 copies, it did include 'Anything But Love', later featured in the Ben Stiller movie, *Flirting With Disaster*, where it was covered by Dr. John. The follow-up collection, *Hot*, was promoted by a limited-edition 7-inch single and the Squirrel Nut Zippers' own blend of coffee, which was made available in cafés in the North Carolina region. Recorded at Daniel Lanois' Kingsway Studios in New Orleans, it featured a guest spot from local trumpet player Duke Heitger to add some regional flavour. With everything recorded in two or three takes, it captured the Squirrel Nut Zippers' lucid sound more succinctly than their debut and saw the band rise in prominence within alternative rock circles, though many radio programmers were bemused at the impact a contemporary 'showband' were making on their listeners.

● ALBUMS: *The Inevitable* (Mammoth 1995)★★, *Hot* (Mammoth 1996)★★★, *Sold Out EP* (Mammoth 1997)★★★, *Perennial Favorites* (Mammoth 1998)★★★.

ST LOUIS BLUES

One of the first talkies, and one of few early films to feature jazz or blues artists, this offers the only screen appearance of Bessie Smith, the Empress of the Blues. Directed by Dudley Murphy (who in the same year made *Black And Tan*), this 1929 film features an extended performance of the title song built around a thin story that fully exploits elements of pathos in the lyrics. There is an excellent accompanying band, including Joe Smith and Kaiser Marshall, mostly drawn from the ranks of Fletcher Henderson's band but led on this occasion by James P. Johnson. For all such attractions, however, this film's value lies in this solitary opportunity to see Smith, one of the greatest figures in the history of American popular music and through it to glean some fleeting understanding of the manner in which she commanded attention and dignified the blues.

NB: The same title was used for a 1939 feature film, which includes performances by Maxine Sullivan, and for the 1958 biopic based upon the life of W.C. Handy and starring Nat 'King' Cole.

STACY, JESS

b. 11 August 1904, Bird's Point, Missouri, USA, d. 1 January 1995, Los Angeles, California, USA. After teaching himself to play piano, Stacy worked the riverboats for a number of years, arriving in Chicago in the mid-20s. There, he played with numerous bands, including that of Paul Mares, on through into the early 30s. In 1935, John Hammond Jnr. brought him to the attention of Benny Goodman and for the next four years Stacy was a member of the latter's band, playing at the 1938 Carnegie Hall concert during which he contributed a remarkable if out-of-context solo in the middle of the gallery-pleasing excesses of 'Sing Sing Sing'. He was with Bob Crosby from 1939-42, then returned to Goodman for a couple of years. He recorded with Lee Wiley, to whom he was married for a while, and directed her accompanying orchestra for a number of years. By the late 40s he was playing in west coast bars. Although he made a few return appearances with Goodman, he drifted towards the periphery of the music business and by 1963 had abandoned playing altogether. In 1974, he performed again, this time at the Newport Jazz Festival, where he was rapturously received by audiences and critics. Thereafter, he resumed his playing career and continued to delight audiences. A distinctive and accomplished pianist, Stacy was capable of playing fearsome, two-fisted stride piano and contrastingly delicate solos, all marked by striking inventiveness.

● ALBUMS: one side only *Stacy 'N' Sutton* (1953)★★, *Tribute To Benny Goodman* (1955)★★★, *The Return Of Jess Stacy* (1962)★★★, *Stacy Still Swings* (Chiaroscuro 1977)★★★.

● COMPILATIONS: *Jess Stacy And Friends* (1944)★★★, *Jess Stacy 1935-1939* (Classics 1996)★★★★.

STAFFORD, TERRELL

b. *c*.1967, Downingtown, Pennsylvania, USA. Stafford first came to widespread attention during a five-year spell playing trumpet with Bobby Watson's Horizon, appearing on the early 90s *Tailor Made*. Coming out of the hard bop school, Stafford's playing is notable for its wide emotional range. He is a fine ballad player with an uncloying romantic touch. He also composes well and has extended his career into teaching, serving as director of bands at Cheyney University in Pennsylvania. Despite an already secure reputation, Stafford is constantly seeking to extend his musical boundaries while never losing touch with the roots of his style of playing.

● ALBUMS: *Time To Let Go* (Candid 1995)★★★, *Centripetal Force* (Candid 1996)★★★.

STAGE DOOR CANTEEN

Released in 1943, this film was a paper-thin excuse for Hollywood to bring onto the screen a stream of mostly front-rank entertainers to alleviate wartime gloom. Alongside screen stars are leading figures from Broadway, vaudeville, popular music and jazz. Benny Goodman And His Orchestra, including Jack Jenney, Conrad Gozzo, Jess Stacy, Louie Bellson and Peggy Lee, perform two numbers. Count Basie And His Orchestra, including Buck Clayton, Freddie Green, Walter Page, Harry Edison, Dicky Wells, Buddy Tate, Don Byas, Earle Warren and Jo Jones, perform one number backing Ethel Waters.

STALLINGS, MARY

b. San Francisco, California, USA. Stallings began singing in public at the age of eight. Encouraged by her saxophonist uncle, Orlando Stallings, she sang in local jazz clubs during her teenage years and while still in high school joined Louis Jordan's band. She began touring, singing in other parts of the USA and also as far afield as Australia. Back in the USA she sang in Chicago with Sonny Stitt, and during an engagement at San Francisco's Blackhawk was heard by Dizzy Gillespie who invited her to appear with him at the 1965 Monterey Jazz Festival. She then joined Billy Eckstine and soon afterwards was with the Grover Mitchell-Earl 'Fatha' Hines band. When Mitchell joined Count Basie he recommended Stallings when the female vocalist spot became vacant. This was in 1969 and she stayed with the band for three years, touring internationally. Stallings then returned home to raise her daughter but was called upon by Gillespie for a tour of South America and also worked in her home-town with pianist Ed Kelly. Eventually, she returned to full-time singing, still based in San Francisco but touring Europe and the Orient. A mature and confident style allows Stallings to deliver her material with flair and skill.

● ALBUMS: *Mary Stallings & Cal Tjader* (Fantasy 1961)★★★, *I Waited For You* (Concord Jazz 1994)★★★, *Spectrum* (Concord Jazz 1995)★★★★, *Manhattan Moods* (Concord Jazz 1997)★★★.

STAMM, MARVIN

b. 23 May 1939, Memphis, Tennessee, USA. After studying trumpet at school and later at North Texas State University, Stamm joined the Stan Kenton Mellophonium Orchestra. In the mid-60s he was with Woody Herman, then became a studio player based in New York. During the next few years he also played many jazz dates, including work with the Thad Jones-Mel Lewis Jazz Orchestra, Frank Foster, Chick Corea and with Duke Pearson's rehearsal band. In the 70s and on into the 80s he continued mixing studio work with jazz, playing with Benny Goodman, leading his own small groups and working with the American Jazz Orchestra and with George Gruntz. Stamm's decision to spend a substantial part of his career to date working in the studios has limited the number of opportunities for the jazz audience to hear him. When those occasions have arisen he has proved to be an interesting and enthusiastic player whose best work is always precise and controlled.

STANDARDS, VOL. 1 - KEITH JARRETT

Not to forget the equal billing of drummer Jack DeJohnette and bassist Gary Peacock, without doubt Keith Jarrett's most critically acclaimed line-up. They just know how to play together and feed off their respective dynamics. Most of Jarrett's best non-solo work has been with these two peerless musicians. Their interpretations are stunning, especially Bobby Troup and Leah Worth's 'Meaning Of The Blues' and an astonishingly good version of Billie Holiday's 'God Bless The Child', which after 15 minutes never once drags. Jarrett also sounds positively buoyant on the tracks he scats. *Standards, Vol. 2* and *Standards Live* are also essential.

● Tracks: *Meaning Of The Blues; All The Things You Are; It Never Entered My Mind; The Masquerade Is Over; God Bless The Child.*

● First released 1983

● UK peak chart position: did not chart

● USA peak chart position: did not chart

STANKO, TOMASZ

b. 11 July 1942, Rzeszow, Poland. Stanko learnt the violin and piano at school and studied trumpet at the music high school in Cracow (1969). He has a wide range and formidable technique. He formed the group Jazz Darings (1962) with Adam Makowicz and played with various other local musicians. In the early 70s he played with the Globe Unity Orchestra and the European Free Jazz Orchestra at Donaueschingen. He then formed a quintet which included Zbigniew Seifert who switched from alto saxophone to violin while he was with the band. Later on he re-formed the Unit with Makowicz, and this band earned widespread praise, being described as a 'white Ornette Coleman'. In fact, the band was more traditionally based, though there was an element of free playing in the music. He has also played as an unaccompanied soloist at the Taj Mahal and Karla Caves Temple as well as performing with Chico Freeman, James Spaulding, Jack DeJohnette, Gary Peacock and the Cecil Taylor Big Band.

● ALBUMS: *Music For K* (Power Bros 1970)★★★, *We'll Remember Komeda* (1973)★★★, *Balladyna* (ECM 1975)★★★★, *Music From The Taj Mahal And Karla Caves* (1980)★★, with Gary Peacock *A Voice From The Past* (1981)★★★, with Cecil Taylor *Winged Serpent* (1985)★★★★, *The Montreux Performance* (ITM 1988)★★★, *Tales For A Girl 12/A Shakey Chica* (Jam 1992)★★★, *Bluish* (Power Bros 1992)★★, *Bosanossa And Other Ballads* (GOWI 1994)★★★, *Matka Joanna* (ECM 1995)★★★, *Leosia* (ECM 1997)★★★★, *Litania: Music Of Krzysztof Komeda* (ECM 1997)★★★.

STARK, BOBBY

b. 6 January 1906, New York City, New York, USA, d. 29 December 1945, New York, USA. After learning to play several instruments Stark settled on trumpet, and by the mid-20s he was well known on the New York club scene. He played briefly with McKinney's Cotton Pickers and Chick Webb, then joined Fletcher Henderson for five years. He followed this with another five-year job, this time with Webb. After Webb's death he continued for a while under Ella Fitzgerald's leadership, then entered the US Army during the early part of World War II. In 1943 he was with Garvin Bushell, then played in various bands, including Benny Morton's, until his early death in December 1945. A strikingly individualistic soloist, Stark's playing changed over the years, from a forceful, extrovert style to one that was thoughtfully melodic.

Staton, Dakota

b. Aliyah Rabia, 3 June 1931, Pittsburgh, Pennsylvania, USA. After singing in clubs in a style modelled on that of such diverse artists as Dinah Washington and Sarah Vaughan, Staton began to attract wider attention in the mid-50s. She extended her repertoire to include popular songs, R&B, soul and gospel and made a number of successful record albums. In the mid-60s she took up residence in the UK and Europe, but was back in the USA early in the following decade. She is at her best with mainstream jazz accompaniment, whether a big band, such as Manny Albam's or Kurt Edelhagen's, or a small group, such as those led by George Shearing and Jonah Jones. Staton's R&B material is less attractive, often performed at feverish tempos and with a deliberate coarsening of her powerful voice.

● ALBUMS: *The Late, Late Show* (Capitol 1957)★★★★, *In The Night* (Capitol 1958)★★★, *Dynamic!* (Capitol 1958)★★★, *Crazy He Calls Me* (Capitol 1959)★★★, *Time To Swing* (Capitol 1959)★★★, *More Than The Most* (Capitol 1959)★★★, *Ballads And The Blues* (Capitol 1960)★★★, *Softly* (Capitol 1960)★★★, *Round Midnight* (Capitol 1961)★★★, *Dakota Staton At Storyville* (Capitol 1961)★★★, *From Dakota With Love* (United Artists 1963)★★★, *Live And Swinging* (United Artists 1963)★★★★, *Dakota Staton With Strings* (United Artists 1964)★★★, with Richard 'Groove' Holmes *Let Me Off Uptown* (1972)★★★, *Dakota Staton With The Manny Albam Big Band* (1973)★★★, *Darling, Please Save Your Love* (1992)★★★.

Stegmeyer, Bill

b. 8 October 1916, Detroit, Michigan, USA, d. 19 August 1968, Long Island, New York, USA. Stegmeyer began playing clarinet and saxophones while still at school, then joined the Austin Wylie band. A colleague there was Billy Butterfield, a friend from his university days. While with the Wylie band Stegmeyer also arranged and worked on local radio. In 1938 he joined Glenn Miller and the following year played in Bob Crosby's band. His interest in arranging gradually superseded his playing and in later decades he worked extensively in radio in Detroit and New York. From time to time he made appearances with jazz groups, among them the band co-led by Yank Lawson and Bob Haggart. Very highly regarded by fellow musicians, the direction taken by Stegmeyer in his career resulted in his being little known except by a few fans.

● ALBUMS: *The Best Of Dixieland: The Legendary Lawson-Haggart Jazz Band 1952-3* (1975)★★★★.

Steig, Jeremy

b. 23 September 1942, New York, USA. Steig began on the recorder when he was six, took up the flute aged 11 and first played professionally when he was 15 while he was still at the High School of Music and Art. Early in his career he played in a band including Paul Bley and Gary Peacock. In the late 60s he played with Richie Havens before joining Tim Hardin's backing band and then forming his own rock-influenced band - Jeremy And The Satyrs. Steig has great technical ability on the whole range of flutes on which he employs a wide performance technique. He has been especially adept at incorporating the use of all sorts of electronics into his music-making, employing devices such as the wah wah peddle and ring modulator. He has continued to work as a soloist and with his own groups, although he has also performed with Eddie Gomez, Art Blakey and Pierre Courbois' Association PC in 1974.

● ALBUMS: *Flute Fever* (1963)★★★, *Jeremy And The Satyrs* (1967)★★★★, *Temple Of Birth* (1974)★★★, *Firefly* (1977)★★, with Eddie Gomez *Outlaws* (1976)★★★, *Lend Me Your Ears* (1978)★★★, *Rain Forest* (1980)★★★.

Stein, Lou

b. Louis Stein, 22 April 1922, Philadelphia, Pennsylvania, USA. Stein played piano as a teenager with several noted musicians, including Buddy De Franco. In the early 40s he was briefly with Ray McKinley, then was inducted into the US Army where he played with Glenn Miller's Army Air Force band. At the end of the war he was again with McKinley, then rejoined another musician from his earlier years, Charlie Ventura, co-composing with him the jazz standard, 'East Of Suez'. Versatile, happily moving between extremes of jazz style, Stein spent the 50s with a similarly wide range of musicians: Billy Butterfield, Kai Winding, Sarah Vaughan, Sauter-Finegan and Louie Bellson. In these years he was a regular sideman with the bands put together by Bob Haggart and Yank Lawson that eventually became the World's Greatest Jazz Band. Towards the end of the decade, Stein played with two outstanding tenor saxophonists, Coleman Hawkins and Lester Young. In the late 60s Stein was often in Europe, playing and recording with Joe Venuti and he continued working through the 70s and into the 80s, playing with important artists such as Joe 'Flip' Phillips, and also resuming his acquaintance with McKinley and the WGJB, with which group he toured Europe. A fine player with a light touch, Stein's eclecticism has tended to deter some listeners from giving him the attention that is so clearly his due. Whether in a Dixieland format, or playing bop, or, at his most comfortable, in a swinging mainstream setting, he is a pianist with taste, subtlety and swing.

● ALBUMS: *Session At Riverside* (Capitol 1956)★★★, with Joe Venuti *Once More With Feeling* (Ovation 1969)★★★★, with Venuti *The Daddy Of The Violin* (MPS 1971)★★, with Venuti *Violinology* (Jump 1971)★★★, *Joe Venuti Quartet* (I Giganti Del Jazz 1971)★★, with Elise Stein *Go Daddy!* (Pullen 1996)★★★.

Steps Ahead

Formed in 1979 under the name Steps, this group was seen by founder and vibes player Mike Mainieri as a way of bringing together some of the virtuoso musicians working in the New York studio scene. Originally comprising Michael Brecker (tenor saxophone), Don Grolnick (keyboards), Eddie Gomez (bass) and Peter Erskine (drums), Steps toured Japan and recorded three albums there. With the departure of Grolnick in 1983, Steps became Steps Ahead, and a series of changes of personnel ensued, including the passing through of David Sancious and Warren Bernhardt. By 1987, the group, now led by Brecker, had stabilized, and included Mike Stern (electric guitar), Darryl Jones (bass) and Steve Smith (drums). Steps Ahead has defined the New York fusion sound for some time, and has been an important vehicle for the hugely influential Brecker.

● ALBUMS: *Step By Step* (Denon 1981)★★★, *Smokin' In The Pit Live* (Denon 1981)★★★, *Paradox* (Denon 1982)★★★, *Steps Ahead* (Elektra 1983)★★★★, *Modern Times* (Elektra 1984)★★★★, *Magnetic* (Elektra 1986)★★★, *Yin-Yang* (NYC 1992)★★★, *Vibe* (NYC 1995)★★★, *Live In Tokyo 1986* (NYC)★★.

STERN, MIKE

b. 10 January 1953, Boston, Massachusetts, USA. While always a rock-orientated electric guitarist, Stern's forays into contemporary jazz have never lacked edge or excitement. A student of Pat Metheny while at Berklee College Of Music, his first break came in 1976, when he joined Blood, Sweat And Tears. He worked with drummer Billy Cobham towards the end of the 70s, before being hired by Miles Davis. Following Davis's band, Stern worked with bass virtuoso Jaco Pastorius's Word Of Mouth, and began touring and recording as a leader in the early 80s. Some of his most exciting recent work has been with extraordinary tenor saxophonist Michael Brecker, in Brecker's own band or with the fast-fingered fusion group Steps Ahead. Recommended recordings include *Time In Place*, which features some of the New York fusion/studio virtuosi with whom Stern has become associated, including Brecker and Bob Berg on tenor saxophones, keyboardist Don Grolnick, fusion drummer Peter Erskine and sought-after percussionist Don Alias. He plays some subtle guitar on Michael Brecker's *Don't Try This At Home*, as part of a line-up that includes pianist Herbie Hancock, drummer Jack DeJohnette and bassist Charlie Haden.

● ALBUMS: *Upside Downside* (Atlantic 1986)★★★, *Time In Place* (Atlantic 1988)★★★★, *Jigsaw* (Atlantic 1989)★★★, *Odds Or Evens* (Atlantic 1991)★★★, *Standards (And Other Songs)* (Atlantic 1992)★★★, *Is What It Is* (Atlantic 1994)★★★, *Between The Lines* (Atlantic 1996)★★★, *Give And Take* (Atlantic 1997)★★★★.

STEVENS, GARRY

b. 21 October 1916, Los Angeles, California, USA. An excellent band singer during the 40s, early in his career Stevens worked as a trumpeter-vocalist with various bands on the US east coast, and spent some time with combos led by Paul Kain and Don Bestor. In the late 30s he became a staff musician-singer on radio in Washington, DC, before joining Charlie Spivak's outfit as vocalist in late 1941. He stayed with Spivak until 1943, and sang on several of his hit records, including 'This Is No Laughing Matter', 'My Devotion', 'I Left My Heart At The Stage Door Canteen' and 'White Christmas'. The Stardusters vocal group, featuring one of the best girl band singers, June Hutton, was with the band at the same time. After military service in World War II, Stevens joined Tex Beneke's Glenn Miller Orchestra in the late 40s, and sang on two of the band's successful sides, 'Anniversary Song' and 'As Long As I'm Dreaming' in 1947. His other records included 'But Beautiful', 'Beyond The Sea' and 'Poinciana' (with Beneke), 'At Last', and 'It's So Peaceful In The Country' (with Spivak).

STEVENS, JOHN

b. 10 June 1940, Brentford, Middlesex, England, d. 13 September 1994, London, England. Stevens, whose father was a tap dancer, studied at Ealing Junior Art School and Ealing College of Higher Education. In 1958 he joined the Air Force, where he played drums in various bands after studying at the RAF's Music School. He spent three and a half years in Cologne, where he was able to see concerts by modern players such as John Coltrane and Eric Dolphy; there he also played with future German *avant gardists*, Manfred Schoof and Alex Von Schlippenbach. The late 50s skiffle boom had awakened his interest in blues and jazz - both New Orleans and modern - and back in England he played with Joe Harriott, Ellsworth 'Shake' Keane and Tubby Hayes. By 1964 he was centrally involved with modern jazz in London, playing with Ronnie Scott and Stan Tracey, then joining a quartet that comprised Jeff Clyne, Ian Carr and Trevor Watts, whom he had met in the RAF in 1958 and who would become one of his most frequent collaborators over the next 10 years. In 1965 he formed a septet that included Kenny Wheeler, Alan Skidmore and Ron Mathewson and, together with Watts and Paul Rutherford (another ex-RAF colleague), he also initiated the Spontaneous Music Ensemble, a launchpad for many free improvising musicians. In 1966, Stevens began organizing concerts at the Little Theatre Club, which rapidly became the epicentre of the new British jazz. Stevens moved back into more mainstream areas with the group Splinters in 1971, which he co-led with fellow-drummer Phil Seamen. In 1971, he formed the John Stevens Dance Orchestra and, in 1974, Away, his jazz-rock group. During this time he recorded and toured with John Martyn. In 1982, he formed Freebop and Folkus (their musical inclinations can be inferred from their names). In 1985, he published a book of workshop techniques, something with which he had been involved since the mid-60s, winning the 1972 Thames Television award for community work. From 1983 he directed the UK Jazz Centre Society's Outreach Community Project, nurturing the talents of prominent figures in the mid-80s jazz revival, including Courtney Pine. In 1988, *Live Tracks* brought together many of his collaborators, including Pine, US trumpeter Bobby Bradford, UK saxophonists Pete King and Evan Parker and trombonist Annie Whitehead, in a celebration of the joys of untrammelled bop-based improvisation. *New Cool*, released in the early 90s, is arguably his finest work.

● ALBUMS: *Springboard* (1967)★★, with Evan Parker *The Longest Night Vols 1 & 2* (1976)★★★★, *Somewhere In Between*

(1976)★★★, *Application, Interaction And* ... (Spotlite 1979)★★★, with Folkus *The Life Of Riley* (Affinity 1983)★★★★, *Freebop* (Affinity 1983)★★★, with Dudu Pukwana *Radebe - They Shoot To Kill* (1987)★★★, with Free Bop *Live Tracks* (1988)★★★★, *A Luta Continua* 1977-1980 recordings (Konnex 1992)★★, *Touching On* (Konnex 1992)★★★, *New Cool* (Jazz Label 1993)★★★★.

STEWARD, HERBIE

b. 7 May 1926, Los Angeles, California, USA. Steward took up clarinet and alto and tenor saxophones while still a youth, but later concentrated on tenor. In the early and mid-40s he gigged in the Los Angeles area, playing with Barney Kessel and then signing on with a succession of big bands, including those of Artie Shaw, Alvino Rey and Butch Stone. In the latter band he played alongside Stan Getz, Shorty Rogers and Don Lamond. In 1947 he played in the Gene Rowland rehearsal band, in which the leader experimented with unusual saxophone voicings using the talents of Steward, Getz, Zoot Sims and Jimmy Giuffre. When the entire section was hired by Woody Herman, Steward became one of the original 'Four Brothers' saxophone team but stayed only three months before moving on. Later in the 40s and in the early 50s he played with more big bands, including those led by Tommy Dorsey, Harry James and Claude Thornhill. During the remainder of the 50s and on through the 60s he worked in show and studio bands, by now usually preferring the alto to the tenor. In these decades and in the 70s he made occasional returns to the jazz scene for record dates. From the early 70s he was resident in San Francisco and could still be heard playing with rehearsal bands. In 1987, he returned to centrestage with appearances on the international festival circuit, playing alto, tenor and soprano saxophones. A highly regarded player, Steward's coolly elegant tone fitted well into the Four Brothers concept and the more introspective small groups. His early work showed few signs of major influences and although his later work displays his awareness of musical developments in jazz, everything is filtered through his highly personal and eminently tasteful style.

● ALBUMS: *Passport To Pimlico* (1950)★★★, with Zoot Sims, Serge Chaloff, Al Cohn *Four Brothers Together Again* (1957)★★, *So Pretty* (1962)★★★, *Herbie Steward With Orchestra Directed By Dick Hazard* (1962)★★, *Barney Plays Kessel* (1975)★★★★, *The Three Horns Of Herbie Steward* (1981)★★★.

● COMPILATIONS: *The Best Of Woody Herman* (1945-47)★★★★.

STEWART, BILL

b. 18 October 1966, Des Moines, Iowa, USA. Percussionist Bill Stewart made his name as the rhythmic force behind guitarist John Scofield's band, working with him for five years between 1990 and 1995. Self-taught on drums, Stewart is also a capable pianist, the instrument on which he composes. He grew up listening to his parents' jazz and R&B record collection, but otherwise jazz was a rare commodity in Iowa in the 70s and he played in a Top 40 covers band in high school as well as the school orchestra. After graduating he enrolled at the University Of Northern Iowa in Cedar Falls, playing in the jazz and marching bands as well as the orchestra. He then transferred to college in Wayne, New Jersey, where he studied with Dave Samuels, Rufus Reid and Harold Mabern. It was here that he met future collaborator, saxophonist Joe Lovano. While still in college he made his recording debut with saxophonist Scott Kreitzer and recorded two further collections with pianist Armen Donelian. After graduation in 1988 he moved to Brooklyn, New York, where he set up home. There he began the slow process of establishing his reputation by regular appearances at jam sessions and by word of mouth, leading to his first gigs with the Larry Goldings trio. At one of their regular sessions at Augie's Club in Manhattan, Maceo Parker attended and invited him to contribute to a forthcoming recording date (for *Roots Revisited*). Afterwards he was invited to join Scofield's band, which also included Lovano, who has featured on both of Stewart's solo albums to date. The first, *Think Before You Think*, was issued on the Japanese label Jazz City and featured Dave Holland on bass and Marc Copland on piano in addition to Lovano. The second, *Snide Remarks*, featured pianist Bill Carrothers, trumpeter Eddie Henderson and bassist Larry Grenadier. This boasted nine original Stewart compositions, highlighting a sophisticated compositional technique that Lovano once analogized as being that of 'a melody player within the concept of rhythm'.

● ALBUMS: *Think Before You Think* (Jazz City 1990)★★★, *Snide Remarks* (Blue Note 1995)★★★★, *Telepathy* (Blue Note 1997)★★★★, *Think Before You Think* (Evidence 1998)★★★.

STEWART, BOB

b. 3 February 1945, Sioux Falls, Dakota, USA. Stewart played trumpet for eight years, then switched to tuba in his second year at the Philadelphia College of Performing Arts. He learned to play in Dixieland bands (where the tuba occupies the role taken in later jazz by the string bass), including a residency at Your Father's Moustache. After graduating with a teaching degree in 1968 he relocated to New York, where he taught and led a junior high school band. He had been jamming with tuba-player Howard Johnson for years; now he joined his tuba ensemble Substructure and was also a founder-member of Gravity. In 1971 he worked with the Collective Black Artists Ensemble and in the early 70s with a variety of artists, including Freddie Hubbard and Taj Mahal. He formed a trio with Arthur Blythe and cellist Abdul Wadud, showing that the tuba could operate at the forefront of post-free explorations of tradition, particularly gripping as he interpreted Monk's left-hand bass lines on the tribute record *Light Blue*. He worked with Gil Evans (recording the tuba solo on Jimi Hendrix's 'Voodoo Chile' on *Live At Royal Festival Hall*) and with Carla Bley. He became a founder-member of Lester Bowie's Brass Fantasy. Indeed, Stewart was there whenever a tuba was needed - as it increasingly was during the 80s period of consolidation, when arrangers looked to jazz history for inspiration. He has also played with the Globe Unity Orchestra and co-leads (with French-horn player John Clark) the Clark-Stewart Quartet. In 1987 he formed his own band, First Line, with guitarist Kelvyn Bell from Defunkt, touring in 1988 and 1991. The band play an amalgam of New Orleans, free jazz and fusion that Stewart calls 'dixie funk'.

● ALBUMS: *First Line* (1988)★★★, with First Line *Going Home* (1990)★★, *Then & Now* (Postcards 1996)★★★, *One Life* (VWC 1997)★★★.

STEWART, LOUIS

b. 5 January 1944, Waterford, Eire. After playing guitar in a succession of show bands, Stewart began playing jazz in the early 60s. By the end of the decade he had achieved a substantial reputation and had worked with such leading jazzmen as Tubby Hayes and Benny Goodman. Throughout the 70s he continued to enhance his standing in both the UK and the USA, recording with Peter Ind and others. He also toured Europe, attracting considerable attention everywhere he played. In the 80s his reputation grew apace, despite his preference for spending a substantial part of his time in his homeland, and he made well-received albums with Martin Taylor, Brian Dunning, Spike Robinson and others. A brilliant sound allied to a crystal-clear tone has helped to make Stewart one of the outstanding guitarists in jazz. A virtuoso technique allows him to realize fully his endless inventiveness.

● ALBUMS: *Louis Stewart In Dublin* (1975)★★★, with Peter Ind *Baubles, Bangles And Beads* (1975)★★★, *Out On His Own* (Livia 1977)★★★, *Milesian Source* (1977)★★★★, with Brian Dunning *Alone Together* (Livia 1979)★★★, *I Thought About You* (Lee Lambert 1979)★★★, with Martin Taylor *Acoustic Guitar Duets* (1985)★★★★, *Good News* (Villa 1986)★★★, with Spike Robinson *Three For The Road* (1989)★★★.

STEWART, REX

b. 22 February 1907, Philadelphia, Pennsylvania, USA, d. 7 September 1967, Los Angeles, California, USA. Stewart began playing cornet in his early teens, having previously tried several other instruments. By 1921 he was in New York where he played in a succession of bands over the next three or four years. A spell with Elmer Snowden in the mid-20s was followed by a job with Fletcher Henderson. Over the next few years he worked in a number of bands, frequently returning to Henderson, and then, in 1934, joined Duke Ellington. He remained with Ellington until 1945, with spells out of the band for engagements with Benny Carter and others. In the late 40s and 50s he led his own bands in the USA and Europe, and was the driving force behind the re-formed Henderson All Stars band at the South Bay Jazz Festival in 1957.

In the 60s Stewart developed a parallel career as a broadcaster and writer. One of the most distinctive cornetists in jazz, Stewart developed the half-valve style of playing into an art form. His featured numbers with Ellington, especially 'Boy Meets Horn', have been frequently imitated but never surpassed. The biting, electrifying solos he played on numerous record dates, notably with the Henderson All Stars reunion band, have enormous energy and constantly display a strikingly original mind.

● ALBUMS: *Ellingtonia* 10-inch album (Dial 1951)★★★, *Rex Stewart & His Orchestra* 10-inch album (X 1954)★★★, *Dixieland On Location* (Concert Hall Jazz 1954)★★★, *Cool Fever* (Urania 1955)★★★, with Illinois Jacquet *Rex Stewart Plays Duke/Uptown Jazz* (Grand Award 1955)★★★, with Jack Teagarden *Big Jazz* (Atlantic 1956)★★★, *Dixieland Free-For-All* (Jazztone 1956)★★★, *Dedicated To Jazz* (Jazztone 1957)★★★, with Cootie Williams *The Big Challenge* (Jazztone 1957)★★★, with Fletcher Henderson *The Big Reunion* (Jazztone 1957)★★★★, *Rendezvous With Rex* (Felsted 1958)★★★, *Porgy And Bess Revisited* (Warners 1958)★★★, with Dicky Wells *Chatter Jazz* (RCA Victor 1959)★★★, *Henderson Homecoming* (United Artists 1959)★★★, *The Happy Jazz Of Rex Stewart* (Swingville 1960)★★★, with Henri Chaix *Rex Stewart Meets Henri Chaix* (1966)★★★, *Rex Stewart Memorial* (1966)★★★.

● FURTHER READING: *Jazz Masters Of The Thirties*, Rex Stewart with Stanley Dance.

STEWART, SLAM

b. Leroy Stewart, 21 September 1914, Englewood, New Jersey, USA, d. 10 December 1987. He studied bass at Boston Conservatory, having earlier played violin. Almost from the start of his career, Stewart was experimenting with his distinctive style in which he bowed the bass while humming in unison, an octave higher. John Chilton suggests that the concept was originally violinist Ray Perry's but certainly Stewart developed this technique into a fine art. In New York in 1937, Stewart met Slim Gaillard and together they became hugely popular on radio and records, their 'Flat Foot Floogie' being an enormous hit. During the late 30s and through the 40s he worked mostly in small groups, accompanying Gaillard, Art Tatum, Lester Young, Benny Goodman and others. In the 50s he played with Tatum, Roy Eldridge and also became a regular accompanist to singer Rose Murphy. In the 60s he added classical music to his repertoire. He continued to tour extensively in the 70s and 80s, playing with a wide range of artists, mostly in the mainstream of jazz. Stewart consistently displayed a comprehensive technique yet always played in an intensely rhythmic manner that he was never afraid to temper with wit.

● ALBUMS: *Slam Stewart* (Black And Blue 1971)★★★, *Slamboree* (1975)★★★, *Slam Stewart/Georges Delerue* (1975)★★, *Fish Scales* (Black And Blue 1975)★★★★, *Two Big Mice* (Black And Blue 1977)★★★★, with Bucky Pizzarelli *Dialogue* (1978)★★★, with Major Holley *Shut Yo' Mouth* (1981)★★★★, *New York New York* (Stash 1981)★★★.

● COMPILATIONS: with Slim Gaillard *Original 1938 Recordings, Volume 1* (1989)★★★.

STILES, DANNY

b. USA. Stiles played trumpet and flügelhorn in the late 60s and early 70s, in a studio band for the Merv Griffin and Dick Cavett shows. On the former, he met Bill Watrous, with whom he began an important musical relationship. He also played lead trumpet in Watrous's Manhattan Wildlife Refuge big band.

STILL LIFE (TALKING) - PAT METHENY

On *Still Life (Talking)*, Pat Metheny's south American influence is strong and the melody is more AOR than jazz. 'Last Train Home' is evocative of its title and has punishing timing throughout for Paul Wertico's drums. Throughout each track Lyle Mays creates a sheet of canvas, utilizing various keyboards and synthesizers, on which Metheny paints his Brazilian excursions. The group is completed by Steve Rodby (bass) and the voices of Armando Marcal, David Blamires and Mark Ledford.

● Tracks: *Minuano; So May It Secretly Begin; Last Train Home; It's Just Talk; Third Wind; Distance; In Her Family.*

● First released 1987

● UK peak chart position: did not chart

● USA peak chart position: 86

STILL WARM - JOHN SCOFIELD

John Scofield has really come of age since this album was released, winning awards and nominations galore, and in doing so has become one of the world's leading jazz guitarists. His popularity increased with this record as his funk and rock influences shone through. 'Techno' is the type of music we might have imagined Jimi Hendrix playing, had he lived. The title track is both romantic and highly erotic, the rhythm is almost Latin and the song builds continuously as the musical scale ascends, yet the listener is completely fooled because the climax is only one octave. It is a brilliant piece of music.

● Tracks: *Techno; Still Warm; High And Mighty; Protocol; Rule Of Thumb; Picks And Pans; Gil B 643.*

● First released 1987

● UK peak chart position: did not chart

● USA peak chart position: did not chart

STINSON, ALBERT

b. Albert Forrest Stinson Jnr., 2 August 1944, Cleveland, Ohio, USA, d. 2 June 1969. Although he played several instruments as a child, by his early teens Stinson had settled on the bass. Still a teenager, he played with Terry Gibbs and then with Chico Hamilton, with whom he recorded several albums including two sessions for Impulse! Records, 1962's *Passin' Thru* and 1965's *El Chico*. He also recorded with fellow Hamilton sideman, Dennis Budimir. Towards the end of the 60s, he played with bands led by John Handy and Larry Coryell. A strikingly gifted player with great technical accomplishment and enormous flair, Stinson's death in his mid-twenties brought to an abrupt end a potentially important career.

STITT, SONNY

b. Edward Stitt, 2 February 1924, Boston, Massachusetts, USA, d. 22 July 1982. Starting out on alto saxophone, Stitt gained his early experience playing in the big bands led by Tiny Bradshaw and Billy Eckstine. Influenced by Charlie Parker and by the many fine young beboppers he encountered on the Eckstine band, Stitt quickly developed into a formidable player. He played with Dizzy Gillespie, Kenny Clarke and others but by the late 40s was concerned that he should develop a more personal style. In pursuit of this he switched to tenor saxophone and formed the first of many bands he was to lead and co-lead over the years. Among his early collaborators was Gene Ammons, whom he had met during the Eckstine stint. In the late 50s he was with Jazz At The Philharmonic and in 1960 was briefly with Miles Davis. Throughout the 60s and 70s Stitt maintained a high level of performances at home and abroad, despite periodic bouts of ill-health generated by his drug addictions. In the early 60s he recorded with Paul Gonsalves, *Salt And Pepper*, and in the early 70s toured with Gillespie as a member of the Giants Of Jazz, continuing to make many fine record albums. His early 80s albums included *Sonny, Sweets And Jaws*, with Harry Edison and Eddie 'Lockjaw' Davis, and a fine set made just weeks before his death. Although his early career was overshadowed by Parker, Stitt was never a copyist. Indeed, his was a highly original musical mind, as became apparent after he switched to tenor and forged a new and appreciative audience for his work. In later years he played alto saxophone as often as he played tenor, by which time it was plain to see that the comparisons to Parker were largely the result of critical pigeonholing.

● ALBUMS: *Sonny Stitt And Bud Powell* 10-inch album aka as *Sonny Stitt With Bud Powell & J.J. Johnson* (New Jazz 1950)★★★★, *Sonny Stitt And Bud Powell* 10-inch album (Prestige 1951)★★★★, with Gene Ammons *Battle Of The Saxes: Ammons Vs. Stitt* 10-inch album (Prestige 1951)★★★, *Mr Saxophone* 10-inch album (Prestige 1951)★★★, *Super Stitt, Volume 1 - Favorites* 10-inch album aka *Stitt's Bits* (Prestige 1952)★★★★, *Super Stitt, Volume 2 - Tenor Sax* 10-inch album (Prestige 1953)★★★, *All Star Series: Sonny Stitt* 10-inch album (Savoy 1952)★★★, *New Trends Of Jazz* 10-inch album (Savoy 1952)★★★★, *New Sounds In Modern Music* 10-inch album (Savoy 1952)★★★★, *Sonny Stitt Plays Arrangements From The Pen Of Johnny Richards* 10-inch album (Roost 1953)★★★, *Jazz At The Hi-Hat* 10-inch album (Roost 1954)★★★, with Eddie Davis *Battle Of Birdland* (Roost 1955)★★★, *Early Modern* (Jazztone 1956)★★★★, *Sonny Stitt* (Roost 1956)★★★★, *Sonny Stitt Plays Arrangements Of Quincy Jones* (Roost 1956)★★★, *37 Minutes And 48 Seconds* (Roost 1957)★★★, *Kaleidoscope* (Prestige 1957)★★★, *Sonny Stitt With The New Yorkers* (Roost 1957)★★★, with Dizzy Gillespie, Sonny Rollins *Duets* reissued as *Dizzy, Rollins & Stitt* (Verve 1958)★★★★, *New York Jazz* (Verve 1958)★★★★, *Only The Blues* (Verve 1958)★★★★, *Sonny Side Up* (Verve 1958)★★★★, *Sonny Stitt* (Argo 1958)★★★, *Burnin'* (Argo 1958)★★★, *The Hard Swing* (Verve 1959)★★★, *Sonny Stitt Plays Jimmy Giuffre Arrangements* (Verve 1959)★★★, *Personal Appearances* (Verve 1959)★★, *The Saxophone Of Sonny Stitt* (Roost 1959)★★★, *Little Bit Of Stitt* (Roost 1959)★★★, *Sonny Stitt Sits In With The Oscar Peterson Trio* (Verve 1959)★★, *Sonny Stitt Blows The Blues* (Verve 1960)★★★, *Saxophone Supremacy* (Verve 1960)★★★, *Sonny Stitt Swings The Most*

(Verve 1960)★★★, *Sonny Side Of Stitt* (Roost 1960)★★, *Stittsville* (Roost 1960)★★★, *Sonny Stitt At The D.J. Lounge* (Argo 1961)★★, *Sonny Stitt And The Top Brass* (Atlantic 1962)★★★, *Rearin' Back* (Argo 1962)★★★, *Low Flame* (Jazzland 1962)★★★, *The Sensual Sound Of Sonny Stitt* (Verve 1962)★★★, *Feelin's* (Roost 1962)★★★, *Autumn In New York* (1962-67)★★★, with Jack McDuff *Sonny Stitt Meets Brother Jack* aka *Nuther Fu'ther* (Prestige 1962)★★, with Ammons *Boss Tenors* (Verve 1962)★★★, with Ammons, McDuff *Soul Summit* (Prestige 1962)★★★, with Ammons *Boss Tenors In Orbit* (Verve 1962)★★★, *Sonny Stitt In Orbit* (Roost 1963)★★★, *Sonny Stitt Goes Latin* (Roost 1963)★, *My Mother's Eyes* (Pacific Jazz 1963)★★★, *Sonny Stitt Now!* (Impulse! 1963)★★★, *Salt And Pepper* (Impulse! 1963)★★★, *Sonny Stitt Plays Bird* (Atlantic 1964)★★★★, *Move On Over* (Argo 1964)★★★, with McDuff *Soul Shack* (Prestige 1964)★★, *Primitivo Soul!* (Prestige 1964)★★★, *Broadway Soul* (Colpix 1964)★★★, *My Main Man* (Argo 1965)★★★, *Soul People* (Prestige 1965)★★, *Interaction* (Cadet 1965)★★, *Soul In The Night* (Cadet 1965)★★★, *The Matadors Meet The Bull* (Roulette 1965)★★★, *Sonny* (1966)★★, *Stardust* (1966)★★, *What's New!!! Sonny Stitt Plays The Varitone* (Roulette 1966)★★★, *I Keep Comin' Back* (Roulette 1966)★★★, with Don Patterson *Night Crawler* (Prestige 1967)★★★, with Ammons *Jug And Sonny* (Cadet 1967)★★★★, *Sonny Stitt . . . Pow!* (Prestige 1967)★★★, *Autumn In New York* (Black Lion 1968)★★★, *Little Green Apples* (Solid State 1969)★★, *Come Together* (Solid State 1969)★★, *Night Letter* (1969)★★★, with Ammons *We'll Be Together Again* (Prestige 1969)★★★★, *Soul Electricity* (Prestige 1969)★★★, *Black Vibrations* (1971)★★★, with Ammons *You Talk That Talk* (Prestige 1971)★★★★, *So Doggone Good* (1972)★★★, *Constellation* (Muse 1972)★★★, *Tune Up!* (Muse 1972)★★★★, *The Champ* (Muse 1973)★★★★, with Ammons *Together Again For The Last Time* (1973)★★★★, *Satan* (1974)★★★, *In Walked Sonny* (Sonet 1975)★★★, *I Remember Bird* (Catalyst 1976)★★, *Moonlight In Vermont* (Denon 1977)★★★, *Back To My Old Home Town* (Black And Blue 1979)★★★, *Groovin' High* (1980)★★★, *Sonny, Sweets And Jaws* (1981)★★★, *At Last* (1982)★★★, *The Last Stitt Sessions* (Muse 1982)★★★, *Made For Each Other* (Delmark 1997)★★★, with Ronnie Scott *The Night Has A Thousand Eyes* (Jazz House 1998)★★★, *Just In Case You Forgot How Bad He Really Was* 1981 recording (32 Jazz 1998)★★★.

● COMPILATIONS: *The Best Of Sonny Stitt With Brother Jack McDuff* (Prestige 1969)★★★, *Soul Classics* (Prestige 1988)★★★.

Stobart, Kathy

b. 1 April 1925, South Shields, Co. Durham, England. Stobart in her long career as a leading jazz saxophonist has recorded and played with countless top musicians, yet her own recorded output is comparatively sparse. From her professional debut at the age of 14 she eventually moved to London where work was more plentiful, playing with Art Pepper (then a serviceman) while posted in the UK during the war. Following a spell with the Vic Lewis Big Band during the late 40s Stobart married trumpeter Bert Courtley and formed her own band in the early 50s. Her work over many years with Humphrey Lyttelton has produced some of her finest playing and Lyttelton rightly regards her as a world-class musician. Her other credits include work with Johnnie Griffin, Al Haig, Earl 'Fatha' Hines, Buddy Tate, Zoot Sims, Harry Beckett and Dick Hyman. Stobart topped the bill at the first British women's jazz festival in 1982 and was a member of Gail Force 17 (the women's big band) during the mid-80s. Additionally she has made a reputation as a music teacher. Still refusing to retire from the road, she was on tour with Lyttelton again throughout the 90s.

● ALBUMS: *Arderia* (1983)★★★, *Saxploitation* (1983)★★★★.

Stockhausen, Markus

b. 1957, Cologne, Germany. Son of the composer Karlheinz Stockhausen, Markus studied piano and trumpet at the Cologne Musikhochschule. He also plays flügelhorn and synthesizer. In 1981 he won the German Music Competition. Since 1974 he has worked regularly with his father, who has written a number of works for him, including 'Sirius'. In particular, the solo trumpet parts in Stockhausen père's massive opera cycle, Licht, were created for Markus. Outside of the contemporary 'classical' field he has played free improvised music with various groups, and currently has a band, Aparis, with his brother Simon on saxophones and keyboards.

● with Gary Peacock: *Cosi Lotano ... Quasi Dentro* (ECM 1989)★★★, *Aparis* (ECM 1990)★★, *Tagtraum* (New Note 1992)★★, *Despite The Fire Fighters' Efforts* (ECM 1993)★★★★, *Possible Worlds* (CMP 1996)★★★, *Sol Mestizo* (Act 1997)★★★★.

Stoller, Alvin

b. 7 October 1925, New York City, USA, d. 19 October 1992, Los Angeles, California, USA. Taking up the drums as a child, Stoller's dues were paid while he was still a teenager with stints in bands led by Raymond Scott, Teddy Powell, Benny Goodman and Charlie Spivak. In 1945 he followed Buddy Rich into the vacated drum stool with the Tommy Dorsey band, bringing with him much of his predecessor's enthusiasm - and not a little of his fiery temperament. Through the late 40s and 50s, Stoller's career found him playing in name bands such as those led by Georgie Auld, Harry James, Billy May, Charlie Barnet, Claude Thornhill and Bob Crosby. This same period saw him in constant demand as a studio musician, especially for Norman Granz, backing artists such as Erroll Garner, Billie Holiday, Ben Webster, Ella Fitzgerald and Benny Carter, with whom he appeared on *Additions To Further Definitions*. Tastefully discreet when backing singers or in a small group setting and powerfully propulsive when driving a big band, Stoller was one of the best late swing era drummers even if he was sometimes overlooked thanks to his long service in film and television studios in later years.

● ALBUMS: with Harry Edison *Sweets At The Haig* (1953)★★★, with Roy Eldridge, John Simmons, Art Tatum *The Art Tatum-Roy Eldridge-Alvin Stoller-John Simmons Quartet* (Clef 1955)★★★, *Around The Horn With Maynard Ferguson* (1956)★★★★, *The Genius Of Coleman Hawkins* (1957)★★★, with Benny Carter *Additions To Further Definitions* (1966)★★★★.

STONE, JESSE

b. 1901, Atchison, Kansas, USA. As a young man, pianist Stone worked extensively in the south-west playing in numerous bands. During the greater part of the 20s he led his own territory band but at the end of the decade became arranger and musical director for other leading territory bands, including those of Terrence Holder, George E. Lee and Thamon Hayes. He returned to bandleading in the mid-30s, continuing in this capacity throughout the next decade before becoming an A&R man. Stone, who made very few recordings, was one of the lesser, but still important, figures in the development of Kansas City Jazz. His arrangements and expertise as leader and director helped to fashion the propulsive swing that marked the style.

STORDAHL, AXEL

b. 8 August 1913, Staten Island, New York, USA, d. 30 August 1963, Encino, California, USA. An accomplished arranger-conductor, and sometime composer, whose name is indelibly linked with Frank Sinatra's Columbia recordings of the 40s. Early in his career, Stordahl played trumpet and arranged for the Bert Block Orchestra, before being hired by Tommy Dorsey in the mid-30s. When Sinatra left Dorsey to go solo in 1943, Stordahl's arrangements played an important role, mainly on the singer's ballad records through to 1949. He also worked with Sinatra on his many radio broadcasts, including the immensely popular *Your Hit Parade*. After Sinatra moved to Capitol Records, and the backings of Nelson Riddle, Gordon Jenkins, Billy May, *et al.*, Stordahl served as arranger-conductor for vocalists such as Giselle Mackenzie, Doris Day, Eddie Fisher, Nanette Fabray, Bing Crosby, Dean Martin, and Stordahl's wife, June Hutton, and was continuously in demand for various television programmes. Stordahl's catalogue of songs and instrumental works included two outstanding romantic ballads, 'I Should Care' and 'Day By Day' (both written with Paul Weston and Sammy Cahn), as well as others such as the pleasant 'Ain'tcha Ever Comin' Back?', 'Neiani', 'Talking To Myself About You', 'Night After Night', 'Return To The Magic Islands', 'Recollections', 'Jasmine And Jade' and 'Ride Off'.

● ALBUMS: *The Strings Of Stordahl* (Capitol 50s)★★★★, *Lure* (Decca 1959)★★★, *Jasmine And Jade* (Dot 1960)★★★, *Magic Islands Revisited* (Decca 1961)★★, *Axel Stordahl* (Decca 1963)★★★.

STORMY WEATHER

Hollywood being what it was then, director Andrew Stone led an almost 'all-white' team behind the cameras for this otherwise 'all-black' musical. Never mind the routine and rather trite backstage storyline, the cast is superb. Led by Bill 'Bojangles' Robinson and Lena Horne, they romp through some magnificent musical numbers including spots by Cab Calloway and his Orchestra, including Shad Collins, Illinois Jacquet and J.C. Heard, Katharine Dunham and her dancers, and the fabulous Nicholas Brothers. For all this remarkable talent, however, the show is stolen by Fats Waller. In addition to acting in a couple of scenes he and an all-star band, including Slam Stewart, Benny Carter, the film's musical director (and the only black person in an off-camera role), and Zutty Singleton, the band's nominal leader, back Ada Brown for one number and are featured in two: 'Ain't Misbehavin'' and 'Moppin' And Boppin''. It was while returning east from Hollywood after appearing in this film that Waller died. Adding to this 1943 film's many marvels is the fact that at the time of its making, Robinson, who was born around 1873, was long past his youthful prime.

STOVALL, DON

b. Donald Stovall, 12 December 1913, St. Louis, Missouri, USA, d. 20 November 1970. Stovall began his musical life playing violin but soon shifted to saxophones and clarinet, playing dance music in the late 20s and early 30s with leaders such as Dewey Jackson and Fate Marable. In the mid- and late 40s he played with Lillian Armstrong and Peanuts Holland before moving to New York and joining Sammy Price. In the early 40s he played in a succession of small groups, then joined the Cootie Williams big band in 1941. The following year he settled into a long spell with Henry 'Red' Allen's small group. He stayed with Allen until almost the end of the decade and early in the 50s he retired from music. A competent player, who also composed, Stovall was one of the many underrated and quickly forgotten names of the swing era.

● ALBUMS: *Sam Price And His Texas Bluesicians* (KM 1940-42)★★★, *Hot Lips Page 1938-1940* (Official 1938-40)★★★★, *Red Allen And His Sextet* (Phoenix/Rarities 1944)★★★, *Pete Johnson's All Stars* (Savoy 1946)★★★.

STRAIGHT, CHARLEY

b. 16 January 1891, Chicago, USA, d. 21 September 1940. On leaving Wendell Phillips High School, Straight was a pianist in vaudeville before entering the band business. Together with Roy Bargy (on second piano) and a saxophonist he formed Straight's Trio aka the Imperial Three, doing unsuccessful recording tests for Victor and Columbia on consecutive days in November 1919. However, a month later the Emerson label released the trio's first records. In 1923, Straight and his new nine-piece band were recording for Paramount, the tracks being simultaneously issued on subsidiary labels as the Frisco Syncopators, Harmograph Dance Orchestra, Manhattan Imperial Orchestra, Broadway Melody Makers and Rendezvous Dance Orchestra. Long resident at the Rainbow Gardens in Chicago, the band was joined by Bix Beiderbecke in 1924. Joseph 'Wingy' Manone also played with Straight, and in 1926, Miff Mole and Wild Bill Davison were on a Brunswick session which produced 'Hobo's Prayer'/'Minor Gaff', also issued on Vocalion as by the Tennessee Tooters. Most of Straight's 1926-27 sides went out on Brunswick under his own name but some were also issued on Vocalion as the Tuxedo Orchestra. He never worked as a leader after his last Brunswick sessions of August 1928, though he is known to have recorded with the Benson Orchestra of Chicago, run by the agency which handled his own band. Straight was a prolific songwriter, though none of his work seems to have endured; he was also musical director of a company making piano rolls, to which he undoubtedly contributed himself. He was born, lived, worked, seldom left, and finally died, in Chicago, in September 1940.

STRANGE, PETE

b. 19 December 1938, London, England. Strange is a self-taught trombonist who started his career with Eric Silk's Southern Jazz Band. He played with a variety of bands before joining Bruce Turner's Jump Band. When that folded he played semi-professionally for a number of years before joining Keith Nichols' Midnite Follies Orchestra in the late 70s. He wrote arrangements for, and played with, the band of trumpeter Digby Fairweather. Strange also organized his own unusual five-trombone band Five-A-Slide and played with Alan Elsdon's band. In 1983 he moved on to Humphrey Lyttelton's band, for which he has written many fine arrangements as well as providing stylish trombone-playing derived principally from Lawrence Brown and Dicky Wells.

● ALBUMS: with Bruce Turner *Going Places* (1963)★★★, with Humphrey Lyttelton *It Seems Like Yesterday* (1983)★★★★, *Echoes Of The Duke* (1984)★★★, *Humph At The Bull's Head* (1985)★★★.

STRAYHORN, BILLY

b. 29 November 1915, Dayton, Ohio, USA, d. 31 May 1967. After studying music at school and privately, Strayhorn began writing music and late in 1938 submitted material to Duke Ellington. Early the following year Ellington recorded the first of these works, and Strayhorn was soon involved in writing original material and arrangements for the Ellington band. The association with Ellington largely excluded all other musical activity during the rest of Strayhorn's life. When he did write arrangements for and play piano with other artists, they were usually present or former Ellingtonians. Although he played piano on record dates with various Ellingtonians and on piano duets with Ellington himself, Strayhorn's greatest contribution to jazz must be the many superb compositions immortalized by the Ellington orchestra. The best-known of these might well be the Ellington theme, 'Take The "A" Train', but his other masterpieces are almost all sumptuous ballads and include 'Day Dream', 'Passion Flower', 'Lotus Blossom', 'Raincheck', 'Chelsea Bridge' and 'Lush Life'. This last piece was written in 1938 but Strayhorn withheld publication for many years, preferring to wait until a singer emerged capable of interpreting the song as he imagined it. The first recording was by Nat 'King' Cole in 1949 but, good as this was, Strayhorn later remarked that he had still to hear the song sung right. The intertwining of Strayhorn's writing with that of Ellington complicates a thorough understanding of his importance, and Brian Priestley is one of several musicians/writers who have indicated the value of intensive research in this area. When Strayhorn was hospitalized in 1967, he continued working almost to the end on his final composition, 'Blood Count'. A few months after his death in May 1967, Ellington recorded a tribute album of Strayhorn compositions, *And His Mother Called Him Bill*.

● ALBUMS: *Billy Strayhorn Trio* (Mercer 1951)★★★, *And The All Stars* (Mercer 1951)★★★, *Billy Strayhorn Septet* (Felsted 1958)★★★, *Cue For Saxophones* (Affinity 1958)★★★, with Duke Ellington *Billy Strayhorn Live!* (1960)★★★, *Billy Strayhorn And The Paris String Quartet* (1961)★★★, *The Peaceful Side* (United Artists 1962)★★★, *The Billy Strayhorn Project* (Stash 1991)★★★, *Lush Life* (Red Baron 1992)★★★★, performed by the Dutch Jazz Orchestra *Portrait Of A Silk Thread: Newly Discovered Works Of Billy Strayhorn* (Kokopelli 1996)★★★.

● COMPILATIONS: various artists *Lush Life: The Billy Strayhorn Songbook* (Verve 1996)★★★★.

● FURTHER READING: *Lush Life: A Biography Of Billy Strayhorn*, David Hadju.

STRING TRIO OF NEW YORK

The band, formed in October 1977 by violinist Billy Bang (b. Billy Walker, 20 September 1947, Mobile, Alabama, USA), James Emery (guitar) and John Lindberg (bass), was an unlikely proposition: three members of the New York *avant garde*, associates of Anthony Braxton, Frank Lowe and Leroy Jenkins, playing café music that ransacked gypsy music, blues, jazz and ragtime for inspiration. During the solos the players would be as 'out' as anything to be heard in New York, but their tunes provided entry points for the listener. They proved to be very popular and recorded prolifically. In May 1986 Bang was replaced by violinist Charles Burnham, a former accomplice of James Blood Ulmer. They had not lost their invention or swing, as was proved by 1990's *Ascendant*. New violinist Regina Carter featured heavily on 1996's *Blues ... ?*, introducing reggae rhythms on the track 'Hurry Up And Wait'.

● ALBUMS: *String Trio Of New York* (1978)★★★, *Area Code 212* (1980)★★★★, *Common Goal* (1982)★★★, *Rebirth Of A Feeling* (1984)★★★, *Natural Balance* (1987)★★★, *Ascendant* (1990)★★★, *Blues ... ?* (Black Saint 1996)★★★★.

STRIP, THE

A would-be jazz drummer, Mickey Rooney, fresh out of the army, tangles with criminals. Directed by Leslie Kardos in 1951, all is very predictable but the pleasures in this film centre upon the band he joins, no less than Louis Armstrong And His All Stars. To meet some Hollywood executive's misconceived ideas on racial integration, apart from Rooney, another white face appears on-screen in the band, behind the string bass. However, part of what you see and all of what you hear is the real All Stars back in the days when Armstrong's group truly merited the term: Jack Teagarden, Barney Bigard, Earl Hines, Arvell Shaw and William 'Cozy' Cole (the last two dubbing for their on-screen counterparts). Armstrong recorded one of the film's songs, 'A Kiss To Build A Dream On', which became a minor hit for him.

He also sings 'Shadrack' and the band plays a handful of other 'good old good ones' including 'Ole Miss'/'Bugle Call Rag' which is a feature for Rooney/Cole. In some scenes without the band Rooney may have played drums himself, something at which he was rather good, although he was no Cozy Cole.

STUDER, FREDY

b. 16 June 1948, Lucerne, Switzerland. Studer is a self-taught musician who started playing drums when he was 16 years old and appeared in a wide range of bands from rock through jazz to experimental. In 1970, he moved to Rome with a rock trio. He became a consultant for the development of Paiste cymbals. Throughout the 70s he was with the jazz/rock band Om and then played in the rock band Hand In Hand. Studer formed a trio with Rainer Bruninghaus and Markus Stockhausen between 1981 and 1984 and then played in the Charlie Mariano/Jasper Van't Hof band. He also performed in the percussion group Singing Drums with Pierre Favre, Paul Motian and Nana Vasconcelos. Studer has toured extensively, including trips to the USA, Central and South America, the Caribbean, North Africa and Japan.

● ALBUMS: with George Gruntz *Percussion Profiles* (1977)★★★, *Om With Dom Um Romao* (1977)★★★, *Continuum* (1983)★★★★, with Singing Drums *Singing Drums* (1985)★★★, as Doran, Studer, Minton, Bates, Ali *Play The Music Of Jimi Hendrix* (Call It Anything 1994)★★.

SUBTERRANEANS, THE

This adaptation of a Jack Kerouac novel came too early for it to be successful. When it was released in 1960, Hollywood was then still hidebound by its own peculiar code of sexual ethics. What could and could not be shown on the screen was a tangle that this film, directed by Ranald MacDougall, failed to unravel. Jazz fans have an excuse for watching it, however, as there are good moments from musicians such as André Previn, the film's musical director, Dave Bailey, Chico Hamilton, Art Farmer, Art Pepper, Bob Enevoldson, Russ Freeman, Red Mitchell, Shelly Manne, Bill Perkins and Gerry Mulligan, who also acts in the film.

SUDHALTER, DICK

b. 28 December 1928, Boston, Massachusetts, USA. Sudhalter played as an amateur while engaged in a career in journalism. Playing cornet in various parts of the USA and UK, he established a quiet reputation mostly amongst musicians. As he expanded his career in music, Sudhalter's virtues as a player and a tireless organizer became more widely apparent. He was involved in the creation of the New Paul Whiteman Orchestra and also worked with Bobby Hackett, Keith Nichols, the New York Jazz Repertory Company and others in faithful but undogmatic recreations of early jazz, in particular the music of Bix Beiderbecke. His interest in the life and career of Beiderbecke led him to write the biography, *Bix: Man And Legend*, and his other writings have extended into the *New York Post*. His late 80s and early 90s playing ventures include performances with Dick Wellstood and Marty Grosz in the band known as the Classic Jazz Quartet, and with Loren Schoenberg and singers Barbara Lea and Daryl Sherman in the group named Mr Tram Associates.

● ALBUMS: *Friends With Pleasure* (Audiophile 1981)★★★, with Mr Tram Associates *Getting Some Fun Out Of Life* (1988)★★, *Get Out And Get Under The Moon* (1989)★★★, *Dick Sudhalter And Connie Jones* (Stomp Off 1992)★★★, *With Pleasure* 1981-1994 recordings (Audiophile 1996)★★★★, *After Awhile* (Challenge 1996)★★★.

SULIEMAN, IDREES

b. Leonard Graham, 7 August 1923, St. Petersburg, Florida, USA. After playing trumpet for a number of years with territory bands, in 1943 Sulieman joined Earl 'Fatha' Hines. After some more dues-paying in minor bands, he came to New York where he played with Thelonious Monk and then began a tour through an impressive succession of big bands, including those led by Cab Calloway, Count Basie and Lionel Hampton. He also played in small groups led by Mal Waldron, Randy Weston and others. In the 60s he moved to Sweden, then settled in Denmark where he has remained. From the mid-60s he played with the Clarke-Boland Big Band and also took up alto saxophone. In the 70s he continued to work in Denmark, mostly with radio big bands, but made occasional record dates as leader and with musicians such as Horace Parlan. Despite being one of the first jazz musicians to play bop, Sulieman's long residency away from the international spotlight has meant that he has had little influence upon others.

● ALBUMS: with Mal Waldron *Mal 1* (1956)★★★, with Horace Parlan *Arrival* (1973)★★★, *Now Is The Time* (Steeplechase 1976)★★, *Bird's Grass* (Steeplechase 1977)★★, *Groovin'* (Steeplechase 1986)★★★.

SULLIVAN, IRA

b. 1 May 1931, Washington, USA. Sullivan is that rare thing, a true multi-instrumentalist, capable of improvising statements of worth on all his instruments. He was taught trumpet by his father, saxophone by his mother and played both in 50s Chicago with such seminal figures as Charlie Parker, Lester Young, Wardell Gray and Roy Eldridge, garnering a reputation as a fearsome bebop soloist. After playing briefly with Art Blakey (1956), and mastering alto and baritone saxophone, Sullivan moved south to Florida and out of the spotlight in the early 60s. His reluctance to travel limited his opportunities to play with musicians of the first rank, but Sullivan continued to play in the Miami area, often in schools and churches. Contact with local younger players, notably Jaco Pastorius and Pat Metheny led to teaching and to a broadening of his own musical roots to include the lessons of John Coltrane's music and elements of jazz rock. With the addition of flute and soprano saxophone to his armoury, Sullivan moved to New York and in 1980 formed a quintet with legendary bop trumpeter Red Rodney. Resisting the temptation to follow current trends and play the music of their youth, Sullivan and Rodney worked on new material and fostered young talent to produce some of the freshest and most stimulating music of the decade.

● ALBUMS: *Nicky's Tune* (Delmark 1958)★★, *Ira Sullivan Quartet* (Delmark 1974)★★★, *Ira Sullivan* (Flying Fish 1976)★★★, *Peace* (1978)★★★, with Red Rodney *Live At The Village Vanguard* (1980)★★★★, *Bird Lives* (Affinity 1981)★★★, *Horizons* (Discovery 1983)★★★, *Does It All* (Muse 1988)★★★, *Tough Town* (Delmark 1992)★★.

SULLIVAN, JOE

b. 4 November 1906, Chicago, Illinois, USA, d. 13 October 1971. After studying piano formally, Sullivan began working in theatres and clubs in and around Chicago while still a teenager. Throughout the 20s he was one of the busiest musicians in Chicago, playing at clubs and on numerous record dates with leading jazzmen, mostly in small groups. He also worked as accompanist to Bing Crosby during the early 30s. At various times in that decade he played in several larger ensembles, among them bands led by Roger Wolfe Kahn and Bob Crosby. Ill-health drove him from the Crosby band just as it hit the big-time. In the 40s he played with Bobby Hackett and Eddie Condon and also worked as a single. He continued playing alone, although not through choice, and in small jazz groups through the 50s. From the early 60s onwards his career was dogged by both poor health and critical disregard. An eclectic pianist, Sullivan's robust style displayed elements of stride but he was at his propulsive best playing in a lively Chicago-style band. Among his compositions are 'Gin Mill Blues' and 'Little Rock Getaway'.

● ALBUMS: *Fats Waller First Editions* (1952)★★, *New Solos By An Old Master* (1953)★★★, *Mr Piano Man* (1955)★★★, *Gin Mill* (Pumpkin 1963)★★★.

● COMPILATIONS: *Joe Sullivan And The All Stars (1950)* (Shoestring 1981)★★★, *At The Piano* (Shoestring 1981)★★★, *Piano Man (1935-40)* (1988)★★.

SULLIVAN, MAXINE

b. Marietta Williams, 13 May 1911, Homestead, Pennsylvania, USA, d. 7 April 1987. Sullivan began singing in and around Pittsburgh, Pennsylvania, before travelling to New York in 1937. She joined the Claude Thornhill band and made a hugely successful record of 'Loch Lomond'. The popularity of this recording led to her making several more jazzed-up folk songs, including 'Annie Laurie', which, for all their frequent banality, she sang with effortless charm. In the late 30s and early 40s she made several feature films and also worked and recorded with her husband John Kirby. After a brief retirement she began appearing again in New York and also travelled to Europe. In the mid-50s she quit singing to take up nursing but returned in 1958. In addition to singing she also played flügelhorn, valve-trombone and pocket trumpet. She continued to work through the 60s, often with Cliff Jackson, who had become her second husband, and with Bob Wilber. Her career blossomed in the late 70s and throughout most of the 80s, thanks to performances with the World's Greatest Jazz Band and Scott Hamilton. In her later years she devoted some of her considerable energy to running the 'House That Jazz Built', a museum she created at her home and dedicated to Jackson's memory. The hallmarks of her singing were charm and delicacy, qualities that were often out of favour and probably accounted for the ups and downs of her career. Her later work, especially the recordings with Wilber, proved that her talent was far greater than public taste had allowed.

● ALBUMS: with others *Seven Ages Of Jazz* (1958)★★★, *Maxine Sullivan* i (1969)★★★★, *Close As Pages In A Book* (1969)★★★, *Queen Of Song* (1970)★★★, *Maxine Sullivan* ii (1971)★★★, *Maxine* (1975)★★★★, *Harlem Butterfly* (1975-77)★★★, *We Just Couldn't Say Goodbye* (1978)★★★, *Maxine Sullivan And Ike Isaacs* (1978)★★★★, *Sullivan, Shakespeare, Hyman* (Audiophile 1979)★★★, *Maxine Sullivan And Her Swedish Jazz All Stars* (1981)★★, *It Was Great Fun!* (1983)★★★, *Good Morning, Life* (1983)★★★, *The Queen; Something To Remember Her By* (Kenneth 1985)★★, *The Great Songs From The Cotton Club By Harold Arlen And Ted Koehler* (Mobile Fidelity 1985)★★, *Uptown* (Concord 1985)★★★, *The Lady's In Love With You* (1985)★★★, *I Love To Be In Love* (1986)★★★, *Maxine Sullivan And Scott Hamilton* (1986)★★★, *Songs Of Burton Lane* (1986)★★★, *Together: Maxine Sullivan Sings Julie Styne* (1986)★★★, *Swingin' Street* (Concord 1987)★★★, *Spring Isn't Everything* (Audiophile 1987)★★★.

● COMPILATIONS: *It's Wonderful* (1992)★★★, *1944 To 1948* (1993)★★, *Say It With A Kiss* (Jasmine 1997)★★★.

SULZMANN, STAN

b. 30 November 1948, London, England. From his mid-teens Sulzmann was playing saxophones on the blues circuit, but in 1964 he joined the first edition of Bill Ashton's National Youth Jazz Orchestra. Following this he worked on the Queen Mary crossing to New York and then returned to London to study at the Royal Academy of Music. Subsequently, as well as winning the *Melody Maker* New Star award, he played with Mike Gibbs, Graham Collier, John Dankworth, John Taylor (with whom he also established a quartet in 1970), John Warren, Clark Terry, Brian Cooper, Alan Cohen, the Clarke-Boland Big Band, Kenny Wheeler, Gordon Beck's Gyroscope and Gil Evans' early 80s London band. Equally adept on soprano, alto and tenor saxophones and flutes and clarinet, Sulzmann was one of the earliest of several distinguished graduates from the NYJO, and his influences range from Frank Zappa, through to Kenny Wheeler (whose compositions he showcased on *Everybody's Song But My Own*) and Miles Davis to Debussy and Delius.

● ALBUMS: with Michael Gibbs *Tanglewood '63* (1971)★★★★, *On Loan With Gratitude* (1977)★★★, *Krark* (1979)★★★, with John Taylor *Everybody's Song But My Own* (1987)★★★, with Tony Hymas *Flying Fortress* (1991)★★, *Feudal Rabbits* (Ah-Um 1991)★★★, with Marc Copland *Never At All* (Future Music 1993)★★★, *Treasure Trove* (ASC 1996)★★★★.

Summers, Andy

b. Andrew Somers, 31 December 1942, Poulton-le-Fylde, Lancashire, England. Raised in Bournemouth, Dorset, Summers was performing in the city's clubs and coffee-bars while still a teenager. He first encountered Zoot Money in the Don Robb Band, a local cabaret attraction, and later joined the ebullient singer in his Big Roll Band. This excellent soul/R&B group became one of the leading acts of the London club circuit during the mid-60s. Summers retained his association with Money in Dantalion's Chariot and the US-based New Animals. When the latter broke up in 1968, the guitarist remained in California where he studied classical styles, joined a Latino-rock band and acted with various Hollywood theatre groups. He returned to England in 1973 and over the next four years Summers toured with Neil Sedaka, David Essex, Kevin Coyne and Kevin Ayers. In May 1977, he played guitar in a temporary unit, Strontium 90, which also included Sting (bass) and Stewart Copeland (drums). Summers so impressed the duo they asked him to join their full-time group, the Police, with whom the guitarist remained until they disbanded. A superbly inventive musician, he did much to popularize the use of the 'flanging' effect, Summers' embarked on several projects; his finely-honed skills were more fully developed on *I Advance Unmasked*, a collaboration with King Crimson's Robert Fripp. Ensuing solo albums have enhanced the guitarist's reputation for both excellence and imagination. Ginger Baker collaborated with him on *Synaesthesia* in 1996.

● ALBUMS: with Robert Fripp *I Advance Unmasked* (A&M 1982)★★★★, with Fripp *Bewitched* (A&M 1984)★★★, *XYZ* (MCA 1987)★★, *Mysterious Barricades* (Private Music 1988)★★★, *The Golden Wire* (Private Music 1989)★★★★, *Charming Snakes* (Private Music 1990)★★★★, *World Gone Strange* (Private Music 1991)★★, with John Etheridge *Invisible Threads* (Mesa 1994)★★★, *Synaesthesia* (CMP 1996)★★★, *The Last Dance Of Mr. X* (RCA Victor 1997)★★★.

Sun Ra

b. Herman P. Blount, 22 May 1914, Birmingham, Alabama, USA, d. 30 May 1993, Birmingham, Alabama, USA. One of the most extraordinary figures in 20th century music who deserves much greater attention, Sun Ra claimed to have arrived here from the planet Saturn on a date that cannot be revealed because of its astrological significance! More down-to-earth researchers have suggested the birth-date above, although this remains unconfirmed. There is a similar uncertainty about his original name: while he sometimes went under the name of Herman 'Sonny' Blount in the 30s and 40s, he also used the name Sonny Lee and claimed that his parents' name was Arman. However, for approximately 40 years he was known as Sun Ra - or, as he announced to countless concert audiences, 'Some call me Mr Ra, some call me Mr Re. You can call me Mr Mystery.' His first musical memories are of hearing classic blues singers such as Bessie Smith and Ethel Waters and he grew up a fan of the swing bands, especially those led by Fletcher Henderson. His early work experience as pianist, arranger and composer included stints with Fess Wheatley and Oliver Bibb in the Chicago area in the mid-30s, but this period of his life remains largely undocumented. In 1946 he was at Chicago's Club DeLisa, playing behind visiting jazz and blues artists such as Joe Williams and LaVern Baker and writing arrangements for his idol, Henderson, who had a 15-month residency at the club. Ra then worked with bassist Eugene Wright's Dukes Of Swing in 1948 and also played with Coleman Hawkins and Stuff Smith. In the early 50s he began to lead his own small groups, which soon featured Pat Patrick and John Gilmore, and by the middle of the decade he had assembled a 10-piece big band, the Arkestra, who recorded their debut, *Sun Song*, in 1956. Originally playing an idiosyncratic bebop, with arrangements that also showed the influence of Duke Ellington and Tadd Dameron, the Arkestra had developed by the early 60s into possibly the era's most advanced and experimental group. Ra was one of the first jazz leaders to use two basses, to employ the electric bass, to play electronic keyboards, to use extensive percussion and polyrhythms, to explore modal music and to pioneer solo and group freeform improvisations.

In addition, he made his mark in the wider cultural context: he proclaimed the African origins of jazz, reaffirmed pride in black history and reasserted the spiritual and mystical dimensions of music (all important factors in the black cultural/political renaissance of the 60s). In the late 50s Ra set up his own label, Saturn Records (aka Thoth), one of the first musician-owned labels, and most of his 100-plus recordings have been released on Saturn, although many have been issued or reissued on other labels (notably Impulse! in the 60s and 70s). Nearly all Saturn albums have been limited-edition pressings that appear in plain white or hand-drawn sleeves and are now valued collector's items. (The facts that they are extremely rare, that they often contain no recording details, that they are sometimes reissued under different titles and that some 'new' releases actually comprise a side each from two older albums, all mean that a complete and accurate Sun Ra discography is almost impossible to compile.)

Despite years of severe poverty and relocations from Chicago to New York (1961) and then to Philadelphia (1968), Sun Ra kept the Arkestra in existence for over three decades, though they played under a different name almost every year: examples include the Astro-Infinity Arkestra, the Blue Universe Arkestra, the Cosmo Jet Set Arkestra and the Year 2000 Myth Science Arkestra. The list of illustrious band members over the years takes in Ahmed Abdullah, Marion Brown, Richard Davis, Robin Eubanks, Craig Harris, Billy Higgins, Frank Lowe, Julian Priester, Pharoah Sanders, James Jacson and James Spaulding (there are dozens more), while occasional guest performers have included Lester Bowie, Don Cherry and Archie Shepp. Many players returned for further stints, though the financial rewards were never great, and a handful remained virtually without a break from the very beginning - notably Gilmore and Marshall Allen. Several core band members lived together in a communal house where Ra reportedly imposed strict discipline: he allowed no drugs, no alcohol and was fond of waking everyone up in the middle of the night for extra rehearsals. (He was also credited as the person who persuaded John Coltrane to give up drugs, and Coltrane took saxophone lessons from Gilmore.) Almost from the outset the band wore exotic costumes, usually with Ancient Egyptian or outer space motifs, and used elements of spectacle in their stage act: light shows, dance, mime and an endearing habit of winding through the audience, chanting about their exploits on other planets ('we travel the spaceways, from planet to planet'). In the 70s Ra began to expand his repertoire to include more traditional material, especially big band numbers by the likes of Ellington, Henderson, Jimmie Lunceford and Jelly Roll Morton. At the same time he kept abreast of jazz-funk and also continued to perform his ear-splitting, freeform synthesizer solos, so any live concert by the Arkestra was likely to span the entire gamut of black creative music. Their recordings proved more erratic (and often very low-fi), but over the years they had accumulated a set of indisputable masterpieces, with apparent creative peaks coming in the early/mid-60s (*Jazz In Silhouette, Rocket Number Nine Take Off For The Planet Venus, The Heliocentric Worlds Of Sun Ra, Volumes 1 & 2, Nothing Is, The Magic City*) and the late 70s (*Media Dreams, Disco 3000, Omniverse, Sleeping Beauty, Strange Celestial Road, Sunrise In Different Dimensions*). The Arkestra made occasional guest appearances (for example, they played on three tracks of Phil Alvin's *Unsung Stories* and contributed 'Pink Elephants' to Hal Willner's Disney tribute, *Stay Awake* - an episode that led to them playing entire sets of Disney tunes in the late 80s) and selected members have occasionally made small-group recordings with Ra: for instance, both *New Steps* and *Other Voices, Other Blues* feature Ra, Gilmore, Michael Ray (trumpet) and Luqman Ali (percussion). Sun Ra himself released a handful of solo piano albums - *Monorails & Satellites, Vols 1 & 2, Aurora Borealis, St Louis Blues Solo Piano* - and the duo *Visions* with Walt Dickerson. His piano style ranged across a variety of influences, including blues, Count Basie's bounce, Thelonious Monk's dissonance and a degree of European impressionism.

A stroke in 1990 left Ra with impaired movement, but the Arkestra's 1991 London concerts proved there had been no diminution of musical quality. His influence has been enormous and has seeped through into every nook and cranny of modern music, from Funkadelic to Karlheinz Stockhausen to the Art Ensemble Of Chicago. 'Musically,' said drummer Roger Blank, 'Sun Ra is one of the unacknowledged legislators of the world.' A poet and philosopher too, Ra published several volumes of writings. In fact, while a few critics have seized on items such as the Arkestra's glitzy costumes and space chants to dismiss them as a circus and Ra himself as a freak or charlatan, most of his ideas and proclamations made perfect sense when viewed in the context of African-American culture. Taking a new name, for instance, is a venerable blues tradition (Muddy Waters, Howlin' Wolf, Lead Belly) and Ra's emphasis on Ancient Egypt was just one of the means he used to focus attention on black history and black achievement. More detailed expositions can be found in the chapters on his music and thought in Chris Cutler's *File Under Popular*, John Litweiler's *The Freedom Principle*, Graham Lock's *Forces In Motion* and Valerie Wilmer's *As Serious As Your Life.* A documentary film, *Sun Ra: A Joyful Noise*, directed by Robert Muge, was released in 1980. Sun Ra was one of the great modern visionaries: he not only had a dream, but lived it to the full for over 40 years. He showed that, with imagination, commitment and a love of beauty, one can create one's own future and make the impossible real. Sun Ra left planet Earth in 1993.

● ALBUMS: *Sun Song* (1957)★★★, *Super-Sonic Jazz* (Saturn 1957)★★★★, *Jazz By Sun Ra* (Transition 1957)★★★, *Angels And Demons At Play* (Evidence 1958)★★★, *Jazz In Silhouette* (Saturn 1958)★★★★, *Sun Ra & His Solar Arkestra Visit Planet Earth* (1958)★★★★, *We Travel The Space Ways* (1960)★★★★, *Fate In A Pleasant Mood* (1961)★★★, *The Nubians Of Plutonia* aka *The Lady With The Golden Stockings* (1962)★★★★, *Rocket Number Nine Take Off For The Planet Venus* aka *Interstellar Low Ways* (1962)★★★, *When Sun Comes Out* (Saturn 1963)★★★★, *Bad & Beautiful* (1963)★★★, *The Futuristic Sounds Of Sun Ra* aka *We Are In The Future* (1963)★★★★, *Art Forms Of Dimensions Tomorrow* (Evidence 1965)★★★, *Secrets Of The Sun* (1965)★★★, *When Angels Speak Of Love* (1965)★★★, *The Heliocentric Worlds Of Sun Ra, Vol 1* (ESP 1965)★★★★, *Cosmic Tones For Mental Therapy* (Evidence 1966)★★★, *The Heliocentric Worlds Of Sun Ra, Vol 2* (ESP 1966)★★★★, *The Magic City* (Evidence 1966)★★★★, *Nothing Is* (ESP 1967)★★★★, *Other Planes Of There* (1967)★★★★, *Sound Of Joy* 1957 recording (1968)★★★, *Sun Ra Visits Planet Earth* (Saturn 1958)★★★★, *Holiday For Soul Dance* (Evidence 1968)★★★★, *Atlantis* (Evidence 1968)★★★★, *Sound Sun Pleasure* (1969)★★★, *My Brother The Wind* (1970)★★★★, *The Night Of The Purple Moon* (1970)★★★, *Continuation* (1970)★★★, *Pictures Of Infinity* 1967 recording (1971)★★★, *Nuits De La Fondation Maeght, Vols 1 & 2* (1971)★★★, *The Solar Myth Approach, Vols 1 & 2* (Affinity 1971)★★★, *It's After The End Of The World* (1971)★★★, *Song Of The Stargazers* (1971)★★★, *Strange Strings* 1968 recording (1972)★★★, *To Nature's God* aka *Sun Ra In Egypt* (1972)★★★, *Horizon* (1972)★★★, *Nidhamu* (1972)★★★, *Space Is The Place* (Blue Thumb 1972)★★★★, *Monorails & Satellites, Vol. 1* 1967 recording (1973)★★★, *Astro Black* (1973)★★★, *Monorails & Satellites, Vol. 2* 1967 recording (1974)★★★, *Discipline 27 - 11* (1974)★★★, *Pathways To Unknown Worlds* (1974)★★★, *Dreams Come True* 50s/60s recordings (1975)★★★, *My Brother The Wind, Vol. 2* (1975)★★★, *The Antique Blacks* (1975)★★★, *Cosmo Earth Fantasy* aka *Temple U* aka *Sub-Underground* (1975)★★★, *Taking A Chance On Chances* (1975)★★★, *The Invisible Shield* 50s/60s recordings (1976)★★★, *Featuring Pharoah Sanders And Black Harold* 1964 recording (1976)★★★, *Live In Paris* aka *Live At The Gibus* (1976)★★★, *Outer Spaceways Incorporated* (Black Lion 1977)★★★, *Primitone* (1977)★★★, *Universe In Blue* (1977)★★★, *Discipline 99* aka *Out Beyond The Kingdom Of* (1977)★★★, *What's*

New (1977)★★★, *Over The Rainbow* (1977)★★★, *Celebrations For Dial Tunes* (1978)★★★, *Cosmos* (1978)★★★, *Live At Montreux* (1978)★★★, *Solo Piano* (1978)★★★★, *Unity* (1978)★★★, *New Steps* (1978)★★★, *Other Voices, Other Blues* (1978)★★★, *Media Dreams* (1978)★★★, *Sound Mirror* (1978)★★★, *Disco 3000* (1978)★★★, *Lanquidity* (1978)★★★, *St Louis Blues* (1979)★★★★, *The Soul Vibrations Of Man* aka *Soul Vibrations* (1979)★★★, *The Other Side Of The Sun* (1980)★★★, *Blithe Spirit Dance* (1980)★★★, *Omniverse* (1980)★★★, *Seductive Fantasy* (1980)★★★, *Of Mythic Worlds* (1980)★★★, *Strange Celestial Road* (1980)★★★, *Sleeping Beauty* (1980)★★★, *Dance Of Innocent Passion* (1980)★★★, *Rose Hued Mansions Of The Sun* aka *Voice Of The Eternal Tomorrow* (1981)★★★, *Sunrise In Different Dimensions* (1981)★★★, *Aurora Borealis* (1981)★★★, *I Pharaoh* (1981)★★★, *Some Blues But Not The Kind That's Blue* aka *My Favourite Things* (1981)★★★, *Beyond The Purple Star Zone* (1981)★★★, *Journey Stars Beyond* (1981)★★★, *Otherness Blue* aka *Just Friends* 50s-80s recordings (1983)★★★, *Hiroshima* (1984)★★★, *Sun Ra Meets Salah Ragab In Egypt* (1984)★★★, *Ra To The Rescue* (1984)★★★, *Live At Praxis '84, Vols 1 - 3* (1984)★★★, *A Fireside Chat With Lucifer* (1985)★★★, *Cosmo Sun Connection* (1985)★★★, *Celestial Love* (1985)★★★, *Children Of The Sun* (1986)★★★, *Stars That Shine Darkly* (1986)★★★, *A Night In East Berlin* (1987)★★★, *Reflections In Blue* (1987)★★★, *Love In Outer Space* 1983 recording (1988)★★★, *Live At Pit-Inn, Tokyo* (1988)★★★, *Blue Delight* (A&M 1989)★★★, *Hours After* (1989)★★★, *Cosmo Omnibus Imaginable Illusion* (DIW 1989)★★★, *Out There A Minute* 60s recordings (1989)★★★, *John Cage Meets Sun Ra* (1989)★★★, *Purple Night* (A&M 1990)★★★★, *Sun Ra & His Year 2000 Myth Science Arkestra - Live In London 1990* (1990)★★★★, *Mayan Temples* (Black Saint 1992)★★★, *Destination Unknown* (Leo 1992)★★★, *Friendly Galaxy* (Leo 1993)★★★, *Pleiades* (Leo 1993)★★★, *The Singles* (Evidence 1996)★★★, various artists *Wavelength Infinity* (Rastascan 1996)★★★★, *Calling Planet Earth* 3-CD box set (Freedom 1998)★★★.

● FURTHER READING: *The Immeasurable Equation*, Sun Ra. *Space Is The Place: The Lives And Times Of Sun Ra*, John F. Szwed, *The Earthly Recordings Of Sun Ra*, Robert Campbell.

SUNSHINE, MONTY

b. 8 April 1928, London, England. After teaching himself to play clarinet, Sunshine became involved in the UK trad jazz scene of the late 40s. He was a founder-member of the Crane River Jazz Band and later teamed up with Chris Barber to form a co-operative group. For a while this band was under the nominal leadership of Ken Colyer, but later reverted to its original democratic status. Sunshine was featured on several records, notably 'Petite Fleur', and helped the band to establish a reputation as one of the best of the UK trad outfits. In 1960 he left Barber to form his own band which, while retaining a high level of popularity for a number of years, never equalled the success of the Barber/Sunshine band. However, Sunshine established a name in Europe, especially in Germany. In the 70s he had occasional reunions with the re-formed Crane River Jazz Band and with Barber. Although a proponent of New Orleans jazz, Sunshine's playing style has always favoured the full, romantic sound of musicians such as Sidney Bechet and Barney Bigard. In the 80s and 90s he was often on tour, still popular with the audience he had known from his earliest days in the business.

● ALBUMS: *A Taste Of Sunshine* (DJM 1976)★★★, *Magic Is The Moonlight* (Telefunken 1978)★★★, *Sunshine In London* (Black Lion 1979)★★★, *On Sunday* (Wam 1987)★★★, *Just A Little While To Stay Here* (Lake 1990)★★, *Gotta Travel On* (Timeless 1992)★★★, *South* (Timeless)★★, *Live At The Worker's Museum Copenhagen* (Music Mecca 1997)★★★★.

● COMPILATIONS: *Monty Sunshine And The Crane River Jazz Band, 1950-53* (Dormouse 1988)★★★,

SUPERSAX

Formed in Los Angeles in 1972 by Buddy Clark and Med Flory, the band's original purpose was to recreate the music of Charlie Parker through sparkling orchestrations of Parker's solos scored for a five-piece saxophone section. The original saxophone line-up comprised Flory, Bill Perkins, Jack Nimitz, Warne Marsh and Jay Migliori with trumpeter Conte Candoli and a rhythm section of Ronnell Bright (piano), Clark, and Jake Hanna. Clark left the band in the mid-70s and other changes took place but under Flory's direction they continued to make club appearances in Los Angeles and to record into the late 80s.

● ALBUMS: *Supersax Plays Bird* (Capitol 1972)★★★★, *Salt Peanuts* (Capitol 1974)★★★★, *Supersax Plays Bird With Strings* (Capitol 1974)★★★, *Chasin' The Bird* (Verve 1977)★★★, *Dynamite!* (MPS 1978)★★★★, *Supersax & L.A. Voices* (Columbia 1982)★★★, *Supersax & L.A. Voices, Vol. 2* (Columbia 1984)★★★, *Supersax & L.A. Voices: Straighten Up And Fly Right* (Columbia 1986)★★★, *Stone Bird* (Columbia 1989)★★★.

SURMAN, JOHN

b. John Douglas Surman, 30 August 1944, Tavistock, Devon, England. Surman, a remarkable player on soprano and baritone saxophones, bass clarinet, bamboo flutes and sometimes tenor saxophone and synthesizers. He was a member of the Jazz Workshop at Plymouth Arts Centre with Mike Westbrook while still at school, and came to London with Westbrook's band in 1962. He studied at London College of Music (1962-65) and London University Institute of Education (1966). By the time he ceased to be a regular member of Westbrook's band in 1968 he was also working in Ronnie Scott's nine-piece outfit (the Band) with Humphrey Lyttelton and had twice been voted the world's best baritone saxophone player by *Melody Maker* readers as well as top instrumentalist at the 1968 Montreux International Jazz Festival. Since then various of his albums have collected awards from all over the world. From 1968-69 he led a group, varying from a quartet to an octet, centring round Mike Osborne, Harry Miller and Alan Jackson. During the 60s and 70s he also played with Alexis Korner's New Church, Mike Gibbs, Graham Collier, Chris McGregor, Dave Holland, John McLaughlin (on the guitarist's acclaimed *Extrapolation*), John Warren and Harry Beckett. Owing to lack of work in the UK, he emigrated to Europe where he formed the Trio with Barre Phillips and Stu Martin. Surman next worked with Terje Rypdal (*Morning Glory*), before the Trio briefly re-formed, augmented by Albert Mangelsdorff to become MUMPS. At this time he first met Jack DeJohnette with whom he was to work regularly in the 80s and 90s. In 1973 he formed another highly impressive and influential trio, S.O.S., with Osborne and Alan Skidmore. He began experimenting with electronics during this period, a facet of his work explored in depth on his albums of the late 70s and 80s. He formed duos with Stan Tracey and Karin Krog in 1978 (the latter becoming a regular musical associate), and from 1979-82 worked with Miroslav Vitous. Surman also composes for all sizes of jazz groups, as well as writing pieces for choirs and for dance companies, notably the Carolyn Carlson Dance Theatre at the Paris Opera, with whom he worked from 1974-79. In 1981, Surman's pivotal album *The Amazing Adventures Of Simon Simon* was released. This was the springboard for a number of beautiful recordings that started with *Upon Reflection* and re-defined the word sparseness. Working solo, save for the contribution of Jack DeJohnette (drums, congas, electric piano) *The Amazing Adventures Of Simon Simon* arguably remains Surman's finest work. That year he also formed the Brass Project, working with the noted arranger John Warren and during the 80s he was a member of Gil Evans' British band and later of his New York band. He also worked with Paul Bley and Bill Frisell and, in 1986, toured with Elvin Jones, Holland and Mangelsdorff. In 1990 the conceptual *Road To St Ives* explored themes of Simon Simon. This was another brilliant and evocative solo excursion travelling through Cornwall from 'Polperro' to 'Bedruthan Steps'. In the early 90s he recorded some memorable albums working with John Abercrombie, Marc Johnson, Krog, Rypdal and Mangelsdorff, although it is his solo work of recent years that has been particularly inspired, notably *Stranger Than Fiction* in 1994 and another conceptual project, *A Biography Of The Rev. Absolom Dave*. Surman is a powerful and resourceful improviser who leaves out more than he puts in. He is without doubt one of the key figures in contemporary jazz over the past three decades.

● ALBUMS: *Release* (1968)★★★, *John Surman* (1968)★★★★, *How Many Clouds Can You See* (1969)★★★, with John McLaughlin *Extrapolation* (1969)★★★, *Marching Song* (1969)★★★, *Where Fortune Smiles* (1970)★★★, *The Trio* (1970)★★★, *Conflagration* (1971)★★★, with John Warren *Tales Of The Algonquin* (1971)★★★, *Westering Home* (1972)★★★, *Morning Glory* (1973)★★★, *S.O.S.* (1975)★★★, *Live At Woodstock Town Hall* (1975)★★★, *Live At Moers Festival* (1975)★★★, *Surman For All Saints* (Ogun 1979)★★★, *Upon Reflection* (ECM 1979)★★★, *The Amazing Adventures Of Simon Simon* (ECM 1981)★★★★, with Karin Krog *Such Winters Of Memory* (ECM 1982)★★★, with Barry Altschul *Irina* (1983)★★★, *Withholding Pattern* (ECM 1984)★★★, with Paul Bley *Fragments* (1986)★★★, with Alexis Korner *Alexis Korner And ... 1961-72* (1986)★★★, with the Trio *By Contact* recorded 1971 (1987)★★★★, *Private City* (ECM 1987)★★★, *The Paul Bley Quartet* (1988)★★★, *The Road To St. Ives* (ECM 1990)★★★★, *Adventure Playground* (ECM 1991)★★★, with John Taylor *Ambleside Days* (1992)★★★, with John Warren *The Brass Project* (ECM 1993)★★★★, with Albert Mangelsdorff *Room 1220* (1993)★★★, with John Abercrombie, Marc Johnson, Peter Erskine *November* (ECM 1994)★★★, *Stranger Than Fiction* (ECM 1994)★★★★, with Krog, Terje Rypdal, Vigleik Storaas *Nordic Quartet* (ECM 1995)★★★, *A Biography Of The Rev. Absolom Dave* (ECM 1995)★★★★, *Proverbs And Songs* (ECM 1998)★★★★, with Anouar Brahem, Dave Holland *Thimar* (ECM 1998)★★★★.

SUTTON, RALPH

b. 4 November 1922, Hamburg, Missouri, USA. After playing piano locally for several years, Sutton joined Jack Teagarden in 1941. During the 40s he attracted widespread attention, thanks to his participation in a series of radio shows hosted by jazz writer Rudi Blesh. From the late 40s through to the mid-50s he played regularly at Eddie Condon's club in New York. In the 60s he worked mostly as a single, but also played in a number of traditional bands and towards the end of the decade was a founder-member of the World's Greatest Jazz Band. Thereafter, Sutton's star rose and remained in the ascendancy with a series of record albums and world tours, solo and in a variety of settings. His musical partners in these ventures included Ruby Braff, Jay McShann, Kenny Davern and Peanuts Hucko. He continues to perform with great panache and a seemingly undiminished level of invention into the early 90s. An outstanding pianist in the great tradition of stride giants such as James P. Johnson and Fats Waller, Sutton's style is both forceful and lightly dancing, as the needs of his repertoire demand. Although drawing from the century-old tradition of jazz piano, from ragtime through the blues to Harlem stride, Sutton brings to his playing such inventive enthusiasm that everything he does seems freshly minted.

● ALBUMS: *Piano Moods* (Columbia 1950)★★★, *Ralph Sutton* (Commodore 1951)★★★★, *Ralph Sutton Plays The Music Of Fats Waller* (1951)★★★★, *Ralph Sutton At The Piano* (1952)★★★, one side only *Stacy 'N' Sutton* (1953) ★★, with Lee Collins *The Hangover All Stars Live 1953* (1953)★★★, *I Got Rhythm* (Decca 1953)★★★★, *Ralph Sutton's Jazzola Six* (1953)★★★, *Ragtime Piano Solos* (Down Home 1953)★★★, *Ralph Sutton And The All Stars* (1954)★★★, *Backroom Piano: The Ragtime Piano Of Ralph Sutton* (Down Home 1955)★★★, *Classic Jazz Piano* (Riverside 1956)★★★★, *A Salute To Fats* (Harmony 1958)★★, *The Ralph Sutton Quartet* i (1959)★★★★, *Ragtime USA* (Roulette 1963)★★★, *The Ralph Sutton Trio* (1966)★★★, with Ruby Braff *On Sunnie's Side Of The Street* (1968)★★★★, *The Night They Raided Sunnie's* (1969)★★★, with Yank Lawson and Bob Wilber *The Ralph Sutton Trio And Guests* (1969)★★★, *Piano Moods* (1975)★★, *Off The Cuff* (1975)★★★, *Suttonly It Jumped* (1975)★★★, *Live!* (1975)★★, *Changes* (1976)★★★, *Jazz At The Forum* (1976)★★, *Live At Haywards Heath* (Flyright 1976)★★★, *The Ralph Sutton Quartet* ii (1977)★★★, with Wild Bill Davison *Together Again* (1977)★★★, *Stomp Off, Let's Go* (1977)★★★★, *The Other Side Of Ralph Sutton* (1980)★★, with Braff *Quartet* (1980)★★★, *Ralph Sutton & Ruby Braff: Duets* (1980)★★★, with

Jay McShann *The Last Of The Whorehouse Piano Players Vols 1 & 2* (Chiaroscuro 1980)★★★, *Ralph Sutton & Kenny Davern Trio Vols 1 & 2* (1980)★★★, *Ralph Sutton And The Jazz Band* (1981)★★, with Eddie Miller *We've Got Rhythm* (1981)★★★, *Ralph Sutton & Jack Lesberg* (1981)★★★, *The Big Noise From Wayzata* (1981)★★★, *Great Piano Solos And Duets* (1982)★★★, *Live At Hanratty's* (1982)★★, *Blowin' Bubbles* (1982)★★★, *Partners In Crime* (Sackville 1983)★★★, *At Cafe Des Copains* (Sackville 1987)★★★, Bix Beiderbecke Suite (Commodore Class 1987)★★★, with the Sackville All Stars *A Tribute To Louis Armstrong* (1988)★★, *Alligator Crawl* (Jazzology 1989)★★★, *Eye Opener* (J&M 1990)★★★, *Maybeck Recital Hall Series Vol 30* (Concord 1993)★★★, *Easy Street* (Sackville 1998)★★★★, *Echoes Of Swing* (Nagel-Heyer 1998)★★★.

● COMPILATIONS: *Piano Solos In The Classic Jazz Tradition* (1949-52)★★★★, *Piano Solos/Beiderbecke Suite* (1950)★★★, *The Ralph Sutton Trio* (1950)★★★.

Swallow, Steve

b. 4 October 1940, Fair Lawn, New Jersey, USA. Swallow started out on trumpet, then took up the double bass at the age of 18. At college he played bebop with Ian Underwood (later saxophonist with Frank Zappa). In 1960, he joined the Paul Bley Trio, later working with Jimmy Giuffre, Art Farmer and George Russell and winning the *Down Beat* critics' poll as new star in 1964. In June 1965 he joined the Stan Getz Quartet, with which he played until 1967. Between 1967 and 1970, he was in Gary Burton's quartet and between 1970 and 1973 he played in San Francisco with pianists Art Lande and Mike Nock before returning to work with Burton. Since the early 70s he has played intermittently with Mike Gibbs, but has worked most regularly with Carla Bley (his current partner), playing in her various groups of the late 70s and 80s. In 1980 he set music to poems by Robert Creeley for the album *Home*. By the mid-70s he was playing nothing but electric bass, using a pick, and producing a sound that was popular with the current arrangers. He is also a prolific composer, with credits on Gibbs, Burton and Chick Corea albums for titles such as 'Arise Her Eyes', 'Chelsea Bells', 'Como En Vietnam' and 'Hotel Hello'. John Scofield, who has recorded and played with Swallow over many years, regards him as his mentor. In the late 80s Swallow recorded a set of duos with Bley and also began to work with UK saxophonist Andy Sheppard, producing his first three albums as a leader and playing with him in 1991 in a trio that also featured Bley. Swallow remains a hugely underrated and highly talented figure in recent jazz.

● ALBUMS: with Gary Burton *Hotel Hello* (ECM 1974)★★★, *Home* (ECM 1980)★★★, with Carla Bley *Carla* (ECM 1987)★★, with Carla Bley *Duets* (ECM 1988)★★★, with Paul Bley, Jimmy Giuffre *The Diary Of A Trio: Saturday* (Owl 1990)★★★★, with Paul Bley, Giuffre *The Diary Of A Trio: Sunday* (Owl 1990)★★★, *Swallow* (ECM/XtraWatt 1991)★★★, with Carla Bley *Go Together* (ECM 1993)★★★, *Real Book* (ECM/XtraWatt 1994)★★★, with Paul Bley, Giuffre *Conversations With A Goose* (Soul Note 1996)★★★★, *Deconstructed* (ECM/XtraWatt 1997)★★★★.

Sweatman, Wilbur

b. 7 February 1882, Brunswick, Missouri, USA, d. 9 March 1961. Sweatman played violin, later clarinet, with various bands at the turn of the century. Often, these were large orchestras that toured with circuses and tent shows. In 1902 he formed his own orchestra, touring with it and sometimes playing residencies at theatres and restaurants in Chicago and New York. In 1923 he played at the opening of Connie's Inn, and in that same year the young Duke Ellington was briefly in his band. Sweatman's virtuoso playing was designed for audience appeal, incorporating elements of showmanship. By the end of the 20s, Sweatman moved out of performing but retained his showbusiness interests, working in booking, publicity and music publishing. In the 40s, he returned to performing, leading a small group in New York. Among his many compositions is 'Down Home Rag'.

Sweet And Low-Down

Only one good reason for staying up late to watch this 1944 film (if it is ever shown on television) and that is Benny Goodman. Fortunately, he and his orchestra and quartet are on-screen rather a lot in this tale of a swing band on tour. Although this was not Goodman's best band, there are still several good musicians on hand. Some are seen, others only heard while actors mime their instruments. Amongst the musicians are Bill Harris, Zoot Sims, Morey Feld, Jess Stacy, Sid Weiss, Allan Reuss, Heinie Beau and Al Klink. (Alternative title: *Moment For Music*).

Sweet Love, Bitter

A film directed by Herbert Daniels in 1966, this is an uneven and slightly self-conscious attempt to examine racial problems in the USA through the life of a jazz musician. Based upon the novel *Night Song*, by John Alfred Williams, the story loosely portrays Charlie Parker's final years. Dick Gregory stars as the saxophone player, dubbed by Charles McPherson. Also heard are Chick Corea and Steve Swallow. The musical director was Mal Waldron. (Alternative title: *It Won't Rub Off, Baby*).

Swift, Duncan

b. 21 February 1943, Rotherham, Yorkshire, England, d. 8 August 1997, Bewdley, Worcestershire, England. Swift was one of the most authentic artisans in the stride piano jazz tradition, even though he came to the style, with its sophisticated musical variations, long after its mass appeal had ended. He had originally trained in classical music, obtaining two diplomas and a degree at the Birmingham School of Music. He started playing jazz by the age of 14, and pursued this interest in the evenings throughout his classical studies. Following in the footsteps of American greats headed by Fats Waller and also including James P. Johnson and Ralph Sutton, Swift established himself as the premier British exponent of the frenetic stride method. The first stride pianists - a style derived from classic ragtime but additionally featuring quick crescendos of rhythm to give the music 'swing' - had originally been recorded on the metal cylinders from which piano rolls were constructed, and aspiring pianists would learn by copying from the patterns of holes drilled through the hammer marks. However, unbeknownst to the early stride pianists, extra holes were later drilled in - saturating already complex piano patterns with new notes. Nevertheless, Swift was one of the pianists who somehow managed to emulate those technically obtuse patterns. After playing with Rotherham's Jazz Hounds, he joined Mike Taylor's Jazz Band and took up the trombone. When he and his family relocated to the Midlands in 1960, he played with trumpeter Jim Simpson. Through Simpson's numerous connections (he also edited a jazz magazine and worked as a promoter), Swift enjoyed a high-profile concert career in the 80s and 90s. He also released a brace of CDs for Simpson's Big Bear label, which brought modest acclaim. As well as working with the Bill Niles Jazz Band, forming his own group, the New Delta Jazzmen, and spending seven years as a member of Kenny Ball's band, Swift augmented his income from the 60s onwards as a music teacher. In 1983 he bought a Worcestershire pub with the intention of retiring from live music. Inevitably, however, he returned to performance by the end of the decade. For the last of his three albums he invoked his own record label; 1993's *The Key Of D Is Daffodil Yellow* featured skilful interpretations of Jelly Roll Morton and Fats Waller material, alongside his own compositions. Despite ailing health in the 90s, he continued to make a series of live concert, television and radio appearances.

● ALBUMS: *Out Looking For The Lion* (Big Bear 1988)★★★, *The Broadwood Concert* (Big Bear 1991)★★★, *The Key Of D Is Daffodil Yellow* (own label 1993)★★.

SWINGLE SINGERS

The commercial success of this French choir undermined many engrained prejudices by pop consumers against serious music, preparing them for Walter Carlos's *Switched-On Bach*, Deep Purple's *Concerto For Group And Orchestra* and the promotion of the Portsmouth Sinfonia as a pop act. In 1963, the Singers were assembled by Ward Lamar Swingle (b. 21 September 1927, Mobile, Alabama, USA), a former conductor of Les Ballets De Paris. Addressing themselves to jazzy arrangements of the classics - particularly Bach - their wordless style had the novel effect of predetermined mass scat-singing. After *Jazz Sebastian Bach* and *Bach's Greatest Hits* made respective inroads into the UK and US Top 20, the outfit was catapulted into an arduous schedule of television and radio appearances during back-to-back world tours that embraced over 2,000 concerts by 1991. While the main choir continued to earn Grammy awards for 1965's *Going Baroque* and similar variations on his original concept, Swingle formed a smaller unit (Swingles II) for more contemporary challenges such as Luciano Berio's *Sinfonia* which was premiered in New York in 1973 - and for *Cries, A-Ronne* and other increasingly more complex works by the same composer.

● ALBUMS: *Bach's Greatest Hits* (1963)★★★, *Jazz Sebastian Bach* (1963)★★★★, *Going Baroque* (1964)★★★, *Anyone For Mozart?* (Philips 1965)★★★, *Place Vendome* (Philips 1966)★★★, *Folio* (1980)★★★, *Swingle Singers Christmas Album* (1980)★★★★, *Anyone For Mozart, Bach, Handel, Vivaldi?* (1986)★★★.

● COMPILATIONS: *Compact Jazz: Best Of The Swingle Singers* (Verve 1987)★★★★.

SYKES, ROOSEVELT

b. 31 January 1906, Elmar, Arkansas, USA, d. 17 July 1983. Sykes learned piano at the age of 12 and by the early 20s was playing in local barrelhouses. He moved to St. Louis in 1928 and his first records for OKeh and Victor were made from 1929-31. During the 30s, Sykes recorded for Decca and acted as a talent scout for the label. Among his most popular compositions were 'Night Time Is The Right Time' and 'The Honeydripper', which was Sykes' nickname. He settled in Chicago in the early 40s, becoming the piano accompanist on numerous city blues records by artists such as St. Louis Jimmy and Lonnie Johnson. In 1954, he moved to New Orleans and continued to record prolifically for Decca, Prestige, Spivey, Folkways, Delmark and other labels. The Prestige album *Honeydripper* featured King Curtis on saxophone. His versatility in different piano styles meant that Sykes was well placed to take advantage of the increased European interest in blues and he made his first visit to the UK in 1961, performing with Chris Barber's jazz band. He returned in 1965 and 1966 with the Folk Blues Festival package and played many US blues and jazz festivals in the 70s. As a result of his popularity with these new audiences, much of his pre-1945 work was reissued in the 70s/80s.

● ALBUMS: *Big Man Of The Blues* (1959)★★★, *Return Of Roosevelt Sykes* (Bluesville 1960)★★★, *Honeydripper* (Bluesville 1961)★★★, *Hard Drivin' Blues* (Delmark 1963)★★★, *Blues From Bar Rooms* (1967)★★★, *Feel Like Blowing My Horn* (Delmark 1973)★★★, *Dirty Double Mother* (1973)★★★, with Victoria Spivey *Grind It!* (Sequel 1996)★★★, *Music Is My Business* 1977 recording (The Blues Alliance 1996)★★★.

● COMPILATIONS: *The Original Honeydripper* (Blind Pig 1988)★★★, *The Honeydripper 1945-1960* (Blues Encore 1992)★★★, *Roosevelt Sykes 1931-1941* (Best Of Blues 1996)★★★.

● VIDEOS: *Roosevelt Sykes/Jay 'Hootie' McShann* (1992).

SYMPHONY IN BLACK

A very short but fascinating film made in 1934 that offers an opportunity to see and hear Duke Ellington And His Orchestra and Billie Holiday. Ellington's musicians include Artie Whetsol, Cootie Williams, Joe Nanton, Lawrence Brown, Johnny Hodges, Harry Carney and Sonny Greer. Holiday, in the first of her few film appearances, sings 'Saddest Tale'.

Syms, Sylvia

b. Sylvia Blagman, 2 December 1917, Brooklyn, USA, d. 10 May 1992, New York, USA. One of America's most distinguished cabaret and jazz singers with a profound appreciation of lyrics, Sylvia Syms overcame polio as a child, and in her teens discovered the delights of jazz in the clubs of New York's 52nd Street. Inspired and trained by Billie Holiday, she made her singing debut in 1941 at Kelly's Stable, and in 1948 was spotted while performing at the Cinderella Club in Greenwich Village by Mae West, who gave her the part of Flo the Shoplifter in a revival of *Diamond Lil*. She subsequently appeared in the regional theatre on many occasions as Bloody Mary in *South Pacific* and as Dolly Levi in *Hello, Dolly!*, and also acted in straight roles. Signed to Decca, she had a million-selling record in 1956 with an up-tempo version of 'I Could Have Danced All Night' from *My Fair Lady*, and enjoyed further success with 'English Muffins And Irish Stew' and 'It's Good To Be Alive'. Frank Sinatra called her the 'Buddha' on account of her short 'beer barrel' stature, but he was one of her greatest admirers, hailing her as 'the best saloon singer in the world'. He also produced her 1982 album *Syms By Sinatra*. In the late 80s and early 90s, Syms still performed occasionally at intimate venues such as Eighty Eight's, Michael's Pub, and Freddy's in New York, where sensitive audiences thrilled to her tasteful selections, which included such delights as 'Skylark', 'You Are Not My First Love', 'I Want To Be Yours', 'Fun To Be Fooled', 'I Guess I'll Hang My Tears Out To Dry', 'It Amazes Me', and 'Pink Taffeta'. She died of a heart attack while performing a tribute programme to Frank Sinatra in the Oak Room of the Algonquin Hotel in Manhattan.

● ALBUMS: *Sings* (Atlantic 50s)★★★, *That Man* (Kapp 1961)★★★★, *Sylvia Syms Is* (Prestige 60s)★★, *In A Sentimental Mood* (Movietone (1967)★★, *For Once In My Life* (Prestige 1967)★★★, *Syms By Sinatra* (Reprise 1982)★★★, *Along Came Bill* (80s)★★★, *You Must Believe In Spring* (Cabaret 1992)★★★, *A Jazz Portrait Of Johnny Mercer* 1984 recording (Koch 1995)★★.

Syncopation

Directed by William Dieterle, this 1942 film offers a Hollywood eye-view of the story of jazz. Predictably, accuracy is a minor consideration but there are some nice musical moments from a band of winners of a poll held by the *Saturday Evening Post*, whose readers seem to have heard of Benny Goodman and a few other swing era musicians but very little else. Apart from Goodman there are Harry James, Jack Jenney, Charlie Barnet, Joe Venuti, Bob Haggart and Gene Krupa. Stan Wrightsman dubbed the soundtrack for Bonia Granville, Bunny Berigan for Jackie Cooper, and Rex Stewart for Todd Duncan.

Szabo, Frank J.

b. 16 September 1952, Budapest, Hungary. Szabo was raised in Los Angeles where he studied trumpet. His first important engagement was with the Harry James band in the early 70s and he also played in a band accompanying Ray Charles on tour. He then spent time with Louie Bellson, Count Basie, Chuck Mangione and the Capp-Pierce Juggernaut. In the 80s he continued to play with big bands, particularly those based in the Los Angeles area and which included Capp-Pierce, Basie and Woody Herman. A fluent musician with remarkable technical resources, he is a first-call trumpeter with many leaders requiring strong players for club, concert and recording dates. On album sleeves his name is sometimes spelled 'Zsabo'.

● ALBUMS: with Frank Capp *In A Hefti Bag* (Concord 1994-95)★★★★.

Szabó, Gabor

b. 1936, Budapest, Hungary, d. 26 February 1982. Guitarist Szabó emigrated to the USA in 1956 to study at the Berklee College Of Music. He came to notice playing with Chico Hamilton and Charles Lloyd. In the late 60s he began to explore a fusion of jazz with the kind of rock that was superficially influenced by Indian music. He introduced a number of Eastern styles into his playing. Although his Hungarian roots probably predisposed him towards an empathy with these elements, they were often seen as mere gimmicks, and he was generally dismissed by the critics. The eclectic albums made under his own name were very much of their time, and he was not an important figure, but in his work with Lloyd and Hamilton, he showed himself capable of warm-toned and subtle playing.

● ALBUMS: with Charles Lloyd *Of Course Of Course* (1965)★★★, *Spellbinder* (1967)★★★★, *The Sorcerer* (1967)★★★, *Bacchanal* (1968)★★★, *Gabor Szabó 1969* (1969)★★★, with Lena Horne *Lena & Gabor* (Skye 1970)★★★★, *Nightflight* (1976)★★★, *Rambler, Wind, Sky And Diamonds* (1977)★★★, *Macho* (1978)★★★, *Mizra* (1978)★★, *Belsta River*, (Four Leaf Clover 1988)★★, with Bobby Womack *High Contrast* (Affinity 1988)★★, *Small World* (Four Leaf Clover 1988)★★★.

● COMPILATIONS: *His Greatest Hits* (1977)★★★.

Tabackin, Lew

b. 26 March 1940, Philadelphia, Pennsylvania, USA. Tabackin studied music extensively - at high school, the Philadelphia Conservatory and privately - before beginning his playing career in 1965. He played tenor saxophone and flute with various bands in and around New York, including those led by Tal Farlow, Maynard Ferguson, Clark Terry, Cab Calloway, the band led by Larry and Les Elgart, the Thad Jones-Mel Lewis Jazz Orchestra and the rehearsal bands of Duke Pearson and Chuck Israels. He also led his own small group and was active in the east coast television studios. In the late 60s he was briefly in Europe, playing and teaching in Germany and Denmark. In 1970 he began a musical, and eventually personal relationship with Toshiko Akiyoshi. After their marriage he was principal soloist with their orchestra, which was based in Los Angeles during the 70s and in New York from the early 80s. In the late 80s and early 90s he was frequently on tour around the world, usually as a single.

A superb technician on tenor saxophone, Tabackin's powerful playing style contains echoes of several of his influences, most strikingly Sonny Rollins. He is, however, a distinctive and accomplished performer in his own right. His solos, often dazzling and lengthy unaccompanied cadenzas interpolated into Akiyoshi's frequently complex charts, are filled with extraordinarily fluent and brilliantly executed ideas. In contrast Tabackin's flute-playing gleams with softly executed yet vivid concepts. In addition to his albums with the Akiyoshi-Tabackin band, he has also recorded with Bill Berry (who was instrumental in introducing Tabackin and Akiyoshi to one another), with Louie Bellson, fellow tenorist Warne Marsh, Toshiyuki Miyama and his New Herd on *Vintage Tenor*, and with his own small groups.

● ALBUMS: *Tabackin* (Inner City 1975)★★★, *Dual Nature* (Inner City 1976)★★★, *Trackin'* (1976)★★★, *Tenor Gladness* (Inner City 1977)★★★, *Rites Of Pan* (Inner City 1977)★★★, *Vintage Tenor* (1978)★★★, *Black And Tan Fantasy* (Ascent 1979)★★★★, *Lew Tabackin Quartet* (1983)★★★, *Angelica* (1984)★★★, *Desert Lady* (Concord Jazz 1989)★★★★, *I'll Be Seeing You* (Concord Jazz 1992)★★★★, *What A Little Moonlight Can Do* (Concord Jazz 1994)★★★★, *Live At Vartan Jazz* (Vartan Jazz 1995)★★★, *Tenority* (Concord Jazz 1997)★★★.

Tacuma, Jamaaladeen

b. Rudy MacDaniel, 11 June 1956, Hempstead, New York, USA. Tacuma grew up in Philadelphia and sang doo-wop as a teenager. He has named his youthful inspirations as James Brown, the Temptations and Stevie Wonder. He started playing double bass at the age of 13 and his first professional gig was with organist Charles Earland. He was brought to the world's attention by his participation in Ornette Coleman's seminal *Dancing In Your Head* in 1977 (his name was still listed as Rudy MacDaniel since this was before his conversion to Islam). He had the ability to combine slick, dance-orientated riffs with an ear open to Coleman's harmolodic weaving of contrasting keys and tempi. He also appeared on *Body Meta* (1978, recorded 1975) and *Of Human Feelings* (1979) as part of Prime Time, Coleman's electric band. In 1978 he played on James Blood Ulmer's thunderous masterpiece *Tales Of Captain Black*. In 1981 he received the highest number of votes ever received for an electric bassist in the 'Talent Deserving Wider Recognition' category of the *Down Beat* critics' poll. His debut for Gramavision in 1983, *Showstopper* presented his own sleek, airbrushed version of harmolodics. The follow-up, *Renaissance Man* (1984), featured a disco version of the 'Dancing In Your Head' theme (on which Coleman guested), a poem for Paul Robeson and an extended suite for string quartet and fretless bass; the album lived up to its name. Having produced the excellent '(I Want To) Squeeze You Hold You' for Willy (Mink) DeVille in 1983, he went on to form a pop/dance band, Cosmetic, who released a cover version of Smokey Robinson's 'Get Ready' for Rough Trade Records and a (stunning) album of out-and-out commercial music, *So Tranquilizin'*. Such attention to the commercial jugular caused Bill Laswell to call him the 'pimp' of harmolodics; Tacuma preferred to call it a 'Trojan horse' operation. In April 1985 he presented his music at Carnegie Recital Hall with the Ebony String Quartet, drummer Anton Fier and an orchestra led by Anthony Davis. The same year Tacuma was back with Prime Time for *Opening At The Caravan Of Dreams* and he also played on the harmolodic half of Coleman's 1987 *In All Languages* double set. *Music World* (1987) and *Juke Box* (1989) confirmed his ability to flit between genres while maintaining his own special flavour. Other involvements have been as a founder-member of Golden Palominos, and backing both guitarist Jeff Beck and poet Jayne Cortez.

● ALBUMS: *Showstopper* (Gramavision 1983)★★★★, with Cosmetic *So Tranquilizin'* (Gramavision 1984)★★★, *Renaissance Man* (1984)★★★, *Music World* (Sonet 1987)★★, *Juke Box* (1989)★★★, *Boss Of The Bass* (Gramavision 1993)★★★★, *Dreamscape* (DIW 1996)★★★.

Takahashi, Tatsuya

b. 24 December 1931, Yamagata, Japan. As a young man Takahashi played saxophones, becoming a professional musician in the early 50s. He became well known in Japan as a tenor player and, eventually, as a bandleader. In 1966 he formed his big band, Tokyo Union, a powerhouse outfit with a strong, rhythmic pulse and often fearsome playing from the brass. Takahashi's solo style is strong, with a mainstream bent. His high standards of musicianship are demonstrated by the well-rehearsed band he leads.

● ALBUMS: *Maiden Voyage* (TMB 1976)★★★, *Scandinavian Suite* (TBM 1977)★★★★, *Funpico With Ueda Chikara* (Warners 1978)★★★, *Black Pearl* (Victor-Zen Zen 1980)★★★, *Chasin' The Duke* (Carnival 1983)★★, *Beauties* (TDK 1984)★★★.

TAKE 6

Initially a quartet known as the Sounds Of Distinction then the Alliance, this highly rated ensemble first formed in northern Alabama, USA, in 1980. The group evolved into a six-piece a cappella gospel group of breathtaking ability. The members are Alvin Chea, Cedric Dent, David Thomas, Mervyn Warren, Mark Kibble and Claude V. McKnight. The combination of their Seventh-day Adventist beliefs and their appreciation of jazz and R&B styles has enabled them to make inroads into both record-buying markets, winning Grammies for best Soul Gospel and best Jazz Vocal categories. Their 1990 appearance with k.d. lang in the movie *Dick Tracy* singing 'Ridin' The Rails' also gave them further valuable exposure. Additionally they have recorded with artists including Dianne Reeves, Quincy Jones and Joe Sample. *Join The Band* marked a new direction for the group as it incorporated live musicians including Greg Phillinganes, Gerald Albright and Herbie Hancock. It also featured lead vocals from Ray Charles, Stevie Wonder and a rap from Queen Latifah. Music writer David Okamota aptly described Take 6 as 'winning over a loyal congregation of secular fans with a soothing, uplifting sound that stirs the soul without twisting the arm'.

● ALBUMS: *Take 6* (Reprise 1988)★★★, *So Much 2 Say* (Reprise 1990)★★★★, *He Is Christmas* (Reprise 1992)★★, *Join The Band* (Reprise 1994)★★★, *Brothers* (Reprise 1996)★★★, *So Cool* (Reprise 1998)★★★★.

TANA, AKIRA

b. 14 March 1952, San Jose, California, USA. A self-taught drummer, Tana played semi-professionally while still at college. He attended Harvard University where he gained a degree in East Asian Studies/Sociology. He then studied at the New England Conservatory of Music, also taking private tuition from percussionists with the Boston Symphony and Boston Pops Orchestras and from jazz drummer Alan Dawson. During his studies he had the opportunity of working with Helen Humes, Milt Jackson, Sonny Rollins, George Russell, Sonny Stitt and other leading jazz musicians. He also played with the Boston Symphony Orchestra and several of the classical music ensembles at the New England Conservatory. In the early 80s he continued to accompany major artists such as Al Cohn, Art Farmer, Benny Golson, Jim Hall, Jimmy Rowles, Zoot Sims and Cedar Walton. He also performed with artists outside the jazz world, including Charles Aznavour and Lena Horne. Tana recorded extensively during these years and in addition to albums with some of the foregoing also appeared with Ran Blake, Chris Connor, Carl Fontana, Jimmy Heath, Tete Montoliu, Spike Robinson, Warne Marsh and many others. In the early 90s Tana worked with James Moody, Dizzy Gillespie, Frank Wess, Ray Bryant and J.J. Johnson. With Rufus Reid he formed the band TanaReid and, with Reid and Kei Akagi, the Asian American Jazz Trio. A technically accomplished drummer, Tana's wide range is hinted at by the musicians with whom he has worked. Comfortably at home accompanying singers and instrumental ballads, Tana is equally in his element playing hard bop. In the bands he co-leads with Reid he generates an excitingly propulsive rhythmic drive. In addition to playing, Tana has also produced and co-produced several albums including those by TanaReid, the Asian American Jazz trio and Project G-7. He regularly conducts workshops and clinics at colleges and universities, including Berklee College Of Music, and is an adjunct professor at two colleges.

● ALBUMS: with Zoot Sims *I Wish I Were Twins* (1983)★★★, with TanaReid *Yours And Mine* (1990)★★★★, with Sumi Tonooka *Taking Time* (1990)★★★, with Asian American Jazz Trio *Sound Circle* (1991)★★★, with Project G-7 *A Tribute To Wes Montgomery Vol. 1* (1991)★★★, *Yours And Mine* (Concord 1991)★★, with TanaReid *Passing Thoughts* (Concord 1992)★★★★, *Blue Motion* (Paddlewheel 1994)★★★, *Looking Forward* (Evidence 1995)★★★★.

TANIA MARIA

b. 9 May 1948, São Luis, Maranhao, Brazil. An excellent pianist, powerful singer and enchanting live performer, Tania Maria combines in her staccato vocal style the rhythmic virtues of bebop and Latin dance, with a strong commitment to spontaneity. She learned classical piano at first, discovered the work of Nat 'King' Cole and Oscar Peterson, and moved to Paris in 1974. Maria's vitality won her a contract at a Paris nightclub for a three-month residency, and she stayed in the city for the next seven years, recording several albums that emphasized her Brazilian roots. She played the 1975 Newport Jazz Festival opposite Sarah Vaughan, was encouraged by the guitarist Charlie Byrd, and in 1981 she recorded *Piquant* for the USA label Concord, moved to the USA and began to develop a successful recording career there. Live recordings have best captured her essence (1984's *Wild!* is one of her most impressive), and recent commercial funk outings have obscured her originality and vividness, but her concert performances still reveal an artist of energy, musicality and originality. *No Comment* is relaxing and smooth while exploring the outer fringes of dance and funk. A lyric sheet is not required to appreciate her work, merely an open mind and open ears.

● ALBUMS: *Brazil With My Soul* (1978)★★★, *Live* (1978)★★, *Tania Maria Et Niels-Henning Ørsted Pedersen* (1979)★★★★, *Piquant* (Concord 1981)★★★, *Taurus* (1982)★★★, *Come With Me* (1983)★★★, *Love Explosion* (1984)★★, *Wild!* (1984)★★★★, *Made In New York* (1985)★★★, *The Lady From Brazil* (1987)★★★, *Outrageous* (1993)★★★, *No Comment* (TKM 1995)★★★★, *Bluesilian* (TKM 1996)★★★.

● COMPILATIONS: *Europe* 1991-93 live recordings (New Note 1997)★★★.

TANKSLEY, FRANCESCA

b. 21 November 1957, Vincenza, Italy. Although born in Italy she grew up in Munich, where she studied music from the age of seven. She went to Boston when she was 16 to study piano and composition at Berklee College Of Music; then two years later she returned to Munich. In 1980 she moved to New York, working with Melba Liston until 1983, when she joined Billy Harper's quintet with whom she toured extensively. She has also worked with Clifford Jordan, Cecil Payne, Bill Hardman and Erica Lindsay, and has led her own quintet and co-leads the Erica Lindsay/Howard Johnson Quintet. She is also a fine composer.

● ALBUMS: with Billy Harper *Destiny Is Yours* (1990)★★★, with Erica Lindsay *Dreamer* (1990)★★★.

TAPSCOTT, HORACE

b. 6 April 1934, Houston, Texas, USA. Tapscott moved to Los Angeles at the age of nine and, although taught piano by his mother (an accomplished stride player), he decided to concentrate on trombone. Helped by bandleader Gerald Wilson, Tapscott began to play professionally, but after army service in Korea, switched back to piano, jamming on LA's Central Avenue scene with musicians such as Sonny Criss, Eric Dolphy, Red Callender, Charles Lloyd and Buddy Collette. For 18 months he was accompanist to singer Lorez Alexandria, then toured briefly with Lionel Hampton before deciding to remain in Los Angeles where, in 1961, he co-founded the UGMA (the Underground Musicians Association) as a community self-help organization based in the Watts area. The UGMA later became the UGMAA (the Union of God's Musicians and Artists Ascension) but has otherwise survived intact for 30 years, providing a testing ground for generations of up-and-coming west coast musicians (alumni include Arthur Blythe, David Murray, Roberto Miranda) as has its offshoot big band, the Pan-Afrikan Peoples Arkestra (motto: 'Our music is contributive rather than competitive'). Although (or perhaps because) Tapscott and the UGMAA served the black community and celebrated the black cultural heritage in much the same way as Muhal Richard Abrams and the AACM would do in Chicago, they found themselves neglected by the media and the mainstream record industry. Until a cluster of albums suddenly appeared in the late 70s, Tapscott had only two appearances on record to show for nearly 20 years of making music. The first, in 1968, was on alto saxophonist Criss's *Sonny's Dream: The Birth Of The New Cool*, for which Tapscott wrote and arranged all the tunes and conducted the 10-piece ensemble; the second was his own *The Giant Is Awakened*, a fiercely exciting quintet session that also marked Arthur Blythe's recording debut. (Long a collector's item, it was reissued in 1991 as part of the Novus Series '70 CD, *West Coast Hot*.) The record's evident Black Power sympathies - the 'Giant' of the title was, said Tapscott, 'the New Black Nation' - perhaps help to explain why it was almost a decade before Tapscott was able to record again, a sudden flurry of activity producing some small-group albums and, notably, a trio of releases with the Pan-Afrikan Peoples Arkestra (*Flight 17*, *The Call*, *Live At The IUCC*) on the small, independent Nimbus label, which also initiated a series of solo piano records (*The Tapscott Sessions*) in the 80s. A dramatic, lyrical pianist - he cites Art Tatum, Thelonious Monk, Andrew Hill, his mother and Vladimir Horowitz as major influences - Tapscott's compositions are, he says, inspired by 'the experience of black people in America'. His tunes celebrate their history, their community, their culture; filled with blues, dance, struggle, dream, they are - as the title of his first solo album declares - the songs of the unsung. By devoting himself to their cause, Tapscott has remained largely unsung himself.

● ALBUMS: *The Giant Is Awakened* (Flying Dutchman 1969)★★★, *West Coast Hot* (Novus 1970)★★, *Songs Of The Unsung* (1978)★★★, *Flight 17* (1978)★★★, *The Call* (1978)★★★, *In New York* (1979)★★★, *Live At The IUCC* (1979)★★, with Everett Brown Jnr. *At The Crossroads* (1980)★★★, *Dial 'B' For Barbra* (1981)★★★, *Live At Lobero* (1982)★★, *Live At Lobero Vol II* (1982)★★, *The Tapscott Sessions Vols. 1-8* 1982-1984 recordings (1985-91)★★★★, *The Dark Tree Vol. 1* 1989 recordings (hatART 1991)★★★★, *The Dark Tree Vol. 2* 1989 recordings (hatART 1991)★★★★, *aiee! The Phantom* (Arabesque 1996)★★★★, *Thoughts Of Dar Es Salaam* (Arabesque 1997)★★★★.

TARTO, JOE

b. Vincent Joseph Tortoriello, 22 February 1902, Newark, New Jersey, USA, d. 24 August 1986. As a child Tarto played trombone before switching to the tuba. He served in the US Army in World War I, being injured, and on his discharge formed a dance band that he continued to lead on a part-time basis for a year or so. He became a full-time musician in the early 20s, touring and often recording with a remarkably wide range of popular artists and dance bands of the era. Among those with whom he played were Cliff Edwards, Eva Taylor, Paul Specht, Sam Lanin, Vincent Lopez, Red McKenzie, Bing Crosby, Ethel Waters, Sophie Tucker, the Boswell Sisters, Tommy and Jimmy Dorsey, Eddie Lang and Bix Beiderbecke. On some of these sessions Tarto played string bass but his speciality was the brass bass or tuba on which he was a master. He also wrote arrangements for a number of popular bands of the day, including those led by Chick Webb and Fletcher Henderson. From the 30s onwards, Tarto took his considerable talent into the recording studios and numerous Broadway pit bands. During these years he was also professionally involved on a fairly regular basis with Paul Whiteman. In the 40s and onwards through to the 80s, Tarto worked in studios, playing occasional jazz gigs for which he sometimes led his own small band, the New Jersey Dixieland Brass Quintet. The growth in popularity of the string bass in jazz, which gradually sidelined the tuba, has tended to make jazz audiences dismissive of the instrument as being somewhat archaic. While this might be true when it is played by lesser musicians it has unfairly thrust into the shadows some exceptional players, among whom Tarto clearly belongs. His string bass playing was also of a high standard, as can be heard on his recordings with Taylor ('Moanin' Low') and Waters ('Am I Blue?'), both in 1929.

● COMPILATIONS: *Miff Mole's Molers '1927'* (Swaggie 1927)★★★, *An Introduction To Ethel Waters* (Best Of Jazz 1921-40)★★.

TATE, BUDDY

b. George Holmes Tate, 22 February 1915, Sherman, Texas, USA. One of the outstanding tenor saxophonists of his generation, Tate paid his dues in a succession of territory bands between 1927 and 1939. Having started out on alto, he quickly developed into a formidable tenor player, lending presence and distinction to the bands of Troy Floyd, Terrence Holder, Andy Kirk and Nat Towles, the latter always regarded by Tate as one of the best in which he ever worked. In 1939 he joined the Count Basie band, having briefly worked with Basie five years earlier. He stayed until the end of the 40s, then played with Lucky Millinder, Oran 'Hot Lips' Page and others, before taking his own band into a residency at the Celebrity Club in Harlem in 1953. He remained there until the mid-70s, taking time out to tour and record extensively with artists such as Jimmy Rushing and Buck Clayton. In 1975 he briefly co-led a band with Paul Quinichette, but from then onwards worked mostly as a solo, occasionally teaming up with mainstream comrades such as Illinois Jacquet, Al Grey, Scott Hamilton and Bobby Rosengarden. Tate was seriously injured in 1981, scalded in a hotel shower, but returned to the fray only to be stricken with serious illness in the late 80s. The early 90s saw him return tentatively to playing again. His full-toned sound, robust 'Texas Tenor' styling and unflagging swing have earned him a significant place in the history of mainstream jazz. A thoroughly delightful individual, charming, sophisticated and thoughtful, he is a true gentleman of jazz and one of the music's most distinguished ambassadors.

● ALBUMS: *Buddy Tate's Celebrity Club Orchestra Vol. 1* (1954)★★★, *Swinging Like Tate* (Felsted 1958)★★★, *Tate's Date* (Swingville 1960)★★★, *Tate-A-Tate* (Swingville 1960)★★★★, *Groovin' With Buddy Tate* (Swingville 1961)★★★★, with Buck Clayton *Buck & Buddy* (Swingville 1961)★★★, with Clayton *Buck & Buddy Blow The Blues* (Vanguard 1962)★★★, with Milt Buckner *Midnight Slows, Volume 1* (Black & Blue 1967)★★★, with Buckner *Crazy Rhythm* (1968)★★★, *Buddy Tate's Celebrity Club Orchestra Vol. 2* (1968)★★★, *Unbroken* (MPS/Pausa 1970)★★★★, *Buddy Tate And His Buddies* (Chiaroscuro 1973)★★★, *Broadway* (Black & Blue 1973)★★★★, with Buckner *Midnight Slows, Volume 5* (1974)★★★, *Swinging Scorpio* (Black Lion 1975)★★★, *The Texas Twister* (New World 1975)★★★★, *After Midnight* (1976)★★★, *Jive At Five* (Storyville 1976)★★★★, *Tate A Tete At La Fontaine, Copenhagen* (Storyville 1976)★★★, with Buckner *Midnight Slows, Volume 7* (Black & Blue 1977)★★★, with Dollar Brand *Buddy Tate Meets Dollar Brand* (Chiaroscuro 1977)★★★, *Sherman Shuffle* (Sackville 1978)★★★, *The Buddy Tate Quartet* (Sackville 1978)★★★, *Hard Blowin': Live At Sandy's* (Muse 1978)★★★★, *The Great Buddy Tate* (Concord Jazz 1981)★★★★, *The Ballad Artistry Of Buddy Tate* (Sackville 1981)★★★★, with Al Cohn, Scott Hamilton *Tour De Force* (Concord Jazz 1981)★★★★, *Swingin' The Forties With The Great Eight* (1983)★★★, *Buddy Tate Meets Torsten Zwingenberger* (1983)★★★, *Just Jazz* (Reservoir 1984)★★★, *After Dark* (Progressive 1986)★★★.

TATE, ERSKINE

b. 19 December 1895, Memphis, Tennessee, USA, d. 17 December 1978. Tate first studied music and the violin with his father who was a music teacher. Later, he studied formally in Jackson, Tennessee, and then in Chicago, Illinois. While in Chicago he played professionally and in 1919 formed his own band which he took into the Vendome Theater. This band was billed as the Erskine Tate Vendome Symphony Orchestra, despite being only a nine-piece ensemble, although it did grow to a 15-piece band after a few years. Tate was resident at the Vendome until 1928, then moved to other theatres in the city, also playing clubs and dance halls there, including those named after more famous venues in other places, among them the Cotton Club and the Savoy. He was resident at the latter throughout the 30s. In these years, the 20s and 30s, Tate's bands were home to many exceptional talents, some of whom gained invaluable early experience there: Louis Armstrong, Buster Bailey, Jimmy Bertrand, Earl 'Fatha' Hines, Milt Hinton, Darnell Howard, Freddie Keppard, Eddie South, Jabbo Smith. In the 40s Tate performed less but retained his musical links through a studio he opened and where he taught a wide range of instruments for the next three decades, continuing until shortly before his death. Although largely a show band, and only rarely recording, the orchestras Tate led at the Vendome and the Savoy were excellent musical aggregations because he insisted upon the highest musical standards. This, together with his work as a teacher make him an important, if often overlooked figure in jazz and popular music.

TATE, FRANK

b. 18 July 1943, Washington, DC. USA. Growing up on Long Island, Tate began playing trumpet and was a neighbour of pianist Art Hodes. When he was 23 he began doubling on bass but played trumpet professionally in North Carolina in a band led by Bert Massengale. When Tate later rejoined the band there was no vacancy for a trumpet player so he played bass instead. He continued to advance his bass playing, studying with Michael Moore. In the late 60s Tate was briefly outside music but in late 1972 he was leader of the house band at Blues Alley in his home-town. A few years later he was working in the Cape Cod area, playing in bands led by Bobby Hackett and Dave McKenna, then he joined Marian McPartland and in the early 80s was with Zoot Sims. He helped organize the Dave McKenna-Scott Hamilton band and also toured with singer Pearl Bailey. In the mid-80s he was with the Howard Alden-Dan Barrett Quintet and in the early 90s played with Ruby Braff. A strong player with a fine sense of swing, Tate has always been a great asset to the rhythm section of any band in which he has played. His understanding of the needs of front-line players is perhaps strengthened through his early experience as a trumpet player.

● ALBUMS: with Marian McPartland *A Fine Romance* (Improv 1975)★★, with Ken Peplowski *Mr Gentle And Mr Cool* (Concord 1992)★★★.

Tate, Grady

b. 14 January 1932, Durham, North Carolina, USA. A self-taught drummer, Tate began playing while still a small child. During his military service he turned to jazz and subsequently worked with Wild Bill Davis. In the early 60s he played in the Quincy Jones big band and then spent time with Count Basie, Duke Ellington and a string of small groups, including those led by Rahsaan Roland Kirk, Oscar Peterson, Zoot Sims, Red Rodney and Ray Brown. He also made some albums as a singer. Tate's interest in singing made him especially sympathetic to vocalists' needs and he has recorded with Ella Fitzgerald, Sarah Vaughan, Lena Horne, as well as Ray Charles among many. Tate's drumming is suited to many areas of jazz and he invariably brings a lithe swing to any band of which he is a member. In recent years he appears to show a preference for singing, not in the jazz idiom but angled towards the popular field.

● ALBUMS: as singer *Feeling Life* (1969)★★, as singer *Master Grady Tate* (1977)★★★, with Roland Kirk *Now Please Don't You Cry Beautiful Edith* (1967)★★★, with Pee Wee Russell, Oliver Nelson *The Spirit Of '67* (1967)★★★, with Quincy Jones *Walking In Space* (1969)★★★, with Oscar Peterson *Silent Partner* (1979)★★★, with Red Rodney *The 3 Rs* (1979)★★★★, with Ray Brown *Don't Forget The Blues* (1985)★★★, *TNT: Grady Tate Sings* (1993)★★★.

Tatum, Art

b. 13 October 1909, Toledo, Ohio, USA, d. 5 November 1956, Los Angeles, California, USA. Born into a musical family, Tatum was handicapped from birth by impaired sight. Blind in one eye and only partially sighted in the other, he nevertheless studied piano formally and learned to read music. By his mid-teens he was playing professionally in Toledo. He played briefly in the Speed Webb band, but was mostly active as a soloist or in small groups working in clubs and playing on radio. He was heard by singer Adelaide Hall, who took him on the road as her accompanist. With Hall he travelled to New York in 1932 and the following year made his first recordings. He spent the next few years playing clubs in Cleveland and Chicago, but in 1937 was back in New York, where his playing in clubs, on radio and on record established his reputation as a major figure in jazz circles. He toured the USA and also played in the UK. In the early 40s he formed a trio with bassist Slam Stewart and guitarist Tiny Grimes that became extremely popular. For the next decade Tatum toured extensively, performing throughout North America. In the early 50s he was signed by Norman Granz who recorded him in a series of remarkable performances, both as soloist (*The Solo Masterpieces*) and in a small group context with Benny Carter, Buddy De Franco, Roy Eldridge, Lionel Hampton, Ben Webster and others (*The Group Masterpieces*). A matchless virtuoso performer, Tatum's impact on the New York jazz scene in the early 30s had extensive repercussions. Even Fats Waller, an acknowledged master and someone to whom Tatum had listened on record in his own formative years, was aware of the phenomenal talent of the newcomer, reputedly declaring onstage - when he spotted Tatum in the audience - 'God is in the house tonight'.

Tatum's dazzling extemporizations on themes from jazz and the classics, but mostly from the popular songbook, became bywords and set standards few of his successors matched and none surpassed. Capable of breathtaking runs, interspersed with striking single notes and sometimes unexpected chords, he developed a unique solo style. His powerful left-hand figures tipped a hat in the direction of stride while he simultaneously explored the limits of an orthodox keyboard like no other pianist in jazz (and few elsewhere). A playful habit of quoting from other melodies, a technique that in unskilled hands can be merely irritating, was developed into a singular stylistic device. Unlike some virtuoso performers, Tatum never sacrificed feeling and swing for effect. Although he continued to develop throughout his career, it is hard to discover any recorded evidence that he was never poised and polished. His prodigious talent allowed him to achieve extraordinary recording successes: his solo sessions for Granz were mostly completed in two days - 69 tracks, all but three needing only one take. Ray Spencer, whose studies of the artist are extensive, has commented that Tatum achieved such a remarkable work rate through constant 'refining and honing down after each performance until an ideal version remained needing no further adjustments'. While this is clearly the case, Tatum's performances never suggest a man merely going through the motions. Everything he did sounded fresh and vital, as if minted especially for the occasion in hand. Although he remains a major figure in jazz piano, Tatum is often overlooked in the cataloguing of those who affected the course of the music. He appears to stand to one side of the developing thrust of jazz, yet his creativity and the manner in which he explored harmonic complexities and unusual chord sequences influenced many musicians, including Bud Powell and Herbie Hancock, and especially non-pianists, among whom can be listed Charlie Parker and John Coltrane. The word genius is often used carelessly but, in assessing Tatum and the manner in which he transformed ideas and the imagined limitations of the piano in jazz, any other word would be inadequate.

● ALBUMS: *Art Tatum Trio* 10-inch album (Dial 1950)★★★★, *Art Tatum* 10-inch album (Asch 1950)★★★★, *Art Tatum Trio* 10-inch album (Stinson 1950)★★★★, *Art Tatum Trio* 10-inch album (Brunswick 1950)★★★★, *Art Tatum Piano Solos* (Brunswick 1950)★★★★, *Tatum Piano* 10-inch album (Remington 1950)★★★★, *Art Tatum Encores* 10-inch album (Capitol 1951)★★★★, *Art Tatum Trio* 10-inch album (Folkways 1951)★★★★, *Gene Norman Concert At Shrine Auditorium, May*

1949 10-inch album (Columbia 1952)★★★★, *Art Tatum Trio* 10-inch album (Capitol 1953)★★★★, *Here's Art Tatum* (Brunswick 1954)★★★★, *An Art Tatum Concert* reissued as *The Tatum Touch* (Columbia 1954)★★★★, *Art Tatum* (Capitol 1955)★★★, with Roy Eldridge, John Simmons, Alvin Stoller *The Art Tatum-Roy Eldridge-Alvin Stoller-John Simmons Quartet* (Clef 1955)★★★, with Louis Bellson, Benny Carter *Tatum-Carter-Bellson* reissued as *The Three Giants* (Clef 1955)★★★, with Lionel Hampton, Buddy Rich *The Hampton-Tatum-Rich Trio* (Clef 1956)★★★, with Buddy De Franco *The Art Tatum-Buddy De Franco Quartet* (American Recording Society 1956)★★★, with Erroll Garner *Giants Of The Piano* (Roost 1956)★★★, with Mary Lou Williams *The King And Queen* (Jazztone 1958)★★★, with Bellson, Carter *Makin' Whoopee* (Verve 1958)★★★, with Ben Webster *The Art Tatum-Ben Webster Quartet* (Verve 1958)★★★★, *Presenting The Art Tatum Trio* (Verve 1961)★★★★.

● COMPILATIONS: *Classic Early Solos (1934-1937)* (GRP)★★★★, *Classic Piano Solos (1934-1939)* (GRP)★★★★, *Art Tatum Standards* 1938-39 recordings (Black Lion)★★★★, *The Genius Of Art Tatum Volumes 1-11* (Clef/Verve 1954-57)★★★★, *The Greatest Piano Hits Of Them All* (Verve 1959)★★★★, *The Incomparable Music Of Art Tatum* (Verve 1959)★★★★, *More Of The Greatest Piano Of Them All* (Verve 1959)★★★★, *Still More Of The Greatest Piano Of Them All* (Verve 1960)★★★★, *The Essential Art Tatum* 1953-56 recordings (Verve 1962)★★★★, *God Is In The House* 1940-41 recordings (Onyx 1973)★★★★, *The Complete Pablo Solo Masterpieces Volumes 1-12* 1953-55 recordings (Pablo 1978)★★★★★, *The Tatum Group Masterpieces Volumes 1-9* 1954-56 recordings (Pablo 1978)★★★★★, *Art Tatum On The Air* (Aircheck 1978)★★★★, *The V Discs* 1944-46 recordings (Black Lion 1979)★★★★, *Masterpieces* 1934-37 recordings (MCA 1979)★★★★, *20th Century Piano Genius* (Emarcy 1987)★★★★, *The Complete Capitol Recordings, Volume One* 1949-52 recordings (Capitol 1989)★★★★, *The Complete Capitol Recordings, Volume Two* 1949-52 recordings (Capitol 1989)★★★★, *Complete Art Tatum Volumes 1 & 2* (Capitol 1990)★★★★, *The Best Of Art Tatum* (Pablo 1990)★★★★, *Art Tatum Standards* (Pablo 1991)★★★★★, *Piano Starts Here* 1933 and 1949 recordings (Columbia/Legacy 1991)★★★★, *The Complete Pablo Solo Masterpieces* 7-CD box set 1953-55 recordings (Pablo 1991)★★★★★, *The Complete Pablo Group Masterpieces* 6-CD box set 1954-56 recordings (Pablo 1992)★★★★★, *20th Century Piano Genius* recorded 1955 (Verve 1992)★★★★, *Complete Brunswick And Decca Sessions 1932-41* (Affinity 1993)★★★★, *Art Tatum 1932-1934* (Classics 1995)★★★, *Art Tatum 1934-1940* (Classics 1995)★★★★, *Art Tatum 1940-1944* (Classics 1995)★★★, *Art Tatum 1944* (Classics 1995)★★★, *20th Century Piano Genius* (Verve 1996)★★★★, *His Best Recordings 1933-1944* (Best Of Jazz 1996)★★★, *The Complete Capitol Recordings* 1949-52 recordings (Blue Note 1997)★★★★.

● FURTHER READING: *Art Tatum, A Guide To His Recorded Music*, Arnold Laubich. *Too Marvellous For Words: The Life And Genius Of*, James Lester.

● FILMS: *The Fabulous Dorseys* (1947).

TAYLOR, 'SAM THE MAN'

b. Leroy Samuel Taylor, 12 July 1916, Lexington, Tennessee, USA. Taylor started on clarinet and played with Paul Taylor in Gary, Indiana, going on to play his tenor saxophone in the bands of Scat Man Crothers (1937-38), Sunset Royals/Doc Wheeler's Sunset Orchestra (1939-42; recording for RCA's Bluebird subsidiary), Cootie Williams (1942-45; recording for Hit/Majestic and Capitol), Lucky Millinder (1945-46; recording for Decca and King/Queen) and Cab Calloway (1946-52; recording for Columbia, Bluebird, Hi-Tone, London and Regal). Leaving the Calloway band upon its demise, several of the band members, notably Taylor, David 'Panama' Francis and Milt Hinton, went on to carve out a lucrative career with their own units separately, and as ubiquitous session musicians together for the rest of the 50s and early 60s on the majority of New York R&B sessions. Taylor played with Alan Freed's Rock 'n' Roll Orchestra, often battling on saxophone with his friend Big Al Sears, and settled into the 60s album market with his own albums on Metrojazz and MGM. In the 70s he took part in several festival tours of Europe and Japan, but little has been heard from him in recent years.

● ALBUMS: with Hal Singer, Paul Williams, Lee Allen and Big Jay McNeely *Honkers & Screamers - The Roots Of Rock 'N' Roll Vol. 6* (1989)★★★★.

TAYLOR, ART

b. 6 April 1929, New York City, New York, USA, d. 6 February 1995, New York City, New York, USA. As a teenager Taylor played drums with Sonny Rollins, Howard McGhee and other young bop musicians in New York. In the early 50s he was also to be heard in mainstream groups, playing with Buddy De Franco and Coleman Hawkins. He continued to play with leading beboppers, including Bud Powell, and later in the decade was with Miles Davis and John Coltrane. From time to time he led his own bands, and toured the USA and Europe with several groups. He became resident in Europe in the early 60s, playing with visiting fellow Americans including Dexter Gordon and Johnny Griffin. During this period, Taylor began recording interviews with musicians, the results of which, often acutely angled towards the racial and political circumstances surrounding jazz, were first published in 1977 under the title *Notes And Tones*. In the mid-80s Taylor returned to the USA and hosted a radio show. His last studio session was with Jimmy Smith in 1995 for the excellent *Damn!*, and the album was dedicated to his memory.

● ALBUMS: *Taylor's Wailers* (Prestige 1957)★★★★, *Taylor's Tenors* (New Jazz 1959)★★★★, *A.T.'s Delight* (Blue Note 1960)★★★, shared with Art Farmer *Hard Cookin'* (Prestige 1964)★★★★, with Dexter Gordon *A Day In Copenhagen* (1969)★★★, *Mr A. T.* (Enja 1992)★★★, *Wailin' At The Vanguard* (Verve 1993)★★★★, with Jimmy Smith *Damn!* (Verve 1995)★★★★, with Steve Grossman, Tyler Mitchell *Bouncing With Mr A.T.* (Dreyfus 1996)★★★.

● FURTHER READING: *Notes And Tones*, Arthur Taylor.

TAYLOR, BILLY

b. 24 July 1921, Greenville, North Carolina, USA. After extensive formal studies, Taylor began playing piano with numerous leading jazzmen of the late swing era/early bebop period. These included Ben Webster, Dizzy Gillespie, Stuff Smith and Charlie Parker. By the early 50s Taylor's high reputation led to his being hired as house pianist at Birdland. His main contribution to jazz in the 50s was as leader of a trio, usually in New York, which continued more or less non-stop for the next three decades. He also appeared regularly on radio and television both as a performer and a presenter of programmes, including a successful regular slot on CBS's *Sunday Morning* program. Taylor also developed an abiding interest in jazz education, writing piano tutors and, in 1965, forming Jazzmobile, the Harlem-based concert group. In 1969 he became band director for *The David Frost Show*, the first black musician to achieve this role on a network television series. Taylor has frequently played and composed music that fuses jazz with the classical form. Among these works are his 'Suite For Jazz Piano And Orchestra', composed in 1973, and 'Homage', a chamber music piece first performed by the Billy Taylor Trio and the Juilliard String Quartet in 1990. An inventive and technically facile player, Taylor's dedication to the development of interest in jazz in the community has sometimes led the wider audience to overlook his undoubted skills. One of the most popular jazz classics of recent years is 'I Wish I Knew (How It Would Feel To Be Free)', a handclapping happy-go-lucky song in the style of Ramsey Lewis's 'Wade In The Water'. Taylor's song is better known as the long-running theme to UK film critic Barry Norman's television programme - a sad fact, that outside the jazz circle, his song is better known than he is. (This artist should not be confused with either Billy Taylor Snr. or Billy Taylor Jnr., father-and-son bass players.)

● ALBUMS: *Piano Panorama* reissued as *The Billy Taylor Touch* (Atlantic 1951)★★★, *Jazz At Storyville* 10-inch album (Roost 1952)★★★, *Taylor Made Jazz* 10-inch album (Roost 1952)★★★, *Billy Taylor Piano* 10-inch album (Savoy 1953)★★★, *Billy Taylor Trio, Volume 1* 10-inch album (Prestige 1953)★★★, *Billy Taylor Trio, Volume 2* 10-inch album (Prestige 1953)★★★, *Billy Taylor Trio, Volume 3* 10-inch album (Prestige 1953)★★★, *Billy Taylor Trio* reissued as *Cross Section* (Prestige 1954)★★★★, *Billy Taylor Trio* reissued as *The Billy Taylor Trio With Candido* (Prestige 1954)★★★★, *Billy Taylor Trio In Concert At Town Hall, December 17, 1954* 10-inch album (Prestige 1955)★★★, *A Touch Of Taylor* (Prestige 1955)★★★, *"Evergreens"* (ABC-Paramount 1956)★★★, *Billy Taylor At The London House* (ABC-Paramount 1956)★★★, *Billy Taylor Introduces Ira Sullivan* (ABC-Paramount 1957)★★★, *My Fair Lady Loves Jazz* (ABC-Paramount 1957)★★★, *The New Trio* (ABC-Paramount 1958)★★★, *Taylor Made Flute* (Argo 1959)★★★, *Custom Taylored* (SeSac 1959)★★★, *Billy Taylor With Four Flutes* (Riverside 1959)★★★★, *One For Fun* (Atlantic 1960)★★★, *Billy Taylor Trio Uptown* (Riverside 1960)★★★, *Warming Up* (Riverside 1960)★★★, *Interlude* (Moodsville 1961)★★★, *Impromptu* (Mercury 1962)★★★, *Right Here, Right Now* (Capitol 1963)★★★, *Midnight Piano* (Capitol 1965)★★★, *Easy Life* (Surrey 1966)★★★, *I Wish I Knew* (Tower 1968)★★★, *Billy Taylor Today/A Sleeping Bee* (MPS 1969)★★★, *OK Billy* (Bell 1970)★★★, *Jazz Alive* (Monmouth Evergreen 1977)★★★, *Live At Storyville* (West 54 1977)★★★★, with Joe Kennedy *Where've You Been?* (Concord Jazz 1981)★★★★, *White Nights And Jazz In Leningrad* (Taylor Made 1988)★★★, *You Tempt Me* 1985 recording (Taylor Made 1989)★★★, *Solo* (Taylor Made 1989)★★★, *Billy Taylor And The Jazzmobile All Stars* (Taylor Made 1989)★★★, *Dr. T* (GRP 1993)★★★★, *It's A Matter Of Pride* (GRP 1993)★★★, *Homage* (GRP 1995)★★★, *Music Keeps Us Young* (Arkadia 1997)★★★★.

● FURTHER READING: *The History And Development Of Jazz Piano*, Billy Taylor.

TAYLOR, CECIL

b. 15 March 1929, New York City, New York, USA. A towering figure in post-war *avant garde* jazz, Taylor has been hailed as the greatest piano virtuoso of the 20th century because of the phenomenal power, speed and intensity of his playing. 'We in black music think of the piano as a percussive instrument,' he told writer John Litweiler, 'we beat the keyboard, we get inside the instrument. . . the physical force going into the making of black music - if that is misunderstood, it leads to screaming'. Taylor grew up in Long Island, studying piano from the age of five and percussion (with a classical tutor) soon afterwards. He attended the New York College of Music and the New England Conservatory in Boston, though he later claimed he had learned more by listening to Duke Ellington records. Despite an early interest in European classical composers, especially Stravinsky, Taylor's major influences come from the jazz tradition, notably big band leaders such as Ellington, drummers Sonny Greer and Chick Webb and a lineage of pianists that runs through Fats Waller, Erroll Garner, Thelonious Monk and Horace Silver. Although his first gigs were with swing era veterans Hot Lips Page, Johnny Hodges and Lawrence Brown, by the mid-50s Taylor was leading his own small groups and laying the basis for a musical revolution that is still in progress. His early associates included Buell Neidlinger, Dennis Charles, Steve Lacy and Archie Shepp (plus a fairly disastrous one-off encounter with John Coltrane) and his first recordings still bore a discernible, if carefully distanced, relationship to the jazz mainstream. By the early 60s, working with Sunny Murray, Alan Silva and his longest-serving colleague, Jimmy Lyons, Taylor's music had shed all direct reference to tonality and regular time-keeping and sounded almost purely abstract. However, the arrival of Ornette Coleman in New York in 1959, playing his own version of 'free jazz', rather overshadowed all other innovators and Taylor's more radical and complex music was largely ignored by the press and public, although a handful of fellow pioneers - the best-known of whom was Albert Ayler - embraced it enthusiastically. (Another admirer was Gil Evans, whose *Into The Hot* actually comprised one side of music by Taylor and one side by Johnny Carisi: Evans himself is not on the album!) Taylor lived in poverty for much of the 60s, even working as a dishwasher on occasion; but gradually his influence began to permeate the scene, particularly after Blue Note Records released two outstanding 1966 sessions. Both featured his regular partners Lyons, Silva, Andrew Cyrille and Henry Grimes; in addition, *Unit Structures* had Ken McIntyre and trumpeter Eddie Gale Stevens and *Conquistador!* had Bill Dixon (with whom Taylor had worked in the Jazz Composers' Guild). In 1968 Taylor made an album with the Jazz Composers' Orchestra and a 1969 concert with a new group of Lyons, Cyrille and Sam Rivers was released on the French label Shandar; but recording opportunities remained scarce. In the early 70s he became involved in education, teaching at Wisconsin University and colleges in Ohio and New Jersey; in 1973 he briefly ran his own label, Unit Core, releasing *Indents (Mysteries)* and *Spring Of Two Blue-Js*. Finally, the trickle of other releases - on Trio in Japan, on Arista's Freedom label in the USA, on Enja in Europe - began to gather momentum and by the early 80s Taylor was recording regularly for the European Soul Note and Hat Hut labels, while later in the decade Leo Records and FMP also championed his work. During this period his ensembles included Lyons (always), Cyrille (often), Silva (occasionally) plus players such as Sirone, Ronald Shannon Jackson, violinist Ramsey Ameer, trumpeter Raphé Malik, Jerome Cooper, William Parker and percussionist Rashid Bak. Their characteristic sound was a torrential flood of full-tilt, densely textured, swirling, churning, flying improvisation that could and usually did last for two to three hours without pause.

Taylor also recorded a series of stunning solo albums, notably *Fly! Fly! Fly! Fly! Fly!* and the live double-set *Garden*, which showed he was one of the most dazzling, dynamic pianists in jazz history, and released two memorable duo albums - *Embraced,* with Mary Lou Williams, and *Historic Concerts*, with Max Roach - that further enhanced his reputation. In 1985 the first recording of Taylor's big band music, *Winged Serpent (Sliding Quadrants)*, was released by Soul Note. In 1986 Jimmy Lyons died of lung cancer; Taylor lost both a close friend and his most dedicated musical collaborator. In 1987 he toured with a new Unit (Parker, Carlos Ward, Leroy Jenkins, Thurman Barker - three of their concerts were released by Leo the following year) but since then has worked mostly in a trio format, usually with Parker and Tony Oxley (sometimes calling themselves the Feel Trio). In 1988, FMP brought 20 European improvisers to Berlin for a month-long festival of concerts and workshops that featured Taylor. Several of these were later released in the lavishly packaged, 11-CD box-set *Cecil Taylor In Berlin '88*, which comprised two discs of Taylor's big band music, one of a big band workshop, one solo concert, one trio set with Tristan Honsinger and Evan Parker, a duo with Derek Bailey and five discs of duos with drummers - Oxley, Günter Sommer, Paul Lovens, Han Bennink and Louis Moholo. The set was released to worldwide acclaim in the music press and sealed Taylor's standing as one of the four or five leading innovators in post-bebop jazz. Although he has few direct imitators, he has proved an inspiration to free players everywhere and in particular to many jazz pianists, from Alex Von Schlippenbach to Marilyn Crispell.

The tremendous energy and sweep of his music has fooled many listeners into believing it has no structural underpinning, but Ekkehard Jost, both in his book *Free Jazz* and in one of the several essays in the booklet that accompanies the FMP box-set, has identified certain formal elements that recur in Taylor's work. (There are also useful chapters on his music in John Litweiler's *The Freedom Principle* and Valerie Wilmer's *As Serious As Your Life*, plus a detailed account of his early career in A.B. Spellman's *Four Lives In The Bebop Business*. Taylor himself has always stressed the spiritual and mystical nature of African American music: 'It's about magic and capturing spirits.') A devotee of dance from Baby Lawrence to contemporary ballet (he once remarked 'I try to imitate on the piano the leaps in space a dancer makes'), Taylor has worked extensively in this field, for example on projects with choreographers/dancers Dianne McIntyre and Mikhail Baryshnikov. A poet too, whose writings often adorn his album sleeves, Taylor's *Chinampus* had him half-reciting, half-chanting a selection of sound-poetry and accompanying himself on various percussion instruments. For many years he has been working on a book about 'methodological concepts of black music', to be entitled *Mysteries*.

● ALBUMS: *Jazz Advance* (Advance 1956)★★★★, *Hard Driving Jazz* reissued as John Coltrane's *Coltrane Time* (United Artists 1959)★★★, *Stereo Drive* (United Artists 1959)★★★, *Love For Sale* (United Artists 1959)★★★★, *Looking Ahead!* (United Artists 1959)★★★★, *The World Of Cecil Taylor* (Candid 1960)★★★★, *Live At The Cafe Montmartre* (Fantasy 1964)★★★★, *Unit Structures* (Blue Note 1966)★★★★, *Conquistador* (Blue Note 1967)★★★★, *Student Studies* (Affinity 1967)★★★, *Great Paris Concert* 3-LP set (Prestige 1969)★★★★, *J For Jazz Broadcasts Present Cecil Taylor* (1971)★★★, with Buell Neidlinger *New York City R&B* 1961 recording (Barnaby 1971)★★★★, *Indent (Mysteries)* (Unit Core/Arista Freedom 1973)★★★, *Akisakila* (Konnex 1973)★★★, *Spring Of Two Blue-Js* (1974)★★★, *Silent Tongues* (Arista Freedom 1975)★★★★, *Dark Unto Themselves* (Enja 1976)★★★, *Air Above Mountains (Buildings Within)* (Enja 1977)★★★★, with Neidlinger *Cecil Taylor All Stars Featuring Buell Neidlinger* 1961 recording (Candid/Victor 1977)★★★★, with Mary Lou Williams *Embraced* (Pablo 1977)★★, *The Cecil Taylor Unit* (New World 1978)★★★★, *Three Phasis* (New World 1979)★★★★, *One Too Many Salty Swifty And Not Goodbye* 1978 recordings (hatART 1980)★★★★, *Spots Circles And Fantasy* (FMP 1979)★★★★, *It Is In The Brewing Luminous* (hatART 1981)★★★★, *Fly! Fly! Fly! Fly! Fly!* (MPS 1981)★★★, *Garden Part One* (hatART 1982)★★★★, *Garden Part Two* (hatART 1982)★★★★, *Praxis* 1968 recording (1982)★★★, *Live In Willisau '83* (1983)★★★, *Calling It The 8th* (hatART 1983)★★★★, with Max Roach *Historic Concerts* 1979 recording (Soul Note 1984)★★★★, *Winged Serpent (Sliding Quadrants)* (Soul Note 1985)★★★★, *The Eighth* 1981 recording (1986)★★★★, *For Olim* (Soul Note

1987)★★★, with Neidlinger *Jumpin' Punkins* 1961 recordings (Candid 1987)★★★★, *Live In Bologna* (Leo 1988)★★★, *Live In Vienna* (Leo 1988)★★★★, *Chinampus* (Leo 1988)★★★★, *Tzotzil Mummers Tzotzil* (1989)★★★, *Cecil Taylor In Berlin '88* 11-CD box set (1989)★★★, *Erzulie Maketh Scent* (FMP 1989)★★★★, with Derek Bailey *Pleistozaen Mit Wasser* (FMP 1989)★★★, *Leaf Palm Hand* (FMP 1989)★★★★, *Regalia* (FMP 1989)★★★, *Remembrance* (FMP 1989)★★★★, *Riobec* (FMP 1989)★★★★, *The Hearth* (FMP 1989)★★★★, *Legba Crossing* (FMP 1989)★★★★, *Alms/Tiergarten* (FMP 1989)★★★★, with Günter Sommer *In East Berlin* (1989)★★★, *Looking (The Feel Trio)*, (FMP 1990)★★★★, *In Florescence* (1990)★★★★, with Tony Oxley, William Parker *Looking (Berlin Version) The Feel Trio* (1990)★★★★, *Looking (Berlin Version) Corona* (1991)★★★★, *Looking (Berlin Version) Solo* (1991)★★★★, with Oxley, Parker *Celebrated Blazons* (FMP 1991)★★★, *Double Holy House* (FMP 1991)★★★, with Art Ensemble Of Chicago *Thelonious Sphere Monk* (DIW 1991)★★★, with Neidlinger *Cecil* 1961 recordings (Maestri Del Jazz 1991)★★★★, *Olu Iwa* 1986 recording (Soul Note 1994)★★★★, *Iwontunwonsi: Live At Sweet Basil* 1986 recording (Sound Hills 1996)★★★, *Nefertiti, The Beautiful One Has Come* 1962 recording (Revenant 1997)★★★★, *The Tree Of Life* 1991 recording (FMP 1998)★★★, *Always A Pleasure* 1993 recording (FMP 1998)★★★, *Qu'a: Live At The Tridium Vol 1* (Cadence 1998)★★★★.

● COMPILATIONS: *In Transition* 1955-1959 recordings (1975)★★★★, with others *Masters Of The Modern Piano* 1957 recordings (1976)★★★, *The Complete Candid Recordings Of Cecil Taylor And Buell Neidlinger* 6-LP/4-CD box set (Mosaic 1989)★★★★.

● FURTHER READING: *Black Music: Four Lives*, A.B. Spellman. *The Freedom Principle: Jazz After 1958*, John Litweiler.

TAYLOR, JAMES, QUARTET

When the Medway Valley's psychedelic-mod hopefuls the Prisoners disbanded in 1986, organist James Taylor vowed to move into the realms of jazz, and away from rock. Assembling a quartet from Kent, England, comprising fellow Prisoner bassist Allan Crockford and ex-Daggermen personnel Simon Howard (drums) and Taylor's brother David (guitar), the band recorded a BBC session for disc jockey John Peel, before Taylor retired to Sweden for a break. However, the broadcast made such an impression that the group were signed to new 'mod' label Re-Elect The President. A mini-album of cover versions, *Mission Impossible*, featured 'organ groovy' 60s soundtrack instrumentals like the single 'Blow Up', with Jimmy Smith and Booker T. And The MGs providing the strongest influences. *The Money Spyder* took the theme a stage further; while the Damned had mocked the psychedelic soundtrack as Naz Nomad And The Nightmares, the JTQ reminisced on the beat and jazz age. Taylor become frustrated with the band's limitations and by the time *Wait A Minute* appeared on Polydor's dance offshoot, Urban, in September 1988, only his brother remained with him in the group. For a powerful remake of the 'Starsky And Hutch Theme', new jazz musicians and ex-James Brown horn-players were recruited, as the JTQ found themselves central to a new, London-based 'acid jazz' movement. Howard and Crockford, meanwhile, provided the rhythm section for ex-Prisoner Graham Day's new project, the Prime Movers. 1989 saw a further development for the JTQ with the recruitment of two rappers for May's 'Breakout'. The single hinted at a move away from jazz towards the dance charts, but *Do Your Own Thing* combined both elements, alongside a continuing debt to the original fusion of jazz/dance and rare groove, not least on their rousing rendition of the 70s club favourite, 'Got To Get Your Own'. While ex-Style Council and Jazz Renegades drummer Steve White served in the JTQ for a time, Taylor himself has also made several guest performances, including appearances for the Wonder Stuff. 'See A Brighter Day', featuring Noel McKoy, saw them bid for chart success in July 1993. Once the spurious 'acid house' bubble had burst, Taylor was able to concentrate on making music without the pressure of following a trend. His mid-90s work took him back to the Hammond groove jazz of Jimmy McGriff and Jimmy Smith. His composition 'Austin's Theme' was featured in the 1997 movie *Austin Powers*.

● ALBUMS: *Mission Impossible* (Re-Elect Pres 1987)★★★, *The Money Spyder* (Re-Elect Pres 1987)★★★, *Wait A Minute* (Urban 1988)★★★, *Get Organized* (Polydor 1989)★★★★, *Do Your Own Thing* (Polydor 1990)★★★★, *Absolute* (1991)★★★, *Supernatural Feeling* (1993)★★★, *In The Hands Of The Inevitable* (Acid Jazz 1995)★★★, *The BBC Sessions* (Nightracks 1995)★★★, *A Few Useful Tips About Living Underground* (Acid Jazz 1996)★★★, *Creation* (Hollywood 1997)★★★.

● COMPILATIONS: *Blow Up! A JTQ Collection* (Music Club 1998)★★★.

TAYLOR, JOHN

b. 25 September 1942, Manchester, England. A self-taught pianist, Taylor had established himself as one of the most respected British jazz pianists by the end of the 60s and has continued to consolidate his reputation ever since. He began his musical career with a dance band until 1964, when he moved to London, and began playing with other young lions of the time, such as John Surman, Alan Skidmore and Norma Winstone, whom he would later marry. He also worked with established stars such as Marian Montgomery, Cleo Laine and John Dankworth. In the late 60s he began to lead his own trio and sextet with Kenny Wheeler, Chris Pyne, Stan Sulzmann, Chris Laurence and Tony Levin. He also played in Sulzmann's quartet, with Winstone in Edge Of Time and with Mike Gibbs. He was a member of Surman's outstanding but short-lived Morning Glory with Terje Rypdal. His collaboration with Surman, which produced some of the most inventive and original jazz-based music of the 70s and 80s, has continued to the present. In the mid-70s he spent some time with the Ronnie Scott quintet. In 1977, with Wheeler and Winstone, he formed Azimuth (not to be confused with Azymuth), for which he writes most of the music. At the end of the decade he played with Jan Garbarek, Arild Andersen and Miroslav Vitous. He has also worked with Lee Konitz, John Warren, Graham Collier, and Harry Beckett. His rich, fluid playing, inspired in part by Bill Evans, is especially distinctive on ballads. He is also an accomplished composer, and credits Gibbs with being a fundamental influence on his writing. In the 90s Taylor continues to work with Azimuth, to play in a regular duo with Winstone and to lead his own trio, with Mick Hutton and Steve Argüelles.

● ALBUMS: *Pause And Think Again* (FMR 1971)★★★★, with Michael Gibbs *Michael Gibbs* (1971)★★★, with John Surman *Morning Glory* (1973)★★★, *Fragment* (1974)★★★, with Miroslav Vitous *Journey's End* (1982)★★★, with Kenny Wheeler *Double Double You* (1983)★★, with Stan Sulzmann *Everybody's Song But My Own* (1987)★★★, with Lee Konitz *Songs Of The Stars* (1988)★★★, *Blue Glass* (Jazz House 1992)★★★★, with Surman *Ambleside Days* (Ah Um 1992)★★★★, with Palle Danielsson, Erskine *You Never Know* (ECM 1993)★★★, with Danielsson, Erskine *Time Being* (ECM 1993)★★★, with Danielsson, Erskine *As It Is* (ECM 1996)★★★★.

TAYLOR, MARTIN

b. 1956. Repeatedly referred to as 'the guitarists' guitarist', Taylor shows an extraordinary flair and natural feel for his instrument that has enabled him to make subtle and profound contributions in a number of different musical styles, and has resulted in a keen and loyal international audience that makes its presence felt on each Taylor tour. An early starter at the age of four, he was playing his first professional performance (in a Harlow, Hertfordshire music shop) at eight, and displaying his genuinely prodigious talent in trad and mainstream bands led by Sonny Dee and Lennie Hastings by 1968. Turning professional at the first opportunity three years later, Taylor spent much of the 70s honing his talents in swing bands and café residencies, and enjoying the occasional opportunity to sit in with and impress visiting Americans, including Count Basie (whom he met on a cruise ship) and Barney Kessel. His first album, a duo with bassist Peter Ind, was released on Ind's Wave label in 1978, and a year later he established his celebrated and continuing relationship with the legendary swing violinist Stéphane Grappelli, touring internationally, recording with Grappelli and classical violin virtuoso Yehudi Menuhin and broadcasting live on the BBC with Grappelli and popular composer Julian Lloyd Webber. Touring with Grappelli, whose previous guitar partners had included the brilliant Django Reinhardt and Joe Pass, helped introduce Taylor's talents to a wider audience, and appearances during 1981 at Carnegie Hall, the Hollywood Bowl, the Royal Opera House and on Johnny Carson's *Tonight Show* marked the beginning of a busy decade - as Taylor concurrently worked at perfecting his solo style while in the UK, and continued steadily to build a solid reputation amongst America's jazz musicians, touring with guitarist Emily Remler, and recording with Toots Thielemans, Buddy De Franco (their album *Groovin'* was voted Jazz Album of the Year by the British Music Retailers Association), Paulinho De Costa and John Patitucci, Chet Atkins, and finally replacing Herb Ellis in the Great Guitars trio with Charlie Byrd and Barney Kessel. Since 1990, Taylor has been touring increasingly under his own name, playing sell-out dates and televised concerts in Australia, Hong Kong and Israel, and enjoying greater recognition in the UK, partly as a result of a fruitful relationship with Linn Records. His 1993 *Artistry* was the culmination of years spent developing a 'complete' solo style. Performing on a custom-made 'stereo guitar' that separates the bass and treble strings into different channels, Taylor accompanies his own swinging improvisations with chords and walking bass lines, providing a record of the kind of performance that has left so many other guitarists stunned in recent years.

● ALBUMS: *Taylor Made* (Wave 1978)★★★, with Stéphane Grappelli *At The Winery* (1980)★★★, with Grappelli, Yehudi Menuhin *Strictly For The Birds* (1980)★★★★, with Grappelli, Menuhin *Top Hat* (1981)★★★, *Skye Boat* (Concord 1981)★★★, with Grappelli *Vintage '81* (1981)★★★, with Grappelli *Live In San Francisco* (1982)★★★, *A Tribute To Art Tatum* (Hep 1984)★★, with Buddy De Franco *Groovin'* (1985)★★★, *Innovations* (1985)★★★, *Sarabanda* (Gala 1986)★★★, with Vassar Clements *Together At Last* (1987)★★, *Don't Fret* (Linn 1990)★★★★, *Matter Of Time* (1991)★★★, *Change Of Heart* (Linn 1991)★★★★, *Artistry* (Linn 1993)★★★★, *Spirit Of Django* (Linn 1994)★★★★, with Grappelli *Reunion* 1993 recording (Honest 1995)★★★, with David Grisman *Tone Poems 2* (Acoustic Disc 1995)★★★, *Years Apart* (Linn 1996)★★★, *Portraits* (Linn 1996)★★★, *Two's Company* (Linn 1997)★★★★, *Gypsy* (Linn 1998)★★★.

TAYLOR, MIKE

b. 1938, London, England, d. 1969. Taylor crammed a great deal of work as performer, arranger and composer into his brief career. He played piano from early childhood and by the time he was in his twenties was active as a bandleader, performing a wide range of music, including contemporary jazz, jazz-rock, and rock/pop. He was frequently linked with the rock band, Cream, and with the individual musicians who formed this group, as both player and arranger. His jazz affiliations included Norma Winstone, for whom he wrote arrangements, and Jon Hiseman who played in one of Taylor's early bands.

● ALBUMS: *Pendulum* (Columbia 1965)★★★, *The Mike Taylor Trio* (Columbia 1966)★★★.

TAYLOR, MONTANA

b. Arthur Taylor, 1903, Butte, Montana, USA. Nicknamed after his birthplace, Taylor was raised in Indianapolis, where he learned piano in 1919. He played at cafés and rent parties there and in Chicago, before recording two 78s for Vocalion in 1929. Although one record was partially spoiled by the vocal antics of the Jazoo Boys, Taylor's percussive, inventive piano playing was of the highest order. Shortly afterwards he stopped playing, discouraged by the absence of royalties. Located by jazz fans in 1946, Taylor made a series of recordings that not only showed he retained all his instrumental abilities, both solo and as accompanist to Bertha 'Chippie' Hill, but also revealed him to be a mov-

ing singer, particularly on slow, introspective pieces such as 'I Can't Sleep'. Discouraged anew, however, Taylor dropped out of sight once more, and his subsequent whereabouts are unknown.
● COMPILATIONS: *Montana's Blues* (Oldie Blues 1988)★★★.

TCHICAI, JOHN

b. 28 April 1936, Copenhagen, Denmark. Tchicai, the son of a Danish mother and Congolese father, was the only major non-American figure in the free jazz movement of the early 60s. He had studied violin at first, but then took up alto saxophone and clarinet. Since 1983 he has switched primarily to tenor saxophone. He spent three years at the Aarhus Academy of Music and then moved to the Copenhagen Academy. In 1962 he met Albert Ayler during Ayler's stay in Copenhagen, led his own band at the World Youth Jazz Festival in Helsinki, and worked with Jorgen Leth's quintet at the Warsaw Jazz Festival. As a result of his meeting in Helsinki with Archie Shepp and Bill Dixon he moved to New York in 1963 and joined the New York Contemporary Five, which included Shepp, Dixon (later replaced by Don Cherry for a tour of Europe), Don Moore and J.C. Moses. On his return to New York he founded the New York Art Quartet with Roswell Rudd, Milford Graves and Lewis Worrell (or sometimes Steve Swallow or Eddie Gomez) on bass. He also joined the Jazz Composers' Guild and worked with the Jazz Composers' Orchestra and Carla Bley. In 1965 he took part in John Coltrane's controversial and epoch-making *Ascension*. On returning to Europe in 1966 he played with Gunter Hampel and Cherry as well as leading groups of his own, including Cadentia Nova Danica. CND was an extremely impressive nine-piece band that grew, reaching 26 pieces for its second recording, and finally split, some of its members forming the rock band Burning Red Ivanhoe. In the 70s he worked frequently with Johnny Dyani, who had emigrated to Denmark, and with the Strange Brothers (1976-81), the Instant Composers Pool, George Gruntz and Irène Schweizer. In the early 80s he played with Pierre Dørge, the New Jungle Orchestra, Chris McGregor's Brotherhood Of Breath (*Yes, Please*), De Zes Winden (an all-saxophone group) and, again, Dyani, with whom he was touring at the time of the bassist's death. An impressive and personal improviser, he was a lyrical altoist with a rich tone, and his sound is equally distinctive since moving over to tenor. He also plays soprano sax and bass clarinet and has essayed occasional vocals and synthesizer programming on some recent sessions.
● ALBUMS: with Archie Shepp *Rufus* (1964)★★★, with the New York Contemporary Five *Consequences* (1964)★★★, *New York Eye And Ear Control* (1964)★★★, *New York Contemporary Five Vols. 1 & 2* (1964)★★★, with Shepp *Four For Trane* (1964)★★★, *New York Art Quartet* (1965)★★★, with the New York Art Quartet *Mohawk* (1965)★★★, with John Coltrane *Ascension* (1965)★★★★, *John Tchicai And Cadentia Nova Danica* (Freedom 1969)★★★★, with CND *Afrodisiaca* (1970)★★★, with Irène Schweizer *Willi The Pig* (1976)★★, *Real Tchicai* (1977)★★★, with Strange Brothers *Darktown Highlights* (Storyville 1977)★★, *Solo* (1977)★★★, *John Tchicai And Strange Brothers* (1978)★★★, with Andre Goudbeck *Duets* (1978)★★★, with Goudbeck *Barefoot Dance* (1979)★★★, with Hartmut Geerken *Continent* (Praxis 1981)★★, *Live In Athens* (Praxis 1981)★★★, with Strange Brothers *Merlin Vibrations* (1983)★★★, *Put Up The Fight* (Storyville 1987)★★★, *Timo's Message* 1984 recording (Black Saint 1987)★★★★, *Clinch* (1991)★★★, with Vitold Rek *Satisfaction* (Enja 1992)★★★★, *Love Is Touching* (B&W 1995)★★★★.

TEAGARDEN, CHARLIE

b. 19 July 1913, Vernon, Texas, USA, d. 10 December 1984. A trumpet-playing member of the prodigious Teagarden family, Charlie played in several territory bands during the 20s. At the end of the decade he was in Ben Pollack's band and during the 30s played in bands led by Red Nichols, Paul Whiteman and others. In the 40s he was with Harry James and, most fruitfully, Jimmy Dorsey. Throughout these years he regularly played and recorded with his brother Jack Teagarden. In the 50s he mingled studio work in Hollywood with appearances in the Bob Crosby band and eventually settled in Las Vegas, playing in casino and hotel bands. A rich-toned trumpeter, with a joyous ring to everything he played, Little T's career was inevitably, if rather unfairly, overshadowed by that of his famous brother.
● ALBUMS: with Jimmy Dorsey *Dorseyland Band* (1950)★★★, *Big Horn* (1962)★★★.

TEAGARDEN, CUB

b. Clois Lee Teagarden, 16 December 1915, Vernon, Texas, USA, d. 1969. Youngest of the noted Teagarden family of jazz musicians, Cub played drums in various territory bands in the 30s. He touched the edge of the big time with the big band led by his brother, Jack Teagarden, at the end of the 30s but this was a short-lived experience. Thereafter, he gigged on the west coast until his eventual retirement from full-time music at the end of the 40s.

TEAGARDEN, JACK

b. Weldon L. Teagarden, 29 August 1905, Vernon, Texas, USA, d. 15 January 1964. One of the giants of jazz, Teagarden began playing trombone and singing in and around his home-town, encouraged by his mother, Helen Teagarden, a pianist. From his early teens he was playing professionally, touring with various bands, notably that led by Peck Kelley. He continued to gain experience with a number of bands, his reputation spreading ahead of him until, by the time he reached New York City in the late 20s, he was ready for the big time. He joined Ben Pollack in 1928 and through his work with this band, and numerous record dates, he frightened just about every other trombone player in the country into either changing their approach or contemplating premature retirement. He recorded extensively with small bands and with Paul Whiteman, and appeared frequently on radio, sometimes forming his own small groups. An attempt at leading a big band was doomed to failure, due in part to Teagarden's casual and unbusinesslike manner and also to his fondness for drink. In 1946 he became a member of Louis Armstrong's All Stars, touring extensively and reaching audiences who had long idolized him through his recordings. In 1951 he left Armstrong to form his own band. During the remainder of his life he led small groups, some of which included his brother and sister, Charlie and Norma Teagarden. He was also co-leader with Earl Hines of an all-star band that included Peanuts Hucko, Cozy Cole and Max Kaminsky. The ceaseless touring and drinking weakened him and he died suddenly in 1964.

Teagarden's trombone playing was smooth and stylish and quite unlike any player before him. Although his consummate skill affected the playing of numerous other trombone players, Teagarden's style was not really developed by his successors. When he played the blues he was much closer to the work of black musicians than any other white musician of his generation. His relaxed sound concealed a thorough command of his instrument and in retrospect it is easy to understand the fear he inspired in musicians like Glenn Miller and Bill Rank. A pointer to the awe with which he was regarded in the profession is the fact that even Tommy Dorsey, himself one of the most technically distinguished trombonists in jazz, refused to play a solo when he found himself on a record date with Teagarden. Heavily influenced by the black blues singers he heard as a child in Texas, Teagarden was also a remarkable singer. He sang in a sleepy drawl and formed a significant bridge in popular music, linking the blues to the white crooning style of Bing Crosby. Despite the success of his blues singing, his later performances with Armstrong inclined more towards the humour and easy-going charm that reflected his personality. Thanks to a succession of definitive recordings, on which he ably demonstrated his superlative trombone technique and lazy vocal charm, Teagarden made many songs his own. These include 'I'm Coming Virginia', 'If I Could Be With You One Hour Tonight', 'Aunt Hagar's Blues', 'The Sheik Of Araby' and, especially, 'Stars Fell On Alabama' and 'Basin Street Blues'.

● ALBUMS: with Benny Goodman *Goodman & Teagarden* 10-inch album (Jazz Panorama 1951)★★★★, *The Blues* 10-inch album (Royale 1951)★★★, with Goodman *Benny Goodman Featuring Jack Teagarden* 10-inch album (Jolly Rogers 1954)★★★★, *Meet The New Jack Teagarden* 10-inch album (Urania 1954)★★★, *Jack Teagarden Sings And Plays* 10-inch album (Urania 1954)★★★, *Meet Me Where They Play The Blues* 10-inch album (Period 1955)★★★, *Original Dixieland* 10-inch album (Period 1955)★★★★, *Jack Teagarden* 10-inch album (Jolly Roger 1955)★★★, *Jazz Great* (Bethlehem 1955)★★★, with Bobby Hackett *Coast Concert* (Capitol 1956)★★★★, *Big T's Jazz* (Decca 1956)★★★, with Rex Stewart *Big Jazz* (Atlantic 1956)★★★, *This Is Teagarden* (Capitol 1956)★★★★, with Van Alexander *Jack Teagarden With Van Alexander's Orchestra* (1956)★★★, with Pee Wee Russell *Jack Teagarden's Big Eight/Pee Wee Russell's Rhythmakers* 1938-1940 recordings (Riverside 1956)★★★, with Earl 'Fatha' Hines*The Jack Teagarden-Earl Hines All Stars In England* (1957)★★★★, with Hines *The Jack Teagarden-Earl Hines All Stars At The Olympia Theatre, Paris* (1957)★★★, *Swing Low Sweet Spiritual* (Capitol 1957)★★★, with Hackett *Jazz Ultimate* (Capitol 1958)★★★★, *The Blues And Dixie* (Rondo-lette 1958)★★★, with Red Allen, Kid Ory *Red Allen, Jack Teagarden & Kid Ory At Newport* (Verve 1958)★★★★, *Big T's Dixieland Band* (Capitol 1959)★★★★, *Shades Of Night* (Capitol 1959)★★★, with Jonah Jones *Dixieland* (Bethlehem 1959)★★★, with Hackett *Jack Teagarden And Bobby Hackett* (Commodore 1959)★★★★, *Jack Teagarden At The Round Table* (Roulette 1960)★★★, *Jazz Maverick* (Roulette 1961)★★★, *Mis'ry And The Blues* (Verve 1961)★★★, *Think Well Of Me* (Verve 1962)★★★, *Jack Teagarden!!* (Verve 1962)★★★, *Dixie Sound* (Roulette 1962)★★★, *Portrait Of Mr. T* (Roulette 1963)★★★, *Hollywood Bowl Concert* (1963)★★★.

● COMPILATIONS: *King Of The Blues Trombone* 3-LP set (Epic 1963)★★★★, *The Golden Horn Of Jack Teagarden* (Decca 1964)★★★, *Jack Teagarden* 3-LP box set (XFL 1979)★★★★, *The Complete Capitol Fifties Jack Teagarden Sessions* 6-LP/4-CD box set (Mosaic 1996)★★★★.

● FURTHER READING: *Jack Teagarden's Music*, H. Walters Jnr. *Jack Teagarden: The Story Of A Jazz Maverick*, Jay D. Smith and Len Guttridge.

● FILMS: *Birth Of The Blues* (1941).

TEAGARDEN, NORMA

b. Norma Louise Teagarden, 28 April 1911, Vernon, Texas, USA, d. 6 June 1996, San Francisco, California, USA. Norma Teagarden was born into the famed Teagarden family of musicians, headed by elder brother and trombonist Jack Teagarden. She took early lessons on piano from her mother, Helen, with whom she played at the 1963 Monterey Jazz Festival, alongside other family members. By that time, however, the family members already had a long track record of jazz performance and composition. As a teenager Norma played professionally in Oklahoma City, before leaving home at the age of 18 to play with territory bands that toured Texas and New Mexico. In 1939 she and her brothers joined the first of Jack's many unsuccessful attempts to form a jazz big band. That group disbanded in 1946 and Norma moved to Long Beach for solo engagements. As well as leading her own unit she also worked in Ada Leonard's All Girl Orchestra. She subsequently took a position at the Hangover Club in San Francisco, where she often played opposite Earl 'Fatha' Hines. In the meantime, Jack had been working with Louis Armstrong's band, but when he left them after five years' service in 1952, he again recruited Norma (and brother Charlie Teagarden) to his new California-based sextet. She married John Friedlander in 1955 after meeting him on tour in Milwaukee. Afterwards she temporarily retired from music, aside from giving irregular piano lessons. It was only when the couple and their children moved to San Francisco that she returned to jazz, working with bands led by Turk Murphy and Pete Daily. Her first solo residency for many years came at the Washington Square Bar And Grill in 1975 - and she remained there for nearly two decades until ill-health forced a permanent retirement in the mid-90s.

Teague, Thurman

b. 1910, Illinois, USA, d. date unknown. Early in his career he played banjo and guitar with various bands in and around Chicago. By the early 30s he had switched to playing bass and subsequently worked with popular bandleaders Ben Pollack and Vincent Lopez. At the end of the 30s he joined Harry James, becoming the mainstay of the band's rhythm section through until the middle of the next decade. After a short spell with Red Nichols, Teague settled in Los Angeles, becoming an in-demand studio musician. His playing with James shows Teague to have been a fine player with good time and technique, qualities that doubtless directed his career choices in later years.

● COMPILATIONS: *The Uncollected Harry James Vols. 1-5* (Hindsight 1939-46)★★★.

Tee, Richard

b. 24 November 1943, New York, USA, d. 21 July 1993, New York, USA. Tee had 12 years of classical training on the piano and went to the High School of Music and Art. When he graduated, a contact obtained him work as house pianist at Motown Records, which was then turning out a string of hits. His first recording was with Marvin Gaye. In time Tee became a staff arranger and as well as playing the piano discovered the orchestral capabilities of the Hammond organ. When he returned to New York he continued to work in the studio. He described his playing thus: 'Chords and rhythm are my meat; even my solos are mostly chords. I try to be an orchestra and I feel most comfortable playing everything I can with 10 fingers.' He played on numerous records with musicians as diverse as Roland Kirk, Carly Simon, Joe Cocker and Herbie Mann. In 1976 he played in the influential funk band Stuff along with other session musicians including Eric Gale and Steve Gadd. The band recorded several well-received albums and Tee's solo career with CBS saw him marketed alongside contemporary 'smooth' jazz artists such as Bob James and Lonnie Liston Smith. Tee was one of the small core of musicians Paul Simon regularly used to record and perform with over the years. In 1991 Tee also played live with Paul Simon on the Rhythm Of The Saints tour. He ascribed his popularity on sessions to a willingness to keep things simple and not to restrict the leader's efforts: 'I play a constant rhythm that doesn't really change, and I try to keep it simple so that it gives others a chance to put their two cents in.'

● ALBUMS: with Stuff *Stuff* (Warners 1977)★★★, with Stuff *Live In Japan* (Warners 1979)★★★, *Strokin'* (1979)★★★, *Natural Ingredients* (1980)★★★, *The Bottom Line* (1985)★★★, *Real Time* (One Voice 1995)★★★.

Temiz, Okay

b. 11 February 1939, Istanbul, Turkey. Temiz first learned Turkish music from his mother and later studied classical percussion and tympani. He started to play drums professionally in 1955 and toured with Turkish show groups in Turkey and North Africa. During 1969-70 he played with the Don Cherry Trio and in 1970 he toured with the famous Turkish musician Binali Selman. He became a founder-member of the Swedish-Turkish group Sevda in 1971 and played with them until 1972. He then participated in the trio Music For Xaba together with Johnny Mbizo Dyani and Mongezi Feza. He rejoined Sevda in 1973 and started his own trio in 1974 with which he recorded Turkish Folk Jaz. In the mid-70s he formed the group Oriental Wind, which has since been the main outlet for his activities. This group mixes modal jazz improvisation with Turkish and Oriental music forms in uneven time signatures. Temiz' drums are of his own design and are made of hand-beaten copper after the ideal of the Turkish drums Dumbukas and Darbukas.

● ALBUMS: with Johnny Dyani, Mongezi Feza *Music For Xaba* (1972)★★★, with Sevda *Jazz I Sverige '72* (1972)★★★, *Live At Jazzhus Montmartre* (1972)★★★, *Live At Fregatten* (1973)★★, with Berndt Rosengren *Notes From Underground* (1974)★★★, *Sankirna* (1975)★★★, *Turkish Folk Jazz* (1975)★★★, with Oriental Wind *Oriental Wind* (1977)★★, with Salih Baysal *The Myth* (1978)★★★, with Don Cherry *Live In Ankara* (1978)★★★, *Music For Xaba Vol. II* (1979)★★★, *Zikir* (1979)★★★, *Chila-Chila* (1979)★★★, with Percussion Summit *Percussion Summit* (1984)★★, *Misket* (1991)★★★, *Magnet Dance* (Enja 1995)★★★.

Temperance 7

Formed in 1955 to play 20s-style jazz, the Temperance 7 consisted at various times of Whispering Paul McDowell (vocals), Captain Cephas Howard (trumpet, euphonium and various instruments), Joe Clark (clarinet), Alan Swainston-Cooper (pedal clarinet, swanee whistle), Philip 'Finger' Harrison (banjo, alto and baritone sax), Canon Colin Bowles (piano, harmonica), Clifford Beban (tuba), Brian Innes (drums), Dr. John Grieves-Watson (banjo), Sheik Haroun el John R.T. Davies (trombone, alto sax) and Frank Paverty (sousaphone). Their debut single, 'You're Driving Me Crazy' (producer George Martin's first number 1), was followed by three more hits in 1961, 'Pasadena', 'Hard Hearted Hannah'/'Chili Bom Bom', and 'Charleston'. In 1963 they appeared in the play *The Bed Sitting Room* written by John Antrobus and Spike Milligan. They split in the mid-60s, but their spirit resurfaced in groups such as the Bonzo Dog Doo-Dah Band and the New Vaudeville Band. The Temperance 7 were re-formed in the 70s by Ted Wood, brother of the Rolling Stones' Ron Wood. Colin Bowles is reported to have died several years ago, but the other members are said to be pursuing a variety of interests, including publishing, film set and graphic designing, acting and antiques.

● ALBUMS: *Temperance 7* (Parlophone 1961)★★★★, *Temperance 7 Plus One* (Argo 1961)★★★, *Hot Temperance 7* (1987)★★★, *Tea For Eight* (1990)★★★, *33 Not Out* (1990)★★★.

● COMPILATIONS: *Pasadena & The Lost Cylinders* (Lake 1997)★★★.

Temperley, Joe

b. 20 September 1929, Cowdenbeath, Scotland. After taking a few lessons on alto saxophone, Temperley began gigging at clubs in Glasgow. When he was 20 he joined the Tommy Sampson band, returning with them to London. He then worked with Harry Parry, Joe Loss, Jack Parnell, Tony Crombie and others, and during this period began playing tenor saxophone. A mid-50s stint with Tommy Whittle brought a further change of instrument, this time onto baritone saxophone. He then joined Humphrey Lyttelton, in whose band he remained for seven years. It was while he was with Lyttelton that he made his first big impression on the international jazz scene and in 1965 he settled in the USA, playing in the bands of Woody Herman, Buddy Rich, Buck Clayton, Duke Pearson and the Thad Jones-Mel Lewis Jazz Orchestra. During the 70s he played in Clark Terry's band and in the Duke Ellington orchestra, which was continuing under the direction of Mercer Ellington. From the late 70s onwards he freelanced, mainly in New York City, but also finding time for touring and recording with several musicians, including Jimmy Knepper, Kathy Stobart and Scott Hamilton. A major saxophonist and one of the outstanding baritone players in jazz, Temperley plays with an enviable sonority, bringing wit and imagination to his solos. The fluidity of his playing shows that in skilled hands this most demanding of instruments is capable not only of power and drive but also of warmth and moving tenderness.

● ALBUMS: with Humphrey Lyttelton *Humph Plays Standards* (1960)★★★★, *Le Vrai Buck Clayton* (1964)★★★, with Clark Terry *Live On 57th Street* (1970)★★★, with Mercer Ellington *Continuum* (1975)★★★, with Jimmy Knepper *Just Friends* (Hep 1978)★★, *Nightingale* (Hep 1993)★★★, *Concerto For Joe* (Hep 1994)★★★, with Dave McKenna *Sunbeam And Thundercloud* (Concord Jazz 1996)★★★, *With Every Breath* (Hep 1998)★★★.

TERRASSON, JACKY

b. 27 November 1966, Berlin, Germany. Born to a music loving French mother and an American father, Terrasson began playing piano at the age of five. His musical upbringing was steeped in the music of the jazz greats, from Billie Holiday and Bill Evans to Miles Davis and Thelonious Monk. Terrasson studied at the Berklee College of Music in Boston before moving to the heart of the action, playing clubs in New York and Chicago. His first break came when Betty Carter hired him at a recording session, after which he spent a year on the road with the legendary jazz vocalist. Terrasson has since become one of the most in demand sideman in jazz, but his big break as a leader came when he one the Thelonious Monk Piano Competition in 1993. The resultant media attention led to a prestigious recording contract with Blue Note Records, and the fêting of Terrasson as one of the new 'Young Lions' on the traditional jazz scene. Working in a trio with bassist Ugonna Okegwo and drummer Leon Parker, Terrasson breathes new life into old standards, including 'I Love Paris' and 'I Fall In Love Too Easily' from 1994's self-titled debut, and 'For Sentimental Reasons' and 'Smoke Gets In Your Eyes' (as a medley with his own 'Reach') on 1996's sophomore set, *Reach*. Following a high profile arranging/recording session for Jimmy Scott's *Heaven*, Terrasson teamed up with one of jazz's brighest new singers, Cassandra Wilson, for the atmospheric *Rendezvous*.

● ALBUMS: *Jacky Terrasson* (Blue Note 1994)★★★, *Reach* (Blue Note 1996)★★★★, with Cassandra Wilson *Rendezvous* (Blue Note 1997)★★★★.

TERRELL, PHA

b. Pha Elmer Terrell, 25 May 1910, Kansas City, Missouri, USA, d. 14 October 1945. He first sang and danced in his home-town and made an impression upon bandleader Andy Kirk who hired him in 1933. Terrell remained with Kirk for seven years, then sang with other bands and also as a single, mostly in the Los Angeles area where he died at 35. Unlike many of the Midwestern instrumentalists in whose work there is a strong thread of the blues, Terrell favoured sentimental ballads which he sang in a high tenor, sometimes using falsetto, a characteristic that was popular among singers of the time. His sophisticated style blended well with the similarly smooth and practised Kirk band. For all the style he projected on records, however, Terrell did have a jazzman's soul. Jo Jones recalled nights in Kansas City, 'with guys like Dick Wilson and Ben Webster, and sometimes Pha Terrell would come right out of the audience and sing right in the middle of a number, and he knew exactly where to start.'

TERRITORY BANDS

Many of the popular dance and jazz orchestras of the late 20s and 30s were based in New York. Even those bands that toured extensively started and ended their trips on the east coast, and thus found the accumulation of musicians in New York particularly helpful when hiring new men. Additionally, most of the leading recording and broadcasting companies had their headquarters in the city. However, New York was far from the whole story. Many fine bands rarely came there, some never at all. Many of the bands that worked extensively, sometimes exclusively in the Midwest, south and south-western states, based themselves in other centres. These bands were referred to by people in the music business as territory bands, a term that should not be regarded as having dismissive connotations. Perhaps the region with the most notable tradition in high-quality dance and jazz orchestras was Texas. Based in Dallas were the fine Alphonso Trent band, generally regarded as the best of the territory bands, plus outfits led by Don Albert, Terrence Holder and Doc Ross, in whose band Jack Teagarden played. The Milt Larkins and Nat Towles units, both bands highly regarded amongst musicians, were based in Houston; and San Antonio had Boots And His Buddies, led by drummer Clifford 'Boots' Douglas, and Troy Floyd. Even smaller towns, such as Amarillo, had exceptional bands, in this case Gene Coy's Happy Black Aces. Texas was not the only state with a musical tradition. In Denver, Colorado, George Morrison led an exceptional band that at times included musicians such as Andy Kirk and

Jimmie Lunceford. St Louis, Missouri was the homebase for Charlie Creath, Dewey Jackson, Frank Trumbauer, the Jeter-Pillars Orchestra, and the Missourians, a band with which Blanche and Cab Calloway were associated. Oklahoma City boasted Eugene Crookes and the Blue Devils, a band led by Walter Page and whose sidemen, and leader, eventually became important in the development of the bands of Bennie Moten and Count Basie. Milwaukee, Wisconsin had Grant Moore; Omaha, Nebraska had Clarence Love, Lloyd Hunter and Red Perkins; and Cincinnati, Ohio was home to Zack Whyte's Chocolate Beau Brummels. Salina, Kansas was the base for Art Bronson's Bostonians. Although the south-west and Midwest is usually thought of as home for the territory bands, those from California and Massachusetts should not be overlooked. These included the Los Angeles-based bands of the Spikes Brothers, Charlie Echols and Les Hite, while outstanding on the north-east coast was Boston-based Sabby Lewis. For all the status and quality of bands such as these, however, Kansas City, Missouri was the single most important centre outside of New York. The city boasted an enviable roster of superb bands, many of which went on to national and international fame, while individual sidemen became important, and in some cases legendary, figures of jazz. Most of the bands already referred to passed through Kansas City (see Kansas City Jazz). A list of sidemen who played in territory bands during their formative years would be almost endless, but amongst those who must be mentioned are Lester Young, Ben Webster, Herschel Evans, Buddy Tate, Oran 'Hot Lips' Page, Jimmy Rushing, Harry Edison, Charlie Christian, Snub Mosley, Peanuts Holland, Gene Ramey, Budd Johnson, Arnett Cobb, Illinois Jacquet and Earl Bostic. Numerous compilation albums have been released, most of which bear confusingly similar titles, such as *The Territory Bands*.

● FURTHER READING: *Jazz Style In Kansas City And The Southwest*, Ross Russell.

TERRY, CLARK

b. 14 December 1920, St. Louis, Missouri, USA. Terry gained invaluable experience playing trumpet in local bands, but developed his remarkable technique while in the US Navy. As he recalled for jazz writer Steve Voce, he practised using a clarinet book, preferring the more fluid sound this generated in his playing. After his military service he joined Charlie Barnet, then became a mainstay of the Count Basie band for three years until 1951, when he joined Duke Ellington for an eight-year stint. At the end of the 50s he went into studio work in New York City, becoming one of the first black musicians regularly to be employed in this way. For a dozen years he was featured in the Doc Severinsen band, which played on the Johnny Carson *Tonight Show*. During this time he continued to play in jazz groups for club and record dates, working with Bob Brookmeyer, J.J. Johnson and others, and also leading his own 'Big B-A-D Band', which featured many leading New York session men. In the early 70s Terry became a member of Norman Granz's Pablo edition of Jazz At The Philharmonic, and began playing flügelhorn, eventually making this his principal instrument. The 70s and 80s found him touring extensively, playing concerts, clubs and festivals around the world, usually as leader but ably blending in with almost any background from late swing style to post-bop. Terry's remarkable technical accomplishment has never overwhelmed the depth of emotion that imbues his playing, and neither of these characteristics has ever dampened his infectious humour. This quality is most readily apparent on his singing of 'Mumbles', for which he created a unique variation on scat. His duets with himself, during which he plays flügelhorn and trumpet, are remarkable displays of his astonishing skills yet never degenerate into mere bravura exercises. Terry remains a major figure in the history of jazz trumpet and is one of the music's most respected and widely admired ambassadors.

● ALBUMS: *Introducing Clark Terry* (EmArcy 1955)★★★, *The Jazz School* (Wing 1955)★★, *Out On A Limb* (Argo 1957)★★, *Serenade To A Bus Seat* (Riverside 1957)★★★★, *Duke With A Difference* (Riverside 1957)★★★★, with Thelonious Monk *In Orbit* reissued as *C.T. Meets Monk* (Riverside 1958)★★★★, *In Orbit* (Riverside 1958)★★★★, *Top And Bottom Brass* (Riverside 1959)★★★★, *Color Changes* (Candid 1960)★★★, *Everything's Mellow* (Moodsville 1961)★★★, *The Jazz Version Of 'All American'* (Moodsville 1962)★★★, *What Makes Sammy Swing!* (20th Century Fox 1963)★★★, with Coleman Hawkins *Eddie Costa Memorial Concert* (Colpix 1963)★★★, shared with Gary Burton, Sonny Rollins *3 In Jazz* (RCA Victor 1963)★★★, *More* (Cameo 1964)★★★, *Tread Ye Lightly* (Cameo 1964)★★★★, *The Happy Horn Of Clark Terry* (Impulse! 1964)★★★★, with Bob Brookmeyer *Clark Terry Tonight* (Mainstream 1965)★★★, *The Power Of Positive Swinging* (Mainstream 1965)★★★, *Mumbles* (Mainstream 1966)★★★, *Spanish Rice* (Impulse! 1966)★★★, with Brookmeyer *Gingerbread Men* (Mainstream 1966)★★★, *It's What's Happenin'* (Impulse! 1968)★★★, *Clark Terry At The Montreux Jazz Festival* (1969)★★★★, *Big B-A-D-Band Live On 57th Street* (1970)★★★, *Big B-A-D-Band Live at The Wichita Jazz Festival* (Vanguard 1974)★★★, *Clark Terry And His Jolly Giants* (Vanguard 1975)★★★, *Ain't Misbehavin'* (Pablo 1976)★★★★, *Wham! Live At The Lighthouse* (1976)★★★, *Big B-A-D-Band Live At Buddy's Place* (Vanguard 1976)★★★, *Clark After Dark* (1977)★★★, *The Globetrotter* (1977)★★★, *Out Of Nowhere* (Bingow 1978)★★★, *Funk Dumplin's* (Matrix 1978)★★★, *Clark Terry's Big Band In Warsaw* (1978)★★★, *Brahms Lullaby* (1978)★★★, *Mother...! Mother...!* (Pablo 1979)★★★, *Clark Terry At Buffalo State* (1979)★★★, *Memories Of Duke* (Pablo 1980)★★★★, *'Yes, The Blues'* (1981)★★★, with Red Mitchell *To Duke And Basie* (Rhino 1986)★★★★, *Take Double* (1986)★★★, with Mitchell *Jive At Five* (Enja 1988)★★★★, *Portraits* (Chesky 1988)★★★★, *The Clark Terry Spacemen* (1989)★★★, with Oliver Jones *Just Friends* (1989)★★★, *Live From The Village Gate* (Chesky 1990)★★★★, *Having Fun* (Delos 1991)★★★, and the De Paul University Big Band *Clark Terry Express* (Reference 1996)★★★, with George Robert 1993 recording *The Good Things In Life* (Mons 1996)★★★, *Express* (Reference 1996)★★★, with Frank Wess and the De Paul Jazz Ensemble *Big Band Basie* (Reference 1996)★★★, with Phil Woods *Lucerne*

1978 (TCOB 1997)★★★, *What A Wonderful World* 1993 recording (Red Baron 1997★★★★), with Carol Sloane *The Songs Ella & Louis Sang* (Concord Jazz 1998)★★.

TESCHEMACHER, FRANK

b. 13 March 1906, Kansas City, Missouri, USA, d. 1 March 1932. Raised in Chicago, Teschemacher first took up violin then played various other instruments before settling on alto saxophone. He played with many of the young emergent Chicagoans, including Jimmy McPartland, making many jazz records while playing in dance bands for a living. In 1925 he began playing clarinet, the instrument on which he made his greatest mark. In the late 20s he played in the bands of Ben Pollack, Ted Lewis and Red Nichols, but continued to work in numerous minor groups. At the end of the 20s he resumed playing alto and violin and also occasionally played cornet. Although he appeared on many fine jazz recordings with Red McKenzie, Eddie Condon and others, usually on clarinet, his contributions here rarely support the enormously high regard in which he was held by his fellow musicians. Shortly after he joined a new band formed by Wild Bill Davison he was killed in a road accident in March 1932.

● COMPILATIONS: with various leaders *Chicago Jazz Vol. 1* (1928-30)★★★.

THELIN, EJE

b. Eilert Ove Thelin, 9 September 1938, Jonkoping, Sweden, d. 18 May 1990. Thelin was one of the strongest voices on the trombone to emerge from Europe in the 60s. His knowledge of every style of jazz helped him to develop an identity for his own groups and gave him the opportunity of playing with illustrious visitors such as George Russell. Thelin moved to Austria where he taught for five years, while still jointly leading a group with Joachim Kuhn; they both appeared on *Eternal Rhythm* by Don Cherry. On his return to Sweden Thelin continued to lead his own groups and obtained a government stipend for life as a leading artist. Sadly, he died in his early 50s in 1990. Thelin will be remembered as one of the most powerful trombonists in modal and free music to come from Europe.

● ALBUMS: with Don Cherry *Eternal Rhythm* (1969)★★★, with Jouck Minor and Pierre Favre *Candles of Vision* (1973)★★★, as leader *Live* (1976)★★★, *Raggruppamento* 1989 recording (Phono Sueccia 90s)★★★★.

THEMEN, ART

b. 26 November 1939, Manchester, England. A self-taught musician, Themen played tenor saxophone with a university jazz band while studying medicine at Cambridge. After qualifying as a doctor, he moved to London and in the early 60s played in several blues and R&B bands and also worked in the backing groups for numerous pop sessions. During this period he worked with Alexis Korner, Phil Seamen, Dick Heckstall-Smith, Rod Stewart, Joe Cocker and Long John Baldry. In the late 60s and early 70s his musical direction shifted towards jazz and he played with Barbara Thompson, Michael Garrick, Henry Lowther and Graham Collier. In 1974 he began a long and particularly fruitful association with Stan Tracey, which has continued into the 90s. He has also accompanied numerous visiting US jazzmen, including Al Haig, Red Rodney, George Coleman and Nat Adderley. A highly individual playing style marks Themen's performances and had he chosen to adopt music as a full-time career he would have doubtless been an international artist of considerable stature. That he has achieved his present high standing in the jazz world while at the same time pursuing his medical career as a consultant surgeon, is testimony to his remarkable gifts.

● ALBUMS: with Stan Tracey *Under Milk Wood* (1976)★★★★, with Al Haig *Expressly Ellington* (1978)★★★, with Tracey *Spectrum* (1982)★★★, *Stan Tracey's Hexad Live At Ronnie Scott's* (1985)★★★.

THERE GOES THE NEIGHBORHOOD - GARY BARTZ

Recorded live at New York's famous Birdland Club in November 1990, *There Goes The Neighborhood* is a vivid record of one of modern jazz's most intense and exciting living saxophonists, playing at his peak. Pianist Kenny Barron, bassist Ray Drummond and drummer Ben Riley offer firm support for Bartz's powerful, plaintive alto, as he powers his way through a well-chosen programme of standards and original tunes. Bartz by this time had got over his bland jazz/pop flirtation, and was playing an intense combination of neo-bop and heavy, Coltrane-influenced shapes. Check out the inspired version of 'Impressions'.

● Tracks: *Racism (Blues In Double Bb Minor); On A Misty Night; Laura; Tadd's Delight; Impressions; I've Never Been In Love Before; Flight Path.*

● First released 1990

● UK peak chart position: did not chart

● USA peak chart position: did not chart

THIELE, BOB

b. 1922, Brooklyn, New York, USA, d. 30 January 1996, New York City, New York, USA. Thiele was one of the most important and prolific jazz and pop producers in US popular music. A teenage jazz fan, Thiele joined the US Decca company after World War II and produced Teresa Brewer and the McGuire Sisters. He became head of A&R for Coral Records in 1958. There he supervised hundreds of records including hits by Jackie Wilson, as well as licensing Buddy Holly material from Norman Petty. In 1961, Thiele set up the Impulse! jazz label with Creed Taylor. Over the rest of the decade he signed and recorded many of the greatest names in the 'new wave' jazz scene, including John Coltrane, Charles Mingus, Dizzy Gillespie, Sonny Rollins, Archie Shepp and Albert Ayler. His biggest hit, however, was with Louis Armstrong's 'What A Wonderful World', which he co-wrote with George David Weiss. Thiele's first independent label had been Signature, during the brief life of which he had released jazz-and-poetry records by beat-poet Jack Kerouac and jazz pianist Art Hodes. In 1969 he set up the Flying Dutchman label with Bernard 'Pretty' Purdie as musical director. Among its signings were Gil Scott-Heron and Lonnie Liston Smith, whose records Thiele continued to produce until the late 80s. He married Teresa Brewer in 1972, some 20 years after he first recorded her. After Flying Dutchman was closed down, Thiele returned to freelance production but in 1983 he founded Dr. Jazz, a company devoted to mainstream jazz from the orchestras of Duke Ellington and Count Basie as well as Brewer. In 1988, Dr. Jazz was sold to CBS but Thiele returned three years later, launching Red Baron Records with albums from Brewer and McCoy Tyner. He died of kidney failure.

● FURTHER READING: *What A Wonderful World*, Bob Golden.

THIELEMANS, TOOTS

b. Jean Baptiste Thielemans, 29 April 1922, Brussels, Belgium. A child prodigy, Thielemans played the accordion at the age of three (a home-made version; a real one would have considerably outweighed him), switching to harmonica in his mid-teens. A few years later he added the guitar to his instrumental roll-call and also became an accomplished whistler. The guitar apart, Thielemans' chosen instruments were not especially suited to jazz, but he displayed enough invention and assurance to be hired by Benny Goodman for a European tour in 1950 and by George Shearing in 1953 for a spell that lasted over five years. In the 60s his popularity increased with a successful recording of his own composition, 'Bluesette', and he worked frequently in clubs in Europe and the USA and at international festivals. His activity continued throughout the following two decades and he played with leading artists such as Oscar Peterson and Dizzy Gillespie. He has also played on the soundtracks of many films. Most distinctive on harmonica, Thielemans has gone far towards correcting the prejudice felt by many jazz fans towards this instrument. A momentary shift in the late 80s into jazz-rock fusion was less than wholly successful; he remains happiest in a bop setting, while displaying a fine command of ballads on his many recordings. Whilst the harmonica has only limited appeal in a jazz setting, Thielemans has made the genre his own.

● ALBUMS: *The Sound* (Columbia 1955)★★★, with George Shearing *On Stage!* (1958)★★★, *Man Bites Harmonica* (Riverside 1958)★★★★, *Time Out For Toots* (Decca 1958)★★★★, *Toots Thielemans And His Orchestra* (1958)★★★, *The Toots Thielemans Quartet* i (1959)★★★, *The Soul Of Toots Thielmans* (Signature 1960)★★★, *Toots Thielemans With Kurt Edelhagen And His Orchestra* (1960)★★★, *The Toots Thielemans Quartet* ii (1960)★★★, *The Toots Thielemans Quartet* iii (1961)★★★, *The Toots Thielemans Trio* (1961)★★★, *Toots Thielemans And Arne Domnerus* (1961)★★★, *Toots Thielemans And Dick Hyman* (1962)★★★, *The Whistler And His Guitar* (ABC 1965)★★, *Contrasts* (c.1967)★★★, *Toots Thielemans With Herbie Hancock* (1968)★★★, *Toots Thielemans With Orchestra* overdubbed (1969)★★, *A Taste Of Toots* (1970)★★★, *Live* (Sonet 1972)★★★, *Toots Thielemans And Friends* (1974)★★★, *Toots Thielemans Captured Alive* (Polydor 1974)★★★, *The Oscar Peterson Big Six At Montreux* (1975)★★★, *Live Two* (1975)★★★, *Old Friends* (1976)★★★, *Live Three* (1976)★★★, *Toots Thielemans* iii (1978)★★★, *Slow Motion* (c.1979)★★★, *Apple Dimple* (Denon 1979)★★★, *Live In The Netherlands* (1980)★★★, *Dizzy Gillespie At Montreux* (1980)★★★, *Jean 'Toots' Thielemans Live!* (1981)★★★, *Nice To Meet You* (c.1981)★★★, *Chiko's Bar* (1985)★★★, *Your Precious Love* (1985)★★★, *Just Friends* (Jazzline 1986)★★★, *Do Not Leave Me* (Stash 1986)★★★, *Only Trust Your Heart* (Concord 1988)★★★, *Footprints* (Emarcy 1989)★★★, *For My Lady* (Emarcy 1992)★★★, *The Brasil Project* (1992)★★★, *Chez Toots* (Windham Hill 1998)★★★★.

● COMPILATIONS: *The Silver Collection* (Polydor 1985)★★★★.

THIGPEN, BEN

b. Benjamin F. Thigpen, 16 November 1908, Laurel, Mississippi, USA, d. 5 October 1971. As a child he first played piano but then switched to drums. Thigpen played drums professionally in local bands, then moved to Chicago where he studied with Jimmy Bertrand. Subsequently, he played in numerous territory bands until 1930 when he joined Andy Kirk. He remained with Kirk's Clouds Of Joy until 1947, around the time that this highly successful and popular band folded. After leaving Kirk, Thigpen settled in St. Louis, Missouri, playing in local bands and sometimes forming his own groups. Thigpen had three musician children, one of whom is Ed Thigpen, a drummer, like his father. Thigpen's playing with Kirk is a fine example of the best of Midwest percussion - subtle, swinging and always supportive of soloists. While it would be wrong to credit Kirk's success to Thigpen (the entire band was an exceptional example of in-depth musicianship, with an outstanding pianist and arranger in Mary Lou Williams), it is difficult to think of more than a tiny handful of drummers of the time who shared the necessary qualities that he brought to the band. Thigpen also sometimes sang with the band, and in his vocal on 'I'se A Muggin'', recorded in 1935, he takes a scat chorus that uses the word 'be-bop', perhaps the first time on record of a later famous term.

● COMPILATIONS: with Andy Kirk *Walkin' And Swingin'* (Affinity 1936-42)★★★, with Kirk *Andy's Jive* (Swing House 1944-45)★★★.

THIGPEN, ED

b. 28 December 1930, Chicago, Illinois, USA. Following in the footsteps of his father Ben (who played drums with Andy Kirk for almost two decades), Thigpen began playing drums as a child. His first big-name engagement came in 1951 when he joined the Cootie Williams band. Later in the 50s he played with Johnny Hodges, Lennie Tristano, John Coltrane, Bud Powell and most often with Billy Taylor. In the 60s he followed his Taylor stint with another long spell accompanying a noted pianist, this time Oscar Peterson. His sensitive playing style endeared him to singers and he accompanied Dinah Washington in the early 50s and Ella Fitzgerald in the late 60s and early 70s. In 1972 he settled in Scandinavia, playing with visitors such as Johnny Griffin and Art Farmer, and teaching in Copenhagen and Malmö. Thigpen's neat and contained style is ideally suited to a small group setting while his inquiring mind has caused him to introduce many unusual effects into his performances, drawing on Eastern musical traditions. He has written several manuals on drumming techniques and is a tireless educator.

● ALBUMS: with John Coltrane *Cattin'* (1957)★★★, *The Oscar Peterson Trio: Live From Chicago* (1961)★★★★, *Out Of The Storm* (1966)★★★, with Johnny Griffin *Blues For Harvey* (1973)★★★, *Ed Thigpen's Action-Re-Action* (Sonet 1974)★★★, with Art Farmer *Manhattan* (1980)★★★, *Young Men And Olds* (Timeless 1989)★★★, *Easy Flight* (Reckless 1990)★★★★, *Mr. Taste* (Justin Time 1992)★★★.

Thilo, Jesper

b. 28 November 1941, Copenhagen, Denmark. Thilo was educated at the Copenhagen Conservatory of Music on clarinet. In the 60s he played in trumpeter Arnvid Meyer's swing band backing American visitors who included Coleman Hawkins and Ben Webster. Thilo's sound on the tenor saxophone, his main instrument, is close to Eddie 'Lockjaw' Davis but is stylistically quite versatile. Thilo has been a member of the Radio Big Band as well as Copenhagen bands led by Thad Jones and Ernie Wilkins. On record Thilo's solos are models of masterly and elegantly integrated melodic playing, avoiding the rambling, getting-ready-to-play string of choruses. In recent years certain mannerisms have become more pronounced in his playing, in particular passages of 'dotted' rhythmic regularity reminiscent of Hawkins. This is evidence of Thilo's allegiance to a great saxophone tradition, which for him, besides Hawkins and Webster, includes Johnny Hodges.

● ALBUMS: *Swingin' Friends* (Storyville 1981)★★★, with Roland Hanna *Live At Slukefter* (Storyville 80s)★★★, *Jesper Thilo Quintet Featuring Harry Edison* (Storyville 1986)★★, *Shufflin'* (Music Mecca 1990)★★★, *Featuring Hank Jones* (Storyville 1991)★★★, *Jesper Thilo Plays Ellington* (Music Mecca 1992)★★★, *Don't Count Him Out* (Music Mecca 1993)★★★, *Movin' Out* (Storyville 1994)★★★, *Together* (Music Mecca 1996)★★★.

Third Ear Band

Described by founder Glenn Sweeny as 'electric-acid-raga', the music of the UK Third Ear Band employed the drone-like figures and improvisatory techniques beloved by fellow pioneers the Soft Machine and Terry Riley. However, the esoteric, almost preternatural sweep of their work gave the group its originality as they studiously invoked an aura of ley-lines, druids and cosmology. Sweeny (drums, percussion) had been part of London's free-jazz circle prior to forming two *avant garde* ensembles, the Sun Trolly and the Hydrogen Jukebox. Paul Minns (oboe) and Richard Koss (violin) completed the early Third Ear Band line-up, although cellist Mel Davis augmented the group on their debut *Alchemy*. The unit was later commissioned to compose a soundtrack to Roman Polanski's film, *Macbeth*. However, although their ethereal music provided the ideal accompaniment to this remarkable project, the group's highly stylized approach proved too specialized for mainstream acceptance. Despite record company indifference, Sweeny has pursued his vision into the 90s, while a late-period member, Paul Buckmaster, has become a successful arranger.

● ALBUMS: *Alchemy* (Harvest 1969)★★★★, *Third Ear Band* (Harvest 1970)★★★, *Music From Macbeth* (Harvest 1972)★★, *Magic Music* (1990)★★.

● COMPILATIONS: *Experiences* (Harvest 1976)★★★.

Thomas, Joe (saxophonist)

b. Joseph Vankert Thomas, 19 June 1909, Uniontown, Pennsylvania, USA, d. 3 August 1986. After starting out on alto saxophone, on which instrument he played with Horace Henderson and others, Thomas switched to tenor saxophone. On this instrument he played with Stuff Smith in 1932 and then joined Jimmie Lunceford for a 14-year-long stay. Heavily featured as an instrumentalist and also as an occasional singer, he was one of several key figures in the band. On Lunceford's death Thomas co-led the band for a while but then formed his own small group. In the early 50s he dropped out of full-time music, but made sporadic appearances at festivals and on recording sessions into the late 70s. A forceful soloist, Thomas's playing steadily improved during his spell with Lunceford where the stern discipline exerted by section leader Willie Smith dramatically affected his work.

NB. This musician should not be confused with several others of the same name in jazz, at least two of whom also play tenor saxophone: Joe Thomas (b. 23 December 1908), the brother of Walter 'Foots' Thomas, and Joe Thomas (b. 16 June 1933).

● ALBUMS: *Raw Meat* (1979)★★.

● COMPILATIONS: *The Complete Jimmie Lunceford* (1939-40)★★★★.

Thomas, Joe (trumpeter)

b. Joseph Lewis Thomas, 24 July 1909, Webster Groves, Missouri, USA, d. 6 August 1984. After playing trumpet in several obscure territory bands during the late 20s and early 30s, Thomas settled in New York City in 1933. There he played with the bands of Fletcher Henderson, Fats Waller, Willie Bryant and Benny Carter. At the start of the 40s he briefly led his own band, then worked with numerous other leaders, including James P. Johnson, Teddy Wilson, Barney Bigard, Roy Eldridge, Don Byas, Cozy Cole and Bud Freeman. He continued to play through succeeding decades, his appearances including a stint in the Fletcher Henderson Reunion band and engagements at Eddie Condon's club and with Claude Hopkins and J.C. Higginbotham. He played into the 70s before ill-health prompted his retirement. A warm, full tone characterized Thomas's playing and the many small group recordings made during his career show a gifted instrumentalist with an inventive solo capacity.

● ALBUMS: with Henderson All Stars *Big Reunion* (1957)★★★, one side only *Mainstream* (1958)★★.

● COMPILATIONS: *The Indispensable Fletcher Henderson* (1927-

36 recordings)★★★★, with Roy Eldridge *The Jazz Greats - Brass* (1944 recordings)★★★, *Don Byas - 1945* (1945 recordings)★★★, *Blowin' In From KC* (Uptown 1983)★★, *Raw Meat* (Uptown 1983)★★, *Jumping With Joe* (Swingtime 1987)★★★.

THOMAS, LEONE

b. 4. October 1937, East St. Louis, Illinois, USA. Thomas studied music at Tennessee State University but he had already started singing, sitting in with the band of Armando Peraza (congas) and bands including Jimmy Forest and Grant Green. During these early years he had been particularly inspired by seeing John Coltrane playing with Miles Davis. In 1959 Thomas moved to New York and sang in Apollo shows with Dakota Staton and Art Blakey's Jazz Messengers among others. In 1961 he joined Count Basie's Orchestra and only left when he was inducted into the army. When he was discharged he worked with Pharoah Sanders, with whom he was free to develop the more unusual elements of his style; in particular, the 'yodelling' he says is derived from the singing of Congo pygmies. It was most apparent at this stage that he sees music as social commentary: 'You just have to be more than an entertainer. How the blazes can you ignore what is happening?'. Since then he has worked solo and appeared with the bands of guitarist Carlos Santana and trumpeter Freddy Hubbard.

● ALBUMS: with Pharoah Sanders *Karma* (1969)★★★, with Santana *Spirits Known And Unknown* (1969)★★, *Leone Thomas Album* (1970)★★, *Three Shades Of Blue* (1971)★★★, *Blues And The Soulful Truth* (1972)★★★, *Full Circle* (1973)★★.

● COMPILATIONS: *Anthology* (Passion Jazz 1998)★★★★.

THOMAS, RENE

b. 25 February 1927, Liege, Belgium, d. 3 January 1975, Santander, Spain. Thomas was a self-taught guitarist at first much influenced by Django Rheinhardt. By the time he moved to Paris in the early 50s, he had adapted to the style of Jimmy Raney. In Paris he played with many visiting Americans including trumpeter Chet Baker in 1955. In 1958 he moved to New York where he worked with the groups of pianist Toshiko Akiyoshi and tenor saxophonist Sonny Rollins, who thought him 'better than any of the American guitarists of the day'. He was an excellent accompanist who soloed with long, flowing lines and a sharp attack. By 1963 he had returned to Paris and was working with Kenny Clarke and others. He played with tenor saxophonist Stan Getz from 1969-72. Thomas died of a heart attack in 1975.

● ALBUMS: with Sonny Rollins *Brass/Trio* (1958)★★★, *Guitar Groove* (Jazzland 1960)★★★★, *Meeting Mr. T* (1963)★★, with Stan Getz *Dynasty* (1971)★★★.

THOMAS, WALTER 'FOOTS'

b. 10 February 1907, Muskogee, Oklahoma, USA, d. 26 August 1981. Accomplished on most of the saxophone family, as well as clarinet and flute, Thomas played professionally while still at high school. In the late 20s he played with several important New York-based musicians, including Jelly Roll Morton and Luis Russell. At the end of the 20s he joined the Missourians, the band later fronted by Cab Calloway. During several years with Calloway he also wrote many of the band's most popular arrangements. In the early 40s he played with Don Redman and led his own bands, but by the end of the decade had stopped playing to concentrate on other aspects of the music business. He died in August 1981. His brother, Joe Thomas (b. 23 December 1908), was also a saxophonist.

● COMPILATIONS: *The Most Important Recordings Of Cab Calloway* (1930-49 recordings)★★★★, one side only *The Walter 'Foots' Thomas All Stars* (1944-45 recordings)★★.

THOMPSON, BARBARA

b. 27 July 1944, Oxford, England. Classically trained at the Royal College of Music in London, where she studied flute, clarinet, piano and composition between 1965 and 1968, Thompson had private tuition on the saxophone before joining Neil Ardley's New Jazz Orchestra in 1965, her first professional jazz gig. She performed and recorded intermittently with the National Jazz Orchestra until 1978, and met her future husband, drummer Jon Hiseman, while both were members of the band. From 1969, Thompson led various groups of her own, working with musicians including John Dankworth, Don Rendell and Manfred Mann. In 1975 she formed the jazz-rock group Paraphernalia, which has been the main outlet for her compositional and performing skills. Mixing a range of musics as diverse as Sri Lankan folk tunes, English country music and modern jazz, Paraphernalia has toured extensively throughout Europe and performed at many of the continent's major jazz festivals. Away from Paraphernalia, Thompson has been a member of the United Rock And Jazz Ensemble since 1975, and an active session musician - performing on the albums of Andrew Lloyd Webber's *Variations*, *Cats* and *Requiem* - and from 1973-80 led a Latin-jazz outfit called Jubiaba. In 1988, her *Concert For Saxophone And Orchestra* was premiered in Germany; she has also written three long works for a 20-piece jazz orchestra. With Hiseman, she tours, she runs Temple Music, a music publishing company, and maintains a 24-track studio at their home in Surrey. The United Jazz & Rock Ensemble, Paraphernalia and her quartet regroups and tours occasionally, always to find a receptive following, especially in Germany where she is rightly appreciated. She collaborated with the Medici Quartet in 1995 on an album of Kurt Weill songs, that also feaured some fine arrangements by Mike Westbrook and John Dankworth. In 1996 she was awarded the MBE for services as an ambassador of UK Jazz.

● ALBUMS: *Barbara Thompson's Paraphernalia* (1978)★★★★, *Jubiaba* (MCA 1978)★★, *Wilde Tales* (MCA 1979)★★★, *Live In Concert* (1980)★★, *Mother Earth* (Verabra 1983)★★★★, *Ghosts* (1983)★★★★, *Pure Fantasy* (TM 1984)★★★, *Shadowshow* (1984)★★★, *Heavenly Bodies* (Verabra 1986)★★★, *Lady Saxophone* (1986)★★★★, *Special Edition* (Verabra 1987)★★★, *A Cry From The Heart* (Verabra 1987)★★★, *Breathless* (Verabra 1991)★★★★, *Songs From The Center Of The Earth* (Black Sun

1991)★★★, *Everlasing Flame* (Verabra 1993)★★★, with the Medici Quartet *Barbara Song* (Virgin 1995)★★.

THOMPSON, BUTCH

b. 28 November 1943, Marine, Minnesota, USA. Thompson began playing piano as a child and in his late teens became a member of a popular New Orleans-style band in Minneapolis. The band regularly accompanied such leading New Orleans jazzmen as George Lewis, Kid Thomas and Pops Foster. Thompson also formed his own small group which worked extensively on radio, achieving considerable popularity. During the 70s Thompson began to tour internationally. He also worked with the New Orleans Ragtime Orchestra and his own band dedicated to the music of King Oliver. Thompson's dedication to a tradition that was vintage long before he was born, has ensured that an important strand of jazz piano history remains extant. A sparkling player in the idiom of New Orleans, Thompson regularly revives the music of Jelly Roll Morton, Oliver and other past masters. In recent years he has often worked with several unsung musicians with similarly dedicated concepts, including cornetist Charles DeVore and drummer Hal Smith.

● ALBUMS: *Kid Thomas At San Jacinto Hall* (1965)★★★, *A'Solas* (1981)★★★, *Echoes From Storyville* (1984)★★★★, *Live From The Shattuck Hotel* (1985)★★, *King Oliver's Centennial Band* (1988)★★★, *New Orleans Joys* (1989)★★★, *Chicago Breakdown* (1989)★★★, *Good Old New York* (1989)★★, *Plays Favorites* (Solo Art 1993)★★★, *Minnesota Wonder* (Daring 1993)★★★, *Lincoln Avenue Blues* (Daring Records 1995)★★★, *Plays Jelly Roll Morton's Piano Solos* (Biograph 1996)★★★★, *Lincoln Avenue Express* (Daring 1997)★★★, *Thompson Plays Joplin* (Daring 1998)★★★.

THOMPSON, CHARLES, SIR

b. 12 March 1918, Springfield, Ohio, USA. After starting out on violin Thompson switched to piano and was playing professionally by his mid-teenage years. During the mid- to late 30s he played with several notable territory bands in the south-west, including that led by Nat Towles. In 1940 he was briefly with Lionel Hampton's big band but preferred small group work, although he regularly wrote arrangements for musicians including Count Basie and Jimmy Dorsey. During the 40s and 50s he worked with leading jazzmen such as Lester Young (who bestowed upon him the title by which he was subsequently known), Coleman Hawkins, Illinois Jacquet, Jimmy Rushing and Buck Clayton, the last an especially important musical associate. Through the 60s he continued playing with Roy Eldridge, Clayton and other major artists, and also led his own groups, often switching to organ.

Poor health slowed his career in the 70s but by the 80s he was back on the scene again, playing at numerous venues around the world. A particularly effective ensemble player, Thompson's work in the Clayton bands of the mid-50s ably demonstrated his understated skills. His solos display a calm assurance, a largely unused affinity for the blues and a delicate touch on ballads. 'Robbins' Nest', a jazz standard, is his composition.

● ALBUMS: *Bop This* (1953)★★★, *Buck Clayton Jam Sessions* (1953-54)★★★★, *The Sir Charles Thompson Quartet/For The Ears* (1954-55)★★★, *Sir Charles Thompson With Coleman Hawkins* (1954)★★★, *The Sir Charles Thompson Trio* (1955)★★★, *The Sir Charles Thompson Quintet* (1960)★★★★, with Buck Clayton *Kansas City Nights* (1960-61)★★★★, *Rockin' Rhythm* (1961)★★★, with Roy Eldridge *Trumpet Summit* (1967)★★★, *Hey, There!* (1974)★★★, *Sweet And Lovely* (1977)★★★, *Portrait Of A Piano* (1984)★★★, *Robbins' Nest* (1993)★★★.

THOMPSON, DANNY

b. April 1939, Teignmouth, Devon, England. An expressive, inventive double bass player, Thompson became established in British jazz circles through his work with Tubby Hayes. In 1964 he joined Alexis Korner's Blues Incorporated where he would forge an intuitive partnership with drummer Terry Cox following John Marshall's departure. Three years later the duo formed the rhythm section in Pentangle, a folk 'supergroup' that featured singer Jacquie McShee and guitarists John Renbourn and Bert Jansch. Thompson remained with this seminal quintet until their demise in 1972 but had forged a concurrent career as a leading session musician. He appeared on releases by Donovan, Cliff Richard ('Congratulations') and Rod Stewart ('Maggie May'), but was acclaimed for peerless contributions to albums by folk-singers Nick Drake and John Martyn. Thompson's collaborations with the latter were particularly of note (as were their legendary drinking sessions), and the working relationship spanned several excellent albums, including *Solid Air*, *Inside Out* and *Live At Leeds*. A notorious imbiber, Thompson then found his workload and confidence diminishing. He successfully conquered his alcohol problem and resumed session work with typically excellent contributions to releases by Kate Bush, David Sylvian and Talk Talk. In 1987 the bassist formed his own group, Whatever, and recorded new age and world music collections. In the 90s his remarkable dexterity was heard on regular tours with Richard Thompson, the only criticism received that he should have also been given a microphone as the inter-song banter was hilarious. In the mid-90s he was the regular bassist with Everything But The Girl, but continued with solo projects, including an album with Richard Thompson. He remains a leading instrumentalist, respected for his sympathetic and emotional style on the stand up bass. Thompson is a giant, both in stature and in his contribution to jazz and rock. Should the music ever desert him, he could carve a career as a stand-up comic. In 1998 he toured with Loreena McKennitt and recorded with Ian McNabb.

● ALBUMS: *Whatever* (Hannibal 1987)★★★★, *Whatever Next* (Antilles/New Direction1989)★★★, with Toumani Diabate, Ketama *Songhai* (Hannibal 1989)★★★, *Elemental* (Antilles/New Direction 1990)★★★★, with Richard Thompson *Live At Crawley 1993* (What Disc 1995)★★★, *Singing The Storm*

(Cooking Vinyl 1996)★★★, with Richard Thompson *Industry* (Parlophone 1997)★★★.

THOMPSON, EDDIE

b. 31 May 1925, London, England, d. 6 November 1986. Born blind, Thompson learned to play piano as a child. In the late 40s he was active in London clubs, playing with Carlo Krahmer, Vic Feldman and others. In the 50s he played on radio, in studio bands, made records under his own name and with Tony Crombie, Tommy Whittle, Freddy Randall and others and by the end of the decade was house pianist at Ronnie Scott's club. In the early 60s he went to the USA to live, playing regularly at the Hickory House in New York. Back in the UK in the early 70s, he led a trio that toured extensively and frequently backed visiting American jazzmen, including Buddy Tate, Ruby Braff and Spike Robinson. A dazzlingly inventive player in his early days, Thompson sometimes delivered bravura performances at the expense of feeling but in his maturity he made many memorable appearances at concerts around the UK. He had an enormous repertoire and when in musical sympathy with a guest he could be the best of accompanists. His solo playing was long overlooked by record companies but Alastair Robertson of Hep Records compensated for this with some excellent sessions in the early 80s. Thompson's death at the age of 61 came when he was at the height of his powers.

● ALBUMS: *I Hear Music* (Dormouse 1956)★★★, *By Myself* (77 1970)★★★, *Some Strings, Some Skins And A Bunch Of Keys* (1975)★★★, *Dutch Treat* (1976)★★, *Ain't She Sweet* (1978)★★★★, *When Lights Are Low* (1980)★★★★, *Memories Of You* (1983)★★★★, with Roy Williams *When The Lights Are Low* (Hep Jazz 1988)★★.

THOMPSON, LUCKY

b. Eli Thompson, 16 June 1924, Columbia, South Carolina, USA. Thompson's professional career began in the early 40s as a sideman in territory bands. After moving to New York in 1943 he played tenor saxophone in the bands of Lionel Hampton, Don Redman, Billy Eckstine, Lucky Millinder and in 1944 joined Count Basie. On the west coast he recorded with Dizzy Gillespie and Charlie Parker, being hired by Gillespie for the famous engagement at Billy Berg's to help make up the numbers when Parker failed to turn up or was late. Indeed, Parker failed to show up for a record date with Ross Russell's Dial label and Thompson sat in. When Parker eventually made a date for Russell, this time with Miles Davis, Thompson was again present. Thompson played briefly with Boyd Raeburn and was also active in the studios. In 1946 he was a member of the Stars Of Swing, a co-operative band masterminded by Charles Mingus and Buddy Collette and which also featured Britt Woodman and John Anderson. This band lasted less than two months and unfortunately was never recorded. Back in New York at the end of the 40s, Thompson formed his own band and in the early 50s headlined at the Savoy Ballroom. After dabbling briefly in R&B he made several jazz albums with Oscar Pettiford, Milt Jackson and, notably, with Miles Davis on the famous Prestige session for which Davis hired Thompson, J.J. Johnson, Horace Silver, Percy Heath and Art Blakey and which resulted in superb performances of 'Walkin'' and 'Blue 'N' Boogie'. In 1956 he visited Europe, recording prodigiously in France under his own name and also touring with Stan Kenton. Thompson took a liking to Europe and resided there for several years in the late 50s/early 60s and again at the end of the 60s.

Between these two sojourns he played little, preferring life on a small farm in Michigan, and after his latest return from Europe in 1973 he taught for a while before retiring from music. Thompson's playing on tenor and soprano saxophone ably straddles the main strands favoured by musicians of his generation. Although identifiably influenced by Coleman Hawkins and Don Byas, he had absorbed the stylistic departures of Lester Young and Charlie Parker. However, he possessed a fertile imagination and the characteristics of his playing were very much his own; indeed, Thompson proved to be one of the most original and inventive saxophonists working in the post-bebop mainstream and his early retirement was a grievous loss to jazz. His departure from music was prompted by his growing dissatisfaction with the way in which musicians were treated by record companies, club owners, promoters and others in the business. He was especially dismayed by discriminatory practices he encountered from bigoted whites who were in positions of power and could control the careers of black musicians. His own relatively small legacy of recordings is probably not unconnected with the fact that he was never afraid to speak out when he felt injustice was being done.

● ALBUMS: *Lucky Thompson Featuring Oscar Pettiford* (1956)★★★★, *Lucky Thompson & Gerard Pochonet Et Son Quartette* (1956)★★★, *Lucky Standards* (1956)★★★, *Lucky Thompson* (1963)★★★, *Lucky Thompson Plays Jerome Kern And No More* (1963)★★★★, *Lucky Strikes* (Original Jazz Classics 1965)★★★★, *Happy Days Are Here Again* (1965)★★★, *Lucky Thompson In Switzerland* (1969)★★, *A Lucky Songbook In Europe* (1969)★★, *I Offer You* (1973)★★★, *Brown Rose* 1956 recordings (1985)★★★★.

● COMPILATIONS: *Dancing Sunbeam* 1956 recording (1975)★★★★, *Body And Soul* 1970 recording (1978)★★★, *Paris 1956 Volume One* 1956 recording (1985)★★★, *Illuminations* (1974)★★★, *Lucky Sessions* (Vogue 1993)★★★, *Tricotism* (Impulse! 1994)★★★.

THORNHILL, CLAUDE

b. 10 August 1909, Terra Haute, Indiana, USA, d. 1 July 1965. Thornhill studied piano formally, playing jazz with a friend, Danny Polo. In the early 30s he was resident in New York City, playing with Hal Kemp, Don Voorhees, Paul Whiteman, Benny Goodman and many other leaders. In the mid-30s he worked with Ray Noble and Andre Kostelanetz. Later in the decade he was busily writing arrangements for several bands and singers, and one song recorded by Maxine Sullivan ('Loch Lomond') was a huge hit. His successes for others led him to form his own band, hiring emerging talents such as Lee Konitz, Red Rodney and Gerry Mulligan, while his arranging staff included Gil Evans, who would later frequently assert how much his time with Thornhill had influenced his writing. In his 1940 band Thornhill sought perfect intonation from his musicians and balance between the sections. He urged his sidemen to eliminate vibrato, aiding this effect by adding French horns, themselves essentially vibratoless instruments. The resulting pastel-shaded musical patterns and sustained chords, against which Thornhill made delicate solo statements on piano, was in striking contrast to the sound of other big bands of the period. Ill-health forced him to disband in 1948, but he returned to playing in the 50s and continued on an occasional basis until his sudden death in July 1965. Lasting testimony to Thornhill lies in the arranging styles of both Evans and Mulligan, both of whom long afterwards pursued concepts and sounds rooted in Thornhill's band of the early 40s.

● ALBUMS: *One Night Stand With Claude Thornhill* (1950)★★★★, *Claude Thornhill And His Orchestra* i (1953)★★★, *Claude Thornhill And His Orchestra* ii (1956)★★★, *Claude On A Cloud* (1958)★★, *Claude Thornhill And His Orchestra* iii (1959)★★, *Claude Thornhill And His Orchestra* iv (1963)★★★.

● COMPILATIONS: *The Real Birth Of The Cool* (1942-47)★★★★, *Claude Thornhill* (1947)★★★, *The Uncollected Claude Thornhill* (1947)★★★, *The Song Is You* 1948-49 recordings (Hep Jazz 1981)★★★★, *Tapestries* 1937-47 recordings (Charly 1987)★★, *Snowfall* (Fresh Sounds 1988)★★★.

THORSON, LISA

b. *c.*1954, USA. Singing professionally from the early 70s, Thorson studied at the Boston Conservatory of Music where she received her bachelor's degree in music theatre. Later, she received her master's degree, this time in jazz vocal performance, at the New England Conservatory. It was at NEC that she encountered Sheila Jordan, who actively encouraged her vocal aspirations. In addition to singing, however, Thorson also writes songs and works as an actress. She has worked throughout eastern USA, performing in clubs and on radio and television. In 1979 Thorson sustained injuries in an accident that limited her mobility thereafter, and she has since used a wheelchair. This change in her physical status redirected her career and she subsequently created the professional theatre company Next Move Unlimited, which specifically addresses the needs of performers with disabilities. In 1982 she created a musical work, *SpokeSong*, which toured the USA educating audiences through entertainment about the issues of art and disability. Through activities such as these, Thorson has become deeply involved with the National Endowment for the Arts and in 1989 received the Humanitarian Entertainer of the Year Award from the Boston Encore Awards for Excellence in Cabaret. Among many other awards and honours, in 1992 she received a Living Legend Award from the Women's International Center in San Diego. Her life and career were documented in a PBS television programme, *Key Changes: A Portrait of Lisa Thorson*. Thorson's singing is filled with glowing sincerity and a deep awareness of the musical potential of her wide-ranging repertoire. Her commitments to other aspects of her many interests have perhaps kept her from wider attention in the world of jazz. Regrettable though this might be for jazz, clearly her decision has been of enormous benefit to many people in other fields. A hint of what the jazz world has lost can be gained from a comment made by Jordan: 'It was a pleasure to have her as a student and it's an even greater pleasure to have her in the jazz world bringing that glorious sound for all to hear'.

● ALBUMS: *My Funny Valentine* (Thorson 1985)★★★, *Passion Flower* (Thorson 1987)★★★, *From This Moment On* (Brownstone 1994)★★.

THOUSANDS CHEER

Another lavish film effort by Hollywood in 1943 to lighten the war years by parading many of the most popular entertainers across the screen with only the most tenuous storyline to hold things together. Paul Jarrico and Richard Collins's script concerns the love affair between a former circus aerialist (Gene Kelly), who becomes a US army private and falls for the colonel's daughter (Kathryn Grayson). John Boles and Mary Astor play her father and mother, and most of MGM's galaxy of stars perform a dazzling array of musical party pieces, including Lena Horne ('Honeysuckle Rose'), Judy Garland, with Jose Iturbi ('The Joint Is Really Jumpin' In Carnegie Hall'), and Virginia O'Brien ('In A Little Spanish Town'). Gene Kelly danced 'The Mop Dance' delightfully, and Kathryn Grayson sang several numbers, notably 'Three Letters In A Mailbox', 'Daybreak', and 'Let There Be Music'. Also cast were Mickey Rooney, Red Skelton, Eleanor Powell, Margaret O'Brien, June Allyson, Gloria De Haven, Lucille Ball, and Frank Morgan. Guest stars included Marilyn Maxwell, Ann Sothern, and Marsha Hunt. Some of the best musical moments were provided by the bands of Bob Crosby, Kay Kyser, and Benny Carter. There were Oscar nominations for George Folsey's colour cinematography, Herbert Stothart's 'scoring of a musical picture', and Cedric Gibbons and Daniel Cathcart's interior direction. George Sidney directed *Thousands Cheer*, which grossed $3.5 million at the box office in the USA and Canada alone, making it one of the most successful musicals of the decade.

THREADGILL, HENRY

b. 15 February 1944, Chicago, Illinois, USA. At college Threadgill shared a saxophone teacher with Anthony Braxton. In the early 60s he played with Roscoe Mitchell and Muhal Richard Abrams in the Experimental Band, the precursor of the AACM. He missed the AACM's beginnings as he spent several years touring America with an Evangelist Camp, contributing saxophone to the gospel services. Two years in the army had him playing everything from marches to classical music to jazz. In the late 60s he returned to Chicago and his AACM colleagues, playing with Amina

Claudine Myers and Abrams and also in the house band of a Chicago blues club. In 1971 he formed Air, a trio with Fred Hopkins (bass) and Steve McCall (percussion) though it was only after 1975 that the group became widely active. Adept on alto, tenor and baritone saxophones as well as clarinet, flute and bass flute, Threadgill's playing was characterized by a pliancy and exceptional freshness. In the late 70s he formed X-75, a nonet of strings and winds, which recorded *Volume One* for Arista/Novus. The unusual line-up bewildered promoters and there was no volume two. In 1977 he recorded on Braxton's *For Trio* and later played in David Murray's Octet (1980-2). His X-75 ensemble evolved into his long-standing 'Sextet' (although it has seven members there are only *six parts*), with a fascinating deployment of Hopkins on bass, Deidre Murray on cello and two percussionists. This group became the vehicle for some of the great jazz records of the 80s: *Just The Facts And Pass The Bucket* (1983), *You Know The Number* (1986) and *Rag, Bush And All* (1988). In December 1987 his composition for strings, percussion and voices, *Run Silent, Run Deep, Run Loud, Run High* (based on the laws of particle physics) was premiered at the Brooklyn Academy of Music. By the end of the 80s he had formed a 19-piece band that played dance tunes, a marching band and a septet, Very Very Circus, with an unusual line-up of two tubas, two electric guitars, trombone, drums plus the leader's alto saxophone and flute. In 1991, Very Very Circus released their debut recording, *Spirit Of Nuff...Nuff*, and in 1992 they toured the UK. In the mid-90s Threadgill put together Make A Move, featuring guitarist Brandon Ross, accordion/harmonium player Tony Cedras, bassist Stomu Takeishi and drummer J.T. Lewis. Together with his AACM colleagues Abrams, Braxton and Mitchell, Threadgill remains on the cutting edge of musical exploration: he is a thrilling improviser and a boldly original composer.

● ALBUMS: with X-75 *Volume One* (1979)★★★, *When Was That* (1982)★★★, *Just The Facts And Pass The Bucket* (1983)★★★★, *Subject To Change* (1985)★★★, *You Know The Number* (RCA 1986)★★★★, *Easily Slip Into Another World* (RCA 1987)★★★, *Rag, Bush And All* (RCA 1988)★★★★, with Very Very Circus *Spirit Of Nuff...Nuff* (Black Saint 1991)★★★, *Live At Koncepts* (Taylor Made 1992)★★, *Too Much Sugar For A Dime* (1993)★★★, *Song Out Of My Trees* (Black Saint 1994)★★★, *Carry The Day* (Columbia 1995)★★★, *Makin' A Move* (Columbia 1996)★★★, with Make A Move *Where's Your Cup?* (Columbia 1997)★★★, *Where's Your Cup?* (Columbia 1998)★★★★.

THREE SOUNDS

Led by self-taught pianist Gene Harris (b. 1 September 1933, Benton Harbour, Michigan, USA), the Three Sounds' smooth mainstream jazz proved highly popular during a recording career that spanned over ten years. After Harris left the army he played with several bands on the midwest circuit, before befriending drummer Bill Dowdy in South Bend, Indiana. The two men formed the Four Sounds with bassist Andrew Simpkins, but after unsuccessfully experimenting with several tenor saxophonists they reverted to the Three Sounds, playing a bluesy style of mainstream jazz. Support slots for soloists including Lester Young, Sonny Stitt, Miles Davis, Kenny Burrell and Nat Adderley established the trio's reputation. A move to New York led to a contract with Blue Note Records. Their 1958 debut *Introducing The Three Sounds* remains one of the label's most successful releases, and was followed by a further nine albums in five years. The trio made further albums for Verve Records, Mercury Records and Limelight before returning to Blue Note in 1966. Dowdy was replaced by Donald Bailey after the same year's *Vibrations*, who was in turn replaced by Carl Burnett for 1968's string-laden *Elegant Soul*. Henry Franklin was brought in to replace the departing Simpkins for 1969's *Soul Symphony*, the last official album by the trio (although numerous sessions have subsequently been released). Monk Montgomery replaced Franklin for live dates, but with 1971's *Gene Harris & The Three Sounds* Harris began a solo career that saw the pianist moving towards a jazz-rock sound.

● ALBUMS: *Introducing The Three Sounds* (Blue Note 1958)★★★★, *Bottoms Up* (Blue Note 1959)★★★★, *Good Deal* (Blue Note 1959)★★★, *Moods* (Blue Note 1960)★★★, *Feelin' Good* (Blue Note 1960)★★★★, *Here We Come* (Blue Note 1961)★★★, *It Just Got To Be* (Blue Note 1962)★★★, *Hey! There* (Blue Note 1962)★★★, *Out Of This World* (Blue Note 1963)★★★, *Black Orchid* (Blue Note 1963)★★★★, *Blue Genes* (Verve 1963)★★★★, with Anita O'Day *Anita O'Day And The Three Sounds* (Verve 1963)★★★, *Jazz On Broadway* (Mercury 1963)★★★, *Some Like It Modern* (Mercury 1963)★★★, *Live At The Living Room* (Mercury 1964)★★★, *Three Moods* (Limelight 1964)★★★, *Beautiful Friendship* (Limelight 1965)★★★, *Today's Sound* (Limelight 1966)★★★, *Vibrations* (Blue Note 1966)★★★, *The Three Sounds Live At The Lighthouse* (Blue Note 1967)★★★★, *Coldwater Flat* (Blue Note 1968)★★★, *Elegant Soul* (Blue Note 1968)★★★, *Soul Symphony* (Blue Note 1969)★★, *Babe's Blues* 1961-1962 recordings (Blue Note 1986), *Live At The 'It' Club* 1970 recording (Blue Note 1995)★★★.

● COMPILATIONS: *The Best Of The Three Sounds* (Blue Note)★★★★, *Standards* 1958-1962 recordings (Blue Note 1998)★★★.

THUNDERING HERDS 1945-1947, THE - WOODY HERMAN

Of all the big band leaders, Woody Herman was one of the most committed to jazz. Hardly ever concerning himself with commerciality, happily ranging from blues to bop, a striking array of jazz soloists adorned his 'Herds'. Whether playing loose-limbed charts by Ralph Burns, the tightly structured arrangements of Jimmy Giuffre, or the rampaging 'heads' by the band, Herman, as soloist, vocalist, leader, catalyst and talent finder, was one of the all-time jazz greats. All these qualities, together with soloists such as Sonny Berman, Bill Harris, Flip Phillips, Red Norvo and Stan Getz, appear on this album which covers his greatest years.

● Tracks: *Woodchopper's Ball; Apple Honey; Goosey Gander; Northwest Passage; The Good Earth; A Jug Of Wine; Your Father's Moustache; Bijou; Wild Root; Panacea; Backtalk; Non-alcoholic;*

Blues Are Brewin'; The Goof And I; Four Brothers; Blue Flame.
- First released 1953
- UK peak chart position: did not chart
- USA peak chart position: did not chart

TIBERI, FRANK

b. 4 December 1928, Camden, New Jersey, USA. A self-taught tenor saxophonist, Tiberi's early career took him through the bands of Bob Chester, Benny Goodman, Urbie Green and Dizzy Gillespie. A period as a studio musician followed, but in 1969 he was back on the road as Woody Herman's leading saxophone soloist. He remained with the band for the rest of the leader's life, sometimes taking over when ill-health affected Herman. A notable section player and an effective soloist, Tiberi was one of the most dominant figures in the later Herds.

- ALBUMS: all with Woody Herman *The Thundering Herd* (1974)★★★★, *50th Anniversary Tour* (1986)★★★, *Woody's Gold Star* (1987)★★★.

TIL THE BUTCHER CUTS HIM DOWN

An excellent documentary film directed by Phillip Spalding in 1971, which shows many of the fine New Orleans veterans still around at the time of its making. Central to the film is Ernest 'Punch' Miller and also seen and heard are Kid Thomas Valentine, Kid Sheik Cola, Raymond Burke, Don Ewell, Emmanuel Sayles and Kid Ory. Amongst non-New Orleans musicians filmed are Bobby Hackett and Dizzy Gillespie. At the time of the film's making, Miller was terminally ill (he died in December 1971), but he plays to a festival audience with astonishing, and inevitably moving, verve and enthusiasm.

TILBROOK, ADRIAN

b. 20 July 1948, Hartlepool, Co. Durham, England. The son of a tenor saxophone/clarinet player, Tilbrook studied drums for two years with Max Abrams. In 1974 he replaced Tony Hicks in the blues-influenced rock trio Back Door and toured extensively in Germany and the UK in the 70s with British blues giant Alexis Korner. Tilbrook formed Full Circle with trombonist Rick Taylor in 1984 and has, throughout his freelance career, played with many American musicians, including Eddie 'Lockjaw' Davis, Al Grey, James Moody, Jimmy Witherspoon and Al Casey, as well as British artists such as Ian Carr, Allan Holdsworth, Don Weller and Stan Tracey. A powerful yet tasteful technician, influenced by Elvin Jones and Billy Higgins, Tilbrook has also taught percussion for many years, and since 1986 has worked with Northern Arts/Yorkshire Arts as Jazz Development Officer based at Jazz Action in Darlington.

- ALBUMS: with Full Circle *Beauty Of The Unexpected* (1986)★★★.

TILTON, MARTHA

b. 12 November *c.*1918. The 'liltin' Martha Tilton', as she was often introduced by radio announcers, spent much of her early life in and around Los Angeles, appearing on local radio during the mid-30s. She sang with various bands including Jimmy Dorsey in 1936, then appeared with a vocal group, Three Hits And A Miss, on Benny Goodman's *Camel Caravan* radio show before joining Goodman as a regular band vocalist in August 1937. During her two-year stay she was featured on well over 40 of the band's tracks, including two US number 1s - 'And The Angels Sing' and 'I Let A Song Go Out Of My Heart'. During World War II she toured US bases with Jack Benny and signed for the Capitol label, having a big hit in 1944 with Sammy Cahn and Jule Styne's 'I'll Walk Alone', only to be beaten to the top of the charts by Jo Stafford's version. Other Top 10 hits included 'I Should Care', 'Stranger In Town', 'I Wonder, I Wonder, I Wonder' and 'How Are Things In Glocca Morra?' from the Broadway hit musical *Finian's Rainbow*. During the 40s and early 50s she worked regularly in radio with Dick Powell, Paul Whiteman, top comedian Milton Berle, and Curt Massey, with whom she recorded the album *We Sing The Old Songs*. Her films included the acclaimed musical *Sunny* (1941), *Strictly In The Groove* (1942), *Crime Inc.* (1945), and a celebration of her old mentor's music in *The Benny Goodman Story* (1955).

- ALBUMS: with Curt Massey *We Sing The Old Songs* (*c.*50s)★★★.

TIME OUT - DAVE BRUBECK

Second only to *Jazz Samba* by Stan Getz, as the most commercially successful jazz record of all time (it even contained a single for the pop charts, Paul Desmond's magnificent 'Take Five'), Brubeck brilliantly popularized jazz and offered it as a palatable alternative to Bobby Vee. This album sold by the trunkload and made Dave Brubeck a popular star. Those jazz critics who shunned him for becoming too commercial must eat their words, as this is a monumental album of the finest modern jazz. 'Blue Rondo A La Turk' and 'Kathy's Waltz' demonstrate this man's graceful, nonchalant class.

- Tracks: *Blue Rondo A La Turk; Strange Meadow Lark; Take Five; Three To Get Ready; Kathy's Waltz; Everybody's Jumpin'; Pick Up Sticks.*
- First released 1959
- UK peak chart position: 11
- USA peak chart position: 2

TIMMONS, BOBBY

b. 19 December 1935, Philadelphia, Pennsylvania, USA, d. 1 March 1974. Timmons studied with an uncle who was a musician, and then attended the Philadelphia Academy for a year. After playing piano around his home-town he joined Kenny Dorham's Jazz Prophets in February 1956. He next played with Chet Baker (April 1956 to January 1957), Sonny Stitt (February to August 1957), Maynard Ferguson (August 1957 to March 1958) and Art Blakey's Jazz Messengers (July 1958 to September 1959). Although this last stint was no longer than the others, it was with the Messengers that he made his name. He replaced Sam Dockery to become part of a classic line-up, with Wayne Shorter on tenor and Lee Morgan on trumpet, and recorded *Like Someone In Love*. His composition 'Moanin'' became a signature for the Messengers, and has remained a definitive example of gospel-inflected hard bop ever since. In October 1959 he joined Cannonball Adderley, for whom he wrote 'This Here' and 'Dat Dere'. He rejoined Blakey briefly in 1961, touring Japan in January (a broadcast was subsequently released as *A Day With Art Blakey* by Eastwind) and recording on some of *Roots & Herbs*. From the early 60s Timmons led his own trios and appeared regularly in Washington, DC. In Spring 1966 he had a residency at the Village Gate in New York and played throughout Greenwich Village in the early 70s. He died of cirrhosis of the liver in 1974. Timmons was a seminal figure in the soul-jazz movement, which did so much to instil jazz with the vitality of gospel. Although best known as a pianist and composer, he also played vibes during the last years of his life.

● ALBUMS: *This Here Is Bobby Timmons* (Riverside 1956)★★★★, with John Jenkins, Clifford Jordan *Jenkins, Jordan & Timmons* (1957)★★★, *Soul Time* (Riverside 1960)★★★, *Easy Does It* (Riverside 1961)★★★, *The Bobby Timmons Trio In Person At The Village Vanguard* (Riverside 1961)★★★★, *Sweet And Soulful Sounds* (Riverside 1962)★★★, *Born To Be Blue* (Riverside 1963)★★★★, *From The Bottom* (1964)★★★, *Workin' Out* (1964)★★★, *Holiday Soul* (1964)★★★, *Chun-king* (Prestige 1964)★★★, *Little Barefoot Soul* (Prestige 1964)★★★, *Chicken And Dumplin's* (Prestige 1965)★★★, *Soul Food* (Prestige 1966)★★★★, *The Soul Man* (Prestige 1966)★★★★, *Got To Get It* (Milestone 1968)★★★, *Do You Know The Way* (Milestone 1968)★★★, *Live At The Connecticut Jazz Party* (Early Bird 1981)★★★, *This Here* (Riverside 1984)★★★.

● COMPILATIONS: *Moanin'* (Milestone 1963)★★★★.

TIPPETT, KEITH

b. Keith Tippetts, 25 August 1947, Bristol, Avon, England. As a child Tippett studied piano and church organ privately, and cornet and tenor horn with the Bristol Youth Band. In 1967 he won a scholarship to the Barry Summer School in Wales. Here he met Elton Dean and Nick Evans and invited them to become members of his band. In 1968 the Keith Tippett Sextet was the first beneficiary of the London Jazz Centre Society's scheme to give six-week residencies to new bands at its Monday sessions at London's 100 Club. Following these exciting and exhilarating gigs the reputation of the band and its individual members (Marc Charig, Evans, Dean, Tippett, Gill Lyons and Alan Jackson) spread rapidly. Pianist Tippett recorded with King Crimson and appeared on their hit single 'Cat Food.' In 1970 he formed the enormous 50-piece Centipede to play his composition *Septober Energy*, and in 1972 founded Ovary Lodge, a free band, with his wife Julie Tippetts (née Driscoll - she decided to retain the 's'). For the rest of the decade he worked with various bands, including those of Dean (Just Us and Ninesense), Charig, Harry Miller (Isipingo), Louis Moholo and John Stevens (Dance Orchestra) and Trevor Watts (Amalgam, with whom he appeared in a revival of Jack Gelber's play *The Connection* in London in autumn 1974). He also formed the duo TNT with Stan Tracey. In 1975 he resurrected Centipede and in 1978 he was back with a big band, Ark. During the 80s through to the present he has worked with a septet, a duo with Julie, the powerful quartet Mujician (with Tony Levin, Paul Dunmall and Paul Rogers) and in a duo with Andy Sheppard. After the acclaim of the 60s and early 70s Tippett seems to have been out of favour with the critics and public in recent years, but he remains one of Britain's most original and provocative talents.

● ALBUMS: *You Are Here I Am There* (Polydor 1969)★★★, *Dedicated To You But You Weren't Listening* (Vertigo 1970)★★★★, *Septober Energy* (1971)★★★, *Blueprint* (RCA 1972)★★★, with Stan Tracey *TNT* (Steam 1974)★★★, *Ovary Lodge* (1975)★★★, *Warm Spirits, Cool Spirits* (Vinyl 1977)★★★, *Frames* (Ogun 1977)★★★, with Marc Charig *Pipedream* (1978)★★, with Louis Moholo *No Gossip* (1980)★★★, *Mujician* (1982)★★★, with Larry Stabbins *Tern* (1983)★★★, duet with Howard Riley *In Focus* (1984)★★★★, *Live - Keith Tippett* (1986)★★, *Mercy Dash* (1986)★★★, *Mujician II* (FMP 1987)★★★★, *A Loose Kite In A Gentle Wind ...* (1988)★★★, duet with Julie Tippetts *Couple In Spirit* (Editions EG 1988)★★★, with Tippetts, Maggie Nicols *Mr Invisible And The Drunken Sheilas* (1989)★★★, *Mujician III (August Air)* (FMP 1989)★★★, duet with Andy Sheppard *66 Shades Of Lipstick* (E.G. 1990)★★★★, *The Dartington Concert* (Editions EG 1992)★★★, with Riley *The Bern Concert* (Future Music 1994)★★★, with Mujician *Birdman* (Cuneiform Rune 1996)★★★★, *Une Croix Dans L'Océan* 1995 recording (Victo 1998)★★★.

TISSENDIER, CLAUDE

b. France. While studying classical clarinet and alto saxophone at Toulouse Conservatory, Tissendier began playing jazz. His interests followed a chronological path, starting with New Orleans music, passing through the mainstream into bop. In 1977 he joined the big band led by Claude Bolling and also worked with Gerard Badini and others. In the early 80s he taught at the Paris School of Jazz and in 1983 formed a sextet especially to recreate the music of John Kirby. In demand for club and festival dates, the band won many awards for both live performances and records. In 1987 Tissendier formed Saxomania, a seven-piece band featuring two alto saxophones, two tenors and three rhythm. Once again he won honours and gained invaluable experience and exposure accompanying visiting American jazzmen including Benny Carter, Buddy Tate, Jimmy Witherspoon and Spike Robinson, with some of whom he also recorded. Tissendier's alto playing is striking for its intensity and driving swing and the high musical standards displayed by the Saxomania band ably demonstrate that his is a major talent.

● ALBUMS: *Tribute To John Kirby* (1986)★★★, *Saxomania Featuring Benny Carter* (Ida 1988)★★★, *Saxomania Presenting Spike Robinson* (Ida 1989)★★★★, *Saxomania Out Of The Woods* (Ida 1993)★★★, *Sax Connection* (Ida 1993)★★★.

TIZOL, JUAN

b. 22 January 1900, San Juan, Puerto Rico, d. 23 April 1984. After playing in concert orchestras in his homeland, Tizol came to the USA in 1920. He played valve trombone in a theatre orchestra in Washington, DC, where he met Duke Ellington. He joined Ellington's band in 1929, immediately becoming a major and unique voice in that ensemble. Tizol's formal training gave him an important musical edge and several of his compositions, most of which had a Latin touch, became standards for the band, among them 'Conga Brava', 'Bakiff', and two jazz immortals, 'Perdido' and 'Caravan'. In 1944 he quit Ellington for the Harry James band, where he remained until 1951, then returned to Ellington for two years before another seven-year spell with James. He made some outside record dates, among them one with Nat 'King' Cole, and then, after a couple more brief stays with Ellington, retired in 1961. He subsequently appeared on a few live record dates, including a session with Louie Bellson, but appeared happy to live out his life off the bandstand.

● ALBUMS: with Nat 'King' Cole *After Hours* (1956)★★.

● COMPILATIONS: *Duke Ellington And His Orchestra* (1941)★★★★.

TJADER, CAL

b. Callen R. Tjader, 16 July 1925, St. Louis, Missouri, USA, d. 5 May 1982. After studying formally, Tjader played drums with various bands on the west coast before joining Dave Brubeck in 1949. In the early 50s he played with Alvino Rey and also led his own small bands. By 1953, the year he joined George Shearing, he had added vibraphone and various other percussion instruments to his roster. In 1954 he again formed a band of his own, concentrating on Latin American music and making numerous records on the Fantasy and Verve labels. He hired his sidemen with care, employing over the years distinguished musicians such as Lalo Schifrin, Willie Bobo, Donald Byrd and Kenny Burrell, while later musical associates included Hank Jones and Scott Hamilton. For all his undoubted skills as an instrumentalist, much of Tjader's solo recorded output lacks urgency and vitality, often slipping gently into well-played but undemanding background music.

● ALBUMS: *The Cal Tjader Trio* 10-inch album (Fantasy 1953)★★★, *Cal Tjader - Vibist* 10-inch album (Savoy 1954)★★★, *Ritmo Caliente* 10-inch album (Fantasy 1954)★★★, *Mambo With Tjader* (Fantasy 1955)★★★, *Tjader Plays Tjazz* (Fantasy 1956)★★★, *Tjader Plays Mambo* (Fantasy 1956)★★★, *Cal Tjader Quartet* i (Fantasy 1956)★★★, *The Cal Tjader Quintet* (Fantasy 1956)★★★, *Jazz At The Blackhawk* (Fantasy 1957)★★★, *Latin Kick* (Fantasy 1957)★★★, *Mass Ritmo Caliente* (Fantasy 1957)★★★, with Stan Getz *Cal Tjader-Stan Getz Sextet* (Fantasy 1958)★★★, *San Francisco Moods* (Fantasy 1958)★★★, *Latin Concert* (Fantasy 1958)★★, *Latin For Lovers* (Fantasy 1958)★★, *Jazz At Blackhawk* (Fantasy 1959)★★★, *Tjader Goes Latin* (Fantasy 1959)★★, *Concert By The Sea* (Fantasy 1959)★★★, *Concert On The Campus* (Fantasy 1960)★★★, *Cal Tjader Quartet* ii (Fantasy 1960)★★★, *Demasado Caliente* (Fantasy 1960)★★★, *West Side Story* (Fantasy 1960)★★★, *Cal Tjader* (Fantasy 1961)★★★, *Cal Tjader Live And Direct* (Fantasy 1961)★★, *Cal Tjader Plays Harold Arlen* (Fantasy 1961)★★★, *Concert By The Sea, Volume 2* (Fantasy 1961)★★★, *In A Latin Bag* (Verve 1961)★★★, *Latino* (Fantasy 1962)★★★, *Saturday Night-Sunday Night At The Blackhawk* (Verve 1962)★★★, *The Contemporary Music Of Mexico & Brazil* (Verve 1962)★★★, *Several Shades Of Jade* (Verve 1963)★★★, *Sona Libre* (Verve 1963)★★★, *Breeze From The East* (Verve 1964)★★, *Warm Wave* (Verve 1964)★★, *Soul Sauce* (Verve 1965)★★★, *Soul Bird/Whiffenpoof* (Verve 1965)★★, *Soul Burst* (Verve 1965)★★, *Latin For Dancers* (Fantasy 1966)★★, with Eddie Palmieri *El Sonid Nuevo - The New Soul Sound* (Verve 1966)★★★★, *Along Comes Cal* (Verve 1966)★★★, *Hip Vibrations* (Verve 1967)★★★, with Palmieri *Bamboleate* (Verve 1967)★★★, *Solar Heat* (Rhapsody 1968)★★, *Cal Tjader Sounds Out Burt Bacharach* (1968)★, *The Prophet* (Verve 1969)★, *Primo* (1971)★★★, *Concert At Hermosa Beach* (1973)★★, *The Cal Tjader Quintet With Strings* (1973)★★★, *Amazonas* (1975)★★★, *Cal Tjader At Grace Cathedral* (1976)★★, *Guarabe* (1976)★★, *Breathe Easy* (1977)★★★, *Here* (1977)★★★, *Huracan* (Crystal Clear 1978)★★★, *La Onda Va Bien* (Concord 1979)★★★, *Gozame! Peroya* (Concord 1980)★★★, *The Shining Sea* (Concord 1981)★★★, *A Fuego Vivo* (Concord 1981)★★, with Carmen McRae *Heat Wave* (1982)★★★, *Good Vibes* (Concord 1984)★★★, *Sounds Out Burt Bacharach* (DCC 1998)★★.

● COMPILATIONS: *Cal Tjader's Greatest Hits* (Fantasy 1965)★★★, *The Best Of Cal Tjader* (Verve 1967)★★★, *Talkin' Verve* (Verve 1997)★★★.

TOBIN, CHRISTINE

b. Eire. After singing in Dublin, Tobin went to London where she studied at the Guildhall School of Music, taking the jazz course. Tobin sang at various London venues, working with musicians such as Jean Toussaint and Django Bates. She also toured Europe, appearing at festivals in Austria and Hungary. Her repertoire is wide-ranging, including, as it does, music from the Irish folk tradition with contemporary world music, Latin overlays, and hints of jazz influence.

● ALBUMS: *Aililiu* (Babel 1994)★★★.

TODD, PHIL

b. 6 August 1956, Borehamwood, Hertfordshire, England. After a two-year music course at Hitchin College, Todd spent three years at the Trinity College of Music in London. He played with the National Youth Jazz Orchestra (1973-7), Jeff Clyne's Turning Point (1978-82), Mike Westbrook's Concert Band (1982) and since then with Ian Carr's Nucleus. He is a fine all-round saxophonist who is one of the few to incorporate successfully the wind synthesizer, which was developed in the late 80s. He is much in demand for studio work of all kinds.

TOGASHI, MASAHIKO

b. 22 March 1940, Tokyo, Japan. A child prodigy on violin and percussion, Togashi became a professional drummer when barely into his teens. He gained a solid reputation in his homeland, playing with Sadao

Watanabe among others and also led his own small groups. At the end of the 60s injuries turned him away from playing drums to other percussion instruments and he extended his interest in writing music. He continued to lead bands, write, and collaborate with Japanese and visiting musicians, appearing with Masabumi Kikuchi and recording a 1981 duo session with Steve Lacy. Togashi's technical expertise on a wide range of percussion instruments allows him to introduce into his performances telling effects that add intriguingly exotic undertones.

● ALBUMS: *Song For Myself* (East Wind 1974)★★★, *Rings* (East Wind 1975)★★★, *Spiritual Nature* (East Wind 1975)★★★, *Essence* (Denon 1976)★★★, *Sketch* (Denon 1977)★★★, *Al-alarf: Improvisation Jazz Orchestra* (Paddle Wheel 1980)★★★, *Flame Up* (Paddle Wheel 1981)★★★, with Steve Lacy *Eternal Duo* 1981 recording (Paddle Wheel/King 1983)★★★, *Follow The Dream* (Paddle Wheel 1984)★★★, *Bura Bura* (ALFA 1986)★★★, *Scene* (Cornelius 1987)★★★, with Jean-Jacques Avenel, Lacy *Voices* (NEC Avenue/Pan 1989)★★★, with Lacy *Twilight* (Nippon Crown 1992)★★★.

TOLLIVER, CHARLES

b. 6 March 1942, Jacksonville, Florida, USA. Tolliver was set on the road to music by his grandmother who gave him a cornet when he was eight years old. He was raised and educated in New York and also studied at Howard University, Washington DC, majoring in pharmacy. By the time he began playing trumpet as a full-time professional he was already committed to bop. During the 60s he worked extensively with several leading bop musicians of the time including Jackie McLean, with whom he recorded the 1964 Blue Note Records session *It's Time*, Art Blakey and Sonny Rollins. He spent the second half of the decade on the west coast playing with Gerald Wilson, in whose band he met Roy Ayers. He recorded with both Wilson and Ayers as leaders and he was a member of the Max Roach Quintet, recording the 1968 Atlantic Records session *Members Don't Get Weary*. At the end of the 60s he was a founder member of the cooperative quartet, Music, Inc. Another member of this band was Stanley Cowell with whom Tolliver formed a record company, Strata-East. Although his business activities were time-consuming, Tolliver continued to play, touring Europe and the far east, and to compose. A melodic yet forceful player with flowing ideas and an endless capacity for invention, Tolliver's international reputation is not as great as his talent merits.

● ALBUMS: *Paper Man* (Arista Freedom 1968)★★★, *The Ringer* (Arista Freedom 1970)★★★★, *Music, Inc. & Big Band* (Strata-East 1971)★★★, *Compassion* (Strata-East 1971)★★★, *Live At Slugs, Vol. 1* 1970 recording (Strata-East 1972)★★★, *Live At Slugs, Vol. 2* 1970 recording (Strata-East 1972)★★★, *Live At The Loosdrecht Jazz Festival* 1972 recording (Strata-East 1973)★★★, *Live In Tokyo* (Strata-East 1973)★★★, *Impact* (Strata-East 1975)★★★★, *Live In Berlin At The Quasimodo, Vol.1* (Strata-East 1988)★★★, *Live In Berlin At The Quasimodo, Vol. 2* (Strata-East 1988)★★★, *Right Now* (Strata-East 1998)★★★, *In The Trenches* (Strata-East 1998)★★★.

TOMKINS, TREVOR

b. 12 May 1941, London, England. As a young teenager Tomkins first took up the trombone before switching to the drums on which he made his first professional appearance. Although he studied extensively, mostly in the classical vein, he was deeply interested in jazz and in the early 60s moved permanently into this field, working often with the small group co-led by Ian Carr and Don Rendell. He spent some time in the USA but from the 70s onwards became one of the most sought-after jazz drummers in the UK, where he has played with Michael Garrick, Barbara Thompson, Mike Westbrook and others. He is also in demand as accompanist to American jazzmen visiting the UK, amongst them Lee Konitz. A gifted mainstream and bop drummer, Tomkins' studies, which encompassed harmony and music theory, allied to a wealth of experience, have given him enviable command. His technical accomplishment is complemented by a subtle sense of swing and the ability to anticipate and fulfil the demands of the musicians he accompanies. He is also a much respected teacher.

● ALBUMS: with Don Rendell-Ian Carr *Shades Of Blue* (1964)★★★★, with Rendell-Carr *Dusk Fire* (1965)★★★, with Tony Coe *Zeitgeist* (1977)★★★, with Pat Crumly *Third World Sketches* (1984)★★★, with Christian Josi *I Walks With My Feet Off The Ground* (Master Mix 1994)★★★.

TOMLINSON, JIM

b. 9 September 1966, Sutton Coldfield, Warwickshire, England. Tomlinson grew up in Northumberland, then attended Oxford University where he studied Philosophy, Politics and Economics. Meanwhile, he was playing clarinet and saxophones, mostly the tenor, and developing his interest in jazz. In his post graduate year he studied at London's Guildhall School of Music and began to establish himself on the local jazz scene. His reputation quickly spread and he was soon working with noted musicians, including Matt Wates, David Newton and Michael Garrick, recording with the latter on his 1997 session *For Love Of Duke And Ronnie*. In the 90s he was frequently leader of his own quartet, touring extensively in the UK. He is often in the musical company of singer Stacey Kent, to whom he is married, appearing on her two very well-received albums for Candid Records. Tomlinson's playing on tenor is immensely satisfying. He has a heartfelt way with ballads, plays with driving intensity of up-tempo pieces, and as an accompanist to Kent has proved himself to be supportive, understanding and lyrically inventive. Clearly, Tomlinson is a musician who will ably carry the flame of mainstream tenor saxophone playing into the new century.

● ALBUMS: *The Jim Tomlinson Quartet* (Candid 1998)★★★.

TOMPKINS, ROSS

b. 13 May 1938, Detroit, Michigan, USA. After formal studies Tompkins began playing piano in various small groups in New York City. Although most often in company with mainstream musicians such as Wes Montgomery, Bob Brookmeyer, Al Cohn, Zoot Sims and Clark Terry, he was also at ease with the more adventurous Eric Dolphy. He spent time working in radio and television studios in New York, later resuming this activity in Los Angeles. He continued to record extensively, appeared at festivals and club dates with musicians such as Marshal Royal, Herb Ellis, Louie Bellson, Joe Venuti, Ray Brown, Conte Candoli and Scott Hamilton. A solid ensemble player and accompanist, Tompkins is also an inventive soloist, developing long, flowing lines of deceptive simplicity.

● ALBUMS: with Herb Ellis *A Pair To Draw To* (Concord Jazz 1976)★★★, *Scrimshaw* (1976)★★★, with Louie Bellson *Prime Time* (1977)★★★, with Joe Venuti *Ross Tompkins And Joe Venuti Live At Concord '77* (Concord Jazz 1977)★★★, *Lost In The Stars* (1977)★★★, *Ross Tompkins And Good Friends* (1978)★★★, with Red Norvo *Red & Ross* (Concord Jazz 1979)★★★★, *Festival Time* (1979)★★★, *Street Of Dreams* (1982)★★, *Symphony* (1984)★★★, *LA After Dark* (1985)★★★, with Jack Sheldon *On My Own* (1992)★★★, *Aka The Phantom* (Progressive 1993)★★★, with Sheldon *Class Act* (Butterfly 1997)★★★.

TONEFF, RADKA

b. 25 June 1952, Oslo, Norway, d. 20 October 1982, Oslo, Norway. Vocalist Toneff, whose father was a Bulgarian folk musician and singer, enrolled at the Oslo Music Conservatory to become a piano teacher. Here she met Arild Andersen, Jon Balke and other Norwegian jazz artists with whom she recorded. Toneff listened closely to Joni Mitchell, Betty Carter and Sarah Vaughan, but insisted on avoiding the nonsensical lyrics of the standards repertoire. She chose hers from poems by Nikki Giovanni, Robert Creeley, and Fran Landesman, and on her second album she also added lyrics of her own. *Fairy Tales* ventured into contemporary rock territory by including songs by Bernie Taupin and Jim Webb as well as standards. Her version of 'Lost In The Stars' was regarded as the definitive version by Sheila Jordan. Toneff's songs and her vocals projected not only a sense of personal desolation and lovelessness but also one of defiance, as heard in her remarkable rendition of Bob Dylan's 'Just Like A Woman' on *Live In Hamburg*.

● ALBUMS: *Winter Poem* reissue by Verve (1977)★★★★, *It Don't Come Easy* reissue by Verve (1979)★★★, *Fairy Tales* (Odin 1982)★★, *Live in Hamburg* (Odin 1993)★★.

TONOLO, PIETRO

b. 30 May 1959, Mirano, Venice, Italy. Tonolo is one of the most interesting of the batch of young Italian musicians broadly grouped under the umbrella of *La Nuova Onda* (New Wave) of the late 80s. Although he took piano lessons at seven and studied the violin between the ages of 10 and 18, Tonolo taught himself saxophone at 16 and has developed an individual voice on the alto. He began in jazz-rock bands then moved over to jazz, getting his first job with his pianist brother, Marcello, in 1978. At the end of 1981 he joined Enrico Rava's band and in 1982 toured with Gil Evans. He has also played with Franco D'Andrea, Massimo Urbani, Luigi Bonafede, Roswell Rudd, Kenny Clarke, Jimmy Owens, Sal Nistico, Lee Konitz, George Lewis and Barry Altschul, and has worked in a duo and quartet with Rita Marcotulli, a collaboration that has produced some highly inventive and adventurous improvization.

● ALBUMS: *Andanada* (1983)★★★, with Marcello Tonolo Trio *D.O.C.* (1985)★★, *Pietro Tonolo Quartet-Quintet-Sextet* (1986)★★★, *Slowly* (Splasch 1996)★★, *Tresse* (Splasch 1997)★★, *Simbiosi* (Splasch 1997)★★★★, *Disguise* (Splasch 1997)★★★★.

TOO LATE BLUES

Director and star John Cassavetes, uncharacteristically turning out a Hollywood studio film in 1961, carefully evokes the personal and professional relationships between members of a jazz group. Cassavetes, who also appeared in the *Johnny Staccato* television series about a jazzman-private eye, not only loves the music but clearly cares for the musicians who play it. Among the participating musicians, mostly off-screen, are Milt Bernhardt, Benny Carter, Slim Gaillard, Shelly Manne, Red Mitchell, Jimmy Rowles and Uan Rasey, who dubs for Bobby Darin who has an acting role.

TORMÉ, MEL

b. 13 September 1925, Chicago, Illinois, USA. A child prodigy, Tormé first sang on radio as a toddler and while still in his teens was performing as a singer, pianist, drummer and dancer. He was also composing songs and wrote arrangements for the band led by Chico Marx. He acted on radio and in films and in addition to singing solo led his own vocal group, the Mel-Tones. In this last capacity he recorded with Artie Shaw, enjoying a hit with 'Sunny Side Of The Street'. By the 50s he was established as one of the leading song stylists, performing the great standards and often working with a jazz backing, notably with the Marty Paich Dektette on albums such as *Lulu's Back In Town*. He headlined concert packages across the USA and in Europe, appeared on television, often producing his own shows, and always delivering performances of impeccable professionalism. He continued in such a vein throughout the 60s and 70s, making many fine albums of superior popular music, on several of which he was accompanied by jazzmen. Among these were Shorty Rogers (*'Round Midnight*), Al Porcino (*Live At The Maisonette*), Buddy Rich (*Together Again - For The First Time*), Gerry Mulligan (*Mel Tormé And Friends*) and Rob McConnell (*Mel Tormé With Rob McConnell And The Boss Brass*). Of all his musical collaborations, however, the best and most satisfying has been a long series of concerts and radio and television shows, many of which were issued on record, with George Shearing. Among these albums are *An Evening At Charlie's*, *An Elegant Evening*, *A Vintage Year* and *Mel And George "Do" World War II*.

In the early 90s Tormé was still drawing rave reviews for records and personal appearances, with Shearing, at festivals in California and the Channel Islands, and with Bill Berry's big band at the Hollywood Bowl. As a songwriter Tormé has several hundred compositions to his credit, of which the best-known by far is 'The Christmas Song' (written with Robert Wells), first recorded by Nat 'King' Cole. As a performer, Tormé often features himself on drums - for many years he used a drum kit that was formerly the property of Gene Krupa - and he plays with unforced swing. As a singer, Tormé's work is touched with elegant charm. His voice, with the characteristic huskiness that earned him the sobriquet 'The Velvet Fog', has deepened over the years and by the early 90s still retained all the qualities of his youth, not least remarkable pitch and vocal control. In his choice of material he has never shown anything other than perfect taste and his repertoire is an object lesson in musical quality. The fact that he also writes almost all the arrangements of the songs he sings adds to his status as a major figure in the story of American popular song. Tormé suffered a stroke during 1996 and a further one in 1998 and it is not yet known whether this will curtail his magnificent career.

● ALBUMS: *California Suite* 10-inch album (Capitol 1950)★★★, *Songs* 10-inch album (MGM 1952)★★★, *Musical Sounds Are The Best Songs* (Coral 1955)★★★, *It's A Blue World* (Bethlehem 1955)★★★★, with Marty Paich *Mel Tormé With The Marty Paich Dek-tette* (Bethlehem 1956)★★★★, *Gene Norman Presents Mel Torme Live At The Crescendo* (Coral 1956)★★★★, *Lulu's Back In Town* (1957)★★★, *Mel Tormé Sings Astaire* (Bethlehem 1957)★★★, *'Round Midnight* i (1957)★★★, with Paich *Tormé* (Verve 1958)★★★, with Paich *Prelude To A Kiss* (Tops 1958)★★★, *Songs For Any Taste* (Bethlehem 1959)★★★, *Olé Tormé - Mel Tormé Goes South Of The Border With Billy May* (Verve 1959)★★★★, with Paich *Back In Town* (Verve 1959)★★★, with Paich *Mel Tormé Swings Schubert Alley* (Verve 1960)★★★★, *Swingin' On The Moon* (Verve 1960)★★★★, *I Dig The Duke, I Dig The Count* (Verve 1960)★★★★, *Mel Tormé Sings* (Strand 1960)★★★, with Margaret Whiting *Broadway Right Now!* (Verve 1961)★★★, *'Round Midnight* ii (1961)★★★, *Mel Tormé At The Red Hill Inn* (Atlantic 1962)★★★, *Comin' Home Baby* (Atlantic 1962)★★★, *Sunday In New York* (Atlantic 1963)★★★★, *I Wished On The Moon* (Metro 1965)★★★, *That's All; A Lush Romantic Album* (Columbia 1965)★★★, *Mel Tormé Right Now* (Columbia 1966)★★★, *A Day In The Life Of Bonnie And Clyde* (Liberty 1968)★★★, *Live At The Maisonette* (1974)★★★, *Tormé A New Album* (Paddlewheel 1978)★★★★, with Buddy Rich *Together Again - For The First Time* (RCA 1978)★★★, *Mel Tormé And Friends* (Finesse 1981)★★★, *Encore At Marty's, New York* (1982)★★★, with George Shearing *An Evening At Charlie's* (Concord Jazz 1983)★★★, with Shearing *An Elegant Evening* (Concord Jazz 1985)★★★, *Mel Tormé With Rob McConnell And The Boss Brass* (Concord Jazz 1986)★★★, with Shearing *A Vintage Year* (Concord Jazz 1987)★★★, with Paich *Reunion* (Concord Jazz 1988)★★★★, with Paich *In Concert Tokyo* (Concord Jazz 1989)★★★★, *Night At The Concord Pavilion* (Concord Jazz 1990)★★★★, with Shearing *Mel And George 'Do' World War II* (Concord Jazz 1991)★★★, *In Hollywood* 1954 recording (1992)★★★, *Live At Fujitsu - Concord Jazz Festival 1992* (1992)★★★, *Christmas Songs* (Telarc 1992)★★, with Cleo Laine *Nothing Without You* (1993)★★★★, *A Tribute To Bing Crosby* (Concord 1994)★★★, *Velvet & Brass* (Concord 1995)★★★★, *A&E - An Evening With Mel Tormé* (Concord Jazz 1996)★★★★, *My Night To Dream* (Concord Jazz 1997)★★★.

● COMPILATIONS: *Verve's Choice The Best Of Mel Tormé* (Verve 1964)★★★, *Walkman Jazz* 1958-61 recordings (Verve 1990)★★★, *Capitol Years* (Capitol 1992)★★★, *The Magic Of ...* (Music Club 1995)★★★, *The Mel Tormé Collection: 1944-1985* 4-CD box set (Rhino 1996)★★★★.

● FURTHER READING: all by Mel Tormé *The Other Side Of The Rainbow-With Judy Garland On The Dawn Patrol. It Wasn't All Velvet: An Autobiography. My Singing Teachers.*

● FILMS: *Girl's Town* aka *The Innocent And The Damned* (1959).

TORN, DAVID

b. 26 May 1953, Amityville, New York, USA. A guitar practitioner of what he describes as 'arrogant ambient music', Torn enjoys the conflict between sounds that are hypnotic and sounds that are 'like giant mosquitoes from hell, attacking.' He says, 'If I play something that's too pretty I feel compelled to go after it with razor-blades.' Jazz-educated, inspired by the minimalism of Terry Riley, a veteran of half a dozen rock and jazz-rock groups, former leader of the Everyman Band, film-music composer and guitarist, Torn is a gifted player still in search of the optimum context. He contributed usefully to Jan Garbarek's and David Sylvian's touring bands; his own records have found him playing idiosyncratic neo-fusion (*Cloud About Mercury*) and, rather ill-advisedly, singing Jimi Hendrix's 'Voodoo Chile' (*Door X*). In 1991, he launched a new 'improvising rock' group with Steve Jansen, Richard Barbieri, and Mick Karn, all ex-members of Japan and Rain Tree Crow. Torn also freelances as a record producer, with albums by Bill Bruford, Mick Karn and others to his credit. *Tripping Over God* in 1995 was a pure solo outing; in his words, it was 'my public meditation on the insanely unspeakable beauty inherent in the harshness of our mortality, a meditation on limitations: no, I take that back, hand me a beer would you?'.

● ALBUMS: *Best Laid Plans* (1985)★★★, *Cloud About Mercury* (1986)★★★, *Door X* (1990)★★★, with Mick Karn, Terry Bozzio *Polytown* (CMP 1994)★★, *Tripping Over God* (CMP 1995)★★★★, *What Means Solid, Traveller?* (CMP 1996)★★★★.

TÖRNQVIST, REBECKA

b. Sweden. Törnqvist spent most of her childhood in Africa where her father worked for the Swedish foreign aid organization SIDA. From an early age she was devoted to music, counting Steely Dan and the Beatles among her favourites. Soon the sound of African music also made an impact on her, before she discovered jazz and gospel singers such as Mahalia Jackson and Errol Garner. When she returned to Stockholm to undertake study at the Swedish Music Conservatory she distilled these influences into dates with various local jazz bands. Soon she decided to launch a solo career. She made a huge impact with her debut 1993 releases - the single, 'Wander Where You Wander', and album, *A Night Like This*. Törnqvist had been signed by EMI Records Sweden after the completion of her first demo, the record label seeing in her the perfect contemporary torch singer. The material included on her debut album, such as 'Easy Come, Easy Go' (the second single to be released from it), confirmed their judgement.

● ALBUMS: *A Night Like This* (EMI 1993)★★★, *Good Thing* (EMI 1996)★★★.

Tough, Dave

b. 26 April 1907, Oak Park, Illinois, USA, d. 9 December 1948. Tough began playing drums as a child and while still at school was a member of the 'Austin High School Gang'. This loosely assembled group of musicians effectively formulated the Chicago style of jazz which became popular in the 20s. Tough, a swinging drummer with a fine sense of musical quality, was a significant member of the group. He travelled to Europe in the 20s and also spent time in New York City making records with Eddie Condon, Red Nichols and others. In 1932 he was forced into temporary inactivity through illness, returning to the scene in 1935. Although his work up to the time of his illness had been primarily in small groups, he now slotted into the big band scene as if made for it. He played first with Tommy Dorsey and later with Red Norvo, Bunny Berigan, Benny Goodman and Dorsey again. Tough then joined Jimmy Dorsey, Bud Freeman, Jack Teagarden, Artie Shaw and others. His employers were a who's who of the best of the white big bands of the swing era. There were a number of reasons for his restlessness, among them his insistence on musical perfection, irritation with the blandness of many of the more commercial arrangements the bands had to play, and his own occasionally unstable personality which was aggravated by his drinking. During World War II he was briefly in the US Navy (where he played with Shaw) but was discharged on medical grounds. On his discharge he joined Woody Herman, with whom he had played briefly before the war. The records of Herman's First Herd demonstrated to fans worldwide that the physically frail and tiny Tough was a powerful giant among drummers. Despite his broad-based style, Tough believed himself unsuited to bop and for much of his career he sought to develop a career as a writer. Sadly, his drinking became uncontrollable and his disaffection with the changing jazz scene accelerated his physical and mental deterioration, leading to fits. Although helped by many people who knew him, among them writers Leonard Feather and John Hammond Jnr., his lifestyle had numbered his days. Walking home one night, he fell, fractured his skull and died from the injury on 9 December 1948. His body lay unrecognized in the morgue for three days. Whether playing in small Chicago-style groups or in any of the big bands of which he was a member, Tough consistently demonstrated his subtle, driving swing. It was with Herman, however, that he excelled, urging along one of the finest of the period's jazz orchestras with sizzling enthusiasm.

Toussaint, Jean

b. St. Thomas, Trinidad. Tenor saxophonist Jean Toussaint has established a wide audience for his rich, expressive straight jazz work throughout the 80s and 90s. As a teenager he formed his own calypso band before moving to Boston, Massachusetts, USA, in 1977 to attend the Berklee College Of Music alongside friends and collaborators Greg Osby, Branford Marsalis and Jeff Watts. Moving to New York in 1982, he joined Art Blakey's Jazz Messengers. As he later recalled, 'I learned more in four years with Art than I'd have learned in ten had I not got through that initial audition.' Other work in New York also paired him with artists of the calibre of Wynton Marsalis, Gil Evans and McCoy Tyner, often by dint of leading jam sessions at the Blue Note club. His extensive touring commitments with the Jazz Messengers took him across the world, and he developed a fondness for London audiences and in particular those at Ronnie Scott's jazz club in London. After leaving the Messengers in 1987 he accepted a three-month commission to teach improvisation at London's Guildhall School of Music and Drama. He has remained in London ever since. From this base he has continued to collaborate with visiting American musicians including Max Roach and Cedar Walton. He continues to teach at Guildhall and also the Northern Ireland Arts Council's summer school at the University of Ulster. His 1996 album, *Life I Want*, made good use of his contacts among Britain's best young jazz musicians, including co-producer Jason Rebello, Tony Remy, Mark Mondesir, Clyo Brown and Wayne Batchelor. It was his first album for Graham Griffiths and Eddie Wilkinson's New Note label.

● ALBUMS: *What Goes Around* (Wild Circuit 1993)★★, *Life I Want* (New Note 1996)★★★★.

Towles, Nat

b. 10 August 1905, New Orleans, Louisiana, USA, d. January 1963. Well-strewn though it is with forgotten names and unjustifiably overlooked musicians, the history of jazz has been particularly unkind to Towles. After learning to play violin and guitar, he switched to playing bass and in the early 20s gained experience playing with musicians such as Henry 'Red' Allen and Buddy Petit. During the mid-20s he led his own bands in southern and south-eastern states, occasionally playing with other leaders. In the early 30s, he formed a band with which he toured the south-west for the next decade or so. It was this band, one of the very best of the territory bands, that most warrants Towles' claims to unrecognized fame. Unfortunately, any attempt to assess the band is necessarily based upon very little factual evidence and a great deal that is either circumstantial or anecdotal or both. Sidemen in the band in those years, whenever interviewed during their years of international fame, inevitably spoke of this band as being the finest in which they had ever played. Among these notable musicians are Sir Charles Thompson, Fred Beckett, Emmett Berry, Harold 'Money' Johnson, Henry Coker, Bob Dorsey, C.Q. Price, Debo Mills and Buddy Tate. The band almost never recorded, at least not as a Towles unit. However, in 1940 Horace Henderson 'borrowed' the band for a four-side recording date and it is these four performances upon which any latter-day assessment must be made. With fine arrangements, by tenor saxophonist Dorsey and Thompson, excellent ensemble playing, strong individual performances (by trumpeters Johnson, Berry, Price and Nat Bates, trombonist Archie Brown, drummer/vocalist Mills), this recording date is one of which any band of the time, Count Basie and Duke Ellington included, could be proud. The reasons why Towles elected to stay away from the main centres of music can only be speculated upon. If among his reasons was the fear that his best men might be stolen by other leaders, it was probably justified. Not long after his recording sessions, Henderson did just that, luring into the big-time most of the band. Although the period, the swing era, was one of intense commercialization of jazz, Towles also appears to have turned his back on fame and possibly fortune. He continued to lead a band through the 40s and into the 50s, making just a few more sides in the early 40s. At the end of the 50s, Towles retired from music, settling on the west coast where he went into the restaurant business.

● ALBUMS: *The Chronological Horace Henderson 1940 - Fletcher Henderson 1941* (Classics 1940-41)★★★★.

TOWNER, RALPH

b. 1 March 1940, Chehalis, Washington, USA. Towner is primarily known as a highly regarded acoustic guitarist, an instrument he did not even take up until he was 23. Towner was born into a musical family and as a child he played trumpet and taught himself piano. He later studied composition at the University of Oregon, but after graduation in 1963 began to play guitar seriously, studying classical technique in Vienna. Back in the USA from 1968, he worked in New York with a number of jazz groups, mainly playing piano, and first came to public notice in 1971 with a fine 12-string guitar solo on Weather Report's *I Sing The Body Electric.* Since 1970, Towner has mainly pursued a solo career, releasing a series of fine albums for ECM Records, some in company with fellow guitarist John Abercrombie or vibraphonist Gary Burton. In 1971 Towner co-formed Oregon and he continues a dual career as a solo artist. He is a prolific composer, and many of his compositions have been performed by orchestras around the world. All are distinguished by their evocative moods and resonant harmonies.

● ALBUMS: *Trios/Solos* (ECM 1972)★★★, *Diary* (ECM 1973)★★★★, with Gary Burton *Matchbook* (ECM 1975)★★★★, *Solstice* (ECM 1975)★★★, with John Abercrombie *Sargasso Sea* (ECM 1976)★★★★, *Sounds And Shadows* (ECM 1977)★★★, *Batik* (ECM 1978)★★★, *Solo Concert* (ECM 1979)★★★★, *Old Friends, New Friends* (ECM 1979)★★★, with Abercrombie *Five Years Later* (ECM 1981)★★★★, *Blue Sun* (ECM 1983)★★, with Burton *Slide Show* (ECM 1986)★★★★, *City Of Eyes* (ECM 1990)★★★, *Open Letter* (ECM 1992)★★★, with Arild Andersen, Nana Vasconcelos *If You Look Far Enough* (ECM 1993)★★★, *Lost And Found* (ECM 1996)★★★★, *Ana* (ECM 1997)★★★, with Bill Bruford, Eddie Gomez *If Summer Had Its Ghosts* (Discipline 1997)★★, with Gary Peacock *A Closer View* (ECM 1998)★★★.

● COMPILATIONS: *Works* (ECM 1983)★★★★.

TOWNS, COLIN

b. *c.*1946, England. A 90s jazz performer with a distinguished history in pop and rock, Towns first rose to prominence as the keyboard player in heavy rockers Gillan. However, he is probably better known for his contributions to television and film soundtracks, which include *Full Circle*, *Vampire's Kiss* and BBC costume drama, *The Buccaneers*. He always yearned to pursue the jazz music that had dominated his youth, and took his chance in 1993 with an album for Danny Thompson's The Jazz Label, a double CD released through New Note/Vital Records. This included some of the UK's foremost modern jazz exponents, including saxophonists Peter King and John Surman and trumpeter Guy Barker. Afterwards there was a lull in the artist's career, until the announcement of a six-date UK tour in early 1995. Following the rave reviews that attended a pre-tour warm-up set at London's Purcell Room in February, Towns' debut was reissued to coincide with the dates. Music from *The Buccaneers* was released by Mercury Records shortly thereafter. The rest of 1995 was taken up with work on a second series of BBC programmes *Pie In The Sky*, ITV's *Brother Cadfael* and feature film *The Puppetmasters*. Plans for a second jazz album were built around a piece entitled 'Short Stories', premiered at his Purcell Room concert. He has also set up the Provocateur label.

● ALBUMS: *The Mask Orchestra* (The Jazz Label 1993)★★★, *The Buccaneers* (Mercury 1995)★★★, with Maria Pia De Vito *Still Life* (Provocateur 1998)★★★.

TRACEY, CLARK

b. 5 February 1961, London, England. Tracey began playing drums at an early age, often working with his father, Stan Tracey. At the start of his professional career, however, Tracey's drumming was rock-orientated and sat uneasily with the jazz groups with which he often associated. By the early 80s, however, in his playing style it was clear that Tracey had absorbed much from the experience of playing with jazz artists such as Red Rodney, Charlie Rouse and James Moody. With visiting Americans, with bands led by contemporaries and by his father, and also as leader of his own groups, Tracey grew with every appearance. By the early 90s he was a major figure among the new and vital group of young British jazz stars. He is married to fellow singer Tina May.

● ALBUMS: with Guy Barker *Suddenly Last Tuesday* (Cadillac 1986)★★★, with Barker *Stiperstones* (Steam 1987)★★★, *We've Been Expecting You* (Charly 1992)★★.

TRACEY, STAN

b. 30 December 1926, London, England. Tracey taught himself to play piano and by his early teens was performing professionally. In the 50s he was deeply involved in the British modern jazz scene, working with musicians such as Tony Crombie and Ronnie Scott. For most of the 60s he was resident at Scott's club, backing numerous visiting jazzmen. In the middle of the decade he formed a regular band, which included in its personnel at one time or another Bobby Wellins, Peter King and for many years Art Themen. Tracey made numerous albums, many of them on his own label, Steam Records, run with the help of his wife Jackie. Some of his recordings are with a quartet, others have him in duo, with the sextet Hexad, as leader of an octet, and with a powerful big band. Amongst his collaborators on concert and record dates have been Don Weller, Keith Tippett, Tony Coe, John Surman and Mike Osborne, whose 1972 encounter with Tracey helped to revive the pianist's flagging faith in music as a career. For the past few years Tracey's regular quartet has included his son, Clark Tracey, Themen and bassist Roy Babbington. He has also taught for several years, including periods at the Guildhall School of Music. A leading jazz composer, Tracey's work includes *Under Milk Wood*, a suite inspired by Dylan Thomas's play for voices. He is also an accomplished arranger and has employed this talent to great effect, notably when acknowledging his admiration for Duke Ellington on *We Love You Madly* and other albums. As a player, his early work showed the influence of Thelonious Monk but over the years he has consistently displayed a distinctive, sometimes quirkily personal, touch. Tracey is one of the outstanding figures Britain has given to the world of jazz.

● ALBUMS: *Under Milk Wood* i (Blue Note 1965)★★★★, *Alice In Jazz Land* (1966)★★★, *Stan Tracey ... In Person* (1966)★★★, *With Love From Jazz* (1967)★★★, *The Latin American Caper* (1968)★★★, *We Love You Madly* (1968)★★★, *Seven Ages Of Man* (1969)★★★, with Mike Osborne *Original* (1972)★★★, *Alone At Wigmore Hall* (Cadillac 1974)★★★, with Keith Tippett *T'N'T* (1974)★★★, *Captain Adventure* (Steam 1975)★★★, *Under Milk Wood* ii (1976)★★★★, *The Bracknell Connection* (Steam 1976)★★★, *Salisbury Suite* (1977)★★★, with John Surman *Sonatinas* (1978)★★★, *'Hello Old Adversary!'* (Steam 1979)★★★, *Spectrum/Tribute To Monk* (c.1979)★★★, *South East Assignment* (Steam c.1980)★★★, *The Crompton Suite* (1981)★★★, *Stan Tracey Now* (1983)★★★, *The Poet's Suite* (1984)★★★, *Stan Tracey Plays Duke Ellington* (Mole 1986)★★★★, *Live At Ronnie Scott's* (Steam 1986)★★★, with Charlie Rouse *Playin' In The Yard* (1987)★★★, *Genesis* (Steam 1987)★★★, *We Still Love You Madly* (Mole 1988)★★★, *Stan Tracey And Don Weller Play Duke, Monk And Bird* (Emanem 1988)★★★, *Stan Tracey Now* (Steam 1988)★★★, *Portraits Plus* (Blue Note 1993)★★★★, *Duets* (Blue Note 1993)★★★★, *Live At The QEH* (Blue Note 1994)★★★, *Solo: Trio* (Cadillac 1998)★★★★.

TRAVELS - PAT METHENY

A double album that flirts with rock, folk, country and Latin - but is emphatically a jazz album. Pat Metheny is equipped with probably his best ever live group; Steve Rodby, Danny Gottlieb, Nana Vasconcelos, and his right arm, keyboard virtuoso Lyle Mays. The recording exudes warmth, and often improves on tracks already issued on studio albums; for example, 'Phase Dance' is played with more verve and 'Song For Bilbao' sounds more passionate in a live context. The diamond in the mine, however, is the shortest piece - the glorious and delicate title track - worth the price of the album alone.

● Tracks: *Are You Going With Me?; The Fields, The Sky; Goodbye; Phase Dance; Straight On Red; Farmer's Trust; Extradition; Goin' Ahead; As Falls Wichita, So Falls Wichita Falls; Travels; Song For Bilbao; San Lorenzo.*
● First released 1983
● UK peak chart position: did not chart
● USA peak chart position: 62

TRENT, ALPHONSO

b. 24 August 1905, Fort Smith, Arkansas, USA, d. 14 October 1959. Born into a middle-class family, Trent learned piano at an early age and by his teens was playing regularly in local dance bands. He formed his own band while in his late teens, then worked briefly for another local leader before taking over his small band and securing a long residency at a hotel in Dallas, Texas. For this engagement he expanded the band to 10 pieces; among the excellent musicians he hired were Snub Mosley, James Jeter, Hayes Pillars (who later teamed up to form the Jeter-Pillars Orchestra), drummer A.G. Godley, generally acclaimed as the father of Kansas City-style drumming, Stuff Smith, Peanuts Holland and Sy Oliver. Thanks to regular broadcasts from the hotel, Trent's popularity spread throughout the south-western states. He paid high wages and offered his sidemen exceptionally good conditions which included smart uniforms and personal limousines. The line-up of the band remained remarkably constant and the musicians enthusiastic, well aware that they were envied by less fortunate members of other territory bands. This consistency, allied to ample rehearsal time and excellent arrangements (aside from Oliver, the band's arrangers included Gus Wilson, brother of Teddy Wilson), helped to build the orchestra into the outstanding territory band of the pre-swing era. Although the band occasionally played in the east, including an appearance at New York's Savoy Ballroom, Trent preferred to remain in the south-west. This parochial attitude, coupled with the fact that the band made only a tiny handful of records, prevented it from making an impact upon the national jazz scene. Worse still, the band's management was inept and in 1933, on the eve of the explosion of interest in big band jazz, Trent was obliged to fold. For the rest of the 30s he continued to play with small groups, for one of which he unearthed the unknown Charlie Christian, but by the early part of the following decade music was only a part-time interest. He died in October 1959. During its existence the Trent band displayed standards of musicianship on a par with those of more famous bands, such as Fletcher Henderson's and Jimmie Lunceford's, but his few records give only a tantalizing glimpse of its qualities.

● COMPILATIONS: with others *Sweet And Low Blues: Big Bands And Territory Bands Of The 20s* (1928-33)★★★.

TRIO, THE

Not to be confused with the German electronic pop band of the early 80s who had a big UK hit with 'Da Da Da', this Trio were an ambitious meeting ground between jazz and rock musicians in the early 70s. The group featured Stu Martin (drums), Barre Phillips (b. 27 October 1934, San Francisco, California, USA; bass) and John Surman (b. John Douglas Surman, 30 August 1944, Tavistock, Devon, England; saxophone). Trio made their debut in 1970 with an ambitious double album for Dawn Records. The follow-up, *Conflagration*, featured many renowned contributors, including Chick Corea, who was an early supporter of the group. However, neither managed to break the band in the rock mainstream.

● ALBUMS: *The Trio* (Dawn 1970)★★★, *Conflagration* (Dawn 1971)★★★★, *Live At Woodstock Town Hall* 1974 recording (Dawn 1976)★★.

TRISTANO, LENNIE

b. 19 March 1919, Chicago, Illinois, USA, d. 18 November 1978. Encouraged by his mother, Tristano learned piano and various reed instruments while still a very small child, despite steadily deteriorating eyesight (he was born during a measles epidemic). By the age of 11 he was completely blind but, overcoming this handicap, he studied formally at the American Conservatory in Chicago, graduating in 1943. Before graduation he had already established a reputation as a session musician and teacher, including among his pupils outstanding talents such as Lee Konitz and Bill Russo. He also made a handful of records with Earl Swope. Based in New York from 1946, he worked with Charlie Parker and other leading bop musicians and attracted considerable attention within the jazz community, even if his work was little known outside (his first recordings were not released until many years later). In New York Tristano continued to teach; Warne Marsh was one of his important pupils from this period. The extent of his teaching increased so much that by the early 50s he had founded the first important jazz school in New York, a development that kept him still further away from the wider public. By the mid-50s he had returned to private teaching and although he made a few recordings and some public appearances, including a mid-60s tour of Europe, he lived out the remaining years of his life in undeserved, but presumably intentional obscurity. An exceptionally original thinker, Tristano's work follows a path that, while related to the development of bop, traces different concepts. He was an early experimenter in playing jazz free from traditional notions of time signatures, but the results were very different from the later free jazz movement developed by Ornette Coleman and others. Among the lessons Tristano imparted to his pupils were those of strict precision in ensemble playing, complete command of the instrument and the ability to play complex shifts of time signature within a piece. He also lay particular significant stress upon listening - 'ear training'. In his own playing he preferred a pure sound and line, devoid of emotional content, and persuaded his pupils to follow this example so that, in Brian Priestley's words, their performances would 'stand or fall on the quality of their construction and not on emotional coloration'. Despite this almost puritanical attitude towards jazz, Tristano's teaching encouraged detailed study of solos by emotional players such as Louis Armstrong, Roy Eldridge and Charlie Parker. Clearly, Tristano was a powerful influence upon the many musicians he taught and through them upon countless more, especially through the work of such pupils as Peter Ind and Konitz, himself an important teacher.

● ALBUMS: *Live In Toronto* (Jazz Records 1952)★★★, *Lines* (1955), *Lennie Tristano* (Atlantic 1955)★★★, *New York Improvisations* (1956)★★★, *The New Tristano* (Rhino 1962)★★★★, *Manhattan Studio* (Elektra 1983)★★★★.

● COMPILATIONS: *Live At Birdland 1949* (Jazz Records 1945-49)★★★, *The Lost Session* (1946)★★★, *The Rarest Trio/Quartet Sessions 1946/7* (1946-47)★★★★, *Cool In Jam* (1947)★★★, *Crosscurrents* (1949)★★★, *Wow* (Jazz Records 1950 recording)★★★★, *Descent Into The Maelstrom* (1951-66)★★★★, *Note To Note* (Jazz Records 1997)★★★★, with Lee Konitz, Warne Marsh *The Complete Atlantic Recordings Of Lennie Tristano, Lee Konitz & Warne Marsh* 6-CD box set (Mosaic 1997)★★★★.

TROTMAN, LLOYD NELSON

b. 25 May 1923, Boston, Massachusetts, USA. Lloyd and elder brother Ernie learned music at school and went on to more advanced studies at both New England Conservatory and their father's own Music Lovers' School Of Music. Lloyd played the double bass and, inspired by Slam Stewart and Jimmy Blanton, began touring with a jazz band in 1941. He went on to play with Blanche Calloway, Billie Holiday, Stuff Smith, Eddie Heywood, Hazel Scott, Duke Ellington, Pete Brown and other artists. His most famous period was as bassist with the Johnny Hodges-Al Sears breakaway group from the early 50s on such recordings as 'Castle Rock.' He subsequently joined Alan Freed's Rock 'n' Roll Orchestra. In the 40s and 50s, Lloyd was a popular session musician, his bass forming the dance foundation for many jazz and R&B sessions from Viola Watkins, Cousin Joe and Champion Jack Dupree to Lucky Millinder, Mickey And Sylvia, Ray Charles and Ben E. King (he plays the distinctive bass on 'Stand By Me'). He made some quartet recordings with Oscar Pettiford (who named Lloyd as his favourite bass player) in 1950 for Mercer and had a couple of singles released under his own name on Tuxedo and Brunswick. Today he lives on Long Island, New York, but has retired from the music business.

TRUEHEART, JOHN

b. *c*.1900, Baltimore, Maryland, USA, d. 1949. Trueheart started out playing banjo and guitar with local bands, where another young hopeful was his close friend, Chick Webb. When Webb went to New York, Trueheart also uprooted and remained with Webb, apart from a long illness, until the drummer's death. Trueheart stayed on with the band which continued under the nominal leadership of Ella Fitzgerald. He then teamed up with Art Hodes and others for a short time before illness prevailed and he retired from music. A solid and dependable (and clearly very loyal) musician,

Trueheart's playing on his many records with Webb is rarely clearly audible given the technical shortcomings of the period. Nevertheless, he was an ideal big band player, helping to provide a strong rhythmic pulse to one of the best of the era's bands.

● COMPILATIONS: *The Chronological Chick Webb 1929-1934* (Classics 1929-34)★★★★, *The Chronological Chick Webb 1935-1938* (Classics 1935-38)★★★★.

TRUMBAUER, FRANK

b. 30 May 1901, Carbondale, Illinois, USA, d. 11 June 1956. As a teenager Trumbauer played various instruments, including piano and trombone, before concentrating on the 'C' melody saxophone. He began leading a band while still in his teens and after military service in World War I played with several Midwestern dance bands. In the mid-20s he joined the Jean Goldkette organization, leading a band that included Bix Beiderbecke. Trumbauer and Beiderbecke made a number of fine small group recordings during this association, which continued until 1927 when they both joined a big band formed by Adrian Rollini. They then moved on together to the Paul Whiteman band, where Trumbauer remained until the early 30s. He briefly led his own band and was co-leader with Jack and Charlie Teagarden of the Three T's band. By the end of the decade he was working on the west coast. He quit music in 1939, taking up work in the aviation industry. He briefly led a band in 1940 and then, during World War II, he became a test pilot. After the war he played in a number of bands, mostly in the studios, sometimes playing alto saxophone, but by 1947 was back working in aviation. He made occasional appearances at jazz dates, including a special tribute to Beiderbecke held in 1952. He died in June 1956. The precision and control displayed by Trumbauer was greatly admired by other saxophonists, including Benny Carter and Buddy Tate. As a soloist his work was somewhat less relaxed and swinging than his contemporaries but the association with Beiderbecke resulted in several recordings that remain among the classics of 20s jazz.

● ALBUMS: with Jean Goldkette, Paul Whiteman, Bix Beiderbecke *Bixology Vols 2,3,6,7,8* (1924-28)★★★★, with Beiderbecke *The Studio Groups - Late 1927* (1927)★★★★, *Bix And Tram* (1927)★★★, *The Essential Frank Trumbauer Vol. 4* (1929-30)★★★★, with Jack Teagarden *T'N'T* (1933-36)★★★, *Frankie Trumbauer 1937-38* (IAJRC 1991)★★★★.

● FURTHER READING: *Tailspin*, Frank Trumbauer.

TUCK AND PATTI

Tuck Andress (b. 28 October 1952, Tulsa, Oklahoma, USA) and Patti Cathcart (b. 4 October 1950, San Francisco, California, USA) are a totally fresh and innovative duo making their own subtle versions of contemporary pop in a jazz setting. Tuck's remarkably sparse electric guitar is set against Patti's strong and soulful voice. Their intuitive interplay comes from their close domestic and musical intimacy. On *Tears Of Joy* they tackle Cyndi Lauper's 'Time After Time', Rodgers And Hart's 'My Romance' and Wes Montgomery's 'Up And At It', as well as their own sparkling composition, 'Love Is The Key'. Similarly on *Love Warriors*, their blend was as inspired as it was broad, with the Beatles' 'Honey Pie', and the classic 'They Can't Take That Away From Me'. Another bold move was daring to attempt 'Castles Made Of Sand'/'Little Wing' by Jimi Hendrix; it was a total success, with some exceptional guitar playing from Andress. Patti stated, 'We're willing to take chances and throw each other a curve; that's why we keep growing and the music stays fresh. We risk messing up in front of everybody, but you have to take chances because if you don't, that's the beginning of the end'.

● ALBUMS: *Tears Of Joy* (1988)★★★★, *Love Warriors* (1989)★★★★, *Dream* (Windham Hill 1991)★★★, *Learning How To Fly* (Sony 1995)★★★, *Paradise Found* (Windham Hill 1998)★★.

Solo: Tuck Andress *Hymns, Carols And Songs About Snow* (1989)★★, *Reckless Precision* (1989)★★.

● COMPILATIONS: *The Best Of Tuck And Patti* (Windham Hill 1994)★★★★.

TURNBULL, ALAN

b. Alan Lawrence Turnbull, 23 November 1943, Melbourne, Victoria, Australia. Turnbull began playing drums as a child and was working professionally while still in his early teens. During the 60s he played with several of Australia's leading jazz musicians, including Don Burrows, with whom he continued to play during succeeding decades making appearances at festivals in Europe and the USA. Turnbull is a skilled bop mainstreamer and is in much demand as an accompanist to jazz stars, including Milt Jackson, Phil Woods and George Cables.

TURNER, 'BIG' JOE

b. Joseph Vernon Turner, 18 May 1911, Kansas City, Missouri, USA, d. 24 November 1985, Los Angeles, California, USA. 'Big' Joe Turner (aka Big Vernon) began singing in local clubs in his early teens upon the death of his father, and at the age of 15 teamed up with pianist Pete Johnson. Their professional relationship lasted on-and-off for over 40 years. During the late 20s and early 30s, Turner toured with several of Kansas City's best black bands, including those led by George E. Lee, Bennie Moten, Andy Kirk and Count Basie. However, it was not until 1936 that he left his home ground and journeyed to New York City. Making little impression on his debut in New York, Turner, with Johnson, returned in 1938 to appear in John Hammond Jnr.'s *From Spirituals To Swing* concerts and on Benny Goodman's *Camel Caravan* CBS radio show, and this time they were well received. Johnson teamed up with Albert Ammons and Meade Lux Lewis as the Boogie Woogie Boys and sparked the boogie-woogie craze that subsequently swept the nation and the world. Turner's early recordings depicted him as both a fine jazz singer and, perhaps more importantly, a hugely influential blues shouter. He appeared on top recording sessions by Benny Carter, Coleman Hawkins and Joe Sullivan as well as his own extensive recording for Vocalion (1938-40) and Decca (1940-44), which featured accompaniment by artists such as Willie 'The Lion' Smith, Art Tatum, Freddie Slack or Sammy Price, when Johnson, Ammons or Lewis were unavailable. After World War II, Turner continued to make excellent records in the jazz-blues/jump-blues styles for the burgeoning independent labels - National (1945-47), Aladdin (1947, which included a unique *Battle Of The Blues* session with Turner's chief rival, Wynonie Harris), Stag and RPM (1947), Down Beat/Swing Time and Coast/DooTone (1948), Excelsior and Rouge (1949), Freedom (1949-50), and Imperial/Ba'you (1950), as well as a west coast stint in 1948-49 with new major MGM Records. As the 40s wore on, these recordings, often accompanied by the bands of Wild Bill Moore, Maxwell Davis, Joe Houston and Dave Bartholomew, took on more of an R&B style which began to appeal to a young white audience by the early 50s. In 1951 'Big' Joe started the first of 13 years with the fledgling Atlantic Records, where he became one of the very few jazz/blues singers of his generation who managed to regain healthy record sales in the teenage rock 'n' roll market during the mid- to late 50s. His early Atlantic hits were largely blues ballads such as 'Chains Of Love' and 'Sweet Sixteen', but 1954 witnessed the release of Turner's 'Shake Rattle And Roll' which, covered by artists such as Bill Haley and Elvis Presley, brought the 43-year-old blues shouter some belated teenage adoration. This was maintained with such irresistible (and influential) classics as 'Hide And Seek' (1954), 'Flip, Flop And Fly', 'The Chicken And The Hawk' (1955), 'Feelin' Happy' (1956) and 'Teenage Letter' (1957). At the height of rock 'n' roll fever, Atlantic had the excellent taste to produce a retrospective album of Turner singing his old Kansas City jazz and blues with a peerless band, featuring his old partner Pete Johnson. The album, *The Boss Of The Blues*, has since achieved classic status.

In the late 50s, Atlantic's pioneering rock 'n' roll gave way to over-production, vocal choirs and symphonic string sections. In 1962 Turner left this fast-expanding independent company and underwent a decade of relative obscurity in the clubs of Los Angeles, broken by the occasional film appearance or sporadic single release on Coral and Kent. The enterprising Bluesway label reintroduced 'Big' Joe to the general public. In 1971 he was signed to Pablo Records, surrounded by old colleagues such as Count Basie, Eddie Vinson, Pee Wee Crayton, Jay McShann, Lloyd Glenn and Jimmy Witherspoon. He emerged irregularly to produce fine one-off albums for Blues Spectrum and Muse, and stole the show in Bruce Ricker's essential jazz film, *The Last Of The Blue Devils*. Turner's death in 1985 was as a result of 74 years of hard living, hard singing and hard drinking, but he was admired and respected by the musical community and his funeral included musical tributes by Etta James and Barbara Morrison.

● ALBUMS: *Sings Kansas City Jazz* (Decca 1953)★★★, *The Boss Of The Blues* (Atlantic 1956)★★★★, *Joe Turner And The Blues* (Savoy 1958)★★★★, *Joe Turner* (Atlantic 1958)★★★★, *Big Joe Rides Again* (Atlantic 1959)★★★★, *Rockin' The Blues* (Atlantic 1959)★★★★, *Big Joe Is Here* (Atlantic 1959)★★★★, *Careless Love* (Savoy 1963)★★★, with Buck Clayton *Buck Clayton Meets Joe Turner* (Black Lion 1965)★★★, *Big Joe Singing The Blues* (Bluesway 1967)★★★, *Texas Style* (Black & Blue 1971)★★, with Count Basie *The Bosses* (Pablo 1974)★★★, with Pee Wee Crayton *Every Day I Have The Blues* (1976)★★★, with Jimmy Witherspoon *Nobody In Mind* (Pablo 1976)★★★, *Things That I Used To Do* (Pablo 1977)★★★, with Basie, Eddie Vinson *Kansas City Shout* (1978)★★★, *The Midnight Special* (Pablo 1980)★★★, *Have No Fear, Joe Turner Is Here* (Pablo 1981)★★★★, *In The Evening* (Pablo 1982)★★★, *The Trumpet Kings Meet Joe Turner* (Pablo 1982)★★★, *Boogie Woogie Jubilee* (1982)★★★, *Big Joe Turner & Roomful Of Blues* (1983)★★★★, *Life Ain't Easy* (Pablo 1983)★★★, *Blues Train* (Muse 1983)★★★, *Kansas City Here I Come* (Pablo 1984)★★★, with Witherspoon *Patcha, Patcha All Night Long: Joe Turner Meets Jimmy Witherspoon* (Pablo 1986)★★★, *I Don't Dig It* (Jukebox 1986)★★★, *Honey Hush* (Magnum Force 1988)★★★, *Steppin' Out* (Ace 1988)★★★, with Basie *Flip, Flop & Fly* 1972 recording (Pablo 1989)★★★, *Bosses Of The Blues* (Bluebird 1989)★★★, *I've Been To Kansas City* (1991)★★★, *Every Day In The Week* (1993)★★★, with the Memphis Blues Caravan *Jackson On My Mind* (Mystic 1997)★★.

● COMPILATIONS: *The Best Of Joe Turner* (Atlantic 1953)★★★★, *Jumpin' The Blues* (Arhoolie 1981)★★★, *Great R&B Oldies* (Carosello 1981)★★★, *Boss Blues* (Intermedia 1982)★★, *The Very Best Of Joe Turner* (Intermedia 1982)★★★, *Roll Me Baby* (Intermedia 1982)★★, *Rock This Joint* (Intermedia 1982)★★★, *Jumpin' With Joe* (Charly 1984)★★★, *Jumpin' Tonight* (Pathé Marconi 1985)★★★, *Big Joe Turner Memorial Album: Rhythm & Blues Years* (Atlantic 1987)★★★★, *Big Joe Turner: Greatest Hits* (Atlantic 1987)★★★★, *The Complete 1940-1944 Recordings* (1990)★★★★, *Shouting The Blues* (Specialty/Ace 1993)★★★★, *Jumpin' With Joe - The Complete Aladdin And Imperial Recordings* (EMI 1994)★★★★, *Greatest Hits* (Sequel 1994)★★★★, *The Very Best Of 'Big' Joe Turner* (Atlantic 1998)★★★★.

TURNER, BRUCE

b. 5 July 1922, Saltburn, Yorkshire, England, d. 28 November 1993, Newport Pagnell, Buckinghamshire, England. A self-taught clarinettist, Turner took up alto saxophone during military service in World War II. In the immediate post-war years, Turner showed himself to be a thoroughly eclectic and accommodating musician, playing both bebop and Dixieland with equal aplomb and ability. Significantly, he also played these diverse forms of jazz with considerable integrity. At the start of the 50s he joined a current trend among British musicians and played aboard transatlantic liners in order to visit New York. While there he studied with Lee Konitz (this at a time when Konitz was himself studying with Lennie Tristano). Despite this exposure to contemporary thought in jazz, on his return to the UK Turner joined Freddy Randall, with whom he had played in the late 40s, and then began a long association with Humphrey Lyttelton. His tenure with Lyttelton was marked at its outset by one of the more extreme examples of the division in loyalties among UK jazz audiences of the era; a banner bearing the words 'Go home, dirty bopper' was waved at a concert and the phrase entered the vocabulary even if, subsequently, it was not always used with defamatory intent. In 1957 Turner formed his own 'jump' band, a move that appears to have given him the most suitable setting for his quirky, driving playing style, which reflects the work of predecessors such as Pete Brown while remaining distinctively personal. With this band, Turner toured extensively, often accompanying visiting American jazzmen such as Ben Webster, Ray Nance, Bill Coleman and Don Byas. Some of these tours brought personality clashes and led to Turner's decision to fold the jump band. In the mid-60s Turner then returned to a more traditional setting with Acker Bilk. In the early 70s his relationship with Lyttelton was resumed, although Turner continued to lead his own small bands and to work in a richly varied selection of bands, from the traditional, with Keith Smith, to the modern, with Dave Green (notably in the group Fingers). Late in his career Turner also took up soprano saxophone, displaying an effective command of the instrument. One of the outstanding British musicians of his generation, Turner's eclecticism might well have limited the spread of his reputation. Certainly, this enormously talented and well-liked figure deserved to be better represented on records and on the international festival and club circuits.

● ALBUMS: with Humphrey Lyttelton *Live At The Royal Festival Hall* (1954)★★★★, *Accent On Swing* i (1959)★★★, *Jumping At The NFT* (1961)★★★, *Accent On Swing* ii (1962)★★★, *Going Places* (1962)★★, *Bruce Turner-John Barnes: Jazz Masters* (1975)★★★, with Keith Smith *Up Jumped The Blues* (1978)★★★, with Dave Green *Fingers Remembers Mingus* (1979)★★, *The Dirty Bopper* (Calligraph 1985)★★★, *New Orleans* (Metronome 1990)★★★, *Fishmouth* (Decca 1991)★★★, *Shiek Of Araby* (Decca 1991)★★★.

● FURTHER READING: *Hot Air, Cool Music*, Bruce Turner.

TURNER, DANNY

b. James Daniel Turner, 8 March 1920, Farrell, Pennsylvania, USA, d. 14 April 1995. Raised in upstate New York, he studied music, then began playing alto saxophone while living in Philadelphia in the late 40s; he associated with many distinguished jazzmen including John Coltrane and Philly Joe Jones. He occasionally led his own small groups and also worked with other leaders including Johnny Lynch and the Four Kings And A Queen vocal group. In 1950 he was a member of the Gerald Wilson big band that accompanied Billie Holiday on a disastrous tour of southern states. He was a member of the Milt Buckner small group for four years in the 50s and also played and recorded with Dakota Staton, Jimmy McGriff, Ray Charles and others throughout the 60s, sometimes playing alto, sometimes tenor saxophone. He spent some time with Machito and then, in the early 70s, became an on-call substitute with Count Basie. From the mid-70s he was permanently with Basie, usually playing alto and eventually becoming section leader. A fluid, elegant soloist, Turner's style always charmed and often sparked with boppish fire. After Basie died, Turner continued to play in alumni bands and was a member of the continuing Count Basie Orchestra until shortly before his death.

● ALBUMS: with Milt Buckner *Rockin' With Milt* (Capitol 1955)★★, *First Time Out* (Hemisphere 1983)★★★.

TURNER, JOE

b. 3 November 1907, Baltimore, Maryland, USA, d. 21 July 1990. Taught piano by his mother, Turner began playing professionally in his late teens. Mostly based in New York City, he worked with many leading jazz artists of the 20s, including Hilton Jefferson, June Clark, Louis Armstrong and Benny Carter. He was instrumental in introducing Art Tatum to Adelaide Hall and was himself for many years accompanist to the singer. In 1931 he visited Europe, returning there later in the decade for tours and residencies. He visited France, Turkey and Hungary, where he married a local girl. After military service in World War II, Turner played with Rex Stewart, but before the 40s were over he was back in Europe to be reunited with his wife and daughter. He visited various countries, eventually settling in France, where he remained for the rest of his life. From 1962 he was resident at the Calvados club in Paris, playing Harlem stride piano, singing, and leavening his repertoire with music for the tourists. He made occasional visits to the USA, playing at the Newport Jazz Festival in 1973 and at The Cookery in New York City.

● ALBUMS: *Stridin' In Paris* (1952)★★★, *Sweet And Lovely* (RCA Vogue 1952)★★★★, *Joe Turner* i (1955)★★★, *Joe Turner* ii (1959)★★★, *Stride By Stride* (Solo Art 1960)★★★★, *Smashing Thirds* (1961)★★★, *The Joe Turner Trio* (1971)★★★, *Joe's Back In Town* (1974)★★★, *Harlem Strut* (1974)★★★, *King Of Stride* (1975)★★★, *Another Epoch: Stride Piano Vols 1 & 2* (1975-76)★★★, *Homage A Hugues Panassié* (1976)★★, *Effervescent* (1976)★★, *Joe Turner* iii (1976)★★, *I Understand* (Black And Blue 1979)★★★, *Jazz In Tagi '82* (1982)★★★, *Walking Through Heaven* (1983)★★★.

TURNEY, NORRIS

b. 8 September 1921, Wilmington, Ohio, USA. Turney began playing alto saxophone as a child, emulating the sound of Johnny Hodges and nurturing a dream of one day playing in the Duke Ellington orchestra. In the late 30s and early 40s he played in Fate Marable's riverboat band and several territory bands, including the popular Jeter-Pillars Orchestra. In 1945 he was briefly with Tiny Bradshaw and Billy Eckstine. Through the late 40s and much of the following decade he was content to work outside the main centres. Late in the 60s he appeared in the band accompanying Ray Charles on a tour of the Far East and Australia. At the end of the 60s he finally achieved his lifelong ambition and stepped into the Ellington band when Hodges was sick; later, when his idol died, Turney took the altoist's seat permanently. After Ellington's death Turney worked mostly in New York, playing occasional jazz dates but more often in pit bands along Broadway. In the 80s he became a member of the accomplished band assembled by David 'Panama'

Francis under the name the Savoy Sultans. He also played a number of festivals as a member of the George Wein Newport Festival All Stars. Turney, who also plays flute and clarinet, is a marvellous ballad player and his liquid sound on alto saxophone amply demonstrates his love for the playing style of Hodges, although he has his own stylistic leanings. Among his compositions is 'Chequered Hat', a song dedicated to Hodges.

● ALBUMS: with Duke Ellington *Seventieth Birthday Concert* (1969)★★★★, with Ellington *Toga Brava Suite* (1971)★★★, one side only *The Boys From Dayton* (1975)★★, *I Let A Song* (1979)★★, with Panama Francis *Gettin' In The Groove* (1979)★★★, with George Wein *The Newport Festival All Stars* (1984)★★★.

TURNHAM, EDYTHE

b. Edythe Payne, *c.*1890, Topeka, Kansas, USA, d. 1950. She first played piano as a tiny child and before she reached her teens was accompanying a minstrel group in Spokane, Idaho, where her family had moved. She married in her late teens and eventually formed a family band with her husband on drums and her son on saxophone. She mostly played as a single, however, working in various states in the north-west and in Canada. Eventually, she settled in Los Angeles where she re-formed a band, naming it the Dixie Aces. The outfit, which sometimes broadcast, included her husband, Floyd Turnham Snr., her son, Floyd Jnr., and Teddy Buckner. By the mid-30s and early 40s, she no longer led a band and had no real interest in pursuing her career.

TURRÉ, STEVE

b. 12 September 1948, Omaha, Nebraska, USA. Early in his professional career Turré played trombone with jazzman Rahsaan Roland Kirk and with Santana, the Latin-tinged rock band. This was in California where he was raised and by which time he had studied music at North Texas State University. He toured with Ray Charles's band, was briefly with Woody Shaw, joined Art Blakey's Jazz Messengers, and had a spell with the Thad Jones-Mel Lewis Jazz Orchestra. In the mid-70s he was with Chico Hamilton, also playing electric bass, and had musically profitable reunions with both Kirk and Shaw. For a post-bop group, the Shaw band had an unusual front line of trumpet and trombone. It attracted a good deal of attention and proved to be popular with audiences. The pair teamed up again in the early 80s and in all about a dozen albums resulted, among them *Moontrane* (Muse 1974) and *Master Of The Art* (Elektra Musician 1982). Turré also spent some time working with Slide Hampton's World Of Trombones band and with Max Roach and Cedar Walton. In 1989 he was at London's Royal Festival Hall with Dizzy Gillespie's United Nations Orchestra for a concert that was recorded on audio and video, by Enja Records and Our Video respectively. By the end of the 80s and on into the 90s, Turré was mostly active as leader of his own bands, recording and writing original music and charts. He also performs with his Sanctified Shells, where trombonists double on exotic shells. An eager seeker after perfection, Turré's playing is notable for its purity of sound and fullness of tone. His admiration for past masters, such as Tommy Dorsey, and more recent trombone giants such as J.J. Johnson, with whom he has often worked, is evident in the care he continues to take in honing what many might see as an already perfect technique. However, notwithstanding the painstaking attention to his playing style and sound, Turré's performances are replete with excitement, energy and fluid swing.

● ALBUMS: *Viewpoint* (Stash 1987)★★★★, *Fire And Ice* (Stash 1988)★★★, *Right There* (Antilles 1991)★★★, *Sanctified Shells* (Antilles 1992)★★★, *Rhythm Within* (Verve 1995)★★★★, *Steve Turré* (Verve 1996)★★★★.

TURRENTINE, STANLEY

b. 5 April 1934, Pittsburgh, Pennsylvania, USA. After playing cello Turrentine took up the tenor saxophone before reaching his teenage years. Born into a musical family (his father, Thomas Turrentine, played tenor with Al Cooper's Savoy Sultans), Turrentine quickly became proficient enough to turn professional. He began playing with blues and R&B bands including those led by Lowell Fulson and Earl Bostic, but in the early 50s he played in a band led by Tadd Dameron. In the late 50s he worked with Max Roach and also began leading his own bands, quickly establishing a reputation for live and recorded performances. For some years he was married to Shirley Scott, with whom he also made records. He also recorded with Jimmy Smith and in such organ/saxophone soul-jazz settings he has achieved considerable commercial success. His series of albums for Blue Note Records during the 60s produced some of the finest ever soul-jazz. Although his early professional experience has left a considerable mark on his playing, evident in his strong affinity for the blues, Turrentine has been able to adapt his style to appeal to the crossover audience for jazz-inflected popular dance music of the late 80s. Some of his albums, such as *Wonderland* with tunes by Stevie Wonder, are tailored for this market, while others are aimed at the hardcore jazz audience.

● ALBUMS: *Stan The Man* (Time 1960)★★★, *Look Out!* (Blue Note 1960)★★★★, *Blue Hour* (Blue Note 1961)★★★, *Comin' Your Way* (Blue Note 1961)★★★, *Up At Minton's, Volume 1* (Blue Note 1961)★★★★, *Up At Minton's, Volume 2* (Blue Note 1961)★★★★, *Dearly Beloved* (Blue Note 1961)★★★, *That's Where It's At* (Blue Note 1962)★★★, *Z.T.'s Blues* (Blue Note 1962)★★★, *Never Let Me Go* (Blue Note 1963)★★★★, *A Chip Off The Old Block* (Blue Note 1963)★★★, *Mr Natural* (1964)★★★, *Hustlin'* (Blue Note 1964)★★★, *Tiger Tail* (Mainstream 1965)★★★, *Joyride* (Blue Note 1965)★★★★, *Let It Go* (Impulse! 1966)★★★, *Rough And Tumble* (Blue Note 1966)★★★, *New Time Shuffle* (1967)★★★, *Easy Walker* (Blue Note 1967)★★★★, *The Spoiler* (Blue Note 1967)★★★, *In The Look Of Love* (Blue Note 1968)★★★, *Always Something There* (Blue Note 1968)★★★, *Common Touch!* (Blue Note 1969)★★★, *Another Story* (Blue Note 1969)★★★, *Salt Song* (CTI 1971)★★★★, *Flipped Out* (Polydor 1972)★★★, *Sugar* (CTI

1973)★★★, *Cherry* (CTI 1973)★★★, *Yester Me, Yester You/Another Fine Mess* (1974)★★★, *Pieces Of Dreams* (Fantasy 1974)★★★★, *Everybody Come On Out* (1976)★★★, *Nightwings* (Fantasy 1977)★★★, *West Side Highway* (Fantasy 1977)★★★, *What About You* (Fantasy 1978)★★★, *Soothsayer* (1979)★★★, *Inflation* (Elektra 1980)★★★, *Tender Togetherness* (Elektra 1981)★★★, *Home Again* (Elektra 1982)★★★, *Straight Ahead* (1984)★★★, *Wonderland* (Blue Note 1986)★★★, *Comin' Your Way* (Blue Note 1988)★★★, *La Place* (Blue Note 1989)★★★, *If I Could* (Limelight 1994)★★★, with Three Of A Kind *Three Of A Kind Meets Mr T* (Koch 1995)★★★, *T Time* (Music Masters 1995)★★★.

● COMPILATIONS: with Shirley Scott *The Best Of Shirley Scott And Stanley Turrentine* (Prestige 1969)★★★, *Best Of Stanley Turrentine The Blue Note Years* (Blue Note 1990)★★★★.

TURRENTINE, TOMMY

b. Thomas Walter Turrentine Jnr., 22 April 1928, Pittsburgh, Pennsylvania, USA. Born into a musical family, his father was a member of Al Cooper's Savoy Sultans, and he started playing trumpet as a youth. In the mid-40s he played with Benny Carter and during the 50s was with several popular and distinguished bandleaders, including Earl Bostic, Charles Mingus, Count Basie, Max Roach and Dizzy Gillespie. In the 60s he was frequently in demand for record dates, performing with Jackie McLean, Lou Donaldson and several others, including his younger brother, Stanley Turrentine. Little was heard from Turrentine after the 60s, a fact that, given his rich and melodious playing, can be construed as a loss to the jazz scene of these later years.

● ALBUMS: *Tommy Turrentine* (Time 1960)★★★.

TURTLE ISLAND STRING QUARTET

If one of the most interesting developments in popular music during the late 80s and early 90s has been the blurring of boundaries within genres, arguably the most extreme example of cross-fertilization has been the melding of rock, pop or jazz with classical music. Among the most popular and exciting musical ensembles to fall under this category are the Turtle Island String Quartet. Founded in 1985, the two sustained elements in the quartet since that time have been Darol Anger (violin, baritone violin) and Mark Summer (cello). Anger already had something of an illustrious past in 'new acoustic music'. He founded both the David Grisman Quintet and the Montreux band. He had also recorded as a solo artist (releasing an album, *Fiddlistics*), as well as collaborating with guitarist/mandolin player Mike Marshall. With fellow TISQ founder David Balakrishan and Matt Glaser he was part of an award-winning triple violin team, and he has contributed to recordings by Suzanne Vega, Holly Near, Bela Fleck and John Gorka. His extensive *curriculum vitae* also includes performances with fellow Windham Hill artists Psychograss and Anger/Marshall And Hands On, and he has been pivotal in the development of synthesizer violin technology. Summer, meanwhile, is a graduate of the Cleveland Institute Of Music and has worked with the Winnipeg Symphony, the Oakland Symphony and the Chamber Symphony of San Francisco. He has also ventured outside of classical music into pop, rock and jazz. He has recorded with Will Ackerman and Toni Childs, and also works concurrently with San Francisco ensemble Trio Con Brio. His most enduring composition remains 'Julie-O' (from *Metropolis*), which has become a staple of the modern cello repertoire. This central duo were joined by Pittsburgh native Danny Seidenberg in January 1993, when he took over the viola role vacated by Katrina Wreede, who in turn had replaced founding member Irene Sazer. Schooled at Juilliard, and a member of Pittsburgh's Symphony Orchestra from the age of 16, Seidenburg has performed as principal violist for the Joffrey Ballet, Brooklyn Philharmonic, Soviet Emigre Orchestra and Juilliard Chamber Orchestra. His forays into rock and pop in the 70s included spells with rock band Spy and progressive fusion outfit Szobel. He has toured with a diverse array of artists ranging from Liza Minnelli and Steve Reich to Village People and James Brown. Founding violinist David Balakrishnan also retired from Turtle Island in 1993, though he chose to maintain his involvement as a composer and arranger. New York-born violinist Tracy Silverman replaced him. Silverman made his debut with the Chicago Symphony Orchestra at the age of 13, and has gone on to perform with Luciano Pavarotti as well as several ballets and acclaimed orchestras, and pop artists including Michael Bolton and Linda Ronstadt. Both New York band Stradivarius and Minneapolis trio Gutbucket allowed him to explore his rock instincts. The two new additions joined in time for Turtle Island's residency at the Stanford Jazz Workshop in the summer of 1993, collaborating with David Baker. The subsequent *Who Do We Think We Are?* featured guest appearances from drummer Scott Morris, guitarist Steve Erquiaga and vocalist Vicki Randle (the regular percussionist on US television's *The Tonight Show*). The material was largely drawn from the jazz tradition, with cover versions of Miles Davis's 'Seven Steps To Heaven', Charlie Parker's 'Moose The Mooch' and Thelonious Monk's 'Ruby My Dear'. Ample stylistic variation was offered in an adaptation of Jimi Hendrix's 'Gipsy Eyes'.

● ALBUMS: *Turtle Island String Quartet* (Windham Hill)★★★, *Skylife* (Windham Hill 1990)★★★, *On the Town* (Windham Hill 1991)★★★, *Spider Dreams* (Windham Hill 1991)★★★, *Metropolis* (Windham Hill 1992)★★★, soundtrack *A Shock To The System* (Windham Hill 1992)★★★, *Who Do We Think We Are?* (Windham Hill 1993)★★★, *By The Fireside* (Windham Hill 1995)★★★.

TUTU - MILES DAVIS

Where else can you put Miles Davis? Folk? Soul? Rap? This is funky and very electronically tested with synthesizers everywhere, and is one of the great trumpeter's least jazzy albums. Marcus Miller played most of the instruments and arranged where the syn drums would go. Although this sounds derogatory, this is, in fact, a hypnotic and brilliant record that seeps into you after one or two plays - once you accept that this is light years away from even *Bitches Brew*. It wanders and flows like one long suite and Davis plays with the class that we took for granted. In building a Miles Davis collection this is the best of his later work, but it ain't no *Kind Of Blue*.

● Tracks: *Tutu; Tomaas; Portia; Splatch; Backyard Ritual; Perfect Way; Don't Lose Your Mind; Full Nelson.*

● First released 1986

● UK peak chart position: 74

● USA peak chart position: 141

Twardzik, Dick

b. 30 April 1931, Boston, Massachusetts, USA, d. 1955. Twardzik was an original pianist and composer whose promising career was cut short by his untimely death. His meagre discography suggests that, had he survived, he would have flourished in the young *avant garde* movement of the late 50s. Twardzik started playing when he was nine years old. He pursued an education in classical music at the Longy School of Music in Cambridge, Massachusetts, and the New England Conservatory, but from the age of 14 he played professionally with many of the great names of swing and bop, including Charlie Parker, Lionel Hampton, Chet Baker and Serge Chaloff. He recorded with Chaloff and Baker in 1954/5, contributing compositions to the former, and in no small way ensuring the classic status of both discs. Twardzik recorded only once under his own name, a trio session including the composition 'Albuquerque Social Swim' which in its extraordinary percussive attack and bizarre creativity emphasizes the pianist's originality. Twardzik summed up his approach: 'Development is not my primary consideration. The ability to project ever-changing emotions or moods, plus rhythmic freedom, is far more important to me'.

● ALBUMS: *The Last Set* (Pacific Jazz 1962)★★★.

29th Street Saxophone Quartet

Jim Hartog (baritone saxophone), Ed Jackson (alto saxophone), Rich Rothenburg (tenor saxophone) and Bobby Watson (alto saxophone). The 29th Street Saxophone Quartet first came together for a European tour in 1983, though the idea for the group had been mooted by Hartog and Jackson in the late 70s, and partly put into practice in the early 80s, when the pair had jammed with other New York-based saxophonists both in and outside Hartog's 29th Street loft apartment. In 1983 the arrival of Watson, already a player with a growing international reputation and several years' experience of working with Art Blakey, really launched the group on the road to worldwide success. A popular live act, the quartet's core allegiance to hard bop secured them their particular niche among comparable ensembles (such as the World and ROVA Saxophone Quartets) and also helped to fuel their direct emotional power and danceability. All four are outstanding soloists, but their records are also characterized by what one writer has called 'a state of integrated motion', the horns threading together in quickfire counterpoint or complex rhythmic interweavings. As early as *Watch Your Step*, the group had introduced rap onto one track and *Underground* in 1991 left or diluted (according to one's point of view) the original saxophone quartet concept with guest appearances by vocalist Pamela Watson, pianist Benny Green and trumpeter Hugh Masekela among others.

● ALBUMS: *Pointillistic Groove* (Osmosis 1984)★★★, *Watch Your Step* (Antilles 1985)★★★★, *The Real Deal* (Antilles 1987)★★★★, *Live* (Red 1988)★★★, *Underground* (Antilles 1991)★★★, *Your Move* (Antilles 1992)★★★, *Milano/New York Bridge* (Red 1994)★★★.

Tyler, Charles

b. 1941, Cadiz, Kentucky, USA. Tyler learned clarinet as a child, alto and baritone saxophone in his teens and played in an army band. He met and played with Albert Ayler in Cleveland and then moved to New York where he recorded with Ayler and played with many of the young stars of the free movement, including Ornette Coleman, Sunny Murray and the bass player Errol Henderson. Tyler also played with local R&B groups during this period and developed as an individual composer. He recorded his first album as a leader before gaining a scholarship to study at the University of Indiana from 1966-68. In the early 70s after a second period of study in California, Tyler formed his own record label, Ak-Ba. A series of recordings followed throughout the 70s exploring idioms as diverse as 16th century European music and tone poems inspired by western movies. During the 80s Tyler continued to produce in a variety of musical situations, most recently working with the Hal Russell NRG ensemble. He has moved to Europe and now lives in Stockholm.

● ALBUMS: *The Charles Tyler Ensemble* (ESP-Disk 1966)★★★, *Eastern Man Alone* (ESP-Disk 1968)★★★, *Sixty Minute Man* (1979)★★, *Definites Vols 1 & 2* (1981)★★★, *Autumn In Paris* 1988 recording (Silkheart 90s)★★★★.

Tyner, McCoy

b. 11 December 1938, Philadelphia, Pennsylvania, USA. Beginning in his early teens, Tyner studied piano formally for several years before joining the jazztet led by Benny Golson and Art Farmer in 1959. The following year he joined John Coltrane, with whom he had previously gigged in Philadelphia. He remained with Coltrane until 1965 in what became known as the tenorman's 'classic quartet', touring internationally and recording numerous albums, including celebrated works such as *Impressions* (1963) and *A Love Supreme* (1965). In the late 60s he led his own trio, backed many artists of jazz and popular music, and began to record under his own name. Throughout the 70s Tyner toured and recorded, usually with a quartet or quintet. Several of his albums achieved considerable critical and popular success, some winning awards. He continued touring and recording through the 80s, most often as leader but he also played with Sonny Rollins in the Milestone Jazzstars. Early in his career Tyner was influenced by Bud Powell, Thelonious Monk and Art Tatum, but during his years with Coltrane he developed his own distinctive style. Tyner was not content simply to 'comp' with his left hand, but played in a vigorous two-handed manner that echoed the vibrancy and rhythmic excitement of his influences. His playing and, especially, his composing also displayed an advanced harmonic awareness. In some of his later work Tyner has adopted stylistic devices from other fields of music, incorporating African and Asian ethnic music and elements of the European classical tradition. More surprising was his 1997 album of Burt Bacharach music, displaying Tyner's affection for the composer's lush melodic pop.

● ALBUMS: *Inception* (Impulse! 1962)★★★★, *Reaching Fourth* (Impulse! 1963)★★★★, *A Night Of Ballads* (Impulse! 1963)★★★★, *Today And Tomorrow* (Impulse! 1964)★★★★, *McCoy Tyner Live At Newport* (Impulse! 1963)★★★★, *McCoy Tyner Plays Ellington* (Impulse! 1965)★★★★, *The Real McCoy* (Blue Note 1967)★★★★★, *Tender Moments* (Blue Note 1968)★★★★, *Time For Tyner* (Blue Note 1969)★★★, *Expansions* (Blue Note 1969)★★★★★, *Extensions* (Blue Note 1970)★★★★, *Asante* (Blue Note 1971)★★★, *Sahara* (Milestone 1972)★★★★, *Song For My Lady* (Milestone 1973)★★★★, *Echoes Of A Friend* (Milestone 1973)★★★★, *Song Of The New World* (Milestone 1973)★★★, *Enlightenment* (Milestone 1974)★★★★★, *Sama Layuca* (Milestone 1974)★★★★, *Atlantis* (Milestone 1975)★★★★, *Trident* (Milestone 1975)★★★★, *Cosmos* 1969/1970 recording (Blue Note 1976)★★★, *Fly With The Wind* (Milestone 1976)★★★, *Focal Point* (Milestone 1977)★★★, *Supertrios* (Milestone 1977)★★★★, *Inner Voices* (Milestone 1978)★★★, *The Greeting* (Milestone 1978)★★★, *Passion Dance* (Milestone 1979)★★★, *Together* (Milestone 1979)★★★★, *Horizon* (Milestone 1979)★★★, *4 x 4* (Milestone 1980)★★★★, *13th House* (Milestone 1981)★★★, *La Leyenda De La Hora* (Columbia 1982)★★★, *Looking Out* (Columbia 1982)★★★, *Dimensions* (Elektra Musician 1983)★★★★, with Jackie McLean *It's About Time* (Blue Note 1985)★★★, *Double Trios* (Denon 1986)★★★, *Bon Voyage* (Timeless 1988)★★★, with others *A Tribute To John Coltrane: Blues For Coltrane* (Impulse! 1988)★★★, *Revelations* (Blue Note 1989)★★★, *Uptown/Downtown* (Milestone 1989)★★★, *Live At Sweet Basil, Vols. 1 & 2* (King 1989)★★★★, *Things Ain't What They Used To Be* (Blue Note 1990)★★★, *Just Feelin'* (Palo Alto 1991)★★★, *Autumn Mood* (Delta 1991)★★★, *Soliloquy* (Blue Note 1991)★★★, *Remembering John* (Enja 1991)★★★, with Joe Henderson *New York Reunion* (Chesky 1991)★★★, *44th Street Suite* (Red Baron 1992)★★★, *The Turning Point* (Verve 1992)★★★★, *Journey* (Verve 1994)★★★, with Bobby Hutcherson *Manhattan Moods* (Blue Note 1994)★★★, *Prelude And Sonata* (Milestone 1995)★★★, with Michael Brecker *Infinity* (Impulse! 1995)★★★★, *What The World Needs Now: The Music Of Burt Bacharach* (Impulse! 1997)★★★.

● COMPILATIONS: *Great Moments* 1962-1964 recordings (1981)★★★, *Jazz Profile* (Blue Note)★★★★.

● FURTHER READING: *Fly With The Wind*, McCoy Tyner.

Ulmer, James 'Blood'

b. 2 February 1942, St. Matthews, South Carolina, USA. Although taking up guitar in childhood, between the ages of seven and 13 Ulmer's primary musical activity was as a singer in a gospel group, the Southern Sons. In 1959 he moved to Pittsburgh, then to Detroit in 1967, and then eventually to New York in 1971, where he played in the house band at the famous bebop venue, Minton's Playhouse, for nine months. In the 70s he worked or recorded with Art Blakey, 'Big' John Patton, Larry Young, Joe Henderson and Paul Bley. His big break came in 1974 when he began studying and playing with Ornette Coleman, and in 1977 became a member of Coleman's controversial sextet that later became Prime Time. He also plays with the Music Revelation Ensemble, whose members have included David Murray, Amin Ali and Ronald Shannon Jackson, and Phalanx, with saxophonist George Adams, drummer Rashied Ali and bassist Sirone. He sings like Jimi Hendrix, but his guitar playing is quite different: choppy, rhythmic, harmonically inventive, with a cutting, ringing tone that slices through the harmolodic contexts in which he frequently works. Over the last few years, he has toured with a power blues trio (comprising permutations of Jamaaladeen Tacuma or Amin Ali on electric bass and Grant Calvin Weston or Ronald Shannon Jackson on drums), capable of producing fiercely visceral and danceable music or, as on the group's spring 1991 visit to London, relatively mainstream funk-fusion. Most of the time he creates an intense, brooding momentum that is irresistible.

● ALBUMS: *Revealing* (In + Out 1977)★★★, *Tales Of Captain Black* (Artists House 1978)★★★★, with the Music Revelation Ensemble *Elec. Jazz* (DIW 1980)★★★, with the Music Revelation Ensemble *No Wave* (Moers 1980)★★★, *Are You Glad To Be In America?* (Rough Trade 1980)★★★★, *Freelancing* (Columbia 1981)★★★, *Black Rock* (Columbia 1982)★★★, *Part Time* (Rough Trade 1984)★★★, *Got Something Good For You* (Moers 1985)★★, *Live At The Caravan Of Dreams* (Caravan Of Dreams 1987)★★★, *America: Do You Remember The Love?* (Blue Note 1987)★★★, with Phalanx *Original Phalanx* (DIW 1987)★★★, with Phalanx *In Touch* (DIW 1988)★★★, with the Music Revelation Ensemble *Music Revelation Ensemble* (DIW 1988)★★★, with Grant Calvin Weston *Dance Romance* (In + Out 1989)★★★, *Blues Allnight* (In + Out 1990)★★★, *Black And Blues* (DIW 1991)★★, *Blues Preacher* (DIW/Columbia 1993)★★★, *Odyssey* (Columbia 1993)★★★★, with the Music Revelation Ensemble *In The Name Of The Music Revelation* (Columbia 1994)★★★, *The James Blood Ulmer Blues Experience* (In + Out 1996)★★★, with the Music Revelation Ensemble *Knights Of Power* (DIW 1996)★★★, *Plays The Music Of Ornette Coleman: Music Speaks Louder Than Words* (Koch 1997)★★, with the Music Revelation Ensemble *Cross Fire* (DIW 1998)★★★, *Forbidden Blues* (DIW 1998)★★★★.

United Jazz And Rock Ensemble

The Ensemble was founded in 1975 by pianist Wolfgang Dauner and television director Werner Schretzmeier and, through being featured on a Schretzmeier series, its resulting popularity led the Ensemble to start touring in 1977. Not a fusion band in the usual sense, the Ensemble draws on the technical complexity of jazz and the communicative directness of rock to produce an accessible and rhythmic setting for sophisticated compositions and improvisations. The definitive personnel was Dauner, Kenny Wheeler, Ian Carr, Ack Van Rooyen, Albert Mangelsdorff, Charlie Mariano (the only non-European in the band), Barbara Thompson, Volker Kriegel, Eberhard Weber and Jon Hiseman.

● ALBUMS: *Live In Schutzenhaus* (1977)★★★, *Teamwork* (1978)★★★, *The Break Even Point* (1980)★★, *Live In Berlin* (1981)★★, *United Live Opus Sechs* (1984)★★★.

Unity - Larry Young

During the mid-60s the Hammond organ was enjoying a particularly popular time, especially with the host of soulful jazz organists. The leaders were Jimmy Smith and Jimmy McGriff, and they were followed by 'Big' John Patton, Lonnie Smith and, for many the best of all, Larry Young. *Unity*, his second Blue Note album, features Woody Shaw (trumpet), Joe Henderson (tenor) and Elvin Jones on drums. The playing is polished, clever and occasionally breathtaking. Young never approached the quality of this album again, even though he went on to work with Miles Davis and John McLaughlin. He died at the age of 38.

● Tracks: *Zoltan; Monk's Dream; If; The Moontrane; Softly As A Morning Sunrise; Beyond All Limits.*

● First released 1966

● UK peak chart position: did not chart

● USA peak chart position: did not chart

Urban Knights

A jazz collective formed in 1995 by combining the talents of Grover Washington Jr., Omar Hakim, Victor Bailey and Ramsey Lewis. Their debut was one of the most successful contemporary jazz releases of the year.

● ALBUMS: *Urban Knights* (GRP 1995)★★★★.

Urbaniak, Michal

b. 22 January 1943, Warsaw, Poland. Urbaniak learnt the violin from the age of six and took up the alto saxophone in his teens. He studied at the Academy of Music in Warsaw and although he started playing with Dixieland-style jazz bands, he quickly moved on to bop. He played with various bands including that of alto saxophonist Zbigniew Namyslowski while he continued to perform classical violin. In 1965 he moved to Scandinavia with a band that included vocalist Urzsula

Dudziak, whom he later married, before returning to Poland to form Constellation, including pianist Adam Makowicz. In 1971 he won a scholarship to the Berklee College Of Music in Boston, Massachusetts, and moved to New York in 1974. There, Urbaniak formed a band called Fusion, the music of which was enlivened by melodies and irregular rhythms derived from Polish folk music. Urbaniak also attracted contributions from accomplished players such as guitarist John Abercrombie, drummers Steve Jordan and Steve Gadd, a young Kenny Kirkland and bassist Anthony Jackson. During the 80s Urbaniak performed with Larry Coryell, and later formed a new group, Urbanator. He plays a personalized five-string violin and violin synthesizer and also the lyricon, a saxophone-like electronic instrument that triggers a synthesizer.

● ALBUMS: *Polish Jazz* (Muza 1971)★★★★, with Constellation *Super Constellation* (Columbia 1973)★★★, with Constellation *Constellation In Concert* (Muza 1973)★★★★, *The Beginning* (Catalyst 1973)★★★, with Fusion *Fusion* (Columbia 1974)★★★, with Fusion *Atma* (Columbia 1974)★★★★, with Fusion *Fusion III* (Columbia 1975)★★★, *Paratyphus B* 1973 recording (Spiegelei 1975)★★★, *Inactin'* 1973 recording (Spiegelei 1975)★★★, *Body English* (Arista 1976)★★, *Tribute To Komeda* (BASF 1976)★★★, *Urbaniak* (Inner City 1977)★★★, *Urban Express* (East West 1979)★★★, *Heritage* 1977 recording (Pausa 1980)★★★, *Daybreak* (Pausa 1980)★★★, *Music For Violin And Jazz Quartet* (JAM 1981)★★★★, *Jam At Sandy's* (JAM 1981)★★★★, *My One And Only Love* (Steeple Chase 1982)★★★, *Take Good Care Of My Heart* (Steeple Chase 1984)★★★★, *Folk Songs* (Antilles 1988)★★★, *Cinemode* (Rykodisc 1988)★★★★, *Songbird* (Steeple Chase 1991)★★★★, *Live In New York* (L And R 1991)★★★, *Manhattan Man* (Milan 1992)★★★, with Urbanator *Urbanator* (Hip Bop 1994)★★★, *Friday Night At The Village Vanguard* 1985 recording (Storyville 1994)★★★, with Urbanator *Urbanator II* (Hip Bop 1996)★★★.

Us3

One of 1993's most intriguing musical experiments, UK-based Us3 comprise Geoff Wilkinson and Mel Simpson. Wilkinson was best known for his Jazz DJ work, and met Simpson at his own Flame studio, where they discovered mutually inclusive tastes. Together they struck upon the idea of sampling some of their favourite old jazz tunes and mixing them in with their own material. The resultant 'And The Band Played Boogie' was released on Coldcut's Ninja Tune imprint, featuring the rapping of Born 2B, and created a critical buzz. By hook or by crook the record came to the attention of executives at jazz label Blue Note Records, who quickly deduced that most of the samples were lifted directly from their own catalogue. The miscreants were summoned, but then Capitol Records took the wholly laudable and progressive step of working out a deal whereby the duo could enjoy unlimited access to the Blue Note label archives. The result was an album of richly textured jazz and hip-hop, with guests including rappers Tukka Yoot (b. Jamaica), Kobie Powell and Rahsaan (all three of whom would secure deals with Capitol in the wake of the album's success), and jazzmen Gerald Presencer, Dennis Rollins, Tony Remy and Steve Williamson. The album, which was preceded by the singles, 'Cantaloop' and 'Riddim', proved a worldwide hit, selling particularly strongly in the USA. The foresight of the copyright holders at Blue Note has been amply rewarded too: since the release of *Hand On The Torch* interest in Blue Note back-catalogue has escalated and sales have doubled. Even Herbie Hancock, on whose 'Cantalope Island' the single 'Cantaloop' was loosely based, expressed his appreciation for their efforts. It would be used on the soundtrack to the *Super Mario Bros* movie, and Barry Levinson's *Jimmy Hollywood.* They were also enlisted for Stephen Spielberg's *Flintstones*. In the wake of their success, especially in the US and Europe, Wilkinson was asked by Toshiba/EMI to A&R a compilation of new London jazz musicians. In 1994 Us3 released a remix album, and embarked on collaborative material with the Ragga Twins (famed for their contributions to Shut Up And Dance).

● ALBUMS: *Hand On The Torch* (Blue Note 1993)★★★★, *Us3 The Jazz Mixes* (Blue Note 1994)★★★, *Broadway & 52nd* (Blue Note 1997)★★★★.

Vaché, Allan

b. New Jersey, USA. A gifted clarinettist, Vaché was raised in a very musical family; his father played bass and his brother is Warren Vaché Jnr. For many years Allan Vaché played in Jim Cullum's Jazz Band in San Antonio, Texas, and was thus less well known on the international circuit than might otherwise have been the case. In the late 80s and throughout the 90s he appeared regularly in Europe, playing solo tours and appearing at clubs and festivals. He also began making records both under his own name and in partnership with pianist Johnny Varro and fellow clarinettist Antti Sarpilå. Fluid and emotional, his playing is most rewarding when faced with challenging music, such as his features on Cullum's *Porgy And Bess*. His repertoire is wide, although much of his latter-day work centres upon recreations of swing era music and continues a fine tradition of skilled musicianship in the Benny Goodman mould.

● ALBUMS: *Jazz Moods* (Audiophile 1982)★★★★, *High Speed Swing* (Audiophile 1984)★★★, *At The Atlanta Jazz Party* (Audiophile 1992)★★★★, *Jazz Im Amerika Haus, Vol. 3* (Nagel-Heyer 1994)★★★, with Antti Sarpilå *Swing Is Here* (Nagel-Heyer 1995)★★★, with Ken Peplowski, Sarpilå *Summit Meeting* (Nagel-Heyer 1995)★★★★, *Allan Vaché's Florida Jazz All-Stars* (Nagel-Heyer 1996)★★★, *Swing And Other Things* (Arbors 1997)★★★★,with Antti Sarpila *Swing Is Here* (Nagel-Heyer 1998)★★★.

Vaché, Warren, Jnr.

b. 21 February 1951, Rahway, New Jersey, USA. Vaché grew up in New Jersey, hearing jazz, thanks to his bass-playing father who led a Dixieland band. Vaché took up the cornet and studied formally with, amongst others, George 'Pee Wee' Erwin. He played in his father's band, but from the mid-70s was attracting critical acclaim elsewhere. He played with the New York Jazz Repertory Orchestra and with the house band at Eddie Condon's club and was on regular call whenever Benny Goodman formed a band for special engagements. During this period Vaché met and began working with Scott Hamilton; the two men gained the reverent attention of audiences who thought that the mainstream had dried up. In the late 70s and throughout the 80s Vaché worked as a single, in harness with Hamilton, in bands such as George Wein's Newport Jazz Festival All-Stars and the Concord Super Band. Touring extensively across the USA, Europe and Japan, Vaché continued to enhance his reputation as a major jazz talent. Stylistically, he echoes the post-Louis Armstrong tradition, playing with eloquent charm and ably developing the fruitful ground tilled by melodic players such as Bobby Hackett and Ruby Braff. Vaché's style has allowed him to blend comfortably in seemingly disparate company, as witnessed by his *Warm Evenings* album with the Beaux-Arts String Quartet. His brother, Allan Vaché, plays clarinet with the Jim Cullum Jazz Band.

● ALBUMS: *Jersey Jazz At Midnight* (New Jersey Jazz Society 1975)★★★, *First Time Out* (Monmouth 1977)★★★★, *Blues Walk* (Dreamstreet 1977)★★★, *Jillian* (Concord Jazz 1978)★★★, with Scott Hamilton *Skyscrapers* (Concord Jazz 1979)★★★, *Polished Brass* (Concord Jazz 1979)★★★★, *Iridescence* (Concord Jazz 1981)★★★, *Midtown Jazz* (Concord Jazz 1982)★★★, *Easy Going* (Concord Jazz 1987)★★★, *Warm Evenings* (Concord Jazz 1989)★★★, *Horn Of Plenty* (Muse 1994)★★★, *Jazz Im Amerika Haus, Vol. 2* (Nagel-Heyer 1994)★★★, *Talk To Me Baby* (Muse 1996)★★★, *Warren Vaché Trio Live At The Vineyard* (Challenge 1997)★★★, *. . . Plays Harry Warren: An Affair To Remember* (Zephyr 1997)★★★★, with Kenny Baker *Ain't Misbehavin'* (Zephyr 1998)★★★★, *Shine* (Zephyr 1998)★★★★.

Valdambrini, Oscar

b. 11 May 1924, Turin, Italy. Valdambrini learnt the trumpet and violin as a child and studied at Turin Conservatory. He worked with a variety of local groups in the 40s and played in a jam session with Rex Stewart in 1948. He formed a quintet with saxophonist Gianni Basso in 1955; this band has played in various guises intermittently right through to the late 80s. It has always been one of the most highly rated Italian bands, in which Valdambrini has been able to display an excellent technique in the bop-orientated playing he favours. He has also worked with various big bands including those of Lionel Hampton and Maynard Ferguson. In 1967 and 1968 he joined Duke Ellington's Orchestra for concerts in Milan. Since 1972 he has also played with the Television Orchestra of Rome.

● ALBUMS: *Gin Blues* (1952)★★★, *Bassi/Valdambrini Quintet* (1959)★★★★, *Best Modern Jazz In Italy* (1962)★★, *Afrodite* (1976)★★★.

Valentine, Kid Thomas

b. 3 February 1896, Reserve, Louisiana, USA, d. 16 June 1987. His father, Fernand 'Pete' Valentine, was a talented player of most brass instruments and was bandmaster of the Pickwick Brass Band. Kid Thomas began playing trumpet at an early age and when he was in his twenties moved to Algiers, across the river from New Orleans, where he joined the Elton Theodore Band. He quickly became the band's star attraction and in 1926 took over as leader. Valentine chose to stay in Algiers, content to be the town's leading player in jazz. Perhaps as a result of this small but important distancing from New Orleans, Valentine also remained largely independent of the developing trends in jazz trumpet playing, and was one of a small number who displayed little influence of Louis Armstrong. His band, the Algiers Stompers, played on through the decades, often resident at the town's Moulin Rouge. Despite his comparative isolation from the centres of jazz, he was swept up by the second wave of revivalism and in the 60s made many overseas visits to Europe and Japan. He continued to play, often back in Algiers, into the 80s. A confident, assertive player with incisive attack, his many recordings offer an intriguing insight into the sometimes overlooked variety of styles within the early jazz tradition.

● ALBUMS: *At Hope Ball* (1951)★★★, *At The Moulin Rouge* (Center 1954)★★★, *At San Jacinto Hall* (1965)★★, *Red Wing* (1966)★★★, *Kid Thomas At Moose Hall* (GHB 1967)★★★★, *At Kohlman's Tavern* (GHB 1968)★★★, *At London's 100 Club* (1968)★★, *Same Old Soupbone* (Jazz Crusade 1969)★★★, *Kid Thomas In California* (GHB 1970)★★★, *In Scandinavia* (Rarities 1974)★★★, *Featuring Alton Purnell* (1975)★★★, *His New Orleans Jazz Bird* (Arhoolie 1975)★★★, *Kid Thomas Valentine's Creole Jazz Band* (77 1979)★★★, *In England* (1981)★★★, *In Lugano* (1983)★★, *Kid Thomas And Chester Vardis Visit The Maryland* (1983)★★, *At The Old Grist Mill* (GHB 1986)★★★, *And The New Black Eagle Jazz Band* (GHB 1986)★★★, *Love Songs Of The Nile* (GHB 1987)★★★, *With Sammy Rimington 1981* (Black Label 1988)★★★, *On Stage* (GHB 1988)★★★, *Kid Thomas* (American Music 1993)★★, *Dance Hall Years* (American Music 1994)★★★.

● COMPILATIONS: *The 1957 Lost Sessions Vol 1* (1990)★★★★, *Portrait Of Kid Thomas Valentine* (Storyville 1990)★★★★.

VAN EPS, GEORGE

b. 7 August 1913, Plainfield, New Jersey, USA, d. 29 November 1998, Newport Beach, California, USA. The son of the famous banjoist Fred Van Eps, George played the banjo professionally before he was a teenager. At the age of 13 he heard Eddie Lang, decided to switch to guitar and within a couple of years was earning a reputation as a teacher. In the late 20s and early 30s he worked with a number of bands, including those of Benny Goodman and Ray Noble, and also played with his idol, Lang, in the Smith Ballew band. During the late 30s and for much of the following two decades he did studio work in Hollywood, radio dates, wrote a textbook on guitar and devised his own seven-string instrument, appeared in various bands (including Noble's) and made infrequent records with artists such as Matty Matlock, Wild Bill Davison, Jess Stacy and Ralph Sutton. In the 60s and 70s his playing activities were restricted through poor health but in the 80s he made a return to the jazz scene, playing at festivals in the USA and Europe. In the 90s he recorded sessions with the modern virtuoso Howard Alden. A marvellously gifted technician with an inventive mind, Van Eps was very much a musician's musician. In contrast, his popularity with audiences was limited, owing in part to the comparative obscurity in which he chose to spend the greater part of his working life.

● ALBUMS: *Mellow Guitar* (Columbia 1956)★★★, *My Guitar* (Capitol 1966)★★★, *George Van Eps' Seven-String Guitar* (Capitol 1967)★★★★, *Soliloquy* (Capitol 1968)★★★, with Howard Alden *13 Strings* (Concord Jazz 1991)★★★, with Alden *Hand-Crafted Swing* (Concord Jazz 1992)★★★, with Alden *Seven And Seven* (Concord Jazz 1993)★★★★, with Alden *Keepin' Time* (Concord Jazz 1995)★★★★.

VAN HOVE, FRED

b. 19 February 1937, Antwerp, Belgium. As a child Van Hove studied piano formally but in his teens was diverted from the classics by be-bop. Ever forward-thinking in his approach, he responded to new concepts, including modality and in the late 60s began a long association with Peter Brötzmann that also involved Han Bennink. These three played as a trio into the mid-70s, although during this period Van Hove also continued to develop a reputation as a soloist and for his performances in duo with saxophonists Cel Overbeghe (early 70s) and Lol Coxhill (late 70s/early 80s). During the 80s he continued his contemporary jazz-playing alongside a successful career as a composer of music for motion pictures and also for the theatre. In addition to playing piano, he also occasionally plays organ. Although not as readily accessible as many pianists of his era, Van Hove's work repays the commitment needed by his audiences fully to engage with its often deeply introspective complexities.

● ALBUMS: with Peter Brötzmann, Han Bennink *Outspan No. 2* (FMP 1974)★★★★, *Live At The University* (Vogel 1974)★★★, *Verloren Maandag* (FMP 1977)★★★, *Church Organ* (FMP 1979)★★★, *Suite For B City* (FMP 1998)★★★★.

VAN STRATEN, ALFRED

b. 20 September 1905, London, England, d. 4 December 1988, London, England. Van Straten was one of three musician brothers (Alf on tenor saxophone, Joe on alto and Leon on violin). They played under Leon's leadership, first recording as Van's Ten on the Edison Bell Winner label in 1926. The personnel also included Max Goldberg (trumpet), Max Bacon (drums) and Jay Wilbur (piano). The band, now known simply as Van Straten And His Orchestra, opened at the Ambassador Club in London, recording on Duophone, then at the Riviera Club and the Green Park Hotel (1926-8) and at Claridge's (1929-30), by which time they had returned to Edison Bell for three tracks. Leon gave up the leadership in 1931 to become an osteopath, handing the reins to Alf, who took the band into Quaglino's Restaurant for a 10-year residency, and making one Parlophone record in 1939. A few years into the engagement Joe left to form his own outfit for the Carlton Hotel. During World War II, Alf Van Straten was musical director at the Embassy Club and the Piccadilly Hotel, also touring with his band. After the war, although only in his early 40s, he decided to retire from active playing, and formed a cabaret and band agency which remained in operation until his death in 1988.

VAN'T HOF, JASPER

b. 30 June 1947, Enschede, Netherlands. Both Van't Hof's parents were musicians and he had six years of classical piano lessons. He was a founder-member of Association PC (1970-72) before starting his own band, Pork Pie, with Charlie Mariano and Philip Catherine in the mid-70s. He continued playing with Mariano right through the 80s, as well as with, among others, Archie Shepp, Jean-Luc Ponty and Alphonze Mouzon. He led the band Eyeball including Didier Lockwood, and then Pili Pili, which included African percussion and computers. Van't Hof is a pianist of great technical facility who has enthusiastically incorporated into his music synthesizers and the possibilities of electronic music of all kinds.

● ALBUMS: *Selfkicker* (1974)★★★, with Pork Pie *The Door Is Open* (1975)★★★★, with Mariano/Catherine *Sleep My Love* (1979)★★★, *My World Of Music* (1981)★★★, with Archie Shepp *Mama Rose* (1982)★★★, *Balloons* (1982)★★★, *Pili Pili* (1984)★★, *Eyeball* (CMP 1991)★★★.

VAN, GARWOOD

b. USA. Garwood served his musical apprenticeship in several dance bands, including those led by Hal Grayson, Eddie Oliver, Victor Young, Lennie Hayton and various studio ensembles. He formed his own orchestra, heavily orientated towards hotel and supper dance work, in Los Angeles, California, USA, in 1936. The band was alternately led by featured vocalists Maxine Conrad or Gail Storm. The Garwood band found good bookings at venues such as the St. Francis and Mark Hopkins hotels in San Francisco, the Chase in St. Louis, the Hotel Utah in Salt Lake City and the Muehlebach in Kansas City. In California they usually found themselves based at the Trocadero Ciro's or Florentine Gardens. Garwood helped to pioneer the rise of dance band music in Las Vegas when he appeared at the El Rancho. The rich pickings the city offered strong entertainment troupes was reflected in Garwood's decision to base himself there for the next several years, including a long engagement at the Frontier Hotel. This booking lasted for five years from 1952, before he opened a record store in his adopted state. The venture brought him great personal wealth, so much so that he was able to retire from the business in 1962.

VANCE, DICK

b. Richard Thomas Vance, 28 November 1915, Mayfield, Kentucky, USA, d. July 1985. Vance took up the trumpet after first playing the violin. He played professionally with various bands in Cleveland, where he was raised, and in the north-east. His first name-band engagement came in 1934 when he joined Lillian Armstrong, and he then played with Willie Bryant and others before joining Fletcher Henderson in 1936. In 1939 he joined Chick Webb shortly before the leader's death and stayed on with the band under Ella Fitzgerald. By this time Vance was writing arrangements extensively and during the 40s this activity took precedence over his playing. His arrangements, meanwhile, were being performed by bands led by Cab Calloway, Redman, Harry James and Earl 'Fatha' Hines. In the early 50s he played in and wrote arrangements for Duke Ellington's orchestra. In the mid-50s he formed his own band, occasionally sharing leadership with Taft Jordan, with which he played several residencies, including one at the Savoy Ballroom in Harlem. He also played on numerous recording sessions with many leaders. A competent player, Vance's most important contribution to jazz and, in particular, to big band jazz, was his talent for arranging.

● ALBUMS: with Fletcher Henderson *Sextet* (Alamac 1950)★★★★, as arranger *Ellington '55* (Capitol 1953)★★★★, with the Henderson All Stars *The Big Reunion* (Jazztone 1957)★★★.

VAPIROV, ANATOLY

b. 24 November 1947, Berdyansk, Ukraine. Vapirov studied clarinet at the Leningrad Conservatory and later became a professor of saxophone, pursuing parallel careers as an academic, classical saxophonist (with the Leningrad State Symphony Orchestra and the Kirov Opera and Ballet Theatre) and, increasingly, as a virtuoso jazz performer. Initially working with the jazz-rock Music-Hall Orchestra in the late 60s, Vapirov rapidly broadened his repertoire to include all styles of jazz, from big band swing to the borders of free-form and contemporary composition. By the early 80s he had established himself as the leading saxophonist in the USSR, winning critics' polls in the Russian jazz magazine *Kvadrat* (*Chorus*) and releasing *Misteriya* for jazz soloist and symphony orchestra, on the state-owned label Melodiya. Although he did not lead a regular group, he worked frequently with Sergey Kuryokhin (piano), Alexander Alexandrov (bassoon), Vladimir Volkov (bass) and Valentina Ponomareva (vocals). In August 1982 Vapirov's career was abruptly halted by a two-year prison term for 'private enterprise', but he was released before serving his full sentence, possibly because his records had started to appear in the West, on the London-based Leo Records. In 1986 he moved to Bulgaria, where he had strong family ties. A prolific and versatile musician, Vapirov's recordings include improvised duos with Kuryokhin (*Document*) and pieces for a big band (*Conspiracy*), for tenor saxophone plus chamber orchestra (*Macbeth*) and a chamber jazz trio composition (*De Profundis*).

● ALBUMS: *Misteriya* (1980)★★★, with Sergey Kuryokhin *Sentenced To Silence* 1981 recording (1983)★★★★, *Invocations* (1984)★★★, *Macbeth* (1986)★★★, *De Profundis* (1988)★★★★, with others *Document* 8-CD box set (1990)★★★★, with others *Conspiracy* 4-CD box set (1991)★★★★.

VASCONCELOS, NANA

b. Juvenal de Hollanda Vasconcelos, 2 August 1944, Recife, Brazil. Vasconcelos began playing bongos and maracas with his guitarist father's group at the age of 12, later joining a bossa nova band on the drums. His big break came in the mid-60s when he was offered a place in singer Milton Nascimento's band and he moved to Rio De Janeiro. He learned the berimbau, a traditional Brazilian instrument with a single wire that is repeatedly buzzed and a gourd resonator that is tapped. In 1971 Gato Barbieri brought him to New York and then to Europe. At the end of the tour he stayed on in Europe for two years, recording and playing and also working with handicapped children. During this period he met jazz trumpeter Don Cherry, who was then living in Sweden and exploring all aspects of world folk music. Vasconcelos also recorded with Egberto Gismonti for ECM Records, notably on the inspiring 1976 album *Danca Das Cabeças*. In 1976 he relocated to New York and since then has become much in demand as a percussionist, appearing on albums by Pat Metheny, Talking Heads, Keith Jarrett and B.B. King. He played in the trio Codona with Cherry and Collin Walcott before the latter's death, recording three albums with them, and later toured as part of Cherry's Nu in 1988. His own group, Bush Dance, included Cyro Baptista, a Brazilian percussionist who has recorded with Derek Bailey. In the late 80s Vasconcelos was a member of the Jan Garbarek group; in the 90s he has played with Ralph Towner and Andy Sheppard, and recorded on Paul Simon's *Rhythm Of The Saints*. Vasconcelos has also contributed to the film soundtracks of Susan Seidelman and Jim Jarmusch, notably the latter's *Down By Law*.

● ALBUMS: with Perry Robinson, Badal Roy *Kundalini* (Improvising Artists 1978)★★★, *Saudades* (ECM 1980)★★★★, *Lester* (Soul Note 1986)★★★★, *Bush Dance* (Antilles 1986)★★★★, *Rain Dance* (Antilles 1989)★★★, with Arild Andersen, Ralph Towner *If You Look Far Enough* (ECM 1993)★★★★, *Storytelling* (EMI Hemisphere 1995)★★★, *Fragments: Modern Tradition* (Tzadik 1997)★★★.

VAUGHAN, SARAH

b. Sarah Lois Vaughan, 27 March 1924, Newark, New Jersey, USA, d. 3 April 1990, Los Angeles, California, USA. Although she was not born into an especially musical home environment (her father was a carpenter and her mother worked in a laundry), the young Sarah Vaughan had plenty of contact with music-making. As well as taking piano lessons for nearly 10 years, she sang in her church choir and became the organist at the age of 12. Her obvious talent for singing won her an amateur contest at Harlem's Apollo Theater in 1942, and opportunities for a musical career quickly appeared. Spotted by Billy Eckstine, who was at the time singing in Earl Hines' big band, she was invited to join Hines' band as a female vocalist and second pianist in 1943. Eckstine had been sufficiently impressed by Vaughan to give her a place in his own band, formed a year later. It was here that she met fellow band members and pioneers of modern jazz Charlie Parker and Dizzy Gillespie. Recording with Eckstine's band in 1945, full as it was of modern stylists, gave her a fundamental understanding of the new music that characterized her entire career. After leaving Eckstine, she spent a very short time with John Kirby's band, and then decided to perform under her own name. In 1947 she married trumpeter George Treadwell, whom she had met at the Cafe Society. Recognizing his wife's huge potential, Treadwell became her manager, as she began a decade of prolific recording and worldwide tours. She began by recording with Miles Davis in 1950, and then produced a torrent of albums in either a popular vein for Mercury Records, or more jazz-orientated material for their subsidiary label EmArcy. On the EmArcy recordings she appeared with Clifford Brown, Cannonball Adderley and members of the Count Basie band; these remain some of her most satisfying work.

By the 60s, as Vaughan rose to stardom, her jazz activity decreased slightly, and the emphasis remained on commercial, orchestra-backed recordings. It was not until the 70s that she began to perform and record with jazz musicians again on a regular basis. Vaughan performed at the 1974 Monterey Jazz Festival and made an album in 1978 with a quartet consisting of Oscar Peterson, Joe Pass, Ray Brown, and Louis Bellson. The following year she recorded the *Duke Ellington Song Book*, on which a large number of top jazz players appeared, including Zoot Sims, Frank Foster, Frank Wess, J.J. Johnson, and Pass. In 1980 she appeared in a much-heralded concert at Carnegie Hall, and returned to the Apollo to sing with Eckstine in a show recorded and broadcast by NBC-TV. She recorded an album of Latin tunes in 1987, and around this time appeared in another televised concert, billed as *Sass And Brass*. With a rhythm section featuring Herbie Hancock, Ron Carter, and Billy Higgins, as well as a collection of trumpeters including Dizzy Gillespie, Don Cherry, Maynard Ferguson, and Chuck Mangione, she proved herself still a musical force to be reckoned with. Tragically, she died of lung cancer in April 1990.

Sarah Vaughan won the *Esquire* New Star poll in 1945, the *Down Beat* poll (1947-52) and the *Metronome* poll (1948-52). She also sang at the White House as early as 1965; Vaughan's name was synonymous with jazz singing for two generations. Gifted with an extraordinary range and perfect intonation, she would also subtly control the quality of her voice to aid the interpretation of a song, juxtaposing phrases sung in a soft and warm tone with others in a harsh, nasal vibrato or throaty growl. Her knowledge of bebop, gained during her time with Eckstine's band, enabled her to incorporate modern passing tones into her sung lines, advancing the harmonic side of her work beyond that of her contemporaries. Her recordings will continue to influence vocalists for many years to come. Vaughan probably ranks as a close second only to Ella Fitzgerald in terms of influence, vocal range and sheer, consistent brilliance.

● ALBUMS: *Sarah Vaughan* reissued as *Sarah Vaughan In Hi Fi* (Columbia 1950)★★★★, *Sarah Vaughan Sings* 10-inch album (MGM 1951)★★★, *Tenderly* 10-inch album (MGM 1952)★★★, *Hot Jazz* 1944 recordings (Remington 1953)★★★, *Early Sarah* 10-inch album (Allegro 1953)★★★, *Images* reissued as *Swingin' Easy* (EmArcy 1954)★★★★, *Sarah Vaughan* (Allegro 1955)★★★, *My Kinda Love* (MGM 1955)★★★, *After Hours With Sarah Vaughan* (Columbia 1955)★★★★, *Sarah Vaughan Sings With John Kirby* 10-inch album (Riverside 1955)★★★, *Divine Sarah* 10-inch album (Mercury 1955)★★★, *Sarah Vaughan In The Land Of Hi-Fi* (EmArcy 1956)★★★★, *Sarah Vaughan At The Blue Note* (Mercury 1956)★★★, *Linger Awhile* (Columbia 1956)★★★★, *Sassy* (EmArcy 1956)★★★★, *Great Songs From Hit Shows* (Mercury 1957)★★★★, *Sarah Vaughan Sings George Gershwin* (Mercury 1957)★★★★, *Wonderful Sarah* (Mercury

1957)★★★★, *In A Romantic Mood* (Mercury 1957)★★★★, *Sarah Vaughan Concert* (Concord 1957)★★★, *Close To You* (Mercury 1957)★★★, *Sarah Vaughan And Billy Eckstine Sing The Best Of Irving Berlin* (Mercury 1958)★★★★, *Vaughan And Violins* (Mercury 1958)★★★, *Sarah Vaughan And Her Trio At Mr. Kelly's* (Mercury 1958)★★★, *After Hours At The London House* (Mercury 1958)★★★, *Tenderly* (Lion 1958)★★, *Sarah Vaughan And Her Trio At Mr Kelly's* (Mercury 1958)★★★, *No 'Count Sarah* (Mercury 1959)★★★, with Eckstine *Billy And Sarah* (Lion 1959)★★★, *The Magic Of Sarah Vaughan* (Mercury 1959)★★★, *Misty* (EmArcy 1959)★★★★, *Dreamy* (Roulette 1960)★★★, *The Divine Sarah Vaughan* (Mercury 1960)★★★★, with Count Basie *Count Basie/Sarah Vaughan* (Roulette 1960)★★★★, *Divine One* (Roulette 1960)★★★, *My Heart Sings* (Mercury 1961)★★★, *After Hours* (Roulette 1961)★★★★, *You're Mine, You* (Roulette 1962)★★★, *Snowbound* (Roulette 1962)★★★, *The Explosive Side Of Sarah* (Roulette 1962)★★★, *Star Eyes* (Roulette 1963)★★★, *The Lonely Hours* (Roulette 1963)★★★, *Sarah Sings Soulfully* (Roulette 1963)★★★★, *Sassy Swings The Tivoli* (Mercury 1963)★★★, *Vaughan With Voices* (Mercury 1964)★★★, *Viva Vaughan* (Mercury 1964)★★★, with Dinah Washington, Joe Williams *We Three* (Roulette 1964)★★★, *The World Of Sarah Vaughan* (Roulette 1964)★★★, *Sweet 'N' Sassy* (Roulette 1964)★★★, *Sarah Plus Two* (Roulette 1965)★★★, *Sarah Vaughan Sings The Mancini Songbook* (Mercury 1965)★★★★, *The Pop Artistry Of Sarah Vaughan* (Mercury 1966)★★★, *The New Scene* (Mercury 1966)★★★, *Sassy Swings Again* (Mercury 1967)★★★, *I'm Through With Love* (Xtra 1970)★★★, *A Time In My Life* (Mainstream 1972)★★★, with Michel Legrand *Sarah Vaughan/Michel Legrand* (Mainstream 1972)★★★★, *Feelin' Good* (Mainstream 1973)★★★, *The Summer Knows* (Mainstream 1973)★★★, *Live In Japan* (Mainstream 1974)★★★, with Jimmy Rowles *Sarah Vaughan And The Jimmy Rowles Quintet* (Mainstream 1975)★★★, *More Sarah Vaughan - Live In Japan* (Mainstream 1976)★★★, *I Love Brazil* (Pablo 1977)★★★, with Louis Bellson, Ray Brown, Joe Pass, Oscar Peterson *How Long Has This Been Going On?* (Pablo 1978)★★★, *Live At Ronnie Scott's* (Pye/Ronnie Scott's 1978)★★★, *Duke Ellington Song Book One* (Pablo 1980)★★★★, *Duke Ellington Song Book Two* (Pablo 1981)★★★, *Songs Of The Beatles* (Atlantic 1981)★★★, with Joe Comfort, Barney Kessel *The Two Sounds Of Sarah* (Vogue 1981)★★★, *Send In The Clowns* (Pablo 1981)★★★, *Crazy And Mixed Up* (Pablo 1982)★★★★, *O, Some Brasileiro De* (RCA 1984)★★★, *Jazz Fest Masters* 1969 recording (Jazz Masters 1992)★★★★, *One Night Stand: Town Hall Concert 1947* (Blue Note 1997)★★★★.

● COMPILATIONS: *Sarah Vaughan's Golden Hits!!!* (Mercury 1961)★★★★, *Recorded Live* (EmArcy 1977)★★★★, with Billy Eckstine (coupled with a Dinah Washington and Brook Benton collection) *Passing Strangers* (Mercury 1978)★★★, shared with Ella Fitzgerald, Billie Holiday, Lena Horne *Billie, Ella, Lena, Sarah!* (Columbia 1980)★★★★, *The Divine Sarah* 1946/1947 recordings (Musicraft 1980)★★★★, *Spotlight On Sarah Vaughan* (PRT 1984)★★★, *The Sarah Vaughan Collection* (Deja Vu 1985)★★★, *The Rodgers And Hart Songbook* (Pablo 1985)★★★★, *The Best Of Sarah Vaughan - Walkman Series* (Verve 1987)★★★★, *The Complete Sarah Vaughan On Mercury, Vol. 1 (1954-1956)* 6-CD box set (Mercury 1988)★★★★★, *The Complete Sarah Vaughan On Mercury, Vol. 2: Sings Great American Songs (1956-1957)* 5-CD box set (Mercury 1988)★★★★★, *The Complete Sarah Vaughan On Mercury, Vol. 3: Great Show On Stage (1954-1956)* 6-CD box set (Mercury 1988)★★★★★, *The Complete Sarah Vaughan On Mercury, Vol. 4 (1963-1967)* 6-CD box set (Mercury 1988)★★★★★, *I'll Be Seeing You* 1949-1962 recordings (Vintage Jazz Classics 1990)★★★★, *The Singles Sessions* (Capitol/Blue Note 1991)★★★★, *The Roulette Years* 1960-1964 recordings (Roulette 1991)★★★★, *The Columbia Years* 1949-1953 recordings (Columbia 1991)★★★★, *The Best Of Sarah Vaughan* 1978-1981 recordings (Pablo 1992)★★★★, *The Essential Sarah Vaughan: The Great Songs* (Verve 1992)★★★★, *16 Most Requested Songs* 1949-1953 recordings (Columbia 1993)★★★★, *The Essence Of Sarah Vaughan* (Columbia 1994)★★★★, *Verve Jazz Masters 18: Sarah Vaughan* (Verve 1994)★★★, *Verve Jazz Masters, Vol. 42* (Verve/PolyGram 1995)★★★, *Everything I Have Is Yours* 1945-1947 recordings (Drive Archive 1997)★★★, *Ultimate Sarah Vaughan* (Verve 1997)★★★★, *Sarah Vaughan 1944-1946* (Collectables 1997)★★★, *Sarah Vaughan 1946-1947* (Collectables 1998)★★★, *Very Best Of Sarah Vaughan: 'Round Midnight* (Collectables 1998)★★★, *Gold Collection* (Fine Tune 1998)★★, *Jazz Profile* (Blue Note 1998)★★★, *Time After Time* 1944-1947 recordings (Drive Archive)★★★, *The Man I Love* 1945-1948 recordings (Musica Jazz)★★★★, *Sarah Vaughan* 1944-1954 recordings (Musica Jazz)★★★★, *Compact Jazz: Sarah Vaughan Live* 1957-1963 recordings (Verve)★★★.

● VIDEOS: *Sass And Brass* (Excalibur 1990), *The Divine One* (1993).

● FURTHER READING: *Sassy - The Life Of Sarah Vaughan*, Leslie Gourse.

VENTURA, CHARLIE

b. 2 December 1916, Philadelphia, Pennsylvania, USA, d. 17 January 1992, Pleasantville, New Jersey, USA. After playing C melody and alto saxophones during his childhood, Ventura settled on tenor saxophone and in 1942 joined the Gene Krupa band. He was briefly with Teddy Powell during Krupa's enforced disbandment before rejoining his old boss, where he was featured with the big band and as a member of the band-within-the-band, the trio. In 1946 he formed his own big band, cut back to a small group, then increased in size again, this time playing a commercially orientated form of bebop under the banner of 'Bop For The People'. During this period he also began playing baritone saxophone, but the group eventually disbanded in 1951. He then formed the Big Four with Marty Napoleon, Chubby Jackson and Buddy Rich. For most of the following two decades he alternated between running his own night-club, the Open House in Philadelphia (which closed in 1954), reunions with Krupa, leading big and small bands at Las Vegas hotels and battles with poor health. Although usually thought of as an exuberant, sometimes exhibitionistic soloist, Ventura was fundamentally a straightahead, swinging soloist whose coarser side was encouraged for commercial reasons. Similarly in conflict with his natural playing instincts was his apparent predilection for the complexities of bop. Indeed, in his Bop For The People band, which at one time or another included Conte Candoli, Kai Winding, Bennie Green, Boots Mussulli and the singers Jackie Cain and

Roy Kral, Ventura's swing-styled playing was something of an exception to the prevailing musical atmosphere. He continued playing throughout the 70s and into the early 80s, delighting small but approving audiences with his stomping performances. He later died of lung cancer in 1992.

● ALBUMS: *Charlie Boy* (Phoenix 1946)★★★, *Stomping With The Sax* 10-inch album (Crystalette 1950)★★★, *Open House* 10-inch album (Coral 1952)★★★, *Charlie Ventura Collates* reissued as *In A Jazz Mood* (Mercury 1952)★★★, *Charlie Ventura Quartet* reissued as *Blue Saxophone* (Norgran 1953)★★★, *Charlie Ventura And His Sextet* 1946 recordings (Imperial 1953)★★★, *F.Y.I. Ventura* reissued as *East Of Suez* 1947 recording (EmArcy 1954)★★★, *Charlie Ventura Concert* 1949 recording (Decca 1954)★★★★, *Charlie Ventura In Concert* 1949 recording (GNP 1954)★★★★, with Mary Ann McCall *An Evening With Mary Ann McCall & Charlie Ventura* 10-inch album (Norgran 1954)★★★★, with McCall *Another Evening With Charlie Ventura & Mary Ann McCall* (Norgran 1954)★★★, *Jumping With Ventura* 1946 recording (EmArcy 1955)★★★, *It's All Bop To Me* (RCA Victor 1955)★★★, *Charlie Ventura's Carnegie Hall Concert* 1947 recording (Norgran 1955)★★★★, *Charley's Parley* 1951-1954 recordings (Norgran 1956)★★★, *Charlie Ventura Quintet In Hi Fi* (Harlequin 1956)★★★★, *Here's Charlie* 1954 recording (Brunswick 1957)★★★, *New Charlie Ventura In Hi Fi* (Baton 1957)★★★, with Charlie Kennedy *Crazy Rhythms* (Regent 1957)★★★, *Adventures With Charlie Ventura* (King 1958)★★★, *Charlie Ventura Plays Hi Fi Jazz* reissued as *Charlie Ventura Plays For The People* (Tops 1958)★★★★, *Chazz* (Famous Door 1977)★★★.

● COMPILATIONS: *Euphoria* 1945-1948 recordings (Savoy)★★★★.

VENUTI, JOE

b. Giuseppi Venuti, 16 September 1903, Philadelphia, Pennsylvania, USA, d. 14 August 1978, Seattle, Washington, USA. According to legend, Venuti took up violin when he and a friend, Eddie Lang, tossed a coin to see who would play which of two instruments they had bought from a Philadelphia pawn shop. Lang got the guitar. Similarly legendary are tales of Venuti's birth and early career. The former has been placed in both Italy and Philadelphia, with a favourite in-between location on board a ship filled with Italian immigrants as it sailed into New York harbour. The date varies too, with a range of anything up to five years either way. More prosaically, Venuti spent his early life working in bands in and around Philadelphia, often in company with Lang, before joining Bert Estlow's band in Atlantic City. By 1924 he had graduated to leading one of Jean Goldkette's bands. Later in the 20s, often still with Lang, he played in the bands of Roger Wolfe Kahn and Adrian Rollini and made many records, including the classic Venuti-Lang Blue Four sides. In 1929 he joined Paul Whiteman shortly before the making of the film *The King Of Jazz* (1930). During a rehearsal for the film he surreptitiously emptied a bag of flour into the bell of a tuba so that when the unfortunate musician eventually managed to puff out a note the entire band disappeared under a drifting white cloud. While with Whiteman he survived a serious car crash and also befriended Bix Beiderbecke, whom he once tipped, drunk and unconscious, into a bath of purple Jell-O. During the early 30s Venuti appeared on numerous recording sessions with artists such as Red McKenzie, Jack Teagarden, Tommy and Jimmy Dorsey, Frank Trumbauer, Bing Crosby, Lee Wiley and the Boswell Sisters. Depressed by the sudden death of his friend Lang in 1933, Venuti drifted for a while, visiting Europe and recording in the UK, alternating on violin and guitar. Back in the USA he formed a big band in 1935 but enjoyed only limited success, refusing to take seriously the duties of a bandleader. He folded the big band in 1943 and for a while he played in film and radio studios, becoming a regular on Crosby's show. Throughout the 50s he appeared at clubs and made records, but by the 60s was struggling against alcoholism. In 1967 he was invited to attend a Dick Gibson Colorado Jazz Party; this sparked a revival of interest in his work. He began recording again as leader and in duo with jazzmen such as Earl 'Fatha' Hines; the following year he appeared at the Newport Jazz Festival and the year after that was in England for the Jazz Expo. In 1970 he discovered he had cancer but fought back; during these traumatic years he made some superb recordings with George Barnes, Ross Tompkins, Dave McKenna, Zoot Sims, Marian McPartland, Scott Hamilton and others, defying age, ill-health and a lifetime of hard-living. Throughout his career Venuti played with sparkling invention and enormous vitality, bringing to his playing a sense of urgency and excitement which, on his chosen instrument, was only matched by Stuff Smith. Venuti's was a massive talent, and although his private life was often disastrous - he was often racist and had a propensity for cruel practical jokes - he was still an outstanding musician. Had he chosen to play a more popular instrument, he might have been judged a giant of jazz.

● ALBUMS: *Fiddle On Fire* (Grand Award 1956)★★★, *Joe Venuti Plays Gershwin* (Golden Crest 1959)★★★, *Joe Venuti Plays Jerome Kern* (Golden Crest 1959)★★★, *Once More With Feeling* (Ovation 1969)★★★, *The Daddy Of The Violin* (MPS 1971)★★★, *Joe Venuti In Milan* (Vanguard 1971)★★★, with Marian McPartland *The Maestro And Friend* (Halcyon 1974)★★★, with Zoot Sims *Joe And Zoot* (Chiaroscuro 1974)★★★★, with Sims *The Joe Venuti Blue Four* (Chiaroscuro 1974)★★★★, *Jazz Violin* (Vanguard 1975)★★★, with Sims *Joe Venuti And Zoot Sims* (Chiaroscuro 1975)★★★★, with George Barnes *Gems* (Concord Jazz 1976)★★★, with Earl Hines *Hot Sonatas* (Chiaroscuro 1976)★★★★, with Barnes *Joe Venuti-George Barnes Live At The Concord Summer Festival* (Concord Jazz 1976)★★★★, *'S Wonderful: Four Giants Of Swing* (Flying Fish 1976)★★★, *Sliding By* (Gazell 1977)★★★, with Dave McKenna *Alone At The Palace* (Chiaroscuro 1977)★★★★, with Ross Tompkins *Ross Tompkins And Joe Venuti Live At Concord '77* (Concord Jazz 1977)★★★, *Joe In Chicago* (Flying Fish 1978)★★★, with Tony Romano *Never Before ... Never Again* 1954 recording (Dobre 1979)★★★, *The Mad Fiddler From Philly* 1953-1954 recordings (Shoestring)★★★, *Pretty Trix* 1934 recordings (IAJRC)★★★.

● COMPILATIONS: with Eddie Lang *Joe Venuti And Eddie Lang* (X 1955)★★★★, with Lang *The Golden Days Of Jazz: Stringing*

The Blues 1926-1933 recordings (Columbia 1976)★★★★, with Lang *Joe Venuti And Eddie Lang* 1926-1928 recordings (JSP 1983)★★★★, with Lang *Joe Venuti And Eddie Lang* 1928-1931 recordings (JSP 1983)★★★★, *The Big Bands Of Joe Venuti, Vol. 1* 1928-1930 recordings (JSP 1987)★★★, *The Big Bands Of Joe Venuti, Vol. 2* 1930-1933 recordings (JSP 1987)★★★, *The Essential Joe Venuti* (Vanguard 1995)★★★★, *Violin Jazz* 1927-1934 recordings (Yazoo)★★★, with Lang *Joe Venuti And Eddie Lang* 1926-1933 recordings (ABC)★★★★, with Lang *Joe Venuti And Eddie Lang 1926-1930* (Swaggie)★★★★, with Lang *Joe Venuti And Eddie Lang 1930-1933* (Swaggie)★★★★, *Fiddlesticks* 1931-1939 recordings (Conifer)★★★★.

● FILMS: *The King Of Jazz* (1930).

VER PLANCK, MARLENE

b. Marlene Pampinella, Newark, New Jersey, USA. Ver Planck began singing at the age of 19, having previously considered a career in journalism. Her first important engagement was with the big band of Tex Beneke. She later joined Charlie Spivak, where she met trombonist-arranger Billy Ver Planck. Later, the couple met again, this time in the Tommy Dorsey band, and shortly afterwards were married. In the early 60s the Ver Plancks worked in radio in New York, and set up their own Mounted Records label. During this period Ver Planck sang with many major artists, including Frank Sinatra, but throughout the decade and into the 70s the bulk of her work consisted of singing jingles for countless commercials. She also began to sing in some of New York's best-known jazz clubs. As her reputation spread she appeared at Carnegie Hall and the Kool Jazz Festival, among numerous prestigious venues and events, and attracted the attention of composers such as Loonis McGlohon and Alec Wilder. An outstanding interpreter of ballads, Ver Planck has recorded about a dozen albums, all of which have proved enormously popular and have drawn lavish praise from critics. She sings with great wit, imagination, flawless diction, understanding and sparkling technique. Her huge repertoire includes the songs of Jerome Kern, Alan J. Lerner, Burt Bacharach, Harry Warren, Johnny Mercer, Benny Carter, Wilder, McGlohon and countless others. Although not strictly a jazz singer, she fits easily into a jazz setting, usually working with piano, bass and drums, but also happily blending with jazz musicians such as Spike Robinson, Sonny Costanzo and Bill Berry. By the 90s Ver Planck was beginning to be heard internationally, proving conclusively that she is one of the finest living interpreters of the Great American Songbook. All of the reissues of her Audiophile albums include newly recorded bonus tracks.

● ALBUMS: *I Think Of You With Every Breath I Take* (Savoy 1955)★★★★, *A Breath Of Fresh Air* (Mounted/Audiophile 1968)★★★, *You'd Better Love Me* (Audiophile 1976)★★★, *Marlene Ver Planck Loves Johnny Mercer* (Audiophile 1978/88)★★★★, *A New York Singer* (Audiophile 1980/95)★★, *Marlene Ver Planck Sings Alec Wilder* (Audiophile 1986/91)★★★★, *Pure And Natural* (Audiophile 1987/92)★★★, *A Quiet Storm* (Audiophile 1990)★★★, *Meets Saxomania* (Audiophile 1994)★★★★, *Live! In London* (Audiophile 1994)★★★★, *You Gotta Have Heart: The Songs Of Richard Adler* (Varese Sarabande 1997)★★★.

VERCKYS

b. Kiamuangana Matesa, 1944, Kinshasa, Zaire. Saxophonist and businessman Verckys began playing music professionally in 1965, when he joined Franco's group, OK Jazz. He left to form his own band, L'Orchestre Veve, in 1969. During the 70s the group became one of Zaire's most successful recording and live acts, but by mid-decade Verckys himself was onstage more in name than in person, preferring to spend most of his time building up a network of clubs, recording studios and labels. By 1980 Verckys was threatening Franco and Rochereau for control of the Zairean music business, and produced and released albums by a myriad of stars including Empire Bakuba, Eleison Victoria and Langa Langa Stars. By the mid-80s his own empire was as large and influential as Franco's and Rochereau's, with his EVVI label being one of the most successful in central Africa.

● ALBUMS: *Dynamite* (1970)★★★, *Les Grand Success* (1978)★★★★, *Selibva* (1982)★★★★, *L'Immortelle Veve* (1985)★★★, *Puissant Totale* (1987)★★★.

VERRELL, RONNIE

b. 21 February 1926, Rochester, Kent, England. While playing in a boy's club band Verrell heard a professional drummer and immediately decided this was what he wanted to do. Seeing and hearing Gene Krupa in a film confirmed his ambition. In 1939 he took one lesson from Max Abrams, the noted British drummer and teacher, but was too impatient to take further lessons. Thereafter, he taught himself and was given his first chance to play in public in Wales, where he had been evacuated when the bombing of London began. On his return to Kent he joined the Claude Giddings band in Gillingham. The outfit was well known for the quality of its young musicians, who included Tommy Whittle and pianist Arthur Greenslade, who later worked with Vic Lewis and Shirley Bassey. Verrell also played with Carl Barriteau and the Londonaires band which was briefly popular in Germany. In 1948 Verrell auditioned for the Ted Heath band when Jack Parnell was considering moving on.

He failed the audition but was hired instead by Cyril Stapleton. Three years later Parnell finally left Heath, and was replaced briefly by Basil Kirchin before Verrell took over the drum chair. This was the time when the Heath band reached its peak and as cracks appeared in the UK Musicians Union ban on visiting Americans, Heath was one of the first to tour the USA (on a reciprocal arrangement that brought Stan Kenton to the UK). The Heath band was part of a package that included June Christy, the Four Freshmen and Nat 'King' Cole and it culminated in a concert at Carnegie Hall. The band was a huge success and many of the individual musicians, Verrell among them, attracted favourable attention from critics and fans alike. Apart from the US tour, Verrell was with the Heath band on its

Australasian tour. During his stint with the band Verrell was partly responsible for at least two of their chart successes in the UK. His solo feature on 'Skin Deep' helped the record to reach number 9 in 1954, and his lithely swinging backing assisted 'Swingin' Shepherd Blues' to its number 3 spot in 1958.

The band also had a Top 20 album success in 1962 with *Big Band Percussion*. After leaving Heath, Verrell worked extensively in television studio bands, among them the house band at ATV which was directed by Parnell. Subsequently, Verrell played in the Syd Lawrence band but continued to be active on television where he gained a kind of anonymous fame as 'Animal', the drummer on *The Muppet Show*. In the late 80s Verrell began playing occasionally with the Pizza Express All Stars in London and made infrequent appearances backing visiting American jazzmen, including Buddy Tate and Clark Terry. He also played in the recreated Ted Heath band led by Don Lusher. In the 90s he continued to divide his time between studio and jazz work. A solid danceband drummer and excellent timekeeper, Verrell was also explosive when it mattered and his work with the Heath band remains a high spot in the story of big band drumming in the UK.

● ALBUMS: with Ted Heath *Ted Heath At Carnegie Hall* (London 1957)★★★, with Heath *Big Band Percussion* (Decca 1962)★★★.

VERVE RECORDS

One of the leading modern jazz labels, Verve was started in 1957 by promoter and producer Norman Granz (b. 6 August 1918, Los Angeles, California, USA). Early in the decade, Granz had issued records on Clef and Norgran, which was added to the Verve catalogue. Verve's roster included most of the top jazz names of the era, such as Ella Fitzgerald (whom Granz managed), Dizzy Gillespie, Sarah Vaughan, Oscar Peterson and Count Basie. In 1961 Verve was sold to MGM Records for $3 million. It continued to record jazz, but under Creed Taylor, Verve had a more commercial policy, gaining pop hits with Stan Getz's bossa nova records, Count Basie's versions of Beatles tunes and Jimmy Smith's 'Walk On The Wild Side'. In the early 60s, A&R chief Jerry Schoenbaum began to sign New York folk and rock artists. Among these were Blues Project, Velvet Underground and (on the Verve-Folkways and Verve-Forecast labels) an impressive roster of solo artists like Tim Hardin, Janis Ian, Richie Havens and Laura Nyro. From the west coast came Frank Zappa's Mothers Of Invention and the Righteous Brothers. Tom Wilson, previously with CBS Records, produced many Verve albums, notably those by Zappa and the Velvet Underground. In 1969 MGM and Verve were purchased by Transcontinental Music which in turn sold out to PolyGram Records a few years later. During the 70s there was little emphasis on new jazz recordings and the Verve label became primarily a reissue company. In later years more resources were put into Verve and the company gained a reputation for bringing back veteran artists like Getz, Abbey Lincoln and Maceo Parker. In the 90s Verve also began to release albums of 'world music' artists like Simon Nkabinde Mahtahlini from South Africa.

● COMPILATIONS: *Jazz On Verve (Volumes 1 and 2)* (Verve 1988)★★★★, *Have Yourself A Jazzy Little Christmas* (1989)★★★★, *A Verve Christmas Album* (Verve 1996)★★★★.

VESALA, EDWARD

b. Martti Vesala, 15 February 1945, Eastern Finland. Easily the most influential Finnish jazz musician of his generation, drummer-composer Vesala did not begin to play until he was 20 years old. Growing up in the middle of the Finnish forest, his only access to music was in the dancehalls of neighbouring villages where Nordic tango was available. After a season of playing for country dances he advanced rapidly through psychedelic rock and free jazz, then checked into Helsinki's Sibelius Academy for courses in orchestration, only to drop out impatiently after a year. He roamed through Asia in the early 70s, collecting instruments and soaking up local music in India, Bali and Java. In 1972 he formed a short-lived co-operative trio with Jan Garbarek and Arild Andersen (*Triptykon*), and in 1975 a more compatible quartet co-led with Tomasz Stanko. By this point, Vesala's compositional direction was established. Melody and emotional expression are of prime importance in his work, and his melodies and emotions are complex. He formed Sound And Fury from one of his workshop groups in 1985 and it has come to be one of the outstanding European ensembles, its disciplined young musicians totally committed to Vesala's visions. Although several of his albums have appeared on ECM Records, Vesala also runs his own record label, Leo (not to be confused with the London-based Leo Records), which has released many of his sessions with various European and - notably on *Heavy Life* - American guest musicians.

● ALBUMS: *Soulset* (1969)★★, *Edward Vesala Jazz Band* (1969)★★, *Nana* (1970)★★★, *I'm Here* (1973)★★★, with Peter Brötzmann *Hot Lotta* (1974)★★★, *Nan Madol* (ECM 1975)★★★, with Jasper Van't Hof, Toto Blanke *Electric Circus* (1976)★★★★, with Tomasz Stanko *Live At Remont* (1977)★★★, with Stanko *Twet* (1977)★★★, *Rodina* (1977)★★★, *Satu* (1977)★★★, *Neitsytmatka* (1980)★★★, *Heavy Life* (1980)★★★, with Charlie Mariano, Arild Andersen, Van't Hof *Tea For Four* (1982)★★, *Mau-Mau* (1982)★★★, *Bad Luck, Good Luck* (1984)★★★★, *Kullervo* (1985)★★★, *Lumi* (ECM 1987)★★★★, *Afrikan Tähoet* (1989)★★★, *Ode To The Death Of Jazz* (ECM 1990)★★★★, *Invisible Storm* (ECM 1992)★★★, *Sound And Fury* (1993)★★★, *Nordic Gallery* (ECM 1995)★★★.

VINNEGAR, LEROY

b. 13 July 1928, Indianapolis, Indiana, USA. After teaching himself to play bass, Vinnegar worked in clubs in the Chicago area, accompanying jazz musicians such as Charlie Parker, before moving to the west coast in 1954. He immediately made an impact on the local music scene, then in the middle of the 'cool jazz' boom. He played and recorded with just about everyone; a short list might include Jack Sheldon, Stan Levey, Shorty Rogers, Dexter Gordon, Cy Touff, Russ Freeman, Elmo

Hope, Stan Getz, Harold Land, Carl Perkins (with whom he had gone to school), Art Pepper and Teddy Edwards. He was also a member of the Shelly Manne trio (the third man being André Previn) which recorded the 1956 hit album *My Fair Lady*. Vinnegar continued to work with a variety of bands, sometimes as leader, at home in large and small groups. He sometimes appeared in non-jazz contexts and his eclecticism allowed him to play comfortably alongside musicians as diverse as Howard McGhee and Les McCann, or Serge Chaloff and film actor George Segal's Dixieland jazz group, Panama Hats. After several years of ill-health, Vinnegar returned to recording with a 1992 session for Contemporary. An outstanding exponent of the 'walking bass' technique, Vinnegar always plays with a wonderful plangency, bringing a zestful swing to any performance.

● ALBUMS: *Leroy Walks!* (Contemporary 1957)★★★★, *Leroy Walks Again!!* (Contemporary 1962)★★★★, *Jazz's Great Walker* (Vee Jay 1965)★★★, *Walkin' The Basses* (Contemporary 1992)★★★, *Integrity* (Jazz Focus 1995)★★★.

VINSON, EDDIE 'CLEANHEAD'

b. 18 December 1917, Houston, Texas, USA, d. 2 July 1988, Los Angeles, California, USA. Taking up the alto saxophone as a child, his proficiency at the instrument attracted local bandleaders even while young Vinson was still at school, and he began touring with Chester Boone's territory band during school holidays. Upon his graduation in 1935, Vinson joined the band full-time, remaining when the outfit was taken over by Milton Larkins the following year. During his five-year tenure with the legendary Larkins band he met T-Bone Walker, Arnett Cobb, and Illinois Jacquet, who all played with Larkins in the late 30s. More importantly the band's touring schedule brought Vinson into contact with Big Bill Broonzy, who taught him how to shout the blues, and Jay 'Hootie' McShann's Orchestra whose innovative young alto player, Charlie Parker, was 'kidnapped' by Vinson for several days in 1941 in order to study his technique. After being discovered by Cootie Williams in late 1941, Vinson joined the Duke Ellington trumpeter's new orchestra in New York City and made his recording debut for OKeh Records in April 1942, singing a solid blues vocal on 'When My Baby Left Me'. With Williams' orchestra, Vinson also recorded for Hit Records (1944), Capitol Records (1945) and appeared in a short film, *Film-vodvil no 2* (1943), before leaving to form his own big band in late 1945 and recording for Mercury Records. At Mercury he recorded small-group bop and blasting band instrumentals, but his main output was the fine body of suggestive jump-blues sung in his unique wheezy Texas style. Hits such as 'Juice Head Baby', 'Kidney Stew Blues' and 'Old Maid Boogie' were the exceptions, however, as most of Vinson's no-holds-barred songs, including 'Some Women Do', 'Oil Man Blues' and 'Ever-Ready Blues', were simply too raunchy for airplay. After the 1948 union ban, Vinson began recording for King Records in a largely unchanged style ('I'm Gonna Wind Your Clock', 'I'm Weak But Willing', 'Somebody Done Stole My Cherry Red'), often with all-star jazz units. However, his records were not promoted as well as King's biggest R&B stars, such as Wynonie Harris and Roy Brown, and he left to return to Mercury in the early 50s, rejoining Cootie Williams' small band briefly in the mid-50s. In 1957 he toured with Count Basie's Orchestra and made some recordings with a small Basie unit for King's jazz subsidiary, Bethlehem Records, after which he retired to Houston. In 1961 he was rediscovered by fellow-alto saxophonist Cannonball Adderley, and a fine album resulted on Riverside Records with the Adderley brothers' small band. From then until his death in 1988 (of a heart attack), Vinson found full-time employment at worldwide jazz and blues festivals, a steady international touring schedule and dozens of credible albums on jazz and blues labels such as Black & Blue, Bluesway, Pablo, Muse and JSP.

● ALBUMS: *Back In Town* (Bethlehem 1957)★★★★, *Back Door Blues* (Riverside 1965)★★★★, *Cherry Red* (Bluesway 1967)★★★, *Wee Baby Blues* reissued as *Kidney Stew Is Fine* (Black & Blue/Delmark 1969)★★★★, *You Can't Make Love Alone* (Mega 1971)★★★, *The Original Cleanhead* 1969 recording (Philips 1972)★★★ *Eddie 'Cleanhead' Vinson* 1946-1947 recordings (Trip 1973)★★★, *Jamming The Blues* (Black Lion 1975)★★★, *Live In Blue Note, Göttingen* (1976)★★★, *The Clean Machine* (Muse 1978)★★★, *Hold It Right There!* (Muse 1978)★★★★, *Live At Sandy's* (Muse 1978)★★★★, *Fun In London* (JSP 1980)★★★, *I Want A Little Girl* (Pablo 1981)★★★, with Roomful Of Blues *Eddie 'Cleanhead' Vinson & Roomful Of Blues* (Muse 1982)★★★★, *Eddie 'Cleanhead' Vinson Sings The Blues* (Muse 1987)★★★, with Cannonball Adderley *Cleanhead & Cannonball* 1961/1962 recordings (Landmark 1988)★★★★, *Meat's Too High* (JSP 1989)★★★, *Eddie Vinson Sings* 1957 recording (Bethlehem 1997)★★★.

● COMPILATIONS: *Cherry Red Blues* 1949-1952 recordings (King/Gusto 1976)★★★★, with Jimmy Witherspoon *Battle Of The Blues, Vol. 3* 1949-1952 recording (King).

● FILMS: *Film-vodvil no 2* (1943).

VINTAGE JAZZ AND BLUES BAND

One of Australia's best traditional jazz bands was formed in Brisbane in 1973 by saxophonist Andy Jenner (b. 12 July 1943, Cheshire, England). Early personnel also included John Braben (cornet), Mike Hawthorne (trombone), Jo Bloomfield (piano), Vic Sanderson (banjo), Ron Hawkins (bass), and Duke McMaster (drums), and at the start of their career they held a residency at the Brisbane Carlton Hotel. In March 1974 the band formed the Vintage Jazz Society of Brisbane and operated successfully at the Twelfth Night Theatre Club for six years. In 1975 the band released their debut - *At Home With The Band Of The Vintage Jazz Society Of Brisbane*. The album was well received and featured the driving, vital sound of the unit playing classic early jazz standards. In 1981 the band opened their own jazz club, Jabbo's, in Brisbane, where they were regularly featured with many guests including Bob Barnard, John Sangster, Graeme Bell, Paul Furniss, Acker Bilk, Tom Baker and John R.T. Davies. The unit also supported many international visitors including Stéphane Grappelli, Kenny Baker and the Dutch Swing

College Band. The Vintage Jazz And Blues Band's success peaked in the mid-80s when the essential line-up was Tich Bray (b. 22 December 1924, Geelong, Victoria, Australia, d. 1988) who replaced Jenner, John Braben, Mike Hawthorne, Bob Watson (drums), John Cox (banjo), and Paula Cox (vocals). Jabbo's closed in 1985 and the band then enjoyed a long residency at the St. Pauls Tavern. In the 90s the outfit performed less frequently, usually for special engagements and reunions. The Vintage Jazz And Blues Band was one of Australia's most durable groups in the traditional jazz genre. Performing classic early jazz and blues with feeling and authenticity, it was never less than inspiring and was often dynamic.

● ALBUMS: *At Home With The Band Of the Vintage Jazz Society Of Brisbane* (VJS 1975)★★★, *The Vintage Jazz Society Band* (VJS 1978)★★★, *Eight To The Bar* (VJS 1982)★★.

Vinx

A multi-talented American percussionist, singer and songwriter, Vinx grew up in a suburb of Kansas City and later attended the state university. He then travelled to Montreux, Switzerland, as part of the K.S.U. band, and met Taj Mahal. He found many willing employers for his session music skills in and around Los Angeles. Among his notable musical engagements have been a Grammy Award-winning Ernie Watts album, live work with Rickie Lee Jones, and Herbie Hancock's 1990 *Showtime* special. Sting overheard one of Vinx's studio tracks and signed him as a solo artist through his A&M Records subsidiary, Pangaea. *Rooms In My Fatha's House*, released in 1992, was an auspicious debut, merging samba, funk and hip-hop with the artist's highly individual rhythmic instincts. 1994's *The Storyteller* was a 15-song collection that included a collaboration with Stevie Wonder ('I Will Always Care'), an a cappella rendition of Van Morrison's 'Moondance' and guest vocals from Omar. A breezy, upbeat record signatured with great musical skill, it was premiered on UK tour dates supporting Sting.

● ALBUMS: *Rooms In My Fatha's House* (Pangaea 1992)★★★, *The Storyteller* (Pangaea 1994)★★★.

Vitous, Miroslav

b. 6 December 1947, Prague, Czechoslovakia. After studying bass at the Prague Conservatory (where he played in a trio with Jan Hammer) and then the Berklee College Of Music in Boston, Massachusetts, Vitous had played or recorded with an astonishing list of major jazz artists by 1970, including Freddie Hubbard, Miles Davis, Chick Corea and Wayne Shorter. A founder-member of the influential Weather Report, with Shorter and Joe Zawinul, he left in 1973 to study a custom-made instrument combining electric bass and guitar. Forming a brilliant new group in 1979, with John Surman (saxophone), Kenny Kirkland or John Taylor (piano), and Jon Christensen (drums), Vitous's melodic, folk-influenced bass was important in the creation of the European style recorded by ECM Records.

● ALBUMS: *Infinite Search* reissued as *Mountain In The Clouds* (Embryo/Atlantic 1969)★★★★★, *Miroslav* (Freedom 1978)★★★, *Guardian Angels* (Evidence 1979)★★★, *First Meeting* (ECM 1980)★★★★, *Miroslav Vitous Group* (ECM 1981)★★★★, *Journey's End* (ECM 1983)★★★★, *Emergence* (ECM 1986)★★★★, with Peter Erskine, Jan Garbarek *Star* (ECM 1991)★★★, *Return* (FNAC 1992)★★★, with Garbarek *Atmos* (ECM 1993)★★★, with Tom McKinley *Miroslav Vitous/Tom McKinley* (MMC 1996)★★★.

Voice

Initially conceived as a vocal and instrument free-jazz ensemble, this product of the South London Oval Arts Lab was brought together in 1971 by vocalist Maggie Nicols and Harry Vince (trumpet) and also comprised Brian Eley (b. 22 June 1952, Hackney, London, England; vocals), Dave Mitchell (tenor saxophone), Chris Francis (alto saxophone, congas), Frank Roberts (electric piano), Georg Jensen (bass), David Nash (drums) and Mike Cousins (trombone). After performing on the London jazz circuit to critical acclaim, this extremely weighty line-up collapsed and folded in 1972. Three years later the band name re-emerged for the purposes of an appearance at the Polish Jazz Festival, only this time stripped down to an a cappella quartet comprising Nicols and Eley plus the introduction of Julie Tippetts (a former comrade of Nicols in Keith Tippett's Ark) and ex-Mike Westbrook singer Phil Minton (b. 2 November 1940, Torquay, Devon, England). The group lasted barely 18 months, but recorded one album, live at the Phoenix jazz club in London's Cavendish Square in 1977. A major source of inspiration came from African musical culture and the use of Nicols' 'non-language'. This gave the sound an original dimension with the track 'Yilf Kofla' wonderfully capturing their technique. This eclecticism prompted the noted jazz critic Brian Case to state: 'Jazz? Gawd knows - but check it out. More arresting than Jack Warner!'. With the exception of Tippetts, Voice were also used in the recording of Ken Hyder's group Talisker's 1977 album, *Land Of Stone*. Brian Eley retired to the world of graphic art while the remaining three continued to explore free jazz.

● ALBUMS: *Voice* (1977)★★★.

Von Ohlen, John

b. 13 May 1941, Indianapolis, Indiana, USA. Taking up the drums in his teens, Von Ohlen's first major job was with Billy Maxted's Manhattan Jazz Band which he joined in 1967. The following year he played with Woody Herman and then joined Stan Kenton. He was with the Kenton band for two years before settling in Cincinnati, Ohio, where he formed a big band to play at the Blue Wisp club. The band included several highly talented young musicians, such as pianist Steve Schmidt and trumpeters Al Kiger and Tim Hagans. Extensively recorded by Helen Y. Morr of the Cincinnati-based MoPro Records, the Blue Wisp Big Band is an exceptionally fine example of an American rehearsal band. Although Von Ohlen's international reputation rests largely upon his former association with Kenton, his playing with his own big band and with small groups assembled especially for record dates or to accompany such visiting jazzmen as Cal Collins and Bill Berry, shows him to be a versatile drummer capable of great sensitivity and unflagging swing.

● ALBUMS: *WKRC-TV & The Blue Wisp Jazz Club Presents The Blue Wisp Big Band Of Cincinnati* (1981)★★★, *The John Von Ohlen-Steve Allen Big Band* (1982)★★★★, with the Blue Wisp Big Band *Butterfly* (1982)★★★, with Blue Wisp *The Smooth One* (1983)★★, with Cal Collins *Crack'd Rib* (1984)★★, with Blue Wisp *Live At Carmelo's* (1984)★★★, with Blue Wisp *Rollin' With Von Ohlen* (1985)★★★.

VON SCHLIPPENBACH, ALEX

b. Alexander von Schlippenbach, 7 March 1938, Berlin, Germany. Schlippenbach studied piano and composition at school, and his early jazz-related interests were in boogie-woogie and blues piano. After a period influenced by musicians such as Oscar Peterson, Bud Powell and Thelonious Monk, he began playing free jazz in the 60s. He worked with Gunter Hampel in 1963 and Manfred Schoof (1964-67) and in 1966 set up the Globe Unity Orchestra to play his composition *Globe Unity* at the Berlin Jazz Festival. The orchestra's impact enabled him to resuscitate it the following year and on frequent occasions since; over the 70s and 80s, the Orchestra has established itself as the world's leading free jazz big band, its ranks including many outstanding European players (Schoof, Kenny Wheeler, Peter Brötzmann, Albert Mangelsdorff, Peter Kowald) as well as occasional US guests, such as Steve Lacy and Anthony Braxton. In 1970, Schlippenbach formed a quartet with Evan Parker, with whom he has since produced much challenging music both in and out of the Globe Unity Orchestra and in a regular trio (with Paul Lovens). He has also worked frequently in a duo with drummer Sven Ake Johansson. In 1988 Schlippenbach formed the Berlin Jazz Composers' Orchestra and in 1990 recorded the remarkable duo *Smoke* with Sunny Murray. A tireless organizer and electrifying improviser - whose speed and power of execution recall Cecil Taylor - Schlippenbach has long been one of the major figures of the European free jazz scene.

● ALBUMS: *Globe Unity* (1966)★★★★, *The Living Music* (1969)★★★, *Payan* (1972)★★★, *Pakistani Pomade* (1972)★★★, with Globe Unity Orchestra *Live In Wuppertal* (1973)★★, with GUO *Hamburg '74* (1974)★★★, *Three Nails Left* (1975)★★★, with GUO *Evidence* (1975)★★★, with GUO *Into The Valley* (1975)★★★, with GUO *Local Fair* (1976)★★★, with Sven Ake Johansson *Live At The Quartier Latin* (1976)★★, with GUO *Pearls* (1977)★★★, *The Hidden Peak* (1977)★★★, with GUO *Improvisations* (1977)★★★★, *Piano Solo* (1977)★★★, with Johansson *Kung Bore* (1978)★★, with GUO *Compositions* (1979)★★★, with Johansson *Drive* (1980)★★★, with RAI Big Band *Jelly Roll* (1981)★★★, with Johansson *Kalfactor A. Falke Und Andere Lieder* (1982)★★★, *Detto Fra Di Noi* (1982)★★★★, *Anticlockwise* (1983)★★★, with GUO *Intergalactic Blow* (1983)★★★, with Martin Theurer *Rondo Brillante* (1983)★★★, with Paul Lovens *Stranger Than Love* (1985)★★★, *Berlin Jazz Composers' Orchestra* (1990)★★★, with Sunny Murray *Smoke* (FMP 1990)★★★★, *Elf Bagatellen* (FMP 1991), *Physics* (FMP 1992)★★★★, *The Morlocks* (FMP 1994)★★★.

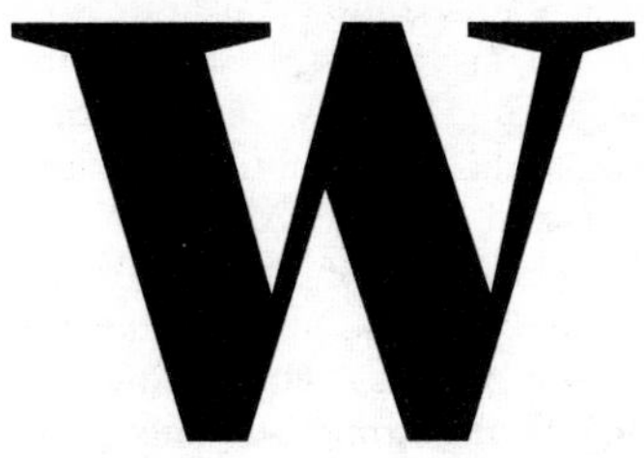

WACHSMANN, PHIL

b. 5 August 1944, Kampala, Uganda. Violinist Wachsmann was born into a musical family: his mother sang and his father studied Ugandan traditional music and played violin. After studying music at Durham University, he won a scholarship to Bloomington University, Indiana. In 1968 he studied for a year in Paris with Nadia Boulanger. Between 1969 and 1970 he lectured on music at Durham University and also set up an improvisation workshop. In the early 70s he worked with Yggdrasil, a group that played compositions by John Cage and Morton Feldman, and led his own group Chamberpot. Since then he has involved himself in the UK free-jazz scene, playing with Tony Oxley, Derek Bailey and Barry John Guy. He started his own record label, Bead, which documented free improvisations at the outer limits. He cites Joe Venuti and classical violinist Itzhak Perlman as influences on his playing, although traces of Gustav Mahler and the Second Viennese School are also apparent: Wachsmann is interested in electronics and in the possibilities of strict 12-tone improvisation (rather than simply 'atonal' playing). In 1989 he formed an especially productive duo with singer Vanessa Mackness.

● ALBUMS: with Ian Brighton *Marsh Gas* (1975)★★★, *Chamberpot* (1976)★★★, *Sparks Of The Desire Magneto* (1977)★★★, with Tony Oxley *February Papers* (1977)★★★, with Harry de Wit *For Harm* (1979)★★, *Was Macht Ihr Denn* (1982)★★★, *Writing In Water* (1985)★★★.

WADUD, ABDUL

b. Ronald DeVaughan, 30 April 1947, Cleveland, Ohio, USA. After studying cello as a child Wadud continued playing this instrument, and while some of his work was in classical music he also took up jazz. Although the cello has rarely been used in jazz, his accomplished technique and strong feeling for the form allowed him to make a significant contribution during the 70s and 80s. After a spell with the New Jersey Symphony Orchestra he worked fruitfully with leading members of the *avant-garde*, including Julius Hemphill, with whom he recorded 1972's *Dogon, A. D.*, Arthur Blythe, Sam Rivers, Cecil Taylor, David Murray and Chico Freeman. Also in the 80s he worked with several small- and medium-size groups of his own and also collaborated with James Newton and Anthony Davis. In the 90s he resumed his association with Hemphill, performing and recording as a duo. Wadud's playing of the cello is notable for his richness of tone and rhythmic flexibility.

● ALBUMS: *By Myself* (Bishara Music 1977)★★★, with Julius Hemphill *Live In New York* (Red Pepper 1979)★★★, with Anthony Davis, James Newton *I've Known Rivers* (Gramavision 1982)★★★★, with Davis, Newton *Trio - Volume 2* (Gramavision 1990)★★★,with Hemphill *Oakland Duets* (Music & Arts Program Of America 1993)★★★.

WAIN, BEA

b. Beatrice Wain, 30 April 1917, New York City, New York, USA. A vocalist, with a warm, easy and very musical style, Wain was at the peak of her popularity with the Larry Clinton Band in the late 30s. She played the piano as a child, and sang on NBC Radio's *Children's Hour*. Later, after broadcasting with vocal groups led by Fred Waring, Ted Straeter and Kay Thompson, and spending some time with Gene Kardos And His Orchestra, she joined ex-Tommy Dorsey arranger Larry Clinton when he formed his first band, late in 1937. During the next year she sang on all the band's vocal hits, including 'True Confession', 'The One Rose (That's Left My Heart)', 'I Double Dare You', 'Always And Always', 'Martha', 'Heart And Soul', 'Summer Souvenirs', 'Old Folks', 'Who Blew Out The Flame?', '(I'm Afraid) The Masquerade Is Over', 'I Want My Share Of Love', 'My Heart Belongs To Daddy', 'Over The Rainbow', 'Deep Purple' (one of the biggest Wain/Clinton smash hits) and Clinton's own composition, 'My Reverie'. After being voted the number 1 female band vocalist in the 1939 *Billboard* magazine college poll, Wain left Clinton to go solo in May of that year, and had several hits in the early 40s, including 'I'm Nobody's Baby', 'Do I Worry?', 'My Sister And I' and 'Kiss the Boys Goodbye'. At around the same time, she also appeared on radio in the *Quaker Party* and *Your Hit Parade* shows, and later co-starred with ex-Carmen Cavallaro vocalist Larry Douglas, who played a featured role in the Broadway musical *The King And I* in 1951, when he and Doretta Morrow introduced 'We Kiss In A Shadow' and 'I Have Dreamed'. After Wain married radio announcer Andre Bruch, the couple had their own record programme, *Mr And Mrs Music*, on New York radio, and later moved to Florida, where they worked together into the 70s.

WALCOTT, COLLIN

b. 24 April 1945, New York City, USA, d. 8 November 1984, Magdeburg, Germany. Walcott played the violin at school and later studied percussion at Indiana University. In 1967 he studied the sitar with the famous Indian sitarist Ravi Shankar and the tabla with Alla Rakha. He began a lifelong association with Oregon in 1971, playing sitar and tabla. In the mid-70s he recorded two albums under his own name with jazz musicians such as John Abercrombie, Dave Holland, Jack DeJohnette and the influential trumpet player Don Cherry. In the late 70s he formed Codona with Cherry and the virtuoso Brazilian berimbau player and percussionist Nana Vasconcelos. The trio toured widely and recorded three albums for ECM Records. Walcott's luminous compositions, which defy easy classification, are among the most subtle and significant attempts to explore the interconnectedness of various world musical traditions. Walcott died in a car crash in Magdeburg, Germany, in 1984 while on tour with Oregon.

● ALBUMS: *Cloud Dance* (ECM 1975)★★★★, *Grazing Dreams* (ECM 1977)★★★★, with Steven Eliovson *Dawn Dance* (ECM 1981)★★★★.

● COMPILATIONS: *Works* 1975-1984 recordings (ECM 1989)★★★★.

WALD, JERRY

b. USA. Clarinettist Jerry Wald formed his dance band orchestra in 1941 in New York City, New York, USA. The group's musical sidemen included Larry Elgart, Bob Dukoff, Les Robinson, Art Ryerson and Sid Weiss, with arrangers Ray Conniff and Jerry Gray. An early booking at Child's Spanish Garden, then an extended visit to the Lincoln Hotel, augured well for their long term future. As the group established its popularity in the 40s they expanded their repertoire from its original Artie Shaw inspired style to swing and jazz. Records such as 'Call Of The Wild' were issued on Majestic, Columbia Records and Decca Records, with radio appearances on *The Robert Q. Lewis Show* and television alongside Jackie Gleason. A reduced aggregation emerged after World War II, regularly appearing at Wald's own club in Hollywood. In Los Angeles in 1951 he established his second big band, which toured the country to limited success. Eventually Wald settled back in New York where he found opportunities in radio and television, though his band was kept together in some form or another for semi-professional engagements thereafter.

● ALBUMS: *Listen To The Music Of Jerry Wald* (Kapp 1956)★★★, *Tops In Pops - Designed For Dancing* (Lion 1958)★★★.

WALDEN, NARADA MICHAEL

b. 23 April 1952, Kalamazoo, Michigan, USA. Though best known for his percussion skills, Walden is also a talented multi-instrumentalist (notably proficient on keyboards) as well as vocalist, composer, arranger and producer. He grew up the eldest of six children in Plainwell, Michigan. Taking his first music lessons at the age of 10, his favoured early listening included rock bands such as the Who and the soulful R&B of the Temptations. His first group was a duo, the Ambassadors, before Distance In The Far and the Electric Flagstyled Promise. He enrolled at Western Michigan University in 1970 as a music major. By 1972 he had joined progressive rock trio the New McGuire Sisters, led by Sandy Torano, formerly of the Edgar Winter Band. By the following year he had made his debut with the Mahavishnu Orchestra, travelling to London, England, were he helped to record *Apocalypse*. Major UK dates in support of the album, co-headlining with Jeff Beck, took up most of 1973. The guitarist then invited him back to London for sessions with George Martin that produced *Wired*, a Beck collection including four Walden compositions. Afterwards he would find work writing for Carlos Santana and the Pointer Sisters. With the dissolution of the Mahavishnu Quartet in 1975 he embarked on work on his first solo album for Atlantic Records, before joining Tommy Bolin's group until the guitarist's death. Walden then found employment with Roy Buchanan, and produced Don Cherry's *Here & Now* album. His second solo album for Atlantic emerged the following year, before he put together his own band to tour throughout America. Though his first three albums, each imbued with strong religious overtones and built around a solidly professional jazz funk backdrop, failed to sell, he made an unexpected breakthrough in 1980. Two singles, 'Tonight I'm Alright' and 'I Shoulda Loved You', both hit the UK charts in the wake of the disco boom, with the latter reaching number 8 and finding international acceptance. Afterwards his influence waned, though he did achieve a US R&B hit in 1985 with 'Gimme, Gimme, Gimme', a duet with Patti Austin. In 1988 he returned to the UK charts with another number 8 single, 'Divine Emotions', but once again failed to capitalize on its impact.

● ALBUMS: *Garden Of Love Light* (Atlantic 1975)★★★, *I Cry, I Smile* (Atlantic 1977)★★, *Awakening* (Atlantic 1979)★★, *The Dance Of Life* (Atlantic 1980)★★★, *Victory* (Atlantic 1980)★★, *Nature Of Things* (Atlantic 1985)★★★.

WALDMAN, HERMAN

b. USA. Herman Waldman And His Orchestra formed in Texas, USA, in the late 20s. The group was composed of sidemen including Rex Preis, Bill Clemens, Ken Sweitzer, Jim Segars, Bob Harris, Tink Nauratal, Tom Blake, Vernon Mills, Barney Dodd, Reggie Kaughlin, Arnold Wadsworth and Jimmie Mann. From their base in Dallas they became one of the earliest and most popular of the dance bands working the south west states of America. Major hotel engagements at the Baker and Adolphus Hotels (Dallas), the Peabody (Memphis) and Muehlebach (Kansas City) ensued. While playing a one-night engagement in Beaumont, Texas, Waldman auditioned trumpet player Harry James. He passed with flying colours and took his first professional touring engagements with the orchestra. However, they could not contain his talent for long, and despite recording contracts with Bluebird and Brunswick Records, the orchestra broke up during the late 30s.

WALDRON, MAL

b. Malcolm Earl Waldron, 16 August 1926, New York City, New York, USA. After studying piano and composition formally, Waldron began playing professionally with a succession of R&B bands. He also recorded with Ike Quebec and from 1954 was a regular associate of Charles Mingus. Waldron's own mid-50s band enjoyed a measure of success in live performances and on record, and he also led the house band for the Prestige label, playing and arranging on sessions for artists such as John Coltrane and Art Farmer. Late in the decade Waldron became Billie Holiday's regular accompanist, remaining with her for nearly two and a half years. After Holiday's death in 1959 he accompanied Abbey Lincoln, but was mainly active in studio work. In the early 60s he played with leading jazz musicians such as Eric Dolphy, Booker Little and Max Roach, but suffered a serious illness that set back his career. From the late 60s Waldron was resident in Europe, finally settling in Munich, where he helped to launch both the ECM Records and Enja labels by recording their debut releases. Although originally a bop pianist in the mould of Thelonious Monk, Waldron has proved adept at free jazz, most notably in various group sessions that feature soprano saxophonist Steve Lacy, with whom he has also recorded a series of duos. He has written for films, is the composer of a number of pieces for the ballet and for many years enjoyed the distinction of being the best-selling jazz album artist in Japan, where he has recorded with many local musicians. In 1998 he recorded *Soul Eyes*, an all-star celebration of his career featuring Joe Henderson, Steve Coleman and Abbey Lincoln.

● ALBUMS: *Mal-1* (Prestige 1957)★★★★, *Mal-2* (Prestige 1957)★★★★, *Mal 3: Sounds* (New Jazz 1958)★★★, *Mal 4: Trio* (New Jazz 1959)★★★, *Impressions* (New Jazz 1959)★★★★, *Left Alone* (Bethlehem 1960)★★★, with Eric Dolphy *The Quest* (New Jazz 1961)★★★★, *Les Nuits De La Negritude* (1964)★★★, *All Alone* (1966)★★★, *Trio* (1966)★★★, *Sweet Love, Bitter* (1967)★★★, *Ursula* (1969)★★★, *Free At Last* (ECM 1969)★★★, *Set Me Free* (1970)★★★, *Tokyo Reverie* (1970)★★★, *Tokyo Bound* (1970)★★★, *Blood And Guts* (1970)★★★, *Spanish Bitch* (1971)★★, *Number Nineteen* (1971), *The Opening* (1971), *The Call* (1971), *Live: 4 To 1* (1971)★★★, *First Encounter* (Catalyst 1971)★★★, *Plays The Blues* (Enja 1971)★★★, *Black Glory* (Enja 1971)★★★, *Signals* (Freedom 1971)★★★, with Steve Lacy *Journey Without End* (Victor 1971)★★★, *Blues For Lady Day* (Freedom 1972)★★★★, *A Little Bit Of Miles* (1972)★★, with Lacy *Mal Waldron With The Steve Lacy Quintet* (America 1972)★★★, *Mal Waldron On Steinway* (1972)★★★, *Up Popped The Devil* (Enja 1974)★★★, *Hard Talk* (Enja 1975)★★★, with Jackie McLean *Like Old Times* (1976)★★★, *One-Upmanship* (Enja 1977)★★★, *Moods* (Enja 1978)★★★, *Mingus Lives* (1979)★★★, *Mal 81* (1981)★★, *What It Is* (1981)★★★, *One Entrance, Many Exits* (Palo Alto 1982)★★★★, with Lacy *Snake Out* (hatART 1982)★★★, *In Retrospect* (1982)★★★, *Breaking New Ground* (1983)★★★, with Lacy *Herbe De L'Oubli* 1981 recording (hatART 1983)★★★, *Plays Erik Satie* (1984)★★★★, *You And The Night And The Music* (1984)★★★, with David Friesen *Encounters* (1984)★★★, with Marion Brown *Songs Of Love And Regret* (Freelance 1985)★★★, *Dedication* (Soul Note 1986)★★★, *Update* (Soul Note 1986)★★★★, with Sumiko Yoseyama *Duo* (1986)★★★★, *Space* (Vent Du Sud 1986)★★★★, with Lacy *Let's Call This* 1981 recordings (hatART 1986)★★★, with Lacy *Sempre Amore* (Soul Note 1987)★★★★, *Eric Dolphy And Booker Little Remembered* (1987)★★★, with McLean *Left Alone '86* (Evidence 1987)★★★★, *The Git Go: Live At The Village Vanguard* (Soul Note 1987)★★★★, with Lacy *Live At Sweet Basil* (King 1987)★★★, with Jim Pepper *Art Of The Duo* (Tutu 1988)★★★, *Seagulls Of Kristiansund* (Soul Note 1988)★★★, *Both Sides Now* (1988)★★★★, *Our Collines's A Tresure* (Soul Note 1988)★★★, with Brown *Much More!* (Freelance 1988)★★★, *Mal, Dance And Soul* (Tutu 1988)★★★, *Quadrologue At Utopia, Volume 1* (Tutu, 1990)★★★, *The Git-Go At Utopia Volume 2* (Tutu 1990)★★★★, with Lacy *Hot House* (Novus 1991)★★★★, *Crowd Scene* 1989 recording (Soul Note 1992)★★★★, *Where Are You* 1989 recording (Soul Note 1992)★★★★, with Chico Freeman *Up And Down* 1989 recording (Black Saint 1992)★★★, with Lacy *Lets Call This ... Esteem* (Slam 1993)★★★, with George Haslam *Waldron-Haslam* (Slam 1994)★★★★, *Two New* (Slam 1995)★★★★, with Lacy *Live At The Dreher, Paris 1981: Round Midnight Vol. 1* (hatART 1996)★★★★, with Lacy *I Remember Thelonious* 1992 recording (Nel Jazz 1996)★★★, with Lacy *Communiqué* 1994 recordings (Soul Note 1997)★★★, with Lacy *Live At The Dreher, Paris 1981: The Peak Vol. 2* (hatART 1997)★★★★, *Soul Eyes* (RCA Victor 1998)★★★.

WALLACE, BENNIE

b. 18 November 1946, Chatanooga, Tennessee, USA. In his teens Wallace played jazz saxophone and sat in with local country and R&B bands. He studied clarinet at Tennessee University, then moved to New York in the early 70s, working with West Indian-born pianist Monty Alexander and singer Sheila Jordan. Wallace's affinity to Ornette Coleman's new jazz language is shown by his later neglect of the piano: he prefers to work in trios, unconfined by the piano's tempered scales. Mostly playing tenor saxophone, his first trio consisted of Glen Moore (bass) and Eddie Moore (drums), who were replaced in 1978 by Eddie Gomez and Dannie Richmond. His debut with this trio - *The Fourteen Bar Blues*, recorded for Enja Records in 1978 - was a revelation. Playing with a loose bravado usually heard from musicians with gospel backgrounds, he had found a way to translate Coleman's concept to tenor, on the way picking up echoes of Eric Dolphy and Albert Ayler. The album won the Deutscher Schallenplattenpreis and he was invited to play at the 1979 Berlin Jazz festival with the George Gruntz band. In 1981, at the festival, Wallace fronted the North German Radio Band. *Live At The Public Theatre* (1978) gave him more room to stretch out and confirmed his stature. In 1982 he recorded with Dave Holland and Elvin Jones (*Big Jim's Tango*) and in 1984 reaffirmed his southern roots with a magnificent gospel track featuring the Wings Of Song vocalists (*Sweeping Through the City*). His Blue Note Records debut, *Twilight Time*, explored his southern background even more extensively, and featured guest appearances by Dr. John and Stevie Ray Vaughan. In the 90s he began film work, scoring the music for *White Men Can't Jump*. Garrulous, inventive and full of the blues, without a trace of the ubiquitous, studied John Coltrane-influenced sound, Wallace's sound is a rejuvenating force for the tenor saxophone.

● ALBUMS: *The Fourteen Bar Blues* (Enja 1978)★★★★, *Live At The Public Theatre* (Enja 1978)★★★, *Plays Monk* (Enja 1981)★★★, *Big Jim's Tango* (Enja 1982)★★★★, *The Free Will* (Enja 1982)★★★★, *The Bennie Wallace Trio And Chick Corea* (Enja 1983)★★★, *Sweeping Through The City* (Enja 1984)★★★★, *Twilight Time* (Blue Note 1985)★★★★, *The Art Of The Saxophone* (Denon 1988)★★★, with Yosuke Yamashita *Brilliant Corners* 1986 recording (Denon 1988)★★★★, *Bordertown* (Blue Note 1989)★★★, *The Wings Of Song* (Enja 1991)★★★, *The Talk Of The Town* (Enja 1993)★★★, *The Old Songs* (AudioQuest 1993)★★★★, *Bennie Wallace* (AudioQuest 1998)★★★★.

WALLER, FATS

b. Thomas Wright Waller, 21 May 1904, Waverley, New York, USA, d. 15 December 1943, Kansas City, Missouri, USA. Influenced by his grandfather, a violinist, and his mother, Waller was playing piano at students' concerts and organ in his father's church by the time he was 10 years old. In 1918, while still in high school, he was asked to fill in for the regular organist at the Lincoln Theatre, and subsequently gained a permanent seat at the Wurlitzer Grand. A year later he won a talent contest, playing ragtime pianist James P. Johnson's 'Carolina Shout'. While a protégé of Johnson's, Waller adopted the Harlem stride style of piano playing, 'the swinging left hand', emphasizing tenths on the bass, to which Waller added his own distinctive touch. In 1919, while on tour as a vaudeville pianist, he composed 'Boston Blues' which, when the title was later changed to 'Squeeze Me', with a lyric by Clarence Williams, became one of his best-known songs. In the early 20s, with the USA on the brink of the 'jazz age', and Prohibition in force, Waller's piano playing was much in demand at rent-parties, bootleg joints, in cabaret and vaudeville. Inevitably, he mixed with gangsters, and it is said that his first 100 dollar bill was given to him by Al Capone, who fortunately enjoyed his piano playing. Around this time Waller made his first records as accompanist to one of the leading blues singers, Sara Martin. He also recorded with the legendary Bessie Smith, and toured with her in 1926. His first solo piano recording was reputedly 'Muscle Shoal Blues'.

From 1926-29 he made a series of pipe organ recordings in a disused church in Camden, New Jersey. Having studied composition from an early age with various teachers, including Leopold Godowski and Carl Bohm, Waller collaborated with James P. Johnson and Clarence Todd on the music for the Broadway revue *Keep Shufflin'* (1928). This was a follow-up to Noble Sissle and Eubie Blake's smash hit *Shuffle Along* (1921), which starred Joséphine Baker, and was the show that is credited with making black music acceptable to Broadway audiences. Although not on stage in *Keep Shufflin'*, Waller made a considerable impression with his exuberant piano playing from the show's orchestra pit at Daly's Theatre. Andy Razaf, who wrote most of the show's lyrics, including the outstanding number, 'Willow Tree', would become Waller's regular collaborator, and his closest friend. Just over a year later, in June 1929, Waller again combined with Razaf for *Hot Chocolates*, another Negro revue, revised for Broadway. In the orchestra pit this time was trumpeter Louis Armstrong, whose role was expanded during the show's run. The score for *Hot Chocolates* also contained the plaintive '(What Did I Do To Be So) Black, And Blue?', and one of the team's most enduring standards, 'Ain't Misbehavin'', an instrumental version of which became Waller's first hit, and years later, was selected for inclusion in the NARAS Hall of Fame. Both *Keep Shufflin'* and *Hot Chocolates* were first staged at Connie's Inn, in Harlem, one of the biggest black communities in the world. Waller lived in the middle of Harlem, until he really hit the big-time and moved to St. Albans, Long Island, where he installed a built-in Hammond organ.

In the late 20s and early 30s he was still on the brink of that success. Although he endured some bleak times during the Depression he was writing some of his most effective songs, such as 'Honeysuckle Rose', 'Blue, Turning Grey Over You' and 'Keepin' Out Of Mischief Now' (all with Razaf); 'I've Got A Feeling I'm Falling' (with Billy Rose and Harry Link); and 'I'm Crazy 'Bout My Baby' (with Alexander Hill). In 1932 he toured Europe in the company of fellow composer Spencer Williams, and played prestigious venues such as London's Kit Kat Club and the Moulin Rouge in Paris. Worldwide fame followed with the formation of Fats Waller And His Rhythm in 1934. The all-star group featured musicians such as Al Casey (b. 15 September 1915, Louisville, Kentucky, USA; guitar), Herman Autrey (b. 4 December 1904, Evergreen, Alabama, USA, d. 14 June 1980; trumpet), Gene Sedric (b. 17 June 1907, St. Louis, Missouri, USA, d. 3 April 1963; reeds), Billy Taylor or Charles Turner (string bass), drummers Harry Dial (b. 17 February 1907, Birmingham, Alabama, USA, d. 25 January 1987) or Yank Porter (b. Allen Porter, *c.*1895, Norfolk, Virginia, USA, d. 22 March 1944, New York, USA) and Rudy Powell (b. Everard Stephen Powell, 28 October 1907, New York City, New York, USA, d. 30 October 1976; clarinet). Signed for Victor Records, the ensemble made over 150 78 rpm records between May 1934 and January 1943, in addition to Waller's output of piano and organ solos, and some big-band tracks. The Rhythm records were a revelation: high-class musicianship accompanied Waller's exuberant vocals, sometimes spiced with sly, irreverent asides on popular titles such as 'Don't Let It Bother You', 'Sweetie Pie', 'Lulu's Back In Town', 'Truckin'', 'A Little Bit Independent', 'It's A Sin To Tell A Lie', 'You're Not That Kind', 'Until The Real Thing Comes Along', 'The Curse Of An Aching Heart', 'Dinah', 'S'posin', 'Smarty', 'The Sheik Of Araby', 'Hold Tight' and 'I Love To Whistle'.

Waller had massive hits with specialities such as 'I'm Gonna Sit Right Down And Write Myself A Letter', 'When Somebody Thinks You're Wonderful', 'My Very Good Friend The Milkman' and 'Your Feet's Too Big'. He recorded ballads including 'Two Sleepy People' and 'Then I'll Be Tired Of You', and several of his own compositions, including 'Honeysuckle Rose' and 'The Joint Is Jumpin'' (written with Razaf and J.C. Johnson). In 1935, Waller appeared in the first of his three feature films, *Hooray For Love*, which also featured Bill 'Bojangles' Robinson. In the following year he received excellent reviews for his rendering of 'I've Got My Fingers Crossed' in *King Of Burlesque*. In 1938, he toured Europe again for several months, this time as a big star. He played concerts in several cities, performed at the London Palladium, and appeared in an early television broadcast from Alexandra Palace. Waller also became the first - and probably the only - jazz musician to play the organ of the Notre Dame de Paris. He returned to England and Scotland the following year. Back in the USA, Waller toured with a combo for a while, and during the early 40s performed with his own big band, before again working as a solo artist. In 1942 he tried to play serious jazz in concert at Carnegie Hall - but was poorly received. In 1943, he returned to Broadway to write the score, with George Marion, for the bawdy musical *Early To Bed*. The comedy high-spot proved to be 'The Ladies Who Sing With The Band'. Waller teamed with 'Bojangles' Robinson once again in 1943 for the film of *Stormy Weather*, which included a version of 'Ain't Misbehavin''. Afterwards, he stayed in California for an engagement at the Zanzibar Club in Los Angeles. On his way back to New York on the Santa Fe Chief railway express, he died of pneumonia as it was pulling into Kansas City. His life had been one of excess. Enormous amounts of food and liquor meant that his weight varied between 285 and 310 lbs - 'a girthful of blues'. Days of carousing were followed by equal amounts of sleeping, not necessarily alone. Jazz continually influenced his work, even when he was cajoled into recording inferior material. He worked and recorded with leading artists such as Fletcher Henderson, Ted Lewis, Alberta Hunter, Jack Teagarden, Gene Austin and Lee Wiley. Waller felt strongly that he did not receive his fair share of the songwriting royalties. He was said to have visited the Brill Building, which housed New York's most prominent music publishers, and obtained advances from several publishers for the same tune. Each, however, had a different lyric. He sold many numbers outright, and never received credit for them. Two songs that are sometimes rumoured to be his, but are always definitely attributed to Jimmy McHugh and Dorothy Fields - 'I Can't Give You Anything But Love' and 'On The Sunny Side Of The Street' - were included in the 1978 Broadway show *Ain't Misbehavin'*. Most of the numbers in that production were genuine Waller, along with a few others like 'Mean To Me', 'It's A Sin To Tell A Lie', 'Fat And Greasy' and 'Cash For Your Trash', which, in performance, he had made his own. The majority of his recordings have been reissued and appear on a variety of labels such as RCA Records, Saville, Halcyon, Living Era, President, Swaggie (Australia) and Vogue (France).

● COMPILATIONS: *Fats Waller 1934-42* 10-inch album (RCA Victor 1951)★★★, *Fats Waller Favorites* 10-inch album (RCA Victor 1951)★★★, *Swingin' The Organ* 10-inch album (RCA Victor 1953)★★★, *Rediscovered Fats Waller Piano Solos* 10-inch album (Riverside 1953)★★★, *Fats Waller At The Organ* 10-inch album (Riverside 1953)★★★, *Jiving With Fats Waller* 10-inch album (Riverside 1953)★★★, *Fats Waller Plays And Sings* (RCA Victor 1954)★★★, *Fats Waller Radio Transcriptions* 2-LP box set (RCA Victor 1955)★★★, *Rhythm And Romance With Fats Waller* (HMV 1954)★★★, *The Young Fats Waller* 10-inch album (X 1955)★★★, *Fun With Fats* (HMV 1955)★★★, *The Amazing Mr Waller* 10-inch album (Riverside 1955)★★★, *Thomas Fats Waller Vols. 1 And 2* (HMV 1955)★★★, *Ain't Misbehavin'* (RCA Victor 1956)★★★, *Handful Of Keys* (RCA Victor 1957)★★★, *Spreadin' Rhythm Around* (HMV 1957)★★★, *Fats* (RCA Victor 1960)★★★, *The Real Fats Waller* (RCA Victor 1965)★★★, *Fats Waller '34/'35* (RCA Victor 1965)★★★, *Valentine Stomp* (RCA Victor 1965)★★★, *Smashing Thirds* (RCA Victor 1966)★★★, *African Ripplets* (RCA Victor 1966)★★★, *Fine Arabian Stuff* 1939 recording (Muse 1981)★★★, *20 Golden Pieces* (Bulldog 1982)★★★, *Piano Solos (1929-1941)* (RCA 1983)★★★, *Live At The Yacht Club, Vol. 1* (Giants Of Jazz 1984)★★★, *Live At The Yacht Club, Vol. 2* (Giants Of Jazz 1984)★★★, *Fats Waller In London* 1922-1939 recordings (Disques Swing 1985)★★★, *My Very Good Friend The Milkman* (President 1986)★★★, *Armful O'Sweetness* (Saville 1987)★★★, *Dust Off That Old Piano* (Saville 1987)★★★, *Complete Early Band Works* 1927-1929 recordings (Halcyon 1987)★★★, *Take It Easy* (Saville 1988)★★★, *Fats Waller And His Rhythm 1934-1936 (Classic Years In Digital Stereo)* (BBC 1988)★★★, *Spreadin' Rhythm Around* (Saville 1989)★★★, *Ragtime Piano Entertainer* (Vogue 1989)★★★, *Loungin' At The Waldorf* (1990)★★★, *1939/40 - Private Acetates And Film Soundtracks* (1993)★★★, *The Ultimate Collection* (Pulse 1997)★★★★, *Piano Masterworks, Vol. 1* 1922-1929 recordings (EPM)★★★, *Giants Of Jazz* 3-LP box set (Time-Life)★★★★, *Classic Jazz From Rare Piano Rolls* 1923-1929 recordings (Music Masters)★★★, *Fats At The Organ* 1923-1927 recordings (ASV/Living Era)★★★, *Turn On The Heat: The Fats Waller Piano Solos* 1927-1941 recordings (Bluebird)★★★★, *Fats Waller And His Buddies* 1927-1929 recordings (Bluebird)★★★, *Greatest Hits* 1929-1943 recordings (RCA Victor)★★★, *Here 'Tis* 1929-1943 recordings (Jazz Archives)★★★, *Jugglin' Jive Of Fats Waller And His Orchestra* 1938 recordings (Sandy Hook)★★★, *Breakin' The Ice: The Early Years, Part 1* 1934/1935 recordings (Bluebird)★★★★, *I'm Gonna Sit Right Down: The Early Years, Part 2* 1935/1936 recordings (Bluebird)★★★★, *Fractious Fingering: The Early Years, Part 3* 1936 recordings (Bluebird 1997)★★★★, *Fats Waller And His Rhythm: The Middle Years, Part 1* 1936-1938 recordings (Bluebird)★★★★, *A Good Man Is Hard To Find: The Middle Years, Part 2* 1938-1940 recordings (Bluebird)★★★★, *The Last Years* 1940-1943 recordings (Bluebird)★★★★, *Last Testament: 1943* (Drive Archive)★★★, *The Definitive Fats Waller, Vol. 1: His Piano His Rhythm* 1935-1939 recordings (Stash)★★★★, *The Definitive Fats Waller, Vol. 2: Hallelujah* 1935-1939 recordings (Stash)★★★★.

● FURTHER READING: *The Music Of Fats Waller*, John R.T. Davies. *Fats Waller*, Charles Fox. *Fats Waller*, Maurice Waller and Anthony Calabrese. *Ain't Misbehavin': The Story Of Fats Waller*, E.W Kirkeby, D.P. Schiedt and S. Traill. *Fats Waller: His Life And Times*, Joel Vance. *Stride: The Music Of Fats Waller*, Paul S. Machlin. *Fats Waller: His Life & Times*, Alyn Shipton. *Misbehavin' With Fats*, Harold D. Sill.

● FILMS: *Hooray For Love* (1935), *King Of Burlesque* (1936) *Stormy Weather* (1943).

WALLINGTON, GEORGE

b. Giacinto Figlia, 27 October 1924, Palermo, Sicily, Italy, d. 15 February 1993, New York City, New York, USA. His family emigrated in 1925 and so Wallington was brought up in the USA. In the 40s he worked with Dizzy Gillespie on Manhattan's 42nd Street and went on to play piano for many other leaders. Although the flowing lines of his playing were reminiscent of Bud Powell, his style was developed independently and as well as being an accomplished pianist he was an interesting composer. He wrote 'Lemon Drop', which was a bestseller for Gene Krupa and 'Godchild' which was recorded by the Miles Davis Nonet. In 1953 he travelled to Europe with Lionel Hampton and then led a series of groups of his own including musicians such as Jackie McLean, Phil Woods and Donald Byrd. Wallington withdrew from the music business in 1960, but made something of a comeback in the 80s when he played at the Kool Festival (1985) and recorded several albums prior to his death in 1993.

● ALBUMS: *The George Wallington Trio* 10-inch album (Progressive 1952)★★★, *The George Wallington Trio* 10-inch album (Prestige 1952)★★★★, *The George Wallington Trio, Volume 2* 10-inch album (Prestige 1953)★★★★, *George Wallington And His All Star Band* 10-inch album (Blue Note 1954)★★★★, *The Workshop Of The George Wallington Trio* 10-inch album (Norgran 1954)★★★, *George Wallington With Strings* (Norgran 1954)★★★, *George Wallington Quintet At The Bohemia* (Progressive 1955)★★★★, *Variations* (Verve 1956)★★★, *Jazz For The Carriage Trade* (Prestige 1956)★★★★, *Jazz At Hotchkiss* (Savoy 1957)★★★★, *Knight Music* (Atlantic 1958)★★★, *The New York Scene* (New Jazz 1958)★★★★, with Jimmy Raney *Swingin' In Sweden* (EmArcy 1958)★★★, *The Prestidigitator* (East West 1964)★★★, *Virtuoso* (Interface 1984)★★★, *The Pleasure Of A Jazz Inspiration* (VSOP 1986)★★★, *The Symphony Of A Jazz Piano* (Denon 1988)★★★, with Jimmy Jones *Trios* (Vogue 1993)★★★.

WALLIS, BOB

b. 3 June 1934, Bridlington, Yorkshire, England. Wallis started his first band in Bridlington in 1950, which lasted right through to 1957. Later he joined Papa Bue's Viking Jazz Band (1956), Diz Disley's Jazz Band (1957) and, briefly, Acker Bilk's Band (1958). From 1958 he had his own Storyville Jazzmen who were very popular throughout the 'trad' boom of the late 50s. His own trumpet playing and singing forcefully reflected the influence of Henry 'Red' Allen. He had two minor UK hits with 'I'm Shy Mary Ellen I'm Shy' (1961, number 44) and 'Come Along Please' (1962, number 33). Change in popular taste brought the demise of the Storyville Jazzmen but Wallis played with a variety of bands including Monty Sunshine's. He then moved to Switzerland, where he played throughout the 80s.

● ALBUMS: *Everybody Loves Saturday Night* (Top Rank 1960)★★★★, *Bob Wallis's Storyville Jazzmen* (Storyville 1973)★★★★, *Live* (Storyville 1975)★★, *Jazz Doctor* (Storyville 1975)★★★, *Doctor Jazz* (Storyville 1988)★★★.

WALRATH, JACK

b. Jack Arthur Walrath, 5 May 1946, Stuart, Florida, USA. A hugely underrated modern jazz trumpeter, Walrath was one of the most talented instrumentalists to work with bassist Charles Mingus during the later part of the great bandleader's career. Like so many major figures in contemporary jazz, he is a graduate of Boston's Berklee College Of Music, which he attended in the early 60s. After graduating, he crossed from east to west and sunnier, Californian climes, and began to earn a reputation for his big tone and sure technique, touring with Ray Charles (for whom he did a certain amount of arranging) and working locally with bassist Gary Peacock. Moving back to New York in the early 70s, he worked commercially backing singers in soul and R&B bands, before he was discovered by Mingus, who helped revive the Jazz Workshop with Walrath's charismatic musical presence in 1974. Mingus allowed him more opportunity to stretch his composition and arrangement skills - many of Mingus's last recordings carry credits for Walrath's arrangements and direction. After Mingus's death in 1979, Walrath continued to work with Jazz Workshop drummer Dannie Richmond, co-leading the last Mingus band formation featuring saxophonist Ricky Ford, pianist Bob Neloms and Cameron Brown taking over the bass chair, as well as touring and recording under his name (with his band: the Masters Of Suspense). Walrath is a gifted, confident bop improviser with an infectious sense of humour. Recommended recordings must include the recent *Serious Hang*, a lively quintet performance featuring fellow ex-Mingus man Don Pullen on Hammond, guitarist David Fluczysnki, bassist Michael Formanek and drummer Cecil Brooks III.

● ALBUMS: *Demons In Pursuit* (Gatemouth 1979)★★★★, with Dannie Richmond *Dannie Richmond Plays Charles Mingus* (Timeless 1980)★★★, *Revenge Of The Fat People* (Stash 1981)★★★, *A Plea For Sanity* (Stash 1982)★★★★, *At The Umbria Jazz Festival, Vol. 1* (Red 1983)★★★, *At The Umbria Jazz Festival, Vol. 2* (Red 1983)★★★, *Wholly Trinity* (Muse 1986)★★★★, *Master Of Suspense* (Blue Note 1987)★★★, *Neohippus* (Blue Note 1988)★★★, *Out Of The Tradition* (Muse 1990)★★★★, *Serious Hang* (Muse 1992)★★★★, *In Montana* (Jazz Alliance 1996)★★★, with the Masters Of Suspense *Hipgnosis* (TCB 1996)★★, *Solidarity* (ACT 1997)★★★★.

WALTON, CEDAR

b. 17 January 1934, Dallas, Texas, USA. After being taught piano by his mother, Walton studied music formally. In the mid-50s his early career was interrupted by military service, but he was fortunate in that this allowed him to meet and play with several emerging jazz musicians, including Don Ellis. After leaving the armed forces, he played in and around New York with important bop artists such as Kenny Dorham, J.J. Johnson and Art Blakey. He proved an adept accompanist to singers as well as to instrumentalists and in the mid-60s was frequently performing with Abbey Lincoln. Later in the decade he worked with artists such as Lee Morgan, Hank Mobley and George Coleman. In the 70s he worked briefly with Blakey again, and played frequently with Clifford Jordan, but was mostly active as co-leader of groups such as Eastern Rebellion and Soundscapes. A gifted soloist and able accompanist, at home mainly in bop and post-bop settings, Walton's reputation with the public still lags behind the high regard with which he is held by his fellow artists.

● ALBUMS: *Cedar!* (Timeless 1967)★★★★, *Spectrum* (Prestige 1968)★★★, *Soul Cycle* (Prestige 1969)★★★, *The Electric Boogaloo Song* (Prestige 1969)★★★, *Breakthrough* (Muse 1972)★★★★, *A Night At Boomer's, Vol. 1* (Muse 1973)★★★, *A*

Night At Boomer's, Vol. 2 (Muse 1973)★★★, *Firm Roots* (1974)★★★, *Pit Inn* (1974)★★★, *Mobius* (1975)★★★★, *Eastern Rebellion* (Timeless 1975)★★★, *The Pentagon* (East Wind/Inner City 1976)★★★, *First Set* (Steeple Chase 1977)★★★★, *Second Set* (Steeple Chase 1977)★★★★, *Third Set* (Steeple Chase 1977)★★★★, *Animation* (Columbia 1977)★★★, *Soundscapes* (1979)★★★, *Piano Solos* (Clean Cuts 1981)★★★, *The Maestro* (Muse 1980)★★★★, *Firm Roots* (Muse 1981)★★★, *Among Friends* (Theresa 1982)★★★★, *Bluesville Time* (Criss Cross 1985)★★★★, *Cedar* (Timeless 1985)★★★★, *The Trio, Vol. 1* (Red 1985)★★★, *The Trio, Vol. 2* (Red 1985)★★★, *The Trio, Vol. 3* (Red 1985)★★★, *Blues For Myself* (Red 1986)★★★★, *Cedar Walton Plays* (Delos 1987)★★★, *Love* (Red 1987)★★★, *Cedar Walton Plays The Music Of Billy Strayhorn* (1988)★★★★, *Maybeck Recital Hall Series, Vol. 25* (1993)★★★, *Manhattan Afternoon* (Criss Cross 1993)★★★★, *As Long As There's Music* (Muse 1993)★★, *Ironclad* (Monarch 1995)★★★, *The Composer* (Astor Place 1996)★★★★, *Live At Yoshi's: Ironclad* (Monarch 1996)★★★, *The Art Blakey Legacy* (Evidence 1997)★★★.

WALTZ FOR DEBBY - BILL EVANS

Recorded on the same night as *Sunday At The Village Vanguard*, *Waltz For Debby* captures one of the most important and well-integrated piano trios in the history of jazz, working on a superbly inspired night. It is clear, listening to this record, that bassist Scott La Faro had a very special rapport with Evans, and drummer Paul Motian's subtle, improvised accompaniments and eccentric, quirkily quiet swing was the perfect engine for this subtle, impressionistic pianist. Check out the lovely, gentle 'My Foolish Heart', and the lively 'Milestones' and, of course, 'Waltz For Debby'.

- Tracks: *My Foolish Heart; Waltz For Debby; Detour Ahead; My Romance; Some Other Time; Milestones.*
- First released 1961
- UK peak chart position: did not chart
- USA peak chart position: did not chart

WARD, ALEX

b. 1974, Grantham, Lincolnshire, England. Ward is an impressive young clarinettist and alto saxophonist who demonstrates a remarkable maturity of musical thought. Ward first made his name while still at school, when he earned a reputation as the *enfant terrible* of Grantham's vibrant music scene. Notable from this period was the seminal one-off gig played by his much talked-about group, Commercial Suicide. He cites figures as diverse as Frank Zappa, Anthony Braxton and Olivier Messiaen among his influences. Ward followed his interest in improvisation under the guidance of Derek Bailey, performing with him at the 1988 Company season at London's Institute of Contemporary Arts, where he produced thoughtful and well-crafted improvisations in a variety of contexts. In 1991, Ward recorded a duo album with Steve Noble for the Incus label. On moving to Oxford in 1992 to study music at Worcester College, Ward met electronics FX-meister The Switch, with whom he has been collaborating on an ongoing basis ever since. As well as his current rock project, Camp Blackfoot, Ward has recently performed live as a member of innovative Oxford band Nought. Ward and The Switch's exciting improvisation outfit, the Thirteen Ghosts, takes the form of a duo augmented by a number of guest musicians, who have included Pat Thomas, Barbara Darling, Derek Bailey, Andrew Clare, and, for the *Legend Of The Blood Yeti* album, Sonic Youth's Thurston Moore. Ward has continued to display his rare talent for intelligent and well-crafted improvisation in solo and group contexts, recently touring with Eugene Chadbourne in Europe (1997, from which an album was issued) and Canada (1998). He has also taken part in a Company session for BBC Radio 3's *Music In Our Time* and has appeared on Channel 4 television. In 1997 he toured the UK with Butch Morris's Conduction project, which culminated in an impressive finale at the South Bank's Queen Elizabeth Hall.

- ALBUMS: with Steve Noble *Ya Boo, Reel & Rumble* (1991)★★★, with the Thirteen Ghosts *Giganti Reptilicus Destructo Beam* (Scatter 1995)★★★★, *Legend Of The Blood Yeti* (Infinite Chug 1997)★★★.

WARD, CARLOS

b. 1 May 1940, Ancon, Panama. Ward moved to Seattle at the age of 13 and started playing clarinet, switching to alto saxophone in 1955. While in the US Army he attended the Navy School of Music in Washington, DC, and played in military bands in Germany, also sitting in with *avant garde* outfits led by Albert Mangelsdorff and Karl Berger and hearing Eric Dolphy (a revelation) in Frankfurt. On returning to Seattle he sat in with John Coltrane, who invited him to join his octet. He moved to New York to do so (unfortunately this group was never recorded). In 1969 he toured and recorded with the funk band B.T. Express. Other engagements included work with Sam Rivers, Sunny Murray, Rashied Ali and a two-year stint in the late 70s with Carla Bley (*Social Studies*). He had met Abdullah Ibrahim and Don Cherry in Copenhagen in 1964: both encounters led to musical associations. In the 70s and early 80s he played with Ibrahim in a variety of ensembles - from duos to big bands to the pianist's group, Ekaya - and in 1985 he formed the co-operative Nu with Cherry, Ed Blackwell, Mark Helias (bass) and Nana Vasconcelos, lending astringent bebop lines to the world-music mix. In 1986 he replaced Jimmy Lyons in the Cecil Taylor Unit (*Live In Bologna*, *Live In Vienna* and *Tzotzil Mummers Tzotzil*). In 1987 he formed a quartet with Ronnie Burrage on drums. The live album *Lito*, recorded at the North Sea Jazz Festival in July 1988, features a guest appearance by Woody Shaw, on what proved to be one of the trumpeter's final recordings.

- ALBUMS: *Lito* (Leo 1988)★★★★, *Faces* (Puell Music 1995)★★★.

WARD, HELEN

b. 19 September 1916, New York City, New York, USA, d. 21 April 1998, Arlington, Virginia, USA. Ward studied piano as a child before taking up singing, and by her early teens was on radio in New York. When she was 17 she worked with the Latin band of violinist Enric Madriguera. In 1934 she was working as a staff singer at NBC's studios where Benny Goodman was playing on the Nabisco *Let's Dance* radio show. When the show ended and Goodman set out on his coast-to-coast tour, Ward went along as the band's singer and was thus on hand for his spectacular breakthrough in August 1935. However, by 1936 she had had enough of one-night stands and the other hassles of touring. She continued to make records with swing era bands and small groups, singing with Gene Krupa, Harry James, Teddy Wilson (all ex-Goodman sidemen) and Red Norvo. She married impresario-producer Albert Marx who reputedly recorded Goodman's 1938 Carnegie Hall concert as a gift for his wife, a record that, since its release in the mid-50s, has never been out of catalogue. She sang on through the 50s but then retired until the 80s and comeback recordings. Ward was a lively, engaging singer with an easy swing that demonstrated her rhythmical sense. Unlike some other big band singers, she stood the passage of time well and her records from the 30s are well worth hearing again.

● ALBUMS: *It's Been So Long* 10-inch album (Columbia 1954)★★★, with Wild Bill Davison *Wild Bill Davison With Helen Ward* 10-inch album (Pax 1954)★★★, *The Helen Ward Songbook* (Lyricon 1981)★★★.

WARDELL, ANITA

b. 1961, Guildford, Surrey, England. When Wardell was 12 years old, she and her family emigrated to Australia, where in due time she completed a four-year performance course in jazz and improvised music at Adelaide University. She began singing professionally and appeared at jazz festivals with Richie Cole and with James Morrison and Don Burrows, with whom she later sang on tracks on two albums. In 1989 she returned to the UK where she studied at the Guildhall School of Music and Drama. While there she was heard by Norma Winstone who declared, 'She sings without affectation, and with clarity of voice, which I love.' In the early 90s Wardell worked extensively in Europe and also visited the USA, singing at festivals at San José, Edinburgh and in Finland. She formed a close working relationship with John Stevens, performing drums/voice duos and they recorded together in 1994. Her debut album under her own name, in 1995, was an exceptional set of duets with pianist Liam Noble. A rich, expressive and agile voice allows her to excel not only with the great ballad standards, which she sings with remarkable expressiveness, but also with bop classics. The guru of contemporary jazz singers, Mark Murphy, has extolled the quality of her bop singing, stating that it is 'always so clear and accurate in its linearism'. Wardell also makes considerable use of scat singing in her programming and while many young singers launch into scat with only a faint notion of its strengths and limitations, she is an exceptionally gifted user of the form.

● ALBUMS: *Why Do I Cry?* (FMR-Ultimate Groove 1995)★★★★.

WARE, DAVID S.

b. David Spencer Ware, 7 November 1949, Plainfield, New Jersey, USA. Before studying at the Berklee College Of Music in the late 60s, Ware had already begun playing several members of the saxophone family. He formed his own band, Apogee, and played in the USA and Europe with both Cecil Taylor and Andrew Cyrille, recording 1978's *Metamusicians' Stomp* with the latter. In his playing style, Ware makes few concessions to any expectations of melodic and lyrical performances. Rather, there is a forceful and aggressively upfront attitude akin to contemporaneous styles in pop and rock. As a consequence, therefore, Ware's following tends to be strongest among members of his generation who are attuned to the dynamics of his style. There is often a thunderous presence to his music invoking aural images of Albert Ayler as torrents of notes pour forth threatening to overwhelm the unprepared listener. His mid-90s quartet featured players such as pianist Matthew Shipp and bassist William Parker. In 1998, Ware was signed by Branford Marsalis to Columbia Records, marking a potentially significant moment in the career of this leading figure in the *avant garde*.

● ALBUMS: *From Silence To Music* (Palm 1978)★★★, *The Birth Of A Being* (hatART 1979)★★★, *Passage To Music* (Silkheart 1989)★★★, *Great Bliss Vol. 1* (Silkheart 1991)★★★, *Flight Of i* (DIW 1992)★★★★, *Third Ear Recitation* (DIW 1993)★★★★, *Earthquation* (DIW 1994)★★★★, *Cryptology* (Homestead 1995)★★★, *DAO* (Homestead 1996)★★★, *Godspelized* (DIW 1998)★★★★, *Go See The World* (Columbia 1998)★★★.

WARE, WILBUR

b. 8 September 1923, Chicago, Illinois, USA, d. 9 September 1979, Philadelphia, Pennsylvania, USA. When Ware's multi-instrumentalist foster-father organized church music Wilbur became interested, and learned to play the banjo and double bass. He then performed in amateur string groups in Chicago. In the 40s he was playing with Stuff Smith (violin), Roy Eldridge (trumpet) and Sonny Stitt (alto saxophone) in the midwest. He started leading his own groups in 1953 at the Bee Hive Club and the Flame Lounge in Chicago, and also gigged with Thelonious Monk and Johnny Griffin. Between 1954 and 1955 he toured with the bebop-altoist-cum-R&B-singer Eddie 'Cleanhead' Vinson and with the Jazz Messengers in the summer of 1956. He and Art Blakey formed the rhythm section of the renowned Monk group that included both Coleman Hawkins and John Coltrane (1957). He also played with Buddy De Franco that year and recorded with Sonny Rollins. In 1959 he returned to Chicago and was inactive for a while. In the late 60s he went back to New York, playing with Monk (1970) and recording with longtime associate, tenor saxophonist Clifford Jordan in 1969 and 1976. Ware participated in some of the crucial music of his time and developed the bass as a force both in solo and ensemble work.

● ALBUMS: *Chicago Sounds* reissued as *The Chicago Cookers* (Riverside 1957)★★★★.

WARING, FRED

b. Frederic Malcolm Waring, 9 June 1900, Tyrone, Pennsylvania, USA, d. 29 July 1984, Danville, Pennsylvania, USA. Waring began playing banjo at the age of 16 and soon formed his own dance band. He graduated to violin and was still at school when, after being turned down for membership of the Glee Club, he augmented his band to give it greater vocal content. This unit he called the Pennsylvanians and, conceived though it may have been as an act of reprisal, it certainly outlived its original purpose. By the 30s Waring's Pennsylvanians, by now boasting a fully-fledged choir, were a popular broadcasting group, had appeared on Broadway and made a film. In addition, the ensemble was in the cast of the 1930 musical *The New Yorkers*, which had a score by Cole Porter. The band had a number of hit recordings, their popularity contin through the 40s and into the early 50s. Although musical tastes had changed drastically and Waring's music, redolent as it was of straw hats, lazy summer days and automobiles with running boards, was out of fashion, he soldiered on. Eventually, he made his farewell appearance in 1980 with a concert at Carnegie Hall. In 1981 he was awarded the Medal of Honour by President Ronald Reagan. Waring was a musical perfectionist and, as one writer has observed, laboured long and mightily on material which was seldom worthy of the care he lavished upon it.

● ALBUMS: *Fred Waring And The Pennsylvanians In Hi-Fi* (1957)★★★, *Now Is The Caroling Season* (1957)★★★, *South Pacific* (1958)★★, *All Through The Night* (1958)★★★, with Frank Sinatra and Bing Crosby *America, I Hear You Singing* (1964)★★, *White Christmas* (1964)★★★.

WARLOP, MICHEL

b. 23 January 1911, Douai, France, d. 20 March 1947. A thoroughly schooled violinist, Warlop spent much of his early career playing with popular entertainers of the day. During the early years of World War II he turned more towards classical music both as a performer and composer. However, during the late 30s he played with some of Europe's leading jazz musicians and also with visiting Americans, sometimes appearing with them on recording dates. Particularly noteworthy are his records with Django Reinhardt and Stéphane Grappelli, where his playing is technically superior to that of Grappelli (whose technique was to improve out of all recognition as the years passed). He also played in a violin trio with Grappelli and Eddie South where his classical background fitted well with South's similar training. In 1938 Warlop also played with pianist Garland Wilson.

● COMPILATIONS: *The Chronological Django Reinhardt 1937-1938* (Classics 1937-38)★★★★, *Eddie South In Paris* (DRG 1929, 1937)★★★.

WARREN, EARLE

b. Earle Ronald Warren, 1 July 1914, Springfield, Ohio, USA, d. 4 June 1994, Springfield, Ohio, USA. As a child Warren played a number of instruments in a family band, but by his teens had settled on the alto saxophone. From 1930 he played in numerous territory bands until, in 1937, he joined Count Basie. Playing lead alto and nicknamed 'Smiley', he stayed with Basie until 1945 and thereafter returned several times in between leading his own band for short engagements. Throughout the 50s he played in various all-star bands, often teamed with other former Basie musicians, among them Buck Clayton, Jimmy Rushing and Dicky Wells. He only left Basie's side for good when his wife became ill, and went on to join vocal group the Platters (on baritone sax). He also managed Johnny Otis' show band. In the 70s and on through the 80s Warren continued to perform, sometimes as a soloist, sometimes in packages featuring other swing era veterans. A striking player with a rich tone, Warren's many years as section leader with Basie have sometimes obscured his importance. Although he was often subordinated in this setting to the solo voices of artists such as Lester Young and Buddy Tate, his solos were always worthy of attention and displayed both an inventive mind and great musical skill. After living in Switzerland for nearly a decade he returned to his home town of Springfield in 1992 for the last two years of his life.

● ALBUMS: *Earle Warren And The Anglo-American All Stars* (1974)★★★, *Earle Warren* (1974)★★★, *Earle Warren & The Counts Men* (Muse 1985)★★★.

● FILMS: *Born To Swing* (1970).

WARREN, GUY

b. Kofi Ghanaba, 1923, Accra, Ghana. Warren was a visionary musician so far ahead of his time that he was for most of his career obliged to scrape a living on the margins of the jazz and African music scenes. As early as the 40s Warren was playing the sort of tough-edged African-jazz fusion which only really took off in the 70s and 80s. In 1938, already well on his way to becoming a master of traditional West African percussion and Afro-American kit drums, he joined the Accra Rhythmic Orchestra, with whom he stayed (after his first visit to the USA in 1939) until 1945. In 1947, he spent a few months with E.T. Mensah's Tempos, but found their mixture of highlife and dance band music insufficiently adventurous for his tastes, and made his way to London, where he soon became a member of Kenny Graham's innovative Afro-Cubists. He returned to Accra in 1949, briefly rejoining the Tempos and also working for Kwame Nkrumah's emergent nationalist organization, the Convention People's Party.

After a three-year sojourn in Nigeria and Liberia (where he worked as a radio disc jockey), he returned to the USA in 1953, settling in Chicago, and forming a variety of line-ups, all of which aimed to fuse traditional West African rhythms and songs with jazz sensibilities. He recorded a number of albums, none of which, tragically, remain available. In 1965, he returned once more to Ghana, but his style was by now so far ahead of anyone else in the country that he was unable to find either regular performing opportunities or a sympathetic record label.

He mounted the occasional concert in Accra, and in 1971 performed at the historic Soul To Soul concert featuring black American and African musicians, but spent more and more of his time as a near recluse at his home in Achimota - practising Buddhist meditation and teaching a small number of younger, similarly adventurous Ghanaian musicians, together with visiting overseas jazz musicians keen to learn the profundities of African rhythm. Warren's musical vision has now been taken up and developed by his master-drummer son, Glen.

● ALBUMS: *Africa Speaks America Answers* (1957)★★★, *Theme For African Drums* (1959)★★★, *African Sounds* (1961)★★★, *Third Phase* (1963)★★, *Afro-Jazz* (1963)★★★.

WARREN, JOHN

b. 23 September 1938, Montreal, Canada. Self-taught although he did study music in Canada at the McGill College in the late 50s. After relocating to England he led his own John Warren Big Band which contained the cream of the new British jazz movement including Henry Lowther, Mick and Chris Pyne, Kenny Wheeler, Alan Skidmore and John Surman. A lasting friendship has continued into the 90s, they both share much in common with their love for the baritone saxophone, an instrument that is cruelly neglected. In addirion to working with Mike Westbrook and numerous others he regularly composes and arranges for Surman's ambitious and sometimes glorious Brass Project. In recent years he has subsidised his work as a composer by teaching. He lives at present in Yorkshire.

● ALBUMS: with John Surman *Tales Of The Algonquin* (1971)★★★, with Surman *The Brass Project* (ECM 1993)★★★★.

WARWICK, CARL 'BAMA'

b. William Carl Warwick, 27 October 1917, Brookside, Alabama, USA. One of the many unsung sidemen of the big bands, Warwick grew up in New Jersey. He became a trumpet player and played in New York and also in eastern state bands until the late 30s, when he moved into a succession of name bands, including the Mills Blue Rhythm Band and those led by Don Redman, Bunny Berigan and Teddy Hill. During military service in World War II, Warwick was director of an army band. Upon his release he began another round of big band duties that took him into the orchestras of Woody Herman and Buddy Rich. In the 50s he was busy in big and small bands, even leading his own group. Among the leaders for whom he worked were Lucky Millinder, with whom he had played briefly in the 30s, Brew Moore, Dizzy Gillespie and Louie Bellson. In the early 60s he led a band for a few years and then, in 1966, became music director for the New York City Correctional Institute. In the 70s he made occasional appearances with pick up bands.

WASHINGTON, DINAH

b. Ruth Lee Jones, 29 August 1924, Tuscaloosa, Alabama, USA, d. 14 December 1963, Detroit, Michigan, USA. Raised in Chicago, Dinah Washington first sang in church choirs for which she also played piano. She then worked in local clubs, where she was heard by Lionel Hampton, who promptly hired her. She was with Hampton from 1943-46, recording hits with 'Evil Gal Blues', written by Leonard Feather, and 'Salty Papa Blues'. After leaving Hampton she sang R&B, again achieving record success, this time with 'Blow Top Blues' and 'I Told You Yes I Do'. In the following years Washington continued with R&B, but also sang jazz, blues, popular songs of the day, standards, and was a major voice of the burgeoning, but as yet untitled, soul movement. However, her erratic lifestyle caught up with her and she died suddenly at the age of 39. Almost from the start of her career, Washington successfully blended the sacred music of her childhood with the sometimes earthily salacious secularity of the blues. This combination was a potent brew and audiences idolized her, thus helping her towards riches rarely achieved by black artists of her generation. She thoroughly enjoyed her success, spending money indiscriminately on jewellery, cars, furs, drink, drugs and men. She married many times and had countless liaisons. Physically, she appeared to thrive on her excesses, as can be seen from her performance in the film of the 1958 Newport Jazz Festival, *Jazz On A Summer's Day*. She was settling down happily with her seventh husband when she took a lethal combination of pills, probably by accident, after having too much to drink.

Washington's voice was rich and she filled everything she sang with heartfelt emotion. Even when the material was not of the highest quality, she could make the most trite of lyrics appear deeply moving. Amongst her popular successes were 'What A Diff'rence A Day Makes', her biggest solo hit, which reached number 8 in the USA in May 1959, and 'September In The Rain', which made number 35 in the UK in November 1961. Washington usually sang alone but in the late 50s she recorded some duets with her then husband, Eddie Chamblee. These records enjoyed a measure of success and were followed in 1960 with songs with Brook Benton, notably 'Baby (You've Got What It Takes)' and 'A Rockin' Good Way (To Mess Around And Fall In Love)', both of which proved to be enormously popular, reaching numbers 5 and 7, respectively, in the US charts. Washington left a wealth of recorded material, ranging from *The Jazz Sides*, which feature Clark Terry, Jimmy Cleveland, Blue Mitchell and others, to albums of songs by or associated with Fats Waller and Bessie Smith. On these albums, as on almost everything she recorded, Washington lays claim to being one of the major jazz voices, and probably the most versatile of all the singers to have worked in jazz.

● ALBUMS: *Dinah Washington Songs* 10-inch album (Mercury 1950)★★★★, *Dynamic Dinah* 10-inch album (Mercury 1952)★★★, *Blazing Ballads* 10-inch album (Mercury 1952)★★★, *After Hours With Miss D* 10-inch album (EmArcy 1954)★★★★, *Dinah Jams* (EmArcy 1955)★★★★★, *For Those In Love* (EmArcy 1955)★★★, *Dinah* (EmArcy 1956)★★★, *In The Land Of Hi-Fi* (EmArcy 1956)★★★★, *The Swingin' Miss "D"*

(EmArcy 1956)★★★★, *The Fats Waller Songbook* reissued as *Dinah Washington Sings Fats Waller* (EmArcy 1957)★★★★, *Music For A First Love* (Mercury 1957)★★★, *Music For Late Hours* (Mercury 1957)★★★★, *The Best In Blues* (Mercury 1958)★★★, *Dinah Washington Sings Bessie Smith* (EmArcy 1958)★★★, *Newport '58* (Mercury 1958)★★★★, *The Queen!* (Mercury 1959)★★★★, *What A Difference A Day Makes!* (Mercury 1959)★★★★, *Unforgettable* (Mercury 1960)★★★, with Brook Benton *The Two Of Us* (Mercury 1960)★★★★, *I Concentrate On You* (Mercury 1961)★★, *For Lonely Lovers* (Mercury 1961)★★★, *September In The Rain* (Mercury 1961)★★★, *Tears & Laughter* (Mercury 1962)★★★, *Dinah '62* (Roulette 1962)★★★, *In Love* (Roulette 1962)★★, *Drinking Again* (Roulette 1962)★★★, *I Wanna Be Loved* (Mercury 1962)★★★, *Back To The Blues* (Roulette 1963)★★★, *Dinah '63* (Roulette 1963)★★, *Mellow Mama* 1945 recording (Delmark 1992)★★★★.

● COMPILATIONS: with the Quincy Jones Orchestra *This Is My Story, Volume One* (Mercury 1963)★★★★, *This Is My Story, Volume Two* (Mercury 1963)★★★★, *Dinah Washington's Golden Hits, Volume 1* (Mercury 1963)★★★★, *Dinah Washington's Golden Hits, Volume 2* (Mercury 1963)★★★★, *In Tribute* (Roulette 1963)★★★, *The Good Old Days* (Mercury 1963)★★★, *Stranger On Earth* (Roulette 1964)★★★, *The Best Of Dinah Washington* (Roulette 1965)★★★, *The Queen And Quincy* (Mercury 1965)★★★, *The Original Queen Of Soul* (Mercury 1969)★★★, *The Jazz Sides* (EmArcy 1976)★★★★, *Spotlight On Dinah Washington* (Philips 1977)★★★★, *A Slick Chick: R&B Years* 1943-1954 recordings (EmArcy 1983)★★★★, *The Best Of Dinah Washington* (Mercury 1987)★★★★, *The Complete Dinah Washington On Mercury, Vol. 1* 1946-1949 recordings (Mercury 1990)★★★★, *The Complete Dinah Washington On Mercury, Vol. 2* 1950-1952 recordings (Mercury 1990)★★★★, *The Complete Dinah Washington On Mercury, Vol. 3* 1952-1954 recordings (Mercury 1990)★★★★, *The Complete Dinah Washington On Mercury, Vol. 4* 1954-1956 recordings (Mercury 1990)★★★★, *The Complete Dinah Washington On Mercury, Vol. 5* 1956-1958 recordings (Mercury 1990)★★★★, *The Complete Dinah Washington On Mercury, Vol. 6* 1958-1960 recordings (Mercury 1990)★★★, *The Complete Dinah Washington On Mercury, Vol. 7* 1961 recordings (Mercury 1990)★★★, *Best Of Dinah Washington* (Roulette 1992)★★★★, *The Dinah Washington Story* (Mercury 1993)★★★★, *First Issue: The Dinah Washington Story, The Original Recordings* 1943-1961 recordings (Mercury 1993)★★★★, *Blue Gardenia* (EmArcy/Verve 1995)★★★, *Ultimate Dinah Washington* (Verve 1997)★★★, *Jazz Profile, Vol. 5* 1962-1963 recordings (Blue Note 1997)★★★★, *Verve Jazz Masters 19: Dinah Washington* 1946-1959 recordings (Verve)★★★★.

● FURTHER READING: *Queen Of The Blues: A Biography Of Dinah Washington*, James Haskins.

WASHINGTON, GEORGE

b. 18 October 1907, Brunswick, Georgia, USA. Raised in Jacksonville, Florida. Washington began learning to play trombone at the age of 10, against his parents wishes. After playing professionally with the local band led by Calvin 'Eagle Eye' Shields, Washington went north to Philadelphia in 1925 to play with J.W. Pepper's band, and then went to New York City. There he studied trombone and arrangement at the New York Conservatory of Musical Art by day and played jazz by night with the bands of Luckey Roberts (1926), Charlie 'Fess' Johnson (various times between 1926-29), Don Redman (1931), Benny Carter (1933), Mills Blue Rhythm Band (various times between 1932-36), Fletcher Henderson (1937), and Louis Armstrong (1937-43). In the mid-40s, Washington moved to Los Angeles where he did several stints with Horace Henderson and Benny Carter before joining Johnny Otis's Orchestra in 1945, with whom he demonstrated his other talent; as a vocalist on jump tunes like 'Good Boogie Googie' (1946) and 'It Ain't The Beauty' (1951). Washington remained with Otis throughout the 50s and left to play with Joe Darensbourg's jazz band in 1960, thereafter working freelance in the music and movie industries.

WASHINGTON, GROVER, JNR.

b. 12 December 1943, Buffalo, New York, USA. Growing up in a musical family, Washington was playing tenor saxophone before he was a teenager. He studied formally and also paid his dues gigging locally on tenor and other instruments in the early 60s. After military service in the late 60s he returned to his career, recording a succession of albums under the aegis of producer Creed Taylor which effectively crossed over into the new market for jazz fusion. By the mid-70s, Washington's popular success had begun to direct the course of his music-making and he moved further away from jazz. Commercially, this brought continuing successes. 'The Two Of Us', with vocals by Bill Withers, reached number 2 in the US pop charts in 1981, and *The Best Is Yet To Come* with Patti Labelle. Over the years Washington has had several gold albums, and 1980's *Winelight* sold over a million copies, achieving platinum status and gaining two Grammy awards. Washington's playing displays great technical mastery, and early in his career his often blues-derived saxophone styling sometimes gave his playing greater depths than the quality of the material warranted. The fact that much of his recorded output proved to be popular in the setting of discos tended to smooth out his playing as the years passed, depleting the characteristics that had attracted so much attention at the start of his career. By the late 80s Washington was still enjoying a degree of popular success, although not at the same high level as a few years before.

● ALBUMS: *Inner City Blues* (Motown 1971)★★, *All The King's Horses* (Motown 1972)★★, *Soul Box* (1973)★★, *Mister Magic* (Mister Magic 1975)★★★, *Feels So Good* (Motown 1975)★★★, *A Secret Place* (Motown 1976)★★★, *Live At The Bijou* (Motown 1977)★★★, with Locksmith *Reed Seed* (Motown 1978)★★, *Paradise* (Elektra 1979)★★★★, *Skylarkin'* (Motown 1980)★★★, *Winelight* (Elektra 1980)★★★★, *Come Morning* (Elektra 1981)★★★, *The Best Is Yet To Come* (Elektra 1982)★★★, *Inside Moves* (Elektra 1984)★★★, *Playboy Jazz Festival* (Elektra 1984)★★★, with Kenny Burrell *Togethering* (Blue Note 1984)★★, *Strawberry Moon* (Columbia 1987)★★, *Then And Now* (Columbia 1988)★★, *Time Out Of Mind* (Columbia 1989)★★, *Next Exit* (Columbia 1992)★★, *All My Tomorrows* (Columbia

1994)★★★, *Soulful Strut* (Columbia 1996)★★★, *Breath Of Heaven A Holiday Collection* (Sony Jazz 1997)★★.
● COMPILATIONS: *Baddest* (1980)★★★, *Anthology* (Motown 1981)★★★, *Greatest Performances* (Motown 1983)★★★, *At His Best* (Motown 1985)★★★, *Anthology* (Elektra 1985)★★★.

WASHINGTON, JACK

b. Ronald Washington, 17 July 1910, Kansas City, Kansas, USA, d. 28 November 1964. As a young child Washington began playing saxophones, including the soprano and alto, although it was as a baritone saxophonist that he is best remembered. He played with a number of Kansas City bands including Jesse Stone's and the Bennie Moten band, where he remained for almost eight years. He was then briefly with other leaders before rejoining the band, which had by then become Count Basie's. He stayed with Basie until interrupted by military service, then came back to the band until the end of the 40s. During his military service Washington had played in a service band in Oklahoma and he returned to the region on leaving Basie and took work outside music. He continued to make local appearances and also travelled to recording sessions during the rest of his life. Although the baritone saxophone chair in many big bands is one of comparative anonymity, Washington was an exceptionally gifted player with a distinctive sound and style and his occasional solo spots with Basie and others are worth seeking out. He played the instrument with an airy ease and his tone reflected the cool approach to the saxophone being then propounded by Lester Young, a colleague in the Basie saxophone section.
● ALBUMS: *Count Basie At The Famous Door* (Jazz Archives 1938-39)★★★★, *Count Basie* (RCA 1947-50)★★★★.
● COMPILATIONS: *The Chronological Count Basie 1939-40* (Classics 1939-40)★★★, *The Chronological Count Basie 1940-1941* (Classics 1940-41)★★★.

WASO

In the early 70s Waso emerged from a larger grouping of gypsy musicians headed by Piotto Lindberger (violin). His son Viri was the rhythm guitarist and Michel Verstraeten played bass. The lead role was taken at first by guitarist Fapy Lafertin (who left to pursue a solo career) and then passed to Koen de Cauter who took up the clarinet as well as playing solo guitar. In the 80s the British saxophonist Bill Greenow took over the leadership. The band has always mixed the style of the Quintet of the Hot Club of Paris with Hungarian/Romany styles and has been especially popular playing the club circuits.
● ALBUMS: *Waso Live In Laren* (1980)★★★.

WASSY, BRICE

b. 1958, Yaounde, Cameroon. Already playing percussion with local bands by the age of five, Wassy moved to Paris in 1974, hooking up with other expatriate African musicians and playing with Manu Dibango and Wally Baderou, among others. Wassy acted as band leader for Salif Keita from 1984-90. He also played on the 'Tam Tam Pour Ethiopie' charity single and Talking Heads' *Naked*, as well as working with jazz musicians including Don Cherry, Jean-Luc Ponty and Graham Haynes. *N'ga Funk*, his debut, mixed jazz, funk and African elements. Recorded in Paris with a group of other locally based African musicians, it also featured guests Dibango and Haynes. *Shrine Dance*, the follow-up, was recorded at Real World Studios in England with predominantly British jazz musicians, including Steve Williamson and Byron Wallen.
● ALBUMS: *N'ga Funk* (MELT 2000 1996)★★★, *Shrine Dance* (MELT 2000 1997)★★★.

WATANABE, KAZUMI

b. 14 October 1953, Tokyo, Japan. After studying guitar extensively at Tokyo's Yamaha Music School Watanabe began his professional career playing in jazz-rock bands, sometimes under his own leadership. His bands, which included Kylyn and Mobo, became very popular in Japan and he also took them to the USA. In 1989 he performed at the Montreux Jazz Festival and in 1990 presented a musical drama, *Django 1953*, in which he extolled past virtues of jazz guitar. In the early 90s he toured Europe with pianist Yosuke Yamashita. Watanabe is a powerful performer with free-flowing ideas backed by remarkable technical ability.
● ALBUMS: *Infinite* (Toshiba Express 1971)★★★, *Endless Way* (Columbia 1975)★★★, *Milky Shade* (Teichiku-Union 70s)★★★, *Olives Step* (Columbia/Better Days 1977)★★★, *Kylyn* (Columbia/Better Days 70s)★★★, *To Chi Ka* (Columbia 1980)★★★★, *Dogatana* (Columbia/Better Days 1980)★★★, *Mobo 1 & 2* (Trio/Domo 1983)★★★, *Mobo-Splash* (Polydor/Domo 1985)★★★, *Spice Of Life* (Polydor/Domo 1987)★★★★, *Spice Of Life Too* (Polydor/Domo 1988)★★★, *Dandyism* (Polydor/Domo c.1988)★★★, *Esprit* (Polydor/Domo 1989)★★★, *Kilowatt* (Polydor/Domo 1989)★★★, *Pandora* (Polydor/Domo 1991)★★★, *O Ya Tsu* (Polydor/Domo 1994)★★★, *Mermaid Boulevard* (ALFA 1997)★★★, *Lonesome Cat* (ALFA 1998)★★★.

WATANABE, SADAO

b. 1 December 1933, Tochigi, Japan. His father was a professional music teacher and Watanabe took up the clarinet to play in the school band before moving on to the alto saxophone. He moved to Tokyo in 1951 and took flute lessons with a member of the Tokyo Philharmonic. Watanabe joined the quartet of Toshiko Akiyoshi and became its leader when she left in 1956. He went to study at the Berklee College Of Music in the early 60s and worked with musicians including Gabor Szabo, Chico Hamilton and Gary McFarland. Returning to Tokyo in 1965, he became director of the Yamaha Institute for Popular Music which was modelled on the Berklee College. He has led his own band since and has toured widely. He revealed that two trips to Africa in 1971 and 1974 were particularly influential on his music. In the 70s his music moved towards pop, or at least to a fusion sound which brought him enormous popularity, of which *Fill Up The Night*, a number 1 jazz album in the USA and Japan, is a good example. In 1977 he became the first jazz musician to receive a National Award in Japan. Watanabe plays with a round, polished tone incorporating vocal effects to heighten the emotional intensity. He has recorded more than 60 albums both with his own bands and with other musicians including, McFarland, Hamilton and Chick Corea.

● ALBUMS: with Chico Hamilton *El Chico* (1965)★★, with Chick Corea *Round Trip* (1970)★★, *Plays Ballads* (Denon 1970)★★★, *Bossa Nova Concert* (Denon 1970)★★★★, *Dedicated To Charlie Parker* (Denon 1970)★★★★, *Pastoral* (1970)★★★, *Round Trip* (Vanguard 1974)★★★, *Pamoja* (1975)★★★, *I'm Old Fashioned* (1976)★★, *My Dear Life* (1977)★★, *Bird Of Paradise* (Elektra 1977)★★★★, *California Shower* (Miracle 1978)★★★, *Morning Island* (1979)★★★, *Live At The Budokan* (1980)★★, *Orange Express* (Columbia 1981)★★★, *Fill Up The Night* (1983)★★, *Rendezvous* (1983)★★★, *Maisha* (Warners 1985)★★★★, *Parker's Mood* (Elektra 1986)★★★★, *Tokyo Dating* (Elektra 1986)★★★★, *Good Time For Love* (Elektra 1987)★★, *Birds Of Passage* (Elektra 1987)★★★★, *Modern Jazz Album* (Denon 1988)★★★, *Elis* (Elektra 1988)★★★★, *Made In Coracao* (Elektra 1989)★★★, *Selected* (Elektra 1989)★★★★, *Sweet Deal* (East West 1991)★★★, *Earth Step* (Verve Forecast 1993)★★★, *In Tempo* (WMD 1994)★★★, *A Night With Strings Vol 2* (1995)★★.

WATERS, BENNY

b. 23 January 1902, Brighton, Maryland, USA, d. 11 August 1998, Columbia, Maryland, USA. A talented multi-instrumentalist, by his mid-teenage years Waters was adept on most of the saxophone family and also played piano and sang. During the 20s he played in various bands, studied formally and taught, numbering Harry Carney among his pupils. In these early years he played with Joe 'King' Oliver, Charlie Johnson and Clarence Williams, and in the following decade worked in the bands of Fletcher Henderson, Johnson again, and Oran 'Hot Lips' Page. In the 40s he worked with artists such as Jimmie Lunceford and Claude Hopkins. He led his own band for a while and also worked with some R&B bands. In the early 50s, while touring Europe in Jimmy Archey's traditional band, he decided to settle in France. He continued to tour from this base throughout the 60s and 70s and became a favourite at many UK clubs and festivals, where he appeared frequently into the 80s and 90s. In the early summer of 1991 he was featured at London's Barbican Centre in concert with fellow octogenarian Doc Cheatham, the pair made nonsense of their ages. A spirited soloist, favouring the tenor among the several saxophones he played, Waters possessed a dazzling technique underscored by a fervent feeling for the blues. His enthusiasm, skill and intensity were creditable in a jazzman of any age; coming from a musician in his nineties they were little short of miraculous. Despite an eye operation in 1992 that left him blind, Waters continued playing and recording up until his death in 1998.

● ALBUMS: *Night Sessions In Swing And Dixieland* (1960)★★★, *Benny Waters And The Latin Jazz Band I* (1960)★★★, *Benny Waters And The Latin Jazz Band II* (1960)★★★, *Together On Records For 25 Years* (1961)★★★★, *Benny Waters In Paris* (1967)★★, *Zigging And Zagging* (1968)★★★, *The Many Faces Of Benny Waters* (1969)★★, *The Benny Waters Quartet* (1972)★★★★, *Benny Waters Et Le Jazz De Pique* (1974)★★★, *Jazz Sur Le RTF* (1974)★★★, *Benny Waters And His Swedish Band I* (1974)★★★, *Swinging Along With Benny Waters* (1974)★★★, *Benny Waters And His Swedish Band II* (1975)★★, *The Two Sides Of Benny Waters* (1976)★★★, *Lady Be Good* (1976)★★★, *Bouncing Benny* (1979)★★★, *When You're Smiling* (Hep 1980)★★★, *On The Sunny Side Of The Street* (JSP 1981)★★★, *Live At The Esplanade With Cy Laurie And The Eggy Ley Hot Quintet* (1981)★★, *Live At The Edinburgh Festival* (1982)★★, *Mature* (1983)★★★, *From Paradise (Small's) To Shangri-La* (Muse 1987)★★★★, *Memories Of The Twenties* (Stomp Off 1988)★★★, *Swinging Again* (Jazzpoint 1993)★★★, *Benny Waters Plays Songs Of Love* (Jazzpoint 1993)★★★, *Birdland Birthday: Live At 95* (Enja 1997)★★★.

WATERS, ETHEL

b. 31 October 1896, Chester, Pennsylvania, USA, d. 1 September 1977. One of the most influential of popular singers, Waters' early career found her working in vaudeville. As a consequence, her repertoire was more widely based and popularly angled than those of many of her contemporaries. It is reputed that she was the first singer to perform W.C. Handy's 'St Louis Blues' in public, and she later popularized blues and jazz-influenced songs such as 'Stormy Weather' and 'Travellin' All Alone', also scoring a major success with 'Dinah'. She first recorded in 1921, and on her early dates she was accompanied by artists such as Fletcher Henderson, Coleman Hawkins, James P. Johnson and Duke Ellington. Significantly, for her acceptance in white circles, she also recorded with Jack Teagarden, Benny Goodman and Tommy Dorsey.

From the late 20s, Waters appeared in several Broadway musicals, including *Africana*, *Blackbirds Of 1930*, *Rhapsody In Black*, *As Thousands Cheer*, *At Home Abroad*, and *Cabin In The Sky*, in which she introduced several diverting songs such as 'I'm Coming Virginia', 'Baby Mine', 'My Handy Man Ain't Handy No More', 'Till The Real Thing Comes Along', 'Suppertime', 'Harlem On My Mind', 'Heat Wave', 'Got A Bran' New Suit' (with Eleanor Powell), 'Hottentot Potentate', and 'Cabin In The Sky'. In the 30s she stopped the show regularly at the Cotton Club in Harlem with 'Stormy Weather', and appeared at Carnegie Hall in 1938. She played a few dramatic roles in the theatre, and appeared in several films, including *On With The Show*, *Check And Double Check*, *Gift Of The Gab*, *Tales Of Manhattan*, *Cairo*, *Cabin In The Sky*, *Stage Door Canteen*, *Pinky*, *Member Of The Wedding*, and *The Sound And The Fury* (1959). In the 50s she was also in the US television series *Beulah* for a while, and had her own Broadway show, *An Evening With Ethel Waters* (1957).

Throughout the 60s and on into the mid-70s she sang as a member of the organization which accompanied evangelist Billy Graham. Although less highly regarded in blues and jazz circles than either Bessie Smith or Louis Armstrong, in the 30s Waters transcended the boundaries of these musical forms to far greater effect than either of these artists and spread her influence throughout popular music. Countless young hopefuls emulated her sophisticated, lilting vocal style and her legacy lived on in the work of outstanding and, ironically, frequently better-known successors, such as Connee Boswell, Ruth Etting, Adelaide Hall, Mildred Bailey, Lee Wiley, Lena Horne and Ella Fitzgerald. Even Billie Holiday (with whom Waters was less than impressed, commenting, 'She sings as though her shoes are too tight'), acknowledged her influence. A buoyant, high-spirited singer with a light, engaging voice that frequently sounds 'whiter' than most of her contemporaries, Waters' career was an object lesson in determination and inner drive. Her appalling childhood problems and troubled early life, recounted in the first part of her autobiography, *His Eye Is On The Sparrow*, were overcome through grit and the application of her great talent.

● ALBUMS: *His Eye Is On The Sparrow* (1963)★★★, *Ethel Waters Reminisces* (1963)★★★.

● COMPILATIONS: *Ethel Waters* (1979)★★★, *The Complete Bluebird Sessions (1938-39)* (1986)★★★★, *On The Air (1941-51)* (1986)★★★★, *Ethel Waters On Stage And Screen (1925-40)* (1989)★★★★, *Who Said Blackbirds Are Blue?* (1989)★★★, *Classics 1921-23,* (Classics 1993)★★★, *Classics 1923-25,* (Classics 1993)★★★, *Ethel Waters 1926-29* (Classics 1993)★★★.

● FURTHER READING: *His Eye Is On The Sparrow*, Ethel Waters. *To Me It's Wonderful*, Ethel Waters.

WATES, MATT

b. 7 February 1964, London, England. An exceptionally gifted alto saxophonist and composer, Wates worked with the National Youth Jazz Orchestra and also studied at Berklee College Of Music, graduating from there in 1988. He gained experience playing with a wide range of artists including Humphrey Lyttelton, Paz, Roadside Picnic, Itchy Fingers and Sax Appeal, recording with the last four artists. He formed his own sextet, playing soft and hard bop, many of his own compositions and featuring Martin Shaw and bassist Malcolm Creese, for whose ABCDs label he made two albums in the 90s. This sextet was nominated in the Best Small Group category at the 1997 British Telecom Jazz Awards; Wates was nominated in the Alto Saxophone category, and he won the award as the Year's Rising Star. Surprisingly for an alto saxophonist of his generation and background, Wates plays with a gentle, subtly intriguing sound and style.

● ALBUMS: *Relaxin' At The Cat* (ABCDs 1992)★★★, *Two* (ABCDs 1996)★★★★.

WATKINS, DOUG

b. Douglas Watkins, 2 March 1934, Detroit, Michigan, USA, d. 5 February 1962. Watkins has the rare distinction of having played bass on a Charles Mingus record, *Mingus Oh Yeah*, on which the volatile leader switched to piano. Watkins never achieved the same critical status as his brother-in-law Paul Chambers, although he too was a very fine player, contributing a solid foundation for one of the most important modern jazz albums, Sonny Rollins' *Saxophone Colossus*. He left Detroit to tour with James Moody in 1953, then, after moving to New York, worked with Kenny Dorham and participated in the Horace Silver recording date, which led to the formation of Art Blakey's Jazz Messengers. He rejoined Silver from 1956-7 and then worked with Kenny Dorham again, and with Rollins, Jackie McLean, Lee Morgan, Donald Byrd, and Hank Mobley. He was relocating to San Francisco when he was killed in a car crash.

● ALBUMS: with Jackie McLean *4, 5 And 6* (1956)★★★, with Sonny Rollins *Saxophone Colossus* (1956)★★★★, with Gene Ammons *Funky* (1957)★★★, with the Prestige All-Stars *Two Guitars* (1957)★★★, with Donald Byrd *Two Trumpets* (1957)★★★★, with Art Farmer, Donald Byrd Sextet *Trumpets All Out* (1957)★★★, *Fuego* (1959)★★★, *Bluesnik* (1961)★★★, with Charles Mingus *Mingus Oh Yeah* (1961)★★★★.

WATKINS, JULIUS

b. 10 October 1921, Detroit, Michigan, USA, d. 4 April 1977. Watkins started playing French horn in grammar school at the age of nine. Between 1943 and 1946 he worked with Ernie Fields, lived in Colorado for a year and then returned to Detroit to form his own band. He studied with Francis Hellstein of the Detroit Symphony Orchestra and Robert Schultze of the New York Philharmonic Orchestra and spent three years at the Manhattan School of Music. In 1949, he worked with Milt Buckner. Watkins recorded with Kenny Clarke and Babs Gonzales and gigged with bassist Oscar Pettiford, then in 1954 toured with the Pete Rugolo Orchestra and recorded with Thelonious Monk. In early 1956, he had formed Les Jazz Modes with Charlie Rouse, which lasted for three years, and he also performed on Miles Davis's *Porgy And Bess*. In August 1959, he joined George Shearing's big band and played in the Charles Mingus Workshop in 1965 and 1971. He also recorded with the Jazz Composers' Orchestra in 1968. The French horn came to symbolize the classical aspirations of 'cool' jazz, but Watkins' playing always had the power and edge of a top jazz improviser.

● ALBUMS: with Les Jazz Modes: *Jazzville* (Dawn 1956)★★★, *Les Jazz Modes* (Dawn 1956)★★★, *Mood In Scarlet* reissued as *Smart Jazz For The Smart Set* (Dawn 1957)★★★, *The Most Happy Fella* (Atlantic 1958)★★★, *Les Jazz Modes* 1956 recordings (Biograph)★★★★.

WATKISS, CLEVELAND

b. October 1959, London, England. The Watkiss family arrived in England from Jamaica in 1955 and he grew up with the sounds of bluebeat, ska and reggae at home and sang pop and soul at school talent competitions where he started to play guitar and take classical piano lessons. In his early 20s he was affected by the Bob Marley explosion of Rastafarian reggae, and followed the Fatman Hi-Fi Sound System. A chance encounter with a tape of Charlie Parker playing 'Night In Tunisia' in 1980 led to a conversion to jazz, confirmed by witnessing Charlie Rouse at Ronnie Scott's Club in 1982. His group, Alumni, featuring brother Trevor Watkiss (piano) and Alan Weekes (guitar), played in London's

Covent Garden wine bars and Watkiss also sang with Simon Purcell's Jazz Train, but it was the formation of the Jazz Warriors by Courtney Pine that made his name. Watkiss is an excellent frontman and his skilled, imaginative scatting added a special fire to their turbulent sound (*Out Of Many, One People*). His interest in Thelonious Monk bore fruit with his debut as leader, *Green Chimneys*, where he added delightful words to Monk's tune. Since then, Watkiss has toured with the Who (1989) and mimicked Bob Marley for the Malibu drinks commercial. 'Spend Some Time', produced by Coldcut, was a hilarious compendium of his singing styles, though it failed to reach the sales expected of it. In 1991 he released *Blessing In Disguise*, a dazzling survey of jazz, pop and carnival music. Watkiss has a facility that may be his own worst enemy, but there is no denying the infectious joyousness of his singing.

● ALBUMS: *Green Chimneys* (Polydor 1989)★★★★, *Spend Some Time* (Urban 1989)★★★, *Blessing In Disguise* (Polydor 1991)★★★★.

WATROUS, BILL

b. 8 June 1939, Middletown, Connecticut, USA. Although Watrous took some formal musical tuition and also learned trombone from his father, he was largely self-taught. After playing in semi-professional bands, he studied with Herbie Nichols before turning full-time in the early 60s. He played in bands led by artists such as Billy Butterfield, Kai Winding, Maynard Ferguson and Woody Herman. In the late 60s and early 70s he was a studio musician in New York, but kept his jazz career alive playing in several bands for club and record dates. He also formed his own big band, colourfully named Manhattan Wildlife Refuge Big Band, which included Wayne Andre (trombone), Danny Stiles (trumpet), Dick Hyman (piano) and Ed Soph (drums). Relocated in Los Angeles from the mid-70s onwards, he continued to work in studios but made records with Stiles and others. He also toured Europe, performing and teaching. In 1980 he teamed up with trombonists Winding and Albert Mangelsdorff to form Trombone Summit. A dazzling technician with an endless supply of intriguing ideas and concepts, Watrous is one of the most formidable of all contemporary trombonists. His feeling for jazz runs deep and he has never allowed his work to be tainted by the use of technique for its own sake.

● ALBUMS: *Bone Straight Ahead* (Famous Door 1972)★★★, *Manhattan Wildlife Refuge* (Columbia 1974)★★★★, *The Tiger Of San Pedro* (Columbia 1975)★★★★, *Watrous In Hollywood* (1978)★★, *Funk'n Fun* (1979)★★★, *I'll Play For You* (Famous Door 1980)★★★, *Coronary Trombossa* (Famous Door 1980)★★★, *La Zorra* (1980)★★★, *Bill Watrous In London: Live At The Pizza Express* (Mole 1982)★★★★, *Roarin' Back To New York, New York* (Famous Door 1982)★★★, *Someplace Else* (Soundwings 1986)★★★, *Reflections* (Soundwings 1987)★★★, *Bone-Ified* (GNP 1992)★★★, *Time For Love* (GNP Crescendo 1993)★★★, *Space Available* (Double-Time 1997)★★★★.

● COMPILATIONS: *The Best Of Bill Watrous* (1980)★★★.

WATSON, BOBBY

b. 23 August 1953, Lawrence, Kansas, USA. Watson comes from a musical family; his father played tenor saxophone, as well as working at tuning saxophones and repairing instruments. He played piano from the age of 10, and took up clarinet when he was 12-years-old. In his teens he was playing saxophone in R&B bands, then studied music theory at the University of Miami between 1972 and 1975. In 1976 he relocated to New York and joined Art Blakey's Jazz Messengers the following year, later becoming the group's musical director. By the time Watson left in 1981, he had produced some of the best late-period Messengers music. A number he wrote then, 'ETA (Estimated Time Of Arrival)', became a theme tune for him. Watson's intense, crystalline alto saxophone sound was much in demand and he played with George Coleman (1981 onwards) and Charlie Persip (1982 onwards). In 1983 he co-founded the 29th Street Saxophone Quartet (with Ed Jackson, Jim Hartog and Rich Rothenburg), which has enjoyed worldwide success ever since. In 1984 he worked with Max Roach on the music for playwright Sam Shepard's *Shepard's Sets*. In 1985 he toured with a band, Young Lions, which had Englishman Guy Barker on trumpet, and in 1987 formed the nine-piece High Court Of Swing for a record dedicated to Johnny Hodges, *The Year Of The Rabbit*. After recording several records for the Italian Red label, including the outstanding *Love Remains*, Watson signed to Blue Note Records and formed the group Horizon with drummer Victor Lewis, bringing a rhythmic punch and sense of humour to the music that fully justified the title of their 1991 album, *Post-Motown Bop*. In the mid-90s he recorded some satisfying work for Columbia Records, before attempting to crossover to the urban R&B market with his group Urban Renewal.

● ALBUMS: *Estimated Time Of Arrival* (Roulette 1977)★★★, *All Because Of You* (1981)★★, *Live In Sweden* (1981)★★, *Straight Ahead* (1981)★★★, *Jewel* (Evidence 1983)★★★★, *Perpetual Groove* (1984)★★★, *Appointment In Milano* (1984)★★★, *Round Trip* (1984)★★★, *Gumbo* (Evidence 1984)★★★★, *Advance* (Enja 1984)★★★, with Curtis Lundy *Beatitudes* (1985)★★★, *Love Remains* (Red 1987)★★★★, *No Question About It* (Blue Note 1988)★★★, *The Year Of The Rabbit* (1988)★★★, *The Inventor* (Blue Note 1990)★★★, *Post-Motown Bop* (Blue Note 1991)★★★★, *Present Tense* (Columbia 1992)★★★★, *Tailor Made* (Columbia 1993)★★★★, *This Little Light Of Mine* (Red 1993)★★★, *Midwest Shuffle* (Columbia 1994)★★★, *Urban Renewal* (Kokopelli 1996)★★★, *Advance* 1984 recording (Enja 1998)★★★.

WATSON, HELEN

b. Manchester, England. An always competent, sometimes exhilarating interpreter of soul, jazz and blues songs, Helen Watson began her professional career in the early 80s with two albums of blues standards for EMI Records. Since then her albums have revealed shifts to and from a jazz and blues bedrock, but maintained an elegance and an intelligence which has ensured she continues to be heralded by both the jazz and blues cognoscenti. By the time she had moved to London at the age of nine, she had already succumbed to her father's record collection of Billie Holiday, Ella Fitzgerald and Peggy Lee. This was soon subsumed by a love of the Rolling Stones, and what she herself describes as an 'undistinguished' Drama and English teaching career. At this time she also formed the group Well Knit Frames, with guitarist Martin McGroarty. She continued to sing with friends, however, eventually resulting in a permanent backing vocals slot behind Carmel. She continued to write with McGroarty, until their work attracted the attention of producer Glyn Johns. Watson's first solo albums were recorded with Johns, as well as a stellar cast of musicians, three of them drawn from Little Feat. For 1989's *The Weather Inside* she was joined by Andy Fairweather-Low, who also reappeared on the subsequent collection, *Companion Girl*. This was produced by La's/Graham Parker producer Bob Andrews, and featured a typically enchanting blend of personal and anecdotal narrative. However, despite strong sales in Europe and an extremely favourable critical reaction, it failed to sell in the quantities EMI anticipated and her contract was not renewed. A projected album deal with RCA Records fell through, eventually resulting in the independent release of *Notes On Desire*. In the interim Watson had become a fixture of the British festival scene, again accruing almost universal critical praise for her emphatic and versatile live performances.

● ALBUMS: *Blue Slipper* (EMI 1987)★★★, *The Weather Inside* (EMI 1989), *Companion Girl* (RCA 1993)★★, *Notes On Desire* (Building 1996)★★★.

WATSON, LEO

b. 27 February 1898, Kansas City, Missouri, USA, d. 2 May 1950. Early in his career Watson sang on the black vaudeville circuit, but in the late 20s and early 30s he reached New York as a vocalist in a novelty act. The group, which in 1932 became known as the Spirits Of Rhythm, enjoyed considerable popular success. In 1937 Watson joined John Kirby and then worked with the bands of Artie Shaw and Gene Krupa before returning to the Spirits Of Rhythm in 1939. He stayed with the group until the mid-40s. In 1946 he was briefly with Slim Gaillard, who greatly admired Watson's inspired improvizational skills. Apart from singing, Watson also played drums, trombone and tiple (a guitar-like instrument). His highly original singing style, a form of scat, was ingeniously developed in much the same manner as a trombonist might improvise and he was influential upon many of the 40s hipsters and future singing stars such as Mel Tormé. At the end of the decade Watson was suffering poor health and he died in 1950.

● COMPILATIONS: as the Spirits Of Rhythm *Rhythm Personified (1933-34)* (1985)★★★, *The Scat Man (1937-46)* (1988)★★★.

WATTERS, LU

b. Lucious Watters, 19 December 1911, Santa Cruz, California, USA, d. 5 November 1989. After playing trumpet with several bands, Watters began leading his own combos in the mid-20s and thereafter was rarely out of work. Although his early bands were orientated towards swing and dance music, by the end of the 30s he was more and more dedicated to traditional jazz styles. Inspired by the music of New Orleans, he formed his Yerba Buena Jazz Band with like-minded fellows such as Turk Murphy, Clancy Hayes and Bob Scobey. Watters' band proved to be enormously successful; he played to capacity audiences at clubs, concerts and festivals and made numerous albums which sold extremely well. Briefly interrupted by military service, Watters' career continued into the early 50s, despite the loss of Murphy and Scobey, who formed their own popular bands. From the 50s onwards Watters chose to follow a career outside music, making only an occasional recording date thereafter. Although little of Watters' music was original, the devotion with which he recreated the earlier seminal works of jazz musicians, such as Joe 'King' Oliver, Jelly Roll Morton, Louis Armstrong was of great importance in reviving interest in New Orleans jazz. His example was followed by many others and he proved a key figure in the revival movement of the 40s.

● ALBUMS: *50s Recordings, Volume 1* and *2* (Dawn Club 1979)★★★, *Air Shots From The Dawn Club - Lu Watters' Yerba Buena Jazz Band (1941)* (Homespun 1988)★★★★, *Lu Watters' Yerba Buena Jazz Band Vols 1-6 (1949-64)* (Homespun 1988)★★★★.

WATTS, ERNIE

b. Ernest James Watts, 23 October 1945, Norfolk, Virginia, USA. After studying at the Berklee College Of Music Watts was hired by Buddy Rich with whom he played saxophone, mostly tenor, for two years in the late 60s. He then became a studio musician, working extensively in Los Angeles but also finding time to play, and sometimes tour, with jazz musicians such as Gerald Wilson, Oliver Nelson and Cannonball Adderley. In the mid- and late 70s he showed his versatility by playing comfortably with the jazz-rock band led by Lee Ritenour and accompanying jazz instrumentalists such as Sadao Watanabe and J.J. Johnson and jazz singer Anita O'Day. During these years he appeared on countless recording dates, accompanying scores of pop, rock and jazz artists.

He continued this diversified approach to his work throughout the 80s, playing with the Rolling Stones, Tom Scott, Stanley Clarke, Ritenour, Kazumi Watanabe, Charlie Haden and his own jazz-rock group. Although Watts's playing is often vigorous and forthright, his ballad style is smooth and relaxed. He is also comfortable in a mainstream and bop mode as he showed in a happy 1997 recording collaboration with fellow tenorists Pete Christlieb and Rickey Woodard. In 1982 he was heard by millions when he played on the soundtrack to the motion picture *Chariots Of Fire*, for which he won a Grammy.

● ALBUMS: *Planet Love* (Pacific Jazz 1969)★★★, *The Wonder Bag* (1972)★★★, *Look In Your Heart* (1981)★★★, *Chariots Of Fire* film soundtrack (Qwest 1982)★★★, *Musician* (Qwest 1985)★★★, *Sanctuary* (Qwest 1986)★★, *The Ernie Watts Quartet* (JVC 1988)★★★, *World Class* (JVC 1988)★★★, *Project: Activation Earth* (Amherst 1989)★★★, *Afoxe* (CTI 1991)★★★★, *Reaching Up* (JVC 1993)★★★, *Unity* (JVC 1994)★★★★, with Bob Boykin & FirePower *Hazardous Material* (Legato 1996)★★★, *The Long Road Home* (JVC 1996)★★★, with Peter Christlieb, Rickey Woodard *The Tenor Trio* (JVC 1997)★★★, *Classic Moods* (JVC 1998)★★★.

WATTS, TREVOR

b. 26 February 1939, York, England. A child of jazz-loving parents, Watts was largely self-taught, but he did spend one year in the RAF School of Music. He took up the cornet at the age of 12 and the alto saxophone at 18. From 1958-63 he played in the RAF band. At the end of his National Service, he moved to London to join the New Jazz Orchestra and in 1965 was a founder member of the Spontaneous Music Ensemble (SME). In 1967 he founded the SME's sister band, Amalgam. In 1972 he formed Splinters with Stan Tracey and John Stevens, working with Stevens again in the Dance Orchestra. He also played with Pierre Favre and Bobby Lee Bradford in 1972-73, with Tracey (1973-74), the London Jazz Composers' Orchestra (1972-75), Open Circle and Tentacles (both with Tracey in 1975) and the Universal Music Group in 1978. He formed the Trevor Watts String Ensemble in 1976 and Moire Music and the Moire Music Drum Orchestra in 1978. He won the Thames Television Award for schools teaching in 1972. He plays with a sharp, clear, singing tone and has been one of the most significant figures in the British post-Ornette Coleman school.

●ALBUMS: *Springboard* (1966)★★★, with the SME *Challenge* (1966)★★★, *Prayer For Peace* (1969)★★★, *Amalgam Play Blackwell And Higgins* (1973)★★★, with Bobby Lee Bradford *Love's Dream* (1973)★★★, with John Stevens *Face To Face* (1973)★★★★, *Cynosure* (Ogun 1976)★★★, *Endgame* (1978)★★★, *Application Interaction And* (1979)★★★, with Amalgam *Over The Rainbow* (1979)★★★, *Closer To You* (Ogun 1979)★★★, *Moire Music* (Arc 1985)★★★, *Moire Music Sextet* (Cadillac 1988)★★, with Barry Guy and the London Jazz Composers' Orchestra *Harmos* (1989)★★, *Double Trouble* (1990)★★★, with the Moire Music Drum Orchestra *Live In Latin America Volume 1* (1991)★★, with the MMDO *A Wider Embrace* (ECM 1994)★★★, *Moiré* (Intakt 1997)★★★★.

WAYNE, MABEL

b. 16 July 1904, Brooklyn, New York, USA, d. 19 June 1978. A little-known composer who wrote several important songs during a career which ranged from the mid-20s through to the mid-50s. Mabel Wayne studied at the New York School of Music and in Switzerland before touring the USA and overseas as a concert singer and pianist while still in her teens. Turning her attention to popular music, in 1925 she had some success with 'Don't Wake Me Up (Let Me Dream)', written with L. Wolfe Gilbert and Abel Baer, and recorded by the orchestras of Vincent Lopez and Howard Lanin. In the following year, Paul Whiteman, who would subsequently record several of Wayne's compositions, took her appealing 'In A Little Spanish Town' (written with Sam M. Lewis and Joe Young) to number 1 in the US. The song was later performed by deadpan Virginia O'Brien in the all-star *Thousands Cheer* movie (1943), and successfully revived in 1954 by David Carroll And His Orchestra. In 1927 Wayne collaborated again with L. Wolfe Gilbert on perhaps her most fondly remembered number, the enchanting waltz 'Ramona'. Dedicated to the Mexican film actress Dolores Del Rio, it was played whenever her silent film of the same name was shown. Wayne composed several other popular songs in the late 20s, including 'Cheerie Beerie Bee' (Lewis-Young) and 'Chiquita' (Wolfe Gilbert), before contributing two items to the spectacular early film musical *King Of Jazz* (1930). One of these, 'Ragamuffin Romeo' (Howard da Costa), has long been forgotten, but Wayne's other song in the film, 'It Happened In Monterey' (Billy Rose), which was introduced by John Boles and Jeannette Loff, has endured. It was one of a selection of her hits that Wayne recorded herself, singing and playing piano, in the 30s. During that decade when so many fine songs were being written, Mabel Wayne's output included 'Little Man, You've Had A Busy Day' (Maurice Sigler-Al Hoffman), 'His Majesty The Baby' (Neville Fleeson and Arthur Terker), 'Home Again' (Mabel Wayne) and 'Why Don't You Fall In Love With Me?' (Al Lewis). The latter number, which was published in 1937, proved successful on record in the early 40s for Connee Boswell, Dinah Shore and Dick Jurgens, amongst others. In 1943 it was also featured in the London revue *Hi-De-Hi*, which starred Flanagan And Allen, and the film musical *Hollywood Lodge*. In the 40s Wayne collaborated on at least two songs with veteran lyricist Kim Gannon, 'I Understand' and 'Dreamer's Holiday', and among her other compositions around that time, and through to the 50s, were 'Under A Strawberry Moon', 'The Language Of Love', 'The Right Kind Of Love', 'So Madly In Love' and 'Guessing' (1954).

WE FREE KINGS - ROLAND KIRK

Roland Kirk bought an exciting and original sound to jazz during the early 60s and was quietly influential. Sadly, in recent years his standing has diminished. This is a very 60s jazz album, and one that found imitators in numerous musical scores for dreadful b-movies. Although it sounds dated, Kirk plays his heart out and gives variation by playing flute, stritch, manzello and siren. Kirk looked outrageously awesome, was courted by the rock world and could play three wind instruments at the same time. 'The Haunted Melody' demonstrates his clean blowing style, while 'We Free Kings' allows him to blast into the freer form that gained him such a following. He was an innovator.

● Tracks: *Three For The Festival; Moon Song; Haunted Melody; Blues For Alice; We Free Kings; You Did It, You Did It; Some Kind*

Of Love; My Delight.
- First released 1962
- UK peak chart position: did not chart
- USA peak chart position: did not chart

WEATHER REPORT

Founded by Joe Zawinul (keyboards) and Wayne Shorter (reeds). The highly accomplished Weather Report was one of the groups credited with inventing jazz-rock fusion music in the 70s. The two founders had worked together as members of Miles Davis's band in 1969-71, playing on *Bitches Brew*. The first line-up of Weather Report included Airto Moreira (percussion) and Miroslav Vitous (bass). Signing to CBS Records, the group's first album included compositions by Shorter and Zawinul and the line-up was strengthened by Eric Gravatt (drums) and Um Romao (percussion) on the best-selling *I Sing The Body Electric*. Among the tracks was Zawinul's ambitious 'Unknown Soldier', evoking the experience of war. During the mid-70s, the group adopted more elements of rock rhythms and electronic technology, a process which reached its peak on *Black Market* where Zawinul played synthesizer and the brilliant electric bassist Jaco Pastorius made his first appearance with the group. Pastorius left the group in 1980.

Weather Report's popularity was at its peak in the late 70s and early 80s, when the group was a four-piece, with drummer Peter Erskine joining Pastorius and the two founder members. He was replaced by Omar Hakim from George Benson's band in 1982, and for the first time Weather Report included vocals on *Procession*. The singer was Janis Siegel from Manhattan Transfer. During the mid-80s, Zawinul and Shorter made solo albums before dissolving Weather Report in 1986. Shorter led his own small group while Zawinul formed Weather Update with guitarist Steve Khan and Erskine. Hakim went on to become a touring drummer, highly acclaimed for his work with Sting and Eric Clapton. Plans were afoot in 1996 to re-form the band around the nucleus of Shorter and Zawinul.

- ALBUMS: *Weather Report* i (Columbia 1971)★★★, *I Sing The Body Electric* (Columbia 1972)★★★★, *Sweetnighter* (Columbia 1973)★★★, *Mysterious Traveller* (Columbia 1974)★★★★, *Tail Spinnin'* (Columbia 1975)★★★, *Black Market* (Columbia 1976)★★★★, *Heavy Weather* (Columbia 1977)★★★★, *Mr. Gone* (Columbia 1978), *8:30* (Columbia 1979)★★★, *Night Passages* (Columbia 1980)★★★, *Weather Report* ii (Columbia 1982)★★★, *Procession* (Columbia 1983)★★★, *Domino Theory* (Columbia 1984)★★★, *Sportin' Life* (Columbia 1985)★★★, *This Is This* (Columbia 1986)★★★, *New Album* (Columbia 1988)★★★, *Live In Tokyo* recorded 1972 (Sony 1998)★★★.
- COMPILATIONS: *Heavy Weather: The Collection* (Columbia 1990)★★★★, *The Weather Report Selection* 3-CD box set (Columbia 1992)★★★.

WEATHERFORD, TEDDY

b. 11 October 1903, Pocahontas, Virginia, USA, d. 25 April 1945. While Weatherford was still a child his family moved to New Orleans where he began playing piano as a teenager. He was still in his teens when he joined the great northward migration, ending up in Chicago in 1922. During the next few years he was in much demand in the city but itchy feet took him abroad, travelling to the Far East in 1926 first as a sideman but later as a bandleader. He played in Malaya, the Philippines and China from where he returned in the mid-30s just long enough to persuade Buck Clayton to take a band to Shanghai. From China, Weatherford moved to India, France, Sweden, back to India and Ceylon and then finally to India yet again where he played, mainly in Calcutta, until his death from cholera. A solid, rhythmically intense player, with a deep-rooted instinct for the blues, Weatherford's peripatetic career makes an accurate assessment of his work difficult to determine. Reputedly, Weatherford's time in Chicago saw him as a rival to Earl 'Fatha' Hines and claims are made that Hines learned from him. However, his relatively few and mostly pre-electric recordings, good as they show him to be, make it hard to justify such assertions.

- COMPILATIONS: with Louis Armstrong *Young Louis The Sideman* (1924-27)★★★, included on *Piano And Swing* 1935-38)★★.

WEBB, CHICK

b. William Webb, 10 February 1909, Baltimore, Maryland, USA, d. 19 June 1939. Although crippled soon after his birth, Webb's determination to be a drummer overcame his physical infirmities. After playing in local bands, he travelled to New York while still a teenager and soon formed his own band there. By 1927 he had played at the Savoy Ballroom and other prestigious dance halls. In 1931 he began a residency at the Savoy and quickly became this famous venue's favourite act. He hired fine musicians, among them Johnny Hodges (whom he generously encouraged to take up an offer from Duke Ellington), Benny Carter, Jimmy Harrison, Mario Bauza, Wayman Carver, Taft Jordan, Louis Jordan and Bobby Stark. He also employed a succession of excellent arrangers, including Charlie Dixon, Carter and the outstandingly talented Edgar Sampson. Webb's popularity at the Savoy and through records and radio broadcasts was further enhanced when, in 1935, he hired the recently-discovered Ella Fitzgerald. From this point until Webb's untimely death four years later, the band remained at a musical and commercial peak. Throughout his career Webb's physical condition had given cause for concern; he underwent several spinal operations at Johns Hopkins Hospital in Baltimore, but died there on 19 June 1939. (Reputedly, his last words were, 'I'm sorry, I gotta go now.') One of the outstanding big band drummers, Webb's technical skills and driving yet uplifting beat were essential components of his band's success with audiences, especially the hard-to-please dancers at the Savoy who loved him. Although Jo Jones was concurrently changing perceptions of how big band drummers should play, Webb continued to exert influence and his most enthusiastic successor was Gene Krupa, who altered his style completely after first hearing Webb. As he, in turn, influenced countless thousands of drummers around the world, the Webb style even spread among musicians who perhaps had never heard of him.

● ALBUMS: *Chick Webb 1937-39* (Decca 1958)★★★★, *Midnite In Harlem (1934-39)* (1962)★★★, *The Immortal Chick Webb* (Columbia 1967)★★★★, *A Legend (1929-36)* (1974)★★★★, *King Of The Savoy (1937-39)* (1974)★★★★, *Spinning The Webb* (1974)★★★, with Ella Fitzgerald *Silver Swing* (1976)★★, *In The Groove* (Affinity 1983)★★★, *Rhythm Man 1931-1934* (Hep Jazz 1988)★★★★, *Stomping At The Savoy* (1988)★★★★, *For Radio Only Recordings (1939)* (Tax 1989)★★★★.

WEBB, GEORGE

b. 8 October 1917, London, England. After playing piano in and around London, Webb was attracted by the revival movement and in 1942 formed his own traditional band. The band proved to be highly popular with British fans, including over the next few years leading lights of the UK jazz scene such as Wally Fawkes, Eddie Harvey, Owen Bryce and Humphrey Lyttelton. In 1948 Webb folded the band, several of the members forming the nucleus of Lyttelton's first band, and thereafter he made only occasional appearances as a performer. Among these was a brief return to the scene as a member of Lyttelton's band, but for the most part he concentrated on his activities as agent, manager and promoter. In the 70s he was again performing, leading a band which included Sammy Rimington.

● COMPILATIONS: *George Webb's Dixielanders* (Jazzology 1988)★★★.

WEBB, SPEED

b. Lawrence Arthur Webb, 18 July 1906, Peru, Indiana, USA, d. 4 November 1994. As a child he learned to play both violin and mellophone but eventually took up the drums as his main instrument. After playing locally for a short time, he studied embalming, intent on a career as a funeral director. However, in 1925 he was co-founder of a band, the Hoosier Melody Lads. Soon, he took over full leadership of the band which quickly built an enviable reputation in Indiana and Idaho as one of the very best of the territory bands. The band, which underwent many personal changes over the dozen or so years of its existence, made only a 1916 recording session, recording four sides for Gennett which were rejected, and the masters then lost. The band did, however, appear in some early sound movies: *Riley The Cop*, *Sins Of The Fathers* (both 1928), *His Captive Woman*, *On With The Show* (both 1929). Although Webb recalled making some later sides for OKeh Records, nothing other than these movies allow a taste of what members of the band regarded as an outstanding outfit. Among Webb's sidemen, some of whom contributed lively charts, were Teddy Buckner, Roy Eldridge, Reunald Jones, John Nesbitt (trumpets), Henderson Chambers, Vic Dickenson, Gus Wilson (trombones), Leonard Gay, Joe Eldridge, Jimmy Mundy (reeds), Art Tatum, and Teddy Wilson (piano). Despite his enormous popularity and the acclaim with which his band appears to have been received, by the end of the 30s when the swing era was at its height, Webb's fortunes were at a low ebb. He dissolved his band and resumed his studies in embalming, thereafter building up a large chain of prosperous funeral parlours. While reliance upon hearsay evidence is unwise, the quality of the sidemen named and the arrangers (the Eldridge and the Wilson brothers, Dickenson and Mundy) cannot but support the view that Webb's band was of great importance, and the absence of any recordings, other than the movie appearances, is a great loss to jazz.

WEBER, EBERHARD

b. 22 January 1940, Stuttgart, Germany. Weber's father taught him the cello from the age of six and he only turned to the bass in 1956. He liked the sound of Bill Haley's records, saw an old stand-up bass hanging on the wall in the school gym and tried it out. He played jazz in his spare time from making television commercials and working as a theatre director and only turned professional in 1972. With Wolfgang Dauner (keyboards) he had played in a trio inspired by the Bill Evans Trio and in Dauner's psychedelic jazz-rock band, Etcetera. He worked with the Dave Pike Set and then joined Volker Kriegel's Spectrum, but did not share Kriegel's fascination with rock rhythms and left in 1974. Weber had already recorded *The Colours Of Chloë* for ECM Records and had developed the 5-string bass, which gives him his individual sound, from an old Italian bass with a long neck and a small rectangular soundbox he had seen in an antique shop. His composition style seemed to owe something to minimalist writing but had developed when he realised that he only liked bits and pieces of other people's music and he had concluded 'that when I came to compose I would only use chords and phrases I really liked - and use them over and over'. *The Colours Of Chloë* brought him international recognition and he then worked with guitarist Ralph Towner (1974) and Gary Burton (1974-76). Meanwhile he formed his own band Colours with Rainer Bruninghaus, Charlie Mariano and first Jon Christensen and then John Marshall. He wanted a band that played in an absolutely European way with understated rhythm, spacey, impressionistic keyboard sounds and flowing melody. This European tradition provides 'the feeling for group empathy that I am drawn to' while the jazz tradition gives 'the whole feeling for improvisation . . . knowing when to stretch out or lay out'. He disbanded Colours when he could no longer hold these two traditions in balance and has since played with the United Jazz And Rock Ensemble and as a regular member of saxophonist Jan Garbarek's bands. Since 1985 he has also performed solo bass concerts, where his prodigious technique is evident. He is able to conjure from his electric instrument and a limited array of equipment, some glorious sounds.

● ALBUMS: *The Colours Of Chloë* (ECM 1974)★★★★, *Yellow Fields* (ECM 1975)★★★★, *The Following Morning* (ECM

1976)★★★★, *Silent Feet* (ECM 1977)★★★, *Fluid Rustle* (ECM 1979)★★★★, *Little Movements* (ECM 1980)★★★★, *Later That Evening* (ECM 1982)★★★★, *Chorus* (ECM 1984)★★★★, *Orchestra* (ECM 1988)★★★, *Pendulum* (ECM 1994)★★★.
● COMPILATIONS: *Works* (ECM 1989)★★★★.

WEBSTER, BEN

b. 27 March 1909, Kansas City, Missouri, USA, d. 20 September 1973, Amsterdam, Netherlands. After studying violin and piano, and beginning his professional career on the latter instrument, Webster took up the tenor saxophone around 1930. He quickly became adept on this instrument; within a year he was playing with Bennie Moten and later worked with Andy Kirk and Fletcher Henderson. In the mid-30s he also played briefly with numerous bands mostly in and around New York, including spells with Duke Ellington. In 1940 he became a permanent member of the Ellington band, where he soon became one of its most popular and imitated soloists. Although he was with the band for only three years, he had enormous influence upon it, both through his presence, which galvanized his section-mates, and by his legacy. Thereafter, any new tenor saxophonist felt obliged to play like Webster until they were established enough to exert their own personalities. After leaving Ellington, he led a small group for club and record dates and also played with several small groups led by artists such as Stuff Smith and Red Allen. In the late 40s he rejoined Ellington for a short stay, then played with Jazz At The Philharmonic. From the 50s and on throughout the rest of his life, he worked mostly as a single, touring extensively, especially to Europe and Scandinavia where he attained great popularity. He was briefly resident in Holland before moving to Denmark, where he lived for the rest of his life. He recorded prolifically during his sojourn in Europe, sometimes with just a local rhythm section, occasionally with other leading American jazz musicians, among them Bill Coleman and Don Byas. Like so many tenor players of his generation, Webster's early style bore some of the hallmarks of Coleman Hawkins; but by the time of his arrival in the Ellington band in 1940, and his first important recording with them, 'Cottontail', he was very much his own man. His distinctive playing style, characterized by a breathy sound and emotional vibrato, became in its turn the measure of many of his successors. A consummate performer at any tempo, Webster's fast blues were powerful and exciting displays of the extrovert side of his nature, yet he was at his best with slow, languorous ballads, which he played with deeply introspective feeling and an often astonishing sensuality. This dichotomy in his playing style was reflected in his personality, which those who worked with him have described as veering between a Dr Jekyll-like warmth and a Mr Hyde-ish ferocity. One of the acknowledged masters of the tenor saxophone, Webster made innumerable records, few of them below the highest of standards. As the years passed, he favoured ballads over the flagwavers that had marked his younger days. From his early work with Ellington, through the small group sides of the 40s, a remarkable set of ballad duets with Hawkins, to his late work in Europe, Webster's recorded legacy is irrefutable evidence that he was a true giant of jazz.

● ALBUMS: *Tenor Sax Stylings* 10-inch album (Brunswick 1952)★★★, *Big Tenor* 10-inch album (EmArcy 1954)★★★, *The Consummate Artistry Of Ben Webster* reissued as *King Of The Tenors* (Norgran 1954)★★★★, *Music For Loving* reissued as *Sophisticated Lady - Ben Webster With Strings* (Norgran 1955)★★★, *Ben Webster Plays Music With Feeling* (Norgran 1955)★★★★, with Illinois Jacquet *"The Kid" And "The Brute"* (Clef 1955)★★★★, with Art Tatum *The Art Tatum-Ben Webster Quartet* (Verve 1958)★★★★, *Soulville* (Verve 1958)★★★★, *At The Nuway Club* (1958)★★★, with Coleman Hawkins *Coleman Hawkins Encounters Ben Webster* (Verve 1959)★★★★, with Gerry Mulligan *Gerry Mulligan Meets Ben Webster* (Verve 1959)★★★★★, *Ben Webster And Associates* (Verve 1959)★★★★, with Oscar Peterson *Ben Webster Meets Oscar Peterson* (Verve 1959)★★★★, *The Soul Of Ben Webster* (Verve 1960)★★★★, *Ben Webster At The Renaissance* (Riverside 1960)★★★★, *The Warm Moods Of Ben Webster* (Reprise 1961)★★★★, with Harry 'Sweets' Edison *Ben Webster-Sweets Edison* (Columbia 1962)★★★★, *Live At Pio's* (Enja 1963)★★★, with Joe Zawinul *Soulmates* (Riverside 1964)★★★★, *Layin' Back With Ben* (1964)★★★, *See You At The Fair* (Impulse! 1964)★★★★, *Stormy Weather* (Black Lion 1965)★★★, *Gone With The Wind* (Black Lion 1965)★★★, *Duke's In Bed* (Black Lion 1965)★★★, *Atmosphere For Lovers And Thieves* (Black Lion 1965)★★★, *There Is No Greater Love* (Black Lion 1966)★★★, *The Jeep Is Jumping* (Black Lion 1966)★★★, *Remember* (1967)★★★, with Bill Coleman *Swingin' In London* (Black Lion 1967)★★★, with Don Byas *Ben Webster Meets Don Byas In The Black Forest* (Saba 1968)★★★, *Quiet Days In Clichy* (1969)★★★, *Blow, Ben, Blow* (1969)★★★, *For The Guv'nor (Tribute To Duke Ellington)* (1969)★★★, *Ben Op Zijn Best* (1970)★★★, *No Fool, No Fun* (Spotlite 1970)★★★, *Live At The Haarlemse Jazz Club* (Cat 1972)★★★, *Ben Webster In Hot House* (1972)★★★, *Messenger* (1972)★★★, *Live In Paris* (1972)★★★, *Makin' Whoopee* (Spotlite 1972)★★★, *Autumn Leaves* (1972)★★★, *Did You Call* (Nessa 1973)★★★, *My Man* (Steeple Chase 1973)★★★, *Last Concert* (1973)★★★, *Saturday Night At The Montmarte* 1965 recording (Black Lion 1974)★★★, *Live In Amsterdam* 1969 recording (1989)★★★, *In A Mellow Tone* 1965 recordings (Jazz House 1995)★★★.

● COMPILATIONS: *Alternate And Incomplete Takes* 1944 recording (Circle 1986)★★★, *Ben Webster Plays Duke Ellington* 1967-1971 recordings (Storyville 1989)★★★★, *The Verve Years* (Verve 1989)★★★★, *Cotton Tail* 1932-1946 recordings (RCA Victor 1997)★★★★, *Ultimate Ben Webster* (Verve 1998)★★★★, *Black Lion Presents* 1965-1967 recordings (Black Lion)★★★, *Tribute To A Great Jazzman* 1936-1945 recordings (Jazz Archives)★★★★, *Ben And The Boys* 1944-1958 recordings (Jazz Archives)★★★★, *He Played It That Way* 1943-1969 recordings (IAJRC)★★★★, *The Complete Ben Webster On EmArcy* 1951-1953 recordings (EmArcy)★★★★.

WEBSTER, FREDDIE

b. 1916, Cleveland, Ohio, USA, d. 1 April 1947. A prodigiously talented trumpet player, Webster led his own band while still in his teens. By his early twenties,

Webster's ability had attracted the attention of several name bandleaders and he played with Earl 'Fatha' Hines and Erskine Tate before forming his own professional band. In 1940 he moved to New York where he played with a dizzying array of leading artists including Benny Carter, Lucky Millinder, Jimmie Lunceford, Cab Calloway, Hines, Billy Eckstine, Sarah Vaughan. While with Hines and Eckstine, one of Webster's trumpet section colleagues was Dizzy Gillespie who held him in very high regard. Later, Webster played in Gillespie's band and then joined Norman Granz's Jazz At The Philharmonic. In addition to the impression he made upon Gillespie, Webster is also believed to have been influential upon Miles Davis. Sadly, the recordings on which he appears, and where he is audible on solos, make a balanced judgement difficult. He can be heard playing well on sides recorded by singers Viola 'Miss Rhapsody' Wells ('I Fell For You' Savoy 1945) and Sarah Vaughan ('You're Not The Kind', Muse 1946).

● COMPILATIONS: *Lucky Millinder, 1941-3* (Alamac 1941-43)★★★★.

WECKL, DAVE

b. 1960, St Louis, Missouri, USA. A technically advanced fusion drummer who specialises in applying jazz's rhythmic complexity to the aggressive sound of the rock kit, Weckl rose to prominence as Chick Corea's fearless drummer, hidden behind a huge, towering kit in the popular Elektric Band. The son of an amateur pianist, Weckl was turned onto the drums by (strangely) jazz big band drummer Buddy Rich, eventually studying jazz at the University of Bridgeport Connecticut. His first gigging experience was with the successful fusion outfit Nitesprite, and he soon dropped out of college to take advantage of the opportunities to gig and tour abroad. He impressed leading fusion drummer Peter Erskine, who helped spread the young musician's name further, and Weckl soon found himself busy in the fusion scene and in the studio, recording lucrative dates for Diana Ross, George Benson, Madonna and Robert Plant. He joined keyboardist Chick Corea in the mid-80s, forming a third of the fast-moving, virtuoso rhythm section with bassist John Patitucci that in its seven years came to represent Corea's 80s style. Since the group's disbandment, Weckl has concentrated on his own career, recording as a leader for GRP Records, and powering the All-Star GRP Big Band live and on record.

● ALBUMS: *Heads Up* (GRP 1992)★★★, *Hard-Wired* (1994)★★★, with GRP All-Star Big Band *All Blues* (1995)★★, *Rhythm Of The Soul* (Stretch 1998)★★★.

WEEKEND

After the demise of the Young Marble Giants in 1980, Alison Statton (b. March 1958, Cardiff, Wales; vocals, bass) and fellow Cardiffian Spike (guitarist, viola) moved to London. After teaming up the following year with Simon Booth (b. 12 March 1956), who worked at Mole Jazz record shop, they formed Weekend. Their debut single on Rough Trade Records, 'The View From Her Room', produced by Simon Jeffes of the Penguin Cafe Orchestra, presented a breezy jazz-shuffle driven by Statton's excellent bass-line. Among the studio support were two veterans of the British jazz scene, Harry Beckett (trumpet, flugelhorn) and former Centipede member Larry Stabbins (b. 9 September 1949; tenor sax). Mixed with Statton's introspective lyrics, the band's image of an 'anti-rock' outfit drawing on multicultural jazz influences, from the bossa nova of Gilberto Gill and Astrud Gilberto to the light African guitar style of King Sunny Ade, was quickly picked up by the then-fashionable youthful London 'jazz-club' scene. Later singles 'Past Meets Present' and 'Drumbeat For Baby' gave Weekend further independent chart hits. Their debut *La Varieté* perfectly captured the group's light summery feel. While live performances were few and far between, London was blessed one memorable weekend in 1983 with two concerts, one at the Africa Centre, Covent Garden, and another at the legendary Ronnie Scott's Club in Soho, where they were joined onstage by Keith Tippett. This set was recorded and later released on a posthumous mini-album. Statton's unease with live performances and Booth's desire to lead the group down a harder jazz-dance direction led to the group splitting, with Stabbins and Booth carrying on the bloodline with the formation of Working Week. Statton returned to Cardiff and her college studies, re-emerging in the late 80s with the duo Devine And Statton.

● ALBUMS: *La Varieté* (Rough Trade 1982)★★★, *Live At Ronnie Scott's* mini-album (Rough Trade 1983)★★★.

● COMPILATIONS: with the Young Marble Giants and the Gist *Nipped In The Bud* (Rough Trade 1984)★★★.

WEEKS, ANSON

b. 14 February 1896, Oakland, California, USA, d. 7 February 1969, Sacramento, California, USA. Weeks began leading a dance band in the mid-20s and achieved great popularity in 1928 during an engagement at the Mark Hopkins Hotel in San Francisco. Thereafter, he worked at many of the best hotels in New York, Chicago and New Orleans, introducing the band with his own composition, 'I'm Writing You This Little Melody', and the slogan 'Dancin' with Anson'. The musical policy he operated was geared strictly for dancing and he was largely indifferent to passing vogues such as the swing era. Among the musicians who played in the band was Xaviar Cugat, while his singers included Bob Crosby and Tony Martin. Weeks continued to lead his band through the 50s and 60s, still blithely ignoring musical fads and fancies, and was still working when he died in Sacramento.

● COMPILATIONS: *Dancin' With Anson* (50s)★★, *Memories Of Dancin' With Anson* (50s)★★, *Anson Weeks 1932 - Two Complete Radio Broadcasts (1932)* (1988)★★★★.

WEEMS, TED

b. 26 September 1901, Pitcairn, Pennsylvania, USA, d. 6 May 1963, Tulsa, Oklahoma, USA. After learning to play the violin when he was at high school, Weems switched to trombone while attending the University of

Pennsylvania. That instrument was also favoured by his brother, Art, and in 1923 the brothers formed their own band, and soon afterwards Ted Weems decided to concentrate on simply being the leader. They became very popular during the latter part of the 20s, appealing to dancers mostly in and around Chicago with their sophisticated playing and featured singers. They were also in demand on radio for many years. Among those who sang successfully with the band were future movie star Marilyn Maxwell, Al Jarrett, Parker Gibbs, Country Washburn and Perry Como. Also popular were whistler Elmo Tanner and saxophonist-cum-novelty-vocalist Red Ingle. From 1922-47 the band had a number of big-selling records, among them 'Somebody Stole My Gal', 'Covered Wagon Days', 'A Smile Will Go A Long, Long Way', 'Blue Eyed Sally', 'Love Bound', 'Highways Are Happy Ways', 'You're The Cream In My Coffee', 'Piccolo Pete', 'The Man From the South' (number 1), 'My Baby Just Cares For Me', 'Walkin' My Baby Back Home', 'Talkin' To Myself', 'Knock! Knock! Who's There?', 'Peg O' My Heart', 'I Wonder Who's Kissing Her Now', 'Mickey', and 'Nola'. The latter featured Elmo Tanner, and the whistler also featured on the record of the band's theme, 'Out Of The Night', and 'Heartaches', which was originally released in 1933. It became an unexpected million-selling hit in 1947, shortly after Weems formed his new band following service in the Merchant Marine during World War II. In the 50s and 60s Weems worked as a disc jockey and ran a band agency for a time, but still led his own band occasionally. He was also the co-composer of several songs, including 'Jig Time', 'Three Shifless Skonks', 'Oh Monah', 'The One-Man Band, and 'The Martins And The Coys'.

● ALBUMS: *Remember When* (Strand 50s)★★★, *Golden Hits* (Mercury 1962)★★★★, *Ted Weems* (Decca 1963)★★★★, *Beat The Band Shows (1940-41)* (1979)★★★, *Marvellous* (1984)★★★, *Heartaches (1933-51)* (1988)★★★★.

WEIN, GEORGE

b. 3 October 1925, Boston, Massachusetts, USA. After studying formally, Wein began playing piano professionally in his early teenage years. He led his own band in and around his home town for a period, frequently accompanying visiting jazz musicians. In the early 50s he opened his own club in Boston, the Storyville, formed his own record label (which had the same name) and was thus launched on his second career as a jazz impresario. In 1954 he was invited to organize the first Newport Jazz Festival and subsequently played an important part in establishing other major international festivals, including the annual Grande Parade du Jazz at Nice in the south of France. In addition to his work on festivals around the world, he has also actively promoted such organizations as the New York Jazz Repertory Orchestra, and taught jazz in Boston. Although his work in promotion has been enormously time-consuming, Wein has never lost his desire to play piano and regularly appears with all-star bands on festival programmes and record dates. While his career as a pianist might perhaps be overlooked, his importance to jazz through his non-playing activities has been of great significance. Together with Norman Granz, he has been a major force in maintaining the highest standards of presentation and performance, and in ensuring that his artists are given the respect that is their due.

● ALBUMS: *George Wein And The Newport All-Stars* (1962)★★★, *The Newport Jazz Festival All-Stars* (1984)★★★★, *Magic Horn* (RCA 1993)★★.

WEISS, SAMMY

b. Samuel Weiss, 1 September 1910, New York, USA, d. 18 December 1977. Weiss played drums, and occasionally the vibraphone, in various dance bands in New York while in his late teens and early twenties. He spent most of the 30s working with popular singer/saxophonist Gene Kardos but also played gigs and made records with other leaders, including Benny Goodman, Tommy Dorsey and Artie Shaw. Regularly on call for studio dates, Weiss also recorded with Louis Armstrong. In the 40s he continued in like manner, playing frequently with Johnny Guarnieri, then relocated to Los Angeles where he formed his own dance band. With this band he worked regularly through succeeding decades, appearing on radio and television as well as playing hotel and dance sessions. Like his near contemporary, Stan King, Weiss was an exceptionally good dance band drummer, showing excellent time-keeping. His playing was never quite suited to swing era dynamics, however, as can be heard by contrasting his playing on Goodman's 'Bugle Call Rag', recorded in August 1934, with the same number recorded a few months later with Gene Krupa on drums.

● COMPILATIONS: *Benny Goodman And His Music Hall Orchestra* (Saville 1934)★★★★.

WEISS, SID

b. 30 April 1914, Schenectady, New York, USA, d. 20 March 1994. As a child Weiss played several instruments including violin and clarinet before choosing the bass. He was active in New York from the early 30s onwards, playing with leaders including Louis Prima, Wingy Manone and Joe Marsala, and had stints with swing era giants such as Artie Shaw, Tommy Dorsey and Benny Goodman. From the mid-40s until the mid-50s he played mostly in New York pick-up groups, appearing on numerous record dates including many of Eddie Condon's Town Hall broadcasts. After this, he relocated to the west coast and altough he occasionally played thereafter, often outside jazz music, he earned his living in the electronics industry. A sound and unobtrusive member of the rhythm sections in which he played, Weiss's contribution to swing era jazz was frequently overlooked, a fact exacerbated by his decision to retire from active playing while still very much in his prime.

● COMPILATIONS: *Eddie Condon's Town Hall Concerts* (1944-45)★★★★.

WELLER, DON

b. 19 December 1947, Croydon, Surrey, England. After studying classical clarinet Weller switched to tenor saxophone, playing jazz with Kathy Stobart. By the late 60s he had become an important figure on the UK jazz scene, working extensively with Stan Tracey, Art Themen and others. During the 70s Weller continued to play with Tracey, also led his own jazz-rock group, Major Surgery, and regularly played straight jazz gigs with his quartet. In the 80s he still led his quartet and also worked with Bryan Spring and Bobby Wellins, appearing at London clubs and festivals at venues throughout the UK. A powerful player with a robust sound which reflects his burly physical appearance, Weller is one of the best post-bop tenor saxophonists to emerge in the UK. Although well-known and respected by visiting American jazz musicians, he has yet to make an appreciable impact upon international audiences.

● ALBUMS: with Stan Tracey *The Bracknell Connection* (1976)★★★, *Don Weller* (Affinity 1979)★★★, *Commit No Nuisance* (Affinity 1981)★★★, *Stan Tracey And Don Weller Play Duke, Monk And Bird* (1988)★★★★.

WELLINS, BOBBY

b. 24 January 1936, Glasgow, Scotland. Wellins studied alto saxophone with his father; his mother had been a singer in the Sammy Miller Show Band. (His parents later performed on stage as a double act.) Wellins also studied formally, learning piano and clarinet. In the mid-50s he was active in London, by now settled on tenor saxophone. He played in bands led by Buddy Featherstonhaugh, Tony Crombie and Vic Lewis, with whom he visited the USA, then joined Stan Tracey, having first met him in Crombie's Jazz Incorporated band. He was with Tracey for some years in the early 60s, as a member of the New Departures Quartet which also featured Jeff Clyne and Laurie Morgan. The group made a number of important albums, moving British jazz forward into areas previously considered, at least by critics and audiences, to be the preserve of Americans. For Wellins, the next few years were disastrous. The late 60s and early 70s vanished under a haze of various personal problems but by the late 70s he was again active, as leader and co-leader with Don Weller of a number of fine hard bop groups. The albums from these years were amongst the best of their genre recorded in the UK. Since his return to jazz, Wellins has been busy as a teacher. A distinctive player, with an intensely emotional sound which reflects his passionate approach to music, by the late 80s Wellins had become a respected figure on the British jazz scene. Amongst his compositions is the suite 'Endangered Species' recorded under the title, 'Birds Of Brazil'.

● ALBUMS: with Stan Tracey *Under Milk Wood* (1965)★★★★, *Jubilation* (1978)★★★, *Dreams Are Free* (1979)★★★, *Birds Of Brazil* (Sungai 1989)★★, *Nomad* (Hot House 1994)★★★, *Don't Worry Bout Me* (Cadillac 1997)★★★★, *The Satin Album* (Jazzizit 1997)★★★.

WELLS, DICKY

b. 10 June 1907, Centerville, Tennessee, USA, d. 12 November 1985. After starting out on other instruments, Wells took up the trombone in his mid-teens and a year later was playing in New York City with the band led by brothers Lloyd and Cecil Scott. He later worked with the bands of Elmer Snowden, Benny Carter, Charlie 'Fess' Johnson, Fletcher Henderson and Chick Webb, then toured Europe with Teddy Hill before joining Count Basie in the summer of 1938. He remained with Basie until 1950, taking some months off to play with Sy Oliver's ill-fated big band in 1946/7. During the 50s Wells worked with several bands, often in Europe, and usually in good company: Jimmy Rushing, Earl Hines, Buck Clayton and Bill Coleman. In the early 60s he spent long spells with Ray Charles and Reuben Phillips, but by the middle of the decade was back on the road again, touring extensively and continuing to record. Unfortunately, this period also saw the onset of personal problems as a result of alcoholism which prompted his premature retirement from music. In 1973, however, his autobiography, *The Night People* (co-written with Stanley Dance), was published and this revealing, warm and witty book helped to encourage him back onto the scene. His reappearance was well-received and, although he suffered ill-health and was mugged twice (one attack putting him into a coma for several weeks), he continued to perform into the early 80s. In his playing, Wells chose to adopt a seemingly casual approach, liberally peppering his inventive solos with musical witticisms and deliberately jokey effects. In lesser hands, his style could have mirrored the comic excesses of an earlier generation of trombone players in jazz and popular music. Fortunately, his stylishness and wit, coupled with exemplary technique, allowed him to establish a reputation as one of the finest and most distinctive trombone soloists in jazz.

● ALBUMS: with Rex Stewart *Chatter Jazz* (RCA Victor 1959)★★★, *Lonesome Road* (Uptown 1982)★★★, *Trombone Four-In-Hand (1958-59)* (Affinity 1986)★★★★, *Bones For The King (1958)* (Affinity 1986)★★★, *In Paris* (Affinity 1992)★★★, *Swingin' In Paris* (Le Jazz 1993)★★.

● FURTHER READING: *The Night People*, Dicky Wells with Stanley Dance.

WELLSTOOD, DICK

b. 25 November 1927, Greenwich, Connecticut, USA, d. 24 July 1987, Palo Alto, California, USA. After learning to play piano in his home town, Wellstood came to New York City in 1946 and was soon working with able musicians such as newcomer Bob Wilber and veteran Sidney Bechet. In the early 50s he visited Europe with Jimmy Archey's band, but divided his time between music and law studies. After qualifying as a lawyer he returned to full-time music, working mostly solo, but also in small groups with artists such as Roy Eldridge, Henry 'Red' Allen, Coleman Hawkins and Gene Krupa. In the 70s his solo career expanded, but he also played in the World's Greatest Jazz Band. Throughout his career

Wellstood recorded extensively, displaying a remarkable command of his instrument and a wide taste in jazz, although his clear preference was for the older traditions. He was an accomplished exponent of stride piano. In the 80s he continued to work as a single but also played in a trio, the Blue Three, with Kenny Davern and Bobby Rosengarden, and briefly practised law.

● ALBUMS: *Dick Wellstood* 10-inch album (Riverside 1956)★★★, with Cliff Jackson *Uptown And Downtown* (Swingville 1961)★★★, *Alone* (Solo Art 1971)★★★★, with Kenny Davern *Dick Wellstood And His Famous Orchestra Featuring Kenny Davern* (1973)★★★★, *Fats Waller Revisited* (Classic Jazz 1975)★★★, *This Is The One ... Dig!* (Solo Art 1976)★★★★, *Take Me To The Land Of Jazz* (Aviva 1978)★★★, with the Blue Three *The Blue Three At Hanratty's* (1981)★★★★, *Live At Hanratty's* (Chaz Jazz 1981)★★★★, with Dick Hyman *I Wish I Were Twins* (Swingtime 1983)★★★, *Diane* (Swingtime 1985)★★★, *Live At The Cafe Des Copains* (Unisson 1985)★★★, *After You've Gone* (Unisson 1987)★★★★, *Live At The Sticky Wicket* 1986 recording (Arbors 1997)★★★★.

● COMPILATIONS: with Kenny Davern, Bobby Rosengarden *Dick Wellstood And His Famous Orchestra Featuring Kenny Davern* 1973-1981 recordings (Chiaruscuro 1981)★★★★.

WELSH, ALEX

b. 9 July 1929, Edinburgh, Scotland, d. 25 June 1982. Welsh began his musical career in Scotland playing cornet, and later trumpet, in trad jazz bands. In the early 50s he moved to London and formed a band that quickly became one of the most proficient of its kind. With every chair filled by musicians of great skill and enthusiasm, the Welsh band was a major force in the British trad jazz movement. Eschewing the fancy dress eccentricities and pop music escapades of many of his rivals (although 'Tansy' did reach the UK Top 50 in 1961), Welsh concentrated on creating exciting music that echoed the vitality of the best of Chicago-style Dixieland jazz. Among Welsh's sidemen over the years were Archie Semple, Fred Hunt, Roy Crimmins, Roy Williams, John Barnes, Lennie Hastings and Al Gay. During the 60s and early 70s Welsh toured the UK and Europe, building up a rapturous following, and also made occasional successful sorties to the USA. In common with Chris Barber, Welsh saw the need to maintain a wide repertoire, drawing (as jazz always has) from the best of popular music and thus creating a band that effectively swam in the mainstream. By the mid-70s Welsh's health was poor, but he continued to play for as long as he could. Throughout his career Welsh blew with great exuberance, sometimes sang too and always encouraged his sidemen by his example. Not only popular with audiences, he was also respected and admired by his fellow musicians.

● ALBUMS: *Music Of The Mauve Decade* (1957)★★★, *The Melrose Folio* (1958)★★★, *Alex Welsh In Concert* (Columbia 1961)★★, *Echoes Of Chicago* (1962)★★★, *Strike One* (1966)★★★, *At Home With Alex Welsh* (Dormouse 1967)★★★, *Vintage '69* (1969)★★, *Classic Concert* (Black Lion 1971)★★★★, *An Evening With Alex Welsh, Part 1* (Polydor 1974)★★★, *Dixieland Party* (Black Lion 1975)★★, *If I Had A Talking Picture Of You* (Black Lion 1975)★★★, *The Alex Welsh Showcase, Volume 1* (Black Lion 1976)★★★, *The Alex Welsh Showcase, Volume 2* (Black Lion 1976)★★★, *Alex Welsh In Concert* (Black Lion 1977)★★★, *In A Party Mood* (One-Up 1977)★★★, with Humphrey Lyttelton, Bruce Turner, George Chisholm *Salute To Satchmo* (Black Lion 1979)★★★, *Dixieland To Duke* (Dormouse 1986)★★★★, *Live At The Royal Festival Hall (1954-55)* (Lake 1988)★★★, *Doggin' Around* 1973 recordings (Black Lion 1993)★★★.

WENTZEL, MAGNI

b. 28 June 1945, Norway. Although latterly known primarily as a jazz singer, Wentzel has had a very varied career. Her mother was a singer and her father played the violin with the Oslo Philharmonic Orchestra. When she was five years old she performed in childrens' theatre, then studied classical guitar and also occasionally sang. At the age of 18 she studied singing at the Norwegian School of Opera, then decided to pursue her guitar studies in Spain, Switzerland and England. While in Spain in the late 60s she sang jazz with pianist Tete Montolui and saxophonist Pony Poindexter. Back in Oslo she began performing in clubs and incorporated R&B into her repertoire. As a classical guitarist she appeared on television, recorded and in 1978 performed at the National Gallery of Art in Washington, DC. Also in the late 70s she was singing jazz with the Danish radio Big Band, sang at festivals in Poland and appeared with Charlie Ventura. During the 80s and early 90s her varied career continued. She played guitar on television both as soloist and as a member of chamber music groups; as a classical singer she sang in recitals of operatic music; as a jazz singer she worked in various European countries, singing with musicians such as Art Farmer, Roger Kellaway, Red Mitchell and Neils-Henning Ørsted Pedersen. In 1993 she toured the USA with Kellaway and the following year toured with him and Pedersen. Wentzel sings with a true, clear voice and while classical training is evident in much of her work, she has a good command of phrasing and interprets English-language lyrics with intelligence and feeling. She uses her four-octave range with discretion and her singing swings.

● ALBUMS: all as jazz singer *All Or Nothing At All* (Gemini 1986)★★★, *My Wonderful One* (Gemini 1988)★★★, *New York Nights* (Gemini 1991)★★, *Come Away With Me* (Gemini 1993)★★★.

WESS, FRANK

b. 4 January 1922, Kansas City, Missouri, USA. Wess started out on alto saxophone, playing in bands in and around Washington, DC, where he was raised. Later, he switched to tenor saxophone and worked briefly in the band led by Blanche Calloway. He developed his musical abilities while on military service and, following his discharge at the end of World War II, he played in the bands of artists such as Billy Eckstine and Lucky Millinder. During this period he began to play the flute. In 1953 he joined the Count Basie band, mostly playing tenor and flute, and becoming a featured attraction with the band both as soloist and as duettist with fellow sideman Frank Foster. In the late 50s Wess reverted to alto saxophone but continued to feature his flute playing, becoming the first major jazz soloist to popularize this instrument and proving in the process that it could be used in a gimmick-free fashion. He left Basie in 1964, thereafter working in studios, leading his own small groups, making records and working in groups such as the New York Jazz Quartet and Dameronia, the band led by Philly Joe Jones. Wess also wrote numerous arrangements, for his own groups and for other bands. In the mid-80s he was briefly with Woody Herman and also continued to lead his own small group and to colead a quintet with Foster. In the late 80s and early 90s he was leading a splendid Basie-style big band, which included in its ranks Harry 'Sweets' Edison, Joe Newman, Snooky Young, Al Grey, Benny Powell, Marshal Royal and Billy Mitchell, and which made highly successful appearances in Japan. Albums by this band, *Dear Mr Basie* and *Entre Nous*, showed that Wess had ably assumed the role of big band leader and arranger in the Basie tradition. As a soloist (whichever instrument he uses), Wess plays with uncluttered swing, fashioning his phrases with care. His playing satisfactorily updates the stylistic traditions of the swing era and is always polished and highly sophisticated.

● ALBUMS: *Frank Wess Quintet* 10-inch album (Commodore 1952)★★★, *Frank Wess* 10-inch album (Commodore 1952)★★★, *Wess Of The Moon* (Commodore 1954)★★★, *Flutes And Reeds* (Savoy 1955)★★★, *North, South, East...Wess* (Savoy 1956)★★, with Dorothy Ashby *In A Minor Groove* (New Jazz 1958)★★★, *I Hear Ya Talkin'* (1959)★★★, *Frank Wess Quartet* (Moodsville 1960)★★, *Southern Comfort* (Prestige 1962)★★★, with Kenny Burrell *Steamin'* (Prestige 1963)★★★, *Yo Ho! Poor You, Little Me* (Prestige 1963)★★★, with Thad Jones *Touche* (Status 1965)★★★, with Coleman Hawkins *Commodore Years* (Atlantic 1973)★★★, with Johnny Coles *Two At The Top* (Uptown 1983)★★★★, with Frank Foster *Two For The Blues* (Pablo Jazz 1983)★★★, with Foster *Frankly Speaking* (Pablo Jazz 1984)★★★, *Dear Mr Basie* (Concord Jazz 1989)★★, *Entre Nous* (Concord Jazz 1990)★★★, *Live At The 1990 Concord Jazz Festival* (Concord Jazz 1991)★★★, *Trombones And Flute* (1992)★★★, *Jazz For Playboys* (1992)★★★, with Clark Terry *Big Band Basie* (Reference 1996)★★★, with Gene Harris *It's The Real Soul* (Concord Jazz 1996)★★, *Surprise Surprise* (Chiaroscuro 1998)★★★★.

West, Harold 'Doc'

b. 12 August 1915, Wolford, North Dakota, USA, d. 4 May 1951. In his early years West played several instruments before settling on the drums. During the early 30s he played in several bands including those led by Tiny Parham and Erskine Tate. By the late 30s he had a secure reputation, being called upon on one occasion to substitute for Chick Webb when the drummer-leader was unwell. A few years later he deputized for Jo Jones in Count Basie's band. During this time, the early 40s, he worked with Oran 'Hot Lips' Page but he was also attuned to new developments in jazz and in jazz drumming. West was one of a small number of swing era drummers who adapted readily to the demands of bop. He played at exploratory sessions at Minion's Playhouse and, in the early and mid-40s, backed musicians such as Wardell Gray and Charlie Parker. In these same years he continued to work in more orthodox settings, playing with Don Byas, Lester Young and Erroll Garner. His sudden death came while touring with Roy Eldridge, with whom he had first played in the late 30s.

● COMPILATIONS: *The Chronological Billie Holiday 1939-1940* (Classics 1939-40)★★★★, with Erroll Garner *Bounce With Me* (SPA 1945-47)★★★.

Westbrook, Kate

b. Kate Bernard, Guildford, Surrey, England. Westbrook initially studied as a painter, exhibiting in the UK, Europe and the USA, before joining her future husband in the Mike Westbrook Brass Band (1974). Self-taught as a musician she sings and plays a variety of wind instruments, as well as composing and writing lyrics for many of Mike Westbrook's groups. Independently, she was a guest soloist with the RAI Orchestra in Rome and the Zurich Radio Orchestra during the 70s, and in the 80s worked on projects with Lindsay Cooper. She sings in French, German, Greek and Italian and has performed from the works of poets and songwriters as diverse as D.H. Lawrence, William Blake, Cole Porter, Rossini and Lorca. In conjunction with Mike Westbrook, she organized many multi-media events involving music, performance and painting, which have been performed on television and the theatre. With such a wide variety of experience it is hardly surprising that she has complained: 'I think we've got some way to go before there's an understanding in the musical world of this thing greater than any category: music'.

● ALBUMS: with Mike Westbrook *The Westbrook Blake* (1980)★★★★, with Lindsay Cooper *Music For Other Occasions* (80s)★★★, with Westbrook *Love For Sale* (1985)★★★★, with Westbrook *A Little Westbrook Music* (1983)★★★, with Westbrook *London Bridge Is Broken Down* 3-album box-set (1988)★★★★, with Westbrook *Pierides, The Dance Band* (1989)★★★, with Cooper *Goodbye Peter Lorre* (1992)★★★, with Westbrook *Stage Set* (ASC 1996)★★★.

Westbrook, Mike

b. 21 March 1936, High Wycombe, Buckinghamshire, England. The UK's premier jazz composer, Westbrook grew up in Torquay and tried accountancy, National Service and art school before realizing that music was his first love. He formed his first band in Plymouth in 1958, soon recruiting the teenage John Surman on baritone saxophone, and in 1962 moved to London, where he led numerous groups and played regularly at the Old Place and the Little Theatre Club while working in the day as an art teacher. His first three records - *Celebration*, *Release* and *Marching Song* - were large-scale, big band works that showed Westbrook rapidly expanding his modern jazz base to include blues, rock 'n' roll, brass band marches, 'The Girl From Ipanema' and Lionel Hampton's 'Flying Home' riff in glorious profusion. His composerly skills in blending all of these together was matched by outbursts of brilliant improvisation from soloists such as Surman, Mike Osborne, Malcolm Griffiths and Paul Rutherford. Two unrecorded pieces, 'Earthrise' and the seven-hour 'Copan/Backing Track', were early examples of his continuing interest in multi-media projects, with Cosmic Circus (1970-72). Another early 70s Westbrook group, Solid Gold Cadillac, explored facets of jazz-rock. Reverting to the big band format, he recorded *Citadel Room 315* in 1975 (again featuring Surman), which is considered his first real masterpiece. Orchestral projects have remained a major focus of interest - the subsequent *The Cortege, Westbrook-Rossini* (based on themes from Rossini operas),*On Duke's Birthday* (Duke Ellington tribute taken from a larger work, 'After Smith's Hotel') have all been hailed as outstanding examples of jazz composition. In 1973 Westbrook also formed his Brass Band, featuring old friend and vocalist Phil Minton and his future wife Kate Westbrook (née Bernard), and they toured the UK playing at factories, schools, hospitals and street-theatre festivals. The group later developed into one of Westbrook's most impressive line-ups notably on *Bright As Fire*, a tribute to the poet William Blake, based on music that he had earlier written (and recorded) for the Adrian Mitchell play, *Tyger*. In 1983 Westbrook started a trio with Kate and regular associate Chris Biscoe, which explored the Westbrooks' interest in European cabaret music (*A Little Westbrook Music*). Much of his music is inspired by literary or theatrical sources: for instance, *The Cortege*, widely considered his finest work to date, comprises a series of songs based on texts by poets such as Rimbaud, Hesse, Lorca, Blake and John Clare. More recent albums have included the ambitious, brilliant in parts *London Bridge Is Broken Down* (for voice, jazz orchestra and chamber orchestra) and the Beatles tribute *Off Abbey Road*. Though awarded the OBE in 1988, Westbrook, like many UK jazz musicians, works chiefly on the continent, where he is offered many more opportunities to play and record than he is at home. Proficient on piano and tuba, he is less an instrumentalist than a virtuoso composer, the scope and scale of whose work places him firmly in the lineage of his heroes Ellington, Charles Mingus and Kurt Weill.

● ALBUMS: *Celebration* (Deram 1967)★★★★, *Release* (Deram 1968)★★★★, *Marching Song, Vols. 1 & 2* (Deram 1969)★★★, *Love Songs* (Deram 1970)★★★, *Metropolis* (RCA Neon 1971)★★★★, *Tyger* (RCA 1971)★★★, *Live* (Cadillac 1972)★★★, *Mike Westbrook Live* (1972)★★★, *Citadel Room 315* (Novus 1975)★★★★, *Plays 'For The Record'* (Transatlantic 1976)★★★, *Love/Dreams And Variations* (Transatlantic 1976)★★★★, *Mike Westbrook - Piano* (1978)★★★, *Goose Sauce* (Original 1978)★★★, *Mama Chicago* (1979)★★★, *Bright As Fire - The Westbrook Blake* (Impetus 1980)★★★, *Piano* (1980)★★★, *This Is Their Time - Oh Yes* rec. 1969 (1981)★★★, *The Paris Album* (1981)★★★, *The Cortege* 3-LP set (Enja 1982)★★★, *A Little Westbrook Music* (1983)★★★, *Love For Sale* (hatART 1986)★★★, *Pier Rides* (1986)★★★, *Westbrook-Rossini* (hatART 1987)★★★, *London Bridge Is Broken Down* 3-LP box-set (Venture 1988)★★★, *On Duke's Birthday* rec. 1984 (hatART 1988)★★★, *Pierides, The Dance Band* (Line 1989)★★★, *Off Abbey Road* (Tip Toe 1990)★★★, with Kate Westbrook *Stage Set* (ASC 1996)★★★, *Bar Utopia* (ASC 1998)★★★★.

WESTON, PAUL

b. Paul Wetstein, 12 March 1912, Springfield, Massachusetts, USA, d. 20 September 1996, Santa Monica, California, USA. A leading arranger and conductor, who recorded numerous albums of mood music, and was particularly successful working with female singers such as Lee Wiley, Ella Fitzgerald, Doris Day, Dinah Shore, Kate Smith, Sarah Vaughan, Margaret Whiting, Connee Boswell, Rosemary Clooney, Judy Garland, and Diahann Carroll. Weston first attracted attention arranging for Rudy Vallee in the mid-30s, and made his name during a lengthy spell as one of Tommy Dorsey's staff arrangers after Dorsey had taken over the Joe Haymes band. Among Weston's most notable charts for Dorsey were those featuring Jo Stafford, whom he married in 1952. When Capitol Records were formed in 1943, Weston joined as conductor-arranger, and later became A&R director. Throughout the 40s he served as musical director on various radio shows, and late in the decade began recording mood music, an activity that was boosted by the development of the long-playing record. In 1951 he moved over to Columbia Records, but by the end of the 50s was back at Capitol. The extent of Weston's musicianship is also displayed on a series of records he and Stafford made under the names Jonathan And Darlene Edwards. Stafford's deliberately off-key singing to Weston's out-of-tempo playing is brilliantly executed and the results number among the most hilarious comedy albums ever made. One of them, *Jonathan And Darlene Edwards In Paris*, was awarded a Grammy in 1960. In the 60s and 70s Weston conducted on several top-rated television programmes, starring Danny Kaye and Jonathan Winters. A gifted composer, Weston collaborated on several popular songs, including 'I Should Care' (with Axel Stordahl-Sammy Cahn), 'Day By Day' (Stordahl-Cahn), one of Stafford's biggest hits 'Shrimp Boats' (Paul Mason Howard), 'Autumn In Rome' (Cahn), 'Hey, Mr. Postman' (Don Raye), 'Indiscretion' (Cahn), 'The Gandy Dancers' Ball' (Howard), 'Congratulations' (Sid Robin) and 'No Other Love' (Bob Russell). He also wrote serious works such as 'Mass For Three Voices' and 'Crescent City Suite'. In 1971 Weston received the Trustees Award from the National Academy Of Recording Arts And Science (NARAS) for his 'inspiring and tireless dedication to the Academy's development'. During the 90s, he operated the Corinthian Records label in Beverly Hills, California, formed by himself and Stafford, which released the couple's new recordings and reissued their leased back catalogue. Weston died in September 1996.

● ALBUMS: as Paul Weston And His Orchestra *Crescent City - A Musical Portrait Of New Orleans* (Columbia 1954)★★★★, *Mood For 12* (Columbia 1955)★★★★, *Easy Jazz* (Columbia 1955)★★★, *Solo Mood* (Columbia 1956)★★★★, *Cinema Cameos* (Columbia 1956)★★★, *Reflections Of An Indian Boy* (Columbia 1957)★★, *Music For A Rainy Night* (Columbia 1957)★★★,

Moonlight Becomes You (Columbia 1958)★★★, *The Music Of Jerome Kern* (Columbia 1958)★★★, *Columbia Album Of Romberg* (Columbia 1958)★★★, *Hollywood* (Columbia 1958)★★★, *Carefree* (Capitol 1959)★★★, *Memories That Linger On* (Decca 1959)★★★, *Floatin' Like A Feather* (Capitol 1959)★★★, *Music For Memories* (Capitol 1959)★★★, *Music For Romancing* (Capitol 1959)★★★, *Music For The Fireside* (Capitol 1959)★★★, *Music For Dreaming* (Capitol 1959)★★★, *The Sweet And Swingin'* (Capitol 1960)★★★, *Music For My Love* (Capitol 1961)★★★.
As Jonathan And Darlene Edwards *Sing Along With Jonathan And Darlene Edwards - Only The Chorus Is For Real* (Columbia 1959)★★★, *Jonathan And Darlene's Original Masterpiece* (Columbia 1960)★★★, *Jonathan And Darlene Edwards In Paris* (Columbia 1960)★★★, *Songs For Sheiks And Flappers* (Corinthian 1988)★★, *Darlene Remembers Duke, Jonathan Plays Fats* (Corinthian 1988)★★★.
● COMPILATIONS: *Paul Weston - The Original* (1985)★★★★. With Jo Stafford *Jo And Broadway* (Columbia 1960)★★★, with Stafford *As You Desire Me* (Columbia 1960)★★★, with Stafford *Swingin' Down Broadway* (Columbia 1960)★★★★.
As Jonathan And Darlene Edwards *Jonathan And Darlene's Greatest Hits* (Corinthian 1987)★★★.

Weston, Randy

b. Randolph Weston, 6 April 1926, New York City, New York, USA. Weston grew up in Brooklyn and in the late 40s ran a restaurant that was frequented by many of the city's leading bebop musicians. Deciding to pursue a musical career himself, he played piano with various R&B bands (including a record date with the Clovers) and also worked with Eddie 'Cleanhead' Vinson, Kenny Dorham and Cecil Payne. One of the first artists signed to Riverside Records, his debut session, in April 1954, comprised a set of Cole Porter tunes. Later Riverside dates included a solo album and a trio recording with Art Blakey on drums. Long fascinated by all things African, Weston recorded *Uhuru Afrika* in 1960 - a big band suite with lyrics by Langston Hughes and arrangements by Melba Liston: players included Freddie Hubbard, Yusef Lateef, Max Roach and Babatunde Olatunji. In 1961 he travelled to Nigeria with other USA artists to appear at an arts festival in Lagos, and returned again for a lecture tour in 1963. In the early 60s he led a group that featured Booker Ervin and (later) Ed Blackwell, releasing *Highlife* and *African Cookbook*. He also recorded the solo/trio *Berkshire Blues* for Duke Ellington's projected label, but this never materialized and the sessions finally appeared on the Freedom label some 13 years later. Weston started his own label, Bakton, but it quickly folded and, discouraged by the music scene, he left the USA. After a 14-country tour of North and West Africa, he settled in Tangier in 1968, where he ran the African Rhythms Club for several years. Returning to the USA in the early 70s, he released two big band albums, the jazz-funk *Blue Moses* and *Tanjah*, but subsequent releases have concentrated almost exclusively on solo piano and have included tributes to Ellington and Thelonious Monk, his major piano mentors. Notable exceptions are a duo album with David Murray and his recent *The Spirits Of Our Ancestors*, which again has arrangements by Liston and features guest artists Dizzy Gillespie, Dewey Redman and Pharoah Sanders.
A powerful player (he is over six-and-a-half feet tall!), Weston is adept at using the piano percussively, although he is also a talented melodist who has written several well-known tunes, such as 'Hi Fly' and 'Little Niles', the latter a 1952 waltz named after his son Azadeen, now a skilled percussionist.
● ALBUMS: *Cole Porter In A Modern Mood* 10-inch album (Riverside 1954)★★★, *The Randy Weston Trio* reissued as *Randy Weston Trio And Solo* and *Zulu!* (Riverside 1955)★★★★, *Get Happy* (Riverside 1956)★★★, *With These Hands ...* (Riverside 1956)★★★, with Cecil Payne *Jazz A La Bohemia* reissued as *Greenwich Village Jazz* (Riverside 1957)★★★★, *The Modern Art Of Jazz* (Dawn 1957)★★★, *Piano A La Mode* (Jubilee 1957)★★★, with Lem Winchester *New Faces At Newport* (Metrojazz 1958)★★★, *Little Niles* (United Artists 1959)★★★★, *Destry Rides Again* (United Artists 1959)★★★, *Live At The Five Spot* (United Artists 1959)★★★, *Uhuru Afrika* (Roulette 1960)★★★★, *Highlife* (Colpix 1963)★★★, *Randy!* (1964)★★★, *African Cookbook* (Atlantic 1965)★★★★, *Monterey '66* (Verve 1967)★★★, *Blues* (1967)★★★, *Blues Moses* (CTI 1972)★★★, *Tanjah* (1973)★★★, *Informal Solo Piano* (1974)★★★★, *African Rhythms* (1975)★★★★, *Carnival* (Freedom 1975)★★★★, *Blues To Africa* (Freedom 1975)★★★, *African Nite* (Inner City 1976)★★★, *Perspective* (Denon 1977)★★★, *Berkshire Blues* 1965 recording (1978)★★★★, *Nuits Americaine* (1982)★★★, *Blue* (1984)★★★, with David Murray *The Healers* (Black Saint 1987)★★★, *How High The Moon* (1989)★★, *Portraits Of Duke Ellington* (Verve 1990)★★★, *Portraits Of Thelonious Monk* (Verve 1990)★★★, *Self Portraits* (Verve 1990)★★★, with Melba Liston *The Spirits Of Our Ancestors* (Antilles 1992)★★★★, with Liston *Volcano Blues* (Verve 1993)★★★, *Marrakech In The Cool Of The Evening* (Verve 1993)★★★, *Tanjah* (Verve 1994)★★, *The Splendid Master Gnawa Musicians Of Morocco* (Verve 1995)★★, *Saga* (Verve 1996)★★★★, with Liston *Earth Birth* (Verve 1997)★★★★, with Liston *Khepera* (Verve 1998)★★★★.

Wettling, George

b. 28 November 1907, Topeka, Kansas, USA, d. 6 June 1968, New York City, New York, USA. Resident in Chicago from his early teenage years, Wettling studied drums under various teachers, including the celebrated Roy C. Knapp (who also taught Gene Krupa). While still in his teens Wettling became a professional musician and worked with numerous bands, mostly based in Chicago and all playing dance and popular music of the day. In the mid-30s he worked with Paul Mares and was a member of Jack Hylton's American band. Later in the decade he moved to New York City and was hired by Artie Shaw for his first big band. He later played in the big band led by Bunny Berigan and was also with Red Norvo and Paul Whiteman. His musical inclinations lay in other areas, however, and during this period he made many records with small dixieland-Chicago-style groups. Gradually, he moved into this field of music, although he did spend time in big bands led by Abe Lyman and Benny Goodman during the early 40s. From the mid-40s onwards he was closely associated with

Eddie Condon, playing at Condon's club, touring and recording with Wild Bill Davison, Bud Freeman, Pee Wee Russell, Sidney Bechet and many others. A propulsive and energetic drummer, Wettling played with dash and verve, inspiring his musical companions to give of their best. In addition to his musical career, Wettling was an accomplished painter and his abstract work was exhibited in New York City and has been reproduced in magazines.

● ALBUMS: *George Wettling's High Fidelity Rhythms* (Weathers 1954)★★★★, with Frank Signorelli *Ragtime Duo* (Kapp 1955)★★★, *Jazz Trios* (Kapp 1956)★★★, *George Wettling's Jazz Band* 10-inch album (Columbia 1956)★★★, *Dixieland In Hi-Fi* (Harmony 1957)★★★★, *Is George Really George?* (1962)★★★.

Wheeler, Kenny

b. 14 January 1930, Toronto, Canada. Sometimes known as Weeny Keller, this outstanding jazz composer, trumpet, cornet and flügelhorn player is one of the shyest and most self-effacing artists imaginable. Buddy Rich once said 'show me a humble man and I'll show you a nonentity' which must make Wheeler the world's most respected and influential musical nonentity. Major figures from jazz and improvised music, such as John Surman and Evan Parker, have queued up to work with him since the 60s and continue to do so; witness the line-ups he assembled for Orchestra UK and the Kenny Wheeler Big Band at the start of the 90s. He learned cornet at the age of 12 and studied trumpet and harmony at Toronto Conservatory. He moved to London in 1952, mainly working in big bands such as Roy Fox and Vic Lewis. From 1959-65 he was in the John Dankworth band, but also played with the groups of Tubby Hayes and Joe Harriott. In the 60s he studied for a while with Richard Rodney Bennett and Bill Russo, and came into contact with free music at the Little Theatre Club where he worked with Tony Oxley, John Stevens and the Spontaneous Music Ensemble. He guested with the brilliant John Surman-Mike Osborne Quartet in the late 60s and was so lacking in self-confidence that at one gig he played from behind a stack of equipment, producing thrilling and challenging music nonetheless. His CV demonstrates his versatility and status among his peers: he has played with John Taylor, Mike Pyne, Jan Garbarek, Michael Gibbs, the Clarke-Boland Big Band, John Warren, the Globe Unity Orchestra, Graham Collier, Ronnie Scott, Alan Skidmore (in a quintet which was a highlight of Jazz Expo 69), the United Jazz And Rock Ensemble, Dave Holland and Anthony Braxton and has led, apart from Orchestra UK, several starry bands of his own, including Azimuth (which he co-founded in 1977 with John Taylor and Norma Winstone, and which is not to be confused with Azymuth), Coe (Tony Coe) Wheeler & Co, and the superb Freedom For A Change. In the early 90s he toured with the new Michael Gibbs Band featuring John Scofield. Although Wheeler is highly respected it is as a supporting musician that he has gained most of his praise, save for *Gnu High*. It was therefore a pleasant surprise when the excellent quartet work *Angel Song* was released in 1997. This ethereal album featured Lee Konitz, Bill Frisell and Holland.

● ALBUMS: *Windmill Tilter* (Fontana 1968)★★★★, *Song For Someone* (Incus 1974)★★★, *Gnu High* (ECM 1975)★★★★, *Deer Wan* (ECM 1977)★★★★, *Around 6* (ECM 1980)★★★, *Double, Double You* (ECM 1983)★★★★, *Welcome* (Soul Note 1987)★★★, *Flutter By, Butterfly* (Soul Note 1988)★★★, *Music For Large And Small Ensembles* (ECM 1990)★★★, *The Widow in The Window* (ECM 1991)★★★★, *California Daydream* (Musidisc 1991)★★★, *Kayak* (Ah Um 1993)★★★, with Sonny Greenwich *Live At The Montreal Bistro* (Justin Time 1997)★★★, with Paul Bley *Touché* (Justin Time 1997)★★★, with Bill Frisell, Dave Holland, Lee Konitz *Angel Song* (ECM 1997)★★★★, *Walk Softly* 1987 recording (Wave 1998)★★★, *All The More* (Soul Note 1998)★★★★, with Norma Winstone, John Taylor *Siren's Song* (Justin Time 1998)★★★.

Whetsol, Artie

b. 1905, Punta Gorda, Florida, USA, d. 5 January 1940. Brought up in Washington, DC, Whetsol became a friend and musical associate of Duke Ellington, playing trumpet in Ellington's first band. Together, they visited New York in 1923, but Whetsol then decided to abandon music in favour of a medical career. In 1928 he was persuaded to rejoin Ellington, becoming an important factor in the band's success. He remained in the band until 1937, but thereafter severe ill-health meant that he could play only intermittently. He was a fine lead trumpeter with a pure sound and a gift for melodic, understated solos.

● ALBUMS: *The Indispensable Duke Ellington Vol. 1/2 (1927-29)* (early 80s)★★★★, *The Indispensable Duke Ellington Vol. 3/4 (1930-34)* (early 80s)★★★★, *Duke Ellington 1927-34* (1988)★★★.

Whigham, Jiggs

b. Haydn Whigham, 20 August 1943, Cleveland, Ohio, USA. Whigham studied extensively as a young man, learning trombone, harmony and composing. In the early 60s he joined the Glenn Miller band led by Ray McKinley, remaining until the middle of the decade. He was then briefly with Stan Kenton before joining Kurt Edelhagen in Germany. Whigham decided to stay on in Germany, freelancing and teaching throughout the 70s and into the early 80s, eventually becoming a member of the faculty of the Cologne Music School. He also recorded *The Third Stone* with Bill Holman and the West German Radio big band. In the mid- to late 80s Whigham occasionally toured as a single, visiting the UK and recording with Vic Lewis. He also made some appearances in duo with Mundell Lowe. Technically faultless, Whigham exudes power tempered with finesse and is greatly respected by his fellow musicians.

● ALBUMS: *Hope* (Mons 1976)★★★, *The Third Stone* (1982)★★★, *The Jiggs Up* (Capri 1989)★★★, with Gene Bertoncini *Jiggs And Gene* (Azica 1998)★★★.

White, Andrew

b. 6 September 1942, Washington, DC, USA. White's uncle played saxophone, flute and guitar. He studied saxophone himself with John Reed in Nashville (1954-

60) and music theory with Brenton Banks (1958-60), then attended Howard University, Washington (1960-64), playing with the University Band and Symphonietta. Early work experience was gained with pianist Don Pullen in the late 50s, by which time White was playing alto and tenor saxophones and double bass. During 1964/5 he played tenor saxophone with Kenny Clarke in Paris. In 1965 he led the New Jazz Trio in Buffalo. Next came stints playing electric bass with Stanley Turrentine and tenor saxophone with the Cyclones and Otis Redding (1967). Between 1968 and 1970 White played electric bass with Stevie Wonder and was the principal oboist and English horn player for New York's American Ballet Theatre Orchestra. He played bass in the popular singing group Fifth Dimension from 1971-76, and in a production of *Hair* in 1971. The following year he guested on Weather Report's *I Sing The Body Electric*, and in 1973 played electric bass and English horn on their historic *Sweetnighter*. In September 1973 he completed a catalogue of 209 transcribed John Coltrane solos, for which he had set up (in 1971) his own publishing imprint, Andrew's Music. In 1977 he published a further series of 212 transcribed Coltrane solos. Peter Ochiogrosso described White's work as 'doing for 'Trane what Kirschel did for Mozart'. Albums of Coltrane solos, trio work with the artists including Buell Neidlinger, and orchestral works - *Concerto* and *Concertino* - have been produced since, along with books, articles and further transcriptions (including Eric Dolphy and Charlie Parker solos). In 1991 White's catalogue of products for sale totalled 1600 items. In 1984 he stunned the jazz world by producing *Andrew's X-Rated Band Stories*, the first in a series of four X-rated comedy books.

In the 80s White played with the Elvin Jones Jazz Machine (1980-81), the Beaver Harris All-Stars (1983) and, since 1987, has worked with Julius Hemphill on several saxophone-based projects. His 1981 classical record, *Petite Suite Francaise*, was, he claims, the 'first-ever feature album recorded by a black oboist', but since the mid-80s he has released no new albums, preferring to concentrate on his voluminous activities as writer, teacher, transcriber and live performer - not to mention single-handedly running Andrew's Music and continuing his unstaunchable dedication to the music of John Coltrane.

● ALBUMS: *Andrew Nathaniel White III* (1971)★★, *Live At The New Thing In Washington DC* (1973)★★, *Live In Bucharest* (1973)★★★, *Who Got De Funk?* (1973)★★★, *Passion Flower* (1974)★★★, *Sings For A French Lady* (1974)★★, *Theme* (1974)★★★, *Live At The Foolery, Vols 1-6* (1975)★★, *Collage* (1975), *Marathon '75, Vols 1-9* (1976)★★, *Spotts, Maxine And Brown* (1977)★★★, *Countdown* (1977)★★★, *Red Top* (1977)★★★, *Trinkle, Trinkle* (1977)★★★, *Ebony Glaze* (1977)★★★, *Miss Ann* (1977)★★★, *Seven Giant Steps For John Coltrane* (1977)★★★★, *Live In New York At The Ladies Fort* (1977)★★, *Live In New York, Volumes 1 & 2* (1977)★★, *Bionic Saxophone* (1978)★★★, *The Coltrane Interviews, Volumes One and Two* (1979)★★★, *Saxophonitis* (1979)★★★, *Funk Update* (1979)★★★, *I Love Japan* (1979)★★, *Have Band, Will Travel* (1979)★★★, *Petite Suite Francaise: Andrew White Plays The Oboe* (1981)★★★, *Seven More Giant Steps For John Coltrane* (1983)★★★, *Profile* (1984)★★★.

WHITE, LENNY

b. 19 December 1949, New York City, New York, USA. White took up the drums when he was 14-years-old and by the late 60s was playing in the band of Jackie McLean. He joined the sessions to record *Bitches Brew* with Miles Davis in 1969 and in the next couple of years played with many other leaders - Freddie Hubbard, Woody Shaw, Gato Barbieri, Joe Henderson, Stan Getz, Stanley Clarke and Gil Evans. He had a spell with the Latin rock band Azteca before joining Chick Corea's Return To Forever (1973-6). His bold, assertive playing was well-suited to the rock-influenced music of the 70s which he thought of as a music 'where you improvise more, like traditional jazz, but you use different instruments'. *Present Tense* in 1995 was his first solo album for many years and featured an impressive guest list including John Scofield (guitar), Chick Corea (keyboards), Marcus Miller (bass) and Michael Brecker (saxophone). On *Renderers Of Spirit* featured cover versions of Bacharach And David's 'Walk On By' as well as the Christopher Cross pop song 'Sailing'.

● ALBUMS: *Venusian Summer* (1975)★★, *Big City* (1977)★★★, with Twennynine *Twennynine With Lenny White* (1980)★★★, *Streamline* (1978)★★★, *The Adventures Of Astral Pirates* (1978)★★★, *Just Like Dreaming* (1981)★★★, *Present Tense* (Hip Bop 1995)★★★, *Renderers Of Spirit* (Hip Bop 1997)★★★.

WHITE, MICHAEL

b. Michael Walter White, 24 May 1933, Houston, Texas, USA. White, (not to be confused with the New Orleans clarinettist) was raised in California and took up the violin when he was nine years old. He first came to public attention when he played with the John Handy Quintet at the Monterey Jazz Festival in 1965. He has a formidable technique regularly including passages of double-stopping in his solos. He has been able to incorporate into his playing influences and techniques from classical and eastern music. In the late 60s he moved in a new direction joining jazz rock group, Fourth Way. In the early 70s he returned to *avant garde* jazz working with artists such as tenor saxophone players Pharoah Sanders and Joe Henderson and pianist McCoy Tyner as well as leading his own bands.

● ALBUMS: with John Handy *Live At The Monterey Jazz Festival* (Columbia 1965)★★★, with Fourth Way *The Sun And Moon Have Come Together* (Harvest 1969)★★, *Werewolf* (1970)★★★, *The Fourth Way* (1970)★★, with Pharoah Sanders *Thembi* (Impulse! 1970)★★★, with McCoy Tyner *Song For My Lady* (Milestone 1972)★★★, *The Land Of Spirit And Light* (Impulse! 1973)★★★, *Father Music, Mother Dance* (Impulse! 1974)★★, *Spirit Dance* (1975)★★★, *The X Factor* (Elektra 1978)★★.

WHITE, SONNY

b. Ellerton Oswald White, 11 November 1917, Panama, d. 28 April 1971. White first came to localized attention in the mid-30s playing piano for Jesse Stone, the Kansas

City-based bandleader. Thereafter, he worked with several small groups and also some big bands, including those led by Willie Bryant and Frankie Newton. With Newton he played at the opening of the Café Society in New York on 30 December 1938. During this engagement White's duties also included accompanying Billie Holiday. He also backed her on record dates that included the session at which she made her famous recording of 'Strange Fruit'. White's relationship with Holiday extended beyond music and throughout most of 1939 they had an intense affair but, as Holiday told *Down Beat*, 'Like me, he lives with his mother . . . our plans for marriage didn't jell.' White recorded again with Holiday in 1940 and that year was also briefly with Benny Carter. He then joined Artie Shaw for a short spell before serving in the armed forces during World War II. Later, after a return to Carter's band, he settled into several long residencies in New York's clubland. In the 60s he played and sometimes recorded with the bands of Wilbur De Paris, Louis Metcalf, Eddie Barefield and Jonah Jones. White was a solid section player and a sensitive accompanist with a delicate touch. His career epitomizes the overlooked contribution made to jazz by musicians other than soloists.

WHITEHEAD, ANNIE

b. Lena Annie Whitehead, 16 July 1955, Oldham, Lancashire, England. Whitehead joined her school's brass band wanting to play tuba, but - an indication of the patronising attitudes she continues to suffer from as an adult, professional musician - was not allowed to, because it was felt a girl could not cope with the large instrument. She was therefore forced to choose cornet, but after a year took up the euphonium and baritone sax as well. Finally, she was allowed to switch to trombone, on which she has since proved her skill and versatility with rock, reggae and jazz groups. Leaving school at the age of 16, she joined Ivy Benson's all-woman big band to tour Germany where, to Ivy's disapproval, she would sneak off to jam with local musicians. She stayed with Benson for two years, then moved to Jersey, giving up playing almost completely for six years as she was disillusioned with music as a job. In 1979, she formed her own ska band, and two years later moved to London to work as a session musician, re-kindling her interest in jazz at jam sessions in a Finsbury Park, north London pub. In 1983 she toured Africa with Chris McGregor's Brotherhood Of Breath and the USA with Fun Boy Three. In the mid-80s she ran her own band including Louise Elliott, a fine saxophonist with bands like Zubop, and pianist Laka Daisical, and was one of the Sisterhood Of Spit: at the end of the decade she was again the only sister in the Brotherhood Of Breath. She has also worked with John Stevens (duelling memorably with Evan Parker), Charlie Watts Orchestra, Guest Stars, Working Week, Jah Wobble, Lydia D'Ustbyn's Swing Orchestra, Native Hipsters, District Six, and Smiley Culture. At the end of the 80s she set up a new band, Dance.

● ALBUMS: with John Stevens' Folkus *The Life Of Riley* (1984),★★★ *Mix-Up* (Paladin 1985)★★★, with Charlie Watts *Live At Fulham Town Hall* (1986)★★, *Naked* (EFZ 1996)★★★.

WHITEHEAD, TIM

b. 12 December 1950, Liverpool, England. Whitehead had clarinet lessons as a child and played in a folk group at school before reading law at university. In 1976 he turned professional playing tenor saxophone and in the following year formed South Of The Border, which he led with Glenn Cartledge (guitar), which won the Greater London Arts Association jazz competition. In the years that followed he worked with Nucleus and Graham Collier's Band before forming his own outfit Borderline (1980) for which he writes much of the music. He has continued to play and record with a wide range of musicians and in 1984 joined Loose Tubes.

● ALBUMS: with Borderline *English People* (1982)★★★, with Harry Beckett *Pictures Of You* (1985)★★★, with Loose Tubes *Loose Tubes* (1984)★★★★, *Open Letter* (1988)★★★, *Silence Between Waves* (Jazz House 1994)★★★, *Authentic* (Jazz House 1996)★★★.

WHITEMAN, PAUL

b. 28 March 1890, Denver, Colorado, USA, d. 29 December 1967, Doylestown, Pennsylvania, USA. Whiteman's father was a distinguished music teacher and a career in music seemed the most natural thing for the youngster to follow. A tall, heavily-built individual, Whiteman first learned classical violin, and in his teens was a member of the local symphony orchestra. During World War I he organized bands in the US Navy and thereafter led his own bands in Los Angeles, Atlantic City and eventually New York City. By 1920, he already had a recording contract with RCA Victor; in 1923 he took a band to London, and in the following year presented a spectacular concert at New York's Aeolian Hall. Billed as an 'Experiment In Modern Music', the occasion was later hailed, inaccurately, as the first jazz concert. It was typical of what was to become the Whiteman trademark: lavish presentation, many musicians, and music of all kinds mixed together, whether compatible or not. The concert also saw the premiere of a work specially commissioned for the occasion, George Gershwin's 'Rhapsody In Blue', with the composer at the piano. Whiteman's star rose and he performed concerts at Carnegie Hall and in capital cities across Europe. He always took a highly commercial view of the music business, and when he saw the growing popularity of jazz (allied to the fact that he loved this kind of music), he decided to hire the best white jazz musicians money could buy. Amongst those he employed over the years were Joe Venuti, Jack Teagarden, Frank Trumbauer, Jimmy and Tommy Dorsey, Bunny Berigan, Red Norvo and, most significant of all, Bix Beiderbecke. Whiteman also hired good singers, including Mildred Bailey and Bing Crosby. Although he subsequently took much criticism for his outrageous publicity claims (he angered many when he was labelled as 'The King of Jazz'), Whiteman was genuinely enthusiastic about jazz and the manner in which he treated his sidemen was exemplary. Musically, Whiteman's recordings of the late 20s and early 30s are often zesty, and many of the arrangements, notably those by Bill Challis, are worthy attempts to showcase the jazz talents in this often cumbersome orchestra. During this period he had numerous hit records, including 'Whispering' (reported sales in excess of two million), 'The Japanese Sandman', 'Wang Wang Blues', 'Bright Eyes', 'My Mammy', 'Make Believe', 'Cherie', 'Song Of India', 'Say It With Music', 'Canadian Capers', 'When Buddha Smiles', 'Do It Again', 'Stumbling', 'Hot Lips', 'Three O'Clock In The Morning', 'I'll Build A Stairway To Paradise', 'When Hearts Are Young', 'Parade Of The Wooden Soldiers', 'Bambalina', 'Last Night On The Back Porch', 'Linger Awhile', 'What'll I Do?', 'Somebody Loves Me', 'All Alone', 'Oh! Lady Be Good. 'Valencia', 'The Birth Of The Blues', 'In A Little Spanish Town', 'My Blue Heaven', 'Among My Souvenirs', 'Together', 'Ramona', 'Ol' Man River', and 'My Angel'. Most important of all, however, Whiteman's efforts helped to make jazz acceptable to the wider public. He may have misjudged the true nature of jazz, and did it little good by sanitizing the earthier aspects of the developing music, but he did it all the same. As Harry Carney observed, Whiteman 'made a lady out of jazz'. Because of the nature of his music, Whiteman was never a part of the swing era, despite making some good records with the Swing Wing and the Bouncing Brass, featuring Jack and Charlie Teagarden and Miff Mole in the late 30s. Instead, he continued to present musical stage and film extravaganzas. Among the cast of one of his movies, *King Of Jazz* (1930), were the Rhythm Boys, a vocal trio which included Bing Crosby and was resident with the Orchestra for a time. Whiteman's other films included *Thanks A Million* (1935), *Strike Up The Band* (1940), *Atlantic City* (1944), and *Rhapsody In Blue* (1945), He was also in the Broadway musical shows *George White's Scandals Of 1922*, *Lucky* (1927), and *Jumbo* (1935), and remained immensely popular on radio throughout the 30s. In the 40s Whiteman retired from music to become musical director of ABC radio. He later made occasional appearances with specially formed orchestras. In the 70s, some years after Whiteman's death, Dick Sudhalter formed the New Paul Whiteman Orchestra, which effectively recreated the music if not the glitz of the original. Latterly, most of Whiteman's recorded output is readily available although it is usually released under the name of Beiderbecke, his star sideman.

● ALBUMS: *50th Anniversary* (1956).

● COMPILATIONS: *Jazz A La King 1920-36* (RCA 1983)★★★, *Shakin' The Blues Away 1920-27* (Halcyon 1983)★★★, *Wang Dang Blues* (Astan 1986)★★★, *The Paul Whiteman Collection - 20 Golden Greats* (Deja Vu 1987)★★★, *Whiteman Stomp 1923-36* (Halcyon 1987)★★★. The New Paul Whiteman Orchestra *Runnin' Wild* (1975)★★★, *Number 2* (Monmouth 1979)★★★, *In Concert At The Queen Elizabeth Hall* (1979)★★★, *The Complete Capitol Recordings* (Capitol 1995)★★★.

● FURTHER READING: *A Paul Whiteman Chronology, 1890-1967*, Carl Johnson.

WHITFIELD, MARK

b. 1967, Long Island, New York, USA. Whitfield began his musical life playing bass but switched to guitar in his mid-teens, later taking up a scholarship at the Berklee College Of Music. Back in New York from 1986, he played with several leading musicians, including Donald Harrison and Terence Blanchard, spent two years in Brother Jack McDuff's group, and also met George Benson who became his mentor and helped him land a record deal. On subsequent recording dates, Whitfield performed with top-flight artists, among them Nicholas Payton, Branford Marsalis, Stephen Scott, Christian McBride, Tommy Flanagan and Courtney Pine, appearing with the latter on the 1997 sessions for *Underground*. In 1996 he appeared in the film, *Kansas City* playing the part of guitarist Freddie Green, a task which prompted him to reassess the role of the guitarist in earlier forms of jazz. Whitfield's playing often suggests that he is a stylistic descendant of Wes Montgomery, and there is also more than a hint of a strong feeling for the blues. His sound is warm and mellow, and he solos with admirable fluency. When joined by rhythm players of the calibre gathered for some of his record dates, and rubbing front line shoulders with distinguished horns, he is a strong and inventive soloist and a fast-thinking accompanist. By the time of his third album for Verve Records a decision was made, presumably to broaden his audience appeal, to record with strings. The result was very good music but with the jazz content diluted from the earthier sound and style that had marked his earlier albums.

● ALBUMS: *The Marksman* (Warners 1990)★★★, *Patrice* (Warners 1991)★★★, *Mark Whitfield* (Warners 1993)★★★, *True Blue* (Verve 1994)★★★★, *7th Avenue Stroll* (Verve 1995)★★★, *Forever Love* (Verve 1997)★★★, with Christian McBride, Nicholas Payton *Fingerpainting: The Music Of Herbie Hancock* (Verve 1997)★★★★.

● FILMS: *Kansas City* (1996).

WHITFIELD, WESLIA

b. California, USA. Whitfield first sang at the age of four as a member of a trio with her sisters, and three years later began studying the piano and, at 14, voice, studying both classical and bel canto methods. As an adult she sang professionally both in opera, as a member of the San Fransciso Opera Chorus, and in church as both chorister and soloist. She was encouraged to turn to jazz by Mike Greensill, a highly gifted pianist and arranger, whom she later married. She developed an extensive repertoire, drawing from the great standards of pop and jazz, and attracted a great deal of attention in her home base of San Francisco. Although she has declared unequivocally that she does not consider herself a jazz singer, she is frequently close to the elusive boundaries between jazz and superior cabaret work. Her eclectic tastes are borne out by her influences, which include diverse singers such as Frankie Laine, Julie Andrews, Peggy Lee, Ray Charles and Rosemary Clooney. Gradually, word of her talent spread and thanks to the encouragement of Eileen Farrell, Michael Feinstein, Margaret Whiting and others, together with several admirable albums it became possible for audiences far away to enjoy her singing. In considering her work it is almost impossible to separate what she does from what is done by Greensill. Their collaboration is a true meeting of minds, hearts and talents. Song treatments are often unexpected, as Greensill puts it, 'We've always liked to swim against the current.' Unusual tempos are sought and moulded to fit; sometimes the verse is interpolated into the middle of the song rather than in its written place at the start. Allied to a strong, sinewy and very distinctive voice, these treatments make Whitfield one of the more interesting singers working in the 90s.

● ALBUMS: *Seeker Of Wisdom And Truth* (Cabaret 1993)★★★, *Nice Work* (Landmark 1994)★★★, *Nobody Else But Me* (Landmark 1996)★★★, *My Shining Hour* (HighNote 1996)★★★, *Teach Me Tonight* (HighNote 1997)★★★.

Whittle, Tommy

b. 13 October 1926, Grangemouth, Scotland. Whittle began playing tenor saxophone while in his early teens and, in 1942, moved to Chatham, England, where he joined a dance band led by Claude Giddings. Also in the band was Ronnie Verrell and Whittle soon found himself playing with guest artists such as Ralph Sharon and Stéphane Grappelli. He also played with Johnny Claes, Carl Barriteau and, in 1946, joined the Ted Heath band. He remained with Heath for six years before moving on to play in Tony Kinsey's small group. Throughout the 50s he played with several small bands, sometimes leading or co-leading, and his associates included Dill Jones, Kenny Wheeler and Joe Temperley. From the 60s on through to the early 90s, Whittle has remained a prominent figure on the UK jazz scene, playing club and festival dates, and making records with a wide range of jazzmen from the UK and USA, including Benny Goodman. A quiet and introspective individual offstage, Whittle's playing reflects these personal characteristics and his warm, caressing sound is particularly well-suited to ballads. His many records include several with his wife, the singer Barbara Jay.

● ALBUMS: *New Horizons* (1959)★★★, *Jigsaw* (1977)★★★, *Why Not* (Jam 1979)★★, *The Nearness Of You* (1982)★★★, *Straight Eight* (Miles Music 1986)★★★, *The Warm Glow* (Teejay 1992)★★.

● COMPILATIONS: *Waxing With Whittle (1953-54)* (Esquire 1979)★★★, *More Waxing With Whittle (1954-55)* (Esquire 1987)★★★.

Whyte, Ronny

b. 12 May 1937, Seattle, Washington, USA. An excellent interpreter of song lyrics and a good jazz-influenced pianist, he has also worked as an actor and dancer. Mostly based in the New York area, he has performed in many of the city's intimate supper clubs, night clubs and superior hotel lounges. Amongst the venues are Michael's Pub, The Village Gate, the Sherry Netherland, the St. Regis and the Oak Room of the Algonquin Hotel. He has also worked elsewhere in the USA, including Los Angeles, San Francisco, Chicago and Washington while overseas engagements have taken him to Paris, Tokyo, Johannesburg and São Paulo. His concert performances include New York's Town Hall and Carnegie Hall and he has also appeared at jazz festivals. In addition to his singing he has acted in Shakespeare and has played the lead in a production of *Pal Joey*. He also makes appearances with symphony orchestras and in performances of music by George Gershwin including 'Rhapsody In Blue', and his own arrangement of *Porgy And Bess*. Whyte's singing style is delightful and he delivers lyrics with masterly interpretative skills and crystal-clear diction, always displaying acute understanding of the songwriters' intentions. His piano playing is of a similarly high order and his performances are always beautifully crafted, polished and supremely professional.

● ALBUMS: *Ronny Whyte* (Bandbox 1967)★★★, with Travis Hudson *We Like A Gershwin Tune* (Monmouth-Evergreen 1973)★★★★, *It's Smooth, It's Smart, It's Rodgers, It's Hart* (Monmouth-Evergreen 1974)★★★★, *New York State Of Mind* (Monmouth-Evergreen 1978)★★★, *I Love A Piano* (Audiophile 1978)★★★, *At The Conservatory* (Audiophile 1980)★★★, *Soft Whyte* (Audiophile 1982)★★★, *Something Wonderful* (Progressive 1985)★★, *All In A Night's Work* (Audiophile 1988)★★, *Walk On The Weill Side* (Audiophile 1996)★★★, with Hudson *The Songs Of Rodgers And Hart* 1974 recording (Audiophile 1998)★★★.

Wickman, Dick

b. USA. Bandleader Dick Wickman inaugurated his first orchestra in 1941 in Omaha, Nebraska, USA. However, only a year later his career was interrupted when he was called up for military service. Following the end of World War II Wickman embarked on a series of business ventures before returning to leading his dance band. Throughout the remainder of the 40s and into the 50s the Dick Wickman Orchestra proved one of the most popular playing the Midwest hotel and ballroom circuit. He also established an independently operated record label to release the band's songs, including their theme tune, 'I Want To Be Happy'. Despite the fall off in revenues affecting dance bands during the late 50s and early 60s, Wickman's group maintained their stature with engagements in Iowa and the Dakotas as well as Nebraska. In 1965 they were the central attraction on a television show launched from Lincoln, Nebraska, which ran for three years on KOLN TV. The group continued to be active in the 70s, although by now Wickman was also diverting much of his time to separate business ventures.

Wickman, Putte

b. Hans-Olof Wickman, 10 September 1924, Borlänge, Sweden. He played clarinet from childhood, emerging in the years after World War II as a distinguished player in the swing era style of Benny Goodman. Soon, however, he began to adapt to the new sounds of bop, and was thus one of very few clarinettists to make the move. By the early 50s he was sufficiently well regarded to be on regular call to support visiting American jazz musicians and he also played with fellow-countryman Lars Gullin. In the 60s he moved into more commercial music, forming a dance band that became successful. In the 70s he returned to jazz, playing with increasing technical mastery as the years passed. His recordings of the 90s demonstrate a sometimes clinical accuracy, although Wickman never fails to swing.

● ALBUMS: *The Sound Of Surprise* (Dragon 1969)★★★, *Happy New Year!* (Odeon 1973)★★★, *Putte Wickman Quartet Live In Stockholm* (Out 1977)★★, *Mr Clarinet* (Four Leaf Clover 1985)★★★, *Some O' This And Some O' That* 1989 recording (Dragon 1992)★★★★, *In Trombones* (Phontastic 1992)★★★, *In Silhouette* (Phontastic 1994)★★★.

Wiedoft, Herb

b. USA, d. May 1928, Kiamath Falls, Oregon, USA. An accomplished trumpet player as well as bandleader, Herb Wiedoft formed his own dance band in the early 20s in Los Angeles, California, USA. The brother of renowned saxophonist Rudy Wiedoft, who played in the band, his orchestra also included two other members of the family, Adolph and Guy. The other musical sidemen were Jess Stafford, Joe Nemoli, Gene Secrest, Larry Abbott, Fred Bibesheimer, Vincent Rose, Jose Sucedo, Clyde Lucas, Dub Kirkpatrick, Gene Rose, Leon Lucas and Art Winters. The group established itself by means of an extended run at the Cinderella Roof in Los Angeles. A contract to record with Brunswick Records followed, with the label soon playing host to material including the group's theme tune, 'Cinderella Blues', a song written in tribute to their first home. However, Rudy Wiedoft left shortly before the band embarked on east coast dates to find significant solo fame in his own right. He never saw his brother again. Herb was driving between Medford and Kimath Falls in Oregon when he was involved in a car accident. He died from his injuries in 1928. His band continued, however, with trombone player Jess Stafford taking over its leadership. He relocated the orchestra to San Francisco, where they played a three year run at the Palace Hotel, before taking a series of dates in local theatres. When Stafford died of a heart attack in 1947 the orchestra finally disbanded.

Wiggins, Gerry

b. 12 May 1922, New York City, New York, USA. One of Wiggins's first professional jobs was playing piano for the club act of film actor-comedian Stepin Fetchit (Lincoln Perry). After hearing Art Tatum he turned to jazz and, following a spell with Les Hite, worked with Louis Armstrong and Benny Carter. In the mid-40s Wiggins settled in Los Angeles and established a reputation as a reliable accompanist for singers. During the 50s and 60s he worked for Lena Horne, Kay Starr, Nat 'King' Cole, Lou Rawls and Eartha Kitt. Also in the 60s he was active in film and television soundtrack work but he played with several jazz groups too, including Gerald Wilson's big band. In the mid-70s he toured Europe with Helen Humes, then in the 80s worked with Red Callender and also appeared on the international festival circuit. He continued to serve singers well, playing with Linda Hopkins. He also regularly returned to work with Wilson and occasionally led his own small groups. A solid, dependable pianist with eclectic tastes, Wiggins remains relatively unknown despite his many qualities.

● ALBUMS: *The Gerry Wiggins Trio* i (1950)★★★, *The Gerry Wiggins Trio* ii (1956)★★★, *The Gerry Wiggins Trio* iii (1956)★★★★, *Gerry Wiggins* (1958)★★★, with Helen Humes *Sneakin' Around* (1974)★★, *Wig Is Here* (Black And Blue 1975)★★★, with Red Callender *Night Mist Blues* (1983)★★★, *King And I* (Fresh Sounds 1988)★★★, *Live At Maybeck Recital Hall* (Concord 1990)★★★★, *Soulidarity* (Concord Jazz 1996)★★★.

Wiggs, Johnny

b. John Wigginton Hyman, 25 July 1899, New Orleans, Lousiana, USA, d. 9 October 1977. Although he played violin for some years, Wiggs was concurrently developing a reputation as a cornet player. After playing briefly in New York in the mid-20s he settled in his home town, concentrating now on cornet. Active as a teacher throughout the 30s and early 40s, Wiggs resumed full-time playing in the late 40s. He led his own bands, made some records and worked with Eddie Miller and others but by the 60s was again playing part time. He continue to work into the 70s, recording with Maxine Sullivan. A strong and effective player, the nature of Wiggs's career kept him in largely unwarranted shadows.

●ALBUMS: *Johnny Wiggs And His Bayou Stompers* (1968)★★.

Wilber, Bob

b. 15 March 1928, New York City, New York, USA. After studying clarinet as a child, Wilber began leading his own band and while still a teenager became a student of Sidney Bechet. He recorded with Bechet, grew adept on the soprano saxophone, and was clearly at home in a traditional jazz setting. Nevertheless, Wilber's avid desire to expand his knowledge and expertise led him to further studies under Lennie Tristano. A mid-50s band Wilber led blended traditional with modern concepts in jazz and, perhaps predictably, fell between the two audiences for such music. During the late 50s and on through the 60s, Wilber played and recorded with distinguished leaders, such as Bobby Hackett, Benny Goodman, Bechet, Jack Teagarden and Eddie Condon. At the close of the 60s (at this time also playing alto saxophone), he became one of the original members of the World's Greatest Jazz Band. In the early 70s, he teamed up with Kenny Davern to form Soprano Summit, a band which brought him to the attention of new audiences around the world. This group stayed in existence until 1979 and soon afterwards he formed the Bechet Legacy band, recording extensively, often on his own record label, Bodeswell. Active in jazz education, Wilber has also been musical director of the Smithsonian Jazz Repertory Ensemble, the house band for some of the Duke Ellington conventions, and has written for films, most notably the recreation of Ellington's music for *The Cotton Club* (1984). He continued leading his Bechet Legacy band throughout the 80s, making records (including a fine set which set out to recapture the essence of the King Oliver band), and accompanying his wife, singer Joanne 'Pug' Horton. He also recreated a Benny Goodman band for anniversary performances of the 1938 Carnegie Hall concert and published his autobiography, *Music Was Not Enough* (in collaboration with Derek Webster). In the early 90s Wilber was reunited with Davern for concert appearances and was still keenly exploring new ways of presenting older musical styles to a contemporary audience.

● ALBUMS: *Bob Wilber Jazz Band* 10-inch album (Circle 1951)★★★, *Young Men With Horns* 10-inch album (Riverside 1952)★★★, *Spreadin' Joy* (1957)★★★★, *Bob Wilber And His All Star Band* i (1959)★★★, *Bob Wilber And His All Star Band* ii (1959)★★★, *New Clarinet In Town* (1960)★★★, *Evolution Of The Blues* (1960)★★★★, *Blowin' The Blues Away* (1960)★★★, *The Music Of Hoagy Carmichael* (Monmouth 1969)★★★★, with Soprano Summit *Soprano Summit* (World Jazz 1973)★★★★, with Soprano Summit *Soprano Summit II* (World Jazz 1974)★★★★, with Soprano Summit *Chalumeau Blue* (Chiaroscuro 1976)★★★, with Soprano Summit *Soprano Summit At The Big Horn Jazzfest* (Concord Jazz 1976)★★★★, with Soprano Summit *Soprano Summit In Concert* (Concord Jazz 1976)★★★★, with Scott Hamilton *Bob Wilber And The Scott Hamilton Quartet* (Chiaroscuro 1977)★★★★, *At Thatchers* (J&M 1977)★★, with Soprano Summit *Soprano Summit Live At Concord* (Concord Jazz 1977)★★★★, *Rapturous Reeds* (Phontastic 1978)★★★, with Joanne 'Pug' Horton *The Many Faces Of Bob Wilber And Pug Horton* (1978)★★★, *Groovin' At The Grunewald* (Phontastic 1978)★★★, *Original Wilber* (1978)★★, *In The Mood For Swing* (Phontastic 1979)★★★★, *The Music Of Fats Waller And James P. Johnson* (1979)★★★, *Dizzy Fingers* (Bodeswell 1980)★★★, with Bechet Legacy *Bob Wilber And The Bechet Legacy* (Bodeswell 1981)★★★, *The Music Of King Oliver's Creole Jazz Band* (GHB 1981)★★★, with Bechet Legacy *On The Road* (Bodeswell 1981)★★★, with Horton *Don't Go Away* (1981)★★★, with Bechet Legacy *Ode To Bechet* (Bodeswell 1982)★★★★, *Reflections* (Bodeswell 1983)★★★, with Dick Wellstood *The Bob Wilber-Dick Wellstood Duet* (Progressive 1984)★★★★, *The Cotton Club* soundtrack (1984)★★★★, with Soprano Summit *Summit Reunion* (Chiaroscuro 1990)★★★, *Dancing On A Rainbow* (Circle 1990)★★, with Soprano Summit *Summit Reunion 1992* (Chiaroscuro 1992)★★★, *Moments Like This* (Phontastic 1992)★★, with Soprano Summit *Jazz Im Amerika Haus, Vol. 5* (Nagel-Heyer 1995)★★★, with Bechet Legacy *Bob Wilber & Bechet Legacy* 1984 recording (Challenge 1995)★★★, with Soprano Summit *Yellow Dog Blues* (Chiaroscuro 1995)★★★★, with Bechet Legacy *The Hamburg Concert* (Nagel-Heyer 1996)★★★, with Soprano Summit *Soprano Summit* 1976 recording (Storyville 1996)★★★, *Bean: Tribute To Coleman Hawkins* (Arbors 1996)★★★★, *Bufadora Blow-Up: At The March Of Jazz '96* (Arbors 1997)★★★, *Nostalgia* (Arbors 1997)★★★, with Dick Hyman *A Perfect Match* (Arbors 1998)★★★★, with Kenny Davern *Reunion At Arbors* (Arbors 1998)★★★, *What Swing Is All About* (Nagel-Heyer 1998)★★★.

● FURTHER READING: *Music Was Not Enough*, Bob Wilber with Derek Webster.

WILD PARTY, THE

Football players, drop-outs, petty criminals and jazz musicians team up in an unlikely Hollywood farrago made in 1956 and directed by Harry Horner and starring Anthony Quinn and Nehemiah Persoff. Jazz, on-screen and off, is provided by a host of talented studio-cum-jazz musicians. Amongst them are Georgie Auld, Teddy Buckner, Pete Candoli, Bob Cooper, Buddy De Franco, Maynard Ferguson, Frank Rosolino, Bud Shank and Alvin Stoller. Persoff's on-screen piano playing was dubbed by Pete Jolly.

WILDER, ALEC

b. Alexander LaFayette Chew Wilder, 16 February 1907, Rochester, New York, USA, d. 23 December 1980, Gainesville, Florida, USA. A composer of popular ballads, illustrative works, jazz and classical pieces, Wilder attended Collegiate School, New York, and studied privately at the Eastman School of Music. He became an active composer in 1930 when his first popular song, 'All The King's Horses', was interpolated into the Arthur Schwartz and Howard Dietz revue *Three's A Crowd*. Thereafter, he is reputed to have written several hundred popular songs, including 'Stop That Dancin' Up There', 'It's So Peaceful In The Country', 'J.P. Dooley III' (a jazz piece recorded by Harry James), 'Who Can I Turn To?', 'Soft As Spring', 'Moon And Sand', 'At The Swing Shift Ball', 'While We're Young', 'I'll Be Around', 'The Long Night', 'One More Road', 'All The Cats Join In' (featured by Benny Goodman And His Orchestra in the 1946 Walt Disney cartoon *Make Mine Music*), 'Kalamazoo To Timbuktu', 'Goodbye John', 'Crazy In The Heart', 'Winter Of My Discontent', 'You're Free', 'Is It Always Like This?', 'Summer Is A-Comin' In', and 'April Age'. Artists who have recorded from his popular catalogue include Frank Sinatra, Mabel Mercer, Bing Crosby, Mildred Bailey, Marlene Dietrich, Peggy Lee, Nat 'King' Cole, Jeri Southern, and Anita O'Day.

Singer Elaine Delmar devoted an album, *Elaine Sings Wilder*, to him. Among his serious works were sonatas for flute, tuba and bassoon, a concerto for saxophone and chamber orchestra, quintets and trios for various musical instruments, piano works, four operas, the *Juke Box* ballet, and several unorthodox pieces, such as 'A Debutante's Diary', 'Sea Fugue Mama', 'She'll Be Seven In May', 'Neurotic Goldfish', 'Dance Man Buys A Farm', 'Concerning Etchings', 'Walking Home In The Spring', 'Amorous Poltergeist' and 'The Children Met The Train'. For over 50 years of his life he lived in the Algonquin Hotel, Manhattan, and the Sheraton in Rochester, New York City. His memoir of the period he spent at the Algonquin was unpublished at the time of his death from lung cancer in 1980. Two of his books that did emerge are *Letter I Never Mailed* (1975), a collection of imaginary letters to real people, and *American Popular Song: The Great Innovators 1900-1950* (with James T. Maher) (1972). He hosted a weekly series based on the latter book for the National Public Radio.

● ALBUMS: *Alec Wilder And His Octet* 10-inch album (Mercury

1949)★★★, *Alec Wilder Octet* 10-inch album (Columbia 1951)★★★, *The Music Of Alec Wilder Conducted By Alec Wilder* (Columbia 1974)★★★.

● FURTHER READING: *Alec Wilder And His Friends*, Whitney Balliett.

WILDER, JOE

b. 22 February 1922, Colwyn, Pennsylvania, USA. After studying music in his home town, Wilder joined the trumpet section of the Les Hite band in his late teens. From Hite he graduated to the Lionel Hampton band and, before the 40s were over, had played with leaders such as Dizzy Gillespie, Jimmie Lunceford, Lucky Millinder and Sam Donahue. In the 50s he mostly worked in theatre bands but spent several months with Count Basie, and by the end of the decade had embarked upon a long stint as a staff musician in US radio and television studios. During this period, which extended into the early 70s, he found time to play with Benny Goodman on a tour of the Soviet Union. Later in the 70s and throughout the 80s he continued to play in studio orchestras, making occasional recordings, including a fine set with Benny Carter. A top-rank lead trumpeter, Wilder's technical command has ensured his successful career in the studios but that, in turn, has necessarily overshadowed his jazz playing.

● ALBUMS: with Count Basie *Dance Session* (1953)★★★★, *Wilder 'N' Wilder* (Savoy 1956)★★★★, with Benny Carter *A Gentleman And His Music* (1985)★★★, *Alone With Just My Dreams* (Evening Star 1992)★★★, with Britt Woodman and John LaPorta *Playing For Keeps* (GM 1996)★★★★.

WILEN, BARNEY

b. Bernard Jean Wilen, 4 March 1937, Nice, France, d. 25 May 1996. Born of an American father and French mother, Wilen spent his first 10 years in Arizona, USA, before returning to the Côte d'Azur and serious saxophone study. Initially a follower of Lester Young, by the mid-50s Wilen had his own voice and was fast becoming one of the most respected European musicians. From 1955-60 he played with Bud Powell and John Lewis, joined the Miles Davis band and Art Blakey's Jazz Messengers. Lewis classed Wilen as one of his four favourite saxophonists, with Lester Young, Stan Getz and Eli 'Lucky' Thompson. During the early 60s Wilen experimented with jazz rock, and from 1968-73 he lived in Africa, an experience that influenced his work during the late 70s and early 80s. Wilen returned to Nice and back to the hard bop style of playing that made him famous in the 50s. He recorded his final album in 1995 in the company of Kenny Barron, Ira Coleman and Lewis Nash.

● ALBUMS: *New York Romance* (Columbia 1995)★★★.

WILEY, LEE

b. 9 October c.1910, Fort Gibson, Oklahoma, USA, d. 11 December 1975. While still in her early teens, Wiley left home to begin a career singing with the Leo Reisman band. Her career was interrupted when, following a fall while horse-riding, she suffered temporary blindness. She recovered her sight and at the age of 19 was back with Reisman again. She also sang with Paul Whiteman and later, the Casa Loma Band. A collaboration with composer Victor Young resulted in several songs for which Wiley wrote the lyrics, including 'Got The South In My Soul' and 'Anytime, Anyday, Anywhere', the latter becoming an R&B hit in the 50s. In the early 40s Wiley began a long succession of fine recording dates, singing many classic songs, usually with backing from small jazz groups, which included musicians such as Bud Freeman, Max Kaminsky, Fats Waller, Billy Butterfield, Bobby Hackett, Eddie Condon, and Jess Stacy, the latter to whom she was married for a while. In 1943 she sang with Stacy's big band and subsequently continued to perform with small groups, notably with Condon-directed jazzmen, and pursued her prolific recording career.

Although she had only a small voice, she possessed a wistful and charming sound and delivered lyrics with a low-key sensuality. The warmth and intimacy she projected resulted in many of her performances becoming definitive versions of the songs. 'I've Got A Crush On You', from 1939 with Waller and Freeman in support, 'How Long Has This Been Going On?', 'Baby's Awake Now' and 'You Took Advantage Of Me', all from 1939 and 1940, and 'I've Got The World On A String', from 1945, with Condon and Ernie Caceres, are all excellent examples of her distinctively delicate singing style. She made fewer appearances and records in the 50s and 60s, although a 1963 television film, *Something About Lee Wiley*, which told a version of her life story, boosted interest in her work. One of her final appearances came in 1972 at the New York Jazz Festival, where she was rapturously received by audiences who were beginning to appreciate what her fellow musicians had known all along: that she was one of the best jazz singers the music had known even if, by this time, her always fragile-sounding voice was no longer at its best.

● ALBUMS: *Night In Manhattan* (1950)★★★, *Lee Wiley Sings Vincent Youmans* (1951)★★, *Lee Wiley Sings Irving Berlin* (1951)★★★★, *Lee Wiley Sings Rodgers And Hart* (1954)★★★, *Duologue* (1954)★★★, *West Of The Moon* (1957)★★★, *A Touch Of The Blues* (1957)★★★★, *One And Only Lee Wiley* (1965)★★, *Back Home Again* (Monmouth Evergreen 1971)★★, *I Got The World On A String* (1972)★★.

●COMPILATIONS: *Lee Wiley On The Air, Volume 1 (1932-36)* (Totem 1988)★★★★, *Lee Wiley On The Air, Volume 2 (1944-45)* (Totem 1989)★★★, *Rarites* (Jass 1989)★★★, *I Got A Right To Sing The Blues* (Jass 1990)★★★, *As Time Goes By* (Bluebird 1991)★★★✻, *Lee Wiley 1931-37* (Original Jazz Classics 1991)★★★★.

WILKINS, DAVE

b. 25 September 1914, Barbados. Wilkins learned to play the trumpet playing in Salvation Army Bands in his native Barbados. In 1935 he moved to Trinidad to play with the well-known Blue Rhythm Orchestra which he had often heard on the radio. A couple of years later, in 1937, a small group of young West Indian musicians came to London to join Ken 'Snake Hips' Johnson's

West Indian Swing Band. In the 40s Wilkins played with the bands of Ted Heath, Harry Parry and Joe Daniels before retiring from music altogether.

Wilkins, Ernie

b. 20 July 1922, St. Louis, Missouri, USA. Wilkins studied formally, learning piano and violin before taking up the saxophone. He played locally before military service and in the post-war years played in the Jeter-Pillars Orchestra and that led by Earl 'Fatha' Hines. He then freelanced as player, composer and arranger until in 1952 he joined Count Basie, remaining with the band until 1955, playing alto and tenor saxophones. He returned to freelancing, concentrating on writing arrangements for many bands, including those of Basie, Tommy Dorsey, Dizzy Gillespie and Harry James. Wilkins's charts for the James band were outstanding and helped to create one of the best bands the trumpeter led. In many respects these arrangements, loosely swinging and with tight section work, closely resembled similar work that Wilkins did for Basie and which was partly responsible for boosting the Basie band into its second period of greatness. Whether James or Basie was the first to play in this manner remains a matter of some contention. In the 60s Wilkins's career stalled due to addiction problems but he still wrote for several big bands, including that led by Clark Terry. In the early 70s he was A&R director for Mainstream Records and later in the decade worked again with Terry before settling in Denmark. In the 80s he formed his own Almost Big Band. As a big band arranger, Wilkins belongs firmly in the post-Sy Oliver tradition and has consistently adhered to the characteristics of a style which concentrates upon presenting an uncluttered ensemble sound that effectively frames the soloists.

● ALBUMS: *Ernie Wilkins /Kenny Clarke Septet* (Savoy 1956)★★★★, *The Trumpet Album* (1957)★★★, *Here Comes The Swinging Mr Wilkins* (1960)★★★, *The Big New Band Of The 60s* (1960)★★★, *A Time For The Blues* (1973)★★★, *Ernie Wilkins And The Almost Big Band* (1980)★★★, *Ernie Wilkins' Almost Big Band Live* (Matrix 1981)★★, *Montreux* (1983)★★★, *K.a.l.e.i.d.o.d.u.k.e.* (Birdology 1991)★★★.

Wilkinson, Alan

b. 22 August 1954, Ilford, Essex, England. Wilkinson played guitar from the age of 12 and received formal education on trumpet between the ages of eight and 11. He attended a course in librarianship in Manchester for a year, then left to attend art school in Leeds. In 1978 he acquired a saxophone and played in Crow alongside alto-player Matthew Coe (aka Xero Slingsby), Richard Bostock (bass) and Paul Hession (drums). He involved himself with the British and European free improvisation scene and appeared at the Antwerp Free Music Festival in 1983 in a trio with Hession and Akemi Kuniyoshi-Kuhn. Wilkinson played with Derek Bailey's Company in Italy in 1987 and with Company Week in London in 1988. In 1988 he also recorded with the Leeds busking band Bassa Bassa. Between 1984 and 1990 he ran the Termite Club in Leeds, which presented international improvisers as well as members Wilkinson, Hession, Paul Buckton (guitar) and industrial-*bruitiste* John McMillan. Also in 1988 he led a quartet featuring pianist Alex Maguire and a German rhythm section. This quartet toured in 1991 and appeared at the Crawley Outside In Festival. In 1989 Wilkinson toured with pianist Maguire's big band Cat O'Nine Tails (whose concert *Live At Leeds Trades Club* was issued on cassette by *Wire* magazine). The same year he toured and recorded with Sheffield improviser Mick Beck's big band, Feetpackets. He also formed a trio with Hession and bassist/composer Simon Fell, which was branded as 'punkjazz' by enthusiasts. Wilkinson cites as inspirations Ornette Coleman, John Coltrane and Albert Ayler as well as Europeans Peter Brötzmann, Mike Osborne and Evan Shaw Parker. Wilkinson looks set to become a leading saxophonist of his generation, playing alto, baritone and soprano with startling weight and imagination.

● ALBUMS: with Bassa Bassa *Bassa Bassa* (1988)★★★, with Feetpackets *Listen Feetpackets* (1989)★★, with Simon Fell *Compilation II* (1991)★★★.

Williams, Buster

b. Charles Anthony Williams, 17 April 1942, Camden, New Jersey, USA. Williams was taught to play bass by his father and later studied formally in Philadelphia. In the early 60s he played and recorded with Jimmy Heath, Sonny Stitt and others, and was also in demand for sessions with singers, notably Betty Carter, Sarah Vaughan and Nancy Wilson. Towards the end of the 60s he settled briefly in Los Angeles, where he played with Miles Davis, Bobby Hutcherson and others, but by the end of the decade he had moved to New York and joined Herbie Hancock. In the early and mid-70s he toured and recorded with Hancock and also worked with Mary Lou Williams and fellow bassist Ron Carter. In the late 70s and through the 80s Williams was in constant demand as a session musician, recording with Kenny Barron, Sathima Bea Benjamin, Sphere and the Timeless All Stars. Apart from his exemplary work as an accompanist, Williams is also an accomplished soloist.

● ALBUMS: *Crystal Reflections* (1976)★★★, *Heartbeat* (Muse 1978)★★★, *Toku Do* (Denon 1978)★★★★, *Dreams Come True* (1981)★★★, *Pinnacle* (Muse 1981)★★★, with Sphere *Four In One* (Elektra Musician 1982)★★★★, with Sphere *Flight Path* (Elektra Musician 1982)★★★, with Sphere *Sphere On Tour* (Red 1985)★★★, with Sphere *Four For All* (Verve 1987)★★★, with Sphere *Bird Songs* (Verve 1988)★★★★, *Something More* (In And Out 1989)★★★★, with Sphere *Sphere* (Verve 1998)★★★.

Williams, Clarence

b. 8 October 1893, Plaquemine, Louisiana, USA, d. 6 November 1965. Although Williams first made his mark as a pianist, singer and dancer, it was as a composer, record producer, music publisher and entrepreneur that he made a lasting impact on jazz. Before he was in his teens he had decided upon a career in showbusiness and had run away from home to work with a travelling minstrel show. By the time he was 21 he had started composing, formed his first publishing company, and was married to blues singer Eva Taylor. His early associates, as perfomers and/or in business, included Armand Piron and W.C. Handy. First in New Orleans, then Chicago and finally in New York City, Williams established himself as a successful publisher, an energetic record producer and a tireless accompanist to some of the finest jazz and blues artists of the day. Among Williams' most notable recording sessions are those on which he was joined by Louis Armstrong and Sidney Bechet, while his sensitive accompaniment enhanced many record dates with singers such as Bessie Smith, Beulah 'Sippie' Wallace and his wife. He was a dedicated promoter of the music of such leading pianist-composers as James P. Johnson and Fats Waller, his name often appearing as co-composer on works to which he may have contributed little that was creative but a great deal of enthusiastic effort in their promotion. By the late 30s he had decided to concentrate upon composing and, for a while, ran a business outside music. Even an accident that robbed him of his sight did not deter him and he worked steadily until his death in 1965. Williams' legacy to jazz includes many songs that bear his name as composer or co-composer and that became standards, among them 'Baby, Won't You Please Come Home', "Tain't Nobody's Biz-ness If I Do', 'Everybody Loves My Baby', 'Royal Garden Blues', 'West End Blues' and 'I Ain't Gonna Give Nobody None Of This Jelly Roll'.

● COMPILATIONS: *Clarence Williams And His Orchestra* (London 1954)★★★, *Back Room Special* (Columbia 1955)★★★, *Clarence Williams And His Orchestra Vol. 2* (London 1957)★★★, *Sidney Bechet Memorial* (Fontana 1960)★★★, *Clarence Williams Volume 1 1927-1935* (Philips 1962)★★★, *Clarence Williams Jazz Kings (1927-29)* (1979)★★★, *Clarence Williams And His Washboard Band, Volume 1 (1933-35)* (1983)★★★, *Clarence Williams And His Orchestra (1929-31)* (1986)★★★, *WNYC Jazz Festival* (1986)★★★, *Clarence Williams (1927-34)* (1988)★★★, *The Washboard Bands* (1988)★★★, *Jazz Classics In Digital Stereo* (1989)★★★, *Clarence Williams 1926-27* (Original Jazz Classics 1993)★★★, *Clarence Williams And The Blues Singers, Volumes 1 & 2* (Document 1996)★★★.

● FURTHER READING: *Clarence Williams*, Tom Lord.

WILLIAMS, CLAUDE

b. 22 February 1908, Muskogee, Oklahoma, USA. Williams started out playing violin in local dance bands, including one led by Oscar Pettiford. In the late 20s he joined Terrence Holder's band, staying on after Holder was replaced by Andy Kirk. He also spent time in the fine territory band led by Alphonso Trent and was briefly with the band co-led by Eddie and Nat 'King' Cole. In the mid-30s Williams switched to guitar to join Count Basie, but was replaced by Freddie Green. Williams continued to play guitar, working with the Four Shades Of Rhythm, Frank Martin, Roy Milton and other R&B bands, though he preferred to play the rarely fashionable violin. By the early 50s Williams was resident in Kansas City, but had drifted onto the sidelines. In the early 70s he returned to the spotlight, once again playing violin, and recording with Jay McShann, B.B. King and under his own name. A gutsy violinist with an energetic, swinging style, Williams has rarely attracted the attention he deserves.

● ALBUMS: with Jay McShann *The Man From Muskogee* (1971)★★★, *Call For The Fiddler* (1976)★★★, *Fiddler's Dream* (1977)★★★, *Kansas City Giants* (1982)★★, *Swing Time In New York* (Progressive 1996)★★★★.

WILLIAMS, COOTIE

b. Charles Melvin Williams, 10 July 1911, Mobile, Alabama, USA, d. 15 September 1985. A self-taught trumpeter, Williams first played professionally in the mid-20s, when he was barely into his teens, appearing in the band run by the family of Lester Young. He later played in several New York bands, including those led by Chick Webb and Fletcher Henderson. In 1929 he replaced Bubber Miley in Duke Ellington's orchestra, remaining there for 11 years. During this stint he made a number of records with other leaders, notably Lionel Hampton and Teddy Wilson (on some of whose sessions he accompanied Billie Holiday). He also led the Rug Cutters, one of the many small groups drawn from within the Ellington band. In 1940 Williams left Ellington and was briefly with Benny Goodman before forming his own big band. In later years, asked about his drinking habits, Williams remarked that he had not been a drinker until he had his own band. Given that his band included unpredictable musicians such as Bud Powell and Charlie Parker it is easy to understand why he turned to the bottle. For all the undoubted qualities of the band, which also featured Eddie 'Lockjaw' Davis and Eddie 'Cleanhead' Vinson, and the high standard of his own playing, by the late 40s Williams was forced to cut the band down in size.

In the early 50s he moved into the currently popular R&B field. For the next few years he continued playing R&B, leading small bands and making record dates - notably, a 1957 session, on which he was co-leader with Rex Stewart, by a band which boasted Coleman Hawkins, Bud Freeman, Lawrence Brown and Hank Jones within its ranks. In 1962 he rejoined Ellington, remaining in the band after the leader's death and during its brief, post-Ducal life, under Mercer Ellington. Although Williams was brought into the 1929 Ellington band to take over the so-called 'jungle effects' originally created by Miley, he quickly became an outstanding soloist in his own right. His full, rich tone and powerful style was showcased by Ellington on 'Concerto For Cootie' ('Do Nothing Till You Hear From Me'), recorded in 1940. Throughout his years with Ellington, and on many occasions under his own name, Williams readily displayed the command and vigour of his distinctive playing.

● ALBUMS: with Rex Stewart *The Big Challenge* (Jazztone 1957)★★★, *The Solid Trumpet Of Cootie Williams* (1962)★★★, *Salute To Duke Ellington* (1976)★★★.

● COMPILATIONS: *Cootie Williams And The Boys From Harlem, 1937-40* (1974)★★★, *Cootie Williams And His Rug Cutters, 1937-*

40 (1974)★★★, *Big Band Bounce* (1974)★★★, *Cootie Williams And Oran 'Hot Lips' Page* (1974)★★★, *New York 1944 - Sextet And Big Band* (1977)★★★, *Sextet And Orchestra* (1981)★★★, *Echoes From Harlem* (Affinity 1986)★★★, *Typhoon* (Swingtime 1986)★★★, *Memorial* (RCA 1986)★★★, *From Films, 1944-46* (Harlequin 1988)★★★.

WILLIAMS, FESS

b. Stanley R. Williams, 10 April 1894, Danville, Kentucky, USA, d. 17 December 1975. As a child Williams played several instruments, receiving formal tuition from N. Clark-Smith at Tuskegee University. By his late teens he had settled on clarinet, and soon afterwards formed the first of many bands he was to lead over the coming years. In New York City in the mid-20s, he became one of the first bands to hold a residency at the Savoy Ballroom where, resplendent in top hat and diamond-studded suit, he was a great popular success. However, his music was well-laced with amiable hokum and he was soon overtaken in popularity by the more swinging bands, which were better suited to the Savoy's demanding dancers. He continued to lead a band throughout the 30s but, despite the presence of some good musicians, among them Rex Stewart and Albert Nicholas, he failed to match the successes enjoyed by other bands. Although he continued to lead bands periodically in the 40s and beyond, his later career was mostly outside music. In 1962 Williams was invited to attend a concert at New York's Town Hall, where the orchestra was directed by his nephew, Charles Mingus.

● COMPILATIONS: *Fess Williams And His Royale Flush Orchestra* (1978)★★★, *Fess Williams, Volume One (1929)* (1985)★★★, *Fess Williams, Volume Two (1929-30)* (1986)★★★, *Rare Masters* (1989)★★★.

WILLIAMS, GENE

b. USA. Gene Williams first entered the entertainment industry as vocalist with the Claude Thornhill Orchestra, before forming his own dance band in 1950 in New York City, New York, USA. The musical sidemen enrolled included Harry Wegbreit, Jack Mootz, Don Josephs, Harry Di Vito, Dick Hoch, Sam Marowitz, Charlie O'Cain, Mickey Folus, Joe Reisman, Teddy Napoleon, Russ Saunders and Mel Zelnick. While Gene Williams himself and Adele Castle were the featured vocalists, Gil Evans, Hubie Wheeler, Chico O'Farrill and Joe Reisman served as the band's arrangers.

Their initial contracts came from college dates, before the membership elected to put the group on a more permanent footing. Mixing bebop instrumentals with the smooth style inherited from Williams' time with Claude Thornhill, by 1952 they had secured engagements at such venues as the Glen Island Casino. Thereafter, however, they struggled to make any headway, hamstrung by the reduced air time available to dance bands with the advent of rock 'n' roll.

WILLIAMS, GRIFF

b. La Grande, Oregon, USA, d. February 1959, Chicago, Illinois, USA. Williams studied at Stanford University and formed his first dance band on campus. His first professional employment came alongside Anson Weeks during his tenure at the Mark Hopkins Hotel, playing second piano. The experience encouraged him to put together his own orchestra, which was founded in San Francisco. The musical sidemen in this first incarnation of the band included Gene McDonald, Horace Perazzi, Ray Anderson, Albert Arnold, Jack Buck, Paul Hare, Buddy Moreno, Walter Kelsey, Bob Logan and Warren Luce. Williams himself played piano, with the featured vocalist Coralee Scott, later replaced by a succession of singers including Buddy Moreno, Lois Lee and 'the Williams trio'. Their first engagement came at Edgewater Beach, where the group opened in October 1933. From the outset they styled themselves so as to appeal to hotel audiences, touring such venues almost exclusively during their active life. Included in these engagements were frequent visits to the Mark Hopkins Hotel where Williams had once played with Weeks. They also played regularly at the Stevens Hotel after the band had settled in the Chicago area during 1939. They continued to play there throughout the war years. By the end of the 30s a radically different ensemble had been recruited with Bill Clifford, Don Mulford, Walter King, Bob Kirk and Lyle Gardner among the personnel. During this time contracts with Varsity, OKeh and Columbia Records produced a number of recordings including the band's theme tune, 'Dream Music'. Williams stayed with the band until their playing opportunities began to dwindle in 1953. At that point he joined the Haywood Publishing Company, taking charge of the launch of several successful business magazines. However, he continued to appear occasionally with impromptu versions of the orchestra, before his professional commitments prevented further engagements. He became vice president of Haywood and then one of its directors, before dying of a heart attack in 1959.

WILLIAMS, JESSICA

b. 17 March 1948, Baltimore, Maryland, USA. Learning to play piano as a child and studying classical music at the Peabody Conservatory of Music, Williams turned to jazz and was playing professionally at the age of 14. In Philadelphia, she was a member of the Philly Joe Jones Quartet and also worked with Joe Morello and singer Ethel Ennis. In 1977 she relocated to the west coast which remained her base into the 90s. Her reputation grew in San Francisco, Sacramento and other centres but despite playing in bands led by Stan Getz, Tony Williams, Bobby Hutcherson, Charlie Rouse, Airto Moreira, John Abercrombie and others, and some early recordings, the wider world of jazz remained largely unaware of her existence. All this began to change from the mid-80s when a succession of fine recordings began to appear. Received ecstatically by the jazz press in the USA and UK, awards followed and frequent overseas tours and appearances at international festivals helped consolidate her burgeoning reputation. By the early 90s she was widely accepted as one of the best pianists currently playing jazz and high on the list of all-time greats. In 1994 she had the distinction of seeing two albums appear in the top eight of *Jazz Journal International*'s critics poll for the best records of the year. That same year she was awarded a Guggenhein Fellowship for composition. A brilliantly incisive player, with a deft and sure touch, Williams command of her instrument is outstanding. But she is far from merely a superb technician. Her intelligent, strikingly original improvisations are built upon a sure knowledge of the meaning of jazz and the role of the solo piano in the music's development. Her playing reveals not only her admiration for the likes of Thelonious Monk and Bud Powell but also the genius of earlier giants such as Earl 'Fatha' Hines and Art Tatum. Nevertheless, her style is distinctively her own and by the mid-90s admiration for her talent was widespread and the long years of obscurity were finally behind her.

● ALBUMS: *Jessica Williams* (1976)★★, *The Portal Of Antrim* (Adelphi 1978)★★★, *Rivers Of Memory* (Clean Cuts 1979)★★, *Portraits* (Adelphi 1981)★★, *Orgonomic Music* (Clean Cuts 1981)★★★, *Nothin' But The Truth* (Blackhawk 1986)★★★, with Charlie Rouse *Epistrophy/The Charlie Rouse Memorial Concert* (Landmark 1989)★★★, *The Golden Light* (Quanta 1989)★★★, *Heartland* (Ear-Art 1990)★★★, *And Then, There's This* (Timeless 1991)★★★★, *In The Pocket* (Hep 1993)★★★★, *Live At Maybeck Recital Hall* (Concord 1992)★★★, *The Next Step* (Hep 1992)★★★, *Arrival* (Jazz Focus 1993)★★★★, *Momentum* (Jazz Focus 1993)★★★, *Encounters* (Jazz Focus 1994)★★★, *Inspiration* (Jazz Focus 1995)★★★, *In The Pocket* (Hep 1995)★★★, *Gratitude* (Candid 1996)★★★, *The Victoria Concert* (Jazz Focus 1997)★★, *Jazz In The Afternoon* (Candid 1998)★★★★, *Higher Standards* (Candid 1997)★★★★ and Leroy Vinnegar Trio *Encounters II* (Jazz Focus 1998)★★★.

WILLIAMS, JOE

b. 12 December 1918, Cordele, Georgia, USA. Williams began his musical career singing in a gospel group in Chicago and by the late 30s was performing regularly as a solo singer. He had short-lived jobs with bands led by Jimmie Noone and others, was encouraged by Lionel Hampton, who employed him briefly in the early 40s, and in 1950 was with Count Basie for a short spell. In 1951 he had a record success with 'Every Day I Have The Blues', but he did not make his breakthrough into the big time until he rejoined Basie in 1954. For the next few years, records by the band with Williams in powerful voice were hugely successful and, coming at a period when Basie's band was at a low commercial ebb, it is hard to say with any certainty who needed whom the most. By the time Williams moved on, in 1961, both the band and the singer had reached new heights of popularity, and they continued to make occasional concert appearances together during the following decades. In the 60s Williams worked mostly as a single, often accompanied by top-flight jazzmen, including Harry Edison, Clark Terry, George Shearing and Cannonball Adderley. He toured and recorded throughout the 70s and 80s, his stature growing as he matured and his voice seemingly growing stronger and more mellow with age. A highly sophisticated artist, whose blues singing has a burnished glow which can contrast vividly with the harsh edge of the lyrics he sings, Williams has built a substantial and devoted audience. His later appearances, with bands such as the Capp-Pierce Juggernaut, frequently contain popular songs which he performs with more than a tinge of blues feeling. He also favours material which allows him to display the good humour which is a characteristic of the man himself. (This artist should not be confused with the singer-pianist Big Joe Williams.)

● ALBUMS: with Count Basie *A Night At Count Basie's* (Vanguard 1955)★★★, with Basie *Count Basie Swings/Joe Williams Sings* (Clef 1955)★★★★, with Basie *The Greatest! Count Basie Swings/Joe Williams Sings Standards* (Verve 1956)★★★★, with Basie, Ella Fitzgerald *One O'Clock Jump* (Columbia 1956)★★★★, with Basie *Memories Ad Lib* (Roulette 1959)★★★, with Basie *Everyday I Have The Blues* (Roulette 1959)★★★★, *Joe Williams Sings About You* (1959)★★★, *That Kind Of Woman* (1959)★★★, with Basie *Just The Blues* (Roulette 1960)★★★★, *Have A Good Time* (1961)★★★, *Together* (1961)★★★, *A Swinging Night At Birdland* (Roulette 1962)★★★, *One Is A Lonesome Number* (1962)★★★, *Me And The Blues* (1963)★★★★, *Joe Williams At Newport* (1963)★★★★, *The Song Is You* (1964)★★★, *Then And Now* (1965)★★★, *Mister Excitement* (1965)★★★, *Presenting Joe Williams And The Thad Jones-Mel Lewis Jazz Orchestra* (1966)★★★, *Something Old, New And Blue* (1968)★★, *Having The Blues Under European Skies* (1971)★★, *Joe Williams Live* (1973)★★★, with Juggernaut *Live At The Century Plaza* (1977)★★★, with Dave Pell *Prez & Joe* (1979)★★, *Nothin' But The Blues* (1983)★★★★, *Then And Now* (1983)★★★, *I Just Want To Sing* (1985)★★★, *Ballad And Blues Master* (Verve 1987)★★★, *Live At Vine Street* (Verve 1987)★★★, *Every Night* (1987)★★★, *In Good Company* (Verve 1989)★★★, *A Man Ain't Supposed To Cry* (1989)★★★, *That Holiday Feelin'* (Verve 1990)★★, *Jump For Joy* (Bluebird 1993)★★★.

● COMPILATIONS: *Joe Williams Sings Every Day* (1950-51)★★★★, *The Overwhelming Joe Williams* (Bluebird 1989)★★★★.

● FILMS: *Jamboree a.k.a. Disc Jockey Jamboree* (1957).

WILLIAMS, JOHN

b. 28 January 1928, Windsor, Vermont, USA. He took piano lessons as a child and at the age of 12 played in a high school danceband. Four years later he joined the popular Mal Hallett band at a time when many big bands were suffering from sidemen being called into the armed forces. Later that same year, 1945, Williams returned to complete his education, then played locally until 1948 when he joined the Johnny Bothwell big band. The next year he moved to New York, mostly playing bop in nightclubs which included gigging with Charlie Parker. Called into the armed forces at the time of the Korean war, he returned to New York and promptly joined Charlie Barnet then in early 1953 began the first of two long stints with Stan Getz. Throughout the 50s he continued to play clubs, making records with Cannonball Adderley, Phil Woods, Al Cohn, Zoot Sims and many others. He also found time to continue his musical studies and helped pay the rent by playing second piano in the Vincent Lopez band at the Hotel Taft. He also played briefly with Gerry Mulligan then continued his round of New York club engagements until the end of the 50s when he moved to Florida where he remained, leading a trio at local clubs and also becoming involved in politics. He might have remained there in relative and contended obscurity had it not been for the joint efforts of Spike Robinson, who hired him to play on a Florida date, and Steve Voce, who interviewed Williams for *Jazz Journal International* in 1994. This all helped bring Williams back to the attention of the jazz world and plans were soon in hand for a resumption of his recording career. Inventive, forceful, with a commanding sense of swing and, importantly, a workmanlike view of the true role of the pianist in both mainstream and bop settings, Williams' long absence from the spotlight has been a considerable loss to jazz.

● ALBUMS: *Stan Getz At The Shrine Auditorium* (Norgran 1954)★★★, *John Williams Trio* i (Mercury 1954)★★★★, *John Williams Trio* ii (Emarcy 1955)★★★★, with Al Cohn *The Saxophone Section* (Epic 1956)★★.

WILLIAMS, MARY LOU

b. Mary Elfrieda Scruggs, 8 May 1910, Atlanta, Georgia, USA, d. 28 May 1981, Durham, North Carolina, USA. A child prodigy, Williams played in public at the age of six and by the time she reached her teenage years was already a seasoned professional piano player. At the age of 16 she married saxophonist John Williams, playing in his band throughout the mid-west. When her husband left to join Terrence Holder's band, Mary Lou took over the leadership of the band before eventually she too joined Holder. After this band had metamorphosed into Andy Kirk and his Clouds Of Joy, Williams assumed additional responsibilities as the group's chief arranger. During the 30s, while still with Kirk, her arrangements were also used by Earl 'Fatha' Hines, Tommy Dorsey, Louis Armstrong and Benny Goodman, who had a hit with her composition 'Roll 'Em'. After her marriage to John Williams ended, she married Harold 'Shorty' Baker and co-led a band with him before he joined Duke Ellington. She continued to lead the band but also contributed some arrangements to Ellington. Williams was instrumental in informing John Hammond (senior) about the talents of Charlie Christian.

Throughout the 40s and early 50s she played at clubs in the USA and Europe, sometimes as a solo artist, at other times leading a small group. For a few years in the mid-50s she worked outside music, but returned to the scene in the autumn of 1957 and thereafter played clubs, concerts and festivals for the rest of her life. As an arranger, Williams's greatest contribution to jazz was her work with the Kirk band. Her charts were exemplary, providing this fine group with a distinctive voice and ably employing the individual talents of the band's members. Although her arrangements for other groups were necessarily somewhat impersonal, they were invariably first-class examples of straightforward swinging big band music. Many of her arrangements were of her own compositions and the breadth of her work in this area was such that, in the mid-40s, a classical piece, 'Zodiac Suite', was performed by the New York Philharmonic Orchestra. During this same period, she extended her writing into bop, providing charts for the Dizzy Gillespie big band.

Her deep religious beliefs, which had led to her leaving music for a few years in the 50s, surfaced in some of her longer compositions, which included cantatas and masses. As a pianist, her range was similarly wide, encompassing stride and boogie-woogie, swing and early bop; she even recorded a duo concert with *avant gardist* Cecil Taylor, though this was not an unqualified success. Throughout the later years of her career, Williams extended her repertoire still further, offering performances which, interpreted through the piano, told the story of jazz from its origins to the present day. Williams was a highly articulate and intellectually gifted individual. In interviews she displays a complex and decidedly ambivalent attitude towards life and music, perhaps fostered by the racial antagonism she encountered early in her career and dissatisfaction with the manner in which the entertainment industry demonstrated that it cared more for money than for music. Williams's importance to the fabric of jazz was recognised towards the end of her life and she was honoured by several universities.

● ALBUMS: *Mary Lou Williams Trio* 10-inch album (Asch 1950)★★★★, *Mary Lou Williams* 10-inch album (Stinson 1950)★★★★, *Jazz Variation* 10-inch album (Stinson 1950)★★★★, *Rehearsal - Jazz Session/Footnotes To Jazz, Vol. 3* 10-inch album (Folkways 1951)★★★★, *Piano Panorama* 10-inch album (Atlantic 1951)★★★★, *Piano Contempo* 10-inch album (Circle 1951)★★★★, *Progressive Piano Stylings* 10-inch album (King 1953)★★★, *Piano '53* 10-inch album (Contemporary 1953)★★★, with Al Haig *Piano Moderns* 10-inch album (Prestige 1953)★★★, *Mary Lou* 10-inch album (EmArcy 1954)★★★★, *A Keyboard History* (Jazztone 1955)★★★, with Ralph Burns *Composers - Pianists* (Jazztone 1956)★★★, with Don Byas, Buck Clayton, Alix Combelle *Messin' Round In Montmarte* (Storyville 1956)★★★, with Art Tatum *The King And Queen* (Jazztone 1958)★★★, *Black Christ Of The Andes* (Mary 1964)★★, *Music For Peace* (Mary 1964)★★★, *Zoning* (Smithsonian/Folkways 1974)★★★★, *Free Spirits* (Steeple Chase 1975)★★★, *Live At The Cookery* (Chiaroscuro 1976)★★★, with Cecil Taylor *Embraced* (Pablo 1977)★★, *My Mama Pinned A Rose On Me* (Pablo 1978)★★★, *Solo Recital At Montreux* (Pablo 1978)★★★, *Zodiac Suite* 1945 recordings (Smithsonian/Folkways 1995)★★★★.

● COMPILATIONS: *The Best Of Mary Lou Williams* (Pablo 1982)★★★, *1927-40* (Classics)★★★★, *Asch Recordings* 1944-1947 recordings (Smithsonian/Folkways)★★★★.

WILLIAMS, MIDGE

b. *c.*1908, California, USA, d. date unk. Despite a short period of fame, little is known about her origins, background, or even her dates of birth and death. Williams sang with a family vocal group before starting to sing professionally in the late 20s. During the early 30s she visited China and Japan, with residencies in Shanghai and Tokyo. She also recorded while in the Orient, performing popular American songs in Japanese. In 1934 she returned to the USA and for a time had her own regular radio show in Los Angeles. She then teamed up with Fats Waller and also sang on a radio show featuring the popular entertainer Rudy Vallee. She made a number of records, sometimes using leading jazz musicians of the day, including Miff Mole and John Kirby. In 1938 she was hired as a vocalist with Louis Armstrong's big band, a job she retained until 1941. After that she returned to her solo career but soon drifted from sight. Williams sang in an engaging manner with a light, finely textured voice. Her style was relatively straightforward and on her records the chief jazz interest lies in the solos heard from the musicians such as Frankie Newton, Pete Brown, Charlie Shavers, Buster Bailey and Russell Procope. Her records are therefore worth seeking out and she certainly does not harm the proceedings.

● COMPILATIONS: *Midge Williams And Her Jazz Jesters* (Classics 1937-38)★★★.

WILLIAMS, PAMELA

b. *c.*1969, Philadelphia, Pennsylvania, USA. Williams began playing tenor saxophone while still very young and played in the Martin Luther King Jazz Ensemble at King High School in her hometown. In her teens she was already leading her own band, playing local clubs and building a wide-ranging repertoire that encompassed jazz, Latin, R&B and hip-hop. When she was 20 she began touring with Patti LaBelle, an engagement that lasted almost six years. In 1996 Williams's recording of 'Secret Garden', a single from *Saxtress*, which featured singers Teena Marie and LaBelle, spent four months on the *Billboard* Top 25. Williams has also worked with Prince and has made videos with Barry White. An immensely talented player, Williams has built an enviable following among a younger generation of listeners and has created a satisfying blend of smooth jazz and contemporary pop.

● ALBUMS: *Saxtress* (Heads Up 1996)★★, *Eight Days Of Ecstasy* (Heads Up 1997)★★★.

WILLIAMS, ROY

b. 7 March 1937, Bolton, Lancashire, England. Williams first played trombone with a Manchester-based traditional jazz band. After moving to London he became a well-known figure during the trad jazz boom of the late 50s and early 60s. He played and recorded with Monty Sunshine and other leading lights of the era, earning praise from the many visiting American jazz stars whom he accompanied. In 1965, he joined the Alex Welsh band where he remained for more than a dozen years. After leaving Welsh he joined Humphrey Lyttelton, staying with the band until the early 80s when he began freelancing. As a member of the Pizza Express All Stars, Five-A-Slide and other mainstream bands, touring with various visitors, recording with Spike Robinson and others, and broadcasting, he became one of the most familiar figures on the UK jazz scene. The respect he earned travelled well and in the 80s he was invited to play at one of Dick Gibson's famous Colorado Jazz Parties and he also worked in New York. Superb technical accomplishment, allied to impeccable phrasing, fluid swing and innate good taste, have combined to make Williams one of the best mainstream jazz trombonists in the world.

● ALBUMS: *The Melody Maker Tribute To Louis Armstrong* (1970)★★, *Something Wonderful* (Hep Jazz 1981)★★★, with Benny Waters *When You're Smiling* (Hep Jazz 1981)★★★, *Royal Trombone* (Phontastic 1983)★★, *Again! Roy Williams In Sweden* (1983)★★, with Spike Robinson *It's A Wonderful World* (1985)★★★★, *A Jazz Concert With Roy Williams* (1985)★★★, *Standard Time* (Sine 1996)★★★★, *Interplay* (Sine 1997)★★★.

WILLIAMS, RUDY

b. 1909, Newark, New Jersey, USA, d. September 1954. Williams played alto saxophone as a child and in the late 30s joined the Savoy Sultans, the very popular band led by Al Cooper at the Savoy Ballroom in Harlem. Williams was one of the Sultans' principal soloists and was a favourite of the Savoy's discerning patrons. After leaving the Sultans he played in bands led by Oran 'Hot Lips' Page, Luis Russell and others. In the mid-40s he was still active in New York, although often with lesser-known bands, and he also played with several leading bop musicians, including Tadd Dameron and Oscar Pettiford. From the end of the 40s into the early 50s he sometimes led bands of his own, playing alto, tenor and baritone saxophones as well as clarinet. Mostly, he worked on the east coast but occasionally toured farther afield, making trips to the west coast (where he played with Gene Ammons) and to US military bases in the Orient with Pettiford. During his career, Williams made several records with the Sultans and with leaders such as Howard McGhee, Dameron, Eddie 'Lockjaw' Davis, Ammons and Johnny Hodges. Although steeped in the music of the swing era and an able performer in jump band tradition, Williams made the transition to bop better than most of his contemporaries. His playing style has been likened to that of Don Byas, another musician who made the adjustment. Williams's career might have developed interestingly had he not drowned accidentally in 1954.

● ALBUMS: *Lifetime* (1964)★★★, *Spring* (1965)★★★, with Miles Davis *Miles In The Sky* (1968)★★★★, *Emergency* (1969)★★★, *Civilization* (1986)★★, *Angel Street* (1988)★★★, *Native Heart* (1989)★★★.

WILLIAMS, SANDY

b. Alexander Balos Williams, 24 October 1906, Summerville, South Carolina, USA. After dabbling with the tuba he began playing trombone and quickly found professional work with theatre pit bands in Washington, DC, where he was raised. At the end of the 20s he began a tour of some of the best bands of the day including Claude Hopkins, Horace and Fletcher Henderson, and Chick Webb. He joined Webb in 1933 and remained there until after the leader's death when the band continued with Ella Fitzgerald. In the 40s Williams was in other big bands, among them Benny Carter, Fletcher Henderson and Cootie Williams. With the decline in the fortunes and the numbers of big bands, Williams turned to small groups, working in the mid- to late 40s with Sidney Bechet, Wild Bill Davison, Pete Brown, Oran 'Hot Lips' Page, Roy Eldridge, Rex Stewart and many others. During this period, in 1943, he spent almost a year with Duke Ellington. In the late 40s, Williams' lifestyle caught up with him and he was in and out of music, and hospital, for some years and by the early 50s was forced into retirement. In later years, during which he earned his living as an elevator operator, he occasionally played again. Williams drew his remarkable playing style largely from that of Jimmy Harrison, although it is clear that like so many musicians of his generation, regardless of instrument, he was also influenced by Louis Armstrong. Williams could outshine anyone when he was in the mood to do so, providing dazzling solo displays even when playing in bands led by forceful personalities such as Webb and Eldridge. Although rooted in early swing style, as the years passed William's playing took on many of the influences of later swing era music and even adopted elements of bop.

● COMPILATIONS: *The Chronological Chick Webb 1929-1934* (Classics 1929-34)★★★★, *The Chronological Chick Webb 1935-1938* (Classics 1935-38)★★★★.

WILLIAMS, SPENCER

b. *c.*1889, New Orleans, Louisiana, USA, d. 14 July 1965, New York, USA. Believed to be a nephew of Lulu White, who operated Mahogany Hall, one of the most notorious brothels in New Orleans, Williams began playing piano as a child. After living in Atlanta for a while, he moved to Chicago, playing piano in an amusement park, but by 1916 was resident in New York and had embarked upon a hugely successful career as a songwriter. Among his songs, many of which became hits and have remained popular with singers and jazz instrumentalists to the present day, are 'I Ain't Got Nobody', 'Basin Street Blues', 'Tishomingo Blues', 'I Found A New Baby', 'Everybody Loves My Baby', 'Shimme-sha-wabble', 'Mahogany Hall Stomp', 'I Ain't Gonna Give Nobody None Of My Jelly Roll' and 'Royal Garden Blues' (these last two with the unrelated Clarence Williams). He also composed 'Fireworks' and 'Skip The Gutter', which were recorded in 1928 by Louis Armstrong's Hot Five, as was 'Squeeze Me', which Williams co-composed with Fats Waller. In the mid-20s he visited Paris to write special material for Joséphine Baker. He remained in Europe for a few years, visiting London and working with local and visiting American musicians. Around the end of the decade he was tried and acquitted on a charge of murder, and thereafter, soon moved to England, living in London until the early 50s. He then moved to Stockholm, Sweden, where he lived until 1957; finally he returned to New York, where he died.

WILLIAMS, TONY

b. 12 December 1945, Chicago, Illinois, USA, d. 23 February 1997. Williams was raised in Boston, Massachusetts, where his father, an amateur musician, encouraged him to take up drums. Williams studied with Alan Dawson and was sitting in at local clubs before he entered his teens. At the age of 15, he was freelancing in and around Boston and had already earned the admiration of leading drummers, including Max Roach. In the early 60s he went to New York, where he played with Jackie McLean and in 1963 joined Miles Davis. With Davis, Williams's rhythm section colleagues were Herbie Hancock and Ron Carter and together they made a formidable team which is still widely admired and often cited as Davis' greatest unit. During this period, both with Davis and on his many Blue Note recordings as leader, and sideman, Williams began reshaping modern jazz drumming, developing concepts created by some of his immediate predecessors such as Elvin Jones. Notably, Williams advanced the manner in which drummers could play freely yet retain a recognizable pulse. With Williams in a band, free jazz improvisers could dispense with time but were not entirely cut off from a basic rhythmic impulse. At the end of the 60s Williams left Davis to form a jazz-rock band with John McLaughlin. The band, named Lifetime, together with Larry Young and Jack Bruce set the standards to which most subsequent bands in the genre aspired but, insofar as the drumming was concerned, few achieved their aim. After McLaughlin moved on, Williams continued to lead jazz-rock bands but gradually moved back into jazz circles. In the late 70s he was with Hancock again in the V.S.O.P. quintet and also recorded with Gil Evans and Wynton Marsalis. In the late 80s Williams was leading a band with a stable personnel that included saxophonist Billy Pierce and Mulgrew Miller. In the mid-90s he signed to Miles Copeland's Ark 21 label and issued *Wilderness* with support from Michael Brecker, Pat Metheny, Stanley Clarke and Herbie Hancock. He also recorded with Derek Bailey and Bill Laswell as Arcana. Williams died after suffering a heart attack while undergoing gall bladder surgery.

● ALBUMS: *Life Time* (Blue Note 1964)★★★, *Spring* (Blue Note 1965)★★★, *Emergency* (Polydor 1969)★★★★, *Turn It Over* (Polydor 1970)★★★, *Ego* (Polydor 1971)★★★, *The Old Bum's Rush* (Polydor 1972)★★★, *Believe It* (Columbia 1975)★★★, *The Joy Of Flying* (Columbia 1979)★★★, *Foreign Intrigue* (Blue Note 1985)★★★, *Civilization* (Blue Note 1986)★★★, *Angel Street* (Blue Note 1988)★★★, *Native Heart* (Blue Note 1989)★★★, *Story Of Neptune* (Blue Note 1992)★★★, *Tokyo Live, Vol. 1* (Blue Note 1993)★★★, with Wayne Shorter, Ron Carter, Wallace Roney, Herbie Hancock *A Tribute To Miles* (QWest/Reprise 1994)★★★, *Wilderness* (Ark 21 1996)★★★, as Arcana *The Last Wave* (DIW 1996)★★★, *Young At Heart* (Columbia 1998)★★.

● COMPILATIONS: *Lifetime: The Collection* (Columbia 1992)★★★.

WILLIAMSON, CLAUDE

b. 18 November 1926, Brattleboro, Texas, USA. After studying piano formally at the New England Conservatory in Boston, Massachusetts, Williamson turned to playing jazz in the late 40s. He first worked with Charlie Barnet, where he was featured on 'Claude Reigns', then with Red Norvo and also briefly led his own small group. In the early 50s he toured with Bud Shank before settling in Los Angeles, where he led a trio for many years. He played too with Tal Farlow, appeared in the second edition of the Lighthouse All-Stars with Shank, Rolf Ericson, Bob Cooper and Max Roach, and recorded with Art Pepper. Amongst Williamson's better-known compositions is 'Aquarium', recorded by the All-Stars in 1954. His trio work kept him busy but musically static for several years. However, in the late 70s and early 80s he toured Japan and the records he made there spurred his career. Although he began as mainstream player, Williamson later adapted to bop and most of his subsequent work reflects this interest. Although little known on the international scene, Japan apart, his work bears much closer attention than it has usually enjoyed.

● ALBUMS: *The Lighthouse All Stars Vol. 3* (1953)★★★, *The Lighthouse All Stars Vol. 4: Flute And Oboe* (1954)★★★, with Art Pepper *Discoveries* (1954)★★★, *Salute To Bud* (Affinity 1954)★★★★, *Keys West* (Affinity 1955)★★★★, *The Claude Williamson Trio* (1956)★★★★, *'Round Midnight* (1957)★★★★, *Claude Williamson In Italy* (1958)★★, *The Claude Williamson Quintet* i (1958)★★★, *The Claude Williamson Quintet* ii (1961)★★★, *New Departure* (1978)★★★, *Holography* (Interplay 1979)★★★, *La Fiesta* (Interplay 1979)★★★, *Tribute To Bud* (1981)★★★★, *Theatre Party* (Fresh Sounds 1988)★★★, *Mulls The Mulligan Scene* (Fresh Sounds 1988)★★★.

WILLIAMSON, STEVE

b. 1964, London, England. This tenor saxophonist has never received the media attention that near-contemporary colleague Courtney Pine has had and, as a very shy person, has never sought it. This may well have been to Williamson's advantage, since it meant he could develop at his own pace and on his own terms. It also meant, on the minus side, that he did not issue an album under his own name until 1990, but when the opportunity came he was in a position to make demands, such as that the album should be cut in New York - Steve Coleman produced the album and Abbey Lincoln was guest vocalist on the title track. Williamson is a mature and versatile player who convinces whether playing turbo-charged hard bop (such as at the Wembley Nelson Mandela 70th birthday concert where, accompanying dancers IDJ, he and Pine reached their biggest-ever audience), in a free jam, locking horns with the likes of Evan Parker in Joe Gallivan's New Soldiers Of The Road, or contributing to the glorious exuberance of Louis Moholo's *Viva La Black*.

He played for a week with Art Blakey at Ronnie Scott's club, and produced some of his finest work on a 1989 four track demo disc with Wayne Batchelor's Quartet which, sadly, is currently not publicly available. His first saxophone was an alto, but he switched to tenor after hearing John Coltrane. On occasions he also plays soprano. Of the many talented young black musicians to emerge from the London jazz scene in the late 80s, Williamson looks set to prove one of the most original and durable if he can shake off the Coltrane shadow that haunts him.

● ALBUMS: with Louis Moholo *Viva La Black* (1988)★★★★, *A Waltz For Grace* (Polydor 1990)★★★★, *Rhyme Time* (Polydor 1991)★★★, *Journey To Truth* (Verve 1995)★★★.

WILSON, CASSANDRA

b. 4 December 1955, Jackson, Mississippi, USA. Wilson started piano and guitar lessons at the age of nine. In 1975 she began singing professionally, primarily folk and blues, working in various R&B and Top 20 cover version bands. She emerged as a jazz singer while studying with drummer Alvin Fielder and singing with the Black Arts Music Society in her hometown. In 1981 she moved to New Orleans and studied with saxophonist Earl Turbinton. In 1982 she relocated to New York at the suggestion of trumpeter Woody Shaw and began working with David Holland and Abbey Lincoln. In 1985 she guested on Steve Coleman's *Motherland Pulse* and was asked by the JMT label to record her own albums. Her debut was *Point Of View*, which featured Coleman and guitarist Jean-Paul Bourelly. New York's finest wanted to work with her. She sang with New Air, Henry Threadgill's trio, and he returned the compliment by helping with arrangements on her second, more powerful album, *Days Aweigh*. Her mix of smoky, knowing vocals and expansive, lush music that travelled between psychedelia and swing was transfixing. The more conservative American audience was won over by her record of standards, *Blue Skies* (1988), which was named jazz album of the year by *Billboard* magazine. The follow-up, the innovative sci-fi epic *Jumpworld* (1990), showed that Cassandra Wilson was not to be easily categorised: it included raps and funk as well as jazz and blues. This stylistic diversity was maintained on 1991's *She Who Weeps*. In the meantime, Wilson has continued to record on Steve Coleman's albums and has also made guest appearances with other musicians associated with Coleman's M-Base organisation, such as Greg Osby and Robin Eubanks. Her latest recordings on Blue Note Records have exposed her to a much wider market. *New Moon Daughter* (a number 1 album in the USA jazz chart) featured songs by the Monkees, U2, Hank Williams, Son House and Neil Young.

● ALBUMS: *Point Of View* (JMT 1986)★★★, *Days Aweigh* (JMT 1987)★★★, *Blue Skies* (JMT 1988)★★★★, *Jumpworld* (JMT 1990)★★★, *She Who Weeps* (JMT 1991)★★★, *Cassandra Wilson Live* (JMT 1991)★★★, *Dance To The Drums Again* (DIW 1992)★★★, *After The Beginning Again* (JMT 1993)★★★, *Blue Light 'Til Dawn* (Blue Note 1993)★★★★, *New Moon Daughter* (Blue Note 1996)★★★★, with Jacky Terrasson *Rendezvous* (Blue Note 1997)★★★★.

WILSON, DICK

b. Richard Wilson, 11 November 1911, Mount Vernon, Illinois, USA, d. 24 November 1941. Born into a musical family, Wilson was raised in the north-western states where he was taught to play alto saxophone by Joe Darensbourg. He began playing professionally in 1929, having meantime switched to tenor saxophone. He played with various bands, including Darensbourg's, Gene Coy's and Zack Whyte's. These engagements took him through into the mid-30s when he joined Andy Kirk and his Clouds Of Joy. Wilson quickly became the band's most impressive soloist, playing with technical assurance and advanced thinking. Although there is a strong swing era affiliation in his playing, it is also evident that he was reaching out to as yet unknown areas of music. Had Wilson not died when he did, there can be little doubt that he would have become a major influence upon a new generation of saxophonists, in the same way as his contemporary, Lester Young. Any one of his solos recorded with Kirk is an artistic gem, fully formed, note perfect, yet musically adventurous. Even so, there is a smooth, uncluttered aspect to his playing which makes it highly accessible to latter-day musicians.

● COMPILATIONS: *The Chronological Andy Kirk 1936-1937, 1937-1938, 1938, 1939-1940, 1940-1942* (Classics 1936-42)★★★★.

WILSON, ED

b. Edward John Wilson, 22 June 1944, Sydney, New South Wales, Australia. In the 50s Wilson played trombone with several jazz and dance bands in various parts of Australia and also broadcast extensively. In the late 60s he teamed up with Warren Daly to form a big band using seasoned jazz and studio musicians. This band remained active on and off into the early 80s. Subsequently, Wilson led his own band and also became musical director for show bands at hotels and casinos. A strong player with a direct uncluttered style, Wilson echoed the tradition of swing era players.

● ALBUMS: with Warren Daly *The Daly-Wilson Big Band On Tour* (Reprise 1973)★★★.

WILSON, GARLAND

b. 13 June 1909, Martinsburg, West Virginia, USA, d. 31 May 1954. Wilson began playing piano as a child and, when he was 20, moved to New York City, where he enjoyed some success playing in Harlem clubs. His records were very well received and in 1932 he became accompanist to the popular entertainer Nina Mae McKinney, with whom he toured Europe. He stayed in Europe, playing long residencies in Paris and also appearing in London with Jack Payne and his band. With the outbreak of war he returned to the USA, finding work in clubs in New York and Los Angeles, but in 1951 he was back in Europe, travelling between London and Paris, where he later died in 1954.

● COMPILATIONS: *The Way I Feel (1932-51)* (Collectors Items 1986)★★★, *Piano Solos* (Neovox 1990)★★★.

WILSON, GERALD

b. 4 September 1918, Shelby, Mississippi, USA. After starting out on piano, Wilson switched to trumpet while at Manassa high school. He studied formally at Cass Tech, Detroit, before joining Jimmie Lunceford in 1939, where he had the unenviable job of replacing Sy Oliver. Like Oliver, Wilson's duties in the Lunceford band not only required him to play trumpet but also to write arrangements. He composed original material for the band, including 'Hi Spook' and 'Yard Dog Mazurka'. After leaving Lunceford in 1942 he settled in Los Angeles, served in the US Navy, where he played in the band directed by Willie Smith (and which included Clark Terry), and also played briefly in bands led by Les Hite and Benny Carter. He formed his first band in 1945, recording and touring with a measure of success. The band included trombonist-arranger Melba Liston, whom Wilson married. He folded the band in 1947 and resumed his studies, this time in composition. During the 50s he was active as an arranger/writer, for Dizzy Gillespie, Count Basie and Duke Ellington ('You Gotta Crawl Before You Walk', 'You're Just An Old Antidisestablishmentarianist') among others, and also wrote for films and television. In 1961 he formed a new big band which recorded and played concerts and festivals, including Monterey in 1963 where the band included Teddy Edwards, Joe Pass and Harold Land. In 1969, he began teaching and also presented a radio series on jazz which lasted for six years. During this period he also worked extensively with singers, arranging for and accompanying Ella Fitzgerald, Carmen McRae, Sarah Vaughan, Ray Charles (*Modern Sounds In Country And Western*) and others. In 1970, El Chicano's cover version of Wilson's 'Viva Tirado' reached number 28 on the *Billboard* pop charts.

In 1972 he composed a classical piece, which was performed by the Los Angeles Philharmonic Orchestra under Zubin Mehta, and in later years continued to work in this field. In 1976 he directed the all-star festival band at Monterey in a programme of music that recalled the Lunceford band of the 30s and early 40s. In 1977 he continued his association with Monterey when he directed the Airmen Of Note, the US Air Force's jazz orchestra, in the premiere of his suite, 'The Happy Birthday Monterey Suite', commissioned for the festival. His orchestras have continued to present his own music, compositions and arrangements, and feature top class musicians, both veterans and newcomers, in well-rehearsed, effective performances. A sound, if little-known trumpet player in his earlier years, Wilson's contribution to jazz lies in the many fine bands he has led, in the example he has set by his undiminished enthusiasm and impeccably high standards of musicianship and, perhaps most important of all, in his distinctive writing.

His son, Anthony Wilson, is an accomplished guitarist who has recorded two acclaimed sets for MAMA Records in the late 90s. The elder Wilson continues to record, as demonstrated by *State Street Sweet* at the age of 77. He has also taught jazz since 1970, and is currently resident at U.C.L.A.

● ALBUMS: *Gerald Wilson* reissued as *Big Band Modern* (Federal 1953)★★★, *You Better Believe It!* (Pacific Jazz 1961)★★★, *Moment Of Truth* (Pacific Jazz 1962)★★★★, *Portraits* (Pacific Jazz 1963)★★★, *Gerald Wilson On Stage* (Pacific Jazz 1964)★★, *Feelin' Kinda Blue* (Pacific Jazz 1965)★★★, *The Golden Sword* (Pacific Jazz 1966)★★★, *Live And Swinging* (Pacific Jazz 1967)★★★, *Everywhere* (Pacific Jazz 1967)★★★, *California Soul* (Pacific Jazz 1968)★★★, *Eternal Equinox* (Pacific Jazz 1969)★★★, *Lomelin* (Discovery 1981)★★★, *Groovin' High* (Hep Jazz 1981)★★★, *Jessica* (Trend 1982)★★★, *Calafia* (Trend 1984)★★, *Love You Madly* (Discovery 1988)★★★, *Jenna* (Discovery 1989)★★★, *State Street Sweet* (MAMA 1995)★★★★, *Suite Memories* spoken word (MAMA 1997)★★, *Theme For Monterey* (MAMA 1998)★★★.

● COMPILATIONS: *Gerald Wilson And His Orchestra 1945-46* (Classics 1998)★★★★.

WILSON, JUICE

b. Robert Edward Wilson, 21 January 1904, St. Louis, Missouri, USA. Raised in Chicago, Wilson played drums in a boys' band, then took up the violin. He played in various bands in clubs in Chicago and also on pleasure boats. In the 20s he was mostly in the north-east, eventually playing in New York at the end of the decade. He visited Europe with Noble Sissle's band and remained there for many years, playing with local bands and also with visiting fellow countrymen. He worked in Germany, Spain, Holland, France and North Africa, the latter region with a band led by 'Little Mike' McKendrick. He held residencies as a featured artist in Malta where he remained until the mid-50s. He continued to tour the Mediterranean region for a few more years before visiting Paris en route to the USA.

WILSON, NANCY

b. 20 February 1937, Chillicothe, Ohio, USA. Wilson began singing in clubs in and around Columbus, Ohio. She attracted attention among jazz musicians, made her first records in 1956, and in the late 50s toured with a band led by Rusty Bryant. At the end of the decade she sang with George Shearing, with whom she recorded, and Cannonball Adderley. It was at Adderley's insistence that she went to New York, where she was soon signed by Capitol. During the next few years Wilson made numerous albums, toured extensively, and built a substantial following among the popular audience but always retained a connection, if sometimes tenuously so, with jazz. In the early 80s she was again working more closely with jazz musicians, including Hank Jones, Art Farmer, Benny Golson and Ramsey Lewis. Later in the decade she was active around the world, performing at major concert venues and singing in a style that revealed that the long years in the more flamboyant atmosphere of popular music had given her a taste for slightly over-dramatizing songs. Nevertheless, when backed by top-flight musicians she could still deliver a rhythmic and entertaining performance.

● ALBUMS: *Like Love* (Capitol 1959)★★★★, *Something Wonderful* (Capitol 1960)★★★★, *Nancy Wilson With Billy May's Orchestra* (1959)★★★★, *Nancy Wilson* (1960)★★★★, with George Shearing *The Swingin's Mutual* (Capitol 1961)★★★★, *Nancy Wilson With Gerald Wilson's Orchestra* (1961)★★★, *Nancy Wilson/Cannonball Adderley* (Capitol 1962)★★★, *Hello Young Lovers* (Capitol 1962)★★★★, *Broadway - My Way* (Capitol 1963)★★★★, *Hollywood - My Way* (Capitol 1963)★★★, *Nancy Wilson With Jimmy Jones's Orchestra* (1963)★★★★, *Yesterday's Love Songs, Today's Blues* (Capitol 1963)★★★★, *Today, Tomorrow, Forever* (Capitol 1964)★★★, *Nancy Wilson With Kenny Dennis's Group* (Capitol 1964)★★★, *How Glad I Am* (Capitol 1964)★★★, *The Nancy Wilson Show!* (Capitol 1965)★★★★, *Today - My Way* (Capitol 1965)★★★, *Gentle Is My Love* (Capitol 1965)★★★, *From Broadway With Love* (Capitol 1966)★★★★, *A Touch Of Today* (Capitol 1966)★★★, *Tender Loving Care* (Capitol 1966)★★★, *Nancy Wilson With Oliver Nelson's Orchestra* (Capitol 1967)★★★★, *Nancy - Naturally* (Capitol 1967)★★★, *Just For Now* (1967)★★★, *Nancy Wilson With H. B. Barnum's Orchestra* (Capitol 1967)★★★, *Lush Life* aka *The Right To Love* (Capitol 1967)★★★★, *Welcome To My Love* (Capitol 1968)★★★★, *Easy* (Capitol 1968)★★★, *The Sound Of Nancy Wilson* (Capitol 1968)★★★★, *Nancy Wilson With The Hank Jones Quartet* (Capitol 1969)★★★, *Nancy* (Capitol 1969)★★★, *Son Of A Preacher Man* (Capitol 1969)★★★, *Hurt So Bad* (Capitol 1969)★★★, *Can't Take My Eyes Off You* (Capitol 1970)★★★★, *Now I'm A Woman* (Capitol 1970)★★★, *But Beautiful* (Capitol 1971)★★★, *Kaleidoscope* (Capitol 1971)★★★, *All In Love Is Fair* (Capitol 1974)★★★, *Come Get To This* (Capitol 1975)★★★, *This Mother's Daughters* (Capitol 1976)★★★, *I've Never Been To Me* (Capitol 1977)★★★, *What's New?* (1982)★★★, *Nancy Wilson In Performance At The Playboy Jazz Festival* (1982)★★★, with Ramsey Lewis *The Two Of Us* (Capitol 1984)★★★, *Godsend* (1984)★★★, *Keep You Satisfied* (1985)★★★, *Forbidden Love* (1987)★★★, *If I Had My Way* (Columbia 1997)★★★★.

● COMPILATIONS: *The Best Of Nancy Wilson* (Capitol 1968)★★★★, *Nancy Wilson's Greatest Hits* (Capitol 1988)★★★★, *The Capitol Years* (Capitol 1992)★★★★.

WILSON, PHIL

b. Phillip Sanford Wilson, 8 September 1941, St. Louis, Missouri, USA, d. 25 March 1992, New York City, New York, USA. A strong drummer who also studied violin, Wilson was a professional from the age of 16 and worked with soul singers such as Solomon Burke and Jackie Wilson as well as with trumpeter Lester Bowie and saxophonists Julius Hemphill and David Sanborn. In 1965 he went to Chicago, where he worked with Otis Rush and played alongside Sanborn again in the Paul Butterfield Blues Band, a mixed-race outfit which featured often frantic versions of blues classics. During this period he became a member of the AACM and joined Roscoe Mitchell's group. He was one of the early, transient occupants of the drum stool in the Art Ensemble Of Chicago (AEC), which grew out of Mitchell's quartet, and Wilson was reunited with Bowie in both of these bands. In 1972 he moved to New York and worked with Anthony Braxton, another AACM alumnus and his association with colleagues from the AACM continued through the 70s and 80s. In 1978 he joined a quintet led by Lester Bowie and until the early 90s (when replaced by Don Moye, his successor in the AEC) he was the one non-brass-playing member of Bowie's Brass Fantasy, where he provided a solid but flexible backbone for the group's rich and witty mixture of doo-wop, blues, marching band pastiches and straight ahead jazz. He also played in the gospel group, From The Root To The Scource (with Fontella Bass and David Peaston) and led his own groups, including a quartet with Frank Lowe and Olu Dara that recorded at the Moers Festival. Wilson was killed in a shooting incident in 1992.

● ALBUMS: with Paul Butterfield *The Resurrection Of Pigboy Crabshaw* (1967)★★★, *Fruits* (1977)★★, with Lester Bowie *Duet* (1978)★★★.

WILSON, SHADOW

b. Rossiere Wilson, 25 September 1919, New York City, New York, USA, d. 11 July 1959. Early in his career, Wilson played drums with bands in the eastern states, in particular around Philadelphia. In 1939 he began an impressive swing through many of the important big bands of the period, including those led by Lucky Millinder, Benny Carter, Lionel Hampton, Earl 'Fatha' Hines, Billy Eckstine, County Basie and, in the late 40s, Woody Herman. In the 50s he played mostly in small groups, working comfortably with swing era stars and rising bop names: Illinois Jacquet, Erroll Garner, Ella Fitzgerald, Thelonious Monk, Sonny Stitt, Lee Konitz, John Coltrane. Wilson's playing style was subtle and driving, always supportive and with unfailing good taste.

●ALBUMS: with Count Basie *The Master's Touch* (Savoy 1944-49)★★★★, with Tadd Dameron *Fontainebleau* (Prestige 1956)★★★★, with Phil Woods, Gene Quill *Phil And Quill* (RCA 1956)★★★, *Thelonious Monk With John Coltrane* (Jazzland 1957)★★★.

WILSON, TEDDY

b. 24 November 1912, Austin, Texas, USA, d. 31 July 1986, New Britain, Connecticut, USA. Born into a middle-class family, Wilson grew up in Tuskegee where his parents moved to take up teaching posts at the university. He studied violin and piano at Tuskegee and later extended his studies at college in Alabama. In 1929, by now concentrating on piano, he became a professional musician in Detroit. He played in bands led by Speed Webb and others in the Midwest until he settled in Chicago, where he worked with Erskine Tate, Eddie Mallory, Louis Armstrong and Jimmie Noone. In the early 30s he played with Art Tatum, holding his own in duets, a feat of considerable distinction. In 1933 he was heard by John Hammond, who encouraged him to move to New York to play in Benny Carter's band, and he also played with Willie Bryant. During this period in his career Wilson made a succession of outstanding records, with Carter in the Chocolate Dandies, leading small bands for which he hired the best available sidemen, and accompanying Billie Holiday on sessions that produced numerous masterpieces of jazz. Back in Chicago he guested with Benny Goodman, made records with Goodman and Gene Krupa and, in April 1936, became a member of the Goodman entourage, where he was featured as a member of the Benny Goodman Trio.

He remained with Goodman until 1939, usually playing as a member of the trio and later the quartet, before leaving to form his own big band. Wilson set high standards of musicianship, which militated against the band's commercial success, and it survived for barely a year. He then formed a sextet, for which he adopted similarly high standards, but fortunately this group attained a measure of success with long residencies and some excellent recordings. After a brief return visit to Goodman, Wilson worked in the studios, taught, toured and recorded over the next dozen years. By the 60s he had become a deserved elder statesman of jazz, a role which he maintained throughout the rest of his life, touring internationally as either a single or in small groups such as the Gentlemen Of Swing, in which he was joined by Harry Edison and Benny Carter.

Although the playing style Wilson adopted early in his career owed much to the influence of Earl 'Fatha' Hines, by the mid-30s he was a highly distinctive performer in his own right. A naturally restrained musician, Wilson's fleet playing and the elegant poise of his solos (the latter a facet that was reflected in his personal demeanour), combined to make him an influential figure in the development of jazz piano. His influence is most directly noticeable in the work of Nat 'King' Cole. His accompaniments to many of Billie Holiday's classic performances were an important factor in the singer's success. The quality of the setting he provided, especially on some of the earlier sessions when Holiday's talent was still unpolished, are object lessons in their deceptive simplicity. The excellence of the arrangements, which aid the instrumental soloists as much as the singer, display his prowess, while his seemingly effortless obbligato and solo contributions add to the quality of these timeless recordings. His performances with the Goodman trio and quartet are scarcely less important, providing a brilliantly intuitive counterpoint to the leader's playing. A noted stickler for quality, Goodman never failed to praise Wilson in a manner that contrasted strikingly with his often dismissive attitude towards other important musicians. Wilson's big band was another musical landmark, although the band's failure to attain commercial success was something which still clearly rankled with its leader four decades after it had folded. The sextet of the early 40s, which included at times artists such as Benny Morton, Jimmy Hamilton, 'Big' Sid Catlett, Bill Coleman, Emmett Berry, Slam Stewart and Edmond Hall, was yet another demonstration of his subtle and understated musicianship. Among important recording dates in later years were sessions with Lester Young and Roy Eldridge in 1956, with Carter in Japan in 1980, and several outstanding solo albums. Although a shy and retiring man, Wilson had no illusions about his musical stature. Late in his life, when an interviewer asked who was his favourite pianist, he answered, with only a hint of a disarming grin, 'I am.'

● ALBUMS: *Teddy Wilson Featuring Billie Holiday* 10-inch album (Columbia 1949)★★★★, *Teddy Wilson And His Piano* 10-inch album (Columbia 1950)★★★★, *Piano Moods* 10-inch album (Columbia 1950)★★★★, *Teddy Wilson All Stars* 10-inch album (Dial 1950)★★★★, *Runnin' Wild* 10-inch album (MGM 1951)★★★★, *Town Hall Concert* 10-inch album (Commodore 1952)★★★★, *Piano Pastries* 10-inch album (Mercury 1953)★★★, *The Didactic Mr Wilson* 10-inch album (Clef 1953)★★★, *All Star Sextet* 10-inch album (Allegro 1954)★★★★, *Soft Moods With Teddy Wilson* 10-inch album (Clef 1954)★★★, *The Creative Teddy Wilson* reissued as *For Quiet Lovers* (Norgran 1955)★★★★, *Intimate Listening* (Verve 1956)★★★, with Lester Young *Pres And Teddy* (American Recording Society/Verve 1956)★★★★, *I Got Rhythm* (Verve 1957)★★★, *The Impeccable Mr. Teddy Wilson* (Verve 1958)★★★★, with Gerry Mulligan *The Teddy Wilson Trio And The Gerry Mulligan Quartet At Newport* (Verve 1958)★★★★, *These Tunes Remind Me Of You* (Verve 1959)★★★, *The Touch Of Teddy Wilson* (Verve 1959)★★★, *"Gypsy" In Jazz* (Columbia 1959)★★★, *Teddy Wilson 1964* (Cameo 1964)★★★, *Stompin' At The Savoy* (Black Lion 1967)★★★, *Air Mail Special* (Black Lion 1968)★★★, *The Teddy Wilson Trio In Europe* (Prestige 1969)★★★, *Swedish Jazz My Way* (Sonet 1970)★★★, *Elegant Piano* (1970)★★★, with Eiji Kitamura *Teddy Wilson Meets Eiji Kitamura* (Storyville 1970)★★★, *With Billie In Mind* (Chiaroscuro 1972)★★★★, *Teddy Wilson And The Dutch Swing College Band* (Everest 1973)★★★★, *Runnin' Wild* (Black Lion 1973)★★★, *Piano Solos* (Affinity 1973)★★★, *Concert In Argentina* (1974)★★, *Blues For Thomas Waller* (Black Lion 1974)★★★, *Teddy Wilson In Tokyo* (Sackville 1976)★★★, *Teddy Wilson And His All-Stars* (Chiaroscuro 1976)★★★, *Three Little Words* (Classic Jazz 1976)★★★, *The Teddy Wilson Trio In Milan* (1976)★★★, *Teddy Wilson Revamps Rodgers And Hart* (Chiaroscuro 1977)★★, *Cole Porter Classics* (Black Lion 1977)★★★★, *Lionel Hampton Presents Teddy Wilson* (Who's Who 1977)★★★, *Teddy Wilson Revisits The Goodman Years* (Storyville 1980)★★★, with Benny Carter *Gentlemen Of Swing* (1980)★★★, *Traces* (1983)★★★, *Solo Piano: Keystone Transcriptions 1939-1940* (Storyville 1997)★★★, *How High The Moon* 1945 recording (Tradition/Rykodisc 1997)★★★, *B Flat Swing* 1944 recording (Jazz Archives)★★★★, *Teddy Wilson Sextet: 1944, Vol. 2* (Jazz Archives)★★★★.

● COMPILATIONS: *Masters Of Jazz, Vol. 11* 1968-1980 recordings (Storyville 1968)★★★★, *Too Hot For Words (1935)* (Hep 1986)★★★★, *Of Thee I Swing* 1936-1937 recordings (Hep)★★★, *America Dances Broadcasts (1939)* (Fanfare 1988)★★★, *Fine And Dandy* 1937 recordings (Hep 1991)★★★★, *Blue Mood* 1937-1938 recordings (Hep 1991)★★★★, *Complete All Star And V-Disc Sessions* (Victorious 1991)★★★★, *Teddy Wilson And His Orchestra 1934-1935* (Classics 1996)★★★★, *Teddy Wilson And His Orchestra 1935-1936* (Classics 1996)★★★★, *Teddy Wilson And His Orchestra 1936-1937* (Classics 1996)★★★★, *Teddy Wilson And His Orchestra 1937* (Classics 1996)★★★★, *Teddy Wilson And His Orchestra 1937-1938* (Classics 1996)★★★★, *Teddy Wilson And His Orchestra 1938* (Classics 1996)★★★★, *Teddy Wilson And His Orchestra 1939* (Classics 1996)★★★★, *Teddy Wilson And His Orchestra 1939-1941* (Classics 1996)★★★★, *Teddy Wilson And His Orchestra 1942-1945* (Classics 1997)★★★★, *An Introduction To Teddy Wilson* 1935-1945 recordings (Best Of Jazz 1997)★★★, *The Complete Verve Recordings Of The Teddy Wilson Trio* 5-CD/8-LP box set (Mosaic 1998)★★★★, *The Complete Associated Transcriptions* 1944 recordings (Storyville 1998)★★★★, *The Keystone Transcriptions, c. 1939-1949* (Storyville 1998)★★★.

● FURTHER READING: *The Genius Of Teddy Wilson*, no author listed. *Teddy Wilson Talks Jazz*, Artie Ligthart and Humphrey Van Loo.

WINDHURST, JOHNNY

b. 5 November 1926, New York City, New York, USA, d. November 1981. After teaching himself to play trumpet, Windhurst first played in public, at Nick's in New York, while still in his early teens. Before he was out of his teenage years, he was playing professionally with Sidney Bechet, Art Hodes and James P. Johnson. In the late 40s he played in bands led by Edmond Hall, Hilton 'Nappy' Lamare and Louis Armstrong. He also led his own bands, but in these ventures chose to stay out of the main east coast centres. In the early 50s he worked with Eddie Condon, Ruby Braff and, later in the decade, with Jack Teagarden.

He also accompanied a number of singers who found his unassuming nature, as reflected in his discreet playing, an ideal accompaniment. During the 60s and 70s he played mostly in obscure, out-of-the-way corners of the USA, seemingly content to hide his considerable talent from the bigtime spotlight. Very much a musician's musician, highly regarded by all who heard him, Windhurst's chosen lifestyle might have robbed jazz of an important figure but, at least, he lived the life he wanted.

● ALBUMS: *The Imaginative Johnny Windhurst* (1956)★★★.

WINDING, KAI

b. Kai Chresten Winding, 18 May 1922, Arhus, Denmark, d. 7 May 1983, Spain. Winding's family emigrated to the USA in 1934, and soon thereafter he began teaching himself to play trombone. In the late 30s and early 40s he was with a number of big bands including those of Sonny Dunham and Alvino Rey. After serving in the US Coast Guard during the war, he began frequenting New York clubs, including Minton's Playhouse, and eagerly assimilating bop. He played in Benny Goodman's mid-40s bebop-inclined band, and then he joined Stan Kenton in 1946. Although he moved on the following year, his impact was substantial and he was now both a name to be reckoned with and popular with audiences. He next played with Charlie Ventura, Charlie Parker and Miles Davis, appearing on the *Birth Of The Cool* album. He also developed a penchant for working with other trombonists, starting with J.J. Johnson, with whom he formed a successful quintet in 1954. Later in the 50s he toured with his own bands, including a four-trombone and rhythm line-up, and in the 60s was musical director of the Playboy Club in New York. In the 70s he was leader, co-leader or sideman of various groups, including the Giants Of Jazz with Dizzy Gillespie, Giant Bones with Curtis Fuller, and the Lionel Hampton All-Star Big Band. One of the first trombone players to fully assimilate bop, Winding was an accomplished musician who could readily blend into most musical styles. His playing, in such diverse settings as Kenton's brassy powerhouse band and Davis's coolly restrained group, was always appropriate. His duets with Johnson were exquisitely formed and displayed his total command of the instrument. Towards the end of his life Winding played only when he chose to do so, spending time in semi-retirement in Spain where he died in 1983.

● ALBUMS: with J.J. Johnson *Modern Jazz Trombones, Volume 1* 10-inch album (Prestige 1951)★★★★, *Kai Winding All Stars* 10-inch album (Roost 1952)★★★, *New Trends Of Jazz* 10-inch album (Savoy 1952)★★★, with Bennie Green, Johnson *Jazz Workshop, Vol. 1* 10-inch album (Debut 1953)★★★, with Green, Johnson *Jazz Workshop, Vol. 2* 10-inch album (Debut 1953)★★★, with Johnson *Jay And Kai* i 10-inch album (Prestige 1954)★★★★, with Johnson *Jay And Kai* i 10-inch album (Savoy 1954)★★★★, with Johnson *Jay And Kai, Volume 2* 10-inch album (Savoy 1955)★★★★, with Johnson *Jay And Kai, Volume 3* 10-inch album (Savoy 1955)★★★★, with Johnson *An Afternoon At Birdland* (Vik 1955)★★★★, with Johnson *Kai Winding & J.J. Johnson* (Bethlehem 1955)★★★, with Johnson *Kai + J.J.* 10-inch album (Columbia 1956)★★★, with Johnson *Trombone For Two* (Columbia 1956)★★★, with Johnson *J.J. Johnson/Kai Winding + Six* (Columbia 1956)★★★, with Green, Johnson *Trombone By Three* (Prestige 1956)★★★★, with Green, Johnson *J.J. Johnson, Kai Winding, Bennie Green* (Prestige 1956)★★★★, *Trombone Sound* (Columbia 1956)★★★, shared with Dave Brubeck *American Jazz Festival At Newport '56* (Columbia 1956)★★★, with Brew Moore, Fats Navarro *In The Beginning ... Bebop* (Savoy 1957)★★★★, with Stan Getz, Red Rodney *Lestorian Mode* (Savoy 1957)★★★, *Trombone Panorama* (Columbia 1957)★★★, *Swingin' State* (Columbia 1958)★★★, *Dance To The City Beat* (Columbia 1959)★★★★, *The Incredible Kai Winding Trombones* (Impulse! 1960)★★★★, with Johnson *The Great Kai & J.J.* (Impulse! 1961)★★★★, *The Great Kai Winding Sound* (Harmony 1962)★★★, *Kai Ole'* (Verve 1962)★★★, *Suspense Themes In Jazz* (Verve 1962)★★★, with Johnson *Looking Back* (Prestige 1963)★★★, *Kai Winding Solo* (Verve 1963)★★★, with Kenny Burrell *More!!!* aka *Soul Surfin'* (Verve 1963)★★★, *The Lonely One* (Verve 1963)★★★, *Mondo Cane #2* (Verve 1964)★★★, *Modern Country* (Verve 1964)★★★, *The Rainy Day* (Verve 1965)★★★, *The 'In' Instrumentals* (Verve 1965)★★★, with Gerry Mulligan, Red Rodney *Broadway* (Status 1965)★★★, *More Brass* (Verve 1966)★★★, *Dirty Dog* (Verve 1966)★★★, *Penny Lane & Time* (Verve 1967)★★★, with Johnson *Israel* (A&M 1968)★★★, with Johnson *Betwixt And Between* (A&M 1969)★★★, with Johnson *Stonebone* (A&M 1970)★★★★, *Giants Of Jazz* (1971)★★★, *Kai Winding's Caravan* (1974)★★★, *Danish Blue* (1977)★★, *Showcase* (1977)★★★, *Lionel Hampton Presents Kai Winding* (1977)★★, *Duo Bones* (1978)★★★, *Giant Bones* (1979)★★★, *Trombone Summit* (1980)★★★, *Giant Bones At Nice* (1980)★★★, *Giant Bones 90* (Sonet 1980)★★★.

● COMPILATIONS: *Kai's Krazy Kats* (1945)★★★, *Kai Winding* (1989)★★★.

WINSTONE, ERIC

b. 1 January 1915, London, England. d. 2 May 1974, Pagham, Sussex, England. A popular bandleader and composer from the 30s through to the 70s, Winstone worked as a clerk at the Gas Light and Coke Company in Westminster, and played the piano in his spare time, before leaving to become a full time musician. After leading his first band at the Spanish Club in Cavendish Square, London in 1935, he learned to play the accordion, and eventually founded an accordion school. He became an accomplished arranger for the instrument, and formed his renowned Accordion Quintet and Swing Quartet. The latter outfit consisted of himself on accordion, with string bass, vibraphone, guitar and vocalist Julie Dawn.

During World War II he led the Eric Winstone Dance Orchestra and toured throughout Europe entertaining the troops. After the war his highly popular stage show played theatres and ballrooms, and was resident at Butlin's Holiday Camps in the summer for more than 20 years. Among the musicians associated with his various line-ups were Ralph Dollimore, Alan Moorhouse, Roy Marsh, Frank Deniz, Norman Payne, Bill Shakespeare, Ernie Shear, Ronnie Priest, Jimmy Skidmore, Kenny Graham, Pat Dodd, Carl Barriteau, Freddy Gardner, Harry Bence, and many more, along with vocalists Alan Kane, Michael Holliday, Elizabeth Batey and Marion Williams. For some years Winstone was the musical director for Southern Television, and he also ran an entertainment agency for a time. His best-remembered compositions include the atmospheric 'Stage Coach' (his signature tune), 'Oasis', 'Bottle Party', 'Mirage', 'Pony Express', and he also wrote several light pieces and some background music for films.

● ALBUMS: *Happy Beat For Happy Feet* (Top Rank 1961)★★★, *Eric Winstone And His Band* (President 1993)★★★.

WINSTONE, NORMA

b. 23 September 1941, London, England. Although she studied formally as a pianist, Winstone decided to sing as a career and by her mid-teens was a professional vocalist. Although her earliest work was in the mainstream of jazz and jazz-influenced popular song, she was soon orientated towards the modern end of the jazz spectrum. In the 60s she became known for her musical associations with Michael Garrick, her singing developing into a frequently wordless instrumental style. In the late 60s, 70s and early 80s her reputation spread and she was a member of the trio, Azimuth, with Kenny Wheeler and her husband John Taylor. She continued to work with leading contemporary musicians, including Ralph Towner, Mike Westbrook and Eberhard Weber.

In the late 80s and early 90s Winstone's repertoire underwent a slight shift and she was again performing many classic songs of earlier decades, often accompanied by Tony Coe. Although her new repertoire is rather more orthodox, Winstone brought to her material overtones of the free form work of her middle period, thus creating intriguing musical blends. In 1994 she was heard in the varied settings of London's Barbican, performing her own English lyrics to *The Songs of the Auvergne,* and as the singing voice for actress Geraldine James and in Alan Plater's BBC Television play, *Doggin' Around.* In this same year she also recorded *Well Kept Secret* with veteran pianist Jimmy Rowles. In February 1995 she launched her band New Friends in a concert at Ronnie Scott's. An exceptionally gifted and highly original singer, Winstone's chosen path has sometimes restricted her acceptance by the wider jazz audience, but those who have followed her work have been rewarded by the consistently high standards and indubitable integrity of her performances.

● ALBUMS: with Mike Westbrook *Love Songs* (1970)★★★★, with Michael Garrick *The Heart Is A Lotus* (1970)★★★, *Edge Of Time* (1972)★★★, *Somewhere Called Home* (ECM 1987)★★★, *In Concert* (Enodoc 1988)★★★, *Well Kept Secret* (Hot House 1994)★★★★, *Manhattan In The Rain* (Enodoc 1998)★★★.

WINTER, PAUL

b. 31 August 1939, Altoona, Pennsylvania, USA. While Winter was at Northwestern University, Chicago, he played the alto saxophone and the sextet he led won the Intercollegiate Jazz Festival of 1961. John Hammond Jnr. signed the group to CBS Records. The group toured Latin America in 1962 and became the first jazz group to play at the White House. The tour 'absolutely exploded our conception of what the world was' and the music Winter had heard led to the gradual change of the Sextet into the Consort. This was a band with a wholly new instrumentation - classical guitar, English horn, cello, ethnic percussion. The combination of jazz, classical and ethnic instruments has remained constant through numerous personnel changes over the following 20 years. It was difficult at the time for Winter to explain just what it was he was trying to produce and record companies found it hard to categorize. Winter now sees it as 'celebrating the convergence of both roots of American music - European and African'. He has had a series of talented musicians pass through the Consort - Collin Walcott, Paul McCandless, David Darling and Ralph Towner among them. *Icarus* was produced by George Martin and described by him as 'the finest album I have made'. Through the 70s Winter showed an increasing concern with conservation and became an active supporter of Greenpeace. He has recorded music accompanied by the sounds of whales off the Canadian coast and wolves in the mountains of California and Minnesota. He recorded Canyon Lullaby live in the Grand Canyon.

● ALBUMS: *Jazz Premiers: Washington* (1962)★★★, *Jazz Meets The Bossa Nova* (1962)★★★, *New Jazz On Campus* (1963)★★★★, *Something In The Wind* (1969)★★, *Icarus* (1971)★★, *Earthdance* (1977)★★★★, *Callings* (1980)★★★, *Missa Gaia/Earth Mass* (1982)★★, *Concert For The Earth* (1985)★★★, *Canyon* (1985)★★★, *Whales Alive* (1987)★★, *Earthbeat* (Living Music 1988)★★, *Canyon Lullaby* (Living Music 1997)★★★.

WINTERS, TINY

b. Frederick Winters, 24 January 1909, London, England, d. 7 February 1996. A largely self-taught bass player, Winters played in many of the leading British dance bands of the 30s. He was briefly with Roy Fox and Bert Ambrose before spending five years with Lew Stone's band, helping to provide the immaculate timekeeping for which this excellent orchestra was renowned. In the late 30s he was again with Ambrose and throughout the decade took time to make records, both under his own name and with Ray Noble, Coleman Hawkins and Nat Gonella. In the post-war years he played again for Stone and became a familiar figure in clubs and in theatrical pit bands. During the 60s he played often with George Chisholm and, after a short retirement in the mid-70s, was back on the scene again playing with musicians of his own age group and with those of younger generations, notably John Barnes and Digby Fairweather. Solid, dependable, in the best sense of that sometimes pejorative term, and highly regarded by his peers, he was a source of delight and information for many generations of UK musicians.

● COMPILATIONS: with Lew Stone *Coffee In The Morning (1933-34)* (1983)★★★.

WINTHER, JENS

b. 29 October 1960, Næstved, Denmark. Trumpeter and composer Winther was still in his teens when he enrolled in John Tchicai's and Hugh Steinmetz's 'school' of free jazz and ethnic music, the Cadentia Nova Danica big band. In the 80s he joined Erling Kroner's band which played a fusion of Argentinian tango and American jazz. Winther has made frequent visits to New York, USA where he has received encouragement from musicians including Bob Brookmeyer and has also sat in with local groups. Winther is thoroughly at home with all current styles of black American popular music and tends to eschew so-called Scandinavian 'coolness'. His lines are rhythmically exciting and avoids melodic clichés by employing unusual interval leaps. He is one among a handful of Danish jazz musicians who has recorded his own compositions with the Danish Radio Big Band. Winther's admiration for the sound of Chet Baker and Miles Davis is particularly apparent on the broodingly desolate music in parts of *The Planets.*

● ALBUMS: *Jens Winther Quintet* (Stunt 1986)★★★★, *Jens Winther And The Danish Radio Big Band* (Olufsen 1991)★★★, *Scorpio Dance* (Storyville 1991)★★★, *Nomads Of Tomorrow* (Olufsen 1993)★★★, *Looking Through* (Storyville 1993)★★, *The Planets* (Stunt 1995)★★.

WISEMAN, VAL

b. 15 August 1942, West Bromwich, West Midlands, England. Wiseman began singing as a young girl and at the age of 18 joined a local jazz band. In 1963 she joined Monty Sunshine where she remained for three years and also sang at clubs, concerts and on radio with many other bands, including Alex Welsh, Humphrey

Lyttelton and the Al Fairweather-Sandy Brown Allstars. In 1986 she sang with Eggy Ley's Hot Shots, appearing with the band at that year's Birmingham International Jazz Festival. This performance resulted in an invitation to headline the following year's festival tribute to Billie Holiday. Entitled *Lady Sings The Blues*, this show subsequently toured regularly throughout the UK and Europe and featured several leading jazz instrumentalists, including Digby Fairweather, Roy Williams, Alan Barnes and Len Skeat. She has also appeared in the touring package *Drummin' Man*, singing the Anita O'Day songs from the Gene Krupa repertoire. Wiseman has also recorded extensively, appearing on albums by King Pleasure And The Biscuit Boys, Sunshine, and the Midland Youth Jazz Orchestra. In addition to packages and as singer with several bands, Wiseman has also toured as a solo artist and in these settings broadens her repertoire to include the great standards. Although popular in various parts of the UK, Netherlands, Belgium, Germany and Canada, Wiseman is not as well known as her skill and stylishness so clearly warrants. Her vocal sound, warm, relaxed and with effortless swing, makes her one of the best singers working in the UK jazz field in the late 90s.

● ALBUMS: *Lady Sings The Blues* (Big Bear 1990)★★★.

WITHERSPOON, JIMMY

b. 8 August 1923, Gurdon, Arkansas, USA, d. 18 September 1997, Los Angeles, California, USA. Witherspoon crossed over into rock, jazz and R&B territory, but his deep and mellow voice placed him ultimately as a fine blues singer. He sang in his local Baptist church from the age of seven. From 1941-43 he was in the Merchant Marines and, during stopovers in Calcutta, he found himself singing the blues with a band led by Teddy Weatherford. In 1944, he replaced Walter Brown in the Jay McShann band at Vallejo, California, and toured with it for the next four years. In 1949 he had his first hit, 'Tain't Nobody's Business If I Do', which stayed on the *Billboard* chart for 34 weeks. Other recordings at the time with bands led by Jimmy 'Maxwell Street' Davis are fine examples of rollicking west coast R&B (collected as *Who's Been Jivin' You*). Witherspoon's popularity as an R&B singer faded during the course of the 50s, but he made a great impression on jazz listeners at the Monterey Jazz Festival in October 1959, performing with a group that included Ben Webster. Other collaborations with jazz artists included *Some Of My Best Friends Are The Blues*, with horns and strings arranged and conducted by Benny Golson, and a guest performance on Jon Hendricks' *Evolution Of The Blues Song*. He won the *Down Beat* critics' poll as a 'new star' in 1961. Frequent tours of Europe followed, beginning in 1961 with a Buck Clayton group and later with Coleman Hawkins, Roy Eldridge, Earl Hines and Woody Herman. He also did community work, including singing in prisons.

In the early 70s he gave up touring for a sedentary job as a blues disc jockey on the radio station KMET in Los Angeles, but resumed active music thanks to the encouragement of Eric Burdon. During his touring with Burdon he introduced a young Robben Ford as his guitarist and toured Japan and the Far East. In 1974 his 'Love Is A Five Letter Word' was a hit, though some fans regretted his neglect of the blues. A record with the Savoy Sultans in 1980 was a spirited attempt to recall a bygone era. *The Blues, The Whole Blues And Nothin' But The Blues* was the first album release for Mike Vernon's new label Indigo. Witherspoon has been revered by generations during different eras, and his name was often cited as a major influence during the 60s beat boom; his work is destined to endure.

● ALBUMS: *New Orleans Blues* (1956)★★★, *Goin' To Kansas City Blues* (RCA Victor 1957)★★★★, with Eddie Vinson *Battle Of The Blues, Volume 3* (1959)★★★, *At The Monterey Jazz Festival* (Hifi 1959)★★★★, with Gerry Mulligan *Mulligan With Witherspoon* (1959)★★★, *Jimmy Witherspoon* (Crown 1959)★★★, *Feelin' The Spirit* (Hifi 1959)★★★★, *Jimmy Witherspoon At The Renaissance* (Hifi 1959)★★★, *Singin' The Blues* reissued as *There's Good Rockin' Tonight* (World Pacific 1959)★★★★, *Jimmy Witherspoon Sings The Blues* (Crown 1960)★★★, *Spoon* (Reprise 1961)★★★, *Hey, Mrs. Jones* (Reprise 1962)★★★, *Roots* (Reprise 1962)★★★, *Baby, Baby, Baby* (Prestige 1963)★★★, *Evenin' Blues* (Prestige 1964)★★★, *Goin' To Chicago Blues* (Prestige 1964)★★★, *Blues Around The Clock* (1964)★★★, *Blue Spoon* (Prestige 1964)★★★, *Some Of My Best Friends Are The Blues* (Prestige 1964)★★★, *Take This Hammer* (Constellation 1964)★★★, *Blues For Spoon And Groove* (Surrey 1965)★★★, *Spoon In London* (Prestige 1965)★★★, *Blues Point Of View* (Verve 1967)★★★, with Jack McDuff *The Blues Is Now* (Verve 1967)★★★, *Blues For Easy Livers* (Prestige 1967)★★★, *A Spoonful Of Soul* (Verve 1968)★★★, *The Blues Singer* (Stateside 1969)★★★, *Back Door Blues* (Polydor 1969)★★★, *Hunh!* (1970)★★★, *Handbags & Gladrags* (Probe 1970)★★★, *Blues Singer* (Stateside 1970)★★★, with Eric Burdon *Guilty!* (United Artists 1971)★★★, *Ain't Nobody's Business* (Polydor 1974)★★★, *Love Is A Five Letter Word* (Capitol 1975)★★★, *Jimmy Witherspoon And Ben Webster (That's Jazz)* (Warners 1977)★★★, with New Savoy Sultans *Sings The Blues* (Muse 1980)★★★, with Buck Clayton *Live In Paris, Big Blues* (Vogue 1981)★★★, *Midnight Lady Called The Blues* (1986)★★★, *Call My Baby* (1991)★★★, *The Blues, The Whole Blues And Nothin' But The Blues* (Indigo 1992)★★★, with Robben Ford *Live At The Notodden Blues Festival* (1993)★★★★, *Spoon's Blues* (Stony Plain 1995)★★★, with Howard Scott *American Blues* (Avenue/Rhino 1995)★★★, with Robben Ford *Ain't Nothin' New But The Blues* 1977 recording (AIM 1996)★★★★, with Robben Ford *Live At The Mint* (On The Spot 1996)★★★, *Spoonful* (ARG Jazz 1997)★★★.

● COMPILATIONS: *The Best Of Jimmy Witherspoon* (Prestige 1969)★★★★, *Never Knew This Kind Of Hurt Before: The Bluesway Sessions* 1969-1971 recordings (Charly 1988)★★★, *Meets The Jazz Giants* 1959 recordings (1989)★★★, *Blowin' In From Kansas* (Ace 1991)★★★★, *Jimmy Witherspoon & Jay McShann* 40s recordings (1992)★★★, *Jazz Me Blues* (Prestige 1998)★★★.

WOLVERINES

The Wolverine Orchestra was an early white jazz group, modelled loosely upon the New Orleans Rhythm Kings.

Formed in the mid-west in 1923, the group played in clubs and restaurants in Chicago, at the Stockton Club in Hamilton, Ohio, in Cincinnati, and in Richmond, Indiana, where they recorded for the Gennett label. The recording sessions, which took place between March and November, produced 13 tracks. The personnel comprised Dick Voynow (piano), Al Gandee (trombone, appearing on two tracks only), trombonist Georg Brunis (trombone, appearing on two later tracks), Jimmy Hartwell (clarinet), George Johnson (tenor saxophone), and a rhythm section of Bob Gillette (banjo), Min Leibrook (tuba), Vic Moore (drums). The final member of the band, and the reason why the short-lived Wolverines warrant an important place in jazz history, was Bix Beiderbecke. The records were not only commercially successful, they were also influential upon jazz musicians, particularly whites, and include classic performances of 'Jazz Me Blues' and 'Riverboat Shuffle'. Subsequently, some personnel changes took place and the band recorded again with Jimmy McPartland replacing Beiderbecke. Between 1927 and 1929 a band named the Original Wolverines led by McPartland, but with only Voynow and Moore from the original group, recorded for Vocalion. Two sides from a 1926 recording date by a small band featuring Red Nichols and Miff Mole were issued on Brunswick under the name of the Wolverines but were more accurately labelled on Vocalion issues as being by the Tennessee Tooters, a band derived from the Original Memphis Five. By 1930, the Wolverines had passed into history but, thanks to Beiderbecke, their records remain a constant source of interest and pleasure.

● COMPILATIONS: *The Wolverines Orchestra (1924)* (1979)★★★.

WOOD, BOOTY

b. Mitchell Wood, 27 December 1919, Dayton, Ohio, USA, d. June 1987. Wood took up the trombone in his teens, beginning his professional career towards the end of the 30s. In the early 40s he was a member of the bands of Tiny Bradshaw and Lionel Hampton. While serving in the US Navy during World War II he played in the band that included Willie Smith and Clark Terry. After the war Wood returned briefly to Hampton, then worked in bands led by Arnett Cobb, Erskine Hawkins and Count Basie. After a spell outside music he returned to the scene in 1959, joining Duke Ellington with whom he played intermittently during the next dozen years. He also appeared with Earl 'Fatha' Hines and in the late 70s and early 80s was with Basie again. A forceful player with a rich open tone, Wood's spell with Ellington ensured that he also became adept at using the mute, performing with colourful effect on many of the band's standards.

● ALBUMS: with Duke Ellington *Blues In Orbit* (1959)★★★★, with Ellington *Nutcracker Suite* (1960)★★★★, *The Booty Wood All Stars* (1960)★★★.

WOODARD, RICKEY

b. 5 August 1950, Nashville, Tennessee, USA. After studying saxophones under Bill Green and majoring in music at Tennessee State University, Woodard worked extensively with a wide range of performers. He worked with jazz artists such as Jimmy Smith, Billy Higgins, Frank Capp and Al Grey and also backed singers from the jazz and pop worlds including Ella Fitzgerald, Ernestine Anderson, Barbara McNair and Prince. He also recorded with Capp and with the big band co-led by Jeff Clayton and Jeff Hamilton. Mostly playing tenor saxophone, he established a solid if localized reputation in the USA before venturing onto the international jazz festival circuit. By the early 90s Woodard was fast becoming a popular visitor to Europe and the UK. Playing alto and soprano saxophones in addition to tenor (he also plays clarinet, flute and guitar), Woodard is a vibrant and forceful soloist, his tenor saxophone styling hinting at an affection for the work of Wardell Grey, Dexter Gordon and, especially, Hank Mobley. For all such stylistic mentors, however, Woodard is very much his own man and this, allied to his playing skills and an engaging personality, assures him of a continuing welcome at jazz venues at home and abroad.

● ALBUMS: *The Frank Capp Trio Presents Rickey Woodard* (Concord 1991)★★★, *California Cookin'!* (Candid 1991)★★★★, *Night Mist* (1992)★★★, *The Tokyo Express* (Candid 1993)★★★, *Yazoo* (Concord 1994)★★, with Frank Capp *Quality Time* (Concord 1996)★★★, *The Silver Strut* (Concord Jazz 1996)★★★, with Peter Christlieb, Ernie Watts *The Tenor Trio* (JVC 1997)★★★.

WOODE, JIMMY

b. 23 September 1928, Philadelphia, Pennsylvania, USA. After extensive studies on both piano and bass, Woode settled on the latter instrument. Military service delayed the start of his professional career, but in 1946 he formed his own band which worked in the Boston area. Among his early musical associates were Nat Pierce, Joe 'Flip' Phillips and Zoot Sims, and he was also accompanist to Ella Fitzgerald and Sarah Vaughan. In the early 50s he was a member of the house band at George Wein's Storyville Club in Boston, where he played with numerous visiting jazz stars. By 1955 his reputation was such that he was invited to join Duke Ellington, a job he held for five years. After leaving Ellington he settled in Europe, becoming a member of the Clarke-Boland Big Band throughout most of its existence. The 60s and 70s were busy years for Woode; in addition to playing with various bands on a regular basis, he gigged with visiting Americans, including Don Byas and Johnny Griffin, ran his own music publishing company, and worked in radio, television and recording studios. This pattern continued throughout the 80s, with appearances in the Paris Reunion Band, led by Nathan Davis, and at Ellington reunions, including Ellington '88 at Oldham, England, where he was reunited with former Ellington rhythm-section partner Sam

Woodyard. A solid section player, Woode continues to draw the respect of his fellow musicians.

● ALBUMS: with Duke Ellington *Such Sweet Thunder* (1957)★★★★, *The Colorful Strings Of Jimmy Woode* (1957)★★★.

WOODING, SAM

b. 17 June 1895, Philadelphia, Pennsylvania, USA, d. 1 August 1985. Largely self-taught, Wooding began playing piano professionally around 1912, before playing in clubs in New York City. After military service in World War I he formed his own band for an engagement in Atlantic City, then played other east coast venues before taking a band to Europe in 1925. He was resident in Berlin with the *Chocolate Kiddies* show, which featured some of Duke Ellington's earliest music, then toured throughout central and eastern Europe, Russia, Scandinavia, and the UK. On the way back to the USA the band visited South America. After a few months in the USA, Wooding formed another band with which to tour Europe, this time returning in 1931. In the early 30s he led a band in the USA, but by the middle of the decade, and on the eve of the swing era, he abandoned performing in order to study music. In the late 30s and early 40s he taught, and also directed a gospel choir, then formed a small vocal group. In the 50s and 60s he toured as a single and in partnership with singer Rae Harrison. He continued a round of teaching and frequent appearances as a performer into old age. In 1976, as part of America's Bicentennial celebrations, he led a 10-piece band at concerts and for a recording session. Despite his popularity in other lands, Wooding never gained real success in his own country. By the time he tried to establish himself in the USA, musical times were changing and the style on which he had built his overseas reputation was out of fashion. Nevertheless, Wooding was enormously important in spreading awareness of jazz and his was a significant role in helping to make jazz a truly international music. The music he played to European audiences was much closer to true jazz than was, say, the earlier music offered to Europeans by James Reese Europe; and Wooding's sidemen on his early visits included leading jazzmen such as Tommy Ladnier, Willie Lewis and Gene Sedric.

● ALBUMS: *Bicentennial* (1976)★★★.

● COMPILATIONS: *Sam Wooding And His Chocolate Kiddies Orchestra (1925-29)* (1974)★★★.

WOODMAN, BRITT

b. 4 June 1920, Los Angeles, California, USA. Following in the footsteps of his trombone-playing father, Woodman took up the instrument in childhood to play in his father's band. In the late 30s he worked mostly on the west coast, usually in lesser-known bands, although he ended the decade with Les Hite. After military service in World War II he played in Boyd Raeburn's musically adventurous band and was then with Lionel Hampton. At the end of the 40s he formalized his musical education, studying at Westlake College in Los Angeles, and then joined the Duke Ellington orchestra as lead trombonist. In the mid-50s he found time for record dates with Charles Mingus, a friend from childhood, and Miles Davis. His tenure with Ellington ended in 1960 and thereafter he worked in studio and theatre bands in Los Angeles and New York City. He has continued with his film and television work, but has appeared on record leading his own small band and with small groups led by Bill Berry and Benny Carter. He has also played in the big bands of Berry, Toshiko Akiyoshi and the Capp-Pierce Juggernaut. Woodman's playing style reflects his career-long immersion in big band music, but is shot through with intriguing glimpses of his interest in bop.

● ALBUMS: with Duke Ellington *Seattle Concert* (1952)★★★, with Ellington *Such Sweet Thunder* (1957)★★★, with Charles Mingus *Mingus!* (1960)★★★, with Bill Berry *For Duke* (1977)★★★, *Britt Woodman In LA* (1977)★★★, with Joe Wilder and John LaPorta *Playing For Keeps* (GM 1996)★★★★.

WOODS, PHIL

b. 2 November 1931, Springfield, Massachusetts, USA. Woods began playing alto saxophone as a child, studied later at the Juilliard School of Music in New York and by his early 20s had already made a significant mark on jazz. Playing hard bop and acknowledging Charlie Parker but never slavishly so, Woods became a vital force in jazz in the late 50s. He led his own small groups, co-led a band with Gene Quill, played in bands led by artists such as Buddy Rich, Cecil Payne, Thelonious Monk, Quincy Jones and Benny Goodman, and worked as a studio musician and recorded extensively, including appearing on Benny Carter's 1961 *Further Definitions*. During the 60s he was also active as a teacher and towards the end of the decade became resident in France, where he formed the European Rhythm Machine with pianist George Gruntz, bassist Henri Texler and drummer Daniel Humair. Woods led this band until his return to the USA in the early 70s where, in 1973, he formed a new acoustic quartet (pianist Mike Melillo, bassist Steve Gilmore, drummer Bill Goodwin) which met with great critical and commercial acclaim. This group stayed in operation for the next few years and Woods's stature continued to grow. He also made a dynamic if somewhat anonymous impact on the pop music scene with his solo on Billy Joel's hit single, 'I Love You Just The Way You Are'. In the early 80s Woods was active in the USA, touring internationally, and continuing to record albums of exceptional quality. His quartet had expanded with the addition of Tom Harrell, while Melillo was replaced by Hal Galper. He also recorded with Dizzy Gillespie, Rob McConnell and Budd Johnson Although identified with the post-Parker school of alto saxophone playing, Woods has always had his own style. Early records, such as *Bird Calls*, reveal a highly sophisticated performer belying his age with the maturity of his improvisations. He plays with a rich, full sound, avoiding the harshness favoured by some of his contemporaries. By the late 80s Woods was firmly established as a major jazz musician and one of the most successful alto saxophonists the music had known. In the 90s his standards of performance remain outstanding. Although this decade saw him entering his 60s the depth of his imagination was unimpaired and his playing was still filled with the enthusiasm and vitality of his youth.

● ALBUMS: *Phil Woods New Jazz Quintet* 10-inch album (New Jazz 1954)★★★, *Phil Woods New Jazz Quartet* 10-inch album (Prestige 1954)★★★, *Woodlore* (Prestige 1956)★★★★, *Pairing Off* (Prestige 1956)★★★★, with Gene Quill *The Woods-Quill Sextet* (RCA Victor 1956), with Donald Byrd *The Young Bloods* (Prestige 1957)★★★★, with Quill, Sahib Shihab, Hal Stein *Four Altos* (Prestige 1957)★★★, with Quill *Phil & Quill With Prestige* (Prestige 1957)★★★★, *Bird Calls, Volume 1* (1957)★★★, *Warm Woods* (Epic 1958)★★★, with Quill, Jackie McLean, John Jenkins, Hal McKusick *Bird Feathers* (New Jazz 1958)★★★, with Quill *Phil Talks With Quill* (Epic 1959)★★★, *Rights Of Swing* (Candid 1960)★★★★, *Pot Pie* (New Jazz 1962)★★★, *Sugan* (Status 1965)★★★, *Greek Cooking* (Impulse! 1967)★★, *Alive And Well In Paris* (1968)★★, *The Birth Of The European Rhythm Machine* (1968)★★★, *Early Quintets* (Prestige 1969)★★, *Stolen Moments* (JMY 1969)★★★, *Round Trip* (Verve 1969)★★★, *1968 Jazz* (EMI 1969)★★, *Phil Woods And His European Rhythm Machine At The Montreux Jazz Festival* (1970)★★★, *Phil Woods And His European Rhythm Machine At The Frankfurt Jazz Festival* (Embryo 1970)★★★, *Chromatic Banana* (1970)★★★, *Musique Du Bois* (Muse 1974)★★★, *Images* (RCA 1975)★★★, *Live From The Showboat* (RCA 1976)★★★, *Songs For Sisyphus* (RCA 1979)★★, *I Remember ...* (Telefunken 1978)★★★, *Crazy Horse* (1979)★★★, *European Tour, Live* (Mobile Fidelity 1980)★★, *The Macerata Concert* (1980)★★, *Birds Of A Feather* (1981)★★★, *Three For All* (Enja 1982)★★★, *At The Vanguard* (Antilles 1982)★★★, *Piper At The Gates Of Dawn* (1984)★★★, *Integrity* (Red 1984)★★★, with Budd Johnson *The Ole Dude And The Fundance Kid* (Uptown 1984)★★★, with Rob McConnell *Boss Brass And Woods* (MCA 1985)★★★, *More Mistletoe Magic* (1985)★★, *Gratitude* (Denon 1986)★★★, with Dizzy Gillespie *Dizzy Gillespie Meets The Phil Woods Quintet* (Timeless 1987)★★★, *Bouquet* (Concord 1987)★★★, *Bop Stew* (Concord 1987)★★★, *Evolution* (Concord 1988)★★★, *Here's To My Lady* (Chesky 1988)★★★, *Phil's Mood* (Philology 1988)★★, *Flash* (Concord 1989)★★★, *Phil On Etna* (Philology 1989)★★, *Embraceable You* (Philology 1989)★★★, *Real Life* (Chesky 1990)★★★, *All Bird's Children* (Concord Jazz 1990)★★★, *Flowers For Hodges* (Concord 1992)★★★, *Elsa* (Philology 1992)★★★, *Full House* (Milestone 1992)★★★, *Live At The Corridonia Jazz Festival* (Philology 1992)★★, *An Affair To Remember* (Evidence 1995)★★★★, *Our Monk* (Philology 1995)★★★, *The Phil Woods Quintet Plays The Music Of Jim McNeely* (TCB 1996)★★★, with Benny Carter *Another Time, Another Place* (Evening Star 1996)★★★★, *For Astor & Elis* (Chesky 1996)★★★, *Mile High Jazz: Live In Denver* (Concord Jazz 1997)★★★, with Gordon Beck *Live At The Wigmore Hall - The Complete Concert* (JMS 1997)★★★★, with Clark Terry *Lucerne 1978* (TCOB 1997)★★★, with the Festival Orchestra *Celebration!* (Concord Jazz 1997)★★★★, with Johnny Griffin *The Rev And I* (Blue Note 1998)★★.

● COMPILATIONS: *Into The Woods: The Best Of Phil Woods* (Concord Jazz 1996)★★★★.

● CD-ROMS: *Jazz Tutor Featuring Phil Woods* (Masterclass Productions).

● VIDEOS: *The Phil Woods Quartet* (Rhapsody 1995).

Woodyard, Sam

b. 7 January 1925, Elizabeth, New Jersey, USA, d. 20 September 1988, Paris, France. A self-taught drummer, Woodyard played in several small bands in his home state in the 40s and early 50s. In 1952 he joined Roy Eldridge and the following year played with Milt Buckner. In 1955 he joined Duke Ellington, a job he retained with occasional lay-offs through ill-health and personal waywardness, until the late 60s. He subsequently worked with Ella Fitzgerald and as an extra percussionist with Ellington and Buddy Rich. Occasional gigs with Bill Berry helped his sagging career, but by 1975 he had decided to relocate to Europe. Based in Paris, he played and recorded with local musicians such as Guy Lafitte, other ex-patriates including Buckner, and visitors like Teddy Wilson, Buddy Tate and Slam Stewart. By the 80s Woodyard's earlier years of hard drinking and wild living had begun to take their toll. The theft of his drum kit added to his decline, but in the mid-summer of 1988 he was a welcome guest at the Ellington '88 convention held at Oldham, England. Although his health was clearly at a very low ebb, he was rejuvenated by the renewal of contact with other ex-Ellingtonians, Berry, Buster Cooper and Jimmy Woode, and by the gift from the assembled delegates of a new drum kit. His playing at the convention was inevitably more tentative than of old, but he enjoyed himself and performed such crowd-pleasing favourites as 'Limbo Jazz' with his eccentric vocal. A short while later, on 20 September 1988, he died in Paris. A vigorous and skilful drummer, Woodyard's erratic temperament sometimes showed itself in his playing and he occasionally slipped into musical extravagances. At his best, however, whether in subtle accompaniments to Ellington's piano solos, or driving the big band along in thunderous performances such as the classic 1956 Newport concert, behind Paul Gonsalves's legendary solo on 'Diminuedo And Crescendo In Blue', or the 1971 UK tour recording of 'La Plus Belle Africaine', he was unmatched.

● ALBUMS: *Ellington At Newport* (1956)★★★★, *Duke Ellington Plays Mary Poppins* (1964)★★★, with Ellington *Soul Call* (1966)★★★, *Duke Ellington - The Pianist* (1966)★★★, with Ellington *Togo Brava Suite* (1971)★★★, *Sam Woodyard In Paris* (1975)★★★.

Working Week

The band was formed in 1983 around the nucleus of Simon Booth (guitar) and Larry Stabbins (saxophone) as an off-shoot of the soft jazz-influenced group Weekend. Adopting a harder jazz/Latin direction, Working Week commanded much music press attention and, in particular, 'style' magazines (*Blitz* and *The Face*), who latched on to the band's connection with the London jazz dance teams. Their radical image was strengthened by Booth and Stabbins left-wing allegiances, borne out on their 1984 debut single on Paladin/Virgin Records, 'Venceremos (We Will Win)'. The song, dedicated to the Chilean protest singer Victor Jara, included guest vocals from Tracey Thorn, Robert Wyatt and Claudia Figueroa. The follow-up, 'Storm Of Light' featured Julie Tippetts on lead vocals. In time, the group recruited a permanent lead vocalist in Juliet Roberts. After her departure in 1988, Working Week reverted back to the system of guest vocalists until the addition of a new vocalist in Yvonne Waite for 1991's *Black And Gold*. Although Working Week has centred around Booth and Stabbins for recordings and live appearances they have employed a vast array of respected UK jazz musicians who, on various occasions, have included Harry Beckett (trumpet), Keith Tippett (piano), Kim Burton (piano), Cleveland Watkiss (vocals), Mike Carr (organ), Richard Edwards and Paul Spong (brass), Dave Bitelli (reeds), Annie Whitehead (trombone) and Nic France (drums). Since then, the group has continued to work, turning out quality recordings, although that initial wave of interest and impetus in the mid-80s has somewhat subsided.

●ALBUMS: *Working Nights* (Virgin 1985)★★★, *Companeros* (Virgin 1986)★★★, *Knocking On Your Door* (Virgin 1987)★★★, *Fire In The Mountain* (Ten 1989)★★★, *Black And Gold* (Ten 1991)★★★.

●COMPILATIONS: *Payday* (Venture 1988)★★★.

WORKMAN, REGGIE

b. 26 June 1937, Philadelphia, Pennsylvania, USA. One of the premier bassists in post-war jazz, Workman's first involvement in music was 'singing doo-wop at a YMCA'. Piano lessons failed to interest him, but a cousin introduced him to the bass and he was hooked - though his high school's lack of an instrument meant he had to play bass lines on tuba and euphonium for a while. By the time he left school, he was working as a professional bassist playing R&B and jazz standards. At the end of the 50s he moved to New York and played with Gigi Gryce, Eric Dolphy and his mentor, John Coltrane, with whom he'd previously been in contact. Workman toured and recorded with Coltrane in 1961, then joined the leading hard bop group of the time, Art Blakey's Jazz Messengers, remaining for two years and also recording with both the group's tenor saxophonist Wayne Shorter, on his own Blue Note dates such as *Night Dreamer*, *Juju* and *Adam's Apple*, and the group's trumpeter Freddie Hubbard. Workman next played with the radical New York Art Quartet and later worked with a variety of leaders, including Yusef Lateef and Thelonious Monk. Increasingly involved in education, in the 70s he led the Collective Black Arts organization in New York - a community self-help project that for a while published its own newspaper, *Expansions*. He also worked with Max Roach, Marion Brown, Archie Shepp and Charles Tolliver. In the 80s Workman recorded with David Murray, Steve Lacy and Mal Waldron, toured with Alice Coltrane and Rashied Ali in the Coltrane Legacy band, was a founder member of both the all-string Black Swan Quartet and Trio Transition and became a regular member of pianist Marilyn Crispell's groups, playing on her *Gaia*, *Circles* and *Live In Zurich*. He has also recorded a solo album, *The Works Of Workman*, and since the mid-80s led his own ensemble, whose members over the years have included Crispell, singer Jeanne Lee, drummers Andrew Cyrille or Gerry Hemingway and saxophonists Joseph Jarman, Oliver Lake or, most recently, Don Byron: their two albums are *Images* and *Synthesis*. One of the most versatile and adventurous of bass players, Workman is married to the well-known choreographer and poet Maya Milenovic.

● ALBUMS: *Conversation* (1977)★★★, *The Works Of Workman* (Denon 1979)★★★, *Synthesis* (Leo 1986)★★★★, *Black Swan Quartet* (1986)★★★, *Trio Transition* (1988)★★★, *Trio Transition With Oliver Lake* (1989)★★★, *Images* (Music And Arts 1990)★★★, *Altered Spaces* (Leo 1993)★★★★, *Cerebral Caverns* (Postcards 1995)★★★★, with Oliver Lake, Andrew Cyruille *Live In Willisau* (Dizim 1998)★★★.

WORLD SAXOPHONE QUARTET

In 1974, Anthony Braxton recorded a composition for a saxophone quartet on his *New York Fall 1974*. The other three players involved - Julius Hemphill, Oliver Lake and Hamiet Bluiett - must have liked the format as in 1977 they and David Murray formed the World Saxophone Quartet. The proud name was no idle boast: these really were four pre-eminent saxophone voices. All the players are multi-instrumentalists, but in general Hemphill and Lake played alto, Murray tenor and Bluiett baritone saxophone. Wearing tuxedos as a reference to the era of big band sophistication, they became sure-fire festival favourites, starting regular European tours in 1978. They all contributed compositions, though perhaps Hemphill and Bluiett have shown most interest in the quartet's possibilities, producing thoughtful arrangements that examine ballads, bop and blues with understanding and affection. Originally located on the jazz *avant garde*, their later albums have looked back at aspects of the black music tradition (*Plays Duke Ellington*, *Rhythm And Blues*), while the new *Metamorphosis* introduced African drums into the musical mix. In 1991, Hemphill left the group and was replaced by altoist Arthur Blythe, who marked his debut on *Metamorphosis*. Senegalese drummers Chief Bey, Mor Thiam and Mar Gueye contributed to *Four Now*, a much more cohesive fusion set that also featured new member John Purcell on saxello.

● ALBUMS: *Point Of No Return* (Moers 1977)★★★★, *Steppin' With* (Black Saint 1979)★★, *WSQ* (Black Saint 1981)★★★, *Revue* (Black Saint 1982)★★★★, *Live In Zurich* (Black Saint 1984)★★★, *Live At The Brooklyn Academy Of Music* (Black Saint 1986)★★, *Plays Duke Ellington* (Elektra/Nonesuch 1986)★★★★, *Dances And Ballads* (Elektra/Nonesuch 1987)★★★★, *Rhythm And Blues* (Elektra/Nonesuch 1989)★★★★, *Metamorphosis* (Elektra/Nonesuch 1991)★★★, *Breath Of Life* (Elektra/Nonesuch 1994)★★★, *Moving Right Along* (Black Saint 1994)★★★★, with African Drums *Four Now* (Justin Time 1996)★★★★, with Donald Blackman, Ronnie Burrage, Calvin Jones *Takin' It 2 The Next Level* (Justin Time 1997)★★★, with Jack DeJohnette *Selim Sivad: A Tribute To Miles Davis* (Justin Time 1998)★★★.

WORLD'S GREATEST JAZZ BAND

The World's Greatest Jazz Band was formed from musicians who played at Dick Gibson's Colorado Jazz Parties in the mid-to-late 60s. Led by Yank Lawson and Bob Haggart and encouraged and supported by Gibson, these players formed a semi-regular group known as the Ten Greats Of Jazz (the name changing as the numbers varied). In 1968 the band became a full-time organization and settled on the name by which they were known for the next decade. In its earliest form, the World's Greatest Jazz Band included Lawson, Billy Butterfield, Lou McGarity, Carl Fontana, Bob Wilber, Bud Freeman, Ralph Sutton, Clancy Hayes, Haggart and Morey Feld. Successful concerts and records kept the band busy and subsequent personnel changes maintained the high standards set by the originals. Later sidemen included Gus Johnson, Eddie Hubble, Bobby Hackett, George Masso, Al Klink, Peanuts Hucko, Bobby Rosengarden, Eddie Miller, Nick Fatool and John Bunch. Playing sophisticated dixieland and mainstream jazz, with well-rehearsed tight arrangements interspersed with vigorous solos, the band found and filled a niche in public demand for unpretentious music played by a superior selection of musicians. In 1978, with Lawson and Haggart now in their late 60s, the band broke up. However, the call remained too strong to ignore completely and thereafter the two veterans occasionally reformed a band to make special appearances and records.

● ALBUMS: *The World's Greatest Jazz Band* (World Jazz 1968)★★★, *Jazz At The Troc* (World Jazz 1969)★★, *At The Roosevelt Grill* (World Jazz 1970)★★, *What's New?* (World Jazz 1970)★★★, *Century Plaza* (World Jazz 1972)★★★, *Hark The Herald Angels Swing* (World Jazz 1972)★★★, *In Concert At Massey Hall* (World Jazz 1972)★★, *In Concert At Carnegie Hall* (World Jazz 1973)★★★, *On Tour* (World Jazz 1975)★★, *Plays Cole Porter* (World Jazz 1975)★★★, *Plays Rodgers And Hart* (World Jazz 1975)★★★, *Plays Duke Ellington* (World Jazz 1976)★★★, *Plays George Gershwin* (World Jazz 1977)★★★, *The World's Greatest Jazz Band Of Yank Lawson And Bob Haggart* (1986)★★★.

WRIGHT, ELLY

b. Austria. Singing since childhood, Wright has established a considerable following in and around Vienna. She has also toured throughout Austria, sometimes working with local musicians such as pianist-composer-arranger Erwin Schmidt and guitarist Christian Havel. She has also worked with Rolf Ericson and Ed Thigpen, both of whom appeared on *A World Of My Own*. Wright's singing style is sleekly professional and she builds her repertoire from an intriguing blend of standards, jazz pieces by Duke Ellington, Dave Brubeck and others, compositions by her regular associates and a sprinkling of songs for which she herself has written either the music, the lyrics, or both.

● ALBUMS: *A World Of My Own* (RST 1994)★★★.

WRIGHT, FRANK

b. 9 July 1935, Grenada, Mississippi, USA, d. 17 June 1990, Wuppertal, Germany. Wright grew up in Memphis and, later, in Cleveland alongside Albert Ayler, whose influence persuaded him to switch to tenor saxophone from double bass (on which instrument he had backed visiting blues stars such as B.B. King and Bobby Bland). He developed a ferocious, vocalized saxophone style that was rooted in Ayler's innovations and, on moving to New York in 1965, associated with John Coltrane, Sunny Murray and Cecil Taylor, as well as recording two albums for the *avant garde* ESP label. In 1969 he moved to Europe with Noah Howard, settled in Paris with a band that included pianist Bobby Few, drummer Muhammad Ali and (later) Alan Silva and for many years helped to run the Center Of The World record label. Nicknamed 'the Reverend', Wright stayed in Europe for most of the 70s and 80s: and continued to play the intense, squealing, all-out free music for which he was best-known.

In the early 80s he renewed his acquaintance with Cecil Taylor, touring in the pianist's Orchestra Of Two Continents and recording on his 1984 *Winged Serpent (Sliding Quadrants)*. In 1988 when he appeared at London's ICA with Jeanne Lee and Lawrence 'Butch' Morris, Wright's playing was as exciting as ever. He died of a heart attack in 1990.

● ALBUMS: *Frank Wright Trio* (ESP 1965)★★★★, *Your Prayer* (1967)★★★★, *One For John* (1970)★★★, *Center Of The World* (1972)★★★, *Last Polka In Nancy* (1973)★★, with Muhammad Ali *Adieu Little Man* (1974)★★★, with Bobby Few and Alan Silva *Solos Et Duets, Volumes 1 & 2* (1975)★★★, with Cecil Taylor *Winged Serpent (Sliding Quadrants)* (1984)★★★★.

WRIGHT, LAMMAR

b. 20 June 1907, Texarkana, Texas, USA, d. 13 April 1973. Wright was raised in Kansas City where he took up the trumpet. In his mid-teens he played with Bennie Moten's band, staying with the group until 1927 when he joined the Missourians. With this band he came to New York, remaining with the band through its metamorphosis into the Cab Calloway orchestra. In the 40s he played with Don Redman, Claude Hopkins, Calloway again, Cootie Williams, Lucky Millinder and others. Wright was also in demand for session and studio work and as a teacher.

During the 50s these activities occupied much of his time although he still played jazz gigs with Count Basie, Sauter-Finegan and others, and worked briefly at the end of the decade with a band organized by George Shearing. Wright's technical mastery and the ease and fluency of his playing made him a valued and respected member of the jazz community. His skills were passed on to many other trumpeters through his teaching and in particular to his sons. Lammar Wright Jnr. (1927-1983) played trumpet with Lionel Hampton, Dizzy Gillespie and Charlie Barnet. Elmon Wright (1929-1984) also played trumpet with Gillespie, Roy Eldridge, Earl Bostic, Buddy Rich and Milt Jackson.

● ALBUMS: with George Shearing *Satin Brass* (Capitol 1959)★★★★.

● COMPILATIONS: *The Chronological Bennie Moten 1923-1927* (Classics 1923-27)★★★, *The Chronological Cab Calloway 1930-1931* (Classics 1930-31)★★★★.

WRIGHT, LEO

b. Leo Nash Wright, 14 December 1933, Wichita Falls, Texas, USA. After studying alto saxophone with his father and with jazzman John Hardee, Wright began a professional career which took him swiftly into stellar company. Among early engagements were spells with bands led by Charles Mingus and Dizzy Gillespie. With the latter he appeared at several major international festivals and made records including *A Musical Safari*. During the early 60s he worked with many musicians, sometimes as leader, and in the middle of the decade performed in Europe with George Gruntz and Lee Konitz's Alto Summit, recording with both. From the end of the 60s he lived in Europe where he played with various bands but then, at the end of the 70s, he retired. In the mid-80s he returned to music to perform and sometimes record with Nat Adderley, Kenny Drew, and others, and also lead his own groups. Although he sometimes plays clarinet and flute it is on alto that he has made his greatest mark, finding a tasteful blend between lush romaticism and earthy blues-influenced drive.

● ALBUMS: *Blues Shout* (Atlantic 1960)★★★, *Suddenly The Blues* (Atlantic 1962)★★★, *Modern Jazz Studies No. 4* (Amiga 1965)★★★, *It's All-Wright* (MPS 1972)★★★.

WRUBEL, ALLIE

b. 15 January 1905, Middletown, Connecticut, USA, d. 13 December 1973, Twentynine Palms, California, USA. A popular songwriter from the 30s through to the 50s, who frequently wrote both music and lyrics. After studying medicine at Columbia University, Wrubel played the saxophone with several dance bands, including a one-year stint with Paul Whiteman in the 20s, and toured England with his own band in 1924. He spent some time working as a theatre manager before having his first song published in 1931. 'Now You're In My Arms' (written with Morton Downey), was followed by 'As You Desire Me', 'I'll Be Faithful' (Jan Garber) and 'Farewell To Arms' (Paul Whiteman). In 1934, like many of his contemporaries, Wrubel began to write songs for films, often with lyricist Mort Dixon. Their 'Try To See It My Way' was interpolated into the Dubin-Warren score for *Dames*. During the 30s Wrubel also contributed to *Happiness Ahead* ('Pop! Goes Your Heart'), *Flirtation Walk* ('Mr And Mrs Is The Name'), *I Live For Love* ('Mine Alone'), *In Caliente* ('The Lady In Red'), *Sweet Music* ('Fare Thee Well, Annabelle' and 'I See Two Lovers'), *The Toast Of New York* ('The First Time I Saw You'), *Life Of The Party* ('Let's Have Another Cigarette'), and *Radio City Revels* ('Goodnight Angel' and 'There's A New Moon Over The Old Mill'). The films featured some of the biggest stars of the day, such as Dick Powell, Ruby Keeler, and Rudy Vallee. Around that time Wrubel also collaborated with Herb Magidson on 'Gone With The Wind' (an all-time standard), 'The Masquerade Is Over' (popularized by Dick Robertson, Sarah Vaughan and Patti Page), and 'Music Maestro Please', one of the most popular songs of the 30s in versions by Tommy Dorsey and Lew Stone. During the 40s and 50s Wrubel continued to write songs for movies such as *Sing Your Way Home*, in which Anne Jeffreys sang Wrubel and Madgison's Oscar-nominated 'I'll Buy That Dream' ('A honeymoon in Cairo, in a brand-new autogiro/Then, home by rocket in a wink'), *Song Of The South* (the Oscar-winning 'Zip-A-Dee-Doo-Dah', written with Ray Gilbert), *Duel In The Sun* ('Gotta Get Me Somebody To Love'), *The Fabulous Dorseys* ('To Me'), *I Walk Alone* ('Don't Call It Love'), and two full-length Walt Disney cartoons, *Make Mine Music* , in which the Andrews Sisters sang his 'Johnny Fedora And Alice Blue Bonnet', and *Melody Time*, the Andrews Sisters again, with Wrubel's story about a tiny tugboat, 'Little Toot'.

During the 50s Wrubel's output declined, although he did contribute several numbers to *Never Steal Anything Small* (1959), which featured an ageing James Cagney duetting with Cara Williams on 'I'm Sorry, I Want A Ferrari'. He also wrote 'What Does A Woman Do?' for the thriller *Midnight Lace* (1960). During a career spanning nearly 30 years, his other songs included 'Gypsy Fiddler', 'The You And Me That Used To Be', 'I Can't Love You Anymore', 'I'm Home Again', 'I'm Stepping Out With A Memory Tonight' (a hit for Glenn Miller and Kate Smith), 'Where Do I Go From You?'), 'There Goes That Song Again' (revived by Gary Miller in the UK in 1961), 'The Lady From Twentynine Palms', '1400 Dream Street', 'Please, My Love' and 'Corabelle'. Among his collaborators were Walter Bullock, Nat Shilkret, Ned Washington, Abner Silver, and Charles Newman. Wrubel was a Charter member of the Composers Hall of Fame. He died from a heart attack in 1973 at the location mentioned in one of his popular songs - Twentynine Palms, in the state of California.

WYANDS, RICHARD

b. 2 July 1928, Oakland, California, USA. In mid-teenage, he was playing piano in San Francisco jazz clubs, accompanying local musicians and visitors. In the late 50s he moved to New York where he worked with many jazz artists in both bop and mainstream. By the mid-60s he had settled into a long spell with Kenny Burrell with whom he toured extensively. In 1974 he left Burrell to join JPJ Trio, replacing co-founder Dill Jones. In the late 70s and through the 80s, he continued to play a discreet supporting role with a wide range of jazzmen. Despite such diffidence, however, Wyands is an accomplished and inventive soloist with a light touch and a subtly engaging sense of swing as can be heard on *There Here And Now*, a rare instance of Wyands as leader.

● ALBUMS: *Roamin' With Jerome Richardson* (1959)★★, with Elvin Jones *Don't Go To Strangers* (1960)★★★, with Kenny Burrell *The Tender Gender* (1966)★★★, *Then Here And Now*

(Storyville 1978)★★★★, with Cecil Payne *Casbah* (1985)★★★, *The Arrival* (DIW 1992)★★★.

WYLIE, AUSTIN

b. USA. Although the Austin Wylie Orchestra essentially played at only one location, the Golden Pheasant in Cleveland, Ohio, USA, the orchestra was notable for the number of key personnel to pass through its ranks. Claude Thornhill, Spud Murphy, Tony Pastor, Artie Shaw, Clarence Hutchenrider, Joe Bishop, Billy Butterfield, Bill Stegmeyer, Vaughn Monroe and many others were among Wylie's personnel at one stage or another. Their sound, fashioned so as to make the best possible appeal to the hotel's supper dance clientele, was emblazoned with the vocals of Helen O'Connell and Vaughn Monroe. Their best moments were captured on labels including Beltoba and Vocalion Records. They were gainfully employed at the Golden Pheasant for over 10 years from the early 20s onwards, before Wylie gave up bandleading to take over management duties for Artie Shaw's group in the 40s. He briefly returned to the baton but these ventures proved unsuccessful. He eventually entered Chicago's business community instead.

Yamashita, Yosuke

b. 26 February 1942, Tokyo, Japan. Although he had played professionally at the age of 17, pianist Yamashita went on to study at the Kunitachi College of Music (1962-67). He established himself playing in the quartets of Masahiko Togashi and Sadao Watanabe. The earliest influence of Bill Evans soon gave way to the influence of Cecil Taylor. When Yamashita formed his own trio with Akira Sakata (alto saxophone) and Takeo Moriyama (drums) and toured Europe (1974) the music was so wild the group was known as the Kamikaze Trio. For inspiration Yamashita looked back to 'the beginning of jazz - Europe had the system but Africa had all the feeling. All the material I use belongs to the system, but as long as I can stand on the outside and approach things from the outside, I will never be suffocated'. He kept a trio going throughout the 70s and continued to play as a sideman with the bands of Kazumi Takeda (tenor saxophone) and Seuchi Nakamura (tenor saxophone). From 1974 he made regular trips to Europe with the trio in Germany as well as playing with Manfred Schoof (1975), then as a soloist and in 1977 in a duo with bassist Adellard Roidinger. He disbanded the trio in 1983 when he felt that he had achieved as much as he could in that format. Yamashita formed a big band with an eclectic style and performed in many varied situations including solo performances of his own versions of classical pieces, playing with Kodo, a Japanese drum choir, and having pieces performed by the Ozaka Philharmonic Orchestra. In the early 90s he was again playing with a trio and touring Europe.

● ALBUMS: *Clay* (Enja 1974)★★★, *Distant Thunder* (1975)★★★, *Banslikana* (Enja 1976)★★★, *Ghosts By Albert Ayler* (West Wind 1977)★★★★, *A Tribute To Mal Waldron* (Enja 1980)★★★, *In Europe* (1983)★★, *It Don't Mean A Thing* (DIW 1984)★★★, *Breath With Hozan Tagoshi* (1984)★★★, *Sentimental* (1985)★★★, *Asian Games* (Verve 1988)★★★★, *Kurdish Dance* (Verve 1993)★★★★, *Dazzling Days* (Verve 1994)★★★★, *Ways Of Time* (Verve 1995)★★★★, *Spider* (Verve 1996)★★★, *Canves In Quiet* (Verve 1995)★★★★, *Canves In Vigor* (Verve 1997)★★★★, *Wind Of The Age* (Verve 1998)★★★.

Yancey, Jimmy

b. 20 February 1898, Chicago, Illinois, USA, d. 17 September 1951. While still a small child Yancey appeared in vaudeville as a tap dancer and singer. After touring the USA and Europe he abandoned this career and, just turned 20, settled in Chicago where he taught himself to play piano. He began to appear at rent parties and informal club sessions, gradually building a reputation. Nevertheless, in 1925, he decided that music was an uncertain way to earn a living and took a job as groundsman with the city's White Sox baseball team. He continued to play piano and was one of the prime movers in establishing the brief popularity of boogie-woogie. He made many records and played clubs and concerts, often accompanying his wife, singer Estella 'Mama' Yancey, but retained his job as groundsman until shortly before his death in 1951. Although Yancey's playing style was elementary, he played with verve and dash, and if he fell behind such contemporaries as Albert Ammons and Pete Johnson in technique, he made up most of the deficiencies through sheer enthusiasm.

● COMPILATIONS: *Piano Solos* (1939)★★★, *The Immortal Jimmy Yancey* 1940-1943 recordings (Oldie Blues 1977)★★★★, *Jimmy Yancey Vol 1 1939-40* (Oldie Blues 1988)★★★★, *In The Beginning* (Jazzology 1990)★★★, *Jimmy Yancey Vol 2 1943-50* (Document 1992)★★★★.

Yellowjackets

Over two decades, the Yellowjackets have achieved a formidable reputation for their live performances and critical and commercial success with their recordings of electric pop jazz. The members of the band are accomplished musicians in their own right and perhaps this accounts for the Yellowjackets' two Grammys and six nominations. The band originally included Robben Ford (b. Robben Lee Ford, 16 December 1951, Woodlake, California, USA; guitar), Russell Ferrante (keyboards), Michael Franks (b. 1944, La Jolla, California, USA; vocals) and Ricky Lawson (drums). Their recording career began in 1980 with *The Inside Story*, when Ford heard Jimmy Haslip (bass) playing with veterans Airto Moreira and Flora Purim and decided to use them on his solo project. By the time of 1982's *Mirage á Trois*, Ford's presence was declining. Saxophonist, Marc Russo featured prominently on *Samurai Samba* (1983) and *Shades* in 1986 rewarded the band's steady touring with a Grammy and six-figure sales. Drummer William Kennedy was the next addition to the line-up and this prompted the band to explore some new territory. *Politics* (1988) was another Grammy winner and the band took another radical change of direction. Their next project, *The Spin* was recorded in Oslo, Norway with well-known engineer, Jan Erik Konshaug, and was a more acoustic, resolutely jazz album. *Greenhouse* featured new saxophonist Bob Mintzer (b. 27 January 1953, New Rochelle, Westchester, New York, USA; saxophone), replacing Russo who had departed to work with Kenny Loggins. *Live Wires*, the band's 1992 release successfully demonstrated the multifaceted approach the Yellowjackets like to adopt. Indeed, the simplicity of the band's sound belies the diversity of their influences: 'We spend hours experimenting, studying and listening to music from all over the world. You can't be afraid to take chances . . . '. The line-up in 1997 comprised Mintzer, William Kennedy, Haslip and Ferrante.

● ALBUMS: *Yellowjackets* (Warners 1981)★★★, *Mirage à Trois*

(Warners 1982)★★★, *Samurai Samba* (Warners 1983)★★★, *Shades* (MCA 1986)★★★★, *Four Corners* (MCA 1987)★★★, *Politics* (MCA 1988)★★★★, *The Spin* (MCA 1990)★★★, *Greenhouse* (GRP 1991)★★★, *Live Wires* (GRP 1992)★★★, *Like A River* (GRP 1992)★★, *Run For Your Life* (GRP 1994)★★★, *Dreamland* (Warners 1995)★★★, *Blue Hats* (Warners 1997)★★★, *Club Nocturne* (Warners 1998)★★.
● COMPILATIONS: *Collection* (GRP 1994)★★★★.

YORKE, PETER

b. 4 December 1902, London, England, d. 2 February 1966, England. A highly respected composer, conductor and arranger, Yorke was well known in Britain through his hundreds of broadcasts, and his themes have been widely used on television and radio. In the 30s he was one of the finest dance band orchestrators in England, working with Percival Mackey, Jack Hylton, Louis Levy and many others. After World War II he established himself as a light music composer and conductor through BBC radio shows such as *Sweet Serenade*, *Our Kind Of Music* and *The Peter Yorke Melody Hours*. From the late 40s onwards he made numerous 78s for EMI's Columbia, including some legendary titles with saxophonist Freddy Gardner (1911-50), which are regarded as models of their genre: 'I'm In The Mood For Love', 'I Only Have Eyes For You', 'Roses Of Picardy', 'These Foolish Things', 'Body And Soul' and 'Valse Vanite'. Yorke also recorded an early composition, 'Sapphires And Sables', which he used as his theme music, and his other notable pieces included 'Melody Of The Stars', 'Dawn Fantasy', 'Quiet Countryside', 'Caravan Romance', 'Carminetta', 'Faded Lilac', 'Fireflies', 'Flyaway Fidles', 'Golden Melody', 'Oriental Bazaar', 'In My Garden' - suite, 'Midnight In Mexico', 'Parade Of The Matadors', 'Royal Mile', 'Highdays And Holidays', 'Brandy Snaps', 'Miss In Mink', 'Lazy Piano', and 'Ladies Night'. From 1957-67 'Silks And Satins' was used to close the popular British television soap *Emergency Ward 10*. Most of Yorke's original works were written for various London mood music libraries especially Chappells, Francis Day & Hunter, Bosworth, Harmonic, Conroy, Paxton, Southern and Josef Weinberger. He also conducted several albums of popular songs, mainly for the American market.
● ALBUMS: *Music For Sweethearts - Romantic Compositions Of Victor Herbert* (Brunswick 1956)★★★, *Sapphires And Sables - Music In The Peter Yorke Manner* (Delyse-Envoy 1959)★★★, *Mood For Love* (EMI-World Records 1979)★★★★.

YOUNG MAN WITH A HORN

Directed by Michael Curtiz, this film made in 1950 follows broadly upon Dorothy Baker's novel which was in its turn very loosely based on the life of Bix Beiderbecke. Any chance of reality went out the window with the casting of Kirk Douglas and the choice of Harry James to dub the character's trumpet playing. Hoagy Carmichael appears as a pianist but despite the fact that he actually did play piano with Bix he was ghosted by Buddy Cole. Amongst other musicians involved, mostly off-screen, are Babe Russin, Nick Fatool, Jack Jenney, Willie Smith, Stan Wrightsman and Jimmy Zito. Doris Day plays Douglas's long-suffering girlfriend and has a chance to sing between the melodramatics. (Alternative title: *Young Man Of Music*).

YOUNG, DAVE

b. Winnipeg, Manitoba, Canada. This highly gifted bass player studied in Toronto and quickly made a great impression on fellow musicians and audiences alike. In 1962 he attended Berklee College Of Music, subsequently returning to Toronto. For several years he performed with guitarist Lenny Breau, a Toronto nightclub set in the early 80s being recorded and released under Breau's name on the Guitarchives label almost 15 years later as *Live At Bourbon Street, 1983*. In the 90s, Young has frequently displayed a penchant for working in duos and in particular has recorded a series of duets with a roster of distinguished pianists. Among his partners on record are Kenny Barron and Cyrus Chestnut, fellow countrymen Oliver Jones and Oscar Peterson, with whom he has toured Japan, Barry Harris and Tommy Flanagan. A very melodic musician, Young produces a beautiful tone and his arco playing is especially adept and swinging.
● ALBUMS: *Fables And Dreams* (Justin Time 1993)★★★, *Two By Two: Piano-Bass Duets, Volume One* (Justin Time 1995)★★★, *Two By Two: Piano-Bass Duets, Volume Two* (Justin Time 1996)★★, *Side By Side: Piano-Bass Duets, Volume Three* (Justin Time 1997)★★★, *Inner Urge* (Justin Time 1998)★★★★.

YOUNG, ELDEE

b. 7 January 1936, Chicago, Illinois, USA. Young studied bass at high school and at advanced level before starting to play professionally. His early engagements were frequently with blues players and singers including Big Joe Turner and Joe Williams. In the mid-50s he became a member of the Ramsey Lewis Trio, with drummer Redd Holt, making many recordings including 1965's Grammy Award-winning Argo Records session, *The In Crowd*. He also recorded with James Moody on 1959's *Hey! It's James Moody*. Subsequently he played with various small groups, sometimes leading his own bands. In the early 60s he was in Holt's Unlimited band, recording *Look Out! Look Out!* (Argo/Cadet 1961). Later in the decade he and Holt formed Young-Holt Unlimited. This was a soul band and, in addition to bass, Young sometimes played electric bass guitar. In 1983 Young, Holt and Lewis made a reunion album and in the early 90s the trio toured the USA and Israel. At times a vigorously swinging player, Young plays with subtle flair in appropriate settings, such as with the Lewis group, where he would occasionally switch to cello with pleasing results.

YOUNG, IRMA

b. *c.*1913, Thebedux, Louisiana, USA. Born into a highly musical family, she was encouraged to play the alto saxophone and joined the family band which was led by her father, W.H. Young, and which included her younger brother, Lee Young, on drums, and her older brother, Lester Young, on tenor saxophone. Her mother also played in the outfit, as did several cousins, and Ben Webster is reputed to have played piano with the band for a time. According to Paul Quinchette, himself a devoted admirer of Lester Young, Irma Young was an exceptionally fine musician and would happily jam with her brother and other jazzmen. In addition to the alto, she also played baritone and soprano saxophones. However, her preference was for none of these instruments and in the 30s she gave them all up to concentrate on dancing. Thereafter, she worked as a dancer and occasional singer until her retirement in the mid-50s. She was still living in California in the early 80s. Her daughter, Martha Young, is a professional pianist.

YOUNG, LA MONTE

b. 1935, USA. A composer since the mid-50s, although primarily considered within the contemporary classical sphere, Young is well known within popular music for his work with John Cale, who appeared in his Theatre Of Eternal Music band before joining Velvet Underground. He was also acknowledged by Lou Reed on the sleevenotes to *Metal Machine Music* as a major influence. Theatre Of Eternal Music also included other collaborators such as his wife Marian Zazeela, Terry Riley, jazz saxophonist Lee Konitz, Andy Warhol associate Billy Linich and Jon Hassell. Though his output has been sporadic, Young's experiments with 'overtones', or the range of frequencies that make up individual notes, has been acknowledged by artists as diverse as Sonic Youth, Spacemen 3, the Orb and the Future Sound Of London. Since the early 60s he has pioneered minimalist expression in his work, composing much of his work in a New York loft to the sound of a sine-wave generator to engender a 'drone' mentality. Little of his work with Theatre Of Eternal Music was ever officially released due to his well-publicized perfectionism, but he was persuaded to issue a portion of his monolithic 'life work', *The Well-Tuned Piano*, in 1987. This employed his self-customised Bosendorfer grand piano. Over five albums it expresses perfectly the linear manifesto he previously related in his 'Composition 1960 No. 10' - 'Draw a straight line and follow it'. Previous releases had included two albums recorded with his wife (with contributions from Theatre Of Eternal Music). In 1992 he founded a travelling 'rock orchestra', the Forever Bad Blues Band, whose *Just Stompin' Live At The Kitchen* is easily Young's most accessible recording.

●ALBUMS: with Marian Zazeela *The Black Record* (WG 1969)★★★★, with Zazeela *Dream House 78'17'* (Shandar 1974)★★★, *The Well-Tuned Piano* quintuple album (Gramavision 1987)★★★★, *The Melodic Version Of The Second Dream Of the High-Tension Line Stepdown Transformer From The Four Dreams Of China* (Gramavision 1991)★★★, *The Forever Bad Blues Band: Just Stompin': Live At The Kitchen* (Gramavision 1993)★★★.

YOUNG, LARRY

b. 7 October 1940, Newark, New Jersey, USA, d. 30 March 1978. His father was an organ player but at first Young played piano instead. In 1957 he joined an R&B group in Elizabeth, New Jersey and, switching to Hammond organ, recorded with tenor saxophonist Jimmy Forrest in 1961. In 1962 he made his record debut as leader with *Groove Street*. He procured the services of top guitarist Grant Green and, signed to Blue Note, made classic records with artists such as Joe Henderson, Woody Shaw, Donald Byrd and Lee Morgan. In 1964 he visited Europe, playing piano on Nathan Davis's *Happy Girl*. Affected by John Coltrane's expansion of hard bop, he recorded with Coltrane and inducted drummer Elvin Jones into his band, recording *Unity* with him in 1965. He played electric piano on Miles Davis's *Bitches Brew* in 1970, the album which launched the jazz rock genre, worked briefly with John McLaughlin in 1970 and then played in Lifetime, the band run by drummer Anthony Williams. His own *Lawrence Of Newark* featured James 'Blood' Ulmer, making one of his earlier appearances on record. In 1977 Young co-led a group with drummer Joe Chambers, recording *Double Exposure*. Young also worked under his Islamic name of Khalid Yasin. His death at the age of 38 deprived the world of an innovative and passionate player.

● ALBUMS: *Testifying* (New Jazz 1961)★★★★, *Young Blues* (New Jazz 1961)★★★★, *Groove Street* (Prestige 1962)★★★, *Into Somethin'*, (Blue Note 1964)★★★, *Of Love And Peace* (Blue Note 1966)★★★, *Contrasts* (1965)★★★, *Unity* (Blue Note 1966)★★★★★, *Heaven On Earth* (Blue Note 1968)★★★, *Lawrence Of Newark* (1973)★★, *Spaceball* (1975)★★, with Joe Chambers *Double Exposure* (1977)★★.

●COMPILATIONS: *The Art Of Larry Young* (Blue Note 1990)★★★★.

YOUNG, LEE

b. 7 March 1917, New Orleans, Louisiana, USA. Before settling on drums Young studied piano and various reed and brass instruments. As a child he played in the family band led by his father and which also included his brother Lester Young. In the early 30s he moved to Los Angeles, playing in a variety of musical settings with bands led by Mutt Carey, Buck Clayton, Fats Waller and others. He was one of the first black musicians to be hired on a regular basis for film studio work but continued to appear in jazz groups in the early 40s, including those led by Lionel Hampton and Nat 'King' Cole. Young also led his own small groups, one of which featured his brother, and he backed many leading artists including Dinah Washington. He was a regular with Norman Granz's Jazz At The Philharmonic in the mid-40s and later in the decade he was with Benny Goodman. In the 50s, still working in the studios, he belatedly rejoined Cole. In the 60s he was active in record production, mostly as producer and administrator with Vee Jay Records, and in the late 70s was briefly with Motown Records. A solid player with a good sense of time, Young's career outside jazz, as both studio musician and record company executive, occupied the best of his years.

●ALBUMS: *Jazz At The Philhamonic 1944-1946* (1944-46)★★★, *Jazz At The Philharmonic 1946* (1946)★★★.

YOUNG, LESTER

b. 27 August 1909, Woodville, Mississippi, USA, d. 15 March 1959, New York City, New York, USA. Born into a musical family, Young was taught several instruments by his father. As a child he played drums in the family's band, but around 1928 he quit the group and switched to tenor saxophone. His first engagements on this instrument were with Art Bronson, in Phoenix, Arizona. He stayed with Bronson until 1930, with a brief side trip to play again with the family, then worked in and around Minneapolis, Minnesota, with various bands. In the spring of 1932 he joined the Original Blue Devils, under the leadership of Walter Page, and was one of several members of the band who joined Bennie Moten in Kansas City towards the end of 1933. During the next few years Young played in the bands of Moten, George E. Lee, King Oliver, Count Basie, Fletcher Henderson, Andy Kirk and others. In 1936 he rejoined Basie, with whom he remained for the next four years, touring, broadcasting and recording. He also recorded in small groups directed by Teddy Wilson and others and appeared on several classic record dates, backing Billie Holiday, with whom he forged a special and lasting relationship. (She nicknamed him 'Pres' or 'Prez', for president, while he bestowed on her the name 'Lady Day'.) In the early 40s he played in, and sometimes led, small groups in the Los Angeles area alongside his brother, Lee Young, and musicians such as Red Callender, Nat 'King' Cole and Al Sears. During this period he returned briefly to the Basie band, making some excellent recordings, and also worked with Dizzy Gillespie. Late in 1944 he was conscripted into the US Army but was discharged in mid-summer the following year, having spent part of his military service in hospital and part in an army prison. In the mid-40s he was filmed by Gjon Mili in the classic jazz short, *Jammin' The Blues*, a venture which was co-produced by Norman Granz. At this time he also joined Granz's Jazz At The Philharmonic package, remaining with the organization for a number of years. He also led small groups for club and record dates, toured the USA and visited Europe. From the mid-40s onwards Young's health was poor and in the late 50s his physical decline became swift. He continued to record and make concert and festival appearances and was featured on television's *The Sound Of Jazz* in 1957. In these final years his deteriorating health was exacerbated by a drinking problem, and some close observers suggest that towards the end he lost the will to live. He died on 15 March 1959.

One of the seminal figures in jazz history and a major influence in creating the musical atmosphere in which bop could flourish, Young's early and late career was beset by critical bewilderment. Only his middle period appears to have earned unreserved critical acclaim. In recent years, however, thanks in part to a more enlightened body of critical opinion, allied to perceptive biographies (by Dave Gelly and Lewis Porter), few observers now have anything other than praise for this remarkable artist's entire output. In the early 30s, when Young appeared on the wider jazz scene, the tenor saxophone was regarded as a forceful, barrel-toned, potentially dominating instrument. In the early years of jazz none of the saxophone family had met with favour and only the clarinet among the reed instruments maintained a front-line position. This position had been challenged, almost single-handedly, by Coleman Hawkins, who changed perceptions of the instrument and its role in jazz. Despite his authority, Hawkins failed to oust the trumpet from its dominating role. Nevertheless, his example spawned many imitators who attempted to replicate his rich and resonant sound. When Young appeared, favouring a light, acerbic, dry tone, he was in striking contrast to the majestic Hawkins, and many people, both musicians and audiences, disliked what they heard. Only the more perceptive listeners of the time, and especially younger musicians, heard in Young's floating melodic style a distinctive and revolutionary approach to jazz.

The solos he recorded with the Basie band included many which, for all their brevity - some no more than eight bars long - display an astonishing talent in full and magnificent flight. On his first record date, on 9 October 1936, made by a small group drawn from the Basie band under the name of Jones-Smith Inc., he plays with what appears at first hearing to be startling simplicity. Despite this impression, the performances, especially of 'Shoe Shine Swing' and 'Lady Be Good', are undisputed masterpieces seldom equalled, let alone bettered (perhaps not even by Young himself). He recorded many outstanding solos - with the full Basie band on 'Honeysuckle Rose', 'Taxi War Dance' and 'Every Tub'; with the small group, the Kansas City Seven, on 'Dickie's Dream' and 'Lester Leaps In'. On all of these recordings, Young's solos clearly indicate that, for all their emotional depths, a massive intellectual talent is at work. In 1940 he made some excellent records with a small band assembled under the nominal leadership of Benny Goodman which featured Basie, Buck Clayton and Charlie Christian and was clearly at ease in such illustrious company. His sessions with Billie Holiday belong to a higher level again. The empathy displayed by these two frequently-troubled people is always remarkable and at times magical. Almost any of their recordings would serve as an example, with 'Me, Myself And I', 'Mean To Me', 'When You're Smiling', 'Foolin' Myself' and 'This Year's Kisses' being particularly rewarding examples of their joint and separate artistry. Even late in their lives, after they had seen little of one another for several years (theirs was an extremely close although almost certainly platonic relationship), their appearance on the television show *The Sound Of Jazz* produced a moment of astonishing emotional impact. In a performance of 'Fine And Mellow', just after Holiday has sung, Young plays a brief solo of achingly fragile tenderness that is packed with more emotion than a million words could convey.

After Young left the army his playing style was demonstrably different, a fact which led many to declare that his suffering at the hands of the military had broken his artistic will. While Young's time in the army was clearly unpleasant, and the life was something for which he was physically and psychologically unsuited, it seems unlikely that the changes in his playing were directly attributable to his army service. On numerous record dates he demonstrated that his talent was not damaged by his spell in the stockade. His playing had changed but the differences were almost certainly a result of changes in the man himself. He had matured, moved on, and his music had too. Those critics who like their musicians to be trapped in amber were unprepared for the new Lester Young. Adding to the confusion was the fact that, apart from the faithful Hawkins-style devotees, most other tenor players in jazz were imitating the earlier Lester. His first recordings after leaving the army, which include 'DB Blues' and 'These Foolish Things', are not the work of a spent spirit but have all the elegance and style of a consummate master, comfortably at one with his world. A 1956 session with Teddy Wilson, on which Young is joined by Roy Eldridge and an old comrade from his Basie days, Jo Jones, is another striking example of a major figure who is still in full command of all his earlier powers; and a long-overlooked set of records made at about the same time with the Bill Potts Trio, a backing group that accompanied him during an engagement in a bar in Washington, D.C., show him to be as musically alert and inventive as ever.

A withdrawn, moody figure with a dry and slightly anarchic sense of humour, Young perpetuated his own mythology during his lifetime, partly through a personal use of words which he developed into a language of his own (among other things he coined the use of 'bread' to denote money). His stoicism and a marked preference for his own company - or, at best, for a favoured few who shared his mistrustful view of life - set him apart even from the jazz musicians who admired him. It is impossible to overstate Young's importance in the development of jazz. From the standpoint of the 90s, when the tenor saxophone is the dominant instrument in jazz, it is easy to imagine that this is the way it always was. That the tenor has come to hold the place it does is largely a result of Young's influence, which inspired so many young musicians to adopt the instrument or to turn those who already played it into new directions. Most of the developments in bop and post-bop owe their fundamentals to Young's concern for melody and the smooth, flowing lines with which he transposed his complex musical thoughts into beautiful, articulate sounds. Although other important tenor saxophonists have come, and in some cases gone, during the three decades since Lester Young died, few have had the impact of this unusual, introspective, sensitive and musically profound genius of jazz.

● ALBUMS: with Count Basie *Lester Young Quartet And Count Basie Seven* 10-inch album (Mercury 1950)★★★★, *Lester Young* reissued as *The Immortal Lester Young* (Savoy 1951)★★★★, with Nat 'King' Cole, Buddy Rich *The Lester Young Trio* 10-inch album (Mercury 1951)★★★★, with Basie *Count Basie And Lester Young* 10-inch album (Jazz Panorama 1951)★★★★, *Lester Young Collates* reissued as *Pres* (Mercury/Norgran 1951)★★★★, *Kansas City Style* 10-inch album (Commodore 1952)★★★, with Illinois Jacquet *Battle Of The Saxes* 10-inch album (Aladdin 1953)★★★★, with Red Callender, Cole *King Cole-Lester Young-Red Callender Trio* reissued as *Lester Young-Nat King Cole Trio* (Aladdin/Score 1953)★★★★, *Lester Young - His Tenor Sax* 10-inch album (Aladdin 1953)★★★, with Cole, Rich *The Lester Young Trio* ii (Clef 1953)★★★★, *The President Plays* (Verve 1953)★★★★, with Oscar Peterson *Lester Young With The Oscar Peterson Trio* i (Norgran 1954)★★★★, with Peterson *Lester Young With The Oscar Peterson Trio* ii (Norgran 1954)★★★★, with Paul Quinichette *Pres Meets Vice-Pres* 10-inch album (EmArcy 1954)★★★, *The President* reissued as *Lester Swings Again* (Norgran 1954)★★★★, with Harry 'Sweets' Edison *Pres And Sweets* (Norgran 1955)★★★★, with Peterson *The Pres-ident Plays With The Oscar Peterson Trio* (Norgran 1955)★★★★, *Lester Young* reissued as *It Don't Mean A Thing (If It Aint't Got That Swing)* (Norgran/Verve 1955)★★★★, *The Jazz Giants '56* (Verve 1956)★★★★, with Chu Berry *Tops On Tenor* (Jazztone 1956)★★★, *Lester Young And His Tenor Sax, Volume 1* (Aladdin 1956)★★★★, *Lester Young And His Tenor Sax, Volume 2* (Aladdin 1956)★★★★, *The Masters Touch* (Savoy 1956)★★★, *Lester's Here* (Norgran 1956)★★★, with Teddy Wilson *Pres And Teddy* (American Recording Society/Verve 1956)★★★★, with Cole, Rich *Lester Young-Nat 'King' Cole-Buddy Rich Trio* (Norgran 1956)★★★★, *Swingin' Lester Young* (Intro 1957)★★★, *The Greatest* (Intro 1957)★★★, with Edison, Roy Eldridge *Going For Myself* (Verve 1959)★★★★, with Edison, Roy Eldridge *Laughin' To Keep From Cryin'* (Verve 1959)★★★★, *The Lester Young Story* (Verve 1959)★★★★, *Lester Young Memorial Album* (Epic 1959)★★★★, *Lester Young In Paris* (Verve 1960)★★★, *The Essential Lester Young* (Verve 1961)★★★★, *Lester Warms Up - Jazz Immortals Series, Vol. 2* (Savoy 1961)★★★★, *Pres* (Charlie Parker 1961)★★★, *Pres Is Blue* 1950-1952 recordings (Charlie Parker 1961)★★, with Coleman Hawkins, Howard McGhee *A Date With Greatness* (Imperial 1962)★★★★, *The Immortal Lester Young, Volume 1* (Imperial 1962)★★★★, *The Immortal Lester Young, Volume 2* (Imperial 1962)★★★★, *The Influence Of Five* (Mainstream 1965)★★★, *Town Hall Concert* (Mainstream 1965)★★★, *Chairman Of The Board* (Mainstream 1965)★★★, *52nd Street* (Mainstream 1965)★★★, *Prez* (Mainstream 1965)★★★, *Pres And His Cabinet* (Verve 1966)★★★, *Lester Young In Washington, D.C., Vol. 1* 1956 recordings (Pablo 1980)★★★★, *Lester Young In Washington, D.C., Vol. 2* 1956 recordings (Pablo 1980)★★★★, *Lester Young In Washington, D.C., Vol. 3* 1956 recordings (Pablo 1980)★★★★, *Lester Young In Washington, D.C., Vol. 4* 1956 recordings (Pablo 1980)★★★★.

● COMPILATIONS: *Prez's Hat Vols 1-4* (Philology 1988)★★★★, *Lester Leaps In* (ASV 1995)★★★★, *The Complete Aladdin Sessions* 1942-1948 recordings (Blue Note 1996)★★★★★, *The Immortal Lester Young* (Savoy Jazz 1996)★★★★, *The 'Kansas City' Sessions* 1938-1944 recordings (GRP/Commodore 1997)★★★★, *Ultimate Lester Young* 1950-1958 recordings (Verve 1998)★★★★, *Lester Young And Charlie Christian* 1939-1940 recordings (Jazz Archives)★★★★, *Historical Prez* 1940-1944 recordings (Everybody's)★★★★, *The Complete Lester Young On Keynote* 1943/1944 recordings (Verve)★★★★, *Master Takes* 1944-1949 recordings (Savoy)★★★★, *Pres: The Complete Savoy Recordings* 1944-1949 recordings (Savoy)★★★★, *Jammin' With Lester* 1944-1946 recordings (Jazz Archives)★★★★, *Prez Conferences* 1946-1958 recordings (Jass)★★★★, *Ultimate Lester Young* (Verve 1998)★★★★.

● FURTHER READING: *Lester Young*, Lewis Porter. *The Tenor Saxophone And Clarinet Of Lester Young, 1936-1949*, Jan Evensmo. *You Got To Be Original Man! The Music of Lester Young*, Frank Buchmann-Moller. *You Just Fight For Your Life: The Story of Lester Young*, Frank Buchmann-Moller. *A Lester Young Reader*, Lewis Porter.

YOUNG, SNOOKY

b. Eugene Howard Young, 3 February 1919, Dayton, Ohio, USA. Young began playing trumpet while still a small child and by his early teens was working in territory bands. He was heard by Gerald Wilson, who was then playing in the Jimmie Lunceford band, and on his recommendation Young was hired. Young stayed with the Lunceford band until 1942 and in that year played with Count Basie, Lionel Hampton, Les Hite and Benny Carter. In the following year, after a brief return visit to Basie, he joined Wilson's big band in California. In the late 40s he was again with Hampton and Basie, and he was back yet again in the Basie band in the late 50s and early 60s. From the early 60s he worked in television studios in New York City, and was a member of the Thad Jones-Mel Lewis Jazz Orchestra from its inception. Subsequently, Young continued to play in the studios, mostly in Los Angeles, and also appeared at jazz festivals, with occasional return visits to Basie in the late 70s and early 80s. He also made a handful of records as sideman with Ray Bryant, and as either leader or co-leader (with Marshal Royal). A strong lead trumpeter, his solo gifts were frequently underused by his employers. Content to work in the studios for more than a quarter of a century, Young's infrequent jazz excursions in the past three decades have shown him to be an interesting soloist, whether on open horn or with the plunger mute.

● ALBUMS: with Count Basie *Chairman Of The Board* (1959)★★★, one side only *The Boys From Dayton* (1971)★★, with Marshal Royal *Snooky And Marshal's Album* (Concord 1978)★★★, *Horn Of Plenty* (1979)★★★.

YOUNG, TRUMMY

b. James Osborne Young, 12 January 1912, Savannah, Georgia, USA, d. 10 September 1984. As a child Young played trumpet and drums but by his teens was concentrating on trombone. Resident in Washington, DC, he played in local bands before relocating to Chicago and working with Earl 'Fatha' Hines. He remained with Hines for four years, making occasional visits to other bands. In 1937 he began a five-year stint with Jimmie Lunceford, becoming an important member of the band as both trombone soloist and singer. He also had a number of hit records with the band, among them 'Margie' and his own composition, 'Tain't What You Do, It's The Way That You Do It'. In the 40s he worked with bands covering a wide stylistic range, including those led by Boyd Raeburn and Roy Eldridge. He also played with Jazz At The Philharmonic before settling for a while in Hawaii. In 1952 he became a member of Louis Armstrong's All Stars, a job he held for 12 years. After leaving Armstrong he returned to Hawaii, leading his own bands, playing with visiting musicians, and making occasional visits to the mainland for concert and festival appearances. A superbly gifted trombonist, Young's early playing style showed him to be a completely rounded soloist with an approach to his instrument that was, in many respects, very advanced for a 30s big band musician. His playing style changed after he joined Armstrong, with whom he used a deceptively simple approach. The change was highly appropriate for Armstrong's band and Young was in many ways a more suitable partner than his predecessor, the sublime Jack Teagarden, had been. His blistering solos and delightfully melodic ensemble lines, allied to his engagingly casual singing, helped to give the band a strength of character that it lacked after he departed.

● ALBUMS: *Louis Armstrong Plays W.C. Handy* (1954)★★★★, *Satch Plays Fats* (1955)★★★, *Trummy Young And His Fifty-Fifty Band* (1955)★★★, *A Man And His Horn* (1975)★★★, *Yours Truly: Trummy Young And Friends* (1975)★★, *Struttin' With Some Barbecue* (1979)★★★.

● COMPILATIONS: *The Complete Jimmie Lunceford 1939-40* (1939-40)★★★★.

YOUNG, VICTOR

b. 8 August 1900, Chicago, Illinois, USA, d. 11 November 1956, Palm Springs, California, USA. A violinist, conductor, bandleader, arranger and composer, Young is said to have been responsible for over 300 film scores and themes. He studied at the Warsaw Conservatory in 1910 before joining the Warsaw Philharmonic as a violinist, and touring Europe. He returned to the USA at the outbreak of World War I, and later, in the early 20s, toured as a concert violinist, and then became a concert master in theatre orchestras. On 'defecting' to popular music, he served for a while as violinist-arranger with the popular pianist-bandleader Ted Fio Rito. During the 30s, Young worked a great deal on radio, conducting for many artists including Al Jolson, Don Ameche and Smith Ballew. He also started recording with his own orchestra, and had a string of hits from 1931-54, including 'Gems From "The Band Wagon"', 'The Last Round-Up', 'Who's Afraid Of The Big Bad Wolf', 'The Old Spinning Wheel', 'This Little Piggie Went To Market' (featuring Jimmy Dorsey, Bunny Berigan and Joe Venuti), 'Flirtation Walk', 'Ev'ry Day', 'Way Back Home', 'About A Quarter To Nine' and 'She's A Latin From Manhattan' (both from the Jolson movie *Go Into Your Dance*), 'It's A Sin To Tell A Lie', 'Mona Lisa', 'The Third Man Theme', 'Ruby', 'Limelight Theme', and 'The High And The Mighty'. He also provided the orchestral accompaniments for other artists, such as Dick Powell, Eddie Cantor, Deanna Durbin, Helen Forrest, Frances Langford, trumpet virtuoso Rafael Mendez, Cliff

Edwards, the Boswell Sisters, and western movies singer Rex Allen. Most notably, it was Young's orchestra that backed Judy Garland on her record of 'Over The Rainbow', the Oscar-winning song from the legendary 1939 film *The Wizard Of Oz*. He also backed Bing Crosby on two of his million-sellers: 'Too-Ra-Loo-Ra-Loo-Ral (That's An Irish Lullaby)', from *Going My Way* (the 'Best Picture' of 1944), and British doctor Arthur Colahan's somewhat unconventional song, 'Galway Bay' (1948).
Young's extremely successful and prolific career as a film composer, musical director, conductor, and arranger, began in the early 30s with Paramount. Some of his best-known film works included *Wells Fargo* (1937), *Swing High, Swing Low* (1937), *Breaking The Ice* (1938), *Golden Boy* (1939), *Man Of Conquest* (1939), *Arizona* (1940), *I Wanted Wings* (1941), *Hold Back The Dawn* (1941), *Flying Tigers* (1942), *Silver Queen* (1942), *The Glass Key* (1942), *Take A Letter, Darling* (1942), *For Whom The Bell Tolls* (1943), *The Uninvited* (1944), *Samson And Delilah* (1949), *Rio Grande* (1950), *Scaramouche* (1952), *The Greatest Show On Earth* (1952), *Shane* (1953) and *Three Coins In The Fountain* (1954). In 1956, Young was awarded a posthumous Academy Award for his score for Mike Todd's spectacular film *Around The World In Eighty Days*. His record of the title song made the US charts in 1957, and had a vocal version by Bing Crosby on the b-side. He also wrote some television themes, including 'Blue Star' for the US *Medic* series, and contributed music to two minor Broadway shows, *Pardon Our French* (1950) and *Seventh Heaven* (1955). Young's popular songs were written mostly with lyricist Ned Washington. These included 'Can't We Talk It Over?', 'A Hundred Years From Today' (from the revue *Blackbirds Of 1933/34*), and three beautiful and enduring ballads: 'A Ghost Of A Chance' (co-writer, Bing Crosby), 'Stella By Starlight' and 'My Foolish Heart' (film title song). Young's other lyricists included Will J. Harris ('Sweet Sue'), Wayne King, Haven Gillespie, and Egbert Van Alstyne ('Beautiful Love'), Sam M. Lewis ('Street Of Dreams'), Edward Heyman ('When I Fall In Love' and 'Love Letters') and Sammy Cahn (the film title song, 'Written On The Wind'). Young also wrote 'Golden Earrings' with the songwriting team of Jay Livingston and Ray Evans.

● ALBUMS: *April In Paris* (c.50s)★★★, *Cinema Rhapsodies* (c.50s)★★★, *Gypsy Magic* (c.50s)★★, *Imagination* (c.50s)★★★, *Night Music* (c.50s)★★★, *Pearls On Velvet* (c.50s)★★, *Themes From 'For Whom The Bell Tolls' And 'Golden Earrings'* (c.50s)★★★, *Valentino Tangos* (c.50s)★★, *Hollywood Rhapsodies* (c.50s)★★★, *Around The World In 80 Days* film soundtrack (1957)★★★★, *Forever Young* (1959)★★★, *Love Themes From Hollywood* (1959)★★★, *Wizard Of Oz/Pinocchio* (Ace Of Hearts/Decca 1966)★★, *The Quiet Man/Samson And Delilah* film soundtracks (Varese International 1979)★★★.

Ysaguirre, Bob

b. Robert Ysaguirre, 22 February 1897, Belize, British Honduras, d. 27 March 1982. As a young man he played tuba in military-style brass bands. In his early 20s he went to New Orleans where he played both tuba and string bass with various dance bands; he then moved to New York with Armand Piron's orchestra. In New York during the 20s, he played with Elmer Snowden and Alex Jackson, then was briefly with bands led by Fletcher and Horace Henderson. He spent most of the following decade with Don Redman. From the 40s onwards, Ysaguirre continued to play but no longer on a full-time basis.

● COMPILATIONS: *The Chronological Don Redman 1931-1933* (Classics 1931-33).

Yukl, Joe

b. Joseph Yukl, 5 March 1909, New York, USA, d. March 1981. After first playing violin he switched to trombone and played in college dance bands. In New York in the 20s he joined the staff of CBS Records but also appeared from time to time on record with jazzmen such as Red Nichols and Tommy and Jimmy Dorsey. In the 30s he was with Joe Haymes and Jimmy Dorsey, also playing dates and sometimes recording with a wide range of popular and jazz artists, including Bing Crosby, Louis Armstrong, Frankie Trumbauer and Ted Fio Rito. By this time he had relocated to the west coast where he again worked in studios. He continued these activities into the 40s and 50s, playing jazz dates with Wingy Manone and others. He also played on soundtracks or appeared in at least two motion pictures: *Rhythm Inn* (1951), which also featured Manone, Pete Daily and Barrett Deems, and *The Glenn Miller Story* (1953). In the latter film, together with Murray McEachern, he both coached and ghosted for James Stewart in his role as Miller. Yukl played with skill and a pleasing sound.

Z

ZARCHY, ZEKE

b. Rubin Zarchy, 12 June 1915, New York City, New York, USA. Zarchy began playing trumpet as a child and was playing semi-professionally while still at high school. He first came to note as a member of the excellent dance band led by Joe Haymes. In 1936 he joined Benny Goodman and thereafter played with Artie Shaw, Bob Crosby, Red Norvo and Tommy Dorsey, before joining Glenn Miller in 1940. Zarchy then moved into studio work but appeared on a number of Miller recordings and during World War II played in Miller's army band. He resumed studio work in the post-war years, and also made recording dates with many leading big bands throughout the 50s and 60s. In the early 80s he began making appearances with the Great Pacific Jazz Band (comprised mostly of musicians from the Walt Disney studio orchestra) and also toured Australia and the UK with a Miller reunion band. Zarchy never risked improvising, admitting to interviewer Ralph Gulliver, 'I would have been scared witless', but he enjoyed a reputation as being one of the best and most reliable lead trumpeters of the swing era.

ZARDIS, CHESTER

b. 27 May 1900, New Orleans, Louisiana, USA, d. 1990. Zardis began playing double bass in 1916, going against the prevailing preference for brass instruments to play bass lines. In the 20s he performed with many of the leading New Orleans jazzmen, including Chris Kelly and Kid Rena. Throughout the 30s he played in his hometown and on Mississippi riverboats, also recording with Kid Howard. In 1942 he took part in recording dates with the rediscovered Bunk Johnson and the following year recorded with George Lewis. In the late 40s and early 50s he played in New Orleans and after a spell away from music returned to the local scene to become a member of the Preservation Hall Jazz Band. He visited Europe with this band in the mid-60s. Zardis spent the 70s in New Orleans but found time for another trip to Europe, this time with the New Orleans Joymakers in 1972. In the following decade he was still playing regularly, visiting Europe again with Kid Thomas Valentine. A firm player with a lovely tone, Zardis maintained a steady yet fluid beat. One of the best of the New Orleans bass players.

ZAWINUL, JOE

b. Josef Erich Zawinul, 7 July 1932, Vienna, Austria. After studying music at the Vienna Conservatory Zawinul's musical ambitions soon outgrew the limited opportunities for a jazz musician in Austria shortly after the war. But financial necessity meant that he spent the 50s almost exclusively involved in local session work. Playing piano in dance and radio orchestras, and working as the house pianist for Polydor Records, he played only briefly with the talented saxophonist Hans Koller in 1952. However, his fortunes improved suddenly in 1959, when he won a scholarship to Berklee College Of Music in Boston. Emigrating to the USA, he immediately received a huge amount of attention, and decided to spend the rest of 1959 touring with Maynard Ferguson. Two years with Dinah Washington followed this, and then in 1961 he began a musical collaboration with Cannonball Adderley (*Mercy, Mercy, Mercy!*, recorded 1966) which was to last nine years. Although he recorded with other musicians during this period - most notably Miles Davis (*In A Silent Way* and *Bitches Brew*) - it was his work with Adderley that spread his reputation as an inventive improviser and talented writer. His composition 'Mercy, Mercy, Mercy' won a Grammy Award for the group. At the end of 1970 he joined Wayne Shorter to form the highly influential Weather Report, the band with which he will always be primarily associated. When the group disbanded in 1985, after 15 years of phenomenal success, Zawinul began touring Europe and the USA again as a soloist. More recently forming Weather Update and Zawinul Syndicate, his dark and ominous chord voicings and electric piano sound will remain a distinctive part of fusion for many years to come. Recorded in Germany in 1997, *World Tour* showcased a particularly stunning performance.

● ALBUMS: with Ben Webster *Soulmates* (Riverside 1964)★★★★, *Money In The Pocket* (Atlantic 1966)★★★, *The Rise And Fall Of The 3rd Stream* (Vortex 1967)★★★, *Zawinul* (Atlantic 1970)★★★, *Dialects* (Columbia 1986)★★★, *The Immigrants* (Columbia 1988)★★★, *Black Water* (Columbia 1989)★★★, *The Beginning* 1959 recording (Fresh Sounds 1990)★★, *Stories Of The Danube* (Philips 1996)★★★, *My People* (Escapade 1996)★★★, *World Tour* (Escapade 1998)★★★★.

● COMPILATIONS: and the Austrian All Stars *His Majesty Swinging Nephews 1954-1957* (RST 1997)★★★.

ZEITLIN, DENNY

b. 10 April 1938, Chicago, Illinois, USA. Zeitlin had a classical music training before studying medicine at Johns Hopkins University and then Columbia. In 1963 he successfully auditioned for the record producer John Hammond Jnr. but then moved to San Francisco where he studied psychiatry and played the piano. In 1965 he was involved in a trio with bassist Charlie Haden. His interest in the use of the prepared piano (in which the sound of the piano is changed by attaching nuts, bolts and screws to the strings) encouraged him to experiment with sounds available from synthesizers as these became more readily available in the late 60s. Along with his keyboard playing, he has written instrumental scores, including a film score for Philip Kaufman's *Invasion Of The Bodysnatchers* in 1978.

● ALBUMS: *Cathexis* (Columbia 1964)★★★, *Carnival*

(Columbia 1965)★★★, *Live At The Trident* (Columbia 1966)★★★, *Shining Hour* (Columbia 1966)★★★★, *Zeitgeist* (Columbia 1966)★★★, *Expansion* (Arch 1973)★★★, *Syzygy* (Arch 1977)★★★, *Soundings* (Arch 1978)★★★, *Tidal Wave* (Palo Alto 1981)★★★, with Charlie Haden *Time Remembers One Time Once* (ECM 1983)★★★★, *Homecoming* (Living Music 1986)★★★★, *Trio* (Windham Hill Jazz 1988)★★★, *In The Moment* (Windham Hill Jazz 1989)★★, with David Friesen *In Concert* (TM Pacific 1992)★★, *Live At Maybeck Recital Hall - Vol. 27* (Concord Jazz 1993)★★★, *As Long As There's Music* (Venus 1998)★★★.

ZENTNER, SI

b. Simon H. Zentner, 13 June 1917, New York City, New York, USA. After learning to play the trombone as a child, Zentner played in and around New York before joining Les Brown in 1940. During the 40s he played in a number of bands, including those led by Harry James and Jimmy Dorsey, and at the end of the decade entered a long period of studio work. From 1957 onwards, he periodically formed a big band for studio sessions and gained a substantial following among the record-buying public. For these bands he employed studio musicians, many with strong leanings to jazz; among them were Don Fagerquist, Don Lodice, Joe and Ray Triscari, Alvin Stoller, Lanny Morgan, Frank Capp and Gene Goe. Perhaps the most important among the regular members of the bands Zentner formed was pianist Bob Florence, whose arrangements were influential in establishing Zentner's reputation among big band fans. Zentner continued his series of recordings until 1968, and thereafter continued to form big bands to accompany leading singers and also for appearances at important venues in Los Angeles and Las Vegas. Leading by example, Zentner has consistently shown that there is a substantial and enthusiastic audience for big band music, and that such music need not be repetitious or confined to recreations of old favourites.

● ALBUMS: *Introducing Si Zentner And His Dance Band/Si Zentner, His Trombone And Orchestra* i (Liberty 1957)★★★★, *Si Zentner And His Orchestra* (Liberty 1957)★★★, *Swing Fever/Si Zentner, His Trombone And Orchestra* ii (Liberty 1957)★★★★, *Sleepy Lagoon: Si Zentner With Russell Garcia* (Liberty 1957)★★, *A Thinking Man's Band* (Liberty 1959)★★★, *Suddenly It's Swing* (Liberty 1960)★★★★, with the Johnny Mann Singers *Great Band With Great Voices Vols 1 & 2* (Liberty 1961)★★★★, *The Si Zentner Big Band Plays The Big Hits* (Liberty 1961)★★, *Up A Lazy River (Big Band Plays The Big Hits: Vol. 2)* (Liberty 1962)★★★, *The Stripper And Other Big Band Hits* (Liberty 1962)★★, *Waltz In Jazz Time* (Liberty 1962)★★★, *Rhythm And Blues* (Liberty 1962)★★, *Exotica Suite* (Liberty 1962)★★, *Desafinado* (Liberty 1963)★★★, *In Full Swing* (Liberty 1963)★★★, *From Russia With Love* (Liberty 1963)★★★, *Si Zentner Plays The Big Big-Band Hits* (Liberty 1964)★★★, *It's Nice To Go Trav'ling* (Liberty 1965)★★★, *Put Your Hand On My Shoulder* (Liberty 1965)★★★, *Swingin' Country* (Liberty 1966)★★, *Warning Shot* (Liberty 1967)★★★, *Right Here* (Liberty 1969)★★★.

ZETTERLUND, MONICA

b. 20 September 1938, Hagfors, Sweden. During the 50s Zetterlund sang in various parts of Scandinavia, often in good jazz company such as an orchestra led by Arne Domnérus with whom she recorded. She toured elsewhere in the late 50s and early 60s, including trips to the UK and the USA. Once again, her accompanists were of the highest order and a distinguished record date with Bill Evans was one such example. Like her fellow countrywoman, Alice Babs, she also sang traditional folk songs of Sweden and studied and sang music from the classical repertoire. Zetterlund's singing is clean and well ordered and she has a nice sense of swing. Her interpretation of lyrics is also good and she copes comfortably with the idioms of what is to her a foreign language. In addition to singing, she has also acted, working in this capacity mostly in her homeland.

● ALBUMS: *Hajman* (Odeon 1975)★★★, *It Only Happens Every Time* (EMI 1977)★★★.

ZOLLER, ATTILA

b. 13 June 1927, Visegard, Hungary, d. 25 January 1998, Townsend, Vermont, USA. Zoller learnt to play the violin and trumpet as a child and only turned to the guitar when he chose to make a career in music. He played in a variety of bands in Budapest after the war before political unrest at home sent him to Austria and then, in the mid-50s, to Germany. There he played with Hans Koller and accompanied visiting Americans like Oscar Pettiford. In 1959 he won a scholarship to the Lennox School of Jazz and went to the USA. Zoller was a technically skilful guitarist who performed in a restrained style, with a keen harmonic sense which sometimes revealed his east European background. He joined Chico Hamilton's Quintet in 1960 and then played with Herbie Mann until 1965. He performed in a group specializing in modal jazz with Dave Friedman before playing with Red Norvo and then Benny Goodman. In 1968 he was a co-leader in a trio with Albert Mangelsdorff and Lee Konitz. In the early 80s he played with Jimmy Raney. In 1971 he patented a bi-directional pick-up for the guitar and later developed a magnetic pick-up which could be used with a vibraphone.

● ALBUMS: with Albert Mangelsdorff, Lee Konitz *Z0-KO-MA* (MPS 1967)★★★★, *The Horizon Beyond* (EmArcy 1968)★★★, *Gypsy Cry* (1971)★★★★, *The K & K In New York* (L+R 1980)★★★★, *Memories Of Pannonia* (1987)★★★, *Common Cause* (1992)★★★, *Live Highlights '92* (Bhakti 1992)★★★, *When It's Time* (Enja 1995)★★★★, with Don Friedman, Lee Konitz *Thingin* (hatArt 1996)★★★, *Lasting Love* (Acoustic Music 1998)★★★.

ZORN, JOHN

b. 2 September 1953, New York City, New York, USA. Zorn trained in classical composition, initial inspirations being the American composer-inventors Charles Ives, John Cage and Harry Partch. He developed an interest in jazz when he attended a concert given by trumpeter Jacques Coursil, who was teaching him

French at the time. His later jazz idols have included Anthony Braxton, Ornette Coleman, Jimmy Giuffre and Roscoe Mitchell. Since 1974 he has been active on New York's Lower East Side, a leading representative of the 'downtown' *avant garde*, applying 'game theory' to structure-free improvisation, a parallel technique to Butch Morris's 'conduction'. Zorn's keen study of bebop and his razor-sharp alto saxophone technique gained him respect from the jazz players: in 1977 he and guitarist Eugene Chadbourne were included in an 11-piece ensemble playing Frank Lowe's compositions (*Lowe & Behold*). A record collector, Zorn was inspired by Derek Bailey's Incus releases, and in 1983 recorded *Yankees* with him and trombonist George Lewis. The same year he wrote some music for Hal Willner's tribute to Thelonious Monk, *That's The Way I Feel Now*. In 1985 he contributed to Willner's Kurt Weill album *Lost In The Stars* and made a commercial breakthrough with *The Big Gundown*, which interpreted Ennio Morricone's themes by deploying all kinds of unlikely musicians (including 'Big' John Patton and Toots Thielemans). *News For Lulu* (1987), with Lewis and Bill Frisell, presented classic hard bop tunes from the 60s with Zorn's customary steely elegance: it was his second bebop venture, following *Voodoo* by the Sonny Clark Memorial Quartet (Zorn, Wayne Horvitz, Ray Drummond, Bobby Previte). Declaring that hardcore rock music had the same intensity as 60s free jazz, he championed Nottingham's Napalm Death and recorded hardcore versions of Ornette Coleman's tunes on the provocative *Spy Vs Spy* (1989). Naked City (Frisell - guitar, Horvitz - keyboards, Fred Frith - bass, Joey Baron - drums) became his vehicle for skipping between sleaze-jazz, surf rock and hardcore: they made an impressive debut for Nonesuch/Elektra Records in 1990, and have continued to record challenging work throughout the 90s (with the addition of Boredoms vocalist Yamatsuka Eye). In 1991 he formed Pain Killer with bassist/producer Bill Laswell and Mick Harris (the drummer from Napalm Death) and released *The Guts Of A Virgin* on Earache Records, the Nottingham hardcore label. He played at Company Week 1991, proving by his commitment and enthusiasm that (relative) commercial success has not made him turn his back on free improvisation. Zorn's genre transgression seems set to become the commonsense of creative music in the 90s. He also runs his own Tzadik record label.

● ALBUMS: *School* (Parachute 1978)★★★, *Pool* (Parachute 1980)★★★, *Archery* (Parachute 1981)★★★, *The Classic Guide To Strategy Volume One* (Lumina 1983)★★★, *Locus Solus* (Eva/Wave 1983)★★★, with Derek Bailey, George Lewis *Yankees* (Celluloid 1983)★★★★, with Jim Staley *OTB* (1984)★★★, with Michihiro Sato *Ganryu Island* (Yukon 1985)★★★, *The Big Gundown* (Elektra 1985)★★★★, *The Classic Guide To Strategy Volume Two* (Lumina 1986)★★★, with the Sonny Clark Memorial Quartet *Voodoo: The Music Of Sonny Clark* (Black Saint 1986)★★★, *Cobra* recorded 1985 (hatART 1987)★★★, with Lewis, Bill Frisell *News For Lulu* (hatART 1987)★★★★, *Spillane* (Elektra 1988)★★★★, *Spy Vs Spy: The Music Of Ornette Coleman* (Elektra 1989)★★★★, with Pain Killer *The Guts Of A Virgin* (Earache 1991)★★★, with Lewis, Frisell *More News For Lulu* (hatART 1992)★★★★, *Filmworks 1986-1990* (Elektra 1992)★★★★, *Masada* (DIW 1994)★★★★, *Vav* (DIW 1996)★★★, *Hei* (DIW 1996)★★★, *Redbird (For Agnes Martin)* (Tzadik 1996)★★★, *Bar Kokhba* (Tzadik 1996)★★★, *Downtown Lullaby* (Depth Of Field 1998)★★★, with Bobby Previte *Euclid's Nightmare* (Depth Of Field 1998)★★★★, *Masada Tet* (DIW 1998)★★★★, *Duras: Duchamp* (Tzadik 1998)★★, *Angelus Novus* (Tzadik 1998)★★★.

● COMPILATIONS: *The Parachute Years 1977-1980* (Tzadik 1998)★★★★.

ZOTTOLA, GLENN

b. 28 April 1947, Port Chester, New York, USA. Zottola first played trumpet at the age of three, his early start explained by the fact that his father not only played trumpet but was also a manufacturer of trumpet mouthpieces (his brother, Bob Zottola, played with the bands of Charlie Barnet, Maynard Ferguson and Billy May). At the age of nine Glenn was playing in public, and within three years was performing regularly on television and had made an appearance at the Atlantic City Jazz Festival. In the early 60s he played a leading role in a documentary film, *Come Back*. In 1967 he joined the Glenn Miller Orchestra, then under the direction of Buddy De Franco. In 1970 Zottola was briefly with Lionel Hampton and then began a fruitful decade that saw him backing a wide range of artists including Bob Hope, Al Martino, Patti Page, Tony Martin, Robert Merrill and Mel Tormé. Towards the end of the 70s Zottola played lead trumpet in the orchestra accompanying the touring version of *Chicago*. In 1979 he joined Tex Beneke and that same year became a member of the Benny Goodman Sextet for a national tour. Zottola began the 80s in fine style, playing, singing and acting in *Swing*, a musical presented at the Kennedy Center in Washington, DC, before playing in the pit bands of several Broadway shows including *Evita*, *Annie* and *Barnum*, and also for the Stratford, Connecticut revival of *Anything Goes*, which starred Ginger Rogers. In the early 80s he joined Bob Wilber's Bechet Legacy band, playing on record dates and international tours. Zottola has also recorded with Butch Miles, George Masso, Keith Ingham and Maxine Sullivan. In the mid-80s, in addition to his regular appearances with Wilber, Zottola led his own big band at the Rainbow Room in New York City and then joined forces with Bobby Rosengarden to co-lead a big band at the Hyatt Regency Hotel in Greenwich, Connecticut. He toured overseas, playing jazz festivals in Ireland, Holland and Finland, while his US festival appearances have included St. Louis, Sacramento and the Kool Jazz Festival in New York. In 1988 he was featured soloist in Wilber's recreation of Benny Goodman's 1938 Carnegie Hall concert. In 1990 Zottola was headlining at the Clearwater Jazz Festival in Florida and late in 1991 toured the UK and Europe with a band led by Peanuts Hucko. Unusually among brass players, Zottola is also an accomplished saxophonist, playing alto with flair. Although rooted in the mainstream of jazz and with a marked kinship for the swing era, his playing shows flashes of a deep awareness of bop and postbop developments in the music. The exceptional talent he displayed as a child has not been dissipated but has been nurtured into an impressive all-round ability.

● ALBUMS: *Live At Eddie Condon's* (1980)★★★, *Secret Love* (1981)★★★, with Bob Wilber *Ode To Bechet* (1982), with George Masso *Pieces Of Eight* (1982), with Butch Miles *Butch Miles Salutes Gene Krupa* (1982), *Stardust* (1983)★★★, with Maxine Sullivan *The Lady's In Love With You* (1985), *Christmas In Jazztime* (Dreamstreet 1986)★★.

Zurke, Bob

b. 17 January 1912, Detroit, Michigan, USA, d. 17 February 1944. Learning piano as a child, Zurke displayed a remarkable talent and by his teenage years was playing semi-professionally. He worked regularly in and around Philadelphia in the late 20s and 30s, playing in numerous small bands and also as a single. In 1937 he joined the Bob Crosby band, achieving great success that was due in part to his ability to play convincingly sophisticated boogie-woogie during the brief craze for that style. The band's recording of 'Honky Tonk Train Blues', a feature for Zurke, was a hit. He left Crosby in 1939 to form his own band but this proved unsuccessful and he returned to solo work, playing clubs in Detroit, Chicago, Los Angeles and elsewhere. Although noted particularly for his boogie-woogie playing, Zurke had a much wider range and was an important, if erratic, factor in the Crosby band's success.

● ALBUMS: *Tom Cat On The Keys* (RCA Victor 1955)★★★.

● COMPILATIONS: with Bob Crosby *South Rampart Street Parade* 1935-42 recordings (MCA), with Crosby *Big Noise From Winnetka* 1937-42 recordings (MCA), *Bob Zurke And His Delta Rhythm Band* 1939-40 recordings (Meritt 1988)★★★.

Zwerin, Mike

b. 18 May 1930, New York, USA. Zwerin was educated at the High School of Music and Art before going to the University of Miami. During one holiday he played trombone on club dates at the Royal Roost with the Miles Davis nonet which later produced *Birth Of The Cool*. Zwerin moved to Paris in the early 50s but returned to New York in 1958 and worked with the big bands of Claude Thornhill, Maynard Ferguson and Bill Russo. Later he played with Eric Dolphy and John Lewis as well as in Orchestra USA (1962-65) and in the sextet drawn from its ranks. He toured the USSR with Earl Hines's band in 1966. During the early 60s Zwerin was president of his father's steel fabrication company and afterwards became the jazz critic for the *Village Voice* (1964-66) and was subsequently appointed its European Editor. Since then he has been music correspondent for the *International Herald Tribune*. He settled in Paris where he promotes jazz concerts for the American Centre, writes books and contributes articles to music magazines.

● ALBUMS: radio broadcast with Miles Davis *Pre-Birth Of The Cool* (1948), *Jazz Versions Of The Berlin Theatre Songs Of Kurt Weill* (1964)★★★, with Celestial Communication Orchestra *Desert Mirage* (1982)★★★, *Not Much Noise* (Spotlite 1983)★★★.

● FURTHER READING: *Too Close For Jazz*, Mike Zwerin.

Zwingenberger, Axel

b. 7 May 1955, Hamburg, Germany. After studying classical piano for more than a decade, Zwingenberger began playing boogie-woogie in 1973. Although this was more than 30 years after the style had enjoyed its brief period of popular success, Zwingenberger's technical prowess brought him immediate public recognition in Germany. He released a successful album and was invited to tour and record in the USA, appearing with Joe Turner. By the end of the 70s he had established a reputation throughout Europe and was featured at concerts and festivals, sometimes as a single and also with visiting jazz luminaries such as Lionel Hampton. In the 80s he continued his touring and recording, working with Beulah 'Sippie' Wallace, Mama Yancey, Joe Newman and others. Although rightly praised for his remarkable technique, Zwingenberger has shown himself to be a sensitive accompanist to the blues singers with whom he has performed: this, allied to his mastery of his instrument, suggests that he has even more to offer the jazz world.

● ALBUMS: *Boogie Woogie Breakdown* (Vagabond 1977)★★★, with Joe Turner *Let's Boogie All Night Long* (Vagabond 1978)★★★★, with Turner, Joe Newman *Between Hamburg And Hollywood* (1978-85)★★★, *Powerhouse Boogie* (Vagabond 1979)★★★★, *Boogie Woogie Live* (Vagabond 1979)★★★★, *Boogie Woogie Jubilee* (Vagabond 1981)★★★★, *Axel Zwingenberger And The Friends Of Boogie Woogie Volumes 1 & 2* (Vagabond 1982)★★★★, *Lionel Hampton Introduces Axel Zwingenberger: The Boogie Woogie Album* (Vagabond 1982)★★★★, *Axel Zwingenberger With Sippie Wallace And The Friends Of Boogie Woogie* (1983)★★★, *An Evening With Sippie Wallace* (1984)★★★★, *Axel Zwingenberger And Sippie Wallace 'Live'* (Vagabond 1986)★★★★, *Axel Zwingenberger 'Live'* (1986)★★, *Axel Zwingenberger And The Blues Of Mama Yancey* (Vagabond 1988)★★★, *Axel Zwingenberger And The Friends Of Boogie Woogie: Vol 6* (Vagabond 1988)★★★, *Boogie Woogie Bros* (Vagabond 1989)★★★★, *Axel Zwingenberger And The Friends Of Boogie Woogie Volume 7 - Champion Jack Dupree Sings Blues Classics* (Vagabond 1991)★★★.

Bibliography by Artist

Allen, Henry 'Red'
Evensmo, Jan, *The Trumpet And Vocal Of Henry Red Allen, 1927-1942*, Evensmo.

Allison, Mose
Jones, Patti, *One Man's Blues: The Life And Music Of Mose Allison*, Quartet Books (UK), 1996.

Armstrong, Louis
Armstrong, Louis, *Satchmo: My Life In New Orleans*, Da Capo (USA), 1986.
Bergreen, Laurence, *Louis Armstrong: An Extravagant Life*, Broadway Books (USA), 1997.
Bigard, B., *With Louis And The Duke*, London, 1985.
Boujut, Michel, *Pour Armstrong*, Filipacchi, 1976.
Collier, James Lincoln, *Louis Armstrong: An American Genius*, Oxford University Press, 1983.
Collier, James Lincoln, *Louis Armstrong: An American Success Story*, Macmillan (USA).
Giddins, Gary, *Satchmo*, Doubleday (USA), 1988.
Jones, Max, and John Chilton, *J. Louis: The Louis Armstrong Story, 1900-1971*, London, 1971.
Jones, Max, John Chilton and Leonard Feather, *Salute To Satchmo*, London, 1955.
Meryman, Richard, *Louis Armstrong: A Self-Portrait*, Eakins Press (USA), 1971.
Pinfold, Mike, *Louis Armstrong, His Life And Times*, Universe Books (UK).
Schiff, Ronny S., *Louis Armstrong, A Jazz Master*, MCA Music.
Stratemann, Klaus, *Louis Armstrong On The Screen*, Copenhagen, 1997.
Tanenhaus, Sam, *Louis Armstrong*, Chelsea House.
Westerberg, Hans, *Boy From New Orleans: Louis 'Satchmo' Armstrong*, Copenhagen, 1981.

Bailey, Pearl
Bailey, Pearl, *Talking To Myself*, New York, 1971.
Bain, *The Raw Pearl*, New York, 1968.

Baker, Chet
Wulff, Ingo, *Chet Baker In Concert*, Nielswand Verlag, 1992.
Wulff, Ingo (ed.), *Chet Baker In Europe 1975 - 1988*, Nieswand Verlag, 1993.

Barker, Danny
Barker, Danny, *A Life In Jazz*, London, 1986.

Barnet, Charlie
Barnet, Charlie, with Stanley Dance, *Those Swinging Years: The Autobiography Of Charlie Barnet*, Tulane, Louisiana, 1984.

Barron, Kenny
Barron, Kenny, *Kenny Barron (Interviewed by Marian McPartland)*.

Basie, Count
Dance, Stanley, *The World Of Count Basie*, Charles Scribner (USA).
Horricks, Raymond, *Count Basie And His Orchestra: Its Music and Its Musicians*, Citadel Press, 1957.
Morgan, A., *Count Basie*, Tunbridge Wells (UK), 1984.
Murray, Albert, *Good Morning Blues: The Autobiography Of Count Basie*, William Heinemann (UK), 1986.
Sheridan, Chris, *Count Basie: A Biodiscography*, Greewood, Westport (USA), 1986.

Bechet, Sidney
Bechet, Sidney, *Treat It Gentle*, Da Capo (USA), 1996.
Chilton, John, *Sidney Bechet, The Wizard Of Jazz*, Da Capo (USA), 1996.
Hippenmeyer, Jean Roland, *Sidney Bechet, Ou, L'Extraordinaire Odyssee D'Un Musicien De Jazz*, Tribune Editions.

Beiderbecke, Bix
Berton, R., *Remembering Bix*, New York, 1974.
James, B., *Bix Beiderbecke*, London, 1959.
Sudhalter, Richard M., Philip R. Evans with Dean-Myatt, *Bix, Man & Legend*, New Rochelle (USA), Arlington House (UK), 1974.

Bennink, Han
Whitehead, Kevin, *New Dutch Swing*, Billboard Books (USA), 1998.

Berigan, Bunny
Dupuis, Robert, *Bunny Berigan: Elusive Legend Of Jazz*, Louisiana State University Press, 1992.

BERNHARDT, CLYDE
Harris, Sheldon E.B., (ed.), *I Remember Clyde Bernhardt*, Philadelphia, 1986.

BILK, ACKER
Leslie, P., and P. Gwynn-Jones, *The Book Of Bilk*, London, 1961.

BISHOP, WALTER, JNR.
Bishop, Walter, *Walter Bishop (Interviewed by Marian McPartland)*.

BLAKE, EUBIE
Rose, A., *Eubie Blake*, Schirmer Books (USA).

BLEY, PAUL
Kluck, Henk, *Bley Play*, 1996.

BLUE NOTE RECORDS
Marsh, Graham, Glyn Callingham and Felix Cromey (eds.), *The Cover Art Of Blue Note Records*, Chronicle Books (USA), Collins Brown (UK), 1991.
Marsh, Graham, and Glyn Callingham (eds.), *The Cover Art Of Blue Note Records Volume 2*, Chronicle Books (USA), Collins Brown (UK), 1997.

BOLDEN, BUDDY
Marquis, D., *In Search Of Buddy Bolden, First Man Of Jazz*, Baton Rouge (USA), 1978.

BRAXTON, ANTHONY
Braxton, Anthony, *Tri-axium Writings*, Synthesis Music, 1985.
Lock, Graham, *Forces In Motion: Anthony Braxton & The Meta-reality Of Creative Music*, Quartet Books (UK), 1989.
Radno, Ronald M., *New Musical Figurations: Anthony Braxton's Cultural Critique*, University Of Chicago Press (USA), 1993.

BREUKER, WILLEM
Whitehead, Kevin, *New Dutch Swing*, Billboard Books (USA), 1998.

BRIDGES, HENRY
Evensmo, Jan, *The Tenor Saxophones Of Henry Bridges, Robert Carroll, Herschal Evans*, J. Evensmo, 1976.

BROWN, CLEO
Brown, Cleo, *Cleo Brown, Interviewed By Marion McPartland Plus Cleo Sings-Plays Piano*.

BROWN, RUTH
Brown, Ruth, with Andrew Yule, *Miss Rhythm*, Dutton (USA), Fine Books (UK), 1995.

BROWN, SANDY
Brown, Sandy, *The Jazz Manuscripts*, London, 1979.

BROZMAN, BOB
Brozman, Bob, *Rhythm In The Blues: The Bluesman's Bag Of Tricks And Licks*, Crossroads Music, 1996.

BRUBECK, DAVE
Brubeck, Dave, *Blue Rondo*, Columbia Pictures.
Brubeck, Dave, *Deluxe Piano Album*, C. Hansen II.
Brubeck, Dave, *The Genius Continues*, Columbia Pictures.
Brubeck, Dave, *The Genius Of Dave Brubeck*, Columbia Pictures.
Hall, Fred M., *It's About Time: The Dave Brubeck Story*, University Of Arkansas, Fayetteville (USA), 1996.

CALLENDER, RED
Callender, Red, and Elaine Cohen, *Unfinished Dream: The Musical World Of Red Callender*, London, 1985.

CALLOWAY, CAB
Calloway, Cab, *Of Minnie The Moocher & Me*, Thomas Crowell (USA).
Calloway, Cab, *The New Cab Calloway's Catologue*.
Calloway, Cab, *The New Cab Calloway's Hepster's Dictionary*, Derby, Connecticut (USA), 1945.

CARR, IAN
Carr, Ian, *Music Outside-Contemporary Jazz In Britain*, Latimer New Dimensions, 1973.

CARTER, BENNY
Berger, M. and E., *Benny Carter: A Life In American Music*, Metuchen, New Jersey, 1982.
Evensmo, Jan, *The Alto Saxophone, Trumpet And Clarinet Of Benny Carter, 1927-1946*, J. Evensmo, 1982.

CARTER, RON
Carter, Ron, *Building A Jazz Bass Line*, R. Carter Music , 1971.
Carter, Ron, *Spielmethode Fur Jazz-Bass*, Munchen: Edition Modern, 1968.

CARVER, WAYMAN
Evensmo, Jan, *The Flute Of Wayman Carver*, Jan Evensmo, 1983.

CHEATHAM, DOC
Cheatham, Adolphus 'Doc', *I Guess I'll Get The Papers And Go Home: The LIfe Of Doc Cheatham*, Cassell (UK), 1996.

CHRISTIAN, CHARLIE
Broadbent, Peter, *Charlie Christian: The Story Of The Seminal Electric Guitarist*, Ashley Mark, 1997.

CLARKE, KENNY 'KLOOK'
Hennessey, Mike, *Klook: The Story Of Kenny Clarke*, Quartet Books (UK), 1990.

CLAYTON, BUCK
Clayton, Buck, *Buck Clayton's Jazz World*, Macmillan, 1986.

CLOONEY, ROSEMARY
Clooney, Rosemary, *This For Remembrance*, New York.

COLEMAN, BILL
Chilton, John, *Bill Coleman On Record*, Steve Lane, 1966.
Coleman, Bill, *Trumpet Story*, Macmillan.

COLEMAN, ORNETTE
Coleman, Ornette, *A Collection Of 26 Ornette Coleman Compositions*, MJQ Music.
Litweiler, John, *Ornette Coleman: A Harmolodic Life*, W. Morrow (USA), 1995.
McRae, Barry, *Ornette Coleman*, Apollo (USA), 1988.
Spellman, A.B., *Four Lives In The Bebop Business*, Pantheon (USA), 1966.

COLLINS, LEE
Collins, Lee, *Oh, Didn't He Ramble: The Autobiography of Lee Collins*, University Of Illinois (USA), 1974.

COLTRANE, JOHN
Cole, Bill, *John Coltrane*, Da Capo (USA), 1993.
Cole, William Shadrack, *The Style Of John Coltrane*, Middletown, Connecticut (USA), 1974.
Coltrane, John, *The Artistry Of John Coltrane*, Big 3.
Davis, Brian, *John Coltrane, Discography*, B. Davis & R. Smith.
Fujioka, Yasuhiro, *John Coltrane*, Scarecrow Press (USA), 1996.
Gelatt, Tim (ed.), *About John Coltrane*, New York Jazz Museum (USA).
Nisenson, Eric, *Ascension: John Coltrane And His Quest*, Da Capo (USA), 1995.
Porter, Lewis, *John Coltrane: His Life And Music*, University Of Michigan Press (USA), 1998.
Priestley, Brian, *John Coltrane*, Apollo, 1990.
Simpkins, Cuthbert Ormond, *Coltrane*, Herndon House (USA), 1975.
Thomas, J.C., *Chasin' The Trane*, Doubleday (USA), 1975.
White, Andrew Nathaniel, *Trane 'N' Me*, Andrew's Musical Enterprises.

CONDON, EDDIE
Condon, Eddie, and Hank O'Neal, *The Eddie Condon Scrapbook Of Jazz*, Galahad Books (USA), 1973.
Condon, Eddie, and T. Sugrue, *We Called It Music*, New York, 1947.
No editor listed, *Eddie Condon's Treasury Of Jazz*, London, 1957.

COREA, CHICK
Corea, Chick, *Chick Corea*, Warner Brothers (USA).

COXHILL, LOL
Nuttall, Jeff, *The Bald Soprano*, London, 1991.

CROSBY, BOB
Chilton, John, *Stomp Off, Let's Go! The Story Of Bob Crosby's Bob Cats & Big Band*, London, 1983.

DANIELS, MIKE
Bowen, Mike, *The Mike Daniels Delta Jazz Band*, North Ferriby, 1982.

DANKWORTH, JOHN
Dankworth, John, *Jazz In Revolution*, Constable (UK), 1998.

DARENSBOURG, JOE
Darensbourg, Joe, *Jazz Odyssey: The Autobiography Of Joe Darensbourg*, Louisiana State University Press (USA), 1987.
Darensbourg, Joe, and Peter Vacher, *Telling It Like It Is*, London, 1987.

DAVIS, FRANCIS
Davis, Francis, *Bebop And Nothingness: Jazz And Pop At The End Of The Century*, Schirmer Books (USA), 1996.

DAVIS, MILES
Carner, Gary (ed.), *The Miles Davis Companion*, Schirmer (USA), Omnibus Press (UK), 1998.
Carr, Ian, *Miles Davis: A Critical Biography*, Grafton (UK), 1990.
Chambers, J., *Milestones: 1. Miles Davis, 1945-60*, Toronto, 1983.
Chambers, J., *Milestones: 2. Miles Davis Since 1960*, Toronto, 1985.
Chambers, Jack, *Milestones: The Life And Times Of Miles Davis*, Da Capo (USA), 1998.
Cole, Bill, *Miles Davis: The Early Years*, Da Capo (USA), 1995.
Davis, Miles, *Miles Davis Transcribed Solos*, J. Aebersold.
Davis, Miles, *Miles: The Autobiography*, Simon & Schuster (USA), Macmillan (UK).
Kirchner, Bill (ed.), *A Miles Davis Reader*, Smithsonian Institute Press (USA), 1998.
Long, Daryl, *Miles Davis For Beginners*, Writers & Readers (USA), 1992.
McRae, Barry, *Miles Davis*, Apollo, 1990.
Nisenson, Eric, *'Round About Midnight: A Portrait Of Miles Davis*, Da Capo (USA), 1996.
Williams, Richard, *The Man In The Green Shirt: Miles Davis*, Bloomsbury (UK), 1993.

DAVISON, WILD BILL
Willard, Hal, *The Wildest One*, Avondale Press (USA), 1997.

DEARIE, BLOSSOM
Dearie, Blossom, *Blossom Dearie (Interviewed by Marian McPartland)*.

DIAL, HARRY
Dial, Harry, *All This Jazz About Jazz*, Storyville.

DICKENSON, VIC
Selchow, Manfred, *Ding! Ding! A Bio-Discographical Scrapbook On Vic Dickenson*, Germany, 1998.

DODDS, BABY
Dodds, Warren 'Baby', and Larry Gara, *The Baby Dodds Story*, Los Angeles, 1959.

DODDS, JOHNNY
Lambert, G.E., *Johnny Dodds*, A.S. Barnes (USA), 1961.

DOLPHY, ERIC
Horricks, Raymond, *The Importance Of Being Eric Dolphy*, Costello (UK), 1990.
Reichardt, Eric, *Like A Human Voice - The Eric Dolphy Discography*.
Simosko, Vladimir, and Barry Tepperman, *Eric Dolphy: A Musical Biography & Discography*, Da Capo (USA), 1996.

DORSEY, JIMMY
Dorsey, Jimmy, *Beebs*, Robbins Music.
Dorsey, Jimmy, *Contrasts From The Solo Oodles Of Noodles*, Robbins Music.
Dorsey, Jimmy, *Dixieland Detour*, Robbins Music.
Dorsey, Jimmy, *Mood Hollywood*, Robbins Music.
Dorsey, Jimmy, *Tap Dancer's Nightmare*, Robbins Music, 1946.

DORSEY, TOMMY
Haines, Connie, with Robert B. Stone, *For Once In My Life*, Warner Books (USA), 1976.
Sanford, H., *Tommy And Jimmy: The Dorsey Years*, Arlington House (USA), 1972.

DUNBAR, TED
Dunbar, Ted, *New Approaches To Jazz Guitar*.
Dunbar, Ted, *A System Of Tonal Convergence*.

ECM RECORDS
No editor listed, *ECM: Sleeves Of Desire*, Lars Muller (Germany), Princeton Architectural Press (USA), 1996.

ELLINGTON, DUKE
Collier, James Lincoln, *Duke Ellington: Life And Times Of A Restless Genius Of Jazz*, Michael Joseph (UK), 1987.
Dance, Stanley, *The World Of Duke Ellington*, Charles Scribner (USA), 1970.
Dodson, Leon, *Adapting Selected Compositions And Arrangements Of Duke Ellington*, 1979.
Ellington, Duke, *Music Is My Mistress*, W.H. Allen (UK), 1974.
Ellington, Duke, *Autobiographie*, P. List, 1974.
Ellington, Duke, *Duke Ellington At The Piano*, Big 3.
Ellington, Mercer, *Duke Ellington In Person*, Houghton Mifflin (USA), 1978.
Franki, Ron, *Duke Ellington*, Chelsea House.
Gammond, Peter, *Duke Ellington: His Life And Music*, Apollo, 1987.
George, Don R., *Sweet Man, The Real Duke Ellington*, Putnam.
Gleason, Ralph J., *Celebrating The Duke*, Dell (USA), Little, Brown (USA), 1975.
Hasse, John Edward, *Beyond Category: The Life And Genius Of Duke Ellington*, Simon & Schuster (USA), 1993.
Jackson, Quentin Leonard, *Duke Ellington (Sound Recording)*, Duke Ellington Society, 1976.
Jewell, Derek, *Duke: A Portrait Of Duke Ellington*, London, 1977.
Rattenbury, Ken, *Duke Ellington: Jazz Composer*, Yale University Press (USA), 1991.
Schaaf, Martha E., *Duke Ellington: Young Music Master*, Bobbs-Merrill.
Timner, W.E., *Ellingtonia: The Recorded Music Of Duke Ellington & His Sidesman*, Scarecrow, 1988.
Travis, Dempsey J., *The Duke Ellington Primer*, Urban Research Press (USA), 1996.
Tucker, Mark, *The Duke Ellington Reader*, Oxford University Press, 1993.
Tucker, Michael, *Duke Ellington: The Early Years*, Bayou Press (USA), 1991.
Ulanov, Barry, *Duke Ellington*, New York: Creative Age, 1946.

ELLIS, DON
Ellis, Don, *Notebooks On Indic Music*.

EVANS, BILL (PIANIST)
Pettinger, Peter, *How My Heart Sings*, Yale University Press (USA), 1998.

EVANS, GIL
Horricks, Raymond, *Svengali, Or The Orchestra Called Gill Evans*, Hippocrene Books (USA), 1984.

EWELL, DON
Colinson, John, and Eugene Kramer, *Jazz Legacy Of Don Ewell*, Storyville, 1991.

FEATHER, LEONARD
Feather, Leonard, *Jazz Years: Earwitness To An Era*, Quartet Books (UK), 1990.
Feather, Leonard, *The Encyclopedia Of Jazz.*, Horizon Press (USA), 1955.

FEINSTEIN, MICHAEL
Feinstein, Michael, *Nice Work If You Can Get It: My Life In Rhythm And Rhyme*, Hyperion (USA), 1995.

FELDMAN, VICTOR
Schiff, Ronny S. (ed.), *Victor Feldman Fake Book*, Dick Grove.

FERGUSON, MAYNARD
Lee, William F., *Maynard Ferguson's Life In Music: The Authorized Biography*, M.F. Music (USA), 1998.

FITZGERALD, ELLA
Colin, Sid, *Ella: The Life And Times Of Ella Fitzgerald*, Elm Tree Books (UK), 1990.
Fidelman, Mark, *First Lady Of Song*, Birch Lane Press (USA), 1995.
Haskins, Jim, *Ella Fitzgerald: A Life Through Jazz*, Hodder & Stoughton (UK), 1991.
Nicholson, Stuart, *Ella Fitzgerald*, Gollancz (UK), Da Capo (USA), 1993.

FOSTER, GEORGE 'POPS'
Foster, G.M., T. Stoddard and R. Russell, *Pops Foster: The Autobiography Of A New Orleans Jazzman*, Berkeley (USA), 1971.

FREEMAN, BUD
Freeman, Bud, *Crazeology*, University Of Illinois Press (USA).

GARNER, ERROLL
Doran, James M., *Erroll Garner, The Most Happy Piano*, Rutgers University (USA), 1985.

GETZ, STAN
Astrup, Arne, *The Stan Getz Discography*, A. Astrup, 1978.
Kirkpatrick, Ron, *Stan Getz: An Appreciation Of His Recorded Work*, Zany Publications (UK), 1992.
Maggin, Donald, *Stan Getz: A Life In Jazz*, W. Morrow (USA), 1996.
Palmer, Richard, *Stan Getz*, Apollo, 1988.

GILLESPIE, DIZZY
Evensmo, Jan, *The Trumpets Of Dizzy Gillespie, 1937-1943*, Irving Randolph, Joe Thomas, Jan Evensmo, 1982.
Frazer, Alan, *Dizzy: To Be Or Not To Bop*, Quartet Books (UK), 1990.
Gillespie, Dizzy, *Dizzy Gillespie Blows Kerouac*, Thornwood Music.
Horricks, Raymond, *Dizzy Gillespie And The Be-Bop Revolution*, Spellmount, 1984.
James, M., *Dizzy Gillespie*, New York, 1978.
Lees, Gene, *Waiting for Dizzy*, Oxford University Press, 1992.
McRae, Barry, *Dizzy Gillespie: His Life & Times*, Universe Books, 1988.
Tanner, Lee (ed.), *Dizzy: John Birks Gillespie In His 75th Year*, Pomegranate Artbooks, 1993.

GLASS, PHILIP
Kostelanetz, Richard (ed.), *Writings On Glass: Essays, Original Writings, Interviews, Criticism*, Schirmer Books (USA), 1997.

GOLSON, BENNY
Golson, Benny, *The Genius Of Benny Golson*, Columbia Pictures.

GONELLA, NAT
Brown, Ron, and Cyril Brown, *The Nat Gonella Story*, Milestone, 1985.
Gonella, Nat, *Modern Style Of Trumpet Playing*, London, 1935.

GOODMAN, BENNY
Collier, James Lincoln, *Benny Goodman And The Swing Era* , Oxford University Press, 1990.
Connor, D. Russell, *Benny Goodman: Listen To His Legacy*, Metuchen (USA), 1988.
Connor, D. Russell and Warren W. Hicks, *BG On The Record: A Bio-Discography Of Benny Goodman*, Arlington House (UK), 1969.
Crowther, Bruce, *Benny Goodman*, Apollo, 1988.
Firestone, Ross, *Swing, Swing, Swing: The Life And Times Of Benny Goodman*, Hodder & Stoughton (UK), 1992.
Goodman, Benny, *Benny, King Of Swing*, Thames & Hudson, 1979.
Goodman, Benny, and Irving Kolodin, *The Kingdom Of Swing*, New York, 1939.

GORDON, DEXTER
Britt, Stan, *Long Tall Dexter*, Quartet Books (UK), 1989.

GRAPPELLI, STÉPHANE
Horricks, Raymond, *Stephane Grappelli, Or, The Violin With Wings*, Da Capo (USA).
Smith, Geoffrey, *Stephane Grappelli: A Biography*, Pavilion (USA), 1990.

HAMPTON, LIONEL
Hampton, Lionel, *Hamp*, Warner Books (USA), 1989.

HARVEY, EDDIE
Harvey, Eddie, *Jazz Piano*, Hodder & Stoughton, 1977.

HAWKINS, COLEMAN
Chilton, John, *The Song Of The Hawk*, Quartet Books (UK), 1990.
James, Burnett, *Coleman Hawkins*, Hippocrene Books (USA), 1984.
Villetard, Jean François, *Coleman Hawkins Volume 1 (1922-44), Volume 2 (1945-57)*.

HECKSTALL-SMITH, DICK
Heckstall-Smith, Dick, *The Safest Place In The World*, Quartet Books (UK), 1989.

HENDERSON, FLETCHER
Allen, W., *Hendersonia: The Music Of Fletcher Henderson And His Musicians*, Highland Park, New Jersey (USA), 1973.

HERMAN, WOODY
Herman, Woody, *The Woodchopper's Ball*, E.P. Dutton.
Herman, Woody, *Your Father's Moustache*, Mayfair Music.
Morrill, Dexter, *Woody Herman: A Guide To The Big Band Recordings, 1936-87*, Greenwood Press, 1991.
Voce, Steve, *Woody Herman*, Apollo, 1990.

HINES, EARL 'FATHA'
Courlander, Harold, *The World Of Earl Hines*, Scribners (USA).

HINTON, MILT
Hinton, Milt, and David G. Berger, *Bass Line*, Temple University Press (USA), 1988.

HODES, ART
Hansen, Chadwick (ed.), *Hot Man: The Life Of Art Hodes*, Bayou Press (USA), 1992.
Hodes, Art, and Chadwick Hansen (ed.), *Selections From The Gutter*, University Of California Press (USA).

HORN, PAUL
Horn, Paul, with Lee Underwood, *Inside Paul Horn: The Spiritual Odessey Of A Universal Traveller*, Harper Collins (USA), 1991.

HORN, SHIRLEY
Horn, Shirley, *Shirley Horn (Interviewed By Marian McPartland)*.

HORNE, LENA
Haskins J., and K. Benson, *Lena: A Personal And Professional Biography.*, New York.
Horne, Lena, *In Person.*
Horne, Lena, with Richard Schikel, *Lena*, New York, 1966.

HUGHES, SPIKE
Hughes, Spike, *Opening Bars*, London, 1946.
Hughes, Spike, *Second Movement*, London, 1952.

JAMES, BOB
James, Bob, *Bob James And His Music*, Columbia Pictures.

JARRETT, KEITH
Carr, Ian, *Keith Jarrett: The Man And His Music*, Grafton (UK), 1991.

JOHNSON, BUDD
Evensmo, Jan, *The Tenor Saxophones Of Budd Johnson, Cecil Scott, Elmer Williams, Dick Wilson*, Evensmo, 1977.

JOHNSON, BUNK
Hillman, Christopher, *Bunk Johnson: His Life & Times*, Universe Books, 1988.
Sonnier, Austin H., *Willie Geary Bunk 'Johnson'*, Crescendo.

JOHNSON, JAMES P.
Brown, Scott E., *James P. Johnson*, Rutgers University (USA), 1986.
Trolle, Frank H., *James P. Johnson: Father Of The Stride Piano*, Micrography, 1981.

JOHNSON, PETE
Mauerer, Hans J., *The Pete Johnson Story*, Hans J. Mauerer, 1965.

JONES, QUINCY
Horricks, Raymond, *Quincy Jones*, Hippocrene Books (USA), 1985.

JOPLIN, SCOTT
Gammond, Peter, *Scott Joplin And The Ragtime Era*, London, 1975.
Reed, A.W., *The Life And Works Of Scott Joplin*, University Of North Carolina (USA), 1973.

KEANE, ELLSWORTH 'SHAKE'
Keane, Shake, *The Volcano Suite*, 1979.
Keane, Shake, *One A Week With Water.*

KENTON, STAN
Arganian, Lillian, *Stan Kenton: The Man And His Music*, East Lansing, 1990.
Easton, Carol, *Straight Ahead: The Story Of Stan Kenton*, W. Morrow (USA), 1973.
Gabel, Edward F., *Stan Kenton: The Early Years*, Balboa Books (USA), 1995.
Lee, William F., *Stan Kenton*, Creative Press Of Los Angeles (USA), 1980.

KIRK, ANDY
Kirk, Andy, *Twenty Years On Wheels*, University Of Michigan Press (USA), 1989.

KRUPA, GENE
Crowther, Bruce, *Gene Krupa*, Omnibus Press (UK), 1988.

LACY, STEVE
Lacy, Steve, *Findings: My Experience With The Soprano Saxophone*, Outre Mesure (France), 1996.

LAINE, CLEO
Collier, Graham (ed.), *Cleo And John*, Quartet Books (UK), 1976.
Laine, Cleo, *Cleo*, Simon & Schuster (UK), 1994.
Stoller, Lee, with Pete Chaney, *Cristy Lane: One Day At A Time*, St. Martins Paperbacks (USA), 1993.

LEE, PEGGY
Lee, Peggy, *Miss Peggy Lee*, Donald I. Fine (USA), 1990.

LEWIS, GEORGE (CLARINET)
Bethell, T., *George Lewis: A Jazzman From New Orleans*, Berkeley (USA), 1977.

LEWIS, VIC
Lewis, Vic, and Tony Barrow, *Music & Maiden Overs: My Show Business Life*, Chatto & Windus (UK), 1987.

LIEBMAN, DAVE
Fisher, Larry, *Miles Davis And David Liebman: Jazz Connections*, Edward Mellen Press (USA), 1996.
Liebman, David, *David Liebman: Self-Portrait Of A Jazz Artist*, Advance Music, Rottenburg (Germany), 1996.

LUNCEFORD, JIMMIE
Lyttkens, Bertil, *The Jimmie Lunceford Legacy*, Lyttkens, Grevgatan (Sweden), 1998.

LYTTELTON, HUMPHREY
Lyttelton, Humphrey, *Take It From The Top*, Robson Books (UK), 1975.
Lyttelton, Humphrey, *I Play As I Please*, Pan Books (UK), 1958.
Lyttelton, Humphrey, *Second Chorus*, London.
Lyttelton, Humphrey, *The Best Of Jazz, i: Basin Street To Harlem*, London, 1978.
Purser, Julian, *Humph*, Collectors Items, 1985.

MAIRANTS, IVOR
Mairants, Ivor, *Great Jazz Guitarists*, Music Maker Books (UK), 1994.
Mairants, Ivor, *My Fifty Fretting Years*, 1980.

MAKEBA, MIRIAM
Makeba, Miriam, with James Hall, *Makeba: My Story*, Bloomsbury (UK), 1988.

MANNE, SHELLY
Brand, Jack, and Bill Korst, *Shelly Manne: Sounds Of The Different Drummer*, Percussion Express, 1998.

MARSALIS, WYNTON
Marsalis, Wynton, and Frank Stewart, *Sweet Swing Blues On The Road*, W. Norton (USA), 1994.

MCGREGOR, CHRIS
McGregor, Maxine, *Chris McGregor And The Brotherhood Of Breath*, Bamberger Books (USA), 1997.

MCKINNEY'S COTTON PICKERS
Chilton, John, *McKinney's Music: A Bio-Discography Of McKinney's Cotton Pickers*, London, 1978.

MCLAUGHLIN, JOHN
McLaughlin, John, *John McLaughlin And The Mahavishnu Orchestra*, Warner Brothers (USA), 1976.

MCPARTLAND, MARIAN
McPartland, Marian, *All In Good Time*, Oxford University Press, 1987.

MCRAE, CARMEN
McRae, Carmen, *Carmen McRae (Interviewed by Marian McPartland).*

MELLY, GEORGE
Melly, George, *Scouse Mouse*, Futura (UK), 1985.
Melly, George, *Rum, Bum & Concertina*, Weidenfeld & Nicholson (UK), 1977.
Melly, George, *Mellymobile, 1970-1981*, Robson Books (UK), 1982.
Melly, George, *Owning-Up*, Penguin, 1970.
Melly, George, *Revolt Into Style*, Oxford University Press, 1990.

MENGELBERG, MISHA
Whitehead, Kevin, *New Dutch Swing*, Billboard Books (USA), 1998.

MILLER, GLENN
Butcher, Geoffrey, *Next To A Letter From Home*, Sphere (UK), 1990.
Polic, Edward F., *Sustineo Alas/I Sustain The Wings*, Scarecrow Methchen (USA), 1989.
Simon, George Thomas, *Glenn Miller & His Orchestra*, Thomas Crowell (USA), 1974.

MINGUS, CHARLES
Coleman, Janet, *Mingus/Mingus*, Creative Arts Book, 1989.
Mingus, Charles, *Beneath The Underdog*, Payback Press (USA), 1995.
Mingus, Charles, *Revelations*, Margun Music.
Priestley, Brian, *Mingus: A Critical Biography*, Quartet Books (UK), 1982.
Weber, Horst, *Charles Mingus, Sein Leben, Seine Musik, Seine Schallplatten*, Oreos, 1984.

MONK, THELONIOUS
Bijl, L., and F. Canté, *Monk On Records: A Discography Of Thelonious Monk.*
De Wilde, Laurent, *Monk*, Marlowe & Co. (USA), 1997.
Fitterling, Thomas, *Thelonious Monk: His Life And Music*, Berkeley Hills (USA), 1987.
Gourse, Leslie, *Straight, No Chaser: The Life And Genius Of Thelonious Monk*, Schirmer Books (USA), 1997.
Monk, Thelonious, *Thelonious Monk*, Consolidated Music.
Monk, Thelonious, *Works, Instrumental*, Consolidated Music.

MONTEREY JAZZ FESTIVAL
Minor, William, *Monterey Jazz Festival: Forty Legendary Years*, Angel City Press (USA), 1997.

MONTGOMERY, WES
Ingram, Adrian, *Wes Montgomery*, Ashley Mark, 1985.

MOORE, DUDLEY
Donovan, Paul, *Dudley*, W.H. Allen (UK), 1988.
Moore, Dudley, *Off Beat: Dudley Moore's Book Of Musical Anecdotes*, Robson Books (UK), 1992.
Paskin, Barbara, *Dudley Moore: The Authorized Biography*, Sidgwick & Jackson (UK), 1997.

MORTON, JELLY ROLL
Balliett, Whitney, *Jelly Roll, Jabbo, And Fats*, Oxford University Press, 1983.
Charters, Samuel B., *Jelly Roll Morton's Last Night At The Jungle Inn*, Marion Boyars (UK), 1989.
Kennedy, Rick, *Jelly Roll, Bix And Hoagy: Gennett Studios And The Birth Of Recorded Jazz*, Indiana University Press (USA), 1994.
Lomax, Alan, *Mister Jelly Roll*, Berkeley: University Of California Press (USA), 1950.
Williams, M., *Jelly Roll Morton*, London, 1962.

MULLIGAN, GERRY
Horricks, Raymond, *Gerry Mulligan's Ark*, Apollo, 1986.
Klinkowitz, Jerome, *Listen: Gerry Mulligan: An Aural Narrative In Jazz*, Schirmer Books (USA), 1991.

NEWTON, JAMES
Newton, James, *Improvising Flute*, 1990.

NICHOLS, HERBIE
Spellman, A.B., *Four Lives In The Bebop Business.*

O'DAY, ANITA
O'Day, Anita, with George Eells, *High Times Hard Times*, New York, 1981.

OLIVER, JOE 'KING'
Albertson, Chris, and Brian Rust, *King Joe Oliver*, Walter C. Allen, 1955.
Williams, M., *King Oliver And Kings Of Jazz*, London and Newark, 1960.
Wright, Laurie, *King Oliver*, London, 1987.

PARKER, CHARLIE 'BIRD'
Giddins, Gary, *Celebrating Bird: The Triumph Of Charlie Parker*, Hodder & Stoughton (UK), 1987.
Harrison, M., *Charlie Parker*, London, 1960.
Isacoff, Stuart, *Charlie Parker*, Amsco, 1984.
Jepsen, Jorgen Grunnet, *Discography Of Charlie Parker*, Debut Records.

Koch, Lawrence O., *Yardbird Suite*, Bowling Green State University Popular Press.
Miller, Mark, *Cool Blues*, Nightwood Editions.
Parker, C., and F. Paudras, *To Bird With Love*, Poitiers, 1981.
Parker, Charles Christopher, *Charlie Parker Omnibook*, Joe Goldfeder Music.
Priestley, Brian, *Charlie Parker*, Tunbridge Wells (UK), 1984.
Reisner, R, *Bird: The Legend Of Charlie Parker*, New York, 1961.
Russell, Ross, *Bird Lives! The High Life & Hard Times Of Charlie (Yardbird) Parker*, Da Capo (USA), 1996.
Watts, Charlie, *From One Charlie to Another*, UFO Jazz (UK), 1991.
Woideck , Carl, *Charlie Parker: His Music And Life*, University Of Michigan (USA), 1997.

PARKER, ERROL
Parker, Errol, *A Flat Tire On My Ass*, Cadence Jazz Books (USA), 1996.

PASTORIUS, JACO
Milkowski, Bill, *Jaco: The Extraordinary And Tragic Life Of Jaco Pastorius*, Miller Freeman (USA), 1995.

PAYNE, JACK
Payne, Jack, *Signature Tune.*
Payne, Jack, *This Is Jack Payne.*

PEPPER, ART
Pepper, Art and Laurie, *Straight Life: The Story Of Art Pepper*, Da Capo (USA), 1979.

PETERSON, OSCAR
Lees, Gene, *Oscar Peterson: The Will To Swing*, Lester & Orpen Dennys, 1988.
Peterson, Oscar, *Oscar Peterson Highlights Jazz Piano*, Hansen House, 1980.

PONTY, JEAN-LUC
Ponty, Jean-Luc, *The Musical Styles Of Jean-Luc Ponty*, Warner Brothers (USA).

PORTER, ROY
Porter, Roy, *There And Back*, Bayou Press (USA), 1991.

POWELL, BUD
Groves, Alan with Shipton, Alyn, *The Glass Enclosure: The Life Of Bud Powell*, Bayou (USA), 1993.
Paudras, Francis, *Dance Of The Infidels: A Portrait Of Bud Powell*, Da Capo (USA), 1998.
Safane, Clifford Jay (ed.), *Bud Powell*, Consolidated Music.

PREVIN, ANDRÉ
Previn, Andre, *No Minor Chords (My Days In Hollowood)*, Doubleday (USA), 1992.

PRICE, SAMMY
Price, Sammy, and Caroline Richmond (ed.), *What Do They Want? A Jazz Autobiography*, Bayou Press (USA), 1990.

RAZAF, ANDY
Singer, Barry, *Black And Blue: The Life And Lyrics Of Andy Razaf*, Schirmer (USA), 1992.

REINHARDT, DJANGO
Abrams, M., *The Book Of Django*, Los Angeles, 1973.
Cruickshank, Ian (ed.), *Django's Gypsies: The Mystique Of Django Reinhardt*, Ashley Mark Publishing (UK), 1996.
Delaunay, C., *Django Reinhardt*, London.

RICH, BUDDY
Balliett, Whitney, *Improvising.*
Meriwether, Doug, *Mister, I Am The Band!: Buddy Rich His Life And Travels*, National Drum Association (USA), 1998.

ROLLINI, ARTHUR
Rollini, Arthur, *Thirty Years With The Big Bands*, London, 1987.

ROLLINS, SONNY
Baker, David N., *The Jazz Style Of Sonny Rollins*, Studio Publications/Recordings.
Blancq, Charles Clement, *Sonny Rollins: The Journey Of A Jazzman*, Twayne, 1983.
Gerard, Charley (ed.), *Sonny Rollins*, Consolidated Music.

RÜEGG, MATTHIAS
No author listed, *Vienna Art Orchestra 1977-1997*, Falter Verlag, 1997.

RUSSELL, PEE WEE
Hilbert, Robert, *Pee Wee Russell: The Life Of A Jazzman*, Oxford University Press, 1993.
Hilbert, Robert, with David Niven, *Pee Wee Speaks: A Discography Of Pee Wee Russell*, Scarecrow Press (USA), 1993.

SAMPLE, JOE
Sample, Joe, *Joe Sample*, IMP (UK).

SCHULLER, GUNTHER
Schuller, Gunther, *Early Jazz: Its Roots And Musical Delevopment*, New York, 1968.
Schuller, Gunther, *The Swing Era: The Development Of Jazz 1930-1945*, New York, 1989.

SCOTT, RONNIE
Fordham, John, *Let's Join Hands And Contact The Living*, Elm Tree Books (UK), 1986.
Fordham, John, *Jazz Man: The Amazing Story Of Ronnie Scott And His Club*, Kyle Cathie (UK), 1994.
Grime, Kitty (ed.), *Jazz At Ronnie Scott's*, Robert Hale (UK), 1979.

SCOTT, TOM
No author listed, *Tom Scott*, Warner Brothers (USA).

SCOTT-HERON, GIL
Scott-Heron, Gil, *The Vulture And The Nigger Factory*, Payback Press (USA), 1996.

SHAPIRO, HELEN
Janson, John S., *Helen Shapiro: Pop Princess*, Four Square (UK), 1963.
Shapiro, Helen, *Walking Back To Happiness*.

SHORE, DINAH
Cassidy, B., *Dinah!*, New York, 1979.

SHORT, BOBBY
Short, Bobby, *Black & White Baby*, New York, 1971.
Short, Bobby with Robert Mackintosh, *The Life And Times Of A Saloon Slinger*, Clarkson Potter (USA), 1996.

SIDRAN, BEN
Sidran, Ben, *Black Talk*, Payback Press (USA), 1995.

SIMONE, NINA
Simone, Nina, with Stephen Cleary, *I Put A Spell On You: The Autobiography Of Nina Simone*, Ebury Press (UK), 1991.

SIMS, ZOOT
Astrup, Arne, *The John Haley Sims (Zoot Sims) Discography*, Dansk Historisk Handbogsforlag.

SMITH, STUFF
Barnett, Anthony, *Desert Sands: The Recordings And Performances Of Stuff Smith*, Allardyce Books (UK), 1995.

SOFT MACHINE
Allen, Daevid, *Gong Dreaming*, Gong Appreciation Society (UK), 1995.

STEWART, REX
Stewart, Rex, with Stanley Dance, *Jazz Masters Of The Thirties*, New York and London, 1972.
Stewart, Rex, *Rex Stewart's 'Warm-Up' Book*, Leeds Music.

STRAYHORN, BILLY
Hadju, David, *Lush Life: A Biography Of Billy Strayhorn*, Farrar, Straus & Giroux (USA), Granta (UK), 1996.

SUN RA
Campbell, Robert, *The Earthly Recordings Of Sun Ra*, Cadence Jazz Books (USA).
Sun Ra, *The Immeasurable Equation*.
Szwed, John E., *Space Is The Place: The Lives And Times Of Sun Ra*, Pantheon (USA), Payback Press (UK), 1997.

TATUM, ART
Distler, Jed (ed.), *Art Tatum*, Music Sales.
Laubich, Arnold, *Art Tatum, A Guide To His Recorded Music*, Scarecrow (USA), 1982.
Lester, James, *Too Marvellous For Words: The Life And Genius Of*, Oxford University Press, 1994.

TAYLOR, BILLY
Taylor, Billy, *Jazz Combo Arranging*, C. Hansen Educational Music & Books.
Taylor, Billy, *Jazz Piano*, W.C. Brown, 1983.
Taylor, Billy, *Jazz Piano: History And Development*, Dubuque, 1982.
Taylor, Billy, *Piano Solos*, C. Hansen.
Taylor, Billy, *Sketches For Jazz Trio*, Duane Music.
Taylor, Billy, *The History And Development Of Jazz Piano*, Amherst, Massachusetts (USA), 1975.

TEAGARDEN, JACK
Smith, Jay D., and Len Guttridge, *Jack Teagarden: The Story Of A Jazz Maverick*, Cassell (UK), 1960.
Walters Jnr., H., *Jack Teagarden's Music*, Stanhope, New Jersey (USA), 1960.

THIELE, BOB
Golden, Bob, *What A Wonderful World*, (USA), 1994.

TORMÉ, MEL
Tormé, Mel, *The Other Side Of The Rainbow*, W. Morrow (USA), 1970.
Tormé, Mel, *Mel Tormé: It Wasn't All Velvet*, Viking (USA), 1988.

TRUMBAUER, FRANK
Trumbauer, Frank, *Tailspin*, Robbins Music.

TURNER, BRUCE
Turner, Bruce, *Hot Air, Cool Music*, London, 1984.

TYNER, MCCOY
Tyner, McCoy, *Fly With The Wind*, Fantasy, 1986.

VAUGHAN, SARAH
Gourse, Leslie, *Sassy - The Life Of Sarah Vaughan*, Mainstream, 1993.

WALLER, FATS
Davies, R.T., *The Music Of Fats Waller*.
Fox, Charles, *Fats Waller*, Barnes, 1961.
Kirkeby, E.W., D.P. Schiedt and S. Traill, *Ain't Misbehavin': The Story Of Fats Waller*, Dodd Mead & Co./Da Capo (USA).
Machlin, Paul S., *Stride, The Music Of Fats Waller*, Macmillan, 1985.
Shipton, Alyn, *Fats Waller: His Life & Times*, Universe Books, 1988.
Sill, Harold D., *Misbehavin' With Fats*, Addison-Wesley.
Vance, Joel, *Fats Waller: His Life And Times*, Contemporary Books (USA), 1977.
Waller, Maurice, and Anthony Calabrese, *Fats Waller*.

WALLINGTON, GEORGE
Wallington, George, *George Wallington (Interviewed by Marian McPartland)*.

WASHINGTON, DINAH
Haskins, James, *Dinah Washington: Queen Of The Blues*, New York, 1987.

WATERS, ETHEL
Waters, Ethel, and C. Samuels, *His Eye Is On The Sparrow*, London, 1951.

WEATHER REPORT
Zawinul, Josef, *The Best Of Weather Report*, Warner Brothers (USA).

WEBSTER, BEN
Langhorn, Peter, and Thorbjorn Sjogren, *Ben Webster: A Discography*, Jazzmedia (USA), 1998.

WELK, LAWRENCE
No author listed, *Welk, Laurence, Wunnerful, Wunnerful*, New York, 1971.
Welk, Lawrence, *Ah-One, Ah-Two: Life With My Musical Family*, New York, 1974.

WELLS, DICKY
Wells, Dicky, as told to Stanley Dance, *The Night People*, Crescendo, Boston (USA), 1971.

WHITEMAN, PAUL
Johnson, Carl, *A Paul Whiteman Chronology, 1890-1967*, Williams College, 1978.

WILBER, BOB
Wilber, Bob, with Derek Webster, *Music Was Not Enough*, New York and London, 1987.

WILDER, ALEC
Balliett, Whitney, *Alec Wilder And His Friends*, Houghton Mifflin (USA), 1974.

WILLIAMS, CLARENCE
Lord, Tom, *Clarence Williams*, Storyville, 1976.

WILSON, TEDDY
Ligthart, Artie, and Humphrey Van Loo, *Teddy Wilson Talks Jazz*, Cassell (UK/USA), 1997.
No author listed, *The Genius Of Teddy Wilson*, Big 3.

YOUNG, LESTER
Buchmann-Moller, Frank, *You Got To Be Original Man! The Music of Lester Young*, Greenwood Press, 1989.
Buchmann-Moller, Frank, *You Just Fight For Your Life: The Story Of Lester Young*, Greenwood Press, 1989.
Evensmo, Jan, *The Tenor Saxophone And Clarinet Of Lester Young, 1936-1949*, Jan Evensmo, 1983.
Gelly, Dave, *Lester Young*, Tunbridge Wells (UK), 1984.
Luckey, Robert A., *A Study Of Lester Young And His Influence Upon His Contemporaries.*
Porter, Lewis, *A Lester Young Reader*, Smithsonian Institution Press (USA), 1992.
Porter, Lewis, *Lester Young*, Twayne.

Bibliography by Author

Abe, K., *Jazz Giants*, Billboard (USA), 1988.
Adderly, Julian, *Cannonball Adderly's Complete Jazz Fake Book*, Silhouette Music, 1976.
Aebersold, Jamey, *A New Approach To Jazz Improvisation*, Jamey Aebersold.
Agostinelli, Anthony J., *The Newport Jazz Festival, Rhode Island, 1954-1971*, Agostinelli.
Akiyoshi, Toshiko, *Transience*, Kendor Music.
Akiyoshi, Toshiko, *Notorious Tourist From The East*, Kendor Music.
Akiyoshi, Toshiko, *American Ballad*, Kendor Music.
Alkyer, Frank (ed.), *Down Beat 60 Years Of Jazz*, Hal Leonard Publications (USA), 1995.
Allen, Daniel, *78-RPM Phonorecords In The Jazz Archive*, Toronto, 1972.
Allen, W.C., *Studies In Jazz Discography*, New Brunswick, 1971.
Almeida, Laurindo, *Bossa Guitarra*, Criterion.
Amstell, Billy, *Don't Fuss, Mr. Ambrose*, Spellmount, 1986.
Andriessen, Jurriaan, *Pasticcio-Finale Voor Symfonieorkest*, Donemus.
Angstmann, Freddy J., *Jazz*, Silva-Verlag.
Araque, Luis, *Defensa De La Musica De Jazz*, Ediciones Alguero, 1946.
Archambault, Gilles, *Discographie De Jazz*, Service De Publicite-Radio De Radio-Canada, 1982.
Arkansas Arts Center, *Catalog Of The John D. Reid Collection Of Early American Jazz*, Arkansas Arts Center, Little Rock (USA), 1975.
Arkansas Arts Center, Catalog Of The John D. Reid Collection, *Arkansas Arts Center*, Little Rock (USA), 1975.
Asbury, H., *The French Quarter: An Informal History Of The New Orleans Underworld*, New York, 1937.
Asch, Glenn, and David Reiner, *Mel Bay's Deluxe Anthology Of Jazz Violin Styles*, Mel Bay, 1982.
Attali, Jacques, *Noise: The Political Economy Of Music*, Manchester University Press, 1986.
Averill, Gage, *A Day For The Hunter, A Day For The Prey: Popular Music And Power In Haiti*, University Of Chicago Press (USA), 1997.
Ayoub, Nick, *Joey's Place*, Dorn.
Baats, Harry, *All Kind Of Music*, Muziekuitgeverij Van Teeseling.
Backus, R., *A Political History Of Jazz*, Chicago, 1977.
Backus, Rob, *Fire Music*, Vanguard Books (USA), 1976.
Baker, David, *Improvisational Patterns, The Bepop Era*, Charles Colin.
Baker, David N., *Contemporary Techniques For The Trombone*, C. Colin.
Baker, David N. (ed.), *New Perspectives On Jazz*, Smithsonian Institution (USA), 1991.
Balcerak, Jozef, *Magia Jazzu*, Krajowa Agenija Wydawnicza, 1981.
Balliett, Whitney, *Goodbye And Other Messages*, Oxford University Press (UK), 1992.
Balliett, Whitney, *Night Creature: Journal Of Jazz 1975-80*, Oxford University Press, 1981.
Balliett, Whitney, *New York Notes*, Houghton Mifflin (USA), 1976.
Balliett, Whitney, *Improvising: Sixteen Jazz Musicians And Their Art*, Oxford, 1990.
Balliett, Whitney, *Goodbyes And Other Messages: Journal Of Jazz 1981-1990*, Oxford University Press, 1992.
Balliett, Whitney, *Ecstasy At The Onion*, Bobbs-Merrill, 1971.
Balliett, Whitney, *American Singers: Twenty-Seven Portraits In Song*, Oxford University Press, 1988.
Balliett, Whitney, *American Musicians: Fifty-Six Portraits In Jazz*, Oxford University Press, 1990.
Balliett, Whitney, *Ecstasy At The Onion*, Bobbs-Merrill (USA), 1971.
Baraka, Imamu Amiri, *The Music*, W. Morrow (USA).
Baraka, Imamu Amiri, *Blues People: Negro Music In White America*, W. Morrow (USA), 1963.
Barlow, William, and Thomas L. Morgan, *From Cakewalks To Concert Halls*, Elliott & Clark Publishing (USA), 1992.
Barnet, Charles, *Those Swinging Years*, Louisiana State University Press (USA).
Barr, Walter Laning, *The Jazz Studies Curriculum*, Tempe, Arizona (USA), 1974.
Barreto, Jorge Lima, *Revolucao Do Jazz*, Editorial Inova Limitada, 1972.
Barreto, Jorge Lima, *Grande Musica Negro*, Edicoes RES, 1975.
Barreto, Jorge Lima, *Anarqueologia Do Jazz*, Regra Do Jogo, 1984.
Bart, Teddy, *Inside Music City USA Nashville*, Aurora (USA), 1970.
Basie, Bill 'Count', *Good Morning Blues*, Grafton, 1990.
Batashev, Aleksei Nikolaevich, *Sovetskii Dzhaz. Ist. Ocherk. Pod Red.*, Moskva, Muzyka, 1972.

Baumgartel, Willy, *Rhythmisch-Stilistische Studien Fur Jazzposaune*, Deutscher Verlag Fur Musik.
Beckman, Monica, *Gimnasia Jazz*, Editorial Stadium.
Beeftink, Herman, *Jazz For Flute*, Muziekuiktgeverij van Teeseling.
Bellson, Louis, *Guide To Big Band Drumming*, C. Hansen.
Benham, Patrick, *Mostly Jazz*, G. Ricordi.
Berendt, Joachim E., *Jazz Book: From Ragtime To Fusion And Beyond*, L. Hill Books, (USA), 1993.
Berendt, Joachim Ernst, *The New Jazz Book, A History And Guide*, Hill and Wang, 1962.
Berendt, Joachim Ernst, *The Jazz Book*, Lawrence Hill (USA) Granada (UK), 1975.
Berendt, Joachim Ernst, *Photo-Story Des Jazz*, Kruger.
Berendt, Joachim Ernst, *Die Story Des Jazz*, Deutsche Verlags-Anstalt.
Berendt, Joachim Ernst, *Jazz, A Photo History*, Schirmer (USA).
Berendt, Joachim Ernst, *Das Grosse Jazzbuch*, Fischer Taschenbuch (Germany), 1986.
Berger, E. (ed.), *Annual Review Of Jazz*, Scarecrow Press (USA), 1994.
Bergerot, Franck, and Arnaud Merlin, *Story Of Jazz, Bop And Beyond*, Thames & Hudson (UK), 1993.
Berigan, Bunny, *Modern Trumpet Studies*, Robbins Music.
Berindei, Mihai, *Dictionar De Jazz*, Editura Stiintifica Si Enciclopedica, 1976.
Berle, Arnie, *Complete Handbook For Jazz Improvisation*, Music Sales, 1972.
Berlin, Irving, *Blue Skies*, Blue Note.
Berliner, Paul F., *Thinking In Jazz: The Infinite Art Of Improvisation*, University Of Chicago Press (USA), 1993.
Bernhardt, Clyde, *I Remember: Eighty Years Of Black Entertainment Big Band And Blues*, Pennsylvania University Press (USA), 1986.
Bernstein, Leonard, *Prelude, Fugue And Riffs*, Schirmer (USA).
Berry, Jason, *Up from the Cradle Of Jazz: New Orleans Music Since The War*, Da Capo (USA), 1992.
Best, William, *For Sentimental Reasons*, Capitol.
Bettonville, A., *Paranoia Du Jazz*, Brussels, 1939.
Biderbost, Marc, *Le Guide Marabout De La Musique Et Du Disque De Jazz*, Marabout.
Bird, Christiane, *The Jazz & Blues Lover's Guide To The U.S.*, Addison Wesley (UK), 1991.
Bisceglia, Jacques, *Black And White Fantasy*, Corps 9 Editions.
Bisset, Andrew, *Black Roots, White Flowers*, Golden Press, 1979.
Blackstone, O., *Index To Jazz*, Fairfax, Virginia (USA).
Blake, Ran, *A Collection Of Third Stream Compositions*, Margun Music.
Blanq, Charles Clement, *Melodic Improvisation In American Jazz*, 1977.
Blatny, Pavel, *In Mod Classico*, Editio Supraphon, 1982.
Blesh, Rudi, *Eight Lives In Jazz*, Hayden (USA), 1971.
Blesh, Rudi, *Combo*, Chilton Book, 1971.
Blesh, Rudi, *Shining Trumpets*, Da Capo (USA), 1975.
Blesh, Rudi, and Harriet Janis, *They All Played Ragtime*, Alfred A. Knopf (USA), 1971.
Bohlander, Carlo, *Reclams Jazzfuhrer*, Reclam, 1970.
Bolelli, Franco, *Musica Creativa*, Squilibri, 1978.
Bolling, Claude, *Jazz Piano Course*, Hansen House, 1980.
Bolocan, David, *Jazz, Jazz, Jazz, Jazz*, Tab Books, 1985.
Bonnemere, Eddie, *Papers*, 1940.
Bonnemere, Eddie, *Help Me, Jesus*.
Bonnemere, Eddie, *Educational Cross Section*.
Boogaard, Bernard Van Den, *Panta Rhei*, Donemus.
Borneman, E., *Boogie-Woogie*, Just Jazz (UK), 1957.
Bragaglia, A.G., *Jazz Band*, Milan, 1929.
Brandman, Russella, *The Evolution Of Jazz Dance From Folk Origins To Concert Stage*, 1977.
Breton, Marcela, *Hot And Cool: Jazz Short Stories*, Bloomsbury (UK), 1991.
Britt, Stan, *The Jazz Guitarist*, Sterling, 1984.
Broadbent, Alan, *Adam's Apple*.
Brooks Fox, Jules and Jo, *The Melody Lingers On*, Fifthian Press (USA), 1996.
Broonzy, William, *Big Bill Blues*, Oak Publications (USA), 1964.
Brown, Chris, *The Family Album*, Hitman, 1980.
Brown, Marion, *Faces And Places*, 1976.
Brown, Marion, *Recollections*, Juergen A. Schmitt .
Brown, Ray, *An Introduction To Jazz Improvisation*, Edward B. Marks.
Brown, Ron, *Georgia On My Mind*, Milestone.
Brown, Sandy, *The McJazz Manuscripts*, Faber & Faber (UK), 1979.
Brown, Theodore Dennis, *A History And Analysis Of Jazz Drumming To 1942*, 1976.
Brun, H., *The Story Of The Original Dixieland Jazz Band*, Baton Rouge (USA), 1960.
Bruyninckx, W., *60 Years Of Recorded Jazz: 1917-77*, Mechelen.
Bryant, Lance, *The Touch*, 1988.
Budds, M.J., *Jazz In The Sixties: The Expansion Of Musical Resources And Techniques*, Iowa City (USA), 1978.
Buerkle, J.V, and D. Barker, *Bourbon Street Black: The New Orleans Black Jazzman*, New York: Oxford University Press, 1973.
Burns, Ralph, *Bijou*, Mayfair Music.
Burton, Jack, *The Blue Book Of Tin Pan Alley*, Century House.
Bushell, Garvin, *Jazz From The Beginning*, University Of Michigan Press (USA).
Cabanowski, Marek, *Polska Dyskografia Jazzowa*, M. Cabanowski, H. Cholinski, 1974.
Cacibauda, Joe, *No Nonsense Electric Bass*, Studio P/R.
Caldwell, Hansonia L., *African American Music: A Chronolgy, 1619-1995*, Ikoro Communications (USA), 1997.
Camarata, Salvador, *What Makes Sammy Run*, Robbins Music.
Campbell, James (ed.), *The Picador Book Of Blues And Jazz*, Picador (UK), 1995.
Cane, Giampiero, *Canto Nero*, Clueb, 1982.
Caraceni, A., *Il Jazz Delle Origini Ad Oggi*, Milan.
Carey, David Arthur (ed.), *The Directory Of Recorded Jazz And Swing Music*, Delphic Press.
Carey, Joseph Kuhn, *Big Noise From Notre Dame*, University Of Notre Dame Press.
Carisi, John, *Israel*, Margun Music.
Carles, Philippe, *Free Jazz/Black Power*, Editions Champ Libre, 1971.

Carner, Gary, *Jazz Performers: An Annotated Bibliography Of Biographical Materials*, Greenwood Press (UK), 1990.
Carr, Ian, Digby Fairweather and Brian Priestley, *Jazz: The Rough Guide*, Rough Guides (UK), 1995.
Carr, Ian, Digby Fairweather and Brian Priestley, *Jazz: The Essential Companion*, Grafton (UK), 1987.
Carr, Roy, *The Hip*, Faber & Faber (UK), 1986.
Carr, Roy (ed.), *Jazz On CD*, Mitchell Beazley (UK), 1995.
Carruth, Hayden, *Sitting In*, University Of Iowa Press (USA), 1986.
Carter, Willliam, *Preservation Hall*, Bayou Press (USA), 1992.
Case, Brian, *The Illustrated Encyclopedia Of Jazz*, Salamander Books (UK), 1978.
Case, Brian, *The Harmony Illustrated Encyclopedia Of Jazz*, Harmony Books (USA).
Castelli, Vittorio, *Il Jazz Su Disco*, A. Mondadori, 1983.
Castellucci, Stella, *An Approach To Jazz And Popular Music For Harp*, Miranda.
Caston, Leonard, *From Blues To Pop*, John Edwards Memorial Foundation, 1974.
Cayou, Dolores Kirton, *Modern Jazz Dance*, National Press Books, 1971.
Cerri, Livio, *Mezzo Secolo Di Jazz*, Nistri-Lischi, 1981.
Chambers, Jack, *Milestones*, Beech Tree Books.
Charters, S.B., and L. Kunstadt, *Jazz: A History Of The New York Scene, Garden City*, New York, 1962.
Charters, Samuel Barclay, *Jazz: New Orleans 1885-1963*, Oak Publications (USA), 1963.
Chaumier, J., *La Litterature Du Jazz*, Le Mans, 1963.
Chesky, David, *Contemporary Jazz Rock Rhythms*, C. Colin.
Chevigny, Paul, *After The Law: Jazz And The Cabaret Laws In New York City*, Routledge (UK), 1992.
Chilton, John, *Who's Who Of British Jazz*, Cassell Academe, New York (USA), 1997.
Chilton, John, *Who's Who Of Jazz*, Macmillan, 1990.
Chilton, John, *McKinney's Music*, Bloomsbury Book Shop, 1978.
Chilton, John, *Jazz*, Sevenoaks, 1979.
Chilton, John, *The Song Of The Hawk*, Quartet Books (UK), 1990.
Christian, Charley, *The Art Of The Jazz Guitar*, Cherry Lane Music.
Cichero, Augusto, *Guia Del Jazz*, Editorial Huemul, 1976.
Claghorn, Charles Eugene, *Biographical Dictionary Of Jazz*, Prentice-Hall (USA).
Clark, C., *Jazz Readers' Guide*, London, 1982.
Claxton, William, *Jazz*, Twelvetrees Press.
Clayton, Peter, *Jazz A-Z*, Guinness Publishing (UK).
Clayton, Peter, and Peter Gammond, *Guinness Jazz Companion*, Guinness Publishing (UK), 1989.
Clement, Raymond, *Jazz Im/Expressions*, RTL Editions, 1980.
Closson, David L., *One Life In Black Music*, Philadelphia (USA).
Cogno, Enrico, *Jazz Inchiesta*, Cappelli, 1971.
Cohan, Robert, *The Dance Workshop*, G. Allen & Unwin (USA), 1986.
Coker, Jerry, *The Jazz Idiom*, Englewood Cliffs (USA), 1975.
Coker, Jerry, *Patterns For Jazz*, Studio Editions.
Coker, Jerry, *Listening To Jazz*, Prentice-Hall (USA).
Coker, Jerry, *Improvising Jazz*, Simon & Schuster (USA), 1986.
Collier, Graham, *Jazz*, Cambridge University Press (UK), 1975.
Collier, Graham, *Inside Jazz*, Quartet Books (UK), 1973.
Collier, Graham, *Compositional Devices Vol. 1*, Berklee Press (USA).
Collier, James Lincoln, *The Reception Of Jazz In America*, Institute For Studies In American Music (USA).
Collier, James Lincoln, *The Making Of Jazz: A Comprehensive History*, Houghton Mifflin (USA), Macmillan (UK), 1978.
Collier, James Lincoln, *The Great Jazz Artists*, Four Winds Press (USA).
Collier, James Lincoln, *Jazz: The American Theme Song*, Oxford University Press (USA), 1994.
Collins, L., *Oh, Didn't He Ramble?*, Urbana (USA), 1974.
Cook, Richard, and Brian Morton, *Penguin Guide To Jazz On CD, LP & Cassette*, Penguin (UK), 1992.
Cook, Richard, and Brian Morton, *Penguin Guide To Jazz On CD, LP & Cassette, Third Edition*, Penguin (UK), 1996.
Cooper, David Edwin, *International Bibliography Of Discographies*, Libraries Unlimited, 1975.
Coryell, Julie, and Laura Friedman, *Jazz-Rock Fusion: The People, The Music*, Marion Boyars (UK), 1978.
Courtioux, Jean, *Les Quatre Elements*, Dorn.
Coyner, Lou, *South Rampart Street Revisited*, Dorn, 1981.
Cracker, Chris, *Get Into Jazz*, Bantam (USA), 1994.
Crawford, Ralston, *Music In The Street*, Historic New Orleans Collection.
Crouch, Stanley, *The All-American Skin Game Or The Decoy Of Race*, Pantheon (USA), 1996.
Crow, Bill, *Jazz Anecdotes*, Oxford University Press, 1990.
Crow, Bill, *From Birdland To Broadway: Scenes From A Jazz Life*, Oxford University Press, 1992.
Crowder, Henry, *As Wonderful As All That?*, Wild Trees Press.
Crowther, Bruce, and Mike Pinfold, *The Jazz Singers*, Javelin, 1988.
Crowther, Bruce, and Mike Pinfold, *Jazz Singing: The Singers And Their Styles*, Blandford (UK), Miller-Freeman (USA), 1997.
Crowther, Bruce, and Mike Pinfold, *The Big Band Years*, David & Charles (UK), 1986.
Crump, Janice D. Lapointe, and Kimberly T. Staley, *Discovering Jazz Dance: America's Energy And Soul*, W.C. Brown (USA), 1992.
Cushman, Jerome, *Tom B. And The Joyful Noise*, Westminster Press, 1970.
Czompo, Ann I., *Recreational Jazz Dance*, AC.
D'Rozario, Rico, *North Sea Jazz Festival, 1976-1985*, 1985.
Dahl, Linda, *Stormy Weather*, Quartet Books (UK), 1988.
Dalaunay, Charles, *Hot Discography: Edited By Hot Jazz*, Commodore Record, 1943.
Dale, Rodney, *The World Of Jazz*, Phaidon (UK), 1980.
Dallas, Karl F., *Singers Of An Empty Day*, Kahn & Averill, 1971.
Danca, Vince, *Bunny*, Danca.
Dance Masters Of America, *Jazz Syllabus*.
Dance, Stanley, *The World Of Swing*, Scribners (USA), 1974.

Dankworth, Avril, *Jazz: An Introduction To Its Musical Basis*, Oxford University Press, 1968.
Darrell, R.D., *Black Beauty*, Philadelphia (USA), 1933.
Dauer, A.M., and S. Longstreet, *Knaur's Jazz Lexikon*, Munich, 1957.
Dauer, Alfons M., *Der Jazz, Seine Ursprunge Und Seine Entwicklung*, E. Roth-Verlag, 1958.
David, Ron, *Jazz For Beginners*, Writers & Readers, 1995.
Davis, Francis, *Outcats*, Oxford University Press, 1990.
Davis, Francis, *In The Moment*, Oxford University Press.
Davis, Francis, *Bebop And Nothingness: Jazz And Pop At The End Of The Century*, Schirmer Books (USA), 1996.
Davis, Nathan Tate, *Writings In Jazz*, Gorsuch Scarisbrick.
De Fatto, Guy, *Aux Rythmes De Dieu*, Editions Du Cerf, 1978.
De Graef, Jack, *De Swingperiode (1935-1947)*, Dageraad, 1980.
De Roque, Pedro, *El Jazz*, Editorial Convergencia, 1977.
De Ruyter, Michiel, *Michiel De Ruyter, Een Leven Met Jazz*, Van Gennep, 1984.
De Stefano, Gildo, *Trecento Anni Di Jazz*, Sugar Edizioni, 1986.
De Toledano, Ralph, *Frontiers Of Jazz*, F. Ungar, 1962.
De Veaux, Scott, *The Birth Of Bebop: A Social And Musical History*, University Of California (USA), 1998.
Dean, Roger, *New Structures In Jazz And Improvised Music Since 1960*, Open University Press (UK), 1991.
Deffaa, Chip, *Voices Of The Jazz Age: Profiles Of Eight Vintage Jazzmen*, Bayou Press (USA), 1990.
Deffaa, Chip, *Swing Legacy*, Scarecrow Press (USA), 1989.
Deffaa, Chip, *Blue Rhythms: Six Lives In Rhythm And Blues*, University Of Illinois Press (USA), 1997.
Deffaa, Chip, *In The Mainstream: 18 Portraits In Jazz*, Scarecrow Press (USA), 1992.
Delaunay, Charles, *New Hot Discography*, Criterion.
Delaunay, Charles, *Hot Discographie 1943*, Collection Du Hot Club De France, 1944.
Deutsch, Maury, *Improvisational Concepts And Jazz Patterns*, C. Colin.
DeVeaux, Scott Knowles, *Jazz In Transition*, 1985.
Dexter Jnr., Dave, *The Jazz Story: From The '90s To The '60s* , Prentice-Hall (USA), 1964.
Dexter Jnr., Dave, *Jazz Cavalcade: The Inside Story Of Jazz*, Criterion Music, 1946.
Dollase, Rainer, *Das Jazzpublikum*, Schott.
Dorigne, Michel, *Jazz 2*, New York.
Doruzka, Lubomir, *Ceskoslovensky Jazz*, Praha, 1967.
Dow, Allen, *The Official Guide To Jazz Dancing*, Chartwell Books.
Driggs, F., and H. Lewine, *Black Beauty*, White Heat (USA), 1982.
Dulfer, Hans, *Jazz In China En Andere Perikels Uit De Geimproviseerde Muziek*, Bakker, 1980.
Dyer, Georff, *But Beautiful*, Jonathan Cape (UK), 1991.
Ebbesen, Niels Fink, *Dansk Jazzlitteratur: Litteratur Om Dansk Jazz*, Kobenhavns Universitet, 1980.
Edmonds, Hank, *Great Jazz Lines*, C. Colin.
Edwards, Ernie, *Jazz Discographies Unlimited Presents Bill Harris*, Erngeobil, 1966.
Ehle, Robert C., *Love*, Dorn.
Eldridge, Roy, *The Nifty Cat*, New World Records, 1986.
Elings, A., *Bibliografie Van De Nederlandse Jazz*, Nijmegen, 1966.
Elite Special Schallplatten, *Generalkatalog*, E. & W. Buhler, 1946.
Ellison, Mary, *Extensions Of The Blues*, Calder, 1990.
Ellison, R., *Shadow And Act*, New York, 1964.
Encyclopedia Of Jazz Duets, *For All Instruments*, C. Colin.
Englund, Bjorn, *Jazz Pa Cupol*, Svenskt Visarkiv.
Enstice, Wayne, and Paul Rubin, *Jazz Spoken Here*, Da Capo (USA), 1994.
Erb, Donald, *The Hawk*, Galaxy Music.
Erenberg, Lewis A., *Swingin' The Dream: Big Band Jazz And The Rebirth Of American Culture*, University Of Chicago Press (USA), 1998.
Erlich, Lillian, *What Jazz Is All About*, Julian Messner, 1962.
Escher, Wolf, *Die Trompete Im Jazz*, Universal.
European Jazz Directory, *Jazz World*.
European Jazz Federation, *List Of EJF Jazz-Clubs*, European Jazz Federation, 1976.
Evans, Lee, *The Jazz Tetrachord Approach To Keyboard Jazz Improvisation*, Belwin Mills, 1982.
Evans, Lee, *Modes And Their Use In Jazz*, E.B. Marks Music (USA).
Ewen, David, *The Life And Death Of Tin Pan Alley*, Funk & Wagnall (USA), 1964.
Faas, Hugo, *Der Jazz In Der Schweiz*, Pro Helvetia, 1976.
Fairbairn, Ann, *Call Him George*, Crown (USA), 1961.
Fark, Reinhard, *Die Missachtete Botschaft*, Spiess, 1971.
Fayenz, Franco, *Jazz & Jazz*, Laterza, 1981.
Fayenz, Franco, *Il Jazz Dal Mito All'Avanguardia*, Sapere, 1970.
Feather, Leonard, *The Pleasures Of Jazz*, Horizon Press (USA), 1976.
Feather, Leonard, *The Passion For Jazz*, Horizon Press (USA), 1980.
Feather, Leonard, *The New Edition Of The Encyclopedia Of Jazz*, Horizon Press (USA), 1960.
Feather, Leonard, *The Jazz Years*, Da Capo (USA), 1987.
Feather, Leonard, *The Encyclopedia Of Jazz In The Sixties*, Horizon Press (USA), 1966.
Feather, Leonard, *The Encyclopedia Of Jazz In The Seventies*, Quartet Books (UK), 1978.
Feather, Leonard, *The Encyclopedia Of Jazz*, New York.
Feather, Leonard, *Panacea*, Mayfair Music.
Feather, Leonard, *Inside Jazz, Inside Be-Bop*, Da Capo (USA), 1990.
Feather, Leonard, *The Book Of Jazz*, Horizon Press (USA), 1965.
Feather, Leonard, *Laughter From The Hip: The Lighter Side Of Jazz*, Da Capo (USA), 1990.
Feather, Leonard, *From Satchmo To Miles*, Da Capo (USA), 1990.
Feather, Leonard, *Encyclopedia Yearbook Of Jazz (1956)*, Da Capo (USA), 1993.
Feather, Leonard, *New Yearbook Of Jazz (1958)*, Da Capo (USA), 1993.
Feather, Leonard (intro. by), *Jazz Guitarists*, Guitar Player (USA).
Feigin, Leo, *Russian Jazz: New Identity*, Quartet Books (UK), 1985.

Feinstein, Sascha, *Jazz Poetry: From The 1920s To The Present*, Praeger, Westport (USA), 1997.
Ferguson, *Mainstream Jazz Reference And Price Guide, 1949-1965, Caroline House*, Ferguson.
Fernett, Gene, *Swing Out: Great Negro Dance Bands*, Da Capo (USA), 1993.
Finkelstein, Sidney Walter, *Jazz: A People's Music*, (USA).
Fischer-Munstermann, Uta, *Von Der Jazzgymnastik Zum Jazztanz*, Pohl.
Floyd, Samuel A., *Black Music In The Harlem Renaissance: A Collection Of Essays*, Afro-American & African Studies/Greenwood Press, 1990.
Fordham, John, *The Sound Of Jazz*, Hamlyn (UK), 1989.
Fordham, John, *Let's Join Hands And Contact The Living*, Elm Tree Books (UK), 1986.
Fordham, John, *Jazz On CD: The Essential Guide*, Kyle Cathie (UK), 1991.
Fordham, John, *Jazz: History, Instruments, Musicians, Recordings*, Dorling Kindersley (UK), 1993.
Fordham, John, *Shooting From The Hip: Changing Tunes In Jazz 1970-95*, Kyle Cathie (UK), 1995.
Foreman, Ronald Clifford, *Jazz And Race Records, 1920-1932* (USA), 1968.
Fortunato, Joanne Alba, *Major Influences Affecting The Development Of Jazz Dance, 1950-1971*.
Foss, Peter (ed.), *Jazz 'N' Blues*, Busker S., 1994.
Foster, Frank Benjamin, *In Defense Of Be-Bop*, F. Foster Music, 1979.
Fox, Charles, *The Jazz Scene*, Hamlyn (UK), 1972.
Fox, Charles, *Jazz In Perspective*, London, 1969.
Fox, Roy, *Hollywood, Mayfair, And All That Jazz*, Frewin, 1975.
Francis, Andre, *Jazz*, Paris.
Frankenstein, A., *Syncopating Saxophones*, Chicago, 1925.
Fredrickson, Scott, *Scat Singing Method*.
Freeman, Bud, *Crazeology*, Bayou Press (USA), 1989.
Freeman, Lawrence, *You Don't Look Like A Musician*, Belamp.
Freeman, Lawrence, *If You Know Of A Better Life Please Tell Me*, B. Eaves, 1976.
Freeman, Lawrence, *Atomic Era*, Robbins Music.
Freeman, Lawrence, *The Eel's Nephew*, E.B. Marks Music (USA).
Freeman, Lawrence, *The Barracuda*, Robbins Music.
Freeman, Lawrence, *Dr. Peycer's Dilemma*, E.B. Marks Music (USA).
Freeman, Lawrence, *Disenchanted Trout*, E.B. Marks Music (USA).
Frich, Elisabeth, *The Matt Mattox Book Of Jazz Dance*, Sterling (USA).
Friedman, Carol, *A Moment's Notice*, Macmillan.
Friedwald, Will, *Jazz Singing*, Scribners (USA).
Gamble, Peter, *Focus On Jazz*, R. Hale.
Gammond, Peter, *Fourteen Miles On A Clear Night*, Greenwood Press, 1978.
Ganfield, J., *Books And Periodical Artricles On Jazz In America From 1926-1932*, New York, 1933.
Garwood, Donald, *Masters Of Instrumental Blues Guitar*, Oak Publications (USA), 1968.
Gayford, Martin, *The Best Of Jazz: The Essential CD Guide*, Orion (UK), 1993.
Gelly, Dave, and Weef, *The Giants Of Jazz*, Aurum Press (USA).
Gershwin, George, *Embraceable You*, Harms.
Giddins, G., *The Sax Section*, New York Jazz Museum (USA).
Giddins, G., *Celebrating Bird*, W. Morrow (USA), 1987.
Giddins, G., *Riding On A Blue Note: Jazz And American Pop*, New York and Oxford, 1981.
Giddins, G., *Rhythm-a-ning*, New York, 1985.
Giddins, Gary, *Visions Of Jazz: The First Century*, Oxford University Press (USA), 1998.
Giddins, Gary, *Faces In The Crowd*, New York, 1992.
Gillenson, Lewis W., *Esquire's World Of Jazz*, Esquire (USA), 1962.
Gillespie, D, and A. Fraser, *To Be, Or Not To Bop*, New York, 1976.
Gillespie, Dizzy, *Groovin' High*, MCA Music.
Gilmore, John, *Who's Who Of Jazz In Montreal*, University Of Toronto Press (Canada).
Gilmore, John, *Swinging In Paradise*, University Of Toronto Press (Canada), 1988.
Gioia, Ted, *West Coast Jazz: Modern Jazz In California 1945-60*, Oxford University Press (UK), 1992.
Gioia, Ted, *The Imperfect Art*, Oxford University Press, 1988.
Gioia, Ted, *The History Of Jazz*, Oxford University Press (USA), 1997.
Giordano, Gus, *Anthology Of American Jazz Dance*, Orion (UK).
Gitler, Ira, *Swing To Bop*, Oxford University Press, 1985.
Gitler, Ira, *Jazz Masters Of The Forties*, Da Capo (USA), 1990.
Gleason, Jackie, *Bulova Presents Time*, Bulova Watch.
Gleason, Ralph J., *Celebrating The Duke, And Louis, Bessie, Billie, Bird, Carmen, Miles, Dizzy*, Little, Brown, 1975.
Gleason, Ralph J., *Jam Session: An Anthology Of Jazz*, Putnams (USA), 1958.
Godbolt, Jim, *World Of Jazz: Through Printed Ephemera And Collectables*, Studio Editions (UK), 1990.
Godbolt, Jim, *All This And Many A Dog*, Quartet Books (UK), 1986.
Godbolt, Jim, *A History Of Jazz In Britain 1950-70*, Quartet Books (UK), 1989.
Godbolt, Jim, *A History Of Jazz In Britain 1919-50*, Quartet Books (UK).
Godrich, John, *Blues & Gospel Records, 1902-1942*, Storyville, 1969.
Gold, R., *A Jazz Lexicon*, New York.
Gold, Robert S., *Jazz Talk*, Bobbs-Merrill (USA).
Goldberg, Joe, *Jazz Masters Of The Fifties*, Da Capo (USA), 1990.
Goldblatt, Burt, *Newport Jazz Festival*, Dial Press (USA).
Goldson, Elizabeth (ed.), *Seeing Jazz: Artists And Writers On Jazz*, Chronicle Books (USA), 1998.
Goldstein, Gil, *Introduction To Jazz History*, Music Sales.
Golson, Benny, *Killer Joe.*, USA.
Gonda, Janos, *Jazz: Tortenet, Elmelet, Gyakorlat, Zenemukiado (Budapest)*.
Gonda, Janos (ed.), *Who's Who In Hungarian Jazz*, European Jazz Federation, 1973.
Gonzales, Babs, *I Paid My Dues*, Expubidence.
Gonzales, Babs, *Movin On Down De Line*, Expubidence.
Gordon, Robert, *Jazz West Coast*, Quartet Books (UK), 1990.

Gottlieb, Robert, *Reading Jazz: A Gathering Of Autobiography, Reportage And Criticism From 1919*, Bloomsbury (UK), 1998.
Gottlieb, W., *The Golden Age Of Jazz*, Pomegranate (USA), 1995.
Gounelle Kline, P., *Le Theatre De Pagnol*, P. Lang.
Gourse, Leslie, *Louis' Children*, W. Morrow (USA), 1984.
Gourse, Leslie, *Every Day*, Quartet Books (UK), 1985.
Granholm, Ake, *Finnish Jazz*, Finnish Music Information Centre, 1974.
Gras, Pim, *Jazz Uit Het Historisch Archief*, Tango, 1974.
Gray, John, *Fire Music: A Bibliography of the New Jazz 1959-1990*, Greenwood Press, 1992.
Green, Benny, *The Reluctant Art: Five Studies In The Growth Of Jazz*, MacGibbon & Kee (UK), 1962.
Green, Benny, *Drums In My Ears*, Davis-Poynter (UK), 1973.
Green, John Waldo, *Murder At The Vanities. I Cover The Waterfront*, Harms.
Green, John Waldo, *Body And Soul*, Harms.
Greene, Ted, *Jazz Guitar*, Zdenek.
Gregor, Carl, Duke Of Mecklenburg, *Die Theorie Des Blues Im Modernen Jazz*, V. Koerner, 1971.
Gregor, Carl, *Stilformen Des Jazz. Vom Ragtime Zum Chicago-Stil*, Universal Edition.
Gregor, Carl, *International Jazz Bibliography: Jazz Books From 1919 To 1968*, P.H. Heitz Strasbourg.
Gregor, Carl, *International Jazz Bibliography (ijb) & Selective Bibli (1971/72/73 Supplement)*, Institute For Jazz Research/Universal Edition, 1975.
Gregor, Carl, *International Jazz Bibliography & International Drum & Perc. (1970 Supplement)*, Universal Edition, 1971.
Gregor, Carl, *International Bibliography Of Jazz Books*, Verlag Valentin Koerner, 1983.
Gridley, Mark C., *Jazz Styles: History & Analysis*, Prentice-Hall (USA), 1988.
Griffin, N., *To Bop Or Not To Bop?*, New York, 1948.
Griffiths, Paul, *New Sounds, New Personalites*, Faber & Faber (UK), 1986.
Grime, Kitty, *Jazz Voices*, Quartet Books (UK).
Grindley, Mark, *Concise Guide To Jazz*, Prentice-Hall (USA), 1992.
Gross, Louis D., *The Jazz Singer, A. Yokel For Lewis And Gordon*.
Grossman, S., *Ragtime Blues Guitarists*, New York, 1965.
Grundmann, Jan, *Jazz Aus Den Trummern*, Der Jazzfreund.
Gubaidulina, Sofia Asgatovna, *Kontsert Dlia Dvukh Orkestrov*, Sov. Kompozitor, 1985.
Gullickson, Gordon, *Numerical Index To Delaunay's Hot Discography*, 1941.
Gunter, John Osbon, *Good Players*, 1980.
Gunther, Helmut, *Jazz Dance*, Heinrichshofen, 1980.
Hadlock, R., *Jazz Masters Of The Twenties*, New York.
Haerle, Dan, *The Jazz Language*, Studio 224.
Hald, Jon, *10 Blues'er*, W. Hansen/Chester Music.
Hamilton, James, *Slapstick*, Robbins Music.
Hamilton, James, *Blues In My Music Room*, Robbins Music.
Hamilton, James, *Blues For Clarinet*, Robbins Music.
Hamm, C., *Music In The New World*, New York, 1983.
Hamm, C., B. Nettl and R. Byrnside, *Contemporary Music And Music Cultures*, Englewood Cliffs, 1975.
Harding, John Ralph, *A Survey Of The Evolution Of Jazz For The General Reader*, 1981.
Harris, Howard C., *The Complete Book Of Improvistion*, DeMos Music.
Harris, Rex, *Jazz*, Penguin (UK), 1952.
Harris, Steve, *Jazz On Compact Disc*, Harmony Books (USA).
Harris, William J., *The Poetry And Poetics Of Amiri Baraka*, University Of Missouri Press (USA), 1985.
Harrison, M., *Kings Of Jazz*, New York, 1978.
Harrison, M., *Boogie Woogie*, Jazz: New Perspectives, New York.
Harrison, M., and others, *Modern Jazz: The Essential Records (1945-1970)*, London, 1975.
Harrison, Max, *Jazz: Retrospect*, Quartet Books (UK), 1991.
Hartmann, Walter, *Duette In Swing Und Beat*, Deutscher Verlag Fur Musik.
Haselgrove, J.R., *Readers' Guide To Books On Jazz*, Library Association (County Libraries Section), 1965.
Haskins, James, *The Cotton Club*, Random House (USA).
Hasse, J.E., *Ragtime: Its History, Composers And Music*, New York, 1985.
Hawes, H., *Raise Up Off Me*, New York, 1973.
Hayakawa, S.I., *Reflections On The History Of Jazz*, 1945.
Hayes, M., R. Scribner and P. Magee, *Encyclopedia Of Australian Jazz*, Eight Mile Plains, 1976.
Heen, Carol Louise, *Procedures For Style Analysis Of Jazz*, 1981.
Hefele, Bernhard, *Jazz-Bibliography*, Saur, 1981.
Hellhund, Herbert, *Cool Jazz*, Schott.
Hennessey, Thomas J., *From Jazz To Swing: African American Jazz Musicians And Their Music*, Wayne State University Press (USA), 1995.
Hentoff, Nat, *Jazz Is*, Random House (USA), 1976.
Hentoff, Nat, *Boston Boy*, Random House (USA), 1986.
Hentoff, Nat, *Listen To The Stories*, Harper Collins (USA), 1995.
Hentoff, Nat, and Albert J. McCarthy, *The Jazz Life*, Dial Press (USA).
Hentoff, Nat, and Albert J. McCarthy, *Jazz: New Perspectives On The History Of Jazz*, Rinehart (USA), 1959.
Herman, Woody, Chubby Jackson and Ralph Burns, *Northwest Passage*, Mayfair Music.
Hinton, Milt, David D. Berger and Holly Maxson, *Overtime: The Jazz Photographs Of Milt Hinton*, Pomegranate Artbooks, 1996.
Hippenmeyer, Jean Roland, *Le Jazz En Suisse, 1930-1970*, Editions De La Thiele, 1971.
Hippenmeyer, Jean Roland, *Jazz Sur Films*, Editions De La Thiele, 1973.
Hobbs, Christopher, *Three For Redlands*, Dorn.
Hobson, Wilder, *American Jazz Music*, W.W. Norton (USA), 1939.
Hodeir, Andre, *Toward Jazz*, New York.
Hodeir, Andre, *The Worlds Of Jazz*, New York, 1972.
Holcombe, Bill, *Creative Arranging At The Piano*, Musicians.
Holmes, John Clellon, *The Horn*, Penguin, 1990.

Holmes, Lowell Don, *Jazz Greats*, Holmes & Meier, 1986.
Hoskyns, Barney, *From A Whisper To A Scream*, Fontana (UK), 1991.
Houghton, Steve, *A Guide For The Modern Jazz Rhythm Section*, C.L. Barnhouse.
Howe, M., *Blue Jazz*, Bristol, 1934.
Huber, L., *New Orleans: A Pictorial History*, New York, 1971.
Hughes, Langston, *Jazz/Langston Hughes*, F. Watts, 1982.
Hughes, Langston, *Jazu, Huzu*, Showa 35 Nen, 1960.
Hughes, Langston, *Das Buch Vom Jazz*, Buchheim Verlag.
Hughes, Langston, *The First Book Of Jazz*, W.W. Norton (USA), 1996.
Hughes, Langston, *The Book Of Rhythms*, Oxford University Press (USA), 1996.
Iakushenko, Igor Vasilevich, *Dzhazovyi Albom*, Muzyka, 1984.
Internationales Festival New Jazz, *Presseschau*, Stadt Moers Kulturamt.
Isadora, Rachel, *Ben's Trumpet*, Greenwillow Books.
Ita, Bassey, *Jazz In Nigeria*, Atiaya Communications.
Itoh, Kimiko, *For Lovers Only*, Columbia, 1987.
Jacquet, Illinois, *Jacquet Mood.*, Apollo, 1940.
Jalard, Michel-Claude, *Le Jazz Est-Il Encore Possible?*, Parentheses.
James, B., *Essays On Jazz*, London.
James, M., *Ten Modern Jazzmen*, London, 1960.
Jasen, D.A., and T.J. Tichenor, *Rags And Ragtime: A Musical History*, New York, 1978.
Jepsen, J. Grunnet, *Jazz Records, 1942-1969: A Discography*, Holte & Copenhagen.
Johnson, Bruce, *The Oxford Companion To Australian Jazz*, Oxford University Press, 1987.
Johnson, J.J., *Trombone*, Hansen House.
Johnson, Tom, *The Voice Of New Music: New York City 1972-1982*, Het Apollobuis, 1991.
Jones, Max, *Talking Jazz*, Macmillan (UK), 1987.
Jones, R.P., *Jazz* , Methuen (UK), 1963.
Jost, Ekkehard, *Jazzmusiker*, Ullstein, 1982.
Jost, Ekkehard, *Free Jazz*, Da Capo (USA), 1994.
Jouvin, Georges, *Dix Etudes Speciales Pour Trompette Si b*, A. Leduc.
Kaminsky, M., and V.E. Hughes, *My Life In Jazz*, New York, 1963.
Karpa, Gunther, *Rhythmisch-Stilistische Studien Fur Jazztrompete*, Deutscher Verlag Fur Musik.
Kater, Michael H., *Different Drummers: Jazz In The Culture Of Nazi Germany*, Oxford University Press, 1992.
Katscher, Robert, *When Day Is Done*, Harms.
Kaufman, Fredrick, *The African Roots Of Jazz*, Alfred Knopf (USA).
Kaufman, H., *From Jehovah To Jazz*, New York, 1937.
Keepnews, Orrin, *The View From Within: Jazz Writings, 1948-1987*, Oxford University Press, 1991.
Keepnews, Orrin, and B. Grauer, *A Pictorial History Of Jazz*, New York.
Kennedy, Rick, *Jelly Roll, Bix And Hoagy: Gennett Studios And The Birth Of Recorded Jazz*, Indiana University Press (USA), 1994.
Kennington, Donald, *The Literature Of Jazz: A Critical Guide*, Library Association, 1980.
Kernfeld, Barry (ed.), *Blackwell Guide To Recorded Jazz*, Blackwell (UK), 1992.
Kernfeld, Barry (ed.), *The New Grove Dictionary Of Jazz*, Macmillan (UK), 1990.
Kernfield, Barry, *What To Listen For In Jazz*, Yale University Press (USA), 1998.
King, Jonny, *What Jazz Is: An Insider's Guide To Understanding And Listening To Jazz*, Walker & Co. (USA), 1998.
Kington, Miles, *Jazz Anthology*, Harper Collins (UK), 1992.
Kinkle, Roger D., *The Complete Encyclopedia Of Popular Music And Jazz. 1900-1950 (4 vols)*, Arlington House, 1974.
Kirk, Andy, *Twenty Years On Wheels*, Bayou Press (USA), 1989.
Kjellberg, Erik, *Svensk Jazz Historia*, Norstedt.
Klaasse, Piet, *Jam Session*, David & Charles (UK), 1985.
Kleberg, L., *Svensk Jazzbibliografi*, Stockholm, 1964.
Knowles, Richard H., *Fallen Heroes: A History Of New Orleans Brass Bands*, Jazzology Press, New Orleans (USA), 1997.
Koebner, F.W., *Jazz And Shimmy*, Berlin, 1921.
Konen, V., *Rozhdenie Dzhaza*, Kompozitor, 1984.
Konowitz, Bert, *The Bert Konowitz Vocal Improvisation Method*, Alfred Music.
Korall, Burt, *Drummin' Men: Heartbeat Of Jazz: The Swing Years*, Schirmer (USA), 1990.
Korte, Karl, *I Think You Would Have Understood*, Seesaw Music.
Kotek, Josef, *Kronika Ceske Synkopy*, Editio Supraphon, 1975.
Krahenbuhl, Peter, *Der Jazz Und Seine Menschen*, Francke, 1968.
Kraines, Minda Goodman, *Jump Into Jazz*, Mayfield, 1983.
Kraner, Dietrich Heinz, *Jazz In Austria*, Universal Edition, 1972.
Kreutz, Arthur, *Study In Jazz*, Mercury Music.
Kristensen, S.M., *Hvad Jazz*, Copenhagen, 1938.
Kroger, Ed, *Die Posaune Im Jazz*, Universal Edition, 1972.
Kukla, Barbara J., *Swing City: Newark Nightlife 1925-1950*, Temple University Press, Philadelphia (USA), 1992.
Kumpf, Hans, *Posterserielle Musik Und Free Jazz*, Musikverlag G.F. Doring.
La Porta, John, *Tonal Organization Of Improvisational Techniques*, Kendor Music.
La Porta, John, *A Guide To Jazz Phrasing And Interpretation*, Berklee Press (USA).
La Porta, John, *A Guide To Improvisation*, Berklee Press (USA).
Lacy, Steve, *Prospectus*, Margun Music.
Laing, R.D., and C. Sheridan, *Jazz Records: The Specialist Labels*, Copenhagen, 1981.
Laird, Ross, *Tantalizing Tingles*, Greenwood Press (USA), 1997.
Lane, Christy, *All That Jazz And More*, Leisure Press.
Lang, Iain, *Jazz In Perspective: The Background Of The Blues*, Jazz Book Club, 1957.
Lange, Horst, *Jazz In Deutshland: Die Deutsche Jazz-Chronik*, Berlin.
Lange, Horst Heinz, *Die Deutsche 78er Discographie Der*

Hot-Dance Und Jazz-Musik, 1903-1958, Colloquium Verlag, 1978.
Langridge, D., *Your Jazz Collection*, London, 1970.
Larkin, Colin (ed.), *Guinness Who's Who Of Jazz*, Guinness Publishing (UK), 1992.
Larkin, Colin (ed.), *Guinness Who's Who Of Jazz Second Edition*, Guinness Publishing (UK), 1995.
Larkin, Colin (ed.), *The Virgin Encyclopedia Of Jazz*, Virgin Books (UK), 1999.
Larkin, Philip, *All What Jazz*, Faber & Faber (UK), 1985.
Lassen, Anni, *Jazzmusik Og Jazznoder*, Denmarks Biblioteksskole, 1975.
Lateef, Yusef A., *Yusef Lateef's Is Is*, Fana Music.
Lateef, Yusef A., *Transcribed Solos For Flute, Oboe & Tenor Saxophone*, Alnur Music.
Lawn, Richard, and Jeffrey L. Hellmer, *Jazz Theory And Practice*, Wadsworth Publishing Co. (UK), 1993.
Laycock, Ralph, *Swing-a-ling*, T. Presser.
Lea, Barbara, *How To Sing Jazz*, T. Presser.
Leder, Jan, *Women In Jazz*, Greenwood Press.
Lee, Bill, *1002 Jumbo Jazz Album*, Silhouette Music.
Lee, Edward, *Jazz: An Introduction*, Kahn & Averill, 1972.
Lees, Gene, *Meet Me At Jim And Andy's: Jazz Musicians And Their World*, Oxford University Press, 1988.
Lees, Gene, *Waiting For Dizzy*, Oxford University Press, 1994.
Leloir, Jean Pierre, *Du Jazz Plein Les Yeux*, Edica.
Lems-Dworkin, Carol, *World Music Center*, Northwestern University.
Leonard, Herman, *The Eye Of Jazz*, Viking Penguin, 1989.
Leonard, Neil, *Jazz: Myth And Religion*, Oxford University Press, 1987.
Leonard, Neil, *Jazz And The White Americans: The Acceptance Of A New Art Form*, Chicago and London, 1962.
Levey, Joseph, *The Jazz Experience*, Prentice-Hall (USA).
Levi, Ezio, *Introduzione Alla Vera Musica Di Jazz*, Edizione Magazzino Musicale, 1938.
Levine, Mark, *The Jazz Theory Book*, Sher Music (USA), 1996.
Levitt, Rod, *Woodmen Of The World*, Associated Music.
Levy, Henry J., *The Time Revolution*, Creative World.
Lewis, Alwyn, *Join 'Em On The Riff: Jazz Musings In Metre*, K'vrie Press (USA), 1998.
Lindroth, Scott, *Chasing The Trane Out Of Darmstadt*, Dorn.
Linehan, Norm, *Norm Linehan's Australian Jazz Picture Book*, Child & Henry, 1980.
Link, Harry, *These Foolish Things*, Aladdin.
Litchfield, J., *The Canadian Jazz Discography, 1916-1980*, Toronto, 1982.
Litweiler, John, *The Freedom Principle*, W. Morrow (USA), 1984.
Lock, Graham, *Chasing The Vibration*, Stride (UK), 1994.
Locke, Alain LeRoy, *The Negro And His Music*, The Associates In Negro Folk Education, 1936.
Longstreet, Stephen, *Sportin' House: A History Of The New Orleans Sinners And The Birth Of Jazz*, Sherbourne Press, 1965.
Longstreet, Stephen, *Jazz From A To Z: A Graphic Dictionary*, Catbird Press, 1989.
Longstreet, Stephen, *Storyville To Harlem*, Rutgers University Press (USA).
Lotz, Rainer E., *The AFRS 'Jubilee' Transcription Programs*, N. Ruecker, 1985.
Lotz, Rainer E., *German Ragtime & Prehistory Of Jazz*, Storyville, 1985.
Lowe, Jacques, *Jazz: Photographs Of The Masters*, Artisan Press (USA), 1995.
Lowinger, Gene, *Jazz Violin*, Schirmer (USA).
Lucas, John, *Basic Jazz On Long Play*, Carleton College, 1954.
Lucas, Paul, *Jazz Chording For The Rock-Blues Guitarist*, Sole Distributorship.
Ludwig, Siegfried, *Rhythmisch-Stilistische Studien Fur Drums*, Deutscher Verlag Fur Musik.
Luigi, *The Luigi Jazz Dance Technique*, Doubleday (USA), 1981.
Lydon, Michael, *Boogie Lightning*, Dial Press (USA), 1974.
Lykiard, Alexis, *Living Jazz*, Tenormen Press, 1992.
Lyons, Len, *The Great Jazz Pianists*, Da Capo (USA), 1990.
Lyons, Leonard, *The 101 Best Jazz Albums*, W. Morrow (USA), 1980.
Lyons, Leonard, *Jazz Portraits: The Lives And Music Of The Jazz Masters*, W. Morrow (USA).
Lyttelton, Humphrey, *Why No Beethoven?*, Robson Books (UK), 1984.
Lyttelton, Humphrey, *Best Of Jazz Vol 2: Enter The Giants*, Robson (UK), 1990.
Mackenzie, Harry, *AFRS Downbeat Series*, Joyce Record Club, 1986.
Manone, W., and P. Vandervoort, *Trumpet On The Wing*, New York, 1948.
Margulis, Max, *Present State Of Jazz And Swing*.
Mariano, Charlie, *Jazz Originals*, Berklee Press (USA).
Marinelli, Joseph, *Jomars LP Price Guide*, J. Marinelli, 1973.
Markewich, Reese, *The New Expanded Bibliography Of Jazz Compositions*, Markewich, 1974.
Markewich, Reese, *Jazz Publicity II*, Markewich, 1974.
Markewich, Reese, *Jazz Publicity*, Riverdale, 1973.
Marsh, Graham, and Glyn Callingham, *California Cool*, Collins & Brown (UK), 1992.
Martin, Henry, *Enjoying Jazz*, Schirmer (USA), 1986.
Martin, Henry John, *Jazz Harmony*, 1980.
Martin, Stephen Harvey, *Music In Urban East Africa*.
Martinez, Raymond J., *Portraits Of New Orleans Jazz; Its Peoples And Places*, Hope, 1971.
Matzner, Antonin, *Encyklopedie Jazzu A Moderni Popularni Hudby*, Editio Supraphon, 1983.
Mauriello, Joseph G., *The First Annual Greenwich Village Jazz Guide*, Bleecker Street (USA).
Mauro, Walter, *Jazz E Universo Negro*, Rizzoli (USA), 1972.
McCalla, James, *Jazz, A Listener's Guide*, Prentice-Hall (USA), 1995.
McCarthy, Albert, *The Dance Band Era*, Spring Books (UK), 1971.
McCarthy, Albert, *Big Band Jazz*, Putnams (USA), 1974.
McCarthy, Albert, Paul Oliver and Max Harrison, *Jazz On Record: A Critical Guide To The First Fifty Years: 1917-67*, London, 1968.

McGhee, Howard, *Blues Duende*, E.B. Marks Music (USA).
McKee, M., and F. Chisenhall, *Beale Stret Black And Blue*, Baton Rouge (USA), 1981.
McRae, Barry, *The Jazz Handbook*, Longman (UK), 1987.
McSloy, Peter, *For Jazz*, Hit & Run Press (USA), 1995.
Meadows, Eddie S., *Jazz Reference And Research Materials*, Garland, 1981.
Meeker, D., *Jazz In The Movies*, London.
Megill, Donald D., *Introduction To Jazz History*, Prentice-Hall (USA).
Mehegan, John F., *Jazz Improvisation*, New York.
Mehegan, John F., *Contemporary Styles For The Jazz Pianist*, S. Fox.
Mellers, W., *Music In A New Found Land*, London, 1964.
Meltzer, David (ed.), *Reading Jazz*, Mercury House, 1995.
Mendl, R., *The Appeal Of Jazz*, London, 1927.
Merod, Jim, *Jazz As A Cultural Archive*, Duke UP (USA), 1995.
Merriam, A.P., and R.J. Benford, *A Bibliography Of Jazz*, Philadelphia.
Miller, M., *Jazz In Canada*, Toronto, 1982.
Miller, Mark, *Boogie, Pete & The Senator*, Nightwood Editions, 1987.
Miller, Norma, and Evette Jensen, *Swingin' At The Savoy: The Memoir Of A Jazz Dancer*, Temple University Press (USA), 1996.
Mingus, Charles, *Beneath The Underdog*, New York: Alfred A. Knopf (USA), 1971.
Mitchell, Jack, *Australian Jazz On Record, 1925-80*, Australian Government (Australia), 1988.
Mohr, K., *Discographie Du Jazz*, Geneva, 1945.
Moller, B., *Dansk Jazz Discography*, Copenhagen, 1945.
Monson, Ingrid, *Saying Something: Jazz Improvisation And Interaction*, University Of Chicago Press (USA), 1998.
Montgomery, Michael R., *Studies In Jazz Style For The Double Bassist*, 1984.
Moody, Bill, *Jazz Exiles: American Musicians Abroad*, University Of Nevada Press (USA), 1993.
Morgenstern, D., *Jazz People*, New York, 1976.
Morris, Ronald L., *Wait Until Dark: Jazz And The Underworld, 1880-1940*, Bowling Green University Popular Press (USA), 1980.
Morse, Jim, *Big Band Era*, Hiawatha Publishers (USA), 1993.
Mosness, Terje, *Jazz I Molde*, Nordvest-Informasjon.
Muckenberger, Heiner, *Meet Me Where They Play The Blues*, Oreos.
Murphy, Turk, *When The Saints Go Marching In*, E.B. Marks Music (USA).
Murray, James Briggs, *Black Visions '88: Lady Legends In Jazz, February 1-March 11, 1988*, Mayor's Office Of Minority Affairs (USA), 1988.
Musica Jazz Presenta Harlem, *Musica Jazz: Rusconi Editore*, 1984.
Namyslowski, Zbigniew, *Utwory Jazzowe Na Rozny Sklad Instrumentow*, Polskie Wydawn. Muzyczne.
Nanry, C., *American Music: From Storyville To Woodstock*, E.P. Dutton (USA), 1972.
Nanry, C., and Berger, E., *The Jazz Text*, New York, 1979.
National Portrait Gallery, Washington, D.C., *A Glimmer Of Their Own Beauty*, Washington, 1971.
New York Jazz Festival, *The First Annual New York Jazz Fest*, New York, 1956.
Nicholson, Stuart, *Jazz: The Modern Resurgence*, Simon & Schuster (USA), 1990.
Nicholson, Stuart, *Jazz: The 1980s Resurgence*, Da Capo (USA), 1995.
Nicholson, Stuart, *Jazz-Rock: A History*, Schirmer Books (USA), 1998.
Niemoeller, A., *Story Of Jazz*, Kansas City, 1946.
Nisenson, Eric, *Blue: The Murder Of Jazz*, St. Martin's (USA), 1998.
Nisenson, Eric, *Round About Midnight*, Dial Press (USA), 1982.
No author listed, *Rhythmisch-Stilistische Studien Fur Gitarre*, Deutscher Verlag Fur Musik, 1971.
No author listed, *Jazz On LP's*, Greenwood Press, 1978.
No author listed, *Dallas Jazz News Letter*, 1977.
No author listed, *Music Master Jazz Catalogue*, Music Master, 1990.
No author listed, *Swing And Sound*, MediaPlus, 1987.
No editor listed, *Vogue's Real Jazz Fake Book*, Golden Press.
No editor listed, *Refrains Populaires D'Amerique*, New York Mills Music.
No editor listed, *Proceedings Of NAJE Research*, NAJE.
No editor listed, *Portraits Of Jazz-Musicians*, Jazzfreund.
No editor listed, *Encyclopedia Of Jazz Standards*, Warner Brothers (USA), 1987.
No editor listed, *Coversations With Jazz Musicians*, Gale Research, 1977.
No editor listed, *All That Jazz*, Warner Brothers (USA).
Noble, James, *Blue Flame*, Mayfair Music.
Noble, Peter, *Transatlantic Jazz, A Short History Of American Jazz*, Citizen Press (USA).
Noll, Dietrich J., *Zur Improvisation Im Deutschen Free Jazz*, Verlag Der Musikalienhandlung Wagner, 1977.
Nordisk Jazzforskning, *Rapport Fran Den Forsta Konferensen 14-16 Februari 1980 i Stockholm*, Svensk Visarkiv, 1981.
Norton, Christopher, *Microjazz: For Trumpet*, Boosey & Hawkes (UK).
Norton, Christopher, *Microjazz: For Flute*, Boosey & Hawkes (UK).
Norton, Christopher, *Microjazz For Clarinet*, Boosey & Hawkes (UK).
Norton, Christopher, *Microjazz*, Boosey & Hawkes (UK).
Ogren, Kathy J., *Jazz Revoloution: Twenties America And The Meaning Of Jazz*, Oxford University Press (USA), 1992.
Oliver, J., *Jazz Classic*, London, 1962.
Oliver, Paul, *Savannah Syncopators*, Stein & Day (USA), 1970.
Oliver, Paul, *The New Grove Gospel, Blues And Jazz*, W.W. Norton (USA), 1986.
Olsen, David C., *Great Jazz Standards*, Columbia Pictures.
Ondaatje, Michael, *Coming Through Slaughter*, Penguin.
Ostransky, Leroy, *The Anatomy Of Jazz*, Seattle, 1960.
Ostransky, Leroy, *Understanding Jazz*, Englewood Cliffs/Prentice-Hall (USA), 1977.
Ostransky, Leroy, *Jazz City: The Impact Of Our Cities On*

the Development Of Jazz, Englewood Cliffs (USA), 1978.
Owens, Thomas, *Bebop: The Music And The Players*, Oxford University Press (USA), 1995.
Page, Drew, *Drew's Blues*, Louisiana State University Press (USA).
Panassie, Hugues, *The Real Jazz*, Smith & Durrell (USA), 1942.
Panassie, Hugues, *Monsieur Jazz*, Stock.
Panassie, Hugues, *Guide To Jazz*, Greenwood Press, 1973.
Panassie, Hugues, *Dictionnaire Du Jazz ... Nouvelle Edition Revue Et Augemtee*, A. Michel (Paris), 1971.
Papademetriou, Sakes, *Themata Kai Prosopa Tes Synchrones Tzaz (1950-1970)*, Ekdoseis Diagoniou, 1974.
Papademetriou, Sakes, *Eisagoge Sten Tzaz*, Ekdoseis Diagoniou, 1975.
Papo, Alfredo, *Jazz Para Cinco Instrumentos*, Distribuido Por Graf. Layetana, 1975.
Parker, Chris (ed.), *B Flat, Bebop, Scat*, Quartet Books (UK), 1986.
Pauer, Fritz, *Modale Suite*, Advance Music.
Pearson, Nathan W., *Goin' To Kansas City*, University Of Illinois Press (USA).
Pellett, Roy (ed.), *Best Of Jazz Score*, BBC (UK), 1992.
Perett, Burton W., *The Creation Of Jazz: Music, Race And Culture In Urban America*, Univeristy Of Illinois Press (USA), 1992.
Perrin, Michel, *Le Jazz A Cent Ans*, Editions France-Empire.
Perry, David, *Jazz Greats*, Phaidon (UK), 1996.
Peter Russell's Hot Record Store, *The Good Noise*, Peter Russell's Hot Record Store, 1974.
Piazza, Tom, *Blues Up And Down: Jazz In Our Time*, St. Martin's (USA), 1998.
Piazza, Tom, *Setting The Tempo: Fifty Years Of Great Jazz Liner Notes*, Anchor Books (USA), 1996.
Piazza, Tom, *The Guide To Classic Recorded Jazz*, University Of Iowa Press (USA), 1995.
Placksin, Sally, *American Women In Jazz: 1900 To The Present*, Wideview Books.
Pohlert, Werner, *Praludium, Fantasie Und Suite In D*, Zimmermann.
Poindexter, Pony, *The Pony Express*, J.A.S.
Polillo, Arrigo, *Stasera Jazz*, A. Mondadori, 1978.
Polillo, Arrigo, *Jazz: La Vicenda E I Protagonisti Della Musica Afro-Americana*, A. Mondadori, 1983.
Polonsky, Bruce, *Hearing Music*, Private Books, 1981.
Poole, G., *Enciclopedia De Swing*, Buenos Aires, 1939.
Porter, Lewis, *Jazz, A Century Of Change: Readings And New Essays*, Schimer Books, 1998.
Porter, Ray, and David Keller (ed.), *There And Back*, Bayou Press (USA), 1991.
Porto, Sergio, *Pequena Historia Do Jazz*, Servico De Documentacao, 1953.
Postgate, John, *A Plain Man's Guide To Jazz*, Hanover Books, 1973.
Price, Sammy, *What Do They Want?*, Bayou Press (USA), 1989.
Priestley, Brian, *Jazz On Record: A History*, Elm Tree (UK), 1988.
Raben, Erik (ed.), *Jazz Records, 1942-80 Vol 3: Bro-Cl*, Stainless/Wintermoon, 1992.
Ragland, Glenn, *Jazz Profiles In Paris*, Minerva, 1995.
Raich, S., *Criticisms Of Jazz*, Casa Provinicial De Caridad, 1958.
Ramsey, Douglas K., *Jazz Matters*, University Of Arkansas Press (USA), 1989.
Ramsey Jnr., F., *A Guide To Longplay Jazz Records*, New York.
Ramsey Jnr., F., and C.E. Smith, *Jazz Record Book*, New York, 1942.
Ramsey Jnr., F., and C.E. Smith, *Jazzmen*, New York, 1939.
Reda, Jacques, *L'Improviste*, Gallimard.
Reda, Jacques, *Anthologie Des Musiciens De Jazz*, Stock.
Redfern, David, *David Redfern's Jazz Album*, Eel Pie (UK), 1980.
Reiff, Carole, *Nights In Birdland*, Simon & Schuster (UK).
Reisner, R., *The Literature Of Jazz*, New York.
Rimler, W., *Not Fade Away: Comparison Of Jazz Age With Rock Era Pop Song Composer*, Pierian Press (UK), 1990.
Rius, Guia, *Incompleta Del Jazz*, Grijalbo, 1987.
Rivelli, Pauline, and Robert Levin, *Black Giants*, World Books, 1970.
Roach, Hildred, *Black American Music*, Crescendo (USA), 1973.
Rockmore, Noel, *Preservation Hall Portraits*, Louisiana State University Press (USA), 1968.
Romijn Meijer, Henk, *Een Blauwe Golf Aan De Kust*, Meulenhoff.
Rose, A., and E. Souchon, *New Orleans Jazz: A Family Album*, Baton Rouge (USA), 1967.
Rose, A., *I Remember Jazz*, Louisiana State University Press (USA).
Rose, A., *Storyville*, University Of Alabama (USA), 1974.
Rosenhain, Sigurd, *Fascination Jazz*, Lied Der Zeit, 1974.
Rosenthal, David H., *Hard Bop: Jazz And Black Music 1955-65*, Oxford University Press (USA), 1992.
Rosenthal, George S., and Frank Zachary, *Jazzways*, Greenberg, 1946.
Rossi, Abner, *Technica Della Chitarra Jazz*, Edizioni Musicali Farfisa.
Rossi, Nick, *Music Of Our Time*, Crescendo, 1970.
Routley, E., *Is Jazz Music Christian?*, London, 1964.
Rublowsky, John, *Black Music In America*, Basic Books (USA), 1971.
Ruppli, Michel, *The Savoy Label*, Greenwood Press, 1980.
Ruppli, Michel, *The Prestige Label*, Greenwood Press, 1980.
Ruppli, Michel, *Atlantic Records*, Greenwood Press, 1979.
Rusch, Robert D., *JazzTalk*, Lyle Stuart.
Rusch, Robert D., *Collection Of (The Periodical Literature Of Jazz) 1918-1972*, New York Public Library (USA), 1974.
Russell, Bill, *New Orleans Style*, Jazzology Press (USA), 1995.
Russell, R., *Jazz Style In Kansas City And The South West*, Berkeley.
Russell, Ross, *The Sound*, E.P. Dutton (USA), 1961.
Russell, William, *Boogie Woogie Jazzmen*, New York, 1959.
Russell, William, *Technical Aspects Of Jazz*.
Russo, William, *Jazz Composition And Orchestration*, Chicago and London, 1968.
Rust, Brian, *The Dance Bands*, Arlington House, 1974.
Rust, Brian, *My Kind Of Jazz*, Hamish Hamilton, 1990.
Rust, Brian, *Jazz Records, 1897-1942*, Storyville, 1982.

Sabat, Hermenegildo, *Scat*, Instituto Salesiano De Artes Graficas.
Sacco, P. Peter, *Three Jazz Preludes*.
Saenz, Miguel, *Jazz De Hoy, De Ahora*, Siglo Veintiuno De Espana, 1971.
Sales, Grover, *Jazz: America's Classical Music*, Da Capo (USA), 1992.
Sandole, Adolph, *The Craft Of Jazz*, A. Sandole.
Sandole, Adolph, *Reflections For Piano*, A. Sandole.
Sandole, Adolph, *Poems Of Granada*, A. Sandole.
Sandole, Adolph, *Jazz Piano Left Hand*, A. Sandole.
Sandole, Adolph, *Jazz Improvisation II*, A. Sandole.
Santisi, Ray, *Jazz Originals For Piano*, Berklee Press.
Santoro, Gene, *Dancing In Your Head: Jazz, Blues, Rock, And Beyond*, Oxford University Press, 1994.
Sargeant, Winthrop, *Jazz Hot & Hybrid*, McGraw Hill/Da Capo (USA), 1975.
Sartori, Afo, *Santi A Dispetto Del Paradiso*, Pacini.
Sbarcea, George, *Jazzul, O Poveste Cu Negri Si Mic Dictionar Al Jazzului*, Editura Muzicala A Uniunii Compozitorilor, 1974.
Schafer, W.J., and J. Riedel, *The Art Of Ragtime*, Baton Rouge (USA).
Schafer, W.J., and R.B. Allen, *Brass Bands And New Orleans Jazz*, Baton Rouge (USA), 1977.
Scheller, Elske, *Jazzdans*, Hollandia.
Schenkel, Steven M., *The Tools Of Jazz*, Prentice-Hall (USA).
Schiedt, D., *The Jazz State Of Indiana*, Pittsboro (USA), 1977.
Schindler, Klaus, *Swinging*, Verlag Vogt & Fritz.
Schleman, H., *Rhythm On Record 1906 To 1936*, London, 1936.
Schmitz, Manfred, *Jazz Parnass*, Deutscher Verlag Fur Musik.
Schreiner, C., *Jazz Aktuell*, Mainz, 1968.
Schuller, Gunther, *The Swing Era: The Development Of Jazz 1930-1945*, Oxford University Press, 1991.
Schuller, Gunther, *Early Jazz: Its Roots & Development*, New York, 1968.
Schulz-kohn, Dietrich, *Kleine Geschichte Des Jazz*, C. Bertelsmann, 1963.
Schwaninger, A., and A. Gurwitsch, *Swing Discographie*, Geneva, 1945.
Scobey, Jan, *Jan Scobey Presents He Rambled! 'Til Cancer Cut Him Down*, Pal, 1976.
Scott, Allen, *Jazz Educated, Man*, American International, 1973.
See, Cees, *Das Schlagzeug Im Jazz*, Universal Edition.
Shapiro, Nat, and Nat Hentoff, *Hear Me Talkin' To Ya: Story Of Jazz By The Men Who Made It*, Dover (USA), Souvenir Press (UK), 1990.
Shapiro, Nat, and Nat Hentoff, *The Jazz Makers*, Rinehart (USA), 1957.
Shaw, Arnold, *The Trouble With Cinderella*, New York, 1952.
Shaw, Arnold, *The Street That Never Slept*, Coward, McCann & Geoghegan, 1971.
Shaw, Arnold, *The Jazz Age*, Oxford University Press, 1990.
Shaw, Arnold, *52nd Street: The Street Of Jazz*, Da Capo (USA), 1971.
Shearing, George Albert, *Piano Music. Selectons*, Warner Brothers (USA).
Sher, Chuck, *The Improviser's Bass Method*, Sher Music.
Sher, Chuck (ed.), *The World's Greatest Fake Book*, Sher Music.
Sidran, Ben, *Talking Jazz: An Illustrated Oral History*, Pomegranate Artbooks (USA), 1992.
Simon, George Thomas, *The Big Bands*, Macmillan (USA), 1967.
Simon, George Thomas, *Simon Says: The Sights And Sounds Of The Swing Era 1935-55*, Arlington House (USA), 1971.
Sinclair, John, *Music And Politics*, World, 1971.
Skaarup, V., and M. Goldstein, *Jazz*, Copenhagen, 1934.
Skvorecky, Josef, *Talkin' Moscow Blues*, Lester & Orpen Dennys, 1988.
Smith, Charles Edward, *Riverside History Of Classic Jazz*, Bill Grauer.
Smith, Charles Edward, with Frederic Ramsey Jnr., *The Jazz Record Book*, Smith & Durrell (USA), 1942.
Smith, W., and G. Hoefer, *Music On My Mind*, New York, 1964.
Sol, Ydo, *Faces Of Jazz*, Nieswand Verlag, 1992.
Somma, Robert (ed.), *No One Waved Good-bye*, Outerbridge & Dienstfrey (USA), 1971.
Southern, Eileen, *The Music Of Black Americans*, New York, 1983.
Southern, Eileen, *Readings In Black American Music*, W.W. Norton (USA), 1971.
Spagnardi, Ronald, *Great Jazz Drummers*, International Music Publishers (UK), 1992.
Spedale, Rhodes, *A Guide To Jazz In New Orleans*, Hope.
Spellman, A.B., *Four Lives In The Behop Business*, Harper & Row (USA), 1985.
Spitzer, D., *Jazzshots*, Miami, 1980.
Stagg, T., and C. Crump, *New Orleans Revival*, Dublin, 1973.
Stanton, Kenneth, *Jazz Theory*, Taplinger, 1982.
Starr, Frederick, *Red And Hot: The Fate Of Jazz In The Soviet Union 1917-1980*, New York and Oxford, 1983.
Stearns, Marshall, and Jean Stearns, *The Story Of Jazz*, Oxford University Press, 1956.
Stearns, Marshall, and Jean Stearns, *The Jazz Dance: The Story Of American Vernacular Dance*, New York, 1968.
Stebbins, Robert Alan, *The Jazz Community*, Minneapolis, 1964.
Steen, Arild, *Molde-jazz*, Gyldendal, 1971.
Stewart, Charles, *Chuck Stewart's Jazz Files*, Little, Brown (USA).
Stewart, Milton Lee, *Structural Development In The Jazz Improvisational Technique Of Clifford Brown*, 1973.
Stewart, Rex, *Jazz Masters Of The 30s*, New York, 1972.
Stewart, Rex, with Claire Gordon, *Boy Meets Horn*, Bayou Press (USA), 1992.
Stock, D., and N. Hentoff, *Jazz Street*, Garden City (USA) 1960.
Stoddard, Tom, *Jazz On The Barbary Coast*, Storyville.
Stoddard, Tom, *An Autobiography Of A New Orleans Jazzman*, University Of California Press (USA), 1971.
Stokes, W. Royal, *Jazz Scene: An Informal History From New Orleans To 1990*, Oxford University Press (USA), 1993.

Stone, Gregory Prentice, *Games, Sport, And Power*, E.P. Dutton (USA), 1971.
Stramacci, Fabrizio, *New Orleans*, Alle Origini Del Jazz Lato Side.
Stratemann, Klaus, *Jazz Ball & Feather On Jazz*, Der Jazzfreund.
Strom Pa Jazzen, *I Kommission Hos Attika*, 1978.
Stuart, Walter, *Encyclopedia Of Modem Jazz*, C. Colin.
Such, David Glen, *Music, Metaphor And Values Among Avant-Garde Jazz Musicians*, 1985.
Sudnow, David, *Ways Of The Hand*, Harvard University Press (USA), 1978.
Summerfield, Maurice Joseph, *Jazz Guitar: Its Evolution, Players And Personalities Since 1900*, A. Mark Publishing, Olsover House, Sackville Road, Newcastle (UK), 1994.
Sweet, Robert E., *Music Universe, Music Mind*, Arborville Publishing (USA), 1997.
Swenson, John, *The Rolling Stone Jazz Record Guide*, Random House (USA).
Sylvester, Peter, *A Left Hand Like God: A Study of Boogie-Woogie*, Quartet Books (UK), 1989.
Szadkowski, Dita von, *Auf Schwarzweissen Flugeln*, Focus Verlag.
Tanner, Lee, *Images Of Jazz*, Friedman/Fairfax (USA), 1997.
Tanner, Leo, *Jazz Address Book*, Pomegranate, 1991.
Tanner, P., and M. Gerow, *A Study Of Jazz*, Dubuque, 1981.
Taylor, Art, *Notes And Tones*, Quartet Books (UK), 1988.
Taylor, Roger, *Art, An Enemy Of The People*, Harvester Press, 1978.
Tenot, F., and P. Carls, *Dictionnaire Du Jazz*, Paris, 1967.
Tenot, Frank, *Le Jazz*, Larousse, 1977.
Terkel, Louis, *Giants Of Jazz, Studs Terkel With Milly Hawk Daniel*, Thomas Y. Crowell (USA), 1975.
Tesser, Neil, *The Playboy Guide To Jazz*, Plume Trade Paperback Original (USA), 1998.
Testoni, G., and others, *Enciclopedia Del Jazz*, Milan, 1953.
Thigpen, Ed, *The Sound Of Brushes*, E. Thigpen/Action-Reaction.
Thomas, Ianthe, *Willie Blows A Mean Horn*, Harper & Row.
Thomas, Neil, *Playing Popular Piano*, Prentice-Hall.
Tichenor, T.J., *Ragtime Rediscoveries*, New York, 1979.
Tirro, Frank, *Jazz: A History*, W.W. Norton (USA), 1993.
Toll, Robert C., *Blacking Up*, Oxford University Press, 1974.
Tracy, Sheila, *Bands, Booze And Broads*, Mainstream Publishing (UK), 1995.
Traill, Sinclair, *Just Jazz (No. 4)*, Souvenir Press, 1960.
Travis, Dempsey, *An Autobiography Of Black Jazz*, Urban Research Institute, 1983.
Turner, Frederick, *Remembering Songs: Encounters With The New Orleans Jazz Tradition*, Da Capo (UK), 1994.
Ulanov, Barry, *A History Of Jazz In America*, Viking (USA).
Ulanov, Barry, *A Handbook Of Jazz*, Viking (USA), 1957.
Umphred, Neil, *Goldmine's Price Guide To Collectible Jazz Records*, Krause Publications (USA), 1991.
Unterbrink, Mary, *Jazz Women At The Keyboard*, McFarland, 1983.
Usinger, F., *Kleine Biographie Des Jazz*, Offenbach Am Main, 1953.
Vail, Ken (ed.), *Jazz Milestones: A Pictorial Chronicle Of Jazz 1900-90*, Castle Communications (UK), 1995.
Valli, Raymond, *Maestro Rag*, R. Valli.
Velebny, Karel, *Jazzova Praktika*, Panton, 1983.
Velez, Ana, *En Torno Al Jazz*, Producciones Don Pedro, 1978.
Vian, Boris, *Chroniques De Jazz*, Union Generale D'Editions, 1971.
Vian, Boris, *Autres Ecrits Sur Le Jazz*, Bourgois.
Vidossich, Edoardo, *Sincretismos Na Musica Afro-Americana*, Edicoss Quiron, 1975.
Viera, Joe, *Neue Formen*, Freies Spiel.
Viera, Joe, *Grundlagen Der Jazzharmonik*, Universal Edition.
Viera, Joe, *Der Free Jazz*, Universal Edition, 1974.
Viera, Joe, *Das Saxophon Im Jazz*, Universal Edition.
Viera, Joe, *Arrangement Und Improvisation*, Universal Edition, 1971.
Vittorini, Tommaso, *Musica In Libera Uscita*, A. Mondadori, 1984.
Voigt, John, *Jazz Music In Print And Jazz Books In Print*, Hornpipe Music.
Von Physter, George, *Destiny*, Down Beat (USA).
Waite, Brian, *Modern Jazz Piano*, Spellmount, 1990.
Waldo, Terry, *This Is Ragtime*, Da Capo (USA), 1991.
Waldron, Mal, *Reflections In Modern Jazz*, S. Fox.
Walker, Leo, *Wonderful Era Of Great Dance Bands*, Da Capo (USA), 1990.
Walker, Leo, *The Big Band Almanac*, Da Capo (USA), 1978.
Wallington, George, *Virtuoso*, Denon, 1984.
Watanabe, Sadao, *Fill Up The Night*, Nichion.
Waterman, G., *The Art Of Jazz '(A Survey Of Ragtime)'*, New York, 1959.
Waterman, G., *Jazz: New Perspectives*, New York.
Wayne, Bennett, *3 Jazz Greats*, Garrard, 1973.
Weinstein, Norman C., *Night In Tunisia: Imaginations Of Africa In Jazz*, Scarecrow Press, 1992.
Welburn, Ronald G., *American Jazz Criticism, 1914-1940*.
Werner, Craig Hansen, *Playing The Changes: From Afro-Modernism To The Jazz Impulse*, University Of Illinois Press (USA), 1997.
Westerberg, Hans, *Suomalaiset Jazzlevytykset 1932-1976*, Suomen Jazzliitto, 1977.
Whannel, P., *Jazz On Film*, London, 1966.
White, Clarence Cameron, *Book Review On Henry O. Osgood's So This Is Jazz*.
White, Mark, *The Observer's Book Of Big Bands*, F. Warne (UK), 1978.
Whitehead, Kevin, *New Dutch Swing*, Billboard Books (USA), 1998.
Whiteman, P., and M.M. McBride, *Jazz*, Arno Press (USA).
Wilber, Bob, *Music Was Not Enough*, Macmillan (UK), 1987.
Wilder, Alec, *Jazz Suite*, Margun Music.
Williams, Clarence, *The Boogie Woogie Blues Folio*, Clarence Williams, 1940.
Williams, M., *The Jazz Heritage*, New York (USA), 1986.
Williams, M., *Jazz Panorama*, New York and London, 1962.

Williams, M., *Jazz Masters Of New Orleans*, New York and London, 1967.
Williams, Martin, *Jazz Tradition*, Oxford University Press, 1993.
Williams, Martin T., *The Art Of Jazz: Essays On The Nature And Development Of Jazz*, Oxford University Press, 1959.
Williams, Martin T., *Jazz In Its Time*, Oxford University Press, 1989.
Williams, Martin T., *Jazz Masters In Transition, 1957-69*, Macmillan, 1970.
Williams, Martin T., *Jazz Changes*, Oxford University Press, 1992.
Williams, Richard, *Jazz: A Photographic Documentary*, Studio Editions (UK), 1995.
Williamson, Ken, *This Is Jazz*, Newnes (UK), 1960.
Williamson, Liz, *Jazz Dance & Jazz Gymnastics*, Sterling (USA).
Willioughby, Bill, *Jazz In L.A.*, Nieswand Verlag, 1992.
Wilmer, Val, *The Face Of Black Music*, Da Capo (USA), 1976.
Wilmer, Val, *Mama Said There'd Be Days Like This*, The Women's Press (UK), 1989.
Wilmer, Val, *As Serious As Your Life: Story Of The New Jazz*, Allison & Busby (UK), 1977.
Winick, S., *Rhythm: An Annotated Bibliography*, Metuchen, New Jersey, 1974.
Wolfer, Jurgen, *Handbuch Des Jazz*, Heyne, 1980.
Wood, Celia, and Steve French (ed.), *Jazz Musicians Guide: National UK Directory Of Jazz*, Jazz Services (UK), 1992.
Woodward, Woody, *Jazz Americana*, Trend Books, 1956.
Wright, Rayburn, *Inside The Score*, Kendor Music, 1982.
Wylie, Floyd E.M., *An Investigation Of Some Aspects Of Creativity Of Jazz Musicians*, Detroit, 1963.
Yates, Tom, *A Boy: A Golden Trombone - And A Dream*, T. Yates.
Young, Al, *Things Ain't What They Used To Be*, Creative Arts Book, 1987.
Young, Al, *Kinds Of Blue*, Creative Arts Books, 1984.
Young, Al, *Bodies & Soul*, Creative Arts Books, 1981.
Zano, Anthony, *Mechanics Of Modern Music*, Berben.
Zinn, David, *Be-Bach*, T. Presser.
Zinsser, William Knowlton, *Willie And Dwike*, Harper & Row (USA).
Zwerin, Michael, *Close Enough For Jazz*, Quartet Books (UK), 1983.
Zwerin, Michael, *La Tristesse De Saint Louis*, Quartet Books (UK), 1985.

Index

B

C

D

F

G

H

I

J

K

L

M

N

O

P

Q

R

S

T

U

V

W

Y

Z